Ready for your satisfaction!

As the best regional partner for strengthening naval forces,
we are ready to satisfy your demands in naval shipbuilding

HOVERCRAFT   FAST PATROL BOAT   CORVETTE   FRIGATE   LANDING SHIP TANK   LANDING PLATFORM HELICOPTER

HANJIN HEAVY INDUSTRIES
& CONSTRUCTION CO., LTD.

Jane's

Fighting Ships
2006-2007

Edited by Commodore Stephen Saunders RN

One Hundred and Ninth Edition

Founded in 1897 by Fred T Jane

ISBN-13 978-0-7106-2753-7
ISBN-10 0 7106 2753X
"Jane's" is a registered trademark

Printed by Cambridge University Press, UK

Face it with confidence

With the right equipment, any mission can be faced
confidently. Thales is known worldwide for its excellent
naval systems and system integration capabilities.
By being alert, navies can act and protect.

www.thalesgroup.com/naval

Contents

Jane's Fighting Ships website: jfs.janes.com

EDITORIAL AND ADMINISTRATION

Director: Ian Kay, e-mail: Ian.Kay@janes.com

New Media Publishing Director: Sean Howe, e-mail: Sean.Howe@janes.com

Publisher: Sara Morgan, e-mail: Sara.Morgan@janes.com

Content Services Director: Anita Slade, e-mail: Anita.Slade@janes.com

Content Systems Manager: Jo Agius, e-mail: Jo.Agius@janes.com

Pre-Press Manager: Christopher Morris, e-mail: Christopher.Morris@janes.com

Content Editor: Emma Donald, e-mail: Emma.Donald@janes.com

Production Controller: Helen Grimley, e-mail: Helen.Grimley@janes.com

Content Update: Jacqui Beard, Information Collection Team Leader
Tel: (+44 20) 87 00 38 08 Fax: (+44 20) 87 00 39 59, e-mail: yearbook@janes.com
Jane's Information Group Limited, Sentinel House, 163 Brighton Road, Coulsdon, Surrey CR5 2YH, UK
Tel: (+44 20) 87 00 37 00 Fax: (+44 20) 87 00 39 00

SALES OFFICES

Europe and Africa
Jane's Information Group Limited, Sentinel House, 163 Brighton Road, Coulsdon, Surrey CR5 2YH, UK
Tel: (+44 20) 87 00 37 50 Fax: (+44 20) 87 00 37 51
e-mail: customerservices.uk@janes.com

North/Central/South America
Jane's Information Group Inc, 110 N Royal Street, Suite 200, Alexandria, Virginia 22314, US
Tel: (+1 703) 683 21 34 Fax: (+1 703) 836 02 97 Telex: 6819193
Tel: (+1 800) 824 07 68 Fax: (+1 800) 836 02 97
e-mail: customerservices.us@janes.com

Asia
Jane's Information Group Asia, 78 Shenton Way, #10-02, Singapore 079120, Singapore
Tel: (+65) 63 25 08 66 Fax: (+65) 62 26 11 85
e-mail: asiapacific@janes.com

Oceania
Jane's Information Group, PO Box 3502, Rozelle Delivery Centre, New South Wales 2039 Australia
Tel: (+61 2) 85 87 79 00 Fax: (+61 2) 85 87 79 01
e-mail: oceania@janes.com

Middle East
Jane's Information Group, PO Box 502138, Dubai, United Arab Emirates
Tel: (+971 4) 390 23 35/36 Fax: (+971 4) 390 88 48
e-mail: mideast@janes.com

Japan
Jane's Information Group, Palaceside Building, 5F, 1-1-1, Hitotsubashi, Chiyoda-ku, Tokyo 100-0003, Japan
Tel: (+81 3) 52 18 76 82 Fax: (+81 3) 52 22 12 80
e-mail: japan@janes.com

ADVERTISEMENT SALES OFFICES

(Head Office)
Jane's Information Group
Sentinel House, 163 Brighton Road,
Coulsdon, Surrey CR5 2YH, UK
Tel: (+44 20) 87 00 37 00 Fax: (+44 20) 87 00 38 59/37 44
e-mail: defadsales@janes.com

Janine Boxall, Global Advertising Sales Director,
Tel: (+44 20) 87 00 38 52 Fax: (+44 20) 87 00 38 59/37 44
e-mail: janine.boxall@janes.com

Richard West, Senior Key Accounts Manager
Tel: (+44 1892) 72 55 80 Fax: (+44 1892) 72 55 81
e-mail: richard.west@janes.com

Nicky Eakins, Advertising Sales Manager
Tel: (+44 20) 87 00 38 53 Fax: (+44 20) 87 00 38 59/37 44
e-mail: nicky.eakins@janes.com

James Austin, Advertising Sales Executive
Tel: (+44 20) 87 00 39 63 Fax: (+44 20) 87 00 38 59/37 44
e-mail: james.austin@janes.com

(US/Canada office)
Jane's Information Group
110 N Royal Street, Suite 200,
Alexandria, Virginia 22314, US
Tel: (+1 703) 683 37 00 Fax: (+1 703) 836 55 37
e-mail: defadsales@janes.com

US and Canada
Robert Silverstein, US Advertising Sales Director
Tel: (+1 703) 236 24 10 Fax: (+1 703) 836 55 37
e-mail: robert.silverstein@janes.com

Sean Fitzgerald
Tel: (+1 703) 683 37 00 Fax: (+1 703) 836 55 37
e-mail: sean.fitzgerald@janes.com

Northern US and Eastern Canada
Linda Hewish, Northeast Region Advertising Sales Manager
Tel: (+1 703) 683 37 00 Fax: (+1 703) 836 55 37
e-mail: linda.hewish@janes.com

Southeastern US
Kristin D Schulze, Advertising Sales Manager
PO Box 270190, Tampa, Florida 33688-0190, US
Tel: (+1 813) 961 81 32 Fax: (+1 813) 961 96 42
e-mail: kristin.schulze@janes.com

Western US and Western Canada
Richard L Ayer
127 Avenida del Mar, Suite 2A, San Clemente, California 92672, US
Tel: (+1 949) 366 84 55 Fax: (+1 949) 366 92 89
e-mail: ayercomm@earthlink.com

Rest of the World

Australia: *Richard West* (see UK Head Office)

Benelux: *Nicky Eakins* (see UK Head Office)

Eastern Europe (excl. Poland): MCW Media & Consulting Wehrstedt
Dr Uwe H Wehrstedt
Hagenbreite 9, D-06463 Ermsleben, Germany
Tel: (+49 03) 47 43/620 90 Fax: (+49 03) 47 43/620 91
e-mail: info@Wehrstedt.org

France: Patrice Février

BP 418, 35 avenue MacMahon,
F-75824 Paris Cedex 17, France
Tel: (+33 1) 45 72 33 11 Fax: (+33 1) 45 72 17 95
e-mail: patrice.fevrier@wanadoo.fr

Germany and Austria: *MCW Media & Consulting Wehrstedt* (see Eastern Europe)

Greece: *Nicky Eakins* (see UK Head Office)

Hong Kong: *James Austin* (see UK Head Office)

India: *James Austin* (see UK Head Office)

Iran: Ali Jahangard
Tel: (+98 21) 88 73 59 23
e-mail: ali.jahangard@eidehinfo.com

Israel: Oreet - International Media
15 Kinneret Street, IL-51201 Bene Berak, Israel
Tel: (+972 3) 570 65 27 Fax: (+972 3) 570 65 27
e-mail: admin@oreet-marcom.com
Defence: Liat Heiblum
e-mail: liat_h@oreet-marcom.com

Italy and Switzerland: Ediconsult Internazionale Srl
Piazza Fontane Marose 3, I-16123 Genoa, Italy
Tel: (+39 010) 58 36 84 Fax: (+39 010) 56 65 78
e-mail: genova@ediconsult.com

Middle East: *James Austin* (see UK Head Office)

Pakistan: *James Austin* (see UK Head Office)

Poland: *James Austin* (see UK Head Office)

Russia: *James Austin*
(see UK Head Office)

Scandinavia: Falsten Partnership
23, Walsingham Road, Hove, East Sussex BN3 4FE, UK
Tel: (+44 1273) 77 10 20 Fax: (+ 44 1273) 77 00 70
e-mail: sales@falsten.com

Singapore: *Richard West/Nicky Eakins* (see UK Head Office)

South Africa: *Richard West* (see UK Head Office)

South Korea: Infonet Group Inc
Sanbu Rennaissance Tower 902, 456 Gongdukdong, Mapogu, Seoul, South Korea
Contact: Mr Jongseog Lee
Tel: (+82 2) 716 99 22 Fax: (+82 2) 716 95 31
e-mail: jslee@infonetgroup.co.kr

Spain: Via Exclusivas SL
c/Albasanz 14 Bis 3 1, E-28037 Madrid, Spain
(+34 91) 448 76 22 Fax: (+34 91) 446 02 14
e-mail: viaexclusivas@viaexclusivas.com

Turkey: *Richard West* (see UK Head Office)

ADVERTISING COPY
Linda Letori (Jane's UK Head Office)
Tel: (+44 20) 87 00 37 42 Fax: (+44 20) 87 00 38 59/37 44
e-mail: linda.letori@janes.com

For North America, South America and Caribbean only:
Tel: (+1 703) 683 37 00 Fax: (+1 703) 836 55 37
e-mail: us.ads@janes.com

Copyright enquiries
e-mail: copyright@janes.com

British Library Cataloguing-in-Publication Data.
A catalogue record for this book is available from the British Library.

Jane's Libraries

To assist your information gathering and to save you money, Jane's has grouped some related subject matter together to form 'ready-made' libraries, which you can access in whichever way suits you best – online, on CD-ROM, via Jane's EIS or through Jane's Data Service.

The entire contents of each library can be cross-searched, to ensure you find every reference to the subjects you are looking for. All Jane's libraries are updated according to the delivery service you choose and can stand alone or be networked throughout your organisation.

www.janes.com

Jane's Defence Equipment Library

Aero-Engines
Air-Launched Weapons
Aircraft Upgrades
All the World's Aircraft
Ammunition Handbook
Armour and Artillery
Armour and Artillery Upgrades
Avionics
C4I Systems
Electro-Optic Systems
Explosive Ordnance Disposal
Fighting Ships
Infantry Weapons
Land-Based Air Defence
Military Communications
Military Vehicles and Logistics
Mines and Mine Clearance
Naval Weapon Systems
Nuclear, Biological and Chemical Defence
Radar and Electronic Warfare Systems
Strategic Weapon Systems
Underwater Warfare Systems
Unmanned Aerial Vehicles and Targets

Jane's Defence Magazines Library

Defence Industry
Defence Weekly
Foreign Report
Intelligence Digest
Intelligence Review
International Defence Review
Islamic Affairs Analyst
Missiles and Rockets
Navy International
Terrorism and Security Monitor

Jane's Market Intelligence Library

Aircraft Component Manufacturers
All the World's Aircraft
Defence Industry
Defence Weekly
Electronic Mission Aircraft
Fighting Ships
Helicopter Markets and Systems
International ABC Aerospace Directory
International Defence Directory
Marine Propulsion
Naval Construction and Retrofit Markets
Police and Security Equipment
Simulation and Training Systems
Space Directory
Underwater Technology
World Armies
World Defence Industry

Jane's Security Library

Amphibious and Special Forces
Chemical-Biological Defense Guidebook
Facility Security
Fighting Ships
Intelligence Digest
Intelligence Review
Intelligence Watch Report
Islamic Affairs Analyst
Police and Security Equipment
Police Review
Terrorism & Security Monitor
Terrorism Watch Report
World Air Forces
World Armies
World Insurgency and Terrorism

Jane's Sentinel Library

Central Africa
Central America and the Caribbean
Central Europe and the Baltic States
China and Northeast Asia
Eastern Mediterranean
North Africa
North America
Oceania
Russia and the CIS
South America
South Asia
Southeast Asia
Southern Africa
The Balkans
The Gulf States
West Africa
Western Europe

Jane's Transport Library

Aero-Engines
Air Traffic Control
Aircraft Component Manufacturers
Aircraft Upgrades
Airport Review
Airports and Handling Agents –
    Central and Latin America (inc. the Caribbean)
    Europe
    Far East, Asia and Australasia
    Middle East and Africa
    United States and Canada
Airports, Equipment and Services
All the World's Aircraft
Avionics
High-Speed Marine Transportation
Marine Propulsion
Merchant Ships
Naval Construction and Retrofit Markets
Simulation and Training Systems
Transport Finance
Urban Transport Systems
World Airlines
World Railways

101

☑ Rodman

Incomparable excellence.
The leading Patrol Boat.

T E C H N I C A L D A T A	
Length	30,00 m.
Beam	6,00 m.
Draught	1,35 m.
Range	800 nm
Crew	9/16 men
Propulsion	2x1.350 / 2x2.000 Hp
Speed	28 / 36 knots

☑ Rodman

Rios - Teis s/nº • P.O. BOX 501 • 36200 VIGO - Spain • Tel.: +34 986 811 811 • Fax: +34 986 811 821 • vpresidencia@rodman.es

pintado et guzmán

Alphabetical list of advertisers

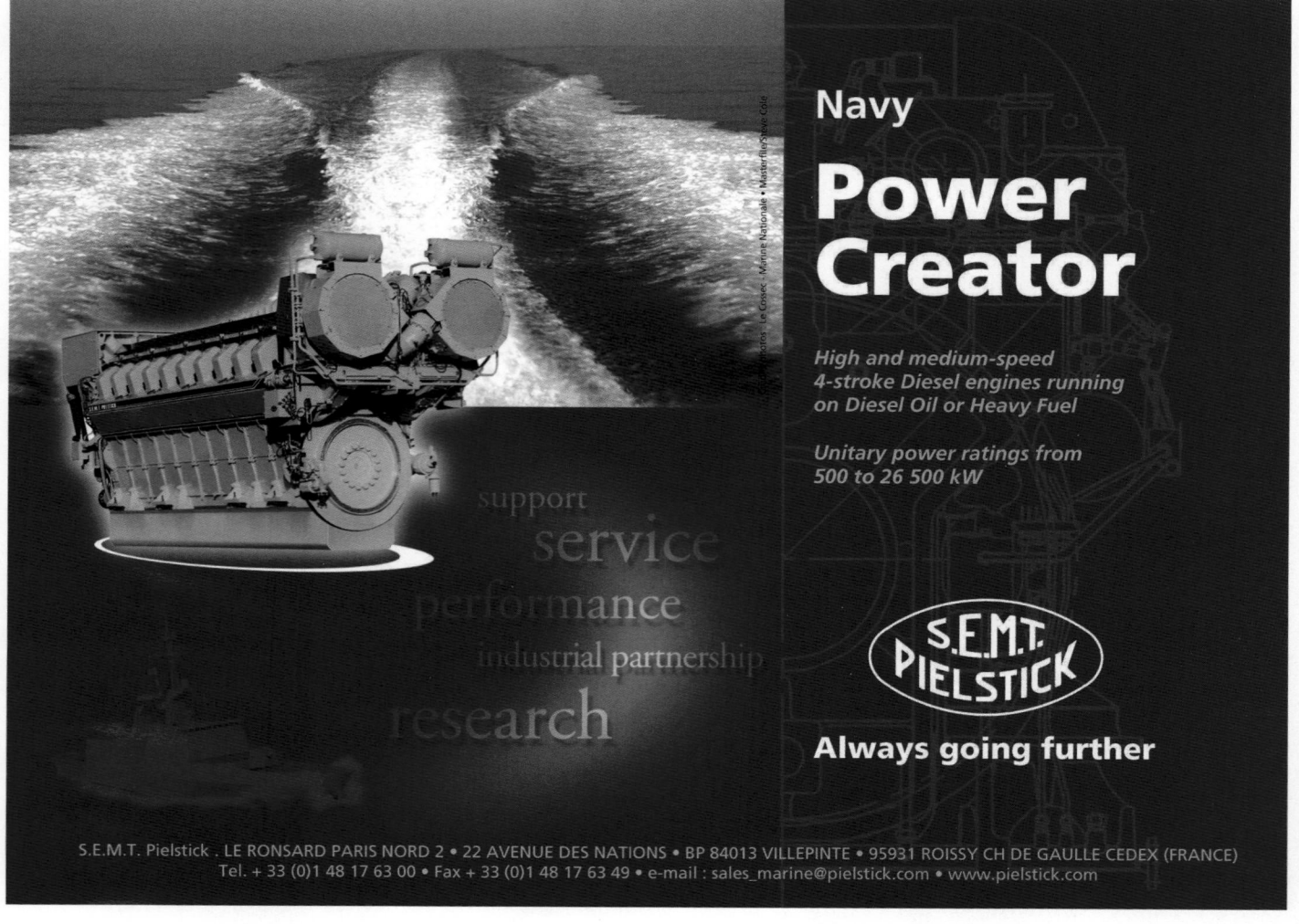

DISCLAIMER

Jane's Information Group gives no warranties, conditions, guarantees or representations, express or implied, as to the content of any advertisements, including but limited to compliance with description and quality or fitness for purpose of the product or service. Jane's Information Group will not be liable for any damages, including without limitation, direct, indirect or consequential damages arising from any use of products or services or any actions or omissions taken in direct reliance on information contained in advertisements.

FREE ENTRY/CONTENT IN THIS PUBLICATION

Having your products and services represented in out titles means that they are being seen by the professionals who matter - both by those involved in the procurement and by those working for the companies that are likely to affect your business. We therefore feel that it is very much in the interest of your organisation, as well as Jane's, to ensure your data is current and accurate.

■ **Don't forget** - You may be missing out on business if your entry in a Jane's product is incorect because you have not supplied the latest information to us.

■ **Ask yourself** - Can you afford not to be represented in Jane's printed and electronic products? And if you are listed, can you afford for your information to be out of date?

■ **And most importantly** - The best part of all is that your entries in Jane's products are TOTALLY FREE OF CHARGE.

Please provide (using a photocopy of this form) the information on the following categories where appropriate:

1. Organisation name: _____

2. Division name: _____

3. Location address: _____

_____

4. Mailing address if different: _____

_____

5. Telephone (please include switchboard and main departmental contact numbers, for example Public Relations, Sales, and so on):

_____

6. Facsimile _____

7. E-mail: _____

8. Web sites: _____

9. Contact name and job title: _____

_____

10. A brief description of your organisation's activities, products and services: _____

_____

_____

11. Jane's publications in which you would like to be included: _____

_____

Please send this information to:
Jacqui Beard, Information Collection, Jane's Information Group
Sentinel House, 163 Brighton Road, Coulsdon, Surrey CR5 2YH, UK
Tel: (+44 20) 87 00 38 08
Fax: (+44 20) 87 00 39 59
e-mail: yearbook@janes.com

Copyright enquiries:
e-mail: copyright@janes.com

Please tick this box if you do not wish your organisation's staff to be included in Jane's mailing lists ☐

JFS

Ensigns and flags of the world's navies

In cases where countries do not have ensigns their warships normally fly the national flag.

Albania
Ensign

Argentina
National Flag and Ensign

Bahrain
National Flag and Ensign

Benin
National Flag and Ensign

Algeria
Ensign

Australia
Ensign

Bangladesh
Ensign

Bermuda
Ensign

Angola
National Flag and Ensign

Austria
Ensign

Barbados
Ensign

Bolivia
Ensign

Anguilla
National Flag

Azerbaijan
Ensign

Belgium
Ensign

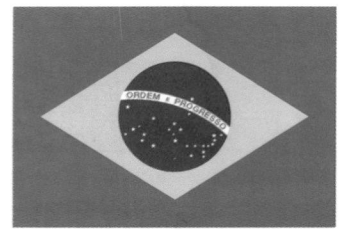

Brazil
National Flag and Ensign

Antigua and Barbuda
Ensign

Bahamas
Ensign

Belize
National Flag and Ensign

Brunei
Ensign

Bulgaria
Ensign

Chile
National Flag and Ensign

Cook Islands
National Flag

Cyprus, Turkish Republic of Northern (Not recognised by United Nations)
National Flag and Ensign

Cambodia
National Flag and Ensign

China
Ensign

Costa Rica
Ensign

Denmark
Ensign

Cameroon
National Flag and Ensign

Colombia
Ensign

Côte d'Ivoire
National Flag and Ensign

Djibouti
National Flag and Ensign

Canada
National Flag and Ensign

Comoros
National Flag and Ensign

Croatia
Ensign

Dominica
National Flag and Ensign

Cape Verde
National Flag

Congo-Brazzaville
National Flag and Ensign

Cuba
National Flag and Ensign

Dominican Republic
Ensign

Cayman Islands
National Flag

Democratic Republic of Congo
National Flag and Ensign

Cyprus
National Flag and Ensign

East Timor
National Flag and Ensign

Ecuador
Ensign

European Union
Flag of the European Union

Gabon
National Flag and Ensign

Grenada
Ensign

Egypt
Ensign

Falkland Islands
Falkland Islands Flag

Gambia
National Flag and Ensign

Guatemala
National Flag and Ensign

El Salvador
National Flag and Ensign

Faroe Islands
Territory Flag

Georgia
Ensign

Guinea
National Flag and Ensign

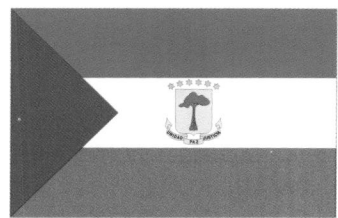

Equatorial Guinea
National Flag and Ensign

Fiji
Ensign

Germany
Ensign

Guinea-Bissau
National Flag and Ensign

Eritrea
National Flag and Ensign

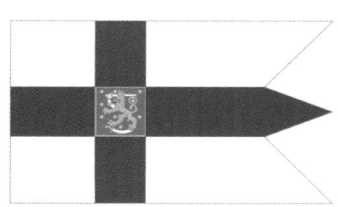

Finland
Ensign

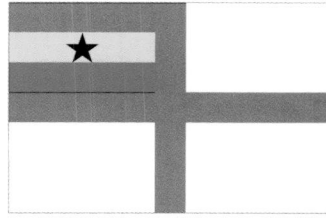

Ghana
Ensign

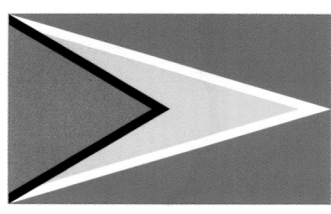

Guyana
National Flag and Ensign

Estonia
Ensign

France
National Flag and Ensign

Greece
National Flag and Ensign

Honduras
Ensign

Hong Kong
Regional Flag and Ensign

Iraq
National Flag

Japan
Japan (MSA) Ensign

Korea, South
National Flag and Ensign

Hungary
National Flag

Ireland
National Flag and Ensign

Jordan
Ensign

Kuwait
National Flag and Ensign

Iceland
Ensign

Israel
Ensign

Kazakhstan
Ensign

Latvia
Ensign

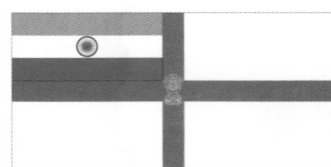

India
Ensign

Italy
Ensign

Kenya
Ensign

Lebanon
National Flag and Ensign

Indonesia
National Flag and Ensign

Jamaica
Ensign

Kiribati
National Flag and Ensign

Liberia
National Flag and Ensign

Iran
National Flag and Ensign

Japan
Japan (Navy) Ensign

Korea, North
National Flag and Ensign

Libya
Ensign

Lithuania
Ensign

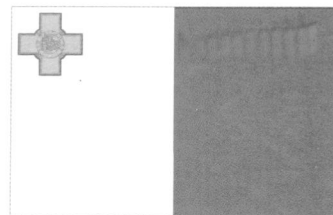

Malta
National Flag and Ensign

Morocco
Ensign

New Zealand
Ensign

Macedonia, Former Yugoslav Republic of
National Flag

Marshall Islands
National Flag and Ensign

Mozambique
National Flag and Ensign

Nicaragua
National Flag and Ensign

Madagascar
National Flag and Ensign

Mauritania
National Flag and Ensign

Myanmar
Ensign

Nigeria
Ensign

Malawi
National Flag

Mauritius
Ensign

Namibia
National Flag and Ensign

Norway
Ensign

Malaysia
Ensign

Mexico
National Flag and Ensign

NATO
Flag of the North Atlantic Treaty Organisation

Oman
Ensign

Maldives
National Flag and Ensign

Federated States of Micronesia
Flag of the Federation

Netherlands
National Flag and Ensign

Pakistan
Ensign

Palau
National Flag and Ensign

Philippines
National Flag and Ensign

Russian Federation
Border Guard Ensign

Senegal
National Flag and Ensign

Panama
National Flag and Ensign

Poland
Ensign

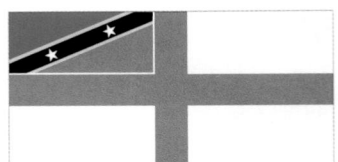

St Kitts and Nevis
Ensign

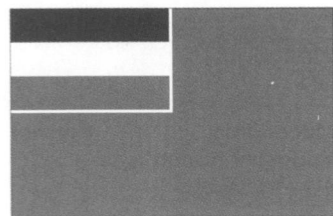

Serbia and Montenegro
Ensign

Papua New Guinea
Ensign

Portugal
National Flag and Ensign

St Lucia
Ensign

Seychelles
National Flag

Paraguay
National Flag and Ensign

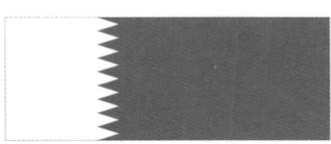

Qatar
National Flag and Ensign

St Vincent and the Grenadines
National Flag and Ensign

Sierra Leone
Ensign

Paraguay
National Flag and Ensign (reverse)

Romania
National Flag and Ensign

Samoa
National Flag and Ensign

Singapore
Ensign

Peru
National Flag and Ensign

Russian Federation
Ensign

Saudi Arabia
National Flag and Ensign

Slovenia
National Flag and Ensign

Solomon Islands
Ensign

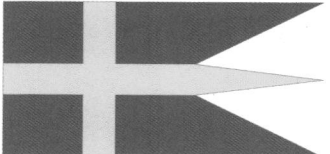
Sweden
Ensign

Thailand
Ensign

Turkmenistan
National Flag

South Africa
Ensign

Switzerland
National Flag

Togo
National Flag and Ensign

Tuvalu
National Flag and Ensign

Spain
National Flag and Ensign

Syria
National Flag and Ensign

Tonga
Ensign

Ukraine
Ensign

Sri Lanka
Ensign

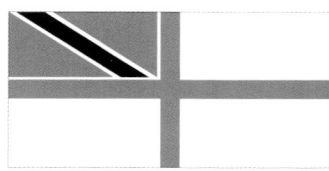
Trinidad and Tobago
Ensign

United Arab Emirates
National Flag and Ensign

Sudan
National Flag and Ensign

Taiwan
National Flag and Ensign

Tunisia
National Flag and Ensign

United Kingdom
Ensign

Suriname
National Flag and Ensign

Tanzania
National Flag and Ensign

Turkey
National Flag and Ensign

United Nations
Flag of the United Nations Organisation

United States
National Flag and Ensign

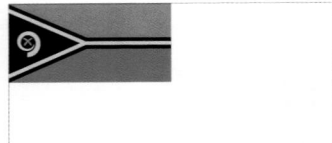

Vanuatu
Ensign

Vietnam
National Flag and Ensign

Yemen
National Flag and Ensign

Uruguay
National Flag and Ensign

Venezuela
Ensign

Virgin Islands (UK)
National Flag

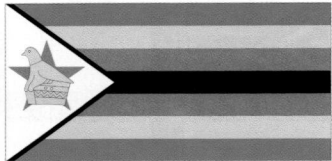

Zimbabwe
National Flag

KALKAN

[27]

Executive Overview

Introduction

The '1,000-ship Navy' concept is one of the more thought-provoking ideas to emerge in the last few years. The call for a global approach to international security in which "policing and protecting the maritime commons against a wide spectrum of threats is a high priority for all nations interested in the economic prosperity and security that comes from a safe and free maritime domain" was first made by Admirals John Morgan and Charles Martoglio at the International Seapower Symposium at Rhode Island in September 2005. It was later published in the November 2005 edition of the US Naval Institute's *Proceedings*. The authors' proposition is that, because such a task would require "substantially more capability than the United States or any individual nation can deliver", there is a need for the voluntary development of a trans-national network that would include navies, the shipping industry and law enforcement agencies. The aim would be to improve maritime awareness and to dispose sea-going units in a way that would enable them to respond to crises or emergencies at sea.

The concept has been generally well received, but there is no disguising the fact that there are significant hurdles to be overcome if the concept is to be implemented. Not least of these is the danger that, despite the best of intentions, this will be seen as a US initiative to bend international maritime forces to an American agenda. To their credit, the authors make it plain that this is not the case. However the US Navy, the natural leaders of such an enterprise, will need to exercise considerable tact and diplomacy both in accommodating other points of view and in addressing national sensitivities. Unless the vital ingredient of trust can be established, it is unlikely that willingness to co-operate on vital matters such as intelligence, command and control and rules of engagement will follow. To some extent, the basic building blocks for naval co-operation are already in place. Navies of NATO and of the various Alliance initiatives have worked together closely for many years and these, together with other regional agreements, have provided the foundations upon which interoperability between a wide group of like-minded nations has been developed. However, the concept is not just about military forces and the same cannot necessarily be said for the miscellaneous law enforcement agencies involved in countering terrorism, weapons proliferation, piracy, organised crime, smuggling, illegal immigration and the drugs trade. Not only is international co-operation in these matters patchy, but even at a national level, co-ordination can be frustrated by bureaucracy, judicial issues and political in-fighting. Moreover, the thorny issue of national sovereignty, whether it be applied to exclusive economic zones or territorial seas, can lead to a defensive mindset that regards any offer of outside help as a threat.

It is because there are obstacles to be overcome that it is easy to dismiss a visionary idea such as the '1,000-ship Navy' as being impractical. However, as the international responses to the Asian tsunami in December 2004 and to Hurricane Katrina in September 2005 have shown, a lot can be achieved if there is sufficient goodwill and political consensus.

United States and Canada

The Quadrennial Defence Review (QDR), published on 6 February 2006, was a disappointment to those who expected a revolutionary document. The Review, the first to be conducted since the attacks of 11 September 2001, emphasised that it was not intended to be a 'new beginning' but rather an indication of the changes of emphasis required amidst current strategic uncertainties. Key recommendations included the necessity "to move from a 'one size fits all' deterrence to tailored deterrence for rogue powers, terrorist networks and near-peer competitors". The need to be able to act proactively using mobile, expeditionary forces was also highlighted. It is because naval forces are inherently expeditionary and mobile that it is easy to dismiss the QDR as something of a 'non-event'. Its vision for Joint Maritime Forces is not a surprise. Development of the capability to "conduct highly distributed operations with a networked fleet that is more capable of projecting power in the 'brown and green waters' of coastal areas" is already being progressed. Nevertheless, the QDR does contain some interesting plans. These include: an adjustment of force posture and basing to provide at least six operationally available and sustainable carriers and 60 per cent of its submarines in the Pacific; the adaptation of ballistic-missile armed submarines to fire conventional weapons and the development of a riverine capability. But the QDR is not a programming document and translation of its priorities into the future size and shape of the US Navy remains a budgetary challenge.

Current plans for the future navy are laid out in the 30-year shipbuilding plan that was presented to Congress on 8 February 2006. The overall aim is ambitious – to grow the current fleet of about 280 ships to one that contains 313 by 2020. This can only be achieved if the Navy is successful in reversing a rising trend of shipbuilding costs. Many of the core units expected to be in service in 2020 are already in commission or being built today. Ten carriers of the Nimitz class will have been joined by the first two new-generation CVN 21 class carriers. This follows a dip in carrier numbers to ten in FY13 when *Enterprise* decommissions. Following an increase in production to two Virginia class submarines per year, a force of about 48 nuclear powered submarines is to be maintained while amphibious forces, which are to include the LHA(R)s and the still to be defined MPF(F) ships,

PELELIU and TOKIWA

6/2005*, Ships of the World / 1154629

are planned to total about 31 vessels. Fifty-five Littoral Combat Ships will have replaced the current frigate force. Perhaps the most contentious issue is the DD(X) destroyer, a programme (now reduced to seven ships) that does not even merit a mention in the QDR. It has always been hard to understand the argument for these vessels given that the US Navy already possesses a proven class of very capable ships. All 62 Arleigh Burke destroyers will still be in service in 2020. The need for yet more land-attack capability is also hard to justify in view of the entry into service of the converted Ohio class SSGNs and of the potential of other platforms to be used to launch cruise missiles. Above all, the astronomical cost of these ships and the difficulty of keeping such a high-risk programme to budget could undermine all the assumptions of the shipbuilding plan.

One of the most interesting, and potentially controversial, decisions of the QDR was to "within two years, deploy an initial capability to deliver precision-guided conventional warheads using long-range Trident Submarine-Launched Ballistic Missiles". The plan is to convert two launch tubes (each missile would carry up to four warheads) on all 12 submarines with a view to becoming capable of launching pre-emptive strikes on hard and deeply buried targets. Typically these might include enemy command bunkers and stockpiles of weapons of mass destruction. Given that the D5 missile has a range of some 12,000 km, it should then be possible to strike any target on the globe within about 30 minutes. While, on the face of it, this seems to be a very sensible initiative, some sort of modus operandi will first need to be worked out with allies and with China and Russia in order to avoid misinterpretation of any ballistic attack and its potentially catastrophic consequences.

Ohio, the first of four ballistic missile submarines converted to carry guided missiles and special operations forces, formally rejoined the fleet on 7 February 2006. The other three are currently undergoing conversion and are to return to service over the next two years. *Ohio* and *Michigan* are to be based at Bangor, Washington, while *Florida* and *Georgia* are to be based at King's Bay, Georgia. The boats are capable of carrying up to 154 cruise missiles, have facilities for up to 66 special operations troops and are equipped with a battle-management centre for planning operations. While none of these roles is new, their scale and sophistication is such that the SSGNs open up a new era of submarine operations; the development and testing of future weapons systems, sensors and operational concepts is to continue. These may include unmanned underwater and air vehicles for reconnaissance, surveillance and other missions.

The requirement to develop a riverine capability is a welcome recognition that an area of expertise built up during the Vietnam War has been lost. Reportedly, much of the river patrol work on Iraq's waterways has been undertaken by the US Marine Corps and US Army using craft of opportunity as the US Navy has lacked the requisite equipment and training. However, development of a new capability will not be easy. It will not just be a question of procuring the right craft but also of developing the tactics and procedures that will be required for operations in a joint war-fighting environment. Moreover, the most serious challenge will be to instigate the culture change required if the current generation of sailors, weaned in the high-tech environment of a modern destroyer, are to adapt to the low-tech and uncomfortable setting of small patrol craft armed with machine-guns.

Cultural issues are also likely to have been the cause of some of the inconsistencies between the QDR and programming decisions. Given the emphasis to be given to littoral warfare, it is surprising that all of the Osprey class mine-hunters are to be decommissioned over the next two years and that the Mine Warfare Command is to be merged with the Fleet ASW Command at San Diego. Despite the fact that some 14 US Navy ships have been damaged by mines since 1945, the US Navy mine-warfare community has always struggled to make its voice heard and the threat continues to be underrated, despite the fact that it is, arguably, the original asymmetric weapon. Until it has been proven that new deployable systems have the capability to replace specialist MCM shipping, it seems an unwise decision.

The persistent refusal by the US Navy to consider the acquisition of diesel submarines, despite the advanced capability of the modern generation of boats, is also a sign that vested interests are hard to overcome. The principal argument for procuring such boats is that they are cheaper and smaller and are, therefore, more suitable for the types of demanding, clandestine operations in shallow waters that might be considered too risky for larger nuclear boats. There is also a strong case for having a non-nuclear 'aggressor' force to act in a training role, as the extended deployment of the Swedish submarine *Gotland* to San Diego suggests. The requirement to keep ASW skills up-to-date and to develop tactics against the type of submarine that might be encountered in littoral waters is likely to remain a high priority. In the context of submarine procurement, the Chief of Naval Operations, Admiral Mullen, commented in January 2006 to *Jane's Defence Weekly* that "if we do not get them down to USD2 billion per submarine, it is not affordable". As about five diesel submarines could be acquired for the same price, there must surely be some merit in boosting submarine numbers and saving money at the same time?

Following the general election in Canada on 23 January 2006, a new minority Conservative government was formed under Prime Minister Stephen Harper. While it is generally expected that there will be changes in foreign and defence policy, particularly in renewing Canada-US relations, it is doubtful whether the Canadian defence budget will be increased significantly. For the Navy, much depends on whether the Standing Contingency Task Force (SCTF) concept, originated by the former government, will be adopted. If it is, the principal naval programmes, the procurement of three Joint Support Ships, to enter service from 2012, and the Single Class Surface Combatant (SCSC) programmes are likely to stand. Acquisition of an amphibious assault ship is also likely to be high on the agenda as the Canadian Navy attempts to adopt the expeditionary posture of other countries. The lease of such a ship from an allied nation may be the next step in proving the concept. The principal new maritime defence issue involves the sovereignty of Canadian northern waters. Under consideration are the installation of a new underwater sensor system and the procurement of three large, armed ice-breakers to be based at a new port at Iqaluit in south-east Baffin Island. The background to these proposals is that, if current predictions of a shrinking polar ice-cap prove to be correct, the Arctic region could become a source of dispute as oil and gas reserves and other mineral resources become more accessible. For the time-being, the quickest (and cheapest) method of achieving an armed presence in the Arctic would be to put naval parties onboard existing Coast Guard icebreakers.

China

Of the major and emerging powers, "China has the greatest potential to compete militarily with the US and field disruptive military technologies" stated the United States' *Quadrennial Defense Review (QDR) Report*. The Report was careful not to exclude the possibility of confrontation with "near-peer" competitors. While the Chinese government may profess annoyance at being singled out in this way, it can hardly be surprised. The *QDR* recalls that "since 1996, China has increased its defense spending by more than ten per cent in real terms in every year except 2003" and that "China continues to invest heavily in its military, particularly in its strategic arsenal and capabilities designed to improve its ability to project power beyond its borders". Nevertheless, the US seems keen not to demonise China in what could easily become a self-fulfilling prophecy. Rather it has sensibly opted for a "hedging strategy". Indeed, it is the only realistic alternative in view of the fact that "secrecy envelops most aspects of Chinese security affairs". As the Pentagon candidly admitted in a previous report, its annual report to Congress *The Military Power of the People's*

MAANSHAN   *6/2005* / 1154635*

Republic of China 2005, "direct insights into China's national strategies are difficult to acquire".

The Chinese naval build-up continued in 2005 although domestic production proceeded at a less feverish pace than in recent years. The aircraft-carrier conundrum resurfaced in mid-year when the former Russian carrier *Varyag*, which had arrived at Dalian on 4th March 2002, emerged from dock painted in Chinese naval colours. This lead to speculation, intensified by the construction of two new Type 051C Luzhou class destroyers in the same dockyard, that deployment of the ship was imminent. Wide discussion of its potential roles included development into a fully operational carrier or amphibious ship or a more modest function as an aviation training vessel (the name of *Shi Lang* has been suggested). In the event, the ship did not go to sea in 2005 and lack of information continues to frustrate objective assessment. In particular, the material state of *Varyag* when it arrived in China is unclear. The outward appearance of the ship suggested that she had not been well maintained and that possibly she was derelict. If this was the case, there would be a requirement for a very large work-package including the checking and/or replacement of wiring, installation of electronic systems, setting to work of main machinery, which did not appear to have been removed before transfer, and raising habitability to acceptable standards. All of this could be achieved, at a cost, but it would probably require longer than the ten weeks spent by the ship in dock during 2005.

Other highlights of the year include the delivery of a third Sovremenny class–destroyer, *Taizhou*, from St Petersburg. A fourth ship is to follow in 2006. These two vessels are to a modified design and their acquisition, together with the indigenously designed and built Types 051C, 052B and 052C classes, brings to ten the number of very capable destroyers that will have entered service over a seven-year period. It is of note that the Chinese navy has chosen to adopt an incremental approach, in which only two ships of each class are built, rather than opt for a longer shipbuilding line with corresponding economies in development and building costs and equipment commonality. A possible explanation is that the navy is on a steep learning curve and that, rather than being cautious about the introduction of new technology, it is keen to ensure that every ship introduced into service reflects the latest developments. The result is a relatively slow process; 12 elderly Luda class remain in service despite being overdue for replacement. Meanwhile, rumours that a further destroyer class (such as Type 052D?) is on the way have not been confirmed. Other surface ship construction has been relatively quiet after a busy few years. Some 30 amphibious vessels have entered service since 2003 but, while work seemed to slow in 2005, the use of some ten shipyards in the building process suggests that a concentrated building programme could be resumed quickly. There have also been unconfirmed reports that a LPD is under construction at Dalian. Production of the Jiangkai (Type 054) frigates has paused, possibly due to technical problems, although building of more advanced variants is expected. Replacement of the aging Jianghu class frigates is likely to be a high priority. Delivery of the first new Wozang class minesweeper, which looks remarkably similar to the 1950s vintage T43 class, took place in 2005 but further units have failed to materialise so far, although mine-

countermeasures is perhaps the weakest part of the Chinese naval inventory. Production of the new Hubei class catamaran-hulled patrol craft has also not been as fast as originally expected. In the submarine flotilla, delivery of all eight Russian-built Type 636 Kilo class missile-armed submarines is likely to be completed in 2006. In contrast, production of the indigenous Song class appears to have slowed while only one of the new Yuan class has been built at Wuhan. Of the nuclear-powered submarines, the first of a new class of Type 093 attack boats is likely to commission in 2006 while the first Type 094 class ballistic missile submarine is on track to enter service in 2008. This programme was boosted by the successful firing of a JL-2 missile from a submerged submarine (probably the converted Golf class trials boat) in June 2005.

Overall, the pattern of development of the Chinese navy changed slightly in 2005 as imported ships and submarines, rather than the indigenous building programme, were in the news. However, a return to domestic production is expected to follow soon. Meanwhile, the Chinese navy continues its evolution into a significant force with the capability both to conduct sea-denial operations and to threaten Taiwan. For the time being, the scope of such operations would be hampered by a relative lack of afloat support, despite the recent commissioning of two new replenishment ships. Information systems are also likely to lag behind those of most western navies although the probable deployment of surveillance equipment onboard *Shenzhou 6*, China's second manned space mission, and the testing of associated communication systems was a reminder of the importance that China attaches to space technology and to information dominance.

United Kingdom

The Royal Navy's future aircraft carrier programme moved a step closer when, on 14 December 2005, agreement on the composition and responsibilities of the Aircraft Carrier Alliance, which is to be charged with building the two ships, was announced and funding was released to undertake the demonstration phase. This period, during which the 65,000 ton 'Delta' design is to be finalised, is due to be completed in late 2006. Thereafter, in what is now to be a split 'Main Gate' process, a separate decision to initiate the manufacturing phase is expected by early 2007. It is not until this stage that the in-service dates are to be announced although it is assumed that the commissioning date of *Queen Elizabeth* has slipped to 2013.

The declared aim of adopting the two-phase process is to "further remove risk from the project and give greater understanding of projected costs". However, this careful approach is probably as much to do with uncertainty about the choice of aircraft as about construction of the ships. Planning assumptions have, since 30 September 2002, been predicated on the acquisition of the F-35B STOVL variant of the Joint Strike Fighter (JSF) to meet the UKs Joint Combat Aircraft (JCA) requirement. However, the demise of the Future Offensive Air System (FOAS) programme in 2005 necessitated a re-appraisal of the JCA requirement, which will now have to subsume some FOAS missions. As a result, the argument, which has always been finely balanced, as to whether to choose the F-35B or the US Navy's F-35C carrier variant, will be even more difficult to resolve. While

TRAFALGAR

6/2005*, B Sullivan / 1154628

Jane's Electronic Solutions

Jane's provides the most comprehensive open-source intelligence resource on the Internet. It is your ultimate resource for subscription-based security, defence, aerospace, transport, and related business information, providing you easy access, extensive content and total control.

Jane's offers you the choice of how you want to receive our information. Whether you want to integrate data into your organisation's network or access the data online, Jane's can provide you with critical information quickly and easily, in a format to suit you.

www.janes.com

Jane's

Intelligence and Insight You Can Trust

operational factors suggest that the F-35C would be the best option, industrial considerations are likely to favour the F-35B.

Unfortunately, this awkward choice may be complicated by the troubling possibility that neither F-35 variant will be available for selection if the UK decides to withdraw from the JSF project; the next milestone is signature of the Production, Sustainment and Follow On Development Memorandum of Understanding in late 2006. UK commitment to this phase is by no means certain, particularly in light of an apparent impasse over technology-transfer issues and of the US DOD's cost-saving proposal to terminate the General Electric/Rolls-Royce F136 alternative engine programme. Disagreement over these matters has been both strong and vocal but, hopefully, common-sense will prevail. At stake is participation in an enormous aircraft programme in which much is to be gained by UK industry. Above all, despite unsubtle hints about having a 'Plan B' (options include Rafale-M and a naval version of the Eurofighter Typhoon), the F-35 is the preferred aircraft choice. It would be a tragedy if, following a long period in which the Royal Navy has had an aircraft without a ship, 2006 were to end with a ship without an aircraft.

The launch on 1 February 2006 of the first of class Type 45 destroyer, *Daring*, was a welcome step forward in upgrading the Royal Navy's fragile air-defences. However, the happiness of the occasion was quickly tempered by the fact that she will not enter service until mid-2009 and that the sixth ship is not planned to commission until 2013. In the meantime, both carrier and amphibious task forces, now without Sea Harrier fighter defences, will continue to be vulnerable to air and missile attack. Even more worryingly, the Type 45 programme, cut only as recently as 2004 from 12 to eight ships, is yet again under threat. A proposal for the construction of the seventh and eighth of class has been made by BAE Systems Naval Ships but pressure on equipment spending could result in postponement or even cancellation of these ships on affordability grounds. The uncertainty over this programme is compounded by the absence of any concrete plans for the remainder of the surface fleet following the termination of the Future Surface Combatant programme. In the long term, the broad requirement is to replace the capability currently provided by frigate and Mine CounterMeasures Vessels (MCMV) with an undefined number of interrelated, multirole ships. In the short term, however, the approach is likely to be more prosaic. Current thoughts are to replace the four Type 22 frigates in about 2016 with a ship derived from an existing design. Options include the Type 45 or the Franco-Italian frigate. There is more scope for innovative thinking when it comes to replacing the Type 23s and MCMVs from about 2023. The future vision for MCM, already announced, is to dispense with specialist vessels altogether and to replace their capability with a mixture of modular deployable systems, an organic mine reconnaissance capability and a suite of unmanned underwater vehicles. It remains to be seen whether technology can meet the challenge. There will be many arguments surrounding the remaining fleet units and, not for the first time, a mixture of small and medium-sized ships is likely to be considered.

The Landing Ship Dock (Auxiliary) programme has been troubled by cost and programme overruns and so there was relief when *Mounts Bay* left the Clyde on sea trials on 8 September 2005. She is to enter service in 2006 and is to be followed by the other three ships in 2007. The new ships, based on the Dutch LPD *Rotterdam* design, will complete the transformation of amphibious forces that began with the commissioning of *Ocean* in 1998 and which has seen the introduction of a strategic sealift force and the commissioning of two Albion class LPDs. Logistic support of these and other deployed forces is to be provided by a future auxiliary force to be procured under the Military Afloat Reach and Sustainability (MARS) project. MARS shipping is to provide three core capabilities, wider in scope

than the current inventory of auxiliaries, as follows: bulk consumables, Joint Sea-Based Logistics (JSBL) and forward aviation support. Current assumptions envisage the acquisition of a total of 11 ships comprising five fleet tankers (for delivery in the period 2011-15), three JSBL vessels (for delivery in 2016, 2017 and 2020), two Fleet Solid Support ships (for delivery in 2017 and 2020) and a single Fleet Tanker (Carrier Strike) for delivery in 2021. The transformation of the fleet auxiliary force is every bit as fundamental as that of the remainder of the fleet and the JSBL ships, in particular, will become core units of future operations.

The revitalisation of the Royal Navy's approach to intelligence was a long overdue but welcome step taken during 2005. In a service in which its front-line units and many of its personnel are regularly involved in intelligence collection, both formal and informal, it is not surprising that the Royal Navy's ad hoc approach was considered for many years to serve it well enough. However, the contraction of the officer corps and a perception that work in intelligence was something of a career backwater, had resulted in the serious dilution of naval expertise in intelligence staff appointments and in the quality of support provided to ships at sea. Maritime intelligence is now to be managed by the fleet operations staff whose N2 branch is to provide the focus both for the support of afloat forces and to the Joint Headquarters. N2 appointments are likely in the future to be filled by officers (of any branch) who have opted to specialise in intelligence. The deployment of the 'Aquila 06' group, including *Illustrious* in a maritime strike configuration, to the Indian Ocean during 2006 will have been a good test for the new organisation.

Europe and the Mediterranean
The intention of the French government to proceed with the construction of a second aircraft carrier (PA2) was confirmed when the 2006 defence budget was increased significantly to accommodate what is the largest item in a programme dominated by naval projects. Equipment spending was raised to EUR15.5 billion, an overall increase of some EUR700 million over the previous year. Agreement was subsequently reached on 24 January 2006 for the French Navy to 'buy in' to the UK carrier programme with a view to adapting the UK design to meet French requirements. These include the need for catapults, arrester gear and national weapons and sensors. Facilities for the storage of nuclear weapons are also required. Assuming satisfactory completion of French design work, a contract for the detailed design and build of the ship is expected in late 2006, at about the same time as similar decisions are to be made in the UK. Against a background of sometimes troubled Anglo-French projects, this procurement approach is a victory for common sense; it would have been silly to have pursued two separate national carrier programmes without any level of co-operation.

Progress in other French surface ship programmes has been mixed. While a contract for a first batch of eight FREMM frigates, six of which are to be the ASW variant, was let on 15 November 2005, it is probable that another Franco-Italian collaborative programme, the Horizon class destroyers, is to be curtailed. The first of class, *Forbin*, was launched on 10 March 2005 and *Chevalier Paul* is likely to follow in July 2006. However it looks as if the planned second pair of ships may now be replaced by AAW variants of FREMM, although it is unclear whether these are to be in addition to the 17 ships already announced. The other principal naval programmes are for submarines and their associated systems. Construction of the next-generation Barracuda class attack submarines is expected to start in 2006 when an order for the first three boats of a class of six is expected to be made. Commissioning of the first of class is planned in 2014 while subsequent units are to be completed at 20-month intervals. Meanwhile, the

ESBERN SNARE

6/2005*, B Sullivan / 1154632

same shipyard at Cherbourg is also progressing construction of *Le Terrible*, the fourth boat of the Le Triomphant class. The submarine is planned to be launched in 2008 and is to be the first to be fitted with the new M51 ballistic missile, an underwater test of which is programmed for 2009. The nuclear weapon payload is also to be upgraded when a new warhead, TNO, replaces the current warhead TN 75 from 2015.

In contrast, the budgetary situation in Italy is much less favourable. The Italian Navy has been affected particularly badly by an overall decrease in defence funding and both operating and procurement budgets have been cut. The most obvious immediate effect is likely to be a reduction in Italian commitments to multinational operations but, looking ahead, it is hard to see how all current procurement programmes will survive intact. While construction of the aircraft carrier *Cavour* and of two Horizon class destroyers, *Andrea Doria* and *Caio Duilio*, are unlikely to be affected, the prospects for a second pair of destroyers are not good and other shipbuilding plans are vulnerable, at the very least, to delay and possibly to cancellation. This comes at just the time when real progress is being made in re-shaping Italian amphibious forces. The Army's Serenissima regiment is to be merged with the Navy's San Marco regiment under one command with the aim of building up to a brigade-sized force, with two assault regiments, by 2010. For such a force, additional amphibious shipping is highly desirable and it was probably with the Spanish Strategic Projection Ship in mind that the Italian Navy has launched studies into the procurement of a 20,000 ton helicopter landing ship. Such a vessel might replace *Giuseppe Garibaldi* when she retires. However, this programme may not now attract the necessary funding. It is also far from certain that the Rinascimento (FREMM) frigate programme will survive in its current form. The order for the first batch of ships was restricted to two despite plans for a class of ten. It also remains to be seen whether the expected order for two further Type 212 submarines will materialise. In order to maintain a flotilla of six boats, two new submarines will be required to replace the two older Improved Sauro class in about 2013. In summary, these are difficult times for the Italian Navy which are unlikely to improve in the short-term.

The Royal Netherlands Navy has had to undergo painful contraction over the last few years as its size and shape has been re-cast to undertake a different spectrum of tasks. This has resulted in a reduction in destroyer and frigate strength from 15 in 2000 to a projected six by about 2008. During this period, both the Jacob van Heemskerck air-defence frigates will have been sold to Chile while, of the Karel Doorman class, two each have been sold to Chile and Belgium and two further are to be disposed of. However, all is not gloom and doom. Expeditionary forces are to be augmented by a second LPD, *Johan de Witt*, which is to be commissioned in 2006 and by a multipurpose logistic support ship, to be capable of both replenishment and strategic sealift, which is to enter service in about 2010. Meanwhile, low-intensity military tasks are to be undertaken by four new 90 m patrol vessels equipped with a medium calibre gun and a NH 90 helicopter. The four De Zeven Provincien class air-defence frigates have all entered service and these already powerful ships are to be further upgraded by the addition of Tactical Tomahawk from 2008; installation of a sea-based Theatre Ballistic Missile Defence (TBMD) capability is also under consideration.

Clearly, there is scope for collaboration with the German Navy which has also announced plans to develop a TBMD role for its three similarly-armed Sachsen class frigates. Germany has no current plans to acquire amphibious forces, but its transformation is typified by the reduction of its patrol forces from 30 to ten craft since 2000 and by the acquisition of five 1,600 ton Braunschweig class corvettes, the first of which is to enter service in 2007. These ocean-going vessels are to be augmented by four multipurpose Type 125 frigates, due to enter service from 2012. Upgrade plans for both the Brandenburg class and the older Bremen class frigates have also been announced. Germany's fourth Type 212A submarine, U34, started sea trials on 14 March 2006. Equipped with air-independent propulsion, she is to enter service in 2007. An order for a second batch of two boats, to a modified design, is expected in 2006.

Of navies worldwide, those of Scandinavia have been faced with the need to adapt more than most to the changed strategic situation. Both Norway and Denmark have had to make painful adjustments but some of their decisions are now bearing fruit. The first of a new class of five Norwegian frigates, *Fridtjof Nansen*, arrived in Norway in mid-2006 to usher in a new era of naval operations. More than twice the size of the Oslo class that they replace, they are to have an ASW bias although their SPY-1 radar and Aegis system will be able to make a significant contribution to area air-defence. The Danish Flyvefisken class pioneered a modular approach to warfare whereby ships could be re-roled with relative ease. It is ironic that, just as a similar concept has been adopted for the US Navy Littoral Combat Ships, the class has been reduced to ten ships and a permanent-role policy has now been introduced. This has probably been driven by the cost of maintaining a pool of containerised weapon-systems. Nevertheless, the modular approach has been carried through to the new Flexible Support Ships, *Absalon* and *Esbern Snare*, both of which are to become operational in

2007, and to a new class of three frigates which are to replace the Niels Juel class from 2011. In common with the Norwegian Navy, the new ships are to be much larger and a great deal more capable than their predecessors. In contrast Sweden, which has the largest defence budget of the three nations, has a navy that is hamstrung by its national defence industrial strategy. The Visby class corvettes, much admired for their technology, are just entering service but clearly have been developed with self-defence rather than international operations in mind. Swedish submarines are also held in high esteem, as exemplified by the continuing deployment of *Gotland* to San Diego for ASW training tasks. However, it is questionable whether the now national A-26 (ex-Viking) submarine programme is affordable without international partners.

The participation of the Russian Slava class cruiser *Moskva*, in training with units of NATO's Operation Active Endeavour during February 2006 might have been seen as paving the way towards expansion of Alliance counter-terrorism patrols into the Black Sea. However, US efforts to initiate this new role are opposed, not only by Russia, but more surprisingly by Turkey, a leading NATO member. Whether this is due to sensitivities over the Montreux convention, the treaty that controls the transit of warships through the Turkish Straits, or whether it is more to do with political differences between Turkey and the US is difficult to discern. Turkey can fairly point to the fact that operations in the Black Sea are already conducted by two naval force structures. BLACKSEAFOR comprises all the Black Sea littoral states (Turkey, Russia, Bulgaria, Romania, Georgia and Ukraine) while Operation Black Sea Harmony is conducted by Turkey, mainly in the western part of the sea. However, it does seem odd that a sea that is already bordered by three NATO members (Turkey, Romania and Bulgaria) and may be joined by a fourth (Ukraine) is not policed by an Alliance force.

A Letter of Intent for the procurement of two further Dolphin class submarines for the Israeli Navy was signed on 21 November 2005. The boats are to be to a modified design that is to incorporate air-independent propulsion. Funding is reportedly to be shared between the Israeli, German and US governments. Given that the navy has always been the poor relation of the Israeli services, it is perhaps surprising that the project has enjoyed such broad support within the IDF. The usefulness of submarines for intelligence, surveillance and reconnaissance, and in protecting a vulnerable coastline, is well known but an expansion of the force to five boats has re-ignited speculation that the submarines also have a 'deterrent' role. The Israeli Navy is understandably tight-lipped about the issue and so it can only be surmised that such a weapon, launched from a submarine in the Mediterranean, would require a range of about 300 n miles to strike targets beyond the Syrian border and of about 600 n miles to strike targets in Iran. The surface fleet is also to be augmented and plans for a bespoke Saar 5+ design look to have been overtaken by ambitions to join the US Navy's Littoral Combat Ship programme. A two-year feasibility study has been launched to this effect with a view to two ships entering service in about 2014.

Russia

It has been another year of mixed fortunes for the Russian Navy but with a new Commander-in-Chief, Admiral Vladimir Masorin, at the helm, there is an opportunity to restore confidence, following a series of embarrassing accidents, and to set clear priorities for the future. The Navy has been busy. According to Russian Defence Minister Sergei Ivanov, the Russian Navy performed 11 exercises and 28 long-range deployments during 2005. Perhaps the most significant of these were carried out in the Pacific region with two emerging regional powers. Exercise 'Peace Mission 2005', which took place 18-25 August 2005, was the first major bilateral exercise to be conducted between Russia and China. Naval aspects included missile firings and an offshore blockade followed by an amphibious landing. These were carried out off the Shandong peninsula and on the Weifang ranges. While the exercises were reportedly more of a fire-power demonstration rather than having any tactical realism, they were a clear demonstration of the strong defence ties between the two nations. Later in the year, the Slava class cruiser *Varyag* led participation in another high-profile event, INDRA-2005. This second biennial, bilateral exercise to be conducted with India took place off Vishakapatnam 14-20 October 2005. Attended by Defence Minister Ivanov and Admiral Masorin, the exercises included extensive surface firings, air defence and anti-submarine warfare serials. The Akula class nuclear submarine *Samara* joined in the latter. Later in the three-month deployment, the squadron paid visits to the Indonesian base at Tanjung Priok and to Singapore, the first by the Russian Navy since 1890.

At about the same time as the Russian-Chinese exercise, the annual Northern Fleet exercises took place in the Barents Sea. Led by the carrier *Admiral Kuznetsov* and by the cruiser *Pyotr Velikiy*, the event was attended by President Putin. The culmination of the exercise was the successful firing on 17 August 2005 of a Sineva (modified SS-N-23) ballistic missile from the Delta IV submarine *Ekaterinburg* to a target in Kamchatka. Later in the year, the first submerged test launch of the new Bulava ballistic missile was

SAINT PETERSBURG   6/2005*, A Sheldon-Duplaix / 1154633

became necessary to conduct the emergency rescue of the crew of the Priz class submersible AS-28 off the naval base at Petropavlovsk-Kamchatski. The boat had become ensnared at a depth of some 200 m by underwater netting which was probably part of a seabed detection system. In marked contrast to the attitude of the Russian authorities during the *Kursk* submarine disaster in 2000, foreign help was sought promptly once it was accepted that national equipment was not up to the task. The response by the Royal Navy and US Navy was rapid and although, in the event, it was the British team that spearheaded the rescue (using the Scorpio 45 ROV) on 7 August, the support of the US Navy was a critical factor in effecting a speedy and successful outcome. Both Japan and Australia also made efforts to assist and the benefit of international collaboration on submarine rescue is a key lesson to be drawn from the incident. But the harsh truth is that, as Admiral Popov, Commander Northern Fleet, is quoted as saying "if the country has modern submarines, then it should have effective rescue capabilities".

On a more positive note, Defence Minister Sergei Ivanov announced in November 2005 that Defence spending in 2006 was to increase by 22 per cent. Surprisingly, this represents a small decrease to 2.75 per cent of gross national product, such has been the increase in revenues from higher oil prices. The immediate impact on the navy is likely to be reflected in increased activity levels and the replenishment of weapon stocks; positive effects on the ship and submarine building programme will take time to filter through. Meanwhile, the ballistic missile submarine force enters a period of change and possible down-sizing. It is expected that the first new Project 955 submarines *Yuri Dolgoruky* will be launched in 2006 with a view to becoming operational in about 2008. The second of class, *Alexander Nevsky*, was laid down on 19 March 2004 and the third, *Vladimir Monomakh*, on 19 March 2006. Assuming all three new submarines become operational by 2011 by when all six Delta III boats are likely to have been paid off, the overall force level will be reduced to 12. It will also be necessary to re-deploy some boats to the Pacific Fleet. Launch of the new attack submarine, *Severodvinsk*, is also expected in 2006 when the first of the Lada class diesel-powered submarines, *St Petersburg*, is expected to become operational. More units are expected to follow. Of surface units, the first of a new class of Project 22350 frigates is reported to have been laid down on 31 June 2005 at Severnaya Verf shipyard. Displacing about 8,000 tons, it is the first major surface combatant to be procured for some 15 years. A class of ten is expected. The third Project 20380 class frigate *Boisky* was laid down on 27 July 2005 while the first of two new Buyan class gunboats *Astrakhan* was launched on 7 October 2005 and is to be followed by the second, *Kaspiysk*, in 2006.

conducted from the Typhoon class submarine *Dmitry Donskoy* on 27 September 2005. During April 2005, the Black Sea Fleet was involved in Black Sea Partnership 2005. The exercise involved ships from the Russian and Turkish Navies as well as from Georgia, Bulgaria, Romania, and Ukraine; the so called BLACKSEAFOR having been established to improve interoperability in the region. In the Mediterranean, the principal unit of the Black Sea Fleet, the Slava class cruiser *Moskva*, took part in NATO's Operation Active Endeavour during February 2006. Participation involved the embarkation of a small NATO team on board the ship during its passage from Sevastopol to Messina, the installation of secure communications and an active phase in the company of *Navarra* and *Nottingham*. This short period of preparatory training should lead to more lengthy assignments in the future.

The accident-prone image of the Russian Navy had begun to fade when on 30 July 2005 a demonstration sea-mine drifted on to the flagship of the St Petersburg Navy Day parade, the Krivak class frigate *Neukrotimy*, and exploded near the ship's side. The ship suffered flooding in its engine room and had to be docked for repairs. While this was a relatively minor story of incompetence and damaged pride, the Russian Navy was confronted with a far more serious situation a few days later when, on 4 August 2005, it

Indian Ocean, Gulf and Caspian

The establishment of closer ties between India and the US was the most important development in the Indian Ocean region over the last year. The agreement in March 2006 that the United States would provide nuclear fuel and expertise to India, despite India not being a signatory to the Nuclear Non-Proliferation Treaty, was a historic step, although ratification in both countries may prove to be difficult hurdles. The agreement followed a visit to Washington in July 2005 by the Indian Prime Minister at the end of which he and President Bush resolved "to transform the relationship between their

MYSORE   10/2005*, Ships of the World / 1154630

Indonesia (Tentara Nasional)

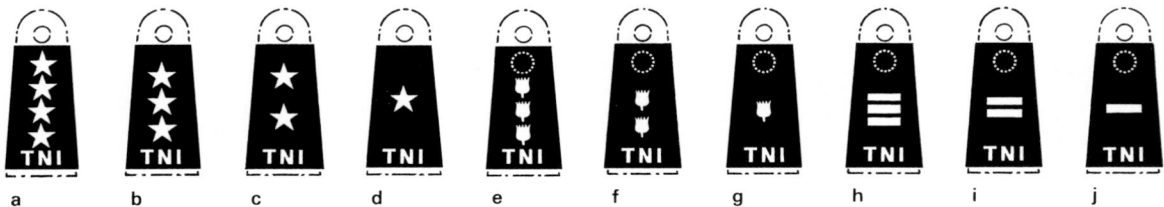

Gold on medium blue.
a: *Laksamana*, Admiral   **b:** *Laksdya*, Vice Admiral   **c:** *Laksda*, Rear Admiral   **d:** *Laksma*, Commodore   **e:** *Kolonel*, Captain
f: *Letnan Kolonel*, Commander   **g:** *Mayor*, Lieutenant Commander   **h:** *Kapten*, Senior Lieutenant   **i:** *Letnan Satu*, Lieutenant
j: *Letnan Dua*, Sub Lieutenant

Iran

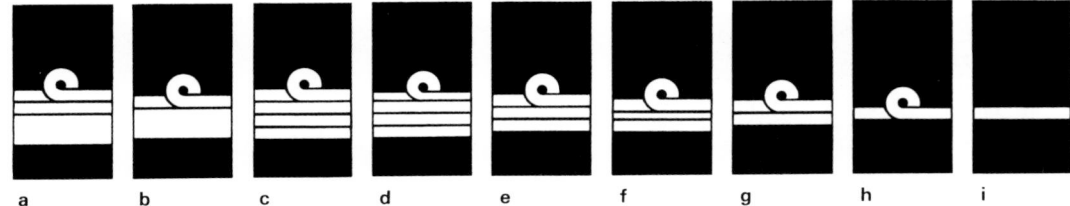

Gold on navy blue.
a: *Daryaban*, Vice Admiral   **b:** *Daryadar*, Rear Admiral   **c:** *Nakhoda Yekom*, Captain   **d:** *Nakhoda Dovom*, Commander
e: *Nakhoda Sevom*, Lieutenant Commander   **f:** *Navsarvan*, Lieutenant   **g:** *Navban Yekom*, Junior Lieutenant   **h:** *Navban Dovom*, Sub Lieutenant
i: *Navban Sevom*, Midshipman.

Iraq

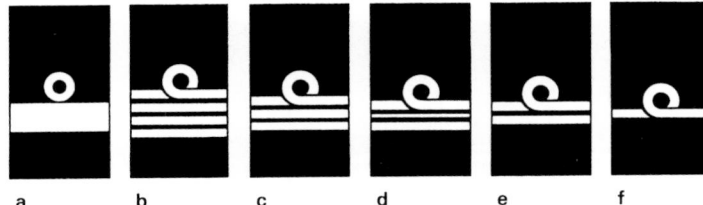

Gold on navy blue.
a: Commodore   **b:** Captain   **c:** Commander   **d:** Lieutenant Commander   **e:** Lieutenant   **f:** Sub Lieutenant

Ireland (An Seirbhis Chabhlaigh)

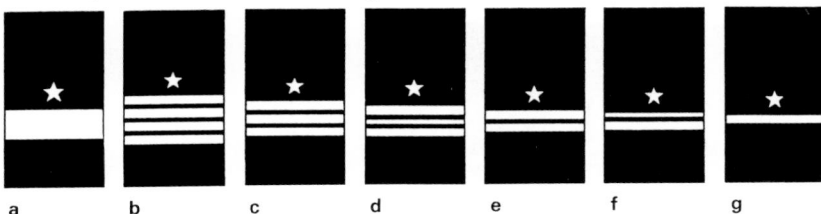

Gold on navy blue.
a: Commodore   **b:** Captain   **c:** Commander   **d:** Lieutenant Commander   **e:** Lieutenant   **f:** Sub Lieutenant   **g:** Ensign

Israel (Heyl Hayam)

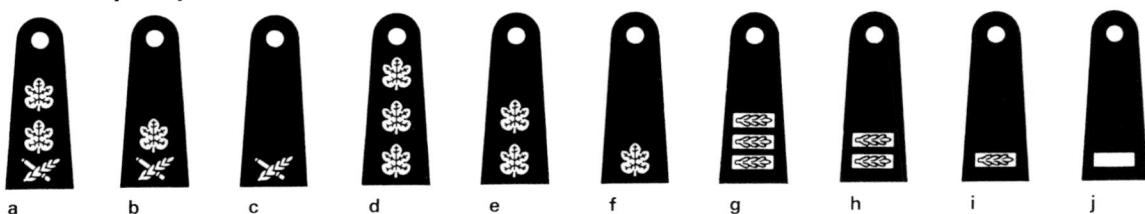

Bright brass or gold generally on dark blue or black. Officer Candidate, white bar.
a: *General (Rav-Aluf)*, Admiral   **b:** *Major General (Aluf)*, Vice Admiral   **c:** *Brigadier (Tat-Aluf)*, Rear Admiral   **d:** *Colonel (Alut-Mishneh)*, Captain
e: *Lieutenant Colonel (Sgan-Aluf)*, Commander   **f:** *Major, (Rav-Seren)*, Lieutenant Commander   **g:** *Captain (Seren)*, Lieutenant
h: *First Lieutenant (Segen)*, Sub Lieutenant   **i:** *Second Lieutenant (Segen-Mishneh)*, Acting Sub Lieutenant   **j:** *Officer Aspirant (Mamak)*, Officer Candidate

Italy (Marina Militare)

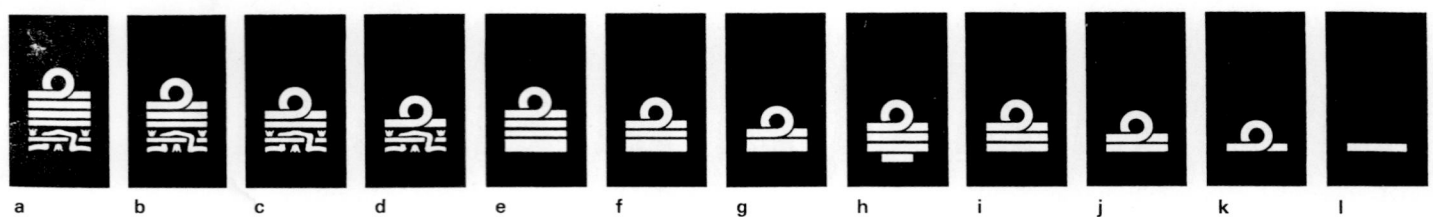

a   b   c   d   e   f   g   h   i   j   k   l

Gold on dark blue.
a: *Ammiraglio di Squadra con Incarichi Speciali,* Admiral Commanding Navy
b: *Ammiraglio di Squadra e Ammiraglio Ispettore Capo,* Admiral and Senior Inspector General (Navy)
c: *Ammiraglio di Divisione e Ammiraglio Ispettore,* Vice Admiral and Inspector General (Navy)   **d:** *Contrammiraglio,* Rear Admiral
e: *Capitano di Vascello,* Captain   **f:** *Capitano di Fregata,* Commander   **g:** *Capitano di Corvetta,* Lieutenant Commander
h: *1° Tenente di Vascello,* First Lieutenant   **i:** *Tenente di Vascello,* Lieutenant   **j:** *Sottotenente di Vascello,* Sub Lieutenant
k: *Guardiamarina,* Acting Sub Lieutenant   **l:** *Aspirante Guardiamarina,* Midshipman

Jamaica (Defence Force Coast Guard)

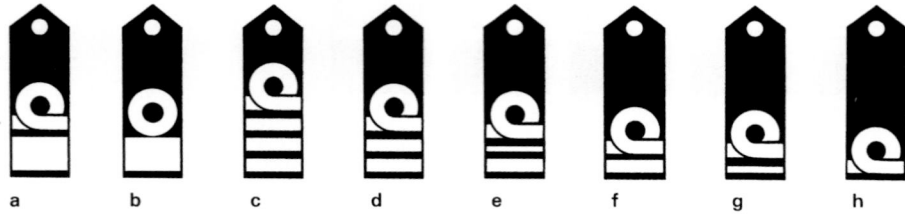

a   b   c   d   e   f   g   h

Gold on black.
a: Rear Admiral   **b:** Commodore   **c:** Captain   **d:** Commander   **e:** Lieutenant Commander   **f:** Lieutenant   **g:** Junior Lieutenant   **h:** Ensign

Japan (Maritime Self Defence Force)

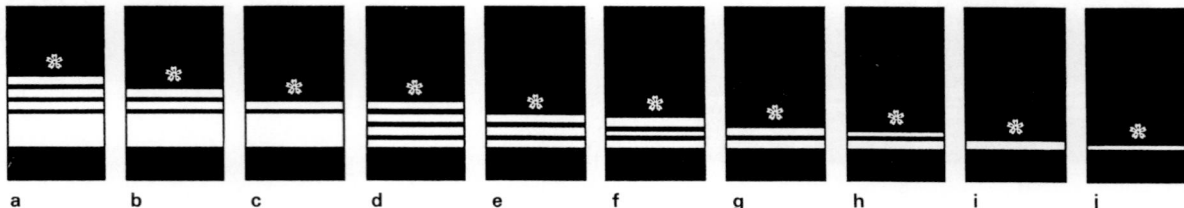

a   b   c   d   e   f   g   h   i   j

Gold on navy blue.
a: Admiral   **b:** Vice Admiral   **c:** Rear Admiral   **d:** Captain   **e:** Commander   **f:** Lieutenant Commander   **g:** Lieutenant   **h:** Sub Lieutenant
i: Acting Sub Lieutenant   **j:** Warrant Officer

Japan (Coast Guard)

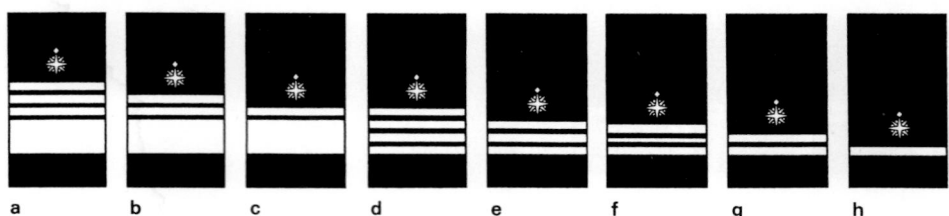

a   b   c   d   e   f   g   h

Gold on navy blue.
a: Commandant   **b:** Vice Commandant   **c:** Superintendent First Grade   **d:** Superintendent Second Grade   **e:** Superintendent Third Grade
f: Officer First Grade   **g:** Officer Second Grade   **h:** Officer Third Grade

Jordan

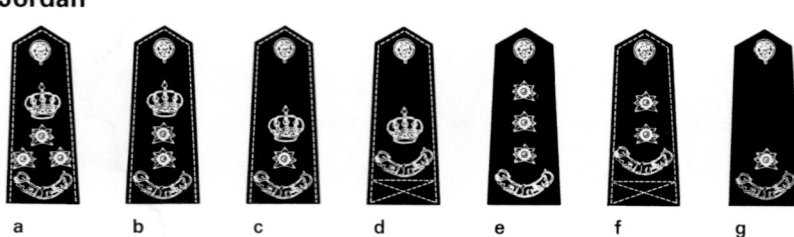

a   b   c   d   e   f   g

Khaki shoulder straps.
a: *'Amid,* Commodore   **b:** *'Aqid,* Captain   **c:** *Muqaddam,* Commander   **d:** *Ra'id,* Lieutenant Commander   **e:** *Naqib,* Lieutenant
f: *Mulazim Awwal,* Sub Lieutenant   **g:** *Mulazim,* Acting Sub Lieutenant

Kenya

a   b   c   d   e   f   g   h   i   j

Gold embroidery on navy blue.
a: *General*, Admiral   **b:** *Lieutenant General*, Vice Admiral   **c:** *Major General*, Rear Admiral   **d:** *Brigadier*, Commodore   **e:** *Colonel*, Captain
f: *Lieutenant Colonel*, Commander   **g:** *Major*, Lieutenant Commander   **h:** *Captain*, Lieutenant   **i:** *Lieutenant*, Sub Lieutenant
j: *Second Lieutenant*, Acting Sub Lieutenant

Korea, North (People's Democratic Republic)

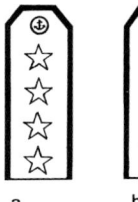        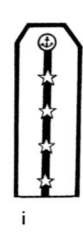   

a   b   c   d   e   f   g   h   i   j   k   l

Black stripes, silver stars on gold.
a: Admiral of the Fleet   **b:** Admiral   **c:** Vice Admiral   **d:** Rear Admiral   **e:** Commodore   **f:** Captain   **g:** Commander   **h:** Lieutenant Commander
i: Senior Lieutenant   **j:** Lieutenant   **k:** Sub Lieutenant   **l:** Acting Sub Lieutenant

Korea, South Republic

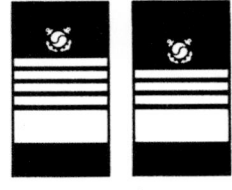          

a   b   c   d   e   f   g   h   i   j   k   l

Gold on navy blue.
a: Admiral of the Fleet (Fleet Admiral)   **b:** Admiral   **c:** Vice Admiral   **d:** Rear Admiral   **e:** Commodore   **f:** Captain   **g:** Commander
h: Lieutenant Commander   **i:** Lieutenant   **j:** Sub Lieutenant   **k:** Acting Sub Lieutenant   **l:** Warrant Officer

Kuwait

a   b   c   d   e   f   g   h   i

Usually gold on tan. Can be gold on dark green or dark blue.
a: *Fariq*, Vice Admiral   **b:** *Liwa'*, Rear Admiral   **c:** *'Amid*, Commodore   **d:** *'Aqid*, Captain   **e:** *Muqaddam*, Commander   **f:** *Ra'id*, Lieutenant Commander
g: *Naqib*, Lieutenant   **h:** *Mulazim Awwal*, Sub Lieutenant   **i:** *Mulazim*, Acting Sub Lieutenant

Latvia (Latvijas Juras Speki)

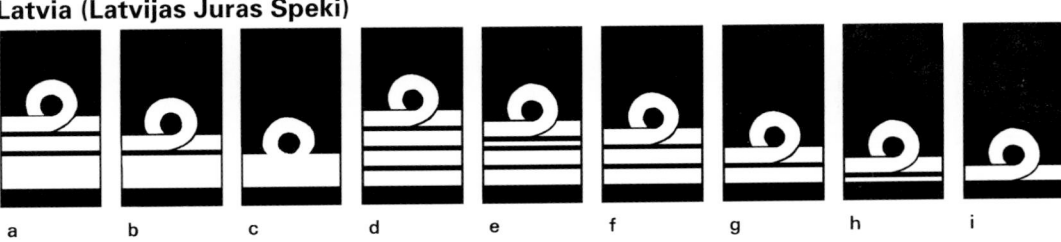

a   b   c   d   e   f   g   h   i

Gold on navy blue.
a: *Vice Admirális*, Vice Admiral   **b:** *Kontra Admirális*, Rear Admiral   **c:** *Flotiles Admirális*, Commodore   **d:** *Jūraskapteinis*, Captain
e: *Kommandkapteinis*, Commander Senior Grade   **f:** *Kommandleitnants*, Commander Junior Grade   **g:** *Kapteinleitnants*, Lieutenant Commander
h: *Virsleitnants*, Lieutenant   **i:** *Leitnants*, Lieutenant Junior Grade

Lebanon

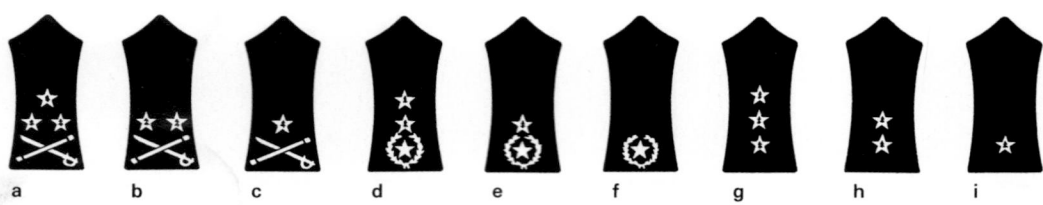

Gold on black.
a: *'Imad*, Vice Admiral   **b:** *Liwa'*, Rear Admiral   **c:** *'Amid*, Commodore   **d:** *'Aqid*, Captain   **e:** *Muqaddam*, Commander   **f:** *Ra'id*, Lieutenant Commander
g: *Ra'is*, Lieutenant   **h:** *Mulazim Awwal*, Sub Lieutenant   **i:** *Mulazim*, Acting Sub Lieutenant

Libya

Gold on navy blue.
a: *'Aqid*, Captain   **b:** *Muqaddam*, Commander   **c:** *Ra'id*, Lieutenant Commander   **d:** *Naqib*, Lieutenant   **e:** *Mulazim Awwal*, Sub Lieutenant
f: *Mulazim*, Acting Sub Lieutenant

Lithuania (Karines Juru Pajegos)

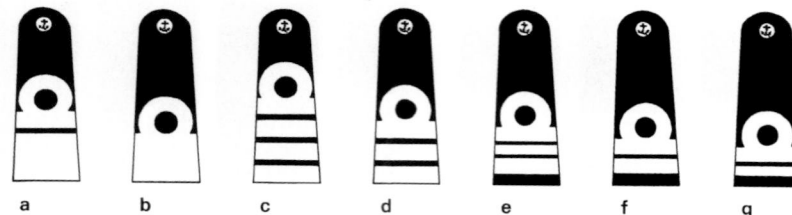

Gold on black.
a: *Kontradmirolas*, Rear Admiral   **b:** *Komandoras*, Commodore   **c:** *Komandoras-Leitenantas*, Captain   **d:** *Jüru Kapitonas*, Commander
e: *Kapitonas-Leitenantas*, Lieutenant Commander   **f:** *Jüru Vyresnysis Leitenantas*, Lieutenant   **g:** *Jüru Leitenantas*, Sub Lieutenant

Madagascar (Malagasy Republic Marine)

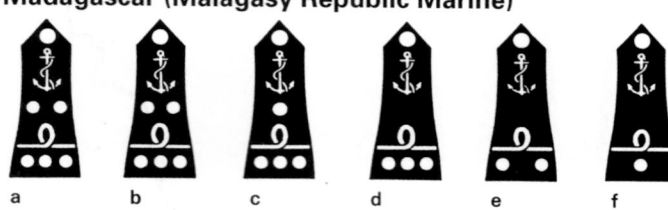

Gold on black. Commander, top two discs silver.
a: *Capitaine de Vaisseau*, Captain   **b:** *Capitaine de Frégate*, Commander   **c:** *Capitaine de Corvette*, Lieutenant Commander
d: *Lieutenant de Vaisseau*, Lieutenant   **e:** *Enseigne de Vaisseau 1re Classe*, Sub Lieutenant   **f:** *Enseigne de Vaisseau 2e Classe*, Acting Sub Lieutenant

Malawi

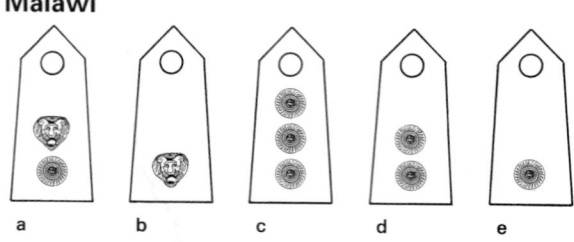

Black on khaki.
a: *Lieutenant Colonel*, Commander   **b:** *Major*, Lieutenant Commander   **c:** *Captain*, Lieutenant   **d:** *Lieutenant*, Sub Lieutenant
e: *2nd Lieutenant*, Acting Sub Lieutenant

Malaysia (Tentera Laut Dira Ja)

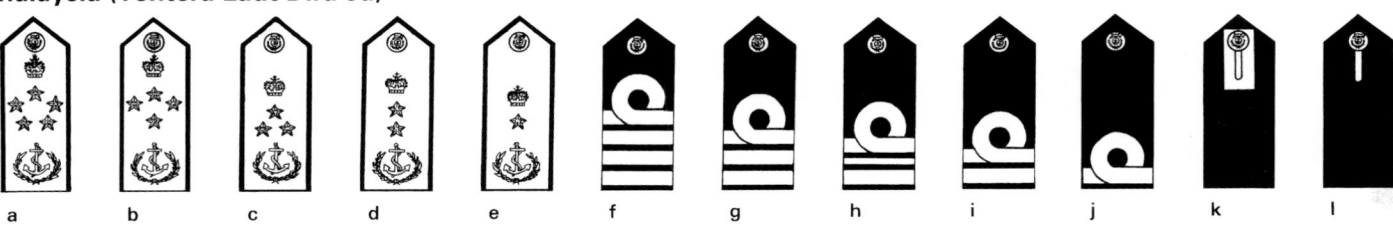

Vice Admiral to Commodore, silver on gold. Remainder gold on navy blue, plus midshipman's white patch.
a: *Laksamana Armada*, Admiral of the Fleet   **b:** *Laksamana*, Admiral   **c:** *Laksamana Madya*, Vice Admiral   **d:** *Laksamana Muda*, Rear Admiral
e: *Laksamana Pertama*, Commodore   **f:** *Kapeten*, Captain   **g:** *Komander*, Commander   **h:** *Leftenan Komander*, Lieutenant Commander
i: *Leftenan*, Lieutenant   **j:** *Leftenan Madya and Leftenan Muda*, Sub Lieutenant and Acting Sub Lieutenant   **k:** *Kadet Kanan*, Midshipman   **l:** *Kadet*, Cadet

Maldives

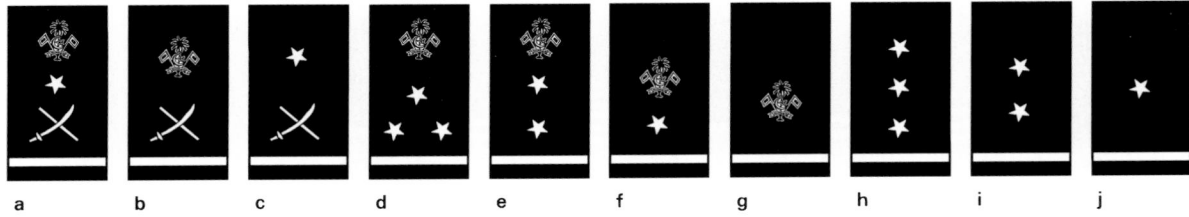

Yellow on light olive.
a: General   **b:** Lieutenant General   **c:** Major General   **d:** Brigadier   **e:** Colonel   **f:** Lieutenant Colonel   **g:** Major   **h:** Captain   **i:** First Lieutenant
j: Lieutenant

Malta (Maritime Squadron, AFM)

White on dark blue.
a: *Major*, Lieutenant Commander   **b:** *Captain*, Lieutenant   **c:** *Lieutenant*, Sub Lieutenant   **d:** *2nd Lieutenant*, Acting Sub Lieutenant

Mauritania (Marine Mauritanienne)

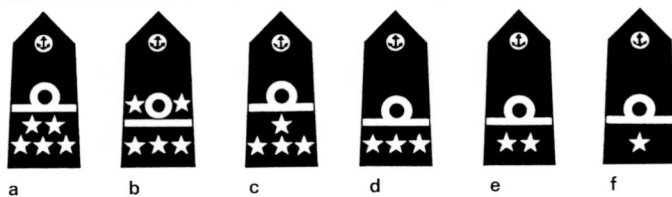

Gold on blue or green. Exception is two silver stars above lace for commander.
a: *Colonel*, Captain   **b:** *Lieutenant Colonel*, Commander   **c:** *Major*, Lieutenant Commander   **d:** *Captain*, Lieutenant   **e:** *Lieutenant*, Sub Lieutenant
f: *2nd Lieutenant*, Acting Sub Lieutenant

Mexico (Marina Nacional)

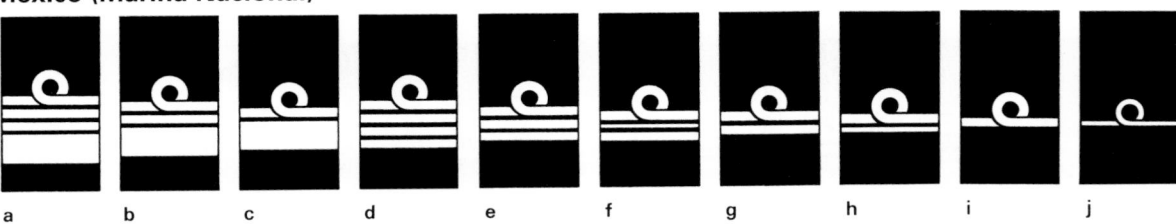

Gold on navy blue.
a: *Almirante*, Admiral   **b:** *Vicealmirante*, Vice Admiral   **c:** *Contraalmirante*, Rear Admiral   **d:** *Capitán de Navío*, Captain
e: *Capitán de Fragata*, Commander   **f:** *Capitán de Corbeta*, Lieutenant Commander   **g:** *Teniente de Navío*, Lieutenant
h: *Teniente de Fragata*, Sub Lieutenant   **i:** *Teniente de Corbeta*, Acting Sub Lieutenant   **j:** *Guardiamarina*, Midshipman

Morocco (Marine Royale Marocaine)

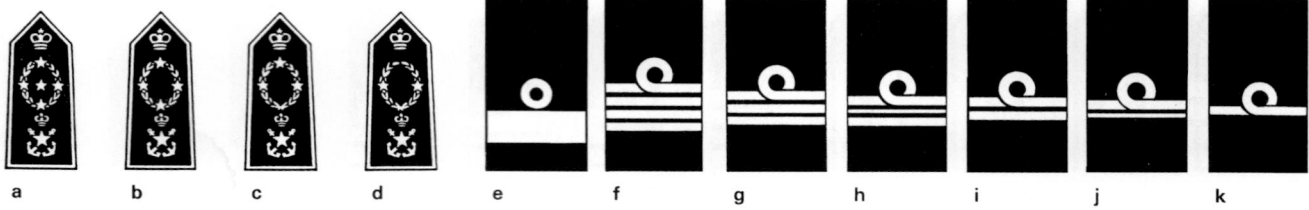

a b c d e f g h i j k

Gold on black. Flag ranks silver stars.
a: *Amiral*, Admiral of the Fleet **b:** *Amiral d'Escadre*, Admiral **c:** *Vice Amiral*, Vice Admiral **d:** *Contre Amiral*, Rear Admiral
e: *Capitaine de Vaisseau Major*, Commodore **f:** *Capitaine de Vaisseau*, Captain **g:** *Capitaine de Frégate*, Commander
h: *Capitaine de Corvette*, Lieutenant Commander **i:** *Lieutenant de Vaisseau*, Lieutenant **j:** *Enseigne de Vaisseau 1re Classe*, Sub Lieutenant
k: *Enseigne de Vaisseau 2e Classe*, Acting Sub Lieutenant

Mozambique (Marina Moçambique)

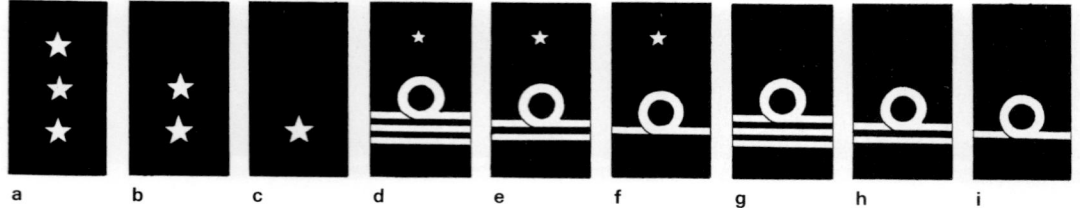

a b c d e f g h i

Gold insignia on dark blue slip-ons.
a: *Almirante*, Admiral **b:** *Vice-Almirante*, Vice Admiral **c:** *Contra-Almirante*, Rear Admiral **d:** *Capitão-de-Mar-e-Guerra*, Captain
e: *Capitão-de-Fragate*, Commander **f:** *Capitão-Tenente, Lieutenant Commander* **g:** *Primerio-Tenente*,Lieutenant **h:** *Segundo-Tenente*, Sub Lieutenant
i: *Guarda-Marinha*, Midshipman

Myanmar (Tatmadaw Yay)

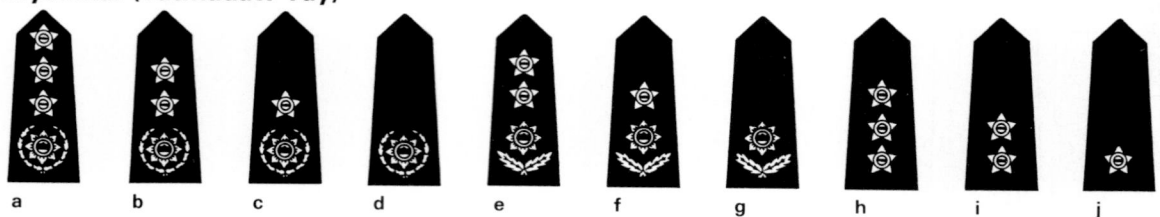

a b c d e f g h i j

Gold on dark blue. All three services have same rank insignia based on the army.
a: Admiral **b:** Vice Admiral **c:** Rear Admiral **d:** Commodore **e:** Captain **f:** Commander **g:** Lieutenant Commander **h:** Lieutenant
i: Sub Lieutenant **j:** Acting Sub Lieutenant

Netherlands

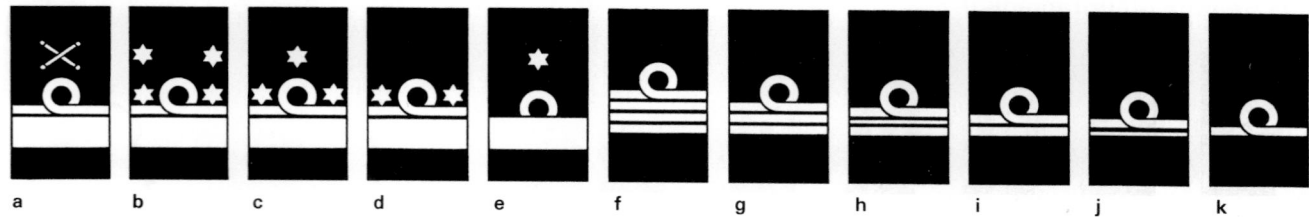

a b c d e f g h i j k

Gold on navy blue. Stars and crossed batons, silver.
a: *Admiraal*, Admiral of the Fleet **b:** *Luitenant-Admiraal*, Admiral **c:** *Vice-Admiraal*, Vice Admiral **d:** *Schout-bij-nacht*, Rear Admiral
e: *Commandeur*, Commodore **f:** *Kapitein ter zee*, Captain **g:** *Kapitein-luitenant ter zee*, Commander
h: *Luitenant ter zee der eerste klasse*, Lieutenant Commander **i:** *Luitenant ter zee der tweede klasse oudste categorie*, Lieutenant
j: *Luitenant ter zee der tweede klasse*, Sub Lieutenant **k:** *Luitenant ter zee der derde klasse*, Acting Sub Lieutenant

New Zealand

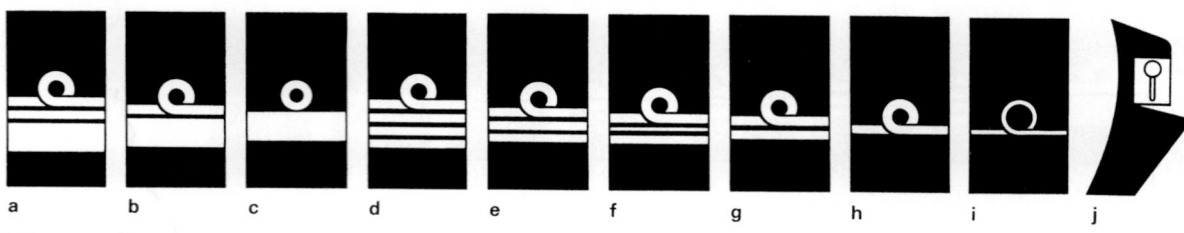

a b c d e f g h i j

Gold on navy blue.
a: Vice Admiral **b:** Rear Admiral **c:** Commodore **d:** Captain **e:** Commander **f:** Lieutenant Commander **g:** Lieutenant **h:** Sub Lieutenant **i:** Ensign
j: Midshipman

Nicaragua (la Fuerza Naval)

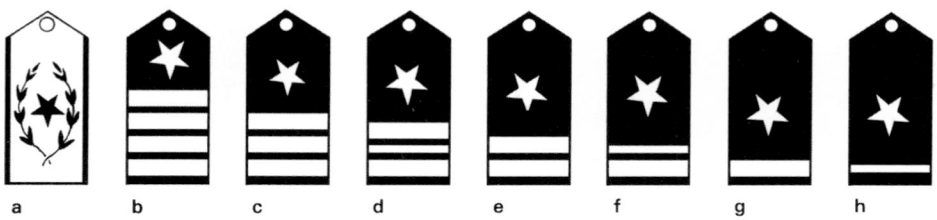

a   b   c   d   e   f   g   h

Gold button and star. Green wreath on gold brocade, navy blue edges. Gold lace and stars on navy blue.
a: *Contraalmirante*, Rear Admiral **b:** *Capitán de Navío*, Captain **c:** *Capitán de Fragata*, Commander **d:** *Capitán de Corbeta*, Lieutenant Commander
e: *Teniente de Navío*, Lieutenant **f:** *Teniente de Fragata*, Sub Lieutenant **g:** *Teniente de Corbeta*, Acting Sub Lieutenant **h:** *Alférez*, Midshipman

Nigeria

a   b   c   d   e   f   g   h   i   j   k

Gold on navy blue. Eagles, red. Stars and crossed battons, silver.
a: Admiral of the Fleet **b:** Admiral **c:** Vice Admiral **d:** Rear Admiral **e:** *Brigadier*, Commodore **f:** *Colonel*, Captain
g: *Lieutenant Colonel*, Commander **h:** *Major*, Lieutenant Commander **i:** *Captain*, Lieutenant **j:** *Lieutenant*, Sub Lieutenant
k: *Second Lieutenant*, Midshipman

Norway

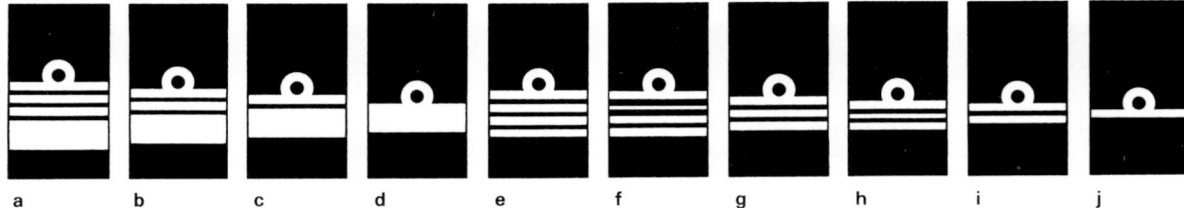

a   b   c   d   e   f   g   h   i   j

Gold on navy blue. The Coast Guard is manned by naval personnel on secondment. They wear a distinguishing shoulder insignia on the upper left sleeve.
a: *Admiral*, Admiral **b:** *Viseadmiral*, Vice Admiral **c:** *Kontreadmiral*, Rear Admiral **d:** *Flaggkommandør*, Commodore **e:** *Kommandør*, Captain
f: *Kommandørkaptein*, Commander Senior Grade **g:** *Orlogskaptein*, Commander **h:** *Kapteinløytnant*, Lieutenant Commander **i:** *Løytnant*, Lieutenant
j: *Fenrik*, Sub Lieutenant

Oman

a   b   c   d   e   f   g   h   i

Gold on navy blue. White stripe, midshipman.
a: *Liwaa Bahry*, Rear Admiral **b:** *'Amid Bahry*, Commodore **c:** *'Aqid Bahry*, Captain **d:** *Muqaddam Bahry*, Commander
e: *Ra'id Bahry*, Lieutenant Commander **f:** *Naqib Bahry*, Lieutenant **g:** *Mulazim Awwal Bahry*, Sub Lieutenant
h: *Mulazim Tanin Bahry*, Acting Sub Lieutenant **i:** *Dabit Murashshah*, Midshipman

Pakistan

a   b   c   d   e   f   g   h   i   j

Gold on dark blue shoulder boards. Flag ranks: gold shoulder boards edged blue, silver devices.
a: Admiral **b:** Vice Admiral **c:** Rear Admiral **d:** Commodore **e:** Captain **f:** Commander **g:** Lieutenant Commander **h:** Lieutenant
i: Sub Lieutenant **j:** Midshipman

Panama (Servicio Maritime Nacional)

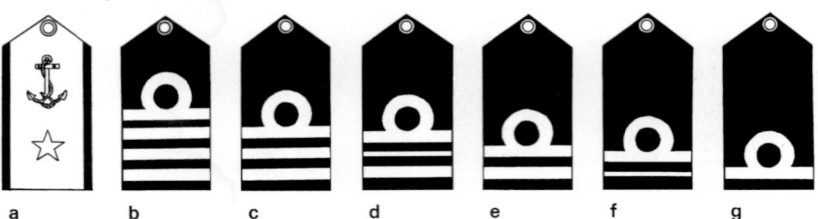

a   b   c   d   e   f   g

Gold on navy blue.
a: *Director General*, Rear Admiral   **b:** *Capitán de Navío*, Captain   **c:** *Capitán de Fragata*, Commander   **d:** *Capitán de Corbeta*, Lieutenant Commander
e: *Teniente de Navío*, Lieutenant   **f:** *Teniente de Fragata*, Lieutenant (JG)   **g:** *Alférez de Navío*, Sub Lieutenant

Paraguay (Armada Nacional)

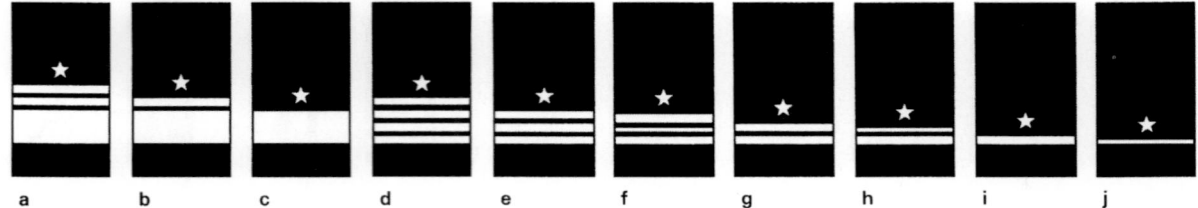

a   b   c   d   e   f   g   h   i   j

Gold on navy blue.
a: *Vicealmirante*, Vice Admiral   **b:** *Contralmirante*, Rear Admiral   **c:** *Contraalmirante Medio Inferior*, Rear Admiral Lower Half (Commodore)
d: *Capitán de Navío*, Captain   **e:** *Capitán de Fragata*, Commander   **f:** *Capitán de Corbeta*, Lieutenant Commander   **g:** *Teniente de Navío*, Lieutenant
h: *Teniente de Fragata*, Sub Lieutenant   **i:** *Teniente de Corbeta*, Acting Sub Lieutenant   **j:** *Guardiamarinha*, Midshipman

Peru (Armada Perúana)

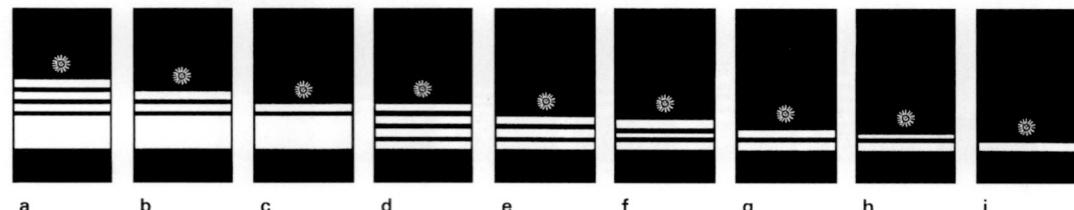

a   b   c   d   e   f   g   h   i

Gold on navy blue.
a: *Almirante*, Admiral   **b:** *Vicealmirante*, Vice Admiral   **c:** *Contraalmirante*, Rear Admiral   **d:** *Capitán de Navío*, Captain
e: *Capitán de Fragata*, Commander   **f:** *Capitán de Corbeta*, Lieutenant Commander   **g:** *Teniente Primero*, Lieutenant
h: *Teniente Segundo*, Sub Lieutenant   **i:** *Alférez de Fragata*, Acting Sub Lieutenant

Philippines

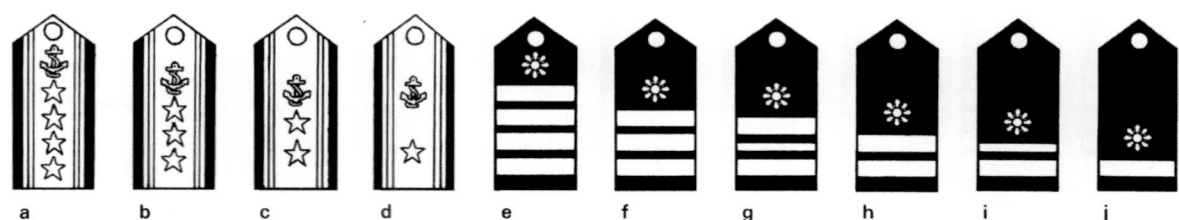

a   b   c   d   e   f   g   h   i   j

Gold on black. Commodore, dark blue edged, silver devices on gold.
a: Admiral   **b:** Vice Admiral   **c:** Rear Admiral   **d:** Commodore   **e:** Captain   **f:** Commander   **g:** Lieutenant Commander   **h:** Lieutenant
i: Lieutenant Junior Grade   **j:** Ensign

Philippines (Coast Guard)

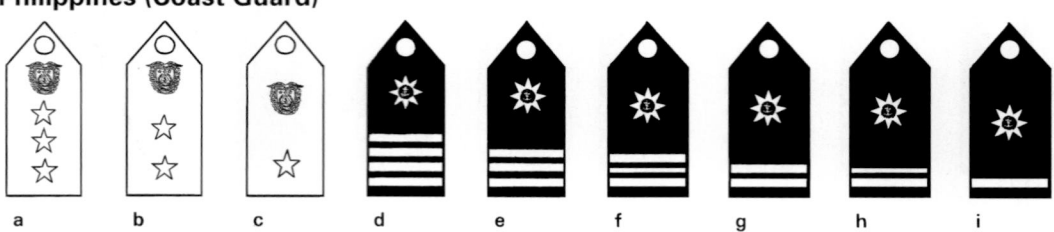

a   b   c   d   e   f   g   h   i

a: Vice Admiral   **b:** Rear Admiral   **c:** Commodore   **d:** Captain   **e:** Commander   **f:** Lieutenant Commander   **g:** Lieutenant Senior Grade
h: Lieutenant Junior Grade   **i:** Ensign

Poland (Marynarka Wojenna)

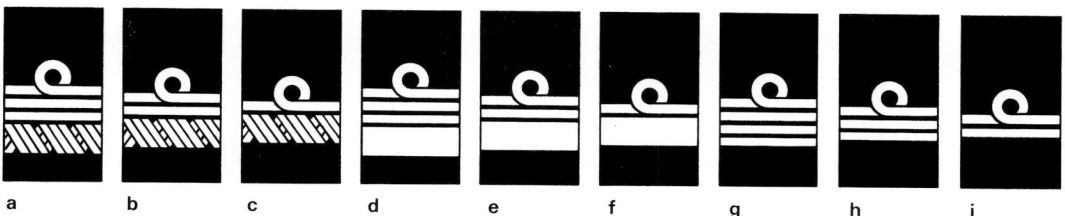

a   b   c   d   e   f   g   h   i

Gold on dark blue. The Sea Department of the Border Guard (MOSG) use the same insignia up to the rank of Rear Admiral.
a: *Admiral*, Admiral   **b:** *Vice-Admiral*, Vice Admiral   **c:** *Kontradmiral*, Rear Admiral   **d:** *Komandor*, Captain   **e:** *Komandor Porucznik*, Commander
f: *Komandor Podporucznik*, Lieutenant Commander   **g:** *Kapitan Marynarki*, Lieutenant   **h:** *Porucznik Marynarki*, Sub Lieutenant
i: *Podporucznik Marynarki*, Acting Sub Lieutenant

Portugal (Marinha Portuguesa)

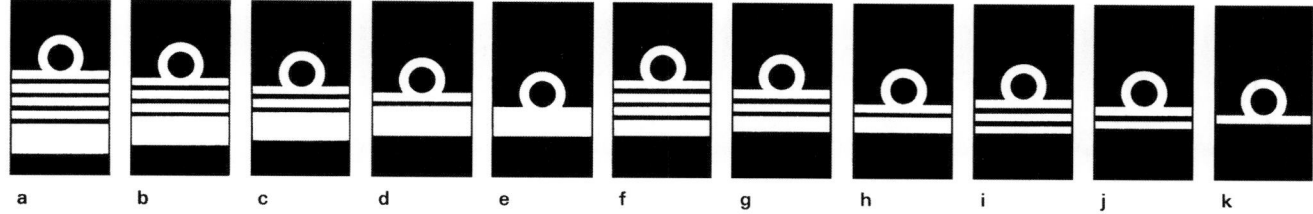

a   b   c   d   e   f   g   h   i   j   k

Gold on navy blue.
a: *Almirante da Armada*, Admiral of the Fleet   **b:** *Almirante*, Admiral   **c:** *Vice-Almirante*, Vice Admiral   **d:** *Contra-Almirante*, Rear Admiral
e: *Comodoro*, Commodore   **f:** *Capitão-de-Mar-e-Guerra*, Captain   **g:** *Capitão-de-Fragata*, Commander   **h:** *Capitão-Tenente*, Lieutenant Commander
i: *Primeiro-Tenente*, Lieutenant   **j:** *Segundo-Tenente*, Sub Lieutenant   **k:** *Guarda-Marinha-ou-Subtenente*, Midshipman or Acting Sub Lieutenant

Qatar

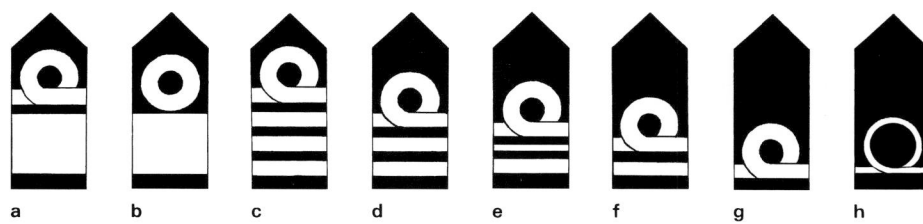

a   b   c   d   e   f   g   h

Gold bullion lace on navy blue.
a: Rear Admiral   **b:** Commodore   **c:** Captain   **d:** Commander   **e:** Lieutenant Commander   **f:** Lieutenant   **g:** Sub Lieutenant   **h:** Acting Sub Lieutenant

Romania (Marină Română)

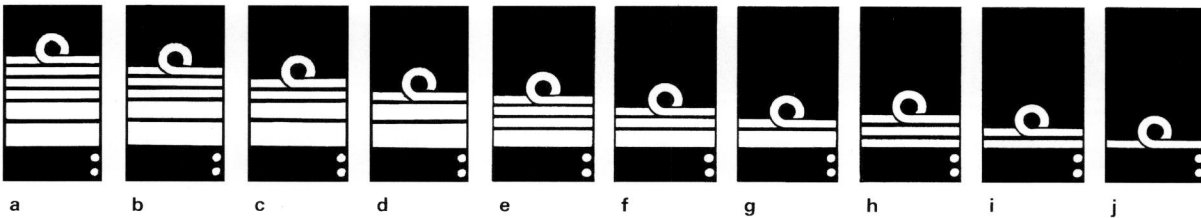

a   b   c   d   e   f   g   h   i   j

Gold on dark blue.
a: *Amiral*, Admiral   **b:** *Viceamiral*, Vice Admiral   **c:** *Contraamiral*, Rear Admiral   **d:** *Contraamiral de Flotilă*, Commodore   **e:** *Comandor*, Captain
f: *Căpitan Commander*, Commander   **g:** *Locotenent Comandor*, Lieutenant Commander   **h:** *Căpitan*, Lieutenant   **i:** *Locotenent*, Sub Lieutenant
j: *Aspirant*, Midshipman

Russian Federation (Rosiyskiy Voennomorsky Flot) (Seaman and Marine Engineer Officers)

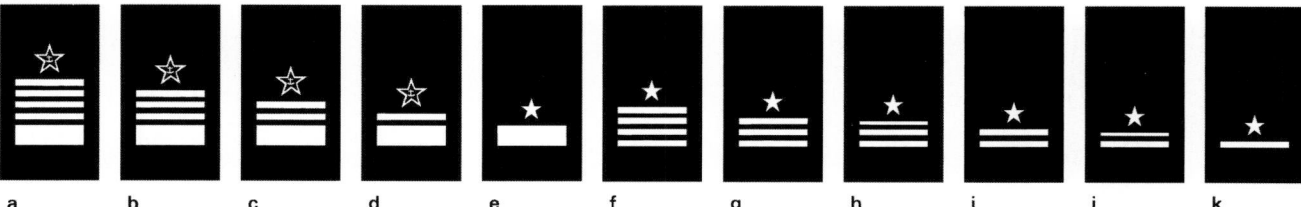

a   b   c   d   e   f   g   h   i   j   k

Gold on black. Not worn by aviation and specialist officers.
a: *Admiral Flota*, Admiral of the Fleet   **b:** *Admiral*, Admiral   **c:** *Vitse-Admiral*, Vice Admiral   **d:** *Kontr-Admiral*, Rear Admiral
e: *Kapitan Pervogo Ranga*, Captain   **f:** *Kapitan Vtorogo Ranga*, Commander   **g:** *Kapitan Tretyego Ranga*, Lieutenant Commander
h: *Kapitan-Leytenant*, Lieutenant   **i:** *Starshiy Leytenant*, Junior Lieutenant   **j:** *Leytenant*, Sub Lieutenant   **k:** *Mladshiy Leytenant*, Acting Sub Lieutenant

RANKS AND INSIGNIA OF THE WORLD'S NAVIES

Russian Federation (Aviation and specialist officers, shoulder insignia)

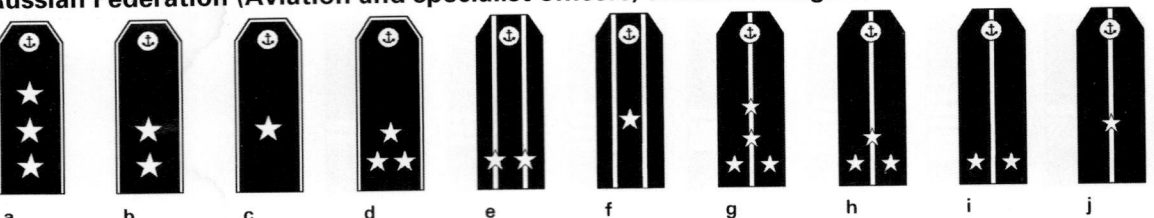

a: *Colonel General*, Admiral   **b:** *Lieutenant General*, Vice Admiral   **c:** *Major General*, Rear Admiral   **d:** *Colonel*, Captain
e: *Lieutenant Colonel*, Commander   **f:** *Major*, Lieutenant Commander   **g:** *Captain*, Lieutenant   **h:** *Senior Lieutenant*, Junior Lieutenant
i: *Lieutenant*, Sub Lieutenant   **j:** *Junior Lieutenant*, Acting Sub Lieutenant

Saudi Arabia (Royal Saudi Naval Forces)

Gold buttons, sabres and Arabic titles, light green stars and crowns on black.
a: *Lieutenant General (Navy)*, Vice Admiral   **b:** *Major General (Navy)*, Rear Admiral   **c:** *Brigadier General (Navy)*, Commodore   **d:** *Colonel (Navy)*, Captain
e: *Lieutenant Colonel (Navy)*, Commander   **f:** *Major (Navy)*, Lieutenant Commander   **g:** *Captain (Navy)*, Lieutenant   **h:** *Lieutenant (Navy)*, Sub Lieutenant
i: *Second Lieutenant (Navy)*, Acting Sub Lieutenant

Senegal (Marine Sénégalaise)

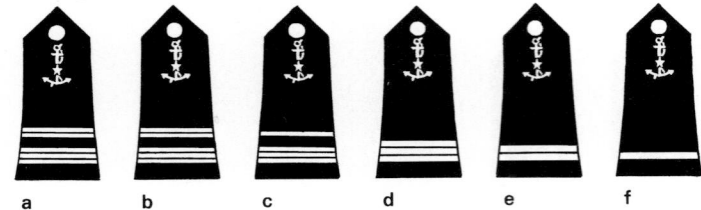

Gold on black. Captain, three gold and two silver stripes.
a: *Contre-Amiral*, Rear Admiral   **b:** *Capitaine de Vaisseau*, Captain   **c:** *Capitaine de Frégate*, Commander   **d:** *Capitaine de Corvette*, Lieutenant Commander
e: *Lieutenant de Vaisseau*, Lieutenant   **f:** *Enseigne de Vaisseau*, Sub Lieutenant

Serbia and Montenegro

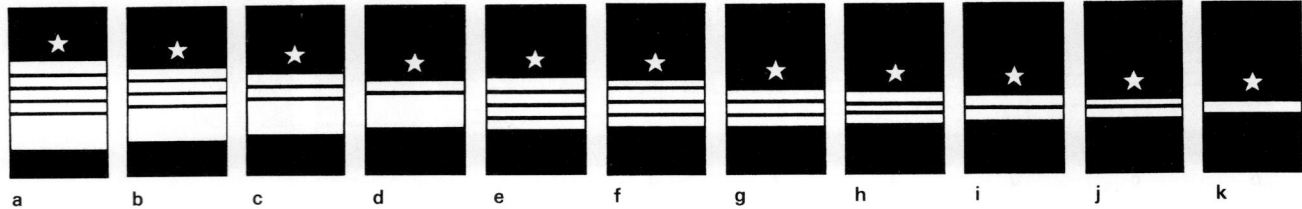

Gold on dark blue.
a: *Admiral Flote*, Admiral of the Fleet   **b:** *Admiral*, Admiral   **c:** *Viceadmiral*, Vice Admiral   **d:** *Kontraadmiral*, Rear Admiral
e: *Kapetan Bojnog Broda*, Captain   **f:** *Kapetan Fregate*, Commander   **g:** *Kapetan Korvete*, Lieutenant Commander
h: *Poručnik Bojnog Broda*, Lieutenant (Senior)   **i:** *Poručnik Fregate*, Lieutenant   **j:** *Poručnik Korvete*, Sub Lieutenant   **k:** *Potporučnik*, Acting Sub Lieutenant

Seychelles

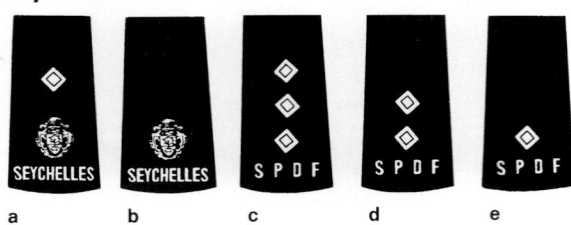

Gold embroidered on dark blue.
a: *Lieutenant Colonel*, Commander   **b:** *Major*, Lieutenant Commander   **c:** *Captain*, Lieutenant   **d:** *Lieutenant*, Sub Lieutenant
e: *Second Lieutenant*, Acting Sub Lieutenant

Singapore (Republic of Singapore Navy)

a　b　c　d　e　f　g　h　i

Gold on navy blue. Senior officers only have naval titles.
a: Vice Admiral　**b:** Rear Admiral　**c:** Commodore　**d:** Colonel　**e:** Lieutenant Colonel　**f:** Major　**g:** Captain　**h:** Lieutenant　**i:** Second Lieutenant

Slovenia (Slovenska Mornarical)

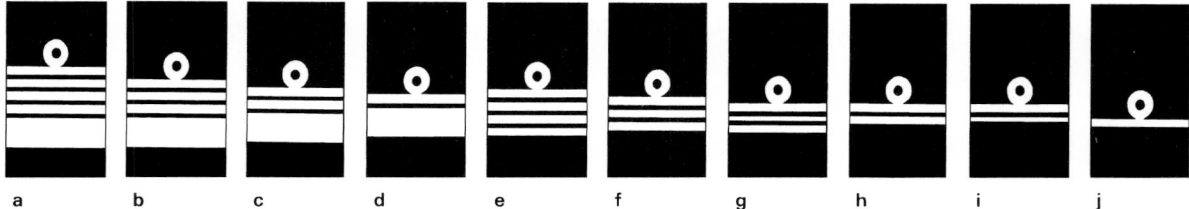

a　b　c　d　e　f　g　h　i　j

Gold on dark blue.
a: *Admiral*, Admiral of the Fleet　**b:** *Admiral*, Admiral　**c:** *Viceadmiral*, Vice Admiral　**d:** *Kapitan*, Commodore　**e:** *Kapitan Bojne Ladje*, Captain
f: *Kapitan Fregate*, Commander　**g:** *Kapitan Korvete*, Lieutenant Commander　**h:** *Poročnik Fregate*, Lieutenant　**i:** *Poročnik Korvete*, Sub Lieutenant
j: *Podporočnik*, Acting Sub Lieutenant

South Africa

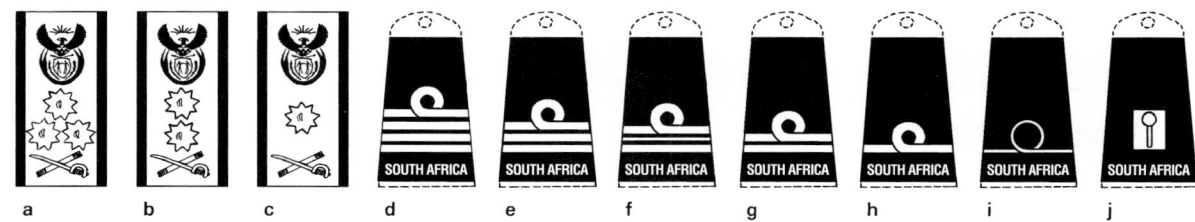

a　b　c　d　e　f　g　h　i　j

Gold on navy blue. Flag Officers gold brocade with blue piping and silver devices.
a: Vice Admiral　**b:** Rear Admiral　**c:** Rear Admiral (JG)　**d:** Captain　**e:** Commander　**f:** Lieutenant Commander　**g:** Lieutenant　**h:** Sub Lieutenant
i: Ensign　**j:** Midshipman

Spain (Armada Española)

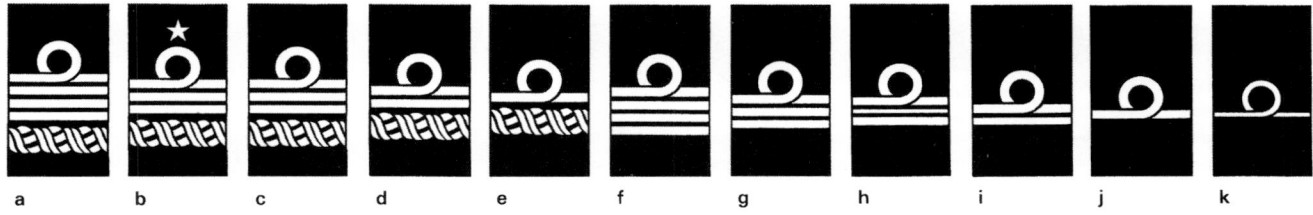

a　b　c　d　e　f　g　h　i　j　k

Gold on navy blue. Rank of Capitán General held by the monarch only. Rank of Almirante General held by Chief of Naval Staff and Chief of Defence Staff when post held by a naval officer.
a: *Capitán General a la Armada*, Captain General　**b:** *Almirante General*, Admiral　**c:** *Almirante*, Admiral　**d:** *Vicealmirante*, Vice Admiral
e: *Contraalmirante*, Rear Admiral　**f:** *Capitán de Navío*, Captain　**g:** *Capitán de Fragata*, Commander　**h:** *Capitán de Corbeta*, Lieutenant Commander
i: *Teniente de Navío*, Lieutenant　**j:** *Alférez de Navío*, Sub Lieutenant　**k:** *Alférez de Fragata*, Acting Sub Lieutenant

Sri Lanka

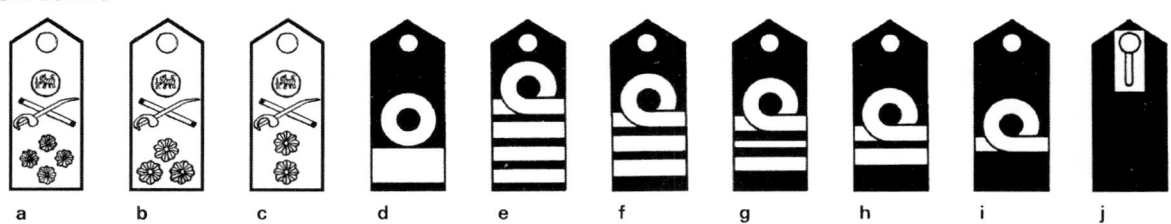

a　b　c　d　e　f　g　h　i　j

Gold on navy blue.
a: Admiral　**b:** Vice Admiral　**c:** Rear Admiral　**d:** Commodore　**e:** Captain　**f:** Commander　**g:** Lieutenant Commander　**h:** Lieutenant
i: Sub Lieutenant　**j:** Midshipman

Sudan

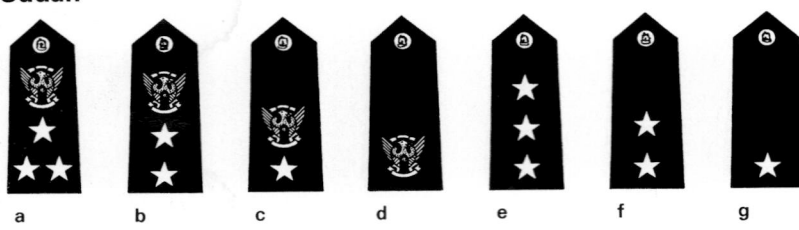

Gold on black.
a: *'Amid*, Commodore **b:** *'Aqid*, Captain **c:** *Muqaddam*, Commander **d:** *Ra'id Lieutenant*, Commander **e:** *Naqib*, Lieutenant
f: *Mulazim Awwal*, Sub Lieutenant **g:** *Mulazim Thani*, Acting Sub Lieutenant

Suriname

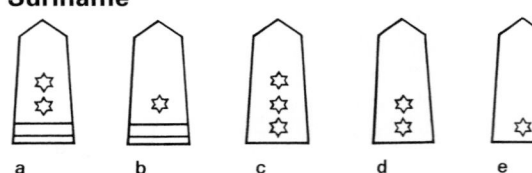

Gold on white.
a: *Kapitein Ter Zee*, Commander **b:** *Kapitein-Luitenant Ter Zee*, Lieutenant Commander **c:** *Luitenant Ter Zee Der 1e Klasse*, Lieutenant
d: *Luitenant Ter Zee Der 2e Klasse Oudste Categorie*, Sub Lieutenant **e:** *Luitenant Ter Zee Der 3e Klasse*, Acting Sub Lieutenant

Sweden (Svenska Marinen)

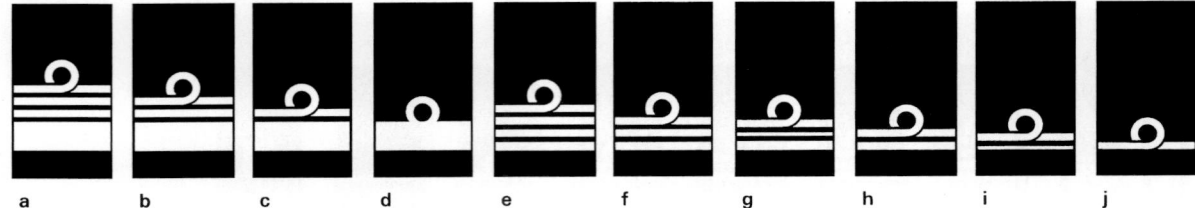

Gold on dark blue.
a: *Amiral*, Admiral **b:** *Viceamiral*, Vice Admiral **c:** *Konteramiral*, Rear Admiral **d:** *Kommendör av 1. gr*, Commodore **e:** *Kommendör*, Captain
f: *Kommendörkapten*, Commander **g:** *Örlogskapten*, Lieutenant Commander **h:** *Kapten, Lieutenant* **i:** *Löjnant*, Sub Lieutenant
j: *Fänrik*, Acting Sub Lieutenant

Sweden Coast Guard (Kustbevakning)

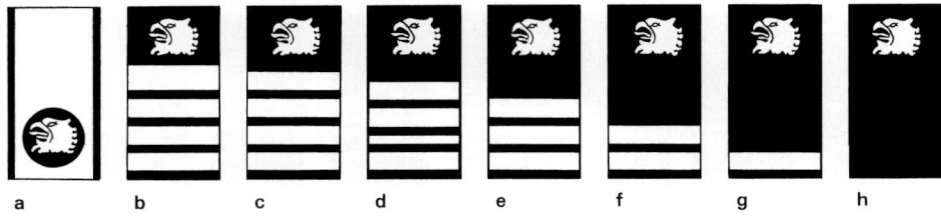

Gold on navy blue.
a: *Generaldirektör*, Rear Admiral **b:** *Kustbevakningsdirektör*, Commodore
c: *Kustbevakningsöverinspectör Överingenjör*, Captain and Senior Engineer Officer **d:** *Förste Kustbevakningsinspektör*, Commander
e: *Kustbevakningsinspektör*, Lieutenant Commander **f:** *Kustbevakningassistent*, Lieutenant **g:** *Kustuppsyningsman*, Sub Lieutenant
h: *Kustbevakningsaspirant*, Midshipman

Syria

Gold on black.
a: *Fariq*, Vice-Admiral **b:** *Liwa*, Rear Admiral **c:** *Amid*, Commodor **d:** *'Aqid*, Captain **e:** *Muqaddam*, Commander **f:** *Ra'id*, Lieutenant Commander
g: *Naqib*, Lieutenant **h:** *Mulazim Awwal*, Sub Lieutenant **i:** *Mulazim*, Acting Sub Lieutenant

Taiwan (Republic of China)

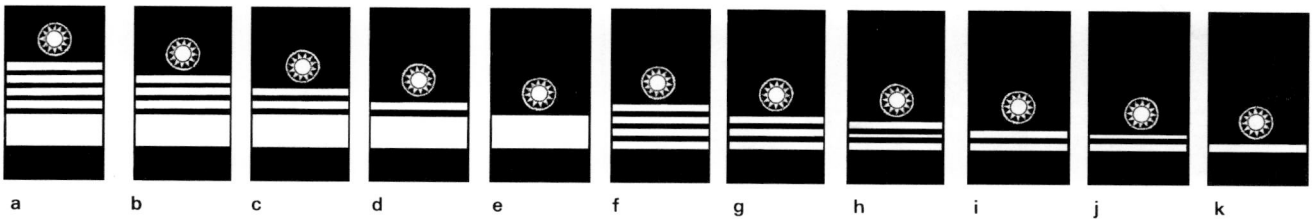

Gold on navy blue.
a: Admiral of the Fleet   **b:** Admiral   **c:** Vice Admiral   **d:** Rear Admiral   **e:** Commodore   **f:** Captain   **g:** Commander   **h:** Lieutenant Commander
i: Lieutenant   **j:** Lieutenant JG (II)   **k:** Sub Lieutenant

Tanzania

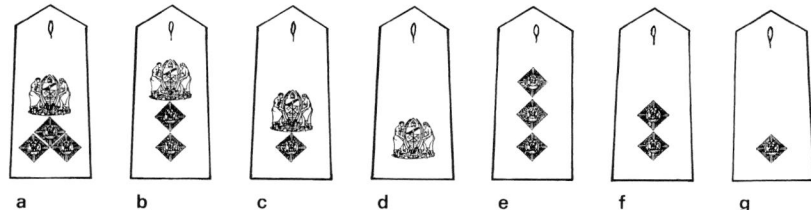

Gold coloured devices on light tan shoulder straps.
a: *Brigadier Head of the Navy*, Commodore   **b:** *Colonel*, Captain   **c:** *Lieutenant Colonel*, Commander   **d:** *Major*, Lieutenant Commander
e: *Captain*, Lieutenant   **f:** *Lieutenant*, Sub Lieutenant   **g:** *Second Lieutenant*, Acting Sub Lieutenant

Thailand (Royal Thai Navy)

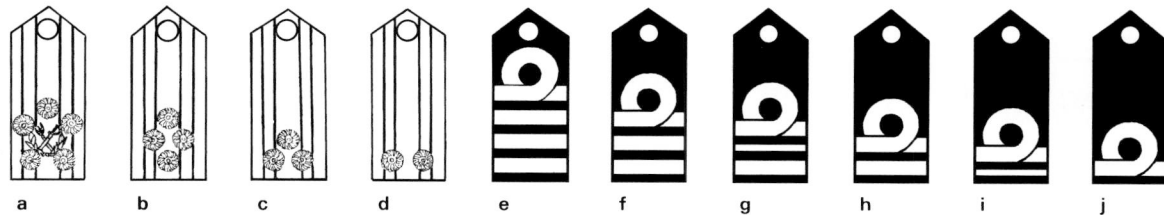

Admirals wear gold brocaded shoulder straps with silver insignia. Gold lace and buttons on black.
a: Admiral of the Fleet   **b:** Admiral   **c:** Vice Admiral   **d:** Rear Admiral   **e:** Captain   **f:** Commander   **g:** Lieutenant Commander   **h:** Lieutenant
i: Sub Lieutenant   **j:** Acting Sub Lieutenant

Togo (Marine du Togo)

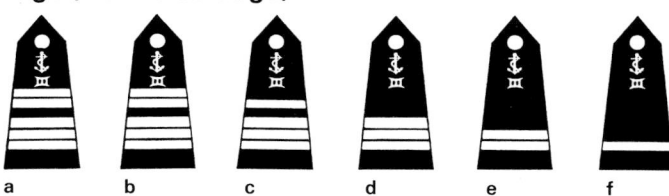

Gold on black. Commander, three gold two silver stripes.
a: *Capitaine de Vaisseau*, Captain   **b:** *Capitaine de Frégate*, Commander   **c:** *Capitaine de Corvette*, Lieutenant Commander
d: *Lieutenant de Vaisseau*, Lieutenant   **e:** *Enseigne de Vaisseau 1re Classe*, Sub Lieutenant   **f:** *Enseigne de Vaisseau 2e Classe*, Acting Sub Lieutenant

Tonga

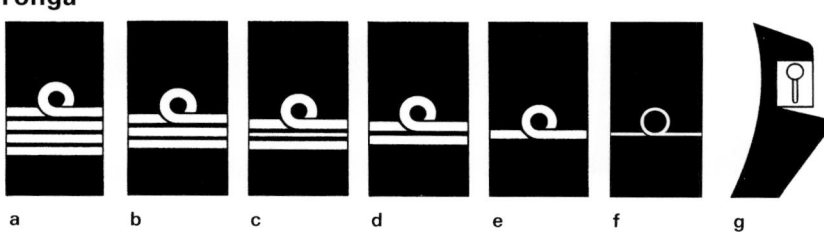

Gold on navy blue.
a: Captain   **b:** Commander   **c:** Lieutenant Commander   **d:** Lieutenant   **e:** Sub Lieutenant   **f:** Ensign   **g:** Midshipman

Trinidad and Tobago Coast Guard

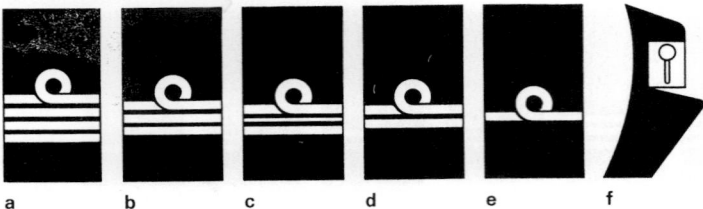

Gold on navy blue.
a: Captain   **b:** Commander   **c:** Lieutenant Commander   **d:** Lieutenant   **e:** Sub Lieutenant   **f:** Midshipman

Tunisia

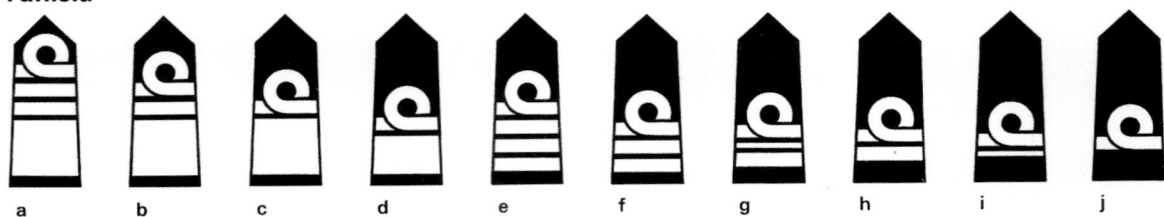

Gold on navy blue. Silver on navy blue (Lieutenants and below).
a: *Vice-Amiral d'Escadre*, Admiral   **b:** *Vice-Amiral*, Vice Admiral   **c:** *Contre-Amiral*, Rear Admiral   **d:** *Capitaine de Vaisseau Major*, Commodore
e: *Capitaine de Vaisseau*, Captain   **f:** *Capitaine de Frégate*, Commander   **g:** *Capitaine de Corvette*, Lieutenant Commander
h: *Lieutenant de Vaisseau*, Lieutenant   **i:** *Enseigne de Vaisseau 1ere Classe*, Sub Lieutenant   **j:** *Enseigne de Vaisseau 2eme Classe*, Acting Sub Lieutenant

Turkey (Türk Deniz Kuvvetleri)

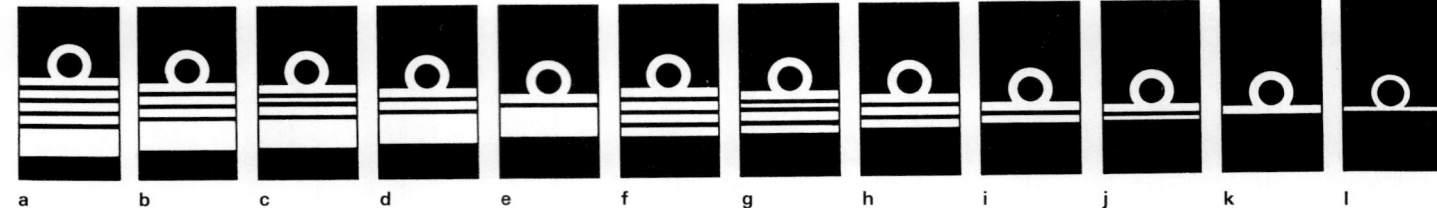

Gold on black. The Coast Guard is manned by naval personnel on secondment. They wear a distinguishing shoulder title 'Sahil Guvenlik Kiligi' at the top of each sleeve.
a: *Büyükamiral*, Admiral of the Fleet   **b:** *Oramiral*, Admiral   **c:** *Koramiral*, Vice Admiral   **d:** *Tümamiral*, Rear Admiral   **e:** *Tugamiral*, Commodore
f: *Albay*, Captain   **g:** *Yarbay*, Commander   **h:** *Binbasi*, Lieutenant Commander   **i:** *Yüzbasi*, Lieutenant   **j:** *Üstegmen*, Sub Lieutenant
k: *Tegmen*, Acting Sub Lieutenant   **l:** *Astegmen*, Warrant Officer

Ukraine

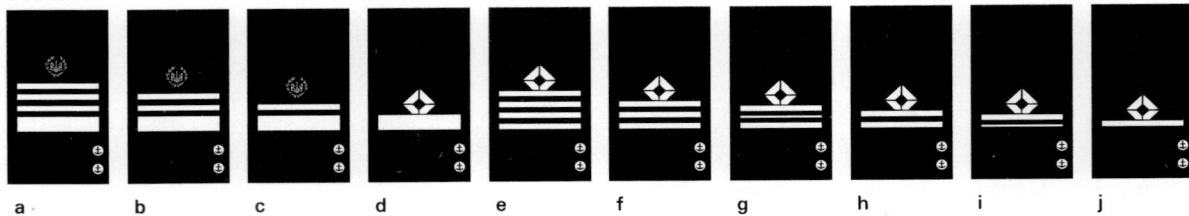

Gold on black.
a: *Admiral*, Admiral   **b:** *Vitse-Admiral*, Vice Admiral   **c:** *Kontr-Admiral*, Rear Admiral   **d:** *Kapitan Pervogo Ranga*, Captain
e: *Kapitan Vtorogo Ranga*, Commander   **f:** *Kapitan Tretyego Ranga*, Lieutenant Commander   **g:** *Kapitan-Leytenant*, Lieutenant
h: *Starshiy-Leytenant*, Junior Lieutenant   **i:** *Leytenant*, Sub Lieutenant   **j:** *Mladshiy-Leytenant*, Acting Sub Lieutenant

United Arab Emirates

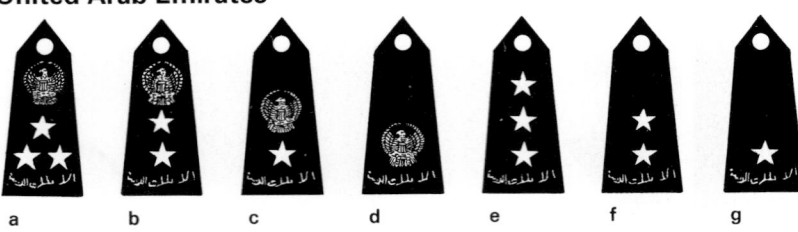

Gold on black.
a: *'Amid*, Commodore   **b:** *'Aqid*, Captain   **c:** *Muqaddam*, Commander   **d:** *Ra'id*, Lieutenant Commander   **e:** *Naqib*, Lieutenant
f: *Mulazim Awwal*, Sub Lieutenant   **g:** *Mulazim Thani*, Acting Sub Lieutenant

United Kingdom

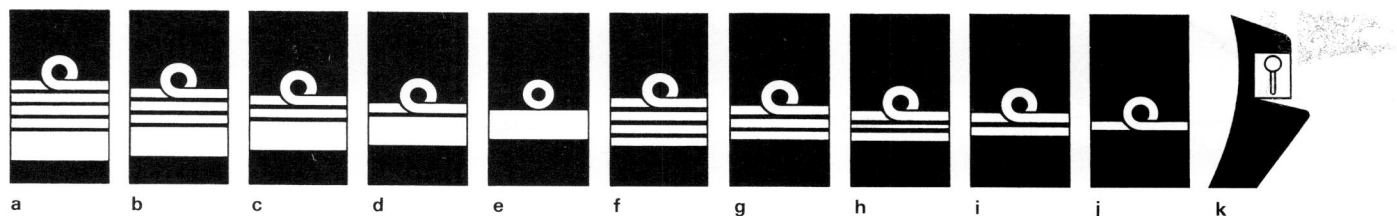

a b c d e f g h i j k

Gold on navy blue. Rank **a**: This rank is now in abeyance in peacetime.
a: Admiral of the Fleet   **b**: Admiral   **c**: Vice Admiral   **d**: Rear Admiral   **e**: Commodore   **f**: Captain   **g**: Commander   **h**: Lieutenant Commander
i: Lieutenant   **j**: Sub Lieutenant   **k**: Midshipman

United Kingdom (Royal Fleet Auxiliary)

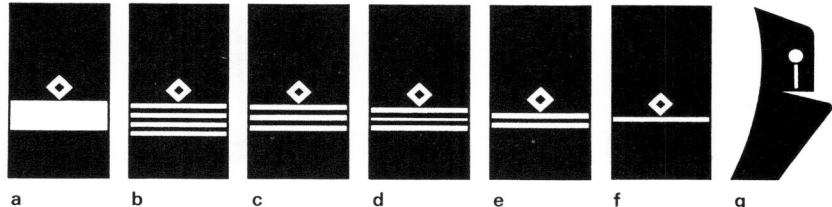

a b c d e f g

Gold on navy blue.
a: Commodore   **b**: Captain   **c**: Chief Officer   **d**: First Officer   **e**: 2nd Officer   **f**: 3rd Officer   **g**: Deck Cadet

United States

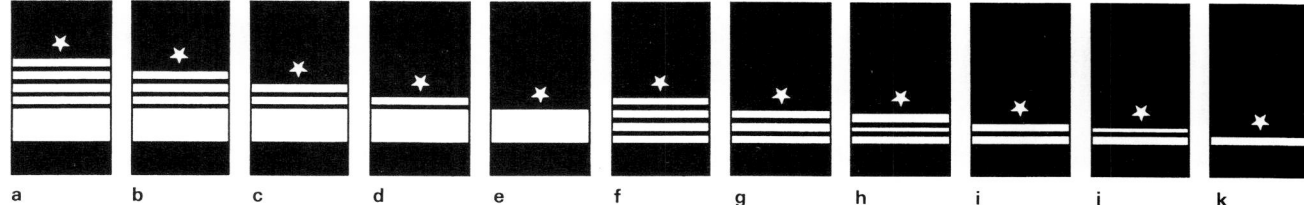

a b c d e f g h i j k

Gold on navy blue.
a: *Fleet Admiral*, Admiral of the Fleet   **b**: *Admiral*, Admiral   **c**: *Vice Admiral*, Vice Admiral   **d**: *Rear Admiral (Upper Half)*, Rear Admiral
e: *Rear Admiral (Lower Half)*, Commodore   **f**: *Captain*, Captain   **g**: *Commander*, Commander   **h**: *Lieutenant Commander*, Lieutenant Commander
i: *Lieutenant*, Lieutenant   **j**: *Lieutenant Junior Grade*, Sub Lieutenant   **k**: *Ensign*, Acting Sub Lieutenant

United States Coast Guard

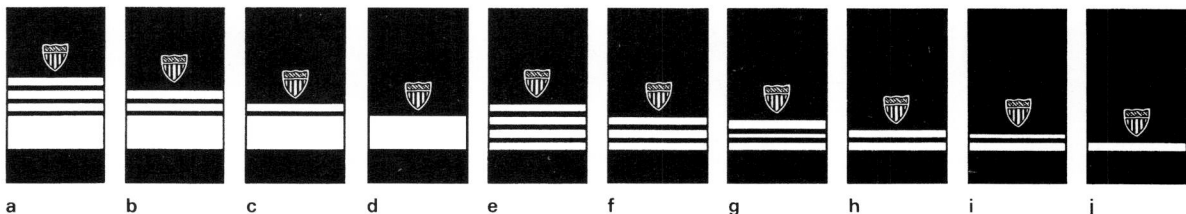

a b c d e f g h i j

Gold on navy blue.
a: *Admiral*, Admiral   **b**: *Vice Admiral*, Vice Admiral   **c**: *Rear Admiral*, Rear Admiral   **d**: *Rear Admiral Lower Half*, Commodore   **e**: *Captain*, Captain
f: *Commander*, Commander   **g**: *Lieutenant Commander*, Lieutenant Commander   **h**: *Lieutenant*, Lieutenant   **i**: *Lieutenant Junior Grade*, Sub Lieutenant
j: *Ensign*, Acting Sub Lieutenant

Uruguay (Armada Nacional)

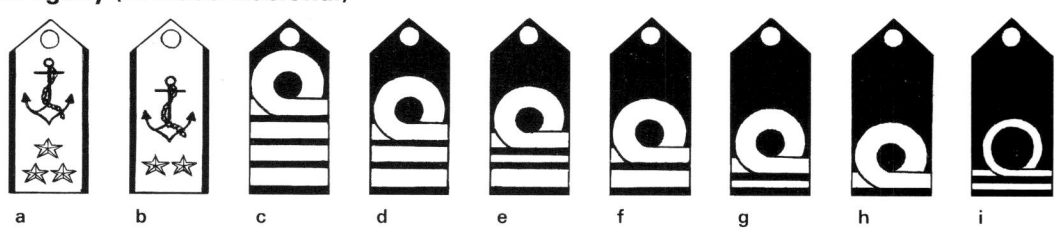

a b c d e f g h i

Gold on navy blue. Flag Officer's insignia in silver on gold brocade
a: *Vicealmirante*, Vice Admiral   **b**: *Contraalmirante*, Rear Admiral   **c**: *Capitán de Navío*, Captain   **d**: *Capitán de Fragata*, Commander
e: *Capitán de Corbeta*, Lieutenant Commander   **f**: *Teniente de Navío*, Lieutenant   **g**: *Alférez de Navío*, Sub Lieutenant
h: *Alférez de Fragata*, Acting Sub Lieutenant   **i**: *Guardiamarina*, Midshipman

Venezuela (Armada de Venezuela)

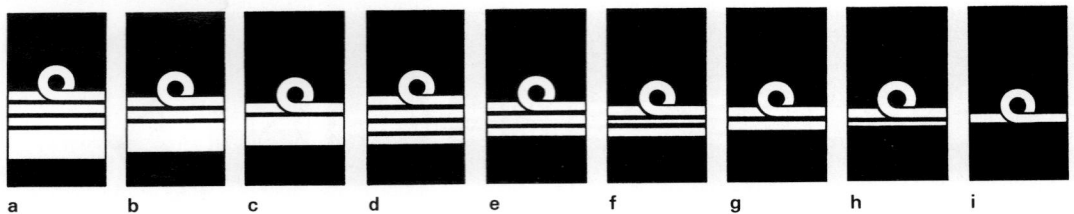

a   b   c   d   e   f   g   h   i

Gold on navy blue.
a: *Almirante*, Admiral   **b:** *Vicealmirante*, Vice Admiral   **c:** *Contraalmirante*, Rear Admiral   **d:** *Capitán de Navío*, Captain
e: *Capitán de Fragata*, Commander   **f:** *Capitán de Corbeta*, Lieutenant Commander   **g:** *Teniente de Navío*, Lieutenant
h: *Teniente de Fragata*, Sub Lieutenant   **i:** *Alférez de Navío*, Acting Sub Lieutenant

Vietnam

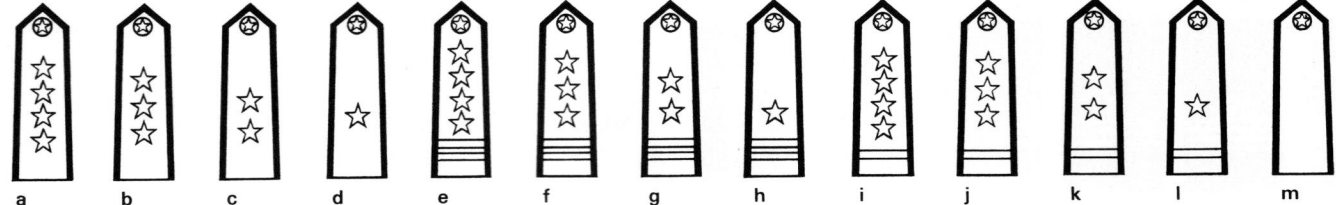

a   b   c   d   e   f   g   h   i   j   k   l   m

Gold shoulder straps. Generals, edged red gold stars. Remainder, silver stars and lace.
a: *Senior General*, Admiral of the Fleet   **b:** *Colonel General*, Admiral   **c:** *Lieutenant General*, Vice Admiral   **d:** *Major General*, Rear Admiral
e: *Senior Colonel*, Commodore   **f:** *Colonel*, Captain   **g:** *Lieutenant Colonel*, Commander   **h:** *Major*, Lieutenant Commander
i: *Senior Captain*, Senior Lieutenant   **j:** *Captain*, Lieutenant   **k:** *Senior Lieutenant*, Sub Lieutenant   **l:** *2nd Lieutenant*, Acting Sub Lieutenant
m: *Student Officer*, Midshipman

Virgin Islands (UK) (Police - Marine Branch)

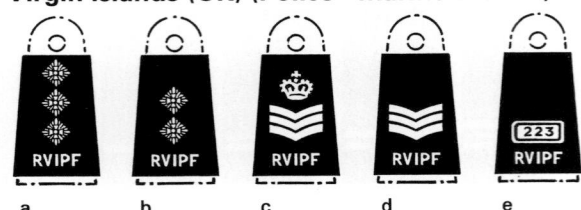

a   b   c   d   e

Silver on black.
a: Chief Inspector   **b:** Inspector   **c:** Station Sergeant   **d:** Sergeant   **e:** Constable

Yemen

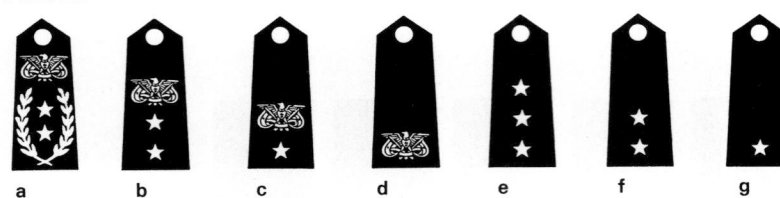

a   b   c   d   e   f   g

Gold on black.
a: *'Amid*, Commodore   **b:** *'Aqid*, Captain   **c:** *Muqaddam*, Commander   **d:** *Ra'id*, Lieutenant Commander   **e:** *Naqib*, Lieutenant
f: *Mulazim Awwal*, Sub Lieutenant   **g:** *Mulazim Thani*, Acting Sub Lieutenant

Pennant list of major surface ships

Type abbreviations

Notes: Designations specific to one nationality are followed by Country abbreviations.
The prefix W denotes a vessel of the Coastguard Service. Suffixes to type indicators are as follows:
F denotes a vessel capable of speeds in excess of 35 kt.
G denotes a vessel with a force guided missile system, including SAM, USM and SUM, usually with a range exceeding 20 miles.
H denotes a vessel equipped with a helicopter, or with a platform for operating one.
J denotes an air cushion or surface effect design.
K denotes a vessel equipped with hydrofoils.
M denotes a Combatant vessel with a close-range guided missile system.

Submarines

AGSS	Submarine, auxiliary, nuclear-powered (USA)
DSRV	Deep submergence rescue vehicle
DSV	Deep submergence vehicle
SDV	Swimmer delivery vehicle
SNA	Submarine, attack, nuclear-powered (Fra)
SNLE	Ballistic missile nuclear-powered submarine (Fra)
SS	Submarine, general
SSA(N)	Submarine, auxiliary, nuclear-powered
SSA	Submarine with ASW capability (Jpn)
SSB	Ballistic missile submarine (CPR)
SSBN	Ballistic missile nuclear-powered submarine
SSC	Submarine, coastal
SSGN	Submarine, surface-to-surface missile, nuclear-powered
SSK	Patrol submarine with ASW capability
SSW	Submarine, midget
SSN	Submarine, attack, nuclear-powered

Aircraft Carriers

CV (M)	Aircraft carrier (guided missile system)
CVH (G)	Helicopter carrier (guided missile system)
CVN (M)	Aircraft carrier, nuclear-powered guided missile system)
PAN	Aircraft carrier, nuclear-powered (Fra)

Cruisers

CG	Guided missile cruiser
CGH	Guided missile cruiser with helicopter
CGN	Guided missile cruiser, nuclear-powered
CLM	Guided missile cruiser (Per)

Destroyers

DD	Destroyer
DDG (M)	Guided missile destroyer
DDGH (M)	Guided missile destroyer with helicopter, or helicopter platform
DDK	Destroyer (Jpn)

Frigates

DE	Destroyer escort (Jpn)
FF (L) (H)	Frigate (Light) (Helicopter)
FFG (M)	Guided missile frigate
FFGH (M)	Guided missile frigate with helicopter, or helicopter platform
FS (G) (H) (M)	Corvette (guided missile) (helicopter) (missile)

Patrol Forces

CF	River gunboat (Per)
CM	Corvette (guided missile) (Per)
HSIC	High Speed Interception Craft with speeds in excess of 55 kt
PB	Coastal patrol vessel under 45 m without heavy armament
PB (F) (I) (R)	Patrol boat (fast) (inshore) (river)
PBO (H)	Offshore patrol vessel between 45 and 60 m (helicopter)
PC	Vessel 35–55 m primarily for ASW role
PCK	As for PC but fitted with hydrofoils
PG	Vessel 45–85 m equipped with at least 76 mm (3-in) gun
PGG	As for PG but with force guided missile system
PGGJ	As for PGG but air cushion or ground effect design
PGGK	As for PGG but fitted with hydrofoils
PSO (H)	Offshore patrol vessel over 60 m (helicopter)
PTK	Attack boat torpedo fitted with hydrofoils
PTGK	Attack boat guided missile fitted with hydrofoils
SOC	Special operations craft (US)

Landing Ships

AAAV	Advanced Amphibious Assault Vehicle
ACV	Landing craft air cushion (Rus)
AGC	Amphibious command ship (RoC)
ASDS	Advanced Swimmer-Seal Delivery System
EDCG	Landing craft, utility (Brz)
LCA	Landing craft, assault
LCAC	Landing craft air cushion
LCC	Amphibious command ship
LCH	Landing craft, heavy (Aust)
LCM	Landing craft, mechanised
LCP (L)	Landing craft, personnel (large)
LCT	Landing craft, tank
LCU	Landing craft, utility
LCVP	Landing craft, vehicle/personnel with bow ramp
LHA	Amphibious assault ship general purpose with flooded well
LDW	Swimmer delivery vehicle
LHD (M)	Amphibious assault ship (multipurpose), can operate VSTOL aircraft and helicopters
LKA	Amphibious cargo ship with own landing craft
LLP	Assault ship, personnel
LPD	Amphibious transport, dock with own LCMs and helicopter deck
LPH	Amphibious assault ship, helicopter
LSD (H)	Landing ship dock with own landing craft, helicopter
LSL (H)	Landing ship logistic (Aust, UK, Sin), helicopter
LSM (H)	Landing ship medium with bow doors and/or landing ramp, helicopter
LST (H)	Landing ship tank with bow doors and/or landing ramp, helicopter
LSV	Landing ship vehicle with bow doors and/or landing ramp
RCL	Ramped craft, logistic (UK)
TCD	Landing ship, dock (Fra)
UCAC	Utility craft air cushion

Mine Warfare Ships

MCAC	Mine clearance air cushion
MCD	Mine countermeasures vessel, diving support
MCDV	Maritime coast defence vessel (Can)
MCMV	Mine countermeasures vessel
MCS	Mine countermeasures support ship
MH (I) (C) (O)	Minehunter (inshore) (coastal) (ocean)
MHCD	Minehunter coastal with drone
MHSC	Minehunter/sweeper coastal
ML (I) (C) (A)	Minelayer (inshore) (coastal) (auxiliary)
MS (I) (C) (R)	Minesweeper (inshore) (coastal) (river)
MSA (T)	Minesweeper, auxiliary (tug)
MSB	Minesweeper, boat
MSCD	Coastal minesweeper capable of controlling drones
MSD	Minesweeper, drone
MSO	Minesweeper, ocean
SRMH	Single role minehunter (UK)

Auxiliaries

ABU (H)	Buoy tender (helicopter)
AD	Destroyer tender
ADG	Degaussing/deperming ship
AE (L)	Ammunition ship capable of underway replenishment (small)
AEM	Missile support ship
AET (L)	Ammunition transport (small)
AF (L)	Stores ship (small)
AFS	Combat stores ship, capable of underway replenishment
AG (H)	Auxiliary miscellaneous (helicopter)
AGB	Icebreaker
AGDS	Deep submergence support ship
AGE (H)	Research ship (helicopter)
AGF (H)	Auxiliary Flag or command ship (helicopter)
AGI (H)	Intelligence collection ship (helicopter)
AGM (H)	Missile range instrumentation ship (helicopter)
AGOB	Polar research ship
AGOR (H)	Oceanographic research ship (helicopter)
AGOS (H)	Ocean surveillance ship (helicopter)
AGP	Patrol craft tender
AGS (C) (H)	Surveying ship (coastal) (helicopter)
AH	Hospital ship
AK (L) (R) (H)	Cargo ship (light) (Ro-Ro) (helicopter)
AKE	Armament stores carrier
AKR	Roll on/roll off sealift ship
AKS (L) (H)	Stores ship (light) (helicopter)
ANL	Boom defence/cable/netlayer
AO	Replenishment oiler (US)
AOE	Fast combat support ship, primarily for POL replenishment
AOR (L) (H)	Replenishment oiler (small) (helicopter)
AOT (L)	Transport oiler (small)
AP (H)	Personnel transport (helicopter)
APB	Barracks ship
APCR	Primary casualty receiving ship
AR (L)	Repair ship (small)
ARC	Submarine cable repair ship
ARS (D) (H)	Salvage ship (heavy lift) (helicopter)
AS (L)	Submarine tender (small)
ASE	Research ship (Jpn)
ASR	Submarine rescue ship
ATA	Auxiliary ocean tug
ATF	Fleet ocean tug and supply ship
ATR	Fleet ocean tug (firefighting and rescue)
ATS	Salvage and rescue ship
AVB	Aviation support ship
AVM	Aviation and missile support
AWT (L)	Water tanker (small)
AX (L) (H)	Training ship (small) (helicopter)
AXS	Sail training ship
AXT	Training tender
HSS	Helicopter support ship
HSV	High speed logistic support vessel (catamaran)
TV	Training ship (Jpn)

Service Craft

ASY	Auxiliary yacht (Jpn)
SAR	Search and rescue vessel
WFL	Water/fuel lighter (Aust)
YAC	Royal yacht
YAG	Service craft, miscellaneous
YAGK	Surface effect craft, experimental
YDG	Degaussing vessel
YDT	Diving tender
YE	Ammunition lighter
YF	Covered personnel transport under 40 m
YFB (H)	Ferry (helicopter)
YFL	Launch
YFRT	Range safety vesel
YFU	Former LCU used for cargo
YGS	Survey launch
YH	Ambulance boat
YM	Dredging craft
YO (G)	Fuel barge (gasolene)
YP	Harbour patrol craft
YPB	Floating barracks
YPC	Oil pollution control vessel
YPT	Torpedo recovery vessel
YT (B) (M) (L)	Harbour tug (large) (medium) (small)
YTR	Harbour fire/rescue craft with several monitors
YTT	Torpedo trials craft
YW	Water barge

Pennant numbers of major surface ships in numerical order

Number	Ship's name	Type	Country	Page
001	Guria	LCU	Georgia	266
001	President H I Remeliik	PB	Palau	559
001	San Juan	WPBO	Philippines	579
001	KBV	WPSO	Sweden	742
LRG 001	Constancia	PBR	Venezuela	939
LSM 001	Punta Macolla	PB	Venezuela	939
002	Atia	LCU	Georgia	266
002	Edsa II	WPBO	Philippines	579
002	KBV	WPSO	Sweden	742
LRG 002	Perseverancia	PBR	Venezuela	939
LSM 002	Farallón Centinela	PB	Venezuela	939
003	Pampanga	WPBO	Philippines	579
AF 003	Amougna	PBR	Côte d'Ivoire	166
LRG 003	Honestidad	PBR	Venezuela	939
LSM 003	Charagato	PB	Venezuela	939
004	Batangas	WPBO	Philippines	579
AF 004	Monsekela	PBR	Côte d'Ivoire	166
LRG 004	Tenacidad	PBR	Venezuela	939
LSM 004	Bajo Brito	PB	Venezuela	939
LRG 005	Integridad	PBR	Venezuela	939
LSM 005	Bajo Araya	PB	Venezuela	939
LRG 006	Lealtad	PBR	Venezuela	939
LSM 006	Carecare	PB	Venezuela	939
LSM 007	Vela De Cobo	PB	Venezuela	939
LSM 008	Cayo Macereo	PB	Venezuela	939
01	Adelaide	FFGHM	Australia	25
01	Pohjanmaa	ML	Finland	221
01	Tarangau	PB	Papua New Guinea	562
A 01	Paluma	AGSC	Australia	32
A 01	Salema	WPB	Spain	719
ADR 01	Banderas	YM	Mexico	501
AMP 01	Huasteco	APH/AK/AH	Mexico	501
ARE 01	Otomi	ATF	Mexico	502
ATQ 01	Aguascalientes	YOG/YO	Mexico	502
ATR 01	Maya	AKS	Mexico	501
ASV 01	Wyatt Earp	YGS	Australia	32
B 01	Ejdern	MSI	Sweden	737
BACS 01	Almirante Hess	YPT	Brazil	79
BE 01	Cuauhtémoc	AXS	Mexico	502
BI 01	Alejandro De Humboldt	AGOR	Mexico	500
BNVC 01	Cabo Schram	YTB	Brazil	80
CSL 01	Wattle	YE	Australia	34
F 01	Abu Dhabi	FFGHM	UAE	816
FL 01	Hiryu	FL/YTR	Japan	430
FM 01	Presidente Eloy Alfaro	FFGHM	Ecuador	192
FSM 01	Palikir	PB	Micronesia	503
G 01	Mazzei	PB/YXT	Italy	396
HL 01	Shoyo	AGS	Japan	431
KA 01	Kristaps	WPB	Latvia	460
LC 01	Yopito	LCM	Venezuela	939
LF 01	Cacine	PC	Guinea-Bissau	306
LL 01	Tsushima	AKSL	Japan	431
LP 01	Marlim	PB	Brazil	71
M 01	Viesturs	MSC	Latvia	459
MRF 01	Sökaren	MSD	Sweden	738
MS 01	Kinugasa	YPC	Japan	432
OR 01	Shirasagi	YAG	Japan	433
P 01	Liberta	PB	Antigua and Barbuda	9
P 01	Trident	PB	Barbados	54
P 01	Salamis	PBM	Cyprus	172
P 01	Antonio Zara	PB	Italy	396
P 01	Zibens	PB	Latvia	458
P 01	Oryx	PBO	Namibia	516
P 01	Capitán Cabral	PBR	Paraguay	564
P 01	Alphonse Reynolds	PB	St Lucia	669
P 01	Jarabakka	PB	Suriname	728
PB 01	Tyrrel Bay	PB	Grenada	304
PC 01	Matsunami	PC/PB	Japan	429
PL 01	Oki	PL/PSOH	Japan	423
PLH 01	Soya	PLH/PSOH	Japan	422
PM 01	Natsui	PM/PSO	Japan	426
PS 01	Shinzan	PS/PBF	Japan	427
Q 01	Damsah	PGGF	Qatar	603
S 01	Gladan	AXS	Sweden	739
SSN-2 01	Aldebaran	ABU	Brazil	76
SSN-4 01	Vega	ABU	Brazil	76
SVG 01	Captain Mulzac	PB	St Vincent	669
TNBH 01	Xavier Pinto Telleria	YAG	Bolivia	61
TNR 01	Jose Manuel Pando	YAG	Bolivia	61
U 01	Zaporizya	SS	Ukraine	807
02	Tukoro	PB	Vanuatu	933
A 02	Mermaid	AGSC	Australia	32
A 02	Rio Guadiaro	WPB	Spain	720
ADR 02	Magdalena	YM	Mexico	501
ARE 02	Yaqui	ATF	Mexico	502
ATQ 02	Tlaxcala	YOG/YO	Mexico	502
B 02	Krickan	MSI	Sweden	737
BI 02	Onjuku	AGS	Mexico	499
CAMR 02	Suboficial Oliveira	AGSC	Brazil	76
CPSP 02	Achernar	ABU	Brazil	76
CSL 02	Boronia	YE	Australia	34
F 02	Al Emirat	FFGHM	UAE	816
FL 02	Shoryu	FL/YTR	Japan	430
FM 02	Moran Valverde	FFGHM	Ecuador	192
FSM 02	Micronesia	PB	Micronesia	503
G 02	Vaccaro	PB/YXT	Italy	396
HL 02	Takuyo	AGS	Japan	431
KAL-IV-02	Baruna Jaya I	AGS/AGOR	Indonesia	349
LF 02	Cacheu	PC	Guinea-Bissau	306
M 02	Imanta	MSC	Latvia	459
MP 02	Zapoteco	APH/AK/AH	Mexico	501
MS 02	Saikai	YPC	Japan	432
OR 02	Shiratori	YAG	Japan	433
P 02	Palmetto	PB	Antigua and Barbuda	9
P 02	Waspada	PTG	Brunei	81
P 02	Kyrenia	PBM	Cyprus	173
P 02	Giuseppe Vizzari	PB	Italy	396
P 02	Lode	PB	Latvia	458
P 02	Nanawa	PBR	Paraguay	563
P 02	Defender	PB	St Lucia	669
PB 02	Levera	PB	Grenada	304
PL 02	Erimo	PL/PSOH	Japan	423
PLH 02	Tsugaru	PLH/PSOH	Japan	422
PM 02	Kitakami	PM/PSO	Japan	426
PS 02	Saroma	PS/PBF	Japan	427
Q 02	Al Ghariyah	PGGF	Qatar	603
S 02	Falken	AXS	Sweden	739
SSN-4 02	Denébola	ABU	Brazil	76
TNR 02	Nicolas Suarez	YAG	Bolivia	61
03	Sydney	FFGHM	Australia	25
03	Lomor	PB	Marshall Islands	486
03	Seeadler	PB	Papua New Guinea	562
03	Lata	PB	Solomon Islands	695
A 03	Shepparton	AGSC	Australia	32
A 03	Rio Pisuerga	WPB	Spain	720
ADR 03	Kino	YM	Mexico	501
ARE 03	Seri	ATF	Mexico	502
ATR 03	Tarasco	AK	Mexico	501
B 03	Svärtan	MSI	Sweden	737
BHMN 03	Camocim	YGS	Brazil	76
BI 03	Altair	AGOR	Mexico	500
BNRJ 03	Comandante Marroig	YTB	Brazil	80
CPCE-03	Mucuripe	PB	Brazil	72
CPES 03	Capella	ABU	Brazil	76
CSL 03	Telopea	YE	Australia	34
FL 03	Nanryu	FL/YTR	Japan	430
FSM 03	Paluwlap	PB	Micronesia	503
G 03	Di Bartolo	PB/YXT	Italy	396
HL 03	Meiyo	AGS	Japan	431
KA 03	Cometa	WPB	Latvia	460
KAL-IV-03	Baruna Jaya I	AGS/AGOR	Indonesia	349
M 03	Nemejs	MHC	Latvia	459
MS 03	Katsuren	YPC	Japan	432
OR 03	Mizunangi	YAG	Japan	433
P 03	Yellow Elder	PB	Bahamas	39
P 03	Commander Tsomakis	PB	Cyprus	173
P 03	Giovanni Denaro	PB	Italy	396
P 03	Linga	PB	Latvia	458
P 03	Gramorgu	PB	Suriname	728
PL 03	Kudaka	PL/PSOH	Japan	423
PLH 03	Oosumi	PLH/PSOH	Japan	422
PM 03	Echizen	PM/PSO	Japan	426
PS 03	Inasa	PS/PBF	Japan	427
Q 03	Rbigah	PGGF	Qatar	603
SSN-4 03	Paraibano	YGS	Brazil	76
WB 03	Bream	YAG	UK	855
04	Darwin	FFGHM	Australia	25
04	Basilisk	PB	Papua New Guinea	562
04	Auki	PB	Solomon Islands	695
A 04	Benalla	AGSC	Australia	32
A 04	Kahu	AXL	New Zealand	531
A 04	Rio Nalon	WPB	Spain	720
A 04	Martín Posadillo	AKRH	Spain	717
ADR 04	Yavaros	YM	Mexico	501
ARE 04	Cora	ATF	Mexico	502
B 04	Viggen	MSI	Sweden	737
BI 04	Antares	AGOR	Mexico	500
BNRJ 04	Comandante Didier	YTB	Brazil	80
FL 04	Kairyu	FL/YTR	Japan	430
FM 04	Shiraito	FM/YTR	Japan	430
FSM 04	Constitution	PB	Micronesia	503
G 04	Avallone	PB/YXT	Italy	396
HL 04	Tenyo	AGS	Japan	431
KAL-IV-04	Baruna Jaya II	AGS/AGOR	Indonesia	349
M 04	Carlskrona	AXH/MLH	Sweden	736
OR 04	Chidori	YAG	Japan	433
P 04	Port Nelson	PB	Bahamas	39
P 04	Commander Georgiu	PB	Cyprus	173
P 04	Bulta	PB	Latvia	458
P 04	Teniente Farina	PBR	Paraguay	563
P 04	Protector	PB	St Lucia	669
PL 04	Yahiko	PL/PSOH	Japan	423
PLH 04	Hayato	PLH/PSOH	Japan	422
PM 04	Tokachi	PM/PSO	Japan	426
PS 04	Kirishima	PS/PBF	Japan	427
Q04	Barzan	PGGFM	Qatar	604
SSN-4 04	Rio Branco	YGS	Brazil	76
SVG 04	Hairoun	PB	St Vincent	670
TNR 04	Max Paredes	YAG	Bolivia	61
05	Melbourne	FFGHM	Australia	25
05	Uusimaa	ML	Finland	221
A 05	Rio Palma	WPB	Spain	720
A 05	El Camino Español	AKR	Spain	717
ADR 05	Chamela	YM	Mexico	501
ARE 05	Iztaccihuatl	YTL	Mexico	502
BI 05	Rio Suchiate	AKS	Mexico	500
CPPR 05	Fomalhaut	ABU	Brazil	76
CPRJ-05	Rio	PB	Brazil	72
CPSC 05	Betelgeuse	ABU	Brazil	76

Number	Ship's name	Type	Country	Page
D 05	Ukale	PB	Dominica	186
FL 05	Suiryu	FL/YTR	Japan	430
FSM 05	Independence	PB	Micronesia	503
G 05	Oltramonti	PB/YXT	Italy	396
HL 05	Kaiyo	AGS	Japan	431
KAL-IV-05	Baruna Jaya Iv	AGS/AGOR	Indonesia	349
L 05	President El Hadj	LSTH	Gabon	264
OR 05	Isoshigi	YAG	Japan	433
P 05	Samana	PB	Bahamas	39
P 05	Itaipú	PBR	Paraguay	564
PL 05	Hakata	PL/PSOH	Japan	423
PLH 05	Zao	PLH/PSOH	Japan	422
PM 05	Hitachi	PM/PSO	Japan	426
PS 05	Kamui	PS/PBF	Japan	427
Q05	Huwar	PGGFM	Qatar	604
R 05	Invincible	CV	UK	830
SVG 05	George McIntosh	PB	St Vincent	670
TNR 05	Julio Olmos	YAG	Bolivia	61
WB 05	Roach	YAG	UK	855
06	Newcastle	FFGHM	Australia	25
06	Almirante Condell	FFGHM	Chile	111
A 06	Rio Andarax	WPB	Spain	720
ADR 06	Tepoca	YM	Mexico	501
ARE 06	Popocateptl	YTL	Mexico	502
BI 06	Rio Hondo	YGS	Mexico	500
BNA 06	Tenente Magalhães	YTB	Brazil	80
G 06	Barbariso	PB/YXT	Italy	396
KA 06	Gaisma	WPB	Latvia	460
KAL-IV-06	Baruna Jaya Viii	AGOR	Indonesia	349
P 06	Capitán Ortiz	PBF	Paraguay	564
PL 06	Kurikoma	PL/PSOH	Japan	423
PLH 06	Chikuzen	PLH/PSOH	Japan	422
PM 06	Okitsu	PM/PSO	Japan	426
PS 06	Banna	PS/PBF	Japan	427
Q06	Al Udeid	PGGFM	Qatar	604
R 06	Illustrious	CV	UK	830
SSN-5 06	Rigel	ABU	Brazil	76
TNBTL-06	Horacio Ugarteche	YAG	Bolivia	61
WB 06	Perch	YAG	UK	855
07	Almirante Lynch	FFGHM	Chile	111
A 07	Rio Guadalope	WPB	Spain	720
ADR 07	Todo Santos	YM	Mexico	501
ARE 07	Citlaltepl	YTL	Mexico	502
BI 07	Moctezuma I	AGSC	Mexico	500
BNRJ 07	Rio Negro	YFB	Brazil	79
CPSP-07	Espadarte	PB	Brazil	72
G 07	Paolini	PB/YXT	Italy	396
KA 07	Ausma	WPB	Latvia	460
P 07	Général d'Armée Ba-Oumar	PBO	Gabon	263
P 07	Teniente Robles	PBF	Paraguay	564
PL 07	Satauma	PL/PSOH	Japan	423
PLH 07	Settsu	PLH/PSOH	Japan	422
PM 07	Isazu	PM/PSO	Japan	426
PS 07	Ashitaki	PS/PBF	Japan	427
Q07	Al Deebel	PGGFM	Qatar	604
R 07	Ark Royal	CV	UK	830
TNR 07	Thames Crespo	YAG	Bolivia	61
A 08	Rio Almanzora	WPB	Spain	720
ADR 08	Asuncion	YM	Mexico	501
ARE 08	Xinantecatl	YTL	Mexico	502
BNAJ 08	Rio Pardo	YFB	Brazil	79
FM 08	Minoo	FM/YTR	Japan	430
KA 08	Saule	WPB	Latvia	460
L 08	Pono	LCU	Tanzania	761
P 08	Colonel Djoue-Dabany	PBO	Gabon	263
P 08	Yhaguy	PBR	Paraguay	564
PL 08	Motobu	PL/PSOH	Japan	423
PLH 08	Echigo	PLH/PSOH	Japan	422
PM 08	Chitose	PM/PSO	Japan	426
PS 08	Kariba	PS/PBF	Japan	427
SVG 08	Chatham Bay	PB	St Vincent	670
WB 08	Mill Reef	YAG	UK	855
A 09	Manawanui	YDT	New Zealand	531
A 09	Rio Nervion	WPB	Spain	720
ADR 09	Almejas	YM	Mexico	501
ARE 09	Matlalcueye	YTL	Mexico	502
BNRJ 09	Rio Oiapoque	YFB	Brazil	79
FM 09	Ryusei	FM/YTR	Japan	430
KA 09	Klints	WPB	Latvia	460
L 09	Kibua	LCU	Tanzania	761
P 09	Tebicuary	PBR	Paraguay	564
PLH 09	Ryukyu	PLH/PSOH	Japan	422
PM 09	Kuwano	PM/PSO	Japan	426
PS 09	Arase	PS/PBF	Japan	427
A 10	Rio Guadalaviar	WPB	Spain	720
ADR 10	Chacagua	YM	Mexico	501
ARE 10	Tlaloc	YTL	Mexico	502
D 10	Almirante Brown	DDGHM	Argentina	12
FM 10	Kiyotaki	FM/YTR	Japan	430
L 10	Guarapari	EDCG/LCU	Brazil	74
P 10	Piratini	PB	Brazil	72
P 10	Général Nazaire Boulingui	PTM	Gabon	264
PC 10	Firebolt	PBFM	US	892
PLH 10	Daisen	PLH/PSOH	Japan	422
011	Varyag	CGHM	Russian Federation	631
012	Rais Hadj Mubarek	SSK	Algeria	3
012	Olenegorskiy Gorniak	LSTM	Russian Federation	645
013	El Hadj Slimane	SSK	Algeria	3
014	PSKR-714	PTF	Russian Federation	665
016	Georgiy Pobedonosets	LSTM	Russian Federation	645
016	Ural	PBO	Russian Federation	663
017	Podolsk	PGM	Russian Federation	665
018	Murmansk	PGH	Russian Federation	663
020	Mitrofan Moskalenko	LPDHM	Russian Federation	645
021	Tolyatti	PCM	Russian Federation	664
022	Zapolarye	PBO	Russian Federation	663
023	Nakhodka	PCM	Russian Federation	664
023	Nevelsk	PGM	Russian Federation	665
024	Kaliningrad	PCM	Russian Federation	664
026	Yuzhno-Sakhalinsk	PGM	Russian Federation	665
027	Kondopoga	LSTM	Russian Federation	645
028	Sochi	PGM	Russian Federation	665
031	Alexander Otrakovskiy	LSTM	Russian Federation	645
031	Yaroslavl	PCM	Russian Federation	664
035	Victor Kingisepp	PBO	Russian Federation	663
035	Kotlas	LSTM	Russian Federation	645
037	Yastreb	PCM	Russian Federation	664
038	Yenisey	PBO	Russian Federation	663
LP 039	Miguel Ela Edjodjomo	PB	Equatorial Guinea	212
040	Sarych	PCM	Russian Federation	664
041	Grif	PCM	Russian Federation	664
LP 041	Hipolito Micha	PB	Equatorial Guinea	212
042	Siktivkar	PGM	Russian Federation	665
042	Orlan	PCM	Russian Federation	664
042	Madeleine	PB	Lithuania	468
043	Amur	PBO	Russian Federation	663
LP 043	Gaspar Obiang Esono	PBR	Equatorial Guinea	212
044	Yamalets	PGM	Russian Federation	665
044	PSKR-660	PTF	Russian Federation	665
LP 045	Fernando Nuara Engonda	PBR	Equatorial Guinea	212
047	PSKR-700	PTF	Russian Federation	665
048	PSKR-715	PTF	Russian Federation	665
053	Povorino	FFLM	Russian Federation	639
053	Pskr-718	PTF	Russian Federation	665
054	Eisk	FFLM	Russian Federation	639
BA 055	Dorado I	YAG	Panama	562
BA 056	Dorado II	YAG	Panama	562
BA 057	Aguacero	YAG	Panama	562
058	Ladoga	PBO	Russian Federation	663
BA 058	Portobelo	YAG	Panama	562
059	Aleksandrovets	FFLM	Russian Federation	639
BA 059	Fantasma Azul	YAG	Panama	562
060	Vladimirets	PGK	Russian Federation	644
060	Anadyr	FFHM	Russian Federation	662
061	Chang Bogo	SSK	Korea, South	443
062	Yi Chon	SSK	Korea, South	443
063	Choi Muson	SSK	Korea, South	443
063	Sokol	PCM	Russian Federation	664
063	Admiral Kuznetsov	CVGM	Russian Federation	628
064	Muromets	FFLM	Russian Federation	639
065	Park Wi	SSK	Korea, South	443
065	Minsk	PCM	Russian Federation	664
065	Briz	PGM	Russian Federation	665
066	Lee Jongmu	SSK	Korea, South	443
066	Mukhtar Avezov	LSTM	Russian Federation	645
066	Blagoveshchensk	PGR	Russian Federation	666
067	Jung Woon	SSK	Korea, South	443
067	Chukotka	PBO	Russian Federation	663
068	Lee Sunsin	SSK	Korea, South	443
069	Na Daeyong	SSK	Korea, South	443
071	Lee Eokgi	SSK	Korea, South	443
077	Nikolay Kaplunov	PCM	Russian Federation	664
077	Neptun	PGM	Russian Federation	665
077 (II)	Nikolay Korsakov	LSTM	Russian Federation	645
078	Kobchik	PCM	Russian Federation	664
078	MPK 127 (III)	FFLM	Russian Federation	639
078	PSKR-717	PTF	Russian Federation	665
088	Cholmsk	PGM	Russian Federation	665
090	Nikolay Sipyagin	AK	Russian Federation	667
099	Krechet	PCM	Russian Federation	664
099	Pter. Almaz	PGM	Russian Federation	665
1	Seehund	MSD	Germany	280
1	Tangkis	PBF	Malaysia	477
1	Uruguay	FF	Uruguay	929
A 1	Comandante General Irigoyen	PSO	Argentina	16
AFDL 1	Hay Tan	YFD	Taiwan	756
B 1	Patagonia	AORH	Argentina	18
BA 1	Tortuguero	ABU	Dominican Republic	189
C 1	Paraguay	PGR	Paraguay	563
DF 1	Endeavor	YFD	Dominican Republic	190
DSRV 1	Mystic	DSRV	US	906
FSF-1	Sea Fighter	AGE	US	904
H 1	Haras 1	PB	Oman	549
HSV-X1	Joint Venture	HSVH	US	905
KA 1	Trondenes	LCP	Norway	540
KV 1	Titran	WPSOH	Norway	543
LCC 1	Kao Hsiung	AGF	Taiwan	755
LCS 1	Freedom	FFGHM	US	885
LH 1	Suboficial Rogelio Lesme	YGS	Paraguay	565
LHA 1	Tarawa	LHAM	US	895
LHD 1	Wasp	LHDM/MCSM	US	896
LSV 1	Gen Frank S Besson Jr	LSV-ARMY	US	901
MCM 1	Avenger	MCM/MHSO	US	902
PCL 1	Ning Hai	PCF	Taiwan	754
RM 1	Guaroa	YTM/YTL	Dominican Republic	190
S 1	Shabab Oman	AXS	Oman	547
SB 1	Ho Chie	LCU	Taiwan	755
T 1	Teniente Herreros	AKL	Paraguay	565
T 1	Al Sultana	AKS	Oman	547
T-ACS 1	Keystone State	AK	US	917
T-AKE 1	Lewis and Clark	AKEH	US	910
TSV-1X	Spearhead	HSV	US	905
Z1	Dheep Al Bahar 1	PB	Oman	549
Z1	Al Bushra	PBO	Oman	545
Z 1	Baltyk	AORL	Poland	590
2	Seehund	MSD	Germany	280
A 2	Teniente Olivieri	PBO	Argentina	16

Number	Ship's name	Type	Country	Page	Number	Ship's name	Type	Country	Page
A 2	Nasr Al Bahr	LSTH	Oman	546	A 7	Kupang	YTM/YTL	Malaysia	480
AFDL 2	Kim Men	YFD	Taiwan	756	A 7	Al Neemran	LSTH	Oman	547
BA 2	Capotillo	ABU	Dominican Republic	189	BA 7	Nube Del Mar	AXS	Dominican Republic	189
H 2	Haras 2	PB	Oman	549	CG 7	Corozal Point	PB	Trinidad and Tobago	781
HD 2	Viken	YPT/YDT	Norway	542	H 7	Haras 7	PB	Oman	548
HSV-2	Swift	HSV/MCS	US	913	HM 7	Kjeøy	YPT/YDT	Norway	542
KA 2	Hysnes	LCP	Norway	540	KV 7	Åhav	WPSOH	Norway	543
KV 2	Kongsøy	WPSOH	Norway	543	LHD 7	Iwo Jima	LHDM/MCSM	US	896
LCS 2	Independence	FFGHM	US	885	LPD 7	Cleveland	LPD	US	898
LHA 2	Saipan	LHAM	US	895	LSV 7	SSGT Robert T Kuroda	LSV-ARMY	US	901
LHD 2	Essex	LHDM/MCSM	US	896	MCM 7	Patriot	MCM/MHSO	US	902
LSV 2	CW 3 Harold C Clinger	LSV-ARMY	US	901	PC 7	Squall	PBFM	US	892
LSV-2	Cutthroat	DSV	US	905	R 7	Ona	YTB/YTL	Argentina	19
MCM 2	Defender	MCM/MHSO	US	902	R 7	Esperanza	YTM/YTL	Paraguay	565
PCL 2	An Hai	PCF	Taiwan	754	T-ACS 7	Diamond State	AK	US	917
Q 2	Libertad	AXS	Argentina	18	T-AFS 7	San Jose	AFSH	US	910
R 2	Querandi	YTB/YTL	Argentina	19	T-AKR 7	Comet	AKR	US	918
RM 2	Guarionex	YTM/YTL	Dominican Republic	190	T-AOE 7	Rainier	AOEH	US	910
SB 2	Ho Ten	LCU	Taiwan	755	T-ARC 7	Zeus	ARC	US	912
T-ACS 2	Gem State	AK	US	917	8	Seehund	MSD	Germany	280
T-AKE 2	Sacagawea	AKEH	US	910	A 8	Kepah	YTM/YTL	Malaysia	480
WPB 2	Tempest	WPC/PB	US	922	A 8	Saba Al Bahr	LSTH	Oman	546
Z 2	Al Mansoor	PBO	Oman	545	B 8	Astra Federico	AKS/AOTL	Argentina	19
3	Seehund	MSD	Germany	280	CG 8	Crown Point	PB	Trinidad and Tobago	781
3	Montevideo	FF	Uruguay	929	FFG 8	McInerney	FFGHM	US	886
A 3	Francisco de Gurruchaga	PSO	Argentina	16	H 8	Haras 8	PB	Oman	548
AFDL 3	Han Jih	YFD	Taiwan	756	LHD 8	Makin Island	LHDM/MCSM	US	896
B 3	Canal Beagle	AKS	Argentina	19	LPD 8	Dubuque	LPD	US	898
H 3	Haras 3	PB	Oman	549	LSV 8	MG Robert Smails	LSV-ARMY	US	901
HM 3	Torpen	YPT/YDT	Norway	542	MCM 8	Scout	MCM/MHSO	US	902
HT 3	Karlsøy	YPT/YDT	Norway	542	R 8	Toba	YTB/YTL	Argentina	19
KA 3	Hellen	LCP	Norway	540	SB 8	Canal Emilio Mitre	YTL/YTR	Argentina	22
LHD 3	Kearsarge	LHDM/MCSM	US	896	T-ACS 8	Equality State	AK	US	917
LSV 3	Gen Brehon B Somervell	LSV-ARMY	US	901	T-AOE 8	Arctic	AOEH	US	910
MCM 3	Sentry	MCM/MHSO	US	902	Z 8	Meduza	AOTL	Poland	590
PC 3	Hurricane	PBFM	US	892	9	Seehund	MSD	Germany	280
R 3	Tehuelche	YTB/YTL	Argentina	19	B 9	Astra Valentina	AKS/AOTL	Argentina	19
SB 3	Ayanka	ARS/ATA	Russian Federation	661	CG 9	Galera Point	PB	Trinidad and Tobago	781
T-ACS 3	Grand Canyon State	AK	US	917	H 9	Haras 9	PB	Oman	548
T-AFS 3	Niagara Falls	AFSH	US	910	LPD 9	Denver	LPD	US	898
T-AKE 3	Alan Shepard	AKEH	US	910	MCM 9	Pioneer	MCM/MHSO	US	902
T-AVB 3	Wright	AVB	US	915	PC 9	Chinook	PBFM	US	892
YAC 3	Oriole	AXS	Canada	96	SB 9	Canal Costanero	YTL/YTR	Argentina	22
Z 3	Al Najah	PBO	Oman	545	T-ACS 9	Green Mountain State	AK	US	917
Z 3	Dheep Al Bahar 3	PB	Oman	549	T-AFS 9	Spica	AFSH	US	910
4	Seehund	MSD	Germany	280	T-AKR 9	Meteor	AKR	US	918
B 4	Bahia San Blas	AKS	Argentina	19	WPB 8	Zephyr	WPC/PB	US	922
D 4	Melville	PB	Dominica	187	Z 9	Slimak	AOTL	Poland	590
H 4	Haras 4	PB	Oman	549	10	Ngpwb	YFL/YDT	Australia	36
HS 4	Sleipner	YPT/YDT	Norway	542	10	Al Riffa	PB	Bahrain	43
KA 4	Toraas	LCP	Norway	540	10	RV-90	PB	Finland	228
LDM 4	Neiba	LCU	Dominican Republic	190	10	Seehund	MSD	Germany	280
LHA 4	Nassau	LHAM	US	895	10	General Paraschiv Vasilescu	PB	Romania	609
LHD 4	Boxer	LHDM/MCSM	US	896	10	Colonia	PB	Uruguay	930
LPD 4	Austin	LPD	US	898	A 10	Teritup	YTM/YTL	Malaysia	480
LSV 4	LTG William B Bunker	LSV-ARMY	US	901	A 10	Al Temsah	LSTH	Oman	546
MCM 4	Champion	MCM/MHSO	US	902	A 10	Rio Guadalaviar	WPB	Spain	720
R 4	Triunfo	YTM/YTL	Paraguay	565	ACV 10	Roebuck Bay	PB	Australia	37
SI 4	Puerto Buenos Aires	YTL/YTR	Argentina	22	CG 10	Barcolet Point	PB	Trinidad and Tobago	781
T-ACS 4	Gopher State	AK	US	917	H 10	Haras 10	PB	Oman	548
T-AVB 4	Curtiss	AVB	US	915	LPD 10	Juneau	LPD	US	898
WPB 4	Monsoon	WPC/PB	US	922	MCM 10	Warrior	MCM/MHSO	US	902
5	Seehund	MSD	Germany	280	PK 10	Sailfish	PBF	Singapore	693
5	15 de Noviembre	PBO	Uruguay	930	PM 10	Sorachi	PM/PSO	Japan	426
A 5	Ketam	YTM/YTL	Malaysia	480	PS 10	Sanbe	PS/PBF	Japan	427
ARD 5	Fo Wu 5	YFD	Taiwan	756	R 10	Chulupi	YTB/YTL	Argentina	19
B 5	Cabo De Hornos	AKS	Argentina	19	T-ACS 10	Beaver State	AK	US	917
BT 5	Capitán Beotegui	AOTL	Dominican Republic	189	T-AFS 10	Saturn	AFSH	US	910
CG 5	Barracuda	PB	Trinidad and Tobago	781	T-AOE 10	Bridge	AOEH	US	910
H 5	Haras 5	PB	Oman	549	U 10	Aspirante Nascimento	AXL	Brazil	77
HS 5	Mjølner	YPT/YDT	Norway	542	WAGB 10	Polar Star	WAGBH	US	924
KA 5	Møvik	LCP	Norway	540	YTT 10	Battle Point	YTT	US	907
KV 5	Agder	WPSOH	Norway	543	Z 10	Dhofar	PGGF	Oman	546
LHA 5	Peleliu	LHAM	US	895	11	Hawar	PB	Bahrain	43
LHD 5	Bataan	LHDM/MCSM	US	896	11	Smeli	FFLM	Bulgaria	83
LPD 5	Ogden	LPD	US	898	11	Seehund	MSD	Germany	280
LSV 5	MG Charles P Gross	LSV-ARMY	US	901	11	Mahamiru	MHC	Malaysia	478
MCM 5	Guardian	MCM/MHSO	US	902	11	Tempur	PBF	Malaysia	477
PC 5	Typhoon	PBFM	US	892	11	Rio Negro	PB	Uruguay	930
Q 5	Almirante Irizar	AGB/AGOB	Argentina	19	A 11	Endeavour	AORH	New Zealand	531
R 5	Mocovi	YTB/YTL	Argentina	19	A 11	Rio Cabriel	WPB	Spain	720
R 5	Angostura	YTM/YTL	Paraguay	565	AGF 11	Coronado	AGFH	US	894
T-ACS 5	Flickertail State	AK	US	917	AGS 11	Sunjin	AGE	Korea, South	452
T-AFS 5	Concord	AFSH	US	910	BE 11	Simón Bolívar	AXS	Venezuela	937
6	Seehund	MSD	Germany	280	BO 11	Punta Brava	AGOR	Venezuela	936
6	25 de Agosto	PBO	Uruguay	930	C 11	Lieutenant General Dimo Hamaambo	PB	Namibia	516
A 6	Suboficial Castillo	PSO	Argentina	16	CAMR 11	Pollux	ABU	Brazil	76
A 6	Sotong	YTM/YTL	Malaysia	480	CF 11	Amazonas	CF/PGR	Peru	569
ARD 6	Fo Wu 6	YFD	Taiwan	756	CM 11	Esmeraldas	FSGHM	Ecuador	193
CG 6	Cascadura	PB	Trinidad and Tobago	781	D 11	La Argentina	DDGHM	Argentina	12
H 6	Haras 6	PB	Oman	548	F 11	Žemaitis	FFLM	Lithuania	466
KV 6	Garsøy	WPSOH	Norway	543	GC 11	Almirante Clemente	WFS	Venezuela	938
LHD 6	Bonhomme Richard	LHDM/MCSM	US	896	K 11	Felinto Perry	ASRH	Brazil	77
LSV 6	SP/4 James A Loux	LSV-ARMY	US	901	K 11	Stockholm	FSG	Sweden	731
MCM 6	Devastator	MCM/MHSO	US	902	KA 11	Skrolsvik	LCP	Norway	540
PC 6	Sirocco	PBFM	US	892	L 11	Tambaú	EDCG/LCU	Brazil	74
R 6	Calchaqui	YTB/YTL	Argentina	19	LG 11	Los Taques	YAG	Venezuela	939
SB 6	Moshchny	ARS/ATA	Russian Federation	661	LH 11	Gabriela	AGSC	Venezuela	937
T-ACS 6	Cornhusker State	AK	US	917	LL 11	Hokuto	ABU	Japan	432
T-AOE 6	Supply	AOEH	US	910	M 11	Styrsö	MHSDI	Sweden	738
7	RV-37	PB	Finland	228	M 11	Diana	PSOH/MCS/FSGM	Spain	710
7	Seehund	MSD	Germany	280	MCM 11	Gladiator	MCM/MHSO	US	902
7	Comodoro Coé	PBO	Uruguay	930	P 11	Pirajá	PB	Brazil	72

Number	Ship's name	Type	Country	Page
P 11	Mont Arreh	PB	Djibouti	186
P 11	Sea Dog	PB	Gambia	265
P 11	Barceló	PB	Spain	711
PC 11	Hayanami	PC/PB/YTR	Japan	429
PC 11	Whirlwind	PBFM	US	892
PC 11	Constitución	PBG/PG	Venezuela	935
PF 11	Rajah Humabon	FF	Philippines	574
PL 11	Dionysos	PB	Cyprus	173
PM 11	Yubari	PM/PSO	Japan	426
PS 11	Mizuki	PS/PBF	Japan	427
Q 11	Comodoro Rivadavia	AGOR	Argentina	18
R 11	Gniewko	ATS	Poland	591
R 11	Príncipe de Asturias	CV	Spain	704
RA 11	General Francisco de Miranda	ATA	Venezuela	937
RTOP 11	Kralj Petar Kresimir IV	FSG	Croatia	167
SD 11	Wrona	YDG	Poland	591
T-AKR 11	Cape Intrepid	AKR	US	918
U 11	Guarda Marinha Jensen	AXL	Brazil	77
WAGB 11	Polar Sea	WAGBH	US	924
YTT 11	Discovery Bay	YTT	US	907
Z 11	Al Sharqiyah	PGGF	Oman	546
12	Almirante Cochrane	DDGHM	Chile	109
12	Seehund	MSD	Germany	280
12	Jerai	MHC	Malaysia	478
12	Tempur	PBF	Malaysia	477
12	Paysandu	PB	Uruguay	931
12-64	Al Whada	SAR	Morocco	509
12-65	Sebou	SAR	Morocco	509
A 12	São Paulo	CVM	Brazil	64
A 12	Rio Cervantes	WPB	Spain	720
ADR 12	Farrallon	YM	Mexico	501
BI 12	Rio Tuxpan	AGS	Mexico	501
CF 12	Loreto	CF/PGR	Peru	569
CM 12	Manabi	FSGHM	Ecuador	193
D 12	Heroina	DDGHM	Argentina	12
F 12	Aukštaitis	FFLM	Lithuania	466
GC 12	General José Trinidad Moran	WFS	Venezuela	938
K 12	Malmö	FSG	Sweden	731
KA 12	Granata	WPB	Latvia	461
L 12	Ocean	LPH	UK	842
L 12	Camboriú	EDCG/LCU	Brazil	74
LG 12	Los Cayos	YAG	Venezuela	939
LH 12	Lely	AGSC	Venezuela	937
LL 12	Kaiou	ABU	Japan	432
LPD 12	Shreveport	LPD	US	898
M 12	Spårö	MHSDI	Sweden	738
MCM 12	Ardent	MCM/MHSO	US	902
MUL 12	Arkösund	MLC	Sweden	737
P 12	Pampeiro	PB	Brazil	72
P 12	Laya	PB	Spain	711
PC 12	Setogiri	PC/PB/YTR	Japan	429
PC 12	Thunderbolt	PBFM	US	892
PC 12	Federación	PBG/PG	Venezuela	935
PL 12	Kourion	PB	Cyprus	173
PM 12	Motoura	PM/PSO	Japan	426
PS 12	Kouya	PS/PBF	Japan	427
R 12	Mataco	YTB/YTL	Argentina	19
RP 12	Hercules	YTM/YTL	Dominican Republic	190
RTOP 12	Kralj Dmitar Zvonimir	FSG	Croatia	167
U 12	Guarda Marinha Brito	AXL	Brazil	77
YDT 12	Granby	YDT/YAG	Canada	96
Z 12	Al Bat'nah	PGGF	Oman	546
13	Reshitelni	FSM	Bulgaria	84
13	Seehund	MSD	Germany	280
13	Ledang	MHC	Malaysia	478
13	Tempur	PBF	Malaysia	477
A 13	Tunas Samudera	AXS	Malaysia	479
A 13	Rio Ara	WPB	Spain	720
ADR 13	Chairel	YM	Mexico	501
B 13	Ingeniero Julio Krause	AKS/AOTL	Argentina	19
CF 13	Marañon	CF/PGR	Peru	570
CM 13	Los Rios	FSGHM	Ecuador	193
D 13	Sarandi	DDGHM	Argentina	12
GC 13	Delfin	WPSO	Argentina	20
KA 13	Stangenes	LCP	Norway	540
LL 13	Ginga	ABU	Japan	432
LPD 13	Nashville	LPD	US	898
M 13	Skaftö	MHSDI	Sweden	738
MCM 13	Dextrous	MCM/MHSO	US	902
P 13	Parati	PB	Brazil	72
PC 13	Mizunami	PC/PB/YTR	Japan	429
PC 13	Independencia	PBG/PG	Venezuela	935
PL 13	Ilarion	PB	Cyprus	173
PM 13	Kano	PM/PSO	Japan	426
R 13	Semko	ATS	Poland	591
RP 13	Guacanagarix	YTM/YTL	Dominican Republic	190
WPC 13	Shamal	WPC/PB	US	922
14	Bodri	FSM	Bulgaria	84
14	Almirante Latorre	FFGM	Chile	109
14	PV-11	PB	Finland	228
14	Seehund	MSD	Germany	280
14	Kinabalu	MHC	Malaysia	478
14	Tempur	PBF	Malaysia	477
14	Al Hirasa	FFL	Syria	745
A 14	Resolution	AGS	New Zealand	531
A 14	Patiño	AORH	Spain	717
ADR 14	San Andres	YM	Mexico	501
AGOR 14	Melville	AGOR	US	904
CF 14	Ucayali	CF/PGR	Peru	570
CIAW 14	Rio Chui	YFB	Brazil	79
CM 14	El Oro	FSGHM	Ecuador	193
J 14	Nirupak	AGSH	India	332
KA 14	Astra	WPB	Latvia	461
L 14	Albion	LPD	UK	841
LCM 14	Sardelle	LCM	Germany	278
LPD 14	Trenton	LPD	US	898
M 14	Sturkö	MHSDI	Sweden	738
MCM 14	Chief	MCM/MHSO	US	902
P 14	Bolong Kanta	PB	Gambia	264
P 14	Ordóñez	PB	Spain	711
P 14	Penedo	PB	Brazil	72
PC 14	Iyonami	PC/PB/YTR	Japan	429
PC 14	Libertad	PBG/PG	Venezuela	935
PL 14	Karpasia	PB	Cyprus	173
PM 14	Sendai	PM/PSO	Japan	426
R 14	Zbyszko	ARS	Poland	591
WPC 14	Tornado	WPC/PB	US	922
Z 14	Mussandam	PGGF	Oman	546
15	Almirante Blanco Encalada	FFGHM	Chile	110
15	Seehund	MSD	Germany	280
15	Tempur	PBF	Malaysia	477
A 15	Nireekshak	ASR	India	334
A 15	Rio Duero	WPB	Spain	720
ADR 15	San Ignacio	YM	Mexico	501
AGOR 15	Knorr	AGOR	US	904
BA 15	Rambo	AXS	Dominican Republic	189
CM 15	Los Galapágos	FSGHM	Ecuador	193
DF 15	Recalada	WAGH/AHH	Argentina	22
F 15	Abu Bakr	FF/FFT	Bangladesh	48
G 15	Paraguassú	AP	Brazil	77
HP 15	Hitra	YPT/YDT	Norway	542
J 15	Investigator	AGSH	India	332
KA 15	Mørvika	LCP	Norway	540
L 15	Bulwark	LPD	UK	841
LPD 15	Ponce	LPD	US	898
M 15	Aratu	MSC	Brazil	74
M 15	Tineycheide	WPBF	Spain	720
MUL 15	Grundsund	MLC	Sweden	737
P 15	Acevedo	PB	Spain	711
P 15	Poti	PB	Brazil	72
PC 15	Kurinami	PC/PB/YTR	Japan	429
PC 15	Patria	PBG/PG	Venezuela	935
PL 15	Akamas	PB	Cyprus	173
PM 15	Teshio	PM/AGOB	Japan	426
Q 15	Cormoran	AGSC	Argentina	18
R 15	Macko	ARS	Poland	591
U 15	Pará	YFB	Brazil	78
V 15	Imperial Marinheiro	PG/ATR	Brazil	72
Z 15	Zahra 15	PBI	Oman	549
16	Seehund	MSD	Germany	280
ADR 16	Terminos	YM	Mexico	501
BNRJ 16	Intrépido	YTB	Brazil	80
CM 16	Loja	FSGHM	Ecuador	193
F 16	Umar Farooq	FF	Bangladesh	47
J 16	Jamuna	AGSH	India	332
KA 16	Kopaas	LCP	Norway	540
L 16	Absalon	AGF/AKR/AH	Denmark	182
L 16	Nombre De Dios	YAG	Panama	561
M 16	Anhatomirim	MSC	Brazil	74
M 16	Almirante Diaz Pimienta	WPBF	Spain	720
P 16	Cándido Pérez	PB	Spain	711
P 16	Penyerang	PB	Brunei	81
PC 16	Hamanami	PC/PB/YTR	Japan	429
PC 16	Victoria	PBG/PG	Venezuela	935
R 16	Capayan	YTB/YTL	Argentina	19
RP 16	Bohechio	YTM/YTL	Dominican Republic	190
U 16	Doutor Montenegro	AH	Brazil	78
17	Seehund	MSD	Germany	280
ADR 17	Teculapa	YM	Mexico	501
BNRJ 17	Arrojado	YTB	Brazil	80
CPAOR-17	Timbira	PB	Brazil	72
F 17	Ali Haider	FF/FFT	Bangladesh	48
G 17	Potengi	AG	Brazil	79
J 17	Sutlej	AGSH	India	332
KA 17	Tangen	LCP	Norway	540
L 17	Esbern Snare	AGF/AKR/AH	Denmark	182
L 17	Sharabh	LSM/LSMH	India	331
LPD 17	San Antonio	LPDM	US	900
M 17	Atalaia	MSC	Brazil	74
M 17	Rio Arba	PB	Spain	720
PC 17	Shinonome	PC/PB/YTR	Japan	429
TK 17	Arkhangelsk	SSBN	Russian Federation	615
U 17	Parnaiba	PGRH	Brazil	73
Z 17	Zahra 17	PBI	Oman	549
18	Seehund	MSD	Germany	280
BNRJ 18	Valente	YTB	Brazil	80
F 18	Osman	FFG	Bangladesh	46
H 18	Comandante Varella	ABU	Brazil	75
J 18	Sandhayak	AGSH	India	332
K 18	Karelia	SSBN	Russian Federation	616
KA 18	Oddane	LCP	Norway	540
L 18	Cheetah	LSM/LSMH	India	331
LPD 18	New Orleans	LPDM	US	900
M 18	Araçatuba	MSC	Brazil	74
M 18	Rio Caudal	PB	Spain	720
MUL 18	Fårösund	MLC	Sweden	737
P 18	Armatolos	PGG	Greece	296
PC 18	Harunami	PC/PB/YTR	Japan	429
R 18	Chiquilyan	YTB/YTL	Argentina	19
U 18	Oswaldo Cruz	AHH	Brazil	78
Z 18	Zahra 18	PBI	Oman	549
19	Almirante Williams	FFHM	Chile	112
BNRJ 19	Impávido	YTB	Brazil	80
GS 19	Zhigulovsk	AGIM	Russian Federation	651
H 19	Tenente Castelo	ABU	Brazil	75
J 19	Nirdeshak	AGSH	India	332
KA 19	Malmøya	LCP	Norway	540

Number	Ship's name	Type	Country	Page
L 19	Mahish	LSM/LSMH	India	331
LCC 19	Blue Ridge	LCCH/AGFH	US	893
LPD 19	Mesa Verde	LPDM	US	900
M 19	Abrolhos	MSC	Brazil	74
M 19	Rio Bernesga	PB	Spain	720
P 19	Navmachos	PGG	Greece	296
P 19	Ngunguri	PB	Tanzania	761
PC 19	Kiyozuki	PC/PB/YTR	Japan	429
PS 19	Miguel Malvar	FS	Philippines	575
R 19	Morcoyan	YTB/YTL	Argentina	19
RP 19	Cayacca	YTM/YTL	Dominican Republic	190
T-AGOS 19	Victorious	AGOS	US	913
T-AH 19	Mercy	AHH	US	911
U 19	Carlos Chagas	AHH	Brazil	78
20	Ahmad El Fateh	PGGF	Bahrain	43
20	Thomson	SSK	Chile	108
20	Capitán Miranda	AXS	Uruguay	932
ACV 20	Holdfast Bay	PB	Australia	37
CG 20	Nelson	PBO	Trinidad and Tobago	781
F 20	Godavari	FFGHM	India	321
H 20	Comandante Manhães	ABU	Brazil	75
L 20	Magar	LSTH	India	331
LCC 20	Mount Whitney	LCCH/AGFH	US	893
LPD 20	Green Bay	LPDM	US	900
M 20	Albardão	MSC	Brazil	74
M 20	Rio Martin	PB	Spain	720
MUL 20	Furusund	MLC	Sweden	736
P 20	Murature	AX	Argentina	16
P 20	Pedro Teixeira	PBR	Brazil	72
P 20	Anthypoploiarchos Laskos	PGGF/PGG	Greece	295
PC 20	Ayanami	PC/PB/YTR	Japan	429
PK 20	Spearfish	PBF	Singapore	693
PS 20	Magat Salamat	FS	Philippines	575
PT 20	Manta Ray	WPB	Singapore	693
PV 20	Poseidon	PBF	Cyprus	174
Q 20	Puerto Deseado	AGOB	Argentina	18
S 20	Astute	SSN	UK	828
ST 20	Intrépido	SSW	Colombia	156
T-AH 20	Comfort	AHH	US	911
TK 20	Severstal	SSBN	Russian Federation	615
U 20	Cisne Branco	AXS	Brazil	77
WAGB 20	Healy	WAGBH	US	924
Z 20	Seeb	PB	Oman	546
21	Al Jabiri	PGGF	Bahrain	43
21	Simpson	SSK	Chile	108
21	Haixun	PBOH	China	154
21	Kuha 21	MSI	Finland	222
21	Hejaz	LST	Iran	362
21	Cheong Hae Jin	ARS	Korea, South	452
21	Sour	LST	Lebanon	461
21	Tempur	PBF	Malaysia	477
21	Vigilant	PSOH	Mauritius	488
21	Sirius	ABU	Uruguay	932
BP 21	Bredstedt	WPSO	Germany	286
CM 21	Velarde	CM/PGGFM	Peru	569
F 21	Gomati	FFGHM	India	321
F 21	Mariscal Sucre	FFGHM	Venezuela	934
G 21	Ary Parreiras	AKSH	Brazil	77
GC 21	Lynch	WPB	Argentina	20
H 21	Sirius	AGSH	Brazil	75
HPL 21	Ankaran	PBF	Slovenia	694
HS 21	Hamashio	YGS	Japan	431
J 21	Darshak	AGSH	India	332
K 21	Göteborg	FSG	Sweden	733
KA 21	Brettingen	LCP	Norway	540
L 21	Guldar	LSM/LSMH	India	331
L 21	Isla Paridas	YAG	Panama	562
LC 21	Curiapo	LCM	Venezuela	939
LG 21	Polaris	PBF	Venezuela	939
LPD 21	New York	LPDM	US	900
M 21	Rio Guadalobon	PB	Spain	720
P 21	King	AX	Argentina	16
P 21	Raposo Tavares	PBR	Brazil	72
P 21	Plotarchis Blessas	PGGF/PGG	Greece	295
P 21	Emer	PSO	Ireland	367
P 21	Anaga	PB	Spain	712
PC 21	Tokinami	PC/PB/YTR	Japan	429
PF 21	Manaure	PBR	Venezuela	937
PK 21	White Marlin	PBF	Singapore	693
PL 21	Kojima	PL/PSOH	Japan	423
PLH 21	Mizuho	PLH/PSOH	Japan	423
PM 21	Tokara	PM/PBO	Japan	427
PP 21	Giorgi Toreli	WPBF	Georgia	267
PV 21	Evagoras	PBF	Cyprus	174
R 21	Tritão	ATA	Brazil	79
RP 21	Fernando Gomez	AKSL	Venezuela	939
RTOP 21	Šibenik	PTGF	Croatia	168
S 21	Ambush	SSN	UK	828
SSN 21	Seawolf	SSN	US	867
ST 21	Indomable	SSW	Colombia	156
T-AGOS 21	Effective	AGOS	US	913
Y 21	Oilpress	AOTL	UK	851
Z 21	Shinas	PB	Oman	546
22	Abdul Rahman Al Fadel	PGGF	Bahrain	43
22	O'Higgins	SSK	Chile	108
22	Kuha 22	MSI	Finland	222
22	Karabala	LST	Iran	362
22	Damour	LST	Lebanon	461
22	Tempur	PBF	Malaysia	477
22	Oyarvide	AGS	Uruguay	931
AM 22	Óbuda	MSR	Hungary	311
BP 22	Neustrelitz	WPBO	Germany	286
CM 22	Santillana	CM/PGGFM	Peru	569
F 22	Ganga	FFGHM	India	321
F 22	Almirante Brión	FFGHM	Venezuela	934
GC 22	Toll	WPB	Argentina	20
HS 22	Isoshi	YGS	Japan	431
J 22	Sarvekshak	AGSH	India	332
K 22	Gävle	FSG	Sweden	733
KA 22	Løkhaug	LCP	Norway	540
KV 22	Barentshav	WPSOH	Norway	543
L 22	Kumbhir	LSM/LSMH	India	331
LG 22	Sirius	PBF	Venezuela	939
LPD 22	San Diego	LPDM	US	900
M 22	Rio Cedena	PB	Spain	720
P 22	Maharajalela	PB	Brunei	81
P 22	Ayety	WPBO	Georgia	267
P 22	Ypoploiarchos Mikonios	PGGF/PGG	Greece	295
P 22	Aoife	PSO	Ireland	367
P 22	Tagomago	PB	Spain	712
PC 22	Hamagumo	PC/PB/YTR	Japan	429
PF 22	Mara	PBR	Venezuela	937
PK 22	Silver Marlin	PBF	Singapore	693
PL 22	Miura	PL/PSOH	Japan	423
PLH 22	Yashima	PLH/PSOH	Japan	423
PM 22	Fukue	PM/PBO	Japan	427
PS 22	Sultan Kudarat	FS	Philippines	575
PV 22	Odysseus	PBF	Cyprus	173
R 22	Tridente	ATA	Brazil	79
R 22	Viraat	CVM	India	317
RM 22	Enriquillo	PG/ATA	Dominican Republic	188
S 22	Artful	SSN	UK	828
SSN 22	Connecticut	SSN	US	867
T-AGOS 22	Loyal	AGOS	US	913
Z 22	Sadh	PB	Oman	546
23	Al Taweelah	PGGF	Bahrain	43
23	Carrera	SSK	Chile	108
23	Kuha 23	MSI	Finland	222
23	Amir	LST	Iran	362
23	Tempur	PBF	Malaysia	477
A 23	Antares	AGS	Spain	715
AGOR-23	Thomas G Thompson	AGOR	US	904
BP 23	Bad Düben	WPBO	Germany	286
CM 23	De Los Heros	CM/PGGFM	Peru	569
F 23	General Urdaneta	FFGHM	Venezuela	934
G 23	Almirante Gastão Motta	AOR	Brazil	78
H 23	Lokys	PB	Lithuania	468
HS 23	Uzushio	YGS	Japan	431
K 23	Kalmar	FSG	Sweden	733
KA 23	Sørviknes	LCP	Norway	540
L 23	Gharial	LSTH	India	331
LCM 23	Krabbe	LCM	Germany	278
LG 23	Rigel	PBF	Venezuela	939
LPD 23	Anchorage	LPDM	US	900
M 23	Rio Ladra	PB	Spain	720
P 23	Kemaindera	PB	Brunei	81
P 23	Ypoploiarchos Troupakis	PGGF/PGG	Greece	295
P 23	Aisling	PSO	Ireland	367
P 23	Marola	PB	Spain	712
PC 23	Awanami	PC/PB/YTR	Japan	429
PF 23	Guaicaipuro	PBR	Venezuela	937
PK 23	Striped Marlin	PBF	Singapore	693
PM 23	Oirase	PM/PBO	Japan	427
PS 23	Datu Marikudo	FS	Philippines	575
PV 23	Thexas	PB	Cyprus	173
R 23	Triunfo	ATA	Brazil	79
SSN 23	Jimmy Carter	SSN	US	867
T-AGM 23	Observation Island	AGM	US	912
T-AGOS 23	Impeccable	AGOS	US	912
Z 23	Khassab	PB	Oman	546
24	Kuha 24	MSI	Finland	222
24	Farsi	LST	Iran	362
24	Tempur	PBF	Malaysia	477
24	Lieutenant Remus Lepri	MSC	Romania	610
A 24	Rigel	AGS	Spain	715
AGOR-24	Roger Revelle	AGOR	US	904
BP 24	Bad Bramstedt	WPSO	Germany	286
CM 24	Herrera	CM/PGGFM	Peru	569
F 24	General Soublette	FFGHM	Venezuela	934
GC 24	Mantilla	WPSO	Argentina	20
HS 24	Okishio	YGS	Japan	431
K 24	Sundsvall	FSG	Sweden	733
LG 24	Aldebaran	PBF	Venezuela	939
LPD 24	Arlington	LPDM	US	900
M 24	Rio Cervera	PB	Spain	720
P 24	Mouro	PB	Spain	712
P 24	Simeoforos Kavaloudis	PGGF/PGG	Greece	295
PC 24	Uranami	PC/PB/YTR	Japan	429
PF 24	Tamanaco	PBR	Venezuela	937
PK 24	Black Marlin	PBF	Singapore	693
R 24	Almirante Guilhem	ATF	Brazil	79
T-AGM 24	Invincible	T-AGM	US	912
25	Kuha 25	MSI	Finland	222
25	Sardasht	LST	Iran	362
25	Kasturi	FSGH	Malaysia	473
25	Lieutenant Lupu Dunescu	MSC	Romania	610
AGOR-25	Atlantis	AGOR	US	904
AT 25	Ang Pangulo	AP	Philippines	579
BP 25	Bayreuth	WPSO	Germany	286
CM 25	Larrea	CM/PGGFM	Peru	569
F 25	General Salom	FFGHM	Venezuela	934
GC 25	Azopardo	WPSO	Argentina	20
H 25	Tenente Boanerges	ABU	Brazil	75
HS 25	Iseshio	YGS	Japan	431

Number	Ship's name	Type	Country	Page	Number	Ship's name	Type	Country	Page
KV 25	Sjøveien	WPSOH	Norway	543	CN 31	Rosca Fina	AXL	Brazil	77
LCM 25	Muschel	LCM	Germany	278	F 31	Brahmaputra	FFGHM	India	323
LG 25	Antares	PBF	Venezuela	939	G 31	Rio de Janeiro	LSDH	Brazil	73
LPD 25	Somerset	LPDM	US	900	K 31	Visby	FSGH	Sweden	732
M 25	Rio Aragon	PB	Spain	720	KA 31	Osternes	LCP	Norway	540
P 25	Grosa	PB	Spain	712	L 31	Damuan	YFU	Brunei	81
PC 25	Shikinami	PC/PB/YTR	Japan	429	LG 31	Chichiriviche	PB	Venezuela	939
PK 25	Blue Marlin	PBF	Singapore	693	LG 31	25 de Julio	WPB	Ecuador	197
R 25	Almirante Guillobel	ATF	Brazil	79	LM 31	Chipana	PGG	Chile	113
26	Kuha 26	MSI	Finland	222	M 31	Segura	MHC	Spain	715
26	Sab Sahel	LST	Iran	362	M 31	Cattistock	MHSC/PP	UK	844
26	Lekir	FSGH	Malaysia	473	P 31	Rondônia	PBR	Brazil	72
26	Vanguardia	ARS	Uruguay	932	P 31	Ureca	PB	Equatorial Guinea	212
AGOR 26	Kilo Moana	AGOR	US	904	P 31	Bonsu	PBO	Ghana	289
BP 26	Eschwege	WPSO	Germany	286	P 31	Eithne	PSOH	Ireland	366
CM 26	Sanchez Carrión	CM/PGGFM	Peru	569	P 31	Džūkas	PB	Lithuania	467
F 26	Almirante Garcia	FFGHM	Venezuela	934	P 31	Conejera	PB	Spain	712
GC 26	Thompson	WPSO	Argentina	20	PF 31	Terepaima	PBR	Venezuela	937
H 26	Faroleiro Mário Seixas	ABU	Brazil	76	PG 31	Petrel	WPB	Venezuela	938
HS 26	Hayashio	YGS	Japan	431	PL 31	Izu	PL/PSOH	Japan	423
LCM 26	Koralle	LCM	Germany	278	PLH 31	Shikishima	PLH/PSOH	Japan	422
LG 26	Canopus	PBF	Venezuela	939	PS 31	Pangasinan	FS	Philippines	575
M 26	Rio Alfambra	PB	Spain	720	PX 31	Tioman	PBF	Malaysia	480
P 26	Medas	PB	Spain	712	S 31	Salta	SSK	Argentina	10
P 26	Ypoploiarchos Degiannis	PGGF/PGG	Greece	295	S 31	Tamoio	SSK	Brazil	63
					S 31	Vengeance	SSBN	UK	824
PK 26	Jumping Marlin	PBF	Singapore	693	S 31	Sábalo	SSK	Venezuela	934
R 26	Trindade	ATA	Brazil	79	SS 31	Angamos	SSK	Peru	566
T-AE 26	Kilauea	AEH	US	910	V 31	Jaceguay	FSGH	Brazil	69
27	Pyong Taek	ATS	Korea, South	452	32	Guerrico	FFG	Argentina	14
27	Banco Ortiz	YTB	Uruguay	933	32	Zibar	MSC	Bulgaria	86
CG 27	Plymouth	PB	Trinidad and Tobago	781	32	Tempur	PBF	Malaysia	477
D 27	Pará	FFHM	Brazil	68	32	Buna	LSM	Papua New Guinea	562
G 27	Marajo	AOR	Brazil	78	A 32	Al Ahweirif	YTB	Libya	465
GC 27	Prefecto Fique	WPSO	Argentina	20	A 32	Tofiño	AGS	Spain	716
HS 27	Kurushima	YGS	Japan	431	AM 32	Dunafoldvar	MSR	Hungary	311
LG 27	Altair	PBF	Venezuela	939	BG 32	Donbas	PCF	Ukraine	814
M 27	Rio Ulla	PB	Spain	720	C 32	Al Mua'zzar	FSGMH	Oman	544
P 27	Inagua	PB	Bahamas	40	CG 32	Moriah	PB	Trinidad and Tobago	782
P 27	Simeoforos Xenos	PGGF/PGG	Greece	295	CN 32	Voga Picada	AXL	Brazil	77
P 27	Izaro	PB	Spain	712	D 32	Daring	DDGHM	UK	834
PN 27	Sipa	AOTL	Serbia and Montenegro	684	FFG 32	John L Hall	FFGHM	US	886
					K 32	Helsingborg	FSGH	Sweden	732
U 27	Brasil	AXH	Brazil	76	KA 32	Fjell	LCP	Norway	540
Z 27	Zahra 27	YDT	Oman	549	L 32	Puni	YFU	Brunei	81
28	Nakhoda Ragam	FSGH	Brunei	80	LG 32	Caruanta	PB	Venezuela	939
28	Kwang Yang	ATS	Korea, South	452	LG 32	24 de Mayo	WPB	Ecuador	197
CG 28	Caroni	PB	Trinidad and Tobago	781	M 32	Sella	MHC	Spain	715
FFG 28	Boone	FFGHM	US	886	P 32	Amapá	PBR	Brazil	72
G 28	Mattoso Maia	LSTH	Brazil	73	P 32	Selis	PB	Lithuania	467
GC 28	Prefecto Derbes	WPSO	Argentina	20	P 32	Dragonera	PB	Spain	712
KV 28	Nysleppen	WPSOH	Norway	543	PG 32	Alcatraz	WPB	Venezuela	938
M 28	Rio Jucar	PB	Spain	720	PS 32	Iloilo	FS	Philippines	575
P 28	Simeoforos Simitzopoulos	PGGF/PGG	Greece	295	PX 32	Tumpat	PBF	Malaysia	480
					S 32	Timbira	SSK	Brazil	63
P 28	Tabarca	PB	Spain	712	S 32	Caribe	SSK	Venezuela	934
PS 28	Cebu	FS	Philippines	575	SS 32	Antofagasta	SSK	Peru	566
PX 28	Sangitan	PBF	Malaysia	480	T-AE 32	Flint	AEH	US	910
S 28	Vanguard	SSBN	UK	824	V 32	Julio De Noronha	FSGH	Brazil	69
SO 28	Pijao	SS	Colombia	155	Y 32	Moorhen	ARS	UK	851
29	Bendahara Sakam	FSGH	Brunei	80	33	Granville	FFG	Argentina	14
29	Lieutenant Dimitrie Nicolescu	MSC	Romania	610	33	Teraban	LCU	Brunei	81
					33	Dobrotich	MSC	Bulgaria	86
CG 29	Galeota	PB	Trinidad and Tobago	781	33	Vikram	WPSOH	India	336
FFG 29	Stephen W Groves	FFGHM	US	886	33	Tempur	PBF	Malaysia	477
M 29	Rio Santa Eulalia	PB	Spain	720	33	Kotor	FFGM	Serbia and Montenegro	681
P 29	Simeoforos Starakis	PGGF/PGG	Greece	295					
PS 29	Negros Occidental	FS	Philippines	575	33	Fortuna	MSC	Uruguay	931
PX 29	Sabahan	PBF	Malaysia	480	A 33	Hespérides	AGOBH	Spain	715
S 29	Victorious	SSBN	UK	824	AW 33	Lake Bulusan	AWT	Philippines	579
SO 29	Tayrona	SS	Colombia	155	CG 33	Matelot	PB	Trinidad and Tobago	782
U 29	Piraim	YFBH	Brazil	78	CN 33	Leva Arriba	AXL	Brazil	77
30	Al Jarim	PB	Bahrain	43	D 33	Dauntless	DDGHM	UK	834
30	Jerambak	FSGH	Brunei	80	FFG 33	Jarrett	FFGHM	US	886
30	Sub Lieutenant Alexandru Axente	MSC	Romania	610	J 33	Meen	AGS	India	332
					K 33	Juang	PB	Malaysia	481
ACV 30	Botany Bay	PB	Australia	37	K 33	Härnösand	FSGH	Sweden	732
BG 30	Perekop	PCF	Ukraine	814	KA 33	Lerøy	LCP	Norway	540
CG 30	Moruga	PB	Trinidad and Tobago	781	LG-33	10 de Agosto	WPB	Ecuador	197
G 30	Ceará	LSDH	Brazil	73	M 33	Tambre	MHC	Spain	715
LM 30	Casma	PGG	Chile	113	M 33	Brocklesby	MHSC/PP	UK	844
M 30	Rio Ulla	PB	Spain	720	P 33	Abhay	FSM	India	324
M 30	Ledbury	MHSC/PP	UK	844	P 33	Skalvis	PB	Lithuania	467
P 30	Roraima	PBR	Brazil	72	P 33	Espalmador	PB	Spain	712
P 30	Anzone	PBO	Ghana	289	PF 33	Yaracuy	PBR	Venezuela	937
P 30	Bergantin	PB	Spain	712	PG 33	Albatros	WPB	Venezuela	938
PK 30	Billfish	PBF	Singapore	693	PX 33	Segama	PBF	Malaysia	480
PT 30	Eagle Ray	WPB	Singapore	693	S 33	Tapajó	SSK	Brazil	63
PX 30	Dungun	PBF	Malaysia	480	SS 33	Pisagua	SSK	Peru	566
Q 30	Al Mabrukah	FSH/AXL/AGS	Oman	545	T-AE 33	Shasta	AEH	US	910
RPB 30	Kozara	PBR	Serbia and Montenegro	683	V 33	Frontin	FSGH	Brazil	69
					Y 33	Moorfowl	ARS	UK	851
S 30	Tupi	SSK	Brazil	63	34	Serasa	LCU	Brunei	81
S 30	Vigilant	SSBN	UK	824	34	Evstati Vinarov	MSC	Bulgaria	86
V 30	Inhaúma	FSGH	Brazil	69	34	Vijaya	WPSOH	India	336
31	Drummond	FFG	Argentina	14	34	Tempur	PBF	Malaysia	477
31	Al Jasrah	PB	Bahrain	43	34	Novi Sad	FFGM	Serbia and Montenegro	681
31	Iskar	MSC	Bulgaria	86					
31	Salamaua	LSM	Papua New Guinea	562	34	Audaz	MSC	Uruguay	931
31	Temerario	MSC	Uruguay	931	AW 34	Lake Paoay	AWT	Philippines	579
A 31	Ras El Helal	YTB	Libya	465	D 34	Diamond	DDGHM	UK	834
A 31	Malaspina	AGS	Spain	716	H 34	Almirante Graça Aranha	ABUH	Brazil	75
AM 31	Dunaújváros	MSR	Hungary	311					
BB 31	Gorgona	AGSC	Colombia	161	J 34	Mithun	AGS	India	332
C 31	Qahir Al Amwaj	FSGMH	Oman	544	K 34	Pulai	PB	Malaysia	481
CG 31	Kairi	PB	Trinidad and Tobago	782	K 34	Nyköping	FSGH	Sweden	732

Number	Ship's name	Type	Country	Page
L 34	Vasco Da Gama	LSM	India	331
LG-34	3 de Noviembre	WPB	Ecuador	197
LM 34	Angamos	PGG	Chile	113
M 34	Turia	MHC	Spain	715
M 34	Middleton	MHSC/PP	UK	844
P 34	Ajay	FSM	India	324
P 34	Alcanada	PB	Spain	712
PF 34	Sorocaima	PBR	Venezuela	937
PG 34	Pelícano	WPB	Venezuela	938
SS 34	Chipana	SSK	Peru	566
T-AE 34	Mount Baker	AEH	US	910
V 34	Barroso	FSGH	Brazil	68
35	Veera	WPSOH	India	336
D 35	Dragon	DDGHM	UK	834
F 35	Udaygiri	FFH	India	324
H 35	Amorim Do Valle	AGS	Brazil	75
K 35	Karlstad	FSGH	Sweden	732
LG 35	5 de Agosto	WPB	Ecuador	196
M 35	Duero	MHC	Spain	715
P 35	Akshay	FSM	India	324
PS 35	Emilio Jacinto	FS	Philippines	575
SS 35	Islay	SSK	Peru	566
T-AE 35	Kiska	AEH	US	910
Y 35	Mesaha 1	AGSC	Turkey	798
36	Varuna	WPSOH	India	336
36-1	Puerto Quepos	PB	Costa Rica	165
D 36	Defender	DDGHM	UK	834
F 36	Dunagiri	FFH	India	324
FFG 36	Underwood	FFGHM	US	886
H 36	Taurus	AGS	Brazil	75
K 36	Perak	PB	Malaysia	481
LG 36	27 de Febrero	WPB	Ecuador	196
LM 36	Riquelme	PGG	Chile	113
M 36	Tajo	MHC	Spain	715
P 36	Agray	FSM	India	324
PS 36	Apolinario Mabini	FS	Philippines	575
RSRB 36	Sabac	YDG	Serbia and Montenegro	684
SS 36	Arica	SSK	Peru	566
Y 36	Mesaha 2	AGSC	Turkey	798
37	Vajra	WPSOH	India	336
D 37	Duncan	DDGHM	UK	834
F 37	Beas	FFGHM	India	323
FFG 37	Crommelin	FFGHM	US	886
H 37	Garnier Sampaio	ABU	Brazil	75
K 37	Bayu	PB	Malaysia	481
LG 37	9 de Octubre	WPBF	Ecuador	196
LM 37	Orella	PGG	Chile	113
M 37	Chiddingfold	MHSC/PP	UK	844
PS 37	Artemio Ricarte	FS	Philippines	575
38	Vivek	WPSOH	India	336
CG 38	Soldado	PB	Trinidad and Tobago	782
FFG 38	Curts	FFGHM	US	886
K 38	Hijau	PB	Malaysia	481
L 38	Midhur	LSM	India	331
L 38	Galana	LCM	Kenya	435
LG 38	27 de Octubre	WPBF	Ecuador	196
LM 38	Serrano	PGG	Chile	113
M 38	Atherstone	MHSC/PP	UK	844
PS 38	General Mariano Alvares	PB	Philippines	576
WMEC 38	Storis	PSO/WMEC	US	921
Y 38	Yüzbaşi Naşit Öngören	YPB	Turkey	800
39	Vigraha	WPSOH	India	336
AS 39	Emory S Land	ASH	US	907
CG 39	Roxborough	PB	Trinidad and Tobago	782
F 39	Betwa	FFGHM	India	323
FFG 39	Doyle	FFGHM	US	886
GS 39	Syzran	AGIM	Russian Federation	651
L 39	Mangala	LSM	India	331
L 39	Tana	LCM	Kenya	435
LG 39	6 de Diciembre	PBO	Ecuador	196
LM 39	Uribe	PGG	Chile	113
M 39	Hurworth	MHSC/PP	UK	844
WMEC 39	Alex Haley	PSOH/WMEC	US	920
Y 39	Binbaşi Metin Sülüş	YPB	Turkey	800
40	Al Zubara	LCU	Bahrain	44
40	Varad	WPSOH	India	336
A 40	Attock	AOTL	Pakistan	557
ACV 40	Hervey Bay	PB	Australia	37
AS 40	Frank Cable	ASH	US	907
CG 40	Mayaro	PB	Trinidad and Tobago	782
F 40	Niterói	FFGHM	Brazil	67
F 40	Talwar	FFGHM	India	322
FFG 40	Halyburton	FFGHM	US	886
H 40	Antares	AGS	Brazil	75
K 40	Veer	FSGM	India	327
LG 40	11 de Noviembre	PBO	Ecuador	196
P 40	Grajaú	PBO	Brazil	71
PK 40	Swordfish	PBF	Singapore	693
S 40	Vela	SS	India	314
41	Espora	FFGH	Argentina	13
41	Ajeera	YFU	Bahrain	43
41	Drazki	FFGM	Bulgaria	83
41	Letyashti	FS	Bulgaria	84
41	Varaha	WPSOH	India	336
41	Tempur	PBF	Malaysia	477
A 41	Vetra	AGOR/AX	Lithuania	467
AP 41	Aquiles	APH	Chile	116
BP 41	Kustrin-Kiez	WPBR	Germany	287
F 41	Defensora	FFGHM	Brazil	67
F 41	Taragiri	FFH	India	324
FFG 41	McClusky	FFGHM	US	886
K 41	Nirbhik	FSGM	India	327
LG 41	11 de Abril	PBO	Ecuador	196
LSD 41	Whidbey Island	LSDHM and LSD-CV	US	899
M 41	Quorn	MHSC/PP	UK	844
P 41	Guaiba	PBO	Brazil	71
P 41	Orla	PSO	Ireland	367
PL 41	Aso	PL/PSO	Japan	424
PO 41	Espartana	PBO	Colombia	157
S 41	Santa Cruz	SSK	Argentina	11
42	Rosales	FFGH	Argentina	13
42	Mashtan	LCU	Bahrain	44
42	Bditelni	FS	Bulgaria	84
42	Merino	AGP/ASH	Chile	116
42	Samar	WPSOH	India	336
42	Tempur	PBF	Malaysia	477
42-1	Primera Dama	PB	Costa Rica	164
BP 42	Schwedt	WPBR	Germany	287
F 42	Constituição	FFGHM	Brazil	67
F 42	Vindhyagiri	FFH	India	324
FFG 42	Klakring	FFGHM	US	886
K 42	Nipat	FSGM	India	327
L 42	Pizarro	LSTH	Spain	714
LSD 42	Germantown	LSDHM and LSD-CV	US	899
P 42	Graúna	PBO	Brazil	71
P 42	Ciara	PSO	Ireland	367
PL 42	Dewa	PL/PSO	Japan	424
PO 42	Capitán Pablo José De Porto	PBO	Colombia	157
S 42	San Juan	SSK	Argentina	11
S 42	Vagli	SS	India	314
43	Spiro	FFGH	Argentina	13
43	Rubodh	LCU	Bahrain	44
43	Bezstrashni	FS	Bulgaria	84
43	Esmeralda	AXS	Chile	116
43	Sangram	WPSOH	India	336
43	Tempur	PBF	Malaysia	477
43	Novorossiysk	PCM	Russian Federation	663
BP 43	Frankfurt/Oder	WPBR	Germany	287
F 43	Liberal	FFGHM	Brazil	67
F 43	Trishul	FFGHM	India	322
FFG 43	Thach	FFGHM	US	886
GC 43	Mandubi	WAX	Argentina	20
K 43	Nishank	FSGM	India	327
LSD 43	Fort McHenry	LSDHM and LSD-CV	US	899
P 43	Goiana	PBO	Brazil	71
PL 43	Hakusan	PL/PSO	Japan	424
PO 43	Capitán Jorge Enrique Marquez Duran	PBO	Colombia	
44	Parker	FFGH	Argentina	13
44	Suwad	LCU	Bahrain	44
44	Khrabri	FS	Bulgaria	84
44	Sarang	WPSOH	India	336
44	Tempur	PBF	Malaysia	477
A 44	Bholu	YTB	Pakistan	558
BP 44	Aurith	WPBR	Germany	287
F 44	Independência	FFGHM	Brazil	67
F 44	Tabar	FFGHM	India	322
H 44	Ary Rongel	AGOBH	Brazil	74
K 44	Nirghat	FSGM	India	327
K 44	Borisoglebsk	SSBN	Russian Federation	617
LSD 44	Gunston Hall	LSDHM and LSD-CV	US	899
P 44	Guajará	PBO	Brazil	71
P 44	Kirpan	FSGHM	India	326
PO 44	Valle Del Cauca	FLGHM	Colombia	
S 44	Shishumar	SSK	India	315
45	Robinson	FFGH	Argentina	13
45	Jaradah	LCU	Bahrain	44
45	Sagar	WPSOH	India	336
45	Mikhail Kogalniceanu	PGR	Romania	609
A 45	Gama	YTB	Pakistan	558
F 45	União	FFGHM	Brazil	67
FFG 45	De Wert	FFGHM	US	886
K 45	Vibhuti	FSGM	India	327
LSD 45	Comstock	LSDHM and LSD-CV	US	899
P 45	Guaporé	PBO	Brazil	71
S 45	Shankush	SSK	India	315
T-AG 45	Waters	AGM	US	912
46	Gomez Roca	FFGH	Argentina	13
46	Tighatlib	YFL	Bahrain	44
46	I C Bratianu	PGR	Romania	609
AE 46	Cape Bojeador	ABU	Philippines	580
AP 46	Contre-Almirante Oscar Viel Toro	AGS/AGOBH	Chile	115
F 46	Greenhalgh	FFGHM	Brazil	66
F 46	Krishna	AXH	India	333
FFG 46	Rentz	FFGHM	US	886
K 46	Vipul	FSGM	India	327
LSD 46	Tortuga	LSDHM and LSD-CV	US	899
P 46	Gurupá	PBO	Brazil	71
P 46	Kuthar	FSGHM	India	326
S 46	Shalki	SSK	India	315
47	Lascar Catargiu	PGR	Romania	609
A 47	Nasr	AORH	Pakistan	557
FFG 47	Nicholas	FFGHM	US	886
GC 47	Tonina	WARS	Argentina	21
K 47	Vinash	FSGM	India	327
LSD 47	Rushmore	LSDHM and LSD-CV	US	899
P 47	Gurupi	PBO	Brazil	71
P 47	Khanjar	FSGHM	India	326
S 47	Shankul	SSK	India	315
F 48	Bosisio	FFGHM	Brazil	66

Number	Ship's name	Type	Country	Page	Number	Ship's name	Type	Country	Page
FFG 48	Vandegrift	FFGHM	US	886	PH 53	Blue Shark	WPB	Singapore	692
GC 48	Estrellemar	WPB	Argentina	21	Y 53	Kuvvet	YTB/YTM/YTL	Turkey	802
K 48	Vidyut	FSGM	India	327	A 54	Amba	ASH	India	333
LSD 48	Ashland	LSDHM and LSD-CV	US	899	BP 54	Oderbruch	WPB	Germany	287
					CG 54	Antietam	CGHM	US	877
P 48	Guanabara	PBO	Brazil	71	D 54	Ranvir	DDGHM	India	320
SV 48	Behr Paima	AGS/AGOR	Pakistan	557	DDG 54	Curtis Wilbur	DDGHM	US	880
A 49	Gwadar	AOTL	Pakistan	557	FFG 54	Ford	FFGHM	US	886
F 49	Rademaker	FFGHM	Brazil	66	FL 54	Independiente	FLGHM	Colombia	156
FFG 49	Robert G Bradley	FFGHM	US	886	FM 54	Mariategui	FFGHM	Peru	568
GC 49	Remora	WPB	Argentina	21	GC 54	Salmon	WPB	Argentina	21
LSD 49	Harpers Ferry	LSDHM and LSD-CV	US	899	MHC 54	Robin	MHC	US	903
					PC 54	Nunobiki	PC/YTR	Japan	428
P 49	Guarujá	PBO	Brazil	71	PH 54	Tiger Shark	WPB	Singapore	692
P 49	Khukri	FSGHM	India	326	55	BDK-98	LSTM	Russian Federation	645
50	Al Manama	FSGH	Bahrain	42	55	Kasimov	FFLM	Russian Federation	639
50	Kiisla	PB	Finland	221	55	Marshal Ustinov	CGHM	Russian Federation	631
50	RV	YDT	Netherlands	528	BG 55	Galichina	PCK	Ukraine	814
A 50	Alster	AGI	Germany	282	CG 55	Leyte Gulf	CGHM	US	877
ACV 50	Corio Bay	PB	Australia	37	D 55	Ranvijay	DDGHM	India	320
ARS 50	Safeguard	ARS	US	906	DDG 55	Stout	DDGHM	US	880
BG 50	Grigory Kuropiatnikov	PC	Ukraine	814	FFG 55	Elrod	FFGHM	US	886
FFG 50	Taylor	FFGHM	US	886	FM 55	Aguirre	FFGHM	Peru	568
GC 50	Congrio	WPB	Argentina	21	FV 55	Indaw	PBO	Myanmar	511
L 50	Tobruk	LSLH	Australia	30	GC 55	Bigua	WPB	Argentina	21
LSD 50	Carter Hall	LSDHM and LSD-CV	US	899	MHC 55	Oriole	MHC	US	903
					P 55	Sharada	PSOH	India	330
N 50	Tyr	ML	Norway	541	PH 55	Basking Shark	WPB	Singapore	692
P 50	Guaratuba	PBO	Brazil	71	S 55	Sindhughosh	SSK	India	315
P 50	Sukanya	PSOH	India	330	Y 55	Atil	YTB/YTM/YTL	Turkey	802
PH 50	Hammerhead Shark	WPB	Singapore	692	56	Kajava	AX	Finland	222
PK 50	Spikefish	PBF	Singapore	693	CG 56	San Jacinto	CGHM	US	877
T-ARS 50	Grasp	ARS	US	911	DDG 56	John S Mccain	DDGHM	US	880
Y 50	Gölcük	YO	Turkey	800	FFG 56	Simpson	FFGHM	US	886
51	Al Muharraq	FSGH	Bahrain	42	FM 56	Palacios	FFGHM	Peru	568
51	Kurki	PB	Finland	221	GC 56	Foca	WPB	Argentina	21
A 51	Gaj	YTM/YTL	India	335	P 56	Sujata	PSOH	India	330
A 51	Lidaka	YDT	Latvia	460	PH 56	Sandbar Shark	WPB	Singapore	692
A 51	Mahón	ATA	Spain	719	S 56	Sindhudhvaj	SSK	India	315
A 51	Temsah	YTM	UAE	819	Y 56	Pendik	YTB/YTM/YTL	Turkey	802
BG 51	Poltava	PC	Ukraine	814	57	Lokki	AX	Finland	222
BP 51	Vogtland	WPB	Germany	287	57	Chun Jee	AORH	Korea, South	452
D 51	Rajput	DDGHM	India	320	A 57	Shakti	AORH	India	313
DDG 51	Arleigh Burke	DDGHM	US	880	BG 57	Mikolaiv	PCF	Ukraine	814
FFG 51	Gary	FFGHM	US	886	CG 57	Lake Champlain	CGHM	US	877
FL 51	Almirante Padilla	FLGHM	Colombia	156	DDG 57	Mitscher	DDGHM	US	880
FM 51	Carvajal	FFGHM	Peru	568	FFG 57	Reuben James	FFGHM	US	886
GC 51	Mero	WPB	Argentina	21	FV 57	Inya	PBO	Myanmar	511
K 51	Verchoture	SSBN	Russian Federation	616	GC 57	Tiburon	WPB	Argentina	21
L 51	Kanimbla	LCCH/LLP	Australia	29	MHC 57	Cormorant	MHC	US	903
L 51	Galicia	LPD	Spain	713	P 57	Pyrpolitis	PGG	Greece	296
L 51	Al Feyi	LCU	UAE	820	PH 57	Thresher Shark	WPB	Singapore	692
LSD 51	Oak Hill	LSDHM and LSD-CV	US	899	S 57	Sindhuraj	SSK	India	315
					58	Dae Chung	AORH	Korea, South	452
M 51	Kuršis	MHC	Lithuania	467	A 58	Jyoti	AORH	India	333
MHC 51	Osprey	MHC	US	903	CG 58	Philippine Sea	CGHM	US	877
P 51	Gravataí	PBO	Brazil	71	DDG 58	Laboon	DDGHM	US	880
P 51	Subhadra	PSOH	India	330	FFG 58	Samuel B Roberts	FFGHM	US	886
PC 51	Yodo	PC/YTR	Japan	428	GC 58	Melva	WPB	Argentina	21
PH 51	Mako Shark	WPB	Singapore	692	MHC 58	Black Hawk	MHC	US	903
PL 51	Hida	PL/PSO	Japan	424	PH 58	Whitetip Shark	WPB	Singapore	692
Y 51	Söndæren 1	YTB/YTM/YTL	Turkey	802	S 58	Sindhuvir	SSK	India	315
52	Cheboksary	PCM	Russian Federation	664	59	Rajkiran	WPB	India	337
A 52	Oste	AGI	Germany	282	59	Hwa Chun	AORH	Korea, South	452
A 52	Las Palmas	AGOB	Spain	715	A 59	Aditya	AORH/AS	India	334
A 52	Ugaab	YTM	UAE	819	CG 59	Princeton	CGHM	US	877
ARS 52	Salvor	ARS	US	906	DDG 59	Russell	DDGHM	US	880
B 52	Hercules	DDGHM	Argentina	11	FFG 59	Kauffman	FFGHM	US	886
BG 52	Grigory Gnatenko	PC	Ukraine	814	GC 59	Lenguado	WPB	Argentina	21
BP 52	Rhön	WPB	Germany	287	MHC 59	Falcon	MHC	US	903
CG 52	Bunker Hill	CGHM	US	877	PH 59	Blacktip Shark	WPB	Singapore	692
D 52	Rana	DDGHM	India	320	S 59	Sindhuratna	SSK	India	315
DDG 52	Barry	DDGHM	US	880	60	Vidal Gormaz	AGOR	Chile	115
FFG 52	Carr	FFGHM	US	886	ACV 60	Arnhem Bay	PB	Australia	37
FL 52	Caldas	FLGHM	Colombia	156	CG 60	Normandy	CGHM	US	877
FM 52	Villavisencio	FFGHM	Peru	568	D 60	Mysore	DDGHM	India	318
GC 52	Marsopa	WPB	Argentina	21	DDG 60	Paul Hamilton	DDGHM	US	880
L 52	Manoora	LCCH/LLP	Australia	29	FFG 60	Rodney M Davis	FFGHM	US	886
L 52	Castilla	LPD	Spain	713	GC 60	Orca	WPB	Argentina	21
L 52	Dayyinah	LCU	UAE	820	M 60	Erato	MHC/MSC	Greece	298
LSD 52	Pearl Harbor	LSDHM and LSD-CV	US	899	MHC 60	Cardinal	MHC	US	903
					P 60	Bahamas	NONE	Bahamas	39
M 52	Sūduvis	MHC	Lithuania	467	P 60	Bracui	PBO	Brazil	72
MHC 52	Heron	MHC	US	903	PH 60	Goblin Shark	WPB	Singapore	692
P 52	Suvarna	PSOH	India	330	S 60	Sindhukesari	SSK	India	315
PC 52	Kotobiki	PC/YTR	Japan	428	61	Briz	MSC	Bulgaria	86
PH 52	White Shark	WPB	Singapore	692	61	Rajkamal	WPB	India	337
PL 52	Akaishi	PL/PSO	Japan	424	61	Ashdod	LCT	Israel	374
Y 52	Doğanarslan	YTB/YTM/YTL	Turkey	802	CG 61	Monterey	CGHM	US	877
A 53	Oker	AGI	Germany	282	D 61	Delhi	DDGHM	India	318
A 53	Matanga	ATA/ATR	India	335	DDG 61	Ramage	DDGHM	US	880
A 53	Virsaitis	MCCS/AG	Latvia	459	FFG 61	Ingraham	FFGHM	US	886
A 53	La Graña	ATA	Spain	719	GC 61	Pinguino	WPB	Argentina	21
AO 53	Araucano	AOR	Chile	116	M 61	Pondicherry	MSO	India	331
BP 53	Spreewald	WPB	Germany	287	MHC 61	Raven	MHC	US	903
CG 53	Mobile Bay	CGHM	US	877	P 61	Baradero	PB	Argentina	16
D 53	Ranjit	DDGHM	India	320	P 61	Nassau	NONE	Bahamas	39
DDG 53	John Paul Jones	DDGHM	US	880	P 61	Benevente	PBO	Brazil	72
FFG 53	Hawes	FFGHM	US	886	P 61	Polemistis	PGG	Greece	296
FL 53	Antioquia	FLGHM	Colombia	156	P 61	Kora	FSGHM	India	325
FM 53	Montero	FFGHM	Peru	568	P 61	Chilreu	PSO	Spain	711
GC 53	Petrel	WPB	Argentina	21	PG 61	Agusan	PB	Philippines	580
L 53	Jananah	LCU	UAE	820	PH 61	School Shark	WPB	Singapore	692
MHC 53	Pelican	MHC	US	903	Q 61	Ciudad De Zarate	ABU	Argentina	19
P 53	Savitri	PSOH	India	330	S 61	Sindhukirti	SSK	India	315
PC 53	Nachi	PC/YTR	Japan	428	T 61	Trinkat	PBO	India	330

PENNANT LIST

Number	Ship's name	Type	Country	Page	Number	Ship's name	Type	Country	Page
T 61	Capana	LSTH	Venezuela	936	P 69	Ypoploiarchos Kristallidis	PGGM	Greece	295
TR 61	Hualcopo	LST	Ecuador	194	70	Avvaiyyar	WPBO	India	337
62	Shkval	MSC	Bulgaria	86	70	Rauma	PTGM	Finland	220
62	Oulu	PTGM	Finland	220	70	Steadfast	FFGHM	Singapore	688
CG 62	Chancellorsville	CGHM	US	877	ACV 70	Dame Roma Mitchell	PB	Australia	37
D 62	Mumbai	DDGHM	India	318	CG 70	Lake Erie	CGHM	US	877
DDG 62	Fitzgerald	DDGHM	US	880	CVN 70	Carl Vinson	CVNM	US	871
M 62	Evropi	MHSC	Greece	298	DDG 70	Hopper	DDGHM	US	880
M 62	Porbandar	MSO	India	331	GC 70	Rio de la Plata	WPB	Argentina	21
MHC 62	Shrike	MHC	US	903	M 70	Kakinada	MSO	India	331
P 62	Barranqueras	PB	Argentina	16	MHV 70	Saturn	PB	Denmark	185
P 62	Bocaina	PBO	Brazil	72	P 70	Ypoploiarchos Grigoro Poulos	PGGM	Greece	295
P 62	Niki	FS	Greece	294	PS 70	Quezon	FS	Philippines	575
P 62	Kirch	FSGHM	India	325	71	Raahe	PTGM	Finland	220
P 62	Alboran	PSOH	Spain	712	71	Tara Bai	WPBO	India	336
PG 62	Catanduanes	PB	Philippines	580	71	Alvand	FFG	Iran	356
Q 62	Ciudad De Rosario	ABU	Argentina	19	71	Suzdalets	FFLM	Russian Federation	639
S 62	Sindhuvijay	SSK	India	315	71	Tenacious	FFGHM	Singapore	688
T 62	Esequibo	LSTH	Venezuela	936	A 71	Juan Sebastián De Elcano	AXS	Spain	716
TR 62	Calicuchima	AETL	Ecuador	195	AT 71	Mangyan	ABU	Philippines	580
63	Priboy	MSC	Bulgaria	86	CG 71	Cape St George	CGHM	US	877
63	Kotka	PTGM	Finland	220	CVN 71	Theodore Roosevelt	CVNM	US	871
BP 63	Uckermark	WPB	Germany	286	DDG 71	Ross	DDGHM	US	880
BP 63	Altmark	WPB	Germany	286	GC 71	La Plata	WPB	Argentina	21
BRS 63	George Slight Marshall	ABU	Chile	115	M 71	Kozhikode	MSO	India	331
CG 63	Cowpens	CGHM	US	877	M 71	Landsort	MHSCDM	Sweden	737
DDG 63	Stethem	DDGHM	US	880	MHV 71	Scorpius	PB	Denmark	185
M 63	Kallisto	MHSC	Greece	298	P 71	Anthypoploiarchos Ritsos	PGGM	Greece	295
M 63	Bedi	MSO	India	331	P 71	Serviola	PSOH	Spain	711
P 63	Clorinda	PB	Argentina	16	PSG 71	Micalvi	PB/AEM	Chile	114
P 63	Babitonga	PBO	Brazil	72	S 71	Galerna	SSK	Spain	702
P 63	Doxa	FS	Greece	294	T 71	Margarita	LCU	Venezuela	936
P 63	Kulish	FSGHM	India	325	72	Porvoo	PTGM	Finland	220
P 63	Arnomendi	PSOH	Spain	712	72	Ahalya Bai	WPBO	India	336
PG 63	Romblon	PB	Philippines	580	72	Alborz	FFG	Iran	356
Q 63	Punta Alta	ABU	Argentina	19	72	Stalwart	FFGHM	Singapore	688
S 63	Sindhurakshak	SSK	India	315	A 72	Arosa	AXS	Spain	716
T 63	Tarasa	PBO	India	330	AF 72	Lake Taal	YO	Philippines	579
T 63	Goajira	LSTH	Venezuela	936	BS 72	Andrija Mohorovičić	AX	Croatia	169
TR 63	Atahualpa	AWT	Ecuador	195	CG 72	Vella Gulf	CGHM	US	877
64	Shtorm	MSC	Bulgaria	86	CVN 72	Abraham Lincoln	CVNM	US	871
64	Jija Bai	WPBO	India	337	DDG 72	Mahan	DDGHM	US	880
BP 64	Börde	WPB	Germany	286	GC 72	Buenos Aires	WPB	Argentina	21
CG 64	Gettysburg	CGHM	US	877	M 72	Konkan	MSO	India	331
DDG 64	Carney	DDGHM	US	880	M 72	Arholma	MHSCDM	Sweden	737
GC 64	Mar Del Plata	WPB	Argentina	21	P 72	Ypoploiarchos Votsis	PGGF	Greece	296
M 64	Bhavnagar	MSO	India	331	P 72	Centinela	PSOH	Spain	711
P 64	Concepciãn Del Uruguay	PB	Argentina	16	PC 72	Urayuki	PC/SAR	Japan	428
P 64	Eleftheria	FS	Greece	294	PSG 72	Ortiz	PB/AEM	Chile	114
P 64	Karmukh	FSGHM	India	325	RB 72	Sangay	YTM/YTL	Ecuador	196
P 64	Tarifa	PSOH	Spain	712	S 72	Siroco	SSK	Spain	702
PG 64	Palawan	PB	Philippines	580	T 72	La Orchila	LCU	Venezuela	936
S 64	Sindhushastra	SSK	India	315	73	Collins	SSK	Australia	24
T 64	Los Llanos	LSTH	Venezuela	936	73	Naantali	PTGM	Finland	220
TR 64	Quisquis	AWT	Ecuador	196	73	Lakshmi Bai	WPBO	India	336
Y 64	Ersev Bayrak	YTB/YTM/YTL	Turkey	802	73	Sabalan	FFG	Iran	356
65	Chand Bibi	WPBO	India	337	73	Supreme	FFGHM	Singapore	688
65-3	Cabo Blanco	PB	Costa Rica	165	BS 73	Faust Vrančič	ASR	Croatia	170
65-4	Isla Burica	PB	Costa Rica	165	CG 73	Port Royal	CGHM	US	877
CG 65	Chosin	CGHM	US	877	CVN 73	George Washington	CVNM	US	871
CVN 65	Enterprise	CVNM	US	876	DDG 73	Decatur	DDGHM	US	880
DDG 65	Benfold	DDGHM	US	880	GC 73	Cabo Corrientes	WPB	Argentina	21
GC 65	Martin Garcia	WPB	Argentina	21	M 73	Koster	MHSCDM	Sweden	737
M 65	Alleppey	MSO	India	331	P 73	Anthypoploiarchos Pezopoulos	PGGF	Greece	296
P 65	Punta Mogotes	PB	Argentina	17	P 73	Vigía	PSOH	Spain	711
T 65	Bangaram	PBO	India	330	PM 73	Bihoro	PM/PSO	Japan	426
66	Kittur Chennamma	WPBO	India	337	PSG 73	Isaza	PB/AEM	Chile	114
ATF 66	Galvarino	ATF	Chile	117	RB 73	Cotopaxi	YTM/YTL	Ecuador	196
CG 66	Hue City	CGHM	US	877	S 73	Mistral	SSK	Spain	702
DDG 66	Gonzalez	DDGHM	US	880	74	Akka Devi	WPBO	India	336
GC 66	Rio Lujan	WPB	Argentina	21	74	Farncomb	SSK	Australia	24
M 66	Ratnagiri	MSO	India	331	A 74	La Graciosa	AXS	Spain	716
P 66	Rio Santiago	PB	Argentina	17	CVN 74	John C Stennis	CVNM	US	871
T 66	Bitra	PBO	India	330	DDG 74	McFaul	DDGHM	US	880
67	Rani Jindan	WPBO	India	337	F 74	Asturias	FFGM	Spain	707
ATF 67	Lautaro	ATF	Chile	117	GC 74	Rio Quequen	WPB	Argentina	21
CG 67	Shiloh	CGHM	US	877	M 74	Kullen	MHSCDM	Sweden	737
DDG 67	Cole	DDGHM	US	880	P 74	Plotarchis Vlahavas	PGGF	Greece	296
GC 67	Rio Uruguay	WPB	Argentina	21	P 74	Atalaya	PSOH	Spain	711
M 67	Karwar	MSO	India	331	PC 74	Asoyuki	PC/PB	Japan	429
P 67	Ypoploiarchos Roussen	PGGM	Greece	295	PS 74	Rizal	FS	Philippines	575
T 67	Batti Malv	PBO	India	330	PSG 74	Morel	PB/AEM	Chile	114
P 67	Mzizi	PB	Tanzania	761	S 74	Tramontana	SSK	Spain	702
68	Habbah Khatun	WPBO	India	337	75	Waller	SSK	Australia	24
68	Formidable	FFGHM	Singapore	688	75	Naiki Devi	WPBO	India	336
ATF 68	Leucoton	AFL/ATF	Chile	117	75	Grigore Antipa	AGOR	Romania	610
CG 68	Anzio	CGHM	US	877	A 75	Tarangini	AXS	India	333
CVN 68	Nimitz	CVNM	US	871	A 75	Sisargas	AXS	Spain	716
DDG 68	The Sullivans	DDGHM	US	880	AU 75	Bessang Pass	PB	Philippines	580
GC 68	Rio Paraguay	WPB	Argentina	21	CVN 75	Harry S Truman	CVNM	US	871
M 68	Cannanore	MSO	India	331	DDG 75	Donald Cook	DDGHM	US	880
P 68	Ypoploiarchos Daniolos	PGGM	Greece	295	F 75	Extremadura	FFGM	Spain	707
P 68	Mzia	PB	Tanzania	761	GC 75	Bahia Blanca	WPB	Argentina	21
T 68	Baratang	PBO	India	330	M 75	Vinga	MHSCDM	Sweden	737
69	Ramadevi	WPBO	India	337	P 75	Plotarchis Maridakis	PGGF	Greece	296
69	Intrepid	FFGHM	Singapore	688	P 75	Descubierta	PSOH/MCS/FSGM	Spain	710
CG 69	Vicksburg	CGHM	US	877	PC 75	Hatagumo	PC/SAR	Japan	428
CVN 69	Dwight D Eisenhower	CVNM	US	871	RB 75	Iliniza	YTM/YTL	Ecuador	196
DDG 69	Milius	DDGHM	US	880	RM 75	Andagoya	YTL	Colombia	162
GC 69	Rio Parana	WPB	Argentina	21	76	Dechaineux	SSK	Australia	24
M 69	Cuddalore	MSO	India	331					

Number	Ship's name	Type	Country	Page
76	Ganga Devi	WPBO	India	336
76	Hang Tuah	FFH/AX	Malaysia	479
76	Storochevik	PGM	Russian Federation	665
A 76	Giralda	AXS	Spain	716
CVN 76	Ronald Reagan	CVNM	US	871
DDG 76	Higgins	DDGHM	US	880
GC 76	Ingeniero White	WPB	Argentina	21
M 76	Ven	MHSCDM	Sweden	737
P 76	Ypoploiarchos Tournas	PGGF	Greece	296
P 76	Sea Wolf	PTGFM	Singapore	690
P 76	Infanta Elena	PSOH/MCS/FSGM	Spain	710
PC 76	Makigumo	PC/SAR	Japan	428
RB 76	Josué Alvarez	YTL	Colombia	162
RB 76	Altar	YTM/YTL	Ecuador	196
77	Sheean	SSK	Australia	24
77	Huvudskär	PBR	Sweden	735
A 77	Sálvora	AXS	Spain	716
CVN 77	George H W Bush	CVNM	US	871
DDG 77	O'Kane	DDGHM	US	880
F 77	Te Kaha	FFHM	New Zealand	529
GC 77	Golfo San Matias	WPB	Argentina	21
M 77	Ulvön	MHSCDM	Sweden	737
P 77	Plotarchis Sakipis	PGGF	Greece	296
P 77	Sea Lion	PTGFM	Singapore	690
P 77	Infanta Cristina	PSOH/MCS/FSGM	Spain	710
PC 77	Hamazuki	PC/SAR	Japan	428
PSG 77	Cabrales	PB/AEM	Chile	114
78	Rankin	SSK	Australia	24
AF 78	Lake Buhi	YO	Philippines	579
DDG 78	Porter	DDGHM	US	880
F 78	Kent	FFGHM	UK	836
G 78	Ottonelli	PB	Italy	396
GC 78	Madryn	WPB	Argentina	21
P 78	Sea Dragon	PTGFM	Singapore	690
P 78	Cazadora	PSOH/MCS/FSGM	Spain	710
PC 78	Isozuki	PC/SAR	Japan	428
PM 78	Ishikari	PM/PSO	Japan	426
PSG 78	Sibbald	PB/AEM	Chile	114
RB 78	Portete	YTL	Colombia	162
RB 78	Quilotoa	YTM/YTL	Ecuador	196
T-AOG 78	Nodaway	AOT	US	917
AE 79	Limasawa	ABU	Philippines	580
DDG 79	Oscar Austin	DDGHM	US	882
F 79	Portland	FFGHM	UK	836
G 79	Barletta	PB	Italy	396
GC 79	Rio Deseado	WPB	Argentina	21
P 79	Sea Tiger	PTGFM	Singapore	690
P 79	Vencedora	PSOH/MCS/FSGM	Spain	710
PC 79	Shimanami	PC/SAR	Japan	428
PM 79	Abukuma	PM/PSO	Japan	426
RB 79	Maldonado	YTL	Colombia	162
80	Hamina	PTGM	Finland	220
ACV 80	Storm Bay	PB	Australia	37
BG 80	Dunai	AGF	Ukraine	814
G 80	Bigliani	PB	Italy	396
GC 80	Ushuaia	WPB	Argentina	21
P 80	Sea Hawk	PTGFM	Singapore	690
PC 80	Yuzuki	PC/SAR	Japan	428
PM 80	Isuzu	PM/PSO	Japan	426
81	Zhenghe	AXH	China	147
81	Tornio	PTGM	Finland	220
81	Bayandor	FS	Iran	357
81	Tapper	PBR	Sweden	734
A 81	Brambleleaf	AOR	UK	848
BG 81	Lubny	PGR	Ukraine	815
CLM 81	Almirante Grau	CG/CLM	Peru	567
DBM 81	Cetina	LCT/ML	Croatia	169
DF 81	Rio Amazonas	YFD	Ecuador	196
F 81	Santa María	FFGHM	Spain	708
F 81	Sutherland	FFGHM	UK	836
G 81	Cavaglia	PB	Italy	396
GC 81	Canal De Beagle	WPB	Argentina	21
P 81	Sea Scorpion	PTGFM	Singapore	690
P81	Toralla	PB	Spain	712
PC 81	Tamanami	PC/SAR	Japan	428
PM 81	Kikuchi	PM/PSO	Japan	426
RF 81	Capitán Castro	YTL	Colombia	162
T 81	Ciudad Bolívar	AORH	Venezuela	937
T-AOG 81	Alatna	AOT	US	917
82	Shichang	HSS/AHH	China	146
82	Hanko	PTGM	Finland	220
82	Naghdi	FS	Iran	357
82	Resilience	PCM/PGM	Singapore	689
82	Djärv	PBR	Sweden	734
A 82	Guardiamarina Salas	AXL	Spain	716
BG 82	Kaniv	PGR	Ukraine	815
DBV 82	Krka	LCT/ML	Croatia	169
DF 82	Rio Napo	YFD	Ecuador	196
F 82	Victoria	FFGHM	Spain	708
F 82	Somerset	FFGHM	UK	836
G 82	Galiano	PB	Italy	396
P 82	Formentor	PB	Spain	712
PC 82	Awagiri	PC/SAR	Japan	428
PM 82	Kuzuryu	PM/PSO	Japan	426
T-AOG 82	Chattahoochee	AOT	US	917
83	Armidale	PB	Australia	30
83	Unity	PCM/PGM	Singapore	689
83	Dristig	PBR	Sweden	734
A 83	Guardiamarina Godínez	AXL	Spain	716
A 83	Melton	YAG	UK	854
BG 83	Nizyn	PGR	Ukraine	815
F 83	Numancia	FFGHM	Spain	708
F 83	St Albans	FFGHM	UK	836
G 83	Macchi	PB	Italy	396
K 83	Nashak	FSGM	India	327
M 83	Mahé	MSI	India	332
PC 83	Shimagiri	PC/PB	Japan	428
PM 83	Horobetsu	PM/PSO	Japan	426
RF 83	Joves Fiallo	YTL	Colombia	162
84	Larrakia	PB	Australia	30
84	Norman	MHC	Australia	31
84	Slava	SS	Bulgaria	82
84	Sovereignty	PCM/PGM	Singapore	689
84	Händig	PBR	Sweden	734
A 84	Guardiamarina Rull	AXL	Spain	716
A 84	Menai	YAG	UK	854
BG 84	Izmayl	PGR	Ukraine	815
F 84	Enymiri	FSM	Nigeria	533
F 84	Reina Sofía	FFGHM	Spain	708
G 84	Smalto	PB	Italy	396
K 84	Ekaterinburg	SSBN	Russian Federation	616
PC 84	Okinami	PC/PB	Japan	428
PM 84	Shirakami	PM/PSO	Japan	426
RF 84	Capitán Alvaro Ruiz	YTL	Colombia	162
85	Bathurst	PB	Australia	30
85	Gascoyne	MHC	Australia	31
85	Justice	PCM/PGM	Singapore	689
85	Trygg	PBR	Sweden	734
A 85	Guardiamarina Chereguini	AXL	Spain	716
F 85	Navarra	FFGHM	Spain	708
F 85	Cumberland	FFGHM	UK	835
G 85	Fortuna	PB	Italy	396
P 85	Intrepida	PGGF	Argentina	17
PC 85	Hayagiri	PC/PB	Japan	428
PM 85	Matsuura	PM/PSO	Japan	426
RF 85	Miguel Silva	YTL	Colombia	162
86	Albany	PB	Australia	30
86	Diamantina	MHC	Australia	31
86	Freedom	PCM/PGM	Singapore	885
86	Modig	PBR	Sweden	734
A 86	Tir	AXH	India	332
F 86	Canarias	FFGHM	Spain	708
F 86	Campbeltown	FFGHM	UK	835
G 86	Buonocore	PB	Italy	396
H 86	Gleaner	YGS	UK	845
LT 86	Zamboanga Del Sur	LST	Philippines	578
M 86	Malpe	MSI	India	332
P 86	Indomita	PGGF	Argentina	17
PC 86	Natsugiri	PC/PB	Japan	429
RF 86	Capitan Rigoberto Giraldo	YTL	Colombia	162
87	Pirie	PB	Australia	30
87	Yarra	MHC	Australia	31
87	Independence	PCM/PGM	Singapore	689
87	Hurtig	PBR	Sweden	734
A 87	Meon	YAG	UK	854
F 87	Chatham	FFGHM	UK	835
G 87	Squitieri	PB	Italy	396
H 87	Echo	AGSH	UK	845
PC 87	Suganami	PC/PB	Japan	429
PM 87	Misasa	PM/PSO	Japan	426
RF 87	Vladimir Valek	YTL	Colombia	162
S 87	Turbulent	SSN	UK	826
88	Rapp	PBR	Sweden	734
G 88	La Malfa	PB	Italy	396
GC 88	Medusa	WPB	Argentina	21
H 88	Enterprise	AGSH	UK	845
P 88	Victory	FSGM	Singapore	687
PM 88	Natori	PM/PSO	Japan	426
RF 88	Teniente Luis Bernal	YTL	Colombia	162
S 88	Tireless	SSN	UK	826
89	Stolt	PBR	Sweden	734
AG 89	Kalinga	AKLH	Philippines	580
D 89	Exeter	DDGH	UK	832
F 89	Aradu	FFGHM	Nigeria	533
G 89	Rosati	PB	Italy	396
GC 89	Perca	WPB	Argentina	21
P 89	Valour	FSGM	Singapore	687
PM 89	Takatori	PM/PBO	Japan	426
90	Sabha	FFGHM	Bahrain	41
90	Elicura	LSM	Chile	114
90	Ärlig	PBR	Sweden	734
A 90	Varonis	AKS/AXL	Latvia	460
D 90	Southampton	DDGH	UK	832
G 90	Corrubia	PBF	Italy	397
GC 90	Calamar	WPB	Argentina	21
MHV 90	Bopa	PB	Denmark	185
P 90	Vigilance	FSGM	Singapore	687
PM 90	Chikugo	PM/PSO	Japan	426
S 90	Torbay	SSN	UK	826
91	Munter	PBR	Sweden	734
A 91	Astrolabio	YGS	Spain	716
ASY 91	Hashidate	ASY/YAC	Japan	421
BE 91	Guayas Debe Ser Consierado	AXS	Ecuador	195
BI 91	Orion	YGS	Ecuador	195
D 91	Nottingham	DDGH	UK	832
G 91	Giudice	PBF	Italy	397
GC 91	Hipocampo	WPB	Argentina	21
K 91	Pralaya	FSGM	India	327
M 91	Sagar	MSO	Bangladesh	51
MHV 91	Brigaden	PB	Denmark	185
P 91	Valiant	FSGM	Singapore	687
PM 91	Yamakuni	PM/PSO	Japan	426
PO 91	Lubin	AKR	Serbia and Montenegro	683

Number	Ship's name	Type	Country	Page	Number	Ship's name	Type	Country	Page
R 91	Charles De Gaulle	CVNM/PAN	France	234	102	Kihu	PB	Lithuania	468
RF 91	Teniente Alejandro Baldomero Salgado	YTL	Colombia	162	D 102	Netzahualcoyotl	DDH	Mexico	490
					DD 102	Harusame	DDGHM	Japan	408
S 91	Trenchant	SSN	UK	826	F 102	Almirante Don Juan de Borbón	FFGHM	Spain	706
92	Rancagua	LSTH	Chile	114					
92	Putsaari	ANL	Finland	224	FNH 102	Honduras	PB	Honduras	307
92	Orädd	PBR	Sweden	734	G 102	Miccoli	PBF	Italy	397
A 92	Escandallo	YGS	Spain	716	GC 102	Betelgeuse	PB	Dominican Republic	188
D 92	Liverpool	DDGH	UK	832	P 102	Atauro	PB	East Timor	190
G 92	Alberti	PBF	Italy	397	P 102	Calamar	PB	Panama	561
GC 92	Robaldo	WPB	Argentina	21	PC 102	Murozuki	PC/PB	Japan	429
K 92	Prabal	FSGM	India	327	PG 102	Bagong Lakas	PB	Philippines	576
MHV 92	Holger Danske	PB	Denmark	185	PL 102	Esan	PL/PSO	Japan	424
P 92	Vigour	FSGM	Singapore	687	PM 102	Rafael Del Castillo Y Rada	PB	Colombia	158
PM 92	Katsura	PM/PSO	Japan	426					
RF 92	Carlos Rodriguez	YTL	Colombia	162	PO 102	Juan de la Barrera	PG/PGH	Mexico	497
S 92	Talent	SSN	UK	826	PS 102	Tsukuba	PS/PB	Japan	427
G 93	Angelini	PBF	Italy	397	S 102	Huancavilca	SSK	Ecuador	191
GC 93	Camaron	WPB	Argentina	21	WTGB 102	Bristol Bay	WTGB	US	924
MHV 93	Hvidsten	PB	Denmark	185	103	Burya	PTFG	Bulgaria	85
P 93	Vengeance	FSGM	Singapore	687	103	Al Maks	ATA	Egypt	208
PM 93	Ooyodo	PM/PSO	Japan	426	103	King Abdullah	PB	Jordan	433
RF 93	Sejeri	YTL	Colombia	162	103	Kedrov	FFHM	Russian Federation	662
S 93	Triumph	SSN	UK	826	103	Don	PBO	Russian Federation	663
94	Orompello	LSM	Chile	114	DD 103	Yuudachi	DDGHM	Japan	408
94	Fearless	PCM/PGM	Singapore	689	DDG 103	Truxtun	DDGHM	US	882
G 94	Cappelletti	PBF	Italy	397	F 103	Blas De Lezo	FFGHM	Spain	706
GC 94	Gaviota	WPB	Argentina	21	FNH 103	Hibueras	PB	Honduras	307
MHV 94	Ringen	PB	Denmark	185	G 103	Trezza	PBF	Italy	397
PM 94	Kumano	PM/PBO	Japan	426	GC 103	Procion	PB	Dominican Republic	188
RF 94	Ciudad De Puerto López	YTL	Colombia	162	H 103	Guama	ABU	Cuba	172
					M 103	Comandante Arandia	YFL	Bolivia	61
95	Brave	PCM/PGM	Singapore	689	P 103	L'Audacieux	PBO	Cameroon	89
D 95	Manchester	DDGH	UK	833	PB 103	Alimamy Rassin	PB	Sierra Leone	685
G 95	Ciorlieri	PBF	Italy	397	PC 103	Wakagumo	PC/PB	Japan	429
GC 95	Abadejo	WPB	Argentina	21	PL 103	Wakasa	PL/PSO	Japan	424
M 95	Shapla	MHSC/PBO/AGS	Bangladesh	51	PM 103	José Maria Palas	PB	Colombia	158
MHV 95	Speditøren	PB	Denmark	185	PO 103	Mariano Escobedo	PG/PGH	Mexico	497
PM 95	Amami	PM/PBO	Japan	426	PS 103	Kongou	PS/PB	Japan	427
Y 95	Torpido Tenderi	YPT	Turkey	801	PVL 103	Pikker	PB	Estonia	216
96	Pikkala	YFB	Finland	225	WTGB 103	Mobile Bay	WTGB	US	924
D 96	Gloucester	DDGH	UK	833	104	Grum	PTFG	Bulgaria	85
G 96	D'amato	PBF	Italy	397	DD 104	Kirisame	DDGHM	Japan	408
M 96	Saikat	MHSC/PBO/AGS	Bangladesh	51	DDG 104	Sterett	DDGHM	US	882
					F 104	Mendez Nuñez	FFGHM	Spain	706
PM 96	Kurokami	PM/PBO	Japan	426	FNH 104	Tegucigalpa	PB	Honduras	308
RF 96	Inirida	YTL	Colombia	162	G 104	Apruzzi	PBF	Italy	397
97	Gallant	PCM/PGM	Singapore	689	GC 104	Aldebarán	PB	Dominican Republic	188
D 97	Edinburgh	DDGH	UK	833	M 104	Walney	MHC/SRMH	UK	844
G 97	Fais	PBF	Italy	397	P 104	Bakassi	PBO	Cameroon	89
M 97	Surovi	MHSC/PBO/AGS	Bangladesh	51	PC 104	Naozuki	PC/PB	Japan	429
					PG 104	Bagong Silang	PB	Philippines	576
PM 97	Kunashiri	PM/PBO	Japan	426	PL 104	Kii	PL/PSO	Japan	424
R 97	Jeanne D'arc	CVHG	France	236	PM 104	Medardo Monzon	PB	Colombia	158
98	Mursu	AKSL	Finland	222	PO 104	Manuel Doblado	PG/PGH	Mexico	497
98	Daring	PCM/PGM	Singapore	689	PS 104	Katsuragi	PS/PB	Japan	427
D 98	York	DDGH	UK	833	S 104	Sceptre	SSN	UK	828
G 98	Feliciani	PBF	Italy	397	WTGB 104	Biscayne Bay	WTGB	US	924
K 98	Prahar	FSGM	India	327	105	Jinan	DDGM/DDGHM	China	131
M 98	Shaibal	MHSC/PBO/AGS	Bangladesh	51	105	Al Agami	ATA	Egypt	208
					105	Baykal	PBO	Russian Federation	663
PM 98	Minabe	PM/PBO	Japan	426	105	Ivan Yevteyev	AK	Russian Federation	667
Y 98	Takip 1	YPT	Turkey	801	105	Mou Hsing	WPSO	Taiwan	759
99	Kustaanmiekka	AGF/AGI	Finland	222	105	Antares	PB	Dominican Republic	189
99	Dauntless	PCM/PGM	Singapore	689	105	Isla Del Coco	PB	Costa Rica	165
F 99	Cornwall	FFGHM	UK	833	DD 105	Inazuma	DDGHM	Japan	408
G 99	Garzoni	PBF	Italy	397	DDG 105	Dewey	DDGHM	US	882
Y 99	Takip 2	YPT	Turkey	801	G 105	Ballali	PBF	Italy	397
100	Stavropol	PGM	Russian Federation	665	L 105	Arromanches	RCL	UK	855
100	Shun Hu 5	WPBO	Taiwan	758	M 105	Bedok	MHC	Singapore	692
G 100	Lippi	PBF	Italy	397	PC 105	Hamayuki	PC/PBF	Japan	428
S 100	Saint Petersburg	SSK	Russian Federation	624	PM 105	Jaime Gómez Castro	PB	Colombia	159
101	Mulnaya	FSGM	Bulgaria	84					
101	Levuka	PB	Fiji	219	PS 105	Bizan	PS/PB	Japan	427
101	Tskaltubo	PB	Georgia	266	PVL 105	Torm	PB	Estonia	216
101	Fouque	LSL	Iran	362	WTGB 105	Neah Bay	WTGB	US	924
101	Al Hussein	PB	Jordan	433	106	Xian	DDGM/DDGHM	China	131
101	Lilian	PB	Lithuania	468	106	Derbent	PGM	Russian Federation	665
101	General Matrosov	PBO	Russian Federation	663	106	Shkval	PGR	Russian Federation	666
101	Ho Hsing	WPSO	Taiwan	758	106	Fu Hsing	WPSO	Taiwan	759
101	Raif Denktaş	WPBI	Turkey	805	106	Nirolhu	PB	Maldives	484
101	Aries	PB	Dominican Republic	189	DD 106	Samidare	DDGHM	Japan	408
A 101	Mar Caribe	ATF/AGDS	Spain	718	DDG 106	Stockdale	DDGHM	US	882
DD 101	Murasame	DDGHM	Japan	408	G 106	Bovienzo	PBF	Italy	397
F 101	Alvaro De Bazán	FFGHM	Spain	706	GC 106	Bellatrix	PB	Dominican Republic	188
FNH 101	Guaymuras	PB	Honduras	307	M 106	Kallang	MHC	Singapore	692
G 101	Lombardi	PBF	Italy	397	M 106	Penzance	MHC/SRMH	UK	844
GC 101	Dorado	WPB	Argentina	21	P 106	Akwayafe	PB	Cameroon	90
LM 101	Zuiun	AKSL	Japan	432	PC 106	Murakumo	PC/PBF	Japan	428
LP 101	Paz Zamora	PBR	Bolivia	61	PM 106	Juan Nepomuceno Peña	PB	Colombia	158
M 101	Almirante Grau	YFL	Bolivia	61					
P 101	Panama	PB	Panama	561	PO 106	Santos Degollado	PG/PGH	Mexico	497
P 101	Oecussi	PB	East Timor	190	PS 106	Shizuki	PS/PB	Japan	427
PC 101	Asogiri	PC/PB	Japan	429	PVL 106	Maru	PB	Estonia	215
PL 101	Shiretoko	PL/PSO	Japan	424	WTGB 106	Morro Bay	WTGB	US	924
PS 101	Akagi	PS/PB	Japan	427	107	Yinchuan	DDGM/DDGHM	China	131
S 101	Shyri	SSK	Ecuador	191	107	Al Antar	ATA	Egypt	208
WTGB 101	Katmai Bay	WTGB	US	924	107	BT 88	MHSC/MHSCM	Russian Federation	648
Y 101	Ponton 1	YFB/YE	Turkey	800	107	Pao Hsing	WPBO	Taiwan	759
102	Uragon	PTFG	Bulgaria	85	DD 107	Ikazuchi	DDGHM	Japan	408
102	Lautoka	PB	Fiji	219	G 107	Carreca	PBF	Italy	397
102	Akhmeta	PB	Georgia	266	GC 107	Cristobal Colon	PB	Dominican Republic	188
102	Al Hassan	PB	Jordan	433	L 107	Andalsnes	RCL	UK	855
102	Kizljar	PGM	Russian Federation	665	M 107	German Busch	YFL	Bolivia	61
102	Wei Hsing	WPSO	Taiwan	758	M 107	Katong	MHC	Singapore	692

Number	Ship's name	Type	Country	Page	Number	Ship's name	Type	Country	Page
M 107	Pembroke	MHC/SRMH	UK	844	DD 114	Suzunami	DDGHM	Japan	407
P 107	Jabanne	PB	Cameroon	90	G 114	Puleo	PBF	Italy	397
PC 107	Izunami	PC/PBF	Japan	428	K 114	Tula	SSBN	Russian Federation	616
PL 107	Matsushima	PL/PSO	Japan	424	LG 114	Rio Chone	WPBR	Ecuador	197
PS 107	Takachiho	PS/PB	Japan	427	LM 114	Tokuun	AKSL	Japan	432
S 107	Trafalgar	SSN	UK	826	P 114	Akhisar	PBO	Turkey	794
WTGB 107	Penobscot Bay	WTGB	US	924	P 114	Rangamati	PBR	Bangladesh	51
Y 107	Layter 7	YFB/YE	Turkey	800	PG 114	Salvador Abcede	PBF	Philippines	577
108	Xining	DDGM/ DDGHM	China	131	PL 114	Tosa	PL/PSO	Japan	424
					PM 114	Juan Nepomuceno Eslava	PB	Colombia	158
108	Chin Hsing	WPBO	Taiwan	759	PO 114	Jesus Gonzalez Ortega	PG/PGH	Mexico	497
DD 108	Akebono	DDGHM	Japan	408					
G 108	Conversano	PBF	Italy	397	Y 114	Pinar 4	YW	Turkey	800
GC 108	Capella	PB	Dominican Republic	188	YFB 114	Grumete Perez	YFB	Chile	96
M 108	Punggol	MHC	Singapore	692	115	Shenyang	DDGHM	China	126
M 108	Grimsby	MHC/SRMH	UK	844	115	Emil Racovita	AGS	Romania	610
PO 108	Juan N Alvares	PG/PGH	Mexico	497	115	Ivan Lednev	AK	Russian Federation	667
PS 108	Takatsuki	PS/PBF	Japan	427	115	Burevi	PB	Maldives	484
S 108	Sovereign	SSN	UK	828	G 115	Zannotti	PBF	Italy	397
WTGB 108	Thunder Bay	WTGB	US	924	LG 115	Rio Daule	WPBR	Ecuador	197
109	Kaifeng	DDG	China	132	PG 115	Ramon Aguirre	PBF	Philippines	577
109	Al Dekheila	ATA	Egypt	208	PL 115	Noto	PL/PSO	Japan	424
109	Teh Hsing	WPBO	Taiwan	759	PM 115	Tecim Jaime E Cárdenas Gomez	PB	Colombia	159
A 109	Bayleaf	AOR	UK	848					
DD 109	Ariake	DDGHM	Japan	408	Y 115	Pinar 5	YW	Turkey	800
G 109	Inzerilli	PBF	Italy	397	116	Shijiazhuang	DDGHM	China	126
GC 109	Orion	PB	Dominican Republic	188	116	Pisagua	AKSL	Chile	117
L 109	Akyab	RCL	UK	855	116	Taipei	WPSO	Taiwan	758
M 109	Bangor	MHC/SRMH	UK	844	G 116	Laganà	PB	Italy	396
PL 109	Shikine	PL/PSO	Japan	424	LG 116	Rio Babahoyo	WPBR	Ecuador	197
PO 109	Manuel Gutierrez Zamora	PG/PGH	Mexico	497	PG 116	Nicolas Mahusay	PBF	Philippines	577
PS 109	Nobaru	PS/PBF	Japan	427	S 116	Poseidon	SSK	Greece	291
PVL 109	Valvas	AGF	Estonia	215	Y 116	Pinar 6	YW	Turkey	800
S 109	Superb	SSN	UK	828	117	Ras Al Fulaijah	MSO	Libya	465
110	Dalian	DDG	China	132	117	MPK 197	FFLM	Russian Federation	639
110	Karelia	PBO	Russian Federation	663	117	Taichung	WPSO	Taiwan	758
110	Sirius	PB	Dominican Republic	189	G 117	Sanna	PB	Italy	396
A 110	Orangeleaf	AOR	UK	848	K 117	Briansk	SSBN	Russian Federation	616
DD 110	Takanami	DDGHM	Japan	407	PL 117	Iwami	PL/PSO	Japan	424
G 110	Letizia	PBF	Italy	397	PO 117	Mariano Matamoros	PG/PGH	Mexico	497
L 110	Aachen	RCL	UK	855	S 117	Amphitrite	SSK	Greece	291
M 110	Ramsey	MHC/SRMH	UK	844	118	Korsakov	PGM	Russian Federation	665
PG 110	Tomas Batilo	PBF	Philippines	577	118	Keelung	WPSO	Taiwan	758
PL 110	Suruga	PL/PSO	Japan	424	ACP 118	Noguera	YW/YO	Peru	571
PO 110	Valentin Gomez Farias	PG/PGH	Mexico	497	G 118	Inzucchi	PB	Italy	396
					GC 118	Alumine	PB	Argentina	22
S 110	Glavkos	SSK	Greece	291	PL 118	Shimokita	PL/PSO	Japan	424
111	Svetkavitsa	PTFG	Bulgaria	85	S 118	Okeanos	SSK	Greece	291
111	Al Iskandarani	ATA	Egypt	208	119	Minsk	LSTM	Russian Federation	646
111	Al Tiyar	MSO	Libya	465	119	Nikolay Starshinov	AK	Russian Federation	667
111	Marasesti	FFGH	Romania	607	119	Hualien	WPSO	Taiwan	758
111	Dareen	YTB/YTM	Saudi Arabia	676	G 119	Vitali	PB	Italy	396
A 111	Alerta	AGI/AGOR	Spain	715	GC 119	Traful	PB	Argentina	22
A 111	Oakleaf	AOR	UK	847	K 119	Voronezh	SSGN	Russian Federation	620
D 111	Comodoro Manuel Azueta	FF/AX	Mexico	502	PL 119	Suzuka	PL/PSO	Japan	424
					S 119	Pontos	SSK	Greece	291
DD 111	Oonami	DDGHM	Japan	407	120	Penhu	WPSO	Taiwan	758
F 111	Te Mana	FFHM	New Zealand	529	G 120	Calabrese	PB	Italy	396
G 111	Mazzarella	PBF	Italy	397	GC 120	Lacar	PB	Argentina	22
L 111	Arezzo	RCL	UK	855	PL 120	Kunisaki	PL/PSO	Japan	424
LG 111	Rio Puyango	WPBR	Ecuador	197	S 120	Papanikolis	SSK	Greece	291
M 111	Blyth	MHC/SRMH	UK	844	U 120	Skadovsk	PB	Ukraine	810
P 111	Ladse	PBF	Slovenia	694	121	Vahakari	AKSL	Finland	222
P 111	Pabna	PBR	Bangladesh	51	121	Moskva	CGHM	Russian Federation	631
PG 111	Bonny Serrano	PBF	Philippines	577	G 121	Urso	PB	Italy	396
PGM 111	Rio Chira	PB	Peru	573	GC 121	Fontana	PB	Argentina	22
PL 111	Rebun	PL/PSO	Japan	424	LG121	Rio Esmeraldas	WPBR	Ecuador	197
PVL 111	Vapper	PB	Estonia	216	P121	PGM 104	PC	Turkey	795
S 111	Nereus	SSK	Greece	291	PF 121	Diligente	PBR	Colombia	160
Y 111	Pinar 1	YW	Turkey	800	PL 121	Amagi	PL/PSO	Japan	424
112	Typfun	PTFG	Bulgaria	85	PO 121	Cadete Virgilio Uribe	PSOH	Mexico	496
112	Harbin	DDGHM	China	130	S 121	Matrozos	SSK	Greece	291
112	Altair	PB	Dominican Republic	189	Y 121	Havuz 1	YAC	Turkey	802
DD 112	Makinami	DDGHM	Japan	407	DD 122	Hatsuyuki	DDGHM	Japan	410
G 112	Nioi	PBF	Italy	397	G 122	La Spina	PB	Italy	396
LG 112	Rio Mataje	WPBR	Ecuador	197	GC 122	Mascardi	PB	Argentina	22
M 112	Shoreham	MHC/SRMH	UK	844	LG 122	Rio Santiago	WPBR	Ecuador	197
P 112	Noakhali	PBR	Bangladesh	51	P122	PGM 105	PC	Turkey	795
PG 112	Bienvenido Salting	PBF	Philippines	577	PF 122	Juan Lucio	PBR	Colombia	160
					PL 122	Goto	PL/PSO	Japan	424
PM 112	Quitasueño	PGF	Colombia	158	PO 122	Teniente José Azueta	PSOH	Mexico	496
S 112	Triton	SSK	Greece	291	S 122	Pipinos	SSK	Greece	291
T-AKR 112	Cape Texas	AKR	US	918	Y 122	Havuz 2	YAC	Turkey	802
Y 112	Pinar 2	YW	Turkey	800	123	Ras Al Massad	MSO	Libya	465
113	Smerch	PTFG	Bulgaria	85	ARB 123	Guardian Rios	ATS	Peru	572
113	Qingdao	DDGHM	China	130	DD 123	Shirayuki	DDGHM	Japan	410
113	Al Isar	MSO	Libya	465	G 123	Salone	PB	Italy	396
113	Menzhinsky	FFHM	Russian Federation	662	GC 123	Viedna	PB	Argentina	22
113	PSKR-665	PTF	Russian Federation	665	NL 123	Sarucabey	LSTH/ML	Turkey	796
113	Yunga	FFLM	Russian Federation	639	P123	PGM 106	PC	Turkey	795
113	Barcaza Cisterna De Agua	YW/YO	Peru	571	PF 123	Alfonso Vargas	PBR	Colombia	160
					PL 123	Koshiki	PL/PSO	Japan	424
113	Tuwaig	YTB/YTM	Saudi Arabia	676	PO 123	Capitán de Fragata Pedro Sáinz de Baranda	PSOH	Mexico	496
T-AKR 113	Cape Taylor	AKR	US	918					
DD 113	Sazanami	DDGHM	Japan	407					
G 113	Partipilo	PBF	Italy	397	S 123	Katsonis	SSK	Greece	291
L 113	Audemer	RCL	UK	855	Y 123	Havuz 3	YAC	Turkey	802
LG 113	Rio Zarumilla	WPBR	Ecuador	197	124	Sakhalin	PBO	Russian Federation	663
P 113	Patuakhali	PBR	Bangladesh	51	DD 124	Mineyuki	DDGHM	Japan	410
PM 113	José Maria Garcia Y Toledo	PB	Colombia	158	G 124	Cavatorto	PB	Italy	396
					GC 124	San Martin	PB	Argentina	22
PO 113	Ignacio L Vallarta	PG/PGH	Mexico	497	NL 124	Karamürselbey	LSTH/ML	Turkey	796
S 113	Proteus	SSK	Greece	291	P124	PGM 107	PC	Turkey	795
Y 113	Pinar 3	YW	Turkey	800	PF 124	Fritz Hagale	PBR	Colombia	160
114	Arcturus	PB	Dominican Republic	189	PL 124	Hateruma	PL/PSO	Japan	424

Number	Ship's name	Type	Country	Page	Number	Ship's name	Type	Country	Page
PO 124	Comodoro Carlos Castillo Bretãn	PSOH	Mexico	496	Y 137	Ponton 7	YFB/YE	Turkey	800
Y 124	Havuz 4	YAC	Turkey	802	138	Taizhou	DDGHM	China	127
125	Ras Al Hani	MSO	Libya	465	138	Naryan-Mar	FFLM	Russian Federation	639
DD 125	Sawayuki	DDGHM	Japan	410	B 138	Obninsk	SSN	Russian Federation	619
G 125	Fusco	PB	Italy	396	GC 138	Cisne	WPB	Argentina	21
GC 125	Buenos Aires	PB	Argentina	22	S 138	Saad	SSK	Pakistan	550
NL 125	Osman Gazi	LSTH/ML	Turkey	796	139	PSKR-659	PTF	Russian Federation	665
PF 125	Vengadora	PBR	Colombia	160	GC 139	Pejerrey	WPB	Argentina	21
PL 125	Katori	PL/PSO	Japan	424	K 139	Belgorod	SSGN	Russian Federation	620
PO 125	Vicealmirante Othón P Blanco	PSOH	Mexico	496	S 139	Hamza	SSK	Pakistan	550
Y 125	Havuz 5	YAC	Turkey	802	Y 139	Yakit	YFB/YE	Turkey	800
126	PSKR-657	PTF	Russian Federation	665	A 140	Tornado	YDT/YPT	UK	852
DD 126	Hamayuki	DDGHM	Japan	410	GC 140	Yehuin	PB	Argentina	22
GC 126	Musters	PB	Argentina	22	P 140	Rajshahi	PB	Pakistan	555
L 126	Balikpapan	LCH/LSM	Australia	30	PG 140	Emilio Aguinaldo	PBO	Philippines	576
PF 126	Humberto Cortez	PBR	Colombia	160	Y 140	H 500	YW	Turkey	800
PL 126	Kunigami	PL/PSO	Japan	424	141	Vyborg	PGM	Russian Federation	665
PO 126	Contralmirante Angel Ortiz Monasterio	PSOH	Mexico	496	DDH 141	Haruna	DDHM	Japan	411
Y 126	Havuz 6	YAC	Turkey	802	DT 141	Paitá	LSTH	Peru	570
DD 127	Isoyuki	DDGHM	Japan	410	GC 141	Quillen	PB	Argentina	22
L 127	Brunei	LCH/LSM	Australia	30	P 141	Mubarraz	PGGFM	UAE	819
PL 127	Etomo	PL/PSO	Japan	424	PG 141	Antonio Luna	PBO	Philippines	576
DD 128	Haruyuki	DDGHM	Japan	410	PM 141	Cabo Corrientes	PB	Colombia	158
L 128	Labuan	LCH/LSM	Australia	30	PO 141	Justo Sierra Mendez	PSOH	Mexico	494
PF 128	Carlos Galindo	PBR	Colombia	160	Y 141	H 501	YW	Turkey	800
PL 128	Yonakuni	PL/PSO	Japan	424	142	Aldan	PBO	Russian Federation	663
Y 128	Havuz 8	YAC	Turkey	802	142	Novocherkassk	LSTM	Russian Federation	645
YW 128	Calayeras	YW/YO	Peru	571	A 142	Tormentor	YDT/YPT	UK	852
129	MPK 139	FFLM	Russian Federation	639	DDH 142	Hiei	DDHM	Japan	411
129	PSKR-690	PTF	Russian Federation	665	DT 142	Pisco	LSTH	Peru	570
DD 129	Yamayuki	DDGHM	Japan	410	GC 142	Surel	WPBF	Argentina	21
GC 129	Colhue	PB	Argentina	22	P 142	Makasib	PGGFM	UAE	819
L 129	Tarakan	LCH/LSM	Australia	30	PM 142	Cabo Manglares	PB	Colombia	158
PB-129	Merjen	WPB	Turkmenistan	805	Y 142	H 502	YW	Turkey	800
PF 129	Capitán Jaime Rook	PBR	Colombia	159	143	PSKR-723	PTF	Russian Federation	665
130	Ibn Al Idrisi	LCT	Libya	464	143	Almaz	PGM	Russian Federation	665
DD 130	Matsuyuki	DDGHM	Japan	410	143	Sergey Sudetsky	AK	Russian Federation	667
GC 130	Maria L Pendo	PB	Argentina	22	DDH 143	Shirane	DDHM	Japan	406
H 130	Roebuck	AGS	UK	845	DT 143	Callao	LSTH	Peru	570
L 130	Wewak	LCH/LSM	Australia	30	GC 143	Surubi	WPB	Argentina	21
PF 130	Manuela Saenz	PBR	Colombia	159	PM 143	Cabo Tiburon	PB	Colombia	158
U 130	Hetman Sagaidachny	FFHM	Ukraine	807	PO 143	Guillermo Prieto	PSOH	Mexico	494
Y 130	Havuz 10	YAC	Turkey	802	DDH 144	Kurama	DDHM	Japan	406
131	Ingeniero Mery	YFD	Chile	116	DT 144	Eten	LSTH	Peru	570
131	Nanjing	DDGM/DDGHM	China	131	GC 144	Boga	WPB	Argentina	21
131	Ibn Marwan	LCT	Libya	464	PM 144	Cabo de la Vella	PB	Colombia	158
ATC 131	Mollendo	AOR	Peru	571	PO 144	Matias Romero	PSOH	Mexico	494
DD 131	Setoyuki	DDGHM	Japan	410	F 145	Amatola	FFGHM	South Africa	696
GC 131	Roca	PB	Argentina	22	GC 145	Sabalo	WPB	Argentina	21
H 131	Scott	AGSH	UK	845	A 146	Waterman	AWT	UK	852
NF 131	Socorro	YAG	Colombia	162	F 146	Isandlwana	FFGHM	South Africa	696
PO 131	Capitán De Navio Sebastian José Holzinger	PSOH	Mexico	494	GC 146	Huala	WPB	Argentina	21
132	Mutilla	YFD	Chile	116	A 147	Frances	YTL	UK	853
132	Hefei	DDGM/DDGHM	China	131	F 147	Spioenkop	FFGHM	South Africa	696
132	El Kobayat	LCT	Libya	464	GC 147	Pacu	WPB	Argentina	21
132	PSKR-712	PTF	Russian Federation	665	148	Orsk	LSTM	Russian Federation	646
A 132	Diligence	ARH	UK	849	F 148	Mendi	FFGHM	South Africa	696
DD 132	Asayuki	DDGHM	Japan	410	149	Kuban	PCM	Russian Federation	663
GC 132	Puelo	PB	Argentina	22	A 149	Florence	YTL	UK	853
NF 132	Hernando Gutiérrez	YAG	Colombia	162	GC 149	Corvina	WPB	Argentina	21
PO 132	Capitán De Navio Blas Godinez	PSOH	Mexico	494	150	Anzac	FFGHM	Australia	26
133	Talcahuano	YFD	Chile	116	150	Saratov	LSTM	Russian Federation	646
133	Chongqing	DDGM/DDGHM	China	131	A 150	Genevieve	YTL	UK	853
133	Havouri	AKSL	Finland	223	GC 150	Fagnano	PB	Argentina	22
133	PSKR-641	PTF	Russian Federation	665	151	Arunta	FFGHM	Australia	26
133	Kaani	PB	Maldives	484	GC 151	Nahuel Huapi	PB	Argentina	22
GC 133	Futalaufquen	PB	Argentina	22	LR 151	Hamal	PB	Dominican Republic	189
L 133	Betano	LCH/LSM	Australia	30	P 151	Espadarte	PB	Cape Verde	106
PO 133	Brigadier José Mariá de la Vega	PSOH	Mexico	494	P 151	Ban Yas	PGGF	UAE	818
134	Zunyi	DDGM/DDGHM	China	131	PO 151	Durango	PSOH	Mexico	495
134	Ibn Harissa	LSTH	Libya	464	152	Warramunga	FFGHM	Australia	26
134	PSKR-725	PTF	Russian Federation	665	152	Nikolay Filchenkov	LSTM	Russian Federation	646
F 134	Laksamana Hang Nadim	FSGM	Malaysia	474	152	Berkut	PCM	Russian Federation	664
GC 134	Falkner	PB	Argentina	22	ATP 152	Talara	AOT	Peru	571
PO 134	General Felipe B Berriozábal	PSOH	Mexico	494	K 152	Nerpa	SSN	Russian Federation	622
Y 134	Havuz 11	YAC	Turkey	802	LR 152	Vega	PB	Dominican Republic	189
135	Brest	PBO	Russian Federation	663	M 152	Podgora	MSC/MHC	Serbia and Montenegro	683
A 135	Argus	HSS/APCR	UK	849	P 152	Marban	PGGF	UAE	818
F 135	Laksamana Tun Abdul Jamil	FSGM	Malaysia	474	PO 152	Sonora	PSOH	Mexico	495
PF 135	Riohacha	PBR	Colombia	158	153	Stuart	FFGHM	Australia	26
S 135	Hashmat	SSK	Pakistan	551	153	Perantau	AGS	Malaysia	478
Y 135	Havuz 12	YAC	Turkey	802	ATP 153	Lobitos	AOT	Peru	571
136	Hangzhou	DDGHM	China	127	BH 153	Quindio	AGOR	Colombia	161
F 136	Laksamana Muhammad Amin	FSGM	Malaysia	474	DD 153	Yuugiri	DDGHM	Japan	409
GC 136	Colhue Huapi	PB	Argentina	22	LR 153	Deneb	PB	Dominican Republic	189
S 136	Hurmat	SSK	Pakistan	551	M 153	Blitvenica	MSC/MHC	Serbia and Montenegro	683
Y 136	Havuz 13	YAC	Turkey	802	P 153	Rodqm	PGGF	UAE	818
137	Fuzhou	DDGHM	China	127	PO 153	Guanajuato	PSOH	Mexico	495
137	PSKR-631	PTF	Russian Federation	665	U 153	Priluki	PGGK	Ukraine	810
137	Anatoly Kopolev	PGM	Russian Federation	665	154	Parramatta	FFGHM	Australia	26
F 137	Laksamana Tan Pusmah	FSGM	Malaysia	474	154	Vasiliy Suntzov	AK	Russian Federation	667
GC 137	Cormoran	WPB	Argentina	21	DD 154	Amagiri	DDGHM	Japan	409
PF 137	Arauca	PBR	Colombia	158	K 154	Tigr	SSN	Russian Federation	622
S 137	Khalid	SSK	Pakistan	550	LR 154	Acamar	PB	Dominican Republic	189
					P 154	Shaheen	PGGF	UAE	818
					PO 154	Veracruz	PSOH	Mexico	495
					U 154	Kahovka	PGGK	Ukraine	810
					155	Ballarat	FFGHM	Australia	26
					BO 155	Providencia	AGOR	Colombia	161
					DD 155	Hamagiri	DDGHM	Japan	409
					P 155	Sagar	PGGF	UAE	818
					U 155	Pridneprovye	FSGM	Ukraine	809
					156	Toowoomba	FFGHM	Australia	26
					156	Orel	FFHM	Russian Federation	662

Number	Ship's name	Type	Country	Page	Number	Ship's name	Type	Country	Page
156	Yamal	LSTM	Russian Federation	645	PRF 176	Rio Magdalena	PBR	Colombia	160
BO 156	Malpelo	AGOR	Colombia	161	177	Opanez	PGR	Romania	609
D 156	Nazim	DD	Pakistan	558	B 177	Lipetsk	SSK	Russian Federation	626
DD 156	Setogiri	DDGHM	Japan	409	DDG 177	Atago	DDGHM	Japan	404
157	Perth	FFGHM	Australia	26	L 177	Rodos	LSTH	Greece	297
ATP 157	Supe	AOT	Peru	571	PRF 177	Rio Cauca	PBR	Colombia	160
DD 157	Sawagiri	DDGHM	Japan	409	SFP 177	Akademik Isanin	AGS	Russian Federation	650
K 157	Vepr	SSN	Russian Federation	622	178	Smardan	PGR	Romania	609
P 157	Larkana	PB	Pakistan	556	178	Kosmaj	PCM	Serbia and	681
158	Tsesar Kunikov	LSTM	Russian Federation	645				Montenegro	
158	Yung Chuan	MSC	Taiwan	756	A 178	Husky	YTM	UK	852
DD 158	Umigiri	DDGHM	Japan	409	L 178	Naxos	LCU	Greece	298
BE 160	Gloria	AXS	Colombia	161	MB 178	Saturn	ARS/ATA	Russian Federation	661
Y 160	Önder	YTB/YTM/YTL	Turkey	802	P 178	Ekpe	PGF	Nigeria	534
161	Changsha	DDGM/DDGHM	China	131	PRF 178	Rio Atrato	PBR	Colombia	160
161	Aisberg	PGH	Russian Federation	663	S 178	U 29	SSK	Germany	270
161	Korshun	PCM	Russian Federation	664	PRF 179	Rio Sinú	PBR	Colombia	160
BL 161	Cartagena De Indias	AGP	Colombia	161	L 179	Paros	LCU	Greece	298
P 161	Muray Jib	FSGHM	UAE	817	P 179	Damisa	PGF	Nigeria	534
PO 161	Oaxaca	PSOH	Mexico	495	S 179	U 30	SSK	Germany	270
Y 161	Öncü	YTB/YTM/YTL	Turkey	802	180	Rovine	PGR	Romania	609
162	Nanning	DDGM/DDGHM	China	131	L 180	Kefallinia	LCUJ	Greece	298
162	Yung Fu	MSC	Taiwan	756	P 180	Agu	PGF	Nigeria	534
BL 162	Buenaventura	AGP	Colombia	161	PRF 180	Rio San Jorge	PBR	Colombia	160
P 162	Das	FSGHM	UAE	817	D 181	Tariq	FFHM/FFGH	Pakistan	552
PO 162	Baja California	PSOH	Mexico	495	L 181	Ithaki	LCUJ	Greece	298
Y 162	Özgen	YTB/YTM/YTL	Turkey	802	PRF 181	Tenerife	PBR	Colombia	159
163	Nanchang	DDGM/DDGHM	China	131	S 181	U 31	SSK	Germany	269
163	Voron	PCM	Russian Federation	664	T-AOT 181	Potomac	AOT	US	917
M 163	Muhafiz	MHSC	Pakistan	556	A 182	Saluki	YTM	UK	852
P 163	Express	PB/AXL	UK	846	D 182	Babur	FFHM/FFGH	Pakistan	552
Y 163	Ödev	YTB/YTM/YTL	Turkey	802	L 182	Kerkira	LCUJ	Greece	298
164	Guilin	DDGM/DDGHM	China	131	P 182	Ayam	PGGF	Nigeria	534
164	Onega	FFLM	Russian Federation	639	PRF 182	Tarapaca	PBR	Colombia	159
M 164	Mujahid	MHSC	Pakistan	556	S 182	U 32	SSK	Germany	269
P 164	Explorer	PB/AXL	UK	846	183	Volga	PGH	Russian Federation	663
S 164	Barracuda	SSK	Portugal	595	D 183	Khaibar	FFHM/FFGH	Pakistan	552
Y 164	Özgür	YTB/YTM/YTL	Turkey	802	L 183	Zakynthos	LCUJ	Greece	298
165	Zhanjiang	DDG	China	132	PRF 183	Mompox	PBR	Colombia	159
MB 165	Serdity	ARS/ATA	Russian Federation	661	S 183	U 33	SSK	Germany	269
P 165	Example	PB/AXL	UK	846	SFP 183	Akademik Seminikhin	AGS	Russian Federation	650
M 166	Munsif	MHSC	Pakistan	556	184	Mikhail Konovalov	AK	Russian Federation	667
167	Shenzhen	DDGHM	China	129	D 184	Badr	FFHM/FFGH	Pakistan	552
167	Yung Ren	MSC	Taiwan	756	PRF 184	Orocué	PBR	Colombia	159
L 167	Ios	LCU	Greece	298	S 184	U 34	SSK	Germany	269
P 167	Exploit	PB/AXL	UK	846	A 185	Salmoor	ARSD	UK	851
WMEC 167	Acushnet	PSO/WMEC	US	920	D 185	Tippu Sultan	FFHM/FFGH	Pakistan	552
168	Guangzhou	DDGHM	China	128	PRF 185	Calamar	PBR	Colombia	159
168	Yung Sui	MSC	Taiwan	756	D 186	Shahjahan	FFHM/FFGH	Pakistan	552
DDG 168	Tachikaze	DDGM	Japan	411	K 186	Omsk	SSGN	Russian Federation	620
T-ATF 168	Catawba	ATF	US	911	PRF 186	Magangue	PBR	Colombia	159
169	Wuhan	DDGHM	China	128	A 187	Salmaid	ARSD	UK	851
DDG 169	Asakaze	DDGM	Japan	411	PRF 187	Monclart	PBR	Colombia	159
L 169	Irakleia	LCU	Greece	298	T-AO 187	Henry J Kaiser	AOH	US	909
MB 169	Pochetnyy	ARS/ATA	Russian Federation	661	188	Zborul	FSG	Romania	609
SSV 169	Tavriya	AGIM	Russian Federation	651	PRF 188	Caucaya	PBR	Colombia	159
T-ATF 169	Navajo	ATF	US	911	T-AO 188	Joshua Humphries	AOH	US	909
170	Lanzhou	DDGHM	China	129	189	Pescarusul	FSG	Romania	609
170	Neva	PGH	Russian Federation	663	PRF 189	Mitú	PBR	Colombia	159
A 170	Kitty	YTL	UK	852	T-AO 189	John Lenthall	AOH	US	909
DDG 170	Sawakaze	DDGM	Japan	411	190	Lastunul	FSG	Romania	609
DF 170	Mayor Jaime	ASL	Colombia	162	190	Monchegorsk	FFLM	Russian Federation	639
	Arias Arango				PRF 190	Rio Putumayo	PBR	Colombia	160
L 170	Folegandros	LCU	Greece	298	A 191	Bovisand	YFB	UK	854
171	Haikou	DDGHM	China	129	PRF 191	Rio Caquetá	PBR	Colombia	160
171	Kedah	FSGHM	Malaysia	476	A 192	Cawsand	YFB	UK	854
171	MPK 113	FFLM	Russian Federation	639	LSD 193	Shiu Hai	LSDH	Taiwan	754
A 171	Endurance	AGOBH	UK	840	PRF 193	Rio Orteguaza	PBR	Colombia	160
AH 171	Carrasco	AGSC/EH	Peru	570	T-AO 193	Walter S Diehl	AOH	US	909
DDG 171	Hatakaze	DDGHM	Japan	406	PRF 194	Rio Vichada	PBR	Colombia	160
MB 171	Loksa	ARS/ATA	Russian Federation	661	S 194	U 15	SSK	Germany	270
S 171	U 22	SSK	Germany	270	T-AO 194	John Ericsson	AOH	US	909
T-ATF 171	Sioux	ATF	US	911	L 195	Serifos	LCU	Greece	298
YO 171	Gauden	YW/YO	Peru	571	O 195	Westralia	AORH/AOT	Australia	34
172	Pahang	FSGHM	Malaysia	476	PRF 195	Rio Guaviare	PBR	Colombia	160
172	Primorye	PBO	Russian Federation	663	S 195	U 16	SSK	Germany	270
A 172	Lesley	YTL	UK	852	T-AG 195	Hayes	AGE	US	911
AGOR 172	Quest	AGORH	Canada	96	T-AO 195	Leroy Grumman	AOH	US	909
AHI 172	Stiglich	AGSC/AH	Peru	571	196	Zabaykalye	PBO	Russian Federation	663
DDG 172	Shimakaze	DDGHM	Japan	406	196	Sneznogorsk	FFLM	Russian Federation	639
S 172	U 23	SSK	Germany	270	P 196	Andromeda	PT	Greece	295
T-ATF 172	Apache	ATF	US	911	S 196	U 17	SSK	Germany	270
173	Perak	FSGHM	Malaysia	476	T-AO 196	Kanawha	AOH	US	909
173	MPK 56	FFLM	Russian Federation	639	S 197	U 18	SSK	Germany	270
DDG 173	Kongou	DDGHM	Japan	405	T-AO 197	Pecos	AOH	US	909
L 173	Chios	LSTH	Greece	297	198	Kamchatka	PBO	Russian Federation	663
S 173	U 24	SSK	Germany	270	A 198	Helen	YTL	UK	853
174	Terengganu	FSGHM	Malaysia	476	P 198	Kyknos	PT	Greece	295
174	Učka	PCM	Serbia and	681	T-AO 198	Big Horn	AOH	US	909
			Montenegro		199	Brest	FFLM	Russian Federation	639
AEH 174	Macha	AGSC/EH	Peru	570	A 199	Myrtle	YTL	UK	852
DDG 174	Kirishima	DDGHM	Japan	405	P 199	Pigasos	PT	Greece	295
L 174	Samos	LSTH	Greece	297	T-AO 199	Tippecanoe	AOH	US	909
S 174	U 25	SSK	Germany	270	200	Yan Ion Aung	YDT	Myanmar	515
175	Kelantan	FSGHM	Malaysia	476	200	Oljevern 01	AGS	Norway	541
AEH 175	Carrillo	AGSC/EH	Peru	570	200	Oljevern 02	AGS	Norway	541
DDG 175	Myoukou	DDGHM	Japan	405	200	Oljevern 03	AGS	Norway	541
L 175	Ikaria	LSTH	Greece	297	200	Oljevern 04	AGS	Norway	541
SSV 175	Odograf	AGIM	Russian Federation	651	200	Shun Hu 6	WPBO	Taiwan	758
176	Kala 6	LCU/AKSL	Finland	223	T-AO 200	Guadalupe	AOH	US	909
176	Selangor	FSGHM	Malaysia	476	U 200	Lutsk	FFLM	Ukraine	808
176	Rahova	PGR	Romania	609	201	Kula	PB	Fiji	218
176	Vyacheslav Denisov	AK	Russian Federation	667	201	Kujang	WPB	Indonesia	353
AEH 176	Melo	AGSC/EH	Peru	570	A 201	Orion	AGIH	Sweden	739
DDG 176	Choukai	DDGHM	Japan	405	A 201	Spaniel	YTM	UK	852
L 176	Lesbos	LSTH	Greece	297	LM 201	Shoun	AKSL	Japan	432

PENNANT LIST

Number	Ship's name	Type	Country	Page
P 201	Cabo Fradera	PBR	Spain	712
P 201	Ruposhi Bangla	PB	Bangladesh	50
PS 201	Tsuruugi	PS/PBOF	Japan	427
SSV 201	Priazove	AGIM	Russian Federation	651
T-AO 201	Patuxent	AOH	US	909
UAM 201	Creoula	AXS	Portugal	601
VS 201	Idabato	PB	Cameroon	89
WLB 201	Juniper	WLB/ABU	US	925
202	Kikau	PB	Fiji	218
202	Parang	WPB	Indonesia	353
202	Azadi	PB	Iran	359
LM 202	Seiun	AKSL	Japan	432
P 202	Pangai	PB	Tonga	780
PC 202	Kitagumo	PC/PB	Japan	428
PC 202	Matias De Cordova	PB	Mexico	497
PS 202	Hotaka	PS/PBOF	Japan	427
T-AO 202	Yukon	AOH	US	909
U 202	Ternopil	FFLM	Ukraine	808
VS 202	Isongo	PB	Cameroon	89
WLB 202	Willow	WLB/ABU	US	925
203	Kiro	PB	Fiji	218
203	Celurit	WPB	Indonesia	353
203	Mehran	PB	Iran	359
203	El Wacil	PB	Morocco	506
LDG 203	Bacamarte	LCU	Portugal	601
LM 203	Sekiun	AKSL	Japan	432
P 203	Cacique Nome	PB	Panama	560
P 203	Savea	PB	Tonga	780
PC 203	Yukigumo	PC/PB	Japan	428
PS 203	Norikura	PS/PBOF	Japan	427
T-AO 203	Laramie	AOH	US	909
VS 203	Mouanco	PB	Cameroon	89
WLB 203	Kukui	WLB/ABU	US	925
204	Cundrik	WPB	Indonesia	353
204	El Jail	PB	Morocco	506
204	Apsheron	AKH/AGF	Russian Federation	653
BH 204	El Idrissi	AGS	Algeria	6
LM 204	Houun	AKSL	Japan	432
P 204	Remada	PB	Tunisia	783
P 204	3 de Noviembre	PB	Panama	560
PS 204	Kaimon	PS/PBOF	Japan	427
T-AO 204	Rappahannock	AOH	US	909
VS 204	Campo	PB	Cameroon	89
WLB 204	Elm	WLB/ABU	US	925
205	Townsville	PB	Australia	31
205	Belati	WPB	Indonesia	353
205	El Mikdam	PB	Morocco	506
LM 205	Reiun	AKSL	Japan	432
PC 205	Hayagumo	PC/PBF	Japan	428
PS 205	Asama	PS/PBOF	Japan	427
T 205	Kassir	PBR	Kuwait	457
U 205	Chernigiv	FFLM	Ukraine	808
WLB 205	Walnut	WLB/ABU	US	925
206	Kapitan 1st Rank Dimitri Dobrev	ADG/AX	Bulgaria	88
206	Golok	WSAR	Indonesia	353
206	El Khafir	PB	Morocco	506
LM 206	Genun	AKSL	Japan	432
P 206	10 de Noviembre	PB	Panama	560
PC 206	Akigumo	PC/PB	Japan	428
PC 206	Ignacio López Rayón	PB	Mexico	497
PS 206	Houou	PS/PBOF	Japan	427
U 206	Vinnitsa	FFLM	Ukraine	808
WLB 206	Spar	WLB/ABU	US	925
207	Launceston	PB	Australia	31
207	Panan	WSAR	Indonesia	353
207	El Haris	PB	Morocco	506
F 207	Bremen	FFGHM	Germany	274
L 207	Endurance	LPDM	Singapore	691
LM 207	Ayabane	AKSL	Japan	432
P 207	Utique	PB	Tunisia	783
P 207	28 de Noviembre	PB	Panama	560
PC 207	Yaegumo	PC/PB	Japan	428
PC 207	Manuel Crescencio Rejon	PB	Mexico	497
WLB 207	Maple	WLB/ABU	US	925
208	Pedang	WSAR	Indonesia	353
208	El Essahir	PB	Morocco	506
208	Sevan	AKH/AGF	Russian Federation	653
F 208	Niedersachsen	FFGHM	Germany	274
L 208	Resolution	LPDM	Singapore	691
LM 208	Koun	AKSL	Japan	432
P 208	Jerba	PB	Tunisia	783
P 208	Separacion	PG	Dominican Republic	187
P 208	4 de Noviembre	PB	Panama	560
PC 208	Natsugumo	PC/PB	Japan	428
PC 208	Juan Antonio de la Fuente	PB	Mexico	497
SSV 208	Kurily	AGIM	Russian Federation	651
TK 208	Dmitriy Donskoy	SSBN	Russian Federation	615
U 208	Khmelnitsky	PCM	Ukraine	809
WLB 208	Aspen	WLB/ABU	US	925
209	Ipswich	PB	Australia	31
209	Kapak	WSAR	Indonesia	353
209	Erraid	WPB	Morocco	509
F 209	Rheinland-Pfalz	FFGHM	Germany	274
L 209	Persistence	LPDM	Singapore	691
P 209	Kuriat	PB	Tunisia	783
P 209	5 de Noviembre	PB	Panama	560
PC 209	Leon Guzman	PB	Mexico	497
WLB 209	Sycamore	WLB/ABU	US	925
210	Erracea	WPB	Morocco	509
F 210	Emden	FFGHM	Germany	274
F 210	Mussa Ben Nussair	FSG	Iraq	365
L 210	Endeavour	LPDM	Singapore	691
P 210	Tsotne Dadiani	WPB	Georgia	267
PC 210	Kawagiri	PC/PB	Japan	428
PC 210	Ignacio Ramirez	PB	Mexico	497
PI 210	Rio Supe	PBF/PB	Peru	573
T 210	Dastoor	PBR	Kuwait	457
WLB 210	Cypress	WLB/ABU	US	925
211	Bendigo	PB	Australia	31
211	Parvin	PC	Iran	359
211	El Kaced	WPB	Morocco	509
F 211	Köln	FFGHM	Germany	274
F 211	Ignacio Allende	FFHM	Mexico	491
K 211	Petropavlosk Kamchatsky	SSBN	Russian Federation	617
M 211	Alkyon	MSC	Greece	299
P 211	Meghna	PB	Bangladesh	51
P 211	General Mazniashvili	WPB	Georgia	267
PC 211	Tosagiri	PC/PB	Japan	428
PC 211	Ignacio Mariscal	PB	Mexico	497
WLB 211	Oak	WLB/ABU	US	925
212	Gawler	PB	Australia	31
212	Atabarah	AOTL/AWTL	Egypt	206
212	Bahram	PC	Iran	359
212	Essaid	WPB	Morocco	509
212	Yamal	AKH/AGF	Russian Federation	653
212	Al Qiaq	YFU	Saudi Arabia	676
A 212	Ägir	YDT/AGF	Sweden	740
DCB 212	Mancora	PBF/PB	Peru	573
F 212	Karlsruhe	FFGHM	Germany	274
F 212	Tariq Ibn Ziad	FSG	Iraq	365
F 212	Mariano Abasolo	FFHM	Mexico	491
GS 212	Alchevsk	AGS	Ukraine	812
P 212	Jamuna	PB	Bangladesh	51
PC 212	Natsuzuki	PC/PB	Japan	428
PC 212	Heriberto Jara Corona	PB	Mexico	497
PF 212	Al Hani	FFGM	Libya	463
WLB 212	Hickory	WLB/ABU	US	925
213	Nahid	PC	Iran	359
A 213	Nordanö	YDT	Sweden	740
DCB 213	Huaura	PBF/PB	Peru	573
F 213	Augsburg	FFGHM	Germany	274
F 213	Guadaloupe Victoria	FFHM	Mexico	491
M 213	Klio	MSC	Greece	299
PF 213	Al Qirdabiyah	FFGM	Libya	463
WLB 213	Fir	WLB/ABU	US	925
214	Akdu	AOTL/AWTL	Egypt	206
214	Ghazee	PB	Maldives	484
214	Al Sulayel	YFU	Saudi Arabia	676
A 214	Belos III	ARSH	Sweden	740
DCB 214	Quilca	PBF/PB	Peru	573
F 214	Lübeck	FFGHM	Germany	274
F 214	Francisco Javier Mina	FFHM	Mexico	491
M 214	Avra	MSC	Greece	299
PC 214	Nijigumo	PC/PB	Japan	428
PC 214	Colima	PB	Mexico	497
WLB 214	Hollyhock	WLB/ABU	US	925
215	Geelong	PB	Australia	31
F 215	Brandenburg	FFGHM	Germany	272
PC 215	Tatsugumo	PC/PB	Japan	428
PC 215	Pucusana	PBF/PB	Peru	573
PC 215	Jose Joaquin Fernandez De Lizardi	PB	Mexico	497
T 215	Mahroos	PBR	Kuwait	457
WLB 215	Sequoia	WLB/ABU	US	925
216	Gladstone	PB	Australia	31
216	Ayeda 3	AOTL/AWTL	Egypt	206
216	Al Ula	YFU	Saudi Arabia	676
F 216	Schleswig-Holstein	FFGHM	Germany	272
PC 216	Iseyuki	PC/PB	Japan	428
PC 216	Chicama	PBR	Peru	573
PC 216	Francisco J Mugica	PB	Mexico	497
WLB 216	Alder	WLB/ABU	US	925
F 217	Bayern	FFGHM	Germany	272
PC 217	Isonami	PC/PB	Japan	428
PC 217	Huanchaco	PBR	Peru	573
218	Maryut	AOTL/AWTL	Egypt	206
218	Aleksin	FFLM	Russian Federation	638
218	Afif	YFU	Saudi Arabia	676
218	Chung Chi	LST	Taiwan	755
F 218	Mecklenburg-Vorpommern	FFGHM	Germany	272
PC 218	Nagozuki	PC/PB	Japan	428
PC 218	Chorrillos	PBR	Peru	573
PC 218	Jose Maria Del Castillo Velasco	PB	Mexico	497
219	RT 233	MHC	Russian Federation	648
F 219	Sachsen	FFGHM	Germany	276
PC 219	Yaezuki	PC/PB	Japan	428
PC 219	Chancay	PBR	Peru	573
220	Al Nil	AOTL/AWTL	Egypt	206
220	Dheba	YFU	Saudi Arabia	676
F 220	Hamburg	FFGHM	Germany	276
PC 220	Hamayuki	PC/PB	Japan	428
PC 220	Camana	PBR	Peru	573
PC 220	Jose Natividad Macias	PB	Mexico	497
221	Jupiter	ATS	Bulgaria	88
221	Priyadarshini	WPBO	India	336
221	Sobat	AFL	Sudan	727
F 221	Hessen	FFGHM	Germany	276
P 221	Kaman	PGGF	Iran	358
PC 221	Komayuki	PC/PB	Japan	428
PC 221	Chala	PBR	Peru	573
PR 221	Capitán palomeque	PBR	Bolivia	60
222	Razia Sultana	WPBO	India	336
222	MPK 213	FFLM	Russian Federation	638
222	Umlus	YFU	Saudi Arabia	676
222	Dinder	AFL	Sudan	727

Number	Ship's name	Type	Country	Page	Number	Ship's name	Type	Country	Page
A 222	Nimble	YTB	UK	852	PC 241	Démocrata	PBO	Mexico	496
P 222	Zoubin	PGGF	Iran	358	F 242	Fatih	FFGHM	Turkey	789
PC 222	Umigiri	PC/PB	Japan	428	M 242	Kissa	MSC	Greece	299
PC 222	Zorritos	PBR	Peru	573	PC 242	Rio Piura	PBR	Peru	573
223	Annie Besant	WPBO	India	336	243	Mpk 227	FFLM	Russian Federation	638
223	Iskandhar	PB	Maldives	484	F 243	Yildirim	FFGHM	Turkey	789
A 223	Powerful	YTB	UK	852	PC 243	Rio Nepeña	WPB	Peru	572
K 223	Podolsk	SSBN	Russian Federation	617	244	Bashkortostan	FFLM	Russian Federation	638
M 223	Libertador	YFL	Bolivia	61	F 244	Barbaros	FFGHM	Turkey	790
P 223	Khadang	PGGF	Iran	358	PC 244	Rio Tambo	WPB	Peru	572
PC 223	Asagiri	PC/PB	Japan	428	245	MPK 105	FFLM	Russian Federation	638
PC 223	Tamaulipas	PB	Mexico	497	A 245	Leeuwin	AGS	Australia	32
224	Proteo	ARS	Bulgaria	88	F 245	Orucreis	FFGHM	Turkey	790
224	Al Furat	AOTL/AWTL	Egypt	206	PC 245	Rio Ocoña	WPB	Peru	572
224	Kamla Devi	WPBO	India	336	A 246	Melville	AGS	Australia	32
224	Al Leeth	YFU	Saudi Arabia	676	F 246	Salihreis	FFGHM	Turkey	790
A 224	Adept	YTB	UK	852	LD 246	Morrosquillo	LCU	Colombia	161
M 224	Trinidad	YFL	Bolivia	61	PC 246	Rio Huarmey	WPB	Peru	572
P 224	Peykan	PGGF	Iran	358	A 247	Pelikanen	YPT	Sweden	741
PC 224	Punta Arenas	PBR	Peru	573	F 247	Kemalreis	FFGHM	Turkey	790
PC 224	Yucatan	PB	Mexico	497	M 247	Dafni	MSC	Greece	299
225	Amrit Kaur	WPBO	India	336	PC 247	Rio Zaña	WPB	Peru	572
A 225	Bustler	YTB	UK	852	A 248	Pingvinen	YPT	Sweden	741
PC 225	Santa Rosa	PBR	Peru	573	LD 248	Bahía Honda	LCU	Colombia	161
PC 225	Tabasco	PB	Mexico	497	M 248	Pleias	MSC	Greece	299
226	Kanak Lata Baura	WPBO	India	336	LD 249	Bahía Portete	LCU	Colombia	161
226	Al Quonfetha	YFU	Saudi Arabia	676	A 250	Sheepdog	YTM	UK	852
A 226	Capable	YTB	UK	852	F 250	Muavenet	FFGH	Turkey	792
DE 226	Ishikari	FFG/DE	Japan	412	251	Wodnik	AXTH	Poland	589
P 226	Falakhon	PGGF	Iran	358	A 251	Achilles	ATA/AGB	Sweden	742
PC 226	Pacasmayo	PBR	Peru	573	CG 251	Savannah Point	PB	Jamaica	399
PC 226	Cochimie	PB	Mexico	497	GC 251	El Mouderrib I	AXL	Algeria	7
227	Bhikaji Cama	WPBO	India	336	LD 251	Bahía Solano	LCU	Colombia	161
A 227	Careful	YTB	UK	852	CG 252	Belmont Point	PB	Jamaica	399
B 227	Tur	SSK	Russian Federation	626	GC 252	El Mouderrib II	AXL	Algeria	7
DE 227	Yuubari	FFG/DE	Japan	412	LD 252	Bahía Cupica	LCU	Colombia	161
P 227	Shamshir	PGGF	Iran	358	253	Iskra	AXS	Poland	590
PC 227	Barranca	PBR	Peru	573	A 253	Hermes	YTM	Sweden	742
228	Sucheta Kripalani	WPBO	India	336	C 253	Stalwart	PB	St Kitts and Nevis	668
A 228	Faithful	YTB	UK	852	F 253	Zafer	FFGH	Turkey	792
DE 228	Yuubetsu	FFG/DE	Japan	412	GC 253	El Mouderrib III	AXL	Algeria	7
P 228	Gorz	PGGF	Iran	358	LD 253	Bahía Utria	LCU	Colombia	161
P 228	Toxotis	PT	Greece	295	GC 254	El Mouderrib IV	AXL	Algeria	7
PC 228	Coishco	PBR	Peru	573	LD 254	Bahía Malaga	LCU	Colombia	161
PC 228	Puebla	PB	Mexico	497	F 255	Karadeniz	FFGH	Turkey	792
229	Sarojani Naidu	WPBO	India	337	GC 255	El Mouderrib V	AXL	Algeria	7
A 229	Colonel Templer	AGOR	UK	851	GC 256	El Mouderrib VI	AXL	Algeria	7
DE 229	Abukuma	FFGM/DE	Japan	412	GC 257	El Mouderrib VII	AXL	Algeria	7
F 229	Lancaster	FFGHM	UK	836	P 257	Clyde	PSO	UK	840
P 229	Gardouneh	PGGF	Iran	358	258	MPK 216	FFLM	Russian Federation	638
P 229	Tolmi	PGM	Greece	294	260	Admiral Petre Barbuneanu	FS	Romania	608
PC 229	Independencia	PBR	Peru	573	B 260	Razboynik	SSK	Russian Federation	626
230	Durgabai Deshmukh	WPBO	India	337	F 260	Braunschweig	FSGHM	Germany	277
A 230	Admiral Pitka	FFLH/AGFH/AGE	Estonia	214	PF 260	Rio Hullaga	PBR	Peru	573
DE 230	Jintsu	FFGM/DE	Japan	412	F 261	Magdeburg	FSGHM	Germany	277
P 230	Khanjar	PGGF	Iran	358	GC 261	El Mourafik	WARL	Algeria	7
P 230	Ormi	PGM	Greece	294	262	Nawigator	AGI	Poland	590
PC 230	San Nicolas	PBR	Peru	573	F 262	Erfurt	FSGHM	Germany	277
PC 230	Leona Vicario	PB	Mexico	497	F 262	Zulfiquar	SSW	Pakistan	554
231	Kasturba Gandhi	WPBO	India	337	263	Hydrograf	AGI	Poland	590
A 231	Dexterous	YTB	UK	852	263	Vice Admiral Eugeniu Rosca	FS	Romania	608
DE 231	Ooyodo	FFGM/DE	Japan	412	F 263	Oldenburg	FSGHM	Germany	277
F 231	Argyll	FFGHM	UK	836	264	Contre Admiral Eustatiu Sebastian	FSH	Romania	608
GC 231	El Mounkid I	SAR	Algeria	7	A 264	Trossö	AGP	Sweden	740
P 231	Neyzeh	PGGF	Iran	358	F 264	Ludwigshafen	FSGHM	Germany	277
PC 231	Josefa Ortiz De Dominguez	PB	Mexico	497	LIF 264	Rio Napo	PBR	Peru	573
SSV 231	Vassily Tatischev	AGIM	Russian Federation	651	P 264	Archer	PB/AXL	UK	846
232	Hauki	AKSL	Finland	223	265	Heweliusz	AGS	Poland	589
232	Aruna Asaf Ali	WPBO	India	337	265	Admiral Horia Macelariu	FSH	Romania	608
232	Kalmykia	FFLM	Russian Federation	638	A 265	Visborg	AKH	Sweden	740
A 232	Adamant	YFB	UK	854	LIF 265	Rio Yavari	PBR	Peru	573
DE 232	Sendai	FFGM/DE	Japan	412	M 265	Alanya	MHSC	Turkey	797
GC 232	El Mounkid II	SAR	Algeria	7	P 265	Dumbarton Castle	PSOH	UK	840
P 232	Tabarzin	PGGF	Iran	358	266	Arctowski	AGS	Poland	589
233	Subhdra Kumari Chauhan	WPBO	India	337	K 266	Orel	SSGN	Russian Federation	620
A 233	Maistros	AXS	Greece	299	LIF 266	Rio Matador	PBR	Peru	573
DE 233	Chikuma	FFGM/DE	Japan	412	M 266	Amasra	MHSC	Turkey	797
GC 233	El Mounkid III	SAR	Algeria	7	P 266	Machitis	PGG	Greece	297
234	Meera Behan	WPBO	India	337	M 267	Ayvalik	MHSC	Turkey	797
A 234	Sorokos	AXS	Greece	299	P 267	Nikiforos	PGG	Greece	297
DE 234	Tone	FFGM/DE	Japan	412	M 268	Akãçkoca	MHSC	Turkey	797
F 234	Iron Duke	FFGHM	UK	836	P 268	Aittitos	PGG	Greece	297
GC 234	El Mounkid IV	SAR	Algeria	7	M 269	Anamur	MHSC	Turkey	797
PC 234	Matarani	PBR	Peru	573	P 269	Krateos	PGG	Greece	297
235	Hirsala	AKSL	Finland	223	LIF 270	Rio Itaya	PBR	Peru	573
235	Savitri Bai Phule	WPBO	India	337	M 270	Akçay	MHSC	Turkey	797
F 235	Monmouth	FFGHM	UK	836	P 270	Biter	PB/AXL	UK	846
F 236	Montrose	FFGHM	UK	836	A 271	Gold Rover	AORLH	UK	848
237	Hila	AKSL	Finland	223	LIF 271	Rio Patayacu	PBR	Peru	573
F 237	Westminster	FFGHM	UK	836	PC 271	Cabo Corrientes	PB	Mexico	496
238	Haruna	AKSL	Finland	223	LIF 272	Rio Zapote	PBR	Peru	573
F 238	Northumberland	FFGHM	UK	836	P 272	Smiter	PB/AXL	UK	846
PC 238	Sama	PBR	Peru	573	PC 272	Cabo Corzo	PB	Mexico	496
F 239	Richmond	FFGHM	UK	836	A 273	Black Rover	AORLH	UK	848
240	Kaszub	FSM	Poland	585	LIF 273	Rio Chambira	PBR	Peru	573
F 240	Yavuz	FFGHM	Turkey	789	P 273	Pursuer	PB/AXL	UK	846
M 240	Aidon	MSC	Greece	299	PC 273	Cabo Catoche	PB	Mexico	496
U 240	Feodosiya	YDT/YFL/YPT	Ukraine	813	274	Vice Admiral Constantin Balescu	ML/MCS	Romania	610
241	Askeri	YFB	Finland	224	P 274	Tracker	PB/AXL	UK	846
DBM 241	Krk	LCT/ML	Serbia and Montenegro	682	P 275	Raider	PB/AXL	UK	846
F 241	Turgutreis	FFGHM	Turkey	789	K 276	Kostroma	SSN	Russian Federation	623
M 241	Kichli	MSC	Greece	299					

PENNANT LIST

Number	Ship's name	Type	Country	Page	Number	Ship's name	Type	Country	Page
278	Bukhansan	PBO	Korea, South	453	304	Saqa	PB	Fiji	219
279	Chulmasan	PBO	Korea, South	453	304	Byblos	PB	Lebanon	462
P 279	Blazer	PB/AXL	UK	846	304	El Khattabi	PGG	Morocco	506
280	Iroquois	DDGHM	Canada	94	304	MPK 192	FFLM	Russian Federation	638
A 280	Newhaven	YFL	UK	854	304	Al Riyadh	WPBF	Saudi Arabia	676
P 280	Dasher	PB/AXL	UK	846	F 304	Narvik	FFGM	Norway	537
281	Piast	ARS	Poland	591	OR 304	Success	AORH	Australia	35
281	Constanta	AETLMH	Romania	611	P 304	Mobark	PB	Kuwait	456
A 281	Nutbourne	YFL	UK	854	P 304	Monastir	PBOM	Tunisia	783
P 281	Tyne	PSO	UK	840	S 304	Uthaug	SSK	Norway	536
PC 281	Punta Morro	PB	Mexico	496	T-AKR 304	Pililaau	AKR	US	914
282	Athabaskan	DDGHM	Canada	94	Y 304	Thurø	PB	Denmark	180
282	Lech	ARS	Poland	591	305	Commandant Boutouba	PGG	Morocco	506
A 282	Netley	YFL	UK	854	305	Beirut	PB	Lebanon	462
P 282	Severn	PSO	UK	840	305	Zulurab	WPBF	Saudi Arabia	676
PC 282	Punta Mastun	PB	Mexico	496	P 305	AG 5	ABU	Turkey	801
283	Algonquin	DDGHM	Canada	94	P 305	Al Shaheed	PB	Kuwait	457
283	Midia	AETLMH	Romania	611	P 305	Escudo De Veraguas	PB	Panama	560
A 283	Oban	YFL	UK	854	S 305	Uredd	SSK	Norway	536
P 283	Mersey	PSO	UK	840	T-AKR 305	Brittin	AKR	US	914
A 284	Oronsay	YFL	UK	854	Y 305	Vejrø	PB	Denmark	180
A 285	Omagh	YFL	UK	854	306	Commandant El Harty	PGG	Morocco	506
A 286	Padstow	YFL	UK	854	306	Sidon	PB	Lebanon	462
P 286	Diopos Antoniou	PB	Greece	296	ABH 306	Puno	AH	Peru	572
P 287	Kelefstis Stamou	PB	Greece	296	P 306	Bayan	PB	Kuwait	457
T-AKR 287	Algol	AKRH	US	914	P 306	Taboga	PB	Panama	560
288	Mircea	AXS	Romania	610	P 306	AG 6	ABU	Turkey	801
T-AKR 288	Bellatrix	AKRH	US	914	T-AKR 306	Benavidez	AKR	US	914
T-AKR 289	Denebola	AKRH	US	914	Y 306	Farø	PB	Denmark	180
PL 290	Rio Ramis	PBR	Peru	573	307	Sarafand	PB	Lebanon	462
T-AKR 290	Pollux	AKRH	US	914	307	Commandant Azouggarh	PGG	Morocco	506
WIX 290	Gentian	WLB/ABU	US	924	A 307	Thetis	ANL	Greece	300
291	Orzeł	SSK	Poland	582	P 307	Dasman	PB	Kuwait	457
P 291	Puncher	PB/AXL	UK	846	Y 307	Laesø	PB	Denmark	180
PL 291	Rio Ilave	PBR	Peru	573	308	El Hahiq	PBO	Morocco	506
T-AKR 291	Altair	AKRH	US	914	308	Zelenodolsk	FFLM	Russian Federation	638
B 292	Perm	SSN	Russian Federation	619	P 308	Subahi	PB	Kuwait	456
P 292	Charger	PB/AXL	UK	846	Y 308	Romø	PB	Denmark	180
T-AKR 292	Regulus	AKRH	US	914	309	El Tawfiq	PBO	Morocco	506
P 293	Ranger	PB/AXL	UK	846	P 309	Jaberi	PB	Kuwait	456
PL 293	Juli	PBR	Peru	573	310	L V Rabhi	PBO	Morocco	506
T-AKR 293	Capella	AKRH	US	914	F 310	Fridtjof Nansen	FFGHM	Norway	538
P 294	Trumpeter	PB/AXL	UK	846	P 310	Saad	PB	Kuwait	456
PL 294	Moho	PBR	Peru	573	T-AKR 310	Watson	AKR	US	915
T-AKR 294	Antares	AKRH	US	914	U 310	Zhovti Vody	MSO	Ukraine	811
K 295	Samara	SSN	Russian Federation	622	W 310	Eigun	WPBO	Norway	543
T-AKR 295	Shughart	AKR	US	913	311	Errachiq	PBO	Morocco	506
296	Electronica	ADG/AGI	Romania	611	311	Kazanets	FFLM	Russian Federation	638
T-AKR 296	Gordon	AKR	US	914	311	Prabparapak	PTFG	Thailand	770
T-AKR 297	Yano	AKR	US	913	F 311	Roald Amundsen	FFGHM	Norway	538
298	Magnetica	ADG/AGI	Romania	611	M 311	Wambola	MHC	Estonia	214
T-AKR 298	Gilliland	AKR	US	914	P 311	Bishkhali	PB	Bangladesh	51
P 300	Rayyan	PB	Kuwait	456	P 311	Ahmadi	PB	Kuwait	456
S 300	Ula	SSK	Norway	536	P 311	Weeraya	PB	Sri Lanka	723
T-AKR 300	Bob Hope	AKR	US	914	T-AKR 311	Sisler	AKR	US	915
Y 300	Barsø	PB	Denmark	180	U 311	Cherkasy	MSO	Ukraine	811
301	Denden	LST	Eritrea	213	312	El Akid	PBO	Morocco	506
301	Hamzeh	YDT	Iran	363	312	Hanhak Sattru	PTFG	Thailand	770
301	Huracan	PTG	Mexico	498	F 312	Otto Sverdrup	FFGHM	Norway	538
301	Teanoai	PB	Kiribati	436	M 312	Sulev	MHC	Estonia	214
301	Tripoli	PB	Lebanon	462	P 312	Padma	PB	Bangladesh	50
301	MPK 67	FFLM	Russian Federation	638	P 312	Naif	PB	Kuwait	456
A 301	Drakensberg	AORH	South Africa	700	T-AKR 312	Dahl	AKR	US	915
M 301	Rio Guaporé	YFL	Bolivia	61	W 312	Ålesund	WPBO	Norway	543
MSO 301	Yaeyama	MSO	Japan	416	313	El Maher	PBO	Morocco	506
P 301	Almirante Didiez Burgos	PBO/WMEC	Dominican Republic	187	313	Suphairin	PTFG	Thailand	770
P 301	Batumi	PBF	Georgia	265	ALY 313	Marte	AXS	Peru	572
P 301	Inttisar	PB	Kuwait	456	F 313	Helge Ingstad	FFGHM	Norway	538
P 301	Panquiaco	PB	Panama	559	P 313	Surma	PB	Bangladesh	50
P 301	Bizerte	PBOM	Tunisia	783	P 313	Thafir	PB	Kuwait	456
P 301	Kozlu	MSC/AGS/PBO	Turkey	797	P 313-1	Fath	PTFG	Iran	358
PR 301	General Banzer	PBR	Bolivia	60	P 313-2	Nasr	PTFG	Iran	358
S 301	Utsira	SSK	Norway	536	P 313-3	Saf	PTFG	Iran	358
T-AKR 301	Fisher	AKR	US	914	P 313-4	Ra'd	PTFG	Iran	358
Y 301	Drejø	PB	Denmark	180	P 313-5	Fajr	PTFG	Iran	358
302	Atiya	AORL	Bulgaria	87	P 313-6	Shams	PTFG	Iran	358
302	Tbilisi	PGGK	Georgia	265	P 313-7	Me'raj	PTFG	Iran	358
302	Jounieh	PB	Lebanon	462	P 313-8	Falaq	PTFG	Iran	358
302	Tormenta	PTG	Mexico	498	P 313-9	Hadid	PTFG	Iran	358
302	Okba	PG	Morocco	506	P 313-10	Qadr	PTFG	Iran	358
ABH 302	Morona	AGSC/AH	Peru	571	T-AKR 313	Red Cloud	AKR	US	915
F 302	Trondheim	FFGM	Norway	537	W 313	Tromsö	WPBO	Norway	543
MSO 302	Tsushima	MSO	Japan	416	WLI 313	Bluebell	WLI/ABU	US	925
P 302	Almirante Juan Alexandro Acosta	PBO/WMEC	Dominican Republic	187	314	El Majid	PBO	Morocco	506
P 302	Aman	PB	Kuwait	456	F 314	Thor Heyerdahl	FFGHM	Norway	538
P 302	Ligia Elena	PB	Panama	559	P 314	Karnaphuli	PC	Bangladesh	50
P 302	Horria	PBOM	Tunisia	783	P 314	Marzoug	PB	Kuwait	456
P 302	Kuşadasi	MSC/AGS/PBO	Turkey	797	T-AKR 314	Charlton	AKR	US	915
PR 302	Antofagasta	PBR	Bolivia	60	315	Al Khyber	SS	Libya	462
S 302	Utstein	SSK	Norway	536	315	El Bachir	PBO	Morocco	506
T-AKR 302	Seay	AKR	US	914	C 315	Late	PB	Tonga	780
Y 302	Romsø	PB	Denmark	180	P 315	Jagatha	PB	Sri Lanka	723
303	Saku	PB	Fiji	219	P 315	Mash'noor	PB	Kuwait	456
303	Dioscuria	PTFG	Georgia	266	P 315	Tista	PC	Bangladesh	50
303	Batroun	PB	Lebanon	462	T-AKR 315	Watkins	AKR	US	915
303	Triki	PG	Morocco	506	W 315	Nordsjøbas	WPBO	Norway	543
LPD 303	Ocoa	YTM/YTL	Dominican Republic	190	WLIC 315	Smilax	WLIC	US	926
MSO 303	Hachijyo	MSO	Japan	416	316	Al Hunain	SS	Libya	462
P 303	Maimon	PB	Kuwait	456	316	El Hamiss	PBO	Morocco	506
P 303	Naos	PB	Panama	560	316	RT 57	MHC	Russian Federation	648
S 303	Utvaer	SSK	Norway	536	P 316	Wadah	PB	Kuwait	456
T-AKR 303	Mendonca	AKR	US	914	P 316	Abeetha II	PB	Sri Lanka	723
W 303	Svalbard	WPSOH	Norway	543	T-AKR 316	Pomeroy	AKR	US	915
Y 303	Samsø	PB	Denmark	180	W 316	Malene Østervold	WPBO	Norway	543

Number	Ship's name	Type	Country	Page
317	El Karib	PBO	Morocco	506
317	Assir	WPB	Saudi Arabia	676
K 317	Pantera	SSN	Russian Federation	622
P 317	Edithara II	PB	Sri Lanka	723
T-AKR 317	Soderman	AKR	US	915
W 317	Lafjord	WPBO	Norway	543
318	Raïs Bargach	PSO	Morocco	507
318	Aldhahran	WPB	Saudi Arabia	676
K 317	Pantera	SSN	Russian Federation	622
P 317	Edithara Ii	PB	Sri Lanka	723
T-AKR 317	Soderman	AKR	US	915
W 317	Lafjord	WPBO	Norway	543
318	Raïs Bargach	PSO	Morocco	507
318	Aldhahran	WPB	Saudi Arabia	676
P 318	Wickrama Ii	PB	Sri Lanka	723
W 318	Harstad	WPBO	Norway	543
319	Raïs Britel	PSO	Morocco	507
319	MPK 178 (III)	FFLM	Russian Federation	639
319	Alkahrj	WPB	Saudi Arabia	676
W 319	Thorsteinson	WPSOH	Norway	543
320	Raïs Charkaoui	PSO	Morocco	507
320	Arar	WPB	Saudi Arabia	676
321	Arar	WPB	Saudi Arabia	676
321	Raïs Maaninou	PSO	Morocco	507
321	Ratcharit	PGGF	Thailand	770
322	Arar	WPB	Saudi Arabia	676
322	Raïs Al Mounastiri	PSO	Morocco	507
322	Witthayakhom	PGGF	Thailand	770
A 322	Heros	YTM	Sweden	742
ART 322	San Lorenzo	YPT	Peru	572
K 322	Kashalot	SSN	Russian Federation	622
P 322	Ranarisi	PB	Sri Lanka	723
323	Metel	FFLM	Russian Federation	639
323	Udomdet	PGGF	Thailand	770
AK 323	TSGT John A Chapman	AK	US	915
A 324	Protea	AGSH	South Africa	699
GC 325	El Hamil	PBF	Algeria	7
GC 326	El Assad	PBF	Algeria	7
P 326	Pelikan	PTGF	Turkey	795
GC 327	Markhad	PBF	Algeria	7
WIX 327	Eagle	WIX/AXS	US	926
GC 328	Etair	PBF	Algeria	7
K 328	Leopard	SSN	Russian Federation	622
K 329	Severodvinsk	SSN/SSGN	Russian Federation	617
330	Halifax	FFGHM	Canada	92
F 330	Vasco Da Gama	FFGHM	Portugal	597
P 330	Ranajaya	PB	Sri Lanka	723
U 330	Melitopol	MHSC	Ukraine	811
331	Wallaby	WFL/AOTL	Australia	34
331	Vancouver	FFGHM	Canada	92
331	Sri Gaya	AP	Malaysia	479
331	RT 341	MHC	Russian Federation	648
331	Chon Buri	PG	Thailand	770
F 331	Alvares Cabral	FFGHM	Portugal	597
K 331	Magadan	SSN	Russian Federation	622
M 331	Nestin	MSR	Serbia and Montenegro	683
P 331	Ranadeera	PB	Sri Lanka	723
332	Wombat	WFL/AOTL	Australia	34
332	Ville De Québec	FFGHM	Canada	92
332	Sri Tiga	AP	Malaysia	479
332	MPK 107	FFLM	Russian Federation	639
332	Songkhla	PG	Thailand	770
F 332	Corte Real	FFGHM	Portugal	597
M 332	Motajica	MSR	Serbia and Montenegro	683
P 332	Ranawickrama	PB	Sri Lanka	723
333	Warrigal	WFL/AOTL	Australia	34
333	Toronto	FFGHM	Canada	92
333	Phuket	PG	Thailand	770
M 333	Belegiš	MSR	Serbia and Montenegro	683
P 333	Tufan	PGGF	Turkey	794
334	Regina	FFGHM	Canada	92
334	Hankoniemi	AKSL	Finland	223
334	Wyulda	WFL/AOTL	Australia	34
M 334	Bosut	MSR	Serbia and Montenegro	683
P 334	Meltem	PGGF	Turkey	794
335	Calgary	FFGHM	Canada	92
K 335	Gepard	SSN	Russian Federation	622
M 335	Vučedol	MSR	Serbia and Montenegro	683
P 335	Imbat	PGGF	Turkey	794
336	Montreal	FFGHM	Canada	92
K 336	Pskov	SSN	Russian Federation	618
M 336	Djerdap	MSR	Serbia and Montenegro	683
P 336	Zipkin	PGGF	Turkey	794
337	Fredericton	FFGHM	Canada	92
K 337	Cougar	SSN	Russian Federation	622
P 337	Atak	PGGF	Turkey	794
338	Winnipeg	FFGHM	Canada	92
P 338	Bora	PGGF	Turkey	794
339	Charlottetown	FFGHM	Canada	92
340	St John's	FFGHM	Canada	92
M 340	Oksøy	MHCM/MSCM	Norway	541
P 340	Prathpa	PB	Sri Lanka	724
341	El Yadekh	PG	Algeria	5
341	Ottawa	FFGHM	Canada	92
341	Samadikun	FF	Indonesia	341
M 341	Ingeniero Gumucio	YFL	Bolivia	61
M 341	Novi Sad	MSR	Serbia and Montenegro	683
P 341	Udara	PB	Sri Lanka	724
342	El Mourakeb	PG	Algeria	5

Number	Ship's name	Type	Country	Page
342	Martadinata	FF	Indonesia	341
M 342	Jorge Villarroel	YFL	Bolivia	61
M 342	Måløy	MHCM/MSCM	Norway	541
P 342	Tayfun	PGGF	Turkey	795
343	El Kechef	PG	Algeria	5
A 343	Sleipner	AKR	Sweden	740
M 343	Hinnøy	MHCM/MSCM	Norway	541
P 343	Volkan	PGGF	Turkey	795
344	El Moutarid	PG	Algeria	5
A 344	Loke	AKL	Sweden	741
A 344	Impulse	YTL	UK	853
P 344	Rüzgar	PGGF	Turkey	795
Y 344	Arvak	YTL	Denmark	184
345	El Rassed	PG	Algeria	5
A 345	Impetus	YTL	UK	853
P 345	Poyraz	PGGF	Turkey	795
Y 345	Alsin	YTL	Denmark	184
346	El Djari	PG	Algeria	5
P 346	Gurbet	PGGF	Turkey	795
347	El Saher	PG	Algeria	5
P 347	Firtina	PGGF	Turkey	795
S 347	Atilay	SSK	Turkey	787
348	El Moukadem	PG	Algeria	5
348	RT 248	MHC	Russian Federation	648
P 348	Yildiz	PGGF	Turkey	795
S 348	Saldiray	SSK	Turkey	787
P 349	Karayel	PGGF	Turkey	795
S 349	Batiray	SSK	Turkey	787
350	El Kanass	PG	Algeria	5
350	Leninskaya Kuznitsa	FFLM	Russian Federation	639
M 350	Alta	MHCM/MSCM	Norway	541
S 350	Yildiray	SSK	Turkey	787
351	Djebel Chenoua	FSG	Algeria	5
351	Ahmad Yani	FFGHM	Indonesia	340
351	Al Jouf	WPBF	Saudi Arabia	677
LP 351	Raider	PBR	Bolivia	61
M 351	Otra	MHCM/MSCM	Norway	541
S 351	Doğanay	SSK	Turkey	787
352	El Chihab	FSG	Algeria	5
352	Slamet Riyadi	FFGHM	Indonesia	340
352	Turaif	WPBF	Saudi Arabia	677
S 352	Dolunay	SSK	Turkey	787
353	Al Kirch	FSG	Algeria	5
353	Yos Sudarso	FFGHM	Indonesia	340
353	Hail	WPBF	Saudi Arabia	677
S 353	Preveze	SSK	Turkey	788
354	Oswald Siahaan	FFGHM	Indonesia	340
354	Stelyak	FFLM	Russian Federation	639
354	Najran	WPBF	Saudi Arabia	677
F 354	Niels Juel	FFGM	Denmark	176
S 354	Sakarya	SSK	Turkey	788
355	Abdul Halim Perdanakusuma	FFGHM	Indonesia	340
F 355	Olfert Fischer	FFGM	Denmark	176
S 355	18 Mart	SSK	Turkey	788
356	Karel Satsuitubun	FFGHM	Indonesia	340
F 356	Peter Tordenskiold	FFGM	Denmark	176
S 356	Anafartalar	SSK	Turkey	788
F 357	Thetis	FFHM	Denmark	175
S 357	Gür	SSK	Turkey	788
F 358	Triton	FFHM	Denmark	175
P 358	Hessa	AXL	Norway	542
S 358	Çanakkale	SSK	Turkey	788
A 359	Ostria	AXS	Greece	299
F 359	Vaedderen	FFHM	Denmark	175
P 359	Vigra	AXL	Norway	542
S 359	Burakreis	SSK	Turkey	788
F 360	Hvidbjørnen	FFHM	Denmark	175
P 360	Viana Do Castelo	PSOH	Portugal	599
S 360	Birinci Inönü	SSK	Turkey	788
U 360	Genichesk	MHC	Ukraine	811
361	Fatahillah	FFG/FFGH	Indonesia	342
P 361	Figueira Da Foz	PSOH	Portugal	599
362	Malahayati	FFG/FFGH	Indonesia	342
362	MPK 17	FFLM	Russian Federation	639
P 362	Ponta Delgada	PSOH	Portugal	599
363	Nala	FFG/FFGH	Indonesia	342
364	Ki Hajar Dewantara	FFGH/FFT	Indonesia	339
364	Geofjord	AGS	Norway	541
A 367	Newton	AG	UK	851
A 368	Warden	YFRT	UK	853
369	MPK 191 (III)	FFLM	Russian Federation	639
P 370	Rio Minho	PBR	Portugal	600
PG 370	José Andrada	PB	Philippines	577
371	Kapitan Patimura	FS	Indonesia	343
M 371	Ohue	MHSC	Nigeria	535
PG 371	Enrique Jurado	PB	Philippines	577
372	RT 234	MHC	Russian Federation	648
372	Untung Suropati	FS	Indonesia	343
M 372	Barama	MHSC	Nigeria	535
PG 372	Alfredo Peckson	PB	Philippines	577
373	Nuku	FS	Indonesia	343
374	Lambung Mangkurat	FS	Indonesia	343
A 374	Prometheus	AORH	Greece	300
PG 374	Simeon Castro	PB	Philippines	577
375	MPK 82	FFLM	Russian Federation	639
375	Cut Nyak Dien	FS	Indonesia	343
A 375	Zeus	AOTL	Greece	300
PG 375	Carlos Albert	PB	Philippines	577
376	Sultan Thaha Syaifuddin	FS	Indonesia	343
A 376	Orion	AOTL	Greece	300
PG 376	Heracleo Alano	PB	Philippines	577
377	Sutanto	FS	Indonesia	343
PG 377	Liberato Picar	PB	Philippines	577
378	Sutedi Senoputra	FS	Indonesia	343

Number	Ship's name	Type	Country	Page
PG 378	Hilario Ruiz	PB	Philippines	577
PG 379	Rafael Pargas	PB	Philippines	577
PG 380	Nestor Reinoso	PB	Philippines	577
PG 381	Dioscoro Papa	PB	Philippines	577
PG 383	Ismael Lomibao	PB	Philippines	577
PG 384	Leovigildo Gantioque	PB	Philippines	577
A 385	Fort Rosalie	AFSH	UK	849
PG 385	Federico Martir	PB	Philippines	577
A 386	Fort Austin	AFSH	UK	849
PG 386	Filipino Flojo	PB	Philippines	577
Y 386	Agdlek	PB	Denmark	180
A 387	Fort Victoria	AORH	UK	848
PG 387	Anastacio Cacayorin	PB	Philippines	577
Y 387	Agpa	PB	Denmark	180
A 388	Fort George	AORH	UK	848
B 388	Snezhnogorsk	SSN	Russian Federation	619
PG 388	Manuel Gomez	PB	Philippines	577
Y 388	Tulugaq	PB	Denmark	180
A 389	Wave Knight	AORH	UK	847
PG 389	Testimo Figuracion	PB	Philippines	577
390	Korets	FFLM	Russian Federation	639
A 390	Wave Ruler	AORH	UK	847
PG 390	José Loor Sr	PB	Philippines	577
PG 392	Juan Magluyan	PB	Philippines	577
PG 393	Florenca Nuno	PB	Philippines	577
PG 394	Alberto Navaret	PB	Philippines	576
PG 395	Felix Apolinario	PB	Philippines	577
PG 396	Brigadier Abraham Campo	PB	Philippines	576
400	Vitse Admiral Kulakov	DDGHM	Russian Federation	634
400	Shun Hu 2	WPBO	Taiwan	758
400	Shun Hu 3	WPBO	Taiwan	758
U 400	Rivne	LST	Ukraine	810
401	Admiral Branimir Ormanov	AGS	Bulgaria	86
401	Lieutenant Malghagh	LCU	Morocco	507
401	Rade Končar	PTFG	Serbia and Montenegro	681
401	Ho Chi	LCU	Taiwan	755
A 401	Independencia	PBO	Panama	559
L 401	Al Soumood	LCU	Kuwait	458
L 401	Ertuğrul	LSTH/ML	Turkey	796
M 401	Coati	YFL	Bolivia	61
P 401	Cassiopea	PSOH	Italy	388
PG 401	Gavion	WPB	Venezuela	938
U 401	Kirovograd	LSM	Ukraine	810
402	Daoud Ben Aicha	LSMH	Morocco	507
402	BT 97	MHSC/MHSCM	Russian Federation	648
402	Ho Huei	LCU	Taiwan	755
A 402	Manzanillo	AP	Mexico	499
A 402	Flamenco	YO	Panama	561
B 402	Vologda	SSK	Russian Federation	626
L 402	Al Tahaddy	LCU	Kuwait	458
L 402	Serdar	LSTH/ML	Turkey	796
M 402	Cobija	YFL	Bolivia	61
P 402	Libra	PSOH	Italy	388
PG 402	Alca	WPB	Venezuela	938
U 402	Konstantin Olshansky	LST	Ukraine	810
403	Ahmed Es Sakali	LSMH	Morocco	507
403	Ho Yao	LCU	Taiwan	755
L 403	Jalbout	LCU	Kuwait	458
P 403	Spica	PSOH	Italy	388
PG 403	Bernacla	WPB	Venezuela	938
Y 403W	RP 101	YTM	Italy	395
404	Abou Abdallah El Ayachi	LSMH	Morocco	507
404	Hasan Zafirović-Laca	PTFG	Serbia and Montenegro	681
P 404	Vega	PSOH	Italy	388
PG 404	Chaman	WPB	Venezuela	938
Y 404	RP 102	YTM	Italy	395
405	El Aigh	AKS	Morocco	508
P 405	Esploratore	PB	Italy	388
PG 405	Cormoran	WPB	Venezuela	938
LP 406	General Bejar	PBR	Bolivia	61
P 406	Sentinella	PB	Italy	388
PG 406	Colimbo	WPB	Venezuela	938
Y 406	RP 103	YTM	Italy	395
K 407	Novomoskovsk	SSBN	Russian Federation	616
P 407	Vedetta	PB	Italy	388
PG 407	Fardela	WPB	Venezuela	938
Y 407	RP 104	YTM	Italy	395
P 408	Staffetta	PB	Italy	388
PG 408	Fumarel	WPB	Venezuela	938
Y 408	RP 105	YTM	Italy	395
LP 409	Mariscal De Zapita	PBR	Bolivia	61
P 409	Sirio	PSOH	Italy	387
PG 409	Negron	WPB	Venezuela	938
A 410	Atromitos	YTM/YTL	Greece	301
K 410	Smolensk	SSGN	Russian Federation	620
LP 410	Capitán Bretel	PBR	Bolivia	61
P 410	Orione	PSOH	Italy	387
PG 410	Pigargo	WPB	Venezuela	938
Y 410	RP 106	YTM	Italy	395
411	Kangan	AWT	Iran	363
411	BT 22	MHSC/MHSCM	Russian Federation	648
A 411	Adamastos	YTM/YTL	Greece	301
A 411	Rio Papaloapan	LSTH	Mexico	499
LP 411	Teniente Soliz	PBR	Bolivia	61
P 411	Shaheed Daulat	PC	Bangladesh	49
P 411	Ennasr	PB	Mauritania	487
PG 411	Pagaza	WPB	Venezuela	938
412	Taheri	AWT	Iran	363
A 412	Aias	YTM/YTL	Greece	301
MSC 412	Addriyah	MHSC	Saudi Arabia	675
P 412	Shaheed Farid	PC	Bangladesh	49
PG 412	Serreta	WPB	Venezuela	938
A 413	Pilefs	YTM/YTL	Greece	301
P 413	Shaheed Mohibullah	PC	Bangladesh	49
Y 413	Porto Fossone	YTB	Italy	395
B 414	Danil Moskovskiy	SSN	Russian Federation	619
LA 414	Guaqui	PBR	Bolivia	61
MSC 414	Al Quysumah	MHSC	Saudi Arabia	675
P 414	Shaheed Aktheruddin	PC	Bangladesh	49
A 415	Evros	AEL	Greece	300
M 415	Olev	MSI	Estonia	214
416	Tariq Ibn Ziyad	FSGM	Libya	463
A 416	Ouranos	AOTL	Greece	300
LP 416	Independencia	PBR	Bolivia	61
M 416	Vaindlo	MSI	Estonia	214
MSC 416	Al Wadeeah	MHSC	Saudi Arabia	675
Y 416	Porto Torres	YTB	Italy	395
A 417	Hyperion	AOTL	Greece	300
Y 417	Porto Corsini	YTB	Italy	395
418	Inej	FSG	Russian Federation	641
418	BT 152	MHSC/MHSCM	Russian Federation	648
MSC 418	Safwa	MHSC	Saudi Arabia	675
SSV 418	Ekvator	AGI/AGIM	Russian Federation	651
A 419	Pandora	AP	Greece	301
K 419	Kuzbass	SSN	Russian Federation	622
420	Rastoropny	DDGHM	Russian Federation	635
420	Al Jawf	MHC	Saudi Arabia	675
A 420	Pandrosos	AP	Greece	301
421	Olev Blagoev	ATS	Bulgaria	87
421	Bandar Abbas	AORLH	Iran	364
421	Cornwall	PB	Jamaica	398
421	Orkan	FSGM	Poland	585
C 421	Ardent	PB	St Kitts and Nevis	668
PB 421	Antares	PBI	Colombia	160
Y 421	Porto Empedocle	YTB	Italy	395
422	Boushehr	AORLH	Iran	364
422	Piorun	FSGM	Poland	585
422	Shaqra	MHC	Saudi Arabia	675
A 422	Kadmos	YTM/YTL	Greece	301
AOE 422	Towada	AOE/AORH	Japan	420
PB 422	Capricornio	PBI	Colombia	160
Y 422	Porto Pisano	YTB	Italy	395
423	Grom	FSGM	Poland	585
423	Smerch	FSG	Russian Federation	641
A 423	Heraklis	YTB	Greece	301
AOE 423	Tokiwa	AOE/AORH	Japan	420
PB 423	Acuario	PBI	Colombia	160
Y 423	Porto Conte	YTB	Italy	395
424	Al Kharj	MHC	Saudi Arabia	675
A 424	Iason	YTB	Greece	301
AOE 424	Hamana	AOE/AORH	Japan	420
PB 424	Piscis	PBI	Colombia	160
U 424	Artemivsk	ACV/LCUJM	Ukraine	811
425	BT 226	MHSC/MHSCM	Russian Federation	648
A 425	Odisseus	YTB	Greece	301
AOE 425	Mashuu	AOE/AORH	Japan	420
PB 425	Aries	PBI	Colombia	160
Y 425	Porto Ferraio	YTB	Italy	395
426	BT 241	MHSC/MHSCM	Russian Federation	648
AOE 426	Oumi	AOE/AORH	Japan	420
PB 426	Tauro	PBI	Colombia	160
Y 426	Porto Venere	YTB	Italy	395
PB 427	Géminis	PBI	Colombia	160
A 428	Nestor	YTM/YTL	Greece	301
PB 428	Deneb	PBI	Colombia	160
Y 428	Porto Salvo	YTB	Italy	395
A 429	Perseus	YTM/YTL	Greece	301
PB 429	Rigel	PBI	Colombia	160
430	Al Nour	PC	Egypt	204
431	Kharg	AORH	Iran	364
431	Świnoujście	PTFGM	Poland	587
A 431	Ahti	YDT	Estonia	215
PB 431	Aldebarán	PBI	Colombia	160
A 432	Gigas	YTM/YTL	Greece	301
433	Al Hady	PC	Egypt	204
433	Władysławowo	PTFGM	Poland	587
A 433	Kerkini	AWT	Greece	300
K 433	Syvatoy Giorgiy Pobedonosets	SSBN	Russian Federation	617
434	Marshal Ushakov	DDGHM	Russian Federation	635
A 434	Prespa	AWT	Greece	300
PB 434	Spica	PBI	Colombia	160
A 435	Kekrops	YTM/YTL	Greece	301
PB 435	Denebola	PBI	Colombia	160
436	Al Wakil	PC	Egypt	204
436	Metalowiec	FSGM	Poland	586
A 436	Minos	YTM/YTL	Greece	301
PB 436	Libra	PBI	Colombia	160
437	Rolnik	FSGM	Poland	586
A 437	Pelias	YTM/YTL	Greece	301
PB 437	Escorpión	PBI	Colombia	160
438	BT 40	MHSC/MHSCM	Russian Federation	648
A 438	Aegeus	YTM/YTL	Greece	301
PB 438	Alpheraz	PBI	Colombia	160
439	Al Hakim	PC	Egypt	204
A 439	Atrefs	YTM/YTL	Greece	301
PB 439	Bellatrix	PBI	Colombia	160
A 440	Diomidis	YTM/YTL	Greece	301
PB 440	Canopus	PBI	Colombia	160
441	Rattanakosin	FSGM	Thailand	766
A 441	Theseus	YTM/YTL	Greece	301
PB 441	Procyon	PBI	Colombia	160
442	Sukhothai	FSGM	Thailand	766
A 442	Romaleos	YTM/YTL	Greece	301
K 442	Cheliabinsk	SSGN	Russian Federation	620
PB 442	Tulcán	PBI	Colombia	160

Number	Ship's name	Type	Country	Page		Number	Ship's name	Type	Country	Page
PB 446	Capella	PBI	Colombia	160		489	Ho Chuan	LCU	Taiwan	755
B 448	Tambov	SSN	Russian Federation	619		490	Ho Seng	LCU	Taiwan	755
F 450	Elli	FFGHM	Greece	293		F 490	Gaziantep	FFGHM	Turkey	791
451	Al Rafa	PC	Egypt	204		P 490	Comandante Cigala Fulgosi	PSOH	Italy	387
F 451	Limnos	FFGHM	Greece	293						
PC 451	Andrómeda	PBI	Colombia	160		491	Ho Meng	LCU	Taiwan	755
F 452	Hydra	FFGHM	Greece	292		F 491	Giresun	FFGHM	Turkey	791
PC 452	Casiopea	PBI	Colombia	160		P 491	Comandante Borsini	PSOH	Italy	387
Y 452	RP 108	YTM	Italy	395						
F 453	Spetsai	FFGHM	Greece	292		492	Ho Mou	LCU	Taiwan	755
PC 453	Centauro	PBI	Colombia	160		F 492	Gemlik	FFGHM	Turkey	791
454	BT 50	MHSC/MHSCM	Russian Federation	648		P 492	Comandante Bettica	PSOH	Italy	387
C 454	Prestol Botello	PG	Dominican Republic	188		493	Ho Shou	LCU	Taiwan	755
F 454	Psara	FFGHM	Greece	292		F 493	Gelibolu	FFGHM	Turkey	791
PC 454	Dragón	PBI	Colombia	160		P 493	Comandante Foscari	PSOH	Italy	387
455	Chao Phraya	FFG/FFGH	Thailand	764		494	Ho Chun	LCU	Taiwan	755
F 455	Salamis	FFGHM	Greece	292		B 494	Ust-bolsheretsk	SSK	Russian Federation	626
PC 455	Vela	PBI	Colombia	160		F 494	Gökçeada	FFGHM	Turkey	791
456	Bangpakong	FFG/FFGH	Thailand	764		495	Ho Yung	LCU	Taiwan	755
K 456	Vilyachinsk	SSGN	Russian Federation	620		F 495	Gediz	FFGHM	Turkey	791
PC 456	Polaris	PBI	Colombia	160		F 496	Gokova	FFGHM	Turkey	791
Y 456	RP 109	YTM	Italy	395		K 496	Ryazan	SSBN	Russian Federation	617
457	Kraburi	FFG/FFGH	Thailand	764		F 497	Göksu	FFGHM	Turkey	791
PC 457	Fenix	PBI	Colombia	160		A 498	Lana	AGS	Nigeria	535
458	Saiburi	FFG/FFGH	Thailand	764		Y 498	Mario Marino	YDT	Italy	388
PC 458	Regulus	PBI	Colombia	160		A 499	Commander Apayi Joe	YTB/YTL	Nigeria	535
Y 458	RP 110	YTM	Italy	395						
F 459	Adrias	FFGHM	Greece	293		Y 499	Alcide Pedretti	YDT	Italy	388
PC 459	Aquila	PBI	Colombia	160		500	Grozavu	ATA	Romania	612
A 460	Evrotas	YPT	Greece	301		F 500	Bozcaada	FFGM	Turkey	793
F 460	Aegeon	FFGHM	Greece	293		M 500	Foça	MSI	Turkey	798
PC 460	Perseus	PBI	Colombia	160		501	Teluk Langsa	LST	Indonesia	347
Y 460	RP 111	YTM	Italy	395		501	Eilat	FSGHM	Israel	370
A 461	Arachthos	YPT	Greece	301		501	Lieutenant Colonel Errhamani	FFGM	Morocco	504
F 461	Navarinon	FFGHM	Greece	293						
K 461	Volk	SSN	Russian Federation	622		501	BT 244	MHSC/MHSCM	Russian Federation	648
PC 461	Ramadan	PBI	Colombia	160		501	Hercules	ATA	Romania	612
A 462	Strymon	YPT	Greece	301		501	La Galité	PGGF	Tunisia	783
F 462	Kountouriotis	FFGHM	Greece	293		A 501	Kyanwa	PBO	Nigeria	534
PC 462	Apolo	PBR	Colombia	159		F 501	Bodrum	FFGM	Turkey	793
Y 462	RP 112	YTM	Italy	395		HQ 501	Tran Khanh Du	LST	Vietnam	944
A 463	Nestos	YPT	Greece	301		LT 501	Laguna	LST	Philippines	578
F 463	Bouboulina	FFGHM	Greece	293		M 501	Fethiye	MSI	Turkey	798
MST 463	Uraga	MSTH/ML	Japan	416		502	Teluk Bayur	LST	Indonesia	347
PC 463	Zeus	PBR	Colombia	159		502	Lahav	FSGHM	Israel	370
Y 463	RP 113	YTM	Italy	395		502	Kurmuk	PBR	Sudan	727
A 464	Axios	ARL/AOTL	Greece	300		A 502	Ologbo	PBO	Nigeria	534
B 464	Ust-kamshats	SSK	Russian Federation	626		F 502	Bandirma	FFGM	Turkey	793
F 464	Kanaris	FFGHM	Greece	293		HQ 502	Vung Tau	LST	Vietnam	944
MST 464	Bungo	MSTH/ML	Japan	416		M 502	Fatsa	MSI	Turkey	798
PC 464	Sagitario	PBR	Colombia	159		503	Hanit	FSGHM	Israel	370
Y 464	RP 114	YTM	Italy	395		503	Teluk Amboina	LSTH	Indonesia	347
F 465	Themistocles	FFGHM	Greece	293		503	Qaysan	PBR	Sudan	727
PC 465	Lince	PBR	Colombia	159		503	Carthage	PGGF	Tunisia	783
Y 465	RP 115	YTM	Italy	395		A 503	Nwamba	PBO	Nigeria	534
466	BT 111	MHSC/MHSCM	Russian Federation	648		F 503	Beykoz	FFGM	Turkey	793
F 466	Nikiforos Fokas	FFGHM	Greece	293		HQ 503	Qui Nonh	LST	Vietnam	944
A 466	Trichonis	AWT	Greece	300		M 503	Finike	MSI	Turkey	798
Y 466	RP 116	YTM	Italy	395		504	Teluk Kau	LST	Indonesia	347
A 467	Doirani	AWT	Greece	300		504	Rumbek	PBR	Sudan	727
Y 467	RP 123	YTM	Italy	395		A 504	Obula	PBO	Nigeria	534
A 468	Kalliroe	AWT	Greece	300		F 504	Bartin	FFGM	Turkey	793
Y 468	RP 118	YTM	Italy	395		LT 504	Lanao Del Norte	LST	Philippines	578
469	BT 211	MHSC/MHSCM	Russian Federation	648		505	Mayom	PBR	Sudan	727
A 469	Stimfalia	AWT	Greece	300		F 505	Bafra	FFGM	Turkey	793
A 470	Aliakmon	ARL/AOTL	Greece	300		506	Dauriya	AKH/AGF	Russian Federation	653
Y 470	RP 119	YTM	Italy	395		J 506	Yongxingdao	ASRH	China	148
471	Maga	PTG	Myanmar	510		K 506	Zelenograd	SSBN	Russian Federation	617
B 471	Magneto-gorsk	SSK	Russian Federation	626		507	Daqahliya	MSO	Egypt	205
F 471	Antonio Enes	FSH	Portugal	598		508	Teluk Tomini	LST	Indonesia	347
Y 471	RP 120	YTM	Italy	395		509	Chang De	FFG	China	134
472	Kalaat Beni Hammad	LSTH	Algeria	6		509	Teluk Ratai	LST	Indonesia	347
472	Saittra	PTG	Myanmar	510		AOR 509	Protecteur	AORH	Canada	97
Y 472	RP 121	YTM	Italy	395		510	Shaoxing	FFG	China	134
473	Kalaat Beni Rached	LSTH	Algeria	6		510	Teluk Saleh	LST	Indonesia	347
473	Duwa	PTG	Myanmar	510		510	BT 230	MHSC/MHSCM	Russian Federation	648
Y 473	RP 122	YTM	Italy	395		AOR 510	Preserver	AORH	Canada	97
474	Zeyda	PTG	Myanmar	510		U 510	Slavutich	AGFHM	Ukraine	813
A 474	Pytheas	AGOR	Greece	299		511	Nantong	FFG	China	134
F 475	João Coutinho	FSH	Portugal	598		511	Jymy	YFB	Finland	224
A 476	Strabon	AGSC	Greece	299		511	Teluk Bone	LST	Indonesia	347
F 476	Jacinto Candido	FSH	Portugal	598		511	Hengam	LSLH	Iran	362
F 477	General Pereira D'eça	FSH	Portugal	598		511	Kontradmiral X Czernicki	AKHM/APHM/AGI	Poland	590
Y 477	RP 124	YTM	Italy	395						
A 478	Naftilos	AGS	Greece	299		511	Al Siddiq	PGGF	Saudi Arabia	674
Y 478	RP 125	YTM	Italy	395		511	Pattani	PBOH	Thailand	766
A 479	I Karavoyiannos	ABUH	Greece	301		A 511	Elbe	ARLHM	Germany	283
Y 479	RP 126	YTM	Italy	395		A 511	Shaheed Ruhul Amin	PBO/AX	Bangladesh	49
F 480	Comandante João Belo	FF	Portugal	596		U 511	Simferopol	AGS	Ukraine	811
Y 480	RP 127	YTM	Italy	395		512	Wuxi	FFG	China	134
481	Ho Shun	LCU	Taiwan	755		512	Raju	YFB	Finland	224
A 481	St Lykoudis	ABUH	Greece	301		512	Teluk Semangka	LSTH	Indonesia	347
Y 481	RP 128	YTM	Italy	395		512	Larak	LSLH	Iran	362
Y 482	RP 129	YTM	Italy	395		512	Narathiwat	PBOH	Thailand	766
F 483	Comandante Sacadura Cabral	FF	Portugal	596		A 512	Shahayak	YR	Bangladesh	52
						A 512	Mosel	ARLHM	Germany	283
Y 483	RP 130	YTM	Italy	395		513	Huayin	FFG	China	134
484	Ho Chung	LCU	Taiwan	755		513	Sinai	MSO	Egypt	205
Y 484	RP 131	YTM	Italy	395		513	Teluk Penyu	LSTH	Indonesia	347
Y 485	RP 132	YTM	Italy	395		513	Tonb	LSLH	Iran	362
F 486	Baptista De Andrade	FSH	Portugal	598		513	Al Zuara	PTFG	Libya	464
Y 486	RP 133	YTM	Italy	395		513	Al Farouq	PGGF	Saudi Arabia	674
F 487	João Roby	FSH	Portugal	598		A 513	Shahjalal	AG	Bangladesh	52
Y 487	RP 134	YTM	Italy	395		A 513	Rhein	ARLHM	Germany	283
488	Ho Shan	LCU	Taiwan	755		514	Zhenjiang	FFG	China	134
F 488	Afonso Cerqueira	FSH	Portugal	598						

Number	Ship's name	Type	Country	Page
514	Teluk Mandar	LSTH	Indonesia	347
514	Lavan	LSLH	Iran	362
A 514	Werra	ARLHM	Germany	283
M 514	Silifke	MSC	Turkey	798
515	Xiamen	FFG	China	134
515	Teluk Sampit	LSTH	Indonesia	347
515	Al Ruha	PTFG	Libya	464
515	Abdul Aziz	PGGF	Saudi Arabia	674
A 515	Khan Jahan Ali	AOTL	Bangladesh	52
A 515	Main	ARLHM	Germany	283
M 515	Saros	MSC	Turkey	798
516	Jiujiang	FFG	China	134
516	Assiyut	MSO	Egypt	205
516	Teluk Banten	LSTH	Indonesia	347
A 516	Iman Gazzali	AOTL	Bangladesh	52
A 516	Donau	ARLHM	Germany	283
LT 516	Kalinga Apayao	LST	Philippines	578
M 516	Sigacik	MSC	Turkey	798
517	Nanping	FFG	China	134
517	Teluk Ende	LSTH	Indonesia	347
517	Faisal	PGGF	Saudi Arabia	674
M 517	Sapanca	MSC	Turkey	798
518	Jian	FFG	China	134
518	Sharaba	PGGF	Libya	464
M 518	Sariyer	MSC	Turkey	798
519	Changzhi	FFG	China	134
519	Khalid	PGGF	Saudi Arabia	674
520	Bisma	PBO	Indonesia	354
520	Rassvet	FSG	Russian Federation	641
A 520	Sagres	AXS	Portugal	601
M 520	Karamürsel	MSC/AGS/PBO	Turkey	797
S 520	Leonardo Da Vinci	SSK	Italy	376
521	Jiaxin	FFGHM	China	133
521	Kiiski 1	MSI	Finland	222
521	Baladewa	PBO	Indonesia	354
521	Amyr	PGGF	Saudi Arabia	674
A 521	Schultz Xavier	ABU	Portugal	602
M 521	Kerempe	MSC/AGS/PBO	Turkey	797
P 521	Vigilante	PBO	Cape Verde	106
522	Lianyungang	FFGHM	China	133
522	Kiiski 2	MSI	Finland	222
522	Shehab	PGGF	Libya	464
522	BT 213	MHSC/MHSCM	Russian Federation	648
A 522	D. Carlos I	AGS	Portugal	600
M 522	Kilimli	MSC/AGS/PBO	Turkey	797
S 522	Salvatore Pelosi	SSK	Italy	377
523	Sanming	FFGHM	China	133
523	Kiiski 3	MSI	Finland	222
523	Al Fikah	PTFG	Libya	464
523	Tariq	PGGF	Saudi Arabia	674
A 523	Almirante Gago Coutinho	AGS	Portugal	600
S 523	Giuliano Prini	SSK	Italy	377
524	Balchik	PB	Bulgaria	85
524	Putian	FFGHM	China	133
524	Kiiski 4	MSI	Finland	222
524	Wahag	PGGF	Libya	464
524	Yuen Feng	AKM	Taiwan	757
S 524	Primo Longobardo	SSK	Italy	377
525	Sozopol	PB	Bulgaria	85
525	Maanshan	FFGHM	China	132
525	Kiiski 5	MSI	Finland	222
525	Al Mathur	PTFG	Libya	464
525	BT 232	MHSC/MHSCM	Russian Federation	648
525	Oqbah	PGGF	Saudi Arabia	674
525	Wu Kang	AKM	Taiwan	757
S 525	Gianfranco Gazzana Priaroggia	SSK	Italy	377
526	Nesebar	PB	Bulgaria	85
526	Wenzhou	FFGHM	China	132
526	Kiiski 6	MSI	Finland	222
526	Nakat (IV)	FSG	Russian Federation	641
526	Hsin Kang	AKM	Taiwan	757
K 526	Tomsk	SSGN	Russian Federation	620
S 526	Salvatore Todaro	SSK	Italy	376
527	Luoyang	FFGHM	China	133
527	Kiiski 7	MSI	Finland	222
527	Abu Obaidah	PGGF	Saudi Arabia	674
S 527	Scirè	SSK	Italy	376
528	Mianyang	FFGHM	China	133
528	Shouaiai	PGGF	Libya	464
M 528	Suarez Arana	YFL	Bolivia	61
A 530	Horten	ASH/AGP	Norway	542
530	Giza	MSO	Egypt	205
530	Wu Yi	AOEHM	Taiwan	757
P 530	Trabzon	PBO/AGI	Turkey	794
531	Syöksy	YFB	Finland	224
531	Al Bitar	PTFG	Libya	464
P 531	Terme	PBO/AGI	Turkey	794
532	Shoula	PGGF	Libya	464
533	Ningbo	FFG	China	134
533	Aswan	MSO	Egypt	205
533	Al Sadad	PTFG	Libya	464
533	Tusha	FSG	Russian Federation	641
533	BT 245	MHSC/MHSCM	Russian Federation	648
A 533	Norge	YAC	Norway	542
534	Jinhua	FFG	China	134
534	Shafak	PGGF	Libya	464
K 534	Nizhny Novgorod	SSN	Russian Federation	618
535	Aysberg	FSG	Russian Federation	641
A 535	Valkyrien	ASH/AGP	Norway	542
536	Qena	MSO	Egypt	205
538	Rad	PGGF	Libya	464
539	Anqing	FFGHM	China	133
539	Sohag	MSO	Egypt	205
A 540	Dannebrog	YAC	Denmark	181

Number	Ship's name	Type	Country	Page
A 540	Hansaya	LCP	Sri Lanka	727
U 540	Chigirin	AXL	Ukraine	812
541	Huaibei	FFGHM	China	133
541	Vinha	YFB	Finland	224
541	Hua Hin	PSO	Thailand	769
P 541	Aboubekr Ben Amer	PBO	Mauritania	487
U 541	Smila	AXL	Ukraine	812
542	Tongling	FFGHM	China	133
542	Laheeb	PGGF	Libya	464
542	BT 114	MHSC/MHSCM	Russian Federation	648
542	Klaeng	PSO	Thailand	769
TB 542	Playa Blanca	YDT/YAG	Colombia	162
U 542	Darnicha	AXL	Ukraine	812
543	Dandong	FFG	China	134
543	Marshal Shaposhnikov	DDGHM	Russian Federation	634
543	Si Racha	PSO	Thailand	769
544	Siping	FFGH	China	137
TB 544	Bell Salter	YDT/YAG	Colombia	162
545	Linfen	FFG	China	134
TB 545	Maldonado	YDT/YAG	Colombia	162
TB 546	Orion	YDT/YAG	Colombia	162
TB 547	Pegasso	YDT/YAG	Colombia	162
548	Admiral Panteleyev	DDGHM	Russian Federation	634
TB 548	Almirante I	YDT/YAG	Colombia	162
TB 549	Almirante II	YDT/YAG	Colombia	162
LC 550	Bacolod City	LSVH	Philippines	578
TB 550	Ara	YDT/YAG	Colombia	162
551	Maoming	FFG	China	134
551	Liven	FSG	Russian Federation	641
A 551	Danbjørn	AGB	Denmark	184
ATF 551	Ta Wan	ATF/ARS	Taiwan	757
B 551	Voum-Legleita	PBO	Mauritania	487
C 551	Giuseppe Garibaldi	CVGM	Italy	378
F 551	Minerva	FSM	Italy	385
LC 551	Dagupan City	LSVH	Philippines	578
P 551	Sadd	PBF	Pakistan	558
TB 551	Valerosa	YDT/YAG	Colombia	162
WLM 551	Ida Lewis	WLM/ABU	US	925
552	Yibin	FFG	China	134
A 552	Isbjørn	AGB	Denmark	184
C 552	Cavour	CV	Italy	380
F 552	Urania	FSM	Italy	385
P 552	Havkatten	PGGM/MHCD/MLC/AGSC	Denmark	179
P 552	Shabhaz	PBF	Pakistan	558
TB 552	Luchadora	YDT/YAG	Colombia	162
WLM 552	Katherine Walker	WLM/ABU	US	925
553	Shaoguan	FFG	China	134
553	Andrea Doria	DDGHM	Italy	382
A 553	Thorbjørn	AGB/AGS	Denmark	184
ATF 553	Ta Han	ATF/ARS	Taiwan	757
F 553	Danaide	FSM	Italy	385
P 553	Laxen	PGGM/MHCD/MLC/AGSC	Denmark	179
P 553	Vaqar	PBF	Pakistan	558
WLM 553	Abigail Burgess	WLM/ABU	US	925
554	Anshun	FFG	China	134
554	Caio Duilio	DDGHM	Italy	382
ATF 554	Ta Kang	ATF/ARS	Taiwan	757
F 554	Sfinge	FSM	Italy	385
P 554	Makrelen	PGGM/MHCD/MLC/AGSC	Denmark	179
P 554	Burq	PBF	Pakistan	558
TB 554	Orca	YDT/YAG	Colombia	162
WLM 554	Marcus Hanna	WLM/ABU	US	925
555	Zhaotong	FFG	China	134
555	Geyzer	FSG	Russian Federation	641
ATF 555	Ta Fung	ATF/ARS	Taiwan	757
F 555	Driade	FSM	Italy	385
P 555	Støren	PGGM/MHCD/MLC/AGSC	Denmark	179
WLM 555	James Rankin	WLM/ABU	US	925
YTM 555	Tillicum	YTB/YTL	Canada	97
F 556	Chimera	FSM	Italy	385
WLM 556	Joshua Appleby	WLM/ABU	US	925
557	Jishou	FFG	China	134
F 557	Fenice	FSM	Italy	385
P 557	Glenten	PGGM/MHCD/MLC/AGSC	Denmark	179
WLM 557	Frank Drew	WLM/ABU	US	925
558	Zigong	FFG	China	134
F 558	Sibilla	FSM	Italy	385
P 558	Gribben	PGGM/MHCD/MLC/AGSC	Denmark	179
WLM 558	Anthony Petit	WLM/ABU	US	925
559	Kangding	FFG	China	134
A 559	Sleipner	AKS	Denmark	181
P 559	Lommen	PGGM/MHCD/MLC/AGSC	Denmark	179
WLM 559	Barbara Mabrity	WLM/ABU	US	925
560	Dongguan	FFG	China	134
560	Won San	MLH	Korea, South	451
560	Zyb	FSG	Russian Federation	641
560	BT 256	MHSC/MHSCM	Russian Federation	648
A 560	Gunnar Thorson	YPC/ABU	Denmark	183
D 560	Luigi Durand de la Penne	DDGHM	Italy	381
P 560	Ravnen	PGGM/MHCD/MLC/AGSC	Denmark	179
WLM 560	William Tate	WLM/ABU	US	925
561	Shantou	FFG	China	134
561	Multatuli	AGFH	Indonesia	350
561	Kang Kyeong	MHSC	Korea, South	451
561	BT 115	MHSC/MHSCM	Russian Federation	648
A 561	Gunnar Seidenfaden	YPC/ABU	Denmark	183
D 561	Francesco Mimbelli	DDGHM	Italy	381

Number	Ship's name	Type	Country	Page
P 561	Skaden	PGGM/MHCD/MLC/AGSC	Denmark	179
WLM 561	Harry Claiborne	WLM/ABU	US	925
YTR 561	Firebird	YTB/YTL	Canada	97
562	Jiangmen	FFG	China	134
562	Kang Jin	MHSC	Korea, South	451
A 562	Mette Miljø	AKL	Denmark	183
P 562	Viben	PGGM/MHCD/MLC/AGSC	Denmark	179
WLM 562	Maria Bray	WLM/ABU	US	925
YTR 562	Firebrand	YTB/YTL	Canada	97
563	Zhaoqing	FFG	China	134
563	Ko Ryeong	MHSC	Korea, South	451
563	BT 44	MHSC/MHSCM	Russian Federation	648
A 563	Marie Miljø	AKL	Denmark	183
ATF 563	Ta Tai	ATF/ARS	Taiwan	757
P 563	Søløven	PGGM/MHCD/MLC/AGSC	Denmark	179
WLM 563	Henry Blake	WLM/ABU	US	925
564	Yichang	FFGHM	China	133
564	Admiral Tributs	DDGHM	Russian Federation	634
WLM 564	George Cobb	WLM/ABU	US	925
565	Yulin	FFGHM	China	133
565	Kim Po	MHSC	Korea, South	451
565	BT 100	MHSC/MHSCM	Russian Federation	648
566	Huaihua	FFGHM	China	133
566	Ko Chang	MHSC	Korea, South	451
567	Xiangfan	FFGHM	China	133
567	Kum Wha	MHSC	Korea, South	451
568	BT 94	MHSC/MHSCM	Russian Federation	648
A 570	Taşkizak	AOTL	Turkey	799
570	Passat	FSG	Russian Federation	641
F 570	Maestrale	FFGHM	Italy	383
571	Yang Yang	MSC/MHC	Korea, South	451
A 571	Albay Hakki Burak	AOT	Turkey	799
F 571	Grecale	FFGHM	Italy	383
572	Ongjin	MSC/MHC	Korea, South	451
572	Admiral Vinogradov	DDGHM	Russian Federation	634
A 572	Yuzbasi Ihsan Tolunay	AOT	Turkey	799
F 572	Libeccio	FFGHM	Italy	383
573	Hae Nam	MSC/MHC	Korea, South	451
A 573	Binbaşi Sadettin Gürcan	AORL	Turkey	800
F 573	Scirocco	FFGHM	Italy	383
F 574	Aliseo	FFGHM	Italy	383
F 575	Euro	FFGHM	Italy	383
A 576	Değirmendere	ATA	Turkey	802
F 576	Espero	FFGHM	Italy	383
577	BT 262	MHSC/MHSCM	Russian Federation	648
A 577	Sokullu Mehmet Paşa	AG/AX	Turkey	799
F 577	Zeffiro	FFGHM	Italy	383
A 578	Darica	ATR	Turkey	803
A 579	Cezayirli Gazi Hasan Paşa	AG/AX	Turkey	799
580	Dore	LCU	Indonesia	348
A 580	Akar	AORH	Turkey	799
A 581	Darshak	LCU/LCP	Bangladesh	53
A 581	Çinar	AWT	Turkey	800
F 581	Carabiniere	AGEHM	Italy	391
582	Kupang	LCU	Indonesia	348
A 582	Tallashi	LCU/LCP	Bangladesh	53
A 582	Kemer	MSC/AGS/PBO	Turkey	797
F 582	Artigliere	FFGHM	Italy	384
583	Dili	LCU	Indonesia	348
A 583	Agradoot	AGS	Bangladesh	52
F 583	Aviere	FFGHM	Italy	384
SS 583	Harushio	SSK	Japan	403
584	Nusa Utara	LCU	Indonesia	348
F 584	Bersagliere	FFGHM	Italy	384
SS 584	Natsushio	SSK	Japan	403
F 585	Granatiere	FFGHM	Italy	384
SS 585	Hayashio	SSK	Japan	403
586	BT 325	MHSC/MHSCM	Russian Federation	648
A 586	Akbaş	YTB/YTM/YTL	Turkey	802
SS 586	Arashio	SSK	Japan	403
A 587	Gazal	ATF	Turkey	802
SS 587	Wakashio	SSK	Japan	403
A 588	Çandarli	AGS	Turkey	798
SS 588	Fuyushio	SSK	Japan	403
A 589	Işin	ARS	Turkey	801
590	Meteor	FSG	Russian Federation	641
SS 590	Oyashio	SSK	Japan	402
YTL 590	Lawrenceville	YTB/YTL	Canada	97
SS 591	Michishio	SSK	Japan	402
YTL 591	Parksville	YTB/YTL	Canada	97
A 592	Karadeniz Ereğlisi	AKS/AWT	Turkey	801
SS 592	Uzushio	SSK	Japan	402
YTL 592	Listerville	YTB/YTL	Canada	97
593	BT 215	MHSC/MHSCM	Russian Federation	648
A 593	Eceabat	AKS/AWT	Turkey	801
SS 593	Makishio	SSK	Japan	402
YTL 593	Merrickville	YTB/YTL	Canada	97
A 594	Çubuklu	AGS	Turkey	798
SS 594	Isoshio	SSK	Japan	402
YTL 594	Granville	YTB/YTL	Canada	97
A 595	Yarbay Kudret Güngör	AORH	Turkey	799
SS 595	Narushio	SSK	Japan	402
A 596	Ulubat	AWT	Turkey	800
SS 596	Kuroshio	SSK	Japan	402
A 597	Van	AWT	Turkey	800
SS 597	Takashio	SSK	Japan	402
A 598	Sögüt	AWT	Turkey	800
SS 598	Yaeshio	SSK	Japan	402
A 599	Çesme	AGS	Turkey	798
SS 599	Setoshio	SSK	Japan	402
A 600	Kavak	AWT	Turkey	800
601	Ras El Blais	PBO	Tunisia	785
A 601	Oberst Brecht	PBR	Austria	37
A 601	Monge	AGMH	France	254
NF 601	Filigonio Hichamón	YDT/YAG	Colombia	162
P 601	Élorn	PB	France	262
P 601	Limam El Hadrami	PB	Mauritania	487
P 601	Jayasagara	PB	Sri Lanka	723
S 601	Rubis	SSN/SNA	France	232
602	Junon	PB	Seychelles	685
602	Ras Ajdir	PBO	Tunisia	785
NF 602	Ssim Manuel A Moyar	YDT/YAG	Colombia	162
P 602	Verdon	PB	France	262
S 602	Saphir	SSN/SNA	France	232
603	Aiyar Lulin	PB	Myanmar	513
603	Jin Chiang	PCG	Taiwan	753
603	Ras El Edrak	PBO	Tunisia	785
D 603	Duquesne	DDGM	France	240
NF 603	Igaraparaná	YDT/YAG	Colombia	162
P 603	Adour	PB	France	262
S 603	Casabianca	SSN/SNA	France	232
604	Aiyar Mai	LCU	Myanmar	514
604	Fortune	PB	Seychelles	684
604	Ras El Manoura	PBO	Tunisia	785
A 604	Niederösterreich	PBR	Austria	37
NF 604	Ssim Julio Correa Hernández	YDT/YAG	Colombia	162
P 604	Scarpe	PB	France	262
S 604	Émeraude	SSN/SNA	France	232
605	Aiyar Maung	LCU	Myanmar	514
605	Admiral Levchenko	DDGHM	Russian Federation	634
605	Andromache	PB	Seychelles	684
605	Ras Enghela	PBO	Tunisia	785
NF 605	Manacacías	YDT/YAG	Colombia	162
P 605	Vertonne	PB	France	262
S 605	Améthyste	SSN/SNA	France	232
606	Aiyar Minthamee	LCU	Myanmar	514
606	Hsin Chiang	PCG	Taiwan	753
606	Ras Ifrikia	PBO	Tunisia	785
NF 606	Cotuhe	YDT/YAG	Colombia	162
P 606	Dumbéa	PB	France	262
S 606	Perle	SSN/SNA	France	232
607	Aiyar Minthar	LCU	Myanmar	514
607	Feng Chiang	PCG	Taiwan	753
A 607	Meuse	AORHM	France	256
NF 607	SSCIM Senen Alberto Arango	YDT/YAG	Colombia	162
P 607	Yser	PB	France	262
608	Tseng Chiang	PCG	Taiwan	753
A 608	Var	AORHM	France	256
NF 608	CPCIM Guillermo Londoño Vargas	YDT/YAG	Colombia	162
P 608	Argens	PB	France	262
609	Kao Chiang	PCG	Taiwan	753
NF 609	Ariarí	YDT/YAG	Colombia	162
P 609	Hérault	PB	France	262
610	Nastoychivy	DDGHM	Russian Federation	635
610	Jing Chiang	PCG	Taiwan	753
D 610	Tourville	DDGHM	France	241
NF 610	Mario Villegas	YDT/YAG	Colombia	162
P 610	Gravona	PB	France	262
611	Dokdo	LPD	Korea, South	450
611	Mohammed V	FFGHM	Morocco	505
611	Hsian Chiang	PCG	Taiwan	753
M 611	Vulcain	MCD	France	253
NF 611	Tony Pastrana Contreras	YDT/YAG	Colombia	162
P 611	Tawheed	PC	Bangladesh	49
P 611	Odet	PB	France	262
612	Hassan II	FFGHM	Morocco	505
612	Badr	FFGHM	Saudi Arabia	671
612	Tsi Chiang	PCG	Taiwan	753
D 612	De Grasse	DDGHM	France	241
NF 612	Ctcim Jorge Moreno Salazar	YDT/YAG	Colombia	162
P 612	Tawfiq	PC	Bangladesh	49
P 612	Maury	PB	France	262
A 613	Achéron	MCD	France	253
P 613	Tamjeed	PC	Bangladesh	49
P 613	Charente	PB	France	262
614	Al Yarmook	FFGHM	Saudi Arabia	671
614	Po Chiang	PCG	Taiwan	753
D 614	Cassard	DDGHM	France	237
M 614	Styx	MCD	France	253
P 614	Tanveer	PC	Bangladesh	49
P 614	Tech	PB	France	262
615	Bora	PGGJM	Russian Federation	640
615	Chan Chiang	PCG	Taiwan	753
A 615	Loire	AGH/AR	France	256
D 615	Jean Bart	DDGHM	France	237
P 615	Panfeld	PB	France	262
S 615	L'Inflexible	SSBN/SNLE	France	230
616	Hitteen	FFGHM	Saudi Arabia	671
A 616	Le Malin	YDT	France	257
P 616	Trieux	PB	France	262
S 616	Le Triomphant	SSBN/SNLE-NG	France	231
617	Mirazh	FSG	Russian Federation	641
617	Chu Chiang	PCG	Taiwan	753
P 617	Vésubie	PB	France	262
S 617	Le Téméraire	SSBN/SNLE-NG	France	231
618	Tabuk	FFGHM	Saudi Arabia	671
P 618	Escaut	PB	France	262
S 618	Le Vigilant	SSBN/SNLE-NG	France	231
619	Severomorsk	DDGHM	Russian Federation	634
P 619	Huveaune	PB	France	262
S 619	Le Terrible	SSBN/SNLE-NG	France	231
620	Bespokoiny	DDGHM	Russian Federation	635

Number	Ship's name	Type	Country	Page
620	Shtyl	FSG	Russian Federation	641
A 620	Jules Verne	ADH	France	256
D 620	Forbin	DDGHM	France	240
P 620	Sévre	PB	France	262
P 620	Sayura	PSOH	Sri Lanka	722
621	Mandau	PTFG	Indonesia	344
621	Flaming	MHCM	Poland	588
D 621	Chevalier Paul	DDGHM	France	240
P 621	Aber-Wrach	PB	France	262
P 621	Samudura	PSOH	Sri Lanka	722
622	Rencong	PTFG	Indonesia	344
M 622	Pluton	MCD	France	253
P 622	Estéron	PB	France	262
623	Badik	PTFG	Indonesia	344
623	Mewa	MHCM	Poland	588
P 623	Mahury	PB	France	262
624	Keris	PTFG	Indonesia	344
624	Czajka	MHCM	Poland	588
P 624	Organabo	PB	France	262
630	Goplo	MHC	Poland	588
A 630	Marne	AORHM	France	256
631	Gardno	MHC	Poland	588
A 631	Somme	AORHM	France	256
632	Bukowo	MHC	Poland	588
633	Dabie	MHC	Poland	588
633	LatYa	MHSC	Thailand	773
A 633	Taape	AG/ATS/YDT/YPC/YPT	France	257
634	Jamno	MHC	Poland	588
634	Tha Din Daeng	MHSC	Thailand	773
A 634	Rari	AFL	France	257
635	Mielno	MHC	Poland	588
A 635	Revi	AFL	France	257
636	Wicko	MHC	Poland	588
A 636	Maito	YTM	France	260
637	Resko	MHC	Poland	588
A 637	Maroa	YTM	France	260
638	Sarbsko	MHC	Poland	588
A 638	Manini	YTM	France	260
639	Necko	MHC	Poland	588
640	Naklo	MHC	Poland	588
D 640	Georges Leygues	DDGHM	France	238
641	Druzno	MHC	Poland	588
A 641	Esterel	YTM	France	259
D 641	Dupleix	DDGHM	France	238
M 641	Éridan	MHC	France	252
642	Hancza	MHC	Poland	588
A 642	Lubéron	YTM	France	259
D 642	Montcalm	DDGHM	France	238
M 642	Cassiopée	MHC	France	252
643	Mamry	MHSCM	Poland	588
D 643	Jean De Vienne	DDGHM	France	238
M 643	Andromède	MHC	France	252
644	Wigry	MHSCM	Poland	588
D 644	Primauguet	DDGHM	France	238
M 644	Pégase	MHC	France	252
645	Sniardwy	MHSCM	Poland	588
A 645	Alize	YDT	France	257
D 645	La Motte-Picquet	DDGHM	France	238
M 645	Orion	MHC	France	252
646	Wdzydze	MHSCM	Poland	588
D 646	Latouche-Tréville	DDGHM	France	238
M 646	Croix Du Sud	MHC	France	252
M 647	Aigle	MHC	France	252
M 648	Lyre	MHC	France	252
A 649	L'étoile	AXS	France	255
M 649	Persée	MHC	France	252
A 650	La Belle Poule	AXS	France	255
M 650	Sagittaire	MHC	France	252
651	Singa	PBO	Indonesia	345
FNH 651	Nacaome	PB	Honduras	308
GC 651	Tecun Uman	PB	Guatemala	305
M 651	Verseau	MHC	France	252
A 652	Mutin	AXS	France	255
FNH 652	Goascoran	PB	Honduras	308
GC 652	Kaibil Balan	PB	Guatemala	305
M 652	Céphée	MHC	France	252
653	Ajak	PBO	Indonesia	345
A 653	La Grand Hermine	AXS	France	255
FNH 653	Patuca	PB	Honduras	308
GC 653	Azumanche	PB	Guatemala	305
M 653	Capricorne	MHC	France	252
FNH 654	Ulua	PB	Honduras	308
GC 654	Tzacol	PB	Guatemala	305
FNH 655	Choluteca	PB	Honduras	308
GC 655	Bitol	PB	Guatemala	305
FNH 656	Rio Coco	PB	Honduras	308
BH 656	Gucumaz	PB	Guatemala	305
661	Letuchy	FFM	Russian Federation	637
A 664	Malabar	ATA	France	259
MSC 668	Yurishima	MHSC	Japan	416
A 669	Tenace	ATA	France	259
MSC 669	Hikoshima	MHSC	Japan	416
670	Ramadan	PGGF	Egypt	203
MSC 670	Awashima	MHSC	Japan	416
671	Un Bong	LST	Korea, South	450
MSC 671	Sakushima	MHSC	Japan	416
P 671	Glaive	PB	France	262
672	Khyber	PGGF	Egypt	203
MSC 672	Uwajima	MHSC	Japan	416
P 672	Épée	PB	France	262
MSC 673	Ieshima	MHSC	Japan	416
674	El Kadessaya	PGGF	Egypt	203
MSC 674	Tsukishima	MHSC	Japan	416
P 674	D'Entrecasteaux	AG/AX	France	256
A 675	Fréhel	YTM	France	260
MSC 675	Maejima	MHSC	Japan	416
P 675	Arago	PBO	France	247
676	El Yarmouk	PGGF	Egypt	203
676	Wee Bong	LST	Korea, South	450
A 676	Saire	YTM	France	260
MSC 676	Kumejima	MHSC	Japan	416
P 676	Flamant	PBO	France	248
677	Su Yong	LST	Korea, South	450
A 677	Armen	YTM	France	260
MSC 677	Makishima	MHSC	Japan	416
P 677	Cormoran	PBO	France	248
678	Badr	PGGF	Egypt	203
678	Buk Han	LST	Korea, South	450
678	Admiral Kharlamov	DDGHM	Russian Federation	634
A 678	La Houssaye	YTM	France	260
MSC 678	Tobishima	MHSC	Japan	416
P 678	Pluvier	PBO	France	248
A 679	Kéréon	YTM	France	260
MSC 679	Yugeshima	MHSC	Japan	416
P 679	Grèbe	PBO	France	248
680	Hettein	PGGF	Egypt	203
A 680	Sicié	YTM	France	260
MSC 680	Nagashima	MHSC	Japan	416
P 680	Sterne	PBO	France	248
681	Kojoon Bong	LSTH	Korea, South	450
A 681	Taunoa	YTM	France	260
MSC 681	Sugashima	MHC	Japan	417
P 681	Albatros	PSO	France	248
682	Biro Bong	LSTH	Korea, South	450
A 682	Rascas	YTM	France	260
MSC 682	Notojima	MHC	Japan	417
P 682	L'Audacieuse	PBO	France	247
683	Hyangro Bong	LSTH	Korea, South	450
MSC 683	Tsunoshima	MHC	Japan	417
P 683	La Boudeuse	PBO	France	247
MSC 684	Naoshima	MHC	Japan	417
P 684	La Capricieuse	PBO	France	247
685	Seongin Bong	LSTH	Korea, South	450
MSC 685	Toyoshima	MHC	Japan	417
P 685	La Fougueuse	PBO	France	247
MSC 686	Ukushima	MHC	Japan	417
P 686	La Glorieuse	PBO	France	247
687	Marshal Vasilevsky	DDGHM	Russian Federation	634
MSC 687	Izushima	MHC	Japan	417
P 687	La Gracieuse	PBO	France	247
MSC 688	Aishima	MHC	Japan	417
P 688	La Moqueuse	PBO	France	247
SSN 688	Los Angeles	SSN	US	868
MSC 689	Aoshima	MHC	Japan	417
P 689	La Railleuse	PBO	France	247
MSC 690	Miyajima	MHC	Japan	417
P 690	La Rieuse	PBO	France	247
SSN 690	Philadelphia	SSN	US	868
691	Tatarstan	FFGM	Russian Federation	638
MSC 691	Shishijima	MHC	Japan	417
P 691	La Tapageuse	PBO	France	247
SSN 691	Memphis	SSN	US	868
MSC 692	Kuroshima	MHC	Japan	417
A 693	Acharné	YTM	France	260
A 695	Bélier	YTB	France	259
A 696	Buffle	YTB	France	259
A 697	Bison	YTB	France	259
SSN 698	Bremerton	SSN	US	868
SSN 699	Jacksonville	SSN	US	868
700	Kingston	MM	Canada	95
700	R 160	FSGM	Russian Federation	642
A 700	Khaireddine	AGS	Tunisia	784
SSN 700	Dallas	SSN	US	868
SSV 700	Temryuk	AGS/AGI/AGE	Russian Federation	649
701	Sirius	LSM	Bulgaria	85
701	Glace Bay	MM	Canada	95
701	Thar	WPB	Egypt	209
P 701	Nandimithra	PGG	Sri Lanka	723
SSN 701	La Jolla	SSN	US	868
702	Antares	LSM	Bulgaria	85
702	Nanaimo	MM	Canada	95
702	Pylky	FFM	Russian Federation	637
702	Borovsk	PGGK	Russian Federation	644
702	Madina	FFGHM	Saudi Arabia	672
L 702	Chikoko I	LCU	Malawi	470
P 702	Suranimala	PGG	Sri Lanka	723
703	Edmonton	MM	Canada	95
703	Nur	WPB	Egypt	209
P 703	Lilas	PB	France	263
P 703	Kasungu	PB	Malawi	470
704	Shawinigan	MM	Canada	95
704	Hofouf	FFGHM	Saudi Arabia	672
P 704	Bégonia	PB	France	263
P 704	Kaning'a	PB	Malawi	470
705	Whitehorse	MM	Canada	95
705	Stupinets	FSGM	Russian Federation	642
SSN 705	City of Corpus Christi	SSN	US	868
706	Yellowknife	MM	Canada	95
706	R 25	PGGK	Russian Federation	644
706	Abha	FFGHM	Saudi Arabia	672
SSN 706	Albuquerque	SSN	US	868
707	Goose Bay	MM	Canada	95
708	Moncton	MM	Canada	95
708	Taif	FFGHM	Saudi Arabia	672
SSN 708	Minneapolis-Saint Paul	SSN	US	868
709	Saskatoon	MM	Canada	95
P 709	MDLC Richard	PB	France	263
SSN 709	Hyman G Rickover	SSN	US	868
710	Brandon	MM	Canada	95
F 710	La Fayette	FFGHM	France	242
P 710	General Delfosse	PB	France	263

Number	Ship's name	Type	Country	Page	Number	Ship's name	Type	Country	Page
SSN 710	Augusta	SSN	US	868	759	Mok Po	FS/FSG	Korea, South	448
711	Summerside	MM	Canada	95	A 759	Dupuy De Lôme	AGIH	France	253
711	Pulau Rengat	MHSC	Indonesia	348	SSN 759	Jefferson City	SSN	US	868
F 711	Surcouf	FFGHM	France	242	SSN 760	Annapolis	SSN	US	868
P 711	Barkat	PC	Bangladesh	50	761	Kim Chon	FS/FSG	Korea, South	448
SSN 711	San Francisco	SSN	US	868	P 761	Mimosa	PB	France	262
712	Pulau Rupat	MHSC	Indonesia	348	P 761	Kara	PB	Togo	780
712	Neustrashimy	FFHM	Russian Federation	636	SSN 761	Springfield	SSN	US	868
A 712	Athos	YFRT	France	258	762	Chung Ju	FS/FSG	Korea, South	448
F 712	Courbet	FFGHM	France	242	762	V Gumanenko	MHOM	Russian Federation	648
P 712	Salam	PB	Bangladesh	50	L 762	Lachs	LCU	Germany	278
713	Nisr	WPB	Egypt	209	P 762	Mono	PB	Togo	780
A 713	Aramis	YFRT	France	258	SSN 762	Columbus	SSN	US	868
F 713	Aconit	FFGHM	France	242	763	Jin Ju	FS/FSG	Korea, South	448
P 713	Capitaine Moulié	PB	France	263	SSN 763	Santa Fe	SSN	US	868
P 713	Sangu	PBO/AX	Bangladesh	49	SSN 764	Boise	SSN	US	868
SSN 713	Houston	SSN	US	868	765	Yo Su	FS/FSG	Korea, South	448
714	R 101	FSGM	Russian Federation	642	L 765	Schlei	LCU	Germany	278
F 714	Guépratte	FFGHM	France	242	SSN 765	Montpelier	SSN	US	868
P 714	Lieut Jamet	PB	France	263	766	Jin Hae	FS/FSG	Korea, South	448
P 714	Turag	PBO/AX	Bangladesh	49	SSN 766	Charlotte	SSN	US	868
SSN 714	Norfolk	SSN	US	868	767	Sun Chon	FS/FSG	Korea, South	448
715	Bystry	DDGHM	Russian Federation	635	SSN 767	Hampton	SSN	US	868
P 715	Bellis	PB	France	263	768	Yee Ree	FS/FSG	Korea, South	448
SSN 715	Buffalo	SSN	US	868	A 768	Élan	AG/ATS/YDT/ YPC/YPT	France	257
P 716	MDLS Jacques	PB	France	263					
SSN 717	Olympia	SSN	US	868	SSN 768	Hartford	SSN	US	868
SSN 718	Honolulu	SSN	US	868	769	Won Ju	FS/FSG	Korea, South	448
719	Nimr	WPB	Egypt	209	SSN 769	Toledo	SSN	US	868
SSN 719	Providence	SSN	US	868	770	Yangjiang	PTG	China	139
P 720	Géranium	PB	France	262	770	Yevgeniy Kocheshkov	ACVM/LCUJM	Russian Federation	646
SSN 720	Pittsburgh	SSN	US	868	770	Valentin Pikul	MSOM	Russian Federation	647
A 721	Khadem	ATA	Bangladesh	53	A 770	Glycine	AXL	France	255
P 721	Jonquille	PB	France	262	M 770	Antaès	MHI	France	252
SSN 721	Chicago	SSN	US	868	SSN 770	Tucson	SSN	US	868
722	Vaarlahti	AKSL	Finland	222	771	Shunde	PTG	China	139
722	Al Munjed	ARS	Libya	465	771	Kampela 1	LCU/AKSL	Finland	223
A 722	Sebak	YTM	Bangladesh	53	771	An Dong	FS/FSG	Korea, South	448
A 722	Poséidon	YDT	France	258	771	Anawrahta	FS	Myanmar	510
P 722	Violette	PB	France	262	A 771	Eglantine	AXL	France	255
SSN 722	Key West	SSN	US	868	M 771	Altaïr	MHI	France	252
723	Vänö	AKSL	Finland	222	SSN 771	Columbia	SSN	US	868
A 723	Rupsha	YTM	Bangladesh	53	772	Nanhai	PTG	China	139
P 723	Jasmin	PB	France	262	772	Kampela 2	LCU/AKSL	Finland	223
SSN 723	Oklahoma City	SSN	US	868	772	Chon An	FS/FSG	Korea, South	448
A 724	Shibsha	YTM	Bangladesh	53	M 772	Aldébaran	MHI	France	252
SSN 724	Louisville	SSN	US	868	SSN 772	Greeneville	SSN	US	868
MCL 725	Kamishima	MCSD	Japan	416	773	Panyu	PTG	China	139
SSN 725	Helena	SSN	US	868	773	Song Nam	FS/FSG	Korea, South	448
MCL 726	Ogishima	MCSD	Japan	416	P 773	Njambuur	PBO	Senegal	678
SSGN 726	Ohio	SSGN	US	866	SSN 773	Cheyenne	SSN	US	868
SSGN 727	Michigan	SSGN	US	866	A 774	Chevreuil	AG/ATS/YDT/ YPC/YPT	France	257
SSGN 728	Florida	SSGN	US	866					
SSGN 729	Georgia	SSGN	US	866	SSN 774	Virginia	SSN	US	870
730	Haukipää	YTM	Finland	226	775	Bu Chon	FS/FSG	Korea, South	448
F 730	Floréal	FFGHM	France	244	A 775	Gazelle	AG/ATS/YDT/ YPC/YPT	France	257
SSBN 730	Henry M Jackson	SSBN	US	865					
731	Hakuni	AKSL	Finland	223	SSN 775	Texas	SSN	US	870
731	Neukrotimy	FFM	Russian Federation	637	776	Jae Chon	FS/FSG	Korea, South	448
F 731	Prairial	FFGHM	France	244	P 776	Sténia	PB	France	262
SSBN 731	Alabama	SSBN	US	865	SSN 776	Hawaii	SSN	US	870
F 732	Nivôse	FFGHM	France	244	777	Porkkala	MLI	Finland	221
SSBN 732	Alaska	SSBN	US	865	777	Dae Chon	FS/FSG	Korea, South	448
F 733	Ventôse	FFGHM	France	244	SSN 777	North Carolina	SSN	US	870
SSBN 733	Nevada	SSBN	US	865	778	Sok Cho	FS/FSG	Korea, South	448
F 734	Vendémiaire	FFGHM	France	244	778	Burny	DDGHM	Russian Federation	635
SSBN 734	Tennessee	SSBN	US	865	P 778	Réséda	PB	France	262
F 735	Germinal	FFGHM	France	244	SSN 778	New Hampshire	SSN	US	870
SSBN 735	Pennsylvania	SSBN	US	865	779	Yong Ju	FS/FSG	Korea, South	448
SSBN 736	West Virginia	SSBN	US	865	SSN 779	New Mexico	SSN	US	870
SSBN 737	Kentucky	SSBN	US	865	781	Nam Won	FS/FSG	Korea, South	448
SSBN 738	Maryland	SSBN	US	865	781	Man Nok	LCU	Thailand	772
739	Hästö	AKSL	Finland	223	782	Kwan Myong	FS/FSG	Korea, South	448
SSBN 739	Nebraska	SSBN	US	865	782	Mordoviya	ACVM/LCUJM	Russian Federation	646
P 740	Fulmar	PB	France	262	782	Man Klang	LCU	Thailand	772
SSBN 740	Rhode Island	SSBN	US	865	783	Sin Hung	FS/FSG	Korea, South	448
SSBN 741	Maine	SSBN	US	865	783	Man Nai	LCU	Thailand	772
SSBN 742	Wyoming	SSBN	US	865	785	Kong Ju	FS/FSG	Korea, South	448
SSBN 743	Louisiana	SSBN	US	865	A 785	Thétis	MCD/BEGM	France	254
A 748	Léopard	AXL	France	255	F 789	Lieutenant De Vaisseau Le Hénaff	FFGM	France	243
A 749	Panthère	AXL	France	255					
A 750	Jaguar	AXL	France	255	P 789	Melia	PB	France	262
SSN 750	Newport News	SSN	US	868	A 790	Coralline	YDT	France	258
751	Dong Hae	FS	Korea, South	448	F 790	Lieutenant De Vaisseau Lavallée	FFGM	France	243
A 751	Lynx	AXL	France	255					
SSN 751	San Juan	SSN	US	868	P 790	Vétiver	PB	France	262
752	Lohm	LCU	Finland	223	A 791	Lapérouse	AGS	France	254
752	Su Won	FS	Korea, South	448	F 791	Commandant L'herminier	FFGM	France	243
A 752	Guépard	AXL	France	255					
SSN 752	Pasadena	SSN	US	868	P 791	Hortensia	PB	France	262
753	Kang Reung	FS	Korea, South	448	792	Träskö	YFB	Finland	224
A 753	Chacal	AXL	France	255	A 792	Borda	AGS	France	254
SSN 753	Albany	SSN	US	868	F 792	Premier Maître L'Her	FFGM	France	243
754	Bezboyaznennyy	DDGHM	Russian Federation	635	793	Hai Lung	SSK	Taiwan	748
A 754	Tigre	AXL	France	255	A 793	Laplace	AGS	France	254
SSN 754	Topeka	SSN	US	868	F 793	Commandant Blaison	FFGM	France	243
755	An Yang	FS	Korea, South	448	794	Hai Hu	SSK	Taiwan	748
A 755	Lion	AXL	France	255	F 794	Enseigne De Vaisseau Jacoubet	FFGM	France	243
SSN 755	Miami	SSN	US	868					
756	Po Hang	FS/FSG	Korea, South	448	F 795	Commandant Ducuing	FFGM	France	243
SSN 756	Scranton	SSN	US	868	F 796	Commandant Birot	FFGM	France	243
757	Kun San	FS/FSG	Korea, South	448	F 797	Commandant Bouan	FFGM	France	243
SSN 757	Alexandria	SSN	US	868	798	Matelot Brice Kpomasse	PB	Benin	59
758	Kyong Ju	FS/FSG	Korea, South	448					
A 758	Beautemps-Beaupré	AGOR	France	253	799	La Sota	PB	Benin	59
SSN 758	Asheville	SSN	US	868	799	Hylje	YPC	Finland	225

PENNANT LIST

Number	Ship's name	Type	Country	Page	Number	Ship's name	Type	Country	Page
800	Shun Hu 1	WPBO	Taiwan	758	828	Umitaka	PGGF	Japan	414
B 800	Kaluga	SSK	Russian Federation	626	F 828	Van Speijk	FFGHM	Netherlands	520
L 800	Rotterdam	LPD	Netherlands	524	829	Shirataka	PGGF	Japan	414
801	Rais Hamidou	PTGM	Algeria	5	F 829	Willem Van Der Zaan	FFGHM	Netherlands	520
801	Pandrong	PBO	Indonesia	345	830	Högsära	AKSL	Finland	223
801	Pusan	AGOR	Korea, South	451	831	Kallanpää	YTM	Finland	226
801	Ladny	FFM	Russian Federation	637	831	Kangwon	AGOR	Korea, South	451
801	Te Mataili	PB	Tuvalu	806	831	Komendor	MSOM	Russian Federation	647
L 801	Johan De Witt	LPD	Netherlands	524	831	Sava	SSC	Serbia and Montenegro	680
MHV 801	Aldebaran	PB	Denmark	185					
TRV 801	Tuna	YPT	Australia	34	F 831	Van Amstel	FFGHM	Netherlands	520
802	Salah Rais	PTGM	Algeria	5	A 832	Zuiderkruis	AORH	Netherlands	527
802	Sura	PBO	Indonesia	345	F 833	Van Nes	FFGHM	Netherlands	520
802	Pusan	AGOR	Korea, South	451	F 834	Van Galen	FFGHM	Netherlands	520
A 802	Snellius	AGSH	Netherlands	525	836	Houtskär	AKSL	Finland	223
F 802	De Zeven Provincien	FFGHM	Netherlands	522	A 836	Amsterdam	AORH	Netherlands	526
MHV 802	Carina	PB	Denmark	185	L 836	Ranavijaya	LCM	Sri Lanka	726
S 802	Walrus	SSK	Netherlands	519	L 839	Ranagaja	LCM	Sri Lanka	726
TRV 802	Trevally	YPT	Australia	34	PG 840	Conrado Yap	PBF	Philippines	577
803	Rais Ali	PTGM	Algeria	5	841	Beidiao	AGI	China	146
803	Todak	PBO	Indonesia	345	841	Karabane	LCT	Senegal	679
803	Pusan	AGOR	Korea, South	451	P 841	Chiriqui	PB	Panama	560
A 803	Luymes	AGSH	Netherlands	525	P 842	Veraguas	PB	Panama	560
F 803	Tromp	FFGHM	Netherlands	522	PG 842	Tedorico Dominado Jr	PBF	Philippines	577
MHV 803	Aries	PB	Denmark	185	P 843	Bocas Del Toro	PB	Panama	560
S 803	Zeeleeuw	SSK	Netherlands	519	PG 843	Cosme Acosta	PBF	Philippines	577
TRV 803	Tailor	YPT	Australia	34	PG 844	José Artiaga Jr	PBF	Philippines	577
804	Hiu	PBO	Indonesia	345	PG 846	Nicanor Jimenez	PBF	Philippines	577
A 804	Pelikaan	AP	Netherlands	526	847	Sibarau	PB	Indonesia	346
A 804	Tabarka	ABU	Tunisia	784	PG 847	Leopoldo Regis	PBF	Philippines	577
F 804	De Ruyter	FFGHM	Netherlands	522	848	Siliman	PB	Indonesia	346
MHV 804	Andromeda	PB	Denmark	185	PG 848	Leon Tadina	PBF	Philippines	577
805	Layang	PBO	Indonesia	345	PG 849	Loreto Danipog	PBF	Philippines	577
805	Pusan	AGOR	Korea, South	451	851	KD 11	LCU	Poland	589
A 805	Taguermess	ABU	Tunisia	784	A 851	Cerberus	YDT	Netherlands	527
F 805	Evertsen	FFGHM	Netherlands	522	GC 851	Utatlan	PB	Guatemala	305
MHV 805	Gemini	PB	Denmark	185	PG 851	Apollo Tiano	PBF	Philippines	577
806	Lemadang	PBO	Indonesia	345	852	KD 12	LCU	Poland	589
806	Pusan	AGOR	Korea, South	451	852	R 129	FSGM	Russian Federation	642
806	Motorist	MSOM	Russian Federation	647	A 852	Argus	YDT	Netherlands	527
MHV 806	Dubhe	PB	Denmark	185	GC 852	Subteniente Osorio Saravia	PB	Guatemala	305
807	Boa	PB	Indonesia	346					
807	Yay Bo	AGSC	Myanmar	514	853	KD 13	LCU	Poland	589
807	Phraongkamrop	PB	Thailand	778	A 853	Nautilus	YDT	Netherlands	527
MHV 807	Jupiter	PB	Denmark	185	M 853	Haarlem	MHC	Netherlands	525
808	Welang	PB	Indonesia	346	PG 853	Sulpicio Fernandez	PBF	Philippines	577
808	Pytlivy	FFM	Russian Federation	637	A 854	Hydra	YDT	Netherlands	527
808	Picharnpholakit	PB	Thailand	778	855	R 187	FSGM	Russian Federation	642
B 808	Jaroslavl	SSK	Russian Federation	626	855	Kontradmiral Vlasov	MSOM	Russian Federation	647
MHV 808	Lyra	PB	Denmark	185	855	Samaesan	YTR	Thailand	777
S 808	Dolfijn	SSK	Netherlands	519	856	Raet	YTR	Thailand	777
809	Suluh Pari	PB	Indonesia	346	M 856	Maassluis	MHC	Netherlands	525
809	Ramintra	PB	Thailand	778	857	Sigalu	PB	Indonesia	346
MHV 809	Antares	PB	Denmark	185	M 857	Makkum	MHC	Netherlands	525
810	Katon	PB	Indonesia	346	858	Silea	PB	Indonesia	346
810	Pusan	AGOR	Korea, South	451	M 858	Middelburg	MHC	Netherlands	525
810	Smetlivy	DDGM	Russian Federation	632	859	Siribua	PB	Indonesia	346
MHV 810	Luna	PB	Denmark	185	M 859	Hellevoetsluis	MHC	Netherlands	525
P 810	Jaguar	PB	Netherlands	528	M 860	Schiedam	MHC	Netherlands	525
S 810	Bruinvis	SSK	Netherlands	519	M 861	Urk	MHC	Netherlands	525
811	Kakap	PBOH	Indonesia	345	862	Siada	PB	Indonesia	346
MHV 811	Apollo	PB	Denmark	185	M 862	Zierikzee	MHC	Netherlands	525
P 811	Panter	PB	Netherlands	528	863	Sikuda	PB	Indonesia	346
U 811	Balta	ADG	Ukraine	812	M 863	Vlaardingen	MHC	Netherlands	525
812	Krapu	PBOH	Indonesia	345	864	Sigurot	PB	Indonesia	346
812	Al Riyadh	FFGHM	Saudi Arabia	673	M 864	Willemstad	MHC	Netherlands	525
812	Suk	AGOR	Thailand	774	867	Kobra	PB	Indonesia	346
MHV 812	Hercules	PB	Denmark	185	868	Anakonda	PB	Indonesia	346
P 812	Nirbhoy	PC	Bangladesh	49	869	Patola	PB	Indonesia	346
P 812	Poema	PB	Netherlands	528	870	Taliwangsa	PB	Indonesia	346
813	Tongkol	PBOH	Indonesia	345	870	R 2	FSGM	Russian Federation	642
813	Burespadoongkit	PB	Thailand	778	871	Similan	AORH	Thailand	776
MHV 813	Baunen	PB	Denmark	185	B 871	Alrosa	SSK	Russian Federation	626
814	Barakuda	PBOH	Indonesia	345	874	Kala 4	LCU/AKSL	Finland	223
814	Makkah	FFGHM	Saudi Arabia	673	874	Morshansk	FSGM	Russian Federation	642
MHV 814	Budstikken	PB	Denmark	185	A 874	Linge	YTM	Netherlands	527
815	Sanca	PB	Indonesia	346	A 875	Regge	YTM	Netherlands	527
MHV 815	Kureren	PB	Denmark	185	A 876	Hunze	YTM	Netherlands	527
816	Warakas	PB	Indonesia	346	877	Kampela 3	LCU/AKSL	Finland	223
816	Al Dammam	FFGHM	Saudi Arabia	673	A 877	Rotte	YTM	Netherlands	527
MHV 816	Patrioten	PB	Denmark	185	A 878	Gouwe	YTM	Netherlands	527
817	Panana	PB	Indonesia	346	879	Valas	AKSL	Finland	222
MHV 817	Partisan	PB	Denmark	185	L 880	Shakthi	LSM	Sri Lanka	726
818	Kalakae	PB	Indonesia	346	886	Fuchi	AORH	China	147
MHV 818	Sabotøren	PB	Denmark	185	887	Qiandaohu	AORH	China	147
819	Tedong Naga	PB	Indonesia	346	AG 891	Corregidor	ABU	Philippines	579
819	R 47	FSGM	Russian Federation	642	894	Alskär	YFB	Finland	224
821	Misairutei-ichi-gou	PTGK	Japan	414	899	Halli	YPC	Finland	225
821	Ch'ungnam	AGOR	Korea, South	451	A 900	Mercuur	ASL/YTT	Netherlands	526
821	Lublin	LST/ML	Poland	588	L 900	Shah Amanat	LSL	Bangladesh	53
821	Heroj	SSC	Serbia and Montenegro	680	901	Mourad Rais	FFLM	Algeria	4
					901	Tareq	SSK	Iran	355
821	Suriya	ABU	Thailand	777	901	Balikpapan	AOTL	Indonesia	350
822	Misairutei-ni-gou	PTGK	Japan	414	901	A Zheleznyakov	MHOM	Russian Federation	648
822	Gniezno	LST/ML	Poland	588	901	Sriyanont	PB	Thailand	778
823	Misairutei-san-gou	PTGK	Japan	414	CP 901	Saettia	SAR	Italy	398
823	Krakow	LST/ML	Poland	588	L 901	Shah Poran	LCU	Bangladesh	53
824	Hayabusa	PGGF	Japan	414	MHV 901	Enø	PB	Denmark	184
824	Poznan	LST/ML	Poland	588	902	Rais Kellich	FFLM	Algeria	4
SSV 824	Liman	AGI/AGIM	Russian Federation	651	902	Noor	SSK	Iran	355
825	Wakataka	PGGF	Japan	414	902	Sambu	AOTL	Indonesia	350
825	Torun	LST/ML	Poland	588	902	Boraida	AORH	Saudi Arabia	675
825	Dmitrovgrad	FSGM	Russian Federation	642	A 902	Van Kinsbergen	AXL	Netherlands	525
826	Ootaka	PGGF	Japan	414	CP 902	Ubaldo Diciotti	SAR	Italy	398
827	Kumataka	PGGF	Japan	414	L 902	Shah Makhdum	LCU	Bangladesh	53
F 827	Karel Doorman	FFGHM	Netherlands	520	MHV 902	Manø	PB	Denmark	184

Number	Ship's name	Type	Country	Page
P 902	Liberation	PBR/YFLB	Belgium	57
903	Rais Korfou	FFLM	Algeria	4
903	Yunes	SSK	Iran	355
903	Arun	AORLH	Indonesia	350
CP 903	Luigi Dattilo	SAR	Italy	398
MHV 903	Hjortø	PB	Denmark	184
904	Yunbou	AORH	Saudi Arabia	675
CP 904	Michele Fiorillo	SAR	Italy	398
MHV 904	Lyø	PB	Denmark	184
CP 905	Antonio Peluso	SAR	Italy	398
MHV 905	Askø	PB	Denmark	184
CP 906	Orazio Corsi	SAR	Italy	398
MHV 906	Faenø	PB	Denmark	184
907	R 442	FSGM	Russian Federation	642
909	Vitseadmiral Zhukov	MSOM	Russian Federation	647
909	R 271	FSGM	Russian Federation	642
F 910	Wielingen	FFGM	Belgium	55
911	Sorong	AOTL	Indonesia	350
911	N K Golubets	MSOM	Russian Federation	647
911	Chakri Naruebet	CVM	Thailand	762
F 911	Westdiep	FFGM	Belgium	55
P 911	Madhumati	PSO	Bangladesh	48
912	Turbinist	MSOM	Russian Federation	647
P 912	Shetland	PBO/AX	Bangladesh	49
913	Kovrovets	MSOM	Russian Federation	647
913	Zeta	SSW	Serbia and Montenegro	680
P 913	Karatoa	PBO/AX	Bangladesh	49
P 914	Gomati	PBO/AX	Bangladesh	49
915	Kupa	SSW	Serbia and Montenegro	680
M 915	Aster	MHC/AEL	Belgium	57
916	R 29	FSGM	Russian Federation	642
916	Vardar	SSW	Serbia and Montenegro	680
M 916	Bellis	MHC/AEL	Belgium	57
M 917	Crocus	MHC/AEL	Belgium	57
PVM 917	Al Manoud	YDT	Libya	465
919	Snayper	MSOM	Russian Federation	647
920	Dazhi	AS	China	148
921	El Fateh	AXT	Egypt	207
921	Jaya Wijaya	ARL	Indonesia	351
921	R 20	FSGM	Russian Federation	642
M 921	Lobelia	MHC/AEL	Belgium	57
SB 921	Paradoks	ATS	Russian Federation	660
922	Rakata	AKL	Indonesia	351
SB 922	Shakhter	ATS	Russian Federation	660
923	Soputan	ATF	Indonesia	351
M 923	Narcis	MHC/AEL	Belgium	57
924	R 14	FSGM	Russian Federation	642
M 924	Primula	MHC/AEL	Belgium	57
931	Tariq	AXT	Egypt	207
931	Burujulasad	AGORH	Indonesia	349
932	Dewa Kembar	AGSH	Indonesia	349
933	Jalanidhi	AGOR	Indonesia	349
934	Lampo Batang	YTM	Indonesia	352
935	Tambora	YTM	Indonesia	352
936	Bromo	YTM	Indonesia	352
937	R 18	FSGM	Russian Federation	642
940	R 11	FSGM	Russian Federation	642
F 941	Abu Qir	FFGM	Egypt	200
946	R 24	FSGM	Russian Federation	642
F 946	El Suez	FFGM	Egypt	200
947	Blåtunga	LCPFM	Sweden	735
950	Dynamic	AFDL	US	908
A 950	Valcke	YTM	Belgium	58
951	Najim Al Zaffer	FFG	Egypt	201
951	Ulsan	FFG	Korea, South	446
951	R 297	FSGM	Russian Federation	642
952	Nusa Telu	AKL	Indonesia	351
952	Seoul	FFG	Korea, South	446
952	R 109	FSGM	Russian Federation	642
A 952	Wesp	YTL	Belgium	58
953	Chung Nam	FFG	Korea, South	446
953	Groza	FSGM	Russian Federation	642
954	Ivanovets	FSGM	Russian Federation	642
A 954	Zeemeeuw	YTL	Belgium	58
955	Masan	FFG	Korea, South	446
955	Zadorny	FFM	Russian Federation	642
955	Burya	FSGM	Russian Federation	642
A 955	Mier	YTL	Belgium	58
956	El Nasser	FFG	Egypt	201
956	Kyong Buk	FFG	Korea, South	446
957	Chon Nam	FFG	Korea, South	446
958	Che Ju	FFG	Korea, South	446
A 958	Zenobe Gramme	AXS	Belgium	57
959	Teluk Mentawai	AKL	Indonesia	351
959	Pusan	FFG	Korea, South	446
960	Karimata	AKL	Indonesia	351
A 960	Godetia	AGFH	Belgium	58
P 960	Skjold	PTGMF	Norway	540
961	Wagio	AKL	Indonesia	351
961	Chung Ju	FFG	Korea, South	446
P 961	Storm	PTGMF	Norway	540
962	R 71	FSGM	Russian Federation	642
A 962	Belgica	AGOR/PBO	Belgium	57
P 962	Skudd	PTGMF	Norway	540
A 963	Stern	AGFH	Belgium	58
P 963	Steil	PTGMF	Norway	540
P 964	Glimt	PTGMF	Norway	540
P 965	Gnist	PTGMF	Norway	540
966	R 44	PGGK	Russian Federation	644
HQ 966	Truong	AKL	Vietnam	945
971	Kwanggaeto Daewang	DDGHM	Korea, South	445
971	R 298	FSGM	Russian Federation	642

Number	Ship's name	Type	Country	Page
972	Tanjung Dalpele	LPD/APCR	Indonesia	346
972	Euljimundok	DDGHM	Korea, South	445
973	Tanjung Nusanive	AP	Indonesia	346
973	Yangmanchun	DDGHM	Korea, South	445
974	Tanjung Fatagar	AP	Indonesia	346
975	Chungmugong Yi Sun-shin	DDGHM	Korea, South	444
976	Moonmu Daewang	DDGHM	Korea, South	444
977	Daejoyoung	DDGHM	Korea, South	444
978	Wang Geon	DDGHM	Korea, South	444
978	R 19	FSGM	Russian Federation	642
979	Gang Gam Chan	DDGHM	Korea, South	444
980	Chae Yeon	DDGHM	Korea, South	444
P 986	Hauk	PTGM	Norway	539
P 987	Ørn	PTGM	Norway	539
P 988	Terne	PTGM	Norway	539
P 989	Tjeld	PTGM	Norway	539
P 990	Skarv	PTGM	Norway	539
991	R 261	FSGM	Russian Federation	642
P 991	Teist	PTGM	Norway	539
P 992	Jo	PTGM	Norway	539
993	Torsö	YFB	Finland	224
P 993	Lom	PTGM	Norway	539
P 994	Stegg	PTGM	Norway	539
995	R 79	FSGM	Russian Federation	642
P 995	Falk	PTGM	Norway	539
A 996	Albatros	YTM	Belgium	58
P 996	Ravn	PTGM	Norway	539
P 997	Gribb	PTGM	Norway	539
P 998	Geir	PTGM	Norway	539
P 999	Erle	PTGM	Norway	539
DDG 1000	Zumwalt	DDGH	US	884
T-AKR 1001	Adm Wm H Callaghan	AKR	US	918
1005	Fantome	YGS	Australia	32
PC 1005	Han Kang	PG	Korea, South	453
1006	Meda	YGS	Australia	32
PC 1006	Sumjinkang	PSO	Korea, South	452
1008	Duyfken	YGS	Australia	32
1009	Tom Thumb	YGS	Australia	32
1010	John Gowlland	YGS	Australia	32
1011	Geographe	YGS	Australia	32
P 1011	Titas	PTF	Bangladesh	50
1012	Casuarina	YGS	Australia	32
P 1012	Kusiyara	PTF	Bangladesh	50
P 1013	Chitra	PTF	Bangladesh	50
P 1014	Dhansiri	PTF	Bangladesh	50
1021	Conder	YGS	Australia	32
1023	Jurrat	PTG	Pakistan	556
1026	Essequibo	PBO	Guyana	307
1028	Quwwat	PTG	Pakistan	556
1029	Jalalat	PTG	Pakistan	556
1030	Shujaat	PTG	Pakistan	556
D 1051	Al Gaffa	YDT	UAE	819
GC 1051	Kukulkán	PB	Guatemala	305
M 1052	Mühlhausen	MCD	Germany	280
M 1058	Fulda	MHC	Germany	280
M 1059	Weilheim	MHC	Germany	280
1060	Barkat	PBO	Pakistan	558
1061	Rehmat	PBO	Pakistan	558
M 1061	Rottweil	MHC	Germany	280
1062	Nusrat	PBO	Pakistan	558
M 1062	Sulzbach-rosenberg	MHC	Germany	280
1063	Vehdat	PBO	Pakistan	558
M 1063	Bad Bevensen	MHC	Germany	280
M 1064	Grömitz	MHC	Germany	280
M 1065	Dillingen	MHC	Germany	280
P 1066	Subqat	PB	Pakistan	558
M 1067	Bad Rappenau	MHC	Germany	280
M 1068	Datteln	MHC	Germany	280
P 1068	Rafaqat	PB	Pakistan	558
M 1069	Homburg	MHC	Germany	280
M 1090	Pegnitz	MHCD	Germany	280
M 1091	Kulmbach	MHC	Germany	280
M 1092	Hameln	MHCD	Germany	280
M 1093	Auerbach	MHCD	Germany	280
M 1094	Ensdorf	MHCD	Germany	280
M 1095	Überherrn	MHC	Germany	280
M 1096	Passau	MHC	Germany	280
M 1097	Laboe	MHC	Germany	280
M 1098	Siegburg	MHCD	Germany	280
M 1099	Herten	MHC	Germany	280
1101	Cheng Kung	FFGHM	Taiwan	751
1101	Chasanyabadee	PB	Thailand	778
PI 1101	Polaris	PBF	Mexico	497
1102	Chawengsak Songkram	PB	Thailand	778
PI 1102	Sirius	PBF	Mexico	497
1103	Cheng Ho	FFGHM	Taiwan	751
1103	Phromyothee	PB	Thailand	778
PI 1103	Capella	PBF	Mexico	497
PI 1104	Canopus	PBF	Mexico	497
1105	Kaoh Chhlam	PBR	Cambodia	88
1105	Chi Kuang	FFGHM	Taiwan	751
PI 1105	Vega	PBF	Mexico	497
1106	Kaoh Rong	PBR	Cambodia	88
1106	Yueh Fei	FFGHM	Taiwan	751
PI 1106	Achernar	PBF	Mexico	497
1107	Tzu-I	FFGHM	Taiwan	751
PI 1107	Rigel	PBF	Mexico	497
1108	Pan Chao	FFGHM	Taiwan	751
PI 1108	Arcturus	PBF	Mexico	497
1109	Chang Chien	FFGHM	Taiwan	751
PI 1109	Alpheratz	PBF	Mexico	497
1110	Tien Tan	FFGHM	Taiwan	751
PI 1110	Procyón	PBF	Mexico	497

Number	Ship's name	Type	Country	Page	Number	Ship's name	Type	Country	Page
PI 1111	Avior	PBF	Mexico	497	WPB 1313	Edisto	WPB	US	923
PI 1112	Deneb	PBF	Mexico	497	WPB 1314	Sapelo	WPB	US	923
PI 1113	Fomalhaut	PBF	Mexico	497	WPB 1315	Matinicus	WPB	US	923
PI 1114	Pollux	PBF	Mexico	497	WPB 1316	Nantucket	WPB	US	923
PI 1115	Régulus	PBF	Mexico	497	WPB 1317	Attu	WPB	US	923
PI 1116	Acrux	PBF	Mexico	497	WPB 1318	Baranof	WPB	US	923
PI 1117	Spica	PBF	Mexico	497	WPB 1319	Chandeleur	WPB	US	923
PI 1118	Hadar	PBF	Mexico	497	WPB 1320	Chincoteague	WPB	US	923
PI 1119	Shaula	PBF	Mexico	497	WPB 1321	Cushing	WPB	US	923
PI 1120	Mirfak	PBF	Mexico	497	WPB 1322	Cuttyhunk	WPB	US	923
PI 1121	Ankaa	PBF	Mexico	497	WPB 1323	Drummond	WPB	US	923
PI 1122	Bellatrix	PBF	Mexico	497	WPB 1324	Key Largo	WPB	US	923
PI 1123	Elnath	PBF	Mexico	497	WPB 1325	Metompkin	WPB	US	923
PI 1124	Alnilán	PBF	Mexico	497	WPB 1326	Monomoy	WPB	US	923
PI 1125	Peacock	PBF	Mexico	497	WPB 1327	Orcas	WPB	US	923
PI 1126	Betelgeuse	PBF	Mexico	497	WPB 1328	Padre	WPB	US	923
PI 1127	Adhara	PBF	Mexico	497	WPB 1329	Sitkinak	WPB	US	923
PI 1128	Alioth	PBF	Mexico	497	WPB 1330	Tybee	WPB	US	923
PI 1129	Rasalhague	PBF	Mexico	497	WPB 1331	Washington	WPB	US	923
PI 1130	Nunki	PBF	Mexico	497	WPB 1332	Wrangell	WPB	US	923
1131	Mondolkiri	PBF	Cambodia	88	WPB 1333	Adak	WPB	US	923
PI 1131	Hamal	PBF	Mexico	497	WPB 1334	Liberty	WPB	US	923
PI 1132	Suhail	PBF	Mexico	497	WPB 1335	Anacapa	WPB	US	923
PI 1133	Dubhe	PBF	Mexico	497	WPB 1336	Kiska	WPB	US	923
1134	Ratanakiri	PBF	Cambodia	88	WPB 1337	Assateague	WPB	US	923
PI 1134	Denebola	PBF	Mexico	497	WPB 1338	Grand Isle	WPB	US	923
PI 1135	Alkaid	PBF	Mexico	497	WPB 1339	Key Biscayne	WPB	US	923
PI 1136	Alphecca	PBF	Mexico	497	WPB 1340	Jefferson Island	WPB	US	923
PI 1137	Eltanin	PBF	Mexico	497	WPB 1341	Kodiak Island	WPB	US	923
PI 1138	Kochab	PBF	Mexico	497	WPB 1342	Long Island	WPB	US	923
PI 1139	Enif	PBF	Mexico	497	WPB 1343	Bainbridge Island	WPB	US	923
P 1140	Cacine	PBO	Portugal	599	WPB 1344	Block Island	WPB	US	923
PI 1140	Schedar	PBF	Mexico	497	WPB 1345	Staten Island	WPB	US	923
PI 1141	Markab	PBF	Mexico	497	WPB 1346	Roanoke Island	WPB	US	923
M 1142	Umzimkulu	MHC	South Africa	698	WPB 1347	Pea Island	WPB	US	923
PI 1142	Megrez	PBF	Mexico	497	WPB 1348	Knight Island	WPB	US	923
PI 1145	Acamar	PBF	Mexico	497	WPB 1349	Galveston Island	WPB	US	923
P 1146	Zaire	PBO	Portugal	599	AM 1353	Coral Snake	LCM	Australia	36
PI 1146	Diphda	PBF	Mexico	497	PI 1401	Miaplacidus	PBF	Mexico	498
PI 1147	Menkar	PBF	Mexico	497	A 1409	Wilhelm Pullwer	YAG	Germany	281
PI 1148	Sabik	PBF	Mexico	497	A 1411	Berlin	AFSH	Germany	282
P 1150	Argos	PBR	Portugal	600	A 1412	Frankfurt Am Main	AFSH	Germany	282
P 1151	Dragão	PBR	Portugal	600	A 1425	Ammersee	AOL	Germany	283
P 1152	Escorpião	PBR	Portugal	600	A 1426	Tegernsee	AOL	Germany	283
P 1153	Cassiopeia	PBR	Portugal	600	A 1435	Westerwald	AEL	Germany	283
P 1154	Hidra	PBR	Portugal	600	A 1437	Planet	AGE	Germany	281
P 1155	Centauro	PBR	Portugal	600	A 1439	Baltrum	ATS/YDT	Germany	285
P 1156	Orion	PBR	Portugal	600	A 1440	Juist	ATS/YDT	Germany	285
P 1157	Pégaso	PBR	Portugal	600	A 1441	Langeoog	ATS/YDT	Germany	285
P 1158	Sagitario	PBR	Portugal	600	A 1442	Spessart	AOL	Germany	283
1161	Maroub	PBR	Sudan	727	A 1443	Rhön	AOL	Germany	283
P 1161	Save	PBO	Portugal	599	A 1451	Wangerooge	ATS/YDT	Germany	285
1162	Fijab	PBR	Sudan	727	A 1452	Spiekeroog	ATS/YDT	Germany	285
1163	Salak	PBR	Sudan	727	A1455	Maldonado	PBO/AG	Uruguay	930
1164	Halote	PBR	Sudan	727	A 1456	Alliance	AGOR	NATO	517
P 1165	Aguia	PBR	Portugal	599	A 1458	Fehmarn	ATR	Germany	285
P 1167	Cisne	PBR	Portugal	599	FNH 1491	Punta Caxinas	LCU	Honduras	308
1201	Baklan	HSIC	Yemen	946	M 1499	Umkomaas	MHC	South Africa	698
PI 1201	Isla Coronado	PBF	Mexico	497	1501	Jaemin I	ARSH	Korea, South	454
1202	Kang Ding	FFGHM	Taiwan	752	1502	Jaemin II	ARS	Korea, South	454
1202	Siyan	HSIC	Yemen	946	1503	Sri Indera Sakti	AOR/AE/AXH	Malaysia	480
PI 1202	Isla Lobos	PBF	Mexico	497	1503	Jaemin III	ARSH	Korea, South	455
1203	Si Ning	FFGHM	Taiwan	752	1504	Mahawangsa	AOR/AE/AXH	Malaysia	480
1203	Zuhrab	HSIC	Yemen	946	A 1542	Söndüren 2	YTB/YTM/YTL	Turkey	802
PI 1203	Isla Guadalupe	PBF	Mexico	497	A 1543	Söndüren 3	YTB/YTM/YTL	Turkey	802
1204	Akissan	HSIC	Yemen	946	A 1544	Söndüren 4	YTB/YTM/YTL	Turkey	802
PI 1204	Isla Cozumel	PBF	Mexico	497	P 1552	Tobie	PB	South Africa	697
1205	Kun Ming	FFGHM	Taiwan	752	P 1553	Tern	PB	South Africa	697
1205	Hunaish	HSIC	Yemen	946	P 1554	Tekwane	PB	South Africa	697
1206	Di Hua	FFGHM	Taiwan	752	P 1565	Isaac Dyobha	PGG	South Africa	697
1206	Zakr	HSIC	Yemen	946	P 1567	Galeshewe	PGG	South Africa	697
1207	Wu Chang	FFGHM	Taiwan	752	P 1569	Makhanda	PGG	South Africa	697
1208	Chen Te	FFGHM	Taiwan	752	A 1600	Iskenderun	AK	Turkey	799
M 1212	Umhloti	MHC	South Africa	698	1601	Ta Kuan	AGOR	Taiwan	757
M 1213	Umgeni	MHC	South Africa	698	LEP 1601	Ona	WPB	Chile	118
M1223	Kapa	MSCD	South Africa	698	LEP 1602	Yagan	WPB	Chile	118
M1225	Tekwini	MSCD	South Africa	698	LEP 1603	Alacalufe	WPB	Chile	118
1301	Yung Feng	MHC	Taiwan	756	LEP 1604	Hallef	WPB	Chile	118
PI 1301	Acuario	PBF	Mexico	493	LSG 1609	Aysen	WPB	Chile	118
WPB 1301	Farallon	WPB	US	923	LSG 1610	Corral	WPB	Chile	118
1302	Yung Chia	MHC	Taiwan	756	LSG 1611	Concepcion	WPB	Chile	118
PI 1302	Aguila	PBF	Mexico	493	LSG 1612	Caldera	WPB	Chile	118
WPB 1302	Manitou	WPB	US	923	LSG 1613	San Antonio	WPB	Chile	118
1303	Yung Ting	MHC	Taiwan	756	LSG 1614	Antofagasta	WPB	Chile	118
PI 1303	Aries	PBF	Mexico	493	LSG 1615	Arica	WPB	Chile	118
WPB 1303	Matagorda	WPB	US	923	LSG 1616	Coquimbo	WPB	Chile	118
PI 1304	Auriga	PBF	Mexico	493	LSG 1617	Puerto Natales	WPB	Chile	118
WPB 1304	Maui	WPB	US	923	LSG 1618	Valparaíso	WPB	Chile	118
1305	Yung Shun	MHC	Taiwan	756	LSG 1619	Punta Arenas	WPB	Chile	118
PI 1305	Cancer	PBF	Mexico	493	LSG 1620	Talcahuano	WPB	Chile	118
WPB 1305	Monhegan	WPB	US	923	LSG 1621	Quintero	WPB	Chile	118
1306	Yung Yang	MSO	Taiwan	756	LSG 1622	Chiloé	WPB	Chile	118
PI 1306	Capricorno	PBF	Mexico	493	LSG 1623	Puerto Montt	WPB	Chile	118
WPB 1306	Nunivak	WPB	US	923	LSG 1624	Iquique	WPB	Chile	118
1307	Yung Tzu	MSO	Taiwan	756	Y 1643	Bottsand	YPC	Germany	284
PI 1307	Centauro	PBF	Mexico	493	Y 1644	Eversand	YPC	Germany	284
WPB 1307	Ocracoke	WPB	US	923	Y 1656	Wustrow	YTM	Germany	285
1308	Yung Ku	MSO	Taiwan	756	Y 1658	Dranske	YTM	Germany	285
PI 1308	Geminis	PBF	Mexico	493	Y 1685	Aschau	YFL	Germany	284
WPB 1308	Vashon	WPB	US	923	Y 1686	Ak 2	YFL	Germany	284
1309	Yung Teh	MSO	Taiwan	756	Y 1687	Borby	YFL	Germany	284
WPB 1309	Aquidneck	WPB	US	923	Y 1689	Bums	YAG	Germany	281
WPB 1310	Mustang	WPB	US	923	LSR 1700	Tokerau	SAR	Chile	118
WPB 1311	Naushon	WPB	US	923	LSR 1703	Pelluhue	WPB	Chile	118
LST 1312	Ambe	LST	Nigeria	534	LSR 1704	Arauco	WPB	Chile	118
WPB 1312	Sanibel	WPB	US	923	LSR 1705	Chacao	WPB	Chile	118

Number	Ship's name	Type	Country	Page	Number	Ship's name	Type	Country	Page
LSR 1706	Queitao	WPB	Chile	118	P 3302	Zurara	PB	UAE	819
LSR 1707	Guaiteca	WPB	Chile	118	P 3303	Murban	PB	UAE	819
LSR 1708	Curaumila	WPB	Chile	118	P 3304	Al Ghullan	PB	UAE	819
1770	Adept	AFDL	US	908	P 3305	Radoom	PB	UAE	819
DT 1801	Quokka	YTL	Australia	35	P 3306	Ghanadhah	PB	UAE	819
1802	Damrong Rachanuphap	PBO	Thailand	777	3501	Perdana	PTFG	Malaysia	477
1803	Lopburi Rames	PBO	Thailand	777	3501	Ilocos Norte	PB	Philippines	580
1804	Srinakarin	PSO	Thailand	777	A 3501	Annad	YTB	UAE	819
1814	Diaz	PB	Chile	114	3502	Serang	PTFG	Malaysia	477
LPC 1814	Grumete Diaz	PB	Chile	117	3502	Nueva Vizcaya	PB	Philippines	580
1815	Bolados	PB	Chile	114	3503	Ganas	PTFG	Malaysia	477
LPC 1815	Grumete Bolados	PB	Chile	117	3503	Romblon	PB	Philippines	580
1816	Salinas	PB	Chile	114	3504	Ganyang	PTFG	Malaysia	477
LPC 1816	Grumete Salinas	PB	Chile	117	3504	Davao Del Norte	PB	Philippines	580
1817	Tellez	PB	Chile	114	3505	Jerong	PB	Malaysia	478
LPC 1817	Grumete Tellez	PB	Chile	117	3506	Todak	PB	Malaysia	478
1818	Bravo	PB	Chile	114	3507	Paus	PB	Malaysia	478
LPC 1818	Grumete Bravo	PB	Chile	117	3508	Yu	PB	Malaysia	478
1819	Campos	PB	Chile	114	TV 3508	Kashima	AXH/TV	Japan	419
LPC 1819	Grumete Campos	PB	Chile	117	3509	Baung	PB	Malaysia	478
1820	Machado	PB	Chile	114	3510	Pari	PB	Malaysia	478
LPC 1820	Grumete Machado	PB	Chile	117	3511	Handalan	PTFG	Malaysia	477
1821	Johnson	PB	Chile	114	3512	Perkasa	PTFG	Malaysia	477
LPC 1821	Grumete Johnson	PB	Chile	117	3513	Pendekar	PTFG	Malaysia	477
1822	Troncoso	PB	Chile	114	TV 3513	Shimayuki	AXGHM/TV	Japan	418
LPC 1822	Grumete Troncoso	PB	Chile	117	3514	Gempita	PTFG	Malaysia	477
1823	Hudson	PB	Chile	114	TV 3515	Yamagiri	AX/TV	Japan	419
LPC 1823	Grumete Hudson	PB	Chile	117	TV 3516	Asagiri	AX/TV	Japan	419
LPM 1901	Maule	WPB	Chile	118	P 3553	Moa	PB	New Zealand	530
LPM 1902	Rapel	WPB	Chile	118	P 3554	Kiwi	PB	New Zealand	530
LPM 1903	Aconcagua	WPB	Chile	118	P 3555	Wakakura	PB	New Zealand	530
LPM 1904	Lauca	WPB	Chile	118	P 3556	Hinau	PB	New Zealand	530
LPM 1905	Isluga	WPB	Chile	118	TSS 3601	Asashio	SSK	Japan	403
LPM 1906	Loa	WPB	Chile	118	TSS 3605	Yukishio	SSK	Japan	401
LPM 1907	Maullín	WPB	Chile	118	P 3711	Um Almaradim	PBM	Kuwait	455
LPM 1908	Copiapó	WPB	Chile	118	P 3713	Ouha	PBM	Kuwait	455
LPM 1909	Cau-cau	WPB	Chile	118	P 3715	Failaka	PBM	Kuwait	455
LPM 1910	Pudeto	WPB	Chile	118	P 3717	Maskan	PBM	Kuwait	455
LPM 1911	Robinson Crusoe	WPB	Chile	118	P 3719	Al-Ahmadi	PBM	Kuwait	455
1963	Hudson	AXL	Canada	105	P 3721	Alfahaheel	PBM	Kuwait	455
1967	Vector	AXL	Canada	105	P 3723	Al-Yarmouk	PBM	Kuwait	455
1968	Limnos	AXL	Canada	105	P 3725	Garoh	PBM	Kuwait	455
1971	Shark	AXL	Canada	105	LST 4001	Oosumi	LPD/LSTH	Japan	415
1975	Shamook	AXL	Canada	105	LST 4002	Shimokita	LPD/LSTH	Japan	415
1985	John P Tully	AXL	Canada	105	LST 4003	Kunisaki	LPD/LSTH	Japan	415
1986	Pandalus III	AXL	Canada	105	LSU 4171	Yura	LSU/LCU	Japan	414
1986	F C G Smith	AXL	Canada	105	LSU 4172	Noto	LSU/LCU	Japan	414
1988	Frederick G Creed	AXL	Canada	105	SSN 4201	Regulus	ABU	Brazil	76
1989	Opilio	AXL	Canada	105	ATS 4202	Kurobe	AVM/TV	Japan	419
1990	Matthew	AXL	Canada	105	ATS 4203	Tenryu	AVHM/TV	Japan	419
1991	Calanus II	AXL	Canada	105	T-AK 4296	Capt Steven L Bennett	AK	US	916
1996	Teleost	AXL	Canada	105	AMS 4301	Hiuchi	YTT	Japan	421
2001	Seal	YDT/PB	Australia	35	AMS 4302	Suou	YTT	Japan	421
2001	Neocaligus	AXL	Canada	105	AMS 4303	Amakusa	YTT	Japan	421
LCU 2001	Yusoutei-ichi-go	LCU	Japan	414	T-AK 4396	Maj Bernard F Fisher	AK	US	915
LCU 2002	Yusoutei-ni-go	LCU	Japan	414	P 4505	Al Sanbouk	PGGF	Kuwait	455
2003	Malu Baizam	YDT/PB	Australia	35	T-AK 4543	LTC John U D Page	AK	US	916
2004	Shark	YDT/PB	Australia	35	T-AK 4544	SSGT Edward A Carter	AK	US	916
2013	Almaty	PB	Kazakhstan	434	T-AK 4638	A1C William H Pitsenbarger	AK	US	915
2023	Aktau	PB	Kazakhstan	434	AGB 5002	Shirase	AGBH	Japan	421
2033	Atyrau	PB	Kazakhstan	434	T-AK 5029	Cape Jacob	AK/AKR/AE	US	917
T-AK 2039	Cape Girardeau	AK/AKR/AE	US	917	T-AK 5051	Cape Gibson	AK/AKR/AE	US	917
2043	Schambyl	PB	Kazakhstan	434	T-AKR 5051	Cape Ducato	AKR	US	918
T-AKR 2044	Cape Orlando	AKR	US	918	T-AKR 5052	Cape Douglas	AKR	US	918
LCAC 2101-6	Air Cushion-tei (1-6) Gou	LCAC	Japan	414	T-AKR 5053	Cape Domingo	AKR	US	918
GN 2301	Utique	PB	Tunisia	785	T-AKR 5054	Cape Decision	AKR	US	918
2344	Al Amane	SAR	Morocco	508	T-AKR 5055	Cape Diamond	AKR	US	918
2345	Ait Baâmrane	SAR	Morocco	508	T-AKR 5062	Cape Isabel	AKR	US	918
DT 2601	Tammar	YTL	Australia	35	T-AKR 5063	Cape May	AK/AP/AKR	US	917
T-AK 3000	CPL Louis J Hauge, Jr	AKRH	US	916	T-AKR 5066	Cape Hudson	AKR	US	918
3001	Tae Pung Yang I	ARSH	Korea, South	454	T-AKR 5067	Cape Henry	AKR	US	918
T-AK 3001	PFC William B Baugh	AKRH	US	916	T-AKR 5068	Cape Horn	AKR	US	918
3002	Tae Pung Yang II	ARSH	Korea, South	454	T-AKR 5069	Cape Edmont	AKR	US	918
T-AK 3002	PFC James Anderson, Jr	AKRH	US	916	T-AKR 5076	Cape Inscription	AKR	US	918
T-AK 3003	1st Lt Alex Bonnyman	AKRH	US	916	T-AKR 5077	Cape Lambert	AKR	US	918
L 3004	Sir Bedivere	LSLH	UK	850	T-AKR 5078	Cape Lobos	AKR	US	918
T-AK 3004	PVT Franklin J Phillips	AKRH	US	916	T-AKR 5082	Cape Knox	AKR	US	918
L 3005	Sir Galahad	LSLH	UK	850	T-AKR 5083	Cape Kennedy	AKR	US	918
T-AK 3005	SGT Matej Kocak	AKRH	US	917	T-AOT 5084	Chesapeake	AOT	US	917
L 3006	Largs Bay	LSD	UK	850	AGS 5102	Futami	AGS	Japan	418
T-AK 3006	PFC Eugene A Obregon	AKRH	US	917	AGS 5103	Suma	AGS	Japan	417
L 3007	Lyme Bay	LSD	UK	850	AGS 5104	Wakasa	AGS	Japan	418
T-AK 3007	MAJ Stephen W Pless	AKRH	US	917	AGS 5105	Nichinan	AGS	Japan	417
L 3008	Mounts Bay	LSD	UK	850	A 5201	Vega	AXL	Portugal	601
T-AK 3008	2nd Lt John P Bobo	AKRH	US	917	AOS 5201	Hibiki	AGOSH	Japan	417
L 3009	Cardigan Bay	LSD	UK	850	AOS 5202	Harima	AGOSH	Japan	417
T-AK 3009	PFC Dewayne T Williams	AKRH	US	917	A 5203	Andromeda	AGSC	Portugal	600
T-AK 3010	1st Lt Baldomero Lopez	AKRH	US	917	A 5204	Polar	AXL	Portugal	601
T-AK 3011	1st Lt Jack Lummus	AKRH	US	917	A 5205	Auriga	AGSC	Portugal	600
T-AK 3012	SGT William R Button	AKRH	US	917	A 5210	Bérrio	AORLH	Portugal	602
T-AK 3015	1st Lt Harry L Martin	AKR	US	916	A 5302	Caroly	AXS	Italy	392
T-AK 3016	L/CPL Roy M Wheat	AKR	US	916	A 5303	Ammiraglio Magnaghi	AGSH	Italy	391
T-AK 3017	GYSGT Fred W Stockham	AKR	US	916	A 5304	Aretusa	AGS	Italy	391
P 3100	Mamba	PB	Kenya	435	A 5308	Galatea	AGS	Italy	391
P 3126	Nyayo	PGGF	Kenya	435	A 5309	Anteo	ARSH	Italy	394
P 3127	Umoja	PGGF	Kenya	435	A 5311	Palinuro	AXS	Italy	392
P 3130	Shujaa	PBO	Kenya	435	A 5312	Amerigo Vespucci	AXS	Italy	392
P 3131	Shupavu	PBO	Kenya	435	A 5313	Stella Polare	AXS	Italy	392
3224	Siangin	PB	Malaysia	483	A 5315	Raffaele Rossetti	AG/AGOR	Italy	391
					A 5316	Corsaro II	AXS	Italy	392
					A 5318	Prometeo	ATR	Italy	395
					A 5319	Ciclope	ATR	Italy	395
					A 5320	Vincenzo Martellotta	AG/AGE	Italy	392

Number	Ship's name	Type	Country	Page
A 5322	Capricia	AXS	Italy	392
A 5323	Orsa Maggiore	AXS	Italy	392
A 5324	Titano	ATR	Italy	395
A 5325	Polifemo	ATR	Italy	395
A 5326	Etna	AORH	Italy	393
A 5327	Stromboli	AORH	Italy	393
A 5328	Gigante	ATR	Italy	395
A 5329	Vesuvio	AORH	Italy	393
A 5330	Saturno	ATR	Italy	395
A 5340	Elettra	AGORH/AGE/ AGI	Italy	391
A 5347	Gorgona	AKL	Italy	394
A 5348	Tremiti	AKL	Italy	394
A 5349	Caprera	AKL	Italy	394
A 5351	Pantelleria	AKL	Italy	394
A 5352	Lipari	AKL	Italy	394
A 5353	Capri	AKL	Italy	394
A 5359	Bormida	AWT	Italy	393
A 5364	Ponza	ABU	Italy	394
A 5365	Tenace	ATR	Italy	395
A 5366	Levanzo	ABU	Italy	394
A 5367	Tavolara	ABU	Italy	394
A 5368	Palmaria	ABU	Italy	394
A 5376	Ticino	AWT	Italy	393
A 5377	Tirso	AWT	Italy	393
A 5379	Astice	AXL	Italy	392
A 5380	Mitilo	AXL	Italy	392
A 5382	Porpora	AXL	Italy	392
A 5383	Procida	ABU	Italy	394
A 5390	Leonardo	AGOR (C)	NATO	517
S 5509	Qaruh	AGH	Kuwait	458
M 5550	Lerici	MHSC	Italy	390
M 5551	Sapri	MHSC	Italy	390
M 5552	Milazzo	MHSC	Italy	390
M 5553	Vieste	MHSC	Italy	390
M 5554	Gaeta	MHSC	Italy	390
M 5555	Termoli	MHSC	Italy	390
M 5556	Alghero	MHSC	Italy	390
M 5557	Numana	MHSC	Italy	390
M 5558	Crotone	MHSC	Italy	390
M 5559	Viareggio	MHSC	Italy	390
M 5560	Chioggia	MHSC	Italy	390
M 5561	Rimini	MHSC	Italy	390
ASE 6102	Asuka	AGEH	Japan	418
P 6121	Gepard	PGGFM	Germany	278
P 6122	Puma	PGGFM	Germany	278
P 6123	Hermelin	PGGFM	Germany	278
P 6124	Nerz	PGGFM	Germany	278
P 6125	Zobel	PGGFM	Germany	278
P 6126	Frettchen	PGGFM	Germany	278
P 6127	Dachs	PGGFM	Germany	278
P 6128	Ozelot	PGGFM	Germany	278
P 6129	Wiesel	PGGFM	Germany	278
P 6130	Hyäne	PGGFM	Germany	278
7000	Reliance	AFDL	US	908
Y 8005	Nieuwediep	YFL	Netherlands	527
Y 8018	Breezand	YTL	Netherlands	528
Y 8019	Balgzand	YTL	Netherlands	528
Y 8050	Urania	AXS	Netherlands	526
Y 8055	Schelde	YTL	Netherlands	528
Y 8056	Wierbalg	YTL	Netherlands	528
Y 8057	Malzwin	YTL	Netherlands	528
Y 8058	Zuidwal	YTL	Netherlands	528
Y 8059	Westwal	YTL	Netherlands	528
P 8111	Durbar	PTFG	Bangladesh	49
P 8112	Duranta	PTFG	Bangladesh	49
P 8113	Durvedya	PTFG	Bangladesh	49
P 8114	Durdam	PTFG	Bangladesh	49
P 8125	Durdharsha	PTFG	Bangladesh	48
P 8126	Durdanta	PTFG	Bangladesh	48
8127	Sir William Roe	YFRT	UK	853
P 8128	Dordanda	PTFG	Bangladesh	48
P 8131	Anirban	PTFG	Bangladesh	48
P 8141	Uttal	PTFG	Bangladesh	49
FNH 8501	Chamelecon	PB	Honduras	308
8611	Tarv	YAG	UK	853
8612	Ohms Law	YAG	UK	853
8614	Sapper	YAG	UK	853
L 9011	Foudre	LSDH/TCD 90	France	250
L 9012	Siroco	LSDH/TCD 90	France	250
L 9013	Mistral	LHDM/BPC	France	249
L 9014	Tonnerre	LHDM/BPC	France	249
L 9022	Orage	LSDH/TCD	France	251
L 9031	Francis Garnier	LSTH	France	248
L 9032	Dumont D'urville	LSTH	France	248
L 9033	Jacques Cartier	LSTH	France	248
L 9034	La Grandière	LSTH	France	248
L 9051	Sabre	LCT	France	251
L 9052	Dague	LCT	France	251
L 9061	Rapière	LCT	France	251
L 9062	Hallebarde	LCT	France	251
L 9077	Bougainville	AGIH	France	254
L 9090	Gapeau	LSL	France	257
T-AOT 9109	Petersburg	AOT	US	917
9423	Nesbitt	YGS	UK	845
9424	Pat Barton	YGS	UK	845
9425	Cook	YGS	UK	845
9426	Owen	YGS	UK	845
T-AKR 9678	Cape Rise	AKR	US	918
T-AKR 9711	Cape Trinity	AKR	US	918
T-AKR 9961	Cape Washington	AKR	US	918
T-AKR 9962	Cape Wrath	AKR	US	918
L 9892	San Giorgio	LPD	Italy	389
L 9893	San Marco	LPD	Italy	389

Number	Ship's name	Type	Country	Page
L 9894	San Giusto	LPD	Italy	389
WLI 65400	Bayberry	WLI/ABU	US	925
WLI 65401	Elderberry	WLI/ABU	US	925
WLR 65501	Ouachita	WLR	US	925
WLR 65502	Cimarron	WLR	US	925
WLR 65503	Obion	WLR	US	925
WLR 65504	Scioto	WLR	US	925
WLR 65505	Osage	WLR	US	925
WLR 65506	Sangamon	WLR	US	925
WYTL 65601	Capstan	WYTL	US	927
WYTL 65602	Chock	WYTL	US	927
WYTL 65604	Tackle	WYTL	US	927
WYTL 65607	Bridle	WYTL	US	927
WYTL 65608	Pendant	WYTL	US	927
WYTL 65609	Shackle	WYTL	US	927
WYTL 65610	Hawser	WYTL	US	927
WYTL 65611	Line	WYTL	US	927
WYTL 65612	Wire	WYTL	US	927
WYTL 65614	Bollard	WYTL	US	927
WYTL 65615	Cleat	WYTL	US	927
WLIC 75301	Anvil	WLIC	US	926
WLIC 75302	Hammer	WLIC	US	926
WLIC 75303	Sledge	WLIC	US	926
WLIC 75304	Mallet	WLIC	US	926
WLIC 75305	Vise	WLIC	US	926
WLIC 75306	Clamp	WLIC	US	926
WLR 75307	Wedge	WLR	US	926
WLIC 75309	Hatchet	WLIC	US	926
WLIC 75310	Axe	WLIC	US	926
WLR 75401	Gasconade	WLR	US	926
WLR 75402	Muskingum	WLR	US	926
WLR 75403	Wyaconda	WLR	US	926
WLR 75404	Chippewa	WLR	US	926
WLR 75405	Cheyenne	WLR	US	926
WLR 75406	Kickapoo	WLR	US	926
WLR 75407	Kanawha	WLR	US	926
WLR 75408	Patoka	WLR	US	926
WLR 75409	Chena	WLR	US	926
WLR 75500	Kankakee	WLR	US	926
WLR 75501	Greenbriar	WLR	US	926
87301	Barracuda	WPB	US	923
87302	Hammerhead	WPB	US	923
87303	Mako	WPB	US	923
87304	Marlin	WPB	US	923
87305	Stingray	WPB	US	923
87306	Dorado	WPB	US	923
87307	Osprey	WPB	US	923
87308	Chinook	WPB	US	923
87309	Albacore	WPB	US	923
87310	Tarpon	WPB	US	923
87311	Cobia	WPB	US	923
87312	Hawksbill	WPB	US	923
87313	Cormorant	WPB	US	923
87314	Finback	WPB	US	923
87315	Amberjack	WPB	US	923
87316	Kittiwake	WPB	US	923
87317	Blackfin	WPB	US	923
87318	Bluefin	WPB	US	923
87319	Yellowfin	WPB	US	923
87320	Manta	WPB	US	923
87321	Coho	WPB	US	923
87322	Kingfisher	WPB	US	923
87323	Seahawk	WPB	US	923
87324	Steelhead	WPB	US	923
87325	Beluga	WPB	US	923
87326	Blacktip	WPB	US	923
87327	Pelican	WPB	US	923
87328	Ridley	WPB	US	923
87329	Cochito	WPB	US	923
87330	Manowar	WPB	US	923
87331	Moray	WPB	US	923
87332	Razorbill	WPB	US	923
87333	Adelie	WPB	US	923
87334	Gannet	WPB	US	923
87335	Narwhal	WPB	US	923
87336	Sturgeon	WPB	US	923
87337	Sockeye	WPB	US	923
87338	Ibis	WPB	US	923
87339	Pompano	WPB	US	923
87340	Halibut	WPB	US	923
87341	Bonito	WPB	US	923
87342	Shrike	WPB	US	923
87343	Tern	WPB	US	923
87344	Heron	WPB	US	923
87345	Wahoo	WPB	US	923
87346	Flyingfish	WPB	US	923
87347	Haddock	WPB	US	923
87348	Brant	WPB	US	923
87349	Shearwater	WPB	US	923
87350	Petrel	WPB	US	923
87352	Sea Lion	WPB	US	923
87353	Skipjack	WPB	US	923
87354	Dolphin	WPB	US	923
87355	Hawk	WPB	US	923
87356	Sailfish	WPB	US	923
87357	Sawfish	WPB	US	923
87358	Swordfish	WPB	US	923
87359	Tiger Shark	WPB	US	923
87360	Blue Shark	WPB	US	923
87361	Sea Horse	WPB	US	923
87362	Sea Otter	WPB	US	923
87363	Manatee	WPB	US	923
87364	Ahi	WPB	US	923
87365	Pike	WPB	US	923
87366	Terrapin	WPB	US	923

WORLD NAVIES

A—Z

Albania
FORCE DETAR

Country Overview

After being governed by a communist regime since 1946, democratic elections in the Republic of Albania took place in 1991 although since then there have been periods of instability. Situated in western part of the Balkan Peninsula, the country has an area of 11,100 square miles and is bordered to the north by Serbia and Montenegro and to the south by Greece. There is a coastline of 195 n miles with the Adriatic Sea on which Durrës and Vlorë are the principal ports. The capital and largest city is Tirana. Territorial waters (12 n miles) are claimed but an EEZ has not been claimed. Italy provides strong operational, training and administrative support. Joint Coast Guard and Customs patrols are mounted within territorial waters while other personnel training is conducted in Italy. Turkey has established a 60-strong detachment at Vlorë to provide support and training, Greece assists with the support of navigational aids and the US also provides training.

Headquarters Appointments

Commander of the Navy:
Captain Gerveni Kristaq

Personnel

2006: 1,000 approximately

Bases

HQ: Durrës
Districts: Durrës (1st), Vlorë (2nd).
Bases: Shengyin, Himarë, Saranda, Vlorë.

PATROL FORCES

Notes: (1) Pennant numbers beginning with '1' indicate units from the Durrës district. Those beginning with '2' are from the Vlorë district.
(2) There are six inshore patrol craft of 12 – 15 m length.

1 SHANGHAI II CLASS (FAST ATTACK CRAFT — GUN) (PC)

P 115

Displacement, tons: 113 standard; 134 full load
Dimensions, feet (metres): 127.3 × 17.7 × 5.6 *(38.8 × 5.4 × 1.7)*
Main machinery: 2 Type L-12V-180 diesels; 2,400 hp(m) *(1.76 MW)* (forward)
2 Type 12-D-6 diesels; 1,820 hp(m) *(1.34 MW)* (aft); 4 shafts
Speed, knots: 30
Range, n miles: 700 at 16.5 kt
Complement: 34
Guns: 4 China 37 mm/63 (2 twin); 180 rds/min to 8.5 km *(4.6 n miles)*; weight of shell 1.42 kg.
4 USSR 25 mm/60 (2 twin); 270 rds/min to 3 km *(1.6 n miles)*; weight of shell 0.34 kg.
Torpedoes: 2 – 21 in *(533 mm)* tubes; Yu-1; 9.2 km *(5 n miles)* at 39 kt; warhead 400 kg.
Depth charges: 2 projectors; 8 depth charges in lieu of torpedo tubes.
Mines: Rails can be fitted; probably only 10 mines.
Radars: Surface search/fire control: Skin Head; I-band.
Sonars: Hull-mounted set probably fitted.

Comment: Four transferred from China in mid-1974 and two in 1975. One ship escaped to Italy in early 1997, returned in early 1998 and was reported repaired in 2000. Has torpedo tubes on the stern taken from deleted Huchuan class. Seldom seen at sea.

SHANGHAI II (China colours)   *6/1992* / 0081445

2 PO 2 CLASS (COASTAL PATROL CRAFT) (PB)

A 120   **A 212**

Displacement, tons: 56 full load
Dimensions, feet (metres): 70.5 × 11.5 × 3.3 *(21.5 × 3.5 × 1)*
Main machinery: 1 Type 3-D-12 diesel; 300 hp(m) *(220 kW)* sustained; 1 shaft
Speed, knots: 12
Complement: 8
Guns: 2 – 12.7 mm MGs. At least one of the class has a twin 25 mm/60.
Radars: Surface search: I-band.

Comment: Two survive from a total of 11 transferred from USSR 1957-60. Previous minesweeping gear has been removed and the craft are used for utility roles. All escaped to Italy in early 1997 and returned, two in early 1998 and one in late 1998. Two others were towed back as being beyond repair. One other *A 451* was sunk in a collision with an Italian corvette in March 1997. Seldom seen at sea.

PO 2 (old number)   *7/1992, Terje Nilsen* / 0056447

MINE WARFARE FORCES

2 T 43 CLASS (MINESWEEPERS-OCEAN) (MSO)

M 111-112

Displacement, tons: 500 standard; 580 full load
Dimensions, feet (metres): 190.2 × 27.6 × 6.9 *(58 × 8.4 × 2.1)*
Main machinery: 2 Kolomna Type 9-D-8 diesels; 2,000 hp(m) *(1.47 MW)* sustained; 2 shafts
Speed, knots: 15
Range, n miles: 3,000 at 10 kt; 2,000 at 14 kt
Complement: 65
Guns: 4 – 37 mm/63 (2 twin); 160 rds/min to 9 km *(5 n miles)*; weight of shell 0.7 kg.
8 – 12.7 mm MGs.
Depth charges: 2 projectors.
Mines: 16.
Radars: Air/surface search: Ball End; E/F-band.
Navigation: Furuno; I-band.
Sonars: Stag Ear; hull-mounted set probably fitted.

Comment: Transferred from USSR in 1960. All escaped to Italy in early 1997 and were returned in 1998. M 111 refitted in Italy in 2002 and M 112 is expected to follow.

T 43   *5/1996*, Piet Cornelis* / 1153014

AUXILIARIES

Notes: In addition there are a Poluchat survey and torpedo recovery craft of 20 tons *(A 110)*, an old ex-USSR Shalanda class tender *Marinza*, a water-barge, two tugs and a floating dock *(Vlorë)*.

1 LCT 3 CLASS (REPAIR SHIP) (ARL)

A 223 (ex-MOC 1203)

Displacement, tons: 640 full load
Dimensions, feet (metres): 192 × 31 × 7 *(58.6 × 9.5 × 2.1)*
Main machinery: 2 diesels; 1,000 hp *(746 kW)*; 2 shafts
Speed, knots: 8
Complement: 24

Comment: 1943 built LCT converted in Italian use as a repair craft. Refitted in Italy, transferred in 1999 and used for moored technical support. To be decommissioned in late 2005 following improvements to naval base facilities.

LCT 3 (Italian colours)   *10/1998, Diego Quevedo* / 0017507

COAST GUARD (ROJA BREGDETARE)

Notes: (1) Coast Guard vessel pennant numbers are prefixed by the letter 'R'.
(2) A 'Nyryat 1' diving tender (R 218) was transferred from the Navy in 2003.

2 COASTAL PATROL CRAFT (PB)

R 117   R 217

Displacement, tons: 18 full load
Dimensions, feet (metres): 45.6 × 13 × 3 *(13.9 × 4 × 0.9)*
Main machinery: 2 diesels; 1,300 hp *(942 kW)*; 2 waterjets
Speed, knots: 34
Range, n miles: 200 at 30 kt
Complement: 4
Guns: 2 — 12.7 mm MGs.
Radars: Surface search: Raytheon; I-band.

Comment: Transferred from the US on 27 February 1999. Reported operational.

CPC (US colours)   *6/1994, PBI* / 0056448

4 TYPE 227 INSHORE PATROL CRAFT (PBR)

R 123 (ex-CP 229)   R 124 (ex-CP 235)   R 225 (ex-CP 234)   R 226 (ex-CP 236)

Displacement, tons: 16 full load
Dimensions, feet (metres): 44.0 × 15.7 × 4.3 *(13.4 × 4.8 × 1.3)*
Main machinery: 2 AIFO 8281-SRM diesels; 1,770 hp *(1.32 MW)*; 2 shafts
Speed, knots: 24
Range, n miles: 400 at 24 kt
Complement: 5
Radars: Surface search: I-band.

Comment: Wooden construction. Built in Italy 1966-69. Transferred from Italian Coast Guard to Albanian Coast Guard in 2002.

3 SEA SPECTRE MK III (PB)

R 118   R 215   R 216

Displacement, tons: 41 full load
Dimensions, feet (metres): 65 × 18 × 5.9 *(19.8 × 5.5 × 1.8)*
Main machinery: 3 Detroit 8V-71 diesels; 690 hp *(515 kW)* sustained; 3 shafts
Speed, knots: 28
Range, n miles: 450 at 25 kt
Complement: 9
Guns: 2 — 25 mm. 2 — 12.7 mm MGs.
Radars: Surface search: Raytheon; I-band.

Comment: Transferred from the US on 27 February 1999.

SEA SPECTRE (US colours)   *4/1991, Giorgio Arra* / 0056446

7 TYPE 2010 INSHORE PATROL CRAFT (PBR)

R 125 (ex-CP 2008)   R 127 (ex-CP 2021)   R 224 (ex-CP 2010)   R 228 (ex-CP 2023)
R 126 (ex-CP 2020)   R 128 (ex-CP 2034)   R 227 (ex-CP 2007)

Displacement, tons: 15 full load
Dimensions, feet (metres): 41.0 × 11.8 × 3.6 *(12.5 × 3.6 × 1.1)*
Main machinery: 2 AIFO diesels; 1,072 hp *(800 kW)*; 2 shafts
Speed, knots: 24. **Range, n miles:** 533 at 20 kt
Complement: 5
Radars: Surface search: I-band.

Comment: Former harbour launches built in Italy in the 1970s. GRP construction. One transferred from Italian Coast Guard to Albanian Coast Guard in 2002 and a further six in 2004.

1 TYPE 303 COASTAL PATROL CRAFT (PB)

R 122 (ex-CP 303)

Displacement, tons: 20 full load
Dimensions, feet (metres): 44.0 × 12.5 × 3.6 *(13.4 × 3.8 × 1.1)*
Main machinery: 2 GM6V53 diesels; 730 hp *(544 kW)*; 2 shafts
Speed, knots: 13
Range, n miles: 350 at 13 kt
Complement: 5
Radars: Surface search: I-band.

Comment: Built in US in 1965. Transferred from Italian Coast Guard to Albanian Coast Guard in 2002.

Algeria
MARINE DE LA REPUBLIQUE ALGERIENNE

Country Overview

Formerly a French colony, the People's Democratic Republic of Algeria gained independence in 1962. Situated in north Africa, it has an area of 919,595 square miles and is bordered to the east by Tunisia and Libya, to the south by Niger, Mali, and Mauritania and to the west by Morocco. It has a 540 n mile coastline with the Mediterranean. The capital, largest city and principal port is Algiers. Territorial seas (12 n miles) and Fishery zones (32/52 n miles) have been claimed but an EEZ has not been claimed.

Headquarters Appointments

Commander of the Navy:
    Lieutenant General Malek Necib
Inspector General of the Navy:
    General Major Abdelmadjid Taright

Personnel

(a)   2006: 7,500 (500 officers) (Navy) (includes at least 600 naval infantry); 500 (Coast Guard)
(b)   Voluntary service

Bases

Algiers (1st Region), Mers-el-Kebir (2nd Region), Jijel (3rd Region), Annaba (CG HQ)

Coast Defence

Four batteries of truck-mounted SS-C-3 Styx twin launchers. Permanent sites at Algiers, Mers-el-Kebir and Jijel linked by radar.

SUBMARINES

Notes: One decommissioned Romeo class is used for training.

2 KILO CLASS (PROJECT 877E) (SSK)

Name	No	Builders	Laid down	Launched	Commissioned
RAIS HADJ MUBAREK	012	Admiralty Yard, Leningrad	1985	1986	Oct 1987
EL HADJ SLIMANE	013	Admiralty Yard, Leningrad	1985	1987	Jan 1988

Displacement, tons: 2,325 surfaced; 3,076 dived
Dimensions, feet (metres): 238.2 × 32.5 × 21.7 *(72.6 × 9.9 × 6.6)*
Main machinery: Diesel-electric; 2 diesels; 3,650 hp(m) *(2.68 MW)*; 2 generators; 1 motor; 5,900 hp(m) *(4.34 MW)*; 1 shaft; 2 auxiliary MT-168 motors; 204 hp(m) *(150 kW)*; 1 economic speed motor; 130 hp(m) *(95 kW)*

Speed, knots: 17 dived; 10 surfaced; 9 snorting
Range, n miles: 6,000 at 7 kt snorting; 400 at 3 kt dived
Complement: 52 (13 officers)

Torpedoes: 6 — 21 in *(533 mm)* tubes. Combination of Russian TEST-71ME; anti-submarine active/passive homing to 15 km *(8.2 n miles)* at 40 kt; warhead 205 kg and 53 — 65;

anti-surface ship passive wake homing to 19 km *(10.3 n miles)* at 45 kt; warhead 300 kg. Total of 18 weapons.
Mines: 24 in lieu of torpedoes.
Countermeasures: ESM: Brick Pulp; radar warning.
Weapons control: MVU 110 TFCS.
Radars: Surface search: Snoop Tray; I-band.
Sonars: MGK 400 Shark Teeth/Shark Fin; hull-mounted; passive/active search and attack; medium frequency. MG 519 Mouse Roar; active attack; high frequency.

Programmes: New construction hulls, delivered as replacements for the Romeo class.
Modernisation: Both submarines are to undergo a two-year refit at Admiralty Yard, St Petersburg. Work on the first boat began in November 2005.
Structure: Diving depth, 790 ft *(240 m)*. 9,700 kWh batteries. Pressure hull 169.9 ft *(51.8 m)*. May be fitted with SA-N-5/8 portable SAM launcher.

Operational One in refit at St Petersburg from June 1993, returned to service in May 1995. Second in refit in late 1993 and back in March 1996. Both are active.

RAIS HADJ MUBAREK   *3/1996* / 0056450

FRIGATES

3 MOURAD RAIS (KONI) CLASS (PROJECT 1159.2) (FFLM)

Name	No	Builders	Commissioned
MOURAD RAIS	901	Zelenodolsk Shipyard	20 Dec 1980
RAIS KELLICH	902	Zelenodolsk Shipyard	24 Mar 1982
RAIS KORFOU	903	Zelenodolsk Shipyard	3 Jan 1985

Displacement, tons: 1,440 standard; 1,900 full load
Dimensions, feet (metres): 316.3 × 41.3 × 11.5
(96.4 × 12.6 × 3.5)
Main machinery: CODAG; 1 SGW, Nikolayev, M8B gas
turbine (centre shaft); 18,000 hp(m) *(13.25 MW)* sustained;
2 Russki B-68 diesels; 15,820 hp(m) *(11.63 MW)* sustained;
3 shafts
Speed, knots: 27 gas; 22 diesel
Range, n miles: 1,800 at 14 kt
Complement: 130

Missiles: SAM: SA-N-4 Gecko twin launcher ❶; semi-active
radar homing to 15 km *(8 n miles)* at 2.5 Mach; height
envelope 9—3,048 m *(29.5—10,000 ft)*; warhead 50 kg;
20 missiles. Some anti-surface capability.
Guns: 4—3 in *(76 mm)*/60 (2 twin) ❷; 90 rds/min to
15 km *(8 n miles)*; weight of shell 6.8 kg.
4—30 mm/65 (2 twin) ❸; 500 rds/min to 5 km *(2.7 n miles)*;
weight of shell 0.54 kg.
A/S mortars: 2—12-barrelled RBU 6000 ❹; range 6,000 m;
warhead 31 kg.
Torpedoes: 4—533 mm (2 twin) (in 903 only) ❺.
Depth charges: 2 racks.
Mines: Rails; capacity 22.
Countermeasures: Decoys: 2 PK 16 chaff launchers.
ESM: Watch Dog. Cross Loop D/F.
Weapons control: 3P-60 UE.
Radars: Air/surface search: Pozitiv-ME1.2 ❻; I-band. (Strut
Curve); E/F-band (in 901 and 902).
Navigation: Don 2; I-band.
Fire Control: Drum tilt ❼; H/I-band (for search/
acquisition/FC).
Pop Group ❽; F/H/I-band (for missile control).
Hawk screech (901 and 902) ❾; I-band.
IFF: High Pole B. 2 Square Head.

MOURAD RAIS   *Scale 1 : 900, Ian Sturton* / 0567433

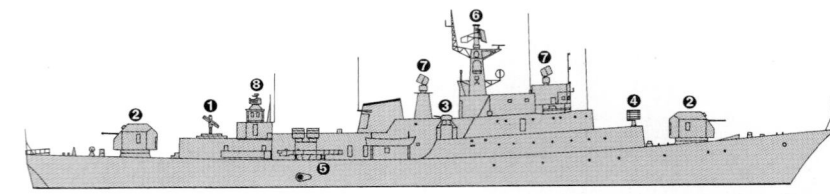

RAIS KORFOU   *Scale 1 : 900, Ian Sturton* / 0104159

Sonars: Hercules (MG 322) hull-mounted; active search
and attack; medium frequency.

Programmes: New construction ships built in USSR with
hull numbers 5, 7 and 10 in sequence. Others of the class
built for Cuba, Yugoslavia, East Germany and Libya.
Interest was shown in ex-GDR ships in 1991 but sale was
rejected by the German government.

Modernisation: New generators fitted 1992-94. *Rais Korfou*
in refit at Kronstadt from 1997 to November 2000. The
refit included replacement of Strut Curve radar, removal
of Hawk screech fire-control radar, fitting of torpedo
tubes and a new electronic suite. The contract for refit of
a second ship and a 'Nanuchka' is expected in 2006.
Structure: The deckhouse aft in Type II Konis houses air
conditioning machinery.
Operational: All have been used for Training cruises.

RAIS KORFOU   *8/2004, B Prézelin* / 1044062

MOURAD RAIS   *8/2004, Schaeffer/Marsan* / 1044063

CORVETTES

3 + (1) DJEBEL CHENOUA (C 58) CLASS (PROJECT 802) (FSG)

Name	No	Builders	Launched	Commissioned
DJEBEL CHENOUA	351	ECRN, Mers-el-Kebir	3 Feb 1985	Nov 1988
EL CHIHAB	352	ECRN, Mers-el-Kebir	Feb 1990	June 1995
AL KIRCH	353	ECRN, Mers-el-Kebir	July 2000	2002

Displacement, tons: 496 standard; 540 full load
Dimensions, feet (metres): 191.6 × 27.9 × 8.5 *(58.4 × 8.5 × 2.6)*
Main machinery: 3 MTU 20V 538 TB92 diesels; 12,800 hp(m) *(9.4 MW);* 3 shafts
Speed, knots: 31
Complement: 52 (6 officers)

Missiles: SSM: 4 China C 802 (CSS-N-8 Saccade) (2 twin); active radar homing to 120 km *(66 n miles)* at 0.9 Mach; warhead 165 kg.
Guns: 1 Russian 3 in *(76 mm)*/60; 90 rds/min to 15 km *(8 n miles);* weight of shell 6.8 kg.
  1—30 mm/65 AK 630; 6 barrels per mounting; 3,000 rds/min combined to 2 km.
Countermeasures: Decoys 2 chaff launchers.
Weapons control: Optronic director.
Radars: Surface search: Racal Decca 1226; I-band.

Programmes: Ordered July 1983. Project 802 built with Bulgarian assistance. First one completed trials in 1988. Work on the second of class was suspended in 1992 due to shipyard debt problems but the ship completed in 1995. Main guns were fitted at a later date. Construction of a fourth ship is reported to be under consideration.
Modernisation: First two ships fitted with main armaments comprising SSMs and 76 mm guns.
Structure: Hull size suggests association with Bazán Cormoran class.

AL KIRCH   *6/2005*, Marian Ferrette* / 1127285

EL CHIHAB   *7/2005*, B Prézelin* / 1129990

3 NANUCHKA II (BURYA) CLASS (PROJECT 1234) (MISSILE CORVETTES) (PTGM)

Name	No	Builders	Commissioned
RAIS HAMIDOU	801	Petrovsky, Leningrad	4 July 1980
SALAH RAIS	802	Petrovsky, Leningrad	9 Feb 1981
RAIS ALI	803	Petrovsky, Leningrad	8 May 1982

Displacement, tons: 660 full load
Dimensions, feet (metres): 194.5 × 38.7 × 8.5 *(59.3 × 11.8 × 2.6)*
Main machinery: 6 M 504 diesels; 26,112 hp(m) *(19.2 MW);* 3 shafts
Speed, knots: 33
Range, n miles: 2,500 at 12 kt; 900 at 31 kt
Complement: 42 (7 officers)

Missiles: SSM: 16 Zvezda SS-N-25 (in 802) (4 quad) (Kh 35E Uran); active radar homing to 130 km *(70.2 n miles)* at 0.9 Mach; warhead 145 kg; sea skimmer.
  4 SS-N-2C (in 801 and 803); active radar or IR homing to 46 km *(25 n miles)* at 0.9 Mach; warhead 513 kg.
SAM: SA-N-4 Gecko twin launcher; semi-active radar homing to 15 km *(8 n miles)* at 2.5 Mach; height envelope 9—3,048 m *(29.5—10,000 ft);* warhead 50 kg; 20 missiles. Some anti-surface capability.
Guns: 2—57 mm/80 (twin); 120 rds/min to 6 km *(3.3 n miles);* weight of shell 2.8 kg.
  1—30 mm/65 AK 630 (in 802); 6 barrels per mounting; 3,000 rds/min combined to 2 km.
Countermeasures: Decoys: 2 PK 16 16-barrelled chaff launchers.
ESM: Bell Tap. Cross Loop; D/F.
Radars: Surface search: Square Tie (Radome) (801 and 803); I-band. Pozitiv-ME1.2 (802); I-band.
Navigation: Don 2; I-band.
Fire control: Pop Group; F/H/I-band (SA-N-4). Muff Cob or Drum Tilt (802); G/H-band. Plank Shave; E-band (SS-N-25).
IFF: Two Square Head. High Pole.

Programmes: Delivered as new construction.
Modernisation: *Salah Rais* refitted at Kronstadt 1997 to November 2000 with refurbished diesels, a replacement SSM system and electronic suite. The contract for refit of a second ship and a 'Koni' is expected by 2006.

SALAH RAIS (SS-N-25 not fitted)   *4/2005*, Rafael Cabrera* / 1151080

RAIS HAMIDOU   *5/2002, Globke Collection* / 0529554

LAND-BASED MARITIME AIRCRAFT

Numbers/Type: 2 Beechcraft Super King Air 200T.
Operational speed: 282 kt *(523 km/h).*
Service ceiling: 35,000 ft *(10,670 m).*
Range: 2,030 n miles *(3,756 km).*
Role/Weapon systems: Operated by air force for crew training and for close-range EEZ operations. Sensors: Weather radar only. Weapons: Unarmed.

Numbers/Type: 3 Fokker F27-400/600.
Operational speed: 250 kt *(463 km/h).*
Service ceiling: 25,000 ft *(7,620 m).*
Range: 2,700 n miles *(5,000 km).*
Role/Weapon systems: Visual reconnaissance duties in support of EEZ, particularly offshore platforms. Sensors: Weather radar and visual means only. Weapons: Limited armament.

PATROL FORCES

13 KEBIR CLASS (FAST ATTACK CRAFT—GUN) (PG)

EL YADEKH 341	EL RASSED 345	—349	—357
EL MOURAKEB 342	EL DJARI 346	EL KANASS 350	—358
EL KECHEF 343	EL SAHER 347	—356	
EL MOUTARID 344	EL MOUKADEM 348		

Displacement, tons: 166 standard; 200 full load
Dimensions, feet (metres): 123 × 22.6 × 5.6 *(37.5 × 6.9 × 1.7)*
Main machinery: 2 MTU 12V 538 TB92 diesels; 5,110 hp(m) *(3.8 MW);* 2 shafts (see Structure)
Speed, knots: 27
Range, n miles: 3,300 at 12 kt; 2,600 at 15 kt
Complement: 27 (3 officers)

Guns: 1 OTO Melara 3 in *(76 mm)*/62 compact (341—342); 85 rds/min to 16 km *(9 n miles)* anti-surface; 12 km *(6.5 n miles)* anti-aircraft; weight of shell 6 kg.
  4 USSR 25 mm/60 (2 twin) (remainder); 270 rds/min to 3 km *(1.6 n miles);* weight of shell 0.34 kg.
  2 USSR 14.5 mm (twin) (in first five).
Weapons control: Lawrence Scott optronic director (in 341 and 342).
Radars: Surface search: Racal Decca 1226; I-band.

Programmes: Design and first pair ordered from Brooke Marine in June 1981. First left for Algeria without armament in September 1982, second arrived Algiers 12 June 1983. A further seven were then assembled or built at ECRN, Mers-el-Kebir. Of these, 346 commissioned 10 November 1985 and 347—349 delivered by 1993. After a delay two further craft were completed; 350 in late 1997 followed by 354 in 1998. 356—358 have since been added and original plans for a class of 15 may be achieved.
Structure: Same hull as Barbados *Trident.* There are some variations in armament.
Operational: Six of the class have been transferred to the Coast Guard.

KEBIR 358   *4/2005*, Rafael Cabrera* / 1151079

KEBIR 350 (with 25 mm guns)   *6/1998* / 0017511

9 OSA II CLASS (PROJECT 205)
(FAST ATTACK CRAFT—MISSILE) (PTGF)

644-652

Displacement, tons: 245 full load
Dimensions, feet (metres): 126.6 × 24.9 × 8.8 *(38.6 × 7.6 × 2.7)*
Main machinery: 3 Type M 504 diesels; 10,800 hp(m) *(7.94 MW)* sustained; 3 shafts
Speed, knots: 37
Range, n miles: 500 at 35 kt
Complement: 30

Missiles: SSM: 4 SS-N-2B; active radar or IR homing to 46 km *(25 n miles)* at 0.9 Mach; warhead 513 kg.
Guns: 4—30 mm/65 (2 twin); 500 rds/min to 5 km *(2.7 n miles)*; weight of shell 0.54 kg.
Radars: Surface search: Square Tie; I-band.
Fire control: Drum Tilt; H/I-band.
IFF: 2 Square Head. High Pole B.

Programmes: Osa II transferred 1976-77 (four), fifth in September 1978, sixth in December 1978, next pair in 1979 and one from the Black Sea on 7 December 1981.
Modernisation: Plans to re-engine were reported as starting in late 1992 but there has been no confirmation.
Operational: At least six Osa IIs are active.

OSA 652   *1989* / 0505953

AMPHIBIOUS FORCES

2 LANDING SHIPS (LOGISTIC) (LSTH)

Name	No	Builders	Commissioned
KALAAT BENI HAMMAD	472	Brooke Marine, Lowestoft	Apr 1984
KALAAT BENI RACHED	473	Vosper Thornycroft, Woolston	Oct 1984

Displacement, tons: 2,450 full load
Dimensions, feet (metres): 305 × 50.9 × 8.1 *(93 × 15.5 × 2.5)*
Main machinery: 2 MTU 16V 1163 TB82 diesels; 8,880 hp(m) *(6.5 MW)* sustained; 2 shafts
Speed, knots: 15
Range, n miles: 3,000 at 12 kt
Complement: 81
Military lift: 240 troops; 7 MBTs and 380 tons other cargo; 2 ton crane with athwartships travel

Guns: 2 Breda 40 mm/70 (twin); 300 rds/min to 12.5 km *(6.8 n miles)*; weight of shell 0.96 kg.
4 USSR 25 mm/60 (2 twin); 270 rds/min to 3 km *(1.6 n miles)*; weight of shell 0.34 kg.
Countermeasures: Decoys: Wallop Barricade double layer chaff launchers.
ESM: Racal Cutlass; intercept.
ECM: Racal Cygnus; jammer.
Weapons control: CSEE Naja optronic.
Radars: Navigation: Racal Decca TM 1226; I-band.
Fire control: Marconi S 800; J-band.

Helicopters: Platform only for one Sea King.

Programmes: First ordered in June 1981, and launched 18 May 1983; second ordered 18 October 1982 and launched 15 May 1984. Similar hulls to Omani *Nasr Al Bahr*.
Structure: These ships have a through tank deck closed by bow and stern ramps. The forward ramp is of two sections measuring length 18 m (when extended) × 5 m breadth, and the single section stern ramp measures 4.3 × 5 m with the addition of 1.1 m finger flaps. Both hatches can support a 60 ton tank and are winch operated. In addition, side access doors are provided on each side forward. The tank deck side bulkheads extend 2.25 m above the upper deck between the forecastle and the forward end of the superstructure, and provide two hatch openings to the tank deck below. Additional 25 mm guns have been fitted either side of the bridge.
Operational: Both are reported active.

KALAAT BENI HAMMAD   *8/2004, B Prézelin* / 1044061

KALAAT BENI RACHED   *7/2005*, Marco Ghiglino* / 1129989

1 POLNOCHNY B CLASS (PROJECT 771) (LSM)

471

Displacement, tons: 760 standard; 834 full load
Dimensions, feet (metres): 246.1 × 31.5 × 7.5 *(75 × 9.6 × 2.3)*
Main machinery: 2 Kolomna Type 40-D diesels; 4,400 hp(m) *(3.2 MW)* sustained; 2 shafts
Speed, knots: 18
Range, n miles: 1,000 at 18 kt
Complement: 42
Military lift: 180 troops; 350 tons including up to 6 tanks
Guns: 2—30 mm/65 (twin) AK 230; 500 rds/min to 5 km *(2.7 n miles)*; weight of shell 0.54 kg.
2—140 mm 18-tubed rocket launchers.
Radars: Navigation: Don 2; I-band.
Fire control: Drum Tilt; H/I-band.
IFF: Square Head. High Pole B.

Comment: Class built in Poland 1968-70. Transferred from USSR in August 1976. Tank deck covers 237 m². Operational and employed on training tasks.

POLNOCHNY 471   *1990, van Ginderen Collection* / 0505954

MINE WARFARE FORCES

Notes: (1) The Coast Guard support ship *El Mourafik* may have a minelaying capability.
(2) Two MCMV are expected to be out to tender in due course.

SURVEY SHIPS

1 SURVEY SHIP (AGS)

EL IDRISSI BH 204 (ex-A 673)

Displacement, tons: 540 full load
Complement: 28 (6 officers)

Comment: Built by Matsukara, Japan and delivered 17 April 1980. Based at Algiers.

EL IDRISSI   *9/1990* / 0056453

2 SURVEY CRAFT (YFS)

RAS TARA   **ALIDADE**

Comment: *Ras Tara* is of 16 tons displacement, built in 1980 and has a crew of four. *Alidade* is of 20 tons, built in 1983 and has a crew of eight.

AUXILIARIES

1 POLUCHAT I CLASS (PROJECT 638) (YPT)

A 641

Displacement, tons: 70 standard; 100 full load
Dimensions, feet (metres): 97.1 × 19 × 4.8 *(29.6 × 5.8 × 1.5)*
Main machinery: 2 Type M 50F diesels; 2,200 hp(m) *(1.6 MW)* sustained; 2 shafts
Speed, knots: 20
Range, n miles: 1,500 at 10 kt
Complement: 15

Comment: Transferred from USSR in early 1970s. Has been used for SAR.

POLUCHAT   *1989* / 0506183

0 + 1 DAXIN CLASS (AXH)

Name	No	Builders	Launched	Commissioned
—	937	Hudong Shipyard, Shanghai	Mar 2005	2006

Displacement, tons: 5,470 full load
Dimensions, feet (metres): 426.5 × 52.5 × 15.7 *(130.0 × 16.0 × 4.8)*
Main machinery: 2 6PC2-5L diesels; 7,800 hp(m) *(5.73 MW)*; 2 shafts
Speed, knots: 15. **Range, n miles:** 5,000 at 15 kt
Complement: 170 plus 30 instructors plus 200 Midshipmen
Guns: 2 China 57 mm/70 (2 twin). 2—30 mm/65 AK 630; 6 barrels per mounting; 3,000 rds/min combined to 2 km.
Radars: Air/surface search: Eye Shield; E-band.
Surface search: China Type 756; I-band.
Navigation: Racal Decca 1290; I-band.
Fire control: Round Ball; I-band.
Sonars: Echo Type 5; hull-mounted; active; high frequency.

Helicopters: Platform only.

Comment: Very similar to Chinese training ship of same class.

DAXIN CLASS 937   *12/2005*, A Sheldon-Duplaix* / 1153015

TUGS

Notes: There are a number of harbour tugs of about 265 tons. These include *Kader* A 210, *El Chadid* A 211 and *Mazafran* 1-4 Y 206-209.

MAZAFRAN 4   *6/1994* / 0056454

COAST GUARD

Notes: (1) Six Kebir class were transferred from the Navy for Coast Guard duties but may have naval crews.
(2) There are also up to 12 small fishery protection vessels in the GC 301 series.

1 SUPPORT SHIP (WARL)

EL MOURAFIK GC 261

Displacement, tons: 600 full load
Dimensions, feet (metres): 193.6 × 27.6 × 6.9 *(59 × 8.4 × 2.1)*
Main machinery: 2 diesels; 2,200 hp(m) *(1.6 MW)*; 2 shafts
Speed, knots: 14
Complement: 54
Guns: 2—12.7 mm MGs.
Radars: Surface search: I-band.

Comment: Delivered by transporter ship from China in April 1990. The design appears to be a derivative of the T43 minesweeper but with a stern gantry. May have a minelaying capability. Based at Algiers.

EL MOURAFIK   *6/2003, B Lemachko* / 0569789

7 EL MOUDERRIB (CHUI-E) CLASS (AXL)

EL MOUDERRIB I-VII GC 251-257

Displacement, tons: 388 full load
Dimensions, feet (metres): 192.8 × 23.6 × 7.2 *(58.8 × 7.2 × 2.2)*
Main machinery: 3 PCR/Kolomna diesels; 6,600 hp(m) *(4.92 MW)*; 3 shafts
Speed, knots: 24
Range, n miles: 1,400 at 15 kt
Complement: 42 including 25 trainees
Guns: 4 China 14.5 mm (2 twin).
Radars: Surface search: Type 756; I-band.

Comment: Two delivered by transporter ship from China in April 1990 and described as training vessels. Two more acquired in January 1991, the last three in July 1991. Hainan class hull with modified propulsion and superstructure similar to some Chinese paramilitary vessels. Used for training when boats are carried aft in place of the second 14.5 mm gun.

EL MOUDERRIB I   *6/1992, Diego Quevedo* / 0056456

4 BAGLIETTO TYPE 20 (PBF)

EL HAMIL GC 325   **EL ASSAD** GC 326   **MARKHAD** GC 327   **ETAIR** GC 328

Displacement, tons: 44 full load
Dimensions, feet (metres): 66.9 × 17.1 × 5.5 *(20.4 × 5.2 × 1.7)*
Main machinery: 2 CRM 18DS diesels; 2,660 hp(m) *(2 MW)*; 2 shafts
Speed, knots: 36
Range, n miles: 445 at 20 kt
Complement: 11 (3 officers)
Guns: 1 Oerlikon 20 mm.

Comment: The first pair delivered by Baglietto, Varazze in August 1976 and six further in pairs at two monthly intervals. Fitted with radar and optical fire control. Four others of the class cannibalised for spares.

BAGLIETTO 20 GC CRAFT   *1978, Baglietto* / 0505955

4 EL MOUNKID CLASS (SAR)

EL MOUNKID I GC 231	**EL MOUNKID** III GC 233
EL MOUNKID II GC 232	**EL MOUNKID** IV GC 234

Comment: First three delivered by transporter ship from China which arrived in Algiers in April 1990, a fourth followed a year later. Used for SAR.

GC 231-233   *1991* / 0056457

CUSTOMS

Notes: The Customs service is a paramilitary organisation employing a number of patrol craft armed with small MGs. These include *Bouzagza*, *Djurdjura*, *Hodna*, *Aures* and *Hoggar*. The first three are P 1200 class 39 ton craft capable of 33 kt. The next pair are P 802 class. They were built by Watercraft, Shoreham and delivered in November 1985.

Angola
MARINHA DE GUERRA

Country Overview

Formerly known as Portuguese West Africa, the Republic of Angola became independent in 1975 but has been ravaged by civil war ever since. With an area of 481,354 square miles it has borders to the south with Namibia, to the east with Zambia and to the north and east with the Democratic Republic of the Congo which separates a small exclave, Cabinda, from the rest of the country. Angola has a coastline with the south Atlantic Ocean of some 864 n

miles. The capital, largest city and principal port is Luanda. Territorial seas (12 n miles) and a fisheries zone (200 n miles) are claimed. A 200 n mile Exclusive Economic Zone (EEZ) has been claimed but the limits have not been published. In 2004, there were no operational vessels in the Navy.

Personnel

(a) 2006: 890
(b) Voluntary service

Bases

Luanda, Lobito, Namibe. (There are other good harbours available on the 1,000 mile coastline.) Naval HQ at Luanda on Ila de Luanda is in an old fort, as is Namibe.

Anguilla

Country Overview

British dependency since 1971 following secession from associated state of St Kitts-Nevis-Anguilla. With an area of 35 square miles, the island is situated at the northern end of the Leeward Islands in the Lesser Antilles and bordered by the Caribbean to the west and Atlantic to the east.

Territorial seas (3 n miles) and a fishery zone (200 n miles) are claimed.

Headquarters Appointments

Commissioner of Police:
  Keithly Benjamin

Personnel

2006: 79

POLICE

1 HALMATIC M160 CLASS (INSHORE PATROL CRAFT) (PB)

DOLPHIN

Displacement, tons: 18 light
Dimensions, feet (metres): 52.5 × 15.4 × 4.6 *(16 × 4.7 × 1.4)*
Main machinery: 2 MAN V10 diesels; 820 hp *(610 kW)* sustained; 2 shafts
Speed, knots: 34
Range, n miles: 575 at 23 kt
Complement: 8
Guns: 1 — 12.7 mm MG.
Radars: Surface search: JRC 2254; I-band.

Comment: Built by Halmatic and delivered 22 December 1989. Identical craft to Qatar. GRP hull. Rigid inflatable boat launched by gravity davit. Returned to service on 30 August 2004 after refit.

1 BOSTON WHALER (INSHORE PATROL CRAFT) (PB)

LAPWING

Displacement, tons: 2.2 full load
Dimensions, feet (metres): 27 × 10 × 1.5 *(8.2 × 3 × 0.5)*
Main machinery: 2 Johnson outboards; 300 hp *(225 kW)*
Speed, knots: 38
Complement: 4

Comment: Delivered in 1990 and re-engined in 2005.

LAPWING
6/2005*, Anguilla Police
1129153

DOLPHIN

6/2005*, Anguilla Police / 1129152

Antigua and Barbuda

Country Overview

Independent since 1981, the British monarch, represented by a governor-general, is head of state. Situated at the southern end of the Leeward Islands in the Lesser Antilles chain, the country comprises Antigua (108 square miles), Barbuda to the north and uninhabited Redonda to the southwest. The capital, largest town, and main port is St John's. An archipelagic state, territorial seas (12 n miles)

and a fishery zone (200 n miles) are claimed. A 200 n mile Exclusive Economic Zone (EEZ) has also been claimed but the limits are not defined. The Antigua Barbuda Defence Force (ABDF) took over the Coast Guard on 1 May 1995.

Headquarters Appointments

Commanding Officer, Coast Guard:
  Lieutenant Auden Nicholas

Personnel

2006: 50 (3 officers)

Bases

HQ: Deepwater Harbour, St Johns
Maintenance: Camp Blizzard

COAST GUARD

Notes: (1) In addition there is a Hurricane RIB, *CG 081* with a speed of 35 kt and two Boston Whalers, *CG 071-2*, with speeds of 30 kt. All were acquired in 1988/90.
(2) A 920 Zodiac RHIB, CG 091, was donated by the US government in 2003. It is capable of over 40 kt.

CG 091   *9/2004*, ABDFCG* / 0587690

CG 081   *9/2004*, ABDFCG* / 0587691

1 SWIFT 65 FT CLASS (PB)

Name	No	Builders	Commissioned
LIBERTA	P 01	Swiftships, Morgan City	30 Apr 1984

Displacement, tons: 36 full load
Dimensions, feet (metres): 65.5 × 18.4 × 5 *(20 × 5.6 × 1.5)*
Main machinery: 2 Detroit Diesel 12V-71TA diesels; 840 hp *(616 kW)* sustained; 2 shafts
Speed, knots: 22
Range, n miles: 250 at 18 kt
Complement: 9
Guns: 1—12.7 mm MG. 2—7.62 mm MGs.
Radars: Surface search: Furuno; I-band.

Comment: Ordered in November 1983. Aluminium construction. Funded by US. Refitted in 2001.

LIBERTA   *5/2003* / 0568341

1 DAUNTLESS CLASS (PB)

Name	No	Builders	Commissioned
PALMETTO	P 02	SeaArk Marine, Monticello	7 July 1995

Displacement, tons: 11 full load
Dimensions, feet (metres): 40 × 14 × 4.3 *(12.2 × 4.3 × 1.3)*
Main machinery: 2 Caterpillar 3208TA diesels; 870 hp *(650 kW)* sustained; 2 shafts
Speed, knots: 27
Range, n miles: 600 at 18 kt
Complement: 4
Guns: 1—7.62 mm MG.
Radars: Surface search: Raytheon R40; I-band.

Comment: Funded by USA. Similar craft delivered to several Caribbean countries in 1994-98.

PALMETTO   *9/2004*, ABDFCG* / 0587689

Argentina

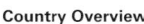

ARMADA ARGENTINA

Country Overview

The Argentine Republic is situated in southern South America. With an area of 1,068,302 square miles it has borders to the north with Bolivia and Paraguay, to the east with Brazil and Uruguay and to the south and west with Chile. The country includes the Tierra del Fuego territory which comprises the eastern half of the Isla Grande de Tierra del Fuego and a number of adjacent islands to the east, including Isla de los Estados. It also claims sovereignty of the Falkland Islands. The capital, largest city and principal port is Buenos Aires. There are further ports at La Plata, Bahia Blanca, Comodoro Rivadavia and a river port at Rosario. There are some 5,940 n miles of navigable internal waterways. Territorial Seas (12 n miles) are claimed. An EEZ (200 n miles) is claimed but its limits are only partly defined by boundary agreements.

Headquarters Appointments

Chief of Naval General Staff:
  Vice Admiral Jorge Omar Godoy
Deputy Chief of Naval Staff:
  Rear Admiral Benito Ítalo Rótolo
Naval Operations Commander:
  Rear Admiral Eduardo Luis Avilés

Senior Appointments

Commander Fleet:
  Rear Admiral Francisco Antonio Galia
Commander, Marine Infantry:
  Rear Admiral Juan Roberto Marín
Commander Naval Aviation:
  Captain Luis Alberto de Vincenti
Commander, Naval Area Austral:
  Commodore Guillermo José Estévez
Commander, Atlantic:
  Commodore Andres Roque di Vincenzo
Commander, Naval Area Fluvial:
  Captain Waldemar Abel Sanginetti

Personnel

2006: 16,371 (2,485 officers)

Organisation

Naval Area Austral covers coastal area from latitude 46° to 60° south.

Naval Area Atlantic covers coastal area from latitude 36° 18' to 46° south.
Naval Area Fluvial includes the rivers Paraná, Uruguay and Plate.
Naval Area Antarctica is activated when *Almirante Irizar* deploys.

Special Forces

Consists of tactical divers who operate from submarines and other naval units, and amphibious commandos who are trained in parachuting and behind the lines operations. Both groups consist of about 150.

Bases

Buenos Aires (Dársena Norte): Some naval training.
Rio Santiago (La Plata): Schools.
Mar del Plata: Submarine base plus three frigates.
Puerto Belgrano: Main naval base, schools. Fleet Marine Force.
Ushuaia, Deseado, Dársena Sur, Zárate, Caleta Paula; Small naval bases.

Coast Guard (Prefectura Naval Argentina)

In January 1992 the Coast Guard was limited to operations inside 12 mile territorial seas but this legislation was then cancelled in favour of the previous 200 mile operating zone. In May 1994 a Community Protection Secretariat was formed to include the Coast Guard, Border Guard and Federal Police. In June 1996 the Coast Guard and Border Guard were placed under the Interior Ministry.

Prefix to Ships' Names

ARA (Armada Republica Argentina)

Naval Aviation

Personnel: 2,500
The Naval Air Command is at Puerto Belgrano.
  1st Naval Air Wing (Punta Indio Naval Air Base): 1st Naval Attack Squadron with Aeromacchi MB-326; Naval Photographic Reconnaissance Group with Beech 200s. Naval Aviation School with Beech T-34s and Turbo Mentor.
2nd Naval Air Wing (Comandante Espora Naval Air Base): ASW Squadron with Grumman S-2T Trackers; 2nd Naval Helicopter Squadron with Agusta/Sikorsky SH-3H and AS-61D Sea Kings; 2nd Naval Attack Squadron with

Super Etendards; 1st Naval Helicopter Squadron with Alouette III and Fennecs; 3rd Naval Helicopter Squadron with Bell UH-1Hs.
3rd Naval Air Wing (Almirante Zar Naval Air Base, Trelew): 6th Naval Reconnaissance and Surveillance Squadron with Lockheed P-3B Orions, Lockheed Electra L-188E, Beech 200s and Pilatus PC-6B.
52 Logistic Support Flight (Almirante Izar Naval Air Base): Fokker F-28s.

Marine Corps

Personnel: 2,800
2nd Marine Infantry Battalion (Puerto Belgrano)
3rd Marine Infantry Battalion (Zarate)
4th Marine Infantry Battalion (Ushuaia)
5th Marine Infantry Battalion (Training) (Rio Grande)
Marine Field Artillery Battalion (Puerto Belgrano)
Command and Logistics Support Battalion (Puerto Belgrano)
Amphibious Vehicles Battalion (Puerto Belgrano)
Communications Battalion (Puerto Belgrano)
Marine A/A Battalion (Puerto Belgrano)
Amphibious Engineers Company (Puerto Belgrano)
Amphibious Commandos Group (Puerto Belgrano)
There are Marine Security Battalions at Naval Bases in Buenos Aires and Puerto Belgrano.

There are Marine Security Companies at Naval Bases in Mar del Plata, Trelew, Ushuaia, Punta Indio and Zarate.

Strength of the Fleet

Type	Active (Reserve)	Building
Patrol Submarines	3	—
Destroyers	5	—
Frigates	9	—
Patrol Ships	7	—
Fast Attack Craft (Gun/Missile)	2	—
Coastal Patrol Craft	6	—
LSDs	—	1 (1)
Survey/Oceanographic Ships	4	—
Survey Launches	1	—
Transports/Tankers	10	—
Training Ships	6	—

DELETIONS

Destroyers

2003   *Santisima Trinidad*

PENNANT LIST

Submarines		
S 31	Salta	
S 41	Santa Cruz	
S 42	San Juan	

Destroyers		
B 52	Hercules	
D 10	Almirante Brown	
D 11	La Argentina	
D 12	Heroina	
D 13	Sarandi	

Frigates		
31	Drummond	
32	Guerrico	
33	Granville	

41	Espora	
42	Rosales	
43	Spiro	
44	Parker	
45	Robinson	
46	Gomez Roca	

Patrol Forces		
A 1	Comandante General Irigoyen	
A 2	Teniente Olivieri	
A 3	Francisco de Gurruchaga	
A 6	Suboficial Castillo	
A 9	Alferez Sobral	
P 20	Murature	
P 21	King	
P 61	Baradero	
P 62	Barranqueras	
P 63	Clorinda	

P 64	Concepción del Uruguay	
P 65	Punta Mogotes	
P 66	Rio Santiago	
P 85	Intrepida	
P 86	Indomita	

Auxiliaries		
B 1	Patagonia	
B 3	Canal Beagle	
B 4	Bahia San Blas	
B 5	Cabo de Hornos	
B 8	Astra Federico	
B 9	Astra Valentina	
B 13	Ingeniero Julio Krause	
Q 2	Libertad	
Q 5	Almirante Irizar	
Q 11	Comodoro Rivadavia	
Q 15	Cormoran	

Q 20	Puerto Deseado	
Q 61	Ciudad de Zarate	
Q 62	Ciudad de Rosario	
Q 63	Punta Alta	
Q 73	Itati	
Q 74	Fortuna I	
Q 75	Fortuna II	
Q 76	Fortuna III	
R 2	Querandi	
R 3	Tehuelche	
R 5	Mocovi	
R 6	Calchaqui	
R 7	Ona	
R 8	Toba	
R 10	Chulupi	
R 12	Mataco	
R 16	Capayan	
R 18	Chiquilyan	
R 19	Morcoyan	

SUBMARINES

Notes: Cosmos and Havas underwater chariots in service. Cosmos types are capable of carrying limpet or ground mines.

1 SALTA (209) (TYPE 1200) CLASS (SSK)

Name	No	Builders	Laid down	Launched	Commissioned
SALTA	S 31	Howaldtswerke, Kiel	30 Apr 1970	9 Nov 1972	7 Mar 1974

Displacement, tons: 1,140 surfaced; 1,248 dived
Dimensions, feet (metres): 183.4 × 20.5 × 17.9 *(55.9 × 6.3 × 5.5)*
Main machinery: Diesel-electric; 4 MTU 12V 493 AZ80 diesels; 2,400 hp(m) *(1.76 MW)* sustained; 4 alternators; 1.7 MW; 1 motor; 4,600 hp(m) *(3.36 MW)*; 1 shaft
Speed, knots: 10 surfaced; 22 dived; 11 snorting
Range, n miles: 6,000 at 8 kt surfaced; 230 at 8 kt; 400 at 4 kt dived
Complement: 31 (5 officers)

Torpedoes: 8—21 in *(533 mm)* bow tubes. 14 AEG SST 4 Mod 1; wire-guided; active/passive homing to 12/28 km *(6.5/15 n miles)* at 35/23 kt; warhead 260 kg or US Mk 37;

wire-guided; active/passive homing to 8 km *(4.4 n miles)* at 24 kt; warhead 150 kg. Swim-out discharge.
Mines: Capable of carrying ground mines.
Countermeasures: ESM: DR 2000; radar warning.
Weapons control: Signaal M8 digital; computer-based; up to 3 targets engaged simultaneously.
Radars: Navigation: Thomson-CSF Calypso II.
Sonars: Atlas Elektronik CSU 3 (AN 526/AN 5039/41); active/passive search and attack; medium frequency.
  Thomson Sintra DUUX 2C and DUUG 1D; passive ranging.

Programmes: Ordered in 1968. Built in sections by Howaldtswerke Deutsche Werft AG, Kiel from the IK 68 design of Ingenieurkontor, Lübeck. Sections were

shipped to Argentina for assembly at Tandanor, Buenos Aires. Second of class *(San Luis)* has been used for spares since 1997 but remains in preservation at Domecq Garcia. The boat may be reactivated subject to funding.
Modernisation: *Salta* completed a mid-life modernisation at the Domecq Garcia Shipyard. New engines, weapons and electrical systems fitted and the ship was relaunched on 4 October 1994 and recommissioned in May 1995. Installation of new batteries began at Domecq Garcia in 2004 and completed in August 2005.
Structure: Diving depth, 250 m *(820 ft)*.
Operational: Operational and based at Mar del Plata.

SALTA   *12/2002, A E Galarce* / 0529819

2 SANTA CRUZ (TR 1700) CLASS (SSK)

Name	No	Builders	Laid down	Launched	Commissioned
SANTA CRUZ	S 41	Thyssen Nordseewerke	6 Dec 1980	28 Sep 1982	18 Oct 1984
SAN JUAN	S 42	Thyssen Nordseewerke	18 Mar 1982	20 June 1983	19 Nov 1985

Displacement, tons: 2,116 surfaced; 2,264 dived
Dimensions, feet (metres): 216.5 × 23.9 × 21.3
(66 × 7.3 × 6.5)
Main machinery: Diesel-electric; 4 MTU 16V 6,720 hp diesels; 6,720 hp(m) *(4.94 MW)* sustained; 4 alternators; 4.4 MW; 1 Siemens Type 1HR4525 + 1HR 4525 4-circuit DC motor; 6.6 MW; 1 shaft
Speed, knots: 15 surfaced; 12 snorting; 26 dived
Range, n miles: 12,000 at 8 kt surfaced; 20 at 25 kt dived; 460 at 6 kt dived
Complement: 29 (5 officers)

Torpedoes: 6—21 in *(533 mm)* bow tubes. 22 AEG SST 4; wire-guided; active/passive homing to 12/28 km *(6.5/15 n miles)* at 35/23 kt; warhead 260 kg; automatic reload in 50 seconds or US Mk 37; wire-guided; active/passive homing to 8 km *(4.4 n miles)* at 24 kt; warhead 150 kg.

Swim-out discharge. Mk 48 to replace Mk 37 in due course.
Mines: Capable of carrying 34 ground mines.
Countermeasures: ESM: Sea Sentry III; radar warning.
Weapons control: Signaal Sinbads; can handle 5 targets and 3 torpedoes simultaneously.
Radars: Navigation Thomson-CSF Calypso IV; I-band.
Sonars: Atlas Elektronik CSU 3/4; active/passive search and attack; medium frequency.
Thomson Sintra DUUX 5; passive ranging.

Programmes: Contract signed 30 November 1977 with Thyssen Nordseewerke for two submarines to be built at Emden. Parts and technical oversight were also to be provided for the construction of four further boats in Argentina by Astilleros Domecq Garcia, Buenos Aires. Work on units three and four was initiated and

S 43 *(Santa Fe)* was reported as 70 per cent complete by 2004. However, although completion of the boat is being kept under review, funding is likely to prove difficult in the current financial climate. Work on S 44 *(Santiago del Estero)* was reported as 30 per cent complete in 1996 but further work since then has not been reported. Equipment for numbers five and six has been used for spares.
Modernisation: *Santa Cruz* underwent mid-life update in Brazil between September 1999 and 2002. Refit includes new main motors and sonar upgrade. *San Juan* is to start a refit at Domecq Garcia in 2006.
Structure: Diving depth, 270 m *(890 ft)*.
Operational: Maximum endurance is 70 days. Both can be used for Commando insertion operations. They are based at Mar del Plata.

SANTA CRUZ   *7/2004, A E Galarce* / 1044064

SAN JUAN   *5/2004, A E Galarce* / 1044065

DESTROYERS

1 HERCULES (TYPE 42) CLASS (DDGHM)

Name	No	Builders	Laid down	Launched	Commissioned
HERCULES	B 52 (ex-D 1, ex-28)	Vickers, Barrow	16 June 1971	24 Oct 1972	12 July 1976

Displacement, tons: 3,150 standard; 4,100 full load
Dimensions, feet (metres): 412 × 47 × 19 (screws)
(125.6 × 14.3 × 5.8)
Flight deck, feet (metres): 85.3 × 42.66 *(26 × 13)*
Main machinery: COGOG; 2 RR Olympus TM3B gas turbines; 50,000 hp *(37.3 MW)* sustained
2 RR Tyne RM1A gas-turbines; 9,900 hp *(7.4 MW)* sustained; 2 shafts; cp props
Speed, knots: 29; 18 (Tynes)
Range, n miles: 4,000 at 18 kt
Complement: 280

Missiles: SAM: British Aerospace Sea Dart Mk 30 twin launcher ❶; semi-active radar homing to 40 km *(21.5 n miles)* at 2 Mach; height envelope 100—18,300 m *(328—60,042 ft)*; 22 missiles; limited anti-ship capability.
Guns: 1 Vickers 4.5 in *(115 mm)*/55 Mk 8 automatic ❷; 25 rds/min to 22 km *(12 n miles)*; weight of shell 21 kg; also fires chaff and illuminants.
2 Oerlikon 20 mm Mk 7 ❸. 4—12.7 mm MGs.
Countermeasures: Decoys: Graseby towed torpedo decoy. Knebworth Corvus 8-tubed trainable launchers for chaff.
ESM: Racal RDL 257; radar intercept.
ECM: Racal RCM 2; jammer.
Combat data systems: Plessey-Ferranti ADAWS-4; Link 10.
Radars: Air search: Marconi Type 965P with double AKE2 array and 1010/1011 IFF ❹; A-band.
Surface search: Marconi Type 992Q ❺; E/F-band.
Navigation, HDWS and helicopter control: Kelvin Hughes Type 1006; I-band.
Fire control: Marconi Type 909 ❻; I/J-band (for Sea Dart missile control).
Sonars: Graseby Type 184M; hull-mounted; active search and attack; medium frequency 6—9 kHz.
Kelvin Hughes Type 162M classification set; sideways looking; active; high frequency.

Helicopters: 2 Sea King ❼.

Programmes: Contract signed 18 May 1970 between the Argentine government and Vickers Ltd.

HERCULES   *(Scale 1 : 1,200), Ian Sturton* / 0528400

HERCULES   *6/2001, Argentine Navy* / 0130745

Modernisation: Combat Data System has been improved with local modifications. Refitted in Chile from November 1999 to July 2000 to make flight deck and hanger Sea King capable. Further modifications included removal of MM38 launchers to be replaced by assault boats and possible adaptation of the Sea Dart magazine to accommodate 150 marines. The second of class,

Santisima Trinidad, has been decommissioned and is to be converted into a museum.
Operational: Based at Puerto Belgrano. SAM and Type 909 fire-control radars are probably non-operational. Officially described as an Amphibious command and control ship.

4 ALMIRANTE BROWN (MEKO 360 H2) CLASS (DDGHM)

Name	No	Builders	Laid down	Launched	Commissioned
ALMIRANTE BROWN	D 10	Blohm + Voss, Hamburg	8 Sep 1980	28 Mar 1981	26 Jan 1983
LA ARGENTINA	D 11	Blohm + Voss, Hamburg	30 Mar 1981	25 Sep 1981	4 May 1983
HEROINA	D 12	Blohm + Voss, Hamburg	24 Aug 1981	17 Feb 1982	31 Oct 1983
SARANDI	D 13	Blohm + Voss, Hamburg	9 Mar 1982	31 Aug 1982	16 Apr 1984

Displacement, tons: 2,900 standard; 3,630 full load
Dimensions, feet (metres): 413.1 × 46 × 19 (screws)
 (125.9 × 14 × 5.8)
Main machinery: COGOG; 2 RR Olympus TM3B gas
 turbines; 50,000 hp *(37.4 MW)* sustained
 2 RR Tyne RM1C gas turbines; 9,900 hp *(7.4 MW)*
 sustained; 2 shafts; cp props
Speed, knots: 30.5; 20.5 cruising. **Range, n miles:** 4,500 at 18 kt
Complement: 200 (26 officers)

Missiles: SSM: 8 Aerospatiale MM 40 Exocet (2 quad)
 launchers ❶; inertial cruise; active radar homing to
 70 km *(40 n miles)*; warhead 165 kg; sea-skimmer.
 SAM: Selenia/Elsag Albatros octuple launcher ❷; 24 Aspide;
 semi-active homing to 13 km *(7 n miles)* at 2.5 Mach; height
 envelope 15—5,000 m *(49.2—16,405 ft)*; warhead 30 kg.
Guns: 1 OTO Melara 5 in *(127 mm)*/54 automatic ❸;
 45 rds/min to 23 km *(12.42 n miles)* anti-surface; 7 km
 (3.6 n miles) anti-aircraft; weight of shell 32 kg; also
 fires chaff and illuminants.
 8 Breda/Bofors 40 mm/70 (4 twin) ❹; 300 rds/min to 12.6 km
 (6.8 n miles) anti-surface; 4 km *(2.2 n miles)* anti-aircraft;
 weight of shell 0.96 kg; 2 Oerlikon 20 mm.
Torpedoes: 6—324 mm ILAS 3 (2 triple) tubes ❺. Whitehead A
 244; anti-submarine; active/passive homing to 7 km *(3.8 n
 miles)* at 33 kt; warhead 34 kg (shaped charge); 18 reloads.
Countermeasures: Decoys: CSEE Dagaie double mounting;
 Graseby G1738 towed torpedo decoy system.
 2 Breda 105 mm SCLAR chaff rocket launchers; 20 tubes
 per launcher; can be trained and elevated; chaff to 5 km
 (2.7 n miles); illuminants to 12 km *(6.6 n miles)*.
 ESM/ECM: Sphinx/Scimitar.
Combat data systems: Signaal SEWACO; Link 10/11.
 SATCOMs can be fitted.
Weapons control: 2 Signaal LIROD radar/optronic systems
 ❻ each controlling 2 twin 40 mm mounts; Signaal WM25
 FCS ❼.
Radars: Air/surface search: Signaal DA08A ❽; F-band;
 range 204 km *(110 n miles)* for 2 m² target.
 Surface search: Signaal ZW06 ❾; I-band.
 Navigation: Decca 1226; I-band.
 Fire control: Signaal STIR ❿; I/J/K-band; range 140 km
 (76 n miles) for 1 m² target.
Sonars: Atlas Elektronik 80 (DSQS-21BZ); hull-mounted;
 active search and attack; medium frequency.

Helicopters: AS 555 Fennec ⓫.

Programmes: Six were originally ordered in 1978, but later
 restricted to four when Meko 140 frigates were ordered
 in 1979. Similar to Nigerian frigate *Aradu*.
Modernisation: Block II Exocet MM 40 may be fitted when
 funds are available.
Operational: *Almirante Brown* took part in allied Gulf
 operations in late 1990. Fennec helicopters delivered in
 1996 provide over the horizon targeting for SSMs and
 have the potential to improve ASW capability. All are
 active and form 2nd Destroyer Squadron based at Puerto
 Belgrano. All can be used as Flagships. Half-life refits
 planned, subject to funding.

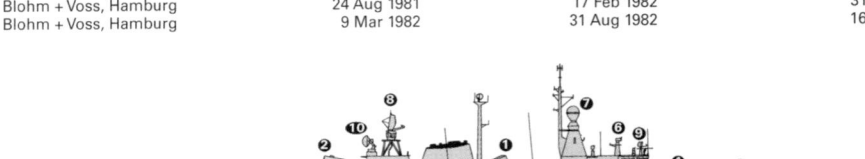

ALMIRANTE BROWN

(Scale 1 : 1,200), Ian Sturton / 0569252

LA ARGENTINA

11/2002, Mario R V Carneiro / 0528303

ALMIRANTE BROWN

10/2005*, Mario R V Carneiro / 1151089

FRIGATES

6 ESPORA (MEKO 140 A16) CLASS (FFGH)

Name	No	Builders	Laid down	Launched	Commissioned
ESPORA	41	AFNE, Rio Santiago	3 Oct 1980	23 Jan 1982	5 July 1985
ROSALES	42	AFNE, Rio Santiago	1 July 1981	4 Mar 1983	14 Nov 1986
SPIRO	43	AFNE, Rio Santiago	4 Jan 1982	24 June 1983	24 Nov 1987
PARKER	44	AFNE, Rio Santiago	2 Aug 1982	31 Mar 1984	17 Apr 1990
ROBINSON	45	AFNE, Rio Santiago	8 June 1983	15 Feb 1985	28 Aug 2000
GOMEZ ROCA	46	AFNE, Rio Santiago	1 Dec 1983	14 Nov 1986	20 May 2004

Displacement, tons: 1,470 standard; 1,850 full load
Dimensions, feet (metres): 299.1 × 36.4 × 11.2
(91.2 × 11.1 × 3.4)
Main machinery: 2 SEMT-Pielstick 16 PC2-5 V 400 diesels;
20,400 hp(m) (15 MW) sustained; 2 shafts
Speed, knots: 28
Range, n miles: 4,000 at 18 kt
Complement: 93 (11 officers)

Missiles: SSM: 4 Aerospatiale MM 38 Exocet ❶ inertial
cruise; active radar homing to 42 km (23 n miles);
warhead 165 kg; sea-skimmer.
Guns: 1 OTO Melara 3 in (76 mm)/62 compact ❷; 85 rds/min
to 16 km (8.7 n miles) anti-surface; 12 km (6.5 n miles)
anti-aircraft; weight of shell 6 kg; also fires chaff and
illuminants.
4 Breda 40 mm/70 (2 twin) ❸; 300 rds/min to 12.5 km
(6.8 n miles); weight of shell 0.96 kg; ready ammunition
736 (or 444) using AP tracer, impact or proximity fuzing.
2—12.7 mm MGs.
Torpedoes: 6—324 mm ILAS 3 (2 triple) tubes ❹. Whitehead
A 244/S; anti-submarine; active/passive homing to 7 km
(3.8 n miles) at 33 kt; warhead 34 kg (shaped charge).
Countermeasures: Decoys: CSEE Dagaie double mounting;
10 or 6 replaceable containers; trainable; chaff to 12 km
(6.5 n miles); illuminants to 4 km (2.2 n miles); decoys in
H- to J-bands.
ESM: Racal RQN-3B; radar warning.
ECM: Racal TQN-2X; jammer.
Combat data systems: Signaal SEWACO.
Weapons control: Signaal WM22/41 integrated system;
1 LIROD 8 optronic director ❺ (plus 2 sights-1 on each
bridge wing).
Radars: Air/surface search: Signaal DA05 ❻; E/F-band;
range 137 km (75 n miles) for 2 m² target.
Navigation: Decca TM 1226; I-band.
Fire control: Signaal WM28 ❼; I/J-band; range 46 km
(25 n miles).
IFF: Mk 10.
Sonars: Atlas Elektronik ASO 4; hull-mounted; active search
and attack; medium frequency.

Helicopters: 1 SA 319B Alouette III or AS 555 Fennec ❽
(in 44—46).

Programmes: A contract was signed with Blohm + Voss on
1 August 1979 for this group of ships which are scaled down
Meko 360s. All have been fabricated in AFNE, Rio Santiago.
The last pair were to have been scrapped, but on 8 May
1997 a decision was taken to complete them some 14 years
after each was first launched. A formal restart ceremony
was held on 18 July 1997 and Robinson became operational
in 2001. Gomez Roca became operational in late 2005.
Modernisation: Plans to fit MM 40 Exocet from Meko 360.
Flight deck extensions for AS 555 helicopters. Robinson
and Gomez Roca may have different EW suite.
Structure: Parker retro-fitted with a telescopic hangar
which has been fitted on build to the last two ships. The
first three ships may be retro-fitted at a later date.
Operational: Mostly used for offshore patrol and fishery
protection duties but Spiro and Rosales sent to the Gulf
in 1990-91. Form 2nd Frigate Squadron based at Puerto
Belgrano.

PARKER
(Scale 1 : 900), Ian Sturton / 0012007

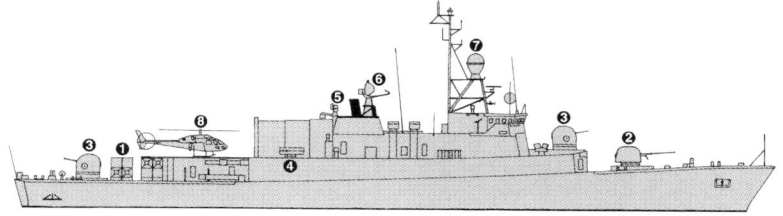

PARKER
5/2004, A E Galarce / 1044067

ROBINSON
10/2005, Mario R V Carneiro*
1151090

SPIRO

7/2005, A E Galarce* / 1151091

3 DRUMMOND (TYPE A 69) CLASS (FFG)

Name	No	Builders	Laid down	Launched	Commissioned
DRUMMOND (ex-*Good Hope*, ex-*Lieutenant de Vaisseau le Hénaff* F 789)	31	Lorient Naval Dockyard	12 Mar 1976	5 Mar 1977	Mar 1978
GUERRICO (ex-*Transvaal*, ex-*Commandant l'Herminier* F 791)	32	Lorient Naval Dockyard	1 Oct 1976	13 Sep 1977	Oct 1978
GRANVILLE	33	Lorient Naval Dockyard	1 Dec 1978	28 June 1980	22 June 1981

Displacement, tons: 950 standard; 1,170 full load
Dimensions, feet (metres): 262.5 × 33.8 × 9.8; 18 (sonar)
(80 × 10.3 × 3; 5.5)
Main machinery: 2 SEMT-Pielstick 12 PC2.2 V 400 diesels;
12,000 hp(m) (8.82 MW) sustained; 2 shafts; LIPS cp props
Speed, knots: 23
Range, n miles: 4,500 at 15 kt; 3,000 at 18 kt
Complement: 93 (10 officers)

Missiles: SSM: 4 Aerospatiale MM 38 Exocet (2 twin)
launchers ❶; inertial cruise; active radar homing to
42 km (23 n miles); warhead 165 kg; sea-skimmer.
Guns: 1 Creusot-Loire 3.9 in (100 mm)/55 Mod 1953 ❷; 80°
elevation; 60 rds/min to 17 km (9 n miles) anti-surface;
8 km (4.4 n miles) anti-aircraft; weight of shell 13.5 kg.
2 Breda 40 mm/70 (twin) ❸; 300 rds/min to 12.5 km
(6.8 n miles); weight of shell 0.96 kg; ready ammunition
736 (or 444) using AP tracer, impact or proximity fuzing.
2 Oerlikon 20 mm ❹. 2—12.7 mm MGs.
Torpedoes: 6—324 mm Mk 32 (2 triple) tubes ❺. Whitehead A
244; anti-submarine; active/passive homing to 7 km
(3.8 n miles) at 33 kt; warhead 34 kg.
Countermeasures: Decoys: CSEE Dagaie double mounting;
10 or 6 replaceable containers; trainable; chaff to 12 km
(6.5 n miles); illuminants to 4 km (2.2 n miles); decoys in
H- to J-bands or Corvus sextuple launchers for chaff.
ESM: DR 2000/DALIA 500; radar warning.
ECM: Thomson-CSF Alligator; jammer.
Combat data systems: MINIACO.
Weapons control: Thomson-CSF Vega system. CSEE Panda
Mk 2 optical director ❻. Naja optronic director (for 40 mm
guns).
Radars: Air/surface search: Thomson-CSF DRBV 51A ❼ with
UPX12 IFF; G-band.
Navigation: Decca 1226; I-band.
Fire control: Thomson-CSF DRBC 32E ❽; I/J-band (for
100 m gun).
Sonars: Thomson Sintra Diodon; hull-mounted; active
search and attack.

Programmes: The first pair was originally built for the
French Navy and sold to the South African Navy in 1976
while under construction. As a result of a UN embargo
on arms sales to South Africa this sale was cancelled.
Purchased by Argentina in Autumn 1978. Both arrived

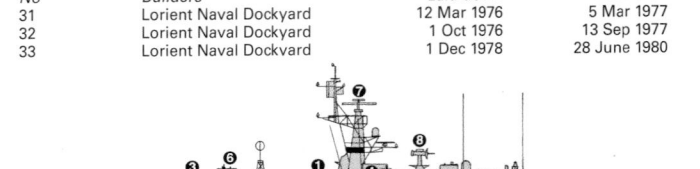

GRANVILLE *(Scale 1 : 900), Ian Sturton* / 0506262

DRUMMOND *5/2004, A E Galarce* / 1044066

in Argentina 2 November 1978 (third ship being ordered
shortly afterwards) and all have proved very popular
ships in the Argentine Navy. The transfer of a further
three of the class from the French Navy is very unlikely.
Modernisation: *Drummond* has had her armament
updated to the same standard as the other two, replacing

the Bofors 40/60. It is reported that a SENIT combat
data system may have been installed but this is not
confirmed.
Operational: Endurance, 15 days. Very economical in fuel
consumption. Assisted in UN operations off Haiti in 1994.
All based at Mar del Plata.

GRANVILLE *12/2002, A E Galarce* / 0529818

SHIPBORNE AIRCRAFT

Numbers/Type: 5 Aerospatiale SA 316B Alouette III.
Operational speed: 113 kt (210 km/h).
Service ceiling: 10,500 ft (3,200 m).
Range: 290 n miles (540 km).
Role/Weapon systems: ASW Helicopter; used for liaison in peacetime; wartime role
includes commando assault and ASW/ASVW. Sensors: Nose-mounted search radar.
Weapons: ASW; 2 × Mk 44 torpedoes. ASV; 2 × AS12 missiles.

Numbers/Type: 4 Aerospatiale AS 555 Fennec.
Operational speed: 121 kt (225 km/h).
Service ceiling: 13,125 ft (4,000 m).
Range: 389 n miles (722 km).
Role/Weapon systems: Principal role OTHT with potential ASW capability. Delivered in
1996. More are wanted. Sensors: Bendix RDR 1500 radar; Mk 3 MAD. Weapons: ASW;
2 × A 244 torpedoes or 4 depth bombs may be fitted.

ALOUETTE III *7/2004, A E Galarce* / 1044070

FENNEC *7/2004*, A E Galarce* / 1044071

Numbers/Type: 2/5 Agusta-Sikorsky ASH-3H/AS-61D Sea King.
Operational speed: 120 kt *(222 km/h)*.
Service ceiling: 12,205 ft *(3,720 m)*.
Range: 630 n miles *(1,165 km)*.
Role/Weapon systems: ASW Helicopter; with limited surface search capability. Can operate from *Hercules*. Sensors: APS-705 search radar, Bendix AQS 18 sonar. Weapons: ASW; up to 4 × A 244 torpedoes or 4 × depth bombs. ASV: 1 AM 39 Exocet ASM.

SEA KING *8/2002, A E Galarce* / 0529816

Numbers/Type: 7 Bell UH-1H.
Operational speed: 110 kt *(204 km/h)*.
Service ceiling: 15,000 ft *(4,570 m)*.
Range: 250 n miles *(463 km)*.
Role/Weapon systems: First pair acquired for the Marines in 1999. Six more in 2000. Seven remain in service. Sensors: none. Weapons: 2—7.62 mm MGs.

UH-1H *3/2001* / 0126382

LAND-BASED MARITIME AIRCRAFT

Notes: (1) In addition there are three Fokker F28 for Logistic Support; one Pilatus PC-6B for reconnaissance and nine Beech T-34 Turbo Mentor training aircraft. The four Lockheed Electra L-188 are no longer in service.
(2) Thirty-six ex-US Navy A4M Skyhawk with radar APG-66 acquired by the Air Force by July 1998. First 18 delivered in crates in 1995-96 and remainder modernised before delivery in 1997-98.
(3) Acquisition of second-hand Mirage 2000 aircraft is reported to be under consideration.

Numbers/Type: 5 + (6) Dassault-Breguet Super Etendard.
Operational speed: Mach 1.
Service ceiling: 44,950 ft *(13,700 m)*.
Range: 920 n miles *(1,700 km)*.
Role/Weapon systems: Strike Fighter with anti-shipping ability. In the past have flown from US or Brazilian aircraft carriers. Five aircraft are operational out of a total of eleven. Strike, air defence and ASV roles. Hi-lo-hi combat radius 460 n miles *(850 km)*. Sensors: Thomson-CSF Agave multimode radar, ECM. Weapons: Strike; 2.1 tons of 'iron' bombs. ASVW; 1 AM 39 Exocet or 1 × Martin Pescador missiles. Self-defence; 2 × Magic AAMs. Standard; 2 × 30 mm cannon.

SUPER ETENDARD *7/1999, A E Galarce* / 0056474

Numbers/Type: 5 Grumman S-2ET Tracker.
Operational speed: 130 kt *(241 km/h)*.
Service ceiling: 25,000 ft *(7,620 m)*.
Range: 1,350 n miles *(2,500 km)*.
Role/Weapon systems: Used for MR and EEZ patrol. One shipped to Israel in 1989 for Garrett turboprop installation. Prototype for fleet conversion in Argentina when completed in 2000. Sensors: EL/M-2022 search radar up to 32 sonobuoys, ALD-2B or AES 210/E ESM, echo-ranging depth charges. Weapons: ASW; A 244 torpedoes, bombs and depth charges.

S-2 TRACKER (landing on São Paulo) *5/2002, Walter Lastra/Fuerzas Navales* / 0528430

Numbers/Type: 6 Aermacchi MB-326GB.
Operational speed: 468 kt *(867 km/h)*.
Service ceiling: 47,000 ft *(14,325 m)*.
Range: 1,320 n miles *(2,446 km)*.
Role/Weapon systems: Light Attack; supplements anti-shipping/strike; also has training role. Weapons: ASV; 1.8 tons of 'iron' bombs. Strike; 6 × rockets. Recce; underwing camera pod.

AERMACCHI 326 *4/2004** / 0051048

Numbers/Type: 4 Beechcraft B 200M Cormoran.
Operational speed: 260 kt *(482 km/h)*.
Service ceiling: 31,000 ft *(9,448 m)*.
Range: 2,000 n miles *(3,705 km)*.
Role/Weapon systems: Multipurpose converted to Cormoran version for maritime patrol. There are three other unconverted aircraft. Sensors: Search radar. Weapons: Unarmed.

BEECH CORMORAN *5/2004* / 0570789

Numbers/Type: 6 Lockheed P-3B Orion.
Operational speed: 410 kt *(760 km/h)*.
Service ceiling: 28,300 ft *(8,625 m)*.
Range: 4,000 m *(7,410 km)*.
Role/Weapon systems: Two acquired in 1997 from US; four more in 1998, and two for spares in 1999. Sensors: APS-115 radar; ESM. Weapons: ASW equipment may be carried in due course. ASV weapons may be fitted in due course. Electronic equipment from L-188E may be fitted in one aircraft.

ORION *6/2002, Argentine Navy* / 0528429

PATROL FORCES

Notes: Project PAM (Patrulleros de Alta Mar) is for up to five 1,800 ton offshore patrol vessels. With a length of over 80 m, the ships are to have diesel propulsion and to be armed with a 40 mm gun. The project has been delayed by funding problems but a call for bids is expected in 2006.

3 CHEROKEE CLASS (PATROL SHIPS) (PSO)

Name	No	Builders	Commissioned
COMANDANTE GENERAL IRIGOYEN (ex-*Cahuilla*)	A 1	Charleston SB and DD Co	10 Mar 1945
FRANCISCO DE GURRUCHAGA (ex-*Luiseno* ATF 156)	A 3	Charleston SB and DD Co	16 June 1945
SUBOFICIAL CASTILLO (ex-*Takelma* ATF 113)	A 6	United Engineering Co, Alameda	3 Aug 1944

Displacement, tons: 1,235 standard; 1,731 full load
Dimensions, feet (metres): 205 × 38.5 × 17 *(62.5 × 11.7 × 5.2)*
Main machinery: Diesel-electric; 4 GM 12−278 diesels; 4,400 hp *(3.28 MW)*; 4 generators; 1 motor; 3,000 hp *(2.24 MW)*; 1 shaft
Speed, knots: 16
Range, n miles: 6,500 at 15 kt; 15,000 at 8 kt
Complement: 85
Guns: 4 Bofors 40/60 (2 twin). 2 Oerlikon 20 mm; 4 Bofors 40 mm/60 (2 twin) (A 1); 2 Bofors 40 mm/60 (A 3); 1 Bofors 40 mm/60 (A 6); 2 Oerlikon 20 mm/70 (A 1); 4 Oerlikon 20 mm (A 3, A 6); 2−12.7 mm MGs (A 6).
Radars: Surface search: Racal Decca 626; I-band.
Navigation: Racal Decca 1230; I-band.

Comment: Fitted with powerful pumps and other salvage equipment. *Comandante General Irigoyen* transferred by the US at San Diego, California, on 9 July 1961. Classified as a tug until 1966 when she was rerated as patrol ship. *Francisco De Gurruchaga* transferred on 24 July 1975 by sale, *Suboficial Castillo* on 30 September 1993 by grant aid. Armament has been reduced. All operational and based at Mar del Plata.

SUBOFICIAL CASTILLO 7/2004*, A E Galarce / 1044072

2 KING CLASS (PATROL SHIPS) (AX)

Name	No	Builders	Launched	Commissioned
MURATURE	P 20	Base Nav Rio Santiago	5 July 1943	12 Apr 1945
KING	P 21	Base Nav Rio Santiago	2 Nov 1943	28 July 1946

Displacement, tons: 913 standard; 1,000 normal; 1,032 full load
Dimensions, feet (metres): 252.7 × 29.5 × 13.1 *(77 × 9 × 4)*
Main machinery: 2 Werkspoor diesels; 2,500 hp(m) *(1.8 MW)*; 2 shafts
Speed, knots: 18
Range, n miles: 9,000 at 12 kt
Complement: 130
Guns: 3 Vickers 4 in *(105 mm)*/45; 16 rds/min to 19 km *(10 n miles)*; weight of shell 16 kg. 4 Bofors 40 mm/60 (1 twin, 2 single); 120 rds/min/barrel to 10 km *(5.5 n miles)*; weight of shell 0.89 kg. 5−12.7 mm MGs.
Radars: Surface search: Racal Decca 1226; I-band.

Comment: Named after Captain John King, an Irish follower of Admiral Brown, who distinguished himself in the war with Brazil, 1826-28; and Captain Jose Murature, who performed conspicuous service against the Paraguayans at the Battle of Cuevas in 1865. *King* laid down June 1938. *Murature* March 1940. Both used for cadet training.

KING 7/2003, A E Galarce / 0572404

1 OLIVIERI CLASS (PATROL SHIP) (PBO)

Name	No	Builders	Commissioned
TENIENTE OLIVIERI (ex-*Marsea 10*)	A 2	Quality SB, Louisiana	1981

Displacement, tons: 1,640 full load
Dimensions, feet (metres): 184.8 × 40 × 14 *(56.3 × 12.2 × 4.3)*
Main machinery: 2 GM/EMD 16-645 E6; 3,230 hp *(2.4 MW)* sustained; 2 shafts; bow thruster
Speed, knots: 14
Range, n miles: 2,800 at 10 kt
Complement: 15 (4 officers)
Guns: 2−12.7 mm MGs.

Comment: Built by Quality Shipyards, New Orleans, as an oilfield support ship but rated as an Aviso. Acquired from US Maritime Administration 15 November 1987. Capable of carrying 600 tons of stores and 800 tons of liquids. Based at Puerto Belgrano.

TENIENTE OLIVIERI 3/2000 / 0104168

1 SOTOYOMO CLASS (PATROL SHIP) (PBO)

Name	No	Builders	Commissioned
ALFEREZ SOBRAL (ex-*Salish* ATA 187)	A 9	Levingstone, Orange	9 Sep 1944

Displacement, tons: 800 full load
Dimensions, feet (metres): 143 × 33.9 × 13 *(43.6 × 10.3 × 4)*
Main machinery: Diesel-electric; 2 GM 12-278A diesels; 2,200 hp *(1.64 MW)*; 2 generators; 1 motor; 1,500 hp *(1.12 MW)*; 1 shaft
Speed, knots: 12.5
Range, n miles: 16,500 at 8 kt
Complement: 49
Guns: 1 Bofors 40 mm/60. 2 Oerlikon 20 mm.
Radars: Surface search: Decca 1226; I-band.

Comment: Former US ocean tug transferred on 10 February 1972. Paid off in 1987 but back in service by 1996. Armament has been reduced.

ALFEREZ SOBRAL 2/2001*, Eric Grove / 1127024

4 BARADERO (DABUR) CLASS (COASTAL PATROL CRAFT) (PB)

Name	No	Builders	Commissioned
BARADERO	P 61	Israel Aircraft Industries	1978
BARRANQUERAS	P 62	Israel Aircraft Industries	1978
CLORINDA	P 63	Israel Aircraft Industries	1978
CONCEPCIÓN DEL URUGUAY	P 64	Israel Aircraft Industries	1978

Displacement, tons: 33.7 standard; 39 full load
Dimensions, feet (metres): 64.9 × 18 × 5.8 *(19.8 × 5.5 × 1.8)*
Main machinery: 2 GM 12V-71TA diesels; 840 hp *(627 kW)* sustained; 2 shafts
Speed, knots: 19
Range, n miles: 450 at 13 kt
Complement: 9
Guns: 2 Oerlikon 20 mm. 4−12.7 mm MGs.
Depth charges: 2 portable rails.
Radars: Navigation: Decca 101; I-band.

Comment: Of all-aluminium construction. Employed in 1991 and 1992 as part of the UN Central American peacekeeping force. Based at Ushuaia.

BARADERO CLASS 12/2000*, Eric Grove / 1044073

2 INTREPIDA CLASS (TYPE TNC 45)
(FAST ATTACK CRAFT—GUN/MISSILE) (PGGF)

Name	No	Builders	Launched	Commissioned
INTREPIDA	P 85	Lürssen, Bremen	2 Dec 1973	20 July 1974
INDOMITA	P 86	Lürssen, Bremen	8 Apr 1974	12 Dec 1974

Displacement, tons: 268 full load
Dimensions, feet (metres): 147.3 × 24.3 × 7.9 *(44.9 × 7.4 × 2.4)*
Main machinery: 4 MTU MD 16V 538 TB90 diesels; 12,000 hp(m) *(8.82 MW)*; 4 shafts
Speed, knots: 38
Range, n miles: 1,450 at 20 kt
Complement: 39 (5 officers)
Missiles: SSM: 2 Aerospatiale Exocet mm 38 *(Intrepida)*; active radar homing to 42 km *(23 n miles)*; warhead 165 kg.
Guns: 1 OTO Melara 3 in *(76 mm)*/62 compact; 85 rds/min to 16 km *(9 n miles)* anti-surface; 12 km *(6.5 n miles)* anti-aircraft; weight of shell 6 kg.
 1 or 2 Bofors 40 mm/70; 330 rds/min to 12 km *(6.5 n miles)* anti-surface; 4 km *(2.2 n miles)* anti-aircraft; weight of shell 0.89 kg.
 2—12.7 mm MGs.
 2 Oerlikon 81 mm rocket launchers for illuminants.
Torpedoes: 2—21 in *(533 mm)* launchers. AEG SST-4; wire-guided; active/passive homing to 28 km *(15 n miles)* at 23 kt; warhead 250 kg.
Countermeasures: ESM: Racal RDL 1; radar warning.
Weapons control: Signaal WM22 optronic for guns/missiles. Signaal M11 for torpedo guidance and control.
Radars: Surface search: Decca 626; I-band.

Comment: These two vessels were ordered in 1970. Both are painted with a brown/green camouflage. Camouflage netting can also be fitted. Exocet SSM fitted vice the forward of the two Bofors guns in *Intrepida* in 1998. There have been unconfirmed reports that *Indomita* was similarly refitted in 2004.

INTREPIDA   *6/2001, Argentine Navy* / 0130735

INTREPIDA (with camouflage netting)   *3/2001* / 0126381

2 POINT CLASS (PB)

Name	No	Builders	Commissioned
PUNTA MOGOTES (ex-*Point Hobart*)	P 65 (ex-82377)	J Martinac, Tacoma	13 July 1970
RIO SANTIAGO (ex-*Point Carrew*)	P 66 (ex-82374)	USCG Yard, Curtis Bay	18 May 1970

Displacement, tons: 67 full load
Dimensions, feet (metres): 83 × 17.2 × 15.8 *(25.3 × 5.2 × 1.8)*
Main machinery: 2 Caterpillar diesels; 1,600 hp *(1.19 MW)*; 2 shafts
Speed, knots: 22
Range, n miles: 1,200 at 8 kt
Complement: 10
Guns: 2—12.7 mm MGs.
Radars: Surface search: Raytheon SPS 64; I-band.

Comment: *Punta Mogotes* transferred from US Coast Guard on 8 July 1999 and is based at Mar del Plata. *Rio Santiago* transferred 22 August 2000.

RIO SANTIAGO   *10/2004*, A E Galarce* / 1151100

AMPHIBIOUS FORCES

Notes: (1) Marine Corps acquired two Guardian craft in October 1999 and two more in February 2000. Powered by twin 150 hp Johnson outboards. Carry 1—12.7 mm MG and 4—7.62 mm MGs, Raytheon radar.
(2) A new class of indigenously built LCVPs is to start entering service in 2005.

GUARDIAN 35   *5/2004, A E Galarce* / 1044075

0 + 1 (1) OURAGAN CLASS (LANDING SHIPS DOCK) (LSDH)

Name	No	Builders	Laid down	Launched	Commissioned
GIACHINO (ex-*Ouragan*)	— (ex-L 9021)	Brest Naval Dockyard	June 1966	22 Apr 1967	1 Apr 1968

Displacement, tons: 5,800 light; 8,500 full load; 14,400 when fully docked down
Dimensions, feet (metres): 488.9 × 75.4 × 17.7 (28.5 flooded) *(149 × 23 × 5.4 (8.7))*
Main machinery: 2 SEMT-Pielstick diesels; 8,640 hp(m) *(6.35 MW) (Ouragan)*; 9,400 hp(m) *(6.91 MW) (Orage)*; 2 shafts; LIPS cp props
Speed, knots: 17
Range, n miles: 9,000 at 15 kt
Complement: 205 (12 officers)
Military lift: 343 troops (plus 129 short haul only); 2 LCTs (EDIC) with 11 light tanks each or 8 loaded CTMs; logistic load 1,500 tons; 2 cranes (35 tons each)
Missiles: SAM: 2 Matra Simbad twin launchers; Mistral; IR homing to 4 km *(2.2 n miles)*; warhead 3 kg; anti-sea-skimmer.
Guns: 2 Breda/Mauser 30 mm/70. 4—12.7 mm MGs.
Weapons control: 2 Sagem VIGY-105 optronic systems.
Radars: Air/surface search: Thomson-CSF DRBV 51A; G-band.
Navigation: 2 Racal Decca DRBN 34A; I-band.

Helicopters: 4 SA 321G Super Frelon or 10 SA 319B Alouette III.

Programmes: Intentions to acquire ex-French Navy Ouragan class assault ships confirmed in 2005. It is expected that ex-*Ouragan* is to be transferred in 2006 with ex-*Orage* to follow, probably as a source of spares, in 2007.
Modernisation: While in French service, Simbad SAM and new search radars fitted in 1993. It is not known whether Sagem VIGY-105 optronic fire-control system and 30 mm guns, fitted to replace the 40 mm gun, are to be transferred to Argentina. Ex-*Orage* has an enclosed Flag bridge. Ex-*Ouragan* sonar has been removed.
Structure: Bridge is on the starboard side. Three LCVPs can also be carried. Extensive workshops. Flight deck is 900 m²; docking well 120 × 13.2 m with 3 m of water. Two 35 ton cranes.
Operational: A 400 ton ship can be docked. Command facilities for directing amphibious and helicopter operations.

OURAGAN CLASS   *9/2005*, B Prézelin* / 1151099

4 LCM 6 CLASS (LCM) and 16 LCVPS

EDM 1, 2, 3, 4	EDVP 30-37	+ 8

Displacement, tons: 56 full load
Dimensions, feet (metres): 56 × 14 × 3.9 *(17.1 × 4.3 × 1.2)*
Main machinery: 2 Gray 64 HN9 diesels; 330 hp *(246 kW)* sustained; 2 shafts
Speed, knots: 11
Range, n miles: 130 at 10 kt
Military lift: 30 tons
Guns: 2—12.7 mm MGs.

Comment: Details given are for the LCMs acquired from the US in June 1971. The LCVPs are split between those acquired from the USA in 1970 and a smaller variant built locally since 1971.

MINE WARFARE FORCES

Notes: Options for the replacement of the deleted Ton class MCMV are under consideration.

SURVEY AND RESEARCH SHIPS

Notes: (1) There are also two Fisheries Research Ships employed by the government. These are *Oca Balda* and *Eduardo Holmberg*.
(2) Two 10 m hydrographic launches, *Monte Blanco* and *Kualchink* entered service in 2004.

1 SURVEY SHIP (AGOB)

Name	No	Builders	Commissioned
PUERTO DESEADO	Q 20 (ex-Q 8)	Astarsa, San Fernando	26 Feb 1979

Displacement, tons: 2,133 standard; 2,400 full load
Dimensions, feet (metres): 251.9 × 51.8 × 21.3 *(76.8 × 15.8 × 6.5)*
Main machinery: 2 Fiat-GMT diesels; 3,600 hp(m) *(2.65 MW)*; 1 shaft
Speed, knots: 15
Range, n miles: 12,000 at 12 kt
Complement: 61 (12 officers) plus 20 scientists
Radars: Navigation: Decca 1629; I-band.

Comment: Laid down on 17 March 1976 for Consejo Nacional de Investigaciones Tecnicas y Scientificas. Launched on 4 December 1976. For survey work fitted with: four Hewlett-Packard 2108-A, gravimeter, magnetometer, seismic systems, high-frequency sonar, geological laboratory. Omega and NAVSAT equipped. Painted with an orange hull in late 1996 for Antarctic deployments.

PUERTO DESEADO   *11/2004*, A E Galarce* / 1151098

1 RESEARCH SHIP (AGOR)

Name	No	Builders	Commissioned
COMODORO RIVADAVIA	Q 11	Mestrina, Tigre	6 Dec 1974

Displacement, tons: 820 full load
Dimensions, feet (metres): 171.2 × 28.9 × 8.5 *(52.2 × 8.8 × 2.6)*
Main machinery: 2 Stork Werkspoor RHO-218K diesels; 1,160 hp(m) *(853 kW)*; 2 shafts
Speed, knots: 12
Range, n miles: 6,000 at 12 kt
Complement: 34 (8 officers)

Comment: Laid down on 17 July 1971 and launched on 2 December 1972. Used for research.

COMODORO RIVADAVIA   *3/2001* / 0126380

1 SURVEY CRAFT (AGSC)

Name	No	Builders	Commissioned
CORMORAN	Q 15	AFNE, Rio Santiago	20 Feb 1964

Displacement, tons: 102 full load
Dimensions, feet (metres): 83 × 16.4 × 5.9 *(25.3 × 5 × 1.8)*
Main machinery: 2 GM 6—71 diesels; 440 hp(m) *(323 kW)*; 2 shafts
Speed, knots: 11
Complement: 19 (3 officers)
Radars: Navigation: Decca TM1226; I-band.

Comment: Launched 10 August 1963. Classified as a coastal launch.

CORMORAN   *5/2003, A E Galarce* / 0572406

TRAINING SHIPS

Notes: There are also three small yachts: *Itati* (Q 73), *Fortuna I* (Q 74) and *Fortuna II* (Q 75) plus a 25 ton yawl *Tijuca* acquired in 1993. *Fortuna III* was commissioned in 2004. A further yacht, *Irene* was acquired in 2005.

1 SAIL TRAINING SHIP (AXS)

Name	No	Builders	Commissioned
LIBERTAD	Q 2	AFNE, Rio Santiago	28 May 1963

Displacement, tons: 3,025 standard; 3,765 full load
Dimensions, feet (metres): 262 wl; 301 oa × 45.3 × 21.8 *(79.9; 91.7 × 13.8 × 6.6)*
Main machinery: 2 Sulzer diesels; 2,400 hp(m) *(1.76 MW)*; 2 shafts
Speed, knots: 13.5 under power
Range, n miles: 12,000 at 8 kt
Complement: 200 crew plus 150 cadets
Guns: 4 Hotchkiss 47 mm saluting guns.
Radars: Navigation: Decca; I-band.

Comment: Launched 30 May 1956. She set record for crossing the North Atlantic under sail in 1966. Sail area, 26,835 m². Based at Puerto Belgrano. Undergoing mid-life refit 2004-06.

LIBERTAD   *8/2003, Derek Fox* / 0569147

AUXILIARIES

Notes: A project for the acquisition of an Antarctic support vessel has been initiated.

1 DURANCE CLASS (AORH)

Name	No	Builders	Launched	Commissioned
PATAGONIA (ex-*Durance*)	B 1 (ex-A 629)	Brest Naval Dockyard	6 Sep 1975	1 Dec 1976

Displacement, tons: 17,900 full load
Dimensions, feet (metres): 515.9 × 69.5 × 38.5 *(157.3 × 21.2 × 10.8)*
Main machinery: 2 SEMT-Pielstick 16 PC2.5 V 400 diesels; 20,800 hp(m) *(15.3 MW)* sustained; 2 shafts; LIPS cp props
Speed, knots: 19
Range, n miles: 9,000 at 15 kt
Complement: 164 (10 officers) plus 29 spare
Cargo capacity: 9,000 tons fuel; 500 tons Avcat; 130 distilled water; 170 victuals; 150 munitions; 50 naval stores
Guns: 2 Bofors 40 mm/60. 4—12.7 mm MGs.
Countermeasures: ESM/ECM.
Radars: Navigation: 2 Racal Decca 1226; I-band.
Helicopters: 1 Alouette III.

Comment: Acquired from France on 12 July 1999 having been in reserve for two years. Entered Argentine Navy service in July 2000 after short refit.

PATAGONIA   *5/2000, A E Galarce* / 0104175

3 CHARTERED SHIPS (AKS/AOTL)

Name	No	Builders	Commissioned	Chartered
INGENIERO JULIO KRAUSE	B 13	Astarsa, Tigre	1981	1992
ASTRA FEDERICO	B 8	Astarsa, Tigre	1981	1992
ASTRA VALENTINA	B 9	Astarsa, Tigre	1982	1992

Comment: Taken over by the Navy but also used for commercial trading. *Krause* is a 10,000 ton oiler, the other pair are 30,000 ton cargo ships. All have civilian crews.

ASTRA VALENTINA   *5/2000, Hartmut Ehlers* / 0104174

3 COSTA SUR CLASS (TRANSPORT) (AKS)

Name	No	Builders	Commissioned
CANAL BEAGLE	B 3	Astillero Principe y Menghi SA	29 Apr 1978
BAHIA SAN BLAS	B 4	Astillero Principe y Menghi SA	27 Nov 1978
CABO DE HORNOS	B 5	Astillero Principe y Menghi SA	28 June 1979
(ex-*Bahia Camarones*)			

Measurement, tons: 5,800 dwt; 4,600 gross
Dimensions, feet (metres): 390.3 × 57.4 × 21 *(119 × 17.5 × 6.4)*
Main machinery: 2 AFNE-Sulzer diesels; 6,400 hp(m) *(4.7 MW)*; 2 shafts
Speed, knots: 16.5
Complement: 40

Comment: Ordered December 1975. Laid down 10 January 1977, 11 April 1977 and 29 April 1978. Launched 19 October 1977, 29 April 1978 and 4 November 1978. Used to supply offshore research installations in Naval Area South. One operated in the Gulf in 1991. *Bahia San Blas* painted grey in 1998 indicating an active naval role in amphibious support operations. Capable of carrying up to eight LCVPs on deck. 132 troops can be accommodated in containers. The ship is to be fitted with a helicopter deck.

BAHIA SAN BLAS (LCVPs embarked)   *5/2000, A E Galarce* / 0104176

CANAL BEAGLE   *8/1999, P Marsan* / 0081446

3 RED CLASS (BUOY TENDERS) (ABU)

Name	No	Builders	Commissioned
PUNTA ALTA (ex-*Red Birch*)	Q 63 (ex-WLM 687)	CG Yard, Maryland	19 Feb 1965
CIUDAD DE ZARATE	Q 61 (ex-WLM 688)	CG Yard, Maryland	1 Aug 1970
(ex-*Red Cedar*)			
CIUDAD DE ROSARIO	Q 62 (ex-WLM 685)	CG Yard, Maryland	4 Apr 1964
(ex-*Red Wood*)			

Displacement, tons: 525 full load
Dimensions, feet (metres): 161.1 × 33 × 6 *(49.1 × 10.1 × 1.8)*
Main machinery: 2 Caterpillar D398 diesels; 1,800 hp *(1.34 MW)*; 2 shafts; cp props; bow thruster
Speed, knots: 12. **Range, n miles:** 2,248 at 11 kt
Complement: 31 (6 officers)
Guns: 2 — 12.7 mm MGs.

Comment: Ex-USCG buoy tenders. First one transferred on 10 June 1998 and recommissioned on 17 November 1998. Two more transferred 30 July 1999. Strengthened hull for light ice breaking. Equipped with a 10 ton boom. *Punta Alta* used as supply ship in the southern archipelago. The other pair are used as river supply ships.

CIUDAD DE ZARATE   *11/2004*, A E Galarce* / 1151097

2 FLOATING DOCKS

Number	Dimensions, feet (metres)	Capacity, tons
Y 1 (ex-ARD 23)	492 × 88.6 × 56 *(150 × 27 × 17.1)*	3,500
3	215.8 × 46 × 45.5 *(65.8 × 14 × 13.7)*	750

Comment: First one is at Mar del Plata naval base, the second at Puerto Belgrano. The ex-USN ARD was transferred 8 September 1993 by grant aid. All other docks have been sold.

ICEBREAKERS

1 SUPPORT SHIP (AGB/AGOB)

Name	No	Builders	Launched	Commissioned
ALMIRANTE IRIZAR	Q 5	Wärtsilä, Helsinki	3 Feb 1978	15 Dec 1978

Displacement, tons: 14,900 full load
Dimensions, feet (metres): 398.1 × 82 × 31.2 *(121.3 × 25 × 9.5)*
Main machinery: Diesel-electric; 4 Wärtsilä-SEMT-Pielstick 8 PC2.5 L diesels; 18,720 hp(m) *(13.77 MW)* sustained; 4 generators; 2 Stromberg motors; 16,200 hp(m) *(11.9 MW)*; 2 shafts
Speed, knots: 17
Complement: 135 ship's company plus 45 passengers
Radars: Air/surface search: Plessey AWS 2; E/F-band.
Navigation: 2 Decca; I-band.
Helicopters: 2 ASH-3H Sea King.

Comment: Fitted for landing craft with two 16 ton cranes, fin stabilisers, Wärtsilä bubbling system and a 60 ton towing winch. RAST helicopter securing system. Red hull with white upperworks and red funnel. Designed for Antarctic support operations and able to remain in polar regions throughout the Winter with 210 people aboard. Used as a transport to South Georgia in December 1981 and as a hospital ship during the Falklands war April to June 1982. Has been used as a Patagonian supply ship, and for other activities associated with the Navy in the region. The ship completed a major refit including the installation of Satcom, by early 2005. 40 mm guns have been removed.

ALMIRANTE IRIZAR   *11/2004*, A E Galarce* / 1151096

TUGS

11 TUGS (YTB/YTL)

QUERANDI R 2	CALCHAQUI R 6	CHULUPI R 10	CHIQUILYAN R 18
TEHUELCHE R 3	ONA R 7	MATACO R 12	MORCOYAN R 19
MOCOVI R 5	TOBA R 8	CAPAYAN R 16	

Comment: R 2-3 and R 7-8 and R 12 are coastal tugs of about 250 tons. The remainder are harbour tugs transferred from the USA.

MATACO   *5/2000, A E Galarce* / 0104177

PREFECTURA NAVAL ARGENTINA – COAST GUARD

Headquarters Appointments

Commander:
Prefecto General Carlos Edgardo Fernández
Vice Commander:
Prefecto General Ricardo Rodriguez

Personnel

2006: 11,900 (1,600 officers)

Tasks

Under the General Organisation Act the PNA is charged with:
(a) Enforcement of Federal Laws on the high seas and waters subject to the Argentine Republic.
(b) Enforcement of environmental protection laws in Federal waters.
(c) Safety of ships in EEZ. Search and Rescue.
(d) Security of waterfront facilities and vessels in port.
(e) Operation of certain Navaids.

(f) Operation of some Pilot Services.
(g) Management and operation of Aviation Service; Coastguard Vessels; Salvage, Fire and Anti-Pollution Service; Yachtmaster School; National Diving School; several Fire Brigades and Anti-Narcotics Department.
(h) Operation of some Customs activities.

Organisation

Formed in 10 districts; High Parana River, Upper Parana and Paraguay Rivers, Lower Parana River, Upper Uruguay River, Lower Uruguay River, Delta, River Plate, Northern Argentine Sea, Southern Argentine Sea, Lakes and Comahue.

History

The Spanish authorities in South America established similar organisations to those in Spain. In 1756 the Captainship of the Port came into being in Buenos Aires- in 1810 the Ship Registry office was added to this title. On 29 October 1896 the title of Capitania General de Puertos

was established by Act of Congress, the beginning of the PNA. Today, as a security and safety force, it has responsibilities throughout the rivers of Argentina, the ports and harbours as well as within territorial waters out to the 200 mile EEZ. An attempt was made in January 1992 to restrict operations to a 12 mile limit but the legislation was cancelled.

Identity markings

Two unequal blue stripes with, superimposed, crossed white anchors followed by the title Prefectura Naval.

Strength of Prefectura

Patrol Ships	6
Large Patrol Craft	3
Coastal Patrol Craft	20
Inshore Patrol Craft	77
Training Ships	4
Pilot Stations	1
Pilot and Patrol Craft	5

PATROL FORCES (PC)

Notes: In addition to the ships and craft listed below the PNA operates 400 craft, including floating cranes, runabouts and inflatables of all types.

1 PATROL SHIP (WPSO)

Name	No	Builders	Commissioned
DELFIN	GC 13	Ijsselwerf, Netherlands	14 May 1957

Displacement, tons: 700 standard; 1,000 full load
Dimensions, feet (metres): 193.5 × 29.8 × 13.8 *(59 × 9.1 × 4.2)*
Main machinery: 2 MAN diesels; 2,300 hp(m) *(1.69 MW)*; 2 shafts
Speed, knots: 15
Range, n miles: 6,720 at 10 kt
Complement: 27
Guns: 1 Oerlikon 20 mm (fitted for). 2—12.7 mm Browning MGs.
Radars: Navigation Decca; I-band.

Comment: Whaler acquired for PNA in 1969. Commissioned 23 January 1970.

DELFIN   *7/2003, A E Galarce* / 0572409

2 LYNCH CLASS (LARGE PATROL CRAFT) (WPB)

Name	No	Builders	Commissioned
LYNCH	GC 21	AFNE, Rio Santiago	20 May 1964
TOLL	GC 22	AFNE, Rio Santiago	7 July 1966

Displacement, tons: 100 standard; 117 full load
Dimensions, feet (metres): 98.4 × 21 × 6.9 *(30 × 6.4 × 2.1)*
Main machinery: 2 MTU Maybach diesels; 2,700 hp(m) *(1.98 MW)*; 2 shafts
Speed, knots: 22
Range, n miles: 2,000
Complement: 14 (3 officers)
Guns: 1 Oerlikon 20 mm (can be carried). 1—7.62 mm MG.
Radars: Surface search: Decca; I-band.

LYNCH   *1/1997, Prefectura Nava* / 0012018

5 HALCON (TYPE B 119) CLASS (WPSO)

Name	No	Builders	Commissioned
MANTILLA	GC 24	Bazán, El Ferrol	20 Dec 1982
AZOPARDO	GC 25	Bazán, El Ferrol	28 Apr 1983
THOMPSON	GC 26	Bazán, El Ferrol	20 June 1983
PREFECTO FIQUE	GC 27	Bazán, El Ferrol	29 July 1983
PREFECTO DERBES	GC 28	Bazán, El Ferrol	20 Nov 1983

Displacement, tons: 910 standard; 1,084 full load
Dimensions, feet (metres): 219.9 × 34.4 × 13.8 *(67 × 10.5 × 4.2)*
Main machinery: 2 Bazán-MTU 16V 956 TB91 diesels; 7,500 hp(m) *(5.52 MW)* sustained; 2 shafts
Speed, knots: 20
Range, n miles: 5,000 at 18 kt
Complement: 33 (10 officers)
Guns: 1 Breda 40 mm/70; 300 rds/min to 12.5 km *(7 n miles)*; weight of shell 0.96 kg. 2—12.7 mm MGs.
Radars: Navigation: Decca 1226 ARPA; I-band.
Helicopters: Platform for 1 Dauphin 2.

Comment: Ordered in 1979 from Bazán, El Ferrol, Spain. All have Magnavox MX 1102 SATNAV. Hospital with four beds. Carry one rigid rescue craft *(6 m)* with a 90 hp MWM diesel powering a Hamilton water-jet and a capacity for 12 and two inflatable craft *(4.1 m)* with Evinrude outboard. Refits of these ships started in 2005.

MANTILLA   *6/2005*, A E Galarce* / 1151095

1 LARGE PATROL CRAFT (WAX)

Name	No	Builders	Commissioned
MANDUBI	GC 43	Base Naval Rio Santiago	1940

Displacement, tons: 270 full load
Dimensions, feet (metres): 108.9 × 20.7 × 6.2 *(33.2 × 6.3 × 1.9)*
Main machinery: 2 MAN G6V-23.5/33 diesels; 500 hp(m) *(367 kW)*; 1 shaft
Speed, knots: 14
Range, n miles: 800 at 14 kt; 3,400 at 10 kt
Complement: 12
Guns: 2—12.7 mm Browning MGs.
Radars: Surface search: Decca; I-band.

Comment: Since 1986 has acted as training craft for PNA Cadets School carrying 20 cadets.

MANDUBI   *8/1994, Mario Diaz* / 0056488

1 RIVER PATROL SHIP (WARS)

Name	No	Builders	Commissioned
TONINA	GC 47	SANYM SA San Fernando, Argentina	30 June 1978

Displacement, tons: 103 standard; 153 full load
Dimensions, feet (metres): 83.8 × 21.3 × 10.1 (25.5 × 6.5 × 3.3)
Main machinery: 2 GM 16V-71TA diesels; 1,000 hp (746 kW) sustained; 2 shafts
Speed, knots: 10. **Range, n miles:** 2,800 at 10 kt
Complement: 11 (3 officers)
Guns: 1 Oerlikon 20 mm.
Radars: Navigation: Decca 1226; I-band.

Comment: Served as training ship for PNA Cadets School until 1986. Now acts as salvage ship with salvage pumps and recompression chamber. Capable of operating divers and underwater swimmers. Also used as a patrol ship.

TONINA   *1/1998, Hartmut Ehlers* / 0017541

18 MAR DEL PLATA CLASS (COASTAL PATROL CRAFT) (WPB)

MAR DEL PLATA GC 64	RIO DE LA PLATA GC 70	INGENIERO WHITE GC 76
MARTIN GARCIA GC 65	LA PLATA GC 71	GOLFO SAN MATIAS GC 77
RIO LUJAN GC 66	BUENOS AIRES GC 72	MADRYN GC 78
RIO URUGUAY GC 67	CABO CORRIENTES GC 73	RIO DESEADO GC 79
RIO PARAGUAY GC 68	RIO QUEQUEN GC 74	USHUAIA GC 80
RIO PARANA GC 69	BAHIA BLANCA GC 75	CANAL DE BEAGLE GC 81

Displacement, tons: 81 full load
Dimensions, feet (metres): 91.8 × 17.4 × 5.2 (28 × 5.3 × 1.6)
Main machinery: 2 MTU 8V-331-TC92 diesels; 1,770 hp(m) (1.3 MW) sustained; 2 shafts
Speed, knots: 22
Range, n miles: 1,200 at 12 kt; 780 at 18 kt
Complement: 14 (3 officers)
Guns: 1 Oerlikon 20 mm. 2—12.7 mm Browning MGs.
Radars: Navigation: Decca 1226; I-band.

Comment: Ordered 24 November 1978 from Blohm + Voss to a Z-28 design. First delivered in June 1979 and then at monthly intervals. Steel hulls. GC 82 and 83 were captured by the British Forces in 1982.

CABO CORRIENTES   *7/2005*, A E Galarce* / 1151094

1 COASTAL PATROL CRAFT (WPB)

Name	No	Builders	Commissioned
DORADO	GC 101	Base Naval, Rio Santiago	17 Dec 1939

Displacement, tons: 43 full load
Dimensions, feet (metres): 69.5 × 14.1 × 4.9 (21.2 × 4.3 × 1.5)
Main machinery: 2 GM 6071-6A diesels; 360 hp (268 kW); 1 shaft
Speed, knots: 12
Range, n miles: 1,550
Complement: 7 (1 officer)
Radars: Navigation: Furuno; I-band.

DORADO   *12/1999, R O Rivero* / 0056490

35 SMALL PATROL CRAFT (WPB)

ESTRELLEMAR GC 48	SALMON GC 54	ORCA GC 60	ROBALDO GC 92
REMORA GC 49	BIGUA GC 55	PINGUINO GC 61	CAMARON GC 93
CONGRIO GC 50	FOCA GC 56	MEDUSA GC 88	GAVIOTA GC 94
MERO GC 51	TIBURON GC 57	PERCA GC 89	ABADEJO GC 95
MARSOPA GC 52	MELVA GC 58	CALAMAR GC 90	GC 102-114
PETREL GC 53	LENGUADO GC 59	HIPOCAMPO GC 91	

Displacement, tons: 15 full load
Dimensions, feet (metres): 41 × 11.8 × 3.6 (12.5 × 3.6 × 1.1)
Main machinery: 2 GM diesels; 514 hp (383 kW); 2 shafts
Speed, knots: 20
Range, n miles: 400 at 18 kt
Complement: 3
Guns: 12.7 mm Browning MG.
Radars: Navigation: I-band.

Comment: First delivered September 1978. First 14 built by Cadenazzi, Tigre 1977-79, most of the remainder by Ast Belen de Escobar 1984-86. *GC 102-114* are slightly smaller.

PERCA   *11/2004*, A E Galarce* / 1151093

1 BAZAN TYPE (WPBF)

SUREL GC 142

Displacement, tons: 14.5 full load
Dimensions, feet (metres): 39 × 12.4 × 2.2 (11.9 × 3.8 × 0.7)
Main machinery: 2 MAN D2848 LXE diesels; 1,360 hp(m) (1 MW) sustained; 2 Hamilton 362 waterjets
Speed, knots: 38
Range, n miles: 300 at 25 kt
Complement: 4
Guns: 1—12.7 mm MG.
Radars: Navigation: Furuno; I-band.

Comment: Acquired in 1997 from Bazán, San Fernando. Similar to Spanish Bazán 39 class for Spanish Maritime Police. Plans to acquire further craft were not fulfilled.

SUREL   *12/2001, A E Galarce* / 0529809

10 ALUCAT 1050 CLASS (WPB)

CORMORAN GC 137	SURUBI GC 143	HUALA GC 146	MANDURUYU GC 148
CISNE GC 138	BOGA GC 144	PACU GC 147	CORVINA GC 149
PEJERREY GC 139	SABALO GC 145		

Displacement, tons: 9 full load
Dimensions, feet (metres): 37.7 × 12.5 × 2 (11.5 × 3.8 × 0.6)
Main machinery: 2 Volvo 61 ALD; 577 hp(m) (424 kW); 2 Hamilton 273 waterjets
Speed, knots: 18
Complement: 4
Radars: Navigation: Furuno 12/24; I-band.

Comment: First three delivered in September 1994. Seven more ordered in 1999.

HUALA   *4/2000, Hartmut Ehlers* / 0104180

4 ALUCAT 850 CLASS (WPB)

GC 152-184 (ex-LS 9201-9233)

Displacement, tons: 7 full load
Dimensions, feet (metres): 30.2 × 10.8 × 2 *(9.2 × 3.3 × 0.6)*
Main machinery: 2 Volvo TAMD 41B; 400 hp(m) *(294 kW);* 2 waterjets
Speed, knots: 26
Complement: 4
Radars: Navigation Furuno; I-band.

Comment: Alucat 850 class built by Damen. First six delivered in 1995, six more in February 1996, five more in December 1996 and five in December 1997. Five more ordered in 1999.

GC 181   *10/2005*, A E Galarce* / 1151092

4 TRAINING SHIPS (WAXL/WAXS)

ESPERANZA   ADHARA II   TALITA II   DR BERNARDO HOUSSAY (ex-*El Austral*)

Displacement, tons: 33.5 standard
Dimensions, feet (metres): 62.3 × 14.1 × 8.9 *(19 × 4.3 × 2.7)*
Main machinery: 1 VM diesel; 90 hp(m) *(66 kW);* 1 shaft
Speed, knots: 6; 15 sailing
Complement: 6 plus 6 cadets

Comment: Details given are for *Esperanza* built by Ast Central de la PNA. Launched and commissioned 20 December 1968 as a sail training ship. The 30 ton training craft *Adhara II* and *Talita II* are of similar dimensions. *Dr Bernardo Houssay* is a Danish-built ketch built in 1930. Displacement 460 tons and has a crew of 25 (five officers). Acquired by the PNA in 1996.

TALITA II   *6/1998, Prefectura Naval* / 0017545

DR BERNARDO HOUSSAY   *5/2000, Harald Carstens* / 0104181

6 SERVICE CRAFT (YTL/YTR)

PUERTO BUENOS AIRES SI 4   — SB 5   **CANAL COSTANERO** SB 9
— SB 3   **CANAL EMILIO MITRE** SB 8   — SB 10

Comment: *Canal Emilio Mitre* is a small tug of 53 tons full load, it has a speed of 10 kt and was built by Damen Shipyard, Netherlands in 1982.

PILOT VESSELS

1 PILOT STATION (WAGH/AHH)

Name	No	Builders	Commissioned
RECALADA (ex-*Rio Limay*)	DF 15	Astillero Astarsa	30 May 1972

Displacement, tons: 10,070 full load
Dimensions, feet (metres): 482.3 × 65.6 × 28 *(147 × 20 × 8.5)*
Speed, knots: 13
Complement: 28 (3 officers)

Comment: Commissioned as a Coast Guard ship 24 December 1991. Painted red with a white superstructure. Has a helicopter deck forward and a 20 bed hospital. After an extensive conversion and refit the ship replaced *Lago Lacar* in 1995.

RECALADA   *8/1994, Marcelo Campodonico* / 0056494

22 PILOT CRAFT (PB)

ALUMINE GC 118 (ex-SP 14)
TRAFUL GC 119 (ex-SP 15)
LACAR GC 120 (ex-SP 24)
MASCARDI GC 122 (ex-SP 17)
FONTANA GC 121 (ex-SP 32)
VIEDNA GC 123 (ex-SP 20)
SAN MARTIN GC 124 (ex-SP 21)
BUENOS AIRES GC 125 (ex-SP 22)
MUSTERS GC 126 (ex-SP 26)

COLHUE GC 129 (ex-SP 16)
MARIA L PENDO GC 130 (ex-SP 18)
ROCA GC 131 (ex-SP 28)
PUELO GC 132 (ex-SP 29)
FUTALAUFQUEN GC 133 (ex-SP 30)
FALKNER GC 134 (ex-SP 31)
HESS (ex-*Huechulafquen*) GC 135 (ex-SP 34)

COLHUE HUAPI GC 136 (ex-SP 33)
YEHUIN GC 140 (ex-SP 30, ex-SP 35)
QUILLEN GC 141 (ex-SP 27)
FAGNANO GC 150 (ex-SP 23)
NAHUEL HUAPI GC 151 (ex-SP 19)
CARDIEL — (ex-SP 25)

(All names preceded by **LAGO**)

Comment: There are five different types of named pilot and patrol craft. SP 14-15 of 33.7 tons built in 1981; SP 16-18 of 47 tons built since 1981; SP 19-23 of 51 tons built since 1981; SP 25-27 of 20 tons built in 1981; SP 28-30 of 16.5 m built in 1983; SP 31-35 of 7 tons built in 1986-1991. Most built by Damen SY, Netherlands. The last one built by Astillero Mestrina, Tigre. No armament. Six were transferred to patrol duties in 1993 and 11 more in 1995 and all have GC numbers. SP 19, 23, 25, 27 and 30 are the pilot craft.

HESS   *12/1997, Hartmut Ehlers* / 0017546

LAND-BASED MARITIME AIRCRAFT

Notes: In addition to the aircraft listed, there are two Piper Warrior II/Archer II training aircraft and five Schweizer 300C training helicopters.

Numbers/Type: 2/3 Casa C-212 S 68/A 68 Aviocar.
Operational speed: 190 kt *(353 km/h).*
Service ceiling: 24,000 ft *(7,315 m).*
Range: 1,650 n miles *(3,055 km).*
Role/Weapon systems: Two S 68 acquired in 1989, three A 68 in 1990. Medium-range reconnaissance and coastal surveillance duties in EEZ. Sensors: Bendix RDS 32 surface search radar. Omega Global GNS-500. Weapons: ASW; can carry torpedoes, depth bombs or mines. ASV; 2 × rockets or machine gun pods not normally fitted.

CASA C-212   *6/2002, CASA/EADS* / 0528295

Numbers/Type: 1 Aerospatiale SA 330 Super Puma.
Operational speed: 151 kt *(279 km/h)*.
Service ceiling: 15,090 ft *(4,600 m)*.
Range: 335 n miles *(620 km)*.
Role/Weapon systems: Support and SAR helicopter for patrol work. Updated in France in 1996. Sensors: Omera search radar. Weapons: Can carry pintle-mounted machine guns but is usually unarmed.

Numbers/Type: 3 Aerospatiale AS 365 Dauphin 2.
Operational speed: 150 kt *(278 km/h)*.
Service ceiling: 15,000 ft *(4,575 m)*.
Range: 410 n miles *(758 km)*.
Role/Weapon systems: Acquired in 1995-96 to replace the Super Puma during the latter's update but have been retained. Sensors: Agrion search radar. Weapons: Unarmed.

SUPER PUMA   11/1996, Luis O Zunino / 0056495

DAUPHIN 2   10/1996, Prefectura Naval / 0012022

Australia

Country Overview

The Commonwealth of Australia comprises the island continent and the island of Tasmania which are separated by the Bass Strait. The British monarch, represented by a governor-general, is head of state. With an overall area of 2,966,151 square miles, it has a 13,910 n mile coastline with the Pacific (Coral and Tasman Seas) and Indian Oceans, the Timor Sea, Arafura Sea and the Torres Strait. External dependencies are the Australian Antarctic Territory, Christmas Island, the Cocos Islands, the Territory of Heard Island and McDonald Islands, Norfolk Island, the Ashmore and Cartier Islands and the Coral Sea Islands Territory. Canberra is the capital while Sydney is the largest city and a major port. There are further ports at Melbourne, Fremantle, Newcastle, Port Kembla, Geelong, Brisbane, Gladstone, Port Hedland and Port Walcott. Territorial Seas (12 n miles) are claimed. An EEZ (200 n miles) is also claimed.

Headquarters Appointments

Chief of Navy:
   Vice Admiral Russ Shalders, AO, CSC
Maritime Commander, Australia:
   Rear Admiral D R Thomas, AM, CSC
Commander Navy Systems Command:
   Commodore G J Geraghty
Commodore Flotillas:
   Commodore D R Thomas AM, CSC

Senior Appointments

Head of Maritime Systems Division:
   Commodore T B Ruting AM, CSC
Head Defence Personnel Executive:
   Rear Admiral B L Adams, AO
Deputy Chief of Joint Operations:
   Rear Admiral R C Moffitt
Commander Joint Offshore Protection Command:
   Rear Admiral J Goldrick

Diplomatic Representation

Head Australian Defence Staff, Washington:
   Rear Admiral R W Gates
Head Australian Defence Staff, London:
   Brigadier V Williams
Defence Attaché in Washington:
   Commodore J R Stapleton, AM
Defence Adviser in Kuala Lumpur:
   Captain D L Garnock, CSC
Defence Attaché in Bangkok:
   Captain B A Fraser
Defence Attaché in Paris:
   Captain W R Haynes
Naval Attaché in Jakarta:
   Captain J B Dudley, CSC
Naval Adviser in London:
   Captain V S Jones
Defence Attaché in Phnom Penh:
   Captain T R Jenkinson
Defence Attaché in Singapore:
   Captain M T Jerrett

Personnel

(a) 2006: 13,155 officers and sailors
(b) 7,015 (2,495 active, 4,520 standby)

RAN Reserve

The Naval Reserve is integrated into the Permanent Force. Personnel are either Active Reservists with regular commitments or Inactive Reservists with periodic or contingent duty. The missions undertaken by the Reserve include Coordination and Guidance of Psychology, Public Relations, Intelligence, Diving and patrol boat/landing craft operations. In addition, members of the Ready Reserve (a component of the Active Reserve) are shadow posted to selected major fleet units.

Offshore Protection

A Joint Offshore Protection Command was established on 30 March 2005 to coordinate and manage offshore maritime security. This integrates the resources of the Australian Defence Force (ADF) and the Australian Customs Service. The ADF has assumed responsibility for offshore counter-terrorism prevention, interdiction and response capabilities and activities, including the protection of offshore oil and gas facilities and the offshore interdiction of ships, while the Australian Customs Service has retained responsibility for civil maritime surveillance and regulatory roles undertaken by its Coastwatch Division. The Commander is accountable to the Chief of the Defence Force for its military functions and to the Chief Executive of Customs for its civil functions.

It was also announced that a Maritime Identification Zone, extending up to 1,000 n miles from the Australian coastline, was to be established. On entering this zone, vessels proposing to enter Australian ports are required to identify themselves and their intended port of arrival. The aim is to be capable of identifying all vessels, other than recreational boats, within the 200 n mile EEZ.

Principal day-to-day assets of the Command are the Armidale and Fremantle class patrol craft, the Customs Service Bay class and the Coastwatch surveillance aircraft.

Shore Establishments

Canberra: Navy Headquarters, Navy Systems Command Headquarters, *Harman* (Communications, Administration).
Sydney: Maritime Headquarters, Fleet Base East (Garden Island), *Waterhen* (Mine Warfare and Clearance Diving), *Watson* (Warfare Training), *Penguin* (Diving, Hospital), *Kuttabul* (Administration).
Wollongong Hydrographic Headquarters.
Jervis Bay Area: *Albatross* (Air Station), *Creswell* (Leadership and Management Training and Fleet Support), Jervis Bay Range Facility.
Cockburn Sound (WA): Fleet Base West, *Stirling* (Administration and Maintenance Support, Submarines, Communications).
Darwin: Minor warship base, *Coonawarra* (Administration).
Cairns: *Cairns* (Administration), Minor Warship Base.
Adelaide: Regional Naval Headquarters, South Australia.
Brisbane: Regional Naval Headquarters, South Queensland.
Hobart: Regional Naval Headquarters, Tasmania.

Fleet Deployment

Fleet Base East (and other Sydney bases): 3 FFG, 1 FFH, 1 AOR, 2 LPA, 1 LSH, 1 ASR, 6 MHC, 3 MSA.
Fleet Base West: 6 SS, 3 FFG, 3 FFH, 1 AO.
Darwin Naval Base: 10 PTF, 1 LCH.
Cairns: 5 PTF, 4 LCH, 4 AGS.

Fleet Air Arm (see *Shipborne Aircraft* section).

Squadron	Aircraft
723	Squirrel AS 350B, Utility, FFG embarked flights, SAR
	HS 748, Fixed-wing, EW operations and training
	Bell 206B, survey support
805	Seasprite SH-2G
817	Sea King Mk 50, Utility
816	Seahawk S-70B-2, ASW, ASST

Prefix to Ships' Names

HMAS. Her Majesty's Australian Ship

Strength of the Fleet

Type	Active	Building (Projected)
Patrol Submarines	6	—
Destroyers	—	(3)
Frigates (FFG)	12	1
Minehunters (Coastal)	6	—
Minesweepers (Auxiliary)	2	—
Large Patrol Craft	10	11
Assault Ships	—	(2)
Amphibious Heavy Lift Ship	1	—
Amphibious Transports	2	1
Landing Craft	10	—
Survey Ships	6	—
Replenishment Ships	2	1
Training Ships	7	—

DELETIONS

Frigates

2005   *Canberra*

Patrol Forces

2005   *Cessnock, Whyalla, Warrnambool, Bunbury, Wollongong*
2006   *Dubbo, Geraldton, Fremantle*

Mine Warfare Forces

2003   *Brolga*
2006   *Huon, Hawkesbury* (both in preservation)

PENNANT LIST

Submarines

73	Collins
74	Farncomb
75	Waller
76	Dechaineux
77	Sheean
78	Rankin

Frigates

01	Adelaide
03	Sydney
04	Darwin
05	Melbourne
06	Newcastle
150	Anzac
151	Arunta
152	Warramunga
153	Stuart
154	Parramatta
155	Ballarat
156	Toowoomba
157	Perth (bldg)

Mine Warfare Forces

M 84	Norman
M 85	Gascoyne
M 86	Diamantina
M 87	Yarra
Y 298	Bandicoot
Y 299	Wallaroo

Patrol Forces

83	Armidale
84	Larrakia
85	Bathurst
86	Albany
87	Pirie
205	Townsville
207	Launceston
209	Ipswich
211	Bendigo
212	Gawler
215	Geelong
216	Gladstone

Amphibious Forces

L 50	Tobruk
L 51	Kanimbla
L 52	Manoora
L 126	Balikpapan
L 127	Brunei
L 128	Labuan
L 129	Tarakan
L 130	Wewak
L 133	Betano

Survey Ships

A 01	Paluma
A 02	Mermaid
A 03	Shepparton
A 04	Benalla
A 245	Leeuwin
A 246	Melville

Auxiliaries

O 195	Westralia
OR 304	Success

SUBMARINES

Notes: Stirling 4V-275R (75 kW) engines supplied for AIP trials ashore.

6 COLLINS CLASS (SSK)

Name	No	Builders	Laid down	Launched	Commissioned
COLLINS	73	Australian Submarine Corp, Adelaide	14 Feb 1990	28 Aug 1993	27 July 1996
FARNCOMB	74	Australian Submarine Corp, Adelaide	1 Mar 1991	15 Dec 1995	31 Jan 1998
WALLER	75	Australian Submarine Corp, Adelaide	19 Mar 1992	14 Mar 1997	10 July 1999
DECHAINEUX	76	Australian Submarine Corp, Adelaide	4 Mar 1993	12 Mar 1998	23 Feb 2001
SHEEAN	77	Australian Submarine Corp, Adelaide	17 Feb 1994	1 May 1999	23 Feb 2001
RANKIN	78	Australian Submarine Corp, Adelaide	12 May 1995	7 Nov 2001	29 Mar 2003

Displacement, tons: 3,051 surfaced; 3,353 dived
Dimensions, feet (metres): 255.2 × 25.6 × 23 *(77.8 × 7.8 × 7)*
Main machinery: Diesel-electric; 3 Hedemora/Garden Island
Type V18B/14 diesels; 6,020 hp *(4.42 MW)*; 3 Jeumont
Schneider generators; 4.2 MW; 1 Jeumont Schneider
motor; 7,344 hp(m) *(5.4 MW)*; 1 shaft; 1 MacTaggart Scott
DM 43006 hydraulic motor for emergency propulsion
Speed, knots: 10 surfaced; 10 snorting; 20 dived
Range, n miles: 9,000 at 10 kt (snort); 11,500 at 10 kt
(surfaced)
400 at 4 kt (dived)
Complement: 45 (8 officers)

Missiles: SSM: McDonnell Douglas Sub Harpoon; active
radar homing to 130 km *(70 n miles)* at 0.9 Mach;
warhead 227 kg.
Torpedoes: 6-21 in *(533 mm)* fwd tubes. Gould Mk 48 Mod 4;
dual purpose; wire-guided; active/passive homing to
38 km *(21 n miles)* at 55 kt or 50 km *(27 n miles)* at 40
kt; warhead 267 kg. Air turbine pump discharge. Total of
22 weapons including Mk 48 and Sub Harpoon.
Mines: 44 in lieu of torpedoes.
Countermeasures: Decoys: 2 SSE.
ESM: Condor CS-5600; intercept and warning.
Weapons control: AN-BYG 1. Link 11.
Radars: Navigation: Kelvin Hughes Type 1007; I-band.
Sonars: Thomson Sintra Scylla active/passive bow array
and passive flank, intercept and ranging arrays.
GEC-Marconi Kariwara (first pair) or Thomson Marconi
Narama or Allied Signal TB 23; retractable passive towed
array.

Programmes: Contract signed on 3 June 1987 for
construction of six Swedish-designed Kockums Type 471.

WALLER *4/2003, Mick Prendergast* / 0569124

Fabrication work started in June 1989; bow and midships
(escape tower) sections of the first submarines built in
Sweden.
Structure: Stirling air independent propulsion (AIP) has
been tested on a shore rig. Scylla is an updated Eledone
sonar suite. Diving depth, 300 m *(984 ft)*. Anechoic
tiles are fitted during build to all but *Collins* which is
retrofitted. Pilkington Optronics CK 43 search and CH 93
attack periscopes fitted. Plans for an external mine belt
have been abandoned.
Modernisation: The Replacement Combat System AN-BYG 1
is based on Raytheon's CCS Mk 2. The shore facilities
version was established in mid-2005 and the first
seagoing system in *Waller* in 2006. The other boats will
follow by 2010. Meanwhile, following trials in *Collins* to
improve the performance of the current combat system,
the systems in *Dechaineux* and *Sheean* have been
augmented. The remaining boats will not receive this

upgrade. In parallel, significant improvements to noise
signature have been achieved following modifications
to propellers and casing sections and improvements to
the hydraulics system and engine reliability. These have
been made to all six boats. Collaborative development
of the US Mk 48 ADCAP torpedo is being progressed
following the signature of a 'Statement of Principles'
agreement which promotes interoperability with US
Navy. Three boats have been fitted with the Condor
CS 5600 ESM system with the remainder to follow in
due course. *Collins* has received a set of modifications to
facilitate the deployment and recovery of special forces.
Operational: *Dechaineux* and *Sheean* have achieved interim
operational capability but full operational capability will
not be achieved until the Replacement Combat System
has been installed. All submarines are based at Fleet
Base West with one or two deploying regularly to the
east coast.

DECHAINEUX *1/2006*, Chris Sattler* / 1153845

RANKIN *9/2003, Chris Sattler* / 0569122

DECHAINEUX *2/2004*, John Mortimer* / 1121117

BALLARAT *6/2005*, Bob Fildes* / 1153862

ANZAC *6/2005*, Michael Nitz* / 1153841

TOOWOOMBA *10/2005*, Chris Sattler* / 1153840

SHIPBORNE AIRCRAFT

Notes: (1) Five Bell 206B Kiowa utility helicopters transferred to the Army in 2001.
(2) 12 Eurocopter MRH 90 troop lift helicopters are planned to enter Army service from 2007. Fully navalised, they are to be capable of operating from *Kanimbla* and *Manoora* and from future amphibious ships. Further aircraft may be procured to replace the Sea King utility helicopter and Seahawk.

Numbers/Type: 11 Kaman Seasprite SH-2G(A).
Operational speed: 130 kt *(241 km/h)*.
Service ceiling: 10,000 ft *(3,048 m)*.
Range: 350 n miles *(650 km)*.
Role/Weapon systems: Contract placed in June 1997 for eleven aircraft for Anzac frigates. Refurbished USN aircraft delivered from 2003-2005. First aircraft provisionally accepted in October 2003 and all delivered by March 2005. Handover of first operational aircraft expected in 2006. Sensors: Telephonics APS 143(V)3 radar; Raytheon AAQ-27 FLIR; AAR 54/AES 210/LWS 20 ESM; ALE 47 chaff and IR flares; Link 11, SATCOM. Weapons: ASW; 2 Mk 46 (to be replaced by MU 90) torpedoes. ASV: 2 Penguin Mk 2 Mod 7; 1—7.62 mm MG.

SH-2G(A)   *6/2002, Royal Australian Navy* / 0528405

Numbers/Type: 7 Westland Sea King HAS 50/50A.
Operational speed: 125 kt *(230 km/h)*.
Service ceiling: 14,500 ft *(4,400 m)*.
Range: 490 n miles *(908 km)*.
Role/Weapon systems: Utility helicopter; embarked periodically for operations from *Success*, *Tobruk* and the LPAs. Life extension to 2008 completed in November 1996 for six aircraft. One more acquired from UK in 1996 and upgraded to 50LEP (Mk 50) standard. Sensors: AW 391(A) radar. Weapons: MAG 58 7.62 mm MG.

SEA KING   *2/2005*, Paul Jackson* / 1153848

Numbers/Type: 16 Sikorsky S-70B-2 Seahawk.
Operational speed: 135 kt *(250 km/h)*.
Service ceiling: 10,000 ft *(3,050 m)*.
Range: 600 n miles *(1,110 km)*.
Role/Weapon systems: Seahawk SH-60F derivative aircraft designed by Sikorsky to meet RAN specifications for ASW and ASST operations. Eight assembled by ASTA in Victoria. Helicopters embarked in FFG-7 and used temporarily in ANZAC frigates. Upgrades from 2004 include Raytheon AAQ 27 FLIR, Tracor ALE 47 countermeasures and Elisra AES 210 ESM. Sensors: MEL Surface surveillance radar, CDC Sonobuoy Processor and Barra Side Processor, and CAE Magnetic Anomaly Detector Set controlled by a versatile Tactical Display/Management System. Weapons: ASW; two Mk 46 Mod 5 (to be replaced by MU 90) torpedoes. ASV; one Mag 58 MG, possibly ASM after 2005.

SEAHAWK   *7/2005*, Mick Prendergast* / 1153861

Numbers/Type: 13 Aerospatiale AS 350B Squirrel.
Operational speed: 125 kt *(232 km/h)*.
Service ceiling: 10,000 ft *(3,050 m)*.
Range: 275 n miles *(510 km)*.
Role/Weapon systems: Support helicopter for utility tasks and training duties. Regularly embarked at sea. Sensors: None. Weapons: ASV; two Mag 58 MGs.

SQUIRREL   *2/2005*, Paul Jackson* / 1153869

LAND-BASED MARITIME AIRCRAFT

Notes: (1) Replacement of the P3-C maritime patrol aircraft fleet from about 2013 is being taken forward under Project Air 7000. Interoperability with the US is a major factor and almost certainly points to selection of the Boeing 737 MMA. Such a choice would also offer significant logistical advantages as both the AEW and maritime patrol aircraft would then be based on a common airframe. In the meantime, procurement of high altitude, long endurance unmanned aerial vehicles for broad area surveillance over maritime and land environments is planned. Trials of the Northrop Grumman RQ-4B Global Hawk and General Atomics Mariner are to start in 2006.
(2) Australia joined the System Design and Development phase of the Joint Strike Fighter in October 2002. Up to 100 aircraft are required to replace the F/A-18 Hornet and F-111 aircraft fleets. Entry into service is scheduled to begin in 2012.

Numbers/Type: 6 Boeing 737 AEW&C 'Wedgetail'.
Operational speed: to be confirmed.
Service ceiling: 41,000 ft *(12,500 m)*.
Range: to be confirmed.
Role/Weapon systems: Contract for four aircraft (adaptation of Boeing Business Jet) signed on 20 December 2000. Two additional aircraft, under option, were added in 2004. Delivery of first aircraft scheduled in November 2006 and the other four by 2008. IOC to be achieved late 2008. AAR capable. Sensors: Details unconfirmed but likely to include Northrop Grumman ESSD L-band multirole electronically scanned array (MESA) radar (fuselage mounted); electronic warfare self-protection (EWSP) system (including IR countermeasures, chaff and flares); Links 11 and 16; Satcom.

BOEING WEDGETAIL   *7/2004, Boeing* / 0566617

Numbers/Type: 17/4/15 General Dynamics F-111C/RF-111C/F-111G.
Operational speed: 793 kt *(1,469 km/h)*.
Service ceiling: 60,000 ft *(18,290 m)*.
Range: 2,540 n miles *(4,700 km)*.
Role/Weapon systems: Air Force operates the F-111 for anti-shipping strike and its small force of RF-111 for coastline surveillance duties using EW/ESM and photographic equipment underwing. To be replaced by upgraded F/A-18 Hornet from 2010. Sensors: GE AN/APG-144, podded EW. Weapons: ASV; 4 × Harpoon missiles. Strike; 4 × Snakeye bombs. Self-defence; 2 × AIM-9P.

F-111C   *2/2003, Paul Jackson* / 0552764

Numbers/Type: 68 McDonnell Douglas F/A-18 Hornet.
Operational speed: 1,032 kt *(1,910 km/h)*.
Service ceiling: 50,000 ft *(15,240 m)*.
Range: 1,000 n miles *(1,829 km)*.
Role/Weapon systems: Air defence and strike aircraft operated by Air Force but with fleet defence and anti-shipping secondary roles. An upgrade programme is being conducted in three phases. Phase 1 modifications, completed in 2002, included new radios, upgraded mission computers, EW upgrade and GPS. Phase 2-1, completed in 2003, included installation of the AN/APG-73 radar and upgraded aircraft software. In Phase 2-2, to be completed by 2007, the aircraft are to be equipped with Link 16 and improved avionics. In Phase 2-3, the EW suite (RWR and jammer) is to be upgraded and in Phase 2-4, a new target designation system (HTDS) is to be installed. Phase 3, structural modifications, is to be completed by 2010. Upgraded aircraft are to replace the F-111 in 2010. Sensors: APG-73 attack radar, AAS-38 FLIR/ALR-67 radar warning receiver. Weapons: ASV; 4 × Harpoon missiles. Strike; 1 × 20 mm cannon, up to 7.7 tons of 'iron' bombs. Fleet defence; 4 × AIM-7 Sparrow and 4 × AIM-9L Sidewinder.

Numbers/Type: 18 Lockheed P-3C/AP-3C Orion.
Operational speed: 410 kt *(760 km/h)*.
Service ceiling: 28,300 ft *(8,625 m)*.
Range: 4,000 n miles *(7,410 km)*.
Role/Weapon systems: Operated by Air Force for long-range ocean surveillance and ASW. Three more aircraft (plus one for spare parts) without armament or sensors acquired for training. Six aircraft upgraded to AP-3C standard with remaining 12 delivered by late 2004. Sensors: Elta EL/M-2022A(V)3 radar, AQS-901 processor, AQS-81 MAD FLIR systems Star Safire electro-optic system, ECM, Elta/IAI, ALR 2001 ESM, 80 × BARRA sonobuoys. Weapons: ASW; 8 × Mk 46 (Mod 5 after upgrade) torpedoes, Mk 25 mines, 8 × Mk 54 depth bombs. ASV; up to 6 AGM-84A/C Harpoon.

ORION AP-3C
2/2005*, Paul Jackson
1153868

AMPHIBIOUS FORCES

Notes: Replacements for the current Amphibious capability are being procured under Joint Project 2048. *Tobruk* and one of the LPA amphibious transports (*Kanimbla* and *Manoora*) are to be replaced by two helicopter capable amphibious ships (LHD) of approximately 20,000 tons from 2012. These are to be named *Canberra* and *Adelaide*. The second LPA is to be replaced by a 'strategic sealift'

capability by 2018. This is likely to be a conventional monohull vessel with a docking well. Short listed LHD designs are those based on the French Mistral class BPC (LHD) and the Spanish Navantia Strategic Projection Ship. JP 2048 is also to deliver replacement of the watercraft capability represented by the current LCH, LCM 8 and LCVP and other ship-to-shore assets required

to integrate with the new LHDs. LCHs and LCM 8s are to be decommissioned as the new capability enters service in 2012-2014. Invitations to tender are to be made by mid-2006. Likely bidders include joint ventures formed by Tenix-Navantia, ADI-Armaris and Austal-Raytheon. Following evaluation of the tenders, a contract is expected in mid-2007.

2 KANIMBLA (NEWPORT) CLASS (LCCH/LLP)

Name	No	Builders	Laid down	Launched	Commissioned	Recommissioned
KANIMBLA (ex-*Saginaw*)	L 51 (ex-1188)	National Steel & Shipbuilding	24 May 1969	7 Feb 1970	23 Jan 1971	29 Aug 1994
MANOORA (ex-*Fairfax County*)	L 52 (ex-1193)	National Steel & Shipbuilding	28 Mar 1970	19 Dec 1970	16 Oct 1971	25 Nov 1994

Displacement, tons: 4,975 light; 8,450 full load
Dimensions, feet (metres): 552 × 69.5 × 17.5 (aft) *(168.2 × 21.2 × 5.3)*
Main machinery: 6 ALCO 16-251 diesels; 16,500 hp *(12.3 MW)* sustained; 2 shafts; cp props; bow thruster
Speed, knots: 20
Range, n miles: 14,000 at 15 kt
Complement: 213 (12 officers)
Military lift: 450 troops (25 officers); 229 lane-metres of vehicles; 2 LCM 8; 250 tons aviation fuel

Guns: 1 General Electric/General Dynamics 20 mm Vulcan Phalanx Mk 15 can be fitted ❶. 4 — 12.7 mm MGs. Fitted for but not with army-operated RBS 70 launchers. To receive 2 Typhoon 25 mm guns in 2004-05.
Countermeasures: 2 SRBOC Mk 36 chaff and IR launchers.
Radars: Surface search: Kelvin Hughes 1007 ❷; I-band. Navigation: Kelvin Hughes ❸; I-band.

Helicopters: 4 Army Black Hawks or 3 Sea Kings or 1 Chinook.

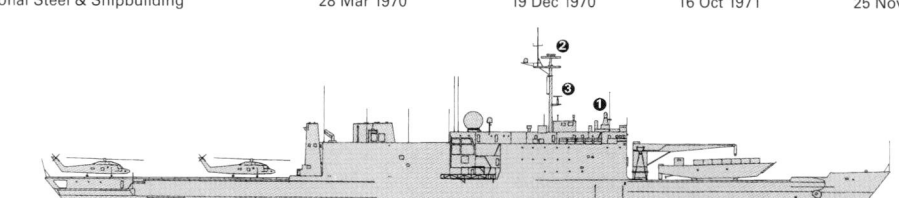

MANOORA *(Scale 1 : 1,500), Ian Sturton* / 0569257

Programmes: Acquired by sale from USA on 25 August and 27 September 1994.
Modernisation: Conversion contract let to Forgacs Shipbuilding, Newcastle in May 1995. Both ships modified by fitting a hangar to take four Black Hawk helicopters, to incorporate a third landing spot forward, to increase aviation fuel capacity and to dispense with the bow landing ramp. The after flight deck is Chinook capable. A stern

gate to the tank deck is retained. Two Army LCM 8 class are carried on the deck forward of the bridge and handled by a 70 ton crane. A classroom and improved medical facilities are installed. Installation of communications and command support system to support a deployable JTFHQ was undertaken in both ships in 2001.
Operational: Both based at Sydney. To be replaced in 2013 and 2016.

MANOORA *5/2005*, Chris Sattler* / 1153858

MANOORA *5/2005*, Chris Sattler* / 1153857

KANIMBLA *4/2005*, Chris Sattler* / 1153859

1 HEAVY LIFT SHIP (LSLH)

Name	No	Builders	Laid down	Launched	Commissioned
TOBRUK	L 50	Carrington Slipways Pty Ltd	7 Feb 1978	1 Mar 1980	23 Apr 1981

Displacement, tons: 3,300 standard; 5,700 full load
Dimensions, feet (metres): 417 × 60 × 16
(127 × 18.3 × 4.9)
Main machinery: 2 Mirrlees Blackstone KDMR8 diesels;
9,600 hp *(72 MW)*; 2 shafts
Speed, knots: 18
Range, n miles: 8,000 at 15 kt
Complement: 148 (13 officers)
Military lift: 314 troops (prolonged embarkation); 1,300 tons
cargo or 330 lane-metres of vehicles; 70 tons capacity
derrick; 2—4.25 ton cranes; 2 LCVP; 2 LCM 8

Guns: 2—12.7 mm MGs. To be fitted with 2 Typhoon 25 mm
guns in 2004-05.
Radars: Surface search: Kelvin Hughes Type 1006; I-band.
Navigation: Kelvin Hughes 1007; I-band.

Helicopters: Platform for one Sea King. Second Chinook
capable spot on forward flight deck (clear of cargo).

Structure: The design is an update of the British Sir
Bedivere class and provides facilities for the operation of
helicopters, landing craft, amphibians for ship-to-shore

movement. A special feature is the ship's heavy lift
derrick system for handling heavy loads. Able to embark
a squadron of Leopard tanks plus a number of wheeled
vehicles and artillery in addition to its troop lift. Bow and
stern ramps are fitted. Two LCM 8 carried on deck and
two LCVPs at davits.
Operational: A basic communications fit enables
participation in amphibious operations but not in
command role. Based at Sydney. To be replaced in
2012.

TOBRUK   *1/2006*, Chris Sattler* / 1153856

4 LANDING CRAFT (LIGHT) (LCVP)

T 4-7

Displacement, tons: 6.5 full load
Dimensions, feet (metres): 43.3 × 11.5 × 2.3 *(13.2 × 3.5 × 0.7)*
Main machinery: 2 Volvo Penta Sterndrives; 400 hp(m) *(294 kW)*
Speed, knots: 22; 15 (fully laden)
Complement: 3
Military lift: 4.5 tons cargo or 1 Land Rover or 36 troops

Comment: Prototype built by Geraldton, Western Australia. Trials conducted in late 1992.
Three more delivered in July 1993. Two for *Tobruk*, one for *Success* (T 7) and one spare
attached to the shore base, *Penguin*.

WEWAK   *4/2004*, Chris Sattler* / 1042103

T5   *8/1999, van Ginderen Collection* / 0104188

6 LANDING CRAFT (HEAVY) (LCH/LSM)

Name	No	Builders	Commissioned
BALIKPAPAN	L 126	Walkers Ltd, Queensland	8 Dec 1971
BRUNEI	L 127	Walkers Ltd, Queensland	5 Jan 1973
LABUAN	L 128	Walkers Ltd, Queensland	9 Mar 1973
TARAKAN	L 129	Walkers Ltd, Queensland	15 June 1973
WEWAK	L 130	Walkers Ltd, Queensland	10 Aug 1973
BETANO	L 133	Walkers Ltd, Queensland	8 Feb 1974

Displacement, tons: 358 light; 509 full load
Dimensions, feet (metres): 146 × 33 × 6.5 *(44.5 × 10.1 × 2)*
Main machinery: 2 GM 6—71 diesels; 348 hp *(260 kW)* sustained; 2 shafts
Speed, knots: 10
Range, n miles: 3,000 at 10 kt
Complement: 16 (2 officers)
Military lift: 3 medium tanks or equivalent
Guns: 2—12.7 mm MGs.
Radars: Navigation: Racal Decca Bridgemaster; I-band.

Comment: Originally this class was ordered for the Army but only *Balikpapan* saw Army
service until being commissioned into the Navy on 27 September 1974. The remainder
were built for the Navy. *Balikpapan* based at Darwin. The remainder are based at Cairns.
All have been given a life extension refit, which started with *Wewak* in 2000, and
completed with *Brunei* in 2002, for retention until at least 2008. *Buna* and *Salamaua*
transferred to Papua New Guinea Defence Force in November 1974.

PATROL FORCES

3 + 11 ARMIDALE CLASS (PATROL CRAFT) (PB)

Name	No	Builders	Commissioned
ARMIDALE	83	Austal Ships, Fremantle	24 June 2005
LARRAKIA	84	Austal Ships, Fremantle	10 Feb 2006
BATHURST	85	Austal Ships, Fremantle	10 Feb 2006
ALBANY	86	Austal Ships, Fremantle	2006
PIRIE	87	Austal Ships, Fremantle	2006
MAITLAND	—	Austal Ships, Fremantle	2006
ARARAT	—	Austal Ships, Fremantle	2006
BROOME	—	Austal Ships, Fremantle	2007
BUNDABERG	—	Austal Ships, Fremantle	2007
WOLLONGONG	—	Austal Ships, Fremantle	2007
CHILDERS	—	Austal Ships, Fremantle	2007
LAUNCESTON	—	Austal Ships, Fremantle	2008

Displacement, tons: 270
Dimensions, feet (metres): 184.6 × 31.8 × 8.8 *(56.8 × 9.7 × 2.7)*
Main machinery: 2 MTU 4000 16V diesels; 6,225 hp *(4.64 MW)*; 2 shafts
Speed, knots: 25
Range, n miles: 3,000 at 12 kt
Complement: 21

Guns: 1—25 mm Rafael M242 Bushmaster. 2—12.7 mm MGs.
Weapons control: Rafael Toplite optronic director.
Radars: Surface search/navigation: To be announced.

Comment: Austal Ships in conjunction with Defence Maritime Services contracted on
17 December 2003 to supply patrol boats to replace the Fremantle class under Project
Sea 1444. The craft are of monohull design and are capable of carrying two RHIBs.
Delivery of the whole class is to be achieved by 2008. DMS will provide through-life
logistics and maintenance support over 15 years. The craft are named after Australian
cities and towns. Eight of the craft are to be based at Darwin, Northern Territory, and the
other four at Cairns, Queensland. Two further craft are to be procured for operations off
north-west West Australia. They are to be based at Dampier or Port Hedland.

ARMIDALE   *1/2006*, Chris Sattler* / 1153853

7 FREMANTLE CLASS (LARGE PATROL CRAFT) (PB)

Name	No	Builders	Commissioned
TOWNSVILLE	205	NQEA Australia, Cairns	18 July 1981
LAUNCESTON	207	NQEA Australia, Cairns	1 Mar 1982
IPSWICH	209	NQEA Australia, Cairns	13 Nov 1982
BENDIGO	211	NQEA Australia, Cairns	28 May 1983
GAWLER	212	NQEA Australia, Cairns	27 Aug 1983
GEELONG	215	NQEA Australia, Cairns	2 June 1984
GLADSTONE	216	NQEA Australia, Cairns	8 Sep 1984

Displacement, tons: 245 full load
Dimensions, feet (metres): 137.1 × 23.3 × 5.9 *(41.8 × 7.1 × 1.8)*
Main machinery: 2 MTU 16V 538TB91 diesels; 6,140 hp(m) *(4.5 MW)* sustained; 2 shafts
Speed, knots: 30
Range, n miles: 1,450 at 30 kt
Complement: 24 (4 officers)

Guns: 1 Bofors AN 4—40 mm/60; 120 rds/min to 10 km *(5.5 n miles)*. The 40 mm mountings were designed by Australian Government Ordnance Factory and although the guns are of older manufacture, this mounting gives greater accuracy particularly in heavy weather.
1—81 mm mortar. 3—12.7 mm MGs.
Countermeasures: ESM: AWA Defence Industries Type 133 PRISM.
Radars: Navigation: Kelvin Hughes Type 1006; I-band.

Programmes: The decision to buy these patrol craft was announced in September 1977. The design is by Brooke Marine, Lowestoft which built the lead ship.
Modernisation: Original 15 year life was extended to 19 years and is now extended again. ESM added in 1994-95. The cruise diesel on a centre line shaft has been deleted.
Operational: Bases: Darwin: P 207, P 212, P 215. Carins: P 205, P 209, P 211, P 216. To be replaced by Armidale class. Decommissioning plan: *Gawler* and *Geelong* (June 2006); *Launceston* and *Bendigo* (August 2006); *Townsville* and *Ipswich* (December 2006); *Gladstone* (February 2007).

IPSWICH   *8/2005*, John Mortimer* / 1153852

MINE WARFARE FORCES

4 HUON (GAETA) CLASS (MINEHUNTERS—COASTAL) (MHC)

Name	No	Builders	Launched	Commissioned
NORMAN	84	ADI, Newcastle	3 May 1999	26 Aug 2000
GASCOYNE	85	ADI, Newcastle	11 Mar 2000	2 June 2001
DIAMANTINA	86	ADI, Newcastle	2 Dec 2000	4 May 2002
YARRA	87	ADI, Newcastle	19 Jan 2002	1 Mar 2003

Displacement, tons: 720 full load
Dimensions, feet (metres): 172.2 × 32.5 × 9.8 *(52.5 × 9.9 × 3.0)*
Main machinery: 1 Fincantieri GMT diesel; 1,986 hp(m) *(1.46 MW)*; 1 shaft; LIPS cp prop; 3 Isotta Fraschini 1300 diesels; 1,440 hp(m) *(1,058 kW)*; 3 electrohydraulic motors; 506 hp(m) *(372 kW)*; Riva Calzoni retractable/rotatable APUs
Speed, knots: 14 diesel; 6 APUs
Range, n miles: 1,600 at 12 kt
Complement: 38 (6 officers) plus 11 spare

Guns: 1 MSI DS 30B 30 mm/75. 650 rds/min to 10 km *(5.4 n miles)* anti-surface; 3 km *(1.6 n miles)* anti-aircraft; weight of shell 0.36 kg.
Countermeasures: MCM systems: 2 Bofors SUTEC Double-Eagle Mk 2 mine disposal vehicles with DAMDIC charges; ADI double Oropesa mechanical sweep and capable of towing the Australian developed Mini-Dyad influence sweep.
Decoys: 2 MEL Aviation Super Barricade; chaff launchers.
ESM: AWADI Prism.
Combat data systems: GEC-Marconi Nautis 2M with Link 11 receive only.
Weapons control: Radamec 1400N optronic surveillance system.
Radars: Navigation: Kelvin Hughes 1007; I-band.
Sonars: GEC-Marconi Type 2093; VDS; VLF-VHF multifunction with five arrays; mine search and classification.

Programmes: The Force Structure Review of May 1991 recommended the acquisition of coastal minehunters of proven design. These ships would be required to operate in deeper and more exposed waters, to achieve lower transit times and remain on station longer than the two inshore minehunters which have now been paid off. A contract was signed with Australian Defence Industries (ADI) on 12 August 1994 to build six Intermarine designed Gaeta class derivatives. The hull of the first ship was constructed at Intermarine's Sarzana Shipyard in Italy and arrived in Australia as deck cargo on 31 August 1995 for fitting out in Newcastle, where the remaining five ships were being built at ADI's Throsby Basin. Local content for this project is about 69 per cent.
Structure: Monocoque GRP construction. A recompression chamber, one RIB and an inflatable diving boat are carried to support a six-man diving team.
Operational: This class which is named after Australian rivers, is based at HMAS *Waterhen* in Sydney. *Huon* and *Hawkesbury* laid up in preservation in 2006.

DIAMANTINA   *10/2005*, Mick Prendergast* / 1153867

2 MINESWEEPERS AUXILIARY (TUGS) (MSCD/YTB)

BANDICOOT (ex-*Grenville VII*) Y 298   **WALLAROO** (ex-*Grenville V*) Y 299

Displacement, tons: 412 full load
Dimensions, feet (metres): 95.8 × 28 × 11.3 *(29.6 × 8.5 × 3.4)*
Main machinery: 2 Stork Werkspoor diesels; 2,400 hp(m) *(1.76 MW)*; 2 shafts
Speed, knots: 11
Range, n miles: 6,300 at 10 kt
Complement: 10
Radars: Navigation: Furuno 7040D; I-band.

Comment: Built in Singapore 1982 and operated by Maritime (PTE) Ltd. Purchased by the RAN and refurbished prior to delivery 11 August 1990. Used for minesweeping trials towing large AMASS influence and mechanical sweeps. No side scan sonar. Also used as berthing tugs. Bollard pull, 30 tons. Both are expected to decommission in 2006.

BANDICOOT   *9/2005*, Chris Sattler* / 1153849

3 MINESWEEPING DRONES (MSD)

MSD 02-04

Dimensions, feet (metres): 24 × 9.2 × 2 *(7.3 × 2.8 × 0.6)*
Main machinery: 2 Yamaha outboards; 300 hp(m) *(221 kW)*
Speed, knots: 45; 8 (sweeping)

Comment: Built by Hamil Haven in 1991-92. Remote-controlled drones. GRP hulls made by Hydrofield. Used for sweeping ahead of the MSA craft. Differential GPS navigation system with Syledis Vega back-up.

MSD 03   *11/1992, John Mortimer* / 0505956

SURVEY SHIPS (HYDROGRAPHIC SURVEY)

Notes: In addition to the ships listed below there are four civilian survey vessels; *Icebird, Franklin, Rig Seismic* and *Lady Franklin*. Also an arctic supply ship *Aurora Australis* started operating in the Antarctic in 1990; this vessel carries 70 scientists and has a helicopter hangar.

AURORA AUSTRALIS   *2/2003, Brian Morrison* / 0569131

2 LEEUWIN CLASS (AGS)

Name	No	Builders	Launched	Commissioned
LEEUWIN	A 245	NQEA, Cairns	19 July 1997	27 May 2000
MELVILLE	A 246	NQEA, Cairns	23 June 1998	27 May 2000

Displacement, tons: 2,170 full load
Dimensions, feet (metres): 233.6 × 49.9 × 14.1 (71.2 × 15.2 × 4.3)
Main machinery: Diesel-electric; 4 GEC Alsthom 6RK 215 diesel generators; 4,290 hp
(3.2 MW) sustained; 2 Alsthom motors; 1.94 MW; 2 shafts; 1 Schottel bow thruster
Speed, knots: 14. **Range, n miles:** 18,000 at 9 kt
Complement: 60 (8 officers)
Radars: Navigation: STN Atlas 9600 ARPA; I-band.
Sonars: C-Tech CMAS 36/39; hull mounted; high frequency active.

Helicopters: 1 AS 350B (not permanently embarked).

Comment: Contract awarded 2 April 1996 to North Queensland Engineers & Agents
(NQEA). Fitted with Atlas Fansweep-20 multibeam echo sounder and one AD 25 single
beam echo sounder. Also fitted with Klein 2000 towed light-weight sidescan sonar. The
ships carry three SMBs, two light utility boats and one RHIB. All repainted grey. Based
at Cairns.

MELVILLE   *11/2003, John Mortimer* / 0569143

4 PALUMA CLASS (AGSC)

Name	No	Builders	Commissioned
PALUMA	A 01	Eglo, Adelaide	27 Feb 1989
MERMAID	A 02	Eglo, Adelaide	4 Dec 1989
SHEPPARTON	A 03	Eglo, Adelaide	24 Jan 1990
BENALLA	A 04	Eglo, Adelaide	20 Mar 1990

Displacement, tons: 320 full load
Dimensions, feet (metres): 118.9 × 42.0 × 8.6 (36.6 × 12.8 × 2.65).
Main machinery: 2 Detroit 12V-92TA diesels; 1,100 hp (820 kW) sustained; 2 shafts
Speed, knots: 11
Range, n miles: 3,600 at 11 kt
Complement: 14 (3 officers)
Radars: Navigation: Kelvin Hughes 1007; I-band.
Sonars: Skipper S113; hull-mounted; active; high frequency. ELAC LAZ 72; hull-mounted
side scan; active; high frequency.

Comment: Catamaran design based on Prince class ro-ro passenger ferries. Steel hulls and
aluminium superstructure. Contract signed in November 1987. Also fitted with two ELAC
LAX 4700 dual-frequency echo sounders and GEONAV data logging and processing
system utilising Teramodel data display. All ships based at Cairns and operate in pairs
when undertaking survey operations.

SHEPPARTON   *1/2005** / 1153865

9 SURVEY MOTOR BOATS (YGS)

FANTOME 1005	TOM THUMB 1009	CASUARINA 1012
MEDA 1006	JOHN GOWLLAND 1010	CONDER 1021
DUYFKEN 1008	GEOGRAPHE 1011	WYATT EARP ASV 01

Dimensions, feet (metres): 35.1 × 9.5 × 5.6 (10.7 × 2.9 × 1.7)
Main machinery: 2 Volvo Penta AQAD-41A diesel stern drives; 400 hp(m) (294 kW);
2 props
Speed, knots: 24
Range, n miles: 300 at 12 kt
Complement: 4 (1 officer)
Radars: Navigation: JRC; I-band.

Comment: Six survey motor boats built by Pro Marine, Victoria between October 1992
and 1993. Two additional SMBs (CAS and GEO) were built in 1997 to supplement the
new AGSs. One craft has been taken out of service. The remaining seven are equipped
with an Atlas Fansweep-20 multibeam echo sounder and one AD 15 single beam echo
sounder, as well as a KLEIN 2000 towed lightweight side scan sonar. All collected data
is fed to the Hydrographic Survey System provided by STN Atlas. Five of the class are
allocated to the Leeuwin class hydrographic ships, two to the hydrographic school at
HMAS *Penguin*. In addition, *Wyatt Earp* is a 9 m craft fitted for Antarctic service and
allocated to the Hydrographic Office (Wollongong) Detached Survey Unit. It is fitted with
the ODOM Hydrotrac Single Beam Echo Sounder and GEONAV/Terramodel. *Conder* has
been built as a prototype replacement SMB.

GEOGRAPHE   *6/2002, Royal Australian Navy* / 0528409

RESCUE VEHICLES

1 RESCUE SUBMERSIBLE (DSRV)

REMORA

Displacement, tons: 16.5
Dimensions, feet (metres): 19.7 × 7.9 × 13.4 (with skirt); 7.9 (without skirt) (6.0 × 2.4 × 4.1; 2.4)
Main machinery: 2 electric motors; 150 hp (112 kW); 4 axial thrusters; 4 vertical thrusters;
2 transverse thrusters
Speed, knots: 3 dived
Complement: 1 operator and 6 survivors

Comment: Manufactured in 1995 by Can Dive Marine Services, Canada for Australian
Submarine Corporation and subsequently in 2001 wholly owned by the RAN, *Remora* is
operated and maintained (at 12 hours notice) by Fraser Diving, West Australia. Capable
of operating to depths in excess of 500 m in a current of 3 kt, it can evacuate six personnel
at a time and transfer them under pressure of up to 5 Bar directly to two 36-man
decompression chambers for medical and hyperbaric treatment. A Remotely Operated
Vehicle (ROV), *Remora* is flown and powered from the surface giving it unlimited
endurance (emergency life support onboard is 240 man-hours). It is launchable from
a craft of opportunity in up to sea state 5 using a Launch And Recovery System (LARS)
that is part of the deployable suite. The skirt on the vehicle can be remotely manipulated
to achieve mating angles up to 60°.
  Communications are by fibre-optic cable. The entire suite of *Remora*, LARS and all
associated equipment can be fitted into ISO containers to facilitate rapid worldwide
deployment. The USN replacement system, SRDRS, is based on the Remora system
and is to enter service in 2007.

REMORA   *6/2002, K Bristow, RAN* / 0528408

TRAINING SHIPS

Notes: In addition to *Young Endeavour* and *Salthorse* there are five Fleet class yachts. Of 36.1 ft *(11 m)*. GRP yachts named *Charlotte of Cerberus, Friendship of Leeuwin, Scarborough of Cerberus, Lady Penrhyn of Nirimba* and *Alexander of Creswell*. The names are a combination of Australia's first colonising fleet and the training base to which each yacht is allocated.

1 SAIL TRAINING SHIP (AXS)

Name	Builders	Launched	Commissioned
YOUNG ENDEAVOUR	Brooke Yachts, Lowestoft	2 June 1987	25 Jan 1988

Displacement, tons: 239 full load
Dimensions, feet (metres): 144 × 26 × 13 *(44 × 7.8 × 4)*
Main machinery: 2 Perkins V8 diesels; 334 hp *(294 kW)*; 2 shafts
Speed, knots: 14 sail; 10 diesel
Range, n miles: 2,500 at 7 kt
Complement: 33 (9 RAN, 24 youth)

Comment: Built to Lloyds 100 AI LMC yacht classification by Brooke Yachts, Lowestoft. Sail area 707.1 m². Presented to Australia by UK Government as a bicentennial gift. Operated by RAN on behalf of the Young Endeavour Youth Scheme.

YOUNG ENDEAVOUR *1/2004*, Chris Sattler* / 1042109

1 SAIL TRAINING SHIP (AXS)

SALTHORSE

Displacement, tons: 32 full load
Dimensions, feet (metres): 65.0 × 16.7 × 7.5 *(19.8 × 5.1 × 2.3)*
Main machinery: 2 Ford Lehman diesel; 120 hp *(89 kW)*
Speed, knots: 8
Range, n miles: 1,400 at 6 kt
Complement: 1 JRC JMA-2253; I-band

Comment: Ketch with steel hull and aluminium masts. Acquired in 1999 for officer training at HMAS *Creswell*.

SALTHORSE *6/2002, Royal Australian Navy* / 0528411

1 TRAINING SHIP (AXL)

Name	No	Builders	Commissioned
SEAHORSE MERCATOR	—	Tenix Shipbuilding, Henderson WA	15 Oct 1998

Displacement, tons: 165 full load.
Dimensions, feet (metres): 103.3 × 26.9 × 7.9 *(31.5 × 8.2 × 2.4)*
Main machinery: 2 Caterpillar 3412 diesels; 2 shafts
Speed, knots: 16
Range, n miles: 2,700 at 10 kt
Complement: 8 plus 18 trainees

Comment: Operated by Defence Maritime Services as a Navigation training ship based at Sydney. Similar to Pacific class patrol craft.

SEAHORSE MERCATOR *6/2005*, Mick Prendergast* / 1153866

AUXILIARIES

Notes: (1) *Success* is due to be replaced in about 2015.
(2) Since 1998 all other support vessels have been contracted to the Defence Maritime Services. These craft have blue hulls and buff superstructures, and are chartered as required.
(3) In addition to the vessels listed there are some 24 workboats (AWB and NWB numbers), a VIP launch *Tresco II* and an admiral's barge *Green Parrot*.

0 + 1 SIRIUS CLASS (REPLENISHMENT TANKER) (AORH)

Name	No	Builders	Laid down	Launched	Commissioned
SIRIUS (ex-*Delos*)	—	Hyundai Mipo Dockyard, Korea	—	2004	2006

Measurement, tons: 37,000 dwt
Dimensions, feet (metres): 598.9 × 89.6 × 36.7 *(182.55 × 27.3 × 11.2)*
Main machinery: 1 Burmeister & Wain diesel; 1 shaft
Speed, knots: 15
Complement: To be announced
Guns: 1—25 mm Rafael M242 Bushmaster (fitted for).
Helicopter: 1 medium.

Comment: New ship of double-hulled construction procured in June 2004 as replacement, following refit and conversion for military use, for *Westralia*. Modifications are likely to include the installation of replenishment-at-sea equipment, a flight deck (with one landing spot) and hangar aft and changes to accommodation and habitability arrangements. The ship is also likely to be fitted for but not with a 25 mm gun and possibly a 20 mm Vulcan Phalanx. A contract for the refit and initial logistic support of the ship was let to Tenix Defence on 15 March 2005. The first RAN ship to carry the name *Sirius;* she is named after the flagship of the First Fleet.

SIRIUS (before conversion) *7/2004, Royal Australian Navy* / 0566629

2 TRIALS AND SAFETY VESSELS (ASR)

Name	No	Builders	Commissioned
SEAHORSE STANDARD (ex-*British Viking*)	—	Marystown Shipyard, Newfoundland	1980
SEAHORSE SPIRIT (ex-*British Magnus*)	—	Marystown Shipyard, Newfoundland	1980

Measurement, tons: 2,090 grt; 1,635 dwt
Dimensions, feet (metres): 236.2 × 52.5 × 17.4 *(72 × 16 × 5.3)*
Main machinery: 2 MLW-ALCO Model 251 V-12 diesels; 5,480 hp(m) *(4.03 MW)*; 1 shaft; cp prop; 2 stern and 2 bow thrusters
Speed, knots: 9
Complement: 20 plus 44 spare

Comment: Acquired 2 December 1998 by Defence Maritime Services to support RAN trials in Western and Southern Australian waters. Dynamic Positioning system. These ships are also used for weapon recovery and can embark the 'Remora' submarine rescue suite.

SEAHORSE STANDARD *12/2002, G Hainsworth, RAN* / 0569128

1 TRIALS AND SAFETY VESSEL (ASR)

Name	No	Builders	Commissioned
SEAHORSE HORIZON	— (ex-ASR 241)	Stirling Marine Services, WA	1984
(ex-*Protector*, ex-*Blue*, *Nabilla*, ex-*Osprey*)			

Displacement, tons: 670 full load
Dimensions, feet (metres): 140.1 × 31.2 × 9.8 *(42.7 × 9.5 × 3)*
Main machinery: 2 Detroit 12V-92TA diesels; 2,440 hp *(1.82 MW)* sustained; 2 Heimdal cp props
Speed, knots: 11.5. **Range, n miles:** 10,000 at 11 kt
Complement: 6 civilian or 9 navy (for training)
Radars: Navigation: JRC 310; I-band. Decca RM 970BT; I-band.
Sonars: Klein; side scan; high frequency.

Helicopters: Platform for 1 light.

Comment: A former National Safety Council of Australia vessel commissioned into the Navy in November 1990. Used to support contractor's sea trials of the Collins class submarines, and for mine warfare trials and diving operations. LIPS dynamic positioning, two ROVs and a recompression chamber. Helicopter deck and a submersible were removed in 1992. Based at Jervis Bay. Decommissioned in early 1998 and run as part of the commercial support programme. Also used for junior officer training.

SEAHORSE HORIZON   *12/2004*, Ian Edwards* / 1042392

3 FISH CLASS (TORPEDO RECOVERY VESSELS) (YPT)

TUNA TRV 801	TREVALLY TRV 802	TAILOR TRV 803

Displacement, tons: 91.6 full load
Dimensions, feet (metres): 88.5 × 20.9 × 4.5 *(27 × 6.4 × 1.4)*
Main machinery: 3 GM diesels; 890 hp *(664 kW)*; 3 shafts
Speed, knots: 13
Complement: 9
Radars: Navigation: I-band.

Comment: All built at Williamstown completed between January 1970 and April 1971. Can transport eight torpedoes. Based at Jervis Bay, Sydney and Fleet Base West respectively. Run as part of the commercial support programme from 1997. Blue hulls and buff superstructures.

TREVALLY   *4/2004*, Chris Sattler* / 1042101

4 SELF-PROPELLED LIGHTERS (WFL/AOTL)

WARRIGAL 333 (ex-WFL 8001)	WOMBAT 332 (ex-WFL 8003)
WALLABY 331 (ex-WFL 8002)	WYULDA 334 (ex-WFL 8004)

Displacement, tons: 265 light; 1,206 full load
Dimensions, feet (metres): 124.6 × 33.5 × 12.5 *(38 × 10.2 × 3.8)*
Main machinery: 2 Harbourmaster outdrives (1 fwd, 1 aft)
Speed, knots: 8
Cargo capacity: 560 tons dieso and 200 tons water

Comment: First three were laid down at Williamstown in 1978. The fourth, for HMAS *Stirling*, was ordered in 1981 from Williamstown Dockyard. Used for water/fuel transport. Steel hulls with twin, swivelling, outboard propellers. Based at Jervis Bay and Stirling (WFL 8001, 8004), other pair at Sydney. Run as part of the commercial support operation from 1997.

WARRIGAL   *8/2005*, John Mortimer* / 1153876

3 WATTLE CLASS STORES LIGHTERS (YE)

WATTLE CSL 01	BORONIA CSL 02	TELOPEA CSL 03

Displacement, tons: 147 full load
Dimensions, feet (metres): 79.4 × 32.8 × 5.4 *(24.2 × 10.0 × 1.66)*
Main machinery: 2 Caterpillar D333C diesels; 600 hp *(447 kW)*
Speed, knots: 8
Range, n miles: 320 at 8 kt
Radars: 1 JRC JMA-2253; I-band.

Comment: Built by Cockatoo DY, Sydney and delivered in 1972. Employed to transport ammunition and stores. Equipped with 3-ton electric crane. CSL 02 and 03 based at Sydney and CSL 01 at Darwin.

WATTLE   *8/2005*, John Mortimer* / 1153875

1 LEAF CLASS (UNDER WAY REPLENISHMENT TANKER) (AORH/AOT)

Name	No	Builders	Laid down	Launched	Commissioned
WESTRALIA (ex-*Appleleaf*, ex-*Hudson Cavalier*)	O 195 (ex-A 79)	Cammell Laird, Birkenhead	1974	24 July 1975	Nov 1979

Displacement, tons: 40,870 full load
Measurement, tons: 20,761 gross; 10,851 net; 33,595 dwt
Dimensions, feet (metres): 560 × 85 × 38.9
(170.7 × 25.9 × 11.9)
Main machinery: 2 SEMT-Pielstick 14 PC2.2 V 400 diesels; 14,000 hp(m) *(10.3 MW)* sustained; 1 shaft
Speed, knots: 16 (11 on 1 engine). **Range, n miles:** 7,260 at 15 kt
Complement: 89 (8 officers) plus 9 spare berths

Cargo capacity: 20,000 tons dieso; 3,000 tons aviation fuel; 1,500 tons water
Countermeasures: ESM: Matilda; radar warning.
Radars: Navigation: 2 Kelvin Hughes; 1007 ARPA (I-band) and Radpak (E/F-band).

Comment: Part of an order by the Hudson Fuel and Shipping Co which was subsequently cancelled. Leased by the RN from 1979 until transferred on 9 October 1989 on a five year lease to the RAN, arriving in Fremantle 20 December 1989. Purchased in 1994. Has three 3 ton cranes and two 5 ton derricks. Hospital facilities. Two beam replenishment stations. Stern refuelling restored in 1995. Based at *Stirling*. Also modified to provide a large Vertrep platform aft. Lifeboats have been replaced by liferafts. To be replaced in 2006 by *Sirius*.

WESTRALIA   *1/2006*, Chris Sattler* / 1153878

1 DURANCE CLASS (UNDERWAY REPLENISHMENT TANKER) (AORH)

Name	No	Builders	Laid down	Launched	Commissioned
SUCCESS	OR 304	Cockatoo Dockyard, Sydney	9 Aug 1980	3 Mar 1984	19 Feb 1986

Displacement, tons: 17,933 full load
Dimensions, feet (metres): 515.7 × 69.5 × 30.6
(157.2 × 21.2 × 8.6)
Main machinery: 2 SEMT-Pielstick 16 PC2.5 V 400 diesels;
20,800 hp(m) *(15.3 MW)* sustained; 2 shafts; LIPS cp
props
Speed, knots: 20
Range, n miles: 8,616 at 15 kt
Complement: 237 (25 officers)
Cargo capacity: 10,200 tons: 8,707 dieso; 975 Avcat; 116
distilled water; 57 victuals; 250 munitions including
SM1 missiles and Mk 46 torpedoes; 95 naval stores and
spares

Guns: Provision for 2 Vulcan Phalanx Mk 15 CIWS.
4 — 12.7 mm MGs. Due to receive Rafael Typhoon 25 mm
guns in 2004/05.
Radars: Navigation. 2 Kelvin Hughes Type 1006; I-band.
Helicopters: 1 AS 350B Squirrel, Sea King or Seahawk.

Comment: Based on French Durance class design.
Replenishment at sea from four beam positions (two
having heavy transfer capability) and vertrep. One LCVP
is carried on the starboard side aft. Hangar modified to
take Sea Kings. Phalanx guns fitted aft in 1997.

SUCCESS *5/2005*, Chris Sattler* / 1153877

4 DIVING TENDERS (YDT/PB)

SEAL 2001   **MALU BAIZAM** 2003   **SHARK** 2004   **DUGONG**

Displacement, tons: 22 full load
Dimensions, feet (metres): 65.5 × 18.5 × 4.6 *(20 × 5.6 × 1.4)*
Main machinery: 2 MTU 8V 183 diesels; 2 shafts
Speed, knots: 26
Range, n miles: 450 at 20 kt
Complement: 6 plus 16 divers

Comment: Built by Geraldton Boat Builders, Western Australia and completed in August
1993. Carry 2 tons of diving equipment to support 24 hour diving operations in depths
of 54 m. *Shark* based at *Stirling*, *Seal* at *Waterhen* and *Dugong* at Sydney, *Malu Baizam*
is used for patrol duties at Thursday Island. *Porpoise* grounded in 1995 and was
assessed as being beyond economical repair. Replacement built in 1996. Run as part
of the commercial support operation from 1997. Sister craft *Coral Snake* and *Red Viper*
are operated by the Army.

DUGONG *5/2005*, Chris Sattler* / 1153874

TUGS

Notes: In addition the two MSCD are used as tugs. Details under Mine Warfare Forces.

7 HARBOUR TUGS (YTL)

TAMMAR DT 2601   **BRONZEWING** HTS 501 (152)   **MOLLYMAWK** HTS 504 (154)
QUOKKA DT 1801   **CURRAWONG** HTS 502 (153)   **SEAHORSE CHUDITCH**
SEAHORSE QUENDA

Comment: *Tammar* has a bollard pull of 35 tons and is based at *Stirling*; *Quokka* bollard
pull 8 tons, is based at Darwin. The three HTS vessels have a bollard pull of 5 tons.
Run as part of the commercial support programme from 1997. *Seahorse Chuditch* and
Seahorse Quenda were built in Malaysia and delivered in 2003. 23 m long they have a
bollard pull of 16 tons.

SEAHORSE QUENDA *6/2005*, Mick Prendergast* / 1153863

QUOKKA *8/2003, John Mortimer* / 0569142

ARMY

Notes: (1) Operated by Royal Australian Army Corps of Transport. Personnel: About 300
as required.
(2) In addition to the craft listed below there are 159 assault boats 16.4 ft *(5 m)* in length
and capable of 30 kt. Can carry 12 troops or 1,200 kg of equipment. Also there are 12
ex-US Army LARC-V amphibious wheeled lighters for service with *Manoora* and *Kanimbla*.

6 AMPHIBIOUS WATERCRAFT (LCM)

AB 2000-2005

Displacement, tons: 135 full load
Dimensions, feet (metres): 83.3 × 24.9 × 3.3 *(25.4 × 7.6 × 1.0)*
Main machinery: 2 Detroit 6062 diesels; 2 Doen waterjets
Speed, knots: 11
Range, n miles: 720 at 10 kt
Complement: To be announced
Guns: 2 — 12.7 mm MGs.

Comment: Contract signed with ADI in June 2002 to provide watercraft to operate in
conjunction with the LPAs. Two carried by each ship. Of aluminium construction, they
have through-deck, roll-on/roll-off design and bow and stern ramps. With 65 tonne
cargo capacity, the craft can carry one Leopard tank or five armoured vehicles. An
innovative feature is a pontoon system to mate with LPA stern ramp to facilitate vehicle
transfer.

AB 2000 *12/2004*, Bob Fildes* / 1153864

4 LCM 8 CLASS

AB 1050, 1051, 1053, 1056, 1058-1067

Displacement, tons: 107 full load
Dimensions, feet (metres): 73.5 × 21 × 5.2 *(22.4 × 6.4 × 1.6)*
Main machinery: 2 8V92GM diesels; 720 hp *(547 kW)*; 2 shafts
Speed, knots: 11
Range, n miles: 290 at 10 kt
Complement: 4
Military lift: 55 tons
Guns: 2—12.7 mm MGs.

Comment: Built by North Queensland Engineers, Cairns and Dillinghams, Fremantle to US design. Based at Townsville and Darwin. *AB 1057* transferred to Tonga 1982, *AB 1052* and *AB 1054* sold to civilian use in 1992. All upgraded to Mod 2 standard by late 1999 with new engines and with endurance increased.

AB 1056   *10/2002, John Mortimer* / 0528383

2 SAFCOL CRAFT

CORAL SNAKE AM 1353   **RED VIPER**

Displacement, tons: 22 full load
Dimensions, feet (metres): 65.5 × 20.0 × 4.6 *(20 × 6.1 × 1.4)*
Main machinery: 2 General Motors Detroit 8V92 diesels; 1,800 hp *(1.34 MW)*
Speed, knots: 28
Range, n miles: 350 at 25 kt
Complement: 3

Comment: Sister to Seal class built at Geraldton Boat Builders. *Coral Snake* delivered in 1994 and *Red Viper* in 1996. Used as Special Action Forces Craft Offshore Large (SAFCOL) to support dives and transport of stores and personnel.

RED VIPER   *9/2005*, Chris Sattler* / 1153873

9 EXPRESS SHARK CAT CLASS (PB)

AM 237-244   **AM 428**

Comment: Built by NoosaCat, Queensland and delivered by 1995. Trailer transportable. Similar craft in service with Navy and Police. Multihulls 30.8 ft *(9.4 m)* in length overall with twin Johnson outboards; 450 hp *(336 kW)* total power output, giving 40 kt maximum speed.

AM 243   *11/1997, van Ginderen Collection* / 0012946

NON-NAVAL PATROL CRAFT

Notes: (1) In addition to the commercial support craft already listed, various State and Federal agencies, including some fishery departments, have built offshore patrol craft up to 25 m and 26 kt.
(2) Cocos Island patrol carried out by *Sir Zelman Cowan* of 47.9 × 14 ft *(14.6 × 4.3 m)* with two Cummins diesels; 20 kt, range 400 n miles at 17 kt, complement 13 (3 officers). Operated by West Australian Department of Harbours and Lights.
(3) All previously listed RAAF craft have been sold for civilian use.

4 SHARK CAT 800 CLASS (WORKBOATS) (YFL)

0801   0802   0803   0805

Displacement, tons: 13.7 full load
Dimensions, feet (metres): 27.4 × 9.2 × 3.3 *(8.35 × 2.8 × 1.0)*
Main machinery: 2 Mercury outboard engines
Speed, knots: 30
Complement: 1 plus 11 passengers

Comment: Built by Shark Cat, Noosaville, Queensland and delivered in 1980s. GRP construction. Used for target-towing, naval police and range clearance duties. Based at Sydney with the exception of *0805* which is based at HMAS *Creswell*.

SHARK CAT 0803   *6/2004, Chris Sattler* / 1042107

4 NOOSACAT 930 WORKBOATS (YFL)

0901-0904

Dimensions, feet (metres): 30.5 × 11.5 × 2.3 *(9.3 × 3.5 × 0.7)*
Main machinery: 2 Volvo Penta ADQ41DP diesels; 2 props
Speed, knots: 30
Range, n miles: 240 at 20 kt

Comment: Built by Noosacat, Queensland and delivered in 1994. GRP hulled craft for general purpose stores and personnel transport. *0903* and *0904* based at Sydney, *0902* at HMAS *Creswell* and 0901 at HMAS *Cerberus*.

NOOSACAT 0904   *6/2002, Royal Australian Navy* / 0528412

10 STEBER CLASS WORKBOATS (YFL/YDT)

NGPWB 01-10

Displacement, tons: 13.7 full load
Dimensions, feet (metres): 43.3 × 15.4 × 4.4 *(13.2 × 4.7 × 1.3)*
Main machinery: 2 diesels (01—06). 1 diesel (07—10)
Speed, knots: 25 (01—06). 20 (07—10)

Comment: Built by Steber craft and delivered in 1997. GRP hulled craft for general purpose stores and personnel transport and for use as diving tenders. Most have radars 01, 02, 07 and 08 based at Sydney, 03 at HMAS *Creswell*, 04 and 09 at Fleet Base West and 06 at HMAS *Cerberus*.

STEBER CRAFT   *10/2005*, John Mortimer* / 1153872

CUSTOMS

Notes: (1) The Australian Customs Service operates a number of inshore vessels between 4.3 m and 6.4 m in length. All larger vessels have been sold and the Bay class are the only sea-going vessels.
(2) The Customs Service operates a number of surveillance aircraft. Six Pilatus Britten-Norman Islanders and one Shrike AC 500 Aero Commander are used for visual surveillance, five de Havilland Dash 8-200 are equipped with radar, IR and EO sensors and three Reims F406 are radar and night vision equipped. There are one Bell 412 and one Bell Longranger helicopters.

DASH 8-200   6/2005*, Massimo Annati / 1153871

8 BAY CLASS (PB)

ROEBUCK BAY ACV 10	**CORIO BAY** ACV 50
HOLDFAST BAY ACV 20	**ARNHEM BAY** ACV 60
BOTANY BAY ACV 30	**DAME ROMA MITCHELL** ACV 70
HERVEY BAY ACV 40	**STORM BAY** ACV 80

Displacement, tons: 134
Dimensions, feet (metres): 125.3 × 23.6 × 7.9 *(38.2 × 7.2 × 2.4)*
Main machinery: 2 MTU 16V 2000M 70 diesels; 2,856 hp(m) *(2.1 MW)* sustained; 2 shafts. 1 Vosper Thornycroft bow thruster
Speed, knots: 24
Range, n miles: 1,000 at 20 kt
Complement: 12
Radars: Surface search: Racal Decca; E/F- and I-band.
Sonars: Wesmar SS 390E dipping sonar.

Comment: Built by Austal Ships and delivered from February 1999 to August 2000. The craft carry two RIBs capable of 35 kt.

ROEBUCK BAY   7/2005*, Chris Sattler / 1153870

Austria

ÖSTERREICHISCHE PATROUILLEN BOOT STAFFER

Country Overview

A landlocked central European country, the Republic of Austria has an area of 83,859 square miles and is bordered by the Czech Republic, Slovakia, Hungary, Slovenia, Italy, Switzerland, Liechtenstein and Germany. Vienna is the country's capital and largest city. The principal river is the Danube whose Austrian tributaries include the Inn, Traun, Enns and Ybbs. Among other important rivers are the Mur and Mürz. Additionally, there are numerous lakes including Bodensee (Lake Constance) and Neusiedler.

Commanding NCO

WO II Sgarz

Diplomatic Representation

Defence Attaché in London:
  Brigadier Michael Derman

Personnel

(a) 2006: 24 (cadre personnel and national service), plus a small shipyard unit
(b) 6 months' national service

Bases

Marinekaserne Tegetthof, Wien-Kuchelau (under command of Austrian School of Military Engineering)

PATROL FORCES

1 RIVER PATROL CRAFT (PBR)

Name	No	Builders	Commissioned
OBERST BRECHT	A 601	Korneuberg Werft AG	14 Jan 1958

Displacement, tons: 10 full load
Dimensions, feet (metres): 40.3 × 8.2 × 2.5 *(12.3 × 2.5 × 0.75)*
Main machinery: 2 MAN 6-cyl diesels; 290 hp(m) *(213 kW)*; 2 shafts
Speed, knots: 18
Complement: 5
Guns: 1 — 12.7 mm MG. 1 — 84 mm PAR 66 Carl Gustav AT mortar.

Comment: Refit in 2004 included overhaul of hull and electrical equipment, a redesigned superstructure and new paint scheme.

OBERST BRECHT   7/2004, HBF / 0589831

1 RIVER PATROL CRAFT (PBR)

Name	No	Builders	Launched	Commissioned
NIEDERÖSTERREICH	A 604	Korneuberg Werft AG	26 July 1969	16 Apr 1970

Displacement, tons: 78 full load
Dimensions, feet (metres): 96.8 × 17.8 × 3.6 *(29.4 × 5.4 × 1.1)*
Main machinery: 2 MWM V16 diesels; 1,640 hp(m) *(1.2 MW)*; 2 shafts
Speed, knots: 22
Complement: 9 (1 officer)
Guns: 1 — 20 mm Oerlikon SPz Mk 66. 1 — 12.7 mm MG. 1 — 7.62 mm MG. 1 — 84 mm PAR 66 'Carl Gustav' AT mortar.

Comment: Fully welded. Only one built of a projected class of 12. Main machinery and electrical equipment overhauled in 2000.

NIEDERÖSTERREICH   7/2001, HBF / 0114504

Azerbaijan

Country Overview

Formerly part of the USSR, the Republic of Azerbaijan declared its independence in 1991. Situated in the Transcaucasia region of western Asia, the country, which includes the disputed region of Nagorno-Karabakh, has an area of 33,400 square miles and is bordered to the north by Russia and Georgia and to the south with Iran. Armenia to the west includes the exclave of Nakhichevan. Azerbaijan has a coastline of 398 n miles with the Caspian Sea on which Baku, the capital and largest city, is the principal port. Maritime claims in the Caspian Sea have yet to be resolved. Coast Guard formed in July 1992 with ships transferred from the Russian Caspian Flotilla and Border Guard. Operational control and maintenance was assumed by Russia 1995-99 but since then, the Azeri Navy has taken back full responsibility. During 2003 there were increasing signs of a drive to improve effectiveness, reflecting heightened tensions in the Caspian Sea.

Headquarters Appointments

Commander of Navy:
  Rear Admiral Sahin Sultanov

Personnel

2006: 2,200

Bases

Baku

PATROL FORCES

Notes: An Osa II class (without SSM) and a Svetlyak are reported non-operational.

1 TURK (AB 25) CLASS (PB)

ARAZ (ex-AB 34)

Displacement, tons: 170 full load
Dimensions, feet (metres): 132 × 21 × 5.5 (40.2 × 6.4 × 1.7)
Main machinery: 4 SACM-AGO V16CSHR diesels; 9,600 hp(m) (7.06 MW); 2 cruise diesels; 300 hp(m) (220 kW); 2 shafts
Speed, knots: 22
Complement: 31 (3 officers)
Guns: 1 or 2 Bofors 40 mm/70.
  1 Oerlikon 20 mm (if only 1 — 40 mm fitted). 2 — 12.7 mm MGs.
Depth charges: 1 rack.
Radars: Surface search: Racal Decca; I-band.

Comment: Ex-AB 34 transferred from Turkey July 2000.

TURK CLASS (Turkish colours)   *11/1998, Selim San* / 0050287

1 POINT CLASS (PB)

Name	No	Builders	Commissioned
—(ex-*Point Brower*)	S-201 (ex-82372)	USCG Yard, Curtis Bay	21 Apr 1970

Displacement, tons: 67 full load
Dimensions, feet (metres): 83 × 17.2 × 5.8 (25.3 × 5.3 × 1.8)
Main machinery: 2 Caterpillar diesels; 1,600 hp (1.19 MW); 2 shafts
Speed, knots: 22
Range, n miles: 1,200 at 8 kt
Complement: 10
Guns: 2 — 12.7 mm MGs.
Radars: Surface search: Hughes/Furuno SPS-73; I-band.

Comment: Transferred from US Coast Guard on 28 February 2003.

POINT CLASS (Jamaica colours)   *10/1999, JDFCG* / 0080127

2 STENKA (PROJECT 205P) CLASS (PBF)

—(ex-AK 234)   —(ex-AK 374)

Displacement, tons: 253 full load
Dimensions, feet (metres): 129.3 × 25.9 × 8.2 (39.4 × 7.9 × 2.5)
Main machinery: 3 diesels; 14,100 hp(m) (10.36 MW); 3 shafts
Speed, knots: 37
Range, n miles: 2,300 at 14 kt
Complement: 25
Guns: 4 — 30 mm/65 (2 twin) AK 230.
Radars: Surface search: Pot Drum; H/I-band.
Fire control: Drum Tilt; H/I-band.
Navigation: Palm Frond; I-band.

Comment: Ex-Russian craft built in the 1970s. Sonar and torpedo tubes removed.

STENKA CLASS (Georgia colours)   *7/1999* / 0088747

1 ZHUK (GRIF) CLASS (PROJECT 1400M) (PB)

137 (ex-AK 55)

Displacement, tons: 39 full load
Dimensions, feet (metres): 78.7 × 16.4 × 3.9 (24 × 5 × 1.2)
Main machinery: 2 Type M 401B diesels; 2,200 hp(m) (1.6 MW) sustained; 2 shafts
Speed, knots: 30
Range, n miles: 1,100 at 15 kt
Complement: 13
Guns: 2 — 14.5 mm (twin). 1 — 12.7 mm MG.
Radars: Surface search: Spin Trough; I-band.

Comment: Ex-Russian craft built in the 1970s.

ZHUK CLASS (Ukraine colours)   *7/2000, Hartmut Ehlers* / 0106655

2 PETRUSHKA (UK-3) CLASS (PB/AXL)

P 215   **+1**

Displacement, tons: 335 full load
Dimensions, feet (metres): 129.3 × 27.6 × 7.2 (39.4 × 8.4 × 2.2)
Main machinery: 2 Wola H12 diesels; 756 hp(m) (556 kW); 2 shafts
Speed, knots: 11
Range, n miles: 1,000 at 11 kt
Complement: 13 plus 30

Comment: Built as training ships at Wisla Shipyard, Poland. Probably operated both in the training and patrol ship role.

PETRUSHKA CLASS   *6/2003, E & M Laursen* / 0570909

1 WODNIK II CLASS (PROJECT 888) (PB/AXT)

T 710 (ex-*Oka*)

Displacement, tons: 1,697 standard; 1,820 full load
Dimensions, feet (metres): 234.3 × 38.1 × 14.8 (71.4 × 11.6 × 4.5)
Main machinery: 2 Zgoda-Sulzer 6TD48 diesels; 2,650 hp(m) (1.95 MW) sustained; 2 shafts; cp props
Speed, knots: 16
Range, n miles: 7,200 at 11 kt
Complement: 56 (24 officers)
Guns: 4 ZU-23-2MR Wrobel 23 mm (2 twin).
Radars: Navigation: 2 Don 2; I-band.

Comment: Built at Gdansk, Poland in 1976-77. Of same general design as Polish ships with an extra deck and a larger superstructure. Probably employed in both training and patrol ship roles.

AMPHIBIOUS FORCES

Notes: (1) Two Vydra class are reported non-operational.
(2) A T4 LCM has also been reported.

1 POLNOCHNY B CLASS (PROJECT 771) (LSM)

D 431 (ex-MDK 107)

Displacement, tons: 760 standard; 834 full load
Dimensions, feet (metres): 246.1 × 31.5 × 7.5 (75 × 9.6 × 2.3)
Main machinery: 2 Kolomna Type 40-D diesels; 4,400 hp(m) (3.2 MW) sustained; 2 shafts
Speed, knots: 18
Range, n miles: 1,000 at 18 kt
Complement: 42
Military lift: 180 troops; 350 tons including up to 6 tanks
Guns: 2 — 30 mm/65 (twin) AK 230; 500 rds/min to 5 km (2.7 n miles); weight of shell 0.54 kg.
  2 — 140 mm 18-tubed rocket launchers.
Radars: Navigation: Don 2; I-band.
Fire control: Drum Tilt; H/I-band.
IFF: Square Head. High Pole B.

Comment: Built in Poland 1968-70. Tank deck covers 237 m².

2 POLNOCHNY A (PROJECT 770) CLASS (LSM)

D 432 (ex-MDK 36)   **D 433** (ex-MDC 37)

Displacement, tons: 800 full load
Dimensions, feet (metres): 239.5 × 27.9 × 5.8 *(73 × 8.5 × 1.8)*
Main machinery: 2 Kolomna Type 40-D diesels; 4,400 hp(m) *(3.2 MW)* sustained; 2 shafts
Speed, knots: 19
Range, n miles: 1,000 at 18 kt
Complement: 40
Military lift: 6 tanks; 350 tons
Guns: 2 USSR 30 mm/65 (twin); 500 rds/min to 5 km *(2.7 n miles);* weight of shell 0.54 kg. 2—140 mm rocket launchers; 18 barrels to 9 km *(4.9 n miles).*
Radars: Surface search: Decca; I-band.
Fire control: Drum Tilt; H/I-band.

Comment: Built at Northern Shipyard, Gdansk in the late 1960s.

POLNOCHNY CLASS (Egyptian colours)   *10/2000, F Sadek* / 0103742

AUXILIARIES

Notes: A variety of auxiliary craft is reported to be in Azerbaijan service although operational status has not been confirmed. Vessels include a Petrushka class training vessel, a Shelon class torpedo recovery craft, an Emba class cable ship and four survey ships (one Kamenka, one Finik, one Vadim Popov and one Valeryan Uryvayev). There is also an ex-commercial (possible oil-rig support) craft with pennant number S 701.

1 VIKHR (IVA) (PROJECT B-99) CLASS (FIREFIGHTING TUGS) (ARS)

S 703

Displacement, tons: 2,300 full load
Dimensions, feet (metres): 237.2 × 46.9 × 15.1 *(72.3 × 14.3 × 4.6)*
Main machinery: 2 diesels; 5,900 hp(m) *(4.4 MW);* 2 shafts; cp props; 2 bow thrusters
Speed, knots: 16
Range, n miles: 2,500 at 12 kt
Complement: 25

Comment: Built in Gdansk, Poland, in mid-1980s.

MINE WARFARE FORCES

Notes: Three Sonya class are reported non-operational.

2 YEVGENYA CLASS (PROJECT 1258) (MINEHUNTERS) (MHC)

237   **+1**

Displacement, tons: 77 standard; 90 full load
Dimensions, feet (metres): 80.7 × 18 × 4.9 *(24.6 × 5.5 × 1.5)*
Main machinery: 2 Type 3-D-12 diesels; 600 hp(m) *(440 kW)* sustained; 2 shafts
Speed, knots: 11
Range, n miles: 300 at 10 kt
Complement: 10
Guns: 2—14.5 mm (twin) MGs.
Countermeasures: Minehunting gear is lowered on a crane at the stern.
Radars: Navigation: Don 2; I-band.
Sonars: MG 7 lifted over the stern.

Comment: Ex-Russian craft built in the 1970s.

YEVGENYA (Russian colours)   *1991* / 0506087

Bahamas

Country Overview

The Commonwealth of the Bahamas gained independence in 1971; the British monarch, represented by a governor-general, is head of state. Situated in the west Atlantic Ocean, it comprises about 700 islands and islets, and nearly 2,400 cays and rocks which stretch between Florida and Hispaniola. About 30 of the islands are inhabited. The capital, Nassau, is on New Providence Island which contains more than half of the total population. Grand Bahama, the most northerly of the group, is the second major island. An archipelagic regime, territorial seas (12 n miles) and a fishery zone (200 n miles) are claimed. A 200 n mile Exclusive Economic Zone (EEZ) has been claimed but the limits are not defined.

Headquarters Appointments

Commander Royal Bahamas Defence Force:
   Commodore Davy F Rolle
Squadron Commanding Officer:
   Commander Albert Armbrister

Bases

HMBS *Coral Harbour* (New Providence Island)
HMBS *Matthew Town* (Great Inagua Island)

Personnel

2006: 922

Prefix to Ships' Names

HMBS (Her Majesty's Bahamian Ship)

PATROL FORCES

2 BAHAMAS CLASS

Name	No	Builders	Commissioned
BAHAMAS	P 60	Moss Point Marine, Escatawpa	27 Jan 2000
NASSAU	P 61	Moss Point Marine, Escatawpa	27 Jan 2000

Displacement, tons: 375 full load
Dimensions, feet (metres): 198.8 × 29.2 × 8.5 *(60.6 × 8.9 × 2.6)*
Main machinery: 3 Caterpillar 3516B diesels; 6,600 hp(m) *(4.85 MW);* 3 shafts
Speed, knots: 24
Range, n miles: 3,000 at 10 kt
Complement: 35 plus 28 spare
Guns: 1 Bushmaster 25 mm. 3—12.7 mm MGs.
Radars: Surface search/Navigation: Decca Bridgemaster Type 656-14/CAB; I-band.

Comment: Order placed 14 March 1997 with Halter Marine Group. Aluminium superstructures fabricated at Equitable Shipyards while hulls built at Moss Point. The design is an adapted Vosper International Europatrol 250 with a RIB and launching crane at the stern. Based at Nassau.

BAHAMAS   *6/2003*, Marco Ghiglino* / 1129991

3 PROTECTOR CLASS (PB)

Name	No	Builders	Commissioned
YELLOW ELDER	P 03	Fairey Marine, Cowes	20 Nov 1986
PORT NELSON	P 04	Fairey Marine, Cowes	20 Nov 1986
SAMANA	P 05	Fairey Marine, Cowes	20 Nov 1986

Displacement, tons: 110 standard; 180 full load
Dimensions, feet (metres): 108.3 × 22 × 6.9 *(33 × 6.7 × 2.1)*
Main machinery: 3 Detroit 16V-149TI diesels; 3,483 hp *(2.6 MW)* sustained; 3 shafts
Speed, knots: 30
Range, n miles: 300 at 24 kt; 600 at 14 kt on 1 engine
Complement: 20 (3 officers) plus 5 spare
Guns: 1 Rheinmetall 20 mm. 3—7.62 mm MGs.
Radars: Surface search: Furuno; I-band.

Comment: Ordered December 1984. Steel hulls. One RIB is carried and can be launched by a trainable crane. Based at Coral Harbour.

SAMANA   *4/1996, RBDF* / 0056527

1 CHALLENGER CLASS (PB)

P 41

Displacement, tons: 8 full load
Dimensions, feet (metres): 27 × 5.5 × 1 *(8.2 × 1.7 × 0.3)*
Main machinery: 2 Evinrude outboards; 450 hp *(330 kW)*
Speed, knots: 26
Complement: 4
Guns: 1—7.62 mm MG.

Comment: Built by Boston Whaler Edgewater, Florida and delivered in September 1995. GRP hull.

P 41   *9/1996, RBDF* / 0056530

1 ELEUTHERA (KEITH NELSON) CLASS (PB)

Name	No	Builders	Commissioned
INAGUA	P 27	Vosper Thornycroft	10 Dec 1979

Displacement, tons: 30 standard; 37 full load
Dimensions, feet (metres): 60 × 15.8 × 4.6 *(18.3 × 4.8 × 1.4)*
Main machinery: 2 Caterpillar 3408BTA diesels; 1,070 hp *(800 kW)* sustained; 2 shafts
Speed, knots: 20
Range, n miles: 650 at 16 kt
Complement: 11
Guns: 3—7.62 mm MGs.
Radars: Surface search Furuno; I-band.

Comment: The survivor of a class of five. Light machine guns mounted in sockets either side of the bridge. One more is used as a museum. Main engine replaced in 1990.

INAGUA   *6/1998, RBDF* / 0017574

2 DAUNTLESS CLASS (INSHORE PATROL CRAFT) (PB)

P 42   **P 43**

Displacement, tons: 11 full load
Dimensions, feet (metres): 40.4 × 14 × 4.3 *(12.3 × 4.3 × 1.3)*
Main machinery: 2 Caterpillar 3208TA diesels; 870 hp *(650 kW)* sustained; 2 shafts
Speed, knots: 25
Range, n miles: 600 at 18 kt
Complement: 5
Guns: 2—7.62 mm MGs.
Radars: Surface search: Furuno 1761; I-band.

Comment: Built by SeaArk Marine, Monticello, Arkansas and delivered in January 1996. Aluminium construction. Used primarily for medium-range search and rescue missions. Based at Coral Harbour.

P 43   *6/1999, RBDF* / 0081453

4 BOSTON WHALERS (PBF)

P 110-111   **P 112-113**

Displacement, tons: 1.5 full load
Dimensions, feet (metres): 20 × 7.2 × 1.1 *(6.1 × 2.2 × 0.4)*
Main machinery: 2 Evinrude outboards; 180 hp *(134 kW)* (P 110-111); 2 Mariner outboards; 150 hp *(120 kW)* (P 112-113)
Speed, knots: 45 *(P 110-111)*; 38 *(P 112-113)*
Complement: 3

Comment: *P 110* and *111* are Impact designs commissioned 25 September 1995. *P 112* and *113* are Wahoo types commissioned 23 October 1995.

P 110 and P 111   *9/1997, RBDF* / 0012053

P 113   *6/1999, RBDF* / 0081454

Bahrain

Country Overview

Formerly under British control from 1861, Bahrain gained its independence in 1971. Situated in the southern Gulf, with which it has a coastline of 87 n miles, the country comprises a group of 33 islands between the Qatar Peninsula to the east and Saudi Arabia to the west. The principal islands include Bahrain (217 square miles), Al Muharraq; Umm an Na'san; Sitrah; Jiddah and the Hawar group. The capital, largest city and principal port is Manama. Territorial seas (12 n miles) are claimed. An EEZ has not been claimed.

Headquarters Appointments

Chief of Staff:
   Major General Shaikh Abdullah Bin Salman Bin Khalid Al Khalifa
Commander of Navy:
   Colonel Abdulla al Mansoori
Director of Coast Guard:
   Colonel Yousef Ahmed al Ghatam

Personnel

(a)   2006: 1,000 (Navy), 770 (Coast Guard 260 seagoing)
(b)   Voluntary service

Bases

Mina Sulman (Navy)
Bandar-Dar (CG HQ)
Muharraq (CG base)

Coast Guard

This unit is under the direction of the Ministry of the Interior.

Prefix to Ships' Names

BRNS (Bahrain Royal Navy Ship)

FRIGATES

1 + (1) OLIVER HAZARD PERRY CLASS (FFGHM)

Name	No	Builders	Laid down	Launched	Commissioned	Recommissioned
SABHA (ex-*Jack Williams*)	90 (ex-FFG 24)	Bath Iron Works	25 Feb 1980	30 Aug 1980	19 Sep 1981	25 Feb 1997

Displacement, tons: 2,750 light; 3,638 full load
Dimensions, feet (metres): 445 × 45 × 14.8; 24.5 (sonar)
(135.6 × 13.7 × 4.5; 7.5)
Main machinery: 2 GE LM 2500 gas turbines; 41,000 hp
(30.59 MW) sustained; 1 shaft; cp prop
2 auxiliary retractable props; 650 hp *(484 kW)*
Speed, knots: 29. **Range, n miles:** 4,500 at 20 kt
Complement: 206 (13 officers) including 19 aircrew

Missiles: SSM: 4 McDonnell Douglas Harpoon; active radar
homing to 130 km *(70 n miles)* at 0.9 Mach; warhead
227 kg.
SAM: 36 GDC Standard SM-1MR; command guidance; semi-
active radar homing to 46 km *(25 n miles)* at 2 Mach.
1 Mk 13 Mod 4 launcher for both SSM and SAM
missiles **❶**.
Guns: 1 OTO Melara 3 in *(76 mm)*/62 Mk 75 **❷**; 85 rds/min
to 16 km *(8.7 n miles)* anti-surface; 12 km *(6.6 n miles)*
anti-aircraft; weight of shell 6 kg.
1 General Electric/General Dynamics 20 mm/76
6-barrelled Mk 15 Vulcan Phalanx **❸**; 3,000 rds/min (4,500
in Block 1) combined to 1.5 km.
4—12.7 mm MGs.
Torpedoes: 6—324 mm Mk 32 Mod 7 (2 triple) tubes **❹**.
24 Honeywell Mk 46; anti-submarine; active/passive
homing to 11 km *(5.9 n miles)* at 40 kt; warhead 44 kg.
Countermeasures: Decoys: 2 Loral Hycor SRBOC 6-barrelled
fixed Mk 36 **❺**; IR flares and chaff to 4 km *(2.2 n miles)*.
SLQ-25 Nixie; torpedo decoy.

SABHA *(Scale 1 : 1,200), Ian Sturton* / 0056532

ESM/ECM: SLQ-32(V)2 **❻**; radar warning. Sidekick
modification adds jammer and deception system.
Combat data systems: NTDS with Link 14. INMARSAT.
Weapons control: SWG-1 Harpoon LCS. Mk 92 (Mod 4).
The Mk 92 is the US version of the Signaal WM28
system. Mk 13 weapon direction system. 2 Mk 24 optical
directors.
Radars: Air search: Raytheon SPS-49(V)4 **❼**; C-band; range
457 km *(250 n miles)*.
Surface search: ISC Cardion SPS-55 **❽**; I-band.
Fire control: Lockheed STIR (modified SPG-60); I/J-band;
range 110 km *(60 n miles)*.
Sperry Mk 92 (Signaal WM28) **❿**; I/J-band.
Tacan: URN 25.

Sonars: Raytheon SQS-56; hull-mounted; active search and
attack; medium frequency.

Helicopters: 1 Eurocopter BO 105 **⓫**. Space for 2 SH-2G.

Programmes: *Sabha* transferred from the US by grant
18 September 1996. Arrived in the Gulf in June 1997 for
a work-up and training period. Transfer of a second ship
is a possibility.
Structure: Apart from the removal of the US SATCOM
aerials there are no visible changes from US
service.
Operational: A transfer of helicopters is required if the
ASW potential of the ship is to be realised.

SABHA *4/2000, Guy Toremans* / 0104200

SABHA *6/2003, A Sharma* / 0568881

For details of the latest updates to *Jane's Fighting Ships* online and to discover the additional
information available exclusively to online subscribers please visit
jfs.janes.com

CORVETTES

2 AL MANAMA (MGB 62) CLASS (FSGH)

Name	No	Builders	Commissioned
AL MANAMA	50	Lürssen	14 Dec 1987
AL MUHARRAQ	51	Lürssen	3 Feb 1988

Displacement, tons: 632 full load
Dimensions, feet (metres): 206.7 × 30.5 × 9.5
(63 × 9.3 × 2.9)
Main machinery: 4 MTU 20V 538 TB92 diesels; 12,820 hp(m)
(9.42 MW) sustained; 4 shafts
Speed, knots: 32. **Range, n miles:** 4,000 at 16 kt
Complement: 43 (7 officers)

Missiles: SSM: 4 Aerospatiale MM 40 Exocet launchers
(2 twin) **❶**; inertial cruise; active radar homing to 70 km
(40 n miles) at 0.9 Mach; warhead 165 kg; sea-skimmer.
Guns: 1 OTO Melara 3 in *(76 mm)*/62 compact **❷**;
85 rds/min to 16 km *(8.7 n miles)* anti-surface; 12 km
(6.5 n miles) anti-aircraft; weight of shell 6 kg.
2 Breda 40 mm/70 (twin) **❸**; 300 rds/min to 12.5 km
(6.8 n miles); weight of shell 0.96 kg.
2—7.62 mm MGs.
Countermeasures: Decoys: CSEE Dagaie **❹**; chaff and IR
flares.
ESM/ECM: Racal Decca Cutlass/Cygnus **❺**; intercept and
jammer.
Weapons control: CSEE Panda Mk 2 optical director. Philips
TV/IR optronic director **❻**.

AL MANAMA   *(Scale 1 : 600), Ian Sturton* / 0104201

Radars: Air/surface search: Philips Sea Giraffe 50 HC **❼**;
G-band.
Navigation: Racal Decca 1226; I-band.
Fire control: Philips 9LV 331 **❽**; J-band.

Helicopters: 1 Eurocopter BO 105 **❾**.

Programmes: Ordered February 1984.

Modernisation: Upgrade planned to include a SAM self-
defence system.
Structure: Similar to Singapore and UAE designs. Steel
hull, aluminium superstructure. Fitted with a helicopter
platform which incorporates a lift to lower the aircraft
into the hangar.
Operational: Planned SA 365F helicopters were not
acquired.

AL MANAMA   *3/1999, Maritime Photographic* / 0056536

AL MANAMA   *11/2001, Royal Australian Navy* / 0526836

SHIPBORNE AIRCRAFT

Notes: SH-2G helicopters may be acquired for the frigate in due course.

Numbers/Type: 2 Eurocopter BO 105.
Operational speed: 113 kt *(210 km/h)*.
Service ceiling: 9,845 ft *(3,000 m)*.
Range: 407 n miles *(754 km)*.
Role/Weapon systems: Acquired in August 1994 as the first aircraft of a Naval Air Arm. Sensors: Bendix RDR 1500B radar. Weapons: Unarmed.

BO 105 *6/1995* / 0056541

PATROL FORCES

4 AHMAD EL FATEH (TNC 45) CLASS
(FAST ATTACK CRAFT—MISSILE) (PGGF)

Name	No	Builders	Commissioned
AHMAD EL FATEH	20	Lürssen	5 Feb 1984
AL JABIRI	21	Lürssen	3 May 1984
ABDUL RAHMAN AL FADEL	22	Lürssen	10 Sep 1986
AL TAWEELAH	23	Lürssen	25 Mar 1989

Displacement, tons: 228 half load; 259 full load
Dimensions, feet (metres): 147.3 × 22.9 × 8.2 *(44.9 × 7 × 2.5)*
Main machinery: 4 MTU 16V 538 TB92 diesels; 13,640 hp(m) *(10 MW)* sustained; 4 shafts
Speed, knots: 40
Range, n miles: 1,600 at 16 kt
Complement: 36 (6 officers)

Missiles: SSM: 4 Aerospatiale MM 40 Exocet (2 twin); inertial cruise; active radar homing to 70 km *(40 n miles)* at 0.9 Mach; warhead 165 kg; sea-skimmer.
Guns: 1 OTO Melara 3 in *(76 mm)*/62; dual purpose; 85 rds/min to 16 km *(8.7 n miles)* anti-surface; 12 km *(6.5 n miles)* anti-aircraft; weight of shell 6 kg.
2 Breda 40 mm/70 (twin); 300 rds/min to 12.5 km *(6.8 n miles)*; weight of shell 0.96 kg.
3 — 7.62 mm MGs.
Countermeasures: Decoys: CSEE Dagaie launcher; trainable mounting; 10 containers firing chaff decoys and IR flares.
ESM: Thales Sealion.
ECM: Racal Cygnus (not in 20 and 21); jammer.
Weapons control: 1 Panda optical director for 40 mm guns.
Radars: Air/surface search: Philips Sea Giraffe 50 HC; G-band.
Fire control: Philips 9LV 226/231; J-band.
Navigation: Racal Decca 1226; I-band.

Programmes: First pair ordered in 1979, second pair in 1985. Similar craft in service with Ecuador, Kuwait and UAE navies.
Structure: Only the second pair have the communication radome on the after superstructure.
Operational: Refits from 2000 by Lürssen at Abu Dhabi.

AHMAD EL FATEH *4/2003, A Sharma* / 0568844

AL TAWEELAH *4/2000, Guy Toremans* / 0104203

2 AL RIFFA (FPB 38) CLASS (FAST ATTACK CRAFT—GUN) (PB)

Name	No	Builders	Commissioned
AL RIFFA	10	Lürssen	3 Mar 1982
HAWAR	11	Lürssen	3 Mar 1982

Displacement, tons: 188 half load; 205 full load
Dimensions, feet (metres): 126.3 × 22.9 × 7.2 *(38.5 × 7 × 2.2)*
Main machinery: 2 MTU 16V 538 TB92 diesels; 6,810 hp(m) *(5 MW)* sustained; 2 shafts
Speed, knots: 32
Range, n miles: 1,100 at 16 kt
Complement: 27 (3 officers)
Guns: 2 Breda 40 mm/70 (twin); dual purpose; 300 rds/min to 12 km *(6.5 n miles)* anti-surface; 4 km *(2.2 n miles)*; weight of shell 0.96 kg.
1 — 57 mm Starshell rocket launcher.
Mines: Mine rails fitted.
Countermeasures: Decoys: 1 Wallop Barricade chaff launcher.
ESM: Racal RDL-2 ABC; radar warning.
Weapons control: CSEE Lynx optical director with Philips 9LV 126 optronic system.
Radars: Surface search: Philips 9GR 600; I-band.
Navigation: Racal Decca 1226; I-band.

Comment: Ordered in 1979. *Al Riffa* launched April 1981. *Hawar* launched July 1981.

HAWAR *6/2003, A Sharma* / 0568880

2 AL JARIM (FPB 20) CLASS (FAST ATTACK CRAFT—GUN) (PB)

Name	No	Builders	Commissioned
AL JARIM	30	Swiftships, Morgan City	9 Feb 1982
AL JASRAH	31	Swiftships, Morgan City	26 Feb 1982

Displacement, tons: 33 full load
Dimensions, feet (metres): 63 × 18.4 × 6.5 *(19.2 × 5.6 × 2)*
Main machinery: 2 Detroit 12V-71TA diesels; 840 hp(m) *(627 kW)* sustained; 2 shafts
Speed, knots: 30
Range, n miles: 1,200 at 18 kt
Guns: 1 Oerlikon GAM-BO1 20 mm.
Radars: Surface search: Decca 110; I-band.

Comment: Aluminium hulls.

AL JARIM *5/2003, A Sharma* / 0568879

AUXILIARIES

Notes: There are also two RTK Medevac boats and one Diving Boat (512).

1 AJEERA CLASS (SUPPLY SHIPS) (YFU)

Name	No	Builders	Commissioned
AJEERA	41	Swiftships, Morgan City	21 Oct 1982

Displacement, tons: 420 full load
Dimensions, feet (metres): 129.9 × 36.1 × 5.9 *(39.6 × 11 × 1.8)*
Main machinery: 2 Detroit 16V-71 diesels; 811 hp *(605 kW)* sustained; 2 shafts
Speed, knots: 13
Range, n miles: 1,500 at 10 kt
Complement: 21
Guns: 2 — 12.7 mm MGs.
Radars: Navigation: Racal Decca; I-band.

Comment: Used as general purpose cargo ships and can carry up to 200 tons of fuel and water. Built to an LCU design with a bow ramp and 15 ton crane.

AJEERA *4/2003, A Sharma* / 0568843

4 LCU 1466 CLASS (LCU)

MASHTAN 42	**RUBODH** 43	**SUWAD** 44	**JARADAH** 45

Displacement, tons: 360 full load
Dimensions, feet (metres): 119 × 34 × 6 *(36.3 × 10.4 × 1.8)*
Main machinery: 3 Gray Marine 64 YTL diesels; 675 hp *(504 kW)*; 3 shafts
Speed, knots: 8
Range, n miles: 800 at 8 kt
Complement: 15
Cargo capacity: 167 tons
Guns: 2 — 12.7 mm MGs.
Radars: Navigation: Racal Decca; I-band.

Comment: Transferred from US in 1991. Capable of carrying 150 tons of cargo.

RUBODH   *4/2003, A Sharma* / 0568842

1 PERSONNEL TRANSPORT CRAFT (YFL)

TIGHATLIB 46

Comment: Details not confirmed.

TIGHATLIB   *6/2003, A Sharma* / 0568877

1 LOADMASTER II CLASS (LCU)

AL ZUBARA (ex-*Sabha*) 40

Displacement, tons: 150 full load
Dimensions, feet (metres): 73.8 × 24.6 × 3.9 *(22.5 × 7.5 × 1.2)*
Main machinery: 2 General Motors 8V92N diesels; 780 hp *(575 kW)*; 2 props
Speed, knots: 6
Radars: Navigation: I-band.

Comment: Built by Fairey Marine Cowes, UK and entered service in 1981.

AL ZUBARA   *4/2003*, A Sharma* / 0568839

COAST GUARD

Notes: (1) In addition to the craft listed below about 14 small open fibreglass boats are used for patrol duties.
(2) Procurement of new patrol craft was expected in 2004 but has not been confirmed.

1 WASP 30 METRE CLASS (WPB)

AL MUHARRAQ

Displacement, tons: 90 standard; 103 full load
Dimensions, feet (metres): 98.5 × 21 × 5.5 *(30 × 6.4 × 1.6)*
Main machinery: 2 Detroit 16V-149TI diesels; 2,322 hp *(1.73 MW)* sustained; 2 shafts
Speed, knots: 25
Range, n miles: 500 at 22 kt
Complement: 9
Guns: 2 — 7.62 mm MGs.
    1 Hughes chain 7.62 mm.
Radars: Surface search: Racal Decca; I-band.

Comment: Ordered from Souters, Cowes, Isle of Wight in 1984. Laid down November 1984, launched 12 August 1985, shipped 21 October 1985. GRP hull.

AL MUHARRAQ   *4/2003, A Sharma* / 0568841

4 HALMATIC 20 METRE CLASS (WPB)

DERA'A 2, 6, 7 and **8**

Displacement, tons: 31.5 full load
Dimensions, feet (metres): 65.9 × 19.4 × 5.1 *(20.1 × 5.9 × 1.5)*
Main machinery: 2 Detroit 12V-71TA diesels; 840 hp *(626 kW)* sustained; 2 shafts
Speed, knots: 25
Range, n miles: 500 at 20 kt
Complement: 7
Guns: 2 — 7.62 mm MGs.

Comment: Three delivered in late 1991, the last in early 1992. GRP hulls.

DERA'A 2   *7/2003, A Sharma* / 0568878

2 WASP 20 METRE CLASS (WPB)

DERA'A 4 and **5**

Displacement, tons: 36.3 full load
Dimensions, feet (metres): 65.6 × 16.4 × 4.9 *(20 × 5 × 1.5)*
Main machinery: 2 Detroit 12V-71TA diesels; 840 hp *(626 kW)* sustained; 2 shafts
Speed, knots: 24.5
Range, n miles: 500 at 20 kt
Complement: 8
Guns: 2 — 7.62 mm MGs.
Radars: Surface search: Racal Decca; I-band.

Comment: Built by Souters, Cowes, Isle of Wight. Delivered 1983. GRP hulls.

DERA'A 4   *6/2000, Bahrain Coast Guard* / 0104206

6 HALMATIC 160 CLASS (WPB)

SAIF 5, 6, 7, 8, 9 and **10**

Displacement, tons: 17 full load
Dimensions, feet (metres): 47.2 × 12.8 × 3.9 *(14.4 × 3.9 × 1.2)*
Main machinery: 2 Detroit 6V-92TA diesels; 520 hp *(388 kW)* sustained; 2 shafts
Speed, knots: 20. **Range, n miles:** 500 at 20 kt
Complement: 4
Guns: 1 — 7.62 mm MG.
Radars: Surface search: Furuno; I-band.

Comment: Built by Halmatic, UK, and delivered in 1990-91. GRP hulls.

SAIF 5   *4/2001, Guy Toremans* / 0114683

2 HAWAR CLASS (PB)

HAWAR 1   **HAWAR 2**

Displacement, tons: 10.5 full load
Dimensions, feet (metres): 40.7 × 13.0 × 2.3 *(12.4 × 4.0 × 0.7)*
Main machinery: 2 Cummins 6CTA8.3 diesels
Speed, knots: 30
Guns: 1 — 7.62 mm MG.

Comment: Entered service in 2003.

HAWAR 1   *6/2003, John Fidler* / 0567903

4 FAIREY SWORD CLASS (WPB)

SAIF 1, 2, 3 and **4**

Displacement, tons: 15
Dimensions, feet (metres): 44.9 × 13.4 × 4.3 *(13.7 × 4.1 × 1.3)*
Main machinery: 2 GM 8V-71 diesels; 590 hp *(440 kW)* sustained; 2 shafts
Speed, knots: 22
Complement: 6
Radars: Navigation: Furuno; I-band.

Comment: Purchased in 1980. Built by Fairey Marine Ltd.

SAIF 3   *11/1999, Bahrain Coast Guard* / 0056543

3 WASP 11 METRE CLASS (WPB)

SAHAM 1   **SAHAM 2**   **SAHAM 3**

Displacement, tons: 7 full load
Dimensions, feet (metres): 36.1 × 10.5 × 2.6 *(11 × 3.2 × 0.8)*
Main machinery: 2 Yamaha outboards; 400 hp(m) *(294 kW)*
Speed, knots: 25
Range, n miles: 125 at 20 kt
Complement: 3
Radars: Navigation: Koden; I-band.

Comment: Built by Souters, Cowes in 1983. *Saham 2* re-engined with outboards and recommissioned in August 1997. *Saham 1* similarly back in service in 1998. *Saham 3* awaits upgrade.

SAHAM 2   *10/1997, Bahrain Coast Guard* / 0012061

1 SUPPORT CRAFT (YAG)

SAFRA 3

Displacement, tons: 165 full load
Dimensions, feet (metres): 85 × 25.9 × 5.2 *(25.9 × 7.9 × 1.6)*
Main machinery: 2 Detroit 16V-92TA diesels; 1,380 hp *(1.03 MW)*; 2 shafts
Speed, knots: 13. **Range, n miles:** 700 at 12 kt
Complement: 6
Radars: Navigation: Racal Decca; I-band.

Comment: Built by Halmatic, Havant and delivered in early 1992. Logistic support work boat equipped for towing and firefighting. Can carry 15 tons.

SAFRA 3   *4/2003, A Sharma* / 0568840

Bangladesh

Country Overview

The People's Republic of Bangladesh, formerly East Pakistan, proclaimed independence in 1971. Situated in south Asia and with an area of 55,598 square miles, most of its land border is with India (cutting off north-east India from the rest). There is a short border with Myanmar to the south-east. Its 313 n mile coastline is with the Bay of Bengal on which the principal port of Chittagong is situated. The capital and largest city is Dhaka. Territorial waters (12 n miles) are claimed. An EEZ (200 n miles) has been claimed but the limits have not been defined.

Headquarters Appointments

Chief of Naval Staff:
  Rear Admiral Mohammad Hasan Ali Khan
Assistant Chief of Naval Staff (Operations):
  Commodore M Atiqur Rahman
Assistant Chief of Naval Staff (Personnel):
  Commodore S H M Kalimullah
Assistant Chief of Naval Staff (Logistics):
  Commodore B Rahman
Assistant Chief of Naval Staff (Materials):
  Commodore M A Haque

Senior Appointments

Naval Administrative Authority, Dhaka:
  Commodore Mohammad Emdadul Islam
Commodore Commanding BN Flotilla:
  Commodore A S M A Awal
Commodore Commanding Chittagong:
  Commodore M S Kabir
Commodore Commanding Khulna:
  Commodore M M Rahman
Director General Coast Guard:
  Commodore S J Nizam
Commodore Superintendent, Dockyard:
  Commodore M S Kabir

Bases

Chittagong (BNS *Issa Khan*, BN Dockyard, Naval Stores Depot, Chittagong, BNS *Ulka*, Bangladesh. Naval Academy, BNS *Patenga*, BNS *Bhatiary*, Naval Units *Cox's Bazar*, *Chanua* and *St Martins*), Kaptai (BNS *Shaheed Moazzam*). Dhaka (NHQ, BNS *Haji Mohsin* and Naval Unit *Pagla*). Khulna (BNS *Titumir*, BNS *Mongla*, BNS *Upasham*, Forward Bases *Khepupara* and *Hiron Point*.

Personnel

(a) 2006: 12,709 (1,177 officers)
(b) Voluntary service

Strength of the Fleet

Type	Active	Building
Frigates	5	–
Fast Attack Craft (Missile)	9	–
Fast Attack Craft (Torpedo)	8	–
Fast Attack Craft (Gun)	13	–
Large Patrol Craft	7	–
Coastal Patrol Craft	9	–
Riverine Patrol Craft	5	–
Minesweepers	4	–
Training Ships	1	–
Repair Ship	1	–
Tankers	2	–
Survey Craft	4	–

Coast Guard

Formed on 19 December 1995 with two ships on loan from the Navy. Bases at Chittagong (East Zone) and Khulna (West Zone). Personnel 721 (54 officers). Colours thick red and thin blue diagonal stripes on hull with COAST GUARD on ships side.

Prefix to Ships' Names

Navy: BNS
Coast Guard: CGS

PENNANT LIST

Frigates		P 411	Shaheed Daulat	P 8113	Durvedya	Auxiliaries	
		P 412	Shaheed Farid	P 8114	Durdam		
F 15	Abu Bakr	P 413	Shaheed Mohibullah	P 8125	Durdharsha	A 511	Shaheed Ruhul Amin
F 16	Umar Farooq	P 414	Shaheed Aktheruddin	P 8126	Durdanta	A 512	Shahayak
F 17	Ali Haider	P 611	Tawheed (CG)	P 8128	Dordanda	A 513	Shahjalal
F 18	Osman	P 612	Tawfiq	P 8131	Anirban	A 515	Khan Jahan Ali
F 25	DW 2000H	P 613	Tamjeed	P 8141	Uttal	A 516	Imam Gazzali
		P 614	Tanveer	P 8221	TB 1	A 581	Darshak
Patrol Forces		P 711	Barkat	P 8222	TB 2	A 582	Tallashi
		P 712	Salam	P 8223	TB 3	A 583	Agradoot
P 111	Pabna (CG)	P 713	Sangu	P 8224	TB 4	A 584	LCT-101
P 112	Noakhali (CG)	P 714	Turag	P 8235	TB 35	A 585	LCT-102
P 113	Patuakhali (CG)	P 811	Nirbhoy	P 8236	TB 36	A 587	LCT-104
P 114	Rangamati (CG)	P 911	Madhumati	P 8237	TB 37	A 711	Sundarban
P 115	Bogra (CG)	P 912	Kapatakhaya	P 8238	TB 38	A 721	Khadem
P 201	Ruposhi Bangla (CG)	P 913	Karatoa			A 722	Sebak
P 211	Meghna	P 914	Gomati	Mine Warfare Forces		A 723	Rupsha
P 212	Jamuna	P 1011	Titas			A 724	Shibsha
P 311	Bishkhali	P 1012	Kusiyara	M 91	Sagar	A 731	Balaban
P 312	Padma	P 1013	Chitra	M 95	Shapla	L 900	Shah Amanat
P 313	Surma	P 1014	Dhansiri	M 96	Saikat	L 901	Shah Paran
P 314	Karnaphuli	P 8111	Durbar	M 97	Surovi	L 902	Shah Makhdum
P 315	Tista	P 8112	Duranta	M 98	Shaibal		

SUBMARINES

Notes: Plans to acquire a submarine service by 2012 were announced by the Defence Minister in April 2004.

FRIGATES

Notes: Replacement of the Salisbury and Leopard class frigates is under consideration although timescales have not been announced.

1 OSMAN (JIANGHU I) CLASS (TYPE 053 H1) (FFG)

Name	No	Builders	Laid down	Launched	Commissioned
OSMAN (ex-*Xiangtan*)	F 18 (ex-556)	Hudong Shipyard, Shanghai	1986	Dec 1988	4 Nov 1989

Displacement, tons: 1,425 standard; 1,702 full load
Dimensions, feet (metres): 338.6 × 35.4 × 10.2
(103.2 × 10.7 × 3.1)
Main machinery: 2 Type 12 E 390V diesels; 16,000 hp(m)
(11.9 MW) sustained; 2 shafts
Speed, knots: 26. **Range, n miles:** 2,700 at 18 kt
Complement: 300 (27 officers)

Missiles: SSM: 4 Hai Ying 2 (2 twin) launchers ❶; active
radar or IR homing to 80 km *(43.2 n miles)* at 0.9 Mach;
warhead 513 kg.
Guns: 4 China 3.9 in *(100 mm)* /56 (2 twin) ❷; 18 rds/min to
22 km *(12 n miles)*; weight of shell 15.9 kg.
8 China 37 mm/76 (4 twin) ❸; 180 rds/min to 8.5 km
(4.6 n miles) anti-aircraft; weight of shell 1.42 kg.
A/S mortars: 2 RBU 1200 5-tubed fixed launchers ❹; range
1,200 m; warhead 34 kg.
Depth charges: 2 BMB-2 projectors; 2 racks.
Mines: Can carry up to 60.
Countermeasures: Decoys: 2 Loral Hycor SRBOC Mk 36
6-barrelled chaff launchers.
ESM: Watchdog; radar warning.
Weapons control: Wok Won director (752A) ❺.
Radars: Air/surface search: MX 902 Eye Shield (922-1) ❻;
G-band.

Surface search/fire control: Square Tie (254) ❼; I-band.
Navigation: Fin Curve (352); I-band.
IFF: High Pole A.
Sonars: Echo Type 5; hull-mounted; active search and
attack; medium frequency.

Programmes: Transferred 26 September 1989 from China,
arrived Bangladesh 8 October 1989. Second order
expected in 1991 was cancelled.

OSMAN

(Scale 1 : 900), Ian Sturton / 0130383

Structure: This is a Jianghu Type I (version 4) hull with
twin 100 mm guns (vice the 57 mm in the ships sold
to Egypt), Wok Won fire-control system and a rounded
funnel.
Operational: Damaged in collision with a merchant
ship in August 1991. One 37 mm mounting uprooted
and SSM and RBU mountings misaligned. Repaired in
1992-93.

OSMAN

10/2003, Hartmut Ehlers / 0569148

1 MODIFIED ULSAN CLASS

Name	No	Builders	Laid down	Launched	Commissioned
–	F 25	Daewoo Heavy Industries	12 May 1999	29 Aug 2000	20 June 2001

Displacement, tons: 2,170 standard; 2,370 full load
Dimensions, feet (metres): 340.3 × 41 × 12.5
(103.7 × 12.5 × 3.8)
Main machinery: CODAD: 4 SEMT-Pielstick 12V PA6V280
STC diesels; 22,501 hp *(16.78 MW)* sustained; 2 shafts
Speed, knots: 25
Range, n miles: 4,000 at 18 kt
Complement: 186 (16 officers)

Missiles: SSM: 4 Otomat Mk 2 ❶; command guidance;
active radar homing to 180 km *(97.2 n miles)*, at 0.9 Mach;
warhead 210 kg; sea-skimmer.
Guns: 1 Otobreda 3 in *(76 mm)*/62 Super Rapid ❷; 120 rds/
min to 16 km *(8.7 n miles)*; weight of shell 6 kg.
4 Otobreda 40 mm/70 (2 twin) compact ❸; 300 rds/min to
12.5 km *(6.8 n miles)*; weight of shell 0.96 kg.
Torpedoes: 6—324 mm B-515 (2 triple) tubes ❹; Whitehead
A244S; anti-submarine; active/passive homing to 7 km
(3.8 n miles); warhead 34 kg (shaped charge).
Countermeasures: Decoys: 2 Super Barricade launchers ❺
ESM: Racal Cutlass 242; intercept.
ECM: Racal Scorpion; jammer.
Combat data systems: Thales TACTICOS.
Weapons control: Signaal Mirador optronic director ❻.

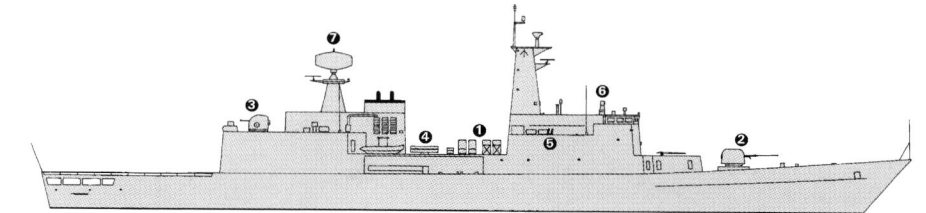

DW 2000H

(Scale 1 : 900), Ian Sturton / 0130076

Radars: Air search: Signaal DA08 ❼; F-band.
Surface search: Thales Variant; G-band.
Fire control: Signaal Lirod Mk 2; K-band.
Navigation: 2 KH-1007; I-band.
Sonars: STN Atlas ASO 90; hull-mounted; active search;
medium frequency.

Helicopters: Hangar and platform for operation of 'Lynx'
sized helicopter.

Programmes: Modified Ulsan class ordered from Daewoo
in March 1998. Arrived at Chittagong on 16 June 2001.
Operational: The ship was decommissioned on 13 February
2002 for design modification, warranty repairs and
capability upgrades. It was expected that the ship would
be recommissioned on completion of these programmes
but there have been no reports of progress and the
future of the ship is uncertain. The ship is known by the
builder's designation DW 2000H.

DW 2000H

6/2001 / 0111271

DW 2000H

6/2001, Daewoo / 0094449

1 SALISBURY CLASS (TYPE 61) (FF)

Name	No
UMAR FAROOQ (ex-*Llandaff*)	F 16

Displacement, tons: 2,170 standard; 2,408 full load
Dimensions, feet (metres): 339.8 × 40 × 15.5 (screws)
(103.6 × 12.2 × 4.7)
Main machinery: 8 16 VTS ASR 1 diesels; 14,400 hp
(10.7 MW) sustained; 2 shafts
Speed, knots: 24
Range, n miles: 2,300 at 24 kt; 7,500 at 16 kt
Complement: 237 (14 officers)

Guns: 2 Vickers 4.5 in *(115 mm)*/45 (twin) Mk 6 ❶; dual
purpose; 20 rds/min to 19 km *(10 n miles)* anti-surface;
6 km *(3.3 n miles)* anti-aircraft; weight of shell 25 kg.
2 Bofors 40 mm/60 Mk 9 ❷; 120 rds/min to 3 km
(1.6 n miles) anti-aircraft; 10 km *(5.5 n miles)* maximum.
A/S mortars: 1 triple-barrelled Squid Mk 4 ❸; fires pattern
of 3 depth charges to 300 m ahead of ship.
Countermeasures: Decoys: Corvus chaff launchers.
Weapons control: 1 Mk 6M gun director.
Radars: Air search: Marconi Type 965 with double AKE 2
array ❹; A-band.
Air/surface search: Plessey Type 993 ❺; E/F-band.

Builders	Laid down	Launched	Commissioned
Hawthorn Leslie Ltd	27 Aug 1953	30 Nov 1955	11 Apr 1958

UMAR FAROOQ

(Scale 1 : 900), Ian Sturton / 0505957

Heightfinder: Type 278M ❻; E-band.
Surface search: Decca Type 978 ❼; I-band.
Navigation: Decca Type 978; I-band.
Fire control: Type 275 ❽; F-band.
Sonars: Type 174; hull-mounted; active search; medium
frequency.
Graseby Type 170B; hull-mounted; active attack; 15 kHz.

Programmes: Transferred from UK at Royal Albert Dock,
London 10 December 1976.
Operational: The radar Type 982 aerial is still retained on
the after mast but the set is non-operational. The ship
has been modified as a training ship and is expected to
remain in service for some years.

UMAR FAROOQ

12/2005*, Chris Sattler / 1153833

2 LEOPARD CLASS (TYPE 41) (FF/FFT)

Name	No	Builders	Laid down	Launched	Commissioned
ABU BAKR (ex-*Lynx*)	F 15	John Brown & Co Ltd, Clydebank	13 Aug 1953	12 Jan 1955	14 Mar 1957
ALI HAIDER (ex-*Jaguar*)	F 17	Wm Denny & Bros Ltd, Dumbarton	2 Nov 1953	30 July 1957	12 Dec 1959

Displacement, tons: 2,300 standard; 2,520 full load
Dimensions, feet (metres): 339.8 × 40 × 15.5 (screws)
(103.6 × 12.2 × 4.7)
Main machinery: 8 16 VTS ASR 1 diesels; 14,400 hp *(10.7 MW)*
sustained; 2 shafts; F 17 fitted with cp props
Speed, knots: 24
Range, n miles: 2,300 at full power; 7,500 at 16 kt
Complement: 235 (15 officers)

Guns: 4 Vickers 4.5 in *(115 mm)*/45 (2 twin) Mk 6 ❶;
dual purpose; 20 rds/min to 19 km *(10 n miles)* anti-
surface; 6 km *(3.3 n miles)* anti-aircraft; weight of shell
25 kg.
1 Bofors 40 mm/60 Mk 9 ❷; 120 rds/min to 3 km
(1.6 n miles) anti-aircraft; 10 km *(5.5 n miles)*.
2—7.62 mm MGs.
Countermeasures: Decoys: Corvus chaff launchers.
ESM: Radar warning.
Weapons control: Mk 6M gun director.
Radars: Air search: Marconi Type 965 with single AKE 1
array ❸; A-band.
Air/surface search: Plessey Type 993 ❹; E/F-band.

ABU BAKR

Navigation: Decca Type 978; Kelvin Hughes 1007; I-band.
Fire control: Type 275 ❺; F-band.

Programmes: *Ali Haider* transferred from UK 16 July 1978
and *Abu Bakr* on 12 March 1982. *Ali Haider* refitted at
Vosper Thornycroft August-October 1978. *Abu Bakr*
extensively refitted in 1982.

(Scale 1 : 900), Ian Sturton / 0505958

Structure: All welded. Fitted with stabilisers. Sonars
removed while still in service with RN. Fuel tanks have a
water compensation system to improve stability.
Operational: Both to remain in service until replacements
have been acquired.

ALI HAIDER   *2/2001, Michael Nitz* / 0529082

PATROL FORCES

Notes: Plans to acquire an offshore patrol vessel, four missile-firing craft and six further
patrol boats were announced by the Defence Minister in April 2004.

1 MADHUMATI (SEA DRAGON) CLASS
(LARGE PATROL CRAFT) (PSO)

Name	No	Builders	Commissioned
MADHUMATI	P 911	Hyundai, Ulsan	18 Feb 1998

Displacement, tons: 635 full load
Dimensions, feet (metres): 199.5 × 26.2 × 8.9 *(60.8 × 8 × 2.7)*
Main machinery: 2 SEMT-Pielstick 12 PA6 diesels; 9,600 hp(m) *(7.08 MW)* sustained;
2 shafts
Speed, knots: 24
Range, n miles: 6,000 at 15 kt
Complement: 43 (7 officers)
Guns: 1 Bofors 57 mm/70 Mk 1; 220 rds/min to 17 km *(9.3 n miles)*; weight of shell 2.4 kg.
1 Bofors 40 mm/70. 2 Oerlikon 20 mm.
Weapons control: Optronic director.
Radars: Surface search: Kelvin Hughes KH 1007; I-band.
Navigation: GEM Electronics SPN 753B; I-band.

Comment: Ordered in 1995 and delivered in October 1997. Very similar to the South Korean
Coast Guard vessels, but with improved fire-control equipment. Vosper stabilisers.

4 DURDHARSHA (HUANGFEN) CLASS (TYPE 021)
(FAST ATTACK CRAFT—MISSILE) (PTFG)

DURDHARSHA P 8125		**DORDANDA** P 8128	
DURDANTA P 8126		**ANIRBAN** P 8131	

Displacement, tons: 171 standard; 205 full load
Dimensions, feet (metres): 126.6 × 24.9 × 8.9 *(38.6 × 7.6 × 2.7)*
Main machinery: 3 diesels; 12,000 hp(m) *(8.8 MW)*; 3 shafts
Speed, knots: 35
Range, n miles: 800 at 30 kt
Complement: 35 (5 officers)
Missiles: SSM: 4 HY-2; active radar or IR homing to 80 km *(43.2 n miles)* at 0.9 Mach;
warhead 513 kg.
Guns: 4 USSR 30 mm/65 (2 twin).
Radars: Surface search: Square Tie; I-band.
Fire control: Rice Lamp; H/I-band.
IFF: High Pole A.

Comment: Built in China. First four commissioned in Bangladesh Navy on 10 November
1988. Chinese equivalent of the Soviet Osa class which started building in 1985. All
damaged in April 1991 typhoon but recovered and repaired (*Durnibar* was converted
to a patrol craft). A fifth vessel *Anirban* was delivered in June 1992. Original main
machinery replaced.

MADHUMATI   *2/1998, Bangladesh Navy* / 0017589

DORDANDA   *6/2003, Bangladesh Navy* / 0572413

6 ISLAND CLASS
(COASTAL PATROL CRAFT/TRAINING CRAFT) (PBO/AX)

Name	No	Builders	Commissioned	Recommissioned
SHAHEED RUHUL AMIN (ex-*Jersey*)	A 511 (ex-P 295)	Hall Russell, Aberdeen	15 Oct 1976	1994
KAPATAKHAYA (ex-*Shetland*)	P 912 (ex-P 298)	Hall Russell, Aberdeen	14 July 1977	4 May 2003
KARATOA (ex-*Alderney*)	P 913 (ex-P 278)	Hall Russell, Aberdeen	6 Oct 1979	4 May 2003
GOMATI (ex-*Anglesey*)	P 914 (ex-P 277)	Hall Russell, Aberdeen	1 June 1979	3 Oct 2004
SANGU (ex-*Guernsey*)	P 713 (ex-P 297)	Hall Russell, Aberdeen	28 Oct 1977	3 Oct 2004
TURAG (ex-*Lindisfarne*)	P 714 (ex-P 300)	Hall Russell, Aberdeen	3 Mar 1978	3 Oct 2004

Displacement, tons: 925 standard; 1,260 full load
Dimensions, feet (metres): 176 wl; 195.3 oa × 36 × 15 *(53.7; 59.5 × 11 × 4.5)*
Main machinery: 2 Ruston 12RKC diesels; 5,640 hp *(4.21 MW)* sustained; 1 shaft; cp prop
Speed, knots: 16.5
Range, n miles: 7,000 at 12 kt
Complement: 39
Guns: 1 Bofors 40 mm/60 Mk 3. 2 FN 7.62 mm MGs.
Countermeasures: ESM: Orange Crop; intercept.
Combat data systems: Racal CANE DEA-1 action data automation.
Radars: Navigation: Kelvin Hughes Type 1006; I-band.

Comment: *Shaheed Ruhul Amin* transferred as a training craft in 1993. Five further former UK Island class acquired as patrol craft. *Kapatakhaya* transferred 31 July 2002, *Karatoa* 31 October 2002, *Gomati* on 12 September 2003 and *Sangu* and *Turag* on 29 January 2004.

TURAG   *3/2004, Derek Fox* / 1042116

5 DURBAR (HEGU) CLASS (TYPE 024)
(FAST ATTACK CRAFT—MISSILE) (PTFG)

DURBAR P 8111	DURVEDYA P 8113	UTTAL P 8141
DURANTA P 8112	DURDAM P 8114	

Displacement, tons: 68 standard; 79.2 full load
Dimensions, feet (metres): 88.6 × 20.7 × 4.3 *(27 × 6.3 × 1.3)*
Main machinery: 4 Type L-12V-180B diesels; 4,800 hp(m) *(3.57 MW)*; 4 shafts
Speed, knots: 37.5
Range, n miles: 400 at 30 kt
Complement: 17 (4 officers)
Missiles: SSM: 2 SY-1; active radar or IR homing to 45 km *(24.3 n miles)* at 0.9 Mach; warhead 513 kg.
Guns: 2—25 mm/80 (twin); 270 rds/min to 3 km *(1.6 n miles)*; weight of shell 0.34 kg.
Radars: Surface search: Square Tie; I-band.

Comment: Built in China. First pair commissioned in Bangladesh Navy on 6 April 1983, second pair on 10 November 1983. Two badly damaged in April 1991 typhoon but were repaired. *Uttal* was delivered in June 1992. Missiles are seldom embarked. All have been refitted with new versions of original engines.

UTTAL   *3/1998* / 0017590

4 HUCHUAN CLASS (TYPE 026)
(FAST ATTACK CRAFT—TORPEDO) (PTK)

TB 35 P 8235	TB 36 P 8236	TB 37 P 8237	TB 38 P 8238

Displacement, tons: 46 full load
Dimensions, feet (metres): 73.8 × 16.4 × 6.9 (foil) *(22.5 × 5 × 2.1)*
Main machinery: 3 Type L-12V-180 diesels; 3,600 hp(m) *(2.64 MW)*; 3 shafts
Speed, knots: 50
Range, n miles: 500 at 30 kt
Complement: 23 (3 officers)
Guns: 4 China 14.5 mm (2 twin); 600 rds/min to 7 km *(3.8 km)*.
Torpedoes: 2—21 in *(533 mm)* China YU-1; anti-ship; to 9.2 km *(5 n miles)* at 39 kt or 3.7 km *(2.1 n miles)* at 51 kt; warhead 400 kg.
Radars: Surface search: China Type 753; I-band.

Comment: Chinese Huchuan class. Two damaged in April 1991 typhoon but were repaired. All reported operational.

TB 38   *6/2003, Bangladesh Navy* / 0572415

1 DURJOY (HAINAN) CLASS
(TYPE 037) (LARGE PATROL CRAFT) (PC)

NIRBHOY P 812

Displacement, tons: 375 standard; 392 full load
Dimensions, feet (metres): 192.8 × 23.6 × 7.2 *(58.8 × 7.2 × 2.2)*
Main machinery: 4 diesels; 4,000 hp(m) *(2.94 MW)* sustained; 4 shafts
Speed, knots: 30.5
Range, n miles: 1,300 at 15 kt
Complement: 70
Guns: 4 China 57 mm/70 (2 twin); 120 rds/min to 12 km *(6.5 n miles)*; weight of shell 6.31 kg.
4—25 mm/60 (2 twin); 270 rds/min to 3 km *(1.6 n miles)* anti-aircraft.
A/S mortars: 4 RBU 1200 fixed 5-barrelled launchers; range 1,200 m; warhead 34 kg.
Depth charges: 2 racks; 2 throwers. 18 DCs.
Mines: Fitted with rails for 12 mines.
Radars: Surface search: Pot Head; I-band.
IFF: High Pole.
Sonars: Tamir II; hull-mounted; short-range attack; high frequency.

Comment: Transferred from China and commissioned 1 December 1985. Forms part of Escort Squadron 81 at Chittagong. *Durjoy* damaged beyond repair by cyclone in 1991. *Nirbhoy* refitted with new main machinery.

NIRBHOY   *6/2003, Bangladesh Navy* / 0572414

8 SHAHEED (SHANGHAI II) (TYPE 062) CLASS
(FAST ATTACK CRAFT—GUN) (PC)

SHAHEED DAULAT P 411	SHAHEED AKTHERUDDIN P 414	TAMJEED P 613
SHAHEED FARID P 412	TAWHEED P 611	TANVEER P 614
SHAHEED MOHIBULLAH P 413	TAWFIQ P 612	

Displacement, tons: 113 standard; 134 full load
Dimensions, feet (metres): 127.3 × 17.7 × 5.6 *(38.8 × 5.4 × 1.7)*
Main machinery: 4 Type L 12—180 diesels; 4,400 hp(m) *(3.2 MW)* sustained; 4 shafts
Speed, knots: 30
Range, n miles: 800 at 16.5 kt
Complement: 36 (4 officers)
Guns: 4—37 mm/63 (2 twin); 180 rds/min to 8.5 km *(4.6 n miles)*; weight of shell 1.4 kg.
4—25 mm/80 (2 twin); 270 rds/min to 3 km *(1.6 n miles)* anti-aircraft.
Depth charges: 2 throwers; 8 charges.
Mines: 10 can be carried.
Radars: Surface search: Skin Head/Pot Head; E-band.
Sonars: Hull-mounted; active; short range; high frequency. Some reported to have VDS.

Comment: Transferred from China March 1982. Different engine arrangement from Chinese craft. P 411—414 form Patrol Squadron 41 based at Khulna. P 611—614 form Patrol Squadron 61 based at Chittagong. P 611 operated by the Coast Guard.

TAMJEED   *3/1998* / 0017591

4 SEA DOLPHIN CLASS (FAST ATTACK CLASS—GUN) (PTF)

TITAS P 1011	**KUSIYARA** P 1012	**CHITRA** P 1013	**DHANSIRI** P 1014

Displacement, tons: 143 full load
Dimensions, feet (metres): 107.9 × 22.6 × 7.9 *(32.9 × 6.9 × 2.4)*
Main machinery: 2 MTU MD 16V 538 TB90 diesels; 4,500 hp(m) *(3.35 MW)* sustained; 2 shafts
Speed, knots: 37
Range, n miles: 600 at 20 kt
Complement: 28 (4 officers)
Guns: 1—40 mm.
  2—30 mm (1 twin).
  2—20 mm.
Weapons control: Optical director.
Radars: Surface search: Raytheon 1645; I-band.

Comment: Built by Korea SEC in the 1980s and transferred from South Korea as a gift. First pair (P 1011, 1012) recommissioned on 27 May 2000 and second pair (P 1013, 1014) on 3 October 2004. All form 101 Patrol Squadron based at Chittagong.

TITAS   *6/2001, Bangladesh Navy* / 0529005

1 RUPOSHI BANGLA CLASS (COASTAL PATROL CRAFT) (PB)

Name	No	Builders	Launched	Commissioned
RUPOSHI BANGLA	P 201	Hong Leong-Lürssen	28 June 1999	23 Jan 2000

Displacement, tons: 195 full load
Dimensions, feet (metres): 126.3 × 23 × 13.5 *(38.5 × 7 × 4.1)*
Main machinery: 2 Paxman 12VP 185 diesels; 6,729 hp(m) *(4.95 MW)* sustained; 2 shafts
Speed, knots: 30
Complement: 27 (5 officers)
Guns: 1 Oto Melara 25 mm KBA. 2—7.62 mm MGs.
Radars: Surface search: Furuno; I-band.

Comment: Ordered in June 1998 and laid down 11 August 1998. Based on the PZ design for the Malaysian Police. Operated by the Coast Guard.

RUPOSHI BANGLA   *10/1999, Hong Leong-Lürssen* / 0064625

1 COASTAL PATROL CRAFT (PB)

Name	No	Builders	Commissioned
SALAM (ex-*Durnibar*)	P 712 (ex-*P 8127*)	Khulna Shipyard	19 Mar 2002

Displacement, tons: 185 standard; 216 full load
Dimensions, feet (metres): 126.6 × 24.9 × 8.9 *(38.6 × 7.6 × 2.7)*
Main machinery: 2 Paxman 12V 185 diesels; 4,800 hp *(3.6 MW)* sustained; 2 shafts
Speed, knots: 24
Range, n miles: 3,460 at 13 kt
Complement: 27 (5 officers)
Guns: 1 Bofors 40 mm/60; 120 rds/min 20 3 km (1.6 n miles).
  2 GCM AO2 30 mm (twin).
Radars: Surface search: Furuno HR 2010; E/F-band.
Navigation: Anritsu; I-band.

Comment: Former Huangfen class missile craft transferred from China in 1988. Sunk in River Kamaphuli in 1991 during cyclone and later recovered. Renovated and converted to patrol craft role and recommissioned in 2002.

1 HAIZHUI (TYPE 062/1) CLASS (COASTAL PATROL CRAFT) (PC)

BARKAT P 711

Displacement, tons: 139 full load
Dimensions, feet (metres): 134.5 × 17.4 × 5.9 *(40.9 × 5.3 × 1.8)*
Main machinery: 4 Chinese L12-180A diesels; 4,800 hp(m) *(35.3 MW)*; 4 shafts
Speed, knots: 28
Range, n miles: 750 at 17 kt
Complement: 43 (4 officers)
Guns: 4 China 37 mm/63 (2 twin); 180 rds/min to 8.5 km *(4.6 n miles)*; weight of shell 1.42 kg.
  4 China 25 mm/80 (2 twin).
Depth charges: 2 rails.
Radars: Surface search: Anitsu 726; I-band.
Sonars: Stag Ear; active; high frequency.

Comment: Acquired from China in 1995. This is the Shanghai III, the larger and slower version of the Shanghai II which in Chinese service has anti-submarine mortars. An inclined pole mast and platform behind the bridge are distinguishing features.

BARKAT   *3/1998* / 0017592

2 KARNAPHULI (KRALJEVICA) CLASS
(LARGE PATROL CRAFT) (PC)

Name	No	Builders	Commissioned
KARNAPHULI (ex-*PBR 502*)	P 314	Yugoslavia	1956
TISTA (ex-*PBR 505*)	P 315	Yugoslavia	1956

Displacement, tons: 195 standard; 245 full load
Dimensions, feet (metres): 141.4 × 20.7 × 5.7 *(43.1 × 6.3 × 1.8)*
Main machinery: 2 Paxman 12V P185 (P 314); 2 MTU 12V 396 TE84 (P 315); 2 shafts
Speed, knots: 24
Range, n miles: 1,500 at 12 kt
Complement: 44 (4 officers)
Guns: 2 Bofors 40 mm/70. 2 Oerlikon 20 mm. 2—128 mm rocket launchers (5 barrels per mounting).
Depth charges: 2 racks; 2 Mk 6 projectors.
Radars: Surface search: Decca 1229; I-band.
Sonars: QCU 2; hull-mounted; active; high frequency.

Comment: Transferred and commissioned 6 June 1975. *Karnaphuli* re-engined in 1995, *Tista* in 1998.

TISTA   *6/1999, Bangladesh Navy* / 0056550

2 AKSHAY CLASS (COASTAL PATROL CRAFT) (PB)

Name	No	Builders	Commissioned
PADMA (ex-*Akshay*)	P 312	Hooghly D & E Co, Calcutta	Jan 1962
SURMA (ex-*Ajay*)	P 313	Hooghly D & E Co, Calcutta	Apr 1962

Displacement, tons: 120 standard; 150 full load
Dimensions, feet (metres): 117.2 × 20 × 5.5 *(35.7 × 6.1 × 1.7)*
Main machinery: 2 Paxman YHAXM diesels; 1,100 hp *(820 kW)*; 2 shafts
Speed, knots: 18
Range, n miles: 500 at 12 kt
Complement: 35 (3 officers)
Guns: 4 or 8 Oerlikon 20 mm 1 or (2 quad). 2 Bofors 40 mm/60 (twin) *(Surma)*.
Radars: Surface search: Racal Decca; I-band.

Comment: Transferred from India and commissioned 12 April 1973 and 26 July 1974 respectively. *Surma* has a 40 mm gun aft vice the second quad 20 mm.

PADMA   *6/1997, Bangladesh Navy* / 0012065

2 MEGHNA CLASS (COASTAL PATROL CRAFT) (PB)

Name	No	Builders	Commissioned
MEGHNA	P 211	Vosper Private, Singapore	19 Jan 1984
JAMUNA	P 212	Vosper Private, Singapore	19 Mar 1984

Displacement, tons: 410 full load
Dimensions, feet (metres): 152.5 × 24.6 × 6.6 *(46.5 × 7.5 × 2)*
Main machinery: 2 Paxman Valenta 12CM diesels; 5,000 hp *(3.73 MW)* sustained; 2 shafts
Speed, knots: 20
Range, n miles: 2,000 at 16 kt
Complement: 47 (3 officers)
Guns: 1 Bofors 57 mm/70 Mk 1; 200 rds/min to 17 km *(9.3 n miles)*; weight of shell 2.4 kg.
　1 Bofors 40 mm/70; 300 rds/min to 12 km *(6.5 n miles)*; weight of shell 0.96 kg.
　2—7.62 mm MGs; launchers for illuminants on the 57 mm gun.
Weapons control: Selenia NA 18 B optronic system.
Radars: Surface search: Decca 1229; I-band.

Comment: Built for EEZ work under the Ministry of Agriculture. Both completed late 1984. Both damaged in April 1991 typhoon but have been repaired. P 212 damaged by container ship at Chittagong in September 2003.

MEGHNA *6/2003, Bangladesh Navy* / 0572416

4 TYPE 123K (CHINESE P4) CLASS
(FAST ATTACK CRAFT—TORPEDO) (PTL)

TB 1 P 8221　　**TB 2** P 8222　　**TB 3** P 8223　　**TB 4** P 8224

Displacement, tons: 25 full load
Dimensions, feet (metres): 62.3 × 10.8 × 3.3 *(19 × 3.3 × 1)*
Main machinery: 2 Type L-12V-180 diesels; 2,400 hp(m) *(1.76 MW)*; 2 shafts
Speed, knots: 50
Range, n miles: 410 at 30 kt
Complement: 12 (1 officer)
Guns: 2—14.5 mm (twin) MG.
Torpedoes: 2—17.7 in *(450 mm)*; anti-ship.

Comment: Transferred from China 6 April 1983. Three reported to be operational.

TB 4 *6/2003, Bangladesh Navy* / 0572417

1 RIVER CLASS (COASTAL PATROL CRAFT) (PB)

Name	No	Builders	Commissioned
BISHKHALI (ex-*Jessore*)	P 311	Brooke Marine Ltd	20 May 1965

Displacement, tons: 115 standard; 143 full load
Dimensions, feet (metres): 107 × 20 × 6.9 *(32.6 × 6.1 × 2.1)*
Main machinery: 2 MTU 12V 538 TB90 diesels; 4,500 hp(m) *(3.3 MW)* sustained; 2 shafts
Speed, knots: 24
Complement: 30
Guns: 2 Breda 40 mm/70; 300 rds/min to 12.5 km *(6.8 n miles)*; weight of shell 0.96 kg.
Radars: Surface search: Racal Decca; I-band.

Comment: PNS *Jessore*, which was sunk during the 1971 war, was salvaged and extensively repaired at Khulna Shipyard and recommissioned as *Bishkhali* on 23 November 1978.

BISHKHALI *6/1996, Bangladesh Navy* / 0056554

5 PABNA CLASS (RIVERINE PATROL CRAFT) (PBR)

Name	No	Builders	Commissioned
PABNA	P 111	DEW Narayangonj, Dhaka	12 June 1972
NOAKHALI	P 112	DEW Narayangonj, Dhaka	8 July 1972
PATUAKHALI	P 113	DEW Narayangonj, Dhaka	7 Nov 1974
RANGAMATI	P 114	DEW Narayangonj, Dhaka	11 Feb 1977
BOGRA	P 115	DEW Narayangonj, Dhaka	15 July 1977

Displacement, tons: 69.5 full load
Dimensions, feet (metres): 75 × 20 × 3.5 *(22.9 × 6.1 × 1.1)*
Main machinery: 2 Cummins diesels; 2 shafts
Speed, knots: 10.8
Range, n miles: 700 at 8 kt
Complement: 33 (3 officers)
Guns: 1 Bofors 40 mm/60 or Oerlikon 20 mm.

Comment: The first indigenous naval craft built in Bangladesh. Form River Patrol Squadron 11 at Mongla. All operated by the Coast Guard from 2003.

PABNA *6/2003, Bangladesh Navy* / 0572418

MINE WARFARE FORCES

4 SHAPLA (RIVER) CLASS (MINESWEEPERS/PATROL CRAFT/ SURVEY SHIPS) (MHSC/PBO/AGS)

Name	No	Builders	Commissioned
SHAPLA (ex-*Waveney*)	M 95	Richards, Lowestoft	12 July 1984
SAIKAT (ex-*Carron*)	M 96	Richards, Great Yarmouth	30 Sep 1984
SUROVI (ex-*Dovey*)	M 97	Richards, Great Yarmouth	30 Mar 1985
SHAIBAL (ex-*Helford*)	M 98	Richards, Great Yarmouth	7 June 1985

Displacement, tons: 890 full load
Dimensions, feet (metres): 156 × 34.5 × 9.5 *(47.5 × 10.5 × 2.9)*
Main machinery: 2 Ruston 6RKC diesels; 3,100 hp *(2.3 MW)* sustained; 2 shafts; cp props
Speed, knots: 14
Range, n miles: 4,500 at 10 kt
Complement: 30 (7 officers)
Guns: 1 Bofors 40 mm/60 Mk 3.
Radars: Navigation: 2 Racal Decca TM 1226C; I-band.

Comment: These ships are four of a class of 12 of which seven are in service with Brazil. Transferred from the UK on 3 October 1994 and recommissioned on 27 April 1995. Steel hulled for deep-armed team sweeping with wire sweeps, and intended for use both as minesweepers and as patrol craft. Fitted with Racal Integrated Minehunting System. *Shaibal* converted for hydrographic survey duties but retains minesweeping gear. Fitted with echo sounders, side-scan sonar and a laboratory.

SUROVI *3/1998* / 0017593

1 SAGAR (T 43) CLASS (MINESWEEPER) (MSO)

Name	No	Builders	Commissioned
SAGAR	M 91	Wuhan Shipyard	27 Apr 1995

Displacement, tons: 520 standard; 590 full load
Dimensions, feet (metres): 196.8 × 27.6 × 6.9 *(60 × 8.8 × 2.3)*
Main machinery: 2 CXZ MAN B&W Type 9L 20—27 diesels; 2,400 hp *(1.8 MW)* sustained; 2 shafts; cp props
Speed, knots: 14
Range, n miles: 3,000 at 10 kt
Complement: 70 (10 officers)

Guns: 4 China 37 mm/63 (2 twin); 180 rds/min to 8.5 km *(4.6 n miles)*; weight of shell 1.42 kg.
　4—25 mm/60 (2 twin); 270 rds/min to 3 km *(1.6 n miles)*.
　4 China 14.5 mm/93 (2 twin); 600 rds/min to 7 km *(3.8 n miles)*.
Depth charges: 2 BMB-2 projectors; 20 depth charges.
Mines: Can carry 12—16.
Countermeasures: MCMV; MPT-1 paravanes; MPT-3 mechanical sweep; acoustic and magnetic gear.
Radars: Surface search: Fin Curve; I-band.
Sonars: Celcius Tech CMAS 36/39; active high frequency mine detection.

Programmes: Ordered from China in 1993.
Modernisation: New sonar fitted in 1998.
Structure: Based on Type 010G minesweeper design.
Operational: Used mostly as a patrol ship.

SAGAR *3/1998* / 0017594

SURVEY AND RESEARCH SHIPS

1 SURVEY SHIP (AGS)

Name	No	Builders	Commissioned
AGRADOOT (ex-*Kodan*)	A 583	Khulna Shipyard	19 Mar 2002

Displacement, tons: 687 full load
Dimensions, feet (metres): 157.0 × 25.6 × 11.5 *(47.8 × 7.8 × 3.5)*
Main machinery: 2 Baudouin diesels
Speed, knots: 12.5
Complement: 70 (8 officers)
Guns: 1 Oerlikon 20 mm.
Radars: Furuno HR 2110. Kelvin Hughes HR-3000A.

Comment: Former Thai trawler converted into a Survey vessel by Khulna shipyard. Fitted with two dual frequency digital hydrographic echo sounders, side-scan sonar and laboratories. Carries a survey launch.

AGRADOOT   *6/2003, Bangladesh Navy* / 0572419

AUXILIARIES

Notes: Floating Dock A 711 (*Sundarban*) acquired from Brodogradiliste Joso Lozovina-Mosor, Trogir, Yugoslavia in 1980; capacity 3,500 tons. Has a complement of 85 (5 officers). Floating crane A 731 (*Balaban*) is self-propelled at 9 kt and has a lift of 70 tons; built at Khulna Shipyard and commissioned 18 May 1988, she has a complement of 29 (two officers).

1 TANKER (AOTL)

KHAN JAHAN ALI A 515

Displacement, tons: 2,900 full load
Measurement, tons: 1,343 gross
Dimensions, feet (metres): 250.8 × 37.5 × 18.4 *(76.4 × 11.4 × 5.6)*
Main machinery: 1 diesel; 1,350 hp(m) *(992 kW)*; 1 shaft
Speed, knots: 12
Complement: 26 (3 officers)
Cargo capacity: 1,500 tons
Guns: 2 Oerlikon 20 mm.

Comment: Completed in Japan in 1983. Can carry out stern replenishment at sea but is seldom used in this role.

KHAN JAHAN ALI   *3/1998* / 0017595

1 TANKER (AOTL)

IMAN GAZZALI A 516

Displacement, tons: 213 full load
Dimensions, feet (metres): 146.8 × 23 × 11.2 *(44.8 × 7 × 3.4)*
Main machinery: 1 Cummins diesel; 1 shaft
Speed, knots: 8
Complement: 30 (2 officers)

Comment: An oil tanker of some 600,000 litres capacity acquired in 1996.

IMAN GAZZALI   *6/1999, Bangladesh Navy* / 0056556

1 REPAIR SHIP (YR)

SHAHAYAK A 512

Displacement, tons: 477 full load
Dimensions, feet (metres): 146.6 × 26.2 × 6.6 *(44.7 × 8 × 2)*
Main machinery: 1 Cummins 12 VTS 6 diesel; 425 hp *(317 kW)*; 1 shaft
Speed, knots: 11.5
Range, n miles: 3,800 at 11.5 kt
Complement: 45 (1 officer)
Guns: 1 Oerlikon 20 mm.

Comment: Re-engined and modernised at Khulna Shipyard and commissioned in 1978 to act as repair vessel.

SHAHAYAK   *6/1996, Bangladesh Navy* / 0056557

1 TENDER (AG)

SHAHJALAL A 513

Displacement, tons: 600 full load
Dimensions, feet (metres): 131.8 × 29.7 × 12.6 *(40.2 × 9.1 × 3.8)*
Main machinery: 1 V 16-cyl type diesel; 1 shaft
Speed, knots: 12
Range, n miles: 7,000 at 12 kt
Complement: 55 (3 officers)
Guns: 2 Oerlikon 20 mm.

Comment: Ex-Thai fishing vessel SMS *Gold 4*. Probably built in Tokyo. Commissioned on 15 January 1987 and used as a diving/salvage tender.

SHAHJALAL   *6/1996, Bangladesh Navy* / 0056558

1 HARBOUR TENDER (YAG)

SANKET

Displacement, tons: 80 full load
Dimensions, feet (metres): 96.5 × 20 × 5.9 *(29.4 × 6.1 × 1.8)*
Main machinery: 2 Deutz diesels; 2,400 hp(m) *(1.76 MW)*; 2 shafts
Speed, knots: 16
Range, n miles: 1,000 at 16 kt
Complement: 16 (1 officer)
Guns: 1 Oerlikon 20 mm.

Comment: A former MFV taken over in 1989 and used as a utility harbour craft. No pennant number has been allocated. A second vessel of this type *Shamikha* is in civilian service.

SANKET   *3/1996* / 0056559

1 LANDING CRAFT LOGISTIC (LSL)

SHAH AMANAT L 900

Displacement, tons: 366 full load
Dimensions, feet (metres): 154.2 × 34.1 × 8 *(47 × 10.4 × 2.4)*
Main machinery: 2 Caterpillar D 343 diesels; 730 hp *(544 kW)* sustained; 2 shafts
Speed, knots: 9.5
Complement: 31 (3 officers)
Military lift: 150 tons
Guns: 2—12.7 mm MGs.

Comment: Australian civil vessel confiscated by the Navy while engaged in smuggling in 1988. Transferred to the Navy and commissioned in 1990.

SHAH AMANAT　　　　*6/1996, Bangladesh Navy* / 0056562

2 LCU 1512 CLASS (LCU)

SHAH PORAN (ex-*Cerro Gordo*) L 901　　**SHAH MAKHDUM** (ex-*Cadgel*) L 902

Displacement, tons: 375 full load
Dimensions, feet (metres): 134.9 × 29 × 6.1 *(41.1 × 8.8 × 1.9)*
Main machinery: 4 Detroit 6—71 diesels; 696 hp *(508 kW)* sustained; 2 shafts
Speed, knots: 11
Range, n miles: 1,200 at 8 kt
Complement: 14 (2 officers)
Military lift: 170 tons
Guns: 2—12.7 mm MGs.
Radars: Navigation: LN 66; I-band.

Comment: Ex-US Army landing craft transferred in April 1991 and commissioned 16 May 1992 after refit.

SHAH MAKHDUM　　　　*6/1996, Bangladesh Navy* / 0056563

5 YUCH'IN CLASS (TYPE 068/069) (LCU/LCP)

DARSHAK A 581　　**TALLASHI** A 582
LCT 101 A 584　　**LCT 102** A 585　　**LCT 104** A 587

Displacement, tons: 85 full load
Dimensions, feet (metres): 81.2 × 17.1 × 4.3 *(24.8 × 5.2 × 1.3)*
Main machinery: 2 Type 12V 150 diesels; 600 hp(m) *(440 kW)*; 2 shafts
Speed, knots: 11.5
Range, n miles: 450 at 11.5 kt
Complement: 23
Military lift: Up to 150 troops *(L 101-104)*
Guns: 4 China 14.5 mm (2 twin) MGs can be carried.

Comment: Named craft transferred from China in 1983 fitted with survey equipment and used as inshore survey craft. Second pair transferred 4 May 1986; third pair 1 July 1986. Probably built in the late 1960s. Two badly damaged in April 1991 typhoon and LCT 103 was subsequently scrapped.

TALLASHI (survey)　　　　*6/2003, Bangladesh Navy* / 0572421

LCT 101　　　　*2/1992, Bangladesh Navy* / 0056561

3 LCVP

L 011　　　**L 012**　　　**L 013**

Displacement, tons: 83 full load
Dimensions, feet (metres): 69.9 × 17.1 × 4.9 *(21.3 × 5.2 × 1.5)*
Main machinery: 2 Cummins diesels; 730 hp *(544 kW)*; 2 shafts
Speed, knots: 12
Complement: 10 (1 officer)

Comment: First two built at Khulna Shipyard and *013* at DEW Narayangong; all completed in 1984.

L 011　　　　*6/1996, Bangladesh Navy* / 0056564

TUGS

1 HUJIU CLASS (OCEAN TUG) (ATA)

KHADEM A 721

Displacement, tons: 1,472 full load
Dimensions, feet (metres): 197.5 × 38 × 16.1 *(60.2 × 11.6 × 4.9)*
Main machinery: 2 LVP 24 diesels; 1,800 hp(m) *(1.32 MW)*; 2 shafts
Speed, knots: 14
Range, n miles: 7,200 at 14 kt
Complement: 56 (7 officers)
Guns: 2—12.7 mm MGs.
Radars: Navigation: China Type 756; I-band.

Comment: Commissioned 6 May 1984 after transfer from China.

KHADEM　　　　*6/1996, Bangladesh Navy* / 0056565

3 COASTAL TUGS (YTM)

SEBAK A 722　　　**RUPSHA** A 723　　　**SHIBSHA** A 724

Displacement, tons: 330 full load
Dimensions, feet (metres): 99.9 × 28.1 × 1.6 *(30.0 × 8.4 × 3.5)*
Main machinery: 2 Caterpillar 12V 3512B diesels; 2,700 hp *(2.0 MW)*; 2 shafts
Speed, knots: 12
Range, n miles: 1,800 at 12 kt
Complement: 23 (3 officers)
Guns: 2—7.62 mm MGs (fitted for).

Comment: Details are for *Rupsha* and *Shibsha* built to a Damen Stan Tug 3008 design by Khulna Shipyard. Construction started in 2001, completed in 2003 and commissioned on 3 October 2004. *Sebak* built in Narayangang Dockyard in 1993 and commissioned on 23 December 1993.

SHIBSHA　　　　*6/2003, Bangladesh Navy* / 0572422

Barbados

Country Overview

Barbados gained independence in 1966; the British monarch, represented by a governor-general, is head of state. The easternmost island of the Windward Islands of the Lesser Antilles chain, it consists of a single island of 166 square miles. The capital, largest town and principal port is Bridgetown, located on the southwestern coast. Territorial seas (12 n miles) are claimed. A 200 n mile Exclusive Economic Zone (EEZ) has also been claimed but the limits are not defined. A Coast Guard was formed in 1973 and became the naval arm of the Barbados Defence Force in 1979.

Headquarters Appointments

Chief of Staff, Barbados Defence Force:
  Colonel Alvin Quintyne
Commanding Officer Coast Guard Squadron:
  Lieutenant Commander Errington Shurland

Personnel

(a)   2006: 96 (11 officers)
(b)   Voluntary service

Bases

Bridgetown (HMBS *Willoughby Fort*)

Prefix to Ships' Names

HMBS

PATROL FORCES

2 INSHORE PATROL CRAFT (PB)

Comment: Two Boston Whaler *(P 08* and *P 09)* 22 ft craft; speed 25 kt; commissioned early 1989. One Zodiac Hurricane 24 ft, speed 25 kt commissioned July 1995. A third *(PO 10)* Boston Whaler acquired in late 1996. A Zodiac 920 RHIB was donated by the US in 2004. All used for law enforcement.

1 KEBIR CLASS (LARGE PATROL CRAFT) (PB)

Name	No	Builders	Launched	Commissioned
TRIDENT	P 01	Brooke Marine	14 Apr 1981	Nov 1981

Displacement, tons: 155.5 standard; 190 full load
Dimensions, feet (metres): 123 × 22.6 × 5.6 *(37.5 × 6.9 × 1.7)*
Main machinery: 2 Paxman Valenta 12CM diesels; 5,000 hp *(3.73 MW)* sustained; 2 shafts
Speed, knots: 29
Range, n miles: 3,000 at 12 kt
Complement: 28
Guns: 2—12.7 mm MGs.
Radars: Surface search: Racal Decca Bridgemaster; I-band.

Comment: Refitted by Bender Shipyard in 1990 when the old guns were removed. Refitted again by Cable Marine in 1998 after a main engine seized. Same hull as Algerian Kebir class.

2 DAUNTLESS CLASS (INSHORE PATROL CRAFT) (PB)

Name	No	Builders	Commissioned
ENDEAVOUR	P 04	SeaArk Marine, Monticello	Dec 1997
EXCELLENCE	P 05	SeaArk Marine, Monticello	Apr 1999

Displacement, tons: 11 full load
Dimensions, feet (metres): 40 × 14 × 4.3 *(12.2 × 4.3 × 1.3)*
Main machinery: 2 Caterpillar 3208TA diesels; 870 hp *(650 kW)*; 2 shafts
Speed, knots: 27. **Range, n miles:** 600 at 18 kt
Complement: 4
Guns: 1—12.7 mm MG. 1—7.62 mm MG.
Radars: Surface search Raytheon R40; I-band.

Comment: Aluminium construction.

ENDEAVOUR   *12/2002, Judy Ross* / 0528291

TRIDENT   *12/2002, Judy Ross* / 0528292

Belgium

Country Overview

The Kingdom of Belgium is situated in north-western Europe. With an area of 11,787 square miles, it is bordered to the north by the Netherlands and to the south by France. It has a 35 n mile coastline with the North Sea. The capital and largest city is Brussels while the principal port is Antwerp which is accessible via the Schelde and Meuse estuaries, which lie within the Netherlands. Antwerp is also connected to an extensive canal system. Territorial seas (12 n miles) are claimed and an EEZ has also been claimed.

Headquarters Appointments

Commander, Maritime Command:
  Rear Admiral Jean Paul Robyns
Deputy Commander, Maritime Command:
  Captain E Verbrugghe

Personnel

(a)   2006: 2,566
(b)   Voluntary service

Bases

Zeebrugge: Frigates, MCMV, Reserve Units, Training Ships, Logistics, Diving Centre. Mine Warfare Operational Sea Test centre (MOST).
Oostende: Belgium-Netherlands Mine-warfare school (EGUERMIN).
Koksijde: Naval aviation.
Brugge: Naval training centre.

DELETIONS

Frigates

2004   *Wandelaar* (to Bulgaria)

Mine Warfare Forces

2004   *Myosotis*

Patrol Forces

2005   *Barbara*

Auxiliaries

2003   *Zinnia* (reserve)

FRIGATES

2 WIELINGEN CLASS (TYPE E-71) (FFGM)

Name	No	Builders	Laid down	Launched	Commissioned
WIELINGEN	F 910	Boelwerf, Temse	5 Mar 1974	30 Mar 1976	20 Jan 1978
WESTDIEP	F 911	Cockerill, Hoboken	2 Sep 1974	8 Dec 1975	20 Jan 1978

Displacement, tons: 1,940 light; 2,430 full load
Dimensions, feet (metres): 349 × 40.3 × 18.4
  (106.4 × 12.3 × 5.6)
Main machinery: CODOG; 1 RR Olympus TM3B gas-turbine;
  25,440 hp (19 MW) sustained; 2 Cockerill 240 CO V 12
  diesels; 6,000 hp(m) (4.4 MW); 2 shafts; LIPS; cp props
Speed, knots: 26; 15 on 1 diesel; 20 on 2 diesels
Range, n miles: 4,500 at 18 kt; 6,000 at 15 kt
Complement: 159 (13 officers)

Missiles: SSM: 4 Aerospatiale MM 38 Exocet (2 twin)
  launchers ❶; inertial cruise; active radar homing to
  42 km (23 n miles) at 0.9 Mach; warhead 165 kg; sea-
  skimmer.
SAM: Raytheon Sea Sparrow RIM-7P; Mk 29 octuple
  launcher ❷; semi-active radar homing to 14.6 km
  (8 n miles) at 2.5 Mach; warhead 39 kg.
Guns: 1 Creusot-Loire 3.9 in (100 mm)/55 Mod 68 ❸;
  80 rds/min to 17 km (9 n miles) anti-surface; 8 km
  (4.4 n miles) anti-aircraft; weight of shell 13.5 kg.
Torpedoes: 2—21 in (533 mm) launchers. ECAN L5 Mod 4;
  anti-submarine; active/passive homing to 9.5 km (5 n miles)
  at 35 kt; warhead 150 kg; depth to 550 m (1,800 ft).
A/S Mortars: 1 Creusot-Loire 375 mm 6-barrelled trainable
  launcher ❹; Bofors rockets to 1,600 m; warhead 107 kg.
Countermeasures: Decoys: 2 Tracor MBA SRBOC 6-barrelled
  Mk 36 launchers; chaff (Mk 214 Seagnat) and IR flares to
  4 km (2.2 n miles).
  Nixie SLQ-25; towed anti-torpedo decoy.
ESM: Argos AR 900; intercept.
Combat data systems: Signaal SEWACO IV action data
  automation; Link 11. SATCOM.
Weapons control: Sagem EOMS optronic director ❺.
Radars: Air/surface search: Signaal DA05 ❻; E/F-band.
Surface search/fire control: Signaal WM25 ❼; I/J-band.
Navigation: Signaal Scout; I/J-band.
IFF: Mk XII.
Sonars: Computing Devices Canada SQS 510; hull-
  mounted; active search and attack; medium frequency.

Programmes: This compact, well-armed class of frigate was
  designed by the Belgian Navy and built in Belgian yards.
  The programme was approved on 23 June 1971 and an
  order placed in October 1973.

Modernisation: A rolling programme of upgrades started
in 1996 and was completed in 2005. Sea Sparrow
has been updated from 7M to 7P. WM25 radar has
been modified to include improved ECCM and MTI
capabilities and a new navigation radar and sonar
have been fitted. New optronic director, IFF and
communications facilities have also been installed. Plans
to install new diesel engines (2 ABC 12V DZC (2,915 kW

each)) but alternators are unlikely to be implemented.
Hull modernisation has included measures to reduce
RCS.
Structure: Fully air conditioned. Fin stabilisers fitted.
Operational: Based at Zeebrugge.
Sales: *Wandelaar* to Bulgaria in 2005. *Wielingen* and
Westdiep may follow in 2007/08 as they are replaced by
two Karel Doorman class frigates.

WESTDIEP   (Scale 1 : 900), Ian Sturton / 1047857

WIELINGEN   1/2005*, B Prézelin / 1151101

WESTDIEP   6/2005*, M Declerck / 1151236

WESTDIEP   8/2005*, B Prézelin / 1151103

0 + 2 KAREL DOORMAN CLASS (FFGHM)

Name	No	Builders	Laid down	Launched	Commissioned
— (ex-*Karel Doorman*)	— (ex-F 827)	Koninklijke Maatschappij De Schelde, Flushing	26 Feb 1985	20 Apr 1988	31 May 1991
— (ex-*Willem Van Der Zaan*)	— (ex-F 829)	Koninklijke Maatschappij De Schelde, Flushing	6 Nov 1985	21 Jan 1989	28 Nov 1991

Displacement, tons: 3,320 full load
Dimensions, feet (metres): 401.2 oa; 374.7 wl × 47.2 × 14.1
(122.3; 114.2 × 14.4 × 4.3)
Flight deck, feet (metres): 72.2 × 47.2 *(22 × 14.4)*
Main machinery: CODOG; 2 RR Spey SM1C; 33,800 hp
(25.2 MW) sustained; 2 Stork-Wärtsilä 12SW280 diesels;
9,790 hp(m) *(7.2 MW)* sustained; 2 shafts; LIPS cp props
Speed, knots: 30 (Speys); 21 (diesels)
Range, n miles: 5,000 at 18 kt
Complement: 156 (16 officers) (accommodation for 163)

Missiles: SSM: 8 McDonnell Douglas Harpoon Block 1C
(2 quad) launchers; active radar homing to 130 km
(70 n miles) at 0.9 Mach; warhead 227 kg.
SAM: Raytheon Sea Sparrow Mk 48 vertical launchers;
semi-active radar homing to 14.6 km *(8 n miles)* at
2.5 Mach; warhead 39 kg; 16 missiles. Canisters mounted
on port side of hangar.
Guns: 1—3 in *(76 mm)* /62 OTO Melara compact Mk 100;
100 rds/min to 16 km *(8.6 n miles)* anti-surface; 12 km
(6.5 n miles) anti-aircraft; weight of shell 6 kg. 1 Signaal
SGE-30 Goalkeeper with General Electric 30 mm
7-barrelled; 4,200 rds/min combined to 2 km. 2 Oerlikon
20 mm; 800 rds/min to 2 km.

Torpedoes: 4—324 mm US Mk 32 Mod 9 (2 twin) tubes
(mounted inside the after superstructure). Honeywell
Mk 46 Mod 5; anti-submarine; active/passive homing to
11 km *(5.9 n miles)* at 40 kt; warhead 44 kg.
Countermeasures: Decoys 2 Loral Hycor SRBOC 6-tubed
fixed Mk 36 quad launchers; IR flares and chaff to 4 km
(2.2 n miles).
SLQ-25 Nixie towed torpedo decoy.
ESM/ECM: Argo APECS II (includes AR 700 ESM); intercept
and jammers.
Combat data systems: Signaal SEWACO VIIB action data
automation; Link 11. SATCOM. WSC-6 twin aerials.
Weapons control: Signaal IRSCAN infra-red detector.
Signaal VESTA helo transponder.
Radars: Air/Surface search: Signaal SMART; 3D; F-band.
Air search: Signaal LW08; D-band.
Surface search: Signaal Scout; I-band.
Navigation: Racal Decca 1226; I-band.
Fire control: 2 Signaal STIR; I/J/K-band; range 140 km
(76 n miles) for 1 m² target.
Sonars: Signaal PHS-36; hull-mounted; active search and
attack; medium frequency.
Thomson Sintra Anaconda DSBV 61; towed array;
passive low frequency.

Helicopters: 1 medium.

Programmes: The intended purchase of the two
ex-Netherlands frigates was approved by Belgium's
Council of Ministers on 20 July 2005 and a contract for
the supply of the two ships, a support package, weapons
transfer, joint upgrades and crew training was signed
on 21 December 2005. Given the close co-operation that
already exists between the Belgian Navy and the RNLN,
it is expected that spares support and crew training of
the ships will remain at Den Helder. The ships are to
replace the two remaining Wielingen class frigates and
the first transfer is expected to take place in 2007 and the
second in 2008.
Modernisation: A modernisation package is expected to be
implemented before transfer.
Structure: The VLS SAM is similar to Canadian Halifax and
Greek MEKO classes. The ship is designed to reduce radar
and IR signatures and has extensive NBCD arrangements.
Full automation and roll stabilisation fitted. The APECS
jammers are mounted starboard forward of the bridge
and port aft corner of the hangar.

KAREL DOORMAN CLASS

10/2005*, Derek Fox / 1151102

SHIPBORNE AIRCRAFT

Notes: Ten NH Industries NH-90 multirole helicopters are to enter service from 2008. Of
these, three are to replace the Sea King SAR helicopters, two are to operate from the Karel
Doorman class frigates and five are to act as troop transports.

Numbers/Type: 3 Aerospatiale SA 316B Alouette III.
Operational speed: 113 kt *(210 km/h)*.
Service ceiling: 10,500 ft *(3,200 m)*.
Range: 290 n miles *(540 km)*.
Role/Weapon systems: CG helicopter; used for close-range search and rescue and support
for commando forces. Sensors: Carries Thomson-CSF search radar. Weapons: Unarmed.
It is planned to upgrade these aircraft with new navigation and communications
systems.

LAND-BASED MARITIME AIRCRAFT

Numbers/Type: 4 Westland Sea King Mk 48.
Operational speed: 140 kt *(260 km/h)*.
Service ceiling: 10,500 ft *(3,200 m)*.
Range: 630 n miles *(1,165 km)*.
Role/Weapon systems: SAR helicopter; operated by air force; used for surface search
and combat rescue tasks. Upgraded in 1995 with new radar, FLIR and GPS. One
decommissioned in 2005 and two reported operational. Sensors: Bendix RDR 1500B
search radar. FLIR 2000F. Weapons: Unarmed.

ALOUETTE III

7/2001, van Ginderen Collection / 0114692

SEA KING

7/2001, van Ginderen Collection / 0114691

PATROL FORCES

Notes: (1) Three 7 m RIC were acquired in May 1994 from RIBTEC, Swanwick.
(2) A range safety craft A 998 has replaced the hovercraft *Barbara* A 999.

A 998   *6/2005*, M Declerck* / 1151239

1 RIVER PATROL CRAFT (PBR/YFLB)

Name	No	Builders	Launched	Commissioned
LIBERATION	P 902	Hitzler, Regensburg	29 July 1954	4 Aug 1954

Displacement, tons: 45 full load
Dimensions, feet (metres): 85.5 × 13.1 × 3.2 *(26.1 × 4 × 1)*
Main machinery: 2 MWM diesels; 440 hp(m) *(323 kW)*; 2 shafts
Speed, knots: 19
Complement: 7
Guns: 2 — 12.7 mm MGs.
Radars: Navigation: Racal Decca; I-band.

Comment: Laid down 12 March 1954. Paid off 12 June 1987 but put back in active service 15 September 1989 after repairs. Last of a class of 10 used for patrol and personnel transport. Replacement planned when funds are available.

LIBERATION   *6/2005*, M Declerck* / 1151237

MINE WARFARE FORCES

6 FLOWER CLASS (TRIPARTITE)
(MINEHUNTERS — COASTAL) (MHC/AEL)

Name	No	Builders	Launched	Commissioned
ASTER	M 915	Beliard, Ostend	6 June 1985	17 Dec 1985
BELLIS	M 916	Beliard, Ostend	14 Feb 1986	14 Aug 1986
CROCUS	M 917	Beliard, Ostend	6 Aug 1986	5 Feb 1987
LOBELIA	M 921	Beliard, Ostend	6 Jan 1988	9 May 1989
NARCIS	M 923	Beliard, Ostend	30 Mar 1990	27 Sep 1990
PRIMULA	M 924	Beliard, Ostend	17 Dec 1990	29 May 1991

Displacement, tons: 562 standard; 595 full load
Dimensions, feet (metres): 168.9 × 29.2 × 8.2 *(51.5 × 8.9 × 2.5)*
Main machinery: 1 Stork Wärtsilä A-RUB 215W-12 diesel; 1,860 hp(m) *(1.37 MW)* sustained; 1 shaft; LIPS cp prop; 2 motors; 240 hp(m) *(176 kW);* 2 active rudders; 2 bow thrusters
Speed, knots: 15
Range, n miles: 3,000 at 12 kt
Complement: 46 (5 officers)

Guns: 1 DCN 20 mm/20; 720 rds/min to 10 km *(5.5 n miles)*. 2 — 12.7 mm MGs.
Countermeasures: MCM: 2 PAP 104 remote-controlled mine locators; 39 charges. Mechanical sweep gear (medium depth).
Combat data systems: Atlas Elektronic IMCMS.
Radars: Navigation: Racal Decca 1229; I-band.
Sonars: Thales TSM 2022 Mk III; hull-mounted; active minehunting; 100, 200 and 400 kHz.

Programmes: Developed in co-operation with France and the Netherlands. A 'ship factory' for the hulls was built at Ostend and the hulls were towed to Rupelmonde for fitting out. Each country built its own hulls but France provided all MCM gear and electronics, Belgium electrical installation and the Netherlands the engine room equipment.
Modernisation: Propulsion system upgrade completed in 1999 for all of the class. Capability upgrade to extend service life of six ships to 2020 is in progress at Zeebrugge. Modifications include an MCM command and control system, an Integrated Mine Countermeasures System (comprising hull-mounted and self-propelled variable-depth sonar (installed in Double Eagle Mk III Mod 1 ROV)) and a Mine-Identification and Disposal System (MIDS) based on the STN Atlas Seafox. Linked to the ship by a 3,000 m fibre optic tether, one variant (Seafox-C) is used for mine disposal and another (Seafox-I) is used for identification. The equipment was first installed in HrMS *Hellevoetsluis*. BNS *Lobelia* is the first Belgium ship to have been upgraded and operational evaluation is to begin in 2006. All six ships are to be completed by late 2008.
Structure: GRP hull fitted with active tank stabilisation, full NBC protection and air conditioning. Has automatic pilot and buoy tracking.
Operational: A 5 ton container can be carried, stored for varying tasks-HQ support, research, patrol, extended diving, drone control. The ship's company varies from 33 to 46 depending on the assigned task. Six divers are carried when minehunting. All of the class are based at Zeebrugge.
Sales: Three of the class paid off for sale in July 1993 and were bought by France in 1997.

NARCIS   *6/2005*, Derek Fox* / 1151104

LOBELIA   *9/2005*, Guy Toremans* / 1151238

SURVEY SHIPS

Notes: In addition to *Belgica* there are five small civilian manned survey craft: *Ter Streep, Scheldewacht II, De Parel II, Veremans* and *Prosper*.

1 SURVEY SHIP (AGOR/PBO)

Name	No	Builders	Launched	Commissioned
BELGICA	A 962	Boelwerf, Temse	6 Jan 1984	5 July 1984

Displacement, tons: 1,085 full load
Dimensions, feet (metres): 167 × 32.8 × 14.4 *(50.9 × 10 × 4.4)*
Main machinery: 1 ABC 6M DZC diesel; 1,600 hp(m) *(1.18 MW)* sustained; 1 Kort nozzle prop
Speed, knots: 13.5. **Range, n miles:** 5,000 at 12 kt
Complement: 26 (11 civilian)
Radars: Navigation: Racal Decca 1229; I-band.

Comment: Ordered 1 December 1982. Laid down 17 October 1983. Used for hydrography, oceanography, meteorology and fishery control. Marisat fitted. Based at Zeebrugge. Painted white.

BELGICA   *6/2004, B Prézelin* / 1044079

TRAINING SHIPS

1 SAIL TRAINING VESSEL (AXS)

Name	No	Builders	Commissioned
ZENOBE GRAMME	A 958	Boel and Zonen, Temse	27 Dec 1961

Displacement, tons: 149 full load
Dimensions, feet (metres): 92 × 22.5 × 7 *(28 × 6.8 × 2.1)*
Main machinery: 1 MWM diesel; 200 hp(m) *(147 kW)*; 1 shaft
Speed, knots: 10
Complement: 14 (2 officers)
Radars: Navigation: Racal Decca; I-band.

Comment: Auxiliary sail ketch. Laid down 7 October 1960 and launched 23 October 1961. Designed for scientific research but now only used as a training ship.

ZENOBE GRAMME   *7/2003, P Marsan* / 1044080

AUXILIARIES

Notes: It is planned to acquire a Command and Support Ship (MCS) to replace BNS *Godetia* in about 2012.

1 SUPPORT SHIP (AGFH)

Name	No	Builders	Commissioned
STERN (ex-KBV 171)	A 963	Karlskronavarvet	3 Sep 1980

Displacement, tons: 375 full load
Dimensions, feet (metres): 164 × 27.9 × 7.9 *(50 × 8.5 × 2.4)*
Main machinery: 2 Hedemora V16A diesels; 4,480 hp(m) *(3.28 MW)* sustained; 2 shafts; cp props
Speed, knots: 18 **Range, n miles:** 3,000 at 12 kt
Complement: 13
Radars: Navigation: 2 Kelvin Hughes; E/F- and I-band.
Helicopters: Platform for 1 light.

Comment: Transferred from Swedish Coast Guard on 6 October 1998. GRP hull indentical to Landsort class. In Swedish service the ship carried a 20 mm gun, and had a Subsea sonar. Used for fishery protection and SAR duties.

STERN *6/2005*, Frank Findler* / 1151106

1 COMMAND AND SUPPORT SHIP (AGFH)

Name	No	Builders	Launched	Commissioned
GODETIA	A 960	Boelwerf, Temse	7 Dec 1965	23 May 1966

Displacement, tons: 2,000 standard; 2,260 full load
Dimensions, feet (metres): 301 × 46 × 11.5 *(91.8 × 14 × 3.5)*
Main machinery: 4 ACEC-MAN diesels; 5,400 hp(m) *(3.97 MW)*; 2 shafts; cp props
Speed, knots: 19. **Range, n miles:** 8,700 at 12.5 kt
Complement: 105 (8 officers)
Guns: 6 — 12.7 mm MGs.
Radars: Surface search: Racal Decca 1229; I-band.
Helicopters: 1 Alouette III.

Comment: Laid down 15 February 1965. Rated as Command and Logistic Support Ship. Refit (1979-80) and mid-life conversion (1981-82) included helicopter deck and replacement cranes. Refitted again in 1992. Minesweeping cables fitted either side of helo deck have been removed. Can also serve as a Royal Yacht. To be replaced by new ship in about 2012.

TUGS

2 COASTAL TUGS (YTM)

VALCKE (ex-*Steenbank*, ex-*Astroloog*) A 950   ALBATROS (ex-*Westgat*) A 996

Displacement, tons: 183 full load
Dimensions, feet (metres): 99.7 × 24.9 × 11.8 *(30.4 × 7.6 × 3.6)*
Main machinery: Diesel-electric; 2 Deutz diesel generators; 1,240 hp(m) *(911 kW)*; 1 shaft; 1 bow thruster
Speed, knots: 11
Complement: 8

Comment: Details given are for A 950 which was launched in 1960. A 996 is 206 tons and was launched in 1967.

ALBATROS *6/2005*, B Prézelin* / 1151105

3 HARBOUR TUGS (YTL)

WESP A 952   ZEEMEEUW A 954   MIER A 955

Displacement, tons: 195 full load
Dimensions, feet (metres): 86.5 × 24.7 × 10.7 *(26.23 × 7.5 × 3.25)*
Main machinery: 2 ABC 6 MDUS diesels; 1,000 hp *(746 kW)*
Speed, knots: 11
Complement: 4

Comment: Details given are for A 952 and A 955. A 954 is 146 tons.

MIER *7/2005*, Guy Toremans* / 1151241

GODETIA *6/2005*, Maritime Photographic* / 1151240

Belize

Country Overview

Formerly known as British Honduras, Belize became an independent state in 1981. The British monarch, represented by a governor-general, is head of state. With an area of 8,867 square miles, it has borders with Mexico to the north and Guatemala to the west; its 208 n mile coastline is on the Caribbean Sea and fringed by numerous coral barrier reefs and cays. The capital city is Belmopan while the largest city and major port is Belize City. Territorial seas (12 n miles) are claimed. A 200 n mile Exclusive Economic Zone (EEZ) has been claimed but the limits are not defined. Transformation of the Defence Force Maritime Wing into a Coast Guard awaits legislation.

Headquarters Appointments

Commanding Officer Defence Force Maritime Wing:
Major J F Teck

Personnel

(a) 2006: 45 (2 officers)
(b) The Maritime Wing of the Belize Defence Force comprises volunteers from the Army.

Bases

Ladyville, Hunting Cay, Calabash Cay (planned)

Maritime Patrol

Two Pilatus Britten-Norman Defenders are used for maritime surveillance.

PATROL FORCES

Notes: Transformation of the Maritime Wing into a Coast Guard awaits legislation. Current assets include:
- Two Halmatic 22 ft RIBs with twin Yamaha 115 hp outboards. Names *Stingray Commando* and *Blue Marlin Ranger*.
- Two Pelikan 35 ft craft with twin Yamaha 200 hp outboards. Built at Bradleys Boatyard in 1996 and called *Ocean Sentinel* and *Reef Sniper*.
- Six Colombian 32 ft skiffs with twin Yamaha 200 hp outboards, confiscated and commissioned in service 1995-97.
- One 36 ft skiff.

PELIKAN CRAFT
6/2001, Belize Defence Force
0109932

Benin

FORCES NAVALES

Country Overview

Formerly part of French West Africa, the republic gained full independence in 1960 as the Republic of Dahomey; it was renamed The Republic of Benin in 1975. With an area of 43,484 square miles it has borders to the east with Nigeria and to the west with Togo. Benin has a short coastline of 65 n miles with the Gulf of Guinea. The capital is Porto-Novo while Cotonou is the largest city and principal port. Benin has not claimed an Exclusive Economic Zone (EEZ) but is one of a few coastal states which claims a 200 n miles territorial sea. The naval force was established in 1978.

Headquarters Appointments

Commander Navy:
  Capitaine de Vaisseau Soulémane Marcos

Aircraft

Dornier Do 128 and a DHC-6 Twin Otter reconnaissance aircraft are used for surveillance.

Bases

Cotonou

Personnel

2006: 220 (30 officers)

PATROL FORCES

Notes: There are two French-built 6 m river patrol craft with hydrojet propulsion.

2 CHINESE 27 METRE CLASS (PATROL CRAFT) (PB)

MATELOT BRICE KPOMASSE 798   **LA SOTA** 799

Displacement, tons: 55
Dimensions, feet (metres): 88.6 × 13.1 × 3.9 *(27 × 4 × 1.2)*
Main machinery: 2 diesels; 1,000 hp *(746 kW)*
Complement: 13
Guns: 4–14.5 mm (2 twin) MGs.
Radars: Navigation: I-band.

Comment: Understood to have been transferred from China in 2000.

KPOMASSE and SOTA
2001, Benin Navy
0114348

Bermuda

Country Overview

A British self-governing dependency, a Governor, appointed by the British Crown, is responsible for external affairs, internal security, defence, and the police. Situated in the north Atlantic Ocean some 650 n miles southeast of Cape Hatteras, the country consists of six principal islands, of which the largest is 14 miles long, linked by bridges and a causeway; there are some 150 other small islands, islets, and rocks, of which about 20 are inhabited. Hamilton is the capital, chief port and largest town. Territorial seas (12 n miles) and an Exclusive Economic Zone (EEZ) (200 n miles) are claimed.

Headquarters Appointments

Commanding Officer:
  Inspector Mark Bothello

Bases

Hamilton

POLICE

Notes: In addition to patrol craft, three tugs, *Powerful, Faithful* and *Refit* are operated by the Department of Marine and Port Services.

0 + 1 AUSTAL PATROL CRAFT (PB)

Displacement, tons: To be announced
Dimensions, feet (metres): 53.5 × 16.1 × 3.9 *(16.3 × 4.9 × 1.2)*
Main machinery: 2 Caterpillar C12 diesels; 1,300 hp *(970 kW)*; 2 shafts
Speed, knots: 28
Range, n miles: 400 at 25 kt
Complement: 3 plus 8 passengers

Comment: Contract with Austal Ships in August 2005 to build aluminium hull replacement craft for *Blue Heron* for operations up to 200 n miles from shore. Similar to craft operated by the New South Wales police. Delivery is expected by mid-2006.

AUSTAL 16
7/2000, Austal*
1127929

1 PATROL CRAFT (PBI)

BLUE HERON

Comment: Donated by the US Drug Enforcement Agency in May 1996 to replace the original craft of the same name. 46 ft *(14 m)* in length and fitted with a Furuno radar. Complement six. The craft is used by the Joint Marine Interdiction Team to patrol inshore waters to intercept drug runners. To be replaced by a new 16 m craft in 2006.

HERON II   *6/1997, Bermuda Police* / 0012079

SAR CRAFT (SAR)

RESCUE I   RESCUE II

Comment: *Rescue I* replaced the craft of the same name in November 1998 and *Rescue II* replaced the craft of the same name in 2001. Both are Halmatic 24 ft Arctic RIBs with twin 200 hp Yamaha outboards and a complement of three.

BLUE HERON   *5/1996, Bermuda Police* / 0056583

4 PATROL CRAFT (PBI)

HERON I   **HERON II**   **HERON III**   **HERON IV**

Comment: *Heron I*, delivered in July 1997 to replace the previous craft of the same name, and *Heron III* delivered in June 1992 are 22 ft Boston Whalers fitted with twin Yamaha 225 hp and twin Yamaha 115 hp outboards, respectively. *Heron II* delivered in August 1996 to replace the previous craft of the same name, is a 27 ft Boston Whaler with twin Yamaha 250 hp(m) outboard engines. *Heron IV*, delivered in 2001, is a further 22 ft Boston Whaler with twin 115 hp outboards.

HALMATIC ARCTIC RIB   *2001, Bermuda Police* / 0109933

Bolivia

ARMADA BOLIVIANA

Country Overview

The Republic of Bolivia is one of two landlocked countries in South America; Paraguay is the other. With an area of 424,165 square miles, it has borders to the north and east with Brazil, to the southeast with Paraguay, to the south with Argentina, and to the west with Chile and Peru. It has a 211 n mile shoreline with Lake Titicaca. The constitutional capital is Sucre while the administrative capital and seat of government is La Paz which is connected by railway to the Chilean port of Antofagasta.

The Bolivian Navy was founded in 1963 and received its present name in 1982. Its purpose is to patrol some 10,000 miles in three geographical areas. The Amazon basin includes the rivers Ichilo, Mamore, Itenez, Yacuma, Orthon, Abuna, Beni and Madre de Dios. The central basin comprises Lake Titicaca while the Del Plata basin includes the rivers Paraguay and Bermejo. Most advanced training is carried out in Argentina and Peru.

Headquarters Appointments

Commandant General of the Navy:
  Vice Admiral Jorge Botello Monje

Chief of the Naval Staff:
  Rear Admiral Ismael Schabib Montero
Inspector General:
  Rear Admiral Jose Alba Arnez

Personnel

(a)   2006: 6,659 (including Marines)
(b)   12 months' selective military service

Organisation

The country is divided into six naval districts, three naval areas and a Fuerza de Tareas Especiales.
1st Naval District (Beni) (HQ Riberalta). River Beni.
2nd Naval District (Mamore) (HQ Trinidad). Rivers Ichilo and Mamore.
3rd Naval District (Madera) (HQ Puerto Guayamerin). Rivers Madera and Itenez.
4th Naval District (Titicaca) (HQ San Pedro de Tiquina). Lake Titicaca.
5th Naval District (Santa Cruz de la Sierra) (HQ Puerto Quijarro). River Paraguay.

Organisation — *continued*

6th Naval District (Pando) (HQ Cobija). Rivers Acre, Madre dos Dios and Tahuamanu.
1st Naval Area (Cochabamba) (Puerto Villarroel). Naval yard and oil transport.
2nd Naval Area (Santa Cruz). Support duties.
3rd Naval Area (Bermejo).
4th Naval Area (La Paz).
Fuerza de Tareas Especiales consists of five task groups (based at Guayamerin, Cobija, Riberalta, Puerto Suarez and Copacabana) to provide support in counter-drug operations.

Marine Corps

The Bolivian Navy has seven marine corps battalions (BIM I-VII). Two are located in 4th Naval District and one in each of the remainder.

Prefix to Ships' Names

ARB

PATROL FORCES

3 RIVER PATROL CRAFT (PBR)

CAPITÁN PALOMEQUE PR 221   **ANTOFAGASTA** PR 302   **GENERAL BANZER** PR 301

Displacement, tons: 8 full load
Dimensions, feet (metres): 42.7 × 10.5 × 1.6 *(13 × 3.2 × 0.5)*
Main machinery: 2 diesels; 2 shafts
Speed, knots: 27
Complement: 4
Guns: 1–7.62 mm MG.

Comment: Details given are for *Capitán Palomeque* acquired in 1993. The others are similar in appearance and all are less than ten years old. Operate in the 2nd and 3rd Districts.

CAPITÁN PALOMEQUE
1996, Bolivian Navy
0056585

1 SANTA CRUZ CLASS (PBR)

SANTA CRUZ DE LA SIERRA PR 501

Displacement, tons: 46 full load
Dimensions, feet (metres): 68.9 × 19 × 3.9 *(21 × 5.8 × 1.2)*
Main machinery: 2 Detroit diesels; 2 shafts
Speed, knots: 20
Range, n miles: 800 at 16 kt
Complement: 10
Guns: 2 — 12.7 mm MGs.
Radars: Surface search: Furuno; I-band.

Comment: Built by Hope Shipyards, Louisiana, in 1985. Used both as a patrol craft and supply ship. Operates in the 5th District on the river Paraguay.

SANTA CRUZ DE LA SIERRA (old number)   *1996, Bolivian Navy* / 0056584

8 RIVER PATROL CRAFT (PBR)

PAZ ZAMORA LP 101	**MARISCAL DE ZAPITA** LP 409	**GUAQUI** LA 414
RAIDER LP 351	**CAPITÁN BRETEL** LP 410	**INDEPENDENCIA** LP 416
GENERAL BEJAR LP 406	**TENIENTE SOLIZ** LP 411	

Displacement, tons: 5 full load
Dimensions, feet (metres): 42.3 × 12.7 × 3.3 *(12.9 × 3.9 × 1)*
Main machinery: 2 diesels; 2 shafts
Speed, knots: 15
Complement: 5
Guns: 1 — 12.7 mm MG.
Radars: Surface search: Raytheon; I-band.

Comment: Details given are for *Capitán Bretel, Teniente Soliz* and *Guaqui* which is used as a logistic craft. The remainder are Boston Whaler types. All operate in the 4th District except *Paz Zamora* (1st) and *Raider* (5th).

CAPITÁN BRETEL alongside TENIENTE SOLIZ   *1996, Bolivian Navy* / 0056587

42 RIVER PATROL CRAFT (PBR)

LP 01-42

Comment: Thirty-two Piranas were delivered from 1992-96. Fitted with one 12.7 mm MG and has twin outboards. Ten more craft delivered by the US 1998-99.

PIRANA Mk II   *1996, Bolivian Navy* / 0056588

AUXILIARIES

Notes: (1) Approximately 30 Rodman craft are used for transport and logistic support. A mixture of 17 m, 11 m, 8 m and 6 m were commissioned on 11 February 1999. The 17 m craft are reported to have pennant numbers M 342, M 343, M 401, M 402 and M 529.
(2) *Guayamerin* (TNTB-01) is an LCM used as a transport vessel on Lake Titicaca. Built in Bolivia she was commissioned on 22 July 1998.
(3) A dredge *Pirai II* (FNDR-01) was commissioned on 11 August 2001.

11 RIVER TRANSPORTS (YFL)

ALMIRANTE GRAU M 101	**INGENIERO GUMUCIO** M 341
COMANDANTE ARANDIA M 103	**JORGE VILLARROEL** M 342
GERMAN BUSCH M 107	**COATI** M 401
LIBERTADOR M 223	**COBIJA** M 402
TRINIDAD M 224	**SUAREZ ARANA** M 528 (ex-M 501)
RIO GUAPORÉ M 301	

Displacement, tons: 70 full load
Dimensions, feet (metres): 78.7 × 21.3 × 4.6 *(24 × 6.5 × 1.4)*
Speed, knots: 12
Range, n miles: 500 at 12 kt
Complement: 11
Radars: Navigation: Raytheon; I-band.

Comment: Details given are for *Ingeniero Gumucio* which is a troop transport and supply ship. The remainder are craft of various types, some acquired from China.

INGENIERO GUMUCIO   *1996, Bolivian Navy* 0056589

6 LOGISTIC VESSELS (YAG)

JOSE MANUEL PANDO TNR 01	**JULIO OLMOS** TNR 05
NICOLAS SUAREZ TNR 02	**HORACIO UGARTECHE** TNBTL-06
MAX PAREDES TNR 04	**THAMES CRESPO** TNR 07

Comment: TNR-01 is a tug. The remainder are pusher/lighter combinations. There are eight lighters TNBTP-02A, -02B, -04A, -04B, -05A, -06A, -06B and -07A

MAX PAREDES   *6/2000, Bolivian Navy* / 0104222

2 HOSPITAL SHIPS

Name	No	Tonnage
JULIAN APAZA	TNBH 401	150
XAVIER PINTO TELLERIA	TNBH 01	–

Comment: *Julian Apaza* given by the US; assembled in 1972 and based at Lake Titicaca. *Telleria* was built in 1997 and is based at Puerto Villarod.

TELLERIA   *6/2000, Bolivian Navy* / 0104223

1 TRAINING VESSEL

BUQUE ESCUELA NAVAL MILITAR

Displacement, tons: 80 full load
Dimensions, feet (metres): 117.3 × 29.5 × 3.9 *(35.7 × 9.0 × 1.2)*
Main machinery: 2 diesels; 1,300 hp *(969 kW)*
Speed, knots: 18
Complement: 15 plus 50 trainees

Comment: Catamaran design. Launched at Tiquina, Lake Titicaca on 9 May 2001. Commissioned on 24 April 2004.

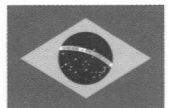

Brazil
MARINHA DO BRASIL

Country Overview

The Federal Republic of Brazil is the largest country in South America. With an area of 3,286,500 square miles it has borders to the north with Colombia, Venezuela, Guyana, Suriname and French Guiana, to the south with Uruguay and to the west with Argentina, Paraguay, Bolivia, and Peru. It has a coastline of 4,045 n miles with the south Atlantic Ocean. There are some 23,220 n miles of internal waterways that consist primarily of the Amazon and its tributaries; the river is navigable by ocean-going ships from its mouth to Iquitos in Peru. The capital is Brasilia while the largest city is São Paulo. The principal ports are the former capital, Rio de Janeiro, Santos, Paranaguá, Recife, and Vitória. Manaus is an important river port. Territorial seas (12 n miles) are claimed. An EEZ (200 n miles) is claimed and its limits have been partly defined by boundary agreements.

Headquarters Appointments

Commander of the Navy:
Admiral Roberto de Guimarães Carvalho
Chief of Naval Staff:
Admiral Rayder Alencar da Silveira
Chief of Naval Operations:
Admiral Mauro Magalhães de Souza Pinto
Commandant General Brazilian Marine Corps:
Admiral (Marine Corps) Marcelo Gaya Cardoso Tosta
General Director of Personnel:
Admiral Julio Soares de Moura Neto
General Director of Material:
Admiral Euclides Duncan Janot de Matos
General Secretary of Navy:
Admiral Kleber Luciano de Assis
Vice Chief of Naval Staff:
Vice Admiral Gerson Carvalho Ravanelli

Senior Officers

Commander-in-Chief, Fleet:
Vice Admiral Carlos Augusto Vasconcelos Saraiva Ribeiro
Commander, Fleet Marine Force:
Vice Admiral (Marine Corps) Álvaro Augusto Dias Monteiro
Commander, I Naval District:
Vice Admiral José Eduardo Pimental de Oliveira
Commander, II Naval District:
Vice Admiral Álvaro Luiz Pinto
Commander, III Naval District:
Vice Admiral Afonso Barbosa
Commander, IV Naval District:
Vice Admiral Marcus Vinicius Oliveira dos Santos
Commander, V Naval District:
Vice Admiral Luiz Umberto de Mendonça
Commander, VI Naval District:
Rear Admiral Carlos Augusto de Sousa
Commander, VII Naval District:
Rear Admiral Newton Cardoso
Commander, VIII Naval District:
Vice Admiral Marcelio Carmo de Castro Pereira
Commander, IX Naval District:
Rear Admiral Marcus Vinícius Iório Hollanda

Diplomatic Representation

Naval Attaché in USA and Canada:
Rear Admiral Edison Lawrence Mariath Dantas
Naval Attaché in United Kingdom, Sweden and Norway:
Captain Paulo Fontes da Rocha Vianna
Naval Attaché in Uruguay:
Captain Hamilton Jorge da Gama Henrique

Diplomatic Representation — *continued*

Naval Attaché in France and Belgium:
Captain Carlos Alberto Pêgas
Naval Attaché in Italy:
Captain Moacyr Cavichiolo Filho
Naval Attaché in Germany and Netherlands:
Commander Ernesto Martins Tavares de Souza
Naval Attaché in South Africa and Mozambique:
Captain José Carlos Mathias
Naval Attaché in Bolivia:
Captain (Marine Corps) Augusto Cesar Lobato Pousada
Naval Attaché in Argentina:
Captain Julio Cesar da Costa Fonseca
Naval Attaché in Venezuela:
Captain (Marine Corps) Jorge de Oliveira Carlos
Naval Attaché in Peru:
Captain (Marine Corps) Alexandre José Barreto da Mattos
Naval Attaché in Portugal:
Captain Girlano Bezerra Santiago Freitas
Naval Attaché in Chile:
Captain Marco Antônio Soares Garrido
Defence Attaché in Japan and Indonesia:
Captain Carlos Alberto Auffinger
Defence Attaché in China and South Korea:
Captain Bernardo Augusto Cunha de Hollanda
Defence Attaché in Russia:
Captain Sergio Luiz Coutinho

Personnel

a) 2006: 36,700 (5,900 officers) Navy; (including 1,300 naval air)
14,600 (690 officers) Marines
b) One year's national service

Bases

Arsenal de Marinha do Rio de Janeiro - Rio de Janeiro (Naval shipyard with three dry docks and one floating dock with graving docks of up to 70,000 tons capacity)
Base Naval do Rio de Janeiro – Rio de Janeiro (Main Naval Base with two dry docks)
Base Almirante Castro e Silva – Rio de Janeiro (Naval Base for submarines)
Base Naval de Aratu – Bahia (Naval Base and repair yard with one dry dock and synchrolift)
Base Naval de Val-de-Cães – Pará (Naval River and repair yard with one dry dock)
Base Naval de Natal – Rio Grande do Norte (Small Naval Base and repair yard with one floating dock)
Base Fluvial de Ladário – Mato Grosso do Sul (Small Naval River Base and repair yard with one dry dock)
Base Aérea Naval de São Pedro d'Aldeia – Rio de Janeiro (Naval Air Station)
Estação Naval do Rio Negro – Amazonas (Small Naval River Station and repair yard with one floating dock)
Estação Naval do Rio Grande – Rio Grande do Sul (Small Naval Station and repair yard)

Organisation

Naval Districts as follows:
I Naval District (HQ Rio de Janeiro)
II Naval District (HQ Salvador)
III Naval District (HQ Natal)
IV Naval District (HQ Belém)
V Naval District (HQ Rio Grande)
VI Naval District (HQ Ladário)
VII Naval District (HQ Brasilia)
VIII Naval District (HQ São Paulo)
IX Naval District (HQ Manaus)

Naval Aviation

Squadrons: São Pedro da Aldeira; HA-1 Super Lynx; HS-1 Sea King; HI-1 JetRanger; HU-1 Ecureuil 1 and 2; HU-2 Super Puma/Cougar; VF 1 Skyhawk AF1.
Manaus; HU-3 Ecureuil.
Ladário; HU-4 Jet Ranger.
Rio Grande; HU-5 Ecureuil.

Prefix to Ships' Names

These vary, indicating the type of ship for example, N Ae = Aircraft Carrier; CT = Destroyer.

Pennant Numbers

As a result of cuts in Officer numbers, ships are sometimes formally decommissioned from the Navy and lose their pennant numbers. They are then retained in service as tenders to Naval establishments and are commanded by Warrant Officers.

Marines (Corpo de Fuzileiros Navais)

Headquarters at Fort São José, Rio de Janeiro
Divisão Anfibia: 3 Infantry Battalions (Riachuelo, Humaita and Paissandu), 1 Artillery Battalion, 1 HQ Company, 1 Air Defence Battery, 1 Tank Company.
Tropa de Reforço: 1 Engineer Battalion, 1 Amphib Vehicles Battalion, 1 Logistic Battalion.
Special Forces Battalion (Tonelero).
Grupamentos Regionais: One security group in each naval district and command (Rio de Janeiro, Salvador, Natal, Belém, Rio Grande, Ladário, Manaus, Brasilia).

Strength of the Fleet

Type	Active	Building (Planned)
Submarines (Patrol)	5	–
Aircraft Carrier	1	–
Frigates	10	–
Corvettes	4	1
Patrol Forces	34	(14)
LSD/LST	3	–
Minesweepers (Coastal)	6	–
Survey and Research Ships	9	–
Buoy Tenders	17	–
S/M Rescue Ship	1	–
Tankers	2	–
Hospital Ships	3	–
Training Ships	8	–

DELETIONS

Frigates

2004   *Dodsworth, Pernambuco* (both reserve)

Patrol Forces

2003   *Solimóes* (museum)
2004   *Angostura, Caboclo*

Survey Ships and Tenders

2003   *Almirante Câmara*
2004   *Caravelas, Itacurassá, Nogueira da Gama, Argus*

Auxiliaries

2005   *Atlantico Sud*

PENNANT LIST

Submarines

S 30	Tupi
S 31	Tamoio
S 32	Timbira
S 33	Tapajó
S 34	Tikuna (bldg)

Aircraft Carriers

A 12	São Paulo

Destroyers/Frigates

D 27	Pará
F 40	Niteroi
F 41	Defensora
F 42	Constituição
F 43	Liberal
F 44	Independência
F 45	União
F 46	Greenhalgh
F 48	Bosisio
F 49	Rademaker

Corvettes

V 30	Inhaúma
V 31	Jaceguay
V 32	Julio de Noronha
V 33	Frontin
V 34	Barroso (bldg)

Amphibious Forces

G 28	Mattoso Maia
G 30	Ceará
G 31	Rio de Janeiro
L 10	Guarapari
L 11	Tambaú
L 12	Camboriú

Patrol Forces

V 15	Imperial Marinheiro
P 10	Piratini
P 11	Pirajá
P 12	Pampeiro
P 13	Parati
P 14	Penedo
P 15	Poti
P 20	Pedro Teixeira
P 21	Raposo Tavares
P 30	Roraima
P 31	Rondônia
P 32	Amapá
P 40	Grajaú
P 41	Guaiba
P 42	Graúna
P 43	Goiana
P 44	Guajará
P 45	Guaporé
P 46	Gurupá
P 47	Gurupi
P 48	Guanabara
P 49	Guarujá
P 50	Guaratuba
P 51	Gravataí
P 60	Bracui
P 61	Benevente
P 62	Bocaina
P 63	Babitonga

Mine Warfare Forces

M 15	Aratú
M 16	Anhatomirim
M 17	Atalaia
M 18	Araçatuba
M 19	Abrolhos
M 20	Albardão

Survey Ships and Tenders

H 18	Comandante Varella
H 19	Tenente Castelo
H 20	Comandante Manhães
H 21	Sirius
H 25	Tenente Boanerges
H 26	Faroleiro Mário Seixas
H 34	Almirante Graça Aranha
H 35	Amorim do Valle
H 36	Taurus
H 37	Garnier Sampaio
H 40	Antares
H 44	Ary Rongel
SSN-4 03	Paraibano
SSN-4 04	Rio Branco
BHMN 03	Camocin

Auxiliaries

G 15	Paraguassú
G 17	Potengi
G 21	Ary Parreiras
G 23	Almirante Gastao Motta
G 27	Marajo
K 11	Felinto Perry
R 21	Tritão
R 22	Tridente
R 23	Triunfo
R 24	Almirante Guilhem
R 25	Almirante Guillobel
R 26	Trindade
U 10	Aspirante Nascimento
U 11	Guarda Marinha Jensen
U 12	Guarda Marinha Brito
U 15	Para
U 16	Doutor Montenegro
U 17	Parnaiba
U 18	Oswaldo Cruz
U 19	Carlos Chagas
U 20	Cisne Branco
U 27	Brasil
U 29	Piraim

SUBMARINES

Notes: (1) Plans for the construction of nuclear-powered submarines continue although the programme has been constrained by lack of funding. The prototype nuclear reactor IPEN/MB-1 built at Aramar, Iperó, São Paulo is reportedly awaiting installation in a land-based prototype submarine although the programme for this work has not been released. An uranium enrichment plant was inaugurated at Iperó in April 1988. Published plans of the prototype SSN (SNAC-2) are of a boat of about 2,825 tons with power plant developing 48 MW for a speed of 28 kt. Entry into service is not expected before 2020.

(2) Design of a new SSK, designated S-MB-10 is in progress. Five boats of about 2,500 tons, 67 m length and 8 m beam are planned. The construction programme has not been published although all five are required by 2018.

(3) On 28 September 2005, the US Congress was advised of the possible sale of 30 Raytheon Mk 48 Mod 6 torpedoes to the Brazilian Navy.

1 + (1) TIKUNA CLASS (SSK)

Name	No
TIKUNA (ex-*Tocantins*)	S 34

Builders	Laid down	Launched	Commissioned
Arsenal de Marinha, Rio de Janeiro	11 June 1996	9 Mar 2005	2006

Displacement, tons: 1,490 surfaced; 1,620 dived
Dimensions, feet (metres): 200.2 × 20.3 × 18
(61 × 6.2 × 5.5)
Main machinery: Diesel-electric; 4 MTU 12V 396 diesels; 3,760 hp(m) *(2.76 MW)*; 4 alternators; 1 motor; 1 shaft
Speed, knots: 11 surfaced/snorting; 22 dived
Range, n miles: 11,000 at 8 kt surfaced; 400 at 4 kt dived
Complement: 36 (7 officers)

Torpedoes: 8—21 in *(533 mm)* bow tubes. Bofors Torpedo 2000; wire guided active/passive homing to 50 km *(27 n miles)* at 20—50 kt; warhead 250 kg. Swim-out discharge. IPqM designed A/S torpedoes may also be carried; 18 km *(9.7 n miles)* at 45 kt. Total of 16 torpedoes.
Mines: 32 IPqM/Consub MCF-01/100 carried in lieu of torpedoes.
Countermeasures: ESM: Thomson-CSF DR-4000; intercept.
Weapons control: STN Atlas Electronik ISUS 83-13; 2 Kollmorgen Mod 76 periscopes.

Radars: Navigation: Terma Scanter; I-band.
Sonars: Atlas Elektronik CSU-83/1; hull-mounted; passive/active search and attack; medium frequency.

Programmes: Planned intermediate stage between Tupi class and the first SSN. Designed by the Naval Engineering Directorate. Contract effective with HDW in October 1995. A second of class, possibly to be named *Tapuia* is likely to be built. Construction is expected to start in 2006 and delivery in 2012.
Structure: Improved Tupi design similar to Turkish Gur class. Diving depth, 300 m *(985 ft)*. Very high-capacity batteries with GRP lead-acid cells by Microlite. More powerful engines than *Tupi*. Fitted with two Kollmorgen Mod 76 non-penetrative optronic masts.
Operational: Endurance, 60 days. Sea trials began on 10 November 2005.

TIKUNA
3/2005*, AMRJ
1127026

4 TUPI CLASS (209 TYPE 1400) (SSK)

Name	No
TUPI	S 30
TAMOIO	S 31
TIMBIRA	S 32
TAPAJÓ	S 33

Builders	Laid down	Launched	Commissioned
Howaldtswerke-Deutsche Werft, Kiel	8 Mar 1985	28 Apr 1987	6 May 1989
Arsenal de Marinha, Rio de Janeiro	15 July 1986	18 Nov 1993	12 Dec 1994
Arsenal de Marinha, Rio de Janeiro	15 Sep 1987	5 Jan 1996	16 Dec 1996
Arsenal de Marinha, Rio de Janeiro	6 Mar 1996	5 June 1998	16 Nov 1999

Displacement, tons: 1,453 surfaced; 1,590 dived
Dimensions, feet (metres): 200.8 × 20.3 × 18
(61.2 × 6.2 × 5.5)
Main machinery: Diesel-electric; 4 MTU 12V 493 AZ80 GA31L diesels; 2,400 hp(m) *(1.76 MW)*; 4 alternators; 1.7 MW; 1 Siemens motor; 4,600 hp(m) *(3.36 MW)* sustained; 1 shaft
Speed, knots: 11 surfaced/snorting; 21.5 dived
Range, n miles: 8,200 at 8 kt surfaced; 400 at 4 kt dived
Complement: 36 (7 officers)

Torpedoes: 8—21 in *(533 mm)* bow tubes. 16 Marconi Mk 24 Tigerfish Mod 1 or 2; wire-guided; active homing to 13 km *(7 n miles)* at 35 kt; passive homing to 29 km *(15.7 n miles)* at 24 kt; warhead 134 kg. IPqM anti-submarine torpedoes may also be carried; range 18 km *(9.7 n miles)* at 45 kt. Swim-out discharge.
Countermeasures: ESM: Thomson-CSF DR-4000; radar warning.
Weapons control: Ferranti KAFS-A10 action data automation. 2 Kollmorgen Mod 76 periscopes.
Radars: Navigation: Terma Scanter; I-band.
Sonars: Atlas Elektronik CSU-83/1; hull-mounted; passive/active search and attack; medium frequency.

Programmes: Contract signed with Howaldtswerke in February 1984. Financial negotiations were completed with the West German Government in October 1984. Original plans included building four in Brazil followed by two improved Tupis for a total of six. In the end only three were constructed in Brazil.

TAPAJÓ   *10/2005*, Mario R V Carneiro* / 1153025

Modernisation: A programme (Mod Sub) to upgrade auxiliary machinery, sonars, weapon control, countermeasures and navigation systems was announced in 2003. Refit work on S 31 was completed in June 2005 when work on S 32 began. The programme is to be completed in 2008. Tigerfish torpedoes may be replaced by Mk 48 Mod 6 if sale approved by US government.

Structure: Hull constructed of HY 80 steel. Single hull. Diving depth, 250 m *(820 ft)*. Equipped with Sperry Mk 29 Mod 3 SINS.
Operational: Based at Niteroi, Rio de Janeiro.

TUPI   *6/2003, Mario R V Carneiro*/ 0569159

AIRCRAFT CARRIERS

1 CLEMENCEAU CLASS (CVM)

Name	No	Builders	Laid down	Launched	Commissioned
SÃO PAULO (ex-*Foch*)	A 12 (ex-R 99)	Chantiers de l'Atlantique, St. Nazaire	15 Feb 1957	23 July 1960	15 July 1963

Displacement, tons: 27,307 standard; 33,673 full load
Dimensions, feet (metres): 869.4 oa; 780.8 pp × 104.1 hull
(168 oa) × 28.2 *(265; 238 × 31.7; 51.2 × 8.6)*
Flight deck, feet (metres): 850 × 154 *(259 × 47)*
Main machinery: 6 boilers; 640 psi *(45 kg/cm²)*; 840°F
(450°C); 2 GEC Alsthom turbines; 126,000 hp(m) *(93 MW)*;
2 shafts
Speed, knots: 30
Range, n miles: 7,000 at 18 kt; 4,800 at 24 kt; 3,500 at full
power
Complement: 1,220 (80 officers); 358 (80 officers) aircrew

Missiles: SAM: 2 AESN Albatros Mk 2 (8 cells, 2 reloads);
Aspide 2000 missiles; semi-active homing to 21 km
(11 n miles) at 2.5 Mach; warhead 30 kg (to be fitted).
Guns: 2 Bofors SAK 40 mm/L 70—600 Mk 3 Sea Trinity;
330 rds/min to 4 km *(2.2 n miles)* (to be fitted).
5—12.7 mm MGs.
Countermeasures: 2 CSEE AMBL 2A Sagai (10 barrelled
trainable launchers); chaff and IR flares.
Combat data systems: To be fitted with IPqM/Elebra
SICONTA Mk 1 tactical system; Links YB and 14.
Radars: Air search: Thomson-CSF DRBV 23B ❶; D-band.
Air/surface search: Thomson-CSF DRBV 15 ❷; E/F-band.
Height finder: 2 DRBI 10 ❸; E/F-band.
Navigation: Racal Decca 1226; I-band.
Fire control: 2 AESN Orion RTN 30X; I/J-band (to be fitted).
Tacan: NRBP-2B.
Landing approach control: NRBA 51 ❹; I-band.

Fixed-wing aircraft: 15-18 A-4 Skyhawks.
Helicopters: 4-6 Agusta SH-3A/D Sea Kings; 3 Aerospatiale
UH-12/13; 2 UH-14 Cougar.

Programmes: Acquired from France on 15 November 2000
and following modifications in Brest, arrived in Brazil in
February 2001.
Modernisation: A foldable mini ski-jump has been fitted
to both catapults. The jet deflectors are enlarged (this
implies reducing the area of the forward lift). Crotale and
Sadral systems disembarked before transfer. A point-
defence system, possibly Aspide SAM, may be fitted.
An Umkhonto VLS system is also reported to be under
consideration. Upgrade/replacement of some sensors
may also be undertaken subject to funding. Refit in
2003 included re-tubing of boilers and refurbishment of
catapults.
Structure: Flight deck, island superstructure and bridges,
hull (over machinery spaces and magazines) are all
armour plated. There are three bridges: Flag, Command
and Aviation.

SÃO PAULO *9/2003, S C Neto/Mario R V Carneiro* / 0569158

Two Mitchell-Brown steam catapults; Mk BS 5; able to
launch 20 ton aircraft at 110 kt. The flight deck is angled
at 8°. Two lifts 52.5 × 36 ft *(16 × 10.97 m)* one of which is
on the starboard deck edge. Dimensions of the hangar
are 590.6 × 78.7 × 23 ft *(180 × 24 × 7 m)*.

Operational: Oil fuel capacity is 3,720 tons. The aircraft
complement for the helicopter carrier role includes
between 30 and 40 with a mixture of Sea Kings, Super
Puma, Super-Lynx, Ecureuil and Jet Ranger III.

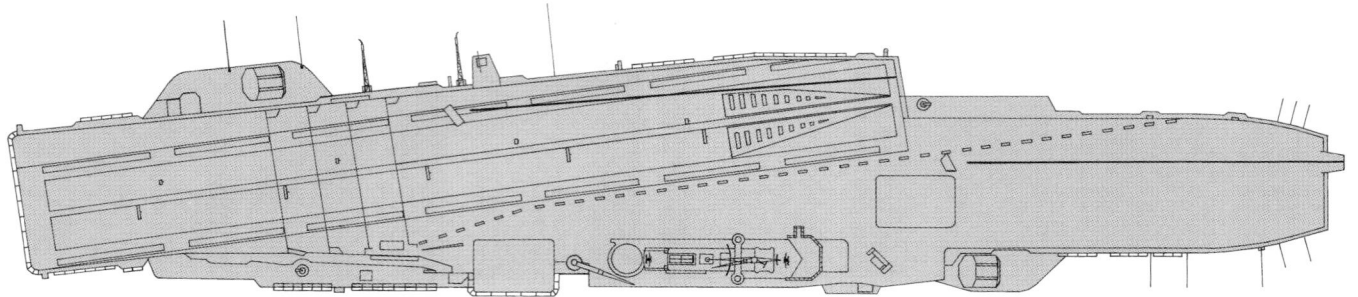

SÃO PAULO *(Scale 1 : 1,500), Ian Sturton* / 0529159

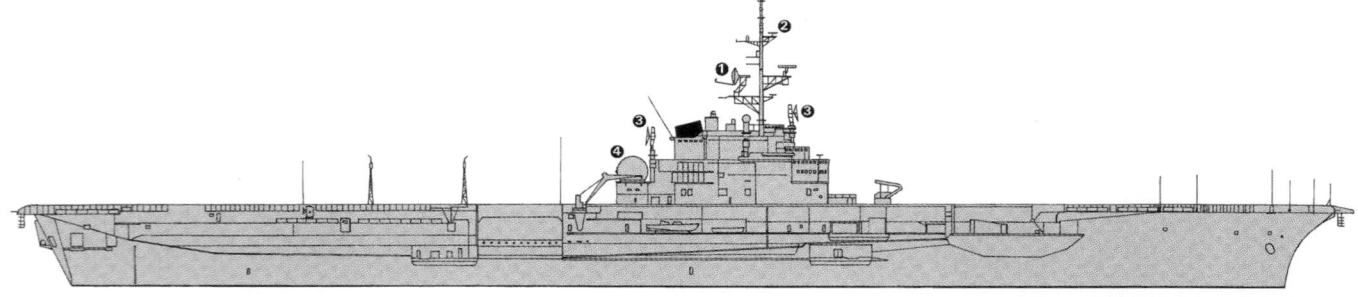

SÃO PAULO *(Scale 1 : 1,500), Ian Sturton* / 0130381

SÃO PAULO *2/2001, Mario R V Carneiro* / 0059751

SÃO PAULO *2/2001, Mario R V Carneiro* / 0059752

SÃO PAULO

2/2001, Mario R V Carneiro / 0059750

FRIGATES

3 BROADSWORD CLASS (TYPE 22) (FFGHM)

Name	No	Builders	Laid down	Launched	Commissioned	Recommissioned
GREENHALGH (ex-*Broadsword*)	F 46 (ex-F 88)	Yarrow Shipbuilders, Glasgow	7 Feb 1975	12 May 1976	3 May 1979	30 June 1995
BOSISIO (ex-*Brazen*)	F 48 (ex-F 91)	Yarrow Shipbuilders, Glasgow	18 Aug 1978	4 Mar 1980	2 July 1982	31 Aug 1996
RADEMAKER (ex-*Battleaxe*)	F 49 (ex-F 89)	Yarrow Shipbuilders, Glasgow	4 Feb 1976	18 May 1977	28 Mar 1980	30 Apr 1997

Displacement, tons: 3,500 standard; 4,731 full load
Dimensions, feet (metres): 430 oa; 410 wl × 48.5 × 19.9
(screws) *(131.2; 125 × 14.8 × 6)*
Main machinery: COGOG; 2 RR Olympus TM3B gas turbines;
50,000 hp *(37.3 MW)* sustained; 2 RR Tyne RM1C gas
turbines; 9,900 hp *(7.4 MW)* sustained; 2 shafts; cp props
Speed, knots: 30; 18 on Tynes
Range, n miles: 4,500 at 18 kt on Tynes
Complement: 239 (17 officers)

Missiles: SSM: 4 Aerospatiale MM 38 Exocet ❶; inertial
cruise; active radar homing to 42 km *(23 n miles)*
at 0.9 Mach; warhead 165 kg; sea-skimmer.
SAM: 2 British Aerospace 6-barrelled Seawolf GWS 25
Mod 4 ❷; command line of sight (CLOS) TV/radar
tracking to 5 km *(2.7 n miles)* at 2+ Mach; warhead
14 kg; 32 rounds.
Guns: 2 Bofors SAK 40 mm/L 70—350 A-3 ❸ (F 46, F 49);
300 rds/min to 12 km *(6.5 n miles)*
2 Oerlikon BMARC 20 mm GAM-BO1; 1,000 rds/min
to 2 km.
Torpedoes: 6—324 mm Plessey STWS Mk 2 (2 triple) tubes
❹. Honeywell Mk-46 Mod 5; active/passive homing to
11 km *(5.9 n miles)* at 40 kt; warhead 44 kg.
Countermeasures: Decoys: 4 Loral Hycor SRBOC Mk 36;
6-barrelled fixed launchers ❺; for chaff.
Graseby Type 182; towed torpedo decoy.
ESM: MEL UAA-2; intercept.
ECM: Type 670; jammers.

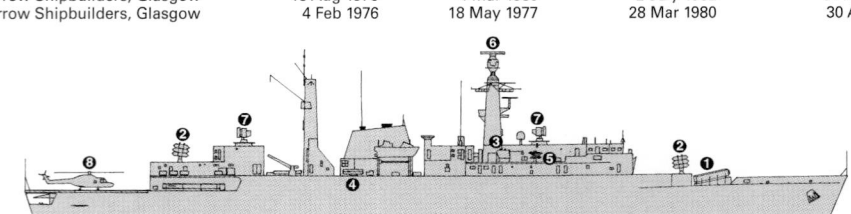

GREENHALGH

(Scale 1 : 1,200), Ian Sturton / 0012084

Combat data systems: CAAIS; Link YB being fitted.
Inmarsat.
Weapons control: GWS 25 Mod 4 (for SAM); GWS 50
(Exocet).
Radars: Air/surface search: Marconi Type 967/968 ❻;
D/E-band.
Navigation: Kelvin Hughes Type 1006; I-band.
Fire control: Two Marconi Type 910 ❼; I/Ku-band (for
Seawolf).
Sonars: Plessey Type 2050; hull-mounted; search and
attack; medium frequency.

Helicopters: 2 Westland Super Lynx AH-11A ❽.

Programmes: Contract signed on 18 November 1994 to
transfer four Batch I Type 22 frigates from the UK, one

in 1995, two in 1996 and one in 1997. It is not planned to
buy more Type 22s.
Modernisation: Plans to fit a single 57 mm gun on
the bow were shelved in favour of a 40 mm gun
on each beam. These guns are being taken from the
Niteroi class. The modernisation programme has
been suspended due to lack of funds. F 46 has not
been upgraded with Exocet MM 40 as previously
reported.
Structure: Accommodation modified in UK service to take
65 officers under training.
Operational: Primary role is ASW. Form part of Second
Frigate Squadron at Niteroi, Rio de Janeiro. F 47
placed in reserve in 2004. F 46 may be placed in reserve
in 2006.

BOSISIO

10/2005*, Mario R V Carneiro / 1153024

RADEMAKER

10/2005*, Mario R V Carneiro / 1153023

6 NITERÓI CLASS (FFGHM)

Name	No	Builders	Laid down	Launched	Commissioned
NITERÓI	F 40	Vosper Thornycroft Ltd	8 June 1972	8 Feb 1974	20 Nov 1976
DEFENSORA	F 41	Vosper Thornycroft Ltd	14 Dec 1972	27 Mar 1975	5 Mar 1977
CONSTITUIÇÃO	F 42	Vosper Thornycroft Ltd	13 Mar 1974	15 Apr 1976	31 Mar 1978
LIBERAL	F 43	Vosper Thornycroft Ltd	2 May 1975	7 Feb 1977	18 Nov 1978
INDEPENDÊNCIA	F 44	Arsenal de Marinha, Rio de Janeiro	11 June 1972	2 Sep 1974	3 Sep 1979
UNIÃO	F 45	Arsenal de Marinha, Rio de Janeiro	11 June 1972	14 Mar 1975	12 Sep 1980

Displacement, tons: 3,200 standard; 3,707 full load
Dimensions, feet (metres): 424 × 44.2 × 18.2 (sonar)
  (129.2 × 13.5 × 5.5)
Main machinery: CODOG; 2 RR Olympus TM3B gas
  turbines; 50,880 hp *(37.9 MW)* sustained; 4 MTU 20V
  1163 TB 93 diesels; 20,128 hp(m) *(14.8 MW)* sustained;
  2 shafts; cp props
Speed, knots: 30 gas; 22 diesels
Range, n miles: 5,300 at 17 kt on 2 diesels; 4,200 at 19 kt on
  4 diesels; 1,300 at 28 kt on gas
Complement: 209 (22 officers)

Missiles: SSM: 4 Aerospatiale MM 40 Exocet (2 twin)
  launchers **❶**; inertial cruise; active radar homing to 70 km
  (40 n miles) at 0.9 Mach; warhead 165 kg; sea-skimmer.
  SAM: AESN Albatros (8 cell, 2 reloads) **❷**; Aspide 2000; semi-
  active radar homing to 21 km *(11 n miles)* at 2.5 Mach.
Guns: 1 Vickers 4.5 in *(115 mm)*/55 Mk 8 **❸**; 25 rds/min to
  22 km *(12 n miles)* anti-surface; 6 km *(3.2 n miles)* anti-
  aircraft; weight of shell 21 kg.
  2 Bofors SAK 40 mm/L 70—600 Mk 3 Sea Trinity **❹**;
  330 rds/min to 4 km *(2.2 n miles)*.
Torpedoes: 6—324 mm Plessey STWS-1 (2 triple) tubes **❺**.
  Honeywell Mk 46 Mod 5; anti-submarine; active/passive
  homing to 11 km *(5.9 n miles)* at 40 kt; warhead 44 kg.
A/S mortars: 1 Bofors 375 mm trainable rocket launcher
  (twin-tube) **❻**; automatic loading; range 1,600 m.
Countermeasures: Decoys: 4 IPqM/Elebra MDLS octuples
  chaff launchers **❼**.
  ESM: Racal Cutlass B-1B; intercept.
  ECM: Racal Cygnus or IPqM/Elebra ET/SLQ-2X; jammer.
Combat data systems: IPqM/Elebra Siconta II. Link YB.

Weapons control: Saab/Combitech EDS-400/10B optronic
  director. WSA 401. FCS.
Radars: Air/surface search: AESN RAN 20 S (3L) **❽**; D-band.
  Surface search: Terma Scenter MiP **❾**; I-band.
  Fire control: 2 AESN RTN 30X **❿**; I/J-band.
  Navigation: Furuno FR-1942 Mk 2; I-band.
Sonars: EDO 997F; hull-mounted; active search and attack;
  medium frequency.
  EDO 700E VDS (F 40 and 41); active search and attack;
  medium frequency.

Helicopters: 1 Westland Super Lynx AH-11A **⓫**.

Programmes: A contract announced on 29 September
1970 was signed between the Brazilian Government and
Vosper Thornycroft for the design and building of six
Vosper Thornycroft Mark 10 frigates. Seventh ship with

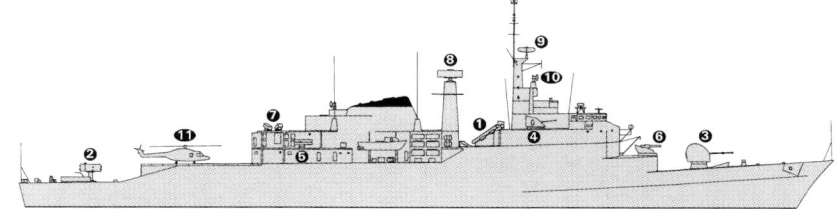

LIBERAL (after modernisation)   *(Scale 1 : 1,200), Ian Sturton* / 0529160

differing armament was ordered from Navyard, Rio de
Janeiro in June 1981 and is used as a training ship.
Modernisation: The modernisation plan (Mod Frag) first
signed in March 1995 included replacing Seacat by
Aspide, Plessey AWS 2 radar by Alenia RAN 20S, RTN
10X by RTN 30X, ZW06 radar by Terma Scanter, new
40 mm mountings, new EW equipment, combat data
system and hull-mounted sonar. Ikara removed. Work
was undertaken by Elebra. *Liberal* completed 2001.
Defensora (2002), *Independência* (2004) and *Niterói*
(2004). *Constituição* and *União* were completed in 2005.
Structure: Originally F 40, 41, 44 and 45 were of the A/S
configuration. F 42 and 43 general purpose design. Fitted
with retractable stabilisers.
Operational: Endurance, 45 days' stores, 60 days'
provisions. The helicopter has Sea Skua ASM. All are
based at Niterói and form the First Frigate Squadron.

LIBERAL   *10/2005*, Mario R V Carneiro* / 1153021

INDEPENDÊNCIA   *10/2005*, Mario R V Carneiro* / 1153022

1 PARÁ (GARCIA) CLASS (FFHM)

Name	No	Builders	Laid down	Launched	Commissioned	Recommissioned
PARÁ (ex-*Albert David*)	D 27 (ex-FF 1050)	Lockheed SB & Construction Co	29 Apr 1964	19 Dec 1964	19 Oct 1968	18 Sep 1989

Displacement, tons: 2,620 standard; 3,560 full load

Dimensions, feet (metres): 414.5 × 44.2 × 24 sonar; 14.5 keel *(126.3 × 13.5 × 7.3; 4.4)*

Main machinery: 2 Foster-Wheeler boilers; 1,200 psi *(83.4 kg/cm²)*; 950°F *(510°C)*; 1 Westinghouse or GE turbine; 35,000 hp *(26 MW)*; 1 shaft

Speed, knots: 27.5

Range, n miles: 4,000 at 20 kt

Complement: 286 (18 officers) + 25 spare

Missiles: A/S Honeywell ASROC Mk 116 Mod 3 octuple launcher ❶; inertial guidance to 1.6—10 km *(1—5.4 n miles)*; payload Mk 46 torpedo. *Pará* has automatic ASROC reload system.

Guns: 2 USN 5 in *(127 mm)*/38 Mk 30 ❷; 15 rds/min to 17 km *(9.3 n miles)*; weight of shell 25 kg.
2—12.7 mm MGs.

Torpedoes: 6—324 mm Mk 32 (2 triple) tubes ❸. 14 Honeywell Mk 46 Mod 5; anti-submarine; active/passive homing to 11 km *(5.9 n miles)* at 40 kt; warhead 44 kg.

Countermeasures: Decoys: 2 Loral Hycor Mk 33 RBOC 4 barrelled chaff launchers. T-Mk 6 Fanfare; torpedo decoy system. Prairie/Masker; hull/blade rate noise suppression. ESM: WLR-1; WLR-6; radar warning.
ECM: ULQ-6; jammer.

Combat data systems: IPqH/Elebra Mini-Siconta.

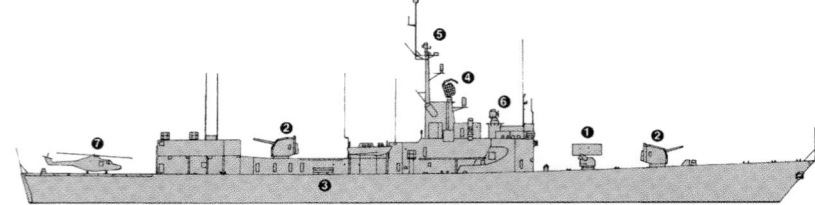

PARÁ   *(Scale 1 : 1,200), Ian Sturton* / 0505960

Weapons control: Mk 56 GFCS (*127 mm*). Mk 114 ASW FCS. SATCOM.

Radars: Air search: Lockheed SPS-40B ❹; B-band; range 320 km *(175 n miles)*.
Surface search: Raytheon SPS-10C ❺; G-band.
Navigation: Marconi LN66; I-band.
Fire control: General Electric Mk 35 ❻; I/J-band.
Tacan: SRN 15. IFF: UPX XII.

Sonars: SQS-26B; bow-mounted; active search and attack; medium frequency.

Helicopters: Westland Super Lynx AH-11 ❼.

Programmes: Last remaining ship of four transferred from USA in 1989. Classified as Destroyer in the Brazilian Navy. The lease was renewed in 1994.

Structure: Enlarged hangar capable of taking a helicopter the size of a Sea King. In USN service had the flight deck area converted to take SQR-15 towed array which was removed on transfer.

Operational: Part of Second Frigate Squadron at Niterói, Rio de Janeiro. Operational readiness is proving difficult to maintain. D 28 and D 29 decommissioned and D 30 placed in reserve.

PARÁ CLASS   *2/2001, Mario R V Carneiro* / 0130424

CORVETTES

0 + 1 BARROSO CLASS (FSGH)

Name	No	Builders	Laid down	Launched	Commissioned
BARROSO	V 34	Arsenal de Marinha, Rio de Janeiro	21 Dec 1994	20 Dec 2002	Dec 2008

Displacement, tons: 1,785 standard; 2,350 full load

Dimensions, feet (metres): 339.3 × 37.4 × 13.0; 17.4 (sonar) *(103.4 × 11.4 × 3.95; 5.3)*

Main machinery: CODOG; 1 GE LM 2500 gas turbine; 27,500 hp *(20.52 MW)* sustained; 2 MTU 20V 1163 TB83 diesels; 11,780 hp(m) *(8.67 MW)* sustained; 2 shafts; Kamewa cp props

Speed, knots: 29. **Range, n miles:** 4,000 at 15 kt

Complement: 160 (15 officers)

Missiles: SSM 4 Aerospatiale MM 40 Exocet ❶; inertial cruise; active radar homing to 70 km *(40 n miles)* at 0.90 Mach; warhead 165 kg; sea-skimmer.

Guns: 1 Vickers 4.5 in *(115 mm)* Mk 8 ❷; 55° elevation; 25 rds/min to 22 km *(12 n miles)* anti-surface; 6 km *(3.3 n miles)* anti-aircraft; weight of shell 21 kg.
1 Bofors SAK Sea Trinity CIWS 40 mm/70 Mk 3 ❸; 330 rds/min to 4 km *(2.2 n miles)*; anti-aircraft; 2.5 km *(1.4 n miles)* anti-missile; weight of shell 0.96 kg; with '3P' improved ammunition.
2—12.7 mm MGs.

Torpedoes: 6—324 mm Mk 32 (2 triple) tubes ❹; Honeywell Mk 46 Mod 5; anti-submarine; active/passive homing to 11 km *(5.9 n miles)* at 40 kt; warhead 44 kg.

Countermeasures: Decoys: 2 IPqM octuple chaff launchers ❺. ESM: IPqM/Elebra ET/SLQ-1A ❻; radar warning.
ECM: IPqM/Elebra ET/SLQ-2 ❼; jammer.

Combat data systems: IPqM/Esca Siconta Mk III with Link YB.

Weapons control: Saab/Combitech EOS-400 FCS with optronic director ❽; two OFDLSE optical directors ❾.

Radars: Surface search: AESN RAN-20S ❿; F-band.
Navigation: Terma Scanter; I-band.
Fire control: AESN RTN-30-X ⓫; I/J-band (for Albatross and guns).

Sonars: EDO 997(F); hull-mounted; active; medium frequency.

Helicopters: 1 AH-11A Westland Super Lynx ⓬.

Programmes: Ordered in 1994 as a follow-on to the Inhauma programme. The building programme has been beset by funding difficulties and although a class of six ships is projected by 2018, construction of furthers units has not started.

Structure: The hull is some 4.2 m longer than the Inhauma class to improve sea-keeping qualities and allow extra space in the engine room. The design allows the use of containerised equipment to aid modernisation. Efforts have been made to incorporate stealth technology. Vosper stabilisers.

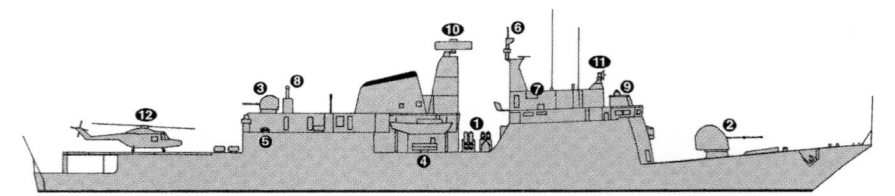

BARROSO   *(Scale 1 : 900), Ian Sturton* / 0506270

BARROSO   *10/2004*, A E Galarce* / 1153020

4 INHAÚMA CLASS (FSGH)

Name	No	Builders	Laid down	Launched	Commissioned
INHAÚMA	V 30	Arsenal de Marinha, Rio de Janeiro	23 Sep 1983	13 Dec 1986	12 Dec 1989
JACEGUAY	V 31	Arsenal de Marinha, Rio de Janeiro	15 Oct 1984	8 June 1987	2 Apr 1991
JULIO DE NORONHA	V 32	Verolme, Angra dos Reis	8 Dec 1986	15 Dec 1989	27 Oct 1992
FRONTIN	V 33	Verolme, Angra dos Reis	14 May 1987	6 Feb 1992	11 Mar 1994

Displacement, tons: 1,600 standard; 1,970 full load
Dimensions, feet (metres): 314.2 × 37.4 × 12.1; 17.4 (sonar) *(95.8 × 11.4 × 3.7; 5.3)*
Main machinery: CODOG; 1 GE LM 2500 gas turbine; 27,500 hp *(20.52 MW)* sustained; 2 MTU 16V 396 TB94 diesels; 5,800 hp(m) *(4.26 MW)* sustained; 2 shafts; Kamewa cp props
Speed, knots: 27
Range, n miles: 4,000 at 15 kt
Complement: 133 (20 officers)

Missiles: SSM: 4 Aerospatiale MM 40 Exocet ❶; inertial cruise; active radar homing to 70 km *(40 n miles)* at 0.9 Mach; warhead 165 kg; sea-skimmer.
Guns: 1 Vickers 4.5 in *(115 mm)* Mk 8 ❷; 55° elevation; 25 rds/min to 22 km *(12 n miles)* anti-surface; 6 km *(3.3 n miles)* Santi-aircraft, weight of shell 21 kg.
2 Bofors 40 mm/70 ❸; 300 rds/min to 12 km *(6.5 n miles)* anti-surface; 4 km *(2.2 n miles)* anti-aircraft; weight of shell 0.96 kg.
Torpedoes: 6—324 mm Mk 32 (2 triple) tubes ❹. Honeywell Mk 46 Mod 5; anti-submarine; active/passive homing to 11 km *(5.9 n miles)* at 40 kt; warhead 44 kg.
Countermeasures: Decoys: 2 Plessey Shield chaff launchers ❺; fires chaff and IR flares in distraction, decoy or centroid patterns.
ESM/ECM: Racal Cygnus B1 radar intercept ❻ and IPqM SDR-7 or Elebra SLQ-1; jammer ❼.

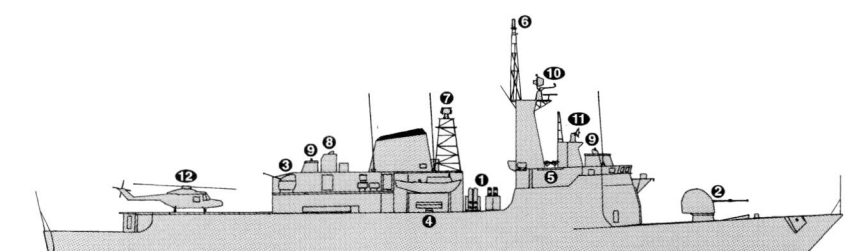

INHAÚMA *(Scale 1 : 900), Ian Sturton* / 0017617

Combat data systems: Ferranti CAAIS 450/WSA 421; Link YB.
Weapons control: Saab EOS-400 FCS with optronic director ❽ and two OFDLSE optical ❾ directors.
Radars: Surface search Plessey AWS 4 ❿; E/F-band.
Navigation: Kelvin Hughes Type 1007; I/J-band.
Fire control: Selenia Orion RTN 10X ⓫; I/J-band.
Sonars: Atlas Elektronik DSQS-21C; hull-mounted; active; medium frequency.

Helicopters: 1 Westland Super Lynx ⓬ or UH-12/13 Ecureuil.

Programmes: Designed by Brazilian Naval Design Office with advice from West German private Marine Technik design company. Signature of final contract on 1 October 1981. First pair ordered on 15 February 1982 and second pair 9 January 1986. In mid-1986 the government approved, in principle, construction of a total of 16 ships but this was reduced to four.
Modernisation: Plans to fit Simbad SAM have been shelved.
Operational: Form part of First Frigate Squadron based at Niterói, Rio de Janeiro.

JACEGUAY *10/2005*, Mario R V Carneiro* / 1153017

JULIO DE NORONHA *10/2005*, Mario R V Carneiro* / 1153018

SHIPBORNE AIRCRAFT (FRONT LINE)

Notes: It is planned to acquire up to three AEW aircraft. Options include Grumman S-2 Trackers. McDonnell Douglas AF-1 Skyhawk.

Numbers/Type: 20/3 McDonnell Douglas AF-1/AF-1A Skyhawk.
Operational speed: 560 kt *(1,040 km/h)*.
Service ceiling: 45,000 ft *(13,780 m)*.
Range: 1,060 n miles *(1,965 km)*.
Role/Weapon systems: Acquired from Kuwait Air Force in September 1998 to restore carrier fixed wing flying. Sensors: APQ 145B radar; ESM/ECM. Weapons: AAM; 4 MAA-1 or 4 AIM 9H; 2 Colt 20 mm cannon; ASVW; bombs and rocket pods.

AF-1   *10/2001, S C Neto/Mario R V Carneiro* / 0569157

Numbers/Type: 4/3/3/3 Sikorsky ASH-3D/SH-3D/SH-3G/SH-3H.
Operational speed: 125 kt *(230 km/h)*.
Service ceiling: 12,200 ft *(3,720 m)*.
Range: 400 n miles *(740 km)*.
Role/Weapon systems: ASW helicopter; carrierborne and shore-based for medium-range ASW, ASVW and SAR. Sixteen delivered between 1970 and 1997. Three have been lost. Seven are reported operational. Sensors: SMA APS-705(V)II or APS-24 search radar; Bendix AQS 13F or AQS 18(V) dipping sonar. Weapons: ASW; up to 4 × Mk 46 torpedoes, or 4 Mk II depth bombs. ASVW; 2 × AM 39 Exocet missiles.

SH-3B   *2/2001, Mario R V Carneiro* / 0130466

Numbers/Type: 2/5 Aerospatiale UH-14 (AS 332F1 Super Puma)/(AS 532 SC Cougar).
Operational speed: 100 kt *(182 km/h)*.
Service ceiling: 20,000 ft *(6,100 m)*.
Range: 345 n miles *(635 km)*.
Role/Weapon systems: SAR, troop transport and ASVW. Sensors: Bendix RDR-1400C search radar. Weapons: None.

UH-14   *6/2003, S C Neto/Mario R V Carneiro* / 0569155

Numbers/Type: 12 AH-IIA Westland Super Lynx.
Operational speed: 125 kt *(232 km/h)*.
Service ceiling: 12,000 ft *(3,650 m)*.
Range: 160 n miles *(296 km)*.
Role/Weapon systems: ASW/ASV roles. First batch upgraded in 1994-97 to Super Lynx standard with Mk 3 radar and Racal Kestrel EW suite. Sensors: Sea Spray Mk 1/Mk 3 radar; Racal MIR 2 ESM. Weapons: ASW; 2 × Mk 46 torpedoes, or Mk II depth bombs. ASV; 4 × BAe/Ferranti Sea Skua missiles.

AH-11A   *5/2005*, Julio Montes* / 1153019

Numbers/Type: 18 Aerospatiale UH-12 Esquilo (AS-350BA Ecureuil).
Operational speed: 140 kt *(260 km/h)*.
Service ceiling: 10,000 ft *(3,050 m)*.
Range: 240 n miles *(445 km)*.
Role/Weapon systems: Support helicopters for Fleet liaison and Marine Corps transportation. Sensors: None. Weapons: 2 × axial 7.62 mm MGs or 1 × lateral MG or 1 × rocket pod.

UH-12   *12/2002, Mario R V Carneiro* / 0569156

Numbers/Type: 8 Aerospatiale UH-13 Esquilo (AS 355F2 Ecureuil 2).
Operational speed: 121 kt *(224 km/h)*.
Service ceiling: 11,150 ft *(3,400 m)*.
Range: 240 n miles *(445 km)*.
Role/Weapon systems: SAR, liaison and utility in support of Marine Corps. Seven more ordered in 1998. Sensors: Search radar. Weapons: 2 × axial 7.62 mm MGs or 1 × lateral MG or 1 × rocket pod.

UH-13   *8/2002, Mario R V Carneiro* / 0528966

Numbers/Type: 18 IH-6B (Bell JetRanger III).
Operational speed: 115 kt *(213 km/h)*.
Service ceiling: 20,000 ft *(6,100 m)*.
Range: 368 n miles *(682 km)*.
Role/Weapon systems: Utility and training helicopters. One lost in June 2005. Sensors: None. Weapons: 2 × 7.62 mm MGs or 2 × rocket pods.

IH-6B   *12/2002, Mario R V Carneiro* / 0569154

LAND-BASED MARITIME AIRCRAFT (FRONT LINE)

Numbers/Type: 6 Lockheed P-3BR Orion.
Operational speed: 411 kt *(761 km/h).*
Service ceiling: 28,300 ft *(8,625 m).*
Range: 4,000 m *(7,410 km).*
Role/Weapon systems: Twelve P-3 A/B acquired by the Air Force from the US Navy in 2002. Eight to be upgraded to P-3BR standard by EADS/CASA. Contract awarded in April 2005. The aircraft are to be fitted with CASA Fully Integrated Tactical System (FITS) mission suite. The remaining four aircraft are to be used for spare parts.

P-3BR *2002, Brazilian Navy* / 0536045

Numbers/Type: 10/9 Bandeirante P-95A/P-95B (EMB-111(B)).
Operational speed: 194 kt *(360 km/h).*
Service ceiling: 25,500 ft *(7,770 m).*
Range: 1,590 n miles *(2,945 km).*
Role/Weapon systems: Air Force operated for coastal surveillance role by four squadrons. Sensors: MEL search radar, searchlight pod on starboard wing, EFIS-74 (electronic flight instrumentation) and Collins APS-65 (autopilot); ESM Thomson-CSF DR2000A/Dalia 1000A Mk II, GPS (Trimble). Weapons: 4 or 6 × 127 mm rockets, or up to 28 × 70 mm rockets.

EMB-111 *6/1995* / 0503428

Numbers/Type: 53 A-1 (Embraer/Alenia/Aermacchi) AMX.
Operational speed: 493 kt *(914 km/h).*
Service ceiling: 42,650 ft *(13,000 m).*
Range: 1,800 n miles *(3,336 km).*
Role/Weapon systems: Air Force operated for strike, reconnaissance and anti-shipping attack; shore-based for fleet air defence and ASV primary roles; operated by 3rd/10th Group at Santa Maria Air Base (KS) and Santa Cruz Air Base. Sensors: Tecnasa/SMA SCP-01 Scipio radar. ECM suite/ESM flares and chaffs; GPS and IFF. Weapons: Strike; up to 3,800 kg of 'IRON' bombs; Self-defence; AAM; 2 × MAA-1 Piranha or 2 × AIM-9 Sidewinder missiles; 2 DEFA 30 mm cannon.

AMX *6/1998* / 0013614

Numbers/Type: 8 Tucano AT-27 (EMB-312A).
Operational speed: 247 kt *(457 km/h).*
Service ceiling: 32,570 ft *(9,936 m).*
Range: 995 n miles *(1,844 km).*
Role/Weapon systems: Air Force operated for liaison and attack by 2 ELO. Sensors: None. Weapons: 6 or 8 × 127 mm rockets or bombs and 1 × 7.62 mm MG pod in each wing.

PATROL FORCES

Notes: (1) Four 1,000 ton offshore patrol craft and five 500 ton patrol craft are planned.
(2) There are 115 LAEP series Instruction and Support craft. 24 LAEP-10 are 10 m long and 91 LAEP-7 are 7 m long.
(3) There are 182 LPN series River patrol craft of 3 to 15 m length.
(4) There are ten Swift class patrol boats operated by port authorities.
(5) Fifteen 8 m aluminium hulled LAR (fast insertion craft) have entered service with the Brazilian Marines. Further orders are expected. There are two other variants of the class: LIN are operated by port authorities and LAM are ambulance craft.

1 + (15) MARLIM (MEATINI) CLASS (PB)

MARLIM LP 01

Displacement, tons: 40 full load
Dimensions, feet (metres): 74.8 × 17.1 × 3.3 *(22.8 × 5.2 × 1)*
Main machinery: 2 CRM 18D/52 diesels; 2,500 hp(m) *(1.84 MW);* 2 shafts
Speed, knots: 34. **Range, n miles:** 550 at 20 kt
Complement: 11 (1 officer)
Guns: 1—12.7 mm MG.
Radars: Surface search: 1 GEM 1210; I-band.

Comment: The first of a new class of patrol craft that entered service in 2005. Slightly longer version of Italian Meatini class design in service with Guardia di Finanzia. Built by Inace Shipyard, Brazil. Aluminium hull. Up to 15 further craft may be ordered. Details are for those in service in Italy and may be different.

MARLIM *6/2005*, INACE* / 1153026

12 GRAJAÚ CLASS (LARGE PATROL CRAFT) (PBO)

Name	No	Builders	Launched	Commissioned
GRAJAÚ	P 40	Arsenal de Marinha	21 May 1993	1 Dec 1993
GUAIBA	P 41	Arsenal de Marinha	10 Dec 1993	12 Sep 1994
GRAÚNA	P 42	Estaleiro Mauá, Niteroi	10 Nov 1993	15 Aug 1994
GOIANA	P 43	Estaleiro Mauá, Niteroi	26 Jan 1994	26 Feb 1997
GUAJARÁ	P 44	Peenewerft, Germany	24 Oct 1994	28 Apr 1995
GUAPORÉ	P 45	Peenewerft, Germany	23 Jan 1995	29 Aug 1995
GURUPÁ	P 46	Peenewerft, Germany	11 May 1995	8 Dec 1995
GURUPI	P 47	Peenewerft, Germany	6 Sep 1995	23 Apr 1996
GUANABARA	P 48	Inace, Fortalesa	5 Nov 1997	9 July 1999
GUARUJÁ	P 49	Inace, Fortalesa	24 Apr 1998	25 Nov 1999
GUARATUBA	P 50	Peenewerft, Germany	16 June 1999	1 Dec 1999
GRAVATAÍ	P 51	Peenewerft, Germany	26 Aug 1999	17 Feb 2000

Displacement, tons: 263 full load
Dimensions, feet (metres): 152.6 × 24.6 × 7.5 *(46.5 × 7.5 × 2.3)*
Main machinery: 2 MTU 16V 396 TB94 diesels; 5,800 hp(m) *(4.26 MW)* sustained; 2 shafts
Speed, knots: 26. **Range, n miles:** 2,200 at 12 kt
Complement: 29 (4 officers)
Guns: 1 Bofors 40 mm/70. 2 Oerlikon 20 mm (P 40—44). 2 Oerlikon BMARC 20 mm GAM-BO1 (P 45—51).
Weapons control: Radamec 1000N optronic director may be fitted in due course.
Radars: Surface search: Racal Decca 1290A; I-band.

Comment: Two ordered in late 1987 to a Vosper QAF design similar to Bangladesh Meghna class. Technology transfer in February 1988 and construction started in July 1988 for the first pair; second pair started construction in September 1990. Class name changed in 1993 when the first four were renumbered to reflect revised delivery dates. Building problems are also reflected in the replacing of the order for the third pair with Peenewerft in November 1993 and the fourth pair in August 1994. Two more ordered from Inace in September 1996 and from Peenewerft in 1998. Used for patrol duties and diver support. Carry one RIB and telescopic launching crane.

GUAPORÉ *2/2001, Mario R V Carneiro* / 0130468

GUAJARÁ *3/1999* / 0056606

1 IMPERIAL MARINHEIRO CLASS
(COASTAL PATROL SHIPS) (PG/ATR)

Name	No	Builders	Commissioned
IMPERIAL MARINHEIRO	V 15	Smit, Kinderdijk, Netherlands	8 June 1955

Displacement, tons: 911 standard; 1,025 full load
Dimensions, feet (metres): 184 × 30.5 × 11.7 *(56 × 9.3 × 3.6)*
Main machinery: 2 Sulzer 6TD36 diesels; 2,160 hp(m) *(1.59 MW)*; 2 shafts
Speed, knots: 16
Complement: 64 (6 officers)
Guns: 1—3 in *(76 mm)*/50 Mk 33; 50 rds/min to 12.8 km *(6.9 n miles)*; weight of shell 6 kg.
2 or 4 Oerlikon 20 mm.
Radars: Surface search: Racal Decca; I-band.

Comment: Fleet tugs classed as corvettes. Equipped for firefighting. *Imperial Marinheiro* has acted as a submarine support ship but gave up the role in 1990. V 21 and V 23 withdrawn from service in 2002, V 24 in 2003 and V 19 and V 20 in 2004.

IMPERIAL MARINHEIRO CLASS   *2/2000, van Ginderen Collection* / 0104229

2 PEDRO TEIXEIRA CLASS (RIVER PATROL SHIPS) (PBR)

Name	No	Builders	Launched	Commissioned
PEDRO TEIXEIRA	P 20	Arsenal de Marinha	14 Oct 1970	17 Dec 1973
RAPOSO TAVARES	P 21	Arsenal de Marinha	11 June 1972	17 Dec 1973

Displacement, tons: 690 standard
Dimensions, feet (metres): 208.7 × 31.8 × 5.6 *(63.6 × 9.7 × 1.7)*
Main machinery: 4 MAN V6 V16/18TL diesels; 3,840 hp(m) *(2.82 MW)*; 2 shafts
Speed, knots: 16. **Range, n miles:** 6,800 at 13 kt
Complement: 60 (6 officers)
Guns: 1 Bofors 40 mm/60; 300 rds/min to 12 km *(6.5 n miles)*.
6—12.7 mm MGs. 2—81 mm Mk 2 mortars.
Radars: Surface search: 2 Racal Decca; I-band.
Helicopters: 1 Bell JetRanger or UH-12 Esquilo.

Comment: Built in Rio de Janeiro. Belong to Amazon Flotilla. Can carry two armed LCVPs and 85 marines in deck accommodation. Both ships to be re-engined.

PEDRO TEIXEIRA   *6/1997, Brazilian Navy* / 0012091

3 RORAIMA CLASS (RIVER PATROL SHIPS) (PBR)

Name	No	Builders	Launched	Commissioned
RORAIMA	P 30	Maclaren, Niteroi	2 Nov 1972	21 Feb 1975
RONDÔNIA	P 31	Maclaren, Niteroi	10 Jan 1973	3 Dec 1975
AMAPÁ	P 32	Maclaren, Niteroi	9 Mar 1973	12 Jan 1976

Displacement, tons: 340 standard; 365 full load
Dimensions, feet (metres): 151.9 × 27.9 × 4.6 *(46.3 × 8.5 × 1.4)*
Main machinery: 2 MAN V6 V16/18TL diesels; 1,920 hp(m) *(1.41 MW)*; 2 shafts
Speed, knots: 14. **Range, n miles:** 3,000 at 12 kt
Complement: 48 (5 officers)
Guns: 1 Bofors 40 mm/60; 300 rds/min to 12 km *(6.5 n miles)*.
2 Oerlikon 20 mm. 2—81 mm mortars. 6—12.7 mm MGs.
Radars: Surface search: 2 Racal Decca; I-band.

Comment: Carry two armed LCVPs. Belong to Amazon Flotilla. P 32 re-engined with Volvo engines and P 30 and P 31 to be similarly refitted.

RORAIMA   *6/1998, Brazilian Navy* / 0017623

4 BRACUI (RIVER) CLASS (COASTAL PATROL CRAFT) (PBO)

Name	No	Builders	Commissioned
BRACUI (ex-*Itchen*)	P 60 (ex-M 2009)	Richards, Lowestoft	12 Oct 1985
BENEVENTE (ex-*Blackwater*)	P 61 (ex-M 2008)	Richards, Great Yarmouth	5 July 1985
BOCAINA (ex-*Spey*)	P 62 (ex-M 2013)	Richards, Lowestoft	4 Apr 1986
BABITONGA (ex-*Arun*)	P 63 (ex-M 2014)	Richards, Lowestoft	29 Aug 1986

Displacement, tons: 770 standard; 890 full load
Dimensions, feet (metres): 156 × 34.5 × 9.5 *(47.5 × 10.5 × 2.9)*
Main machinery: 2 Ruston 6 RKC diesels; 3,100 hp(m) *(2.3 MW)* sustained; 2 shafts
Speed, knots: 14. **Range, n miles:** 4,500 at 10 kt
Complement: 32 (4 officers)
Guns: 1 Bofors 40 mm/60.
2—7.62 mm MGs.
Mines: Rails for up to 20.
Radars: Surface search: 2 Racal Decca TM 1226C; I-band.

Comment: Second batch of ex-UK River class minesweepers transferred in 1998. These four were converted as patrol craft in UK service. Recommissioned 6 April, 10 July and 9 September respectively. Three others transferred in 1995 are listed as Survey Ships and as a Buoy Tender.

BOCAINA   *7/1998, Maritime Photographic* / 0056608

6 PIRATINI CLASS (COASTAL PATROL CRAFT) (PB)

Name	No	Builders	Commissioned
PIRATINI (ex-PGM 109)	P 10	Arsenal de Marinha, Rio de Janeiro	30 Nov 1970
PIRAJÁ (ex-PGM 110)	P 11	Arsenal de Marinha, Rio de Janeiro	8 Mar 1971
PAMPEIRO (ex-PGM 118)	P 12	Arsenal de Marinha, Rio de Janeiro	16 June 1971
PARATI (ex-PGM 119)	P 13	Arsenal de Marinha, Rio de Janeiro	29 July 1971
PENEDO (ex-PGM 120)	P 14	Arsenal de Marinha, Rio de Janeiro	30 Sep 1971
POTI (ex-PGM 121)	P 15	Arsenal de Marinha, Rio de Janeiro	29 Oct 1971

Displacement, tons: 105 standard; 146 full load
Dimensions, feet (metres): 95 × 19 × 6.5 *(29 × 5.8 × 2)*
Main machinery: 4 Cummins VT-12M diesels; 1,100 hp *(820 kW)*; 2 shafts
Speed, knots: 17. **Range, n miles:** 1,700 at 12 kt
Complement: 16 (2 officers)
Guns: 1 Oerlikon 20 mm. 2—12.7 mm MGs.
Radars: Surface search: Racal Decca 1070; I-band.
Navigation: Furuno 3600; I-band.

Comment: Built under offshore agreement with the USA and similar to the US Cape class. 81 mm mortar removed in 1988. Carries an inflatable launch. P 10, P 11, P 14 and P 15 are based at Ladário Fluvial Base, Mato Grosso, the other two at Amazonas.

POTI   *6/1998, Brazilian Navy* / 0017624

4 TRACKER II (LPAN-21) CLASS (COASTAL PATROL CRAFT) (PB)

RIO CPRJ-05 (ex-P 8002)		TIMBIRA CPAOR-17 (ex-P 8005)	
MUCURIPE CPCE-03 (ex-P 8004)		ESPADARTE CPSP-07 (ex-P 8003)	

Displacement, tons: 31 standard; 45 full load
Dimensions, feet (metres): 68.6 × 17 × 4.8 *(20.9 × 5.2 × 1.5)*
Main machinery: 2 MTU 8V 396 TB83 diesels; 2,100 hp(m) *(1.54 MW)* sustained; 2 shafts
Speed, knots: 25. **Range, n miles:** 600 at 15 kt
Complement: 8 (2 officers)
Guns: 2—12.7 mm MGs.
Radars: Surface search: Racal Decca RM 1070A; I-band.

Comment: Ordered in February 1987 to a Fairey design and built at Estaleiro Shipyard, Porto Alegre. National input is 60 per cent. First of class completed building 22 February 1990. All entered service in May 1991. Employed as Police patrol boats.

RIO   *10/2003, Gomel/Marsan* / 0569150

1 PARNAIBA CLASS (RIVER MONITOR) (PGRH)

Name	No	Builders	Commissioned
PARNAIBA	U 17 (ex-P 2)	Arsenal de Marinha, Rio de Janeiro	6 Nov 1938

Displacement, tons: 620 standard; 720 full load
Dimensions, feet (metres): 180.5 × 33.3 × 5.1 *(55 × 10.1 × 1.6)*
Main machinery: 2 diesels; 2 shafts
Speed, knots: 12. **Range, n miles:** 1,350 at 10 kt
Complement: 74 (6 officers)
Guns: 1 US 76 mm. 2 Bofors 40 mm/70. 6 Oerlikon 20 mm.
Radars: Surface search: Racal Decca; I-band.
Navigation: Furuno 3600; I-band.
Helicopters: Platform for one Esquilo.

Comment: Laid down 11 June 1936. Launched 2 September 1937. In Mato Grosso Flotilla. Re-armed with new guns in 1960. 3 in *(76 mm)* side armour and partial deck protection. Refitted in 1995/96 with improved armament, and with diesel engines replacing the steam reciprocating propulsion plant. Converted again in 1998 with Bofors 40 mm/70 guns taken from Niterói class frigates and a helo deck at the stern. Facilities to refuel and re-arm a UH-12 helicopter. Recommissioned 6 May 1999.

PARNAIBA   *5/2000, Hartmut Ehlers* / 0087859

AMPHIBIOUS FORCES

Notes: (1) Replacement of the two Ceará class LSDs is under consideration. Four LCU and eight LCM are also required.
(2) There are 8 EDVP II class landing craft of 13 tons built by BFL, Ladario and capable of carrying 3.7 tons or 37 troops at 9 kt. These are based at Ladario.
(3) There are 32 RIBs for special operations.

1 NEWPORT CLASS (LSTH)

Name	No	Builders	Laid down	Launched	Commissioned	Recommissioned
MATTOSO MAIA (ex-*Cayuga*)	G 28 (ex-LST 1186)	National Steel & Shipbuilding Co	28 Sep 1968	12 July 1969	8 Aug 1970	30 Aug 1994

Displacement, tons: 4,975 light; 8,750 full load
Dimensions, feet (metres): 522.3 (hull) × 69.5 × 17.5 (aft) *(159.2 × 21.2 × 5.3)*
Main machinery: 6 ALCO 16—251 diesels; 16,500 hp *(12.3 MW)* sustained; 2 shafts; cp props; bow thruster
Speed, knots: 20. **Range, n miles:** 14,250 at 14 kt
Complement: 257 (20 officers)
Military lift: 351 (33 officers); 500 tons vehicles; 3 LCVPs and 1 LCPL on davits

Guns: 1 General Electric/General Dynamics 20 mm Vulcan Phalanx Mk 15. 8—12.7 mm MGs.
Radars: Surface search: Raytheon SPS-10F; G-band.
Navigation: Raytheon SPS-64(V)6 and Furuno FR 2120; I-band.

Helicopters: Platform only.

Programmes: Transferred from the USN by lease 26 August 1994, arriving in Brazil in late October. Purchased outright on 19 September 2000.
Structure: The ramp is supported by twin derrick arms. A stern gate to the tank deck permits unloading of amphibious tractors into the water, or unloading of other vehicles into an LCU or onto a pier. Vehicle stowage covers 19,000 sq ft. Length over derrick arms is 562 ft *(171.3 m)*; full load draught is 11.5 ft forward and 17.5 ft aft.

MATTOSO MAIA   *6/2003, S C Neto/Mario R V Carneiro* / 0569153

2 CEARÁ (THOMASTON) CLASS (LSDH)

Name	No	Builders	Laid down	Launched	Commissioned	Recommissioned
CEARÁ (ex-*Hermitage*)	G 30 (ex-LSD 34)	Ingalls, Pascagoula	11 Apr 1955	12 June 1956	14 Dec 1956	28 Nov 1989
RIO DE JANEIRO (ex-*Alamo*)	G 31 (ex-LSD 33)	Ingalls, Pascagoula	11 Oct 1954	20 Jan 1956	24 Aug 1956	21 Nov 1990

Displacement, tons: 6,880 light; 12,150 full load
Dimensions, feet (metres): 510 × 84 × 19 *(155.5 × 25.6 × 5.8)*
Main machinery: 2 Babcock & Wilcox boilers; 580 psi *(40.8 kg/cm²)*; 2 GE turbines; 24,000 hp *(17.9 MW)*; 2 shafts
Speed, knots: 22.5
Range, n miles: 10,000 at 18 kt
Complement: 345 (20 officers)
Military lift: 340 troops; 21 LCM 6s or 3 LCUs and 6 LCMs or 50 LVTs; 30 LVTs on upper deck

Guns: 6 USN 3 in *(76 mm)*/50 (3 twin) Mk 33; 50 rds/min to 12.8 km *(7 n miles)*; weight of shell 6 kg.
4—12.7 mm MGs.
Radars: Surface search: Raytheon SPS-10F; G-band.
Air/Surface search: Plessey AWS-2 (G 30); E/F-band.
Navigation: Raytheon CRP 3100; I-band.
Helicopters: Platform for Super Puma.

Programmes: The original plan to build a 4,500 ton LST was overtaken by the acquisition of these two LSDs from the US initially on a lease and finally by purchase on 24 January 2001.
Structure: Has two 50 ton capacity cranes and a docking well of 391 × 48 ft *(119.2 × 14.6 m)*. SATCOM fitted. Phalanx guns and SRBOC chaff launchers removed before transfer. Air search radars removed.

RIO DE JANEIRO   *4/2000, Hartmut Ehlers* / 0104231

3 LCU 1610 CLASS (EDCG/LCU)

Name	No	Builders	Commissioned
GUARAPARI	L 10 (ex-GED 10)	Arsenal de Marinha, Rio de Janeiro	27 Mar 1978
TAMBAÚ	L 11 (ex-GED 11)	Arsenal de Marinha, Rio de Janeiro	27 Mar 1978
CAMBORIÚ	L 12 (ex-GED 12)	Arsenal de Marinha, Rio de Janeiro	6 Jan 1981

Displacement, tons: 390 full load
Dimensions, feet (metres): 134.5 × 27.6 × 6.6 *(41 × 8.4 × 2.0)*
Main machinery: 2 GM 12V-71 diesels; 874 hp *(650 kW)* sustained; 2 shafts; cp props
Speed, knots: 11
Range, n miles: 1,200 at 8 kt
Complement: 14 (2 officers)
Military lift: 172 tons
Guns: 3—12.7 mm MGs.
Radars: Navigation: Furuno 3600; I-band.

Comment: Original pennant numbers restored in 2004. Based at Niteroi.

CAMBORIÚ   *6/2001, Brazilian Navy* / 0130473

3 EDVM 17 CLASS (LCM)

301-303

Displacement, tons: 55 full load
Dimensions, feet (metres): 55.8 × 14.4 × 3.9 *(17 × 4.4 × 1.2)*
Main machinery: 2 Saab Scania diesels; 470 hp(m) *(345 kW)*; 2 shafts
Speed, knots: 9
Complement: 3
Military lift: 80 troops plus 31 tons equipment

Comment: LCM 6 type acquired from the US.

301   *1985, Ronaldo S Olive* / 0505961

5 EDVM 25 CLASS (LCM)

801-805

Displacement, tons: 61 standard; 130 full load
Dimensions, feet (metres): 71 × 21 × 4.8 *(21.7 × 6.4 × 1.5)*
Main machinery: 2 Detroit diesels; 400 hp *(294 kW)* sustained; 2 shafts
Speed, knots: 9
Range, n miles: 95 at 9 kt
Complement: 5
Military lift: 150 troops plus 72 tons equipment

Comment: First of class launched 18 January 1994 by AMRJ, remainder by Inace. LCM 8 type. Based at Niteroi.

801   *6/2001, Brazilian Navy* / 0130472

MINE WARFARE FORCES

6 ARATU (SCHÜTZE) CLASS
(MINESWEEPERS—COASTAL) (MSC)

Name	No	Builders	Commissioned
ARATU	M 15	Abeking & Rasmussen, Lemwerder	5 May 1971
ANHATOMIRIM	M 16	Abeking & Rasmussen, Lemwerder	30 Nov 1971
ATALAIA	M 17	Abeking & Rasmussen, Lemwerder	13 Dec 1972
ARAÇATUBA	M 18	Abeking & Rasmussen, Lemwerder	13 Dec 1972
ABROLHOS	M 19	Abeking & Rasmussen, Lemwerder	25 Feb 1976
ALBARDÃO	M 20	Abeking & Rasmussen, Lemwerder	25 Feb 1976

Displacement, tons: 230 standard; 280 full load
Dimensions, feet (metres): 154.9 × 23.6 × 6.9 *(47.2 × 7.2 × 2.1)*
Main machinery: 2 MTU Maybach diesels; 4,500 hp(m) *(3.3 MW)*; 2 shafts; 2 Escher-Weiss cp props
Speed, knots: 24. **Range, n miles:** 710 at 20 kt
Complement: 32 (4 officers)
Guns: 1 Bofors 40 mm/70.
Radars: Surface search: Bridge Master E; I-band.
Navigation: Furuno FR 1831; I-band.

Comment: Wooden hulled. First four ordered in April 1969 and last pair in November 1973. Same design as the now deleted German Schütze class. Can carry out wire, magnetic and acoustic sweeping. A life-extension refit programme started in 2001. M 15 completed in 2002 and M17, 18 and 19 by 2005. Work on M 16 began in 2005 and on M 20 in 2006. Modifications include replacement of the surface search radar, communications upgrade and hull preservation measures. Based at Aratu, Bahia.

ABROLHOS   *3/1998, Brazilian Navy* / 0017625

SURVEY AND RESEARCH SHIPS

Notes: (1) Survey ships are painted white except for those operating in the Antarctic which have red hulls.
(2) There are also 21 buoy tenders of between 15 and 26 m: nine LB-15, two LB-17 (*Lufanda* and *Piracema*), four LB-19, two LB-23 and four LB-26.

1 POLAR RESEARCH SHIP (AGOBH)

Name	No	Builders	Commissioned
ARY RONGEL (ex-*Polar Queen*)	H 44	Eides, Norway	22 Jan 1981

Displacement, tons: 3,628 full load
Dimensions, feet (metres): 247 × 42.7 × 17.4 *(75.3 × 13 × 5.3)*
Main machinery: 2 MAK 6M-453 diesels; 4,500 hp(m) *(3.3 MW)*; 1 shaft; cp prop; 2 bow thrusters; 1 stern thruster
Speed, knots: 14.5
Range, n miles: 17,000 at 12 kt
Complement: 70 (19 officers) + 22 scientists
Radars: Navigation: Sperry; I-band Racal-Decca; I/J-band.
Cargo capacity: 2,400 m³
Helicopters: Platform for Ecureuil 2.

Comment: Acquired by sale 19 April 1994. Ice-strengthened hull fitted with Simrad Albatross dynamic positioning system.

ARY RONGEL   *6/2002, Carlos Veras, Brazilian Navy* / 0572424

1 RESEARCH SHIP (AGS)

Name	No	Builders	Commissioned
ANTARES (ex-M/V *Lady Harrison*)	H 40	Mjellem and Karlsen A/S, Bergen	Aug 1984

Displacement, tons: 1,076 standard; 1,248 full load
Dimensions, feet (metres): 180.3 × 33.8 × 14.1 *(55 × 10.3 × 4.3)*
Main machinery: 1 Burmeister & Wain Alpha diesel; 1,860 hp(m) *(1.37 MW)*; 1 shaft; bow thruster
Speed, knots: 13.5
Range, n miles: 10,000 at 12 kt
Complement: 58 (12 officers) + 12
Radars: Navigation: 2 Racal Decca; I-band.

Comment: Research vessel acquired from Racal Energy Resources. Used for seismographic survey. Recommissioned 6 June 1988.

ANTARES *4/2000, Hartmut Ehlers* / 0104233

1 SIRIUS CLASS (SURVEY SHIP) (AGSH)

Name	No	Builders	Launched	Commissioned
SIRIUS	H 21	Ishikawajima Co Ltd, Tokyo	30 July 1957	17 Jan 1958

Displacement, tons: 1,463 standard; 1,741 full load
Dimensions, feet (metres): 255.7 × 39.3 × 12.2 *(78 × 12.1 × 3.7)*
Main machinery: 2 Sulzer 7T6-36 diesels; 2,700 hp(m) *(1.98 MW)*; 2 shafts; cp props
Speed, knots: 15.7
Range, n miles: 12,000 at 11 kt
Complement: 116 (16 officers) plus 14 scientists
Radars: Navigation: Racal Decca TM 1226C; I-band.
Helicopters: 1 Bell JetRanger or UH-12.

Comment: Laid down 1955-56. Special surveying apparatus, echo-sounders, Raydist equipment, sounding machines installed, and landing craft (LCVP), jeep, and survey launches carried. All living and working spaces are air conditioned.

SIRIUS *8/1999* / 0056615

2 AMORIM DO VALLE (RIVER) CLASS (SURVEY SHIPS) (AGS)

Name	No	Commissioned
AMORIM DO VALLE (ex-*Humber*)	H 35 (ex-M 2007)	7 June 1985
TAURUS (ex-*Helmsdale/Jorge Leite*)	H 36 (ex-M 2010)	1 Mar 1986

Displacement, tons: 890 full load
Dimensions, feet (metres): 156 × 34.5 × 9.5 *(47.5 × 10.5 × 2.9)*
Main machinery: 2 Ruston 6RKC diesels; 3,100 hp *(2.3 MW)* sustained; 2 shafts
Speed, knots: 14
Range, n miles: 4,500 at 10 kt
Complement: 36 (4 officers)
Radars: Navigation: 2 Racal Decca TM 1226C; I-band.

Comment: H 35 and H 36 were two of the three ships transferred from the UK on 31 January 1995. The contract was signed on 18 November 1994. Steel hulled for deep-armed team sweeping with wire sweeps. All minesweeping gear and the 40 mm gun removed on transfer. Used as hydrographic ships. H 35 has a stern gantry and second crane amidships for oceanographic research. Four others of the class transferred in 1998 are listed under Patrol Forces. The class is also in service with the Bangladesh Navy.

AMORIM DO VALLE *6/2005*, David Cullen* / 1153035

1 LIGHTHOUSE TENDER (ABUH)

Name	No	Builders	Launched	Commissioned
ALMIRANTE GRAÇA ARANHA	H 34	Ebin, Niteroi	23 May 1974	9 Sep 1976

Displacement, tons: 2,440 full load
Dimensions, feet (metres): 245.3 × 42.6 × 13.8 *(74.8 × 13 × 4.2)*
Main machinery: 1 diesel; 2,440 hp(m) *(1.8 MW)*; 1 shaft; bow thruster
Speed, knots: 13
Complement: 80 (13 officers)
Radars: Navigation: 2 Racal Decca; I-band.
Helicopters: 1 Bell JetRanger.

Comment: Laid down in 1971. Fitted with telescopic hangar, 10 ton crane, two landing craft, GP launch and two Land Rovers. Omega navigation system.

ALMIRANTE GRAÇA ARANHA *4/2000, Hartmut Ehlers* / 0104234

1 GARNIER SAMPAIO (RIVER) CLASS (BUOY TENDER) (ABU)

Name	No	Builders	Commissioned
GARNIER SAMPAIO (ex-*Ribble*)	H 37 (ex-M 2012)	Richards, Great Yarmouth	19 Feb 1986

Displacement, tons: 890 full load
Dimensions, feet (metres): 156 × 34.5 × 9.5 *(47.5 × 10.5 × 2.9)*
Main machinery: 2 Ruston 6RKC diesels; 3,100 hp *(2.3 MW)* sustained; 2 shafts
Speed, knots: 14. **Range, n miles:** 4,500 at 10 kt
Complement: 36 (6 officers)
Radars: Navigation: 2 Racal Decca TM 1226C; I-band.

Comment: One of three ships transferred from UK in 1995. Steel hulled for deep-armed team sweeping with wire sweeps. All minesweeping gear and the 40 mm gun removed on transfer and used as light buoy tender. Four others of the class transferred in 1998 are listed under Patrol Forces. The class is also in service with the Bangladesh Navy.

GARNER SAMPAIO *6/2002, Brazilian Navy* / 0529149

4 BUOY TENDERS (ABU)

Name	No	Builders	Commissioned
COMANDANTE VARELLA	H 18	Arsenal de Marinha, Rio de Janeiro	20 May 1982
TENENTE CASTELO	H 19	Estanave, Manaus	15 Aug 1984
COMANDANTE MANHÃES	H 20	Estanave, Manaus	15 Dec 1983
TENENTE BOANERGES	H 25	Estanave, Manaus	29 Mar 1985

Displacement, tons: 420 full load
Dimensions, feet (metres): 123 × 28.2 × 8.5 *(37.5 × 8.6 × 2.6)*
Main machinery: 2—8-cyl diesels; 1,300 hp(m) *(955 kW)*; 2 shafts
Speed, knots: 12. **Range, n miles:** 2,880 at 9 kt
Complement: 28 (2 officers)
Radars: Navigation: Racal Decca; I-band.

Comment: Dual-purpose minelayers. *Tenente Castelo* is based at Santana, *Tenente Boanerges* at Salvador.

COMANDANTE VARELLA *1/2000, van Ginderen Collection* / 0104235

1 BUOY TENDER (ABU)

FAROLEIRO MÁRIO SEIXAS (ex-*Mestre Jerânimo*) H 26

Displacement, tons: 294 full load
Dimensions, feet (metres): 116.4 × 21.8 × 11.8 *(35.5 × 6.6 × 3.6)*
Main machinery: 2 Scania DSI 14 MO3 diesels, 2 shafts
Speed, knots: 10
Complement: 18 (2 officers)
Radars: Navigation: Furuno FR 1831; I-band

Comment: Former fishing vessel built in Vigo, Spain. Acquired by Brazilian Navy in 1979 and rebuilt as a buoy tender. Commissioned 31 January 1984.

FAROLEIRO MÁRIO SEIXAS   *6/2002, Brazilian Navy* / 0529148

10 LB 20 CLASS BUOY TENDERS (ABU)

ACHERNAR CPSP 02   **CAPELLA** CPES 03   **RIGEL** SSN-5 06 (ex-SSN 409)
ALDEBARAN SSN-2 01   **DENÉBOLA** SSN-4 02   **VEGA** SSN-4 01 (ex-SSN 506)
BETELGEUSE CPSC 05   **FOMALHAUT** CPPR 05   **POLLUX** CAMR 11
   (ex-SUL 03)   **REGULUS** SSN 4201 (ex-SSN 4204)

Displacement, tons: 102
Dimensions, feet (metres): 65 × 19.7 × 5.9 *(19.8 × 6 × 1.8)*
Main machinery: 2 Cummins NT 855M diesels; 720 hp(m) *(530 kW)*; 2 shafts
Speed, knots: 10
Range, n miles: 1,000 at 10 kt
Complement: 6
Radars: Navigation: Furuno; I-band.

Comment: Built by Damen, Gorichen and assembled by Wilson, Sao Paolo. First one commissioned 20 December 1995 and the last on 29 December 1997. The pennant numbers correspond to naval facilities in which they are stationed.

RIGEL   *2/2000, van Ginderen Collection* / 0104236

3 SURVEY LAUNCHES (YGS)

PARAIBANO SSN-4 03 (ex-H 11)   **CAMOCIM** BHMN 03 (ex-H 16)
RIO BRANCO SSN-4 04 (ex-H 12)

Displacement, tons: 32 standard; 50 full load
Dimensions, feet (metres): 52.5 × 15.1 × 4.3 *(16 × 4.6 × 1.3)*
Main machinery: 2 GM diesels; 330 hp *(246 kW)*; 2 shafts
Speed, knots: 11
Range, n miles: 600 at 11 kt
Complement: 10 (1 officer)
Radars: Navigation: Racal Decca 110; I-band.

Comment: Built by Bormann, Rio de Janeiro and commissioned 1969-72. Majority work in Amazon Flotilla. Wooden hulls. All decommissioned in 1991 but retained in service as support to naval establishments and reclassified AvHi (inshore survey craft). Three decommissioned in 2004.

PARAIBANO (old number)   *1985, Brazilian Navy* / 0505963

1 OCEAN SURVEY VESSEL (AGSC)

Name	No	Builders	Commissioned
SUBOFICIAL OLIVEIRA	CAMR 02 (ex-DHN 02, ex-U 15)	Inace	22 May 1981

Displacement, tons: 170 full load
Dimensions, feet (metres): 116.4 × 22 × 15.7 *(35.5 × 6.7 × 4.8)*
Main machinery: 2 diesels; 740 hp(m) *(544 kW)*; 2 shafts
Speed, knots: 8
Range, n miles: 1,400 at 8 kt
Complement: 10 (2 officers)
Radars: Navigation: Racal Decca 110; I-band.

Comment: Commissioned at Fortaleza for Naval Research Institute. Decommissioned in 1991 but retained in service as an AvPqOc (ocean survey craft). Based at Niterói.

SUBOFICIAL OLIVEIRA (old number)   *1990, Brazilian Navy* / 0056618

TRAINING SHIPS

Notes: (1) There are 10 small sail training ships.
(2) One new training vessel *Braz de Aguiar* (ex-*Calha Norte*) has been reported.

1 MODIFIED NITERÓI CLASS (AXH)

Name	No	Builders	Commissioned
BRASIL	U 27	Arsenal de Marinha, Rio de Janeiro	21 Aug 1986

Displacement, tons: 2,548 light; 3,729 full load
Dimensions, feet (metres): 430.7 × 44.3 × 13.8 *(131.3 × 13.5 × 4.2)*
Main machinery: 2 Pielstick/Ishikawajima (Brazil) 6 PC2.5 L 400 diesels; 7,020 hp(m) *(5.17 MW)* sustained; 2 shafts
Speed, knots: 18
Range, n miles: 7,000 at 15 kt
Complement: 218 (27 officers) plus 201 midshipmen
Guns: 2 Bofors 40 mm/70. 4 saluting guns.
Countermeasures: Decoys: 2 CBV 50.8 mm flare launchers.
ESM: Racal RDL-2 ABC; radar intercept.
Weapons control: Saab Scania TVT 300 optronic director.
Radars: Surface search: Racal Decca RMS 1230C; E/F-band.
Navigation: Racal Decca TM 1226C and TMS 1230; I-band.
Helicopters: Platform for 1 Sea King.

Comment: A modification of the Vosper Thornycroft Mk 10 Frigate design ordered in June 1981. Laid down 18 September 1981, launched 23 September 1983. Designed to carry midshipmen and other trainees from the Naval and Merchant Marine Academies. Minimum electronics as required for training. There are four 51 mm launchers for flares and other illuminants.

BRASIL   *9/2005*, Michael Nitz* / 1153034

3 NASCIMENTO CLASS (AXL)

Name	No	Builders	Commissioned
ASPIRANTE NASCIMENTO	U 10	Ebrasa, Santa Catarina	13 Dec 1980
GUARDA MARINHA JENSEN	U 11	Ebrasa, Santa Catarina	22 July 1981
GUARDA MARINHA BRITO	U 12	Ebrasa, Santa Catarina	22 July 1981

Displacement, tons: 108.5 standard; 136 full load
Dimensions, feet (metres): 91.8 × 21.3 × 5.9 *(28 × 6.5 × 1.8)*
Main machinery: 2 Mercedes Benz OM-352A diesels; 650 hp(m) *(478 kW)*; 2 shafts
Speed, knots: 10
Range, n miles: 700 at 10 kt
Complement: 6 (2 officers) + 10 midshipmen
Guns: 1 — 12.7 mm MG.
Radars: Navigation: Racal Decca; I-band.

Comment: Can carry 10 trainees overnight. All of the class are attached to the Naval Academy at Rio de Janeiro.

GUARDA MARINHA JENSEN   *5/2003, A E Galarce* / 0572425

3 ROSCA FINA CLASS (AXL)

ROSCA FINA CN 31   **VOGA PICADA** CN 32   **LEVA ARRIBA** CN 33

Displacement, tons: 50 full load
Dimensions, feet (metres): 61 × 15.4 × 3.9 *(18.6 × 4.7 × 1.2)*
Main machinery: 1 diesel; 650 hp(m) *(477 kW)*; 1 shaft
Speed, knots: 11. **Range, n miles:** 200
Complement: 5 plus trainees
Radars: Navigation: Racal Decca 110; I-band.

Comment: Built by Carbrasmar, Rio de Janeiro. All commissioned 21 February 1984. All attached to the Naval college at Angra dos Reis.

VOGA PICADA (old number)   *1984, Brazilian Navy* / 0505964

1 SAIL TRAINING SHIP (AXS)

Name	No	Builders	Launched	Commissioned
CISNE BRANCO	U 20	Damen Shipyards, Gorinchem	4 Aug 1999	28 Feb 2000

Displacement, tons: 1,038 full load
Dimensions, feet (metres): 249.3 × 34.4 × 15.7 *(76 × 10.5 × 4.8)*
Main machinery: 1 Caterpillar 3508B DI-TA diesel; 1,015 hp(m) *(746 kW)* sustained; 1 shaft; Berg cp prop; bow thruster; 408 hp(m) *(300 kW)*
Speed, knots: 17 (sail); 11 (diesel)
Complement: 41 (10 officers) + 30 midshipmen
Radars: Navigation: Furuno FR 1510 Mk 3; I-band.

Comment: Ordered in 1998. Maximum sail area 2,195 m².

CISNE BRANCO   *6/2005*, John Mortimer* / 1153033

AUXILIARIES

Notes: Future procurement plans include two support transport ships to replace *Ary Parreiras* and *Marajó* 2005-08.

1 SUBMARINE RESCUE SHIP (ASRH)

Name	No	Builders	Commissioned
FELINTO PERRY	K 11	Stord Verft, Norway	Dec 1979
(ex-*Holger Dane*, ex-*Wildrake*)			

Displacement, tons: 1,380 standard; 3,850 full load
Dimensions, feet (metres): 256.6 × 57.4 × 15.1 *(78.2 × 17.5 × 4.6)*
Main machinery: Diesel-electric; 2 BMK KVG B12 and 2 KVG B16 diesels; 11,400 hp(m) *(8.4 MW)*; 2 motors; 7,000 hp(m) *(5.15 MW)*; 2 shafts; cp props; 2 bow thrusters; 2 stern thrusters
Speed, knots: 14.5
Complement: 65 (9 officers)
Radars: Navigation: 2 Raytheon; I-band.
Helicopters: Platform only.

Comment: Former oilfield support ship acquired 28 December 1988. Has an octagonal heliport (62.5 ft diameter) above the bridge. Equipped with a moonpool for saturation diving, and rescue and recompression chambers as the submarine rescue ship. Dynamic positioning system. Based at Niteroi, Rio de Janeiro.

FELINTO PERRY   *2/2003, Mario R V Carneiro* / 0569152

1 BARROSO PEREIRA CLASS (TRANSPORT) (AKSH)

Name	No	Builders	Commissioned
ARY PARREIRAS	G 21	Ishikawajima, Tokyo	6 Mar 1957

Displacement, tons: 4,800 standard; 7,300 full load
Measurement, tons: 4,200 dwt; 4,879 gross (Panama)
Dimensions, feet (metres): 362 pp; 391.8 oa × 52.5 × 20.5 *(110.4; 119.5 × 16 × 6.3)*
Main machinery: 2 Ishikawajima boilers and turbines; 4,800 hp(m) *(3.53 MW)*; 2 shafts
Speed, knots: 15
Complement: 159 (15 officers)
Military lift: 1,972 troops (overload); 497 troops (normal)
Cargo capacity: 425 m³ refrigerated cargo space; 4,000 tons
Guns: 2 — 3 in *(76 mm)* Mk 33; 50 rds/min to 12.8 km *(6.9 n miles)* anti-aircraft; weight of shell 6 kg.
2 or 4 Oerlikon 20 mm.
Radars: Navigation: Two Racal Decca; I-band.
Helicopters: Platform for one medium.

Comment: Transport and cargo vessel. Helicopter landing platform aft. Medical, hospital and dental facilities. Working and living quarters are mechanically ventilated with partial air conditioning. Refrigerated cargo space 15,500 cu ft. Operates commercially from time to time. Likely to be decommissioned by 2008.

BARROSO PEREIRA CLASS   *4/2000, Hartmut Ehlers* / 0104239

1 RIVER TRANSPORT SHIP (AP)

Name	No	Builders	Commissioned
PARAGUASSÚ (ex-*Garapuava*)	G 15	Amsterdam Drydock	1951

Displacement, tons: 285 full load
Dimensions, feet (metres): 131.2 × 23 × 6.6 *(40 × 7 × 2)*
Main machinery: 3 diesels; 2,505 hp(m) *(1.84 MW)*; 1 shaft
Speed, knots: 13. **Range, n miles:** 2,500 at 10 kt
Complement: 43 (4 officers)
Military lift: 178 troops
Guns: 6 — 7.62 mm MGs.
Radars: Navigation: Furuno 3600; I-band.

Comment: Passenger ship converted into a troop carrier in 1957 and acquired on 20 June 1972.

PARAGUASSÚ   *5/2000, Hartmut Ehlers* / 0104240

1 RIVER TRANSPORT (YFBH)

Name	No	Builders	Commissioned
PIRAIM (ex-*Guaicuru*)	U 29	Estaleiro SNBP, Mato Grosso	10 Mar 1982

Displacement, tons: 91.5 full load
Dimensions, feet (metres): 82.0 × 18.0 × 3.2 *(25.0 × 5.5 × 0.97)*
Main machinery: 2 MWM diesels; 400 hp(m) *(294 kW)*; 2 shafts
Speed, knots: 7
Range, n miles: 700 at 7 kt
Complement: 17 (2 officers)
Guns: 4 — 7.62 mm MG.
Radars: Navigation: Furuno 3600; I-band.
Helicopters: Platform for UH-12.

Comment: Used as a logistics support ship for the Mato Grosso Flotilla. Can carry 2 platoons of marines and 2 rigid inflatable boats.

PIRAIM　　　　　　　　　　　*6/1998, Brazilian Navy* / 0017635

1 REPLENISHMENT TANKER (AOR)

Name	No	Builders	Commissioned
ALMIRANTE GASTÃO MOTTA	G 23	Ishibras, Rio de Janeiro	26 Nov 1991

Displacement, tons: 10,320 full load
Dimensions, feet (metres): 442.9 × 62.3 × 24.6 *(135 × 19 × 7.5)*
Main machinery: Diesel-electric; 2 Wärtsilä 12V32 diesel generators; 11,700 hp(m) *(8.57 MW)* sustained; 1 motor; 1 shaft; Kamewa cp prop
Speed, knots: 20
Range, n miles: 9,000 at 15 kt
Complement: 121 (13 officers)
Cargo capacity: 5,000 tons liquid; 200 tons dry
Guns: 2 — 12.7 mm MGs.

Comment: Ordered March 1987. Laid down 11 December 1989 and launched 1 June 1990. Fitted for abeam and stern refuelling.

ALMIRANTE GASTÃO MOTTA　　　　　　*3/2002, Robert Pabst* / 0528968

1 HOSPITAL SHIP (AH)

Name	No	Builders	Commissioned
DOUTOR MONTENEGRO	U 16	CONAVE Shipyard, Manaus	17 May 2000

Displacement, tons: 347 full load
Dimensions, feet (metres): 137.8 × 36 × 7.9 *(42 × 11 × 2.4)*
Main machinery: 2 diesels; 600 hp(m) *(448 kW)*; 2 shafts
Speed, knots: 10
Complement: 50 (8 officers) plus 11 (8 doctors/dentists)
Radars: Navigation: Furuno 1942 Mk 2.

Comment: U 16 was built in January 1997 and belonged to the government of the Acre state before transfer to the Brazilian Navy. The ship has two wards, a pediatric ICU, an operating theatre, an X-ray room, a dentist office, a lab for clinical analysis, a trauma room and a pharmacy.

DOUTOR MONTENEGRO　　　　　　*6/2002, Brazilian Navy* / 0529147

2 HOSPITAL SHIPS (AHH)

Name	No	Builders	Commissioned
OSWALDO CRUZ	U 18	Arsenal de Marinha, Rio de Janeiro	29 May 1984
CARLOS CHAGAS	U 19	Arsenal de Marinha, Rio de Janeiro	7 Dec 1984

Displacement, tons: 500 full load
Dimensions, feet (metres): 154.2 × 26.9 × 5.9 *(47.2 × 8.5 × 1.8)*
Main machinery: 2 Volvo diesels; 714 hp(m) *(525 kW)*; 2 shafts
Speed, knots: 12
Range, n miles: 4,000 at 9 kt
Complement: 27 (5 officers) plus 21 medical (6 doctors/dentists)
Radars: Navigation: Racal Decca; I-band.
Helicopters: 1 Helibras HB-350B.

Comment: *Oswaldo Cruz* launched 11 July 1983, and *Carlos Chagas* 16 April 1984. Has two sick bays, a dental surgery, a laboratory, two clinics and X-ray centre. The design is a development of the Roraima class with which they operate in the Amazon Flotilla. Since 1992 both ships painted grey with dark green crosses on the hull.

OSWALDO CRUZ　　　　　　*6/2004*, Brazilian Navy* / 1044086

1 PARÁ CLASS (RIVER TRANSPORT SHIP) (YFB)

PARÁ U 15

Displacement, tons: 1,060 full load
Dimensions, feet (metres): 184.1 × 70.2 × ? *(56.1 × 21.4 × ?)*
Main machinery: To be announced
Speed, knots: 11
Complement: 66 (7 officers)
Guns: 4 Oerlikon 20 mm.

Comment: Ex-civilian catamaran hull vessel that was commissioned into the navy on 19 January 2005. Capable of carrying 175 marines. A further six similar vessels are likely to enter service in the Amazon and Mato Grosso flotillas.

1 REPLENISHMENT TANKER (AOR)

Name	No	Builders	Launched	Commissioned
MARAJO	G 27	Ishikawajima do Brasil	31 Jan 1968	8 Jan 1969

Displacement, tons: 10,500 full load
Dimensions, feet (metres): 440.7 × 63.3 × 24 *(134.4 × 19.3 × 7.3)*
Main machinery: 1 Sulzer GRD 68 diesel; 8,000 hp(m) *(5.88 MW)*; 1 shaft
Speed, knots: 13
Range, n miles: 9,200 at 13 kt
Complement: 80 (13 officers)
Cargo capacity: 6,600 tons fuel

Comment: Fitted for abeam replenishment with two stations on each side. Was to have been replaced by *Gastão Motta* but is to be retained in service until 2008.

MARAJO　　　　　　*1/1999* / 0056623

1 RIVER TENDER (AG)

Name	No	Builders	Commissioned
POTENGI	G 17	Papendrecht, Netherlands	28 June 1938

Displacement, tons: 600 full load
Dimensions, feet (metres): 178.8 × 24.5 × 6 *(54.5 × 7.5 × 1.8)*
Main machinery: 2 diesels; 550 hp(m) *(404 kW)*; 2 shafts
Speed, knots: 10
Range, n miles: 600 at 8 kt
Complement: 19 (2 officers)
Cargo capacity: 450 tons dieso and avcat
Guns: 4—7.62 mm MGs.
Radars: Navigation: Furuno 3600; I-band.

Comment: Launched 16 March 1938. Employed in the Mato Grosso Flotilla on river service. Converted to logistic support ship and recommissioned 6 May 1999.

POTENGI   *5/2000, Hartmut Ehlers* / 0104241

4 RIO PARDO CLASSES (YFB)

RIO PARDO BNAJ 08 (ex-U 40)   RIO CHUI CIAW 14 (ex-U 42)
RIO NEGRO BNRJ 07 (ex-U 41)   RIO OIAPOQUE BNRJ 09 (ex-U 43)

Displacement, tons: 150 full load
Dimensions, feet (metres): 120 × 21.3 × 6.2 *(36.6 × 6.5 × 1.9)*
Main machinery: 2 Sulzer 6TD24; 900 hp(m) *(661 kW)*; 2 shafts
Speed, knots: 14
Range, n miles: 700 at 14 kt
Complement: 10
Radars: Navigation: Racal Decca; 110; I-band.

Comment: Can carry 600 passengers. Built by Inconav de Niterói in 1975-76. Pennant numbers removed in 1989.

1 TORPEDO RECOVERY VESSEL (YPT)

Name	No	Builders	Commissioned
ALMIRANTE HESS	BACS 01 (ex-U 30)	Inace, Fortaleza	2 Dec 1983

Displacement, tons: 91 full load
Dimensions, feet (metres): 77.4 × 19.7 × 6.6 *(23.6 × 6 × 2)*
Main machinery: 2 diesels; 2 shafts
Speed, knots: 13
Complement: 14
Radars: Navigation: Racal Decca; 110; I-band.

Comment: Attached to the Submarine Naval Base. Can transport up to four torpedoes. Decommissioned in 1991 but retained in service as an AvPpCo (coast support craft). BACS (Base Almirante Castro y Silva).

ALMIRANTE HESS   *6/1997, Brazilian Navy* / 0012096

4 FLOATING DOCKS

CIDADE DE NATAL (ex-G 27, ex-AFDL 39)   ALMIRANTE JERONIMO GONÇALVES
ALMIRANTE SCHIECK   (ex-G 26, ex-*Goiaz* AFDL 4)
ALFONSO PENA (ex-ARD 14)

Comment: The first two are floating docks loaned to Brazil by US Navy in the mid-1960s and purchased 11 February 1980. Ship lifts of 2,800 tons and 1,000 tons respectively. *Cidade de Natal* based at Natal and *Almirante Jeronimo Gonçalves* at Manaus. *Almirante Schieck* of 3,600 tons displacement was built by Arsenal de Marinha, Rio de Janeiro and commissioned 12 October 1989. *Alfonso Pena* acquired from US and based at Val-de-Caes (Para).

TUGS

Notes: (1) In addition to the vessels listed below there are two harbour tugs: *Olga* (CASOP 01) and *Alves Barbosa* (AMRJ 11).
(2) There are plans to procure six ocean tugs from 2007-14. These are also to serve as offshore patrol ships.

2 ALMIRANTE GUILHEM CLASS (FLEET OCEAN TUGS) (ATF)

Name	No	Builders	Commissioned
ALMIRANTE GUILHEM	R 24	Sumitomo, Uraga	1976
(ex-*Superpesa 4*)			
ALMIRANTE GUILLOBEL	R 25	Sumitomo, Uraga	1976
(ex-*Superpesa 5*)			

Displacement, tons: 2,400 full load
Dimensions, feet (metres): 207 × 44 × 14.8 *(63.2 × 13.4 × 4.5)*
Main machinery: 2 GM EMD 20-645F7B diesels; 7,120 hp *(5.31 MW)* sustained; 2 shafts; cp props; bow thruster
Speed, knots: 14
Range, n miles: 10,000 at 10 kt
Complement: 40 (4 officers)
Guns: 2 Oerlikon 20 mm (not always carried)
Radars: Navigation: Racal Decca; I-band. Furuno; I-band.

Comment: Originally built as civilian tugs. Bollard pull, 84 tons. Commissioned into the Navy 22 January 1981.

ALMIRANTE GUILLOBEL   *5/2003, A E Galarce* / 0572426

3 TRITÃO CLASS (FLEET OCEAN TUGS) (ATA)

Name	No	Builders	Commissioned
TRITÃO (ex-*Sarandi*)	R 21	Estanave, Manaus	19 Feb 1987
TRIDENTE (ex-*Sambaiba*)	R 22	Estanave, Manaus	8 Oct 1987
TRIUNFO (ex-*Sorocaba*)	R 23	Estanave, Manaus	5 July 1986

Displacement, tons: 1,680 full load
Dimensions, feet (metres): 181.8 × 38.1 × 11.2 *(55.4 × 11.6 × 3.4)*
Main machinery: 2 Vilares-Burmeister and Wain Alpha diesels; 2,480 hp(m) *(1.82 MW)*; 2 shafts; bow thruster
Speed, knots: 12
Complement: 43 (6 officers)
Guns: 2 Oerlikon 20 mm.
Radars: Navigation: 2 Racal Decca; I-band.

Comment: Offshore supply vessels acquired from National Oil Company of Brazil and converted for naval use. Assumed names of previous three ships of Sotoyomo class. Fitted to act both as tugs and patrol vessels. Bollard pull, 23.5 tons. Firefighting capability. Endurance, 45 days.

TRIDENTE   *10/2004*, A E Galarce* / 1153016

1 TARGET TOWING TUG (ATA)

Name	No	Builders	Commissioned
TRINDADE (ex-*Nobistor*)	R 26 (ex-U 16)	J G Hitzler, Lavenburg	1969

Displacement, tons: 590 light; 1,308 full load
Dimensions, feet (metres): 176.1 × 36.1 × 11.1 *(53.7 × 11 × 3.4)*
Main machinery: 2 MWM diesels; 2,740 hp(m) *(2 MW)* sustained; 2 shafts
Speed, knots: 12.7
Complement: 22 (2 officers)
Guns: 2—12.7 mm MGs.
Radars: Navigation: Furuno 1830; I-band.

Comment: Ex-Panamanian tug seized for smuggling in 1989 and commissioned in the Navy 31 January 1990. Used for target towing.

TRINDADE (old number)   *1990, Mário R V Carneiro* / 0056625

8 COASTAL TUGS (YTB)

COMANDANTE MARROIG BNRJ 03 (ex-R 15)	**CABO SCHRAM** BNVC 01 (ex-R 18)	**VALENTE** BNRJ 18
COMANDANTE DIDIER BNRJ 04 (ex-R 16)	**INTRÉPIDO** BNRJ 16	**IMPÁVIDO** BNRJ 19
TENENTE MAGALHÃES BNA 06 (ex-R 17)	**ARROJADO** BNRJ 17	

Comment: BNRJ 16-19 are StanTug 2207s of 200 tons with a bollard pull of 22.5 tons, built in 1992. BNRJ 03-04 and BNA 06 are 115 tons and built in 1981.

ARROJADO
2/2003, Mario R V Carneiro
0569151

Brunei

ANGKATAN TENTERA LAUT DIRAJA BRUNEI

Country Overview

Formerly a British dependency, the Nation of Brunei is a sultanate that gained full independence in 1984. Situated on the northern coast of the island of Borneo, the country has a total area of 2,226 square miles and is bordered and divided into two halves by the Malaysian state of Sarawak. It has an 87 n mile coastline with the South China Sea. The capital and largest town is Bandar Seri Begawan which also has port facilities. There are further ports at Kuala Belait and Muara. Territorial seas (3 n miles) and an EEZ (200 n mile) are claimed.

Headquarters Appointments

Commander of the Navy:
　Colonel Joharie Bin Haji Matusin
Fleet Commander:
　Lieutenant Colonel Haji Saied Hussain

Bases

Muara

Personnel

(a) 2006: 747 (58 officers)
　This total, which includes the River Division, is planned to rise to 1,200 but will require concomitant enhancements to training infrastructure.
(b) Voluntary service

Prefix to Ships' Names

KDB (Kapal Di-Raja Brunei)

CORVETTES

3 BRUNEI CLASS (FSGH)

Name	No	Builders	Laid down	Launched	Commissioned
NAKHODA RAGAM	28	BAE System Marine (Scotstoun)	16 Mar 1999	13 Jan 2001	2006
BENDAHARA SAKAM	29	BAE System Marine (Scotstoun)	15 Nov 1999	23 June 2001	2006
JERAMBAK	30	BAE System Marine (Scotstoun)	5 Apr 2000	22 June 2002	2006

Displacement, tons: 1,940 full load
Dimensions, feet (metres): 311.7 oa; 294.9 wl × 42 × 11.8
　(95; 89.9 × 12.8 × 3.6)
Main machinery: CODAD; 4 MAN 20 RK270 diesels; 2 shafts; cp props
Speed, knots: 30
Range, n miles: 5,000 at 12 kt
Complement: 79 plus 24 spare

Missiles: SSM: 8 MBDA Exocet MM 40 Block II ❶; active radar homing to 70 km *(40 n miles)* at 0.9 Mach.
SAM: BAe 16 cell VLS ❷. BAe Sea Wolf; Command Line Of Sight (CLOS) radar/TV tracking to 6 km *(3.3 n miles)* at 2.5 Mach; warhead 14 kg; 16 missiles.
Guns: Otobreda 76 mm Super Rapid ❸. 120 rds/min to 16 km *(8.7 n miles)*; weight of shell 6 kg.
2 MSI 30 mm/75. 650 rds/min to 10 km *(5.4 n miles)* ❹.
Torpedoes: 6 Marconi 324 mm (2 triple) tubes ❺.
Countermeasures: Decoys: 2 Super Barricade chaff launchers ❻.
ECM: Thales Scorpion; jammer.
ESM: Thales Cutlass 242; intercept.
CESM: Falcon DS 300; intercept.
Combat data systems: Nautis Mk 2 with Link Y.
Weapons control: Radamec 2500 optronic director ❼.
Radars: Air/Surface search: Plessey AWS 9 ❽; E/F-band.
Surface search: Kelvin Hughes 1007 ❾; I-band.
Fire control: 2 Marconi 1802 ❿; I/J-band.
Sonars: Thomson Marconi 4130C1; hull mounted.

Helicopters: Platform for 1 medium.

Programmes: Tenders requested on 28 April 1995. Yarrow Shipbuilders selected in August 1995. Detailed design done in 1996 with final contract signed 14 January 1998. Long-term support contract signed with BAE Systems in May 2002.
Structure: Scaled down version of Malaysian Lekiu class. Facilities to land and refuel S-70A and Bell 212 helicopters.
Operational: Sea trials of first of class began in January 2002. Training for all three crews provided by Flagship Training. *Jerambak* conducted acceptance trials in late 2004. Formal acceptance of all three is not expected until contractual issues which are the subject of legal proceedings, have been resolved. Meanwhile, the ships remain at Scotstoun under care and maintenance.

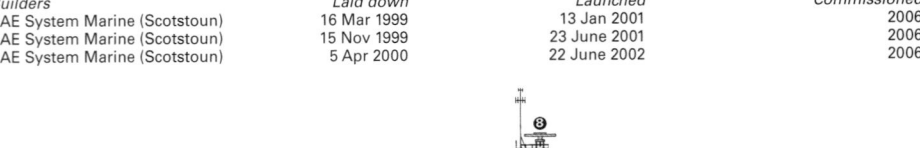

NAKHODA RAGAM
(Scale 1 : 900), Ian Sturton / 0526842

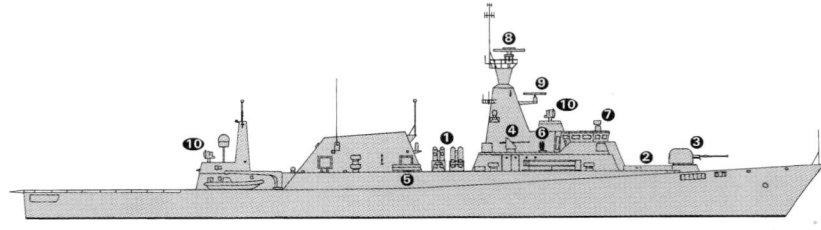

NAKHODA RAGAM (on trials)
6/2002, H M Steele / 0533228

BENDAHARA SAKAM
4/2004, John Brodie
1044352

PATROL FORCES

Notes: There are also up to 15 Rigid Raider assault boats operated by the River Division for infantry battalions. These boats are armed with 1 — 7.62 mm MG.

3 WASPADA CLASS (FAST ATTACK CRAFT—MISSILE) (PTG)

Name	No	Builders	Launched	Commissioned
WASPADA	P 02	Vosper (Singapore)	3 Aug 1977	2 Aug 1978
PEJUANG	P 03	Vosper (Singapore)	15 Mar 1978	25 Mar 1979
SETERIA	P 04	Vosper (Singapore)	22 June 1978	22 June 1979

Displacement, tons: 206 full load
Dimensions, feet (metres): 121 × 23.5 × 6 *(36.9 × 7.2 × 1.8)*
Main machinery: 2 MTU 20V 538 TB91 diesels; 7,680 hp(m) *(5.63 MW)* sustained; 2 shafts
Speed, knots: 32. **Range, n miles:** 1,200 at 14 kt
Complement: 24 (4 officers)

Missiles: SSM: 2 Aerospatiale MM 38 Exocet; inertial cruise; active radar homing to 42 km *(23 n miles)* at 0.9 Mach; warhead 165 kg.
Guns: 2 Oerlikon 30 mm GCM-B01 (twin); 650 rds/min to 10 km *(5.5 n miles)*; weight of shell 1 kg.
2 — 7.62 mm MGs. 2 MOD(N) 2 in launchers for illuminants.
Countermeasures: ESM: Decca RDL; radar warning.
Weapons control: Sea Archer system with Sperry Co-ordinate Calculator and 1412A digital computer. Radamec 2500 optronic director.
Radars: Surface search: Kelvin Hughes Type 1007; I-band.
Modernisation: Started in 1988 and included improved gun fire control and ESM equipment. Further improvements in 1998-2000 included Type 1007 radar and a Radamec 2500 optronic director.
Structure: Welded steel hull with aluminium alloy superstructure. *Waspada* has an enclosed upper bridge for training purposes.
Operational: Reported active.

SETERIA   *5/1998* / 0017639

PEJUANG (with optronic director)   *7/2000* / 0104244

3 PERWIRA CLASS (COASTAL PATROL CRAFT) (PB)

Name	No	Builders	Launched	Commissioned
PERWIRA	P 14	Vosper (Singapore)	5 May 1974	9 Sep 1974
PEMBURU	P 15	Vosper (Singapore)	30 Jan 1975	17 June 1975
PENYERANG	P 16	Vosper (Singapore)	20 Mar 1975	24 June 1975

Displacement, tons: 38 full load
Dimensions, feet (metres): 71 × 20 × 5 *(21.7 × 6.1 × 1.2)*
Main machinery: 2 MTU MB 12V 331 TC81 diesels; 2,450 hp(m) *(1.8 MW)* sustained; 2 shafts
Speed, knots: 32. **Range, n miles:** 600 at 22 kt; 1,000 at 16 kt
Complement: 14 (2 officers)
Guns: 2 Oerlikon/BMARC 20 mm GAM-BO1; 800 rds/min to 2 km; weight of shell 0.24 kg.
2 — 7.62 mm MGs.
Radars: Surface search: Racal Decca RM 1290; I-band.

Comment: Of all-wooden construction on laminated frames. Fitted with enclosed bridges-modified July 1976. A high speed RIB is launched from a stern ramp. New guns fitted in mid-1980s. P 15 may not be operational.

PENYERANG   *6/1999, Royal Brunei Armed Forces* / 0056628

LAND-BASED MARITIME AIRCRAFT

Notes: (1) There are also five BO-105, two S-70A and ten Bell 212 utility helicopters.
(2) The requirement for maritime patrol aircraft was to have been met by three CN-235 MPA but these were not acquired. A decision on the way-ahead is awaited.
(3) The requirement for shipborne helicopters, to operate from the corvettes, appears to be in abeyance.

AUXILIARIES

2 TERABAN CLASS (LCU)

Name	No	Builders	Commissioned
TERABAN	33	Transfield, Perth	8 Nov 1996
SERASA	34	Transfield, Perth	8 Nov 1996

Displacement, tons: 220 full load
Dimensions, feet (metres): 119.8 × 26.2 × 4.9 *(36.5 × 8 × 1.5)*
Main machinery: 2 diesels; 2 shafts
Speed, knots: 12
Complement: 12
Military lift: 100 tons
Radars: Navigation: Racal; I-band.

Comment: Ordered in November 1995 and delivered in December 1996. Used as utility transports. Bow and side ramps are fitted. Reported active.

TERABAN   *5/1998, John Mortimer* / 0056629

2 CHEVERTON LOADMASTERS (YFU)

Name	No	Builders	Commissioned
DAMUAN	L 31	Cheverton Ltd, Isle of Wight	May 1976
PUNI	L 32	Cheverton Ltd, Isle of Wight	Feb 1977

Displacement, tons: 60; 64 *(Puni)* standard
Dimensions, feet (metres): 65 × 20 × 3.6 *(19.8 × 6.1 × 1.1)* (length 74.8 *(22.8)* Puni)
Main machinery: 2 Detroit 6-71 diesels; 442 hp *(305 kW)* sustained; 2 shafts
Speed, knots: 9
Range, n miles: 1,000 at 9 kt
Complement: 8
Military lift: 32 tons
Radars: Navigation: Racal Decca RM 1216; I-band.

DAMUAN   *6/1997, Royal Brunei Armed Forces* / 0012141

POLICE

Notes: In addition to the vessels listed below there are two 12 m Rotork type *Behagia* 07 and *Selamat* 10 and four River Patrol Craft *Aman* 01, *Damai* 02, *Sentosa* 04 and *Sejahtera* 06.

3 BENDEHARU CLASS (PB)

BENDEHARU P 21   **MAHARAJALELA** P 22   **KEMAINDERA** P 23

Displacement, tons: 68 full load
Dimensions, feet (metres): 93.5 × 17.8 × 5.6 *(28.5 × 5.4 × 1.7)*
Main machinery: 2 MTU diesels; 2,260 hp *(1.7 MW)*; 2 shafts
Speed, knots: 29
Guns: 1 — 12.7 mm MG.
Radars: Navigation: I-band.

Comment: Constructed by PT Pal, Surabaya, and entered service in 1991.

7 INSHORE PATROL CRAFT

PDB 11-15	PDB 63	PDB 68

Displacement, tons: 20 full load
Dimensions, feet (metres): 47.7 × 13.9 × 3.9 *(14.5 × 4.2 × 1.2)*
Main machinery: 2 MAN D 2840 LE diesels; 1,040 hp(m) *(764 kW)* sustained; 2 shafts
Speed, knots: 30
Range, n miles: 310 at 22 kt
Complement: 7
Guns: 1 — 7.62 mm MG.
Radars: Surface search: Furuno; I-band.

Comment: Built by Singapore SBEC. First three handed over in October 1987, second pair in 1988, last two in 1996. Aluminium hulls.

PDB 15
3/1999, John Webber
0056631

Bulgaria

VOENNOMORSKI SILI

Country Overview

Situated in the Balkan Peninsula, the Republic of Bulgaria has an area of 42,823 square miles and is bordered to the north by Romania and to the south by Turkey and Greece. The River Danube forms much of the northern border. Bulgaria has a coastline of 191 n miles with the Black Sea on which Varna and Burgas are the principal ports. The capital is Sofia. Territorial waters (12 n miles) are claimed. An Exclusive Economic Zone (EEZ) was declared in 1987 but the precise limits have yet to be fully agreed and defined.

Headquarters Appointments

Commander of the Navy and Chief of Staff:
 Rear Admiral Neiko Petrov Atanasov

Diplomatic Representation

Defence Attaché, London:
 Brigadier V T Taankov

Organisation

Four squadrons: Submarine, Surface, MCMV and Auxiliary, with Headquarters at Varna and Burgas. There is also a Border Guard Unit.

Personnel

(a) 2006: 4,140 (695 officers)
(b) 12 months' national service
(c) Reserves 10,000

Bases

Varna; Naval HQ (North Zone), Naval Base, Air Station
Burgas: Naval HQ (South Zone)
Sozopol, Atiya, Balchik, Vidin (Danube); Naval Bases
Higher Naval School *(Nikola Yonkov Vaptsarov)* at Varna.

Coast Defence

One battalion with six truck-mounted SS-C-3 Styx twin launchers. Two Army regiments of coastal artillery with 100 mm and 130 mm guns.

SUBMARINES

Notes: Procurement of a second-hand submarine, possibly from Denmark, is reported to be under consideration.

1 ROMEO CLASS (PROJECT 633) (SS)

SLAVA 84

Displacement, tons: 1,475 surfaced; 1,830 dived
Dimensions, feet (metres): 251.3 × 22 × 16.1
 (76.6 × 6.7 × 4.9)
Main machinery: Diesel-electric; 2 Type 37-D diesels; 4,000 hp(m) *(2.94 MW)*; 2 motors; 2,700 hp(m) *(1.98 MW)*; 2 creep motors; 2 shafts
Speed, knots: 16 surfaced; 13 dived
Range, n miles: 9,000 at 9 kt surfaced
Complement: 54

Torpedoes: 8 — 21 in *(533 mm)* tubes (6 bow, 2 stern). 14 SAET-60; passive homing to 15 km *(8.1 n miles)* at 40 kt; warhead 400 kg.
Mines: Can carry up to 28 in lieu of torpedoes.
Countermeasures: ESM: Stop Light; radar warning.
Radars: Surface search: Snoop Plate; I-band.
Sonars: Hull-mounted; active/passive search and attack; high frequency.

Programmes: Built in 1961. Transferred from the USSR in 1986. An order for two Kilo class was subsequently cancelled.
Operational: Restricted to diving to about 50 m *(165 ft)*. Based at Varna. Attempts have been made to keep this last boat operational by cannibalising others of the class and operational status is doubtful.

SLAVA

6/1997 / 0012100

FRIGATES

1 KONI CLASS (PROJECT 1159) (FFLM)

SMELI (ex-*Delfin*) 11

Displacement, tons: 1,440 standard; 1,900 full load
Dimensions, feet (metres): 316.3 × 41.3 × 11.5
(96.4 × 12.6 × 3.5)
Main machinery: CODAG; 1 SGW, Nikolayev M8B gas turbine (centre shaft); 18,000 hp(m) *(13.25 MW)* sustained; 2 Russki B-68 diesels; 15,820 hp(m) *(11.63 MW)* sustained; 3 shafts
Speed, knots: 27 gas; 22 diesel
Range, n miles: 1,800 at 14 kt
Complement: 110

Missiles: SAM: SA-N-4 Gecko twin launcher ❶; semi-active radar homing to 15 km *(8 n miles)* at 2.5 Mach; warhead 50 kg; altitude 9.1–3,048 m *(30—10,000 ft)*; 20 missiles.
Guns: 4—3 in *(76 mm)*/60 (2 twin) ❷; 60 rds/min to 15 km *(8 n miles)*; weight of shell 7 kg.
  4—30 mm/65 (2 twin) ❸; 500 rds/min to 5 km *(2.7 n miles)*; weight of shell 0.54 kg.
A/S mortars: 2 RBU 6000 12-tubed trainable ❹; range 6,000 m; warhead 31 kg.
Depth charges: 2 racks.
Mines: Capacity for 22.

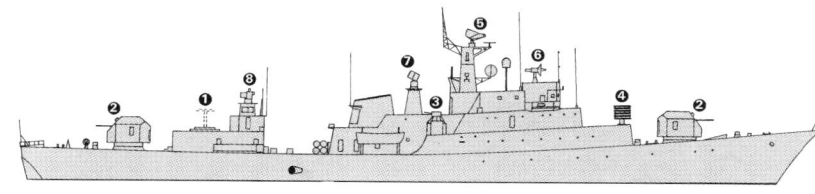

SMELI *(Scale 1 : 900), Ian Sturton* / 0114505

Countermeasures: Decoys: 2 PK 16 chaff launchers.
ESM: 2 Watch Dog; radar warning.
Radars: Air search: Strut Curve ❺; F-band; range 110 km *(60 n miles)* for 2 m² target.
Surface search: Don 2; I-band.
Fire control: Hawk Screech ❻; I-band (for 76 mm). Drum Tilt ❼; H/I-band (for 30 mm). Pop Group ❽; F/H/I-band (for SA-N-4).
IFF: High Pole B.
Sonars: Hercules (MG 322); hull-mounted; active search and attack; medium frequency.

Programmes: First reported in the Black Sea in 1976. Type I retained by the USSR for training foreign crews but transferred in February 1990 when the Koni programme terminated. Others of the class acquired by the former East German Navy (now deleted), Yugoslavia, Algeria, Cuba and Libya.
Modernisation: Marisat fitted in 1996. Reported to be RAS capable. Communications upgrade planned to achieve NATO interoperability.
Operational: Based at Varna. Likely to be decommissioned as *Drusky* enters service.

SMELI *6/2004, C D Yaylali* / 0587693

1 + 2 WIELINGEN CLASS (TYPE E-71) (FFGM)

Name	No	Builders	Laid down	Launched	Commissioned
DRAZKI (ex-*Wandelaar*)	41 (ex-F 912)	Boelwerf, Temse	28 Mar 1975	21 June 1977	27 Oct 1978

Displacement, tons: 1,940 light; 2,430 full load
Dimensions, feet (metres): 349 × 40.3 × 18.4
(106.4 × 12.3 × 5.6)
Main machinery: CODOG; 1 RR Olympus TM3B gas-turbine; 25,440 hp *(19 MW)* sustained; 2 Cockerill 240 CO V 12 diesels; 6,000 hp(m) *(4.4 MW)*; 2 shafts; LIPS cp props
Speed, knots: 26; 15 on 1 diesel; 20 on 2 diesels
Range, n miles: 4,500 at 18 kt; 6,000 at 15 kt
Complement: 159 (13 officers)

Missiles: SSM: 4 Aerospatiale MM 38 (2 twin) launchers; inertial cruise; active radar homing to 42 km *(23 n miles)* at 0.9 Mach; warhead 165 kg; sea-skimmer.
SAM: Raytheon Sea Sparrow RIM-7P; Mk 29 octuple launcher; semi-active radar homing to 14.6 km *(8 n miles)* at 2.5 Mach; warhead 39 kg.
Guns: 1 Creusot-Loire 3.9 in *(100 mm)*/55 Mod 68; 80 rds/min to 17 km *(9 n miles)* anti-surface; 8 km *(4.4 n miles)* anti-aircraft; weight of shell 13.5 kg.
Torpedoes: 2—21 in *(533 mm)* launchers. ECAN L5 Mod 4; anti-submarine; active/passive homing to

9.5 km *(5 n miles)* at 35 kt; warhead 150 kg; depth to 550 m *(1,800 ft)*.
A/S mortars: 1 Creusot-Loire 375 mm 6-barrelled trainable launcher; Bofors rockets to 1,600 m; warhead 107 kg.
Countermeasures: Decoys: 2 Tracor MBA SRBOC 6-barrelled launchers; chaff (Mk 214 Seagnat) and IR flares to 4 km *(2.2 n miles)*. Nixie SLQ-25; towed anti-torpedo decoy.
ESM: Argos AR 900; intercept.
Combat data systems: Signaal SEWACO IV action data automation; Link 11. SATCOM.
Weapons control: Sagem Vigy 105 optronic director.
Radars: Air/Surface search: Signaal DA05; E/F-band.
Surface search/fire control: Signaal WM25; I/J-band.
Navigation: Signaal Scout; I/J band.
IFF: Mk XII.
Sonars: Computing Devices Canada SQS 510; hull-mounted; active search and attack; medium frequency.

Programmes: A compact, well-armed class of frigate originally designed by and for the Belgian Navy.

Following the signature of a letter of intent on 4 December 2004, the Bulgarian government gave final approval on 17 March 2005 for transfer of the ship to Bulgarian service in October 2005. Acquisition of two further Wielingen class by 2008 is under consideration.
Modernisation: The ship completed a major upgrade programme before leaving Belgian service. This included update of Sea Sparrow to 7P, modification of WM25 radar to include improved ECCM and MTI capabilities and a new navigation radar and sonar. A new optronic director, IFF and communications facilities were also installed. Platform improvements included new diesel engines and alternators.
Structure: Fully air conditioned. Fin stabilisers fitted.
Operational: It is intended that the ship is to be used for surveillance missions in the Black Sea, maritime interdiction and contributions to international peace-support operations, both under the NATO flag and as part of the Black Sea Naval Co-operation Task Group (BLACKSEAFOR).

DRAZKI *10/2005*, Guy Toremans* / 1133237

CORVETTES

Notes: A plan to procure a new class of multirole corvettes is understood to be a high priority within a wider modernisation programme to meet NATO requirements. A class of six ships is planned of which the first is expected to be built by a strategic shipbuilding partner with a further five to be built at the Navy Maintenance and Repair Shipyard near Varna. Requests for proposals have reportedly been sent to Navantia, Armaris, Fincantieri, Lürssen, Blohm + Voss, VT Shipbuilding and Schelde Shipbuilding. However, funding of the programme has not been confirmed.

1 TARANTUL II CLASS (PROJECT 1241.1M) (FSGM)

MULNAYA 101

Displacement, tons: 385 standard; 455 full load
Dimensions, feet (metres): 184.1 × 37.7 × 8.2 *(56.1 × 11.5 × 2.5)*
Main machinery: COGAG; 2 Nikolayev Type DR 77 gas turbines; 16,016 hp(m) *(11.77 MW)* sustained; 2 Nikolayev Type DR 76 gas turbines with reversible gearboxes; 4,993 hp(m) *(3.67 MW)* sustained; 2 shafts
Speed, knots: 36 on 4 turbines
Range, n miles: 400 at 36 kt; 2,000 at 20 kt
Complement: 34 (5 officers)

Missiles: SSM: 4 Raduga SS-N-2C Styx (2 twin) launchers; active radar or IR homing to 83 km *(45 n miles)* at 0.9 Mach; warhead 513 kg; sea-skimmer.
SAM: SA-N-5 Grail quad launcher; manual aiming; IR homing to 6 km *(3.2 n miles)* at 1.5 Mach; altitude to 2,500 m *(8,000 ft)*; warhead 1.5 kg.
Guns: 1—3 in *(76 mm)*/60; 120 rds/min to 15 km *(8.1 n miles)*; weight of shell 7 kg.
2—30 mm/65; 6 barrels per mounting; 3,000 rds/min to 2 km.
Countermeasures: Decoys: 2 PK 16 chaff launchers.
ESM: 2 Half Hat; intercept.
Weapons control: Hood Wink optronic director. Band Stand datalink for SSM.
Radars: Air/Surface search: Plank Shave; E-band.
Navigation: Kivach; I-band.
Fire control: Bass Tilt; H/I-band.
IFF: Square Head. High Pole.

Programmes: Built at Volodarski, Rybinsk. Transferred from USSR in December 1989. Name means Thunderbolt.
Operational: Based at Sozopol.

MULNAYA *7/2000, van Ginderen Collection* / 0104245

2 RESHITELNI (PAUK I) (PROJECT 1241P) CLASS (FSM)

RESHITELNI 13 **BODRI** 14

Displacement, tons: 440 full load
Dimensions, feet (metres): 195.2 × 33.5 × 10.8 *(59.5 × 10.2 × 3.3)*
Main machinery: 2 Type 521 diesels; 16,180 hp(m) *(11.9 MW)* sustained; 2 shafts
Speed, knots: 32
Range, n miles: 2,200 at 14 kt
Complement: 38

Missiles: SAM: SA-N-5 Grail quad launcher; manual aiming; IR homing to 6 km *(3.2 n miles)* at 1.5 Mach; altitude to 2,500 m *(8,000 ft)*; warhead 1.5 kg; 8 missiles.
Guns: 1—3 in *(76 mm)*/60; 120 rds/min to 15 km *(8 n miles)*; weight of shell 7 kg.
1—30 mm/65; 6 barrels; 3,000 rds/min combined to 2 km.
Torpedoes: 4—16 in *(406 mm)* tubes. Type 40; anti-submarine; active/passive homing up to 15 km *(8 n miles)* at up to 40 kt; warhead 100—150 kg.
A/S mortars: 2 RBU 1200 5-tubed fixed; range 1,200 m; warhead 34 kg.
Depth charges: 2 racks (12).
Countermeasures: Decoys: 2 PK 16 chaff launchers.
ESM: 3 Brick Plug; intercept.
Radars: Air/Surface search: Peel Cone; E-band.
Surface search: Spin Trough; I-band.
Fire control: Bass Tilt; H/I-band.
Sonars: Foal Tail VDS (mounted on transom); active attack; high frequency.

Programmes: *Reshitelni* transferred from USSR in September 1989, *Bodri* in December 1990.
Operational: Based at Varna. *Reshitelni* is non-operational with propulsion problems.

BODRI *12/2004*, C D Yaylali* / 1129549

4 LETYASHTI (POTI) CLASS (PROJECT 204) (FS)

LETYASHTI 41 **BDITELNI** 42 **BEZSTRASHNI** 43 **KHRABRI** 44

Displacement, tons: 545 full load
Dimensions, feet (metres): 196.8 × 26.2 × 6.6 *(60 × 8 × 2)*
Main machinery: CODAG; 2 gas-turbines; 30,000 hp(m) *(22.4 MW)*; 2 Type M 503A diesels; 5,350 hp(m) *(3.91 MW)* sustained; 2 shafts
Speed, knots: 32. **Range, n miles:** 3,000 at 18 kt; 500 at 37 kt
Complement: 80

Guns: 2 USSR 57 mm/80 (twin); 120 rds/min to 6 km *(3 n miles)*; weight of shell 2.8 kg.
Torpedoes: 4—16 in *(406 mm)* tubes. SAET-40; anti-submarine; active/passive homing to 10 km *(5.4 n miles)* at 30 kt; warhead 100 kg.
A/S mortars: 2 RBU 6000 12-tubed trainable launchers; range 6,000 m; warhead 31 kg.
Countermeasures: ESM: 2 Watch Dog; radar warning.
Radars: Air search: Strut Curve; F-band.
Surface search: Don; I-band.
Fire control: Muff Cob; G/H-band.
IFF: Square Head. High Pole.
Sonars: Hull-mounted; active search and attack; high frequency.

Programmes: Series built at Zelenodolsk between 1961 and 1968. Three transferred from USSR December 1975, the fourth at the end of 1986 and the last two in 1990. Two deleted in 1993. Names: 41 Flying, 42 Vigilant, 43 Fearless and 44 Gallant.
Operational: Based at Atiya and probably non-operational.

LETYASHTI *6/1996, Bulgarian Navy* / 0506271

LAND-BASED MARITIME AIRCRAFT (FRONT LINE)

Notes: (1) A number of Air Force MiG-23s have AS-7 Kerry ASMs.
(2) Three Hormone B helicopters are non-operational.

Numbers/Type: 3 Mil Mi-14PL 'Haze A'.
Operational speed: 120 kt *(222 km/h)*.
Service ceiling: 15,000 ft *(4,570 m)*.
Range: 240 n miles *(445 km)*.
Role/Weapon systems: Primary role as inshore/coastal ASW and Fleet support helicopter; one converted as transport. Based at Asparukhovo airport. Sensors: Search radar, MAD, sonobuoys, dipping sonar. Weapons: ASW; up to 2 × torpedoes, or mines, or depth bombs.

HAZE *1994, A Mladenov* / 0056632

PATROL FORCES

Notes: Customs craft operate on the Danube. Vessels include three Boston Whalers donated by the US and RIBs given by the UK in 1992-93.

9 ZHUK (PROJECT 1400M) CLASS
(COASTAL PATROL CRAFT) (PB)

511-513 **521-523** **531-533**

Displacement, tons: 39 full load
Dimensions, feet (metres): 78.7 × 16.4 × 3.9 *(24 × 5 × 1.2)*
Main machinery: 2 Type M 401B diesels; 2,200 hp(m) *(1.6 MW)* sustained; 2 shafts
Speed, knots: 30. **Range, n miles:** 1,100 at 15 kt
Complement: 11 (3 officers)
Guns: 4 USSR 14.5 mm (2 twin) MGs.
Radars: Surface search: Spin Trough; I-band.

Comment: Transferred from USSR 1980-81. Belong to the Border Police under the Minister of the Interior and have 'Border Guard' insignia on the ships side. Based at Atiya and at Varna.

ZHUK 512 (and others) *6/1996, Bulgarian Navy* / 0506272

6 OSA (PROJECT 205) CLASS
(FAST ATTACK CRAFT—MISSILE) (PTFG)

URAGON 102	**SVETKAVITSA** 111
BURYA 103 (Osa I)	**TYPFUN** 112 (Osa 1)
GRUM 104	**SMERCH** 113

Displacement, tons: 245 full load; 210 (Osa I)
Dimensions, feet (metres): 126.6 × 24.9 × 8.8 (38.6 × 7.6 × 2.7)
Main machinery: 3 Type M 504 diesels; 10,800 hp(m) (7.94 MW) sustained; 3 shafts (Osa II)
3 Type 503A diesels; 8,025 hp(m) (5.9 MW) sustained; 3 shafts (Osa I)
Speed, knots: 37 (Osa II); 35 (Osa I)
Range, n miles: 500 at 35 kt
Complement: 26 (3 officers)
Missiles: SSM: 4 SS-N-2A/B Styx; active radar/IR homing to 46 km (25 n miles) at 0.9 Mach; warhead 513 kg. SS-N-2A in Osa I.
Guns: 4 USSR 30 mm/65 (2 twin); 500 rds/min to 5 km (2.7 n miles); weight of shell 0.54 kg.
Radars: Surface search/fire control: Square Tie; I-band.
Fire control: Drum Tilt; H/I-band.
IFF: High Pole. Square Head.

Comment: Four Osa IIs built between 1965 and 1970, and transferred from USSR between 1977 and 1982. Two Osa Is transferred in 1972 and survived longer than expected. Names: 102 Hurricane, 103 Storm, 104 Thunder, 111 Lightning, 112 Typhoon and 113 Tornado. All based at Sozopol and seldom go to sea.

GRUM   6/2002, A Sheldon-Duplaix / 0524968

BURYA   6/2002, A Sheldon-Duplaix / 0524970

3 NEUSTADT CLASS (PB)

SOZOPOL (ex-Rosenheim) 525 (ex-BG 18)	**NESEBAR** (ex-Neustadt) 526 (ex-BG 11)
BALCHIK (ex-Duderstadt) 524 (ex-BG 14)	

Displacement, tons: 218 full load
Dimensions, feet (metres): 127.1 × 23 × 5 (38.5 × 7 × 2.2)
Main machinery: 2 MTU MD diesels; 6,000 hp(m) (4.41 MW); 1 MWM diesel; 685 hp(m) (500 kW); 3 shafts
Speed, knots: 30
Range, n miles: 450 at 27 kt
Complement: 17
Guns: 2—7.62 mm MGs.
Radars: Surface search: Selenia ARP 1645; I-band.
Navigation: Racal Decca Bridgemaster MA 180/4; I-band.

Comment: Built in 1970 by Lürssen, Vegesack. 525 transferred from German Border Guard in June 2002, 526 on 16 April 2004 and 524 in December 2004. Operated by the Border Police.

NESEBAR   5/2004, Martin Mokrus / 0587692

3 COASTAL PATROL CRAFT (PB)

BURGAS	**VARNA**	**KABAPHA**

Displacement, tons: 50 standard
Dimensions, feet (metres): 68.9 × 19.0 × 4.6 (21.0 × 5.8 × 1.4)
Main machinery: 2 Deutz MWM TBD 616 diesels; 2,970 hp(m) (2.2 MW); 2 shafts
Speed, knots: 30

Comment: Contract awarded in November 2002 to Lürssen, Berne-Bardenfleth. Delivery of the first two craft made in 2003 and of the third in October 2005. Operated by Border Police.

KABAPHA (in foreground)   9/2005*, Michael Nitz /1133236

AMPHIBIOUS FORCES

2 POLNOCHNY A (PROJECT 770) CLASS (LSM)

SIRIUS (ex-Ivan Zagubanski) 701	**ANTARES** 702

Displacement, tons: 750 standard; 800 full load
Dimensions, feet (metres): 239.5 × 27.9 × 5.8 (73 × 8.5 × 1.8)
Main machinery: 2 Kolomna Type 40-D diesels; 4,400 hp(m) (3.2 MW) sustained; 2 shafts
Speed, knots: 19. **Range, n miles:** 1,000 at 18 kt
Complement: 40
Military lift: 350 tons including 6 tanks; 180 troops
Guns: 2 USSR 30 mm (twin). 2—140 mm 18-barrelled rocket launchers.
Radars: Navigation: Spin Trough; I-band.

Comment: Built 1963 to 1968. Transferred from USSR 1986-87. Not fitted either with the SA-N-5 Grail SAM system or with Drum Tilt fire-control radars. Plans to convert them to minelayers have been shelved and both are now used as transports. Based at Atiya.

ANTARES   4/2005*, C D Yaylali / 1129550

7 VYDRA (PROJECT 106K) CLASS (LCU)

205	**703-707**	**712**

Displacement, tons: 425 standard; 550 full load
Dimensions, feet (metres): 179.7 × 25.3 × 6.6 (54.8 × 7.7 × 2)
Main machinery: 2 Type 3-D-12 diesels; 600 hp(m) (440 kW) sustained; 2 shafts
Speed, knots: 12
Range, n miles: 2,500 at 10 kt
Complement: 20
Military lift: 200 tons or 100 troops or 3 MBTs
Radars: Navigation: Don 2; I-band.
IFF: High Pole.

Comment: Built 1963 to 1969. Ten transferred from the USSR in 1970, the remainder built in Bulgaria between 1974 and 1978. In 1992-93 703-707 and 712 converted to be used as minelayers. Many deleted. 205 based at Varna, the remainder at Atiya.

VYDRA 706 (and others)   7/1995, Alexander Mladenov / 0056636

MINE WARFARE FORCES

Notes: (1) Six Vydra class (see *Amphibious Forces*) converted to minelayers in 1992-93. Some are in reserve.
(2) Negotiations to procure Tripartite class minehunters from Belgium reportedly took place in 2005.

4 BRIZ (SONYA) (PROJECT 12650) CLASS
(MINESWEEPERS — COASTAL) (MSC)

BRIZ 61	SHKVAL 62	PRIBOY 63	SHTORM 64

Displacement, tons: 450 full load
Dimensions, feet (metres): 157.4 × 28.9 × 6.6 *(48 × 8.8 × 2)*
Main machinery: 2 Kolomna Type 9-D-8 diesels; 2,000 hp(m) *(1.47 MW)* sustained; 2 shafts
Speed, knots: 15. **Range, n miles:** 1,500 at 14 kt
Complement: 43 (5 officers)
Guns: 2 USSR 30 mm/65 (twin); 500 rds/min to 5 km *(2.7 n miles)*; weight of shell 0.54 kg.
2 USSR 25 mm/80 (twin); 270 rds/min to 3 km *(1.6 n miles)*; weight of shell 0.34 kg.
Mines: 5.
Radars: Surface search/Navigation: Kivach; I-band.
IFF Two Square Head. High Pole B.
Sonars: MG 69/79; hull-mounted; active minehunting; high frequency.

Comment: Wooden hulled ships transferred from USSR in 1981-84. Based at Atiya.

PRIBOY **7/2000** / 0114506

4 ISCAR (VANYA) (PROJECT 257D) CLASS
(MINESWEEPERS — COASTAL) (MSC)

ISKAR 31	ZIBAR 32	DOBROTICH 33	EVSTATI VINAROV 34

Displacement, tons: 245 full load
Dimensions, feet (metres): 131.2 × 23.9 × 5.9 *(40 × 7.3 × 1.8)*
Main machinery: 2 M 870 diesels; 2,502 hp(m) *(1.84 MW)*; 2 shafts; cp props
Speed, knots: 16. **Range, n miles:** 2,400 at 10 kt
Complement: 36
Guns: 2 USSR 30 mm/65 (twin); 500 rds/min to 5 km *(2.7 n miles)*; weight of shell 0.54 kg.
Mines: Can carry 8.
Radars: Surface search: Don 2; I-band.
Sonars: MG 69/79; hull-mounted; active minehunting; high frequency.

Comment: Built 1961 to 1973. Transferred from the USSR-two in 1970, two in 1971 and two in 1985. Can act as minehunters. Two paid off in 1992, but back in service in 1994 and then finally scrapped in 1995. Based at Varna.

EVSTATI VINAROV **8/2000** / 0114508

2 YEVGENYA (PROJECT 1258) CLASS
(MINESWEEPERS — COASTAL) (MSC)

65	66

Displacement, tons: 77 standard; 90 full load
Dimensions, feet (metres): 80.4 × 18 × 4.6 *(24.5 × 5.5 × 1.4)*
Main machinery: 2 Type 3-D-12 diesels; 600 hp(m) *(440 kW)* sustained; 2 shafts
Speed, knots: 11. **Range, n miles:** 300 at 10 kt
Complement: 10 (1 officer)
Guns: 2 — 25 mm/80 (twin).
Mines: 8 racks.
Radars: Surface search: Spin Trough; I-band.
IFF: High Pole.
Sonars: MG-7 lifted over stern; active; high frequency.

Comment: GRP hulls built at Kolpino. Transferred from USSR 1977. Based at Varna.

YEVGENYA 66 **6/1996, Bulgarian Navy** / 0506273

1 PO 2 (PROJECT 501) CLASS
(MINESWEEPERS — INSHORE) (MSB)

57

Displacement, tons: 56 full load
Dimensions, feet (metres): 70.5 × 11.5 × 3.3 *(21.5 × 3.5 × 1)*
Main machinery: 1 Type 3-D-12 diesel; 300 hp(m) *(220 kW)* sustained; 2 shafts
Speed, knots: 12
Complement: 8

Comment: Built in Bulgaria. First units completed in early 1950s and last in early 1960s. Originally a class of 24 and this is the last to survive. Occasionally carries a 12.7 mm MG, when used for patrol duties. Both based at Balchik.

PO 2 58 **7/2000, van Ginderen Collection** / 0104252

6 OLYA (PROJECT 1259) CLASS
(MINESWEEPERS — INSHORE) (MSB)

51	52	53	54	55	56

Displacement, tons: 64 full load
Dimensions, feet (metres): 84.6 × 14.9 × 3.3 *(25.8 × 4.5 × 1)*
Main machinery: 2 Type 3D 6S11/235 diesels; 471 hp(m) *(346 kW)* sustained; 2 shafts
Speed, knots: 12. **Range (miles):** 300 at 10 kt
Complement: 15
Guns: 2 — 12.7 mm MGs (twin).
Radars: Navigation: Pechora; I-band.

Comment: First five built between 1988 and 1992 in Bulgaria to the Russian Olya design. *56* completed in 1996. Minesweeping equipment includes AT-6, SZMT-1 and 3 PKT-2 systems. *55* based at Varna, the remainder at Balchik.

OLYA 52 **7/2000, van Ginderen Collection** / 0104250

SURVEY SHIPS

1 MOMA (PROJECT 861) CLASS (AGS)

ADMIRAL BRANIMIR ORMANOV 401

Displacement, tons: 1,580 full load
Dimensions, feet (metres): 240.5 × 36.8 × 12.8 *(73.3 × 11.2 × 3.9)*
Main machinery: 2 Zgoda-Sulzer 6TD48 diesels; 3,300 hp(m) *(2.43 MW)* sustained; 2 shafts; cp props
Speed, knots: 17. **Range, n miles:** 9,000 at 12 kt
Complement: 37 (5 officers)
Radars: Navigation: 2 Don-2; I-band.

Comment: Built at Northern Shipyard, Gdansk, Poland in 1977. Based at Varna. Two others of the class belonging to Russia were refitted in Bulgaria in 1995-96.

ADMIRAL BRANIMIR ORMANOV **7/2000, van Ginderen Collection** / 0104253

2 COASTAL SURVEY VESSELS (PROJECT 612) (AGSC)

231   331

Displacement, tons: 114 full load
Dimensions, feet (metres): 87.6 × 19 × 4.9 (26.7 × 5.8 × 1.5)
Main machinery: 2 Type 3-D-12 diesels; 600 hp(m) (440 kW) sustained; 2 shafts
Speed, knots: 12
Range, n miles: 600 at 10 kt
Complement: 9 (2 officers)
Radars: Navigation: I-band.

Comment: Built in Bulgaria in 1986 and 1988 respectively. Can carry 2 tons of equipment. *231* is based at Varna and *331* at Atiya.

AGSC 331   *6/1996, Bulgarian Navy* / 0506274

AUXILIARIES

1 SUPPORT TANKER (AOTL)

203

Displacement, tons: 1,250 full load
Dimensions, feet (metres): 181.8 × 36.1 × 11.5 (55.4 × 11 × 3.5)
Main machinery: 2 Sulzer 6AL-20-24 diesels; 1,500 hp(m) (1.1 MW); 2 shafts
Speed, knots: 12
Range, n miles: 1,000 at 8 kt
Complement: 23
Cargo capacity: 650 tons fuel
Guns: 2 ZU-23-2F Wrobel 23 mm (twin).
Radars: Navigation: I-band.

Comment: Laid down 1989, launched 1993 and completed in 1994 at Burgas Shipyards, Burgas. Based at Varna.

203   *1/1998* / 0017648

1 MESAR CLASS (PROJECT 102) (SUPPORT TANKER) (AORL)

ATIYA 302

Displacement, tons: 3,240 full load
Dimensions, feet (metres): 319.8 × 45.6 × 16.4 (97.5 × 13.9 × 5)
Main machinery: 2 diesels; 12,000 hp(m) (8.82 MW); 2 shafts
Speed, knots: 18
Range, n miles: 12,000 at 15 kt
Complement: 32 (6 officers)
Cargo capacity: 1,593 tons
Guns: 4 USSR 30 mm/65 (2 twin).
Radars: Navigation: 2 Don 2; I-band.

Comment: Built in Bulgaria in 1987. Abeam fuelling to port and astern fuelling. Mount 1.5 ton crane amidships. Also carries dry stores. Based at Atiya.

ATIYA   *7/2002, S Breyer* / 0568845

1 DIVING TENDER (PROJECT 245) (YDT)

223

Displacement, tons: 112 full load
Dimensions, feet (metres): 91.5 × 17.1 × 7.2 (27.9 × 5.2 × 2.2)
Main machinery: Diesel-electric; 2 MCK 83 — 4 diesel generators; 1 motor; 300 hp(m) (220 kW); 1 shaft
Speed, knots: 10
Range, n miles: 400 at 10 kt
Complement: 6 + 7 divers
Radars: Navigation: Don 2; I-band.

Comment: Built in Bulgaria in mid-1980s. A twin 12.7 mm MG can be fitted. Capable of bell diving to 60 m. Based at Varna.

YDT 223   *6/1998, S Breyer collection* / 0017650

6 AUXILIARIES (ATS)

KALIAKRA   OLEV BLAGOEV 421   224   312   313   321

Comment: *Olev Blagoev* is a survey vessel converted to a training ship. *224* and *321* are firefighting vessels. *312* and *313* are tugs. *Kaliakra* is a 380 ton barquentine used for sail training.

OLEV BLAGOEV   *6/2003, Schaeffer/Marsan* / 0567877

224   *7/2000, van Ginderen Collection* / 0104254

KALIAKRA   *5/2005*, C D Yaylali* / 1129551

1 BEREZA (PROJECT 130) CLASS (ADG/AX)

KAPITAN 1st RANK DIMITRI DOBREV 206

Displacement, tons: 2,051 full load
Dimensions, feet (metres): 228 × 45.3 × 13.1 *(69.5 × 13.8 × 4)*
Main machinery: 2 Zgoda-Sulzer 8 AL 25/30 diesels; 2,925 hp(m) *(2.16 MW)* sustained;
2 shafts; cp props
Speed, knots: 13. **Range, n miles:** 1,000 at 13 kt
Complement: 48
Radars: Navigation: Kivach; I-band.

Comment: New construction built in Poland and transferred July 1988. Used as a degaussing ship. Fitted with an NBC citadel and upper deck wash-down system. The ship has three laboratories. Has also been used as a training ship. Based at Varna.

KAPITAN 1st RANK DIMITRI DOBREV   *6/2004*, Giorgio Ghiglione* / 0587694

1 TYPE 700 SALVAGE TUG (ATS)

JUPITER 221

Displacement, tons: 792 full load
Dimensions, feet (metres): 146.6 × 35.1 × 12.7 *(44.7 × 10.7 × 3.9)*
Main machinery: 2—12 KVD 21 diesels; 1,760 hp(m) *(1.3 MW)*; 2 shafts
Speed, knots: 12.5
Range, n miles: 3,000 at 12 kt
Complement: 39 (6 officers)
Guns: 4—25 mm/70 (2 twin) automatic (can be carried).
Radars: Navigation: I-band.

Comment: Built at Peenewerft Shipyard and completed 20 March 1964. Bollard pull, 16 tons. Based at Varna.

JUPITER   *8/1996* / 0056638

1 SALVAGE SHIP (ARS)

Name	No	Builders	Commissioned
PROTEO (ex-*Perseo*)	224 (ex-A 5310)	Cantieri Navali Riuniti, Ancona	24 Aug 1951

Displacement, tons: 1,865 standard; 2,147 full load
Dimensions, feet (metres): 248 × 38 × 21 *(75.6 × 11.6 × 6.4)*
Main machinery: 2 Fiat diesels; 4,800 hp(m) *(3.53 MW)*; 1 shaft
Speed, knots: 16. **Range, n miles:** 7,500 at 13 kt
Complement: 122 (8 officers)
Radars: Navigation: SMA-748; I-band.

Comment: Transferred to Bulgaria on 3 June 2004 having been decommissioned from the Italian Navy in 2002. Originally laid down in 1943, construction was suspended until restarted in 1949. Details are those of the ship when in Italian service.

224   *6/2004, Giorgio Ghiglione* / 0580523

Cambodia

Country Overview

Formerly a French protectorate, the south-east Asian Kingdom of Cambodia was ravaged by the Vietnam War and then by the Khmer Rouge regime before relative stability followed the nation's first multiparty elections in 1993. With an overall land area of 69,898 square miles, the country is bordered to the north by Thailand and Laos and to the east by Vietnam. There is a 239 n mile coastline with the Gulf of Thailand. The capital and largest city is Phnom Penh while the principal port is Kompong Som. There are extensive inland waterways. Territorial seas (12 n miles) are claimed. An EEZ (200 n miles) is claimed but the limits have not been fully defined.

Headquarters Appointments

Commander of Navy:
Vice Admiral Ung Samkhan

Personnel

2006: 2,800 (780 officers) including marines

Bases

Ream (ocean), Phnom Penh (river), Kompongson (civil)

Organisation

Ocean Division has nine battalions and the River Division seven battalions. Command HQ is at Phnom Penh.

PATROL FORCES

Notes: (1) There are also about 170 motorised and manual canoes.
(2) Six patrol craft of unknown type were donated by China on 9 January 2005.

2 KAOH CLASS (RIVER PATROL CRAFT) (PBR)

KAOH CHHLAM 1105   **KAOH RONG** 1106

Displacement, tons: 44 full load
Dimensions, feet (metres): 76.4 × 20 × 3.9 *(23.3 × 6.1 × 1.2)*
Main machinery: 2 Deutz/MWM TBD 616 V16 diesels; 2,992 hp(m) *(2.2 MW)*; 2 shafts
Speed, knots: 34
Range, n miles: 400 at 30 kt
Complement: 13 (3 officers)
Guns: 2—14.5 mm MG (twin). 2—12.7 mm MGs.
Radars: Surface search: Racal Decca Bridgemaster; I-band.

Comment: Ordered from Hong Leong Shipyard, Butterworth to a German design in 1995 and delivered 20 January 1997. Aluminium construction.

KAOH CHHLAM   *1/1997, Hong Leong Shipyard* / 0056667

2 MODIFIED STENKA CLASS (PROJECT 205P)
(FAST ATTACK CRAFT—PATROL) (PBF)

MONDOLKIRI 1131   **RATANAKIRI** 1134

Displacement, tons: 211 standard; 253 full load
Dimensions, feet (metres): 129.3 × 25.9 × 8.2 *(39.4 × 7.9 × 2.5)*
Main machinery: 3 Caterpillar diesels; 14,000 hp(m) *(10.29 MW)*; 3 shafts
Speed, knots: 37. **Range, n miles:** 800 at 24 kt; 500 at 35 kt
Complement: 25 (5 officers)
Guns: 2—23 mm/87 (twin). 1 Bofors 40 mm/70.
Radars: Surface search: Racal Decca Bridgemaster; I-band.
Fire control: Muff Cob; G/H-band.
Navigation: Racal Decca; I-band.
IFF: High Pole. 2 Square Head.

Comment: Four transferred from USSR in November 1987. Export model without torpedo tubes and sonar. One pair were modernised in Hong Leong Shipyard, Butterworth, from early 1995 to April 1996. New engines, guns and radars were fitted. The second pair similarly refitted by August 1997. By late 1998 only two were operational although it was reported in 2000 that a third may have undergone a further refit. Pennant numbers changed for UN operations but changed back again in November 1993.

MONDOLKIRI   *8/1997, Hong Leong Shipyard* / 0056666

Cameroon

MARINE NATIONALE RÉPUBLIQUE

Country Overview

The Republic of Cameroon became a unitary republic in 1972 and replaced the federation of East Cameroon (formerly French Cameroons) and West Cameroon (formerly part of British Cameroons). With an area of 183,569 square miles, the country has borders to the west with Nigeria and to the south with Gabon and Equatorial Guinea. It has a 217 n mile coastline with Atlantic Ocean on the Bight of Bonny. The capital is Yaoundé while Douala is the principal port which also serves adjacent landlocked states. Kribi is the country's second port. Cameroon is the only coastal state to claim territorial seas of 50 n miles. It has not been declared an Exclusive Economic Zone (EEZ) and claims to jurisdiction would be complicated by the offshore islands of Bioko (Equatorial Guinea), São Tomé and Principe.

Headquarters Appointments

Chief of Naval Staff:
    Commander Guillaume Ngouah Ngally

Personnel

2006: 1,250

Bases

Douala (HQ), Limbe, Kribi
Construction of new maintenance facilities at Douala started in 2003.

PATROL FORCES

Notes: (1) Ten Rodman 6.5 m craft were delivered in 2000. All have speeds in excess of 25 kt. (2) There are some eight Simmoneau 10 m craft in service and a further 15 are reported to have been ordered from Raidco Marine, Lorient.

1 BIZERTE (TYPE PR 48) CLASS (LARGE PATROL CRAFT) (PBO)

Name	No	Builders	Commissioned
L'AUDACIEUX	P 103	SFCN, Villeneuve-La-Garenne	11 May 1976

Displacement, tons: 250 full load
Dimensions, feet (metres): 157.5 × 23.3 × 7.5 *(48 × 7.1 × 2.3)*
Main machinery: 2 SACM 195 V12 CZSHR diesels; 6,000 hp(m) *(4.41 MW)* sustained; 2 shafts; cp props
Speed, knots: 23
Range, n miles: 2,000 at 16 kt
Complement: 25 (4 officers)
Guns: 2 Bofors 40 mm/70; 300 rds/min to 12.8 km *(7 n miles)*; weight of shell 0.96 kg.

Comment: *L'Audacieux* ordered in September 1974. Laid down on 10 February 1975, launched on 31 October 1975. Similar to Bizerte class in Tunisia. Operational status doubtful and not reported at sea since 1995. Fitted for SS 12M missiles but these are not embarked.

BIZERTE CLASS (Tunisian colours)   *1993, van Ginderen Collection* / 0056668

1 COASTAL PATROL CRAFT (PB)

QUARTIER MAÎTRE ALFRED MOTTO

Displacement, tons: 96 full load
Dimensions, feet (metres): 95.4 × 20.3 × 6.3 *(29.1 × 6.2 × 1.9)*
Main machinery: 2 Baudouin diesels; 1,290 hp(m) *(948 kW)*; 2 shafts
Speed, knots: 14
Complement: 17 (2 officers)
Guns: 2—7.62 mm MGs.
Radars: Surface search: I-band.

Comment: Built at Libreville, Gabon in 1974. Discarded as a derelict hulk in 1990 but refurbished and brought back into service with assistance from the French Navy in 1995-96.

QUARTIER MAÎTRE ALFRED MOTTO   *2/1996, French Navy* / 0056670

4 RODMAN 46 CLASS (PB)

IDABATO VS 201	ISONGO VS 202	MOUANCO VS 203	CAMPO VS 204

Displacement, tons: 12.5
Dimensions, feet (metres): 45.9 × 12.5 × 2.9 *(14.0 × 3.8 × 0.9)*
Main machinery: 2 Caterpillar diesels; 900 hp *(671 kW)*; 2 Hamilton waterjets
Speed, knots: 30
Complement: 4

Comment: GRP hull. Built in 2000 by Rodman, Vigo.

1 BAKASSI (TYPE P 48S) CLASS (OFFSHORE PATROL CRAFT) (PBO)

Name	No	Builders	Launched	Commissioned
BAKASSI	P 104	SFCN, Villeneuve-La-Garenne	22 Oct 1982	9 Jan 1984

Displacement, tons: 308 full load
Dimensions, feet (metres): 172.5 × 23.6 × 7.9 *(52.6 × 7.2 × 2.4)*
Main machinery: 2 SACM 195 V16 CZSHR diesels; 8,000 hp(m) *(5.88 MW)* sustained; 2 shafts
Speed, knots: 25
Range, n miles: 2,000 at 16 kt
Complement: 39 (6 officers)
Guns: 2 Bofors 40 mm/70; 300 rds/min to 12.8 km *(7 n miles)*; weight of shell 0.96 kg.
Weapons control: 2 Naja optronic systems. Racal Decca Cane 100 command system.
Radars: Navigation/surface search: 2 Furuno; I-band.

Comment: Ordered January 1981. Laid down 16 December 1981. Six month major refit by Raidco Marine (Lorient) in 1999. This included removing the Exocet missile system and EW equipment, and fitting new propellers and a funnel aft of the mainmast to replace the waterline exhausts. New radars were also installed. Two RIBs are carried.

BAKASSI   *7/1999, H M Steele* / 0121304

2 SWIFT PBR CLASS (RIVER PATROL CRAFT) (PBR)

PR 001	PR 005

Displacement, tons: 12 full load
Dimensions, feet (metres): 38 × 12.5 × 3.2 *(11.6 × 3.8 × 1)*
Main machinery: 2 Stewart and Stevenson 6V-92TA diesels; 520 hp *(388 kW)* sustained; 2 shafts
Speed, knots: 32
Range, n miles: 210 at 20 kt
Complement: 4
Guns: 2—12.7 mm MGs. 2—7.62 mm MGs.

Comment: Built by Swiftships and supplied under the US Military Assistance Programme. First 10 delivered in March 1987, second 10 in September 1987 and the remainder in March 1988. These last survivors are used by the gendarmerie. Several others have been cannibalised for spares.

PBR class   *4/1992* / 0056671

2 RODMAN 101 (COASTAL PATROL CRAFT) (PB)

AKWAYAFE P 106   JABANNE P 107

Displacement, tons: 63 full load
Dimensions, feet (metres): 98.4 × 19 × 5.9 *(30 × 5.8 × 1.8)*
Main machinery: 2 diesels; 2,800 hp(m) *(2.06 MW)*; 2 shafts
Speed, knots: 26. **Range, n miles:** 800 at 18 kt
Complement: 9
Guns: 2 — 12.7 mm MGs.
Radars: Surface search: Furuno; I-band.

Comment: Delivered in late 2000.

AKWAYAFE   *7/2001, Adolfo Ortigueira Gil* / 0524974

AMPHIBIOUS FORCES

2 YUNNAN CLASS (TYPE 067) (LCU)

DEBUNDSHA   KOMBO A JANEA

Displacement, tons: 135 full load
Dimensions, feet (metres): 93.8 × 17.7 × 4.9 *(28.6 × 5.4 × 1.5)*
Main machinery: 2 diesels; 600 hp(m) *(441 kW)*; 2 shafts
Speed, knots: 12. **Range, n miles:** 500 at 10 kt
Complement: 22 (2 officers)
Military lift: 46 tons
Guns: 2 — 14.5 mm (1 twin) MGs.
Radars: Surface search: Fuji; I-band.

Comment: Acquired from China in 2002.

YUNNAN CLASS   *8/2000*, Hachiro Nakai* / 0103675

Canada

Country Overview

Canada is the world's second-largest country. The British monarch, represented by a governor-general, is head of state. With an area of 3,849,652 square miles, it occupies most of northern North America and is bordered to the south by the United States and to the west by the US state of Alaska. It has a coastline of 131,647 n miles with the Pacific, Arctic and Atlantic Oceans and with Baffin Bay and the Davis Strait. Numerous coastal islands include the Arctic Archipelago to the north, Newfoundland, Cape Breton, Prince Edward, and Anticosti to the east and Vancouver Island and the Queen Charlotte Islands to the west. Hudson Bay contains Southampton Island and many smaller islands. The 2,035 n mile St Lawrence-Great Lakes navigation system enables ocean-going vessels to sail between the Atlantic Ocean and the Great Lakes via the St Lawrence Seaway (opened 1959). Ottawa is the capital while Toronto is the largest city. Major ports include Vancouver, Montreal, Halifax, Sept-Iles, Port-Cartier, Quebec City, Saint John (New Brunswick), Thunder Bay, Prince Rupert, and Hamilton. Territorial seas (12 n miles) are claimed. A 200 n mile EEZ has been claimed but the limits have only been partly defined by boundary agreements.

Headquarters Appointments

Vice Chief of Defence Staff:
  Vice Admiral R D Buck, CMM, CD
Assistant Chief of Maritime Staff:
  Commodore J R Sylvester, CD
Director General Maritime Personnel and Readiness:
  Commodore R D Murphy, CD
Director General Maritime Force Development:
  Captain P A Maddison, CD

Flag Officers

Chief of Maritime Staff:
  Vice Admiral D W Robertson, OMM, MSM, CD
Commander, Maritime Forces, Atlantic:
  Rear Admiral D G McNeil, CD
Commander, Maritime Forces, Pacific:
  Rear Admiral R Girouard, OMM, CD
Commander, Canadian Fleet Atlantic:
  Commodore P D McFadden, CD
Commander, Canadian Fleet Pacific:
  Commodore A B Donaldson, CD
Commander, Naval Reserves:
  Commodore R Blakely, CD

Diplomatic Representation

Defence Attaché, Washington:
  Captain W S Truelove, CD
Naval Adviser, London:
  Captain N H Jolin, CD
Defence Adviser, Canberra:
  Captain R R Town, MSM, CD
Defence Attaché, Tokyo:
  Captain S E King, OMM, CD
Naval Attaché, Paris:
  Commander C Gauthier, CD
Defence Attaché, Warsaw:
  Captain K M Carlé, CD
Defence Attaché, Berlin:
  Captain S D Andrews, XD
Defence Attaché, The Hague:
  Commander K A Heemskerk, CD
Defence Attaché, Bogotá:
  Commander B R Struthers, CD

Establishment

The Royal Canadian Navy (RCN) was officially established on 4 May 1910, when Royal Assent was given to the Naval Service Act. On 1 February 1968 the Canadian Forces Reorganisation Act unified the three branches of the Canadian Forces and the title 'Royal Canadian Navy' was dropped.

Personnel

2006: 11,352 (Regular), 4,041 (Reserves)

Prefix to Ships' Names

HMCS

Bases

Halifax and Esquimalt

Fleet Deployment

Atlantic
Canadian Fleet Atlantic (destroyers, frigates, AOR)
Maritime Operations Group Five (maritime warfare forces, submarines)

Pacific
Canadian Fleet Pacific (destroyers, frigates, AOR)

Maritime Operations Group Four (maritime warfare forces, submarines)

Maritime Air Components (MAC)

Commander MAC (Atlantic)-based in Halifax
Commander MAC (Pacific)-based in Esquimalt

Squadron/ Unit	Base	Aircraft	Function
MP 404	Greenwood, NS	Aurora/ Arcturus	LRMP/ Training
MP 405	Greenwood, NS	Aurora	LRMP
HT 406	Shearwater, NS	Sea King	Training
MP 407	Comox, BC	Aurora	LRMP
MP 415	Greenwood, NS	Aurora	LRMP
MH 423	Shearwater, NS	Sea King	General
MH 443	Victoria, BC	Sea King	General
HOTEF	Shearwater, NS	Sea King	Test
MPEU	Greenwood, NS	Aurora	Test

Notes

(a) Detachments from 423 and 443 meet ships' requirements in Atlantic and Pacific Fleets respectively. Sea King helicopters are now classified as General Purpose vice the former ASW designation.
(b) 413 Squadron based in Greenwood, NS, and 442 Squadron based in Comox, BC, are two maritime search and rescue squadrons under the command of 1 Canadian Air Division (CAD).
(c) Combat training support provided by commercial contract from March 2002.

Strength of the Fleet

Type	Active	Building
Submarines	4	—
Destroyers	3	—
Frigates	12	—
Mine Warfare Forces	12	—
Survey Ships	1	—
Support Ships	2	—

DELETIONS

Destroyers

2004 *Huron*

PENNANT LIST

Submarines		
876	Victoria	
877	Windsor	
878	Corner Brook	
879	Chicoutimi	

Destroyers		
280	Iroquois	
282	Athabaskan	
283	Algonquin	

Frigates		
330	Halifax	
331	Vancouver	
332	Ville de Québec	
333	Toronto	
334	Regina	
335	Calgary	
336	Montreal	
337	Fredericton	
338	Winnipeg	
339	Charlottetown	
340	St John's	
341	Ottawa	

Mine Warfare Forces		
700	Kingston	
701	Glace Bay	
702	Nanaimo	
703	Edmonton	
704	Shawinigan	
705	Whitehorse	
706	Yellowknife	
707	Goose Bay	
708	Moncton	
709	Saskatoon	
710	Brandon	
711	Summerside	

Training Ships		
55	– (bldg)	
56	– (bldg)	
57	– (bldg)	
58	– (bldg)	
59	– (bldg)	
60	– (bldg)	

Auxiliaries		
172	Quest	
509	Protecteur	
510	Preserver	
610	Sechelt	
611	Sikanni	
612	Sooke	
613	Stikine	

SUBMARINES

4 VICTORIA (UPHOLDER) CLASS (TYPE 2400) (SSK)

Name	No	Builders	Start date	Launched	Commissioned	Recommissioned
VICTORIA (ex-*Unseen*)	876 (ex-S 41)	Cammell Laird, Birkenhead	Jan 1986	14 Nov 1989	7 June 1991	2 Dec 2000
WINDSOR (ex-*Unicorn*)	877 (ex-S 43)	Cammell Laird, Birkenhead (VSEL)	Feb 1989	16 Apr 1992	25 June 1993	4 Oct 2003
CORNER BROOK (ex-*Ursula*)	878 (ex-S 42)	Cammell Laird, Birkenhead (VSEL)	Aug 1987	28 Feb 1991	8 May 1992	29 June 2003
CHICOUTIMI (ex-*Upholder*)	879 (ex-S 40)	Vickers Shipbuilding and Engineering, Barrow	Nov 1983	2 Dec 1986	9 June 1990	2 Oct 2004

Displacement, tons: 2,168 surfaced; 2,455 dived
Dimensions, feet (metres): 230.6 × 25 × 17.7
   (70.3 × 7.6 × 5.5)
Main machinery: Diesel-electric; 2 Paxman Valenta 16SZ
   diesels; 3,620 hp *(2.7 MW)* sustained; 2 GEC alternators;
   2.8 MW; 1 GEC motor; 5,400 hp *(4 MW)*; 1 shaft
Speed, knots: 12 surfaced; 20 dived; 12 snorting
Range, n miles: 8,000 at 8 kt snorting
Complement: 48 (7 officers) plus 11 spare

Torpedoes: 6—21 in *(533 mm)* bow tubes. 18 Gould Mk 48
   Mod 4; dual purpose; active/passive homing to 50 km
   (27 n miles)/38 km *(21 n miles)* at 40/55 kt; warhead
   267 kg. Air turbine pump discharge.
Countermeasures: Decoys: 2 SSE launchers.
   ESM: AR 900; intercept.
Weapons control: Lockheed Martin SFCS.
Radars: Navigation: Kelvin Hughes Type 1007; I-band.
   Furuno (portable); I-band.
Sonars: Thomson Sintra Type 2040; hull-mounted; passive
   search and intercept; medium frequency.
   BAE Type 2007; flank array; passive; low frequency.
   Thales Type 2046; towed array; passive very low
   frequency.
   Thales Type 2019; passive/active range and intercept
   (PARIS).

Programmes: First ordered 2 November 1983. Further three
   ordered on 2 January 1986. Laid up after post Cold War
   defence cuts in 1994 and acquired from the UK on 6 April
   1998. Refitted at Vickers, Barrow, for delivery from June
   2000.
Modernisation: The Canadianisation Work Period (CWP)
   includes the installation of Mk 48 torpedoes and its
   associated fire-control system and new communications
   and ESM systems. There are also plans to modernise/
   replace the Mk 48 torpedo and possibly to add a surface-
   to-surface missile capability.
Structure: Single-skinned NQ1 high tensile steel hull, tear
   dropped shape 9:1 ratio, five man lock-out chamber in
   fin. Fitted with elastomeric acoustic tiles. Diving depth,
   greater than 200 m *(650 ft)*. Fitted with Pilkington
   Optronics CK 35 search and CH 85 attack optronic
   periscopes.
Operational: Reactivation of the four submarines took
   longer than originally planned. *Victoria* arrived in
   Canada in October 2000 and, following an extended CWP
   during which repairs to exhaust valves and replacement
   of seawater valves were also made, transferred to
   Esquimault, British Columbia in August 2003. The other
   boats are based at Halifax, NS. *Windsor* was accepted in
   2002 and completed CWP in 2003. *Corner Brook* arrived
   in mid-2003 and, having completed CWP, is expected to
   become operational in mid-2006. *Chicoutimi* suffered
   a serious fire on 5 October 2004 while on passage to
   Canada. Extensive repairs are being carried out in Halifax,
   NS, and are to be completed by late 2007. Mid-life refits
   for the whole class and the possible transfer of a second
   submarine to the Pacific are under consideration.

VICTORIA   *10/2000*, **CDF** / 0104257

WINDSOR   *6/2004*, **Ships of the World** / 1042121

VICTORIA   *10/2000*, **CDF** / 0094514

FRIGATES

12 HALIFAX CLASS (FFGHM)

Name	No	Builders	Laid down	Launched	Commissioned
HALIFAX	330	Saint John SB Ltd, New Brunswick	19 Mar 1987	30 Apr 1988	29 June 1992
VANCOUVER	331	Saint John SB Ltd, New Brunswick	19 May 1988	8 July 1989	23 Aug 1993
VILLE DE QUÉBEC	332	Marine Industries Ltd, Sorel	17 Jan 1989	16 May 1990	14 July 1994
TORONTO	333	Saint John SB Ltd, New Brunswick	24 Apr 1989	18 Dec 1990	29 July 1993
REGINA	334	Marine Industries Ltd, Sorel	6 Oct 1989	25 Oct 1991	30 Sep 1994
CALGARY	335	Marine Industries Ltd, Sorel	15 June 1991	28 Aug 1992	12 May 1995
MONTREAL	336	Saint John SB Ltd, New Brunswick	8 Feb 1991	28 Feb 1992	21 July 1994
FREDERICTON	337	Saint John SB Ltd, New Brunswick	25 Apr 1992	13 Mar 1993	10 Sep 1994
WINNIPEG	338	Saint John SB Ltd, New Brunswick	19 Mar 1993	5 Dec 1993	23 June 1995
CHARLOTTETOWN	339	Saint John SB Ltd, New Brunswick	5 Dec 1993	10 July 1994	9 Sep 1995
ST JOHN'S	340	Saint John SB Ltd, New Brunswick	24 Aug 1994	12 Feb 1995	26 June 1996
OTTAWA	341	Saint John SB Ltd, New Brunswick	29 Apr 1995	22 Nov 1995	28 Sep 1996

Displacement, tons: 4,770 full load
Dimensions, feet (metres): 441.9 oa; 408.5 pp × 53.8 × 16.4; 23.3 (screws) *(134.7; 124.5 × 16.4 × 5; 7.1)*
Main machinery: CODOG; 2 GE LM 2500 gas turbines; 47,494 hp *(35.43 MW)* sustained
1 SEMT-Pielstick 20 PA6 V 280 diesel; 8,800 hp(m) *(6.48 MW)* sustained; 2 shafts; cp props
Speed, knots: 29
Range, n miles: 9,500 at 13 kt (diesel); 3,930 at 18 kt (gas)
Complement: 198 (17 officers) plus 17 (8 officers) aircrew

Missiles: SSM: 8 McDonnell Douglas Harpoon Block 1C (2 quad) launchers ❶; active radar homing to 130 km *(70 n miles)* at 0.9 Mach; warhead 227 kg.
SAM: 2 Mk 48 octuple vertical launchers ❷; semi-active radar homing to 14.6 km (ESSM 18 km) *(8 (10) n miles)* at 2.5 (ESSM 3.6) Mach; warhead 39 kg; 16 missiles.
Guns: 1 Bofors 57 mm/70 Mk 2 ❸; 220 rds/min to 17 km *(9 n miles)*; weight of shell 2.4 kg.
1 GE/GDC 20 mm Vulcan Phalanx Mk 15 Mod 1 ❹; anti-missile; 3,000 rds/min (6 barrels combined) to 1.5 km.
6—12.7 mm MGs.
Torpedoes: 4—324 mm Mk 32 Mod 9 (2 twin) tubes ❺. 24 Honeywell Mk 46 Mod 5; anti-submarine; active/passive homing to 11 km *(5.9 n miles)* at 40 kt; warhead 44 kg.
Countermeasures: Decoys: 4 Plessey Shield Mk 2 decoy launchers ❻; sextuple mountings; fires P8 chaff and P6 IR flares in distraction, decoy or centroid modes.
Nixie SLQ-25; towed acoustic decoy.
ESM: MEL/Lockheed Canews SLQ-501 ❼; radar intercept; (1—18 GHz). SRD 502; intercept. Sea Search AN/ULR 501.
ECM: MEL/Lockheed Ramses SLQ-503 ❽; jammer.
Combat data systems: UYC-501 SHINPADS action data automation with UYQ-504 and UYK-505 or 507 (336-341) processors. Links 11 and 14.
Weapons control: AHWCS for Harpoon. CDC UYS-503(V); sonobuoy processing system.
Radars: Air search: Raytheon SPS-49(V)5 ❾; C-band.
Air/surface search: Ericsson Sea Giraffe HC 150 ❿; G/H-band.
Fire control: Two Signaal SPG-503 (STIR 1.8) ⓫; K/I-band.
Navigation: Sperry Mk 340 being replaced by Kelvin Hughes 1007; I-band.
Tacan: URN 25. IFF Mk XII.
Sonars: Westinghouse SQS-510; hull-mounted; active search and attack; medium frequency.
General Dynamics SQR-501 CANTASS towed array (uses part of Martin Marietta SQR-19 TACTASS).

Helicopters: 1 CH-124A ASW ⓬.

Programmes: On 29 June 1983 Saint John Shipbuilding Ltd won the competition for the first six of a new class of patrol frigates. Combat system design and integration was subcontracted to Loral Canada (formerly Paramax, a subsidiary of Unisys). Three ships were subcontracted to Marine Industries Ltd in Lauzon and Sorel. On 18 December 1987 six additional ships of the same design were ordered from Saint John SB Ltd.
Modernisation: The Frigate Life Extension (FELEX) programme is to subsume all maintenance, sustainment and stand-alone projects planned to ensure the continued operation of the class for the duration of its life. In general, combat system enhancements are to reflect increasing emphasis on littoral operations in a joint and coalition context and the integration of the

HALIFAX *(Scale 1 : 1,200), Ian Sturton* / 0528399

HALIFAX *9/2005, Martin Mokrus* / 1151107

Cyclone helicopter. Key components are the upgrade or replacement of the combat data and communication systems, including the fitting of Link 22. Projects already underway include modifications to receive Evolved Sea Sparrow (ESSM) (completed in 339 and 340) the upgrade of Vulcan Phalanx to Block 1B (from 2003) and the fitting of Wescam 14PS-MAR optronics (from 2004). Other enhancements under consideration include upgrade of the Bofors 57 mm Mk 2 gun to Mk 3 standard and Harpoon to Block II. SPS-49, Sea Giraffe and STIR 1.8 radars are also likely to be upgraded or replaced. Following the completion of the Sirius Infra-Red Search-and-Track (IRST) trials in 2003, Sirius is being fitted throughout the class. Of the EW suite, SLQ-501 is likely to be modernised while SLQ-503 and Plessey Shield decoy system are

likely to be replaced. ASW projects include improvement of torpedo defence and the integration of active and passive sensors. All ships are undergoing maintenance programmes to achieve a common equipment and systems baseline before beginning the FELEX upgrade.
Structure: Much effort has gone into stealth technology. Gas turbine engines are raft mounted. Dresball IR suppression is fitted. Indal RAST helicopter handling system.
Operational: Problems on first of class trials included higher than designed radiated noise levels which were reported as speed associated. These have been rectified and the ships are stable and quiet in all sea conditions. *Vancouver, Regina, Calgary, Winnipeg* and *Ottawa* are Pacific based.

MONTREAL *6/2005, Michael Nitz* / 1151248

REGINA *7/2004, Michael Nitz* 1042128

VANCOUVER *9/2005, Nicola Mazumdar* / 1151247

OTTAWA *6/2002, John Chaney* / 0529806

DESTROYERS

Notes: A Single Class Surface Combatant (SCSC), to replace both the Iroquois class destroyers and the Halifax class frigates, is under consideration. The first batch of SCSC ships is expected to enter service in 2016 and are planned, as a minimum, to replace the capabilities of the Iroquois class. SCSCs are to be multipurpose vessels of about 7,500 tons and will be built to a modular design.

3 IROQUOIS CLASS (DDGHM)

Name	No	Builders	Laid down	Launched	Commissioned
IROQUOIS	280	Marine Industries Ltd, Sorel	15 Jan 1969	28 Nov 1970	29 July 1972
ATHABASKAN	282	Davie Shipbuilding, Lauzon	1 June 1969	27 Nov 1970	30 Sep 1972
ALGONQUIN	283	Davie Shipbuilding, Lauzon	1 Sep 1969	23 Apr 1971	3 Nov 1973

Displacement, tons: 5,300 full load
Dimensions, feet (metres): 398 wl; 426 oa × 50 × 15.5 keel/21.5 screws (121.4; 129.8 × 15.2 × 4.7/6.6)
Main machinery: COGOG; 2 Pratt & Whitney FT4A2 gas turbines; 50,000 hp (*37 MW*); 2 GM Allison 570-KF gas turbines; 12,700 hp (*9.5 MW*) sustained; 2 shafts; LIPS cp props
Speed, knots: 27
Range, n miles: 4,500 at 15 kt (cruise turbines)
Complement: 255 (23 officers) plus 30 (9 officers) aircrew

Missiles: SAM: 1 Martin Marietta Mk 41 VLS ❶ for 29 GDC Standard SM-2MR Block III; command/inertial guidance; semi-active radar homing to 167 km (*90 n miles*) at Mach 2.
Guns: 1 OTO Melara 3 in (*76 mm*)/62 Super Rapid ❷; 120 rds/min to 16 km (*8.7 n miles*); weight of shell 6 kg. 6−12.7 mm MGs.
1 GE/GDC 20 mm/76 6-barrelled Vulcan Phalanx Mk 15 ❸; 3,000 rds/min combined to 1.5 km.
Torpedoes: 6−324 mm Mk 32 (2 triple) tubes ❹. Honeywell Mk 46 Mod 5; anti-submarine; active/passive homing to 11 km (*5.9 n miles*) at 40 kt; warhead 44 kg.
Countermeasures: Decoys: 4 Plessey Shield Mk 2 6-tubed fixed launchers ❺. P 8 chaff or P 6 IR flares.
BAe Nulka offboard decoys in quad pack launchers.
SLQ-25 Nixie; torpedo decoy.
ESM: MEL SLQ-501 Canews ❻; radar warning.
ECM: BAe Nulka.
Combat data systems: SHINPADS, automated data handling with UYQ-504 and UYK-507 processors. Links 11, 14 and 16. GCCS-M and Marconi Matra SHF SATCOM ❼.
Weapons control: Signaal LIROD 8 ❽ optronic director. UYS-503(V) sonobuoy processor.
Radars: Air search: Signaal SPQ-502 (LW08) ❾; D-band.

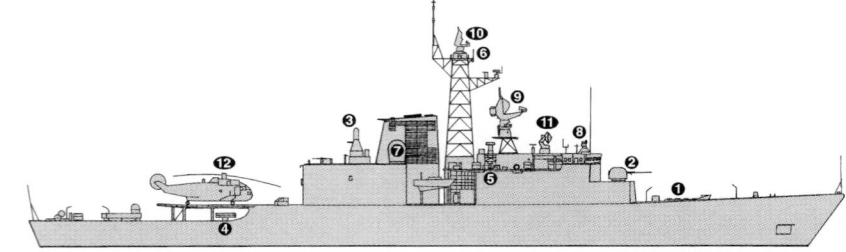

IROQUOIS *(Scale 1 : 1,200), Ian Sturton* / 0056677

Surface search: Signaal SPQ-501 (DA08) ❿; E/F-band.
Fire control: 2 Signaal SPG-501 (STIR 1.8) ⓫; I/J-band.
Navigation: 2 Raytheon Pathfinder; I-band.
Koden MD 373 (*Iroquois* only, on hangar roof); I-band.
Tacan: URN 26.
Sonars: General Dynamics SQS-510; combined VDS and hull-mounted; active search and attack. 2 sets.

Helicopters: 2 CH-124A Sea King ASW ⓬.

Modernisation: A contract for the Tribal Class Update and Modernisation Project (TRUMP) was awarded to Litton Systems Canada Limited in June 1986. The equipment reflected the changing role of the ship and replaced systems that did not meet the air defence requirement. *Algonquin* completed modernisation in October 1991, followed by *Iroquois* in May 1992 and *Athabaskan* in

August 1994. Sonar upgraded from 1998. Nulka system replaced ULQ-6 in 1999. JMCIS has been fitted vice JOTS II, with SHF SATCOM in all three ships. Wescan 14 optronics to be fitted in all. Vulcan Phalanx to be upgraded to Block 1B from 2003.
Structure: These ships are also fitted with a landing deck equipped with double hauldown and Beartrap, pre-wetting system to counter NBC conditions, enclosed citadel and bridge control of machinery. The flume type anti-roll tanks have been replaced during modernisation with a water displaced fuel system. Design weight limit has been reached.
Operational: Helicopters can carry 12.7 mm MGs and ESM/FLIR instead of ASW gear. After five years at extended notice, *Huron* was decommissioned in 2005. The remaining three ships are planned to remain in service until 2015.

ALGONQUIN *7/2004, Michael Nitz* / 1042129

ALGONQUIN *9/2005, M Mazumdar* / 1151245

SHIPBORNE AIRCRAFT

Notes: The Maritime Helicopter Project to procure up to 28 new aircraft, to replace the Sea King, was given government approval in mid-2000. The Sikorsky H-92 Superhawk, to be designated CH-148 Cyclone, was selected on 22 July 2004. Two contracts were signed on 23 November 2004. The first covers the acquisition of 28 fully integrated, certified and qualified helicopters and will include modifications to the 12 Halifax class frigates. The second is for 20 years in service support which includes construction of a training facility as well as a simulation and training suite. Delivery of the first aircraft planned for November 2008. The retirement of the CH-124 Sea Kings is to take place in 2012.

Numbers/Type: 23/5 Sikorsky CH-124A ASW Sea King/CH-124B Helicopter Towed Array Support (HELTAS) Sea King.
Operational speed: 110 kt *(203 km/h)*
Service ceiling: 10,000 ft *(3,030 m)*
Range: 380 n miles *(705 km)*
Role/Weapon systems: ASW, surface surveillance and support, convertible for carriage of six troops; deployed from shore or from three classes of ships (Halifax class FFG (1 aircraft), Iroquois class DDG (2 aircraft) and 'Protecteur' AOR (3 aircraft)); Sensors: CH-124A/B: APS-903 radar, ASN-123 mission computer, GPS, ARA-5 direction finder, APX-77A IFF, HF/VHF/UHF comms (with secure voice capability), ALQ-144 IR countermeasures (fitted for but not with). CH-124A: AQS-502 dipping sonar, ARR-52A sono receiver and ARR-1047 OTPI. CH-124B: UYS-503 sono processor, ARR-75 sono receiver, ASQ-504 MAD. Weapons: Two Mk 46 torpedoes and C6 light machine gun for both aircraft types.

CH-124A   *4/2005*, Martin Mokrus* /1151108

LAND-BASED MARITIME AIRCRAFT (FRONT LINE)

Numbers/Type: 18/2 Lockheed CP-140 Aurora/CP-140A Arcturus.
Operational speed: 405 kt *(750 km/h)*
Service ceiling: 34,000 ft *(9,930 m)*
Range: 4,000 n miles *(7,410 km)*
Role/Weapon systems: Aurora operated for long-range maritime surveillance over Atlantic, Pacific and Arctic Oceans; roles include ASW/ASV and SAR; Arcturus for unarmed Arctic patrol, maritime surveillance, SAR and training. Arcturus fitted with same equipment as Aurora but without the ASW fit. Incremental modernisation programme to upgrade avionics and communications scheduled 2000-2010. Contract for update of navigation and flight instruments awarded to CMC Electronics in late 2000 and to MacDonald Dettwiler in January 2003 for replacement of AN/APS 506 radar by Telephonics AN/APS-143(V)3. Aurora sensors: APS-506 radar, IFF, ALR-502 ESM, ECM, FLIR OR 5008 (to be replaced by L-3 Wescam MX-20), ASQ-502 MAD, OL 5004 acoustic processor. Weapons: 8 Mk 46 Mod 5 torpedoes. Arcturus sensors: APS-507 radar, IFF.

AURORA   *7/2003, Paul Jackson* / 0569161

AMPHIBIOUS FORCES

Notes: Following publication of the Defence Policy Statement by the Canadian government on 19 April 2005, acquisition of an amphibious capability is under consideration. Acting in concert with the new Joint Support Ships, amphibious assault ship(s) would be part of an emerging Canadian concept known as the Standing Contingency Task Force. The broad requirement is for a ship capable of prepositioning and deploying a force of about 800 regular troops and special forces. It is likely that offload would be enabled by landing craft, operating from a well-deck, and by helicopters. Studies to refine amphibious requirements, including development of the necessary operational skills, began in 2005. Options include the acquisition of new-build or second-hand ships or lease/loan arrangements with an allied nation.

MINE WARFARE FORCES

Notes: Development of a remote minehunting capability is in progress and current plans involve delivery of two production remote minehunting and disposal systems 2010-2013. Until 2010, the Remote Minehunting System – Technology Demonstrator (RMS-TD) is to provide an interim operational capability whilst also developing the personnel, training and the technical database to support the production systems when they are introduced into service. The RMS-TD (prime contractor MacDonald Dettwiler and Associates) successfully demonstrated in 2003 the technology for a remote-controlled, semi-submersible drone (based on the DORADO developed by International Submarine Engineering Limited) to tow a sensor suite within a variable depth towfish capable of minehunting down to 200 m. The projected operational system would be deployable from a ship (displacing more than 900 tons), transportable by air and operable from a shore position.

12 KINGSTON CLASS (MM)

Name	No	Builders	Laid down	Launched	Commissioned
KINGSTON	700	Halifax Shipyards	15 Dec 1994	12 Aug 1995	21 Sep 1996
GLACE BAY	701	Halifax Shipyards	28 Apr 1995	22 Jan 1996	26 Oct 1996
NANAIMO	702	Halifax Shipyards	11 Aug 1995	17 May 1996	10 May 1997
EDMONTON	703	Halifax Shipyards	8 Dec 1995	16 Aug 1996	21 June 1997
SHAWINIGAN	704	Halifax Shipyards	26 Apr 1996	15 Nov 1996	14 June 1997
WHITEHORSE	705	Halifax Shipyards	26 July 1996	24 Feb 1997	17 Apr 1998
YELLOWKNIFE	706	Halifax Shipyards	7 Nov 1996	5 June 1997	18 Apr 1998
GOOSE BAY	707	Halifax Shipyards	22 Feb 1997	4 Sep 1997	26 July 1998
MONCTON	708	Halifax Shipyards	31 May 1997	5 Dec 1997	12 July 1998
SASKATOON	709	Halifax Shipyards	5 Sep 1997	30 Mar 1998	21 Nov 1998
BRANDON	710	Halifax Shipyards	6 Dec 1997	3 Sep 1998	5 June 1999
SUMMERSIDE	711	Halifax Shipyards	28 Mar 1998	4 Oct 1998	18 July 1999

Displacement, tons: 962 full load
Dimensions, feet (metres): 181.4 × 37.1 × 11.2
(55.3 × 11.3 × 3.4)
Main machinery: Diesel-electric; 4 Wärtsilä UD 23V12 diesels; 4 Jeumont ANR-53-50 alternators; 7.2 MW; 2 Jeumont Cl 560L motors; 3,000 hp(m) *(2.2 MW);* 2 LIPS Z drive azimuth thrusters
Speed, knots: 15; 10 sweeping
Range, n miles: 5,000 at 8 kt
Complement: 31 (Patrol); 37 (MCM)

Guns: 1 Bofors 40 mm/60 Mk 5C. 2—12.7 mm MGs.
Countermeasures: MCM: 1 of 4 modular payloads: (a) Indal Technologies SLQ 38 deep mechanical minesweeping system; (b) MDA Ltd AN/SQS 511 Route Survey System (RSS); (c) ISE Ltd TB 25 Bottom Object Inspection Vehicle (BOIV) System; (d) Fullerton and Sherwood Containerised Diving System. The RSS and BOIV systems can be carried at the same time.
Radars: Surface search: Kelvin Hughes 6000; E/F-band.
Navigation: Kelvin Hughes; I-band.
Sonars: AN/SQS 511 towed side scan; high frequency active; minehunting.

Programmes: Contract awarded to Fenco MacLaren on 15 May 1992. Halifax Shipyards is owned by Saint John Shipbuilding. Known as Maritime Coastal Defence Vessels (MCDV) combining MCM with general patrol duties.
Structure: MacDonald Dettwiler combat systems integration, MCM systems and integrated logistics support. Modular payloads comprising two MMS, four Route Survey and one ISE Trail Blazer 25 ROV. The Z drives can be rotated through 360°. Options for diving and minehunting equipment are being considered.
Operational: Predominantly manned by reservists. Six on each coast (700, 701, 704, 707, 708 and 711 Atlantic, remainder Pacific). One ship per coast is kept at extended readiness on a rotational basis.

NANAIMO   *10/2004, Frank Findler* / 1042120

2 MCM DIVING TENDERS (YDT/YAG)

YDT 11   **GRANBY** YDT 12

Displacement, tons: 110
Dimensions, feet (metres): 99 × 20 × 8.5 *(27.3 × 6.2 × 2.6)*
Main machinery: Diesel; 228 hp (170 kW); 1 shaft
Speed, knots: 11
Complement: 13 (2 officers)
Radars: Navigation: Racal Decca; I-band.
Sonar: fitted for AN/SQQ 505(V); side scan.

Comment: Fitted with a two-compartment recompression chamber and for 100 m surface
supplied diving and underwater maintenance. Both ships are due for replacement by 2010.

GRANBY   *11/1995, CDF* / 0056682

SURVEY AND RESEARCH SHIPS

1 RESEARCH SHIP (AGORH)

Name	No	Builders	Launched	Commissioned
QUEST	AGOR 172	Burrard, Vancouver	9 July 1968	21 Aug 1969

Displacement, tons: 2,130 full load
Dimensions, feet (metres): 235 × 42 × 15.5 *(71.6 × 12.8 × 4.6)*
Main machinery: Diesel-electric; 4 Fairbanks-Morse 38D8-1/8-9 diesel generators;
4.37 MW sustained; 2 GE motors; 2 shafts; cp props
Speed, knots: 16. **Range, n miles:** 10,000 at 12 kt
Complement: 55
Helicopters: Platform only.

Comment: Built for the Naval Research Establishment of the Defence Research Board for
acoustic, hydrographic and general oceanographic work. Capable of operating in heavy ice
in the company of an icebreaker. Launched on 9 July 1968. Based at Halifax and does line
array acoustic research in the straits of the northern archipelago. Mid-life update in 1997-99
included new communications and navigation equipment and improved noise insulation.

QUEST   *6/2000, CDF* / 0104261

TRAINING SHIPS

0 + 6 ORCA CLASS (TRAINING SHIPS) (AXL)

55	56	57	58	59	60

Measurement, tons: 210 full load
Dimensions, feet (metres): 108.3 × 27.4 × 7.9 *(33.0 × 8.3 × 2.4)*
Main machinery: 2 Caterpillar 3516 diesels; 5,000 hp *(3.7 MW)*; 2 shafts
Speed, knots: 20
Range, n miles: 660 at 12 kt
Complement: 4 plus 16 trainees

Comment: Contract awarded to Victoria Shipyards, BC, on 8 November 2004 for the
construction of six (with the option for a further two) training vessels. Based on the
Australian *Seahorse Mercator* design (on which dimensions are based), delivery of
the first ship is expected in October 2006, with the sixth and final vessel to be delivered
in late 2008. All vessels are to be based at Esquimalt.

ORCA CLASS (artist's impression)   *1/2005, CDF* / 1042397

1 SAIL TRAINING SHIP (AXS)

Name	No	Builders	Commissioned
ORIOLE	YAC 3	Owens	4 June 1921

Displacement, tons: 92 full load
Dimensions, feet (metres): 102 × 19 × 9 *(31.1 × 5.8 × 2.7)*
Main machinery: 1 Cummins diesel; 165 hp *(123 kW)*; 1 shaft
Speed, knots: 8
Complement: 6 (1 officer) plus 18 trainees

Comment: Commissioned in the Navy in 1948 and based at Esquimalt. Sail area (with
spinnaker) 11,000 sq ft. Height of mainmast 94 ft *(28.7 m)*, mizzen 55.2 ft *(16.8 m)*.

ORIOLE   *12/1997, van Ginderen Collection* / 0017662

AUXILIARIES

0 + 3 JOINT SUPPORT SHIPS (AFSH/AGFH/APCR)

Displacement, tons: 28,000 full load
Dimensions, feet (metres): 656.2 × 105 × 27.9 *(200 × 32 × 8.5)*
Main machinery: To be decided. Podded propulsion under investigation
Speed, knots: 21. **Range, n miles:** 10,800 at 15 kt
Complement: 165 + 210
Cargo capacity: 8,000 tons fuel; 500 tons aviation fuel; 300 tons ammunition and 230 tons
of drinking water; combination of up to 120 × 20 ft containers and vehicles/equipment
occupying 2,500 lane-metres (1,500 covered) of cargo space
Guns: Self-defence system.
Countermeasures: Likely to include active and passive missile and torpedo self-defence
systems.
Radars: Air/surface search: E/F-band.
Navigation: I-band.
Helicopters: 4 medium.

Comment: Following an announcement by the Canadian government on 14 April 2004, it
is planned to acquire three multirole ships, combining afloat support, sealift and shore
support functions, to replace the current AORs between 2012 and 2015. There will be
two RAS stations on each side, a modular onboard hospital that could include up to 60
beds and facilities for a Joint Task Force Headquarters. The double-hulled vessels will be
capable of navigation in first-year ice (up to 0.7 m thick) while the hangar will be capable
of providing second-line helicopter servicing. A flexible cargo system will consist of a
container handling system, ramps, cranes and a capability to transfer cargo (single unit
loads of up to 30 tonnes) from the ship to a destination ashore using landing craft in Sea
State 1. A well-dock is unlikely to be included.

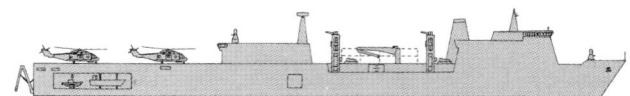

JOINT SUPPORT SHIP   *(Scale 1 : 2, 400), Ian Sturton* / 1151085

4 SECHELT CLASS (YTT/YPT/YDT)

Name	No	Builders	Commissioned
SECHELT	YDT 610	West Coast Manly	10 Nov 1990
SIKANNI	YPT 611	West Coast Manly	10 Nov 1990
SOOKE	YDT 612	West Coast Manly	10 Nov 1990
STIKINE	YPT 613	West Coast Manly	10 Nov 1990

Displacement, tons: 290 full load
Dimensions, feet (metres): 108.5 × 27.8 × 7.8 *(33.1 × 8.5 × 2.4)*
Main machinery: 2 Caterpillar 3412T diesels; 1,080 hp *(806 kW)* sustained; 2 shafts
Speed, knots: 12.5
Complement: 4 or 12 (610 and 612)
Sonar: fitted for AN/SQQ 505(V); side scan.

Comment: *Sikanni* and *Stikine* based at the Nanoose Bay Maritime Experimental and
Test Range. *Sechelt* and *Sooke* converted to diving tenders in 1997 with a 6 place
recompression chamber embarked. Diving operations supported to 80 m. *Sechelt* based
at Halifax, Novia Scotia, *Sooke* at Esquimault, British Columbia.

SOOKE (with containerised diving system)   *6/2002, CDF* / 0528415

2 PROTECTEUR CLASS (AORH)

Name	No	Builders	Laid down	Launched	Commissioned
PROTECTEUR	AOR 509	St John Dry Dock Co, NB	17 Oct 1967	18 July 1968	30 Aug 1969
PRESERVER	AOR 510	St John Dry Dock Co, NB	17 Oct 1967	29 May 1969	30 July 1970

Displacement, tons: 8,380 light; 24,700 full load
Dimensions, feet (metres): 564 × 76 × 33.3 *(171.9 × 23.2 × 10.1)*
Main machinery: 2 Babcock & Wilcox boilers; 1 GE Canada turbine; 21,000 hp *(15.7 MW)*; 1 shaft; bow thruster
Speed, knots: 21
Range, n miles: 4,100 at 20 kt; 7,500 at 11.5 kt
Complement: 365 (27 officers) including 45 aircrew
Cargo capacity: 14,590 tons fuel; 400 tons aviation fuel; 1,048 tons dry cargo; 1,250 tons ammunition; 2 cranes (15 ton lift)

Guns: 2 GE/GDC 20 mm/76 6-barrelled Vulcan Phalanx Mk 15.
6 – 12.7 mm MGs.
Countermeasures: Decoys: 6 Loral Hycor SRBOC chaff launchers.
ESM: Racal Kestrel SLQ-504; radar warning.
Combat data systems: EDO Link 11; SATCOM WSC-3(V).
Radars: Surface search: Norden SPS-502 with Mk XII IFF.
Navigation: Racal Decca 1630 and 1629; I-band.
Tacan URN 20.

Helicopters: 3 CH-124A ASW.

Comment: Four replenishment positions. Both have been used as Flagships and troop carriers. They can carry anti-submarine helicopters, military vehicles and bulk equipment for sealift purposes; also four LCVPs.

PRESERVER *4/2003, Declerck & Steeghers* / 1042119

TUGS AND TENDERS

13 COASTAL TUGS (YTB/YTL)

GLENDYNE YTB 640	LAWRENCEVILLE YTL 590	FIREBIRD YTR 561
GLENDALE YTB 641	PARKSVILLE YTL 591	FIREBRAND YTR 562
GLENEVIS YTB 642	LISTERVILLE YTL 592	TILLICUM YTM 555
GLENBROOK YTB 643	MERRICKVILLE YTL 593	
GLENSIDE YTB 644	GRANVILLE (ex-*Marysville*) YTL 594	

Comment: Glen class are 255 ton tugs built in the mid-1970s. Ville class are 70 ton tugs built in 1974. The two YTRs are firefighting craft of 130 tons. The YTM is a 140 ton tug.

GLENEVIS *6/2001, CDF* / 0126371

6 DIVING SUPPORT VESSELS (YDT)

FORTUNE	RESOLUTE	TONNERRE
ABALONE	DUNGENESS	SCULPIN

Displacement, tons: 2.2 full load
Dimensions, feet (metres): 39 × 12.5 × 2.3 *(11.9 × 3.8 × 0.7)*
Main machinery: 2 Caterpillar 3126TA diesels; 740 hp(m) *(548 kW)*; 2 WMC 357 waterjets
Speed, knots: 36. **Range, n miles:** 600 at 29 kt
Complement: 3 plus 14 divers

Comment: Built by Celtic Shipyards and delivered in early 1997. Landing craft bows for launching unmanned submersibles. Bollard pull 6,560 lb. *Fortune, Resolute* and *Tonnerre* based at Halifax, Nova Scotia, and the remainder at Esquimault, British Columbia.

DSVs *6/1997, CDF* / 0012131

COAST GUARD

Administration

Acting Commissioner Canadian Coast Guard Marine:
George Da Pont
Deputy Commissioner:
Kate Fawkes

Establishment

In January 1962, the ships owned and operated by the Department of Transport along with vessels operated by some other government agencies were amalgamated into a new organisation to be known as the Canadian Coast Guard. This reflected the increase in duties that had occurred since 1945, especially in the Arctic. Further expansion and diversification followed: notably the dedicated search and rescue facilities, vessel traffic management and pollution prevention and response. On 1 April 1995, the fleet of the Department of Fisheries and Oceans was merged with the Coast Guard under the direction of the Minister of Fisheries and Oceans. Its headquarters are in Ottawa while operations are administered from regional offices in Vancouver, British Columbia (Pacific Region); Sarnia, Ontario (Central and Arctic Region); Quebec, Quebec (Quebec Region); Dartmouth, Nova Scotia, (Maritimes Region) and St John's, Newfoundland (Newfoundland Region).

Missions

The Canadian Coast Guard carries out the following missions:

(a) Provides services for the safe, economical and efficient movement of ships in Canadian waters through the provision of aids to navigation systems, marine communication and traffic management and channel maintenance.
(b) Provides icebreaking services and vessel escort through ice in the Arctic and, in Winter, in the Gulf and River St Lawrence and the Great Lakes.
(c) Contributes to the marine component of the Search and Rescue programme and participates with the Department of National Defence in Joint Rescue Coordination Centres in Victoria, British Columbia; Trenton, Ontario and Halifax, Nova Scotia. Sponsors a Coast Guard Auxiliary and promotes pleasure craft safety.
(d) Participates (from April 2005) as a Special Operating Agency in joint patrols with the Royal Canadian Mounted Police to combat organised crime and terrorism.
(e) Carries out fisheries patrols and enforcement of fishery regulations.
(f) Provides and operates hydrographic survey, oceanographic and fisheries research vessels.

(g) Supports other departments, boards and agencies of the government through the provision of ships, aircraft and other maritime services.

Shipborne Aircraft

A total of 26 helicopters can be embarked in ships with aircraft facilities. These include six Bell 206, four Bell 212 and 16 MBB BO 105s. A long range Sikorsky S-61N is based ashore. All have Coast Guard markings.

Small Craft

In addition to the ships listed there are numerous lifeboats, surfboats, self-propelled barges and other small craft which are carried on board the larger vessels. Also excluded are shore-based work boats, floating oil spill boats, oil slick-lickers or any of the small boats which are available for use at the various Canadian Coast Guard Bases and lighthouse stations.

DELETIONS

2003	*Westfort, Parizeau,* CG 045
2004	*Navicula, Souris,* CG 141
2005	*Namao, Partridge Island, Advent, Kestrel,* CG 106, *Tobermory,* CGR 100, *Bittern, Sora, J L Hart*

HEAVY GULF ICEBREAKERS

1 GULF CLASS (TYPE 1300)

Name	Builders	Launched	Commissioned
LOUIS S ST LAURENT	Canadian Vickers Ltd, Montreal	3 Dec 1966	Oct 1969

Displacement, tons: 14,500 full load
Measurement, tons: 11,441 grt; 5,370 net
Dimensions, feet (metres): 392.7 × 80.1 × 32.2 (119.7 × 24.4 × 9.8)
Main machinery: Diesel-electric; 5 Krupp MaK 16 M 453C diesels; 39,400 hp(m) (28.96 MW); 5 Siemens alternators; 3 GE motors; 27,000 hp(m) (19.85 MW); 3 shafts; bow thruster
Speed, knots: 18. **Range, n miles:** 23,000 at 17 kt
Complement: 47 (13 officers) plus 38 scientists
Radars: Navigation: 3 Kelvin Hughes; I-band.
Helicopters: 2 BO 105 CBS.

Comment: Larger than any of the former Coast Guard icebreakers. Two 49.2 ft (15 m) landing craft embarked. Mid-life modernisation July 1988 to early 1993 included replacing main engines with a diesel-electric system, adding a more efficient *Henry Larsen* type icebreaking bow (adds 8 m to length) with an air bubbler system and improving helicopter facilities with a fixed hangar. In addition the complement was reduced. Based in the Maritimes Region at Dartmouth, NS. On 22 August 1994 became the first Canadian ship to reach the North Pole, in company with USCG *Polar Sea*.

LOUIS S ST LAURENT   6/1998, Harald Carstens / 0017665

LOUIS S ST LAURENT   6/1998, Harald Carstens / 0056691

MEDIUM GULF/RIVER ICEBREAKERS

3 R CLASS (TYPE 1200)

Name	Builders	Launched	Commissioned
PIERRE RADISSON	Burrard, Vancouver	3 June 1977	June 1978
AMUNDSEN (ex-*Vancouver*, ex-*Sir John Franklin*)	Burrard, Vancouver	10 Mar 1978	Mar 1979
DES GROSEILLIERS	Port Weller, Ontario	20 Feb 1982	Aug 1982

Displacement, tons: 6,400 standard; 8,180 (7,594, *Des Groseilliers*) full load
Measurement, tons: 5,910 gross; 1,678 net
Dimensions, feet (metres): 322 × 64 × 23.6 (98.1 × 19.5 × 7.2)
Main machinery: Diesel-electric; 6 Montreal Loco 251V-16F diesels; 17,580 hp (13.1 MW); 6 GEC generators; 11.1 MW sustained; 2 motors; 13,600 hp (10.14 MW); 2 shafts; bow thruster
Speed, knots: 16. **Range, n miles:** 15,000 at 13.5 kt
Complement: 38 (12 officers)
Radars: Navigation: Sperry; E/F- and I-band.
Helicopters: 1 Bell 212.

Comment: Based in the Quebec Region at Quebec. *Amundsen* underwent a major refit in 2003 to convert her to an Arctic research role.

AMUNDSEN   6/2003, P Dionne / 0572428

1 MODIFIED R CLASS (TYPE 1200)

Name	Builders	Launched	Commissioned
HENRY LARSEN	Versatile Pacific SY, Vancouver, BC	3 Jan 1987	29 June 1988

Displacement, tons: 5,798 light; 8,290 full load
Measurement, tons: 6,172 gross; 1,756 net
Dimensions, feet (metres): 327.3 × 64.6 × 24 (99.8 × 19.7 × 7.3)
Main machinery: Diesel-electric; 3 Wärtsilä Vasa 16V32 diesel generators; 17.13 MW/60 Hz sustained; 3 motors; 16,320 hp(m) (12 MW); 3 shafts
Speed, knots: 16
Range, n miles: 15,000 at 13.5 kt
Complement: 52 (15 officers) plus 20 spare berths
Radars: Navigation: Racal Decca Bridgemaster; I-band.
Helicopters: 1 Bell 212.

Comment: Contract date 25 May 1984, laid down 23 August 1985. Although similar in many ways to the R class she has a different hull form particularly at the bow and a very different propulsion system. Fitted with Wärtsilä air bubbling system. Based at St John's in the Newfoundland and Labrador Region. Engine room fire in 1998 put her out of commission for some time.

HENRY LARSEN   *3/1999, Canadian Coast Guard* / 0056707

MAJOR NAVAIDS TENDERS/LIGHT ICEBREAKERS

6 MARTHA L BLACK CLASS (TYPE 1100)

Name	Builders	Commissioned
MARTHA L BLACK	Versatile Pacific, Vancouver, BC	30 Apr 1986
GEORGE R PEARKES	Versatile Pacific, Vancouver, BC	17 Apr 1986
EDWARD CORNWALLIS	Marine Industries Ltd, Tracy, Quebec	14 Aug 1986
SIR WILLIAM ALEXANDER	Marine Industries Ltd, Tracy, Quebec	13 Feb 1987
SIR WILFRID LAURIER	Canadian Shipbuilding Ltd, Ontario	15 Nov 1986
ANN HARVEY	Halifax Industries Ltd, Halifax, NS	29 June 1987

Displacement, tons: 4,662 full load
Measurement, tons: 3,818 (*Martha L Black*); 3,809 (*George R Pearkes*); 3,812 (*Sir Wilfrid Laurier*); 3,727 (*Edward Cornwallis* and *Sir William Alexander*); 3,823 (*Ann Harvey*) gross
Dimensions, feet (metres): 272.2 × 53.1 × 18.9 (83 × 16.2 × 5.8)
Main machinery: Diesel-electric; 3 Bombardier/Alco 12V-251 diesels; 8,019 hp (6 MW) sustained; 3 Canadian GE generators; 6 MW; 2 Canadian GE motors; 7,040 hp (5.25 MW); 2 shafts; bow thrusters
Speed, knots: 15.5. **Range, n miles:** 6,500 at 15 kt
Complement: 25 (10 officers)
Radars: Navigation: Racal Decca Bridgemaster; I-band.
Helicopters: 1 light type, such as Bell 206L.

Comment: *Black* based in the Quebec Region at Quebec, *Cornwallis* and *Alexander* in the Maritimes Region at Dartmouth, *Ann Harvey* and *Pearkes* in the Newfoundland and Labrador Region at St Johns and *Laurier* in the Pacific Region at Victoria. The feasibility of converting *Cornwallis* to a survey ship was investigated but not taken forward.

GEORGE R PEARKES   *4/1996, van Ginderen Collection* / 0056692

SIR WILLIAM ALEXANDER   *8/1998, M B MacKay* / 0017668

1 GRIFFON CLASS (TYPE 1100)

Name	Builders	Commissioned
GRIFFON	Davie Shipbuilding, Lauzon	Dec 1970

Displacement, tons: 3,096 full load
Measurement, tons: 2,212 gross; 752 net
Dimensions, feet (metres): 233.9 × 49 × 15.5 *(71.3 × 14.9 × 4.7)*
Main machinery: Diesel-electric; 4 Fairbanks-Morse 38D8-1/8-12 diesel generators; 5.8 MW sustained; 2 motors; 3,982 hp(m) *(2.97 MW);* 2 shafts
Speed, knots: 14
Range, n miles: 5,500 at 10 kt
Complement: 25 (9 officers)
Radars: Navigation: 2 Kelvin Hughes; I-band.
Helicopters: Platform for 1 light type, such as Bell 206L.

Comment: Based in the Central and Arctic Region at Prescott, Ontario.

GRIFFON   *7/1998, van Ginderen Collection* / 0017669

HEAVY ICEBREAKER/SUPPLY TUG

1 TERRY FOX CLASS (TYPE 1200)

Name	Builders	Launched	Commissioned
TERRY FOX	Burrard Yarrow, Vancouver	1982	1983

Displacement, tons: 7,100 full load
Measurement, tons: 4,233 gross; 1,955 net
Dimensions, feet (metres): 288.7 × 58.7 × 27.2 *(88 × 17.9 × 8.3)*
Main machinery: 4 Werkspoor 8-cyl 4SA diesels; 23,200 hp(m) *(17 MW);* 2 shafts; cp props; bow and stern thrusters
Speed, knots: 16
Range, n miles: 1,920 at 15 kt
Complement: 23 (10 officers)
Radars: Navigation: 2 Racal Decca ARPA; 1 Furuno 1411; E/F- and I-bands.

Comment: Initially leased for two years from Gulf Canada Resources during the completion of *Louis S St Laurent* conversion but has now been retained. Commissioned in Coast Guard colours 1 November 1991 and purchased 1 November 1993. Based in the Maritimes Region at Dartmouth.

TERRY FOX   *7/1997, M B MacKay* / 0012133

MAJOR NAVAIDS TENDERS/LIGHT

1 J E BERNIER CLASS (TYPE 1100)

Name	Builders	Commissioned
J E BERNIER	Davie Shipbuilding, Lauzon	Aug 1967

Displacement, tons: 3,096 full load
Measurement, tons: 2,457 gross; 705 net
Dimensions, feet (metres): 218.9 × 49 × 16 *(66.7 × 14.9 × 4.9)*
Main machinery: Diesel-electric; 4 Fairbanks-Morse 4SA 8-cyl diesels; 5,600 hp *(4.12 MW);* 4 generators; 3.46 MW; 2 motors; 4,250 hp *(3.13 MW);* 2 shafts
Speed, knots: 13.5
Range, n miles: 4,000 at 11 kt
Complement: 21 (9 officers)
Radars: Navigation: 2 Kelvin Hughes; I-band.
Helicopters: 1 Bell 206L/L-1.

Comment: Based in Newfoundland and Labrador Region at St Johns. Plans to decommission the ship have been deferred and, following a refit in 2005-06, is expected to remain in service until 2008.

J E BERNIER   *7/1996, van Ginderen Collection* / 0056693

MEDIUM NAVAIDS TENDERS/ICE STRENGTHENED

2 PROVO WALLIS CLASS (TYPE 1000)

Name	Builders	Commissioned
BARTLETT	Marine Industries, Sorel	Dec 1969
PROVO WALLIS	Marine Industries, Sorel	Oct 1969

Displacement, tons: 1,620 full load *(Bartlett)*
Measurement, tons: 1,317 gross; 491 net
Dimensions, feet (metres): 189.3; 209 *(Provo Wallis)* × 42.5 × 15.4 *(57.7; 63.7 × 13 × 4.7)*
Main machinery: 2 National Gas 6-cyl diesels; 2,100 hp *(1.55 MW);* 2 shafts; LIPS cp props
Speed, knots: 12.5
Range, n miles: 3,300 at 11 kt
Complement: 24 (9 officers)
Radars: Navigation: 2 Kelvin Hughes; I-band.

Comment: *Bartlett* based in Pacific Region at Victoria, *Provo Wallis* in the Maritimes Region at Dartmouth, Nova Scotia. *Bartlett* was modernised in 1988 and *Provo Wallis* completed one year modernisation at Marystown, Newfoundland at the end of 1990. Work included lengthening the hull by 6 m, installing new equipment and improving accommodation.

BARTLETT   *5/1999, Hartmut Ehlers* / 0056695

0 + (3) TYPE 1000

Displacement, tons: 2,013 full load
Dimensions, feet (metres): 213.3 × 45.9 × 11.8 *(65 × 14 × 3.6)*
Main machinery: 2 diesels; 2 shafts
Speed, knots: 14
Range, n miles: 6,000 at 12 kt
Complement: 34

Comment: Designated as a shallow draft, multitaskable utility vessel. The long-term plan is to order three first followed by four more to replace all existing Type 1000 ships. Construction dates have not been decided.

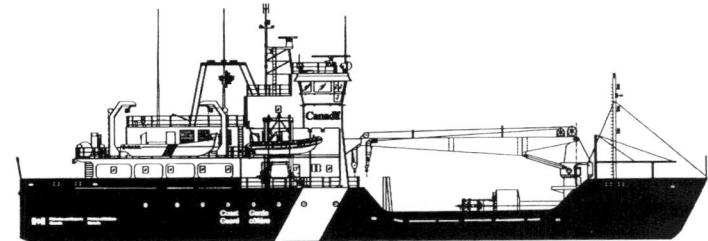

TYPE 1000   *1998, Canadian Coast Guard* / 0017670

1 TRACY CLASS (TYPE 1000)

Name	Builders	Commissioned
TRACY	Port Weller Drydocks, Ontario	17 Apr 1968

Displacement, tons: 1,300 full load
Measurement, tons: 963 gross; 290 net
Dimensions, feet (metres): 181.1 × 38 × 12.1 *(55.2 × 11.6 × 3.7)*
Main machinery: Diesel-electric; 2 Fairbanks-Morse 38D8-1/8-8 diesel generators; 1.94 MW sustained; 2 motors; 2,000 hp *(1.49 MW)*; 2 shafts
Speed, knots: 13
Range, n miles: 5,000 at 11 kt
Complement: 23 (8 officers)
Radars: Navigation: Kelvin Hughes; I-band.

Comment: Based in Quebec Region at Sorel.

TRACY *4/1999, Canadian Coast Guard* / 0056716

1 SIMCOE CLASS (TYPE 1000)

Name	Builders	Commissioned
SIMCOE	Canadian Vickers Ltd, Montreal	Oct 1962

Displacement, tons: 1,390 full load
Measurement, tons: 961 gross; 361 net
Dimensions, feet (metres): 179.5 × 38 × 12.5 *(54.7 × 11.6 × 3.8)*
Main machinery: Diesel-electric; 2 Paxman 4SA 12-cyl diesels; 3,000 hp *(2.24 MW)*; 2 motors; 2,000 hp *(1.49 MW)*; 2 shafts
Speed, knots: 13. **Range, n miles:** 5,000 at 10 kt
Complement: 27 (10 officers)
Radars: Navigation: 2 Kelvin Hughes; I-band.

Comment: Based in Central and Arctic Region at Prescott, Ontario. Modernised in 1988.

SIMCOE *4/1999, Canadian Coast Guard* / 0056712

MEDIUM NAVAIDS TENDERS/LIGHT ICEBREAKERS

2 SAMUEL RISLEY CLASS (TYPE 1050)

Name	Builders	Commissioned
SAMUEL RISLEY	Vito Construction Ltd, Delta, BC	4 July 1985
EARL GREY	Pictou Shipyards Ltd, Pictou, NS	30 May 1986

Displacement, tons: 2,935 full load
Measurement, tons: 1,988 gross *(Grey)*; 1,967 gross *(Risley)*; 642 net *(Grey)*; 649.5 net *(Risley)*
Dimensions, feet (metres): 228.7 × 44.9 × 19 *(69.7 × 13.7 × 5.8)*
Main machinery: Diesel-electric; 4 Wärtsilä 4SA 12-cyl diesels; 8,644 hp(m) *(6.4 MW)* *(Samuel Risley)*; 4 Deutz 4SA 9-cyl diesels; 8,836 hp(m) *(6.5 MW)* *(Earl Grey)*; 2 shafts; cp props
Speed, knots: 13
Range: 18,000 at 12 kt
Complement: 22
Radars: Navigation: 2 Racal Decca; I-band.

Comment: *Risley* based in the Central and Arctic Region at Pary Sound, Ontario, *Grey* in the Maritimes Region at Charlottetown, PEI.

SAMUEL RISLEY *4/1993, Canadian Coast Guard* / 0056694

SMALL NAVAIDS TENDERS

6 COVE ISLAND CLASS (TYPE 800)

Name	Builders	Commissioned
COVE ISLE	Canadian D and D, Kingston, Ontario	1980
GULL ISLE	Canadian D and D, Kingston, Ontario	1980
TSEKOA II	Allied Shipbuilders, Vancouver	1984
ILE DES BARQUES	Breton Industries, Port Hawkesbury, NS	26 Nov 1985
ILE SAINT-OURS	Breton Industries, Port Hawkesbury, NS	15 May 1986
CARIBOU ISLE	Breton Industries, Port Hawkesbury, NS	16 June 1986

Displacement, tons: 138 full load
Measurement, tons: 92 gross; 36 net
Dimensions, feet (metres): 75.5 × 19.7 × 4.4 *(23 × 6 × 1.4)*
Main machinery: 2 Detroit 8V-92 diesels; 475 hp *(354 kW)*; 2 shafts
Speed, knots: 11. **Range, n miles:** 1,800 at 11 kt
Complement: 5
Radars: Navigation: Sperry 1270; I-band.

Comment: Details given are for the last three. *Cove Isle* and *Gull Isle* are 3 m shorter in length; *Tsekoa II* is 3.7 m longer. *Cove Isle, Gull Isle* and *Caribou Isle* are based in the Central and Arctic Region at Parry Sound, Amherstburg and *Prescott* respectively. *Tsekoa II* is based in the Pacific at Victoria. *Ile Saint-Ours* is based in the Quebec Region at Sorel and *Ile des Barques*, which may be decommissioned in 2006, is laid up in the Maritime Region at Dartmouth. Can carry 20 tons of stores.

ILE SAINT-OURS *9/1994, van Ginderen Collection* / 0056696

1 VAKTA CLASS

Name	Builders	Commissioned
VAKTA	Hike Metal Products Ltd, Wheatley, Ontario	2004

Measurement, tons: 34 gross; 26 net
Dimensions, feet (metres): 53.5 × 14.8 × 9.8 *(16.3 × 4.5 × 3.0)*
Main machinery: 2 Caterpillar diesels; 980 hp *(731 kW)*; 2 shafts
Speed, knots: 21
Complement: 3

Comment: Replaced *Namao* in 2005. Provides navigational aids and SAR services on Lake Winnipeg. Based in the Central and Arctic Region at Gimli, Manitoba.

VAKTA *6/2005*, Canadian Coast Guard* / 1151242

SPECIAL RIVER NAVAIDS TENDERS

1 NAHIDIK CLASS (TYPE 700)

Name	Builders	Commissioned
NAHIDIK	Allied Shipbuilders Ltd, N Vancouver	1974

Displacement, tons: 1,125 full load
Measurement, tons: 856 gross; 392 net
Dimensions, feet (metres): 175.2 × 49.9 × 6.6 *(53.4 × 15.2 × 2)*
Main machinery: 2 Detroit diesels; 4,290 hp *(3.2 MW)*; 2 shafts
Speed, knots: 14
Range, n miles: 5,000 at 10 kt
Complement: 15

Comment: Based in Central and Arctic Region at Hay River, North West Territories.

NAHIDIK   *6/2004, Canadian Coast Guard* / 1042126

1 DUMIT CLASS (TYPE 700)

Name	Builders	Commissioned
DUMIT	Allied Shipbuilders Ltd, N Vancouver	July 1979

Displacement, tons: 629 full load
Measurement, tons: 569 gross; 176 net
Dimensions, feet (metres): 160.1 × 40 × 5.2 *(48.8 × 12.2 × 1.6)*
Main machinery: 2 Caterpillar 3512TA; 2,420 hp *(1.8 MW)* sustained; 2 shafts
Speed, knots: 12
Range, n miles: 8,500 at 10 kt
Complement: 10

Comment: Similar to *Eckaloo*. Based in Central and Arctic Region at Hay River, North West Territories.

DUMIT   *7/1996, Canadian Coast Guard* / 0017671

1 TEMBAH CLASS (TYPE 700)

Name	Builders	Commissioned
TEMBAH	Allied Shipbuilders Ltd, N Vancouver	Oct 1963

Measurement, tons: 189 gross; 58 net
Dimensions, feet (metres): 123 × 25.9 × 3 *(37.5 × 7.9 × 0.9)*
Main machinery: 2 Cummins diesels; 500 hp *(373 kW)*; 2 shafts
Speed, knots: 12
Range: 1,300 at 10 kt
Complement: 9

Comment: Based in Central and Arctic Region at Hay River, North West Territories.

TEMBAH   *4/1999, Canadian Coast Guard* / 0056714

1 ECKALOO CLASS (TYPE 700)

Name	Builders	Commissioned
ECKALOO	Vancouver SY Ltd	31 Aug 1988

Displacement, tons: 534 full load
Measurement, tons: 661 gross; 213 net
Dimensions, feet (metres): 160.8 × 44 × 4 *(49 × 13.4 × 1.2)*
Main machinery: 2 Caterpillar 3512TA; 2,420 hp *(1.8 MW)* sustained; 2 shafts
Speed, knots: 13. **Range:** 2,500 at 12 kt
Complement: 10
Helicopters: Platform for 1 Bell 206L/L-1.

Comment: Replaced vessel of the same name. Similar design to *Dumit*. Based in Central and Arctic Region at Hay River, North West Territories.

ECKALOO   *9/1994, van Ginderen Collection* / 0056697

OFFSHORE MULTITASK PATROL CUTTERS

1 SIR WILFRED GRENFELL (TYPE 600)

Name	Builders	Commissioned
SIR WILFRED GRENFELL	Marystown SY, Newfoundland	1987

Displacement, tons: 3,753 full load
Measurement, tons: 2,403 gross; 664.5 net
Dimensions, feet (metres): 224.7 × 49.2 × 16.4 *(68.5 × 15 × 5)*
Main machinery: 4 Deutz 4SA (2—16-cyl, 2—9-cyl) diesels; 12,862 hp(m) *(9.46 MW)*; 2 shafts; cp props
Speed, knots: 16
Range: 11,000 at 14 kt
Complement: 20

Comment: Built on speculation in 1984-85. Modified to include an 85 tonne towing winch and additional SAR accommodation and equipment. Ice strengthened hull. Based in the Newfoundland Region and Labrador at St John's.

SIR WILFRED GRENFELL   *8/1997, M B MacKay* / 0012137

For details of the latest updates to *Jane's Fighting Ships* online and to discover the additional
information available exclusively to online subscribers please visit
jfs.janes.com

1 LEONARD J COWLEY CLASS (TYPE 600)

Name	Builders	Commissioned
LEONARD J COWLEY	Manly Shipyard, RivTow Ind, Vancouver BC	June 1985

Displacement, tons: 2,080 full load
Measurement, tons: 2,244 grt; 655 net
Dimensions, feet (metres): 236.2 × 45.9 × 16.1 *(72 × 14 × 4.9)*
Main machinery: 2 Wärtsilä Nohab F 312A diesels; 2,325 hp(m) *(1.71 MW)*; 1 shaft; bow thruster
Speed, knots: 12
Range, n miles: 12,000 at 12 kt
Complement: 20
Guns: 2−12.7 mm MGs.
Radars: Surface search: Sperry 340; E/F-band.
Navigation: Sperry ARPA; I-band.
Helicopters: Capability for 1 light.

Comment: Based in Newfoundland and Labrador Region at St John's.

LEONARD J COWLEY   *9/1996, D Maginley* / 0056698

2 CAPE ROGER CLASS (TYPE 600)

Name	Builders	Commissioned
CYGNUS	Marystown SY, Newfoundland	May 1981
CAPE ROGER	Ferguson Industries, Pictou NS	Aug 1977

Displacement, tons: 1,465 full load
Measurement, tons: 1,255 grt; 357 net
Dimensions, feet (metres): 205 × 40 × 13 *(62.5 × 12.2 × 4.1)*
Main machinery: 2 Wärtsilä Nohab F 212V diesels, 4,461 hp(m) *(3.28 MW)*; 1 shaft; bow thruster
Speed, knots: 13
Range, n miles: 10,000 at 12 kt
Complement: 19
Guns: 2−12.7 mm MGs.
Helicopters: Capability for 1 light.

Comment: *Cygnus* based in Maritimes Region at Dartmouth and *Cape Roger* in Newfoundland and Labrador Region at St John's. Half-life refits completed in 1995-97.

CYGNUS   *9/1999, Canadian Coast Guard* / 0056704

INTERMEDIATE MULTITASK PATROL CUTTERS

1 TANU CLASS (TYPE 500)

Name	Builders	Commissioned
TANU	Yarrows Ltd, Victoria BC	Sep 1968

Displacement, tons: 925 full load
Measurement, tons: 746 grt; 203 net
Dimensions, feet (metres): 164.3 × 3.2 × 15.1 *(50.1 × 9.8 × 4.6)*
Main machinery: 2 Fairbanks-Morse diesels; 2,624 hp *(1.96 MW)*; 1 shaft
Speed, knots: 11. **Range, n miles:** 4,000 at 11 kt
Complement: 18 plus 16 spare
Guns: 2−12.7 mm MGs.

Comment: Based in Pacific Region at Patricia Bay.

TANU   *7/2004, M K Mitchell* / 1042125

2 LOUISBOURG CLASS (TYPE 500)

Name	Builders	Commissioned
LOUISBOURG	Breton Industries, Port Hawkesbury, NS	1977
LOUIS M LAUZIER	Breton Industries, Port Hawkesbury, NS	1976
(ex-*Cape Harrison*)		

Displacement, tons: 460 full load
Measurement, tons: 295 grt; 65 net
Dimensions, feet (metres): 125 × 27.2 × 8.5 *(38.1 × 8.3 × 2.6)*
Main machinery: 2 MTU 12V 538TB91 diesels; 4,600 hp(m) *(3.38 MW)*; 2 shafts
Speed, knots: 13. **Range, n miles:** 6,200 at 12 kt
Complement: 14
Guns: 2−12.7 mm MGs.

Comment: Both based in the Quebec Region. *Louis M Lauzier* returned to service from charter (to Memorial University) in 2005.

LOUISBOURG   *9/1999, Canadian Coast Guard* / 0056708

1 QUÉBÉCOIS CLASS

Name	Builders	Commissioned
E P LE QUÉBÉCOIS	Les Chantiers Maritimes, Paspebiac, Quebec	1968

Measurement, tons: 186 gross; 32 net
Dimensions, feet (metres): 78.1 × 23.3 × ? *(28.3 × 7.1 × ?)*
Main machinery: 1 Caterpillar 3509 diesel; 509 hp *(380 kW)*; 1 shaft
Speed, knots: 11. **Range, n miles:** 2,800 at 9 kt
Complement: 8 (4 officers)

Comment: Based at Sept Îles, Quebec. Refitted in 1994.

E P LE QUÉBÉCOIS   *6/2002, Canadian Coast Guard* / 0529823

1 GORDON REID CLASS (TYPE 500)

Name	Builders	Commissioned
GORDON REID	Versatile Pacific, Vancouver	Oct 1990

Measurement, tons: 836 gross; 247 net
Dimensions, feet (metres): 163.9 × 36.1 × 13.1 *(49.9 × 11 × 4)*
Main machinery: 4 Deutz SBV-6M-628 diesels; 2,475 hp(m) *(1.82 MW)* sustained; 2 shafts; bow thruster; 400 hp *(294 kW)*
Speed, knots: 15. **Range, n miles:** 2,500 at 15 kt
Complement: 14 plus 8 spare

Comment: Designed for long-range patrols along the British Columbian coast out to 200 mile limit. Has a stern ramp for launching Zodiac Hurricane 733 rigid inflatables in up to Sea State 6. The Zodiac has a speed of 50 kt and is radar equipped. Based in the Pacific Region at Victoria.

GORDON REID   *6/2004, M K Mitchell* / 1042122

1 ARROW POST CLASS

Name	Builders	Commissioned
ARROW POST	Hike Metal Products, Wheatley, Ontario	1991

Measurement, tons: 228 gross; 93.1 net
Dimensions, feet (metres): 94.8 × 28.9 × ? *(28.9 × 8.8 × ?)*
Main machinery: 1 Caterpillar 3512 diesel; 711 hp *(954 kW)*; 1 shaft
Speed, knots: 12
Range, n miles: 2,800 at 11 kt
Complement: 6 (3 officers). 6 additional

Comment: Based in Pacific Region at Prince Rupert, British Columbia.

ARROW POST   *6/2004, M K Mitchell* 1/ 1042124

SMALL MULTITASK CUTTERS

4 CUTTERS (TYPE 400)

Name	Builders	Commissioned
POINT HENRY	Breton Industrial and Machinery, Pt Hawkesbury, NS	1980
ISLE ROUGE	Breton Industrial and Machinery, Pt Hawkesbury, NS	1980
POINT RACE	Breton Industrial and Machinery, Pt Hawkesbury, NS	1982
CAPE HURD	Breton Industrial and Machinery, Pt Hawkesbury, NS	1982

Displacement, tons: 97 full load
Measurement, tons: 57 gross; 14 net
Dimensions, feet (metres): 70.8 × 18 × 5.6 *(21.6 × 5.5 × 1.7)*
Main machinery: 2 MTU 8V 396 TC82 diesels; 1,740 hp(m) *(1.28 MW)* sustained; 2 shafts
Speed, knots: 20. **Range, n miles:** 950 at 12 kt
Complement: 5

Comment: Aluminium alloy hulls. *Point Henry* and *Point Race* based in Pacific Region at Prince Rupert and Campbell River respectively; *Cape Hurd* in Central and Arctic Region at Amherstburgh; *Isle Rouge* in the Quebec Region at Quebec.

POINT RACE   *6/2001, Canadian Coast Guard* / 0126356

3 POST CLASS

Name	Builders	Commissioned
ATLIN POST	Philbrooks Shipyard Ltd, Sidney, BC	1975
KITIMAT II	Philbrooks Shipyard Ltd, Sidney, BC	1974
SOOKE POST	Philbrooks Shipyard Ltd, Sidney, BC	1973

Measurement, tons: 57 gross; 15 net
Dimensions, feet (metres): 65.0 × 17.1 × ? *(19.8 × 5.2 × ?)*
Main machinery: 2 General Motors V12-71 diesels; 800 hp *(596 kW)*; 2 shafts
Speed, knots: 15. **Range, n miles:** 400 at 12 kt
Complement: 4 (3 officers)

Comment: *Atlin Post* based at Patricia Bay, British Columbia, *Kitimat II* at Prince Rupert, British Columbia and *Sooke Post* at Port Hardy, BC.

ATLIN POST   *6/2001, Canadian Coast Guard* / 0126355

1 CUMELLA CLASS

Name	Builders	Commissioned
CUMELLA	A F Theriault & Son, Meteghan, NS	1983

Measurement, tons: 80 gross; 19 net
Dimensions, feet (metres): 76.1 × 15.7 × ? *(23.2 × 4.8 × ?)*
Main machinery: 2 General Motors V6-24L diesels; 1,680 hp *(1.25 MW)*; 2 shafts
Speed, knots: 15. **Range, n miles:** 600 at 12 kt
Complement: 4 (2 officers)

Comment: Based in Maritimes Region at Grand Manaan, New Brunswick.

CUMELLA   *6/2001, Canadian Coast Guard* / 0126354

SMALL SAR CUTTERS/ICE STRENGTHENED

1 CUTTER (TYPE 200)

Name	Builders	Commissioned
HARP	Georgetown SY, PEI	12 Dec 1986

Displacement, tons: 225 full load
Measurement, tons: 179 gross; 69 net
Dimensions, feet (metres): 76.1 × 24.9 × 8.2 *(23.2 × 7.6 × 2.5)*
Main machinery: 2 Caterpillar 3408 diesels; 850 hp *(634 kW)*; 2 Kort nozzle props
Speed, knots: 10. **Range, n miles:** 500 at 10 kt
Complement: 7 plus 10 spare berths
Radars: Navigation: Sperry Mk 1270; I-band.

Comment: Ordered 26 April 1985. Ice strengthened hull. Based in Newfoundland and Labrador Region at St Anthony.

TYPE 200 CUTTER   *3/1999, Canadian Coast Guard* / 0056706

SMALL SAR UTILITY CRAFT

Notes: There are also at least 15 Inshore Rescue boats with CG numbers.

5 SAR CRAFT (TYPE 100)

Name	Builders	Commissioned
CG 119	Eastern Equipment, Montreal	1973
MALLARD	Matsumoto Shipyard, Vancouver, BC	Feb 1986
SKUA	Matsumoto Shipyard, Vancouver, BC	Mar 1986
OSPREY	Matsumoto Shipyard, Vancouver, BC	May 1986
STERNE	Matsumoto Shipyard, Vancouver, BC	Mar 1987

Measurement, tons: 15 gross
Dimensions, feet (metres): 40.8 × 13.2 × 4.2 *(12.4 × 4.1 × 1.3)*
Main machinery: 2 Mitsubishi diesels; 637 hp *(475 kW)*; 2 shafts
Speed, knots: 26. **Range, n miles:** 200 at 16 kt
Complement: 3

Comment: CG 119 based in Central and Arctic Region at Prescott; *Sterne* (laid up) is based in Quebec Region at Quebec and *Mallard*, *Skua* and *Osprey* in the Pacific Region at Powell River, Ganges and Kitsilano respectively. CG 119 is structurally different to and slower than the remainder.

CG 119   *1990, van Ginderen Collection* / 0505968

MULTITASK LIFEBOATS

10 LIFEBOATS (TYPE 300A)

Name	Builders	Commissioned
BICKERTON	Halmatic, Havant	Aug 1989
SPINDRIFT	Georgetown, PEI	Oct 1993
SPRAY	Industrie Raymond, Quebec	Sep 1994
COURTENAY BAY (ex-*Spume*)	Industrie Raymond, Quebec	Oct 1994
W JACKMAN (ex-*Cap Aux Meules*)	Industrie Raymond, Quebec	Sep 1995
W G GEORGE	Industrie Raymond, Quebec	Sep 1995
CAP AUX MEULES	Hike Metal Products Ltd, Ontario	Oct 1996
CLARK'S HARBOUR	Hike Metal Products Ltd, Ontario	Sep 1996
SAMBRO	Hike Metal Products Ltd, Ontario	Jan 1997
WESTPORT	Hike Metal Products Ltd, Ontario	May 1997

Measurement, tons: 34 gross
Dimensions, feet (metres): 52 × 17.5 × 4.6 *(15.9 × 5.3 × 1.5)*
Main machinery: 2 Caterpillar 3408BTA diesels; 1,070 hp *(786 kW)* sustained; 2 shafts
Speed, knots: 16—20
Range: 100—150 m
Complement: 5
Radars: Navigation: Furuno; I-band.

Comment: Seven based in Martimes Region, two in Newfoundland and Labrador Region, one in Quebec Region. *Bickerton* has GRP hull, remainder aluminium.

CLARKS HARBOUR   *8/1996, Kathy Johnson* / 0056702

31 LIFEBOATS (TYPE 300B)

Name	Builders	Commissioned
THUNDER CAPE	Metalcraft Marine, Kingston	Aug 2000
CAPE SUTIL	Metalcraft Marine, Kingston	Dec 1998
CAPE CALVERT	Metalcraft Marine, Kingston	Aug 1999
CAPE ST JAMES	Metalcraft Marine, Kingston	Nov 1999
CAPE MERCY	Metalcraft Marine, Kingston	Dec 2000
CAPE LAMBTON	Metalcraft Marine, Kingston	July 2001
CAPE STORM	Metalcraft Marine, Kingston	Nov 2002
CAPE FOX	Victoria Shipyard Co Ltd, Victoria, BC	May 2003
CAPE NORMAN	Victoria Shipyard Co Ltd, Victoria, BC	May 2003
CAP DE RABAST	Victoria Shipyard Co Ltd, Victoria, BC	Aug 2003
CAP ROZIER	Victoria Shipyard Co Ltd, Victoria, BC	Aug 2003
CAPE MUDGE	Victoria Shipyard Co Ltd, Victoria, BC	Nov 2003
CAPE FAREWELL	Victoria Shipyard Co Ltd, Victoria, BC	Nov 2003
CAPE COCKBURN	Victoria Shipyard Co Ltd, Victoria, BC	Jan 2004
CAPE SPRY	Victoria Shipyard Co Ltd, Victoria, BC	Apr 2004
CAP NORD	Victoria Shipyard Co Ltd, Victoria, BC	Apr 2004
CAP BRETON	Victoria Shipyard Co Ltd, Victoria, BC	Apr 2004
CAPE MCKAY	Victoria Shipyard Co Ltd, Victoria, BC	June 2004
CAPE CHAILLON	Victoria Shipyard Co Ltd, Victoria, BC	Oct 2004
CAPE PROVIDENCE	Victoria Shipyard Co Ltd, Victoria, BC	Oct 2004
CAPE COMMODORE	Victoria Shipyard Co Ltd, Victoria, BC	Oct 2004
CAPE ANN	Victoria Shipyard Co Ltd, Victoria, BC	Nov 2004
CAPE CAUTION	Victoria Shipyard Co Ltd, Victoria, BC	Dec 2004
CAPE DISCOVERY	Victoria Shipyard Co Ltd, Victoria, BC	Jan 2005
CAPE HEARNE	Victoria Shipyard Co Ltd, Victoria, BC	Feb 2005
CAPE DUNDAS	Victoria Shipyard Co Ltd, Victoria, BC	Mar 2005
CAP TOURMENTE	Victoria Shipyard Co Ltd, Victoria, BC	Apr 2005
CAP D'ESPOIR	Victoria Shipyard Co Ltd, Victoria, BC	June 2005
CAP PERCÉ	Victoria Shipyard Co Ltd, Victoria, BC	Aug 2005
CAPE EDENSAW	Victoria Shipyard Co Ltd, Victoria, BC	Sep 2005
CAPE KUPER	Victoria Shipyard Co Ltd, Victoria, BC	Oct 2005

Measurement, tons: 33.8 gross
Dimensions, feet (metres): 47.9 × 14 × 4.5 *(14.6 × 4.27 × 1.37)*
Main machinery: 2 Caterpillar 3196 diesels; 905 hp *(675 kW)* sustained; 2 shafts
Speed, knots: 22—25. **Range, n miles:** 200 n miles
Complement: 4
Radars: Navigation: Furuno 1942; I-band.

Comment: Multitask medium endurance lifeboat.

THUNDER CAPE   *2000, Canadian Coast Guard* / 0104265

HOVERCRAFT

1 API-88/200 TYPE

Name	Builders	Commissioned
WABAN-AKI	Westland Aerospace	15 July 1987

Displacement, tons: 47.6 light
Dimensions, feet (metres): 80.4 × 36.7 × 19.6 *(24.5 × 11.2 × 6.6)* (height on cushion)
Main machinery: 4 Deutz diesels; 2,394 hp(m) *(1.76 MW)*
Speed, knots: 50; 35 cruising
Complement: 3
Cargo capacity: 12 tons

Comment: *Waban-Aki* is based at Trois Rivières and capable of year round operation as a Navaid Tender for flood control operations in the St Lawrence. Fitted with a hydraulic crane. The name means People of the Dawn.

WABAN-AKI   *4/1999, Canadian Coast Guard* / 0056717

2 AP. I-88/400 TYPE

SIPU MUIN   SIYAY

Displacement, tons: 69 full load
Dimensions, feet (metres): 93.5 × 39.4 *(28.5 × 12)*
Main machinery: 4 Caterpillar 3412 TTA diesels; 3,650 hp(m) *(2.68 MW)* sustained
Speed, knots: 50; 35 cruising
Complement: 4
Cargo capacity: 22.6 tons

Comment: Contract awarded to GKN Westland in May 1996. Built at Hike Metal Products, Wheatley, Ontario and completed in August and December 1998 respectively. Well-deck size 8.2 × 4.6 m. There is a 5,000 kg load crane. *Sipu Muin* is based at Trois Rivières and the second at Sea Island, BC.

SIPU MUIN   *5/1998, Canada Coast Guard* / 0017672

1 AP.I-88/100S TYPE (TRAINING SHIPS) (AXL)

PENAC (ex-*Liv Viking*)

Displacement, tons: 45.5 full load
Dimensions, feet (metres): 80.4 × 39.0 *(24.5 × 11.9)*
Main machinery: 2 Deutz BF 12L513 diesels; 1,050 hp(m) *(785 kW)*. 2 MTU 12V 183TB32 diesels; 1,640 hp(m) *(1.25 MW)* sustained
Speed, knots: 50; 35 cruising
Complement: 7
Cargo capacity: 5.3 tons

Comment: Built by Hoverworks Ltd, Isle of Wight, UK in 1984. Procured by Canadian Coast Guard in 2004. Based in Vancouver, BC.

PENAC   *6/2004, Canadian Coast Guard* / 1042123

ROYAL CANADIAN MOUNTED POLICE

Notes: The Marine Branch of the Royal Canadian Mounted Police is responsible for enforcement of Customs, Immigration, Shipping and Drug regulations as well as for standard policing duties in areas that are difficult to access by land. Of five 17—19 m catamaran-design patrol craft, *Inkster, Nadon, Higgitt* and *Lindsay* are stationed on the West Coast while *Simmonds* is based in Newfoundland on the East Coast. In addition there are some 377 smaller craft for use on inland waterways.

FISHERY RESEARCH SHIPS

10 RESEARCH SHIPS

Name	Commissioned	Based	Measurement, tons
ALFRED NEEDLER	Aug 1982	Dartmouth, NS	925 grt
WILFRED TEMPLEMAN	Mar 1982	St John's, NL	925 grt
W E RICKER (ex-*Callistratus*)	Dec 1978	Nanaimo, BC	1,040 grt
TELEOST	1996	St John's, NL	
PANDALUS III	1986	St Andrew's, NB	13 grt
SHAMOOK	1975	St John's, NL	187 grt
OPILIO	1989	Shippagan, NB	74 grt
SHARK	1971	Burlington, ON	19 grt
CALANUS II	1991	Rimouski, QC	160 grt
NEOCALIGUS	2001	Nanaimbo, QC	98 grt

Comment: First four are classified as Offshore Fishery Research vessels, remainder as Inshore Fishery Research vessels. *Shark* is to be decommissioned in 2006.

TELEOST   *4/1999, Canadian Coast Guard* / 0056713

SURVEY AND RESEARCH SHIPS

7 RESEARCH SHIPS

Name	Commissioned	Based	Displacement, tons
MATTHEW	1990	Dartmouth, NS	950
F C G SMITH	1986	Quebec, QC	300
HUDSON	1963	Dartmouth, NS	3,740
JOHN P TULLY	1985	Patricia Bay, BC	1,800
VECTOR	1967	Patricia Bay, BC	520
LIMNOS	1968	Burlington, ON	–
FREDERICK G CREED	1988	Rimouski, QC	81

Comment: The one ship in the Central and Arctic Region is employed on Limnology, and the remainder on Oceanographic Research. *Hudson* and *Tully* are classified as Offshore vessels, and the remainder are Coastal. *Smith* and *Creed* are multihulled. *R B Young* is in reserve, and *Tully* and *Vector* only operate for part of the year.

F C G SMITH   *7/1998, C D Maginley* / 0017673

Cape Verde

Country Overview

A former Portuguese colony, the Republic of Cape Verde became independent in 1975. Situated in the Atlantic Ocean some 335 n miles due west of the western point of Africa, it consists of ten islands and five islets, which are divided into the northerly windward (Barlavento) and southerly leeward (Sotavento) groups. The windward group includes Santo Antâo, São Vicente, Santa Luzia, São Nicolau, Sal and Boa Vista; the leeward group includes São Tiago, Brava, Fogo and Maio. Mindelo, on São Vicente, is the principal port and economic centre while Praia on São Tiago is the capital and largest town. An archipelagic state, territorial seas (12 n miles) are claimed. A 200 n mile Exclusive Economic Zone (EEZ) has been claimed but the limits are not fully defined.

Personnel

2006: 50

Bases

Praia, main naval base.
Porto Grande (Isle de São Vicente), naval repair yard.

Maritime Aircraft

One EMB-111 and one Dornier Do 328 are used for maritime surveillance.

PATROL FORCES

Notes: (1) One Zhuk class may still be in service but seldom goes to sea.
(2) There is a 25 m patrol boat *Tainha* P 262.

TAINHA   *6/2004* / 1044089

1 KONDOR I CLASS (COASTAL PATROL CRAFT) (PBO)

Name	No	Builders	Commissioned
VIGILANTE	P 521	Peenewerft, Wolgast	1970
(ex-*Kühlungsborn*)	(ex-BG 32, ex-GS 07)		

Displacement, tons: 377 full load
Dimensions, feet (metres): 170.3 × 23.3 × 7.2 *(51.9 × 7.1 × 2.2)*
Main machinery: 2 Russki/Kolomna Type 40DM diesels; 4,408 hp(m) *(3.24 MW)* sustained; 2 shafts; cp props
Speed, knots: 20
Range, n miles: 1,800 at 15 kt
Complement: 25 (3 officers)
Guns: 2—25 mm (twin).
Radars: Surface search: Racal Decca; I-band.

Comment: Former GDR minesweeper taken over by the German Coast Guard, and then acquired by Cape Verde in September 1998. Armament is uncertain. Reported refitted in Germany in 1999-2000.

KONDOR I (Malta colours)   *6/1997, Robert Pabst* / 0017674

1 ESPADARTE CLASS (PETERSON MK 4 TYPE)
(COASTAL PATROL CRAFT) (PB)

Name	No	Builders	Commissioned
ESPADARTE	P 151	Peterson Builders Inc	19 Aug 1993

Displacement, tons: 22 full load
Dimensions, feet (metres): 51.3 × 14.8 × 4.3 *(15.6 × 4.5 × 1.3)*
Main machinery: 2 Detroit 6V-92TA diesels; 520 hp *(388 kW)* sustained; 2 shafts
Speed, knots: 24
Range, n miles: 500 at 20 kt
Complement: 6 (2 officers)
Guns: 2—12.7 mm MGs (twin). 2—7.62 mm MGs.
Radars: Surface search: Raytheon; I-band.

Comment: Ordered from Peterson Builders Inc, under FMS programme on 25 September 1992. Option on three more not taken up. Aluminium hulls. The 12.7 mm mounting is aft with the smaller guns on the bridge roof.

Mk 4 CPC (US colours)   *11/1993, Peterson Builders* / 0081500

Cayman Islands

Country Overview

A British dependency since 1962, the island group is situated south of Cuba in the Caribbean Sea. It comprises three islands: Grand Cayman, containing the capital George Town, Little Cayman and Cayman Brac, located about 80 miles northeast of Grand Cayman. Territorial seas (12 n miles) and a Fishery Zone (200 n miles) are claimed. A governor, appointed by the British Crown, is responsible for external affairs, internal security, defence and the police. The Marine section is a division of the Royal Cayman Islands Police (RCIP) and UK Customs Drugs Task Force. Its roles are Maritime Drug Interdiction, SAR, Safety, Conservation and Fishery Protection.

Headquarters Appointments

Commander Royal Cayman Islands Police (Marine):
 Bruce D Smith

Personnel

2006: 15 (mixture of police and customs)

Bases

Grand Cayman (main), Little Cayman, Cayman Brac.

POLICE

Notes: A Concept pursuit craft, *Derry's Pride*, with twin 225 hp Johnson outboards is based at Grand Cayman together with *Intrepid*, an 'Eduardono' Colombian craft, and *Typhoon*, a 24 ft RIB. Two Boston Whalers, *Lima 1* and *Miss Molly*, are based at Little Cayman and Cayman Brac respectively.

DERRY'S PRIDE   *6/2001, RCIP* / 0121307

LIMA 1   *6/2001, RCIP* / 0121306

1 DAUNTLESS CLASS (PB)

CAYMAN PROTECTOR

Displacement, tons: 17 full load
Dimensions, feet (metres): 47.9 × 14.1 × 3.3 *(14.6 × 4.3 × 1)*
Main machinery: 2 Caterpillar 3208TA diesels; 720 hp(m) *(529 kW)* sustained; 2 shafts
Speed, knots: 26
Range, n miles: 400 at 20 kt
Complement: 11
Guns: 2—7.62 mm MGs.
Radars: Surface search: Raytheon R40; I-band.

Comment: Built by SeaArk Marine, Monticello and acquired in July 1994. Aluminium construction. Based at Grand Cayman.

CAYMAN PROTECTOR   *6/2001, RCIP* / 0121305

Chile

ARMADA DE CHILE

Country Overview

The Republic of Chile is situated in western South America. With an area of 292,135 square miles it has borders to the north with Peru and to the east with Bolivia and Argentina. Off the 2,305 n mile coastline with the Pacific Ocean lie the Chonos Archipelago, Wellington Island and the western portion of Tierra del Fuego. Chilean islands in the south Pacific include the Juan Fernández Islands, Easter Island, and Sala y Gómez. The capital, largest city and principal port is Santiago. There are further ports at Talcahuano, Tomé, Antofagasta, San Antonio, Arica, Iquique, Coquimbo, San Vicente, Puerto Montt, and Punta Arenas. Territorial seas (12 n miles) and an EEZ (200 n miles) are claimed.

Headquarters Appointments

Commander-in-Chief:
    Admiral Rodolfo Codina Diaz
Naval Operations Command:
    Vice Admiral Gerardo Covacevich Castex
Director General, Naval Personnel:
    Vice Admiral Gudelio Mondaca Oyarzún
Director General, Naval Services:
    Vice Admiral Juan Illanes Laso
Director General Maritime Territory and Merchant Marine:
    Vice Admiral Francisco Martínez Villarroel
Flag Officer, Fleet:
    Rear Admiral Cristián Gantes Young
Flag Officer, Submarines:
    Commodore Eduardo Junge Pumpin
Commander, Naval Infantry:
    Rear Admiral Arturo Fuenzalida Prado
Flag Officer, 1st Naval Zone:
    Rear Admiral Gustavo Jordán Astaburuaga
Flag Officer, 2nd Naval Zone:
    Rear Admiral Roberto Carvajal Gacitúa
Flag Officer, 3rd Naval Zone:
    Rear Admiral Edmundo Gonzales Robles
Flag Officer, 4th Naval Zone:
    Rear Admiral Percy Richter Silberstein
Flag Officer, Aviation:
    Rear Admiral Jorge Raby Brieva

Diplomatic Representation

Naval Attaché in Ottawa:
    Captain Kenneth Pugh Olavarria
Naval Attaché in Beijing:
    Captain Sergio Cabezas Ferrari
Naval Attaché in London:
    Captain Charles Le-May Vizcaya
Naval Attaché in Washington:
    Rear Admiral Roberto Carvajal Gacitúa
Naval Attaché in Paris:
    Captain Matías Purcell Echeverría

Diplomatic Representation — *continued*

Naval Attaché in Buenos Aires:
    Captain Julian Elorrieta Grimalt
Naval Attaché in Seoul:
    Captain Roggero Cozzi Paredes
Naval Attaché in Lima:
    Captain Humberto Ramirez Navarro
Naval Attaché in Madrid:
    Captain Gastón Massa Barros
Naval Attaché in Brasilia:
    Captain Luis Catalan Cruz
Naval Attaché in Quito:
    Captain Alejandro Campos Calvo
Naval Attaché in Panama:
    to be announced

Personnel

(a) 2006: 19,829 (1,988 officers)
(b) 4,500 Marines
(c) 2 years' national service (1,300)

Command Organisation

1st Naval Zone. HQ at Valparaiso. From 26° 00′ S to 34° 09′ S.
2nd Naval Zone. HQ at Talcahuano. From 34° 09′ S to 46° 00′ S.
3rd Naval Zone. HQ at Punta Arenas. From 46° 00′ S to South Pole.
4th Naval Zone. HQ at Iquique. From 18° 21′ S to 26° 00′S.
Coast Guard is fully integrated with the Navy.

Naval Air Stations and Organisation

Having won the battle to own all military aircraft flying over the sea, a fixed-wing squadron of about 20 CASA/ENAER Halcón is envisaged when finances permit.
Viña del Mar (Valparaiso); *Almirante Von Schroeders* (Punta Arenas); *Guardiamarina Zañartu* (Puerto Williams).
    Four Squadrons: VP1: EMB-111, P-3A
    HA1: NAS 332C Cougar
    VC1: EMB-110, CASA 212, PC-7
    HU1: Bell 206B, BO 105C
    VP1: Mod Skymaster

Infanteria de Marina

Organisation: 4 detachments each comprising Amphibious Warfare, Coast Defence and Local Security. Also embarked are detachments of commandos, engineering units and a logistic battalion.
1st Marine Infantry Detachment 'Patricio Lynch'. At Iquique.
2nd Marine Infantry Detachment 'Miller'. At Viña del Mar.

Infanteria de Marina — *continued*

3rd Marine Infantry Detachment 'Sargento Aldea'. At Talcahuano.
4th Marine Infantry Detachment 'Cochrane'. At Punta Arenas.
51 Commando Group. At Valparaiso.
Some embarked units, commando and engineering units and a logistics battalion.

Bases

Valparaiso. Main naval base, schools, repair yard. HQ 1st Naval Zone. Air station.
Talcahuano. Naval base, schools, major repair yard (two dry docks, three floating docks), two floating cranes. HQ 2nd Naval Zone. Submarine base.
Punta Arenas. Naval base. Dockyard with slipway having building and repair facilities. HQ 3rd Naval Zone. Air station.
Iquique. Small naval base. HQ 4th Naval Zone.
Puerto Montt. Small naval base.
Puerto Williams (Beagle Channel). Small naval base. Air station.
Dawson Island (Magellan Straits). Small naval base.

Strength of the Fleet (including Coast Guard)

Type	Active	Building
Patrol Submarines	3	1
Destroyers	1	—
Frigates	6	4
Landing Ships (Tank)	3	—
Landing Craft	2	—
Fast Attack Craft (Missile)	7	—
Large Patrol Craft	6	—
Coastal Patrol Craft	40	—
Survey Ships	3	—
Training Ships	1	—
Transports	1	—
Tankers	1	—
Tenders	5	—

DELETIONS

Destroyers

2003	*Blanco Encalada* (old)	
2006	*Capitán Prat* (old)	

Patrol Forces

2005	*Guacolda*	

PENNANT LIST

Notes: From 1997 pennant numbers have been painted on major warship hulls.

Submarines

20	Thomson
21	Simpson
22	O'Higgins
23	Carrera

Destroyers

12	Cochrane

Frigates

06	Condell
07	Lynch
14	Almirante Latorre
15	Almirante Riveros
19	Almirante Williams

Patrol Forces

30	Casma
31	Chipana
34	Angamos
36	Riquelme
37	Orella
38	Serrano
39	Uribe
73	Isaza
74	Morel
77	Cabrales

78	Sibbald
1601	Ona (CG)
1602	Yagan (CG)
1603	Alacalufe (CG)
1604	Hallef (CG)
1608	Fresia
1609	Aysen (CG)
1610	Corral (CG)
1611	Concepcion (CG)
1612	Caldera (CG)
1613	San Antonio (CG)
1614	Antofagasta (CG)
1615	Arica (CG)
1616	Coquimbo [1616] (CG)
1617	Natales (CG)
1618	Valparaiso (CG)
1619	Punta Arenas (CG)
1620	Talcahuano (CG)
1621	Quintero (CG)
1622	Chiloe (CG)
1623	Puerto Montt (CG)
1624	Iquique
1814	Diaz
1815	Bolados
1816	Salinas
1817	Tellez
1818	Bravo
1819	Campos
1820	Machado
1821	Johnson
1822	Troncoso
1823	Hudson
1901	Maule (CG)
1902	Rapel (CG)
1903	Aconcagua (CG)
1904	Lauca (CG)
1905	Isluga (CG)
1906	Loa (CG)
1907	Maullín (CG)
1908	Copiapó (CG)
1909	Cau-Cau (CG)
1910	Pudeto (CG)
1911	Robinson Crusoe (CG)

Survey Ships

46	Contre-almirante Oscar Viel Toro
60	Vidal Gormaz
63	George Slight Marshall

Training Ships

43	Esmeralda

Amphibious Forces

90	Elicura
92	Rancagua
93	Valdivia
94	Orompello
95	Chacabuco

Auxiliaries

41	Aquiles
42	Merino
53	Araucano
71	Micalvi
72	Ortiz
YFB 114	Grumete Perez
116	Pisagua

Tugs/Supply Ships

ATF 66	Galvarino
ATF 67	Lautaro
ATF 68	Leucoton

SUBMARINES

Notes: There are some Swimmer Delivery Vehicles French Havas Mk 8 in service. This is the two-man version.

1 + 1 SCORPENE CLASS (SSK)

Name	No	Builders	Laid down	Launched	Commissioned
O'HIGGINS	22	DCN Cherbourg/IZAR	18 Nov 1999	1 Nov 2003	8 Sep 2005
CARRERA	23	IZAR, Cartagena/DCN	Nov 2000	24 Nov 2004	2006

Displacement, tons: 1,668 dived
Dimensions, feet (metres): 217.8 × 20.3 × 19 (66.4 × 6.2 × 5.8)
Main machinery: Diesel electric; 4 MTU 16V 396 SE84 diesels; 2,992 hp(m) (2.2 MW); 1 Jeumont Schneider motor; 3,808 hp(m) (2.8 MW); 1 shaft
Speed, knots: 20 dived; 12 surfaced
Range, n miles: 550 at 4 kt dived; 6,500 at 8 kt surfaced
Complement: 31 (6 officers)

Torpedoes: 6—21 in (533 mm) tubes. 18 WASS Black Shark torpedoes; active/passive homing at 52 kt.
Countermeasures: ESM; Argos AR 900; intercept.
Weapons control: UDS International SUBTICS.
Radars: Navigation: Sagem; I-band.
Sonars: Hull mounted; active/passive search and attack, medium frequency.

Programmes: Project Neptune. Contract awarded to DCN and Bazán on 18 December 1997 and became effective in April 1998. The bows of both boats were built at Cherbourg and the sterns at Cartagena. First steel cut for the first of class on 22 July 1998 and final assembly by DCN began on 15 November 2002 when the stern arrived at Cherbourg. Final assembly of the second of class began on 22 March 2004 when the bow arrived at Cartagena. *O'Higgins* arrived at Valparaiso on 10 December 2005.
Structure: Equipped with Sagem APS attack periscope, an SMS optronic search periscope and SISDEF datalink terminal. Diving depth more than 300 m (984 ft). AIP is not fitted.
Operational: Sea trials of *Carrera* started on 11 November 2005. She is expected to enter service in 2006.

O'HIGGINS *9/2004, B Prézelin* / 1044092

CARRERA
11/2004, Diego Quevedo
1121118

2 THOMSON (TYPE 209) CLASS (TYPE 1300) (SSK)

Name	No	Builders	Laid down	Launched	Commissioned
THOMSON	20	Howaldtswerke	1 Nov 1980	28 Oct 1982	31 Aug 1984
SIMPSON	21	Howaldtswerke	15 Feb 1982	29 July 1983	18 Sep 1984

Displacement, tons: 1,260 surfaced; 1,390 dived
Dimensions, feet (metres): 195.2 × 20.3 × 18 (59.5 × 6.2 × 5.5)
Main machinery: Diesel-electric; 4 MTU 12V 493 AZ80 GA31L diesels; 2,400 hp(m) (1.76 MW) sustained; 4 Piller alternators; 1.7 MW; 1 Siemens motor; 4,600 hp(m) (3.38 MW) sustained; 1 shaft
Speed, knots: 11 surfaced; 21.5 dived
Range, n miles: 400 at 4 kt dived; 16 at 21.5 kt dived; 8,200 at 8 kt snorkel
Complement: 32 (5 officers)

Torpedoes: 8—21 in (533 mm) bow tubes. 14 AEG SUT Mod 1; wire-guided; active homing to 12 km (6.5 n miles)

at 35 kt; passive homing to 28 km (15 n miles) at 23 kt; warhead 250 kg.
Countermeasures: ESM: Thomson-CSF DR 2000U; radar warning.
Radars: Surface search: Thomson-CSF Calypso II; I-band.
Sonars: Atlas Elektronik CSU 3; hull-mounted; active/passive search and attack; medium frequency.

Programmes: Ordered from Howaldtswerke, Kiel in 1980.
Modernisation: *Thomson* refit completed at Talcahuano in late 1990, *Simpson* in 1991. Refit duration about 10 months each. A major programme to upgrade and extend the service life of both boats to 2025 has been initiated. The work is to include the fitting of a

UDS Subtics combat management system and a new fire-control system. Torpedo tubes are to be upgraded to enable the Whitehead Black Shark torpedoes and anti-ship missiles to be fired while platform improvements are likely to include a new engine-control system and battery set. Work on *Simpson* started in 2005 and is to complete in 2008. Modernisation of *Thomson* is to run approximately 18 months behind. The CSU 90 sonars from the 'Oberons' may have been transferred.
Structure: Fin and associated masts lengthened by 50 cm to cope with wave size off Chilean coast.

THOMSON *7/2001, Maritime Photographic* / 0121308

DESTROYERS

1 PRAT (COUNTY) CLASS (DDGHM)

Name	No
ALMIRANTE COCHRANE (ex-*Antrim*)	12

Builders	Laid down	Launched	Commissioned
Fairfield SB & Eng Co Ltd, Govan	20 Jan 1966	19 Oct 1967	14 July 1970

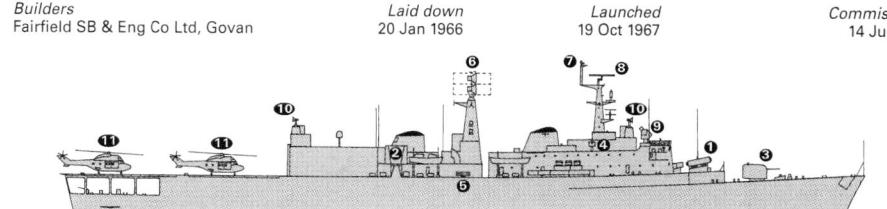

ALMIRANTE COCHRANE *(Scale 1 : 1,500), Ian Sturton* / 0529544

Displacement, tons: 6,200 standard; 6,800 full load
Dimensions, feet (metres): 520.5 × 54 × 20.5
(158.7 × 16.5 × 6.3)
Main machinery: COSAG; 2 Babcock & Wilcox boilers; 700 psi *(49.2 kg/cm²)*; 950°F *(510°C)*; 2 AEI steam turbines; 30,000 hp *(22.4 MW)*; 4 English Electric G6 gas turbines; 30,000 hp *(22.4 MW)*; 2 shafts
Speed, knots: 28
Range, n miles: 3,500 at 28 kt
Complement: 470 (36 officers)

Missiles: SSM: 4 Aerospatiale MM 38 Exocet ❶; inertial cruise; active radar homing to 42 km *(23 n miles)* at 0.9 Mach; warhead 165 kg; sea-skimmer.
2 octuple IAI/Rafael Barak I ❷ command line of sight radar or optical guidance to 10 km *(5.5 n miles)* at 2 Mach; warhead 22 kg.
Guns: 2 Vickers 4.5 in *(115 mm)* Mk 6 semi-automatic (twin) ❸; 20 rds/min to 19 km *(10.3 n miles)* anti-surface; 6 km *(3.2 n miles)* anti-aircraft; weight of shell 25 kg.
2 or 4 Oerlikon 20 mm Mk 9 ❹; 800 rds/min to 2 km.
Torpedoes: 6—324 mm Mk 32 (2 triple) tubes ❺; Honeywell Mk 46 Mod 2; active/passive homing to 11 km *(5.9 n miles)* at 40 kt; warhead 44 kg.
Countermeasures: ESM: Elisra 9003, intercept. Elta IR sensor.
ECM: Type 667; jammer.
Decoys: SLQ-25 Nixie; noisemaker.
Combat data systems: Sisdef Imagen SP 100 with datalink. SATCOM.
Weapons control: Gunnery MRS 3 system.
Radars: Air search: Marconi Type 966 ❻; A-band.
Elta LM 2228S ❼; E/F-band (for Barak).
Surface search: Marconi Type 992 Q or R ❽; E/F-band; range 55 km *(30 n miles)*.
Navigation: Decca Type 978/1006; I-band.
Fire control: Plessey Type 903 ❾; I-band (for Guns).
Two Elta EL/M-2221GM ❿; I/J/K-band (for Barak).
Sonars: Kelvin Hughes Type 162 M; hull-mounted; sideways looking classification; high-frequency.
Graseby Type 184 M; hull-mounted; active search and attack; medium range; 7 to 9 kHz.

Helicopters: 2 (1 in *Prat*) NAS-332SC Cougar ⓫.

ALMIRANTE COCHRANE *7/2001, Maritime Photographic* / 0121309

Programmes: Transferred from UK on 22 June 1984. Extensive refits carried out after transfer.
Modernisation: Converted to carry two Super Puma helicopters and completed in May 1994. Fitted with the Israeli Barak I and new communications, optronic directors and EW equipment. Imagen combat data system fitted. Indal Assist helo recovery system also fitted and magazine stowage increased.
Structure: Enlarged flight deck (617 m²) continued right aft to accommodate two large helicopters simultaneously, making them effectively flush-decked. The hangar has also been completely rebuilt (dimensions 16.9 × 11.7 m) and the foremast extended. Indal ASIST helo handling system. Chaft launchers have been removed.
Operational: *Latorre* paid off in 1998, *Blanco Encalada* in 2003 and *Prat* in 2006. *Cochrane* is to be decommissioned in 2007.

FRIGATES

2 JACOB VAN HEEMSKERCK CLASS (FFGM)

Name	No
ALMIRANTE LATORRE (ex-*Jacob van Heemskerck*)	14 (ex-F 812)
CAPITÁN PRAT (ex-*Witte de With*)	(ex-F 813)

Builders	Laid down	Launched	Commissioned
Koninklijke Maatschappij De Schelde, Flushing	21 Jan 1981	5 Nov 1983	15 Jan 1986
Koninklijke Maatschappij De Schelde, Flushing	15 Dec 1981	25 Aug 1984	17 Sep 1986

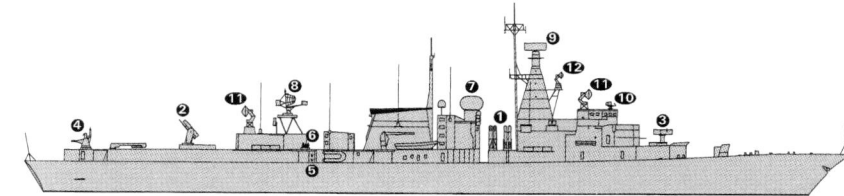

JACOB VAN HEEMSKERCK CLASS *(Scale 1 : 1,200), Ian Sturton* / 0114748

Displacement, tons: 3,750 full load
Dimensions, feet (metres): 428 × 47.9 × 14.1 (20.3 screws) *(130.5 × 14.6 × 4.3; 6.2)*
Main machinery: COGOG; 2 RR Olympus TM3B gas turbines; 50,880 hp *(37.9 MW)* sustained
2 RR Tyne RM1C gas turbines; 9,900 hp *(7.4 MW)* sustained; 2 shafts; LIPS cp props
Speed, knots: 30. **Range, n miles:** 4,700 at 16 kt on Tynes
Complement: 197 (23 officers)

Missiles: SSM: 8 McDonnell Douglas Harpoon (2 quad) launchers ❶; active radar homing to 130 km *(70 n miles)* at 0.9 Mach; warhead 227 kg.
SAM: 40 GDC Pomona Standard SM-1MR; Block IV; Mk 13 Mod 1 launcher ❷; command guidance; semi-active radar homing to 46 km *(25 n miles)* at 2 Mach.
Raytheon Sea Sparrow Mk 29 octuple launcher ❸; semi-active radar homing to 14.6 km *(8 n miles)* at 2.5 Mach; warhead 39 kg; 24 missiles.
Guns: 1 Signaal SGE-30 Goalkeeper ❹ with General Electric 30 mm 7-barrelled; 4,200 rds/min combined to 2 km.
2 Oerlikon 20 mm.
Torpedoes: 4—324 mm US Mk 32 (2 twin) tubes ❺. Honeywell Mk 46 Mod 5; anti-submarine; active/passive homing to 11 km *(5.9 n miles)* at 40 kt; warhead 44 kg.
Countermeasures: Decoys: 2 Loral Hycor Mk 36 SRBOC 6-tubed fixed quad launchers ❻; IR flares and chaff to 4 km *(2.2 n miles)*. SLQ-25 Nixie towed torpedo decoy.
ESM/ECM: Ramses; intercept and jammer.
Combat data systems: Signaal SEWACO VI action data automation; Link 11. SHF SATCOM ❼. JMCIS.
Radars: Air search: Signaal LW08 ❽; D-band; range 264 km *(145 n miles)* for 2 m² target.
Air/surface search: Signaal Smart; 3D ❾; F-band.
Surface search: Signaal Scout ❿; I-band.
Fire control: 2 Signaal STIR 240 ⓫; I/J/K-band; range 140 km *(76 n miles)* for 1 m² target.
Signaal STIR 180 ⓬; I/J/K-band.
Sonars: Westinghouse SQS-509; hull-mounted; active search and attack; medium frequency.

Programmes: Contract signed on 26 March 2004 for the acquisition of two air-defence frigates. *Latorre* transferred on 16 December 2005 and is to arrive in Chile in 2006. *Prat* is to be transferred in August 2006. 200 SM-1 missiles also reported acquired.
Operational: Command facilities for a task group commander and his staff.

ALMIRANTE LATORRE *12/2005*, Piet Cornelis* / 1153044

1 + 1 KAREL DOORMAN CLASS (FFGHM)

Name	No	Builders	Laid down	Launched	Commissioned
ALMIRANTE RIVEROS (ex-*Tjerk Hiddes*)	— (ex-F 830)	Koninklijke Maatschappij De Schelde, Flushing	28 Oct 1986	9 Dec 1989	3 Dec 1992
ALMIRANTE BLANCO ENCALADA	15 (ex-F 832)	Koninklijke Maatschappij De Schelde, Flushing	8 Feb 1989	7 Sep 1991	15 Dec 1993
(ex-*Abraham van der Hulst*)					

Displacement, tons: 3,320 full load
Dimensions, feet (metres): 401.2 oa; 374.7 wl × 47.2 × 14.1 *(122.3; 114.2 × 14.4 × 4.3)*
Flight deck, feet (metres): 72.2 × 47.2 *(22 × 14.4)*
Main machinery: CODOG; 2 RR Spey SM1C; 33,800 hp *(25.2 MW)* sustained (early ships of the class will initially only have SM1A gas generators and 30,800 hp *(23 MW)* sustained available); 2 Stork-Wärtsilä 12SW280 diesels; 9,790 hp(m) *(7.2 MW)* sustained; 2 shafts; LIPS cp props
Speed, knots: 30 (Speys); 21 (diesels)
Range, n miles: 5,000 at 18 kt
Complement: 156 (16 officers) (accommodation for 163)

Missiles: SSM: 8 McDonnell Douglas Harpoon Block 1C (2 quad) launchers ❶; active radar homing to 130 km *(70 n miles)* at 0.9 Mach; warhead 227 kg (to be confirmed).
SAM: Raytheon Sea Sparrow Mk 48 vertical launchers ❷; semi-active radar homing to 14.6 km *(8 n miles)* at 2.5 Mach; warhead 39 kg; 16 missiles. Canisters mounted on port side of hangar.
Guns: 1—3 in *(76 mm)*/62 OTO Melara compact Mk 100 ❸; 100 rds/min to 16 km *(8.6 n miles)* anti-surface; 12 km *(6.5 n miles)* anti-aircraft; weight of shell 6 kg. This is the version with an improved rate of fire.
1 Signaal SGE-30 Goalkeeper with General Electric 30 mm 7-barrelled ❹; 4,200 rds/min combined to 2 km.
2 Oerlikon 20 mm; 800 rds/min to 2 km.
Torpedoes: 4—324 mm US Mk 32 Mod 9 (2 twin) tubes (mounted inside the after superstructure) ❺; Honeywell Mk 46 Mod 5; anti-submarine; active/passive homing to 11 km *(5.9 n miles)* at 40 kt; warhead 44 kg.
Countermeasures: Decoys: 2 Loral Hycor SRBOC 6-tubed fixed Mk 36 quad launchers; IR flares and chaff to 4 km *(2.2 n miles)*.
SLQ-25 Nixie towed torpedo decoy.
ESM/ECM: Argo APECS II (includes AR 700 ESM) ❻; intercept and jammers.
Combat data systems: Signaal SEWACO VIIB action data automation; Link 11. WSC-6 twin aerials.
Weapons control: Signaal IRSCAN infra-red detector (fitted in F 829 for trials and may be retrofitted in all in due course). Signaal VESTA helo transponder.
Radars: Air/surface search: Signaal SMART ❼; 3D; F-band.
Air search: Signaal LW08 ❽; D-band.
Surface search: Signaal Scout ❾; I-band.
Navigation: Racal Decca 1226; I-band.
Fire control: 2 Signaal STIR 180 ❿; I/J/K-band; range 140 km *(76 n miles)* for 1 m² target.
Sonars: Signaal PHS-36; hull-mounted; active search and attack; medium frequency.

KAREL DOORMAN CLASS *(Scale 1 : 1,200), Ian Sturton* / 1044090

ALMIRANTE BLANCO ENCALADA *12/2005*, Piet Cornelis* / 1153045

Thomson Sintra Anaconda DSBV 61; towed array; passive low frequency. LFAS may be fitted in due course.

Helicopters: 1 NAS 332SC Cougar.

Programmes: Contract signed on 26 March 2004 for the acquisition of two frigates. *Blanco Encalada* transferred on 16 December 2005 and is to arrive in Chile in 2006. *Riveros* is to be transferred in April 2007.

Structure: The VLS SAM is similar to Canadian Halifax and Greek MEKO classes. Both ships modified to operate Cougar helicopters. This includes lengthening and partly raising the helicopter hangar and replacement of the flight-deck grid with the ASIST system which includes 35 m traverse rails. A new horizon bar has also been installed.

0 + 3 DUKE CLASS (TYPE 23) (FFGHM)

Name	No	Builders	Laid down	Launched	Commissioned
—(ex-*Norfolk*)	—(ex-F 230)	Yarrow Shipbuilders, Glasgow	14 Dec 1985	10 July 1987	1 June 1990
—(ex-*Marlborough*)	—(ex-F 233)	Swan Hunter Shipbuilder, Wallsend-on-Tyne	22 Oct 1987	21 Jan 1989	14 June 1991
—(ex-*Grafton*)	—(ex-F 80)	Yarrow Shipbuilders, Glasgow	13 May 1993	5 Nov 1994	29 May 1997

Displacement, tons: 3,500 standard; 4,200 full load
Dimensions, feet (metres): 436.2 × 52.8 × 18 (screws); 24 (sonar) *(133 × 16.1 × 5.5; 7.3)*
Main machinery: CODLAG; 2 RR Spey SM1A (ex-F 230 and F 233) or SM1C (ex-F 80) gas turbines (see *Structure*); 31,100 hp *(23.2 MW)* sustained; 4 Paxman 12CM diesels; 8,100 hp *(6 MW)*; 2 GEC motors; 4,000 hp *(3 MW)*; 2 shafts
Speed, knots: 28; 15 on diesel-electric
Range, n miles: 7,800 miles at 15 kt
Complement: 181 (13 officers)

Missiles: SSM: 8 McDonnell Douglas Harpoon (2 quad) launchers; active radar homing to 130 km *(70 n miles)* at 0.9 Mach; warhead 227 kg (84C). 4 normally carried.
SAM: British Aerospace Seawolf GWS 26 Mod 1 VLS; Command Line Of Sight (CLOS) radar/TV tracking to 6 km *(3.3 n miles)* at 2.5 Mach; warhead 14 kg; 32 canisters.
Guns: 1 Vickers 4.5 in *(114 mm)*/55 Mk 8; 25 rds/min to 22 km *(11.9 n miles)*; 27.5 km *(14.8 n miles)* Mod 1 anti-surface; weight of shell 21 kg. Mk 8 Mod 1 being progressively fitted.

2 DES/MSI DS 30B 30 mm/75; 650 rds/min to 10 km *(5.4 n miles)* anti-surface; 3 km *(1.6 n miles)* anti-aircraft; weight of shell 0.36 kg.
Torpedoes: 4 Cray Marine 324 mm fixed (2 twin) tubes. Marconi Stingray; active/passive homing to 11 km *(5.9 n miles)* at 45 kt; warhead 35 kg (shaped charge); depth to 750 m *(2,460 ft)*. Reload in 9 minutes.
Countermeasures: Decoys: Outfit DLH; 4 Sea Gnat 6-barrelled 130 mm/102 mm launchers. DLF 2/3 offboard decoys.
ESM: Racal UAT; intercept.
Combat data systems: BAeSEMA Surface Ship Command System (DNA); Link 11.
Weapons control: BAe GSA 8B/GPEOD optronic director. GWS 60 (for SSM). GWS 26 (for SAM).
Radars: Air/surface search: Plessey Type 996(I); 3D; E/F-band.
Surface search: Racal Decca Type 1008; E/F-band.
Navigation: Kelvin Hughes Type 1007; I-band.
Fire control: 2 Marconi Type 911 ⓬; I/Ku-band.
IFF: 1010/1011 or 1018/1019.
Sonars: Ferranti/Thomson Sintra Type 2050; bow-mounted; active search and attack.

Helicopters: 1 NAS 332C Cougar.

Programmes: Formerly in UK Royal Navy service, letter of intent for purchase of the three ships signed by Chilean government in December 2004 followed by formal agreement on 7 September 2005. The contract includes purchase of the three ships, pre-sale sanitisation and maintenance and a package of operator and maintainer training. BAE Systems to act as lead contractor with Fleet Support Limited to undertake overhauls in Portsmouth. Work started on ex-*Norfolk* in late 2005; she is due to arrive in Chile in September 2006. Ex-*Marlborough* and *Grafton* are to follow in April 2007 and January 2008 respectively.
Modernisation: Most of the pre-transfer work is to be focused on the ships' power plants, with both diesel engines and gas turbines being removed for scheduled maintenance. Main gearwheel changes will also be effected on ex-*Marlborough* and ex-*Grafton*.
Structure: Incorporates stealth technology to minimise acoustic, magnetic, radar and IR signatures. The design includes a 7° slope to all vertical surfaces, rounded edges, reduction of IR emissions and a hull bubble system to reduce radiated noise.

TYPE 23 CLASS *6/2005*, Michael Nitz* / 1153047

2 LEANDER CLASS (FFGHM)

Name	No	Builders	Laid down	Launched	Commissioned
ALMIRANTE CONDELL	06	Yarrow & Co, Scotstoun	5 June 1971	12 June 1972	21 Dec 1973
ALMIRANTE LYNCH	07	Yarrow & Co, Scotstoun	6 Dec 1971	6 Dec 1972	25 May 1974

Displacement, tons: 2,500 standard; 2,962 full load
Dimensions, feet (metres): 372 oa; 360 wl × 43 × 18 (screws) *(113.4; 109.7 × 13.1 × 5.5)*
Main machinery: 2 Babcock & Wilcox boilers; 550 psi *(38.7 kg/cm²)*; 850°F *(450°C)*; 2 White/English Electric turbines; 30,000 hp *(22.4 MW)*; 2 shafts
Speed, knots: 27
Range, n miles: 4,500 at 12 kt
Complement: 263 (20 officers)

Missiles: SSM: 4 Aerospatiale MM 40 Exocet ❶; inertial cruise; active radar homing to 70 km *(40 n miles)* (MM 40) at 0.9 Mach; warhead 165 kg; sea-skimmer.
SAM: Short Brothers Seacat GWS 22 quad launcher (06); optical/radar guidance to 5 km *(2.7 n miles)*; warhead 10 kg; 16 reloads.
Guns: 2 Vickers 4.5 in *(115 mm)*/45 Mk 6 (twin) semi-automatic ❸; 20 rds/min to 19 km *(10 n miles)* anti-surface; 6 km *(3.2 n miles)* anti-aircraft; weight of shell 25 kg.
4 Oerlikon 20 mm Mk 9 (2 twin) ❹; 800 rds/min to 2 km.
1 GE/GD 20 mm/76 Mk 15 Vulcan Phalanx (07) ❺; 6 barrels per mounting; 3,000 rds/min combined to 1.5 km.
Torpedoes: 6—324 mm Mk 32 (2 triple) tubes ❻. Honeywell Mk 46 Mod 2; active/passive homing to 11 km *(5.9 n miles)* at 40 kt; warhead 44 kg.

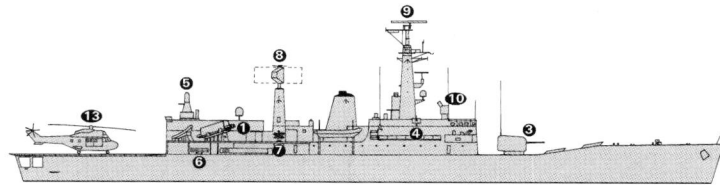

ALMIRANTE LYNCH   *(Scale 1 : 1,200), Ian Sturton* / 0534087

Countermeasures: Decoys: 2 Corvus 8-barrelled trainable chaff rocket launchers ❼; distraction or centroid patterns to 1 km. Wallop Barricade double layer chaff launchers.
ESM/ECM: Elta EW system; intercept and jammer.
Combat data systems: Sisdef Imagen SP 100 includes datalink. Link 11 receive.
Weapons control: Maiten-1/CH for gunnery. GWS 22 system for Seacat.
Radars: Air search: Marconi Type 965/966 ❽; A-band.
Surface search: Marconi Type 992 Q ❾; E/F-band.
Navigation: Kelvin Hughes Type 1006; I-band.
Fire control: Plessey Type 903 ❿; I-band (for guns).
Plessey Type 904 (06); I-band (for Seacat).

Sonars: Graseby Type 184 M/P; hull-mounted; active search and attack; medium frequency (6/9 kHz).
Graseby Type 170 B; hull-mounted; active attack; high frequency (15 kHz).
Kelvin Hughes Type 162 M; hull-mounted; sideways-looking classification; high frequency.

Helicopters: 1 Cougar ⓭.

Programmes: Ordered from Yarrow & Co Ltd, Scotstoun in the late 1960s.
Modernisation: The first major modernisations of *Lynch* (1989) and *Condell* (1993) were undertaken by ASMAR, Talcahuano. Upgrades included enlargement of the hangar and flight deck to operate a Cougar helicopter, the fitting of the Indal Assist helicopter recovery system, mounting of two twin MM 40 Exocet launchers on each side of the hangar (instead of the MM 38 aft) and moving the torpedo tubes down one deck. Other modifications include a new combat data system, improvements to the fire-control radars and the installation of Israeli EW systems. A second major modernisation of *Lynch* was completed in 2002. Upgrades included complete overhaul of propulsion and machinery systems, improvements to habitability, replacement of the Seacat system with a Phalanx 20 mm CIWS and modernisation of the communications systems.
Operational: A fourth of class paid off in 1998. Both remaining ships are to be decommissioned as the ex-UK Type 23 frigates enter service. *Zenteno* decommissioned in March 2006.

ALMIRANTE CONDELL
7/2001, Maritime Photographic
0121313

ALMIRANTE LYNCH   *7/2002, Chris Sattler* / 0534045

1 BROADSWORD CLASS (TYPE 22) (FFHM)

Name	No	Builders	Laid down	Launched	Commissioned
ALMIRANTE WILLIAMS (ex-*Sheffield*)	19 (ex-F 96)	Swan Hunter Shipbuilders, Wallsend-on-Tyne	29 Mar 1984	26 Mar 1986	26 July 1988

Displacement, tons: 4,100 standard; 4,800 full load
Dimensions, feet (metres): 480.5 × 48.5 × 21
(146.5 × 14.8 × 6.4)
Main machinery: COGOG: 2 RR Olympus TM3B gas turbines; 50,000 hp *(37.3 MW)* sustained; 2 RR Tyne RM1C gas turbines; 9,900 hp *(7.4 MW)*; 2 shafts; cp props
Speed, knots: 30; 18 on Tynes
Complement: 273 (30 officers) (accommodation for 296)

Missiles: SSM: To be announced.
SAM: 2 British Aerospace Seawolf GWS 25 Mod 3; Command Line Of Sight (CLOS) with 2 channel radar tracking to 5 km *(2.7 n miles)* at 2+ Mach; warhead 14 kg.
Guns: 1 Vickers 4.5 in *(114 mm)* 55 Mk 8; 25 rds/min to 22 km *(11.9 n miles)*; weight of shell 21 kg. 2 Oerlikon 20 mm.
Torpedoes: to be announced.
Countermeasures: to be announced.
Combat data systems: CACS 1.
Weapons control: to be announced.
Radars: Air/Surface search: Marconi Type 967/968; D/E-band.
Surface search: Racal Decca Type 2008; E/F-band.
Navigation: Kelvin Hughes Type 1008; I-band.
Fire control: 2 Marconi Type 911; I-Ku-band (for Seawolf).
Sonars: Ferranti/Thomson Sintra Type 2050; hull-mounted; active search and attack.

Helicopters: 1 NAS 332SC Cougar.

Programmes: Originally successors to the UK Leander class, these ships entered RN service in 1987 but were withdrawn, half-way through their ships' lives, as a result of the 1998 UK Defence Review. Agreement for transfer to Chile ratified by the Chilean government in April 2003.

ALMIRANTE WILLIAMS   *9/2003, B Sullivan* / 0567435

Modernisation: The ship is to undergo a modernisation programme which is to start in late 2006 at ASMAR-Talcahuano Yard. This will include installation of a new combat data system, surface-to-surface missiles, and a medium calibre gun. Further upgrades are under consideration.

Structure: Broadsword Batch 2 ships were stretched versions of Batch 1. The flight deck may be modified to allow operation of the Cougar replacement helicopter.
Operational: The ship entered service on 5 September 2003 when it replaced the former *Almirante Blanco Encalada*.

SHIPBORNE AIRCRAFT

Notes: Replacement of the four Cougar helicopters by a specialist ASW helicopter is under consideration. Ex-USN SH-60 Seahawks are reported to be the preferred option.

Numbers/Type: 4 Nurtanio (Aerospatiale) NAS 332C Cougar.
Operational speed: 151 kt *(279 km/h)*.
Service ceiling: 15,090 ft *(4,600 m)*.
Range: 335 n miles *(620 km)*.
Role/Weapon systems: ASV/ASW helicopters for DLG conversions; surface search and SAR secondary roles. Sensors: Thomson-CSF Varam radar and Thomson Sintra HS-312 dipping sonar. DR 2000 ESM. Weapons: ASW; 2 × Alliant Mk 46 Mod 2 torpedoes or depth bombs. ASV; 1 or 2 × Aerospatiale AM 39 Exocet missiles.

COUGAR   *7/2001, Maritime Photographic* / 0121314

Numbers/Type: 4 MBB BO105C.
Operational speed: 113 kt *(210 km/h)*.
Service ceiling: 9,845 ft *(3,000 m)*.
Range: 407 n miles *(754 km)*.
Role/Weapon systems: Coastal patrol helicopter for patrol, training and liaison duties; SAR as secondary role. Sensors: Bendix search radar. Weapons: Unarmed.

Numbers/Type: 4 Bell 206B JetRanger.
Operational speed: 115 kt *(213 km/h)*.
Service ceiling: 13,500 ft *(4,115 m)*.
Range: 368 n miles *(682 km)*.
Role/Weapon systems: Some tasks and training carried out by torpedo-armed liaison helicopter; emergency war role for ASW. To be replaced by Bell 412. Weapons: ASW; 1 × Mk 46 torpedo or 2 depth bombs.

JETRANGER   *7/2001, Maritime Photographic* / 0121315

Numbers/Type: 2 Bell Textron 412.
Operational speed: 122 kt *(226 km/h)*.
Service ceiling: 6,300 ft *(1,920 m)*.
Range: 500 n miles *(744 km)*.
Role/Weapon systems: Multipurpose aircraft to replace Bell 206B in training, SAR and surveillance roles. Further aircraft are likely to follow.

BO 105C   *11/2001, Freddie Philips* / 0534054

BELL 412   *4/2002, Mario R V Carniero* / 0534103

LAND-BASED MARITIME AIRCRAFT (FRONT LINE)

Notes: (1) In addition there are two EMB-110, and three Casa Aviocar 212/300 support aircraft.
(2) The Air Force has one Boeing 707 converted for AEW duties.

Numbers/Type: 6 Embraer EMB-111 Bandeirante.
Operational speed: 194 kt *(360 km/h)*.
Service ceiling: 25,500 ft *(7,770 m)*.
Range: 1,590 n miles *(2,945 km)*.
Role/Weapon systems: Designated EMB-111N for peacetime EEZ and wartime MR. Sensors: Eaton-AIL AN/APS-128 search radar, Thomson-CSF DR 2000 ESM, searchlight. Weapons: Strike; 6 × 127 mm or 28 × 70 mm rockets.

Numbers/Type: 7 Pilatus PC-7 Turbo-Trainer.
Operational speed: 270 kt *(500 km/h)*.
Service ceiling: 32,000 ft *(9,755 m)*.
Range: 1,420 n miles *(2,630 km)*.
Role/Weapon systems: Training includes simulated attacks to exercise ships' AA defences; emergency war role for strike operations. Sensors: None. Weapons: 4 × 127 mm or similar rockets and machine gun pods.

Numbers/Type: 4 Lockheed P-3A Orion.
Operational speed: 410 kt *(760 km/h)*.
Service ceiling: 28,300 ft *(8,625 m)*.
Range: 4,000 n miles *(7,410 km)*.
Role/Weapon systems: Long-range MR for surveillance and SAR. First one delivered from USA in March 1993 followed by seven more of which one has been modified for transport, two are in reserve and two are used for spares. Sensors: Three aircraft upgraded with new radar, ESM and FLIR. APS-115 radar. Weapons: Weapon systems removed but to be replaced in due course including ASMs.

ORION *6/2003, Chilean Navy* / 0569794

Numbers/Type: 8 Cessna 0-2A Skymaster.
Operational speed: 130 kt *(241 km/h)*.
Service ceiling: 5,000 ft *(1,524 m)*.
Range: 550 n miles *(1,019 km)*.
Role/Weapon systems: Maritime coastal patrol and training acquired in 1998/99. Sensors: None. Weapons: May be equipped with 4 weapons stations in due course.

SKYMASTER *6/1999, Chilean Navy* / 0056723

PATROL FORCES

Notes: It is planned to procure three new corvettes, possibly derived from the Fassmer OPV (Coast Guard) design. Such ships would be more heavily armed and would replace the Casma class fast attack craft.

3 CASMA (SAAR 4) CLASS
(FAST ATTACK CRAFT — MISSILE) (PGG)

Name	No	Builders	Commissioned
CASMA (ex-*Romah*)	LM 30	Haifa Shipyard	Mar 1974
CHIPANA (ex-*Keshet*)	LM 31	Haifa Shipyard	Oct 1973
ANGAMOS (ex-*Reshef*)	LM 34	Haifa Shipyard	Apr 1973

Displacement, tons: 415 standard; 450 full load
Dimensions, feet (metres): 190.7 × 24.9 × 9.2 *(58.1 × 7.6 × 2.8)*
Main machinery: 4 MTU 16V 396 diesels; 13,029 hp(m) *(9.58 MW)* (30 and 31); 4 MTU 16V 596 TB91 diesels; 15,000 hp(m) *(11.3 MW)* (34); 4 shafts
Speed, knots: 32
Range, n miles: 1,650 at 30 kt; 3,700 at 18 kt
Complement: 46 (8 officers)

Missiles: SSM: 4 IAI Gabriel I or II; radar or optical guidance; semi-active radar homing to 20 km *(10.8 n miles)* (I) or 36 km *(20 n miles)* (II); at 0.7 Mach; warhead 75 kg HE.
Guns: 2 OTO Melara 3 in *(76 mm)*/62 compact; 85 rds/min to 16 km *(8.7 n miles)* anti-surface; 12 km *(6.5 n miles)* anti-aircraft; weight of shell 6 kg.
2 Oerlikon 20 mm; 800 rds/min to 2 km.
2 — 12.7 mm MGs.
Countermeasures: Decoys: 4 Rafael LRCR chaff decoy launchers.
ESM: Elta Electronics MN-53; intercept.
ECM: Elta Rattler; jammer.
Radars: Surface search: Elta EL-2208C; E/F-band.
Navigation: Raytheon 20X; I-band.
Fire control: Selenia Orion RTN 10X; I/J-band.

Programmes: One transferred from Israel December 1979 and second in January 1981. Two more acquired from Israel 1 June 1997 but one (ex-*Tarshish*) was cannibalised for spares in 1998.
Modernisation: New engines fitted in the first pair in 2000. Weapons control systems have been upgraded in LM 30 and LM 34. Similar refit of LM 31 completed by 2003.
Operational: All operate in Third Naval Zone (Beagle Channel).

CASMA *9/2000, MTU* / 0094035

4 RIQUELME (TIGER) CLASS (TYPE 148)
(FAST ATTACK CRAFT — MISSILE) (PGG)

Name	No	Builders	Commissioned
RIQUELME (ex-*Wolf*)	LM 36 (ex-P 6149)	CMN Cherbourg	26 Feb 1974
ORELLA (ex-*Elster*)	LM 37 (ex-P 6154)	CMN Cherbourg	14 Nov 1974
SERRANO (ex-*Tiger*)	LM 38 (ex-P 6141)	CMN Cherbourg	30 Oct 1972
URIBE (ex-*Luchs*)	LM 39 (ex-P 6143)	CMN Cherbourg	9 Apr 1973

Displacement, tons: 234 standard; 265 full load
Dimensions, feet (metres): 154.2 × 23 × 8.9 *(47 × 7 × 2.7)*
Main machinery: 4 MTU 16V 396 diesels; 13,029 hp(m) *(9.58 MW)* sustained; 4 shafts
Speed, knots: 31
Range, n miles: 570 at 30 kt; 1,600 at 15 kt
Complement: 30 (4 officers)

Missiles: SSM: 4 Aerospatiale MM 38 Exocet (2 twin) launchers; inertial cruise; active radar homing to 42 km *(23 n miles)* at 0.9 Mach; warhead 165 kg; sea-skimmer.
Guns: 1 OTO Melara 3 in *(76 mm)*/62 compact; 85 rds/min to 16 km *(8.6 n miles)* anti-surface; 12 km *(6.5 n miles)* anti-aircraft; weight of shell 6 kg.
1 Bofors 40 mm/70; 330 rds/min to 12 km *(6.5 n miles)* anti-surface; 4 km *(2.2 n miles)* anti-aircraft; weight of shell 0.96 kg; fitted with GRP dome (1984).
2 — 12.7 mm MGs.
Mines: Laying capability.
Countermeasures: Decoys: Wolke chaff launcher.
Combat data systems: PALIS and Link 11.
Weapons control: CSEE Panda optical director. Thomson-CSF Vega PCET system, controlling missiles and guns.
Radars: Air/surface search: Thomson-CSF Triton; G-band; range 33 km *(18 n miles)* for 2 m² target.
Navigation: SMA 3 RM 20; I-band; range 73 km *(40 n miles)*.
Fire control: Thomson-CSF Castor; I/J-band.

Programmes: First pair transferred from Germany on 27 August 1997 and sailed in a transport ship on 2 September 1997. Four more transferred on 22 September 1998 and sailed 11 October. These four were all damaged during a storm in transit, and the two best were taken into service, with the other pair (*Pelikan* and *Kranich*) being used for spares. The ship names have prefixed ranks but these are not used.
Modernisation: New engines fitted in 2000. Speed reduced to 31 kt.
Structure: Similar to Combattante II craft. EW equipment was removed prior to transfer.
Operational: Operate in 4th Naval Zone (Iquique). Exocet missiles were not part of the transfer but have been acquired separately.

URIBE *7/2001, Maritime Photographic* / 0121316

SERRANO *7/2001, Maritime Photographic* / 0121317

10 GRUMETE DIAZ (DABUR) CLASS
(COASTAL PATROL CRAFT) (PB)

DIAZ 1814	**BRAVO** 1818	**JOHNSON** 1821
BOLADOS 1815	**CAMPOS** 1819	**TRONCOSO** 1822
SALINAS 1816	**MACHADO** 1820	**HUDSON** 1823
TELLEZ 1817		

Displacement, tons: 39 full load
Dimensions, feet (metres): 64.9 × 18 × 5.9 (19.8 × 5.5 × 1.8)
Main machinery: 2 Detroit 12V 71TA diesels; 840 hp (627 kW) sustained; 2 shafts
Speed, knots: 19
Range, n miles: 450 at 13 kt
Complement: 8 (2 officers)
Guns: 2 Oerlikon 20 mm.
Radars: Surface search: Racal Decca Super 101 Mk 3; I-band.

Comment: All have LPC numbers and Grumete precedes the ships' names. First six transferred from Israel and commissioned 3 January 1991. Second batch of four more transferred and commissioned 17 March 1995. A fast inflatable boat is carried on the stern. Five deployed in 4th Naval Zone (Iquique) and five in 2nd Naval Zone and operate in the Chiloé area. All underwent life extension refits in 2001-02 at Valparaiso and Puerto Montt. Service lives end by 2012.

HUDSON　　　　　　　　　*7/2001, Maritime Photographic* / 0121321

6 MICALVI CLASS (LARGE PATROL CRAFT) (PB/AEM)

Name	No	Builders	Launched	Commissioned
MICALVI	PSG 71	ASMAR, Talcahuano	12 Sep 1992	30 Mar 1993
ORTIZ	PSG 72	ASMAR, Talcahuano	23 July 1993	15 Dec 1993
ISAZA	PSG 73	ASMAR, Talcahuano	7 Jan 1994	31 May 1994
MOREL	PSG 74	ASMAR, Talcahuano	21 Apr 1994	11 Aug 1994
CABRALES	PSG 77	ASMAR, Talcahuano	4 Apr 1996	29 June 1996
SIBBALD	PSG 78	ASMAR, Talcahuano	5 June 1996	29 Aug 1996

Displacement, tons: 518 full load
Dimensions, feet (metres): 139.4 × 27.9 × 9.5 (42.5 × 8.5 × 2.9)
Main machinery: 2 Caterpillar 3512TA diesels; 2,560 hp(m) (1.88 MW) sustained; 2 shafts
Speed, knots: 15
Range, n miles: 4,200 at 12 kt
Complement: 23 (5 officers) plus 10 spare
Guns: 1 Bofors 40 mm/60. 2 Oerlikon 20 mm.
Radars: Surface search: Racal Decca; I-band.

Comment: First four built under design project Taitao. Last pair built for export but bought by the Navy. Multipurpose patrol vessels with a secondary mission of transport and servicing navigational aids. Provision for bow thruster, sonar and mine rails. Can carry 35 tons cargo in holds and 18 tons in containers. Crane lift of 2.5 tons. The ships' names all have prefixed ranks but these are not used. *Micalvi* and *Ortiz* were classified as missile tenders in 1999 but reclassified as patrol craft in 2004. *Cabrales* is also used as a survey vessel.

ORTIZ　　　　　　　　　*7/2001, Maritime Photographic* / 0534129

MICALVI　　　　　　　　　*11/2001, Freddie Philips* / 0534131

1 GUACOLDA CLASS (COASTAL PATROL CRAFT) (PB)

Name	No	Builders	Commissioned
FRESIA	1608 (ex-81)	Bazán, San Fernando	9 Dec 1965

Displacement, tons: 134 full load
Dimensions, feet (metres): 118.1 × 18.4 × 7.2 (36 × 5.6 × 2.2)
Main machinery: 2 Caterpillar diesels; 3,200 hp(m) (2.35 MW) sustained; 2 shafts
Speed, knots: 22
Range, n miles: 1,500 at 15 kt
Complement: 20
Guns: 1 Bofors 40 mm/70.
Radars: Navigation: Decca 505; I-band.

Comment: Built to West German Lürssen design from 1963 to 1966. Launched 1964. By mid-1998 had been converted to coastal patrol craft with torpedo tubes and after gun removed. Two deleted 2001-02 and a third in 2005.

FRESIA　　　　　　　　　*7/2001, Maritime Photographic* / 0121322

AMPHIBIOUS FORCES

2 MAIPO (BATRAL) CLASS (LSTH)

Name	No	Builders	Launched	Commissioned
RANCAGUA	92	ASMAR, Talcahuano	6 Mar 1982	8 Aug 1983
CHACABUCO	95 (ex-93)	ASMAR, Talcahuano	16 July 1985	15 Apr 1986

Displacement, tons: 873 standard; 1,409 full load
Dimensions, feet (metres): 260.4 × 42.7 × 8.2 (79.4 × 13 × 2.5)
Main machinery: 2 Caterpillar diesels; 4,012 hp(m) (2.95 MW) sustained; 2 shafts; cp props
Speed, knots: 16. **Range, n miles:** 3,500 at 13 kt
Complement: 43 (5 officers)
Military lift: 180 troops; 12 vehicles; 350 tons
Guns: 2 Bofors 40 mm/60. 1 Oerlikon 20 mm. 2—81 mm mortars.
Radars: Navigation: Decca 1229; I/J-band.
Helicopters: Platform for 1 Bell 206B or BO 105C.

Comment: First laid down in 1980 to standard French design with French equipment. Have 40 ton bow ramps and vehicle stowage above and below deck. Both ships underwent life-extension refits in 2002-03.

CHACABUCO　　　　　　　　　*12/2004, Globke Collection* / 1047869

2 ELICURA CLASS (LSM)

Name	No	Builders	Commissioned
ELICURA	90	Talcahuano	10 Dec 1968
OROMPELLO	94	Dade Dry Dock Co, MI	15 Sep 1964

Displacement, tons: 290 light; 750 full load
Dimensions, feet (metres): 145 × 34 × 12.8 (44.2 × 10.4 × 3.9)
Main machinery: 2 Cummins VT-17-700M diesels; 900 hp (660 kW); 2 shafts
Speed, knots: 10.5
Range, n miles: 2,900 at 9 kt
Complement: 20
Military lift: 350 tons
Guns: 3 Oerlikon 20 mm (can be carried).
Radars: Navigation: Raytheon 1500B; I/J-band.

Comment: Two of similar class operated by Chilean Shipping Co. Oil fuel, 77 tons.

ELICURA　　　　　　　　　*10/2001, Freddie Philips* / 0534132

1 NEWPORT CLASS (LSTH)

Name	No	Builders	Laid down	Launched	Commissioned	Recommissioned
VALDIVIA (ex-*San Bernardino*)	93 (ex-LST 1189)	National Steel & Shipbuilding Co	12 July 1969	28 Mar 1970	27 Mar 1971	30 Sep 1995

Displacement, tons: 4,975 light; 8,450 full load
Dimensions, feet (metres): 522.3 (hull) × 69.5 × 17.5 (aft) *(159.2 × 21.2 × 5.3)*
Main machinery: 6 ALCO 16-251 diesels; 16,500 hp *(12.3 MW)* sustained; 2 shafts; cp props; bow thruster
Speed, knots: 20
Range, n miles: 14,250 at 14 kt
Complement: 257 (13 officers)
Military lift: 400 troops; 500 tons vehicles; 3 LCVPs and 1 LCPL on davits
Radars: Surface search: Raytheon SPS-67; G-band.
Navigation: Marconi LN66; I/J-band.

Helicopters: Platform only.

Programmes: Transferred from the US by lease on 30 September 1995. A second of class was offered but not accepted due to its poor condition.
Structure: The hull form required to achieve 20 kt would not permit bow doors, thus these ships unload by a 112 ft ramp over their bow. The ramp is supported by twin derrick arms. A ramp just forward of the superstructure connects the lower tank deck with the main deck and a vehicle passage through the superstructure provides access to the parking area amidships. A stern gate to the tank deck permits unloading of amphibious tractors into the water, or unloading of other vehicles into an LCU or on to a pier. Vehicle stowage covers 19,000 sq ft. Length over derrick arms is 562 ft *(171.3 m)*; full load draught is 11.5 ft forward and 17.5 ft aft. Bow thruster fitted to hold position offshore while unloading amphibious tractors.
Operational: Damaged by grounding in mid-1997, but subsequently repaired. Vulcan Phalanx removed in 2002 and fitted in *Almirante Lynch*.

VALDIVIA *1/1999, van Ginderen Collection* / 0056726

SURVEY SHIPS

1 TYPE 1200 CLASS (AGS/AGOBH)

Name	No	Builders	Commissioned
CONTRE-ALMIRANTE OSCAR VIEL TORO (ex-*Norman McLeod Rogers*)	AP 46	Canadian Vickers, Montreal	Oct 1960

Displacement, tons: 6,320 full load
Measurement, tons: 4,179 gross; 1,847 net
Dimensions, feet (metres): 294.9 × 62.5 × 20 *(89.9 × 19.1 × 6.1)*
Main machinery: 4 Fairbanks-Morse 38D8-1/8-12 diesels; 8,496 hp *(6.34 MW)* sustained; 4 GE generators; 4.8 MW; 2 Ruston RK3CZ diesels; 7,250 hp *(5.6 MW)* sustained; 2 GE generators; 2.76 MW; 2 GE motors; 12,000 hp *(8.95 MW)*; 2 shafts
Speed, knots: 15
Range, n miles: 12,000 at 12 kt
Complement: 33
Guns: 2 Oerlikon 20 mm.
Helicopters: 1 BO 105C.

Comment: Acquired from the Canadian Coast Guard on 16 February 1995. The ship was formerly based on the west coast at Victoria, BC, and was laid up in 1993. Has replaced the deleted *Piloto Pardo* as the Antarctic patrol and survey ship.

CONTRE-ALMIRANTE OSCAR VIEL TORO *6/2004, Chilean Navy* / 1044093

1 ROBERT D CONRAD CLASS (AGOR)

Name	No	Builders	Commissioned
VIDAL GORMAZ (ex-*Thomas Washington*)	60 *(ex-AGOR 10)*	Marinette Marine, WI	27 Sep 1965

Displacement, tons: 1,370 full load
Dimensions, feet (metres): 208.9 × 40 × 15.3 *(63.7 × 12.2 × 4.7)*
Main machinery: Diesel-electric; 2 Cummins diesel generators; 1 motor; 1,000 hp *(746 kW)*; 1 shaft
Speed, knots: 13.5
Range, n miles: 12,000 at 12 kt
Complement: 41 (9 officers, 15 scientists)
Guns: 2 Oerlikon 20 mm.
Radars: Navigation: TM 1660/12S; I-band.

Comment: Transferred from US on 28 September 1992. This is the first class of ships designed and built by the US Navy for oceanographic research. Fitted with instrumentation and laboratories to measure gravity and magnetism, water temperature, sound transmission in water, and the profile of the ocean floor. Special features include a 10 ton capacity boom and winches for handling over-the-side equipment; 620 hp gas turbine (housed in funnel structure) for providing 'quiet' power when conducting experiments; can propel the ship at 6.5 kt. Ships of this class are in service with several other navies.

VIDAL GORMAZ *7/2001, Maritime Photographic* / 0121325

1 BUOY TENDER (ABU)

Name	No	Builders	Commissioned
GEORGE SLIGHT MARSHALL (ex-*M V Vigilant*)	BRS 63	Netherlands	July 1978

Displacement, tons: 816 full load
Dimensions, feet (metres): 173.9 × 36.7 × 11.5 *(53 × 11.2 × 3.5)*
Main machinery: 2 Ruston 6AP230 diesels; 1,360 hp *(1 MW)*; 2 shafts; bow thruster
Speed, knots: 12
Complement: 20
Guns: 2 Oerlikon 20 mm.

Comment: Acquired from the UK Mersey Harbour Board and recommissioned 5 February 1997. Carries a 15 ton derrick.

GEORGE SLIGHT MARSHALL *1/1999, van Ginderen Collection* / 0050081

TRAINING SHIPS

1 SAIL TRAINING SHIP (AXS)

Name	No	Builders	Commissioned
ESMERALDA	43	Bazán, Cadiz	15 June 1954
(ex-*Don Juan de Austria*)			

Displacement, tons: 3,420 standard; 3,754 full load
Dimensions, feet (metres): 269.2 pp; 360 oa × 44.6 × 23 *(82; 109.8 × 13.1 × 7)*
Main machinery: 1 Burmeister & Wain diesel; 1,400 hp(m) *(1.03 MW)*; 1 shaft
Speed, knots: 11. **Range, n miles:** 8,000 at 8 kt
Complement: 271 plus 80 cadets
Guns: 2 Hotchkiss saluting guns.

Comment: Four-masted schooner originally intended for the Spanish Navy. Near sister ship of *Juan Sebastian de Elcano* in the Spanish Navy. Refitted Saldanha Bay, South Africa, 1977. Sail area, 26,910 sq ft.

ESMERALDA   *7/2005*, A E Galarce* / 1153046

AUXILIARIES

1 TRANSPORT SHIP (APH)

Name	No	Builders	Launched	Commissioned
AQUILES	AP 41	ASMAR, Talcahuano	4 Dec 1987	15 July 1988

Displacement, tons: 2,767 light; 4,550 full load
Dimensions, feet (metres): 337.8 × 55.8 × 18 *(103 × 17 × 5.5; max)*
Main machinery: 2 Krupp MaK 8 M 453B diesels; 7,080 hp(m) *(5.10 MW)* sustained; 1 shaft; bow thruster
Speed, knots: 18
Complement: 80
Military lift: 250 troops
Helicopters: Platform for up to Cougar size.

Comment: Ordered 4 October 1985. Can be converted rapidly to act as hospital ship.

AQUILES   *7/2001, Maritime Photographic* / 0121327

1 ÄLVSBORG CLASS (SUPPORT SHIP) (AGP/ASH)

Name	No	Builders	Launched	Commissioned
MERINO (ex-*Älvsborg*)	42 (ex-A 234, ex-M 02)	Karlskronavarvet	11 Nov 1969	6 Apr 1971

Displacement, tons: 2,660 full load
Dimensions, feet (metres): 303.1 × 48.2 × 13.2 *(92.4 × 14.7 × 4)*
Main machinery: 2 Nohab-Polar 112 VS diesels; 4,200 hp(m) *(3.1 MW)*; 1 shaft; cp prop; bow thruster; 350 hp(m) *(257 kW)*
Speed, knots: 16
Complement: 52 (accommodation for 205)
Guns: 3 Bofors 40 mm/70 SAK 48.
Countermeasures: Decoys: 2 Philax chaff/IR launchers.
Radars: Surface search: Raytheon; E/F-band.
Fire control: Philips 9LV 200 Mk 2; I/J-band.
Navigation: Terma Scanter 009; I-band.
Helicopters: Platform for 1 medium.

Comment: Ordered in 1968 as a minelayer. Transferred from the Swedish Navy in November 1996, having been paid off in 1995. Recommissioned 7 February 1997. Originally designed as a minelayer with a capacity of 300 mines. Converted to act as a general support ship with improved accommodation and workshops. Acts as a depot ship for submarines and attack craft. The full name is *Almirante José Toribio Merino Castro*.

MERINO   *7/2001, Maritime Photographic* / 0121328

1 REPLENISHMENT SHIP (AOR)

Name	No	Builders	Commissioned
ARAUCANO	AO 53	Burmeister & Wain, Copenhagen	10 Jan 1967

Displacement, tons: 23,000 full load
Dimensions, feet (metres): 497.6 × 74.9 × 28.8 *(151.7 × 22.8 × 8.8)*
Main machinery: 1 Burmeister & Wain Type 62 VT 2BF140 diesel; 10,800 hp(m) *(7.94 MW)*; 1 shaft
Speed, knots: 17
Range, n miles: 12,000 at 15.5 kt
Complement: 130 (14 officers)
Cargo capacity: 21,126 m³ liquid; 1,444 m³ dry
Guns: 4 Bofors 40 mm/60 (2 twin).
Radars: Navigation: Racal Decca; I-band.

Comment: Launched on 21 June 1966. Single-hulled design.

ARAUCANO   *7/2001, Chilean Navy* / 0121329

1 HARBOUR TRANSPORT (YFB)

Name	No	Builders	Commissioned
GRUMETE PEREZ	YFB 114	ASMAR, Talcahuano	12 Dec 1975

Displacement, tons: 165 full load
Dimensions, feet (metres): 80 × 22 × 8.5 *(24.4 × 6.7 × 2.6)*
Main machinery: 1 diesel; 370 hp(m) *(272 kW)*; 1 shaft
Speed, knots: 10
Complement: 6
Guns: 1 Oerlikon 20 mm can be carried.
Radars: Navigation: Furuno; I-band.

Comment: Transferred to Seaman's School as harbour transport. Modified fishing boat design.

GRUMETE PEREZ   *8/1997, Chilean Navy* / 0012168

3 FLOATING DOCKS (YFD)

Name	No	Lift	Commissioned
INGENIERO MERY (ex-ARD 25)	131	3,000 tons	1944 (1973)
MUTILLA (ex-ARD 32)	132	3,000 tons	1944 (1960)
TALCAHUANO (ex-ARD 5)	133	3,000 tons	1944 (1999)

Comment: There is also a Floating Dock *Marinero Gutierrez* with a 1,200 ton lift. Built in 1991.

1 SUPPLY SHIP (AKSL)

Name	No	Builders	Commissioned
PISAGUA	116	SIMAR, Santiago	11 July 1995

Displacement, tons: 195 full load
Dimensions, feet (metres): 73.2 × 19.7 × 4.9 *(22.3 × 6 × 1.5)*
Main machinery: 1 diesel; 1 shaft
Speed, knots: 8
Range, n miles: 500 at 8 kt
Cargo capacity: 50 tons
Radars: Navigation: Furuno; I-band.

Comment: LCU design operated by the Seaman's School, Quiriquina Island as a general purpose stores ship.

PISAGUA   *8/1997, Chilean Navy* / 0012169

TUGS

Notes: Small harbour tugs *Reyes, Cortés* (both 100 tons and built in 1960) and *Galvez* (built in 1975), and the small personnel transport *Buzo Sobenes* BRT 112 are also in commission.

BUZO SOBENES   *7/1997, Chilean Navy* / 0012170

1 SMIT LLOYD CLASS (TUG/SUPPLY VESSEL) (AFL/ATF)

Name	No	Builders	Commissioned
LEUCOTON (ex-*Smit Lloyd* 44)	ATF 68	de Waal, Zaltbommel	1972

Displacement, tons: 1,750 full load
Dimensions, feet (metres): 174.2 × 39.4 × 14.4 *(53.1 × 12 × 4.4)*
Main machinery: 2 Burmeister & Wain Alpha diesels; 4,000 hp(m) *(2.94 MW)*; 2 shafts
Speed, knots: 13
Complement: 12
Guns: 2 Bofors 40 mm/60.
Radars: Surface search: E/F-band.

Comment: Acquired in February 1991. Modified at Punta Arenas and now used mainly as a supply ship.

LEUCOTON   *11/2001, Freddie Philips* / 0534134

2 VERITAS CLASS (TUG/SUPPLY VESSELS) (ATF)

Name	No	Builders	Commissioned
GALVARINO (ex-*Maersk Traveller*)	ATF 66	Aukra Bruk, Aukra	1974
LAUTARO (ex-*Maersk Tender*)	ATF 67	Aukra Bruk, Aukra	1973

Displacement, tons: 941 light; 2,380 full load
Dimensions, feet (metres): 191.3 × 41.4 × 12.8 *(58.3 × 12.6 × 3.9)*
Main machinery: 2 Krupp MaK 8 M 453AK diesels; 6,400 hp(m) *(4.7 MW)*; 2 shafts; cp props; bow thruster
Speed, knots: 14
Complement: 11 plus 12 spare berths
Cargo capacity: 1,400 tons
Guns: 1 Bofors 40 mm/70 can be carried.
Radars: Navigation: Terma Pilot 7T-48; Furuno FR 240; I-band.

Comment: First one delivered from Maersk and commissioned into Navy 26 January 1988. Third one delivered in 1991. *Janequero* since deleted. Bollard pull, 70 tonnes; towing winch, 100 tons. Fully air conditioned. Designed for towing large semi-submersible platform in extreme weather conditions. Ice strengthened.

GALVARINO   *7/2001, Maritime Photographic* / 0121330

COAST GUARD

Notes: There are also large numbers of harbour and SAR craft.

0 + 2 (2) OFFSHORE PATROL VESSELS (PSO)

Displacement, tons: 1.850 full load
Dimensions, feet (metres): 262.5 × 42.6 × 12.5 *(80.0 × 13.0 × 3.8)*
Main machinery: 2 Wärtsilä 12V26 diesels; 10,950 hp *(8.2 MW)*; 2 shafts; LIPS cp props; 2 bow thrusters
Speed, knots: 21
Range, n miles: 8,600 at 12 kt
Complement: 30 + 30 passengers
Guns: 1 — 40 mm.
Radars: Surface search: To be announced.
Navigation: To be announced.
Fire control: To be announced.
Helicopters: Platform for NAS 332SC Cougar.

Programmes: Project Danubio IV. Contract signed on 20 May 2005 with Fassmer GmbH & Co. and Astilleros y Maestranzas de la Armada (ASMAR) for the design and construction of two patrol vessels. Fassmer is to provide the design and construction assistance for the vessels which are to be built at Talcahuano Yard. The ships are to be delivered in 2008 and 2009. Two further units are planned for delivery in 2010 and 2011.
Structure: Steel construction. The design includes stealth features. Upper-deck layout features a helicopter launching platform, crane, two 7 m RIBs, container storage and a special rescue zone.

OPV   *6/2005*, Fassmer GmbH* / 1116081

10 DABUR CLASS (PATROL CRAFT) (PB)

GRUMETE DIAZ LPC 1814	**GRUMETE CAMPOS** LPC 1819	
GRUMETE BOLADOS LPC 1815	**GRUMETE MACHADO** LPC 1820	
GRUMETE SALINAS LPC 1816	**GRUMETE JOHNSON** LPC 1821	
GRUMETE TELLEZ LPC 1817	**GRUMETE TRONCOSO** LPC 1822	
GRUMETE BRAVO LPC 1818	**GRUMETE HUDSON** LPC 1823	

Displacement, tons: 33.7 standard; 39 full load
Dimensions, feet (metres): 64.9 × 18.0 × 5.8 *(19.8 × 5.5 × 1.8)*
Main machinery: 2 GM 12V-71TA diesels; 840 hp *(627 kW)*; 2 shafts
Speed, knots: 19
Range, n miles: 450 at 13 kt
Complement: 8 (2 officers)
Guns: 2 Oerlikon 20 mm. 2 — 12.7 mm MGs.
Radars: Navigation: Decca; I-band.

Comment: Built by Israeli Aircraft Industries, Ramta. First six purchased in 1990 and commissioned in early 1991. Four further craft purchased and commissioned in 1995. Carry a RIB inspection boat. 20 mm guns replaced by 12.7 mm machine guns in some.

18 PROTECTOR CLASS (WPB)

ALACALUFE LEP 1603	**COQUIMBO** LSG 1616
HALLEF LEP 1604	**PUERTO NATALES** LSG 1617
AYSEN LSG 1609	**VALPARAÍSO** LSG 1618
CORRAL LSG 1610	**PUNTA ARENAS** LSG 1619
CONCEPCION LSG 1611	**TALCAHUANO** LSG 1620
CALDERA LSG 1612	**QUINTERO** LSG 1621
SAN ANTONIO LSG 1613	**CHILOÉ** LSG 1622
ANTOFAGASTA LSG 1614	**PUERTO MONTT** LSG 1623
ARICA LSG 1615	**IQUIQUE** LSG 1624

Displacement, tons: 120 full load
Dimensions, feet (metres): 107.3 × 22 × 6.6 *(33.1 × 6.6 × 2)*
Main machinery: 2 MTU diesels; 5,200 hp(m) *(3.82 MW)*; 2 shafts
Speed, knots: 22. **Range, n miles:** 800 at 16 kt
Complement: 10 (2 officers)
Guns: 1 Hornicon.50.

Comment: All built under licence from FBM at ASMAR, Talcahuano, in conjunction with FBM Marine. There are minor differences between LEP 1603-4 and the rest. First commissioned 24 June 1989 and last on 10 March 2004. A class of 19 (Project Danube) is envisaged. All conduct coastal patrols between Arica and Puerto Williams.

ARICA   *12/2004, Globke Collection* / 1047868

ALACALUFE   *6/2003, Chilean Navy* / 0569805

1 ASMAR 1160 (SEARCH AND RESCUE CRAFT) (SAR)

TOKERAU LSR 1700

Displacement, tons: 7.8 standard; 10 full load
Dimensions, feet (metres): 41.5 × 12.8 × 3.6 *(12.7 × 3.9 × 1.1)*
Main machinery: 2 Volvo Penta TAMD-61A diesels; 612 hp *(456 kW)*; 2 Hamilton waterjets
Speed, knots: 25. **Range, n miles:** 310 at 20 kt
Complement: 4 plus 32 survivors
Radars: Navigation: Decca; I-band.

Comment: Built by Asmar Talcahuano and entered service in 1992. GRP hull and superstructure with inflatable surrounding bulwark. Carries extensive naviation, diving and first-aid equipment.

6 TYPE 44 CLASS (WPB)

PELLUHUE LSR 1703	**CHACAO** LSR 1705	**GUAITECA** LSR 1707
ARAUCO LSR 1704	**QUEITAO** LSR 1706	**CURAUMILA** LSR 1708

Displacement, tons: 18 full load
Dimensions, feet (metres): 44 × 12.8 × 3.6 *(13.5 × 3.9 × 1.1)*
Main machinery: 2 Detroit 6V-38 diesels; 185 hp *(136 kW)*; 2 shafts
Speed, knots: 14. **Range, n miles:** 215 at 10 kt
Complement: 3

Comment: Acquired from the US and recommissioned on 31 May 2001.

TYPE 44 (Uruguay Colours)   *5/2000, Hartmut Ehlers* / 0105801

2 COASTAL PATROL CRAFT (WPB)

ONA LEP 1601   **YAGAN** LEP 1602

Displacement, tons: 79 full load
Dimensions, feet (metres): 80.7 × 17.4 × 9.5 *(24.6 × 5.3 × 2.9)*
Main machinery: 2 MTU 8V 331 TC82 diesels; 1,300 hp(m) *(960 kW)* sustained; 2 shafts
Speed, knots: 22
Complement: 5
Guns: 2 — 12.7 mm MGs.

Comment: Built by Asenav and commissioned in 1980.

YAGAN   *6/2003, Chilean Navy* / 0569804

11 INSHORE PATROL CRAFT (WPB)

MAULE LPM 1901	**ISLUGA** LPM 1905	**CAU-CAU** LPM 1909
RAPEL LPM 1902	**LOA** LPM 1906	**PUDETO** LPM 1910
ACONCAGUA LPM 1903	**MAULLÍN** LPM 1907	**ROBINSON CRUSOE** LPM 1911
LAUCA LPM 1904	**COPIAPÓ** LPM 1908	

Displacement, tons: 14 full load
Dimensions, feet (metres): 43.3 × 11.5 × 3.5 *(13.2 × 3.5 × 1.1)*
Main machinery: 2 MTU 6V 331 TC82 diesels; 1,300 hp(m) *(960 kW)* sustained; 2 shafts
Speed, knots: 18
Guns: 1 — 12.7 mm MG.
Radars: Surface search: I-band.

Comment: LPM 1901-1910 ordered in August 1981. Completed by Asenav 1982-83. LPM 1911 is a smaller 12 m craft built by Ast Sitecna, Puerto Montt, and commissioned 19 July 2000.

ACONCAGUA   *12/2004, Globke Collection* / 1047867

18 RODMAN 800 CLASS (WPB)

PM 2031-2048

Dimensions, feet (metres): 29.2 × 9.8 × 3.6 *(8.9 × 3 × 0.8)*
Main machinery: 2 Volvo diesels; 300 hp(m) *(220 kW)*; 2 shafts
Speed, knots: 28
Range, n miles: 150 at 25 kt
Complement: 3
Guns: 1 — 12.7 mm MG.

Comment: Built by Rodman Polyships, Vigo and all delivered by 17 May 1996.

PM 2034   *7/2001, Maritime Photographic* / 0121331

China
PEOPLE'S LIBERATION ARMY NAVY (PLAN)

Country Overview

The People's Republic of China, proclaimed on 1 October 1949, is the world's third-largest country by area (3,695,000 square miles) and the largest by population. It is bordered to the north by Kyrgyzstan, Kazakhstan, Mongolia and Russia, to the south by Vietnam, Laos, Myanmar, India, Bhutan, Nepal and North Korea and to the west by Pakistan, Afghanistan and Tajikistan. It has a 7,830 n mile coastline with the Yellow, East China and South China seas. There are more than 3,400 offshore islands of which Hainan is the largest. Sovereignty over Taiwan, still formally a province of China, is also claimed. Ownership of some or all of the Spratly Islands is disputed between China, Brunei, Taiwan, Vietnam, Malaysia and the Philippines although a code of conduct was mutually brokered in 2002. The principal ports are Shanghai (largest city), Fuzhou, Qingdao, Tianjin, Guangzhou and Hangzhou which is linked to the capital Beijing by the Grand Canal. Overall there are 54,000 n miles of navigable inland waterways including the Yangtze River on which the port of Wuhan is situated. Territorial seas (12 n miles) are claimed. A 200 n mile EEZ has also been claimed but the limits have not been defined.

Headquarters Appointments

Commander-in-Chief of the Navy:
    Admiral Zhang Dingfa
Political Commissar of the Navy:
    Admiral Hu Yianlin
Deputy Commanders-in-Chief of the Navy:
    Vice Admiral Zhao Xingta
    Vice Admiral Wang Shouye
    Vice Admiral Zhang Yongyi
    Rear Admiral Zheng Baohua
Chief of Naval Staff:
    Vice Admiral Sun Jianguo

Fleet Commanders

North Sea Fleet:
    Vice Admiral Zhang Zhannan
East Sea Fleet:
    Vice Admiral Zhao Guojun
South Sea Fleet:
    Vice Admiral Gu Wengen

Personnel

(a) 2006: 250,000 officers and men, including 25,000 naval air force, 8–10,000 marines (28,000 in time of war) and 28,000 for coastal defence
(b) 2 years' national service for sailors afloat; 3 years for those in shore service. Some stay on for up to 15 years. 41,000 conscripts

Operational Numbers

Because numbers of vessels are kept in operational reserve, the Chinese version of the order of battle tends to show fewer ships than are counted by Western observers.

Organisation

Each of the North, East and South Sea Fleets has two submarine divisions, three DD/FF divisions and one MCMV division. The North also has one Amphibious Division, and the other Fleets have two each. The South has two Marine Infantry Brigades.

Bases

North Sea Fleet. Major bases: Qingdao (HQ), Huludao, Jianggezhuang, Guzhen Bay, Lushun, Xiaopingdao. Minor bases: Weihai Wei, Qingshan, Luda, Lianyungang, Ling Shan, Ta Ku Shan, Changshandao, Liuzhuang, Dayuanjiadun, Dalian
East Sea Fleet. Major bases: Ningbo (HQ), Zhoushan, Shanghai, Daxie, Fujan. Minor bases: Zhenjiangguan, Wusong, Xinxiang, Wenzhou, Sanduao, Xiamen, Xingxiang, Quandou, Wen Zhou SE, Wuhan, Dinghai, Jiaotou
South Sea Fleet. Major bases: Zhanjiang (HQ), Yulin, Huangfu, Hong Kong, Guangzhou (Canton). Minor bases: Haikou, Shantou, Humen, Kuanchuang, Tsun, Kuan Chung, Mawai, Beihai, Ping Tan, San Chou Shih, Tang-Chiah Huan, Longmen, Bailong, Dongcun, Baimajing, Xiachuandao, Yuchi

Coast Defence

A large number of HY-2 (CSSC-3) and HY-3 (CSSC-301) SSMs in 20 semi-fixed armoured sites. 35 Coastal Artillery regiments.

Equipment Procurement

Although often listed under the name of the designer, equipment has not necessarily been supplied direct from the parent company. It may have been acquired from a third party or by reverse engineering.

Training

The main training centres are:

Dalian: First Surface Vessel Academy
Guangzhou (Canton): Second Surface Vessel Academy
Qingdao: Submarine Academy
Wuhan: Engineering College
Nanjing: Naval Staff College, Electronic Engineering College
Yan Tai: Aviation Engineering College
Tianjin: Logistic School

Marines

There are two brigades based at Heieu and subordinate to the Navy. Each has three Infantry regiments and one Artillery regiment.

Naval Air Force

With 25,000 officers and men and over 800 aircraft, this is a considerable naval air force primarily land-based. There is a total of eight Divisions with 27 Regiments split between the three Fleets. Some aircraft are laid up unrepaired.

Air bases include:

North Sea Fleet: Dalian, Qingdao, Jinxi, Jiyuan, Laiyang, Jiaoxian, Xingtai, Laishan, Anyang, Changzhi, Liangxiang and Shan Hai Guan
East Sea Fleet: Danyang, Daishan, Shanghai (Dachang), Ningbo, Luqiao, Feidong and Shitangqiao
South Sea Fleet: Foluo, Haikou, Lingshui, Sanya, Guiping, Jialaishi and Lingling

Strength of the Fleet

Type	Active (Reserve)	Building (Planned)
SSBN	1	2 (2)
SSB	1	–
SSN	4	2 (3)
SSG	20	7
Patrol Submarines	56	–
Destroyers	26	3
Frigates	47	–
Fast Attack Craft (Missile)	41	–
Fast Attack Craft (Gun)	35	–
Fast Attack Craft (Patrol)	118	–
Patrol Craft	17	2
Minesweepers (Ocean)	19 (26)	–
Mine Warfare Drones	4 (42)	–
Minelayer	1	–
Hovercraft	10	(8)
LPD	–	(1)
LSTs	26	2
LSMs	47	–
LCMs-LCUs	150	–
Training Ships	2	–
Troop Transports (AP/AH)	6	–
Submarine Support Ships	11	–
Salvage and Repair Ships	3	1
Supply Ships	68+	–
Fleet Replenishment Ships	5	–
Icebreakers	4	–

DELETIONS

Submarines

2003 *Han* 401

Patrol Forces

2003 14 'Houkou', 15 'Huchuan'

PENNANT LIST

Submarines

406	Xia

Destroyers

105	Jinan
106	Xian
107	Yinchuan
108	Xining
109	Kaifeng
110	Dalian
112	Harbin
113	Qingdao
115	Shenyang
116	Shijiazhuang
131	Nanjing
132	Hefei
133	Chongqing
134	Zunyi
136	Hangzhou
137	Fuzhou
138	Taizhou
161	Changsha
162	Nanning
163	Nanchang
164	Guilin
165	Zhanjiang
166	Zhuhai
167	Shenzhen
168	Guangzhou
169	Wuhan
170	Lanzhou
171	Haikou

Frigates

509	Chang De
510	Shaoxing
511	Nantong
512	Wuxi
513	Huayin
514	Zhenjiang
515	Xiamen
516	Jiujiang
517	Nanping
518	Jian
519	Changzhi
521	Jiaxing
522	Lianyungang
523	Sanming
524	Putian
525	Maanshan
527	Luoyang
528	Mianyang
533	Ningbo
534	Jinhua
535	Huangshi
536	Wuhu
537	Zhoushan
539	Anqing
540	Huainan
541	Huaibei
542	Tongling
543	Dandong
544	Siping
545	Linfen
551	Maoming
552	Yibin
553	Shaoguan
554	Anshun
555	Zhaotong
557	Jishou
558	Zigong
559	Kangding
560	Dongguan
561	Shantou
562	Jiangmen
563	Zhaoqing
564	Yichang
565	Yulin
566	Huaihua
568	Wenzhou

Principal Auxiliaries

81	Zhenghe
82	Shichang
920	Dazhi
121	Changxingdao
302	Chongmingdao
506	Yongxingdao
891	Dagushan
881	Taicang
882	Fengcang
885	Nancang
886	Fuchi
887	Qiandaohu

For details of the latest updates to *Jane's Fighting Ships* online and to discover the additional information available exclusively to online subscribers please visit

jfs.janes.com

SUBMARINES

Strategic Missile Submarines

Notes: The successful flight-testing of a JL-2 missile took place on about 12 June 2005. The firing was made from a submarine, probably the Golf class SSB, off Qingdao and impacted in the western desert.

0 + 2 (2) JIN CLASS (TYPE 094) (SSBN)

Name	No	Builders	Laid down	Launched	Commissioned
–	–	Huludao Shipyard	2001	28 July 2004	2008
–	–	Huludao Shipyard	2003	2006	2010

Displacement, tons: 8,000
Dimensions, feet (metres): 449.5 × 36 × 7.5
(137.0 × 11.0 × 7.5)
Main machinery: Nuclear: 2 PWR; 150 MW; 2 turbines; 1 shaft
Speed, knots: To be announced
Complement: 140

Missiles: SLBM; 12 JL-2 (CSS-NX-5); 3-stage solid-fuel rocket; stellar inertial guidance to over 8,000 km *(4,320 n miles);* single nuclear warhead of 1 MT or 3—8 MIRV of smaller yield. CEP 300 m approx.

Torpedoes: 6—21 in (533 mm tubes).
Countermeasures: Decoys: ESM.
Radars: Surface search.
Sonars: Hull mounted passive/active; flank and towed arrays.

Programmes: The in-service date for the first boat is expected to be 2008 but deployment of the system will be dependent on successful testing of the missile. Further units are expected, probably at two-year intervals and an overall class of 4—6 boats is expected.
Structure: Details of both the boat and the SLBM are speculative. Likely to be based on the Type 093 SSN

design which in turn is believed to be derived from the Russian Victor III design. The dimensions of the hull assume the incorporation of a 30 m 'missile plug' of 12 tubes for the 42 ton JL-2 missiles.
Operational: Likely to be based at Jianggezhuang. The long range of the missile may prompt a change in operating concept to a 'bastion' patrol approach.

1 XIA CLASS (TYPE 092) (SSBN)

Name	No	Builders	Laid down	Launched	Commissioned
XIA	406	Huludao Shipyard	1978	30 Apr 1981	1987

Displacement, tons: 6,500 dived
Dimensions, feet (metres): 393.6 × 33 × 26.2
(120 × 10 × 8)
Main machinery: Nuclear; turbo-electric; 1 PWR; 90 MW; 1 shaft
Speed, knots: 22 dived
Complement: 140

Missiles: SLBM: 12 JL-1 (CSS-N-3); inertial guidance to 2,150 km *(1,160 n miles);* warhead single nuclear 250 kT.
Torpedoes: 6—21 in *(533 mm)* bow tubes. Yu-3 (SET-65E); active/passive homing to 15 km *(8.1 n miles)* at 40 kt; warhead 205 kg.

Countermeasures: ESM: Type 921-A; radar warning.
Radars: Surface search: Snoop Tray; I-band.
Sonars: Trout Cheek; hull-mounted; active/passive search and attack; medium frequency.

Programmes: A second of class was reported launched in 1982 and an unconfirmed report suggests that one of the two was lost in an accident in 1985.
Modernisation: Started major update in late 1995 at Huludao, thought to include fitting improved JL-1A missile with increased range but this has not been confirmed.
Structure: Diving depth 300 m *(985 ft).*

Operational: First test launch of the JL-1 missile took place on 30 April 1982 from a submerged pontoon near Huludao (Yellow Sea). Second launched on 12 October 1982, from the Golf class trials submarine. The first firing from *Xia* was in 1985 and was unsuccessful (delaying final acceptance into service of the submarine) and it was not until 27 September 1988 that a satisfactory launch took place. Based in the North Sea Fleet at Jianggezhuang. Following a refit which completed in late 1998, was reported to be operational again in 2003 although firing of a JL-1 missile has not been reported.

XIA　　　　　　　　　　　　　　　　　　　　　　*2002, Ships of the World* / 0529138

1 GOLF CLASS (TYPE 031) (SSB)

200

Displacement, tons: 2,350 surfaced; 2,950 dived
Dimensions, feet (metres): 319.9 × 28.2 × 21.7
(97.5 × 8.6 × 6.6)
Main machinery: Diesel-electric; 3 Type 37-D diesels; 6,000 hp(m) *(4.41 MW)*; 3 motors; 5,500 hp(m) *(4 MW)*; 3 shafts
Speed, knots: 17 surfaced; 13 dived
Range, n miles: 6,000 surfaced at 15 kt
Complement: 86 (12 officers)

Missiles: SLBM: 1 JL-2 (CSS-NX-5); 3-stage solid fuel; stellar inertial guidance to 8,000 km *(4,320 n miles);* single nuclear warhead of 1 MT or 3—8 MIRV of smaller yield. CEP 300 m approx.
Torpedoes: 10—21 in *(533 mm)* tubes (6 bow, 4 stern). 12 Type Yu-4 (SAET-60); passive homing to 15 km *(8.1 n miles)* at 40 kt; warhead 400 kg.
Radars: Navigation: Snoop Plate; I-band.
Sonars: Pike Jaw; hull-mounted; active/passive search; medium frequency.

Programmes: Ballistic missile submarine similar but not identical to the deleted USSR Golf class. Built at Dalian and launched in September 1966.
Modernisation: Refitted in 1995 to take the JL-2 missile.
Operational: This was the trials submarine for the JL-1 ballistic missile which was successfully launched to 1,800 km in October 1982. Continues to be available as a trials platform for the successor missile JL-2 and probably conducted a test firing on 12 June 2005. Based in the North Sea Fleet.

GOLF 200　　　　　　　　　　　　　　　　　　*2002, Ships of the World* / 0529137

Attack Submarines (SSN)

0 + 2 (3) SHANG CLASS (TYPE 093) (SSN)

Name	No	Builders	Laid down	Launched	Commissioned
–	–	Huludao Shipyard	1994	24 Dec 2002	2006
–	–	Huludao Shipyard	2000	2003	2007

Displacement, tons: 6,000 dived
Dimensions, feet (metres): 351 × 36 × 24.6
 (*107 × 11 × 7.5*)

Main machinery: Nuclear: 2 PWR; 150 MW; 2 turbines; 1 shaft
Speed, knots: 30 dived
Complement: 100

Missiles: SLCM; SSM.
Torpedoes: 6—21 in *(533 mm tubes)*.
Countermeasures: Decoys: ESM.
Radars: Surface search.
Sonars: Hull mounted passive/active; flank and towed arrays.

Programmes: Designed in conjunction with Russian experts. Prefabrication started in late 1994 and the first launch took place in late 2002. The in-service date of the first of class is expected to be 2006 with a second boat to follow in 2007. Construction of a third boat may have started but has not been confirmed. Five boats of the class are expected.
Structure: Details given are speculative, based on the double-hulled Russian Victor III design from which this submarine is reported to be derived.
Operational: Sea trials of the first of class are reported to have started in 2005.

TYPE 093   *1997, US Navy* / 0012178

4 HAN CLASS (TYPE 091) (SSN)

No	Builders	Laid down	Launched	Commissioned
402	Huludao Shipyard	1974	1977	Jan 1980
403	Huludao Shipyard	1980	1983	21 Sep 1984
404	Huludao Shipyard	1984	1987	Nov 1988
405	Huludao Shipyard	1987	8 Apr 1990	Dec 1990

Displacement, tons: 4,500 surfaced; 5,550 dived
Dimensions, feet (metres): 321.5; 347.8 (*403* onwards) × 32.8 × 24.2
 (*98; 106 × 10 × 7.4*)

Main machinery: Nuclear; turbo-electric; 1 PWR; 90 MW; 1 shaft
Speed, knots: 25 dived; 12 surfaced
Complement: 75

Missiles: SSM: YJ-801Q (C-801); inertial cruise; active radar homing to 40 km *(22 n miles)* at 0.9 Mach; warhead 165 kg; sea-skimmer may be carried.
Torpedoes: 6—21 in *(533 mm)* bow tubes; combination of Yu-3 (SET-65E); active/passive homing to 15 km *(8.1 n miles)* at 40 kt; warhead 205 kg and Yu-1 (Type 53-51) to 9.2 km *(5 n miles)* at 39 kt or 3.7 km *(2 n miles)* at 51 kt; warhead 400 kg. 20 weapons.
Mines: 36 in lieu of torpedoes.
Countermeasures: ESM: Type 921-A; radar warning.
Radars: Surface search: Snoop Tray; I-band.
Sonars: Trout Cheek; hull-mounted; active/passive search and attack; medium frequency.
 DUUX-5; passive ranging and intercept; low frequency.

Programmes: First of this class delayed by problems with the power plant. Although completed in 1974 she was not fully operational until the 1980s.
Modernisation: The basic Russian ESM equipment was replaced by a French design. A French intercept sonar set has been fitted.
Structure: From *403* onwards the hull has been extended by some 8 m although this was not to accommodate missile tubes as previously reported. SSMs may be fired from the torpedo tubes. Diving depth 300 m *(985 ft)*.
Operational: In North Sea Fleet based at Jianggezhuang. *403* and *404* started mid-life refits in 1998 which completed in early 2000. *405* started mid-life refit in 2000 and was reported completed in 2002. Torpedoes are a combination of older straight running and more modern Russian homing types. The first of class *401* was reported to have been decommissioned in 2003 and it is expected that others will follow as the Type 093 enter service.

HAN 404
5/1996, Ships of the World
0506277

HAN 402   *1990* / 0506276

Patrol Submarines

Notes: An unknown number of midget submarines are reported building.

1 + 1 YUAN CLASS (TYPE 041) (SSG)

Name	No	Builders	Laid down	Launched	Commissioned
–	330	Wuhan Shipyard	–	31 May 2004	2006
–	–	Wuhan Shipyard	–	2006	2008

Displacement, tons: To be announced.
Dimensions, feet (metres): 236.2 × 27.5 × ?
(72.0 × 8.4 × ?)
Main machinery: To be announced
Speed, knots: To be announced
Complement: To be announced

Missiles: Anti-ship (possibly Klub or indigenous missile).
Torpedoes: 6—21 in *(533 mm)* bow tubes.
Countermeasures: To be announced.

Weapons control: To be announced.
Radars: To be announced.
Sonars: To be announced.

Programmes: A new class of submarine of which the first of class was launched in May 2004. A second of class is expected to be launched in 2006.
Structure: There are few details at present but the design appears to exhibit some features of the Song class, although it appears to be shorter and broader, and possibly also of the Russian Kilo class. The design of the fin is similar to that of the former while a distinctive 'hump' on top of a teardrop shaped hull is characteristic of the latter. It is possible therefore that the boat is of double-hulled construction. Fitted with a seven-bladed propeller. It is not known whether an AIP system has been incorporated.
Operational: Sea trials of the first of class started in 2005.

YUAN CLASS

4/2005*, Ships of the World / 0581580

10 + 3 SONG CLASS (TYPE 039/039G) (SSG)

No	Builders	Laid down	Launched	Commissioned
320	Wuhan Shipyard	1991	25 May 1994	June 1999
321	Wuhan Shipyard	1995	11 Nov 1999	Apr 2001
322	Wuhan Shipyard	1996	28 June 2000	Dec 2001
323	Wuhan Shipyard	1998	May 2002	Nov 2003
324	Wuhan Shipyard	1999	28 Nov 2002	Dec 2003
325	Wuhan Shipyard	2001	3 Dec 2002	2004
314	Wuhan Shipyard	2001	19 May 2003	2004
315	Wuhan Shipyard	2002	29 Sep 2003	2004
316	Wuhan Shipyard	2002	2004	2005
326	Wuhan Shipyard	2002	July 2004	2005
328	Jiangnan Shipyard, Shanghai	2002	Aug 2004	2005
327	Wuhan Shipyard	2003	Sep 2004	2006
329	Jiangnan Shipyard, Shanghai	2003	Nov 2004	2006

Displacement, tons: 1,700 surfaced; 2,250 dived
Dimensions, feet (metres): 246 × 24.6 × 17.5
(74.9 × 7.5 × 5.3)
Main machinery: Diesel-electric; 4 MTU 16V 396 SE; 6,092 hp(m) *(4.48 MW)* diesels; 4 alternators; 1 motor; 1 shaft
Speed, knots: 15 surfaced; 22 dived
Complement: 60 (10 officers)

Missiles: SSM: YJ-801Q (C-801); radar active homing to 40 km *(22 n miles)* at 0.9 Mach; warhead 165 kg.
Torpedoes: 6—21 in *(533 mm)* tubes. Combination of Yu-4 (SAET-60); passive homing to 15 km *(8.1 n miles)* at 40 kt; warhead 400 kg and Yu-1 (Type 53—51) to 9.2 km *(5 n miles)* at 39 kt or 3.7 km *(2.1 n miles)* at 51 kt; warhead 400 kg.
Mines: In lieu of torpedoes.
Countermeasures: ESM: Type 921-A; radar warning.
Radars: Surface search: I-band.
Sonars: Bow-mounted; passive/active search and attack; medium frequency.
Flank array; passive search; low frequency.

Programmes: First of class (Type 039) started sea trials in August 1995, as a result of which substantial modifications were made. Second of class (Type 039G) trials started in early 2000 and third in early 2001. Fourth commissioned in 2003 while fifth and sixth were conducting trials in late 2003. Construction of the seventh hull is understood to have started in 2001 and of the eighth, ninth and tenth hulls in 2002. The twelfth hull is reported to have started construction at Wuhan in 2003. The building programme appears to have been switched to Jiangnan Shipyard, Shanghai, where the eleventh and thirteenth boats are being built but it is unclear whether there will be any further units of the class.
Structure: Comparable in size to Ming class but with a single skew propeller and an integrated spherical bow sonar. The forward hydroplanes are mounted below the bridge, which is on a step lower than the part of the fin that contains the masts in earlier boats. The fin is of a different shape (no cutaway) in later boats. Some of the details are speculative and the latest hulls of the class may have benefited from experience gained with the Kilos. The diesel engines are likely to be reverse engineered. Sonars are reported to be of French design.
Operational: The YJ-82 is the submarine launched version of the C-801 and is fired from torpedo tubes. Reports of an anti-submarine CY-1 air flight weapon are not confirmed.

SONG CLASS

4/2004, Ships of the World / 1042142

SONG CLASS

6/2004 / 1042169

SONG CLASS 315 and 316
6/2005*, Hachiro Nakai
1153050

3 + 1 (2) SOVREMENNY CLASS (PROJECT 956E/956EM) (DDGHM)

Name	No	Builders	Laid down	Launched	Commissioned
HANGZHOU (ex-*Vazhny*, ex-*Yekaterinburg*)	136 (ex-698)	North Yard, St Petersburg	4 Nov 1988	23 May 1994	25 Dec 1999
FUZHOU (ex-*Alexandr Nevsky*)	137	North Yard, St Petersburg	22 Feb 1989	16 Apr 1999	16 Jan 2001
TAIZHOU	138	North Yard, St Petersburg	27 June 2002	27 Apr 2004	28 Dec 2005
–	139	North Yard, St Petersburg	2003	23 July 2004	2006

Displacement, tons: 7,940 full load
Dimensions, feet (metres): 511.8 × 56.8 × 21.3
(156 × 17.3 × 6.5)
Main machinery: 4 KVN boilers; 2 GTZA-674 turbines; 99,500 hp(m) *(73.13 MW)* sustained; 2 shafts; bow thruster
Speed, knots: 32
Range, n miles: 2,400 at 32 kt; 4,000 at 14 kt
Complement: 296 (25 officers) plus 60 spare

Missiles: SSM: 8 Raduga SS-N-22 Sunburn (Moskit 3M-80E) (2 quad) launchers ❶; active/passive radar homing to 160 km *(87 n miles)* at 2.5 (4.5 for attack) Mach; warhead 300 kg; sea-skimmer.
SAM: 2 SA-N-7 Gadfly (Uragan) ❷ 9M38M1 Smerch; command/semi-active radar and IR homing to 25 km *(13.5 n miles)* at 3 Mach; warhead 70 kg; altitude 15–14,020 m *(50–46,000 ft)*; 44 missiles. Multiple channels of fire.
2 CADS-N-1 (Kashtan); each has 30 mm gatling combined with 8 SA-N-11 (Grisson) and Hot Flash/Hot Spot radar/optronic director. Laser beam guidance for missiles to 8 km *(4.4 n miles)*; warhead 9 kg; 9,000 rds/min to 1.5 km for guns.
Guns: 4 (2 (138, 139)) 130 mm/70 (2 (1) twin) AK 130 ❸; 35–45 rds/min to 29.5 km *(16 n miles)*; weight of shell 33.4 kg.
4–30 mm/65 AK 630 (136, 137) ❹; 6 barrels per mounting; 3,000 rds/min combined to 2 km.
Torpedoes: 4–21 in *(533 mm)* (2 twin) tubes ❺.
A/S mortars: 2 RBU 1000 6-barrelled ❻; range 1,000 m; warhead 55 kg; 120 rockets carried. Torpedo countermeasure.
Mines: Mine rails for up to 40.
Countermeasures: Decoys: 8 PK 10 and 2 PK 2 chaff launchers.
ESM/ECM: 4 Foot Ball. 6 Half Cup laser warner.
Weapons control: 1 China optronic director and laser rangefinder ❼. Band Stand ❽ datalink for SS-N-22. Bell Nest, 2 Light Bulb and 2 Tee Pump datalinks.
Radars: Air search: Top Plate ❾; 3D; E-band.
Surface search: 3 Palm Frond ❿; I-band.
Fire control: 6 Front Dome ⓫; H/I-band (for SA-N-7). Kite Screech ⓬; H/I/K-band (for 130 mm guns). 2 Bass Tilt ⓭; H/I-band (for 30 mm guns).
Sonars: Bull Horn (Platina) and Whale Tongue; hull-mounted; active search and attack; medium frequency.

Helicopters: 1 Harbin Zhi-9C Haitun ⓮ or Kamov Ka-28 Helix.

Programmes: After prolonged negotiations, a contract was signed in September 1996 for two uncompleted Russian Sovremenny class destroyers. These were hulls 18 and 19. Progress was held up for a time because China wanted KA-28 helicopters included, and the Russians demanded extra payment for the aircraft. Deleted Russian units of the class may have been cannibalised for some equipment. A contract for the procurement of two more ships was signed on 3 January 2002. The keel of the first modified Sovremenny class was laid down on 27 June 2002. An option for two further ships was also agreed although these could be to a modified design.
Structure: These are the first Chinese warships to have a data system link. The optronic director is probably a Chinese version of Squeeze Box. The modified 'Sovremenny' include variations in weapon fit including replacement of the AK 630 system with 'Kashtan' (with associated Cross Dome target indication

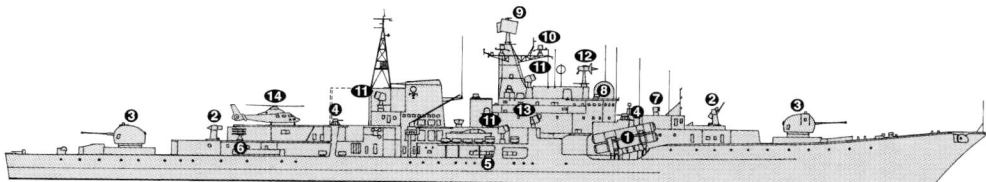

HANGZHOU   *(Scale 1 : 1,200), Ian Sturton* / 0103652

TAIZHOU   *1/2006*, B Prézelin* / 1154273

HANGZHOU   *2/2004, Ships of the World* / 1042158

radar) CIWS and a reduction to one forward AK 130 turret. The flight deck is to be extended. Two single-armed launchers for SA-N-7 are to be retained. An uprated SS-N-22 system with 200 km range may also be fitted.
Operational: 136 arrived Dinghai on 16 February 2000 and 137 in February 2001. SS-N-22 test fired on 15 September

2001. Both based in the East Sea Fleet. 138 was delivered on 28 December 2005 and 139 is expected in mid-2006.
Opinion: The main role of these ships is anti-surface warfare although they also possess a good AAW capability. Together with the new AAW destroyers, they represent a step-change in Chinese naval capabilities.

FUZHOU   *12/2005*, Ships of the World* / 1153060

2 LUYANG I (TYPE 052B) CLASS (DDGHM)

Name	No
GUANGZHOU	168
WUHAN	169

Builders	Laid down	Launched	Commissioned
Jiangnan Shipyard, Shanghai	2001	25 May 2002	18 July 2004
Jiangnan Shipyard, Shanghai	2001	9 Sep 2002	18 July 2004

Displacement, tons: 7,000 full load
Dimensions, feet (metres): 508.5 × 55.8 × 19.7 (155 × 17 × 6)
Main machinery: CODOG: 2 Ukraine DA80 gas turbines; 48,600 hp(m) (35.7 MW); 2 diesels; 8,840 hp(m) (6.5 MW); 2 shafts; cp props
Speed, knots: 29
Range, n miles: 4,500 at 15 kt
Complement: 280 (40 officers)

Missiles: SSM: 16 C-803 (YJ-83/C SS-N-8 Saccade) 4 quad ❶; mid-course guidance and active radar homing to 150 km (81 n miles) at 0.9 Mach; warhead 165 kg; sea skimmer.
SAM: SA-N-12 Grizzly (Shtil-1) 9M38M2 ❷; command/semi-active radar and IR homing to 35 km (18.9 n miles) at 3 Mach; warhead 70 kg; 2 magazines (forward and aft). 48 missiles.
Guns: 1—3.9 in (100 mm)/56 ❸; 60—80 rds/min to 17 km (9.3 n miles); weight of shell 13.5 kg.
2—30 mm Type 730 ❹; 7 barrels per mounting; 4,200 rds/min combined to 1.5 km.
A/S mortars: 4 multiple rocket launchers (possibly multirole) ❺.
Countermeasures: Decoys: 4—18 tube 100 mm launchers.
ESM: SRW 210A.
ECM: Type 984 (I-band jammer). Type 985 (E/F-band jammer).
Combat data systems: To be announced. SATCOM.
Weapons control: Band Stand ❻ datalink (for C-803).
Radars: Air search: Top Plate ❼; E/F-band.
Air/Surface search: Type 364 Seagull C ❽; G-band.
Fire control: 4 Front Dome (Orekh) ❾; H/I-band (for SA-N-12).
Type 344 (MR 34) ❿; I-band (for SSM and 100 mm).
2 Type 347G(1) Rice Bowl; I-band (for Type 730).
Navigation: To be announced.
Sonars: Bow mounted. To be announced.

Helicopters: 1 Harbin Zhi-9A Haitun or Kamov KA-28 Helix ⓫.

Programmes: Construction of new multirole destroyers with medium-range air defence capability started in 2001.
Structure: Based on 'Luhai' design but with more advanced stealth features. The aft superstructure contains the hangar on the port side and aft missile magazine to starboard. Details of both the hull and its weapon systems are speculative.
Operational: Names are unconfirmed. Sea trials of 168 began on 24 July 2003. Likely to be based in the South Sea Fleet.

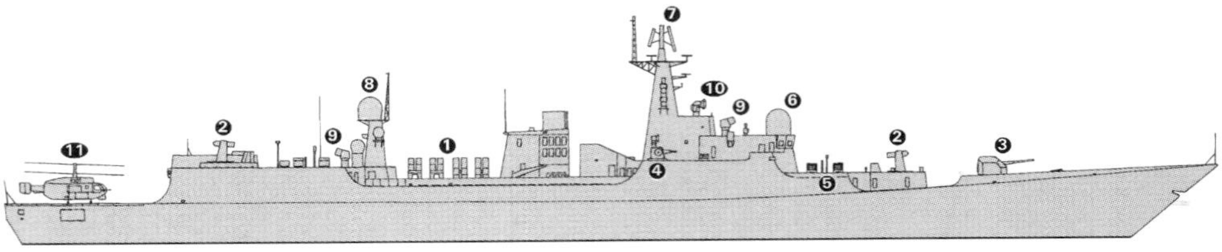

GUANGZHOU

(Scale 1 : 1,200), Ian Sturton / 1153007

GUANGZHOU *6/2004* / 1042168

WUHAN *7/2004*
0583664

GUANGZHOU

11/2004, Ships of the World / 1042157

2 LUYANG II (TYPE 052C) CLASS (DDGHM)

Name	No	Builders	Laid down	Launched	Commissioned
LANZHOU	170	Jiangnan Shipyard, Shanghai	June 2002	29 Apr 2003	18 July 2004
HAIKOU	171	Jiangnan Shipyard, Shanghai	Nov 2002	29 Oct 2003	2005

Displacement, tons: 7,000 full load
Dimensions, feet (metres): 508.5 × 55.8 × 19.7
 (155 × 17 × 6)
Main machinery: CODOG: 2 Ukraine DA80 gas turbines;
48,600 hp(m) *(35.7 MW);* 2 diesels; 8,840 hp(m) *(6.5 MW);*
2 shafts; cp props
Speed, knots: 29
Range, n miles: 4,500 at 15 kt
Complement: 280 (40 officers)

Missiles: SSM: 8 YJ-62 ❶ 2 quad; inertial-GPS guidance
 and terminal active radar homing to 280 km *(151 n miles)*
 at 0.8 Mach; warhead 300 kg.
SAM: HHQ-9 ❷; 8 vertical revolving sextuple launchers
 (6 forward, 2 aft); command guidance; semi-active radar
 homing to 100 km *(54 n miles)* at 3 Mach; warhead
 90 kg; 48 missiles.
Guns: 1—3.9 in *(100 mm)*/56 ❸; 60—80 rds/min to 17 km
 (9.3 n miles); weight of shell 13.5 kg.
 2—30 mm Type 730 ❹; 7 barrels per mounting; 4,200 rds/
 min combined to 1.5 km.
A/S mortars: 4 multiple rocket launchers (possibly
 multirole) ❺.
Countermeasures: To be announced.

Combat data systems: To be announced. SATCOM.
Weapons control: Band Stand ❻ datalink for YJ-62.
Radars: Air search: Type 517 Knife Rest ❼; A-band.
 Air search/fire control: Type 382 phased arrays ❽; 3D; G-band.
 Air/Surface search: Type 364 Seagull C ❾; G-band.
 Fire control: Type 344 (MR 34) ❿; I-band (for SSM and
 100 mm).
 2 Type 347G(1) Rice Bowl; I-band (for Type 730).
Navigation: To be announced.
Sonars: Bow mounted. To be announced.

Helicopters: 2 Harbin Zhi-9A Haitun or Kamov KA-28
 Helix ⓫.

Programmes: The second phase of the destroyer
 construction programme which introduces the long-
 range HHQ-9 missile system into service.
Structure: Appears to share the same basic hull design as
 the Type 052B destroyers which in turn are based on the
 Luhai class. As well as incorporating stealth features,
 the design includes a taller forward superstructure
 in which the four phased array antennas are installed.
 The helicopter hangar is on the port side of the aft
 superstructure. Details are speculative and firm details of

both the SAM and SSM systems are yet to be confirmed.
The CIWS systems are on raised platforms forward and
on top of the hangar.
Operational: Likely to be based in the South Sea Fleet.

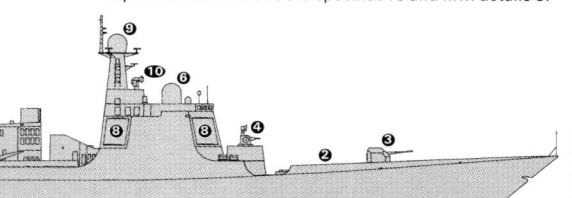

LANZHOU *(Scale 1 : 1,200), Ian Sturton* / 1153008

LANZHOU *7/2004* / 0583665

LANZHOU *12/2004, Ships of the World* / 1042156

1 LUHAI CLASS (TYPE 051B) (DDGHM)

Name	No	Builders	Laid down	Launched	Commissioned
SHENZHEN	167	Dalian Shipyard	July 1996	16 Oct 1997	4 Jan 1999

Displacement, tons: 6,000 full load
Dimensions, feet (metres): 505 × 52.5 × 19.7
 (154 × 16 × 6)
Main machinery: CODOG: 2 Ukraine gas turbines; 48,600
 hp(m) *(35.7 MW);* 2 MTU 12V 1163 TB 83 diesels; 8,840
 hp(m) *(6.5 MW)* sustained; 2 shafts; cp props
Speed, knots: 29. **Range, n miles:** 4,500 at 14 kt
Complement: 250 (42 officers)

Missiles: SSM: 16 C-803 (YJ-83/CSS-N-8 Saccade) ❶; mid-
 course guidance and active radar homing to 150 km
 (81 n miles) at 0.9 Mach; warhead 165 kg; sea skimmer.
SAM: 1 HQ-7 (Crotale) octuple launcher ❷; CSA-N-4 line
 of sight guidance to 13 km *(7 n miles)* at 2.4 Mach;

warhead 14 kg. Possible reloading hatch aft of the HQ-7
 launcher.
Guns: 2—3.9 in *(100 mm)*/56 (twin) ❸; 18 rds/min to 22 km
 (12 n miles); weight of shell 15 kg.
 8—37 mm/63 Type 76A (4 twin) ❹; 180 rds/min to
 8.5 km *(4.6 n miles)* anti-aircraft; weight of shell 1.42 kg.
Torpedoes: 6—324 mm B515 (2 triple) tubes ❺ Yu-2/5/6;
 active/passive homing to 11 km *(5.9 n miles)* at 40 kt;
 warhead 44 kg.
Countermeasures: Decoys: 2 Type 946 15-tube 100 mm
 chaff launchers ❻.
 2 Type 947 10-tube 130 mm chaff launchers.
ESM: Type 826.

ECM: Type 984; I-band jammer; Type 985; E/F-band jammer.
Combat data systems: Thomson-CSF Tavitac; SATCOM.
Weapons control: 2 GDG 776 optronic directors.
Radars: Air search: Type 517 Knife Rest ❼; A-band.
 Air search: Type 381C Rice Shield ❽; E/F-band.
 Air/surface search: Type 360 Seagull S ❾; E/F-band.
 Fire control: Type 344 (MR 34) ❿; I-band (for SSM and
 100 mm).
 2 Type 347G(1) Rice Bowl ⓫; I-band (for 37 mm).
 Type 345 (MR 35) ⓬; I/J-band (for HQ-7).
Navigation: Racal/Decca 1290; I-band.
Sonars: DUBV-23; hull mounted; active search and attack;
 medium frequency.

Helicopters: 2 Harbin Zhi-9C Haitun ⓭ or Kamov Ka-28 Helix.

Programmes: Follow-on from the Luhu class. Although the
 only ship of its class, it would appear to be the baseline
 design for the Type 052B and 052C destroyers.
Structure: Apart from the second funnel and octuple SSM
 launchers, there are broad similarities with the smaller
 Luhu. Anti-aircraft guns are all mounted aft allowing
 more space in front of the bridge which seems to show a
 reloading hatch for HQ-7.
Operational: Based at Zhanjiang in South Sea Fleet. Out of
 area deployment to Europe in 2001.

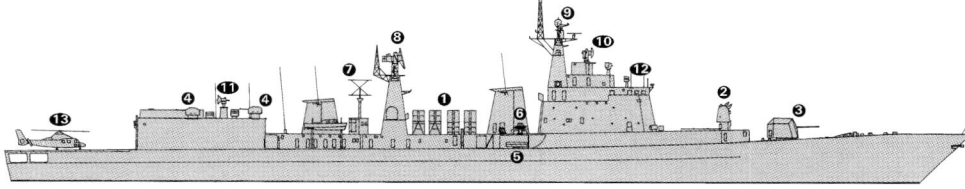

SHENZHEN *(Scale 1 : 1,200), Ian Sturton* / 0569249

SHENZHEN *10/2001, Derek Fox* / 0126287

2 LUHU (TYPE 052) CLASS (DDGHM)

Name	No
HARBIN	112
QINGDAO	113

Builders	Laid down	Launched	Commissioned
Jiangnan Shipyard, Shanghai	Nov 1990	Oct 1991	July 1994
Jiangnan Shipyard, Shanghai	Jan 1993	Oct 1993	Mar 1996

Displacement, tons: 4,600 full load
Measurement, tons: 472.4 × 52.5 × 16.7 *(144 × 16 × 5.1)*
Main machinery: CODOG: 2 GE LM 2500 gas turbines (112); 55,000 hp *(41 MW)* sustained or 2 Ukraine gas turbines (113) 48,600 hp(m) *(35.7 MW)*; 2 MTU 12V 1163 TB83 diesels; 8,840 hp(m) *(6.5 MW)* sustained; 2 shafts; cp props
Speed, knots: 31
Range, n miles: 5,000 at 15 kt
Complement: 266 (38 officers)

Missiles: SSM: 16 C-803 (YJ 83/CSS-N-8) Saccade ❶; mid-course guidance and active radar homing to 150 km *(81 n miles)* at 0.9 Mach; warhead 165 kg; sea-skimmer.
SAM: 1 HQ-7 (Crotale) octuple launcher ❷; CSA-4; line of sight guidance to 13 km *(7 n miles)* at 2.4 Mach; warhead 14 kg. 32 missiles.
Guns: 2—3.9 in *(100 mm)*/56 (twin) ❸; 18 rds/min to 22 km *(12 n miles)*; weight of shell 15 kg.
8—37 mm/63 Type 76A (4 twin) ❹; 180 rds/min to 8.5 km *(4.6 n miles)* anti-aircraft; weight of shell 1.42 kg.
Torpedoes: 6—324 mm Whitehead B515 (2 triple) tubes ❺. Yu-2 (Mk 46 Mod 1); active/passive homing to 11 km *(5.9 n miles)* at 40 kt; warhead 44 kg.
A/S mortars: 2 FQF 2500 ❻ 12-tubed fixed launchers; range 1,200 m; warhead 34 kg. 120 rockets.
Countermeasures: Decoys: 2 Type 946; 15 barrelled 100 mm chaff launchers.
ESM: Rapids.
ECM: Ramses.
Combat data systems: Thomson-CSF Tavitac action data automation. SATCOM. Link W.
Weapons control: 2 GDG-775 optronic directors ❼.
Radars: Air search: Type 518 (navalised REL-1) ❽; D-band.
Air/surface search: Type 363S Sea Tiger ❾; E/F-band.
Surface search: Type 362 (ESR 1) ❿; I-band.
Fire control: Type 344 (MR 34) ⓫; I-band (for SSM and 100 mm).
2 Type 347G(2) Rice Bowl ⓬; I-band (for 37 mm).
Type 345 (MR 35) ⓭; I/J-band (for Crotale).
Navigation: Racal Decca 1290; I-band.
Sonars: DUBV-23; Hull-mounted; active search and attack; medium frequency.
DUBV-43 VDS; active attack; medium frequency.

Helicopters: 2 Harbin Zhi-9C Haitun ⓮.

Programmes: Class of two ordered in 1985 but delayed by priority being given to export orders for Thailand.
Modernisation: *Harbin* completed refit in early 2003. It has been fitted with a new low radar profile 100 mm gun turret. *Qingdao* reported to have completed similar refit in 2005.
Structure: The most notable features are the SAM launcher, improved radar and fire-control systems and a modern 100 mm gun. Gas turbines for the second of class came from the Ukraine. The HQ-7 launcher is a Chinese copy of Crotale. DCN Samahe 110N helo handling system. *Harbin* has a dome-shaped radome on the superstructure while *Qingdao* has cylindrical antennae in the same position. Both are likely to be ECM systems.
Operational: First of class based in North Sea Fleet at Guzhen Bay, second in the East Sea Fleet at Jianggezhuang.

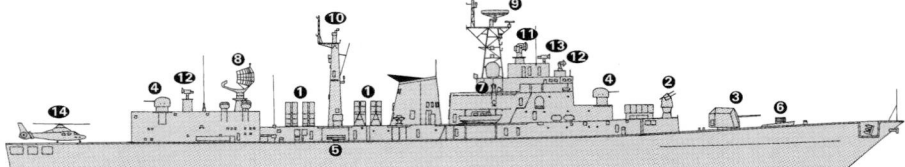

HARBIN

(Scale 1 : 1,200), Ian Sturton / 0569255

HARBIN

2/2003, Y Chang / 0531594

HARBIN
6/2005*, Hachiro Nakai
1153051

HARBIN

11/2004, Ships of the World / 1042144

12 LUDA (TYPES 051/051D/051Z) CLASS (DDGM/DDGHM)

Name	No	Name	No	Name	No
JINAN	105	NANJING	131	CHANGSHA	161
XIAN	106	HEFEI	132	NANNING	162
YINCHUAN	107	CHONGQING	133	NANCHANG	163
XINING	108	ZUNYI	134	GUILIN	164

Displacement, tons: 3,250 standard; 3,670 full load
Dimensions, feet (metres): 433.1 × 42 × 15.1
(132 × 12.8 × 4.6)
Main machinery: 2 or 4 boilers; 2 turbines; 72,000 hp(m)
(53 MW); 2 shafts
Speed, knots: 32. **Range, n miles:** 2,970 at 18 kt
Complement: 280 (45 officers)

Missiles: SSM: 6 HY-2 (C-201) (CSS-C-3A Seersucker)
(2 triple) launchers ❶; active radar or IR homing to 95 km
(51 n miles) at 0.9 Mach; warhead 513 kg.
Guns: 4 USSR 5.1 in *(130 mm)*/58 (2 twin) ❷; 17 rds/min to
29 km *(16 n miles);* weight of shell 33.4 kg.
8 China 57 mm/70 (4 twin); 120 rds/min to 12 km
(6.5 n miles); weight of shell 6.31 kg or 8 China 37 mm/63
(4 twin) ❸; 180 rds/min to 8.5 km *(4.6 n miles);* weight
of shell 1.42 kg.
8 USSR 25 mm/60 (4 twin) ❹; 270 rds/min to 3 km
(1.6 n miles) anti-aircraft; weight of shell 0.34 kg.
Torpedoes: 6—324 mm Whitehead B515 (2 triple tubes)
(fitted in some); Yu-2 (Mk 46 Mod 1); active/passive
homing to 11 km *(5.9 n miles)* at 40 kt; warhead 44 kg.
A/S mortars: 2 FQF 2500 12-tubed fixed launchers ❺; 120
rockets; range 1,200 m; warhead 34 kg. Similar in design
to the RBU 1200.
Depth charges: 2 or 4 BMB projectors; 2 or 4 racks.
Mines: 38.
Combat data systems: ZKJ-1 (132).
Radars: Air search: Type 515 Bean Sticks ❻; A-band.
Type 381 Rice Shield ❼ (132); 3D; G-band. Similar to
Hughes SPS-39A.
Surface search: Type 354 Eye Shield ❽; G-band.
Type 352 Square Tie (not in all); I-band.
Navigation: Fin Curve or Racal Decca 1290; I-band.
Fire control: Wasp Head (also known as Wok Won) or Type
343 Sun Visor B (series 2) ❾; I-band.
2 Type 347G Rice Bowl ❿; I-band.
IFF: High Pole.
Sonars: Pegas 2M and Tamir 2; hull-mounted; active search
and attack; high frequency.

Helicopters: 2 Harbin Z-9C (Dauphin) (105).

Programmes: The first Chinese-designed destroyers of
such a capability to be built. First of class completed in
1971. 105 to 108 built at Luda; 131 to 134 at Shanghai and

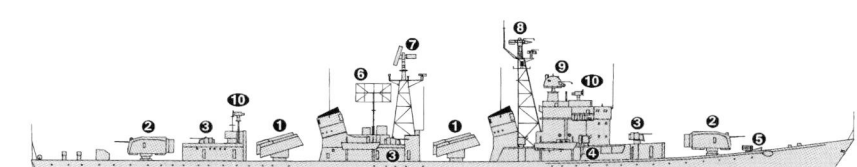

HEFEI *(Scale 1 : 1,200), Ian Sturton* / 0056749

JINAN with helicopter deck *1/1994* / 0056753

161 to 164 at Dalian. Similar to the deleted USSR Kotlin
class. The programme was much retarded after 1971 by
drastic cuts in the defence budget. In early 1977 building
of series two of this class was put in hand and includes
those after 108, with the latest 164 completed in April
1990. The order of completion was 105, 160 (scrapped),
106, 161, 107, 162, 131, 108, 132, 163, 133, 134 and 164.
Modernisation: Equipment varies considerably from ship
to ship. The original Type 051 ships are 105, 106, 107, 131,
161 and 162. Of these 105 was converted in 1987 to act as
a trials ship; a twin helicopter hangar and deck replaced
the after armament. Type 051D ships are 108, 133, 134,
163 and 164. 132 is a command ship (Type 051Z) fitted

with ZKJ-1 command system and Rice Screen (Type
381A) 3-D radar although this has been temporarily
replaced by a SATCOM terminal.
Structure: Electronics vary in later ships. Some ships
have 57 mm guns, others 37 mm. 105 may have Alcatel
'Safecopter' landing aid. SAM is fitted in *Kaifeng* and
Dalian in X gun position.
Operational: Capable of foreign deployment, although
command and control is limited. Underway refuelling is
practised. Deployment; 105 series in North Sea Fleet at
Yuchi; 131 series in East Sea Fleet at Dalian; 161 series
in South Sea Fleet at Zhanjiang. 160 was damaged by an
explosion in 1978, and was scrapped.

HEFEI *6/1999, Ships of the World* / 0056752

YINCHUAN *8/1999, Ships of the World* / 0056754

4 LUDA CLASS (TYPE 051DT/051G/051G II) (DDG)

Name	No	Builders	Laid down	Launched	Commissioned
KAIFENG	109	Dalian Shipyard	–	–	–
DALIAN	110	Dalian Shipyard	–	–	–
ZHANJIANG	165	Dalian Shipyard	1988	1990	1991
ZHUHAI	166 (168 out of area)	Dalian Shipyard	1988	1990	1991

Displacement, tons: 3,250 standard; 3,730 full load
Dimensions, feet (metres): 433.1 × 42 × 15.3
(132 × 12.8 × 4.7)
Main machinery: 2 boilers; 2 turbines; 72,000 hp(m)
(53 MW); 2 shafts
Speed, knots: 32
Range, n miles: 2,970 at 18 kt
Complement: 280 (45 officers)

Missiles: SSM: 16 C 801A (YJ 81/CSS-N-4) (Sardine) ❶;
active radar homing to 95 km *(51 n miles)* at 0.9 Mach;
warhead 165 kg; sea-skimmer.
SAM: 1 HQ-7 (Crotale) octuple launcher ❷; line of sight
guidance to 13 km *(7 n miles)* at 2.4 Mach; warhead 14 kg.
Guns: 2 USSR 5.1 in *(130 mm)* (109, 110) ❸; 17 rds/min to
29 km *(16 n miles)*; weight of shell 33.4 kg.
4—3.9 in *(100 mm)*/56 (2 twin) (165, 166) ❹; 18 rds/min to
22 km *(12 n miles)*; weight of shell 15 kg.
6 China 57 mm/63 (3 twin) (109,110) ❺; 120 rds/min to
12 km *(6.5 n miles)*; weight of shell 6.31 kg.
6 China 37 mm/63 Type 76A (3 twin) (165, 166) ❻; 180 rds/
min to 8.5 km *(4.6 n miles)*; weight of shell 1.42 kg.
Torpedoes: 6—324 mm Whitehead B515 (2 triple tubes) ❼;
Yu-2 (Mk 46 Mod 1); active/passive homing to 11 km
(5.9 n miles) at 40 kt; warhead 44 kg.
A/S mortars: 2 FQF 2500 12-tubed fixed launchers ❽; 120
rockets; range 1,200 m; warhead 34 kg. Similar in design
to the RBU 1200.
Countermeasures: Decoys: 2 Type 946; 15 barrelled 100 mm
chaff launchers.
ESM: Type 825; intercept.
ECM: Type 981; jammer.
Combat data systems: Thomson-CSF Tavitac with Vega FCS
(109); ZKJ-1 (110); ZKJ 4A (165); ZKJ 4B (166).
Radars: Air search: Type 517 Knife Rest ❾; A-band.
Surface search: Type 363 Sea Tiger S (109). Type 354 Eye
Shield (165, 166) ❿; E/F-band.
Navigation: Racal Decca 1290; I-band.
Fire control: Type 344 (MR 34) (165, 166) ⓫; I-band
(for SSM and 100 mm).
Type 343G Sun Visor (109, 110) ⓬; I-band.
Type 347G Rice Bowl ⓭; I-band (for 57/37 mm).
Type 345 (MR 35) ⓮; I/J-band (for Crotale).
IFF: High Pole.
Sonars: DUBV 23 (165, 166); hull-mounted; active search
and attack; medium frequency.

Programmes: Updated Luda designs sometimes known
collectively as the Luda III class.

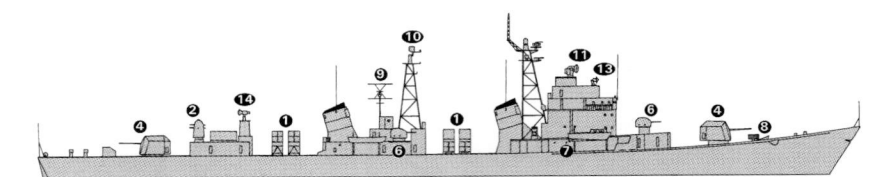

ZHANJIANG *(Scale 1 : 1,200)*, Ian Sturton / 0572402

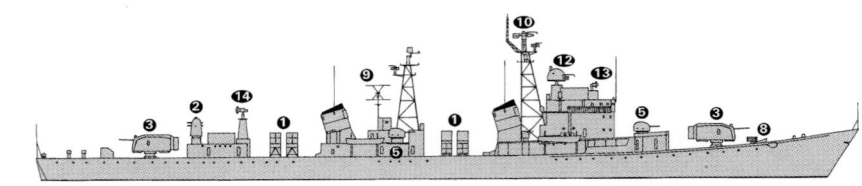

KAIFENG *(Scale 1 : 1,200)*, Ian Sturton / 0126350

KAIFENG (with C-801) *1/2000, Ships of the World* / 0103654

Modernisation: 109 redesignated Type 051DT after being
fitted with Tavitac, Sea Tiger radar and HQ-7 (Crotale).
In 1999, she was further modified to receive 16 C0801A
missiles, Type 825 ESM, Type 981 ECM and Type 946 chaff
launchers. 110 subsequently modernised with ZKJ-1
command system and an otherwise similar configuration
as 109. 166 underwent extensive modernisation 2001-03.
Principal enhancements include the replacement of YJ-1
by four quadruple YJ-81 missiles, the installation of an
octuple HQ-7 SAM launcher in place of the aft (X turret)
37 mm gun and the replacement of the 130 mm guns
with twin 100 mm guns fore and aft. 165 is reported to
have undergone a similar upgrade.
Structure: The VDS sonar is a copy of DUBV 43.
Operational: South Seas Fleet based at Zhanjiang. 166 has
used different pennant number on foreign deployments.

FRIGATES
2 JIANGKAI (TYPE 054) CLASS (FFGHM)

Name	No	Builders	Laid down	Launched	Commissioned
MAANSHAN	525	Hudong Shipyard, Shanghai	Dec 2001	11 Sep 2003	18 Feb 2005
WENZHOU	526	Huangpu Shipyard, Guangzhou	Feb 2002	Nov 2003	26 Sep 2005

Displacement, tons: 3,500 standard; 3,900 full load
Dimensions, feet (metres): 433.2 × 49.2 × 16.4
(132.0 × 15.0 × 5.0)
Main machinery: CODAD; 4 SEMT-Pielstick diesels; 2 shafts
Speed, knots: 27
Range, n miles: 3,800 at 18 kt
Complement: 190

Missiles: SSM: 8 C-803 (YJ-83/CSS-N-8 Saccade) ❶; mid-
course guidance and active radar homing to 150 km
(81 n miles) at 0.9 Mach; warhead 165 kg; sea skimmer.
SAM: 1 HQ-7 (Crotale) ❷; CSA-N-4 line-of-sight guidance to
13 km *(7 n miles)* at 2.4 Mach; warhead 14 kg.
Guns: 1—3.9 in *(100 mm)*/56 ❸; 18 rds/min to 22 km
(12 n miles); weight of shell 15 kg.
4—300 mm/65 AK 630 ❹; 6 barrels per mounting;
3,000 rds/min combined to 2km.
Torpedoes: 6—324 mm B515 (2 triple) tubes; Yu-2/6/7;
active/passive homing to 11 km *(5.9 n miles)* at 40 kt;
warhead 44 kg.
Countermeasures: to be announced.
Combat data systems: to be announced.

Radars: Air/surface search: Type 360 Seagull S ❺; E/F-band.
Surface search: Type 364 Seagull C ❻; G-band.
Fire control: Type 344 (MR 34) ❼; I-band (for SSM and
100 mm).
Type 345 (MR 35) ❽; I/J-band (for HQ-7).
Type 347G(1) Rice Bowl ❾; I-band (for AK 630).
Sonars: to be announced.

Helicopters: 1 Harbin Zhi-9C Haitun ❿.

Programmes: The first two vessels of a new general-
purpose frigate class to follow the Jiangwei II class and
to replace the Jianghu class. A third ship was believed
to be under construction at Huangpu Shipyard but this
has not been confirmed. A more advanced variant (Type
054A) with a VLS system is a possibility.
Structure: A new design incorporating stealth features.
Operational: Reports of possible engineering (shaft
alignment) problems have not been confirmed.

MAANSHAN *(Scale 1 : 1,200)*, Ian Sturton / 1042084

MAANSHAN *7/2004* / 0583666

4 JIANGWEI I (TYPE 053 H2G) CLASS (FFGHM)

Name	No	Builders	Laid down	Launched	Commissioned
ANQING	539	Hudong Shipyard, Shanghai	Nov 1990	July 1991	Dec 1991
HUAINAN	540 (548 out of area)	Hudong Shipyard, Shanghai	Jan 1991	Oct 1991	July 1992
HUAIBEI	541	Hudong Shipyard, Shanghai	July 1992	Apr 1993	Aug 1993
TONGLING	542	Hudong Shipyard, Shanghai	Dec 1992	Sep 1993	Apr 1994

Displacement, tons: 2,250 full load
Dimensions, feet (metres): 366.5 × 40.7 × 15.7
  (111.7 × 12.4 × 4.8)
Main machinery: 2 Type 18E 390 diesels; 24,000 hp(m)
  (17.65 MW) sustained; 2 shafts
Speed, knots: 27
Range, n miles: 4,000 at 18 kt
Complement: 170

Missiles: SSM: 6 YJ-1 (Eagle Strike) (C-801) (CSS-N-4 Sardine) or C-803 (YJ-83) (2 triple) launchers ❶; active radar homing to 40 km *(22 n miles)* or 150 km *(81 n miles)* (C-803) at 0.9 Mach; warhead 165 kg; sea-skimmer.
SAM: 1 HQ-61 sextuple launcher ❷; RF 61 (CSA-N-2); semi-active radar homing to 10 km *(5.5 n miles)* at 2 Mach. Similar to Sea Sparrow. May be replaced in due course.
Guns: 2 China 3.9 in *(100 mm)*/56 (twin) ❸; 18 rds/min to 22 km *(12 n miles)*; weight of shell 15.9 kg.
  8 China 37 mm/63 Type 76A (4 twin) ❹; 180 rds/min to 8.5 km *(4.6 n miles)* anti-aircraft; weight of shell 1.42 kg.
A/S mortars: 2 Type 87 ❺ 6-tubed launchers.
Countermeasures: Decoys: 2 China Type 945 26-barrelled chaff launchers ❻.
  ESM: RWD8; intercept.
  ECM: NJ81-3; jammer. Similar to Scimitar.
Radars: Air search: Type 517 Knife Rest ❼; A-band.
  Air/surface search: Type 360 Seagull S ❽; E/F-band.
  Fire control: Type 343 (Wok Won) (Wasp Head) ❾; I-band.
    Fog Lamp ❿; I/J-band (for SAM).
    Type 347G Rice Bowl ⓫; I/J-band (for 37 mm).
  Navigation: Racal Decca 1290 and China Type 360; I-band.
Sonars: Echo Type 5; hull-mounted; active search and attack; medium frequency.

Helicopters: 2 Harbin Z-9C (Dauphin) ⓬.

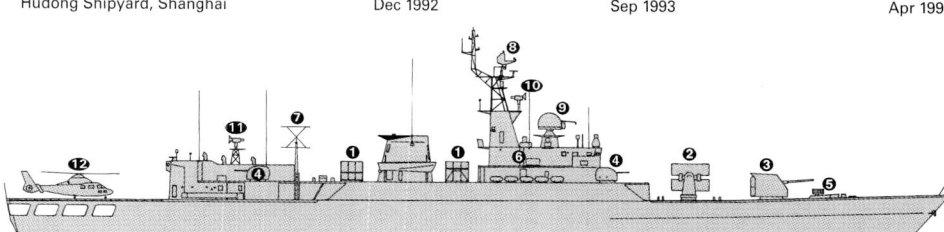

HUAIBEI *(Scale 1 : 900), Ian Sturton* / 0130723

HUAIBEI *4/2000, Ships of the World* / 0103659

Programmes: Programme started in 1988. First one conducted sea trials in late 1991. Four of the class built before the design moved on to the Jiangwei II.
Modernisation: SAM system has been unsatisfactory and may be replaced in due course.

Structure: The sextuple launcher is a multiple launch SAM system using the CSA-N-2 missile.
Operational: All based in the East Sea Fleet at Dinghai.

10 JIANGWEI II (TYPE 053H3) CLASS (FFGHM)

Name	No	Builders	Laid down	Launched	Commissioned
JIAXIN	521 (ex-597)	Hudong Shipyard, Shanghai	Oct 1996	10 Aug 1997	Nov 1998
LIANYUNGANG	522	Hudong Shipyard, Shanghai	Dec 1996	8 Aug 1997	Feb 1999
SANMING	523	Hudong Shipyard, Shanghai	June 1997	10 Aug 1998	Oct 1999
PUTIAN	524	Hudong Shipyard, Shanghai	Dec 1997	Dec 1998	Nov 1999
YICHANG	564	Huangpu Shipyard, Guangzhou	Dec 1997	Oct 1998	Dec 1999
YULIN	565	Huangpu Shipyard, Guangzhou	May 1998	Apr 1999	Mar 2000
HUAIHUA (ex-*Yuxi*)	566	Hudong Shipyard, Shanghai	May 2000	Jan 2001	Mar 2002
XIANGFAN	567	Huangpu Shipyard, Guangzhou	Mar 2001	Aug 2001	Sep 2002
LUOYANG	527	Hudong Shipyard, Shanghai	2003	1 Oct 2004	2005
MIANYANG	528	Huangpu Shipyard, Guangzhou	2003	30 May 2004	2005

Displacement, tons: 2,250 full load
Dimensions, feet (metres): 366.5 × 40.7 × 15.7
  (111.7 × 12.4 × 4.8)
Main machinery: 2 Type 18E 390 diesels; 24,000 hp(m)
  (17.65 MW) sustained; 2 shafts
Speed, knots: 27
Range, n miles: 4,000 at 18 kt
Complement: 170

Missiles: SSM: 8 YJ-1 (Eagle Strike) (C-801) (CSS-N-4 Sardine) or C-803 (YJ-83) (2 quad) launchers ❶; active radar homing to 40 km *(22 n miles)* or 150 km *(81 n miles)* (C-803) at 0.9 Mach; warhead 165 kg; sea-skimmer.
SAM: 1 HQ-7 (Crotale) octuple launcher ❷; CSA-N-4 line of sight guidance to 13 km *(7 n miles)* at 2.4 Mach; warhead 14 kg.
Guns: 2 China 3.9 in *(100 mm)*/56 (twin) ❸; 18 rds/min to 22 km *(12 n miles)*; weight of shell 15 kg.
  8 China 37 mm/63 Type 76A (4 twin) ❹; 180 rds/min to 8.5 km *(4.6 n miles)* anti-aircraft; weight of shell 1.42 kg.
A/S mortars: 2 RBU 1200 ❺; 5-tubed fixed launchers; range 1,200 m; warhead 34 kg.
Countermeasures: Decoys: 2 SRBOC Mk 36 6-barrelled chaff launchers ❻; 2 China 26-barrelled chaff launchers ❼.
  ESM: SR-210; intercept.
  ECM: 981-3 noise jammer. RWD-8 deception jammer.
Combat data systems: ZKJ 3C.
Weapons control: JM-83H optronic director.
Radars: Air search: Type 517 Knife Rest ❽; A-band.
  Air/surface search: Type 360 Seagull S ❾; E/F-band.
  Fire control: Type 343G ❿; I-band (for SSM and 100 mm).
    Type 345 (MR 35) ⓫; I/J-band (for SAM).
    Type 347G Rice Bowl ⓬; I/J-band (for 37 mm).
  Navigation: 2 RM-1290; I-band.
Sonars: Echo Type 5; hull-mounted; active search and attack; medium frequency.

Helicopters: 2 Harbin Z-9C (Dauphin) ⓭.

Programmes: Follow-on to the Jiangwei class, building some four years later. The building programme appeared to have been terminated after eight ships but reports indicate that two further ships are under construction. Further units are possible.
Structure: An improved SAM system, updated fire-control radars and a redistribution of the after anti-aircraft guns are the obvious differences from the original Jiangwei. New Type 99 turret fitted in 567 and to be retro-fitted to the remainder of the class.
Operational: 521-524 assigned to East Sea Fleet and 564-566 to South Sea Fleet.
Sales: Possibly two for Pakistan in due course, but with some changes in equipment fitted.

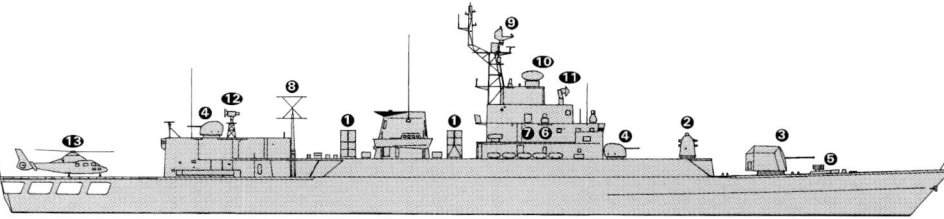

JIANGWEI II *(Scale 1 : 900), Ian Sturton* / 0569248

LIANYUNGANG *6/2005* / 1153075

LUOYANG *10/2004*
1042167

27 JIANGHU I/V (TYPE 053H) CLASS (FFG)

Name	No	Name	No	Name	No
CHANG DE	509	JIAN	518	ANSHUN	554
SHAOXING	510	CHANGZHI	519	ZHAOTONG	555
NANTONG	511	NINGBO	533	JISHOU	557
WUXI	512	JINHUA	534	ZIGONG	558
HUAYIN	513	DANDONG	543	KANGDING	559
ZHENJIANG	514	LINFEN	545	DONGGUAN	560
XIAMEN	515	MAOMING	551	SHANTOU	561
JIUJIANG	516	YIBIN	552	JIANGMEN	562
NANPING	517	SHAOGUAN	553	ZHAOQING	563

Displacement, tons: 1,425 standard; 1,702 full load
Dimensions, feet (metres): 338.5 × 35.4 × 10.2
(103.2 × 10.8 × 3.1)
Main machinery: 2 Type 12E 390V diesels; 14,400 hp(m)
(10.6 MW) sustained; 2 shafts
Speed, knots: 26
Range, n miles: 4,000 at 15 kt; 2,700 at 18 kt
Complement: 200 (30 officers)

Missiles: SSM: 4 HY-2 (C-201) (CSSC-3 Seersucker)
(2 twin) launchers ❶; active radar or IR homing to 80 km
(43.2 n miles) at 0.9 Mach; warhead 513 kg.
Guns: 2 or 4 China 3.9 in *(100 mm)*/56 (2 single ❷ or
2 twin ❸); 18 rds/min to 22 km *(12 n miles)*; weight of
shell 15.9 kg.
12 China 37 mm/63 (6 twin) ❹ (8 (4 twin), in some);
180 rds/min to 8.5 km *(4.6 n miles)* anti-aircraft; weight
of shell 1.42 kg.
A/S mortars: 2 RBU 1200 5-tubed fixed launchers
(4 in some) ❺; range 1,200 m; warhead 34 kg.
Depth charges: 2 BMB-2 projectors; 2 racks (in some).
Mines: Can carry up to 60.
Countermeasures: Decoys: 2 RBOC Mk 33 6-barrelled chaff
launchers or 2 China 26-barrelled launchers.
ESM: Jug Pair or Watchdog; radar warning.
Weapons control: Wok Won director (in some) ❻.
Radars: Air search: Type 517 Knife Rest ❼; A-band.
Air/surface search: Type 354 Eye Shield (MX 902) ❽;
G-band.
Type (unknown) ❾; I-band.
Surface search/fire control: Type 352 Square Tie ❿; I-band.
Navigation: Don 2 or Fin Curve or Racal Decca; I-band.
Fire control: Type 347G Rice Bowl (in some) ⓫; I/J-band.
Type 343 (Wok Won) (Wasp Head) (in some) ⓬; I-band.
IFF: High Pole A. Yard Rake or Square Head.
Sonars: Echo Type 5; hull-mounted; active search and
attack; medium frequency.

Programmes: Pennant numbers changed in 1979. All built
in Shanghai starting in the mid-1970s at the Hudong,
Jiangnan and Huangpu shipyards. Ships were completed
in the following order: 515, 516, 517, 511, 512, 513, 514,
518, 509, 510, 519, 520, 551, 552, 533, 534, two for Egypt,
543, 553, 554, 555, 545, 556 (to Bangladesh), 557, 544,
558, 560, 561, 559, 562 and 563. The last of class 563
completed in February 1996. Reports that construction
had restarted in 1997 were incorrect.
Modernisation: Equipment varies considerably from ship
to ship. The Type 053H ships are 509—519 and 551 and
552. These are equipped with SY-1 or SY-2 SSM, a single
100 mm gun and SJD-3 sonar. Type 053H1 ships are 533,
534, 543, 544, 553, 554, 555 and 557. These are similar to
Type 053H but are equipped with twin 100 mm guns and
SJD-5 (Echo 5) sonar. Type 053H1G ships are 558—563.
These are similar to Type 053H1 but are equipped with
37 mm enclosed gun mounts. A larger bridge structure
suggests a possible CIC compartment. The designation
of the Air/Surface search radar in Type 053H1G is not
yet known but it bears similarities to the I-band MR-36A
which has been promoted as a replacement for Type 352
'Square Tie'. 516 appears to have been modified for a
shore bombardment role having been fitted with a new
twin 100 mm mounting and seven 122 mm MLRs. This is
known as Jianghu V class.
Structure: All of the class have the same hull dimensions.
Previously reported Type numbers have been superseded
by the following designations:
Type I has at least five versions. Version 1 has an oval
funnel and square bridge wings; version 2 a square
funnel with bevelled bridge face; version 3 an octagonal
funnel; version 4 reverts back to the oval funnel and
version 5 has a distinctive fluting arrangement with
cowls on the funnel, as well as gunhouses on the 37 mm
guns. Some have bow bulwarks.
Type II. See separate entry.

ZHENJIANG (single 100 mm gun) *(Scale 1 : 900), Ian Sturton* / 0529151

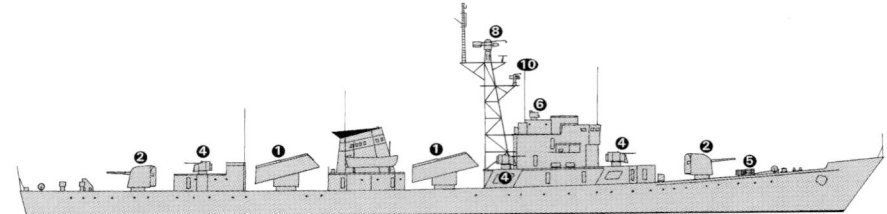

NINGBO (Rice Lamp FC radar) *(Scale 1 : 900), Ian Sturton* / 0130728

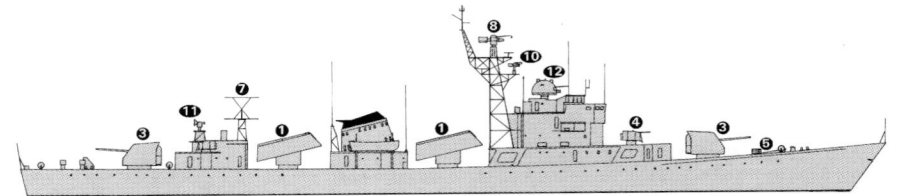

DONGGUAN (37 mm gunhouses) *(Scale 1 : 900), Ian Sturton* / 0130727

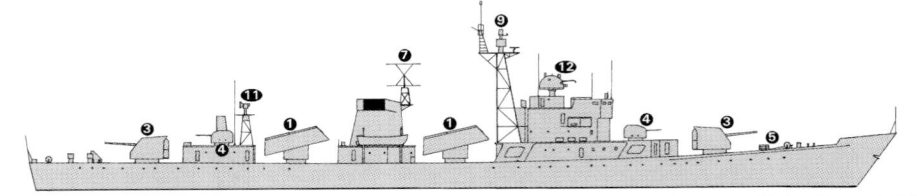

SHANTOU *9/2000* / 0103662

Types III and IV. See separate entry.
Operational: 520 paid off in 1993. Ten are based in the
Eastern Fleet, three in the North and the remainder in
the South.

Sales: Two have been transferred to Egypt, one in
September 1984, the other in March 1985, and one,
Xiangtan 556, to Bangladesh in November 1989.

XIAMEN *12/2005*, Ships of the World* / 1153059

JIUJIANG *7/2004, Ian Edwards* / 1042409

KANGDING *1/1999, 92 Wing RAAF* / 0056763

WUXI *5/2004* / 1042132

3 JIANGHU III AND IV (TYPE 053 H2) CLASS (FFG)

HUANGSHI 535 (Type III)	WUHU 536 (Type III)	ZHOUSHAN 537 (Type IV)

Displacement, tons: 1,924 full load
Dimensions, feet (metres): 338.5 × 35.4 × 10.2
(103.2 × 10.8 × 3.1)
Main machinery: 2 Type 18E 390V diesels; 14,400 hp(m)
(10.6 MW) sustained; 2 shafts
Speed, knots: 26
Range, n miles: 4,000 at 15 kt; 2,700 at 18 kt
Complement: 200 (30 officers)

Missiles: SSM: 8 YJ-1 (Eagle Strike) (C-801) (CSS-N-4
Sardine) ❶; active radar homing to 40 km *(22 n miles)*
at 0.9 Mach; warhead 165 kg. Type IV is fitted with C-803
(YJ-83) (CSS-N-8 Saccade) with an extended range to
150 km *(81 n miles)*.
Guns: 4 China 3.9 in *(100 mm)*/56 (2 twin) ❷; 18 rds/min to
22 km *(12 n miles)*; weight of shell 15.9 kg.
8 China 37 mm/63 (4 twin) ❸; 180 rds/min to 8.5 km
(4.6 n miles) anti-aircraft; weight of shell 1.42 kg.
A/S mortars: 2 RBU 1200 5-tubed fixed launchers ❹; range
1,200 m; warhead 34 kg.
Depth charges: 2 BMB-2 projectors; 2 racks.
Mines: Can carry up to 60.
Countermeasures: Decoys: 2 China 26-barrelled chaff
launchers.
ESM: Elettronica Newton; radar warning.
ECM: Elettronica 929 (Type 981); jammer.
Combat data systems: ZKJ-3.
Radars: Air search: Type 517 Knife Rest ❺; A-band.

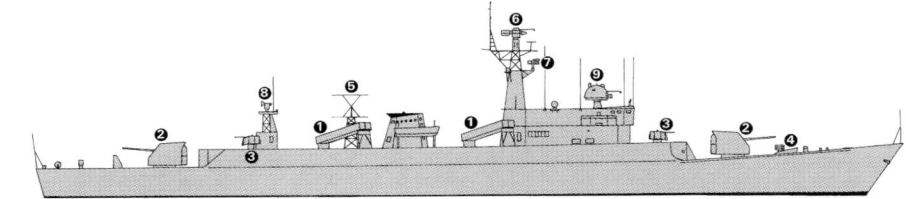

Air/surface search: Type 354 Eye Shield (MX 902) ❻;
G-band.
Surface search/fire control: Type 352 Square Tie ❼; I-band.
Navigation: Fin Curve; I-band.
Fire control: Type 347G Rice Bowl ❽; I/J-band.
Type 343G (Wok Won) (Wasp Head) ❾; I-band.
IFF: High Pole A. Square Head.
Sonars: Echo Type 5; hull-mounted; active search and
attack; medium frequency.

Programmes: These ships are Jianghu hulls 27, 28 and 30
and are referred to as New Missile Frigates. *Huangshi*
commissioned 14 December 1986, *Wuhu* in 1987,
and *Zhoushan* completed in 1989. They were the first

(Scale 1 : 900), Ian Sturton / 0130726

Chinese warships to be equipped with a computerised
combat system. A fourth of class 538 was reported in
1991 but may have been confused with one of the Thai
ships.
Structure: The main deck is higher in the midships section
and the lower part of the mast is solid. Type IV has an
improved SSM missile which is probably the turbojet
C-802. The arrangement of the launchers is side by side,
as opposed to the staggered pairings in Type III. These
are the first all-enclosed, air conditioned ships built in
China.
Operational: Based in East Sea Fleet at Dinghai.
Sales: Four modified Type III to Thailand in 1991-92.

ZHOUSHAN

10/1992, Ships of the World / 0056766

HUANGSHI

2/2001, Ships of the World / 0126362

1 JIANGHU II (TYPE 053) CLASS (FFGH)

Name	No	Builders	Laid down	Launched	Commissioned
SIPING	544	Hudong Shipyard, Shanghai	1984	Sep 1985	Nov 1986

Displacement, tons: 1,550 standard; 1,865 full load
Dimensions, feet (metres): 338.5 × 35.4 × 10.2
(*103.2 × 10.8 × 3.1*)
Main machinery: 2 Type 12E 390V diesels; 14,400 hp(m)
(*10.6 MW*) sustained; 2 shafts
Speed, knots: 26
Range, n miles: 4,000 at 15 kt; 2,700 at 18 kt
Complement: 185 (30 officers)

Missiles: SSM: 2 HY-2 (C-201) (CSSC-3 Seersucker) (twin)
launchers ❶; active radar or IR homing to 80 km (*43.2 n
miles*) at 0.9 Mach; warhead 513 kg.
Guns: 1 Creusot-Loire 3.9 in (*100 mm*)/55 ❷; 60—80 rds/min
to 17 km (*9.3 n miles*); weight of shell 13.5 kg.
8 China 37 mm/63 (4 twin) ❸; 180 rds/min to 8.5 km
(*4.6 n miles*) anti-aircraft; weight of shell 1.42 kg.
Torpedoes: 6—324 mm ILAS (2 triple) tubes ❹. Yu-2 (Mk 46
Mod 1) active/passive homing to 11 km (*5.9 n miles*) at 40 kt;
warhead 44 kg.
A/S mortars: 2 RBU 1200 5-tubed fixed launchers ❺; range
1,200 m; warhead 34 kg.
Countermeasures: Decoys: 2 SRBOC Mk 33 6-barrelled
chaff launchers or 2 China 26-barrelled launchers.
ESM: Jug Pair or Watchdog; radar warning.
Weapons control: CSEE Naja optronic director for 100 mm
gun.
Radars: Air/surface search: Type 354 Eye Shield (MX 902)
❻; G-band.
Surface search/fire control: Type 352 Square Tie ❼; I-band.
Navigation: Don 2 or Fin Curve; I-band.
IFF: High Pole A. Yard Rake or Square Head.
Sonars: Echo Type 5; hull-mounted; active search and
attack; medium frequency.

Helicopters: Harbin Z-9C (Dauphin) ❽.

Programmes: Built as a standard Jianghu I and
then converted, probably as a helicopter trials ship

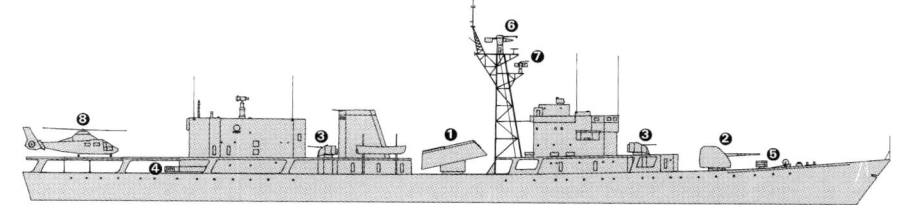

SIPING   (*Scale 1 : 900*), *Ian Sturton* / 0572397

SIPING   *6/2003* / 0569166

for the Luhu and Jiangwei classes, before being
commissioned.
Structure: The after part of the ship has been rebuilt to take
a hangar and flight deck for a single helicopter. Alcatel

'Safecopter' landing aid. This ship also has a French
100 mm gun and optronic director, and Italian triple
torpedo tubes mounted on the quarterdeck.
Operational: Based in North Sea Fleet at Guzhen Bay.

SHIPBORNE AIRCRAFT

Numbers/Type: 20 Changhe Z-8 Super Frelon.
Operational speed: 134 kt (*248 km/h*).
Service ceiling: 10,000 ft (*3,100 m*).
Range: 440 n miles (*815 km*).
Role/Weapon systems: ASW helicopter; SA 321G delivered from France in 1977 but
supplemented by locally built Zhi-8, of which the first operational aircraft was delivered
in late 1991. Thomson Sintra HS-12 in four SA 321Gs for SSBN escort role. Sensors:
HS-12 dipping sonar and processor, some have French-built search radar. Weapons:
ASW; Whitehead A244 or Yu-2 (Mk 46 Mod 1) torpedo. ASV; C-802K ASM.

Z-8   *9/2002, Paul Jackson* / 0525833

Numbers/Type: 25 Hai Z-9C Haitun (Dauphin 2).
Operational speed: 140 kt (*260 km/h*).
Service ceiling: 15,000 ft (*4,575 m*).
Range: 410 n miles (*758 km*).
Role/Weapon systems: China has an option to continue building. Sensors: Thomson-CSF
Agrion; HS-12 dipping sonar; Crouzet MAD. Weapons: ASV; up to four locally built radar-
guided anti-ship missiles and Whitehead A244 torpedoes or Yu-2 (Mk 46 Mod 1).

Z-9C   *4/2002* / 0106480

Numbers/Type: 6/4 Kamov Ka 28PL/28PS Helix A.
Operational speed: 135 kt (*250 km/h*).
Service ceiling: 19,685 ft (*6,000 m*).
Range: 432 n miles (*800 km*).
Role/Weapon systems: First pair are (Ka 28PL) ASW helicopters acquired in 1997 for
evaluation. Four more ASW versions and four (Ka 28PS) for SAR delivered in late
1999. Sensors: Splash Drop radar; VGS-3 dipping sonar; MAD; ESM. Weapons: three
torpedoes or depth bombs or mines.

Ka-28   *6/2004* / 1042165

LAND-BASED MARITIME AIRCRAFT (FRONT LINE)

Notes: In addition to those listed there are about 170 training and transport aircraft.

Numbers/Type: 3 KJ-2000 AWACS.
Operational speed: 425 kt (*785 km/h*).
Service ceiling: 34,440 ft (*10,500 m*).
Range: 2,753 n miles (*5,100 km*).
Role/Weapon systems: Airborne Warning And Control System (AWACS) aircraft based
on the Russian-made A-50 (Mainstay) airframe. The non-rotating radome houses
three Chinese-made (ESA) phased array antennas in a triangular configuration.
A SATCOM antenna may be installed inside a fairing on top of forward cabin. At least
three prototypes have been built since 2002 and are undergoing tests at China Flight
Test Establishment (CFTE) in Yanliang, Shaanxi Province and Nanjing, Jiangsu Province
where the main contractor for the radar system, Nanjing Research Institute of Electronic
Technology (also known as 14 Institute), is based. The aircraft is expected to be ready for
operational deployment by 2007.

KJ-2000   *8/2005*, Jane's* / 1046316

Numbers/Type: 48 Sukhoi Su-30 MKK 2 Flanker.
Operational speed: 1,345 kt *(2,500 km/h)*.
Service ceiling: 59,000 ft *(18,000 m)*.
Range: 2,160 n miles *(4,000 km)*.
Role/Weapon systems: 24 delivered in 2004 and delivery of a further 24 expected. The air force operates at least 130 of the similar Su-27 which also might be used for fleet air-defence. Sensors: Doppler radar. Weapons: One 30 mm cannon; 10 AAMs. Kh-35 anti-ship missiles may be fitted to some aircraft in due course.

Su-27 *5/2003* / 0114638

Numbers/Type: 18 XAC JH-7.
Operational speed: 653 kt *(1,210 km/h)*.
Service ceiling: 51,180 ft *(15,600 m)*.
Range: 891 n miles *(1,650 km)*.
Role/Weapon systems: All-weather dual seat 'Fencer' type attack fighter first revealed in 1988 and being redesigned for export market (FBC-1). A second batch of JH-7A is expected. Further domestic orders not thought likely. Sensors: Letri JL-10A Shen-Ying pulse Doppler fire-control radar capable of tracking four targets to 29 n miles *(54 km)* in look-down mode simultaneously. Weapons: AAM; PL-5b, PL-7 and 23 mm gun. ASM; Two C-801 or C-802 anti-ship missiles; C-701 anti-ship missile and 500 kg LGBs. AS-17 (Kh-31) may be fitted in due course.

JH-7 *5/2003* / 0114641

Numbers/Type: 4 Harbin SH-5.
Operational speed: 243 kt *(450 km/h)*.
Service ceiling: 23,000 ft *(7,000 m)*.
Range: 2,563 n miles *(4,750 km)*.
Role/Weapon systems: Multipurpose amphibian introduced into service in 1986. Final total of about 20 planned with ASW and avionics upgrade. Sensors: Doppler radar; MAD; sonobuoys. Weapons: ASV; four C 101, two gun turret, bombs. ASW; Yu-2 (Mk 46 Mod 1) torpedoes, mines, depth bombs.

SH-5 *6/2004* / 1042160

Numbers/Type: 3 SAC Y-8X (Cub).
Operational speed: 351 kt *(650 km/h)*.
Service ceiling: 34,120 ft *(10,400 m)*.
Range: 3,020 n miles *(5,600 km)*.
Role/Weapon systems: Maritime patrol version of An-12 Cub transport; first flown 1985. There are reported to be two Y-8J variants equipped with Searchwater radar in a dropped nose radome. In addition a Y-8DZ Elint variant was reported undergoing trials in 2004. Sensors: Litton APSO-504(V)3 search radar in undernose radome. Two Litton LTN 72R INS and Omega/Loran. Weapons: No weapons carried.

Y-8X *7/1997* / 0012195

Numbers/Type: 100 Harbin H-5 (Il-28 Beagle).
Operational speed: 487 kt *(902 km/h)*.
Service ceiling: 40,350 ft *(12,300 m)*.
Range: 1,175 n miles *(2,180 km)*.
Role/Weapon systems: Overwater strike aircraft with ASW/ASVW roles. Numbers are doubtful as some have been phased out and others moved into second line roles such as target towing and ECM training. Weapons: ASW; two torpedoes or four depth bombs. ASVW; one torpedo + mines. Standard; four 23 mm cannon.

Numbers/Type: 50/50/20 SAC J-8-I Finback A/J-8-II Finback B/J-8-IV Finback D.
Operational speed: 701 kt *(1,300 km/h)*.
Service ceiling: 65,620 ft *(20,000 m)*.
Range: 1,187 n miles *(2,200 km)*.
Role/Weapon systems: Dual role, all-weather fighter introduced into service in 1990 and production continues. There are at least 450 more in service with the Air Force. Weapons: 23 mm twin-barrel cannon; PL-2/7 AAM; ASM. PL-2 has some ASM capability.

J-8-II *4/2002* / 0116938

Numbers/Type: 40 Nanchang A-5 (Fantan-A).
Operational speed: 643 kt *(1,190 km/h)*.
Service ceiling: 52,500 ft *(16,000 m)*.
Range: 650 n miles *(1,188 km)*.
Role/Weapon systems: Strike aircraft developed from Shenyang J-6; operated in the beachhead and coastal shipping attack role. A-5M version adapted to carry two torpedoes or C-801 ASM. Weapons: Two 23 mm cannon, two cluster bombs, one or two air-to-air missiles. Capable of carrying 1 ton warload.

FANTAN-A *6/2002, Ships of the World* / 0554726

Numbers/Type: 200 Shenyang J-6 (MiG-19 Ffarmer).
Operational speed: 831 kt *(1,540 km/h)*.
Service ceiling: 58,725 ft *(17,900 m)*.
Range: 1,187 n miles *(2,200 km)*.
Role/Weapon systems: Strike fighter for Fleet air defence and anti-shipping strike. Weapons: Fleet air defence role; four AA-1 ('Alkali') beam-riding missiles. Attack; some 1,000 kg of underwing bombs or depth charges, PL-2 missile has anti-ship capability.

Numbers/Type: 30/1 XAC H-6D/H-6X (Tu-16 Badger).
Operational speed: 535 kt *(992 km/h)*.
Service ceiling: 40,350 ft *(12,300 m)*.
Range: 2,605 n miles *(4,800 km)*.
Role/Weapon systems: Three regiments of H-6D bomber and maritime reconnaissance aircraft. Some converted as tankers. H-6s now believed to be out of service and deliveries of new version H-6X, armed with ASM, have begun. Sensors: Search/attack radar; ECM. Weapons: ASV; two underwing anti-shipping missiles of local manufacture, including C-801. Up to five 23 mm cannon; bombs.

H-6X *6/2004* / 1042161

Numbers/Type: 200 CAC J-7.
Operational speed: 1,175 kt *(2,175 km/h)*.
Service ceiling: 61,680 ft *(18,800 m)*.
Range: 804 n miles *(1,490 km)*.
Role/Weapon systems: Land-based Fleet air defence fighter with limited strike role against enemy shipping or beachhead. Most are J-7 but also some J-7E in service. Sensors: Search attack radar, some ECM. Weapons: ASV; 500 kg bombs or 36 rockets. Standard; two 30 mm cannon. AD; two 'Atoll' AAMs.

J-7E *6/2002, Ships of the World* / 0554725

PATROL FORCES

Notes: (1) Many patrol craft carry the HN-5 shoulder-launched Chinese version of the SA-N-5 SAM.
(2) More Patrol Craft are listed under Paramilitary vessels at the end of the Chinese section.

4 HOUBEI CLASS (FAST ATTACK CRAFT—MISSILE) (PGGF)

2208-2211

Displacement, tons: 220 full load
Dimensions, feet (metres): 141.1 × 39.4 × 4.9 *(43.0 × 12.0 × 1.5)*
Main machinery: 2 diesels; 6,865 hp *(5.1 MW)*; 4 waterjet propulsors
Speed, knots: 36
Complement: 12
Missiles: 4 SSM.
Guns: 1—30 mm/65 AK 630; 6 barrels; 3,000 rds/min combined to 2 km; 12 missiles.
Weapons control: Optronic director.
Radars: Surface search Type: 362 (ESR-1); I-band.
Navigation: I-band.

Comment: A new fast attack craft, the first of which was launched at Qiuxin Shipyard, Shanghai in April 2004. The design is believed to be based on a 42 m hull developed by AMD Marine Consulting, Sydney. This was further progressed by its joint venture company in Guangzhou, Sea Bus International (SBI), into a patrol boat configuration which was selected by the Chinese Navy after a five-year investigation into various platform contenders. The craft has a wave-piercing catamaran hull form and a centre bow. Likely to be of aluminium alloy construction, the design clearly incorporates RCS reduction measures. Following extensive first of class trials, three further craft have been constructed and it is likely that full production has started at other shipyards. Large numbers are expected to replace the ageing patrol boat inventory. Dimensions are based on the original AMD design and other details are speculative.

HOUBEI 2210 *11/2004* / 1042171

HOUBEI 2208 *6/2005*, Massimo Annati* / 1153108

16 HOUXIN (TYPE 037/1G) CLASS
(FAST ATTACK CRAFT—MISSILE) (PTG)

751-760   764-769

Displacement, tons: 478 full load
Dimensions, feet (metres): 203.4 × 23.6 × 7.5 *(62.8 × 7.2 × 2.4)*
Main machinery: 4 China PR 230ZC diesels; 4,000 hp(m) *(2.94 MW)*; 4 shafts
Speed, knots: 28
Range, n miles: 750 at 18 kt
Complement: 71

Missiles: SSM: 4 YJ-1 (Eagle Strike) (C-801) (CSS-N-4 Sardine) (2 twin); active radar homing to 40 km *(22 n miles)* at 0.9 Mach; warhead 165 kg; sea-skimmer. C-802 in due course.
Guns: 4—37 mm/63 (Type 76A) (2 twin); 180 rds/min to 8.5 km *(4.6 n miles)* anti-aircraft; weight of shell 1.42 kg.
4—14.5 mm (Type 69) (2 twin); 600 rds/min to 7 km *(3.8 n miles)*.
Countermeasures: ESM/ECM: Intercept and jammer.
Radars: Surface search: Square Tie; I-band.
Fire control: Rice Lamp; I-band.
Navigation: Anritsu Type 723; I-band.

Programmes: First seen in 1991 and built at the rate of up to three per year at Qiuxin and Huangpu Shipyards to replace the Houku class and for export. Building may have stopped in mid-1999.
Structure: This is a missile armed version of the Hainan class. There are some variations in the bridge superstructure in later ships of the class.
Operational: Split between the East and South Sea Fleets.
Sales: Two to Burma in December 1995, two in July 1996 and two in late 1997.

HOUXIN 758 *3/2003, Bob Fildes* / 0569184

HOUXIN 765 *5/2004** / 1042140

2 HAIJIU CLASS (LARGE PATROL CRAFT) (PC)

688   697

Displacement, tons: 490 full load
Dimensions, feet (metres): 210 × 23.6 × 7.2 *(64 × 7.2 × 2.2)*
Main machinery: 4 diesels; 8,800 hp(m) *(6.47 MW)*; 4 shafts
Speed, knots: 28
Range, n miles: 750 at 18 kt
Complement: 72
Guns: 4 China 57 mm/70 (2 twin); 120 rds/min to 12 km *(6.5 n miles)*; weight of shell 6.31 kg.
2 USSR 30 mm/65 (1 twin); 500 rds/min to 5 km *(2.7 n miles)* anti-aircraft; weight of shell 0.54 kg.
A/S mortars: 4 RBU 1200 5-tubed fixed launchers; range 1,200 m; warhead 34 kg.
Depth charges: 2 rails.
Radars: Surface search: Pot Head; I-band.
Fire control: Round Ball; I-band.
Sonars: Stag Ear or Thomson Sintra SS 12.

Comment: A lengthened version of the Hainan class probably used as a prototype for the Houxin class. *697* seen with a Thomson Sintra SS 12 VDS Sonar. Both in East Sea Fleet. Two others have been scrapped.

HAIJIU CLASS *4/1990, John Mapletoft* / 0056768

7 HOUJIAN (OR HUANG) (TYPE 037/2) CLASS
(FAST ATTACK CRAFT—MISSILE) (PTG)

Name	No	Builders	Launched	Commissioned
YANGJIANG	770	Huangpu Shipyard	Jan 1991	May 1991
SHUNDE	771	Huangpu Shipyard	July 1994	Feb 1995
NANHAI	772	Huangpu Shipyard	Feb 1995	Apr 1995
PANYU	773	Huangpu Shipyard	May 1995	July 1995
–	774	Huangpu Shipyard	Sep 1998	Feb 1999
–	775	Huangpu Shipyard	Apr 1999	Nov 1999
–	776	Huangpu Shipyard	–	2000

Displacement, tons: 520 standard
Dimensions, feet (metres): 214.6 × 27.6 × 7.9 *(65.4 × 8.4 × 2.4)*
Main machinery: 3 SEMT-Pielstick 12 PA6 280 diesels; 15,840 hp(m) *(11.7 MW)* sustained; 3 shafts
Speed, knots: 32
Range, n miles: 1,800 at 18 kt
Complement: 75

Missiles: SSM: 6 YJ-1 (Eagle Strike) (C-801) (CSS-N-4 Sardine) (2 triple); inertial cruise; active radar homing to 40 km *(22 n miles)* at 0.9 Mach; warhead 165 kg or C-802 (CSS-N-8 Saccade); range 120 km *(66 n miles)*.
Guns: 2—37 mm/63 (twin) Type 76A; 180 rds/min to 8.5 km *(4.6 n miles)* anti-aircraft; weight of shell 1.42 kg.
4—30 mm/65 (2 twin) Type 69; 500 rds/min to 5 km *(2.7 n miles)*; weight of shell 0.54 kg.
Countermeasures: Decoys: 2 Type 945G 26-barrelled launcher.
ESM: Type 928; intercept.
Weapons control: Type JM-83 optronic director.
Radars: Surface search: Type 348 (MR 36); I-band.
Fire control: Type 347G Rice Bowl; I-band.
Navigation: Type 765; I-band.

Programmes: First of class laid down in 1989 and built in a very short time. Sometimes called the Huang class.
Modernisation: Some may be fitted with Type 363 search radar and Type 344 (MR 34) fire-control radar rather than Type 347G.
Operational: Based in South Sea Fleet at Hong Kong from mid-1997. One possibly sunk in late 1997.

YANGJIANG *12/2002, Ian Edwards* / 1042408

98 HAINAN (TYPE 037) CLASS
(FAST ATTACK CRAFT—PATROL) (PC)

275-285, 290, 302, 305, 609, 610, 618-622, 626-629, 636-643, 646-681, 683-687, 689-692, 695-699, 701, 707, 723-733, 740-742

Displacement, tons: 375 standard; 392 full load
Dimensions, feet (metres): 192.8 × 23.6 × 7.2 *(58.8 × 7.2 × 2.2)*
Main machinery: 4 PCR/Kolomna Type 9-D-8 diesels; 4,000 hp(m) *(2.94 MW)* sustained; 4 shafts
Speed, knots: 30.5
Range, n miles: 1,300 at 15 kt
Complement: 78

Missiles: Can be fitted with 4 YJ-1 launchers in lieu of the after 57 mm gun.
Guns: 4 China 57 mm/70 (2 twin); 120 rds/min to 12 km *(6.5 n miles)*; weight of shell 6.31 kg.
  4 USSR 25 mm/60 (2 twin); 270 rds/min to 3 km *(1.6 n miles)* anti-aircraft; weight of shell 0.34 kg.
A/S mortars: 4 RBU 1200 5-tubed fixed launchers; range 1,200 m; warhead 34 kg.
Depth charges: 2 BMB-2 projectors; 2 racks. 18 DCs.
Mines: Rails fitted for 12.
Radars: Surface search: Pot Head or Skin Head; E/F-band.
IFF: High Pole.
Sonars: Stag Ear; hull-mounted; active search and attack; high frequency.
  Thomson Sintra SS 12 (in some); VDS.

Programmes: A larger Chinese-built version of the former Soviet SO 1. Low freeboard. Programme started 1963-64 and continued with new hulls replacing the first ships of the class. There are at least six variants with minor differences.
Structure: Later ships have a tripod or solid foremast in place of a pole and a short stub mainmast. Two trials SS 12 sonars fitted in 1987.
Operational: Divided between the three Fleets.
Sales: Two to Bangladesh, one in 1982 and one in 1985; eight to Egypt in 1983-84; six to North Korea 1975-78; four to Pakistan, two in 1976 and two in 1980; six to Burma in 1991 and four in 1993.

HAINAN 685   *5/2004* / 1042138

HAINAN 686   *3/2001, Ships of the World* / 0126358

14 HUANGFEN (TYPE 021) (OSA I TYPE) and 1 HOLA CLASS
(FAST ATTACK CRAFT—MISSILE) (PTGF)/(FAST ATTACK CRAFT—MISSILE) (PCFG)

3100 series   **6100** series   **7100** series

Displacement, tons: 171 standard; 205 full load
Dimensions, feet (metres): 126.6 × 24.9 × 8.9 *(38.6 × 7.6 × 2.7)*
Main machinery: 3 Type 42—160 diesels; 12,000 hp(m) *(8.8 MW)* sustained; 3 shafts
Speed, knots: 35
Range, n miles: 800 at 30 kt
Complement: 28

Missiles: SSM: 4 HY-2 (CSS-N-3 Seersucker) (2 twin) launchers; active radar or IR homing to 80 km *(43.2 n miles)* at 0.9 Mach; warhead 513 kg.
Guns: 4 USSR 25 mm/60 (2 twin); 270 rds/min to 3 km *(1.6 n miles)* anti-aircraft.
  Replaced in some by 4 USSR 30 mm/65 (2 twin) AK 230.
Radars: Surface search: Square Tie; I-band.
Fire control: Round Ball or Rice Lamp; H/I-band.
IFF: 2 Square Head; High Pole A.

Programmes: First reported in 1985.
Structure: The only Hola class has a radome aft, four launchers, no guns, slightly larger dimensions (137.8 ft *(42 m)* long) and a folding mast. This radome is also fitted in others which carry 30 mm guns. Pennant numbers: Hola, 5100 and the remainder 3100/7100 series.
Operational: China credits this class with a speed of 39 kt. Split between the Fleets. Numbers continue to be reduced.
Sales: Four to North Korea, 1980; four to Pakistan, 1984; four to Bangladesh, 1988; and one more in 1992. Three of a variant were transferred to Yemen in June 1995, delivery having been delayed by the Yemen civil war. A variant called the Houdong class has been built for Iran. Five delivered to Iran in September 1994, five more in March 1996.

HUANGFEN 6120   *3/2002, Ships of the World* / 0529118

20 HAIQING (TYPE 037/1) CLASS
(FAST ATTACK CRAFT—PATROL) (PC)

710-717, 743-744, 761-763, 786-792

Displacement, tons: 478 full load
Dimensions, feet (metres): 206 × 23.6 × 7.9 *(62.8 × 7.2 × 2.4)*
Main machinery: 4 Chinese PR 230ZC diesels; 4,000 hp(m) *(2.94 MW)* sustained; 4 shafts
Speed, knots: 28. **Range, n miles:** 1,300 at 15 kt
Complement: 71

Guns: 4 China 37 mm/63 (2 twin) Type 76. 4 China 14.5 mm (2 twin) Type 69.
A/S mortars: 2 Type 87 6-tubed launchers.
Radars: Surface search: Anritsu RA 723; I-band.
Sonars: Hull mounted; active search and attack; medium frequency Thomson Sintra SS 12; VDS.

Programmes: Starting building at Qiuxin Shipyard in 1992 and replaced the Hainan class programme. First one completed in November 1993. Production continued at Qingdao, Chongqing and Huangpu as well as Qiuxin.
Structure: Based on the Hainan class, but the large A/S mortars suggest a predominantly ASW role, and this may explain the rapid building rate.
Operational: In service in all three Fleets. Some pennant numbers may have changed.
Sales: One to Sri Lanka in December 1995.

HAIQING 713   *6/2003, Ships of the World* / 0569183

15 HAIZHUI/SHANGHAI III (TYPE 062/1) CLASS
(COASTAL PATROL CRAFT) (PC)

1203	2327	4339	4341	4345-4348
1204	2329	4340	4342	+3

Displacement, tons: 170 full load
Dimensions, feet (metres): 134.5 × 17.4 × 5.9 *(41 × 5.3 × 1.8)*
Main machinery: 4 Chinese L12-180A diesels; 4,400 hp(m) *(3.22 MW)* sustained; 4 shafts
Speed, knots: 25
Range, n miles: 750 at 17 kt
Complement: 43

Guns: 4 China 37 mm/63 (2 twin); 180 rds/min to 8.5 km *(4.6 n miles)*; weight of shell 1.42 kg.
  4 China 14.5 mm (2 twin) Type 69 or 4 China 25 mm (2 twin).
Radars: Surface search: Pot Head or Anritsu 726; I-band.
Sonars: Stag Ear; hull-mounted; active search; high frequency (in some).

Programmes: First seen in 1992 and built for Chinese use and for export. Sometimes referred to as Shanghai III class when not fitted with ASW equipment.
Structure: Lengthened Shanghai II hull. Inclined pole mast and a pronounced step at the back of the bridge superstructure are recognition features. Much reduced top speed. Some may be equipped with RBU 1200 launchers in place of other armament.
Operational: Based in the North and East Sea Fleets.
Sales: Three of a variant to Tunisia in 1994, three to Sri Lanka in August 1995, three more in May 1996 and three more in August 1998. One to Bangladesh in mid-1996. One to Sierra Leone in 1997.

HAIZHUI 1203   *12/2005*, A Sheldon-Duplaix* / 1153107

HAIZHUI 1204   *4/2004* / 1042139

35 SHANGHAI II (TYPE 062) CLASS
(FAST ATTACK CRAFT—GUN) (PC)

Displacement, tons: 113 standard; 134 full load
Dimensions, feet (metres): 127.3 × 17.7 × 5.6 *(38.8 × 5.4 × 1.7)*
Main machinery: 2 Type L-12V-180 diesels; 2,400 hp(m) *(1.76 MW)* (forward); 2 Type 12-D-6 diesels; 1,820 hp(m) *(1.34 MW)* (aft); 4 shafts
Speed, knots: 30
Range, n miles: 700 at 16.5 kt on 1 engine
Complement: 38

Guns: 4 China 37 mm/63 (2 twin); 180 rds/min to 8.5 km *(4.6 n miles)*; weight of shell 1.42 kg.
4 USSR 25 mm/60 (2 twin); 270 rds/min to 3 km *(1.6 n miles)* anti-aircraft; weight of shell 0.34 kg.
Some are fitted with a twin 57 mm/70, some have a twin 75 mm Type 56 recoilless rifle mounted forward and some have a twin 14.5 mm MG.
Depth charges: 2 projectors; 8 weapons.
Mines: Mine rails can be fitted for 10 mines.
Radars: Surface search: Skin Head; E/F-band or Pot Head; I-band.
IFF: High Pole.
Sonars: Hull-mounted active sonar or VDS in some.

Programmes: Construction began in 1961 and continued at Shanghai and other yards at rate of about 10 a year for 30 years before being replaced by the Type 062/1G Haizhui class.
Structure: The five versions of this class vary slightly in the outline of their bridges. A few of the class have been reported as fitted with RBU 1200 anti-submarine mortars.
Operational: Evenly divided between the three Fleets. Reported but not confirmed that up to 20 have been converted to sweep mines. Numbers continue to decline.
Sales: Eight to North Vietnam in May 1966, plus Romanian craft of indigenous construction. Seven to Tanzania in 1970-71, six to Guinea, 12 to North Korea, 12 to Pakistan, five to Sri Lanka in 1972, two to Tunisia in 1977, six to Albania, eight to Bangladesh in 1980-82, three to Congo, four to Egypt in 1984, three to Sri Lanka in 1991, two to Tanzania in 1992. Many of the earlier craft have since been deleted.

SHANGHAI II Sri Lankan colours   *1992* / 0012772

4 HARBOUR PATROL CRAFT (PBI)

Displacement, tons: 80 full load
Dimensions, feet (metres): 82 × 13.3 × 4.5 *(25 × 4.1 × 1.4)*
Main machinery: 2 diesels; 2 shafts
Speed, knots: 28
Guns: 2—14.5 mm (twin).
Radars: Surface search: I-band.

Comment: Four new patrol craft arrived at Hong Kong on 1 July 1997. There may be more of the class, which are similar to some of the paramilitary patrol craft, but much faster.

HARBOUR PATROL CRAFT   *6/1999, Ships of the World* / 0056772

AMPHIBIOUS FORCES

Notes: (1) There have been reports that construction of an LPD began in 2005, possibly at Dalian. These have not been confirmed.
(2) In addition to the ships listed below there are up to 500 minor LCM/LCVP types used to transport stores and personnel.
(3) Eight Yuchai class (USSR T 4 design) and ten T4 LCMs are still in reserve in the South Sea Fleet.
(4) A 20 m WIG (wing-in-ground effect) craft assembled at Shanghai and completed in late 1997. Resembles Russian Volga II passenger ferry and may enter naval service if it proves to be reliable.

1 YUDENG (TYPE 073) CLASS (LSM)

No	Builders	Launched	Commissioned
990	Zhonghua Shipyard	Mar 1991	Aug 1994

Displacement, tons: 1,850 full load
Dimensions, feet (metres): 285.4 × 42.7 × 12.5 *(87 × 13 × 3.8)*
Main machinery: 2 diesels; 2 shafts
Speed, knots: 14
Complement: 35
Military lift: 500 troops; 9 tanks
Guns: 2 China 57 mm/50 (twin). 4—25 mm (2 twin).
Radars: Navigation: China Type 753; I-band.

Comment: The only one of the class. Based in the South Sea Fleet. Production may have been for export or the design was overtaken by the smaller Wuhu-A class.

YUDENG 990   *1999, China Shipbuilding Ltd* / 0105535

10 YUTING I (TYPE 072 IV) CLASS (LSTH)

No	Builders	Launched	Commissioned
991	Zhonghua Shipyard, Shanghai	Sep 1991	Sep 1992
934	Zhonghua Shipyard, Shanghai	Apr 1995	Sep 1995
935	Zhonghua Shipyard, Shanghai	July 1995	Dec 1995
936	Zhonghua Shipyard, Shanghai	Dec 1995	May 1996
937	Zhonghua Shipyard, Shanghai	Apr 1996	Aug 1996
908 (ex-938)	Zhonghua Shipyard, Shanghai	Aug 1996	Jan 1997
909 (ex-939)	Zhonghua Shipyard, Shanghai	Nov 1999	Apr 2000
910	Zhonghua Shipyard, Shanghai	May 2000	Dec 2001
939	Zhonghua Shipyard, Shanghai	Apr 2001	Aug 2001
940	Zhonghua Shipyard, Shanghai	Dec 2001	Apr 2002

Displacement, tons: 3,770 standard; 4,800 full load
Dimensions, feet (metres): 393.7 × 52.5 × 10.5 *(120 × 16 × 3.2)*
Main machinery: 2 diesels; 2 shafts
Speed, knots: 17
Range, n miles: 3,000 at 14 kt
Complement: 120
Military lift: 250 troops; 10 tanks; 4 LCVP
Guns: 6 China 37 mm/63 (3 twin); 180 rds/min to 8.5 km *(4.6 n miles)*; weight of shell 1.42 kg.
Radars: Navigation: 2 China Type 753; I-band.
Helicopters: Platform for 2 medium.

Comment: To augment amphibious lift capabilities and provide helicopter lift. Bow and bridge structures are very similar to the Yukan class but there is a large helicopter deck. *934-937* and *991* based in South Sea Fleet. *908-910* based in East Sea Fleet.

YUTING 909   *5/2004* / 1042136

YUTING 908   *11/2004, Ships of the World* / 1042143

9 + 2 YUTING II CLASS (LSTH)

No	Builders	Launched	Commissioned
913	Zhonghua Shipyard, Shanghai	Mar 2003	Oct 2003
911	Dalian Shipyard	May 2003	2003
992	Wuhan Shipyard	June 2003	2003
993	Zhonghua Shipyard, Shanghai	July 2003	Jan 2004
912	Dalian Shipyard	Sep 2003	2004
994	Wuhan Shipyard	2004	2004
995	Zhonghua Shipyard, Shanghai	2004	2004
996	Dalian Shipyard	2004	2004
997	Wuhan Shipyard	2004	2004

Displacement, tons: 3,770 standard; 4,800 full load
Dimensions, feet (metres): 393.7 × 53.8 × 10.5 (120 × 16.4 × 3.2)
Main machinery: 2 diesels; 2 shafts
Speed, knots: 17
Range, n miles: 3,000 at 14 kt
Complement: 120
Military lift: 250 troops; 10 tanks; 4 LCVP
Guns: To be announced.
Radars: Navigation: 2 China Type 753; I-band.
Helicopters: Platform for 2 medium.

Comment: Details are speculative but reported to be an improved version of the Yuting I class with similar dimensions. Design differences include modifications to the stern, including the ramp and a taller funnel. A tunnel in the centre of the superstructure connects the main and after decks. With construction undertaken at three shipyards, this appears to be a very active programme. Two more are reported to be under construction.

YUTING II 911 and 912   *6/2005*, Hachiro Nakai* / 1153049

YUTING II 995   *4/2004, Ships of the World* / 1042147

7 YUKAN (TYPE 072) CLASS (LST)

927	928	929	930	931	932	933

Displacement, tons: 3,110 standard; 4,170 full load
Dimensions, feet (metres): 393.6 × 50 × 9.5 (120 × 15.3 × 2.9)
Main machinery: 2 Type 12E 390 diesels; 14,400 hp(m) (10.6 MW) sustained; 2 shafts
Speed, knots: 18
Range, n miles: 3,000 at 14 kt
Complement: 109
Military lift: 200 troops; 10 tanks; 2 LCVP; total of 500 tons
Guns: 2 China 57 mm/50 (1 twin); 120 rds/min to 12 km (6.5 n miles); weight of shell 6.31 kg.
4, 6 or 8—37 mm (2, 3 or 4 twin); 180 rds/min to 8.5 km (4.6 n miles); weight of shell 1.42 kg.
4—25 mm/60 (2 twin) (some also have 4—25 mm (2 twin) mountings amidships above the tank deck); 270 rds/min to 3 km (1.6 n miles).
Radars: Navigation: 2 China Type 753; I-band.

Comment: First completed in 1980 at Wuhan Shipyard. Building appeared to terminate in November 1995. Bow and stern ramps fitted. Carry two LCVPs. Bow ramp maximum load 50 tons, stern ramp 20 tons. Five based in the East and two in South Sea Fleets.

YUKAN 933   *12/2005*, A Sheldon-Duplaix* / 1153104

YUKAN 930   *3/2001, Ships of the World* / 0126363

0 + (8) POMORNIK (ZUBR) (PROJECT 1232.2) CLASS (ACVM/LCUJM)

Displacement, tons: 550 full load
Dimensions, feet (metres): 189 × 84 (57.6 × 25.6)
Main machinery: 5 Type NK-12MV gas-turbines; 2 for lift, 23,672 hp(m) (17.4 MW) nominal; 3 for drive, 35,508 hp(m) (26.1 MW) nominal
Speed, knots: 63. **Range, n miles:** 300 at 55 kt
Complement: 31 (4 officers)
Military lift: 3 MBT or 10 APC plus 230 troops (total 130 tons)

Missiles: SAM: 2 SA-N-5 Grail quad launchers; manual aiming; IR homing to 6 km (3.2 n miles) at 1.5 Mach; altitude to 2,500 m (8,000 ft); warhead 1.5 kg.
Guns: 2—30 mm/65 AK 630; 6 barrels per mounting; 3,000 rds/min combined to 2 km.
2—140 mm A-22 Ogon 22-barrelled rocket launchers.
Mines: 2 rails can be carried for 80.
Countermeasures: Decoys: MS227 chaff launcher.
ESM: Tool Box; intercept.
Weapons control: Quad Look (DWU-3) (modified Squeeze Box) optronic director.
Radars: Surface search: Curl Stone; I-band.
Fire control: Bass Tilt; H/I-band.
IFF: Salt Pot A/B. Square Head.

Comment: Negotiations with Almaz, St Petersburg, for the procurement of an initial two air cushion landing craft were reported to be in progress during 2005. Up to eight craft may ultimately be acquired. The craft, which first entered service in 1986, are operated by the Russian and Ukrainian navies and four had also been exported to Greece by 2005. The world's largest air cushion craft have bow and stern ramps for Ro-Ro working. Details of the craft are as for those in Russian service and Chinese requirements may be different.

22 YULIANG (TYPE 079) CLASS (LSM)

Displacement, tons: 1,100 full load
Dimensions, feet (metres): 206.7 × 32.8 × 7.9 (63 × 10 × 2.4)
Main machinery: 2 diesels; 2 shafts
Speed, knots: 14
Complement: 60
Military lift: 3 tanks
Guns: 4—25 mm/60 (2 twin); 270 rds/min to 3 km (1.6 n miles).
2 BM 21 MRL rocket launchers; range about 9 km (5 n miles).
Radars: Navigation: Fin Curve; I-band.

Comment: Production started in 1980 in three or four smaller shipyards. Numbers have been overestimated in the past and production stopped in favour of Yuhai class. Four in the North Sea Fleet, remainder based in the South Sea Fleet.

YULIANG 1122   *5/2004* / 1042135

10 YUNSHU CLASS (LSM)

No	Builders	Launched	Commissioned
946	Hudong Zhonghua Shipyard, Shanghai	June 2003	2004
947	Qingdao Naval Dockyard	July 2003	2004
948	Lushun Shipyard	July 2003	2004
–	Wuhu Shipyard	July 2003	2004
–	Lushun Shipyard	Oct 2003	2004
941	Hudong Zhonghua Shipyard, Shanghai	Dec 2003	2004
949	Lushun Shipyard	Feb 2004	2004
942	Wuhu Shipyard	2004	2004
943	Qingdao Naval Dockyard	2004	2004
950	Hudong Zhonghua Shipyard, Shanghai	Mar 2004	2004

Displacement, tons: 1,460 standard; 1,850 full load
Dimensions, feet (metres): 285.4 × 41.3 × 7.4 (87.0 × 12.6 × 2.25)
Main machinery: 2 diesels; 2 shafts
Speed, knots: 17. **Range, n miles:** 1,500 at 14 kt
Complement: 70
Military lift: 6 tanks or 12 trucks or 250 tons dry stores
Guns: 2—57 mm.
Radars: Navigation: I-band.

Comment: A new class of LSM, based on the Yudeng class, built at Zhonghua, Wuhu, Qingdao and Lushun. Series production at four shipyards suggests that further ships may be built.

YUNSHU 950   *7/2004*, Ian Edwards* / 1153057

YUNSHU 941   *7/2004*, Ian Edwards* / 1153058

10 YUBEI CLASS (LCU)

No	Builders	Launched	Commissioned
3128	Qingdao Naval Dockyard	Sep 2003	2004
3315	Zhanjiang Shipyard North	2003	2004
3232	Shanghai Shipyard International	Sep 2003	2004
3129	Qingdao Naval Dockyard	Dec 2003	2004
3316	Dinghai Naval Dockyard	Sep 2003	2004
3317	Dinghai Naval Dockyard	Nov 2003	2004
3318	Dinghai Naval Dockyard	Jan 2004	2004
3233	Qingdao Naval Dockyard	2004	2004
3235	–	2004	2005
–	–	2004	2005

Displacement, tons: To be announced.
Dimensions, feet (metres): 213.2 × 36.1 × 88.6 *(65.0 × 11.0 × 2.7)*
Main machinery: 2 diesels; 2 shafts
Speed, knots: To be announced
Complement: To be announced
Military lift: 10 tanks; 150 troops
Guns: To be announced.
Radars: To be announced.

Comment: A new class of LCU built at Qingdao, Zhanjiang, Shanghai and Dinghai. Series production at four shipyards suggests that further ships are expected.

YUBEI 3315 *8/2003* / 1042164

YUBEI 3232 *7/2004, Ian Edwards* / 1042407

13 YUHAI (TYPE 074) (WUHU-A) CLASS (LSM)

481	6562	7579	7595	+9

Displacement, tons: 799 full load
Dimensions, feet (metres): 191.6 × 34.1 × 8.9 *(58.4 × 10.4 × 2.7)*
Main machinery: 2 MAN-8L 20/27 diesels; 4,900 hp(m) *(3.6 MW)*; 2 shafts
Speed, knots: 14
Complement: 56
Military lift: 2 tanks; 250 troops
Guns: 2—25 mm/80 (1 twin).
Radars: Navigation: I-band.

Comment: First one completed in Wuhu Shipyard in 1995. One sold to Sri Lanka in December 1995. Three based in the North, four in the East and six in the South Sea Fleet.

YUHAI 7595 *12/2002, Ian Edwards* / 1042406

120 YUNNAN CLASS (TYPE 067) (LCU)

Displacement, tons: 135 full load
Dimensions, feet (metres): 93.8 × 17.7 × 4.9 *(28.6 × 5.4 × 1.5)*
Main machinery: 2 diesels; 600 hp(m) *(441 kW)*; 2 shafts
Speed, knots: 12
Range, n miles: 500 at 10 kt
Complement: 12
Military lift: 46 tons
Guns: 4—14.5 mm (2 twin) MGs.
Radars: Navigation: Fuji; I-band.

Comment: Built in China 1968-72 although a continuing programme was reported in 1982. Pennant numbers in 3000 series (3313, 3321, 3344 seen). 5000 series (5526 seen) and 7000 series (7566 and 7568 seen). The majority of the operational hulls are based in the South Sea Fleet. One to Sri Lanka in 1991 and a second in 1995. Estimation of numbers is difficult but most are believed to be in reserve or in non-naval service. Some may have 12.7 mm MGs. Twelve in the East Sea Fleet, remainder in the South.

YUNNAN 3003 *8/2000, Hachiro Nakai* / 0103675

1 YUDAO CLASS (TYPE 073) (LSM)

965

Displacement, tons: 1,650 full load
Dimensions, feet (metres): 253.9 × 34.1 × 9.8 *(77.4 × 10.4 × 3)*
Speed, knots: 18. **Range, n miles:** 1,000 at 16 kt
Complement: 60
Guns: 4—25 mm/60 (2 twin); 270 rds/min to 3 km *(1.6 n miles)*.
Radars: Navigation: Fin Curve; I-band.

Comment: First entered service in early 1980s. *965* is the only one left and is in the East Fleet.

YUDAO 965 *6/1995* / 0056781

20 YUCH'IN (TYPE 068/069) CLASS (LCM)

Displacement, tons: 58 standard; 85 full load
Dimensions, feet (metres): 81.2 × 17.1 × 4.3 *(24.8 × 5.2 × 1.3)*
Main machinery: 2 Type 12V 150C diesels; 600 hp(m) *(441 kW)*; 2 shafts
Speed, knots: 11.5. **Range, n miles:** 450 at 11.5 kt
Complement: 12
Military lift: Up to 150 troops
Guns: 4—14.5 mm (2 twin) MGs.

Comment: Built in Shanghai 1962-72. Smaller version of Yunnan class with a shorter tank deck and longer poop deck. Primarily intended for personnel transport. Based in South Sea Fleet. Six sold to Bangladesh and two to Tanzania in 1995.

YUCH'IN 4507 *5/2000, van Ginderen Collection* / 0103674

10 JINGSAH II CLASS (HOVERCRAFT) (UCAC)

452	+9

Displacement, tons: 70
Dimensions, feet (metres): 72.2 × 26.2 *(22 × 8)*
Main machinery: 2 propulsion motors; 2 lift motors
Speed, knots: 55
Military lift: 15 tons
Guns: 4—14.5 mm (2 twin) MGs.

Comment: The prototype was built at Dagu in 1979. This may now have been scrapped and been superseded by this improved version which has a bow door for disembarkation. Numbers are uncertain and may be conditional on progress with WIG craft.

JINGSAH II *1993, Ships of the World* / 0056783

MINE WARFARE FORCES

Notes: There are also some 50 auxiliary minesweepers of various types including trawlers and motor-driven junks. Up to 20 Shanghai II class, known as the Fushun class, may be used.

0 + 1 WOZANG CLASS (MCMV)

Name	No	Builders	Launched	Commissioned
–	804	Qiuxin Shipyard, Shanghai	Apr 2004	July 2005

Displacement, tons: 575 full load
Dimensions, feet (metres): 180.4 × 30.5 × 8.5 *(55.0 × 9.3 × 2.6)*
Main machinery: To be announced
Speed, knots: To be announced
Complement: To be announced
Guns: 8—37 mm (4 twin).
Countermeasures: To be announced.
Combat data system: To be announced.
Radars: To be announced.
Sonars: To be announced.

Comment: A new class of mine-countermeasures vessel which is likely to be a successor to the T43 class. Sea trials started in 2005. Little is known about the capabilities of the vessel. 10—15 units are expected.

WOZANG 804   *7/2005* / 1153086

14 (+ 26 RESERVE) T 43 CLASS (TYPE 010)
(MINESWEEPERS—OCEAN) (MSO)

830	831	832	833	+10

Displacement, tons: 520 standard; 590 full load
Dimensions, feet (metres): 196.8 × 27.6 × 6.9 *(60 × 8.8 × 2.3)*
Main machinery: 2 PCR/Kolomna Type 9-D-8 diesels; 2,000 hp(m) *(1.47 MW)*; 2 shafts
Speed, knots: 14
Range, n miles: 3,000 at 10 kt
Complement: 70 (10 officers)

Guns: 2 or 4 China 37 mm/63 (1 or 2 twin) (3 of the class have a 65 mm/52 forward instead of one twin 37 mm/63); dual purpose; 180 rds/min to 8.5 km *(4.6 n miles)*; weight of shell 1.42 kg.
  4 USSR 25 mm/60 (2 twin); 270 rds/min to 3 km *(1.6 n miles)*.
  4 China 14.5 mm/93 (2 twin); 600 rds/min to 7 km *(3.8 n miles)*.
  Some also carry 1—85 mm/52 Mk 90K; 18 rds/min to 15 km *(8 n miles)*; weight of shell 9.6 kg.
Depth charges: 2 BMB-2 projectors; 20 depth charges.
Mines: Can carry 12-16.
Countermeasures: MCMV; MPT-1 paravanes; MPT-3 mechanical sweep; acoustic and magnetic gear.
Radars: Surface search: Fin Curve or Type 756; F-band.
IFF: High Pole or Yard Rake.
Sonars: Tamir II; hull-mounted; active search and attack; high frequency.

Programmes: Started building in 1956 and continued intermittently until the late 1980s at Wuhan and at Guangzhou.
Structure: Based on the USSR T 43s, some of which transferred in the mid-1950s but have all now been deleted.
Operational: Some are used as patrol ships with sweep gear removed. Three units reported as having a 65 mm/52 gun forward. There are 26 of the class in reserve.
Sales: One to Bangladesh in 1995.

T 43 833   *12/2005*, *Massimo Annati* / 1153106

T 43 830   *3/2004, L-G Nilsson* / 1042145

1 WOLEI CLASS (MINELAYER) (ML/MST)

814

Displacement, tons: 3,100 full load
Dimensions, feet (metres): 307.7 × 47.2 × 13.1 *(93.8 × 14.4 × 4)*
Main machinery: 4 diesels; 6,400 hp(m) *(4.7 MW)*; 2 shafts
Speed, knots: 18
Range, n miles: 7,000 at 14 kt
Complement: 180
Guns: 2 China 57 mm/50 (twin).
  6 China 37 mm/63 (3 twin); 180 rds/min to 8.5 km *(4.6 n miles)*; weight of shell 1.42 kg.
Mines: 300.
Radars: Surface search. Fire control. Navigation.

Comment: Built at Dalian Shipyard and completed successful sea trials in 1988. Resembles the deleted Japanese Souya class and may be used as a support ship as well as a minelayer. Based in the North Sea Fleet.

WOLEI 814   *6/2002* / 0529145

4 WOSAO (TYPE 082) CLASS
(MINESWEEPERS—COASTAL) (MSC)

800-803

Displacement, tons: 320 full load
Dimensions, feet (metres): 147 × 22.3 × 7.5 *(44.8 × 6.8 × 2.3)*
Main machinery: 4 M 50 diesels; 4,400 hp(m) *(3.23 MW)*; 4 shafts
Speed, knots: 25
Range, n miles: 500 at 15 kt
Complement: 40 (6 officers)
Guns: 4 China 25 mm/60 (2 twin); 270 rds/min to 3 km *(1.6 n miles)*.
Mines: 6.
Countermeasures: Acoustic, magnetic and mechanical sweeps.
Radars: Navigation: China Type 753; I-band.
Sonars: Hull-mounted; active minehunting.

Comment: Building started in 1986. First of class commissioned in 1988 but second, with modified bridge structure, not seen until 1997. There are further craft but numbers have not been confirmed. Steel hull with low magnetic properties. Equipped with mechanical (Type 316), magnetic (Type 317), acoustic (Type 318) and infrasonic (Type 319) sweeps. Based in the East Sea Fleet. Pennant numbers changed.

WOSAO 800   *12/2005*, *A Sheldon-Duplaix* / 1153105

4 (+ 42 RESERVE) FUTI CLASS (TYPE 312)
(DRONE MINESWEEPERS) (MSD)

Displacement, tons: 47 standard
Dimensions, feet (metres): 68.6 × 12.8 × 6.9 *(20.9 × 3.9 × 2.1)*
Main machinery: Diesel-electric; 1 Type 12V 150C diesel generator; 300 hp(m) *(220 kW)*; 1 motor; cp prop
Speed, knots: 12
Range, n miles: 144 at 12 kt
Complement: 3

Comment: A large number of these craft, similar to the German Troikas, has been built since the early 1970s. Fitted to carry out magnetic and acoustic sweeping under remote control up to 5 km *(2.7 n miles)* from shore control station. Most are kept in reserve.

DRONE Type 312   *1988, CSSC* / 0056775

SURVEY AND RESEARCH SHIPS

Notes: (1) In addition to the naval ships shown in this section there are large numbers of civilian marine survey ships. The majority belong to the **National Marine Bureau** and have funnel markings of a red star with light blue wave patterns on either side. There are about 37 ships with names *Zhong Guo Hai Jian* or *Xiang Yang Hong* followed by a pennant number. The **National Land Resources Department** has two Geological Survey Squadrons and these ships have a red star and light blue ring on a white or yellow background. The **State Education Department** Science section owns ships with funnel markings of yellow and blue lines either side of a circular blue design. Also there are a few nationalised companies such as the **China Marine Oil Company** which have a band of light blue round the top of the funnel.

(2) There is a large number of ocean surveillance fishing trawlers. These sometimes engage in fishing activities and are not easily distinguishable from civilian fishing vessels.

(3) A new research ship, possibly known as Haiyang 20, has been reported.

AGI 201 (converted trawler) *6/1997, A Sharma* / 0017746

XIANG YANG HONG 14 (National Marine Bureau) *4/2004, Ships of the World* / 1042141

ZHONG GUO HAI JIAN 51 *12/2005*, A Sheldon-Duplaix* / 1153099

FENDOU SHIHAO (National Land Resources) *6/1999, Ships of the World* / 0056795

DONG FANG HONG 2 (State Education Department) *4/2004, Ships of the World* / 1042130

HAI YING 12 HAO (China Marine Oil Company) *6/1997, A Sharma* / 0006690

HAIYANG 20 *12/2005*, Massimo Annati* / 1153098

1 DAHUA CLASS (AGOR/AGE)

891 (ex-970, ex-909)

Displacement, tons: 6,000 full load
Dimensions, feet (metres): 433.1 × 58.1 × 23 *(132 × 17.7 × 7)*
Main machinery: 2 diesels; 2 shafts
Speed, knots: 20
Complement: 80

Comment: Launched on 9 March 1997 with pennant number 909 at Zhonghua, and completed in August 1997 with new pennant number. There is a helicopter deck aft. This is a key unit which has been involved in a number of trials including those for the HQ-9 phased array radar. Large cylindrical launch tubes have been fitted midships.

891 *6/2003* / 0572429

4 SPACE EVENT SHIPS (AGMH/AGI)

YUAN WANG 1   YUAN WANG 2   YUAN WANG 3   YUAN WANG 4

Displacement, tons: 17,100 standard; 18,400 full load
Dimensions, feet (metres): 610.2 × 74.1 × 24.6 *(186 × 22.6 × 7.5)*
Main machinery: 1 Sulzer diesel; 17,400 hp(m) *(12.78 MW)*; 1 shaft
Speed, knots: 20
Range, n miles: 18,000 at 20 kt
Complement: 470

Comment: Built by Shanghai Jiangnan Yard. First two commissioned in 1979, the third in April 1995. The fourth is a former survey ship of 11,000 tons. Have helicopter platform but no hangar. Extensive communications, SATNAV and meteorological equipment fitted in the first pair in Jiangnan SY in 1986-87. Both refitted in 1991-92. Based in the East Sea Fleet, but all belong to the National Marine Bureau.

YUAN WANG 4 *12/2003, M Back, RAN* / 0569178

YUAN WANG 3 *10/2003, Robert Pabst* / 0569171

1 SPACE EVENT SHIP (AGM/AGI)

DONGDIAO 851 (ex-232)

Displacement, tons: 6,000 full load
Dimensions, feet (metres): 426.5 × 53.8 × 21.3 *(130 × 16.4 × 6.5)*
Main machinery: 2 diesels; 2 shafts
Speed, knots: 20
Complement: 250
Guns: 1—37 mm. 2—14.5 mm.

Comment: First seen fitting out in 1999. A larger version of Dadie class with extensive space monitoring equipment. In service in March 2000.

DONGDIAO *12/2005*, Ships of the World* / 1153055

1 DADIE CLASS (AGI)

BEIDIAO 841

Displacement, tons: 2,550 full load
Dimensions, feet (metres): 308.4 × 37.1 × 13.1 *(94 × 11.3 × 4)*
Main machinery: 2 diesels; 2 shafts
Speed, knots: 17
Complement: 170 (18 officers)
Guns: 4—14.5 mm (2 twin)
Radars: Navigation: 2 Type 753; I-band.

Comment: Built at Wuhan shipyard, Wuchang and commissioned in 1986. North Sea Fleet and seen regularly in Sea of Japan and East China Sea.

BEIDIAO *10/1997* / 0017748

2 KAN CLASS (AGOR)

101   102

Displacement, tons: 1,100 full load
Dimensions, feet (metres): 225 × 22.5 × 9 *(68.6 × 6.9 × 2.7)*
Main machinery: 2 diesels; 2 shafts
Speed, knots: 18
Complement: 150
Radars: Navigation: Fin Curve; I-band.

Comment: Details given are for *102* which is believed built in 1985-87, possibly at Shanghai. Large open stern area. Aft main deck area covered and may have cable reel system. *101* is similar but slightly larger and may have been built in 1965 as an ASR. Operate in East China Sea and Sea of Japan.

KAN 101 *5/2000, van Ginderen Collection* / 0103684

1 BIN HAI CLASS (AGOR)

HAI 521

Displacement, tons: 550 full load
Dimensions, feet (metres): 164 × 32.8 × 11.5 *(50 × 10 × 3.5)*
Main machinery: 2 Niigata Type 6M26KHHS diesels; 1,600 hp(m) *(1.18 MW);* 2 shafts; bow thruster
Speed, knots: 14. **Range, n miles:** 5,000 at 11 kt
Complement: 15 (7 officers) plus 25 scientists
Radars: Navigation: Japanese AR-M31; I-band.

Comment: A purpose-built research ship built by Niigata Engineering Co, Niigata (Japan) in 1974-75. Launched 10 March 1975. Commissioned July 1975. First operated by the China National Machinery Export-Import Corporation on oceanographic duties. Operates on East and South China research projects but based in North Sea Fleet. For small vessel, has cruiser stern with raked bow and small funnel well aft. Capability to operate single DSRV and the Chinese Navy has a number of Japanese-built KSWB-300 submersibles. Painted white. This ship may belong to the China Marine Oil Company and further vessels may be in service.

1 SHUGUANG CLASS (EX-T-43) (AGOR/AGS)

203

Displacement, tons: 500 standard; 570 full load
Dimensions, feet (metres): 190.3 × 28.9 × 11.5 *(58 × 8.8 × 3.5)*
Main machinery: 2 PRC/Kolomna Type 9-D-8 diesels; 2,000 hp(m) *(1.47 MW)* sustained; 2 shafts
Speed, knots: 15. **Range, n miles:** 5,300 at 8 kt
Complement: 55-60

Comment: Converted from ex-Soviet T-43 minesweeper in late 1960s. Painted white. This last survivor is based in the North Sea Fleet.

SHUGUANG 203 *10/1997, van Ginderen Collection* / 0012980

1 GANZHU CLASS (AGS)

420

Displacement, tons: 1,000 full load
Dimensions, feet (metres): 213.2 × 29.5 × 9.7 *(65 × 9 × 3)*
Main machinery: 4 diesels; 4,400 hp(m) *(3.23 MW)*; 2 shafts
Speed, knots: 20
Complement: 125
Guns: 4—37 mm/63 (2 twin); 8—14.5 mm (4 twin).

Comment: Built at Zhujiang in 1973-75. Long refit in 1996 for up to two years.

GANZHU 420 *8/1998* / 0056802

5 YENLAI CLASS (AGS)

226   227   420   427   943

Displacement, tons: 1,040 full load
Dimensions, feet (metres): 241.8 × 32.1 × 9.7 *(73.7 × 9.8 × 3)*
Main machinery: 2 PRC/Kolomna Type 9-D-8 diesels; 2,000 hp(m) *(1.47 MW)* sustained; 2 shafts
Speed, knots: 16. **Range, n miles:** 4,000 at 14 kt
Complement: 25
Guns: 4 China 37 mm/63 (2 twin). 4—25 mm/80 (2 twin).
Radars: Navigation: Fin Curve; I-band.

Comment: Built at Zhonghua Shipyard, Shanghai in early 1970s. Carries four survey motor boats.

YENLAI 226 *6/2005*, Hachiro Nakai* / 1153052

TRAINING SHIPS

1 SHICHANG CLASS (HSS/AHH)

Name	No	Builders	Launched	Commissioned
SHICHANG	82	Qiuxin, Shanghai	Apr 1996	27 Jan 1997

Displacement, tons: 10,000 full load
Dimensions, feet (metres): 393.7 × 59.1 × 23 *(120 × 18 × 7)*
Main machinery: 2 diesels; 2 shafts
Speed, knots: 17.5. **Range, n miles:** 8,000 at 17 kt
Complement: 170 plus 200 trainees
Military lift: 300 containers
Helicopters: 2 Zhi-9A Haitun.

Comment: China's first air training ship described officially as a defence mobilisation vessel which can be used for civilian freight, for helicopter or navigation training, or as a hospital ship. The vessel looks like a scaled down version of the UK *Argus* with the bridge superstructure forward and an after funnel on the starboard side of the flight deck. There are two landing spots. Based in the South Sea Fleet and deployed to Australia in mid-1998.

SHICHANG *5/1998, Sattler/Steele* / 0017738

SHICHANG *5/1998, RAN* / 0017739

1 DAXIN CLASS (AXH)

Name	No	Builders	Launched	Commissioned
ZHENGHE	81	Qiuxin, Shanghai	12 July 1986	27 Apr 1987

Displacement, tons: 5,470 full load
Dimensions, feet (metres): 426.5 × 52.5 × 15.7 *(130.0 × 16.0 × 4.8)*
Main machinery: 2 6PC2-5L diesels; 7,800 hp(m) *(5.73 MW)*; 2 shafts
Speed, knots: 15. **Range, n miles:** 5,000 at 15 kt
Complement: 170 plus 30 instructors plus 200 Midshipmen
Guns: 4 China 57 mm/70 (2 twin). 4—30 mm AK 230 (2 twin). 4—12.7 mm MGs.
A/S mortars: 2 FQF 2500 fixed 12-tubed launchers; range 1,200 m; warhead 34 kg.
Radars: Air/surface search: Eye Shield; E-band.
Surface search: China Type 756; I-band.
Navigation: Racal Decca 1290; I-band.
Fire control: Round Ball; I-band.
Sonars: Echo Type 5; hull-mounted; active; high frequency.
Helicopters: Platform only.

Comment: Resembles a small cruise liner. Subordinate to the Naval Academy and replaced *Huian*. Based in the North Sea Fleet.

ZHENGHE *9/2000, B Lemachko* / 0126258

AUXILIARIES

Notes: (1) There is a water-tanker with similar characteristics to the Fuzhou class with pennant number 1101.
(2) There is a water tanker of unknown dimensions with pennant number 1102.

1102 *9/2001, Ian Edwards* / 1042405

1101 *7/2003, Ian Edwards* / 1042404

2 FUQING CLASS (REPLENISHMENT SHIPS) (AORH)

TAICANG 881 (ex-575)   **FENGCANG** (ex-*Dongyun*) 882 (ex-615)

Displacement, tons: 7,500 standard; 21,750 full load
Dimensions, feet (metres): 552 × 71.5 × 30.8 *(168.2 × 21.8 × 9.4)*
Main machinery: 1 Sulzer 8RL B66 diesel; 15,000 hp(m) *(11 MW)* sustained; 1 shaft
Speed, knots: 18. **Range, n miles:** 18,000 at 14 kt
Complement: 130 (24 officers)
Cargo capacity: 10,550 tons fuel; 1,000 tons dieso; 200 tons feed water; 200 tons drinking water; 4 small cranes
Guns: 8—37 mm (4 twin) (fitted for but not with).
Radars: Navigation: Fin Curve or Racal Decca 1290; I-band.
Helicopters: Platform for 1 medium.

Comment: Operational in late 1979. This is the first class of ships built for underway replenishment in the Chinese Navy. Helicopter platform but no hangar. Both built at Dalian. Two liquid replenishment positions each side with one solid replenishment position each side by the funnel. A third of the class *Hongcang* (X 950) was converted to merchant use in 1989 and renamed *Hai Lang*, registered at Dalian. A fourth (X 350) was sold to Pakistan in 1987. One based in the North and one in the East. Both ships deployed out of area in 2001 and *Fengcang* appears to have a command role.

TAICANG *6/2005*, Hachiro Nakai* / 1153048

FENGCANG *3/2004, L-G Nilsson* / 1042154

1 NANYUN CLASS (REPLENISHMENT SHIP) (AORH)

Name	No	Builders	Launched	Commissioned
NANCANG (ex-*Vladimir Peregudov*)	885 (ex-953)	Kherson/Dalian	Apr 1992	2 June 1996

Displacement, tons: 37,000 full load
Measurement, tons: 28,750 dwt
Dimensions, feet (metres): 586.9 × 83 × 36.1 *(178.9 × 25.3 × 11)*
Main machinery: 1 B&W diesel; 11,600 hp(m) *(8.53 MW)*; 1 shaft
Speed, knots: 16
Complement: 125
Cargo capacity: 9,630 tons fuel
Helicopters: 1 Super Frelon.

Comment: Sometimes referred to as Fusu class. One of a class of 11 built at Kherson Shipyard, Crimea. Laid down in January 1989. Sailed from Ukraine to Dalian Shipyard in 1993. Completed fitting out in China and joined the South Sea Fleet. RAS rigs on both sides and stern refuelling. Similar to Indian *Jyoti* but with better helicopter facilities. Deployed out of area with DDG 167 in 2000.

NANCANG *6/2005*, A Sheldon-Duplaix* / 1153101

NANCANG (old number) *8/2000, Robert Pabst* / 0103677

2 FUCHI CLASS (REPLENISHMENT SHIPS) (AORH)

Name	No	Builders	Laid down	Launched	Commissioned
FUCHI	886	Hudong Shipyard, Shanghai	2002	29 Mar 2003	30 Apr 2004
QIANDAOHU	887	Guangzou Shipyard	—	June 2003	2004

Displacement, tons: 23,000 full load
Dimensions, feet (metres): 585.6 × 81.4 × 28.5 *(178.5 × 24.8 × 8.7)*
Main machinery: 2 SEMT-Pielstick diesels; 24,000 hp *(17.9 MW)*; 2 shafts
Speed, knots: 19. **Range, n miles:** 10,000 at 14 kt
Complement: 130
Cargo capacity: 10,500 tons fuel, 250 tons of water, 680 tons of ammunition and stores
Guns: 8—37 mm (4 twin).
Radars: To be announced.
Helicopters: Platform for 1 medium.

Comment: New ships which bear a marked resemblance to Type R22T Similan class tanker built for Thailand in 1996. Fitted with two RAS stations (one liquids, one solids) on each side. In view of the Chinese Navy's increasing requirement for underway replenishment, further ships are likely.

FUCHI *12/2005*, Ships of the World* / 1153056

QIANDAOHU *12/2005*, Ships of the World* / 1153054

6 QIONGSHA CLASS (4 AP + 2 AH)

Y 830	Y 831	Y 832	Y 833	Y 834	Y 835

Displacement, tons: 2,150 full load
Dimensions, feet (metres): 282.1 × 44.3 × 13.1 *(86 × 13.5 × 4)*
Main machinery: 3 SKL 8 NVD 48 A-2U diesels; 3,960 hp(m) *(2.91 MW)* sustained; 3 shafts
Speed, knots: 16
Complement: 59
Military lift: 400 troops; 350 tons cargo
Guns: 8 China 14.5mm/93 (4 twin); 600 rds/min to 7 km *(3.8 n miles).*
Radars: Navigation: Fin Curve; I-band.

Comment: Personnel attack transports begun about 1980. Previous numbers of this class were overestimated. All South Sea Fleet. Has four sets of davits, light cargo booms serving forward and aft. No helicopter pad. Twin funnels. Carries a number of LCAs. *Y 833* and *Y 834* converted to Hospital Ships (AH) and painted white.

QIONGSHA 831 *2/1999* / 0056784

3 DAJIANG CLASS (SUBMARINE SUPPORT SHIPS) (ASRH)

CHANGXINGDAO 861 (ex-J 121)	CHONGMINGDAO 862 (ex-J 302)	YONGXINGDAO J 506

Displacement, tons: 11,975 full load
Dimensions, feet (metres): 511.7 × 67.2 × 22.3 *(156 × 20.5 × 6.8)*
Main machinery: 2 MAN K9Z60/105E diesels; 9,000 hp(m) *(6.6 MW)*; 2 shafts
Speed, knots: 20
Complement: 308
Guns: Light MGs. Can carry 6—37 mm (3 twin).
Radars: Surface search: Eye Shield; E-band.
Navigation: 2 Fin Curve; I-band.
Helicopters: 2 Aerospatiale SA 321G Super Frelon.

Comment: Submarine support and salvage ships built at Shanghai. First launched in mid-1973, operational in 1976. *Yongxingdao* has a smoke deflector on funnel. Provision for DSRV on forward well-deck aft of launching crane. A fourth and fifth of the class are listed under *Research Ships*. Foremast on *Yongxingdao* suggests long-range communications capability, possibly for submarine command. One based in each Fleet.

CHONGMINGDAO (with DSRV) *12/2005*, Ships of the World* / 1153053

1 DAZHI CLASS (SUBMARINE SUPPORT SHIP) (AS)

DAZHI 920

Displacement, tons: 5,600 full load
Dimensions, feet (metres): 350 × 50 × 20 *(106.7 × 15.3 × 6.1)*
Main machinery: Diesel-electric; 2 diesel generators; 3,500 hp(m) *(2.57 MW)*; 2 shafts
Speed, knots: 14
Range, n miles: 6,000 at 14 kt
Complement: 290
Cargo capacity: 500 tons dieso
Guns: 4 China 37 mm/63 (2 twin). 4—25 mm/60 (2 twin).
Radars: Navigation: Fin Curve; I-band.

Comment: Built at Hudong, Shanghai 1963-65. Has four electrohydraulic cranes. Carries large stock of torpedoes and stores. Based in East Sea Fleet but ship has not been seen at sea in recent years and may have been withdrawn from service.

DAZHI *(not to scale)* / 0505972

1 DADONG CLASS and 1 DADAO CLASS (SALVAGE SHIPS) (ARS)

304	+1

Displacement, tons: 1,500 full load
Dimensions, feet (metres): 269 × 36.1 × 8.9 *(82 × 11 × 2.7)*
Main machinery: 2 diesels; 7,400 hp(m) *(5.44 MW)*; 2 shafts
Speed, knots: 18
Complement: 150
Guns: 4—25 mm/80 (2 twin).
Radars: Navigation: Type 756; F-band.

Comment: *304* reported to have been built at Hudong. Has a large and conspicuous crane aft. Principal role is wreck location and salvage. A similar ship called the Dadao class was launched in January 1986. This vessel is slightly larger (84 × 12.4 m) and is civilian manned. Both ships are in the East Sea Fleet.

DADAO class *1989, Gilbert Gyssels* / 0505970

5 DALANG CLASS (SUBMARINE SUPPORT SHIPS) (AS)

503	122	911	428	332

Displacement, tons: 3,700 standard; 4,200 full load
Dimensions, feet (metres): 367 × 47.9 × 14.1 *(111.9 × 14.6 × 4.3)*
Main machinery: 2 diesels; 4,000 hp(m) *(2.94 MW)*; 2 shafts
Speed, knots: 16. **Range, n miles:** 8,000 at 14 kt
Complement: 180
Guns: 2—25 mm/80 (1 twin) or 2—14.5 mm/93 (1 twin).
Radars: Navigation: Fin Curve; I-band.

Comment: Details given are for the first two built at Guangzhou Shipyard. *503* commissioned November 1975, *122* in 1986. *911* built at Wuhu Shipyard, commissioning in late 1986, and *428* was launched in June 1996. Sometimes called Dalang I and Dalang II classes. Have been used as AGIs. Upper deck modifications (which may include a decompression chamber) have been incorporated in *332*. A further ship was launched in May 2005.

DALANG 911 *3/2004, L-G Nilsson* / 1042151

DALANG 332 *5/2000, M Declerck* / 0103679

2 DAZHOU CLASS (SUBMARINE TENDERS) (ASL)

502	504

Displacement, tons: 1,100 full load
Dimensions, feet (metres): 259.2 × 31.2 × 8.5 *(79 × 9.5 × 2.6)*
Main machinery: 2 diesels; 2 shafts
Speed, knots: 18
Complement: 130
Guns: 2 China 37 mm/63 (twin). 4—14.5 mm/93 (2 twin).
Radars: Navigation: Fin Curve; I-band.

Comment: Built in 1976-77. One in South Sea Fleet, one in the North and both have been used as AGIs.

DAZHOU 504 *12/1990, DTM* / 0505971

2 DSRV (SALVAGE SUBMARINES) (DSRV)

Displacement, tons: 35 full load
Dimensions, feet (metres): 48.9 × 8.5 × 8.5 *(14.9 × 2.6 × 2.6)*
Main machinery: 2 silver-zinc batteries; 1 mortar; 1 shaft
Speed, knots: 4
Range, n miles: 40 at 2 kt
Complement: 3

Comment: First tested in 1986 and can be carried on large salvage ships. Capable of 'wet'
rescue at 200 m and of diving to 600 m. Capacity for six survivors. Underwater TV,
high-frequency active sonar and a manipulator arm are all fitted. Life support duration
is 1,728 man-hours. An upgrade of submarine rescue capabilities may be planned
following attendance at international conferences in 2001 and talks with industry. Up to
three modern DSRV may be required.

DSRV *1991, CSSC* / 0056786

2 YANTAI CLASS SUPPLY SHIPS (AK)

800   801

Displacement, tons: 3,330 full load
Dimensions, feet (metres): 255.9 × 37.7 × 9.8 *(78.0 × 11.5 × 3.0)*
Main machinery: 2 diesels; 9,600 hp(m) *(7.06 MW)*; 2 shafts
Speed, knots: 17
Range, n miles: 3,000 at 16 kt
Complement: 100
Guns: 2 China 37 mm/63 (twin).
Radars: Navigation: Type 756; I-band.

Comment: First seen in 1992. Appears to be based on a landing ship design but without a
bow door. Fitted with cargo-handling cranes fore and aft. A ship with pennant number
938 has been reported unloading missile containers but it is not known whether this is
an additional ship. Based in South Sea Fleet.

YANTAI 800 *6/1996* / 0056789

2 DAYUN (TYPE 904) CLASS SUPPLY SHIPS (AKH)

883 (ex-951)   884 (ex-952)

Displacement, tons: 8,500 full load
Dimensions, feet (metres): 407.5 × 42 × 12.5 *(124.2 × 12.8 × 3.8)*
Main machinery: 2 diesels; 9,000 hp(m) *(6.6 MW)*; 2 shafts
Speed, knots: 22
Complement: 240
Guns: 4—37 mm/63 (2 twin). 4—25 mm/80 (2 twin).
Radars: Navigation: 2 Type 756; I-band.
Helicopters: 2 SA 321 Super Frelon.

Comment: First of class completed at Hudong Shipyard in March 1992, second in August
1992. Four landing craft are embarked. Both based in South Sea Fleet. A reported third
of class was in fact the first of the larger Nanyun class. Pennant numbers may have
changed.

DAYUN CLASS *6/2005*, A Sheldon-Duplaix* / 1153100

3 DANLIN CLASS SUPPLY SHIPS (AK/AOT)

531	591	592	594	794	+3
827	834	835	972	975	

Displacement, tons: 1,290 full load
Dimensions, feet (metres): 198.5 × 29.5 × 13.1 *(60.5 × 9 × 4)*
Main machinery: 1 USSR/PRC Type 6DRN 30/50 diesel; 750 hp(m) *(551 kW)*; 1 shaft
Speed, knots: 15
Complement: 35
Cargo capacity: 750-800 tons
Guns: 4—25 mm/80 (2 twin). 4—14.5 mm (2 twin).
Radars: Navigation: Fin Curve or Skin Head; I-band.

Comment: Built in China in early 1960-62. The six AKs have refrigerated stores capability
and serve in the South Sea Fleet. The seven AOTs are split between the Fleets. Not all
are armed.

DANLIN 794 *5/1992, Henry Dodds* / 0056790

3 DANDAO CLASS (AK/AOT)

599   802   803

Displacement, tons: 1,600 full load
Dimensions, feet (metres): 215.6 × 41 × 13 *(65.7 × 12.5 × 4)*
Main machinery: 1 diesel; 1 shaft
Speed, knots: 12
Complement: 40
Guns: 4 China 37 mm/63 (2 twin). 4 China 14.5 mm/93 (2 twin).
Radars: Navigation: Fin Curve; I-band.

Comment: Built in the late 1970s. Similar to the Danlin class. Two in the North and one in
the East Sea Fleet.

DANDAO 802 *5/2000, van Ginderen Collection* / 0126255

5 HONGQI CLASS (AK)

443   528   755   756   771

Displacement, tons: 1,950 full load
Dimensions, feet (metres): 203.4 × 39.4 × 14.4 *(62 × 12 × 4.4)*
Main machinery: 1 diesel; 1 shaft
Speed, knots: 14. **Range, n miles:** 2,500 at 11 kt
Complement: 35
Guns: 4 China 25/80 (2 twin).

Comment: Used to support offshore military garrisons. A further ship, L 202, appears
to be similar but carries no armament. Others of this type in civilian use. Three in the
North, two in the East Sea Fleet.

HONGQI 755 *3/2003, Bob Fildes* / 0569175

For details of the latest updates to *Jane's Fighting Ships* online and to discover the additional
information available exclusively to online subscribers please visit
jfs.janes.com

10 LEIZHOU CLASS (AWT/AOT)

| 728 | 755 | 793 | 826 | 973 |
| 736 | 792 | 823 | 828 | 974 |

Displacement, tons: 900 full load
Dimensions, feet (metres): 173.9 × 32.2 × 10.5 *(53 × 9.8 × 3.2)*
Main machinery: 1 diesel; 500 hp(m) *(367 kW)*; 1 shaft
Speed, knots: 12
Range, n miles: 1,200 at 10 kt
Complement: 25–30
Cargo capacity: 450 tons
Guns: 4—14.5 mm/93 (2 twin).
Radars: 2 navigation; I-band.

Comment: Built in late 1960s at Qingdao and Wudong. Split between the Fleets. Some have been converted to carry water, others carry oil. Many deleted or in civilian use.

LEIZHOU 755　　　　　　　　　*7/2004, Ian Edwards* / 1042403

16 FULIN CLASS (REPLENISHMENT SHIPS) (AOT)

560	589	620	629
563	606	623	630
582	607	625	632
583	609	628	633

Displacement, tons: 2,300 standard
Dimensions, feet (metres): 216.5 × 42.6 × 13.1 *(66 × 13 × 4)*
Main machinery: 1 diesel; 600 hp(m) *(441 kW)*; 1 shaft
Speed, knots: 10
Range, n miles: 1,500 at 8 kt
Complement: 30
Guns: 4—14.5 mm/93 (2 twin).
Radars: Navigation: Fin Curve; I-band.

Comment: A total of 20 of these ships built at Hudong, Shanghai, beginning 1972. Naval ships painted grey. Both in South Sea Fleet. Many others of the class are civilian but may carry pennant numbers.

FULIN 632　　　　　　　　　*3/2004, L-G Nilsson* / 1042150

2 SHENGLI CLASS (AOT)

| 620 | 621 |

Displacement, tons: 3,300 standard; 4,950 full load
Dimensions, feet (metres): 331.4 × 45.3 × 18 *(101 × 13.8 × 5.5)*
Main machinery: 1 6 ESDZ 43/82B diesel; 2,600 hp(m) *(1.91 MW)*; 1 shaft
Speed, knots: 14
Range, n miles: 2,400 at 11 kt
Complement: 48
Cargo capacity: 3,400 tons dieso
Guns: 2—37 mm/63 (twin). 4—25 mm/80 (2 twin).
Radars: Navigation: Fin Curve; I-band.

Comment: Built at Hudong SY, Shanghai in late 1970s. Others of the class in commercial service.

SHENGLI 621　　　　　　　　　*7/2004, Ian Edwards* / 1042402

3 JINYOU CLASS (AOT)

| 622 | 625 | 675 |

Displacement, tons: 4,800 full load
Dimensions, feet (metres): 324.8 × 104.3 × 187.0 *(99.0 × 31.8 × 5.7)*
Main machinery: 1 SEMT-Pielstick 8PC2.2L diesel; 3,000 hp *(2.24 MW)*; 1 shaft
Speed, knots: 15. **Range, n miles:** 4,000 at 10 kt
Complement: 40
Radars: Navigation: I-band.

Comment: Built by Kanashashi Shipyard, Japan and entered service 1989-90.

JINYOU 625　　　　　　　　　*6/2004, Ian Edwards* / 1042401

9 FUZHOU CLASS (AOT/AWT)

Displacement, tons: 2,100 full load
Dimensions, feet (metres): 208.3 × 41.3 × 12.5 *(63.5 × 12.6 × 3.8)*
Main machinery: 1 diesel; 600 hp(m) *(441 kW)*; 1 shaft
Speed, knots: 11
Complement: 35
Cargo capacity: 600 tons
Guns: 4—25 mm/80 (2 twin). 4—14.5 mm/93 (2 twin).
Radars: Navigation: Fin Curve; I-band.

Comment: Built 1964-70. At least 18 others of the class are civilian and used as transport oilers but may carry pennant numbers. Not all are armed.

FUZHOU 1104　　　　　　　　　*4/2003, Bob Fildes* / 0569173

5 GUANGZHOU CLASS (AOTL/AWTL)

| 412 | 555 | 558 | 645 | +1 |

Displacement, tons: 530 full load
Dimensions, feet (metres): 160.8 × 24.6 × 9.8 *(49 × 7.5 × 3)*
Main machinery: 1 diesel; 1 shaft
Speed, knots: 10
Complement: 19
Guns: 4—14.5 mm/93 (2 twin).

Comment: Coastal tankers built in the 1970s and 1980s. At least 18 others of the class are civilian but may carry pennant numbers.

GUANGZHOU 645　　　　　　　　　*7/2004, Ian Edwards* / 1042400

7 YANNAN CLASS (BUOY TENDER) (ABU)

| 124 | 263 | 463 | 982 | 983 | B-22 | B-25 |

Displacement, tons: 1,750 standard
Dimensions, feet (metres): 237.2 × 38.7 × 13.1 *(72.3 × 11.8 × 4)*
Main machinery: 2 diesels; 2,640 hp(m) *(1.94 MW)*; 2 shafts
Speed, knots: 12
Complement: 95
Radars: Navigation: Fin Curve; I-band.

Comment: Built 1978-79; commissioned 1980.

YANNAN B-25　　　　　　　　　*3/2004, L-G Nilsson* / 1042153

4 YEN PAI CLASS (ADG)

735	736	746	863

Displacement, tons: 746 standard
Dimensions, feet (metres): 213.3 × 29.5 × 8.5 (65 × 9 × 2.6)
Main machinery: Diesel-electric; 2 12VE 230ZC diesels; 2,200 hp(m) (1.62 MW); 2 ZDH-99/57 motors; 2 shafts
Speed, knots: 16
Range, n miles: 800 at 15 kt
Complement: 55
Guns: 4—37 mm/63 (2 twin). 4—25 mm/80 (2 twin).
Radars: Navigation: Type 756; I-band.

Comment: Enlarged version of T 43 MSF with larger bridge and funnel amidships. Reels on quarterdeck for degaussing function. Not all the guns are embarked.

YEN PAI 736　　　*3/2004, L-G Nilsson* / 1042152

ICEBREAKERS

1 YANBING (MOD YANHA) CLASS (AGB/AGI)

723

Displacement, tons: 4,420 full load
Dimensions, feet (metres): 334.6 × 56 × 19.5 (102 × 17.1 × 5.9)
Main machinery: Diesel-electric; 2 diesel generators; 2 motors; 2 shafts
Speed, knots: 17
Complement: 95
Guns: 8—37 mm/63 Type 61/74 (4 twin).
Radars: Navigation: 2 Fin Curve; I-band.

Comment: Enlarged version of Yanha class icebreaker, built in 1982, with greater displacement, longer and wider hull, added deck level and curved upper funnel. In October 1990, painted white while operating in Sea of Japan. Used as an AGI in the North Sea Fleet.

YANBING 723　　　*12/2001, Ships of the World* / 0529115

3 YANHA CLASS (AGB/AGI)

519	721	722

Displacement, tons: 3,200 full load
Dimensions, feet (metres): 290 × 53 × 17 (88.4 × 16.2 × 5.2)
Main machinery: Diesel-electric; 2 diesel generators; 1 motor; 1 shaft
Speed, knots: 17.5
Complement: 90
Guns: 8—37 mm/63 Type 61/74 (4 twin). 4—25 mm/80 Type 61.
Radars: Navigation: Fin Curve; I-band.

Comment: 721 and 722 built in 1969-70. 519 commissioned in 1989. Used as AGIs in the North Sea Fleet.

519　　　*10/1991, G Jacobs* / 0505974

TUGS

Notes: The vessels below represent a cross-section of the craft available.

4 TUZHONG CLASS (ATF)

154	710	830	890

Displacement, tons: 3,600 full load
Dimensions, feet (metres): 278.5 × 46 × 18 (84.9 × 14 × 5.5)
Main machinery: 2 10 ESDZ 43/82B diesels; 8,600 hp(m) (6.32 MW); 2 shafts
Speed, knots: 18.5
Complement: 120
Radars: Navigation: Fin Curve; I-band.

Comment: Built in late 1970s. Can be fitted with twin 37 mm AA armament and at least one of the class (710) has been fitted with a Square Tie radar. 35 ton towing winch. One in each Fleet and one in reserve.

TUZHONG　　　*11/1996, A Sharma* / 0012228

1 DAOZHA CLASS (ATF)

Displacement, tons: 4,000 full load
Dimensions, feet (metres): 275.6 × 41.3 × 17.7 (84 × 12.6 × 5.4)
Main machinery: 2 diesels; 8,600 hp(m) (6.32 MW); 2 shafts
Speed, knots: 18
Complement: 125

Comment: Built in 1993-94 probably as a follow-on to the Tuzhong class. Based in South Sea Fleet.

DAOZHA　　　*9/1993, Hachiro Nakai* / 0506142

17 GROMOVOY CLASS (ATF)

149	156	166	167	680	683	684	716	802
809	811	813	814	817	822	824	827	

Displacement, tons: 795 standard; 890 full load
Dimensions, feet (metres): 149.9 × 31.2 × 15.1 (45.7 × 9.5 × 4.6)
Main machinery: 2 diesels; 1,300 hp(m) (956 kW); 2 shafts
Speed, knots: 11
Range, n miles: 7,000 at 7 kt
Complement: 25—30 (varies)
Guns: 4—14.5 mm (2 twin) or 12.7 mm (2 twin) MGs.
Radars: Navigation: Fin Curve or OKI X-NE-12 (Japanese); I-band.

Comment: Built at Luda Shipyard and Shanghai International, 1958-62. Four in North Sea Fleet, nine in East Sea Fleet and four in South Sea Fleet.

GROMOVOY 802　　　*5/1992, Henry Dodds* / 0056805

10 HUJIU CLASS (ATF)

147	155	622	711	717	837	842	843	875	877

Displacement, tons: 1,470 full load
Dimensions, feet (metres): 197.5 × 38.1 × 14.4 *(60.2 × 11.6 × 4.4)*
Main machinery: 2 LVP 24 diesels; 1,800 hp(m) *(1.32 MW)*; 2 shafts
Speed, knots: 15
Range, n miles: 7,200 at 14 kt
Complement: 56
Radars: Navigation: Fin Curve or Type 756; I-band.

Comment: Built at Wuhu in 1980s. One sold to Bangladesh in 1984 and a second in 1995. Three based in the North and East, three in the South Sea Fleet.

HUJIU 877   *3/2004*, L-G Nilsson* / 1042149

19 ROSLAVL CLASS (ATA/ARS)

153	159	161-164	168	518	604	613
618	646	707	852-854	862	863	867

Displacement, tons: 670 full load
Dimensions, feet (metres): 149.9 × 31 × 15.1 *(45.7 × 9.5 × 4.6)*
Main machinery: Diesel-electric; 2 diesel generators; 1,200 hp(m) *(882 kW)*; 1 motor; 1 shaft
Speed, knots: 12. **Range, n miles:** 6,000 at 11 kt
Complement: 28
Guns: 4 — 14.5 mm (2 twin) MGs.

Comment: Built in China in mid-1960s to the USSR design. One carries diving bell and submarine rescue gear on stern and is classified as ARS. Split evenly between the fleets.

ROSLAVL 854   *9/2002, Ian Edwards* / 1042398

MARITIME MILITIA (MBDF)

Notes: (1) China has four regular paramilitary maritime Security Forces: the Customs Service *(Hai Guan)*; the maritime section of the Public Security Bureau *(Hai Gong)*; the maritime command *(Gong Bian)* of the Border Security Force (which is itself a part of the PLA-subordinated People's Armed Police); and the Border Defence *(Bian Jian)*.

These four organisations patrol extensively with a variety of vessels. In recent years the better disciplined and centrally controlled *Hai Guan* has received a significant number of new vessels, many of them with offshore capabilities. A number of Haitun helicopters are also in service.

There have been many reports of Chinese paramilitary vessels committing acts of piracy in the South China Sea, particularly *Gong Bian* vessels. *Gong Bian* and *Hai Guan* patrol vessels have been operating as far as the coasts of Luzon and Taiwan.

(2) Types of vessels vary from Huxins, Shanghai IIs and Huludaos to a number of other designs spread across all forces. For example Huxin and Huludao classes can show the markings of all four services.

(3) From December 1999 pennant numbers have been standardised to show the vessels' legitimate operating area. This is an attempt to crack down on illegal activities by making it easier for merchant ships to report violations to the Maritime Police (Hai Gong), who have taken overall responsibility.

a. 海关   HAI GUAN (HOI KWAN) – CUSTOMS

b. 海公   HAI GONG (HOI KUNG) – MARITIME POLICE

c. 公边   GONG BIAN (KUNG BIN) – BORDER SECURITY

d. 边检   BIAN JIAN (PIN KAM) – BORDER DEFENCE

BORDER SECURITY FORCE MARITIME COMMAND (GONG BIAN)

HUXIN CLASS (PB)

Displacement, tons: 165 full load
Dimensions, feet (metres): 91.9 × 13.8 × 5.2 *(28 × 4.2 × 1.6)*
Main machinery: 2 diesels; 1,000 hp(m) *(735 kW)*; 2 shafts
Speed, knots: 17
Range, n miles: 400 at 10 kt
Complement: 26
Guns: 2 China 14.5 mm/93 (twin).
Radars: Surface search: Skin Head; I-band.

Comment: This is a class of modified Huangpu design with a greater freeboard and a slightly larger displacement. First seen in 1989 and now in series production. Huxin 178 is a modified command vessel with a forward superstructure extension.

HUXIN   *4/2003, Bob Fildes* / 0569179

COASTAL PATROL CRAFT (NEW) (PB)

Displacement, tons: 58 full load
Dimensions, feet (metres): 73.8 × 15.7 × 5.2 *(22.5 × 4.8 × 1.6)*
Main machinery: 2 diesels; 1,600 hp(m) *(1.18 MW)*; 2 shafts
Speed, knots: 22
Range, n miles: 850 at 11 kt
Complement: 13
Guns: 2 — 14.5 mm (twin).
Radars: Surface search: I-band.

Comment: Large numbers of this type in all Fleet areas. Sometimes involved in piracy and other illegal activities, although whether as official policy or as a result of private enterprise is unknown. Armaments vary.

GONG BIAN 4401   *6/1999* / 0056807

GONG BIAN 4407   *6/1997* / 0017754

COASTAL PATROL CRAFT (OLD) (PB)

Displacement, tons: 82 full load
Dimensions, feet (metres): 82 × 13.5 × 4.6 *(25 × 4.1 × 1.4)*
Main machinery: 2 diesels; 900 hp(m) *(662 kW)*; 2 shafts
Speed, knots: 14
Range, n miles: 900 at 11 kt
Complement: 12
Guns: 4 — 14.5 mm/93 2 (twin).
Radars: Surface search: Fin Curve; I-band.

Comment: Large numbers of this type still extensively used although numbers are declining in favour of Huxin and the newer CPC design.

GONG BIAN 1301   *3/1995, van Ginderen Collection* / 0056808

STEALTH CRAFT (PBF)

Comment: Since 1996 large numbers of low profile stealth craft have been active in the South Sea areas, and have been reported as far away as the Philippines. Sizes vary from 30 to 60 m in length and many are capable of speeds in excess of 30 kt. Most are paramilitary vessels but some may be privately owned.

STEALTH   *8/1996* / 0012232

INSHORE PATROL CRAFT (PBI)

Displacement, tons: 32 full load
Dimensions, feet (metres): 62 × 13.1 × 3.6 *(18.9 × 4 × 1.1)*
Main machinery: 2 diesels; 900 hp(m) *(662 kW)*; 2 shafts
Speed, knots: 15
Complement: 5
Guns: 1 — 12.7 mm MG.

Comment: Details given are for the standard small patrol craft. In addition there are a number of speedboats confiscated from smugglers and used for interception duties.

GONG BIAN 3110   *4/1998* / 0017755

GONG BIAN SPEEDBOAT   *2/1995, T Hollingsbee* / 0056809

CUSTOMS (HAI GUAN) AND PUBLIC SECURITY BUREAU (HAI GONG) AND BORDER DEFENCE (BIAN JIAN)

Notes: A new class of 20-24 Qui-M class offshore patrol craft is reported to have entered service. Armed with twin 30 mm guns, a distinguishing feature is a stern ramp to facilitate the handling of high-speed interceptor craft. At 100 m length, they are substantially larger than previous Customs vessels and, despite appearances, there has been some speculation as to whether these craft are manned by naval personnel.

HULUDAO CLASS (TYPE 206)
(FAST ATTACK CRAFT—PATROL) (PC)

Displacement, tons: 180 full load
Dimensions, feet (metres): 147.6 × 21 × 5.6 *(45 × 6.4 × 1.7)*
Main machinery: 3 MWM TBD604BV12 diesels; 5,204 hp(m) *(3.82 MW)* sustained; 3 shafts
Speed, knots: 29. **Range, n miles:** 1,000 at 15 kt
Complement: 24 (6 officers)
Guns: 6 China 14.5 mm Type 82 (3 twin); 600 rds/min to 7 km *(3.8 n miles)*; weight of shell 1.42 kg.

Comment: EEZ patrol craft first seen at Wuxi Shipyard in 1988. The craft is sometimes referred to as the Wuting class.

HAI GONG HULUDAO   *6/1995* / 0056810

7 TYPE P 58E (COMMAND SHIPS) (AGF)

901-907

Displacement, tons: 435 full load
Dimensions, feet (metres): 190.3 × 24.9 × 7.5 *(58 × 7.6 × 2.3)*
Main machinery: 4 MTU diesels; 8,720 hp(m) *(6.4 MW)* sustained; 4 shafts
Speed, knots: 27. **Range, n miles:** 1,500 at 12 kt
Complement: 50
Guns: 2 China 14.5 mm/93 (twin) MGs.
Radars: Surface search: I-band.

Comment: First one built at Guangzhou in 1990, last one in 1998. Less well armed but similar to those in service with Pakistan's MSA. Used as command ships.

HAI GUAN 901   *1993, T Hollingsbee* / 0056811

42 COASTAL PATROL CRAFT (NEW) (PB)

801-842

Displacement, tons: 98 full load
Dimensions, feet (metres): 101.7 × 15.4 × 4.6 *(31 × 4.7 × 1.4)*
Main machinery: 2 diesels; 2 shafts
Speed, knots: 32
Complement: 15
Guns: 2 China 14.5 mm/93 (twin).
Radars: Surface search: Racal Decca ARPA; I-band.

Comment: Building in Shanghai at about six a year since 1992. More may follow.

HAI GUAN 812   *1993, T Hollingsbee* / 0506223

COASTAL PATROL CRAFT (OLD) (PB)

Comment: Shanghai type hull but with a different superstructure. Two twin 14.5 mm MGs. Being phased out and replaced by the 800 series of patrol craft.

HAI GUAN 62   *6/1995* / 0056812

2 COMBATBOAT 90E (PBF)

Displacement, tons: 9 full load
Dimensions, feet (metres): 39 × 9.5 × 2.3 *(11.9 × 2.9 × 0.7)*
Main machinery: 1 Scania AB DSI 14 diesel; 398 hp(m) *(293 kW)*; waterjet
Speed, knots: 40
Complement: 2

Comment: Two delivered to Hai Guan in April 1997. This is the transport version of the Swedish raiding craft and can lift two tons of stores or 6-10 troops.

COMBATBOAT 90E (Swedish colours)   *5/1999, Per Körnefeldt* / 0056813

COAST GUARD

Notes: The China Coast Guard (Maritime Safety Administration), part of the Ministry of Communications, was established in 1998 and is responsible for safety at sea, security and pollution control in Chinese offshore waters, ports and inland rivers. The agency reportedly operates some 150 vessels which are painted white with a large diagonal red stripe and four thin blue stripes.

1 + (2) HAIXUN CLASS (PBOH)

HAIXUN 21

Displacement, tons: 1,500 full load
Dimensions, feet (metres): 305.8 × 40.0 × 17.7 *(93.2 × 12.2 × 5.4)*
Main machinery: 2 diesels; 2 shafts
Speed, knots: 22
Radars: Navigation.
Helicopters: Platform for one medium.

Comment: The first of possibly three patrol ships. Conducted joint exercises with the Japanese Coast Guard in May 2004.

HAIXUN 21
5/2004, Hachiro Nakai
0589002

Colombia

ARMADA DE LA REPUBLICA

Country Overview

The Republic of Colombia is the only South American country that fronts both the Caribbean Sea and the Pacific Ocean with coastlines of 950 n miles and 782 n miles respectively. With an area of 440,831 square miles, it is bordered to the north by the Caribbean Sea, to the east by Venezuela and Brazil and to the south by Peru and Ecuador. The capital and largest city is Bogotá. Buenaventura and Tumaco are the main Pacific ports while Cartagena, Santa Marta and Barranquilla, which is near the mouth of the principal river and transport artery, the Magdalena, are on the Caribbean side. Territorial seas (12 n miles) are claimed but while it has claimed a 200 n mile EEZ, its limits have not been fully defined.

Headquarters Appointments

Commander of the Navy:
  Admiral Mauricio Soto Gomez
Deputy Commander and Chief of Staff of the Navy:
  Vice Admiral David René Moreno Moreno
Inspector General:
  Vice Admiral Fernando Elías Román Campos
Chief of Naval Operations:
  Vice Admiral Guillermo Enrique Barrera Hurtado
Commander Caribbean Force:
  Rear Admiral Alfonso Díaz Gutiérrez de Piñerez
Chief of Logistics:
  Rear Admiral José Sanabria Fonseca
Commander Marine Corps:
  Rear Admiral Luis Fernando Yance Villamil
Commander Pacific Force:
  Captain Jairo Javier Peña Gómez
Commander South Force:
  Captain Fernando Ortiz Polanía
Chief of Naval Intelligence:
  Rear Admiral Alvaro Echandia Duran

Personnel

(a) 2006: 12,000 (Navy); 9,000 (Marines); 200 (Coast Guard); 100 (Aircrew)
(b) 2 years' national service (few conscripts in the Navy)

Organisation

Caribbean Force Command: HQ at Cartagena.
Pacific Force Command: HQ at Bahia Malaga.
Naval Force South: HQ at Puerto Leguízamo.
Riverine Brigade: HQ at Bogotá, DC.
Coast Guard: HQ at Bogotá.

Bases

ARC Bolivar, Cartagena, Main naval base (floating dock, 1 slipway), schools.
ARC Bahía Málaga: Major Pacific base.
ARC Barranquilla: Naval training base.
ARC Puerto Leguízamo: Putumayo River base.
ARC Leticia: Minor River base.
Puerto López: Minor River base.
Puerto Carreño: Minor River base.
Barrancabermeja: Minor River base.
San Andrés y Providencia: Specific Command

Marine Corps

Organisation: First Brigade (Sincelejo):
31, 32, 33 Battalions (Sincelejo)
No. 3 Battalion (Malaga)
No. 21 MP Battalion (Cartagena de Indias)
No. 5 Battalion (Corozal)
No. 43 Training Battalion, (Coveñas)
No. 23 MP Battalion (Coveñas)
No. 41 Training Battalion (Coveñas)
Special Forces Battalion (Cartagena de Indias)
Second Brigade (Buenaventura).
No. 6 Battalion (Bahía Solano)
No. 40 training Battalion (Tumaco)
No. 2 Battalion (Tumaco)
No. 4 Battalion (Leguizano)
Riverine Brigade (Bogotá DC)
Five battalions at Turbo (20 Bn), Yati (30 Bn), Puerto Carreno (40 Bn),
Puerto Leguizamo (60 Bn) and Puerto Inirida (50 Bn).

Strength of the Fleet

Type	Active
Patrol Submarines	2
Midget Submarines	2
Frigates	4
Patrol Ships and Fast Attack Craft (Gun)	12
Coast Patrol Craft	45
Amphibious Forces	8
River Patrol Craft	32
River Patrol Craft Support	11
River Assault Boats	150
Survey Vessels	8
Auxiliaries	27
Training Ships	4

Prefix to Ships' Names

ARC (Armada Republica de Colombia)

Dimar

Maritime authority in charge of hydrography and navigational aids.

Coast Guard and Customs (DIAN)

The Coast Guard was established in 1979 but then gave way to the Customs Service before being re-established in January 1992 under the control of the Navy. Headquarters at Bogotá. Main bases are Cartagena, Buenaventura y Turbo and Valle. Ships have a red and yellow diagonal stripe on the hull and patrol craft have a PM number. Customs craft were absorbed into the Coast Guard but by 1995 were again independent as part of the DIAN (Direccion de Impuestos y Aduanas Nacionales). Customs craft have Aduana written on the ship's side, a thick and two thin diagonal stripes and have AN numbers.

PENNANT LIST

Submarines

SO 28   Pijao
SO 29   Tayrona
ST 20   Intrépido
ST 21   Indomable

Frigates

FL 51   Almirante Padilla
FL 52   Caldas
FL 53   Antioquia
FL 54   Independiente

Patrol Forces

PO 41	Espartana
PO 42	Capitán Pablo José de Porto
PO 43	Capitán Jorge Enrique Marques Duran
PO 44	Valle del Cauca
PM 102	Rafael del Castillo y Rada
PM 103	TN José María Palas
PM 104	CN Medardo Monzon Coronado
PM 105	S2 Jaime Gómez Castro
PM 106	S2 Juan Nepomuceno Peña
PM 112	Quitasueño
PM 113	José María García y Toledo
PM 114	Juan Nepomuceno Eslava
PM 115	TECIM Jaime E Cárdenas Gomez
PM 141	Cabo Corrientes
PM 142	Cabo Manglares
PM 143	Cabo Tiburon
PM 144	Cabo de la Vella
PG 401	Altair
PG 402	Castor
PG 403	Pollux
PG 404	Vega
PB 421	Antares
PB 422	Capricornio
PB 423	Acuario
PB 424	Piscis
PB 425	Aries
PB 426	Tauro
PB 427	Géminis
PB 428	Deneb
PB 429	Rigel
PB 430	Júpiter
PB 431	Aldebarán
PB 433	Neptuno
PB 434	Spica
PB 435	Denebola
PB 436	Libra
PB 437	Escorpión
PB 438	Alpheraz
PB 439	Bellatrix
PB 440	Canopus
PB 441	Procycom
PB 442	Tulcán
PB 443	Halley
PB 444	Hooker Bay
PB 445	Isla Bolívar
PB 446	Capella
PC 451	Andrómeda
PC 452	Casiopea
PC 453	Centauro
PC 454	Dragón

PC 455	Vela
PC 456	Polaris
PC 457	Fenix
PC 458	Regulus
PC 459	Aquila
PC 460	Perseus
PC 461	Ramadan
PC 462	Apolo
PC 463	Zeus
PC 464	Sagitario
PC 465	Lince
PF 121	Diligente
PF 122	Juan Lucio
PF 123	Alfonso Vargas
PF 124	Fritz Hagale
PF 125	Vengadora
PF 126	Humberto Cortez
PF 128	Carlos Galindo
PF 129	Capitán Jaime Rook
PF 130	Manuela Saenz
PF 135	Riohacha
PF 137	Arauca
PRF 176	Río Magdalena
PRF 177	Rio Cauca
PRF 178	Rio Atrato
PRF 179	Río Sinú
PRF 180	Río San Jorge
PRF 181	Tenerife
PRF 182	Tarapaca
PRF 183	Mompox
PRF 184	Orocué
PRF 185	Calamar
PRF 186	Magangue
PRF 187	Monclart
PRF 188	Caucaya
PRF 189	Mitú
PRF 190	Rio Putumayo
PRF 191	Río Caquetá
PRF 193	Río Orteguaza
PRF 194	Río Vichada
PRF 195	Río Guaviare
PRF 320-322	

Amphibious Forces

LD 240	Bahía Zapzurro
LD 246	Morrosquillo
LD 248	Bahía Honda
LD 249	Bahía Portete
LD 251	Bahía Solano
LD 252	Bahía Cupica
LD 253	Bahía Utría
LD 254	Bahía Málaga

Auxiliaries

BL 161	Cartagena de Indias
BL 162	Buenaventura
TM 501	Bocachica
TM 502	Arturus
TM 503	Pedro David Salas
TM 504	Sirius
TM 506	Tolú
TM 507	Calima
TM 508	Bahí Santa Catalina
TM 509	Móvil I

TM 510	Móvil II
TM 511	Renacer del Pacifico
TM 512	Jhonny Cay
TM 513	Punta Evans
TB 542	Playa Blanca
TB 544	Bell Salter
TB 545	Maldonado
TB 546	Orion
TB 547	Pegasso
TB 548	Almirante I
TB 549	Almirante II
TB 550	Ara
TB 551	Valerosa
TB 552	Luchadora
TB 554	Orca
DF 170	Mayor Jaime Arias Arango
NF 601	Filigonio Hichamón
NF 602	SSIM Manuel Antonio Moyar
NF 603	Igaraparaná
NF 604	SSIM Julio Correa Hernández
NF 605	Manacacías
NF 606	Cotuhe
NF 607	SSCIM Senen Alberto Araujo
NF 608	CPCIM Guillermo Londoño Vargas
NF 609	Ariari
NF 610	Mario Villegas
NF 611	Tony Pastrana Contreras
NF 131	Socorro
NF 132	Hernando Gutiérrez

Survey Vessels

BO 155	Providencia
BO 156	Malpelo
BH 153	Quindio
BB 31	Gorgona
BB 32	Capitán Binney
BB 33	Abadia Médez
BB 34	Ciénaga de Mayorquin
BB 35	Isla Palma

Training Ships

BE 160	Gloria
YT 230	Comodoro
YT 231	Tridente
YT 232	Cristina

Tugs

RM 75	Andagoya
RM 76	Josué Alvarez
RB 78	Portete
RB 79	Maldonado
RF 81	Capitán Castro
RF 83	Joves Fiallo
RF 84	Capitán Alvaro Ruiz
RF 85	Miguel Silva
RF 86	Capitán Rigoberto Giraldo
RF 87	Vladimir Valek
RF 88	Teniente Luis Bernal
RF 91	TN Alejandro Baldomero Salgado
RF 92	Carlos Rodriguez
RF 93	Sejeri
RF 94	Ciudad de Puerto López
RF 96	Inirida

SUBMARINES

Notes: There are three Swimmer Delivery Vehicles: *Defensora, Poderosa* and *Protectora*.

2 PIJAO (209 TYPE 1200) CLASS (SS)

Name	No	Builders	Laid down	Launched	Commissioned
PIJAO	SO 28	Howaldtswerke, Kiel	1 Apr 1972	10 Apr 1974	18 Apr 1975
TAYRONA	SO 29	Howaldtswerke, Kiel	1 May 1972	16 July 1974	16 July 1975

Displacement, tons: 1,180 surfaced; 1,285 dived
Dimensions, feet (metres): 183.4 × 20.5 × 17.9
  (55.9 × 6.3 × 5.4)
Main machinery: Diesel-electric; 4 MTU 12V 493 AZ80 diesels; 2,400 hp(m) *(1.76 MW)* sustained; 4 AEG alternators; 1.7 MW; 1 Siemens motor; 4,600 hp(m) *(3.38 MW)* sustained; 1 shaft
Speed, knots: 22 dived; 11 surfaced
Range, n miles: 8,000 at 8 kt surfaced; 4,000 at 4 kt dived
Complement: 34 (7 officers)

Torpedoes: 8—21 in *(533 mm)* bow tubes. 14 AEG SUT; dual purpose; wire-guided; active/passive homing to 12 km *(6.5 n miles)* at 35 kt; 28 km *(15 n miles)* at 23 kt; warhead 250 kg. Swim-out discharge.
Countermeasures: ESM: Thomson-CSF DR 2000; intercept.
Weapons control: Signaal M8/24 TFCS.
Radars: Surface search: Thomson-CSF Calypso II; I-band.
Sonars: Krupp Atlas PSU 83—55; hull-mounted; active/passive search and attack; medium frequency.
  Atlas Elektronik PRS 3-4; passive ranging; integral with CSU 3.

Programmes: Ordered in 1971. Both refitted by HDW at Kiel; *Pijao* completed refit in July 1990 and *Tayrona* in September 1991. Main batteries were replaced.
Structure: Single-hulled. Diving depth, 820 ft *(250 m)*.
Operational: Refitted 1999-2002. Both boats employed on counter-drug operations.

PIJAO
2000, Colombian Navy
0103689

2 MIDGET SUBMARINES (SSW)

Name	No	Builders	Launched	Commissioned
INTRÉPIDO	ST 20	Cosmos, Livorno	1 Jan 1972	17 Apr 1973
INDOMABLE	ST 21	Cosmos, Livorno	1 Jan 1972	17 Apr 1973

Displacement, tons: 58 surfaced; 70 dived
Dimensions, feet (metres): 75.5 × 13.1 *(23 × 4)*
Main machinery: Diesel-electric; 1 diesel; 1 motor; 300 hp(m) *(221 kW)*; 1 shaft
Speed, knots: 11 surfaced; 6 dived
Range, n miles: 1,200 surfaced; 60 dived
Complement: 4
Mines: 6 Mk 21 with 300 kg warhead. 8 Mk 11 with 50 kg warhead.

Comment: They can carry eight swimmers with 2 tons of explosive as well as two swimmer delivery vehicles (SDVs). Built by Cosmos, Livorno and commissioned at 40 tons, but subsequently enlarged in the early 1980s. Listed by the Navy as 'Tactical Submarines'.

INTRÉPIDO
2000, Colombian Navy
0103690

FRIGATES

4 ALMIRANTE PADILLA CLASS (TYPE FS 1500) (FLGHM)

Name	No	Builders	Laid down	Launched	Commissioned
ALMIRANTE PADILLA	FL 51	Howaldtswerke, Kiel	17 Mar 1981	6 Jan 1982	31 Oct 1983
CALDAS	FL 52	Howaldtswerke, Kiel	14 June 1981	23 Apr 1982	14 Feb 1984
ANTIOQUIA	FL 53	Howaldtswerke, Kiel	22 June 1981	28 Aug 1982	30 Apr 1984
INDEPENDIENTE	FL 54	Howaldtswerke, Kiel	22 June 1981	21 Jan 1983	24 July 1984

Displacement, tons: 1,500 standard; 2,100 full load
Dimensions, feet (metres): 325.1 × 37.1 × 12.1 *(99.1 × 11.3 × 3.7)*
Main machinery: 4 MTU 20V 1163 TB92 diesels; 23,400 hp(m) *(17.2 MW)* sustained; 2 shafts; cp props
Speed, knots: 27; 18 on 2 diesels
Range, n miles: 7,000 at 14 kt; 5,000 at 18 kt
Complement: 94

Missiles: SSM: 8 Aerospatiale MM 40 Exocet ❶; inertial cruise; active radar homing to 70 km *(40 n miles)* at 0.9 Mach; warhead 165 kg; sea-skimmer.
SAM: ❷ 2 Matra Simbad twin launchers; Mistral; IR homing to 4 km *(2.2 n miles)*; warhead 3 kg; anti-sea-skimmer.
Guns: 1 OTO Melara 3 in *(76 mm)*/62 compact ❸; 85 rds/min to 16 km *(8.7 n miles)*; weight of shell 6 kg.
2 Breda 40 mm/70 (twin) ❹; 300 rds/min to 12.5 km *(6.8 n miles)* anti-surface; weight of shell 0.96 kg.
Torpedoes: 6 – 324 mm ILAS 3 (2 triple) tubes ❺; Whitehead A244S; anti-submarine; active/passive homing to 7 km *(3.8 n miles)*; warhead 38 kg (shaped charge).
Countermeasures: Decoys: 1 CSEE Dagaie double mounting; IR flares and chaff decoys (H- to J-band).
ESM: Argo AC672; radar warning.
ECM: Racal Scimitar; jammer.
Combat data systems: Thomson-CSF TAVITAC action data automation. Possibly Link Y fitted.
Weapons control: 2 Canopus optronic directors. Thomson-CSF Vega II GFCS.
Radars: Air/surface search: Thomson-CSF Sea Tiger ❻; E/F-band; range 110 km *(60 n miles)* for 2 m² target.
Navigation: Furuno; I-band.
Fire control: Castor II B ❼; I/J-band; range 15 km *(8 n miles)* for 1 m² target.
IFF: Mk 10.
Sonars: Atlas Elektronik ASO 4-2; hull-mounted; active attack; medium frequency.

Helicopters: 1 MBB BO 105 CB ❽ or 1 Bell 412.

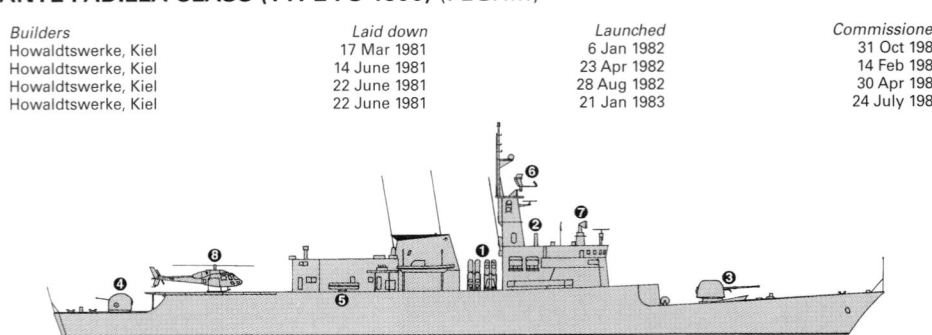

ALMIRANTE PADILLA
(Scale 1 : 900), Ian Sturton / 0056815

CALDAS
5/2003 / 0568909

Programmes: Order for four Type FS 1500 placed late 1980. Reclassified as light frigates in 1999. Similar to Malaysian Kasturi class frigates.

Modernisation: Mistral SAM system reported to have been fitted. Helicopter deck lengthened by 2 m to take Bell 412 aircraft. There have also been minor modifications to ship systems and superstructure.

ANTIOQUIA
5/2003 / 0587696

SHIPBORNE AIRCRAFT

Numbers/Type: 2 MBB BO 105CB. (FLGHM)
Operational speed: 113 kt *(210 km/h)*.
Service ceiling: 9,854 ft *(3,000 m)*.
Range: 407 n miles *(754 km)*.
Role/Weapon systems: Surface search and limited ASW helicopter. Sensors: Search/weather radar. Weapons: ASW; provision to carry depth bombs. ASV; light attack role with machine gun pods.

BO 105   *2000, Colombian Navy* / 0103692

Numbers/Type: 2 Eurocopter AS 555 Fennec.
Operational speed: 121 kt *(225 km/h)*.
Service ceiling: 13,125 ft *(4,000 m)*.
Range: 389 n miles *(722 km)*.
Role/Weapon systems: OTHT capability for surface-to-surface role. Also used for logistic support. More are being acquired. Sensors: Bendix RDR 1500B radar. Weapons: Torpedoes may be fitted in due course.

AS 555   *6/2000, Colombian Navy* / 0103693

Numbers/Type: 4 Bell 412.
Operational speed: 122 kt *(226 km/h)*.
Service ceiling: 10,000 ft *(3,300 m)*.
Range: 500 n miles *(744 km)*.
Role/Weapon systems: Multipurpose used mostly for surveillance, troop transport and logistic support. Sensors: Weather radar. Weapons: ASV 7.62 mm MG can be carried.

BELL 412   *6/1999, Colombian Navy* / 0056820

LAND-BASED MARITIME AIRCRAFT

Notes: The Navy operates the following fixed-wing aircraft for maritime surveillance and transport: four RC690, two PA-31, one Cessna 206, one Beech B-350, one Gulfstream I and two PA-28 Cherokee. There are also one R22, one Bell 212 and five Bell Huey II helicopters for training and transport.

Numbers/Type: 2 Casa CN-235 200.
Operational speed: 210 kt *(384 km/h)*.
Service ceiling: 24,000 ft *(7,315 m)*.
Range: 2,000 n miles *(3,218 km)*.
Role/Weapon systems: EEZ surveillance. Delivered in 2003. Sensors: Search radar Bendix APS 504(V)5; FLIR. Weapons: Unarmed.

CN-235   *6/2003, CASA* / 0587695

PATROL FORCES

Notes: At least three Orca class 12 m fast intercept craft, capable of 40 kt, are reported to be in service.

1 RELIANCE CLASS

Name	No	Builders	Commissioned
VALLE DEL CAUCA (ex-*Durable*)	PO 44 (ex-*WMEC 628*)	Coast Guard Yard, Baltimore	8 Dec 1967

Displacement, tons: 1,129 full load
Dimensions, feet (metres): 210.5 × 34 × 10.5 *(64.2 × 10.4 × 3.2)*
Main machinery: 2 Alco 16V-251 diesels; 6,480 hp *(4.83 MW)* sustained; 2 shafts; LIPS cp props
Speed, knots: 18. **Range, n miles:** 6,100 at 14 kt; 2,700 at 18 kt
Complement: 75 (12 officers)
Guns: 1 Boeing 25 mm/87 Mk 38 Bushmaster; 200 rds/min to 6.8 km *(3.4 n miles)*. 2—12.7 mm MGs.
Radars: Surface search: Hughes/Furuno SPS-73; I-band.
Helicopters: Platform for one medium.

Comment: Transferred to Colombia on 4 September 2003. During 34 years in USCG service, underwent Major Maintenance Availability (MMA) in 1989. The exhausts for main engines, ship service generators and boilers were run in a vertical funnel which reduced flight deck size. Capable of towing ships up to 10,000 tons. Based in the Pacific.

RELIANCE CLASS (USCG colours)   *10/2002, M Mazumdar* / 0530032

2 LAZAGA CLASS (FAST ATTACK CRAFT—GUN) (PBO)

Name	No	Builders	Commissioned
CAPITÁN PABLO JOSÉ DE PORTO (ex-*Recalde*)	PO 42 (ex-PM 116, ex-P 06)	Bazán, La Carraca	17 Dec 1977
CAPITÁN JORGE ENRIQUE MARQUEZ DURAN (ex-*Cadarso*)	PO 43 (ex-PM 117, ex-P 03)	Bazán, La Carraca	10 July 1976

Displacement, tons: 393 full load
Dimensions, feet (metres): 190.6 × 24.9 × 8.5 *(58.1 × 7.6 × 2.6)*
Main machinery: 2 MTU/Bazán 16V 956 TB 91 diesels; 7,500 hp(m) *(5.5 MW)* sustained; 2 shafts
Speed, knots: 26. **Range, n miles:** 2,400 at 15 kt
Complement: 40 (4 officers)
Guns: 1 Breda 40 mm/70. 1 Oerlikon 20 mm L85. 1—12.7 mm MG.
Weapons control: CSEE optical director.
Radars: Surface search: Furuno; E/F-band.
Navigation: Furuno; I-band.

Comment: Paid off from the Spanish Navy in 1993 and put into reserve. Acquired by Colombia in March 1997 for extensive refurbishment at Bazán, San Fernando. Recommissioned 25 April 1998 and 25 June 1998 respectively. Radars have been changed and the 76 mm gun replaced by a 20 mm cannon. These ships may be used to carry troops. Four more of the class are available and more may be acquired in due course.

CAPITÁN JORGE ENRIQUE MARQUEZ DURAN   *6/2001, Maritime Photographic* / 0114510

1 CORMORAN CLASS (FAST ATTACK CRAFT—GUN) (PBO)

Name	No	Builders	Commissioned
ESPARTANA (ex-*Cormoran*)	PO 41	Bazán, San Fernando	27 Oct 1989

Displacement, tons: 358 full load
Dimensions, feet (metres): 185.7 × 24.7 × 6.5 *(56.6 × 7.5 × 2)*
Main machinery: 3 MTU-Bazán 16V 956 TB91 diesels; 11,250 hp(m) *(8.27 MW)* sustained; 3 shafts
Speed, knots: 32. **Range, n miles:** 2,500 at 15 kt
Complement: 31 (5 officers)
Guns: 1 Bofors 40/70 SP 48. 1 Oerlikon 20 mm.
Weapons control: Alcor C optronic director.
Radars: Surface search: Raytheon; I-band.

Comment: Built with overseas sales in mind, this ship was launched in October 1985, but from 1989 served in the Spanish Navy until April 1994 when she was laid up at Cartagena. Transferred in September 1995, she was then refitted at Cadiz, before sailing for Colombia in mid-1996. Based at San Andres Island and belongs to the Coast Guard.

ESPARTANA   *10/1996, Colombian Navy* / 0056822

4 POINT CLASS (PB)

Name	No	Builders	Commissioned
CABO CORRIENTES	PM 141 (ex-82368)	J M Martinac, Tacoma	14 Aug 1967
(ex-*Point Warde*)			
CABO MANGLARES	PM 142 (ex-82343)	USCG Yard, Curtis Bay	20 Nov 1963
(ex-*Point Wells*)			
CABO TIBURON	PM 143 (ex-82344)	USCG Yard, Curtis Bay	11 Dec 1963
(ex-*Point Estero*)			
CABO DE LA VELLA	PM 144 (ex-82352)	J M Martinac, Tacoma	5 Dec 1966
(ex-*Point Sal*)			

Displacement, tons: 66; 69 full load
Dimensions, feet (metres): 83 × 17.2 × 5.8 *(25.3 × 5.2 × 1.8)*
Main machinery: 2 Caterpillar 3412 diesels; 1,600 hp *(1.19 MW)*; 2 shafts
Speed, knots: 23.5
Range, n miles: 1,500 at 8 kt
Complement: 10 (1 officer)
Guns: 2—12.7 mm MGs.
Radars: Surface search: Hughes/Furuno SPS-73; I-band.

Comment: Steel hulled craft with aluminium superstructure built in United States 1960-70. *Cabo Corrientes* transferred on 29 June 2000 followed by *Cabo Manglares* on 13 October 2000. *Cabo Tiburon* and *Cabo de la Vella* transferred on 8 February 2001 and 29 May 2001 respectively.

CABO CORRIENTES   *2000, Colombian Navy* / 0103695

2 ARAUCA CLASS (RIVER GUNBOATS) (PBR)

Name	No	Builders	Commissioned
RIOHACHA	PF 135 (ex-35)	Union Industrial de Barranquilla	6 Sep 1956
ARAUCA	PF 137 (ex-37)	Union Industrial de Barranquilla	6 Sep 1956

Displacement, tons: 275 full load
Dimensions, feet (metres): 163.5 × 27.2 × 8.9 *(49.9 × 8.3 × 2.7)*
Main machinery: 2 Caterpillar diesels; 916 hp *(683 kW)*; 2 shafts
Speed, knots: 14
Range, n miles: 1,890 at 14 kt
Complement: 43; 39 plus 6 orderlies
Guns: 2 USN 3 in *(76 mm)*/50 Mk 26. 4 Oerlikon 20 mm.

Comment: Launched in 1955. Based in Naval Force South.

ARAUCA   *1991, Colombian Navy* / 0056821

2 JOSÉ MARIA PALAS (SWIFT 110) CLASS
(LARGE PATROL CRAFT) (PB)

Name	No	Builders	Commissioned
JOSÉ MARIA PALAS	PM 103 (ex-GC 103)	Swiftships Inc, Berwick	Sep 1989
MEDARDO MONZON CORONADO	PM 104 (ex-GC 104)	Swiftships Inc, Berwick	July 1990

Displacement, tons: 99 full load
Dimensions, feet (metres): 109.9 × 24.6 × 6.6 *(33.5 × 7.5 × 2)*
Main machinery: 4 Detroit 12V-71TI diesels; 2,400 hp *(1.79 MW)*; 4 shafts
Speed, knots: 25
Range, n miles: 2,250 at 15 kt
Complement: 19 (3 officers)
Guns: 1 Bofors 40 mm/70. 1—12.7 mm MG. 2—7.62 mm MGs.
Radars: Surface search: Furuno FR 8100D; I-band.

Comment: Acquired under US FMS programme. These ships belong to the Coast Guard.

JOSÉ MARIA PALAS   *1/1996, van Ginderen Collection* / 0056824

1 ASHEVILLE CLASS (FAST ATTACK CRAFT—GUN) (PGF)

Name	No	Builders	Commissioned
QUITASUEÑO	PM 112	Tacoma Boat Building	14 July 1969
(ex-*Tacoma*)			

Displacement, tons: 225 standard; 245 full load
Dimensions, feet (metres): 164.5 × 23.8 × 9.5 *(50.1 × 7.3 × 2.9)*
Main machinery: CODOG; 2 Cummins VT12-875M diesels; 1,450 hp *(1.08 MW)*; 1 GE LM 1500 gas turbine; 13,300 hp *(9.92 MW)*; 2 shafts; cp props
Speed, knots: 40
Range, n miles: 1,700 at 16 kt on diesels; 325 at 37 kt
Complement: 24
Guns: 1 US 3 in *(76 mm)*/50 Mk 34; 50 rds/min to 12.8 km *(7 n miles)*; weight of shell 6 kg.
1 Bofors 40 mm/56; 160 rds/min to 11 km *(5.9 n miles)* anti-aircraft; weight of shell 0.96 kg.
2—12.7 mm (twin) MGs.
Radars: Surface search: Raytheon 3100; I-band.

Comment: Transferred from US by lease 16 May 1983 and recommissioned 6 September 1983 and by sale August 1989. Fire-control system removed. Unreliable propulsion system prevented further transfers of this class and it is unlikely the gas turbine is operational, which reduces the top speed to 16 kt. Belongs to the Coast Guard.

QUITASUEÑO   *2000, Colombian Navy* / 0103696

2 TOLEDO CLASS (LARGE PATROL CRAFT) (PB)

Name	No	Builders	Commissioned
JOSÉ MARIA GARCIA Y TOLEDO	PM 113	Bender Marine, Mobile	15 July 1994
JUAN NEPOMUCENO ESLAVA	PM 114	Bender Marine, Mobile	25 May 1994

Displacement, tons: 142 full load
Dimensions, feet (metres): 116 × 24.9 × 7 *(35.4 × 7.6 × 2.1)*
Main machinery: 2 MTU 12V 396 TE94 diesels; 8,240 hp(m) *(6.1 MW)*; 2 shafts
Speed, knots: 25
Range, n miles: 1,200 at 15 kt
Complement: 25 (5 officers)
Guns: 1 Bushmaster 25 mm/87 Mk 96. 2—12.7 mm MGs.
Radars: Surface search: Furuno FR 151OD; I-band.

Comment: Acquired under US FMS programme. These ships belong to the Coast Guard.

JUAN NEPOMUCENO ESLAVA   *6/2001, Maritime Photographic* / 0114511

2 RAFAEL DEL CASTILLO Y RADA (SWIFT 105) CLASS (LARGE PATROL CRAFT) (PB)

Name	No	Builders	Commissioned
RAFAEL DEL CASTILLO Y RADA	PM 102 (ex-GC 102, ex-AN 202)	Swiftships Inc, Berwick	28 Feb 1983
TECIM JAIME E CÁRDENAS GOMEZ (ex-*Olaya Herrera*)	PM 115 (ex-AN 21, ex-AN 201)	Swiftships Inc, Berwick	16 Oct 1981

Displacement, tons: 115 full load
Dimensions, feet (metres): 105 × 22 × 7 *(31.5 × 6.7 × 2.1)*
Main machinery: 4 MTU 12V 331 TC92 diesels; 5,320 hp(m) *(3.97 MW)* sustained; 4 shafts
Speed, knots: 25. **Range, n miles:** 1,200 at 18 kt
Complement: 19 (3 officers)
Guns: 1 Bofors 40 mm/60 Mk 3 (PM 102). 2—12.7 mm MGs.
Weapons control: 1 COAR optronic director.
Radars: Surface search: Raytheon; I-band.

Comment: Delivered for the Customs service. PM 102 is part of the Coast Guard. PM 115 was paid off, but returned unarmed as part of the resurrected Customs service until being transferred back to the Coast Guard in 1997.

RAFAEL DEL CASTILLO Y RADA   *6/1999, Colombian Navy* / 0056826

2 JAIME GÓMEZ (MK III PB) CLASS (COASTAL PATROL CRAFT) (PB)

Name	No	Builders	Commissioned
JAIME GÓMEZ CASTRO	PM 105 (ex-GC 105)	Peterson Builders	1975
JUAN NEPOMUCENO PEÑA	PM 106 (ex-GC 106)	Peterson Builders	1977

Displacement, tons: 34 full load
Dimensions, feet (metres): 64.9 × 18 × 5.1 *(19.8 × 5.5 × 1.6)*
Main machinery: 3 Detroit 8V-71 diesels; 690 hp *(515 kW)* sustained; 3 shafts
Speed, knots: 28
Range, n miles: 450 at 26 kt
Complement: 7 (1 officer)
Guns: 2—12.7 mm MGs. 2—7.62 mm MGs. 1 Mk 19 grenade launcher.
Radars: Surface search: 2 Furuno FR 1510D; I-band.

Comment: Acquired from the USA. Recommissioned in December 1989 and February 1990 respectively. Original 40 mm and 20 mm guns replaced by lighter armament. Both based at Leticia, Rio Amazonas, under coast guard control.

JAIME GÓMEZ CASTRO   *2000, Colombian Navy* / 0103697

3 SWIFTSHIPS CLASS (RIVER PATROL CRAFT) (PBR)

PRF 320-322

Displacement, tons: 17 full load
Dimensions, feet (metres): 45.5 × 11.8 × 1.8 *(13.9 × 3.6 × 0.6)*
Main machinery: 2 Detroit 6V-92TA diesels; 900 hp *(671 kW)*; 2 Hamilton water-jets
Speed, knots: 22
Range, n miles: 600 at 22 kt
Complement: 4
Guns: 2 M2HB 12.7 mm MGs; 2 M60D 7.62 mm MGs.
Radars: Surface search: Raytheon 40; I-band.

Comment: Acquired in 2000. Hard chine modified V hull form. Can carry up to eight troops.

SWIFTSHIPS CLASS   *6/2001, Ecuador Coast Guard* / 0114516

2 ROTORK 412 CRAFT (RIVER PATROL CRAFT) (PBR)

CAPITÁN JAIME ROOK PF 129 (ex-PM 107)   **MANUELA SAENZ** PF 130 (ex-PM 108)

Displacement, tons: 9 full load
Dimensions, feet (metres): 41.7 × 10.5 × 2.3 *(12.7 × 3.2 × 0.7)*
Main machinery: 2 Caterpillar diesels; 240 hp *(179 kW)*; 2 shafts
Speed, knots: 25
Complement: 4
Military lift: 4 tons or 8 marines
Guns: 1—12.7 mm MG. 2—7.62 mm MGs.
Radars: Surface search: Raytheon; I-band.

Comment: Acquired in 1989-90. Capable of transporting eight fully equipped marines but used as river patrol craft.

CAPITÁN JAIME ROOK   *1990, Colombian Navy* / 0056828

9 TENERIFE CLASS (RIVER PATROL CRAFT) (PBR)

TENERIFE PRF 181	OROCUÉ PRF 184	MONCLART PRF 187
TARAPACA PRF 182	CALAMAR PRF 185	CAUCAYA PRF 188
MOMPOX PRF 183	MAGANGUE PRF 186	MITÚ PRF 189

Displacement, tons: 12 full load
Dimensions, feet (metres): 40.7 × 9.5 × 2 *(12.4 × 2.9 × 0.6)*
Main machinery: 2 Caterpillar 3208 TA diesels; 850 hp *(634 kW)* sustained; 2 shafts
Speed, knots: 29
Range, n miles: 530 at 15 kt
Complement: 5 plus 12 troops
Guns: 3—12.7 mm MGs (1 twin, 1 single). 1 Mk 19 grenade launcher. 1—7.62mm MGs.
Radars: Surface search: Raytheon 1900; I-band.

Comment: Built by Bender Marine, Mobile, Alabama. Acquired in October 1993 for anti-narcotics patrols. Aluminium hulls. Can be transported by aircraft.

MITÚ   *2000, Colombian Navy* / 0103698

13 INSHORE PATROL CRAFT

ALTAIR PG 401	NEPTUNO PB 433	APOLO PC 462
CASTOR PG 402	HALLEY PB 443	ZEUS PC 463
POLLUX PG 403	HOOKER BAY PB 444	SAGITARIO PC 464
VEGA PG 404	ISLA BOLIVAR PB 445	LINCE PC 465
JÚPITER PB 430		

Comment: All are of about 10 tons. PG 401-404 (Altair class) have a speed of 10 kt and are armed with 2—7.62 mm MGs. The remainder (Bay class and Sea Ark class) have outboard engines and are capable of speeds in excess of 30 kt.

VEGA   *6/1999, Colombian Navy* / 0056830

11 ANDRÓMEDA CLASS (INSHORE PATROL CRAFT) (PBI)

ANDRÓMEDA PC 451	VELA PC 455	AQUILA PC 459
CASIOPEA PC 452	POLARIS PC 456	PERSEUS PC 460
CENTAURO PC 453	FENIX PC 457	RAMADAN PC 461
DRAGÓN PC 454	REGULUS PC 458	

ANDROMEDA   *2000, Colombian Navy* / 0103699

10 RIO CLASS (RIVER PATROL CRAFT) (PBR)

RIO MAGDALENA PRF 176	RIO SAN JORGE PRF 180	RIO ORTEGUAZA PRF 193
RIO CAUCA PRF 177	RIO PUTUMAYO PRF 190	RIO VICHADA PRF 194
RIO ATRATO PRF 178	RIO CAQUETÁ PRF 191	RIO GUAVIARE PRF 195
RIO SINÚ PRF 179		

Displacement, tons: 7 full load
Dimensions, feet (metres): 31 × 11.1 × 2 *(9.8 × 3.5 × 0.6)*
Main machinery: 2 Detroit 6V-53 diesels; 296 hp *(221 kW)* sustained; 2 water-jets
Speed, knots: 24
Range, n miles: 150 at 22 kt
Complement: 4
Guns: 2—12.7 mm (twin) MGs. 1—7.62 mm MG. 1—60 mm mortar.
Radars: Surface search: Raytheon 1900; I-band.

Comment: Acquired in 1989-90. Ex-US PBR Mk II built by Uniflite in 1970. All recommissioned in September 1990. GRP hulls.

RIO MAGDALENA   *2000, Colombian Navy* / 0103700

7 RIVER PATROL CRAFT (PBR)

DILIGENTE	ALFONSO VARGAS	VENGADORA	CARLOS GALINDO
PF 121 (ex-LR 121)	PF 123	PF 125 (ex-LR 125)	PF 128
JUAN LUCIO	FRITZ HAGALE	HUMBERTO CORTEZ	
PF 122	PF 124	PF 126	

Comment: All between 31 and 40 tons. Various designs and ages, but all are armed with two 12.7 mm MGs and most have 7.62 mm MGs as well.

VENGADORA (old number)   *2000, Colombian Navy* / 0103701

20 DELFIN CLASS (INSHORE PATROL CRAFT) (PBI)

ANTARES PB 421	TAURO PB 426	SPICA PB 434	BELLATRIX PB 439
CAPRICORNIO PB 422	GÉMINIS PB 427	DENEBOLA PB 435	CANOPUS PB 440
ACUARIO PB 423	DENEB PB 428	LIBRA PB 436	PROCYON PB 441
PISCIS PB 424	RIGEL PB 429	ESCORPIÓN PB 437	TULCÁN PB 442
ARIES PB 425	ALDEBARÁN PB 431	ALPHERAZ PB 438	CAPELLA PB 446

Displacement, tons: 5.4 full load
Dimensions, feet (metres): 25.9 × 8.5 × 3.1 *(7.9 × 2.6 × 0.9)*
Main machinery: 2 Evinrude outboards; 400 hp *(294 kW)*
Speed, knots: 40
Complement: 4
Guns: 1—12.7 mm MG. 2—7.62 mm MGs.
Radars: Surface search: Raytheon; I-band.

Comment: First two built by Mako Marine, Miami and delivered in December 1992. Remainder acquired locally from 1993-94.

DELFIN CLASS   *6/2001, Maritime Photographic* / 0114512

AMPHIBIOUS FORCES

150 RIVER ASSAULT BOATS (RAB) (PBR)

Comment: These are 6.8 m river assault boats acquired from Boston Whaler for use by Marines. Armed with 1-12.7 mm and 2-7.62 mm MGs. 14 patrol units each operate with one Rio or Tenerife class and three Pirañas. Capable of 25 to 30 kt depending on load. Some have been damaged beyond repair. There are also about 110 small river assault boats.

RAB   *2000, Colombian Navy* / 0103703

1 LCM 8

BAHÍA ZAPZURRO LD 240

Displacement, tons: 125 full load
Dimensions, feet (metres): 71.9 × 20.7 × 9.9 *(21.9 × 6.3 × 3)*
Main machinery: 1 diesel; 285 hp *(213 kW)*; 1 shaft
Speed, knots: 12
Complement: 5
Military lift: 60 tons or 150 troops

Comment: Transferred in 1993.

BAHÍA ZAPZURRO   *6/1999, Colombian Navy* / 0056832

7 MORROSQUILLO (LCU 1466A) CLASS (LCU)

MORROSQUILLO LD 246	BAHÍA SOLANO LD 251	BAHÍA UTRIA LD 253
BAHÍA HONDA LD 248	BAHÍA CUPICA LD 252	BAHÍA MALAGA LD 254
BAHÍA PORTETE LD 249		

Displacement, tons: 347 full load
Dimensions, feet (metres): 119 × 34 × 6 *(36.3 × 10.4 × 1.8)*
Main machinery: 3 Detroit 6-71 diesels; 522 hp *(389 kW)* sustained; 3 shafts
Speed, knots: 7. **Range, n miles:** 700 at 7 kt
Complement: 14
Cargo capacity: 167 tons or 300 troops
Guns: 2—12.7 mm MGs.
Radars: Navigation: Raytheon; I-band.

Comment: Former US Army craft built in 1954 and transferred in 1991 and 1992 with new engines. Used as inshore transports. Speed quoted is fully laden. Numbers split between each coast.

MORROSQUILLO   *1/1993* / 0056833

SURVEY SHIPS

Notes: There are also four small buoy tenders: *Capitán Binney* BB 32, *Abadía Médez* BB 33, *Ciénaga de Mayorquin* BB 34, and *Isla Palma* BB 35.

2 PROVIDENCIA CLASS (AGOR)

Name	No	Builders	Commissioned
PROVIDENCIA	BO 155	Martin Jansen SY, Leer	24 July 1981
MALPELO	BO 156	Martin Jansen SY, Leer	24 July 1981

Displacement, tons: 1,157 full load
Dimensions, feet (metres): 164.3 × 32.8 × 13.1 *(50.3 × 10 × 4)*
Main machinery: 2 MAN-Augsburg diesels; 1,570 hp(m) *(1.15 MW)*; 1 Kort nozzle prop; bow thruster
Speed, knots: 13. **Range, n miles:** 15,000 at 12 kt
Complement: 48 (5 officers) plus 6 scientists
Radars: Navigation: Raytheon; I-band.

Comment: Both launched in January 1981. *Malpelo* employed on fishery research and *Providencia* on geophysical research. Both are operated by DIMAR, the naval authority in charge of hydrographic, pilotage, navigational and ports services. Painted white.

MALPELO   *2000, Colombian Navy* / 0103704

1 BUOY TENDER

Name	No	Builders	Commissioned
QUINDIO (ex-YFR 443)	BH 153	Niagara SB Corporation	11 Nov 1943

Displacement, tons: 600 full load
Dimensions, feet (metres): 131 × 29.8 × 9 *(40 × 9.1 × 2.7)*
Main machinery: 2 Union diesels; 600 hp *(448 kW)*; 2 shafts
Speed, knots: 10
Complement: 17 (2 officers)

Comment: Transport ship transferred by lease from the US in July 1964 and by sale on 31 March 1979. Used as a buoy tender.

QUINDIO   *2000, Colombian Navy* / 0103705

1 SURVEY SHIP (AGSC)

Name	No	Builders	Commissioned
GORGONA	BB 31 (ex-BO 154, ex-BO 161, ex-FB 161)	Lidingoverken, Sweden	28 May 1954

Displacement, tons: 574 full load
Dimensions, feet (metres): 135 × 29.5 × 9.3 *(41.2 × 9 × 2.8)*
Main machinery: 2 Wärtsilä Nohab diesels; 910 hp(m) *(669 kW)*; 2 shafts
Speed, knots: 13
Complement: 45 (2 officers)

Comment: Paid off in 1982 but after a complete overhaul at Cartagena naval base was back in service in late 1992.

GORGONA (old number)   *1993, Colombian Navy* / 0056835

TRAINING SHIPS

Notes: There are also three sail training yachts *Comodoro* YT 230, *Tridente* YT 231 and *Cristina* YT 232.

1 SAIL TRAINING SHIP (AXS)

Name	No	Builders	Launched	Commissioned
GLORIA	BE 160	AT Celaya, Bilbao	6 Sep 1966	16 May 1969

Displacement, tons: 1,250 full load
Dimensions, feet (metres): 249.3 oa; 211.9 wl; × 34.8 × 21.7 *(76; 64.6 × 10.6 × 6.6)*
Main machinery: 1 auxiliary diesel; 530 hp(m) *(389 kW)*; 1 shaft
Speed, knots: 10.5
Complement: 51 (10 officers) plus 88 trainees

Comment: Sail training ship. Barque rigged. Hull is entirely welded. Sail area, 1,675 sq yds *(1,400 sq m)*. Endurance, 60 days. Similar to Ecuador, Mexico and Venezuelan vessels.

GLORIA   *6/2005*, John Mortimer* / 1129554

AUXILIARIES

2 LUNEBURG CLASS (TYPE 701) (SUPPORT SHIPS) (AGP)

Name	No	Builders	Commissioned
CARTAGENA DE INDIAS (ex-*Luneburg*)	BL 161 (ex-A 1411)	Flensburger	31 Jan 1966
BUENAVENTURA (ex-*Nienburg*)	BL 162 (ex-A 1416)	Bremer Vulcan	1 Aug 1968

Displacement, tons: 3,483 full load
Dimensions, feet (metres): 341.2 × 43.3 × 13.8 *(104 × 13.2 × 4.2)*
Main machinery: 2 MTU MD 16V 538 TB90 diesels; 6,000 hp(m) *(4.1 MW)* sustained; 2 shafts; cp props; bow thruster
Speed, knots: 16. **Range, n miles:** 3,200 at 14 kt
Complement: 70 (9 officers)
Cargo capacity: 1,100 tons
Guns: 4 Bofors 40 mm/70 (2 twin).
Radars: Navigation: I-band.

Comment: BL 161 paid off from the German Navy in 1994. Taken in hand for refit by HDW, Kiel in August 1997. Recommissioned on 2 November 1997. Guns were cocooned in German service. The ship acts as a depot ship for patrol craft. BL 162 paid off and was transferred the same day on 27 March 1998. She is now based at Cartagena.

BUENAVENTURA   *5/1998, Michael Nitz* / 0056836

2 RIVER SUPPORT CRAFT (YAG)

Name	No	Builders	Commissioned
HERNANDO GUTIÉRREZ	NF 132 (ex-BD 35, ex-TF 52)	Ast Naval, Cartagena	1955
SOCORRO (ex-*Alberto Gomez*)	NF 131 (ex-BD 33, ex-TF 53)	Ast Naval, Cartagena	1956

Displacement, tons: 190 full load
Dimensions, feet (metres): 98.4 × 18 × 3.9 *(30 × 5.5 × 1.2)*
Main machinery: 2 Lister 8KB FRAPIL diesels; 260 hp *(194 kW)*; 2 shafts
Speed, knots: 6. **Range, n miles:** 650 at 9 kt
Complement: 20 plus berths for 48 troops and medical staff
Guns: 2 — 12.7 mm MGs.

Comment: River transports. Named after Army officers. *Socorro* was converted in July 1967 into a floating surgery. *Hernando Gutierrez* was converted into a dispensary ship in 1970. Both used as support river patrol craft.

HERNANDO GUTIÉRREZ   *1/2002, van Ginderen Collection* / 0533239

12 RIVER SUPPORT CRAFT (YDT/YAG)

FILIGONIO HICHAMÓN NF 601 (ex-NF 141)	**CPCIM GUILLERMO LONDOÑO**
SSIM MANUEL A MOYAR NF 602 (ex-NF 144)	**VARGAS** NF 608 (ex-NF 146)
IGARAPARANÁ NF 603 (ex-RR 92, LR 92)	**ARIARÍ** NF 609 (ex-PF-127, RR 97)
SSIM JULIO CORREA HERNÁNDEZ NF 604 (ex-NF 143)	**MARIO VILLEGAS** NF 610
MANACACÍAS NF 605 (ex-RR 95, LR 95)	**TONY PASTRANA**
COTUHE NF 606 (ex-RR 98)	**CONTRERAS** NF 611 (ex-NF 149)
SSCIM SENEN ALBERTO ARANGO NF 607 (ex-NF 147)	**CTCIM JORGE MORENO SALAZAR** NF 612

Displacement, tons: 260
Dimensions, feet (metres): 126.0 × 31.2 × 3.1 *(38.4 × 9.5 × 0.95)*
Main machinery: Diesels
Speed, knots: 9
Complement: 18 plus 82 troops
Guns: 8 — 12.7 mm MGs.
Helicopters: Platform (NF 610, 611) for 1 small.

Comment: Details are for the Londoño class (NF 607, 608, 610, 611 and 612) which were built by COTECMAR, Cartagena de Indias and delivered 2000-2005. Five further are projected. The remainder have various characteristics and are deployed as river patrol craft, command and support ships.

TONY PASTRANA CONTRERAS   *3/2004, Colombian Navy* / 0563761

12 TRANSPORTS

BOCACHICA TM 501	**TOLÚ** TM 506	**MÓVIL II** TM 510
ARTURUS TM 502	**CALIMA** TM 507 (ex-TM 49)	**RENACER DEL PACIFICO** TM 511
PEDRO DAVID SALAS	**BAHÍA SANTA CATALINA**	**JOHNNY CAY** TM 512
TM 503 (ex-TM 101)	TM 508	**PUNTA EVANS** TM 513
SIRIUS TM 504 (ex-TM 62)	**MÓVIL I** TM 509	

Comment: Small supply ships of various characteristics from 300 tons (TM 506) to 3 tons (TM 508-513). The others are mostly about 30 tons with a speed of 10 kt.

CALIMA (old number)   *6/1999, Colombian Navy* / 0056838

11 BAY SUPPORT CRAFT

PLAYA BLANCA TB 542	**PEGASSO** TB 547	**LUCHADORA** TB 552
ALMIRANTE I TB 548	**ORCA** TB 554	**BELL SALTER** TB 544
ALMIRANTE II TB 549	**MALDONADO** TB 545	**ARA** TB 550
ORION TB 546	**VALEROSA** TB 551	

Comment: Mostly small craft of less than 10 tons. The largest is TB 544 which is 87 tons and has previously been listed as an Admiral's Yacht.

BELL SALTER   *6/1999, Colombian Navy* / 0056840

1 FLOATING DOCK (ASL)

MAYOR JAIME ARIAS ARANGO DF 170 (ex-DF 41, ex-170)

Comment: Capacity of 165 tons, length 140 ft *(42.7 m)*, displacement 700 tons. Used as a non-self-propelled depot ship for the midget submarines.

MAYOR JAIME ARIAS ARANGO   *6/2001, Maritime Photographic* / 0114513

TUGS

16 TUGS (YTL)

ANDAGOYA RM 75	**CAPITAN RIGOBERTO GIRALDO** RF 86
JOSUÉ ALVAREZ RB 76	**VLADIMIR VALEK** RF 87
PORTETE RB 78	**TENIENTE LUIS BERNAL** RF 88
MALDONADO RB 79	**TENIENTE ALEJANDRO BALDOMERO SALGADO** RF 91
CAPITÁN CASTRO RF 81	**CARLOS RODRIGUEZ** RF 92
JOVES FIALLO RF 83	**SEJERI** RF 93
CAPITÁN ALVARO RUIZ RF 84	**CIUDAD DE PUERTO LÓPEZ** RF 94
MIGUEL SILVA RF 85	**INIRIDA** RF 96

Comment: River craft of various types described as 'Remolcador Bahia (RB), Fluvial (RF) or Mar (RM)'. Used for transport and ferry duties in harbours and rivers. RM 75 and RM 76 are harbour tugs.

JOSUÉ ALVAREZ   *6/1999, Colombian Navy* / 0056841

Comoros

Country Overview

A former French territory, the Federal Islamic Republic of the Comoros declared independence in 1975. The islands are situated at the northern entrance to the Mozambique Channel, between the African mainland and the island of Madagascar. There are three islands: Njazidja (formerly known as Grande Comore), Mwali (Mohéli), and Nzwani (Anjouan). A fourth island in the archipelago, Mayotte (Mahoré), is formally claimed by Comoros but chose to remain a French dependency. The largest town, capital and principal port is Moroni on southwestern Njazidja. This archipelagic state claims 12 n miles of territorial seas. A 200 n mile Exclusive Economic Zone (EEZ) has been claimed but the limits are not fully defined.

Bases

Moroni.

PATROL FORCES

2 YAMAYURI CLASS (PBI)

Name	No	Builders	Commissioned
KARTHALA	–	Ishihara Dockyard Co Ltd	Oct 1981
NTRINGUI	–	Ishihara Dockyard Co Ltd	Oct 1981

Displacement, tons: 26.5 standard; 41 full load
Dimensions, feet (metres): 59 × 14.1 × 3.6 *(18 × 4.3 × 1.1)*
Main machinery: 2 Nissan RD10TA06 diesels; 900 hp(m) *(661 kW)* maximum; 2 shafts
Speed, knots: 20
Complement: 6
Guns: 2 — 12.7 mm (twin) MGs.
Radars: Surface search: FRA 10; I-band.

Comment: These two patrol vessels of the MSA type (steel-hulled), supplied under Japanese government co-operation plan. Used for fishery protection services. Due to be replaced.

KARTHALA
10/1981, Ishihara DY
0056842

Democratic Republic of Congo

Country Overview

Formerly known as the Belgian Congo until it became independent in 1960, the Democratic Republic of the Congo was known as Zaire from 1971-97. With an area of 905,568 square miles, it has borders to the north with the Republic of the Congo. A 22 n mile coastline with the Atlantic Ocean separates Angola, to the south, from its Cabinda province. The capital and largest city is Kinshasa (formerly Léopoldville) while the principal ports are Matadi and Boma, on the lower Congo, and Banana, at its mouth. Territorial seas (12 n miles) are claimed. An EEZ has reportedly been claimed but the details have not been published. A cease fire in the civil war was declared in September 1999 although some fighting continued until January 2001. In July 2003, the Transitional National Government was established as part of the evolving peace process.

Headquarters Appointments

Chief of the Navy:
   Major General Dieudonne Amuli Bahigwa

Personnel

(a)   2006: 1,000 (70 officers)
(b)   Voluntary service

Organisation

There are four commands which came under the Army in 1997: Matadi (coastal), Kinshasa (riverine), Kalémié (Lake Tanganyika) and Goma (Lake Kivu).

Bases

Matadi, Kinshasa, Kalémié (Lake Tanganyika), Goma.

PATROL FORCES

Notes: Some barges and small patrol craft have been mounted with guns.

1 SHANGHAI II (TYPE 062) CLASS (FAST ATTACK CRAFT — GUN) (PC)

102

Displacement, tons: 113 standard; 134 full load
Dimensions, feet (metres): 127.3 × 17.7 × 5.6 *(38.8 × 5.4 × 1.7)*
Main machinery: 2 Type L-12V-180 diesels; 2,400 hp(m) *(1.76 MW)* (forward); 2 Type 12-D-6 diesels; 1,820 hp(m) *(1.34 MW)* (aft); 4 shafts
Speed, knots: 30

Range, n miles: 700 at 16.5 kt on 1 engine
Complement: 38

Guns: 4 China 37 mm/63 (2 twin); 180 rds/min to 8.5 km *(4.6 n miles)*; weight of shell 1.42 kg.
4 USSR 25 mm/60 (2 twin); 270 rds/min to 3 km *(1.6 n miles)* anti-aircraft; weight of shell 0.34 kg.

Radars: Surface search: Furuno; I-band.

Comment: Four craft were originally delivered from China 1976-78. Two of these were replaced in 1987. All craft were reported derelict after the civil war but, following the refurbishment of *102*, more may be restored to operational use.

SHANGHAI II 102

3/2005*, M Declerck / 1151082

Congo-Brazzaville

Country Overview

Formerly known as the Middle Congo, part of a French colony, the Republic of Congo gained independence in 1960. An unstable political period followed, culminating in civil war between 1997 and 2000 when a Transitional Council was created. A new constitution was approved by referendum in 2002. With an area of 132,000 square miles, it is situated in west-central Africa and has borders to the north with Cameroon and the Central African Republic, to the south-west with Angola (Cabinda enclave) and to the west with Gabon. The River Congo, a major transport artery, provides the southern and much of the eastern

border with the Democratic Republic of Congo (formerly Zaire). It has a 91 n mile coastline with the Atlantic Ocean. Brazzaville is the capital and largest city while Pointe Noire is the principal port and centre of the offshore oil industry. Congo has not claimed an EEZ but is one of a few coastal states which claims a 200 n mile territorial sea. The navy consists mainly of riverine craft but acquisition of offshore patrol vessels to protect offshore resources is a possibility.

Headquarters Appointments

Chief of the Navy:
Capitaine de Vaisseau Fulgort Ongobo

Organisation

There are two commands: Brazzaville (riverine) and Pointe Noire (coastal).

Bases

Pointe Noire, Brazzaville, Impfondo.

Cook Islands

Country Overview

The Cook Islands are a South Pacific island group which became self-governing in 1965; defence and external affairs remain the responsibility of the New Zealand government. Situated some 2,430 n miles south of Hawaii, they comprise two groups of widely scattered islands. The Southern Group includes Rarotonga, Aitutaki, Atiu, Mangaia, Mauke, Mitiaro, Manuae and Takutea.

The Northern Group is composed of low-lying coral islands and includes Pukapuka, Tongareva (also called Penrhyn), Manihiki, Palmerston, Rakahanga, Suwarrow and Nassau. The port of Avarua on the island of Rarotonga is the administrative centre. Territorial seas (12 n miles) are claimed. An Exclusive Economic Zone (EEZ) (200 n miles) is claimed but limits have not been fully defined by boundary agreements.

Headquarters Appointments

Maritime Commander:
Chief Inspector Pira Wichman

Bases

Avatiu Wharf, Rarotonga

PATROL FORCES

1 PACIFIC CLASS
(LARGE PATROL CRAFT) (PB)

Name	Builders	Commissioned
TE KUKUPA	Australian Shipbuilding Industries	1 Sep 1989

Displacement, tons: 162 full load
Dimensions, feet (metres): 103.3 × 26.6 × 6.9 *(31.5 × 8.1 × 2.1)*
Main machinery: 2 Caterpillar 3516TA diesels; 2,820 hp *(2.1 MW)* sustained; 2 shafts
Speed, knots: 20
Range, n miles: 2,500 at 12 kt
Complement: 17 (3 officers)
Radars: Surface search: Furuno 1011; I-band.

Comment: Laid down 16 May 1988 and launched 27 January 1989. Cost, training and support provided by Australia under defence co-operation. Acceptance date was 9 March 1989 but the handover was deferred another six months because of the change in local government. Has Furuno D/F equipment, SATNAV and a Stressl seaboat with a 40 hp outboard engine. A half-life refit was conducted in 1997 and, following the announcement by the Australian government to extend the Pacific Patrol Boat programme to a 30 year ship life, *Te Kukupa* is due to undertake a life extension refit at Townsville in 2006.

TE KUKUPA   *6/1995, van Ginderen Collection* / 0506281

Costa Rica

SERVICIO NACIONAL GUARDACOSTAS

Country Overview

The Republic of Costa Rica is an independent Central American State which lies between Nicaragua to the north and Panama to the south-east. With an area of 19,652 square miles, it has a 584 n mile coastline with the North Pacific Ocean

and of 112 n miles with the Caribbean. The uninhabited Cocos Island, about 290 n miles southwest of Burrica Point, is also under Costa Rican sovereignty. The country's capital is San José while other important cities are the Caribbean port of Limón and the Pacific port of Puntarenas. Territorial seas (12 n miles) are claimed.

While a 200 n mile EEZ has been claimed, the limits have only been partly defined by boundary agreements.

Personnel

(a)   2006: 350 officers and men
(b)   Voluntary service

Bases

Pacific: Golfito, Punta Arenas, Cuajiniquil, Quepos.
Atlantic: Limon, Moin.

PATROL FORCES

Notes: Three Boston Whalers, *Tauro* (20-1), *Villa Mar* (20-2) and *Cocori* (22-1) are operational. The first of six Costa Rican-built Apex RIBs, *Escorpion* (24-1), entered service in 2001.

APEX RIB
5/2001, Julio Montes
0109935

1 SWIFT 42 FT CLASS (INSHORE PATROL CRAFT) (PB)

PRIMERA DAMA 42-1

Comment: Probably ex-*Donna Margarita* (ex-*Puntarena*), completed in 1986 and formerly used as a hospital ship.

1 SWIFT 105 ft CLASS (FAST PATROL CRAFT) (PB)

Name	No	Builders	Commissioned
ISLA DEL COCO	105-1 (ex-1055)	Swiftships, Morgan City	Feb 1978

Displacement, tons: 118 full load
Dimensions, feet (metres): 105 × 23.3 × 7.2 *(32 × 7.1 × 2.2)*
Main machinery: 3 MTU 12V 1163 TC92 diesels; 10,530 hp(m) *(7.74 MW)*; 3 shafts
Speed, knots: 33
Range, n miles: 1,200 at 18 kt; 2,000 at 12 kt
Complement: 17 (3 officers)
Guns: 1—12.7 mm MG. 4—7.62 mm (2 twin) MGs. 1—60 mm mortar.
Radars: Navigation: Furuno; I-band.

Comment: Aluminium construction. Refitted in 1985-86 under FMS funding. The twin MGs are fitted abaft the bridge and the mortar is on the stern. Based at Punta Arenas.

ISLA DEL COCO (old number)   *2/1989* / 0056844

3 POINT CLASS (COASTAL PATROL CRAFT) (PB)

Name	No	Builders	Commissioned
SANTAMARIA (ex-*Point Camden*)	82-2 (ex-82373)	J Martinac, Tacoma	4 May 1970
JUAN RAFAEL MORA (ex-*Point Chico*)	82-3 (ex-82339)	US Coast Guard Yard, Curtis Bay	29 Oct 1962
PANCHA CARRASCO (ex-*Point Bridge*)	82-4 (ex-82338)	US Coast Guard Yard, Curtis Bay	10 Oct 1962

Displacement, tons: 67 full load
Dimensions, feet (metres): 83 × 17.2 × 5.8 *(25.3 × 5.2 × 1.8)*
Main machinery: 2 Caterpillar 3412 diesels; 1,600 hp *(1.19 MW)*; 2 shafts
Speed, knots: 23
Range, n miles: 1,200 at 8 kt
Complement: 10
Guns: 2—12.7 mm MGs.
Radars: Navigation: Raytheon SPS-64/Hughes SPS-73; I-band.

Comment: First transferred from USCG on 15 December 1999. A second transferred on 22 June 2001 and third on 28 September 2001.

SANTAMARIA   *2/2000, Julio Montes* / 0109937

2 SWIFT 65 ft CLASS (COASTAL PATROL CRAFT) (PB)

CABO BLANCO 65-3   **ISLA BURICA** 65-4

Displacement, tons: 35 full load
Dimensions, feet (metres): 65.5 × 18.4 × 6.6 *(20 × 5.6 × 2)*
Main machinery: 2 MTU 8V 331 TC92 diesels; 1,770 hp(m) *(1.3 MW)*; 2 shafts
Speed, knots: 23
Range, n miles: 500 at 18 kt
Complement: 7 (2 officers)
Guns: 1—12.7 mm MG. 4—7.62 mm (2 twin) MGs. 1—60 mm mortar.
Radars: Navigation: Furuno; I-band.

Comment: Built by Swiftships, Morgan City in 1979. Refitted 1985-86 under FMS funding. 65-3 is based at Limon.

CABO BLANCO   *11/2003, A A de Kruijf* / 0587697

1 SWIFT 36 ft CLASS (INSHORE PATROL CRAFT) (PB)

PUERTO QUEPOS (ex-*Telamanca*) 36-1

Displacement, tons: 11 full load
Dimensions, feet (metres): 36 × 10 × 2.6 *(11 × 3.1 × 0.8)*
Main machinery: 2 Detroit diesels; 500 hp *(373 kW)*; 2 shafts
Speed, knots: 24
Range, n miles: 250 at 18 kt
Complement: 4 (1 officer)
Guns: 1—12.7 mm MG. 1—60 mm mortar.
Radars: Navigation: Raytheon 1900; I-band.

Comment: Built by Swiftships, Morgan City and completed in March 1986.

PUERTO QUEPOS   *2/2000, Julio Montes* / 0109936

Côte d'Ivoire

MARINE CÔTE D'IVOIRE

Country Overview

Formerly a French colony, The Republic of Côte d'Ivoire gained full independence in 1960. Located in west Africa, the country has an area of 133,425 square miles and a 281 n mile coastline with the Gulf of Guinea. It is bordered to the east by Ghana and to the west by Liberia and Guinea. The capital is Yamoussoukro while the former capital, Abidjan, is the largest city, principal port and commercial centre. A further port at San Pedro is linked to Mali by rail. Territorial seas (12 n miles) are claimed. A 200 n mile EEZ has been claimed but the limits have not been defined by boundary agreements.

Following the rebellion of September 2002, a Government of National Conciliation has restored a level of stability although internal tensions continue. While the navy remains unchanged, operational effectiveness is likely to have suffered.

Headquarters Appointments

Chief of Naval Staff:
   Colonel Vagba Faussgnaux

Bases

Use made of ports at Locodjo (Abidjan), Sassandra, Tabouand San-Pédro

Personnel

2006: 950 (75 officers)

PATROL FORCES

Notes: Two Rodman 890 craft delivered in late 1997 for the Police.

1 PATRA CLASS (LARGE PATROL CRAFT) (PBO)

Name	No	Builders	Launched	Commissioned
L'INTRÉPIDE	–	Auroux, Arcachon	21 July 1978	6 Oct 1978

Displacement, tons: 147.5 full load
Dimensions, feet (metres): 132.5 × 19.4 × 5.2 *(40.4 × 5.9 × 1.6)*
Main machinery: 2 SACM AGO 195 V12 CZSHR diesels; 4,340 hp(m) *(3.19 MW)* sustained; 2 shafts; cp props
Speed, knots: 26
Range, n miles: 1,750 at 10 kt; 750 at 20 kt
Complement: 19 (2 officers)
Guns: 1 Breda 40 mm/70. 1 Oerlikon 20 mm. 2—7.62 mm MGs.
Radars: Surface search: Racal Decca 1226; I-band.

Comment: Of similar design to French Patra class. Laid down 7 July 1977. Patrol endurance of five days. SS-12M missiles are no longer carried. Sister ship *L'Ardent* decommissioned in 2003 to provide spares.

L'ARDENT　　　　　　　　　　　　　　　*3/1994* / 0080123

AUXILIARIES

Notes: (1) There are also some Rotork 412 craft supplied in 1980. Some are naval, some civilian.
(2) Two French harbour tugs *Merisier* and *Meronnior* were acquired in September 1999.
(3) A Yunnan class LCM *Atchan* may still be in limited service.

2 CTM (LCM)

ABY (ex-CTM 15)　　　　　　**TIAGHA** (ex-CTM 16)

Displacement, tons: 150 full load
Dimensions, feet (metres): 78 × 21 × 4.2 *(23.8 × 6.4 × 1.3)*
Main machinery: 2 Poyaud 520 V8 diesels; 225 hp(m) *(165 kW)*; 2 shafts
Speed, knots: 9.5
Range, n miles: 350 at 8 kt
Complement: 6
Military lift: 48 tons

Comment: Transferred from France in March 1999. Built in about 1968. Bow ramps are fitted. Probably not operational.

CTM (French colours)　　　　　　　　　*6/1995* / 0012960

AFFAIRES MARITIMES

2 RODMAN 890 (PBR)

AMOUGNA AF 003　　　　　　**MONSEKELA** AF 004

Dimensions, feet (metres): 29.2 × 9.8 × 3.6 *(8.9 × 3 × 0.8)*
Main machinery: 2 Volvo diesels; 300 hp(m) *(220 kW)*; 2 shafts
Speed, knots: 28
Range, n miles: 150 at 25 kt
Complement: 3
Guns: 1—7.62 mm MG.
Radars: Surface search: I-band.

Comment: Two craft delivered by Rodman in 1997. Employed on Fishery Protection duties.

AMOUGNA　　　　　　　　　　　　　*6/1997, Rodman* / 0583296

Croatia

HRVATSKA RATNA MORNARICA

Country Overview

Formerly a constituent republic of the Federal Republic of Yugoslavia, Croatia declared its independence in 1991. With an area of 21,829 square miles, it is situated in southeast Europe in the Balkan Peninsula and bordered to the north by Slovenia and Hungary, to the east and south by Bosnia and Herzegovina and to the east by Serbia and Montenegro. There is a coastline of 3,127 n miles with the Adriatic Sea on which Dubrovnik, Split, Ploče and Rijeka are the principal ports. The capital and largest city is Zagreb. Territorial waters (12 n miles) are claimed but an EEZ has not been claimed.

Headquarters Appointments

Commander of the Navy:
Rear Admiral Zdravko Kardum
Deputy Commander of the Navy:
Commodore Zdenko Simićić
Chief of Staff, Navy HQ:
Captain Ante Urlić
Commander of the Fleet:
Commodore Ivica Tolić

Personnel

(a) 2006: 1,850 (620 officers)
(b) Reserve: 8,000

General

The Navy was established on 12 September 1991. Ships captured from the Yugoslav Federation form the bulk of the Fleet. Plans to establish a Coast Guard were revived in 2005. Its roles would include fishery protection, counter-drugs and smuggling operations and environmental protection. Some naval units would almost certainly be transferred to such a force.

Bases and Organisation

Headquarters: Lora-Split.
Main base: Split.
Minor bases: Sibenik, Pula, Ploče, Lastovo, Vis.
River Patrol Flotillas: Osijek (Drava) and Sisak (Sava).
There are two coastal command sectors: North and South Adriatic. Radar surveillance stations and coastal batteries are established on key islands and peninsulas. All the bases and naval installations of the former federal Navy were taken over with the exception of those in the Gulf of Kotor.

Coast Defence

Three mobile RBS 15 batteries on trucks. Total of 10 coastal artillery batteries. Jadran command system for coastal defence using Italian built and US radars installed in 2003.

Naval Infantry

Headquarters in Split. All in reserve.

DELETIONS

Submarines

2003　*Velebit*

Amphibious Forces

2003　DJC 101, DJC 102, DSM 110

SUBMARINES

Notes: The Una class submarine *Velebit* is not operational.

2 R-2 MALA CLASS (TWO-MAN SWIMMER DELIVERY VEHICLES) (LDW)

Displacement, tons: 1.4
Dimensions, feet (metres): 16.1 × 4.6 × 4.3 *(4.9 × 1.4 × 1.3)*
Main machinery: 1 motor; 4.7 hp(m) *(3.5 kW)*; 1 shaft
Speed, knots: 4.4. **Range, n miles:** 18 at 4.4 kt; 23 at 3.7 kt
Complement: 2
Mines: 250 kg of limpet mines.

Comment: Free-flood craft with the main motor, battery, navigation pod and electronic equipment housed in separate watertight cylinders. Instrumentation includes aircraft type gyrocompass, magnetic compass, depth gauge (with 0 to 100 m scale), echo-sounder, sonar and two searchlights. Constructed of light aluminium and plexiglass, it is fitted with fore and after-hydroplanes, the tail being a conventional cruciform with a single rudder abaft the screw. Large perspex windows give a good all-round view. Operating depth, 60 m *(196.9 ft)*, maximum. Two reported sold to Syria and one to Sweden.

Notes: There is also an R-1 craft which is 3.7 m long and capable of 2.8 kt down to 50 m. It has a range of 4 n miles. There may also be some locally built SDVs.

R-1 *2/2002, RH-Alan* / 0528427

R-2
2/2002, RH-Alan
0528428

CORVETTES

2 KRALJ (TYPE R-03) CLASS (FSG)

Name	No	Builders	Launched	Commissioned
KRALJ PETAR KRESIMIR IV	RTOP 11	Kraljevica Shipyard	21 Mar 1992	7 July 1992
KRALJ DMITAR ZVONIMIR	RTOP 12	Kraljevica Shipyard	30 Mar 2001	June 2002

Displacement, tons: 385 (11), 401 (12) full load
Dimensions, feet (metres): 175.9 × 27.9 × 7.5 *(53.6 × 8.5 × 2.3)*
Main machinery: 3 M 504B-2 diesels; 12,500 hp(m) *(9.2 MW)* sustained; 3 shafts
Speed, knots: 36
Range, n miles: 1,700 at 18 kt
Complement: 29 (11), 30 (12) (5 officers)

Missiles: SSM: 4 or 8 Saab RBS 15B (2 or 4 twin) ❶; active radar homing to 70 km *(37.8 n miles)* at 0.8 Mach; warhead 83 kg.
Guns: 1 Bofors 57 mm/70 (RTOP 11) ❷; 200 rds/min to 17 km *(9.3 n miles)*; weight of shell 2.4 kg. Launchers for illuminants on side of mounting.
  1—30 mm/65 AK 630M ❸; 6 barrels; 3,000 rds/min combined to 4 km.
Mines: 4 AIM-70 magnetic or 6 SAG-1 acoustic in lieu of SSMs.
Countermeasures: Decoys: 2 Wallop Barricade chaff/IR launchers.
Weapons control: PEAB 9LV 249 Mk 2 director.
  Kolonka for AK 630M.
Radars: Surface search: Racal BT 502 ❹; E/F-band.
Fire control: PEAB 9LV 249 Mk 2 ❺; I/J-band.
Navigation: Racal 1290A; I-band.
Sonars: RIZ PP10M; hull-mounted; active search; high frequency.

Programmes: The building of this class (formerly called Kobra by NATO) was officially announced as 'suspended' in 1989 but was restarted in 1991. Designated as a missile Gunboat.
Structure: Derived from the Koncar class with a stretched hull and a new superstructure. Either missiles or mines may be carried. The second of class is 0.6 m longer than the first ship and incorporates modifications to the bridge structure.
Operational: Based at Split.

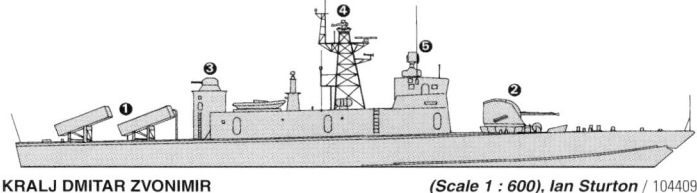

KRALJ DMITAR ZVONIMIR *(Scale 1 : 600), Ian Sturton* / 1044094

KRALJ PETAR KRESIMIR IV *6/2003, Agencija Alan* / 0569185

KRALJ DMITAR ZVONIMIR *2/2002, RH-Alan* / 0528425

KRALJ PETAR KRESIMIR IV *2/2002, Hrvatski Vojnik* / 0528426

For details of the latest updates to *Jane's Fighting Ships* online and to discover the additional information available exclusively to online subscribers please visit

jfs.janes.com

PATROL FORCES

Notes: (1) A requirement for up to ten offshore patrol vessels is unlikely to be realised in the current financial climate.
(2) A new multirole riverine craft, capable of both hydrographic and patrol duties, is under construction at Kraljevica. It is to be transported to Vukovar from where it is to operate on the Danube and Drava rivers.

1 KONČAR (TYPE R-02) CLASS
(FAST ATTACK CRAFT—MISSILE) (PTGF)

Name	No	Builders	Launched	Commissioned
ŠIBENIK	RTOP 21 (ex-402)	Tito SY, Kraljevica	20 Aug 1977	Mar 1978
(ex-*Vlado Cetković*)				

Displacement, tons: 260 full load
Dimensions, feet (metres): 147.6 × 27.6 × 8.5 *(45 × 8.4 × 2.6)*
Main machinery: CODAG; 2 RR Proteus 52-M558 gas turbines; 7,200 hp *(5.37 MW)* sustained; 2 MTU 16V 538 TB91 diesels; 7,200 hp(m) *(5.29 MW)* sustained; 4 shafts; cp props
Speed, knots: 38; 23 (diesels)
Range, n miles: 500 at 35 kt; 880 at 23 kt (diesels)
Complement: 29 (5 officers)

Missiles: SSM: 4 Saab RBS 15B; active radar homing to 70 km *(37.8 n miles)* at 0.8 Mach; warhead 83 kg.
Guns: 1 Bofors 57 mm/70; 200 rds/min to 17 km *(9.3 n miles)*; weight of shell 2.4 kg. 128 mm rocket launcher for illuminants.
1—30 mm/65 AK 630M; 6 barrels; 3,000 rds/min to 4 km.
Countermeasures: Decoys: 2 Wallop Barricade double layer chaff launchers.
Weapons control: PEAB 9LV 202 GFCS.
Radars: Surface search: Decca 1226; I-band.
Fire control: Philips TAB; I/J-band.

Programmes: Type name, Raketna Topovnjaca. Recommissioned into the Croatian Navy on 28 September 1991. Others of the class serve with the Yugoslav Navy.
Modernisation: The original Styx missiles have been replaced by RBS 15 and the after 57 mm gun by a 30 mm AK 630. Fire-control radar was updated in 1994.
Structure: Aluminium superstructure. Designed by the Naval Shipping Institute in Zagreb based on Swedish Spica class with bridge amidships like Malaysian boats.
Operational: Based at Split. Reported operational.

ŠIBENIK   *7/1997, Dario Vuljanić* / 0012240

1 RLM-301 CLASS (RIVER PATROL CRAFT) (PBR)

SLAVONAC PB 91

Displacement, tons: 48 full load
Dimensions, feet (metres): 63.6 × 14.4 × 3.3 *(19.4 × 4.4 × 1)*
Main machinery: 2 Torpedo B 536 diesels; 280 hp(m) *(206 kW)*; 2 shafts
Speed, knots: 12
Complement: 9
Guns: 1 Bofors 40 mm/70. 4—14.5 mm (quad) MGs; 2—12.7 mm MG.
Radars: Surface search: Racal Decca; I-band.

Comment: Former minesweeper launched in 1952 at Mačvanska, Mitrovica. Used as a river patrol vessel. Based at Sisak.

SLAVONAC   *12/1996, Croatian Navy* / 0017764

3 RIVER PATROL CRAFT (PBR)

BREKI	PB 92	DOMAGOJ

Displacement, tons: 48 full load
Dimensions, feet (metres): 59.4 × 13.4 × 3.4 *(19.5 × 4.4 × 3.4)*
Main machinery: 2 Torpedo B 538 diesels; 345 hp(m) *(254 kW)*; 2 shafts
Speed, knots: 8
Guns: 1 Bofors 40 mm/70. 4—14.5 mm (quad) MGs. 2—12.7 mm MGs.

Comment: Details given are for *PB 92* which is based at Sisak. *Breki* is of similar size but unarmed while *Domagoj* is of 30 tons and capable of 6 kt. The latter two craft are based at Osijek.

PB 92   *12/1996, Croatian Navy* / 0017765

4 MIRNA (TYPE 140) CLASS
(FAST ATTACK CRAFT—PATROL) (PCM)

Name	No	Builders	Commissioned
NOVIGRAD	OB 61 (ex-171)	Kraljevica Shipyard	18 Dec 1980
(ex-*Biokovo*)			
ŠOLTA	OB 62 (ex-176)	Kraljevica Shipyard	11 Nov 1982
(ex-*Mukos*)			
CAVTAT	OB 63 (ex-180)	Kraljevica Shipyard	27 Sep 1984
(ex-*Vrlika*, ex-*Cer*)			
HRVATSKA KOSTAJNICA	OB 64 (ex-181)	Kraljevica Shipyard	10 Jan 1985
(ex-*Durmitor*)			

Displacement, tons: 142 full load
Dimensions, feet (metres): 106.9 × 22 × 7.5 *(32.6 × 6.7 × 2.3)*
Main machinery: 2 SEMT-Pielstick 12 PA4 200 VGDS diesels; 5,292 hp(m) *(3.89 MW)* sustained; 2 shafts
Speed, knots: 25
Range, n miles: 600 at 24 kt
Complement: 19 (3 officers)
Missiles: SAM: 1 SA-N-5 Grail quad mounting; manual aiming; IR homing to 6 km *(3.2 n miles)* at 1.5 Mach; altitude to 2,500 m *(8,000 ft)*; warhead 1.5 kg.
Guns: 1 Bofors 40 mm/70. 4 Hispano 20 mm (quad) Type M75. 2—128 mm illuminant launchers.
Depth charges: 8 DCs.
Countermeasures: Decoys: chaff launcher (PB 62).
Radars: Surface search: Racal Decca 1216C; I-band.
Sonars: Simrad SQS-3D/SF; active high frequency.

Comment: An electric outboard motor has been removed. Two were captured after sustaining heavy damage, one by a missile and the other by a torpedo fired from the island of Brač. Both fully repaired and all four are operational and display coast guard markings.

HRVATSKA KOSTAJNICA   *6/2005*, Freivogel Collection* / 1151110

AMPHIBIOUS FORCES

2 CETINA (SILBA) CLASS (LCT/ML)

Name	No	Builders	Launched	Commissioned
CETINA	DBM 81	Brodosplit, Split	18 July 1992	19 Feb 1993
KRKA	DBV 82	Brodosplit, Split	17 Sep 1994	9 Mar 1995

Displacement, tons: 880 full load
Dimensions, feet (metres): 163.1 oa; 144 wl × 33.5 × 10.5 (49.7; 43.9 × 10.2 × 3.2)
Main machinery: 2 Alpha 10V23L-VO diesels; 3,100 hp(m) (2.28 MW) sustained; 2 shafts; cp props
Speed, knots: 12
Range, n miles: 1,200 at 12 kt
Complement: 25 (3 officers)
Military lift: 460 tons or 6 medium tanks or 7 APCs or 4—130 mm guns plus towing vehicles or 300 troops with equipment
Missiles: SAM: 1 SA-N-5 Grail quad mounting (Cetina).
Guns: 4—30 mm/65 (2 twin) AK 230 (Cetina).
2 (Krka) Hispano 20 mm M71.
Mines: 94 (Krka) or 70 (Cetina) SAG-1.
Radars: Surface search: Racal Decca 1290A; I-band.

Comment: Ro-ro design with bow and stern ramps. Krka's 40 mm gun is mounted at the bow; Cetina 's two 30 mm guns are either side of the bridge. Can be used for minelaying, transporting weapons or equipment and personnel. Krka is being used as a water carrier. Both are operational and based at Split.

CETINA *4/2001* / 0528299

KRKA *6/2005*, Freivogel Collection* / 1151109

3 TYPE 21 (LCVP)

DJB 103, 104, DJB 107

Displacement, tons: 38 full load
Dimensions, feet (metres): 69.9 × 14.1 × 5.2 (21.3 × 4.3 × 1.1)
Main machinery: 1 (2 in 103) MTU 12V 331 TC81 diesel; 1,450 hp(m) (1.07 MW); 1 shaft (2 waterjets in 103)
Speed, knots: 21
Range, n miles: 320 at 18 kt
Complement: 6
Military lift: 6 tons or 40 troops
Guns: 1—20 mm M71. 1—30 mm grenade launcher.
Radars: Navigation: Decca 1213; I-band.

Comment: Built at Greben Shipyard 1987-88. DJB 103 upgraded with new main machinery in 1991.

DJB 103 *5/1997, Dario Vuljanić* / 0012246

1 TYPE 22 (LCVPF)

DJC 106 (ex-624)

Displacement, tons: 42 full load
Dimensions, feet (metres): 73.2 × 15.7 × 3.3 (22.3 × 4.8 × 1)
Main machinery: 2 MTU MWM 604 TDV8 diesels; 1,740 hp(m) (1.28 MW); 2 waterjets
Speed, knots: 35
Range, n miles: 320 at 22 kt
Complement: 8
Military lift: 40 troops or 15 tons cargo
Guns: 2 Hispano 20 mm. 1—30 mm grenade launcher.
Radars: Navigation: Decca 150; I-band.

Comment: Built at Greben Shipyard in 1987 of polyester and glass fibre.

DJC 106 *8/1998, N A Sifferlinger* / 0038489

MINE WARFARE FORCES

0 + 1 MPMB CLASS (MINEHUNTER—INSHORE) (MHI)

Name	No	Builders	Launched
–	–	Greben, Vela Luka	–

Displacement, tons: 173 full load
Dimensions, feet (metres): 84.3 × 22.3 × 8.5 (25.7 × 6.8 × 2.6)
Main machinery: 2 MTU 8V 183TE62 diesels; 993 hp(m) (730 kW); 2 Holland Roerpropeler stern azimuth thrusters; bow thruster; 190 hp(m) (140 kW)
Speed, knots: 11.
Range, n miles: 1,000 at 9 kt
Complement: 14 (3 officers)
Guns: 1—20 mm M71.
Countermeasures: Minehunting 1 ECA38 PAP 104; 1 Super Sea Rover (Benthos);
Minesweeping: MDL3 mechanical sweep.
Radars: Navigation: Kelvin Hughes 5000 ARPA, NINAS Mod.
Sonars: Reson mine avoidance; active; high frequency.
Klein 2000 side scan; active for route survey; high frequency.

Comment: Ordered in 1995. The ship has a trawler appearance with a gun on the forecastle and a hydraulic crane on the sweep deck. GRP hull. Due to a shortage of funds, building had stopped by late 1999 but, since then, the contract has been updated and it is planned to complete the ship in 2006.

MINEHUNTER (building) *6/2005*, Freivogel Collection* / 1151113

TRAINING SHIPS

1 MOMA (PROJECT 861) CLASS (AX)

Name	No	Builders	Commissioned
ANDRIJA MOHOROVIČIĆ	BS 72 (ex-PH 33)	Northern Shipyard, Gdansk	1972

Displacement, tons: 1,514 full load
Dimensions, feet (metres): 240.5 × 36.7 × 12.8 (73.3 × 11.2 × 3.9)
Main machinery: 2 Zgoda-Sulzer 6TD48 diesels; 3,300 hp(m) (2.4 MW) sustained; 2 shafts; cp props
Speed, knots: 17
Range, n miles: 9,000 at 11 kt
Complement: 27 (4 officers)
Radars: Navigation: Racal Decca BT 502; I-band.

Comment: Built in 1971 for the Yugoslav Navy as a survey vessel. Based at Split. Has a 5 ton crane and carries a launch. Used as the Naval Academy training ship.

ANDRIJA MOHOROVIČIĆ *4/2001* / 0528297

AUXILIARIES

Notes: In addition there are two harbour tugs *LR-71* and *LR-73*, two diving tenders *BRM-81* and *BRM-83*, auxiliary transport ship *PDS-713*, five harbour transport boats *BMT-1/5*, and two yachts *Učka* (ex-*Podgorka*) and *Jadranka* (ex-civilian *Smile*).

LR 73   *10/2004, E & M Laursen* / 1047866

1 SPASILAC CLASS (ASR)

Name	No	Builders	Commissioned
FAUST VRANČIĆ (ex-*Spasilac*)	BS 73 (ex-PS 12)	Tito Shipyard, Belgrade	10 Sep 1976

Displacement, tons: 1,590 full load
Dimensions, feet (metres): 182 × 39.4 × 12.5 *(55.5 × 12 × 3.8)*
Main machinery: 2 diesels; 4,340 hp(m) *(3.19 MW)*; 2 shafts; Kort nozzle props; bow thruster
Speed, knots: 13
Range, n miles: 4,000 at 12 kt
Complement: 28 (4 officers)
Cargo capacity: 350 tons fuel; 300 tons deck cargo
Radars: Navigation: Kelvin Hughes Nucleus 5000R; I-band.

Comment: Fitted for firefighting and fully equipped for salvage work. Decompression chamber and can support a German built manned rescue submersible. Can be fitted with two quadruple M 75 and two single M 71 20 mm guns. Underwent refit during 2005. Based at Split.

FAUST VRANČIĆ   *6/2000, N A Sifferlinger* / 0103708

1 PT 71 TYPE (TRANSPORT) (AKL)

PT 71 (ex-*Meduza*)

Displacement, tons: 710 full load
Dimensions, feet (metres): 152.2 × 23.6 × 17.1 *(46.4 × 7.2 × 5.2)*
Main machinery: 1 Burmeister & Wain diesel; 930 hp(m) *(684 kW)*; 1 shaft
Speed, knots: 10
Complement: 16 (2 officers)
Guns: 1 Bofors 40 mm/60. 2 Hispano 20 mm M71 can be carried.
Radars: Navigation Racal Decca 1216A; I-band.

Comment: Built in 1953. Reported operational.

PT 71   *6/1996* / 0056850

MINISTRY OF INTERIOR

Notes: (1) A Ministry of Interior maritime force polices inshore waters. These vessels are in five types:
  Type 1: 3—24 m craft capable of 30 kt; P-1 *(Srd)*, P-2 *(Marino)*, P-101 *(Sveti Mihovil)*
  Type 2: 6—13 m craft capable of 23 kt; P-11 to P-16
  Type 3: 6—11 m craft capable of 23 kt; P-111 to P-116
  Type 4: 2—14 m craft capable of 30 kt; P-201 and P-202
  Type 5: Numerous small craft under 10 m; RIB or inflatable construction
(2) In addition there are civilian registered base port craft with PU (Pula), SB (Sibenic), ST (Split) and so on markings.

MARINO   *7/2004*, Martin Mokrus* / 1151112

INSHORE CRAFT   *7/2004*, Martin Mokrus* / 1151111

P-112   *5/2004, Martin Mokrus* / 1044095

Cuba

MARINA DE GUERRA REVOLUCIONARIA

Country Overview

The Republic of Cuba is an independent republic located in the Caribbean Sea with which it has a 2,020 n mile coastline. The most westerly of the Greater Antilles group, the country comprises two main islands, Cuba (40,519 square miles) and Isla de la Juventud (849 square miles), and more than 1,600 small coral cays and islets. To the west, Cuba commands the approaches to the Gulf of Mexico; the Straits of Florida and the Yucatán Channel separate the country from Florida and Mexico respectively. To the east, the Windward Passage separates the island from Hispaniola (Haiti and the Dominican Republic). Jamaica lies to the south and the Bahamas to the north-east. Havana is the capital, largest city and principal port. Territorial seas (6 n miles) are claimed. A 200 n mile EEZ has been claimed but the limits have not been defined.

The Navy is in a parlous state and has no capability to sustain operations beyond territorial waters. The Naval Academy is at Punta Santa Ana.

Headquarters Appointments

Chief of Naval Staff:
  Vice Admiral Pedro Perez Miguel Betancourt

Personnel

2006: 2,000 (approximately) (including 500 marines)

Command Organisation

Western Naval District (HQ Cabanas).
Eastern Naval District (HQ Holguin).

Naval Aviation

Four Kamov Ka-28 and 14 Mi-14PL Haze A have been reported but operational status is not known.

Coast Defence

Truck mounted SS-N-2B Styx.

Bases

Cabanas, Nicaro, Cienfuegos, Havana, Santiago de Cuba, Banes.

DELETIONS

Notes: Some vessels have been disposed of. Others are decaying alongside in harbour.

CORVETTES

1 PAUK II CLASS (PROJECT 1241PE) (FSM)

321

Displacement, tons: 440 full load
Dimensions, feet (metres): 191.9 × 33.5 × 11.2 *(58.5 × 10.2 × 3.4)*
Main machinery: 2 Type M 521 diesels; 16,184 hp(m) *(11.9 MW)* sustained; 2 shafts
Speed, knots: 32
Range, n miles: 2,400 at 14 kt
Complement: 32
Missiles: SAM: SA-N-5 quad launcher; manual aiming, IR homing to 10 km *(5.4 n miles)* at 1.5 Mach; warhead 1.1 kg.
Guns: 1 USSR 76 mm/60; 120 rds/min to 7 km *(3.8 n miles)*; weight of shell 16 kg. 1—30 mm/65; 6 barrels; 3,000 rds/min combined to 2 km. 4—25 mm (2 twin).
A/S mortars: 2 RBU 1200 5-tubed fixed; range 1,200 m; warhead 34 kg.
Countermeasures: 2 PK 16 chaff launchers.
Radars: Air/surface search: Positive E; E/F-band.
Navigation: Pechora; I-band.
Fire control: Bass Tilt; H/I-band.
Sonars: Rat Tail; VDS (on transom); attack; high frequency.

Comment: Built at Yaroslav Shipyard in the USSR and transferred in May 1990. Similar to the ships built for India. Has a longer superstructure than the Pauk I and electronics with a radome similar to the Parchim II class. Torpedo tubes removed. Two twin 25 mm guns fitted on the stern. Based at Havana. Operational status doubtful.

PAUK II (Indian colours) *2/1998* / 0052339

PATROL FORCES

6 OSA II CLASS (PROJECT 205)
(FAST ATTACK CRAFT—MISSILE) (PTGF)

261 262 267 268 271 274

Displacement, tons: 171 standard; 245 full load
Dimensions, feet (metres): 126.6 × 24.9 × 8.8 *(38.6 × 7.6 × 2.7)*
Main machinery: 3 Type M 504 diesels; 10,800 hp(m) *(7.94 MW)* sustained; 3 shafts
Speed, knots: 37
Range, n miles: 500 at 35 kt
Complement: 30
Missiles: SSM: 4 SS-N-2B Styx; active radar or IR homing to 46 km *(25 n miles)* at 0.9 Mach; warhead 513 kg.
Guns: 4—30 mm/65 (2 twin); 500 rds/min to 5 km *(2.7 n miles)*; weight of shell 0.54 kg.
Radars: Surface search: Square Tie; I-band.
Fire control: Drum Tilt; H/I-band.
IFF: Square Head. High Pole B.

Comment: One Osa II delivered in mid-1976, one in January 1977 and one in March 1978. Further two delivered in December 1978, one in April 1979, one in October 1979, two from Black Sea November 1981, four in February 1982. While a few may be seagoing, most have been cannibalised for spares and all have had their missiles disembarked for use in shore batteries. One was sunk as a tourist attraction in 1998. Based at Nicaro and Cabanas.

OSA II (Bulgarian colours) *8/1998, E & M Laursen* / 0017645

MINE WARFARE FORCES

2 SONYA CLASS (PROJECT 1265)
(MINESWEEPERS/HUNTERS) (MSC/MH)

570 578

Displacement, tons: 450 full load
Dimensions, feet (metres): 157.4 × 28.9 × 6.6 *(48 × 8.8 × 2)*
Main machinery: 2 Kolomna Type 9-D-8 diesels; 2,000 hp(m) *(1.47 MW)* sustained; 2 shafts
Speed, knots: 15
Range, n miles: 3,000 at 10 kt
Complement: 43
Guns: 2—30 mm/65 (twin); 500 rds/min to 5 km *(2.7 n miles)*; weight of shell 0.54 kg. 2—25 mm/80 (twin); 270 rds/min to 3 km *(1.6 n miles)*.
Mines: Can carry 8.
Radars: Navigation: Don 2; I-band.
IFF: 2 Square Head. High Pole B.
Sonars: MG 69/79; hull-mounted; active minehunting; high frequency.

Comment: Transferred from USSR in January and December 1985. Two others are non-operational and these two have not been reported at sea since 1999.

SONYA (Russian colours) *5/1990* / 0056851

3 YEVGENYA CLASS (PROJECT 1258) (MINEHUNTERS) (MHC)

501, 510, 511

Displacement, tons: 77 standard; 90 full load
Dimensions, feet (metres): 80.7 × 18 × 4.9 *(24.6 × 5.5 × 1.5)*
Main machinery: 2 Type 3-D-12 diesels; 600 hp(m) *(440 kW)* sustained; 2 shafts
Speed, knots: 11
Range, n miles: 300 at 10 kt
Complement: 10
Guns: 2—14.5 mm (twin) MGs.
Countermeasures: Minehunting gear is lowered on a crane at the stern.
Radars: Navigation: Don 2; I-band.
Sonars: MG 7 lifted over the stern.

Comment: First pair transferred from USSR in November 1977, one in September 1978, two in November 1979, two in December 1980, two from the Baltic on 10 December 1981, one in October 1982 and four on 1 September 1984. There are two squadrons, based at Cabanas and Nicaro although these last three are the only seaworthy units.

YEVGENYA (Russian colours) *1991* / 0506087

AUXILIARIES

Notes: In addition there are two other vessels: *Siboney* H 101 of 535 tons and used for cadet training, and a buoy tender *Taino* H 102 of 1,123 tons. Neither are active.

1 PELYM (PROJECT 1799) CLASS (AXT)

40

Displacement, tons: 1,050 full load
Dimensions, feet (metres): 210.3 × 38.4 × 11.5 *(64.1 × 11.7 × 3.5)*
Main machinery: 1 diesel; 1,540 hp *(1.1 MW)*; 1 shaft
Speed, knots: 13.5
Range, n miles: 1,000 at 13 kt
Complement: 40
Radars: Navigation: Don; I-band.

Comment: Transferred from the USSR in 1982 equipped as deperming vessel. Deperming gear since deleted and now employed as a training ship. Based at Havana.

PELYM CLASS (Russian colours) *9/1998, T Gander* / 0050067

1 BIYA (PROJECT 871) CLASS (ABU)

GUAMA H 103

Displacement, tons: 766 full load
Dimensions, feet (metres): 180.4 × 32.1 × 8.5 *(55 × 9.8 × 2.6)*
Main machinery: 2 diesels; 1,200 hp(m) *(882 kW)*; 2 shafts; cp props
Speed, knots: 13
Range, n miles: 4,700+ at 11 kt
Complement: 29 (7 officers)
Radars: Navigation: Don 2; I-band.

Comment: Has laboratory facilities, one survey launch and a 5 ton crane. Built in Poland and acquired from USSR in November 1980. Subordinate to Institute of Hydrography. Last deployed in 1993, but is used locally as a buoy tender and is based at Havana.

STENKA *1990* / 0056852

18 ZHUK (GRIF) CLASS (PROJECT 1400M)
(COASTAL PATROL CRAFT) (PB)

Displacement, tons: 39 full load
Dimensions, feet (metres): 78.7 × 16.4 × 3.9 *(24 × 5 × 1.2)*
Main machinery: 2 Type M 401B diesels; 2,200 hp(m) *(1.6 MW)* sustained; 2 shafts
Speed, knots: 30
Range, n miles: 1,100 at 15 kt
Complement: 11 (3 officers)
Guns: 4-14.5 mm (2 twin) MGs.
Radars: Surface search Spin Trough; I-band.

Comment: A total of 40 acquired since 1971. Last batch of two arrived December 1989. Some transferred to Nicaragua. The total has been reduced to allow for wastage. In some of the class the after gun has been removed. Most of the remaining vessels are still active.

BIYA CLASS (Russian colours) *10/1993, van Ginderen Collection* / 0506283

BORDER GUARD

Notes: A 5,000 strong force which operates under the Ministry of the Interior at a higher state of readiness than the Navy. Pennant numbers painted in red.

2 STENKA (TARANTUL) CLASS
(PROJECT 205P) (FAST ATTACK CRAFT—PATROL) (PB)

801   816

Displacement, tons: 211 standard; 253 full load
Dimensions, feet (metres): 129.3 × 25.9 × 8.2 *(39.4 × 7.9 × 2.5)*
Main machinery: 3 M 583A diesels; 12,172 hp(m) *(8.95 MW)*; 3 shafts
Speed, knots: 34
Range, n miles: 2,250 at 14 kt
Complement: 25 (5 officers)
Guns: 4—30 mm/65 (2 twin) AK 230; 500 rds/min to 5 km *(2.7 n miles)*; weight of shell 0.54 kg.
Radars: Surface search: Pot Drum; H/I-band.
Fire control: Muff Cob; G/H-band.
IFF: High Pole. Square Head.

Comment: Similar to class operated by Russian border guard with torpedo tubes and sonar removed. Transferred from USSR in February 1985 (two) and August 1985 (one). These two reported to be operational.

ZHUK (Yemen colours) *11/1989* / 0056853

Cyprus

Country Overview

Formerly a British colony, the Republic of Cyprus gained independence in 1960. The United Kingdom retained sovereignty over two military bases on the south coast. The total area of the country is 3,572 square miles but, since 1974, the northern third of the country has been occupied by Turkish troops and has formed, de facto, a separate (not UN recognised) state called the Turkish Republic of Northern Cyprus. Situated in the eastern Mediterranean Sea, with which it has a 351 n mile coastline, the island lies west of Syria and south of Turkey. Nicosia is the capital and largest city while Limassol and Larnaca are the principal ports. Territorial seas (12 n miles) are claimed. An EEZ has not been claimed.

Headquarters Appointments

Commander Navy Command of the National Guard:
  Captain Fotis Kotsis
Director Operations:
  Commander Constantinos Fitiris

General

Raif Denktas KKTC 101, *Erenköy* KKTC 02, KKTC 104 and two KAAN 15 craft, KKTC SG11 and SG12 are patrol craft permanently based at Kyrenia (Girne) flying the North

Cyprus flag. For details of these vessels see Turkey Coast Guard section.

Bases

Limassol
Zyyi

Coast Defence

Twenty-four Exocet MM 40 Block 2. Truck-mounted in batteries of four.

PATROL FORCES

Notes: (1) There are no current plans to transfer Combattante II class fast attack craft from Greece, as previously expected.
(2) There are also three launches and a number of RIBs in use by the Underwater Diving section of the Navy.

1 MODIFIED PATRA CLASS (PBM)

Name	No	Builders	Commissioned
SALAMIS	P 01	Chantiers de l'Esterel	24 May 1983

Displacement, tons: 92 full load
Dimensions, feet (metres): 105.3 × 21.3 × 5.9 *(32.1 × 6.5 × 1.8)*
Main machinery: 2 SACM 195 CZSHRY12 diesels; 4,680 hp(m) *(3.44 MW)* sustained; 2 shafts
Speed, knots: 30
Range, n miles: 1,200 at 15 kt
Complement: 22
Missiles: SAM: 1 Matra Simbad twin launcher; Mistral; IR homing to 4 km *(2.2 n miles)*; warhead 3 kg.
Guns: 1 Rheinmetall Wegmann 20 mm. 2—12.7 mm MGs.
Radars: Surface search: Decca 1226; I-band.

Comment: Laid down in December 1981 for Naval Command of National Guard.

SALAMIS *10/1999, E & M Laursen* / 0056854

1 DILOS CLASS (COASTAL PATROL CRAFT) (PBM)

Name	No	Builders	Commissioned
KYRENIA (ex-*Knossos*)	P 02 (ex-P 268)	Hellenic Shipyards, Skaramanga	1979

Displacement, tons: 92 full load
Dimensions, feet (metres): 95.1 × 16.2 × 5.6 *(29 × 5 × 1.7)*
Main machinery: 2 MTU 12V 331 TC81 diesels; 2,700 hp(m) *(1.97 MW)* sustained; 2 shafts
Speed, knots: 26
Range, n miles: 1,600 at 24 kt
Complement: 17 (4 officers)
Missiles: 1 Matra Simbad twin launcher; Mistral; IR homing to 4 km *(2.2 n miles)*; warhead 3 kg
Guns: 1 Rheinmetall Wegmann 20 mm.
Radars: Surface search: Racal Decca 914C; I-band.

Comment: Ordered in May 1976 to a design by Abeking & Rasmussen. Transferred from Greece in March 2000 and used mainly for SAR. Others of the class are in service in Georgia, and with the Hellenic Coast Guard and Customs services.

KYRENIA (Greek colours)   *61/1998, E M Cornish* / 0052296

2 RODMAN 55HJ CLASS (PBF)

PANAGOS   AGATHOS

Displacement, tons: 15.7 full load
Dimensions, feet (metres): 57.1 × 12.5 × 2.3 *(17.4 × 3.8 × 0.7)*
Main machinery: 2 MAN diesels; 2 waterjets
Speed, knots: 48
Range, n miles: 300 at 35 kt
Complement: 7
Guns: 1—12.7 mm MG. 2—7.62 mm MGs.
Radars: Surface search: Furuno; I-band.

Comment: GRP hulls built by Rodman, Vigo and commissioned on 8 June 2002.

PANAGOS   *9/2002, van Ginderen Collection* / 1044096

2 VITTORIA CLASS (COASTAL PATROL CRAFT) (PB)

Name	No	Builders	Commissioned
COMMANDER TSOMAKIS	P 03	Cantiere Navale Vittoria, Adria	Aug 2004
COMMANDER GEORGIU	P 04	Cantiere Navale Vittoria, Adria	Aug 2004

Displacement, tons: 95 full load
Dimensions, feet (metres): 88.9 × 13.4 × 1.0 *(27.6 × 4.1 × 0.3)*
Main machinery: 2 MTU diesels; 2 shafts
Speed, knots: 45
Range, n miles: 800 at 35 kt
Complement: 12
Guns: 1 Breda 25 mm. 2—12.7 mm MGs.

Comment: Built by Cantiere Navale Vittoria, Italy. Two similar craft are in service with the Police Force.

LAND-BASED MARITIME AIRCRAFT

Notes: There are also three Bell 206 utility helicopters.

Numbers/Type: 1 Pilatus Britten-Norman Maritime Defender BN-2A.
Operational speed: 150 kt *(280 km/h)*.
Service ceiling: 18,900 ft *(5,760 m)*.
Range: 1,500 n miles *(2,775 km)*.
Role/Weapon systems: Operated around southern coastline of Cyprus to prevent smuggling and terrorist activity. Sensors: Search radar, searchlight mounted on wings. Weapons: ASV; various machine gun pods and rockets.

POLICE

Notes: (1) In addition there are five Fletcher Malibu speed boats, *Astrapi I-V*, of 5.3 m with 200 hp engines built in Cyprus in 1986.
(2) Personnel numbers are approximately 330 Maritime Police.

2 VITTORIA CLASS (COASTAL PATROL CRAFT) (PB)

Name	No	Builders	Commissioned
THEXAS	PV 23	Cantiere Navale Vittoria, Adria	2005
–	–	Cantiere Navale Vittoria, Adria	2005

Displacement, tons: 95 full load
Dimensions, feet (metres): 88.9 × 13.4 × 1.0 *(27.6 × 4.1 × 0.3)*
Main machinery: 2 MTU diesels; 2 shafts
Speed, knots: 45
Range, n miles: 800 at 35 kt
Complement: 12
Guns: 2—12.7 mm MGs.

Comment: Built by Cantiere Navale Vittoria, Italy.

THEXAS   *3/2005*, Joly/Marsan* / 1133388

5 SAB 12 TYPE (PB)

KARPASIA PL 14 (ex-G 50/GS 10)		DIONYSOS PL 11 (ex-G 55/GS 12)
ILARION PL 13 (ex-G 52/GS 25)		AKAMAS PL 15 (ex-G 57/GS 28)
KOURION PL 12 (ex-G 54/GS 27)		

Displacement, tons: 14 full load
Dimensions, feet (metres): 41.3 × 13.1 × 3.6 *(12.6 × 4 × 1.1)*
Main machinery: 2 Volvo Penta diesels; 539 hp(m) *(396 kW)*; 2 shafts
Speed, knots: 16
Range, n miles: 300 at 15 kt
Complement: 5
Guns: 1—7.62 mm MG.
Radars: Surface search: Raytheon; I-band.

Comment: Built in 1979 by Veb Yachwerft, Berlin. Harbour patrol craft of the former GDR MAB 12 class transferred in December 1992. New radars fitted.

DIONYSOS   *3/2005*, Joly/Marsan* / 1133389

1 SHALDAG CLASS (PBF)

Name	No	Builders	Commissioned
ODYSSEUS	PV 22	Israel Shipyards	4 Sep 1997

Displacement, tons: 56 full load
Dimensions, feet (metres): 81.4 × 19.7 × 3.9 *(24.8 × 6 × 1.2)*
Main machinery: 2 MTU 12V 396TE diesels; 3,560 hp(m) *(2.62 MW)* sustained; 2 Kamewa waterjets
Speed, knots: 45
Range, n miles: 850 at 16 kt
Complement: 15
Guns: 1 Oerlikon 20 mm; 2—7.62 mm MGs.
Weapons control: Optronic director.
Radars: Surface search: Raytheon; I-band.

Comment: Similar to craft in service with Sri Lankan Navy.

ODYSSEUS   *3/2005*, Joly/Marsan* / 1133387

2 POSEIDON CLASS (PBF)

Name	No	Builders	Commissioned
POSEIDON	PV 20	Brodotehnika SY, Belgrade	21 Nov 1991
EVAGORAS	PV 21	Brodotehnika SY, Belgrade	21 Nov 1991

Displacement, tons: 58 full load
Dimensions, feet (metres): 80.7 × 18.7 × 3.9 *(24.6 × 5.7 × 1.2)*
Main machinery: 2 MTU 12V 396 TE94 diesels; 3,560 hp(m) *(2.62 MW)* sustained; 2 Kamewa 56 water-jets
Speed, knots: 42
Range, n miles: 600 at 20 kt
Complement: 9
Guns: 1 Breda KVA 25 mm; ISBRS rocket launcher. 2—12.7 mm MGs.
Radars: Surface search: JRC; I-band.

Comment: Designated as FAC-23 Jets. Aluminium construction. New radars fitted.

POSEIDON
9/2002, van Ginderen Collection
0569188

Denmark

DEN KONGELIGE DANSKE MARINE

Country Overview

The Kingdom of Denmark is a constitutional monarchy. The southernmost of the Scandinavian countries, it comprises most of the Jutland peninsula and more than 400 islands, the principal of which are Sjaelland (the largest), Fyn, Lolland, Falster, Langeland and Møn. The island of Bornholm lies in the Baltic about 70 n miles east of Sjaelland. With an area of 16,639 square miles, the country is bordered to the south by Germany. Its 1,825 n mile coastline is with the North Sea to the west, the Skagerrak to the north and the Kattegatt, which is linked to the Baltic Sea by the Øresund, to the east. The capital, largest city and principal port is Copenhagen. There are further ports at Århus, Odense and Ålborg. Territorial seas (12 n miles) are claimed. It has claimed a 200 n mile EEZ for the mainland and 200 n mile Fishery Zones for the external territories of the Faroes and Greenland.

Headquarters Appointments

Admiral Fleet:
Rear Admiral Nils Wang
Inspector Naval Home Guard:
Captain K R Andersen

Diplomatic Representation

Defence Attaché, Washington and Ottawa:
Brigadier P J Larsen
Defence Attaché, London, Dublin and The Hague:
Captain N A K Olsen
Defence Attaché, Paris:
Colonel C J D Dirksen
Defence Attaché, Berlin and Prague:
Colonel P O Topp
Defence Attaché, Moscow and Minsk:
Brigadier S B Bojesen
Defence Attaché, Warsaw:
Colonel P E Tranberg
Defence Attaché, Vilnius:
Commander Senior Grade C V Rasmussen
Defence Attaché, Riga:
Lieutenant Colonel O C Grüner
Defence Attaché, Kiev:
Lieutenant Colonel C Mathiesen
Defence Attaché, Helsinki and Tallin:
Lieutenant Colonel E K Praestegaard

Personnel

(a) 2006: 3,770 (874 officers) including 450 national service
Reserves: 4,000.
Naval Home Guard: 4,800.
(b) 4 months' national service

Bases

Korsør (Corvettes, Patrol Craft Stanflex), Frederikshavn (Inspection ships, MCMV, Support Ships), Copenhagen, Grønnedal (Greenland)

Naval Air Arm

Naval helicopters owned and operated by Navy in naval squadron based at Karup, Jutland. All servicing and maintenance by Air Force. LRMP are flown by the Air Force.

Naval Home Guard

Established in 1952 as a separate service under the operational control of the navy. Duties include surveillance, harbour control, search and rescue and the guarding of naval installations ashore. Following the Defence Agreement 2004, the service is to play a greater role in home defence and further tasks include environmental survey, pollution control and support of the police and customs services.

Coast Defence

The coastal radar system is being upgraded with additional sites and with new radars and sensors. The system will comprise 27 sites when completed in 2008.

Command and Control

The Royal Danish Navy, on behalf of the Ministry of Defence, runs and maintains the icebreakers. Likewise, the Navy runs and maintains two environmental protection divisions based in Copenhagen and Korsør respectively. Responsibility for environmental survey, protection and pollution fighting in maritime areas around Denmark is executed by the Royal Danish Navy. Survey ships are run by the Farvandsvæsenet Nautisk Afdeling (Administration of Navigation and Hydrography) under the Ministry of Defence, and the Directorate of Fisheries has four rescue vessels.

Appearance

Ships are painted in six different colours as follows:
Grey: frigates, corvettes and patrol frigates.
Orange: survey vessels.
White: Royal Yacht and the sail training yawls.
Black/yellow: service vessels, tugs and ferryboats.

Strength of the Fleet

Type	Active	Building (Projected)
Frigates	7	3
Large Patrol Craft	22	8 (1)
Coastal Patrol Craft	24	6
Naval Home Guard	12	7
Minehunters and Drones	10	2
Support Ships	2	–
Transport Ship	1	–
Icebreakers	3	–
Royal Yacht	1	–

Prefix to Ships' Names

HDMS

DELETIONS

Submarines

2003	Narhvalen, Nordkaperen
2004	Tumleren, Saelen, Springeren, Kronborg

Patrol Forces

2005	Flyvefisken, Hajen, Svaerdfisken

Mine Warfare Forces

2003	Fyen
2004	Lindormen, Lossen, Møen

Auxiliaries

2003	Hugin, Elbjørn, Nordjylland, Jens Vaever
2004	Munin, Mimer

PENNANT LIST

Frigates

F 354	Niels Juel
F 355	Olfert Fischer
F 356	Peter Tordenskiold
F 357	Thetis
F 358	Triton
F 359	Vaedderen
F 360	Hvidbjørnen

Patrol Forces

P 552	Havkatten
P 553	Laxen
P 554	Makrelen
P 555	Støren
P 557	Glenten
P 558	Gribben
P 559	Lommen
P 560	Ravnen
P 561	Skaden
P 562	Viben
P 563	Søløven
Y 300	Barsø
Y 301	Drejø
Y 302	Romsø
Y 303	Samsø
Y 304	Thurø
Y 305	Vejrø
Y 306	Farø
Y 307	Laesø
Y 308	Rømø
Y 386	Agdlek
Y 387	Agpa
Y 388	Tulugaq

Auxiliaries

A 540	Dannebrog
A 551	Danbjørn
A 552	Isbjørn
A 553	Thorbjørn
A 559	Sleipner
A 560	Gunnar Thorson
A 561	Gunnar Seidenfaden
A 562	Mette Miljø
A 563	Marie Miljø
L 16	Absalon
L 17	Esbern Snare
Y 101	Svanen
Y 102	Thyra

SUBMARINES

Notes: As a consequence of the 2004 Defence Agreement, the submarine force has been disbanded. All submarines have been decommissioned. *Kronborg* (ex-*Näcken*) has been returned to Sweden while *Saelen* and *Springeren* are to be preserved as museum ships at the Naval Station, Copenhagen and at Bagenhop, Langeland respectively.

FRIGATES

4 THETIS CLASS (FFHM)

Name	No	Builders	Laid down	Launched	Commissioned
THETIS	F 357	Svenborg Vaerft	10 Oct 1988	14 July 1989	1 July 1991
TRITON	F 358	Svenborg Vaerft	27 June 1989	16 Mar 1990	2 Dec 1991
VAEDDEREN	F 359	Svenborg Vaerft	19 Mar 1990	21 Dec 1990	9 June 1992
HVIDBJØRNEN	F 360	Svenborg Vaerft	2 Jan 1991	11 Oct 1991	30 Nov 1992

Displacement, tons: 2,600 standard; 3,500 full load

Dimensions, feet (metres): 369.1 oa; 327.4 wl × 47.2 × 19.7 *(112.5; 99.8 × 14.4 × 6.0)*

Main machinery: 3 MAN/Burmeister & Wain Alpha 12V 28/32A diesels; 10,800 hp(m) *(7.94 MW)* sustained; 1 shaft; Kamewa cp prop; bow and azimuth thrusters; 880 hp(m) *(647 kW)*, 1,100 hp(m) *(800 kW)*

Speed, knots: 20; 8 on thrusters

Range, n miles: 8,500 at 15.5 kt

Complement: 60 (12 officers) plus 30 spare berths

Missiles: SAM: 4 Stinger mountings (2 twin) on hangar roof near mast.

Guns: 1 OTO Melara 3 in *(76 mm)*/62; Super Rapid ❶; dual purpose; 120 rds/min to 16 km *(8.7 n miles)*; SAPOMER round weight 12.7 kg.
2 — 12.7 mm MGs.

Depth charges: 2 Rails (door in stern).

Countermeasures: Decoys: 2 Sea Gnat DL-12T 12-barrelled launchers for chaff and IR flares.
ESM: Racal Sabre; intercept.

Combat data systems: Terma TDS; SATCOM ❷.

Weapons control: Bofors 9LV 200 Mk 3 director. FSI Safire surveillance director ❸.

Radars: Air/surface search: Plessey AWS 6 ❹; G-band.
Surface search: Furuno 2135; E/F-band.
Navigation: Furuno 2115; I-band.
Fire control: CelsiusTech 9LV Mk 3 ❺; I/J-band.

Sonars: Thomson Sintra TSM 2640 Salmon; VDS; active search and attack; medium frequency.
C-Teck; hull-mounted; active search; medium frequency.

Helicopters: 1 Westland Lynx Mk 90B ❻.

Programmes: Preliminary study by YARD in 1986 led to Dwinger Marine Consultants being awarded a contract for a detailed design completed in mid-1987. All four ordered in October 1987.

Modernisation: There are plans for a new air search radar and SAM in due course.

Structure: The hull is some 30 m longer than the Hvidbjørnen class to improve sea-keeping qualities and allow considerable extra space for additional armament. The design allows the use of containerised equipment to be shipped depending on role and there is some commonality with the Flex 300 ships. The hull is ice strengthened to enable penetration of 1 m thick ice and efforts have been made to incorporate stealth technology, for instance by putting anchor equipment, bollards and winches below the upper deck. There is a double skin up to 2 m below the waterline. A rigid inflatable boarding craft plumbed by a hydraulic crane is fitted alongside the fixed hangar. The bridge and ops room are combined. *Thetis* was modified in the stern for seismological survey. Since these operations have terminated, the stern has been remodified to facilitate the ability to act as a command ship and to conduct training.

Operational: Primary role is sovereignty patrol and fishery protection in the North Atlantic. *Vaedderen* is to operate in support of the Galathea III oceanographic project in 2006-07.

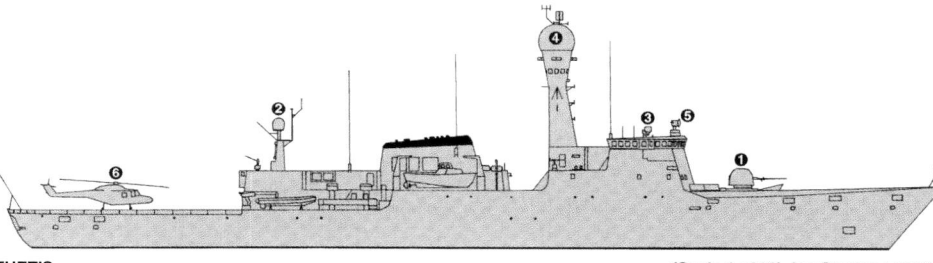

THETIS *(Scale 1 : 900), Ian Sturton* / 0012258

THETIS *9/2005*, Guy Toremans* / 1133412

THETIS
6/2004, P Froud
1121261

THETIS *9/2003, Harald Carstens* / 1044112

3 NIELS JUEL CLASS (FFGM)

Name	No	Builders	Laid down	Launched	Commissioned
NIELS JUEL	F 354	Aalborg Vaerft	20 Oct 1976	17 Feb 1978	26 Aug 1980
OLFERT FISCHER	F 355	Aalborg Vaerft	6 Dec 1978	10 May 1979	16 Oct 1981
PETER TORDENSKIOLD	F 356	Aalborg Vaerft	3 Dec 1979	30 Apr 1980	2 Apr 1982

Displacement, tons: 1,320 full load
Dimensions, feet (metres): 275.5 × 33.8 × 10.2
  (84 × 10.3 × 3.1)
Main machinery: CODOG; 1 GE LM 2500 gas turbine;
  24,600 hp *(18.35 MW)* sustained; 1 MTU 20 V 956 TB82
  diesel; 5,210 hp(m) *(3.83 MW)* sustained; 2 shafts
Speed, knots: 28, gas; 20, diesel
Range, n miles: 2,500 at 18 kt
Complement: 94 (15 officers)

Missiles: SSM: 8 McDonnell Douglas Harpoon (2 quad)
  launchers ❶; active radar homing to 130 km *(70 n miles)*
  at 0.9 Mach; warhead 227 kg.
  SAM: 12 (2 sextuple) Raytheon Sea Sparrow Mk 48 Mod
  3 VLS (12 missiles) or Mk 56 Mod O VLS (24 missiles)
  modular launchers ❷; semi-active radar homing to
  14.6 km *(8 n miles)* at 2.5 Mach; warhead 39 kg;
  12 missiles.
    4 Stinger mountings (2 twin) ❸.
Guns: 1 OTO Melara 3 in *(76 mm)*/62 compact ❹;
  85 rds/min to 16 km *(8.7 n miles)* anti-surface; 12 km
  (6.6 n miles) anti-aircraft; SAPOMER round weight 12.7 kg.
  4—12.7 mm MGs.
Depth charges: 1 rack.
Countermeasures: Decoys: 2 DL-12T Sea Gnat 12-barrelled
  chaff launchers ❺.

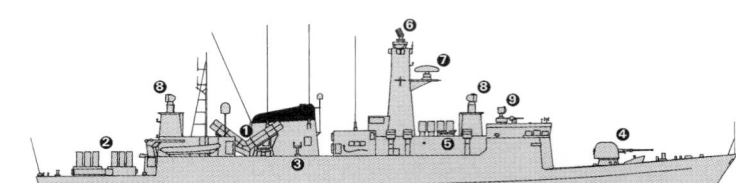

PETER TORDENSKIOLD   *(Scale 1 : 900), Ian Sturton* / 1047859

Combat data systems: CelciusTech 9LV Mk 3. Link 11.
  SATCOMs (can be fitted forward or aft of the funnel).
Weapons control: Philips 9LV 200 Mk 3 GFCS with TV
  tracker. Raytheon Mk 91 Mod 1 MFCS with two directors.
  Harpoon to 1A(V) standard.
Radars: Air search: DASA TRS-3D ❻; G/H-band.
  Surface search: Philips 9GR 600 ❼; I-band.
  Fire control: 2 Mk 95 ❽; I/J-band (for SAM).
  Philips 9LV 200 Mk 1 Rakel 203C ❾; J-band (for guns and
  SSM).
  Navigation: Terma Scanter Mil; I-band.
Sonars: Plessey PMS 26; hull-mounted; active search and
  attack; 10 kHz.

Programmes: YARD Glasgow designed the class to Danish
  order.
Modernisation: Mid-life update from 1996, including a
  NATO Sea Sparrow VLS, and new communications. Air
  search radar replaced by TST TRS-3D. Improved combat
  data system fitted. F 356 completed in May 1998, F 354
  in April 1999, F 355 in December 2001. Stinger SAM
  mounted each side of the funnel.
Operational: Normally only one sextuple SAM launcher
  is carried, but the second set can be embarked in
  a few hours. To be replaced by new frigates
  from 2011.

PETER TORDENSKIOLD   *6/2005*, Frank Findler* / 1133390

OLFERT FISCHER   *9/2004, M Nitz* / 1044119

NIELS JUEL *5/2005*, Guy Toremans* / 1133413

PETER TORDENSKIOLD *5/2005*, M Declerck* / 1133414

NIELS JUEL *4/2005*, Per Körnefeldt* / 1133391

0 + 3 PATROL SHIPS (FFHM)

Name	No	Builders	Laid down	Launched	Commissioned
–	F 361	Odense Shipyard, Lindø	2008	2010	2011
–	F 362	Odense Shipyard, Lindø	2009	2011	2012
–	F 363	Odense Shipyard, Lindø	2010	2011	2012

Displacement, tons: 6,000
Dimensions, feet (metres): 452.5 × 64.0 × 20.7 *(138.7 × 19.8 × 6.1)*
Main machinery: CODAD; 4 MTU 20V M70 diesels; 44,000 hp *(32.8 MW)*; 2 shafts; cp props; bow thruster
Speed, knots: 28
Complement: 100 (accommodation for 165)

Missiles: SSM: 16 Boeing Harpoon Block II (2 octuple AHWCS VLS launchers); active radar homing to 130 km *(70 n miles)* at 0.9 Mach; warhead 227 kg.
SAM: 32 GDC Standard SM-2 MR Block IIIA; command/inertial guidance; semi-active radar homing to 167 km *(90 n miles)* at 2 Mach. Lockheed Martin Mk 41 VLS (32 cells).
24 Evolved Sea Sparrow RIM 162B; semi-active radar homing to 18 km *(9.7 n miles)* at 3.6 Mach; warhead 39 kg. 2 Raytheon Mk 56 VLS (2 × 12 cells).
6 twin Sea Stinger launchers.
Guns: 3 mountings (United Defense 127 mm and/or OTO Melara 76 mm and Oerlikon Contraves 35 mm).
Torpedoes: 6—324 mm (2 triple) launchers; Eurotorp MU 90 Impact.
Countermeasures: Decoys: Terma 130 mm Decoy Launching System; 2 DL-12T and 2 DL-6T launchers (36 barrels).
ESM: To be announced.
Combat data systems: Terma C-Flex Combat Management System.
Weapons control: To be announced.
Radars: Air/Surface search: Thales Smart-L or BAE systems Sampson; 3D.
Fire control: (SAM) Thales APAR or CEA Tech CEA-MOUNT; I/J-band.
Fire control: (guns) Saab Ceros 200; J/K-band.
Navigation: Furuno; E/F/I-bands.
Sonars: Hull-mounted, towed and variable depth.

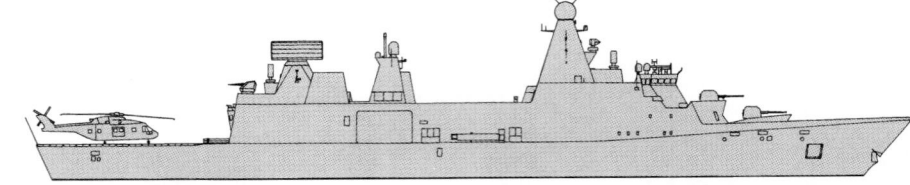

PATROL SHIP (Sampson variant)   *(Scale 1 : 1,200), Ian Sturton* / 1153486

PATROL SHIP (APAR variant)   *(Scale 1 : 1,200), Ian Sturton* / 1153488

Helicopters: 1 medium or 2 Lynx.

Programmes: Construction of three frigates was approved in the 2004 Defence Agreement. Construction contracts are expected to be let in 2006.
Structure: Built to DNV standards. The design is based on the Absalon class Flexible Support Ships and utilises the same hull and the majority of equipment. There are to be dedicated staff facilities for national or NATO task group commanders. Four Stanflex container positions are to be located on the weapons deck and one at B-position. There is to be cargo space for four 20 ft TEU containers. The flight deck is to be capable of operating 20 ton helicopters and prepared to operate UAVs. The radar and gunnery suites are to be selected in 2006.
Operational: The ships are to have a global, expeditionary role and to be capable of providing area air-defence and support of land forces.

SHIPBORNE AIRCRAFT

Notes: The Defence Agreement of 10 June 2004 provided for the procurement of four maritime helicopters to enter service 2008-10. These might be further Merlin aircraft in addition to the 14 utility variants being procured for the Danish Air Force.

Numbers/Type: 8 Westland Lynx Mk 90B.
Operational speed: 125 kt *(232 km/h)*.
Service ceiling: 12,500 ft *(3,810 m)*.
Range: 320 n miles *(593 km)*.
Role/Weapon systems: Shipborne helicopter for EEZ and surface search tasks. All being upgraded to Super Lynx standard with first delivered November 2000. Sensors: Ferranti Seaspray; Racal Kestrel ESM; FLIR 2000. Weapons: Unarmed.

LYNX   *2/2004, Per Körnefeldt* / 1044107

LAND-BASED MARITIME AIRCRAFT

Notes: The Sikorsky S-61 A-1 helicopters are to be replaced 2007-09 by SAR versions of the 14 DMRH-101 helicopters being procured by the Danish Air Force.

Numbers/Type: 3 Challenger 604.
Operational speed: 470 kt *(870 km/h)*.
Service ceiling: 41,000 ft *(12,497 m)*.
Range: 3,769 n miles *(6,980 km)*.
Role/Weapon systems: Maritime reconnaissance for EEZ patrol in the Baltic and off Greenland. Sensors: Terma SLAR radar; IR/UV scanner. Weapons: unarmed.

CHALLENGER 604   *6/2005*, Massimo Annati* / 1153495

Numbers/Type: 8 Sikorsky S-61A-1 Sea King.
Operational speed: 118 kt *(219 km/h)*.
Service ceiling: 14,700 ft *(4,480 m)*.
Range: 542 n miles *(1,005 km)*.
Role/Weapon systems: Land-based SAR helicopter for combat rescue and surface search. Sensors: Bendix weather radar; GEC Avionics FLIR. Weapons: unarmed.

SEA KING   *5/1999, H M Steele* / 0056867

PATROL FORCES

Notes: *Lunden* Y 343 is a 20 m trawler type vessel. Previously thought to have been decommissioned, she remains in service as a target-towing vessel.

0 + 2 (1) ARCTIC PATROL SHIPS (PGBH)

Name	No	Builders	Laid down	Launched	Commissioned
–	P 570	Karstensens Skibsvaerft, Skagen	2006	2007	2008
–	P 571	Karstensens Skibsvaerft, Skagen	2006	2007	2008

Displacement, tons: 1,720
Dimensions, feet (metres): 235.5 × 49.7 × 16.2 *(71.8 × 14.6 × 4.9)*
Main machinery: 2 MAN B&W ALPHA 8L 27/38 diesels; 7,300 hp *(5.4 MW)*; 1 shaft; cp prop
Speed, knots: 17
Complement: 18
Guns: 2—12.7 mm MGs.
Countermeasures: To be announced.
Combat data systems: To be announced.
Radars: Surface/air search: Terma Scanter 4100; I-band.
Fire control: To be announced.
Navigation: Furuno; E/F/I-bands.
Sonars: Reson; hull mounted (retractable).
Helicopters: Platform for 1 medium.

Programmes: Contract for the construction of two ships let in December 2004. Construction is to begin in 2006 to meet an in-service date of 2008. There is an option for a third unit.
Structure: Built to DNV Navy ICE 1A standards. A high-speed long-range rescue craft, an ice-strengthened version of the Combat Boat 90E, can be launched from a bay in the stern. Fitted with four Stanflex container positions for equipment and weapons, the design has the flexibility to operate in its (lightly armed) primary role or in a more heavily armed secondary role.
Operational: To replace Agdlek class. The principal role is sovereignty patrol in the arctic waters off Greenland while secondary roles, such as command and control of a small force, might be exercised globally. Containerised weapons including a 76 mm gun, a Mk 56 launcher with evolved Sea Sparrow missiles and MU 90 torpedoes may be fitted.

ARCTIC PATROL SHIP   *10/2005*, Royal Danish Navy* / 1133410

2 VTS CLASS (COASTAL PATROL CRAFT) (PB)

VTS 3   **VTS 4**

Displacement, tons: 34 full load
Dimensions, feet (metres): 55.8 × 16.1 × 6.9 *(17 × 4.9 × 2.1)*
Main machinery: 2 MWM TBD 616 V12 diesels; 979 hp(m) *(720 kW)*; 2 waterjets
Speed, knots: 33
Range, n miles: 300 at 30 kt
Complement: 3
Guns: 1—7.62 mm MG can be carried.
Radars: Surface search: Furuno FR 1505 Mk 2; I-band.
Navigation: Furuno M1831; I-band.

Comment: Built by Mulder & Rijke, Netherlands. Completed in 1997 and 1998 to replace Botved type.

VTS 3   *6/1999, Royal Danish Navy* / 0056874

14 FLYVEFISKEN CLASS (LARGE PATROL/ATTACK CRAFT AND MINEHUNTERS/LAYERS) (PGGM/MHCD/MLC/AGSC)

Name	No	Builders	Commissioned
HAVKATTEN	P 552	Danyard A/S, Aalborg	1 Nov 1990
LAXEN	P 553	Danyard A/S, Aalborg	22 Mar 1991
MAKRELEN	P 554	Danyard A/S, Aalborg	1 Oct 1991
STØREN	P 555	Danyard A/S, Aalborg	24 Apr 1992
GLENTEN	P 557	Danyard A/S, Aalborg	29 Apr 1993
GRIBBEN	P 558	Danyard A/S, Aalborg	1 July 1993
LOMMEN	P 559	Danyard A/S, Aalborg	21 Jan 1994
RAVNEN	P 560	Danyard A/S, Aalborg	17 Oct 1994
SKADEN	P 561	Danyard A/S, Aalborg	10 Apr 1995
VIBEN	P 562	Danyard A/S, Aalborg	15 Jan 1996
SØLØVEN	P 563	Danyard A/S, Aalborg	28 May 1996

Displacement, tons: 480 full load
Dimensions, feet (metres): 177.2 × 29.5 × 8.2 *(54 × 9 × 2.5)*
Main machinery: CODAG; 1 GE LM 500 gas turbine (centre shaft); 5,450 hp *(4.1 MW)* sustained; 2 MTU 16V 396TB94 diesels (outer shafts); 5,800 hp(m) *(4.26 MW)* sustained; 3 shafts; cp props on outer shafts; bow thruster. Auxiliary propulsion by hydraulic motors on outer gearboxes; hydraulic pumps driven by 1 GM 12V-71 diesel; 500 hp *(375 kW)*
Speed, knots: 30; 20 on diesels; 10 on hydraulic propulsion
Range, n miles: 2,400 at 18 kt
Complement: 19-29 (depending on role) (4 officers)

Missiles: SSM: 8 McDonnell Douglas Harpoon; active radar homing to 130 km *(70 n miles)* at 0.9 Mach; warhead 227 kg. Attack role only. Block II from 2004 gives land attack option.
SAM: Raytheon Sea Sparrow Mk 48 Mod 3 VLS (6 missiles) or Mk 56 Mod 0 VLS (12 missiles); semi-active radar homing to 14.6 km *(8 n miles)* at 2.5 Mach; warhead 32 kg. 12 missiles from 2002. Fitted for Attack, MCM and Minelaying roles. In MCM role one Stinger twin launcher can be fitted instead of Sea Sparrow.
Guns: 1 OTO Melara 3 in *(76 mm)*/62 Super Rapid; dual purpose; 120 rds/min to 16 km *(8.7 n miles)*; SAPOMER round weight 12.7 kg.
2—12.7 mm MGs.
Torpedoes: 4—324 mm tubes; Eurotorp MU 90 Impact.
Depth charges: 4.
Mines: 60. Minelaying role only.
Countermeasures: MCMV: Ibis 43 minehunting system with Thomson Sintra 2061 tactical system and 2054 side scan sonar towed by MSF class drones (see *Mine Warfare Forces* section). Bofors Double Eagle ROV Mk II. Minehunting role only.
Decoys: 2 Sea Gnat 130 mm DL-6T 6-barrelled launcher for chaff and IR flares.
ESM: Racal Sabre; radar warning.
Combat data systems: Terma/CelsiusTech TDS. Link 11.
Weapons control: CelsiusTech 9LV Mk 3 optronic director. Harpoon to 1A(V) standard or AHWCS with Block II.
Radars: Air/surface search: Plessey AWS 6 (552—555); G-band; or EADS TRS-3D (557—563); G/H-band.
Surface search: Terma Scanter Mil; I-band.
Navigation: Furuno; I-band.
Fire control: CelsiusTech 9LV 200 Mk 3; Ku/J-band.

STØREN   *5/2005*, Martin Mokrus* / 1133393

GLENTEN   *9/2005*, Guy Toremans* / 1133408

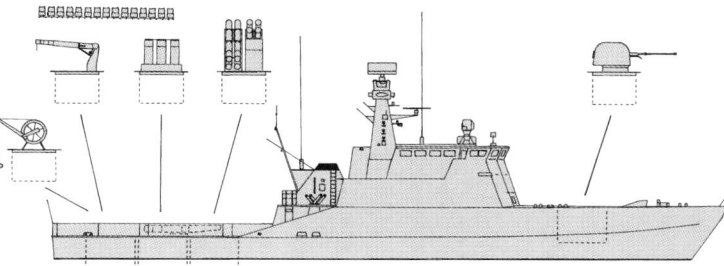

FLYVEFISKEN (composite fit)   *(Scale 1 : 600), Ian Sturton* / 0103718

Sonars: CelsiusTech CTS-36/39; hull-mounted; active search; high frequency.
Thomson Sintra TSM 2640 Salmon; VDS; medium frequency. For ASW only.

Programmes: Standard Flex 300 replaced Daphne class (seaward defence craft), Søløven class (fast attack craft torpedo), and Sund (MCM) class. First batch of seven with option on a further nine contracted with Danyard on 27 July 1985. Second batch of six ordered 14 June 1990 and last one authorised in 1993 to a total of 14, two less than originally planned.
Modernisation: Mk 48 Mod 3 SAM launchers replaced by Mk 56 launchers. Harpoon launchers upgraded to AHWCS version 2 capable of firing Block II missiles. Link 11 fitted.
Structure: GRP sandwich hulls. Four positions prepared to plug in armament and equipment containers in combinations meeting the requirements of the various roles. Torpedo tubes and minerails detachable. Combat data system modular with standard consoles of which three to six are embarked depending on the role. SAV control aerials are mounted on the bridge. TRS-3D radar fitted in last seven.
Operational: Following an operational review of the class, the original concept, to be able to re-role by the interchange of mission-specific containers for different taskings (ASUW, ASW, MCM and Patrol) has been abandoned. Under a revised concept of employment, the class is to be reduced to ten ships. Of these, four ships are to be permanently roled for MCM *(Laxen, Makrelen, Havkatten, Støren)*, four for a combat role (ASW or ASUW) *(Glenten, Skaden, Viben, Ravnen)* and two *(Gribben and Søløven)* for Patrol duties. Three ships *(Svaerdfisken, Flyvefisken, Hajen)* have been decommissioned and *Lommen*, currently operating as a test platform for the Terma C-Flex combat system, is to be decommissioned in 2007. Gas turbines are not fitted in MCM ships.

LOMMEN   *2/2005*, Per Körnefeldt* / 1133392

3 AGDLEK CLASS (LARGE PATROL CRAFT) (PB)

Name	No	Builders	Commissioned
AGDLEK	Y 386	Svendborg Vaerft	12 Mar 1974
AGPA	Y 387	Svendborg Vaerft	14 May 1974
TULUGAQ	Y 388	Svendborg Vaerft	26 June 1979

Displacement, tons: 394 full load
Dimensions, feet (metres): 103 × 25.3 × 11.2 *(31.4 × 7.7 × 3.4)*
Main machinery: 1 Burmeister & Wain Alpha A08-26 VO diesel; 800 hp(m) *(588 kW)*; 1 shaft
Speed, knots: 12
Complement: 14 (3 officers)
Guns: 2—12.7 mm MGs.
Radars: Surface search: Furuno 2135; E/F-band.
Navigation: Furuno 1510; I-band.

Comment: Designed for service off Greenland. Ice strengthened. SATCOM fitted. To be replaced from from 2008 by new 70 m Arctic patrol vessels.

TULUGAQ   *10/2004, Per Körnefeldt* / 1044106

0 + 6 SF MK II CLASS (LARGE PATROL CRAFT) (PB)

P 520-525

Displacement, tons: 276 full load
Dimensions, feet (metres): 141.1 × 26.9 × 7.2 *(43.0 × 8.2 × 2.2)*
Main machinery: 2 MTU 396 16V TB94 diesels; 2,700 hp *(2 MW)*; 2 shafts; cp props
Speed, knots: 18
Complement: 9 (accommodation for 15)
Guns: 2—12.7 mm MGs.
Radars: Navigation: Furuno 2117; I-band.

Comment: GRP vessels to replace the Ø class. Ordered from Faaborg Vaerft, Denmark, the hull, superstructure and machinery are to be built by Kockums, Karlskrona. Fitted with one Stanflex container position. To be delivered 2007-08.

SF MK II   *10/2005*, Royal Danish Navy* / 1133409

9 Ø CLASS (LARGE PATROL CRAFT) (PB)

Name	No	Builders	Commissioned
BARSØ	Y 300	Svendborg Vaerft	13 June 1969
DREJØ	Y 301	Svendborg Vaerft	1 July 1969
ROMSØ	Y 302	Svendborg Vaerft	21 July 1969
SAMSØ	Y 303	Svendborg Vaerft	15 Aug 1969
THURØ	Y 304	Svendborg Vaerft	12 Sep 1969
VEJRØ	Y 305	Svendborg Vaerft	17 Oct 1969
FARØ	Y 306	Svendborg Vaerft	17 May 1973
LAESØ	Y 307	Svendborg Vaerft	23 July 1973
ROMØ	Y 308	Svendborg Vaerft	3 Sep 1973

Displacement, tons: 155 full load
Dimensions, feet (metres): 84 × 19.7 × 9.2 *(25.6 × 6 × 2.8)*
Main machinery: 1 diesel; 385 hp(m) *(283 kW)*; 1 shaft
Speed, knots: 11
Complement: 9 (2 officers)
Guns: 2—12.7 mm MG.
Radars: Navigation: Furuno 1510; I-band.

Comment: Rated as patrol cutters. *Laesø* acts as diver support ship with a recompression chamber and towed acoustic array. The last three have a wheelhouse which extends over the full beam. To be replaced by six new 43 m patrol craft from 2007.

SAMSØ   *8/2001, E & M Laursen* / 0533295

0 + 6 SF MK I CLASS (MULTIROLE CRAFT) (MSD/AXL/AGSC)

A 541	A 542	A 543	A 544	MSD 5	MSD 6

Displacement, tons: 138 full load
Dimensions, feet (metres): 94.8 × 21.0 × 6.6 *(28.9 × 6.4 × 2.0)*
Main machinery: 2 Scania DC 16 diesels; 1,005 hp(m) *(750 kW)*; 2 azimuth thrusters
Speed, knots: 12
Complement: 3 (accommodation for 9)
Radars: Navigation: Furuno 2117; I-band.

Comment: Multirole GRP vessels constructed by Danish Yacht A/S, Skagen. One Stanflex container position. First two vessels to be inshore survey craft launches and to be followed by two training vessels and two MCM drones. To be delivered between 2006 and 2008.

SF MK I   *10/2005*, Royal Danish Navy* / 1133407

MINE WARFARE FORCES

Notes: See also Flyvefisken class under *Patrol Forces*.

4 MSF CLASS (MRD)

MSF 1-4

Displacement, tons: 125 full load
Dimensions, feet (metres): 86.9 × 23 × 6.9 *(26.5 × 7 × 2.1)*
Main machinery: 2 Scania DSI 14 diesels; 1,000 hp(m) *(736 kW)*; 2 Schottel waterjets or 2 Schottel azimuth thrusters
Speed, knots: 12
Complement: 4
Combat data systems: IN-SNEC/INFOCOM.
Radars: Navigation: Raytheon 40 or Terma; I-band.
Sonars: Thomson Marconi STS 2054 side scan active; high frequency.

Comment: MSF (Minor Standard Vessel). Ordered in January 1997 from Danyard, Aalborg, and five delivered June 1998 to January 1999. Used primarily as MCM drones although built as multipurpose platform (with one Stanflex container position). Fitted with containerised MCM gear for working in conjunction with Flyvefisken class minehunters. GRP hulls. IN-SNEC is a high data rate sonar/TV link. INFOCOM is a low data rate command link. Plans for further craft are under consideration. One transferred to Sweden in 2001.

MSF 3   *10/2005*, Martin Mokrus* / 1133396

6 SAV CLASS (MINEHUNTER-DRONES) (MSD)

MRD 1 (ex-MRF 1)	MRD 2 (ex-MRF 2)	MRD 3-6

Displacement, tons: 32 full load
Dimensions, feet (metres): 59.7 × 15.6 × 3.9 *(18.2 × 4.8 × 1.2)*
Main machinery: 2 Detroit diesels; 350 hp(m) *(257 kW)*; 2 Schottel waterjet propulsors
Speed, knots: 12
Complement: 4
Combat data systems: Terma link to Flyvefisken class (in MCMV configuration).
Radars: Navigation: Furuno; I-band.
Sonars: Thomson Sintra TSM 2054 side scan; active minehunting; high frequency.

Comment: Built by Danyard with GRP hulls. First one completed in March 1991, second in December 1991. Four more ordered in mid-1994 and delivered in 1996. The vessels are robot drones (or Surface Auxiliary Vessels (SAV)) operated in pairs by the Flyvefisken class in MCMV configuration. Hull is based on the Hugin class TRVs with low noise propulsion. The towfish with side scan sonar is lowered and raised from the stern-mounted gantry. The first two craft have slightly different funnel designs.

MRD 4 *7/2002, E & M Laursen* / 0526826

TRAINING SHIPS

Notes: There are two small Sail Training Ships, *Svanen* Y 101 and *Thyra* Y 102. Of 32 tons they have a sail area of 480 m² and an auxiliary diesel of 72 hp(m) *(53 kW)*. Built in 1960 by Molich yacht builders, Hundested. Used to train midshipmen before attending the naval academy.

THYRA *6/2005*, Frank Findler* / 1133400

SURVEY SHIPS

6 SURVEY LAUNCHES (YGS)

SKA 11-16

Displacement, tons: 52 full load
Dimensions, feet (metres): 65.6 × 17.1 × 6.9 *(20 × 5.2 × 2.1)*
Main machinery: 1 GM diesel; 540 hp *(403 kW)*; 1 shaft
Speed, knots: 12
Complement: 6 (1 officer)
Radars: Navigation: Furuno; I-band.

Comment: GRP hulls. Built 1981-84 by Rantsausminde. *SKA 11* and *SKA 12* have strengthened hulls and are permanently deployed to Naval Station Grønnedal (Greenland) for surveying of Greenland waters. Multibeam echo sounders are fitted. *SKA 13* and *14* have been modified for other tasks at the Naval Bases. *SKA 15* and *16* are fitted for surveying of Danish waters. The survey launches can work alone, in pairs or in conjunction with Flyvefisken class vessels. All have red hulls and white superstructures.

SKA 16 *7/1997, E & M Laursen* / 0012275

AUXILIARIES

Notes: The Mobile Base (MOBA) and Mobile Logistics (M-LOG) units have been consolidated into one M-LOG detachment. It consists of some 30 vehicles (fuel-trucks, torpedo and helicopter handling facilities, communications, stores, provisions and workshops).

1 ROYAL YACHT (YAC)

Name	No	Builders	Commissioned
DANNEBROG	A 540	R Dockyard, Copenhagen	20 May 1932

Displacement, tons: 1,130 full load
Dimensions, feet (metres): 246 × 34 × 12.1 *(75 × 10.4 × 3.7)*
Main machinery: 2 Burmeister & Wain Alpha T23L-KVO diesels; 1,800 hp(m) *(1.32 MW)*; 2 shafts; cp props
Speed, knots: 14
Complement: 54 (12 officers)
Guns: 2—40 mm saluting guns.
Radars: Navigation: Furuno 2115; I-band.

Comment: Laid down 2 January 1931, launched on 10 October 1931. Major refit 1980 included new engines and electrical gear. Marisat fitted in 1992.

DANNEBROG *9/2005*, Guy Toremans* / 1133404

1 TRANSPORT SHIP (AKS)

Name	No	Builders	Commissioned
SLEIPNER	A 559	Åbenrå Vaerft og A/S	18 July 1986

Displacement, tons: 465 full load
Dimensions, feet (metres): 119.6 × 24.9 × 8.8 *(36.5 × 7.6 × 2.7)*
Main machinery: 1 Callesen diesel; 575 hp(m) *(423 kW)*; 1 shaft
Speed, knots: 11
Range, n miles: 2,400 at 11 kt
Complement: 7 (1 officer)
Cargo capacity: 150 tons
Radars: Navigation: Furuno 2115; I-band.

SLEIPNER *4/2005*, Martin Mokrus* / 1133397

2 ABSALON CLASS (FLEXIBLE SUPPORT SHIPS) (AGF/AKR/AH)

Name	No	Builders	Laid down	Launched	Commissioned
ABSALON	L 16	Odense Shipyard, Lindø	28 Nov 2003	25 Feb 2004	1 July 2004
ESBERN SNARE	L 17	Odense Shipyard, Lindø	2004	24 June 2004	25 Feb 2005

Displacement, tons: 6,300 full load
Dimensions, feet (metres): 449.6 × 64.0 × 20.7
  (137.0 × 19.5 × 6.3)
Main machinery: CODAD. 2 MTU 8000 diesels; 22,300 hp
  (16.63 MW); 2 shafts; CP propellers; bow thruster
Speed, knots: 23
Range, n miles: 9,000 at 15 kt
Complement: 100 + 70 staff

Missiles: SSM: 16 Boeing Harpoon Block II (2 octuple
  AHWCS VLS launchers); active radar homing to 130 km
  (70 n miles) at 0.9 Mach; warhead 227 kg.
  SAM: 36 Evolved Sea Sparrow RIM 162B; semi-active radar
  homing to 18 km *(9.7 n miles)* at 3.6 Mach; warhead
  39 kg. 3 Raytheon Mk 56 VLS (3 × 12 cells).
  4 twin Sea Stinger launchers.
Guns: United Defense 5 in *(127 mm)*/62 Mk 45 Mod 4;
  20 rds/min to 23 km *(12.6 n miles)*; weight of shell 32 kg.
  Prepared for extended range capable munitions.
  2 Oerlikon Contraves 35 mm GDM08 Millenium guns.
  4—12.7 mm MGs.
Torpedoes: 6—324 mm (2 triple) launchers; Eurotorp Mu 90
  Impact.
Countermeasures: Decoys:Terma 130 mm Decoy Launching
  System 2 DL-12T and 2 DL-6T launchers (36 barrels).

FLEXIBLE SUPPORT SHIP *(Scale 1 : 1,500), Ian Sturton* / 0569800

ESM: EDO ES 3701.
Combat data systems: Terma C-Flex.
Radars: Air/Surface search: Thales SMART-S 3D; E/F-band.
Fire control: 4 SaabTech Ceros 200 Mk 3; J/K-band.
Navigation: Furuno; E/F/I-band.
Sonars: Atlas ASO 94 hull mounted. VDS/DTAS/ATAS to be
  decided.
Helicopter: 2 medium.

Programmes: Contract on 16 October 2001 for detailed
  design and construction of two multirole support ships.
  Construction of first of class started on 30 April 2003.

Structure: Built to DNV Navy standards with five Stanflex
  container positions. Ro-Ro ramp aft gives access to
  900 m² of multipurpose deck (vehicles (including 62 ton
  MBT), logistics, ammunition, up to 34 TEU containers).
  2 Combat Boat 90E high-speed insertion craft carried
  on cargo deck. Flight deck capable of operating 20 ton
  helicopters.
Operational: To be capable of acting as a command
  platform, transporting up to 200 personnel and
  equipment, provision of joint logistic support, and as a
  hospital ship. Full operational capabilities to be achieved
  in 2007.

ABSALON *9/2005*, Guy Toremans* / 1133405

ESBERN SNARE *6/2005*, Michael Winter* / 1133399

ESBERN SNARE *6/2005*, E & M Laursen* / 1133398

4 LCP CLASS (COASTAL PATROL CRAFT) (PB)

LCP 1-4

Displacement, tons: 6.5 full load
Dimensions, feet (metres): 39.0 × 9.5 × 2.3 *(11.9 × 2.9 × 0.7)*
Main machinery: 1 Scania DSI 14 V8 diesel; 625 hp *(465 kW)*; 1 Kamewa water-jet
Speed, knots: 38
Complement: 3
Guns: 1 — 12.7 mm or 7.62 mm MG.

Comment: Based on the Swedish Combatboat 90E, these craft were developed as a joint venture between Forsvarets Materielverk and Storebro by whom LCP 1-4 were constructed and completed in 2004. Used as fast landing craft from the Absalon class support ships, they can carry 10 fully equipped soldiers or four stretchers. Two ice-strengthened variants are to be operated by the Arctic Patrol Ships. To be painted orange, they are to have pennant numbers SAR 1 and SAR 2 and are to be delivered in 2006.

LCP 1   *4/2005*, Martin Mokrus* / 1133403

2 POLLUTION CONTROL CRAFT (YPC)

MILJØ 101 and **102**

Displacement, tons: 16 full load
Dimensions, feet (metres): 53.8 × 14.4 × 7.1 *(16.2 × 4.2 × 2.2)*
Main machinery: 1 MWM TBD232V12 diesel; 454 hp(m) *(334 kW)* sustained; 1 shaft
Speed, knots: 15
Range, n miles: 350 at 8 kt
Complement: 3 (1 officer)

Comment: Built by Ejvinds Plastikbodevaerft, Svendborg. Carry derricks and booms for framing oil slicks and dispersant fluids. Naval manned. Delivered 1 November and 1 December 1977.

MILJØ 101   *6/1999, Royal Danish Navy* / 0056890

4 RESCUE VESSELS (PBO)

NORDSØEN   **VESTKYSTEN**   **HAVØRNEN**   **VIBEN**

Measurement, tons: 594 gwt *(Nordsøen)*; 657 gwt *(Vestkysten)*; 188 gwt *(Havørnen)*; 23 gwt *(Viben)*
Dimensions, feet (metres): 174.6 × 33.8 × 10.8 *(53.2 × 10.3 × 3.3)* (Nordsøen)
163.7 × 32.8 × 13.8 *(49.9 × 10 × 4.2)* (Vestkysten)
101.4 × 21.6 × ? *(30.9 × 6.6 × ?)* (Havørnen)
56.4 × 11.8 × 5.2 *(17.2 × 3.6 × 1.6)* (Viben)

Comment: Non-naval ships operated by the Ministry of Food and Fisheries. *Nordsøen* and *Vestkysten* operate primarily in the North Sea and Kattegat area, *Havørnen* in the Baltic Sea around Bornholm and *Viben* in shallow waters. Capable of 14-18 kt.

NORDSØEN   *1/1999, Harald Carstens* / 0056889

2 SEA TRUCKS (AKL)

METTE MILJØ A 562   **MARIE MILJØ** A 563

Displacement, tons: 157 full load
Dimensions, feet (metres): 97.7 × 26.2 × 5.2 *(29.8 × 8 × 1.6)*
Main machinery: 2 Grenaa diesels; 660 hp(m) *(485 kW)*; 2 shafts
Speed, knots: 10
Complement: 9 (1 officer)

Comment: Built by Carl B Hoffmann A/S, Esbjerg and Søren Larsen & Sønners Skibsvaerft A/S, Nykøbing Mors. Delivered 22 February 1980. Have orange and yellow superstructure.

METTE MILJØ   *9/2002, Per Körnefeldt* / 0526824

2 OIL POLLUTION CRAFT (YPC/ABU)

GUNNAR THORSON A 560   **GUNNAR SEIDENFADEN** A 561

Displacement, tons: 750 full load
Dimensions, feet (metres): 183.7 × 40.3 × 12.8 *(56 × 12.3 × 3.9)*
Main machinery: 2 Burmeister and Wain Alpha 8V23L-VO diesels; 2,320 hp(m) *(1.7 MW)*; 2 shafts; cp props; bow thruster
Speed, knots: 12.5
Complement: 16 (7 officers)

Comment: Built by Ørnskov Stålskibsvaerft, Frederikshavn. Delivered 8 May and 2 July 1981 respectively. *G Thorson* at Copenhagen, *G Seidenfaden* at Korsør. Carry firefighting equipment. Large hydraulic crane fitted in 1988 for the secondary task of buoy tending. Orange painted hulls.

GUNNAR THORSON   *4/2005*, Martin Mokrus* / 1133402

GUNNAR SEIDENFADEN   *5/2002, L-G Nilsson* / 0526823

1 RESEARCH SHIP (AGE)

DANA

Displacement, tons: 3,700 full load
Dimensions, feet (metres): 257.5 × 48.6 × 19.7 *(78.5 × 14.8 × 6)*
Main machinery: 2 Burmeister and Wain Alpha 16V23-LU diesels; 4,960 hp(m) *(3.65 MW)*; 1 shaft cp prop; bow and stern thrusters
Speed, knots: 15
Range, n miles: 8,000 at 14 kt
Complement: 27 plus 12 scientists

Comment: Built by Dannebrog, Aarhus in 1982. Used mostly for Fisheries survey and research. Has an ice-strengthened hull and three 6 ton cranes.

DANA   *6/2002, Royal Danish Navy* / 0533223

2 ARVAK CLASS (HARBOUR TUGS) (YTL)

ARVAK Y 344   **ALSIN** Y 345

Displacement, tons: 79 full load
Dimensions, feet (metres): 52.5 × 21.7 × 8.2 *(16.0 × 6.6 × 2.5)*
Main machinery: 1 MTU 12V 183TE62 diesel; 737 hp(m) *(550 kW)*
Speed, knots: 10

Comment: Built by Hvide Sande Skibs & Baadebyggeri and delivered on 18 November 2002. In service at Korsør and Frederikshavn. Fitten with Stanflex container position aft to facilitate transport of containerised stores and equipment between naval bases.

ARVAK   *4/2005*, Martin Mokrus* / 1133401

ICEBREAKERS

Notes: Icebreakers, are controlled by the Navy but have a combined naval and civilian crew. Maintenance is done at Frederikshavn in Summer. Surveying is no longer conducted by these vessels.

1 THORBJØRN CLASS (AGB/AGS)

Name	No	Builders	Commissioned
THORBJØRN	A 553	Svendborg Vaerft	June 1981

Displacement, tons: 2,344 full load
Dimensions, feet (metres): 221.4 × 50.2 × 15.4 *(67.5 × 15.3 × 4.7)*
Main machinery: Diesel-electric; 4 Burmeister & Wain Alpha 16U28L-VO diesels; 6,800 hp(m) *(5 MW)*; 2 motors; 2 shafts
Speed, knots: 16.5
Range, n miles: 22,000 at 16 kt
Complement: 22 (7 officers)

Comment: No bow thruster. Side rolling tanks. Fitted for surveying duties in non-ice periods.

THORBJØRN   *6/2002, Royal Danish Navy* / 0533297

2 DANBJØRN CLASS (AGB)

Name	No	Builders	Commissioned
DANBJØRN	A 551	Lindø Vaerft, Odense	1965
ISBJØRN	A 552	Lindø Vaerft, Odense	1966

Displacement, tons: 3,685 full load
Dimensions, feet (metres): 252 × 56 × 20 *(76.8 × 17.1 × 6.1)*
Main machinery: Diesel-electric; 6 Burmeister and Wain 12-26MT-40V diesels; 10,500 hp(m) *(7.72 MW)*; 8 motors; 5,240 hp(m) *(38.5 MW)*; 4 shafts
Speed, knots: 14
Range, n miles: 11,500 at 14 kt
Complement: 25 (9 officers)

Comment: Two of the four propellers are positioned forward, two aft.

DANBJØRN   *10/2004*, Per Körnefeldt* / 1044099

NAVAL HOME GUARD

4 + 7 MHV 900 CLASS (COASTAL PATROL CRAFT) (PB)

Name	No	Builders	Commissioned
ENØ	MHV 901	Søby Shipyard	Oct 2003
MANØ	MHV 902	Søby Shipyard	Apr 2004
HJORTØ	MHV 903	Søby Shipyard	Jan 2005
LYØ	MHV 904	Søby Shipyard	Nov 2005
ASKØ	MHV 905	Søby Shipyard	2006
FAENØ	MHV 906	Søby Shipyard	2007

Displacement, tons: 95 full load
Dimensions, feet (metres): 89.3 × 18.7 × 8.2 *(27.2 × 5.7 × 2.5)*
Main machinery: 2 Saab Scania DI 16V8 diesels; 980 hp(m) *(730 kW)*; 2 shafts
Speed, knots: 13
Complement: 10
Guns: 2–7.62 mm MGs.

Comment: Similar to but 3.5 m longer than the MHV 800 class. Steel construction. Eleven vessels ordered.

ENØ   *10/2003, Per Körnefeldt* / 0567436

18 MHV 800 CLASS (COASTAL PATROL CRAFT) (PB)

Name	No	Builders	Commissioned
ALDEBARAN	MHV 801	Soby Shipyard	9 July 1992
CARINA	MHV 802	Soby Shipyard	30 Sep 1992
ARIES	MHV 803	Soby Shipyard	30 Mar 1993
ANDROMEDA	MHV 804	Soby Shipyard	30 Sep 1993
GEMINI	MHV 805	Soby Shipyard	28 Feb 1994
DUBHE	MHV 806	Soby Shipyard	1 July 1994
JUPITER	MHV 807	Soby Shipyard	30 Nov 1994
LYRA	MHV 808	Soby Shipyard	30 May 1995
ANTARES	MHV 809	Soby Shipyard	30 Nov 1995
LUNA	MHV 810	Soby Shipyard	30 May 1996
APOLLO	MHV 811	Soby Shipyard	30 Nov 1996
HERCULES	MHV 812	Soby Shipyard	28 May 1997
BAUNEN	MHV 813	Soby Shipyard	17 Dec 1997
BUDSTIKKEN	MHV 814	Soby Shipyard	30 Aug 1998
KUREREN	MHV 815	Soby Shipyard	30 May 1999
PATRIOTEN	MHV 816	Soby Shipyard	25 Feb 2000
PARTISAN	MHV 817	Soby Shipyard	29 Nov 2000
SABOTØREN	MHV 818	Soby Shipyard	13 Oct 2001

Displacement, tons: 83 full load
Dimensions, feet (metres): 77.8 × 18.4 × 6.6 *(23.7 × 5.6 × 2)*
Main machinery: 2 Saab Scania DSI-14 diesels; 900 hp(m) *(661 kW)*; 2 shafts
Speed, knots: 13
Range, n miles: 990 at 11 kt
Complement: 8 + 4 spare
Guns: 2 — 7.62 mm MGs. 2 — 12.7 mm MGs (can be fitted).
Radars: Navigation: Furuno 1505; I-band.

Comment: First six ordered in April 1991, second six in July 1992, six more in 1997. Steel hulls with a moderate ice capability.

PATRIOTEN *8/2004, Per Körnefeldt* / 1044105

GEMINI *5/2005*, Frank Findler* / 1133394

APOLLO *5/2004, E & M Laursen* / 1121263

SABATØREN *5/2005*, Michael Nitz* / 1133406

6 MHV 90 CLASS (COASTAL PATROL CRAFT) (PB)

BOPA MHV 90   **HOLGER DANSKE** MHV 92   **RINGEN** MHV 94
BRIGADEN MHV 91   **HVIDSTEN** MHV 93   **SPEDITØREN** MHV 95

Displacement, tons: 85 full load
Dimensions, feet (metres): 64.9 × 18.7 × 8.2 *(19.8 × 5.7 × 2.5)*
Main machinery: 1 Burmeister & Wain diesel; 400 hp(m) *(294 kW)*; 1 shaft
Speed, knots: 11
Complement: 12
Guns: 2 — 7.62 mm MGs.
Radars: Navigation: Furuno 1505; I-band.

Comment: Built between 1973 and 1975. New radars fitted.

BRIGADEN *6/2005*, Harald Carstens* / 1133395

2 MHV 70 CLASS (COASTAL PATROL CRAFT) (PB)

SATURN MHV 70   **SCORPIUS** MHV 71

Displacement, tons: 125 full load
Dimensions, feet (metres): 64 × 16.7 × 8.2 *(19.5 × 5.1 × 2.5)*
Main machinery: 1 diesel; 200 hp(m) *(147 kW)*; 1 shaft
Speed, knots: 10
Complement: 12
Guns: 2 — 7.62 mm MGs.
Radars: Navigation: Raytheon RM 1290S; I-band.

Comment: Patrol boats and training craft for the Naval Home Guard. Built in the Royal Dockyard, Copenhagen and commissioned in 1958. Formerly designated DMH, but allocated MHV numbers in 1969. MHV 70 to be decommissioned in 2006 and MHV 71 in 2007.

SCORPIUS *10/2003, Per Körnefeldt* / 0567455

Djibouti

Country Overview

Formerly the French territory of French Somaliland and later the Afars and the Issas, Djibouti became independent in 1977. With an area of 8,957 square miles and a coastline of 170 n miles, the country is situated in a strategic position on the Bab el Mandeb, the strait that links the Red Sea with the Gulf of Aden. It is bordered to the north by Eritrea, to the west by Ethiopia and to the south by Somalia. The largest town and capital is also called Djibouti whose port serves as an international transhipment and refuelling centre. It also provides Ethiopia with its only rail link to the sea. Territorial seas (12 n miles) are claimed. A 200 n mile Exclusive Economic Zone (EEZ) has been claimed but the limits are not fully defined.

Personnel

2006: 125

Bases

Djibouti

French Navy

The permanent French naval contingent usually includes up to three frigates and a repair ship.

PATROL FORCES

Notes: (1) One Zhuk and one Boghammar (*Dorra* P 15) patrol craft were transferred from Ethiopia in 1996. Neither is operational.
(2) Up to six RIBs are in use. Zodiac and Avon types.
(3) One LCM (ex-CTM 14) transferred from France in 1999.

1 PLASCOA CLASS (COASTAL PATROL CRAFT) (PB)

Name	No	Builders	Commissioned
MONT ARREH	P 11	Plascoa, Cannes	16 Feb 1986

Displacement, tons: 35 full load
Dimensions, feet (metres): 75.5 × 18 × 4.9 *(23 × 5.5 × 1.5)*
Main machinery: 2 SACM Poyaud V12-520 M25 diesels; 1,700 hp(m) *(1.25 MW)*; 2 shafts
Speed, knots: 25
Range, n miles: 750 at 12 kt
Complement: 15
Guns: 1 Giat 20 mm. 1—12.7 mm MG.
Radars: Navigation: Decca 36; I-band.

Comment: Ordered in October 1984 and transferred as a gift from France. GRP hulls. Refitted in 1988 and 1994. *Moussa Ali* decommissioned in 2001.

MONT ARREH   *1986, Plascoa* / 0056896

1 SAWARI CLASS (INSHORE PATROL CRAFT) (PBR)

P 13

Comment: Acquired from Iraq in 1989. Can be armed with MGs and rocket launchers. Outboard engines give speeds up to 25 kt in calm conditions. Four further craft are no longer operational.

2 BATTALION 17 (PBF)

P 16   P 17

Displacement, tons: 35.5 full load
Dimensions, feet (metres): 55.9 × 17 × 5.2 *(17.05 × 5.2 × 1.6)*
Main machinery: 2 MTU 12V 183 TE 92 diesels
Speed, knots: 35.2
Range, n miles: 680 at 30 kt
Complement: 8
Guns: 2—14.5 mm MGs (1 twin).
Radars: Surface search: Raytheon; I-band.

Comment: Built by Harena Boat Yard at Assab, Eritrea and delivered in 2001. Five similar craft in service in Eritrea.

BATTALION 17 (Eritrean colours)   *6/2000*, Eritrean Navy* / 0103788

Dominica

Country Overview

Formerly a British colony, the Commonwealth of Dominica became an independent republic in 1978. With an area of 290 sq miles and coastline of 80 n miles, it is the largest and most northerly of the Windward Islands in the Lesser Antilles chain and is situated in the Caribbean Sea between the French possessions of Guadeloupe to the north and Martinique to the south. The capital, major town, and port is Roseau. Territorial seas (12 n miles) are claimed. A 200 n mile Exclusive Economic Zone (EEZ) has been claimed but the limits are not fully defined.

Headquarters Appointments

Head of Coast Guard:
Inspector O Frederick

Personnel

2006: 32

Bases

Roseau

COAST GUARD

1 DAUNTLESS CLASS (PB)

Name	No	Builders	Commissioned
UKALE	D 05	SeaArk Marine	8 Nov 1995

Displacement, tons: 11 full load
Dimensions, feet (metres): 40 × 14 × 4.3 *(12.2 × 4.3 × 1.3)*
Main machinery: 2 Caterpillar 3208TA diesels; 870 hp *(650 kW)* sustained; 2 shafts
Speed, knots: 27. **Range, n miles:** 600 at 18 kt
Complement: 6
Guns: 1—7.62 mm MG (can be carried).
Radars: Surface search: Raytheon; I-band.

Comment: Similar to craft delivered by the US to many Caribbean coast guards under FMS. Aluminium construction.

UKALE
11/1995, SeaArk
0056897

1 SWIFT 65 ft CLASS (PB)

Name	No	Builders	Commissioned
MELVILLE	D 4	Swiftships, Morgan City	1 May 1984

Displacement, tons: 33 full load
Dimensions, feet (metres): 64.9 × 18.4 × 6.6 *(19.8 × 5.6 × 2)*
Main machinery: 2 Detroit 12V-71TA diesels; 840 hp *(616 kW)* sustained; 2 shafts
Speed, knots: 23
Range, n miles: 250 at 18 kt
Complement: 10
Guns: 1 — 7.62 mm MG.
Radars: Surface search: Furuno; I/J-band.

Comment: Donated by US government. Similar craft supplied to Antigua and St Lucia. Aluminium construction.

MELVILLE   *11/1993, Maritime Photographic* / 0506143

3 PATROL CRAFT (PBR)

VIGILANCE	OBSERVER	RESCUER

Displacement, tons: 2.4 full load
Dimensions, feet (metres): 27 × 8.4 × 1 *(8.2 × 2.6 × 0.3)*
Main machinery: 1 Evinrude outboard; 225 hp *(168 kW)* sustained or 2 Johnson outboards *(Rescuer)*; 280 hp *(205 kW)*
Speed, knots: 28 or 45 *(Rescuer)*
Complement: 3

Comment: First two are Boston Whalers acquired in 1988. *Rescuer* is of similar size but is an RHIB acquired in 1994.

OBSERVER   *11/1993, Maritime Photographic* / 0506227

Dominican Republic
MARINA DE GUERRA

Country Overview

The Dominican Republic is an independent state whose constitution was promulgated in 1966. With an area of 18,816 square miles, it occupies the eastern two thirds of the island of Hispaniola, which it shares with Haiti to the west. There are also a number of adjacent islands, notably Beata and Saona. It has a 697 n mile coastline and is bordered to the north by the Atlantic Ocean, to the east by the Mona Passage, which separates it from Puerto Rico, and to the south by the Caribbean Sea. Santo Domingo is the capital, largest city and principal port. Territorial seas (6 n miles) are claimed. A 200 n mile EEZ has been claimed but the limits have not been defined by boundary agreements.

Headquarters Appointments

Chief of Naval Staff:
Vice Admiral Cesar Augusto de Windt Ruiz

Personnel

(a) 2006: 3,800 officers and men (including naval infantry)
(b) Selective military service

Bases

27 de Febrero, Santo Domingo: HQ of CNS, Naval School. Supply base.
Las Calderas, Las Calderas, Baní: Naval dockyard, 700 ton synchrolift. Training centre. Supply base.
Haina: Dockyard facility. Supply base.
Puerto Plata. Small naval base.

Organisation

There are three naval zones:
North: Haitian border east to the Mona passage.
South: Mona passage west to the Haitian border.
Santo Domingo: Naval establishments in the capital and its environs.

Naval Aviation

One Bell OH-58A Kiowa was acquired in November 2003.

DELETIONS

Notes: *Melia* still flies an ensign as a museum ship.

PATROL FORCES

Notes: (1) Two Super Dvora class may be acquired from Israel.
(2) One Eduardoño class patrol craft is reported to have been transferred from the US in 2003.

1 COHOES CLASS (PG)

Name	No	Builders	Commissioned
SEPARACION (ex-*Passaconaway* AN 86)	P 208	Marine SB Co	27 Apr 1945

Displacement, tons: 855 full load
Dimensions, feet (metres): 168.6 × 33.8 × 10.8 *(51.4 × 10.3 × 3.3)*
Main machinery: Diesel-electric; 2 Busch-Sulzer BS-539 diesels; 1,500 hp(m) *(1.1 MW)*; 2 generators; 1 motor; 1 shaft
Speed, knots: 12
Complement: 64 (5 officers)
Guns: 2 — 3 in *(76 mm)*/50 Mk 26. 3 Oerlikon 20 mm.
Radars: Surface search: Raytheon SPS-64; I-band.

Comment: Ex-netlayer laid up in reserve in US in 1963. Transferred by sale on 29 September 1976. Now used for patrol duties. Modified in 1980 with the removal of the bow horns. P 209 has been decommissioned and the operational status of P 208 is doubtful.

SEPARACION   *5/1999, A Sheldon-Duplaix* / 0056898

2 BALSAM CLASS (PBO/WMEC)

Name	No	Builders	Commissioned
ALMIRANTE JUAN ALEXANDRO ACOSTA (ex-*Citrus*)	P 302 (ex-C 456, ex-WMEC 300)	Marine Iron, Duluth	30 May 1943
ALMIRANTE DIDIEZ BURGOS (ex-*Buttonwood*)	P 301 (ex-C 457, ex-WLB 306)	Duluth Shipyard, Minnesota	24 Sep 1943

Displacement, tons: 1,034 full load
Dimensions, feet (metres): 180 × 37 × 12 *(54.9 × 11.3 × 3.8)*
Main machinery: Diesel-electric; 2 Cooper Bessemer diesels; 1,402 hp *(1.06 MW)*; 2 motors; 1,200 hp *(895 kW)*; 1 shaft; bow thruster
Speed, knots: 13
Complement: 54 (4 officers)
Guns: 1 — 4 in; 2 — 20 mm (456). 2 — 20 mm; 2 — 12.7 MGs (457).
Radars: Surface search: Raytheon SPS-64(V)1; I-band.

Comment: C 456 built as a buoy tender but served as a US Coast Guard cutter from 1979 to 1994. Transferred by gift on 16 September 1995 and recommissioned in January 1996 after a short refit. C 457 transferred from US Coast Guard on 30 June 2001.

ALMIRANTE JUAN ALEXANDRO ACOSTA   *8/2002, A Sheldon-Duplaix* / 0534105

For details of the latest updates to *Jane's Fighting Ships* online and to discover the additional information available exclusively to online subscribers please visit
jfs.janes.com

1 ADMIRABLE CLASS (PG)

Name	No	Builders	Commissioned
PRESTOL BOTELLO (ex-*Separacion*, ex-*Skirmish* MSF 303)	C 454	Associated SB	16 Aug 1943

Displacement, tons: 650 standard; 905 full load
Dimensions, feet (metres): 184.5 × 33 × 14.4 (*56.3 × 10.1 × 4.4*)
Main machinery: 2 Cooper-Bessemer GSB8 diesels; 1,710 hp (*1.28 MW*); 2 shafts
Speed, knots: 15
Range, n miles: 4,300 at 10 kt
Complement: 90 (8 officers)
Guns: 1—3 in (*76 mm*)/50 Mk 26. 2 Bofors 40 mm/60. 6 Oerlikon 20 mm.
Radars: Surface search: Raytheon SPS-64(V)9; I-band.

Comment: Former US fleet minesweeper. Purchased on 13 January 1965. Sweep-gear removed. Classified as Cañoneros.

PRESTOL   *6/1997, A Sheldon-Duplaix* / 0012278

1 SOTOYOMO CLASS (PG/ATA)

Name	No	Builders	Commissioned
ENRIQUILLO (ex-*Stallion* ATA 193)	RM 22	Levington SB Co, Orange, TX	26 Feb 1945

Displacement, tons: 534 standard; 860 full load
Dimensions, feet (metres): 143 × 33.9 × 13 (*43.6 × 10.3 × 4*)
Main machinery: Diesel-electric; 2 GM 12-278A diesels; 2,200 hp (*1.64 MW*); 2 generators; 1 motor; 1,500 hp (*1.12 MW*); 1 shaft
Speed, knots: 13
Range, n miles: 8,000 at 10kt
Complement: 45
Guns: 1 US 3 in (*76 mm*)/50 Mk 26. 2 Oerlikon 20 mm.
Radars: Surface search: Raytheon SPS-5D; G/H-band.

Comment: Leased from US 30 October 1980, renewed 15 June 1992 and approved for transfer 10 June 1997.

ENRIQUILLO   *8/2002, A Sheldon-Duplaix* / 0534084

1 PGM 71 CLASS (LARGE PATROL CRAFT) (PB)

Name	No	Builders	Commissioned
BETELGEUSE (ex-*PGM 77*)	GC 102	Peterson, USA	1966

Displacement, tons: 130 standard; 145 full load
Dimensions, feet (metres): 101.5 × 21 × 5 (*30.9 × 6.4 × 1.5*)
Main machinery: 2 Caterpillar D 348 diesels; 1,450 hp (*1.08 MW*) sustained; 2 shafts
Speed, knots: 21
Range, n miles: 1,500 at 10 kt
Complement: 20 (3 officers)
Guns: 1 Oerlikon 20 mm. 2—12.7 mm MGs.
Radars: Surface search: Raytheon; I-band.

Comment: Built in the USA and transferred to the Dominican Republic under the Military Aid Programme on 14 January 1966. Re-engined in 1980.

BETELGEUSE (alongside ENRIQUILLO)   *3/2001, A Sheldon-Duplaix* / 0114349

2 CANOPUS (SWIFTSHIPS 110 ft) CLASS
(LARGE PATROL CRAFT) (PB)

Name	No	Builders	Commissioned
CRISTOBAL COLON (ex-*Canopus*)	GC 107	Swiftships, Morgan City	June 1984
ORION	GC 109	Swiftships, Morgan City	Aug 1984

Displacement, tons: 93.5 full load
Dimensions, feet (metres): 109.9 × 23.9 × 5.9 (*33.5 × 7.3 × 1.8*)
Main machinery: 3 Detroit 12V-92TA diesels; 1,020 hp (*760 kW*) sustained; 3 shafts
Speed, knots: 23
Range, n miles: 1,500 at 12 kt
Complement: 19 (3 officers)
Guns: 1—20 mm or 2—12.7 mm MGs.
Radars: Surface search: Raytheon; I-band.

Comment: Built of aluminium. GC 107 completely rebuilt and reconditioned by Swiftships in 2003. GC 109 was similarly refitted in 2004.

CRISTOBAL COLON   *1/2004, Swiftships* / 0587700

4 BELLATRIX CLASS (COASTAL PATROL CRAFT) (PB)

Name	No	Builders	Commissioned
PROCION	GC 103	Sewart Seacraft Inc, Berwick, LA	1967
ALDEBARÁN	GC 104	Sewart Seacraft Inc, Berwick, LA	1972
BELLATRIX	GC 106	Sewart Seacraft Inc, Berwick, LA	1967
CAPELLA	GC 108	Sewart Seacraft Inc, Berwick, LA	1968

Displacement, tons: 60 full load
Dimensions, feet (metres): 85 × 18 × 5 (*25.9 × 5.5 × 1.5*)
Main machinery: 2 GM 16V-71 diesels; 811 hp (*605 kW*) sustained; 2 shafts
Speed, knots: 18.7
Range, n miles: 800 at 15 kt
Complement: 12
Guns: 3—12.7 mm MGs.
Radars: Surface search: Raytheon SPS-64; I-band.

Comment: Transferred to the Dominican Navy by the US. *Procion* was taken out of service in 1995 but returned in 1997 after a long refit. GC 103 and GC 106 completely rebuilt and reconditioned by Swiftships, Morgan City, in 2003. GC 104 and GC 108 were similarly refitted in 2004.

CAPELLA   *8/2002, A Sheldon-Duplaix* / 0534085

BELLATRIX   *6/2004, A Sheldon-Duplaix* / 0587699

4 POINT CLASS (PB)

Name	No	Builders	Commissioned
ARIES	101 (ex-82340)	CG Yard, Maryland	21 Nov 1962
ANTARES	105 (ex-82379)	J Martinac, Tacoma	20 Aug 1970
(ex-*Point Martin*)			
SIRIUS	110 (ex-82349)	J Martinac, Tacoma	25 Oct 1966
(ex-*Point Spencer*)			

Displacement, tons: 67 full load
Dimensions, feet (metres): 83 × 17.2 × 5.8 *(25.3 × 5.2 × 1.8)*
Main machinery: 2 Caterpillar diesels; 1,600 hp *(1.19 MW)*; 2 shafts
Speed, knots: 22
Range, n miles: 1,200 at 8 kt
Complement: 10
Guns: 2–12.7 mm MGs.
Radars: Surface search: Hughes/Furuno SPS-73; I-band.

Comment: *Aries* and *Antares* transferred from US Coast Guard 1 October 1999. *Sirius* transferred 12 December 2000.

SIRIUS   *6/2004, A Sheldon-Duplaix* / 0587698

2 SWIFTSHIPS 35M CLASS (LARGE PATROL CRAFT) (PB)

Name	No	Builders	Commissioned
ALTAIR	112	Swiftships, Morgan City	Oct 2003
ARCTURUS	114	Swiftships, Morgan City	Mar 2004

Displacement, tons: 95 standard
Dimensions, feet (metres): 115.1 × 24.0 × 5.0 *(35.1 × 7.3 × 1.5)*
Main machinery: 3 CAT 3412 diesels; 3,000 hp *(2.2 MW)*; 3 Hamilton HM 651 waterjets
Speed, knots: 25
Range, n miles: To be announced
Complement: To be announced
Guns: 1–25 mm. 2–12.7 mm MGs.

Comment: Two new craft ordered from Swiftships, Morgan City, LA as part of wider programme to increase capability to conduct counter-smuggling and drug-trafficking operations. Fitted with launching ramp for 4.7 m RIB.

ALTAIR   *12/2003, A Sheldon-Duplaix* / 0569189

4 DAMEN 1505 PATROL CRAFT (LARGE PATROL CRAFT) (PB)

Name	No	Builders	Commissioned
HAMAL	LR 151	Astilleros Navales de la Bahia de las Calderas	Dec 2004
VEGA	LR 152	Astilleros Navales de la Bahia de las Calderas	Dec 2004
DENEB	LR 153	Astilleros Navales de la Bahia de las Calderas	14 Apr 2005
ACAMAR	LR 154	Astilleros Navales de la Bahia de las Calderas	14 Apr 2005

Displacement, tons: 16
Dimensions, feet (metres): 49.5 × 14.8 × 3.3 *(15.1 × 4.5 × 1.0)*
Main machinery: 2 MTU diesels; 2,250 hp *(1.7 MW)*
Speed, knots: 34
Range, n miles: To be announced
Complement: 6
Guns: 1–7.62 mm MG (fitted for).

Comment: Damen Stan Patrol 1505 design craft constructed in the Dominican Republic. Aluminium construction. Employed as patrol craft on counter-drugs and illegal immigration duties.

TRAINING SHIPS

2 SAIL TRAINING SHIPS (AXS)

Name	No	Builders	Commissioned
RAMBO (ex-*Jurel*)	BA 15	Ast Navales Dominicanos	1975
NUBE DEL MAR	BA 7	Ast Navales Dominicanos	1979

Displacement, tons: 24
Dimensions, feet (metres): 45 × 13 × 6.6 *(13.7 × 4 × 1.9)*
Main machinery: 1 GM diesel; 101 hp *(75 kW)*; 1 shaft
Speed, knots: 9
Complement: 4
Guns: 1–7.62 mm MG.

Comment: *Rambo* is a slightly smaller sailing craft with a sail area of 750 sq ft and a cargo capacity of 7 tons. *Nube del Mar* is an auxiliary yacht used for sail training at the Naval School.

AUXILIARIES

Notes: (1) There are also two dredgers manned by the Navy.
(2) An ocean tug *Guarocuya* BA 3 has been reported.

DREDGER   *10/1998, A Sheldon-Duplaix* / 0056902

1 HARBOUR TANKER (AOTL)

Name	No	Builders	Commissioned
CAPITÁN BEOTEGUI (ex-*YO 215*)	BT 5	Ira S Bushey, Brooklyn	17 Dec 1945

Displacement, tons: 422 light; 1,400 full load
Dimensions, feet (metres): 174 × 32.9 × 13.3 *(53.1 × 10 × 4.1)*
Main machinery: 1 Union diesel; 525 hp *(392 kW)*; 1 shaft
Speed, knots: 8
Complement: 23
Cargo capacity: 6,570 barrels
Guns: 1 Oerlikon 20 mm.

Comment: Former US self-propelled fuel oil barge. Lent by the USA in April 1964. Lease renewed 31 December 1980 and again 5 August 1992 and approved for transfer 10 June 1997.

CAPITÁN BEOTEGUI   *1/1998, M Mokrus* / 0017794

2 WHITE SUMAC CLASS (ABU)

Name	No	Builders	Commissioned
TORTUGUERO	BA 1 (ex-*WLM 547*)	Erie Concrete and Steel, Erie	11 July 1944
(ex-*White Pine*)			
CAPOTILLO	BA 2 (ex-*WLM 540*)	Niagara Shipbuilding	1943
(ex-*White Sumac*)			

Displacement, tons: 485 full load
Dimensions, feet (metres): 133 × 31 × 9 *(40.5 × 9.5 × 2.7)*
Main machinery: 2 Caterpillar diesels; 600 hp *(448 kW)*; 2 shafts
Speed, knots: 9
Complement: 24

Comment: BA 1 transferred from US Coast Guard in 1999 and BA 2 on 20 September 2002. Fitted with a 10 ton capacity boom.

TORTUGUERO   *12/1999, A Sheldon-Duplaix* / 0056903

1 FLOATING DOCK (YFD)

ENDEAVOR DF 1 (ex-AFDL 1)

Comment: Lift, 1,000 tons. Commissioned in 1943. Transferred from US on loan 8 March 1986 and approved for transfer 10 June 1997. DF 2 (ex-AFDM 2), previously reported, was not acquired.

1 LCU 1600 CLASS (UTILITY LANDING CRAFT) (LCU)

NEIBA (ex-*Commando*) LDM 4 (ex-LCU 1675)

Displacement, tons: 200 light; 375 full load
Dimensions, feet (metres): 134.9 × 29 × 6.1 *(41.1 × 8.8 × 1.9)*
Main machinery: 4 Detroit 6—71 diesels; 696 hp *(519 kW)* sustained; 2 shafts; Kort nozzles
2 Detroit 12V-71 diesels (LCU 1680-1681); 680 hp *(508 kW)* sustained; 2 shafts; Kort nozzles
Speed, knots: 11
Range, n miles: 1,200 at 8 kt
Complement: 14 (2 officers)
Military lift: 134 tons or 400 troops
Guns: 2–12.7 mm MGs.
Radars: Navigation: Furuno; I-band.

Comment: Steel hulled construction. Built by General Ship and Engineering Works in 1978. Formerly operated by the US Army and transferred in 2004.

LCU 1600 CLASS   *8/2004, Hachiro Nakai* / 1043687

TUGS

7 COASTAL/HARBOUR TUGS (YTM/YTL)

GUAROA RM 1	**GUARIONEX** RM 2
HERCULES (ex-*R 2*) RP 12	**BOHECHIO** (ex-*YTL 600*) RP 16
GUACANAGARIX (ex-*R 5*) RP 13	**CAYACCA** RP 19
OCOA LPD 303	

Displacement, tons: 265 full load
Dimensions, feet (metres): 85.6 × 26.0 × 13.3 *(26.1 × 7.9 × 4.05)*
Main machinery: 2 Caterpillar 3512B diesels; 3,500 hp *(2.6 MW)*; 2 shafts
Speed, knots: 12.7
Complement: 6

Comment: Details given are for RM 1 and RM 2, Damen Stantug 2608, built at Astilleros Navales de la Bahia de las Calderas and commissioned in April 2004 and June 2005 respectively. RP 12 and RP 13 are 200 ton tugs built in 1960. RP 16 and 19 are small harbour tugs of about 70 tons. *Ocoa* is an LCU type used as a tug.

HERCULES   *5/1999, A Sheldon-Duplaix* / 0056904

East Timor

Country Overview

The Democratic Republic of Timor-Leste (also known as East Timor) has an area of 7,400 square miles and lies in the eastern part of Timor island, the largest and easternmost of the Lesser Sunda Islands in the Malay Archipelago. Originally settled in the early 16th century, the Portuguese and Dutch competed for influence until boundaries became established. Dutch Timor, in the west, later became part of the Republic of Indonesia in 1950. Portuguese Timor, comprising the region of Dili, in the east, and the small area of Oecussi in the north-west, was annexed by Indonesia in 1975. Following an armed conflict and two and a half years of UN administration, East Timor gained independence on 20 May 2002 and became a UN member on 27 September 2002. The UN mission (UNMISET) was withdrawn on 20 May 2005 when it was succeeded by a political mission (UNOTIL). The capital, principal city and port is Dili. Maritime claims are not known.

The East Timor Defence Force (ETDF) is being trained by multinational staff. The role of the Naval Component of ETDF is to conduct Fishery Protection duties in the East Timorese EEZ and to safeguard the only direct access to the enclave of Oecussi which is by sea.

Headquarters Appointments

Commander in Chief Defence Forces:
  Brigadier General Taur Matan Ruak

Personnel

2006: 150 (under training)

Bases

Hera Harbour

PATROL FORCES

2 ALBATROZ CLASS (RIVER PATROL CRAFT) (PB)

Name	No	Builders	Commissioned
OECUSSI (ex-*Açor*)	P 101 (ex-P 1163)	Arsenal do Alfeite	9 Dec 1974
ATAURO (ex-*Albatroz*)	P 102 (ex-P 1162)	Arsenal do Alfeite	9 Dec 1974

Displacement, tons: 45 full load
Dimensions, feet (metres): 77.4 × 18.4 × 5.2
  (23.6 × 5.6 × 1.6)
Main machinery: 2 Cummins diesels; 1,100 hp *(820 kW)*;
  2 shafts
Speed, knots: 20
Range, n miles: 2,500 at 12 kt
Complement: 8 (1 officer)
Guns: 1 Oerlikon 20 mm/65. 2—12.7 mm MGs.
Radars: Surface search: Decca RM 316P; I-band.

Comment: Transferred by Portugal in 2001 to establish the Naval Component of the ETDF.

ALBATROZ CLASS (Portuguese colours)
10/1994, van Ginderen Collection
0081608

Ecuador
ARMADA DE GUERRA

Country Overview

The Republic of Ecuador is situated in northwestern South America. With an area of 105,037 square miles it straddles the equator and has borders to the north with Colombia and to the south with Peru. It has a coastline of 1,210 n miles with the Pacific Ocean. The country also includes the Galápagos Islands about 520 n miles west of the mainland. The capital is Quito while Guayaquil is the principal port and commercial centre. Ecuador has not claimed an EEZ but is one of a few coastal states which claims a 200 n mile territorial sea.

Headquarters Appointments

Commander-in-Chief of the Navy:
  Vice Admiral Hector Holguin
Chief of Naval Staff:
  Rear Admiral Valdemar Sanchez Vera
Chief of Naval Operations:
  Rear Admiral Galo Moncayo Navarrete
Inspector General:
  Rear Admiral Luis Flores Cazañas

Diplomatic Representation

Naval Attaché in Rome:
  Captain Livio Espinoza Espinoza
Naval Attaché in London and Paris:
  Rear Admiral Louis Merida Galindo
Naval Attaché in Washington:
  Captain Aland Molestina Malta

Personnel

(a) 2006: 4,200 (including 1,500 marines and 250 naval aviation)
(b) 1 year's selective national service

Prefix to Ships' Names

BAE (Buque de Armada de Ecuador)

Bases

Guayaquil (main naval base), Jaramijo, Salinas. San Lorenzo, Galapagos Islands. Guayaquil air base.

Establishments

The Naval Academy and Merchant Navy Academy in Salinas; Naval War College in Guayaquil.

Naval Infantry

A force of marines is based at Guayaquil, Esmeraldas San Lorenzo, Galapagos and Jaramijo.

Coast Guard

Small force formed in 1980. Hull markings include diagonal thick and thin red stripes on the hull.

PENNANT LIST

Submarines

S 101	Shyri
S 102	Huancavilca

Frigates

FM 01	Presidente Eloy Alfaro
FM 02	Moran Valverde

Corvettes

CM 11	Esmeraldas
CM 12	Manabi
CM 13	Los Rios
CM 14	El Oro
CM 15	Los Galápagos
CM 16	Loja

Patrol Forces

LM 21	Quito
LM 23	Guayaquil
LM 24	Cuenca

Amphibious Forces

TR 61	Hualcopo

Survey/Research Vessels

BI 91	Orion
LH 94	Rigel

Tugs

RA 70	Chimborazo
RB 72	Sangay
RB 73	Cotopaxi

RB 75	Iliniza
RB 76	Altar
RB 78	Quilotoa

Auxiliaries

TR 62	Calicuchima
TR 63	Atahualpa
TR 64	Quisquis
TR 65	Taurus
BE 91	Guayas Debe Ser Consierado
DF 81	Rio Amazonas
DF 82	Rio Napo
UT 111	Isla la Plata
UT 112	Isla Puná

Coast Guard

LG 31	25 de Julio
LG 32	24 de Mayo

LG 33	10 de Agosto
LG 34	3 de Noviembre
LG 35	5 de Agosto
LG 36	27 de Febrero
LG 37	9 de Octubre
LG 38	27 de Octubre
LG 39	6 de Diciembre
LG 40	11 de Noviembre
LG 41	11 de Abril
LG 111	Rio Puyango
LG 112	Rio Mataje
LG 113	Rio Zarumilla
LG 114	Rio Chone
LG 115	Rio Daule
LG 116	Rio Babahoyo
LG 121	Rio Esmeraldas
LG 122	Rio Santiago

SUBMARINES

2 TYPE 209 CLASS (TYPE 1300) (SSK)

Name	No	Builders	Laid down	Launched	Commissioned
SHYRI	S 101 (ex-S 11)	Howaldtswerke, Kiel	5 Aug 1974	6 Oct 1976	5 Nov 1977
HUANCAVILCA	S 102 (ex-S 12)	Howaldtswerke, Kiel	2 Jan 1975	15 Mar 1977	16 Mar 1978

Displacement, tons: 1,285 surfaced; 1,390 dived
Dimensions, feet (metres): 195.1 × 20.5 × 17.9 *(59.5 × 6.3 × 5.4)*
Main machinery: Diesel-electric; 4 MTU 12V 493 AZ80 GA31L diesels; 2,400 hp(m) *(1.76 MW)* sustained; 4 Siemens alternators; 1.7 MW; 1 Siemens motor; 4,600 hp(m) *(3.38 MW)* sustained; 1 shaft
Speed, knots: 11 surfaced/snorting; 21.5 dived
Complement: 33 (5 officers)

Torpedoes: 8—21 in *(533 mm)* bow tubes. 14 AEG SUT; dual purpose; wire-guided; active/passive homing to 28 km *(15 n miles)* at 23 kt; 12 km *(6.5 n miles)* at 35 kt; warhead 250 kg.
Countermeasures: ESM: Thomson-CSF DR 2000U; intercept.
Weapons control: Signaal M8 Mod 24.
Radars: Surface search: Thomson-CSF Calypso; I-band.
Sonars: Atlas Elektronik CSU 3; hull-mounted; active/passive search and attack; medium frequency. Thomson Sintra DUUX 2; passive ranging.

Programmes: Ordered in March 1974. *Shyri* underwent major refit in West Germany in 1983; *Huancavilca* in 1984. Second refits by Astinave, Ecuador; *Shyri* in 1994 and *Huancavilca* in 1996.
Operational: Based at Guayaquil. Having been badly damaged by fire on 2 February 2003, *Shyri* returned to service on 21 July 2005. *Huancavilca* reported non-operational. Modernisation of both boats is planned.

TYPE 209   *6/2001, Maritime Photographic* / 0114670

SHYRI   *6/1998* / 0017796

FRIGATES

Notes: Replacement of the two Leander class frigates is reported to be under consideration. Acquisition of two Chilean Leanders, when they are decommissioned is one possibility.

2 LEANDER CLASS (FFGHM)

Name	No	Builders	Laid down	Launched	Commissioned
PRESIDENTE ELOY ALFARO (ex-*Penelope*)	FM 01 (ex-F 127)	Vickers Armstrong, Newcastle	14 Mar 1961	17 Aug 1962	31 Oct 1963
MORAN VALVERDE (ex-*Danae*)	FM 02 (ex-F 47)	HM Dockyard, Devonport	16 Dec 1964	31 Oct 1965	7 Sep 1967

Displacement, tons: 2,450 standard; 3,200 full load
Dimensions, feet (metres): 360 wl; 372 oa × 41 × 14.8 (keel); 19 (screws) (*109.7; 113.4 × 12.5 × 4.5; 5.8*)
Main machinery: 2 Babcock & Wilcox boilers; 38.7 kg/cm²; 850°F (*450°C*); 2 English Electric/White turbines; 30,000 hp (*22.4 MW*); 2 shafts
Speed, knots: 28
Range, n miles: 4,000 at 15 kt
Complement: 248 (20 officers)

Missiles: SSM: 4 Aerospatiale MM 38 Exocet ❶; inertial cruise; active radar homing to 42 km (*23 n miles*) at 0.9 Mach; warhead 165 kg.
SAM: 3 twin Matra Simbad launchers ❷ for Mistral; IR homing to 4 km (*2.2 n miles*); warhead 3 kg.
Guns: 2 Bofors 40 mm/60 Mk 9 ❸; 120 rds/min to 10 km (*5.4 n miles*) anti-surface; 3 km (*1.6 n miles*) anti-aircraft; weight of shell 0.89 kg.
2 Oerlikon/BMARC 20 mm GAM-BO1 can be fitted midships or aft.
Torpedoes: 6—324 mm ILAS-3 (2 triple) tubes ❹ Whitehead A 244; anti-submarine; pattern running to 7 km (*3.8 n miles*) at 33 kt; warhead 34 kg shaped charge.
Countermeasures: Decoys: Graseby Type 182; towed torpedo decoy.

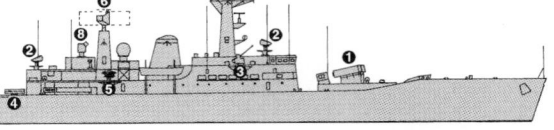

PRESIDENTE ELOY ALFARO   *(Scale 1 : 1,200)*, Ian Sturton / 0056906

4 Mk 36 Mod 2 SRBOC; chaff and IR launchers ❺.
ESM: ELISRA NS-9010; intercept.
ECM: Type 667/668; jammer.
Combat data systems: SISDEF. Link Y.
Radars: Air search: Marconi Type 966 ❻; A-band.
Surface search: Plessey Type 994 ❼; E/F-band.
Navigation: Kelvin Hughes Type 1006; I-band.
Fire control: Selenia ❽ I/J-band.
Sonars: Kelvin Hughes Type 162M; hull-mounted; bottom classification; 50 kHz.
Graseby Type 184P; hull-mounted; active search and attack; 7—9 kHz.

Helicopters: 1 Bell 206B ❾.

Programmes: Both ships acquired from UK 25 April 1991 and sailed for Ecuador after working up in July and August respectively.
Modernisation: Chilean SISDEF command system has been installed. Simbad launchers have replaced Seacat, and the torpedo tubes restored. FM 02 refitted 2002-04 and FM 01 2003-05.
Structure: These are Batch 2 Exocet conversions completed in 1980 and 1982. SRBOC chaff launchers fitted after transfer.
Operational: FM 02 reported to be operational again following refit. FM 01 is expected to be operational again in 2006.

PRESIDENTE ELOY ALFARO   *6/1998* / 0017799

PRESIDENTE ELOY ALFARO   *6/1998* / 0017798

CORVETTES

6 ESMERALDAS CLASS (FSGHM)

Name	No	Builders	Laid down	Launched	Commissioned
ESMERALDAS	CM 11	Fincantieri Muggiano	27 Sep 1979	1 Oct 1980	7 Aug 1982
MANABI	CM 12	Fincantieri Ancona	19 Feb 1980	9 Feb 1981	21 June 1983
LOS RIOS	CM 13	Fincantieri Muggiano	5 Dec 1979	27 Feb 1981	9 Oct 1983
EL ORO	CM 14	Fincantieri Ancona	20 Mar 1980	9 Feb 1981	11 Dec 1983
LOS GALAPÁGOS	CM 15	Fincantieri Muggiano	4 Dec 1980	4 July 1981	26 May 1984
LOJA	CM 16	Fincantieri Ancona	25 Mar 1981	27 Feb 1982	26 May 1984

Displacement, tons: 685 full load
Dimensions, feet (metres): 204.4 × 30.5 × 8
  (62.3 × 9.3 × 2.5)
Main machinery: 4 MTU 20V 956TB92 diesels; 22,140 hp(m)
  (16.27 MW) sustained; 4 shafts
Speed, knots: 37
Range, n miles: 4,400 at 14 kt
Complement: 51

Missiles: SSM: 6 Aerospatiale MM 40 Exocet (2 triple) launchers ❶; inertial cruise; active radar homing to 70 km (40 n miles) at 0.9 Mach; warhead 165 kg; sea-skimmer.
SAM: Selenia Elsag Albatros quad launcher ❷; Aspide; semi-active radar homing to 13 km (7 n miles) at 2.5 Mach; height envelope 15—5,000 m (49.2—16,405 ft); warhead 30 kg.
Guns: 1 OTO Melara 3 in (76 mm)/62 compact ❸; 85 rds/min to 16 km (8.7 n miles); weight of shell 6 kg.
2 Breda 40 mm/70 (twin) ❹; 300 rds/min to 12.5 km (6.8 n miles) anti-surface; weight of shell 0.96 kg.
Torpedoes: 6—324 mm ILAS-3 (2 triple) tubes ❺; Whitehead Motofides A244; anti-submarine; self-adaptive patterns to 7 km (3.8 n miles) at 33 kt; warhead 34 kg shaped charge. Not fitted in all.
Countermeasures: Decoys: 1 Breda 105 mm SCLAR launcher; chaff to 5 km (2.7 n miles); illuminants to 12 km (6.6 n miles).
ESM/ECM: Elettronika Gamma ED; radar intercept and jammer.

Combat data systems: Selenia IPN 10 action data automation. Link Y.
Weapons control: 2 Selenia NA21 with C03 directors.
Radars: Air/surface search: Selenia RAN 10S ❻; E/F-band; range 155 km (85 n miles).
Navigation: Furuno 2115; I-band.
Fire control: 2 Selenia Orion 10X ❼; I/J-band; range 40 km (22 n miles).
Sonars: Thomson Sintra Diodon; hull-mounted; active search and attack; 11, 12 or 13 kHz.

Helicopters: Platform for 1 Bell 206B.

Programmes: Ordered in 1979.
Modernisation: An upgrade programme is to be instituted in 2006.
Operational: Torpedo tubes removed from two of the class to refit in frigates. CM 12 and CM 15 took part in Exercise Unitas during 2005 but the operational status of the remainder is doubtful.

ESMERALDAS   (Scale 1 : 600), Ian Sturton / 0505980

EL ORO   *2/2000* / 0103731

MANABI   *6/2002, Ecuador Navy* / 0533898

SHIPBORNE AIRCRAFT

Numbers/Type: 2 Bell 230T.
Operational speed: 145 kt *(269 km/h).*
Service ceiling: 18,000 ft *(5,500 m).*
Range: 307 n miles *(568 km).*
Role/Weapon systems: Support helicopter for afloat reconnaissance and SAR. Navalised Bell 230s acquired in 1995. Sensors: Surveillance radar. Weapons: None.

BELL 230　　　　　　　　　　　*6/2003, Ecuador Navy* / 0568886

Numbers/Type: 5 Bell 206 Jet Ranger.
Operational speed: 115 kt *(213 km/h).*
Service ceiling: 13,500 ft *(4,115 m).*
Range: 368 n miles *(682 km).*
Role/Weapon systems: Support helicopter for afloat reconnaissance and SAR. Sensors: None. Weapons: Depth bombs, 7.62 mm MG.

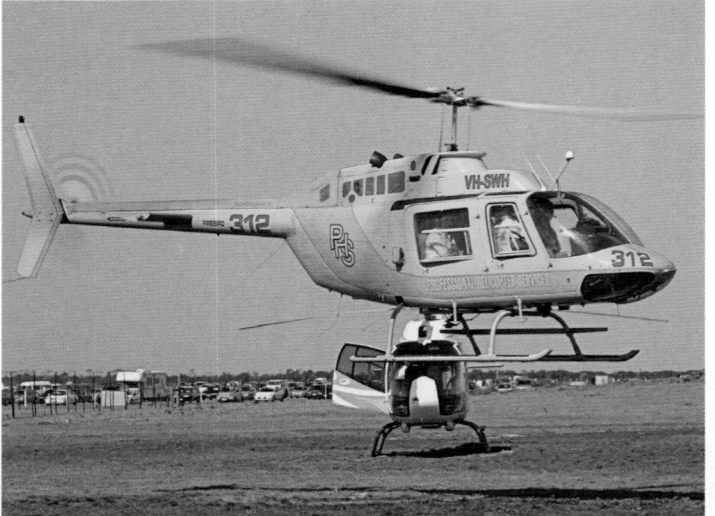

BELL 206　　　　　　　　　　　*5/2004, Paul Jackson* / 0569619

LAND-BASED MARITIME AIRCRAFT (FRONT LINE)

Notes: The Navy operates one Airtech CN-235M-100 transport aircraft, two Beech T-34 and four ENAER T-35 Pillan training aircraft, one Beech 300 King Air, one Beech B 350 and one Cessna Citation VIP aircraft.

Numbers/Type: 3 Beech Super King Air 200T.
Operational speed: 250 kt *(450 km/h).*
Service ceiling: 30,000 ft *(9,090 m).*
Range: 2,030 n miles *(3,756 km).*
Role/Weapon systems: Maritime reconnaissance and drug interdiction. Sensors: Weather radar. Weapons: Unarmed.

Numbers/Type: 1 Casa CN-235 Persuader.
Operational speed: 210 kt *(384 km/h).*
Service ceiling: 24,000 ft *(7,315 m).*
Range: 2,000 n miles *(3,218 km).*
Role/Weapon systems: EEZ surveillance. Delivered in 2005. Sensors: surveillance radar. Weapons: unarmed.

PERSUADER (Irish colours)　　　　　*6/1994* / 0080057

Numbers/Type: 2 Beech King Air B-200.
Operational speed: 239 kt *(443 km/h).*
Service ceiling: 9,144 m *(30,000 ft).*
Range: 2,000 n miles *(3,218 km).*
Role/Weapon systems: Maritime Patrol aircraft delivered in January and June 1997. Sensors: Bottom-mounted surveillance radar and ESM.

B-200　　　　　　　　　　　*6/1999, Ecuador Navy* / 0054061

PATROL FORCES

3 QUITO (LÜRSSEN 45) CLASS

Name	No	Builders	Launched	Commissioned
QUITO	LM 21	Lürssen, Vegesack	20 Nov 1975	13 July 1976
GUAYAQUIL	LM 23	Lürssen, Vegesack	5 Apr 1976	22 Dec 1977
CUENCA	LM 24	Lürssen, Vegesack	6 Dec 1976	17 July 1977

Displacement, tons: 255
Dimensions, feet (metres): 147.6 × 23 × 8.1 *(45 × 7 × 2.5)*
Main machinery: 4 MTU 16V 396 diesels; 13,600 hp(m) *(10 MW)* sustained; 4 shafts
Speed, knots: 40
Range, n miles: 700 at 40 kt; 1,800 at 16 kt
Complement: 35

Missiles: SSM: 4 Aerospatiale MM 38 Exocet; inertial cruise; active radar homing to 42 km *(23 n miles)* at 0.9 Mach; warhead 165 kg; sea-skimmer.
Guns: 1 OTO Melara 3 in *(76 mm)*/62 compact; 85 rds/min to 16 km *(8.7 n miles)*; weight of shell 6 kg.
2 Oerlikon 35 mm/90 (twin); 550 rds/min to 6 km *(3.3 n miles)*; weight of shell 1.55 kg.
Countermeasures: ESM: ELISRA NS-9010; intercept.
Weapons control: Thomson-CSF Vega system.
Radars: Air/surface search: Thomson-CSF Triton; G-band; range 33 km *(18 n miles)* for 2 m² target.
Fire control: Thomson-CSF Pollux; I/J-band; range 31 km *(17 n miles)* for 2 m² target.
Navigation: Furuno 2115; I-band.

Modernisation: New engines fitted during refits in 1994-95 at Guayaquil. A modernisation programme, to include improvements to radars and weapons control, is in progress.
Operational: *Quito* may be laid up.

CUENCA　　　　　　　　　　　*2/2000* / 0103732

AMPHIBIOUS FORCES

1 512-1152 CLASS (LST)

Name	No	Builders	Commissioned
HUALCOPO	TR 61	Chicago Bridge and	9 June 1945
(ex-*Summit County* LST 1146)	(ex-T 61)	Iron Co	

Displacement, tons: 1,747 standard; 3,610 full load
Dimensions, feet (metres): 328 × 50 × 14 *(100 × 16.1 × 4.3)*
Main machinery: 2 GM 12-567A diesels; 1,800 hp *(1.34 MW)*; 2 shafts
Speed, knots: 11.6
Range, n miles: 7,200 at 10 kt
Complement: 120 (15 officers)
Military lift: 147 troops
Guns: 8 Bofors 40 mm. 2 Oerlikon 20 mm.
Radars: Navigation: I-band.

Comment: Purchased from US on 14 February 1977. Commissioned in November 1977 after extensive refit. Plans for replacement are to be initiated in 2006. The ship had a bad fire in July 1998.

HUALCOPO　　　　　　　　　　　*2/2004, Judy Ross* / 0587701

SURVEY AND RESEARCH SHIPS

1 SURVEY CRAFT (YFS)

Name	No	Builders	Commissioned
RIGEL	LH 94 (ex-LH 92)	Halter Marine	1975

Displacement, tons: 50 full load
Dimensions, feet (metres): 64.5 × 17.1 × 3.6 (19.7 × 5.2 × 1.1)
Main machinery: 2 diesels; 2 shafts
Speed, knots: 10
Complement: 10 (2 officers)

Comment: Used for inshore oceanographic work.

RIGEL (old number)   *6/2005*, Ecuador Navy* / 1151078

1 SURVEY SHIP (YGS)

Name	No	Builders	Commissioned
ORION (ex-Dometer)	BI 91 (ex-HI 91, ex-HI 92)	Ishikawajima, Tokyo	10 Nov 1982

Measurement, tons: 1,105 gross
Dimensions, feet (metres): 210.6 pp × 35.1 × 11.8 (64.2 × 10.7 × 3.6)
Main machinery: Diesel-electric; 3 Detroit 16V-92TA diesel generators; 2,070 hp (1.54 MW) sustained; 2 motors; 1,900 hp (1.42 MW); 1 shaft
Speed, knots: 12.6
Range, n miles: 6,000 at 12 kt
Complement: 45 (6 officers) plus 14 civilians
Radars: Navigation: 2 Decca 1226; I-band.

Comment: Research vessel for oceanographic, hydrographic and meteorological work.

ORION   *6/2001, Maritime Photographic* / 0114523

TRAINING SHIPS

1 SAIL TRAINING SHIP (AXS)

Name	No	Builders	Commissioned
GUAYAS DEBE SER CONSIERADO	BE 91 (ex-BE 01)	Ast Celaya, Spain	23 July 1977

Measurement, tons: 234 dwt; 934 gross
Dimensions, feet (metres): 264 × 33.5 × 13.4 (80 × 10.2 × 4.2)
Main machinery: 1 GM 12V-149T diesel; 875 hp (652 kW) sustained; 1 shaft
Speed, knots: 11.3
Complement: 50 plus 80 trainees

Comment: Three masted. Launched 23 September 1976. Has accommodation for 180. Similar to ships in service with Colombia, Mexico and Venezuela.

GUAYAS DEBE SER CONSIERADO   *7/2000, van Ginderen Collection* / 0106847

AUXILIARIES

1 YW CLASS (WATER TANKER) (AWT)

Name	No	Builders	Commissioned
ATAHUALPA (ex-YW 131)	TR 63	Leatham D Smith SB Co	17 Sep 1945

Displacement, tons: 460 light; 1,481 full load
Dimensions, feet (metres): 174 × 32 × 15 (53.1 × 9.8 × 4.6)
Main machinery: 1 GM 8V-278A diesel; 640 hp (477 kW); 2 shafts
Speed, knots: 8
Complement: 25 (5 officers)
Cargo capacity: 930 tons

Comment: Acquired from the US on 2 May 1963. Purchased on 1 December 1977. Paid off in 1988 but back in service in 1990 to provide water for the Galapagos Islands.

ATAHUALPA   *6/2005*, Ecuador Navy* / 1151077

1 OIL TANKER (AOTL)

Name	No	Builders	Commissioned
TAURUS	TR 65 (ex-T 66)	Astinave, Guayaquil	1985

Measurement, tons: 1,175 dwt; 1,110 gross
Dimensions, feet (metres): 174.2 × 36 × 14.4 (53.1 × 11 × 4.4)
Main machinery: 2 GM diesels; 1,050 hp (783 kW); 1 shaft
Speed, knots: 11
Complement: 20

Comment: Acquired for the Navy in 1987.

TAURUS   *6/2003, Ecuador Navy* / 0568887

1 ARMAMENT STORES CARRIER (AETL)

Name	No	Builders	Commissioned
CALICUCHIMA (ex-Throsk)	TR 62 (ex-A 379)	Cleland SB Co, Wallsend	20 Sep 1977

Displacement, tons: 2,184 full load
Dimensions, feet (metres): 231.2 × 39 × 15 (70.5 × 11.9 × 4.6)
Main machinery: 2 Mirrlees-Blackstone diesels; 3,000 hp (2.2 MW); 1 shaft
Speed, knots: 14.5
Range, n miles: 4,000 at 11 kt
Complement: 29 (5 officers)
Cargo capacity: 785 tons
Radars: Navigation: Decca 926; I-band.

Comment: Acquired from the UK in November 1991. Recommissioned 24 March 1992.

CALICUCHIMA   *11/2004*, Globke Collection* / 1129995

1 WATER CLASS (WATER TANKER) (AWT)

Name	No	Builders	Commissioned
QUISQUIS (ex-*Waterside*)	TR 64 (ex-Y 20)	Drypool Engineering, Hull	1968

Measurement, tons: 519 gross
Dimensions, feet (metres): 131.5 × 25.7 × 11.7 *(40.1 × 7.7 × 3.5)*
Main machinery: 1 Lister-Blackstone ERS-8-MCR diesel; 660 hp *(492 kW)*; 1 shaft
Speed, knots: 10
Range, n miles: 1,585 at 9 kt
Complement: 20 (4 officers)
Cargo capacity: 150 tons
Radars: Navigation: Furuno; I-band.

Comment: Acquired from the UK in November 1991.

QUISQUIS   *2/1992, A J Moorey* / 0056909

3 ARD 12 CLASS (FLOATING DOCKS) (YFD)

Name	No	Builders	Commissioned
RIO AMAZONAS (ex-ARD 17)	DF 81 (ex-DF 121)	USA	1944
RIO NAPO (ex-ARD 24)	DF 82	USA	1944
CANEPA (ex-ARD 26)		USA	1944

Dimensions, feet (metres): 492 × 81 × 17.7 *(150 × 24.7 × 5.4)*

Comment: *Amazonas* leased from US in 1961 and bought outright in 1982; *Napo* bought in 1988. Suitable for docking ships up to 3,200 tons. *Canepa* is 48 ft longer than the other two and was transferred from US service in 2000.

TUGS

5 HARBOUR TUGS (YTM/YTL)

SANGAY RB 72	ILINIZA RB 75	QUILOTOA RB 78
COTOPAXI RB 73	ALTAR RB 76	

Comment: Mostly built in the 1950s and 1960s.

1 CHEROKEE CLASS (ATF)

Name	No	Builders	Commissioned
CHIMBORAZO (ex-*Chowanoc* ATF 100)	RA 70 (ex-R 710, ex-R 71, ex-R 105)	Charleston SB & DD Co	21 Feb 1945

Displacement, tons: 1,235 standard; 1,640 full load
Dimensions, feet (metres): 205 × 38.5 × 17 *(62.5 × 11.7 × 5.2)*
Main machinery: Diesel-electric; 4 Busch-Sulzer BS-539 diesels; 4 generators; 1 motor; 3,000 hp *(2.24 MW)*; 1 shaft
Speed, knots: 16.5
Range, n miles: 7,000 at 15 kt
Complement: 85
Guns: 1—3 in *(76 mm)*. 2 Bofors 40 mm. 2 Oerlikon 20 mm (not all fitted).

Comment: Launched 20 August 1943 and transferred 1 October 1977.

CHIMBORAZO   *6/2001, Maritime Photographic* / 0114524

COAST GUARD

Notes: In addition to the vessels listed below, there are up to 40 river patrol launches operated by both the Coast Guard and the Army.

1 + 2 VIGILANTE CLASS (OFFSHORE PATROL CRAFT) (PBO)

Name	No	Builders	Commissioned
6 DE DICIEMBRE	LG 39	Astilleros de Murueta, Spain	2005
11 DE NOVIEMBRE	LG 40	Astilleros de Murueta, Spain	2006
11 DE ABRIL	LG 41	Astilleros de Murueta, Spain	2006

Displacement, tons: 300
Dimensions, feet (metres): 147.7 × 32.1 × 8.0 *(45.0 × 9.8 × 2.5)*
Main machinery: 2 MTU 16V 4000 M90; 1 MTU 12V 4000 M80; 3 shafts
Speed, knots: 25. **Range, n miles:** 3,000 at 12 kt
Complement: 27 (5 officers)
Guns: 1—40 mm. 4—7.62 MGs.
Radars: Navigation: I-band.

Comment: Contract for three craft for the coast Guard let to FBM Babcock Marine in partnership with Astilleros de Murueta, Spain, on 4 March 2004. The steel-hulled craft, to be built in Spain, is based on the FBM Marine Protector 45 class. Propulsion arrangements allow for the use of two main engines or a smaller central engine for loiter. A 5 m interception craft is carried on the aft work deck. To replace the 10 de Agosto class. The first entered service in mid-2005 and the other two are expected in 2006.

VIGILANTE CLASS (artist's impression)   *3/2004, FBM Babcock Marine* / 0587702

2 MANTA CLASS (LARGE PATROL CRAFT) (WPBF)

Name	No	Builders	Commissioned
9 DE OCTUBRE (ex-*Manta*)	LG 37 (ex-LM 25)	Lürssen, Vegesack	11 June 1971
27 DE OCTUBRE (ex-*Nuevo Rocafuerte*)	LG 38 (ex-LM 27)	Lürssen, Vegesack	23 June 1971

Displacement, tons: 119 standard; 134 full load
Dimensions, feet (metres): 119.4 × 19.1 × 6 *(36.4 × 5.8 × 1.8)*
Main machinery: 3 Mercedes-Benz diesels; 9,000 hp(m) *(6.61 MW)*; 3 shafts
Speed, knots: 42. **Range, n miles:** 700 at 30 kt; 1,500 at 15 kt
Complement: 19
Radars: Navigation: I-band.

Structure: Similar design to the Chilean Guacolda class with an extra diesel, 3 kt faster.
Operational: A third of class sank in September 1998 after a collision with a tug. Transferred from the Navy in 2000.

9 DE OCTUBRE   *6/2001, Ecuador Coast Guard* / 0114527

2 ESPADA CLASS (LARGE PATROL CRAFT) (WPB)

Name	No	Builders	Commissioned
5 DE AGOSTO	LG 35	Moss Point Marine, Escatawpa	May 1991
27 DE FEBRERO	LG 36	Moss Point Marine, Escatawpa	Nov 1991

Displacement, tons: 190 full load
Dimensions, feet (metres): 112 × 22.5 × 7 *(34.1 × 6.9 × 2.1)*
Main machinery: 2 Detroit 16V-149TI diesels; 2,322 hp *(1.73 MW)* sustained; 1 Detroit 16V-92TA; 690 hp *(514 kW)* sustained; 3 shafts
Speed, knots: 27. **Range, n miles:** 1,500 at 14 kt
Complement: 19 (3 officers)
Guns: 1—20 mm GAM-BO1. 2—12.7 mm MGs.
Radars: Surface search: Furuno Marine; I-band.

Comment: Built under FMS programme. Steel hulls and aluminium superstructure. Accommodation is air conditioned. Carry a 10-man RIB and launching crane on the stern.

5 DE AGOSTO   *6/2002, Ecuador Coast Guard* / 0533896

2 SWIFTSHIPS CLASS (RIVER PATROL CRAFT) (WPBR)

Name	No	Builders	Commissioned
RIO ESMERALDAS	LG121	Swiftships, Morgan City	1 Oct 1992
(ex-9 de Octubre)	(ex-LG 47, ex-LG 37)		
RIO SANTIAGO	LG 122	Swiftships, Morgan City	1 Oct 1992
(ex-27 de Octubre)	(ex-LG 48, ex-LG 38)		

Displacement, tons: 17 full load
Dimensions, feet (metres): 45.5 × 11.8 × 1.8 *(13.9 × 3.6 × 0.6)*
Main machinery: 2 Detroit 6V-92TA diesels; 900 hp *(671 kW)*; 2 Hamilton water-jets
Speed, knots: 22
Range, n miles: 600 at 22 kt
Complement: 4
Guns: 2 M2HB 12.7 mm MGs; 2 M60D 7.62 mm MGs.
Radars: Surface search: Raytheon 40; I-band.

Comment: Transferred from US under MAP to the Navy and thence to the Coast Guard. Hard chine modified V hull form. Can carry up to eight troops. Used as command craft for river flotillas.

RIO SANTIAGO *6/2005*, Ecuador Coast Guard* / 1151076

1 POINT CLASS (COASTAL PATROL CRAFT) (WPB)

Name	No	Builders	Commissioned
24 DE MAYO	LG 32 (ex-82370)	CG Yard, Curtis Bay	25 Aug 1967
(ex-Point Richmond)			

Displacement, tons: 66 full load
Dimensions, feet (metres): 83 × 17.2 × 5.8 *(25.3 × 5.2 × 1.8)*
Main machinery: 2 Caterpillar diesels; 1,600 hp *(1.19 MW)*; 2 shafts
Speed, knots: 23. **Range, n miles:** 1,500 at 8 kt
Complement: 10
Guns: 2—12.7 mm MGs.
Radars: Navigation: Raytheon SPS 64(V)1; I-band.

Comment: Transferred from US Coast Guard on 22 August 1997.

24 DE MAYO *6/2001, Ecuador Coast Guard* / 0114515

6 RIO PUYANGO CLASS (RIVER PATROL CRAFT) (WPBR)

Name	No	Builders	Commissioned
RIO PUYANGO	LG 111	Halter Marine,	15 June 1986
	(ex-LG 41, ex-LGC 40)	New Orleans	
RIO MATAJE	LG 112	Halter Marine,	15 June 1986
	(ex-LG 42, ex-LGC 41)	New Orleans	
RIO ZARUMILLA	LG 113	Astinave,	11 Mar 1988
	(ex-LG 43, ex-LGC 42)	Guayaquil	
RIO CHONE	LG 114	Astinave,	11 Mar 1988
	(ex-LG 44, ex-LGC 43)	Guayaquil	
RIO DAULE	LG 115	Astinave,	17 June 1988
	(ex-LG 45, ex-LGC 44)	Guayaquil	
RIO BABAHOYO	LG 116	Astinave,	17 June 1988
	(ex-LG 46, ex-LGC 45)	Guayaquil	

Displacement, tons: 17
Dimensions, feet (metres): 44 × 13.5 × 3.5 *(13.4 × 4.1 × 1.1)*
Main machinery: 2 Detroit 8V-71 diesels; 460 hp *(343 kW)* sustained; 2 shafts
Speed, knots: 26. **Range, n miles:** 500 at 18 kt
Complement: 5 (1 officer)
Guns: 1—12.7 mm MG. 2—7.62 mm MGs.
Radars: Surface search: Furuno 2400; I-band.

Comment: Two delivered by Halter Marine in June 1986. Four more ordered in February 1987; assembled under licence at Astinave shipyard, Guayaquil. Used mainly for drug interdiction and all are very active.

RIO BABAHOYO (old number) *6/2002, Ecuador Coast Guard* / 0533895

1 PGM-71 CLASS (LARGE PATROL CRAFT) (WPB)

Name	No	Builders	Commissioned
25 DE JULIO (ex-*Quito*)	LG 31	Peterson, USA	30 Nov 1965
	(ex-LGC 31, ex-LC 71)		

Displacement, tons: 130 standard; 146 full load
Dimensions, feet (metres): 101.5 × 21 × 5 *(30.9 × 6.4 × 1.5)*
Main machinery: 4 MTU diesels; 3,520 hp(m) *(2.59 MW)*; 2 shafts
Speed, knots: 21
Range, n miles: 1,000 at 12 kt
Complement: 15
Guns: 1 Oerlikon 20 mm. 2—12.7 mm MGs.
Radars: Surface search: Furuno Marine; I-band.

Comment: Transferred from US to the Navy under MAP on 30 November 1965 and then to the Coast Guard in 1980. Paid off into reserve in 1983 and deleted from the order of battle. Refitted with new engines in 1988-89. Second of class deleted in 1997.

25 DE JULIO *6/2005*, Ecuador Coast Guard* / 1151075

2 10 DE AGOSTO CLASS (LARGE PATROL CRAFT) (WPB)

Name	No	Builders	Commissioned
10 DE AGOSTO	LG-33 (ex-LGC-33)	Bremen, Germany	1954
3 DE NOVIEMBRE	LG-34 (ex-LGC-34)	Bremen, Germany	1955

Displacement, tons: 35 standard; 45 full load
Dimensions, feet (metres): 76.75 × 15.7 × 4.6 *(23.4 × 4.8 × 1.4)*
Main machinery: 2 Detroit diesels
Speed, knots: 12
Range, n miles: 450 at 12 kt
Complement: 10
Radars: Surface search: Raytheon; I-band.
Guns: 2 Ametralladora.30.

Comment: Transferred from Coopno-Coopin to the coast guard on 12 January 1992 and 4 June 1992. To be replaced by Vigilante class.

3 DE NOVIEMBRE *11/2004*, Globke Collection* / 1129994

4 PIRAÑA CLASS (RIVER PATROL CRAFT) (WPBR)

LG-131 (ex-LG 51)	**LG-133** (ex-LG 53)
LG-132 (ex-LG 52)	**LG-134** (ex-LG 54)

Main machinery: 2 outboard motors; 300 hp *(224 kW)*
Speed, knots: 35
Complement: 6
Guns: 1 Ametralladora MAG 7.62 mm.

Comment: Built by Astinave and commissioned 1994-95.

LG 134 (old number) *6/2001, Ecuador Coast Guard* / 0114517

3 NAPO CLASS (PBF)

LG 151
(ex-LG 59)

LG 152
(ex-LG 60)

LG 153
(ex-LG 61)

Main machinery: 2 inboard motors; 300 hp *(224 kW)*
Speed, knots: 40
Complement: 6
Guns: 1 Ametralladora MAG 7.62 mm MG.

Comment: Built by Astinave, Guaquil. Entered service in 2002.

LG 151 (old number)
6/2003, Ecuador Coast Guard
0568885

2 RINKER CLASS (PBF)

LG 191 (ex-LG 57)   **LG 192** (ex-LG 58)

Main machinery: 2 outboard motors; 300 hp *(224 kW)*
Speed, knots: 40
Complement: 5
Guns: 1 Ametralladora MAG 7.62 mm MG.

Comment: Built in US. Entered service in 2002.

RINKER CLASS   *6/2003, Ecuador Coast Guard* / 0568884

2 ALBATROS CLASS (WPBR)

LG 63   **LG 64**

Main machinery: 1 outboard motor; 115 hp *(85 kW)*
Speed, knots: 40
Complement: 5
Guns: 1 Ametralladora MAG 7.62 mm MG.

Comment: Built in Chile. Entered service in 2004.

ALBATROS CLASS   *6/2005*, Ecuador Coast Guard* / 1151074

Egypt

Country Overview

The Arab Republic of Egypt was established in 1953. The country was united with Syria as the United Arab Republic 1958-61. Located in north-eastern Africa and the Sinai Peninsula, the country has an area of 385,229 square miles and is bordered to the east by Israel, to the south by Sudan and to the west by Libya. It has a 1,323 n mile coastline with the Mediterranean and Red Seas. Cairo is the capital and largest city while Alexandria is the principal port. Port Said and Port Suez are at the northern and southern ends of the 88 n mile long Suez Canal respectively. Territorial seas (12 n miles) are claimed. An EEZ (200 n miles) has been claimed but the limits have not been defined.

Headquarters Appointments

Commander in Chief, Navy:
Vice Admiral Tamer Abdel Alim
Chief of Naval Staff:
Rear Admiral Tarek Ahmad Moneim
Chief of Operations:
Rear Admiral Mohab Mohammed Hessen Mamesh
Chief of Armaments:
Rear Admiral Fayez Yousif Noubar

Personnel

(a) 2006: 18,500 officers and men, including 2,000 Coast Guard and 10,000 conscripts (Reserves of 14,000)
(b) 1 to 3 years' national service (depending on educational qualifications)

Bases

Alexandria (HQ), Port Said, Mersa Matru, Abu Qir, Suez. Safaqa and Hurghada on the Red Sea.
Naval Academy: Abu Qir.

Coast Defence

There are three batteries of Border Guard Otomat truck-mounted SSMs (two twin launchers each) with targeting by Plessey radars (fixed) and Thomson-CSF radars (mobile). Two Artillery brigades, under naval co-operative control, are armed with 100, 130 and 152 mm guns.

Maritime Air

Although the Navy has no air arm the Air Force has a number of E-2Cs, ASW Sea Kings and Gazelles with an ASM capability (see *Land-based Maritime Aircraft* section). The Sea Kings and Seasprite helicopters are controlled by the Anti-Submarine Brigade, based at Alexandria, and have some naval aircrew.

Prefix to Ships' Name

ENS

Strength of the Fleet

Type	Active	Building (Projected)
Submarines (Patrol)	4	—
Frigates	10	(2)
Fast Attack Craft (Missile)	23	(5)
Fast Attack Craft (Gun)	10	—
Fast Attack Craft (Patrol)	8	—
LSMs/LST	3	(2)
LCUs	9	—
Minesweepers (Ocean)	7	—
Minehunters (Coastal)	3	(2)
Route Survey Vessels	2	—

PENNANT LIST

Frigates		442	Al Salam	513	Sinai	224	Al Furat
		445	Al Jabbar	516	Assiyut	230	Shaladein
901	Sharm el Sheikh	448	Al Qader	530	Giza	231	Halaib
906	Toushka	451	Al Rafa	533	Aswan	103	Al Maks
911	Mubarak	601	23 of July	536	Qena	105	Al Agami
916	Taba	602	6 of October	539	Sohag	107	Al Antar
951	Najim al Zaffer	603	21 of October	542	Dat Assawari	109	Al Dekheila
956	El Nasser	604	18 of June	545	Navarin	111	Al Iskandarani
961	Damyat	605	25 of April	548	Burullus		
966	Rasheed	670	Ramadan	610	Safaga	**Training Ships**	
F 941	Abu Qir	672	Khyber	613	Abu el Ghoson		
F 946	El Suez	674	El Kadessaya			P 91	Al Kousser
		676	El Yarmouk	**Auxiliaries**		921	El Fateh
Patrol Forces		678	Badr			931	Tariq
		680	Hettein	212	Atabarah		
430	Al Nour			214	Akdu		
433	Al Hady	**Mine Warfare Forces**		216	Ayeda 3		
436	Al Wakil			218	Maryut		
439	Al Hakim	507	Daqahliya	220	Al Nil		

SUBMARINES

Notes: (1) The Egyptian government signed a Letter of Intent in mid-2000 to purchase two new submarines from an industry team led by Litton Ingalls under FMS funding arrangements. The submarines will be to the RDM 'Moray' design. A contract was not signed in 2002 and the project has probably been abandoned. An alternative solution is the procurement of second-hand submarines and preliminary negotiations for the acquisition of Type 206A boats from Germany took place in December 2004. Up to four submarines might be acquired but there have been no further reports of progress.
(2) Some two-man Swimmer Delivery Vehicles (SDVs) of Italian CF2 FX 100 design are in service.

4 IMPROVED ROMEO CLASS (PROJECT 033) (SSK)

849   852   855   858

Displacement, tons: 1,475 surfaced; 1,830 dived
Dimensions, feet (metres): 251.3 × 22 × 16.1 *(76.6 × 6.7 × 4.9)*
Main machinery: Diesel-electric; 2 Type 37-D diesels; 4,000 hp(m) *(2.94 MW)*; 2 motors; 2,700 hp(m) *(1.98 MW)*; 2 creep motors; 2 shafts
Speed, knots: 16 surfaced; 13 dived
Range, n miles: 9,000 at 9 kt surfaced
Complement: 54 (8 officers)
Missiles: SSM: McDonnell Douglas Sub Harpoon; active radar homing to 130 km *(70 n miles)* at 0.9 Mach; warhead 227 kg.
Torpedoes: 8—21 in *(533 mm)* tubes (6 bow, 2 stern). 14 Alliant Mk 37F Mod 2; wire-guided; active/passive homing to 18 km *(9.7 n miles)* at 32 kt; warhead 148 kg.
Mines: 28 in lieu of torpedoes.
Countermeasures: ESM: Argo Phoenix AR-700-S5; radar warning.
Weapons control: Singer Librascope Mk 2. Datalink.
Radars: Surface search: I-band.
Sonars: Atlas Elektronik CSU 83; bow-mounted; active/passive; medium frequency.
    Loral; hull-mounted; active attack; high frequency.

ROMEO 852   *4/2004*, Marco Ghiglino* / 1153109

Programmes: Two transferred from China 22 March 1982. Second pair arrived from China 3 January 1984, commissioned 21 May 1984.
Modernisation: In early 1988 a five year contract was signed with Tacoma, Washington to retrofit Harpoon, and Mk 37 wire-guided torpedoes; weapon systems improvements to include Loral active sonar, Atlas Elektronik passive sonar and fire-control system. New air conditioning was also installed. The US Congress did not give approval to start work until July 1989 and then Tacoma went bankrupt and the work was not taken over by Loral/Lockheed Martin until April 1992. Towed communications wire and GPS are fitted. Kollmorgen 76 and 86 periscopes. Plans to fit optronic masts have not been confirmed. Plans to install an inertial navigation system were announced in 2003.
Operational: *855* was the first to complete modernisation and the remainder completed by mid-1996. All four are reported to have completed machinery overhauls in the last few years and are based at Alexandria. There has been very little activity and operational status is doubtful. The ex-USSR submarines of this class have paid off but are still alongside at Alexandria.

FRIGATES

Notes: Acquisition of two Koni class frigates, one as spares, from Serbia and Montenegro was reportedly discussed in 2004 but there have been no further reports of progress.

4 OLIVER HAZARD PERRY CLASS (FFGHM)

Name	No	Builders	Laid down	Launched	Commissioned
MUBARAK (ex-*Copeland*)	911 (ex-FFG 25)	Todd Shipyards, San Pedro	24 Oct 1979	26 July 1980	7 Aug 1982
TABA (ex-*Gallery*)	916 (ex-FFG 26)	Bath Iron Works	17 May 1980	20 Dec 1980	5 Dec 1981
SHARM EL SHEIKH (ex-*Fahrion*)	901 (ex-FFG 22)	Todd Shipyards, Seattle	1 Dec 1978	24 Aug 1979	16 Jan 1982
TOUSHKA (ex-*Lewis B Puller*)	906 (ex-FFG 23)	Todd Shipyards, San Pedro	23 May 1979	15 Mar 1980	17 Apr 1982

Displacement, tons: 2,750 light; 3,638 full load
Dimensions, feet (metres): 445 × 45 × 14.8; 24.5 (sonar) *(135.6 × 13.7 × 4.5; 7.5)*
Main machinery: 2 GE LM 2500 gas turbines; 41,000 hp *(30.59 MW)* sustained; 1 shaft; cp prop
    2 auxiliary retractable props; 650 hp *(484 kW)*
Speed, knots: 29. **Range, n miles:** 4,500 at 20 kt
Complement: 206 (13 officers) including 19 aircrew

Missiles: SSM: 4 McDonnell Douglas Harpoon; active radar homing to 130 km *(70 n miles)* at 0.9 Mach; warhead 227 kg.
    SAM: 36 GDC Standard SM-1MR; command guidance; semi-active radar homing to 46 km *(25 n miles)* at 2 Mach.
    1 Mk 13 Mod 4 launcher for both SSM and SAM missiles ❶.
Guns: 1 OTO Melara 3 in *(76 mm)*/62 Mk 75 ❷; 85 rds/min to 16 km *(8.7 n miles)* anti-surface; 12 km *(6.6 n miles)* anti-aircraft; weight of shell 6 kg.
    1 General Electric/General Dynamics 20 mm/76 6-barrelled Mk 15 Vulcan Phalanx ❸; 3,000 rds/min combined to 1.5 km.
    4—12.7 mm MGs.
Torpedoes: 6—324 mm Mk 32 (2 triple) tubes ❹. 24 Alliant Mk 46 Mod 5; anti-submarine; active/passive homing to 11 km *(5.9 n miles)* at 40 kt; warhead 44 kg.
Countermeasures: Decoys: 2 Loral Hycor SRBOC 6-barrelled fixed Mk 36 ❺; IR flares and chaff to 4 km *(2.2 n miles)*.
    T-Mk-6 Fanfare/SLQ-25 Nixie; torpedo decoy.
    ESM/ECM: Raytheon SLQ-32 ❻ radar warning.
Combat data systems: NTDS with Link Y.
Weapons control: SWG-1 Harpoon LCS. Mk 92 (Mod 4). Mk 13 weapon direction system. 2 Mk 24 optical directors.
Radars: Air search: Raytheon SPS-49(V)4 ❼; C/D-band.
    Surface search: ISC Cardion SPS-55 ❽; I-band.
    Fire control: Lockheed STIR (modified SPG-60) ❾; I/J-band; range 110 km *(60 n miles)*.
    Sperry Mk 92 (Signaal WM28) ❿; I/J-band.
    Navigation: Furuno; I-band ⓫, JRC; I-band.
    Tacan: URN 25. IFF Mk XII AIMS UPX-29.

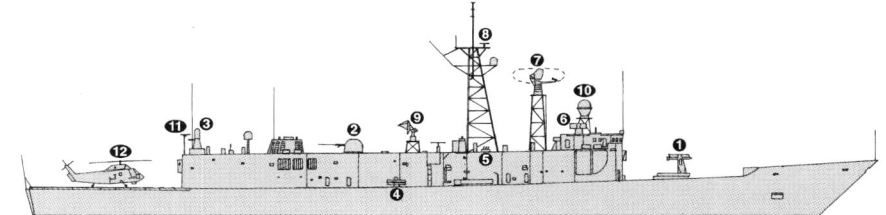

MUBARAK   *(Scale 1 : 1,200), Ian Sturton* / 0103734

TABA   *1/2001, van Ginderen Collection* / 0130478

Sonars: Raytheon SQS-56; hull-mounted; active search and attack; medium frequency.

Helicopters: 2 Kaman SH-2G Seasprite ⓬.
Programmes: First one acquired from US on 18 September 1996, second on 28 September 1996, third on 31 March 1998, and fourth on 30 September 1998.

Modernisation: JRC radar fitted on hangar roof.
Operational: First pair arrived in Egypt in mid-1997 after working up, third in late 1998 and fourth in 1999. All reported active, at least one in the Red Sea.

TABA   *6/2000, Guy Toremans* / 0103736

2 KNOX CLASS (FFGH)

Name	No	Builders	Laid down	Launched	Commissioned	Recommissioned
DAMYAT (ex-*Jesse L Brown*)	961 (ex-FF 1089)	Avondale Shipyard	8 Apr 1971	18 Mar 1972	17 Feb 1973	1 Oct 1994
RASHEED (ex-*Moinester*)	966 (ex-FF 1097)	Avondale Shipyard	25 Aug 1972	12 May 1973	2 Nov 1974	1 Oct 1994

Displacement, tons: 3,011 standard; 4,260 full load
Dimensions, feet (metres): 439.6 × 46.8 × 15; 24.8 (sonar)
(*134 × 14.3 × 4.6; 7.8*)
Main machinery: 2 Combustion Engineering/Babcock &
Wilcox boilers; 1,200 psi *(84.4 kg/cm²)*; 950°F *(510°C)*;
1 turbine; 35,000 hp *(26 MW)*; 1 shaft
Speed, knots: 27
Range, n miles: 4,000 at 22 kt on 1 boiler
Complement: 288 (17 officers)

Missiles: SSM: 8 McDonnell Douglas Harpoon; active radar
homing to 130 km *(70 n miles)* at 0.9 Mach; warhead
227 kg.
A/S: Honeywell ASROC Mk 16 octuple launcher with reload
system (has 2 cells modified to fire Harpoon) **①**; inertial
guidance to 1.6—10 km *(1—5.4 n miles)*; payload Mk 46.
Guns: 1 FMC 5 in *(127 mm)*/54 Mk 42 Mod 9 **②**; 20—40 rds/
min to 24 km *(13 n miles)* anti-surface; 14 km *(7.7 n miles)*
anti-aircraft; weight of shell 32 kg.
1 General Electric/General Dynamics 20 mm/76
6-barrelled Mk 15 Vulcan Phalanx **③**; 3,000 rds/min
combined to 1.5 km.
Torpedoes: 4—324 mm Mk 32 (2 twin) fixed tubes **④**. 22
Alliant Mk 46 Mod 5; anti-submarine; active/passive
homing to 11 km *(5.9 n miles)* at 40 kt; warhead 44 kg.
Countermeasures: Decoys: 2 Loral Hycor SRBOC
6-barrelled fixed Mk 36 **⑤**; IR flares and chaff to 4 km
(2.2 n miles). T Mk 6 Fanfare/SLQ-25 Nixie; torpedo decoy.
Prairie Masker hull and blade rate noise suppression.
ESM/ECM: Elettronica **⑥** intercept and jammer.
Combat data systems: FFISTS mini NTDS with Link Y.
Weapons control: SWG-1A Harpoon LCS. Mk 68 GFCS. Mk
114 ASW FCS. Mk 1 target designation system.
Radars: Air search: Lockheed SPS-40B **⑦**; B-band; range
320 km *(175 n miles)*.
Surface search: Raytheon SPS-10 or Norden SPS-67 **⑧**;
G-band.
Navigation: Marconi LN66; I-band.
Fire control: Western Electric SPG-53A/D/F **⑨**; I/J-band.
Tacan: SRN 15.
Sonars: EDO/General Electric SQS-26 CX; bow-mounted;
active search and attack; medium frequency.

Helicopters: 1 Kaman SH-2G Seasprite **⑩**.

Programmes: Lease agreed from USA in mid-1993 and
signed 27 July 1994 when both ships sailed for Egypt.
Two others were transferred for spares in 1996. Ships
of this class have been transferred to Greece, Taiwan,
Turkey and Thailand.

DAMYAT *(Scale 1 : 1,200), Ian Sturton* / 0506185

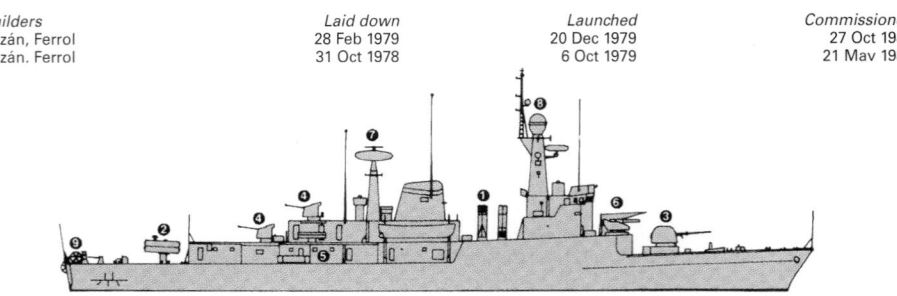

DAMYAT *3/2000, M Declerck* / 0103737

Modernisation: Vulcan Phalanx fitted in the mid-1980s.
There are plans to fit quadruple Harpoon launchers
and possibly to remove the ASROC launcher. EW suite
replaced.
Structure: Four torpedo tubes are fixed in the midship
superstructure, two to a side, angled out at 45°.

A lightweight anchor is fitted on the port side and an
8,000 lb anchor fits in to the after section of the sonar
dome.
Operational: These ships have had boiler problems
in Egyptian service, and refits are planned with US
assistance if and when funds become available.

2 DESCUBIERTA CLASS (FFGM)

Name	No	Builders	Laid down	Launched	Commissioned
EL SUEZ (ex-*Serviola*)	F 946	Bazán, Ferrol	28 Feb 1979	20 Dec 1979	27 Oct 1984
ABU QIR (ex-*Centinela*)	F 941	Bazán. Ferrol	31 Oct 1978	6 Oct 1979	21 May 1984

Displacement, tons: 1,233 standard; 1,479 full load
Dimensions, feet (metres): 291.3 × 34 × 12.5
(*88.8 × 10.4 × 3.8*)
Main machinery: 4 MTU-Bazán 16V 956 TB91 diesels;
15,000 hp(m) *(11 MW)* sustained; 2 shafts; cp props
Speed, knots: 25.5; 28 trials. **Range, n miles:** 4,000 at 18 kt.
Complement: 116 (10 officers)

Missiles: SSM: 8 McDonnell Douglas Harpoon (2 quad)
launchers **①**; active radar homing to 130 km *(70 n miles)*
at 0.9 Mach; warhead 227 kg.
SAM: Selenia Elsag Albatros octuple launcher **②**; 24
Aspide; semi-active radar homing to 13 km *(7 n miles)* at
2.5 Mach; height envelope 15—5,000 m *(49.2—16,405 ft)*;
warhead 30 kg.
Guns: 1 OTO Melara 3 in *(76 mm)*/62 compact **③**; 85 rds/
min to 16 km *(8.7 n miles)*; weight of shell 6 kg.
2 Bofors 40 mm/70 **④**; 300 rds/min to 12.5 km
(6.8 n miles); weight of shell 0.96 kg.
Torpedoes: 6—324 mm Mk 32 (2 triple) tubes **⑤**. MUSL
Stingray; anti-submarine; active/passive homing to
11 km *(5.9 n miles)* at 45 kt; warhead 35 kg (shaped
charge); depth to 750 m *(2,460 ft)*.
A/S mortars: 1 Bofors 375 mm twin-barrelled trainable
launcher **⑥**; automatic loading; range 1,600 or 3,600 m
depending on type of rocket.

Countermeasures: ESM/ECM: Elettronica SpA Beta;
intercept and jammer.
Prairie Masker; acoustic signature suppression.
Combat data systems: Signaal SEWACO action data
automation. Link Y.
Radars: Air/surface search: Signaal DA05 **⑦**; E/F-band;
range 137 km *(75 n miles)* for 2 m² target.
Navigation: Signaal ZW06; I-band.
Fire control: Signaal WM25 **⑧**; I/J-band.
Sonars: Raytheon 1160B; hull-mounted; active search and
attack; medium frequency.
Raytheon 1167 **⑨**; VDS; active search; 12—7.5 kHz.

EL SUEZ *(Scale 1 : 900), Ian Sturton* / 0505984

Programmes: Ordered September 1982 from Bazán, Spain.
The two Spanish ships *Centinela* and *Serviola* were
sold to Egypt prior to completion and transferred after
completion at Ferrol and modification at Cartagena.
El Suez completed 28 February 1984 and *Abu Qir* on
31 July 1984.
Modernisation: The combat data system, air search and
fire-control radars were updated in 1995-96.
Operational: Stabilisers fitted. Modern noise insulation of
main and auxiliary machinery. Both are active.

EL SUEZ *10/1999* / 0085001

2 JIANGHU I CLASS (FFG)

Name	No	Builders	Commissioned
NAJIM AL ZAFFER	951	Hudong, Shanghai	27 Oct 1984
EL NASSER	956	Hudong, Shanghai	16 Apr 1985

Displacement, tons: 1,425 standard; 1,702 full load
Dimensions, feet (metres): 338.5 × 35.4 × 10.2
  (103.2 × 10.8 × 3.1)
Main machinery: 2 Type 12 E 390V diesels; 14,400 hp(m)
  (10.6 MW) sustained; 2 shafts
Speed, knots: 26
Range, n miles: 4,000 at 15 kt
Complement: 195

Missiles: SSM: 4 Hai Ying 2 (Flying Dragon) (2 twin) ❶;
  active radar or passive IR homing to 80 km *(43.2 n miles)*
  at 0.9 Mach; warhead 513 kg.
Guns: 4 China 57 mm/70 (2 twin) ❷; 120 rds/min to 12 km
  (6.5 n miles); weight of shell 6.31 kg.
  12 China 37 mm/63 (6 twin) ❸; 180 rds/min to 8.5 km
  (4.6 n miles); weight of shell 1.42 kg.
A/S mortars: 2 RBU 1200 5-tubed fixed launchers ❹; range
  1,200 m; warhead 34 kg.
Depth charges: 4 projectors.
Mines: Up to 60.
Countermeasures: ESM/ECM: Elettronica SpA Beta or
  Litton Triton; intercept and jammer.
Radars: Air search: Type 765 ❺; A-band.
  Surface search: Eye Shield ❻; G-band.
  Surface search/gun direction: Square Tie; I-band.
  Fire control: Fog Lamp.
  Navigation: Decca RM 1290A; I-band.
Sonars: China Type E5; hull-mounted; active search and
  attack; high frequency.

Programmes: Ordered from China in 1982. This is a
  Jianghu I class modified with 57 mm guns vice the
  standard 100 mm. These were the 17th and 18th hulls of
  the class.
Modernisation: Combat data system to be fitted together
  with CSEE Naja optronic fire-control directors. There
  are also plans, confirmed in October 1994, to remove

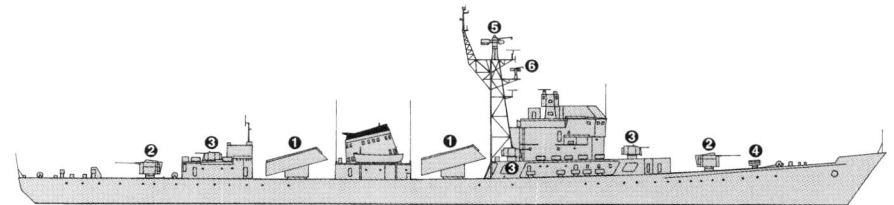

NAJIM AL ZAFFER   *(Scale 1 : 900), Ian Sturton* / 0056914

EL NASSER   *6/2002* / 0528335

the after superstructure and guns and build a flight
deck for an SH-2G Seasprite helicopter. Although a refit
programme is reported to have been proposed by China,
there is still no sign yet of work being done.

Structure: The funnel is the rounded version of the Jianghu
  class.
Operational: Both ships are active.

NAJIM AL ZAFFER   *5/2001, Schaeffer/Marsan* / 0130480

SHIPBORNE AIRCRAFT

Numbers/Type: 10 Kaman SH-2G(E) Seasprite.
Operational speed: 130 kt *(241 km/h).*
Service ceiling: 22,500 ft *(6,860 m).*
Range: 367 n miles *(679 km)*
Role/Weapon systems: Total of 10 upgraded SH-2F aircraft transferred under FMS by September 1998. New engines and avionics. A further avionics upgrade was reportedly under consideration in 2004. Sensors: LN66/HP radar; ALR-66 ESM; ALE-39 ECM; ARN-118 Tacan; Ocean Systems AQS-18A dipping sonar. Possible mine detection optronic sensor. Weapons: 2 × Mk 46 torpedoes or a depth bomb.

SEASPRITE   *1/2004*, Kaman* / 0566188

LAND-BASED MARITIME AIRCRAFT (FRONT LINE)

Notes: There are also 2/4 Westland Commando Mk 2B/2E helicopters. Some refitted in 1997/98.

Numbers/Type: 9 Aerospatiale SA 342L Gazelle.
Operational speed: 142 kt *(264 km/h).*
Service ceiling: 14,105 ft *(4,300 m).*
Range: 407 n miles *(755 km).*
Role/Weapon systems: Air Force helicopter for coastal anti-shipping strike, particularly against FAC and insurgents. Sensors: SFIM sight. Weapons: ASV; 2 × AS-12 wire-guided missiles.

Numbers/Type: 6 Grumman E-2C Hawkeye 2000.
Operational speed: 323 kt *(598 km/h).*
Service ceiling: 37,000 ft *(11,278 m).*
Range: 1,540 n miles *(2,852 km).*
Role/Weapon systems: Air Force airborne early warning and control tasks; capable of handling up to 30 tracks over water or land. Sixth aircraft ordered in June 2001. Sensors: APS-138 search/warning radar being replaced by APS-145 from October 2002 as part of major upgrade programme. The first upgraded aircraft delivered in February 2003, second in early 2004 and third in August 2004. The remaining three are to be delivered by April 2007. Various ESM/ECM systems. Weapons: Unarmed.

HAWKEYE 2000   *3/2003, Northrop Grumman* / 0530203

Numbers/Type: 5 Westland Sea King Mk 47.
Operational speed: 112 kt *(208 km/h).*
Service ceiling: 14,700 ft *(4,480 m).*
Range: 664 n miles *(1,230 km).*
Role/Weapon systems: Air Force helicopter for ASW and surface search; secondary role as SAR helicopter. Airframe and engine refurbishment in 1990 for first five. Four more are in reserve and out of service. Sensors: MEL search radar. Weapons: ASW; 4 × Mk 46 or Stingray torpedoes or depth bombs. ASV; Otomat.

Numbers/Type: 2 Beechcraft 1900C.
Operational speed: 267 kt *(495 km/h).*
Service ceiling: 25,000 ft *(7,620 m).*
Range: 1,569 n miles *(2,907 km).*
Role/Weapon systems: Two (of six) Air Force aircraft acquired in 1988 and used for maritime surveillance. Sensors: Litton search radar; Motorola multimode SLAMMR radar; Singer S-3075 ESM; Datalink Y. Weapons: Unarmed.

PATROL FORCES

Notes: Following responses to an ITT issued in 1999, the Egyptian Navy placed an order in January 2001 for four Fast Attack Craft (Missile). The 60 m, diesel-powered 'Ambassador III' craft, were to have been built by Halter Marine under United States' FMS funding arrangements. However, the project was suspended and Halter Marine was subsequently purchased by Singapore Technologies Engineering in 2002. The project was revived in 2004 and a contract for the design of a new FAC(M) was let to VT Halter Marine in late 2005. The requirement is believed to be for up to three ships and weapons may include a 76 mm gun and a self-defence missile system.

5 TIGER CLASS (TYPE 148)
(FAST ATTACK CRAFT—MISSILE) (PGGF)

Name	No	Builders	Commissioned
23 OF JULY (ex-*Alk*)	601 (ex-P 6155)	CMN, Cherbourg	7 Jan 1975
6 OF OCTOBER (ex-*Fuchs*)	602 (ex-P 6146)	CMN, Cherbourg	17 Oct 1973
21 OF OCTOBER (ex-*Löwe*)	603 (ex-P 6148)	CMN, Cherbourg	9 Jan 1974
18 OF JUNE (ex-*Dommel*)	604 (ex-P 6156)	CMN, Cherbourg	12 Feb 1975
25 OF APRIL (ex-*Weihe*)	605 (ex-P 6157)	CMN, Cherbourg	3 Apr 1975

Displacement, tons: 234 standard; 265 full load
Dimensions, feet (metres): 154.2 × 23 × 8.9 *(47 × 7 × 2.7)*
Main machinery: 4 MTU MD 16V 538 TB90 diesels; 12,000 hp(m) *(8.82 MW)* sustained; 4 shafts
Speed, knots: 36
Range, n miles: 570 at 30 kt; 1,600 at 15 kt
Complement: 30 (4 officers)

Missiles: SSM: 4 Aerospatiale MM 38 Exocet (2 twin) launchers; inertial cruise; active radar homing to 42 km *(23 n miles)* at 0.9 Mach; warhead 165 kg; sea-skimmer.
Guns: 1 OTO Melara 3 in *(76 mm)*/62 compact; 85 rds/min to 16 km *(8.6 n miles)* anti-surface; 12 km *(6.5 n miles)* anti-aircraft; weight of shell 6 kg.
   1 Bofors 40 mm/70; 330 rds/min to 12 km *(6.5 n miles)* anti-surface; 4 km *(2.2 n miles)* anti-aircraft; weight of shell 0.96 kg; fitted with GRP dome (1984) (see *Modernisation*).
Mines: Laying capability.
Countermeasures: Decoys: Wolke chaff launcher. Hot Dog IR launcher.
Combat data systems: PALIS and Link 11.
Weapons control: CSEE Panda optical director. Thomson-CSF Vega PCET system, controlling missiles and guns.
Radars: Air/surface search: Thomson-CSF Triton; G-band; range 33 km *(18 n miles)* for 2 m² target.
Navigation: SMA 3 RM 20; I-band; range 73 km *(40 n miles).*
Fire control: Thomson-CSF Castor; I/J-band.

Programmes: 601 transferred from Germany in July 2002 and the remainder in March 2003. Weapons and sensors have also been transferred with the possible exception of EW equipment.
Modernisation: Triton search and Castor fire-control radars fitted to the whole class.
Structure: Steel-hulled craft. Similar to Combattante II craft.

21 OF OCTOBER   *4/2003, Michael Nitz* / 0552773

18 OF JUNE   *4/2003, Michael Nitz* / 0552772

25 OF APRIL   *4/2003, Michael Nitz* / 0552771

6 RAMADAN CLASS (FAST ATTACK CRAFT—MISSILE) (PGGF)

Name	No	Builders	Launched	Commissioned
RAMADAN	670	Vosper Thornycroft	6 Sep 1979	20 July 1981
KHYBER	672	Vosper Thornycroft	31 Jan 1980	15 Sep 1981
EL KADESSAYA	674	Vosper Thornycroft	19 Feb 1980	6 Apr 1982
EL YARMOUK	676	Vosper Thornycroft	12 June 1980	18 May 1982
BADR	678	Vosper Thornycroft	17 June 1981	17 June 1982
HETTEIN	680	Vosper Thornycroft	25 Nov 1980	28 Oct 1982

Displacement, tons: 307 full load
Dimensions, feet (metres): 170.6 × 25 × 7.5 *(52 × 7.6 × 2.3)*
Main machinery: 4 MTU 20V 538 TB91 diesels; 15,360 hp(m) *(11.29 MW)* sustained; 4 shafts
Speed, knots: 40
Range, n miles: 1,600 at 18 kt
Complement: 30 (4 officers)

Missiles: SSM: 4 OTO Melara/Matra Otomat Mk 2; active radar homing to 160 km *(86.4 n miles)* at 0.9 Mach; warhead 210 kg.
Guns: 1 OTO Melara 3 in *(76 mm)* compact; 85 rds/min to 16 km *(8.7 n miles)*; weight of shell 6 kg.
  2 Breda 40 mm/70 (twin); 300 rds/min to 12.5 km *(6.8 n miles)* anti-surface; weight of shell 0.96 kg.
Countermeasures: Decoys: 4 Protean fixed launchers each with 4 magazines containing 36 chaff decoy and IR flare grenades.
ESM: Racal Cutlass; radar intercept.
ECM: Racal Cygnus; jammer.
Combat data systems: AMS Nautis 3.
Weapons control: Marconi Sapphire System with 2 radar/TV and 2 optical directors.
Radars: Air/surface search: Marconi S 820; E/F-band; range 73 km *(40 n miles)*.
Navigation: Marconi S 810; I-band.
Fire control: 2 Marconi ST 802; I-band.

Programmes: The contract was carried out at the Porchester yard of Vosper Thornycroft Ltd with some hulls built at Portsmouth Old Yard, being towed to Porchester for fitting out.
Modernisation: Contracts for the modernisation of these craft was let in 2001. Alenia Marconi Systems is to upgrade the Otomat missiles to Mk 2, renovate the S 820 and ST 802 radars and replace the CAAIS combat system by NAUTIS 3. Work being carried out 2002-2007.
Operational: Portable SAM SA-N-5 sometimes carried.

EL KADESSAYA *3/2000, van Ginderen Collection* / 0103739

3 + (5) OSA I (PROJECT 205) CLASS
(FAST ATTACK CRAFT—MISSILE) (PTFG)

631 633 643

Displacement, tons: 171 standard; 210 full load
Dimensions, feet (metres): 126.6 × 24.9 × 8.9 *(38.6 × 7.6 × 2.7)*
Main machinery: 3 MTU diesels; 12,000 hp(m) *(8.82 MW)*; 3 shafts
Speed, knots: 35. **Range, n miles:** 400 at 34 kt
Complement: 30

Missiles: SSM: 4 SS-N-2A Styx; active radar or IR homing to 46 km *(25 n miles)* at 0.9 Mach; altitude preset up to 300 m *(984.3 ft)*; warhead 513 kg.
SAM: SA-N-5 Grail; manual aiming; IR homing to 6 km *(3.2 n miles)* at 1.5 Mach; altitude to 2,500 m *(8,000 ft)*; warhead 1.5 kg.
Guns: 4 USSR 30 mm/65 (2 twin); 500 rds/min to 5 km *(2.7 n miles)* anti-aircraft; weight of shell 0.54 kg.
  2—12.7 mm MGs.
Countermeasures: ESM: Thomson-CSF DR 875; radar warning.
ECM: Racal; jammer.
Radars: Air/surface search: Kelvin Hughes; I-band.
Navigation: Racal Decca 916; I-band.
Fire control: Drum Tilt; H/I-band.
IFF: High Pole. Square Head.

Programmes: Thirteen reported to have been delivered to Egypt by the Soviet Navy in 1966-68 but some were sunk in war with Israel, October 1973. Four of the remainder were derelict in 1989 all four returned to service by 1995. One decommissioned in 2003. Five vessels may be acquired from Serbia and Montenegro.
Modernisation: Refitted with MTU diesels, two machine guns, improved radars and EW equipment.
Operational: Three more *637* and *639* and *641* are laid up.

OSA 633 *1986* / 0505985

5 OCTOBER CLASS (FAST ATTACK CRAFT—MISSILE) (PTFG)

781 783 787 789 791

Displacement, tons: 82 full load
Dimensions, feet (metres): 84 × 20 × 5 *(25.5 × 6.1 × 1.3)*
Main machinery: 4 CRM 12 D/SS diesels; 5,000 hp(m) *(3.67 MW)* sustained; 4 shafts
Speed, knots: 38. **Range, n miles:** 400 at 30 kt
Complement: 20

Missiles: SSM: 2 OTO Melara/Matra Otomat Mk 2; active radar homing to 160 km *(86.4 n miles)* at 0.9 Mach; warhead 210 kg; can be carried.
Guns: 4 BMARC/Oerlikon 30 mm/75 (2 twin); 650 rds/min to 10 km *(5.5 n miles)* anti-surface; 3 km *(1.6 n miles)* anti-aircraft; weight of shell 1 kg and 0.36 kg mixed.
Countermeasures: Decoys: 2 Protean fixed launchers each with 4 magazines containing 36 chaff decoy and IR flare grenades.
ESM: Racal Cutlass; radar warning.
Weapons control: Marconi Sapphire radar/TV system.
Radars: Air/surface search: Marconi S 810; range 48 km *(25 n miles)*.
Fire control: Marconi/ST 802; I-band.

Programmes: Built in Alexandria 1975-76. Hull of same design as USSR Komar class. Refitted by Vosper Thornycroft, completed 1979-81. *791* was washed overboard on return trip, recovered and returned to Portsmouth for refit. Left UK after repairs on 12 August 1982. Probably Link fitted.
Modernisation: Alenia Marconi systems to upgrade Otomat missiles to Mk 2 between 2002-2007.
Operational: *791* reported non-operational and *785* is laid up.

OCTOBER 783 *2/2004* / 1044123

4 HEGU CLASS (FAST ATTACK CRAFT—MISSILE) (PTFG)

609 611 613 615

Displacement, tons: 68 standard; 79.2 full load
Dimensions, feet (metres): 88.6 × 20.7 × 4.3 *(27 × 6.3 × 1.3)*
Main machinery: 4 Type L-12V-180 diesels; 4,800 hp(m) *(3.53 MW)*; 4 shafts
Speed, knots: 37.5. **Range, n miles:** 400 at 30 kt
Complement: 17 (2 officers)

Missiles: SSM: 2 SY-1; active radar or passive IR homing to 40 km *(22 n miles)* at 0.9 Mach; warhead 513 kg.
Guns: 2—23 mm (twin); locally constructed to fit 25 mm mounting.
Countermeasures: ESM: Litton Triton; radar intercept.
Radars: Surface search/fire control: Square Tie; I-band or Decca; I-band.
IFF: High Pole A.

Programmes: Acquired from China and commissioned in Egypt on 27 October 1984. The Hegu is the Chinese version of the deleted Komar.
Modernisation: ESM fitted in 1995-96.
Operational: *619* and *617* are reported laid up.

HEGU 609 *3/2000* / 0103740

HEGU 609 *7/1995* / 0050086

6 SHERSHEN CLASS (FAST ATTACK CRAFT—GUN) (PTFM)

751	753	755	757	759	761

Displacement, tons: 145 standard; 170 full load
Dimensions, feet (metres): 113.8 × 22 × 4.9 (34.7 × 6.7 × 1.5)
Main machinery: 3 Type M 503A diesels; 8,025 hp(m) (5.9 MW) sustained; 3 shafts
Speed, knots: 45
Range, n miles: 850 at 30 kt
Complement: 23

Missiles: SAM: SA-N-5 Grail (755—761); manual aiming; IR homing to 6 km (3.2 n miles) at 1.5 Mach; warhead 1.5 kg.
Guns: 4 USSR 30 mm/65 (2 twin); 500 rds/min to 5 km (2.7 n miles); weight of shell 0.54 kg.
2 USSR 122 mm rocket launchers (755—761 in lieu of torpedo tubes); 20 barrels per launcher; range 9 km (5 n miles).
Depth charges: 12.
Countermeasures: ESM: Thomson-CSF DR 875; radar warning.
Radars: Surface search: Pot Drum; H/I-band.
Fire control: Drum Tilt, H/I-band (in some).
IFF: High Pole.

Programmes: Five delivered from USSR in 1967 and two more in 1968. One deleted. 753 completed an extensive refit at Ismailia in 1987; 751 in 1988.
Structure: The last four have had their torpedo tubes removed to make way for multiple BM21 rocket launchers and one SA-N-5 Grail, which are not always carried. Some have Drum Tilt radars removed. The first two have also had their torpedo tubes removed but these may be replaced.
Operational: Based at Alexandria, Port Said and Mersa Matru. All are active.

SHERSHEN 759 *5/2003, A Sharma* / 0552770

8 HAINAN CLASS (FAST ATTACK CRAFT—PATROL) (PC)

AL NOUR 430	AL HADY 433	AL WAKIL 436	AL HAKIM 439
AL SALAM 442	AL JABBAR 445	AL QADER 448	AL RAFA 451

Displacement, tons: 375 standard; 392 full load
Dimensions, feet (metres): 192.8 × 23.6 × 7.2 (58.8 × 7.2 × 2.2)
Main machinery: 4 PRC/Kolomna Type 9-D-8 diesels; 4,000 hp (2.94 MW) sustained; 4 shafts
Speed, knots: 30.5. **Range, n miles:** 1,300 at 15 kt
Complement: 69

Guns: 4 China 57 mm/70 (2 twin); 120 rds/min to 12 km (6.5 n miles); weight of shell 6.31 kg.
4—23 mm (2 twin); locally constructed to fit the 25 mm mountings.
Torpedoes: 6—324 mm (2 triple) tubes (in two of the class). Mk 44 or MUSL Stingray.
A/S mortars: 4 RBU 1200 fixed 5-tubed launchers; range 1,200 m; warhead 34 kg.
Depth charges: 2 projectors; 2 racks. 18 DCs.
Mines: Rails fitted. 12 mines.
Radars: Surface search: Pot Head or Skin Head; I-band.
Navigation: Decca; I-band.
IFF: High Pole.
Sonars: Stag Ear; hull-mounted; active search and attack; high frequency.

Programmes: First pair transferred from China in October 1983, next three in February 1984 (commissioned 21 May 1984) and last three late 1984.
Modernisation: Two fitted with torpedo tubes and with Singer Librascope fire control. No sign of the remainder being similarly equipped. New sonar reported being fitted.
Operational: Based at Alexandria. 436, 439 and 451 reported not operational.

AL SALAM *3/2000* / 0103741

4 SHANGHAI II CLASS (FAST ATTACK CRAFT—GUN) (PB)

793	795	797	799

Displacement, tons: 113 standard; 131 full load
Dimensions, feet (metres): 127.3 × 17.7 × 5.6 (38.8 × 5.4 × 1.7)
Main machinery: 2 Type L12-180 diesels; 2,400 hp(m) (1.76 MW) (forward); 2 Type L12-180Z diesels; 1,820 hp(m) (1.34 MW) (aft); 4 shafts
Speed, knots: 30
Range, n miles: 700 at 16.5 kt
Complement: 34

Guns: 4 China 37 mm/63 (2 twin); 180 rds/min to 8.5 km (4.6 n miles); weight of shell 1.42 kg.
4—23 mm (2 twin); locally constructed to fit the 25 mm mountings.
Mines: Rails can be fitted for 10 mines.
Countermeasures: ESM: Thomson-CSF; radar warning.
Radars: Surface search: Decca; I-band.
IFF: High Pole.

Programmes: Transferred from China in 1984.
Operational: Three based at Suez and one (799) at Mersa Matru. 795 refitted in 1998.

SHANGHAI 797 *6/1997, J W Currie* / 0012295

AMPHIBIOUS FORCES

Notes: (1) Acquisition of LSTs is a high priority.
(2) Ro-Ro ferries are chartered for amphibious exercises.
(3) Rigid Raiders with Johnson outboards are also in service.
(4) Three small hovercraft similar to Slingsby SAH 2200 reported to be in service.

3 POLNOCHNY A (PROJECT 770) CLASS (LSM)

301	303	305

Displacement, tons: 800 full load
Dimensions, feet (metres): 239.5 × 27.9 × 5.8 (73 × 8.5 × 1.8)
Main machinery: 2 Kolomna Type 40-D diesels; 4,400 hp(m) (3.2 MW) sustained; 2 shafts
Speed, knots: 19
Range, n miles: 1,000 at 18 kt
Complement: 40
Military lift: 6 tanks; 350 tons
Guns: 2 USSR 30 mm/65 (twin); 500 rds/min to 5 km (2.7 n miles); weight of shell 0.54 kg.
2—140 mm rocket launchers; 18 barrels to 9 km (4.9 n miles).
Radars: Surface search: Decca; I-band.
Fire control: Drum Tilt; H/I-band.

Comment: Built at Northern Shipyard, Gdansk and transferred from USSR 1973-74. All used for Gulf logistic support in 1990-91. SA-N-5 may be carried. Radar updated. All are active.

POLNOCHNY 303 *10/2000, F Sadek* / 0103742

4 SEAFOX TYPE (SWIMMER DELIVERY CRAFT) (LDW)

21	23	27	30

Displacement, tons: 11.3 full load
Dimensions, feet (metres): 36.1 × 9.8 × 2.6 (11 × 3 × 0.8)
Main machinery: 2 GM 6V-92TA diesels; 520 hp (388 kW) sustained; 2 shafts
Speed, knots: 30
Range, n miles: 200 at 20 kt
Complement: 3
Guns: 2—12.7 mm MGs. 2—7.62 mm MGs.
Radars: Surface search: LN66; I-band.

Comment: Ordered from Uniflite, Washington in 1982. GRP construction painted black. There is a strong underwater team in the Egyptian Navy which is also known to use commercial two-man underwater chariots. Based at Abu Qir and all took part in the 1998 Fleet review. Six others are in various states of repair. RIBs are also in service.

SEAFOX *1999* / 0056917

9 VYDRA CLASS (LCU)

330	332	334	336	338	340	342	344	346

Displacement, tons: 425 standard; 600 full load
Dimensions, feet (metres): 179.7 × 25.3 × 6.6 *(54.8 × 7.7 × 2)*
Main machinery: 2 Type 3-D-12 diesels; 600 hp(m) *(440 kW)* sustained; 2 shafts
Speed, knots: 11. **Range, n miles:** 2,500 at 10 kt
Complement: 20
Military lift: 200 troops; 250 tons.
Guns: 2 or 4—37 mm/63 (1 or 2 twin) (may be fitted).
Radars: Navigation: Decca; I-band.

Comment: Built in late 1960s, transferred from USSR 1968-69. For a period after the Israeli war of October 1973 several were fitted with rocket launchers and two 37 or 40 mm guns, some of which have now been removed. All still in service.

VYDRA 346 *10/2002, F Sadek* / 1044122

MINE WARFARE FORCES

Notes: Procurement of two ex-US Navy Osprey class (*Cardinal* MHC-60 and *Raven* MHC-61) is under consideration.

4 YURKA CLASS (MINESWEEPERS—OCEAN) (MSO)

GIZA 530	ASWAN 533	QENA 536	SOHAG 539

Displacement, tons: 540 full load
Dimensions, feet (metres): 171.9 × 30.8 × 8.5 *(52.4 × 9.4 × 2.6)*
Main machinery: 2 Type M 503 diesels; 5,350 hp(m) *(3.91 MW)* sustained; 2 shafts
Speed, knots: 17. **Range, n miles:** 1,500 at 12 kt
Complement: 45
Guns: 4 USSR 30 mm/65 (2 twin); 500 rds/min to 5 km *(2.7 n miles);* weight of shell 0.54 kg.
Mines: Can lay 10.
Radars: Navigation: Don; I-band.
Sonars: Stag Ear; hull-mounted; active search; high frequency.

Comment: Steel-hulled minesweepers transferred from the USSR in 1969. Built 1963-69. Egyptian Yurka class do not carry Drum Tilt radar and have a number of ship's-side scuttles. The plan to equip them with VDS sonar has been shelved. At least one operates an ROV.

SOHAG *10/2001, F Sadek* / 1044121

2 SWIFTSHIPS TYPE (ROUTE SURVEY VESSELS) (MSI)

Name	No	Builders	Commissioned
SAFAGA	610 (ex-RSV 1)	Swiftships	1 Oct 1994
ABU EL GHOSON	613 (ex-RSV 2)	Swiftships	1 Oct 1994

Displacement, tons: 165 full load
Dimensions, feet (metres): 90 × 24.8 × 8 *(27.4 × 7.6 × 2.4)*
Main machinery: 2 MTU 12V 183 TA61 diesels; 928 hp(m) *(682 kW);* 2 shafts; bow thruster; 60 hp(m) *(44 kW)*
Speed, knots: 12
Range, n miles: 1,500 at 10 kt
Complement: 16 (2 officers)
Guns: 1—12.7 mm MG.
Radars: Navigation: Furuno 2020; I-band.
Sonars: EG & G side scan; active; high frequency.

Comment: Route survey vessels ordered from Swiftships in November 1990 and delivered in September 1993. Two more are planned to be built in Egyptian yards in due course. Unisys improved SYQ-12 command system. Provision for both shallow and deep towed bodies. The names have been taken from the obsolete K 8 class.

SAFAGA *3/2000* / 0103744

3 SWIFTSHIPS TYPE (COASTAL MINEHUNTERS) (MHC)

Name	No	Builders	Launched	Commissioned
DAT ASSAWARI	542 (ex-CMH 1)	Swiftships, Morgan City	4 Oct 1993	13 July 1997
NAVARIN	545 (ex-CMH 2)	Swiftships, Morgan City	13 Nov 1993	13 July 1997
BURULLUS	548 (ex-CMH 3)	Swiftships, Morgan City	4 Dec 1993	13 July 1997

Displacement, tons: 203 full load
Dimensions, feet (metres): 111 × 27 × 8 *(33.8 × 8.2 × 2.3)*
Main machinery: 2 MTU 12V 183 TE61 diesels; 1,068 hp(m) *(786 kW);* 2 Schottel steerable props; 1 White Gill thruster; 300 hp *(224 kW)*
Speed, knots: 12.4. **Range, n miles:** 2,000 at 10 kt
Complement: 25 (5 officers)
Guns: 2—12.7 mm MGs.
Radars: Navigation: Sperry; I-band.
Sonars: Thoray/Thomson Sintra TSM 2022; hull-mounted; active minehunting; high frequency.

Comment: MCM vessels with GRP hulls ordered from Swiftships in December 1990 with FMS funding. First one acceptance trials in June 1994 and completion in August. Fitted with a Unisys command data handling system which is an improved version of SYQ-12. GPS and line of sight navigation system. Dynamic positioning. A side scan sonar body and Gaymarine Pluto ROV can be streamed from a deck crane. Portable decompression chamber carried. Two delivered 29 November 1995 and the third in April 1996. All were finally commissioned after delays caused by problems with the minehunting equipment.

DAT ASSAWARI *3/2000, van Ginderen Collection* / 0088754

3 T 43 CLASS (MINESWEEPERS—OCEAN) (MSO)

DAQAHLIYA 507	SINAI 513	ASSIYUT 516

Displacement, tons: 580 full load
Dimensions, feet (metres): 190.2 × 27.6 × 6.9 *(58 × 8.4 × 2.1)*
Main machinery: 2 Kolomna Type 9-D-8 diesels; 2,000 hp(m) *(1.47 MW)* sustained; 2 shafts
Speed, knots: 15. **Range, n miles:** 3,000 at 10 kt
Complement: 65
Guns: 4—37 mm/63 (2 twin); 160 rds/min to 9 km *(5 n miles);* weight of shell 0.7 kg. 8—12.7 mm (4 twin) MGs.
Mines: Can carry 20.
Radars: Navigation: Don 2; I-band.
Sonars: Stag Ear; hull-mounted; active search; high frequency.

Comment: Delivered in the early 1970s from the USSR. Others of the class have been sunk or used as targets or cannibalised for spares. The plan to fit them with VDS sonars and ROVs has been shelved.

DAQAHLIYA *3/2000* / 0103745

For details of the latest updates to *Jane's Fighting Ships* online and to discover the additional information available exclusively to online subscribers please visit

jfs.janes.com

AUXILIARIES

Notes: (1) There are also two survey launches *Misaha 1* and *2* with a crew of 14. Both were commissioned in 1991.
(2) A small barge *Amira Rama* was donated to the Navy in 1987 and is used as lighthouse tender.
(3) *El Hurreya*, a 6,000 ton transport ship, was launched at Alexandria on 27 January 2004. It was announced in early 2005 that a second ship was to be built. This may be followed by a larger 10,000 ton vessel.

6 TOPLIVO 2 CLASS (TANKERS) (AOTL/AWTL)

ATABARAH 212	**AKDU** 214	**AYEDA 3** 216
MARYUT 218	**AL NIL** 220	**AL FURAT** 224

Displacement, tons: 1,029 full load
Dimensions, feet (metres): 176.2 × 31.8 × 10.5 *(53.7 × 9.7 × 3.2)*
Main machinery: 1 6DR 30/50-5 diesel; 600 hp(m) *(441 kW)*; 1 shaft
Speed, knots: 10
Range, n miles: 400 at 7 kt
Complement: 16
Cargo capacity: 500 tons diesel or water (211–215)
Radars: Navigation: Spin Trough; I-band.

Comment: Built in Alexandria in 1972-77 to a USSR design. Another of the class 217 is laid up.

ATABARAH   *6/1999* / 0080651

1 LÜNEBURG CLASS (TYPE 701) (SUPPORT SHIP) (ARL)

Name	*No*	*Builders*	*Commissioned*
SHALADEIN (ex-*Glücksburg*)	230 (ex-A 1414)	Bremer Vulkan/Flensburger Schiffbau	9 July 1968

Displacement, tons: 3,709 full load
Dimensions, feet (metres): 374.9 × 43.3 × 13.8 *(114.3 × 13.2 × 4.2)*
Main machinery: 2 MTU MD 16V 538 TB90 diesels; 6,000 hp(m) *(4.1 MW)* sustained; 2 shafts; cp props; bow thruster
Speed, knots: 17
Range, n miles: 3,200 at 14 kt
Complement: 71 (9 officers)
Cargo capacity: 1,100 tons
Guns: 4 Bofors 40 mm/70 (2 twin).
Countermeasures: Decoys: 2 Breda 105 mm SCLAR chaff launchers.

Comment: Transferred from Germany in early 2003 to act as support ship, including missile maintenance, of Type 148 patrol craft.

SHALADEIN   *4/2003, Frank Findler* / 0552746

1 WESTERWALD CLASS (TYPE 760) (AMMUNITION TRANSPORT) (AEL)

Name	*No*	*Builders*	*Commissioned*
HALAIB (ex-*Odenwald*)	231 (ex-A 1436)	Orenstein and Koppel, Lübeck	23 Mar 1967

Displacement, tons: 3,460 standard; 4,042 full load
Dimensions, feet (metres): 344.4 × 46 × 15.1 *(105 × 14 × 4.6)*
Main machinery: 2 MTU MD 16V 538 TB90 diesels; 6,000 hp(m) *(4.1 MW)* sustained; 2 shafts; cp props; bow thruster
Speed, knots: 17
Range, n miles: 3,500 at 17 kt
Complement: 31
Cargo capacity: 1,080 tons ammunition
Guns: 2 Bofors 40 mm.
Radars: Navigation: Kelvin Hughes; I-band.

Comment: Transferred from Germany in early 2003.

HALAIB   *4/2003, Frank Findler* / 0552745

1 POLUCHAT 1 CLASS (YPT)

P 937

Displacement, tons: 100 full load
Dimensions, feet (metres): 97.1 × 19 × 4.8 *(29.6 × 5.8 × 1.5)*
Main machinery: 2 Type M 50 diesels; 2,200 hp(m) *(1.6 MW)* sustained; 2 shafts
Speed, knots: 20
Range, n miles: 1,500 at 10 kt
Complement: 15
Radars: Surface search: Spin Trough; I-band.

Comment: Used as Torpedo Recovery Vessel. Unarmed.

POLUCHAT   *3/2000* / 0103779

2 NYRYAT I (PROJECT 522) CLASS (DIVING TENDERS) (YDT)

P 001	P 002

Displacement, tons: 116 full load
Dimensions, feet (metres): 93.8 × 17.1 × 5.6 *(28.6 × 5.2 × 1.7)*
Main machinery: 1 diesel; 450 hp(m) *(331 kW)* sustained; 1 shaft
Speed, knots: 12.5
Range, n miles: 1,500 at 10 kt
Complement: 15
Radars: Surface search: Spin Trough; I-band.

Comment: Transferred in 1964.

TRAINING SHIPS

Notes: *Al Kousser* P 91 is a 1,000 ton vessel belonging to the Naval Academy. *Intishat* is a 500 ton training ship. Pennant number 160 is a USSR Sekstan class used as a cadet training ship. Two YSB training craft acquired from the US in 1989. A 3,300 ton training ship *Aida IV* presented by Japan in 1988 for delivery in March 1992 belongs to the Arab Maritime Transport Academy.

1 PRESIDENTIAL YACHT (YAC/AX)

Name	*Builders*	*Commissioned*
EL HORRIYA (ex-*Mahroussa*)	Samuda, Poplar	1865

Displacement, tons: 4,560 full load
Dimensions, feet (metres): 479 × 42.6 × 17.4 *(146 × 13 × 5.3)*
Main machinery: 3 boilers; 3 turbines; 5,500 hp *(4.1 MW)*; 3 shafts
Speed, knots: 16
Complement: 160

Comment: Became a museum in 1987 but was reactivated in 1992. Used as a training ship as well as a Presidential Yacht.

EL HORRIYA   *3/2000, van Ginderen Collection* / 0103782

1 Z CLASS (AXT)

Name	No	Builders	Laid down	Launched	Commissioned
EL FATEH (ex-*Zenith*, ex-*Wessex*)	921	Wm Denny & Bros, Dumbarton	19 May 1942	5 June 1944	22 Dec 1944

Displacement, tons: 1,730 standard; 2,575 full load
Dimensions, feet (metres): 362.8 × 35.7 × 16
  (110.6 × 10.9 × 4.9)
Main machinery: 2 Admiralty boilers; 2 Parsons turbines;
  40,000 hp *(30 MW)*; 2 shafts
Speed, knots: 24. **Range, n miles:** 2,800 at 20 kt
Complement: 186

Missiles: SAM: 2 SA-N-5 mountings.
Guns: 4 Vickers 4.5 in *(115 mm)*/45 hand-loaded Mk 5
  mounting; 50° elevation; 14 rds/min to 17 km
  (9.3 n miles); weight of shell 25 kg.

8 China 37 mm/63 (4 twin); 180 rds/min to 8.5 km
  (4.6 n miles); weight of shell 1.42 kg.
2 Bofors 40 mm/60 (twin).
Torpedoes: 8—21 in *(533 mm)* (2 quad) tubes.
Depth charges: 4 projectors.
Weapons control: Fly 4 director.
Radars: Air/surface search: Marconi SNW 10; D-band.
Navigation: Racal Decca 916; I-band.
Fire control: Marconi Type 275; F-band.

Programmes: Purchased from the UK in 1955.

Modernisation: Bofors replaced by Chinese 37 mm guns.
  Sonars removed. Boilers renewed in 1993 and SA-N-5
  mountings fitted.
Operational: Used primarily for harbour training, and the
  intention is to keep the ship in service. Last seen at sea
  in 1994. The last survivor of its class, the ship may be
  preserved as a museum.

EL FATEH   *4/1994, van Ginderen Collection* / 0017808

1 BLACK SWAN CLASS (AXT)

Name	No	Builders	Laid down	Launched	Commissioned
TARIQ (ex-*Malek Farouk*, ex-*Whimbrel*)	931	Yarrows, Glasgow	31 Oct 1941	25 Aug 1941	13 Jan 1943

Displacement, tons: 1,925 full load
Dimensions, feet (metres): 299 × 38.5 × 11.5
  (81.2 × 11.7 × 3.5)
Main machinery: 2 Admiralty boilers; 2 Parsons geared
  turbines; 3,600 hp *(2.69 MW)*; 2 shafts
Speed, knots: 18
Complement: 180

Guns: 6 Vickers 4 in *(102 mm)*/45 (3 twin) Mk 19; 16 rds/min
  to 19.5 km *(10.5 n miles)*; weight of shell 15.9 kg.
  4—37 mm (2 twin). 4—12.7 mm MGs.
Depth charges: 4 projectors; 2 racks.
Radars: Surface search: 2 Decca; I-band.

Programmes: Transferred from UK in November 1949.
Structure: Still has the original class appearance with some
  minor modifications to the armament.
Operational: Relegated for a time in the mid-1980s
  to an accommodation ship and offered as part of a
  deal involving the acquisition of two Oberon class
  submarines in 1989. When this project was cancelled,
  the ship resumed service as a training platform and
  was described as 'running like a train' in 1993. Since
  then there has been limited activity but the ship was
  reported at sea again in late 1997. Although seagoing
  days are probably over, the ship still has a limited
  training role. A project to return the ship to Liverpool as a
  museum ship was boosted when, following a survey, the
  ship was declared to be in a sound condition in October
  2005.

TARIQ *3/2000*
0103738

TUGS

Notes: (1) There are also four Coast Guard harbour tugs built by Damen in 1982. Names *Khoufou*, *Khafra*, *Ramses* and *Kreir*. Two other harbour tugs were delivered in 1998. Names *Ajmi* and *Jihad*.
(2) Two former oilfield supply vessels 113 and 115 are probably employed as tugs. They are also fitted with firefighting equipment.
(3) A large Chinese built tug *El Alamein* is reported to be in service.

115
3/2004, Bob Fildes
1044120

5 OKHTENSKY CLASS (ATA)

AL MAKS 103	**AL ANTAR** 107	**AL ISKANDARANI** 111
AL AGAMI 105	**AL DEKHEILA** 109	

Displacement, tons: 930 full load
Dimensions, feet (metres): 156.1 × 34 × 13.4 *(47.6 × 10.4 × 4.1)*
Main machinery: Diesel-electric; 2 BM diesel generators; 1 motor; 1,500 hp(m) *(1.1 MW)*;
   1 shaft
Speed, knots: 13. **Range, n miles:** 6,000 at 13 kt
Complement: 38

Comment: Two transferred from USSR in 1966, others assembled at Alexandria.
   Replacements are needed. 113 may have been deleted.

AL AGAMI   *3/2000, M Declerck* / 0103780

COAST GUARD

Notes: (1) The Coast Guard is controlled by the Navy.
(2) There are four obsolete P 6 craft; pennant numbers 222, 246, 253 and 201.
(3) There is also a minimum of four ex-USN Bollinger type harbour security craft of
3.9 tons capable of 22 kt. Twin diesel engines. Carry a 7.62 mm MG.
(4) There is an unknown number of RIBs for inshore patrols.

9 TYPE 83 CLASS (LARGE PATROL CRAFT) (WPB)

46-54

Displacement, tons: 85 full load
Dimensions, feet (metres): 83.7 × 21.3 × 5.6 *(25.5 × 6.5 × 1.7)*
Main machinery: 2 diesels; 2 shafts
Speed, knots: 24
Complement: 12
Guns: 4—23 mm (2 twin). 1 Oerlikon 20 mm.
Radars: Surface search: Furuno; I-band.

Comment: Two of this class commissioned 13 July 1997. Built locally, these craft are similar
   to the Swiftships 93 ft class. Numbers uncertain but at least three are operational.

TYPE 83 CLASS   *10/1995* / 0056923

21 TIMSAH CLASS (LARGE PATROL CRAFT) (WPB)

01-02   04-22

Displacement, tons: 106 full load
Dimensions, feet (metres): 101.8 × 17 × 4.8 *(30.5 × 5.2 × 1.5)*
Main machinery: 2 MTU 8V 331TC92 diesels; 1,770 hp *(1.3 MW)* sustained; 2 shafts *(01—06)*;
   2 MTU 12V 331TC92 diesels; 2,660 hp(m) *(1.96 MW)* sustained; 2 shafts *(07—19)*
Speed, knots: 25
Range, n miles: 600 at 18 kt
Complement: 13
Guns: 2 Oerlikon 30 mm (twin) or 2 14.5 mm MGs.
Radars: Surface search: Racal Decca; I-band.

Comment: First three Timsah I completed December 1981, second three Timsah I December
   1982 at Timsah SY, Ismailia. These all have funnels but there appear to be minor structural
   differences. *03* sunk in late 1993. Further six Timsah II ordered in January 1985 and
   completed in 1988-89 with a different type of engine and with waterline exhaust vice a
   funnel. Last of this batch in service in 1992, followed by ten more by 1999.

TIMSAH 17   *4/2002, A Sharma* / 0528333

TIMSAH 02 (with funnel)   *6/1995, Ships of the World* / 0056922

TIMSAH 19   *4/2005*, Queun/Marsan* / 1151174

9 SWIFTSHIPS 93 ft CLASS (LARGE PATROL CRAFT) (WPB)

35-43

Displacement, tons: 102 full load
Dimensions, feet (metres): 93.2 × 18.7 × 4.9 *(28.4 × 5.7 × 1.5)*
Main machinery: 2 MTU 12V 331 TC92 diesels; 2,660 hp(m) *(1.96 MW)* sustained; 2 shafts
Speed, knots: 27. **Range, n miles:** 900 at 12 kt
Complement: 14 (2 officers)
Guns: 4—23 mm (2 twin); 1 Oerlikon 20 mm or 2—14.5 mm MG.
Radars: Surface search: Furuno; I-band.

Comment: Ordered November 1983. First three built in US, remainder assembled by
   Osman Shipyard, Ismailia. First four commissioned 16 April 1985, five more in 1986.
   Armament upgraded with 23 mm guns fitted forward in some of the class.

SWIFTSHIPS 343   *2/2003, A Sharma* / 0569931

6 CRESTITALIA MV 70 CLASS
(COASTAL PATROL CRAFT) (WPBF)

Displacement, tons: 36 full load
Dimensions, feet (metres): 68.9 × 17.4 × 3 *(21 × 5.3 × 0.9)*
Main machinery: 2 MTU 12V 331 TC92 diesels; 2,660 hp(m) *(1.96 MW)* sustained; 2 shafts
Speed, knots: 35. **Range, n miles:** 500 at 32 kt
Complement: 10 (1 officer)
Guns: 2 Oerlikon 30 mm A32 (twin). 1 Oerlikon 20 mm.
Radars: Surface search: Racal Decca; I-band.

Comment: Ordered 1980-GRP hulls. Naval manned but still employed on Coast Guard
   duties.

CRESTITALIA 70 ft   *1980, Crestitalia* / 0505986

12 SEA SPECTRE PB MK III CLASS
(COASTAL PATROL CRAFT) (WPB)

Displacement, tons: 37 full load
Dimensions, feet (metres): 64.9 × 18 × 5.9 *(19.8 × 5.5 × 1.8)*
Main machinery: 3 GM 8V-71TI diesels; 1,800 hp *(1.3 MW)*; 3 shafts
Speed, knots: 29
Range, n miles: 450 at 25 kt
Complement: 9 (1 officer)
Guns: 2 – 12.7 mm MGs.
Radars: Surface search: Raytheon; I-band.

Comment: PB Mk III type built by Peterson, Sturgeon Bay and delivered in 1980-81. Used for Customs duties.

SPECTRE   *1981, Peterson Builders* / 0056924

9 PETERSON TYPE (COASTAL PATROL CRAFT) (WPB)

71-79

Displacement, tons: 18 full load
Dimensions, feet (metres): 45.6 × 13 × 3 *(13.9 × 4 × 0.9)*
Main machinery: 2 MTU 8V 183 TE92 diesels; 1,314 hp(m) *(966 kW)* sustained; Hamilton 362 water-jets
Speed, knots: 34
Range, n miles: 200 at 30 kt
Complement: 4
Guns: 2 – 12.7 mm MGs.
Radars: Surface search: Raytheon; I-band.

Comment: Built by Peterson Shipbuilders, Sturgeon Bay and delivered between June and October 1994 under FMS. Replaced Bertram type and used as pilot boats.

PETERSON 72 (US colours)   *6/1994, PBI* / 0056925

5 NISR CLASS (LARGE PATROL CRAFT) (WPB)

THAR 701   **NUR** 703   **NISR** 713   **NIMR** 719   **AL BAHR**

Displacement, tons: 110 full load
Dimensions, feet (metres): 102 × 18 × 4.9 *(31 × 5.2 × 1.5)*
Main machinery: 2 Maybach diesels; 3,000 hp(m) *(2.2 MW)*; 2 shafts
Speed, knots: 24
Complement: 15
Guns: 2 or 4 – 23 mm (twin). 1 BM 21 122 mm 8-barrelled rocket launcher.
Radars: Surface search: Racal Decca 1230; I-band.

Comment: Built by Castro, Port Said on P6 hulls. First three launched in May 1963. Two more completed 1983. The rocket launcher and after 23 mm guns are interchangeable. 701 and 703 were refitted in 1998. Naval manned but employed on Coast Guard duties.

3 PETERSON TYPE (COASTAL PATROL CRAFT) (WPBF)

80-82

Displacement, tons: 20 full load
Dimensions, feet (metres): 51 × 12 × 3 *(15.5 × 3.7 × 0.9)*
Main machinery: 2 MTU diesels; 2,266 hp(m) *(1.66 MW)*; Hamilton 391 water-jets
Speed, knots: 45
Range, n miles: 320 at 30 kt
Complement: 5
Guns: 2 – 12.7 mm MGs.
Radars: Surface search: Raytheon; I-band.

Comment: Built by Peterson Shipbuilders, Sturgeon Bay and delivered between October and December 1996 under FMS. Aluminium construction. Used mostly as pilot boats.

PETERSON 81   *3/2000* / 0103781

29 DC 35 TYPE (YFL)

Displacement, tons: 4 full load
Dimensions, feet (metres): 35.1 × 11.5 × 2.6 *(10.7 × 3.5 × 0.8)*
Main machinery: 2 Perkins T6-354 diesels; 390 hp *(287 kW)*; 2 shafts
Speed, knots: 25
Complement: 4

Comment: Built by Dawncraft, Wroxham, UK, from 1977. Harbour launches. One destroyed in September 1994. About half are laid up at Port Said.

DC 35   *8/1994, F Sadek* / 0056927

1 + 5 (24) SWIFTSHIPS PROTECTOR CLASS
(LARGE PATROL CRAFT) (WPB)

90

Displacement, tons: 116 full load
Dimensions, feet (metres): 85.0 × 20.0 × 4.9 *(26.1 × 6.1 × 1.5)*
Main machinery: 2 Caterpillar 3512B diesels; 2 Hamilton HM651 propulsors
Speed, knots: 40
Complement: 12
Radars: Navigation: I-band.

Comment: Contract awarded in September 2004 to Swiftships, Morgan City, LA, for the construction of six patrol craft under the US government's Foreign Military Sales programme. The contract includes a training package. With an aluminium hull and superstructure and a high-speed RIB launching well, the craft are designed for SAR, law enforcement, and local patrol operations. Details of weapons and sensors have not been confirmed but up to a 30 mm gun with associated fire-control system may be fitted. A FLIR system may also be installed. Delivery of the first craft is to be made in June 2006 and thereafter at two-month intervals until April 2007. A further 24 craft may be procured.

PROTECTOR 90   *1/2006** / 1041657

El Salvador
FUERZA NAVAL DE EL SALVADOR

Country Overview

The Republic of El Salvador is an independent Central American State whose current constitution was established in 1983. With an area of 8,124 square miles, it has a 166 n mile coastline with the Pacific Ocean and is bounded to the north by Honduras and to the west by Guatemala. The country's capital is San Salvador while Acajutla, La Libertad and La Unión are the principal ports. El Salvador has not claimed an Exclusive Economic Zone (EEZ) but is one of a few coastal states which claims a 200 n mile territorial sea.

Senior Officer

Commander of the Navy:
  General Carlos Eduardo Cáceres Flores

Personnel

(a)   2006: 877 (including 133 naval infantry)
(b)   Voluntary service

Bases

Acajutla, La Libertad, El Triunfo y La Union

Air Bases

El Tamarindo Air Station is reported to have been improved to enable the Third Air Brigade to provide air support to naval patrols. The US may donate fixed-wing aircraft and helicopters to assist in this task.

PATROL FORCES

Notes: There are two high-speed RHIBs donated by Taiwan and US.

1 POINT CLASS (PB)

Name	*Builders*	*Commissioned*
PM 12 (ex-GC 12, ex-82358)	J Martinac, Tacoma	17 Mar 1967

Displacement, tons: 67 full load
Dimensions, feet (metres): 83 × 17.2 × 5.8 *(25.3 × 5.2 × 1.8)*
Main machinery: 2 Caterpillar diesels; 1,600 hp *(1.19 MW)*; 2 shafts
Speed, knots: 22
Range, n miles: 1,200 at 8 kt
Complement: 10
Guns: 2—12.7 mm MGs.
Radars: Surface search: Hughes/Furuno SPS-73; I-band.

Comment: Ex-*Point Stuart* transferred from US Coast Guard on 27 April 2001.

PM 12   *11/2001, Julio Montes* / 0130481

3 CAMCRAFT TYPE (COASTAL PATROL CRAFT) (PB)

PM 6-8 (ex-CG 6-8)

Displacement, tons: 100 full load
Dimensions, feet (metres): 100 × 21 × 4.9 *(30.5 × 6.4 × 1.5)*
Main machinery: 3 Detroit 12V-71TA diesels; 1,260 hp *(939 kW)* sustained; 3 shafts
Speed, knots: 25
Range, n miles: 780 at 24 kt
Complement: 10
Guns: 1—20 mm Oerlikon or 1—12.7 mm MG. 2—7.62 mm MGs. 1—81 mm mortar.
Radars: Surface search: Furuno; I-band.

Comment: Aluminium hulled. Delivered 24 October, 8 November and 3 December 1975. Refitted in 1986 at Lantana Boatyard. Sometimes carry a combined 12.7 mm MG/81 mm mortar mounting in the stern. New radars fitted in 1995. Difficult to maintain and may be replaced by ASMAR Protector class.

PM 6 (old number)   *6/2000, Julio Montes* / 0103783

1 SWIFTSHIPS 77 ft CLASS (COASTAL PATROL CRAFT) (PB)

PM 11 (ex-GC 11)

Displacement, tons: 48 full load
Dimensions, feet (metres): 77.1 × 20 × 4.9 *(23.5 × 6.1 × 1.5)*
Main machinery: 3 Detroit 12V-71TA diesels; 1,260 hp *(939 kW)* sustained; 3 shafts
Speed, knots: 26
Complement: 7
Guns: 2—12.7 mm MGs. Aft MG combined with 81 mm mortar.
Radars: Surface search: Furuno; I-band.

Comment: Aluminium hull. Delivered by Swiftships, Morgan City 6 May 1985.

PM 11 (old number)   *9/2000, Von Santos* / 0103784

1 SWIFTSHIPS 65 ft CLASS (COASTAL PATROL CRAFT) (PB)

PM 10 (ex-GC 10)

Displacement, tons: 36 full load
Dimensions, feet (metres): 65.6 × 18.3 × 5 *(20 × 6 × 1.5)*
Main machinery: 2 Detroit 12V-71TA diesels; 840 hp *(626 kW)* sustained; 2 shafts
Speed, knots: 23. **Range, n miles:** 600 at 18 kt
Complement: 6
Guns: 1 Oerlikon 20 mm. 1 or 2—12.7 mm MGs. 1—81 mm mortar.
Radars: Surface search: Furuno; I-band.

Comment: Aluminium hull. Delivered by Swiftships, Morgan City 14 June 1984. Was laid up for a time in 1989-90 but became operational again in 1991. Refitted in 1996.

PM 10   *6/2003, El Salvador Navy* / 0568340

4 TYPE 44 CLASS (PBI)

PRM 01-04

Displacement, tons: 18 full load
Dimensions, feet (metres): 44 × 12.8 × 3.6 *(13.5 × 3.9 × 1.1)*
Main machinery: 2 Detroit 6V-38 diesels; 185 hp *(136 kW)*; 2 shafts
Speed, knots: 14. **Range, n miles:** 215 at 10 kt
Complement: 3

Comment: Ex-USCG craft similar to those transferred to Uruguay.

PRM 04 *11/2001, Julio Montes* / 0130482

6 PIRANHA CLASS (RIVER PATROL CRAFT) (PBR)

PF 01-06 (ex-LOF 021-26) series

Displacement, tons: 8.2 full load
Dimensions, feet (metres): 36 × 10.1 × 1.6 *(11 × 3.1 × 0.5)*
Main machinery: 2 Caterpillar 3208TA diesels; 680 hp *(507 kW)* sustained; 2 shafts
Speed, knots: 26
Complement: 5
Guns: 2 — 12.7 mm (twin) MGs. 2 — 7.62 mm (twin) MGs.
Radars: Surface search: Furuno 3600; I-band.

Comment: Riverine craft with Kevlar hulls used by the Naval Infantry. Completed in March 1987 by Lantana Boatyard, Florida. Same type supplied to Honduras. Five craft reported operational.

PF 06 *6/2003, El Salvador Navy* / 0568339

9 PROTECTOR CLASS (RIVER PATROL CRAFT) (PBR)

PC 01-09

Displacement, tons: 9 full load
Dimensions, feet (metres): 40.4 × 13.4 × 1.4 *(12.3 × 4 × 0.4)*
Main machinery: 2 Caterpillar 3208TA diesels; 680 hp *(507 kW)* sustained; 2 shafts
Speed, knots: 28. **Range, n miles:** 350 at 20 kt
Complement: 4
Guns: 2 — 12.7 mm MGs. 2 — 7.62 mm MGs.
Radars: Surface search: Furuno 3600; I-band.

Comment: Ordered in December 1987 from SeaArk Marine (ex-MonArk). Four delivered in December 1988 and four in February and March 1989. Eight reported operational and one in maintenance.

PC 09 *11/2001, Julio Montes* / 0130483

8 AIR PATROL BOATS (PBI)

PFR 01-08

Comment: Purchased in Miami for SAR on inland waters.

PFR 05 *6/2003, El Salvador Navy* / 0568338

2 MERCOUGAR INTERCEPT CRAFT (PBR)

PA 01-02

Comment: Two remaining of five 40 ft craft delivered by Mercougar in 1988. Powered by two Ford Merlin diesels; 600 hp *(448 kW)* giving speeds of up to 40 kt and range of 556 km *(300 n miles)*. Radar fitted.

PA 02 *5/2001, Julio Montes* / 0109938

1 BALSAM CLASS (AGP)

Name	No	Builders	Commissioned
MANUEL JOSÉ ARCE (ex-*Madrona*)	BL 01 (ex-WLB 302)	Zenith Dredge, Duluth, MN	30 May 1943

Displacement, tons: 1,034 full load
Dimensions, feet (metres): 180 × 37 × 12 *(54.9 × 11.3 × 3.8)*
Main machinery: Diesel electric; 2 diesels; 1,402 hp *(1.06 MW)*; 1 motor; 1,200 hp *(895 kW)*; 1 shaft; bow thruster
Speed, knots: 13
Range, n miles: 8,000 at 12 kt
Complement: 53
Guns: 2 — 12.7 mm MGs.
Radars: Navigation: Raytheon SPS-64(V)1.

Comment: Transferred from the US Coast Guard on 14 June 2002. Used as a mother ship for coastal patrol craft.

ARCE *6/2003, El Salvador Navy* / 0568337

POLICE

Notes: Ten jet-skis are reported to have been delivered in 2002 for SAR.

20 RODMAN 890 (PBR)

L-01-01 to 01-20

Displacement, tons: 3.1 full load
Dimensions, feet (metres): 29.2 × 9.8 × 3.6 *(8.9 × 3 × 0.8)*
Main machinery: 2 Volvo diesels; 300 hp(m) *(220 kW)*; 2 shafts
Speed, knots: 28. **Range, n miles:** 150 at 25 kt
Complement: 3
Guns: 1—7.62 mm MG.
Radars: Surface search: I-band.

Comment: Eleven craft delivered by Rodman in 1998. Operational availability is reported to be constrained by lack of spares.

RODMAN 890   *6/1998, Rodman* / 0576109

AUXILIARIES

3 LCM 8 CLASS

BD 02 (ex-LD 02)   **BD 04-05** (ex-LD 04-05)

Displacement, tons: 45 full load
Dimensions, feet (metres): 64.7 × 14 × 5 *(21.5 × 4.6 × 1.6)*
Main machinery: 2 Detroit 12V 71TA diesels; 840 hp *(626 kW)* sustained; 2 shafts
Speed, knots: 15
Complement: 6
Guns: 2—12.7 mm MGs. 2—7.62 mm MGs.
Radars: Navigation: Furuno; I-band.

Comment: First one delivered by SeaArk Marine in January 1987, second pair in May 1996.

BD 04   *6/2003, El Salvador Navy* / 0568336

Equatorial Guinea

Country Overview

The Republic of Equatorial Guinea became independent in 1968 as a federation of the two former Spanish provinces of Fernando Po and Río Muni. It became a unitary state in 1973. Located in west Africa, the country has an overall area of 10,831 square miles and includes a mainland section which is bordered to the north by Cameroon and to the east and south by Gabon. It has a 160 n mile coastline with the Gulf of Guinea in which lie the islands of Bioko (formerly Fernando Po), Annobón, Corisco, Elobey Grande and Elobey Chico. The administrative capital on the mainland is Bata while Malabo, on the north coast of Bioko, is capital of the republic, largest city and prinicpal port. Territorial waters (12 n miles) are claimed. A 200 n mile Exclusive Economic Zone (EEZ) has been claimed but the boundaries have not been agreed.

Personnel

2006: 120 officers and men

Bases

Malabo, Bata.

PATROL FORCES

Notes: (1) The Lantana 68 class *Isla de Bioko* and 20 m patrol craft *Riowele* are believed to be non-operational.
(2) Two patrol craft of unknown type were reportedly delivered from Israel in mid-2005.

1 DAPHNE CLASS (PB)

Name	No	Builders	Commissioned
URECA (ex-*Nymfen*)	P 31 (ex-P 535)	Royal Dockyard, Copenhagen	4 Oct 1963

Displacement, tons: 170 full load
Dimensions, feet (metres): 121 × 20 × 6.5 *(36.9 × 6.1 × 2.0)*
Main machinery: 3 diesels; 3 shafts
Speed, knots: 20
Complement: 23
Guns: 2—14.5 mm.
Radars: Navigation: Furuno; I-band.

Comment: Acquired in 1999.

2 ZHUK (GRIF) CLASS (PROJECT 1400M) (PB)

MIGUEL ELA EDJODJOMO LP 039   **HIPOLITO MICHA** LP 041

Displacement, tons: 39 full load
Dimensions, feet (metres): 78.7 × 16.4 × 3.9 *(24 × 5 × 1.2)*
Main machinery: 2 diesels; 2 shafts
Speed, knots: 30
Range, n miles: 1,100 at 15 kt
Complement: 13 (1 officer)
Guns: 2—14.5 mm (twin, fwd) MGs. 1—12.7 mm (aft) MG.
Radars: Surface search: Furuno; I-band.

Comment: Reported to have been transferred from Ukraine in 2000.

2 KALKAN (PROJECT 50030) M CLASS (INSHORE PATROL CRAFT) (PBR)

GASPAR OBIANG ESONO LP 043   **FERNANDO NUARA ENGONDA** LP 045

Displacement, tons: 8.5 full load
Dimensions, feet (metres): 38.1 × 10.8 × 2.0 *(11.6 × 3.3 × 0.6)*
Main machinery: 1 Type 475K diesel; 496 hp *(370 kW)*; 1 waterjet
Speed, knots: 34
Complement: 2

Comment: Built by Morye Feodosiya and reportedly acquired in 2001.

KALKAN CLASS   *6/2003, Morye* / 0572655

Eritrea

Country Overview

A British protectorate from 1941, The State of Eritrea was federated with Ethiopia in 1952 and incorporated as a province in 1962. The following war of liberation culminated in independence in 1993. The country is situated on the southwest shore of the Red Sea with which it has a 621 n mile coastline with an area of 46,842 square miles, it is bordered to the north by Sudan, to the west by Ethiopia and to the south by Djibouti. The largest town and capital is Asmara and the principal port is Massawa. There are no claims to maritime jurisdiction over territorial seas or Exclusive Economic Zone (EEZ).

All vessels of the former Ethiopian Navy were put up for sale at Djibouti from 16 September 1996. All were either taken over by Eritrea, sold to civilian firms or scrapped.

Headquarters Appointments

Commander Eritrean Navy:
   Major General Romedan Awliai
Chief of Staff:
   Fitsum Gebrehiwet

Personnel

2006: 1,100 including 500 conscripts

Bases

Massawa, Dahlak.

PATROL FORCES

Notes: There are also about 50 rigid raiding craft.

1 OSA II (PROJECT 205) CLASS
(FAST ATTACK CRAFT—MISSILE) (PTFG)

FMB 161

Displacement, tons: 245 full load
Dimensions, feet (metres): 126.6 × 24.9 × 8.8 *(38.6 × 7.6 × 2.7)*
Main machinery: 3 Type M 504 diesels; 10,800 hp(m) *(7.94 MW)* sustained; 3 shafts
Speed, knots: 37. **Range, n miles:** 800 at 30 kt
Complement: 30

Missiles: SSM: 4 SS-N-2B Styx; active radar or IR homing to 46 km *(25 n miles)* at 0.9 Mach; warhead 513 kg.
Guns: 4—30 mm/65 (2 twin); 500 rds/min to 5 km *(2.7 n miles)* anti-aircraft; weight of shell 0.54 kg.
Radars: Surface search: Square Tie; I-band.
Fire control: Drum Tilt; H/I-band.
IFF: Square Head. High Pole B.

Programmes: Acquired from USSR on 13 January 1981. The rest of the class has been sunk or scuttled. *FMB 161* was refitted from October 1994 to January 1995 and taken over by Eritrea in 1997. A second of class *FMB 163* was acquired for spares. New missiles were reported to have been ordered in 2002 but operational status is doubtful.

FMB 161 *1/1998* / 0017824

4 SUPER DVORA CLASS (FAST ATTACK CRAFT—GUN) (PTF)

P 101   **P 102**   **P 103**   **P 104**

Displacement, tons: 58 full load
Dimensions, feet (metres): 82 × 18.7 × 3 *(25 × 5.7 × 0.9)*
Main machinery: 2 MTU 8V 396 TE 94 diesels; 3,046 hp(m) *(2.24 MW)*; 2 shafts; ASD 14 surface drives
Speed, knots: 40. **Range, n miles:** 1,200 at 17 kt
Complement: 10 (1 officer)
Guns: 2—23 mm (twin). 2—12 mm MGs.
Depth charges: 1 rail.
Weapons control: Optronic sight.
Radars: Surface search: Raytheon; I-band.

Comment: Built by Israel Aircraft Industries and delivered from July 1993 to a modified Super Dvora design. The original order may have been for six of the class. All are based at Massawa and all are active.

SUPER DVORA P 104 *6/2000, Eritrean Navy* / 0103787

1 SWIFTSHIPS 65 ft CLASS (COASTAL PATROL CRAFT) (PB)

P 151   **P 152**   **P 153**

Displacement, tons: 118 full load
Dimensions, feet (metres): 105 × 23.6 × 6.5 *(32 × 7.2 × 2)*
Main machinery: 2 MTU MD 16V 538TB90 diesels; 6,000 hp(m) *(4.41 MW)* sustained; 2 shafts
Speed, knots: 30. **Range, n miles:** 1,200 at 18 kt
Complement: 21
Guns: 4 Emerlec 30 mm (2 twin) *(P 151)*; 600 rds/min to 6 km *(3.3 n miles)*; weight of shell 0.35 kg.
4—23 mm/60 (2 twin) *(P 152/153)*. 2—12.7 mm (twin).
Radars: Surface search: Decca RM 916; I-band.

Comment: Six ordered in 1976 of which four were delivered in April 1977 before the cessation of US arms sales to Ethiopia. Built by Swiftships, Louisiana. One deserted to Somalia and served in that Navy for a time. Based at Massawa and in reasonable condition. All are active.

P 153 *1/1998* / 0017825

5 BATTALION 17 (PBF)

P 084   **P 085**   **P 086**   **P 087**   **P 088**

Displacement, tons: 35.5 full load
Dimensions, feet (metres): 55.9 × 17 × 5.2 *(17.05 × 5.2 × 1.6)*
Main machinery: 2 MTU 12V 183 TE 92 diesels
Speed, knots: 35.2
Range, n miles: 680 at 30 kt
Complement: 8
Guns: 2—14.5 mm MGs (1 twin).
Radars: Surface search: Raytheon; I-band.

Comment: Built by Harena Boat Yard at Assab, Eritrea. Five craft delivered in 2000 with possible further orders since then.

P 086 *6/2000, Eritrean Navy* / 0103788

AMPHIBIOUS FORCES

Notes: Two obsolete ex-USSR T4 LCUs (LST-63 and 64) are in harbour service at Massawa.

1 ASHDOD CLASS (LST)

P 63 (ex-302)

Displacement, tons: 400 standard; 730 full load
Dimensions, feet (metres): 205.5 × 32.8 × 5.8 *(62.7 × 10 × 1.8)*
Main machinery: 3 MWM diesels; 1,900 hp(m) *(1.4 MW)*; 3 shafts
Speed, knots: 10.5
Complement: 20
Guns: 2—23 mm (1 twin). 2—12.7 mm MGs.

Comment: Former Ethiopian commercial LST acquired from Israel in 1993, taken over by Eritrea in 1997 and subsequently transferred to the Navy. Reported operational.

P 63 (Israeli pennant number) *1995, Eritrean Navy* / 0103789

1 CHAMO CLASS (LST)

DENDEN 301

Displacement, tons: 884 full load
Dimensions, feet (metres): 197.5 × 39.3 × 4.7 *(60.2 × 12 × 1.44)*
Main machinery: 2 MTU 6V 396TB 63; 1,350 hp(m) *(1 MW)*; 2 shafts
Speed, knots: 10
Complement: 23
Guns: 2—23 mm (1 twin); 2—12.7 mm MGs.

Comment: German built former Ethiopian commercial LST taken over by Eritrea in 1997 and subsequently transferred to the Navy. Reported operational.

Estonia
EESTI MEREVÄGI

Country Overview

The Republic of Estonia regained independence in 1991 after 51 years as a Soviet republic. Situated in northeastern Europe, the country includes more than 1,500 islands, the largest of which are Saaremaa and Hiiumaa. With an area of 17,462 square miles it has borders to the east with Russia and to the south with Latvia. It has a 750 n mile coastline with the Baltic Sea and Gulf of Finland. Tallinn is the capital, largest city and principal port. Territorial seas (12 n miles) are claimed but while it has claimed a 200 n mile Exclusive Economic Zone (EEZ), its limits have

not been fully defined by boundary agreements.The Navy was founded in 1918 and re-established on 22 April 1994. The Border Guard comes under the Ministry of Internal Affairs and is responsible for SAR and Pollution Prevention.

Headquarters Appointments

Commander in Chief Estonian Defence Forces:
Vice AdmiralTarmo Kõuts
Commander of the Navy and Chief of Staff:
Lieutenant Commander Ahti Piirimägi

Personnel

(a) 2006: 270 (70 officers)
(b) 8—11 months' national service
(c) Border Guard: 300

Bases

Major: Miinisadam (Tallinn)
Minor: Kopli (Tallinn) (Border Guard)

FRIGATES

1 MODIFIED HVIDBJØRNEN CLASS (FFLH/AGFH/AGE)

Name	No	Builders	Laid down	Launched	Commissioned
ADMIRAL PITKA (ex-*Beskytteren*)	A 230 (ex-F 340)	Aalborg Vaerft	11 Dec 1974	29 May 1975	27 Feb 1976

Displacement, tons: 1,970 full load
Dimensions, feet (metres): 245 × 40 × 17.4
(*74.7 × 12.2 × 5.3*)
Main machinery: 3 MAN/Burmeister & Wain Alpha diesels; 7,440 hp(m) (*5.47 MW*); 1 shaft; cp prop
Speed, knots: 18
Range, n miles: 4,500 at 16 kt on 2 engines; 6,000 at 13 kt on 1 engine
Complement: 43 (9 officers)

Guns: 1 USN 3 in (*76 mm*)/50; Mk 22.
Countermeasures: ESM: Racal Cutlass; radar warning.
Radars: Navigation: 2 Litton Decca E; I-band.

Helicopters: Platform for 1 Lynx type.

Programmes: Transferred by gift from Denmark in July 2000 and formally recommissioned on 21 November 2000.
Structure: Strengthened for ice operations.
Operational: Flagship of the Estonian Navy, its primary role is as a Command and Support ship and its secondary role is as a research ship. The vessel was refitted prior to being transferred. Modifications included the replacement of the military radars with Litton Marine radars, and the removal of PMS 26 sonar.

ADMIRAL PITKA   *7/2005*, B Sullivan* / 1129998

MINE WARFARE FORCES

2 FRAUENLOB (TYPE 394) CLASS (MSI)

Name	No	Builders	Commissioned
OLEV (ex-*Diana*)	M 415 (ex-M 2664)	Krogerwerft, Rendsburg	21 Sep 1967
VAINDLO (ex-*Undine*)	M 416 (ex-M 2662)	Krogerwerft, Rendsburg	20 Mar 1967

Displacement, tons: 246 full load
Dimensions, feet (metres): 124.6 × 26.9 × 6.6 (*38 × 8.2 × 2*)
Main machinery: 2 MTU MB 12V 493 TY70 diesels; 2,200 hp(m) (*1.62 MW*) sustained; 2 shafts
Speed, knots: 14. **Range, n miles:** 400 at 12 kt
Complement: 23 (5 officers)
Guns: 1 Bofors 40 mm/70.
Mines: Laying capability.
Radars: Navigation: Atlas Elektronik; I-band.

Comment: *Olev* transferred in June 1997 and *Vaindlo*, which replaced *Kalev*, on 8 October 2002 having paid off from the German Navy in 1995. Capable of influence and mechanical minesweeping.

VAINDLO   *9/2005*, Guy Toremans* / 1129997

OLEV   *6/2000, Findler & Winter* / 0103792

2 LINDAU (TYPE 331) CLASS (MHC)

Name	No	Builders	Commissioned
WAMBOLA (ex-*Cuxhaven*)	M 311 (ex-M 1078)	Burmeister, Bremen	11 Mar 1959
SULEV (ex-*Lindau*)	M 312 (ex-M 1072)	Burmeister, Bremen	24 Apr 1958

Displacement, tons: 463 full load
Dimensions, feet (metres): 154.5 × 27.2 × 9.8 (9.2 Troika) (*47.1 × 8.3 × 3*) (*2.8*)
Main machinery: 2 MTU MD diesels; 4,000 hp(m) (*2.94 MW*); 2 shafts
Speed, knots: 16.5
Range, n miles: 850 at 16.5 kt
Complement: 37 (6 officers)
Guns: 1 Bofors 40 mm/70; 330 rds/min to 12 km (*6.5 n miles*); weight of shell 0.96 kg.
Radars: Navigation: Raytheon SPS 64; I-band.
Sonars: Plessey 193M; minehunting; high frequency (100/300 kHz).

Comment: *Wambola* transferred from Germany on 23 March 2000 and *Sulev* on 29 September 2000. Two PAP 104 ROVs were included in the transfer.

WAMBOLA   *6/2005*, M Declerck* / 1129996

SULEV   *5/2004, Per Körnefeldt* / 0589735

AUXILIARIES

1 MAAGEN CLASS (YDT)

Name	No	Builders	Commissioned
AHTI (ex-*Mallemukken*)	A 431 (ex-Y 385)	Helsingor Dockyard	19 May 1960

Displacement, tons: 190 full load
Dimensions, feet (metres): 88.6 × 23.6 × 9.5 *(27 × 7.2 × 2.9)*
Main machinery: 1 diesel; 385 hp(m) *(283 kW)*; 1 shaft
Speed, knots: 10
Complement: 11
Guns: 2 — 12.7 mm MGs.
Radars: Surface search: Pechora; I-band.
Navigation: Skanter 009; I-band.
Sonars: Sidescan.

Comment: Handed over at Tallinn on 29 March 1994, having decommissioned from the Danish Navy in 1992. Serves as a diving tender and for route surveillance.

AHTI   *6/2003, Hartmut Ehlers* / 0561497

BORDER GUARD (EESTI PIIRIVALVE)

Notes: (1) *Director General:* Colonel Harry Hein
(2) The letters PV are visible on the national flag which is defaced with green and yellow markings.
(3) Three vessels are used for anti-pollution duties. *Triin* (PVL-200) (ex-*Bester*) and *Reet* (PVL-201) (ex-*EVA-200)* are both 34 m vessels which entered Border Guard service in May 2001. *Kati* (PVL-202) (ex-*KBV-003*) is a 40 m vessel transferred from Sweden in May 2002.
(4) PVL-110 is a Slavyanka class LCM acquired in 1997 and used as a harbour utility craft.
(5) *Tiir* (PVL-104) is an ex-Russian Serna class 26 m LCM used as a utility craft.
(6) The Border Guard Aviation Group was formed in February 1993 and includes two L-410 maritime patrol aircraft and two Mi-8 helicopters.

REET   *6/2003, Hartmut Ehlers* / 0561496

PVL-110   *6/2003, Hartmut Ehlers* / 0561495

L-410   *7/2004, Paul Jackson* / 0589739

1 BALSAM CLASS (AGF)

Name	No	Builders	Commissioned
VALVAS (ex-*Bittersweet*)	PVL 109 (ex-WLB 389)	Duluth Shipyard, Minnesota`	11 May 1944

Displacement, tons: 1,034 full load
Dimensions, feet (metres): 180 × 37 × 12 *(54.9 × 11.3 × 3.8)*
Main machinery: Diesel electric; 2 diesels; 1,402 hp *(1.06 MW)*; 1 motor; 1,200 hp *(895 kW)*; 1 shaft; bow thruster
Speed, knots: 13
Range, n miles: 8,000 at 12 kt
Complement: 53
Guns: 2 — 25 mm/L80 (1 twin). 2 — 12.7 mm MGs.
Radars: Navigation: Raytheon SPS-64(V)1.

Comment: Transferred from the US Coast Guard and recommissioned as a Border Guard Headquarters ship on 5 September 1997.

VALVAS   *6/2003, Hartmut Ehlers* / 0561492

1 SILMÄ CLASS (LARGE PATROL CRAFT) (PBO)

Name	No	Builders	Commissioned
KOU (ex-*Silmä*)	PPVL 107	Laivateollisuus, Turku	19 Aug 1963

Displacement, tons: 530 full load
Dimensions, feet (metres): 158.5 × 27.2 × 14.1 *(48.3 × 8.3 × 4.3)*
Main machinery: 1 Werkspoor diesel; 1,800 hp(m) *(1.32 MW)*; 1 shaft
Speed, knots: 15
Complement: 10
Guns: 2 — 25 mm/80 (twin).
Radars: Surface search: I-band.
Sonars: Simrad SS105; active scanning; 14 kHz.

Comment: Transferred from Finland Frontier Guard in January 1995.

KOU   *6/2000, Per Körnefeldt* / 0103793

1 VIIMA CLASS (COASTAL PATROL CRAFT) (PB)

Name	No	Builders	Commissioned
MARU (ex-*Viima*)	PVL 106	Laivateollisuus, Turku	12 Oct 1964

Displacement, tons: 134 full load
Dimensions, feet (metres): 117.1 × 21.7 × 7.5 *(35.7 × 6.6 × 2.3)*
Main machinery: 3 MTU MB diesels; 4,050 hp(m) *(2.98 MW)*; 3 shafts; cp props
Speed, knots: 23
Complement: 9
Guns: 2 — 25 mm/L 80 (1 twin). 2 — 14.5 mm MGs (twin). 1 — 7.62 mm MG.
Radars: Surface search: I-band.

Comment: Acquired from Finland Frontier Guard in January 1995.

MARU   *6/2003, Hartmut Ehlers* / 0589736

1 VAPPER CLASS (COASTAL PATROL CRAFT) (PB)

Name	No	Builders	Commissioned
VAPPER	PVL 111	Baltic Ship Repairers, Tallinn	1 June 2000

Displacement, tons: 117 full load
Dimensions, feet (metres): 103 × 19.7 × 5.9 *(31.4 × 6.0 × 1.8)*
Main machinery: 2 Deutz TBD 620 V12 diesels; 4,087 hp(m) *(3.1 MW)*; 2 shafts
Speed, knots: 27
Complement: 7
Guns: 2 — 25 mm (1 twin). 1 — 14.5 mm.
Radars: Navigation: Furuno; I-band.

Comment: Launched in April 2000. Steel hull and aluminium superstructure. Carries one RIB for SAR and inspection.

VAPPER *8/2000* / 0114351

1 PIKKER CLASS (COASTAL PATROL CRAFT) (PB)

Name	No	Builders	Launched	Commissioned
PIKKER	PVL 103	Talinn	23 Dec 1995	Apr 1996

Displacement, tons: 90 full load
Dimensions, feet (metres): 91.9 × 19 × 4.9 *(28.0 × 5.8 × 1.5)*
Main machinery: 2 12YH 18/20 diesels; 2,700 hp(m) *(1.98 MW)* sustained; 2 shafts
Speed, knots: 23
Complement: 5
Guns: 1 — 14.5 mm MG.
Radars: Surface search/navigation: Kelvin Hughes nucleus; I-band.

Comment: Steel hull and superstructure. Carries a RIB with a hydraulic launch crane aft.

PIKKER *6/2003, Hartmut Ehlers* / 0561494

1 STORM CLASS (PB)

Name	No	Builders	Commissioned
TORM (ex-Arg)	PVL 105 (ex-P968)	Bergens Mek, Verksteder	24 May 1966

Displacement, tons: 100 standard; 135 full load
Dimensions, feet (metres): 120 × 20 × 5 *(36.5 × 6.1 × 1.5)*
Main machinery: 2 MTU MB 16V 538 TB90 diesels; 6,000 hp(m) *(4.41 MW)* sustained; 2 shafts
Speed, knots: 32. **Range, n miles:** 800 at 25 kt
Complement: 8
Guns: 2 — 25 mm/80 (twin). 2 — 14.5 mm MGs (twin).
Radars: Surface search: Racal Decca TM 1226; I-band.

Comment: Built in 1966 and paid off from the Norwegian Navy in 1991. Transferred 16 December 1994 stripped of all weapons and associated sensors. Rearmed in 1995 with light guns. No further transfers are expected.

TORM *6/1999, Estonian Border Guard* / 0056948

3 KBV 236 CLASS (PB)

PVK 001 (ex-KBV 257) **PVK 002** (ex-KBV 259) **PVK 003** (ex-KBV 246)

Displacement, tons: 17 full load
Dimensions, feet (metres): 63 × 13.1 × 4.3 *(19.2 × 4 × 1.3)*
Main machinery: 2 Volvo Penta TAMD120A diesels; 700 hp(m) *(515 kW)*; 2 shafts
Speed, knots: 22
Complement: 5
Guns: 1 — 7.62 mm MG.

Comment: Transferred on 4 April 1992, 20 October 1993 and 6 December 1993. Former Swedish Coast Guard vessel built in 1970. Similar craft to Latvia and Lithuania.

PVK 003 *8/1995, Erki Holm* / 0056949

11 INSHORE PATROL CRAFT (PBI)

PVK 006, 008, 010-013, 016-017, 020-021, 025

Comment: *PVK 010* is a 15 m patrol craft built in 1997, *PVK 011* was commissioned in 1999, *PVK 017* (ex-EVA 203) is a 44 ton MFV type of vessel built in Finland in 1963. *PVK 018* (ex-EVA 204) is a 22 kt craft built in Finland in 1993 and *PVK 008* and *013* are 13.7 ton icebreaking launches acquired from Finland and based on Lake Peipus. There is also a Jet Combi 10 power boat based on Lake Peipus. Further craft under 12 m have numbers *PVK 004, 006, 012, 016, 020-021*. *PVK 025* is an ex-Swedish craft (KBV 275) acquired in January 1997.

PVK 010 *6/2002, Baltic Ship Repairers* / 0526817

1 GRIFFON 2000 TDX MK II (HOVERCRAFT) (UCAC)

PVH 1

Displacement, tons: 6.8 full load
Dimensions, feet (metres): 36.1 × 15.1 *(11 × 4.6)*
Main machinery: 1 Deutz BF8L 513 diesel; 320 hp *(293 kW)* sustained
Speed, knots: 33
Range, n miles: 300 at 25 kt
Complement: 2
Military lift: 16 troops or 2 tons
Guns: 1 — 7.62 mm MG.

Comment: Similar to craft supplied to Finland. Acquired in 1999.

PVH 1 *9/1999, Nick Hall* / 0103794

MARITIME ADMINISTRATION
(EESTI VEETEDE AMET (EVA))

Notes: The Maritime Administration (EVA) was re-established in 1990 and is responsible for hydrographic work, aids to navigation, ice-breaking and control of shipping. The main base is at Tallin. Ships are painted with a blue hull and white superstructure and are as follows:

Tarmo, icebreaker built in 1963 and acquired from Finland in 1992. Fleet flagship.
EVA 010, port control launch built in Finland in 1991
EVA 017, port control launch built in Finland in 1995
EVA 019, port control launch built in Estonia in 1997
EVA 300 (ex-*Tormilind*), hydrographic ship built in Russia in 1983
EVA 303 (ex-*Kaater*), buoy ship built in Poland in 1988
EVA 305, hydrographic launch built in Russia in 1979
EVA 308 (ex-GS-108-93), buoy ship built in Poland in 1968
EVA 309 (ex-BGK-117-93), buoy ship built in Russia in 1967
EVA 316 (ex-*Lonna*), buoy ship built in Finland in 1980
EVA 317-318, buoy ships built in Finland in 1994
EVA 319, buoy ship built in Finland in 1996
EVA 320, hydrographic ship built in Finland in 1997
EVA 321, buoy ship built in Estonia in 1999
EVA 322, launch built in Finland in 1997
EVA 323, launch built in Finland in 1994
EVA 324, workboat built in Japan in 1996
EVA 325, hydrographic ship built in Finland in 2002

EVA-318 *6/2003, Hartmut Ehlers* / 0589737

TARMO *6/2003, Hartmut Ehlers* / 0561491

EVA-308 *6/2003, Hartmut Ehlers* / 0589738

Falkland Islands

Country Overview

The Falkland Islands are a self-governing British dependency administered by a Governor and a legislative council. Situated in the south Atlantic Ocean 323 n miles northeast of Cape Horn, approximately 200 islands are divided into two main groups on the east and west by the narrow Falkland Sound. The two largest islands are West Falkland Island (2,090 square miles) and East Falkland Island (2,610 square miles) on which the capital, largest town and principal port, Stanley, is situated. Territorial waters (12 n miles) are claimed as is a 200 n mile fishery zone.

Maritime Aircraft

There are two Pilatus Britten-Norman Defender unarmed maritime surveillance aircraft.

PATROL FORCES

1 FISHERY PATROL SHIP (PBO)

SIGMA

Measurement, tons: 1,467 grt
Dimensions, feet (metres): 196.92 × 36.2 × 20.7 *(60 × 11.03 × 6.3)*
Main machinery: 1 Wärtsilä 8R32 diesel; 3,680 hp *(2.74 MW)*; 1 shaft; cp prop; 1 Brunvoll bow thruster 500 hp *(373 kW)*
Speed, knots: 14.5
Complement: 12
Radars: Surface search/navigation: 1 Furuno 2100; I-band. 2 Furuno 2115; I-band.

Comment: Stern trawler built in Norway in 1972. Converted in 1982 for seismic work and again in 2000 for Fishery Protection. Chartered from Sigma Marine Ltd in August 2000 and extended in 2003 until August 2006. Carries two RIBs capable of over 30 kt.

1 FISHERY PATROL SHIP (PSO)

DORADA

Measurement, tons: 2,360 grt
Dimensions, feet (metres): 249.3 × 47.9 × 20 *(76 × 14.6 × 6.1)*
Main machinery: 2 Sulzer-Cegielski diesels; 1—2,333 hp *(1,740 kW)*; 1—1,167 hp *(870 kW)*; 1 shaft; cp prop; 1 ABB bow thruster; 340 hp *(250 kW)*
Speed, knots: 15.5
Range, n miles: 14,000 at 12 kt
Complement: 15
Guns: 1 Oerlikon Mk VII A 20 mm.
Radars: Surface search/navigation: 1 Furuno 2100; I-band. 1 Furuno 2115; I-band. 1 Furuno 1500 Mk 3; I-band.

Comment: Stern trawler built in Poland in 1991 and refitted in New Zealand. On long-term charter from Dorada Marine until January 2008. Has a red hull and white superstructure. Carries two RIBs capable of over 30 kt. Took part in multinational operation in 2003 to arrest Uruguayan fishing vessel.

SIGMA *6/2002, Falkland Islands Fisheries* / 0137784

DORADA *6/2002, Falkland Islands Fisheries* / 0137785

Faroe Islands

Country Overview

The Faroe Islands are a self-governing island group that is an integral part of Denmark which retains control of foreign relations. Located in the North Atlantic Ocean, about midway between the Shetland Islands and Iceland, there are 18 islands, of which the most important are Østerø, Suderø, Sandø, Vagø, Bordø and Strømø, on which the capital and principal port, Tórshavn, is situated. Territorial waters (12 n miles) are claimed. A 200 n mile fishery zone

has also been claimed although the limits have only been partly defined by boundary agreements.

The Coast Guard and Fisheries come under the Landsstyri which is the islands' local government. Vessels work closely with the Danish Navy.

Headquarters Appointments

Head of Coast Guard:
  Captain Elmar Hojgaard

Personnel

2006: 60

Bases

Tórshavn (Isle of Streymoy)

COAST GUARD

1 PATROL SHIP (PBO)

TJALDRID

Displacement, tons: 650 full load
Dimensions, feet (metres): 146 × 33.1 × 10.5 *(44.5 × 10.1 × 3.2)*
Main machinery: 2 MWM diesels; 2,400 hp(m) *(1.76 MW)*; 2 shafts
Speed, knots: 14.5
Complement: 18 plus 4 divers
Guns: 1 Oerlikon 20 mm can be carried.
Radars: Surface search: Raytheon TM/TCPA; I-band.

Comment: Originally a commercial tug built in 1976 by Svolvaer, Verksted and acquired by the local government in 1987. The old 57 mm gun has been replaced. A decompression chamber can be carried.

1 PATROL SHIP (PSO)

BRIMIL

Displacement, tons: 2,000 full load
Dimensions, feet (metres): 208.71 × 41.3 × 14.1 *(63.6 × 12.6 × 4.3)*
Main machinery: 2 Bergen diesels; 5,452 hp *(4.06 MW)*
Speed, knots: 17
Complement: 12 with accommodation for 30 including 3 divers
Radars: Surface search: 2 Furuno.

Comment: Built for Faroese government as a patrol vessel by Myclebust Mek. Verksted, Norway. Entered service in April 2001.

TJALDRID   *12/1999, Faroes Coast Guard* / 0080652

BRIMIL   *7/2003, Martin Mokrus* / 0589001

Fiji

Country Overview

A former British colony, the Republic of Fiji gained independence in 1970. Part of Melanesia, it is situated in the south Pacific Ocean some 972 n miles north of New Zealand and comprises more than 300 islands and islets, 100 of which are inhabited. The largest and most important of these are Viti Levu and Vanua Levu, which together contain more than 85 per cent of the total land area. To the southeast lie Taveuni, Kandavu, Koro and the Lau group while to the northwest lie Rotuma and the Yasawa group. The capital, largest town and principal port is Suva. An archipelagic state, territorial seas (12 n miles) are claimed. An Exclusive Economic Zone (EEZ) (200 n miles) is also claimed

but limits have yet to be fully defined by boundary agreements.

Headquarters Appointments

Commander, Navy:
  Commander Mosese Semi

Personnel

2006: 300

Prefix to Ships' Names

RFNS (Republic of Fiji naval ship)

Bases

RFNS *Viti*, at Togalevu (Training).
RFNS *Stanley Brown*.
Operation base at Walu Bay, Suva.
Forward base at Lautoka.

DELETIONS

Patrol Forces

2003   *Vai, Ogo*

PATROL FORCES

3 PACIFIC CLASS (LARGE PATROL CRAFT) (PB)

Name	No	Builders	Commissioned
KULA	201	Transfield Shipbuilding	28 May 1994
KIKAU	202	Transfield Shipbuilding	27 May 1995
KIRO	203	Transfield Shipbuilding	14 Oct 1995

Displacement, tons: 162 full load
Dimensions, feet (metres): 103.3 × 26.6 × 6.9 *(31.5 × 8.1 × 2.1)*
Main machinery: 2 Caterpillar 3516TA diesels; 2,820 hp *(2.09 MW)* sustained; 2 shafts
Speed, knots: 20
Range, n miles: 2,500 at 12 kt
Complement: 17 (4 officers)
Guns: 1—20 mm Oerlikon. 2—12.7 mm MGs.
Radars: Surface search: Furuno; I-band.

Comment: Ordered in December 1992. These are hulls 17, 19 and 20 of the class offered by the Australian government under Defence Co-operation Programme. *Kikau* underwent a half-life refit at Gladstone in 2001 followed by *Kula* and *Kiro* in 2002. Following the decision by the Australian government to extend the Pacific Patrol Boat project until 2025, life extension refits will be required for *Kikau* in 2010 and for *Kula* and *Kiro* in 2011.

KIRO   *9/1998, van Ginderen Collection* / 0017831

2 COASTAL PATROL CRAFT (PB)

Name	No	Builders	Commissioned
LEVUKA	101	Beaux's Bay Craft, Louisiana	22 Oct 1987
LAUTOKA	102	Beaux's Bay Craft, Louisiana	28 Oct 1987

Displacement, tons: 97 full load
Dimensions, feet (metres): 110 × 24 × 5
  (33.8 × 7.4 × 1.5)
Main machinery: 4 GM 12V-71TA diesels; 1,680 hp (1.25 MW) sustained; 4 shafts
Speed, knots: 12
Complement: 12 (2 officers)
Guns: 1 — 12.7 mm MG.
Radars: Surface search: Racal Decca; I-band.

Comment: Built in 1979-80 as oil rig support craft. Purchased in September 1987. All aluminium construction.

LAUTOKA
8/1996, Fiji Navy
0056953

2 VAI (DABUR) CLASS (COASTAL PATROL CRAFT) (PB)

SAKU 303   **SAQA** 304

Displacement, tons: 39 full load
Dimensions, feet (metres): 64.9 × 18 × 5.8
  (19.8 × 5.5 × 1.8)
Main machinery: 4 GM 12V-71TA diesels; 1,680 hp (1.25 MW) sustained; 2 shafts
Speed, knots: 19
Range, n miles: 450 at 13 kt
Complement: 9 (2 officers)
Guns: 2 — 20 mm Oerlikon. 2 — 12.7 mm MGs.
Radars: Surface search: Racal Decca Super 101 Mk 3; I-band.

Comment: Built in mid-1970s by Israel Aircraft Industries and transferred from Israel 22 November 1991. ASW equipment is not fitted. Reported as being no longer required by the Navy and may be used by other government departments.

SAQA *6/1995*
0056954

Finland
SUOMEN MERIVOIMAT

Country Overview

The Republic of Finland is situated in northern Europe. Nearly one third of the country lies north of the Arctic Circle. With an area of 130,559 square miles, which includes some 60,000 lakes, it has borders to the north with Norway and to the east with Russia. It has a 510 n mile coastline with the Baltic Sea and Gulf of Finland. The Ahvenanmaa archipelago (Åland Islands), consisting of some 6,500 islands, lies southwest of the mainland. Helsinki is the capital, largest city and principal port. Territorial Seas and a Fishing Zone, both of 12 n miles, have been claimed but not an EEZ.

Headquarters Appointments

Commander-in-Chief Finnish Navy:
  Vice Admiral Hans Holström
Chief of Staff FNHQ:
  Captain Veli-Juha Pennala

Diplomatic Representation

Defence Attaché in London:
  Lieutenant Colonel Juhani Karjomaa
Defence Attaché in Moscow:
  Colonel Jukka Hellberg

Personnel

(a) 2006: 2,200 regulars
(b) 3,650 conscripts (6-12 months' national service)

Fleet Organisation

Naval Headquarters is to be relocated from Helsinki to Turku by 2008.
Gulf of Finland Naval Command; main base Upinniemi, Helsinki.
Archipelago Sea Naval Command; main base at Pansio, near Turku.
Kotka Coastal Command at Kotka.
Uusimaa Jaeger Brigade at Tammisaari.
Not all ships are fully manned all the time but all are rotated on a regular basis.

Coast Defence

Coastal Artillery and naval infantry troops. RBS 15 truck-mounted quadruple SSM launchers. 155 mm, 130 mm and 100 mm fixed and mobile guns.

Frontier Guard

All Frontier Guard vessels come under the Ministry of the Interior. The ships have dark green hulls with a thick red diagonal stripe superimposed by a thin white stripe. Superstructure is painted grey. Personnel numbers: 600.

Icebreakers

Icebreakers work for the Board of Navigation.

DELETIONS

Patrol Forces

2004   *Tuuli, Helsinki, Turku*

PENNANT LIST

Patrol Forces		05	Uusimaa	235	Hirsala	799	Hylje
		21-26	Kuha 21-26	237	Hila	826	Isku
50	Kiisla	521-527	Kiiski 1-7	238	Haruna	830	Högsåra
51	Kurki	777	Porkkala	241	Askeri	831	Kallanpää
62	Oulu	875	Pyhäranta	334	Hankoniemi	836	Houtskär
63	Kotka	876	Pansio	511	Jymy	874	Kala 4
70	Rauma			512	Raju	877	Kampela 3
71	Raahe	**Auxiliaries**		531	Syöksy	879	Valas
72	Porvoo			541	Vinha	894	Alskär
73	Naantali	56	Kajava	722	Vaarlahti	899	Halli
80	Hamina	57	Lokki	723	Vänö	993	Torsö
81	Tornio	92	Putsaari	730	Haukipää		
82	Hanko	96	Pikkala	731	Hakuni		
83	— (bldg)	98	Mursu	739	Hästö		
		99	Kustaanmiekka	751	Lohi		
Mine Warfare Forces		121	Vahakari	752	Lohm		
		133	Havouri	771	Kampela 1		
01	Pohjanmaa	176	Kala 6	772	Kampela 2		
02	Hämeenmaa	232	Hauki	792	Träskö		

PATROL FORCES

4 RAUMA CLASS (FAST ATTACK CRAFT—MISSILE) (PTGM)

Name	No	Builders	Commissioned
RAUMA	70	Hollming, Rauma	18 Oct 1990
RAAHE	71	Hollming, Rauma	20 Aug 1991
PORVOO	72	Finnyards, Rauma	27 Apr 1992
NAANTALI	73	Finnyards, Rauma	23 June 1992

Displacement, tons: 215 standard; 248 full load
Dimensions, feet (metres): 157.5 × 26.2 × 4.5 *(48 × 8 × 1.5)*
Main machinery: 2 MTU 16V 538 TB93 diesels; 7,510 hp(m) *(5.52 MW)* sustained; 2 Riva Calzoni IRC 115 water-jets
Speed, knots: 30
Complement: 19 (5 officers)

Missiles: SSM: 6 Saab RBS 15SF (could embark 8); active radar homing to 150 km *(80 n miles)* at 0.8 Mach; warhead 200 kg.
SAM: 1 sextuple launcher; Matra Mistral; IR homing to 4 km *(2.2 n miles)*; warhead 3 kg.
Guns: 1 Bofors 40 mm/70; 300 rds/min to 12 km *(6.6 n miles)*; weight of shell 0.96 kg.
6—103 mm rails for rocket illuminants. 2—12.7 mm MGs.
2 Sako 23 mm/87 (twin); can be fitted instead of Mistral launcher.
A/S mortars: 4 Saab Elma LLS-920 9-tubed launchers; range 300 m; warhead 4.2 kg shaped charge.
Depth charges: 1 rail.
Countermeasures: Decoys: Philax chaff and IR flares.
ESM: MEL Matilda; radar intercept.
Weapons control: Bofors Electronic 9LV Mk 3 optronic director with TV camera; infra-red and laser telemetry.
Radars: Surface search: 9GA 208; I-band.
Fire control: Bofors Electronic 9LV 225; J-band.
Navigation: Raytheon ARPA; I-band.
Sonars: Simrad Subsea Toadfish sonar; search and attack; active high frequency.
Finnyards Sonac/PTA towed array; low frequency.

Programmes: Ordered 27 August 1987.
Structure: Developed from Helsinki class. Hull and superstructure of light alloy. SAM and 23 mm guns are interchangeable within the same Sako barbette which has replaced the ZU mounting.
Operational: Primary function is the anti-ship role but there is some ASW capability. Mine rails can be fitted in place of the missile launchers. Towed array cable is 78 m with 24 hydrophones and can be used at speeds between 3 and 12 kt.

PORVOO   *6/2001, Harald Carstens* / 0114728

3 + 1 HAMINA CLASS
(FAST ATTACK CRAFT—MISSILE) (PTGM)

Name	No	Builders	Commissioned
HAMINA	80 (ex-74)	Aker Finnyards, Rauma	24 Aug 1998
TORNIO	81	Aker Finnyards, Rauma	July 2005
HANKO	82	Aker Finnyards, Rauma	Dec 2005
–	83	Aker Finnyards, Rauma	Dec 2006

Displacement, tons: 270 full load
Dimensions, feet (metres): 164 × 26.2 × 6.2 *(50.8 × 8.3 × 2)*
Main machinery: 2 MTU 16V 538 TB93 diesels; 7,510 hp(m) *(5.52 MW)* sustained; 2 Kamewa 90SII waterjets
Speed, knots: 32
Range, n miles: 500 at 30 kt
Complement: 21 (5 officers)

Missiles: SSM: 4 Saab RBS 15SF; active radar homing to 100 km *(54 n miles)* at 0.8 Mach; warhead 200 kg.
SAM: Denel Umkhonto 8 cell VLS; inertial guidance with mid-course guidance and IR homing to 12 km *(6.5 n miles)* at 2.4 Mach; warhead 23 kg.
Guns: Bofors 57 mm/L 70 Mk 3; 220 rds/min to 17 km *(9.2 n miles)*; weight of shell 2.6 kg.
A/S mortars: 4 Saab Elma LLS-920 9-tubed launchers; range 300 m; warhead 4.2 kg shaped charge.
Depth charges: 1 rail.
Countermeasures: Decoys: 2 MASS; softkill launchers.
ESM: Thales SIEWS; radar intercept.
Combat data systems: EADS Advanced Naval Combat System (ANCS 2000).
Weapons control: Saab Ceros electro-optic director. Signaal EOMS IR scanner.
Radars: Air/Surface search: EADS TRS-3D; G-band.
Fire control: SAAB Ceros 200; K-band.
Navigation: Furuno; I-band.
Sonars: Simrad Subsea Toadfish sonar; search and attack; active high frequency.
Finnyards Sonac/PTA towed array; low frequency.

Programmes: First ordered on 31 December 1996, second in February 2000, third on 3 December 2003 and a fourth on 15 February 2005 for delivery in 2006.
Structure: A continuation of the Rauma design with aluminium hull, composite superstructure and RAM coating. Signature reduction is aided by RAM coatings on the superstructure, submerged engine exhausts, upper deck pre-wetting, resilient mountings for all machinery, waterjet propulsion and conductive sealings on doors and hatches to prevent electromagnetic leakage.
Operational: The squadron is to become operational in 2008.

TORNIO   *6/2005*, Finnish Navy* / 1133418

TORNIO   *6/2005*, Finnish Navy* / 1133417

2 HELSINKI CLASS (FAST ATTACK CRAFT—MISSILE) (PTGM)

Name	No	Builders	Commissioned
OULU	62	Wärtsilä, Helsinki	1 Oct 1985
KOTKA	63	Wärtsilä, Helsinki	16 June 1986

Displacement, tons: 280 standard; 300 full load
Dimensions, feet (metres): 147.6 × 29.2 × 9.9 *(45 × 8.9 × 3)*
Main machinery: 3 MTU 16V 538 TB92 diesels; 10,230 hp(m) *(7.52 MW)* sustained; 3 shafts
Speed, knots: 30
Complement: 30

Missiles: SSM: 8 Saab RBS 15; inertial guidance; active radar homing to 70 km *(37.8 n miles)* at 0.8 Mach; warhead 150 kg; sea-skimmer.
SAM: 2 sextuple launchers; Matra Mistral; IR homing to 4 km *(2.2 n miles)*; warhead 3 kg.
Guns: 1 Bofors 57 mm/70; 200 rds/min to 17 km *(9.3 n miles)*; weight of shell 2.4 kg.
6—103 mm rails for rocket illuminants.
4 Sako 23 mm/87 (2 twin); can be fitted in place of Mistral launcher.
Depth charges: 2 rails.
Countermeasures: Decoys: Philax chaff and IR flare launcher.
ESM: Argo; radar intercept.
Weapons control: Saab EOS 400 optronic director.
Radars: Surface search: 9GA 208; I-band.
Fire control: Philips 9LV 225; J-band.
Navigation: Raytheon ARPA; I-band.
Sonars: Simrad Marine SS 304; high-resolution active scanning.
Finnyards Sonac/PTA towed array; low frequency.

Programmes: Both ordered on 13 January 1983.
Modernisation: A Sako barbette can take either twin 23 mm guns or a Sadral SAM launcher. The Sako mounting has replaced the original ZU version.
Structure: The light armament can be altered to suit the planned role. Missile racks can also be replaced by mine rails. Hull and superstructure of light alloy.
Operational: *Helsinki* and *Turku* decommissioned in 2004. The future of *Oulu* and *Kotka* is to be decided in 2006.

KOTKA   *6/2005*, Martin Mokrus* / 1133415

2 KIISLA CLASS (COASTAL PATROL CRAFT) (PB)

Name	No	Builders	Commissioned
KIISLA	50	Hollming, Rauma	25 May 1987
KURKI	51	Hollming, Rauma	Nov 1990

Displacement, tons: 270 full load
Dimensions, feet (metres): 158.5 × 28.9 × 7.2 *(48.3 × 8.8 × 2.2)*
Main machinery: 2 MTU 16V 538TB93 diesels; 7,510 hp(m) *(6.9 MW)* sustained; 2 Kamewa 90 waterjets
Speed, knots: 25
Complement: 10
Guns: 2 USSR 23 mm/60 (twin) or 1 Madsen 20 mm.
Weapons control: Radamec 2100 optronic director.
Sonars: Simrad SS304 hull-mounted and VDS; active search; high frequency.

Comment: First ordered on 23 November 1984 and second on 22 November 1988. Plans for two further craft were cancelled. The design allows for rapid conversion to attack craft, ASW craft, minelayer, minesweeper or minehunter. A central telescopic crane over the engine room casing is used to launch a 5.7 m rigid inflatable sea boat. A fire monitor is mounted in the bows. The Kamewa steerable water-jets extend the overall hull length by 2 m. Transferred from the Frontier Guard in 2004.

KIISLA *6/2004, Finnish Navy* / 0587710

MINE WARFARE FORCES

Notes: Development of a new MCM squadron is in progress. Following Requests for Proposals initiated in Spring 2004, seven responses from potential European prime contractors were received in early 2005. On completion of evaluation, a contract is expected in 2006 with a view to ship deliveries 2009-11. The requirement is for three MCMVs equipped with modern IMCM systems and a variety of remotely controlled or autonomous sensors and effectors to be operational in 2012. In addition, the programme includes a Mine Warfare Data Centre. In a complementary programme, it is planned to acquire remotely controlled mine sweeping systems and to equip clearance/EOD diver units 2009-12.

2 HÄMEENMAA CLASS (MINELAYERS) (ML)

Name	No	Builders	Laid down	Launched	Commissioned
HÄMEENMAA	02	Finnyards, Rauma	2 Apr 1991	11 Nov 1991	15 Apr 1992
UUSIMAA	05	Finnyards, Rauma	12 Nov 1991	June 1992	2 Dec 1992

Displacement, tons: 1,330 full load
Dimensions, feet (metres): 252.6 oa; 228.3 wl × 38.1 × 9.8 *(77; 69.6 × 11.6 × 3)*
Main machinery: 2 Wärtsilä 16V22 diesels; 6,300 hp(m) *(4.64 MW)* sustained; 2 Kamewa cp props; bow thruster; 247 hp(m) *(184 kW)*
Speed, knots: 19
Complement: 70

Missiles: SAM: 1 sextuple launcher; Matra Mistral; IR homing to 4 km *(2.2 n miles)*; warhead 3 kg.
Guns: 2 Bofors 40 mm/70; 300 rds/min to 12 km *(6.6 n miles)*; weight of shell 0.96 kg.
4 or 6 Sako 23 mm/87 (2 or 3 twin) (the third mounting is interchangeable with Mistral launcher).
A/S mortars: 2 RBU 1200 fixed 5-tubed launchers; range 1,200 m; warhead 34 kg.
Depth charges: 2 racks for 16 DCs.
Mines: 4 rails for 100—150.
Countermeasures: Decoys: 2 ML/Wallop Superbarricade multichaff and IR launchers.
ESM: MEL Matilda; intercept.
Weapons control: Radamec System 2400 optronic director; 2 Galileo optical directors.
Radars: Surface search and Navigation: 3 Selesmar ARPA; I-band.
Sonars: Simrad; hull-mounted; active mine detection; high frequency.

Programmes: First one ordered 29 December 1989 after the original order in July from Wärtsilä had been cancelled. Second ordered 13 February 1991.
Modernisation: A mid-life upgrade is planned to be ordered in 2006. Modernisation, to be undertaken in 2007-08, is likely to include EADS ANCS 2000 combat data system, EADS TRS 3D radar, Sagem EOMS and Umkhonto point defence missile system.
Structure: Steel hull and alloy superstructure. Ice strengthened (Ice class 1A) and capable of breaking up to 40 mm ice. Ramps in bow and stern. The Mistral launcher is mounted at the stern. SAM system can be replaced by a third twin 23 mm mounting within the same barbette.
Operational: Dual role as a transport and support ship.

UUSIMAA *6/2001, Findler & Winter* / 0114718

UUSIMAA *6/2001, van Ginderen Collection* / 0114727

1 MINELAYER (ML)

Name	No	Builders	Laid down	Launched	Commissioned
POHJANMAA	01	Wärtsilä, Helsinki	4 May 1978	28 Aug 1978	8 June 1979

Displacement, tons: 1,000 standard; 1,100 full load
Dimensions, feet (metres): 255.8 × 37.7 × 9.8 *(78.2 × 11.6 × 3)*
Main machinery: 2 Wärtsilä Vasa 16V22 diesels; 6,300 hp(m) *(4.64 MW)* sustained; 2 shafts; cp props; bow thruster
Speed, knots: 19. **Range, n miles:** 3,500 at 15 kt
Complement: 90

Missiles: SAM: 2 sextuple launchers; Matra Mistral; IR homing to 4 km *(2.2 n miles)*; warhead 3 kg.
Guns: 1 Bofors 57 mm/70; 200 rds/min to 17 km *(9.3 n miles)*; weight of shell 2.4 kg.
6—103 mm launchers for illuminants fitted to the mounting.
2 Bofors 40 mm/70; 300 rds/min to 12 km *(6.6 n miles)*; weight of shell 0.96 kg.
4 Sako 23 mm/87 (2 twin). 2—12.7 mm MGs.
A/S mortars: 2 RBU 1200 fixed 5-tubed launchers; range 1,200 m; warhead 34 kg.
Depth charges: 2 rails.
Mines: 120 including UK Stonefish.
Countermeasures: Decoys: Philax chaff and IR flare launcher.
ESM: Argo; radar intercept.
Radars: Air search: Signaal DA05; E/F-band.
Fire control: Phillips 9LV 220; J-band.
Navigation: I-band.
Sonars: Simrad; hull-mounted; active search and attack; high frequency.
Bottom classification; search; high frequency.

Programmes: Design completed 1976. Ordered late 1977.
Modernisation: In 1992 the forward 23 mm guns were replaced by 12.7 mm MGs. Major refit in 1996-98 to replace the main gun, improve air defences and minelaying capability. The SAM mounting is interchangeable with 23 mm guns.
Operational: Also serves as training ship. Carries 70 trainees accommodated in Portakabins on the mine deck. Helicopter area on quarterdeck but no hangar.

POHJANMAA *6/2005*, Jurg Kürsener* / 1133416

3 PANSIO CLASS (MINELAYERS—LCU TYPE) (MLI)

Name	No	Builders	Commissioned
PANSIO	876 (ex-576)	Olkiluoto Shipyard	25 Sep 1991
PYHÄRANTA	875 (ex-575, ex-475)	Olkiluoto Shipyard	26 May 1992
PORKKALA	777	Olkiluoto Shipyard	29 Oct 1992

Displacement, tons: 450 standard
Dimensions, feet (metres): 144.3 oa; 128.6 wl × 32.8 × 6.6 *(44; 39.2 × 10 × 2)*
Main machinery: 2 MTU 12V 183 TE62 diesels; 1,500 hp(m) *(1.1 MW)*; 2 shafts; bow thruster
Speed, knots: 10
Complement: 12
Guns: 2 ZU 23 mm/87 (twin). 1—12.7 mm MG.
Mines: 50.
Radars: Navigation: Raytheon ARPA; I-band.

Comment: Ordered in May 1990. Used for inshore minelaying and transport with a capacity of 100 tons. Ice strengthened with ramps in bow and stern. Has a 15 ton crane fitted aft.

PANSIO *6/2001, Finnish Navy* / 0114730

6 KUHA CLASS (MINESWEEPERS—INSHORE) (MSI)

Name	No	Builders	Commissioned
KUHA 21-26	21-26	Laivateollisuus, Turku	1974-75

Displacement, tons: 90 full load
Dimensions, feet (metres): 87.2; 104 × 22.7 × 6.6 *(26.6; 31.7 × 6.9 × 2)*
Main machinery: 2 Cummins MT-380M diesels; 600 hp(m) *(448 kW)*; 1 shaft; cp prop; active rudder
Speed, knots: 12
Complement: 15 (3 officers)
Guns: 2 ZU 23 mm/60 (twin). 1 — 12.7 mm MG.
Radars: Navigation: Decca; I-band.
Sonars: Reson Seabat 6012 mine avoidance; active high frequency.

Comment: All ordered 1972. First one completed 28 June 1974, and last on 13 November 1975. Fitted for magnetic, acoustic and pressure-mine clearance. Hulls are of GRP. May carry a Pluto ROV. Four of the class were lengthened in 1997/98 and remaining two by 2000 to take a new minesweeping control system, and new magnetic and acoustic sweeps. New sonars installed. Armament not fitted in all of the class.

KUHA 21 *6/2001, Finnish Navy* / 0114724

7 KIISKI CLASS (MINESWEEPERS—INSHORE) (MSI)

Name	No	Builders	Commissioned
KIISKI 1-7	521-527	Fiskars, Turku	1983-84

Displacement, tons: 20 full load
Dimensions, feet (metres): 49.9 × 13.4 × 3.3 *(15.2 × 4.1 × 1.2)*
Main machinery: 2 Valmet 611 CSMP diesels; 340 hp(m) *(250 kW)*; 2 Hamilton water-jets
Speed, knots: 11. **Range, n miles:** 260 at 11 kt
Complement: 4

Comment: Ordered January 1983. All completed by 24 May 1984. GRP hull. Built to be used with Kuha class for unmanned teleguided sweeping, but this was not successful and they are now used for manned magnetic and acoustic sweeping operations with crew of four.

KIISKI 5 *6/2001, Finnish Navy* / 0114725

TRAINING SHIPS

2 LOKKI CLASS (AX)

Name	No	Builders	Commissioned
LOKKI	57	Valmet/Lavateollisuus	28 Aug 1986
KAJAVA	56	Valmet/Lavateollisuus	3 Oct 1981

Displacement, tons: 59 *(Lokki)*; 64
Dimensions, feet (metres): 87.9 × 18 × 6.2 *(26.8 × 5.5 × 1.9)*
87.9 × 17.1 × 8.5 *(26.8 × 5.2 × 2.1) (Lokki)*
Main machinery: 2 MTU 8V 396TB82 diesels; 1,740 hp(m) *(1.28 MW)* sustained *(Lokki)*
2 MTU 8V 396TB84 diesels; 2,100 hp(m) *(1.54 MW)* sustained; 2 shafts
Speed, knots: 25
Complement: 6
Guns: 2 ZU 23 mm/60 can be carried.
Sonars: Simrad SS 242; hull-mounted; active search; high frequency.

Comment: Transferred from the Frontier Guard to the Navy in 1999 and used as training vessels. Built in light metal alloy. *Lokki* has a V-shaped hull. A third of class to Lithuania in 1997 and a fourth to Latvia in 2001.

LOKKI *6/2001, Finnish Navy* / 0114723

3 TRAINING SHIPS (AX)

681   683   685

Comment: Naval Academy training ships.

681 *5/1997, N A Sifferlinger* / 0012319

AUXILIARIES

1 KEMIO CLASS (COMMAND SHIP) (AGF/AGI)

KUSTAANMIEKKA (ex-*Valvoja III*) 99

Displacement, tons: 340 full load
Dimensions, feet (metres): 118.1 × 29.5 × 9.8 *(36 × 9 × 3)*
Main machinery: 1 Burmeister & Wain diesel; 670 hp(m) *(492 kW)*; 1 shaft
Speed, knots: 11
Complement: 10
Guns: 2 — 12.7 mm MGs (not always carried).

Comment: Completed in 1963. Former buoy tender transferred from Board of Navigation and converted by Hollming, Rauma in 1989. Bofors 40 mm gun removed in 1988. A ship of the same class transferred to Estonia in 1992.

KUSTAANMIEKKA *6/2001, Finnish Navy* / 0587704

5 VALAS CLASS (GP TRANSPORTS) (AKSL)

VALAS 879   **MURSU** 98   **VAHAKARI** 121   **VAARLAHTI** 722   **VÄNÖ** 723

Displacement, tons: 285 full load
Dimensions, feet (metres): 100.4 × 26.5 × 10.4 *(30.6 × 8.1 × 3.2)*
Main machinery: 1 Wärtsilä Vasa 8V22 diesel; 1,576 hp(m) *(1.16 MW)* sustained; 1 shaft
Speed, knots: 12
Complement: 11
Military lift: 35 tons or 150 troops
Guns: 2 — 23 mm/60 (twin). 1 — 12.7 mm MG.
Mines: 28 can be carried.
Radars: Navigation: Decca 1226; I-band.

Comment: Completed 1979-80. *Mursu* acts as a diving tender. Funnel is offset to starboard. Can be used as minelayers or transport/cargo carriers and are capable of breaking thin ice.

VALAS (old number) *7/1998, van Ginderen Collection* / 0069878

3 KAMPELA CLASS (LCU TRANSPORTS) (LCU/AKSL)

Name	No	Builders	Commissioned
KAMPELA 1	771	Enso Gutzeit	29 July 1976
KAMPELA 2	772	Enso Gutzeit	21 Oct 1976
KAMPELA 3	877	Finnmekano	23 Oct 1979

Displacement, tons: 90 light; 260 full load
Dimensions, feet (metres): 106.6 × 26.2 × 4.9 *(32.5 × 8 × 1.5)*
Main machinery: 2 Scania diesels; 460 hp(m) *(338 kW)*; 2 shafts
Speed, knots: 9
Complement: 10
Guns: 2 or 4 ZU 23 mm/60 (1 or 2 twin).
Mines: About 20 can be carried.

Comment: Can be used as amphibious craft, transports, minelayers or for shore support. Armament can be changed to suit role.

KAMPELA 2 (old number)   *6/2000, Finnish Navy* / 0103800

2 KALA CLASS (LCU TRANSPORTS) (LCU/AKSL)

KALA 4 874   **KALA 6** 176

Displacement, tons: 60 light; 200 full load
Dimensions, feet (metres): 88.6 × 26.2 × 6 *(27 × 8 × 1.8)*
Main machinery: 2 Valmet diesels; 360 hp(m) *(265 kW)*; 2 shafts
Speed, knots: 9
Complement: 10
Guns: 2 Oerlikon 20 mm (not in all).
Mines: 34.
Radars: Navigation: Decca 1226; I-band.

Comment: Completed between 1956 and 4 December 1959 *(Kala 6)*. Can be used as coastal transports, amphibious craft, minelayers or for shore support. Armament can be changed to suit role.

KALA 6   *6/2001, Finnish Navy* / 0114729

6 HAUKI CLASS (TRANSPORTS) (AKSL)

HAVOURI 133	HIRSALA 235	HAKUNI 731
HAUKI 232	HANKONIEMI 334	HOUTSKÄR 836

Displacement, tons: 45 full load
Dimensions, feet (metres): 47.6 × 15.1 × 7.2 *(14.5 × 4.6 × 2.2)*
Main machinery: 2 Valmet 611 CSM diesels; 586 hp(m) *(431 kW)*; 1 shaft
Speed, knots: 12
Complement: 4
Cargo capacity: 6 tons or 40 passengers
Radars: Navigation: I-band.

Comment: Completed 1979. Ice strengthened; two serve isolated island defences. Four converted in 1988 as tenders to the Marine War College, but from 1990 back in service as light transports.

HOUTSKÄR (old number)   *9/1997, Finnish Navy* / 0587703

4 HILA CLASS (TRANSPORTS) (AKSL)

HILA 237   **HARUNA** 238   **HÄSTÖ** 739   **HÖGSÅRA** 830

Displacement, tons: 50 full load
Dimensions, feet (metres): 49.2 × 13.1 × 5.9 *(15 × 4 × 1.8)*
Main machinery: 2 diesels; 416 hp(m) *(306 kW)*; 2 shafts
Speed, knots: 12
Complement: 4

Comment: Ordered from Kotkan Telakka in August 1990. Second pair completed in 1994. Ice strengthened.

HILA   *6/2000, Finnish Navy* / 0103801

1 TRIALS SHIP (MLI)

Name	No	Builders	Launched	Commissioned
ISKU	826 (ex-829, ex-16)	Reposaaron Konepaja	4 Dec 1969	1970

Displacement, tons: 180 full load
Dimensions, feet (metres): 108.5 × 28.5 × 5.9 *(33 × 8.7 × 1.8)*
Main machinery: 4 Type M 50 diesels; 4,400 hp(m) *(3.3 MW)* sustained; 4 shafts
Speed, knots: 18
Complement: 25
Radars: Navigation: Raytheon ARPA; I-band.

Comment: Formerly a missile experimental craft, now used for various equipment trials. Modernised in 1989-90 by Uusikaupunki Shipyard and lengthened by 7 m. Can quickly be converted to a minelayer.

ISKU   *6/2000, Finnish Navy* / 0103798

2 LOHI CLASS (LCU TRANSPORTS) (LCU)

LOHI 751 (ex-351)   **LOHM** 752

Displacement, tons: 38 full load
Dimensions, feet (metres): 65.6 × 19.7 × 3 *(20 × 6 × 0.9)*
Main machinery: 2 WMB diesels; 1,200 hp(m) *(882 kW)*; 2 water-jets
Speed, knots: 20. **Range, n miles:** 240 at 20 kt
Complement: 4
Guns: 2 ZU 23 mm/60 (twin). 1 – 14.5 mm MG.

Comment: Commissioned September 1984. Used as troop carriers and for light cargo. Guns not always carried.

LOHI   *6/2000, Finnish Navy* / 0103802

1 TRANSPORT AND COMMAND LAUNCH (YFB)

ASKERI 241

Displacement, tons: 25 full load
Dimensions, feet (metres): 52.6 × 14.5 × 4.5 (16 × 4.4 × 1.4)
Main machinery: 2 Volvo Penta diesels; 1,100 hp(m) (808 kW); 2 shafts
Speed, knots: 22
Complement: 6
Radars: Surface search: I-band.
Navigation: Raytheon; I-band.

Comment: Completed in 1992. Closely resembles Spanish PVC II class.

COMMAND LAUNCH   *6/2000, Finnish Navy* / 0103804

7 VIHURI CLASS (COMMAND LAUNCHES) (YFB)

JYMY 511	**SYÖKSY** 531	**TRÄSKÖ** 792	**ALSKÄR** 894
RAJU 512	**VINHA** 541	**TORSÖ** 993	

Displacement, tons: 13 full load
Dimensions, feet (metres): 42.7 × 13.1 × 3 (13 × 4 × 0.9)
Main machinery: 2 diesels; 772 hp(m) (567 kW); 2 water-jets
Speed, knots: 30
Complement: 6
Radars: Surface search: I-band.

Comment: First of class *Vihuri* delivered in 1988, the next five in 1991 and the last pair in 1993. *Träskö*, *Torsö* and *Alskär* act as fast transports. The remainder are command launches for Navy squadrons. *Vihuri* was destroyed by fire in late 1991.

VINHA   *5/1993, van Ginderen Collection* / 0069883

30 MERIUISKO CLASS (LCP)

U 201-211	**U 301-312**	**U 400 series**

Displacement, tons: 10 full load
Dimensions, feet (metres): 36 × 11.5 × 2.9 (11 × 3.5 × 0.9)
Main machinery: 2 Volvo TAMD70E diesels; 418 hp(m) (307 kW) sustained; 2 Hamilton waterjets
Speed, knots: 36; 30 full load
Complement: 3
Military lift: 48 troops
Radars: Navigation: (U 401 series): I-band.

Comment: First batch of 11 completed by Alumina Varvet from 1983 to 1986. A further four ordered in 1989. Constructed of light alloy. Fitted with small bow ramp. Two of the class equipped with cable handling system for boom defence work. Batch one has smaller cabins.

U 304   *6/2000, Finnish Army* / 0103805

36 JURMO CLASS (LCP)

U 600 series

Displacement, tons: 10 full load
Dimensions, feet (metres): 43.6 × 11.5 × 2.0 (13.3 × 3.5 × 0.6)
Main machinery: 2 Caterpillar diesels; 2 FF-jet 375 waterjets
Speed, knots: 30+
Complement: 2
Military lift: 21 troops with equipment or 2.5 tons cargo
Guns: 1 — 12.7 mm MG.
Radars: Navigation: I-band.

Comment: Developed from Meriusko class for troop carrying role. Prototype built by Alutech Ltd and delivered in 1999. Thirty-six had been delivered by 2005. Cargo hatch of composite material to provide armoured protection.

U 603   *8/2002, E & M Laursen* / 0534066

23 RAIDING CRAFT (LCVP)

Displacement, tons: 3 full load
Dimensions, feet (metres): 26.2 × 6.9 × 1 (8 × 2.1 × 0.3)
Main machinery: 1 Yanmar 4LHA-STE diesel; 240 hp (179 kW); 1 RR FF-jet 240 waterjet
Speed, knots: 30
Complement: 1
Military lift: 9 troops with equipment

Comment: First batch of 23 units ordered in February 2001. Based on Swedish Gruppbåt and built by Alutech Ltd. Delivered late 2001.

RAIDING CRAFT   *6/2001, Finnish Navy* / 0114721

1 CABLE SHIP (ANL)

PUTSAARI 92

Displacement, tons: 430 full load
Dimensions, feet (metres): 149.5 × 28.6 × 8.2 (45.6 × 8.7 × 2.5)
Main machinery: 1 Wärtsilä diesel; 510 hp(m) (375 kW); 1 shaft; active rudder; bow thruster
Speed, knots: 10
Complement: 20

Comment: Built by Rauma-Repola, Rauma, launched on 15 December 1965 and commissioned in 1966. Modernised by Wärtsilä in 1987. Fitted with two 10 ton cable winches. Strengthened for ice operations.

PUTSAARI   *6/2001, Finnish Navy* / 0114720

1 SUPPORT CRAFT (YFB)

PIKKALA (ex-*Fenno*) 96

Displacement, tons: 66 full load
Dimensions, feet (metres): 75.5 × 14.4 × 6.6 *(23 × 4.4 × 2)*
Main machinery: 1 Valmet diesel; 177 hp(m) *(130 kW)*; 1 shaft
Speed, knots: 10
Complement: 5

Comment: Used for utility and transport roles at Helsinki. Commissioned in June 1946 at Turhu.

PIKKALA *6/2000, Finnish Navy* / 0103806

2 POLLUTION CONTROL VESSELS (YPC)

HYLJE 799   **HALLI** 899

Displacement, tons: 1,500 *(Hylje)*; 1,600 *(Halli)* full load
Dimensions, feet (metres): 164; 198.5 *(Halli)* × 41 × 9.8 *(50; 60.5 × 12.5 × 3)*
Main machinery: 2 Saab diesels; 680 hp(m) *(500 kW)*; 2 shafts; active rudders; bow thruster *(Hylje)*
2 Wärtsilä diesels; 2,650 hp(m) *(19.47 MW)*; 2 shafts; active rudders *(Halli)*
Speed, knots: 7 *(Hylje)*; 13 *(Halli)*

Comment: Painted grey. Strengthened for ice. Owned by Ministry of Environment, civilian-manned but operated by Navy from Turku. *Hylje* commissioned 3 June 1981, *Halli* in January 1987. Capacity is about 550 m³ *(Hylje)* and 1,400 m³ *(Halli)* of contaminated seawater. The ships have slightly different superstructure lines aft.

HALLI *6/2000, Finnish Navy* / 0103812

ICEBREAKERS

Notes: Operation of Finnish icebreakers was transferred from the Finnish Maritime Administration to the new state-owned shipping enterprise, Finstaship, in January 2004. All the ships are based at Helsinki.

2 KARHU 2 CLASS (AGBH)

OTSO   **KONTIO**

Measurement, tons: 9,200 dwt
Dimensions, feet (metres): 324.7 × 79.4 × 26.2 *(99 × 24.2 × 8)*
Main machinery: Diesel-electric; 4 Wärtsilä Vasa 16V32 diesel generators; 22.84 MW 60 Hz sustained; 2 motors; 17,700 hp(m) *(13 MW)*; 2 shafts; 2 thrusters
Speed, knots: 18.5
Complement: 28
Helicopters: 1 light.

Comment: First ordered from Wärtsilä 29 March 1984, completed 30 January 1986. Second ordered 29 November 1985, delivered 29 January 1987. Fitted with Wärtsilä bubbler system. One other transferred to Estonia in 1993.

KONTIO *3/2002, Finstaship* / 0587709

2 URHO CLASS (AGBH)

URHO   **SISU**

Displacement, tons: 7,800 *Urho* (7,900, *Sisu*) standard; 9,500 full load
Dimensions, feet (metres): 349.7 × 78.1 × 27.2 *(106.6 × 23.8 × 8.3)*
Main machinery: Diesel-electric; 5 Wärtsilä-SEMT-Pielstick diesel generators; 25,000 hp(m) *(18.37 MW)*; 4 motors; 22,000 hp(m) *(16.2 MW)*; 4 shafts (2 fwd, 2 aft (cp props))
Speed, knots: 18
Complement: 47
Helicopters: 1 light.

Comment: Built by Wärtsilä and commissioned on 5 March 1975 and 28 January 1976 respectively. Fitted with two screws aft, taking 60 per cent of available power and two forward, taking the remainder. Similar to Swedish Atle class.

SISU *1/2003, Finstaship* / 0587708

2 TARMO CLASS (AGBH)

APU   **VOIMA**

Displacement, tons: 4,890 full load
Dimensions, feet (metres): 283.8 × 69.9 × 23.9 *(86.5 × 21.3 × 7.3)*
Main machinery: Diesel-electric; 4 Wärtsilä-Sulzer diesel generators; 12,000 hp(m) *(8.82 MW)*; 4 shafts (2 screws fwd, 2 aft)
Speed, knots: 17
Range, n miles: 7,000 at 17 kt
Complement: 45–55
Helicopters: 1 light.

Comment: Both built by Wärtsilä. *Voima* commissioned in 1954 and modernised 1978-79. *Apu* commissioned in 1970.

APU *1/2003, Finstaship* / 0587707

For details of the latest updates to ***Jane's Fighting Ships*** online and to discover the additional information available exclusively to online subscribers please visit
jfs.janes.com

2 FENNICA CLASS (AGBH)

FENNICA   **NORDICA**

Measurement, tons: 1,650 (Winter); 3,900 (Arctic); 4,800 (Summer) dwt
Dimensions, feet (metres): 380.5 × 85.3 × 27.6 *(116 × 26 × 8.4)*
Main machinery: Diesel-electric; 2 Wärtsilä Vasa 16V32D/ABB Strömberg diesel generators;
   12 MW; 2 Wärtsilä Vasa 12V32D/ABB Strömberg diesel generators; 9 MW; 2 ABB
   Strömberg motors; 2 Aquamaster US ARC 1 nozzles; 20,400 hp(m) *(15 MW)*; 3 Brunvoll
   bow thrusters; 6,120 hp(m) *(4.5 MW)*
Speed, knots: 16
Complement: 16 + 80 passengers
Radars: Navigation: 2 Selemar; I-band.
Helicopters: 1 light.

Comment: First of class ordered in October 1991, second in May 1992, from Finnyards,
Rauma. *Fennica* launched 10 September 1992 and completed 15 March 1993. *Nordica*
launched July 1993 and completed January 1994. Bollard pull 230 tons. Capable of 8 kt
at 0.8 m level ice and continuous slow speed at 1.8 m arctic level ice. 115 ton A frame
and two deck cranes of 15 and 5 tons each. Combination of azimuth propulsion units
and bow thrusters gives full dynamic positioning capability.

FENNICA   *6/2004, Finstaship* / 0587706

1 BOTNICA CLASS (AGBH)

BOTNICA

Measurement, tons: 6,370 grt
Dimensions, feet (metres): 317.2 × 78.7 × 27.9 *(96.7 × 24.0 × 8.5)*
Main machinery: Diesel-electric; 6 twin Caterpillar 3512B V12 diesels; 16,100 hp *(12 MW)*;
   2 Azipod propulsors
Speed, knots: 15
Complement: 25
Radars: Navigation: I-band.
Helicopters: 1 light.

Comment: Combined icebreaker, tug and supply vessel built at Aker Finnyards to Det
Norske Veritas class standards and delivered in 1998. During Summer, it is chartered
for servicing and intervention work on oil and gas wells in the North Sea. There is a
6.5 × 6.5 m moonpool to enable underwater servicing work.

BOTNICA   *6/2004, Finstaship* / 0587705

TUGS

2 HARBOUR TUGS (YTM)

HAUKIPÄÄ 730   **KALLANPÄÄ** 831

Displacement, tons: 38 full load
Dimensions, feet (metres): 45.9 × 16.4 × 7.5 *(14 × 5 × 2.3)*
Main machinery: 2 diesels; 360 hp(m) *(265 kW)*; 2 shafts
Speed, knots: 9
Complement: 2

Comment: Delivered by Teijon Telakka Oy in December 1985. Similar to Hauki class. Also
used as utility craft.

HAUKIPÄÄ (old number)   *6/2000, Finnish Navy* / 0103813

LAND-BASED MARITIME AIRCRAFT

Numbers/Type: 2 Agusta AB 412 Griffon.
Operational speed: 122 kt *(226 km/h)*.
Service ceiling: 17,000 ft *(5,180 m)*.
Range: 354 n miles *(656 km)*.
Role/Weapon systems: Operated by Coast Guard/Frontier force for patrol and SAR.
   Sensors: Radar and FLIR. Weapons: Unarmed at present but mountings for machine
   guns.

AB 412   *6/2005*, Finnish Navy* / 1133422

Numbers/Type: 3 Eurocopter AS 332L1 Super Puma.
Operational speed: 130 kt *(240 km/h)*.
Service ceiling: 15,090 ft *(4,600 m)*.
Range: 672 n miles *(1,245 km)*.
Role/Weapon systems: Coastal patrol, surveillance and SAR helicopters. Sensors:
   Surveillance radar, FLIR, tactical navigation systems and SAR equipment. Weapons:
   Unarmed.

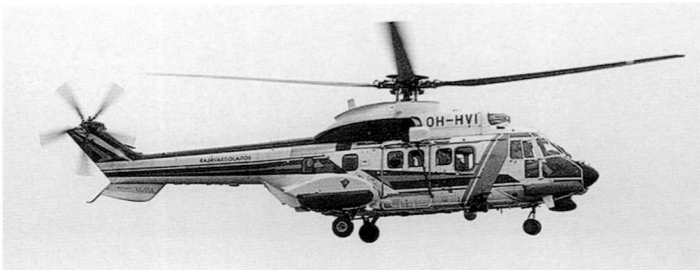

AS 332   *6/2005*, Finnish Navy* / 1133423

Numbers/Type: 2 Agusta AB 206B JetRanger.
Operational speed: 116 kt *(215 km/h)*.
Service ceiling: 13,500 ft *(4,120 m)*.
Range: 364 n miles *(674 km)*.
Role/Weapon systems: Coastal patrol and inshore surveillance helicopters. Sensors:
   Visual means only. FLIR may be fitted in due course. Weapons: Unarmed.

AB 206 (Swedish colours)   *6/2000, Andreas Karlsson, Swedish Defence Image* / 0106563

Numbers/Type: 2 Dornier Do 228-212.
Operational speed: 223 kt *(413 km/h)*.
Service ceiling: 29,600 ft *(9,020 m)*.
Range: 939 n miles *(1,740 km)*.
Role/Weapon systems: Maritime surveillance, SAR and pollution control. Acquired in 1995. Sensors: GEC-Marconi Seaspray radar; Terma Side scan radar; FLIR/TV, SLAR and IR/UV scanner. Weapons: Unarmed.

DORNIER 228 (German colours)   *9/2002, Frank Findler* / 0528878

FRONTIER GUARD

1 IMPROVED TURSAS CLASS
(OFFSHORE PATROL VESSEL) (WPBO)

MERIKARHU

Displacement, tons: 1,100 full load
Dimensions, feet (metres): 189.6 × 36.1 × 15.1 *(57.8 × 11 × 4.6)*
Main machinery: 2 Wärtsilä Vasa 8R26 diesels; 3,808 hp(m) *(2.8 MW)* sustained; 1 shaft; cp prop; bow and stern thrusters
Speed, knots: 15
Range, n miles: 2,000 at 15 kt
Complement: 30
Guns: 2—23 mm/87 (twin) can be carried.
Radars: Surface search. Navigation.

Comment: Ordered 17 June 1993 from Finnyards, and completed 28 October 1994. Capable of 5 kt in 50 cm of ice. Used as an all-weather patrol ship in the Baltic, capable of Command, SAR, tug work with 30 ton bollard pull, and environmental pollution cleaning up. Carries an RIB launched from a hydraulic crane.

MERIKARHU   *6/2005*, Finnish Navy* / 1133421

2 TURSAS CLASS
(OFFSHORE PATROL VESSELS) (WPBO)

TURSAS   **UISKO**

Displacement, tons: 730 full load
Dimensions, feet (metres): 160.8 × 34.1 × 13.1 *(49 × 10.4 × 4)*
Main machinery: 2 Wärtsilä Vasa 8R22 diesels; 3,152 hp(m) *(2.32 MW)* sustained; 2 shafts
Speed, knots: 16
Complement: 32
Guns: 2 Sako 23 mm/60 (twin).
Sonars: Simrad SS105; active scanning; 14 kHz.

Comment: First ordered from Rauma-Repola on 21 December 1984, launched 31 January 1986 and delivered 6 June 1986. Second ordered 20 March 1986, launched 19 June 1986 and delivered 27 January 1987. Operate as offshore patrol craft and can act as salvage tugs. Ice strengthened.

UISKO   *6/2005*, Finnish Navy* / 1133420

1 IMPROVED VALPAS CLASS
(OFFSHORE PATROL VESSEL) (WPBO)

TURVA

Displacement, tons: 550 full load
Dimensions, feet (metres): 159.1 × 28 × 12.8 *(48.5 × 8.6 × 3.9)*
Main machinery: 2 Wärtsilä diesels; 2,000 hp(m) *(1.47 MW)*; 1 shaft
Speed, knots: 15
Complement: 23
Guns: 1 Oerlikon 20 mm.
Sonars: Simrad SS105; active scanning; 14 kHz.

Comment: Built by Laivateollisuus, Turku and commissioned 15 December 1977. Armament changed in 1992.

TURVA   *6/1993, van Ginderen Collection* / 0069889

3 TELKKÄ CLASS (WPBO)

TELKKÄ   **TAVI**   **TIIRA**

Displacement, tons: 400 full load
Dimensions, feet (metres): 160.8 × 24.6 × 11.8 *(49 × 7.5 × 3.6)*
Main machinery: 2 diesels; 6,120 hp(m) *(4.5 MW)*; 2 shafts
Speed, knots: 20
Complement: 17
Guns: 1—20 mm.
Sonars: Sonac PTA; towed array; low frequency.

Comment: *Telkkä* entered service in July 1999, *Tavi* in 2003 and *Tiira* on 27 May 2004.

TAVI   *6/2005*, Finnish Navy* / 1133419

4 SLINGSBY SAH 2200 (HOVERCRAFT) (UCAC)

Displacement, tons: 5.5 full load
Dimensions, feet (metres): 34.8 × 13.8
  (10.6 × 4.2)
Main machinery: 1 Cummins 6CTA-8-3M-1 diesel; 300 hp
  (224 kW)
Speed, knots: 40
Range, n miles: 400 at 30 kt
Complement: 2
Military lift: 2.2 tons or 12 troops
Guns: 1 — 12.7 mm MG.
Radars: Navigation: Raytheon R41; I-band.

Comment: First one acquired from Slingsby Amphibious
  Hovercraft Company in March 1993. Three more ordered
  in February 1998 and delivered in late 1999.

SLINGSBY 2200
6/1993, Slingsby
0069892

3 GRIFFON 2000 TDX(M) (HOVERCRAFT) (UCAC)

Displacement, tons: 6.8 full load
Dimensions, feet (metres): 36.1 × 15.1
  (11 × 4.6)
Main machinery: 1 Deutz BF8L513 diesel; 320 hp *(239 kW)*
  sustained
Speed, knots: 33
Range, n miles: 300 at 25 kt
Complement: 2
Military lift: 16 troops or 2 tons
Guns: 1 — 7.62 mm MG.
Radars: Navigation: I-band.

Comment: First two acquired from Griffon, UK and
  commissioned 1 December 1994; third one bought in
  June 1995. Can be embarked in an LCU. Speed indicated
  is at Sea State 3 with a full load. Similar to those in
  service with the UK Navy.

GRIFFON 2000
6/1994, P Felstead
0080653

39 INSHORE PATROL CRAFT AND TENDERS (PB)

Class	Total	Tonnage	Speed	Commissioned
RV-37	7	20	12	1978-85
RV-90	10	25	12	1992-96
PV-11	14	10	28	1984-90

RV-11 class

6/1993 / 0069894

France
MARINE NATIONALE

Country Overview

The French Republic, which includes the island of Corsica, is situated in western Europe. With an area of 210,026 square miles, the mainland is bordered to the north by Belgium, Luxembourg and Germany, to the south-east by Switzerland and Italy and to the south-west by Spain. It has a 1,852 n mile coastline with the Atlantic Ocean, Mediterranean Sea, North Sea and English Channel. Overseas departments are French Guiana, Martinique, Guadeloupe and Réunion. Dependencies include St Pierre and Miquelon, Mayotte, New Caledonia, French Polynesia, the French Southern and Antarctic Territories, and Wallis and Futuna Islands. The capital and largest city is Paris while the principal ports are Marseille, Le Havre, Dunkirk, St Nazaire and Rouen. Strasbourg is a port on the Rhine. Territorial seas (12 n miles) are claimed. An EEZ (200 n miles) has also been claimed but not all the large number of boundaries have been defined by agreements.

Headquarters Appointments

Chief of the Naval Staff:
Amiral Alain Oudot de Dainville
Inspector General of the Navy:
Amiral Alain Coldefy
Director of Personnel:
Vice-Amiral Pierre Devaux
Major General of the Navy:
Vice-Amiral d'Escadre Pierre-François Forissier

Senior Appointments

C-in-C Atlantic Theatre (CECLANT):
Vice-Amiral d'Escadre Laurent Merer
C-in-C Mediterranean Theatre (CECMED):
Vice-Amiral d'Escadre Jean-Marie Van Huffel
Flag Officer, French Forces Polynesia (ALPACI):
Contre-Amiral Patrick Giaume
Flag Officer, Naval Forces Indian Ocean (ALINDIEN):
Contre-Amiral Hubert de Gaullier des Bordes
Flag Officer, Cherbourg:
Vice-Amiral Hubert Pinon
Flag Officer, Submarines (ALFOST):
Vice-Amiral Yves Boiffin
Flag Officer, Naval Action Force (ALFAN):
Vice-Amiral d'Escadre Philippe Sauter
Deputy Flag Officer, Naval Action Force (TOULON):
Vice-Amiral Jacques Mazars
Deputy Flag Officer, Naval Action Force (BREST):
Contre-Amiral Jean Goursaud
Flag Officer Mine Warfare Force (ALMINES):
Capitaine de Vaisseau Yves-Marie Marechal
Flag Officer Naval Aviation (ALAVIA):
Vice-Amiral Jean-Pierre Tiffou
Flag Officer Lorient and Commandant Marines (Alfusco):
Contre-Amiral Jean-Paul Cabrières

Diplomatic Representation

Defence Attaché in London:
Contre-Amiral Jacques Launay
Naval Attaché in London:
Capitaine de Vaisseau Henri-François Piot
Defence and Naval Attaché in Riyad:
Contre-Amiral Pierre Brunet de Courssou
Head of French Military Delegation to the European Union:
Vice-Amiral d'Escadre Richard Wilmot-Roussel
Head of French Military Mission to HQ SACT:
Capitaine de Vaisseau Jean-Yves Castel
Head of French Military Mission to Joint Force Command Naples:
Contre-Amiral Jean-Marie L'Huissier
Naval Attaché in Washington:
Capitaine de Vaisseau Philippe Alquier

Personnel

(a) 2006: 41,654 (4,767 officers)
(b) military service discontinued November 2001
(c) 2006: civilians in direct support: 8,958
(d) 2006: Active reserve: 6,500

Bases

Brest: Main Atlantic base. SSBN base
Toulon: Mediterranean Command base
Cherbourg: Channel base
Bayonne: Landes firing range
Small bases at Papeete (Tahiti), Fort-de-France (Martinique), Nouméa (New Caledonia), Degrad-des-Cannes (French Guiana), Port-des-Galets (La Réunion).

Shipyards (Naval)

Cherbourg: Submarines and Fast Attack Craft (private shipyard)
Brest: Major warships and refitting
Lorient: Destroyers and Frigates, MCMVs, Patrol Craft
Toulon: Major refits.

Dates

Armement pour essais: After launching when the ship is sufficiently advanced to allow a crew to live on board, and the commanding officer has joined. From this date the ship hoists the French flag and is ready to undertake her first harbour trials.
Armement définitif: On this date the ship has received her full complement and is able to undergo sea trials.
Clôture d'armement: Trials are completed and the ship is now able to undertake her first endurance cruise.
Croisière de longue durée or *traversée de longue durée:* The endurance cruise follows the *clôture d'armement* and lasts until the ship is accepted with all systems fully operational.
Admission au service actif: Commissioning date.

Reserve

A ship in 'Reserve Normale' has no complement but is available at short notice. 'Reserve Speciale' means that a refit will be required before the ship can go to sea again. 'Condamnation' is the state before being broken up or sold; at this stage a Q number is allocated.

Prefix to Ships' Names

FS is used in NATO communications but is not official.

Strength of the Fleet

Type	Active (Reserve)	Building (Projected)
Submarines (SSBN)	4	1
Submarines (SSN)	6	(6)
Aircraft Carriers	1	(1)
Helicopter Carrier	1	—
Destroyers	12	2
Frigates	20	— (17)
Public Service Force	7	—
Patrol Craft	10	—
LPH/LSDs	4	1
LST/LCT	8	—
LCMs	17	—
Route Survey Vessels	3	—
Minehunters	13	—
Diving Tenders	5	—
Survey/Research Ships	6	2
Tankers (AOR)	4	—
Maintenance Ships	2	(2)
Supply Tenders	7	—
Transports	9	—
Training Ships	16	—

DELETIONS

Submarines

2005 *Indomptable*

Patrol Forces

2003 *Stellis*
2005 *Pétulante*

Amphibious Forces

2004 *Champlain*
2006 *Ouragan*

Survey and Research Ships

2006 *Denti*

Auxiliaries

2003 *Garonne*
2004 *Mouette*
2005 *Elfe, Dryade, Ondine*
2006 *Isard*

Tugs

2003 *Mouette*
2004 *Eider*
2005 *Mésange, Papayer*

FLEET AIR ARM BASES

Notes: In addition to the following squadrons, there are two other squadrons operating with mixed Air Force and Navy crews on behalf of both services:
• Helicopter Squadron EH-1/67 "Pyrénées", based at Cazaux AFB, for the combat SAR role, operating seven specialised Aerospatiale SA-330 Puma helicopters. A Eurocopter AS-532 Cougar Mk 2 Resco was delivered in September 1999 for testing in order to settle the equipment suite for the three other machines ordered. All four new Resco helicopters became operational in 2003. Pumas and Cougars regularly embark on *Charles de Gaulle*.
• Training Squadron EAT-319, based at Avord AFB, with Embraer 121 Xingu light transport (some coming from the Navy) for pilot basic training.

Embarked Squadrons

Base/Squadron No	Aircraft	Task
Lann Bihoué/4F	E-2C Hawkeye	AEW
Landivisiau/11F	Super Étendard	Assault, Recce
Landivisiau/12F	Rafale M	Air Defence
Landivisiau/17F	Super Étendard	Assault, Recce
Hyères/31F	Lynx	ASW
Lanvéoc-Poulmic/34F	Lynx	ASW
St-Mandrier/36F	Panther	Surveillance

Support Squadrons

Base/Squadron No	Aircraft	Task
Hyères/CEPA/10S	Various	Research, trials
Lanvéoc-Poulmic/22S (detachments on ships)	Alouette III	Support Atlantic Region
Lanvéoc-Poulmic/32F (detachment at Hyères)	Super Frelon,	Transport, SAR
Hyères/35F (detachments at various locations and ships)	Dauphin 2, Alouette III	Surveillance, SAR, Carrier-borne SAR
Landivisiau/57S	Falcon 10 MER	Support, Training

Maritime Patrol Squadrons

Base/Squadron No	Aircraft	Task
Nîmes-Garons/21F	Atlantique Mk 2	MP
Lann Bihoué/23F	Atlantique Mk 2	MP
Lann Bihoué/24F	Falcon 50M/Xingu Gardian	Surveillance, SAR
Faaa (Papeete)/25F	Gardian	Surveillance, SAR
(detachments at Nouméa, New Caledonia and Fort-de-France, Antilles)		
Nîmes-Garons/28F	Nord 262E/Xingu	Surveillance, SAR, Flying School, liaison

Training Squadrons

Base/Squadron No	Aircraft	Task
Lanvéoc-Poulmic/EIP/50S	MS 880 Rallye/CAP 10	Initial Flying School, Recreational

Approximate Fleet Dispositions 1 May 2006

		Channel	Atlantic	Mediterranean	Indian Ocean*	Pacific	Antilles F. Guiana
Carriers	FAN	—	1 (hel)	1	—	—	—
SSBN	FOST	—	4	—	—	—	—
SSN	FOST	—	—	6	—	—	—
DDG/DDH	FAN	—	5	7	—	—	—
FFG	FAN	—	5	9	2	2	1
MCMV (incl tenders)	FAN	1	14	5	—	—	—
Patrol Forces**	FAN/GM	3	6	1	6	6	4
LPD/LSD	FAN	—	—	4	—	—	—
LST/LCT	FAN	—	—	3	2	2	1
AOR	FAN	—	—	3	1	—	—

FAN = Force d'Action Navale (HQ at Toulon). All surface ships based at Toulon, Brest or overseas.
FOST = Force Océanique Stratégique (HQ at Brest). SSBNs based at l'Île Longue near Brest. All SSNs based at Toulon.
GM = Gendarmerie Maritime
Notes:
* Plus one or two DDG/DDH/FFG regularly deployed from Toulon.
** Patrol forces include vessels manned by the Navy and major craft from the Gendarmerie Maritime.

<h1 style="text-align:center">PENNANT LIST</h1>

Submarines		Mine Warfare Forces					
S 601	Rubis	M 611	Vulcain	P 713	Capitaine Moulié (GM)	A 652	Mutin
S 602	Saphir	M 614	Styx	P 714	Lieut Jamet (GM)	A 653	La Grand Hermine
S 603	Casabianca	M 622	Pluton	P 715	Bellis (GM)	A 664	Malabar
S 604	Émeraude	M 641	Éridan	P 716	MDLC Jacques (GM)	A 669	Tenace
S 605	Améthyste	M 642	Cassiopée	P 720	Géranium (GM)	A 675	Fréhel
S 606	Perle	M 643	Andromède	P 721	Jonquille (GM)	A 676	Saire
S 615	L'Inflexible	M 644	Pégase	P 722	Violette (GM)	A 677	Armen
S 616	Le Triomphant	M 645	Orion	P 723	Jasmin (GM)	A 678	La Houssaye
S 617	Le Téméraire	M 646	Croix du Sud	P 740	Fulmar (GM)	A 679	Kéréon
S 618	Le Vigilant	M 647	Aigle	P 761	Mimosa (GM)	A 680	Sicié
S 619	Le Terrible (bldg)	M 648	Lyre	P 776	Sténia (GM)	A 681	Taunoa
		M 649	Persée	P 778	Réséda (GM)	A 682	Rascas
Aircraft and Helicopter Carriers		M 650	Sagittaire	P 789	Melia (GM)	A 693	Acharné
		M 651	Verseau	P 790	Vétiver (GM)	A 695	Bélier
R 91	Charles de Gaulle	M 652	Céphée	P 791	Hortensia (GM)	A 696	Buffle
R 97	Jeanne d'Arc	M 653	Capricorne			A 697	Bison
		M 770	Antarès	GM = Gendarmerie Maritime		A 712	Athos
Destroyers		M 771	Altaïr			A 713	Aramis
		M 772	Aldébaran	**Amphibious Forces**		A 722	Poséidon
D 603	Duquesne					A 748	Léopard
D 610	Tourville	**Patrol Forces**		L 9011	Foudre	A 749	Panthère
D 612	De Grasse			L 9012	Siroco	A 750	Jaguar
D 614	Cassard	P 601	Elorn (GM)	L 9013	Mistral	A 751	Lynx
D 615	Jean Bart	P 602	Verdon (GM)	L 9014	Tonnerre (bldg)	A 752	Guépard
D 620	Forbin (bldg)	P 603	Adour (GM)	L 9022	Orage	A 753	Chacal
D 621	Chevalier Paul (bldg)	P 604	Scarpe (GM)	L 9031	Francis Garnier	A 754	Tigre
D 640	Georges Leygues	P 605	Vertonne (GM)	L 9032	Dumont D'Urville	A 755	Lion
D 641	Dupleix	P 606	Dumbéa (GM)	L 9033	Jacques Cartier	A 758	Beautemps-Beaupré
D 642	Montcalm	P 607	Yser (GM)	L 9034	La Grandière	A 759	Dupuy de Lôme
D 643	Jean de Vienne	P 608	Argens (GM)	L 9051	Sabre	A 768	Élan
D 644	Primauguet	P 609	Hérault (GM)	L 9052	Dague	A 770	Glycine
D 645	La Motte-Picquet	P 610	Gravona (GM)	L 9061	Rapière	A 771	Églantine
D 646	Latouche-Tréville	P 611	Odet (GM)	L 9062	Hallebarde	A 774	Chevreuil
		P 612	Maury (GM)	L 9090	Gapeau	A 775	Gazelle
Frigates		P 671	Glaive (GM)			A 785	Thétis
		P 672	Épée (GM)	**Major Auxiliaries Survey and Support**		A 791	Lapérouse
F 710	La Fayette	P 675	Arago	**Ships**		A 792	Borda
F 711	Surcouf	P 676	Flamant			A 793	Laplace
F 712	Courbet	P 677	Cormoran	A 601	Monge	L 9077	Bougainville
F 713	Aconit	P 678	Pluvier	A 607	Meuse	P 674	D'Entrecasteaux
F 714	Guépratte	P 679	Grèbe	A 608	Var	Y 613	Faune
F 730	Floréal	P 680	Sterne	A 613	Achéron	Y 638	Lardier
F 731	Prairial	P 681	Albatros	A 615	Loire	Y 639	Giens
F 732	Nivôse	P 682	L'Audacieuse	A 616	Le Malin	Y 640	Mengam
F 733	Ventôse	P 683	La Boudeuse	A 620	Jules Verne	Y 641	Balaguier
F 734	Vendémiaire	P 684	La Capricieuse	A 630	Marne	Y 642	Taillat
F 735	Germinal	P 685	La Fougueuse	A 631	Somme	Y 643	Nividic
F 789	Lieutenant de Vaisseau le Hénaff	P 686	La Glorieuse	A 633	Taape	Y 647	Le Four
F 790	Lieutenant de Vaisseau Lavallée	P 687	La Gracieuse	A 634	Rari	Y 649	Port Cros
F 791	Commandant l'Herminier	P 688	La Moqueuse	A 635	Revi	Y 692	Telenn Mor
F 792	Premier Maître l'Her	P 689	La Railleuse	A 636	Maito	Y 700	Nereide
F 793	Commandant Blaison	P 690	La Rieuse	A 637	Maroa	Y 702	Naiade
F 794	Enseigne de Vaisseau Jacoubet	P 691	La Tapageuse	A 638	Manini	Y 706	Chimère
F 795	Commandant Ducuing	P 703	Lilas (GM)	A 649	L'Étoile	Y 711	Farfadet
F 796	Commandant Birot	P 704	Bégonia (GM)	A 641	Esterel	Y 750	La Persévérante
F 797	Commandant Bouan	P 709	MDLC Richard (GM)	A 642	Lubéron	Y 770	Morse
		P 710	General Delfosse (GM)	A 645	Alize	Y 771	Otarie
				A 650	La Belle Poule	Y 772	Loutre
						Y 773	Phoque

SUBMARINES

Strategic Missile Submarines (SSBN/SNLE)

1 L'INFLEXIBLE M4 CLASS (SSBN/SNLE)

Name	No	Builders	Laid down	Launched	Commissioned
L'INFLEXIBLE	S 615	DCN, Cherbourg	27 Mar 1980	23 June 1982	1 Apr 1985

Displacement, tons: 8,080 surfaced; 8,920 dived
Dimensions, feet (metres): 422.1 × 34.8 × 32.8 *(128.7 × 10.6 × 10)*
Main machinery: Nuclear; turbo-electric; 1 PWR; 2 turbo-alternators; 1 Jeumont Schneider motor; 16,000 hp(m) *(11.76 MW)*; twin SEMT-Pielstick/Jeumont Schneider 8 PA4 V 185 SM diesel-electric auxiliary propulsion; 9.9 MW; 1 emergency motor; 1 shaft
Speed, knots: 20 dived
Range, n miles: 5,000 at 4 kt on auxiliary propulsion only
Complement: 135 (15 officers) (2 crews)

Missiles: SLBM: 16 Aerospatiale M45/TN 75; 3-stage solid fuel rockets; inertial guidance to 6,000 km *(3,240 n miles)*; thermonuclear warhead with 6 MRV each of 100 kT.
SSM: Aerospatiale SM 39 Exocet; launched from 21 in *(533 mm)* torpedo tubes; inertial cruise; active radar homing to 50 km *(27 n miles)* at 0.9 Mach; warhead 165 kg.
Torpedoes: 4—21 in *(533 mm)* tubes. ECAN L5 Mod 3; dual purpose; active/passive homing to 9.5 km *(5.1 n miles)* at 35 kt; warhead 150 kg; depth to 550 m *(1,800 ft)*; and ECAN F17 Mod 2; wire-guided; active/passive homing to 20 km *(10.8 n miles)* at 40 kt; warhead 250 kg; depth 600 m *(1,970 ft)*; total of 18 torpedoes and SSM carried in a mixed load.
Countermeasures: ESM: Thomson-CSF ARUR 12/DR 3000U; intercept.
Weapons control: SAD (Système d'Armes de Dissuasion) strategic data system (for SLBMs); SAT (Système d'Armes Tactique) tactical data system and DLA 1A weapon control system (for SSM and torpedoes).
Radars: Navigation: Thomson-CSF DRUA 33; I-band.
Sonars: Thomson Sintra DSUX 21B 'multifunction' passive bow and flank arrays.
DUUX 5; passive ranging and intercept; low frequency.
DSUV 61B; towed array; very low frequency.

Programmes: With the paying off of Le Redoutable in December 1991, the remaining submarines of the class became known as L'Inflexible class SNLE M4.

L'INFLEXIBLE *7/2004, H M Steele* / 1042262

L'INFLEXIBLE *7/2004, B Prézelin* / 1042173

Modernisation: A successful test firing of an M 45 missile, containing components of the next generation M 51 missile, was conducted on 18 April 2001. L'Inflexible to be refitted in 2005.
Structure: Diving depth, 250 m *(820 ft)* approx.

Operational: L'Inflexible is planned to pay off by 2010. L'Indomptable decommissioned on 19 October 2005. Le Tonnant paid off to reserve in December 1999. Based at Ile Longue, Brest.

3 + 1 LE TRIOMPHANT CLASS (SSBN/SNLE-NG)

Name	No	Builders	Laid down	Launched	Commissioned
LE TRIOMPHANT	S 616	DCN, Cherbourg	9 June 1989	13 July 1993	21 Mar 1997
LE TÉMÉRAIRE	S 617	DCN, Cherbourg	18 Dec 1993	8 Aug 1997	23 Dec 1999
LE VIGILANT	S 618	DCN, Cherbourg	1997	12 Apr 2003	26 Nov 2004
LE TERRIBLE	S 619	DCN, Cherbourg	Nov 2002	2008	July 2010

Displacement, tons: 12,640 surfaced; 14,335 dived
Dimensions, feet (metres): 453 × 41; 55.8 (aft planes) × 41 *(138 × 12.5; 17 × 12.5)*
Main machinery: Nuclear; turbo-electric; 1 PWR Type K15 (enlarged CAS 48); 150 MW; 2 turbo-alternators; 1 motor; 41,500 hp(m) *(30.5 MW)*; diesel-electric auxiliary propulsion; 2 SEMT-Pielstick 8 PA4 V 200 SM diesels; 900 kW; 1 emergency motor; 1 shaft; pump jet propulsor
Speed, knots: 25 dived
Complement: 111 (15 officers) (2 crews)

Missiles: SLBM: 16 Aerospatiale M45/TN 75; 3-stage solid fuel rockets; inertial guidance to 6,000 km *(3,240 n miles)*; thermonuclear warhead with 6 MRV each of 100 kT. To be replaced by M51.1/TN 75 which has a planned range of 8,000 km *(4,300 n miles)* and 6 MRVs (to be fitted first in S 619 in 2010) and from 2015 by M51.2 (to be fitted first in S 618) with the new TNO (Tête Nucléaire Océanique) warhead.
SSM: Aerospatiale SM 39 Exocet; launched from 21 in *(533 mm)* torpedo tubes; inertial cruise; active radar homing to 50 km *(27 n miles)* at 0.9 Mach; warhead 165 kg.
Torpedoes: 4—21 in *(533 mm)* tubes. ECAN L5 Mod 3; dual purpose; active/passive homing to 9.5 km *(5.1 n miles)* at 35 kt; warhead 150 kg; depth to 550 m *(1,800 ft)*; total of 18 torpedoes and SSM carried in a mixed load.
Countermeasures: ESM: Thomson-CSF ARUR 13/DR 3000U; intercept.
Weapons control: SAD (Système d'Armes de Dissuasion) strategic data system (for SLBMs) SAD M5I will be fitted in S 619; SAT (Système d'Armes Tactique) tactical data system and DLA 4A weapon control system (for SSM and torpedoes). SYCOBS to be fitted in S 619.
Radars: Search: Dassault; I-band.
Sonars: Thomson Sintra DMUX 80 'multifunction' passive bow and flank arrays. DUUX 5; passive ranging and intercept; low frequency.
DSUV 61; towed array; very low frequency.

LE VIGILANT *4/2004, H M Steele* / 1042260

Programmes: *Le Triomphant* ordered 10 March 1986. *Le Téméraire* ordered 18 October 1989. *Le Vigilant* ordered 27 May 1993 with first steel cut 9 December 1993. Hull transferred to dock on 12 April 2003 and sea trials began in January 2004. *Le Terrible* ordered 28 July 2000 and first steel cut 24 October 2000. Class of six originally planned, but reduced to four after the end of the Cold War. Sous-marins Nucléaires Lanceurs d'Engins-Nouvelle Génération (SNLE-NG).
Modernisation: Development of the M5 missile discontinued in favour of the less expensive M51 which is planned to equip S 619 (M 51.1) in 2010 and the first three submarines between 2010 and 2015. Warhead TN O on (M 51.2) is to replace TN 75 (on M 51.1) by 2015.
Structure: Built of HLES 100 steel capable of withstanding pressures of more than 100 kg/mm². Diving depth 500 m

(1,640 ft). Height from keel to top of fin is 21.3 m *(69.9 ft)*. Plans to lengthen the hull in later ships of the class have been shelved.
Operational: First sea cruise of *Le Triomphant* 16 July to 22 August 1995. First submerged M45 launch on 14 February 1995, second on 19 September 1996. *Le Téméraire* official trials started April 1998, first submerged M 45 launch 4 May 1999. *Le Triomphant* completed 30 month refit in October 2004 and conducted test launch of M45 missile on 2 February 2005. *Le Téméraire* started refit in early 2006 and is to complete in late 2007. *Le Vigilant* started sea trials on 1 April 2004. The first underwater test launch of the M 51.1 missile is to be conducted from *Le Terrible* in 2009, following land-based tests in 2006 and 2007. All submarines based at Ile Longue, Brest.

LE VIGILANT *5/2004, B Prézelin* / 1042175

LE TÉMÉRAIRE *6/2002, French Navy* / 0529140

Attack Submarines (SSN/SNA)

Notes: (1) The Agosta class submarine *Ouessant* was re-introduced into service on 5 August 2005 following a refit. It is to be used as a training vessel by DCN to support submarine sales to Malaysia.
(2) France signed an MoU with Norway and UK on 5 August 2003 for the procurement of the NATO Submarine Rescue System (NSRS). To be based in UK, it is to become operational in 2007.

6 RUBIS AMÉTHYSTE CLASS (SSN/SNA)

Name	No
RUBIS	S 601
SAPHIR	S 602
CASABIANCA	S 603
ÉMERAUDE	S 604
AMÉTHYSTE	S 605
PERLE	S 606

Builders	Laid down	Launched	Commissioned
Cherbourg Naval Dockyard	11 Dec 1976	7 July 1979	23 Feb 1983
Cherbourg Naval Dockyard	1 Sep 1979	1 Sep 1981	6 July 1984
Cherbourg Naval Dockyard	19 Sep 1979	22 Dec 1984	13 May 1987
Cherbourg Naval Dockyard	4 Mar 1981	12 Apr 1986	15 Sep 1988
Cherbourg Naval Dockyard	31 Oct 1983	14 May 1988	20 Mar 1992
Cherbourg Naval Dockyard	27 Mar 1987	22 Sep 1990	7 July 1993

Displacement, tons: 2,410 surfaced; 2,670 dived
Dimensions, feet (metres): 241.5 × 24.9 × 21 *(73.6 × 7.6 × 6.4)*
Main machinery: Nuclear; turbo-electric; 1 PWR CAS 48; 48 MW; 2 turbo-alternators; 1 motor; 9,500 hp(m) *(7 MW)*; SEMT-Pielstick/Jeumont Schneider 8 PA4 V 185 SM diesel-electric auxiliary propulsion; 450 kW; 1 emergency motor; 1 pump jet propulsor
Speed, knots: 25
Complement: 70 (10 officers) (2 crews)

Missiles: SSM: Aerospatiale SM 39 Exocet; launched from 21 in *(533 mm)* torpedo tubes; inertial cruise; active radar homing to 50 km *(27 n miles)* at 0.9 Mach; warhead 165 kg.
Torpedoes: 4—21 in *(533 mm)* tubes. ECAN F17 Mod 2; wire-guided; active/passive homing to 20 km *(10.8 n miles)* at 40 kt; warhead 250 kg; depth 600 m *(1,970 ft)*. Total of 14 torpedoes and missiles carried in a mixed load.
Mines: Up to 32 FG 29 in lieu of torpedoes.
Countermeasures: ESM: Thomson-CSF ARUR 13/DR 3000U; intercept.
Combat data systems: TIT (Traitement des Informations Tactiques) data system; OPSMER command support system; Syracuse 2 SATCOM. Link 11 (receive only).
Weapons control: LAT (Lancement des Armes Tactiques) system.
Radars: Navigation: Kelvin Hughes 1007; I-band.
Sonars: Thomson Sintra DMUX 20 multifunction; passive search; low frequency.
DSUV 62C; DUUG 7 towed passive array; very low frequency.
DSUV 22 *(Saphir)*; listening suite.

Programmes: The programme was terminated early by defence economies with the seventh of class *Turquoise* and eighth of class *Diamant* being cancelled.
Modernisation: Between 1989 and 1995 the first four of this class converted under operation Améthyste (AMÉlioration Tactique HYdrodynamique Silence Transmission Ecoute) to bring them to the same standard of ASW (included new sonars) efficiency as *Améthyste* and *Perle* rather than that required for the original anti-surface ship role. Two F17 torpedoes can be guided simultaneously against separate targets. *Saphir* recommissioned 1 July 1991, *Rubis* in February 1993; *Casabianca* in June 1994 and *Émeraude* in March 1996. A new radar added on a telescopic mast. A modernisation programme began in 2004. Upgrades include improvements to the tactical system and installation of a pump jet propulsor.
Structure: Diving depth, greater than 300 m *(984 ft)*. There has been a marked reduction in the size of the reactor compared with the L'Inflexible class. On completion of the modernisation programme, all six of the class are virtually identical.

PERLE   *6/2005*, Michael Nitz* / 1153126

CASABIANCA   *4/2005*, B Prézelin* / 1153197

RUBIS   *1/2006*, Derek Fox* / 1151173

Operational: All operational SSNs are assigned to Escadrille des Sous-Marins nucléaires d'attaque (ESNA) based at Toulon but frequently deploy to the Atlantic or overseas. Endurance rated at 45 days, limited by amount of food carried. *Rubis* collided with a tanker on 17 July 1993 and has undergone extensive repairs. *Émeraude* had a bad steam leak on 30 March 1994 which caused casualties amongst the crew. *Saphir* undertook a refit/refuel in September 2000 following reactor problems. The submarine returned to service in late 2001. Modernisation refits completed for *Améthyste* (2005) and scheduled for *Saphir* (2006-07) and *Rubis* (2007-08). Service life of all boats extended to 30 years. To be replaced by the Barracuda class.

0 + 6 BARRACUDA CLASS (SSN)

Name	No
—	—

Builders	Laid down	Launched	Commissioned
DCN, Cherbourg	2006	2013	2014

Displacement, tons: 4,765 surfaced; 5,000 dived
Dimensions, feet (metres): 326.4 × 28.9 × ? *(99.5 × 8.8 × ?)*
Main machinery: Nuclear; turbo-electric; 1 PWR K-15; 1 shaft; pump jet propulsor
Speed, knots: 25 dived
Complement: 60 (8 officers)

Missiles: SLCM: MBDA Scalp land-attack missile launched in capsule from 21 in torpedo tubes; inertial cruise and tercom, electro-optic homing to 400 km *(215 n miles)* at 0.9 Mach; warhead 400 kg.
SSM: Aerospatiale SM 39 Exocet launched from 21 in *(533 mm)* torpedo tubes; inertial cruise; active radar homing to 50 km *(27 n miles)* at 0.9 Mach; warhead 165 kg.
Torpedoes: 4—21 in *(533 mm)* bow tubes. WASS Black Shark torpedoes. Total of 25 torpedoes/missiles in mixed load.
Mines: In lieu of torpedoes.
Countermeasures: ESM.
Combat data systems: SYCOBS.
Radars: Surface search: I-band.
Sonars: Bow sonar, wide aperture flank array and a reelable thin-line towed array.

Programmes: Studies for a new generation SSN (Project Barracuda) funded under the 1997-2002 budget. Programme launched on 14 October 1998. DCN (submarine design authority) expected to present detailed commercial and technical offer in June 2005 for design, development and initial production. A contract for long lead items in 2005 is to be followed by a main contract, covering production of an initial three boats and a 10-year integrated logistic support package by mid-2006. First of class expected to start building at Cherbourg in 2006 with subsequent boats to be built at a rate of one

BARRACUDA CLASS (artist's impression)   *11/2004, DCN* / 0590253

every 20 months to replace Rubis class submarines. The last one is to be delivered in 2024.
Structure: Much of the technology will emanate from the Le Triomphant design as well as new features developed for the Scorpene design. A high level of automation is planned to reduce complement to 60. Diving depth is over 350 m. A hybrid propulsion system will use electric propulsion at cruise speeds and turbo-mechanical propulsion for higher speeds.
Operational: Sea trials for the first of class are scheduled for 2013 and entry into service in 2014/15.

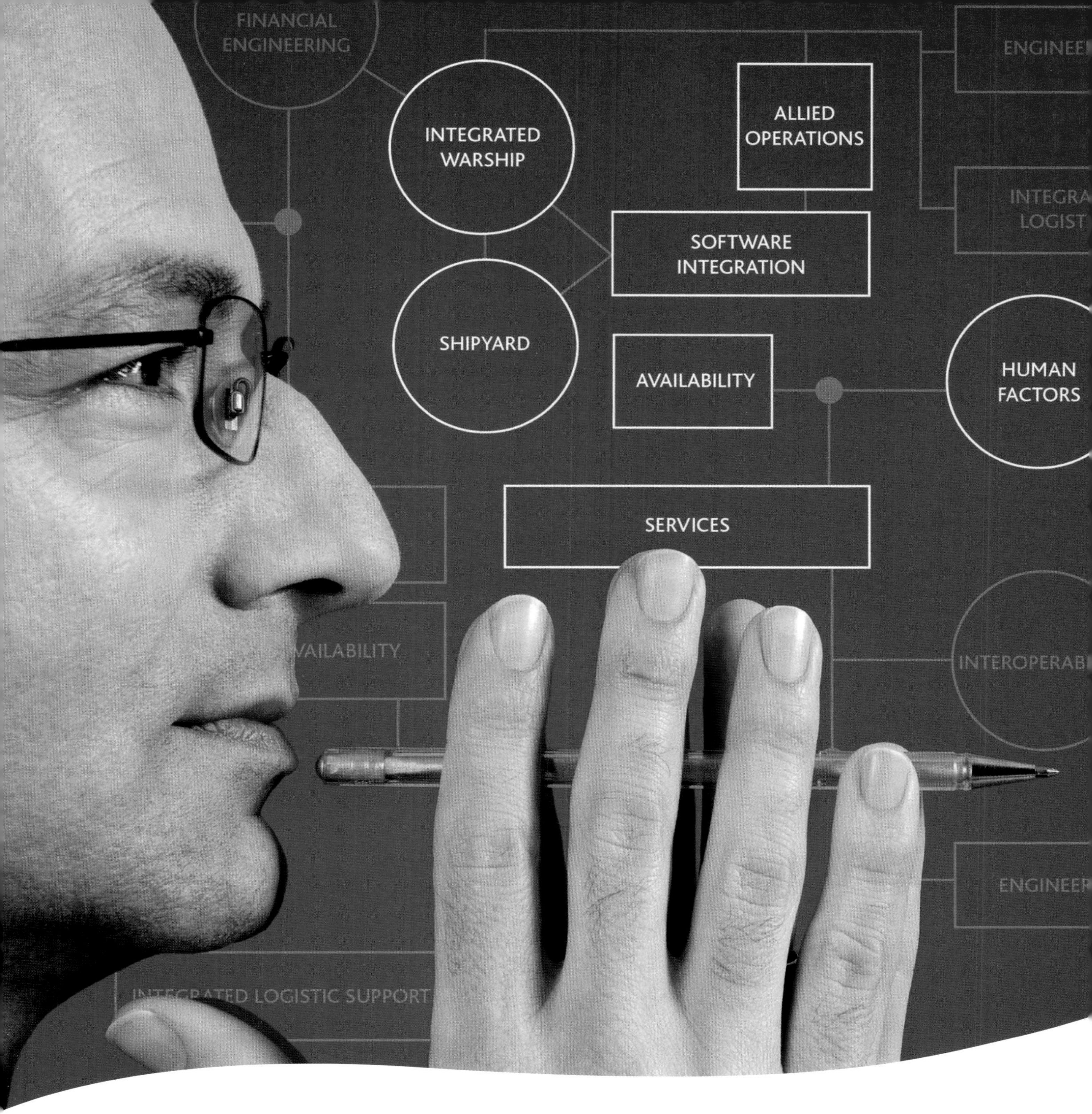

FINANCIAL
ENGINEERING

ENGINEER

INTEGRATED
WARSHIP

ALLIED
OPERATIONS

INTEGRA
LOGIST

SOFTWARE
INTEGRATION

SHIPYARD

AVAILABILITY

HUMAN
FACTORS

AVAILABILITY

SERVICES

INTEROPERAB

INTEGRATED LOGISTIC SUPPORT

ENGINEER

He's the intelligence behind your warships, and he's backed by our unique experience working with the world's most powerful navies. Our warships are intelligent because they're highly interoperable, designed as part of an integrated approach to naval defence and security. As Europe's leading naval defence group, DCN is a prime contractor, naval architect, systems integrator and support specialist. To deliver your warship programmes effectively, from concept to decommissioning. In Europe and around the world. **www.dcn.fr**

I INTEGRATED WARSHIPS **I** STRATEGIC SYSTEMS **I** SERVICES **I** EQUIPMENT **I**

DCN

EXPERTS IN
NAVAL SYSTEMS

AIRCRAFT CARRIERS

1 CHARLES DE GAULLE CLASS (CVNM/PAN)

Name	No	Builders	Laid down	Launched	Commissioned
CHARLES DE GAULLE	R 91	DCN, Brest	14 Apr 1989	7 May 1994	18 May 2001

Displacement, tons: 36,600 standard; 42,000 full load
Dimensions, feet (metres): 857.7 oa; 780.8 wl × 211.3 oa; 103.3 wl × 30.9 *(261.5; 238 × 64.4; 31.5 × 9.4)*
Flight deck, feet (metres): 857.7 × 211.3 *(261.5 × 64.4)*
Main machinery: Nuclear; 2 PWR Type K15; 300 MW; 2 GEC Alsthom turbines; 82,000 hp(m) *(61 MW)* sustained; 2 shafts
Speed, knots: 27
Complement: 1,256 ship's company (94 officers) plus 610 aircrew plus 42 flag staff (accommodation for 1,950) (plus temporary 800 marines)

Missiles: SAM: EUROSAAM SAAM/F system with 4 (2 port, 2 starboard) DCN Sylver A43 octuple VLS launchers ❶; MBDA ASTER 15; inertial guidance and mid-course update; active radar homing at 3 Mach to 30 km *(16.2 n miles)*; warhead 13 kg. 32 weapons.
2 Matra Sadral PDMS sextuple launchers ❷; Mistral; IR homing to 4 km *(2.2 n miles)*; warhead 3 kg; anti-sea-skimmer; able to engage targets down to 10 ft above sea level.
Guns: 4 Giat 20F2 20 mm; 720 rds/min to 8 km *(4.3 n miles)*; weight of shell: 0.25 kg.
Countermeasures: Decoys: 4 CSEE Sagaie AMBL-2A 10-barrelled trainable launchers ❸; medium range; chaff to 8 km *(4.3 n miles)*; IR flares to 3 km *(1.6 n miles)*. Dassault LAD offboard decoys. SLAT torpedo decoys from 2006.
ESM: Thomson-CSF ARBR 21; intercept. 1 SAT DIBV 2A Vampir MB; (IRST) ❹.
ECM: 2 ARBB 33B ❺; jammers.
Combat data systems: SENIT 8; Links 11, 14 and 16. Syracuse 2 and FLEETSATCOM ❻. AIDCOMER and MCCIS command support systems.
Weapons control: 2 DIBC 2A (Sagem VIGY-105) optronic directors.
Radars: Air search: Thomson-CSF DRBJ 11B ❼; 3D; E/F-band; range 366 km *(200 n miles)* for aircraft.
Thales DRBV 26D Jupiter ❽; D-band; range 183 km *(100 n miles)* for 2 m² target.
Air/surface search: Thomson-CSF DRBV 15C Sea Tiger Mk 2 ❾; E/F-band; range 110 km *(60 n miles)* for 2 m² target.
Navigation: Two Racal 1229 (DRBN 34A) ❿; I-band.
Fire control: Thomson-CSF Arabel 3D ⓫; I/J-band (for SAAM); range 70 km *(38 n miles)* for 2 m² target.
Tacan: NRBP 20A ⓬.
Sonars: To include SLAT torpedo attack warning.

Fixed-wing aircraft: 20 Super Étendard, 2 E-2C Hawkeye. 12 Rafale F1.
Helicopters: 2 AS 565 Panther or 2 AS 322 Cougar (AF) or 2 Super Frelon plus 2 Dauphin SAR.

Programmes: On 23 September 1980 the Defence Council decided to build two nuclear-propelled carriers to replace *Clemenceau* in 1996 and *Foch* some years later. First of class ordered 4 February 1986, first metal cut 24 November 1987. Hull floated for technical trials on 19 December 1992, and back in dock on 8 January 1993. A 19.8 m *(65 ft)* long one-twelfth scale model was used for hydrodynamic trials. Building programme delayed three years due to defence budget cuts.
Modernisation: From October 1999 to March 2000 modifications included additional radiation shielding, and lengthening of angled flight deck by 4.4 m. A 43 launchers to be replaced by A 50 (for ASTER 15 and ASTER 30) in due course.

CHARLES DE GAULLE   *6/2005*, Per Körnefeldt* / 1153174

CHARLES DE GAULLE   *5/2001, Ships of the World* / 0130446

Structure: Two lifts 62.3 × 41 ft *(19 × 12.5 m)* of 36 tons capacity. Hangar for 20-25 aircraft; dimensions 454.4 × 96.5 × 20 ft *(138.5 × 29.4 × 6.1 m)*. Angled deck 8.5° and 655.7 ft *(200 m)* overall length. Catapults: 2 USN Type C13-3; length 246 ft *(75 m)* for Super Étendards and up to 23 tonne aircraft. Enhanced weight capability of flight deck to allow operation of AEW aircraft. Island placed well forward so that both lifts can be protected from the weather. CSEE Dallas (Deck Approach and Landing Laser System) fitted, later to be replaced by MLS system. Active fin stabilisers. Bunkerage of 3,000 cum of avgas and 1,500 cum dieso.

Operational: Seven years' continuous steaming at 25 kt available before refuelling (same reactors as *Le Triomphant*). Both reactors self-sustaining by 10 June 1998. Sea trials started 26 January 1999 and after handover to the Navy on 28 September 2000, continued until 9 November 2000 when a large section of the port propeller was lost while steaming at high speed in the west Atlantic. Trials resumed on 26 March 2001 with spare propellers from decommissioned *Clemenceau* (speed limited to 23 kt). Deployed Indian Ocean, December 2001 to June 2002, successful ASTER 15 firing on 30 October 2002. A 15-month refuel/refit is to start in late 2006. New propellers are expected to be installed during this period.

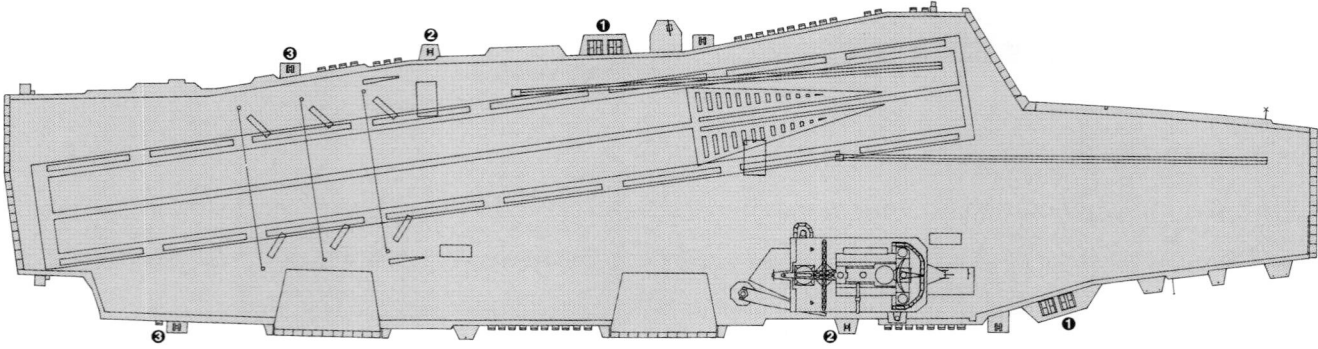

CHARLES DE GAULLE   *(Scale 1 : 1,500), Ian Sturton* / 0104438

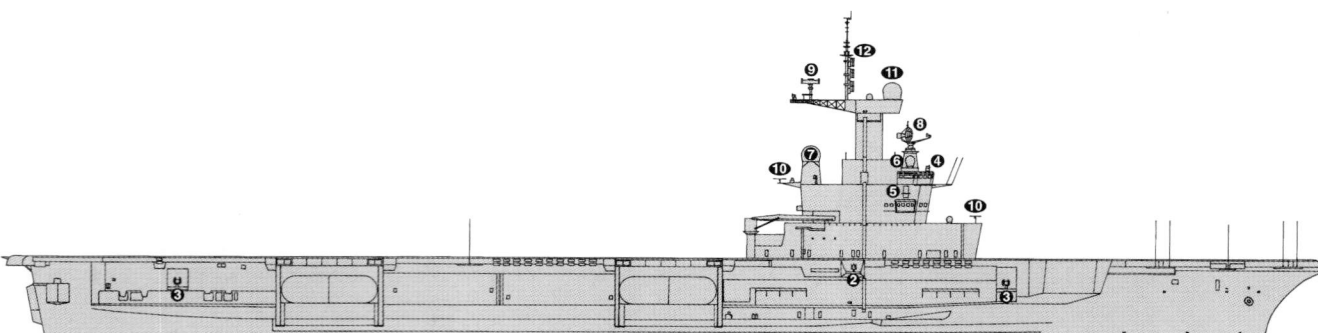

CHARLES DE GAULLE   *(Scale 1 : 1,500), Ian Sturton* / 0069903

CHARLES DE GAULLE

5/2001, Ships of the World / 0130447

CHARLES DE GAULLE

6/2005*, B Sullivan / 1153155

0 + (1) FUTURE AIRCRAFT CARRIER CLASS (CV)

Name	No	Builders	Laid down	Launched	Commissioned
—	—	—	2009	2011	2014

Displacement, tons: 65,000 full load
Dimensions, feet (metres): 928.5 × 255.9 × ?
(283.0 × 78.0 × ?)
Flight deck, feet (metres): To be announced
Main machinery: Integrated Full Electric Propulsion using gas turbines and/or diesels
Speed, knots: 27. **Range, n miles:** To be announced
Complement: 900 approx plus aircrew

Missiles: SAM: ASTER 15.
Guns: To be announced.
Countermeasures: To be announced.
Combat data systems: To be announced.
Weapons control: To be announced.
Radars: Air search: To be announced.
Surface search: To be announced.
Navigation: To be announced.
Fire control: To be announced.
Tacan: To be announced.

Fixed-wing aircraft: Up to 35. A typical mix might include 32 Rafale M and three E-2C Hawkeye.
Helicopters: Up to five NH 90.

Programmes: A second aircraft carrier (PA2) is planned under the 2003-08 Defence Programming Law. The ship is planned to enter service in 2014 before *Charles de Gaulle* undergoes a refuel/refit in 2015. It was announced on 13 February 2004 that the ship was to be built in co-operation with the UK carrier programme and DCN and Thales established a joint venture company, MO PA2 to manage the project at industry level. Studies in 2005 concluded that up to 85 per cent commonality with the British CVF design could be achieved. As a result, a contract for a preliminary definition study for PA2 (or CVF-FR), which would adapt the UK design to meet French requirements, was awarded to MO PA2 on 12 December 2005. Chantiers de l'Atlantique and EADS were also to take part in the work. Formal agreement to share design costs reached between French and UK governments on 24 January 2006. A main contract for detailed design and build of the ship is expected in late 2006.
Structure: The so-called Romeo design, with an all-electric power and propulsion architecture, provided the baseline

PA 2   *10/2004, DCN* / 1042254

for further development of the design and a reference against which industrial co-operation with UK suppliers could proceed. This first concept was followed by a national Juliette design. A further design, CVF-FR, has been adapted from the UK CVF design and is likely to be adopted. The main differences between UK CVF and CVF-FR are the requirement to install two 90 m C-13 steam catapults and a three-wire arrester system, the installation of national combat and data and weapons systems and facilities for the storage of nuclear weapons.

HELICOPTER CARRIERS (CVHG)

1 JEANNE D'ARC CLASS (CVHG)

Name	No	Builders	Laid down	Launched	Commissioned
JEANNE D'ARC (ex-*La Résolue*)	R 97	Brest Naval Dockyard	7 July 1960	30 Sep 1961	16 July 1964

Displacement, tons: 10,575 standard; 13,270 full load
Dimensions, feet (metres): 597.1 × 78.7 hull × 24.6
(182 × 24 × 7.5)
Flight deck, feet (metres): 203.4 × 68.9 *(62 × 21)*
Main machinery: 4 boilers; 640 psi *(45 kg/cm²)*; 840°F *(450°C)*; 2 Rateau-Bretagne turbines; 40,000 hp(m) *(29.4 MW)*; 2 shafts
Speed, knots: 26.5. **Range, n miles:** 6,500 at 16 kt
Complement: 506 (33 officers) plus 13 instructors and 150 cadets

Missiles: SSM: 6 Aerospatiale MM 38 Exocet (2 triple) ❶; inertial cruise; active radar homing to 42 km *(23 n miles)* at 0.9 Mach; warhead 165 kg; sea-skimmer.
Guns: 2 DCN 3.9 in *(100 mm)*/55 Mod 53 CADAM automatic ❷; 60 rds/min to 17 km *(9 n miles)* anti-surface; 8 km *(4.4 n miles)* anti-aircraft; weight of shell 13.5 kg.
4—12.7 mm MGs.
Countermeasures: Decoys: 2 CSEE/VSEL Syllex 8-barrelled trainable launchers for chaff (may not be fitted). 1 AN/SQL-25A Nixie torpedo decoy.
ESM: Thomson-CSF ARBR 16/ARBX 10; intercept.
Weapons control: 3 CT Analogical; 2 Sagem DMAa optical sights. SATCOM ❸.
Radars: Air search Thomson-CSF DRBV 22D ❹; D-band; range 366 km *(200 n miles)*.
Air/surface search: DRBV 51 ❺; G-band.
Navigation: 2 DRBN 34A (Racal-Decca); I-band.
Fire control: 2 (+1 unused) Thomson-CSF DRBC 32A; I-band.
Tacan: SRN-6.
Sonars: Thomson Sintra DUBV 24C; hull-mounted; active search; medium frequency; 5 kHz.

Helicopters: 2 Pumas and 2 Gazelles from the Army and 3 Navy Alouette III for annual training cruises. Up to 8 Super Frelon or 10 mixed heavy/light aircraft in war time.

Modernisation: Long refits in the summers of 1989 and 1990 have allowed equipment to be updated to enable the ship to continue well into the next century. SENIT 2 combat data system was to have been fitted but this was cancelled as a cost-saving measure. Two 100 mm guns were removed from quarterdeck in 2000. A life-extension refit is to start in 2006.
Structure: Flight deck lift has a capacity of 12 tons. Some of the hangar space is used to accommodate officers under training. The ship is almost entirely air conditioned. Carries two LCVPs. Topmast can be removed for passing under bridges or other obstructions.
Operational: Used for training officer cadets. After rapid modification, she could be used as a commando ship, helicopter carrier or troop transport with commando equipment and a battalion of 700 men. Flagship of the Training Squadron on an Autumn/Spring cruise with Summer refit. Army helicopters Super Puma/Cougar and Gazelle are embarked during training cruises. Thirty-three training cruises completed by April 1997 when the ship was docked for extensive propulsion machinery repairs which completed in July 1998. Service life has been extended to at least 2010.

JEANNE D'ARC   *(Scale 1 : 1,500), Ian Sturton* / 0529162

JEANNE D'ARC   *1/2004, Robert Pabst* / 1042183

JEANNE D'ARC   *6/2004, B Prézelin* / 1042182

DESTROYERS

2 CASSARD CLASS (TYPE F 70 (A/A)) (DDGHM)

Name	No	Builders	Laid down	Launched	Commissioned
CASSARD	D 614	Lorient Naval Dockyard	3 Sep 1982	6 Feb 1985	28 July 1988
JEAN BART	D 615	Lorient Naval Dockyard	12 Mar 1986	19 Mar 1988	21 Sep 1991

Displacement, tons: 4,230 standard; 5,000 full load
Dimensions, feet (metres): 455.9 × 45.9 × 21.3 (sonar)
(139 × 14 × 6.5)
Main machinery: 4 SEMT-Pielstick 18 PA6 V 280 BTC diesels;
43,200 hp(m) *(31.75 MW)* sustained; 2 shafts
Speed, knots: 29.5
Range, n miles: 8,000 at 17 kt.
Complement: 245 (25 officers) accommodation for 253

Missiles: SSM: 8 Aerospatiale MM 40 Exocet ❶; inertial
cruise; active radar homing to 70 km *(40 n miles)* at
0.9 Mach; warhead 165 kg; sea-skimmer.
SAM: 40 GDC Pomona Standard SM-1MR; Mk 13 Mod
5 launcher ❷; semi-active radar homing to 46 km
(25 n miles) at 2 Mach; height envelope 45–18,288 m
(150–60,000 ft). Launchers taken from T 47 (DDG) ships.
2 Matra Sadral PDMS sextuple launchers ❸; 39 Mistral;
IR homing to 4 km *(2.2 n miles)*; warhead 3 kg; anti-sea-
skimmer; able to engage targets down to 10 ft above sea
level.
Guns: 1 DCN/Creusot-Loire 3.9 in *(100 mm)*/55 Mod 68
CADAM automatic ❹; 80 rds/min to 17 km *(9 n miles)*
anti-surface; 8 km *(4.4 n miles)* anti-aircraft; weight of
shell 13.5 kg.
2 Oerlikon 20 mm ❺; 720 rds/min to 10 km *(5.5 n miles)*.
4–12.7 mm MGs.
Torpedoes: 2 fixed launchers model KD 59E ❻. 10 ECAN L5
Mod 4; anti-submarine; active/passive homing to 9.5 km
(5.1 n miles) at 35 kt; warhead 150 kg; depth to 550 m
(1,800 ft).
Countermeasures: Decoys: 2 CSEE AMBL 1B Dagaie ❼ and
2 AMBL 2A Sagaie 10-barrelled trainable launchers ❽;
fires a combination of chaff and IR flares. Dassault LAD
offboard decoys. Nixie; towed torpedo decoy.
ESM: Thomson-CSF ARBR 17B ❾; radar warning. DIBV 1A
Vampir ❿; IR detector (integrated with search radar for
active/passive tracking in all weathers). Saigon radio
intercept at masthead.
ECM: Thomson-CSF ARBB 33; jammer; H-, I- and J-bands.
Combat data systems: SENIT 68; Links 11, 14 and 16.
Syracuse 2 SATCOM ⓫. OPSMER command support
system.
Weapons control: DCN CTMS optronic/radar system with
DIBC 1A Piranha II IR/TV tracker; CSEE Najir optronic
secondary director.
Radars: Air search: Thomson-CSF DRBJ 11B ⓬; 3D; E/F-band;
range 366 km *(200 n miles)*.
Air/surface search: Thomson-CSF DRBV 26C ⓭; D-band.
Navigation: 2 Racal DRBN 34A; I-band (1 for close-range
helicopter control ⓮).
Fire control: Thomson-CSF DRBC 33A ⓯; I-band (for
guns).
2 Raytheon SPG-51C ⓰; G/I-band (for missiles).
Sonars: Thomson Sintra DUBA 25A (D 614); DUBA 25C
(D 615); hull-mounted; active search and attack; medium
frequency.

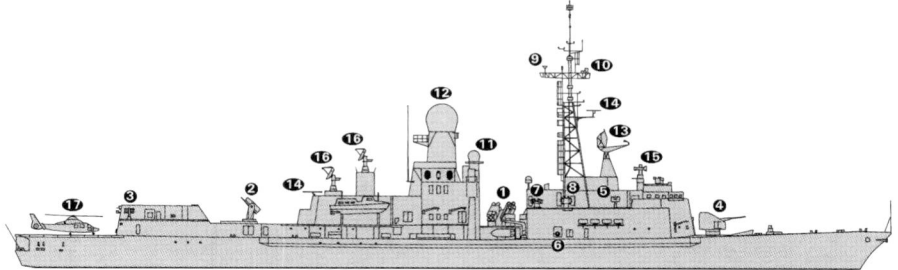

CASSARD *(Scale 1 : 1,200), Ian Sturton* / 0569909

JEAN BART *6/2005*, Martin Mokrus* / 1153195

Helicopters: 1 AS 565SA Panther ⓱.

Programmes: The building programme was considerably
slowed down by finance problems and doubts about the
increasingly obsolescent Standard SM 1 missile system
and was curtailed at two units. Re-rated F 70 (ex-C 70) on
6 June 1988, officially 'frégates anti-aériennes (FAA)'.
Modernisation: DRBJ 15 radar initially fitted in *Cassard* but
this was replaced in 1992 by DRBJ 11. Panther has replaced
Lynx helicopter. *Cassard* refitted 2000-2001. Upgrade
included hull strengthening, fitting of new propellers
and SENIT 68 combat direction system (SENIT 6 core

augmented by SENIT 8 data-link processing component
(for Link 16 and data forwarding). *Jean Bart* similarly
refitted October 2002 to September 2003. Plans to fit
ASTER 30 have been abandoned. *Cassard* to be refitted
2005.
Structure: Samahe 210 helicopter handling system.
Operational: Helicopter used for third party targeting for
the SSM. Both ships are based at Toulon. Service lives:
Cassard, 2018; *Jean Bart*, 2021. Were to have been
replaced by a second batch of Forbin class but AAW
variants of FREMM are a more likely option.

CASSARD *6/2004, Derek Fox* / 1042178

For details of the latest updates to *Jane's Fighting Ships* online and to discover the additional
information available exclusively to online subscribers please visit
jfs.janes.com

7 GEORGES LEYGUES CLASS (TYPE F 70 (ASW)) (DDGHM)

Name	No	Builders	Laid down	Launched	Commissioned
GEORGES LEYGUES	D 640	Brest Naval Dockyard	16 Sep 1974	17 Dec 1976	10 Dec 1979
DUPLEIX	D 641	Brest Naval Dockyard	17 Oct 1975	2 Dec 1978	13 June 1981
MONTCALM	D 642	Brest Naval Dockyard	5 Dec 1975	31 May 1980	28 May 1982
JEAN DE VIENNE	D 643	Brest Naval Dockyard	26 Oct 1979	17 Nov 1981	25 May 1984
PRIMAUGUET	D 644	Brest Naval Dockyard	17 Nov 1981	17 Mar 1984	5 Nov 1986
LA MOTTE-PICQUET	D 645	Brest Naval Dockyard/Lorient	12 Feb 1982	6 Feb 1985	18 Feb 1988
LATOUCHE-TRÉVILLE	D 646	Brest Naval Dockyard/Lorient	15 Feb 1984	19 Mar 1988	16 July 1990

Displacement, tons: 3,880 standard; 4,830 (D 640-643); 4,750 (D 644-646) full load
Dimensions, feet (metres): 455.9 × 45.9 × 18.7; 19.35 (D 640-643)
(139 × 14 × 5.7; 5.9)
Main machinery: CODOG; 2 RR OlympusTM3B gas turbines; 46,200 hp *(34.5 MW)* sustained; 2 SEMT-Pielstick 16 PA6 V280 diesels; 12,800 hp(m) *(9.41 MW)* sustained; 2 shafts; LIPS cp props
Speed, knots: 30; 21 on diesels
Range, n miles: 8,500 at 18 kt on diesels; 2,500 at 28 kt
Complement: 235 (20 officers) (D 644-646); 216 (18 officers) (D 641-643); 183 (18 officers) (D 640)

Missiles: SSM: 4 Aerospatiale MM 40 Exocet (MM 38 in D 640) **❶**; inertial cruise; active radar homing to 42 km *(23 n miles)* at 0.9 Mach (MM 38); active radar homing to 70 km *(40 n miles)* at 0.9 Mach (MM 40); warhead 165 kg; sea-skimmer. 4 additional Exocet MM 40 missiles can be carried as a warload (D 641-646).
SAM:Thomson-CSF Crotale Naval EDIR octuple launcher **❷**; command line of sight guidance; radar/IR homing to 13 km *(7 n miles)* at 2.4 Mach; warhead 14 kg; 26 missiles.
2 Matra Simbad twin launchers mounted in lieu of 20 mm guns (D 644-646); 2 Matra Sadral sextuple launchers being fitted to D 640-643; Mistral; IR homing to 4 km *(2.2 n miles)*; warhead 3 kg.
Guns: 1 DCN/Creusot-Loire 3.9 in *(100 mm)*/55 Mod 68 CADAM automatic **❸**; dual purpose; 78 rds/min to 17 km *(9 n miles)* anti-surface; 8 km *(4.4 n miles)* anti-aircraft; weight of shell 13.5 kg.
2 Breda/Mauser 30 mm (D 641-643) **❹**. 800 rds/min to 3 km; weight of shell 0.37 kg.
2 Oerlikon 20 mm **❺**; 720 rds/min to 10 km *(5.5 n miles)*. 4 M2HB 12.7 mm MGs (D 640, D 644-646).
Torpedoes: 2 fixed launchers. Eurotorp MU 90; anti-submarine; active/passive homing to 12 km *(6.5 n miles)* at 50 kt; warhead 50 kg; depth to 1,000 m *(3,300 ft)*.
Countermeasures: Decoys: 2 CSEE Dagaie Mk 1 or 2 10-barrelled double trainable launcher **❻**; chaff and IR flares; H- to J-band. Dassault LAD offboard decoys.
ESM: ARBR 17 **❼**; radar warning. Sagem DIBV 2A Vampir MB IRST (D 641-643).
ECM: ARBB 32B or Dassault ARBB 36A (D 641-646); jammer.
Combat data systems: SENIT 4 (D 640); STIDAV based on SENIT 8 added (D 641-646) action data automation; Links 11 and 14. Syracuse 2 SATCOM **❽**. OPSMER command support system.
Weapons control: Thomson-CSF Vega (D 640-643) and DCN CTMS (D 644-646) optronic/radar systems. SAT Murène IR tracker being added to CTMS and Vega systems. CSEE Panda optical director. 2 Sagem VIGY-105 optronic systems (for 30 mm guns) fitted 1995-97. DLT L4 (D 640-643) and DLT L5 (D 644-646) torpedo control system. OPS-100F acoustic processor being fitted.
Radars: Air search:Thomson-CSF DRBV 26A (D 640-643) **❾**; D-band; range 182 km *(100 n miles)* for 2 m² target.
Air/surface search:Thales DRBV 15A (D 640, D 641, D 645); Thales DRBV 15B (D 642, D 644, D 646) **❿**; E/F-band.
Navigation: 2 DRBN-34 (Decca 1226) (D 641, D 646); I-band (1 for close-range helicopter control).

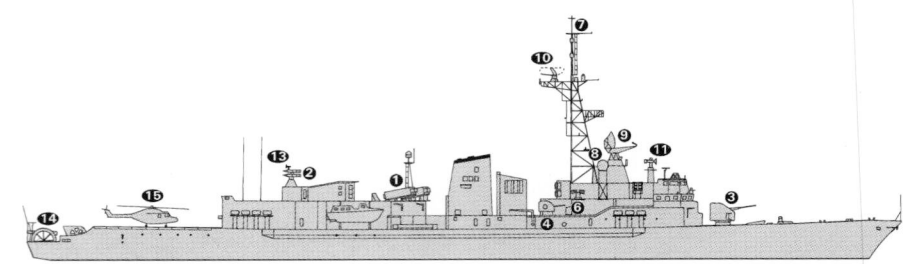

LA MOTTE-PICQUET *(Scale 1 : 1,200), Ian Sturton* / 0569907

DUPLEIX *(Scale 1 : 1,200), Ian Sturton* / 0569908

2 Kelvin Hughes 1007 (D 640, D 642, D 643, D 645); I-band.
2 Decca 1224 (D 644); I-band.
Fire control:Thomson-CSF Vega with DRBC 32E (D 640-643) **⓫**; I-band; DRBC 33A (D 644-646) **⓬**; I-band.
Castor 2 **⓭**; I-band (for SAM).
Sonars: Thomson Sintra DUBV 23D (DUBV 24C in D 644-646); bow-mounted; active search and attack; 5 kHz.
DUBV 43B (43C in D 643-646) **⓮**; VDS; search; medium frequency; paired with DUBV 23D/24; tows at 24 kt down to 200 m *(650 ft)*, *(700 m (3,000 ft)* for 43C). Length of tow 600 m *(2,000 ft)*; being upgraded to 43C.
DSBV 61B (in D 644 onward); passive linear towed array; very low frequency; 365 m *(1,200 ft)*. ATBF 2 lightweight towed array may be fitted in due course.

Helicopters: 2 Lynx Mk 4 **⓯** (except D 640).

Programmes: First three were in the 1971-76 new construction programme, fourth in 1978 estimates, fifth in 1980 estimates, sixth in 1981 estimates, seventh in 1983 estimates. D 645 and 646 were towed from Brest to Lorient for completion. Service lives: *Georges Leygues*, 2009; *Dupleix*, 2012; *Montcalm*, 2013; *Jean de Vienne*, 2015; *Primauguet*, 2018; *La Motte-Picquet*, 2019; *Latouche-Tréville*, 2019. Re-rated F 70 'frégates anti-sous-marines (FASM)' (ex-C 70) on 6 June 1988.
Modernisation: Air defence upgrade (Opération Amélioration Autodéfense Antimissiles, OP3A completed) for six of the class, *Jean de Vienne* (1996),

La Motte-Picquet (1997), *Latouche-Tréville* (1998), *Primauget* (1999), *Dupleix* (1999) and *Montcalm* (2000). Large command structure fitted above the bridge, two Matra Sadral sextuple launchers, two Breda/Mauser 30 mm gun mounts controlled by Sagem Vigy 105 optronic sights, Vampir MB IRST and ARBB 36 jammers (replacing ARBB 32). ASW modernisation of the last six of the class planned but likely to be cancelled in view of plans for multimission frigates. Plans to fit Milas ASW missiles have been shelved. *Georges Leygues* hangar converted for training role in 1999 and crew reduced. Rolling six month refit programme started with *Primauguet* in April 2002, followed by *George Leygues, Dupleix, Montcalm, La Motte-Picquet, Latouche-Tréville* and *Jean de Vienne* which completed in June 2004. Work included hull strengthening, replacement of DRBV 51 with DRBV 15 and replacement of L5 torpedoes with MU 90. *Primauget* completed further refit in March 2005 and *La Motte-Picquet* in January 2006. *Georges Leygues* receives annual upkeep period after training cruise.
Structure: Bridge raised one deck in the last three of the class. Inmarsat aerial can be fitted forward of the funnel or between the Syracuse domes. 210 tons of ballast embarked to improve stability.
Operational: *Primauguet* and *Latouche-Tréville* allocated to ALFAN Brest. *Georges Leygues* has acted since 1990 as a tender to *Jeanne d'Arc* for training cruises. Other ships allocated to ALFAN Toulon.

DUPLEIX *10/2004, Schaeffer/Marsan* / 1042181

PRIMAUGET *5/2005*, John Brodie* / 1153198

GEORGES LEYGUES *12/2004, B Prézelin* / 1042179

LA MOTTE-PICQUET *4/2005*, B Prézelin* / 1153193

0 + 2 FORBIN (HORIZON) CLASS (DDGHM)

Name	No
FORBIN	D 620
CHEVALIER PAUL	D 621

Builders	Laid down	Launched	Commissioned
DCN, Lorient	16 Jan 2004	10 Mar 2005	Dec 2006
DCN, Lorient	13 Jan 2005	July 2006	Mar 2008

Displacement, tons: 7,000 full load
Dimensions, feet (metres): 502.0; 465.0 × 66.6 × 15.7
(153.0; 141.7 × 20.3 × 4.8)
Main machinery: CODOG: 2 Fiat/GE LM 2500 gas turbines;
58,500 hp *(43 MW)*; 2 SEMT-Pielstick 12PA 6STC; 11,700
hp(m) *(8.6 MW)*; 2 shafts; cp props; bow thruster
Speed, knots: 29 (18 on diesels)
Range, n miles: 7,000 at 18 kt
Complement: 190 (accommodation for 230 with up to
20 per cent female crew

Missiles: SSM: 8 Aerospatiale Matra Exocet MM 40 Block III
❶; inertial cruise; active radar homing to 70 km
(40 n miles) at 0.9 Mach; warhead 165 kg; sea-skimmer.
SAM: EUROPAAMS PAAMS with DCN Sylver A50 VLS ❷
for Aerospatiale Matra Aster 15 and Aster 30; 48 cells
(six octuple launcher modules); range (Aster 30): 120 km
(65 n miles) against large aircraft.
2 Aerospatiale Matra Sadral PDMS sextuple launchers ❸
for Mistral SR SAMs; IR homing to 6 km; warhead 3 kg;
anti-sea-skimmer; able to engage targets down to 10 ft
above sea level.
Guns: 2 Otobreda 76 mm/62 Super Rapid ❹. 2 Giat 20 mm ❺.
Torpedoes: 2 EUROTORP TLS fixed launchers ❻. Up to 24
Eurotorp Mu 90 Impact torpedoes; active/passive homing
to 15 km *(8 n miles)* at 29/50 kt.
Countermeasures: SIGEN EW suite comprising 2 EADS
NGDS multifunction decoy launchers ❼, radar warning
equipment, a high-power jammer ❽ and an ESM/ECM
support aid. SLAT torpedo defence system.
Combat data systems: EUROSYSNAV; 2 Link 11 (Link 22
in the future) and Link 16; OPSMER or SIC 21 follow-on
command support system; Syracuse SATCOM ❾.
Weapons control: Sagem Vampir optronic director ❿.
Radars: Air/surface search:Thomson-CSF/Marconi DRBV 27
(S 1850M) Astral ⓫; L-band.
Surveillance/fire control: Alenia Marconi EMPAR ⓬;
C-band; multifunction.
Surface search: 2 SPN 753 ⓭; I-band.
Fire control: Alenia Marconi NA 25 ⓮; J-band.
Sonars: TUS-WASS 4110CL; hull-mounted; active search
and attack; medium frequency.

Helicopters: 1 Eurocopter NH90 ⓯.

Programmes: Classified as 'Frégates antiaériennes' (FAA).
Initially a three-nation project with Italy and UK.
Joint project office established in 1993. After UK
withdrew in April 1999, an agreement was signed on
7 September 1999 between France and Italy to continue.
Following a French/Italian MoU on 22 September
2000 to build four destroyers, the French government
ordered two ships to be built by DCN Lorient and

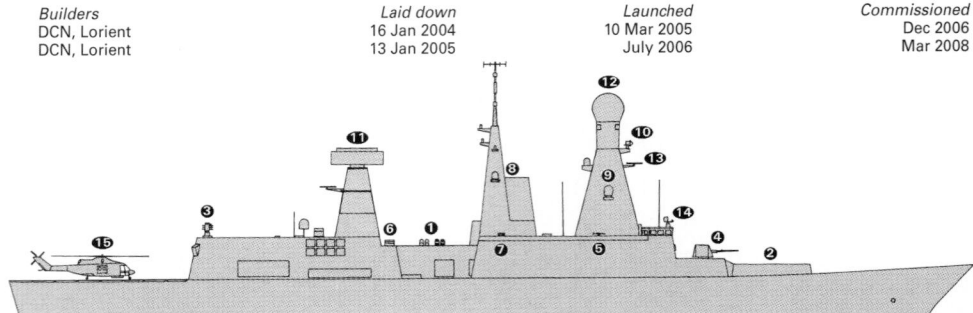

FORBIN *(Scale 1 : 1,200), Ian Sturton* / 1042411

FORBIN *6/2005*, B Prézelin* / 1153194

delivered in December 2006 and April 2008. They are
planned to replace *Suffren* and *Duquesne*. Plans to build
a second pair of ships, to replace *Cassard* and *Jean Bart*,
may be superseded by AAW Variants of the FREMM
design.

Structure: Details given are subject to change. Space
available for two additional missile launcher modules,
possibly with Sylver A70 VLS.
Operational: Sea trials for *Forbin* are to start in 2006. Plans
to build.

---

1 SUFFREN CLASS (DDGM)

Name	No
DUQUESNE	D 603

Builders	Laid down	Launched	Commissioned
Brest Naval Dockyard	1 Feb 1965	12 Feb 1966	1 Apr 1970

Displacement, tons: 5,335 standard; 6,780 full load
Dimensions, feet (metres): 517.1 × 50.9 × 23.8
(157.6 × 15.5 × 7.25)
Main machinery: 4 boilers; 640 psi *(45 kg/cm²)*; 842°F
(450°C); 2 Rateau turbines; 72,500 hp(m) *(53 MW)*;
2 shafts
Speed, knots: 34
Range, n miles: 5,100 at 18 kt; 2,400 at 29 kt
Complement: 355 (23 officers)

Missiles: SSM: 4 Aerospatiale MM 38 Exocet ❶; inertial
cruise; active radar homing to 42 km *(23 n miles)* at
0.9 Mach; warhead 165 kg; sea-skimmer.
SAM: ECAN Ruelle Masurca twin launcher ❷; Mk 2 Mod
3 semi-active radar homers; range 55 km *(30 n miles)*;
warhead 98 kg; 48 missiles.
Guns: 2 DCN/Creusot-Loire 3.9 in *(100 mm)*/55 Mod 1964
CADAM automatic ❸; 80 rds/min to 17 km *(9 n miles)*
anti-surface; 8 km *(4.4 n miles)* anti-aircraft; weight of
shell 13.5 kg.
4 or 6 Oerlikon 20 mm ❹; 720 rds/min to 10 km
(5.5 n miles).
2—12.7 mm MGs.
Torpedoes: 4 launchers (2 each side) ❺. 10 ECAN L5; anti-
submarine; active/passive homing to 9.5 km *(5.1 n miles)*
at 35 kt; warhead 150 kg; depth to 550 m *(1,800 ft)*.
Countermeasures: Decoys: 2 CSEE Sagaie 10-barrelled
trainable launchers; chaff to 8 km *(4.4 n miles)* and IR
flares to 3 km *(1.6 n miles)*. 2 Sagaie launchers ❻.
Dassault LAD offboard decoys.
ESM: ARBR 17 ❼; intercept.
ECM: ARBB 33; jammer.
Combat data systems: SENIT 2 action data automation;
Link 11. Syracuse 2 SATCOM ❽. OPSMER command
support system. Marisat.
Weapons control: DCN CTMS radar/optronic control
system with SAT DIBC 1A Piranha IR and TV tracker.
2 Sagem DMA optical directors.
Radars: Air search (radome): DRBI 23 ❾; D-band.
Air/surface search: DRBV 15A ❿; E/F-band.
Navigation: Racal Decca 1229 (DRBN 34A); I-band.
Fire control: 2 Thomson-CSF DRBR 51 ⓫; G/I-band (for
Masurca).
Thomson-CSF DRBC 33A ⓬; I-band (for guns).
Tacan: URN 20.
Sonars: Thomson Sintra DUBV 23; hull-mounted; active
search and attack; 5 kHz.
DUBV 43 ⓭; VDS; medium frequency 5 kHz; tows at up
to 24 kt at 200 m *(656 ft)*.

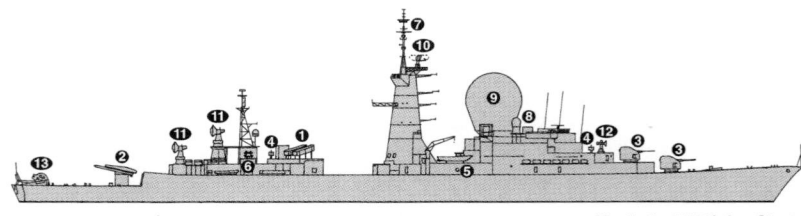

DUQUESNE *(Scale 1 : 1,500), Ian Sturton* / 0069916

DUQUESNE *8/2004, B Prézelin* / 1042186

Programmes: Ordered under the 1960 programme. Service
life 2007.
Modernisation: MM 38 Exocet fitted in 1977; Masurca
modernised in 1984-85 with new computers. DRBV 15A
radars replaced DRBV 50. Major refit from June 1990 to
March 1991: modernisation of the DRBI-23 radar; new
computers for the SENIT combat data system; new
CTMS fire-control system for 100 mm guns fitted (with
DRBC-33A radar, TV camera and DIBC-1A Piranha IR
tracker). New ESM/ECM suite: ARBR 17 radar interceptor,
ARBB 33 jammer and Sagaie decoy launchers. Two 20 mm
guns fitted either side of DRBC 33A.

Structure: Equipped with gyro-controlled stabilisers
operating three pairs of non-retractable fins. NBC
citadel fitted during modernisation. Air conditioning of
accommodation and operational areas.
Operational: Based at Toulon. Officially frégate lance-
missiles (FLM). In refit from September 1998 to July 1999.
Malafon removed having been non-operational since
1997. To be replaced by *Chevalier Paul* in 2008. *Suffren*
decommissioned on 2 April 2001.

2 TOURVILLE CLASS (TYPE F 67) (DDGHM)

Name	No	Builders	Laid down	Launched	Commissioned
TOURVILLE	D 610	Lorient Naval Dockyard	16 Mar 1970	13 May 1972	21 June 1974
DE GRASSE	D 612	Lorient Naval Dockyard	25 July 1972	30 Nov 1974	1 Oct 1977

Displacement, tons: 4,650 standard; 6,100 full load
Dimensions, feet (metres): 501.6 × 51.8 × 21.6
   (152.8 × 15.8 × 6.6)
Main machinery: 4 boilers; 640 psi *(45 kg/cm²)*; 840°F
   (450°C); 2 Rateau turbines; 58,000 hp(m) *(43 MW)*;
   2 shafts
Speed, knots: 32. **Range, n miles:** 5,000 at 18 kt
Complement: 301 (22 officers)

Missiles: SSM: 6 Aerospatiale MM 38 Exocet ❶; inertial
   cruise; active radar homing to 42 km *(23 n miles)* at
   0.9 Mach; warhead 165 kg; sea-skimmer.
SAM: Thomson-CSF Crotale Naval EDIR octuple launcher
   ❷; command line of sight guidance; radar/IR homing to
   13 km *(7 n miles)* at 2.4 Mach; warhead 14 kg.
Guns: 2 DCN/Creusot-Loire 3.9 in *(100 mm)*/55 Mod 68
   CADAM automatic ❸; dual purpose; 80 rds/min to 17 km
   (9 n miles) anti-surface; 8 km *(4.4 n miles)* anti-aircraft;
   weight of shell 13.5 kg.
   2 Giat 20 mm ❹.
   4 – 12.7 mm MGs.
Torpedoes: 2 launchers ❺. 10 ECAN L5; anti-submarine;
   active/passive homing to 9.5 km *(5.1 n miles)* at 35 kt;
   warhead 150 kg; depth to 550 m *(1,800 ft)*. Honeywell
   Mk 46 or Eurotorp Mu 90 Impact torpedoes for helicopters.
Countermeasures: Decoys: 2 CSEE/VSEL Syllex 8-barrelled
   trainable launcher (to be replaced by 2 Dagaie systems)
   ❻; chaff to 1 km in centroid and distraction patterns.
ESM: ARBR 16; radar warning.
ECM: ARBB 32; jammer.
Combat data systems: SENIT 3 action data automation;
   Links 11 and 14. Syracuse 2 SATCOM ❼. OPSMER
   command support system. Inmarsat.
Weapons control: SENIT 3 radar/TV tracker (possibly SAT
   Murène in due course). 2 Sagem DMAa optical directors.
   OPS-100F acoustic processor.
Radars: Air search: DRBV 26A ❽; D-band; range 182 km
   (100 n miles) for 2 m² target.
Air/surface search: Thomson-CSF DRBV 51D ❾; G-band;
   range 29 km *(16 n miles)*.
Navigation: 2 DRBN 34 ❿ (Racal Decca Type 1226); I-band
   (1 for helicopter control).
Fire control: Thomson-CSF DRBC 32D ⓫; I-band.
   Crotale ⓬; J-band (for SAM).
Sonars: Thomson Sintra DUBV 23; bow-mounted; active
   search and attack; medium frequency.
   Thomson Sintra DSBX 1A (ATBF) VDS ⓭; active 1 kHz
   transmitter and 5 kHz transceiver in same 10 tonne towed
   body.
   Thomson Sintra DSBV 62C; passive linear towed array;
   very low frequency.

Helicopters: 2 Lynx Mk 4 ⓮.

Programmes: Originally rated as corvettes but reclassified
   as 'frégates anti-sous-marins (FASM)' on 8 July 1971 and
   given D pennant numbers.

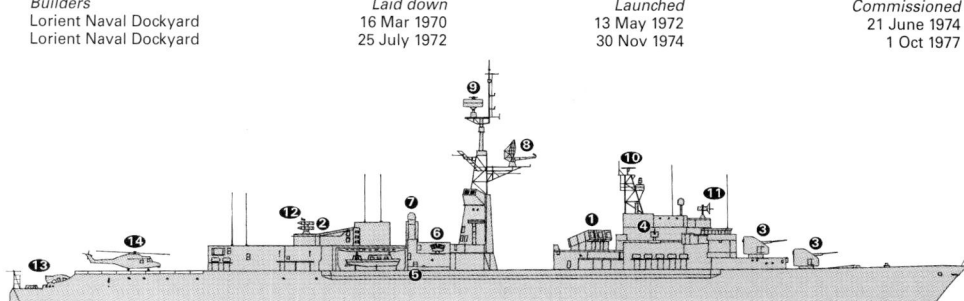

TOURVILLE *(Scale 1 : 1,200), Ian Sturton* / 0569912

DE GRASSE *4/2005*, E & M Laursen* / 1153192

Modernisation: Major communications and combat
data systems updates. The SLASM ASW combat suite
installed in *Tourville* from March 1994 to April 1995,
De Grasse from May 1995 to September 1996. This
included new signal processing for the bow sonar, plus
LF and MF towed active sonar with separate towed
passive array including torpedo warning. Acoustic
processor for helo borne sonobuoys. Milas ASW missile
cancelled. Passive towed arrays fitted in 1990. Malafon
removed from *Tourville* in 1994 and *De Grasse* in 1996.
De Grasse refitted at Brest in 2003.
Operational: Assigned to ALFAN Brest. Helicopters
are now used primarily in the ASW role with sonar or
sonobuoy dispenser, and ASW weapons. Service lives:
Tourville 2011; *De Grasse* 2012.

TOURVILLE *9/2005*, H M Steele* / 1153156

DE GRASSE *5/2005*, M Declerck* / 1153135

FRIGATES

5 LA FAYETTE CLASS (FFGHM)

Name	No	Builders	Laid down	Launched	Commissioned
LA FAYETTE	F 710	DCN, Lorient	15 Dec 1990	13 June 1992	23 Mar 1996
SURCOUF	F 711	DCN, Lorient	3 July 1992	3 July 1993	7 Feb 1997
COURBET	F 712	DCN, Lorient	15 Sep 1993	12 Mar 1994	1 Apr 1997
ACONIT (ex-*Jauréguiberry*)	F 713	DCN, Lorient	1 Aug 1996	8 June 1997	3 June 1999
GUÉPRATTE	F 714	DCN, Lorient	1 Oct 1998	3 Mar 1999	27 Oct 2001

Displacement, tons: 3,300 standard; 3,750 full load
Dimensions, feet (metres): 407.5 oa; 377.3 pp × 50.5 × 19.0 (screws) (*124.2; 115 × 15.4 × 5.8*)
Main machinery: CODAD; 4 SEMT-Pielstick 12 PA6 V 280 STC diesels; 21,107 hp(m) (*15.52 MW*) sustained; 2 shafts; LIPS cp props; bow thruster
Speed, knots: 25. **Range, n miles:** 7,000 at 15 kt; 9,000 at 12 kt
Complement: 140 (13 officers) plus 12 aircrew plus 25 Marines

Missiles: SSM: 8 Aerospatiale MM 40 Block 2 Exocet ❶; inertial cruise; active radar homing to 70 km (*40 n miles*) at 0.9 Mach; warhead 165 kg; sea-skimmer.
SAM: Thomson-CSF Crotale Naval CN 2 (EDIR with V3 in *La Fayette* to be retrofitted with CN 2 in due course) octuple launcher (eighteen missiles in magazine) ❷; VT 1; command line of sight guidance; radar/IR homing to 13 km (*7 n miles*) at 3.5 Mach; warhead 14 kg. 24 missiles. Space for 2 × 8 cell VLS ❸.
Guns: 1 DCN 3.9 in (*100 mm*) /55 TR ❹; 80 rds/min to 17 km (*9 n miles*); weight of shell 13.5 kg.
2 Giat 20F2 20 mm ❺; 720 rds/min to 10 km (*5.5 n miles*).
Countermeasures: Decoys: 2 CSEE Dagaie Mk 2 ❻ 10-barrelled trainable launchers; chaff and IR flares.
ESM: Thomson-CSF ARBR 21 (DR 3000-S) ❼; radar intercept.
ARBG 2 Maigret; comms intercept.
DIBV 10 Vampir ❽; IR detector (can be fitted).
ECM: Dassault ARBB 33; jammer (can be fitted).
Combat data systems: Thomson-CSF TAVITAC 2000. Links 11 and 14. Syracuse 2 SATCOM ❾. OPSMER command support system. INMARSAT.
Weapons control: Thomson-CSF CTM radar/IR system. Sagem TDS 90 VIGY optronic system.
Radars: Air/surface search: Thomson-CSF Sea Tiger Mk 2 (DRBV 15C) ❿; E/F-band; range 110 km (*60 n miles*) for 2 m² target.
Navigation: 2 Racal Decca 1229 (DRBN 34B) ⓫; I-band. One set for helicopter control.
Fire control: Thomson-CSF Castor 2J ⓬; J-band; range 17 km (*9.2 n miles*) for 1 m² target.
Crotale ⓭; J-band (for SAM).

Helicopters: 1 Aerospatiale AS 565MA Panther ⓯ or platform for 1 Super Frelon. NH90 in due course.

Programmes: Originally described as 'Frégates Légères' but this was changed in 1992 to 'Frégates type La Fayette'. First three ordered 25 July 1988; three more 24 September 1992 but the last of these was cancelled in May 1996. The construction timetable was delayed by several months because of funding problems.
Structure: Constructed from high-tensile steel with a double skin from waterline to upperdeck. 10 mm plating protects vital spaces. External equipment and upper deck fittings are concealed or placed in low positions. Superstructure inclined at 10° to vertical to reduce REA. Extensive use of radar absorbent paint. DCN Samahe helicopter handling system. 'Raidco 700' fast assault craft fitted to F 712 and others in due course. The design includes potential to install new and/or replace old weapon systems in the future. Two octuple VLS launchers for ASTER 15 missiles could be installed forward of the bridge while there is space for the associated Arabel radar and also for SLAT anti-torpedo system. Plans to fit a sonar have been dropped and, in view of the FMM frigate programme, it is unlikely that an ASW variant of the ship will be developed.
Operational: *La Fayette* started sea trials 27 September 1993, *Surcouf* 4 July 1994, *Courbet* 14 September 1995, *Aconit* 14 April 1998 and *Guépratte* on 16 January 2001. These frigates are designed for out of area operations on overseas stations and the first three are assigned to FAN for the Indian Ocean. Super Frelon helicopters can land on the flight deck. NH 90 prototype trials in *Courbet* in 1998. The ship can launch inflatable boats from a hatch in the stern which hinges upwards. The Vampir IR detector and ARBB 33 jammer are fitted 'for but not with'. *Courbet* refitted 2005.
Sales: Three of an improved design to Saudi Arabia, six for Taiwan, and six for Singapore.

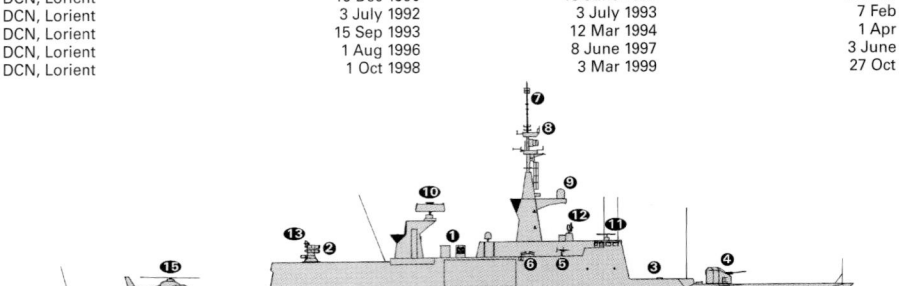

LA FAYETTE *(Scale 1 : 1,200), Ian Sturton* / 0569910

LA FAYETTE *1/2004, B Prézelin* / 1042189

GUÉPRATTE *1/2004, B Prézelin* / 1042191

COURBET *8/2004, B Prézelin* / 1042190

9 D'ESTIENNE D'ORVES (TYPE A 69) CLASS (FFGM)

Name	No	Builders	Laid down	Launched	Commissioned
LIEUTENANT DE VAISSEAU LE HÉNAFF	F 789	Lorient Naval Dockyard	21 Mar 1977	16 Sep 1978	13 Feb 1980
LIEUTENANT DE VAISSEAU LAVALLÉE	F 790	Lorient Naval Dockyard	30 Nov 1977	12 May 1979	8 Oct 1980
COMMANDANT L'HERMINIER	F 791	Lorient Naval Dockyard	29 May 1979	7 Mar 1981	19 Jan 1986
PREMIER MAÎTRE L'HER	F 792	Lorient Naval Dockyard	15 Dec 1978	28 June 1980	5 Dec 1981
COMMANDANT BLAISON	F 793	Lorient Naval Dockyard	15 Nov 1979	7 Mar 1981	28 Apr 1982
ENSEIGNE DE VAISSEAU JACOUBET	F 794	Lorient Naval Dockyard	8 July 1980	26 Sep 1981	23 Oct 1982
COMMANDANT DUCUING	F 795	Lorient Naval Dockyard	1 Oct 1980	26 Sep 1981	17 Mar 1983
COMMANDANT BIROT	F 796	Lorient Naval Dockyard	23 Mar 1981	22 May 1982	14 Mar 1984
COMMANDANT BOUAN	F 797	Lorient Naval Dockyard	12 Oct 1981	23 Apr 1983	31 Oct 1984

Displacement, tons: 1,175 standard; 1,250 (F 789-791), 1,290 (F 792-793), 1,330 (F 794-797) full load
Dimensions, feet (metres): 264.1 × 33.8 × 18 (sonar) *(80.5 × 10.3 × 5.5)*
Main machinery: 2 SEMT-Pielstick 12 PC2 V 400 diesels; 12,000 hp(m) *(8.82 MW)*; 2 shafts; LIPS cp props
2 SEMT-Pielstick 12 PA6 V 280 BTC diesels; 14,400 hp(m) *(10.6 MW)* sustained; 2 shafts; LIPS cp props *(Commandant L'Herminier)*
Speed, knots: 24. **Range, n miles:** 4,500 at 15 kt
Complement: 90 (7 officers) plus 18 marines (in some)

Missiles: SSM: 4 Aerospatiale MM 40 (MM 38 in F 789-791) Exocet ❶; inertial cruise; active radar homing to 70 km *(40 n miles)* (or 42 km *(23 n miles)*) at 0.9 Mach (MM 40); warhead 165 kg; sea-skimmer; active radar homing to 42 km *(23 n miles)* at 0.9 Mach (MM 38).
SAM: Matra Simbad twin launcher for Mistral ❷; IR homing to 4 km *(2.2 n miles)*; warhead 3 kg.
Guns: 1 DCN/Creusot-Loire 3.9 in *(100 mm)*/55 Mod 68 CADAM automatic ❸; 80 rds/min to 17 km *(9 n miles)* anti-surface; 8 km *(4.4 n miles)* anti-aircraft; weight of shell 13.5 kg.
2 Giat 20 mm ❹; 720 rds/min to 10 km *(5.5 n miles)*.
4—12.7 mm MGs.
Torpedoes: 4 fixed tubes ❺. ECAN L5; dual purpose; active/passive homing to 9.5 km *(5.1 n miles)* at 35 kt; warhead 150 kg; depth to 550 m *(1,800 ft)*.
A/S mortars: 1 Creusot-Loire 375 mm Mk 54 6-tubed trainable launcher (F 789, F 790, F 791); range 1,600 m; warhead 107 kg. Removed from others.
Countermeasures: Decoys: 2 CSEE Dagaie 10-barrelled trainable launchers ❻; chaff and IR flares; H- to J-band. Nixie torpedo decoy.
ESM: ARBR 16; radar warning.
Combat data systems: Syracuse 2 SATCOM (F 792, F 793, F 794, F 795, F 796, F 797) ❼. OPSMER command support system with Link 11 (receive only) in MM 40 ships. INMARSAT (F 789, F 790, F 791).
Weapons control: Thomson-CSF Vega system; CSEE Panda optical secondary director.
Radars: Air/surface search: Thomson-CSF DRBV 51A ❽; G-band.
Navigation: Kelvin Hughes 1007; I-band.
Fire control: Thomson-CSF DRBC 32E ❾; I-band.
Sonars: Thomson Sintra DUBA 25; hull-mounted; search and attack; medium frequency.

Programmes: Classified as 'Avisos'.
Modernisation: In 1985 *Commandant L'Herminier*, F 791, fitted with 12PA6 BTC Diesels Rapides as trial for Type F 70. Most have dual MM 38/MM 40 ITL (Installation de Tir Légère) capability. Weapon fit depends on deployment and operational requirement. Those without ITL are fitted with ITS (Installation de Tir Standard). Syracuse 2 SATCOM fitted in F 792-797, vice the A/S mortar, and accommodation provided for commandos. Matra Simbad launchers have been fitted aft of the A/S mortar/Syracuse SATCOM for operations. Fast raiding craft fitted to *Commandant Birot* and to others in due course.
Operational: Endurance, 30 days and primarily intended for coastal A/S operations. Also available for overseas patrols. All assigned to FAN with six ships based at Brest and remaining three at Toulon. F 789 to decommission in 2013 and F 790 in 2014 with remainder to follow by 2018.
Sales: The original *Lieutenant de Vaisseau Le Hénaff* and *Commandant l'Herminier* sold to South Africa in 1976 while under construction. As a result of the UN embargo on arms sales to South Africa, they were sold to Argentina in September 1978 followed by a third, specially built. Six ships were sold to Turkey in October 2000. All delivered by July 2002 after refit at Brest. The last one, *Second Maître Le Bihan*, decommissioned from the French Navy on 26 June 2002. No further sales are planned.

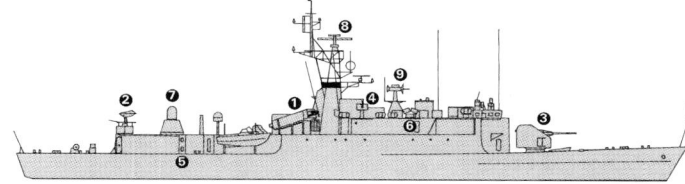

PREMIER MAÎTRE L'HER *(Scale 1 : 900), Ian Sturton* / 0535887

COMMANDANT BLAISON *1/2006*, Marian Ferrette* / 1151172

LIEUTENANT DE VAISSEAU LAVALLÉE *5/2005*, B Prézelin* / 1153190

COMMANDANT L'HERMINIER *7/2005*, B Prézelin* / 1153191

6 FLORÉAL CLASS (FFGHM)

Name	No	Builders	Laid down	Launched	Commissioned
FLORÉAL	F 730	Chantiers de l'Atlantique, St Nazaire	2 Apr 1990	6 Oct 1990	27 May 1992
PRAIRIAL	F 731	Chantiers de l'Atlantique, St Nazaire	11 Sep 1990	16 Mar 1991	20 May 1992
NIVÔSE	F 732	Chantiers de l'Atlantique, St Nazaire	16 Jan 1991	10 Aug 1991	16 Oct 1992
VENTÔSE	F 733	Chantiers de l'Atlantique, St Nazaire	28 June 1991	14 Mar 1992	5 May 1993
VENDÉMIAIRE	F 734	Chantiers de l'Atlantique, St Nazaire	17 Jan 1992	23 Aug 1992	21 Oct 1993
GERMINAL	F 735	Chantiers de l'Atlantique, St Nazaire	17 Aug 1992	14 Mar 1993	18 May 1994

Displacement, tons: 2,600 standard; 2,950 full load
Dimensions, feet (metres): 306.8 × 45.9 × 14.1
 (93.5 × 14 × 4.3)
Main machinery: CODAD; 4 SEMT-Pielstick 6 PA6 L 280 BTC
 diesels; 8,820 hp(m) *(6.5 MW)* sustained; 2 shafts; LIPS
 cp props; bow thruster; 340 hp(m) *(250 kW)*
Speed, knots: 20
Range, n miles: 10,000 at 15 kt
Complement: 90 (11 officers) (including aircrew) plus
 24 Marines + 13 spare

Missiles: SSM: 2 Aerospatiale MM 38 Exocet ❶; inertial
 cruise; active radar homing to 42 km *(23 n miles)* at
 0.9 Mach; warhead 165 kg; sea-skimmer.
 SAM: 1 or 2 Matra Simbad twin launchers can replace
 20 mm guns or Dagaie launcher.
Guns: 1 DCN 3.9 in *(100 mm)*/55 Mod 68 CADAM ❷;
 80 rds/min to 17 km *(9 n miles)*; weight of shell 13.5 kg.
 2 Giat 20 F2 20 mm ❸; 720 rds/min to 10 km *(5.5 n miles)*.
Countermeasures: Decoys: 1 or 2 CSEE Dagaie Mk II;
 10-barrelled trainable launchers ❹; chaff and IR flares.
 ESM: Thomson-CSF ARBR 17 ❺; radar intercept.
 ARBG 1 Saigon; comms intercept (F 730 and F 733).
Weapons control: CSEE Najir optronic director ❻. Syracuse
 2 SATCOM (F 730 and F 733) INMARSAT ❼ (F 731, F 732,
 F 734, F 735).
Radars: Air/surface search: Thomson-CSF Mars DRBV
 21C ❽; D-band.
 Navigation: 2 Racal Decca 1229 (DRBN 34A); I-band (1 for
 helicopter control ❾).

Helicopters: 1 AS 565MA Panther or platform for 1 AS 332F
 Super Puma ❿.

Programmes: Officially described as 'Frégates de
 Surveillance' or 'Ocean capable patrol vessel' and
 designed to operate in the offshore zone in low-intensity
 operations. First two ordered on 20 January 1989; built
 at Chantiers de l'Atlantique, St Nazaire, with weapon
 systems fitted by DCAN Lorient. Second pair ordered
 9 January 1990; third pair in January 1991. Named after
 the months of the Revolutionary calendar.
Structure: Built to merchant passenger marine standards
 with stabilisers and air conditioning. New funnel
 design improves air flow over the flight deck. Has one
 freight bunker aft for about 100 tons cargo. Second-
 hand Exocet MM 38 has been fitted instead of planned
 MM 40.
Operational: Endurance, 50 days. Range proved to be
 better than expected during sea trials. Able to operate a
 helicopter up to Sea State 5. Stations as follows: *Ventose*
 in Antilles, *Germinal* at Brest, *Prairial* in Tahiti. *Floréal*
 and *Nivôse* at Le Réunion and *Vendémiaire* at Noumea
 (New Caledonia). *Floréal* refitted in floating dry-dock at
 Papeete in 2003.
Sales: Two delivered to Morocco in 2002.

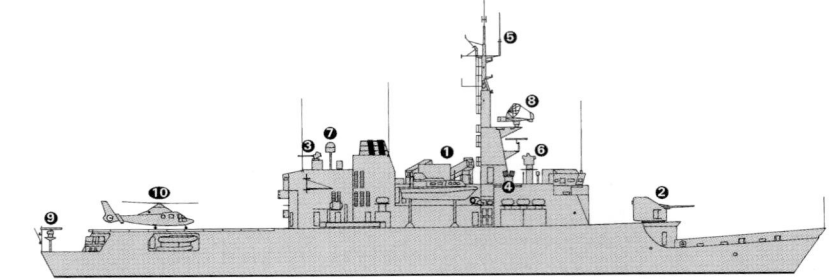

PRAIRIAL

(Scale 1 : 900), Ian Sturton / 0529161

VENDÉMIAIRE

5/2005*, Chris Sattler / 1153139

GERMINAL

8/2004, B Prézelin / 1042241

0 + 8 (9) MULTIMISSION FRIGATES (FFGHM)

No	Builders	Laid down	Launched	Commissioned
—	DCN, Lorient	2007	2009	2011
—	DCN, Lorient	2008	2010	2012
—	DCN, Lorient	2009	2011	2013
—	DCN, Lorient	2009	2011	2013
—	DCN, Lorient	2010	2012	2014
—	DCN, Lorient	2010	2012	2014
—	DCN, Lorient	2011	2013	2015
—	DCN, Lorient	2011	2013	2015

Displacement, tons: 5,800 full load (approx)
Dimensions, feet (metres): 449.8 × 62.3 × 16.4
 (137.1 × 19.0 × 5.0)
Main machinery: CODLOG/CODLAG; 1 (General Electric LM
 2500 or Rolls Royce MT 30) gas turbine; 2 motors; 2 shafts
Speed, knots: 27. **Range, n miles:** 6,000 at 18 kt
Complement: 108 (accommodation for 145)

Missiles: SLCM: 16 cell Sylver A70 VLS for MBDA Scalp-Naval.
SAM: 16 cell Sylver A43 VLS for Aster 15.
SSM: 8 Exocet MM 40 Block 3.
Guns: 1 OTO 127 mm/64 ER (F-AVT). 1-OTO 76 mm SR
 (F-ASM). 4—12.7 mm.
Torpedoes: 4 Eurotorp TLS launchers; Eurotorp MU 90
 torpedoes.
Countermeasures: Decoys: 2 EADS NGDS 12-barrelled
 chaff, IR and anti-torpedo decoy launchers.
 ESM/ECM. SLAT torpedo defence system.
Combat data systems: Horizon class derivative. Links 11
 and 16, 22 and JSAT.
Weapons control: 1 optronic FCS.
Radars: Air/surface search: Thales Herakles 3-D
 multifunction; E/F-band.
Surface search: To be decided.
Navigation: 2 to be decided.
Fire control: Alenia Marconi NA 25; J-band.
Sonars: Thomson Marconi 4110CL; hull mounted (bow
 dome); active search and attack. Thales Captas active/
 passive towed array (F-ASM).

Helicopters: 1 NH-90. ASW aircraft in ASW variant. Transport
 aircraft and tactical UAV in land attack variant.

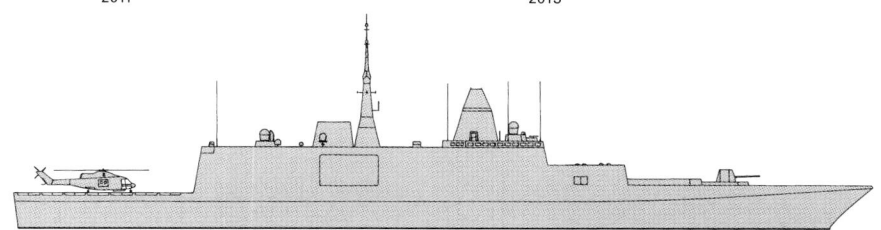

FREMM *(Scale 1 : 1,200), Ian Sturton* / 1153006

Programmes: Agreement reached on 7 November 2002 for a 27 ship collaborative programme with Italy. The French requirement is for 17 'Frégates Européenne multimissions' (FREMM) with common hull and machinery in two variants. Eight ASW ships (F-ASM) are to replace the Tourville and Georges Leygues classes while nine general purpose ships (FMM/F-AVT), with emphasis on land-attack capabilities, are to replace the A 69 Avisos and supplement the La Fayette class frigates. Contract for the first phase awarded on 16 November 2005 to Armaris (DCN/Thales joint venture) for the construction (funded in the 2003-08 Defence Programming Law) of a first batch of eight ships. This is to comprise six F-ASM and two F-AVT, the first of which is to be delivered in 2011. An order for a second batch (2 F-ASM and two F-AVT) is expected by 2008 and thereafter, there will be a third batch of 5 AVT. The 17th ship is to be delivered in 2021. It is also possible that, additionally, two AAW variants of the class will be built to replace *Cassard* and *Jean Bart*, as it is probable that the Horizon destroyer programme is to be curtailed at two ships.

Structure: FREMM has a conventional hull design. The main engine room contains the gas turbine and two diesel generators while the aft machinery space contains the motors. Particular attention has been paid to signature reduction. The radar signature is expected to be comparable to that of the La Fayette class while exhaust cooling measures are expected to achieve a comparatively low IR signature. Acoustic quietening is to be achieved by the rafting of engines and motors and the use of electric propulsion. The original design for a single integrated mast has been abandoned in favour of a two mast configuration. The Herakles radar is housed in the foremast and communications and IFF in the after mast.

SHIPBORNE AIRCRAFT

Notes: (1) Three (out of a total of 13 for all three services) Eurocopter EC 725 Cougar Mk II 725 helicopters for maritime counter-terrorism were ordered for delivery by 2006.
(2) The French Navy and the DGA (Armaments Directorate) have launched two drone demonstration programmes: a rotary wing naval tactical drone, DMT (Drone Maritime Tactique), to be operated from frigates (notably the F-AVT land attack variant of the multimission frigate) up to Sea State 6; a first demonstrator, Hetel, made its maiden flight in December 2002 and is planned for sea trials in 2005 (to enter service by 2009); the second programme concerns a fixed-wing long endurance drone, DELE (Drone Embarqué Longue Endurance), to be operated from aircraft carriers and from Mistral class LHDs; it should have an endurance of 12 hours and be able to operate up to 60 n miles away from carrying ship; sea trials expected in 2006.

Numbers/Type: 16 Dassault Aviation ACM Rafale M.
Operational speed: Mach 2.
Service ceiling: 50,000 ft *(15,240 m)*.
Range: 2,000 n miles *(3,700 km)*.
Role/Weapon systems: Total procurement of up to 60 Rafale M single-seaters (air superiority and ground/surface attack). First of two Rafale M naval prototypes (single seaters) flown 12 December 1992. First deck trials in *Foch* in 1993. First production Rafale M flown 7 July 1999 and assigned to development trials. Second aircraft delivered to the Navy 19 July 2000 and eight more delivered by 2002 to form Flottille 12F. Further deliveries of six (2006), ten (2007) and one (2008). All aircraft at standard F1 for air defence; standard F2 (from 2005) for ground attack; standard F3 (from 2007) for nuclear strike, air to surface and recce capabilities. All aircraft to be brought to this standard later. Sensors: Thales/Dassault Electronique RBE 2 multirole radar; Thales/ Dassault Electronique/Matra SPECTRA EW/IR countermeasure suite, MIDSCO MIDS-LVT voice/data (Link 16), Thales/Sagem OSF optronic surveillance and target acquisition device (Standard F2); Thales Reco NG optronic reconnaissance pod with data link (two-seater F3s). Weapons: Giat M 791 30 mm cannon; up to eight AAMs (air-defence role), including MBDA Magic 2 short range and MICA EM medium range AAMs (standard F1), also MICA IR (standard F2); MBDA Apache stand-off weapon dispenser; Scalp/EG stand-off precision guided ASM; Sagem AASM general-purpose precision bomb; MBDA ASMP-A nuclear ASM and anti-ship missile (standard F3). Up to 8 tons of military load, on 13 hardpoints.

Numbers/Type: 3/6/16 Eurocopter (Aerospatiale) SA 365F Dauphin 2/SA 365N Dauphin 2/AS 565MA Panther.
Operational speed: 165 kt *(305 km/h)*.
Service ceiling: 16,700 ft *(5,100 m)*.
Range: 486 n miles *(900 km)*.
Role/Weapon systems: New-built SA 365F Dauphin 2s acquired to replace Alouette IIIs for carrierborne SAR. They feature the same ORB-32 radars as Panthers. SA 365Ns are second-hand helicopters purchased for SAR, general surveillance and public service roles from various locations in metropolitan France. They do not have any radar. Fifteen AS 565 Panthers purchased in several batches to operate from Cassard class DDGs and Floréal class frigates. 16th aircraft acquired from the Armée de l'Air (French Air Force). All Panthers to be modernised to Standard 2 before 2015 with new avionics, comprehensive countermeasures suite (laser, radar and missile warning systems, decoy dispenser), FLIR and, eventually, lightweight anti-ship missiles. Service life to 2025 (AS 565MA). Sensors: (AS 565MA and SA 365F) Thales ORB-32 radar and (AS 565MA) Thales Chlio FLIR on some helicopters (all fitted for); Titus tactical situation management aid (with encrypted data link). Weapons: (AS 565MA) provision for internally mounted 7.62 mm MG.

SA 365F DAUPHIN 2 *6/2005*, Michael Winter* / 1153189

RAFALE M *7/2003, B Prézelin* / 0569995

SA 565 PANTHER *1/2006*, B Prézelin* / 1151170

Numbers/Type: 51 Dassault-Bréguet Super Étendard.
Operational speed: Mach 1.
Service ceiling: 45,000 ft *(13,700 m)*.
Range: 1,460 n miles *(2,700 km)*.
Role/Weapon systems: Carrierborne strike fighter with nuclear strike capabilities and limited air defence role; tactical recce role to be added. All aircraft still in inventory modernised 1994-1999 to Standard F3. Standard F4 for all the fleet from mid-2000 to early 2005; tactical recce role added; standard 5 under development from 2003 to enter service in 2006; service life extended to 2011. Sensors: Dassault Electronique Anémone radar, DRAX (standard 3) or Thales-Detexis Sherloc-F ESM (standard 4), SAGEM UAT 90 computer, Thomson-CSF Barracuda jammer, Phimat chaff dispenser, Alkan IR decoy dispenser; Thales Optrosys photo/optronic chassis (with Omera 40 panoramic camera and SDS-250 digital camera) in a ventral bay (Standard F4); Thales Atlis 2 FLIR/laser pod designator (Standard F3 and F4) and from late 2002 Thales Damocles day/night FLIR/designator (Standard F4 and F5). Weapons: air defence and self protection: two Matra BAe Dynamic Magic 2 short range AAMs and two DEFA 30 mm cannon; nuclear strike: one Aérospatiale ASMP nuclear ASM; air-to-surface: one Aérospatiale AM 39 Exocet anti-ship missile; air-to-ground: bombs, and (standard 3 aircraft) laser guided bombs (Paveway) or one Aérospatiale AS 30L laser guided missile. 7 hardpoints (from standard 4).

SUPER ÉTENDARD   *6/2005*, Paul Jackson* / 1153141

Numbers/Type: 3 Grumman E-2C Hawkeye Group 2.
Operational speed: 320 kt *(593 km/h)*.
Service ceiling: 37,000 ft *(11,278 m)*.
Range: 1,540 n miles *(2,852 km)*.
Role/Weapon systems: Used for AEW, and direction of AD and strike operations. First pair ordered in May 1995 and delivered in April and December 1998 respectively. Third delivered in December 2003. All aircraft to be upgraded within five years. Sensors: APS-145 radar, ESM, ALR-73 PDS, ALQ-108 airborne tactical data system with Links 11 and 16. Weapons: Unarmed.

HAWKEYE   *6/2004, B Prézelin* / 1042242

Numbers/Type: 3 NH Industries NH 90 NFH.
Operational speed: 162 kt *(300 km/h)*.
Service ceiling: 13,940 ft *(4,250 m)*.
Range: 621 n miles *(1,150 km)*.
Role/Weapon systems: Total of 27 NH-90 ordered 30 June 2000 for the French Navy in two variants: 13 NHS support helicopters with secondary ASuW role; 14 NHC combat helicopters for ASW and ASuW. Three to be delivered in 2007, four in 2008, two in 2009 and two per year thereafter until 2018; all 14 NHC 2009-15; and six last NHS 2016-18. Sensors: both variants: Thales ENR surveillance radar; Sagem OLOSP tactical FLIR; MBDA Saphir decoy dispenser; Link 11; NHC: TUS FLASH dipping sonar, and UMS 2000-TSM 8203 sonobuoy processing system. Weapons: ASM (NHC and NHS); 2 MU 90 Impact torpedoes (NHC).

NH 90   *3/2004, NHI* / 0062373

Numbers/Type: 101 Aérospatiale SA 330Ba Puma.
Operational speed: 139 kt *(257 km/h)*.
Service ceiling: 15,750 ft *(4,800 m)*.
Range: 297 n miles *(550 km)*.
Role/Weapon systems: Troop carrying helicopter owned by French Army and operable from amphibious ships.

SA 330   *6/2005*, FAP* / 0589661

Numbers/Type: 5 Aérospatiale SA 321G Super Frelon.
Operational speed: 135 kt *(250 km/h)*.
Service ceiling: 10,170 ft *(3,100 m)*.
Range: 420 n miles *(778 km)*. 594 n miles *(1,100 km)* with auxiliary tank.
Role/Weapon systems: Formerly ASW helicopter; used for assault and support tasks embarked on carriers and LSDs; radar updated; provision for 27 passengers. Service life extended to 2008 to allow replacement by NH 90. Assigned to Flotille 32F. Sensors: Omera ORB search radar. Thales Chlio FLIR fitted to some. Weapons: Provision for 20 mm gun.

SUPER FRELON   *6/2004, B Prézelin* / 1042243

Numbers/Type: 31 Westland Lynx Mk 4 (FN).
Operational speed: 125 kt *(232 km/h)*.
Service ceiling: 12,500 ft *(3,810 m)*.
Range: 320 n miles *(593 km)*.
Role/Weapon systems: Sole French ASW helicopter, all now of the Mk 4 variant; embarked in destroyers and deployed on training tasks. Service life to 2015. Sensors: Omera 31 search radar, Alcatel (DUAV 4) dipping sonar, sonobuoys, Sextant Avionique MAD. Thales Chlio FLIR. Weapons: ASW; two Mk 46 Mod 1 (or Mu 90 Impact in due course) torpedoes, or depth charges. ASV: 1—7.62 mm MG.

LYNX   *4/2005*, Martin Mokrus* / 1153196

Numbers/Type: 30 Aérospatiale SA 319B Alouette III.
Operational speed: 113 kt *(210 km/h)*.
Service ceiling: 10,500 ft *(3,200 m)*.
Range: 327 n miles *(605 km)*.
Role/Weapon systems: General purpose helicopter; replaced by Lynx for ASW; now used for trials, surveillance and training tasks. Sensors: Some radar. Weapons: Unarmed.

ALOUETTE III   *7/2004, B Prézelin* / 1042246

LAND-BASED MARITIME AIRCRAFT (FRONT LINE)

Numbers/Type: 4 Dassault Falcon 50M.
Operational speed: 475 kt *(880 km/h)*.
Service ceiling: 49,000 ft *(14,930 m)*.
Range: 3,500 n miles *(6,480 km)*.
Role/Weapon systems: Maritime reconnaissance and SAR roles in the Atlantic and overseas stations (replaced deleted Atlantic Mk 1). First aircraft delivered in December 1999 (for Opeval), second in March 2000, third in March 2001; fourth and last one late 2002. Allocated to Flotille 24F (Lann-Bihoué). Sensors: Thales/DASA Ocean Master 100(V) search radar, Thales Chlio FLIR, Inmarsat C. Weapons: Unarmed (two SAR chains). Endurance: six hours 30 minutes at 100 n miles *(185 km)* from base, four hours at 500 n miles *(926 km)* or one hour at 1,200 n miles *(2,222 km)*.

FALCON 50M   *6/2005*, Paul Jackson* / 1153142

Numbers/Type: 4 Boeing E-3F Sentry AWACS.
Operational speed: 460 kt *(853 km/h).*
Service ceiling: 30,000 ft *(9,145 m).*
Range: 870 n miles *(1,610 km).*
Role/Weapon systems: Air defence early warning aircraft with secondary role to provide coastal AEW for the Fleet; 6 hours endurance at the range given above. Sensors: Westinghouse APY-2 surveillance radar, Bendix weather radar, Mk XII IFF, Yellow Gate, ESM, ECM. Weapons: Unarmed. Operated by the Air Force.

E-3F   *6/2002, Armée de l'Air* / 0118289

Numbers/Type: 28 Dassault Aviation Atlantique Mk 2.
Operational speed: 355 kt *(658 km/h).*
Service ceiling: 32,800 ft *(10,000 m).*
Range: 11 hours patrol at 600 n miles from base; 8 hours patrol at 1,000 n miles from base; 4 hours patrol at 1,500 n miles from base.
Role/Weapon systems: Maritime reconnaissance. ASW, ASV, COMINT/ELINT roles. Last one delivered in January 1998. Assigned to Flotilles 21F and 23F. Six aircraft are in long-term storage. Sensors: Thomson-CSF Iguane radar, ARAR 13 ESM, ECM, FLIR, MAD, sonobuoys (with DSAX-1 Thomson-CSF Sadang processing equipment). Link 11 (being fitted in all). COMINT/ELINT equipment optional. Integrated sensor/weapon system built around a CIMSA 15/125X computer. Weapons: Two AM 39 Exocet ASMs in ventral bay, or up to eight lightweight torpedoes (Mk 46 and later Mu 90), or depth charges, mines or bombs. Limited modernisation programme planned to adapt aircraft to Mu 90 torpedoes. More extensive modernisation planned for 2008-2015.

ATLANTIQUE II   *8/2003, Frank Findler* / 0569941

Numbers/Type: 6 Dassault-Aviation Falcon 10MER.
Operational speed: 492 kt *(912 km/h).*
Service ceiling: 35,500 ft *(10,670 m).*
Range: 1,920 n miles *(3,560 km).*
Role/Weapon systems: Primary aircrew/ECM training role but also has overwater surveillance role. Sensors: Search radar. Weapons: Unarmed. Allocated to Flottille 57S (Landivisiau).

FALCON 10MER   *7/2003, Paul Jackson* / 0569996

Numbers/Type: 5 Dassault-Aviation Falcon 20H/Gardian.
Operational speed: 470 kt *(870 km/h).*
Service ceiling: 45,000 ft *(13,715 m).*
Range: 2,425 n miles *(4,490 km).*
Role/Weapon systems: Assigned to Flotilla 25F based at Tahiti with permanent detachments at Tontouta (New Caledonia) and Martinique. Maritime reconnaissance role. Sensors: Thomson-CSF Varan radar, Omega navigation, ECM/ESM pods. Weapons: Unarmed.

Numbers/Type: 15 Aerospatiale N262E.
Operational speed: 226 kt *(420 km/h).*
Service ceiling: 26,900 ft *(8,200 m).*
Role/Weapon systems: Crew training and EEZ surveillance role. All allocated to Flotilla 28F for surveillance, SAR and Flying School. Modified N262A aircraft. Sensors: Omera ORB 32 radar; photo pod. Weapons: Unarmed. Target towing capability.

PATROL FORCES

Notes: 'Sauvegarde Maritime' is the organisation that encompasses the surveillance and traffic control of all maritime approaches around continental France and overseas territories. It also includes pollution control. Although all naval ships could participate in surveillance tasks, specialised vessels include the OPVs manned by the navy, patrol vessels and patrol craft of the 'Gendarmerie Maritime', French Customs and 'Affaires Maritimes'. Also merchant support vessels on long-term charter (see Government Maritime Forces). All these ships, including specialised naval ships, will display blue/white/red stripes on hull sides. Naval patrol ships (OPVs) are sometimes referred to as 'Patrouilleurs Spécialisés de Service Public' (PSSP, Public Service Special Patrol Vessel).

1 LAPÉROUSE CLASS (PBO)

Name	No	Builders	Launched	Commissioned
ARAGO	P 675 (ex-A 795)	Lorient Naval Dockyard	9 Sep 1990	9 July 1991

Displacement, tons: 830 standard; 980 full load
Dimensions, feet (metres): 193.5 × 35.8 × 11.9 *(59 × 10.9 × 3.6)*
Main machinery: 2 Wärtsilä UD 30 V12 M6D diesels; 2,500 hp(m) *(1.84 MW)*; 2 cp props; bow thruster; auxiliary electric motor; 220 hp *(160 kW)*
Speed, knots: 15
Range, n miles: 5,200 at 12 kt
Complement: 30 (3 officers)
Guns: 2 — 12.7 mm MGs.
Radars: Navigation: 1 Decca E 250 (DRBN 38A); 1 Furuno; I-band.

Comment: Ex-survey ship converted for patrol duties. Based at Toulon.

ARAGO   *7/2004, Schaeffer/Marsan* / 1042237

10 P 400 CLASS (LARGE PATROL CRAFT) (PBO)

Name	No	Builders	Commissioned
L'AUDACIEUSE	P 682	CMN, Cherbourg	18 Sep 1986
LA BOUDEUSE	P 683	CMN, Cherbourg	15 Jan 1987
LA CAPRICIEUSE	P 684	CMN, Cherbourg	13 Mar 1987
LA FOUGUEUSE	P 685	CMN, Cherbourg	13 Mar 1987
LA GLORIEUSE	P 686	CMN, Cherbourg	18 Apr 1987
LA GRACIEUSE	P 687	CMN, Cherbourg	17 July 1987
LA MOQUEUSE	P 688	CMN, Cherbourg	18 Apr 1987
LA RAILLEUSE	P 689	CMN, Cherbourg	16 May 1987
LA RIEUSE	P 690	CMN, Cherbourg	13 June 1987
LA TAPAGEUSE	P 691	CMN, Cherbourg	11 Feb 1988

Displacement, tons: 406 standard; 477 full load
Dimensions, feet (metres): 178.6 × 26.2 × 8.5 *(54.5 × 8 × 2.5)*
Main machinery: 2 SEMT-Pielstick 16 PA4 200 VGDS diesels; 8,000 hp(m) *(5.88 MW)* sustained; 2 shafts
Speed, knots: 24.5
Range, n miles: 4,200 at 15 kt
Complement: 26 (3 officers) plus 20 passengers
Guns: 1 Bofors 40 mm/60; 1 Giat 20F2 20 mm; 2 — 7.62 mm MGs.
Radars: Surface search: DRBN 38A; I-band.

Programmes: First six ordered in May 1982, with further four in March 1984. The original propulsion system was unsatisfactory. Modifications were ordered and construction slowed. This class relieved the Patra fast patrol craft which have all transferred to the Gendarmerie.
Structure: Steel hull and superstructure protected by an upper deck bulwark. Design modified from original missile craft configuration. Now capable of transporting personnel with appropriate store rooms. Of more robust construction than previously planned and used as overseas transports. Can be converted for missile armament (MM 38) with dockyard assistance and Sadral PDMS has been considered. L' Audacieuse has done trials with a VDS-12 sonar. Twin funnels replaced the unsatisfactory submerged diesel exhausts in 1990-91. P 682 fitted with new propellers in 2003. If successful the rest of the class will be fitted.
Modernisation: A modernisation programme started in 2002. P 682, 683, 689, 690 and 691 have been refitted. The remainder are to be completed by 2006.
Operational: Deployments: Antilles; P 685, French Guiana; P 682, 684, 687. Nouméa; P 686, 688. La Réunion; P 683 and 690. Tahiti; P 689 and P 691. Endurance, 15 days with 45 people aboard. All are receiving a six month refit in Lorient which means some switching of deployments.
Sales: To Gabon and Oman.

LA MOQUEUSE   *6/2004*, A A de Kruijf* / 1153183

LA GLORIEUSE   *2/2003, Chris Sattler* / 0569954

1 TRAWLER TYPE (PSO)

Name	No	Builders	Commissioned
ALBATROS (ex-*Néve*)	P 681	Ch de la Seine Maritime	1967

Displacement, tons: 1,940 standard; 2,800 full load
Dimensions, feet (metres): 278.1 × 44.3 × 18.4 *(84.8 × 13.5 × 5.6)*
Main machinery: Diesel-electric; 2 SACM UD 33 V12 S4 diesel generators; 3,050 hp(m) *(2.24 MW)* sustained; 2 motors; 2,200 hp(m) *(1.62 MW)*; 1 shaft
Speed, knots: 15
Range, n miles: 14,700 at 14 kt
Complement: 50 (8 officers) plus 15 passengers
Guns: 1 Bofors 40 mm/60. 2—12.7 mm MGs.
Countermeasures: ESM; ARBR 16 radar detector.
Radars: Surface search: 2 DRBN 38A; I-band.

Comment: Former trawler bought in April 1983 from Compagnie Nav. Caennaise for conversion into a patrol ship. Commissioned 19 May 1984. Conducts patrols from Réunion to Kerguelen, Crozet, St Paul and Amsterdam Islands with occasional deployments to South Pacific. Vertrep facilities. Can carry 200 tons cargo, and has 4 tonne telescopic crane. Hospital with six berths and operating room. Major refit in Lorient from June 1990 to March 1991 included new diesel-electric propulsion. A further major overhaul was undertaken August 2001-April 2002. Service life: 2015.

ALBATROS *4/2002, B Prézelin* / 0528841

1 STERNE CLASS (PBO)

Name	No	Builders	Commissioned
STERNE	P 680	La Perrière, Lorient	20 Oct 1980

Displacement, tons: 250 standard; 380 full load
Dimensions, feet (metres): 160.7 × 24.6 × 9.2 *(49 × 7.5 × 2.8)*
Main machinery: 2 SACM 195 V12 CZSHR diesels; 4,340 hp(m) *(3.19 MW)* sustained; electrohydraulic auxiliary propulsion on starboard shaft; 150 hp(m) *(110 kW)*; 2 shafts
Speed, knots: 20; 6 on auxiliary propulsion
Range, n miles: 4,900 at 12 kt; 1,500 at 20 kt
Complement: 18 (3 officers); 2 crews
Guns: 2—12.7 mm MGs.
Radars: Navigation: 1 Racal Decca; 1 Furuno; I-band.

Comment: *Sterne* was the first ship for the FSMC. Has active tank stabilisation. Launched 31 October 1979 and completed 18 July 1980 for the 'Affaires Maritimes' but then transferred and is now manned and operated by the Navy from Brest.

STERNE *11/2004, B Prézelin* / 1042236

1 GRÈBE CLASS (PBO)

Name	No	Builders	Commissioned
GRÈBE	P 679	SFCN, Villeneuve La Garenne	6 Apr 1991

Displacement, tons: 300 standard; 410 full load
Dimensions, feet (metres): 170.6 × 32.2 × 9 *(52 × 9.8 × 2.8)*
Main machinery: 2 Wärtsilä UD 33 V12 M6D diesels; 4,410 hp(m) *(3.24 MW)*; diesel-electric auxiliary propulsion; 245 hp(m) *(180 kW)*; 2 shafts; cp props
Speed, knots: 23; 7.5 on auxiliary propulsion
Range, n miles: 4,500 at 12 kt
Complement: 19 (4 officers); accommodation for 24
Guns: 2—12.7 mm MGs.
Radars: Navigation: Racal Decca; I-band.

Comment: Type Espadon 50 ordered 17 July 1988 and launched 16 November 1989. Serter 'Deep V' hull; stern ramp for craft handling. Large deck area (8 × 8 m) for Vertrep operations. Pollution control equipment and remotely operated water-jet gun for firefighting. Based at Toulon from November 1997.

GRÈBE *6/2004, Schaeffer/Marsan* / 1042235

3 FLAMANT (OPV 54) CLASS (PBO)

Name	No	Builders	Launched	Commissioned
FLAMANT	P 676	CMN, Cherbourg	24 Apr 1995	18 Dec 1997
CORMORAN	P 677	Leroux & Lotz, Lorient	15 May 1995	29 Oct 1997
PLUVIER	P 678	CMN, Cherbourg	2 Dec 1996	18 Dec 1997

Displacement, tons: 314 standard; 390 full load
Dimensions, feet (metres): 179.8 × 32.8 × 9.2 *(54.8 × 10 × 2.8)*
Main machinery: CODAD; 2 Deutz/MWM 16V TBD 620 diesels and 2 MWM 12V TBD 234 diesels; 7,230 hp(m) *(5.32 MW)* sustained; 2 shafts; LIPS cp props
Speed, knots: 23
Range, n miles: 4,500 at 14 kt
Complement: 19 (3 officers)
Guns: 2—12.7 mm MGs.
Radars: Surface search: 1 Racal Decca Bridgemaster 250 (DRBN 38A); I-band.
Navigation: Racal Decca 20V90 (DRBN 34B); I-band.

Comment: Authorised in July 1992 and ordered in August 1993 to a Serter Deep V design. Has a stern door for a 7 m EDL 700 fast assault craft or a Zodiac Hurricane RIB, capable of 30 kt. Two passive stabilisation tanks are fitted, and a remotely operated water-jet gun for firefighting. Deck area of 12 × 9 m for Vertrep. Similar to craft built for Mauritania in 1994. Hulls of all three ships strengthened by DCN Brest by late 2004. *Flamant* and *Pluvier* based at Cherbourg, *Cormoran* at Brest.

PLUVIER *5/2005*, Michael Nitz* / 1153150

AMPHIBIOUS FORCES

Notes: (1) There are plans to acquire new EDA (Engins de Débarquement Amphibie) landing craft to replace CTMs and operate with Mistral class LHDs and Foudre class LSDs. They will be faster than current CTMs and LCMs. L-Cat from CNIM is a candidate.
(2) About 25 LCVPs are still in service (from 59 built). Most are used on board LSDs (Ouragan and Foudre classes), Batral LCTs and AORs.

4 BATRAL TYPE
(LIGHT TRANSPORTS AND LANDING SHIPS) (LSTH)

Name	No	Builders	Commissioned
FRANCIS GARNIER	L 9031	Brest Naval Dockyard	21 June 1974
DUMONT D'URVILLE	L 9032	Français de l'Ouest	5 Feb 1983
JACQUES CARTIER	L 9033	Français de l'Ouest	28 Sep 1983
LA GRANDIÈRE	L 9034	Français de l'Ouest	20 Jan 1987

Displacement, tons: 750 standard; 1,580 full load
Dimensions, feet (metres): 262.4 × 42.6 × 7.9 *(80 × 13 × 2.4)*
Main machinery: 2 SACM AGO 195 V12 diesels; 3,600 hp(m) *(2.65 MW)* sustained; 2 shafts; cp props
Speed, knots: 14.5
Range, n miles: 4,500 at 13 kt
Complement: 52 (5 officers)
Military lift: 180 troops; 12 vehicles; 350 tons load; 10 ton crane

Missiles: SAM: 2 Matra Simbad twin launchers (may be fitted).
Guns: 2 Bofors 40 mm/60 (L 9031). 2 Giat 20F2 20 mm (L 9032-L 9034). 2—12.7 mm MGs.
Radars: Navigation: DRBN 32; I-band.

Helicopters: Platform for Lynx or Panther.

Programmes: Classified as Batral 3F. Bâtiments d'Assaut et de TRAnsport Légers (BATRAL). First two launched 17 November 1973. *Dumont D'Urville* floated out 27 November 1981. *Jacques Cartier* launched 28 April 1982 and *La Grandière* 15 December 1985. *F Garnier* refitted at Brest 2000.
Structure: 40 ton bow ramp; stowage for vehicles above and below decks. One LCVP and one LCPS carried. Helicopter landing platform. Last three of class have bridge one deck higher, a larger helicopter platform and a crane replaces the boom on the cargo deck.
Operational: Deployment: *F Garnier*, Martinique; *D D'Urville*, Papeete; *J Cartier*, New Caledonia; *La Grandière*, Indian Ocean. Service lives of *F Garnier* (2011), *Dumont D' Urville* (2012), *J Cartier* (2013) and *La Grandière* (2014) extended. *Champlain* placed in reserve in Martinique 2004 and later sunk as a target.
Sales: Ships of this class built for Chile, Gabon, Ivory Coast and Morocco. *La Grandière* was also built for Gabon under Clause 29 arrangements but funds were not available.

JACQUES CARTIER *6/2004** / 1153199

1 + 1 MISTRAL CLASS (AMPHIBIOUS ASSAULT SHIPS) (LHDM/BPC)

Name	No	Builders	Laid down	Launched	Commissioned
MISTRAL	L 9013	DCN Brest	10 July 2003	6 Oct 2004	Mar 2006
TONNERRE	L 9014	DCN Brest	26 Aug 2003	26 July 2005	Dec 2006

Displacement, tons: 16,500 standard; 21,500 full load; 32,300 flooded

Dimensions, feet (metres): 653 × 105 × 20.3 *(199 × 32 × 6.2)*

Flight deck, feet (metres): 653 × 105 (199 × 32)

Main machinery: Electric propulsion: 4 (3 Wärtsilä 16V32 and 1 Wärtsilä 18V200) diesel generators provide total of 20.8 MW for propulsion and services. 2 Alstom Mermaid (2 × 7 MW) podded propulsors trainable through 360°; bow thruster

Speed, knots: 19

Range, n miles: 11,000 at 15 kt; 6,000 at 18 kt

Complement: 160 (20 officers) (up to 900 in austerity conditions)

Military lift: 450 troops and 60 armoured vehicles/8 helicopters or 16 helicopters or 230 vehicles. 4 CTM (LCU) or 2 LCACs.

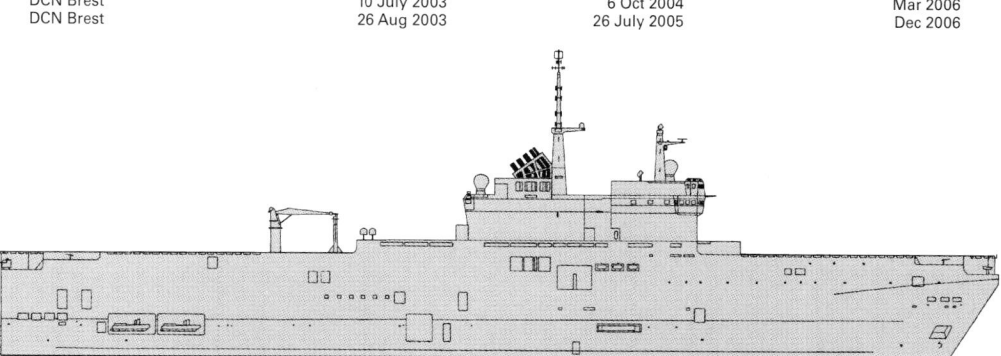

MISTRAL *(Scale 1 : 1,500), Ian Sturton* / 1042093

Missiles: SAM: 2 Simbad twin PDMS launchers for Matra BAE Dynamics Mistral; IR homing to 6 km (3.2 n miles); warhead 3 kg; anti-sea-skimmer.

Guns: 2 Breda Mauser 30 mm. 4 – 12.7 mm MGs.

Countermeasures: ESM: ARBR 21; intercept.

Combat data systems: SENIT combat data system (SENIT 8 derivative) SIC 21 command support system for joint operations; space available for afloat CJTF command; Syracuse III Satcom.

Weapons control: 2 optronic systems.

Radars: Air/surface search: Thales MRR; 3-D; G-band. Navigation: 2 Racal-Decca Bridgemaster E 250 (DRBN 38A); I-band.

Helicopters: Up to 16 NH90 or SA 330 Puma or AS 532U2 Cougar or AS 665 Tigre attack helicopters.

Programmes: Designated BPC (Bâtiment de Projection et de Commandement, support and command ship for force projection, ex-NTCD (new LHDs); to replace *Ouragan* and *Orage*. Design and definition phase launched 12 November 1999; building contract notified 22 December 2000; ordered from DCN (prime contractor) and Alstom Marine-Chantiers de l'Atlantique. Forward sections built at St Nazaire, and middle and aft blocks at Brest where final construction and outfitting is taking place. Sixty per cent of the aft section subcontracted to Stocznia Remontowa, Gdansk, and shipped to Brest by barge. First steel cut for *Mistral* 9 July 2002 and *Tonnerre* 13 December 2002. New landing craft planned to operate with *Mistral* and *Tonnerre*.

TONNERRE *7/2005*, B Prézelin* / 1153186

Structure: Built to merchant marine standards. Flight deck has 6 spots for 16 ton medium/heavy helicopters. Well dock 57.5 × 15.4 × 8.2 m; one 1,800 m² hangar for helicopters or vehicles (with 2 lifts) and one 1,000 m² hangar for vehicles only (1 lift); up to 1,000 tons load on vehicle deck. Hospital: 69 beds; additional modular field hospital may be embarked for humanitarian missions.

Other modular facilities could also be embarked according to missions.

Operational: Roles: forward presence, force projection, logistic support for deployed force (ashore or at sea), humanitarian aid, disaster relief, command ship for combined operations. Endurance: 45 days. Sea trials of *Mistral* began in February 2005.

MISTRAL *9/2005*, B Prézelin* / 1153187

MISTRAL *3/2005*, B Prézelin* / 1153188

2 FOUDRE CLASS (LANDING SHIPS DOCK) (LSDH/TCD 90)

Name	No	Builders	Laid down	Launched	Commissioned
FOUDRE	L 9011	DCN, Brest	26 Mar 1986	19 Nov 1988	7 Dec 1990
SIROCO	L 9012	DCN, Brest	9 Oct 1994	14 Dec 1996	21 Dec 1998

Displacement, tons: 8,190 (L 9011), 8,230 (L 9012) light; 12,400 full load; 17,200 flooded

Dimensions, feet (metres): 551 × 77.1 × 17 (30.2 flooded) *(168 × 23.5 × 5.2; 9.2)*

Main machinery: 2 SEMT-Pielstick 16 PC2.5 V 400 diesels; 20,800 hp(m) *(15.3 MW)* sustained; 2 shafts; LIPS cp props; bow thruster; 1,000 hp(m) *(735 kW)*

Speed, knots: 21

Range, n miles: 11,000 at 15 kt

Complement: 238 (20 officers)

Military lift: 470 (up to 2,000 for 3 days) troops plus 1,880 tons load; 1 EDIC/CDIC plus 4 CTMs (typical) or 2 CDIC or 10 CTMs; 150 vehicles

Missiles: SAM: 2 Matra Simbad twin launchers ❶; Mistral; IR homing to 4 km *(2.2 n miles);* warhead 3 kg.

Guns: 3 Breda/Mauser 30 mm/70 ❷. 4—12.7 mm MGs.

Countermeasures: ECM: 2 Thales ARBB 36 jammers. SLQ-25 Nixie towed torpedo decoy.

Combat data systems: SENIT 8/01 (Siroco); Syracuse SATCOM ❸. OPSMER command support system. Link 11 (receive only).

Weapons control: 2 Sagem DIBC-2A VIGY-105 optronic systems (for 30 mm guns).

Radars: Air/surface search: Thomson-CSF DRBV 21A Mars ❹; D-band.

Surface search: Racal Decca 2459 (Foudre); I-band.

Navigation: 2 Racal-Decca DRBN 34A (L 9012) or Racal-Decca 1229 (L 9011); I-band (1 for helo control) ❺.

Helicopters: 4 AS 532UL Cougar or SA 330B Puma ❻ or 2 Super Frelon.

Programmes: First ordered 5 November 1984, second 11 April 1994. Transports de Chalands de Débarquement (TCD).

Modernisation: Sadral SAM replaced by two lightweight Simbad SAMs either side of bridge. New air search radar. 30 mm guns to replace 40 mm and 20 mm in Foudre and fitted on build in Siroco. Sagem optronic fire control fitted in 1997.

Structure: Designed to take a mechanised regiment of the Rapid Action Force and act as a logistic support ship. Extensive command (OPSMER and other systems) and hospital facilities (500 m²) include two operating suites and 47 beds. Modular field hospital may be embarked on Siroco. Well dock of 122 × 14 m *(1,640 m²)* which can

be used to dock a 400 tons ship. Crane of 37 tons and lift of 52 tons (Foudre) or 38 tons (Siroco). Flight deck of Foudre 1,450 m² with two landing spots (one fitted with landing grid and SAMAHE helo handling system). Additional landing spot on the (removable) well rolling cover. Siroco landing deck extended aft up to the lift to give a 1,740 m² area. Flume stabilisation fitted in 1993 to Foudre.

Operational: Two landing spots on flight deck plus one on deck well rolling cover. Can operate Super Frelons or Super Pumas. Could carry up to 1,600 troops in emergency. Endurance, 30 days (with 700 persons aboard). Assigned to FAN and based at Toulon. Typical loads: one CDIC, four CTM, 10 AMX 10RC armoured cars and 50 vehicles or total of 180 to 200 vehicles (without landing craft). Siroco deployed to East Timor in 1999.

SIROCO

(Scale 1 : 1,500), Ian Sturton / 0529157

SIROCO

6/2002, B Prézelin /0529144

FOUDRE

8/2004, B Prézelin / 1042219

1 OURAGAN CLASS (LANDING SHIP DOCK) (LSDH/TCD)

Name	No	Builders	Laid down	Launched	Commissioned
ORAGE	L 9022	Brest Naval Dockyard	June 1966	22 Apr 1967	1 Apr 1968

Displacement, tons: 5,800 light; 8,500 full load; 14,400 when fully docked down

Dimensions, feet (metres): 488.9 × 75.4 × 17.7 (28.5 flooded)
(149 × 23 × 5.4; 8.7)

Main machinery: 2 SEMT-Pielstick diesels; 9,400 hp(m) *(6.91 MW)*; 2 shafts; LIPS cp props

Speed, knots: 17

Range, n miles: 9,000 at 15 kt

Complement: 205 (12 officers)

Military lift: 343 troops (plus 129 short haul only); 2 LCTs (EDIC) with 11 light tanks each or 8 loaded CTMs; logistic load 1,500 tons; 2 cranes (35 tons each)

Missiles: SAM: 2 Matra Simbad twin launchers; Mistral; IR homing to 4 km *(2.2 n miles)*; warhead 3 kg; anti-sea-skimmer.

Guns: 2 Breda/Mauser 30 mm/70. 4 — 12.7 mm MGs.

Weapons control: 2 Sagem VIGY-105 optronic systems.

Radars: Air/surface search: Thomson-CSF DRBV 51A; G-band.
Navigation: 2 Racal Decca DRBN 34A; I-band.

Helicopters: 4 SA 321G Super Frelon or 10 SA 319B Alouette III.

Modernisation: Simbad SAM and new search radars fitted in 1993. Sagem VIGY-105 optronic fire-control system and 30 mm guns are being fitted to replace the 40 mm. Has enclosed Flag bridge.

Structure: Normal helicopter platform for operating three Super Frelon or 10 Alouette III plus a portable platform for a further one Super Frelon or three Alouette III. Bridge is on the starboard side. Three LCVPs can also be carried. Extensive workshops. Flight deck is 900 m²; docking well 120 × 13.2 m with 3 m of water. Two 35 ton cranes.

ORAGE
4/2003, B Prézelin / 0569949

Operational: Typical loads-18 Super Frelon or 80 Alouette III helicopters or 120 AMX 10 APCs, or 84 DUKWs or 340 Jeeps or 12—50 ton barges. A 400 ton ship can be docked. Command facilities for directing amphibious and helicopter operations. Assigned to FAN and based in Toulon. Typical loads: one CDIC, four CTM, 10 AMX 10RC armoured cars and 21 vehicles or total of 150 to 170 vehicles (without landing craft). *Ouragan* decommissioned in 2006 and to be sold to Argentina. *Orage* to be decommissioned in 2007 and also likely to be sold to Argentina, possibly as spares.

ORAGE
1/2006*, B Prézelin / 1151171

2 EDIC 700 CLASS (LCT)

Name	No	Builders	Commissioned
SABRE	L 9051	SFCN, Villeneuve la Garenne	13 June 1987
DAGUE	L 9052	SFCN, Villeneuve la Garenne	19 Dec 1987

Displacement, tons: 365 (L 9051), 325 (L 9052) standard; 736 full load

Dimensions, feet (metres): 193.6 × 38.1 × 5.8 *(59 × 11.6 × 1.7)*

Main machinery: 2 SACM Uni Diesel UD 30 V12 M3 diesels; 1,200 hp(m) *(882 kW)* sustained; 2 shafts

Speed, knots: 12

Range, n miles: 1,800 at 12 kt

Complement: 10 plus 180 passengers

Military lift: 200 tons, 11 trucks or 5 AMX 30

Guns: 2 Giat 20F2 20 mm. 2 — 12.7 mm MGs.

Radars: Navigation: Racal Decca 1229; I-band.

Comment: Ordered 10 March 1986. Given names on 29 April 1999. Rated as Engins de Débarquement d'Infanterie et Chars (EDIC III). Based at Toulon (L 9051) and Djibouti (L 9052). L 9051 refitted in 2004.

2 CDIC CLASS (LCT)

Name	No	Builders	Commissioned
RAPIÈRE	L 9061	SFCN, Villeneuve la Garenne	28 July 1988
HALLEBARDE	L 9062	SFCN, Villeneuve la Garenne	2 Mar 1989

Displacement, tons: 380 standard; 750 full load

Dimensions, feet (metres): 194.9 × 39 × 5.9 *(59.4 × 11.9 × 1.8)*

Main machinery: 2 SACM Uni Diesel UD 30 V12 M1 diesels; 1,200 hp(m) *(882 kW)* sustained; 2 shafts

Speed, knots: 10.5

Range, n miles: 1,000 at 10 kt

Complement: 12 (1 officer) plus 230 passengers

Military lift: 340 tons

Guns: 2 Giat 20F2 20 mm. 2 — 12.7 mm MGs.

Radars: Navigation: Racal Decca 1229; I-band.

Comment: CDIC (Chaland de Débarquement d'Infanterie et de Chars) built to work with Foudre class. The wheelhouse can be lowered to facilitate docking manoeuvres in the LPDs. Assigned to FAN at Toulon. Given names on 21 July 1997. One other transferred to Senegal in February 1999.

SABRE
4/2005*, B Prézelin / 1153185

RAPIÈRE
4/2005*, B Prézelin / 1153184

15 CTMs (LCM)

CTM 17-31

Displacement, tons: 59 standard; 150 full load
Dimensions, feet (metres): 78 × 21 × 4.2 *(23.8 × 6.4 × 1.3)*
Main machinery: 2 Poyaud V8520NS diesels; 450 hp(m) *(331 kW)*; 2 shafts
Speed, knots: 9.5
Range, n miles: 380 at 8 kt
Complement: 4 + 200 passengers
Military lift: 90 tons (maximum); 48 tons (normal)
Guns: 2 — 12.7 mm MGs.
Radars: Navigation: I-band.

Comment: First series of 16 built 1966 – 70 and all have been deleted. Second series *CTM 17-18* built by Auroux, Arachon; *CTM 19-31* built at CMN, Cherbourg 1982-92. All have a bow ramp. Chalands de Transport de Matériel (CTM). *CTM 17* based at Lorient, *CTM 18* at Mayotte, *CTM 24, 25* at Djibouti, *CTM 26* at Dakar and ten at Toulon. Six others of the class are based at La Rochelle and operated by the French Army Transport Corps (BTI). They include L 14-16 and L 924-925.

L 924 (Army) *9/1997, van Ginderen Collection* / 0012352

CTM 21 *4/2005*, B Prézelin* / 1153182

MINE WARFARE FORCES

3 ANTARÈS (BRS) CLASS (ROUTE SURVEY VESSELS) (MHI)

Name	No	Builders	Commissioned
ANTARÈS	M 770	Socarenam, Boulogne	15 Dec 1993
ALTAÏR	M 771	Socarenam, Boulogne	9 July 1994
ALDÉBARAN	M 772	Socarenam, Boulogne	10 Mar 1995

Displacement, tons: 250 standard; 340 full load
Dimensions, feet (metres): 92.8 × 25.3 × 13.1 *(28.3 × 7.7 × 4)*
Main machinery: 1 Baudouin 12P15-2SR diesel; 800 hp(m) *(590 kW)*; 1 shaft; cp prop; bow thruster
Speed, knots: 12
Range, n miles: 3,600 at 10 kt
Complement: 25 (1 officer)
Guns: 1 — 12.7 mm MG.
Radars: Navigation: 1 Racal-Decca Bridgemaster C 180; I-band.
Sonars: 2 Thomson Sintra DUBM 41B; towed side scan; active search; high frequency.

Comment: Has replaced the Aggressive class for route survey at Brest. BRS Bâtiments Remorqueurs de Sonars. Trawler type similar to Glycine class (see *Training Ships* section). The DUBM 41B towed bodies have been taken from the older MSOs. A mechanical sweep is also carried. There are two 4.5 ton hydraulic cranes. Original dual navigation training role has been lost.

ALDÉBARAN *7/2005*, B Sullivan* / 1153157

13 ÉRIDAN (TRIPARTITE) CLASS (MINEHUNTERS) (MHC)

Name	No	Laid down	Launched	Commissioned
ÉRIDAN	M 641	20 Dec 1977	2 Feb 1979	16 Apr 1984
CASSIOPÉE	M 642	26 Mar 1979	26 Sep 1981	5 May 1984
ANDROMÈDE	M 643	6 Mar 1980	22 May 1982	18 Oct 1984
PÉGASE	M 644	22 Dec 1980	23 Apr 1983	30 May 1985
ORION	M 645	17 Aug 1981	6 Feb 1985	14 Jan 1986
CROIX DU SUD	M 646	22 Apr 1982	6 Feb 1985	14 Nov 1986
AIGLE	M 647	2 Dec 1982	8 Mar 1986	1 July 1987
LYRE	M 648	13 Oct 1983	14 Nov 1986	16 Dec 1987
PERSÉE	M 649	30 Oct 1984	19 Apr 1988	4 Nov 1988
SAGITTAIRE	M 650	1 Feb 1993	14 Jan 1995	2 Apr 1996
VERSEAU (ex-*Iris*)	M 651	20 May 1986	21 June 1987	6 Oct 1988
CÉPHÉE (ex-*Fuchsia*)	M 652	28 Oct 1985	23 Oct 1987	18 Feb 1988
CAPRICORNE (ex-*Dianthus*)	M 653	17 Apr 1985	26 Feb 1987	14 Aug 1987

Displacement, tons: 562 standard; 605 full load
Dimensions, feet (metres): 168.9 × 29.2 × 8.2 *(51.5 × 8.9 × 2.5)*
Main machinery: 1 Stork Wärtsilä A-RUB 215X-12 diesel; 1,860 hp(m) *(1.37 MW)* sustained; 1 shaft; LIPS cp prop
  Auxiliary propulsion; 2 motors; 240 hp(m) *(179 kW)*; 2 active rudders; 2 bow thrusters
Speed, knots: 15; 7 on auxiliary propulsion
Range, n miles: 3,000 at 12 kt
Complement: 49 (5 officers)

Guns: 1 Giat 20F2 20 mm; 1 — 12.7 mm MG.
Countermeasures: MCM: 2 PAP 104 ROVs; OD3 mechanical sweep gear. AP-4 acoustic sweep. Double Eagle ROV from 2001.
Combat data systems: TSM 2061.
Radars: Navigation: Racal Decca 1229; I-band.
Sonars: 2 TUS 2022 Mk III sonars (one hull-mounted and one PVDS on Bofors Double Eagle Mk II UUV; dual frequency.

Programmes: All built in Lorient. Belgium, France and the Netherlands each agreed to build 15 (10 in Belgium with option on five more). Subsequently the French programme was cut to 10. Belgium provided all the electrical installations, France all the minehunting gear and some electronics and the Netherlands the propulsion systems. Replacement for the last of class (sold to Pakistan) was ordered in January 1992. Three Belgian ships of the class acquired between March and August 1997 after being in reserve since 1990.
Modernisation: A modernisation programme started in 2001 and was completed in December 2005. Modernisation included replacement of sonar by TSM 2022 Mk 3, fitting of a Bofors Double Eagle Mk 2 ROV, a new tactical data system and upgrade of radar and comms.
Structure: GRP hull. Equipment includes: autopilot and hovering; automatic radar navigation; navigation aids by Loran and Syledis; Evec data system.
Operational: Minehunting, minesweeping, patrol, training, directing ship for unmanned mine-sweeping, HQ ship for diving operations and pollution control. Prepacked 5 ton modules of equipment embarked for separate tasks. M 645, 651 and 653 based at Toulon, remainder at Brest.
Sales: The original tenth ship of the class, completed in 1989, was transferred to Pakistan 24 September 1992 as part of an order for three; the second built in Lorient, the third in Karachi.

ANDROMÈDE *4/2005*, B Prézelin* / 1153179

CROIX DU SUD *5/2005*, Frank Findler* / 1153180

ÉRIDAN *3/2005*, W Sartori* / 1153181

4 MCM DIVING TENDERS (MCD)

Name	No	Builders	Launched	Commissioned
VULCAIN	M 611	La Perrière, Lorient	17 Jan 1986	11 Oct 1986
PLUTON	M 622	La Perrière, Lorient	13 May 1986	12 Dec 1986
ACHÉRON	A 613	CMN, Cherbourg	9 Nov 1986	17 June 1987
STYX	M 614	CMN, Cherbourg	3 Mar 1987	22 July 1987

Displacement, tons: 375 standard; 505 full load
Dimensions, feet (metres): 136.5 × 24.6 × 12.5 *(41.6 × 7.5 × 3.8)*
Main machinery: 2 SACM MGO 175 V16 ASHR diesels; 2,200 hp(m) *(1.62 MW)*; 2 shafts; bow thruster; 70 hp(m) *(51 kW)*
Speed, knots: 13.7
Range, n miles: 2,800 at 13 kt; 7,400 at 9 kt
Complement: 14 (1 officer) plus 12 divers
Guns: 1 — 12.7 mm MG. 2 — 7.62 mm MGs.
Radars: Navigation: Decca 1226; I-band.

Comment: First pair ordered in December 1984. Second pair ordered July 1985. Designed to act as support ships for clearance divers. (Bâtiments Bases pour Plongeurs Démineurs - BBPD). *Vulcain* based at Cherbourg, *Pluton* at Toulon, *Achéron* at Toulon as a diving school tender and *Styx* at Brest. Modified Chamois (BSR) class design. 5 ton hydraulic crane.

PLUTON   *1/2004, Schaeffer/Marsan* / 1042229

SURVEY AND RESEARCH SHIPS

Notes: (1) These ships are painted white. A total of about 100 officers and technicians with oceanographic and hydrographic training is employed in addition to the ships' companies listed here. They occupy the extra billets marked as 'scientists'.
(2) In addition to the ships listed below there is a civilian-manned 25 m trawler *L'Aventurière II* (launched July 1986) operated by GESMA, Brest for underwater research which comes under DCN.
(3) Two 9 m survey launches, *Matthew* and *Hunter* were built in 1980.

1 BEAUTEMPS-BEAUPRÉ CLASS (BHO HYDROGRAPHIC AND OCEANOGRAPHIC SURVEY SHIP) (AGOR)

Name	No	Builders	Laid down	Launched	Commissioned
BEAUTEMPS-BEAUPRÉ	A 758	Alstom Marine, Lorient	17 July 2001	26 Apr 2002	13 Dec 2003

Displacement, tons: 2,125 standard; 3,330 full load
Dimensions, feet (metres): 264.5 × 48.9 × 23.0 *(80.6 × 14.9 × 7)*
Main machinery: Diesel-electric; four 1,500 hp(m) *(1.1 MW)* Mitsubishi diesels; 2 Alstom electric motors; 2,950 hp *(2.2 MW)*; 1 shaft; 3,000 hp(m) *(2.2 MW)*.
2 active rudders 300 hp(m) *(220 kW)* each; bow thruster 600 hp(m) *(440 kW)*.
Speed, knots: 14
Range, n miles: 8,300 at 12 kt
Complement: 26 (5 officers) (two crews) plus 25 to 30 scientists
Guns: 2 — 7.62 mm MGs.
Radars: Navigation: 2 Kongsberg; I-band.
Sonars: EG & G side looking towed sonar; Kongsberg/Simrad EM 120 deep multipath echo sounder (12 kHz); Kongsberg/Simrad EA 600 deep echo sounder (12 kHz); Kongsberg/Simrad EM 1002S shallow waters multipath echo-sounder (95 kHz); Kongsberg/Simrad EA 400 — 210 shallow waters echo sounder (33 kHz); Kongsber/Simrad SBP 120 (3 to 7 kHz) narrow beam and SHOM 9 TR 109 (3.5 kHz) wide beam sediment echo sounders. Bodenseewerk KSS31 gravimeter; Thales SMM II magnetometer; acoustic current profiler. Most sensor transducers mounted on a removable chassis fixed underneath the hull. Oceanographic buoys; Sippican Mk 21.

Comment: Contracted to Alstom-Leroux Naval 13 March 2001. Derived from the civilian research ship *Thalassa* built in 1995 by Leroux & Lotz (now part of Alstom Marine) for the French government civilian agency IFREMER. 95 per cent funded by the MoD and 5 per cent by the Ministry of civilian research on behalf of IFREMER that will use the ship 10 days per year. First steel cut 17 July 2001. Started builder sea trials 17 October 2002 and official acceptance trials late December. Two 7.85 m survey launches. 10 tonne stern gantry and 10 tonne crane; up to 5 shelters can be shipped and bolted on the deck to increase lab surfaces; up to 4 vehicles can be stored in the hold. Endurance 45 days. Bâtiment hydrographique et océangraphique (BHO, hydrographic and oceanographic survey ship).

BEAUTEMPS-BEAUPRÉ   *7/2003, B Prézelin* / 0569985

---

1 DUPUY DE LÔME INTELLIGENCE COLLECTION SHIP (AGIH)

Name	No	Builders	Laid down	Launched	Commissioned
DUPUY DE LÔME	A 759	Royal Niestern Sander, Delfzijl	1 Dec 2002	27 Mar 2004	31 Mar 2006

Displacement, tons: 3,100 standard; 4,000 full load
Dimensions, feet (metres): 335.9 × 51.7 × 16.1 *(102.4 × 15.8 × 4.9)*
Main machinery: 2 MaK 9M25 diesels; 7,965 hp *(5.94 MW)*; 2 shafts; 2 bow thrusters
Speed, knots: 16
Range, n miles: To be announced
Complement: 32 + 78 specialists
Guns: 2 — 12.7 mm MGs.

Programmes: Programme initiated 29 October 2001. Contract awarded 14 January 2002 to Thales Naval France (for the mission system) and Compagnie Nationale de Navigation to procure and maintain the vessel for initial five year period. Installation of the MINREM mission system started at Toulon in January 2005. After trials, the ship was transferred to the navy in October 2005 and replaced *Bougainville* in April 2006.
Structure: The ship has a design life of 30 years and is fitted with a flight deck and underway replenishment facilities.
Operational: Fitted with both COMINT and ELINT equipment. The ship is to be available for 350 days a year and active for 240 days. There are two complements.

DUPUY DE LÔME   *6/2005*, B Prézelin* / 1127286

1 POURQUOI PAS ? CLASS
(OCEANOGRAPHIC SURVEY SHIP (AGOR)

Name	No	Builders	Laid down	Launched	Commissioned
POURQUOI PAS ?	–	Alstom Marine, St Nazaire	20 Jan 2004	14 Oct 2004	27 Sep 2005

Displacement, tons: 6,600
Dimensions, feet (metres): 353.0 × 65.6 × 22.6 *(107.6 × 20 × 6.9)*
Main machinery: Diesel-electric; four diesel generators; two electric motors; 4,350 hp(m) *(3.2 MW)*; 2 shafts
Speed, knots: 14.5
Range, n miles: 16,000 at 11 kt
Complement: 35 + 40 scientists
Radars: Navigation I-band.
Sonars: Reason Seabat 7111 (100 kHz) and Seabat 7150 (12/24 kHz) multipath echo sounders; Simrad EA 600 (12/38/200 kHz) deep echo sounder; RDI Ocean Surveyor current profiler (38/150 kHz); Eramer/Triton Elics sediment echo sounder (2 — 8 kHz); most sensor transducers mounted on a removable chassis fixed underneath the hull; also optional towed sonars.

Comment: Contract awarded 17 December 2002 to Alstom Marine. Funded 55 per cent by the Ministry of Research and Education, and 45 per cent by the MoD which will use the ship 150 days per year; civilian manned (operated by Genavir on behalf of IFREMER research agency — see Government Maritime Forces), with navy specialists when operating for military campaigns. First steel cut 1 September 2003. Trials in February 2005 and delivery in March 2005. Optional additional labs in containers; helo deck. Able to operate the *Nautile* mini sub, the *Victor 6000* ROV or the future NATO Submarine Rescue System (NSRS); can embark up to three navy VH 8 survey launches (two under davits); stern gantry to handle equipments up to 22 tonnes. Space allocated to embark up to 20 20 ft containers. Endurance 60 days. *Pourquoi Pas?* (Why not?) is the name given by the famous explorer and oceanographer Jean-Baptiste Charcot (1867-1936) to several of his research vessels.

POURQUOI PAS ?   *9/2005*, B Prézelin* / 1153176

7 TYPE VH 8 SURVEY LAUNCHES (YGS)

Displacement, tons: 4
Dimensions, feet (metres): 25.9 × 7.9 × 1.6 *(7.9 × 2.4 × 0.5)*
Main machinery: Volvo Penta Aquamatic Duotrop diesel; Z-drive; 1 shaft; 237 hp(m) *(174 kW)*
Speed, knots: 17
Range, n miles: 109
Complement: 6

Comment: Built by Fr. Frassmer GmbH & Co (Germany); first craft delivered October 2002 and based at Toulon since July 2003. Last craft delivered October 2003. Carried by *Beautemps-Beaupré* and Lapérouse-class survey vessels. Vedette hydrographique de 8m (VH 8). Fitted with two echo sounders, one multipath echo sounder (Simrad EM 3200), side-scan towed sonar and towed magnetometer.

1 BOUGAINVILLE CLASS (AGIH)

Name	No	Builders	Launched	Commissioned
BOUGAINVILLE	L 9077	Chantier Dubigeon, Nantes	3 Oct 1986	25 Mar 1988

Displacement, tons: 3,310 standard; 4,870 full load
Dimensions, feet (metres): 372.3; 344.4 wl × 55.8 × 14.1 *(113.5; 105 × 17 × 4.3)*
Flight deck, feet (metres): 85.3 × 55.8 *(26 × 17)*
Main machinery: 2 SACM AGO 195 V12 RVR diesels; 4,810 hp(m) *(3.6 MW)* sustained;
2 shafts; LIPS cp props; bow thruster; 400 hp(m) *(294 kW)*
Speed, knots: 15
Range, n miles: 6,000 at 12 kt
Complement: 53 (5 officers) plus 10 staff
Military lift: 500 troops for 8 days; 1,180 tons cargo; 2 LCU in support or 10 LCP plus
2 LCM for amphibious role

Missiles: SAM: 2 Matra Simbad twin launchers (may be fitted).
Guns: 2—12.7 mm MGs.
Radars: Navigation: 2 Decca 1226; I-band.

Helicopters: Platform for 2 Super Frelon.

Programmes: Ordered November 1984 for the Direction du Centre d'Experimentations
Nucléaires (DIRCEN). As Chantier Dubigeon closed down after her launch she was
completed by Chantiers de l'Atlantique of the Alsthom group. Bâtiment de Transport
et de Soutien (BTS).
Modernisation: Conversion 30 November 1998, Syracuse II SATCOM and communications
intercept equipment fitted.
Structure: Well size is 78 × 10.2 m *(256 × 33.5 ft)*. It can receive tugs and one BSR or
two CTMs, a supply tender of the Chamois class, containers, mixed bulk cargo. Has
extensive repair workshops and repair facilities for helicopters. Can act as mobile crew
accommodation and has medical facilities. Storerooms for spare parts, victuals and
ammunition. Hull to civilian standards. Carries a 37 ton crane.
Operational: Returned to France from Papeete in November 1998. Can dock a 500 ton
ship. Based at Toulon since November 1999 and replaced *Berry* as an AGI. Replaced
by *Dupuy de Lôme* in April 2006 and may be converted to replace *Loire* as MCM
support ship.

BOUGAINVILLE   *3/2004, B Prézelin* / 1042238

1 RESEARCH SHIP (AGMH)

Name	No	Builders	Launched	Commissioned
MONGE	A 601	Chantiers de l'Atlantique, St Nazaire	6 Oct 1990	5 Nov 1992

Displacement, tons: 17,160 standard; 21,040 full load
Dimensions, feet (metres): 740.1 × 81.4 × 25.3 *(225.6 × 24.8 × 7.7)*
Main machinery: 2 SEMT-Pielstick 8 PC2.5 L 400 diesels; 10,400 hp(m) *(7.65 MW)* sustained;
1 shaft; LIPS cp props; bow thruster; 1,360 hp(m) *(1 MW)*
Speed, knots: 15.8
Range, n miles: 15,000 at 15 kt
Complement: 120 (10 officers) plus 100 military and civilian technicians

Guns: 2 Giat F2 20 mm. 2—12.7 mm MGs.
Combat data systems: Tavitac 2000 for trials.
Radars: Air search: Thomson-CSF DRBV 15C; E/F-band.
Missile tracking Thomson-CSF Stratus; L-band; 2 Gascogne; 2 Armor; Savoie; 5 Antarès.
Navigation: Two Racal Decca (DRBN 34A) (one for helo control); I-band.
Helicopters: 2 Super Frelon or Alouette III.

Comment: Ordered 25 November 1988. Rated as a BEM (Bâtiment d'Essais et de Mesures).
Laid down 26 March 1990, and launched 6 October 1990. She has 14 telemetry antennas;
optronic tracking unit; LIDAR; Syracuse SATCOM. Flume tank stabilisation restricts
the ship to a maximum of 9° roll at slow speed in Sea State 6. Flagship of the Trials
Squadron. Used for space surveillance by the French Space Agency (CNES) and for
M 45 and M 51 ballistic missile tests. To be equipped with new tracking radars, to replace
Savoie and Stratus, by 2009.

MONGE   *4/2004, H M Steele* / 1042256

3 LAPÉROUSE (BH2) CLASS (AGS)

Name	No	Builders	Launched	Commissioned
LAPÉROUSE	A 791	Lorient Naval Dockyard	14 Nov 1986	20 Apr 1988
BORDA	A 792	Lorient Naval Dockyard	14 Nov 1986	16 June 1988
LAPLACE	A 793	Lorient Naval Dockyard	9 Nov 1988	5 Oct 1989

Displacement, tons: 850 standard; 980 full load
Dimensions, feet (metres): 193.5 × 35.8 × 13.8 *(59 × 10.9 × 4.2)*
Main machinery: 2 Unidiesel UD 30 175V12RVR diesels; 2,500 hp(m) *(1.84 MW)*;
2 cp props; auxiliary propulsion; electric motor and 160 hp(m) *(120 kW)* bow thruster
Speed, knots: 15. **Range, n miles:** 6,000 at 12 kt
Complement: 31 (3 officers) plus 11—18 scientists
Guns: 2—7.5 mm MGs.
Radars: Navigation: Decca Bridgemaster (DRBN 38A) (A 791, 792); Furuno (A 793);
I-band.
Sonars: Thomson Sintra DUBM 42 or DUBM 21C (A 791); active search; high frequency.
EG & G towed sidescan sonar.
Kongsberg/Simrad EM 1002 S shallow water multipath echo sounder (95 kHz); Thales
SMM II magnetometer; sediment echo sounder

Comment: Ordered under 1982 and 1986 estimates, first two on 24 July 1984, third
22 January 1986 and fourth (*Arago* — converted in 2002 to patrol craft) on 12 April 1988.
BH2 (Bâtiments Hydrographiques de 2e classe). Carry 2-3 VH 8 survey launches. Based
at Brest.

LAPLACE   *9/2005*, Derek Fox* / 1153177

1 LAPÉROUSE CLASS (MCD/BEGM)

Name	No	Builders	Launched	Commissioned
THÉTIS (ex-*Nereide*)	A 785	Lorient Naval Dockyard	14 Dec 1986	9 Nov 1988

Displacement, tons: 883 standard; 1,015 full load
Dimensions, feet (metres): 183.4 × 35.8 × 12.5 *(55.9 × 10.9 × 3.8)*
Main machinery: 2 Uni Diesel UD 30 V16 M4 diesels; 2,710 hp(m) *(1.99 MW)* sustained;
1 shaft; cp prop
Speed, knots: 15. **Range, n miles:** 6,000 at 12 kt
Complement: 38 (2 officers) plus 7 passengers
Guns: 2—12.7 mm MGs.
Radars: Navigation: Racal Decca Bridgemaster (DRBN 38A); I-band.
Sonars: VDS; Thomson Sintra DUBM 42 and DUBM 60A; active search; high frequency.

Comment: Same hull as Lapérouse class. Classified as Bâtiment Experimental Guerre de
Mines (BEGM). Operated by the Centre d'Études, d'Instruction et d'Entraînement de
la Guerre des Mines (CETIEGM) in Brest. Launched 19 March 1988. Renamed to avoid
confusion with the Y 700. Equipped to conduct trials on all underwater weapons and sensors
for mine warfare. Can lay mines. Can support six divers. Fitted with the Thomson Sintra
Lagadmor mine warfare combat system designed for the cancelled Narvik class. Also
used for experiments with Propelled Variable Depth Sonar system.

THÉTIS   *3/2005*, B Prézelin*/ 1153178

TRAINING SHIPS

2 CHIMERE CLASS (TRAINING SHIPS) (AXL)

CHIMÈRE	Y 706	FARFADET	Y 711

Displacement, tons: 100 full load
Dimensions, feet (metres): 100.1 × 17.1 × 5.7 *(30.5 × 5.2 × 1.75)*
Main machinery: 2 Baudouin DK4 M diesels; 400 hp *(300 kW)*; 1 shaft
Speed, knots: 11
Complement: 7
Radars: Navigation: Decca 1226; I-band.

Comment: Naval school tenders built at Bayonne and which entered service in 1970
(Y 706) and 1971 (Y 711). Due to be decommissioned in 2010.

CHIMÈRE   *7/2002, Per Körnefeldt* / 0528859

8 LÉOPARD CLASS (AXL)

Name	No	Builders	Commissioned
LÉOPARD	A 748	ACM, St Malo	4 Dec 1982
PANTHÈRE	A 749	ACM, St Malo	4 Dec 1982
JAGUAR	A 750	ACM, St Malo	18 Dec 1982
LYNX	A 751	La Perrière, Lorient	18 Dec 1982
GUÉPARD	A 752	ACM, St Malo	1 July 1983
CHACAL	A 753	ACM, St Malo	10 Sep 1983
TIGRE	A 754	La Perrière, Lorient	1 July 1983
LION	A 755	La Perrière, Lorient	10 Sep 1983

Displacement, tons: 335 standard; 463 full load
Dimensions, feet (metres): 141 × 27.1 × 10.5 *(43 × 8.3 × 3.2)*
Main machinery: 2 SACM MGO 175 V16 ASHR diesels; 2,200 hp(m) *(1.62 MW)*; 2 shafts
Speed, knots: 15
Range, n miles: 4,100 at 12 kt
Complement: 14 plus 21 trainees
Guns: 2 — 12.7 mm MGs.
Radars: Navigation: Racal Decca 1226; I-band.

Comment: First four ordered May 1980. Further four ordered April 1981. Form 20ème Divec (Training division) for shiphandling training and occasional EEZ patrols. Based at Brest.

PANTHÈRE *1/2005*, W Sartori* / 1153172

2 LA BELLE POULE CLASS (AXS)

L'ÉTOILE A 649   **LA BELLE POULE** A 650

Displacement, tons: 275 full load
Dimensions, feet (metres): 127 × 24.3 × 12.1 *(37.5 × 7.4 × 3.7)*
Main machinery: 1 Sulzer diesel; 300 hp(m) *(220 kW)*; 1 shaft
Speed, knots: 9 (diesel)
Complement: 20 (1 officer) plus 20 trainees

Comment: Auxiliary sail vessels. Built by Chantiers de Normandie (Fécamp) and launched 7 July 1932 and 8 February 1932 respectively. Accommodation for three officers, 30 cadets, five petty officers, 12 men. Sail area 450 m². Attached to Naval School. A 649 major overhaul in 1994.

LA BELLE POULE *6/2005*, Michael Nitz* / 1153154

2 GLYCINE CLASS (AXL)

Name	No	Builders	Commissioned
GLYCINE	A 770	Socarenam, Boulogne	11 Apr 1992
EGLANTINE	A 771	Socarenam, Boulogne	9 Sep 1992

Displacement, tons: 250 standard; 295 full load
Dimensions, feet (metres): 92.8 × 25.3 × 12.5 *(28.3 × 7.7 × 3.8)*
Main machinery: 1 Baudouin 12P15-2SR diesel; 800 hp(m) *(588 kW)*; 1 shaft; cp prop
Speed, knots: 10
Range, n miles: 3,600 at 10 kt
Complement: 10 + 16 trainees
Radars: Navigation: 4 Furuno; I-band.

Comment: Trawler type. Three more built in 1995-96 as route survey craft (included under *Mine Warfare Forces* section). Based at Brest.

GLYCINE *1/2005*, W Sartori* / 1153173

1 SAIL TRAINING SHIP (AXS)

LA GRAND HERMINE (ex-*La Route est Belle*, ex-*Ménestrel*) A 653

Displacement, tons: 13 full load
Dimensions, feet (metres): 45.9 × 13.5 × 6.6 *(14.0 × 4.1 × 2.0)*
Main machinery: 1 MWM D 225A diesel; 55 hp *(41 kW)*; 1 shaft
Speed, knots: 7
Complement: 7
Radars: Navigation: Decca 1226; I-band.

Comment: Training yawl built in Marseille in 1932. Procured by the French Navy in 1963 and based at Brest.

LA GRAND HERMINE *2/2005*, B Prézelin* / 1153158

1 SAIL TRAINING SHIP (AXS)

Name	No	Builders	Commissioned
MUTIN	A 652	Chaffeteau, Les Sables d'Olonne	18 Mar 1927

Displacement, tons: 57 full load
Dimensions, feet (metres): 108.3 × 21 × 11.2 *(33 × 6.4 × 3.4)*
Main machinery: 1 diesel; 112 hp(m) *(82 kW)*; 1 auxiliary prop
Speed, knots: 6 (diesel)
Range, n miles: 860 at 6 kt
Complement: 12 + 6 trainees

Comment: Attached to the Navigation School. Has a sail area of 312 m². This is the oldest ship in the French Navy. Used by the SOE during the Second World War.

MUTIN *7/2005*, B Prézelin* / 1153159

AUXILIARIES

4 DURANCE CLASS (UNDERWAY REPLENISHMENT TANKERS) (AORHM)

Name	No	Builders	Laid down	Launched	Commissioned
MEUSE	A 607	Brest Naval Dockyard	2 June 1977	2 Dec 1978	21 Nov 1980
VAR	A 608	Brest Naval Dockyard	8 May 1979	1 June 1981	29 Jan 1983
MARNE	A 630	Brest Naval Dockyard	4 Aug 1982	2 Feb 1985	16 Jan 1987
SOMME	A 631	Normed, la Seyne	3 May 1985	3 Oct 1987	7 Mar 1990

Displacement, tons: 7,600 (A 607); 7,800 (others) standard; 17,900 (A 607); 18,500 (others) full load
Dimensions, feet (metres): 515.9 × 69.5 × 38.5 *(157.3 × 21.2 × 10.8)*
Main machinery: 2 SEMT-Pielstick 16 PC2.5 V 400 diesels; 20,800 hp(m) *(15.3 MW)* sustained; 2 shafts; LIPS cp props
Speed, knots: 19
Range, n miles: 9,000 at 15 kt
Complement: 162 (11 officers) plus 29 spare
Cargo capacity: 5,000 tons FFO; 3,200 diesel; 1,800 TR5 Avcat; 130 distilled water; 170 victuals; 150 munitions; 50 naval stores *(Meuse)*. 5,090 tons FFO; 3,310 diesel; 1,090 TR5 Avcat; 260 distilled water; 180 munitions; 15 stores *(Var, Somme* and *Marne)*

Missiles: SAM: 3 (1 in A 607) Matra Simbad twin launchers; Mistral; IR homing to 4 km *(2.2 n miles)*; warhead 3 kg.
Guns: 1—40 mm. 2—20 mm (A 607). 4—12.7 mm MGs.
Countermeasures: ESM/ECM.
Combat data systems: Syracuse 2 SATCOM. OPSMER command support system (fitted for BCR ships).
Radars: Navigation: 2 Racal Decca Bridgemaster (DRBN 38A); I-band.

Helicopters: 1 Dauphin or Lynx Mk 4.

Programmes: One classed as Pétroliers Ravitailleurs d'Escadres (PRE). Three classed as Bâtiments de Commandement et de Ravitaillement (BCR; Command and Replenishment Ships).
Modernisation: EW equipment fitted to improve air defences under the 3A programme in 1996-99. Simbad SAM may be carried at bridge deck level.
Structure: Four beam transfer positions and two astern, two of the beam positions having heavy transfer capability. *Var, Marne* and *Somme* differ from *Meuse* in several respects. The bridge extends further aft, boats are located either side of the funnel and a crane is located between the gantries. Also fitted with Syracuse SATCOM.

MEUSE
6/2005*, Jurg Kürsener / 1153153

VAR
1/2006*, B Prézelin / 1151169

Operational: *Var, Marne* and *Somme* are designed to carry a Maritime Zone staff or Commander of a Logistic Formation and a commando unit of up to 45 men. Capable of accommodating 250 men. Assigned to FAN with one of the three BCR ships deployed to the Indian Ocean as a Flagship. To be replaced after 2010 by new ships.
Sales: One to Australia built locally; two of similar but smaller design to Saudi Arabia. One to Argentina in July 1999.

1 MAINTENANCE AND REPAIR SHIP (ADH)

Name	No	Builders	Launched	Commissioned
JULES VERNE (ex-*Achéron*)	A 620	Brest Naval Dockyard	30 May 1970	17 Sep 1976

Displacement, tons: 7,815 standard; 10,250 full load
Dimensions, feet (metres): 495.4 × 70.5 × 21.3 *(151.0 × 21.5 × 6.5)*
Main machinery: 2 SEMT-Pielstick 12 PC2.2 V 400 diesels; 13,600 hp(m) *(10.1 MW)* sustained; 1 shaft
Speed, knots: 19
Range, n miles: 9,500 at 18 kt
Complement: 132 (16 officers) plus 135 for support
Guns: 2 Bofors 40 mm/60. 4—12.7 mm MGs.
Radars: Navigation: 1 DRBN 34A; 1 DRBN 38A; I-band.
Helicopters: 3 SA 319B Alouette III.

Comment: Ordered in 1961 budget, originally as an Armament Supply Ship. Role and design changed whilst building-now rated as Engineering and Electrical Maintenance Ship. Also equipped with 16-bed hospital. Serves in Indian Ocean, providing general support for all ships, including 40 days supply of food for 300 men and 1,000 tons of dieso. Carries stocks of torpedoes and ammunition. Refit in France November 1988/June 1989 and another refit at Brest from January to June 1995. Based at Toulon from December 1997 and assigned to FAN. Refitted in 1998 after a collision with *Var*. Equipped with two hangars. Flight deck capable of receiving all types of helicopter. Service life 2012.

JULES VERNE
8/2004, B Prézelin / 1042192

1 SUPPORT/TRAINING SHIP (AG/AX)

Name	No	Builders	Commissioned
D'ENTRECASTEAUX	P 674 (ex-A 757)	Brest Naval Dockyard	8 Oct 1971

Displacement, tons: 1,925 standard; 2,450 full load
Dimensions, feet (metres): 292 × 42.7 × 14.4 *(89 × 13 × 4.4)*
Main machinery: Diesel-electric; 2 diesel generators; 2,720 hp(m) *(2 MW)*; 2 motors; 2 shafts; LIPS cp props; auxiliary propulsion; 2 Schottel trainable and retractable props
Speed, knots: 15
Range, n miles: 10,000 at 12 kt
Complement: 55 (5 officers) plus 50 passengers
Radars: Navigation: 1 Racal Decca 1226; 1 DRBN 38A; I-band.
Helicopters: 1 SA 319B Alouette III.

Comment: This ship was originally designed for oceanographic surveys. Telescopic hangar. Based at Brest from September 1995. After being replaced by *Beautemps Beaupré* in her survey role, refitted in 2004 to undertake support role (including pollution control) and training until at least 2007.

D'ENTRECASTEAUX
6/2005*, Harald Carstens / 1153175

1 RHIN CLASS (SUPPORT SHIP) (AGH/AR)

Name	No	Builders	Commissioned
LOIRE	A 615	Lorient Naval Dockyard	17 Oct 1967

Displacement, tons: 2,050 standard; 2,445 full load
Dimensions, feet (metres): 333.0 × 45.3 × 12.5 *(101.5 × 13.8 × 3.8)*
Main machinery: 2 SEMT-Pielstick 12 PA4 V 185VG diesels; 4,000 hp(m) *(2.94 MW)*; 1 shaft
Speed, knots: 16.5
Range, n miles: 13,000 at 13 kt
Complement: 156 (12 officers)
Guns: 3 Bofors 40 mm/60. 3—12.7 mm MGs.
Radars: Navigation: 2 Racal Decca 1226; I-band.
Helicopters: 1—3 SA 310B Alouette III *(Loire)*.

Comment: Has a 5 ton crane and carries two LCPs. Used for minesweeper support at Brest. To decommission in 2008 and may be replaced by *Bougainville*.

LOIRE
6/2004, Michael Nitz / 1042255

4 CHAMOIS CLASS (SUPPLY TENDERS) (AG/ATS/YDT/YPC/YPT)

Name	No	Builders	Commissioned
TAAPE	A 633	La Perrière, Lorient	2 Nov 1983
ÉLAN	A 768	La Perrière, Lorient	7 Apr 1978
CHEVREUIL	A 774	La Perrière, Lorient	7 Oct 1977
GAZELLE	A 775	La Perrière, Lorient	13 Jan 1978

Displacement, tons: 315 (375 A 633) light; 505 full load
Dimensions, feet (metres): 136.1 × 24.6 × 10.5 *(41.5 × 7.5 × 3.2)*
Main machinery: 2 SACM AGO 175 V16 diesels; 2,850 hp(m) *(2.06 MW)*; 2 shafts; cp props; bow thruster
Speed, knots: 14.5
Range, n miles: 7,200 (6,000 A 633) at 12 kt
Complement: 20 plus 12 spare berths
Radars: Navigation: Racal Decca 1226; I-band.

Comment: Similar to the standard fish oil rig support ships. Can act as tugs, oil pollution vessels, salvage craft (two 30 ton and two 5 ton winches), coastal and harbour controlled minelaying, torpedo recovery, diving tenders and a variety of other tasks. Bollard pull 25 tons. Can carry 100 tons of stores on deck or 125 tons of fuel and 40 tons of water or 65 tons of fuel and 120 tons of water. *Taape* ordered in March 1982 from La Perrière-of improved design but basically similar with bridge one deck higher. *Elan* based at Cherbourg, remainder at Toulon. Three paid off so far, one of which (ex-*Chamois*) transferred to Madagascar in May 1996. To be replaced by eight Bâtiments de Soutien et d'Assistance Hauturiers (BSAH) from 2008.

TAAPE *8/2004, Schaeffer/Marsan* / 1042203

1 ALIZE CLASS (DIVING TENDER) (YDT)

Name	No	Builders	Commissioned
ALIZE	A 645	Socarénam, Boulogne	8 Nov 2005

Displacement, tons: 1,100 standard; 1,500 full load
Dimensions, feet (metres): 196.8 × 42.6 × 13.1 *(60.0 × 13.0 × 4.0)*
Main machinery: 2 diesels; 2,800 hp *(2.1 MW)*; 2 shafts; bow thruster
Speed, knots: 14.
Range, n miles: 7,500 at 12 kt
Complement: 17 (3 officers) plus 30 passengers
Guns: 2 – 12.7 mm MGs.
Radars: Navigation: Racal Decca Bridgemaster (DRBN 38A); I-band.
Helicopters: Platform for one medium.

Comment: Ordered in November 2003. Replaced *Isard* in diving support role in early 2006. Based at Toulon.

ALIZE *9/2005*, P Marsan* / 1153169

0 + 1 LE MALIN CLASS (YDT)

LE MALIN (ex-*Apache*) A 616

Displacement, tons: 1,000 full load
Dimensions, feet (metres): 164.0 × 36.1 × ? *(50.0 × 11.0 ×?)*
Main machinery: To be announced
Speed, knots: 14
Complement: 18 (2 officers)
Radars: To be announced.

Comment: Ex-fishing vessel seized on 20 June 2004 and transferred to French Navy 7 September 2005 at Port des Galets (La Réunion). To be refitted at Toulon in 2006 and to enter French naval service as a diving tender on completion. To be based at Toulon.

2 RR 4000 TYPE (SUPPLY TENDERS) (AFL)

Name	No	Builders	Commissioned
RARI	A 634	Breheret, Couéron	21 Feb 1985
REVI	A 635	Breheret, Couéron	9 Mar 1985

Displacement, tons: 900 light; 1,577 full load
Dimensions, feet (metres): 167.3 × 41.3 × 13.1 *(51 × 12.6 × 4)*
Main machinery: 2 SACM-Wärtsilä AGO 195 V12 M6 diesels; 4,410 hp(m) *(3.24 MW)*; 2 shafts; cp props; 2 bow thrusters
Speed, knots: 14.5
Range, n miles: 5,000 at 12 kt
Complement: 22 plus 18 passengers
Guns: 2 – 7.62 mm MGs.
Radars: Navigation: Racal Decca Bridgemaster (DRBN 38A); I-band.

Comment: Two 'remorqueurs ravitailleurs' built for le Centre d'Expérimentation du Pacifique. Can carry 400 tons of cargo on deck. Bollard pull 47 tons. *Rari* refitted at Brest 2004-05. *Revi* based at Papeete and *Rari* at Brest.

RARI *6/2004, B Prézelin* / 1042202

1 TRANSPORT LANDING SHIP (LSL)

Name	No	Builders	Commissioned
GAPEAU	L 9090	Chantier Serra, la Seyne	2 Oct 1987

Displacement, tons: 563 standard; 1,090 full load
Dimensions, feet (metres): 216.5 × 41.0 × 11.2 *(66 × 12.5 × 3.4)*
Main machinery: 2 diesels; 550 hp(m) *(404 kW)*; 2 shafts
Speed, knots: 11
Range, n miles: 1,900 at 10 kt
Complement: 6 + 30 scientists
Cargo capacity: 460 tons
Radars: Navigation: Racal Decca 1226 and Furuno FRS 1000; I-band.

Comment: Supply ship with bow doors. Operates for Centre d'Essais de la Mediterranée, Levant Island (missile range).

GAPEAU *5/2003, Per Körnefeldt* / 0569982

1 MOORING VESSEL (ABU)

TELENN MOR Y 692

Displacement, tons: 392 standard; 520 full load
Dimensions, feet (metres): 135.8 × 29.9 × 6.2 *(41.4 × 9.1 × 1.9)*
Main machinery: 2 Baudouin diesels; 900 hp(m) *(670 kW)*
Radars: 1 Racal Decca; I-band.

Comment: Commissioned on 16 January 1986 and based at Brest. Equipped with 18 ton hydraulic crane.

TELENN MOR *7/2004, B Prézelin* / 1042201

For details of the latest updates to *Jane's Fighting Ships* online and to discover the additional information available exclusively to online subscribers please visit

jfs.janes.com

3 ARIEL CLASS (TRANSPORTS) (YFB)

FAUNE Y 613	**NEREIDE** Y 700	**NAIADE** Y 702

Displacement, tons: 195 standard; 225 full load
Dimensions, feet (metres): 132.8 × 24.5 × 10.8 *(40.5 × 7.5 × 3.3)*
Main machinery: 2 SACM MGO or Poyaud diesels; 1,640 hp(m) *(1.21 MW)* or 1,730 hp(m) *(1.27 MW)*; 2 shafts
Speed, knots: 15.3
Range, n miles: 940 at 14 kt
Complement: 9
Radars: Navigation: Racal Decca 1226; I-band.

Comment: Faune built by Société Française de Construction Naval (ex-Franco-Belge) and *Nereide* and *Naiade* by DCAN Brest. Can carry 400 passengers (250 seated). To be decommissioned by 2007. Based at Brest.

NAIADE   *10/2004, J Y Robert* / 1042252

1 LA PRUDENTE CLASS BUOY TENDER (ABU)

Name	No	Builders	Launched	Commissioned
LA PERSÉVÉRANTE	Y 750	AC de la Rochelle shipyard	14 May 1968	3 Mar 1970

Displacement, tons: 446 tons standard; 626 full load
Dimensions, feet (metres): 142.7 × 32.8 × 9.2 *(43.5 × 10 × 2.8)*
Main machinery: Diesel-electric; 2 diesels; 600 hp *(440 kW)*. 1 motor; 1 shaft
Speed, knots: 10
Range, n miles: 4,000 at 10 kt
Complement: 8
Radars: Decca RM 914; I-band.

Comment: Last survivor of three. *La Fidele* sank off Cherbourg on 30 April 1997 after an explosion while she was destroying old ammunition; *La Prudente* paid off in late 2000. *La Persévérante* was to have been decommissioned in late 2001 but her service life has been extended to 2008. Operates in Toulon area with a reduced crew. Capacity of forward gantry: 25 tonnes.

LA PERSÉVÉRANTE   *2/2004, B Prézelin* / 1042200

1 DIVING TENDER (YDT)

POSÉIDON A 722

Displacement, tons: 240 full load
Dimensions, feet (metres): 132.9 × 23.6 × 7.3 *(40.5 × 7.2 × 2.2)*
Main machinery: 1 diesel; 600 hp(m) *(441 kW)*; 1 shaft
Speed, knots: 13
Complement: 15 (1 officer) plus 27 swimmers
Radars: Navigation: Racal Decca 1226; I-band.

Comment: Base ship for assault swimmers at Toulon. Built in St Malo and completed 6 August 1975.

POSÉIDON   *9/2002, Schaeffer/Marsan* / 0528854

2 RANGE SUPPORT VESSELS (YFRT)

ATHOS A 712	**ARAMIS** A 713

Displacement, tons: 89 standard; 108 full load
Dimensions, feet (metres): 105.3 × 21.3 × 6.2 *(32.1 × 6.5 × 1.9)*
Main machinery: 2 SACM UD 33V12 M5 diesels; 3,950 hp(m) *(2.94 MW)*; 2 shafts
Speed, knots: 28
Range, n miles: 1,500 at 15 kt
Complement: 13 plus 6 passengers
Guns: 1 — 12.7 mm MG.
Radars: Navigation Racal: Decca 1226 (A 712); Furuno (A 713); I-band.

Comment: Built by Chantiers Navals de l'Esterel for Missile Trials Centre of Les Landes (CEL). Based at Bayonne, forming Groupe des Vedettes de l'Adour. A 712 commissioned 20 November 1979 and A 713 on 9 September 1980. Classified as Range Safety Craft from July 1995. *Athos* completed refit at Cherbourg in April 2003.

ATHOS   *1/2005*, B Prézelin* / 1127030

10 VIP 21 DIVING TENDERS (YDT)

CORALLINE A 790	**LISERON** Y 793	**GENÊT** Y 796
DIONÉE Y 790	**MAGNOLIA** Y 794	**GIROFLÉE** Y 797
MYOSOTIS Y 791	**AJONC** Y 795	**ACANTHE** Y 798
GARDÉNIA Y 792		

Displacement, tons: 49 full load
Dimensions, feet (metres): 68.9 × 16.1 × 5.2 *(21.0 × 4.9 × 1.6)*
Main machinery: 2 diesels; 264 hp(m) *(194 kW)*; 2 shafts
Speed, knots: 13
Complement: 4 plus 14 divers
Radars: Racal Decca Bridgemaster (DRBN 38A); I-band.

Comment: Diving tenders built at Lorient. First one delivered in February 1990. *Coralline* is used for radioactive monitoring in Cherbourg. *Y 794* and *Y 798* based at Cherbourg. *Y 790*, *Y 791*, *Y 792*, *Y 795* and *Y 797* based at Toulon. *Y 793* and *Y 796* based at Brest. Rated as 'Vedettes d'Instruction Plongée de 21 m (VIP 21)', divers training craft, and 'Vedettes d'Intervention Plongeurs-Démineurs (VIPD 21)', clearance diving team support craft.

GARDÉNIA   *9/2005*, B Prézelin* / 1153171

2 PHAÉTON CLASS (TOWED ARRAY TENDERS) (YAG)

PHAÉTON Y 656	**MACHAON** Y 657

Displacement, tons: 67 standard; 72 full load
Dimensions, feet (metres): 63.0 × 22.3 × 3.9 *(19.2 × 6.8 × 1.2)*
Main machinery: 2 SACM diesel; 720 hp(m) *(530 kW)*; waterjet
Speed, knots: 9
Range, n miles: 300 at 8 kt
Complement: 4

Comment: 18.6 m catamarans built in 1993-94 at Brest. Water-jet propulsion, speed 8 kt. Hydraulic crane and winch to handle submarine towed arrays. *Phaéton* based at Toulon, *Machaon* at Brest.

MACHAON   *7/2004, B Prézelin* / 1042197

20 HARBOUR CRAFT (YFL/YP/YTR)

Y 603-606	Y 754	Y 765	Y 777	Y 783-787
Y 705	Y 762-763	Y 772 (ex-P 772)	Y 779-781	Y 789

Displacement, tons: 14.5 standard; 19.5 full load
Dimensions, feet (metres): 47.9 × 15.1 × 3.3 *(14.9 × 4.6 × 0.9)*
Main machinery: 2 Baudouin diesels; 1,000-750 hp(m) *(735-551 kW)*; 2 shafts
Speed, knots: 25-17
Range, n miles: 400 at 11 kt
Complement: 4

Comment: Y 772 built in 1975, the remainder between 1988 and 1994. Details are for VPIL 14 class. Y 754 and Y 786 are VSTP 14 class based at Brest. Y 762 and 765 are VSTA 14 class based at Toulon and Brest respectively. Y 763 is a VSC 14 class based at Mayotte. Y 779-781 are VPIL 14 class (pilot craft) based at Cherbourg, Toulon and Brest respectively. Y 783-785 are VIR 14 class (firefighting) based at Brest, Toulon and Cherbourg respectively. Y 787 is a VTP 14 class based at Nouméa. Y 772 is a VPIL 14 class based at Toulon. Y 789 is a VSTP 13 class based at Papeete and Y 777 is a VSR class used for radiological monitoring craft and based at Brest. Y 776 is in reserve. Y 603-606 and Y 705 are ex-Gendarmerie Maritime VSC 10 craft.

Y 777   *12/2004, B Prézelin* / 1042198

Y 784   *9/2005*, Schaeffer/Marsan* / 1153170

42 HARBOUR SUPPORT CRAFT

Comment: There are 11 oil barges (CICGH), one of which is of 1,200 tonnes and the rest between 100 and 800 tonnes, eight 400 tonne oily bilge barges (CIEM), three anti-pollution barges (800 tonne BAPM, and two 400 tonne CIEP), and seven water barges (CIE, 120 to 400 tonnes). Some self-propelled. Also 12 self-propelled YFUs (CHA 27-38), and two 15 m Sea Truck craft.

CHA 30   *10/1999, van Ginderen Collection* / 0069961

1 FLOATING DOCK and 5 FLOATING CRANES

Comment: The dock is of 3,800 tons capacity, built at Brest in 1975. Based at Papeete. 150 × 33 m. Three 15 ton cranes at Toulon (GFA 1, 3 and 4), one at Brest (GFA 6 *Alpaga*) and one 60 ton crane at Cherbourg.

TUGS

2 TYPE RP 50 (COASTAL/HARBOUR TUGS) (YTM)

ESTEREL A 641 (ex-Y 601)   **LUBÉRON** A 642 (ex-Y 602)

Displacement, tons: 510 standard; 670 full load
Dimensions, feet (metres): 119.1 oa; 116.5 wl × 38.1 × 16.4 *(36.3; 35.5 × 11.6 × 5)*
Main machinery: 2 ABC 8 DZ 1000. 179 diesels; 2 Voith-Schneider 28 GII propulsors; 5,120 hp(m) *(3,812 kW)*
Speed, knots: 14
Range, n miles: 1,500 at 12 kt
Complement: 8

Comment: Ordered 15 December 2000; built by SOCARENAM, Boulogne. *Esterel* delivered 27 March 2002 and *Lubéron* 4 July 2002. Based at Toulon to assist *Charles de Gaulle* in harbour. Bollard pull 52 tonnes; 1,350 kN towing winch; fire fighting equipment; 20 cubic metre tank for pollution control dispersal agent. Classified as 'Remorqueurs portuaires de 50 tonnes de traction' (RP 50, 50 tonne bollard pull harbour tugs).

ESTEREL   *8/2004, B Prézelin* / 1042210

2 OCEAN TUGS (ATA)

MALABAR A 664   **TENACE** A 669

Displacement, tons: 1,080 light; 1,454 full load
Dimensions, feet (metres): 167.3 × 37.8 × 18.6 *(51 × 11.5 × 5.7)*
Main machinery: 2 Krupp MaK 9 M 452 AK diesels; 4,600 hp(m) *(3.38 MW)*; 1 shaft; Kort nozzle
Speed, knots: 15
Range, n miles: 9,500 at 13 kt
Complement: 56 (2 officers)
Radars: Navigation: Racal Decca RM 1226 (A 669); Racal Decca 060 (A 664); I-band. Racal Decca 060; I-band.

Comment: *Malabar* and *Tenace* built by J. Oelkers, Hamburg. *Tenace* commissioned 15 November 1973, and *Malabar* on 3 February 1976. Based at Brest. Carry firefighting equipment. Bollard pull, 60 tons. One of the class to Turkey in 1999. To be replaced by BSAH by 2010.

TENACE   *9/2005*, B Prézelin* / 1153160

3 BÉLIER CLASS (YTB)

BÉLIER A 695   **BUFFLE** A 696   **BISON** A 697

Displacement, tons: 356 light; 500 full load
Dimensions, feet (metres): 104.3 × 30.2 × 13.8 *(31.8 × 9.2 × 4.2)*
Main machinery: 2 SACM-Wärtsilä UD 33V12 M4 diesels; 2,600 hp(m) *(1.91 MW)*; 2 Voith-Schneider props
Speed, knots: 11
Complement: 12

Comment: Built by DCN at Cherbourg. *Bélier* commissioned 10 July 1980, *Buffle* on 19 July 1980, *Bison* on 16 April 1981. A 695 and 697 based at Toulon and A 696 at Brest. Bollard pull, 25 tons.

BÉLIER   *8/2004, B Prézelin* / 1042208

3 MAROA CLASS (YTM)

MAITO A 636   **MAROA** A 637   **MANINI** A 638

Displacement, tons: 228 standard; 280 full load
Dimensions, feet (metres): 90.5 × 27.2 × 11.5 (27.6 × 8.3 × 3.5)
Main machinery: 2 SACM-Wärtsilä UD 30 L6 M6 diesels; 1,280 hp(m) (940 kW);
2 Voith-Schneider propulsors
Speed, knots: 11. **Range, n miles:** 1,200 at 11 kt
Complement: 8 + 2 spare
Radar: Navigation: Racal-Decca 1226; I-band.

Comment: Built by SFCN and Villeneuve La Garenne (A 638) and formerly used at the
CEP Nuclear Test Range. *Maito* commissioned 25 July 1984 and is based at Martinique.
Maroa (commissioned 28 July 1984) and *Manini* (commissioned 12 September 1985)
are both based at Papeete, Tahiti. Bollard pull, 12 tons. Fire-fighting water cannon.

MAITO   *3/2003, A Sheldon-Duplaix* / 0569975

1 ACTIF CLASS (YTM)

ACHARNÉ A 693

Displacement, tons: 218 standard; 293 full load
Dimensions, feet (metres): 89.9 × 24.6 × 14.8 (27.4 × 7.5 × 4.5)
Main machinery: 1 SACM MGO diesel; 1,050 hp(m) (773 kW) or 1,450 hp(m) (1.07 MW)
(later ships); 1 shaft
Speed, knots: 11
Range, n miles: 4,100 at 10 kt
Complement: 15

Comment: Last of 12 coastal tugs commissioned 5 July 1974. Bollard pull 13 tons. Not to
be replaced before 2010.

ACHARNÉ   *6/2003, Schaeffer/Marsan* / 0569968

16 + 6 FRÉHEL CLASS (COASTAL TUGS) (YTM)

FRÉHEL A 675	**KÉRÉON** (ex-*Sicie*) A 679	**LARDIER** Y 638	**TAILLAT** Y 642
SAIRE A 676	**SICIÉ** A 680	**GIENS** Y 639	**NIVIDIC** Y 643
ARMEN A 677	**TAUNOA** A 681	**MENGAM** Y 640	**LE FOUR** Y 647
LA HOUSSAYE A 678	**RASCAS** A 682	**BALAGUIER** Y 641	**PORT CROS** Y 649

Displacement, tons: 220 standard; 295 full load
Dimensions, feet (metres): 82 × 27.6 × 11.2 (25 × 8.4 × 3.4)
Main machinery: 2 SACM-Wärtsilä UD 30 V12 M3 diesels (A 675 and 676); 2 Baudouin
P 15 25 (others); 2 Voith-Schneider propulsors; 1,280 hp(m) (941 kW); 1,360 hp(m)
(1 MW) in later vessels
Speed, knots: 11
Range, n miles: 800 at 10 kt
Complement: 8 (coastal); 5 (harbour)
Radars: 1 Racal Decca; I-band.

Comment: Building at Lorient Naval et Industries shipyard (formerly Chantiers et Ateliers
de la Perrière, now part of Leroux et Lotz) and at Boulogne by SOCARENAM. *Fréhel* in
service 23 May 1989, based at Cherbourg, *Saire* 6 October 1989 at Cherbourg, *Armen*
6 December 1991 at Brest, *La Houssaye* 30 October 1992 at Lorient, *Kereon* 5 December
1992 at Brest. *Mengam* 6 October 1994 at Brest and *Sicié* 6 October 1994 at Toulon, *Giens*
2 December 1994 at Toulon, *Lardier* 12 March 1995 at Toulon, *Balaguier* 8 July 1995 at
Toulon, *Taillat* 18 October 1995 at Toulon. *Taunoa* completed 9 March 1996 at Brest,
Nividic on 13 December 1996 at Brest, *Port Cros* on 21 June 1997 at Brest, *Le Four* on
13 March 1998 at Brest and *Rascas* on 12 December 2003. Bollard pull 12 tons. Type RPC
12 coastal tugs, with 'A' pennant numbers and a crew of eight. Type RP12 harbour tugs
with 'Y' pennant numbers and a crew of five. A further order for six craft is expected to
bring the total class number to 22 units.

SAIRE   *6/2005*, E & M Laursen* / 1153161

41 HARBOUR TUGS (YTL/YTR)

MÉSANGE Y 621	**PAPAYE** Y 740	**OTARIE** Y 771	**P 13-24**
BONITE Y 630	**AIGUIÈRE** Y 745	**LOUTRE** Y 772	**P 26-38**
ROUGET Y 634	**EMBRUN** Y 746	**PHOQUE** Y 773	**P 101-104**
MARTINET Y 636	**MORSE** Y 770	**P 6**	

Comment: All between 65 and 100 tons. Those without names are pusher tugs. At least
seven others in reserve. Older 700 hp and 250 hp tugs are being scrapped and replaced
by harbour pushers (with Voith-Schneider propellers) or RPC 12 tugs. One to Senegal in
1998, two to Ivory Coast in 1999. Four new 90 ton RP 10 class tugs (Y 770-773) entered
service on 5 October 2005.

MÉSANGE   *6/2002, Schaeffer/Marsan* / 0528864

PHOQUE   *6/2005*, B Prézelin* / 1153162

GOVERNMENT MARITIME FORCES

Notes: (1) From 29 April 2003, all ships and craft involved in maritime constabulary
operations and public service bear a new livery of blue/white/red on their hull sides. This
has also been applied to some naval vessels and to all those belonging to the Gendarmerie
Maritime, Douanes Français and Affaires Maritimes. It is also to be applied to chartered
vessels involved in pollution control and general support.
(2) All navy and government maritime forces share a common maritime picture network
(Spatio.nav).

AUXILIARIES

Notes: (1) Support vessels are designated Bâtiment de Soutien de Haute Mer (BHSM). An
Invitation to Tender has been issued for the charter of another ship to replace *Carangue*.
(2) It is planned to replace *Alcyon, Ailette*, the ocean-going tugs *Malabar* and *Tenace*,
and the Chamois class tenders by up to eight 65 m Bâtiments de Soutien et d'Assistance
Hauturiers (BSAH) from 2008. These new vessels are to have a bollard pull of 100 tonnes,
to be capable of pollution control and to be fitted with undersea equipment. Some might
be procured by the Navy and others chartered from civilian companies.
(3) In addition to the vessels listed below, the UK tug *Anglian Monarch* (1,480 grt) is
chartered from Klyne Tugs Ltd, under a share agreement with the UK Maritime and Coast
Guard Agency. Based at Dover.
(4) A contract was renewed with Abeilles International in July 2002 for emergency use of
various harbour tugs.
(5) *Langevin* is chartered for submarine associated trials.
(6) Inshore transport duties at Brest and Toulon have been chartered to civilian companies.
At Brest, SMN awarded the contract on 26 January 2004 to transport passengers from
Brest to and from Lanvéoc-Poulmic and the SSBN base at Île Longue. Five high-speed
ships, *Bindy, Tibidy, Trébéron, Arun* and *Térénez* are employed.

2 ULSTEIN UT 515 (SALVAGE AND RESCUE TUGS) (ARS)

ABEILLE BOURBON   ABEILLE LIBERTÉ

Displacement, tons: 3,200 standard; 4,000 full load
Dimensions, feet (metres): 262.5 × 54.1 × 21.3 *(80.0 × 16.5 × 6.5)*
Main machinery: 4 MaK 8M32C diesels; 21,700 hp(m) *(16 MW)*; 2 shafts; 2 cp props; 2 bow
  and 2 stern thrusters
Speed, knots: 19.5
Complement: 12
Radars: Navigation: I-band.

Comment: Contract awarded in November 2003 to Abeilles International for the
  procurement and operation (over eight years) of two Ulstein 515 salvage tugs, classified
  as Remorques d'Intervention, d'Assistance et de Sauvetage (RIAS). Equipped with a
  500 ton towing winch and with extensive fire-fighting and pollution control equipment.
  Vessels built by Myklebust, Norway. The first ship, *Abeille Bourbon*, entered service on
  21 May 2005 and is based at Brest. *Abeille Liberté* entered service on 25 October 2005
  and is based at Cherbourg. There are two crews of 12 per ship.

ABEILLE BOURBON   *5/2005, B Prézelin* / 1127031

1 ULSTEIN UT 710 (SALVAGE AND RESCUE TUG) (ARS)

ARGONAUTE (ex-*Island Patriot*)

Displacement, tons: 2,371 standard; 4,420 full load
Dimensions, feet (metres): 226.0 × 50.8 × 23.0 *(68.9 × 15.5 × 7)*
Main machinery: 2 Rolls Royce Bergen BRM-9 diesels; 10,800 hp(m) *(8.1 MW)*; 2 shafts
Speed, knots: 16
Range, n miles: 19,000 at 10 kt
Complement: 9 plus 22 passengers
Radars: Navigation: I-band.

Comment: Built by Aker-Brevik Construction AS, Norway, the ship was launched on 7 July
  2003 and entered service with Island Offshore on 12 December 2003. Chartered by the
  French government in 2004. Based at Brest.

ARGONAUTE   *3/2005*, B Prézelin* / 1153163

2 ABEILLE FLANDRE CLASS (SALVAGE TUGS) (ARS)

ABEILLE FLANDRE (ex-*Neptun Suecia*)   **ABEILLE LANGEDOC** (ex-*Neptun Gothia*)

Displacement, tons: 3,800 full load
Dimensions, feet (metres): 207.7 × 48.2 × 22.6 *(63.4 × 14.7 × 6.9)*
Main machinery: 4 MaK 8M453AK diesels; 12,800 hp *(9.5 MW)*; 2 cp props; bow thruster
Speed, knots: 17
Complement: 12
Radars: Navigation: 1 Racal Decca Bridgemaster; 1 Racal Decca RMS 2080; I-band.

Comment: Built by Ulstein Hatho A/S, Norway and entered service in 1978 and 1979.
  On long-term charter from Abeilles International since 14 December 1979. Bollard pull
  160 tons. *Abeille Flandre* based at Toulon since 30 May 2005 and *Abeille Langedoc* at
  La Pallice, near La Rochelle, since 25 October 2005. Both ships refitted in 2005.

ABEILLE FLANDRE   *2/2004, B Prézelin* / 0573523

2 ALCYON CLASS (BUOY TENDERS) (ABU)

ALCYON (ex-*Bahram*)   **AILETTE** (ex-*Cyrus*)

Displacement, tons: 1,900 full load
Dimensions, feet (metres): 173.9 × 42.7 × 14.8 *(53.0 × 13.0 × 4.5)*
Main machinery: 2 Bergens-Normo KVMB-12 diesels; 5,200 hp *(3.9 MW)*; 2 cp props;
  2 bow thrusters
Speed, knots: 14.5. **Range, n miles:** 5,400 at 14 kt
Complement: 7 plus 12 passengers
Radars: Navigation: Racal-Decca Bridgemaster and Furuno FR 1830; I-band.

Comment: Built by A & C de la Manche, Dieppe and entered service in 1981 and 1982.
  On long-term charter from SURF (Groupe Bourbon). Former oil-field supply vessels
  (Ulstein UT 711 class) both modernised in 2002-03 at Brest to install dynamic positioning
  system and improve pollution control capabilities. Also fitted with a buoy-handling crane.
  Capable of operating ROVs or TRANSREC 250 sea-skimming system. Deck capacity
  480 tons and bollard pull of 64 tons. *Alcyon* based at Brest and *Aillette* at Toulon.

ALCYON   *10/2004, J Y Robert* / 1042250

1 CARANGUE CLASS (SALVAGE AND RESCUE TUG) (ARS)

CARANGUE (ex-*Pilot Fish*, ex-*Smit Lloyd 119*, ex-*Maersk Handler*)

Displacement, tons: 2,500 full load
Dimensions, feet (metres): 212.3 × 45.3 × 19.7 *(64.7 × 13.8 × 6.0)*
Main machinery: 2 Nohars-Nohab F2116V-D diesels; 7,050 hp *(5.2 MW)*; 2 cp props;
  bow thruster
Speed, knots: 16. **Range, n miles:** 21,000 at 10 kt
Complement: 8
Radars: Navigation: I-band.

Comment: Built by Samsung SB, Koje, South Korea and entered service in 1980. On long-
  term charter from Abeilles International since 1994. Equipped with two fire-pumps, two
  water cannons, anti-pollution equipment and a hydraulic crane. Based at Toulon.

CARANGUE   *4/2005*, B Prézelin* / 1153164

1 AQUITAINE EXPLORER CLASS (SALVAGE VESSEL) (ARS)

AQUITAINE EXPLORER (ex-*Abeille Supporter*, ex-*Seaway Hawk*, ex-*Seaway Devon*)

Displacement, tons: 2,500 full load
Dimensions, feet (metres): 208.7 × 44.0 × 18.9 *(63.6 × 13.4 × 5.75)*
Main machinery: 2 MaK 12M453AK diesels; 8,800 hp *(5.9 MW)*; 2 cp props; bow and stern
  lateral thrusters
Speed, knots: 14
Radars: Navigation: I-band.

Comment: Built by Aukra Bruk, Norway and entered service in 1975. Acquired in 1982 by
  DGA (Armaments Directorate) for support of undersea activities. Operated by Abeilles
  International. Bollard pull 100 tons. Also used in support of pollution control. Based at
  Bayonne.

AQUITAINE EXPLORER   *1/2005*, B Prézelin* / 1153165

RESEARCH SHIPS

Note: Several government agencies use research vessels for various purposes. Most of them are operated by GENAVIR on their behalf. Main agency is IFREMER (Institut Français de Recherche pour l'Exploitation de la Mer) that operates four large ocean-going vessels; *Thalassa* (1996, 3,022 tons), *L'Atalante* (1989, 3,550 tons), *Le Suroît* (1975, modernised 1999, 1,132 tons) and *Nadir* (1974, 1857 tons); and three coastal operations vessels: *L'Europe* (1993, 264 tons catamaran), *Thalia* (1978, 135 grt, trawler type) and *Gwen Drez* (1976, 249 tons, trawler type). *Pourquoi pas?* (5,800 tons) is to replace *Nadir* from 2005. She is partially funded by the MoD, under a general agreement signed in July 2002 for the co-operation between IFREMER and the hydrographic and oceanographic service of the Navy. IRD (Institut de Recherche pour le Développement, ex-ORSTOM) operates in the Pacific two research vessels: *Antéa* (1995, 421 grt, catamaran) and *Alis* (1987, 198 grt UMS, trawler type), and two smaller craft. INSU (Institut National des Sciences de l'Univers) operates five coastal vessels (12.5 to 24.9 m) along the French coasts. TAAF (Administration des Terres Australes et Antarctiques Françaises) uses *Marion Dufresne* (1995, 9,403 GRT UMS, 120 m long), a large support ship for Antarctic operations also fitted for scientific research work, *L'Astrolabe*, (ex-*Austral Fish*, 1986, 1,370 grt) and *La Curieuse* (1989, 150 grt UMS, trawler type).

POLICE (GENDARMERIE MARITIME)

Note: The Gendarmerie Maritime is a force of 1,152 officers and men belonging to the Gendarmerie Nationale (constabulary force) but acting under the operational control of the Marine Nationale. The Gendarmes Maritimes are tasked to protect naval bases and establishments ashore, but also operate 7 large patrol craft (32 to 40 m) and 24 smaller (10 to 24 m) for constabulary tasks in metropolitan France and overseas territories. All ships are procured and maintained on the Navy budget. They display the indication 'Gendarmerie' or Gendarmerie Maritime.

2 PATRA CLASS (COASTAL PATROL CRAFT) (PB)

Name	No	Builders	Commissioned
GLAIVE	P 671	Auroux, Arcachon	2 Apr 1977
ÉPÉE	P 672	CMN, Cherbourg	9 Oct 1976

Displacement, tons: 115 standard; 147.5 full load
Dimensions, feet (metres): 132.5 × 19.4 × 5.2 *(40.4 × 5.9 × 1.6)*
Main machinery: 2 SACM AGO 195 V12 diesels; 4,410 hp(m) *(3.24 MW)*; 2 shafts; cp props
Speed, knots: 26. **Range, n miles:** 1,750 at 10 kt; 750 at 20 kt
Complement: 18 (1 officer)
Guns: 1 Bofors 40 mm/60. 2—7.5 mm MGs.
Radars: Surface search: Racal Decca 1226; I-band.

Comment: *Glaive* based at Cherbourg and *Épée* at Brest. Service life extended to 2006.

ÉPÉE   *1/2005*, B Prézelin* / 1153166

1 STELLIS CLASS (COASTAL PATROL CRAFT) (PB)

Name	No	Builders	Commissioned
STÉNIA	P 776	DCN, Lorient	1 Mar 1993

Displacement, tons: 60 full load
Dimensions, feet (metres): 81.7 × 20 × 5.6 *(24.9 × 6.1 × 1.7)*
Main machinery: 3 diesels; 2,500 hp(m) *(1.8 MW)*; 2 shafts; 1 waterjet
Speed, knots: 28; 10 (water-jet only). **Range, n miles:** 700 at 22 kt
Complement: 8
Guns: 1—12.7 mm MG. 2—7.62 mm MGs.
Radars: Navigation: Racal Decca 1226; I-band.

Comment: Based at Kourou in French Guiana for Guiana launch site duties and for Maroni-Oyapock river patrols. *Stellis* reduced to reserve status in February 2003. GRP hull.

STELLIS CLASS   *6/2000, French Navy* / 0104484

4 GERANIUM CLASS (PB)

Name	No	Builders	Commissioned
GÉRANIUM	P 720	DCN, Lorient	19 Feb 1997
JONQUILLE	P 721	Chantiers Guy Couach Plascoa	15 Nov 1997
VIOLETTE	P 722	DCN, Lorient	4 Dec 1997
JASMIN	P 723	Chantiers Guy Couach Plascoa	15 Nov 1997

Displacement, tons: 80 (P 270, P 722); 82 (P 721, P 723) standard; 96 full load
Dimensions, feet (metres): 105.7 × 20 × 6.2 *(32.2 × 6.1 × 1.9)*
Main machinery: 2 Deutz/MWM TBD 516 V16; 1 Deutz/MWM TBD 516 V12; 3,960 hp *(2.95 MW)*; 2 shafts; 1 Hamilton 422 water-jet
Speed, knots: 30. **Range, n miles:** 1,200 at 15 kt
Complement: 15 (2 officers)
Guns: 1—12.7 mm MG. 1—7.62 mm MG.
Radars: Navigation: Racal-Decca CH 180/6; E/F-band.

Comment: There are some minor differences between the DCN (details shown) and the Plascoa craft. *Géranium* based at Cherbourg; *Jonquille* at Réunion Island; *Violette* at Pointe-à-Pitre, Guadeloupe; *Jasmin* at Papeete, Tahiti. Two similar craft built for Affaires Maritimes.

GÉRANIUM   *9/2003, Marian Ferrette* / 0569970

5 VSC 14 CLASS (PB)

MIMOSA P 761	VÉTIVER P 790	RÉSÉDA P 778
HORTENSIA P 791	MELIA P 789	

Displacement, tons: 21 full load
Dimensions, feet (metres): 47.9 × 15.1 × 3.3 *(14.6 × 4.6 × 1)*
Main machinery: 2 Baudouin 12 F11 SM diesels; 800 hp(m) *(588 kW)*; 2 shafts
Speed, knots: 20. **Range, n miles:** 360 at 18 kt
Complement: 7
Guns: 1—12.7 mm MG. 1—7.5 mm MG.
Radars: Navigation: Furuno; I-band.

Comment: Type V14 SC. Built 1985-87 except P 791 in 1990. Similar to naval tenders with Y pennant numbers. P 790 based at Mayotte, P 761 at Ajaccio, P 778 and P 791 at Brest and P 789 at Toulon. Being replaced in service by VCSM craft.

HORTENSIA   *10/2004, J Y Robert* / 1042249

1 FULMAR CLASS (COASTAL PATROL CRAFT) (PB)

FULMAR (ex-*Jonathan*) P 740

Displacement, tons: 680 full load
Dimensions, feet (metres): 120.7 × 27.9 × 15.4 *(36.8 × 8.5 × 4.7)*
Main machinery: 1 diesel; 1,200 hp(m) *(882 kW)*; 1 shaft. Bow thruster
Speed, knots: 13. **Range, n miles:** 3,500 at 12 kt
Complement: 9 (1 officer)
Guns: 1—12.7 mm MG.
Radars: Surface search: 2 Furuno; I-band.

Comment: Former trawler built in 1990, acquired in October 1996 and converted for patrol duties by April 1997. Recommissioned 28 October 1997 and is based at St Pierre for western Atlantic Fishery Protection duties.

FULMAR   *2000, French Navy* / 0104486

15 + 9 TYPE VCSM (PATROL CRAFT) (PB)

ÉLORN P 601	DUMBÉA P 606	ODET P 611	TRIEUX P 616	ABER-WRACH P 621
VERDON P 602	YSER P 607	MAURY P 612	VÉSUBIE P 617	ESTÉRON P 622
ADOUR P 603	ARGENS P 608	CHARENTE P 613	ESCAUT P 618	MAHURY P 623
SCARPE P 604	HÉRAULT P 609	TECH P 614	HUVEAUNE P 619	ORGANABO P 624
VERTONNE P 605	GRAVONA P 610	PANFELD P 615	SÈVRE P 620	

Displacement, tons: 40
Dimensions, feet (metres): 65.6 × 16.4 × 4.9 *(20.0 × 5.0 × 1.5)*
Main machinery: 2 MAN V12 diesels; 2 shafts; 2,000 hp(m) *(1,470 kW)*
Speed, knots: 25. **Range, n miles:** 530 at 15 kt
Complement: 5
Guns: 1—7.62 mm MG.
Radars: Navigation: Furuno; I-band.

Comment: Designated 'Vedette Côtière de Surveillance Maritime' (VCSM), coastal surveillance craft. Raidco RPB 20. Ordered in two batches of 11 on 6 Dec 2001 and 6 June 2002. Built at l'Herbaudière by Raidco Marine with the co-operation of Chantiers Beneteau. Bear names of rivers. First of class (P 601) entered service on 20 June 2003 followed by P 602-604 in 2003, P 605-610 in 2004 and P 611-615 in 2005. The remainder are to enter service by 2009. To replace VSC 14 and VSC 10 craft. GRP hull and superstructure. One 4.9 m RIB fitted aft on an inclined ramp. Also fitted with water-cannon. P 606 based at Noumea, New Caledonia.

ODET   *7/2005*, Schaeffer/Marsan* / 1153167

8 VSC 10 CLASS (PB)

LILAS P 703   **GENERAL DELFOSSE** P 710   **BELLIS** P 715
BÉGONIA P 704   **CAPITAINE MOULIÉ** P 713   **MDLS JACQUES** P 716
MDLC RICHARD P 709   **LIEUT JAMET** P 714

Comment: 10 m craft capable of 25 kt built 1985-95. Based at Dunkirk, Rochefort, Saint-Malo, Marseilles, Sables d'Olonnes, Dieppe and Pornichet. Six craft transferred to the navy as harbour craft in 2005. P 715 based at Mayotte. To be replaced by VCSM craft as they enter service.

MDLC ROBET   *7/2004, B Prézelin* / 1042226

CUSTOMS (DOUANES FRANÇAISES)

Notes: The French customs service has a number of tasks not normally associated with such an organisation. In addition to the usual duties of dealing with ships entering either its coastal area or ports it also has certain responsibilities for rescue at sea, control of navigation, fishery protection and pollution protection. Operated by about 650 personnel, the fleet comprises 12 large patrol vessels (28 to 35 m), 16 patrol boats (15 to 27 m) and 27 smaller craft. The larger vessels include DF 48 *Arafenua* (105 tons), DF 41 *Avel Gwalarn* (67 tons), DF 42 *Suroît* (67 tons), DF 31 *Alizé* (64 tons), DF 37 *Vent d'Aval* (64 tons), DF 43 *Haize Hegoa* (64 tons), DF 44 *Mervent* (64 tons), DF 45 *Vent d'Autan* (64 tons), DF 46 *Avel Sterenn* (64 tons), DF 47 *Lissero* (64 tons), DF 36 *Kan Avel* (64 tons) and DF 40 *Vent d'Amont* (61 tons). All vessels have DF numbers painted on the bow. There are also four Cessna 404 Titan, and 13 Reims-Cessna F406 patrol aircraft (2 equipped for pollution control) and six AS 350B1 Ecureuil helicopters. A further F 406, configured for pollution control, was delivered late 2002. A 28 m patrol craft is being built by Chantier Naval Guy Couach.

MERVENT   *7/2004, B Prézelin* / 1042225

AFFAIRES MARITIMES

Notes: A force administered and funded by the Ministry of Transport, these vessels are operated by the Préfectures Maritimes. Their duties comprise fishery protection, pollution control, navigation safety and SAR. The vessels are unarmed and manned by civilians and can be identified by a grey/blue hull with blue/red stripes, PM pennant numbers and 'Affaires Maritimes' written on the superstructure. The fleet comprises six large patrol vessels (28 to 46 m), 27 patrol boats (8 to 17 m) and 37 minor craft and service craft (mostly buoy tenders). The larger patrol vessels include PM 41 *Themis* (400 tons), PM 40 *Iris* (230 tons), PM 30 *Gabian* (76 tons), PM 31 *Origan* (70 tons), PM 29 *Mauve* (65 tons) and PM 32 *Armoise* (91 tons). Recent acquisitions include four FPB 50 Mk II patrol boats built by OCEA, Les Stables d'Olonne. These are 22 ton, 16 m craft capable of 25 kt, the first of which, PM 101 *Calisto*, was delivered in December 2000. A further 12 m craft is being built by the same shipyard. Service craft can be identified by 'Phares & Balises' written on the superstructure. Larger vessels include: *Armorique* (500 tons), *Hauts de France* (450 tons), *Provence* (326 tons), *Chef de Caux* (128 tons), *Louis Henin* (73 tons) and *Le Kahouanne* (73 tons).

THEMIS   *9/2004, B Prézelin* / 1042224

ARMOISE   *1/2005*, B Prézelin* / 1153168

HAUTS DE FRANCE   *5/2004, Schaeffer/Marsan* / 1042222

Gabon

MARINE GABONAISE

Country Overview

A former French colony, the Gabonese Republic achieved independence in 1960. Located astride the Equator, the country has an area of 103,347 square miles and has borders to the north with Cameroon and Equatorial Guinea and to the east and south with Congo. It has a 480 n mile coastline with the Atlantic Ocean. The capital, largest city and principal port is Libreville and there is a further port at Port-Gentil. Territorial seas (12 n miles) are claimed. A 200 n mile Exclusive Economic Zone (EEZ) has been claimed but the limits are not defined; jurisdiction is complicated by the offshore islands of Isla de Annobon (Equatorial Guinea) and São Tomé and Principe.

Bases   **Personnel**

Port Gwentil, Mayumba   2006: 600 (65 officers)

PATROL FORCES

2 P 400 CLASS (LARGE PATROL CRAFT) (PBO)

Name	No	Builders	Commissioned
GÉNÉRAL d'ARMÉE BA-OUMAR	P 07	CMN, Cherbourg	27 June 1988
COLONEL DJOUE-DABANY	P 08	CMN, Cherbourg	14 Sep 1990

Displacement, tons: 446 full load
Dimensions, feet (metres): 179 × 26.2 × 8.5 *(54.6 × 8 × 2.5)*
Main machinery: 2 Wärtsilä UD 33 V16 diesels; 8,000 hp(m) *(5.88 MW)* sustained; 2 shafts; cp props
Speed, knots: 24. **Range, n miles:** 4,200 at 15 kt
Complement: 32 (4 officers)
Military lift: 20 troops
Guns: 1 Bofors 57 mm/70 SAK 57 Mk 2 (P 07); 220 rds/min to 17 km *(9 n miles)*; weight of shell 2.4 kg. Not in P 08 which has a second Oerlikon 20 mm.
2 Giat F2 20 mm (P 08).
Weapons control: CSEE Naja optronic director (P 07).
Radars: Surface search: Racal Decca 1226C; I-band.

Programmes: Contract signed May 1985 with CMN Cherbourg. First laid down 2 July 1986, launched 18 December 1987 and arrived in Gabon 6 August 1988 for a local christening ceremony. Second ordered in February 1989 and launched 29 March 1990.
Structure: There is space on the quarterdeck for two MM 40 Exocet surface-to-surface missiles. These craft are similar to the French vessels but with different engines. *Djoue-Dabany* had twin funnels fitted in 1992, similar to French P 400 class conversions.

COLONEL DJOUE-DABANY   *2000, Gabon Navy* / 0104491

1 PATRA CLASS (FAST ATTACK CRAFT—MISSILE) (PTM)

Name	No	Builders	Commissioned
GÉNÉRAL NAZAIRE BOULINGUI (ex-*Président Omar Bongo*)	P 10	Chantiers Naval de l'Estérel	7 Aug 1978

Displacement, tons: 160 full load
Dimensions, feet (metres): 138 × 25.3 × 6.5 *(42 × 7.7 × 1.9)*
Main machinery: 3 SACM 195 V12 CSHR diesels; 5,400 hp(m) *(3.97 MW)* sustained; 3 shafts
Speed, knots: 32. **Range, n miles:** 1,500 at 15 kt
Complement: 20 (3 officers)
Missiles: SSM: 4 Aerospatiale SS 12M; wire-guided to 5.5 km *(3 n miles)* subsonic; warhead 30 kg.
Guns: 1 Bofors 40 mm/60. 1 DCN 20 mm.
Radars: Surface search: Racal Decca RM1226; I-band.

Comment: Re-activated in 2000.

GÉNÉRAL NAZAIRE BOULINGUI *2000, Gabon Navy* / 0104492

POLICE

Notes: The Police have about 12—6.8 m LCVPs and Simonneau 11 m patrol craft, 10 of which were delivered in 1989.

SIMONNEAU SM 360 *1989, Simonneau Marine* / 0069978

LAND-BASED MARITIME AIRCRAFT

Numbers/Type: 1 Embraer Emb-111 Bandeirante.
Operational speed: 194 kt *(360 km/h).*
Service ceiling: 25,500 ft *(7,770 m).*
Range: 1,590 n miles *(2,945 km).*
Role/Weapon systems: Air Force coastal surveillance and EEZ protection tasks are primary roles. Sensors: APS-128 search radar, limited ECM, searchlight. Weapons: ASV; 8 × 127 mm rockets or 28 × 70 mm rockets.

AMPHIBIOUS FORCES

2 SEA TRUCKS (LCVP)

Comment: Built by Tanguy Marine, Le Havre in 1985. One of 12.2 m with two Volvo Penta 165 hp(m) *(121 kW)* engines and one of 10.2 m with one engine.

1 BATRAL TYPE (LSTH)

Name	No	Builders	Launched	Commissioned
PRESIDENT EL HADJ OMAR BONGO	L 05	Français de l'Ouest, Rouen	16 Apr 1984	26 Nov 1984

Displacement, tons: 770 standard; 1,336 full load
Dimensions, feet (metres): 262.4 × 42.6 × 7.9 *(80 × 13 × 2.4)*
Main machinery: 2 SACM Type 195 V12 CSHR diesels; 3,600 hp(m) *(2.65 MW)*; 2 shafts; cp props
Speed, knots: 16
Range, n miles: 4,500 at 13 kt
Complement: 39
Military lift: 188 troops; 12 vehicles; 350 tons cargo
Guns: 1 Bofors 40 mm/60; 300 rds/min to 12 km *(6.5 n miles)*; weight of shell 0.89 kg. 2—81 mm mortars. 2 Browning 12.7 mm MGs. 1—7.62 mm MG.
Radars: Surface search: Racal Decca 1226; I-band.
Helicopters: Capable of operating up to SA 330 Puma size.

Comment: Sister to French *La Grandière*. Carries one LCVP and one LCP. Started refit by Denel, Cape Town in April 1996, and returned to service in 1997 with bow doors welded shut. Completed repair and cleaning at Abidjan during 2000.

PRESIDENT EL HADJ OMAR BONGO *6/1993, Gabon Navy* / 0069977

Gambia

Country Overview

The Republic of Gambia was a British protectorate until 1965 when it gained independence. With an area of 4,361 square miles, it has a short 43 n mile coastline with the Atlantic Ocean but is otherwise completely surrounded by Senegal. The two countries united in 1981 to form the confederation of Senegambia but this collapsed in 1989 when the countries reverted to being separate states. The capital, largest city and principal port is Banjul (formerly Bathurst). Territorial seas (12 n miles) and a 200 n mile fishing zone are claimed. The patrol craft came under 3 Marine Company of the National Army until 1996 when a navy was established.

Headquarters Appointments

Commander, Navy:
Lieutenant Commander M B Sarr

Personnel

(a) 2006: 150
(b) Voluntary service

Bases

Banjul

PATROL FORCES

Notes: Acquisition of new patrol craft is under consideration.

1 PETERSON MK 4 CLASS (PB)

Name	No	Builders	Commissioned
BOLONG KANTA	P 14	Peterson Builders, Sturgeon Bay	15 Oct 1993

Displacement, tons: 24 full load
Dimensions, feet (metres): 50.9 × 14.8 × 4.3 *(15.5 × 4.5 × 1.3)*
Main machinery: 2 Detroit 6V-92A diesels; 520 hp *(388 kW)* sustained; 2 shafts
Speed, knots: 24
Range, n miles: 500 at 20 kt
Complement: 6
Guns: 2—12.7 mm MGs.
Radars: Surface search: Raytheon R41X; I-band.

Comment: Reported seaworthy. Agreement with US government in September 2005 to assist with maintenance and spares. Similar craft in service in Egypt, Cape Verde and Senegal.

PETERSON Mk 4 (Senegal colours) *1/1998* / 0050096

2 PATROL CRAFT (PB)

FATIMAH   **SULAYMAN JUNKUNG**

Displacement, tons: 25
Dimensions, feet (metres): 52.8 × 14.8 × 5.3 *(16.1 × 4.5 × 1.6)*
Main machinery: Caterpillar diesel; 800 hp *(596 kW)*
Speed, knots: 40
Radars: Surface search: Furuno; I-band.

Comment: Procured from Taiwan in 1999.

FATIMAH   *2000, Gambian Navy* / 0104493

1 FAIREY MARINE LANCE CLASS (COASTAL PATROL CRAFT) (PB)

Name	No	Builders	Commissioned
SEA DOG	P 11	Fairey Marine, Cowes	28 Oct 1976

Displacement, tons: 17 full load
Dimensions, feet (metres): 48.7 × 15.3 × 4.3 *(14.8 × 4.7 × 1.3)*
Main machinery: 2 GM 8V-71TA diesels; 650 hp *(485 kW)* sustained; 2 shafts
Speed, knots: 24. **Range, n miles:** 500 at 16 kt
Complement: 9
Guns: 2 — 7.62 mm MGs (not carried).
Radars: Surface search: Racal Decca 110; I-band.

Comment: Delivered 28 October 1976. Unarmed and used for training and personnel transfer. Still seaworthy.

SEA DOG   *1/1990, E Grove* / 0069980

Georgia

Country Overview

Formerly part of the USSR, the Republic of Georgia declared independence in 1991. Situated in the Transcaucasia region of western Asia, the country has an area of 26,900 square miles and is bordered to the north by Russia and to the south by Turkey, Armenia and Azerbaijan. It has a coastline of 167 n miles with the Black Sea on which Poti and Batumi are the principal ports. T'bilisi is the capital and largest city. The country includes two autonomous republics, Abkhazia and Adzharia, and one autonomous region, South Ossetia. USSR legislation appears still to apply to maritime claims.

Territorial waters (12 n miles) are claimed, as is an EEZ (200 n miles) although the limits of the latter are not defined. Naval and Coast Guard Forces (part of the Border Guard) formed 7 July 1993. While merger of the two forces has been considered, they are likely to remain different commands.

Headquarters Appointments

Commander of the Navy:
  Rear Admiral Gennady Khaidarov
Commander of the Border Guard:
  Major General Chkheidze

Personnel

2006: 3,100

Bases

Poti (HQ), Batumi.

PATROL FORCES

Notes: In addition to the vessels listed below, the following vessels are on the Navy List:
(1) A former fishing vessel *Gantiadi* (016) is used as a patrol craft and tender. It is armed with two 23 mm guns and 2 — 12.7 mm MGs.
(2) Three 'Aist' (Project 1398) class patrol launches (10, 12, 14). 14 is active with the Hydrographic Service and has a blue hull.
(3) A 'Nyryat' (DHK-81) and 'Flamingo' (DHK-82) are active with the Hydrographic service and are civilian manned.
(4) A Project 371U patrol launch *Gali* (04).

1 TURK (AB 25) CLASS (PB)

Name	No	Builders	Commissioned
KUTAISI (ex-AB 30)	202 (ex-P 130)	Haliç Shipyard	21 Feb 1969

Displacement, tons: 170 full load
Dimensions, feet (metres): 132 × 21 × 5.5 *(40.2 × 6.4 × 1.7)*
Main machinery: 4 SACM-AGO V16 CSHR diesels; 9,600 hp(m) *(7.06 MW)*; 2 cruise diesels; 300 hp(m) *(220 kW)*; 2 shafts
Speed, knots: 22
Complement: 31
Guns: 1 Bofors 40 mm/60. 2 ZSU 23 mm. 2 — 12.7 mm MGs.
Radars: Surface search: Racal Decca; I-band.

Comment: Transferred from Turkish Navy on 5 December 1998 to the Navy. May retain its active sonar and ASW rocket launcher but this is unlikely.

KUTAISI   *10/2002, Hartmut Ehlers* / 0552754

1 STENKA (PROJECT 205P) CLASS (PBF)

BATUMI (ex-PSKR 638) P301 (ex-648)

Displacement, tons: 253 full load
Dimensions, feet (metres): 129.3 × 25.9 × 8.2 *(39.4 × 7.9 × 2.5)*
Main machinery: 3 diesels; 14,100 hp(m) *(10.36 MW)*; 3 shafts
Speed, knots: 37. **Range, n miles:** 2,300 at 14 kt
Complement: 25
Guns: 2 — 37 mm/L 68.
Radars: Surface search: Pot Drum; H/I-band. Fire control: Drum Tilt; H/I-band.
Navigation: Palm Frond; I-band.

Comment: Transferred from Ukraine in 1998 in a disarmed state. In a poor state of repair at Balaklava and operational status is doubtful.

BATUMI   *9/2004, Hartmut Ehlers* / 1044124

1 MATKA (PROJECT 206MP) CLASS (PGGK)

TBILISI (ex-*Konotop*) 302 (ex-R-15)

Displacement, tons: 225 standard; 260 full load
Dimensions, feet (metres): 129.9 × 24.9 (41 over foils) × 6.9 (13.1 over foils) *(39.6 × 7.6; 12.5 × 2.1; 4)*
Main machinery: 3 Type M 504 diesels; 10,800 hp(m) *(7.94 MW)* sustained; 3 shafts
Speed, knots: 40. **Range, n miles:** 600 at 35 kt foilborne; 1,500 at 14 kt hullborne
Complement: 33
Missiles: SSM: 2 SS-N-2C/D Styx; active radar or IR homing to 83 km *(45 n miles)* at 0.9 Mach; warhead 513 kg; sea-skimmer at end of run.
Guns: 1 — 3 in *(76 mm)*/60; 120 rds/min to 15 km *(8 n miles)*; weight of shell 7 kg. 1 — 30 mm/65 AK 630; 6 barrels per mounting; 3,000 rds/min to 2 km.
Countermeasures: Decoys: 2 PK 16 chaff launchers.
ESM: Clay Brick; intercept.
Weapons control: Hood Wink optronic directors.
Radars: Air/surface search: Plank Shave; E-band.
Navigation: SRN-207; I-band.
Fire control: Bass Tilt; H/I-band.

Comment: Acquired from Ukraine in 1999 with full armament. Based at Poti.

TBILISI   *10/2002, Hartmut Ehlers* / 0552755

1 POLUCHAT 1 CLASS (PB)

AKHMETA 102

Displacement, tons: 100 full load
Dimensions, feet (metres): 97.1 × 19 × 4.8 *(29.6 × 5.8 × 1.5)*
Main machinery: 2 Type M 50 diesels; 2,200 hp(m) *(1.6 MW)* sustained; 2 shafts
Speed, knots: 20
Range, n miles: 1,500 at 10 kt
Complement: 15
Guns: 2—37 mm/L 68. 1—140 mm 17 round rocket launcher.
Radars: Surface search: Spin Trough; I-band.

Comment: Acquired in a disarmed state from commercial sources in Ukraine. Refitted at Metallist Ship Repair Yard, Balaklava 2000-2002.

P 102   *8/2000, Hartmut Ehlers* / 0104494

1 PROJECT 360 PATROL CRAFT (PB)

TSKALTUBO (ex-*Mercuriy*) 101

Displacement, tons: 58; 70 full load
Dimensions, feet (metres): 88.6 × 21.3 × 4.6 *(27 × 6.5 × 1.4)*
Main machinery: 4 diesels; 4,800 hp *(3.58 MW)*; 4 shafts
Speed, knots: 38
Guns: 1—37 mm/L 68.
Radars: 1 navigation.

Comment: Former Black Sea Fleet Flag Officers' Yacht built by Almaz, St Petersburg. Acquired from commercial sources in Ukraine in 1997 and used as a patrol boat.

TSKALTUBO   *10/2002, Hartmut Ehlers* / 0552756

2 DILOS CLASS (PB)

Name	No	Builders	Commissioned
IVERIA (ex-*Lindos*)	201 (ex-P 269)	Hellenic Shipyard, Skaramanga	1978
MESTIA (ex-*Dilos*)	203 (ex-P 267)	Hellenic Shipyard, Skaramanga	1978

Displacement, tons: 86 full load
Dimensions, feet (metres): 95.1 × 16.2 × 5.6 *(29 × 5 × 1.7)*
Main machinery: 2 MTU 12V 331 TC92 diesels; 2,660 hp(m) *(1.96 MW)* sustained; 2 shafts
Speed, knots: 27
Range, n miles: 1,600 at 24 kt
Complement: 15
Guns: 4—23 mm ZSU (2 twin).
Radars: Surface search: Racal Decca 1226C; I-band.

Comment: First one transferred from the Greek Navy in February 1998, second in September 1999. Reported to have been refitted in Greece in 2004.

IVERIA and MESTIA   *10/2002, Hartmut Ehlers* / 0552757

1 ANNINOS (LA COMBATTANTE II) CLASS
(FAST ATTACK CRAFT—MISSILE) (PTFG)

Name	No	Builders	Commissioned
DIOSCURIA (ex-*Ypoploiarchos* *Batsis*, ex-*Calypso*)	303 (ex-P 17)	CMN Cherbourg	Dec 1971

Displacement, tons: 234 standard; 255 full load
Dimensions, feet (metres): 154.2 × 23.3 × 8.2 *(47 × 7.1 × 2.5)*
Main machinery: 4 MTU MD 16V 538 TB90 diesels; 12,000 hp(m) *(8.82 MW)* sustained; 4 shafts
Speed, knots: 36.5. **Range, n miles:** 850 at 25 kt
Complement: 40 (4 officers)

Missiles: SSM: 4 Aerospatiale MM 38 Exocet; inertial cruise; active radar homing to 42 km *(23 n miles)* at 0.9 Mach; warhead 165 kg; sea-skimmer.
Guns: 4 Oerlikon 35 mm/90 (2 twin); 550 rds/min to 6 km *(3.2 n miles)* anti-surface; 5 km *(2.7 n miles)* anti-aircraft; weight of shell 1.55 kg.
Torpedoes: 2—21 in *(533 mm)* tubes. AEG SST-4; wire-guided; active homing to 12 km *(6.5 n miles)* at 35 kt; passive homing to 28 km *(15 n miles)* at 23 kt; warhead 250 kg.
Countermeasures: ESM: Thomson-CSF DR 2000S; intercept.
Weapons control: Thomson-CSF Vega system.
Radars: Surface search: Thomson-CSF Triton; G-band.
Navigation: Decca 1226C; I-band.
Fire control: Thomson-CSF Pollux; I/J-band.
IFF: Plessey Mk 10.

Comment: Transferred from Greece on 23 April 2004. It is likely that torpedoes and EW equipment have also been removed although this has not been confirmed.

DIOSCURIA   *6/2004**, 1127928

AMPHIBIOUS FORCES

2 VYDRA (PROJECT 106K) CLASS (LCU)

GURIA 001   **ATIA** 002

Displacement, tons: 425 standard; 550 full load
Dimensions, feet (metres): 179.7 × 25.3 × 6.6 *(54.8 × 7.7 × 2)*
Main machinery: 2 Type 3-D-12 diesels; 600 hp(m) *(440 kW)* sustained; 2 shafts
Speed, knots: 12. **Range, n miles:** 2,500 at 10 kt
Complement: 20
Military lift: 200 tons or 100 troops or 3 MBTs
Guns: 4—23 mm ZSU (2 twin).
Radars: Navigation: Don 2; I-band.
IFF: High Pole.

Comment: Built at Burgas Shipyard 1974-75. Transferred to Georgia on 6 July 2001.

ATIA   *10/2002, Hartmut Ehlers* / 0552747

2 ONDATRA (PROJECT 1176) CLASS (LCU)

MDK 01   **MDK 02**

Displacement, tons: 145 full load
Dimensions, feet (metres): 78.7 × 16.4 × 4.9 *(24 × 5 × 1.5)*
Main machinery: 1 diesel; 300 hp(m) *(221 kW)*; 1 shaft
Speed, knots: 10. **Range, n miles:** 500 at 5 kt
Complement: 4
Military lift: 1 MBT
Guns: 2—12.7 mm MGs.
Radars: Navigation: Spin Trough; I-band.

Comment: Transferred from USSR January 1983. Has a tank deck of 45 × 13 ft. MDK 02 awaiting refit at Poti.

MDK 02   *10/2002, Hartmut Ehlers* / 0552748

LAND-BASED MARITIME AIRCRAFT

Notes: While there is no naval air arm, two Mi-14 helicopters were reported delivered in April 2004 after five years undergoing refitting in Ukraine. They are believed to be for patrol and SAR duties and to be unarmed.

COAST GUARD

Notes: In addition to the vessels listed below, the following vessels are on the Coast Guard list:
(1) A former fishing vessel *P 101.*
(2) A patrol launch *P 105.*
(3) Nine Aist (Project 1398) class patrol launches *(P 0111-0115, 0212, 702-703).*
(4) One Strizh (Project 1390) class launch *P 0116.*
(5) One 44 m tug *Poti* (ex-*Zorro*) acquired from Ukraine in 1999 for salvage purposes.

1 LINDAU (TYPE 331) CLASS (WPBO)

Name	No	Builders	Commissioned
AYETY (ex-*Minden*)	P 22 (ex-*M1085*)	Burmester, Bremen	22 Jan 1960

Displacement, tons: 463 full load
Dimensions, feet (metres): 154.5 × 27.2 × 9.8 *(47.1 × 8.3 × 2.8)*
Main machinery: 2 MTU MD diesels; 4,000 hp(m) *(2.94 MW)*; 2 shafts
Speed, knots: 16
Range, n miles: 850 at 16 kt
Complement: 43
Guns: 1 Bofors 40 mm/70. 2—12.7 mm MGs.
Radars: Surface search: Atlas Elektronik TRS; I-band.

Comment: Paid off from German Navy in 1997 and transferred 15 November 1998 to the Coast Guard. Former minehunter refitted as a patrol craft in Germany before transfer.

AYETY   *10/2002, Hartmut Ehlers* / 0552749

1 STENKA (TARANTUL) CLASS (PROJECT 205P) (WPBF)

GIORGI TORELI (ex-*Anastasiya*, ex-*PSKR 629*) PP 21

Displacement, tons: 253 full load
Dimensions, feet (metres): 129.3 × 25.9 × 8.2 *(39.4 × 7.9 × 2.5)*
Main machinery: 3 Type M 517 or M 583 diesels; 14,100 hp(m) *(10.36 MW)*; 3 shafts
Speed, knots: 37
Range, n miles: 500 at 35 kt; 1,540 at 14 kt
Complement: 30 (5 officers)
Guns: 2—37 mm/L 68.
Radars: Navigation: Palm Frond; I-band.

Comment: Acquired in a disarmed state from commercial sources in Ukraine.

GIORGI TORELI   *10/2002, Hartmut Ehlers* / 0552750

2 DAUNTLESS CLASS (WPB)

P 106 (ex-P 208)   P 209

Displacement, tons: 11 full load
Dimensions, feet (metres): 40 × 14 × 4.3 *(12.2 × 4.3 × 1.3)*
Main machinery: 2 Caterpillar 3208TA diesels; 870 hp *(650 kW)*; 2 shafts
Speed, knots: 27
Range, n miles: 600 at 18 kt
Complement: 5
Guns: 1—12.7 mm MG.
Radars: Surface search: Raytheon; I-band.

Comment: Aluminium construction. Acquired in July 1999 from SeaArk Marine.

P 209   *10/2002, Hartmut Ehlers* / 0552751

2 POINT CLASS (WPB)

Name	No	Builders	Commissioned
TSOTNE DADIANI	P 210 (ex-82335)	USCG Yard, Curtis Bay	8 Aug 1962
(ex-*Point Countess*)			
GENERAL MAZNIASHVILI	P 211 (ex-82342)	USCG Yard, Curtis Bay	30 Oct 1963
(ex-*Point Baker*)			

Displacement, tons: 66; 69 full load
Dimensions, feet (metres): 83.0 × 17.2 × 5.8 *(25.3 × 5.3 × 1.8)*
Main machinery: 2 Caterpillar 3412 diesels; 1,600 hp *(1.19 MW)*; 2 shafts
Speed, knots: 23.5
Range, n miles: 1,500 at 8 kt
Complement: 10 (1 officer)
Guns: 2—12.7 mm MGs.
Radars: Surface search: Hughes/Furuno SPS-73; I-band.

Comment: Steel hulled craft with aluminium superstructure. First transferred from United States in June 2000 and second on 12 February 2002.

GENERAL MAZNIASHVILI   *10/2002, Hartmut Ehlers* / 0589740

8 ZHUK CLASS (WPB)

P 102-104   P 203-207

Displacement, tons: 25 full load
Dimensions, feet (metres): 49 × 14.8 × 2.4 *(14.9 × 4.5 × 0.7)*
Main machinery: 2 GM diesels; 450 hp *(335 kW)*; 2 shafts
Speed, knots: 12
Range, n miles: 200 at 12 kt
Complement: 7
Guns: 2—23 mm (1 twin) *(P 204, P 205)*.
     2—12.7 mm MGs *(P 203)*.

Comment: P 102-104 constructed at Batumi 1997-99. P 203 transferred from Ukraine in April 1997. P 204-205 acquired from Ukraine and P 206-207 transferred from Georgian Navy in 1998.

P 203   *10/2002, Hartmut Ehlers* / 0552753

Germany
DEUTSCHE MARINE

Country Overview

The Federal Republic of Germany (FRG) is situated in central Europe. The country was re-unified in 1990 when the German Democratic Republic became part of the FRG. With an area of 137,823 square miles, it is bordered to the north by Denmark, to the east by Poland and the Czech Republic, to the south by Austria and Switzerland and to the west by France, Luxembourg, Belgium and the Netherlands. It has a 1,290 n mile coastline with the North and Baltic Seas which are linked by the Kiel Canal. The capital and largest city is Berlin. North Sea ports include Hamburg, Wilhelmshaven, Bremen, Nordenham and Emden, while the main Baltic ports are Lübeck, Wismar, Rostock and Stralsund. The Rhine is the principal inland waterway on which Duisburg is the largest port. Territorial seas (12 n miles) are claimed. An EEZ (200 n miles) has also been claimed.

Headquarters Appointments

Chief of Naval Staff:
  Vice Admiral Lutz Feldt
Chief of Staff:
  Rear Admiral Jörg Auer

Commander-in-Chief

Commander-in-Chief, Fleet:
  Vice Admiral Hans-Joachim Stricker
Deputy Commander-in-Chief, Fleet:
  Rear Admiral Gottfried Hoch

Diplomatic Representation

Defence Attaché in Washington:
  Rear Admiral H von Puttkamer
Naval Attaché in London:
  Captain P Monte
Naval Attaché in Washington:
  Captain M Werner
Naval Attaché in Paris:
  Captain H Walz
Naval Attaché in Moscow:
  Captain K Seemann
Defence Attaché in Brasilia:
  Captain H J Liedke
Defence Attaché in Pretoria:
  Josef Hola
Defence Attaché in Jakarta:
  Commander G Eschle
Defence Attaché in Tokyo:
  Captain R Wallner
Defence Attaché in Kuala-Lumpur:
  Commander G Kramer
Defence Attaché in Oslo:
  Commander V Brügmann
Defence Attaché in Stockholm:
  Commander B Graf von Plettenberg
Naval Attaché in Madrid:
  Commander H Bartels
Naval Attaché in Kiev:
  Commander H-H Schneider

Diplomatic Representation—*continued*

Defence Attaché in Abu Dhabi:
  Commander A Ostermann
Defence Attaché in Tunis:
  Commander R Wittek
Defence Attaché in Copenhagen:
  Commander S Helbig
Defence Attaché in Lisbon:
  Commander G Kleinert
Naval Attaché in Peking:
  Commander C Klenke
Naval Attaché in Tel Aviv:
  Commander W Knipprath
Naval Attaché in Santiago:
  Commander Marusche
Defence Attaché in Ottawa:
  Commander G A Moeller
Defence Attaché in Mexico City:
  Commander H P Lochbaum
Defence Attaché in Canberra:
  Commander F J Birkel
Defence Attaché in Lima:
  Commander W Wirtz

Personnel

(a) 2006: 21,600 (5,017 officers) (including naval air arm) plus 5,600 conscripts
(b) 9 months' national service

Fleet Disposition

1st Task Flotilla (Kiel) 7th FPB Squadron (Warnemünde); Type 143A
3rd and 5th Mine Warfare Squadron (Kiel); Type 332, 333 and 352
1st Submarine Squadron (Eckernförde); Type 206A and Type 212
Fleet Service Ships; Type 423
2nd Task Flotilla (Wilhelmshaven)
2nd Frigate Squadron; Type 123 and 124
4th Frigate Squadron; Type 122
Auxiliary Squadron; Type 702 (AORH), 703 (AOL), 704 (AOL), 720 (ATR), 722 (ATS), 760 (AEL)

Bases

C-in-C Fleet: Glücksburg, Flag Officer Naval Command: Rostock.
Baltic: Kiel, Warnemünde, Eckernförde.
North Sea: Wilhelmshaven.
Naval Arsenal: Wilhelmshaven, Kiel.
Training (other than in bases above): Bremerhaven, List/Sylt (to be closed in 07), Plön, Parow, Neustadt, Flensburg.

Naval Air Arm

MFG 2 (Fighter-Bomber and Reconnaissance Wing at Eggebek) with PA 200 Tornado dissolved in 2005; role transferred to German Air Force.
MFG 3 'Graf Zeppelin' (LRMP Wing at Nordholz) P-3C Orion, remaining in 2 Breguet Atlantic converted for Sigint; Sea Lynx (landbased for embarkation and maintenance). Dornier Do 228 (for pollution control)
MFG 5 (land-based SAR and Fleet Support with embarked helos) Sea King Mk 41.

Strength of the Fleet

Type	Active	Building (Projected)
Submarines—Patrol	12	2 (2)
Frigates	14	1 (4)
Corvettes	—	5
Fast Attack Craft—Missile	10	—
LCM/LCU	4	—
Minehunters	15	—
Minesweepers—Coastal	5	—
Minesweepers—Drones	18	—
Tenders	6	—
Replenishment Tankers	4	—
Ammunition Transports	1	—
Tugs—Icebreaking	3	—
AGIs	3	—
Sail Training Ships	2	—
Diver Support Vessel	1	—

Prefix to Ships' Names

Prefix FGS is used in communications.

Hydrographic Service

This service, under the direction of the Ministry of Transport, is civilian-manned with HQ at Hamburg. Survey ships are listed at the end of the section.

DELETIONS

Submarines

2003	U 11
2004	U 28
2005	U12, U 26

Destroyers

| 2002 | *Mölders* |
| 2003 | *Lütjens* |

Patrol Forces

| 2004 | *Falke, Kondor* |
| 2005 | *Albatros, Bussard, Sperber* (to Tunisia), *Greif* (to Tunisia), *Geier* (to Tunisia), *Seeadler* (to Tunisia), *Habicht* (to Tunisia), *Kormoran* (to Tunisia) |

Mine Warfare Vessels

| 2006 | *Weiden, Frankenthal* |

Survey and Research Ships

| 2004 | *Planet* (old), *Kalkgrund* |

Auxiliaries

2003	*Freiburg* (to Uruguay), *Westensee, Bant*
2004	*Neuende*
2005	*Meersburg*
2006	*Eisvogel*

PENNANT LIST

Submarines

S 171	U 22
S 172	U 23
S 173	U 24
S 174	U 25
S 178	U 29
S 179	U 30
S 181	U 31
S 182	U 32
S 183	U 33 (bldg)
S 184	U 34 (bldg)
S 194	U 15
S 195	U 16
S 196	U 17
S 197	U 18

Frigates

F 207	Bremen
F 208	Niedersachsen
F 209	Rheinland-Pfalz
F 210	Emden
F 211	Köln
F 212	Karlsruhe
F 213	Augsburg
F 214	Lübeck
F 215	Brandenburg
F 216	Schleswig-Holstein
F 217	Bayern
F 218	Mecklenburg-Vorpommern
F 219	Sachsen
F 220	Hamburg
F 221	Hessen

Patrol Forces

P 6121	S 71 Gepard
P 6122	S 72 Puma
P 6123	S 73 Hermelin
P 6124	S 74 Nerz
P 6125	S 75 Zobel
P 6126	S 76 Frettchen
P 6127	S 77 Dachs
P 6128	S 78 Ozelot
P 6129	S 79 Wiesel
P 6130	S 80 Hyäne

Mine Warfare Forces

M 1052	Mühlhausen
M 1058	Fulda
M 1059	Weilheim
M 1061	Rottweil
M 1062	Sulzbach-Rosenberg
M 1063	Bad Bevensen
M 1064	Grömitz
M 1065	Dillingen
M 1067	Bad Rappenau
M 1068	Datteln
M 1069	Homburg
M 1090	Pegnitz
M 1091	Kulmbach
M 1092	Hameln
M 1093	Auerbach
M 1094	Ensdorf
M 1095	Überherrn
M 1096	Passau
M 1097	Laboe
M 1098	Siegburg
M 1099	Herten

Amphibious Forces

| L 762 | Lachs |
| L 765 | Schlei |

Auxiliaries

A 50	Alster
A 52	Oste
A 53	Oker
A 60	Gorch Fock
A 511	Elbe
A 512	Mosel
A 513	Rhein
A 514	Werra
A 515	Main
A 516	Donau
A 1409	Wilhelm Pullwer
A 1411	Berlin
A 1412	Frankfurt Am Main
A 1425	Ammersee
A 1426	Tegernsee
A 1435	Westerwald
A 1437	Planet
A 1439	Baltrum
A 1440	Juist
A 1441	Langeoog
A 1442	Spessart
A 1443	Rhön
A 1451	Wangerooge
A 1452	Spiekeroog
A 1458	Fehmarn
Y 811	Knurrhahn
Y 812	Lütje Hörn
Y 814	Knechtsand
Y 815	Scharhörn
Y 816	Vogelsand
Y 817	Nordstrand
Y 819	Langeness
Y 834	Nordwind
Y 835	Todendorf
Y 836	Putlos
Y 837	Baumholder
Y 838	Bergen
Y 839	Munster
Y 842	Schwimmdock A
Y 855	TF 5
Y 860	Schwedeneck
Y 861	Kronsort
Y 862	Helmsand
Y 863	Stollergrund
Y 864	Mittelgrund
Y 865	Kalkgrund
Y 866	Breitgrund
Y 875	Hiev
Y 876	Griep
Y 891	Altmark
Y 895	Wische
Y 1643	Bottsand
Y 1644	Eversand
Y 1656	Wustrow
Y 1658	Dranske
Y 1671	AK 1
Y 1675	AM 8
Y 1676	MA 2
Y 1677	MA 3
Y 1678	MA 1
Y 1679	AM 7
Y 1683	AK 6
Y 1685	Aschau
Y 1686	AK 2
Y 1687	Borby
Y 1689	Bums

SUBMARINES

2 + 2 (2) TYPE 212A (SSK)

Name	No	Builders	Laid down	Launched	Commissioned
U 31	S 181	HDW, Kiel	Feb 2000	20 Mar 2002	19 Oct 2005
U 32	S 182	TNSW, Emden	Jan 2002	4 Dec 2003	19 Oct 2005
U 33	S 183	HDW, Kiel	Oct 2002	13 Sep 2004	2006
U 34	S 184	TNSW, Emden	June 2003	1 July 2005	2006

Displacement, tons: 1,450 surfaced; 1,830 dived
Dimensions, feet (metres): 183.4 × 23 × 19.7
(55.9 × 7 × 6)
Main machinery: Diesel-electric; 1 MTU 16V 396 diesel; 4,243 hp(m) *(3.12 MW)*; 1 alternator; 1 Siemens Permasyn motor; 3,875 hp(m) *(2.85 MW)*; 1 shaft; 9 Siemens/HDW PEM fuel cell (AIP) modules; 306 kW; sodium sulphide high-energy batteries
Speed, knots: 20 dived; 12 surfaced
Range, n miles: 8,000 at 8 kt surfaced
Complement: 27 (8 officers)

Torpedoes: 6—21 in *(533 mm)* bow tubes; water ram discharge; STN (formerly AEG) DM 2A4. Total 12 weapons.
Countermeasures: Decoys: TAU 2000 (C 303) torpedo countermeasures.
ESM: DASA FL 1800U; radar warning.
Weapons control: Kongsberg MSI-90U weapons control system.
Radars: Navigation: Kelvin Hughes 1007; I-band.
Sonars: STN Atlas Elektronik DBQS-40; passive ranging and intercept; FAS-3 flank and passive towed array.
STN Atlas Elektronik MOA 3070 or Allied Signal ELAK; mine detection; active; high frequency.

Programmes: Design phase first completed in 1992 by ARGE 212 (HDW/TNSW) in conjunction with IKL. Authorisation for the first four of the class was given on 6 July 1994, but the first steel cut was delayed to 1 July 1998 because of modifications needed to achieve commonality with the Italian Navy. Changes included

greater diving depth and improved habitability. HDW Kiel, and TNSW Emden, are sharing the work with the forward half being built by HDW and the stern by TNSW with final assembly alternating between the shipyards. The order for a second batch of two modified boats is expected in 2006 for entry into service in 2011.
Modernisation: The fifth and sixth boats are expected to include IDAS, a missile system to counter ASW helicopters and sea or land targets.
Structure: Equipped with a hybrid fuel cell/battery propulsion based on the Siemens PEM fuel cell technology. The submarine is designed with a partial

U 31   *2/2005*, Michael Nitz* / 1133424

double hull which has a larger diameter forward. This is joined to the after end by a short conical section which houses the fuel cell plant. Two LOX tanks and hydrogen stored in metal cylinders are carried around the circumference of the smaller hull section. Zeiss search and attack periscopes.
Operational: Maximum speed on AIP is 8 kt without use of main battery. Based at Eckernförde as part of the First Submarine Squadron.
Sales: Two identical submarines have been built in Italy. Four Type 214 submarines are being built for Greece and three for South Korea.

U 31   *6/2005*, Frank Findler* / 1133489

U 33   *8/2005*, Martin Mokrus* / 1133488

10 TYPE 206A (SSK)

Name	No	Builders	Laid down	Launched	Commissioned
U 15	S 194	Howaldtswerke, Kiel	1 June 1970	15 June 1972	17 July 1974
U 16	S 195	Rheinstahl Nordseewerke, Emden	1 Nov 1970	29 Aug 1972	9 Nov 1973
U 17	S 196	Howaldtswerke, Kiel	1 Oct 1970	10 Oct 1972	28 Nov 1973
U 18	S 197	Rheinstahl Nordseewerke, Emden	1 Apr 1971	31 Oct 1972	19 Dec 1973
U 22	S 171	Rheinstahl Nordseewerke, Emden	18 Nov 1971	27 Mar 1973	26 July 1974
U 23	S 172	Rheinstahl Nordseewerke, Emden	5 Mar 1973	25 May 1974	2 May 1975
U 24	S 173	Rheinstahl Nordseewerke, Emden	20 Mar 1972	26 June 1973	16 Oct 1974
U 25	S 174	Howaldtswerke, Kiel	1 July 1971	23 May 1973	14 June 1974
U 29	S 178	Howaldtswerke, Kiel	10 Jan 1972	5 Nov 1973	27 Nov 1974
U 30	S 179	Rheinstahl Nordseewerke, Emden	5 Dec 1972	26 Mar 1974	13 Mar 1975

Displacement, tons: 450 surfaced; 498 dived
Dimensions, feet (metres): 159.4 × 15.1 × 14.8
(48.6 × 4.6 × 4.5)
Main machinery: Diesel-electric; 2 MTU 12V 493 AZ80 GA
31L diesels; 1,200 hp(m) (882 kW) sustained; 2 alternators;
810 kW; 1 Siemens motor; 1,800 hp(m) (1.32 MW)
sustained; 1 shaft
Speed, knots: 10 surfaced; 17 dived
Range, n miles: 4,500 at 5 kt surfaced
Complement: 22 (4 officers)

Torpedoes: 8—21 in (533 mm) bow tubes. STN Atlas DM
2A3; wire-guided; active homing to 13 km (7 n miles)
at 35 kt; passive homing to 28 km (15 n miles) at 23 kt;
warhead 260 kg.

Mines: GRP container secured outside hull each side.
Each container holds 12 mines, carried in addition to
the normal torpedo or mine armament (16 in place of
torpedoes).
Countermeasures: ESM: Thomson-CSF DR 2000U with
THORN EMI Sarie 2; intercept.
Weapons control: SLW 83 (TFCS).
Radars: Surface search: Thomson-CSF Calypso II; I-band.
Sonars: Atlas Elektronik DBQS-21D; passive/active search
and attack; medium frequency.
Thomson Sintra DUUX 2; passive ranging.

Programmes: Authorised on 7 June 1969.
Modernisation: Mid-life conversion of the class was a
very extensive one, including the installation of new

sensors (sonar DBQS-21D with training simulator STU-5),
periscopes, weapon control system (LEWA), ESM,
weapons (torpedo Seeal), GPS navigation, and a
comprehensive refitting of the propulsion system, as well
as habitability improvements. Conversion work was shared
between Thyssen Nordseewerke (U 23, 30, 22, 24, 15, 26)
at Emden and HDW (U 29, 16, 25, 17, 18) at Kiel. The work
started in mid-1987 and completed in February 1992.
Structure: Hulls are built of high-tensile non-magnetic
steel.
Operational: First squadron based at Eckernförde. U 25 and
U 30 to be decommissioned in 2008.
Sales: Two unmodernised (Type 206) were to have been
acquired by Indonesia but the sale was cancelled in late
1998.

U 25

6/2005*, Harald Carstens / 1133487

U 29

2/2005*, Michael Nitz / 1133426

U 17
5/2005, **Frank Findler** / 1133456

U 30
8/2005, **Michael Nitz** / 1153499

U 18
7/2005, **B Sullivan** / 1133453

FRIGATES

Notes: The design phase for the next generation Type 125 frigate is to be completed in 2006 with a contract to follow. Four ships are required and the first ship is to enter service in 2012. The design is likely to be based on the requirement to conduct a spectrum of worldwide operations including high-intensity warfare, stabilisation and support roles.

4 BRANDENBURG CLASS (TYPE 123) (FFGHM)

Name	No	Builders	Laid down	Launched	Commissioned
BRANDENBURG	F 215	Blohm + Voss, Hamburg	11 Feb 1992	28 Aug 1992	14 Oct 1994
SCHLESWIG-HOLSTEIN	F 216	Howaldtswerke, Kiel	1 July 1993	8 June 1994	2 Nov 1995
BAYERN	F 217	Thyssen Nordseewerke, Emden	16 Dec 1993	30 June 1994	15 June 1996
MECKLENBURG-VORPOMMERN	F 218	Bremer Vulkan/Thyssen Nordseewerke	23 Nov 1993	8 July 1995	6 Dec 1996

Displacement, tons: 4,900 full load
Dimensions, feet (metres): 455.7 oa; 416.3 wl × 54.8 × 22.3 *(138.9; 126.9 × 16.7 × 6.8)*
Main machinery: CODOG: 2 GE 7LM2500SA-ML gas turbines; 51,000 hp *(38 MW)* sustained; 2 MTU 20V 956 TB92 diesels; 11,070 hp(m) *(8.14 MW)* sustained; 2 shafts; Escher Weiss; cp props
Speed, knots: 29; 18 on diesels
Range, n miles: 4,000 at 18 kt
Complement: 199 (27 officers) plus 19 aircrew

Missiles: SSM: 4 Aerospatiale MM 38 Exocet (2 twin) ❶ (from Type 101A); inertial cruise; active radar homing to 42 km *(23 n miles)* at 0.9 Mach; warhead 165 kg; sea-skimmer.
SAM: Martin Marietta VLS Mk 41 Mod 3 ❷ for 16 NATO Sea Sparrow; semi-active radar homing to 14.6 km *(8 n miles)* at 2.5 Mach; warhead 39 kg.
2 RAM 21 cell Mk 49 launchers ❸; passive IR/anti-radiation homing to 9.6 km *(5.2 n miles)* at 2 Mach; warhead 9.1 kg; 32 missiles.
Guns: 1 OTO Melara 3 in *(76 mm)*/62 Mk 75 ❹; 85 rds/min to 16 km *(8.6 n miles)* anti-surface; 12 km *(6.5 n miles)* anti-aircraft; weight of shell 6 kg.
2 Rheinmetall 20 mm Rh 202 to be replaced by Mauser 27 mm.
Torpedoes: 4—324 mm Mk 32 Mod 9 (2 twin) tubes ❺; anti-submarine. Honeywell Mk 46 Mod 2; anti-submarine; active/passive homing to 11 km *(5.9 n miles)* at 40 kt; warhead 44 kg. To be replaced by Eurotorp MU 90 Impact in due course.
Countermeasures: Decoys: 2 Breda SCLAR ❻. Chaff and IR flares.
ESM/ECM: TST FL 1800S Stage II; intercept and jammers.
Combat data systems: Atlas Elektronik/Paramax SATIR action data automation with Unisys UYK 43 computer; Link 11. Link 16. Matra Marconi SCOT 3 SATCOM ❼.
Weapons control: Signaal MWCS. 2 optical sights. STN Atlas Elektronik WBA optronic sensor.
Radars: Air search: Signaal LW08 ❽; D-band.
Air/Surface search ❾: Signaal SMART; 3D; F-band.
Fire control: 2 Signaal STIR 180 trackers ❿.
Navigation: 2 Raytheon Raypath; I-band.
Sonars: Atlas Elektronik DSQS-23BZ; hull-mounted; active search and attack; medium frequency.
Towed array (provision only); active; low frequency.

Helicopters: 2 Westland Sea Lynx Mk 88A ⓫.

Programmes: Formerly Deutschland class. Four ordered 28 June 1989. Developed by Blohm + Voss whose design was selected in October 1988. Replaced deleted Hamburg class.
Modernisation: SCOT 3 SATCOM and STN optronic sensor fitted from 1998. All four ships are to undergo a major modernisation programme to extend service life to at least 2025. A contract was signed on 21 September 2005 for Phase 1 (2005-11), the replacement of the combat data system by the Thales SABRINA 21 system, which incorporates Tacticos-NC and Sewaco-DDS technology. In Phase 2 (2009-12), ASW capabilities will be upgraded with the installation of the Eurotorp MU 90 lightweight torpedo and modification of the ships to operate the NH90 helicopter and an Atlas Elektronik Low-Frequency Towed Active Sonar (LFTAS). Phase 2 is also likely to include upgrade of the IFF system and replacement of the decoy launchers with Rheinmetall Defence MASS decoy launchers. Phase 3 (2012-14) will improve AAW and ASUW capabilities by installation and integration of RIM-162 Evolved Sea Sparrow (ESSM) and a new surface-to-surface missile, possibly the Saab Bofors Dynamics RBS 15 Mk 3+. New planning and command-and-control systems, such as NATO's MCCIS, Collaboration at Sea (C@S), Link 16 are also to be installed. In a separate contract the DSQS-23BZ bow sonar is to be upgraded 2005-09.
Structure: The design is a mixture of MEKO and improved serviceability Type 122 having the same propulsion as the Type 122. Contemporary stealth features. All steel. Fin stabilisers. Space allocated for a Task Group Commander and Staff.
Operational: 2nd Frigate Squadron based at Wilhelmshaven. One RIB is carried for boarding operations.

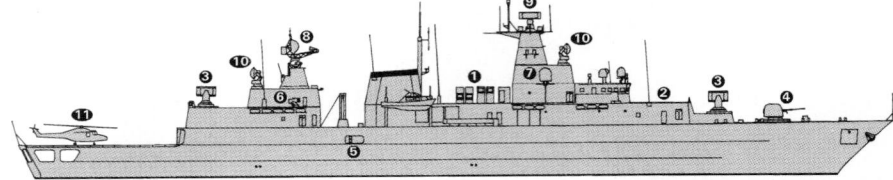

BRANDENBURG   *(Scale 1 : 1,200), Ian Sturton* / 1153487

BAYERN   *9/2005*, M Declerck* / 1133428

MECKLENBURG-VORPOMMERN   *9/2004, John Brodie* / 0587720

BAYERN   *11/2004, John Brodie* / 1044259

MECKLENBURG-VORPOMMERN   *10/2004, B Sullivan* / 0587753

BAYERN   *9/2005*, Martin Mokrus* / 1133486

BRANDENBURG   *4/2002, John Brodie* / 0528871

MECKLENBURG-VORPOMMERN   *8/2005*, Michael Nitz* / 1133430

8 BREMEN CLASS (TYPE 122) (FFGHM)

Name	No	Builders	Laid down	Launched	Commissioned
BREMEN	F 207	Bremer Vulkan	9 July 1979	27 Sep 1979	7 May 1982
NIEDERSACHSEN	F 208	AG Weser/Bremer Vulkan	9 Nov 1979	9 June 1980	15 Oct 1982
RHEINLAND-PFALZ	F 209	Blohm + Voss/Bremer Vulkan	29 Sep 1979	3 Sep 1980	9 May 1983
EMDEN	F 210	Thyssen Nordseewerke, Emden/Bremer Vulkan	23 June 1980	17 Dec 1980	7 Oct 1983
KÖLN	F 211	Blohm + Voss/Bremer Vulkan	16 June 1980	29 May 1981	19 Oct 1984
KARLSRUHE	F 212	Howaldtswerke, Kiel/Bremer Vulkan	10 Mar 1981	8 Jan 1982	19 Apr 1984
AUGSBURG	F 213	Bremer Vulkan	4 Apr 1987	17 Sep 1987	3 Oct 1989
LÜBECK	F 214	Thyssen Nordseewerke, Emden/Bremer Vulkan	1 June 1987	15 Oct 1987	19 Mar 1990

Displacement, tons: 3,680 full load
Dimensions, feet (metres): 426.4 × 47.6 × 21.3
(130 × 14.5 × 6.5)
Main machinery: CODOG; 2 GE LM 2500 gas turbines;
51,000 hp *(38 MW)* sustained; 2 MTU 20V 956 TB92
diesels; 11,070 hp(m) *(8.14 MW)* sustained; 2 shafts;
cp props
Speed, knots: 30; 20 on diesels
Range, n miles: 4,000 at 18 kt
Complement: 219 (26 officers)

Missiles: SSM: 8 McDonnell Douglas Harpoon (2 quad)
launchers ❶; active radar homing to 130 km *(70 n miles)*
at 0.9 Mach; warhead 227 kg.
SAM: 16 Raytheon NATO Sea Sparrow RIM-7M; Mk 29
octuple launcher ❷; semi-active radar homing to 14.6 km
(8 n miles) at 2.5 Mach; warhead 39 kg.
2 GDC RAM 21 cell ❸; passive IR/anti-radiation homing
to 9.6 km *(5.2 n miles)* at 2 Mach; warhead 9.1 kg.
Guns: 1 OTO Melara 3 in *(76 mm)*/62 Compact ❹;
108 rds/min to 16 km *(8.6 n miles)* anti-surface; 12 km
(6.5 n miles) anti-aircraft; weight of shell 6 kg.
2 Rheinmetall 20 mm Rh 202, to be replaced by Mauser
27 mm.
Torpedoes: 4 — 324 mm Mk 32 (2 twin) tubes ❺. 8 Honeywell
Mk 46 Mod 2; anti-submarine; active/passive homing to
11 km *(5.9 n miles)* at 40 kt; warhead 44 kg. To be replaced
by Eurotorp MU 90.
Countermeasures: Decoys: 4 Loral Hycor SRBOC ❻
6-barrelled fixed Mk 36; chaff and IR flares to 4 km
(2.2 n miles).
SLQ-25 Nixie; towed torpedo decoy. Prairie bubble noise
reduction.
ESM/ECM: TST FL 1800 Stage II ❼; intercept and jammer.
Combat data systems: SATIR action data automation; Link
11; Link 16; Matra Marconi SCOT 1A SATCOM ❽ (3 sets
for the class).
Weapons control: Signaal WM25/STIR. STN Atlas Elektronic
WBA optronic sensor.
Radars: Air/surface search: DASA TRS-3D/32 ❾; C-band.
Navigation: SMA 3 RM 20; I-band.
Fire control: Signaal WM25 ❿; I/J-band.
Signaal STIR ⓫; I/J/K-band; range 140 km *(76 n miles)*
for 1 m² target.
Sonars: Atlas Elektronik DSQS-21BZ (BO); hull-mounted;
active search and attack; medium frequency.

Helicopters: 2 Westland Sea Lynx Mk 88A ⓬.

Programmes: Approval given in early 1976 for first six of
this class, a modification of the Netherlands Kortenaer
class. Replaced the deleted Fletcher and Köln classes.
Equipment ordered February 1986 after order placed
6 December 1985 for last pair. Hulls and some engines
provided in the five building yards. Ships were then
towed to the prime contractor Bremer Vulkan where
weapon systems and electronics were fitted and trials
conducted. The three names for F 210-212 were changed
from the names of Länder to take the well known town
names of the Köln class as they were paid off.
Modernisation: RAM fitted from 1993-1996: Updated EW
fit from 1994. 20 mm guns, taken from Type 520 LCUs,
fitted aft of the bridge on each side. TRS-3D/32 radar
has replaced DA 08 in all ships. STN optronic sensor
fitted from 1998. 27 mm guns to replace 20 mm in due
course. All eight ships are to undergo a modernisation
programme to extend service life to at least 2015.
A contract was signed on 21 September 2005 for the
replacement of the combat data system by the Thales
SABRINA 21 system, which incorporates Tacticos-NC
and Sewaco-DDS technology. The work will include
integration of Link 16 which is currently being fitted
throughout the class. The modernisation is also likely
to include upgrade of the IFF system, replacement of
the decoy launchers with Rheinmetall Defence MASS

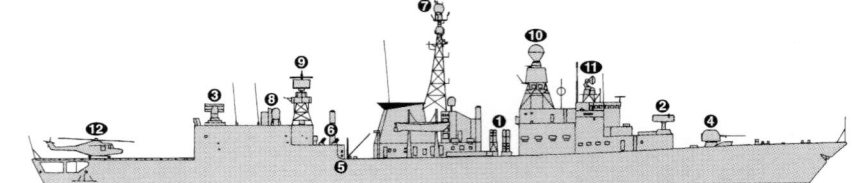

EMDEN *(Scale 1 : 1,200), Ian Sturton* / 0012400

KARLSRUHE *3/2005*, Frank Findler* / 1133485

LÜBECK *11/2004*, B Sullivan* / 1133454

decoy launchers and installation of the Rheinmetall
MSP 500 optronic director. The first ship to be refitted
is to be *Bremen* which will be completed in 2008.
The programme will be completed when *Köln* returns to
the fleet in 2011.

Operational: Form 4th Frigate Squadron based at
Wilhelmshaven. Three containerised SCOT 1A terminals
acquired in 1988 and when fitted are mounted on the
hangar roof.

NIEDERSACHSEN *6/2004*, Marco Ghiglino* / 1133431

Jane's Defence Equipment Intelligence

With a global network of defence experts, Jane's provides unrivalled accurate and authoritative information on commercial and military aerospace systems, ground-based military equipment, naval vessels and weapon systems – a complete resource for market intelligence, threat assessment and recognition.

3 SACHSEN CLASS (TYPE 124) (FFGHM)

Name	No
SACHSEN	F 219
HAMBURG	F 220
HESSEN	F 221

Builders	Laid down	Launched	Commissioned
Blohm + Voss, Hamburg	1 Feb 1999	1 Dec 1999	4 Nov 2004
Howaldtswerke, Kiel	1 Sep 2000	16 Aug 2002	13 Dec 2004
Thyssen Nordseewerke, Emden	14 Sep 2002	27 June 2003	15 Dec 2005

Displacement, tons: 5,600 full load
Dimensions, feet (metres): 469.2 oa; 433.7 wl × 57.1 × 22.7
(143; 132.2 × 17.4 × 6.9)
Main machinery: CODAG; 1 GE LM 2500 gas turbine; 31,514
hp (23.5 MW); 2 MTU 20V 1163 TB 93 diesels; 20,128
hp(m) (14.8 MW); 2 shafts; cp props
Speed, knots: 29
Range, n miles: 4,000 at 18 kt
Complement: 255 (39 officers)

Missiles: SSM: 8 Harpoon ❶ 2 (quad); active radar homing
to 130 km (70 n miles) at 0.9 Mach; warhead 227 kg.
SAM: Mk 41 VLS (32 cells) ❷ 24 GDC Standard SM-2 (Block
IIIA); command/inertial guidance; semi-active radar
homing to 167 km (90 n miles) at 2 Mach. 32 Evolved Sea
Sparrow RIM 162B; semi-active radar homing to 18 km
(9.7 n miles) at 3.6 Mach; warhead 39 kg.
2 RAM launchers ❸. 21 rounds per launcher; passive
IR/anti-radiation homing to 9.6 km (5.2 n miles) at
2 Mach; warhead 9.1 kg.
Guns: 1 Otobreda 76 mm/62 IROF ❹; 85 rds/min to 16 km
(8.6 n miles) anti-surface; 12 km (6.5 n miles) anti-aircraft;
weight of shell 6 kg.
2 Mauser 27 mm ❺.
Torpedoes: 6—324 mm (2 triple) Mk 32 Mod 7 tubes ❻.
Eurotorp Mu 90 Impact.
Countermeasures: Decoys: 6 SRBOC 130 mm chaff
launchers ❼.
ESM/ECM: DASA FI 1800S-II; intercept ❽ and jammer.
Combat data systems: SEWACO FD; Link 11/16.
Weapons control: MSP optronic director ❾.
Radars: Air search: SMART L ❿ 3D; D-band.
Air/surface search: Signaal APAR phased array ⓫;
I/J-band.
Surface search: Thales Triton-G ⓬; G-band.
Navigation: 2 STN Atlas 9600M ARPA ⓭; E/I-band.
IFF: Mk XII.
Sonars: Atlas DSQS-21B (Mod); bow-mounted; active
search; medium frequency.

Helicopters: 2 NH90 NFH ⓮ or 2 Lynx 88A.

Programmes: Type 124 air defence ships built to replace
the Lütjens class. A collaborative design with the

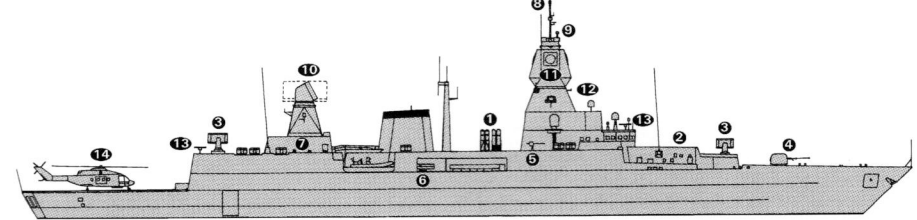

SACHSEN *(Scale 1 : 1, 200), Ian Sturton* / 1153489

HESSEN *2/2005*, Frank Findler* / 1133484

Netherlands. A Memorandum of Understanding (MoU)
was signed in October 1993 between Blohm + Voss,
Royal Schelde and Bazán shipyards. A contract to build
three ships was authorised on 12 June 1996 with an
option on a fourth. *Hessen* started sea trials on
21 January 2005.

Structure: Based on the Type 123 hull with improved stealth
features. MBB-FHS helo handling system.
Operational: Successful sea-firings of Standard SM-2 and
ESSM conducted at USN range off southern California in
July/August 2004. Part of 2nd Frigate Squadron based at
Wilhelmshaven.

SACHSEN *6/2005*, Maritime Photographic* / 1133433

HAMBURG *5/2005*, Michael Nitz* / 1133434

CORVETTES

0 + 5 BRAUNSCHWEIG (K130) CLASS (FSGHM)

Name	No	Builders	Laid down	Launched	Commissioned
BRAUNSCHWEIG	F 260	Blohm + Voss, Hamburg	2005	19 Apr 2006	May 2007
MAGDEBURG	F 261	Lürssen, Vegesack	2005	2006	Nov 2007
ERFURT	F 262	Thyssen Nordseewerke, Emden	2006	2007	Apr 2008
OLDENBURG	F 263	Blohm + Voss, Hamburg	2006	2007	Aug 2008
LUDWIGSHAFEN	F 264	Lürssen, Vegesack	2006	2007	Nov 2008

Displacement, tons: 1,662 full load
Dimensions, feet (metres): 289.8 × 43.4 × 15.7 *(88.3 × 13.2 × 4.8)*
Main machinery: 2 diesels; total of 19,850 hp(m) *(14.8 MW)*; 2 shafts
Speed, knots: 26
Range, n miles: 2,500 at 15 kt
Complement: 50 + 15 spare
Missiles: SSM: 4 Saab RBS-15 Mk 3 ❶; active radar homing to 200 km *(108 n miles)* at 0.9 Mach; warhead 200 kg.
SAM: 2 RAM 21 cell Mk 49 launchers ❷.
Guns: 1 Otobreda 76 mm/62 ❸; 2 Mauser 27 mm ❹.
Countermeasures: Decoys: 2 MASS ❺; softkill launchers.
ESM: EADS SPS-N-5000; intercept.
ECM: DASA SPN/KJS 5000; jammer.
Combat data systems: SEWACO; Link 11/16.
Weapons control: 2 Thales Mirador Trainable Electro-Optical Observation System (TEOOS) ❻.
Radars: Air/surface search: DASA TRS-3D ❼; C-band.
Surface search: E/F-band.
Fire control: I/J-band.

Programmes: Invitations to tender accepted at the end of 1998. Blohm + Voss selected as consortium leader 18 July 2000. Consortium includes Thyssen Nordseewerke and Lürssen. Batch of five ships ordered on 14 December 2001 and first steel cut for the first of class on 19 July 2004. The bow section of the first ship was launched on 6 September 2005. All bow sections are being constructed at Lürssen, the aft sections at Lürssen and the superstructure at Blohm + Voss. There will be no further ships of this class.
Structure: Measures to reduce radar, IR (underwater exhaust system) and noise signatures have been included in the design.

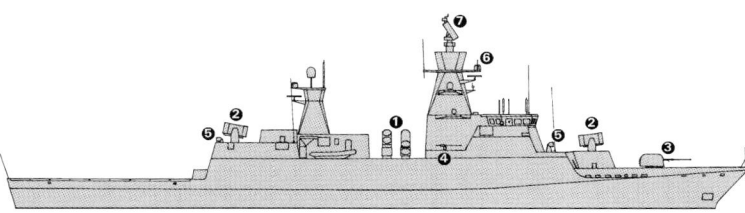

K130 *(Scale 1 : 900), Ian Sturton* / 0529158

BRAUNSCHWEIG *12/2005*, Michael Nitz* / 1153496

BRAUNSCHWEIG *12/2005*, Michael Nitz* / 1154642

SHIPBORNE AIRCRAFT

Notes: (1) NH 90s are required in due course to replace Sea Kings.
(2) Plans to procure a vertical take-off and landing UAV for the K 130 corvette have been abandoned.

Numbers/Type: 21 Westland Sea King Mk 41 KWS.
Operational speed: 140 kt *(260 km/h)*.
Service ceiling: 10,500 ft *(3,200 m)*.
Range: 630 n miles *(1,165 km)*.
Role/Weapon systems: Used in shipborne role for Berlin class AFSH. Land-based roles include SAR, area surveillance and transport. Sensors: Ferranti Sea Spray Mk 3 radar, FLIR, RWR, chaff and flare dispenser. Weapons: 1 – 12.7 mm MG.

SEA KING *6/2005*, Michael Winter* / 1133483

Numbers/Type: 22 Westland Super Lynx Mk 88A.
Operational speed: 125 kt *(232 km/h)*.
Service ceiling: 12,500 ft *(3,010 m)*.
Range: 320 n miles *(593 km)*.
Role/Weapon systems: Shipborne ASW/ASV role. Sensors: GEC Marine Sea Spray 3000 FLIR and Bendix AQS-18 dipping sonar. Weapons: ASW; up to two Mk 46 Mod 2 (or Eurotorp MU 90 Impact in due course) torpedoes. ASV; BAe Sea Skua, 1 – 12.7 mm MG.

LYNX Mk 88A *6/2004, B Prézelin* / 0587747

LAND-BASED MARITIME AIRCRAFT (FRONT LINE)

Notes: The capabilities of former Naval Air Wing 2 (NAW 2) were transferred to the Air Force in 2005. This included 50 Tornado aircraft, weapons and some aircrew and ground staff. The Naval Air Station at Eggebek has been closed.

Numbers/Type: 8 Lockheed P-3C Orion CUP.
Operational speed: 405 kt *(750 km/h)*.
Service ceiling: 30,000 ft *(9,145 m)*.
Range: 4,875 n miles *(9,030 km)*.
Role/Weapon systems: Long-range maritime reconnaissance aircraft procured from the Netherlands 2005-06 and to become fully operational by 2008. Aircraft updated under CUP programme. Sensors: AN/APS-137B(V)5 radar, AAQ 22 Safire FLIR, AN/ALR 95 ESM, AN/ALE 47 chaff dispenser, AN/AAR 47 missile warning system, AN/SSQ 227 central processor, AN/ASQ-78B acoustic processor, AQS 81 MAD. Weapons: 8 Mk 46 torpedoes (or Eurotorp MU 90 Impact in due course).

P-3C *3/2005*, Michael Nitz* / 1133437

Numbers/Type: 4 Dornier DO 228-212.
Operational speed: 156 kt *(290 km/h)*.
Service ceiling: 20,700 ft *(6,300 m)*.
Range: 667 n miles *(1,235 km)*.
Role/Weapon systems: Pollution control. Sensors: Weather radar; SLAR, IR/UR scanner, microwave radiometer, LLL TV camera and data downlink. Weapons: Unarmed.

DORNIER 228 *6/2005*, Paul Jackson* / 1133438

Numbers/Type: 2 Breguet Atlantic 1.
Operational speed: 355 kt *(658 km/h)*.
Service ceiling: 32,800 ft *(10,000 m)*.
Range: 4,850 n miles *(8,990 km)*.
Role/Weapon systems: Long-range Sigint aircraft.

ATLANTIC *8/2003, Frank Findler* / 0570632

Numbers/Type: 50 Panavia Tornado IDS.
Operational speed: Mach 2.2.
Service ceiling: 80,000 ft *(24,385 m)*.
Range: 1,500 n miles *(2,780 km)*.
Role/Weapon systems: Swing-wing strike and recce; shore-based for fleet tactical support (recce, ASUW, limited air defence). Operated by German Air Force. Sensors: Texas Instruments nav/attack system, MBB/Alenia multisensor recce pod. Weapons: ASV; four Kormoran 2 missiles. Fleet AD; two 27 mm cannon, four AIM-9L Sidewinder.

TORNADO
9/2004, Frank Findler / 1044258

PATROL FORCES

Notes: Vessels in this section have an 'S' number as part of their name as well as a 'P' pennant number. The 'S' number is shown in the Pennant List at the front of this country.

10 GEPARD CLASS (TYPE 143 A)
(FAST ATTACK CRAFT—MISSILE) (PGGFM)

Name	No	Builders	Launched	Commissioned
GEPARD	P 6121	AEG/Lürssen	25 Sep 1981	13 Dec 1982
PUMA	P 6122	AEG/Lürssen	8 Feb 1982	24 Feb 1983
HERMELIN	P 6123	AEG/Kröger	8 Dec 1981	5 May 1983
NERZ	P 6124	AEG/Lürssen	18 Aug 1982	14 July 1983
ZOBEL	P 6125	AEG/Kröger	30 June 1982	25 Sep 1983
FRETTCHEN	P 6126	AEG/Lürssen	26 Jan 1983	15 Dec 1983
DACHS	P 6127	AEG/Kröger	14 Dec 1982	22 Mar 1984
OZELOT	P 6128	AEG/Lürssen	7 June 1983	3 May 1984
WIESEL	P 6129	AEG/Lürssen	8 Aug 1983	12 July 1984
HYÄNE	P 6130	AEG/Lürssen	5 Oct 1983	13 Nov 1984

Displacement, tons: 391 full load
Dimensions, feet (metres): 190 × 25.6 × 8.5 *(57.6 × 7.8 × 2.6)*
Main machinery: 4 MTU MA 16V 956 SB80 diesels; 13,200 hp(m) *(9.7 MW)* sustained; 4 shafts
Speed, knots: 40
Range, n miles: 2,600 at 16 kt; 600 at 33 kt
Complement: 34 (4 officers)

Missiles: SSM: 4 Aerospatiale MM 38 Exocet; inertial cruise; active radar homing to 42 km *(23 n miles)* at 0.9 Mach; warhead 165 kg; sea-skimmer.
SAM: GDC RAM 21 cell point defence system; passive IR/anti-radiation homing to 9.6 km *(5.2 n miles)* at 2 Mach; warhead 9.1 kg.
Guns: 1 OTO Melara 3 in *(76 mm)*/62 compact; 85 rds/min to 16 km *(8.6 n miles)* anti-surface; 12 km *(6.5 n miles)* anti-aircraft; weight of shell 6 kg.
Mines: Can lay mines.
Countermeasures: Decoys: Buck-Wegmann Hot Dog/Silver Dog; IR/chaff dispenser.
ESM/ECM: Dasa FL 1800 Mk 2; radar intercept and jammer.
Combat data systems: AEG AGIS with Signaal update; Link 11.
Weapons control: STN Atlas WBA optronic sensor being fitted.
Radars: Surface search/fire control: Signaal WM27; I/J-band; range 46 km *(25 n miles)*.
Navigation: SMA 3 RM 20; I-band.

Programmes: Ordered mid-1978 from AEG-Telefunken with subcontracting to Lürssen (P 6121, 6122, 6124-6128) and Kröger (P 6123, 6129, 6130).
Modernisation: Updated EW fit in 1994-95. RAM fitted in *Puma* in 1992, and to the rest from 1993-98. Combat data system update completed in 1999. Improved EW aerials being fitted from 1999.
Structure: Wooden hulls on aluminium frames.
Operational: Form 7th Squadron based on the tender *Elbe* at Warnemünde. To remain in commission until 2010-12.

DACHS
3/2005, Per Körnefeldt* / 1133482

HYÄNE
5/2005, Michael Nitz* / 1133439

NERZ
7/2005, H M Steele* / 1133455

AMPHIBIOUS FORCES

Notes: Procurement of multirole amphibious shipping is unlikely due to budget restrictions.

4 TYPE 521 (LCM)

SARDELLE LCM 14   **KRABBE** LCM 23   **MUSCHEL** LCM 25   **KORALLE** LCM 26

Displacement, tons: 168 full load
Dimensions, feet (metres): 77.4 × 20.9 × 4.9 *(23.6 × 6.4 × 1.5)*
Main machinery: 2 MWM 8-cyl diesels; 685 hp(m) *(503 kW)*; 2 shafts
Speed, knots: 10.5
Complement: 7
Military lift: 60 tons or 50 troops
Radars: Navigation: Atlas Elektronik; I-band.

Comment: Built by Rheinwerft, Walsam. Completed in 1964-67 and later placed in reserve. All are rated as 'floating equipment' without permanent crews. The design is similar to US LCM 8. LCM 1-11 sold to Greece in April 1991. All but three of the class paid off in 1993-94 but six were brought back into service in 1995 and one paid off again in 1996. Four paid off in 2000. In addition LCM 17 is used by the Bremerhaven Fire Brigade. A new class of LCM is being designed but is not yet funded.

SARDELLE
7/2004, Frank Findler* / 1044265

2 TYPE 520 (LCU)

LACHS L 762   **SCHLEI** L 765

Displacement, tons: 430 full load
Dimensions, feet (metres): 131.2 × 28.9 × 7.2 *(40 × 8.8 × 2.2)*
Main machinery: 2 MWM 12-cyl diesels; 1,020 hp(m) *(750 kW)*; 2 shafts
Speed, knots: 11
Complement: 17
Military lift: 150 tons

Comment: Similar to the US LCU (Landing Craft Utility) type. Provided with bow and stern ramp. Built by Howaldtswerke, Hamburg, 1965-66. Two sold to Greece in November 1989 and six more in 1992. Based at Kiel with Minesweeper Squadron 3. Guns have been removed.

SCHLEI
6/2005, Frank Findler* / 1133481

German Quality at Sea

LÜRSSEN

MINE WARFARE FORCES

Notes: The prototype minesweeping drone *Explorer* was returned to the shipbuilder Abeking and Rasmussen on completion of sea trials in September 2005. Project Minehunting 2000 has been cancelled due to budgetary contraints. *Explorer* is to be sold.

10 FRANKENTHAL CLASS (TYPE 332)
(MINEHUNTERS—COASTAL) (MHC)

Name	No	Builders	Launched	Commissioned
ROTTWEIL	M 1061	Krögerwerft	12 Mar 1992	7 July 1993
BAD BEVENSEN	M 1063	Lürssenwerft	21 Jan 1993	9 Dec 1993
BAD RAPPENAU	M 1067	Abeking & Rasmussen	3 June 1993	19 Apr 1994
GRÖMITZ	M 1064	Krögerwerft	29 Apr 1993	23 Aug 1994
DATTELN	M 1068	Lürssenwerft	27 Jan 1994	8 Dec 1994
DILLINGEN	M 1065	Abeking & Rasmussen	26 May 1994	25 Apr 1995
HOMBURG	M 1069	Krögerwerft	21 Apr 1994	26 Sep 1995
SULZBACH-ROSENBERG	M 1062	Lürssenwerft	27 Apr 1995	23 Jan 1996
FULDA	M 1058	Abeking & Rasmussen	29 Sep 1997	16 June 1998
WEILHEIM	M 1059	Lürssenwerft	26 Feb 1998	3 Dec 1998

Displacement, tons: 650 full load
Dimensions, feet (metres): 178.8 × 30.2 × 8.5 *(54.5 × 9.2 × 2.6)*
Main machinery: 2 MTU 16V 396 TB84 diesels; 5,550 hp(m) *(4.08 MW)* sustained; 2 shafts; cp props; 1 motor (minehunting)
Speed, knots: 18
Complement: 37 (5 officers)

Missiles: SAM: 2 Stinger quad launchers.
Guns: 1 Bofors 40 mm/70; being replaced by Mauser 27 mm.
Combat data systems: STN MWS 80-4.
Radars: Navigation: Raytheon SPS-64; I-band.
Sonars: Atlas Elektronik DSQS-11M; hull-mounted; high frequency.

Programmes: First 10 ordered in September 1988 with STN Systemtechnik Nord as main contractor. M 1066 laid down at Lürssen 6 December 1989. Two ordered 16 October 1995.
Structure: Same hull, similar superstructure and high standardisation as Type 332 and 352. Built of amagnetic steel. Two STN Systemtechnik Nord Pinguin-B3 drones with sonar, TV cameras and two countermining charges, but not Troika control and minelaying capabilities.
Sales: Six of the class being built for Turkey from late 1999. M 1060 and M 1066 decommissioned in 2006 and may be sold to the UAE.

DILLINGEN   *6/2005*, Martin Mokrus* / 1133480

5 KULMBACH CLASS (TYPE 333)
(MINEHUNTERS—COASTAL) (MHC)

Name	No	Builders	Launched	Commissioned
ÜBERHERRN	M 1095	Abeking & Rasmussen	30 Aug 1988	19 Sep 1989
LABOE	M 1097	Krögerwerft	13 Sep 1988	7 Dec 1989
KULMBACH	M 1091	Abeking & Rasmussen	15 June 1989	24 Apr 1990
PASSAU	M 1096	Abeking & Rasmussen	1 Mar 1990	18 Dec 1990
HERTEN	M 1099	Krögerwerft	22 Dec 1989	26 Feb 1991

Displacement, tons: 635 full load
Dimensions, feet (metres): 178.5 × 30.2 × 8.2 *(54.4 × 9.2 × 2.5)*
Main machinery: 2 MTU 16V 538 TB91 diesels; 6,140 hp(m) *(4.5 MW)* sustained; 2 shafts; cp props
Speed, knots: 18
Complement: 37 (4 officers)

Missiles: SAM: 2 Stinger quad launchers.
Guns: 2 Mauser 27 mm.
Mines: 60.
Countermeasures: Decoys: 2 Silver Dog chaff rocket launchers.
ESM: Thomson-CSF DR 2000; radar warning.
Combat data systems: PALIS with Link 11.
Radars: Surface Search/fire control: Signaal WM20/2; I/J-band.
Navigation: Raytheon SPS-64; I-band.
Sonars: Atlas Elektronik DSQS-11M; hull-mounted; high frequency.

Programmes: On 3 January 1985 an STN Systemtechnik Nord-headed consortium was awarded the order. The German designation of 'Schnelles Minenkampfboot' was changed in 1989 to 'Schnelles Minensuchboot'. After modernisation redesignated 'Minenjagdboote'.
Modernisation: Five ships of Hameln class converted to minehunters 1999-2001 and redesignated Kulmbach class (Type 333). Eight to ten disposable ROV Sea Fox I are carried for inspection and up to 30 Sea Fox C for mine disposal. It has a range of 500 m at 6 kt and uses a shaped charge.
Structure: Ships built of amagnetic steel adapted from submarine construction. Signaal M 20 System removed from the deleted Zobel class fast attack craft. PALIS active link.

HERTEN   *5/2005*, Michael Nitz* / 1133443

5 ENSDORF CLASS (TYPE 352)
(MINESWEEPERS—COASTAL) (MHCD)

Name	No	Builders	Launched	Commissioned
HAMELN	M 1092	Lürssenwerft	15 Mar 1988	29 June 1989
PEGNITZ	M 1090	Lürssenwerft	13 Mar 1989	9 Mar 1990
SIEGBURG	M 1098	Krögerwerft	14 Apr 1989	17 July 1990
ENSDORF	M 1094	Lürssenwerft	8 Dec 1989	25 Sep 1990
AUERBACH	M 1093	Lürssenwerft	18 June 1990	7 May 1991

Displacement, tons: 635 full load
Dimensions, feet (metres): 178.5 × 30.2 × 8.2 *(54.4 × 9.2 × 2.5)*
Main machinery: 2 MTU 16V 538 TB91 diesels; 6,140 hp(m) *(4.5 MW)* sustained; 2 shafts; cp props
Speed, knots: 18
Complement: 37 (4 officers)

Missiles: SAM: 2 Stinger quad launchers.
Guns: 2 Mauser 27 mm.
Mines: 60.
Countermeasures: Decoys: 2 Silver Dog chaff rocket launchers.
ESM: Thomson-CSF DR 2000; radar warning.
Combat data systems: PALIS with Link 11. STN C2 remote-control system for minesweeping drone Seehund.
Radars: Surface Search/fire control: Signaal WM20/2; I/J-band.
Navigation: Raytheon SPS-64; I-band.
Sonars: STN ADS DSQS 15A mine-avoidance; active high frequency.

Programmes: On 3 January 1985 an STN Systemtechnik Nord-headed consortium was awarded the order. The German designation of 'Schnelles Minenkampfboot' was changed in 1989 to 'Schnelles Minensuchboot'. After modernisation redesignated 'Hohlstablenkboote'.
Modernisation: Five ships of Hameln class converted to minesweepers 2000-2001 with capability to control up to four remotely controlled minesweeping drones (Seehund). RoV Sea Fox C for mine disposal. Double oropesa system for mechanical sweeping.
Structure: Ships built of amagnetic steel adapted from submarine construction. Signaal M 20 System removed from the deleted Zobel class fast attack craft. PALIS active link.

SIEGBURG   *4/2004, Harald Carstens* / 0587741

18 SEEHUND (MINESWEEPERS—DRONES) (MSD)

SEEHUND 1-18

Displacement, tons: 99 full load
Dimensions, feet (metres): 88.5 × 15 × 4.5 *(26.9 × 4.6 × 1.4)*
Main machinery: 1 Deutz MWM D602 diesel; 446 hp(m) *(328 kW)*; 1 shaft
Speed, knots: 10. **Range, n miles:** 520 at 9 kt
Complement: 3 (passage crew)

Comment: Built by MaK, Kiel and Blohm + Voss, Hamburg between August 1980 and May 1982. Modernised in conjunction with the Type 352 conversion programme 2000-2001.

SEEHUND 18   *6/2005*, Harald Carstens* / 1133479

1 DIVER SUPPORT SHIP (TYPE 742) (MCD)

Name	No	Builders	Commissioned
MÜHLHAUSEN (ex-*Walther von Ledebur*)	M 1052 (ex-A 1410, ex-Y 841)	Burmester, Bremen	21 Dec 1967

Displacement, tons: 775 standard; 825 full load
Dimensions, feet (metres): 206.6 × 34.8 × 8.9 *(63 × 10.6 × 2.7)*
Main machinery: 2 Maybach MTU 16-cyl diesels; 5,200 hp(m) *(3.82 MW)*; 2 shafts
Speed, knots: 19
Complement: 11 plus 10 trials party
Radars: Navigation: I-band.

Comment: Wooden hulled vessel. Launched on 30 June 1966 as a prototype minesweeper but completed as a trials ship. Paid off in April 1994 but reactivated as a diver support ship. Recommissioned in its new role 6 April 1995.

MÜHLHAUSEN   *8/2005*, Martin Mokrus* / 1133478

SURVEY AND RESEARCH SHIPS

Notes: A 12 ton midget submarine *Narwal* was recommissioned in April 1996 for research. Originally built by Krupp Atlas as an SDV.

1 TYPE 751 (AGE)

Name	No	Builders	Commissioned
PLANET	A 1437	Thyssen Nordseewerke, Emden	31 May 2005

Displacement, tons: 3,500 full load
Dimensions, feet (metres): 239.5 × 89.26 × 22.3 *(73 × 27.2 × 6.8)*
Main machinery: Diesel electric; 2 permanent magnet motors; 6,034 hp(m) *(4.5 MW)*; 2 shafts
Speed, knots: 15. **Range, n miles:** 5,000 at 15 kt
Complement: 25 plus 20 trials personnel

Comment: Ex-Type 752 SWATH design which replaced the old *Planet.* The roles of the ship include both research and trials. It is run by Forschungsanstalt für Wasserschall und Geophysik (FWG) in Kiel and Wehrtechmische Dienststelle (WTD 71) in Eckenförde. First authorised in April 1998 and contract placed with TNSW, Emden. After a delay of over two years, firm order finally made in December 2000. Launched on 12 August 2003, the ship has a sonar well, torpedo tubes and can carry five 20 ft containers.

PLANET   *5/2005*, Michael Nitz* / 1127032

3 SCHWEDENECK CLASS (TYPE 748) (MULTIPURPOSE) (AG)

Name	No	Builders	Commissioned
SCHWEDENECK	Y 860	Krögerwerft, Rendsburg	20 Oct 1987
KRONSORT	Y 861	Elsflether Werft	2 Dec 1987
HELMSAND	Y 862	Krögerwerft, Rendsburg	4 Mar 1988

Displacement, tons: 1,018 full load
Dimensions, feet (metres): 185.3 × 35.4 × 17 *(56.5 × 10.8 × 5.2)*
Main machinery: Diesel-electric; 3 MTU 6V 396 TB53 diesel generators; 1,485 kW 60 Hz sustained; 1 motor; 1 shaft
Speed, knots: 13. **Range, n miles:** 2,400 at 13 kt
Complement: 13 plus 10 trials parties
Radars: Navigation: 2 Raytheon; I-band.

Comment: Order for first three placed in mid-1985. One more was planned after 1995 to replace *Mühlhausen* (ex-*Walther von Ledebur*) but was not funded. Based at Eckernförde.

HELMSAND   *8/2005*, Martin Mokrus* / 1133469

3 STOLLERGRUND CLASS (TYPE 745) (MULTIPURPOSE) (AG)

Name	No	Builders	Commissioned
STOLLERGRUND	Y 863	Krögerwerft	31 May 1989
MITTELGRUND	Y 864	Elsflether Werft	23 Aug 1989
BREITGRUND	Y 866	Elsflether Werft	19 Dec 1989

Displacement, tons: 450 full load
Dimensions, feet (metres): 109.9 × 30.2 × 10.5 *(33.5 × 9.2 × 3.2)*
Main machinery: 1 Deutz-MWM BV6M628 diesel; 1,690 hp(m) *(1.24 MW)* sustained; 1 shaft; bow thruster
Speed, knots: 12. **Range, n miles:** 1,000 at 12 kt
Complement: 7 plus 6 trials personnel

Comment: Five ordered from Lürssen in November 1987; two subcontracted to Elsflether. Equipment includes two I-band radars and an intercept sonar. Based at the Armed Forces Technical Centre, Eckernförde. *Bant* decommissioned in 2003 and *Kalkgrund* in 2004. Both ships transferred to Israel.

STOLLERGRUND   *8/2005*, Martin Mokrus* / 1133468

1 TRIALS SHIP (TYPE 741) (YAG)

Name	No	Builders	Commissioned
WILHELM PULLWER	A 1409 (ex-Y 838)	Schürenstadt, Bardenfleth	22 Dec 1967

Displacement, tons: 160 full load
Dimensions, feet (metres): 103.3 × 24.6 × 7.2 *(31.5 × 7.5 × 2.2)*
Main machinery: 2 MTU MB diesels; 700 hp(m) *(514 kW)*; 2 Voith-Schneider props
Speed, knots: 12.5
Complement: 17

Comment: Wooden hulled trials ship for barrage systems.

WILHELM PULLWER   *9/2004, Hartmut Ehlers* / 1044260

1 TRIALS BOAT (TYPE 740) (YAG)

Name	No	Builders	Commissioned
BUMS	Y 1689	Howaldtswerke, Kiel	16 Feb 1970

Dimensions, feet (metres): 86.6 × 22.3 × 4.9 *(26.4 × 6.8 × 1.5)*

Comment: Single diesel engine. Has a 3 ton crane. Based at Eckernförde. To be decommissioned in 2007.

BUMS   *8/1997, N Sifferlinger* / 0012437

For details of the latest updates to ***Jane's Fighting Ships*** online and to discover the additional information available exclusively to online subscribers please visit

jfs.janes.com

INTELLIGENCE VESSELS

3 OSTE CLASS (TYPE 423) (AGI)

Name	No	Builders	Commissioned
ALSTER	A 50	Schiffsbaugesellschaft, Flensburg	5 Oct 1989
OSTE	A 52	Schiffsbaugesellschaft, Flensburg	30 June 1988
OKER	A 53	Schiffsbaugesellschaft, Flensburg	10 Nov 1988

Displacement, tons: 3,200 full load
Dimensions, feet (metres): 273.9 × 47.9 × 13.8 *(83.5 × 14.6 × 4.2)*
Main machinery: 2 Deutz-MWM BV16M728 diesels; 8,980 hp(m) *(6.6 MW)* sustained; 2 shafts; 2 motors (for slow speed)
Speed, knots: 21 (diesels); 8 (motors)
Complement: 36 plus 40 specialists or 51 plus 36 specialists
Missiles: SAM: 2 Stinger launchers.
Guns: 2—12.7 mm Mauser MGs.

Comment: Ordered in March 1985 and December 1986 and replaced the Radar Trials Ships of the same name (old *Oker* and *Alster* transferred to Greece and Turkey respectively). *Oste* launched 15 May 1987, *Oker* 24 September 1987, *Alster* 4 November 1988. Carry Atlas Elektronik passive sonar and optical ELAM and electronic surveillance equipment. Particular attention given to accommodation standards. Reduced to one crew only for each ship in 1994. Fitted for but not with light armaments.

OSTE *6/2005*, Michael Winter* / 1133470

TRAINING SHIPS

Notes: In addition to the two listed below there are 54 other sail training vessels (Types 910-915).

1 SAIL TRAINING SHIP (AXS)

Name	No	Builders	Commissioned
GORCH FOCK	A 60	Blohm + Voss, Hamburg	17 Dec 1958

Displacement, tons: 2,006 full load
Dimensions, feet (metres): 293 × 39.2 × 16.1 *(89.3 × 12 × 4.9)*
Main machinery: Auxiliary 1 Deutz MWM BV6M628 diesel; 1,690 hp(m) *(1.24 MW)* sustained; 1 shaft; Kamewa cp prop
Speed, knots: 11 power; 15 sail
Range, n miles: 1,990 at 10 kt
Complement: 206 (10 officers, 140 cadets)

Comment: Sail training ship of the improved Horst Wessel type. Barque rig. Launched on 23 August 1958. Sail area, 21,141 sq ft. Major modernisation in 1985 at Howaldtswerke. Second major refit in 1991 at Motorenwerke, Bremerhaven included a new propulsion engine and three diesel generators, which increased displacement. Third major refit at Elsfleth-Werft in 2000-2001 included modernisation of electrical distribution system.

GORCH FOCK *8/2005*, Michael Nitz* / 1133448

1 SAIL TRAINING CRAFT (AXSL)

Name	No	Builders	Commissioned
NORDWIND	Y 834 (ex-W 43)	–	1944

Displacement, tons: 110
Dimensions, feet (metres): 78.8 × 21.3 × 8.5 *(24 × 6.5 × 2.6)*
Main machinery: 1 Demag diesel; 150 hp(m) *(110 kW)*; 1 shaft
Speed, knots: 8
Range, n miles: 1,200 at 7 kt
Complement: 10

Comment: Ketch rigged. Sail area, 2,037.5 sq ft. Ex-Second World War patrol craft. Taken over from Border Guard in 1956.

NORDWIND *6/2005*, Frank Findler* / 1133467

AUXILIARIES

2 + (1) BERLIN CLASS (TYPE 702) (AFSH)

Name	No	Builders	Launched	Commissioned
BERLIN	A 1411	Flensburger	30 Apr 1999	11 Apr 2001
FRANKFURT AM MAIN	A 1412	Flensburger	5 Jan 2001	27 May 2002

Displacement, tons: 20,240 full load
Dimensions, feet (metres): 569.9 oa; 527.6 wl × 78.7 × 24.3 *(173.7; 160.8 × 24 × 7.4)*
Main machinery: 2 MAN 12V 32/40 diesels; 14,388 hp(m) *(10.58 MW)* sustained; 2 shafts; cp props; bow thruster; 1,000 hp(m) *(735 kW)*
Speed, knots: 20
Complement: 139 (12 officers) plus 94 for embarked staff
Cargo capacity: 9,540 tons fuel; 450 tons water; 280 tons cargo; 160 tons ammunition
Missiles: SAM: 2 RAM launchers fitted for but not with.
Guns: 4 Mauser 27 mm (fitted for).
Radars: Navigation and aircraft control: I-band.
Helicopters: 2 Sea King Mk 41.

Comment: First ship ordered 15 October 1997, and second 3 July 1998. Hulls built by FSG, superstructure by Kröger and electronics by Lürssen. MBB-FHS helo handling system. Two RAS beam stations and stern refuelling. Two portable SAM launchers are carried. EW equipment may be fitted. These ships are designed to support UN type operations abroad. Twenty-six containers can be mounted in two layers on the upper deck. This could include a containerised hospital unit for 50. A 1411 based at Wilhelmshaven and A 1412 at Kiel. A third ship is planned to enter service in 2011.

BERLIN *5/2004, John Brodie* / 0587739

FRANKFURT AM MAIN *10/2005*, B Sullivan* / 1153497

6 ELBE CLASS (TYPE 404) (TENDERS) (ARLHM)

Name	No	Builders	Launched	Commissioned
ELBE	A 511	Bremer Vulkan	24 June 1992	28 Jan 1993
MOSEL	A 512	Bremer Vulkan	22 Apr 1993	22 July 1993
RHEIN	A 513	Flensburger Schiffbau	11 Mar 1993	22 Sep 1993
WERRA	A 514	Flensburger Schiffbau	17 June 1993	9 Dec 1993
MAIN	A 515	Lürssen/Krögerwerft	15 June 1993	23 June 1994
DONAU	A 516	Lürssen/Krögerwerft	24 Mar 1994	22 Nov 1994

Displacement, tons: 3,114 full load
Dimensions, feet (metres): 329.7 oa; 295.3 wl × 50.5 × 13.5 *(100.5; 90.0 × 15.4 × 4.1)*
Main machinery: 1 Deutz MWM 8V 12M 628 diesel; 3,335 hp(m) *(2.45 MW)*; 1 shaft; bow thruster
Speed, knots: 15. **Range, n miles:** 2,000 at 15 kt
Complement: 40 (4 officers) plus 12 squadron staff plus 38 maintainers
Cargo capacity: 450 tons fuel; 150 tons water; 11 tons luboil; 130 tons ammunition
Missiles: SAM: 2 Stinger (Fliegerfaust 2) quad launchers.
Guns: 2 Rheinmetall 20 mm or Mauser 27 mm.
Radars: Navigation: I-band.
Helicopters: Platform for 1 Sea King.

Comment: Funds released in November 1990 for the construction of six ships to replace the Rhein class. Containers for maintenance and repairs, spare parts and supplies for fast attack craft and minesweepers. Waste disposal capacity: 270 m³ liquids, 60 m³ solids. The use of the Darss class (all sold in 1991) was investigated as an alternative but rejected on the grounds of higher long-term costs because of the age of the ships. Allocated as follows: *Elbe* to 7th Squadron FPBs, *Mosel* to 5th Squadron MSC, *Rhein* to 6th Squadron MSC, *Werra* to 1st Squadron MSC, *Donau* to 2nd Squadron FPBs. *Main* is to undergo conversion to submarine depot ship from November 2005 to November 2006. 20 mm guns are fitted at the break of the forecastle. Converted with helicopter refuelling facilities from July 1996 to July 1997.

RHEIN *5/2005*, Michael Nitz* / 1133447

2 REPLENISHMENT TANKERS (TYPE 704) (AOL)

Name	No	Builders	Commissioned
SPESSART (ex-*Okapi*)	A 1442	Kröger, Rendsburg	1974
RHÖN (ex-*Okene*)	A 1443	Kröger, Rendsburg	1974

Displacement, tons: 14,169 full load
Measurement, tons: 6,103 grt; 10,800 dwt
Dimensions, feet (metres): 427.1 × 63.3 × 26.9 *(130.2 × 19.3 × 8.2)*
Main machinery: 1 MaK 12-cyl diesel; 8,000 hp(m) *(5.88 MW)*; 1 shaft; cp prop
Speed, knots: 16. **Range, n miles:** 7,400 at 16 kt
Complement: 42
Cargo capacity: 11,000 m³ fuel; 400 m³ water
Radars: Navigation: I-band.

Comment: Completed for Terkol Group as tankers. Acquired in 1976 for conversion (*Spessart* at Bremerhaven, *Rhön* at Kröger). The former commissioned for naval service on 5 September 1977 and the latter on 23 September 1977. Has two portable SAM positions. Civilian manned.

RHÖN *10/2005*, Derek Fox* / 1133477

2 WALCHENSEE CLASS (TYPE 703)
(REPLENISHMENT TANKERS) (AOL)

Name	No	Builders	Commissioned
AMMERSEE	A 1425	Lindenau, Kiel	2 Mar 1967
TEGERNSEE	A 1426	Lindenau, Kiel	23 Mar 1967

Displacement, tons: 2,191 full load
Dimensions, feet (metres): 235.9 × 36.7 × 13.8 *(71.9 × 11.2 × 4.2)*
Main machinery: 2 MWM 12-cyl diesels; 1,370 hp(m) *(1 MW)*; 1 Kamewa prop
Speed, knots: 12.6. **Range, n miles:** 3,250 at 12 kt
Complement: 21
Radars: Navigation: Kelvin Hughes; I-band.

Comment: Civilian manned.

TEGERNSEE *9/2005*, B Prézelin* / 1133476

1 KNURRHAHN CLASS (TYPE 730) (APB)

Name	No	Builders	Commissioned
KNURRHAHN	Y 811	Sietas, Hamburg	Nov 1989

Displacement, tons: 1,424 full load
Dimensions, feet (metres): 157.5 × 45.9 × 5.9 *(48 × 14 × 1.8)*

Comment: Accommodation for 200 people.

KNURRHAHN *7/2003, Frank Findler* / 0570616

1 WESTERWALD CLASS (TYPE 760)
(AMMUNITION TRANSPORT) (AEL)

Name	No	Builders	Commissioned
WESTERWALD	A 1435	Orenstein and Koppel, Lübeck	11 Feb 1967

Displacement, tons: 3,460 standard; 4,042 full load
Dimensions, feet (metres): 344.4 × 46 × 11.8 *(105 × 14 × 3.6)*
Main machinery: 2 MTU MD 16V 538 TB90 diesels; 6,000 hp(m) *(4.1 MW)* sustained; 2 shafts; cp props; bow thruster
Speed, knots: 17
Range, n miles: 3,500 at 17 kt
Complement: 63
Cargo capacity: 1,080 tons ammunition
Guns: 2 Bofors 40 mm (cocooned).
Countermeasures: Decoys: 2 Breda SCLAR 105 mm chaff launchers are carried in A 1436.
Radars: Navigation: Kelvin Hughes; I-band.

Comment: Based at Wilhelmshaven. Civilian manned.

WESTERWALD *8/2003, Martin Mokrus* / 0570617

2 OHRE CLASS (ACCOMMODATION SHIPS) (APB)

ALTMARK Y 891 (ex-H 11) **WISCHE** (ex-*Harz*) Y 895 (ex-H 31)

Displacement, tons: 1,320 full load
Dimensions, feet (metres): 231 × 39.4 × 5 *(70.4 × 12 × 1.6)*

Comment: Ex-GDR Type 162 built by Peenewerft, Wolgast. One hydraulic 8 ton crane fitted. First commissioned 1985. Classified as 'Schwimmende Stuetzpunkte'. Propulsion and armament has been removed and they are used as non-self-propelled accommodation ships for crews of vessels in refit. Civilian manned. Both modernised at Wilhelmshaven and to remain in service until further notice. Two others paid off in 2000 later than expected.

ALTMARK *9/2003, Frank Findler* / 0570618

1 BATTERY CHARGING CRAFT (TYPE 718) (YAG)

LP 3

Displacement, tons: 234 full load
Dimensions, feet (metres): 90.6 × 23 × 5.2 *(27.6 × 7.0 × 1.6)*
Main machinery: 1 MTU MB diesel; 250 hp(m) *(184 kW)*; 1 shaft
Speed, knots: 9
Complement: 6

Comment: Built in 1964. Has diesel charging generators for submarine batteries.

LP 3   *6/2001, van Ginderen Collection* / 0130313

6 LAUNCHES (TYPE 946/945) (YFL)

AK 1 Y 1671	**MA 3** Y 1677	**ASCHAU** Y 1685
MA 2 Y 1676	**MA 1** Y 1678	**BORBY** Y 1687

Dimensions, feet (metres): 39.4 × 12.8 × 6.2 *(12.0 × 3.9 × 1.9)*
Main machinery: 1 MAN D2540MTE diesel; 366 hp(m) *(269 kW)*; 1 shaft

Comment: Built by Hans Boost, Trier. All completed in 1985 except *MA 1* and *Aschau* which are larger at 16.2 m and completed in 1992. AK prefix indicates Kiel, and MA Wilhelmshaven.

MA 3   *4/2005*, Frank Findler* / 1133475

5 LAUNCHES (TYPES 743, 744, 744A, 1344) (YFL)

AM 7 Y 1679	**AK 2** Y 1686	**A 41**
AM 8 Y 1675	**AK 6** Y 1683	

Dimensions, feet (metres): 62.3 × 13.1 × 3.9 *(19 × 4 × 1.2)* approx
Main machinery: 1 or 2 diesels

Comment: For personnel transport and trials work. Types 744 *(AK 6)* and 744A *(AK 2)* are radio calibration craft. AM prefix indicates Eckernförde, and AK Kiel. *A 41* is a former GDR tug (Type 1344) used as a diving boat at Warnemünde.

AK 2   *10/2005*, Martin Mokrus* / 1133474

23 PERSONNEL TENDERS (TYPES 934 AND GDR 407) (YFL)

V 3-21	**B 11**	**B 33**	**B 34**	**B 83**

Comment: *V 3-21* built in 1987-88 by Hatecke. The B series are ex-GDR craft built by Yachtwerft, Berlin.

V 13   *6/2005*, Frank Findler* / 1133473

5 RANGE SAFETY CRAFT (TYPE 905) (YFRT)

Name	No	Builders	Commissioned
TODENDORF	Y 835	Lürssen, Vegesack	25 Nov 1993
PUTLOS	Y 836	Lürssen, Vegesack	24 Feb 1994
BAUMHOLDER	Y 837	Lürssen, Vegesack	30 Mar 1994
BERGEN	Y 838	Lürssen, Vegesack	19 May 1994
MUNSTER	Y 839	Lürssen, Vegesack	14 July 1994

Displacement, tons: 126 full load
Dimensions, feet (metres): 91.2 × 19.7 × 4.6 *(27.8 × 6 × 1.4)*
Main machinery: 2 KHD TBD 234 diesels; 2,054 hp(m) *(1.51 MW)*; 2 shafts
Speed, knots: 16
Complement: 15

Comment: Replaced previous Types 369 and 909 craft. Funded by the Army and manned by the Navy.

BAUMHOLDER   *6/2005*, A A de Kruijf* / 1133472

2 OIL RECOVERY SHIPS (TYPE 738) (YPC)

Name	No	Builders	Commissioned
BOTTSAND	Y 1643	Lühring, Brake	24 Jan 1985
EVERSAND	Y 1644	Lühring, Brake	11 June 1988

Measurement, tons: 500 gross; 650 dwt
Dimensions, feet (metres): 151.9 × 39.4 (137.8, bow opened) × 10.2 *(46.3 × 12; 42 × 3.1)*
Main machinery: 1 Deutz BA12M816 diesel; 1,000 hp(m) *(759 kW)* sustained; 2 shafts
Speed, knots: 10
Complement: 6

Comment: Built with two hulls which are connected with a hinge in the stern. During pollution clearance the bow is opened. Ordered by Ministry of Transport but taken over by West German Navy. Normally used as tank cleaning vessels and harbour oilers. Civilian manned. *Bottsand* based at Warnemünde, *Eversand* at Wilhelmshaven. A third of class *Thor* belongs to the Ministry of Transport.

BOTTSAND   *6/2004, Frank Findler* / 0587731

3 FLOATING DOCKS (TYPES 712-715) and
2 CRANES (TYPE 711)

SCHWIMMDOCK 3 Y 842	**HIEV** Y 875
DRUCKDOCK (DOCK C)	**GRIEP** Y 876
DOCK A	

Comment: Schwimmdock 3 is 8,000 tons while Dock C is used for submarine pressure tests. Dock A is 1,000 tons. Y 875 and Y 876 are self-propelled floating cranes with a 100 ton crane.

DOCK C   *4/2003, Frank Findler* / 0570624

1 TORPEDO RECOVERY VESSEL (TYPE 430A) (YPT)

TF 5 Y 855

Comment: Built in 1966 of approximately 56 tons. Provided with stern ramp for torpedo recovery. Two to Greece in 1989 and two more in 1991.

TF 5   *6/2005*, Frank Findler* / 1133471

TUGS

8 HARBOUR TUGS (TYPES 725, 724, 660) (YTM)

Name	No	Builders	Commissioned
VOGELSAND	Y 816	Orenstein und Koppel, Lübeck	14 Apr 1987
NORDSTRAND	Y 817	Orenstein und Koppel, Lübeck	20 Jan 1987
LANGENESS	Y 819	Orenstein und Koppel, Lübeck	5 Mar 1987
LÜTJE HÖRN	Y 812	Husumer Schiffswerft	31 May 1990
KNECHTSAND	Y 814	Husumer Schiffswerft	16 Nov 1990
SCHARHÖRN	Y 815	Husumer Schiffswerft	1 Oct 1990
WUSTROW (ex-*Zander*)	Y 1656	VEB Yachtwerft, Berlin	25 May 1989
DRANSKE (ex-*Kormoran*)	Y 1658	VEB Yachtwerft, Berlin	12 Dec 1989

Displacement, tons: 445 full load
Dimensions, feet (metres): 99.3 × 29.8 × 8.5 *(30.3 × 9.1 × 2.6)*
Main machinery: 2 Deutz MWM BV6M628 diesels; 3,360 hp(m) *(2.47 MW)* sustained; 2 Voith-Schneider props
Speed, knots: 12
Complement: 10

Comment: Details given are for the Type 725 (Y 812—819) which have a bollard pull of 23 tons. Y 1656 and Y 1658 are Type 660 former GDR vessels of 320 tons. Y 823 to Greece in 1998.

SCHARHÖRN   *2/2005*, Frank Findler* / 1133466

DRANSKE   *4/2004, Martin Mokrus* / 0587728

1 HELGOLAND CLASS (TYPE 720B) (ATR)

Name	No	Builders	Commissioned
FEHMARN	A 1458	Unterweser, Bremerhaven	1 Feb 1967

Displacement, tons: 1,310 standard; 1,643 full load
Dimensions, feet (metres): 223.1 × 41.7 × 14.4 *(68 × 12.7 × 4.4)*
Main machinery: Diesel-electric; 4 MWM 12-cyl diesel generators; 2 motors; 3,300 hp(m) *(2.43 MW)*; 2 shafts
Speed, knots: 17
Range, n miles: 6,400 at 16 kt
Complement: 34
Mines: Laying capacity.
Radars: Navigation: Raytheon; I-band.
Sonars: High definition, hull-mounted for wreck search.

Comment: Launched on 9 April 1965. Carry firefighting equipment and has an ice-strengthened hull. Employed as safety ship for the submarine training group. Twin 40 mm guns removed. One of the class to Uruguay in 1998.

FEHMARN   *1/2003, Diego Quevedo* / 0570604

5 WANGEROOGE CLASS (3 TYPE 722 AND 3 TYPE 754)
(ATS/YDT)

Name	No	Builders	Commissioned
WANGEROOGE	A 1451	Schichau, Bremerhaven	9 Apr 1968
SPIEKEROOG	A 1452	Schichau, Bremerhaven	14 Aug 1968
BALTRUM	A 1439	Schichau, Bremerhaven	8 Oct 1968
JUIST	A 1440	Schichau, Bremerhaven	1 Oct 1971
LANGEOOG	A 1441	Schichau, Bremerhaven	14 Aug 1968

Displacement, tons: 854 standard; 1,024 full load
Dimensions, feet (metres): 170.6 × 39.4 × 12.8 *(52 × 12.1 × 3.9)*
Main machinery: Diesel-electric; 4 MWM 16-cyl diesel generators; 2 motors; 2,400 hp(m) *(1.76 MW)*; 2 shafts
Speed, knots: 14
Range, n miles: 5,000 at 10 kt
Complement: 24 plus 33 trainees (A 1439—1441)
Guns: 1 Bofors 40 mm/70 (cocooned in some, not fitted in all).

Comment: First two are salvage tugs with firefighting equipment and ice-strengthened hulls. *Wangerooge* sometimes used for pilot training and *Spiekeroog* as submarine safety ship. The other three were converted 1974-78 to training ships with *Baltrum* and *Juist* being used as diving training vessels at Neustadt, with recompression chambers and civilian crews. A 1455 sold to Uruguay in 2002.

SPIEKEROOG   *5/2005*, Michael Nitz* / 1133449

ARMY

12 BODAN CLASS (RIVER LANDING CRAFT) (LCM)

Displacement, tons: 148 full load
Dimensions, feet (metres): 98.4 × 19 *(30 × 5.8)* (loading area)
Main machinery: 4 diesels; 596 hp(m) *(438 kW)*; 4 Schottel props
Speed, knots: 6
Guns: 1 Oerlikon 20 mm.

Comment: Built of 12 pontoons, provided with bow and stern ramp. Can carry 90 tons. These are the only Army LCMs still in service and are to be decommissioned in 2008.

BODAN *6/1992, Horst Dehnst* / 0505995

COAST GUARD (KÜSTENWACHE)

Notes: The Coast Guard was formed on 1 July 1974 and is a loose affiliation of the forces of several organisations including: seagoing units of the Border Guard (Bundespolizei); Fishery Protection (Fischereischutz); Maritime Police (Wasserschutzpolizei); Water and Navigation Board (Schiffahrtspolizei); Customs (Zoll). These organisations have responsibility for the operation and maintenance of their own craft but all have the inscription *Küstenwache* on the side.

BORDER GUARD (Bundespolizei)

Notes: (1) The force consists of about 600 men. Headquarters at Neustadt and bases at Warnemunde and Cuxhaven. There are three Flotillas; one each at Neustadt, Cuxhaven and Warnemunde. The name of the force was changed from Bundesgrenzschutz-See to Bundespolizei on 1 July 2005.
(2) The force is augmented by a maritime section of the anti-terrorist force GSG 9.
(3) Craft have dark blue hulls and white superstructures with a black, red and yellow diagonal stripe and the inscription Küstenwache painted on the ship's side and Bundespolizei insignia.
(4) There is a total of some 60 helicopters including 13 Eurocopter EC 155, 9 EC 135, 13 Bell UH-1D, 8 Bell 212, 17 BO-105 and a number of AS 330 Puma.
(5) All 40 mm guns removed in 1997.

3 BAD BRAMSTEDT CLASS (WPSO)

Name	No	Builders	Commissioned
BAD BRAMSTEDT	BP 24 (ex-BG 24)	Abeking and Rasmussen, Lemwerder	8 Nov 2002
BAYREUTH	BP 25 (ex-BG 25)	Abeking and Rasmussen, Lemwerder	2 May 2003
ESCHWEGE	BP 26 (ex-BG 26)	Abeking and Rasmussen, Lemwerder	18 Dec 2003

Displacement, tons: 800 standard
Dimensions, feet (metres): 216.3 × 34.8 × 10.5 *(65.9 × 10.6 × 3.2)*
Main machinery: 1 MTU 16V 1163 diesel; 7,000 hp(m) *(5.2 MW)*; 1 shaft; fixed propeller
Speed, knots: 21.5
Complement: 14 + 10 in temporary accommodation
Radars: Surface search: I-band.
Navigation: I-band.
Helicopters: Platform for 1 light.

Comment: Contract awarded in 2000 to Prime Contractor Abeking and Rasmussen for three craft to replace six ships of Neustadt class. Hulls constructed by Yantar, Kaliningrad and completed at Lemwerder. Steel hull with aluminium superstructure. The Russian Federal Border Guard Sprut class offshore patrol vessels is based on this design.

BAYREUTH *9/2005*, Michael Nitz* / 1133450

1 BREDSTEDT CLASS (TYPE PB 60) (WPSO)

Name	No	Builders	Commissioned
BREDSTEDT	BP 21 (ex-BG 21)	Elsflether Werft	24 May 1989

Displacement, tons: 673 full load
Dimensions, feet (metres): 214.6 × 30.2 × 10.5 *(65.4 × 9.2 × 3.2)*
Main machinery: 1 MTU 20V 1163 TB93 diesel; 8,325 hp(m) *(6.12 MW)* sustained; 1 shaft; bow thruster; 1 auxiliary diesel generator; 1 motor
Speed, knots: 25 (12 on motor). **Range, n miles:** 2,000 at 25 kt; 7,000 at 10 kt
Complement: 17 plus 4 spare
Guns: 1 — 40 mm MGs.
Radars: Surface search: Racal AC 2690 BT; I-band.
Navigation: 2 Racal ARPA; I-band.
Helicopters: Platform for 1 light.

Comment: Ordered 27 November 1987, laid down 3 March 1988 and launched 18 December 1988. An Avon Searider rigid inflatable craft can be lowered by a stern ramp. A second RIB on the port side is launched by crane. Based at Cuxhaven.

BREDSTEDT (old number) *6/2002, Michael Nitz* / 0529097

2 SASSNITZ CLASS (TYPE PB 50 ex-TYPE 153) (WPBO)

Name	No	Builders	Commissioned
NEUSTRELITZ (ex-*Sassnitz*)	BP 22 (ex-BG 22, ex-P 6165, ex-591)	Peenewerft, Wolgast	31 July 1990
BAD DÜBEN (ex-*Binz*)	BP 23 (ex-BG 23, ex-593)	Peenewerft, Wolgast	23 Dec 1990

Displacement, tons: 369 full load
Dimensions, feet (metres): 160.4 oa; 147.6 wl × 28.5 × 7.2 *(48.9; 45 × 8.7 × 2.2)*
Main machinery: 2 MTU 12V 595 TE90 diesels; 8,800 hp(m) *(6.48 MW)* sustained; 2 shafts
Speed, knots: 25. **Range, n miles:** 2,400 at 20 kt
Complement: 33 (7 officers)
Guns: 2 — 7.62 mm MGs.
Radars: Surface search: Racal AC 2690 BT; I-band (BG 22 and 23).
Navigation: Racal ARPA; I-band (BG 22 and 23).

Comment: Ex-GDR designated Balcom 10 and seen for the first time in the Baltic in August 1988. The original intention was to build up to 50 for the USSR, Poland and the GDR. In 1991 the first three were transferred to the Border Guard, based at Neustadt. *Neustrelitz* fitted with German engines and electronics in 1992-93 and accommodation improved. *Bad Düben* similarly modified at Peenewerft in 1995-96. The original design had the SS-N-25 SSM and three engines. The third of class, *Sellin*, had been on loan to WTD 71 (weapons trials) at Eckernförde but was sold in 1999.

BAD DÜBEN (old number) *4/2003, Frank Findler* / 0570608

3 BREMSE CLASS (TYPE GB 23) (WPB)

UCKERMARK BP 63 (ex-BG 62, ex-G 34, ex-GS 23)
ALTMARK BP 63 (ex-BG 63, ex-G 21, ex-GS 21)
BÖRDE BP 64 (ex-BG 64, ex-G 35, ex-GS 50)

Displacement, tons: 42 full load
Dimensions, feet (metres): 74.1 × 15.4 × 3.6 *(22.6 × 4.7 × 1.1)*
Main machinery: 2 DM 6VD 18/5 AL-1 diesels; 1,020 hp(m) *(750 kW)*; 2 shafts
Speed, knots: 14
Complement: 6
Radars: Navigation: TSR 333; I-band.

Comment: Built in 1971-72 for the ex-GDR GBK. Five of the class sold to Tunisia, two to Malta and two to Jordan, all in 1992. BG 62 was based on the Danube for WEU embargo operations in 1994-96. All belong to BGSAMT-Rostock.

BÖRDE (old number) *8/2002, Frank Findler* / 0528897

4 SCHWEDT CLASS (WPBR)

SCHWEDT BP 42 (ex-BG 42)	**FRANKFURT/ODER** BP 43 (ex-BG 43)
KUSTRIN-KIEZ BP 41 (ex-BG 41)	**AURITH** BP 44 (ex-BG 44)

Displacement, tons: 6 full load
Dimensions, feet (metres): 33.5 × 10.5 × 2.6 *(10.2 × 3.2 × 0.8)*
Main machinery: 2 Volvo Penta TAMD 42 WJ; 462 hp(m) *(340 kW)*; 2 Hamilton 211 waterjets
Speed, knots: 32
Range, n miles: 200 at 25 km
Complement: 3
Guns: 1 — 7.62 mm MG.
Radars: Navigation: I-band.

Comment: River patrol craft which belong to the BGSAMT-Frankfurt/Oder since 1994.

FRANKFURT/ODER (old number) *12/1998, BGSAMT* / 0056996

4 TYPE SAB 12 (WPB)

VOGTLAND BP 51 (ex-BG 51, ex-G 56, ex-GS 17)
RHÖN BP 52 (ex-BG 52, ex-G 53, ex-GS 26)
SPREEWALD BP 53 (ex-BG 53, ex-G 51, ex-GS 16)
ODERBRUCH BP 54 (ex-BG 54)

Displacement, tons: 14 full load
Dimensions, feet (metres): 41.3 × 13.1 × 3.6 *(12.6 × 4 × 1.1)*
Main machinery: 2 Volvo Penta diesels; 539 hp(m) *(396 kW)*; 2 shafts
Speed, knots: 16
Complement: 5

Comment: Ex-GDR MAB 12 craft based at Karnin, Stralsund and Frankfurt/Oder. Five sold to Cyprus in 1992. Belong to BGSAMT-Rostock.

RHÖN (old number) *6/1998, Hartmut Ehlers* / 0052272

2 EUROPA CLASS (WPBR)

EUROPA 1	**EUROPA 2**

Displacement, tons: 10
Dimensions, feet (metres): 47.2 × 12.5 × 3.1 *(14.4 × 3.8 × 0.9)*
Main machinery: 2 MAN diesels; 240 hp(m) *(180 kW)*
Speed, knots: 22
Radars: Kelvin Hughes; I-band

Comment: River patrol craft.

FISHERY PROTECTION SHIPS (Fischereischutz)

Notes: Operated by Ministry of Food and Agriculture.

3 PATROL SHIPS

MEERKATZE of 2,250 tons and 15 kt. Completed December 1977
SEEFALKE of 2,400 tons gross and 20 kt. Completed August 1981
SEEADLER of 1,600 tons gross (approximately) and 19 kt. Completed 2000

Comment: Fishery Protection Ships. Black hulls with grey superstructure and black, red and yellow diagonal stripes.

MEERKATZE *5/2005*, Michael Nitz* / 1133451

MARITIME POLICE (Wasserschutzpolizei)

Notes: (1) Under the control of regional governments. Most have Küstenwache markings but colours vary from region to region.
(2) There are 13 seaward patrol craft: *WSP 1, 4, 5* and *7, Bremen 2, 3* and *9, Helgoland, Sylt, Fehmarn, Eider, Kieper, Falshöft, Bürgermeister Brauer* and *Bürgermeister Weichmann.*
(3) Harbour craft include *Stegnitz, Greif, Schwansen, Vossbrook, Brunswick, Trave, Wagrien, Bussard* and *Habicht.*

WASSERSCHUTZPOLIZEI 5 *4/2005*, Frank Findler* / 1133464

FALSHÖFT *6/2005*, Michael Winter* / 1133465

CUSTOMS (Zoll)

Notes: (1) Operated by Ministry of Finance with a total of over 100 craft. Green hulls with grey superstructure and sometimes carry machine guns. Some have Küstenwache markings.
(2) Seaward patrol craft include *Hamburg, Bremerhaven, Schleswig-Holstein, Emden, Kniepsand, Priwall, Glückstadt, Oldenburg, Hohwacht, Hiddensee, Rügen* and *Kalkgrund.*

BREMERHAVEN *6/2005*, Frank Findler* / 1133463

GLÜCKSTADT *5/2005*, Frank Findler* / 1133462

WATER AND NAVIGATION BOARD (Schiffahrtspolizei)

Notes: (1) Comes under the Ministry of Transport. Most ships have black hulls with black/red/yellow stripes. Some have Küstenwache markings.
(2) Two icebreakers: *Max Waldeck* and *Stephan Jantzen* (ex-GDR).
(3) Nine buoy tenders: *Walter Körte, Kurt Burkowitz, Otto Treplin, Gustav Meyer, Bruno Illing, Konrad Meisel, Barsemeister Brehme, J G Repsold, Buk* (ex-GDR).
(4) Six oil recovery ships: *Scharhörn, Oland, Nordsee, Mellum, Kiel, Neuwerk.*
(5) Seven SKB 64 and 601 types (ex-GDR). *Golwitz, Ranzow, Landtief, Grasort, Gellen, Darsser Ort, Arkona, Vogelsand.*
(6) One launch: *Friedrich Voss.*

BRUNO ILLING   3/2005*, Frank Findler / 1133461

ALKOR   9/2004*, Frank Findler / 1133459

NEUWERK   10/2004*, Martin Mokrus / 1133460

KOMET   3/2005*, Michael Nitz / 1133452

CIVILIAN SURVEY AND RESEARCH SHIPS

Notes: The following ships operate for the Bundesamt für Seeschiffahrt und Hydrographie (BSH), either under the Ministry of Transport or the Ministry of Research and Technology (*Polarstern, Meteor, Poseidon, Sonne* and *Alkor*).
KOMET (survey and research) 1,590 tons completed by Krögerwerft in October 1998.
ATAIR (survey), **DENEB** (survey), **WEGA** (survey) 1,050 tons, diesel-electric, 11.5 kt. Complement 16 plus 6 scientists. Built by Krögerwerft and Peenewerft *(Deneb)*, completed 3 August 1987, 24 November 1994 and 26 October 1990 respectively.
METEOR (research) 3,500 tons, diesel-electric, 14 kt, range 10,000 n miles. Complement 33 plus 29 research staff. Completed by Schlichting, Travemünde 15 March 1986
GAUSS (survey and research) 1,813 grt, completed 6 May 1980 by Schlichting, speed 13.5 kt. Complement 19 plus 12 scientists. Modernised 1985
WALTHER HERWIG III 2,400 tons. Completed 1993
CAPELLA 455 tons. Completed by Fassmerwerft in 2003.
POLARSTERN (polar research) 10,878 grt. Completed 1982
SONNE (research) 1,200 grt. Completed by Rickmerswerft 1990.
HEINCKE, ALKOR 1,200 tons. Completed 1990
SENCKENBERG 185 tons. Completed in 1977.

CAPELLA   9/2004*, Frank Findler / 1133458

GAUSS   10/2004*, Martin Mokrus / 1133457

Ghana

Country Overview

Formerly a British colony known as the Gold Coast, Ghana gained independence in 1957. Located in west Africa, the country has an area of 92,100 square miles and a 292 n mile coastline with the Gulf of Guinea. It is bordered to the east by Togo and to the west by Ivory Coast. The capital and largest city is Accra which has links to a deep-water port at Tema. There is a second port at Sekondi-Takoradi. Territorial seas (12 n miles) are claimed. A 200 n mile Exclusive Economic Zone (EEZ) has been claimed but the limits are not defined.

Headquarters Appointments

Commander, Navy:
  Rear Admiral A R S Nunoo
Western Naval Command:
  Commodore F Daley

Personnel

(a) 2006: 1,214 (132 officers)
(b) Voluntary service

Bases

Burma Camp, Accra (Headquarters)
Sekondi (Western Naval Command)
Tema (near Accra) (Eastern Naval Command)

Maritime Aircraft

Four Defender aircraft are available for maritime surveillance but only one is used.

PATROL FORCES

Notes: A 20 m patrol craft *David Hansen* has also been reported.

2 BALSAM CLASS (PBO)

Name	No	Builders	Commissioned
ANZONE (ex-*Woodrush*)	P 30 (ex-WLB 407)	Duluth Shipyard, Minnesota	22 Sep 1944
BONSU (ex-*Sweetbrier*)	P 31 (ex-WLB 405)	Duluth Shipyard, Minnesota	26 July 1944

Displacement, tons: 1,034 full load
Dimensions, feet (metres): 180 × 37 × 12
(*54.9 × 11.3 × 3.8*)
Main machinery: Diesel electric; 2 diesels; 1,402 hp *(1.06 MW)*; 1 motor; 1,200 hp *(895 kW)*; 1 shaft; bow thruster
Speed, knots: 13
Range, n miles: 8,000 at 12 kt
Complement: 53
Guns: 2—12.7 mm MGs.
Radars: Navigation: Raytheon SPS-64(V)1.

Comment: *Anzone* transferred from the US Coast Guard on 4 May 2001 and *Bonsu* on 27 August 2001.

ANZONE *5/2002*
0533317

2 LÜRSSEN PB 57 CLASS (FAST ATTACK CRAFT—GUN) (PG)

Name	No	Builders	Commissioned
ACHIMOTA	P 28	Lürssen, Vegesack	27 Mar 1981
YOGAGA	P 29	Lürssen, Vegesack	27 Mar 1981

Displacement, tons: 389 full load
Dimensions, feet (metres): 190.6 × 25 × 9.2
(*58.1 × 7.6 × 2.8*)
Main machinery: 3 MTU 16V 538 TB91 diesels; 9,210 hp(m) *(6.78 MW)* sustained; 3 shafts
Speed, knots: 30
Complement: 55 (5 officers)
Guns: 1 OTO Melara 3 in *(76 mm)* compact; 85 rds/min to 16 km *(8.6 n miles)* anti-surface; 12 km *(6.5 n miles)* anti-air; weight of shell 6 kg; 250 rounds.
1 Breda 40 mm/70; 300 rds/min to 12.5 km *(6.8 n miles)* anti-surface; weight of shell 0.96 kg.
Weapons control: LIOD optronic director.
Radars: Surface search/fire control: Thomson-CSF Canopus A; I/J-band.
Navigation: Decca TM 1226C; I-band.

Comment: Ordered in 1977. *Yogaga* completed a major overhaul at Swan Hunter's Wallsend, Tyneside

ACHIMOTA *12/2001* / 0137789

yard 8 May 1989. *Achimota* started a similar refit at CMN Cherbourg in May 1991 and was joined by *Yogaga* for repairs in late 1991. Both completed by August 1992. Employed on Fishery Protection duties. Planned refit for *Yogaga* at Sekondi in 2000 did not take place.

2 LÜRSSEN FPB 45 CLASS (FAST ATTACK CRAFT—GUN) (PBO)

Name	No	Builders	Commissioned
DZATA	P 26	Lürssen, Vegesack	25 July 1980
SEBO	P 27	Lürssen, Vegesack	25 July 1980

Displacement, tons: 269 full load
Dimensions, feet (metres): 147.3 × 23 × 8.9 (*44.9 × 7 × 2.7*)
Main machinery: 2 MTU 16V 538 TB91 diesels; 6,140 hp(m) *(4.5 MW)* sustained; 2 shafts
Speed, knots: 27

Range, n miles: 1,800 at 16 kt; 700 at 25 kt
Complement: 45 (5 officers)
Guns: 2 Bofors 40 mm/70; 300 rds/min to 12.5 km *(6.8 n miles)*; weight of shell 0.96 kg.
Radars: Surface search: Decca TM 1226C; I-band.

Comment: Ordered in 1976. *Dzata* completed a major overhaul at Swan Hunter's Wallsend, Tyneside yard on 8 May 1989. *Sebo* started a similar refit at CMN Cherbourg in May 1991 which completed in August 1992. Employed in Fishery Protection role. *Dzata* refitted in 2000 at Sekondi.

DZATA *5/2002* / 0533318

Greece

HELLENIC NAVY

Country Overview

The Hellenic Republic is situated in south-eastern Europe and occupies the southernmost part of the Balkan Peninsula. It includes more than 3,000 islands, most of which are in the Aegean Sea. With an area of 50,949 square miles, it has borders to north-west with Albania, to the north with the Former Yugoslav Republic of Macedonia and with Bulgaria, to the north-east with Turkey. It has a 7,387 n mile coastline with the Aegean, Mediterranean and Ionian Seas. The capital and largest city is Athens whose seaport, Piraeus, is also the largest. Other major ports include Thessaloníki, Patras and Iráklion. Territorial seas (6 n miles) are claimed but an EEZ is not claimed.

Headquarters Appointments

Chief of the Hellenic Navy:
  Vice Admiral D Gousis
Deputy Chief of Staff:
  Rear Admiral N Spilianakis
Commander, Navy Training Command:
  Rear Admiral G Ntounis
Commander, Navy Logistics Command:
  Rear Admiral B Dimitropoulos
Inspector General:
  Rear Admiral I Nanos

Fleet Command

Commander of the Fleet:
  Vice Admiral M Tzavaras
Deputy Commander of the Fleet:
  Rear Admiral X Karadimas
Chief of Staff:
  Commodore D Pappagiannidis

Diplomatic Representation

Naval Attaché in Ankara:
  Commander K Tsovos
Naval Attaché in Berlin:
  Captain E Adrobitsaneas
Naval Attaché in Cairo:
  Captain K Leventis
Naval Attaché in London:
  Captain A Papaioannou
Naval Attaché in Paris:
  Commander V Pappas
Naval Attaché in Washington:
  Captain G Konstantinidis
Naval Attaché in Madrid:
  Captain A Giokas
Naval Attaché in Tel Aviv:
  Commander B Tsoutsias
Naval Attaché in Rome:
  Commander S Petrakis
Naval Attaché in Moscow:
  Commander G Riganakos

Diplomatic Representation—*continued*

Naval Attaché in The Hague:
  Captain G Kasmas
Naval Attaché in Tbilisi:
  Captain D Fanourgiakis

Personnel

(a) 2006: 20,752 (4,640 officers) including 5,005 conscripts
(b) 12 months' national service

Bases

Salamis and Suda Bay

Naval Commands

Commander of the Fleet has under his flag all combatant ships. Navy Logistic Command is responsible for the bases at Salamis and Suda Bay, the Supply Centre and all auxiliary ships. Navy Training Command is in charge of the Petty Officers' School, two training centres and one training ship.

Naval Districts

Aegean, Ionian and Northern Greece

Naval Aviation

Alouette III helicopters (Training). AB 212ASW helicopters (No 1 Squadron).
S-70B-6 Seahawk (No 2 Squadron).
P-3B Orions are operated under naval command by mixed Air Force and Navy crews.

Strength of the Fleet

Type	Active	Building (Planned)
Patrol Submarines	8	4
Frigates	14	—
Corvettes	3	—
Fast Attack Craft-Missile	16	4
Fast Attack Craft-Torpedo	4	—
Offshore Patrol Craft	8	—
Coastal Patrol Craft	4	—
LST/LSD/LSM	5	—
LCU/LCM	15	—
Hovercraft	4	—
Minesweepers-Coastal	13	—
Survey and Research Ships	4	—
Support Ships	2	—
Training Ships	4	—
Tankers	5	—
Auxiliary Transports	2	—
Ammunition Ship	1	—

Prefix to Ships' Names

HS (Hellenic Ship)

DELETIONS

Notes: Some of the deleted ships are in unmaintained reserve in anchorages.

Destroyers

2003 *Nearchos*
2004 *Kimon*

Corvettes

2004 *Carteria, Agon*

Patrol Forces

2003 *Ypoploiarchos Konidis*
2004 *Ypoploiarchos Batsis* (to Georgia), *Hesperos, Kyklon, Lelaps, Tyfon*

Amphibious Forces

2003 *Inouse, Kythera, Milos*
2004 *Sikinos*

Mine Warfare Forces

2004 *Evniki, Dafni, Thaleia*

Survey and Research Ships

2003 *Hermis*

Auxiliaries, Training and Survey Ships

2003 *Ariadne, Strymon*
2004 *Aris, Arethusa, Antaios, Atlas, Cyclops, Danaos, Pelops*
2005 *Acchileus*

PENNANT LIST

Submarines

S 110	Glavkos
S 111	Nereus
S 112	Triton
S 113	Proteus
S 116	Poseidon
S 117	Amphitrite
S 118	Okeanos
S 119	Pontos
S 120	Papanikolis
S 121	Matrozos (bldg)
S 122	Pipinos (bldg)
S 123	Katsonis (bldg)

Frigates

F 450	Elli
F 451	Limnos
F 452	Hydra
F 453	Spetsai
F 454	Psara
F 455	Salamis
F 459	Adrias
F 460	Aegeon
F 461	Navarinon
F 462	Kountouriotis
F 463	Bouboulina
F 464	Kanaris
F 465	Themistocles
F 466	Nikiforos Fokas

Corvettes

P 62	Niki
P 63	Doxa
P 64	Eleftheria

Patrol Forces

P 18	Armatolos
P 19	Navmachos

P 20	Anthyploiarchos Laskos
P 21	Plotarchis Blessas
P 22	Ypoploiarchos Mikonios
P 23	Ypoploiarchos Troupakis
P 24	Simeoforos Kavaloudis
P 26	Ypoploiarchos Degiannis
P 27	Simeoforos Xenos
P 28	Simeoforos Simitzopoulos
P 29	Simeoforos Starakis
P 57	Pyrpolitis
P 61	Polemistis
P 67	Ypoploiarchos Roussen
P 68	Ypoploiarchos Daniolos
P 69	Ypoploiarchos Kristallidis
P 70	Ypoploiarchos Grigoro Poulos (bldg)
P 71	Anthypoploiarchos Ritsos (bldg)
P 72	Ypoploiarchos Votsis
P 73	Anthyploiarchos Pezopoulos
P 74	Plotarchis Vlahavas
P 75	Plotarchis Maridakis
P 76	Ypoploiarchos Tournas
P 77	Plotarchis Sakipis
P 196	Andromeda
P 198	Kyknos
P 199	Pigasos
P 228	Toxotis
P 229	Tolmi
P 230	Ormi
P 266	Machitis
P 267	Nikiforos
P 268	Aittitos
P 269	Krateos (bldg)
P 286	Diopos Antoniou
P 287	Kelefstis Stamou

Amphibious Forces

L 167	Ios
L 169	Irakleia
L 170	Folegandros

L 173	Chios
L 174	Samos
L 175	Ikaria
L 176	Lesbos
L 177	Rodos
L 178	Naxos
L 179	Paros
L 180	Kefallinia
L 181	Ithaki
L 182	Kerkira
L 183	Zakynthos
L 195	Serifos

Minesweepers/Hunters

M 60	Erato
M 62	Evropi
M 63	Kallisto
M 211	Alkyon
M 213	Klio
M 214	Avra
M 240	Aidon
M 241	Kichli
M 242	Kissa
M 248	Pleias

Auxiliaries, Training and Survey Ships

A 233	Maistros
A 234	Sorokos
A 307	Thetis
A 359	Ostria
A 373	Gregos
A 374	Prometheus (bldg)
A 375	Zeus
A 376	Orion
A 410	Atromitos
A 411	Adamastos
A 412	Aias
A 413	Pilefs
A 415	Evros
A 416	Ouranos

A 417	Hyperion
A 419	Pandora
A 420	Pandrosos
A 422	Kadmos
A 423	Heraklis
A 424	Iason
A 425	Odisseus
A 428	Nestor
A 429	Perseus
A 432	Gigas
A 433	Kerkini
A 434	Prespa
A 435	Kekrops
A 436	Minos
A 437	Pelias
A 438	Aegeus
A 439	Atrefs
A 440	Diomidis
A 441	Theseus
A 442	Romaleos
A 460	Evrotas
A 461	Arachthos
A 463	Nestos
A 464	Axios
A 466	Trichonis
A 467	Doirani
A 468	Kalliroe
A 469	Stimfalia
A 470	Aliakmon
A 474	Pytheas
A 476	Strabon
A 478	Naftilos
A 479	I Karavoyiannos Theophilopoulos
A 481	St Lykoudis

SUBMARINES

1 + 3 PAPANIKOLIS (TYPE 214) CLASS (SSK)

Name	No	Builders	Laid down	Launched	Commissioned
PAPANIKOLIS	S 120	Howaldtswerke, Kiel	27 Feb 2001	22 Apr 2004	Mar 2006
MATROZOS	S 121	Hellenic Shipyards, Skaramanga	15 Oct 2002	Dec 2006	July 2008
PIPINOS	S 122	Hellenic Shipyards, Skaramanga	1 Apr 2003	Jan 2008	July 2009
KATSONIS	S 123	Hellenic Shipyards, Skaramanga	1 Apr 2004	Dec 2008	July 2010

Displacement, tons: 1,700 (surfaced); 1,800 (dived)
Dimensions, feet (metres): 213.3 × 20.7 × 21.6
  (65 × 6.3 × 6.6)
Main machinery: 2 MTU 16V 396 diesels; 5,600 hp(m)
  (4.17 MW); 1 Siemens Permasyn motor; 1 shaft; 2 HDW
  PEM fuel cells; 240 kW
Speed, knots: 20 dived; 11 surfaced
Complement: 27 (5 officers)

Missiles: SSM: Sub Harpoon.
Torpedoes: 8—21 in *(533 mm)* bow tubes; four (SUT, SST-4,
  DM2A4 or WASS Black Shark) fitted for Sub Harpoon
  discharge; WASS or STN Atlas torpedoes; total of
  16 weapons.
Countermeasures: Decoys: CIRCE torpedo countermeasures.
  ESM. Elbit TIMNEX II.
Weapons control: STN Atlas. ISUS – 90.
Radars: Surface search: Thales Sphynx; I-band.
Sonars: Bow and flank arrays. To be fitted for but not with
  towed array.

Programmes: Decision taken on 24 July 1998 and
  announced on 9 October to order three HDW designed
  submarines with an option for a fourth. The first of class
  is being built at Kiel and subsequent hulls at Hellenic
  Shipyards. Contracts to build signed 15 February 2000
  and the fourth was ordered in 2002.
Structure: Diving depth 400 m *(1,300 ft)*. To be equipped
  with Zeiss optronic mast and SATCOM.
Operational: *Papanikolis* started initial sea trials on
  2 February 2005.

PAPANIKOLIS *2/2005, Michael Nitz* / 1043491

8 GLAVKOS CLASS (209 TYPES 1100 AND 1200) (SSK)

Name	No	Builders	Laid down	Launched	Commissioned
GLAVKOS	S 110	Howaldtswerke, Kiel	1 Sep 1968	15 Sep 1970	6 Sep 1971
NEREUS	S 111	Howaldtswerke, Kiel	15 Jan 1969	7 June 1971	10 Feb 1972
TRITON	S 112	Howaldtswerke, Kiel	1 June 1969	14 Oct 1971	8 Aug 1972
PROTEUS	S 113	Howaldtswerke, Kiel	1 Oct 1969	1 Feb 1972	8 Aug 1972
POSEIDON	S 116	Howaldtswerke, Kiel	15 Jan 1976	21 Mar 1978	22 Mar 1979
AMPHITRITE	S 117	Howaldtswerke, Kiel	26 Apr 1976	14 June 1978	14 Sep 1979
OKEANOS	S 118	Howaldtswerke, Kiel	1 Oct 1976	16 Nov 1978	15 Nov 1979
PONTOS	S 119	Howaldtswerke, Kiel	25 Jan 1977	21 Mar 1979	29 Apr 1980

Displacement, tons: 1,125 surfaced; 1,235 dived (S 110-113)
  1,200 surfaced; 1,285 dived (S 116-119)
Dimensions, feet (metres): 179.5 × 20.3 × 18.5
  (54.4 × 6.2 × 5.6) (S 110-113)
  183.4 × 20.3 × 18.8 *(55.9 × 6.2 × 5.7)* (S 116-119)
Main machinery: Diesel-electric; 4 MTU 12V 493 AZ80 diesels;
  2,400 hp(m) *(1.76 MW)* sustained; 4 Siemens alternators;
  1.7 MW; 1 Siemens motor; 4,600 hp(m) *(3.38 MW)*
  sustained; 1 shaft
Speed, knots: 11 surfaced; 21.5 dived
Complement: 31 (6 officers)

Missiles: McDonnell Douglas Sub Harpoon; active radar
  homing to 130 km *(70 n miles)* at 0.9 Mach; warhead
  258 kg. Can be discharged from 4 tubes only (S 110-113).
Torpedoes: 8—21 in *(533 mm)* bow tubes. 14 AEG SUT Mod 0;
  wire-guided; active/passive homing to 12 km *(6.5 n miles)*
  at 35 kt; warhead 250 kg. Swim-out discharge.
Countermeasures: ESM: Argos AR-700-S5; radar warning
  (S 110—113).
  Thomson Arial DR 2000; radar warning (S 116-119).

Weapons control: Signaal Sinbads (S 116-S 119). Unisys/
  Kanaris with UYK-44 computers (S 110-113).
Radars: Surface search: Thomson-CSF Calypso II (S 116-119).
  Thomson MILNAV (S 110-113); I-band.
Sonars: Atlas Elektronik CSU 83-90 (DBQS-21); (S 110-113);
  Atlas Elektronik CSU 3—4 (S 116-119); hull-mounted;
  active/passive search and attack; medium frequency.
  Atlas Elektronik PRS-3-4; passive ranging.

Programmes: Designed by Ingenieurkontor, Lübeck
  for construction by Howaldtswerke, Kiel and sale by
  Ferrostaal, Essen all acting as a consortium.
Modernisation: Contract signed 5 May 1989 with HDW
  and Ferrostaal to implement a Neptune I update
  programme to bring first four up to an improved
  standard and along the same lines as the German
  S 206A class. Included Sub Harpoon, flank array sonar,
  Unisys FCS, Sperry Mk 29 Mod 3 inertial navigation
  system, GPS and Argos ESM. *Triton* completed refit
  at Kiel in May 1993, *Proteus* at Salamis in December
  1995, *Glavkos* in November 1997, and *Nereus* in

March 2000. A contract signed 31 May 2002 with
Hellenic Shipyards (main sub-contractor HDW) for a
Neptune II modernisation programme for three boats
(plus one option) of S 116-119. *Okeanos* started refit in
December 2004 and is to be completed in November
2007. *Pontos* and *Amphitrite* are to be completed in 2010
and 2012 respectively. The hulls are to receive a 'plug-in'
extension of 6.5 m to incorporate AIP (Siemens PEM fuel
cell system). In addition an STN Atlas ISUS-90 combat
management system, flank array sonar, electro-optic
mast, SATCOM, Link II and Sub Harpoon are to be fitted.
The conversion is expected to take up to three years for
each boat.
Structure: A single-hull design with two ballast tanks and
forward and after trim tanks. Fitted with snort and remote
machinery control. The single screw is slow revving. Very
high-capacity batteries with GRP lead-acid cells and
battery cooling by Wilh Hagen and VARTA. Diving depth,
250 m *(820 ft)*. Fitted with two periscopes.
Operational: Endurance, 50 days. A mining capability is
reported but not confirmed.

POSEIDON *4/2005*, *B Prézelin* / 1133494

FRIGATES

Notes: Procurement of at least two air-defence capable frigates is a high priority and a new programme is expected to be initiated in 2006. Options include new build or acquisition of second-hand ships.

4 HYDRA CLASS (MEKO 200 HN) (FFGHM)

Name	No	Builders	Laid down	Launched	Commissioned
HYDRA	F 452	Blohm + Voss, Hamburg	17 Dec 1990	25 June 1991	12 Nov 1992
SPETSAI	F 453	Hellenic Shipyards, Skaramanga	11 Aug 1992	9 Dec 1993	24 Oct 1996
PSARA	F 454	Hellenic Shipyards, Skaramanga	12 Dec 1993	20 Dec 1994	30 Apr 1998
SALAMIS	F 455	Hellenic Shipyards, Skaramanga	20 Dec 1994	15 May 1997	16 Dec 1998

Displacement, tons: 2,710 light; 3,350 full load
Dimensions, feet (metres): 383.9; 357.6 (wl) × 48.6 × 19.7 *(117; 109 × 14.8 × 6)*
Main machinery: CODOG; 2 GE LM 2500 gas turbines; 60,000 hp *(44.76 MW)* sustained; 2 MTU 20V 956 TB82 diesels; 10,420 hp(m) *(7.66 MW)* sustained; 2 shafts; cp props
Speed, knots: 31 gas; 20 diesel
Range, n miles: 4,100 at 16 kt
Complement: 173 (22 officers) plus 16 flag staff

Missiles: SSM: 8 McDonnell Douglas Harpoon Block 1C; 2 quad launchers ❶; active radar homing to 130 km *(70 n miles)* at 0.9 Mach; warhead 227 kg.
SAM: Raytheon NATO Sea Sparrow Mk 48 Mod 2 vertical launcher ❷; 16 missiles; semi-active radar homing to 14.6 km *(8 n miles)* at 2.5 Mach; warhead 39 kg.
Guns: 1 FMC 5 in *(127 mm)*/54 Mk 45 Mod 2A ❸ 20 rds/min to 24 km *(13 n miles)* anti-surface; 14 km *(7.7 n miles)* anti-aircraft; weight of shell 32 kg.
2 GD/GE Vulcan Phalanx 20 mm Mk 15 Mod 12 ❹; 6 barrels per mounting; 3,000 rds/min combined to 1.5 km.
Torpedoes: 6—324 mm Mk 32 Mod 5 (2 triple) tubes ❺. Honeywell Mk 46 Mod 5; anti-submarine; active/passive homing to 11 km *(5.9 n miles)* at 40 kt; warhead 44 kg.
Countermeasures: Decoys: 4 Mk 36 Mod 2 SRBOC chaff launchers ❻.
SLQ-25 Nixie; torpedo decoy.
ESM: Argo AR 700; Telegon 10; intercept.
ECM: Argo APECS II; jammer.
Combat data systems: Signaal STACOS Mod 2; Links 11 and 14.
Weapons control: 2 Signaal Mk 73 Mod 1 (for SAM). Vesta Helo transponder with datalink for OTHT. SAR-8 IR search. SWG 1 A(V) Harpoon LCS.
Radars: Air search: Signaal MW08 ❼; 3D; F/G-band.
Air Surface search: Signaal/Magnavox; DA08 ❽; G-band.
Navigation: Racal Decca 2690 BT; ARPA; I-band.
Fire control: 2 Signaal STIR ❾; I/J/K-band.
IFF: Mk XII Mod 4.
Sonars: Raytheon SQS-56/DE 1160; hull-mounted and VDS.

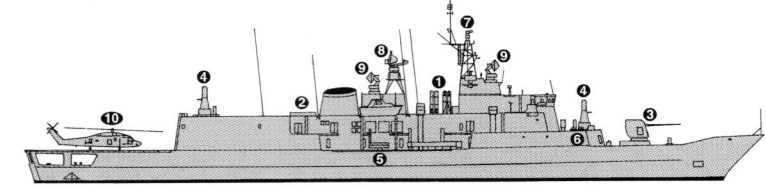

HYDRA   *(Scale 1: 1,200), Ian Sturton* / 0052282

SALAMIS   *5/2005*, C D Yaylali* / 1133493

Helicopters: 1 Sikorsky S-70B-6 Aegean Hawk ❿.

Programmes: Decision to buy four Meko 200 HN announced on 18 April 1988. The first ship ordered 10 February 1989 built by Blohm + Voss, Hamburg and the remainder ordered 10 May 1989 at Hellenic Shipyards, Skaramanga. Programme was delayed by financial problems at Hellenic Shipyards in 1992 and some of the prefabrication of *Spetsai* was done in Hamburg.
Modernisation: A mid-life upgrade programme is to be initiated by 2010.
Structure: The design follows the Portuguese Vasco da Gama class. All steel fin stabilisers.
Operational: Aegean Hawk carried from 1995.

HYDRA   *6/2005*, Michael Winter* / 1133492

HYDRA   *5/2005*, John Brodie* / 1133491

10 ELLI (KORTENAER) CLASS (FFGHM)

Name	No	Builders	Laid down	Launched	Commissioned
ELLI (ex-*Pieter Florisz*)	F 450 (ex-F 812)	Koninklijke Maatschappij de Schelde, Flushing	1 July 1977	15 Dec 1979	10 Oct 1981
LIMNOS (ex-*Witte de With*)	F 451 (ex-F 813)	Koninklijke Maatschappij de Schelde, Flushing	13 June 1978	27 Oct 1979	18 Sep 1982
AEGEON (ex-*Banckert*)	F 460 (ex-F 810)	Koninklijke Maatschappij de Schelde, Flushing	25 Feb 1976	13 July 1978	29 Oct 1980
ADRIAS (ex-*Callenburgh*)	F 459 (ex-F 808)	Koninklijke Maatschappij de Schelde, Flushing	30 June 1975	12 Mar 1977	26 July 1979
NAVARINON (ex-*Van Kinsbergen*)	F 461 (ex-F 809)	Koninklijke Maatschappij de Schelde, Flushing	2 Sep 1975	16 Apr 1977	24 Apr 1980
KOUNTOURIOTIS (ex-*Kortenaer*)	F 462 (ex-F 807)	Koninklijke Maatschappij de Schelde, Flushing	8 Apr 1975	18 Dec 1976	26 Oct 1978
BOUBOULINA (ex-*Pieter Florisz*, ex-*Willem van der Zaan*)	F 463 (ex-F 826)	Koninklijke Maatschappij de Schelde, Flushing	21 Jan 1981	8 May 1982	1 Oct 1983
KANARIS (ex-*Jan van Brakel*)	F 464 (ex-F-825)	Koninklijke Maatschappij de Schelde, Flushing	16 Nov 1979	16 May 1981	14 Apr 1983
THEMISTOCLES (ex-*Philips Van Almonde*)	F 465 (ex-F-823)	Dok en Werfmaatschappij-Fijenoord	3 Oct 1977	11 Aug 1979	2 Dec 1981
NIKIFOROS FOKAS (ex-*Bloys van Treslong*)	F 466 (ex-F-824)	Dok en Werfmaatschappij-Fijenoord	27 Apr 1978	15 Nov 1980	25 Nov 1982

Displacement, tons: 3,050 standard; 3,630 full load
Dimensions, feet (metres): 428 × 47.9 × 20.3 (screws)
  (130.5 × 14.6 × 6.2)
Main machinery: COGOG; 2 RR Olympus TM3B gas turbines; 50,880 hp *(39.7 MW)* sustained; 2 RR Tyne RM1C gas turbines; 9,900 hp *(7.4 MW)* sustained; 2 shafts; LIPS cp props
Speed, knots: 30. **Range, n miles:** 4,700 at 16 kt
Complement: 176 (17 officers)

Missiles: SSM: 8 McDonnell Douglas Harpoon (2 quad) launchers ❶; active radar homing to 130 km *(70 n miles)* at 0.9 Mach; warhead 227 kg.
SAM: Raytheon NATO Sea Sparrow ❷; 24 missiles; semi-active radar homing to 14.6 km *(8 n miles)* at 2.5 Mach; warhead 39 kg.
Portable Redeye; shoulder-launched; short range.
Guns: 1 (459—466) or 2 (450, 451) OTO Melara 3 in *(76 mm)*/62 compact ❸; 85 rds/min to 16 km *(8.6 n miles)* anti-surface; 12 km *(6.5 n miles)* anti-aircraft; weight of shell 6 kg.
1 or 2 (450, 451) GE/GD Vulcan Phalanx 20 mm Mk 15 6-barrelled ❹; 3,000 rds/min combined to 1.5 km. Not fitted in 463—466.
Torpedoes: 4—324 mm Mk 32 (2 twin) tubes ❺. 16 Honeywell Mk 46 Mod 5; anti-submarine; active/passive homing to 11 km *(5.9 n miles)* at 40 kt; warhead 44 kg. Can be fitted.
Countermeasures: Decoys: 2 Loral Hycor Mk 36 SRBOC chaff launchers.
ESM: Elettronika Sphinx and MEL Scimitar; intercept.
ECM: ELT 715; jammer.
Combat data systems: Signaal SEWACO II action data automation; Links 10, 11 and 14.
Radars: Air search: Signaal LW08 ❻; D-band; range 264 km *(145 n miles)* for 2 m² target.
Surface search: Signaal ZW06 ❼; I-band.
Fire control: Signaal WM25 ❽; I/J-band; range 46 km *(25 n miles)*.
Signaal STIR ❾; I/J/K-band; range 39 km *(21 n miles)* for 1 m² target.
Sonars: Canadian Westinghouse SQS-505; hull-mounted; active search and attack; 7 kHz.

Helicopters: 2 AB 212ASW ❿.

Programmes: A contract was signed with the Netherlands on 15 September 1980 for the purchase of one *(Elli)* of the Kortenaer class building for the Netherlands' Navy, and an option on a second of class *(Limnos)*, which was taken up 7 June 1981. A second contract, signed on 9 November 1992, transferred three more of the class. Recommissioning dates for the second batch were *Aegeon* 14 May 1993, *Adrias* 30 March 1994 and *Navarinon* 1 March 1995. *Kountouriotis*, the sixth ship to transfer, recommissioned on 15 December 1997, *Bouboulina*, the seventh, on 14 December 2001, *Kanaris*, the eighth, on 29 November 2002, *Themistocles*, the ninth, on 24 October 2003 and *Nikiforos Fokas*, the tenth, on 17 December 2003.
Modernisation: The original plan was to fit one Phalanx CIWS in place of the after 76 mm gun but this was retained in 450 and 451 during Gulf deployments in 1990-91 and two Phalanx fitted on the deck above the torpedo tubes. Corvus chaff launchers replaced by SRBOC (fitted either side of the bridge). The second batch of three ships were to be similarly modified but the original plan of one Phalanx vice the after 76 mm has been adopted as a cheaper alternative. Mid-life modernisation programme (MLM) is planned for six ships of the class to extend life to 2020. There is an option for two further ships at a later date.
To be undertaken by Hellenic Shipyards with Thales Nederland acting as main sub-contractor, the MLM is to include replacement of the combat data system with Tacticos, replacement of ZW06 surface search radar with Scout, improvements to the tracking performance of LW08 and WM25/STIR and installation of the Mirador optronic director. Upgrades to the EW capability are to include EDO CS-3701 ESM receiver and upgrade of SRBOC. Upgrade of the Sea Sparrow system to RIM 162 ESSM has been postponed indefinitely. F 462 is the first to be modernised and the programme will be completed when F 460 is delivered in 2009.
Structure: Hangar is 2 m longer than in Netherlands' ships to accommodate AB 212ASW helicopters.

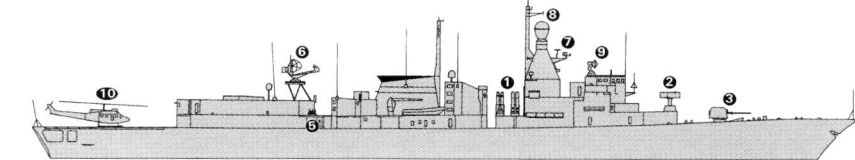

KANARIS   *(Scale 1: 1,200), Ian Sturton* / 1044255

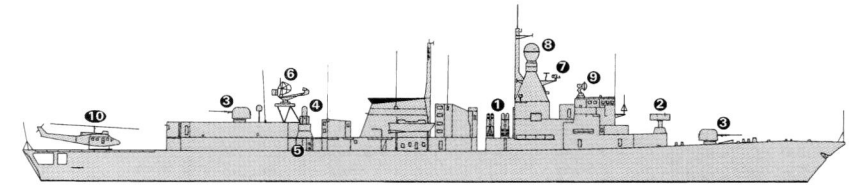

ELLI   *(Scale 1: 1,200), Ian Sturton* / 0126346

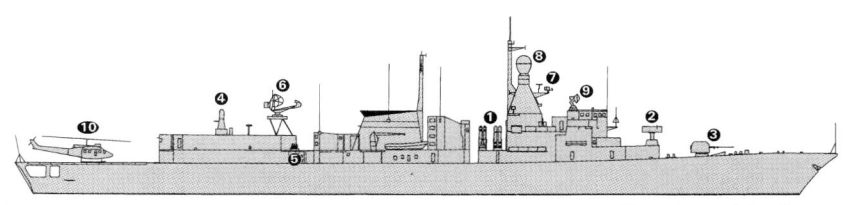

ADRIAS   *(Scale 1: 1,200), Ian Sturton* / 0126345

ELLI   *5/2002, A Sharma* / 0525893

THEMISTOCLES   *9/2005*, H M Steele* / 1153498

AEGEON   *6/2005*, Camil Busquets i Vilanova* / 1133503

CORVETTES

Notes: The corvette programme was cancelled in 2004.

3 NIKI (THETIS) (TYPE 420) CLASS (GUNBOATS) (FS)

Name	No	Commissioned	Recommissioned
NIKI (ex-*Thetis*)	P 62 (ex-P 6052)	1 July 1961	6 Sep 1991
DOXA (ex-*Najade*)	P 63 (ex-P 6054)	12 May 1962	6 Sep 1991
ELEFTHERIA (ex-*Triton*)	P 64 (ex-P 6055)	10 Nov 1962	7 Sep 1992

Displacement, tons: 575 standard; 732 full load
Dimensions, feet (metres): 229.7 × 26.9 × 8.6 *(70 × 8.2 × 2.7)*
Main machinery: 2 MAN V84V diesels; 6,800 hp(m) *(5 MW)*; 2 shafts
Speed, knots: 19.5
Range, n miles: 2,760 at 15 kt
Complement: 48 (4 officers)

Guns: 4 Breda 40 mm/70 (2 twin); 300 rds/min to 12.5 km *(6.7 n miles)*; weight of shell 0.96 kg. 2 Rheinmetall 20 mm.
Torpedoes: 6—324 mm Mk 32 (2 triple) tubes; 4 Honeywell Mk 46 Mod 5; active/passive homing to 11 km *(5.9 n miles)* at 40 kt; warhead 44 kg.
Depth charges: 2 rails.
Countermeasures: ESM: Thomson-CSF DR 2000S; intercept.
Weapons control: Signaal Mk 9 TFCS.
Radars: Surface search: Thomson-CSF TRS 3001; E/F-band.
Navigation: Decca BM-E; I-band.
Sonars: Atlas Elektronik ELAC 1 BV; hull-mounted; active search and attack; high frequency.

Programmes: All built by Rolandwerft, Bremen, and transferred from Germany.
Modernisation: The A/S mortars have been replaced by a second 40 mm gun and single torpedo tubes by triple mountings. Upgrades started in 2000 and completed in 2002 included new diesel generators, two Rheinmetall 20 mm guns to replace the MGs and a new navigation suite.
Structure: *Doxa* has a deckhouse before bridge for sick bay.

DOXA   *7/2002, Ptisi* / 0525866

SHIPBORNE AIRCRAFT

Notes: There are also two Alouette IIIs used for SAR and training.

Numbers/Type: 11 Sikorsky S-70B-6 Aegean Hawk.
Operational speed: 135 kt *(250 km/h)*.
Service ceiling: 10,000 ft *(3,050 m)*.
Range: 600 n miles *(1,110 km)*.
Role/Weapon systems: Five ordered 17 August 1991. First one delivered 14 October 1994, remainder in July 1995. The option was taken up on three more of which one was delivered in 1997, and two more in 1998. Three further more modern aircraft ordered June 2000, all of which have been delivered (differences are indicated in brackets). All of the original eight aircraft are to be similarly upgraded. Sensors: Telephonica APS 143(V)3 search radar and AAQ-22 (or AAS 44) FLIR, AlliedSignal AQS 18(V)3 (or Ocean Systems HELRAS) dipping sonar, MAD, Litton ALR 606(V)2 (or LR 100) ESM, Litton ASN 150(V) tactical data system with CD22 or Link 11. Weapons: ASV; Kongsberg Penguin Mk 2 Mod 7, two AS 12 (or four AGM-114K Hellfire). ASW; two (or three) Mk 46 torpedoes.

AEGEAN HAWK   *10/2001, Diego Quevedo* / 0126292

Numbers/Type: 8/2 Agusta AB 212ASW/212EW.
Operational speed: 106 kt *(196 km/h)*.
Service ceiling: 14,200 ft *(4,330 m)*.
Range: 230 n miles *(425 km)*.
Role/Weapon systems: Shipborne ASW, Elint and surface search role from escorts. Sensors: Selenia APS-705 radar, ESM/ECM (Elint version), AlliedSignal AQS-18 dipping sonar (ASW version). Weapons: ASV; two AS 12. ASW; two Mk 46 or two A244/S homing torpedoes.

AB 212ASW   *6/2003, Adolfo Ortigueira Gil* / 0568866

LAND-BASED MARITIME AIRCRAFT

Notes: (1) A squadron of Air Force Mirage 2000 EG fighters is assigned to the naval strike role using Exocet AM 39 ASMs.
(2) Replacement or upgrade of the six P-3B Orions is under consideration.

Numbers/Type: 6 Lockheed P-3B Orion.
Operational speed: 410 kt *(760 km/h)*.
Service ceiling: 28,300 ft *(8,625 m)*.
Range: 4,000 n miles *(7,410 km)*.
Role/Weapon systems: Four P-3A transferred from the USN in 1992-93 as part of the Defence Co-operation. Four P-3B acquired in 1996 plus two more P-3A. Two more P-3B in 1997. The six P-3B are operational; two P-3A are used for ground training only and the remainder for spares. Sensors: APS 115 radar; sonobuoys; ESM. Weapons: ASW; Mk 46 torpedoes, depth bombs and mines.

ORION   *6/1997, Hellenic Navy* / 0012468

PATROL FORCES

Notes: Eight coastal patrol craft ordered on 24 September 2002 from Motomarine Shipyards. The first was planned to enter service in 2003. Eight further craft ordered by the Hellenic Coast Guard and delivered in 2004.

2 TOLMI (ASHEVILLE) CLASS (COASTAL PATROL CRAFT) (PGM)

Name	No	Builders	Commissioned
TOLMI (ex-*Green Bay*)	P 229	Peterson, Wisconsin	5 Dec 1969
ORMI (ex-*Beacon*)	P 230	Peterson, Wisconsin	21 Nov 1969

Displacement, tons: 225 standard; 245 full load
Dimensions, feet (metres): 164.5 × 23.8 × 9.5 *(50.1 × 7.3 × 2.9)*
Main machinery: 2 MTU 12V 596 TE94 diesels; 4,500 hp *(3.3 MW)*; 2 shafts
Speed, knots: 20
Range, n miles: 1,700 at 16 kt
Complement: 24 (3 officers)
Missiles: SSM: 4 Aerospatiale SS 12M; wire-guided to 5.5 km *(3 n miles)* subsonic; warhead 30 kg.
Guns: 1 USN 3 in *(76 mm)*/50 Mk 34; 50 rds/min to 12.8 km *(7 n miles)*; weight of shell 6 kg.
1 Bofors 40 mm/70 Mk 10. 4—12.7 mm (2 twin) MGs.
Weapons control: Mk 63 GFCS.
Radars: Surface search: Sperry SPS-53; I/J-band.
Fire control: Western Electric SPG-50; I/J-band.

Comment: Transferred from the USA in mid-1990 after a refit and recommissioned 18 June 1991. Both were in reserve from April 1977 having originally been built for the Cuban crisis. Similar craft in Turkish, Colombian and South Korean navies. Original gas-turbine propulsion engine was removed prior to transfer and both craft reported re-engined in 2004.

TOLMI   *9/2001, A Sharma* / 0126331

4 NASTY CLASS (FAST ATTACK CRAFT—TORPEDO) (PT)

Name	No	Builders	Commissioned
ANDROMEDA	P 196	Mandal, Norway	Nov 1966
KYKNOS	P 198	Mandal, Norway	Feb 1967
PIGASOS	P 199	Mandal, Norway	Apr 1967
TOXOTIS	P 228	Mandal, Norway	May 1967

Displacement, tons: 72 full load
Dimensions, feet (metres): 80.4 × 24.6 × 6.9 *(24.5 × 7.5 × 2.1)*
Main machinery: 2 MTU 12V 331 TC92 diesels; 2,660 hp(m) *(1.96 MW)* sustained; 2 shafts
Speed, knots: 25. **Range, n miles:** 676 at 17 kt
Complement: 20
Guns: 1 Bofors 40 mm/70. 1 Rheinmetall 20 mm.
Torpedoes: 4—21 in *(533 mm)* tubes. Mk.14 and Mk.23; anti-surface; straight running to 4.2 km *(2.2 n miles)* at 45 kt; warhead 292 kg.
Radars: Surface search: Decca 1226; I-band.

Comment: Six of the class acquired from Norway in 1967 and paid off into reserve in the early 1980s. Four re-engined and brought back into service in 1988. These craft continue to be active although top speed has been markedly reduced. Torpedo tubes have been removed from P 199.

PIGASOS *7/2004, C D Yaylali* / 0587756

1 + 4 ROUSSEN (SUPER VITA) CLASS
(FAST ATTACK CRAFT—MISSILE) (PGGM)

Name	No	Builders	Commissioned
YPOPLOIARCHOS ROUSSEN	P 67	Elefsis Shipyard	2006
YPOPLOIARCHOS DANIOLOS	P 68	Elefsis Shipyard	2006
YPOPLOIARCHOS KRISTALLIDIS	P 69	Elefsis Shipyard	2006
YPOPLOIARCHOS GRIGORO POULOS	P 70	Elefsis Shipyard	2007
ANTHYPOPLOIARCHOS RITSOS	P 71	Elefsis Shipyard	2007

Displacement, tons: 580 full load
Dimensions, feet (metres): 203.1 × 31.2 × 8.5 *(61.9 × 9.5 × 2.6)*
Main machinery: 4 MTU 16V 595 TE 90 diesels; 4 shafts
Speed, knots: 34
Range, n miles: 1,800 at 12 kt
Complement: 45

Missiles: SSM: 8 MBDA Exocet MM 40 Block 2 (Block 3 in P 70 and P 71) ❶; inertial cruise; active radar homing to 70 km *(40 n miles)* at 0.9 Mach; warhead 165 kg; sea skimmer.
SAM: RAM ❷. Mk 31 Mod 1 launcher with 21 missiles.
Guns: 1 Otobreda 76 mm/62 Super Rapid ❸; 120 rds/min to 16 km *(8.7 n miles)*; weight of shell 6 kg.
2 Oto Melara 30 mm ❹.
Countermeasures: Decoys: 2 Loral Hycor Mk 36 SRBOC chaff launchers ❺.
ESM: Argo AR 900 ❻; intercept.
Combat data systems: Signaal Tacticos. Link 11.
Weapons control: Thales Mirador Trainable Electro-Optical Observation System (TEOOS) ❼.
Radars: Air/surface search: Thomson-CSF MW 08 ❽; G-band.
Surface search: Signaal Scout Mk 2 LPI; I-band.
Navigation: Litton Marine Bridgemaster; I-band.
Fire control: Signaal Sting ❾; I/J-band.
IFF: Mk XII.

Programmes: Design selected 21 September 1999 based on Vosper Thornycroft Vita corvettes in service in Qatar. Contract signed 7 January 2000 for the building of first three vessels which started in March 2000. *Roussen* launched on 13 November 2002 and conducted sea trials in 2004. *Daniolos* launched on 8 July 2003 and *Kristallidis* on 5 April 2004. Contract for a further two ships signed on 23 August 2003 for delivery in 2007.

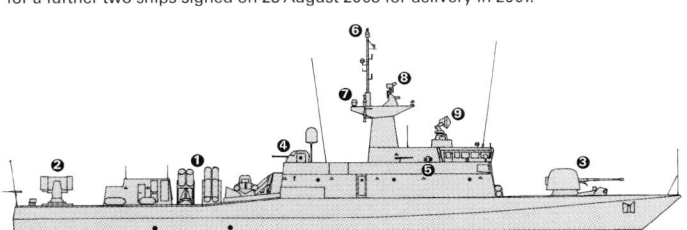

YPOPLOIARCHOS ROUSSEN *(Scale 1: 900), Ian Sturton* / 0126344

DANIOLOS *7/2003, TLV* / 0549881

9 LASKOS (LA COMBATTANTE III) CLASS
(FAST ATTACK CRAFT—MISSILE) (PGGF/PGG)

Name	No	Builders	Commissioned
ANTHYPOPLOIARCHOS LASKOS	P 20	CMN Cherbourg	20 Apr 1977
PLOTARCHIS BLESSAS	P 21	CMN Cherbourg	7 July 1977
YPOPLOIARCHOS MIKONIOS	P 22	CMN Cherbourg	10 Feb 1978
YPOPLOIARCHOS TROUPAKIS	P 23	CMN Cherbourg	8 Nov 1977
SIMEOFOROS KAVALOUDIS	P 24	Hellenic Shipyards, Skaramanga	14 July 1980
YPOPLOIARCHOS DEGIANNIS	P 26	Hellenic Shipyards, Skaramanga	Dec 1980
SIMEOFOROS XENOS	P 27	Hellenic Shipyards, Skaramanga	31 Mar 1981
SIMEOFOROS SIMITZOPOULOS	P 28	Hellenic Shipyards, Skaramanga	June 1981
SIMEOFOROS STARAKIS	P 29	Hellenic Shipyards, Skaramanga	12 Oct 1981

Displacement, tons: 359 standard; 425 full load (P 20-23)
329 standard; 429 full load (P 24-29)
Dimensions, feet (metres): 184 × 26.2 × 7 *(56.2 × 8 × 2.1)*
Main machinery: 4 MTU 20V 538TB92 diesels; 17,060 hp(m) *(12.54 MW)* sustained; 4 shafts (P 20-23)
4 MTU 20V 538TB91 diesels; 15,360 hp(m) *(11.29 MW)* sustained; 4 shafts (P 24-29)
Speed, knots: 36 (P 20-23); 32.5 (P 24-29)
Range, n miles: 700 at 32 kt; 2,700 at 15 kt
Complement: 42 (5 officers)

Missiles: SSM: 4 Aerospatiale MM 38 Exocet (P 20-P 23); inertial cruise; active radar homing to 42 km *(23 n miles)* at 0.9 Mach; warhead 165 kg.
6 Kongsberg Penguin Mk 2 Mod 3 (P 24-P 29); inertial/IR homing to 27 km *(15 n miles)* at 0.8 Mach; warhead 120 kg.
Guns: 2 OTO Melara 3 in *(76 mm)*/62 compact; 85 rds/min to 16 km *(8.6 n miles)* anti-surface; 12 km *(6.5 n miles)* anti-aircraft; weight of shell 6 kg.
4 Emerson Electric 30 mm (2 twin); multipurpose; 1,200 rds/min combined to 6 km *(3.2 n miles)*; weight of shell 0.35 kg.
Torpedoes: 2—21 in *(533 mm)* aft tubes. AEG SST-4; anti-surface; wire-guided; active homing to 12 km *(6.5 n miles)* at 35 kt; passive homing to 28 km *(15 n miles)* at 23 kt; warhead 250 kg.
Countermeasures: Decoys: Wegmann chaff launchers.
ESM: Thomson-CSF DR 2000S; intercept.
Weapons control: 2 CSEE Panda optical directors for 30 mm guns. Thomson-CSF Vega I or II system (P 20-P 23). NFT PFCS-2 (P 24-P 29).
Radars: Surface search: Thomson-CSF Triton; G-band.
Navigation: Decca 1226C; I-band.
Fire control: Thomson-CSF Castor II; I/J-band.
Thomson-CSF Pollux; I/J-band.

Programmes: First four ordered in September 1974. Second group of six ordered 1978.
Modernisation: P 24-29 upgraded to fire Penguin Mk 2 Mod 3 missiles. A contract for the upgrade of P 20-23 was signed on 31 October 2003. Modernisation began in 2004 and is to be completed in 2008. The programme includes installation of the Tacticos Combat Management System, the MIRADOR optronic director, SRBOC launchers, Thales DR 3000 ESM, Link 11 and Variant, Scout Mk 2 and Bridgemaster radars.
Structure: First four fitted with SSM Exocet; remainder have Penguin.
Operational: P 25 sunk after collision with a ferry in November 1996.

YPOPLOIARCHOS TROUPAKIS (with Exocet) *7/2002, Ptisi* / 0525867

SIMEOFOROS SIMITZOPOULOS (with Penguin) *9/2000, A Sharma* / 0126333

SIMEOFOROS STARAKIS (with Penguin) *9/1998, van Ginderen Collection* / 0052292

6 VOTSIS (LA COMBATTANTE IIA) (TYPE 148) CLASS
(FAST ATTACK CRAFT—MISSILE) (PGGF)

Name	No	Builders	Commissioned
YPOPLOIARCHOS VOTSIS (ex-*Iltis*)	P 72 (ex-P 51)	CMN, Cherbourg	8 Jan 1973
ANTHYPOPLOIARCHOS PEZOPOULOS (ex-*Storch*)	P 73 (ex-P 30)	CMN, Cherbourg	17 July 1974
PLOTARCHIS VLAHAVAS (ex-*Marder*)	P 74	CMN, Cherbourg	14 June 1973
PLOTARCHIS MARIDAKIS (ex-*Häher*)	P 75	CMN, Cherbourg	12 June 1974
YPOPLOIARCHOS TOURNAS (ex-*Leopard*)	P 76	CMN, Cherbourg	21 Aug 1973
PLOTARCHIS SAKIPIS (ex-*Jaguar*)	P 77	CMN, Cherbourg	13 Nov 1973

Displacement, tons: 265 full load
Dimensions, feet (metres): 154.2 × 23 × 8.9 *(47 × 7 × 2.7)*
Main machinery: 4 MTU MD 16V 538 TB90 diesels; 12,000 hp(m) *(8.82 MW)* sustained; 4 shafts
Speed, knots: 36. **Range, n miles:** 570 at 30 kt; 1,600 at 15 kt
Complement: 30 (4 officers)

Missiles: SSM: 4 Aerospatiale MM 38 Exocet (2 twin) launchers (P 72-73 and P 76-77); inertial cruise; active radar homing to 42 km *(23 n miles)* at 0.9 Mach; warhead 165 kg; sea-skimmer.
4 McDonnell Douglas Harpoon (2 twin) launchers (P 74-75); active radar homing to 130 km *(70 n miles)* at 0.9 Mach; warhead 227 kg.
Guns: 1 OTO Melara 3 in *(76 mm)*/62 compact; 85 rds/min to 16 km *(8.6 n miles)* anti-surface; 12 km *(6.5 n miles)* anti-aircraft; weight of shell 6 kg.
1 Bofors 40 mm/70; 330 rds/min to 12 km *(6.5 n miles)* anti-surface; 4 km *(2.2 n miles)* anti-aircraft; weight of shell 0.96 kg; fitted with GRP dome (1984).
Mines: Laying capability.
Countermeasures: Decoys: Wolke chaff launcher.
ESM: Thomson-CSF DR 2000S; intercept.
Combat data systems: PALIS and Link 11.
Weapons control: CSEE Panda optical director. Thomson-CSF Vega PCET system, controlling missiles and guns.
Radars: Air/surface search: Thomson-CSF Triton; G-band; range 33 km *(18 n miles)* for 2 m² target.
Navigation: SMA 3 RM 20; I-band.
Fire control: Thomson-CSF Castor; I/J-band.

Programmes: First pair transferred from Germany in September 1993 and recommissioned 17 February 1994. Two more transferred 16 March 1995 and recommissioned 30 June 1995. Third pair transferred from Germany and recommissioned on 27 October 2000.
Modernisation: Mid-life updates in 1980s. P 74-75 fitted with Harpoon. New ESM fitted after transfer. P 76-77 modernised at Lamda Shipyards in 2003-2004.
Structure: Steel hulls. Similar to Combattante II class. Spray rails have been fitted to improve hydrodynamic performance.

YPOPLOIARCHOS TOURNAS   *11/2004*, M Declerck* / 1133495

2 ARMATOLOS (OSPREY 55) CLASS
(LARGE PATROL CRAFT) (PGG)

Name	No	Builders	Commissioned
ARMATOLOS	P 18	Hellenic Shipyards, Skaramanga	27 Mar 1990
NAVMACHOS	P 19	Hellenic Shipyards, Skaramanga	15 July 1990

Displacement, tons: 555 full load
Dimensions, feet (metres): 179.8; 166.7 (wl) × 34.4 × 8.5 *(54.8; 50.8 × 10.5 × 2.6)*
Main machinery: 2 MTU 16V 1163 TB63 diesels; 10,000 hp(m) *(7.3 MW)* sustained; 2 shafts; Kamewa cp props
Speed, knots: 25. **Range, n miles:** 500 at 25 kt, 2,800 at 12 kt
Complement: 36 plus 25 troops
Missiles: SSM: 4 McDonnell Douglas Harpoon (can be fitted).
Guns: 1 OTO Melara 3 in *(76 mm)*/62 compact; 85 rds/min to 16 km *(8.6 n miles)* anti-surface; 12 km *(6.6 n miles)* anti-aircraft; weight of shell 6 kg.
1 Bofors 40 mm/70.
Mines: Rails.
Countermeasures: Decoys: 2 chaff launchers.
ESM: Thomson-CSF DR 2000S; intercept.
Weapons control: Selenia Elsag NA 21.
Radars: Surface search: Thomson-CSF Triton; G-band.
Fire control: Selenia RTNX; I/J-band.

Comment: Built in co-operation with Danyard A/S. Ordered in March 1988. First one laid down 8 May 1989 and launched 19 December 1989. Second laid down 9 November 1989 and launched 16 May 1990. Armament is of modular design and therefore can be changed. 76 mm guns replaced the Bofors 40 mm in 1995, after being taken from decommissioned Gearing class destroyers. Options on more of the class were shelved in favour of the Hellenic 56 design.

NAVMACHOS   *7/2002, Ptisi* / 0525871

2 PYRPOLITIS (HELLENIC 56) CLASS (BATCH 1)
(LARGE PATROL CRAFT) (PGG)

Name	No	Builders	Commissioned
PYRPOLITIS	P 57	Hellenic Shipyard, Skaramanga	4 May 1993
POLEMISTIS	P 61	Hellenic Shipyard, Skaramanga	16 June 1994

Displacement, tons: 555 full load
Dimensions, feet (metres): 185.4 × 32.8 × 8.9 *(56.5 × 10 × 2.7)*
Main machinery: 2 Wärtsilä Nohab 16V25 diesels; 9,200 hp(m) *(6.76 MW)* sustained; 2 shafts
Speed, knots: 24. **Range, n miles:** 2,470 at 15 kt; 900 at 24 kt
Complement: 36 (6 officers) plus 25 spare
Missiles: SSM: 4 McDonnell Douglas Harpoon (can be fitted).
Guns: 1 OTO Melara 3 in *(76 mm)*/62 compact; 85 rds/min to 16 km *(8.6 n miles)* anti-surface; 12 km *(6.6 n miles)* anti-aircraft; weight of shell 6 kg.
1 Bofors 40 mm/70. 2 Rheinmetall 20 mm.
Mines: 2 rails.
Countermeasures: ESM: Thomson-CSF DR 2000S; intercept.
Weapons control: Selenia Elsag NA 21.
Radars: Surface search: Thomson-CSF Triton; I-band.

Comment: First pair ordered 20 February 1990. This is a design by the Hellenic Navy which uses the modular concept so that weapons and sensors can be changed as required. Appearance is similar to Osprey 55 class. *Pyrpolitis* launched 16 September 1992, *Polemistis* 21 June 1993. Completion delayed by the shipyard's financial problems. Alternative guns and Harpoon SSM can be fitted. 25 fully equipped troops can be carried. Engines are resiliently mounted.

POLEMISTIS   *5/2004, Martin Mokrus* / 0587755

POLEMISTIS   *8/2000, van Ginderen Collection* / 0104560

2 COASTAL PATROL CRAFT (PB)

Name	No	Builders	Commissioned
DIOPOS ANTONIOU	P 286	Ch N de l'Esterel	4 Dec 1975
KELEFSTIS STAMOU	P 287	Ch N de l'Esterel	28 July 1975

Displacement, tons: 115 full load
Dimensions, feet (metres): 105 × 19 × 5.3 *(32 × 5.8 × 1.6)*
Main machinery: 2 MTU 12V 331 TC81 diesels; 2,610 hp(m) *(1.92 MW)* sustained; 2 shafts
Speed, knots: 30
Range, n miles: 1,500 at 15 kt
Complement: 17
Missiles: SSM: 4 Aerospatiale SS 12M; wire-guided to 5.5 km *(3 n miles)* subsonic; warhead 30 kg.
Guns: 1 Rheinmetall 20 mm. 1—12.7 mm MG.
Radars: Surface search: Decca 1226; I-band.

Comment: Originally ordered for Cyprus, later transferred to Greece. Wooden hulls. Fast RIB carried on the stern.

DIOPOS ANTONIOU   *11/2004*, Frank Findler* / 1133496

4 MACHITIS CLASS (LARGE PATROL CRAFT) (PGG)

Name	No	Builders	Commissioned
MACHITIS	P 266	Hellenic Shipyards, Skaramanga	29 Oct 2003
NIKIFOROS	P 267	Hellenic Shipyards, Skaramanga	30 Mar 2004
AITTITOS	P 268	Hellenic Shipyards, Skaramanga	5 Aug 2004
KRATEOS	P 269	Hellenic Shipyards, Skaramanga	20 Oct 2005

Displacement, tons: 575 full load
Dimensions, feet (metres): 185.4 × 32.8 × 8.9 *(56.5 × 10 × 2.7)*
Main machinery: 2 Wärtsilä Nohab 16V25 diesels; 9,200 hp(m) *(6.76 MW)* sustained; 2 shafts
Speed, knots: 24. **Range, n miles:** 2,000 at 15 kt; 900 at 24 kt
Complement: 36 (6 officers) plus 37 spare
Missiles: SSM: 4 McDonnell Douglas Harpoon (can be fitted).
Guns: 1 Otobreda 3 in *(76 mm)*/62 compact; 85 rds/min to 16km *(8.6 n miles)* anti-surface; 12 km *(6.6 n miles)* anti-aircraft; weight of shell 6 kg.
1 Otobreda 40 mm/70-520R. 2 Rheinmetall 20 mm.
Mines: 2 rails.
Countermeasures: ESM: Thomson-CSF DR 3000.
Combat data systems: TACTICOS with Link 11.
Weapons control: Thales Mirador Trainable Electro-Optical Observation System (TEOOS).
Radars: Air/surface search: Signaal Variant; E/F-band.
Surface search: Thales Scout Mk 2; I-band.
Navigation: Bridgemaster I-band.

Comment: Contract to build four improved Pyrpolitis class given to Hellenic Shipyard on 21 December 1999. Building started in February 2000 *Machitis* launched in June 2002, *Nikiforos* on 13 December 2002, *Aititos* on 26 February 2003 and *Krateos* on 30 October 2003. An option for a fifth vessel is unlikely to be exercised.

MACHITIS *6/2005*, **Hellenic Navy** / 1133502

15 FAST INTERCEPT CRAFT (HSIC)

SAP 1-9   +6

Displacement, tons: 6.3 full load
Dimensions, feet (metres): 42 × ? × ? *(12.8 × ? × ?)*
Speed, knots: 60+
Complement: 4
Guns: 1—40 mm Mk 19 grenade launcher.
1—12.7 mm MG. 2—7.62 mm MGs.

Comment: Details are for *SAP 7-9*, donated by Angelopoulos family to Hellenic Navy for use by special forces. Rigid Hull Inflatable Boat with removable synthetic armour panels. Built by Italian shipyard Fabio Buzzi. Six smaller craft *(SAP 1-6)* are also in service and there are at least six further similar craft.

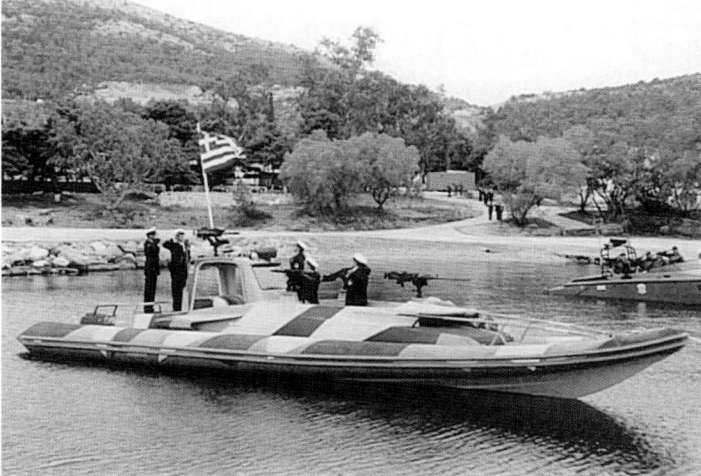

FAST INTERCEPT CRAFT *6/2001, Elias Daloumis* / 0094361

AMPHIBIOUS FORCES

Notes: There is a number of paid off LSTs and LSMs in unmaintained reserve at Salamis.

5 JASON CLASS (LSTH)

Name	No	Builders	Launched	Commissioned
CHIOS	L 173	Eleusis Shipyard	16 Dec 1988	30 May 1996
SAMOS	L 174	Eleusis Shipyard	6 Apr 1989	20 May 1994
LESBOS	L 176	Eleusis Shipyard	5 July 1990	25 Feb 1999
IKARIA	L 175	Eleusis Shipyard	22 Oct 1998	6 Oct 1999
RODOS	L 177	Eleusis Shipyard	6 Oct 1999	30 May 2000

Displacement, tons: 4,400 full load
Dimensions, feet (metres): 380.5 × 50.2 × 11.3 *(116 × 15.3 × 3.4)*
Main machinery: 2 Wärtsilä Nohab 16V25 diesels; 9,200 hp(m) *(6.76 MW)* sustained; 2 shafts
Speed, knots: 16
Military lift: 300 troops plus vehicles; 4 LCVPs
Guns: 1 OTO Melara 76 mm/62 Mod 9 compact; 100 rds/min to 16 km *(8.6 n miles)* anti-surface; 12 km *(6.5 n miles)* anti-aircraft; weight of shell 6 kg.
2 Breda 40 mm/70; 300 rds/min to 12 km *(6.5 n miles)*; weight of shell 0.96 kg.
4 Rheinmetall 20 mm (2 twin).
Weapons control: 1 CSEE Panda optical director. Thomson-CSF Canopus GFCS.
Radars: Thomson-CSF Triton; G-band.
Fire control: Thomson-CSF Pollux; I/J-band.
Navigation: Kelvin Hughes Type 1007; I-band.
Helicopters: Platform for one medium.

Comment: Contract for construction of five LSTs by Eleusis Shipyard signed 15 May 1986. Bow and stern ramps, drive through design. First laid down 18 April 1987, second in September 1987, third in May 1988, fourth April 1989 and fifth November 1989. Completion of all five and in particular the last three, severely delayed by shipyard financial problems which were later overcome, following privatisation. Combat data system is a refurbished German system.

SAMOS *9/2003, Schaeffer/Marsan* / 0568865

LESBOS *8/2001, A Campanera i Rovira* / 0126318

9 TYPE 521 (LCM)

Displacement, tons: 168 full load
Dimensions, feet (metres): 77.4 × 20.9 × 4.9 *(23.6 × 6.4 × 1.5)*
Main machinery: 2 MWM 8-cyl diesels; 685 hp(m) *(503 kW)*; 2 shafts
Speed, knots: 10.5
Range, n miles: 700 at 10 kt
Complement: 7
Military lift: 60 tons or 50 troops

Comment: Built in 1964-67 but spent much of their time in reserve. Transferred from Germany in April 1991 and numbered between ABM 20-30.

TYPE 521 *9/1994, van Ginderen Collection* / 0506192

4 POMORNIK (ZUBR) (PROJECT 1232) HOVERCRAFT (LCUJ)

Name	No	Builders	Commissioned
KEFALLINIA	L 180 (ex-717)	Almaz, St Petersburg	22 Jan 2001
ITHAKI	L 181 (ex-U 421)	Morye Shipyard, Ukraine	2 Mar 2001
ZAKYNTHOS	L 183	Almaz, St Petersburg	5 Oct 2001
KERKIRA	L 182	Almaz, St Petersburg	4 Jan 2005

Displacement, tons: 550 full load
Dimensions, feet (metres): 189 × 84 (57.6 × 25.6)
Main machinery: 5 Type NK-12MV gas-turbines; 2 for lift, 23,672 hp(m) (17.4 MW) nominal;
   3 for drive, 35,508 hp(m) (26.1 MW) nominal
Speed, knots: 60
Range, n miles: 300 at 55 kt
Complement: 27 (4 officers)
Military lift: 3 MBT or 10 APC plus 230 troops (total 130 tons)
Guns: 2—30 mm/65 AK 630; 6 barrels per mounting.
   2 retractable 122 mm rocket launchers.
Mines: 2 rails can be carried for 80.
Countermeasures: ESM: intercept.
Weapons control: Optronic director.
Radars: Air/surface search: Cross Dome; I-band.
   Fire control: Bass Tilt; H/I-band.

Comment: Two ordered from Russia and two from Ukraine on 24 January 2000. First
   delivered late December 2000, the remainder in 2001. L 180 was second-hand, L 181 was
   completion of a half-built vessel and L 183 was new build. The second Ukrainian ship
   was not accepted into service and a replacement (L 182) was ordered from Russia on
   30 September 2002 and launched on 24 June 2004. There are no plans for further craft.

KEFALLINIA — *1/2001, T L Valmas* / 0034713

6 TYPE 520 (LCU)

NAXOS (ex-*Renke*) L 178		**IOS** (ex-*Barbe*) L 167	
PAROS (ex-*Salm*) L 179		**IRAKLEIA** (ex-*Forelle*) L 169	
SERIFOS (ex-*Rochen*) L 195		**FOLEGANDROS** (ex-*Delphin*) L 170	

Displacement, tons: 430 full load
Dimensions, feet (metres): 131.2 × 28.9 × 7.2 (40 × 8.8 × 2.2)
Main machinery: 2 MWM 12-cyl diesels; 1,020 hp(m) (750 kW); 2 shafts
Speed, knots: 11
Range, n miles: 1,200 at 11 kt
Complement: 17
Military lift: 150 tons
Guns: 2 Rheinmetall 20 mm (not all fitted).
Radars: Navigation: Kelvin Hughes; I-band.

Comment: First two transferred from Germany 16 November 1989, remainder on
   31 January 1992. Built by HDW, Hamburg in 1966. Bow and stern ramps similar to US
   Type. One other (ex-*Murane*) used for spares. L 195 modified to act as auxiliary transport
   in 2002.

FOLEGANDROS — *11/1999* / 0081940

FOLEGANDROS — *11/2004*, M Declerck / 1133499

59 LANDING CRAFT

Displacement, tons: 56 full load
Dimensions, feet (metres): 56 × 14.4 × 3.9 (17 × 4.4 × 1.2)
Main machinery: 2 Gray Marine 64 HN9 diesels; 330 hp (264 kW); 2 shafts
Speed, knots: 10
Range, n miles: 130 at 10 kt
Military lift: 30 tons

Comment: Details given are for the 11 LCMs transferred from the USA in 1956-58.
   Twenty-nine LCVPs were also transferred from the USA 1956-71 and the remainder
   (12 LCPs and 7 LCAs) were built in Greece from 1977.

MINE WARFARE FORCES

Notes: Acquisition of two US MHCs (possibly MHCs 52 and 53) was under consideration
in 2005.

2 HUNT CLASS (MHSC)

Name	No	Builders	Commissioned
EVROPI (ex-*Bicester*)	M 62 (ex-M 36)	Vosper Thornycroft	20 Mar 1986
KALLISTO (ex-*Berkeley*)	M 63 (ex-M 40)	Vosper Thornycroft	14 Jan 1988

Displacement, tons: 750 full load
Dimensions, feet (metres): 197 × 34.1 × 10.5 (60 × 10.4 × 3.2)
Main machinery: 2 MTU diesels; 1,900 hp (1.42 MW); 1 Deltic Type 9-55B diesel for pulse
   generator and auxiliary drive; 780 hp (582 kW); 2 shafts; bow thruster
Speed, knots: 15 diesels; 8 hydraulic drive
Range, n miles: 1,500 at 12 kt
Complement: 50 (8 officers)
Guns: 1 DES/MSI DS 30B 30 mm/75; 650 rds/min to 10 km (5.4 n miles) anti-surface;
   3 km (1.6 n miles) anti-aircraft; weight of shell 0.36 kg.
Countermeasures: MCM: 2 PAP 104 remotely controlled submersibles, MS 14 magnetic
   loop, Sperry MSSA Mk 1 Towed Acoustic Generator and conventional Mk 8 Oropesa
   sweeps.
ESM: MEL Matilda UAR 1.
Combat data systems: CAAIS DBA 4 action data automation.
Radars: Navigation: Kelvin Hughes Type 1006; I-band.
Sonars: Plessey 193M Mod 1; hull-mounted; minehunting; 100/300 kHz.
   Mil Cross mine avoidance sonar; hull-mounted; active; high frequency.
   Type 2059 to track PAP 104.

Comment: First one transferred from UK 31 July 2000, second one 28 February 2001. Main
   machinery replaced by MTU units between May 2004 and January 2005. There are no
   further plans for upgrades.

KALLISTO — *3/2001, W Sartori* / 0126329

1 ADJUTANT CLASS
(MINESWEEPER/HUNTER—COASTAL) (MHC/MSC)

ERATO (ex-*Castagno* M 5504) M 60

Displacement, tons: 330 standard; 402 full load
Dimensions, feet (metres): 145 × 27.9 × 8 (44.2 × 8.5 × 2.4)
Main machinery: 2 GM 8-268A diesels; 880 hp (656 kW); 2 shafts
Speed, knots: 14
Range, n miles: 2,500 at 10 kt
Complement: 38 (4 officers)
Guns: 1 Oerlikon 20 mm.
Radars: Navigation: Decca or SMA 3RM 20R; I-band.
Sonars: SQQ-14 or UQS-1D; active; high frequency.

Comment: Bought from Italy on 10 October 1995. Classed as minehunter.

ADJUTANT CLASS — *3/2002, Schaeffer/Marsan* / 0525889

8 ALKYON (MSC 294) CLASS
(MINESWEEPERS—COASTAL) (MSC)

Name	No	Builders	Commissioned
ALKYON (ex-MSC 319)	M 211	Peterson Builders	3 Dec 1968
KLIO (ex-Argo, ex-MSC 317)	M 213	Peterson Builders	7 Aug 1968
AVRA (ex-MSC 318)	M 214	Peterson Builders	3 Oct 1968
AIDON (ex-MSC 314)	M 240	Peterson Builders	22 June 1967
KICHLI (ex-MSC 308)	M 241	Peterson Builders	14 July 1964
KISSA (ex-MSC 309)	M 242	Peterson Builders	1 Sep 1964
DAFNI (ex-MSC 307)	M 247	Peterson Builders	23 Sep 1964
PLEIAS (ex-MSC 310)	M 248	Peterson Builders	13 Oct 1964

Displacement, tons: 320 standard; 370 full load
Dimensions, feet (metres): 144 × 28 × 8.2 *(43.3 × 8.5 × 2.5)*
Main machinery: 2 GM-268A diesels; 1,760 hp *(1.3 MW)*; 2 shafts
Speed, knots: 13
Range, n miles: 2,500 at 10 kt
Complement: 39 (4 officers)
Guns: 2 Oerlikon 20 mm (twin).
Radars: Navigation: Decca; I-band.
Sonars: UQS-1D; active; high frequency.

Comment: Built in the USA for Greece, wooden hulls. Modernisation programme from 1990 to 1995 with replacement main engines and navigation radar. New sonar under consideration but unlikely to be funded.

KISSA   *2/2004, Schaeffer/Marsan* / 0587757

SURVEY AND RESEARCH SHIPS

1 SURVEY SHIP (AGS)

Name	No	Builders	Commissioned
NAFTILOS	A 478	Annastadiades Tsortanides, Perama	3 Apr 1976

Displacement, tons: 1,470 full load
Dimensions, feet (metres): 207 × 38 × 13.8 *(63.1 × 11.6 × 4.2)*
Main machinery: 2 Burmeister & Wain SS28LM diesels; 2,640 hp(m) *(1.94 MW)*; 2 shafts
Speed, knots: 15
Complement: 74 (8 officers)

Comment: Launched 19 November 1975. Of similar design to the two lighthouse tenders.

NAFTILOS   *9/1999, van Ginderen Collection* / 0079497

1 RESEARCH SHIP (AGOR)

Name	No	Builders	Commissioned
PYTHEAS	A 474	Annastadiades Tsortanides, Perama	15 Dec 1983

Displacement, tons: 670 standard; 840 full load
Dimensions, feet (metres): 164.7 × 31.5 × 21.6 *(50.2 × 9.6 × 6.6)*
Main machinery: 2 Detroit 12V-92TA diesels; 1,020 hp *(760 kW)* sustained; 2 shafts
Speed, knots: 14
Complement: 58 (8 officers)

Comment: *Pytheas* ordered in May 1982. Launched 19 September 1983. A similar ship, *Aegeon*, was constructed to Navy specification in 1984 but now belongs to the Maritime Research Institute.

PYTHEAS   *6/2000, Hellenic Navy* / 0104566

1 RESEARCH AND TRAINING CRAFT (AXSL)
OLYMPIAS

Dimensions, feet (metres): 121.4 × 17.1 × 4.9 *(37 × 5.2 × 1.5)*
Main machinery: 170 oars (85 each side in three rows)
Speed, knots: 8
Complement: 180

Comment: Construction started in 1985 and completed in 1987. Made of Oregon pine. Built for historic research and as a reminder of the naval hegemony of ancient Greeks. Part of the Hellenic Navy. Refit in 1992-93.

OLYMPIAS   *6/1996, Hellenic Navy* / 0079500

1 SURVEY SHIP (AGSC)

Name	No	Builders	Commissioned
STRABON	A 476	Emanuil-Maliris, Perama	27 Feb 1989

Displacement, tons: 252 full load
Dimensions, feet (metres): 107.3 × 20 × 8.2 *(32.7 × 6.1 × 2.5)*
Main machinery: 1 MAN D2842LE; 571 hp(m) *(420 kW)* sustained; 1 shaft
Speed, knots: 12.5
Complement: 20 (2 officers)

Comment: Ordered in 1987, launched September 1988. Used as coastal survey vessel.

STRABON   *6/2000, Hellenic Navy* / 0104567

TRAINING SHIPS

3 SAIL TRAINING CRAFT (AXS)

MAISTROS A 233   SOROKOS A 234   OSTRIA A 359

Displacement, tons: 12 full load (A 233 and 234)
Dimensions, feet (metres): 48.6 × 12.8 × 6.9 *(14.8 × 3.9 × 2.1)*

Comment: Sail training ships acquired in 1983-84 (A 233-234) and 1989 (A 359). A 359 is slightly smaller at 12.1 × 3.6 m.

AUXILIARIES

2 FLOATING DOCKS and 5 FLOATING CRANES

Comment: One floating dock is 45 m *(147.6 ft)* in length and has a 6,000 ton lift. Built at Eleusis with Swedish assistance and launched 5 May 1988; delivered 1989. The second is the ex-US AFDM 2 transferred in 1999. This dock was built in 1942 and has a 12,000 ton lift. The cranes were all built in Greece.

1 ETNA CLASS (AORH)

Name	No	Builders	Commissioned
PROMETHEUS	A 374	Elefsis Shipyard	4 July 2003

Displacement, tons: 13,400 full load
Dimensions, feet (metres): 480.6 × 68.9 × 24.3 *(146.5 × 21 × 7.4)*
Flight deck, feet (metres): 91.9 × 68.9 *(28 × 21)*
Main machinery: 2 Sulzer 12 ZAV 40S diesels; 22,400 hp(m) *(16.46 MW)* sustained; 2 shafts; cp props; bow thruster
Speed, knots: 21. **Range, n miles:** 7,600 at 18 kt
Complement: 137 plus 119 spare including flag staff
Cargo capacity: 6,350 tons gas oil; 1,200 tons JP5; 2,100 m³ ammunition and stores
Missiles: SAM: 2 Stinger mountings.
Guns: 4—20 mm guns.
Countermeasures: SLQ-25 Nixie; torpedo decoy.
Radars: Surface search: Raytheon SPS-10D; G-band.
Navigation: GEM LD-1825; I-band.
Helicopters: Aegean Hawk or AB 212.

Comment: Ordered in August 1999 from Fincantieri and from Elefsis on 7 January 2000. First steel cut July 2000, launched 18 February 2002. Almost identical to the Italian Etna class. Two CIWS are to be fitted, one on the hangar roof and forward of the bridge. There is one RAS station on each side and one astern station.

PROMETHEUS   *8/2005*, B Prézelin* / 1133498

2 LÜNEBURG (TYPE 701) CLASS (SUPPORT SHIPS) (ARL/AOTL)

Name	No	Builders	Commissioned	Recommissioned
AXIOS	A 464	Bremer Vulcan	9 July 1968	30 Sep 1991
(ex-*Coburg*)	(ex-A 1412)			
ALIAKMON	A 470	Blohm + Voss	30 July 1968	19 Oct 1994
(ex-*Saarburg*)	(ex-A 1415)			

Displacement, tons: 3,709 full load
Dimensions, feet (metres): 374.9 × 43.3 × 13.8 *(114.3 × 13.2 × 4.2)*
Main machinery: 2 MTU MD 16V 538 TB90 diesels; 6,000 hp(m) *(4.41 MW)* sustained; 2 shafts; cp props; bow thruster
Speed, knots: 17. **Range, n miles:** 3,200 at 14 kt
Complement: 71
Cargo capacity: 1,400 tons fuel; 200 tons ammunition; 130 tons water
Guns: 4 Bofors 40 mm/70 (2 twin); 300 rds/min to 12 km *(6.5 n miles)*; weight of shell 0.96 kg.
Radars: Navigation: Decca; I-band.

Comment: Both ships converted to Fleet oilers by Hellenic Shipyards. Contract signed 21 December 1999. *Axios* completed September 2000 and *Aliakmon* in December 2002.

ALIAKMON   *8/2002, A A de Kruijf* / 0525886

4 OURANOS CLASS (AOTL)

Name	No	Builders	Commissioned
OURANOS	A 416	Kinosoura Shipyard	27 Jan 1977
HYPERION	A 417	Kinosoura Shipyard	27 Apr 1977
ZEUS	A 375 (ex-A 490)	Hellenic Shipyards	21 Feb 1989
ORION	A 376	Hellenic Shipyards	5 May 1989

Displacement, tons: 2,100 full load
Dimensions, feet (metres): 219.8; 198.2 (wl) × 32.8 × 13.8 *(67; 60.4 × 10 × 4.2)*
Main machinery: 1 MAN-Burmeister & Wain 12V 20/27 diesel; 1,632 hp(m) *(1.2 MW)* sustained; 1 shaft
Speed, knots: 11
Complement: 28
Cargo capacity: 1,300 tons oil or petrol
Guns: 2 Rheinmetall 20 mm.

Comment: First two are oil tankers. The others were ordered from Hellenic Shipyards, Skaramanga in December 1986 and are used as petrol tankers. There are some minor superstructure differences between the first two and the last two which have a forward crane instead of kingposts.

ZEUS   *5/2001, E & M Laursen* / 0130738

HYPERION   *9/2001, A Sharma* / 0126326

6 WATER TANKERS (AWT)

KERKINI (ex-German FW 3) A 433	DOIRANI A 467
PRESPA A 434	KALLIROE A 468
TRICHONIS (ex-German FW 6) A 466	STIMFALIA A 469

Comment: All built between 1964 and 1990. Capacity, 600 tons except A 433 and A 466 which can carry 300 tons and A 469 which can carry 1,000 tons. Three in reserve. *Stimfalia* is similar to *Ouranos*. A 433 damaged in collision on 15 April 2002.

KALLIROE   *11/2004*, M Declerck* / 1133497

1 NETLAYER (ANL)

Name	No	Builders	Commissioned
THETIS (ex-AN 103)	A 307	Kröger, Rendsburg	Apr 1960

Displacement, tons: 680 standard; 805 full load
Dimensions, feet (metres): 169.5 × 33.5 × 11.8 *(51.7 × 10.2 × 3.6)*
Main machinery: Diesel-electric; 1 MAN GTV-40/60 diesel generator; 1 motor; 1,470 hp(m) *(1.08 MW)*; 1 shaft
Speed, knots: 12. **Range, n miles:** 6,500 at 10 kt
Complement: 48 (5 officers)
Guns: 1 Bofors 40 mm/60. 3 Rheinmetall 20 mm.
Radars: Navigation: Decca; I-band.

Comment: US offshore order. Launched in 1959. Some guns not always embarked.

THETIS   *9/1998, A Sharma* / 0052305

1 AMMUNITION SHIP (AEL)

Name	No	Builders	Commissioned
EVROS (ex-*Schwarzwald*, ex-*Amaltheé*)	A 415	Ch Dubigeon Nantes	7 June 1956

Displacement, tons: 2,400 full load
Measurement, tons: 1,667 gross
Dimensions, feet (metres): 263.1 × 39 × 15.1 *(80.2 × 11.9 × 4.6)*
Main machinery: 1 Sulzer 6SD60 diesel; 3,000 hp(m) *(2.2 MW)*; 1 shaft
Speed, knots: 15. **Range, n miles:** 4,500 at 15 kt
Guns: 4 Bofors 40 mm/60.

Comment: Bought by FDR from Société Navale Caënnaise in February 1960. Transferred to Greece 6 June 1976.

EVROS   *6/2005*, Hellenic Navy* / 1133500

2 AUXILIARY TRANSPORTS (AP)

Name	No	Builders	Commissioned
PANDORA	A 419	Perama Shipyard	26 Oct 1973
PANDROSOS	A 420	Perama Shipyard	1 Dec 1973

Displacement, tons: 390 full load
Dimensions, feet (metres): 153.5 × 27.2 × 6.2 *(46.8 × 8.3 × 1.9)*
Main machinery: 2 diesels; 2 shafts
Speed, knots: 12
Military lift: 500 troops
Radars: Navigation: Racal Decca; I-band.

Comment: Launched 1972 and 1973.

PANDROSOS *3/2004, Bob Fildes* / 1044257

4 TYPE 430A (TORPEDO RECOVERY VESSELS) (YPT)

EVROTAS (ex-TF 106) A 460 (ex-Y 872)   **STRYMON** (ex-TF 107) A 462 (ex-Y 873)
ARACHTHOS (ex-TF 108) A 461 (ex-Y 874)   **NESTOS** (ex-TF 4) A 463 (ex-Y 854)

Comment: First two acquired from Germany on 16 November 1989, second pair on 5 March 1991. Of about 56 tons with stern ramps for torpedo recovery. Built in 1966. A 461 ran aground on 20 June 2002.

TYPE 430A (German colours) *6/1998, Michael Nitz* / 0052255

2 LIGHTHOUSE TENDERS (ABUH)

Name	No	Builders	Commissioned
I KARAVOYIANNOS THEOPHILOPOULOS	A 479	Perama Shipyard	17 Mar 1976
ST LYKOUDIS	A 481	Perama Shipyard	2 Jan 1976

Displacement, tons: 1,450 full load
Dimensions, feet (metres): 207.3 × 38 × 13.1 *(63.2 × 11.6 × 4)*
Main machinery: 1 Deutz MWM TBD5008UD diesel; 2,400 hp(m) *(1.76 MW)*; 1 shaft
Speed, knots: 15
Complement: 40
Radars: Navigation: Racal Decca; I-band.
Helicopters: Platform for 1 light.

Comment: Similar to *Naftilos*, the survey ship.

I KARAVOYIANNOS THEOPHILOPOULOS *1/1999, van Ginderen Collection* / 0064674

TUGS

16 HARBOUR TUGS (YTM/YTL)

Name	No	Commissioned
ATROMITOS	A 410	1968
ADAMASTOS	A 411	1968
AIAS (ex-*Ankachak* YTM 767)	A 412	1972
PILEFS (ex-*Lütje Horn*)	A 413	1991
KADMOS	A 422	1989
NESTOR (ex-*Wahpeton*)	A 428	1989
PERSEUS	A 429	1989
GIGAS	A 432	1961
KEKROPS	A 435	1989
MINOS (ex-*Mellum*)	A 436	1991
PELIAS (ex-*Knechtsand*)	A 437	1991
AEGEUS (ex-*Schärhorn*)	A 438	1991
ATREFS (ex-*Ellerbek*)	A 439	1971
DIOMIDIS (ex-*Neuwerk*)	A 440	1963
THESEUS (ex-*Heppens*)	A 441	2000
ROMALEOS	A 442	2000

Comment: Some may be armed.

NESTOR *9/1998, M Declerck* / 0064675

PELIAS *1/2002, M Declerck* / 0525884

3 COASTAL TUGS (YTB)

HERAKLIS A 423   **IASON** A 424   **ODISSEUS** A 425

Displacement, tons: 345 full load
Dimensions, feet (metres): 98.5 × 26 × 11.3 *(30 × 7.9 × 3.4)*
Main machinery: 1 Deutz MWM diesel; 1,200 hp(m) *(882 kW)*; 1 shaft
Speed, knots: 12

Comment: Laid down 1977 at Perama Shipyard. Commissioned 6 April, 6 March and 28 June 1978 respectively.

IASON (with Gigas) *8/1997, A Sharma* / 0012482

For details of the latest updates to *Jane's Fighting Ships* online and to discover the additional information available exclusively to online subscribers please visit

jfs.janes.com

COAST GUARD (Limenikon Soma)

Senior Officers

Commander-in-Chief:
Vice Admiral Theodoros Glezakos
Deputy Commander-in-Chief:
Rear Admiral Ilias Sionides

Personnel

2006: 4,000 (1,055 officers)

Bases

HQ: Piraeus
Main bases: Piraeus, Eleusis, Thessalonika, Volos, Patra, Corfu, Rhodes, Mytilene, Heraklion (Crete), Chios, Kavala, Chalcis, Igoumenitsa, Rafina
Minor bases: Every port and island of Greece

Ships and Craft

In general very similar in appearance to naval ships, being painted grey. Since 1990 pennant numbers have been painted white and on both sides of the hull they carry a blue and white band with two crossed anchors. From 1993 ships have been given grey hulls and white superstructures.

Pennant Numbers

OPV: 010-090   FPB: 101-199   FPO: 210-299

General

This force consists of about 150 patrol craft and anti-pollution vessels including 24 inflatables for the 48 man Underwater Missions Squad and 12 anti-pollution vessels. Administration in peacetime is by the Ministry of Merchant Marine. In wartime it would be transferred to naval command. Officers are trained at the Naval Academy and ratings at two special schools.
The pennant numbers are all preceded as in the accompanying photographs by Greek 'Lambda Sigma' for Limenikon Soma.

Duties

The policing of all Greek harbours, coasts and territorial waters, navigational safety, SAR operations, anti-pollution surveillance and operations, supervision of port authorities, merchant navy training, inspection of Greek merchant ships worldwide.

Coast Guard Air Service

In October 1981 the Coast Guard acquired two Cessna Cutlass 172 RG aircraft and in July 1988 two Socata TB 20s. Maintenance and training by the Air Force. Based at Dekelia air base. Four Eurocopter Super Pumas AS 322C1 ordered in August 1998. First pair delivered in December 1999, second pair in May 2000. Being operated by mixed Air Force and Coast Guard crews. Bendix radar fitted. Three Reims Cessna Vigilant maritime patrol aircraft ordered in July 1999. First (F 406) delivered on 7 March 2001 and the other two in 2002. Six AS 365N3 Dauphin 2 helicopters were delivered in mid-2004.

Notes: Three 8 m Boston Whalers were donated by the US government on 26 June 2004.

3 + (1) SAAR 4 CLASS (LARGE PATROL CRAFT) (PB)

FOURNOI LS 060	RO LS 070	A G EFSTRATIOS LS 080

Displacement, tons: 415 standard; 450 full load
Dimensions, feet (metres): 190.6 × 25 × 8 *(58.0 × 7.8 × 2.4)*
Main machinery: 4 MTU 16V956 TB91 diesels; 15,000 hp(m) *(11.03 MW)* sustained; 4 shafts
Speed, knots: 32
Range, n miles: 1,650 at 30 kt; 4,000 at 17.5 kt
Complement: 30
Guns: 1—30 mm. 2—12.7 mm MGs.
Weapons control: Rafael DAFCO.
Radars: Air/Surface search: SIGNAAL variant; E/F-band.
Navigation: Bridgemaster; I-band.

Comment: Three vessels ordered in November 2002. The first two built at Israel Shipyards while the third assembled at Hellenic Shipyards, Skaramanga. The first vessel delivered 23 December 2003, the second in February 2004 and the third in April 2004. A fourth vessel may be ordered. Armament is to be fitted at a later date.

A G EFSTRATIOS   *7/2004, C D Yaylali* / 0583669

A G EFSTRATIOS   *7/2004, C D Yaylali* / 0583668

1 VOSPER EUROPATROL 250 MK 1 (PBF)

LS 050

Displacement, tons: 240 full load
Dimensions, feet (metres): 155.2 × 24.6 × 7.9 *(47.3 × 7.5 × 2.4)*
Main machinery: 3 GEC/Paxman Valenta 16CM diesels; 13,328 hp(m) *(9.8 MW)*; 3 shafts
Speed, knots: 40
Range, n miles: 2,000 at 16 kt
Complement: 21
Radars: Surface search: Racal Decca; I-band.

Comment: Ordered from McTay Marine, Bromborough in July 1993 and completed in November 1994. This is a Vosper International design with a steel hull and aluminium superstructure. Replenishment at sea facilities are provided by light jackstay and the ship carries a 45 kt RIB with water-jet propulsion. A continuous patrol speed of 4 kt is achievable using the centre shaft. Air conditioned accommodation. Similar craft built for the Bahamas. Fitted for a 40 mm gun but this is not carried. Transferred to the Coast Guard in 2004.

LS 050   *5/2004, Martin Mokrus* / 0587762

7 DILOS CLASS (WPB)

LS 010	LS 015	LS 020	LS 025	LS 030	LS 035	LS 040

Displacement, tons: 86 full load
Dimensions, feet (metres): 95.1 × 16.2 × 5.6 *(29 × 5 × 1.7)*
Main machinery: 2 MTU 12V 331 TC92 diesels; 2,660 hp(m) *(1.96 MW)* sustained; 2 shafts
Speed, knots: 27
Range, n miles: 1,600 at 24 kt
Complement: 18
Guns: 2 Rheinmetall 20 mm.
Radars: Surface search: Racal Decca 1226C; I-band.

Comment: Same Abeking and Rasmussen design as the three naval craft and built at Hellenic Shipyards in the early 1980s. Three former Customs craft transferred to the Coast Guard in 2004.

LS 010   *6/2002, C D Yaylali* / 0525872

4 INTERMARINE CRAFT (WPB)

LS 129-132

Displacement, tons: 25 full load
Dimensions, feet (metres): 53.8 × 14.8 × 7.5 *(16.4 × 4.5 × 2.3)*
Main machinery: 2 MAN diesels; 2,000 hp(m) *(1.47 MW)* sustained; 2 shafts
Speed, knots: 36

Comment: Constructed by Intermarine, La Spezia and delivered 1996-97.

39 COLVIC CRAFT (WPB)

LS 114-119   **LS 121-123**   **LS 125-128**   **LS 133**   **LS 137-161**

Displacement, tons: 24 full load
Dimensions, feet (metres): 54.1 × 15.4 × 4.6 *(16.5 × 4.7 × 1.4)*
Main machinery: 2 MAN D2840 LE 401 diesels; 1,644 hp(m) *(1.21 MW)* sustained; 2 shafts
Speed, knots: 34
Range, n miles: 500 at 25 kt
Complement: 5 (1 officer)
Guns: 1 — 12.7 mm MG. 1 — 7.62 mm MG.
Radars: Surface search: Raytheon; I-band.

Comment: Ordered from Colvic Craft, Colchester in 1993. Shipped to Motomarine, Glifada for engine and electronics installation. First 12 completed in mid-1994. The remainder delivered at about 12 per year from 1995. GRP hulls with a stern platform for recovery of divers. Later craft have a higher superstructure sited further forward. Two have been lost in accidents.

LS 119   *11/2004*, M Declerck* / 1133490

3 COMBATBOAT 90H (WPBF)

LS 134-136

Displacement, tons: 19 full load
Dimensions, feet (metres): 52.2 × 12.5 × 2.6 *(15.9 × 3.8 × 0.8)*
Main machinery: 2 Volvo Penta TAMD 163P diesels; 1,500 hp(m) *(1.1 MW)*; 2 waterjets
Speed, knots: 45
Range, n miles: 240 at 30 kt
Complement: 3
Guns: 3 — 12.7 mm MGs.
Radars: Surface search: I-band.

Comment: Built by Dockstavarvet in Sweden and delivered 6 July 1998. Same design as Swedish naval craft but with more powerful engines. GRP construction with armoured protection for cockpit.

LS 136   *7/2004, A Campanera i Rovira* / 0587761

16 OL 44 CLASS (WPB)

LS 55	**LS 95**	**LS 103**	**LS 109**
LS 65	**LS 97**	**LS 106**	**LS 110**
LS 84-88	**LS 101**	**LS 107**	**LS 112**

Displacement, tons: 14 full load
Dimensions, feet (metres): 44.9 × 14.4 × 2 *(13.7 × 4.4 × 0.6)*
Main machinery: 2 diesels; 630 hp(m) *(463 kW)*; 2 shafts
Speed, knots: 23
Complement: 4
Guns: 1 — 7.62 mm MG.
Radars: Surface search: JRC; I-band.

Comment: Built by Olympic Marine. GRP hulls.

LS 101   *5/2000, van Ginderen Collection* / 0104571

8 MOTORMARINE CRAFT (WPB)

LS 601-608

Displacement, tons: To be announced
Dimensions, feet (metres): To be announced
Main machinery: To be announced
Speed, knots: To be announced

Comment: Constructed by Motormarine, Koropi, Greece. *LS 601* delivered November 2003 and remainder by August 2004.

LS 601   *5/2004, Martin Mokrus* / 0587758

4 POLLUTION CONTROL SHIPS (YPC)

LS 401   **LS 413-415**

Displacement, tons: 230 full load
Dimensions, feet (metres): 95.1 × 20.3 × 8.2 *(29 × 6.2 × 2.5)*
Main machinery: 2 CAT 3512 DITA diesels; 2,560 hp(m) *(1.88 MW)* sustained; 2 shafts
Speed, knots: 15
Range, n miles: 500 at 13 kt
Complement: 12
Radars: Navigation: Furuno; I-band.

Comment: Details given are for *LS 413-415*. Built by Astilleros Gondan, Spain in collaboration with Motomarine. Delivered in 1993-94. *LS 401* is an older pollution control ship.

LS 401   *5/2004, Martin Mokrus* / 0587759

10 ARUN 60 CLASS (LIFEBOATS) (SAR)

SAR 511   **SAR 515**   **SAR 516**   **SAR 520**   **+6**

Displacement, tons: 34 tons full load
Dimensions, feet (metres): 59.0 × 17.4 × 4.9 *(18.0 × 5.3 × 1.5)*
Main machinery: 2 Caterpillar 3408 diesels; 2 shafts
Speed, knots: 18
Complement: 5

Comment: Built by Motormarine, Koropi, Greece. GRP hull moulded by Halmatic, UK. A stretched version of the lifeboat used in the UK and Canada. Entered service 1997-98.

SAR 520   *7/2005*, C D Yaylali* / 1133504

16 LS 51 CLASS (WPB)

LS 51	LS 52	LS 155-157	+ 11

Displacement, tons: 13 full load
Dimensions, feet (metres): 44 × 11.5 × 3.3 (13.4 × 3.5 × 1)
Main machinery: 2 diesels; 630 hp(m) (463 kW); 2 shafts
Speed, knots: 25. **Range, n miles:** 400 at 18 kt
Complement: 4
Guns: 1—7.62 mm MG.
Radars: Surface search: Racal Decca; I-band.

Comment: Built by Olympic Marine. GRP hulls.

60 COASTAL CRAFT AND 22 CRISS CRAFT

Comment: Included in the total are 20 of 8.2 m, 17 of 7.9 m, 26 of 5.8 m and 19 ex-US Criss craft. In addition the Coast Guard operates 24 Inflatable craft, and 10 SAR craft (LS 509-518).

LS 130   10/2002, E & M Laursen / 0533891

CUSTOMS

Notes: The Customs service also operates large numbers of coastal and inshore patrol. The craft have a distinctive Alpha Lambda (A/(GL)) on the hull and are sometimes armed with 7.62 mm MGs.

LS 214   7/2004, C D Yaylali / 0587760

AL 20   6/2002, C D Yaylali / 0525874

Grenada

Country Overview

Grenada gained independence in 1974; the British monarch, represented by a governor-general, is the head of state. The southernmost of the Windward Islands in the Lesser Antilles chain, the country comprises the island of Grenada (311 square miles) and some of the southern Grenadines including Carriacou and Petit Martinique. The capital, largest town, and main port is St George's. Territorial seas (12 n miles) are claimed. A 200 n mile Exclusive Economic Zone (EEZ) has been claimed but the limits are not defined. The Coast Guard craft are operated under the direction of the Commissioner of Police.

Headquarters Appointments

Coast Guard Commander:
    Assistant Superintendent Osmond Griffith

Personnel

2006: 30

Bases

Prickly Bay

COAST GUARD

Notes: A 920 Zodiac RHIB, donated by the US government, entered service in 2004.

1 GUARDIAN CLASS (COASTAL PATROL CRAFT) (PB)

Name	No	Builders	Commissioned
TYRREL BAY	PB 01	Lantana, Florida	21 Nov 1984

Displacement, tons: 90 full load
Dimensions, feet (metres): 105 × 20.6 × 7 (32 × 6.3 × 2.1)
Main machinery: 3 Detroit 12V-71TA diesels; 1,260 hp (939 kW) sustained; 3 shafts
Speed, knots: 24
Range, n miles: 1,500 at 18 kt
Complement: 15 (2 officers)
Guns: 2—12.7 mm MGs. 2—7.62 mm MGs.
Radars: Surface search: Furuno 1411 Mk II; I-band.

Comment: Similar to Jamaican and Honduras vessels. Aluminium construction. Refit in 1995/96.

LEVERA   9/1995, SeaArk Marine / 0064683

2 BOSTON WHALERS (PB)

Displacement, tons: 1.3 full load
Dimensions, feet (metres): 22.3 × 7.4 × 1.2 (6.7 × 2.3 × 0.4)
Main machinery: 2 outboards; 240 hp (179 kW)
Speed, knots: 40+
Complement: 4
Guns: 1—12.7 mm MG.

Comment: Acquired in 1988-89.

TYRREL BAY   11/1990, Bob Hanlon / 0064681

1 DAUNTLESS CLASS (PB)

Name	No	Builders	Commissioned
LEVERA	PB 02	SeaArk Marine	8 Sep 1995

Displacement, tons: 11 full load
Dimensions, feet (metres): 40 × 14 × 4.3 (12.2 × 4.3 × 1.3)
Main machinery: 2 Caterpillar 3208TA diesels; 870 hp (650 kW) sustained; 2 shafts
Speed, knots: 27
Range, n miles: 600 at 18 kt
Complement: 5
Guns: 1—7.62 mm MG.
Radars: Surface search: Raytheon R40X; I-band.

Comment: One of many of this type, provided by the US, throughout the Caribbean navies. Aluminium construction.

BOSTON WHALER   11/1990, Bob Hanlon / 0064682

Guatemala

Country Overview

The Republic of Guatemala is situated in Central America between Mexico to the north, Belize to the east and Honduras and El Salvador to the south-east. With an area of 42,042 square miles, it has an 83 n mile coastline with the Caribbean and a 133 n mile coastline with the Pacific Ocean. The capital city is Guatemala City while the principal Caribbean ports are Puerto Barrios and Santo Tomás de Castilla and Pacific ports are Puerto Quetzal, San José and Champerico. Territorial seas (12 n miles) are claimed.

A 200 n mile EEZ has been claimed but the limits are not defined.

Headquarters Appointments

Commander of the Navy:
    Captain Luis Job Garcia Reyes
Commander Caribbean Naval Region:
    Captain Celwin Eduardo Castro Alvarado
Commander Pacific Naval Region:
    Captain Carlos Rene Alvarado Fernandez

Personnel

(a) 2006: 1,250 (130 officers) including 500 Marines (2 battalions) (mostly volunteers)
(b) 2¼ years' national service

Bases

Pacific: Puerto Quetzal (HQ), Puerto San Jose, Champerico
Atlantic: Santo Tomás de Castillo (HQ), Puerto Barrios, Livingston

---

PATROL FORCES

Notes: (1) There is also a naval manned Ferry *15 de Enero* (T 691) and a 69 ft launch *Orca* which was built locally in 1996/97.
(2) Three sail training craft, *Mendieta*, *Margarita* and *Ostuncalco* are based at Santo Thomás de Castilla.
(3) Two launches were reported donated by the Guatemalan government and the US Embassy in 2005.
(4) There are two 11 m personnel landing craft *Picuda* and *Barracuda*.

1 BROADSWORD CLASS (COASTAL PATROL CRAFT) (PB)

Name	No	Builders	Commissioned
KUKULKÁN	GC 1051 (ex-P 1051)	Halter Marine	4 Aug 1976

Displacement, tons: 90.5 standard; 110 full load
Dimensions, feet (metres): 105 × 20.4 × 6.3 *(32 × 6.2 × 1.9)*
Main machinery: 2 Detroit 8V 92TA Model 91; 1,300 hp *(970 kW)*; 2 shafts
Speed, knots: 22
Range, n miles: 1,150 at 20 kt
Complement: 20 (5 officers)
Guns: 2 Oerlikon GAM/204 GK 20 mm. 2—7.62 mm MGs.
Radars: Surface search: Furuno; I-band.

Comment: As the flagship she used to rotate between Pacific and Atlantic bases every two years but has remained in the Pacific since 1989. Rearmed with 20 mm guns in 1989. These were replaced by GAM guns in 1990-91 when the ship received a new radar. Refitted again in 1996 with new engines.

KUKULKÁN   *12/2004*, Julio Montes* / 1129555

2 SEWART CLASS (COASTAL PATROL CRAFT) (PB)

Name	No	Builders	Commissioned
UTATLAN	GC 851 (ex-P 851)	Sewart, Louisiana	May 1967
SUBTENIENTE OSORIO SARAVIA	GC 852 (ex-P 852)	Sewart, Louisiana	Nov 1972

Displacement, tons: 54 full load
Dimensions, feet (metres): 85 × 18.7 × 7.2 *(25.9 × 5.7 × 2.2)*
Main machinery: 2 Detroit 8V 92TA Model 91; 1,300 hp *(970 kW)*; 2 shafts
Speed, knots: 22. **Range, n miles:** 400 at 12 kt
Complement: 17 (4 officers)
Guns: 1 Oerlikon GAM/204 GK 20 mm. 2—7.62 mm MGs.
Radars: Surface search: Furuno; I-band.

Comment: Aluminium superstructure. Both rearmed with 20 mm guns, and 75 mm recoilless removed in 1990. P 851 is based in the Atlantic; P 852 in the Pacific. Refitted in 1995-96 with new engines.

SUBTENIENTE OSORIO SARAVIA   *12/2004*, Julio Montes* / 1129556

6 CUTLASS CLASS
(5 COASTAL PATROL CRAFT AND 1 SURVEY CRAFT) (PB)

Name	No	Builders	Commissioned
TECUN UMAN	GC 651 (ex-P 651)	Halter Marine	26 Nov 1971
KAIBIL BALAN	GC 652 (ex-P 652)	Halter Marine	8 Feb 1972
AZUMANCHE	GC 653 (ex-P 653)	Halter Marine	8 Feb 1972
TZACOL	GC 654 (ex-P 654)	Halter Marine	10 Mar 1976
BITOL	GC 655 (ex-P 655)	Halter Marine	4 Aug 1976
GUCUMAZ	BH 656 (ex-GC 656)	Halter Marine	15 May 1981

Displacement, tons: 45 full load
Dimensions, feet (metres): 64.5 × 17 × 3 *(19.7 × 5.2 × 0.9)*
Main machinery: 2 Detroit 8V 92TA Model 91 diesels; 1,300 hp *(970 kW)*; 2 shafts
Speed, knots: 25. **Range, n miles:** 400 at 15 kt
Complement: 10 (2 officers)
Guns: 2 Oerlikon GAM/204 GK 20 mm. 2 or 3—12.7 mm MGs.
Radars: Surface search: Furuno; I-band.

Comment: First five rearmed with 20 mm guns in 1991. P 651, 654 and 655 are in the Atlantic, remainder in the Pacific. Aluminium hulls. *Gucumaz* was used as a survey craft but by 1996 was again serving as a patrol craft with three MGs. Reverted to survey craft in 2004. 654 and 656 refitted in 1994-95, remainder in 1995-97. New engines fitted.

GUCUMAZ   *12/2004*, Julio Montes* / 1129558

AZUMANCHE   *12/2004*, Julio Montes* / 1129557

1 DAUNTLESS CLASS (PB)

IXIMCHE

Displacement, tons: 11 full load
Dimensions, feet (metres): 40 × 12.66 × 2.3 *(12.19 × 3.86 × 0.69)*
Main machinery: 2 Caterpillar 3208TA diesels; 850 hp *(635 kW)*; 2 shafts
Speed, knots: 28. **Range, n miles:** 400 at 22 kt
Complement: 5
Guns: 1—7.62 mm MG.
Radars: Surface search: Raytheon R40X; I-band.

Comment: Built by SeaArk, Monticello, of aluminium construction. Donated by US government as foreign aid in 1997.

DAUNTLESS CLASS (Cayman Islands colours)   *6/2001*, RCIS* / 0121305

6 VIGILANTE CLASS (PBI)

GC 271-276

Displacement, tons: 3.5 full load
Dimensions, feet (metres): 26.6 × 10 × 1.8 *(8.1 × 3 × 0.5)*
Main machinery: 2 Evinrude outboards; 600 hp *(448 kW)*
Speed, knots: 40+
Complement: 4
Guns: 1 — 12.7 mm MG.
Radars: Surface search: Furuno; I-band.

Comment: Ordered in 1993 from Boston Whaler. Delivered in 1994 and divided three to each coast.

20 RIVER PATROL CRAFT (PBR)

Group A	Group B	Group C	Group D
DENEB	LAGO DE ATITLAN	CHOCHAB	MERO
SIRIUS	MAZATENANGO	ALIOTH	SARDINA
PROCYON	RETALHULEU	MIRFA	PAMPANA
VEGA	ESCUINTLA	SCHEDAR	MAVRO-I
POLLUX		COMAMEFA	
SPICA			
STELLA MARIS			

Comment: Group A are wooden hull craft with a speed of 19 kt. Group B have aluminium hulls and a speed of 28 kt. Group C are probably of Israeli design and Group D are commercial craft caught smuggling and confiscated. All can be armed with 7.62 mm MGs and are used by Marine battalions as well as the Navy.

GC 275   *12/1999* / 0104574

CHOCHAB AND COMAMEFA   *2/1996, Julio Montes* / 0064686

Guinea

Country Overview

A former French colony, The Republic of Guinea became independent in 1958. Located in west Africa, the country has an area of 94,926 square miles, a 173 n mile coastline with the Atlantic Ocean and includes the Iles de Los. It is bordered to the north by Guinea-Bissau and Senegal and to the south by Liberia and Sierra Leone. The capital, largest city and principal port is Conakry. Territorial seas (12 n miles) are claimed. A 200 n mile Exclusive Economic Zone (EEZ) has been claimed but the limits have not been formally agreed. Fishery Protection may be provided by civilian contractors.

Personnel

(a) 2006: 400 officers and men
(b) 2 years' conscript service

Bases

Conakry, Kakanda

Notes: A number of craft, including two Bogomol, two Stinger and two Swiftships (*Vigilante* P 300 and *Intrepide* P 328) are laid up alongside. Some of these might be resurrected to combat piracy problems in the region. A Damen 13 m patrol boat, *Matakang*, is reported to have been delivered in 1999.

Guinea-Bissau

Country Overview

A former Portuguese colony, The Republic of Guinea-Bissau gained independence in 1974. Located in west Africa, the country has an area of 13,948 square miles, a 189 n mile coastline with the Atlantic Ocean and includes about 60 offshore islands, among them the Bijagós (Bissagos) Islands. It is bordered to the north by Senegal and to the south by Guinea. The capital, largest city and principal port is Bissau. Other ports include Cacheu and Bolama. Territorial seas (12 n miles) are claimed. A 200 n mile Exclusive Economic Zone (EEZ) has been claimed and has been partially defined by boundary agreements.

Personnel

(a) 2006: 310 officers and men
(b) Voluntary service

Base

Bissau

Maritime Aircraft

A Cessna 337 patrol aircraft is used for offshore surveillance, when serviceable.

PATROL FORCES

Notes: One Rodman R 800 8.7 m patrol craft with a speed of 28 kt acquired in 1999.

2 ALFEITE TYPE (COASTAL PATROL CRAFT) (PC)

Name	No	Builders	Commissioned
CACINE	LF 01	Arsenal do Alfeite	9 Mar 1994
CACHEU	LF 02	Arsenal do Alfeite	9 Mar 1994

Displacement, tons: 55 full load
Dimensions, feet (metres): 64.6 × 19 × 10.6 *(19.7 × 5.8 × 3.2)*
Main machinery: 3 MTU 12V 183 TE92 diesels; 3,000 hp(m) *(2.2 MW)* maximum; 3 Hamilton MH 521 water-jets
Speed, knots: 28
Complement: 9 (1 officer)
Radars: Navigation: Furuno FR 2010; I-band.

Comment: Ordered from Portugal in 1991. GRP hulls. Used for fishery protection patrols and customs duties. They are the only vessels regularly reported at sea.

CACHEU
3/1994, Arsenal do Alfeite
0064688

Guyana

Country Overview

Formerly known as British Guiana, the Cooperative Republic of Guyana became an independent state in 1966. With an area of 83,000 square miles it has borders to the east with Suriname, to the west with Venezuela and to the south with Brazil; its 248 n mile coastline is on the Atlantic Ocean. The capital, largest city and chief port is Georgetown. Territorial seas (12 n miles) and a fisheries zone (200 n miles) are claimed. A 200 n mile Exclusive Economic Zone (EEZ) has also been claimed but the limits are not defined. Rebuilding of the Coast Guard started in 2001.

Headquarters Appointments

Commanding Officer, Coast Guard:
Commander Terrence Pile

Personnel

(a) 2006: 30 plus 160 reserves
(b) Voluntary service

Bases

Georgetown, Benab (Corentyne)

PATROL FORCES

4 TYPE 44 CLASS (WPB)

BARRACUDA	HYMANA	PIRAI	TIRAPUKA

Displacement, tons: 18 full load
Dimensions, feet (metres): 44 × 12.8 × 3.6 *(13.5 × 3.9 × 1.1)*
Main machinery: 2 Detroit 6V-38 diesels; 185 hp *(136 kW)*; 2 shafts
Speed, knots: 14
Range, n miles: 215 at 10 kt
Complement: 3

Comment: Acquired from the US and recommissioned on 9 August 2003.

1 RIVER CLASS (COASTAL PATROL CRAFT) (PBO)

Name	No	Builders	Commissioned
ESSEQUIBO (ex-*Orwell*)	1026 (ex-M 2011)	Richards, Great Yarmouth	27 Nov 1985

Displacement, tons: 890 full load
Dimensions, feet (metres): 156 × 34.5 × 9.5 *(47.5 × 10.5 × 2.9)*
Main machinery: 2 Ruston 6 RKC diesels; 3,100 hp(m) *(2.3 MW)* sustained; 2 shafts
Speed, knots: 14
Range, n miles: 4,500 at 10 kt
Complement: 32 (4 officers)
Guns: 1 Bofors 40 mm/60.
2 — 7.62 mm MGs.
Radars: Surface search: 2 Racal Decca TM 1226C; I-band.

Comment: Ex-UK River class transferred on 22 June 2001 having previously been employed as patrol ship and then officers' training ship.

TYPE 44 (Uruguay Colours)   *5/2000, Hartmut Ehlers* / 0105801

ESSEQUIBO   *7/2001, Derek Fox* / 0114272

Honduras

FUERZA NAVAL REPUBLICA

Country Overview

The Republic of Honduras is one of the largest Central American republics. With an area of 43,433 square miles, it is situated between El Salvador and Guatemala to the west and Nicaragua to the south and east. It has a 350 n mile coastline with the Caribbean and a 93 n mile coastline with the Pacific Ocean. The capital and largest city is Tegucigalpa while the principal Caribbean ports are La Ceiba and Puerto Cortés and Pacific port is Amapala. Territorial seas (12 n miles) are claimed. A 200 n mile EEZ is claimed and has been partly defined by boundary agreements.

Headquarters Appointments

Commanding Officer, General HQ:
Capitan de Navio D E M N Rolando Gonzalez Flores

Personnel

2006: 1,100 including 450 marines

Bases

Tegucigalpa (General HQ)
Puerto Cortés, Puerto Castilla (Atlantic HQ), Amapala (Pacific HQ), La Ceiba, Puerto Trujillo

PATROL FORCES

Notes: (1) In addition there may be three Piranha river craft still in limited service.
(2) Five 23 m catamarans reported to have been ordered in 2004.
(3) Two 11 m personnel landing craft are used for anti-drug operations.

3 SWIFT 105 ft CLASS (FAST ATTACK CRAFT — GUN) (PB)

GUAYMURAS FNH 101	HONDURAS FNH 102	HIBUERAS FNH 103

Displacement, tons: 111 full load
Dimensions, feet (metres): 105 × 23.6 × 7 *(32 × 7.2 × 2.1)*
Main machinery: 2 MTU 16V 538 TB90 diesels; 6,000 hp(m) *(4.4 MW)* sustained; 2 shafts
Speed, knots: 30
Range, n miles: 1,200 at 18 kt
Complement: 17 (3 officers)
Guns: 6 Hispano-Suiza 20 mm (2 triple). 2 — 12.7 mm MGs.
Weapons control: Kollmorgen 350 optronic director.
Radars: Surface search: Furuno; I-band.

Comment: First delivered by Swiftships, Morgan City in April 1977 and last two in March 1980. Aluminium hulls. Armament changed 1996-98.

HONDURAS and HIBUERAS
12/2004, *Julio Montes*
1129559

1 GUARDIAN CLASS (COASTAL PATROL CRAFT) (PB)

TEGUCIGALPA FNH 104 (ex-FNH 107)

Displacement, tons: 94 full load
Dimensions, feet (metres): 106 × 20.6 × 7 *(32.3 × 6.3 × 2.1)*
Main machinery: 3 Detroit 16V-92TA diesels; 2,070 hp *(1.54 MW)* sustained; 3 shafts
Speed, knots: 30. **Range, n miles:** 1,500 at 18 kt
Complement: 17 (3 officers)
Guns: 1 General Electric Sea Vulcan 20 mm Gatling.
3 Hispano Suiza 20 mm (1 triple). 2—12.7 mm MGs.
Weapons control: Kollmorgen 350 optronic director.
Radars: Surface search: Furuno; I-band.

Comment: Delivered by Lantana Boatyard, Florida August 1986. Second of class, *Copan*, no longer in service. A third of the class, completed in May 1984, became the Jamaican *Paul Bogle*. Aluminium hulls. Operational status doubtful.

GUARDIAN CLASS   *7/1986, Giorgio Arra* / 0506000

6 SWIFT 65 ft CLASS (COASTAL PATROL CRAFT) (PB)

NACAOME (ex-*Aguan*, ex-*Gral*) FNH 651	**ULUA** FNH 654
GOASCORAN (ex-*General J T Cabanas*) FNH 652	**CHOLUTECA** FNH 655
PATUCA FNH 653	**RIO COCO** FNH 656

Displacement, tons: 33 full load
Dimensions, feet (metres): 69.9 × 17.1 × 5.2 *(21.3 × 5.2 × 1.6)*
Main machinery: 2 GM 12V-71TA diesels; 840 hp *(627 kW)* sustained; 2 shafts (FNH 651-2)
2 MTU 8V 396TB93 diesels; 2,180 hp(m) *(1.6 MW)* sustained; 2 shafts (FNH 653-5)
Speed, knots: 25 (FNH 651-2); 36 (FNH 653-6). **Range, n miles:** 2,000 at 22 kt (FNH 651-2)
Complement: 9 (2 officers)
Guns: 2—12.7 mm MGs. 3—7.62 mm MGs.
Radars: Surface search: Racal Decca; I-band.

Comment: First pair built by Swiftships, Morgan City originally for Haiti. Contract cancelled and Honduras bought the two that had been completed in 1973-74. Delivered in 1977. Last four ordered in 1979 and delivered 1980.

PATUCA   *5/1993* / 0064690

1 SWIFT 85 ft CLASS (COASTAL PATROL CRAFT) (PB)

CHAMELECON (ex-*Rio Kuringwas*) FNH 8501

Displacement, tons: 60 full load
Dimensions, feet (metres): 85 × 20 × 5 *(25.9 × 6.1 × 1.8)*
Main machinery: 2 Detroit diesels; 2 shafts
Speed, knots: 25
Complement: 10 (2 officers)
Radars: Surface search: Racal/Decca; I-band.

Comment: Built by Swiftships, Morgan City in about 1967 for Nicaragua from where it was transferred in 1979.

CHAMELECON   *2000, Honduran Navy* / 0105811

5 OUTRAGE CLASS (RIVER PATROL CRAFT) (PBR)

Displacement, tons: 2.2 full load
Dimensions, feet (metres): 24.9 × 7.9 × 1.3 *(7.6 × 2.4 × 0.4)*
Main machinery: 2 Evinrude outboards; 300 hp *(224 kW)*
Speed, knots: 30. **Range, n miles:** 200 at 30 kt
Complement: 4
Guns: 1—12.7 mm MG. 2—7.62 mm MGs.
Radars: Navigation: Furuno 3600; I-band.

Comment: Built by Boston Whaler in 1982. Seven deleted so far. Radar is sometimes embarked.

OUTRAGE   *10/1997, Julio Montes* / 0012491

15 RIVER CRAFT (PBR)

Comment: 4.6 m craft acquired from Taiwan in 1996. Nine based at Castilla, three at Cortes and three at Amapala. Single Mercury outboard engine. Carry a 7.62 mm MG. Three sunk in 1998.

PBR   *10/1997, R Torrento* / 0012492

AUXILIARIES

Notes: In addition there are two ex-US LCM 8 (*Warunta* FNH 7401, *Tansin* FNH 7402) transferred in 1987. Both are used as transport vessels.

LCM 8   *2000, Honduran Navy* / 0105812

1 LANDING CRAFT (LCU)

PUNTA CAXINAS FNH 1491

Displacement, tons: 625 full load
Dimensions, feet (metres): 149 × 33 × 6.5 *(45.4 × 10 × 2)*
Main machinery: 3 Caterpillar 3412 diesels; 1,821 hp *(1.4 MW)* sustained; 3 shafts
Speed, knots: 14. **Range, n miles:** 3,500 at 12 kt
Complement: 18 (3 officers)
Cargo capacity: 100 tons equipment or 50,000 gallons dieso plus 4 standard containers
Radars: Navigation: Furuno 3600; I-band.

Comment: Ordered in 1986 from Lantana, Florida, and commissioned in May 1988.

PUNTA CAXINAS   *12/2004*, Julio Montes* / 1129560

Hong Kong

POLICE MARINE REGION

Country Overview

Formerly a British colony, the Hong Kong Special Administrative Region of China reverted to Chinese sovereignty on 30 June 1997. While China has assumed responsibility for foreign affairs and defence, the territory is to maintain its own legal, social, and economic systems until at least 2047. Hong Kong comprises three main regions, Hong Kong Island (29 sq miles), Kowloon Peninsula and Stonecutters Island (6 sq miles) and the New Territories (380 sq miles). As with the remainder of China, territorial seas (12 n miles) are claimed. An EEZ (200 n mile) is also claimed but the limits have not been defined by boundary agreements. The role of the Marine Police is to maintain the integrity of the sea boundary and territorial waters of Hong Kong, enforce the laws of Hong Kong in territorial waters, prevent illegal immigration by sea, SAR in territorial and adjacent waters, and casualty evacuation.

Headquarters Appointments

Regional Commander:
  Au Hok-Lam
Deputy Regional Commander:
  Kong Shing-shun

Organisation

Marine Police Regional HQ, Sai Wan Ho
Bases at Ma Liu Shui, Tui Min Hoi, Tai Lam Chung, Aberdeen, Sai Wan Ho

Personnel

(a) 2006: 2,600
(b) Voluntary service

DELETIONS

2004 PL 63, PL 65
2005 PL 67, PL 68

POLICE

Notes: The naming of craft has been discontinued.

2 SURVEILLANCE BARGES (YAG)

PB 1-2

Displacement, tons: 227
Dimensions, feet (metres): 98.4 × 42.6 × 2.6 *(30.0 × 13 × 0.8)*
Main machinery: 2 Onan 75 MDGDB
Complement: 10
Radars: Surface search: Decca; I-band.

Comment: Steel-hulled barges constructed by Bonny Fair Ltd and delivered in June 2002. Permanently moored in Deep Bay.

PB 1 *6/2004, Hong Kong Police* / 0589752

1 TRAINING VESSEL (WAX)

PL 3

Displacement, tons: 420 full load
Dimensions, feet (metres): 131.2 × 28.2 × 10.5 *(40 × 8.6 × 3.2)*
Main machinery: 2 Caterpillar 3512TA diesels; 2,420 hp *(1.81 MW)* sustained; 2 shafts
Speed, knots: 14. **Range, n miles:** 1,500 at 14 kt
Complement: 7
Radars: Surface search: 2 Racal Decca ARPA C342/8; I-band.

Comment: Built by Hong Kong SY in 27 July 1987 and commissioned 1 February 1988. Steel hull. Racal ARPA and GPS Electronic Chart system. 12.7 mm MGs removed in mid-1996. Can carry up to 30 armed police for short periods. Former command vessel converted to a training role.

PL 3 *6/2004, Hong Kong Police* / 0589753

6 KEKA CLASS (PATROL CRAFT) (WPB)

PL 60-65

Displacement, tons: 105
Dimensions, feet (metres): 98.4 × 20.6 × 5.6 *(30.0 × 6.3 × 1.7)*
Main machinery: 2 MTU 12V-396 TE 84 diesels
Speed, knots: 25. **Range, n miles:** 360 at 15 kt
Complement: 14
Radars: Surface search: Decca; I-band.

Comment: Aluminium-hulled craft built by Cheoy Lee Shipyards Ltd to replace Damen Mk1 class patrol craft. Delivered in 2002, 2004 and 2005.

PL 62 *6/2004, Hong Kong Police* / 0589751

14 DAMEN MK III CLASS (PATROL CRAFT) (WPB)

PL 70-80   PL 82-84

Displacement, tons: 95 full load
Dimensions, feet (metres): 87 × 19 × 6 *(26.5 × 5.8 × 1.8)*
Main machinery: 2 MTU 12V 396 TC82 diesels; 2,610 hp(m) *(1.92 MW)* sustained; 2 shafts
  1 Mercedes-Benz OM 424A 12V diesel; 341 hp(m) *(251 kW)* sustained; 1 Kamewa 45 water-jet
Speed, knots: 26 on 3 diesels; 8 on water-jet and cruising diesel
Range, n miles: 600 at 14 kt
Complement: 14
Radars: Surface search: Racal Decca; I-band.

Comment: Steel-hulled craft constructed by Chung Wah SB & Eng Co Ltd, 1984-85. 12.7 mm MGs removed in mid-1996.

PL 76 *6/2004, Hong Kong Police* / 0589750

6 PROTECTOR (ASI 315) CLASS
(COMMAND/PATROL CRAFT) (WPB)

PL 51-56

Displacement, tons: 170 full load
Dimensions, feet (metres): 107 × 26.9 × 5.2 *(32.6 × 8.2 × 1.6)*
Main machinery: 2 Caterpillar 3516TA diesels; 4,400 hp *(3.28 MW)* sustained; 2 shafts; 1 Caterpillar 3412TA; 1,860 hp *(1.24 MW)* sustained; Hamilton jet (centreline); 764 hp *(570 kW)*
Speed, knots: 30. **Range, n miles:** 600 at 18 kt
Complement: 19
Weapons control: GEC V3901 optronic director.
Radars: Surface search: Racal Decca; I-band.

Comment: Built by Australian Shipbuilding Industries and completed in 1993. As well as patrol work, the craft provide command platforms for Divisional commanders. 12.7 mm guns removed in 1996 and the optronic director is used for surveillance only.

PL 52 *6/2004, Hong Kong Police* / 0589749

7 HARBOUR PATROL CRAFT (WPB)

PL 11-17

Displacement, tons: 36 full load
Dimensions, feet (metres): 52.5 × 15.1 × 4.9 *(16 × 4.6 × 1.5)*
Main machinery: 2 Cummins NTA-855-M diesels; 700 hp *(522 kW)* sustained; 2 shafts
Speed, knots: 12
Complement: 6
Radars: Surface search: Racal Decca; I-band.

Comment: Built by Chung Wah SB & Eng Co Ltd in 1986-87.

PL 14   *6/2005*, Chris Sattler* / 1127927

5 SEA STALKER 1500 CLASS (INTERCEPTOR CRAFT) (HSIC)

PL 85-89

Displacement, tons: 7.5 full load
Dimensions, feet (metres): 48.6 × 9.5 × 2.6 *(14.8 × 2.9 × 0.8)*
Main machinery: 3 Innovation Marine Sledge Hammers; 1,500 hp(m) *(1.1 MW)*; 3 shafts
Speed, knots: 60; 45 in Sea State 3
Complement: 5
Radars: Surface search: Raytheon; I-band.

Comment: Built by Damen, Gorinchem in 1999. Used by the Small Boat Division.

PL 86   *6/2004, Hong Kong Police* / 0589746

4 SEASPRAY CLASS (LOGISTIC CRAFT) (YFB)

PL 46-49

Displacement, tons: 10.7 full load
Dimensions, feet (metres): 37.4 × 13.8 × 3.9 (11.4 × 4.2 × 1.2)
Main machinery: 2 Caterpillar 3208TA diesels; 550 hp *(410 kW)* sustained; 2 shafts
Speed, knots: 32
Complement: 4
Radars: Navigation: Koden; I-band.

Comment: Built by Seaspray Boats, Fremantle in 1992. Catamaran hulls capable of carrying 16 police officers.

PL 47   *6/2005*, Chris Sattler* / 1127926

11 SEASPRAY CLASS (INSHORE PATROL CRAFT) (WPB)

PL 22-32

Displacement, tons: 8.7 full load
Dimensions, feet (metres): 32.5 × 13.8 × 4.3 *(9.9 × 4.2 × 1.3)*
Main machinery: 2 Caterpillar 3208TA diesels; 680 hp *(508 kW)*; 2 shafts
Speed, knots: 35
Complement: 4
Radars: Surface search: Koden; I-band.

Comment: Built by Seaspray Boats, Fremantle in 1992-93.

PL 22   *6/2004, Hong Kong Police* / 0589744

9 INSHORE PATROL CRAFT (WPB)

PL 20-21   **PL 90-92**   **PL 93-96**

Displacement, tons: 4.5
Dimensions, feet (metres): 27 × 9.2 × 1.6 *(8.3 × 2.8 × 0.5)*
Main machinery: 2 outboards; 540 hp *(403 kW)*
Speed, knots: 40+
Complement: 4
Radars: Surface search: Koden; I-band.

Comment: Details given are for *PL 20-21* which are Sharkcat class of catamaran construction, commissioned in October 1988. *PL 90-92* are Boston Whaler Guardians with 2 Johnson 115 hp outboards, and *PL 93-96* are Boston Whaler Vigilants with 2 Johnson 250 hp outboards. The Whalers were all delivered in 1997 and are capable of speeds in excess of 33 kt.

PL 93   *6/2004, Hong Kong Police* / 0589743

6 CHEOY LEE CLASS (INSHORE PATROL CRAFT) (WPB)

PL 40-45

Displacement, tons: 15
Dimensions, feet (metres): 42.9 × 13 × 2.3 *(13.07 × 3.96 × 0.7)*
Main machinery: 2 MAN D2842LE403 diesels; 720 hp *(537 kW)* sustained; 2 Hamilton water-jets
Speed, knots: 35
Complement: 4
Radars: Surface search: Bridgemaster E 180; I-band.

Comment: Based upon a design from Peterson Shipbuilders, these shallow draft vessels were constructed by Cheoy Lee Shipyards Ltd and delivered in 2000.

PL 43   *6/2004, Hong Kong Police* / 0589742

8 HIGH SPEED INTERCEPTORS (HSIC)

PV 30-37

Displacement, tons: 2.7 full load
Dimensions, feet (metres): 28.3 × 8.7 × 2.4 *(8.5 × 2.6 × 0.7)*
Main machinery: 2 Mercury outboards; 500 hp *(373 kW)*
Speed, knots: 51
Complement: 3

Comment: Built by Queensland Ships in 1997. Used by the Small Boat Division.

PV 36   *6/2005*, Chris Sattler* / 1127925

CUSTOMS (HSIC)

Headquarters Appointments

Senior Superintendent Ports and Marine Command:
  Li Chun-fai

Notes: The Marine Enforcement Group is based at Stonecutters Island. There are five Sector Command launches. Three Damen 26 m craft were completed in 1986 by Chung Wah SB & Eng Co Ltd, Kowloon. In all essentials these craft are sisters of the 14 operated by the Hong Kong Police with the exception of the latter's slow speed waterjet. Names: *Sea Glory* (Customs 6), *Sea Guardian* (Customs 5), *Sea Leader* (Customs 2). Two 32 m launches, *Sea Reliance* (Customs 8) and *Sea Fidelity* (Customs 9) were commissioned in October 2000. With a gross tonnage of 125 tonnes, the craft have a maximum speed of 28 kt. Equipped with a 'sea-rider' they are also fitted with night vision aids and narcotics and explosives scanning devices. There are also two shallow water launches, eight inflatable boats and four fast pursuit craft.

SEA FIDELITY *3/2003, Bob Fildes* / 0568853

FAST PURSUIT CRAFT CE 15 *6/2005*, Ports and Maritime Command* / 1129999

LAND-BASED MARITIME AIRCRAFT

Notes: All aircraft belong to the Government Flying Service based at Hong Kong International Airport.

Numbers/Type: 2 BAE Jetstream J 41.
Operational speed: 260 kt *(482 km/h)*.
Service ceiling: 26,000 ft *(7,925 m)*.
Range: 774 n miles *(1,433 km)*.
Role/Weapon systems: SAR (command and control), airborne surveillance, survey and photography. Sensors: Radar, FLIR, survey camera, VHF/UHF/DF.

Jetstream *6/2005*, Government Flying Service* / 1127924

Numbers/Type: 3 Eurocopter AS 332 L2 Super Puma. (HSIC)
Operational speed: 130 kt *(240 km/h)*.
Service ceiling: 15,090 ft *(4,600 m)*.
Range: 672 n miles *(1,245 km)*.
Role/Weapon systems: SAR/coastal surveillance, Medevac and transport. Sensors: radar, Spectrolab searchlight. Weapons: Unarmed. Medical equipment and up to six stretchers. Ordered on 17 September 1999. The aircraft entered service in April 2002.

AS 332 *6/2005*, Government Flying Service* / 1127922

Numbers/Type: 4 Eurocopter EC 155B1.
Operational speed: 140 kt *(260 km/h)*.
Service ceiling: 16,760 ft *(5,110 m)*.
Range: 432 n miles *(800 km)*.
Role/Weapon systems: SAR, Medevac, VIP transport; enlarged variant of 'Dauphin'. Sensors: Radar, FLIR, searchlight, siren, loudspeaker. Weapons: Unarmed. Two stretchers. Ordered on 17 September 1999; aircraft delivered in late 2002.

EC 155 *6/2005*, Government Flying Service* / 1127923

Hungary

Country Overview

A landlocked central European country, the Republic of Hungary has an area of 35,919 square miles and is bordered by Slovakia, Ukraine, Romania, Yugoslavia, Croatia, Slovenia and Austria. Budapest is the country's capital and largest city. The country is divided into two general regions by the principal river, the Danube, which flows for 145 n miles north-south through the centre of the country and serves as a major artery of the transport system.

Diplomatic Representation

Defence Attaché in London:
  Lieutenant Colonel Árpád Ibolya

Personnel

(a) 2006: 17 (1 officer)
(b) National service replaced by a professional army on 3 November 2004.

Bases

Budapest.

MINE WARFARE FORCES

3 NESTIN CLASS (RIVER MINESWEEPERS) (MSR)

ÓBUDA AM 22   DUNAÚJVÁROS AM 31   DUNAFOLDVAR AM 32

Displacement, tons: 72.3 full load
Dimensions, feet (metres): 87.1 × 21.3 × 3.9 *(26.5 × 6.5 × 1.2)*
Main machinery: 2 Torpedo 12-cyl diesels; 520 hp(m) *(382 kW)*; 2 shafts
Speed, knots: 15. **Range, n miles:** 810 at 11 kt
Complement: 17 (1 officer)
Guns: 6 Hispano 20 mm (1 quad M75 fwd, 2 single M70 aft).
Mines: 24 ground mines.
Radars: Navigation: Decca 101; I-band.

Comment: Built by Brodotehnika, Belgrade in 1979-80. Full magnetic/acoustic and wire sweeping capabilities. Kram minesweeping system employs a towed sweep at 200 m. The ships form the first 'Honved' Ordnance Disposal and Warship Regiment.

ÓBUDA *10/1998, Hungary Maritime Wing* / 0064703

Iceland
LANDHELGISGAESLAN

Country Overview

An island republic, the Republic of Iceland lies just south of the Arctic Circle in the North Atlantic Ocean about 162 n miles southeast of Greenland and 432 n miles northwest of Scotland. With an area of 39,769 square miles, the country has a 2,695 n mile coastline. Reykjavík is the capital, largest city and principal port. Territorial waters (12 n miles) are claimed. A 200 n mile Exclusive Economic Zone (EEZ) has also been claimed although the limits are not fully defined by boundary agreements. The Coast Guard Service deals with fishery protection, salvage, rescue, security, pollution control, hydrographic research, lighthouse duties and bomb disposal.

Headquarters Appointments

Director of Coast Guard:
  Commodore Georg K Lárusson

Personnel

2006: 128 officers and men

Colours

Since 1990 vessels have been marked with red, white and blue diagonal stripes on the ships' side and the Coast Guard name (Landhelgisgaeslan).

Bases

Reykjavík

Research Ships

A number of government Research Ships bearing RE pennant numbers operate off Iceland.

Research Ships

Maritime aircraft include a Fokker Friendship plus AS 332 Super Puma, Dauphin 2 and Ecureuil helicopters

---

COAST GUARD

Notes: Plans to replace *Odinn* are under consideration.

2 AEGIR CLASS (PSOH)

Name	No	Builders	Commissioned
AEGIR	—	Aalborg Vaerft, Denmark	1968
TYR	—	Dannebrog Vaerft, Denmark	15 Mar 1975

Displacement, tons: 1,128 (1,214 *Tyr*) standard; 1,500 full load
Dimensions, feet (metres): 229.1 (233.4 *Tyr*) × 32.8 × 15.1 *(69.8 (71.1) × 10.0 × 4.6)*
Main machinery: 2 MAN/Burmeister & Wain 8L 40/54 diesels; 13,200 hp(m) *(9.68 MW)* sustained; 2 shafts; cp props
Speed, knots: 19 *(Aegir)*; 20 *(Tyr)*. **Range, n miles:** 9,000 at 18 kt
Complement: 19
Guns: 1 Bofors 40 mm/60 Mk 3.
Radars: Surface search/navigation: Sperry; E/F/I-band.

Comment: Similar ships but *Tyr* has a slightly improved design and *Aegir* has no sonar. The hangar is between the funnels. In 1994 a large crane was fitted on the starboard side at the forward end of the flight deck. In 1997 the helicopter deck was extended and a radome fitted on the top of the tower. *Aegir* refitted in Poland in 2005 and *Tyr* in 2006. Work includes extension and modernisation of the bridge area.

AEGIR   *10/2004** / 1129561

1 BALDUR CLASS (AGS)

Name	No	Builders	Commissioned
BALDUR	—	Vélsmiöja Seyöisfjaröar	8 May 1991

Displacement, tons: 54 full load
Dimensions, feet (metres): 67.9 × 17.1 × 5.6 *(20.7 × 5.2 × 1.7)*
Main machinery: 2 Caterpillar 3406TA diesels; 640 hp *(480 kW)*; 2 shafts
Speed, knots: 12
Complement: 5
Radars: Navigation: Furuno; I-band.

Comment: Built in an Icelandic Shipyard. Used for survey work.

BALDUR   *6/2005*, Iceland Coast Guard* / 1153888

1 ODINN CLASS (PSOH)

Name	No	Builders	Commissioned
ODINN	—	Aalborg Vaerft, Denmark	Jan 1960

Displacement, tons: 910 standard; 1,200 full load
Dimensions, feet (metres): 209.0 × 33 × 13 *(63.7 × 10 × 4)*
Main machinery: 2 MAN/Burmeister & Wain diesels; 5,700 hp(m) *(4.19 MW)*; 2 shafts
Speed, knots: 18
Range, n miles: 9,500 at 17 kt

Complement: 19
Guns: 1 Bofors 40 mm/60 Mk 3.
Radars: Surface search/navigation: Sperry; E/F/I-band.

Comment: Refitted in Denmark in late 1975 by Aarhus Flydedock AS with a hangar and helicopter deck which was later adapted in 1989 for the operation of RHIB inspection craft; a crane was fitted at the starboard forward end of the flight deck. The original 57 mm gun was replaced in 1990.

ODINN   *2/2002, L-G Nilsson* / 0561502

India

Country Overview

The Republic of India is a federal democracy which gained independence in 1947. It consists of the entire Indian peninsula and parts of the Asian mainland. With an area of 1,269,219 square miles, it is bordered to the north by Pakistan, Tibet, Nepal, China, and Bhutan and to the east by Burma and Bangladesh, which almost separates north-east India from the rest of the country. The status of Jammu and Kashmir is disputed with Pakistan. It has a 4,104 n mile coastline with the Arabian Sea, the Gulf of Mannar (which separates it from Sri Lanka) and the Bay of Bengal. The capital is New Delhi while the largest city is Mumbai. The principal ports include Mumbai, Calcutta, Madras and Vishakapatnam. Territorial waters (12 n miles) are claimed. A 200 n mile EEZ has been claimed although the limits have only been partly defined by boundary agreements.

Headquarters Appointments

Chief of Naval Staff:
Admiral Arun Prakash, PVSM, AVSM, VrC, VSM
Vice Chief of Naval Staff:
Vice Admiral Venkat Bharathan, PVSM, AVSM, VSM
Deputy Chief of Naval Staff:
Vice Admiral Jagjit Singh Bedi, UYSM, AVSM, VSM
Chief of Personnel:
Vice Admiral Nirmal Verma
Chief of Material:
Vice Admiral Datla Sai Prasad Varma

Senior Appointments

Flag Officer Commanding Western Naval Command:
Vice Admiral Sangram Singh Byce
Flag Officer Commanding Eastern Naval Command:
Vice Admiral Sureesh Mehta, AVSM
Flag Officer Commanding Southern Naval Command:
Vice Admiral Satish Chandra Suresh Bangara
Commander-in-Chief, Andaman and Nicobar:
Vice Admiral Arun Kumar Singh, PVSM, AVSM, NM
Flag Officer Commanding Western Fleet:
Rear Admiral Rustom Faramroze Contractor, AVSM, NM
Flag Officer Commanding Eastern Fleet:
Rear Admiral Sunil K Damle
Flag Officer, Naval Aviation and Goa Area (at Goa):
Rear Admiral Shekar Sinha
Flag Officer, Submarines (Vishakapatnam):
Rear Admiral Krishan Nair Sushil, NM
Flag Officer, Sea Training:
Rear Admiral Vijai Singh Chaudhari

Personnel

(a) 2006: 53,000 (7,500 officers) (including 5,000 Naval Air Arm and 2,000 Marines)
(b) Voluntary service
(c) The Marine Commando Force was formed in 1986.

Naval Air Arm

Squadron	Aircraft	Role
300 (Goa)	Sea Harrier FRS. Mk 51	Fighter/Strike
310 (Goa)	Dornier 228	MRMP
312 (Madras)	Tu-142M 'Bear F'	LRMP/ASW
315 (Goa)	Il-38 May	LRMP/ASW
318 (Goa)	Dornier 228	MRMP
321 (Mumbai)	HAL Chetak	Utility/SAR

Naval Air Arm—*continued*

Squadron	Aircraft	Role
330 (Kochi)	Sea King Mk 42B	ASW
333 (ships) (Goa)	Kamov Ka-28 'Helix'	ASW
336 (Kochi)	Sea King Mk 42A/42B	ASW
339 (Mumbai)	Ka-28 'Helix', Ka-31	ASW/ASVW/AEW
550 (Kochi)	Dornier 228, PBN Defender, Deepak	Training
551 A (Goa)	Kiran Mk I/II	Training
551 B (Goa)	Sea Harrier T Mk 60	Training
552 (Goa)	Sea Harrier T Mk 60	Training
561 (Kochi)	HAL Chetak, Hughes 300	Training

Air Stations

Name	Location	Role
INS *Kunjali*	Mumbai	Helicopters
INS *Garuda*	Willingdon Island, Kochi	Helicopters
INS *Hansa*	Goa	HQ Flag Officer Naval Air Stations, LRMP, Strike/Fighter
	Karwar	Fleet Support
INS *Utkrosh*	Port Blair, Andaman Isles	Maritime Patrol Maritime Patrol Maritime Patrol
INS *Dega*	Vishakapatnam	Fleet support and maritime patrol
INS *Rajali*	Arakonam	LRMP, Helo Training
NAS *Ramnad*	Bangalore	LRMP Naval Air Technical School

Prefix to Ships' Names

INS

Colour Scheme

Surface ship colour scheme was changed from dark grey to light grey in 2004.

Bases and Establishments

Note: Bombay is now referred to as Mumbai, Cochin as Kochi and Madras as Chennai.

New Delhi, Integrated HQ of Ministry of Defence (Navy).
Mumbai, C-in-C **Western Command**, barracks and main Dockyard; with one 'Carrier' dock. Submarine base (INS *Vajrabahu*). Supply school (INS *Hamla*). The region includes Mazagon and Goa shipyards.
Vishakapatnam, C-in-C **Eastern Command**, submarine base (INS *Virbahu*), submarine school (INS *Satyavahana*) and major dockyard built with Soviet support and being extended. Naval Air Station (INS *Dega*). Marine Gas Turbine maintenance facility (INS *Eksila*). New entry training (INS *Chilka*). At Thirunelveli is the submarine VLF W/T station completed in September 1986. Facilities at Chennai and Calcutta. The region includes Hindustan and Garden Reach shipyards.
Kochi, C-in-C **Southern Command**, Naval Air Station, and professional schools (INS *Venduruthy*) (all naval training comes under Southern Command). Ship repair yard. Gunnery Training establishment (INS *Dronacharya*).
There are also limited support facilities including a floating dock at Port Blair in the Andaman Islands.
Goa is HQ Flag Officer Naval Aviation.

Bases and Establishments—*continued*

Karwar (near Goa) is the site for a new naval base; first phase was opened on 31 May 2005 and operations began on 15 December 2005. Alongside berthing for Aircraft Carriers and a naval air station are planned. At Lakshadweep in the Laccadive Islands there is a patrol craft base.
Shipbuilding: Mumbai (submarines, destroyers, frigates, corvettes); Calcutta (frigates, corvettes, LSTs, auxiliaries); Goa (patrol craft, LCU, MCMV facility planned). Vishakapatnam (corvettes, patrol craft).

Marine Commando Force (MCF)

The MCF was formed in 1987. Known as MARCOS, elements are based in the three regional commands. The force is trained in counter-terrorism operations.

Coast Defence

Truck-mounted SS-3-C Styx missiles. At least seven fixed sites.
UAV Squadrons: to be based at Porbandar, Port Blair and Kochi.

Strength of the Fleet

Type	Active	Building (Projected)
Attack Submarine (SSN)	—	2
Patrol Submarines	16	6
Aircraft Carriers	1	2
Destroyers	8	3
Frigates	13	3 (3)
Corvettes	25	6
Patrol Ships	6	—
Patrol Craft	13	(2)
LPD	—	(1)
LST	3	1 (1)
LCM	11	—
Minesweepers-Ocean	12	—
Minesweepers-Inshore	2	—
Minehunters	—	(8)
Research and Survey Ships	11	—
Training Ships	4	—
Submarine Tender	1	—
Diving Support/Rescue Ship	1	—
Replenishment Tankers	3	(1)
Transport Ships	3	—
Support Tankers	6	—
Water Carriers	2	—
Ocean Tugs	1	—

DELETIONS

Frigates

2005 *Himgiri*

Patrol Forces

2003 *Anjadip*
2004 *Sindhudurg*
2005 *Tarmugli* (Seychelles), *Tillan Chang* (Maldives)

Mine Warfare Forces

2003 *Mulki, Malvan*
2004 *Mangrol*

PENNANT LIST

Submarines

S 40	Vela
S 42	Vagli
S 44	Shishumar
S 45	Shankush
S 46	Shalki
S 47	Shankul
S 55	Sindhughosh
S 56	Sindhudhvaj
S 57	Sindhuraj
S 58	Sindhuvir
S 59	Sindhuratna
S 60	Sindhukesari
S 61	Sindhukirti
S 62	Sindhuvijay
S 63	Sindhurakshak
S 64	Sindhushastra

Aircraft Carriers

R 22	Viraat

Destroyers

D 51	Rajput
D 52	Rana
D 53	Ranjit
D 54	Ranvir
D 55	Ranvijay
D 60	Mysore
D 61	Delhi
D 62	Mumbai

Frigates

F 20	Godavari
F 21	Gomati
F 22	Ganga
F 31	Brahmaputra
F 35	Udaygiri
F 36	Dunagiri
F 37	Beas
F 39	Betwa
F 40	Talwar
F 41	Taragiri
F 42	Vindhyagiri
F 43	Trishul
F 44	Tabar
F 46	Krishna (training)

Corvettes

P 33	Abhay
P 34	Ajay
P 35	Akshay
P 36	Agray
P 44	Kirpan
P 46	Kuthar
P 47	Khanjar
P 49	Khukri
P 61	Kora
P 62	Kirch
P 63	Kulish
P 64	Karmukh
K 40	Veer
K 41	Nirbhik
K 42	Nipat
K 43	Nishank
K 44	Nirghat
K 45	Vibhuti
K 46	Vipul
K 47	Vinash
K 48	Vidyut
K 83	Nashak
K 91	Pralaya
K 92	Prabal
K 98	Prahar

Patrol Forces

P 50	Sukanya
P 51	Subhadra
P 52	Suvarna
P 53	Savitri
P 55	Sharada
P 56	Sujata

Mine Warfare Forces

M 61	Pondicherry
M 62	Porbandar
M 63	Bedi
M 64	Bhavnagar
M 65	Alleppey
M 66	Ratnagiri
M 67	Karwar
M 68	Cannanore
M 69	Cuddalore
M 70	Kakinada
M 71	Kozhikode
M 72	Konkan
M 83	Mahé
M 86	Malpe

Amphibious Forces

L 17	Sharabh
L 18	Cheetah
L 19	Mahish
L 20	Magar
L 21	Guldar
L 22	Kumbhir
L 23	Gharial
L 34	—
L 35	—
L 36	—
L 37	—
L 38	—
L 39	—

Auxiliaries and Survey Ships

—	Nicobar
—	Andamans
A 15	Nireekshak
A 53	Matanga
A 54	Amba
A 57	Shakti
A 58	Jyoti
A 59	Aditya
A 72	Torpedo Recovery Vessel
A 74	Sagardhwani
A 75	Tarangini
A 86	Tir
J 14	Nirupak
J 15	Investigator
J 16	Jamuna
J 17	Sutlej
J 18	Sandhayak
J 19	Nirdeshak
J 21	Darshak
J 22	Sarvekshak
J 33	Meen
J 34	Mithun

Seaward Defence Forces

T 58	—
T 59	—
T 61	Trinkat
T 63	Tarasa
T 65	Bangaram
T 66	Bitra
T 67	Batti Malv
T 68	Baratang
J 33	Meen
J 34	Mithun

SUBMARINES

Notes: (1) The Advanced Technology Vessel (ATV) project was initiated in the 1980s. In addition to traditional SSN/SSGN functions, the boat is likely to have a strategic role and, to this end, may also be capable of deploying nuclear-tipped cruise or ballistic missiles in addition to torpedo-tube launched conventional anti-ship and land-attack missiles. Prithvi III, a navalised version of the short-range ballistic missile, was successfully launched at Balasore on 27 October 2004 and the delayed Sagarika cruise missile is also a possibility. Currently led by Vice Admiral Bhasin, the ATV project has facilities in Delhi, Hyderabad, Vishakapatnam and Kalpakkam (where the PWR reactor reportedly achieved criticality in December 2004). Companies in support of the project are reported to be Larsen and Toubro at Hazira, Mazagon Dock Ltd and Bharat Electronics. It is believed that the submarine is a development of a Russian design, derived either from the Project 885 Severodvinsk class SSGN or more probably from the Victor/Akula class generation. The nuclear propulsion system is understood to be an Indo-Russian PWR although reports that it may be a Russian supplied VM-5 PWR have also circulated. In parallel, negotiations for the lease-purchase of one or two nuclear-powered submarines from Russia are believed to be under consideration. Uncertainty remains, however, over key programme dates and given the complexities involved, it is unlikely that the ATV will enter service before 2012. Up to five of the class are expected by 2025.

(2) India has been reported to be interested in the Russian Amur 1650 class SSK. This may also be known as Project 78.

(3) India operates up to 11 Cosmos CE2F/FX100 swimmer delivery vehicles, delivered in 1991.

(4) The upgrade of facilities at Vishakapatnam to undertake refit work on Kilo class submarines is reportedly under consideration.

(5) Procurement of at least two Deep Sea Rescue Vehicles (DSRV) was reported to be in progress in 2005. The Indian Navy currently lacks this capability and would have to rely upon another country, probably the United States, in the event of a submarine emergency.

0 + 6 SCORPENE CLASS (SSK)

Displacement, tons: 1,705 dived
Dimensions, feet (metres): 217.8 × 20.3 × 19
(66.4 × 6.2 × 5.8)
Main machinery: Diesel electric; 4 MTU 16V 396 SE84 diesels; 2,992 hp(m) *(2.2 MW)*; 1 Jeumont Schneider motor; 3,808 hp(m) *(2.8 MW)*; 1 shaft
Speed, knots: 20 dived; 11 surfaced
Range, n miles: 550 at 4 kt dived; 6,500 at 8 kt surfaced
Complement: 31 (6 officers)

Missiles: MBDA Exocet SM 39.
Torpedoes: 6—21 in *(533 mm)* tubes.
Countermeasures: ESM.
Weapons control: UDS International SUBTICS.
Radars: Navigation: Sagem; I-band.
Sonars: Hull mounted; active/passive search and attack, medium frequency.

Programmes: Project 75. Following protracted negotiations which began in 2002, a contract for the licensed production of six submarines at Mazagon Dock Ltd, Mumbai, was signed on 6 October 2005. Building is expected to start in 2006 with full delivery to be achieved by 2017. The agreement is reported to include an option for a further nine boats. Armaris is to supply technical advisers and provide prefabricated hull elements and the combat systems, including the command system, underwater sensors, optronics, and communications. MBDA is to supply Exocet SM39 missiles as part of the package. Details are based on the boats built for Chile. AIP is not to be installed in the first two boats but a reassessment for the remaining submarines will be made at a later date.
Structure: Diving depth more than 300 m *(984 ft)*.

SCORPENE (computer graphic)   *1998, DCN* / 0017689

2 FOXTROT (PROJECT 641) CLASS (SS)

Name	No	Builders	Commissioned
VELA	S 40	Sudomekh, Leningrad	Aug 1973
VAGLI	S 42	Sudomekh, Leningrad	Aug 1974

Displacement, tons: 1,952 surfaced; 2,475 dived
Dimensions, feet (metres): 299.5 × 24.6 × 19.7
(91.3 × 7.5 × 6)
Main machinery: Diesel-electric; 3 Type 37-D diesels; 6,000 hp(m) *(4.4 MW)*; 3 motors (1 × 2,700 and 2 × 1,350); 5,400 hp(m) *(3.97 MW)*; 3 shafts; 1 auxiliary motor; 140 hp(m) *(103 kW)*
Speed, knots: 16 surfaced; 15 dived

Range, n miles: 20,000 at 8 kt surfaced; 380 at 2 kt dived
Complement: 75 (8 officers)

Torpedoes: 10—21 in *(533 mm)* (6 fwd, 4 aft) tubes. 22 SET-65E/SAET-60; active/passive homing to 15 km *(8.1 n miles)* at 40 kt; warhead 205 kg.
Mines: 44 in lieu of torpedoes.
Countermeasures: ESM: Stop Light; radar warning.

Radars: Surface search: Snoop Tray; I-band.
Sonars: Herkules/Fenik; bow-mounted; passive search and attack; medium frequency.

Structure: Diving depth 250 m *(820 ft)*, reducing with age.
Operational: Survivors of an original eight of the class. *Vela* completed refit in 2004. *Vela* is part of the 8th Submarine Squadron at Vishakapatnam. *Vagli* is based at Mumbai.

FOXTROT   *2/2001, Guy Toremans* / 0105814

4 SHISHUMAR (209) CLASS (TYPE 1500) (SSK)

Name	No	Builders	Laid down	Launched	Commissioned
SHISHUMAR	S 44	Howaldtswerke, Kiel	1 May 1982	13 Dec 1984	22 Sep 1986
SHANKUSH	S 45	Howaldtswerke, Kiel	1 Sep 1982	11 May 1984	20 Nov 1986
SHALKI	S 46	Mazagon Dock Ltd, Mumbai	5 June 1984	30 Sep 1989	7 Feb 1992
SHANKUL	S 47	Mazagon Dock Ltd, Mumbai	3 Sep 1989	21 Mar 1992	28 May 1994

Displacement, tons: 1,450 standard; 1,660 surfaced; 1,850 dived
Dimensions, feet (metres): 211.2 × 21.3 × 19.7 *(64.4 × 6.5 × 6)*
Main machinery: Diesel-electric; 4 MTU 12V 493 AZ80 GA31L diesels; 2,400 hp(m) *(1.76 MW)* sustained; 4 Siemens alternators; 1.8 MW; 1 Siemens motor; 4,600 hp(m) *(3.38 MW)* sustained; 1 shaft
Speed, knots: 11 surfaced; 22 dived. **Range, n miles:** 8,000 snorting at 8 kt; 13,000 surfaced at 10 kt
Complement: 40 (8 officers)

Torpedoes: 8—21 in *(533 mm)* tubes. 14 AEG SUT Mod 1; wire-guided; active/passive homing to 28 km *(15.3 n miles)* at 23 kt; 12 km *(6.6 n miles)* at 35 kt; warhead 250 kg.
Mines: External 'strap-on' type for 24 mines.
Countermeasures: Decoys: C 303 acoustic decoys. ESM: Argo Phoenix II AR 700 or Kollmorgen Sea Sentry; radar warning.
Weapons control: Singer Librascope Mk 1.
Radars: Surface search: Thomson-CSF Calypso; I-band.
Sonars: Atlas Elektronik CSU 83; active/passive search and attack; medium frequency. TSM 2272 to be fitted. Thomson Sintra DUUX-5; passive ranging and intercept.

Programmes: Howaldtswerke concluded an agreement with the Indian Navy on 11 December 1981. This was in four basic parts: the building in West Germany of two Type 1500 submarines; the supply of 'packages' for the building of two more boats at Mazagon, Mumbai; training of various groups of specialists for the design and construction of the Mazagon pair; logistic services during the trials and early part of the commissions as well as consultation services in Mumbai. In 1984 it was announced that a further two submarines would be built at Mazagon for a total of six but this was overtaken by events in 1987-88 and the agreement with HDW terminated at four. This was reconsidered in 1992 and again in 1997. Government approval was given in mid-1999 for the construction of further submarines.
Modernisation: Thomson Sintra Eledone sonars may be fitted in due course. Trials for integration of indigenous Panchendriya ATAS developed by NPOL are in progress in Karanj.

Structure: The Type 1500 has a central bulkhead and an IKL designed integrated escape sphere which can carry the full crew of up to 40 men, has an oxygen supply for 8 hours, and can withstand pressures at least as great as those that can be withstood by the submarine's pressure hull. Diving depth 260 m *(853 ft)*.
Operational: Form 10th Submarine Squadron based at Mumbai. *Shishumar* mid-life refit started in 1999 and had been completed by 2001. *Shankul* was undergoing refit in 2005.

SHALKI *2/2001, Sattler/Steele* / 0121373

SHISHUMAR *2/2001, Guy Toremans* / 0105813

10 SINDHUGHOSH (KILO) (PROJECT 877EM/8773) CLASS (SSK)

Name	No	Builders	Commissioned
SINDHUGHOSH	S 55	Sudomekh, Leningrad	30 Apr 1986
SINDHUDHVAJ	S 56	Sudomekh, Leningrad	12 June 1987
SINDHURAJ	S 57	Sudomekh, Leningrad	20 Oct 1987
SINDHUVIR	S 58	Sudomekh, Leningrad	16 May 1988
SINDHURATNA	S 59	Sudomekh, Leningrad	19 Nov 1988
SINDHUKESARI	S 60	Sudomekh, Leningrad	19 Dec 1988
SINDHUKIRTI	S 61	Sudomekh, Leningrad	9 Dec 1990
SINDHUVIJAY	S 62	Sudomekh, Leningrad	17 Dec 1990
SINDHURAKSHAK	S 63	Sudomekh, St Petersburg	24 Dec 1997
SINDHUSHASTRA	S 64	Sudomekh, St Petersburg	19 July 2000

Displacement, tons: 2,325 surfaced; 3,076 dived
Dimensions, feet (metres): 238.2 × 32.5 × 21.7 *(72.6 × 9.9 × 6.6)*
Main machinery: Diesel-electric; 2 Model 4-2AA-42M diesels; 3,650 hp(m) *(2.68 MW)*; 2 generators; 1 motor; 5,900 hp(m) *(4.34 MW)*; 1 shaft; 2 MT-168 auxiliary motors; 204 hp(m) *(150 kW)*; 1 economic speed motor; 130 hp(m) *(95 kW)*
Speed, knots: 10 surfaced; 17 dived; 9 snorting
Range, n miles: 6,000 at 7 kt snorting; 400 at 3 kt dived
Complement: 52 (13 officers)

Missiles: SLCM Novator Alfa Klub SS-N-27 (3M-54E1) (S 55, 57, 59, 60 and 64); active radar homing to 180 km *(97.2 n miles)* at 0.7 Mach (cruise) and 2.5 Mach (attack); warhead 450 kg.
SAM: SA-N-8 portable launcher; IR homing to 3.2 n miles *(6 km)*.
Torpedoes: 6—21 in *(533 mm)* tubes. Combination of Type 53—65; passive wake homing to 19 km *(10.3 n miles)* at 45 kt; warhead 305 kg and TEST 71/96; anti-submarine; active/passive homing to 15 km *(8.1 n miles)* at 40 kt or 20 km *(10.8 n miles)* at 25 kt; warhead 220 kg. Total of 18 weapons. Wire-guided on 2 tubes.
Mines: 24 DM-1 in lieu of torpedoes.

Countermeasures: ESM: Squid Head; radar warning.
Weapons control: Uzel MVU-119EM TFCS.
Radars: Navigation: Snoop Tray; I-band.
Sonars: Shark Teeth/Shark Fin; MGK-400; hull-mounted; active/passive search and attack; medium frequency. Mouse Roar; MG-519; hull-mounted; active search; high frequency.

Programmes: The Kilo class was launched in the former Soviet Navy in 1979 and although India was the first country to acquire one they have since been transferred to Algeria, Poland, Romania, Iran and China. Because of the slowness of the S 209 programme, the original order in 1983 for six Kilo class expanded to 10 but was then cut back again to eight. Two further orders were confirmed in May 1997. S 63 was a spare Type 877 hull built for the Russian Navy, but never purchased. S 64 is a Type 8773 and is fitted for SLCM. She was launched on 14 October 1999. Plans to manufacture the class under licence in India have probably been abandoned in favour of an AMUR 1650 programme.
Modernisation: An engine change is probable during major refits in Russia which started in 1997. A tube launched SLCM capability is also part of the refit. A German designed main battery with a five year life has replaced Russian batteries in all of the class. Battery cooling has been improved.
Structure: Diving depth, 300 m *(985 ft)*. Reported that from *Sindhuvir* onwards these submarines have an SA-N-8 SAM capability. The launcher is shoulder held and stowed in the fin for use when the submarine is surfaced. Two torpedo tubes can fire wire-guided torpedoes and four tubes have automatic reloading. Anechoic tiles are fitted on casings and fins.
Operational: First four form the 11th Submarine Squadron. Based at Vishakapatnam and the remainder of the 12th Squadron based at Mumbai. *Sindhuvir* completed major refit at Severodvinsk from May 1997 to July 1999. *Sindhuraj* and *Sindhukesari* completed similar refits at Admiralty Yard, St Petersburg from May 1999 to November 2001. *Sindhuratna* completed a two-year refit at Severodvinsk in 2002. *Sindhughosh*, following refit work at Vishakapatnam from 1999, started modernisation at Severodvinsk in September 2002 which completed on 22 April 2005. She became the fifth boat to be fitted with SS-N-27. *Sindhuvijay* started a two-year refit at Severodvinsk in May 2005 which is expected to be completed in 2007. Future Kilo class refits may be carried out at Vishakapatnam. All SLCM armed boats may be based in the Western Fleet in future.

SINDHURATNA *10/2002, Diego Quevedo* / 0529550

SINDHURAJ *11/2001, Michael Nitz* / 0534072

AIRCRAFT CARRIERS

0 + 1 MODIFIED KIEV CLASS (PROJECT 1143.4) (CVGM)

Name	Builders	Laid down	Launched	Commissioned
VIKRAMADITYA (ex-*Admiral Gorshkov*, ex-*Baku*)	Nikolayev South	17 Feb 1978	1 Apr 1982	11 Jan 1987

Displacement, tons: 45,400 full load
Dimensions, feet (metres): 928.5 oa; 818.6 wl × 167.3 oa; 107.3 wl × 32.8 *(283; 249.5 × 51; 32.7 × 10)*
Main machinery: 8 KWG4 boilers; 4 GTZA 674 turbines; 200,000 hp(m) *(147 MW)*; 4 shafts
Speed, knots: 29.
Range, n miles: 13,800 at 18 kt
Complement: 1,200 plus aircrew

Missiles: SAM/Guns: 6 CADS-N-1 (Kortik/Kashtan) (3M 87).
Countermeasures: Decoys: 2 PK2 chaff launchers; 2 towed torpedo decoys.
ESM/ECM: Bharat intercept and jammers.
Combat data systems: To be announced.
Radars: Air search: Plate Steer.
Surface search: 2 Strut Pair.
Navigation: Aircraft control.
Sonars: Horse Jaw (MG 355); hull-mounted; active search; medium frequency.

Fixed-wing aircraft: 12 MiG 29K.
Helicopters: 6 Helix 27/28/31.

Programmes: Last of the four Project 1143.4 aircraft carriers built for the Soviet Navy. First offered for sale to India by Russia in 1994. By 1999 the proposal was to gift the ship as long as India pays for the refit. Following a Government to Government agreement on 4 October 2000 and protracted negotiations, contract signed on 20 January 2004 for a five-year refit at a cost estimated to be US$625 million. Most of the work is being undertaken at Severodvinsk and final outfitting is to be undertaken at Cochin. A contract for the procurement of 16 MiG-29 aircraft was also signed in 2004.
Modernisation: New propulsion, power and air conditioning systems to be fitted. All the original Russian weapons systems removed and to be replaced by six Kashtan

VIKRAMADITYA (artist's impression)   *10/2004, Nevskoye Design Bureau* / 1042276

SAM/gun systems. The flight deck is to be converted to a STOBAR configuration with a 14.3° ski-jump.
Structure: The ship has a 198 m angled deck with three arrestor wires. Flight deck lifts are 19.2 × 10.3 m and

18.5 × 4.7 m, and can lift 30 tons (aft) and 20 tons (midships) respectively. The hangar is 130 × 22.5 m.
Operational: The ship is expected to become operational in 2009 and to be based at Karwar.

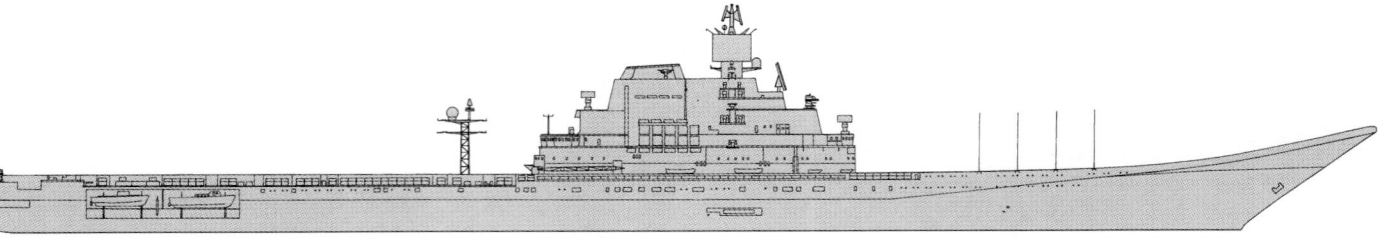

VIKRAMADITYA   *(Scale 1 : 1,500), Ian Sturton* / 1042091

0 + 1 AIR DEFENCE SHIP CLASS (PROJECT 71) (CVM)

Name	No	Builders	Laid down	Launched	Commissioned
—	—	Kochi Shipyard Ltd	2006	2010	2013

Displacement, tons: 37,500 full load
Dimensions, feet (metres): 826.8 oa; 770.1 wl × 190.3 oa; 106.6 wl × 27.6 *(252.3; 235 × 58.0; 32.5 × 8.4)*
Main machinery: 4 General Electric LM 2500 gas turbines; 120,000 hp *(89.5 MW)*; 2 shafts
Speed, knots: 28. **Range, n miles:** 7,500 at 18 kt
Complement: 1,400 (160 officers)

Missiles: SAM.
Guns: CIWS.
Radars: Air search; surface search; fire control.
Sonars: Hull mounted.

Fixed-wing aircraft: 12 MiG-29K.
Helicopters: 10 Ka-31 and ALH.

Programmes: The plan announced in 1989 was to build two new aircraft carriers. The indigenously-built Air Defence Ship (ADS) is to replace the former *Vikrant* while the *Vikramaditya* (ex-*Admiral Gorshkov*) is to replace *Viraat* in 2008. A number of international companies including DCN, IZAR and Fincantieri are believed to have been involved in conceptual and design work of the ADS and it is understood that the shipbuilder, Cochin Shipyard Ltd (CSL), has sub-contracted specialist 'task forces' to collaborate

in building the ship. Two contracts signed in mid-2004 with Fincantieri to finalise the ADS design and its ancillary propulsion systems and main power plants. Fincantieri is likely to provide further assistance during the vessel's construction, tests and sea trials. First steel cut on 11 April 2005 and formal keel-laying is expected in 2006.
Structure: All details are still speculative and the diagrams show an indicative design including a short take off (with 14° ski jump) and arrested recovery (STOBAR) system. The ADS is to have a similar propulsion system as the *Cavour* being built for the Italian Navy.

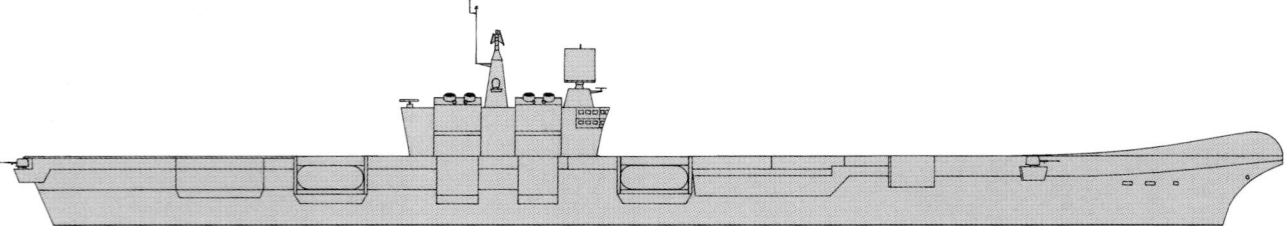

PROJECT 71   *(Scale 1 : 1,500), Ian Sturton (via M Mazumdar)* / 0529540

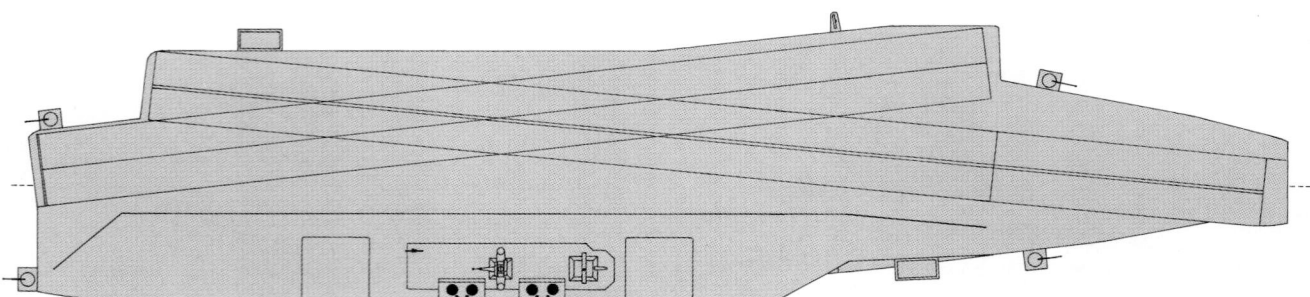

PROJECT 71   *(Scale 1 : 1,500), Ian Sturton (via M Mazumdar)* / 0529542

1 HERMES CLASS (CVM)

Name	No	Builders	Laid down	Launched	Commissioned
VIRAAT (ex-*Hermes*)	R 22	Vickers Shipbuilding Ltd, Barrow-in-Furness	21 June 1944	16 Feb 1953	18 Nov 1959

Displacement, tons: 23,900 standard; 28,700 full load
Dimensions, feet (metres): 685 wl; 744.3 oa × 90; 160 oa × 28.5 (*208.8; 226.9 × 27.4; 48.8 × 8.7*)
Main machinery: 4 Admiralty boilers; 400 psi (*28 kg/cm²*); 700°F (*370°C*); 2 Parsons geared turbines; 76,000 hp (*57 MW*); 2 shafts
Speed, knots: 28
Complement: 1,350 (143 officers)

Missiles: SAM/Guns: 2 Octuple IAI/Rafael Barak VLS **1**, command line of sight radar or optical guidance to 10 km (*5.5 n miles*) at 2 Mach; warhead 22 kg.
Countermeasures: Decoys: 2 Knebworth Corvus chaff launchers **2**.
ESM: Bharat Ajanta; intercept **3**.
Combat data systems: CAAIS action data automation. SATCOM.
Radars: Air search: Bharat RAWL-2 (PLN 517) **4**; D-band.
Air/surface search: Bharat RAWS (PFN 513) **5**; E/F-band.
Fire control: IAI/Elta EL/M-2221 **6**; Ka-band.
Navigation: 2 Bharat Rashmi **7**; I-band.
Tacan: FT 13-S/M.
Sonars: Graseby Type 184M; hull-mounted; active search and attack; 6—9 kHz.

Fixed-wing aircraft: 12 Sea Harriers FRS Mk 51 **8** (capacity for 30).
Helicopters: 7 Sea King Mk 42B/C **9** ASW/ASV/Vertrep and Ka-27 Helix. Ka-31 Helix.

Programmes: Purchased in May 1986 from the UK, thence to an extensive refit in Devonport Dockyard. Life extension of at least 10 years. Commissioned in Indian Navy 20 May 1987.
Modernisation: UK refit included new fire-control equipment, navigation radars and deck landing aids. Boilers were converted to take distillate fuel and the ship was given improved NBC protection. New search radar in 1995. Further modernisation in 1999-2001 refit, improved indigenous RAWL 02 (Mk II) and Rashmi radars for CCA/navigation, EW equipment and new communications systems. A further refit, completed in December 2004, included installation of Barak CIWS. This has replaced the previously fitted 40 mm guns and AK 230 Gatling systems.
Structure: Fitted with 12° ski jump. Reinforced flight deck (0.75 in); 1 to 2 in of armour over magazines and machinery spaces. Four LCVP on after davits. Magazine capacity includes 80 lightweight torpedoes. Barak launchers are recessed in the starboard side of the flight deck, aft of the island.
Operational: The Sea Harrier complement is normally no more than 12 aircraft leaving room for a greater mix of Sea King and Helix helicopters. Based at Mumbai.

VIRAAT

10/2005, Ships of the World* / 1153836

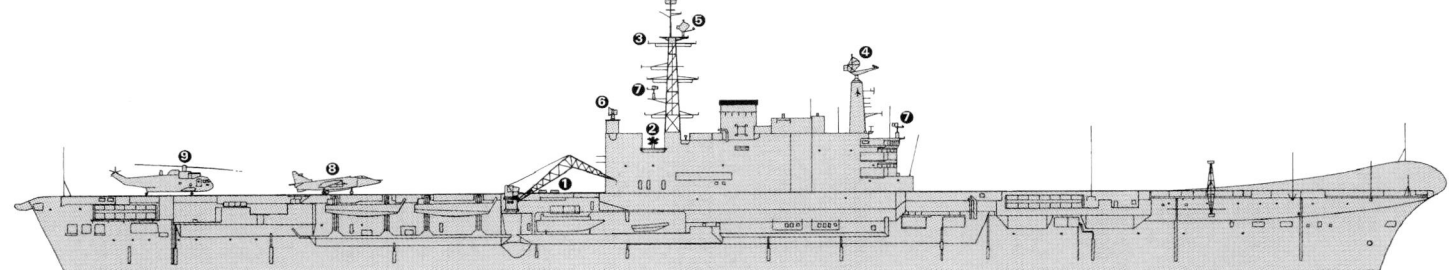

VIRAAT

(Scale 1 : 1,200), Ian Sturton / 1151087

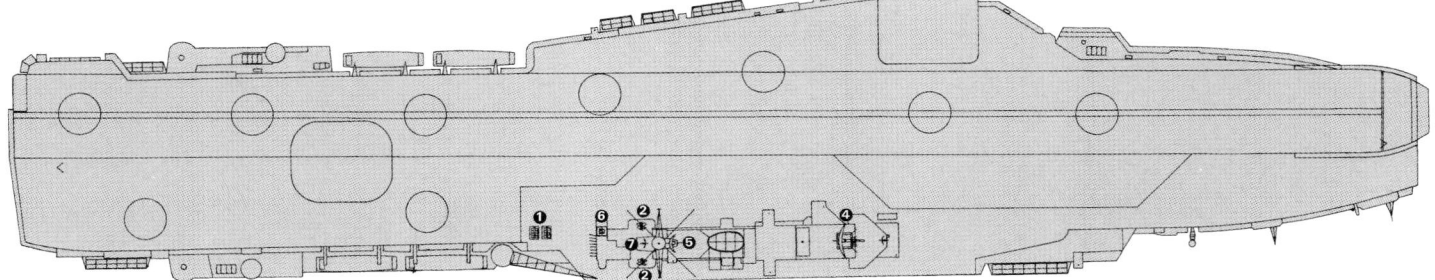

VIRAAT

(Scale 1 : 1,200), Ian Sturton / 1151088

VIRAAT

10/2005, Ships of the World* / 1153835

DESTROYERS

3 DELHI CLASS (PROJECT 15) (DDGHM)

Name	No	Builders	Laid down	Launched	Commissioned
DELHI	D 61	Mazagon Dock Ltd, Mumbai	14 Nov 1987	1 Feb 1991	15 Nov 1997
MYSORE	D 60	Mazagon Dock Ltd, Mumbai	2 Feb 1991	4 June 1993	2 June 1999
MUMBAI	D 62	Mazagon Dock Ltd, Mumbai	14 Dec 1992	20 Mar 1995	22 Jan 2001

Displacement, tons: 6,700 full load
Dimensions, feet (metres): 534.8 × 55.8 × 21.3
(163 × 17 × 6.5)
Main machinery: 4 Zorya/Mashprockt DT-59 gas turbines;
82,820 hp(m) *(61.7 MW)*; 2 shafts; cp props
Speed, knots: 32
Range, n miles: 4,500 at 18 kt
Complement: 360 (40 officers)

Missiles: SSM: 16 Zvezda SS-N-25 (4 quad) (KH 35E Uran) ❶
active radar homing to 130 km *(70.2 n miles)* at
0.9 Mach; warhead 145 kg; sea skimmer.
SAM: 2 SA-N-7 Gadfly (Kashmir/Uragan) ❷ command,
semi-active radar and IR homing to 25 km *(13.5 n miles)*
at 3 Mach; warhead 70 kg. Total of 48 missiles.
4 Octuple IAI/Rafael Barak VLS (D 60, D 61) ❸; command
line of sight radar or optical guidance to 10 km
(5.5 n miles) at 2 Mach; warhead 22 kg.
Guns: 1 USSR 3.9 in *(100 mm)*/59 ❹. AK 100; 60 rds/min to
15 km *(8.2 n miles)*; weight of shell 16 kg.
4 (2 in D 61) USSR 30 mm/65 ❺ AK 630; 6 barrels per
mounting; 3,000 rds/min combined to 2 km.
Torpedoes: 5 PTA 21 in *(533 mm)* (quin) tubes ❻.
Combination of SET 65E; anti-submarine; active/passive
homing to 15 km *(8.1 n miles)* at 40 kt; warhead
205 kg and Type 53-65; passive wake homing to 19 km
(10.3 n miles) at 45 kt; warhead 305 kg.
A/S mortars: 2 RBU 6000 ❼; 12 tubed trainable; range
6,000 m; warhead 31 kg.
Depth charges: 2 rails.
Countermeasures: Decoys: 2 PK2 chaff launchers ❽. Towed
torpedo decoy.

ESM: Bharat Ajanta Mk 2; intercept.
ECM: Elettronica TQN-2; jammer.
Combat data systems: Bharat IPN Shikari (IPN 10).
Radars: Air search: Bharat/Signaal RAWL (LW08) ❾;
D-band.
Air/surface search: Half Plate ❿; E-band.
Fire control: 6 Front Dome ⓫; H/I-band (for SAM); Kite
Screech ⓬; I/J-band (for 100 mm); 2 Bass Tilt (MR-123)
(D 62); I/J-band (for AK 630); EL/M-2221 STGR (D 60,
D 61) ⓭ (for Barak); I/J/K-band; Plank Shave (Granit
Garpun B) ⓮ (for SSM); I/J-band.
Navigation: 3 Nyada MR-212/201; I-band.
Sonars: Bharat HUMVAD; hull-mounted; active search;
medium frequency.
Bharat HUMSA; hull-mounted; medium frequency
(D 62).
Indal/Garden Reach Model 15-750 VDS.
Thales ATAS; active towed array (D 62).

Helicopters: 2 Westland Sea Kings Mk 42B ⓯ or 2 Hindustan
Aeronautics ALH.

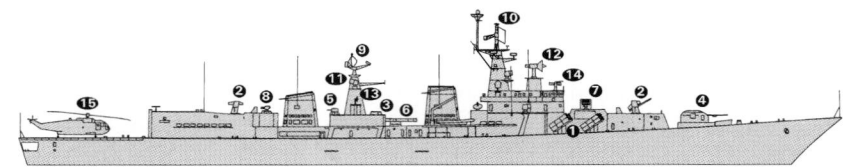

DELHI   *(Scale 1 : 1,500)*, Ian Sturton / 0572398

Programmes: Built with Russian Severnoye Design Bureau
assistance. *Delhi* ordered in March 1986. Programme
is called Project 15. Much delay was caused by the
breakdown in the central control of Russian export
equipment.
Structure: The design is described as a 'stretched *Rajput*
with some *Godavari* features. A combination of
Russian and Indian weapon systems fitted. Missile
blast deflectors indicate an original intention to fit
SS-N-22 Sunburn. Samahé helo handling system.
Forward funnel offset to port and after funnel to
starboard.
Modernisation: Barak has replaced the forward AK-630
mountings in D 60 and D 61. The two Bass Tilt radars
have also been replaced by EL/M-2221 STGR. D 62 is
to be similarly refitted. SS-N-25 may be replaced by
Brahmos.
Operational: Based at Mumbai. Have Flag facilities.

MUMBAI   *6/2005*, Maritime Photographic* / 1151257

MUMBAI   *7/2005*, A A de Kruijf* / 1151116

DELHI (before being fitted with Barak) *2/2001, Sattler/Steele* / 0121369

MYSORE *2/2001, Sattler/Steele* / 0121371

5 RAJPUT (KASHIN II) CLASS (PROJECT 61ME) (DDGHM)

Name	No	Builders	Laid down	Launched	Commissioned
RAJPUT (ex-*Nadezhniy*)	D 51	Nikolayev North (61 Kommuna)	11 Sep 1976	17 Sep 1977	4 May 1980
RANA (ex-*Gubitelyniyy*)	D 52	Nikolayev North (61 Kommuna)	29 Nov 1976	27 Sep 1978	19 Feb 1982
RANJIT (ex-*Lovkiyy*)	D 53	Nikolayev North (61 Kommuna)	29 June 1977	16 June 1979	24 Nov 1983
RANVIR (ex-*Tverdyy*)	D 54	Nikolayev North (61 Kommuna)	24 Oct 1981	12 Mar 1983	21 Apr 1986
RANVIJAY (ex-*Tolkoviyy*)	D 55	Nikolayev North (61 Kommuna)	19 Mar 1982	1 Feb 1986	21 Dec 1987

Displacement, tons: 3,950 standard; 4,974 full load
Dimensions, feet (metres): 480.5 × 51.8 × 15.7
  (146.5 × 15.8 × 4.8)
Main machinery: COGAG; 4 Ukraine gas turbines;
  72,000 hp(m) *(53 MW)*; 2 shafts
Speed, knots: 35. **Range, n miles:** 4,500 at 18 kt; 2,600 at 30 kt
Complement: 320 (35 officers)

Missiles: SSM: 2 (D 51) or 4 SS-N-2D Mod 2 Styx ❶; IR
  homing to 83 km *(45 n miles)* at 0.9 Mach; warhead
  513 kg; sea-skimmer.
  4 (D 51) or 8 (D 52, 53) Brahmos PJ-10; active/passive
  radar terminal homing to 290 km *(157 n miles)* at
  2.6 Mach; warhead 200 kg.
SAM: 2 SA-N-1 Goa twin launchers ❷; command guidance
  to 31.5 km *(17 n miles)* at 2 Mach; height 91—22,860 m
  (300—75,000 ft); warhead 60 kg; 44 missiles. Some SSM
  capability.
  4 octuple IAI/Rafael Barak VLS (D 55); command line of
  sight radar or optical guidance to 10 km *(5.5 n miles)* at
  2 Mach; warhead 22 kg.
Guns: 2—3 in *(76 mm)*/60 (twin, fwd) ❸; 90 rds/min to
  15 km *(8 n miles)*; weight of shell 6.8 kg.
  8—30 mm/65 (4 twin) AK 230 (D 51, 52, 53) ❹; 500 rds/
  min to 5 km *(2.7 n miles)*; weight of shell 0.54 kg.
  2—30 mm/65 AK 630 (6 barrels per mounting) D 54, 55);
  3,000 rds/min combined to 2 km.
Torpedoes: 5—21 in *(533 mm)* (quin) tubes ❺. Combination
  of SET-65E; anti-submarine; active/passive homing to
  15 km *(8.1 n miles)* at 40 kt; warhead 205 kg and
  Type 53-65; passive wake homing to 19 km *(10.3 n miles)*
  at 45 kt; warhead 305 kg.
A/S mortars: 2 RBU 6000 12-tubed trainable ❻; range
  6,000 m; warhead 31 kg.
Countermeasures: 4 PK 16 chaff launchers for radar decoy
  and distraction.
ESM: 2 Bell Squat/Bell Shroud (last pair); Bell Clout/Bell
  Slam/Bell Tap (first three); intercept.
ECM: 2 Top Hat; jammers.
Radars: Air search: Big Net A (D 51-52, 54-55) ❼; C-band;
  range 183 km *(100 n miles)* for 2 m² target.
  Bharat/Signaal RAWL (LW 08) (D 53); D-band.
Air/surface search: Head Net C (D 51-54) ❽; 3D; E-band.
  EL/M-2238 STAR (D 55); 3D; E/F-band.
Navigation: 2 Don Kay; I-band.
Fire control: 2 Peel Group ❾; H/I-band; range 73 km
  (40 n miles) for 2 m² target.
  Owl Screech ❿; G-band.
  2 Drum Tilt ⓫ or 2 Bass Tilt; H/I-band or 2 EL/M-2221
  STGR; I/J/K-band.
IFF: 2 High Pole B.
Sonars: Vycheda MG 311; hull-mounted; active search and
  attack; medium frequency.
  Mare Tail VDS; active search; medium frequency.

Helicopters: 1 Ka-28 Helix ⓬.

Programmes: First batch of three ordered in the mid-1970s.
  Ranvir was the first of the second batch ordered on
  20 December 1982.
Modernisation: New EW equipment installed on all
  ships refitted since 1993. Tenth test-launch of Brahmos
  conducted from D 51 on 15 April 2005. Brahmos is to
  replace SS-N-2D in D 51, D 54 and D 55. D 51 has been
  fitted with four missiles to replace forward SS-N-2D
  mountings. D 54 and D 55 are to be fitted with an 8-cell
  VLS system to replace the aft SA-N-1 system.
Structure: All built as new construction for India at
  Nikolayev with considerable modifications to the

Kashin design. Helicopter hangar, which is reached
by a lift from the flight deck, replaces after 76 mm twin
mount and the SS-N-2D launchers are sited forward of
the bridge. *Ranvir* and *Ranvijay* differ from previous
ships in class by being fitted with AK-630 30 mm guns
and two Bass Tilt fire-control radars. These may in
turn be replaced by EL/M-2221 STGR radars as Barak
is installed to replace the forward AK-630 mountings.
It is possible that an Italian combat data system
compatible with Selenia IPN-10 is installed. Inmarsat
fitted.
Operational: All based at Vishakapatnam. *Dhanush*
(Prithvi) ballistic missile test launched from *Rajput* on
28 December 2005.

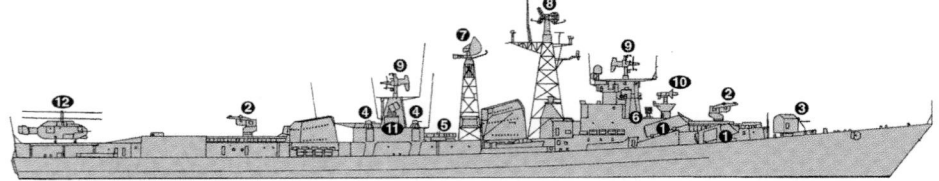

RANA (Scale 1 : 1,200), Ian Sturton / 0506295

RANJIT *10/2004, Toshiyuki Hanta* / 1042266

RANVIJAY *10/2004, Ships of the World* / 1042265

RANA *2/2001, Michael Nitz* / 0534076

0 + 3 KOLKATA (PROJECT 15A) CLASS (DDGHM)

Name	No	Builders	Laid down	Launched	Commissioned
KOLKATA	—	Mazagon Dock Ltd, Mumbai	26 Sep 2003	30 Mar 2006	2007
—	—	Mazagon Dock Ltd, Mumbai	2005	2007	2009
—	—	Mazagon Dock Ltd, Mumbai	2006	2008	2010

Displacement, tons: 7,000 full load
Dimensions, feet (metres): 534.8 × 55.8 × 21.3
(163 × 17 × 6.5)
Main machinery: 4 Zorya/Mashprockt DT-59 gas turbines;
82,820 hp(m) *(61.7 MW)*; 2 shafts; cp props
Speed, knots: 32. **Range, n miles:** 4,500 at 18 kt
Complement: 360 (40 officers)

Missiles: SSM: 16 Brahmos PJ-10 (2 octuple VLS) ❶; active/
passive radar homing to 290 km *(157 n miles)* at 2.6
Mach; warhead 200 kg; sea skimmer in terminal phase.
SAM: SA-N-12 Grizzly (Shtil-1) (9M317ME) ❷; command/
semi-active radar and IR homing to 35 km *(18.9 n miles)* at
3 Mach; warhead 70 kg. 1 × 16 cell VLS launcher (forward),
1 × 32 cell VLS launcher (aft); total of 48 missiles.
SAM/Guns: 2 CADS-N-1 (Kashtan) (may replace AK 630);
each has twin 30 mm Gatling combined with 8 SA-N-11
(Grisson) and Hot Flash/Hot Spot radar/optronic director.
Laser beam guidance for missiles to 8 km *(4.4 n miles)*;
warhead 9 kg; 9,000 rds/min (combined) to 1.5 km for
guns.
4 octuple IAI/Rafael Barak VLS; command line of sight
or optical guidance to 10 km *(5.5 n miles)* at 2 Mach;
warhead 22 kg.
Guns: 1 – 3.9 in *(100 mm)*/59 A 190E ❸; 60 rds/min to
21.5 km *(11.6 n miles)*; weight of shell 16 kg.
2 – 30 mm/AK 630 ❹; 6 barrels per mounting; 3,000 rds/
min combined to 2 km.

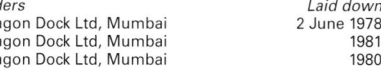

PROJECT 15A — *(Scale 1 : 1,500), Ian Sturton* / 1042090

Torpedoes: 5 PTA 21 in *(533 mm)* (quin) tubes ❺.
Combination of SET 65E; anti-submarine; active/passive
homing to 15 km *(8.1 n miles)* at 40 kt; warhead
205 kg and Type 53-65; passive wake homing to 19 km
(10.3 n miles) at 45 kt; warhead 305 kg.
A/S mortars: 2 RBU 6000 ❻; 12 tubed trainable; range
6,000 m; warhead 31 kg.
Countermeasures: Decoys: 2 PK2 chaff launchers ❼. Towed
torpedo decoy.
ESM: Bharat Ajanta Mk 2; intercept.
ECM: Elettronica TQN-2; jammer.
Combat data systems: BEL EMCCA.
Radars: Air search: Bharat RAWL (LW08) ❽; D-band.
Air/surface search: Top Plate (Fregat M2EM) ❾; 3D; E/F-band.
Fire control: 6 Front Dome (MR 90); H/I-band (for SAM) ❿;
Kite Screech; I/J-band (for 100 mm); Plank Shave (Granit
Garpun B) (for SSM) ⓫; I/J-band.

Navigation: Kelvin Hughes Nucleus 6000; E/F-band.
2 Nyada MR-212/201; I-band.
Sonars: Bharat HUMSA; hull-mounted; medium frequency.
Towed array (to be confirmed).

Helicopters: 2 Westland Sea Kings Mk 42B ⓬ or
2 Hindustan Aeronautics ALH.

Programmes: The first of three modified Delhi class was
laid down in 2003. The launch, due in September 2005,
was delayed until March 2006.
Structure: Designed by the Indian Naval Design Bureau,
the design appears to be a development of the Delhi
class incorporating some features of both the Talwar and
Project 17 frigates.

FRIGATES

3 GODAVARI CLASS (PROJECT 16) (FFGHM)

Name	No	Builders	Laid down	Launched	Commissioned
GODAVARI	F 20	Mazagon Dock Ltd, Mumbai	2 June 1978	15 May 1980	10 Dec 1983
GOMATI	F 21	Mazagon Dock Ltd, Mumbai	1981	19 Mar 1984	16 Apr 1988
GANGA	F 22	Mazagon Dock Ltd, Mumbai	1980	21 Oct 1981	30 Dec 1985

Displacement, tons: 4,209 full load
Dimensions, feet (metres): 414.9 × 47.6 × 14.8 (29.5 sonar)
(126.5 × 14.5 × 4.5; 9)
Main machinery: 2 Babcock & Wilcox boilers; 550 psi
(38.7 kg/cm²); 850°F *(450°C)*; 2 turbines; 30,000 hp
(22.4 MW); 2 shafts
Speed, knots: 28. **Range, n miles:** 4,500 at 12 kt
Complement: 313 (40 officers including 13 aircrew)

Missiles: SSM: 4 SS-N-2D Styx ❶; active radar (Mod 1) or IR
(Mod 2) homing to 83 km *(45 n miles)* at 0.9 Mach; warhead
513 kg; sea-skimmer at end of run. Indian designation.
SAM: SA-N-4 Gecko twin launcher (F 20, F 21) ❷; semi-
active radar homing to 15 km *(8 n miles)* at 2.5 Mach;
height 9.1 – 3,048 m *(130 — 10,000 ft)*; warhead 50 kg;
limited surface-to-surface capability; 20 missiles.
1 Octuple IAI/Rafael Barak VLS (F 22); command line of
sight radar or optical guidance to 10 km *(5.5 n miles)* at
2 Mach; warhead 22 kg.
Guns: 2 – 57 mm/70 (twin) ❸; 120 rds/min to 8 km
(4.4 n miles); weight of shell 2.8 kg.
8 – 30 mm/65 (4 twin) AK 230 ❹; 500 rds/min to 5 km
(2.7 n miles); weight of shell 0.54 kg.
2 – 7.63 mm MGs.
Torpedoes: 6 – 324 mm ILAS 3 (2 triple) tubes ❺. Whitehead
A244S; anti-submarine; active/passive homing to 7 km *(3.8 n
miles)* at 33 kt; warhead 34 kg (shaped charge). *Godavari* has
tube modifications based on the Indian NST 58 version of A244S.
Countermeasures: Decoys: 2 chaff launchers (Super
Barricade). Graseby G738 towed torpedo decoy.
ESM/ECM: Selenia INS-3 (Bharat Ajanta and Elettronica
TQN-2); intercept and jammer.
Combat data systems: Selenia IPN-10 action data
automation. Inmarsat communications (JRC) ❻.
Weapons control: MR 301 MFCS. MR 103 GFCS.
Radars: Air search: Signaal LW08 ❼; D-band.
Air/surface search: Head Net C (F 20, 21) ❽; 3D; E/F-band.
EL/M-2238 STAR (F 22); 3D; E/F-band.
Navigation/helo control: 2 Signaal ZW06 ❾; or Don Kay;
I-band.
Fire control: 2 Drum Tilt ❿; H/I-band (for 30 mm).
Pop Group ⓫; F/H/I-band (for SA-N-4).
Muff Cob ⓬; G/H-band (for 57 mm).

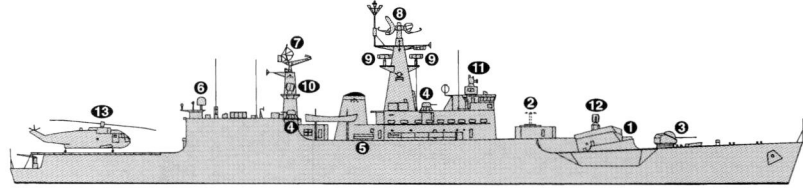

GODAVARI — *(Scale 1 : 1,200), Ian Sturton* / 0052330

GOMATI — *2/2001, Michael Nitz* / 0534079

Sonars: Bharat APSOH; hull-mounted; active panoramic
search and attack; medium frequency.
Fathoms Oceanic VDS.
Thomson Sintra DSBV 62 (in *Ganga*); passive towed
array; very low frequency.
Type 162M; bottom classification; high frequency.

Helicopters: 2 Sea King or 1 Sea King and 1 Chetak ⓭.

Modernisation: Barak launchers have replaced SA-N-4 in
F 22 and are to be fitted to F 20 and F 21.

Structure: A further modification of the original Leander
design with an indigenous content of 72 per cent and
a larger hull. Poor welding is noticeable in *Godavari*.
Gomati is the first Indian ship to have digital electronics
in her combat data system.
Operational: French Samahé helicopter handling equipment
is fitted. Usually only one helo is carried with more
than one crew. These ships have a unique mixture of
Russian, Western and Indian weapon systems which
has inevitably led to some equipment compatibility
problems.

GANGA — *6/2005*, Robert Pabst* / 1151115

3 + (3) TALWAR (PROJECT 1135.6) CLASS (FFGHM)

Name	No	Builders	Laid down	Launched	Commissioned
TALWAR	F 40	Baltic Shipyard, St Petersburg	10 Mar 1999	12 May 2000	18 June 2003
TRISHUL	F 43	Baltic Shipyard, St Petersburg	24 Sep 1999	24 Nov 2000	25 June 2003
TABAR	F 44	Baltic Shipyard, St Petersburg	26 May 2000	25 May 2001	19 Apr 2004

Displacement, tons: 3,620 standard; 4,035 full load
Dimensions, feet (metres): 409.6 × 49.9 × 15.1
(124.8 × 15.2 × 4.6)
Main machinery: COGAG; 2 Zorya DN-59 gas turbines;
43,448 hp/m *(34.2 MW)*; 2 Zorya UGT 6000 gas turbines;
16,628 hp(m) *(12.4 MW)*; 2 shafts; fixed propellers
Speed, knots: 32
Range, n miles: 4,850 at 14 kt; 1,600 at 30 kt
Complement: 180 (18 officers)

Missiles: SSM: 8 SS-N-27 Novator Alfa Klub-N (3K-54-
TE) ❶ active radar homing to 180 km *(97.2 n miles)* at
0.7 Mach (cruise) and 2.5 Mach (attack); warhead 450 kg.
VLS silo.
SAM: SA-N-7 Gadfly (Kashmir/Uragan) single launcher ❷
command, semi-active radar and IR homing to 25 km
(13.5 n miles) at 3 Mach; warhead 70 kg. 24 9M 317
missiles.
SAM/Guns: 2 CADS-N-1 (Kashtan) ❸ each has twin
30 mm Gatling combined with 8 SA-N-11 (Grisson) and
Hot Flash/Hot Spot radar/optronic director. Laser beam
guidance for missiles to 8 km *(4.4 n miles)* warhead 9 kg;
9,000 rds/min (combined) to 1.5 km for guns.
Guns: 1—3.9 in *(100 mm)*/59 A 190E ❹; 60 rds/min to
21.5 km *(11.6 n miles)*; weight of shell 16 kg.
Torpedoes: 4 PTA-53 21 in *(533 mm)* (2 twin) fired
launchers ❺.
A/S mortars: 1 RBU 6000 12-barrelled launcher ❻ range
6 km; warhead 31 kg.
Countermeasures: Decoys: 2 PK 2 chaff launchers (to be
fitted).
ESM: Bharat Ajanta; intercept.
ECM: ASOR 11356; jammer.
Combat data systems: Trebovaniye-M.
Radars: Air search: Top Plate (Fregat-M2EM) ❼ 3D; E/F-band.
Air/surface search: Cross Dome (Positiv-E) ❽; E/F-band.
Fire control: 4 Front Dome (MR-90) ❾; H/I-band (for SA-N-7).
Plank Shave (Garpun-B) ❿; I/J-band (for SSM); Ratep
5P-10E Puma ⓫; I-band (for 100 mm gun).

Navigation: Kelvin Hughes Nucleus 6000 ⓬; E/F-band.
2 Nyada MR 212/201 (Palm Frond) ⓭; I-band.
Sonars: HUMSA; hull mounted; active/passive medium
frequency.
VDS (may be fitted in future).

Helicopters: 1 Ka-28/Ka-31 Helix ⓮ or ALH.

Programmes: Contract placed in 1997 and confirmed 21 July
1998 for three modified Krivak IIIs. Mutual interference
difficulties reportedly delayed entry into service of first of
class by one year. An option for a second batch of three
ships is likely to be exercised in 2006. Construction at
Yantar Shipyard, Kaliningrad, is a possibility.
Structure: The first surface unit to be fitted with SS-N-27
missile. This is likely to be replaced by the Brahmos
missile in Batch 2.

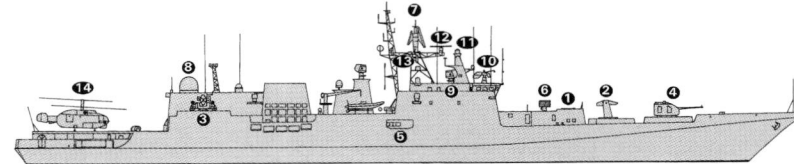

TALWAR *(Scale 1 : 1,200), Ian Sturton* / 0569246

TALWAR *7/2003, H M Steele* / 0554931

TRISHUL *7/2003, Michael Nitz* / 0569191

TABAR *5/2004, Harald Carstens* / 1042274

0 + 3 SHIVALIK (PROJECT 17) CLASS (FFGHM)

Name	No
SHIVALIK	—
SATPURA	—
SAHYADRI	—

Builders	Laid down	Launched	Commissioned
Mazagon Dock Ltd, Mumbai	11 July 2001	18 Apr 2003	2006
Mazagon Dock Ltd, Mumbai	Oct 2002	4 June 2004	2006
Mazagon Dock Ltd, Mumbai	30 Sep 2003	27 May 2005	2007

Displacement, tons: 4,600 standard; 5,300 full load
Dimensions, feet (metres): 469.3 × 55.5 × 17.4
(143.0 × 16.9 × 5.3)
Main machinery: CODOG; 2 GE LM 2,500 gas turbines;
44,000 hp *(32.8 MW)*; 2 SEMT-Pielstick PA6 STC diesels;
15,200 hp *(11.3 MW)*; 2 cp propellers.
Speed, knots: 32
Range, n miles: 4,500 at 18 kt; 1,600 at 30 kt
Complement: 250 (25 officers)

Missiles: SSM: 8 SS-N-27 Novator Alfa Klub (3M-54E1) ❶
active radar homing to 180 km *(97.2 n miles)* at 0.7 Mach
(cruise) and 2.5 Mach (attack); warhead 450 kg. VLS silo.
SAM: SA-N-7 Gadfly (Kashmir/Uragan) single launcher
6 ❷ command, semi-active radar and IR homing to
25 km *(13.5 n miles)* at 3 Mach; warhead 70 kg. 24 9M38M1
missiles.
SAM/Guns: 2 CADS-N-1 (Kashtan) ❸ each has twin 30 mm
Gatling combined with 8 SA-N-11 (Grisson) and Hot
Flash/Hot Spot radar/optronic director. Laser beam
guidance for missiles to 8 km *(4.4 n miles)* warhead 9 kg;
9,000 rds/min (combined) to 1.5 km for guns.
Guns: 1 OTO Melara 3 in *(76 mm)*/62 Super Rapid ❹;
120 rds/min to 16 km *(8.7 n miles)*; weight of shell 6 kg.
Torpedoes: 6—324 mm ILAS 3 (2 triple) ❺.
A/S mortars: 2 RBU 6000 12-barrelled launcher ❻ range
6 km; warhead 31 kg.

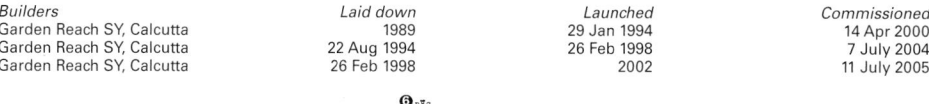

SHIVALIK *(Scale 1 : 1,200), Ian Sturton* / 0569247

Countermeasures: Decoys: 2 PK 2 chaff launchers.
ESM: Bharat Ajanta; intercept.
ECM: ASOR 11356; jammer.
Combat data systems: BEL EMCCA.
Radars: Air search: Bharat RAWL-02 ❼; E/F-band
Air/surface search: Top Plate (Fregat-M2EM) ❽ 3D; D/E-band.
Fire control: 2 BEL Shikari (based on Contraves Seaguard) ❾
(for 76 mm); I/K-bands.
1 Bharat Aparna (modified Plank Shave/Garpun B) ❿
(for SSMs); I/J-bands.
4 Front Dome (MR 90) ⓫ (for SA-N-7); H/I-band.
Navigation: 1 BEL Rashmi; I-band.
Sonars: Bharat HUMSA; hull-mounted; active search and
attack; medium frequency.
VDS; active search; medium frequency.

Helicopters: 1 Sea King Mk 42B ⓬.

Programmes: Three Project 17 ships approved in June 1999
and construction of the first of class began in 2001. The
second and third units are planned to be delivered at one
year intervals, an unprecedented rate of construction.
A class of 12 ships is envisaged.
Structure: An enlarged and modified version of the Talwar
class, the aft section resembles the Delhi class. Signature
reduction (IR and RCS) features are believed to be
incorporated. Details are speculative.

3 BRAHMAPUTRA CLASS (PROJECT 16A) (FFGHM)

Name	No
BRAHMAPUTRA	F 31
BETWA	F 39
BEAS	F 37

Builders	Laid down	Launched	Commissioned
Garden Reach SY, Calcutta	1989	29 Jan 1994	14 Apr 2000
Garden Reach SY, Calcutta	22 Aug 1994	26 Feb 1998	7 July 2004
Garden Reach SY, Calcutta	26 Feb 1998	2002	11 July 2005

Displacement, tons: 4,450 full load
Dimensions, feet (metres): 414.9 × 47.6 × 14.8 (29.5 sonar)
(126.5 × 14.5 × 4.5; 9)
Main machinery: 2 boilers; 550 psi *(38.7 kg/cm²)*; 850°F
(450°C); 2 Bhopal turbines; 30,000 hp *(22.4 MW)*;
2 shafts
Speed, knots: 27. **Range, n miles:** 4,500 at 12 kt
Complement: 351 (31 officers and 13 aircrew)

Missiles: SSM: 16 SS-N-25 (4 quad) (KH-35E Uran) ❶;
active radar homing to 130 km *(70.2 n miles)* at 0.9 Mach;
warhead 145 kg; sea skimmer.
SAM: 1 Octuple IAI/Rafael Barak VLS ❷; command line of
sight radar or optical guidance to 10 km *(5.5 n miles)* at
2 Mach; warhead 22 kg.
Guns: OTO Melara 76 mm/62 ❸; 85 rds/min to 16 km
(8.6 n miles) weight of shell 6 kg.
4—30 mm/65 AK 630 ❹; 6 barrels per mounting;
3,000 rds/min combined to 2 km.
Torpedoes: 6—324 mm ILAS 3 (2 triple) tubes ❺. Whitehead
A244S; anti-submarine; active/passive homing to 7 km
(3.8 n miles) at 33 kt; warhead 34 kg (shaped charge).
Countermeasures: Decoys: 2 chaff launchers (Super Barricade
in due course). Graseby G738 towed torpedo decoy.
ESM/ECM: Selenia INS-3 (Bharat Ajanta and Elettronica
TQN-2) ❻; intercept and jammer.
Combat data systems: BEL EMCCA. Inmarsat
communications (JRC).
Weapons control: MR 103 GFCS.
Radars: Air search: Signaal LW08/Bharat RAWL-02
(PLN 517) ❼; D-band.
Air/surface search: Bharat RAWS-03 (using DA 08 antenna)
(PFN 513) ❽; E/F-band.
Navigation/helo control: Decca Bridgemaster; I-band. BEL
Rashmi (PIN 524) (using ZW 06 antenna); I-band.
Fire control: 2 BEL Shikari (based on Contraves Seaguard) ❾
(for 76 mm and Ak 630); I/K-bands.
EL/M-2221 STGR (for Barak); I/J/K-bands.
Bharat Aparna (modified Plank Shave/Garpun B) ❿ (for
SSM); I/J-band.
Selenia RAN (for SAM); I-band.

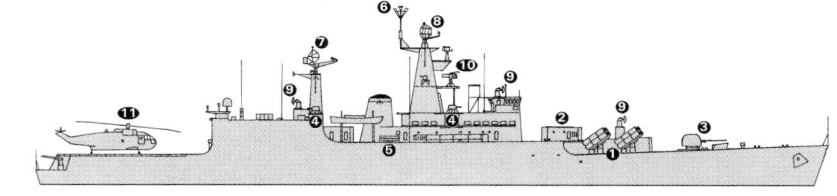

BRAHMAPUTRA *(Scale 1 : 1,200), Ian Sturton* / 0121334

BETWA *12/2005*, Chris Sattler* / 1151258

Sonars: Bharat HUMSA (APSOH); hull-mounted; active
panoramic search and attack; medium frequency.
Thales towed array.

Helicopters: 2 Sea King or 1 Sea King and 1 Chetak ⓫.

Programmes: Project 16A. Progress has been very slow.

Structure: The main difference is the replacement of the
Godavari SS-N-2 by SS-N-25. Following the cancellation
of the Trishul SAM programme, Barak has been fitted in
its place. Gun armament has also improved.
Operational: *Betwa* started sea trials in late 2003 and is
to be commissioned in 2004. *Beas* is also likely to be
commissioned in 2005.

BETWA *12/2005*, Indian Navy* / 1153834

For details of the latest updates to *Jane's Fighting Ships* online and to discover the additional
information available exclusively to online subscribers please visit
jfs.janes.com

Name	No
UDAYGIRI	F 35
DUNAGIRI	F 36
TARAGIRI	F 41
VINDHYAGIRI	F 42

Displacement, tons: 2,962 full load (F 35-F 36). 3,039 full load (F 41-F 42)
Dimensions, feet (metres): 372 × 36.1 (F 35-F 36); 44.3 (F 41 and F 42) × 18 *(113.5 × 11; 13.5 × 5.5)*
Main machinery: 2 Babcock & Wilcox boilers; 550 psi *(38.7 kg/cm²)*; 850°F *(450°C)*; 2 turbines; 30,000 hp *(22.4 MW)*; 2 shafts
Speed, knots: 27; 28 (F 41 and F 42).
Range, n miles: 4,500 at 12 kt
Complement: 267 (17 officers). 300 (20 officers) (F 41 and F 42)

Guns: 2 Vickers 4.5 in *(114 mm)*/45 (twin) Mk 6 ❶; 20 rds/min to 19 km *(10.4 n miles)* anti-surface; 6 km *(3.3 n miles)* anti-aircraft; weight of shell 25 kg.
4—30 mm/65 (2 twin) AK 230 ❷; 500 rds/min to 5 km *(2.7 n miles)*; weight of shell 0.54 kg.
2 Oerlikon 20 mm/70 ❸; 800 rds/min to 2 km.
Torpedoes: 6—324 mm ILAS 3 (2 triple) tubes (F 41 and F 42) ❹. Whitehead A244S or Indian NST 58 version; anti-submarine; active/passive homing to 7 km *(3.8 n miles)* at 33 kt; warhead 34 kg (shaped charge).
A/S mortars: 1 Bofors 375 mm twin-tubed launcher (F 41 and F 42) ❺; range 1,600 m.
1 Limbo Mk 10 triple-tubed launcher (remainder); range 1,000 m; warhead 92 kg.
Countermeasures: Decoys: Graseby 738; towed torpedo decoy.
ESM: Bharat Ajanta; intercept. FH5 Telegon D/F.
ECM: Racal Cutlass; jammer.
Combat data systems: Signaal DS-22.
Radars: Air search: Signaal LW04 ❻; D-band.
Air/surface search: Signaal DA 05 ❼; E/F-band.
Navigation: Signaal ZW 06; I-band.
Fire control: Signaal M 45 ❽; I/J-band.
IFF: Type 944; 954M.
Sonars: Westinghouse SQS-505; Graseby 750 (APSOH fitted in *Himgiri* as trials ship); hull-mounted; active search and attack; medium frequency. Type 170; active attack; high frequency.
Westinghouse VDS (F 36 only); active; medium frequency.
Thomson Diodon VDS in F 41 and F 42.

Helicopters: 1 Chetak or 1 Sea King Mk 42 (in *Taragiri* and *Vindhyagiri*) ❾.

Programmes: The first major warships built in Indian yards to a UK design with a 60 per cent indigenous component. An ex-UK Leander class was acquired in 1995 and is listed under Training Ships.
Modernisation: The VDS arrays are installed inside towed bodies built by Fathom Oceanology Ltd of Canada. The transducer elements in both cases are identical. AK 230 guns have replaced the obsolete Seacat. *Vindhyagiri* modified with UAV control stations above the hangar in order to operate Heron II UAVs.
Structure: In the first two the hangar was provided with telescopic extension to take the Alouette III helicopter while in the last pair, a much-changed

4 NILGIRI (LEANDER) CLASS (FFH)

Builders	Laid down	Launched	Commissioned
Mazagon Dock Ltd, Mumbai	14 Sep 1970	24 Oct 1972	18 Feb 1976
Mazagon Dock Ltd, Mumbai	25 Jan 1973	9 Mar 1974	5 May 1977
Mazagon Dock Ltd, Mumbai	15 Oct 1975	25 Oct 1976	16 May 1980
Mazagon Dock Ltd, Mumbai	5 Nov 1976	12 Nov 1977	8 July 1981

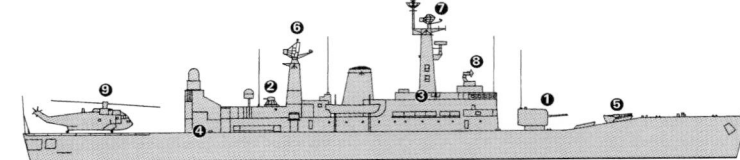

VINDHYAGIRI
(Scale 1 : 1,200), Ian Sturton / 1042089

VINDHYAGIRI
11/2003 / 1042277

DUNAGIRI
2/2001, Michael Nitz / 0534080

design, the Mk 10 Mortar has been removed as well as VDS and the aircraft space increased to make way for a Sea King helicopter with a telescopic hangar and Canadian Beartrap haul-down gear. In these two an open deck has been left below the flight deck for

handling mooring gear and there is a cut-down to the stern.
Operational: *Vindhyagiri* and *Taragiri* have more powerful engines than the remainder. *Himgiri* was decommissioned on 6 May 2005.

CORVETTES

4 ABHAY (PROJECT 1241 PE) (PAUK II) CLASS (FSM)

Name	No	Builders	Commissioned
ABHAY	P 33	Volodarski	10 Mar 1989
AJAY	P 34	Volodarski	24 Jan 1990
AKSHAY	P 35	Volodarski	10 Dec 1990
AGRAY	P 36	Volodarski	30 Jan 1991

Displacement, tons: 485 full load
Dimensions, feet (metres): 191.9 × 33.5 × 11.2; *(58.5 × 10.2 × 3.4)*
Main machinery: 2 Type M 521 diesels; 16,184 hp(m) *(11.9 MW)* sustained; 2 shafts
Speed, knots: 28. **Range, n miles:** 2,400 at 14 kt
Complement: 32 (6 officers)

Missiles: SAM: SA-N-5/8 Grail quad launcher; manual aiming, IR homing to 6 km *(3.2 n miles)* at 1.5 Mach; warhead 1.5 kg.
Guns: 1 USSR 3 in *(76 mm)*/60; 120 rds/min to 15 km *(8 n miles)*; weight of shell 7 kg.
1—30 mm/65 AK 630; 6 barrels; 3,000 rds/min combined to 2 km.
Torpedoes: 4—21 in *(533 mm)* (2 twin) tubes. SET-65E; active/passive homing to 15 km *(8.1 n miles)* at 40 kt; warhead 205 kg.
A/S mortars: 2 RBU 1200 5-tubed fixed; range 1,200 m; warhead 34 kg.
Countermeasures: 2 PK 16 chaff launchers.
Radars: Air/Surface search: Cross Dome; E/F-band.
Navigation: Pechora; I-band.
Fire Control: Bass Tilt; H/I-band.
Sonars: Rat Tail VDS (on transom); attack; high frequency.

Programmes: Modified Pauk II class built in the USSR at Volodarski, Rybinsk for export. Original order in late 1983 but completion of the first delayed by lack of funds and the order for the others was not reinstated until 1987. Names associated with former coastal patrol craft.
Modernisation: There are plans to re-engine all four ships.
Structure: Has a longer superstructure than the Pauk I, larger torpedo tubes and improved electronics.
Operational: Classified as ASW ships. Comprise 23rd Patrol Boat Squadron based at Mumbai.

ABHAY
2/2001, Michael Nitz / 0534082

0 + 4 (8) PROJECT 28 (CORVETTES) (FFG)

Name	No	Builders	Laid down	Launched	Commissioned
—	—	Garden Reach Shipbuilding & Engineering	2006	2008	2009

Displacement, tons: 2,500 full load
Dimensions, feet (metres): 360.9 × 44.3 × ?
(110.0 × 13.5 × ?)
Main machinery: CODAD: 4 diesels
Speed, knots: 29. **Range, n miles:** To be announced
Complement: To be announced

Missiles: SSM: SS-N-27 Novator Alfa Klub-N (3K-54-TE);
active radar homing to 220 km *(119 n miles)* at 0.7 Mach
(cruise) and 2.5 Mach (dive); warhead 450 kg; VLS silo.
SAM: 1—16 cell IAI/Rafael Barak VLS; command line of
sight radar or optical guidance to 10 km *(5.5 n miles)* at
2.0 Mach; warhead 22 kg.
Guns: 1 Otobreda 3 in *(76 mm)*/62 Super Rapid; 120 rds/min
to 16 km *(8.7 n miles)*; weight of shell 6 kg.
2—30 mm/65 AK 630; 6 barrels per mounting; 3,000
rds/min combined to 2 km.

Torpedoes: 6—324 mm ILAS (2 triple); Eurotorp MU-90.
A/S mortars: 1 RBU 6000 12-barrelled launcher; range
6 km; warhead 31 kg.
Countermeasures: Decoys: 4 chaff/flare decoy launchers.
Towed torpedo decoy.
ESM: To be announced.
ECM: To be announced.
Combat data systems: BEL EMCCA. Datalinks. Satcom.
Weapons control: EO director.
Radars: Surveillance: To be announced.
Fire control: Plank Shave (Garpun B); I-band (for SSM).
To be announced (for 76 mm).
2 Elta EL/M-2221 STGR; I/J/K-band (for Barak).
Navigation: Decca Bridgemaster; I-band.
Sonars: Active/passive towed array.

Helicopters: 1 Ka-28PL or HAL Dhruv.

Programmes: Multipurpose corvette designed to operate
in Indian offshore waters. First four units ordered in
2003 and first steel cut for first of class on 12 August
2005. First of class to commission in 2009. Further units
are expected at 18 month intervals and a class of 12 is
planned.
Structure: The design is understood to be the result of a
joint venture by the Indian Navy's DGND SSG (Directorate
General Naval Design Surface Ship Group) and Garden
Reach Shipbuilder's in-house design team. Details have
not been formally released and are speculative. Measures
to reduce acoustic, magnetic, IR and radar cross-section
signatures are reported to have been incorporated. The
hull may use amagnetic steel.

4 KORA CLASS (PROJECT 25A) (FSGHM)

Name	No	Builders	Laid down	Launched	Commissioned
KORA	P 61	Garden Reach SY, Calcutta	10 Jan 1990	23 Sep 1992	10 Aug 1998
KIRCH	P 62	Garden Reach SY, Calcutta/Mazagon Dock	31 Jan 1990	28 Sep 1995	22 Jan 2001
KULISH	P 63	Garden Reach SY, Calcutta	4 Oct 1995	18 Aug 1997	20 Aug 2001
KARMUKH	P 64	Garden Reach SY, Calcutta/Mazagon Dock	27 Aug 1997	6 Apr 2000	4 Feb 2004

Displacement, tons: 1,460 full load
Dimensions, feet (metres): 298.9 × 34.4 × 14.8
(91.1 × 10.5 × 4.5)
Main machinery: 2 SEMT-Pielstick/Kirloskar 18 PA6 V 280
diesels; 14,400 hp(m) *(10.58 MW)* sustained; 2 shafts;
LIPS cp props
Speed, knots: 25. **Range, n miles:** 4,000 at 16 kt
Complement: 134 (14 officers)

Missiles: SSM: 16 Zvezda SS-N-25 (4 quad) (Kh 35E Uran) ❶;
active radar homing to 130 km *(70.2 n miles)* at
0.9 Mach; warhead 145 kg; sea skimmer.
SAM: 2 SA-N-5 Grail ❷; manual aiming; IR homing to 6 km
(3.2 n miles) at 1.5 Mach; altitude to 2,500 m *(8,000 ft)*;
warhead 1.5 kg.
Guns: 1 USSR 3 in *(76 mm)*/60 AK 176 (P 61) ❸; 90 rds/min
to 12 km *(6.4 n miles)*; weight of shell 7 kg. 1 Otobreda
76 mm/62 (P 62, P 63 and P 64).
2—30 mm/65 AK 630 ❹; 6 barrels per mounting; 3,000
rds/min to 2 km.
Countermeasures: Decoys: 2 PK 10 chaff launchers ❺.
2 BEL TOTED; towed torpedo decoys.
ESM: Bharat Ajanta P Mk II intercept ❻.
Combat data systems: Bharat Vympal IPN-10.
Radars: Air search: Cross Dome ❼; E/F-band; range 130 km
(70 n miles).
Air/surface search: Plank Shave (Granit Harpun B) ❽;
I/J-band.
Fire control: Bass Tilt (P 61) ❾; H/I-band; BEL Lynx (P62-64);
I-band.
Navigation: Bharat 1245; I-band.
IFF: Square Head.

Helicopters: Platform only ❿ for Chetak (to be replaced by
Hindustan Aeronautics ALH in due course).

Programmes: First pair ordered in April 1990 and second
pair in October 1994. Programme slowed by delays
in provision of Russian equipment and it is not clear
whether further vessels are to be built.
Structure: Very similar to the original Khukri class except
that SS-N-25 has replaced SS-N-2. Stabilisers fitted.
Operational: Sea trials for *Kirch* and *Kulish* probably took
place in 2000. All 16 SS-N-25 can be fired in one salvo.

KORA

(Scale 1 : 900), Ian Sturton / 0064715

KULISH

1/2004, Ships of the World / 1042275

KIRCH

3/2004, Bob Fildes / 1042273

4 KHUKRI CLASS (PROJECT 25) (FSGHM)

Name	No	Builders	Laid down	Launched	Commissioned
KHUKRI	P 49	Mazagon Dock Ltd, Mumbai	27 Sep 1985	3 Dec 1986	23 Aug 1989
KUTHAR	P 46	Mazagon Dock Ltd, Mumbai	13 Sep 1986	15 Apr 1989	7 June 1990
KIRPAN	P 44	Garden Reach SY, Calcutta	15 Nov 1985	16 Aug 1988	12 Jan 1991
KHANJAR	P 47	Garden Reach SY, Calcutta	15 Nov 1985	16 Aug 1988	22 Oct 1991

Displacement, tons: 1,423 full load
Dimensions, feet (metres): 298.9 × 34.4 × 13.1
  (91.1 × 10.5 × 4)
Main machinery: 2 SEMT-Pielstick/Kirloskar 18 PA6 V 280
  diesels; 14,400 hp(m) *(10.58 MW)* sustained; 2 shafts;
  LIPS cp props
Speed, knots: 24. **Range, n miles:** 4,000 at 16 kt
Complement: 112 (12 officers)

Missiles: SSM: 4 SS-N-2D Mod 1 Styx (2 twin) launchers ❶;
  IR homing to 83 km *(45 n miles)* at 0.9 Mach; warhead
  513 kg.
  SAM: SA-N-5 Grail ❷; manual aiming; IR homing to 6 km
  (3.2 n miles) at 1.5 Mach; altitude to 2,500 m *(8,000 ft)*;
  warhead 1.5 kg.
Guns: 1 USSR 3 in *(76 mm)*/60 AK 176 ❸; 120 rds/min to
  12 km *(6.4 n miles)*; weight of shell 7 kg.
  2—30 mm/65 AK 630 ❹; 6 barrels per mounting; 3,000
  rds/min to 2 km.
Countermeasures: Decoys: 2 PK 16 chaff launchers ❺.
  NPOL; towed torpedo decoy.
  ESM: Bharat Ajanta P; intercept.
Combat data systems: Selenia IPN-10 *(Khukri)*; Bharat
  Vympal IPN-10 (remainder).
Radars: Air search: Cross Dome ❻; E/F-band; range 130 km
  (70 n miles).
  Air/surface search: Plank Shave ❼; I-band.
  Fire control: Bass Tilt ❽; H/I-band.
  Navigation: Bharat 1245; I-band.

Helicopters: Platform only ❾ for Chetak (to be replaced by
  HAL Dhruv in due course).

Programmes: First two ordered December 1983, two in
  1985. The diesels were assembled in India under licence
  by Kirloskar. Indigenous content of the whole ship is
  about 65 per cent.
Structure: The reported plan was to make the first four ASW
  ships, and the remainder anti-aircraft or general purpose.
  However *Khukri* has neither torpedo tubes nor a sonar
  (apart from an Atlas Elektronik echo-sounder), so if the
  plan is correct these ships will rely on an ALH helicopter
  which has dunking sonar and ASW torpedoes and depth
  charges. All have fin stabilisers and full air conditioning.
Operational: All based at Vishakapatnam. The advanced
  light helicopter (ALH) to have Sea Eagle SSM, torpedoes
  and dipping sonar.

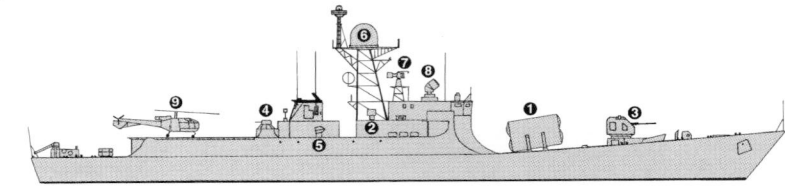

KHUKRI

(Scale 1 : 900), Ian Sturton / 0064713

KHANJAR

10/1998, John Mortimer / 0052335

KUTHAR

3/1996 / 0012974

KIRPAN

2/2001, Michael Nitz / 0534081

13 VEER (TARANTUL I) CLASS (PROJECT 1241RE) (FSGM)

Name	No	Builders	Laid down	Launched	Commissioned
VEER	K 40	Volodarski, Rybinsk	1984	Oct 1986	26 Mar 1987
NIRBHIK	K 41	Volodarski, Rybinsk	1985	Oct 1987	21 Dec 1987
NIPAT	K 42	Volodarski, Rybinsk	1986	Nov 1988	5 Dec 1988
NISHANK	K 43	Volodarski, Rybinsk	1987	June 1989	2 Sep 1989
NIRGHAT	K 44	Volodarski, Rybinsk	1988	Mar 1990	4 June 1990
VIBHUTI	K 45	Mazagon Dock, Mumbai	28 Sep 1987	26 Apr 1990	3 June 1991
VIPUL	K 46	Mazagon Dock, Mumbai	29 Feb 1988	3 Jan 1991	16 Mar 1992
VINASH	K 47	Goa Shipyard	30 Jan 1989	24 Jan 1992	20 Nov 1993
VIDYUT	K 48	Goa Shipyard	27 May 1990	12 Dec 1992	16 Jan 1995
NASHAK	K 83	Mazagon Dock, Mumbai	21 Jan 1991	12 Nov 1993	29 Dec 1994
PRAHAR	K 98	Goa Shipyard	28 Aug 1992	26 Aug 1995	1 Mar 1997
PRABAL	K 92	Mazagon Dock, Mumbai	31 Aug 1998	28 Sep 2000	11 Apr 2002
PRALAYA	K 91	Goa Shipyard	14 Nov 1998	14 Dec 2000	18 Dec 2002

Displacement, tons: 455 full load; 477 full load (K 92 and K 91)
Dimensions, feet (metres): 184.1 × 37.7 × 8.2 *(56.1 × 11.5 × 2.5)*
Main machinery: COGAG (M15E); 2 Nikolayev Type DR 77 (DS 71 in K 92) gas turbines; 16,016 hp(m) *(11.77 MW)* sustained; 2 Nikolayev Type DR 76 gas turbines with reversible gearboxes; 4,993 hp(m)*(3.67 MW)* sustained; 2 shafts
Speed, knots: 36. **Range, n miles:** 2,000 at 20 kt; 400 at 36 kt
Complement: 41 (5 officers)

Missiles: SSM: 4 SS-N-2D Mod 1 Styx; IR homing to 83 km *(45 n miles)* at 0.9 Mach; warhead 513 kg; sea-skimmer at end of run. 16 (4 quad) SS-N-25 (Kh 35 Uran) in K 91 and K 92; active radar homing to 130 km *(70.2 n miles)* at 0.9 Mach; warhead 145 kg; sea skimmer.
SAM: SA-N-5 Grail quad launcher; manual aiming; IR homing to 6 km *(3.2 n miles)* at 1.5 Mach; warhead 1.5 kg.
Guns: 1 USSR 3 in *(76 mm)*/60; 120 rds/min to 15 km *(8 n miles)*; weight of shell 7 kg.
1 OTO Melara 3 in *(76 mm)*/62 Super Rapid (K 91 and K 92); 120 rds/min to 16 km (8.7 n miles); weight of shell 6 kg.
2—30 mm/65 AK 630; 6 barrels per mounting; 3,000 rds/min combined to 2 km. 2—7.62 mm MGs.
Countermeasures: Decoys: PK 16 chaff launcher.
ESM: Bharat Ajanta P Mk II; intercept.
Weapons control: Hood Wink optronic director.
Radars: Air/surface search: Plank Shave; E-band.
Cross Dome (K 91 and K 92); E/F-band.
Navigation: Mius; I-band.
Fire control: Bass tilt: H/I-band.
BEL Lynx (K 91 and K 92) (for guns); I-band; Bharat Aparna (modified Plank Shave/Harpun B) (for SSM); I/J-band.
IFF: Salt Pot, Square Head A.

Programmes: First five are USSR Tarantul I class built for export. Six further of the same type built in India. Two further craft, armed with the SS-N-25 missile were delivered in 2002. It is not clear whether there are to be further vessels.
Structure: K 92 and K 91 are to a modified design to accommodate the SS-N-25 missile. Principal differences are the bridge and mast configurations.
Operational: All form the 22nd Missile Vessel Squadron at Mumbai.

NIRGHAT   *2/2005** / 1151114

PRABAL   *12/2002, Kapil Chandni* / 0529546

SHIPBORNE AIRCRAFT

Notes: (1) The procurement of up to eight second-hand Sea Harriers from the UK was under consideration in early 2006. The aircraft would retain the Blue Vixen radar but would not be equipped with AIM-120 AMRAAM missiles. The aircraft would probably be operated as training aircraft.
(2) Replacement of the Sea King fleet was initiated in January 2006 when Requests for Proposals were issued to eight overseas suppliers. Following evaluation, a contract is expected in 2007-08.

Numbers/Type: 12/4 MIG 29K Fulcrum/MIG 29KUB.
Operational speed: 750 kt *(1,400 km/h)*.
Service ceiling: 57,000 ft *(17,400 m)*.
Range: 1,400 n miles *(2,600 km)*.
Role/Weapon systems: All-weather single-seat fighter with attack capability, optimised for ski-jump take off, is to be main weapon of *Admiral Gorshkov* aircraft carrier. Initial order for 12 aircraft and four trainers to be delivered from 2007 with an option to acquire a further 30 aircraft by 2015. Sensors: Pulse Doppler look down/shoot down radar (Slot Back) able to track 10 targets simultaneously. Weapons: AAM; R77. ASM: CH-31A/P anti-ship and anti-radar. Conventional bombs: KAB-500 Kr. 30 mm cannon.

Numbers/Type: 12 Kamov Ka-28 Helix A.
Operational speed: 110 kt *(204 km/h)*.
Service ceiling: 12,000 ft *(3,660 m)*.
Range: 270 n miles *(500 km)*.
Role/Weapon systems: ASW helicopter embarked in large escorts. Has replaced Ka-25. Sensors: Splash Drop search radar; VGS-3 dipping sonar, sonobuoys. Weapons: ASW; two Whitehead A244S or USSR APR-2 torpedoes or four depth bombs.

MiG-29   *7/2004, Paul Jackson* / 0572477

HELIX A   *8/2002, Arjun Sarup* / 0569192

Numbers/Type: 14/2 British Aerospace Sea Harrier FRS. Mk 51/Mk 60.
Operational speed: 640 kt *(1,186 km/h)*.
Service ceiling: 51,200 ft *(15,600 m)*.
Range: 800 n miles *(1,480 km)*.
Role/Weapon systems: Fleet air defence, strike and reconnaissance STOVL fighter. Three more acquired from UK in 1999 to make good losses. Of total numbers, only about one third are operational. Sensors: Ferranti Blue Fox air interception radar, limited ECM/RWR (Elta 8420 in due course). Weapons: Air defence; two Magic AAMs (possibly ASRAAM in due course), two 30 mm Aden cannon. Plans for a mid-life upgrade have been abandoned. Avionics are to be improved to extend life of aircraft to 2008.

SEA HARRIER   *1994, Indian Navy* / 0012970

Numbers/Type: 2/20/5 Westland Sea King Mk 42A/42B/42C.
Operational speed: 112 kt *(208 km/h)*.
Service ceiling: 11,500 ft *(3,500 m)*.
Range: 664 n miles *(1,230 km)*.
Role/Weapon systems: Mk 42A has primary ASW and 42B primary ASV capability; Mk 42C for commando assault/vertrep. Not all aircraft are operational. Sensors: MEL Super Searcher radar, Thomson Sintra H/S-12 dipping sonar (Mk 42A and B), AQS 902B acoustic processor (Mk 42B); Marconi Hermes ESM (Mk 42B); Bendix weather radar (Mk 42C). Weapons: ASW; 2 Whitehead A244S or USSR APR-2 torpedoes; Mk 11 depth bombs, mines (Mk 42B only). ASV; two Sea Eagle (Mk 42B only). Unarmed (Mk 42C).

SEA KING 42B   *8/2002, Arjun Sarup* / 0569194

Numbers/Type: 9 Kamov Ka-31 Helix B.
Operational speed: 119 kt *(220 km/h)*.
Service ceiling: 11,480 ft *(3,500 m)*.
Range: 325 n miles *(600 km)*.
Role/Weapon systems: AEW helicopter. First two delivered late 2002 with remainder in 2003. Radar antenna folds beneath fuselage. Sensors: OKO E-80/M radar.

Ka-31   *6/2005*, Patrick Allen/Jane's* / 1136991

Numbers/Type: 23 Aerospatiale (HAL) SA 319B Chetak (Alouette III).
Operational speed: 113 kt *(210 km/h)*.
Service ceiling: 10,500 ft *(3,200 m)*.
Range: 290 n miles *(540 km)*.
Role/Weapon systems: Several helicopter roles performed including embarked ASW and carrier-based SAR, utility and support to commando forces. 15 aircraft are operated by Coast Guard. Weapons: ASW; two Whitehead A244S torpedoes.

CHETAK   *2/2001, Wingman Aviation* / 0102181

Numbers/Type: 12 HAL Dhruv.
Operational speed: 156 kt *(290 km/h)*.
Service ceiling: 9,850 ft *(3,000 m)*.
Range: 216 n miles *(400 km)*.
Role/Weapon systems: Formerly known as Advanced Light Helicopter (ALH), full production was delayed by thrust and vibration problems which have now been overcome. The naval variant started trials in March 1995 and the first two were delivered in 2003. Sensors: Dipping sonar, ECM. Weapons: ASW; torpedoes, depth charges. ASV; Sea Eagle ASM.

Dhruv   *2/2001, HAL* / 0095088

LAND-BASED MARITIME AIRCRAFT (FRONT LINE)

Notes: The requirement for future maritime reconnaissance aircraft is being met in the short term by acquisition of up to eight P-3C Orion aircraft from the US. Longer term, the Indian Navy is reported to be considering the Boeing 737 P-8A but is likely also to be investigating non-US MPA manufacturers.

Numbers/Type: 8 Lockheed P-3C Orion.
Operational speed: 410 kt *(760 km/h)*.
Service ceiling: 28,300 ft *(8,625 m)*.
Range: 4,000 n miles *(7,410 km)*.
Role/Weapon systems: Agreement on initial lease of two aircraft reached in late 2005 for delivery in early 2006. A follow-on order for a further six aircraft is expected. These would be transferred after refurbishment. Tenders are to be invited for the upgrade of sensors and weapons. These include: Sensors: APS-115 search radar; up to 100 sonobuoys; ASQ 81 MAD; ESM. Weapons: four torpedoes or depth charges; air-to-surface missiles.

P-3C (US markings)   *3/2005*, Paul Jackson* / 0567125

Numbers/Type: 4 Israel Aircraft Industries Heron.
Operational speed: 125 kt *(231 km/h)*.
Service ceiling: 26,500 ft *(8,075 m)*.
Range: 108 n miles *(200 km)*.
Role/Weapon systems: Capable of performing a variety of missions but primarily a real-time system for intelligence collection, surveillance, target acquisition/tracking, and communications/data relay. Several payloads can be carried simultaneously including real-time TV/FLIR, synthetic aperture radar or camera. Can be controlled from ground station via direct LOS data/command link. Part of UAV squadron commissioned on 6 January 2006. Based at Kochi but operated from other bases. Has conducted sea trials with INS *Vindhyagiri*. Endurance 50 hours.

HERON UAV   *12/2005*, IAI* / 1116200

Numbers/Type: 2 Fokker F27 Friendship.
Operational speed: 250 kt *(463 km/h)*.
Service ceiling: 29,500 ft *(8,990 m)*.
Range: 2,700 n miles *(5,000 km)*.
Role/Weapon systems: Operated by coast guard for long-range patrol. Search radar only. Unarmed.

Numbers/Type: 8 Israel Aircraft Industries Searcher II.
Operational speed: 105 kt *(194 km/h)*.
Service ceiling: 20,000 ft *(6,100 m)*.
Range: 92 n miles *(170 km)*.
Role/Weapon systems: Can be configured for tactical surveillance or as communications relay aircraft. Several payloads can be carried simultaneously including real-time TV/FLIR, synthetic aperture radar or camera. Can be controlled from ground station via direct LOS data/command link. Part of UAV squadron commissioned on 6 January 2006. Based at Kochi but operated from other bases. Endurance 18 hours.

Searcher II   *6/2003*, C Hoyle/Jane's* / 0531011

Numbers/Type: 15 Dornier 228.
Operational speed: 200 kt *(370 km/h)*.
Service ceiling: 28,000 ft *(8,535 m)*.
Range: 940 n miles *(1,740 km)*.
Role/Weapon systems: Coastal surveillance and EEZ protection duties for Navy and Coast Guard. Sensors: MEL Marec or THORN EMI Super Marec search radar with FLIR, cameras and searchlight. Weapons: Unarmed, but may carry anti-ship missiles in due course.

DORNIER 228   *12/2000* / 0121342

Numbers/Type: 3 Ilyushin Il-38 (May).
Operational speed: 347 kt *(645 km/h)*.
Service ceiling: 32,800 ft *(10,000 m)*.
Range: 3,887 n miles *(7,200 km)*.
Role/Weapon systems: Shore-based long-range ASW reconnaissance into Indian Ocean. Following the loss of two aircraft in a mid-air collision in 2002, two replacement aircraft were donated by Russia. All five aircraft being upgraded to Il-38SD standard with improved avionics, radar, ASM and ASW capabilities. Delivery of first refitted aircraft on 15 January 2006. Sensors: Leninets Sea Dragon/Novella radar, MAD, sonobuoys, ESM. Weapons: ASW; various torpedoes, mines and depth bombs.

MAY   *2/2001, Wingman Aviation* / 0121338

Numbers/Type: 3 Pilatus Britten-Norman Maritime Defender.
Operational speed: 150 kt *(280 km/h)*.
Service ceiling: 18,900 ft *(5,760 m)*.
Range: 1,500 n miles *(2,775 km)*.
Role/Weapon systems: Coastal and short-range reconnaissance tasks undertaken in support of Navy (6) and Coast Guard. Six upgraded with turboprop engines 1996-97. Sensors: Search radar, camera. Weapons: Unarmed.

DEFENDER   *2/2001, Wingman Aviation* / 0121339

Numbers/Type: 8 Tupolev Tu-142M (Bear F).
Operational speed: 500 kt *(925 km/h)*.
Service ceiling: 45,000 ft *(13,720 m)*.
Range: 6,775 n miles *(12,550 km)*.
Role/Weapon systems: First entered service in April 1988 for long-range surface surveillance and ASW. Air Force manned. Planned acquisition of further eight in 2001 not confirmed. Sensors: Wet Eye search and attack radars, MAD, cameras. 75 active and passive sonobuoys. Weapons: ASW; 12 torpedoes, depth bombs. ASV; two 23 mm cannon. Avionics, ASM (possibly SS-N-25) and ASW package upgraded in mid-life update from 2001.

BEAR F   *2/2001* / 0121345

Numbers/Type: 8 SEPECAT/HAL Jaguar International.
Operational speed: 917 kt *(1,699 km/h)* (max).
Service ceiling: 36,000 ft *(11,000 m)*.
Range: 760 n miles *(1,408 km)*.
Role/Weapon systems: A maritime strike squadron. Air Force operated. Sensors: Thomson-CSF Agave radar. Weapons: ASV; 2 BAe Sea Eagle; 2 DEFA 30 mm cannon or up to 8-1,000 lb bombs. Can carry 2 Magic AAM overwing.

JAGUAR   *2/2001, Wingman Aviation* / 0121340

PATROL FORCES

5 + (2) SUPER DVORA MK II CLASS (PBF)

No	Builders	Commissioned
T 80	IAI, Ramta	14 May 1998
T 81	Goa Shipyard Ltd	29 May 1999
T 82	IAI, Ramta	9 Oct 2003
T 83	Goa Shipyard Ltd	22 Mar 2004
T 84	Goa Shipyard Ltd	30 Mar 2004

Displacement, tons: 60 full load
Dimensions, feet (metres): 83.3 × 18.4 × 4.9 *(25.4 × 5.6 × 1.5)*
Main machinery: 2 MTU 12V 396 TE94 diesels; 4,570 hp(m) *(3.36 MW)*; 2 Arneson ASD 16 surface drives
Speed, knots: 50
Range, n miles: 700 at 42 kt
Complement: 10 (1 officer)
Guns: 1—20 mm. 1—12.7 mm MG.
Weapons control: Elop MSIS optronic director.
Radars: Surface search: Koden; I-band.

Comment: Collaborative programme involving IAI, Ramta, Israel and Goa Shipyard Ltd. T 80 was built at Ramta and T 82 was procured by the Indian Navy from Israel. The other three were assembled at Goa. An order for a further two craft is expected but has not been confirmed.

SUPER DVORA   *2/2001* / 0126188

6 SUKANYA CLASS (PSOH)

Name	No	Builders	Launched	Commissioned
SUKANYA	P 50	Korea Tacoma, Masan	1989	31 Aug 1989
SUBHADRA	P 51	Korea Tacoma, Masan	1989	25 Jan 1990
SUVARNA	P 52	Korea Tacoma, Masan	22 Aug 1990	4 Apr 1991
SAVITRI	P 53	Hindustan SY, Vishakapatnam	23 May 1990	27 Nov 1990
SHARADA	P 55	Hindustan SY, Vishakapatnam	22 Aug 1990	27 Oct 1991
SUJATA	P 56	Hindustan SY, Vishakapatnam	25 Oct 1991	3 Nov 1993

Displacement, tons: 1,890 full load
Dimensions, feet (metres): 331.7 oa; 315 wl × 37.7 × 14.4
(101.1; 96 × 11.5 × 4.4)
Main machinery: 2 SEMT-Pielstick 16 PA6 V 280 diesels;
12,800 hp(m) *(9.41 MW)* sustained; 2 shafts
Speed, knots: 21. **Range, n miles:** 5,800 at 15 kt
Complement: 140 (15 officers)

Guns: 3 Bofors 40 mm/60. 4—12.7 mm MGs.
A/S mortars: 4 RBU 2500 16-tubed trainable launchers;
range 2,500 m; warhead 21 kg. Two launchers fitted in
forward section.
Radars: Surface search: Racal Decca 2459; I-band

Navigation: Bharat 1245; I-band

Helicopters: 1 Chetak

Programmes: First three ordered in March 1987 from Korea
Tacoma to an Ulsan class design. Second four ordered
in August 1987. The Korean-built ships commissioned at
Masan and then sailed for India where the armament
was fitted. Three others of a modified design have been
built for the Coast Guard. P 54 transferred to Sri Lanka
December 2000.
Structure: Lightly armed and able to 'stage' helicopters,
they are fitted out for offshore patrol work only but

have the capacity to be much more heavily armed. Fin
stabilisers fitted. Firefighting pump on hangar roof aft.
Operational: These ships are used for harbour defence,
protection of offshore installations and patrol of the
EEZ. Potential for role change is considerable. *Subhadra*
modified in early 2000 to test fire Dhanush (naval
version of Prithvi) SRBM from her flight deck. Dhanush
was first successfully fired on 20 September 2001.
On 7 November 2004, a 350 km range Prithvi 3 solid
propellant missile was reportedly fired in the Bay of
Bengal. First three based at Mumbai, last pair at Kochi,
P 53 at Vishakapatnam.
Sales: *Sukanya* transferred to Sri Lanka in 2000.

SUJATA

3/2004, Bob Fildes / 1042272

2 SDB MK 3 CLASS (LARGE PATROL CRAFT) (PB)

T 58-59

Displacement, tons: 210 full load
Dimensions, feet (metres): 124 × 24.6 × 6.2
(37.8 × 7.5 × 1.9)
Main machinery: 2 MTU 16V 538 TB92 diesels; 6,820 hp(m)
(5 MW) sustained; 2 shafts
Speed, knots: 30
Complement: 32
Guns: 2 Bofors 40 mm/60; 120 rds/min to 10 km
(5.5 n miles); weight of shell 0.89 kg.
Radars: Surface search: Bharat 1245; I-band.

Comment: Built at Garden Reach and Goa and completed
1984-86. Employed as seaward defence forces.

SDB MK 3 CLASS
6/2004, Indian Navy
1042279

6 SDB MK 5 (TRINKAT) CLASS (LARGE PATROL CRAFT) (PBO)

TRINKAT T 61	**TARASA** T 63	**BANGARAM** T 65
BITRA T 66	**BATTI MALV** T 67	**BARATANG** T 68

Displacement, tons: 260 full load
Dimensions, feet (metres): 151.0 × 24.6 × 8.2
(46.0 × 7.5 × 2.5)
Main machinery: 2 MTU 16V 538 TB92 diesels; 6,820 hp(m)
(5 MW) sustained; 2 shafts
Speed, knots: 30
Range, n miles: 2,000 at 12 kt
Complement: 34 (4 officers)
Guns: 1 Medak 30 mm 2A42.
Radars: Surface search: Bharat 1245; I-band.

Comment: The first four built at Garden Reach and
commissioned between September 2000 and March
2002. Four of a modified design are under construction.
T 65 was launched on 11 December 2004 and T 66 on
14 December 2004. Both were commissioned in November
2005. T 64 transferred to the Seychelles Coast Guard in
June 2005 and *Tillan Chang* to the Maldives on 16 April
2006. T 67 was launched on 28 June 2005 and T 68 on
6 August 2005. Both are to be commissioned in 2006.

TARASA
5/2005*, Guy Toremans
1127033

AMPHIBIOUS FORCES

Notes: Acquisition of an amphibious assault ship to upgrade sealift capability and from which heavy helicopters could be operated is under consideration. USS *Trenton* (LPD 14) has been offered by the US government and is a strong contender. A refit in a US yard would precede transfer.

3 + 1 (1) MAGAR CLASS (LSTH)

Name	No	Builders	Launched	Commissioned
MAGAR	L 20	Garden Reach	7 Nov 1984	15 July 1987
GHARIAL	L 23	Hindustan/Garden Reach	1 Apr 1991	14 Feb 1997
SHARDUL	—	Hindustan/Garden Reach	3 Apr 2004	2006
KESARI	—	Garden Reach Shipyard	8 June 2005	2007

Displacement, tons: 5,655 full load
Dimensions, feet (metres): 409.4 oa; 393.7 wl × 57.4 × 13.1 *(124.8; 120 × 17.5 × 4)*
Main machinery: 2 SEMT-Pielstick 12 PA6 V280 diesels; 8,560 hp(m) *(6.29 MW)* sustained; 2 shafts
Speed, knots: 15
Range, n miles: 3,000 at 14 kt
Complement: 136 (16 officers)
Military lift: 15 tanks plus 8 APC plus 500 troops
Guns: 4 Bofors 40 mm/60. 2 — 122 mm multibarrel rocket launchers at the bow.
Countermeasures: ESM: Bharat Ajanta; intercept.
Radars: Navigation: Bharat; I-band.
Helicopters: 1 Sea King 42C; platform for 2.

Comment: Based on the *Sir Lancelot* design. *Magar* was built entirely at Garden Reach. *Gharial* ordered in 1985. Built at Hindustan Shipyard but fitted out at Garden Reach. Internal design differs from *Magar*. Carries four LCVPs on davits. Bow door. Can beach on gradients 1 in 40 or more. *Magar* refitted in 1995. Both based at Vishakapatnam. *Shardul* includes major design changes and is expected to be commissioned in late 2005. A fourth ship, *Kesari*, was launched on 9 June 2005. A fifth ship may be built.

MAGAR *2/2001, Guy Toremans* / 0121348

6 MK 2/3 LANDING CRAFT (LSM)

VASCO DA GAMA L 34	— L 36	MIDHUR L 38
— L 35	— L 37	MANGALA L 39

Displacement, tons: 500 full load
Dimensions, feet (metres): 188.6 oa; 174.5 pp × 26.9 × 5.2 *(57.5; 53.2 × 8.2 × 1.6)*
Main machinery: 3 Kirloskar-MAN V8V 17.5/22 AMAL diesels; 1,686 hp(m) *(1.24 MW)*; 3 shafts
Speed, knots: 11
Range, n miles: 1,000 at 8 kt
Complement: 167
Military lift: 250 tons; 2 PT 76 or 2 APC. 120 troops
Guns: 2 Bofors 40 mm/60 (aft).
Mines: Can be embarked.
Radars: Navigation: Decca 1229; I-band.

Comment: L 34 and 35 are Mk 2 craft built by Hooghly D and E Co. The remaining Mk 3 craft were built at Goa Shipyard. First craft commissioned 28 January 1980 and the last one commissioned 25 March 1987. L 36-39 have a considerably modified superstructure and a higher bulwark on the cargo deck.

L 36 *2/1999, 92 Wing RAAF* / 0064719

L 34 *3/1995* / 0064720

5 POLNOCHNY C (PROJECT 773 I) and D CLASS (PROJECT 773 IM) (LSM/LSMH)

SHARABH L 17	CHEETAH L 18	MAHISH L 19
GULDAR L 21	KUMBHIR L 22	

Displacement, tons: 1,150 (C class); 1,190 (D class) full load
Dimensions, feet (metres): 266.7; 275.3 (D class) × 31.8 × 7.9 *(81.3; 83.9 × 9.7 × 2.4)*
Main machinery: 2 Kolomna Type 40-D diesels; 4,400 hp(m) *(3.2 MW)* sustained; 2 shafts
Speed, knots: 16. **Range, n miles:** 3,000 at 12 kt
Complement: 60 (6 officers)
Military lift: 160 troops; 5 MBT or 5 APC or 5 AA guns or 8 trucks
Guns: 4 — 30 mm (2 twin) Ak 230. 2 — 140 mm 18-tubed rocket launchers.
Radars: Navigation: Don 2 or Krivach (SRN 745); I-band
Fire control: Drum Tilt; H/I-band (in D class).
Helicopters: Platform only (in D class).

Comment: A original class of eight built in two batches by Naval Shipyard, Gdynia. *Sharabh* transferred in February 1976, *Cheetah* in February 1985, *Mahish* in July 1985, *Guldar* in March 1986 and *Kumbhir* in November 1986. The last four are Polnochny Ds with the flight deck forward of the bridge and different radars. All are being restricted operationally through lack of spares, but all are seaworthy. Drum Tilt radar removed from some ships. Four Polnochny Ds (L 18-22) form 5th landing Ship Squadron based at Port Blair.

MAHISH *2/2001, Guy Toremans* / 0121353

MINE WARFARE FORCES

Notes: Procurement of up to eight minehunters has been approved. It is anticipated that the ships will be to a foreign design and of GRP construction. Building is expected to take place at Goa Shipyards. The ships are likely to be equipped with a minehunting sonar and with a remote-control mine-disposal system. Requests for proposals are expected to be sought from predominantly European manufacturers. Building of the first of class is due to start in 2008.

12 PONDICHERRY (NATYA I) CLASS (PROJECT 266M) (MINESWEEPERS—OCEAN) (MSO)

Name	No	Builders	Commissioned
PONDICHERRY	M 61	Isora, Leningrad	2 Feb 1978
PORBANDAR	M 62	Isora, Leningrad	19 Dec 1978
BEDI	M 63	Isora, Leningrad	27 Apr 1979
BHAVNAGAR	M 64	Isora, Leningrad	27 Apr 1979
ALLEPPEY	M 65	Isora, Leningrad	10 June 1980
RATNAGIRI	M 66	Isora, Leningrad	10 June 1980
KARWAR	M 67	Isora, Leningrad	14 July 1986
CANNANORE	M 68	Isora, Leningrad	17 Dec 1987
CUDDALORE	M 69	Isora, Leningrad	29 Oct 1987
KAKINADA	M 70	Isora, Leningrad	23 Dec 1986
KOZHIKODE	M 71	Isora, Leningrad	19 Dec 1988
KONKAN	M 72	Isora, Leningrad	8 Oct 1988

Displacement, tons: 804 full load
Dimensions, feet (metres): 200.1 × 33.5 × 10.8 *(61 × 10.2 × 3)*
Main machinery: 2 Type 504 diesels; 5,000 hp(m) *(3.67 MW)* sustained; 2 shafts; cp props
Speed, knots: 16. **Range, n miles:** 3,000 at 12 kt
Complement: 82 (10 officers)

Guns: 4 — 30 mm/65 (2 twin); 500 rds/min to 5 km *(2.7 n miles)*; weight of shell 0.54 kg.
4 — 25 mm/70 (2 twin); 270 rds/min to 3 km *(1.6 n miles)*.
A/S mortars: 2 RBU 1200 5-tubed fixed; range 1,200 m; warhead 34 kg.
Mines: Can carry 10.
Countermeasures: MCM: 1 GKT-2 contact sweep; 1 AT-2 acoustic sweep; 1 TEM-3 magnetic sweep.
Radars: Navigation: Don 2; I-band
Fire control: Drum Tilt; H/I-band
IFF: 2 Square Head. High Pole B
Sonars: MG 69/79; hull-mounted; active mine detection; high frequency

Programmes: Built for export. Last six were delivered out of pennant number order.
Structure: Steel hulls but do not have stern ramp as in Russian class.
Operational: Some are fitted with two quad SA-N-5 systems. *Pondicherry* was painted white and used as the Presidential yacht for the Indian Fleet Review by President R Venkataramen on 15 February 1989; she reverted to her normal role and colour on completion. One serves as an AGI. First six form 19th MCM Squadron based at Mumbai and second batch form 21st MCM Squadron based at Vishakapatnam.

KARWAR *4/2004, John Mortimer* / 1042271

2 MAHÉ (YEVGENYA) CLASS (PROJECT 1258)
(MINESWEEPERS—INSHORE) (MSI)

MAHÉ M 83   **MALPE** M 86

Displacement, tons: 90 full load
Dimensions, feet (metres): 80.7 × 18 × 4.9 *(24.6 × 5.5 × 1.5)*
Main machinery: 2 Type 3-D-12 diesels; 600 hp(m) *(440 kW)* sustained; 2 shafts
Speed, knots: 11. **Range, n miles:** 300 at 10 kt
Complement: 10 (1 officer)
Guns: 2 USSR 25 mm/80 (twin)
Radars: Navigation: Spin Trough; I-band
Sonars: MG 7 small transducer streamed over the stern on a crane

Comment: First batch commissioned 16 May 1983 and second batch on 10 May 1984. A mid-1960s design with GRP hulls built at Kolpino. Form 20th MCM Squadron based at Kochi. *Mulki, Malvan, Magdala* and *Mangrol* have decommissioned.

MAHÉ CLASS   *6/1994* / 0064722

SURVEY AND RESEARCH SHIPS

Notes: The National Institute of Oceanography operates several research and survey ships including *Sagar Kanya, Samudra Manthan, Sagar Sampada, Samudra Sarvekshak, Samudra Nidhi* and *Samudra Sandhari.*

8 SANDHAYAK CLASS (SURVEY SHIPS) (AGSH)

Name	No	Builders	Launched	Commissioned
SANDHAYAK	J 18	Garden Reach, Calcutta	6 Apr 1977	1 Mar 1981
NIRDESHAK	J 19	Garden Reach, Calcutta	16 Nov 1978	4 Oct 1982
NIRUPAK	J 14	Garden Reach, Calcutta	10 July 1981	14 Aug 1985
INVESTIGATOR	J 15	Garden Reach, Calcutta	8 Aug 1987	11 Jan 1990
JAMUNA	J 16	Garden Reach, Calcutta	4 Sep 1989	31 Aug 1991
SUTLEJ	J 17	Garden Reach, Calcutta	1 Dec 1991	19 Feb 1993
DARSHAK	J 21	Goa Shipyard	3 Mar 1999	28 Apr 2001
SARVEKSHAK	J 22	Goa Shipyard	24 Nov 1999	14 Jan 2002

Displacement, tons: 1,929 full load
Dimensions, feet (metres): 288 × 42 × 11.1 *(87.8 × 12.8 × 3.4)*
Main machinery: 2 GRSE/MAN 66V 30/45 ATL diesels; 7,720 hp(m) *(5.67 MW)* sustained; 2 shafts; active rudders
Speed, knots: 16. **Range, n miles:** 6,000 at 14 kt; 14,000 at 10 kt
Complement: 178 (18 officers) plus 30 scientists
Guns: 1 or 2 Bofors 40 mm/60.
Countermeasures: ESM: Telegon IV HF D/F.
Radars: Navigation: Racal Decca 1629; I-band.
Helicopters: 1 Chetak.

Comment: Telescopic hangar. Fitted with three echo-sounders, side scan sonar, extensively equipped laboratories, and carries four GRP survey launches on davits amidships. Painted white with yellow funnels. An active rudder with a DC motor gives speeds of up to 5 kt. First three based at Vishakapatnam and have been used as troop transports. *Investigator* is at Mumbai and *Jamuna* and *Sutlej* at Kochi. The last pair were laid down in May and August 1995 and have a secondary role as casualty holding ships.

DARSHAK   *4/2002, Giorgio Ghiglione* / 0534057

1 SAGARDHWANI CLASS

Name	No	Builders	Commissioned
SAGARDHWANI	A 74	Garden Reach, Calcutta	30 July 1994

Displacement, tons: 2,050 full load
Dimensions, feet (metres): 279.2 × 42 × 12.1 *(85.1 × 12.8 × 3.7)*
Main machinery: 2 GRSE/MAN 66V 30/45 ATL diesels; 3,860 hp(m) *(2.84 MW)* sustained; 2 shafts; 2 auxiliary thrusters
Speed, knots: 16
Range, n miles: 6,000 at 16 kt
Complement: 80 (10 officers) plus 16 scientists
Radars: Navigation: Racal Decca 1629; I-band.
Helicopters: Platform for Alouette III.

Comment: Marine Acoustic Research Ship (MARS) launched in May 1991. The hull and main machinery are very similar to the Sandhayak class survey ships, but there are marked superstructure differences with the bridge positioned amidships and a helicopter platform forward. Aft there are two large cranes and a gantry for deploying and recovering research equipment. The vessel is designed to carry out acoustic and geological research and special attention has been paid to noise reduction. The ship is painted white except for the lift equipment and two boats which are orange. Employed in advanced torpedo trials and missile range support. Based at Kochi.

SAGARDHWANI   *2/2001, Michael Nitz* / 0534058

2 MAKAR CLASS (SURVEY SHIPS) (AGS)

MEEN J 33   **MITHUN** J 34

Displacement, tons: 210 full load
Dimensions, feet (metres): 123 × 24.6 × 6.2 *(37.5 × 7.5 × 1.9)*
Main machinery: 2 diesels; 1,124 hp(m) *(826 kW)*; 2 shafts
Speed, knots: 12
Range, n miles: 1,500 at 12 kt
Complement: 36 (4 officers)
Guns: 1 Bofors 40 mm/60.
Radars: Navigation: Decca 1629; I-band.

Comment: Launched at Goa in 1981-82. Similar hulls to deleted SDB Mk 2 class but with much smaller engines. Employed as seaward defence forces.

MEEN   *4/1992* / 0064723

TRAINING SHIPS

1 TIR CLASS (TRAINING SHIP) (AXH)

Name	No	Builders	Launched	Commissioned
TIR	A 86	Mazagon Dock Ltd, Bombay	15 Apr 1983	21 Feb 1986

Displacement, tons: 3,200 full load
Dimensions, feet (metres): 347.4 × 43.3 × 15.7 *(105.9 × 13.2 × 4.8)*
Main machinery: 2 Crossley-Pielstick 8 PC2 V Mk 2 diesels; 7,072 hp(m) *(5.2 MW)* sustained; 2 shafts
Speed, knots: 18
Range, n miles: 6,000 at 12 kt
Complement: 239 (35 officers) plus 120 cadets
Guns: 2 Bofors 40 mm/60 (twin) with launchers for illuminants. 4 saluting guns.
Countermeasures: ESM: Telegon IV D/F.
Radars: Navigation: Bharat/Decca 1245; I-band.
Helicopters: Platform for Alouette III.

Comment: Second of class reported ordered May 1986 but was cancelled as an economy measure. Built to commercial standards, Decca collision avoidance plot and SATNAV. Can carry up to 120 cadets and 20 instructors. Based at Kochi.

TIR   *2/2001, Michael Nitz* / 0534059

1 LEANDER (BATCH 3A) CLASS (AXH)

Name	No	Builders	Commissioned
KRISHNA (ex-*Andromeda*)	F 46 (ex-F 57)	Portsmouth Dockyard	2 Dec 1968

Displacement, tons: 2,960 full load
Dimensions, feet (metres): 372 × 43 × 18 (screws) *(113.4 × 13.1 × 5.5)*
Main machinery: 2 Babcock & Wilcox boilers; 550 psi *(38.7 kg/cm²)*; 850°F *(454°C)*;
 2 White/English Electric turbines; 30,000 hp *(22.4 MW)*; 2 shafts
Speed, knots: 28. **Range, n miles:** 4,000 at 15 kt
Complement: 260 (19 officers)
Guns: 2 Bofors 40 mm/60. 2 Oerlikon 20 mm.
Radars: Air/surface search: Marconi Type 968; D/E-band.
 Navigation: Kelvin Hughes Type 1006; I-band.
Helicopters: 1 Chetak.

Comment: Laid down 25 May 1966 and launched 24 May 1967. Acquired from the UK in
 April 1995 having paid off in June 1993 to a state of extended readiness. Refitted by
 DML, Devonport, before recommissioning 22 August 1995. The original 114 mm gun
 turret, Seacat SAM and ASW Limbo mortar were removed in 1979-80 when Exocet
 SSM, Seawolf SAM, STWS torpedo tubes and facilities for a Lynx helicopter were fitted.
 Acquired for training purposes to supplement the *Tir*. Armament has been reduced to
 the minimum required for the training role, and now includes 40 mm guns on either
 side, aft of the funnel. Based at Kochi.

KRISHNA *8/1995, H M Steele* / 0064724

2 SAIL TRAINING SHIPS (AXS)

VARUNA TARANGINI A 75

Displacement, tons: 420 full load
Dimensions, feet (metres): 177.2 × 27.9 × 13.1 *(54 × 8.5 × 4)*
Main machinery: 2 diesels; 640 hp(m) *(470 kW)*; 2 shafts; LIPS props
Speed, knots: 10 (diesels)
Complement: 15 (6 officers) plus 45 cadets

Comment: *Varuna* completed in April 1981 by Alcock-Ashdown, Bhavnagar. Can carry 26
 cadets. Details given are for *Tarangini* which is based on a Lord Nelson design by Colin
 Mudie of Lymington and has been built by Goa Shipyard. Launched on 23 December
 1995, and completed in December 1997. Three masted barque, square rigged on forward
 and main mast and 'fore and aft' rigged on mizzen mast. Based at Mumbai.

TARANGINI *6/2005*, Guy Toremans* / 1151260

AUXILIARIES

Notes: (1) There is also a small hospital ship *Lakshadweep* of 865 tons and a crew of 35
 including 16 medics.
(2) *Ambika* is a 1,000 ton oiler commissioned in 1995. Built by Hindustan Shipyard, it is
 based at Vishakhapatnam.

1 UGRA CLASS (SUBMARINE TENDER) (ASH)

Name	No	Builders	Launched	Commissioned
AMBA	A 54	Nikolayev Shipyard	18 Jan 1968	28 Dec 1968

Displacement, tons: 6,750 standard; 9,650 full load
Dimensions, feet (metres): 462.6 × 57.7 × 23 *(141 × 17.6 × 7)*
Main machinery: Diesel-electric; 4 Kolomna Type 2-D-42 diesel generators; 2 motors;
 8,000 hp(m) *(5.88 MW)*; 2 shafts
Speed, knots: 17. **Range, n miles:** 21,000 at 10 kt
Complement: 400
Guns: 4 USSR 3 in *(76 mm)*/60 (2 twin).
Radars: Air/surface search: Slim Net; E/F-band.
 Fire control: 2 Hawk Screech; I-band.
 Navigation: Don 2; I-band.
 IFF: 2 Square Head. High Pole A.

Comment: Acquired from the USSR in 1968. Provision for helicopter. Can accommodate
 750. Two cranes, one of 6 tons and one of 10 tons. Differs from others of the class by
 having 76 mm guns. After extensive repairs, the ship is now deployed on the east coast.

AMBA *2/1998* / 0052348

1 + (1) JYOTI CLASS (REPLENISHMENT TANKER) (AORH)

Name	No	Builders	Launched	Commissioned
JYOTI	A 58	Admiralty Yard, St Petersburg	8 Dec 1995	20 July 1996

Displacement, tons: 35,900 full load
Dimensions, feet (metres): 587.3 × 72.2 × 26.2 *(179 × 22 × 8)*
Main machinery: 1 Burmeister & Wain diesel; 10,948 hp(m) *(8.05 MW)*; 1 shaft
Speed, knots: 15. **Range, n miles:** 12,000 at 15 kt
Complement: 92 (16 officers)
Cargo capacity: 25,040 tons diesel
Radars: Navigation: I-band.
Helicopters: Platform for 1 medium.

Comment: This was the third of a class of merchant tankers, modified for naval use for
 the Indian Navy and acquired in 1995. The ship was laid down in September 1993.
 Based at Mumbai where she arrived in November 1996. There are two replenishment
 positions on each side and stern refuelling is an option. Similar ship sold to China and
 two others are in commercial service. Procurement of another ship is reported to be
 under consideration.

JYOTI *10/2004, Hachiro Nakai* / 1042267

1 DEEPAK CLASS (REPLENISHMENT TANKER) (AORH)

Name	No	Builders	Commissioned
SHAKTI	A 57	Bremer-Vulkan	31 Dec 1975

Displacement, tons: 6,785 light; 15,828 full load
Measurement, tons: 12,013 gross
Dimensions, feet (metres): 552.4 × 75.5 × 30 *(168.4 × 23 × 9.2)*
Main machinery: 2 Babcock & Wilcox boilers; 1 BV/BBC steam turbine; 16,500 hp(m)
 (12.13 MW); 1 shaft
Speed, knots: 18.5. **Range, n miles:** 5,500 at 16 kt
Complement: 169
Cargo capacity: 1,280 tons diesel; 12,624 tons FFO; 1,495 tons avcat; 812 tons FW
Guns: 4 Bofors 40 mm/60. 2 Oerlikon 20 mm can be carried.
Countermeasures: ESM: Telegon IV HF D/F.
Radars: Navigation: 2 Decca 1226; I-band.
Helicopters: 1 Chetak.

Comment: Automatic tensioning fitted to replenishment gear. Heavy and light jackstays.
 Stern fuelling as well as alongside. DG fitted. Based at Mumbai.

SHAKTI *6/2000* / 0104589

1 ADITYA CLASS
(REPLENISHMENT AND REPAIR SHIP) (AORH/AS)

Name	No	Builders	Launched	Commissioned
ADITYA	A 59	Garden Reach, Calcutta	15 Nov 1993	3 Apr 2000
(ex-*Rajaba Gan Palan*)				

Displacement, tons: 24,600 full load
Measurement, tons: 17,000 dwt
Dimensions, feet (metres): 564.3 × 75.5 × 29.9 *(172 × 23 × 9.1)*
Main machinery: 2 MAN/Burmeister & Wain 16V 40/45 diesels; 23,936 hp(m) *(17.59 MW)* sustained; 1 shaft
Speed, knots: 20
Range, n miles: 10,000 at 16 kt
Complement: 156 (16 officers) + 6 aircrew
Cargo capacity: 14,200 m³ diesel and avcat; 2,250 m³ water; 2,170 m³ ammunition and stores.
Guns: 3 Bofors 40 mm/60.
Helicopters: 1 Chetak.

Comment: Ordered in July 1987 to a Bremer-Vulkan design. Lengthened version of Deepak class but with a multipurpose workshop. Four RAS stations alongside. Fully air conditioned. Building progress was very slow and sea trials were curtailed by propulsion problems during 1999. Ship has the capability to carry a Sea King 42B or KA 28 helicopter. First ship to be based at Karwar with effect from 15 December 2005.

ADITYA   *2/2001, Guy Toremans* / 0121357

1 DIVING SUPPORT SHIP (ASR)

Name	No	Builders	Commissioned
NIREEKSHAK	A 15	Mazagon Dock Ltd, Bombay	8 June 1989

Displacement, tons: 2,160 full load
Dimensions, feet (metres): 231.3 × 57.4 × 16.4 *(70.5 × 17.5 × 5)*
Main machinery: 2 Bergen KRM-8 diesels; 4,410 hp(m) *(3.24 MW)* sustained; 2 shafts; cp props; 2 bow thrusters; 2 stern thrusters; 990 hp(m) *(727 kW)*
Speed, knots: 12
Complement: 63 (15 officers)

Comment: Laid down in August 1982 and launched January 1984. Acquired on lease with an option for purchase which was taken up in March 1995, and the ship was recommissioned on 15 September 1995. The vessel was built for offshore support operations but has been modified for naval requirements. Two DSRV, capable of taking 12 men to 300 m, are carried together with two six-man recompression chambers and one three-man bell. Kongsberg ADP-503 Mk II. Dynamic positioning system. The ship is used for submarine SAR. Based at Mumbai.

NIREEKSHAK   *1991* / 0064727

3 TRANSPORT SHIPS (APH)

Name	No	Builders	Commissioned
NICOBAR	—	Szczecin Shipyard, Poland	12 Apr 1990
ANDAMANS	—	Szczecin Shipyard, Poland	5 Oct 1990
(ex-*Nancowry*)			
SWARAJ DEEP	—	Vishakhapatnam	1997

Displacement, tons: 19,000 full load
Measurement, tons: 14,176 grt
Dimensions, feet (metres): 515.1 × 68.9 × 22 *(157 × 21 × 6.7)*
Main machinery: 2 Cegielski-Burmeister am Wain 6L35MC diesels; 72,000 hp *(5.3 MW)*; 2 shafts; bow thruster
Speed, knots: 16
Complement: 160
Cargo capacity: 1,200 troops
Helicopters: Platform for 1 medium.

Comment: The first two ships designed and built in Poland. *Nicobar* delivered to the Shipping Corporation of India (which operated the ship for the Andaman and Nicobar Islands Administration) on 5 June 1991 and subsequently acquired for use by the Indian Navy in April 1998. *Andamans* delivered to the Shipping Corporation of India on 31 March 1992 and acquired for use by the Indian Navy in April 2000. Both ships used to trans-ship stores and personnel to the Andaman and Nicobar Islands. They have large davits capable of operating LCVPs. *Swaraj Deep* is of a similar design.

SWARAJ DEEP   *6/2004, M Mazumdar* / 1042280

6 SUPPORT TANKERS (AOTL)

POSHAK	PURAN	PUSHPA	PRADHAYAK	PURAK	PALAN

Comment: First two built at Mazagon Dock Ltd, Bombay. *Poshak* completed April 1982, and *Puran* in November 1988. *Pushpa* (capacity 650 tons) built at Goa Shipyard and completed in 1990. *Pradhayak, Purak* and *Palan* built at Rajabagan Shipyard, Bombay, the first two in 1977 and *Palan* in May 1986. Cargo capacities vary. Civilian manned.

PUSHPA   *1990, Goa Shipyard* / 0064728

2 WATER CARRIERS (AWT)

AMBUDA	COCHIN

Comment: First laid down Rajabagan Shipyard 18 January 1977. Second built at Mazagon Dock Ltd, Bombay. Civilian manned.

AMBUDA   *4/1992* / 0064729

1 TORPEDO RECOVERY VESSEL (YPT)

A 72

Displacement, tons: 110 full load
Dimensions, feet (metres): 93.5 × 20 × 4.6 *(28.5 × 6.1 × 1.4)*
Main machinery: 2 Kirloskar V12 diesels; 720 hp(m) *(529 kW)*; 2 shafts
Speed, knots: 11
Complement: 13

Comment: Completed in 1981 at Goa Shipyard. Based at Vishakapatnam.

A 72   *2/1989, G Jacobs* / 0506006

3 DIVING TENDERS (YDT)

Displacement, tons: 36 full load
Dimensions, feet (metres): 48.9 × 14.4 × 3.9 *(14.9 × 4.4 × 1.2)*
Main machinery: 2 diesels; 130 hp(m) *(96 kW)*; 2 shafts
Speed, knots: 12

Comment: Built at Cleback Yard. First completed 1979; second and third in 1984.

YDT   *9/1996* / 0012531

TUGS

1 TUG (OCEAN) (ATA/ATR)

MATANGA A 53

Measurement, tons: 1,313 grt
Dimensions, feet (metres): 222.4 × 40.4 × 13.1 *(67.8 × 12.3 × 4)*
Main machinery: 2 GRSE/MAN G7V diesels; 3,920 hp(m) *(2.88 MW)*; 2 shafts
Speed, knots: 15
Range, n miles: 4,000 at 15 kt
Complement: 78 (8 officers)
Guns: 1 Bofors 40 mm/60.
Radars: Navigation: I-band.

Comment: Built by Garden Reach SY. *Matanga* launched 29 October 1977. Bollard pull of 40 tons and capable of towing a 20,000 ton ship at 8 kt. Carries a divers' decompression chamber and other salvage equipment.

MATANGA   *2/2001, Michael Nitz* / 0143309

14 HARBOUR TUGS (YTM/YTL)

AGARAL	BC DUTT	RAJAJI	ANAND	BHIM
SHAMBU SINGH	BALSHIL	MADAN SINGH	BAJARANG	AJRAL
ARJUN	TARAFDAAR	BALRAM	GAJ A 51	

Measurement, tons: 216 grt
Dimensions, feet (metres): 96.1 × 27.9 × 8.5 *(29.3 × 8.5 × 2.6)*
Main machinery: 2 SEMT-Pielstick 8 PA4 V 200 diesels; 3,200 hp(m) *(2.35 MW)*; 2 shafts
Speed, knots: 11
Complement: 12

Comment: First three built by Mazagon Dock Ltd, Bombay in 1973-74. Five more delivered in 1988-89, and four more in 1991 from Mazagon Dock Ltd, Goa. *Gaj* is a 25 ton bollard pull tug built by Hindustan Shipyard and commissioned on 10 October 2002. Details given are for *Balram* and *Bajrang*; *Rajaji* is of comparable size built in 1982; *Bhim*, *Balshil* and *Ajral* were built by Tebma Shipyard, Chennai, the others are of varying types.

MADAN SINGH   *2/2001, Sattler/Steele* / 0121356

COAST GUARD

Senior Appointments

Director General:
Vice Admiral Arun Kumar Singh
Deputy Director General:
Inspector General P Paleri, TM

Personnel

2006: 5,393 (717 officers)

General

The Coast Guard was constituted as an independent paramilitary service on 19 August 1978. It functions under the Ministry of Defence.

Responsibilities include:
(a) Ensuring the safety and protection of artificial islands, offshore terminals and other installations in the Maritime Zones.
(b) Measures for the safety of life and property at sea including assistance to mariners in distress.
(c) Measures to preserve and protect the marine environment and control marine pollution.
(d) Assisting the Customs and other authorities in anti-smuggling operations.
(e) Enforcing the provisions of enactments in force in the Maritime Zones.
(f) Protection of fishermen and assistance to them at sea while in distress.

Bases

The Headquarters of the Coast Guard is located in Delhi with Regional Headquarters in Mumbai, Chennai and Port Blair. West Coast District Headquarters at Mumbai, New Mangalore, Goa, Porbandar, Kavaratti (Lakshadweep), Jakhau, Vizihinjam, Kochi. East Coast District/Headquarters at Vishakapatnam, Chennai, Paradip and Haldia. Andaman and Nicobar District Headquarters at Campbell Bay and Diglipur. Stations at Vadinar, Mandapam, Okha and Tuticorin.

Aviation

Air Squadrons at Daman CGAS 750 (11 Dorniers 228); Kochi CGAS 747 (2 Dornier); Chennai CGAS 744 (7 Dorniers 228); Kolkatta CGAS 700 (2 Dornier 228), Port Blair CGAS 745 (2 Dornier 228); Daman CGAS 841 (4 Chetaks); Mumbai CGAS 842 (3 Chetaks); Goa CGAS 800 (4 Chetaks); Chennai CGAS 848 (3 Chetaks); Port Blair (1 Chetak). Vajra flight (1 Chetak), Veera flight (1 Chetak) and CGEFU Goa (3 ALH).

PATROL FORCES

0 + 1 ADVANCED OFFSHORE PATROL VESSEL (WPSOH)

Name	No	Builders	Laid down	Launched	Commissioned
SANKALP	—	Goa Shipyard	17 July 2004	28 Apr 2006	2007

Displacement, tons: 2,230 full load
Dimensions, feet (metres): 344.5 × 42.3 × 11.8 *(105.0 × 12.9 × 3.6)*
Main machinery: 2 SEMT-Pielstick 20 PA6B stc diesels; 20,900 hp(m) *(15.58 MW)*; 2 shafts; cp props
Speed, knots: 24. **Range, n miles:** 6,500 at 12 kt
Complement: 126 (18 officers)

Guns: 1—3 in *(76 mm)*. 2—30 mm.
Radars: Surface search: To be announced. Navigation: To be announced.

Helicopters: 1 HAL Dhruv.

ADVANCED OPV   *(Scale 1 : 900), Ian Sturton* / 1042088

Comment: Designed and built under ABS and IRS classification by Goa Shipyard for patrol and SAR operations, pollution control and firefighting. Further orders are expected.

0 + 3 POLLUTION CONTROL VESSELS (UT 517 CLASS) (WPSOH)

Name	No	Builders	Laid down	Launched	Commissioned
SAMUDRA PRAHARI	–	ABG Shipyard, Surat	2004	2005	2006
SAMUDRA PAHREDAR	–	ABG Shipyard, Surat	2005	2006	2007
SAMUDRA PAVAK	–	ABG Shipyard, Surat	2006	2007	2008

Displacement, tons: 3,300 full load
Dimensions, feet (metres): 308.4 × 50.9 × 14.8 *(94.0 × 15.5 × 4.5)*
Main machinery: 2 Bergen B32 diesels; 8,050 hp *(6.0 MW)*; 2 shafts; cp props. 1 Ulstein Aquamaster bow thruster; 1,185 hp *(883 kW)*
Speed, knots: 20. **Range, n miles:** 6,000 at 14 kt
Complement: 85 (10 officers)
Guns: 1 – 30 mm.
Radars: Navigation: To be announced.
Helicopters: Platform for 1 medium.

Comment: Rolls-Royce UT 517 design selected on 25 October 2004 for three environmental protection ships. The ships are to feature a range of Rolls-Royce propulsion, steering and motion control equipment and are similar to those selected for use by the French Navy and Norwegian Coast Guard. The ships are to be capable of deploying a boom system to contain oil spillages while additional tasks are to include surveillance and law enforcement, anti-smuggling and fishery protection, search and rescue, collecting data, and assistance with salvage and fire fighting.

UT 517 CLASS (artist's impression) *10/2004, Rolls-Royce* / 1042264

4 SAMAR CLASS (OFFSHORE PATROL VESSELS) (WPSOH)

Name	No	Builders	Laid down	Launched	Commissioned
SAMAR	42	Goa Shipyard	1990	26 Aug 1992	14 Feb 1996
SANGRAM	43	Goa Shipyard	1992	18 Mar 1995	29 Mar 1997
SARANG	44	Goa Shipyard	1993	8 Mar 1997	21 June 1999
SAGAR	45	Goa Shipyard	1999	14 Dec 2001	3 Nov 2003

Displacement, tons: 2,005 full load
Dimensions, feet (metres): 334.6 oa; 315 wl × 37.7 × 11.5 *(102; 96 × 11.5 × 3.5)*
Main machinery: 2 SEMT-Pielstick 16 PA6 V 280 diesels; 12,800 hp(m) *(9.41 MW)* sustained; 2 shafts; LIPS cp props
Speed, knots: 22. **Range, n miles:** 7,000 at 15 kt
Complement: 124 (12 officers)
Guns: 1 OTO Melara 3 in *(76 mm)*/62 Super Rapid; 120 rds/min to 16 km *(8.7 n miles)*; weight of shell 6 kg.
2 – 12.7 mm MGs.
Weapons control: BEL/Radamec optronic 2400 director.
Radars: Surface search: Decca 2459; F/I-band.
Navigation: BEL 1245; I-band.
Helicopters: 1 Chetak.

Programmes: First three ordered in April 1991. Fourth of class ordered 1999.
Structure: Similar to the Navy's Sukanya class but more heavily armed and carrying a helicopter capable of transporting a Marine contingent. Telescopic hangar.

SANGRAM *9/2003, Hachiro Nakai* / 0572431

9 VIKRAM CLASS (OFFSHORE PATROL VESSELS) (WPSOH)

Name	No	Builders	Launched	Commissioned
VIKRAM	33	Mazagon Dock, Mumbai	26 Sep 1981	19 Dec 1983
VIJAYA	34	Mazagon Dock, Mumbai	5 June 1982	12 Apr 1985
VEERA	35	Mazagon Dock, Mumbai	30 June 1984	3 May 1986
VARUNA	36	Mazagon Dock, Mumbai	28 Jan 1986	27 Feb 1988
VAJRA	37	Mazagon Dock, Mumbai	3 Jan 1987	22 Dec 1988
VIVEK	38	Mazagon Dock, Mumbai	5 Nov 1987	19 Aug 1989
VIGRAHA	39	Mazagon Dock, Mumbai	27 Sep 1988	12 Apr 1990
VARAD	40	Goa Shipyard	3 Sep 1989	19 July 1990
VARAHA	41	Goa Shipyard	5 Nov 1990	11 Mar 1992

Displacement, tons: 1,224 full load
Dimensions, feet (metres): 243.1 × 37.4 × 10.5 *(74.1 × 11.4 × 3.2)*
Main machinery: 2 SEMT-Pielstick 16 PA6 V 280 diesels; 12,800 hp(m) *(9.41 MW)* sustained; 2 shafts; cp props
Speed, knots: 22. **Range, n miles:** 4,250 at 12 kt
Complement: 96 (11 officers)
Guns: 1 – 30 mm.
Weapons control: Lynx optical sights.
Radars: Navigation: 2 Decca 1226; I-band.
Helicopters: 1 HAL (Aerospatiale) Chetak.

Comment: Owes something to a NEVESBU (Netherlands) design, being a stretched version of its 750 ton offshore patrol vessels. Ordered in 1979. Fin stabilisers. Diving equipment. 4.5 ton deck crane. External firefighting pumps. Has one GRP boat and two inflatable craft. This class is considered too small for its required task and hence the need for the larger Samar class.

VIJAYA *2/2001, Guy Toremans* / 0121354

8 PRIYADARSHINI CLASS (COASTAL PATROL CRAFT) (WPBO)

Name	No	Builders	Commissioned
PRIYADARSHINI	221	Garden Reach, Calcutta	25 May 1992
RAZIA SULTANA	222	Goa Shipyard	18 Nov 1992
ANNIE BESANT	223	Goa Shipyard	7 Dec 1992
KAMLA DEVI	224	Goa Shipyard	20 May 1992
AMRIT KAUR	225	Goa Shipyard	20 Mar 1993
KANAK LATA BAURA	226	Garden Reach, Calcutta	27 Mar 1997
BHIKAJI CAMA	227	Garden Reach, Calcutta	24 Sep 1997
SUCHETA KRIPALANI	228	Garden Reach, Calcutta	16 Mar 1998

Displacement, tons: 306 full load
Dimensions, feet (metres): 150.9 × 24.6 × 6.2 *(46.0 × 7.5 × 1.9)*
Main machinery: 2 MTU 12V 538 diesels; 4,025 hp(m) *(2.96 MW)* sustained; 2 shafts
Speed, knots: 23
Range, n miles: 2,400 at 12 kt
Complement: 34 (7 officers)
Guns: 1 – 30 mm.
2 – 7.62 mm MGs.
Radars: Surface search: Racal Decca 1226 or BEL 1245/6X (221 – 225); I-band.

Comment: A development of the Tara Bai class. *Razia Sultana* (222), previously thought to have been lost at sea, remains in commission.

KAMLA DEVI *3/2004, Bob Fildes* / 1042270

6 TARA BAI CLASS (COASTAL PATROL CRAFT) (WPBO)

Name	No	Builders	Commissioned
TARA BAI	71	Singapore SBEC	26 June 1987
AHALYA BAI	72	Singapore SBEC	9 Sep 1987
LAKSHMI BAI	73	Garden Reach, Calcutta	20 Mar 1989
AKKA DEVI	74	Garden Reach, Calcutta	9 Aug 1989
NAIKI DEVI	75	Garden Reach, Calcutta	19 Mar 1990
GANGA DEVI	76	Garden Reach, Calcutta	19 Nov 1990

Displacement, tons: 195 full load
Dimensions, feet (metres): 147.3 × 23.0 × 6.23 *(44.9 × 7.0 × 1.9)*
Main machinery: 2 MTU 12V 538 diesels; 4,025 hp(m) *(2.96 MW)* sustained; 2 shafts
Speed, knots: 26
Range, n miles: 2,400 at 12 kt
Complement: 34 (7 officers)
Guns: 1 Bofors 40 mm/60.
2 – 7.6 mm MGs.
Radars: Surface search: Racal Decca 1226 or BEL 1245/6X (221 – 225); I-band.

Comment: Two ordered in June 1986 with license to build further four in India. These were laid down in 1987.

AKKA DEVI *6/2000, Indian Navy* / 1042263

5 + 2 SAROJINI NAIDU CLASS (WPBO)

Name	No	Builders	Commissioned
SAROJANI NAIDU	229	Goa Shipyard	11 Nov 2002
DURGABAI DESHMUKH	230	Goa Shipyard	30 Apr 2003
KASTURBA GANDHI	231	Goa Shipyard	28 Oct 2005
ARUNA ASAF ALI	232	Goa Shipyard	28 Jan 2006
SUBHDRA KUMARI CHAUHAN	233	Goa Shipyard	28 Apr 2006
MEERA BEHAN	234	Goa Shipyard	Jan 2007
SAVITRI BAI PHULE	235	Goa Shipyard	Apr 2007

Displacement, tons: 260 full load
Dimensions, feet (metres): 157.8 × 24.6 × 6.6 *(48.1 × 7.5 × 2)*
Main machinery: 3 MTU-F 16V4000 M90 diesels; total of 10,942 hp(m) *(8.2 MW)* sustained;
   3 Kamewa 71SII waterjets
Speed, knots: 35
Complement: 35
Guns: 1 — 30 mm.
   2 — 12.7 mm MGs.
Radars: Surface search: to be announced.

Comment: A new class of patrol ship designed and developed by Goa Shipyard. Following
   the initial delivery of two vessels, an order for a further five was made in 2004. The first
   of these was launched on 20 October 2005 for delivery in March 2006. The remainder
   are to follow at three month intervals.

SAROJINI NAIDU   *11/2002, Indian Coast Guard* / 0530081

7 JIJA BAI MOD 1 CLASS (TYPE 956)
(COASTAL PATROL CRAFT) (WPBO)

Name	No	Builders	Commissioned
JIJA BAI	64	Sumidagawa, Tokyo	22 Feb 1984
CHAND BIBI	65	Sumidagawa, Tokyo	22 Feb 1984
KITTUR CHENNAMMA	66	Sumidagawa, Tokyo	21 Oct 1983
RANI JINDAN	67	Sumidagawa, Tokyo	21 Oct 1983
HABBAH KHATUN	68	Garden Reach, Calcutta	27 Apr 1985
RAMADEVI	69	Garden Reach, Calcutta	3 Aug 1985
AVVAIYYAR	70	Garden Reach, Calcutta	19 Oct 1985

Displacement, tons: 181 full load
Dimensions, feet (metres): 144.3 × 24.3 × 7.5 *(44 × 7.4 × 2.3)*
Main machinery: 2 MTU 12V 538 TB82 diesels; 4,025 hp(m) *(2.96 MW)* sustained; 2 shafts
Speed, knots: 25. **Range, n miles:** 2,375 at 14 kt
Complement: 34 (7 officers)
Guns: 1 Bofors 40 mm/60. 2 — 7.62 mm MGs.
Radars: Surface search: Racal Decca 1226; I-band.

Comment: All were ordered in 1981 and are similar to those in service with the Philippines
   Coast Guard.

RANI JINDAN   *6/1996, Indian Coast Guard* / 0064732

2 SDB MK 2 RAJ CLASS (COASTAL PATROL CRAFT) (WPB)

Name	No	Builders	Commissioned
RAJKIRAN	59	Garden Reach, Calcutta	29 Mar 1984
RAJKAMAL	61	Garden Reach, Calcutta	19 Sep 1986

Displacement, tons: 203 full load
Dimensions, feet (metres): 123 × 24.6 × 5.9 *(37.5 × 7.5 × 1.8)*
Main machinery: 2 MTU 12V 538 diesels; 4,025 hp(m) *(2.96 MW)* sustained; 2 shafts
Speed, knots: 29. **Range, n miles:** 1,400 at 14 kt
Complement: 28 (4 officers)
Guns: 1 Bofors 40/60 mm.
Radars: Surface search: Racal Decca; I-band.

Comment: Earlier vessels of this class belonged to the Navy but have been scrapped.

RAJKAMAL   *6/2000, Indian Coast Guard* / 0104591

1 SWALLOW 65 CLASS (WPB)

C 63

Displacement, tons: 32 full load
Dimensions, feet (metres): 65.6 × 15.4 × 5 *(20 × 4.7 × 1.5)*
Main machinery: 2 Detroit 12V-71TA diesels; 840 hp *(627 kW)* sustained; 2 shafts
Speed, knots: 20
Range, n miles: 400 at 20 kt
Complement: 9 (1 officer)
Guns: 1 — 7.62 mm MG.
Radars: Navigation: I-band.

Comment: Built by Swallow Craft Co, Pusan, South Korea in early 1980s. Last remaining
   craft in service.

C 63   *1982, Swallow Craft* / 0012534

9 INSHORE PATROL CRAFT (WPB)

C 131-138   C 140

Displacement, tons: 49 full load
Dimensions, feet (metres): 68.2 × 19 × 5.9
Main machinery: 2 Deutz MWM TBD234V12 diesels; 1,646 hp(m) *(1.21 MW)* sustained;
   1 Deutz MWM TBD234V8 diesel; 550 hp(m) *(404 kW)* sustained; 3 Hamilton 402 water-jets
Speed, knots: 25
Range, n miles: 600 at 15 kt
Complement: 8 (1 officer)
Guns: 1 — 12.7 mm MG.
Radars: Navigation: Furuno; I-band.

Comment: Ordered from Anderson Marine, Goa in September 1990 to a P-2000 design
   by Amgram, similar to British Archer class. GRP hull. Official description is 'Interceptor
   Boats'. All built at Goa. Commissioned: *C 131—132* on 16 November 1993, *C 133—134*
   on 20 May 1994, *C 135—136* on 16 February 1995, *C 137—138* on 4 September 1996,
   and *C 139* on 16 October 1997. *C 139* was leased to Mauritius in 2001. C 140, was
   commissioned on 15 November 2003.

C 136 (old number)   *2/2001, Sattler/Steele* / 0121360

2 INSHORE PATROL CRAFT (WPBF)

C 141   C 142

Displacement, tons: To be announced
Dimensions, feet (metres): 85.3 × ? × ? *(26.0 × ? × ?)*
Main machinery: 2 diesels; 2 Kamewa waterjets
Speed, knots: 45
Complement: To be announced
Guns: To be announced.
Radars: Surface search: To be announced.

Comment: Built by ABG Shipbuilding, Surat and commissioned on 8 February 2002.
   Aluminium construction.

C 141   *6/2004, Kapil Chandni* / 1042268

8 INSHORE PATROL CRAFT (WPBF)

C 109-116

Displacement, tons: 5.5 full load
Dimensions, feet (metres): 31.2 × 10.7 × 2.5 *(9.5 × 3.3 × 0.75)*
Main machinery: 2 outboard motors; diesels; 500 hp *(370 kW)*
Speed, knots: 35. **Range, n miles:** 75 at 25 kt
Complement: 2
Guns: 1 — 7.62 mm MG.

Comment: Built by Bristol Boats Ltd, Kochi. The first craft became operational on 1 December 2004.

6 GRIFFON 8000 TD(M) CLASS HOVERCRAFT (UCAC)

H 181-186

Displacement, tons: 18.2; 24.6 full load
Dimensions, feet (metres): 69.5 × 36.1 × 1 *(21.15 × 11 × 0.32)*
Main machinery: 2 MTU 12V 183 TB 32 V12 diesels; 800 hp *(596 kW)*
Speed, knots: 50. **Range, n miles:** 400 at 45 kt
Complement: 13 (2 officers)
Guns: 1 — 12.7 mm MG.
Radar: Raytheon R-80; I-band.

Comment: Six hovercraft were ordered from GRSE Calcutta in May 1999 for construction in technical collaboration with Griffon UK. The first craft H 181 was commissioned on 18 September 2000, four further in 2001, and the final one on 21 March 2002.

H 185

6/2004*, Kapil Chandni / 1042269

Indonesia

TENTARA NASIONAL

Country Overview

The Republic of Indonesia gained full independence from the Netherlands in 1949. Straddling the equator, the country comprises more than 13,670 islands, of which some 6,000 are inhabited. The major islands include Sumatra, Java, Sulawesi (Celebes), southern Borneo (Kalimantan) and western New Guinea (Papua). Smaller islands include Madura, western Timor, Lombok, Sumbawa, Flores, and Bali. The Moluccas and Lesser Sunda Islands are the largest island groups. The coastline of 29,550 n miles is with the South China Sea, the Celebes Sea, the Pacific Ocean and the Indian Ocean. The total land area is 741,903 square miles. The capital, largest city and principal port is Jakarta (Java). Further main ports are at Surabaya (Java), Medan (Sumatra) and Ujung Pandang (Sulawesi). An archipelagic state, territorial seas (12 n miles) are claimed. A 200 n mile EEZ has also been claimed but the limits are only partly defined by boundary agreements.

Headquarters Appointments

Chief of the Naval Staff:
  Admiral Slamet Subijanto
Vice Chief of the Naval Staff:
  Rear Admiral I W R Argawa
Inspector General of the Navy:
  Major General Achmad Rifai
Assistant Chief of Staff, Operations:
  Rear Admiral Ardius Zainuddin

Fleet Command

Commander-in-Chief Western Fleet (Jakarta):
  Rear Admiral Tedjo Edhy Purdijanton
Commander-in-Chief Eastern Fleet (Surabaya):
  Rear Admiral Didik Heru Purnomo

Fleet Command — *continued*

Commandant of Navy Marine Corps:
  Major General Safzen Nurdin
Commander, Military Sealift Command:
  Rear Admiral Djokko Agus Hanung
Commander, Naval Training Command:
  Commodore Waldi Murad

Personnel

(a)   2006: 57,000 (including 20,000 Marine Commando Corps and 1,000 Naval Air Arm)
(b)   Selective national service

Bases

Tanjung Priok (North Jakarta), Ujung (Surabaya), Sabang, Belawan (North Sumatera), Ujung Pandang (South Sulawesi), Balikpapan (East Kalimantan), Jayapura (Irian Jaya), Tanjung Pinang, Bitung (North Sulawesi), Teluk Ratai (South Sumatera), Banjarmasin, South Kalmantan. Naval Air Base at Juanda (Surabaya), Biak (Irian Jaya), Pekan Baru, Sam Ratulangi (North Sulawesi), Sabang, Natuna, P Aru.

Command Structure

Eastern Command (Surabaya)
Western Command (Jakarta)
Training Command
Military Sea Communications Command (Maritime Security Agency)
Military Sealift Command (Logistic Support)

Marine Corps

Reorganisation in March 2001 created the 1st Marine Corps Group (1st, 3rd and 5th battalions) based at Surabaya and the Independent Marine Corps Brigade (2nd, 4th and 6th battalions) based in Jakarta. A new formation (7th, 8th and 9th battalions) is to be based at Teluk Ratai, Sumatra. Equipment includes amphibious tanks, field artillery and anti-aircraft missiles and guns. There are plans to expand the Corps to 22,800 by 2009. Further reorganisation is expected to include relocation of the eastern command from Surabaya to Makassar and the central command from Jakarta to Surabaya.

Strength of the Fleet

Type	Active	Building (Projected)
Patrol Submarines	2	2
Frigates	9	–
Corvettes	19	5 (1)
Fast Attack Craft-Missile	4	–
Large Patrol Craft	21	–
Patrol craft	13	–
LPD	1	4
LST/LSM	26	–
MCMV	12	–
Survey and Research Ships	8	–
Command Ship	1	–
Repair Ship	1	–
Replenishment Tankers	2	–
Coastal Tankers	3	–
Support Ships	6	–
Transports	2	–
Sail Training Ships	2	–

Prefix to Ships' Names

KRI (Kapal di Republik Indonesia)

PENNANT LIST

Submarines							
		379	Wiratno	815	Sanca	514	Teluk Mandar
		380	Memet Sastrawiria	816	Warakas	515	Teluk Sampit
401	Cakra	381	Tjiptadi	817	Panana	516	Teluk Banten
402	Nanggala	382	Hasan Basri	818	Kalakae	517	Teluk Ende
		383	Iman Bonjol	819	Tedong Naga	531	Teluk Gilimanuk
		384	Pati Unus	847	Sibarau	532	Teluk Celukan Bawang
Frigates		385	Teuku Umar	848	Siliman	533	Teluk Cendrawasih
		386	Silas Papare	857	Sigalu	534	Teluk Berau
341	Samadikun			858	Silea	535	Teluk Peleng
342	Martadinata			859	Siribua	536	Teluk Sibolga
351	Ahmad Yani	**Patrol Forces**		862	Siada	537	Teluk Manado
352	Slamet Riyadi			863	Sikuda	538	Teluk Hading
353	Yos Sudarso	621	Mandau	864	Sigurot	539	Teluk Parigi
354	Oswald Siahann	622	Rencong	–	Cucuk	540	Teluk Lampung
355	Abdul Halim Perdanakusuma	623	Badik	867	Kobra	541	Teluk Jakarta
356	Karel Satsuitubun	624	Keris	868	Anakonda	542	Teluk Sangkuring
364	Ki Hajar Dewantara	651	Singa	869	Patola	580	Dore
		653	Ajak	870	Taliwangsa	582	Kupang
		801	Pandrong			583	Dili
Corvettes		802	Sura			584	Nusa Utara
		803	Todak	**Amphibious Forces**			
361	Fatahillah	804	Hiu				
362	Malahayati	805	Layang	501	Teluk Langsa	**Survey Ships**	
363	Nala	806	Lemadang	502	Teluk Bayur		
371	Kapitan Patimura	807	Boa	503	Teluk Amboina	KAL-IV-02	Baruna Jaya I
372	Untung Suropati	808	Welang	504	Teluk Kau	KAL-IV-03	Baruna Jaya II
373	Nuku	809	Suluh Pari	508	Teluk Tomini	KAL-IV-04	Baruna Jaya III
374	Lambung Mangkurat	810	Katon	509	Teluk Ratai	KAL-IV-05	Baruna Jaya IV
375	Cut Nyak Dien	811	Kakap	510	Teluk Saleh	KAL-IV-06	Baruna Jaya VIII
376	Sultan Thaha Syaifuddin	812	Krapu	511	Teluk Bone	931	Burujulasad
377	Sutanto	813	Tongkol	512	Teluk Semangka	932	Dewa Kembar
378	Sutedi Senoputra	814	Barakuda	513	Teluk Penyu	933	Jalanidhi

PENNANT LIST

Mine Warfare Forces		726	Pulau Rusa	561	Multatuli	935	Tambora	
		727	Pulau Rangsang	901	Balikpapan	936	Bromo	
701	Pulau Rani	728	Pulau Raibu	902	Sambu	952	Nusa Telu	
711	Pulau Rengat	729	Pulau Rempang	903	Arun	959	Teluk Mentawai	
712	Pulau Rupat			906	Sungai Gerong	960	Karimata	
721	Pulau Rote	**Auxiliaries**		911	Sorong	961	Wagio	
722	Pulau Raas			921	Jaya Wijaya	972	Tanjung Dalpele	
723	Pulau Romang	543	Teluk Cirebon	922	Rakata	973	Tanjung Nusanive	
724	Pulau Rimau	544	Teluk Sabang	923	Soputan	974	Tanjung Fatagar	
725	Pulau Rondo			934	Lampo Batang			

SUBMARINES

Notes: Two ex-German Type 206 submarines were taken over on 25 September 1997 with plans to refit them, followed by three others. Funds ran out in June 1998 and the whole project was then cancelled. New plans to acquire two submarines from South Korea were announced in October 2003. Delivery from 2008 is a reported requirement and this probably points to a modified Chang Bogo class. Funding is reported to be provided through a counter-trade agreement involving CN-235 aircraft to South Korea. It is possible that this plan may too have been superseded following reported talks with Russia on the purchase of Kilo and/or Amur class submarines in early 2006. Procurement of Chinese boats is yet a further option.

2 CAKRA (209) CLASS (1300 TYPE)

Name	No
CAKRA	401
NANGGALA	402

Builders	Laid down	Launched	Commissioned
Howaldtswerke, Kiel	25 Nov 1977	10 Sep 1980	19 Mar 1981
Howaldtswerke, Kiel	14 Mar 1978	10 Sep 1980	6 July 1981

Displacement, tons: 1,285 surfaced; 1,390 dived
Dimensions, feet (metres): 195.2 × 20.3 × 17.9 *(59.5 × 6.2 × 5.4)*
Main machinery: Diesel-electric; 4 MTU 12V 493 AZ80 GA31L diesels; 2,400 hp(m) *(1.76 MW)* sustained; 4 Siemens alternators; 1.7 MW; 1 Siemens motor; 4,600 hp(m) *(3.38 MW)* sustained; 1 shaft
Speed, knots: 11 surfaced; 21.5 dived
Range, n miles: 8,200 at 8 kt
Complement: 34 (6 officers)

Torpedoes: 8—21 in *(533 mm)* bow tubes. 14 AEG SUT Mod 0; dual purpose; wire-guided; active/passive homing to 12 km *(6.5 n miles)* at 35 kt; 28 km *(15 n miles)* at 23 kt; warhead 250 kg.
Countermeasures: ESM: Thomson-CSF DR 2000U; radar warning.
Weapons control: Signaal Sinbad system.
Radars: Surface search: Thomson-CSF Calypso; I-band.
Sonars: Atlas Elektronik CSU 3-2; active/passive search and attack; medium frequency.
PRS-3/4; (integral with CSU) passive ranging.

Programmes: Ordered on 2 April 1977. Designed by Ingenieurkontor, Lübeck for construction by

NANGGALA   *8/1999, van Ginderen Collection* / 0080001

Howaldtswerke, Kiel and sale by Ferrostaal, Essen-all acting as a consortium.
Modernisation: Major refits at HDW spanning three years from 1986 to 1989. These refits were expensive and lengthy and may have discouraged further orders at that time. *Cakra* refitted again at Surabaya from 1993 completing in April 1997, including replacement batteries and updated Sinbad TFCS. *Nanggala* received a similar refit from October 1997 to mid-1999. *Cakra* began a refit at Daewoo Shipyard, South Korea in 2004. This was completed in 2005. Work is likely to have included new batteries, overhaul of engines and modernisation of the combat system. A similar refit of *Nanggala* is also under consideration subject to funding.
Structure: Have high-capacity batteries with GRP lead-acid cells and battery cooling supplied by Wilhelm Hagen AG. Diving depth, 240 m *(790 ft)*.
Operational: Endurance, 50 days. Operational status of both boats is doubtful until refits have been completed.

FRIGATES

1 KI HAJAR DEWANTARA CLASS (FFGH/FFT)

Name	No
KI HAJAR DEWANTARA	364

Builders	Laid down	Launched	Commissioned
Split SY, Yugoslavia	11 May 1979	11 Oct 1980	31 Oct 1981

Displacement, tons: 2,050 full load
Dimensions, feet (metres): 317.3 × 36.7 × 15.7 *(96.7 × 11.2 × 4.8)*
Main machinery: CODOG; 1 RR Olympus TM3B gas turbine; 24,525 hp *(18.3 MW)* sustained; 2 MTU 16V 956 TB92 diesels; 11,070 hp(m) *(8.14 MW)* sustained; 2 shafts; cp props
Speed, knots: 26 gas; 20 diesels
Range, n miles: 4,000 at 18 kt; 1,150 at 25 kt
Complement: 76 (11 officers) plus 14 instructors and 100 cadets

Missiles: SSM: 4 Aerospatiale MM 38 Exocet ❶; inertial cruise; active radar homing to 42 km *(23 n miles)* at 0.9 Mach; warhead 165 kg; sea-skimmer.
Guns: 1 Bofors 57 mm/70 ❷; 200 rds/min to 17 km *(9.3 n miles)*; weight of shell 2.4 kg.
2 Rheinmetall 20 mm ❸.
Torpedoes: 2—21 in *(533 mm)* tubes ❹. AEG SUT; dual purpose; wire-guided; active/passive homing to 28 km *(15 n miles)* at 23 kt; 12 km *(6.5 n miles)* at 35 kt; warhead 250 kg.
Depth charges: 1 projector/mortar.
Countermeasures: Decoys: 2—128 mm twin-tubed flare launchers.
ESM: MEL Susie; radar intercept.
Combat data systems: Signaal SEWACO-RI action data automation.
Radars: Surface search: Racal Decca 1229 ❺; I-band.
Fire control: Signaal WM28 ❻; I/J-band.
Sonars: Signaal PHS-32; hull-mounted; active search and attack; medium frequency.

Helicopters: Platform ❼ for 1 NBO-105 helicopter.

Programmes: First ordered 14 March 1978 from Split SY, Yugoslavia where the hull was built and engines fitted. Armament and electronics fitted in the Netherlands and Indonesia.
Structure: For the training role there is a classroom and additional wheelhouse, navigation and radio rooms. Torpedo tubes are fixed in the stern transom. Two LCVP-type ship's boats are carried.
Operational: Used for training and troop transport. War roles include escort, ASW and troop transport.

KI HAJAR DEWANTARA   *(Scale 1 : 900), Ian Sturton* / 0506149

KI HAJAR DEWANTARA
12/1992
0080005

6 AHMAD YANI (VAN SPEIJK) CLASS (FFGHM)

Name	No	Builders	Laid down	Launched	Commissioned
AHMAD YANI (ex-*Tjerk Hiddes*)	351	Nederlandse Dok en Scheepsbouw Mij, Amsterdam	1 June 1964	17 Dec 1965	16 Aug 1967
SLAMET RIYADI (ex-*Van Speijk*)	352	Nederlandse Dok en Scheepsbouw Mij, Amsterdam	1 Oct 1963	5 Mar 1965	14 Feb 1967
YOS SUDARSO (ex-*Van Galen*)	353	Koninklijke Maatschappij de Schelde, Flushing	25 July 1963	19 June 1965	1 Mar 1967
OSWALD SIAHAAN (ex-*Van Nes*)	354	Koninklijke Maatschappij de Schelde, Flushing	25 July 1963	26 Mar 1966	9 Aug 1967
ABDUL HALIM PERDANAKUSUMA (ex-*Evertsen*)	355	Koninklijke Maatschappij de Schelde, Flushing	6 July 1965	18 June 1966	21 Dec 1967
KAREL SATSUITUBUN (ex-*Isaac Sweers*)	356	Nederlandse Dok en Scheepsbouw Mij, Amsterdam	5 May 1965	10 Mar 1967	15 May 1968

Displacement, tons: 2,225 standard; 2,835 full load
Dimensions, feet (metres): 372 × 41 × 13.8
(113.4 × 12.5 × 4.2)
Main machinery: 2 Babcock & Wilcox boilers; 550 psi
(38.7 kg/cm²); 850°F *(450°C)*; 2 Werkspoor/English Electric
turbines; 30,000 hp *(22.4 MW)*; 2 shafts
Speed, knots: 28.5. **Range, n miles:** 4,500 at 12 kt
Complement: 180

Missiles: SSM: 8 McDonnell Douglas Harpoon ❶; active
radar homing to 130 km *(70 n miles)* at 0.9 Mach;
warhead 227 kg.
Guns: 1 OTO Melara 3 in *(76 mm)*/62 compact ❷; 85 rds/min
to 16 km *(8.7 n miles)* anti-surface; 12 km *(6.6 n miles)*
anti-aircraft; weight of shell 6 kg. 4—12.7 mm MGs.
Torpedoes: 6—324 mm Mk 32 (2 triple) tubes ❸. Honeywell
Mk 46; anti-submarine; active/passive homing to 11 km
(5.9 n miles) at 40 kt; warhead 44 kg.
Countermeasures: Decoys: 2 Knebworth Corvus 8-tubed
trainable; radar distraction or centroid chaff to 1 km.
ESM: UA 8/9; UA 13 (355 and 356); radar warning. FH5 D/F.
Combat data systems: SEWACO V action data automation
and Daisy data processing.
Weapons control: Signaal LIOD optronic director. Mk 2
fitted in 354, 353 and 356. SWG-1A Harpoon LCS.
Radars: Air search: Signaal LW03 ❹; D-band; range 219 km
(120 n miles) for 2 m² target.
Air/surface search: Signaal DA05 ❺; E/F-band; range 137 km
(75 n miles) for 2 m² target.
Navigation: Racal Decca 1229; I-band.
Fire control: Signaal M 45 ❻; I/J-band (for 76 mm gun and
SSM).
2 Signaal M 44; I/J-band (for Seacat) (being removed).

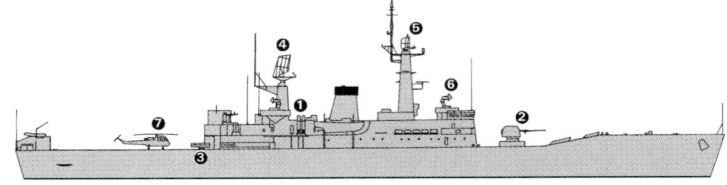

AHMAD YANI   *(Scale 1 : 1,200), Ian Sturton* / 1153005

Sonars: Signaal CWE 610; hull-mounted; active search and
attack; medium frequency. VDS; medium frequency.

Helicopters: 1 NBO-105C ❼.

Programmes: On 11 February 1986 agreement signed with
the Netherlands for transfer of two of this class with
an option on two more. Transfer dates: *Tjerk Hiddes*,
31 October 1986; *Van Speijk*, 1 November 1986; *Van Galen*,
2 November 1987; *Van Nes*, 31 October 1988. Contract
of sale for the last two of the class signed 13 May 1989.
Evertsen transferred 1 November 1989 and *Isaac Sweers*
1 November 1990. Ships provided with all spare parts but
not towed arrays or helicopters.
Modernisation: This class underwent mid-life modernisation
at Rykswerf Den Helder from 1976. This included
replacement of 4.5 in turret by 76 mm, A/S mortar by
torpedo tubes, new electronics and electrics, updating
combat data system, improved communications,
extensive automation with reduction in complement,

enlarged hangar for Lynx and improved habitability.
Harpoon for first two only initially because there was
no FMS funding for the others. However the USN then
provided sufficient SWG 1A panels for all of the class
to be retrofitted with Harpoon missiles. LIOD optronic
directors Mk 2 fitted in 354, 353 and 356 in 1996-97.
Seacat which has probably been removed may be
replaced by Simbad twin launchers when funds are
available. *Ahmad Yani* appears to have some additional
superstructure in place of the Seacat launcher on the
hangar roof. Plans to recondition all six ships were
announced by the Chief of Naval Staff on 31 May 2002
but there have been no firm indications that work has
started.

Operational: Operational availability has been drastically
reduced by propulsion problems. Harpoon missiles are
reported to be time-expired.

KAREL SATSUITUBUN   *10/2004, D Pawlenko, RAN* / 1044131

KAREL SATSUITUBUN   *11/2004, Chris Gee* / 1047873

2 SAMADIKUN (CLAUD JONES) CLASS (FF)

Name	No
SAMADIKUN (ex-*John R Perry* DE 1034)	341
MARTADINATA (ex-*Charles Berry* DE 1035)	342

Builders	Laid down	Launched	Commissioned
Avondale Marine Ways	1 Oct 1957	29 July 1958	5 May 1959
American SB Co, Toledo, OH	29 Oct 1958	17 Mar 1959	25 Nov 1959

Displacement, tons: 1,720 standard; 1,968 full load
Dimensions, feet (metres): 310 × 38.7 × 18
(95 × 11.8 × 5.5)
Main machinery: 2 Fairbanks-Morse 38TD 8-1/8-12 diesels
(not in 343); 7,000 hp *(5.2 MW)* sustained; 1 shaft
Speed, knots: 22
Range, n miles: 3,000 at 18 kt
Complement: 171 (12 officers)

Guns: 1 or 2 US 3 in *(76 mm)*/50 Mk 34; 50 rds/min to 12.8 km
(7 n miles); weight of shell 6 kg.
2 USSR 37 mm/63 (twin); 160 rds/min to 9 km *(5 n miles)*;
weight of shell 0.7 kg.

Torpedoes: 6—324 mm Mk 32 (2 triple) tubes. Honeywell
Mk 46; anti-submarine; active/passive homing to 11 km
(5.9 n miles) at 40 kt; warhead 44 kg.
Depth charges: 2 DC throwers.
Countermeasures: ESM: WLR-1C *(Martadinata)*; radar
warning.
Weapons control: Mk 70 Mod 2 for guns.
Radars: Air search: Westinghouse SPS-6E; D-band; range
146 km *(80 n miles)* (for fighter).
Surface search: Raytheon SPS-5D; G/H-band; range 37 km
(20 n miles).
Navigation: Racal Decca 1226; I-band
Fire control: Lockheed SPG-52; K-band

Sonars: EDO *(Samadikun)*; SQS-45V *(Martadinata)*;
hull-mounted; active search and attack; medium/high
frequency.

Programmes: *Samadikun* transferred from USA 20 February
1973; *Martadinata*, 31 January 1974. Both refitted at Subic
Bay 1979-82.
Modernisation: The Hedgehog A/S mortars have been
removed, as have the 25 mm guns. Some have a second
76 mm gun vice the 37 mm.
Operational: It was planned that the Van Speijk class would
replace these ships. Two have been deleted and the
operational status of these remaining two is doubtful.

SAMADIKUN

10/2001, Chris Sattler / 0121379

CORVETTES

0 + 4 SIGMA CLASS (CORVETTES) (FS)

Name	No
—	—
—	—
—	—
—	—

Builders	Laid down	Launched	Commissioned
Royal Schelde, Vlissengen	2005	2007	2008
Royal Schelde, Vlissengen	2005	2007	2008
Royal Schelde, Vlissengen	2006	2008	2009
Royal Schelde, Vlissengen	2006	2008	2009

Displacement, tons: 1,650 full load
Dimensions, feet (metres): 296.9 × 35.9 × 11.1
(90.5 × 11.0 × 3.4)
Main machinery: 2 diesels; 21,725 hp *(16.2 MW)*; 2 shafts;
cp props
Speed, knots: 28
Range, n miles: 4,000 at 18 kt
Complement: To be announced

Missiles: SAM: 2 quadruple Tetral launchers ❶; MBDA
Mistral; IR homing to 4 km *(2.2 n miles)*❷; warhead 3 kg.
SSM: 4 MBDA MM 40 Exocet Block II ❷; inertial cruise;
active radar homing to 70 km *(40 n miles)* at 0.9 Mach;
warhead 165 kg; sea-skimmer.
Guns: 1 OTO Melara 3 in *(76 mm)*/62 Super Rapid ❸;
120 rds/min to 16 km *(8.7 n miles)*; weight of shell 6 kg.
2 Giat 20 mm ❹.
Torpedoes: 6—324 mm (2 triple) tubes.
Combat data systems: Tacticos including Link Y.
Weapons control: LIROD Mk 2 optronic tracker.
Radars: Surface search: Thales MW 08; G-band.
Navigation: To be announced.
Sonars: Thales Kingclip; hull-mounted.

Helicopters: To be announced.

Programmes: Contract for the construction of two
corvettes, both to be built in the Netherlands, signed on
7 January 2004. The role of the ships is to conduct coastal
security operations. Delivery of the first ship is expected
in 2008. The second ship is to follow four months later.
The option to build two further craft in Indonesia was
exercised on 18 May 2005. These are also to be built in
the Netherlands.

SIGMA CORVETTE (artist's impression)
1/2004, Schelde Naval Shipbuilding
0563344

SIGMA CORVETTE

(Scale 1 : 900), Ian Sturton / 1044125

3 FATAHILLAH CLASS (FFG/FFGH)

Name	No	Builders	Laid down	Launched	Commissioned
FATAHILLAH	361	Wilton Fijenoord, Schiedam	31 Jan 1977	22 Dec 1977	16 July 1979
MALAHAYATI	362	Wilton Fijenoord, Schiedam	28 July 1977	19 June 1978	21 Mar 1980
NALA	363	Wilton Fijenoord, Schiedam	27 Jan 1978	11 Jan 1979	4 Aug 1980

Displacement, tons: 1,200 standard; 1,450 full load
Dimensions, feet (metres): 276 × 36.4 × 10.7
(84 × 11.1 × 3.3)
Main machinery: CODOG; 1 RR Olympus TM3B gas turbine;
25,440 hp *(19 MW)* sustained; 2 MTU 20V 956 TB92
diesels; 11,070 hp(m) *(8.14 MW)* sustained; 2 shafts; LIPS
cp props
Speed, knots: 30. **Range, n miles:** 4,250 at 16 kt
Complement: 89 (11 officers)

Missiles: SSM: 4 Aerospatiale MM 38 Exocet ❶; inertial
cruise; active radar homing to 42 km *(23 n miles)* at
0.9 Mach; warhead 165 kg; sea-skimmer.
Guns: 1 Bofors 4.7 in *(120 mm)*/46 ❷; 80 rds/min to 18.5 km
(10 n miles); weight of shell 21 kg.
1 or 2 Bofors 40 mm/70 (2 in *Nala*) ❸; 300 rds/min to 12 km
(6.6 n miles); weight of shell 0.96 kg.
2 Rheinmetall 20 mm; 1,000 rds/min to 2 km anti-aircraft;
weight of shell 0.24 kg.
Torpedoes: 6—324 mm Mk 32 or ILAS 3 (2 triple) tubes (none in
Nala) ❹. 12 Mk 46 (or A244S); anti-submarine; active/passive
homing to 11 km *(5.9 n miles)* at 40 kt; warhead 44 kg.
A/S mortars: 1 Bofors 375 mm twin-barrelled trainable ❺;
54 Erika; range 1,600 m and Nelli; range 3,600 m.

Countermeasures: Decoys: 2 Knebworth Corvus 8-tubed
trainable chaff launchers ❻; radar distraction or centroid
modes to 1 km. 1 T-Mk 6; torpedo decoy.
ESM: MEL Susie 1 (UAA-1); radar intercept.
Combat data systems: Signaal SEWACO-RI action data
automation.
Weapons control: Signaal LIROD optronic director.
Radars: Air/surface search: Signaal DA05 ❼; E/F-band;
range 137 km *(75 n miles)* for 2 m² target.
Surface search: Racal Decca AC 1229 ❽; I-band.
Fire control: Signaal WM28 ❾; I/J-band; range 46 km
(25 n miles).

Sonars: Signaal PHS-32; hull-mounted; active search and
attack; medium frequency.

Helicopters: 1 Westland Wasp (*Nala* only) ❿.

Programmes: Ordered August 1975. Officially rated as
Corvettes.
Structure: NEVESBU design. *Nala* is fitted with a folding
hangar/landing deck.
Operational: These ships are the busiest of the larger
warships. Three successful Exocet (locally modified after
life-expiry) firings conducted on 25 August 2002.

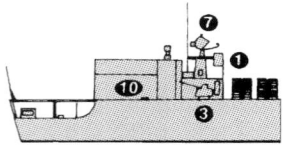

NALA

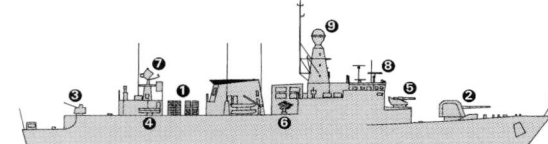

FATAHILLAH   *(Scale 1 : 1,200), Ian Sturton* / 0126692 / 0121374

NALA   *6/2000, van Ginderen Collection* / 0104593

FATAHILLAH   *11/2004, Chris Gee* / 1047876

16 KAPITAN PATIMURA (PARCHIM I) CLASS (PROJECT 1331) (FS)

Name	No	Builders	Commissioned	Recommissioned
KAPITAN PATIMURA (ex-*Prenzlau*)	371 (ex-231)	Peenewerft, Wolgast	11 May 1983	23 Sep 1993
UNTUNG SUROPATI (ex-*Ribnitz*)	372 (ex-233)	Peenewerft, Wolgast	29 Oct 1983	23 Sep 1993
NUKU (ex-*Waren*)	373 (ex-224)	Peenewerft, Wolgast	23 Nov 1982	15 Dec 1993
LAMBUNG MANGKURAT (ex-*Angermünde*)	374 (ex-214)	Peenewerft, Wolgast	26 July 1985	12 July 1994
CUT NYAK DIEN (ex-*Lübz*)	375 (ex-P 6169, ex-221)	Peenewerft, Wolgast	12 Feb 1982	25 Feb 1994
SULTAN THAHA SYAIFUDDIN (ex-*Bad Doberan*)	376 (ex-222)	Peenewerft, Wolgast	30 June 1982	25 Feb 1995
SUTANTO (ex-*Wismar*)	377 (ex-P 6170, ex-241)	Peenewerft, Wolgast	9 July 1981	10 Mar 1995
SUTEDI SENOPUTRA (ex-*Parchim*)	378 (ex-242)	Peenewerft, Wolgast	9 Apr 1981	19 Sep 1994
WIRATNO (ex-*Perleberg*)	379 (ex-243)	Peenewerft, Wolgast	19 Sep 1981	19 Sep 1994
MEMET SASTRAWIRIA (ex-*Bützow*)	380 (ex-244)	Peenewerft, Wolgast	30 Dec 1981	2 June 1995
TJIPTADI (ex-*Bergen*)	381 (ex-213)	Peenewerft, Wolgast	1 Feb 1985	10 May 1996
HASAN BASRI (ex-*Güstrow*)	382 (ex-223)	Peenewerft, Wolgast	10 Nov 1982	10 May 1996
IMAN BONJOL (ex-*Teterow*)	383 (ex-P 6168, ex-234)	Peenewerft, Wolgast	27 Jan 1984	26 Apr 1994
PATI UNUS (ex-*Ludwiglust*)	384 (ex-232)	Peenewerft, Wolgast	4 July 1983	21 July 1995
TEUKU UMAR (ex-*Grevesmühlen*)	385 (ex-212)	Peenewerft, Wolgast	21 Sep 1984	27 Oct 1996
SILAS PAPARE (ex-*Gadebusch*)	386 (ex-P 6167, ex-211)	Peenewerft, Wolgast	31 Aug 1984	27 Oct 1996

Displacement, tons: 769 standard
Dimensions, feet (metres): 246.7 × 32.2 × 11.5
(75.2 × 9.8 × 3.5)
Main machinery: 1 Zvezda M 504A diesel; 4,700 hp *(3.5 MW)*
for centreline cp prop
2 Deutz TBD 620 V16 diesels (372, 373, 374, 377, 378, 381);
6,000 hp *(4.5 MW)*
or 2 MTU 16V 4000 M 90 diesels (371, 379, 380, 382, 383
and 386); 7,300 hp *(5.4 MW)*
or 2 CAT 3516B diesels (355, 376, 384, 385); 5,200 hp
(3.9 MW); 2 outboard shafts
Speed, knots: 24
Range, n miles: 1,750 at 18 kt
Complement: 64 (9 officers)

Missiles: SAM: SA-N-5/8 launchers fitted in some. May be
replaced by twin Simbad launchers.
Guns: 2 USSR 57 mm/80 (twin) ❶ automatic; 120 rds/min to
12 km *(6.4 n miles)*; weight of shell 2.8 kg.
2—30 mm (twin) ❷; 500 rds/min to 5 km *(2.7 n miles)*
anti-aircraft; weight of shell 0.54 kg.
Torpedoes: 4—400 mm tubes ❸.
A/S mortars: 2 RBU 6000 12-barrelled trainable launchers
❹; automatic loading; range 6,000 m; warhead 31 kg.
Depth charges: 2 racks.
Mines: Mine rails fitted.
Countermeasures: Decoys: 2 PK 16 chaff rocket launchers.
ESM: 2 Watch Dog; radar warning.
Radars: Air/surface search: Strut Curve ❺; F-band; range
110 km *(60 n miles)* for 2 m² target.
Navigation: TSR 333; I-band.
Fire control: Muff Cob ❻; G/H-band.
IFF: High Pole B.
Sonars: MG 332T; hull-mounted; active search and attack;
high frequency.
Elk Tail; VDS system on starboard side (in some hulls).

Programmes: Ex-GDR ships mostly paid off in 1991.
Formally transferred on 4 January 1993 and became
Indonesian ships on 25 August 1993. First three arrived
Indonesia in November 1993.
Modernisation: All refitted prior to sailing for Indonesia.
Range increased and air conditioning added to
accommodation. SAM launchers can be carried.
A re-engining programme was completed in 2005.
Structure: Basically very similar to Russian Grisha class but
with a higher freeboard and different armament.
Operational: Some pennant numbers begin with 8 rather
than 3.

KAPITAN PATIMURA *(Scale 1 : 600), Ian Sturton* / 0506007

SILAS PAPARE *5/2005*, Guy Toremans* / 1153204

PATI UNUS *5/2005*, Guy Toremans* / 1153205

For details of the latest updates to *Jane's Fighting Ships* online and to discover the additional
information available exclusively to online subscribers please visit
jfs.janes.com

0 + 1 (1) PT PAL CORVETTE (FS)

Name	No	Builders	Laid down	Launched	Commissioned
—	—	PT Pal, Surabaya	2005	2006	2007

Displacement, tons: 1,500 full load
Dimensions, feet (metres): 263.8 × 40.0 × 11.4
  (80.4 × 12.2 × 3.46)
Main machinery: 2 diesels; 19,850 hp (14.8 MW); 2 shafts;
  cp props
Speed, knots: 25.
Range, n miles: 3,500 at 14 kt
Complement: To be announced

Guns: To be announced.
Combat data systems: To be announced.
Weapons control: To be announced.
Radars: Surface search: To be announced.
Navigation: To be announced.

Helicopters: To be announced.

Programmes: A programme for the construction of corvettes at the PT PAL Shipyard in Surabaya was officially launched on 8 October 2004 when first steel was cut. Designed in collaboration with Orrizonte Sistemi Navali S.P.A (Fincantieri) and Italian Navy Corvette, the design is probably a development of the Comandante class offshore patrol vessels on which outline details are based. Further orders are expected.

SHIPBORNE AIRCRAFT

Notes: (1) One NB 412 helicopter acquired in August 1996. A total of four is reported in service.
(2) Two Mi-17 medium lift helicopters for the Indonesian Marine Corps were reportedly acquired from Russia in 2002.

Numbers/Type: 6 Nurtanio (MBB) NBO 105C.
Operational speed: 113 kt (210 km/h).
Service ceiling: 9,845 ft (3,000 m).
Range: 407 n miles (754 km).
Role/Weapon systems: Surveillance/support aircraft. A further three for SAR. Sensors: Thomson-CSF AMASCOS surveillance system; Chlio FLIR. Weapons: Unarmed.

NBO 105C   11/1990 / 0080007

Numbers/Type: 3 Nurtanio (Aerospatiale) NAS-332 Super Puma.
Operational speed: 151 kt (279 km/h).
Service ceiling: 15,090 ft (4,600 m).
Range: 335 n miles (620 km).
Role/Weapon systems: ASW and assault operations with secondary role in utility and SAR; ASVW development possible with Exocet or similar. Sensors: Thomson-CSF Omera radar and Alcatel dipping sonar in some. Weapons: ASW; two Mk 46 torpedoes or depth bombs.

SUPER PUMA (French colours)   6/1994 / 0080008

LAND-BASED MARITIME AIRCRAFT (FRONT LINE)

Numbers/Type: 7 PZL Mielec M-28 Bryza.
Operational speed: 181 kt (335 km/h).
Service ceiling: 13,770 ft (4,200 m).
Range: 736 n miles (1,365 km).
Role/Weapon systems: Polish built aircraft based on the USSR Cash light transport. Contract on 18 August 2005 for seven maritime patrol aircraft to be delivered in late 2006. Sensors: PIT ARS-400M radar (SAR/ISAR modes).

Numbers/Type: 29/6 GAF Searchmaster Nomad B/Nomad L.
Operational speed: 168 kt (311 km/h).
Service ceiling: 21,000 ft (6,400 m).
Range: 730 n miles (1,352 km).
Role/Weapon systems: Nomad type built in Australia. Short-range maritime patrol, EEZ protection and anti-smuggler duties. 20 more acquired from Australian Army in August 1997 for use in maritime role. Not all are operational and NC-212 replacements are planned. Sensors: Nose-mounted search radar. Weapons: Unarmed.

Numbers/Type: 3 Boeing 737-200 Surveiller.
Operational speed: 462 kt (856 km/h).
Service ceiling: 50,000 ft (15,240 m).
Range: 2,530 n miles (4,688 km).
Role/Weapon systems: Land based for long-range maritime surveillance roles. Air Force manned. Sensors upgraded in 1993-94 to include IFF. Sensors: Motorola APS-135(v) SLAM MR radar, Thomson-CSF Oceanmaster radar. Weapons: Unarmed.

BOEING 737   9/2003, Boeing / 0560018

Numbers/Type: 8 Northrop F-5E Tiger II.
Operational speed: 940 kt (1,740 km/h).
Service ceiling: 51,800 ft (15,790 m).
Range: 300 n miles (556 km).
Role/Weapon systems: Fleet air defence and strike fighter, formed 'naval co-operation unit'. Planned to be replaced by BAe Hawk 200 in due course. Sensors: AI radar. Weapons: AD; two AIM-9 Sidewinder, two 20 mm cannon. Strike; 3,175 tons of underwing stores.

Numbers/Type: 7 IPTN (CASA) NC 212-200.
Operational speed: 240 kt (445 km/h).
Service ceiling: 26,600 ft (8,110 m).
Range: 669 n miles (1,240 km).
Role/Weapon systems: Surveillance aircraft first delivered in 1996. There are nine further transport aircraft. First aircraft augmented with Thales AMASCOS mission system delivered in mid-2005. Sensors: Thomson-CSF Oceanmaster radar. Chlio FLIR. Weapons: ASV; may have Exocet AM 39.

PATROL FORCES

Note: New patrol craft are reportedly under construction.

4 DAGGER CLASS (FAST ATTACK CRAFT—MISSILE) (PTFG)

Name	No	Builders	Commissioned
MANDAU	621	Korea Tacoma, Masan	20 July 1979
RENCONG	622	Korea Tacoma, Masan	20 July 1979
BADIK	623	Korea Tacoma, Masan	Feb 1980
KERIS	624	Korea Tacoma, Masan	Feb 1980

Displacement, tons: 270 full load
Dimensions, feet (metres): 164.7 × 23.9 × 7.5 (50.2 × 7.3 × 2.3)
Main machinery: CODOG; 1 GE LM 2500 gas turbine; 23,000 hp (17.16 MW) sustained; 2 MTU 12V 331 TC81 diesels; 2,240 hp(m) (1.65 MW) sustained; 2 shafts; cp props
Speed, knots: 41 gas; 17 diesel
Range, n miles: 2,000 at 17 kt
Complement: 43 (7 officers)
Missiles: SSM: 4 Aerospatiale MM 38 Exocet; inertial cruise; active radar homing to 42 km (23 n miles) at 0.9 Mach; warhead 165 kg; sea-skimmer.
Guns: 1 Bofors 57 mm/70 Mk 1; 200 rds/min to 17 km (9.3 n miles); weight of shell 2.4 kg. Launchers for illuminants on each side.
  1 Bofors 40 mm/70; 300 rds/min to 12 km (6.6 n miles); weight of shell 0.96 kg.
  2 Rheinmetall 20 mm.
Countermeasures: ESM: Thomson-CSF DR 2000S (in 623 and 624); radar intercept.
Weapons control: Selenia NA-18 optronic director.
Radars: Surface search: Racal Decca 1226; I-band.
Fire control: Signaal WM28; I/J-band.

Programmes: PSMM Mk 5 type craft ordered in 1975.
Structure: Shorter in length and smaller displacement than South Korean units. Mandau has a different shaped mast with a tripod base.

RENCONG   10/1998 / 0052358

4 TODAK (PB 57) CLASS (NAV V)
(LARGE PATROL CRAFT) (PBO)

Name	No	Builders	Commissioned
TODAK	803	PT Pal Surabaya	4 May 2000
HIU	804	PT Pal Surabaya	Sep 2000
LAYANG	805	PT Pal Surabaya	10 July 2002
LEMADANG (ex-Dorang)	806	PT Pal Surabaya	Aug 2004

Displacement, tons: 447 full load
Dimensions, feet (metres): 190.6 × 25 × 9.2 (58.1 × 7.6 × 2.8)
Main machinery: 2 MTU 16V 956 TB92 diesels; 8,850 hp(m) (6.5 MW) sustained; 2 shafts
Speed, knots: 27
Range, n miles: 6,100 at 15 kt; 2,200 at 27 kt
Complement: 53
Guns: 1 Bofors SAK 57 mm/70 Mk 2; 220 rds/min to 14 km (7.6 n miles); weight of shell 2.4 kg.
1 Bofors SAK 40 mm/70; 300 rds/min to 12 km (6.6 n miles); weight of shell 0.96 kg.
2 Rheinmetall 20 mm.
Countermeasures: Decoys: CSEE Dagaie chaff launchers.
ESM: Thomson-CSF DR 3000 S1; intercept.
Combat data systems: TACTICOS type.
Weapons control: Signaal LIOD 73 Ri Mk 2 optronic director.
Radars: Surface search: Thales Variant; G-band.
Fire control: Signaal LIROD Mk 2; K-band.
Navigation: Kelvin Hughes KH 1007; I-band.

Comment: Ordered in mid-1993 from PT Pal Surabaya. Weapon systems ordered in November 1994. Much improved combat data system is fitted. The after gun was intended to be a second 57 mm but this was changed to a 40 mm.

LAYANG *12/2005*, Chris Sattler* / 1153203

4 KAKAP (PB 57) CLASS (NAV III and IV)
(LARGE PATROL CRAFT) (PBOH)

Name	No	Builders	Commissioned
KAKAP	811	Lürssen/PT Pal Surabaya	29 June 1988
KRAPU	812	Lürssen/PT Pal Surabaya	5 Apr 1989
TONGKOL	813	PT Pal Surabaya	Dec 1993
BARAKUDA (ex-Bervang)	814	PT Pal Surabaya	Aug 1995

Displacement, tons: 423 full load
Dimensions, feet (metres): 190.6 × 25 × 9.2 (58.1 × 7.6 × 2.8)
Main machinery: 2 MTU 16V 956 TB92 diesels; 8,850 hp(m) (6.5 MW) sustained; 2 shafts
Speed, knots: 28
Range, n miles: 6,100 at 15 kt; 2,200 at 27 kt
Complement: 49 plus 8 spare berths
Guns: 1 Bofors 40 mm/70; 240 rds/min to 12.6 km (6.8 n miles); weight of shell 0.96 kg.
2—12.7 mm MGs.
Countermeasures: ESM: Thomson-CSF DR 3000 S1; intercept.
Radars: Surface search: Racal Decca 2459; I-band.
Navigation: KH 1007; I-band.
Helicopters: Platform for 1 NBO-105.

Comment: Ordered in 1982. First pair shipped from West Germany and completed at PT Pal Surabaya. Second pair assembled at Surabaya taking longer than expected to complete. The first three are NAV III SAR and Customs versions and by comparison with NAV I are very lightly armed and have a 13 × 7.1 m helicopter deck in place of the after guns and torpedo tubes. Vosper Thornycroft fin stabilisers are fitted. Can be used for Patrol purposes as well as SAR, and can transport two rifle platoons. There is also a fast seaboat with launching crane at the stern and two water guns for firefighting. The single NAV IV version has some minor variations and is used as Presidential Yacht manned by a special unit.

TONGKOL *2/2001, Sattler/Steele* / 0121380

BARAKUDA (NAV IV) *8/1995, van Ginderen Collection* / 0080012

4 SINGA (PB 57) CLASS (NAV I and II)
(LARGE PATROL CRAFT) (PBO)

Name	No	Builders	Commissioned
SINGA	651	Lürssen/PT Pal Surabaya	Apr 1988
AJAK	653	Lürssen/PT Pal Surabaya	5 Apr 1989
PANDRONG	801	PT Pal Surabaya	1992
SURA	802	PT Pal Surabaya	1993

Displacement, tons: 447 full load (NAV I); 428 full load (NAV II)
Dimensions, feet (metres): 190.6 × 25 × 9.2 (58.1 × 7.6 × 2.8)
Main machinery: 2 MTU 16V 956 TB92 diesels; 8,850 hp(m) (6.5 MW) sustained; 2 shafts
Speed, knots: 27
Range, n miles: 6,100 at 15 kt; 2,200 at 27 kt
Complement: 42 (6 officers)
Guns: 1 Bofors SAK 57 mm/70 Mk 2; 220 rds/min to 14 km (7.6 n miles); weight of shell 2.4 kg.
1 Bofors SAK 40 mm/70; 300 rds/min to 12 km (6.6 n miles); weight of shell 0.96 kg.
2 Rheinmetall 20 mm.
Torpedoes: 2—21 in (533 mm) Toro tubes (651 and 653). AEG SUT; anti-submarine; wire-guided; active/passive homing to 12 km (6.6 n miles) at 35 kt; 28 km (15 n miles) at 23 kt warhead 250 kg.
Countermeasures: Decoys: CSEE Dagaie single trainable launcher; automatic dispenser for IR flares and chaff; H/J-band.
ESM: Thomson-CSF DR 2000 S3 with Dalia analyser; intercept. DASA Telegon VIII D/F.
Weapons control: Signaal LIOD 73 Ri optronic director. Signaal WM22 72 Ri WCS (651 and 653).
Radars: Surface search: Racal Decca 2459; I-band; Signaal Scout; H/I-band (801 and 802).
Fire control: Signaal WM22; I/J-band (651 and 653).
Sonars: Signaal PMS 32 (NAV I); active search and attack; medium frequency.

Comment: Class ordered from Lürssen in 1982. First launched and shipped incomplete to PT Pal Surabaya for fitting out in January 1984. Second shipped July 1984. The first two are NAV I ASW versions with torpedo tubes and sonars. The second pair are NAV II AAW versions with an augmented gun armament, an improved surveillance and fire-control radar, but without torpedo tubes and sonars and completed later than expected in 1992-93. Vosper Thornycroft fin stabilisers are fitted.

SINGA (NAV I) *5/1999, G Toremans* / 0080009

AJAK (NAV I) *5/1998, John Mortimer* / 0052359

SURA *5/2000, M Declerck* / 0104597

8 SIBARAU (ATTACK) CLASS (LARGE PATROL CRAFT) (PB)

Name	No	Builders	Commissioned
SIBARAU (ex-Bandolier)	847	Walkers, Australia	14 Dec 1968
SILIMAN (ex-Archer)	848	Walkers, Australia	15 May 1968
SIGALU (ex-Barricade)	857	Walkers, Australia	26 Oct 1968
SILEA (ex-Acute)	858	Evans Deakin	24 Apr 1968
SIRIBUA (ex-Bombard)	859	Walkers, Australia	5 Nov 1968
SIADA (ex-Barbette)	862	Walkers, Australia	16 Aug 1968
SIKUDA (ex-Attack)	863	Evans Deakin	17 Nov 1967
SIGUROT (ex-Assail)	864	Evans Deakin	12 July 1968

Displacement, tons: 146 full load
Dimensions, feet (metres): 107.5 × 20 × 7.3 *(32.8 × 6.1 × 2.2)*
Main machinery: 2 Paxman 16YJCM diesels; 4,000 hp *(2.98 MW)* sustained; 2 shafts
Speed, knots: 21
Range, n miles: 1,220 at 13 kt
Complement: 19 (3 officers)
Guns: 1 Bofors 40 mm/60. 1—12.5 mm MG.
Countermeasures: ESM: DASA Telegon VIII; intercept.
Radars: Surface search: Decca 916; I-band.

Comment: Transferred from Australia after refit- *Bandolier* 16 November 1973, *Archer* in 1974, *Barricade* March 1982, *Acute* 6 May 1983, *Bombard* September 1983, *Attack* 22 February 1985 (recommissioned 24 May 1985), *Barbette* February 1985, *Assail* February 1986. All carry rocket/flare launchers. Two similar craft with pennant numbers 860 and 861 were built locally in 1982/83 but have not been reported for some years.

SIGALU *4/1999* / 0080013

1 PATROL CRAFT (PB)

Name	No	Builders	Launched	Commissioned
CUCUK (ex-Jupiter)	— (ex-A 102)	Singapore SBEC	3 Apr 1990	19 Aug 1991

Displacement, tons: 170 full load
Dimensions, feet (metres): 117.5 × 23.3 × 7.5 *(35.8 × 7.1 × 2.3)*
Main machinery: 2 Deutz MWM TBD234V12 diesels; 1,360 hp(m) *(1 MW)* sustained; 2 shafts; bow thruster
Speed, knots: 14
Range, n miles: 200 at 14 kt
Complement: 33 (5 officers)
Guns: 1 Oerlikon 20 mm GAM-BO1. 4—12.7 mm MGs.
Radars: Navigation: Racal Decca; I-band.

Comment: Designed as an underwater search and salvage craft, decommissioned from the Singapore Navy and transferred on 21 March 2002. Deployed as a patrol craft.

CUCUK (Singapore colours) *6/1994, van Ginderen Collection* / 0084281

13 PC-36 PATROL CRAFT (PB)

Name	No	Builders	Commissioned
KOBRA	867	Fasharkan, Mentigi	31 Mar 2003
ANAKONDA	868	Fasharkan, Jakarta	31 Mar 2003
PATOLA	869	PT Pelindo, Tanjung Pinang	Oct 2003
BOA	807	Fasharkan, Mentigi	6 Aug 2004
WELANG	808	Fasharkan, Mentigi	6 Aug 2004
TALIWANGSA	870	Fasharkan, Manokwari	6 Aug 2004
SULUH PARI	809	Fasharkan, Mentigi	20 Jan 2005
KATON	810	Fasharkan, Mentigi	20 Jan 2005
SANCA	815	Fasharkan, Manokwari	20 Jan 2005
WARAKAS	816	Fasharkan, Jakarta	20 Jan 2005
PANANA	817	Fasharkan, Makassar	20 Jan 2005
KALAKAE	818	Fasharkan, Makassar	20 Jan 2005
TEDONG NAGA	819	Fasharkan, Jakarta	20 Jan 2005

Displacement, tons: 90 full load
Dimensions, feet (metres): 118.1 × 23.0 × 4.4 *(36 × 7.0 × 1.35)*
Main machinery: 3 MAN D2842 LE 410 diesels; 3,300 hp *(2.46 MW)*; or 3 Caterpillar 3412E diesels; 3,600 hp *(2.7 MW)*
Speed, knots: 38
Complement: 18
Guns: 1—20 mm. 1—12.7 mm MG.
Radars: Navigation: I-band.

Comment: *Kobra* was the prototype vessel first demonstrated in late 2002. Glass fibre hull. Some are known as KAL-35 and others as KAL-36 craft. There are some differences in armament and superstructure, some being fitted with a stern ramp for RIB. *Patola* funded by Bali province and others may have been similarly procured. Constructed by variety of shipbuilders and operated by the Indonesian Navy. Further craft are expected.

BOA *7/2004, EPA/Bagus/Indahono* / 0584211

AMPHIBIOUS FORCES

Notes: (1) This section includes some vessels of the Military Sealift Command-Kolinlamil. (2) *Tanjung Kambani* 971 is a converted Ro-Ro ferry which is reported to have a military lift of one battalion and four LCUs. Super Pumas can be operated from a large helicopter deck. Delivered in mid-2000, there may be further vessels.

1 + 4 MULTIROLE VESSEL (LPD/APCR)

Name	No	Builders	Laid down	Launched	Commissioned
TANJUNG DALPELE	972	Daesun Shipbuilders, Pusan	2002	17 May 2003	Sep 2003

Displacement, tons: 11,400
Dimensions, feet (metres): 400.00 × 72.2 × 22.0 *(122.0 × 22.0 × 6.7)*
Main machinery: To be announced
Speed, knots: 15
Range, n miles: 8,600 at 12 kt
Complement: To be announced
Military lift: To be announced
Guns: 1 Bofors 40 mm. 2—20 mm.
Radars: Navigation: 2-I-band.

Helicopters: 2 SH-2G Super Seasprites.

Programmes: Officially designated a Multipurpose Hospital Ship. Following delivery of the first vessel in mid-2003, a contract for a further four vessels, to be delivered 2007-08, was finalised in December 2004. One of these is to have command facilities.
Structure: Has a docking well, capable of accommodating two LCU-23M, stern and side ramps and hospital facilities.

TANJUNG DALPELE *6/2004, Daesun* / 1047875

2 TROOP TRANSPORT SHIPS (AP)

Name	No	Builders	Commissioned
TANJUNG NUSANIVE (ex-Kambuna)	973	Meyer Werft, Papenburg	1984
TANJUNG FATAGAR (ex-Rinjani)	974	Meyer Werft, Papenburg	1984

Measurement, tons: 13,954 grt
Dimensions, feet (metres): 472.4 × 76.8 × 19.4 *(144.0 × 23.4 × 5.9)*
Main machinery: 2 MaK diesels; 16,760 hp *(12.5 MW)*; 2 shafts; bow thruster
Speed, knots: 20
Range, n miles: 5,500 at 12 kt
Complement: 119
Guns: To be announced.
Radars: Navigation: I-band.

Comment: Converted passenger ships originally delivered to the Directorate of Sea Communications, Jakarta, in 1984. Capable of transporting 1,600 passengers and used to serve the Indonesian islands in their civilian configuration. Acquired by the Indonesian Navy in early 2005, converted into troop transports and commissioned on 1 September 2005.

7 LST 1-511 and 512-1152 CLASSES (LST)

Name	No	Builders	Commissioned
TELUK LANGSA (ex-LST 1128)	501	Chicago Bridge	9 Mar 1945
TELUK BAYUR (ex-LST 616)	502	Chicago Bridge	29 May 1944
TELUK KAU (ex-LST 652)	504	Chicago Bridge	1 Jan 1945
TELUK TOMINI (ex-Inagua Crest, ex-Brunei, ex-Bledsoe County, LST 356)	508	Charleston, NY	22 Dec 1942
TELUK RATAI (ex-Inagua Shipper, ex-Presque Isle, APB 44, ex-LST 678, ex-Teluk Sindoro)	509	American Bridge, PA	30 June 1944
TELUK SALEH (ex-Clark County, LST 601)	510	Chicago Bridge	25 Mar 1944
TELUK BONE (ex-Iredell County, LST 839)	511	American Bridge, PA	6 Dec 1944

Displacement, tons: 1,653 standard; 4,080 full load
Dimensions, feet (metres): 328 × 50 × 14 (100 × 15.2 × 4.3)
Main machinery: 2 GM 12-567A diesels; 1,800 hp (1.34 MW); 2 shafts
Speed, knots: 11.6. **Range, n miles:** 11,000 at 10 kt
Complement: 119 (accommodation for 266)
Military lift: 2,100 tons
Guns: 7—40 mm. 2—20 mm (Teluk Langsa). 8—37 mm (remainder).
Radars: Surface search: SPS-21 (Teluk Tomini, Teluk Sindoro). SPS-53 (Teluk Saleh, Teluk Bone). SO-1 (Teluk Kau). SO-6 (Teluk Langsa).

Comment: Teluk Bajur, Teluk Saleh and Teluk Bone transferred from USA in June 1961 (and purchased 22 February 1979). Teluk Kau and Teluk Langsa in July 1970. These ships are used as transports and stores carriers. It was anticipated that they would decay in reserve Fleet anchorages once the Frosch class were in service, but all remain active. Bajur and Tomini serve with the Military Sealift Command.

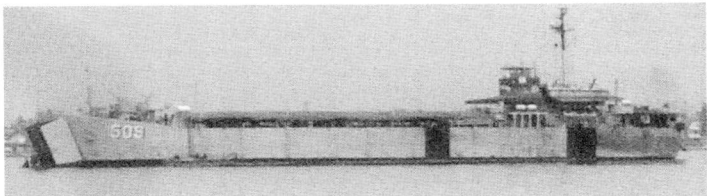

TELUK RATAI   1/2005*, David Boey / 1154407

6 TACOMA TYPE (LSTH)

Name	No	Builders	Commissioned
TELUK SEMANGKA	512	Korea-Tacoma, Masan	20 Jan 1981
TELUK PENYU	513	Korea-Tacoma, Masan	20 Jan 1981
TELUK MANDAR	514	Korea-Tacoma, Masan	July 1981
TELUK SAMPIT	515	Korea-Tacoma, Masan	June 1981
TELUK BANTEN	516	Korea-Tacoma, Masan	May 1982
TELUK ENDE	517	Korea-Tacoma, Masan	2 Sep 1982

Displacement, tons: 3,750 full load
Dimensions, feet (metres): 328 × 47.2 × 13.8 (100 × 14.4 × 4.2)
Main machinery: 2 diesels; 12,800 hp(m) (9.41 MW) sustained; 2 shafts
Speed, knots: 15. **Range, n miles:** 7,500 at 13 kt
Complement: 90 (13 officers)
Military lift: 1,800 tons (including 17 MBTs); 2 LCVPs; 200 troops
Guns: 2 or 3 Bofors 40 mm/70. 2 Rheinmetall 20 mm.
Radars: Surface search: Raytheon; E/F-band (Teluk Banten and Teluk Ende). Navigation: Racal Decca; I-band.
Helicopters: 1 Westland Wasp; 3 NAS-332 Super Pumas can be carried in last pair.

Comment: First four ordered in June 1979, last pair June 1981. No hangar in Teluk Semangka and Teluk Mandar. Two hangars in Teluk Ende. The last pair differ in silhouette having drowned exhausts in place of funnels and having their LCVPs carried forward of the bridge. They also have only two 40 mm guns and an additional radar fitted above the bridge. Battalion of marines can be embarked if no tanks are carried. Teluk Ende and Teluk Banten act as Command ships, the former also able to serve as a hospital ship.

TELUK BANTEN   1/2005*, David Boey / 1154406

TELUK SAMPIT   1/2005*, David Boey / 1154405

TELUK ENDE   5/2001 / 0126190

1 LST

Name	No	Builders	Commissioned
TELUK AMBOINA	503	Sasebo, Japan	June 1961

Displacement, tons: 2,378 standard; 4,200 full load
Dimensions, feet (metres): 327 × 50 × 15 (99.7 × 15.3 × 4.6)
Main machinery: 2 MAN V6V 22/30 diesels; 3,425 hp(m) (2.52 MW); 2 shafts
Speed, knots: 13.1
Range, n miles: 4,000 at 13.1 kt
Complement: 88
Military lift: 212 troops; 2,100 tons; 4 LCVP on davits
Guns: 6—37 mm; anti-aircraft.

Comment: Launched on 17 March 1961 and transferred from Japan in June 1961. A faster copy of US LST 511 class with 30 ton crane forward of bridge. Serves with the Military Sealift Command.

TELUK AMBOINA   8/1995, van Ginderen Collection / 0080018

12 FROSCH I CLASS (TYPE 108) (LSM)

Name	No	Commissioned	Recommissioned
TELUK GILIMANUK (ex-Hoyerswerda)	531 (ex-611)	12 Nov 1976	12 July 1994
TELUK CELUKAN BAWANG (ex-Hagenow)	532 (ex-632)	1 Dec 1976	25 Feb 1994
TELUK CENDRAWASIH (ex-Frankfurt/Oder)	533 (ex-613)	2 Feb 1977	9 Dec 1994
TELUK BERAU (ex-Eberswalde-Finow)	534 (ex-634)	28 May 1977	10 Mar 1995
TELUK PELENG (ex-Lübben)	535 (ex-631)	15 Mar 1978	23 Sep 1993
TELUK SIBOLGA (ex-Schwerin)	536 (ex-612)	19 Oct 1977	15 Dec 1993
TELUK MANADO (ex-Neubrandenburg)	537 (ex-633)	28 Dec 1977	2 June 1995
TELUK HADING (ex-Cottbus)	538 (ex-614)	26 May 1978	12 July 1994
TELUK PARIGI (ex-Anklam)	539 (ex-635)	14 July 1978	21 July 1995
TELUK LAMPUNG (ex-Schwedt)	540 (ex-636)	7 Sep 1979	26 Apr 1994
TELUK JAKARTA (ex-Eisenhüttenstadt)	541 (ex-615)	4 Jan 1979	19 Sep 1994
TELUK SANGKURING (ex-Grimmen)	542 (ex-616)	4 Jan 1979	9 Dec 1994

Displacement, tons: 1,950 full load
Dimensions, feet (metres): 321.5 × 36.4 × 9.2 (98 × 11.1 × 2.8)
Main machinery: 2 diesels; 5,000 hp(m) (3.68 MW); 2 shafts
Speed, knots: 18
Complement: 46
Military lift: 600 tons
Guns: 1—40 mm/60. 2—37 mm/63 (1 twin). 4—25 mm (2 twin).
Mines: Can lay 40 mines through stern doors.
Countermeasures: Decoys: 2 PK 16 chaff launchers.
Radars: Air/surface search: Strut Curve; F-band. Navigation: TSR 333; I-band.

Comment: All built by Peenewerft, Wolgast. Former GDR ships transferred from Germany on 25 August 1993. Demilitarised with all guns removed, but 37 mm guns have replaced the original 57 mm and 30 mm twin guns. All refitted in Germany prior to sailing. First two arrived Indonesia in late 1993, remainder throughout 1994 and 1995. Teluk Lampung damaged by heavy seas during transit in June 1994 but was repaired.

TELUK SANGKURING   1/2005*, David Boey / 1154404

TELUK PELENG   6/2000, M Declerck / 0104598

54 LANDING CRAFT (LCU)

DORE 580   **KUPANG** 582   **DILI** 583   **NUSA UTARA** 584   **+50**

Displacement, tons: 400 full load
Dimensions, feet (metres): 140.7 × 29.9 × 4.6 *(42.9 × 9.1 × 1.4)*
Main machinery: 4 diesels; 2 shafts
Speed, knots: 12. **Range, n miles:** 700 at 11 kt
Complement: 17
Military lift: 200 tons

Comment: Details given are for LCUs 582—584 built at Naval Training Centre, Surabaya in 1978-80. Military Sealift Command. LCU 580 is a smaller ship at 275 tons and built in 1968. About 20 LCM 6 type and 30 LCVPs are also in service.

LCVP   *8/1995, van Ginderen Collection* / 0080020

MINE WARFARE FORCES

9 KONDOR II (TYPE 89) CLASS
(MINESWEEPERS—COASTAL) (MSC)

Name	No	Builders	Commissioned
PULAU ROTE (ex-*Wolgast*)	721 (ex-V 811)	Peenewerft, Wolgast	1 June 1971
PULAU RAAS (ex-*Hettstedt*)	722 (ex-353)	Peenewerft, Wolgast	22 Dec 1971
PULAU ROMANG (ex-*Pritzwalk*)	723 (ex-325)	Peenewerft, Wolgast	26 June 1972
PULAU RIMAU (ex-*Bitterfeld*)	724 (ex-332, ex-M 2672)	Peenewerft, Wolgast	7 Aug 1972
PULAU RONDO (ex-*Zerbst*)	725 (ex-335)	Peenewerft, Wolgast	30 Sep 1972
PULAU RUSA (ex-*Oranienburg*)	726 (ex-341)	Peenewerft, Wolgast	1 Nov 1972
PULAU RANGSANG (ex-*Jüterbog*)	727 (ex-342)	Peenewerft, Wolgast	7 Apr 1973
PULAU RAIBU (ex-*Sömmerda*)	728 (ex-311, ex-M 2670)	Peenewerft, Wolgast	9 Aug 1973
PULAU REMPANG (ex-*Grimma*)	729 (ex-336)	Peenewerft, Wolgast	10 Nov 1973

Displacement, tons: 310 full load
Dimensions, feet (metres): 186 × 24.6 × 7.9 *(56.7 × 7.5 × 2.4)*
Main machinery: 2 Russki Kolomna Type 40-DM diesels; 4,408 hp(m) *(3.24 MW)* sustained; 2 shafts; cp props
Speed, knots: 17.
Range, n miles: 2,000 at 14 kt
Complement: 31 (6 officers)
Guns: 6—25 mm/80 (3 twin).
Mines: 2 rails.
Radars: Navigation: TSR 333; I-band.
Sonars: Bendix AQS 17 VDS; minehunting; active; high frequency (in some).

Comment: Former GDR minesweepers transferred from Germany in Russian dockship *Trans-Shelf* arriving 22 October 1993. MCM is secondary role with EEZ patrol taking priority. ADI Dyads can be embarked for MCM. *Pulau Rondo* was used for trials. Forward 25 mm mounting replaced in 725 by single 12.7 mm MG.

PULAU RIMAU   *4/2004, Chris Sattler* / 1044128

PULAU RONDO   *4/2004*, John Mortimer* / 1153200

PALAU RUSA   *8/1995, van Ginderen Collection* / 0080021

2 PULAU RENGAT (TRIPARTITE) CLASS (MHSC)

Name	No	Builders	Launched	Commissioned
PULAU RENGAT	711	van der Giessen-de Noord	23 July 1987	26 Mar 1988
PULAU RUPAT	712	van der Giessen-de Noord	27 Aug 1987	26 Mar 1988

Displacement, tons: 502 standard; 568 full load
Dimensions, feet (metres): 168.9 × 29.2 × 8.2 *(51.5 × 8.9 × 2.5)*
Main machinery: 2 MTU 12V 396TC82 diesels; 2,610 hp(m) *(1.92 MW)* sustained; 1 shaft; LIPS cp prop; auxiliary propulsion; 3 Turbomeca gas-turbine generators; 2 motors; 2,400 hp(m) *(1.76 MW)*; 2 retractable Schottel propulsors; 2 bow thrusters; 150 hp(m) *(110 kW)*
Speed, knots: 15; 7 auxiliary propulsion
Range, n miles: 3,000 at 12 kt
Complement: 46 plus 4 spare berths

Guns: 2 Rheinmetall 20 mm. Matra Simbad SAM launcher may be added for patrol duties or a third 20 mm gun.
Countermeasures: MCM OD3 Oropesa mechanical sweep gear; Fiskars F-82 magnetic and SA Marine AS 203 acoustic sweeps; Ibis V minehunting system; 2 PAP 104 Mk 4 mine disposal systems.
Combat data systems: Signaal SEWACO-RI action data automation.
Radars: Navigation: Racal Decca AC 1229C; I-band.
Sonars: Thomson Sintra TSM 2022; active minehunting; high frequency.

Programmes: First ordered on 29 March 1985, laid down 22 July 1985, second ordered 30 August 1985 and laid down 15 December 1985. More were to have been built in Indonesia up to a total of 12 but this programme was cancelled by lack of funds.
Structure: There are differences in design between these ships and the European Tripartites, apart from their propulsion. Deckhouses and general layout are different as they are required to act as minehunters, minesweepers and patrol ships. Hull construction is GRP shock-proven.
Operational: Endurance, 15 days. Automatic operations, navigation and recording systems, Thomson-CSF Naviplot TSM 2060 tactical display. A 5 ton container can be shipped, stored for varying tasks-research; patrol; extended diving; drone control.

PULAU RUPAT   *3/2004, Chris Sattler* / 1044129

1 T 43 (PROJECT 244) CLASS (MINESWEEPER—OCEAN) (MSO)

PULAU RANI P701

Displacement, tons: 580 full load
Dimensions, feet (metres): 190.2 × 27.6 × 6.9 *(58 × 8.4 × 2.1)*
Main machinery: 2 Kolomna 9-D-8 diesels; 2,000 hp(m) *(1.6 MW)* sustained; 2 shafts
Speed, knots: 15
Range, n miles: 3,000 at 10 kt
Complement: 55
Guns: 4—37 mm/63 (2 twin). 8—12.7 mm (4 twin) MGs.
Depth charges: 2 projectors.
Radars: Navigation: Decca 110; I-band.
Sonars: Stag Ear; hull-mounted; active search and attack; high frequency.

Comment: Transferred from USSR in 1964. Mostly used as patrol craft. Second of class sunk in collision in May 2000.

PULAU RANI   *1983, P D Jones* / 0506009

SURVEY AND RESEARCH SHIPS

1 RESEARCH SHIP (AGOR)

Name	No	Builders	Commissioned
BARUNA JAYA VIII	KAL-IV-06	Mjellem & Karlsen AS, Bergen	1998

Displacement, tons: 1,476 full load
Dimensions, feet (metres): 174.5 × 41.0 × 14.8 *(53.2 × 12.5 × 4.3)*
Main machinery: 1 Caterpillar 3516BTA diesel; 2,026 bhp *(1.5 MW)*; 1 shaft; cp prop;
 1 Schottel SPJ-82TL bow thruster
Speed, knots: 13
Range, n miles: 7,500 at 12 kt
Complement: 42 (11 officers) plus 23 scientific staff
Radars: Navigation: Furuno FAR-2835S; E/F-band.
 Furuno FR-2110; I-band.

Comment: Multipurpose survey vessel equipped to conduct fisheries research, geophysics and seabed mapping. Delivered to Indonesia on 28 September 1998. Sensors include Simrad SD570 sonar, EM 1000 multibeam echo sounder and EA 500 single beam echo sounder.

BARUNA JAYA VIII *9/1998, Maritime Photographic* / 0044067

4 RESEARCH SHIPS (AGS/AGOR)

Name	No	Builders	Commissioned
BARUNA JAYA I	KAL-IV-02	CMN, Cherbourg	10 Aug 1989
BARUNA JAYA II	KAL-IV-03	CMN, Cherbourg	25 Sep 1989
BARUNA JAYA III	KAL-IV-04	CMN, Cherbourg	3 Jan 1990
BARUNA JAYA IV	KAL-IV-05	CMN, Cherbourg	2 Nov 1995

Displacement, tons: 1,180 (1,425 IV) full load
Dimensions, feet (metres): 198.2 × 39.7 × 13.8 *(60.4 × 12.1 × 4.2)*
Main machinery: 2 Niigata/SEMT-Pielstick 5 PA5 L 255 diesels; 2,990 hp(m) *(2.2 MW)* sustained; 1 shaft; cp prop; bow thruster
Speed, knots: 14. **Range, n miles:** 7,500 at 12 kt
Complement: 37 (8 officers) plus 26 scientists

Comment: First three ordered from La Manche, Dieppe in February 1985 by the office of Technology, Ministry of Industry and Research. Badly delayed by the closing down of the original shipbuilders (ACM, Dieppe) and construction taken over by CMN at Cherbourg. Fourth of class ordered in 1993 to a slightly enlarged design and with a more enclosed superstructure. *Baruna Jaya 1* is employed on hydrography, the second on oceanography and the third combines both tasks. *Baruna Jaya IV* is operated by the Agency responsible for developing new technology. All are part of the Naval Auxiliary Service.

BARUNA JAYA II *4/1998, John Mortimer* / 0052362

BARUNA JAYA IV *11/1995, van Ginderen Collection* / 0080023

1 HECLA CLASS (SURVEY SHIP) (AGSH)

Name	No	Builders	Commissioned
DEWA KEMBAR (ex-*Hydra*)	932	Yarrow and Co, Blythswood	5 May 1966

Displacement, tons: 1,915 light; 2,733 full load
Dimensions, feet (metres): 260.1 × 49.1 × 15.4 *(79.3 × 15 × 4.7)*
Main machinery: Diesel-electric; 3 Paxman 12YJCZ diesels; 3,780 hp *(2.82 MW)*; 3 generators; 1 motor; 2,000 hp(m) *(1.49 MW)*; 1 shaft; bow thruster
Speed, knots: 14. **Range, n miles:** 12,000 at 11 kt
Complement: 123 (14 officers)
Guns: 2—12.7 mm MGs.
Radars: Navigation: Kelvin Hughes Type 1006; I-band.
Helicopters: 1 Westland Wasp.

Comment: Transferred from UK 18 April 1986 for refit. Commissioned in Indonesian Navy 10 September 1986. SATCOM fitted. Two survey launches on davits.

DEWA KEMBAR *11/1997, van Ginderen Collection* / 0012542

1 RESEARCH SHIP (AGORH)

Name	No	Builders	Commissioned
BURUJULASAD	931	Schlichting, Lübeck-Travemünde	1967

Displacement, tons: 2,165 full load
Dimensions, feet (metres): 269.5 × 37.4 × 11.5 *(82.2 × 11.4 × 3.5)*
Main machinery: 4 MAN V6V 22/30 diesels; 6,850 hp(m) *(5.03 MW)*; 2 shafts
Speed, knots: 19.1. **Range, n miles:** 14,500 at 15 kt
Complement: 108 (15 officers) plus 28 scientists
Guns: 4—12.7 mm (2 twin) MGs.
Radars: Surface search: Decca TM 262; I-band.
Helicopters: 1 Bell 47J.

Comment: *Burujulasad* was launched in August 1965; her equipment includes laboratories for oceanic and meteorological research and a cartographic room. Carries one LCVP and three surveying motor boats. A 37 mm gun was added in 1992 but by 1998 had been removed again.

BURUJULASAD *4/1998, John Mortimer* / 0052361

1 RESEARCH SHIP (AGOR)

Name	No	Builders	Commissioned
JALANIDHI	933	Sasebo Heavy Industries	12 Jan 1963

Displacement, tons: 985 full load
Dimensions, feet (metres): 176.8 × 31.2 × 14.1 *(53.9 × 9.5 × 4.3)*
Main machinery: 1 MAN G6V 30/42 diesel; 1,000 hp(m) *(735 kW)*; 1 shaft
Speed, knots: 11.5. **Range, n miles:** 7,200 at 10 kt
Complement: 87 (13 officers) plus 26 scientists
Radars: Navigation: Nikkon Denko; I-band. Furuno; I-band.

Comment: Launched in 1962. Oceanographic research ship with hydromet facilities and weather balloons. 3 ton boom aft. Operated by the Navy for the Hydrographic Office.

JALANIDHI *8/1995, van Ginderen Collection* / 0080024

TRAINING SHIPS

1 SAIL TRAINING SHIP (AXS)

Name	No	Builders	Commissioned
DEWARUCI	–	HC Stülcken & Sohn, Hamburg	9 July 1953

Displacement, tons: 810 standard; 1,500 full load
Dimensions, feet (metres): 136.2 pp; 191.2 oa × 31.2 × 13.9 (41.5; 58.3 × 9.5 × 4.2)
Main machinery: 1 MAN diesel; 600 hp(m) (441 kW); 1 shaft
Speed, knots: 10.5
Complement: 110 (includes 78 midshipmen)

Comment: Barquentine of steel construction. Sail area, 1,305 sq yards (1,091 sq m). Launched on 24 January 1953.

DEWARUCI   *6/2005*, Martin Mokrus* / 1153201

1 SAIL TRAINING SHIP (AXS)

Name	Builders	Launched	Commissioned
ARUNG SAMUDERA (ex-*Adventurer*)	Hendrik Oosterbroek, Tauranga	July 1991	9 Jan 1996

Measurement, tons: 96 grt
Dimensions, feet (metres): 128 oa; 103.7 wl × 21.3 × 8.5 (39; 31.6 × 6.5 × 2.6)
Main machinery: 2 Ford 2725E diesels; 292 hp (218 kW); 2 shafts
Speed, knots: 10 (diesels)
Complement: 20 (includes trainees)

Comment: Three masted schooner acquired from New Zealand. Sail area 433.8 m².

ARUNG SAMUDERA   *5/2000, A Campanera i Rovira* / 0104601

AUXILIARIES

Notes: (1) The Don class depot ship *Ratulangi* 400 is in use as a floating workshop at Surabaya naval base, but is not seaworthy.
(2) There is also a small oiler *Sungai Gerong* 906.

1 COMMAND SHIP (AGFH)

Name	No	Builders	Launched	Commissioned
MULTATULI	561	Ishikawajima-Harima	15 May 1961	Aug 1961

Displacement, tons: 3,220 standard; 6,741 full load
Dimensions, feet (metres): 365.3 × 52.5 × 23 (111.4 × 16 × 7)
Main machinery: 1 Burmeister & Wain diesel; 5,500 hp(m) (4.04 MW); 1 shaft
Speed, knots: 18.5. **Range, n miles:** 6,000 at 16 kt
Complement: 135
Guns: 6 USSR 37 mm/63 (2 twin, 2 single); 160 rds/min to 9 km (5 n miles); weight of shell 0.7 kg.
8 — 12.7 mm MGs.
Radars: Surface search: Ball End; E/F-band.
Navigation: I-band.
Helicopters: 1 Bell 47J.

Comment: Built as a submarine tender. Original after 76 mm mounting replaced by helicopter deck with a hangar added in 1998. Living and working spaces air conditioned. Capacity for replenishment at sea (fuel oil, fresh water, provisions, ammunition, naval stores and personnel). Medical and hospital facilities. Used as fleet flagship (Eastern Force) and is fitted with ICS-3 communications.

MULTATULI   *8/1995, van Ginderen Collection* / 0080025

1 REPLENISHMENT TANKER (AOTL)

Name	No	Builders	Commissioned
SORONG	911	Trogir SY, Yugoslavia	Apr 1965

Displacement, tons: 8,400 full load
Dimensions, feet (metres): 367.4 × 50.5 × 21.6 (112 × 15.4 × 6.6)
Main machinery: 1 diesel; 1 shaft
Speed, knots: 15
Complement: 110
Cargo capacity: 4,200 tons fuel; 300 tons water
Guns: 4 — 12.7 mm (2 twin) MGs.
Radars: Navigation: Don; I-band.

Comment: Has limited underway replenishment facilities on both sides and stern refuelling.

SORONG   *8/1995, van Ginderen Collection* / 0080026

1 ROVER CLASS (REPLENISHMENT TANKER) (AORLH)

Name	No	Builders	Commissioned
ARUN (ex-*Green Rover*)	903	Swan Hunter, Tyneside	15 Aug 1969

Displacement, tons: 4,700 light; 11,522 full load
Dimensions, feet (metres): 461 × 63 × 24 (140.6 × 19.2 × 7.3)
Main machinery: 2 SEMT-Pielstick 16 PA4 diesels; 15,360 hp(m) (11.46 MW); 1 shaft; Kamewa cp prop; bow thruster
Speed, knots: 19
Range, n miles: 15,000 at 15 kt
Complement: 49 (16 officers)
Cargo capacity: 6,600 tons fuel
Guns: 2 Bofors 40 mm/60. 2 Oerlikon 20 mm.
Radars: Navigation: Kelvin Hughes Type 1006; I-band.
Helicopters: Platform for Super Puma.

Comment: Transferred from UK in September 1992 after a refit. Small fleet tanker designed to replenish ships at sea with fuel, fresh water, limited dry cargo and refrigerated stores under all conditions while under way. No hangar but helicopter landing platform is served by a stores lift, to enable stores to be transferred at sea by 'vertical lift'. Capable of HIFR. Used as the Flagship for the Training Commander.

ARUN   *10/2004, Chris Gee* / 1047874

2 KHOBI CLASS (COASTAL TANKERS) (AOTL)

BALIKPAPAN 901		SAMBU 902

Displacement, tons: 1,525 full load
Dimensions, feet (metres): 206.6 × 33 × 14.8 (63 × 10.1 × 4.5)
Main machinery: 2 diesels; 1,600 hp(m) (1.18 MW); 2 shafts
Speed, knots: 13
Range, n miles: 2,500 at 12 kt
Complement: 37 (4 officers)
Cargo capacity: 550 tons dieso
Guns: 4 — 14.5 mm (2 twin) MGs. 2 — 12.7 mm MGs.
Radars: Navigation: Neptun; I-band.

Comment: *Balikpapan* and *Sambu* are Japanese copies of the Khobi class built in the 1960s.

SAMBU   *8/1995, van Ginderen Collection* / 0080028

1 ACHELOUS CLASS (REPAIR SHIP) (ARL)

Name	No	Builders	Commissioned
JAYA WIJAYA (ex-*Askari*, ex-ARL 30, ex-LST 1131)	921	Chicago Bridge and Iron Co	15 Mar 1945

Displacement, tons: 4,325 full load
Dimensions, feet (metres): 328 × 50 × 14 *(100 × 15.3 × 4.3)*
Main machinery: 2 GM 12-567A diesels; 1,800 hp *(1.34 MW)*; 2 shafts
Speed, knots: 12
Range, n miles: 17,000 at 7 kt
Complement: 180 (11 officers)
Cargo capacity: 300 tons; 60 ton crane
Guns: 8 Bofors 40 mm/56 (2 quad); 160 rds/min to 11 km *(5.9 n miles)*; weight of shell 0.9 kg.
Radars: Air/surface search: Sperry SPS-53; I/J-band.
Navigation: Raytheon 1900; I/J-band.
IFF: UPX 12B.

Comment: In reserve from 1956-66. She was recommissioned and reached Vietnam in 1967 to support River Assault Flotilla One. She was used by the US Navy and Vietnamese Navy working up the Mekong in support of the Cambodian operations in May 1970. Transferred from US on lease to Indonesia at Guam on 31 August 1971 and purchased 22 February 1979. Bow doors welded shut. Carries two LCVPs.

JAYA WIJAYA   *9/1998, 92 Wing RAAF* / 0506010

2 FROSCH II CLASS (TYPE 109) (SUPPORT SHIPS) (AKL/ARL)

Name	No	Builders	Commissioned
TELUK CIREBON (ex-*Nordperd*)	543 (ex-E 171)	Peenewerft, Wolgast	3 Oct 1979
TELUK SABANG (ex-*Südperd*)	544 (ex-E 172)	Peenewerft, Wolgast	26 Feb 1980

Displacement, tons: 1,700 full load
Dimensions, feet (metres): 297.6 × 36.4 × 9.2 *(90.7 × 11.1 × 2.8)*
Main machinery: 2 diesels; 4,408 hp(m) *(3.24 MW)* sustained; 2 shafts
Speed, knots: 18
Cargo capacity: 650 tons
Guns: 4—37 mm/63 (2 twin). 4—25 mm (2 twin).
Countermeasures: Decoys: 2 PK 16 chaff launchers.
Radars: Air/surface search: Strut Curve; F-band.
Navigation: I-band.

Comment: Ex-GDR ships disarmed and transferred from Germany 25 August 1993. 5 ton crane amidships. In GDR service these ships had two twin 57 mm and two twin 25 mm guns plus Muff Cob fire-control radar. Both refitted at Rostock and recommissioned 25 April 1995. 37 mm guns fitted after transfer. Rocket launchers are mounted forward of the bridge.

TELUK SABANG   *5/1995, Frank Behling* / 0075856

4 SUPPORT SHIPS (AKL)

NUSA TELU 952	TELUK MENTAWAI 959	KARIMATA 960	WAGIO 961

Displacement, tons: 2,400 full load
Dimensions, feet (metres): 258.4 × 35.4 × 15.1 *(78.8 × 10.8 × 4.6)*
Main machinery: 1 MAN diesel; 1,000 hp(m) *(735 kW)*; 1 shaft
Speed, knots: 12
Range, n miles: 3,000 at 11 kt
Complement: 26
Cargo capacity: 875 tons dry; 11 tons liquid
Guns: 4—14.5 mm (2 twin) MGs.
Radars: Navigation: Spin Trough; I-band.

Comment: 959-961 are Tisza class. Built in Hungary. Transferred in 1963-64. Military Sealift Command since 1978. 952 is much smaller ship of 1950s vintage.

KARIMATA   *1/2005*, David Boey* / 1154403

TUGS

Notes: Two BIMA VIII class of 423 tons completed in 1991 are not naval. Names *Merapi* and *Merbabu*.

1 CHEROKEE CLASS

Name	No	Builders	Commissioned
RAKATA (ex-*Menominee* ATF 73)	922	United Engineering, Alameda	25 Sep 1942

Displacement, tons: 1,235 standard; 1,640 full load
Dimensions, feet (metres): 205 × 38.5 × 17 *(62.5 × 11.7 × 5.2)*
Main machinery: Diesel-electric; 4 GM 12—278 diesels; 4,400 hp *(3.28 MW)*; 4 generators; 1 motor; 3,000 hp *(2.24 MW)*; 1 shaft
Speed, knots: 15
Range, n miles: 6,500 at 15 kt
Complement: 67
Guns: 1 US 3 in *(76 mm)*/50. 2 Bofors 40 mm/60 aft. 4—25 mm (2 twin) (bridge wings).
Radars: Surface search: Racal Decca; I-band.

Comment: Launched on 14 February 1942. Transferred from US at San Diego in March 1961. Used mostly as a patrol ship.

RAKATA   *8/1995, John Mortimer* / 0080030

1 NFI CLASS (ATF)

Name	No	Builders	Commissioned
SOPUTAN	923	Dae Sun SB & Eng, Busan	11 Aug 1995

Measurement, tons: 1,279 grt
Dimensions, feet (metres): 217.2 × 39 × 17.1 *(66.2 × 11.9 × 5.2)*
Main machinery: Diesel-electric; 4 SEMT-Pielstick diesel generators; 1 motor; 12,240 hp(m) *(9 MW)*; 1 shaft; bow thruster
Speed, knots: 13.5
Complement: 42
Radars: Navigation: Racal Decca; I-band.

Comment: Ocean Cruiser class NFI. Bollard pull 120 tons.

SOPUTAN   *8/1995, van Ginderen Collection* / 0080031

3 HARBOUR TUGS (YTM)

Name	No	Builders	Commissioned
LAMPO BATANG	934	Ishikawajima-Harima	Sep 1961
TAMBORA (Army)	935	Ishikawajima-Harima	June 1961
BROMO	936	Ishikawajima-Harima	Aug 1961

Comment: All of 250 tons displacement. There are a number of other naval tugs in the major ports.

CUSTOMS

Notes: Identified by BC (Tax and Customs) preceding the pennant number.

14 COASTAL PATROL CRAFT (WPB)

BC 2001-2007   BC 3001-3007

Displacement, tons: 70.3 full load
Dimensions, feet (metres): 93.5 × 17.7 × 5.5 *(28.5 × 5.4 × 1.7)*
Main machinery: 2 MTU 12V 331 TC92 diesels; 2,660 hp(m) *(1.96 MW)* sustained; 2 shafts
Speed, knots: 28-34
Complement: 19
Guns: 1—20 mm or 1—12.7 mm MG.

Comment: Built CMN Cherbourg. Delivered in 1980 and 1981.

BC 2007   *1/1990, 92 Wing RAAF* / 0506011

10 LÜRSSEN VSV 15 CLASS (WHSIC)

BC 1601-1610

Displacement, tons: 11 full load
Dimensions, feet (metres): 52.5 × 9.2 × 3.3 *(16 × 2.8 × 1)*
Main machinery: 2 MTU diesels; 600 hp(m) *(441 kW)*; 2 shafts
Speed, knots: 50. **Range, n miles:** 750 at 30 kt
Complement: 5 (1 officer)
Guns: 1—7.62 mm MG.

Comment: Built in Germany and delivered between November 1998 and June 1999.

BC 1608   *5/1999, Lürssen* / 0080032

48 LÜRSSEN 28 METRE TYPE (WPB)

BC 4001-3, 5001-3, 6001-24, 7001-6, 8001-6, 9001-6

Displacement, tons: 68 full load
Dimensions, feet (metres): 91.8 × 17.7 × 5.9 *(28 × 5.4 × 1.8)*
Main machinery: 2 Deutz diesels; 2,720 hp(m) *(2 MW)*; or 2 MTU diesels; 2,260 hp(m) *(1.66 MW)*; 2 shafts
Speed, knots: 30
Range, n miles: 1,100 at 15 kt; 860 at 28 kt
Complement: 19 (6 officers)
Guns: 1—12.7 mm MG.

Comment: Lürssen design, some built by Fulton Marine and Scheepswerven van Langebrugge of Belgium, some by Lürssen Vegesack and some by PT Pal Surabaya (which also assembled most of them). Programme started in 1980. Some of these craft are operated by the Navy, the Police and the Maritime Security Agency.

BC 7001   *5/2000, van Ginderen Collection* / 0104602

5 LÜRSSEN NEW 28 METRE TYPE (WHSIC)

BC 10001-10002   BC 20001-20003

Displacement, tons: 85 full load
Dimensions, feet (metres): 92.5 × 21.7 × 4.6 *(28.2 × 6.6 × 1.4)*
Main machinery: 2 MTU 16V 396 TE94 diesels; 2,955 hp(m) *(2.14 MW)* sustained; 2 shafts
Speed, knots: 40
Range, n miles: 1,100 at 30 kt
Complement: 11 (3 officers)
Guns: 2—7.62 mm MGs.
Radars: Surface search: Furuno FR 8731; I-band.

Comment: First pair built in Germany and delivered between May 1999 and November 1999. Last three built by PT Pal Surabaya and delivered between September 1999 and November 1999. Aluminium construction.

BC 10001   *5/1999, Lürssen* / 0080034

BC 20001   *9/1999, PT Pal* / 0075857

COAST AND SEAWARD DEFENCE COMMAND

Notes: (1) Established in 1978 as the Maritime Security Agency to control the 200 mile EEZ and to maintain navigational aids. Comes under the Military Sea Communications Agency. Some craft have blue hulls with a diagonal thick white and thin red stripe plus KPLP on the superstructure. In addition to the craft listed there are large numbers of small harbour boats.
(2) There are also a number of civilian manned vessels used for transport and servicing navigational aids.

2 DISASTER RESPONSE SHIPS (WPSO)

ARDA DEDALI   **ALUGARA**

Measurement, tons: 530 gross
Dimensions, feet (metres): 196.8 × 26.2 × 10.5 *(60.0 × 8.0 × 3.2)*
Main machinery: 2 MTU 16V4000 M60 diesels; 2 shafts; cp props
Speed, knots: 19.3
Range, n miles: 3,000 at 17 kt
Complement: To be announced
Radars: Surface search/navigation: To be announced.

Comment: Built by Niigata Shipbuilding & Repair Inc., a wholly owned subsidiary of Mitsui Engineering & Shipbuilding Co., *Arda Dedali* delivered to the Directorate General of Sea Communication (DGSC) on 27 January 2005. *Alugara* delivered in mid-2005. The ships are designed to undertake disaster relief operations and are equipped to deal with accidents at sea, including rescue and firefighting, and counter-pollution tasks. The ships are likely to be deployed in the Malacca/Singapore Strait region.

ALUGARA   *6/2005*, *Ships of the World* / 1153202

5 KUJANG CLASS (WPB)

KUJANG 201	PARANG 202	CELURIT 203	CUNDRIK 204	BELATI 205

Displacement, tons: 162 full load
Dimensions, feet (metres): 125.6 × 19.6 × 6.8 *(38.3 × 6 × 2.1)*
Main machinery: 2 AGO SACM 195 V12 CZSHR diesels; 4,410 hp(m) *(3.24 MW)*; 2 shafts
Speed, knots: 28
Range, n miles: 1,500 at 18 kt
Complement: 18
Guns: 1 — 12.7 mm MG.

Comment: Built by SFCN, Villeneuve la Garenne. Completed April 1981 *(Kujang* and *Parang)*, August 1981 *(Celurit)*, October 1981 *(Cundrik)*, December 1981 *(Belati)*. Pennant numbers are preceded by PAT.

CUNDRIK　　　　　*11/1998, van Ginderen Collection* / 0052366

4 GOLOK CLASS (WSAR)

GOLOK 206	PANAN 207	PEDANG 208	KAPAK 209

Displacement, tons: 190 full load
Dimensions, feet (metres): 123 pp × 23.6 × 6.6 *(37.5 × 7.2 × 2)*
Main machinery: 2 MTU 16V 652 TB91 diesels; 4,610 hp(m) *(3.39 MW)* sustained; 2 shafts
Speed, knots: 25
Range, n miles: 1,500 at 18 kt
Complement: 18
Guns: 1 Rheinmetall 20 mm.

Comment: All launched 5 November 1981. First pair completed 12 March 1982. Last pair completed 12 May 1982. Built by Deutsche Industrie Werke, Berlin. Fitted out by Schlichting, Travemünde. Used for SAR and have medical facilities. Pennant numbers preceded by PAT.

KAPAK　　　　　*11/1998, van Ginderen Collection* / 0052367

15 HARBOUR PATROL CRAFT (WPB)

PAT 01-15

Displacement, tons: 12 full load
Dimensions, feet (metres): 40 × 14.1 × 3.3 *(12.2 × 4.3 × 1)*
Main machinery: 1 Renault diesel; 260 hp(m) *(191 kW)*; 1 shaft
Speed, knots: 14
Complement: 4
Guns: 1 — 7.62 mm MG.

Comment: First six built at Tanjung Priok Shipyard 1978-79. Four more of a similar design built in 1993-94 by Mahalaya Utama Shipyard and delivered from 1995.

HARBOUR PATROL CRAFT TYPE　　　*11/1998, van Ginderen Collection* / 0052368

NAVAL AUXILIARY SERVICE

Notes: This is a paramilitary force of non-commissioned craft. They have KAL pennant numbers. About 24 vessels operate in the eastern Fleet and 47 in the western Fleet, and three belong to the Naval Academy. In addition, the Baruna Jaya ships listed under Survey Ships are also part of the NAS.

NAS CRAFT　　　　　*4/1999* / 0080035

65 KAL KANGEAN CLASS (COASTAL PATROL CRAFT) (WPB)

Displacement, tons: 44.7 full load
Dimensions, feet (metres): 80.4 × 14.1 × 3.3 *(24.5 × 4.3 × 1)*
Main machinery: 2 diesels; 2 shafts
Speed, knots: 18
Guns: 2 USSR 25 mm/80 (twin). 2 USSR 14.5 mm (twin) MGs.

Comment: Ordered from Tanjung Uban Navy Yard in about 1984 and completed between 1987 and 1996. Numbers are uncertain. Have four figure pennant numbers in the 1101 series.

KAL KANGEAN 1112　　　　*10/1998, Trevor Brown* / 0506008

6 CARPENTARIA CLASS (COASTAL PATROL CRAFT) (WPB)

201-206

Displacement, tons: 27 full load
Dimensions, feet (metres): 51.5 × 15.7 × 4.3 *(15.7 × 4.8 × 1.3)*
Main machinery: 2 MTU 8V 331 TC92 diesels; 1,770 hp(m) *(1.3 MW)* sustained; 2 shafts
Speed, knots: 29
Range, n miles: 950 at 18 kt
Complement: 10
Guns: 2 — 12.7 mm MGs.
Radars: Surface search: Decca; I-band.

Comment: Built 1976-77 by Hawker de Havilland, Australia. Endurance, four to five days. Transferred from the Navy in the mid-1980s to the Police and now with the Naval Auxiliary Service.

CARPENTARIA 203　　　　*8/1995, van Ginderen Collection* / 0080036

ARMY

Notes: The Army (ADRI) craft have mostly been transferred to the Military Sealift Command (Logistic Support).

27 LANDING CRAFT LOGISTICS (LCL)

ADRI XXXII-LVIII

Displacement, tons: 580 full load
Dimensions, feet (metres): 137.8 × 35.1 × 5.9 *(42 × 10.7 × 1.8)*
Main machinery: 2 Detroit 6-71 diesels; 348 hp(m) *(260 kW)* sustained; 2 shafts
Speed, knots: 10. **Range, n miles:** 1,500 at 10 kt
Complement: 15
Military lift: 122 tons equipment

Comment: A variety of LCL built in Tanjung Priok Shipyard 1979-82. Details are for *Adri XL*. XXXI sank in February 1993.

ADRI XXXIII   *10/1999, David Boey* / 0080037

POLICE

Notes: The police operate about 85 craft of varying sizes including 14 Bango class of 194 tons and 32 Hamilton water-jet craft of 7.9 m, 234 hp giving a speed of 28 kt. Lürssen type (619-623) are identical to Customs craft.

POLICE 622   *8/1995* / 0080038

POLICE 620   *3/1997, A Sharma* / 0569198

2 OFFSHORE PATROL CRAFT (PBO)

Name	No	Builders	Commissioned
BISMA	520	Astilleros Gondan, Castropol	May 2003
BALADEWA	521	Astilleros Gondan, Castropol	June 2003

Dimensions, feet (metres): 200.2 × 32.5 × 8.5 *(61.0 × 9.9 × 2.6)*
Main machinery: 2 MTU 12V 595TE 90 diesels; 8,700 hp *(6.5 MW)*
Speed, knots: 22
Range, n miles: 3,500 at 12 kt
Helicopters: Platform for one medium.

Comment: Primary role Search and Rescue.

BISMA   *5/2003, Astilleros Gondan* / 0569201

Iran

Country Overview

Formerly a constitutional monarchy ruled by a shah, The Islamic Republic of Iran was established in 1979. With an area of 636,296 square miles, it is situated in the Middle East and is bordered to the north by Armenia, Azerbaijan and Turkmenistan, to the west by Iraq and Turkey and to the east by Afghanistan and Pakistan. It has a 1,318 n mile coastline with the Gulf, the Gulf of Oman and the Caspian Sea. The capital and largest city is Tehran. The principal Caspian ports are Bandar-e Anzali and Bandar-e Torkeman while those in the Gulf include the oil-shipping facilities on Kharg Island, Khorramshahr, Bandar-Khomeini and Bandar-Abbas on the strategic Strait of Hormuz. Territorial Seas (12 n miles) are claimed. An EEZ (200 n miles) has been claimed but the limits have not been defined.

Headquarters Appointments

Commander of Navy:
    Rear Admiral Abbas Mohtaj
Head of Naval Equipment:
    Rear Admiral Mohammed Hossein Shafii
Head of IRCG(N) (Sepah):
    Rear Admiral Morteza Saffari

Personnel

2006: 18,000 Navy (including 2,000 Naval Air and Marines), 20,000 IRGCN

Bases

Persian Gulf: Bandar Abbas (MHQ and 1st Naval District), Boushehr (2nd Naval District and also a Dockyard), Kharg Island, Qeshm Island, Bandar Lengeh
Indian Ocean: Chah Bahar (Bandar Beheshti) (3rd Naval District and forward base)
Caspian Sea: Bandar Anzali (4th Naval District)
Pasdaran: Al Farsiyah, Halileh, Sirri, Abu Musa, Larak

Coast Defence

Three Navy and one IRGCN brigades with many fixed installations and command posts. Approximately 100 truck-mounted C 802 and 80 CSSC-3 (Seersucker) Chinese SSMs in at least four sites. The indigenously developed Ra'ad cruise missile may be based at launching bases under construction at Bandar Abbas, Bandar Lengeh, Boushehr and Bandar Khomeini.

Mines

Stocks of up to 3,000 mines are reported including Chinese EM 52 rising mines.

Strength of the Fleet

Type	Active	Building
Submarines	3	—
Mini Submarines	1	2
Frigates	3	1
Corvettes	2	—
Fast Attack Craft-Missile	21	1 (1)
Large Patrol Craft	5	—
Coastal Patrol Craft	132+	10
Landing Ships (Logistic)	7	—
Landing Ships (Tank)	6	—
Hovercraft	7	—
Replenishment Ship	1	—
Supply Ships	1 (1)	—
Support Ships	7	—
Water Tankers	4	—
Tenders	13	—

Prefix to Ships' Names

IS

PENNANT LIST

Submarines		Patrol Forces				Amphibious Warfare Forces and Auxiliaries	
901	Tareq	202	Azadi	P 313-1	Fath	21	Hejaz
902	Noor	203	Mehran	P 313-2	Nasr	22	Karabala
903	Yunes	211	Parvin	P 313-3	Saf	23	Amir
		212	Bahram	P 313-4	Ra'd	24	Farsi
		213	Nahid	P 313-5	Fajr	25	Sardasht
Frigates		P 221	Kaman	P 313-6	Shams	26	Sab Sahel
		P 222	Zoubin	P 313-7	Me'raj	101	Fouque
71	Alvand	P 223	Khadang	P 313-8	Falaq	411	Kangan
72	Alborz	P 224	Peykan	P 313-9	Hadid	412	Taheri
73	Sabalan	P 226	Falakhon	P 313-10	Qadr	421	Bandar Abbas
		P 227	Shamshir			422	Boushehr
		P 228	Gorz			431	Kharg
Corvettes		P 229	Gardouneh			511	Hengam
		P 230	Khanjar	**Mine Warfare Forces**		512	Larak
81	Bayandor	P 231	Neyzeh			513	Tonb
82	Naghdi	P 232	Tabarzin	301	Hamzeh	514	Lavan

SUBMARINES

3 KILO CLASS (PROJECT 877 EKM) (SSK)

Name	No	Builders	Laid down	Launched	Commissioned
TAREQ	901	Admiralty Yard, St Petersburg	1988	1991	21 Nov 1992
NOOR	902	Admiralty Yard, St Petersburg	1989	1992	6 June 1993
YUNES	903	Admiralty Yard, St Petersburg	1990	1993	25 Nov 1996

Displacement, tons: 2,356 surfaced; 3,076 dived
Dimensions, feet (metres): 238.2 × 32.5 × 21.7
(72.6 × 9.9 × 6.6)
Main machinery: Diesel-electric; 2 diesels; 3,650 hp(m)
(2.68 MW); 2 generators; 1 motor; 5,500 hp(m) *(4.05 MW)*;
1 economic speed motor; 130 hp(m) *(95 kW)*; 1 shaft;
2 auxiliary propulsion motors; 204 hp(m) *(150 kW)*
Speed, knots: 17 dived; 10 surfaced; 9 snorting
Range, n miles: 6,000 at 7 kt snorting; 400 at 3 kt dived
Complement: 53 (12 officers)

Torpedoes: 6 — 21 in *(533 mm)* tubes; combination of
TEST-71/96; wire-guided active/passive homing to 15 km
(8.1 n miles) at 40 kt; warhead 220 kg and 53-65; passive
wake homing to 19 km *(10.3 n miles)* at 45 kt; warhead
350 kg. Total of 18 weapons.
Mines: 24 in lieu of torpedoes.
Countermeasures: ESM: Squid Head; radar warning. Quad
Loop D/F.
Weapons control: MVU-119EM Murena TFCS.

Radars: Surface search: Snoop Tray MRP-25; I-band.
Sonars: Sharks Teeth MGK-400; hull-mounted; passive/
active search and attack; medium frequency.
Mouse Roar MG-519; active attack; high frequency.

Programmes: Contract signed in 1988 for three of the class.
The first submarine to be transferred sailed from the
Baltic in October 1992 flying the Russian flag and with a
predominantly Russian crew. The second sailed in June
1993. The third completed in 1994 but delivery delayed
by funding problems. She arrived in Iran in mid-January
1997.
Modernisation: Chinese YJ-1 or Russian Novator Alfa SSMs
may be fitted in due course.
Structure: Diving depth, 240 m *(787 ft)* normal. Has a
9,700 kW/h battery. SA-N-10 SAM system may be fitted,
but this is not confirmed.
Operational: Based at Bandar Abbas but planned to move to
Chah Bahar (Bandar Beheshti) on the northern shore of the
Gulf of Oman. So far a jetty has been extended to facilitate

operations. Training is being done with assistance from
Russia. Operational effectiveness has been adversely
affected by technical difficulties and although previously
reported problems with battery cooling and air conditioning
were understood to have been overcome using Indian
batteries, all three submarines are long overdue for refits.
During 2005, negotiations to upgrade the boats were
reported to have taken place with Rosoboronexport, the
Russian arms agency. Potential companies to be involved
include Zvezdochka of Severodvinsk and Admiralty
Shipyards, St Petersburg, who built the boats. Further
speculation that a contract might include installation of
the Klub anti-ship missile system has not been confirmed.
Such a significant enhancement to their capabilities would
have considerable implications for maritime security in
the region.
Opinion: The northern Gulf of Oman and the few deep water
parts of the Persian Gulf are notoriously difficult areas
for anti-submarine warfare. However, these submarines
will be vulnerable to attack when alongside in harbour.

YUNES   *6/1999* / 0080039

1 + 2 COASTAL SUBMARINES (SSC)

Displacement, tons: 120 (approx) surfaced
Dimensions, feet (metres): 98.4 × ? × ? *(30.0 × ? × ?)*
Main machinery: To be announced
Speed, knots: To be announced
Complement: 32
Torpedoes: To be announced.
Sonars: To be announced.

Programmes: Little is known about this submarine whose existence was noted in February
2004. Dimensions are approximate. It is reported that perhaps two further boats have
been constructed or are in manufacture. If this boat has been indigenously built, as
is claimed, this would represent a significant technological development. It is more
likely that another country, possibly North Korea, has been involved in the project. The
submarines are known as *Qadir 1, 2* and *3* and are likely to be employed in shallow
areas of the Gulf such as the Strait of Hormuz.

COASTAL SUBMARINE   *2/2004* / 1044353

1 SWIMMER DELIVERY VEHICLE (LDW)

Comment: On 29 August 2000, the first Iranian-built Swimmer Delivery Vehicle (SDV)
AlSabehat 15 was launched at Bandar Abbas. The 8 m craft can accommodate a two-
man crew and has the capability to carry three additional divers. It is well suited to
coastal reconnaissance, Special Forces insertion/extraction and mining (it can carry
14 limpet mines) of ports and anchorages but not to open water operations. The absence
of further deliveries suggests that first of class difficulties have yet to be overcome.

AL SABEHAT 15   *8/2000* / 0104860

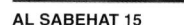

AL SABEHAT 15   *(not to scale), Ian Sturton* / 0104859

FRIGATES

3 + 1 ALVAND (VOSPER MK 5) CLASS (FFG)

Name	No	Builders	Laid down	Launched	Commissioned
ALVAND (ex-*Saam*)	71	Vosper Thornycroft, Woolston	22 May 1967	25 July 1968	20 May 1971
ALBORZ (ex-*Zaal*)	72	Vickers, Barrow	3 Mar 1968	25 July 1969	1 Mar 1971
SABALAN (ex-*Rostam*)	73	Vickers, Newcastle & Barrow	10 Dec 1967	4 Mar 1969	28 Feb 1972
—	—	Bandar Abbas	Oct 2002	2006	

Displacement, tons: 1,350 full load
Dimensions, feet (metres): 310 × 36.4 × 14.1 (screws)
   (94.5 × 11.1 × 4.3)
Main machinery: CODOG; 2 RR Olympus TM2A gas turbines;
   40,000 hp *(29.8 MW)* sustained; 2 Paxman 16YJCM
   diesels; 3,800 hp *(2.83 MW)* sustained; 2 shafts; cp props
Speed, knots: 39 gas; 18 diesel
Range, n miles: 3,650 at 18 kt; 550 at 36 kt
Complement: 125 (accommodation for 146)

Missiles: SSM: 4 China C-802 (2 twin) ❶; active radar
   homing to 120 km *(66 n miles)* at 0.9 Mach; warhead
   165 kg; sea-skimmer.
Guns: 1 Vickers 4.5 in *(114 mm)*/55 Mk 8 ❷; 25 rds/min
   to 22 km *(12 n miles)* anti-surface; 6 km *(3.3 n miles)*
   anti-aircraft; weight of shell 21 kg.
   2 Oerlikon 35 mm/90 (twin) ❸; 550 rds/min to 6 km
   (3.3 n miles); weight of shell 1.55 kg.
   3 Oerlikon GAM-BO1 20 mm ❹. 2–12.7 mm MGs.
Torpedoes: 6–324 mm Mk 32 (2 triple) tubes (71).
A/S mortars: 1–3-tubed Limbo Mk 10 (72 and 73) ❺;
   automatic loading; range 1,000 m; warhead 92 kg.
Countermeasures: Decoys: 2 UK Mk 5 rocket flare launchers.
   ESM: Decca RDL 2AC; radar warning. Racal FH 5-HF/DF.
Radars: Air/surface search: Plessey AWS 1 ❻; E/F-band;
   range 110 km *(60 n miles)*.
   Surface search: Racal Decca 1226 ❼; I-band.
   Navigation: Decca 629; I-band.
   Fire control: Contraves Sea Hunter ❽; I/J-band.
   IFF: UK Mk 10.

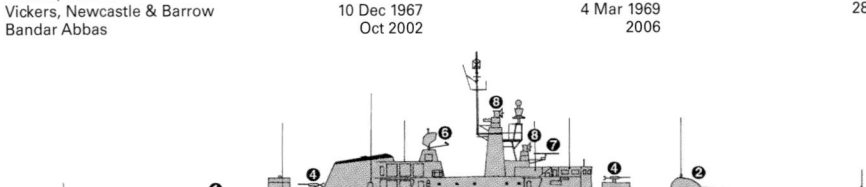

ALBORZ   *(Scale 1 : 900), Ian Sturton* / 0012550

Sonars: Graseby 174; hull-mounted; active search; medium/
   high frequency.
   Graseby 170; hull-mounted; active attack; high frequency.

Programmes: The first three units were ordered from UK
Shipyards on 25 August 1966. A fourth unit, which has
been under construction at Bandar Abbas, was in the
final stages of fitting out in late 2005. Known as the *Mowj*
project, the design is almost certainly very similar to the
original Vosper Mk 5 design. The weapons and sensor fit
is also likely to be similar.
Modernisation: Major refits including replacement of 4.5
in Mk 5 gun by Mk 8 completed 1977. Modifications in
1988 included replacing Seacat with a 23 mm gun and
boat davits with minor armaments. By mid-1991 the
23 mm and both boats had been replaced by GAM-

BO1 20 mm guns and the SSM launcher had effectively
become a twin launcher. In 1996/97 two of the class had
the Sea Killer SSM replaced by C-802 launchers and a
new communications mast fitted between the two fire-
control radars. The third has been similarly modified.
Sabalan appears to be fitted with Rice Screen air/surface
search radar. Torpedo tubes which replaced the mortars
in *Alvand* were probably taken from decommissioned
Babr class.
Structure: Air conditioned throughout. Fitted with Vosper
stabilisers.
Operational: *Sahand* sunk by USN on 18 April 1988. *Sabalan*
had her back broken by a laser-guided bomb in the
same skirmish but was out of dock by the end of 1990
and was operational again in late 1991. ASW mortars
probably unserviceable. All are active.

ALVAND   *1/2002* / 0569203

SABALAN   *2/1998* / 0052371

CORVETTES

2 BAYANDOR (PF 103) CLASS (FS)

Name	No	Builders	Laid down	Launched	Commissioned
BAYANDOR (ex-US PF 103)	81	Levingstone Shipbuilding Co, Orange, TX	20 Aug 1962	7 July 1963	18 May 1964
NAGHDI (ex-US PF 104)	82	Levingstone Shipbuilding Co, Orange, TX	12 Sep 1962	10 Oct 1963	22 July 1964

Displacement, tons: 900 standard; 1,135 full load
Dimensions, feet (metres): 275.6 × 33.1 × 10.2
    (84 × 10.1 × 3.1)
Main machinery: 2 Fairbanks-Morse 38TD8-1/8-9 diesels;
    5,250 hp (3.92 MW) sustained; 2 shafts
Speed, knots: 20
Range, n miles: 2,400 at 18 kt; 4,800 at 12 kt
Complement: 140

Guns: 2 US 3 in (76 mm)/50 Mk 34 ❶; 50 rds/min to 12.8 km
    (7 n miles); weight of shell 6 kg.
    1 Bofors 40 mm/60 (twin) ❷; 120 rds/min to 10 km
    (5.5 n miles); weight of shell 0.89 kg.
    2 Oerlikon GAM-BO1 20 mm ❸. 2 — 12.7 mm MGs.
Weapons control: Mk 63 for 76 mm gun. Mk 51 Mod 2 for
    40 mm guns.
Radars: Air/surface search: Westinghouse SPS-6C ❹;
    D-band; range 146 km (80 n miles) (for fighter).
Surface search: Racal Decca ❺; I-band.
Navigation: Raytheon 1650 ❻; I/J-band.
Fire control: Western Electric Mk 36 ❼; I/J-band.
IFF: UPX-12B.

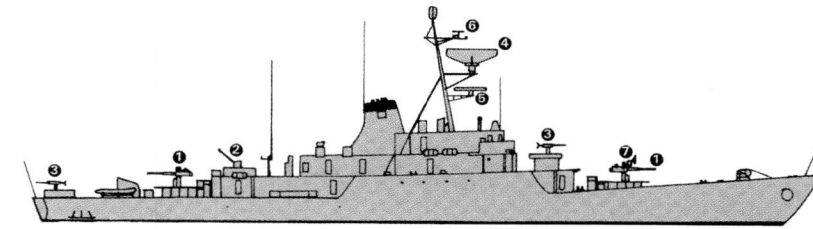

BAYANDOR

(Scale 1 : 900), Ian Sturton / 0506193

Sonars: EDO SQS-17A; hull-mounted; active attack; high
    frequency.

Programmes: Transferred from the USA to Iran under the
    Mutual Assistance programme in 1964.
Modernisation: *Naghdi* change of engines and
    reconstruction of accommodation completed in mid-1988.

23 mm gun and depth charge racks replaced by 20 mm
    guns in 1990.
Operational: *Milanian* and *Khanamuie* sunk in 1982 during
    war with Iraq. Both remaining ships are very active.
    Sonars may have been removed.

BAYANDOR   *2/1998* / 0052372

SHIPBORNE AIRCRAFT

Numbers/Type: 6 Agusta AB 204ASW/212.
Operational speed: 104 kt (193 km/h).
Service ceiling: 11,500 ft (3,505 m).
Range: 332 n miles (615 km).
Role/Weapon systems: Mainly engaged in ASV operations in defence of oil installations.
    Numbers are uncertain. Sensors: APS 705 search radar, dipping sonar (if carried).
    Weapons: ASW; two China YU-2 torpedoes. ASV; two AS 12 missiles.

SEA KING   *3/1997* / 0012549

AB 212 (Spanish colours)   *3/2002, A Campanera I Rovira* / 0529019

Numbers/Type: 8 Agusta-Sikorsky ASH-3D Sea King.
Operational speed: 120 kt (222 km/h).
Service ceiling: 12,200 ft (3,720 m).
Range: 630 n miles (1,165 km).
Role/Weapon systems: Shore-based ASW helicopter to defend major port and oil
    installations. Can be embarked in *Kharg*. Sensors: Selenia search radar, dipping sonar.
    Weapons: ASW; four A244/S torpedoes or depth bombs. ASV; trials of an anti-ship
    missile 'Fajr-e-Darya' are reported to have taken place. Capabilities not known but could
    be a development of Sea Killer.

LAND-BASED MARITIME AIRCRAFT (FRONT LINE)

Notes: (1) The Air Force also has up to six F-4 Phantoms equipped with C 80IK ASMs for
the maritime role.
(2) Four F-27 Fokker Friendship aircraft are used in a utility MPA role.
(3) Five Dornier 228 are also in service but are reported not to be very active.
(4) The Iranian Air Force operates some 14 (plus 18 ex-Iraqi) Su-24 Fencer ground attack,
some of which may be 'marinised' for an anti-ship role.
(5) An-140 transport aircraft are under licensed production at Esfahan. The first aircraft
flew in January 2001. These provide a potential airframe for the replacement of the ageing
P3F fleet.

Numbers/Type: 6 Sikorsky RH/MH-53D Sea Stallion.
Operational speed: 125 kt (232 km/h).
Service ceiling: 11,100 ft (3,385 m).
Range: 405 n miles (750 km).
Role/Weapon systems: Surface search helicopter which could be used for mine clearance
    but so far has only been used for Logistic purposes. Can be carried on Hengam class
    flight deck. Sensors: Weather radar. Weapons: Unarmed.

Numbers/Type: 5 Lockheed C-130H-MP Hercules.
Operational speed: 325 kt (602 km/h).
Service ceiling: 33,000 ft (10,060 m).
Range: 4,250 n miles (7,876 km).
Role/Weapon systems: Long-range maritime reconnaissance role by Air Force which has
    a total of 23 of these aircraft. Sensors: Search/weather radar. Weapons: Unarmed.

Numbers/Type: 3 Lockheed P-3F Orion.
Operational speed: 410 kt *(760 km/h).*
Service ceiling: 28,300 ft *(8,625 m).*
Range: 4,000 n miles *(7,410 km).*
Role/Weapon systems: Air Force manned. One of the remaining aircraft can be used for early warning and control duties for strikes. Replacements are being sought. Sensors: Search radar, sonobuoys. Weapons: ASW; various weapons can be carried. ASV; C-802 SSM.

P3F　　　　　　　　　　　　　　　　　　*12/2001, A Sharma* / 0528307

PATROL FORCES

Notes: (1) At least one 14 m patrol craft, equipped with MLRS, has been reported.
(2) Approximately five 20 m patrol craft have been reported.
(3) A number of 10 m RIB craft are being deployed to ports for maritime law enforcement tasks. Capable of 65 kt and powered by an inboard motor, the craft are armed with a 12.7 mm MG. The design appears to be modern and of possible western origin.

10 THONDOR (HOUDONG) CLASS
(FAST ATTACK CRAFT—MISSILE) (PTFG)

FATH	P 313-1	**FAJR**	P 313-5	**FALAQ**	P 313-8
NASR	P 313-2	**SHAMS**	P 313-6	**HADID**	P 313-9
SAF	P 313-3	**ME'RAJ**	P 313-7	**QADR**	P 313-10
RA'D	P 313-4				

Displacement, tons: 171 standard; 205 full load
Dimensions, feet (metres): 126.6 × 22.3 × 8.9 *(38.6 × 6.8 × 2.7)*
Main machinery: 3 diesels; 8,025 hp(m) *(7.94 MW)* sustained; 3 shafts
Speed, knots: 35
Range, n miles: 800 at 30 kt
Complement: 28 (3 officers)

Missiles: SSM: 4 China C-802; active radar homing to 120 km *(66 n miles)* at 0.9 Mach; warhead 165 kg; sea-skimmer.
Guns: 2—30 mm/65 (twin) AK 230. 2—23 mm/87 (twin).
Radars: Surface search: China SR-47A; I-band.
Navigation: China RM 1070A; I-band.
Fire control: Rice Lamp Type 341; I/J-band.

Programmes: Negotiations for sale started in 1991 but were held up by arguments over choice of missile. Built at Zhanjiang Shipyard. First five delivered in September 1994 by transporter vessel, second batch in March 1996. Original pennant numbers 301-310. More may be built in Iran under licence.
Structure: The hull is a shortened version of the Chinese Huangfen (Osa 1) class but the superstructure has a lattice mast to support two I-band radars and there is a separate director plinth for the fire-control system. A twin 23 mm gun is fitted aft of the mast.
Operational: Manned by the Pasdaran.

SAF　　　　　　　　　　　　　　　　　　*10/1997* / 0052375

ME'RAJ　　　　　　　　　　　　　　　　　　*6/1998* / 0052376

11 + 1 (1) KAMAN (COMBATTANTE II) CLASS
(FAST ATTACK CRAFT—MISSILE) (PGGF)

Name	No	Builders	Commissioned
KAMAN	P 221	CMN, Cherbourg	12 Aug 1977
ZOUBIN	P 222	CMN, Cherbourg	12 Sep 1977
KHADANG	P 223	CMN, Cherbourg	15 Mar 1978
PEYKAN	P 224		2004
FALAKHON	P 226	CMN, Cherbourg	31 Mar 1978
SHAMSHIR	P 227	CMN, Cherbourg	31 Mar 1978
GORZ	P 228	CMN, Cherbourg	22 Aug 1978
GARDOUNEH	P 229	CMN, Cherbourg	11 Sep 1978
KHANJAR	P 230	CMN, Cherbourg	1 Aug 1981
NEYZEH	P 231	CMN, Cherbourg	1 Aug 1981
TABARZIN	P 232	CMN, Cherbourg	1 Aug 1981

Displacement, tons: 249 standard; 275 full load
Dimensions, feet (metres): 154.2 × 23.3 × 6.2 *(47 × 7.1 × 1.9)*
Main machinery: 4 MTU 16V 538 TB91 diesels; 12,280 hp(m) *(9.03 MW)* sustained; 4 shafts
Speed, knots: 37.5
Range, n miles: 2,000 at 15 kt; 700 at 33.7 kt
Complement: 31

Missiles: SSM: 2 or 4 China C-802 (1 or 2 twin); active radar homing to 120 km *(66 n miles)* at 0.9 Mach; warhead 165 kg; sea-skimmer or 4 McDonnell Douglas Harpoon (2 twin); active radar homing to 40 km *(22 n miles)* at 0.9 Mach; warhead 165 kg; sea-skimmer or Standard SM1-MR box launchers *(Gorz).*
Guns: 1 OTO Melara 3 in *(76 mm)*/62 compact; 85 rds/min to 16 km *(8.7 n miles)* anti-surface; 12 km *(6.6 n miles)* anti-aircraft; weight of shell 6 kg; 320 rounds.
1 Breda Bofors 40 mm/70; 300 rds/min to 12 km *(6.6 n miles)*; weight of shell 0.96 kg; 900 rounds. Some have a 23 mm or 20 mm gun in place of the 40 mm.
2—12.7 mm MGs.
Countermeasures: ESM: Thomson-CSF TMV 433 Dalia; radar intercept.
ECM: Thomson-CSF Alligator; jammer.
Radars: Surface search/fire control: Signaal WM28; I/J-band.
Navigation: Racal Decca 1226; I-band.
IFF: UPZ-27N/APX-72.

Programmes: Twelve ordered in February 1974. The transfer of the last three craft was delayed by the French Government after the Iranian revolution. On 12 July 1981 France decided to hand them over. This took place on 1 August, on 2 August they sailed and soon after *Tabarzin* was seized by a pro-Royalist group off Cadiz. After the latter surrendered to the French in Toulon further problems were prevented by sending all three to Iran in a merchant ship. Further indigenously built craft have been developed for operations in the Caspian Sea. Known as the SINA 1 programme, the first vessel was launched on 29 September 2003, a second vessel (possibly to be called *Joshan*) is nearing completion and a third reported to be under construction. *Peykan* has the same name and pennant number of a vessel sunk in 1980 and has similar capabilities.
Modernisation: Most of the class fitted with C-802 SSM in 1996-98. *Gorz* has been used for trials, first with Harpoon, and now with SM 1 launchers taken from the deleted Sumner class destroyers.
Structure: Portable SA-7 launchers may be embarked in some.
Operational: The original *Peykan* P 224 was sunk in 1980 by Iraq; *Joshan* P 225 in April 1988 by the US Navy. The new *Peykan* P 224 is based in the Caspian Sea.

GARDOUNEH (with Harpoon)　　　　　*11/2001, Royal Australian Navy* / 0528433

GORZ (with SM1)　　　　　　　　　　*12/2002* / 0569204

KHANJAR　　　　　　　　　　　　　　　　*6/1998* / 0052374

3 PARVIN (PGM-71) CLASS (LARGE PATROL CRAFT) (PC)

Name	No	Builders	Commissioned
PARVIN (ex-PGM 103)	211	Peterson Builders Inc	1967
BAHRAM (ex-PGM 112)	212	Peterson Builders Inc	1969
NAHID (ex-PGM 122)	213	Peterson Builders Inc	1970

Displacement, tons: 98 standard; 148 full load
Dimensions, feet (metres): 101 × 21.3 × 8.3 *(30.8 × 6.5 × 2.5)*
Main machinery: 8 GM 6-71 diesels; 2,040 hp *(1.52 MW)* sustained; 2 shafts
Speed, knots: 22
Range, n miles: 1,140 at 17 kt
Complement: 20
Guns: 1 Bofors 40 mm/60. 1 GAM-BO1 20 mm. 2—12.7 mm MGs.
Depth charges: 4 racks (8 US Mk 6).
Radars: Surface search: I-band.
Sonars: SQS-17B; hull-mounted active attack; high frequency.

Comment: The heavier 40 mm gun is mounted aft and the 20 mm forward to compensate for the large SQS-17B sonar dome under the bows. Mousetrap A/S mortar removed. Beginning to be difficult to maintain in an operational state.

PARVIN *1/2002, A Sharma* / 0528306

2 KAIVAN (CAPE) CLASS (LARGE PATROL CRAFT) (PB)

AZADI 202   **MEHRAN** 203

Displacement, tons: 98 standard; 148 full load
Dimensions, feet (metres): 95 × 20.2 × 6.6 *(28.9 × 6.2 × 2)*
Main machinery: 24 Cummins NYHMS-1200 diesels; 2,120 hp *(1.58 MW)*; 2 shafts
Speed, knots: 21
Range, n miles: 2,324 at 8 kt
Complement: 15
Guns: 1 Bofors 40 mm/60. 2 USSR 23 mm/80 (twin). 2—12.7 mm MGs.

Comment: Three patrol craft originally built by the US Coast Guard, Curtis Bay, Maryland in the 1950s were withdrawn from Iranian service in approximately 1995. In light of reports that at least two of the craft have been refitted, it is assumed that they have been recommissioned. Details are as for the craft in 1994 but it is likely that machinery and armament may now be different.

6 MIG-S-2600 CLASS (PBF)

Displacement, tons: 85 full load
Dimensions, feet (metres): 80 × 20.3 × 4.6 *(26.2 × 6.2 × 1.4)*
Main machinery: 4 diesels; 4,000 hp(m) *(2.94 MW)*; 4 shafts
Speed, knots: 35
Complement: 12
Guns: 2—23 mm/80 (twin). 1—12-barrelled 107 mm MRL.
Radars: Surface search: I-band.

Comment: Numbers are uncertain. Built by Joolaee Marine Industries, Tehran, to a similar specification as the North Korean Chaho class but with a different superstructure and a raised mast to give an improved radar horizon. Pasdaran manned.

MIG-S-2600 *1996, Joolaee Marine Industries* / 0506298

9 US MK III CLASS (COASTAL PATROL CRAFT) (PB)

Displacement, tons: 41.6 full load
Dimensions, feet (metres): 65 × 18.1 × 6 *(19.8 × 5.5 × 1.8)*
Main machinery: 3 GM 8V-71TI diesels; 690 hp *(515 kW)* sustained; 3 shafts
Speed, knots: 30
Range, n miles: 500 at 28 kt
Complement: 8
Guns: 1—20 mm GAM-BO1. 1—12.7 mm MG.
Radars: Surface search: RCA LN66; I-band.

Comment: Twenty ordered from Marinette Marine Corporation, Wisconsin, USA; the first delivered in December 1975 and the last in December 1976. A further 50 were ordered in 1976 to be shipped out and completed in Iran. It is not known how many were finally assembled. Six lost in the Gulf War, others have been scrapped. These last nine are based at Boushehr and Bandar Abbas. Continue to be active.

US Mk III *5/1999* / 0080041

10 MIG-G-1900 CLASS (COASTAL PATROL CRAFT) (PBF)

Displacement, tons: 30 full load
Dimensions, feet (metres): 64 × 13.8 × 3 *(19.5 × 4.2 × 0.9)*
Main machinery: 2 MWM TBD 234 V12 diesels; 1,646 hp(m) *(1.21 MW)*; 2 shafts
Speed, knots: 36
Complement: 8
Guns: 2—23 mm/80 (twin).
Radars: Surface search: I-band.

Comment: Building in Iran to a modified US Mk II design. Numbers uncertain. Pasdaran craft.

MIG-G-1900 *1992, Iranian Marine Industries* / 0080042

20 MIG-S-1800 CLASS (COASTAL PATROL CRAFT) (PB)

Displacement, tons: 60 full load
Dimensions, feet (metres): 61.3 × 18.9 × 3.4 *(18.7 × 5.8 × 1.1)*
Main machinery: 2 MWM TBD 234 V12 diesels; 1,646 hp(m) *(1.21 MW)*; 2 shafts
Speed, knots: 18
Complement: 10
Guns: 1 Oerlikon 20 mm. 2—7.62 mm MGs.
Radars: Surface search: I-band.

Comment: Assembled in Iran as general purpose patrol craft. Numbers uncertain. Pasdaran craft.

MIG-S-1800 *1996, Joolaee Marine Industries* / 0506299

30 BOGHAMMAR CRAFT (PBF)

Displacement, tons: 6.4 full load
Dimensions, feet (metres): 41.2 × 8.6 × 2.3 *(13 × 2.7 × 0.7)*
Main machinery: 2 Seatek 6-4V-9 diesels; 1,160 hp *(853 kW)*; 2 shafts
Speed, knots: 46. **Range, n miles:** 500 at 40 kt
Complement: 5/6
Guns: 3—12.7 mm MGs. 1 RPG-7 rocket launcher or 106 mm recoilless rifle. 1—12-barrelled 107 mm rocket launcher (MRL).
Radars: Surface search: I-band.

Comment: Ordered in 1983 and completed in 1984-85 for Customs Service. Total of 51 delivered. Used extensively by the Pasdaran. Maximum payload 450 kg. Speed is dependent on load carried. They can be transported by Amphibious Lift Ships and can operate from bases at Farsi, Sirri and Abu Musa Islands with a main base at Bandar Abbas. Re-engined with Seatek diesels from 1991. There are also a further 10-11 m craft with similar characteristics. Known as TORAGH boats and manned by the Pasdaran and the Navy. Numbers approximate.

15 PEYKAAP CLASS (INSHORE PATROL CRAFT) (PTF)

Displacement, tons: 7 approx
Dimensions, feet (metres): 49.2 × 9.8 × 2.3 *(15 × 3 × 0.7)*
Speed, knots: 50 approx
Torpedoes: 2 lightweight

Comment: Up to 15 of this class in service with the Pasdaran. Built in North Korea, six craft were reported to have been delivered on 8 December 2002 on the Iranian freighter *Iran Meead*. An apparently stealthy craft whose unusual armament of lightweight torpedoes suggest a ship-disabling role.

PEYKAAP CLASS   *6/2002, Royal Australian Navy* / 0528431

10 TIR CLASS (INSHORE PATROL CRAFT) (PTF)

Displacement, tons: 30 approx
Dimensions, feet (metres): 65.6 × 16.4 × 3.3 *(20 × 5 × 1)*
Speed, knots: 50 approx
Torpedoes: 2 unknown

Comment: Up to ten of this class in service with the Pasdaran. Built in North Korea, two craft were reported to have been delivered on 8 December 2002 on the Iranian freighter *Iran Meead*. Anti-surface ship role.

TIR CLASS   *6/2002, Royal Australian Navy* / 0528434

3 GAHJAE CLASS (SEMI−SUBMERSIBLE CRAFT) (PTF)

Displacement, tons: 7 approx
Dimensions, feet (metres): 49.2 × 9.8 × 2.3 *(15.0 × 3.0 × 0.7)*
Speed, knots: 50 approx
Torpedoes: 2 lightweight.

Comment: Originally reported as the Taedong-C semi-submersible torpedo boat, three of these craft were reported delivered from North Korea on 8 December 2002 on the Iranian freighter *Iran Meead*. The stealthy design appears to be based on the Peykaap class inshore patrol craft on which the dimensions, which are speculative, are based. The concept of operations is likely to include a high speed surface approach to a target before submerging to a depth of about 3 m to conduct the attack phase using a snort mast.

GAHJAE CLASS (artist's impression)   *10/2005** / 1151265

2 KAJAMI CLASS (SEMI−SUBMERSIBLE CRAFT) (PTF)

Displacement, tons: To be announced
Dimensions, feet (metres): To be announced
Speed, knots: To be announced

Comment: Originally reported as the Taedong-B high-speed infiltration craft, two of these craft were reported delivered from North Korea on 8 December 2002 on the Iranian freighter *Iran Meead*. Little is known about the design of the craft except that it is about 20 m long and that its concept of operations is likely to include a high speed surface approach to a target before submerging to a depth of about 3 m to conduct the attack phase using a snort mast.

KAJAMI (high-speed approach) (artist's impression)   *10/2005** / 1151267

KAJAMI (submerged approach) (artist's impression)   *10/2005** / 1151268

10 TARLAN CLASS (INSHORE PATROL CRAFT) (PTF)

Displacement, tons: To be announced
Dimensions, feet (metres): To be announced
Speed, knots: 50 approx
Complement: 2

Comment: A new class of inshore attack craft, of unknown origin and build, first reported in 2005. Design features include a catamaran hull, probably adapted from a commercial craft, and a 1.5 m high pedestal in the after part of the vessel. This might support a wire/laser guided weapon similar to an Anti-Tank Guided Missile (ATGM). With two surface-piercing propellers, the craft is capable of high-speed of the order of 50 kt. Numbers of craft are uncertain but are likely to increase.

TARLAN CLASS (artist's impression)   *10/2005** / 1151269

6 US MK II CLASS (COASTAL PATROL CRAFT) (PB)

Displacement, tons: 22.9 full load
Dimensions, feet (metres): 49.9 × 15.1 × 4.3 *(15.2 × 4.6 × 1.3)*
Main machinery: 2 GM 8V-71TI diesels; 460 hp *(343 kW)* sustained; 2 shafts
Speed, knots: 28
Range, n miles: 750 at 26 kt
Complement: 8
Guns: 2−12.7 mm MGs.
Radars: Surface search: SPS-6; I-band.

Comment: Twenty-six ordered from Peterson, USA in 1976-77. Six were for the Navy and the remainder for the Imperial Gendarmerie. All were built in association with Arvandan Maritime Corporation, Abadan. The six naval units operate in the Caspian Sea. Of the remaining 20, six were delivered complete and the others were only 65 per cent assembled on arrival in Iran. Some were lost when the Iraqi Army captured Koramshahr. Others have been lost at sea. Numbers uncertain.

US Mk II   *3/1996* / 0080043

30 PBI TYPE (COASTAL PATROL CRAFT) (PBM)

Displacement, tons: 20.1 full load
Dimensions, feet (metres): 50 × 15 × 4 *(15.2 × 4.6 × 1.2)*
Main machinery: 2 GM 8V-71TI diesels; 460 hp *(343 kW)* sustained; 2 shafts
Speed, knots: 28. **Range, n miles:** 750 at 26 kt
Complement: 5 (1 officer)
Missiles: SSM: Tigercat; range 6 km *(3.2 n miles).*
Guns: 2 — 12.7 mm MGs.
Radars: Surface search: I-band.

Comment: Ordered by Iranian Arvandan Maritime Company. First 19 completed by Petersons and remainder shipped as kits for completion in Iran. The SSM is crude and unguided. Numbers are approximate.

PBI *4/1995* / 0080044

11 CHINA CAT (C 14) CLASS (PTGF)

Displacement, tons: 19 full load
Dimensions, feet (metres): 45.9 × 13.1 × 3.4 *(14 × 4 × 1)*
Main machinery: 2 diesels; 2 shafts
Speed, knots: 50
Complement: 10
Missiles: SSM: 4 FL-10 (2 twin) launchers.
Guns: 2 China 25 mm (twin).
Weapons control: Optronic director.
Radars: Surface search: I-band.

Comment: Prototype reported delivered late 2000 and commissioned in February 2001. A further ten have been reported operational and a large class is expected. Catamaran hull. The type of missile has not been confirmed and it is unclear whether it is the FL-10 or Kosar. Missiles have been reported to be fitted to five of the craft all of which are operated by the Pasdaran. Four craft, not equipped with missiles, are operated by the Navy.

CHINA CAT *2001, China State Shipbuilding Corporation* / 0096378

20 MIG-G-0800 (INSHORE PATROL CRAFT) (PBF)

Displacement, tons: 1.3 full load
Dimensions, feet (metres): 22.3 × 7.4 × 1.2 *(6.7 × 2.3 × 0.4)*
Main machinery: 2 outboards; 240 hp *(179 kW)*
Speed, knots: 40+
Complement: 4
Guns: Various, but can include 1 — 12-barrelled 107 mm MRL or 1 — 12.7 mm MG.

Comment: Boston Whaler type craft based on a Watercraft (UK) design. Numerous indigenously constructed GRP hulls. Numbers uncertain. Manned by the Pasdaran and the Navy.

MIG-G-0800 *1988* / 0506014

RIVER ROADSTEAD PATROL AND HOVERCRAFT (PBR)

Comment: Numerous craft used by the Revolutionary Guard include:
Type 2: Dimensions, feet (metres): 22.0 × 7.2 *(6.7 × 2.2)*; single outboard engine; 1 — 12.7 mm MG.
Type 3: Dimensions, feet (metres): 16.4 × 5.2 *(5.0 × 1.6)*; single outboard engine; small arms.
Type 4: Dimensions, feet (metres): 13.1 — 26.2 × 7.9 *(4 — 8 × 1.6)*; two outboard engines; small arms.
Type 5: Dimensions, feet (metres): 24.6 × 9.2 *(7.5 × 2.8)*; assault craft.
Type 6: Dimensions, feet (metres): 30.9 × 11.8 *(9.4 × 3.6)*; single outboard engine; 1 — 12.7 mm MG.
Dhows: Dimensions, feet (metres): 77.1 × 20 *(23.5 × 6.1)*; single diesel engine; mine rails.
Yunus: Dimensions, feet (metres): 27.6 × 9.8 *(8.4 × 3)*; speed 32 kt.
Ashoora: Dimensions, feet (metres): 26.6 × 7.9 *(8.1 × 2.4)*; two outboards; speed 42 kt; 1 — 7.62 mm MG.
Jet Skis: RPGs.

Type 4 *5/1997* / 0012558

JET SKI (with RPG) *5/1999* / 0080046

20 MIG-G-0900 CLASS (INSHORE PATROL CRAFT) (PBI)

Displacement, tons: 3.5 full load
Dimensions, feet (metres): 30.2 × 9.2 × 1.5 *(9.2 × 2.8 × 0.45)*
Main machinery: 2 Volvo Penta diesels; 1,260 hp *(940 kW)*
Speed, knots: 30
Complement: 3
Guns: 3 — 12.7 mm MGs. 1 RPG-7 rocket launcher or 106 mm recoilless rifle. 1 — 12-barrelled 107 mm rocket launcher (MRL).
Radars: Surface search: I-band.

Comment: Built by MiG, the unarmed variant has been produced in relatively large numbers since the mid-1990s. This approximate number of armed variant is believed to be in Pasdaran or naval service.

MIG-G-0900 *2000, MiG* / 0126375

AMPHIBIOUS FORCES

Notes: (1) Commercial LSLs have been built at Bandar Abbas. These include two 1,151 grt ships, *Chavoush* launched in December 1995 and *Chalak* in June 1996.
(2) There are an unknown number of small Wing-In-Ground (WIG) vehicles, possibly for operations in the Caspian Sea.

WIG   *6/2004* / 1044357

4 HENGAM CLASS (LSLH)

Name	No	Builders	Commissioned
HENGAM	511	Yarrow (Shipbuilders) Ltd, Clyde	12 Aug 1974
LARAK	512	Yarrow (Shipbuilders) Ltd, Clyde	12 Nov 1974
TONB	513	Yarrow (Shipbuilders) Ltd, Clyde	21 Feb 1985
LAVAN	514	Yarrow (Shipbuilders) Ltd, Clyde	16 Jan 1985

Displacement, tons: 2,540 full load
Dimensions, feet (metres): 305 × 49 × 7.3 *(93 × 15 × 2.4)*
Main machinery: 4 Paxman 12YJCM diesels *(Hengam, Larak)*; 3,000 hp *(2.24 MW)* sustained; 2 shafts. 4 MTU 16V 652 TB81 diesels *(Tonb, Lavan)*; 4,600 hp(m) *(3.38 MW)* sustained; 2 shafts
Speed, knots: 14.5
Range, n miles: 4,000+ at 12 kt
Complement: 80
Military lift: Up to 9 tanks depending on size; 600 tons cargo; 227 troops; 10 ton crane

Guns: 4 Bofors 40 mm/60 *(Hengam* and *Larak)*. 8 USSR 23 mm/80 (4 twin) *(Tonb* and *Lavan)*. 2 — 12.7 mm MGs.
1 BM-21 multiple rocket launcher.
Countermeasures: Decoys: 2 UK Mk 5 rocket flare launchers.
Radars: Navigation: Racal Decca 1229; I-band.
IFF: SSR 1520 *(Hengam* and *Larak)*.
Tacan: URN 25.
Helicopters: Can embark 1 Sikorsky MH-53D.

Programmes: Named after islands in the Gulf. First two ordered 25 July 1972. Four more ordered 20 July 1977. The material for the last two ships of the second order had been ordered by Yarrows when the order was cancelled in early 1979. *Tonb* carried out trials in October 1984 followed by *Lavan* later in the year and both were released by the UK in 1985 as 'Hospital Ships'.
Structure: Smaller than British *Sir Lancelot* design with no through tank deck. Rocket launcher mounted in the bows.
Operational: Two LCVPs and a number of small landing craft can be carried. Can act as Depot Ships for MCMV and small craft and have been used to ferry Pasdaran small craft around the Gulf.

TONB   *6/2004* / 1044354

TONB   *10/2004** / 1151273

3 IRAN HORMUZ 24 CLASS (LST)

FARSI 24	**SARDASHT** 25	**SAB SAHEL** 26

Displacement, tons: 2,014 full load
Dimensions, feet (metres): 239.8 × 46.6 × 8.2 *(73.1 × 14.2 × 2.5)*
Main machinery: 2 Daihatsu 6DLM-22 diesels; 2,400 hp(m) *(1.76 MW)*; 2 shafts
Speed, knots: 12
Complement: 30 plus 110 berths
Military lift: 9 tanks, 140 troops

Comment: Built at Inchon, South Korea in 1985-86 and as with the Iran Hormuz 21 class officially classed as Merchant Ships. Have been used to support Pasdaran activities.

IRAN HORMUZ 24   *5/1999* / 0080048

3 FOUQUE (MIG-S-3700) CLASS (LSL)

FOUQUE 101	**102**	**103**

Displacement, tons: 276 full load
Dimensions, feet (metres): 121.4 × 26.2 × 4.9 *(37 × 8 × 1.5)*
Main machinery: 2 MWM TBD 234 V8 diesels; 879 hp(m) *(646 kW)*; 2 shafts
Speed, knots: 10
Range, n miles: 400 at 10 kt
Complement: 8
Military lift: 140 tons of vehicles

Comment: *Fouque* assembled in Iran by Martyr Darvishi Marine, Bandar Abbas. Launched in June 1998. Others of the class are in commercial service and more can be taken over by the Navy if required. Two others for the Navy were launched in September 1995.

FOUQUE CLASS   *1994, Iranian Marine Industries* / 0080049

3 IRAN HORMUZ 21 CLASS (LST)

HEJAZ 21	**KARABALA** 22	**AMIR** 23

Displacement, tons: 1,280 full load
Measurement, tons: 750 dwt
Dimensions, feet (metres): 213.3 × 39.4 × 8.5 *(65 × 12 × 2.6)*
Main machinery: 2 MAN V12V-12.5/14 or 2 MWM TBD 604 V12 diesels; 1,460 hp(m) *(1.07 MW)*; 2 shafts
Speed, knots: 9
Complement: 12
Military lift: 600 tons

Comment: Officially ordered for 'civilian use' and built by Ravenstein, Netherlands in 1984-85. 21 and 22 are manned by the Pasdaran. A local version is assembled as the MIG-S-5000 for commercial use. One was launched in mid-1995 at Boushehr and a second in 1997.

6 WELLINGTON (BH.7) CLASS (HOVERCRAFT) (UCAC)

101-106

Displacement, tons: 53.8 full load
Dimensions, feet (metres): 78.3 × 45.6 × 5.6 (skirt) *(23.9 × 13.9 × 1.7)*
Main machinery: 1 RR Proteus 15 M/541 gas turbine; 4,250 hp *(3.17 MW)* sustained
Speed, knots: 70; 30 in Sea State 5 or more. **Range, n miles:** 620 at 66 kt
Guns: 2 Browning 12.7 mm MGs.
Radars: Surface search: Decca 1226; I-band.

Comment: First pair are British Hovercraft Corporation 7 Mk 4 commissioned in 1970-71 and the next four are Mk 5 craft commissioned in 1974-75. Mk 5 craft fitted for, but not with Standard missiles. Some refitted in UK in 1984. Can embark troops and vehicles or normal support cargoes. The Iranian Aircraft Manufacturing Industries (HESA) is reported to be able to maintain these craft in service.

WELLINGTON   *6/1998, HESA* / 0033385

1 IRAN CLASS (HOVERCRAFT) (UCAC)

Displacement, tons: 10 full load
Dimensions, feet (metres): 48.4 × 25.3 × 15.9 *(14.8 × 7.7 × 4.8)*
Main machinery: 1 gas turbine
Speed, knots: 60

Comment: The first of a new Iran class was completed in March 2000 and is probably based on the old SRN-6 class on which the approximate dimensions are based. Reports suggest a military lift of 2 tons and 26 troops.

IRAN CLASS   *6/2004* / 1044355

AUXILIARIES

Notes: (1) There is also an inshore survey vessel *Abnegar*.
(2) Two 65 ton training vessels of Kialas-C-Qasem class are reported to have commissioned mid-2000. There may be further craft. No other details are known.

1 MSC 268/292 CLASS (YDT)

Name	No	Builders	Commissioned
HAMZEH (ex-*Shahrokh*, ex-MSC 276)	301	Bellingham Shipyard	1960

Displacement, tons: 384 full load
Dimensions, feet (metres): 145.8 × 28 × 8.3 *(44.5 × 8.5 × 2.5)*
Main machinery: 4 GM 6—71 diesels; 696 hp *(519 kW)* sustained; 2 shafts
Speed, knots: 13. **Range, n miles:** 2,400 at 10 kt
Complement: 40 (6 officers)
Guns: 2 Oerlikon 20 mm (twin).
Radars: Surface search: Decca; I-band.

Comment: Originally class of four. Transferred from the USA under MAP in 1959-62. Wooden construction. *Hamzeh* in the Caspian Sea was reported scrapped, but has re-emerged as a diving tender with the new name of the former Royal Yacht. *Simorgh*, *Karkas* and *Shabaz* have been deleted.

MSC 268 (Spanish colours)   *4/1999, Diego Quevedo* / 0080047

4 KANGAN CLASS (WATER TANKERS) (AWT)

KANGAN 411	TAHERI 412	SHAHID MARJANI	AMIR

Displacement, tons: 12,000 full load
Measurement, tons: 9,430 dwt
Dimensions, feet (metres): 485.6 × 70.5 × 16.4 *(148 × 21.5 × 5)*
Main machinery: 1 MAN 7L52/55A diesel; 7,385 hp(m) *(5.43 MW)* sustained; 1 shaft
Speed, knots: 15
Complement: 14
Cargo capacity: 9,000 m³ of water
Guns: 2 USSR 23 mm/80 (twin). 2—12.7 mm MGs.
Radars: Navigation: Decca 1229; I-band.

Comment: The first two were built in Mazagon Dock, Bombay in 1978 and 1979. The second pair to a slightly modified design was acquired in 1991-92 but may be civilian manned. Some of the largest water tankers afloat and can be used to supply remote coastal towns and islands. Accommodation is air conditioned. All have a 10 ton boom crane.

TAHERI   *5/1989* / 0506013

12 HENDIJAN CLASS (TENDERS) (PBO)

HENDIJAN	NAYBAND	MOGAM	GAVATAR
GENAVEH	KALAT	MACHAM	ROSTANI
BAHREGAN (ex-*Geno*)	SIRIK	KONARAK	KORAMSHAHR

Displacement, tons: 460 full load
Dimensions, feet (metres): 166.7 × 28.1 × 11.5 *(50.8 × 8.6 × 3.5)*
Main machinery: 2 Mitsubishi S16MPTK diesels; 7,600 hp(m) *(5.15 MW)*; 2 shafts
Speed, knots: 25
Complement: 15 plus 90 passengers
Cargo capacity: 40 tons on deck; 95 m³ of liquid/solid cargo space
Guns: 1—20 mm (sometimes fitted in patrol craft). 2—12.7 mm MGs.
Radars: Navigation: Racal Decca or China RM 1070A; I-band.

Comment: First eight built by Damen, Netherlands 1988-91. Remainder built at Bandar Abbas under the MIG-S-4700 programme. Last pair launched on 25 November 1995. Reports of three more being built may be caused by confusion with new corvettes. Variously described in the Iranian press as 'frigates' or 'patrol ships', they are regularly used for coastal surveillance. One is used as a training ship. Pennant numbers in the 1400 series.

HENDIJAN 1410   *6/2004* / 1044358

10 DAMEN 1550 (PILOT CRAFT)

Displacement, tons: 25 full load
Dimensions, feet (metres): 52.5 × 15.1 × 4.6 *(16 × 4.6 × 1.4)*
Main machinery: 2 MTU diesels; 2 shafts
Speed, knots: 19
Complement: 3
Radars: Navigation: Furuno; I-band.

Comment: Ordered from Damen, Gorinchen in February 1993. Steel hull and aluminium superstructure. Used primarily as pilot craft.

DAMEN 1550   *1993, Damen Shipyards* / 0080051

For details of the latest updates to *Jane's Fighting Ships* online and to discover the additional information available exclusively to online subscribers please visit
jfs.janes.com

2 FLOATING DOCKS

400 (ex-US ARD 29, ex-FD 4)   **DOLPHIN**

Dimensions, feet (metres): 487 × 80.2 × 32.5 *(149.9 × 24.7 × 10)* *(400)*
786.9 × 172.1 × 58.4 *(240 × 52.5 × 17.8)* *(Dolphin)*

Comment: *400* is an ex-US ARD 12 class built by Pacific Bridge, California and transferred in 1977; lift 3,556 tons. *Dolphin* built by MAN-GHH Nordenham, West Germany and completed in November 1985; lift 28,000 tons.

2 FLEET SUPPLY SHIPS (AORLH)

Name	No	Builders	Commissioned
BANDAR ABBAS	421	C Lühring Yard, Brake, West Germany	Apr 1974
BOUSHEHR	422	C Lühring Yard, Brake, West Germany	Nov 1974

Displacement, tons: 4,673 full load
Measurement, tons: 3,250 dwt; 3,186 gross
Dimensions, feet (metres): 354.2 × 54.4 × 14.8 *(108 × 16.6 × 4.5)*
Main machinery: 2 MAN 6L 52/55 diesels; 12,060 hp(m) *(8.86 MW)* sustained; 2 shafts
Speed, knots: 20
Range, n miles: 3,500 at 16 kt
Complement: 59
Guns: 3 GAM-BO1 20 mm can be carried. 2—12.7 mm MGs.
Radars: Navigation: 2 Decca 1226; I-band.
Helicopters: 1 AB 212.

Comment: *Bandar Abbas* launched 11 August 1973, *Boushehr* launched 23 March 1974. Combined tankers and store-ships carrying victualling, armament and general stores. Telescopic hangar. Both carry 2 SA-7 portable SAM and 20 mm guns have replaced the former armament. *Bandar Abbas* damaged by an explosion in early 1999 but has been repaired. Deployment to the Caspian Sea has not taken place.

BANDAR ABBAS   *10/2004** / 1151276

7 DELVAR CLASS (SUPPORT SHIPS) (AEL/AKL/AWT)

CHARAK (AKL)	CHIROO (AKL)	DELVAR (AEL)	DILIM (AWT)
SOURU (AKL)	SIRJAN (AEL)	DAYER (AWT)	

Measurement, tons: 890 gross; 765 dwt
Dimensions, feet (metres): 210 × 34.4 × 10.9 *(64 × 10.5 × 3.3)*
Main machinery: 2 MAN G6V 23.5/33ATL diesels; 1,560 hp(m) *(1.15 MW)*; 2 shafts
Speed, knots: 11
Complement: 20
Guns: 1 GAM-BO1 20 mm. 2—2.7 mm MGs.
Radars: Navigation: Decca 1226; I-band.

Comment: All built by Karachi SY in 1980-82. *Delvar* and *Sirjan* are ammunition ships, *Dayer* and *Dilim* water carriers and the other three are general cargo ships. The water carriers have only one crane (against two on the other types), and have rounded sterns (as opposed to transoms). Re-armed. 424 and 483 have been reported.

CHARAK   *10/1997* / 0012563

DELVAR CLASS 424   *5/2003, A Sharma* / 0569202

1 REPLENISHMENT SHIP (AORH)

Name	No	Builders	Commissioned
KHARG	431	Swan Hunter Ltd, Wallsend	5 Oct 1984

Displacement, tons: 11,064 light; 33,014 full load
Measurement, tons: 9,367 dwt; 18,582 gross
Dimensions, feet (metres): 679 × 86.9 × 30 *(207.2 × 26.5 × 9.2)*
Main machinery: 2 Babcock & Wilcox boilers; 2 Westinghouse turbines; 26,870 hp *(19.75 MW)*; 1 shaft
Speed, knots: 21.5
Complement: 248
Guns: 1 OTO Melara 76 mm/62 compact. 4 USSR 23 mm/80 (2 twin). 2—12.7 mm MGs.
Radars: Navigation: Decca 1229; I-band
Tacan: URN 20.
Helicopters: 3 Sea Kings (twin hangar).

Comment: Ordered October 1974. Laid down 27 January 1976. Launched 3 February 1977. Ship handed over to Iranian crew on 25 April 1980 but remained in UK. In 1983 Iranian Government requested this ship's transfer. The UK Government delayed approval until January 1984. On 10 July 1984 began refit at Tyne Ship Repairers. Trials began 4 September 1984 and ship was then delivered without guns which were subsequently fitted. A design incorporating some of the features of the British Ol class but carrying ammunition and dry stores in addition to fuel. Inmarsat fitted.

KHARG   *5/1997* / 0052379

KHARG   *6/1998* / 0052380

TUGS

17 HARBOUR TUGS (YTB/YTM)

HAAMOON	SEFID-RUD	ATRAK	ABAD
ALBAN	DEHLORAN	ILAM	HANGAM
ASLAM	KHANDAG	ARVAND	KARKHEH
DARYAVAND II	MENAB	HARI-RUD	ARAS
HIRMAND			

Comment: All between 70 and 90 ft in length, built since 1984.

Iraq

Country Overview

The Republic of Iraq was proclaimed in 1958 following a coup d'état. With an area of 168,754 square miles, it is situated in the Middle East and is bordered to the north by Turkey, to the east by Iran (with which it was at war 1980-88), to the west by Jordan and Syria and to the south by Saudi Arabia (with which it jointly administers the Neutral Zone) and Kuwait (which it invaded and occupied 1990-91 until expelled in the Gulf War 1991). It has a 31 n mile coastline with the Gulf. Baghdad is the capital and largest city. There are two ports on the Khawr Abd Allah Channel at Umm Qasr and Khawr al Zubayr. Territorial Seas (12 n miles) are claimed. An EEZ has not been claimed.

In the wake of the US-led occupation in March-April 2003, Iraq remained under coalition control until 30 June 2004 when full authority was handed over to an Iraqi Interim Government. Following elections on 30 January 2005, a new constitution was ratified by public referendum on 15 October 2005. This was followed by a general election on 15 December 2005 to elect a permanent Iraqi National Assembly. All naval coastal defence units, surface ships and aircraft were destroyed or disabled during the war and are unlikely to be resurrected. An oiler *(Agnadeen)* at Alexandria could be reclaimed but this is unlikely to be a high priority. The Iraqi Coastal Defence Force (ICDF), now known as the Iraqi Navy, was formally established at Umm Qasr on 30 September 2004. Key tasks include defence of the offshore oil terminals at Khawr al Amaya and Mina Al Bakr.

Headquarters Appointments

Commander Iraqi Navy:
  Commodore Muhammed Jawad

Bases

Al Basra (Navy HQ), Khor Az Zubayr, Umm Qasr.

Personnel

2006: 1,100 (including 400 naval infantry)

CORVETTES

0 + 2 ASSAD CLASS (FSG)

Name	No	Builders	Laid down	Launched	Commissioned
MUSSA BEN NUSSAIR	F 210	Fincantieri, Muggiano	15 Jan 1982	22 Oct 1982	17 Sep 1986
TARIQ IBN ZIAD	F 212	Fincantieri, Muggiano	20 May 1982	8 July 1983	29 Oct 1986

Displacement, tons: 685 full load
Dimensions, feet (metres): 204.4 × 30.5 × 8.0
  (62.3 × 9.3 × 2.5)
Main machinery: 4 MTU 20V 956 TB92 diesels; 20,120 hp(m) *(14.8 MW)* sustained; 4 shafts
Speed, knots: 37. **Range, n miles:** 4,000 at 18 kt
Complement: 51 (without aircrew)

Missiles: SSM: 2 OTO Melara/Matra Teseo (fitted for).
SAM: 1 Selenia/Elsag Albatros launcher (4 cell-2 reloads) Aspide; semi-active radar homing to 13 km *(7 n miles)* at 2.5 Mach; warhead 30 kg.
Guns: 1 OTO Melara 3 in *(76 mm)*/62 compact; 85 rds/min to 16 km *(8.7 n miles)*; weight of shell 6 kg.

Countermeasures: Decoys: 2 Breda 105 mm 6-tubed fixed multipurpose launchers.
ESM: Selenia INX-3; intercept.
ECM: Selenia TQN-2; jammer.
Combat data systems: Selenia IPN-10.
Weapons control: 2 Selenia 21 (for SAN). Dardo (for guns).
Radars: Air/surface search: Selenia RAN 12L/X; D/I-band.
Fire control: 2 Selenia RTN 10X; I/J-band.
Navigation: SMA SPN-703; I-band.
Sonars: Kae ASO 84-41; hull-mounted; active search and attack.

Helicopters: 1 Agusta AB 212 type.

Programmes: Originally ordered in February 1981 and formally handed over in 1986 without weapon systems. Trials with Iraqi crews began in 1990 but final delivery was halted by the Iraqi invasion of Kuwait and subsequent UN sanctions. Thereafter the ships remained at La Spezia with a caretaker team of about 12. In December 2004, the Italian government announced plans to refurbish both ships and refit work began in 2005. Delivery is expected in 2006. Details are as for original ships and may differ.
Structure: Similar to Malaysian Laksamana class which were originally ordered by Iraq but fitted with flight deck and telescopic hangar.

TARIQ IBN ZIAD   *8/1995, Ships of the World* / 0581387

PATROL FORCES

Notes: (1) 24 fast assault boats were provided by the UAE in 2005. (2) A contract for the construction of six 30 m Al Uboor class patrol craft was signed on 17 February 2005. The vessels are to be built in Iraq and are to be delivered in 2006.

5 PREDATOR CLASS (INSHORE PATROL CRAFT) (PB)

P 101-105

Displacement, tons: To be announced
Dimensions, feet (metres): 88.9 × 9.2 × 5.9 *(27.1 × 2.8 × 1.8)*
Main machinery: 2 MTU 12V 396 TE742; 4,025 hp *(3 MW)*
Speed, knots: 32
Complement: 6
Guns: 1 — 7.62 mm MG.

Comment: Built at Wuhan by Nanhua High-Speed Engineering Company and originally acquired in 2002. Maintained in dry-dock at Jebel Ali, UAE, until the first two were commissioned on 4 April 2004. Three further craft followed in May 2004. Acquisition and refit costs funded by the US. The craft were used initially for training of Iraqi personnel but are to be used increasingly for patrol duties as the navy develops. Based at Umm Qasr.

P 102   *5/2004, US Navy* / 0580527

P 102   *5/2004, US Navy* / 0580528

Ireland

AN SEIRBHIS CHABHLAIGH

Country Overview

The Republic of Ireland comprises about five sixths of the island of Ireland. Situated west of Great Britain, the country consists of the provinces of Leinster, Munster, Connaught and three counties of the province of Ulster. The remaining six counties of Ulster form Northern Ireland, a constituent part of the United Kingdom. With an area of 27,136 square miles, the country has a 783 n mile coastline with the Atlantic Ocean and Irish Sea. Dublin is the capital, largest city and principal port. There is another major port at Cork. Territorial waters (12 n miles) are claimed. A 200 n mile Fishery zone has also been claimed.

Headquarters Appointments

Flag Officer Commanding Naval Service:
  Commodore F Lynch

Bases

Haulbowline Island, Cork Harbour-Naval HQ, Base and Dockyard

Personnel

(a) 2006: 1,144 (189 officers)
(b) Voluntary service
(c) Reserves: 400 (one unit in each of the following cities: Dublin, Waterford, Cork and Limerick)

Fishery Protection

In late 2004 and early 2005, all ships were fitted with the new Lirguard system. This system incorporates the previously separate functions of the database, GIS database display, Vessel Monitoring System (VMS) and legislation browser. This system will be updated several times daily by satellite link from the Fisheries Monitoring Centre (FMC) at Haulbowline. These will provide a near real-time display and analysis tool of fishing activity to allow more intelligent and efficient use of the ships in the Fishery Protection role. Research is also continuing into the incorporation of VMS data with data from Earth Observation (EO) technology.

Prefix to Ships' Names

LÉ (Long Éirennach = Irish Ship)

PATROL FORCES

Notes: Replacement of the P-21 class with more capable vessels is under consideration.

1 EITHNE CLASS (PSOH)

Name	No	Builders	Laid down	Launched	Commissioned
EITHNE	P 31	Verolme, Cork	15 Dec 1982	19 Dec 1983	7 Dec 1984

Displacement, tons: 1,760 standard; 1,910 full load
Dimensions, feet (metres): 265 × 39.4 × 14.1
  (80.8 × 12 × 4.3)
Main machinery: 2 Ruston 12RKC diesels; 6,800 hp *(5.07 MW)* sustained; 2 shafts; cp props
Speed, knots: 20+; 19 normal
Range, n miles: 7,000 at 15 kt
Complement: 73 (10 officers)

Guns: 1 Bofors 57 mm/70 Mk 1; 200 rds/min to 17 km *(9.3 n miles)*; weight of shell 2.4 kg.
  2 Rheinmetall 20 mm/20. 2 — 7.62 mm MGs.
  2 Wallop 57 mm launchers for illuminants.
Weapons control: Signaal LIOD director. 2 Signaal optical sights.
Radars: Air/surface search: Signaal DA05 Mk 4; E/F-band
  Surface search: Kelvin Hughes; E/F-band
  Navigation: 2 Kelvin Hughes; 6000A; I-band
  Tacan: MEL RRB transponder

Helicopters: Not routinely carried.

Programmes: Ordered 23 April 1982 from Verolme, Cork, this was the last ship to be built at this yard.

EITHNE *6/2005*, D Jones, Irish Navy* / 1133508

Structure: Fitted with retractable stabilisers. Closed circuit TV for flight deck operations. Satellite navigation and communications. CTD tactical displays.

Operational: Helicopter no longer operational. Two Delta 7.5 m inboard diesel RIBs fitted in addition to two 5.4 m RIBs in 2003. Long refit (SLEP) in 1998/99.

2 ROISIN CLASS (PSO)

Name	No	Builders	Laid down	Launched	Commissioned
ROISIN	P 51	Appledore Shipbuilders, Bideford	Dec 1998	12 Aug 1999	15 Dec 1999
NIAMH	P 52	Appledore Shipbuilders, Bideford	June 2000	10 Feb 2001	18 Sep 2001

Displacement, tons: 1,700 full load
Dimensions, feet (metres): 258.7 × 45.9 × 12.8
  (78.9 × 14 × 3.9)
Main machinery: 2 Wärtsilä 16V26 diesels; 6,800 hp(m) *(5 MW)* sustained; 2 shafts; LIPS cp props; bow thruster; 462 hp(m) *(340 kW)*
Speed, knots: 23. **Range, n miles:** 6,000 at 15 kt

Complement: 44 (6 officers)
Guns: 1 OTO Melara 3 in *(76 mm)*/62; 85 rds/min to 16 km *(8.6 n miles)*; weight of shell 6 kg.
  2 — 12.7 mm MGs. 4 — 7.62 mm MGs.
Weapons control: Radamec 1500 optronic director.
Radars: Surface search: Kelvin Hughes; E/F-band
  Navigation: Kelvin Hughes; I-band.

Programmes: Contract for first ship signed on 16 December 1997 with 65 per cent of EU funding. Option on a second of class taken up on 6 April 2000.
Operational: Designated Large Patrol Vessel, the design is a modification of the Mauritius ship *Vigilant* but without the hangar or flight deck. Two Delta 6.5 m and one Avon 5.4 m RIBs are carried. CTD tactical displays.

NIAMH *6/2005*, Michael Winter* / 1133507

3 P 21 CLASS (OFFSHORE PATROL VESSELS) (PSO)

Name	No	Builders	Launched	Commissioned
EMER	P 21	Verolme, Cork	4 Aug 1977	16 Jan 1978
AOIFE	P 22	Verolme, Cork	12 Apr 1979	29 Nov 1979
AISLING	P 23	Verolme, Cork	3 Oct 1979	21 May 1980

Displacement, tons: 1,019.5
Dimensions, feet (metres): 213.7 × 34.4 × 14 *(65.2 × 10.5 × 4.4)*
Main machinery: 2 SEMT-Pielstick 6 PA6 L 280 diesels; 4,800 hp *(3.53 MW)*; 1 shaft; bow thruster *(Aoife* and *Aisling)*
Speed, knots: 17
Range, n miles: 4,000 at 17 kt; 6,750 at 12 kt
Complement: 47 (6 officers)

Guns: 1 Bofors 40 mm/L 70; 300 rds/min to 12 km *(6.5 n miles)*; weight of shell 0.88 kg.
2 GAM-B01 20 mm; 900 rds/min to 2 km.
2—12.7 mm MGs. 2—7.62 mm MGs.
Radars: Surface search: Kelvin Hughes I-band
Navigation: Kelvin Hughes Nucleus 6000A; I-band.

Modernisation: New search radars were fitted in 1994-95. CTD tactical display fitted.
Structure: Stabilisers fitted. *Aoife* and *Aisling* are equipped with a bow thruster. Inmarsat SATCOM fitted.
Operational *Emer* refitted in 1995, *Aoife* in 1996/97 and *Aisling* in 1997/98. Sonars have been removed.

AISLING *7/2005*, Guy Toremans* / 1133509

AOIFE *6/2005*, D Jones, Irish Navy* / 1133506

2 P 41 PEACOCK CLASS (COASTAL PATROL VESSELS) (PSO)

Name	No	Builders	Commissioned
ORLA (ex-*Swift*)	P 41	Hall Russell, Aberdeen	3 May 1985
CIARA (ex-*Swallow*)	P 42	Hall Russell, Aberdeen	17 Oct 1984

Displacement, tons: 712 full load
Dimensions, feet (metres): 204.1 × 32.8 × 8.9 *(62.6 × 10 × 2.7)*
Main machinery: 2 Crossley SEMT-Pielstick 18 PA6 V 280 diesels; 14,400 hp(m) *(10.58 MW)* sustained; 2 shafts; auxiliary drive; Schottel prop; 181 hp(m) *(133 kW)*
Speed, knots: 25
Range, n miles: 2,500 at 17 kt
Complement: 39 (5 officers)

Guns: 1—3 in (76 mm)/62 OTO Melara compact; 85 rds/min to 16 km *(8.6 n miles)*; weight of shell 6 kg.
2—12.7 mm MGs. 4—7.62 mm MGs.
Weapons control: Radamec 1500 optronic director (for 76 mm).
Radars: Surface search: Kelvin Hughes; I-band
Navigation: Kelvin Hughes Nucleus 5000A/6000A; I-band.

Programmes: *Orla* launched 11 September 1984 and *Ciara* 31 March 1984. Both served in Hong Kong from mid-1985 until early 1988. Acquired from UK and commissioned 21 November 1988. Others of the class acquired by the Philippines in 1997.
Modernisation: New radars fitted in 1993. CTD tactical display fitted.
Structure: Have loiter drive. Displacement increased after building by the addition of more electronic equipment.

CIARA *6/2005*, D Jones, Irish Navy* / 1133505

SHIPBORNE AIRCRAFT

Numbers/Type: 2 Aerospatiale SA 365F Dauphin 2.
Operational speed: 140 kt *(260 km/h)*.
Service ceiling: 15,000 ft *(4,575 m)*.
Range: 410 n miles *(758 km)*.
Role/Weapon systems: No longer operated from *Eithne*; some shore land-based training by Army Air Corps and SAR. One aircraft lost in 2001. Sensors: Bendix RDR 1500 radar. Weapons: Unarmed

DAUPHIN 2 *6/2002, D Jones, Irish Navy* / 0525904

LAND-BASED MARITIME AIRCRAFT

Notes: Four civilian operated Sikorsky S-61 helicopters provide long-range SAR services.

Numbers/Type: 2 Casa CN-235 Persuader.
Operational speed: 210 kt *(384 km/h)*.
Service ceiling: 24,000 ft *(7,315 m)*.
Range: 2,000 n miles *(3,218 km)*.
Role/Weapon systems: EEZ surveillance. First one delivered in June 1992 but returned to Spain in 1995. Two more delivered in December 1994. Sensors: Search radar Bendix APS 504(V)5; FLIR. Weapons: Unarmed.

CN-235 *7/2003, Paul Jackson* / 0568896

AUXILIARIES

Notes: (1) In addition there are a number of mostly civilian manned auxiliaries including: *Seabhac* a small tug acquired in 1983; *Fainleog, David F* (built in 1962) and *Fiach Dubh* passenger craft, the last two taken over after lease in 1988 and the first in 1983; *Tailte* a Dufour 35 ft sail training yacht bought in 1979 and an elderly training yacht *Creidne*.
(2) *Granuaile* is an 80 m lighthouse tender with a helicopter flight deck forward operated by the Commissioners of Irish Lights. Launched on 14 August 1999 this ship replaced a previous vessel of the same name on 23 March 2000.

GRANUAILE *3/2000, Commissioners of Irish Lights* / 0093593

Israel

HEYL HAYAM

Country Overview

Established in 1948, The State of Israel is situated on the eastern shore of the Mediterranean Sea and has borders to the north with Lebanon, to the north-east with Syria, to the east with Jordan and to the south-west with Egypt. It has coastlines with the Mediterranean (142 n miles) and with the Gulf of Aqaba (5 n miles) in the northern Red Sea. A land area of 8,463 square miles includes East Jerusalem and other territory (including Gaza Strip, the West Bank region of Jordan, the Golan Heights area of south-western Syria) annexed in 1967. Jerusalem is the largest city but, although claimed as the capital, is not so recognised by the United Nations. Many nations maintain embassies at Tel Aviv. Haifa is the principal port. Territorial seas (12 n miles) are claimed but an EEZ is not claimed.

Headquarters Appointments

Commander-in-Chief:
  Vice Admiral David Ben-Ba'ashat

General

Less than 5 per cent of Israeli defence budget is allocated to the Navy.

Personnel

(a)   2006: 6,500 (880 officers) of whom 2,500 are conscripts. Includes a Naval Commando of 300
(b)   3 years' national service for Jews and Druzes

Notes: An additional 5,000 Reserves available on mobilisation.

Bases

Haifa, Ashdod, Eilat
(The repair base at Eilat has a synchrolift)

Coast Defence

There are ten integrated coastal radar stations. These are to be converted to an unmanned, remote-controlled system.

Prefix to Ships' Names

INS (Israeli Naval Ship)

SUBMARINES

Notes: The two decommissioned Gal class submarines arrived in Germany on 18 December 2003. Subsequently, no work on the boats has been reported and it is unclear whether the boats are for sale, to be reactivated or scrapped.

GAL CLASS

4/2004, Martin Mokrus / 0580526

3 + 2 DOLPHIN (TYPE 800) CLASS (SSK)

Name	No	Builders	Laid down	Launched	Commissioned
DOLPHIN	–	Howaldtswerke/Thyssen Nordseewerke	7 Oct 1994	12 Apr 1996	37 July 1999
LEVIATHAN	–	Howaldtswerke/Thyssen Nordseewerke	13 Apr 1995	25 Apr 1997	15 Nov 1999
TEKUMA	–	Howaldtswerke/Thyssen Nordseewerke	12 Dec 1996	26 June 1998	25 July 2000

Displacement, tons: 1,640 surfaced; 1,900 dived
Dimensions, feet (metres): 188 × 22.3 × 20.3
  (57.3 × 6.8 × 6.2)
Main machinery: 3 MTU 16V 396 SE 84 diesels; 4,243 hp(m)
  (3.12 MW) sustained; 3 alternators; 2.91 MW; 1 Siemens
  motor; 3,875 hp(m) *(2.85 MW)* sustained; 1 shaft
Speed, knots: 20 dived; 11 snorting
Range, n miles: 8,000 at 8 kt surfaced; 420 at 8 kt dived
Complement: 30 (6 officers)

Missiles: SSM: Sub Harpoon; UGM-84C; active radar or
  GPS homing to 130 km *(70 n miles)* at 0.9 Mach; warhead
  227 kg.
SAM: Fitted for Triton anti-helicopter system.
Torpedoes: 4—25.6 in *(650 mm)* and 6—21 in *(533 mm)* bow
  tubes. STN Atlas DM2A4 Seehecht; wire-guided active
  homing to 13 km *(7 n miles)* at 35 kt; passive homing to
  28 km *(15 n miles)* at 23 kt; warhead 260 kg. Total of 16
  torpedoes and 5 SSMs. The four 650 mm tubes may be
  for SDVs, but could carry torpedoes if liners are fitted.
Mines: In lieu of torpedoes.
Countermeasures: ESM: Elbit Timnex 4CH(V)2; intercept.
Weapons control: STN/Atlas Elektronik ISUS 90—1 TCS.
Radars: Surface search: Elta; I-band.
Sonars: Atlas Elektronik CSU 90; hull-mounted; passive/
  active search and attack.
  Atlas Elektronik PRS-3; passive ranging.
  FAS-3; flank array; passive search.

Programmes: In mid-1988 Ingalls Shipbuilding Division of
  Litton Corporation was chosen as the prime contractor
  for two IKL-designed Dolphin class submarines to
  be built in West Germany with FMS funds by HDW
  in conjunction with Thyssen Nordseewerke. Funds
  approved in July 1989 with an effective contract date of
  January 1990 but the project was cancelled in November
  1990 due to pressures on defence funds. After the Gulf
  War in April 1991 the contract was resurrected, this time
  with German funding for two submarines with an option
  on a third taken up in July 1994. A letter of intent for
  the construction of two further modified Dolphin class
  submarines was signed on 21 November 2005. The
  new submarines are to be about 10 m longer in order
  to incorporate air-independent propulsion. Subject to
  agreement on a contract, the boats are to be built at
  HDW and TNSW. Funding is likely to be shared equally
  between the Israeli, German and US governments.
Modernisation: Installation of air-independent propulsion
  in the first three boats is under consideration.
Structure: Diving depth, 350 m *(1,150 ft)*. Similar to
  German Type 212 in design but with a 'wet and dry'
  compartment for underwater swimmers. Two Kollmorgen

DOLPHIN   *6/1999, Michael Nitz* / 0080058

periscopes. Probably fitted for Triton anti-helicopter SAM
system.
Operational: Endurance, 30 days. Used for interdiction,
surveillance and special boat operations. Development of
a submarine-launched cruise missile would complete the
final part of a triad of nuclear deterrents. However, while
Israel probably has the expertise and technology to deploy

SLCM, little information exists to confirm or deny such a
programme. Adaptation of the indigenous Delilah and
Popeye groups of missles is a possible option although
encapsulation of the missile would pose a significant
challenge. Painted blue/green to aid concealment in the
eastern Mediterranean. Some other NT 37E torpedoes are
embarked until full Seehecht outfits are available.

TEKUMA   *9/2000, Michael Nitz* / 0104865

CORVETTES

Notes: A Request for Information was issued in September 2003 for the acquisition of up to three multimission corvettes. While this programme was temporarily superseded in 2004 by a proposal to procure a 13,000 ton amphibious ship, it has re-emerged as the priority due to budget realities. Plans for a SAAR 5+ design have been overtaken by ambitions to join the US Navy's Littoral Combat Ship programme. A two year feasibility study was launched in December 2005.

3 EILAT (SAAR 5) CLASS (FSGHM)

Name	No	Builders	Laid down	Launched	Commissioned
EILAT	501	Ingalls, Pascagoula	24 Feb 1992	9 Feb 1993	24 May 1994
LAHAV	502	Ingalls, Pascagoula	25 Sep 1992	20 Aug 1993	23 Sep 1994
HANIT	503	Ingalls, Pascagoula	5 Apr 1993	4 Mar 1994	7 Feb 1995

Displacement, tons: 1,075 standard; 1,295 full load
Dimensions, feet (metres): 278.9 × 39.0 × 10.5
  (85.0 × 11.9 × 3.2)
Main machinery: CODOG; 1 GE LM 2500 gas turbine;
30,000 hp *(22.38 MW)* sustained; 2 MTU 12V 1163 TB82
diesels; 6,600 hp(m) *(4.86 MW)* sustained; 2 shafts;
Kamewa cp props
Speed, knots: 33 gas; 20 diesels
Range, n miles: 3,500 at 17 kt
Complement: 64 (16 officers) plus 10 (4 officers) aircrew

Missiles: SSM: 8 McDonnell Douglas Harpoon (2 quad)
launchers ❶; active radar homing to 130 km *(70 n miles)*
at 0.9 Mach; warhead 227 kg.
SAM: 2 Israeli Industries Barak I (vertical launch) ❷; 2 × 32
cells; command line of sight radar or optical guidance
to 10 km *(5.5 n miles)* at 2 Mach; warhead 22 kg (see
Operational).
Guns: OTO Melara 3 in *(76 mm)*/62 compact ❸; 85 rds/min
to 16 km *(8.7 n miles)*; weight of shell 6 kg.
The main gun is interchangeable with a Bofors 57 mm
gun or Vulcan Phalanx CIWS ❹.
2 Sea Vulcan 20 mm CIWS ❺; range 1 km.
Torpedoes: 6—324 mm Mk 32 (2 triple) tubes ❻. Honeywell
Mk 46; anti-submarine; active/passive homing to 11 km
(5.9 n miles) at 40 kt; warhead 44 kg. Mounted in the
superstructure.
Countermeasures: Decoys: 3 Elbit/Deseaver 72-barrelled
chaff and IR launchers ❼; Rafael ATC-1 towed torpedo
decoy.
ESM: Elisra NS 9003; intercept. Tadiran NATACS.
ECM: 2 Rafael 1010; Elisra NS 9005; jammers.
Combat data systems: Elbit NTCCS using Elta EL/S-9000
computers. Reshet datalink.
Weapons control: 2 Elop MSIS optronic directors ❽.

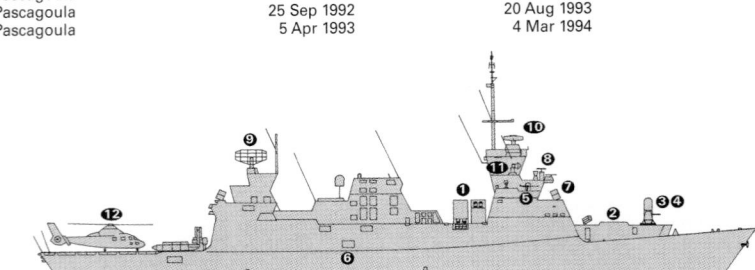

(Scale 1 : 900), Ian Sturton / 1151070

Radars: Air search: Elta EL/M-2218S ❾; E/F-band.
Surface search: Cardion SPS-55 ❿; I-band.
Navigation: I-band.
Fire control: 3 Elta EL/M-2221 GM STGR ⓫; I/K/J-band.
Sonars: EDO Type 796 Mod 1; hull-mounted; search and
attack; medium frequency.
Rafael towed array (fitted for).

Helicopters: 1 Dauphin SA 366G ⓬ or Sea Panther can be
carried.

Programmes: A desi```gn by John J McMullen Associates
Inc for Israeli Shipyards, Haifa in conjunction with Ingalls
Shipbuilding Division of Litton Corporation which was
authorised to act as main contractor using FMS funding.
Contract awarded 8 February 1989. All delivered to Israel
for combat system installation, first two completed
in 1996 and last one in mid-1997. Major refits of these
ships are reported to be under consideration. Plans to
procure a further five new ships (SAAR 5+) under similar

FMS funding are now unlikely to be taken forward in
view of the requirement for multimission ships. The
option for a fourth SAAR 5 is not thought to have been
taken up.
Structure: Steel hull and aluminium superstructure. Stealth
features including resilient mounts for main machinery,
funnel exhaust cooling, Radar Absorbent Material (RAM),
NBC washdown and Prairie Masker Bubbler system. A
secondary operations room is fitted aft. There are some
Flag capabilities. Plans to carry Gabriel SSMs have been
scrapped because of topweight problems. The planned
third MSIS director has not yet been seen on the platform
aft of the air search radar.
Operational: Endurance, 20 days. The main role is to
counter threats in shipping routes. ICS-2 integrated
communications system. The position of the satellite
aerial suggests that the SAM after VLS launchers are not
used. Barak has still to be installed, because of lack of
funds. For the same reason the normal Harpoon load
may be reduced to four.

HANIT

12/2001, M Declerck / 0567460

HANIT

12/2001, M Declerck / 0533267

PATROL FORCES

Notes: (1) There are about 12 'Firefish' type fast attack boats in service with Special Forces.
(2) A 50 ft *(15.2 m)* shallow draft Stealth craft has been built in a Vancouver Shipyard and delivered in late 1998. A second completed by Oregon Iron Works, Portland in 1999 and painted dark green. Two diesels giving 35 kt and a Rafael optronic surveillance system are included. Crew of five.
(3) The Saar 2 class are no longer operational.

8 HETZ (SAAR 4.5) CLASS (FAST ATTACK CRAFT—MISSILE) (PGGM)

Name	Builders	Launched	Commissioned
ROMAT	Israel Shipyards, Haifa	30 Oct 1981	Oct 1981
KESHET	Israel Shipyards, Haifa	Oct 1982	Nov 1982
HETZ (ex-*Nirit*)	Israel Shipyards, Haifa	Oct 1990	Feb 1991
KIDON	Israel Shipyards, Haifa	1993	7 Feb 1994
TARSHISH	Israel Shipyards, Haifa	1995	June 1995
YAFFO	Israel Shipyards, Haifa	1998	1 July 1998
HEREV	Israel Shipyards, Haifa	2002	June 2002
SUFA	Israel Shipyards, Haifa	2002	Aug 2002

Displacement, tons: 488 full load
Dimensions, feet (metres): 202.4 × 24.9 × 8.2
(61.7 × 7.6 × 2.5)
Main machinery: 4 MTU 16V 538 TB93 or 4 MTU 16V 396 TE diesels; 16,600 hp(m) *(12.2 MW)*; 4 shafts
Speed, knots: 31
Range, n miles: 3,000 at 17 kt; 1,500 at 30 kt
Complement: 53

Missiles: SSM: 4 McDonnell Douglas Harpoon ❶; active radar homing to 130 km *(70 n miles)* at 0.9 Mach; warhead 227 kg.
6 IAI Gabriel II ❷; radar or optical guidance; semi-active radar plus anti-radiation homing to 36 km *(19.4 n miles)* at 0.7 Mach; warhead 75 kg.
SAM: Israeli Industries Barak I (vertical launch) ❸; 32 or 16 cells in 2- or 4—8 pack launchers; command line of sight radar or optical guidance to 10 km *(5.5 n miles)* at 2 Mach; warhead 22 kg. Most fitted for but not with.
Guns: 1 OTO Melara 3 in *(76 mm)*/62 ❹; 85 rds/min to 16 km *(8.7 n miles)*; weight of shell 6 kg.
2 Oerlikon 20 mm; 800 rds/min to 2 km.
1 Rafael Typhoon 25 mm (Herev).
1 General Electric/General Dynamics Vulcan Phalanx 6-barrelled 20 mm Mk 15 ❺; 3,000 rds/min combined to 1.5 km anti-missile.
2 or 4—12.7 mm (twin or quad) MGs.
Countermeasures: Decoys: Elbit/Deseaver 72-barrelled launchers for chaff and IR flares ❻.
ESM/ECM: Elisra NS 9003/5; intercept and jammer.
Combat data systems: IAI Reshet datalink.
Weapons control: Galileo OG 20 optical director; Elop MSIS optronic director ❼.
Radars: Air/surface search: Thomson-CSF TH-D 1040 Neptune ❽; G-band.
Fire control: 2 Elta EL/M-2221 GM STGR ❾; I/K/J-band.

Programmes: *Hetz* started construction in 1984 as the fifth of the SAAR 4 class but was not completed, as an economy measure. Taken in hand again in 1989 and fitted out as the trials ship for some of the systems installed in the Eilat class.
Modernisation: *Romat* and *Keshet* were modernised to same standard as *Hetz* in what was called the Nirit programme. The remaining craft were new build and

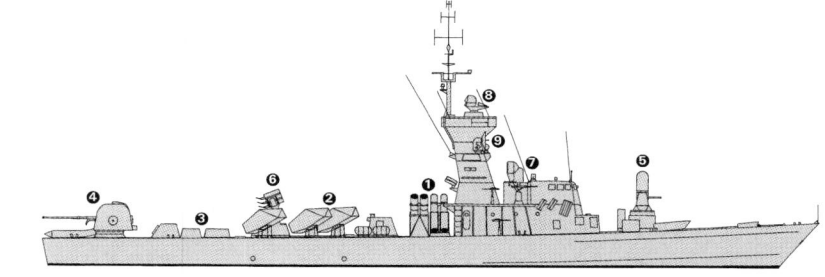

HETZ *(Scale 1 : 600), Ian Sturton* / 0126347

HETZ CLASS *8/2000* / 0105824

some of these have been given names previously allocated to decommissioned/transferred SAAR 4s.
Structure: The CIWS is mounted in the eyes of the ship replacing the 40 mm gun. The eight pack Barak launchers are fully containerised and require no deck penetration or

onboard maintenance. They are fitted aft in place of two of the Gabriel launchers. The fire-control system for Barak is fitted on the platform aft of the bridge on the port side.
Operational: Davits can be installed aft of the Gabriel missiles for special forces boats.

HEREV *6/2002, Israeli Navy* / 0127285

15 DABUR CLASS (COASTAL PATROL CRAFT) (PC)

850	851	853	860-862	864	865	868
873	902	905	906	909	910	

Displacement, tons: 39 full load
Dimensions, feet (metres): 64.9 × 18 × 5.8 *(19.8 × 5.5 × 1.8)*
Main machinery: 2 GM 12V-71TA diesels; 840 hp *(627 kW)* sustained; 2 shafts
About 8 have more powerful GE engines.
Speed, knots: 19; 30 (GE engines). **Range, n miles:** 450 at 13 kt
Complement: 6/9 depending on armament

Guns: 2 Oerlikon 20 mm; 800 rds/min to 2 km.
2—12.7 mm MGs. Carl Gustav 84 mm portable rocket launchers.
Torpedoes: 2—324 mm tubes. Honeywell Mk 46; anti-submarine; active/passive homing
to 11 km *(5.9 n miles)* at 40 kt; warhead 44 kg.
Depth charges: 2 racks in some.
Weapons control: Elop optronic director.
Radars: Surface search: Decca Super 101 Mk 3 or HDWS; I-band.
Sonars: Active search and attack; high frequency.

Programmes: Twelve built by Sewart Seacraft USA and remainder by Israel Aircraft
Industries (RAMTA) between 1973 and 1977. Final total of 34. Likely to be phased out as
new fast attack craft enter service.
Structure: Aluminium hull. Several variations in the armament. Up to eight of the class are
fitted with more powerful General Electric engines to increase speed to 30 kt.
Operational: These craft have been designed for overland transport. Good rough weather
performance. Portable rocket launchers are carried for anti-terrorist purposes. Not
considered fast enough to cope with modern terrorist speedboats and some have been
sold as Super Dvoras commissioned. Two based at Eilat, remainder at Ashdod. To be
replaced by the Super Dvora III as they enter service.
Sales: Four to Argentina in 1978; four to Nicaragua in 1978 and three more in 1996; six to
Chile in 1991 and four more in 1995. Five also given to Lebanon Christian Militia in 1976
but these were returned.

DABUR   *12/1998* / 0075862

2 RESHEF (SAAR 4) CLASS
(FAST ATTACK CRAFT—MISSILE) (PTG)

Name	Builders	Launched	Commissioned
NITZHON	Israel Shipyards, Haifa	10 July 1978	Sep 1978
ATSMOUT	Israel Shipyards, Haifa	3 Dec 1978	Feb 1979

Displacement, tons: 415 standard; 450 full load
Dimensions, feet (metres): 190.6 × 25 × 8 *(58 × 7.8 × 2.4)*
Main machinery: 4 MTU/Bazán 16V 956 TB91 diesels; 15,000 hp(m) *(11.03 MW)* sustained;
4 shafts
Speed, knots: 32. **Range, n miles:** 1,650 at 30 kt; 4,000 at 17.5 kt
Complement: 45

Missiles: SSM: 2—4 McDonnell Douglas Harpoon (twin or quad) launchers; active radar
homing to 130 km *(70 n miles)* at 0.9 Mach; warhead 227 kg.
4—6 Gabriel II; radar or TV optical guidance; semi-active radar plus anti-radiation
homing to 36 km *(20 n miles)* at 0.7 Mach; warhead 75 kg.
Harpoons fitted with Israeli homing systems. The Gabriel II system carries a TV camera
which can transmit a homing picture to the firing ship beyond the radar horizon.
The missile fit currently varies in training boats-2 Harpoon, 5 Gabriel II.
Guns: 2 Oerlikon 20 mm; 800 rds/min to 2 km.
1 General Electric/General Dynamics Vulcan Phalanx 6-barrelled 20 mm Mk 15;
3,000 rds/min combined to 1.5 km anti-missile.
2—12.7 mm MGs.
Torpedoes: Tubes fitted in VDS fitted ship.
Countermeasures: Decoys: 1—45-tube, 4- or 6—24-tube, 4 single-tube chaff launchers.
ESM/ECM: Elisra NS 9003/5; intercept and jammer.
Combat data systems: IAI Reshet datalink.
Radars: Air/surface search: Thomson-CSF TH-D 1040 Neptune; G-band; range 33 km
(18 n miles) for 2 m² target.
Fire control: Selenia Orion RTN 10X; I/J-band.
Sonars: EDO 780; VDS; fitted in one of the class.

Modernisation: Some of the class modernised to Nirit standards and transferred to the
Saar 4.5 class. Gabriel III SSM did not go into production.
Operational: Operational status of last two remaining craft is doubtful. Replacement by
new corvettes is a high priority.
Sales: Nine built for South Africa in Haifa and Durban. One transferred to Chile late 1979,
one in February 1981, and two more in June 1997. Two transferred to Sri Lanka in 2000.

SAAR 4 (with VDS)   *8/2000* / 0105825

SAAR 4   *10/1999* / 0075863

13 SUPER DVORA MK I and MK II CLASSES
(FAST ATTACK CRAFT—GUN) (PTFM)

811-819 (Mk I)	820-823 (Mk II)

Displacement, tons: 54 full load
Dimensions, feet (metres): 71 × 18 × 5.9 screws *(21.6 × 5.5 × 1.8)* (Mk I)
82 × 18.4 × 3.6 *(25 × 5.6 × 1.1)* (Mk II)
Main machinery: 2 Detroit 16V-92TA diesels; 1,380 hp *(1.03 MW)* sustained; 2 shafts (Mk I)
2 MTU 12V 396 TE94 diesels; 4,175 hp(m) *(3.07 MW)* sustained; 2 ASD 16 drives (Mk II)
Speed, knots: 36 or 46 (Mk II)
Range, n miles: 1,200 at 17 kt
Complement: 10 (1 officer)

Missiles: SSM Hellfire; range 8 km *(4.3 n miles)*; can be carried.
Guns: 2 Oerlikon 20 mm/80 or Bushmaster 25 mm/87 Mk 96 or 3 Typhoon 12.7 mm
(triple) MGs.
2—12.7 or 7.62 mm MGs. 1—84 mm rocket launcher.
Depth charges: 2 racks.
Weapons control: Elop MSIS optronic director.
Radars: Surface search: Raytheon; I-band.

Programmes: An improvement on the Dabur design ordered in March 1987 from Israel
Aircraft Industries (RAMTA). First started trials in November 1988, and first two
commissioned in June 1989. First 10 are Mk I. From 820 onwards the ships are fitted
with more powerful engines for a higher top speed and surface drives which greatly
reduce maximum draft. First Mk II commissioned in 1993.
Structure: All gun armament and improved speed and endurance compared with the
prototype Dvora. SSM, depth charges, torpedoes or a 130 mm MRL can be fitted if
required.
Operational: Two (Mk II) are based at Eilat, the remainder at Haifa. The 25 mm or
12.7 mm Gatling guns can be operated by joystick control from the bridge. Hellfire SSM
is sometimes carried.
Sales: Six Mk I sold to Sri Lanka in 1988 and four to Eritrea in 1993. One Mk II to Sri Lanka
in 1995 and three more in 1996. One to Slovenia in 1996 and a second in 1997. Two to
India in 1997, with more building under licence in India.

SUPER DVORA Mk II 820   *1995, IAI* / 0080068

SUPER DVORA Mk I 819   *4/1996* / 0080069

SUPER DVORA Mk I 816   *8/2000* / 0105826

3 + 3 (4) SUPER DVORA MK III CLASS (PTFM)

Displacement, tons: 72 full load
Dimensions, feet (metres): 89.9 × 18.7 × 3.6 *(27.4 × 5.7 × 1.1)*
Main machinery: 2 MTU 12V 4000 diesels; 2 Arneson ASD16 surface drives
Speed, knots: 45
Range, n miles: 1,000 at cruising speed
Complement: 5
Guns: 1 Bushmaster 25 mm M242 chain gun. 1—20 mm. 2—7.62 mm MGs.
Weapons control: ELOP optronic director.
Radars: Surface search: I-band.

Comment: An order for six craft, with an option for a further four, was made with IAI-Ramta on 13 January 2002. The first was delivered in July 2004 and entered service in November 2004. The second and third were delivered on 13 July 2005. Delivery of the remainder is to be completed by December 2006.

SUPER DVORA III   *7/2005*, IAI RAMTA* / 1116348

2 + (2) SHALDAG CLASS (FAST ATTACK CRAFT—GUN) (PBF)

Displacement, tons: 58 full load
Dimensions, feet (metres): 81.4 × 19.7 × 3.9 *(24.8 × 6 × 1.2)*
Main machinery: 2 Deutz 620 TB 16V or MTU 396 TE diesels; 5,000 hp(m) *(3.68 MW)*; 2 LIPS or MJP water-jets
Speed, knots: 50
Range, n miles: 700 at 32 kt
Complement: 10
Guns: 1 Rafael Typhoon 25 mm. 1—20 mm.
Weapons control: ELOP compass optronic director. Typhoon GFCS.
Radars: Surface search: MD 3220 Mk II; I-band.

Comment: Order in January 2002 for two craft, with option for two further hulls, made from Israel Shipyards, Haifa. Details reflect those in Sri Lankan service and are thus speculative. Both delivered in late 2003.

SHALDAG CLASS   *8/2005*, Jane's* / 0589534

3 STINGRAY INTERCEPTOR CLASS (PBF)

Displacement, tons: 10.5 full load
Dimensions, feet (metres): 39.4 × 14.5 × 2.9 *(12 × 4.4 × 0.9)*
Main machinery: 2 Caterpillar marine diesels; 2 shafts
Speed, knots: 35
Range, n miles: 300 at cruising speed
Complement: 5
Radar: Surface search: I-band.

Comment: Catamaran design of GRP construction built by Stingray Marine of Durbanville, Western Cape and delivered in 1997 and 1998.

STINGRAY INTERCEPTOR   *2000, Stingray Marine* / 0104866

4 DEFENDER CLASS (RESPONSE BOATS) (PBF)

Displacement, tons: 2.7 full load
Dimensions, feet (metres): 27.0 × 8.5 × 8.8 *(8.2 × 2.6 × 2.7)*
Main machinery: 2 Honda outboard motors; 450 hp *(335 kW)*
Speed, knots: 46
Range, n miles: 175 at 35 kt
Complement: 4
Guns: 1—12.7 mm MG.
Radars: To be announced.

Comment: High-speed inshore patrol craft of aluminium construction and foam collar built by SAFE Boats International, Port Orchard, Washington. Four delivered in September 2005. To be operated by the port-protection unit on border protection and counter-terrorism operations. The craft are two feet longer than those operated by the USCG. Further orders are expected.

DEFENDER CLASS   *6/2005*, SAFE Boats* / 1116446

0 + 1 RAFAEL PROTECTOR
(UNMANNED SURFACE VEHICLE) (USV)

Displacement, tons: To be announced
Dimensions, feet (metres): 29.5 × ? × ? *(9.0 × ? × ?)*
Main machinery: 1 diesel; 1 waterjet propulsor
Speed, knots: 30+
Guns: 1 Mini-Typhoon stabilised 12.7 mm MG.
Weapons control: Toplite EO sensor pod.

Comment: Developed jointly by Rafael and Aeronautics Defense Systems, Protector was first revealed in June 2003. It is an unmanned patrol craft based on an 9 m Rigid Inflatable Boat (RIB) with composite-materials superstructure that encloses the sensor pod, navigation radar, GPS antenna and gyrostabilised inertial navigation system. Five video channels are used to transmit the outputs from the Toplite and two deck-mounted cameras back to a remote operator. The vessel also carries microphones and loudspeakers, allowing the operator to hail the crew of a suspicious vessel. With an endurance of about eight hours, it can be controlled by line-of-sight communications from ship or shore for various missions such as force protection, anti-terror surveillance and reconnaissance, mine warfare and electronic warfare. Several systems were earmarked to begin evaluation tests with the Israeli Navy but these were subsequently bought by Singapore in 2004. One is expected to begin trials in 2006.

PROTECTOR   *6/2005*, Rafael* / 1116232

AUXILIARIES

Notes: (1) Two new construction landing ships are required by the Navy to transport troops. No funds available. A Newport class *Peoria* LST 1183 was authorised for lease from the US but was sunk as a target in 2004. (2) A Ro-Ro ship *Queshet* is used as a training ship and for research and development. Built in Japan in 1979 and formerly used as a general purpose cargo ship. (3) Two former merchant ships *Nir* and *Naharya* are used as alongside tenders in Haifa and Eilat respectively.
(4) A 19 m Alligator class semi-submersible craft was reported delivered in 1998. It is likely to be used for special forces operations.

2 STOLLERGRUND CLASS (TYPE 745) (AG)

Name	Builders	Launched	Commissioned
BAT YAM (ex-*Kalkgrund*)	— (ex-Y 865)	Krögerwerft	23 Nov 1989
BAT GALIM (ex-*Bant*)	— (ex-Y 867)	Krögerwerft	28 May 1990

Displacement, tons: 450 full load
Dimensions, feet (metres): 126.6 × 30.2 × 10.5
(38.6 × 9.2 × 3.2)
Main machinery: 1 Deutz-MWM BV6M628 diesel; 1,690 hp(m)
(1.24 MW) sustained; 1 shaft; bow thruster
Speed, knots: 12
Range, n miles: 1,000 at 12 kt
Complement: 7 plus 6 trials personnel

Comment: Ex-German Navy trials and support vessels transferred to the Israeli Navy in December 2005. Both ships are fitted with I-band radars and an intercept sonar. Likely to be based at Haifa.

BAT GALIM
12/2005*, Michael Nitz
1153206

1 ASHDOD CLASS (LCT)

Name	Builders	Launched	Commissioned
ASHDOD	61	Israel Shipyards, Haifa	1966

Displacement, tons: 400 standard; 730 full load
Dimensions, feet (metres): 205.5 × 32.8 × 5.8
(62.7 × 10 × 1.8)
Main machinery: 3 MWM diesels; 1,900 hp(m) *(1.4 MW)*;
3 shafts
Speed, knots: 10.5
Complement: 20
Guns: 2 Oerlikon 20 mm.

Comment: Used as a trials ship for Barak VLS. Based at Ashdod but refitted at Eilat in 1999. Operational status doubtful.

ASHDOD
3/1989
0080070

AMPHIBIOUS FORCES

Notes: Plans to acquire an assault ship (LPD) of about 13,000 tons have been suspended.

SHIPBORNE AIRCRAFT

Numbers/Type: 2 Aerospatiale SA 366G Dauphin.
Operational speed: 140 kt *(260 km/h)*.
Service ceiling: 15,000 ft *(4,575 m)*.
Range: 410 n miles *(758 km)*.
Role/Weapon systems: Air Force SAR/MR helicopters acquired in 1985 and primarily SAR/MR. Sensors: Israeli-designed radar/FLIR systems. Integrated Elop MSIS for OTHT. Weapons: Unarmed.

Numbers/Type: 7 Eurocopter AS 565SA Sea Panther.
Operational speed: 165 kt *(305 km/h)*.
Service ceiling: 16,700 ft *(5,100 m)*.
Range: 483 n miles *(895 km)*.
Role/Weapon systems: Built by American Eurocopter in Texas. Three delivered by October 1998 with one more in 1999. Sensors: Telephonics search radar; Elop MSIS for OTHT. Weapons: Unarmed.

AS 565SB   *6/2002, Adolfo Ortigueira Gil* / 0567461

LAND-BASED MARITIME AIRCRAFT

Notes: (1) Army helicopters can be used including Cobras.
(2) Two C-130 aircraft used for maritime surveillance.

Numbers/Type: 17 Bell 212.
Operational speed: 100 kt *(185 km/h)*.
Service ceiling: 13,200 ft *(4,025 m)*.
Range: 224 n miles *(415 km)*.
Role/Weapon systems: SAR and coastal helicopter surveillance tasks undertaken. Sensors: IAI EW systems. Weapons: Unarmed except for self-defence machine guns.

Numbers/Type: 3 IAI 1124N Sea Scan. (LCT)
Operational speed: 471 kt *(873 km/h)*.
Service ceiling: 45,000 ft *(13,725 m)*.
Range: 2,500 n miles *(4,633 km)*.
Role/Weapon systems: Air Force manned. Coastal surveillance tasks with long endurance; used for intelligence gathering. Sensors: Elta EL/M-2022 radar, IFF, MAD, Sonobuoys, and various EW systems of IAI manufacture.

SEA SCAN   *6/1994, R A Cooper* / 0503199

Italy
MARINA MILITARE

Country Overview

Italy is situated in southern Europe and comprises, in addition to the Italian mainland, the islands of Sardinia, Sicily, Elba and many smaller islands. Enclaves within mainland Italy are the independent countries of San Marino and Vatican City. With an area of 116,341 square miles, it is bordered to the north by France, Switzerland, Austria and Slovenia. It has a 2,700 n mile coastline with the Mediterranean, Ionian, Adriatic, Tyrrhenian Sea and Ligurian Seas. The capital and largest city is Rome while the principal ports are Genoa, Naples, Trieste, Taranto, Palermo and Venice. Territorial waters (12 n miles) are claimed but an EEZ has not been claimed.

Headquarters Appointments

Chief of Naval Staff:
Admiral Paulo la Rosa
Vice Chief of Naval Staff:
Admiral Giovanni Vitaloni
Chief of Joint Military Intelligence:
Vice Admiral Andrea Campregher
Chief of Procurement:
Engineer Admiral Dino Nascetti
Chief of Technical Support:
Engineer Admiral Giancarlo Cecchi
Chief of Naval Personnel:
Vice Admiral Vincenzo del Vento

Flag Officers

Commander, Allied Naval Forces, Southern Europe (Naples):
Admiral Roberto Cesaretti
Commander-in-Chief of Fleet (Rome):
Admiral Bruno Branciforte
Commander, Tyrrhenian Sea (La Spezia):
Admiral Quinto Gramellini
Commander, Ionian Sea (Taranto):
Admiral Francesco Ricci
Commander, Adriatic Sea (Ancona):
Vice Admiral Paolo Pagnottella
Commander, Sicily (Augusta):
Vice Admiral Armando Molaschi
Commander, Sardinia (Cagliari):
Vice Admiral Roberto Baggioni
Commander, High Seas Fleet (COMFORAL):
Vice Admiral Andrea Toscano
Commander, Naval Group (COMGRUPNAV) (Taranto):
Rear Admiral Salvatore Ruzzittu
Commander, (1st Frigate Squadron) (Taranto):
Captain Michele Lafortezza
Commander, Naval Group (2nd Frigate Squadron) (La Spezia):
Captain Isidoro Fusco
Commander, MCM Forces (COMFORDRAG) (La Spezia):
Rear Admiral Federico Solari
Commander, Amphibious Force (COMFORSBARC) (Brindisi):
Rear Admiral Michele Saponaro
Commander, Training Command (MARICENTADD) (Taranto):
Vice Admiral Michele De Pinto
Commander, Coastal and Patrol Forces (COMFORPAT) (Augusta):
Captain Francesco De Biase
Commander, Naval Air Arm (COMFORAER) (Rome):
Rear Admiral Giuseppe Cavo Dragone
Commander Submarine Force (COMFORSUB) (Taranto):
Captain Mario Caruso
Commander, Naval Special Forces (COMSUBIN) (La Spezia):
Rear Admiral Roberto Paperini
Commander Coast Guard:
Admiral Eugenio Sicurezza

Diplomatic Representation

Naval Attaché in Bonn:
Captain Gianluca Turilli
Naval Attaché in Peking:
Captain Gianfranco Cucchiaro
Naval Attaché in London:
Rear Admiral Sirio Lanfredini
Naval Attaché in Moscow:
Captain Marco Scano
Naval Attaché in Paris:
Captain Roberto Ive
Naval Attaché in Washington:
Rear Admiral Raffaele Caruso

Bases

Regional Commands: La Spezia (Tyrrhenian Sea), Taranto (Ionian Sea), Ancona (Adriatic Sea), Augusta (Sicily), Cagliari (Sardinia).
Main bases (Major Arsenals/Navy Shipyards): Taranto, La Spezia.
Secondary base (Minor Arsenal/Navy Shipyard): Augusta.
Minor bases: Brindisi.

Organisation

CINCNAV is responsible for all operational activities. There are six subordinate commands:
High-Sea Forces Command (COMFORAL) including all Major and Amphibious Ships. Based in Taranto with subordinated command COMGRUPNAVIT.
Patrol Forces Command (COMFORPAT) Corvettes and OPVs. Based in Augusta.
Naval Air Command. Based at Santa Rosa, Rome.
Submarine Force Command. Based at Taranto.
Mine Countermeasures Command. Based at La Spezia.
COMFORSBARC with San Marco Regiment, Carlotto (logistic) regiment and one assault boat group. Based at Brindisi.
Special Forces Command (COMSUBIN) Commandos and support craft. Based near La Spezia. Controlled directly by Chief of Naval Staff.

Prefix to Ships' Names

ITS (Italian Ship)

Strength of the Fleet

Type	Active	Building (Planned)
Submarines	7	(2)
Aircraft Carriers	1	1
Destroyers	2	2 (2)
Frigates	12	2 (8)
Corvettes	8	–
Offshore Patrol Vessels	10	–
Coastal Patrol Craft	4	–
LPD/LHD	3	(1)
Minehunters/sweepers	12	–
Survey/Research Ships	7	–
Replenishment Tankers	3	–
Coastal Tankers	11	–
Coastal Transports	6	–
Sail Training Ships	7	–
Training Ships	4	–
Lighthouse Tenders	5	–
Salvage Ships	1	–
Repair Ships	1	–

Personnel

(a) 2006: 36,837 (5,050 officers) including 1,550 naval air and 2,100 naval infantry (amphib)
(b) 10 months' national service (about 6,500 are conscripts). The Italian Armed Forces will become all professional from the end of 2006.

Naval Air Arm

Catania (Fontanarossa): AB-212 (2nd), SH-3D (3rd)
Catania (Sigonella): Atlantic (41st)
La Spezia (Luni): AB-212 (1st), SH-3D (5th), EH-101 (5th), EH-101 (OEU)
Taranto (Grottaglie): AV-8B/TAV-8B (7th), AB-212 (4th), AB-212 (Amphib), SH-3 (Amphib)

Naval Infantry and Army Amphibious Units

A Landing Force Command was established in 1998 including a collaborative Spanish/Italian amphibious brigade (SIAF). Landing Force Command is based at Brindisi and comprises the San Marco assault regiment (two assault battalions), the Carlotto support regiment (one logistic and one training battalion) and a Landing Craft Group. The Amphibious assault air squadron has eight modified SH-3D and seven modified AB-212 helicopters.
The Italian Army operates an amphibious regiment named 'Serenissima' which is based at Venice. It is equipped with four LCM, six LCVP and 47 rigid raider and assault craft.
A joint (Army-Navy) amphibious brigade is under development. The army 'Serenissima' regiment is to be added to naval units and joint training began in 2005.

DELETIONS

Submarines

2004   *Fecia di Cossato*

Cruisers

2003   *Vittorio Veneto* (museum)

Destroyers

2005   *Ardito, Audace*

Frigates

2003   *Perseo* (reserve)
2005   *Alpino*

Auxiliaries

2003   *MOC 1204* (to Tunisia), *MOC 1201*
2004   *Basento* (reserve)

PENNANT LIST

Submarines

S 520	Leonardo da Vinci
S 522	Salvatore Pelosi
S 523	Giuliano Prini
S 524	Primo Longobardo
S 525	Gianfranco Gazzana Priaroggia
S 526	Salvatore Todaro
S 527	Scire

Light Aircraft Carriers

C 551	Giuseppe Garibaldi
C 552	Cavour (bldg)

Destroyers

D 560	Luigi Durand de la Penne
D 561	Francesco Mimbelli

Frigates

F 570	Maestrale
F 571	Grecale
F 572	Libeccio
F 573	Scirocco
F 574	Aliseo
F 575	Euro
F 576	Espero
F 577	Zeffiro
F 582	Artigliere
F 583	Aviere
F 584	Bersagliere
F 585	Granatiere

Corvettes

F 551	Minerva
F 552	Urania
F 553	Danaide
F 554	Sfinge
F 555	Driade
F 556	Chimera
F 557	Fenice
F 558	Sibilla

Patrol Forces

P 401	Cassiopea
P 402	Libra
P 403	Spica
P 404	Vega
P 405	Esploratore
P 406	Sentinella
P 407	Vedetta
P 408	Staffetta
P 409	Sirio
P 410	Orione
P 490	Comandante Cigala Fulgosi
P 491	Comandante Borsini
P 492	Comandante Bettica
P 493	Comandante Foscari

Minehunters

M 5550	Lerici
M 5551	Sapri
M 5552	Milazzo
M 5553	Vieste
M 5554	Gaeta
M 5555	Termoli

M 5556	Alghero
M 5557	Numana
M 5558	Crotone
M 5559	Viareggio
M 5560	Chioggia
M 5561	Rimini

Amphibious Forces

L 9892	San Giorgio
L 9893	San Marco
L 9894	San Giusto

Survey and Research Ships

A 5303	Ammiraglio Magnaghi
A 5304	Aretusa
A 5308	Galatea
A 5315	Raffaele Rossetti
A 5320	Vincenzo Martellotta
A 5340	Elettra
F 581	Carabiniere

Auxiliaries

A 5302	Caroly
A 5309	Anteo
A 5311	Palinuro
A 5312	Amerigo Vespucci
A 5313	Stella Polare
A 5316	Corsaro II
A 5318	Prometeo
A 5319	Ciclope
A 5322	Capricia
A 5323	Orsa Maggiore
A 5324	Titano

A 5325	Polifemo
A 5326	Etna
A 5327	Stromboli
A 5328	Gigante
A 5329	Vesuvio
A 5330	Saturno
A 5347	Gorgona
A 5348	Tremiti
A 5349	Caprera
A 5351	Pantelleria
A 5352	Lipari
A 5353	Capri
A 5359	Bormida
A 5364	Ponza
A 5365	Tenace
A 5366	Levanzo
A 5367	Tavolara
A 5368	Palmaria
A 5370-3	MCC 1101-4
A 5376	Ticino
A 5377	Tirso
A 5379	Astice
A 5380	Mitilo
A 5382	Porpora
A 5383	Procida
Y 413	Porto Fossone
Y 416	Porto Torres
Y 417	Porto Corsini
Y 421	Porto Empedocle
Y 422	Porto Pisano
Y 423	Porto Conte
Y 425	Porto Ferraio
Y 426	Porto Venere
Y 428	Porto Salvo
Y 498	Mario Marino
Y 499	Alcide Pedretti

SUBMARINES

2 + (2) TYPE 212A (SSK)

Name	No	Builders	Laid down	Launched	Commissioned
SALVATORE TODARO	S 526	Fincantieri, Muggiano	Jan 2001	6 Nov 2003	29 Mar 2006
SCIRÈ	S 527	Fincantieri, Muggiano	Apr 2002	18 Dec 2004	June 2006

Displacement, tons: 1,450 surfaced; 1,830 dived
Dimensions, feet (metres): 183.4 × 23 × 19.7
(55.9 × 7 × 6)
Main machinery: Diesel-electric; 1 MTU 16V 396 diesel; 4,243 hp(m) *(3.12 MW)*; 1 alternator; 1 Siemens PEM motor; 3,875 hp(m) *(2.85 MW)*; 1 shaft; Siemens/HDW PEM 9 fuel cell (AIP) modules; 306 kW
Speed, knots: 20 dived; 12 surfaced
Range, n miles: 8,000 at 8 kt surfaced
Complement: 27 (8 officers)

Torpedoes: 6—21 in *(533 mm)* bow tubes; water ram discharge; Whitehead A184 Mod 3. Total 12 weapons.
Mines: In lieu of torpedoes.
Countermeasures: Decoys: CIRCE Torpedo countermeasures. ESM: DASA FL 1800U; intercept.

Weapons control: Kongsberg MSI-90U TFCS.
Radars: Navigation: KH 1007; I-band.
Sonars: STN Atlas Elektronik DBQS-40; passive ranging and intercept; FAS-3 Flank and passive towed array.
STN Atlas Moa 3070, mine detection, active, high frequency.

Programmes: German design phase first completed in 1992 by ARGE 212 (HDW/TNSW) in conjunction with IKL. MoU signed with Germany 22 April 1996 for a common design. First pair ordered from Fincantieri in August 1997. First steel cut for first of class 19 July 1999, and for second in July 2000.
Structure: Equipped with a hybrid fuel cell/battery propulsion based on the Siemens PEM fuel cell

technology. The submarine is designed with a partial double hull which has a larger diameter forward. This is joined to the after end by a short conical section which houses the fuel cell plant. Two LOX tanks and hydrogen stored in metal cylinders are carried around the circumference of the smaller hull section. Italian requirements included a greater diving depth, improved external communications, and better submerged escape facilities. The final design is identical to the German submarines. Fitted with Zeiss search and attack periscopes.
Operational: Dived speeds up to 8 kt are projected, without use of main battery. Sea trials of *Salvatore Todaro* started in June 2004.

SALVATORE TODARO
10/2004, Giorgio Ghiglione / 1044359

1 SAURO (TYPE 1081) CLASS

Name	No	Builders	Laid down	Launched	Commissioned
LEONARDO DA VINCI	S 520	Italcantieri, Monfalcone	8 June 1978	20 Oct 1979	23 Oct 1981

Displacement, tons: 1,456 surfaced; 1,631 dived
Dimensions, feet (metres): 210 × 22.5 × 18.9
(63.9 × 6.8 × 5.7)
Main machinery: Diesel-electric; 3 Fincantieri GMT 210.16 NM diesels; 3,350 hp(m) *(2.46 MW)* sustained; 3 alternators; 2.16 MW; 1 motor; 3,210 hp(m) *(2.36 MW)*; 1 shaft. AIP trial in *Fecia di Cossato*
Speed, knots: 11 surfaced; 19 dived; 12 snorting
Range, n miles: 11,000 surfaced at 11 kt; 250 dived at 4 kt
Complement: 49 (6 officers) plus 4 trainees

Torpedoes: 6—21 in *(533 mm)* bow tubes. 12 Whitehead A184 Mod 3; dual purpose; wire-guided; active/passive homing to 25 km *(13.7 n miles)* at 24 kt; 17 km *(9.2 n miles)* at 38 kt; warhead 250 kg. Swim-out discharge.
Countermeasures: ESM: Elettronica BLD 727; radar warning.
Weapons control: SMA BSN 716(V)1 SACTIS data processing and computer-based TMA. CCRG FCS.
Radars: Search/navigation: SMA BPS 704; I-band.
Sonars: Selenia Elsag IPD 70/S; linear passive array; 200 Hz-7.5 kHz; active and UWT transducers in bow (15 kHz).

Programmes: Ordered 12 February 1976.
Modernisation: Modernised in 1993. New batteries have greater capacity, some auxiliary machinery replaced and habitability improved.
Structure: Diving depth, 300 m *(985 ft)* (max) and 250 m *(820 ft)* (normal). Periscopes: Barr & Stroud CK 31 search and CH 81 attack.
Operational: Endurance, 35 days. *Nazario Sauro* paid off in early 2001, *Guglielmo Marconi* in 2002 and *Fecia di Cossato* in 2004. *Leonardo da Vinci* to be paid off in October 2006.

SAURO CLASS
6/2001, H M Steele / 0130519

4 IMPROVED SAURO CLASS (SSK)

Name	No	Builders	Laid down	Launched	Commissioned
SALVATORE PELOSI	S 522	Fincantieri, Monfalcone	24 May 1984	29 Dec 1986	14 July 1988
GIULIANO PRINI	S 523	Fincantieri, Monfalcone	30 May 1985	12 Dec 1987	11 Nov 1989
PRIMO LONGOBARDO	S 524	Fincantieri, Monfalcone	19 Dec 1991	20 June 1992	20 May 1994
GIANFRANCO GAZZANA PRIAROGGIA	S 525	Fincantieri, Monfalcone	12 Nov 1992	26 June 1993	12 Apr 1995

Displacement, tons: 1,476 (1,653, S 524-5) surfaced; 1,662 (1,862, S 524-5) dived
Dimensions, feet (metres): 211.2 (217.8 S 524-5) × 22.3 × 18.4 *(64.4 (66.4) × 6.8 × 5.6)*
Main machinery: Diesel-electric; 3 Fincantieri GMT 210.16 SM diesels; 3,672 hp(m) *(2.7 MW)* sustained; 3 generators; 2.16 MW; 1 motor; 3,128 hp(m) *(2.3 MW)*; 1 shaft
Speed, knots: 11 surfaced; 19 dived; 12 snorting
Range, n miles: 11,000 at 11 kt surfaced; 250 at 4 kt dived
Complement: 51 (7 officers)

Torpedoes: 6 – 21 in *(533 mm)* bow tubes. 12 Whitehead A184 Mod 3; dual purpose; wire-guided; active/passive homing to 25 km *(13.7 n miles)* at 24 kt; 17 km

(9.2 n miles) at 38 kt; warhead 250 kg. Swim-out discharge.
Countermeasures: ESM: Elettronica BLD-727; radar warning; 2 aerials-1 on a mast, second in search periscope.
Weapons control: STN Atlas ISUS 90-20.
Radars: Search/navigation: SMA BPS 704; I-band; also periscope radar for attack ranging.
Sonars: Selenia Elsag IPD 70/S; linear passive array; 200 Hz – 7.5 kHz; active and UWT transducers in bow (15 kHz).

Programmes: The first two were ordered in March 1983 and the second pair in July 1988.
Modernisation: An upgrade programme included replacement of acoustic sensors, weapons control

system (STN Atlas ISUS 90-20) and communications. Work on all four boats was completed in late 2004.
Structure: Pressure hull of HY 80 steel with a central bulkhead for escape purposes. Diving depth, 300 m *(985 ft)* (test) and 600 m *(1,970 ft)* (crushing). The second pair has a slightly longer hull to give space for SSMs.
Periscopes: Kollmorgen; S 76 Mod 322 with laser rangefinder and ESM-attack; S 76 Mod 323 with radar rangefinder and ESM-search. Wave contour snort head has a very low radar profile. The last pair have anechoic tiles.
Operational: Litton Italia PL 41 inertial navigation; Ferranti autopilot (in S 522-3) or Sepa autopilot (S 524-5) Omega and Transit. Endurance, 45 days.

GIULIANO PRINI   *6/2005*, John Brodie* / 1153247

GIULIANO PRINI   *6/2005*, John Mortimer* / 1153233

AIRCRAFT CARRIERS

1 GARIBALDI CLASS (CVGM)

Name	No	Builders	Laid down	Launched	Commissioned
GIUSEPPE GARIBALDI	C 551	Italcantieri, Monfalcone	26 Mar 1981	4 June 1983	30 Sep 1985

Displacement, tons: 10,100 standard; 13,850 full load
Dimensions, feet (metres): 591 × 110.2 × 22
(180 × 33.4 × 6.7)
Flight deck, feet (metres): 570.2 × 99.7 (173.8 × 30.4)
Main machinery: COGAG; 4 Fiat/GE LM 2500 gas turbines; 81,000 hp (60 MW) sustained; 2 shafts
Speed, knots: 30
Range, n miles: 7,000 at 20 kt
Complement: 582 ship plus 230 air group (accommodation for 825 including Flag and staff)

Missiles: SAM: 2 Selenia Elsag Albatros octuple launchers ❶; 48 Aspide; semi-active radar homing to 13 km (7 n miles) at 2.5 Mach; height envelope 15-5,000 m (49.2-16,405 ft); warhead 30 kg.
Guns: 6 Breda 40 mm/70 (3 twin) MB ❷; 300 rds/min to 12.5 km (6.8 n miles) anti-surface; 4 km (2.2 n miles) anti-aircraft; weight of shell 0.96 kg.
Torpedoes: 6—324 mm B-515 (2 triple) tubes ❸. Honeywell Mk 46; anti-submarine; active/passive homing to 11 km (5.9 n miles) at 40 kt; warhead 44 kg. Being replaced by new A 290.
Countermeasures: Decoys: SLQ-25 Nixie; noisemaker. 2 Breda SCLAR 105 mm 20-barrelled launchers; trains and elevates; chaff to 5 km (2.7 n miles); illuminants to 12 km (6.6 n miles). SLAT in 2002.
ESM/ECM: Elettronica Nettuno SLQ-732; integrated intercept and jamming system.
Combat data systems: IPN 20 (SADOC 2) action data automation including Links 11 and 14. SATCOM ❹.
Weapons control: 3 Alenia NA 30E electro-optical back-up for SAM. 3 Dardo NA21 for guns.
Radars: Long-range air search: Hughes SPS-52C ❺; 3D; E/F-band; range 440 km (240 n miles).

Air search: Selenia SPS-768 (RAN 3L) ❻; D-band; range 220 km (120 n miles).
Air/surface search: Selenia SPS-774 (RAN 10S) ❼; E/F-band.
Surface search/target indication: SMA SPS-702 UPX; 718 beacon; I-band.
Navigation: ARPA SPN-753 G(V); I-band.
Fire control: 3 Selenia SPG-75 (RTN 30X) ❽; I/J-band; range 15 km (8 n miles) (for Albatros).
3 Selenia SPG-74 (RTN 20X) ❾; I/J-band; range 13 km (7 n miles) (for Dardo).
CCA: Selenia SPN-728(V)1; I-band.
IFF: Mk XII. Tacan: SRN-15A.
Sonars: Raytheon DE 1160 LF; bow-mounted; active search; medium frequency.

Fixed-wing aircraft: 15 AV-8B Harrier II.
Helicopters: 17 SH-3D Sea King or EH 101 Merlin helicopters (12 in hangar, 6 on deck). The total capacity is either 15 Harriers or 17 helicopters, but this leaves no space for movement. In practice a combination is embarked (see Operational).

Programmes: Contract awarded 21 November 1977. The design work completed February 1980. Started sea trials 3 December 1984.
Modernisation: A major C⁴I upgrade programme, completed in September 2003, has given the ship a Maritime Component Commander (MCC) capability. Improvements to the combat data system include a MCC data system and Link 16. SATCOM domes have replaced the TESEO launchers which have been removed. SHF SATCOM has been installed in the old positions of the chaff launchers while SCLAR-D chaff launchers have been installed on new sponsons aft and below the flight deck. Other work includes modernisation of the ESM/ECM equipment, replacement of the DE 1150F sonar with DMSS 2000 and the fitting of an electro-optic tracking device on the bridge roof in lieu of SPN-728 radar which has been removed. A further upgrade of air defence systems is projected once Andrea Doria has commissioned in 2007 although the scope of this is to be decided. Garibaldi has also been equipped to control RQ-1B Predator UAV and to exploit its imagery.
Structure: Six decks with 13 vertical watertight bulkheads. Fitted with 6.5° ski-jump and VSTOL operating equipment. Two 15 ton lifts 18 × 10 m (59 × 32.8 ft). Hangar size 110 × 15 × 6 m (361 × 49.2 × 19.7 ft). Hangar capacity is for 10 Harriers or 12 Sea Kings. Has a slightly narrower flight deck than UK Invincible class. Two MEN class fast personnel launches (capacity 250) can be embarked for amphibious operations or disaster relief.
Operational: Fleet Flagship. Equipped for Joint Task Force command and control. The long-standing dispute between the Navy and the Air Force concerning the former's operation of fixed-wing aircraft (dating back to pre-Second World War legislation) was finally resolved by legislation passed on 29 January 1989. Embarked aircraft are operated by the Navy with the Air Force providing evaluation and maintenance. The carrier has operated in the assault role with seven SH-3D, four AB 212 and Army helicopters including six AB 205, three A 129 and two CH-47. First operational Harriers embarked for permanent duty in December 1994.

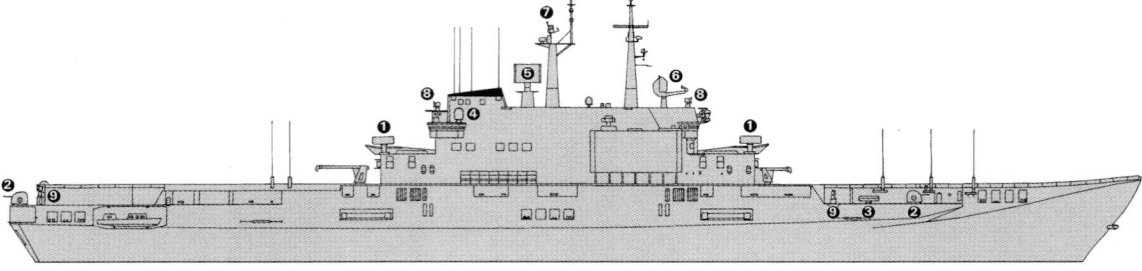

GIUSEPPE GARIBALDI   (Scale 1 : 1,200), Ian Sturton / 1043173

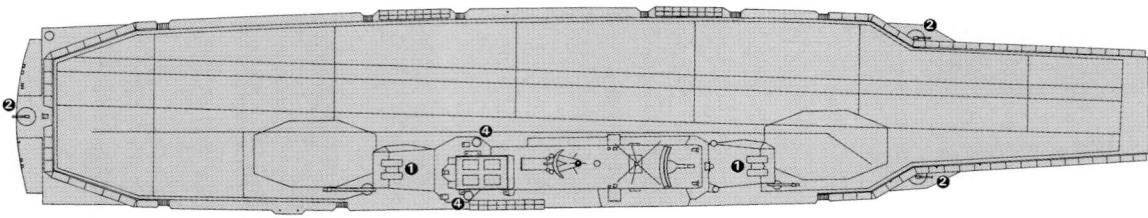

GIUSEPPE GARIBALDI   (Scale 1 : 1,200), Ian Sturton / 1043172

GIUSEPPE GARIBALDI   6/2005*, Marco Ghiglino / 1153230

GIUSEPPE GARIBALDI

7/2004, United States Navy / 1043185

GIUSEPPE GARIBALDI

8/2004, Guy Toremans / 1044368

0 + 1 CAVOUR CLASS (CV)

Name	No	Builders	Laid down	Launched	Commissioned
CAVOUR (ex-*Andrea Doria*)	C 552	Fincantieri Muggiano/Riva Trigoso	17 July 2001	20 July 2004	Sep 2007

Displacement, tons: 27,100 full load
Dimensions, feet (metres): 772.9 oa; 707.3 wl × 128 oa; 96.8 wl × 24.6 *(235.6; 215.6 × 39; 29.5 × 7.5)*
Flight deck, feet (metres): 721.8 × 111.5 *(220 × 34)*
Main machinery: COGAG: 4 GE/Fiat LM 2500 gas turbines; 118,000 hp(m) *(88 MW)* sustained; 2 shafts; cp props; bow and stern thrusters; 6—2.2 MW diesel generators and 2 motors
Speed, knots: 28. **Range, n miles:** 7,000 at 16 kt
Complement: 451 ship plus 203 air group plus 145 staff (CJTF or CATF/CLF) plus 360 marines (90 additional marines for short period). Total accommodation for 1,210
Military lift: (garage only): 100 wheeled vehicles or 60 armoured vehicles or 24 MBTs (Ariete) or mixture

Missiles: 4 Sylver 8 cell VLS for Aster 15.
Guns: 2 OTO Melara 3 in *(76 mm)*/62 Super Rapid. 2 Otobreda 25 mm.
Countermeasures: Decoys: 2 Breda SCLAR-H 20-barrel trainable chaff/decoy launchers.
TCM: 2 SLAT TCM launchers.

ESM: Radar and Comms intercept ❶.
ECM: Jammer.
Combat data systems: 'Horizon' derivative flag and command support system. Links 11 and 16; provision for Link 22. Satcom ❷.
Weapons control: FIAR SSAS optronic director.
Radars: Long-range air search: RAN-40L; D-band ❸.
Air search and missile guidance: EMPAR; G-band ❹.
CCA: SPN-41; J-band.
Surface search: SPS-791; E/F-band ❺.
Navigation: SPN-753G(V); I-band.
Tacan.
Sonars: WASS mine avoidance sonar (bow dome).

Fixed-wing aircraft: 8 AV-8B Harrier II or JSF.
Helicopters: 12 EH 101 (fitted also for AB 212, NH90 and SH-3D).

Programmes: Following a study phase which included significant changes to the initial configuration of the Nuova Unita Maggiore (NUM) design, the Italian government placed a contract with Fincantieri for the construction of a ship to replace *Vittorio Veneto* in 2007. Capabilities include afloat command, air and amphibious operations. The bow section of the ship was constructed at Muggiano and the centre and stern sections at Riva Trigoso. The ship is to be joined, outfitted and tested at Muggiano. A second contract, for the development and supply of the combat system was signed with an AMS-led industrial group in October 2002.

Structure: The flight deck features six helicopter take-off spots, one spot for SAR, eight parking spots and a 12° ski jump. A notional air group includes 12 EH-101 helicopters and 8 AV-8B Harrier IIs. There is provision in the design to operate JSF and UAVs. The hangar/garage can accommodate various combinations of aircraft and vehicles (including MBT and trucks). There are two 30 ton lifts, one forward of the island and the other starboard side aft. Two Ro-Ro ramps are positioned aft and starboard side. Two 15 ton and one 7 ton lifts are fitted for ordnance and logistic needs respectively.

Operational: Sea trials are planned to start in September 2006. Following formal commissioning in 2007, the ship is to become fully operational in 2008.

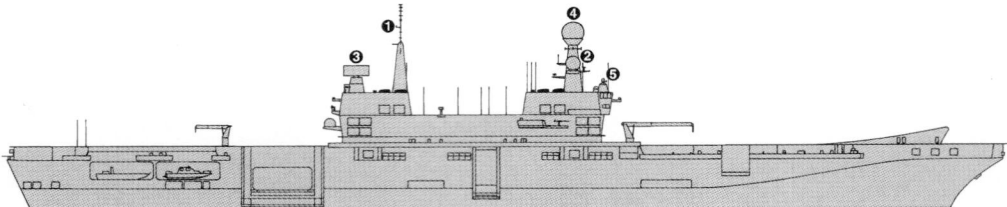

CAVOUR

(Scale 1 : 1,800), Ian Sturton / 0104868

CAVOUR (at launch)

7/2004, Giorgio Ghiglione / 1044361

CAVOUR (artist's impression)

6/2002, Fincantieri / 0528403

DESTROYERS

2 DE LA PENNE (EX-ANIMOSO) CLASS (DDGHM)

Name	No	Builders	Laid down	Launched	Commissioned
LUIGI DURAND DE LA PENNE (ex-*Animoso*)	D 560	Fincantieri, Riva Trigoso/Muggiano	20 Jan 1988	29 Oct 1989	18 Mar 1993
FRANCESCO MIMBELLI (ex-*Ardimentoso*)	D 561	Fincantieri, Riva Trigoso/Muggiano	15 Nov 1989	13 Apr 1991	19 Oct 1993

Displacement, tons: 4,330 standard; 5,400 full load
Dimensions, feet (metres): 487.4 × 52.8 × 28.2 (sonar)
(147.7 × 16.1 × 8.6)
Flight deck, feet (metres): 78.7 × 42.7 *(24 × 13)*
Main machinery: CODOG; 2 Fiat/GE LM 2500 gas turbines;
54,000 hp *(40.3 MW)* sustained; 2 GMT BL 230.20 DVM
diesels; 12,600 hp(m) *(9.3 MW)* sustained; 2 shafts;
cp props
Speed, knots: 31 (21 on diesels). **Range, n miles:** 7,000 at 18 kt
Complement: 331 (25 officers)

Missiles: SSM: 4 or 8 OTO Melara/Matra Teseo Mk 2 (TG 2)
(2 or 4 twin) ❶; mid-course guidance; active radar
homing to 180 km *(98.4 n miles)* at 0.9 Mach; warhead
210 kg; sea-skimmer.
Mk 3 with radar/IR homing to 300 km *(162 n miles)*;
warhead 160 kg in due course.
A/S: OTO Melara/Matra Milas launcher; inertial guidance
with command update to 55 km *(29.8 n miles)* at
0.9 Mach; payload Mk 46 Mod 5 or Mu 90 torpedo;
4 weapons (see *Modernisation*).
SAM: 40 GDC Pomona Standard SM-1MR; Mk 13 Mod 4
launcher ❷; command guidance; semi-active radar
homing to 46 km *(25 n miles)* at 2 Mach.
Selenia Albatros Mk 2 octuple launcher for Aspide ❸;
semi-active radar homing to 13 km *(7 n miles)* at
2.5 Mach; 16 missiles. Automatic reloading.
Guns: 1 OTO Melara 5 in *(127 mm)*/54 ❹; 45 rds/min to
23 km *(12.42 n miles)*; weight of shell 32 kg.
3 OTO Melara 3 in *(76 mm)*/62 Super Rapid ❺; 120 rds/min
to 16 km *(8.7 n miles)*; weight of shell 6 kg. 2—20 mm.
Torpedoes: 6—324 mm B-515 (2 triple) tubes ❻. Honeywell
Mk 46; anti-submarine; active/passive homing to 11 km
(5.9 n miles) at 40 kt; warhead 44 kg. May be replaced by
Whitehead Mu 90 in due course.
Countermeasures: Decoys: 2 CSEE Sagaie chaff launchers ❼.
1 SLQ-25 Nixie anti-torpedo system.
ESM/ECM: Elettronica SLQ-732 Nettuno ❽; integrated
intercept and jamming system. SLC 705.
Combat data systems: Selenia Elsag IPN 20 (SADOC 2);
Links 11 and 14. SATCOM.
Weapons control: 4 Dardo-E systems (3 channels for
Aspide). Milas TFCS.
Radars: Long-range air search: Hughes SPS-52C; 3D ❾;
E/F-band.
Air search: Selenia SPS-768 (RAN 3L) ❿; D-band.
Air/surface search: Selenia SPS-774 (RAN 10S) ⓫; E/F-band.
Surface search: SMA SPS-702 ⓬; I-band.
Fire control: 4 Selenia SPG-76 (RTN 30X) ⓭; I/J-band
(for Dardo).
2 Raytheon SPG-51D ⓮; G/I-band (for SAM).
Navigation: SMA SPN-748; I-band.
IFF: Mk X/XII. Tacan: SRN-15A.
Sonars: Raytheon DE 1164 LF-VDS; integrated bow and
VDS; active search and attack; medium frequency
(3.75 kHz (hull); 7.5 kHz (VDS)).

Helicopters: 2 AB 212ASW ⓯; SH-3D Sea King and EH 101
Merlin capable.

Programmes: Order placed 9 March 1986 with Riva
Trigoso. All ships built at Riva Trigoso are completed at
Muggiano after launching. Names changed on 10 June
1992 to honour former naval heroes. Acceptance dates
were delayed by reduction gear radiated noise problems
which have been resolved.
Modernisation: Milas ASW launchers fitted by late 2004.
New sonar dome fitted in D 560 in 2000 increased draft by
1.5 m. A major 2-year upgrade is planned to be undertaken
in D 561 (starting June 2006) and D 560 (starting in 2008).
SPS-52C is to be removed. SPS-768 is to be replaced by

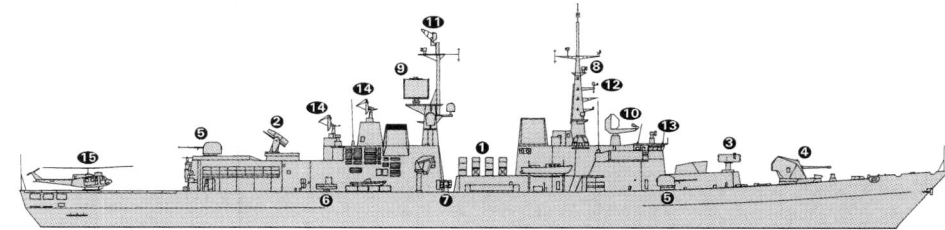

FRANCESCO MIMBELLI *(Scale 1 : 1,200), Ian Sturton* / 0569913

LUIGI DURAND DE LA PENNE *6/2004, John Brodie* / 1044362

LUIGI DURAND DE LA PENNE *5/2004, B Sullivan* / 1044363

AMS RAN-40L (SPS-798) (also to be fitted in *Cavour*); SPS-
774 to be replaced by AMS RAN-21S (SPS-794); SPS-702
to be replaced by SPN-753 ARPA; Dardo-E to be replaced
by four new fire-control systems (Dardo-F with RTN-30X);
Sagem IRST and new combat data system to be installed.
Link 16 is also to be added while Teseo Mk 2 is to be
upgraded to Mk 2a configuration.

Structure: Kevlar armour fitted. Steel alloys used in
superstructure. Prairie Masker noise suppression
system. The 127 mm guns are ex-Audace class B turrets.
Fully stabilised. Hangar is 18.5 m in length.
Operational: GPS and Meteosat receivers fitted. The three
Super Rapid 76 mm guns are used as a combined medium-
range anti-surface armament and CIWS against missiles.

FRANCESCO MIMBELLI *5/2003, A Sharma* / 0570684

0 + 2 (2) ANDREA DORIA (HORIZON) CLASS (DDGHM)

Name	No	Builders	Laid down	Launched	Commissioned
ANDREA DORIA (ex-*Carlo Bergamini*)	553	Fincantieri, Riva Trigoso/Muggiano	19 July 2002	14 Oct 2005	2008
CAIO DUILIO	554	Fincantieri, Riva Trigoso/Muggiano	19 Sep 2003	2007	2010

Displacement, tons: 6,700 full load
Dimensions, feet (metres): 494.1 oa; 464.9 wl × 57.4 × 16.7
  (150.6; 141.7 × 17.5 × 5.1)
Main machinery: CODOG: 2 GE LM 2500 gas turbines;
  55,750 hp(m) *(41 MW)*; 2 SEMT Pielstick 12 PA6B STC
  diesels; 11,700 hp(m) *(8.6 MW)*; 2 shafts; cp props
Speed, knots: 29
Range, n miles: 7,000 at 18 kt
Complement: 200 (35 officers)

Missiles: SSM: 8 (2 quad) Teseo Mk 2A ❶.
  SAM: DCN Sylver VLS ❷ PAAMS (principal anti-air missile
  system); 48 cells for Aster 15 and Aster 30 weapons.
Guns: 3 Otobreda 76 mm/62 Super Rapid ❸.
  2 Breda Oerlikon 25 mm/80 ❹.
Torpedoes: 2 fixed launchers ❺. Eurotorp Mu 90 Impact
  torpedoes.
Countermeasures: Decoys: 2 Otobreda SCLAR-H chaff/IR
  flare launchers ❻. SLAT torpedo defence system.
  ESM/ECM. Elettronica JANEWS ❼.
Combat data systems: DCN/Alenia CMS; Link 16. Link 14
  SATCOM ❽.
Weapons control: Sagem Vampir optronic director ❾.
Radars: Air/surface search: S 1850M ❿; D-band.
  Surveillance/fire control: Alenia EMPAR ⓫; G-band;
  multifunction.
  Surface search: Alenia RASS ⓬; E/F-band.
  Fire control: 2 Alenia Marconi NA 25XP ⓭.
  Navigation: Alenia SPN 753(V) 4; I-band.
Sonars: Thomson Marconi 4110CL; hull-mounted; active
  search and attack; medium frequency.

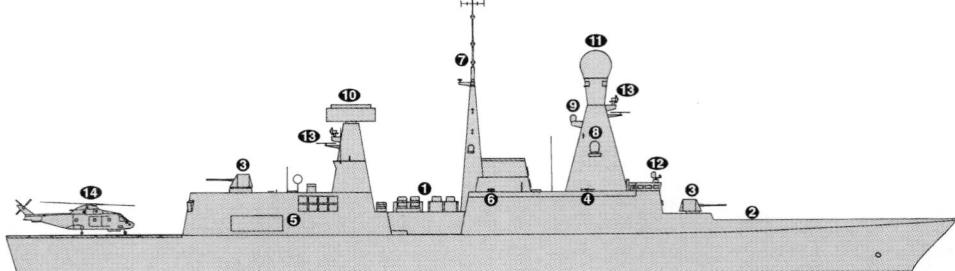

ANDREA DORIA   *(Scale 1 : 1,200), Ian Sturton* / 0104870

Helicopters: 1 Augusta/Westland EH 101 Merlin ⓮ or
  NH-90.

Programmes: Three-nation project for a new air defence
ship with Italy, France and UK. Joint project office
established in 1993. Memorandum of Understanding
for joint development signed 11 July 1994. After UK
withdrew in April 1999, an agreement was signed
on 7 September 1999 between France and Italy to
continue. Following a preliminary agreement on
2 August 2000, a Memorandum of Understanding
was signed by the French and Italian Defence

Ministries on 22 September 2000 for the joint
development of the 'Horizon' destroyer. A Horizon
Joint Venture Company was created by DCN/
Thomson-CSF and Fincantieri/Finmeccanica on
16 October 2000. The first batch of two vessels for each
country was ordered on 27 October 2000. Following
curtailment of the French programme at two ships, it is
possible that the Italian Navy may also consider an AAW
variant of FREMM rather than two further Andrea Doria
class.

Operational: *Andrea Doria* planned to start sea trials in
October 2006.

ANDREA DORIA   *1/2006*, Giorgio Ghiglione* / 1153246

FRIGATES

0 + 2 (8) RINASCIMENTO CLASS (MULTIMISSION FRIGATES) (FFGH)

Displacement, tons: 5,750 full load
Dimensions, feet (metres): 456.0 × 62.3 × 16.4
  (139.0 × 19.0 × 5.0)
Main machinery: CODLOG/CODLAG; 1 Rolls Royce MT30
  or General Electric LM 2500 gas turbine; 40,230 hp
  (30 MW); 4 diesels; 11,270 hp *(8.4 MW)*; 2 motors;
  5,900 hp *(4.4 MW)*; 2 shafts; cp props
Speed, knots: 28. **Range, n miles:** 6,000 at 15 kt
Complement: 123 (accommodation for 165)

Missiles: SLCM: to be decided.
  SAM: 16 Sylver A43 cell VLS for Aster 15/30 ❶.
  SSM: 4 (8 in GP variant) Teseo Mk 2a Block 4 ❷.
Guns: 1 OTO 127 mm/64ER ❸ (GP). 2 (ASW) (1 GP) OTO
  76 mm SR ❹. 2—25 mm.
Torpedoes: 4 (2 twin) tubes; MU-90 ❺.
A/S mortars: 4 MILAS (ASW variant).
Countermeasures: Decoys: 2 Breda SCLAR-H 20-barrel
  trainable chaff/decoy launchers.
  TCM: SLAT launchers.
  ESM: Radar and Comms intercept.
  ECM: jammer.
Combat data systems: Cavour derivative system.
Weapons control: Galileo IRST optronic director ❻.
Radars: Air search: Alenia EMPAR; G-band ❼.
  Surface search: SPS 791; E/F-band ❽.
  Navigation: 1 SPN-753 ❾; I-band.
  SPN-741 ❿; I-band.
  Fire control: Alenia Marconi NA-25XP ⓫; J-band.
Sonars: Thales TUS 4110CL; hull-mounted (bow dome).
  CAPTAS VDS (ASW variant). Mine avoidance sonar.

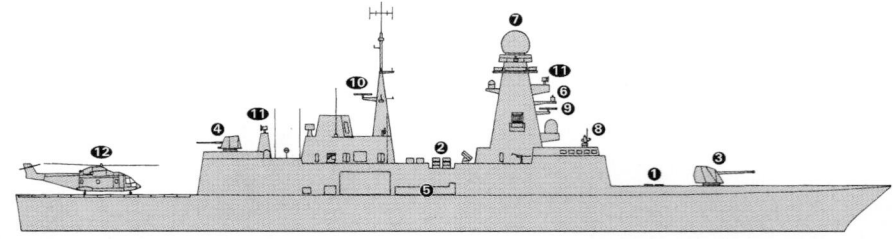

RINASCIMENTO (GP variant)   *(Scale 1 : 1,200), Ian Sturton* / 1153004

Helicopters: 2 NH 90 or 1 NH 90 ⓬ plus 1 EH 101.

Programmes: Agreement reached on 7 November 2002
for a 27 ship collaborative programme with France. The
Italian requirement is for ten 'Rinascimento' (FREMM for
French units) frigates with common hull and machinery
in two variants. Four ASW and six GP (general purpose/
land-attack) ships are to replace the Lupo and Maestrale
classes. Contract for the first phase awarded on
16 November 2005 to Orizzonte Sistemi Navali (Fincantieri/
Finmeccanica joint venture) for the construction of a first
batch of two ships. Steel for the first Italian vessel is
likely to be cut at Fincantieri's Riva Trigoso shipyard in
the second half of 2007. The first of class is to be named
Bergamini. It is also possible that two AAW variants of

the class may be considered if the Horizon destroyer
programme were to be curtailed at two ships.
Structure: The Rinascimento class has a conventional hull
design. The main engine room contains the gas turbine
and two diesel generators while the aft machinery space
contains the motors. The Italian variants have a higher
foredeck (an extra deck) than their French counterparts.
Particular attention has been paid to signature reduction.
The radar signature is expected to be comparable to
that of the French La Fayette class while exhaust cooling
measures are expected to achieve a comparatively low
IR signature. Acoustic quietening is to be achieved by
the rafting of engines and motors and the use of electric
propulsion. The Italian variants are to be fitted with
controllable pitch propellers.

8 MAESTRALE CLASS (FFGHM)

Name	No	Builders	Laid down	Launched	Commissioned
MAESTRALE	F 570	Fincantieri, Riva Trigoso	8 Mar 1978	2 Feb 1981	6 Mar 1982
GRECALE	F 571	Fincantieri, Muggiano	21 Mar 1979	12 Sep 1981	5 Feb 1983
LIBECCIO	F 572	Fincantieri, Riva Trigoso	1 Aug 1979	7 Sep 1981	5 Feb 1983
SCIROCCO	F 573	Fincantieri, Riva Trigoso	26 Feb 1980	17 Apr 1982	20 Sep 1983
ALISEO	F 574	Fincantieri, Riva Trigoso	10 Aug 1980	29 Oct 1982	7 Sep 1983
EURO	F 575	Fincantieri, Riva Trigoso	15 Apr 1981	25 Apr 1983	24 Jan 1984
ESPERO	F 576	Fincantieri, Riva Trigoso	29 July 1982	19 Nov 1983	4 May 1984
ZEFFIRO	F 577	Fincantieri, Riva Trigoso	15 Mar 1983	19 May 1984	4 May 1985

Displacement, tons: 2,500 standard; 3,200 full load
Dimensions, feet (metres): 405 × 42.5 × 15.1
(122.7 × 12.9 × 4.6)
Flight deck, feet (metres): 89 × 39 *(27 × 12)*
Main machinery: CODOG; 2 Fiat/GE LM 2500 gas turbines;
50,000 hp *(37.3 MW)* sustained; 2 GMT B 230.20 DVM
diesels; 11,000 hp(m) *(8.1 MW)* sustained; 2 shafts;
LIPS cp props
Speed, knots: 32 gas; 21 diesels
Range, n miles: 6,000 at 16 kt
Complement: 205 (16 officers)

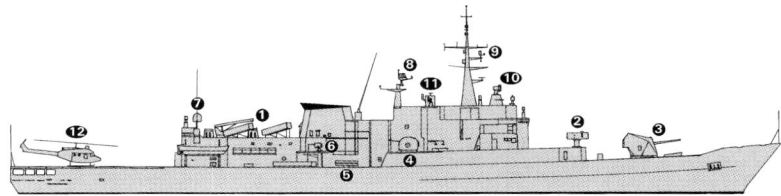

Missiles: SSM: 4 OTO Melara Teseo Mk 2 (TG 2) ❶;
mid-course guidance; active radar homing to 180 km
(98.4 n miles); warhead 210 kg; sea-skimmer. Mk 3
with radar/IR homing to 300 km *(162 n miles)*; warhead
160 kg in due course.
SAM: Selenia Albatros octuple launcher; 16 Aspide ❷;
semi-active homing to 13 km *(7 n miles)* at 2.5 Mach;
height envelope 15–5,000 m *(49.2–16,405 ft)*; warhead
30 kg.
Guns: 1 OTO Melara 5 in *(127 mm)*/54 automatic ❸;
45 rds/min to 23 km *(12.42 n miles)* anti-surface; 7 km
(3.8 n miles) anti-aircraft; weight of shell 32 kg; fires chaff
and illuminants.
4 Breda 40 mm/70 (2 twin) compact ❹; 300 rds/min
to 12.5 km *(6.8 n miles)* anti-surface; 4 km *(2.2 n miles)*
anti-aircraft; weight of shell 0.96 kg.
2 Oerlikon 20 mm fitted for Gulf deployments in 1990-91.
2 Breda Oerlikon 25 mm/90 (twin) tested in *Espero*.
Torpedoes: 6—324 mm US Mk 32 (2 triple) tubes ❺.
Honeywell Mk 46; anti-submarine; active/passive homing
to 11 km *(5.9 n miles)* at 40 kt; warhead 44 kg.
Countermeasures: Decoys: 2 Breda 105 mm SCLAR
20-tubed trainable chaff rocket launchers ❻; chaff to 5 km
(2.7 n miles); illuminants to 12 km *(6.6 n miles)*. 2 Dagaie
chaff launchers.

SLQ-25; towed torpedo decoy. Prairie Masker; noise
suppression system.
ESM: Elettronica SLR-4; intercept.
ECM: 2 SLQ-D; jammers.
Combat data systems: IPN 20 (SADOC 2) action data
automation; Link 11. SATCOM ❼.
Weapons control: NA 30 for Albatros and 5 in guns.
2 Dardo for 40 mm guns.
Radars: Air/surface search: Selenia SPS-774 (RAN 10S) ❽;
E/F-band.
Surface search: SMA SPS-702 ❾; I-band.
Navigation: SMA SPN-703; I-band.
Fire control: Selenia SPG-75 (RTN 30X) ❿; I/J-band (for
Albatros and 12.7 mm gun).
2 Selenia SPG-74 (RTN 20X) ⓫; I/J-band; range 15 km
(8 n miles) (for Dardo).
IFF: Mk XII.
Sonars: Raytheon DE 1164; hull-mounted; VDS; active/
passive attack; medium frequency. VDS can be towed at
up to 28 kt. Maximum depth 300 m. Modified to include
mine detection active high frequency.

Helicopters: 2 AB 212ASW ⓬.

MAESTRALE *(Scale 1 : 1,200), Ian Sturton* / 0569915

Programmes: First six ordered December 1976 and last
pair in October 1980. All Riva Trigoso ships completed at
Muggiano after launch.
Modernisation: Hull and VDS sonars modified from
1994 to give better shallow water performance and a mine
detection capability. A major upgrade is planned
to be undertaken in F 573 and F 577 (starting 2005)
and F 572 and F 576 (starting 2007). SPS-774 to
be replaced by AMS RAN-21S (SPS-794), SPN-703 to
be replaced by SPN-753 ARPA, Dardo to be replaced by
two new fire-control systems (Dardo-F with RTN-30X),
Sagem IRST and new combat data system to be
installed.
Structure: There has been a notable increase of 34 ft
in length and 5 ft in beam over the Lupo class to provide
for the fixed hangar and VDS, the result providing more
comfortable accommodation but a small loss of top
speed. Fitted with stabilisers.
Operational: A towed passive LF array may be attached
to the VDS body. Aft A 184 torpedo tubes have been
removed. F 572, F 573, F 576 and F 577 to remain in
service until 2015-2018. F 570, F 571, F 574 and F 575 are
to be decommissioned from 2010.

LIBECCIO *10/2004, Giorgio Ghiglione* / 1044365

ESPERO *9/2003, B Prézelin* / 0570683

For details of the latest updates to *Jane's Fighting Ships* online and to discover the additional
information available exclusively to online subscribers please visit
jfs.janes.com

4 ARTIGLIERE (LUPO) CLASS (FLEET PATROL SHIPS) (FFGHM)

Name	No	Builders	Laid down	Launched	Commissioned
ARTIGLIERE (ex-*Hittin*)	F 582 (ex-F 14)	Fincantieri, Ancona	31 Mar 1982	27 July 1983	28 Oct 1994
AVIERE (ex-*Thi Qar*)	F 583 (ex-F 15)	Fincantieri, Ancona	3 Sep 1982	19 Dec 1984	4 Jan 1995
BERSAGLIERE (ex-*Al Yarmouk*)	F 584 (ex-F 17)	Fincantieri, Riva Trigoso	12 Mar 1984	18 Apr 1985	8 Nov 1995
GRANATIERE (ex-*Al Qadisiya*)	F 585 (ex-F 16)	Fincantieri, Ancona	1 Dec 1983	1 June 1985	20 Mar 1996

Displacement, tons: 2,208 standard; 2,525 full load
Dimensions, feet (metres): 371.3 × 37.1 × 12.1
(113.2 × 11.3 × 3.7)
Main machinery: CODOG; 2 Fiat/GE LM 2500 gas turbines;
50,000 hp *(37.3 MW)* sustained; 2 GMT BL 230.20 M
diesels; 7,800 hp(m) *(5.7 MW)* sustained; 2 shafts; LIPS
cp props
Speed, knots: 35 turbines; 21 diesels
Range, n miles: 5,000 at 15 kt on diesels
Complement: 177 (13 officers)

Missiles: SSM: 8 OTO Melara Teseo Mk 2 (TG 2) ❶;
mid-course guidance; active radar homing to 180 km
(98.4 n miles) at 0.9 Mach; warhead 210 kg; sea-skimmer.
SAM: Selenia Elsag Aspide octuple launcher ❷; semi-active
radar homing to 14.6 km *(8 n miles)* at 2.5 Mach; warhead
39 kg. 8 reloads.
Guns: 1 OTO Melara 5 in *(127 mm)*/54 ❸; 45 rds/min to
23 km *(12.42 n miles)* anti-surface; 7 km *(3.8 n miles)*
anti-aircraft; weight of shell 32 kg.
4 Breda 40 mm/70 (2 twin) compact ❹; 300 rds/min to
12.5 km *(6.8 n miles)* anti-surface; 4 km *(2.2 n miles)*
anti-aircraft; weight of shell 0.96 kg.
2 Oerlikon 20 mm can be fitted.
Countermeasures: Decoys: 2 Breda 105 mm SCLAR
20-tubed trainable ❺; chaff to 5 km *(2.7 n miles)*;
illuminants to 12 km *(6.6 n miles)*.
ESM/ECM: Selenia SLQ-747 (INS-3M); intercept and jammer.
Combat data systems: IPN 10 mini SADOC action data
automation; Link 11. SATCOM.

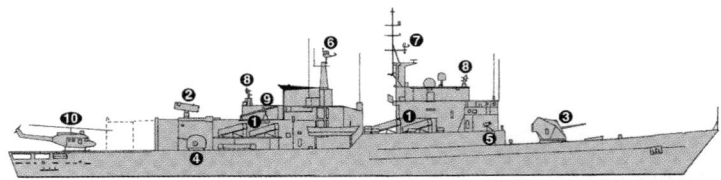

ARTIGLIERE

(Scale 1 : 1,200), Ian Sturton / 0506300

Weapons control: 2 Elsag Mk 10 Argo with NA 21 directors
for missiles and 5 in gun. 2 Dardo for 40 mm guns.
Radars: Air search: Selenia SPS-774 (RAN 10S) ❻;
E/F-band.
Surface search: Selenia SPQ-712 (RAN 12 L/X) ❼; I-band.
Navigation: SMA SPN-703; I-band.
Fire control: 2 Selenia SPG-70 (RTN 10X) ❽; I/J-band; range
40 km *(22 n miles)* (for Argo).
2 Selenia SPG-74 (RTN 20X) ❾; I/J-band; range 15 km
(8 n miles) (for Dardo).
IFF: Mk XII.

Helicopters: 1 AB 212 ❿.

Programmes: On 20 January 1992 it was decided to transfer
the four ships built for Iraq to the Italian Navy. The original
sale to Iraq was first delayed by payment problems and
then cancelled in 1990 when UN embargoes were placed

on military sales to Iraq. After several attempts by the
Italian Defence Committee to cancel the project, finance
was finally authorised in July 1993.
Modernisation: The details given are for the ships as
modernised for Italian service. All ASW equipment
removed, new combat and communications systems
to Italian standards and a major upgrading of damage
control and accommodation facilities. F 584 was fitted
with the lightweight 127 mm/54 gun in late 2000 for trials
which were successfully concluded in 2002.
Operational: The first two commissioned with only
machinery, damage control and accommodation
upgraded. The weapon systems' changes were made
during 1995. The last pair entered service fully modified.
Official designation is Fleet Patrol Ships. *Bersagliere*
replaced *Alpino* in the MCMV control for two deployments
in 2005 but is not permanently assigned to MCM forces.
All based at Taranto.

ARTIGLIERE

2/2002, Giorgio Ghiglione / 0528350

BERSAGLIERI

1/2005*, Camil Busquets i Vilanova / 1153225

CORVETTES

8 MINERVA CLASS (FSM)

Name	No	Builders	Laid down	Launched	Commissioned
MINERVA	F 551	Fincantieri, Riva Trigoso	11 Mar 1985	3 Apr 1986	10 June 1987
URANIA	F 552	Fincantieri, Riva Trigoso	4 Apr 1985	21 June 1986	1 June 1987
DANAIDE	F 553	Fincantieri, Muggiano	26 June 1985	18 Oct 1986	9 Sep 1987
SFINGE	F 554	Fincantieri, Muggiano	2 Sep 1986	16 May 1987	13 Feb 1988
DRIADE	F 555	Fincantieri, Riva Trigoso	18 Mar 1988	11 Mar 1989	19 Apr 1990
CHIMERA	F 556	Fincantieri, Riva Trigoso	21 Dec 1988	7 Apr 1990	15 Jan 1991
FENICE	F 557	Fincantieri, Riva Trigoso	6 Sep 1988	9 Sep 1989	11 Sep 1990
SIBILLA	F 558	Fincantieri, Muggiano	16 Oct 1989	15 Sep 1990	16 May 1991

Displacement, tons: 1,029 light; 1,285 full load
Dimensions, feet (metres): 284.1 × 34.5 × 10.5
(86.6 × 10.5 × 3.2)
Main machinery: 2 Fincantieri GMT BM 230.20 DVM diesels;
11,000 hp(m) *(8.1 MW)* sustained; 2 shafts; cp props
Speed, knots: 24. **Range, n miles:** 3,500 at 18 kt
Complement: 106 (8 officers)

Missiles: SAM: Selenia Elsag Albatros octuple launcher
(F 555-558) ❶; 8 Aspide; semi-active radar homing to
13 km *(7 n miles)* at 2.5 Mach; height envelope 15—5,000 m
(49.2—16,405 ft); warhead 30 kg. Capacity for larger
magazine.
Guns: 1 OTO Melara 3 in *(76 mm)*/62 Compact ❷;
85 rds/min to 16 km *(8.7 n miles)* anti-surface; 12 km
(6.6 n miles) anti-aircraft; weight of shell 6 kg.
Torpedoes: 6-324 mm Whitehead B 515 (2 triple) tubes
(F 555-558) ❸. Honeywell Mk 46; active/passive homing
to 11 km *(5.9 n miles)* at 40 kt; warhead 44 kg. Being
replaced by Whitehead Mu 90.
Countermeasures: Decoys: 2 Wallop Barricade double layer
launchers for chaff and IR flares. SLQ-25 Nixie; towed
torpedo decoy.

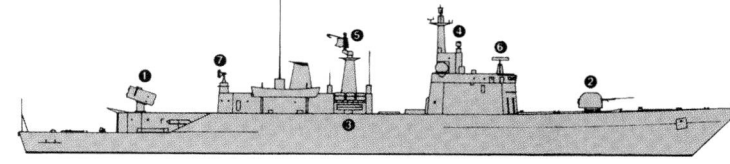

DRIADE

(Scale 1 : 900), Ian Sturton / 0506019

ESM/ECM: Selenia SLQ-747 intercept and jammer.
Combat data systems: Selenia IPN 10 Mini SADOC action
data automation; Link 11. SATCOM.
Weapons control: 1 Elsag Dardo E system. Selenia/Elsag
NA 18L Pegaso optronic director ❹. Elmer TLC system.
Radars: Air/surface search: Selenia SPS-774 (RAN 10S) ❺;
E/F-band.
Navigation: SMA SPN-728(V)2 ❻; I-band.
Fire control: Selenia SPG-76 (RTN 30X) ❼; I/J-band (for
Albatros and gun).
Sonars: Raytheon/Elsag DE 1167; hull-mounted; active
search and attack; 7.5—12 kHz.

Programmes: First four ordered in November 1982, second
four in January 1987. A third four were planned, but this
plan was overtaken by the acquisition of the Artigliere
class. The ships are not fitted for or with SSM.
Structure: The funnels remodelled to reduce turbulence
and IR signature. Two fin stabilisers.
Operational: Omega transit fitted. Intended for a number
of roles including EEZ patrol, fishery protection and
Commanding Officers' training. SAM launchers and
torpedo tubes removed from first four units. All based
at Augusta, Sicily.

DRIADE

4/2002, Schaeffer/Marsan / 0528348

SFINGE

9/2003, Giorgio Ghiglione / 0570674

SHIPBORNE AIRCRAFT

Notes: It is planned to procure up to 26 STOVL variants (F-35B) of the Joint Strike Fighter to enter service 2012-15.

Numbers/Type: 15/2 AV-8B Harrier II Plus/TAV-8B Harrier II Plus.
Operational speed: 562 kt *(1,041 km/h).*
Service ceiling: 50,000 ft *(15,240 m).*
Range: 800 n miles *(1,480 km).*
Role/Weapon systems: Two trainers delivered in July 1991 plus 15 front-line aircraft from 1994 to December 1997. Sensors: Radar derived from Hughes APG-65, FLIR, ALQ-164 ESM. Weapons: Maverick ASM; AMRAAM AIM-120B AAM; JDAM bombs and 25 mm cannon.

HARRIER PLUS   *6/2005*, Paul Jackson* / 1153222

Numbers/Type: 20 Agusta/Westland EH 101 Merlin.
Operational speed: 160 kt *(296 km/h).*
Service ceiling: 15,000 ft *(4,572 m).*
Range: 550 n miles *(1,019 km).*
Role/Weapon systems: Primary anti-submarine role with secondary anti-surface and troop carrying capabilities. 16 ordered in October 1995 and approved in July 1997. Six delivered by mid-2002 and further 10 by June 2004. Total of eight for ASW/ASV, four for AEW and four amphibious support (ASH). Four further special operations aircraft ordered in 2002 for delivery 2005-06. Two additional ASV variants ordered in 2005. Sensors: APS-784 (ASW/ASV version); Eliradar HEW-784 (AEW version) radar, L-3 HELRAS dipping sonar, Galileo FLIR, ALR 735 ESM, ELT 156X ESM, Marconi RALM 1 decoys, Link 11, sonobuoy acoustic processor. Weapons: ASW; four Mk 46 or Mu 90 torpedoes. ASV; four Marte Mk 2/S ASM capability for guidance of ship-launched SSM.

MERLIN   *11/2005*, MBDA Italia* / 1123497

Numbers/Type: 1 NH Industries NH 90 NFH.
Operational speed: 157 kt *(291 km/h).*
Service ceiling: 13,940 ft *(4,250 m).*
Range: 621 n miles *(1,150 km).*
Role/Weapon systems: Total of 56 NFH-90 ordered 30 June 2000 for the Italian Navy in two variants to replace the AB-212: 46 combat helicopters for ASW/ASV; 10 TTH utility/assault helicopters. First aircraft to be delivered in 2007. Sensors and weapons to be announced.

NH 90   *3/2004, NHI* / 0062373

Numbers/Type: 36 Agusta-Bell 212.
Operational speed: 106 kt *(196 km/h).*
Service ceiling: 17,000 ft *(5,180 m).*
Range: 360 n miles *(667 km).*
Role/Weapon systems: ASW/ECM/Assault helicopter; mainly deployed to escorts, but also shore-based for ASW support duties and nine used for assault. Five are for EW. To be replaced by NFH-90. Sensors: Selenia APS 705 (APS 707 in five Artigliere class aircraft) search/attack radar, Safire II EO turret (in some), AQS-13B dipping sonar or GUFO (not in Artigliere aircraft) ESM/ECM. Weapons: ASW; two Mk 46 torpedoes. Assault aircraft have an armoured cabin, no sensors and are armed with two 7.62 mm MGs and two 70 mm MRLs.

AB-212   *6/2001, Adolfo Ortigueira Gil* / 0528387

Numbers/Type: 19 Agusta-Sikorsky SH-3D/H Sea King.
Operational speed: 120 kt *(222 km/h).*
Service ceiling: 12,200 ft *(3,720 m).*
Range: 630 n miles *(1,165 km).*
Role/Weapon systems: ASW helicopter; embarked in larger ASW ships, including CVL; also shore-based for medium ASV-ASW in Mediterranean Sea; nine are fitted for ASV, 12 with ASW and EW equipment, six transport/assault. To be replaced by EH-101. Sensors: Selenia APS 705 search radar, AQS-13B dipping sonar, sonobuoys. ESM/ECM. Weapons: ASW; four Mk 46 torpedoes. ASV; two Marte 2 missiles. Assault aircraft have armoured cabins, no sensors, and are armed with two 7.62 mm MGs.

SEA KING   *6/2003, Adolfo Ortigueira Gil* / 0570676

LAND-BASED MARITIME AIRCRAFT

Notes: (1) It is planned to procure up to eight P-8A (MMA) maritime patrol aircraft for entry into service in about 2015.
(2) It is planned to procure three Boeing 737 AEW aircraft (with option for one further) to be operated by a joint Navy/Air Force Squadron.
(3) One Agusta A 109 transport helicopter procured in 2002 for liaison duties. Three further aircraft may be acquired.
(4) Five RQ-1B Predator are owned and maintained by the Italian Air Force. These can be controlled from the carrier *Giuseppe Garibaldi.*

Numbers/Type: 18 Bréguet Atlantic 1.
Operational speed: 355 kt *(658 km/h).*
Service ceiling: 22,800 ft *(10,000 m).*
Range: 4,855 n miles *(8,995 km).*
Role/Weapon systems: Air Force shore-based for long-range MR and shipping surveillance; wartime role includes ASW support to helicopters. Sensors: Thomson-CSF Iguane radar, ECM/ESM, MAD, sonobuoys; Marconi ASQ-902 acoustic system. Weapons: ASW; nine torpedoes (including Mk 46 torpedoes) or depth bombs or mines.

ATLANTIC   *6/2005*, Paul Jackson* / 1153221

Numbers/Type: 16 Panavia Tornado IDS.
Operational speed: 2.2 Mach.
Service ceiling: 80,000 ft *(24,385 m).*
Range: 1,500 n miles *(2,780 km).*
Role/Weapon systems: Air Force swing wing strike and recce; part of a force of a total of 100 aircraft of which 16 are used for maritime operations based near Bari. Sensors: Texas Instruments nav/attack systems. Weapons: ASV; four Kormoran missiles; two 27 mm cannon. AD; four AIM-9L Sidewinder.

TORNADO IDS   *8/2001, C Hoyle/Jane's* / 0034970

Numbers/Type: 3 Piaggio P-180 Avanti Maritime.
Operational speed: 260 kt *(482 km/h)*.
Service ceiling: 39,000 ft *(11,885 m)*.
Range: 1,195 n miles *(2,213 km)*.
Role/Weapon systems: Maritime version of business aircraft. Two aircraft procured in 2002 for liaison duties since retrofitted with FLIR to conduct surveillance. Third aircraft ordered in 2005. Sensors: FLIR.

Numbers/Type: 4 EADS ATR-42.
Operational speed: 300 kt *(556 km/h)*.
Service ceiling: 18,000 ft *(5,485 m)*.
Range: 1,600 n miles *(2,963 km)*.
Role/Weapon systems: Four aircraft ordered in 2005 for operation by the Navy in surveillance and SAR roles. Sensors: Airborne Tactical Observation and Surveillance System (ATOS), with two tactical consoles and one communication console; SV-2022 radar, Galileo EOST-23 FLIR, Elettronica ALR-733 ESM. Link-11 datalink, defensive suite with chaffs/flare launchers. Weapons: pod-mounted MG.

P-180 MARITIME   *7/2005*, Massimo Annati* / 1127625

ATR-42   *6/2005*, Paul Jackson* / 1127626

PATROL FORCES

6 COMANDANTE CLASS PATROL VESSELS (PSOH)

Name	No	Builders	Launched	Commissioned
COMANDANTE CIGALA FULGOSI	P 490	Fincantieri, Riva Trigoso	7 Oct 2000	31 July 2001
COMANDANTE BORSINI	P 491	Fincantieri, Riva Trigoso	17 Feb 2001	4 Dec 2001
COMANDANTE BETTICA	P 492	Fincantieri, Riva Trigoso	23 June 2001	4 Apr 2002
COMANDANTE FOSCARI	P 493	Fincantieri, Riva Trigoso	24 Nov 2001	1 Aug 2002
SIRIO	P 409	Fincantieri, Riva Trigoso	11 May 2002	31 May 2003
ORIONE	P 410	Fincantieri, Riva Trigoso	24 July 2002	1 Aug 2003

Displacement, tons: 1,520 full load
Dimensions, feet (metres): 290.0 × 40 × 15.1 (screws) *(88.4 × 12.2 × 4.6)*
Main machinery: 2 GM Trieste-Wärtsilä W18-V 26 XIV diesels; 17,600 hp(m) *(13.2 MW)*; 2 shafts; cp props; bow thruster
2 Wärtsilä 12V26X diesels (P409–410); 11,585 hp *(8.64 MW)*; 2 shafts; cp props; bow thruster
Speed, knots: 26 (22 kt for P 409–410)
Range, n miles: 3,500 at 14 kt
Complement: 60 (5 officers)

Guns: 1 Otobreda 3 in *(76 mm)*/62 compact (P 490-493) ❶.
2 Otobreda 25 mm/90 ❷.
Countermeasures: Decoys: chaff launcher.
ESM/ECM: Selenia SLQ-747; intercept and jammer.
Combat data systems: AMS IPNS.
Weapons control: 1 optronic director ❸.
Radars: Surface search ❹: SPS 703; I/J-band.
Fire control ❺: SPG 76 (RTN 25X); I/J-band.
Navigation: SPS 753 ❻; I-band.

Helicopters: 1 AB 212 ❼ or NH90 in due course.

Programmes: Four (P 490–493) for the Navy, and two funded by the Ministry of Transport, manned by the Navy, but equipped with more simple command data systems for anti-pollution and SAR tasks.
Structure: Stealth features include IR suppression and reduced radar cross-section. P 493 has a superstructure of composite material. P 409-410 have less powerful engines, no hangar, no countermeasures and MGs vice 25 mm guns.
Operational: Based in La Spezia until facilities made available at Augusta, Sicily.

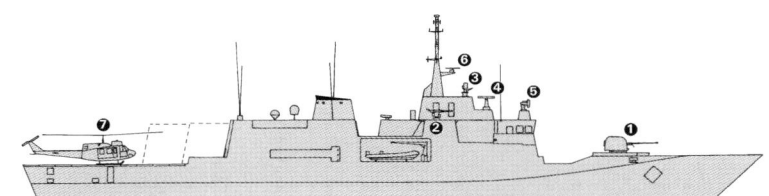

COMANDANTE FOSCARI   *(Scale 1 : 900), Ian Sturton* / 0589003

COMANDANTE BETTICA   *5/2005*, Giorgio Ghiglione* / 1153245

ORIONE   *7/2003, Giorgio Ghiglione* / 0570679

4 CASSIOPEA CLASS (OFFSHORE PATROL VESSELS) (PSOH)

Name	No	Builders	Laid down	Launched	Commissioned
CASSIOPEA	P 401	Fincantieri, Muggiano	16 Dec 1987	20 July 1988	6 July 1989
LIBRA	P 402	Fincantieri, Muggiano	17 Dec 1987	27 July 1988	28 Nov 1989
SPICA	P 403	Fincantieri, Muggiano	5 Sep 1988	27 May 1989	3 May 1990
VEGA	P 404	Fincantieri, Muggiano	20 June 1989	24 Feb 1990	25 Oct 1990

Displacement, tons: 1,002 standard; 1,475 full load
Dimensions, feet (metres): 261.8 × 38.7 × 11.5
(79.8 × 11.8 × 3.5)
Flight deck, feet (metres): 72.2 × 26.2 *(22 × 8)*
Main machinery: 2 Fincantieri/GMT BL 230.16 M diesels;
7,940 hp(m) *(5.84 MW)* sustained; 2 shafts; LIPS cp props
Speed, knots: 20. **Range, n miles:** 3,300 at 17 kt
Complement: 65 (5 officers)

Guns: 1 OTO Melara 3 in *(76 mm)*/62; 60 rds/min to 16 km
(8.7 n miles); weight of shell 6 kg. Breda Oerlikon 25 mm/90.
2—12.7 mm MGs.
Weapons control: Argo NA 10.
Radars: Surface search: SMA SPS-702(V)2; I-band.
Navigation: SMA SPN-748(V)2; I-band.
Fire control: Selenia SPG-70 (RTN 10X); I/J-band.

Helicopters: 1 AB 212ASW.

Programmes: Ordered in December 1986 for operations
in EEZ. Officially 'pattugliatori marittimi'. Funded by the
Ministry of Transport but all operated by the Navy.
Structure: Fitted for firefighting, rescue and supply tasks.
Telescopic hangar. The 20 mm guns were old stock taken
from deleted Bergamini class and have been replaced
by 25 mm guns. There is a 500 m³ tank for storing oil
polluted water.
Operational: All based at Augusta.

VEGA — *3/2001, Giorgio Ghiglione* / 0130329

4 ESPLORATORE CLASS (PB)

Name	No	Builders	Launched	Commissioned
ESPLORATORE	P 405	Coinaval, La Spezia	4 Nov 1996	26 June 1997
SENTINELLA	P 406	Coinaval, La Spezia	13 Nov 1997	10 July 1998
VEDETTA	P 407	Coinaval, La Spezia	11 Jan 1997	29 July 1999
STAFFETTA	P 408	Coinaval, La Spezia/Oromare	Nov 2002	6 July 2005

Displacement, tons: 165 full load
Dimensions, feet (metres): 122 × 23.3 × 6.2
(37.2 × 7.1 × 1.9)
Main machinery: 2 Isotta Fraschini M1712T2 diesels; 3,810
hp(m) *(2.8 MW)*; 2 shafts
Speed, knots: 20. **Range, n miles:** 1,200 at 20 kt
Complement: 14 (2 officers)
Guns: 1 Oerlikon 20 mm/70. 2—7.62 mm MGs.
Weapons control: AESN Medusa optronic director to be fitted.
Radars: Surface search: 2 SPS-753B/C; F/I-band.

Comment: Ordered from Ortona Shipyard in December 1993
but the contract was then transferred to Coinaval Yards,
La Spezia in 1994 which caused inevitable delays and
construction did not start until 1995. An option on a fourth
of class, was taken up in February 1998 but shipbuilding
programme delayed launch until January 2001 when it
was transferred to Oromare shipyard for completion
which was further delayed by financial problems. Based
in Red Sea for Multinational Force Observer (MFO)
operations. To return to Adriatic on completion.

STAFFETTA — *5/2005*, Giorgio Ghiglione* / 1153244

AMPHIBIOUS FORCES

Notes: (1) Initial studies for a new multipurpose Landing
Helicopter Dock (LHD) ship are in progress. Although an
unfunded programme, the aim is to establish options to
improve helicopter assault capability, to provide better
medical support and to act as a co-ordination centre for
disaster relief operations. Broad requirements are for
a ship of the order of 20,000 tons with the capability to
operate helicopters and amphibious craft and with a
vehicle transport capacity of 1,500 lane metres. A well-
dock would be incorporated in the stern. The ship would
be able to accommodate an embarked military force of
750 (comprising a landing force of 600 and a command
staff of 150) and to act as CJTF. If the ship were to emerge
as a replacement for *Giuseppe Garibaldi*, a continuous
flight deck to operate AV-8B and the F-35B would also
be required. (2) A Ro-Ro ship MV *Major* built in 1984 is
on long term charter to the Army Mobility and Transport
Command. 6,830 tons displacement with 1,240 m of
vehicle lanes. Can carry 3,955 tons of cargo. (3) There
are also 54 Rigid Raider Craft in service with Amphibious
Forces.

9 MTM 217 CLASS (LCM)

MEN 217-222	MEN 227-228	MEN 551

Displacement, tons: 64.6 full load
Dimensions, feet (metres): 60.7 × 16.7 × 3 *(18.5 × 5.1 × 0.9)*
Main machinery: 2 Fiat diesels; 560 hp(m) *(412 kW)*; 2 shafts
Speed, knots: 9. **Range, n miles:** 300 at 9 kt
Complement: 3
Military lift: 30 tons

Comment: First six built at Muggiano, La Spezia by Fincantieri. Three completed 9 October
1987 for *San Giorgio*, three completed 8 March 1988 for *San Marco*. Three more ordered
in March 1991 from Balzamo Shipyard and completed in 1993 for *San Giusto*. Others of
this class are also in service with the Army.

MEN 219 and 220 — *2000, M Annati* / 0104881

2 PEDRETTI CLASS
(SPECIAL OPERATIONS SUPPORT CRAFT) (YDT)

Name	No	Builders	Commissioned
ALCIDE PEDRETTI	Y 499 (ex-MEN 213)	Crestitalia-Ameglia	23 Oct 1984
MARIO MARINO	Y 498 (ex-MEN 214)	Crestitalia-Ameglia	21 Dec 1984

Displacement, tons: 75.4 *(Alcide Pedretti)*, 69.5 *(Mario Marino)* full load
Dimensions, feet (metres): 86.6 × 22.6 × 3.3 *(26.4 × 6.9 × 1)*
Main machinery: 2 Isotta Fraschini ID 36 SS 12V diesels; 2,640 hp(m) *(1.94 MW)* sustained;
2 shafts
Speed, knots: 25. **Range, n miles:** 450 *(Alcide Pedretti)*, 250 *(Mario Marino)* at 23 kt
Complement: 8 (1 officer)
Radars: Navigation: I-band.

Comment: Both laid down 8 September 1983. For use by assault swimmers of COMSUBIN.
Both have decompression chambers. *Alcide Pedretti* has a floodable dock aft and is
used for combat swimmers and special operations, while *Mario Marino* is fitted for
underwater work and rescue missions. Based at Varignano, La Spezia. A similar but
more heavily equipped vessel serves with the UAE Navy.

ALCIDE PEDRETTI — *10/1999, Giorgio Ghiglione* / 0080088

3 SAN GIORGIO CLASS (LPD)

Name	No	Builders	Laid down	Launched	Commissioned
SAN GIORGIO	L 9892	Fincantieri, Riva Trigoso	27 June 1985	25 Feb 1987	9 Oct 1987
SAN MARCO	L 9893	Fincantieri, Riva Trigoso	28 June 1986	21 Oct 1987	18 Mar 1988
SAN GIUSTO	L 9894	Fincantieri, Riva Trigoso	30 Nov 1992	2 Dec 1993	9 Apr 1994

Displacement, tons: 6,687 standard; 7,960 (8,000 *San Giusto*) full load
Dimensions, feet (metres): 449.5 *(San Giusto)*; 437.2 × 67.3 × 17.4 *(137; 133.3 × 20.5 × 5.3)*
Flight deck, feet (metres): 328.1 × 67.3 *(100 × 20.5)*
Main machinery: 2 Fincantieri GMT A 420.12 diesels; 16,800 hp(m) *(12.35 MW)* sustained; 2 shafts; LIPS cp props; bow thruster
Speed, knots: 21
Range, n miles: 7,500 at 16 kt; 4,500 at 20 kt
Complement: 168 (12 officers); 167 (15 officers) *(San Giusto)*
Military lift: Battalion of 400 plus 30—36 APCs or 30 medium tanks. 2 LCMs in stern docking well. 2 LCVPs on upper deck *(San Marco)* or 3 LCVPs on sponsons *(San Giusto and San Giorgio)*. 1 LCPL

Guns: 1 OTO Melara 3 in *(76 mm)*/62 (Compact in *San Giusto*); 60 rds/min to 16 km *(8.7 n miles)*; weight of shell 6 kg. 2 Breda Oerlikon 25 mm/90. 2 — 12.7 mm MGs.
Countermeasures: ESM; SLR 730; intercept. ESM/ECM: SLQ-747 *(San Giusto)*.
Combat data systems: Selenia IPN 20 *(San Giusto)*. Marisat. SATCOM.
Weapons control: Elsag NA 10.
Radars: Surface search: SMA SPS-702; I-band
Navigation: SMA SPN-748; I-band
Fire control: Selenia SPG-70 (RTN 10X); I/J-band

Helicopters: 3 SH-3D Sea King or EH 101 Merlin or 5 AB 212.

Programmes: *San Giorgio* ordered 26 November 1983, *San Marco* on 5 March 1984 and *San Giusto* 1 March 1991. Launching dates of the first two are slightly later than the 'official' launching ceremony because of poor weather and for the third because of industrial problems.
Modernisation: 25 mm guns replaced 20 mm from 1999. Modifications to *San Giorgio* include removal of the 76 mm gun, movement of LCVPs from davits to a new sponson, and lengthening and enlargement of the flight deck to allow two Merlin and two AB 212 to operate simultaneously on deck. Work completed in early 2003. Similar work on *San Marco* completed in March 2004. *San Giusto* has been fitted with an MCC data system to enable her to act as CJTF.
Structure: Aircraft carrier type flight deck with island to starboard. Following modernisation, *San Giorgio* and *San Marco* have four landing spots, a stern docking well

SAN GIORGIO — *8/2003, C D Yaylali /* 0570661

SAN GIORGIO — *2/2002, Italian Navy /* 0570697

(20.5 × 7 m), LCVPs on a port side sponson, a 30 ton lift and two 40 ton travelling cranes for LCMs. *San Giusto* is of similar design, but was 300 tons heavier on build to include extra accommodation and a slightly longer island. Bow doors and beaching capability removed from *San Marco* in refit.

Operational: *San Marco* was paid for by the Ministry of Civil Protection, is specially fitted for disaster relief but is run by the Navy. All are based at Brindisi and assigned to COMFORAL. One of the three ships carries out the annual Summer cruise for officer and petty officer cadets.

SAN GIUSTO — *9/2004, John Brodie /* 1044369

17 MTP 96 CLASS (LCVP)

MDN 94-104   MDN 108-109   MDN 114-117

Displacement, tons: 14.3 full load
Dimensions, feet (metres): 44.9 × 12.5 × 2.3 *(13.7 × 3.8 × 0.7)*
Main machinery: 2 diesels; 700 hp(m) *(515 kW)*; 2 shafts or 2 water-jets
Speed, knots: 29 or 22
Range, n miles: 100 at 12 kt
Complement: 3

Comment: Built by Technomatic Ancona in 1985 (two), Technomatic Bari in 1987-88 (six) and Technoplast Venezia 1991-94 (nine). Can carry 45 men or 4.5 tons of cargo. These craft have Kevlar armour. The most recent versions have water-jet propulsion which gives a top speed of 29 kt (22 kt fully laden). This is being backfitted to all GRP LCVPs.

MDN 101
10/2001, Chris Sattler
0130326

MINE WARFARE FORCES

Notes: Plans for future MCM vessels have been shelved and replacement vessels are not expected before 2010.

12 LERICI/GAETA CLASS (MINEHUNTERS/SWEEPERS) (MHSC)

Name	No	Builders	Launched	Commissioned
LERICI	M 5550	Intermarine, Sarzana	3 Sep 1982	22 Mar 1985
SAPRI	M 5551	Intermarine, Sarzana	5 Apr 1984	4 June 1985
MILAZZO	M 5552	Intermarine, Sarzana	4 Jan 1985	6 Aug 1985
VIESTE	M 5553	Intermarine, Sarzana	18 Apr 1985	2 Dec 1985
GAETA	M 5554	Intermarine, Sarzana	28 July 1990	3 July 1992
TERMOLI	M 5555	Intermarine, Sarzana	15 Dec 1990	13 Nov 1992
ALGHERO	M 5556	Intermarine, Sarzana	11 May 1991	31 Mar 1993
NUMANA	M 5557	Intermarine, Sarzana	26 Oct 1991	30 July 1993
CROTONE	M 5558	Intermarine, Sarzana	11 Apr 1992	19 Jan 1994
VIAREGGIO	M 5559	Intermarine, Sarzana	3 Oct 1992	1 July 1994
CHIOGGIA	M 5560	Intermarine, Sarzana	9 May 1994	19 May 1996
RIMINI	M 5561	Intermarine, Sarzana	17 Sep 1994	26 Nov 1996

Displacement, tons: 620 (697, *Gaeta* onwards) full load
Dimensions, feet (metres): 164 (172.1 *Gaeta*) × 32.5 × 8.6 *(50 (52.5) × 9.9 × 2.6)*
Main machinery: 1 Fincantieri GMT BL 230.8 M diesel (passage); 1,985 hp(m) *(1.46 MW)* sustained; 1 shaft; LIPS cp prop; 3 Isotta Fraschini ID 36 SS 6V diesels (hunting); 1,481 hp(m) *(1.1 MW)* sustained; 3 hydraulic 360° rotating thrust props; 506 hp(m) *(372 kW)* (1 fwd, 2 aft)
Speed, knots: 14; 6 hunting. **Range, n miles:** 1,500 at 14 kt
Complement: 44 (4 officers) including 7 divers

Guns: 1 Oerlikon 20 mm/70.
Countermeasures: Minehunting: 1 Plutogigas and 1 Pluto standard RoV; 1 MIN Mk 2 and 1 Pluto Plus (*Gaeta* onwards); diving equipment and Galeazzi recompression chamber; Galeazzi Z1 two-man recompression chamber (*Gaeta* onwards).

Minesweeping: Oropesa Mk 4 wire sweep.
Combat data systems: Motorola MRS III/GPS Eagle precision navigation system with Datamat SMA SSN-714V(3) automatic plotting and radar indicator IP-7113. Datamat SMA SSN-714 V(2) (*Gaeta* onwards).
Radars: Navigation: SMA SPN-728V(3); I-band.
Sonars: FIAR SQQ-14(IT) VDS (lowered from keel forward of bridge); classification and route survey; high frequency.

Programmes: First four (Lerici class) ordered 7 January 1978 under Legge Navale. Next six ordered from Intermarine 30 April 1988 and two more in 1991. From No 5 onwards (Gaeta class) ships are 2 m longer and are of an improved design. Construction of Gaetas started in 1988. The last pair delayed by budget cuts but re-ordered on 17 September 1992.
Modernisation: Improvements to Gaeta class include a better minehunting sonar system which was

backfitted to the Lerici class in 1991. Other Gaeta upgrades include a third hydraulic system, improved electrical generators, Pluto Gigas ROV, a new type of recompression chamber, and a reduced magnetic signature. Plans to replace the guns with 25 mm have been shelved.
Structure: Of heavy GRP throughout hull, decks and bulkheads, with frames eliminated. All machinery is mounted on vibration dampers and main engines made of a magnetic material. Fitted with crane for launching RoVs and for diving operations.
Operational: Endurance, 12 days. For long passages passive roll-stabilising tanks can be used for extra fuel increasing range to 4,000 miles at 12 kt.
Sales: Four to Malaysia, two to Nigeria and two to Thailand. 12 of a modified design built by the US and six by Australia.

CHIOGGIA

1/2003, Giorgio Ghiglione / 0570673

VIAREGGIO

4/2005, Giorgio Ghiglione* / 1153243

SURVEY AND RESEARCH SHIPS

1 SURVEY SHIP (AGORH/AGE/AGI)

Name	No	Builders	Commissioned
ELETTRA	A 5340	Fincantieri, Muggiano	2 Apr 2003

Displacement, tons: 3,180 full load
Dimensions, feet (metres): 305.1 × 49.9 × 17.1 *(93 × 15.2 × 5.2)*
Main machinery: Diesel electric; 2 Wartsila CW 12V 200 diesel generators; 5,750 kVA. 2 ABB motors; 4,023 hp *(3 MW)*; 2 shafts; bow thruster
Speed, knots: 17
Range, n miles: 8,000 at 12 kt
Complement: 94 (12 officers)
Radars: Navigation: I-band.
Helicopters: Platform for one medium.

Comment: Ordered on 1 December 1999; construction started in March 2000 and launch on 24 July 2002. The design is derived from that of the NATO *Alliance* but is equipped as an intelligence collector. The propulsion system, based on two multi permanent magnet electric motors, is the first of its type to be fitted in a surface vessel.

ELETTRA *5/2003, Giorgio Ghiglione* / 0570671

1 ALPINO CLASS (AGEHM)

Name	No	Builders	Commissioned
CARABINIERE (ex-*Climene*)	F 581	Fincantieri, Riva Trigoso	28 Apr 1968

Displacement, tons: 2,400 standard; 2,700 full load
Dimensions, feet (metres): 371.7 × 43.6 × 12.7 *(113.3 × 13.3 × 3.9)*
Main machinery: 4 Tosi OTV-320 diesels; 16,800 hp(m) *(12.35 MW)*; 2 shafts
Speed, knots: 20
Range, n miles: 3,500 at 18 kt
Complement: 158 (13 officers)

Missiles: SAM: Alenia/DCN 8-cell VLS for Aster 15 trials; radar homing to 30 km *(16.2 n miles)* at 4.5 Mach; warhead 13 kg.
A/S: OTO Melara/Matra Milas launcher; command guidance to 55 km *(29.8 n miles)* at Mach 0.9; payload Mu 90 or Mk 46 Mod 5 torpedo.
Guns: 1 OTO Melara 3 in *(76 mm)*/62; 60 rds/min to 16 km *(8.7 n miles)*; weight of shell 6 kg.
Torpedoes: 6 – 324 mm Whitehead (2 triple tubes).
Countermeasures: ESM/ECM: Selenia SLQ-747; integrated intercept and jammer.
Combat data systems: SADOC 3 for EMPAR trials.
Weapons control: 2 Argo 'O' for 3 in guns.
Radars: Air search: RCA SPS-12; D-band.
Surface search: SMA SPS-702(V)3; I-band.
Navigation: SMA SPN-748; I-band.
Fire control: 2 Selenia SPG-70 (RTN 10X); I/J-band.
Alenia/Marconi EMPAR SPY 790; for PAAMS; G-band; range 50 km *(27 n miles)* for 0.1 m² target.

Modernisation: Modified as a trials ship. B gun turret and the Whitehead mortar removed and, following a refit which completed in October 2000, fitted with an eight cell A43 vertical launch system aft of the forward gun and an upgrade of the communication system. The A43 VLS module was then replaced by an A50 module (for Aster 30) in late 2003. An oil rig style mast on the flight deck carries the EMPAR SPY 790 radar that was installed in 1995.
Operational: Since 1993, served as testbed for the Milas anti-submarine missile and EMPAR radar. EMPAR serves as surveillance, acquisition and missile guidance system for the SAAM/IT point defence system on which final qualification firings with Aster 15 missiles were conducted during 2002 and early 2003. SLAT soft-kill anti-torpedo system trials were conducted at the same time. Full PAAMS combat system trials (for the French, Italian and UK navies) began off Toulon from mid-2004.

CARABINIERE *4/2005*, Giorgio Ghiglione* / 1153241

1 SURVEY SHIP (AGSH)

Name	No	Builders	Commissioned
AMMIRAGLIO MAGNAGHI	A 5303	Fincantieri, Riva Trigoso	2 May 1975

Displacement, tons: 1,700 full load
Dimensions, feet (metres): 271.3 × 44.9 × 11.5 *(82.7 × 13.7 × 3.5)*
Main machinery: 2 GMT B 306 SS diesels; 3,000 hp(m) *(2.2 MW)*; 1 shaft; cp prop; auxiliary motor; 240 hp(m) *(176 kW)*; bow thruster
Speed, knots: 16. **Range, n miles:** 6,000 at 12 kt (1 diesel); 4,200 at 16 kt (2 diesels)
Complement: 148 (14 officers, 15 scientists)
Guns: 1 Breda 40 mm/70 (not fitted).
Radars: Navigation: SMA 3 RM 20; I-band.
Helicopters: Platform only.

Comment: Ordered under 1972 programme. Laid down 13 June 1973. Launched 11 October 1974. Full air conditioning, bridge engine controls, flume-type stabilisers. Equipped for oceanographical studies including laboratories and underwater TV. Two Qubit Trac V integrated navigation and logging systems and a Chart V data processing system installed in 1992 to augment the existing Trac 100-based HODAPS. Carries six surveying motor boats.

AMMIRAGLIO MAGNAGHI *3/2002, Giorgio Ghiglione* / 0528354

2 SURVEY SHIPS (AGS)

Name	No	Builders	Commissioned
ARETUSA	A 5304	Intermarine	10 Jan 2002
GALATEA	A 5308	Intermarine	10 Jan 2002

Displacement, tons: 415 full load
Dimensions, feet (metres): 128.6 × 41.3 × 8.2 *(39.2 × 12.6 × 2.5)*
Main machinery: Diesel electric; 2 Isotta Fraschini V170812 ME diesels; 2 ABB generators 1,904 hp(m) *(1.4 MW)*; 2 shafts; Schottel props; 2 bow thrusters
Speed, knots: 13. **Range, n miles:** 1,700 at 13 kt
Complement: 29 (4 officers)
Guns: 2 – 7.62 mm MGs.
Radars: 2 Navigation; I-band.

Comment: GRP catamaran design. Ordered in January 1998. *Aretusa* launched 8 May 2000 and *Galatea* 7 June 2000. Fitted with Kongsberg EA 500 single-beam echo sounder, towed sidescan sonar and dynamic positioning system.

GALATEA *1/2004, Giorgio Ghiglione* / 1044371

1 RESEARCH SHIP (AG/AGOR)

Name	No	Builders	Launched	Commissioned
RAFFAELE ROSSETTI	A 5315	Picchiotti, Viareggio	12 July 1986	20 Dec 1986

Displacement, tons: 320 full load
Dimensions, feet (metres): 146.3 × 25.9 × 6.9 *(44.6 × 7.9 × 2.1)*
Main machinery: 2 Fincantieri Isotta Fraschini ID 36 N 6V diesels; 3,520 hp(m) *(2.55 kW)* sustained; 2 shafts; cp props; bow thruster
Speed, knots: 17.5. **Range, n miles:** 700 at 15 kt
Complement: 17 (2 officers)

Comment: Five different design torpedo tubes fitted for above and underwater testing and trials. Other equipment for research into communications, surface and air search as well as underwater weapons. There is a stern doorway which is partially submerged and the ship has a set of 96 batteries to allow 'silent' propulsion. Operated by the Permanent Commission for Experiments of War Materials at La Spezia.

RAFFAELE ROSSETTI *4/2005*, Giorgio Ghiglione* / 1153242

1 RESEARCH SHIP (AG/AGE)

Name	No	Builders	Commissioned
VINCENZO MARTELLOTTA	A 5320	Picchiotti, Viareggio	22 Dec 1990

Displacement, tons: 340 full load
Dimensions, feet (metres): 146.3 × 25.9 × 7.5 *(44.6 × 7.9 × 2.3)*
Main machinery: 2 Fincantieri Isotta Fraschini ID 36 SS 16V diesels; 3,520 hp(m) *(2.59 MW)* sustained; 2 shafts; cp props; bow thruster
Speed, knots: 17
Range, n miles: 700 at 15 kt
Complement: 19 (2 officers)

Comment: Launched on 28 May 1988. Has one 21 in *(533 mm)* and three 12.75 in *(324 mm)* torpedo tubes and acoustic equipment to operate a 3-D tracking range for torpedoes or underwater vehicles. Like *Rossetti* she is operated by the Commission for Experiments at La Spezia.

VINCENZO MARTELLOTTA   *9/2002, Giorgio Ghiglione* / 0528352

TRAINING SHIPS

Notes: (1) In addition to the ships listed the LPDs are used in a training role.
(2) There is a requirement for new training ships to replace the Aragosta class but the programme is not funded.

1 SAIL TRAINING SHIP (AXS)

Name	No	Builders	Commissioned
AMERIGO VESPUCCI	A 5312	Castellammare	15 May 1931

Displacement, tons: 3,543 standard; 4,146 full load
Dimensions, feet (metres): 229.5 pp; 270 oa hull; 330 oa bowsprit × 51 × 22 *(70; 82.4; 100 × 15.5 × 7)*
Main machinery: Diesel-electric; 2 Fiat B 306 ESS diesel generators; 2 Marelli motors; 2,000 hp(m) *(1.47 MW)*; 1 shaft
Speed, knots: 10
Range, n miles: 5,450 at 6.5 kt
Complement: 243 (13 officers)
Radars: Navigation: 2 SMA SPN-748; I-band.

Comment: Launched on 22 March 1930. Hull, masts and yards are of steel. Sail area, 22,604 sq ft. Extensively refitted at La Spezia Naval Dockyard in 1973 and again in 1984. Used for Naval Academy Summer cruise with up to 150 trainees.

AMERIGO VESPUCCI   *7/2004, Ships of the World* / 1044364

1 SAIL TRAINING SHIP (AXS)

Name	No	Builders	Commissioned
PALINURO (ex-*Commandant Louis Richard*)	A 5311	Ch Dubigeon, Nantes	1934

Displacement, tons: 1,042 standard; 1,450 full load
Measurement, tons: 858 gross
Dimensions, feet (metres): 193.5 × 32.8 × 15.7 *(59 × 10 × 4.8)*
Main machinery: 1 GMT A 230.6N diesel; 600 hp *(447 kW)*; 1 shaft
Speed, knots: 7.5
Range, n miles: 5,390 at 7.5 kt
Complement: 69 (6 officers)
Radars: Navigation: SPN-748; I-band.

Comment: Barquentine launched in 1934. Purchased in 1951. Rebuilt in 1954-55 and commissioned in Italian Navy on 1 July 1955. Sail area, 1,152 sq ft. She was one of the last two French Grand Bank cod-fishing barquentines. Owned by the Armement Glâtre she was based at St Malo until bought by Italy. Used for seamanship basic training.

PALINURO   *7/2004, Diego Quevedo* / 1044376

3 ARAGOSTA (HAM) CLASS (AXL)

ASTICE A 5379	MITILO A 5380	PORPORA A 5382

Displacement, tons: 188 full load
Dimensions, feet (metres): 106 × 21 × 6 *(32.5 × 6.4 × 1.8)*
Main machinery: 2 Fiat-MTU 12V 493 TY7 diesels; 2,200 hp(m) *(1.62 MW)* sustained; 2 shafts
Speed, knots: 14
Range, n miles: 2,000 at 9 kt
Complement: 13 (2 officers)
Radars: Navigation: BX 732; I-band.

Comment: Builders: CRDA, Monfalcone: *Astice*. Picchiotti, Viareggio: *Mitilo*. Costaguta, Voltri: *Porpora*. Similar to the late UK Ham class. All constructed to the order of NATO in 1955-57. Designed armament of one 20 mm gun not mounted. Originally class of 20. Remaining three converted for training 1986. *Porpora* used by the Naval Academy. *Astice* has a modified bridge structure. Plans for transfer to Albania have been shelved. There are no funded replacement plans.

ASTICE   *7/2003, Giorgio Ghiglione* / 0570667

5 SAIL TRAINING YACHTS (AXS)

Name	No	Builders	Commissioned
CAROLY	A 5302	Baglietto, Varazze	1948
STELLA POLARE	A 5313	Sangermani, Chiavari	8 Oct 1965
CORSARO II	A 5316	Costaguta, Voltri	5 Jan 1961
CAPRICIA	A 5322	Bengt-Plym	1963
ORSA MAGGIORE	A 5323	Tencara, Venezia	1994

Comment: The first three are sail training yachts between 40 and 60 tons with a crew including trainees of about 16. *Capricia* is a yawl of 55 tons and was donated by the Agnelli foundation as replacement for *Cristoforo Colombo II* which was not completed when the shipyard building her went bankrupt. *Capricia* commissioned in the Navy 23 May 1993. *Orsa Maggiore* is a ketch of 70 tons.

ORSA MAGGIORE   *7/2003, J Cislak* / 0570669

AUXILIARIES

1 ETNA CLASS (REPLENISHMENT TANKER) (AORH)

Name	No	Builders	Laid down	Launched	Commissioned
ETNA	A 5326	Fincantieri, Riva Trigoso	4 July 1995	12 July 1997	29 Aug 1998

Displacement, tons: 13,400 full load
Dimensions, feet (metres): 480.6 × 68.9 × 24.3
(146.5 × 21 × 7.4)
Flight deck, feet (metres): 91.9 × 68. 9 *(28 × 21)*
Main machinery: 2 Sulzer 12 ZAV 40S diesels; 22,400 hp(m)
(16.46 MW) sustained; 2 shafts; bow thruster
Speed, knots: 21
Range, n miles: 7,600 at 18 kt

Complement: 162 (14 officers) plus 81 spare
Cargo capacity: 6,350 tons gas oil; 1,200 tons JP5; 2,100 m³
ammunition and stores
Guns: 1 OTO Melara 76 mm/62. 2 Breda Oerlikon
25 mm/93.
Radars: Surface search: SMA SPS-702(V)3; I-band.
Navigation: GEM SPN-753; I-band.
Helicopters: 1 EH 101 Merlin or SH-3D or 2 AB 212.

Comment: Details revised in 1992 for an order 29 July 1994. Construction authorised on 3 January 1995. The main gun is not fitted, and the specification includes a CIWS on the hangar roof. Two RAS stations on each side. A similar ship has been built for Greece. A major upgrade to C⁴I capability has given the ship a Maritime Component Commander capability.

ETNA   *6/2001, M Declerck* / 0132012

2 STROMBOLI CLASS (REPLENISHMENT TANKERS) (AORH)

Name	No	Builders	Launched	Commissioned
STROMBOLI	A 5327	Fincantieri, Riva Trigoso	20 Feb 1975	20 Nov 1975
VESUVIO	A 5329	Fincantieri, Muggiano	4 June 1977	18 Nov 1978

Displacement, tons: 3,556 light; 8,706 full load
Dimensions, feet (metres): 423.1 × 59 × 21.3 *(129 × 18 × 6.5)*
Main machinery: 2 GMT C428 SS diesels; 9,600 hp(m) *(7.06 MW)*; 1 shaft; LIPS cp prop
Speed, knots: 18.5
Range, n miles: 5,080 at 18 kt
Complement: 131 (10 officers)
Cargo capacity: 3,000 tons FFO; 1,000 tons dieso; 400 tons JP5; 300 tons other stores
Guns: 1 OTO Melara 3 in *(76 mm)*/62.
2 Oerlikon 20 mm/70.
Weapons control: Argo NA 10 system.
Radars: Surface search: SMA SPQ-2; I-band.
Navigation: SMA SPN-748; I-band.
Fire control: Selenia SPG-70 (RTN 10X); I/J-band.
Helicopters: Platform for 1 medium.

Comment: *Vesuvio* was the first large ship to be built at Muggiano (near La Spezia) since the Second World War and the first with funds under Legge Navale 1975. Beam and stern refuelling stations for fuel and stores. Also Vertrep. The two ships have different midships crane arrangements. Similar ship built for Iraq and laid up in Alexandria since 1986. 20 mm guns replaced by 25 mm from 2002.

VESUVIO   *11/2005*, Manuel Declerck* / 1153213

1 BORMIDA CLASS (WATER TANKER) (AWT)

BORMIDA (ex-GGS 1011) A 5359

Displacement, tons: 736 full load
Dimensions, feet (metres): 131.9 × 23.6 × 10.5 *(40.2 × 7.2 × 3.2)*
Main machinery: 1 diesel; 130 hp(m) *(95.6 kW)*; 1 shaft
Speed, knots: 7
Complement: 11 (1 officer)
Cargo capacity: 260 tons

Comment: Converted at La Spezia in 1974.

BORMIDA   *9/2002, Giorgio Ghiglione* / 0528367

4 MCC 1101 CLASS (WATER TANKERS) (AWT)

MCC 1101 A 5370	**MCC 1102** A 5371	**MCC 1103** A 5372	**MCC 1104** A 5373

Displacement, tons: 898 full load
Dimensions, feet (metres): 155.2 × 32.8 × 10.8 *(47.3 × 10 × 3.3)*
Main machinery: 2 Fincantieri Isotta Fraschini ID 36 SS 6V diesels; 1,320 hp(m) *(970 kW)*
sustained; 2 shafts
Speed, knots: 13. **Range, n miles:** 1,500 at 12 kt
Complement: 12 (2 officers)
Cargo capacity: 550 tons
Radars: Navigation: SPN-753; I-band.

Comment: Built by Ferrari, La Spezia and completed one in 1986, two in May 1987, one in May 1988.

MCC 1103   *7/2003, Giorgio Ghiglione* / 0570663

2 SIMETO CLASS (WATER TANKERS) (AWT)

Name	No	Builders	Commissioned
TICINO	A 5376	Poli Shipyard, Pellestrina	10 June 1994
TIRSO	A 5377	Poli Shipyard, Pellestrina	12 Mar 1994

Displacement, tons: 1,858 full load; 1,968 *(Ticino* and *Tirso)* full load
Dimensions, feet (metres): 229 × 33.1 × 14.4 *(69.8 × 10.1 × 4.1)*
Main machinery: 2 GMT B 230.6 BL diesels; 2,530 hp(m) *(1.86 MW)* sustained; 2 shafts;
cp props; bow thruster; 300 hp(m) *(220 kW)*
Speed, knots: 13. **Range, n miles:** 1,800 at 12 kt
Complement: 36 (3 officers)
Cargo capacity: 1,130 tons; 1,200 tons *(Ticino* and *Tirso)*
Guns: 1 — 20 mm/70. 2 — 7.62 mm MGs can be carried.
Radars: Navigation: 2 SPN-753B(V); I-band.

Comment: Guns are not normally carried. *Simeto* transferred to Tunisia on 30 June 2003.

TICINO   *2/2006*, Maritime Photographic* / 1154402

7 DEPOLI CLASS TANKERS (AOTL/AWT)

GGS 1012-1014   **GRS/G 1010-1012**   **GRS/J 1013**

Dimensions, feet (metres): 128.3 × 27.9 × 10.2 *(39.1 × 8.5 × 3.1)*
Main machinery: 2 diesels; 748 hp(m) *(550 kW)*; 2 shafts
Speed, knots: 11
Complement: 12
Cargo capacity: 500 m³ liquids
Radars: Navigation: I-band.

Comment: Built by DePoli and delivered between February 1990 and February 1991. The GGS series is for water, GRS/G for fuel and GRS/J for JP5.

GGS 1012   *5/2005*, Giorgio Ghiglione* / 1153240

6 MTC 1011 CLASS (RAMPED TRANSPORTS) (AKL)

Name	No	Builders	Commissioned
GORGONA (1011)	A 5347	CN Mario Marini	23 Dec 1986
TREMITI (1012)	A 5348	CN Mario Marini	2 Mar 1987
CAPRERA (1013)	A 5349	CN Mario Marini	10 Apr 1987
PANTELLERIA (1014)	A 5351	CN Mario Marini	26 May 1987
LIPARI (1015)	A 5352	CN Mario Marini	10 July 1987
CAPRI (1016)	A 5353	CN Mario Marini	16 Sep 1987

Displacement, tons: 631 full load
Dimensions, feet (metres): 186 × 32.8 × 8.2 *(56.7 × 10 × 2.5)*
Main machinery: 2 CRM 12D/SS diesels; 1,760 hp(m) *(1.29 MW)*; 2 shafts
Speed, knots: 14.5. **Range, n miles:** 1,500 at 14 kt
Complement: 32 (4 officers)
Guns: 1 Oerlikon 20 mm (fitted for). 2—7.62 mm MGs.
Radars: Navigation: SMA SPN-748; I-band.

Comment: As well as transporting stores, oil or water they can act as support ships for Light Forces, salvage ships or minelayers. Stern ramp fitted. 1011 based at La Spezia, 1012 at Ancona, 1013 at La Maddalena and 1014 at Taranto.

CAPRERA   *8/2005*, Marco Ghiglino* / 1153212

1 SALVAGE SHIP (ARSH)

Name	No	Builders	Launched	Commissioned
ANTEO	A 5309	C N Breda-Mestre	11 Nov 1978	31 July 1980

Displacement, tons: 3,200 full load
Dimensions, feet (metres): 322.8 × 51.8 × 16.7 *(98.4 × 15.8 × 5.1)*
Main machinery: 2 GMT A 230.12 diesels; 5,000 hp(m) *(3.68 MW)*; 2 motors; 6,000 hp(m) *(4.41 MW)*; 1 shaft; 2 bow thrusters; 1,000 hp(m) *(735 kW)*
Speed, knots: 20. **Range, n miles:** 4,000 at 14 kt
Complement: 121 (including salvage staff)
Guns: 2 Oerlikon 20 mm/70 fitted during deployments.
Radars: Surface search: SMA SPN-751; I-band.
Navigation: SMA SPN-748; I-band.
Helicopters: 1 AB 212.

Comment: Ordered mid-1977. Comprehensively fitted with flight deck and hangar, extensive salvage gear, including rescue bell and recompression chambers. Carries four lifeboats of various types. Three firefighting systems. Full towing equipment. Carries midget submarine, *Usel*, of 13.2 tons dived with dimensions 26.2 × 6.2 × 8.9 ft *(8 × 1.9 × 2.7 m)*. Carries two men and can dive to 600 m. Endurance, 120 hours at 5 kt. Also has a McCann rescue chamber.

ANTEO   *5/2000, Giorgio Ghiglione* / 0104889

5 PONZA CLASS (LIGHTHOUSE TENDERS) (ABU)

Name	No	Builders	Commissioned
PONZA	A 5364	Morini Yard, Ancona	9 Dec 1988
LEVANZO	A 5366	Morini Yard, Ancona	24 Jan 1989
TAVOLARA	A 5367	Morini Yard, Ancona	12 Apr 1989
PALMARIA	A 5368	Morini Yard, Ancona	12 May 1989
PROCIDA	A 5383	Morini Yard, Ancona	14 Nov 1990

Displacement, tons: 608 full load
Dimensions, feet (metres): 186 × 35.4 × 8.2 *(56.7 × 10.8 × 2.5)*
Main machinery: 2 Fincantieri Isotta Fraschini ID 36 SS 8V diesels; 1,760 hp(m) *(1.29 MW)* sustained; 2 shafts; cp props; bow thruster; 120 hp(m) *(88 kW)*
Speed, knots: 14.5. **Range, n miles:** 1,500 at 14 kt
Complement: 34 (2 officers)
Guns: 2—7.62 mm MGs.
Radars: Navigation: SPN-732; I-band.

Comment: MTF 1304—1308. Similar to MTC 1011 class.

PALMARIA   *6/2004, Giorgio Ghiglione* / 1044375

1 MEN 212 CLASS (YPT)

MEN 212

Displacement, tons: 32 full load
Dimensions, feet (metres): 58.4 × 16.7 × 3.3 *(17.8 × 5.1 × 1)*
Main machinery: 2 HP diesels; 1,380 hp(m) *(1.01 MW)*; 2 shafts
Speed, knots: 22
Range, n miles: 250 at 20 kt
Complement: 4
Radars: Navigation: SPN-732; I-band.

Comment: Torpedo Recovery Vessel completed in October 1983 by Crestitalia. GRP construction with a stern ramp. Capacity for up to three torpedoes.

MEN 212   *8/2003, P Marsan* / 0570664

2 MEN 215 CLASS (YFU/YFB)

MEN 215   **MEN 216**

Displacement, tons: 82 full load
Dimensions, feet (metres): 89.6 × 23 × 3.6 *(27.3 × 7 × 1.1)*
Main machinery: 2 Isotta Fraschini ID 36 SS 12V diesels; 2,640 hp(m) *(1.94 MW)* sustained; 2 shafts
Speed, knots: 28. **Range, n miles:** 250 at 14 kt
Complement: 4
Radars: Navigation: SPN-732; I-band.

Comment: Fast personnel launches completed in June 1986 by Crestitalia. Can also be used for amphibious operations or disaster relief. One is based at La Spezia and one in Taranto, where they are used as local ferries.

MEN 216   *3/1998, Giorgio Ghiglione* / 0052424

HARBOUR CRAFT

Comment: There are large numbers of naval manned harbour craft with MDN, MCN, MBN and MEN numbers. *Argo* (ex-MEN 209) is being used as a Presidential yacht. There is also a ferry *Cheradi* Y 402 at Taranto. Craft with VF numbers are non-naval.

MCN 1634　　　　　　　　　　　*5/2001, L-G Nilsson* / 0130349

ARGO　　　　　　　　　　　*5/2000, Giorgio Ghiglione* / 0104891

19 FLOATING DOCKS

Number	Date	Capacity-tons
GO 1	1942	1,000
GO 5	1893	100
GO 8	1904	3,800
GO 10	1900	2,000
GO 11	1920	2,700
GO 17	1917	500
GO 18A	1920	800
GO 18B	1920	600
GO 20	1935	1,600
GO 22-23	1935	1,000
GO 51	1971	2,000
GO 52-54	1988-93	6,000
GO 55-57	1995-96	850
GO 58	1995	2,000

Comment: Stationed at La Spezia *(GO 52)*, Augusta *(GO 53)* and Taranto *(GO 54)*.

TUGS

7 OCEAN TUGS (ATR)

PROMETEO A 5318	**POLIFEMO** A 5325	**SATURNO** A 5330
CICLOPE A 5319	**GIGANTE** A 5328	**TENACE** A 5365
TITANO A 5324		

Displacement, tons: 658 full load
Dimensions, feet (metres): 127.6 × 32.5 × 12.1 *(38.9 × 9.9 × 3.7)*
Main machinery: 2 GMT B 230.8 M diesels; 3,970 hp(m) *(2.02 MW)* sustained; 2 shafts; LIPS cp props
Speed, knots: 14.5. **Range, n miles:** 3,000 at 14 kt
Complement: 12
Radars: Navigation: SPN-748; I-band.

Comment: Details given are for all except A 5318. Built by CN Ferrari, La Spezia. Completed *Ciclope*, 5 September 1985; *Titano*, 7 December 1985; *Polifemo*, 21 April 1986; *Gigante*, 18 July 1986; *Saturno* 5 April 1988 and *Tenace* 9 July 1988. All fitted with firefighting equipment and two portable submersible pumps. Bollard pull 45 tons. *Prometeo* was completed 14 August 1975 and is slightly larger at 746 tons and has single engine propulsion.

TITANO　　　　　　　　　　*4/2005*, Giorgio Ghiglione* / 1153239

9 COASTAL TUGS (YTB)

PORTO FOSSONE Y 413	**PORTO EMPEDOCLE** Y 421	**PORTO FERRAIO** Y 425
PORTO TORRES Y 416	**PORTO PISANO** Y 422	**PORTO VENERE** Y 426
PORTO CORSINI Y 417	**PORTO CONTE** Y 423	**PORTO SALVO** Y 428

Displacement, tons: 412 full load
Measurement, tons: 122 dwt
Dimensions, feet (metres): 106.3 × 27.9 × 12.8 *(32.4 × 8.5 × 3.9)*
Main machinery: 1 GMT B 230.8 M diesels; 1,600 hp(m) *(1.18 MW)* sustained; 1 shaft; cp prop
Speed, knots: 12.7. **Range, n miles:** 4,000 at 12 kt
Complement: 13
Radars: Navigation: GEM BX 132; I-band.

Comment: Details given are for all except Y 436 and 443. Six ordered from CN De Poli (Pellestrina) and further three from Ferbex (Naples) in 1986.
Delivery dates *Porto Salvo* (13 September 1985), *Porto Pisano* (22 October 1985), *Porto Ferraio* (20 July 1985), *Porto Conte* (21 November 1985), *Porto Empedocle* (19 March 1986), *Porto Venere* (16 May 1989), *Porto Fossone* (24 September 1990), *Porto Torres* (16 January 1991) and *Porto Corsini* (4 March 1991).
Fitted for firefighting and anti-pollution. Carry a 1 ton telescopic crane. Based at Taranto, La Spezia, Augusta and La Maddalena. *Porto d'Ischia* transferred to Tunisia in 2002 and *Riva Trigoso* decommissioned.

PORTO TORRES　　　　　　　*5/2001, Giorgio Ghiglione* / 0130337

32 HARBOUR TUGS (YTM)

RP 101 Y 403W (1972)	**RP 113** Y 463 (1978)	**RP 125** Y 478 (1983)
RP 102 Y 404 (1972)	**RP 114** Y 464 (1980)	**RP 126** Y 479 (1983)
RP 103 Y 406 (1974)	**RP 115** Y 465 (1980)	**RP 127** Y 480 (1984)
RP 104 Y 407 (1974)	**RP 116** Y 466 (1980)	**RP 128** Y 481 (1984)
RP 105 Y 408 (1974)	**RP 118** Y 468 (1980)	**RP 129** Y 482 (1984)
RP 106 Y 410 (1974)	**RP 119** Y 470 (1980)	**RP 130** Y 483 (1985)
RP 108 Y 452 (1975)	**RP 120** Y 471 (1980)	**RP 131** Y 484 (1985)
RP 109 Y 456 (1975)	**RP 121** Y 472 (1984)	**RP 132** Y 485 (1985)
RP 110 Y 458 (1975)	**RP 122** Y 473 (1981)	**RP 133** Y 486 (1985)
RP 111 Y 460 (1975)	**RP 123** Y 467 (1981)	**RP 134** Y 487 (1985)
RP 112 Y 462 (1975)	**RP 124** Y 477 (1981)	

Displacement, tons: 120 full load
Dimensions, feet (metres): 64.9 × 17.1 × 6.9 *(19.8 × 5.2 × 2.1)*
Main machinery: 1 Fiat diesel; 368 hp *(270 kW)*; 1 shaft
Speed, knots: 9.5

Comment: *RP 101—124* built by Visitini, Dorada 1972-81. *RP 125—134* are larger tugs as shown in details.

RP 129　　　　　　　　　　*11/2004, Declerck/Cracco* / 1043182

RP 109　　　　　　　　　　*3/2004, Giorgio Ghiglione* / 1044377

ARMY

Notes: The following units are operated by the 'Serenissima Amphibious Regiment' in the Venice Lagoons area. EIG means Italian Army Craft and is part of the hull number. Four LCM (EIG 28—31), 60 tons; two LCVP (EIG 26, 27), 13 tons; four recce craft (EIG 32, 33, 48, 49), 5 tons; two command craft (EIG 208, 210), 21.5 tons; one rescue tug (EIG 209), 45 tons; one inshore tanker (EIG 44), 95 tons; one ambulance and rescue craft (EIG 142) and about 70 minor craft (ferries, barges, river boats, rigid inflatable raiders).

ARMY CRAFT *7/1993, van Ginderen Collection* / 0075865

GOVERNMENT MARITIME FORCES

Notes: Consideration has been given to combine all these forces into one Coast Guard.

CUSTOMS (SERVIZIO NAVALE GUARDIA DI FINANZA)

Notes: (1) This force is operated by the Ministry of Finance but in time of war would come under the command of the Marina Militare. It is divided into 16 naval stations, 30 operational sectors and 28 squadrons. Their task is to patrol ports, lakes and rivers. The total manpower is 5,400. Nearly all the larger craft are armed. There are 12 P-166 and 3 ATR 42 patrol aircraft plus 53 Hughes NH 500, 21 Agusta A 109 and 18 Agusta Bell AB 412 helicopters.
(2) A contract for 25—30 m craft to replace the Meatini class is expected in 2006.
(3) In addition to the classes detailed, there is a large number of smaller (under 15 m) craft. These include: 82 V 5500 class, 34 V 5800 class, 4 V 5900 class, 2 V 5300 class, 8 V 4000 class, 14 V 2000 class, 86 VAI 200 class, 5 VAI 500 class and 6 VAI 400 class.

ATR-42 *7/2003, Adolfo Ortigueira Gil* / 0570665

1 TRAINING SHIP (AX)

GIORGIO CINI

Displacement, tons: 800 full load
Dimensions, feet (metres): 172.2 × 32.8 × 9.5 *(54.0 × 10.0 × 2.9)*
Main machinery: 1 Fiat B306-SS diesel; 1,500 hp *(1.1 MW)*; 1 shaft
Speed, knots: 14. **Range, n miles:** 800 at 14 kt
Radars: Navigation: 2 BX-732; I-band.

Comment: Former merchant navy training ship acquired in 1981 for training role.

GIORGIO CINI *3/2002, Adolfo Ortigueira Gil* / 0570670

3 ANTONIO ZARA CLASS (PB)

Name	No	Builders	Commissioned
ANTONIO ZARA	P 01	Fincantieri, Muggiano	23 Feb 1990
GIUSEPPE VIZZARI	P 02	Fincantieri, Muggiano	27 Apr 1990
GIOVANNI DENARO	P 03	Fincantieri, Muggiano	20 Mar 1998

Displacement, tons: 340 full load
Dimensions, feet (metres): 167 × 24.6 × 6.2 *(51 × 7.5 × 1.9)*
Main machinery: 2 GMT BL 230.12 M diesels; 5,956 hp(m) *(4.38 MW)* sustained; 2 shafts
  4 MTU 16V 396 TB94 diesels; 13,029 hp(m) *(9.58 MW)* sustained; 2 shafts (P 03)
Speed, knots: 27; 35 (P 03). **Range, n miles:** 3,800 at 15 kt
Complement: 33 (3 officers)
Guns: 1 or 2 Breda 30 mm/70 (single or twin). 2—7.62 mm MGs.
Weapons control: Selenia Pegaso or AESN Medusa (P 03) optronic director.
Radars: Surface search: Gemant 2 ARPA and SPN 749; I-band.

Comment: Similar to the Ratcharit class built for Thailand in 1976-79. First pair ordered in August 1987. Third ordered in October 1995 with more powerful engines and with a modified armament of a single 30 mm gun with a Medusa optronic director. All are being fitted with an infra-red search and surveillance sensor (AMS SVIR).

ANTONIO ZARA *6/2001, L-G Nilsson* / 0130338

7 + 2 MAZZEI CLASS (PB/YXT)

Name	No	Builders	Commissioned
MAZZEI	G 01	Intermarine, Sarzana	Apr 1998
VACCARO	G 02	Intermarine, Sarzana	May 1998
DI BARTOLO	G 03	Intermarine, Sarzana	Oct 2003
AVALLONE	G 04	Intermarine, Sarzana	Dec 2003
OLTRAMONTI	G 05	Intermarine, Sarzana	Apr 2004
BARBARISO	G 06	Intermarine, Sarzana	2005
PAOLINI	G 07	Intermarine, Sarzana	2005

Displacement, tons: 115 full load
Dimensions, feet (metres): 116.5 × 24.8 × 3.6 *(35.5 × 7.6 × 1.1)*
Main machinery: 2 MTU 16V 396 TB94 diesels; 5,800 hp(m) *(4.26 MW)* sustained; 2 shafts
Speed, knots: 35. **Range, n miles:** 700 at 18 kt
Complement: 17 plus 18 trainees
Guns: 1 Breda Mauser 30 mm/70. 2—7.62 mm MGs.
Weapons control: Elsag Medusa optronic director.
Radars: Surface search: GEM 3072A ARPA; I-band.
Navigation: GEM 1410; I-band.

Comment: Based on the Bigliani class but with an extended hull. G 01 and G 02 used as training ships. G 03—07 are patrol craft. All are being fitted with an infra-red search and surveillance sensor (AMS SVIR). Two further craft are on order.

MAZZEI *7/2005*, Marco Ghiglino* / 1153211

24 + 5 BIGLIANI CLASS (PB)

OTTONELLI G 78	SMALTO G 84	LAGANÀ G 116	LA SPINA G 122
BARLETTA G 79	FORTUNA G 85	SANNA G 117	SALONE G 123
BIGLIANI G 80	BUONOCORE G 86	INZUCCHI G 118	CAVATORTO G 124
CAVAGLIA G 81	SQUITIERI G 87	VITALI G 119	FUSCO G 125
GALIANO G 82	LA MALFA G 88	CALABRESE G 120	— G 126
MACCHI G 83	ROSATI G 89	URSO G 121	— G 127

Displacement, tons: 87 full load
Dimensions, feet (metres): 86.6 × 23 × 3.6 *(26.4 × 7 × 1.1)*
Main machinery: 2 MTU 16V 396 TB94 diesels; 6,850 hp(m) *(5.12 MW)* sustained; 2 shafts
Speed, knots: 42. **Range, n miles:** 770 at 18 kt
Complement: 12
Guns: 1 Breda Mauser 30 mm/80. 2—7.62 mm MGs.
Combat data systems: AMS IPNS.
Weapons control: Elsag Medusa Mk 4 optronic director.
Radars: Surface search: GEM 3072A ARPA; I-band.
Navigation: GEM 1410; I-band.

Comment: First eight built by Crestitalia and delivered from October 1987 to September 1992. Three more were ordered from Crestitalia/Intermarine in October 1994 and were delivered from December 1996 to April 1997. A fourth was delivered in late 1999. There are minor structural differences between Series I (G 80-81), Series II (G 82-87) and Series III (G 78-79, G 88-89). Twelve series IV (G 116-127) craft ordered from Intermarine, Sarzana, for delivery in 2004-06. These include Kevlar armour and are fitted with a remote-control Breda 12.7 mm gun and 40 mm grenade launcher. All are being fitted with an infra-red search and surveillance sensor (AMS SVIR). A further five craft (G 128-132) have been ordered.

SANNA *1/2005*, Giorgio Ghiglione* / 1153238

26 CORRUBIA CLASS (PBF)

CORRUBIA G 90	**FAIS** G 97	**APRUZZI** G 104	**LETIZIA** G 110
GIUDICE G 91	**FELICIANI** G 98	**BALLALI** G 105	**MAZZARELLA** G 111
ALBERTI G 92	**GARZONI** G 99	**BOVIENZO** G 106	**NIOI** G 112
ANGELINI G 93	**LIPPI** G 100	**CARRECA** G 107	**PARTIPILO** G 113
CAPPELLETTI G 94	**LOMBARDI** G 101	**CONVERSANO** G 108	**PULEO** G 114
CIORLIERI G 95	**MICCOLI** G 102	**INZERILLI** G 109	**ZANNOTTI** G 115
D'AMATO G 96	**TREZZA** G 103		

Displacement, tons: 92 full load
Dimensions, feet (metres): 87.9 × 24.9 × 3.9 *(26.8 × 7.6 × 1.2)*
Main machinery: 2 Isotta Fraschini ID 36 SS 16V diesels; 6,400 hp(m) *(4.7 MW)*; 2 shafts (G 90—91)
2 MTU 16V 396 TB94; 5,800 hp(m) *(4.26 MW)* sustained; 2 shafts (G 92—103)
Speed, knots: 43
Range, n miles: 700 at 20 kt
Complement: 12 (1 officer)
Guns: 1 Breda Mauser 30 mm/70 (G 90—103). 1 Astra 20 mm (G 104—115). 2—7.62 mm MGs.
Weapons control: Elsag Medusa optronic director.
Radars: Surface search: GEM 3072A ARPA; I-band.
Navigation: GEM 1210; I-band.

Comment: First two built by Cantieri del Golfo, Gaeta and delivered in 1990. Others built by Cantieri del Golfo (G 92-100), and Crestitalia (G 101—103), and Intermarine from 1995 onwards. G 115 completed in 1999. There are minor structural differences between the first series (G 90—91), the second series (G 92—103) and the third batch (G 104—115). All are being fitted with an infra-red search and surveillance sensor (AMS SVIR).

CONVERSANO *6/2005*, Marco Ghiglino* / 1153210

24 MEATINI CLASS

G 13-66 series

Displacement, tons: 40 full load
Dimensions, feet (metres): 65.9 × 17.1 × 3.3 *(20.1 × 5.2 × 1)*
Main machinery: 2 CRM 18D/52 diesels; 2,500 hp(m) *(1.84 MW)*; 2 shafts
Speed, knots: 34
Range, n miles: 550 at 20 kt
Complement: 11 (1 officer)
Guns: 1—12.7 mm MG.
Radars: Surface search: 1 GEM 1210; I-band.

Comment: Fifty-six of the class built from 1970 to 1978. Numbers are reducing. Replacement by new craft is in progress.

DARIDA *4/2004, Giorgio Ghiglione* / 1044378

36 V 5000/6000 CLASS (FAST PATROL CRAFT) (HSIC)

V 5000-5020	**V 5100**	**V 6000-6012**	**V 6100**

Displacement, tons: 16 (V 6000), 27 (V 5000) full load
Dimensions, feet (metres): 53.8 × 9.2 × 2.6 *(16.4 × 2.8 × 0.8)*
Main machinery: 4 Seatek 6-4V-10D diesels; 2,856 hp(m) *(2.13 MW)* sustained; 4 surface-piercing propellers
2 MTU 8V 396 TE94 diesels (V 5000)
Speed, knots: 70 (V 6000); 52 (V 5000)
Complement: 4
Radars: Surface search: I-band.

Comment: V 6003-6012 were delivered in 2002-03. V 6001-6002 are smaller prototype craft with three engines and a top speed of 64 kt.

V 6006 *6/2005*, Marco Ghiglino* / 1153209

V 5006 *6/2001, Guardia di Finanzia* / 0130143

33 V 600 FALCO CLASS (FAST PATROL CRAFT) (PCF)

V 600 series

Displacement, tons: 4 full load
Dimensions, feet (metres): 33.5 × 9.2 × 2.6 *(10.2 × 2.8 × 0.8)*
Main machinery: 2 VM MD 706 diesels
Speed, knots: 54
Range, n miles: 200 at 33 kt
Complement: 4
Radars: Surface search: I-band.

Comment: FB design RIB designed for high-speed interception work. First prototype delivered in 2001.

V 607 *5/2005*, B Prézelin* / 1153237

POLICE (SERVIZIO NAVALE CARABINIERI)

Notes: (1) The Carabinieri established its maritime force in 1969 and has some 600 personnel. There are 179 craft in service or building which operate in coastal waters within the 3 mile limit and in inshore waters. Craft currently in service include: 20—800 class of 28 tons; 4—700 class of 22 tons; 6—600 class of 12 tons; 27 N 500 class of 6 tons; 3 S 500 class of 18 tons; 65—200 class of 2 tons, 28 minor craft and 30 RHIBs.
Most are capable of 20 to 25 kt except the 800 class at 35 kt.
(2) There is also a Sea Police Force of the State. All craft have POLIZIA written on the side. Vessels include 37 Squalo class of 14 tons, 4 Nelson class of 11 tons, 7 Intermarine class of 8.4 tons, 37 Crestitalia class of 6 tons and 25 Aquamaster/Drago classes of 3 tons. Speeds vary between 23 and 45 kt.
(3) 59—700 class are on order. These are to replace other coastal craft by 2012.

820 *9/2005*, P Marsan* / 1153235

COAST GUARD (GUARDIA COSTIERA—CAPITANERIE DI PORTO)

Notes: This is a force which is affiliated with the Marina Militare under whose command it would be placed in an emergency. The Coast Guard denomination was given after the Sea Protection Law in 1988. The force is responsible for the Italian Maritime Rescue Co-ordination Centre (MRCC) in Rome and 13 sub-centres (MRSC). The SAR network consists of 109 stations, three air stations and one helicopter station. All vessels have a red diagonal stripe painted on the white hull and many are armed with 7.62 mm MGs. There are some 10,500 naval personnel including 1,200 officers of which about half are doing national service. Ranks are the same as the Navy. In addition to the Saettia class (detailed separately), the following craft are in service. All have the prefix CP (Capitaneria di Porto):

(a) SAR craft: *Giulio Ingianni* CP 409 (205 tons); *Antonio Scialoja* CP 406, *Michele Lolini* CP 407, *Mario Grabar* CP 408 (136 tons), *Oreste Cavallari* CP 401, *Renato Pennetti* CP 402, *Walter Fachin* CP 403, *Gaetano Magliano* CP 404 (100 tons), *Bruno Gregoretti* CP 312 (65 tons); *Dante Novaro* CP 313 (57 tons); CP 314-318 (45 tons).

(b) Fast patrol craft: CP 265-292 (54 tons), CP 262 (30 tons), CP 246-253 (23 tons), CP 254-260 (22 tons), CP 454-456 (19.4 tons).

(c) Inshore Patrol craft: 408 craft of between 3 and 15 tons. CP 2201-2205 (15 tons), CP 2084-2103 (12 tons), CP 2001-2009, 2011-2015, 2017-2083, 2201-2205 (15 tons), CP 829-831, 836-838 (14.6 tons); CP 825-828, 832-835 (12.5 tons); CP 839, 862, 872-881, 884-889 (13.3 tons), CP 863, 871, 882-883, 890-892 (10 tons); CP 814-824 (12.5 tons), CP 801-813 (9 tons), CP 701-712 (6 tons), CP 512-523, 540-564 (7.5 tons); CP 6001-6022 (3.7 tons), CP 1001-1006 (5.4 tons), CP 601-605 (3 tons), CG 101 class, 64 CG 20 RHIB.

(d) Aircraft include 14 Piaggio P 166 DL3-SEM and three ATR 42MP maritime patrol and 12 Griffon AB-412-CP helicopters.

(e) CP 451 is a 1,278 ton training ship (ex-US ATF *Bannock*); *Barbara* CP 452 (190 tons) is a former naval Range Safety patrol craft which recommissioned in late 1999.

(f) CP 210 and CP 211 are airboats used for SAR in the Venice Lagoon area.

CP 557   *5/2005*, Ann Saunders* / 1153236

6 SAETTIA CLASS (SAR)

Name	No	Builders	Commissioned
SAETTIA	CP 901	Fincantieri, Muggiano	Dec 1985
UBALDO DICIOTTI	CP 902	Fincantieri, Muggiano	20 July 2002
LUIGI DATTILO	CP 903	Fincantieri, Muggiano	28 Nov 2002
MICHELE FIORILLO	CP 904	Fincantieri, Muggiano	7 Apr 2003
ANTONIO PELUSO	CP 905	Fincantieri, Muggiano	2 July 2003
ORAZIO CORSI	CP 906	Fincantieri, Muggiano	7 Feb 2004

Displacement, tons: 427 full load
Dimensions, feet (metres): 173.3 × 26.6 × 6.6 *(52.8 × 8.1 × 2.0)*
Main machinery: 4 Isotta Fraschini V1716T2MSD diesels; 12,660 hp *(9.44 MW)*; 4 cp props; bow thruster
Speed, knots: 29. **Range, n miles:** 1,800 at 18 kt
Complement: 30 (2 officers)
Guns: 1 Oerliken 20 mm/70.
Weapons control: Eurocontrol optronic sensor.
Radars: Surface search: SPN 753; I-band.

Comment: Details are for CP 902-906 which were ordered on 29 June 2000. CP 901 was built as an attack missile craft demonstrator by Fincantieri in 1984 and was later taken over by the Coast Guard on 20 July 1999. 30 tons lighter and with some structural differences, she is powered by 4 MTU 16V538TB93 engines providing 17,598 hp and a top speed of 40 kt. She is armed with an Otobreda 25 mm gun. All the vessels form a 'Squadrilla' based at Messina, Sicily, whose role is fishery protection and immigration control.

ANTONIO SCIALOJA   *8/2004, Paolo Marsan* / 1044379

CP 269   *7/2005*, Marco Ghiglino* / 1153208

MICHELE FIORILLO   *5/2005*, Marco Ghiglino* / 1153207

Jamaica

Country Overview

Jamaica gained independence in 1962; the British monarch, represented by a governor-general, is head of state. The island country (area 4,244 square miles), third-largest of the Greater Antilles, is situated south of Cuba and has a 552 n mile coastline with the Caribbean Sea. Kingston is the capital, largest town and principal port. An archipelagic state, territorial seas (12 n miles) are claimed. A 200 n mile Exclusive Economic Zone (EEZ) has been claimed but the limits are not defined.

Headquarters Appointments

Commanding Officer Coast Guard:
   Commander Sydney R Innis, MVO

Aviation

Three fixed-wing aircraft (Cessna 21-M, Pilatus-Britten-Norman BN-2A and a Beech 100) are used for coastal patrol and seven helicopters (three Bell 412 and four Eurocopter AS 355N) are used for SAR.

Personnel

(a) 2006: 216 (18 officers) Regulars
(b) 55 (14 officers) Reserve Forces

Bases

Main: HMJS *Cagway*, Port Royal
Coastguard: Discovery Bay, Pedro Cays, Port Antonio, Montego Bay and Black River

---

COAST GUARD

Notes: There are also two Guardian 27 Boston Whalers CG 091 and CG 092 built in 1992.

2 + 1 DAMEN STAN PATROL 4207 (PB)

Name	No	Builders	Commissioned
CORNWALL	421	Damen Shipyard, Gorinchem	27 Oct 2005
MIDDLESEX	—	Damen Shipyard, Gorinchem	7 Apr 2006
SURREY	—	Damen Shipyard, Gorinchem	June 2006

Displacement, tons: 205
Dimensions, feet (metres): 140.4 × 23.3 × 8.3 *(42.8 × 7.11 × 2.52)*
Main machinery: 2 Caterpillar 3516B DI-TA; 5,600 hp *(4.17 MW)*; 2 cp props
Speed, knots: 26
Complement: To be announced
Guns: To be announced

Comment: Contract signed on 21 April 2004 with Damen Shipyard Gorinchem for construction of three Damen 4207 offshore patrol craft. *Cornwall* delivered in late 2005 and following vessels at six month intervals. Details are based on those in UK Customs service.

MIDDLESEX   *11/2005*, A A de Kruijf* / 1151117

1 FORT CLASS (PB)

Name	No	Builders	Commissioned
FORT CHARLES	P 7	Sewart Seacraft Inc, Berwick	Sep 1974

Displacement, tons: 130 full load
Dimensions, feet (metres): 116 × 22 × 7 *(35.3 × 6.7 × 2.1)*
Main machinery: 2 MTU 16V 538 TB90 diesels; 6,000 hp(m) *(4.41 MW)* sustained; 2 shafts
Speed, knots: 32. **Range, n miles:** 1,200 at 18 kt
Complement: 16 (3 officers)
Guns: 1 Oerlikon 20 mm. 2 – 12.7 mm MGs.
Radars: Surface search: Sperry 4016; I-band.

Comment: Of all-aluminium construction, launched July 1974. Underwent refit at Jacksonville, Florida, in 1980-81 which included extensive modifications to the bow resulting in increased length. Refitted again in 1987-88. Accommodation for 18 soldiers and may be used as 18-bed mobile hospital in an emergency. To be decommissioned as new Damen craft enter service.

FORT CHARLES   *6/1999, JDFCG* / 0080125

1 HERO CLASS (PB)

Name	No	Builders	Commissioned
PAUL BOGLE	P 8	Lantana Boatyard Inc, FL	17 Sep 1985

Displacement, tons: 93 full load
Dimensions, feet (metres): 105 × 20.6 × 7 *(32 × 6.3 × 2.1)*
Main machinery: 3 MTU 8V 396 TB93 diesels; 3,270 hp(m) *(2.4 MW)* sustained; 3 shafts
Speed, knots: 32
Complement: 20 (4 officers)
Guns: 1 Oerlikon 20 mm. 2 – 12.7 mm MGs.
Radars: Surface search: Furuno 2400; I-band.
Navigation: Sperry 4016; I-band.

Comment: Of all-aluminium construction, launched in 1984. *Paul Bogle* was originally intended for Honduras as the third of the Guardian class. Similar to patrol craft in Honduras and Grenada navies. Refitted in March 1998 at Network Marine, Louisiana and further refitted in 2004-05 by Damen Shipyards, Gorinchem.

PAUL BOGLE   *6/1999, JDFCG* / 0080126

2 POINT CLASS (PB)

Name	No	Builders	Commissioned
SAVANNAH POINT (ex-*Point Nowell*)	CG 251 (ex-82363)	CG Yard, Maryland	1 June 1967
BELMONT POINT (ex-*Point Barnes*)	CG 252 (ex-82371)	J Martinac, Tacoma	21 Apr 1970

Displacement, tons: 67 full load
Dimensions, feet (metres): 83 × 17.2 × 5.8 *(25.3 × 5.3 × 1.8)*
Main machinery: 2 Caterpillar diesels; 1,600 hp *(1.19 MW)*; 2 shafts
Speed, knots: 22. **Range, n miles:** 1,200 at 8 kt
Complement: 10
Guns: 2 – 12.7 mm MGs.
Radars: Surface search: Hughes/Furuno SPS-73; I-band.

Comment: Transferred from US Coast Guard on 15 October 1999 and 21 January 2000 respectively. To be decommissioned as new Damen craft enter service.

SAVANNAH POINT   *10/1999, JDFCG* / 0080127

3 FAST COASTAL INTERCEPTORS (PBF)

CG 131, 132, 133

Displacement, tons: 11 full load
Dimensions, feet (metres): 44 × 10.5 × 3 *(13.4 × 3.2 × 0.92)*
Main machinery: 2 Caterpillar 3196 diesels; 1,140 hp *(850 kW)*; two twin disc waterjets
Speed, knots: 37. **Range, n miles:** 400 at 20 kt
Complement: 6
Guns: 1 – 7.62 mm M60 MG.
Radars: Surface search: Raytheon Pathfinder; I-band.

Comments: Aluminium construction. Built by Silver Ships, Mobile, Alabama. Funded by the US State Department, Narcotics Affairs Section. Delivered in March 2003.

CG 131   *6/2003, JDFCG* / 0568335

4 DAUNTLESS CLASS (INSHORE PATROL CRAFT) (PB)

CG 121	CG 122	CG 123	CG 124

Displacement, tons: 11 full load
Dimensions, feet (metres): 40 × 14 × 4.3 *(12.2 × 4.3 × 1.3)*
Main machinery: 2 Caterpillar 3208TA diesels; 870 hp *(650 kW)*; 2 shafts
Speed, knots: 27. **Range, n miles:** 600 at 18 kt
Complement: 5
Guns: 1 – 7.62 mm MG (can be carried).
Radars: Surface search: Raytheon 40X; I-band.

Comment: Delivered in September and November 1992, January 1993 and May 1994. Built by SeaArk Marine, Monticello. Aluminium construction. Craft of this class have been distributed throughout the Caribbean under FMS funding.

CG 121   *10/2000* / 0121383

3 OFFSHORE PERFORMANCE TYPE
(INSHORE PATROL CRAFT) (HSIC)

CG 101	CG 102	CG 103

Displacement, tons: 3 full load
Dimensions, feet (metres): 33 × 8 × 1.8 *(10.1 × 2.4 × 0.6)*
Main machinery: 2 Johnson OMC outboards; 450 hp *(336 kW)*
Speed, knots: 48
Complement: 3
Guns: 1 – 7.62 mm MG (can be carried).
Radars: Surface search: Raytheon 40X; I-band.

Comment: Delivered in April 1992. Built by Offshore Performance Marine, Miami. Used in the anti-narcotics role.

CG 102   *5/1992, JDFCG* / 0506022

Japan
MARITIME SELF-DEFENCE FORCE (MSDF)
KAIJOU JIEI-TAI

Country Overview

Japan is a constitutional monarchy in East Asia that comprises four main islands: Hokkaido, Honshu, Shikoku and Kyushu. It also includes the Ryukyu Islands to the southwest and more than 1,000 lesser islands. The sovereignty of the South Kuril Islands (Etorofu, Kunashiri, Shikotan and the Habomai Group) is disputed with Russia. With an overall area of 145,850 square miles it has a coastline of 16,065 n miles, with the Pacific Ocean, Sea of Japan, the La Perouse Strait (which separates it from Sakhalin Island), Sea of Okhotsk, East China Sea and the Korea Strait (which separates it from South Korea). The capital and largest city is Tokyo while the principal ports are Yokohama, Osaka and Kobe. Territorial seas of 12 n miles (3 n miles in Korea Strait) are claimed. A 200 n mile EEZ has also been claimed but the limits have not been defined.

Headquarters Appointments

Chief of Staff, Maritime Self-Defence Force:
  Admiral Takashi Saitou
Commander-in-Chief, Self-Defence Fleet:
  Vice Admiral Kazunari Douke

Senior Appointments

Commander Fleet Escort Force:
  Vice Admiral Nobuharu Yasui
Commander Fleet Air Force:
  Vice Admiral Keiji Akahoshi
Commander Fleet Submarine Force:
  Vice Admiral Masahiko Sugimoto

Diplomatic Representation

Defence (Naval) Attaché in London:
  Captain Takaki Mizuma

Personnel

2006: 45,806 (including Naval Air) plus 3,530 civilians

Organisation of the Major Surface Units of Japan (MSDF)

In addition to the Escort Force, there are two Submarine Flotillas (Kure and Yokosuka), one Minesweeper Flotilla (Yokosuka), which are to be merged, and five District Flotillas (Yokosuka, Maizuru, Ohminato, Sasebo and Kure). The District Flotillas are comprised of three or five destroyers, an AMS or a LSU and a number of MSC and patrol craft.

Fleet Escort Force (Yokosuka)
  Tachikaze (DDG 168) Flagship

Escort Flotilla 1 (Yokosuka)
  Shirane (DDH 143)
1st Destroyer Division (Y)
  Murasame (DD 101)
  Harusame (DD 102)
  Ikazuchi (DD 107)
5th Destroyer Division (Y)
  Takanami (DD 110)
  Oonami (DD 111)
61st Destroyer Division (Y)
  Hatakaze (DDG 171)
  Kirishima (DDG 174)
Escort Flotilla 3 (Maizuru)
  Haruna (DDH 141)
3rd Destroyer Division (M)
  Suzunami (DD 114)
  Amagiri (DD 154)
7th Destroyer Division (O)
  Yuugiri (DD 153)
  Hamagiri (DD 155)
  Setogiri (DD 156)
63rd Destroyer Division (M)
  Shimakaze (DDG 172)
  Myoukou (DDG 175)

Escort Flotilla 2 (Sasebo)
  Kurama (DDH 144)
2nd Destroyer Division (S)
  Yuudachi (DD 103)
  Makinami (DD 112)
  Sawagiri (DD 157)
6th Destroyer Division (S)
  Kirisame (DD 104)
  Ariake (DD 109)
62nd Destroyer Division (S)
  Sawakaze (DDG 170)
  Kongou (DDG 173)
Escort Flotilla 4 (Kure)
  Hiei (DDH 142)
4th Destroyer Division (K)
  Inazuma (DD 105)
  Samidare (DD 106)
  Akebono (DD 108)
8th Destroyer Division (K)
  Sazanami (DD 113)
  Umigiri (DD 158)
64th Destroyer Division (S)
  Asakaze (DDG 169)
  Choukai (DDG 176)

Bases

Naval-Yokosuka, Kure, Sasebo, Maizuru, Ohminato
NavalAir-Atsugi, Hachinohe, Iwakuni, Kanoya, Komatsujima, Naha, Ozuki, Ohminato, Ohmura, Shimofusa, Tateyama, Tokushima, Ioujima

Coast Defence

The Army controls 92 SSM-1 truck-mounted sextuple launchers.

Strength of the Fleet (31 March 2006)

Type	Active (Auxiliary)	Building (Projected)
Submarines	15 (2)	4 (1)
Destroyers	44	3 (1)
Frigates	9	—
Patrol Forces	9	—
LSTs	3	—
LCUs	4	—
LCACs	6	—
Landing Craft (LCM)	12	—
MCM Tenders/Controllers	4	—
Minesweepers-Ocean	3	(1)
Minesweepers-Coastal	24	3
Major Auxiliaries	33	(2)

New Construction Programme (Warships)

2004 1—13,500 ton DDH, 1—2,900 ton SS, 1—570 ton MSC.
2005 1—2,900 ton SS, 1—570 ton MSC, 2—980 ton AMS.
2006 1—13,500 ton DDH, 1—2,900 ton SS, 1—570 ton MSC

Naval Air Force

16 Air Patrol Sqns: P-3C, EP-3, OP-3C, SH-60J/K
Six Air Training Sqns: P-3C, YS-11, TC-90, T-5, OH-6D, SH-60J
One Air Training Support Squadron: U-36A, UP-3D, LC-90
One Transport Sqn: YS-11, LC-90
One MCM Sqn: MH-53E
Air Training Command (Shimofusa)
Air Wings at Kanoya (Wing 1), Hachinohe (Wing 2), Atsugi (Wing 4), Naha (Wing 5), Tateyama (Wing 21), Ohmura (Wing 22), Iwakuni (Wing 31)

DELETIONS and CONVERSIONS

Submarines

2003 *Okishio*
2004 *Akishio*
2005 *Takeshio*
2006 *Sachisio, Yukishio* (converted), *Hamashio*

Destroyers

2003 *Kikuzuki*
2005 *Asagiri* (converted), *Yuugumo*

Frigates

2003 *Noshiro*

Amphibious Forces

2005 *Nemuro*

Mine Warfare Forces

2004 *Yakushima*
2005 *Himeshima, Moroshima*
2006 *Hahajima, Ogishima* (converted)

Auxiliaries

2003 *Aokumo*
2005 *Sagami,* YF 2075

Training Ships

2005 *Akigumo*

PENNANT LIST

Submarines—Patrol

SS 501	— (bldg)
SS 502	— (bldg)
SS 503	— (bldg)
SS 583	Harushio
SS 584	Natsushio
SS 585	Hayashio
SS 586	Arashio
SS 587	Wakashio
SS 588	Fuyushio
SS 590	Oyashio
SS 591	Michishio
SS 592	Uzushio
SS 593	Makishio
SS 594	Isoshio
SS 595	Narushio
SS 596	Kuroshio
SS 597	Takashio
SS 598	Yaeshio
SS 599	Setoshio (bldg)

Submarines—Auxiliary

TSS 3601	Asashio
TSS 3605	Yukishio

Destroyers

DD 101	Murasame
DD 102	Harusame
DD 103	Yuudachi
DD 104	Kirisame
DD 105	Inazuma
DD 106	Samidare
DD 107	Ikazuchi
DD 108	Akebono
DD 109	Ariake
DD 110	Takanami
DD 111	Oonami
DD 112	Makinami
DD 113	Sazanami
DD 114	Suzunami
DD 122	Hatsuyuki
DD 123	Shirayuki
DD 124	Mineyuki
DD 125	Sawayuki

DD 126	Hamayuki
DD 127	Isoyuki
DD 128	Haruyuki
DD 129	Yamayuki
DD 130	Matsuyuki
DD 131	Setoyuki
DD 132	Asayuki
DDH 141	Haruna
DDH 142	Hiei
DDH 143	Shirane
DDH 144	Kurama
DDH 145	— (bldg)
DD 153	Yuugiri
DD 154	Amagiri
DD 155	Hamagiri
DD 156	Setogiri
DD 157	Sawagiri
DD 158	Umigiri
DDG 168	Tachikaze
DDG 169	Asakaze
DDG 170	Sawakaze
DDG 171	Hatakaze
DDG 172	Shimakaze
DDG 173	Kongou
DDG 174	Kirishima
DDG 175	Myoukou
DDG 176	Choukai
DDG 177	Atago (bldg)
DDG 178	— (bldg)

Frigates

DE 226	Ishikari
DE 227	Yuubari
DE 228	Yuubetsu
DE 229	Abukuma
DE 230	Jintsu
DE 231	Ooyodo
DE 232	Sendai
DE 233	Chikuma
DE 234	Tone

Patrol Forces

PG 821	PG 01
PG 822	PG 02

PG 823	PG 03
PG 824	Hayabusa
PG 825	Wakataka
PG 826	Ootaka
PG 827	Kumataka
PG 828	Umitaka
PG 829	Shirataka

Minehunters/Sweepers—Ocean

MSO 301	Yaeyama
MSO 302	Tsushima
MSO 303	Hachijyo

Minesweepers—Coastal

MSC 668	Yurishima
MSC 669	Hikoshima
MSC 670	Awashima
MSC 671	Sakushima
MSC 672	Uwajima
MSC 673	Ieshima
MSC 674	Tsukishima
MSC 675	Maejima
MSC 676	Kumejima
MSC 677	Makishima
MSC 678	Tobishima
MSC 679	Yugeshima
MSC 680	Nagashima
MSC 681	Sugashima
MSC 682	Notojima
MSC 683	Tsunoshima
MSC 684	Naoshima
MSC 685	Toyoshima
MSC 686	Ukushima
MSC 687	Izushima
MSC 688	Aishima
MSC 689	Aoshima
MSC 690	Miyajima
MSC 691	Shishijima
MSC 692	Kuroshima (bldg)
MSC 693	— (bldg)
MSC 694	— (bldg)

MCM Tenders/Control Ships

MCL 725	Kamishima
MCL 726	Ogishima

MST 463	Uraga
MST 464	Bungo

Amphibious Forces

LCU 2001	Yusotei-Ichi-Go
LCU 2002	Yusotei-Ni-Go
LST 4001	Oosumi
LST 4002	Shimokita
LST 4003	Kunisaki
LSU 4171	Yura
LSU 4172	Noto

Submarine Depot/Rescue Ships

AS 405	Chiyoda
ASR 403	Chihaya

Fleet Support Ships

AOE 422	Towada
AOE 423	Tokiwa
AOE 424	Hamana
AOE 425	Mashuu
AOE 426	Oumi

Training Ships

TV 3508	Kashima
TV 3513	Shimayuki
TV 3515	Yamagiri
TV 3516	Asagiri

Training Support Ships

ATS 4202	Kurobe
ATS 4203	Tenryu
AMS 4301	Hiuchi
AMS 4302	Suou
AMS 4303	Amakusa
AMS 4304	— (bldg)
AMS 4305	— (bldg)

Cable Repair Ship

ARC 482	Muroto

PENNANT LIST

Icebreakers		Survey and Research Ships		Ocean Surveillance Ships		Tenders	
AGB 5002	Shirase	AGS 5102	Futami	AOS 5201	Hibiki	ASY 91	Hashidate
AGB 5003	— (bldg)	AGS 5103	Suma	AOS 5202	Harima	YDT 01-06	—
		AGS 5104	Wakasa				
		AGS 5105	Nichinan				
		ASE 6101	Kurihama				
		ASE 6102	Asuka				

SUBMARINES

0 + 2 (1) IMPROVED OYASHIO CLASS (SSK)

Name	No	Builders	Laid down	Launched	Commissioned
—	SS 502	Mitsubishi, Kobe	31 Mar 2005	Oct 2007	Mar 2009
—	SS 503	Mitsubishi, Kobe	2006	2008	2010

Displacement, tons: 2,900 standard; 4,200 dived
Dimensions, feet (metres): 275.6 × 29.9 × 25.9
  (84.0 × 9.1 × 7.9)
Main machinery: Diesel-stirling-electric; 2 diesels; 4 Kockums Stirling AIP; 1 motor; 1 shaft
Speed, knots: 20 dived; 12 surfaced
Range, n miles: To be announced
Complement: 65

Missiles: SSM: McDonnell Douglas Sub-Harpoon; active radar homing to 130 km *(70 n miles)* at 0.9 Mach; warhead 227 kg.
Torpedoes: 6—21 in *(533 mm)* bow tubes. Japanese Type 89; wire-guided (option); active/passive homing to 50 km *(27 n miles)* at 40/55 kt; warhead 267 kg. Type 80 ASW. SSM and torpedoes (total unknown).
Countermeasures: To be announced.
Weapons control: To be announced.
Radars: Surface search: JRS ZPS 6; I-band.

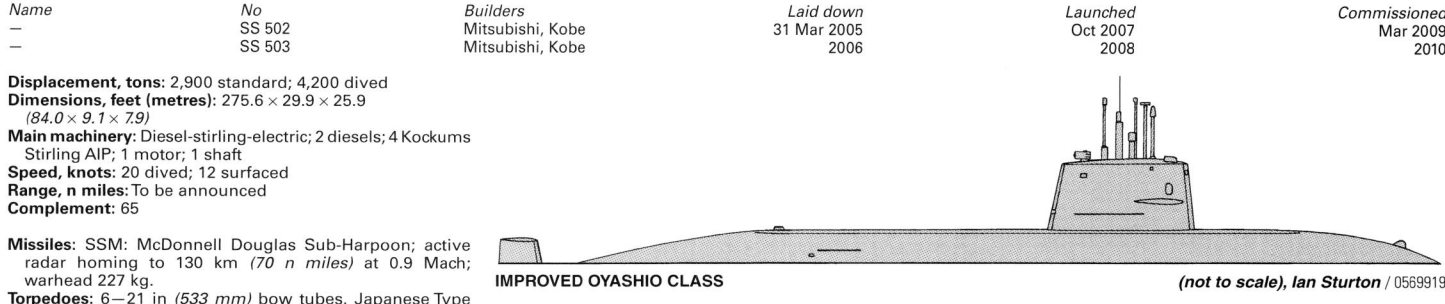

IMPROVED OYASHIO CLASS   *(not to scale), Ian Sturton* / 0569919

Sonars: Hughes/OKI ZQQ 5B/6; hull and flank arrays; active/passive search and attack; medium/low frequency. ZQR 1 (BQR 15). Towed array.

Programmes: First of new class authorised in FY04 budget, second in FY05 budget and third in FY06 budget.

Structure: The hull design incorporates the Swedish Stirling air-independent propulsion system. Components of this system are provided by Kockums for assembly by KHI.

1 YUUSHIO CLASS

Name	No	Builders	Laid down	Launched	Commissioned
YUKISHIO	TSS 3605 (ex-SS 581)	Mitsubishi, Kobe	11 Apr 1985	23 Jan 1987	11 Mar 1988

Displacement, tons: 2,250 standard; 2,900 dived
Dimensions, feet (metres): 249.3 × 32.5 × 24.3
  (76 × 9.9 × 7.4)
Main machinery: Diesel-electric; 2 Kawasaki V8V24/30ATL diesels; 6,800 hp(m) *(5 MW)*; 2 Fuji motors; 7,200 hp(m) *(5.3 MW)*; 1 shaft
Speed, knots: 12 surfaced; 20 dived
Complement: 75 (10 officers)

Missiles: SSM: McDonnell Douglas Sub-Harpoon; active radar homing to 130 km *(70 n miles)* at 0.9 Mach; warhead 227 kg.

Torpedoes: 6—21 in *(533 mm)* tubes amidships. Japanese Type 89; active/passive homing to 50 km *(27 n miles)*/ 38 km *(21 n miles)* at 40/55 kt; warhead 267 kg; depth to 900 m and Type 80 ASW. Total of 20 SSM and torpedoes.
Countermeasures: ESM: ZLR 5, 6; radar warning.
Radars: Surface search: JRC ZPS 5, 6; I-band.
Sonars: Hughes/Oki ZQQ 5 (modified BQS 4); bow-mounted; passive/active search and attack; medium/low frequency.
  ZQR 1 towed array similar to BQR 15 (in most of the class); passive search; very low frequency.

Programmes: First of class approved in FY75 and nine further commissioned by 1989.
Structure: An enlarged version of the Uzushio class with improved diving depth to 450 m *(1,470 ft)*. Double hull construction. The towed array is stowed in a conduit on the starboard side of the casing.
Operational: *Yukishio* was assigned as a training submarine on 9 March 2006. It is likely that the torpedo compartment has been converted into a training area. *Sachisio* decommissioned on 10 April 2006.

YUUSHIO CLASS   *7/2003, Hachiro Nakai* / 0570840

9 + 2 OYASHIO CLASS (SSK)

Name	No	Builders	Laid down	Launched	Commissioned
OYASHIO	SS 590	Kawasaki, Kobe	26 Jan 1994	15 Oct 1996	16 Mar 1998
MICHISHIO	SS 591	Mitsubishi, Kobe	16 Feb 1995	18 Sep 1997	10 Mar 1999
UZUSHIO	SS 592	Kawasaki, Kobe	6 Mar 1996	26 Nov 1998	9 Mar 2000
MAKISHIO	SS 593	Mitsubishi, Kobe	26 Mar 1997	22 Sep 1999	29 Mar 2001
ISOSHIO	SS 594	Kawasaki, Kobe	9 Mar 1998	27 Nov 2000	14 Mar 2002
NARUSHIO	SS 595	Mitsubishi, Kobe	2 Apr 1999	4 Oct 2001	3 Mar 2003
KUROSHIO	SS 596	Kawasaki, Kobe	27 Mar 2000	23 Oct 2002	8 Mar 2004
TAKASHIO	SS 597	Mitsubishi, Kobe	30 Jan 2001	1 Oct 2003	9 Mar 2005
YAESHIO	SS 598	Kawasaki, Kobe	15 Jan 2002	4 Nov 2004	9 Mar 2006
SETOSHIO	SS 599	Mitsubishi, Kobe	23 Jan 2003	5 Oct 2005	Mar 2007
—	SS 501	Kawasaki, Kobe	23 Feb 2004	Oct 2006	Mar 2008

Displacement, tons: 2,750 standard; 3,000 dived
Dimensions, feet (metres): 268 × 29.2 × 24.3 *(81.7 × 8.9 × 7.4)*
Main machinery: Diesel-electric; 2 Kawasaki 12V25S diesels; 5,520 hp(m) *(4.1 MW)*; 2 Kawasaki alternators; 3.7 MW; 2 Toshiba motors; 7,750 hp(m) *(5.7 MW)*; 1 shaft
Speed, knots: 12 surfaced; 20 dived
Complement: 70 (10 officers)

Missiles: SSM: McDonnell Douglas Sub-Harpoon; active radar homing to 130 km *(70 n miles)* at 0.9 Mach; warhead 227 kg.

Torpedoes: 6—21 in *(533 mm)* tubes; Type 89; wire-guided; active/passive homing to 50 km *(27 n miles)*/38 km *(21 n miles)* at 40/55 kt; warhead 267 kg and Type 80 ASW. Total of 20 SSM and torpedoes.
Countermeasures: ESM: NZLR-1B; radar warning.
Weapons control: SMCS type TFCS.
Radars: Surface search: JRC ZPS 6; I-band.
Sonars: Hughes/Oki ZQQ 5B/6; hull and flank arrays; active/passive search and attack; medium/low frequency.
ZQR 1 (BQR 15) towed array; passive search; very low frequency.

Programmes: First of a new class approved in the 1993 budget and then one a year up to FY03.
Structure: Fitted with large flank sonar arrays which are reported as the reason for the increase in displacement over the Harushio class. Double hull sections forward and aft and anechoic tiles on the fin. A new type of deck casing and faired fin are other distinguishing features. Diving depth 650 m *(2,130 ft)*.

YAESHIO   *11/2005*, Hachiro Nakai* / 1153251

MICHISHIO   *7/2005*, Hachiro Nakai* / 1153252

TAKASHIO   *3/2005*, Hachiro Nakai* / 1153253

7 HARUSHIO CLASS (SSK)

Name	No	Builders	Laid down	Launched	Commissioned
HARUSHIO	SS 583	Mitsubishi, Kobe	21 Apr 1987	26 July 1989	30 Nov 1990
NATSUSHIO	SS 584	Kawasaki, Kobe	8 Apr 1988	20 Mar 1990	20 Mar 1991
HAYASHIO	SS 585	Mitsubishi, Kobe	9 Dec 1988	17 Jan 1991	25 Mar 1992
ARASHIO	SS 586	Kawasaki, Kobe	8 Jan 1990	17 Mar 1992	17 Mar 1993
WAKASHIO	SS 587	Mitsubishi, Kobe	12 Dec 1990	22 Jan 1993	1 Mar 1994
FUYUSHIO	SS 588	Kawasaki, Kobe	12 Dec 1991	16 Feb 1994	7 Mar 1995
ASASHIO	TSS 3601 (ex-SS 589)	Mitsubishi, Kobe	24 Dec 1992	12 July 1995	12 Mar 1997

Displacement, tons: 2,450 (2,900, TSS 3601) standard; 3,200 (3,700, TSS 3601) dived
Dimensions, feet (metres): 252.6; 285.5 (TSS 3601) × 32.8 × 25.3 *(77; 87 × 10 × 7.7)*
Main machinery: Diesel-electric; 2 Kawasaki 12V25/25S diesels; 5,520 hp(m) *(4.1 MW)*; 2 Kawasaki alternators; 3.7 MW; 2 Fuji motors; 7,200 hp(m) *(5.3 MW)*; 1 shaft 4 Stirling engines (TSS 3601) Kockums V4-275R Mk 2; 348 hp *(260 kW)*
Speed, knots: 12 surfaced; 20 dived
Complement: 75 (10 officers); 70 (10 officers) (TS 3601)

Missiles: SSM: McDonnell Douglas Sub-Harpoon; active radar homing to 130 km *(70 n miles)* at 0.9 Mach; warhead 227 kg.

Torpedoes: 6—21 in *(533 mm)* tubes. Japanese Type 89; wire-guided (option); active/passive homing to 50 km *(27 n miles)*/38 km *(21 n miles)* at 40/55 kt; warhead 267 kg; depth to 900 m, and Type 80 ASW. Total of 20 SSM and torpedoes.
Countermeasures: ESM: NZLR-1; radar warning.
Radars: Surface search: JRC ZPS 6; I-band.
Sonars: Hughes/Oki ZQQ 5B; hull-mounted; active/passive search and attack; medium/low frequency.
ZQR 1 towed array similar to BQR 15; passive search; very low frequency.

Programmes: First approved in 1986 estimates and then one per year until 1992.
Structure: The slight growth in all dimensions is a natural evolution from the Yuushio class and includes more noise reduction, towed sonar and wireless aerials, as well as anechoic coating. Double hull construction. *Asashio* had a slightly larger displacement on build and a small cutback in the crew as a result of greater systems automation for machinery and snorting control. The hull was extended in 2001 to accommodate an AIP module (Stirling engine) which was fitted by Mitsubishi, Kobe. Diving depth 550 m *(1,800 ft)*.
Operational: A remote periscope viewer is fitted in *Asashio. Asashio* is an experimental submarine for test of AIP propulsion.

NATSUSHIO   *7/2005*, Hachiro Nakai* / 1153248

HARUSHIO   *7/2005*, Hachiro Nakai* / 1153249

WAKASHIO   *7/2005*, Hachiro Nakai* / 1153250

DESTROYERS

0 + 2 FUTURE DESTROYER CLASS (DDHM)

Name	No	Builders	Laid down	Launched	Commissioned
–	145	IHI Marine United, Yokohama	May 2006	Aug 2007	May 2009
–	146		2008	2009	Mar 2011

Displacement, tons: 13,500 standard; 18,000 full load
Dimensions, feet (metres): 646.3 × 108.3 × 31.8
(197.0 × 33.0 × 9.7)
Main machinery: COGAG; 4 LM 2500 gas turbines; 2 shafts
Speed, knots: 30.
Range, n miles: 6,000 at 20 kt
Complement: 322 (+25 HQ staff)

Missiles: SAM: Raytheon Sea Sparrow RIM-7P; Lockheed
Martin Marietta Mk 41 Mod 5 sixteen cell vertical launcher ❶;
semi-active radar homing to 14.6 km (8 n miles) at
2.5 Mach; warhead 39 kg.
A/S: Vertical launch ASROC.

Guns: 2 GE 20 mm/76 Sea Vulcan 20 ❷; 3 barrels
per mounting; 1,500 rds/min.
2–20 mm. 2–12.7 mm MGs.
Torpedoes: 6–324 mm (2 triple) HOS-303 tubes ❸.
Countermeasures: Decoys: 4 Hycor Mk 137 sextuple RBOC
chaff launchers.
ESM/ECM: NOLQ-3C.
Combat data system: Link 16.
Radars: Air search/Fire control: Melco FCS-3; G/H/I-band.
Navigation: JRC OPS-20C; I-band.
Sonars: Bow-mounted sonar. OQS 21.

Helicopters: 3 SH-60K, 1 MCH-101.

Programmes: Two new aviation capable ships to replace
the Haruna class authorised in the FY01-05 and FY05-09
programmes. The first authorised in the FY04 budget and
the second in the FY06 budget.
Structure: Broadly similar to the Spanish light carrier
Príncipe de Asturias although not fitted with a ski jump
and VSTOL capability. The flight deck has two lifts and
four helicopter spots. The Mk 41 VLS launcher is situated
on the starboard quarter.
Operational: To be capable of acting as Command Vessels
to replace Haruna and Hiei.

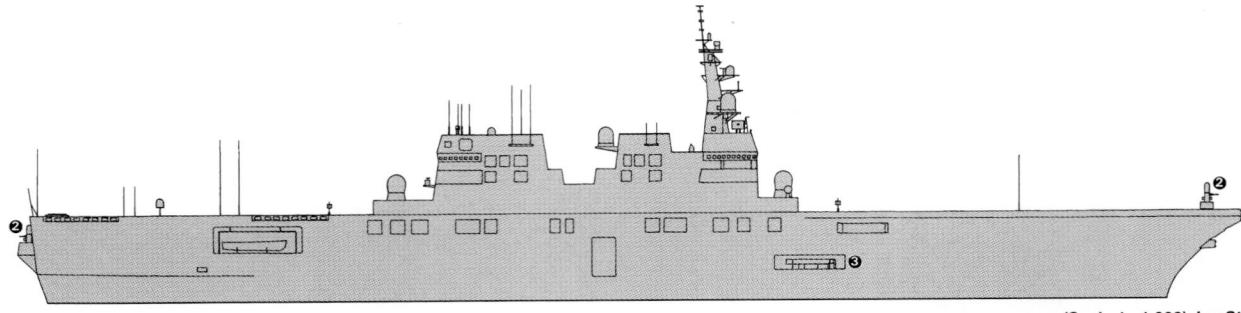

DDH *(Scale 1 : 1,200), Ian Sturton* / 1153013

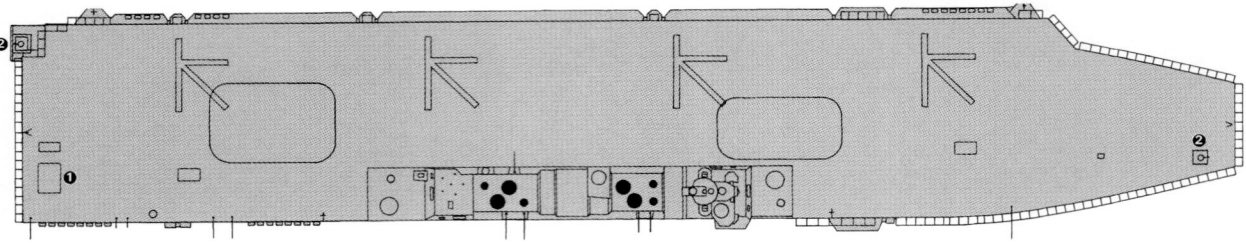

DDH *(Scale 1 : 1,200), Ian Sturton* / 1153012

0 + 2 ATAGO CLASS (DDGHM)

Name	No	Builders	Laid down	Launched	Commissioned
ATAGO	DDG 177	Mitsubishi, Nagasaki	5 Apr 2004	24 Aug 2005	Mar 2007
–	DDG 178	Mitsubishi, Nagasaki	6 Apr 2005	Aug 2006	Mar 2008

Displacement, tons: 7,700 standard; 10,000 full load
Dimensions, feet (metres): 540.1 × 68.9 × 20.3
(164.9 × 21.0 × 6.2)
Main machinery: COGAG; 4 GE LM 2500 gas turbines;
102,160 hp (76.21 MW) sustained; 2 shafts; cp props
Speed, knots: 30
Range, n miles: 4,500 at 20 kt
Complement: 309 (27 officers)

Missiles: SSM: 8 Mitsubishi Type 90 SSM-1B (2 quad) ❶.
SAM: Standard SM-2MR. FMC Mk 41 VLS; 64 cells forward ❷
32 cells aft ❸.
A/S: Vertical launch ASROC.
Guns: 1 United States Mk 45 Mod 4 5 in (127 mm)/62 ❹.
2 GE/GD 20 mm/76 Mk 15 Vulcan Phalanx Block IB ❺.
Torpedoes: 6–324 mm (2 triple) HOS 302 tubes ❻.
Countermeasures: Decoys: 4 Mk 36 SRBOC ❼ 6-barrelled
Mk 36 chaff launchers; Type 4 towed torpedo decoy.
ESM/ECM: NOLQ-2.
Radars: Air search: RCA SPY 1D(V) ❽; 3D; F-band.
Surface search: JRC OPS-28D ❾; G-band.
Navigation: JRC OPS-20; I-band.
Fire control: 3 SPG-62 ❿; 1 Mk 2/21 ⓫; I/J-band.

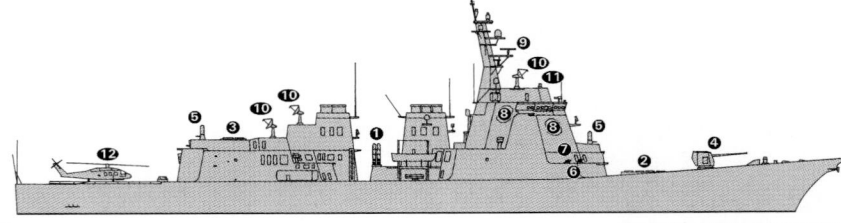

ATAGO *(Scale 1 : 1,500), Ian Sturton* / 1153011

Sonars: SQS-53C bow sonar.

Helicopters: 1 Mitsubishi/Sikorsky SH-60J ⓬.

Programmes: Two ships authorised in the FY01-05
program9*me. The first authorised in the FY02 budget
and the second in FY03 budget.

Structure: The upgrade from the Kongou class includes one
hangar for embarked helicopters. Vertical launchers are
increased by three cells at each end.

ATAGO *8/2005*, Hachiro Nakai* / 1153254

4 KONGOU CLASS (DDGHM)

Name	No	Builders	Laid down	Launched	Commissioned
KONGOU	DDG 173	Mitsubishi, Nagasaki	8 May 1990	26 Sep 1991	25 Mar 1993
KIRISHIMA	DDG 174	Mitsubishi, Nagasaki	7 Apr 1992	19 Aug 1993	16 Mar 1995
MYOUKOU	DDG 175	Mitsubishi, Nagasaki	8 Apr 1993	5 Oct 1994	14 Mar 1996
CHOUKAI	DDG 176	Ishikawajima Harima, Tokyo	29 May 1995	27 Aug 1996	20 Mar 1998

Displacement, tons: 7,250 standard; 9,485 full load
Dimensions, feet (metres): 528.2 × 68.9 × 20.3; 32.7 (sonar)
(161 × 21 × 6.2; 10)
Main machinery: COGAG; 4 GE LM 2500 gas turbines;
102,160 hp (76.21 MW) sustained; 2 shafts; cp props
Speed, knots: 30. **Range, n miles:** 4,500 at 20 kt
Complement: 300 (27 officers)

Missiles: SSM: 8 McDonnell Douglas Harpoon (2 quad) ❶
launchers; active radar homing to 130 km (70 n miles) at
0.9 Mach; warhead 227 kg.
SAM: GDC Pomona Standard SM-2MR (SM-3 in due course).
FMC Mk 41 VLS (29 cells) forward ❷. Martin Marietta
Mk 41 VLS (61 cells) aft ❸; command/inertial guidance;
semi-active radar homing to 167 km (90 n miles) at
2 Mach. Total of 90 Standard and ASROC weapons.
A/S: Vertical launch ASROC; inertial guidance to 1.6—10 km
(1—5.4 n miles); payload Mk 46 Mod 5 Neartip.
Guns: 1 OTO Melara 5 in (127 mm)/54 Compatto ❹;
45 rds/min to 23 km (12.42 n miles); weight of shell 32 kg.
2 GE/GD 20 mm/76 Mk 15 Vulcan Phalanx Block IB ❺
6 barrels per mounting; 3,000 rds/min combined to 1.5 km.
Torpedoes: 6—324 mm (2 triple) HOS 302 tubes ❻.
Honeywell Mk 46 Mod 5 Neartip; anti-submarine; active/
passive homing to 11 km (5.9 n miles) at 40 kt; warhead
44 kg.
Countermeasures: Decoys: 4 Mk 36 SRBOC ❼ 6-barrelled
Mk 36 chaff launchers; Type 4 towed torpedo decoy.
ESM/ECM: Melko NOLQ 2; intercept/jammer.
Combat data systems: Aegis NTDS with Link 11. SATCOM
WSC-3/OE-82C ❽. OQR-1 helicopter datalink ❾.
Weapons control: 3 Mk 99 Mod 1 MFCS. Type 2—21 GFCS.
Mk 116 Hitachi OYQ 102 (Mod 7 for ASW).

KONGOU *(Scale 1 : 1,500), Ian Sturton* / 0130387

Radars: Air search: RCA SPY 1D ❿; 3D; F-band.
Surface search: JRC OPS-28D ⓫; G-band.
Navigation: JRC OPS-20; I-band.
Fire control: 3 SPG-62 ⓬; 1 Mk 2/21 ⓭; I/J-band.
IFF: UPX 29.
Sonars: Nec OQS 102 (SQS-53B/C) bow-mounted; active
search and attack.
Oki OQR 2 (SQR-19A (V)) TACTASS; towed array; passive;
very low frequency.

Helicopters: Platform ⓮ and fuelling facilities for SH-60J.

Programmes: Proposed in the FY87 programme; first one
accepted in FY88 estimates, second in FY90, third in
FY91, fourth in FY93. Designated as destroyers but these
ships are of cruiser size. The combination of cost and US
Congressional reluctance to release Aegis technology
slowed the programme down. The ships' names were

last used by battleships and cruisers of the Second World
War era.
Modernisation: It is likely that these ships will be equipped
with Standard SM-3 Block 1A anti-ballistic missiles
as they become available. Upgrade of the first ship is
expected to start in 2006, with the others following at
one year intervals.
Structure: This is an enlarged and improved version
of the USN *Arleigh Burke* with a lightweight version
of the Aegis system. There are two missile magazines.
OQS 102 plus OQR 2 towed array is the equivalent
of SQQ-89. Prairie-Masker acoustic suppression
system.
Operational: As well as air defence of the Fleet, these
ships contribute to the air defences of mainland
Japan. Standard SM-3 Block 0 to be fitted in due
course.

KONGOU *2/2005*, Hachiro Nakai* / 1153256

CHOUKAI *7/2005*, Hachiro Nakai* / 1153255

2 HATAKAZE CLASS (DDGHM)

Name	No	Builders	Laid down	Launched	Commissioned
HATAKAZE	DDG 171	Mitsubishi, Nagasaki	20 May 1983	9 Nov 1984	27 Mar 1986
SHIMAKAZE	DDG 172	Mitsubishi, Nagasaki	30 Jan 1985	30 Jan 1987	23 Mar 1988

Displacement, tons: 4,600 (4,650, DDG 172) standard; 5,900 full load

Dimensions, feet (metres): 492 × 53.8 × 15.7 *(150 × 16.4 × 4.8)*

Main machinery: COGAG; 2 RR Olympus TM3B gas turbines; 49,400 hp *(36.8 MW)* sustained; 2 RR Spey SM1A gas turbines; 26,650 hp *(19.9 MW)* sustained; 2 shafts; Kamewa cp props

Speed, knots: 30

Complement: 260 (23 officers)

Missiles: SSM: 8 McDonnell Douglas Harpoon ❶; active radar homing to 130 km *(70 n miles)* at 0.9 Mach; warhead 227 kg.

SAM: 40 GDC Pomona Standard SM-1MR; Mk 13 Mod 4 launcher ❷; command guidance; semi-active radar homing to 46 km *(25 n miles)* at 2 Mach; height envelope 45–18,288 m *(150–60,000 ft)*.

A/S: Honeywell ASROC Mk 112 octuple launcher ❸; inertial guidance to 1.6–10 km *(1–5.4 n miles)* at 0.9 Mach; payload Mk 46 Mod 5 Neartip. Reload capability.

Guns: 2 FMC 5 in *(127 mm)*/54 Mk 42 automatic ❹; 20–40 rds/min to 24 km *(13 n miles)* anti-surface; 14 km *(7.6 n miles)* anti-aircraft; weight of shell 32 kg.
2 General Electric/General Dynamics 20 mm Phalanx Mk 15 CIWS ❺; 6 barrels per mounting; 3,000 rds/min combined to 1.5 km.

Torpedoes: 6–324 mm Type 68 or HOS 301 (2 triple) tubes ❻. Honeywell Mk 46 Mod 5 Neartip; anti-submarine;

active/passive homing to 11 km *(5.9 n miles)* at 40 kt; warhead 44 kg.

Countermeasures: Decoys: 2 Loral Hycor SRBOC 6-barrelled Mk 36 chaff launchers; range 4 km *(2.2 n miles)*.
ESM/ECM: Melco NOLQ-1; intercept/jammer. Fujitsu OLR 9B; intercept.

Combat data systems: OYQ-4 Mod 1 action data automation; Link 11. SATCOM ❼.

Weapons control: Type 2–21C for 127 mm guns. General Electric Mk 74 Mod 13 for Standard.

Radars: Air search: Hughes SPS-52C ❽; 3D; E/F-band.
Melco OPS-11C ❾; B-band.
Surface search: JRC OPS-28B ❿; G/H-band.

Fire control: 2 Raytheon SPG-51C ⓫; G-band.
Melco 2–21 ⓬; I/J-band. Type 2–12 ⓭; I-band.
Sonars: Nec OQS 4 Mod 1; bow-mounted; active search and attack; medium frequency.

Helicopters: Platform for 1 SH-60J Seahawk ⓮.

Programmes: DDG 171 provided for in 1981 programme. DDG 172 provided for in 1983 programme, ordered 29 March 1984.

HATAKAZE　　　　　　　　　　　　　*(Scale 1 : 1,200), Ian Sturton* / 0506023

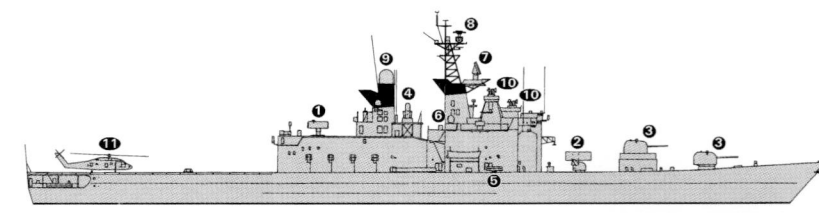

SHIMAKAZE　　　　　　　　　　　　　*4/2004, Hachiro Nakai* / 1044388

2 SHIRANE CLASS (DDHM)

Name	No	Builders	Laid down	Launched	Commissioned
SHIRANE	DDH 143	Ishikawajima Harima, Tokyo	25 Feb 1977	18 Sep 1978	17 Mar 1980
KURAMA	DDH 144	Ishikawajima Harima, Tokyo	17 Feb 1978	20 Sep 1979	27 Mar 1981

Displacement, tons: 5,200 standard; 7,200 full load

Dimensions, feet (metres): 521.5 × 57.5 × 17.5 *(159 × 17.5 × 5.3)*

Main machinery: 2 IHI boilers; 850 psi *(60 kg/cm²)*; 900°F *(480°C)*; 2 IHI turbines; 70,000 hp(m) *(51.5 MW)*; 2 shafts

Speed, knots: 31 (144). 32 (143)

Complement: 350; 360 (DDH 144) plus 20 staff

Missiles: SAM: Raytheon Sea Sparrow RIM-7M; Type 3 launcher ❶; semi-active radar homing to 14.6 km *(8 n miles)* at 2.5 Mach; warhead 39 kg; 24 missiles.

A/S: Honeywell ASROC Mk 112 octuple launcher ❷; inertial guidance to 10 km *(5.4 n miles)* at 0.9 Mach; payload Mk 46 Mod 5 Neartip.

Guns: 2 FMC 5 in *(127 mm)*/54 Mk 42 automatic ❸; 20–40 rds/min to 24 km *(13 n miles)* anti-surface; 14 km *(7.6 n miles)* anti-aircraft; weight of shell 32 kg.
2 General Electric/General Dynamics 20 mm Phalanx Mk 15 CIWS ❹; 6 barrels per mounting; 3,000 rds/min combined to 1.5 km.

Torpedoes: 6–324 mm HOS 301 (2 triple) tubes ❺. Honeywell Mk 46 Mod 5 Neartip; anti-submarine; active/passive homing to 11 km *(5.9 n miles)* at 40 kt; warhead 44 kg.

Countermeasures: Decoys: 4 Mk 36 SRBOC chaff launchers. Prairie Masker; blade rate suppression system.
ESM/ECM: Melco NOLQ 1; intercept/jammer. Fujitsu OLR 9B; intercept.

Combat data systems: OYQ-3B; Links 11 and 14. SATCOM ❻.

Weapons control: Singer Mk 114 for ASROC and TFCS; Type 72-1A GFCS.

Radars: Air search: Nec OPS-12 ❼; 3D; D-band.
Surface search: JRC OPS-28 ❽; G-band.
Navigation: JRC OPS-20; I-band.
Fire control: Type 2–12 ❾; I/J-band.
2 Type 72-1A FCS ❿; I/J-band.
Tacan: ORN-6C/6C-Y.

Sonars: EDO/Nec SQS-35(J); VDS; active/passive search; medium frequency.
Nec OQS 101; bow-mounted; low frequency.
EDO/Nec SQR-18A; towed array; passive; very low frequency.

Helicopters: 3 SH-60J Seahawk ⓫.

SHIRANE　　　　　　　　　　　　　*(Scale 1 : 1,500), Ian Sturton* / 1153010

SHIRANE　　　　　　　　　　　　　*5/2005*, Hachiro Nakai* / 1153259

Programmes: One each in 1975 and 1976 programmes.
Modernisation: DDH 143 refit in 1989-90. Both fitted with CIWS and towed array sonars by mid-1990. DDH 144 upgraded with Type 3 launcher to fire RIM-7M during 2003-04 refit at Mitsubishi, Nagasaki. DDH 143 similarly upgraded at IHI Yokohama in 2004.

Structure: Fitted with Vosper Thornycroft fin stabilisers. The after funnel is set to starboard and the forward one to port. The crane is on the starboard after corner of the hangar. Bear Trap helicopter hauldown gear.
Operational: Both ships carry SH-60J helicopters.

5 TAKANAMI CLASS (DDGHM)

Name	No	Builders	Laid down	Launched	Commissioned
TAKANAMI	DD 110	IHI Marine United, Yokosuka (Uraga)	25 Apr 2000	26 July 2001	12 Mar 2003
OONAMI	DD 111	Mitsubishi, Nagasaki	17 May 2000	20 Sep 2001	13 Mar 2003
MAKINAMI	DD 112	IHI Marine United, Yokohama	7 July 2001	8 Aug 2002	18 Mar 2004
SAZANAMI	DD 113	Mitsubishi, Nagasaki	4 Apr 2002	29 Aug 2003	16 Feb 2005
SUZUNAMI	DD 114	IHI Marine United, Yokohama	24 Sep 2003	26 Aug 2004	16 Feb 2006

Displacement, tons: 4,650 standard; 6,300 full load
Dimensions, feet (metres): 495.4 × 57.1 × 17.4
(151 × 17.4 × 5.3)
Main machinery: COGAG; 2 RR Spey SM1C gas turbines;
26,600 hp (19.9 MW) sustained; 2 GE LM 2500 gas
turbines; 32,500 hp (24.3 MW) sustained; 2 shafts
Speed, knots: 30
Complement: 176

Missiles: SSM: 8 Mitsubishi Type 90 SSM-1B (2 quad) ❶;
active radar homing to 150 km (81 n miles) at 0.9 Mach;
warhead 225 kg.
SAM: Mk 41 VLS 32 cells ❷ Sea Sparrow RIM-7M (PIP); semi-
active radar homing to 14.6 km (8 n miles) at 2.5 Mach;
warhead 39 kg and VL ASROC; internal guidance to 1.6—
10 km (1—5.4 n miles); payload Mk 46 Mod 5 Neartip.
Guns: 1 Otobreda 5 in (127 mm)/54 ❸; 45 rds/min to 24 km
(12.42 n miles); weight of shell 32 kg.
2 General Electric/General Dynamics 20 mm Phalanx
Mk 15 CIWS ❹; 6 barrels per mounting; 3,000 rds/min
combined to 1.5 km.
Torpedoes: 6—324 mm HOS-302 (2 triple) tubes ❺ Mk 46
Mod 5; anti-submarine; active/passive homing to 11 km
(5.9 n miles) at 40 kt; warhead 44 kg.
Countermeasures: Decoys: 4 Mk 36 SRBOC chaff launchers ❻.
SLQ-25 Nixie towed torpedo decoy.
ESM/ECM: Nec NOLQ 3; intercept and jammer.

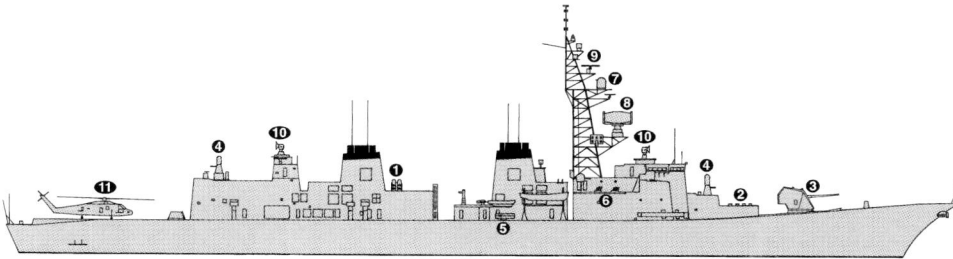

TAKANAMI CLASS   (Scale 1 : 1,200), Ian Sturton / 0080138

Combat data systems: OYQ-9 with Link 11. ORQ-1B
helicopter datalink ❼.
Weapons control: Hitachi OYQ-103 ASW control system.
Radars: Air search: Melco OPS-24B ❽; 3D; D-band.
Surface search: JRC OPS-28D ❾; G-band.
Fire control: Two FCS 2-31B ❿.
Navigation: OPS-20; I-band.
Sonars: OQS-5; Bow-mounted; active search and attack;
low frequency.
OQR-2; towed array; passive search; very low frequency.

Helicopters: 1 Mitsubishi/Sikorsky SH-60J/K ⓫.

Programmes: First two approved in FY98, then one a year
up to FY01.
Modernisation: Evolved Sea Sparrow (ESSM) (RIM-162) to
be fitted in due course.
Structure: Murasame class modified to fit a Mk 41 VLS,
improved missile fire control and new sonar.

SAZANAMI   *2/2005*, Hachiro Nakai* / 1153257

MAKINAMI   *2/2005*, Hachiro Nakai* / 1153258

9 MURASAME CLASS (DDGHM)

Name	No	Builders	Laid down	Launched	Commissioned
MURASAME	DD 101	Ishikawajima Harima, Tokyo	18 Aug 1993	23 Aug 1994	12 Mar 1996
HARUSAME	DD 102	Mitsui, Tamano	11 Aug 1994	16 Oct 1995	24 Mar 1997
YUUDACHI	DD 103	Marine United (Sumitomo, Uraga)	18 Mar 1996	19 Aug 1997	4 Mar 1999
KIRISAME	DD 104	Mitsubishi, Nagasaki	3 Apr 1996	21 Aug 1997	18 Mar 1999
INAZUMA	DD 105	Mitsubishi, Nagasaki	8 May 1997	9 Sep 1998	15 Mar 2000
SAMIDARE	DD 106	Marine United (Ishikawajima Harima, Tokyo)	11 Sep 1997	24 Sep 1998	21 Mar 2000
IKAZUCHI	DD 107	Hitachi, Maizuru	25 Feb 1998	24 June 1999	14 Mar 2001
AKEBONO	DD 108	Marine United (Ishikawajima Harima, Tokyo)	29 Oct 1999	25 Sep 2000	19 Mar 2002
ARIAKE	DD 109	Mitsubishi, Nagasaki	18 May 1999	16 Oct 2000	6 Mar 2002

Displacement, tons: 4,550 standard; 6,200 full load
Dimensions, feet (metres): 495.4 × 57.1 × 17.1
(151 × 17.4 × 5.2)
Main machinery: COGAG; 2 RR Spey SM1C gas turbines;
26,600 hp *(19.9 MW)* sustained; 2 GE LM 2500 gas
turbines; 32,500 hp *(24.3 MW)* sustained; 2 shafts
Speed, knots: 30
Complement: 165

Missiles: SSM: 8 Type 90 SSM-1B ❶ (Harpoon); active radar
homing to 130 km *(70 n miles)* at 0.9 Mach; warhead
227 kg.
SAM: Raytheon Mk 48 VLS 16 cells ❷ Sea Sparrow
RIM-7M; semi-active radar homing to 14.6 km *(8 n miles)*
at 2.5 Mach; warhead 39 kg.
A/S: Mk 41 VL ASROC 16 cells ❸. Total of 29 missiles can
be carried.
Guns: 1 Otobreda 3 in *(76 mm)*/62 compact ❹; 85 rds/min
to 16 km *(8.6 n miles)* anti-surface; 12 km *(6.5 n miles)*
anti-aircraft; weight of shell 6 kg.
2 General Electric/General Dynamics 20 mm Phalanx
Mk 15 CIWS ❺; 6 barrels per mounting; 3,000 rds/min
combined to 1.5 km.
Torpedoes: 6—324 mm HOS 302 (2 triple) tubes ❻ Mk 46
Mod 5; anti-submarine; active/passive homing to 11 km
(5.9 n miles) at 40 kt; warhead 44 kg.
Countermeasures: Decoys: 4 Mk 36 SRBOC chaff launchers ❼.
Type 4 towed torpedo decoy.
ESM/ECM: Nec NOLQ 3; intercept and jammer.
Combat data systems: OYQ-9B with Link 11. ORQ-1
helicopter datalink ❽.
Weapons control: Hitachi OYQ-103 ASW control system.
Radars: Air search: Melco OPS-24B ❾; 3D; D-band.
Surface search: JRC OPS-28D ❿; G-band.
Fire control: Two Type 2-31 ⓫.
Navigation: OPS-20; I-band.
Sonars: Mitsubishi OQS-5; hull-mounted; active search and
attack; low frequency.
OQR-1 towed array; passive search; very low frequency.

Helicopters: 1 SH-60J Seahawk ⓬.

Programmes: First one approved in FY91 as an addition
to the third Aegis-type destroyer. Second approved in
FY92. Two more approved in FY94, two in FY95, one in
FY96 and two in FY97. The programme was given added

priority as the Kongou class was reduced to four ships
because of the cost of Aegis.
Modernisation: Evolved Sea Sparrow (ESSM) to be fitted
in due course.
Structure: More like a mini-Kongou than an enlarged
Asagiri class, with VLS and a much reduced

complement. Stealth features are evident in sloping
sides and rounded superstructure. Indal RAST helicopter
hauldown.
Operational: ASROC missiles are not carried. *Kirisame*
deployed to Indian Ocean in November 2001 to provide
non-combatant support to US forces.

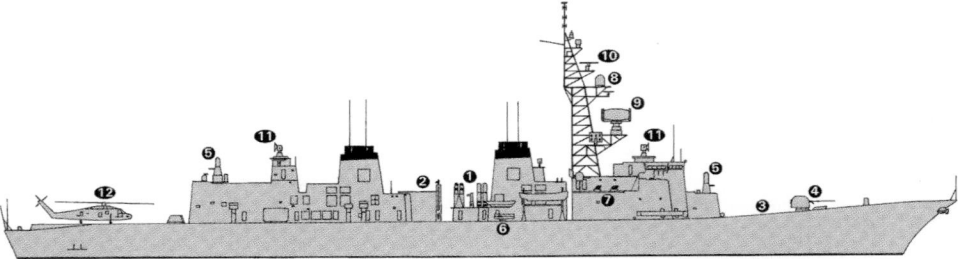

MURASAME   *(Scale 1 : 1,200), Ian Sturton* / 0506235

IKAZUCHI   *5/2005*, Hachiro Nakai* / 1153260

MURASAME   *7/2005*, Michael Nitz* / 1153361

HARUSAME   *5/2005*, Hachiro Nakai* / 1153261

6 ASAGIRI CLASS (DDGHM)

Name	No	Builders	Laid down	Launched	Commissioned
YUUGIRI	DD 153	Sumitomo, Uraga	25 Feb 1986	21 Sep 1987	28 Feb 1989
AMAGIRI	DD 154	Ishikawajima Harima, Tokyo	3 Mar 1986	9 Sep 1987	17 Mar 1989
HAMAGIRI	DD 155	Hitachi, Maizuru	20 Jan 1987	4 June 1988	31 Jan 1990
SETOGIRI	DD 156	Sumitomo, Uraga	9 Mar 1987	12 Sep 1988	14 Feb 1990
SAWAGIRI	DD 157	Mitsubishi, Nagasaki	14 Jan 1987	25 Nov 1988	6 Mar 1990
UMIGIRI	DD 158	Ishikawajima Harima, Tokyo	31 Oct 1988	9 Nov 1989	12 Mar 1991

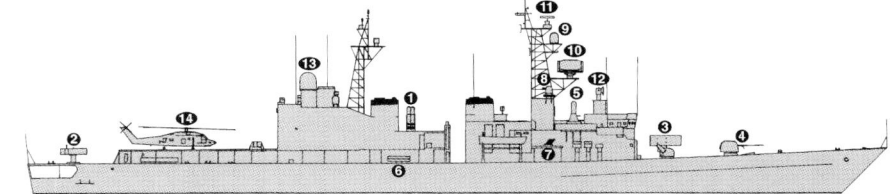

UMIGIRI   *(Scale 1 : 1,200), Ian Sturton* / 0012635

Displacement, tons: 3,500 (DD 153-154), (3,550, DD 155-158) standard; 4,900 (DD 153-154) (4,950 DD 155-158) full load

Dimensions, feet (metres): 449.4 × 48 × 14.6 *(137 × 14.6 × 4.5)*

Main machinery: COGAG; 4 RR Spey SM1A gas turbines; 53,300 hp *(39.8 MW)* sustained; 2 shafts; cp props

Speed, knots: 30+

Complement: 220

Missiles: SSM: 8 McDonnell Douglas Harpoon (2 quad) launchers ❶; active radar homing to 130 km *(70 n miles)* at 0.9 Mach; warhead 227 kg.

SAM: Raytheon Sea Sparrow Mk 29 (Type 3/3A) octuple launcher ❷; semi-active radar homing to 14.6 km *(8 n miles)* at 2.5 Mach; warhead 39 kg; 20 missiles.

A/S: Honeywell ASROC Mk 112 octuple launcher ❸; inertial guidance to 1.6—10 km *(1—5.4 n miles)* at 0.9 Mach; payload Mk 46 Mod 5 Neartip. Reload capability.

Guns: 1 Otobreda 3 in *(76 mm)*/62 compact ❹; 85 rds/min to 16 km *(8.6 n miles)* anti-surface; 12 km *(6.5 n miles)* anti-aircraft; weight of shell 6 kg.
2 General Electric/General Dynamics 20 mm Phalanx Mk 15 CIWS ❺; 6 barrels per mounting; 3,000 rds/min combined to 1.5 km.

Torpedoes: 6—324 mm Type 68 (2 triple) HOS 301 tubes ❻. Honeywell Mk 46 Mod 5 Neartip; anti-submarine; active/passive homing to 11 km *(5.9 n miles)* at 40 kt; warhead 44 kg.

Countermeasures: Decoys: 2 Loral Hycor SRBOC 6-barrelled Mk 36 chaff launchers ❼; range 4 km *(2.2 n miles)*.
1 SLQ-25 Nixie or Type 4; towed torpedo decoy.
ESM: Nec NOLR 6C or NOLR 8 (DD 152) ❽; intercept.
ECM: Fujitsu OLT-3; jammer.

Combat data systems: OYQ-7B data automation; Link 11/14. SATCOM. ORQ-1 helicopter datalink ❾ for SH-60J.
Radars: Air search: Melco OPS-14C (DD 151—154); D-band. Melco OPS-24 (DD 155—158) ❿; 3D; D-band.
Surface search: JRC OPS-28C ⓫; G-band (DD 151, 152, 155—158).
JRC OPS-28C-Y; G-band (DD 153—154).
Fire control: Type 2—22 (for guns) ⓬. Type 2-12E (for SAM) (DD 151—154); Type 2-12G (for SAM) ⓭ (DD 155—158).
Tacan: ORN-6D (URN 25).
Sonars: Mitsubishi OQS 4A (II); hull-mounted; active search and attack; low frequency.
OQR-1; towed array; passive search; very low frequency.

Helicopters: 1 SH-60J Seahawk ⓮.

Programmes: DD 153—154 in 1984 estimates, DD 155-157 in 1985 and DD 158 in 1986.
Modernisation: The last four were fitted on build with improved air search radar, updated fire-control radars and

a helicopter datalink. Plans to fit the first four may have been postponed. *Umigiri* also commissioned with a sonar towed array which has been fitted to the rest of the class.
Structure: Because of the enhanced IR signature and damage to electronic systems on the mainmast caused by after funnel gases there have been modifications to help contain the problem. The mainmast is now slightly higher than originally designed and has been offset to port, more so in the last four of the class. The forward funnel is also offset slightly to port and the after funnel to the starboard side of the superstructure. The hangar structure is asymmetrical extending to the after funnel on the starboard side but only to the mainmast to port. SATCOM is fitted at the after end of the hangar roof.
Operational: Beartrap helicopter hauldown system. Sea Kings have been phased out. *Sawagiri* deployed to Indian Ocean in November 2001 to provide non-combatant support of US forces. *Yamagiri* (D 152) converted to training ship on 18 March 2004 and *Asagiri* (D 151) on 16 February 2005.

YUUGIRI   *7/2005*, Michael Nitz* / 1153360

AMAGIRI   *5/2005*, Hachiro Nakai* / 1153262

11 HATSUYUKI CLASS (DDGHM)

Name	No	Builders	Laid down	Launched	Commissioned
HATSUYUKI	DD 122	Sumitomo, Uraga	14 Mar 1979	7 Nov 1980	23 Mar 1982
SHIRAYUKI	DD 123	Hitachi, Maizuru	3 Dec 1979	4 Aug 1981	8 Feb 1983
MINEYUKI	DD 124	Mitsubishi, Nagasaki	7 May 1981	19 Oct 1982	26 Jan 1984
SAWAYUKI	DD 125	Ishikawajima Harima, Tokyo	22 Apr 1981	21 June 1982	15 Feb 1984
HAMAYUKI	DD 126	Mitsui, Tamano	4 Feb 1981	27 May 1982	18 Nov 1983
ISOYUKI	DD 127	Ishikawajima Harima, Tokyo	20 Apr 1982	19 Sep 1983	23 Jan 1985
HARUYUKI	DD 128	Sumitomo, Uraga	11 Mar 1982	6 Sep 1983	14 Mar 1985
YAMAYUKI	DD 129	Hitachi, Maizuru	25 Feb 1983	10 July 1984	3 Dec 1985
MATSUYUKI	DD 130	Ishikawajima Harima, Tokyo	7 Apr 1983	25 Oct 1984	19 Mar 1986
SETOYUKI	DD 131	Mitsui, Tamano	26 Jan 1984	3 July 1985	11 Dec 1986
ASAYUKI	DD 132	Sumitomo, Uraga	22 Dec 1983	16 Oct 1985	20 Feb 1987

Displacement, tons: 2,950 (3,050 from DD 129 onwards) standard; 4,000 (4,200) full load

Dimensions, feet (metres): 426.4 × 44.6 × 13.8 (14.4 from 129 onwards) (130 × 13.6 × 4.2) (4.4)

Main machinery: COGOG; 2 Kawasaki-RR Olympus TM3B gas turbines; 49,400 hp (36.8 MW) sustained; 2 RR Type RM1C gas turbines; 9,900 hp (7.4 MW) sustained; 2 shafts; cp props

Speed, knots: 30; 19 cruise

Complement: 195 (200, DD 124 onwards)

Missiles: SSM: 8 McDonnell Douglas Harpoon (2 quad) launchers ❶; active radar homing to 130 km (70 n miles) at 0.9 Mach; warhead 227 kg.
SAM: Raytheon Sea Sparrow Mk 29 Type 3A launcher ❷; semi-active radar homing to 14.6 km (8 n miles) at 2.5 Mach; warhead 39 kg; 12 missiles.
A/S: Honeywell ASROC Mk 112 octuple launcher ❸; inertial guidance to 1.6—10 km (1—5.4 n miles) at 0.9 Mach; payload Mk 46 Mod 5 Neartip.

Guns: 1 Otobreda 3 in (76 mm)/62 compact ❹; 85 rds/min to 16 km (8.6 n miles) anti-surface; 12 km (6.5 n miles) anti-aircraft; weight of shell 6 kg.
2 General Electric/General Dynamics 20 mm Phalanx Mk 15 CIWS ❺; 6 barrels per mounting; 3,000 rds/min combined to 1.5 km.

Torpedoes: 6—324 mm Type 68 or HOS 301 (2 triple) tubes ❻. Honeywell Mk 46 Mod 5 Neartip; anti-submarine; active/passive homing to 11 km (5.9 n miles) at 40 kt; warhead 44 kg.

Countermeasures: Decoys: 2 Loral Hycor SRBOC 6-barrelled Mk 36 chaff launchers; range 4 km (2.2 n miles).
ESM: Nec NOLR 6C; intercept.
ECM: Fujitsu OLT 3; jammer.

Combat data systems: OYQ-5B action data automation. SATCOM.

Radars: Air search: Melco OPS-14B ❼; D-band.
Surface search: JRC OPS-18-1 ❽; G-band.
Fire control: Type 2-12 A ❾; I/J-band (for SAM).
2 Type 2-21/21A ❿; I/J-band (for guns).

Tacan: ORN-6C-Y (DD 122, 125 and 132); ORN-6C (remainder).

Sonars: Nec OQS 4A (II) (SQS-23 type); bow-mounted; active search and attack; low frequency.
OQR 1 TACTASS (in some); passive; low frequency.

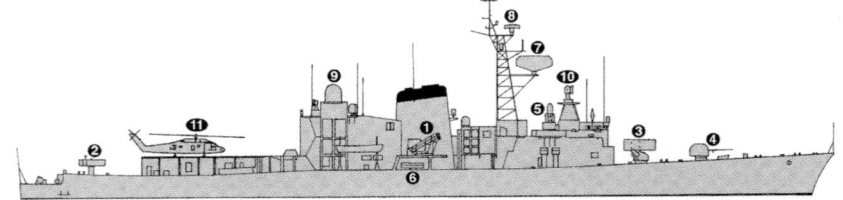

HATSUYUKI *(Scale 1 : 1,200), Ian Sturton* / 0506301

SETOYUKI *6/2005*, Hachiro Nakai* / 1153263

Helicopters: 1 SH-60J Seahawk ⓫.

Modernisation: *Shirayuki* retrofitted with Phalanx in early 1992, and the rest of the class by 1996. *Matsuyuki* first to get sonar towed array in 1990 and *Hatsuyuki* in 1994; the others are being fitted. All of the class converted to carry Seahawk helicopters.

Structure: Fitted with fin stabilisers. Steel in place of aluminium alloy for bridge etc after DD 129 which increased displacement.

Operational: Canadian Beartrap helicopter landing aid. Improved ECM equipment in the last two of the class. Last of class *Shimayuki* converted to a training ship 18 March 1999.

HAMAYUKI *5/2005*, Hachiro Nakai* / 1153264

MATSUYUKI *3/2005*, Hachiro Nakai* / 1153265

3 TACHIKAZE CLASS (DDGM)

Name	No
TACHIKAZE	DDG 168
ASAKAZE	DDG 169
SAWAKAZE	DDG 170

Builders	Laid down	Launched	Commissioned
Mitsubishi, Nagasaki	19 June 1973	17 Dec 1974	26 Mar 1976
Mitsubishi, Nagasaki	27 May 1976	15 Oct 1977	27 Mar 1979
Mitsubishi, Nagasaki	14 Sep 1979	4 June 1981	30 Mar 1983

Displacement, tons: 3,850 (3,950, DDG 170) standard; 5,200 full load

Dimensions, feet (metres): 469 × 47 × 15.1 *(143 × 14.3 × 4.6)*

Main machinery: 2 Mitsubishi boilers; 600 psi *(40 kg/cm²)*; 850°F *(454°C)*; 2 Mitsubishi turbines; 60,000 hp(m); *(44.7 MW)*; 2 shafts

Speed, knots: 32

Complement: 230—255

Missiles: SSM: 8 McDonnell Douglas Harpoon (DDG 170); active radar homing to 130 km *(70 n miles)* at 0.9 Mach; warhead 227 kg HE.
SAM: GDC Pomona Standard SM-1MR; Mk 13 Mod 1 or 4 launcher **❶**; command guidance; semi-active radar homing to 46 km *(25 n miles)* at 2 Mach; height envelope 45—18,288 m *(150—60,000 ft)*; 40 missiles (SSM and SAM combined).
A/S: Honeywell ASROC Mk 112 octuple launcher **❷**; inertial guidance to 1.6—10 km *(1—5.4 n miles)* at 0.9 Mach; payload Mk 46 Mod 5 Neartip. Reloads in DDG 170 only.

Guns: 1 or 2 FMC 5 in *(127 mm)*/54 Mk 42 automatic **❸**; 20—40 rds/min to 24 km *(13 n miles)* anti-surface; 14 km *(7.6 n miles)* anti-aircraft; weight of shell 32 kg.
2 General Electric/General Dynamics 20 mm Phalanx CIWS Mk 15 **❹**; 6 barrels per mounting; 3,000 rds/min combined to 1.5 km.

Torpedoes: 6—324 mm Type 68 or HOS 301 (2 triple) tubes **❺**. Honeywell Mk 46 Mod 5 Neartip; anti-submarine; active/passive homing to 11 km *(5.9 n miles)* at 40 kt; warhead 44 kg.

Countermeasures: Decoys: 4 Loral Hycor SRBOC Mk 36 multibarrelled chaff launchers. SLQ-25 towed torpedo decoy.
ESM: Nec NOLR 6 (DDG 168); Nec NOLQ 1 (others); intercept.
ECM: Fujitsu OLT 3; jammer.

Combat data systems: OYQ-1B (DDG 168), OYQ-2B (DDG 169), OYQ-4 (DDG 170) action data automation; Links 11 and 14. SATCOM.

Weapons control: 2 Mk 74 Mod 13 missile control directors. US Mk 114 ASW control. GFCS-2-21 for gun (DDG 170). GFCS-72-1A for gun (others).

Radars: Air search: Melco OPS-11C **❻**; B-band.
Hughes SPS-52B **❼** or 52C (DDG 170); 3D; E/F-band.
Surface search: JRC OPS-16D **❽**; G-band (DDG 168).
JRC OPS-28 (DDG 170); G-band.
JRC OPS-18-3; G-band (DDG 169).
Fire control: 2 Raytheon SPG-51 **❾**; G/I-band.
Type 2 FCS **❿**; I/J-band.
IFF: NYPX-2.

Sonars: Nec OQS-3A (Type 66); bow-mounted; active search and attack; low frequency.

Modernisation: CIWS added to DDG 168 in 1983, DDG 169 and 170 in 1987. After gun removed to allow increased Flag accommodation in *Tachikaze* in 1998.

Operational: *Tachikaze* is the Escort Force Flagship.

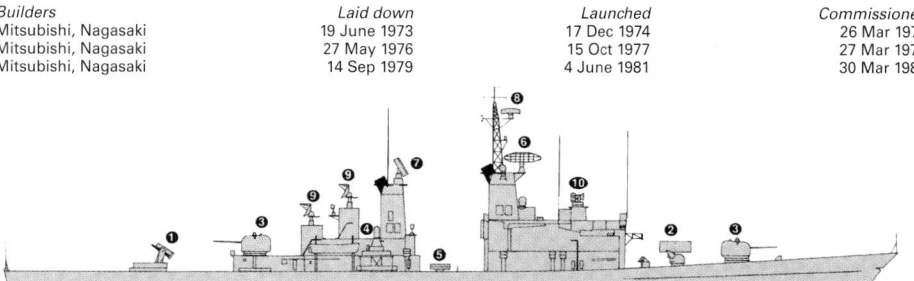

ASAKAZE   *(Scale 1 : 1,200), Ian Sturton* / 0506024

SAWAKAZE   *8/2005*, Hachiro Nakai* / 1153267

TACHIKAZE   *7/2005*, Hachiro Nakai* / 1153266

2 HARUNA CLASS (DDHM)

Name	No
HARUNA	DDH 141
HIEI	DDH 142

Builders	Laid down	Launched	Commissioned
Mitsubishi, Nagasaki	19 Mar 1970	1 Feb 1972	22 Feb 1973
Ishikawajima Harima, Tokyo	8 Mar 1972	13 Aug 1973	27 Nov 1974

Displacement, tons: 4,950 (5,050, DDH 142) standard; 6,900 full load

Dimensions, feet (metres): 502 × 57.4 × 17.1 *(153 × 17.5 × 5.2)*

Main machinery: 2 Mitsubishi (DDH 141) or IHI (DDH 142) boilers; 850 psi *(60 kg/cm²)*; 900°F *(480°C)*; 2 Mitsubishi (DDH 141) or IHI (DDH 142) turbines; 70,000 hp *(51.5 MW)*; 2 shafts

Speed, knots: 31

Complement: 370 (360, DDH 141) (36 officers)

Missiles: SAM: Raytheon Sea Sparrow Mk 29 (Type 3A) octuple launcher **❶**; semi-active radar homing to 14.6 km *(8 n miles)* at 2.5 Mach; warhead 39 kg; 24 missiles.
A/S: Honeywell ASROC Mk 112 octuple launcher **❷**; inertial guidance to 1.6—10 km *(1—5.4 n miles)* at 0.9 Mach; payload Mk 46 Mod 5 Neartip.

Guns: 2 FMC 5 in *(127 mm)*/54 Mk 42 automatic **❸**; 20—40 rds/min to 24 km *(13 n miles)* anti-surface; 14 km *(7.6 n miles)* anti-aircraft; weight of shell 32 kg.
2 General Electric/General Dynamics 20 mm Phalanx Mk 15 CIWS **❹**; 6 barrels per mounting; 3,000 rds/min combined to 1.5 km.

Torpedoes: 6—324 mm HOS 301 (2 triple) tubes **❺**. Honeywell Mk 46 Mod 5 Neartip; anti-submarine; active/passive homing to 11 km *(5.9 n miles)* at 40 kt; warhead 44 kg.

Countermeasures: Decoys: 4 Loral Hycor SRBOC Mk 36 multibarrelled chaff launchers.
ESM/ECM: Melco NOLQ 1; intercept/jammer. Fujitsu OLR 9; intercept.

Combat data systems: OYQ-7B action data automation; Links 11 and 14; US SATCOM **❻**.

Weapons control: 2 Type 2-12 FCS (1 for guns, 1 for SAM).

Radars: Air search: Melco OPS-11C **❼**; B-band.
Surface search: JRC OPS-28C/28C-Y **❽**; G-band.
Fire control: 1 Type 1A **❾**; I/J-band (guns).
1 Type 2-12 **❿**; I/J-band (SAM).
Navigation: Koden OPN-11; I-band.
IFF: YPA-2. YPX-3.
Tacan: Nec ORN-6D/6C.

Sonars: Sangamo/Mitsubishi OQS 3; bow-mounted; active search and attack; low frequency with bottom bounce.

Helicopters: 3 SH-60J Seahawk **⓫**.

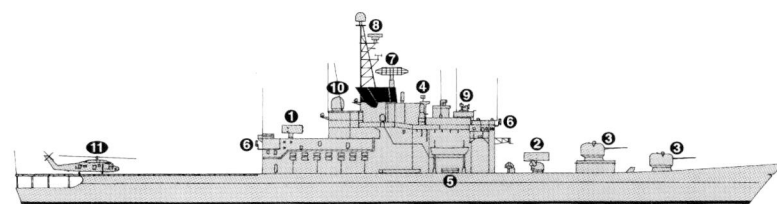

HARUNA   *(Scale 1 : 1,500), Ian Sturton* / 0012641

HARUNA   *7/2005*, Hachiro Nakai* / 1153268

Programmes: Ordered under the third five-year defence programme (from 1967-71). The ships' names were last used by capital ships of the Second World War era.

Modernisation: DDH 141 taken in hand from 31 March 1986 to 31 October 1987 for FRAM at Mitsubishi, Nagasaki; DDH 142 received FRAM from 31 August 1987 to 30 March 1989 at IHI, Tokyo; included Sea Sparrow, two CIWS and chaff launchers.

Structure: The funnel is offset slightly to port. Fitted with fin stabilisers. A heavy crane has been fitted on the top of the hangar, starboard side.

Operational: Fitted with Canadian Beartrap hauldown gear.

FRIGATES

Notes: The MSDF classifies these ships as Destroyer Escorts.

6 ABUKUMA CLASS (FFGM/DE)

Name	No
ABUKUMA	DE 229
JINTSU	DE 230
OOYODO	DE 231
SENDAI	DE 232
CHIKUMA	DE 233
TONE	DE 234

Builders	Laid down	Launched	Commissioned
Mitsui, Tamano	17 Mar 1988	21 Dec 1988	12 Dec 1989
Hitachi, Maizuru	14 Apr 1988	31 Jan 1989	28 Feb 1990
Mitsui, Tamano	8 Mar 1989	19 Dec 1989	23 Jan 1991
Sumitomo, Uraga	14 Apr 1989	26 Jan 1990	15 Mar 1991
Hitachi, Maizuru	14 Feb 1991	22 Jan 1992	24 Feb 1993
Sumitomo, Uraga	8 Feb 1991	6 Dec 1991	8 Feb 1993

Displacement, tons: 2,000 standard; 2,550 full load
Dimensions, feet (metres): 357.6 × 44 × 12.5
(109 × 13.4 × 3.8)
Main machinery: CODOG; 2 RR Spey SM1A gas turbines;
26,650 hp (19.9 MW) sustained; 2 Mitsubishi S12U-MTK
diesels; 6,000 hp(m) (4.4 MW); 2 shafts
Speed, knots: 27
Complement: 120

Missiles: SSM: 8 McDonnell Douglas Harpoon (2 quad)
launchers ❶; active radar homing to 130 km (70 n miles)
at 0.9 Mach; warhead 227 kg.
A/S: Honeywell ASROC Mk 112 octuple launcher ❷; inertial
guidance to 1.6—10 km (1—5.4 n miles) at 0.9 Mach;
payload Mk 46 Mod 5 Neartip.
Guns: 1 Otobreda 3 in (76 mm)/62 compact ❸; 85 rds/min
to 16 km (8.6 n miles) anti-surface; 12 km (6.5 n miles)
anti-aircraft; weight of shell 6 kg.
1 General Electric/General Dynamics 20 mm Phalanx
CIWS Mk 15 ❹; 6 barrels per mounting; 3,000 rds/min
combined to 1.5 km.
Torpedoes: 6—324 mm HOS 301 (2 triple) tubes ❺. Honeywell
Mk 46 Mod 5 Neartip; anti-submarine; active/passive
homing to 11 km (5.9 n miles) at 40 kt; warhead 44 kg.
Countermeasures: Decoys: 2 Loral Hycor SRBOC
6-barrelled Mk 36 chaff launchers.

ABUKUMA *(Scale 1 : 900), Ian Sturton* / 0506197

ESM: Nec NOLR-8; intercept.
Combat data systems: OYQ-6. SATCOM.
Weapons control: Type 2-21; GFCS.
Radars: Air search: Melco OPS-14C ❻; D-band.
Surface search: JRC OPS-28D (DE 233-234); JRS OPC-28C
(remainder) ❼; G-band.
Fire control: Type 2-21 ❽.
Sonars: Hitachi OQS-8; hull-mounted; active search and
attack; medium frequency.
SQR-19A towed passive array in due course.

Programmes: First pair of this class approved in
1986 estimates, ordered March 1987; second pair in
1987 estimates, ordered February 1988; last two in 1989
estimates, ordered 24 January 1989. The name of the first
of class commemorates that of a light cruiser which was
sunk in the battle of Leyte Gulf in October 1944.
Structure: Stealth features include non-vertical and rounded
surfaces. German RAM PDMS may be fitted later, although
this now seems unlikely, and space has been left for a
towed sonar array. SATCOM fitted aft of the after funnel.

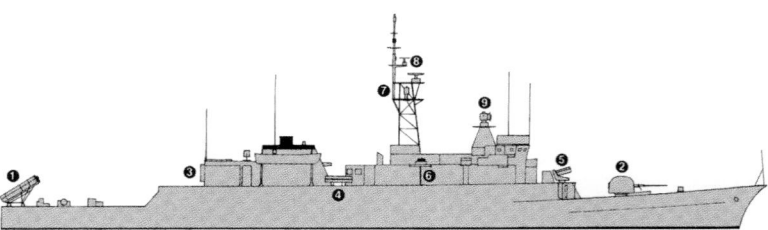

TONE *5/2005*, Hachiro Nakai* / 1153270

3 ISHIKARI/YUUBARI CLASS (FFG/DE)

Name	No
ISHIKARI	DE 226
YUUBARI	DE 227
YUUBETSU	DE 228

Builders	Laid down	Launched	Commissioned
Mitsui, Tamano	17 May 1979	18 Mar 1980	28 Mar 1981
Sumitomo, Uraga	9 Feb 1981	22 Feb 1982	18 Mar 1983
Hitachi, Maizuru	14 Jan 1982	25 Jan 1983	14 Feb 1984

Displacement, tons: 1,470 (1,290 (DE 226)) standard; 1,690
(1,450 (DE 226)) full load
Dimensions, feet (metres): 278.9 × 34.8 × 11.5 (DE 226)
(85.0 × 10.6 × 3.5)
298.5 × 35.4 × 11.8 (DE 227-228)
(91.0 × 10.8 × 3.6)
Main machinery: CODOG; 1 Kawasaki/RR Olympus TM3B gas
turbine; 24,700 hp (18.4 MW) sustained; 1 Mitsubishi/MAN
6DRV diesel; 4,700 hp(m) (3.45 MW); 2 shafts; cp props
Speed, knots: 25
Complement: 95

Missiles: SSM: 8 McDonnell Douglas Harpoon (2 quad)
launchers ❶; active radar homing to 130 km (70 n miles)
at 0.9 Mach; warhead 227 kg.
Guns: 1 Otobreda 3 in (76 mm)/62 compact ❷; 85 rds/min to
16 km (8.6 n miles) anti-surface; 12 km (6.5 n miles) anti-
aircraft; weight of shell 6 kg. 1 General Electric/General
Dynamics 20 mm Phalanx (unlikely to be fitted) ❸.
Torpedoes: 6—324 mm Type 68 (2 triple) tubes ❹. Honeywell
Mk 46 Mod 5 Neartip; anti-submarine; active/passive
homing to 11 km (5.9 n miles) at 40 kt; warhead 44 kg.
A/S mortars: 1—375 mm Bofors Type 71 4 to 6-barrelled
trainable rocket launcher ❺; automatic loading; range
1.6 km.
Countermeasures: Decoys: 2 Loral Hycor SRBOC 6-barrelled
Mk 36 chaff launchers ❻; range 4 km (2.2 n miles).
ESM: Nec NOLR 6B ❼; intercept.
Combat data systems: OYQ-5.
Weapons control: Type 2—21 system for 76 mm gun.
Radars: Surface search: JRC OPS-28B/28-1 ❽; G-band.
Navigation: Fujitsu OPS-19B; I-band.
Fire control: Type 2—21 ❾; I/J-band.
Sonars: Nec SQS-36J; hull-mounted; active/passive;
medium frequency.

Programmes: The name Yuubari commemorates that of a
light cruiser sunk in the Second World War.
Structure: Yuubari and Yuubetsu were slightly larger
versions of Ishikari. The increased space for the same
weapons systems as Ishikari has meant improved
accommodation and an increase in fuel oil carried.

YUUBARI *(Scale 1 : 900), Ian Sturton* / 0506026

YUUBETSU *6/2005*, Hachiro Nakai* / 1153269

SHIPBORNE AIRCRAFT

Notes: Agusta Westland MCH-101 selected on 5 June 2003 to replace MH-53E Sea Dragon minesweeping aircraft and S-61A utility aircraft. Of 14 aircraft to be acquired, 11 are expected to be in the minesweeping configuration. The maiden flight of the first aircraft, built in UK, took place on 15 February 2005. Aircraft kits for the remaining thirteen aircraft are being assembled in Japan by Kawasaki Heavy Industries. Delivery of the first aircraft is expected in 2006.

Numbers/Type: 84/7 Sikorsky/Mitsubishi SH-60J/SH-60K (Seahawk).
Operational speed: 143 kt *(264 km/h)*.
Service ceiling: 13,500 ft *(4,090 m)*.
Range: 600 n miles *(1,110 km)*.
Role/Weapon systems: ASW helicopter; started replacing HSS-2B in July 1991; built in Japan; prototypes fitted by Mitsubishi with Japanese avionics and mission equipment. Overall requirement for 103 aircraft. Half of force land-based. SH-60K are upgraded aircraft with an improved tactical data processing system. Sensors: Texas Instruments APS 124 search radar; sonobuoys plus datalink; Bendix AQS 18/Nippon HQS 103 dipping sonar, ECM, HLR 108 ESM. Weapons: ASW; two Mk 46 torpedoes or depth bombs. 2 Hellfire ASM (SH-60K).

SH-60J   *5/2005*, Hachiro Nakai* / 1153271

Numbers/Type: 2 Mitsubishi-Sikorsky S-61A.
Operational speed: 144 kt *(267 km/h)*.
Service ceiling: 14,700 ft *(4,280 m)*.
Range: 542 n miles *(1,005 km)*.
Role/Weapon systems: Support helicopter based on Sea King airframe. Deployed in ice-patrol ship *Shirase*.

S-61A   *10/2003, Hachiro Nakai* / 0570732

LAND-BASED MARITIME AIRCRAFT

Notes: Aircraft type names are not used by the MSDF.

Numbers/Type: 13 NAMC YS-11.
Operational speed: 230 kt *(425 km/h)*.
Service ceiling: 21,500 ft *(6,580 m)*.
Range: 1,960 n miles *(3,629 km)*.
Role/Weapon systems: First flew in 1962. Of 182 aircraft constructed, 13 believed to remain in service. Of these, two YS-11EA are EW trainers while there are believed to be four YS-11B configured for Sigint operations. These are equipped with dorsal and ventral blade antennas and with radomes. These aircraft may be designated YS-11EL. Other variants include two YS-11FC flight checkers, a YS-11NT navigational trainer and YS-11C transport aircraft.

YS-11   *11/2005*, Hachiro Nakai* / 1153273

Numbers/Type: 80/5/1/3/3 Lockheed/Kawasaki P-3C/EP-3/UP-3C/UP-3D/OP-3C.
Operational speed: 395 kt *(732 km/h)*.
Service ceiling: 28,300 ft *(8,625 m)*.
Range: 3,300 n miles *(6,100 km)*.
Role/Weapon systems: Long-range MR/ASW and surface surveillance and attack. Most maritime surveillance is done by these aircraft. Four EW version EP-3. Sensors: APS-115 radar, ASQ-81 MAD, AQA 7 processor, Unisys CP 2044 computer, IFF, ECM, ALQ 78, ESM, ALR 66, sonobuoys. Weapons: ASW; eight Mk 46 torpedoes, depth bombs or mines, four underwing stations for Harpoon and ASM-1.

P-3C   *4/2005*, Hachiro Nakai* / 1153274

EP-3   *9/2005*, Hachiro Nakai* / 1153275

Numbers/Type: 7/2 Shinmeiwa US-1A Rescue/Shinmeiwa US-2.
Operational speed: 265 kt *(491 km/h)*.
Service ceiling: 30,000 ft *(9,144 m)*.
Range: 2,300 n miles *(4,260 km)*.
Role/Weapon systems: Turboprop amphibian designed for maritime patrol and SAR missions. Crew of 12. Accommodation for 16 survivors or 12 stretchers. The US-1A Kai is undertaking trials with a view to entering service in 2007. A second test vehicle is expected by 2005. Sensors: Raytheon AN/APS-115-2 search radar.

US-1A   *9/2005*, Shinmaywa Industries Ltd* / 1153276

US-2   *6/2004, Hachiro Nakai* / 1044404

Numbers/Type: 10 Sikorsky/Mitsubishi S-80M-1 (Sea Dragon) (MH53E).
Operational speed: 170 kt *(315 km/h)*.
Service ceiling: 18,500 ft *(5,640 m)*.
Range: 1,120 n miles *(2,000 km)*.
Role/Weapon systems: Three-engined AMCM helicopter tows Mk 103, 104, 105 and 106 MCM sweep equipment; self-deployed. Weapons: Two 12.7 mm guns for mine disposal.

MH-53E   *9/2005*, Hachiro Nakai* / 1153272

PATROL FORCES

6 HAYABUSA CLASS (PGGF)

Name	No	Builders	Launched	Commissioned
HAYABUSA	824	Mitsubishi, Shimonoseki	13 June 2001	25 Mar 2002
WAKATAKA	825	Mitsubishi, Shimonoseki	13 Sep 2001	25 Mar 2002
OOTAKA	826	Mitsubishi, Shimonoseki	13 May 2002	24 Mar 2003
KUMATAKA	827	Mitsubishi, Shimonoseki	2 Aug 2002	24 Mar 2003
UMITAKA	828	Mitsubishi, Shimonoseki	21 May 2003	24 Mar 2004
SHIRATAKA	829	Mitsubishi, Shimonoseki	8 Aug 2003	24 Mar 2004

Displacement, tons: 200 standard; 240 full load
Dimensions, feet (metres): 164.4 × 27.6 × 13.8 *(50.1 × 8.4 × 4.2)*
Main machinery: 3 LM 500-G07 gas turbines 16,200 hp *(12.08 MW)*; 3 water jets
Speed, knots: 44
Complement: 18 (+3 staff)
Missiles: 4 Mitsubishi Type 90 SSM-1B; active radar homing to 130 km *(70 n miles)* at 0.9 Mach; warhead 227 kg.
Guns: 1 OTO Melara 3 in *(76 mm)*/62 compact; 85 rds/min to 16 km *(8.7 n miles)* anti-surface; 12 km *(6.6 n miles)* anti-aircraft; weight of shell 6 kg.
2 — 12.7 mm MGs.
Countermeasures: Decoys: chaff launchers.
ESM/ECM: NOLR-9B.
Radars: Surface search: OPS-18-3; G-band.
Fire control: Type 2 — 31C.
Navigation: OPS-20; I-band.

Comment: First pair authorised in FY99 budget, second pair in FY00 and third pair in FY01. Single hull.

KUMATAKA   *5/2005*, Hachiro Nakai* / 1153290

3 PG 01 (SPARVIERO) CLASS
(FAST ATTACK HYDROFOIL — MISSILE) (PTGK)

Name	No	Builders	Launched	Commissioned
MISAIRUTEI-ICHI-GOU	821	Sumitomo, Uraga	17 July 1992	25 Mar 1993
MISAIRUTEI-NI-GOU	822	Sumitomo, Uraga	17 July 1992	25 Mar 1993
MISAIRUTEI-SAN-GOU	823	Sumitomo, Uraga	15 June 1994	13 Mar 1995

Displacement, tons: 50 standard; 60 full load
Dimensions, feet (metres): 71.5 × 22.9 × 4.6 *(21.8 × 7 × 1.4)* (hull)
80.7 × 23.1 × 14.4 *(24.6 × 7 × 4.4)* (foilborne)
Main machinery: 1 GE/IHI LM 500 gas turbine; 5,000 hp *(3.72 MW)* sustained; 1 pumpjet (foilborne); 1 diesel; 1 retractable prop (hullborne)
Speed, knots: 46; 8 (diesel)
Range, n miles: 400 at 40 kt; 1,000 at 8 kt
Complement: 11 (3 officers)
Missiles: SSM: 4 Mitsubishi Type 90 SSM-1B (derivative of land-based system); range 150 km *(81 n miles)*.
Guns: 1 GE 20 mm/76 Sea Vulcan; 3 barrels per mounting; 1,500 rds/min combined to 4 km *(2.2 n miles)*.
Countermeasures: Decoys: 2 Loral Hycor Mk 36 SRBOC chaff launchers.
ESM/ECM: intercept and jammer.
Combat data systems: Link 11.
Radars: Surface search: JRC OPS-28-2; G-band.

Comment: Classified as Guided Missile Patrol Boats. First two approved in FY90 and both laid down 25 March 1991. One more approved in FY92, laid down 8 March 1993. A fourth was asked for but not authorised in FY95 and the programme is now complete. Built with Italian assistance from Fincantieri. Planned to improve the Navy's interceptor capabilities, this was an ambitious choice of vessel bearing in mind the falling popularity of the hydrofoil in the few navies (US, Italy and Russia) that built them.

MISAIRUTEI-SAN-GOU   *7/2003, Hachiro Nakai* / 0570739

AMPHIBIOUS FORCES

2 YURA CLASS (LSU/LCU)

Name	No	Builders	Commissioned
YURA	LSU 4171	Sasebo Heavy Industries	27 Mar 1981
NOTO	LSU 4172	Sasebo Heavy Industries	27 Mar 1981

Displacement, tons: 590 standard
Dimensions, feet (metres): 190.2 × 31.2 × 5.6 *(58 × 9.5 × 1.7)*
Main machinery: 2 Fuji 6L27.5XF diesels; 3,250 hp(m) *(2.39 MW)*; 2 shafts; cp props
Speed, knots: 12
Complement: 31
Military lift: 70 troops
Guns: 1 GE 20 mm/76 Sea Vulcan 20; 3 barrels per mounting; 1,500 rds/min combined to 4 km *(2.2 n miles)*.
Radars: Navigation: Fujitsu OPS-9B; I-band.

Comment: Both laid down 23 April 1980. 4171 launched 15 October 1980 and 4172 on 12 November 1980.

YURA   *6/2004, Hachiro Nakai* / 1044406

2 YUSOUTEI CLASS (LCU)

Name	No	Builders	Commissioned
YUSOUTEI-ICHI-GOU	LCU 2001	Sasebo Heavy Industries	17 Mar 1988
YUSOUTEI-NI-GOU	LCU 2002	Sasebo Heavy Industries	11 Mar 1992

Displacement, tons: 420 standard; 540 full load
Dimensions, feet (metres): 170.6 × 28.5 × 5.2 *(52 × 8.7 × 1.6)*
Main machinery: 2 Mitsubishi S6U-MTK diesels; 3,000 hp(m) *(2.23 MW)*; 2 shafts
Speed, knots: 12
Complement: 28
Guns: 1 GE 20 mm/76 Sea Vulcan; 3 barrels per mounting; 1,500 rds/min combined to 4 km *(2.2 n miles)*.
Radars: Navigation: OPS-9B/26; I-band.

Comment: First approved in 1986 estimates, laid down 11 May 1987, launched 9 October 1987. Second approved in FY90 estimates, laid down 17 May 1991, launched 7 October 1991; plans for a third have been scrapped. Official names are *LCU 01* and *LCU 02*.

YUSOUTEI-ICHI-GOU   *5/2005*, Hachiro Nakai* / 1153279

6 LANDING CRAFT AIR CUSHION (LCAC)

AIR CUSHION-TEI – (1 — 6) – GOU LCAC 2101-2106

Displacement, tons: 100 standard; 180 full load
Dimensions, feet (metres): 88 oa (on cushion) (81 between hard structures) × 47 beam (on cushion) (43 beam hard structure) × 2.9 draught (off cushion) *(26.8 (24.7) × 14.3 (13.1) × 0.9)*
Main machinery: 4 Avco-Lycoming TF-40B gas turbines; 2 for propulsion and 2 for lift; 16,000 hp *(12 MW)* sustained; 2 shrouded reversible-pitch airscrews (propulsion); 4 double entry fans, centrifugal or mixed flow (lift)
Speed, knots: 40 (loaded)
Range, n miles: 300 at 35 kt; 200 at 40 kt
Complement: 5
Military lift: 24 troops; 1 MBT or 60 — 75 tons
Radars: Navigation: LN-66; I-band.

Comment: Built by Textron Marine, New Orleans for embarkation in LPDs. Approval for sale given by US on 8 April 1994. First one authorised in FY93, second in FY95, third and fourth in FY99 and fifth and sixth in FY00. Cargo space capacity is 1,809 sq ft.

AIR CUSHION-TEI-3-GOU   *7/2005*, Hachiro Nakai* / 1153281

10 LCM TYPE (LCM)

| YF 2121 | 2124-25 | 2127-29 | 2132 | 2135 | 2138 | 2141 |

Displacement, tons: 25 standard
Dimensions, feet (metres): 55.8 × 14 × 2.3 (17.0 × 4.3 × 0.7)
Main machinery: 2 Isuzu E120-MF6R diesels; 480 hp(m) (353 kW); 2 shafts
Speed, knots: 10. **Range, n miles:** 130 at 9 kt
Complement: 3
Military lift: 34 tons or 80 troops

Comment: Built in Japan. YF 2127-29 commissioned in March 1992, 2132 in March 1993, 2135 in March 1995, 2138 in March 1996 and 2141 in March 1997. YF 2150-51 are 50 ton vessels built by Yokohama Yacht and completed in March 2003. With a military lift of 100 tons they are capable of 16 kt.

YF 2124 *11/2005*, Hachiro Nakai* / 1153280

2 YF 2150 CLASS LCM (LCM)

YF 2150-51

Displacement, tons: 50 standard
Dimensions, feet (metres): 121.4 × 22.0 × 11.2 (19.8 × 5.4 × 2.3)
Main machinery: 2 Mitsubishi S12R-MTK diesels; 3,000 hp (2.24 MW): 2 waterjets
Speed, knots: 16
Complement: 4
Military lift: 100 troops or 1 vehicle

Comment: Built in Japan by Universal, Keihin and commissioned on 19 March 2003.

YF 2150 *3/2003, Universal* / 0570727

3 OOSUMI CLASS (LPD/LSTH)

Name	No	Builders	Laid down	Launched	Commissioned
OOSUMI	LST 4001	Mitsui, Tamano	6 Dec 1995	18 Nov 1996	11 Mar 1998
SHIMOKITA	LST 4002	Mitsui, Tamano	30 Nov 1999	29 Nov 2000	12 Mar 2002
KUNISAKI	LST 4003	Universal, Maizuru	7 Sep 2000	13 Dec 2001	26 Feb 2003

Displacement, tons: 8,900 standard; 14,000 full load
Dimensions, feet (metres): 584 × 84.6 × 19.7 (178 × 25.8 × 6)
Flight deck, feet (metres): 426.5 × 75.5 (130 × 23)
Main machinery: 2 Mitsui 16V 42MA diesels; 26,000 hp(m) (19.4 MW); 2 shafts; 2 bow thrusters
Speed, knots: 22
Complement: 135
Military lift: 330 troops; 2 LCAC; 10 Type 90 tanks or 1,400 tons cargo

Guns: 2 GE/GD 20 mm Vulcan Phalanx Mk 15 ❶. 6 barrels per mounting; 3,000 rds/min combined to 1.5 km.
Countermeasures: ESM/ECM.
Radars: Air search: Mitsubishi OPS-14C ❷; C-band.
Surface search: JRC OPS-28D ❸; G-band.
Navigation: JRC OPS-20; I-band.

Helicopters: Platform for 2 CH-47J.

Programmes: A 5,500 ton LST was requested and not approved in the 1989 or 1990 estimates. The published design resembled the Italian San Giorgio with a large flight deck and a stern dock. No further action was taken for two years but the FY93 request included a larger ship showing the design of a USN LPH, although smaller in size. This vessel, with some modifications, was authorised in the 1993 estimates. A second of class approved in FY98 and third in FY99.
Structure: Through deck, flight deck and stern docking well make this more like a mini LHA than an LST, except that the ship is described as providing only 'platform and refuelling facilities for helicopters'.

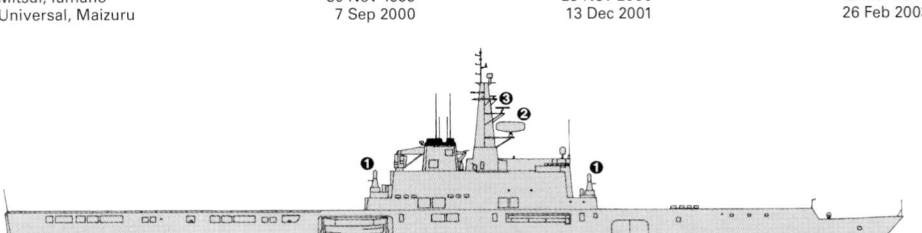

OOSUMI *(Scale 1 : 1,500), Ian Sturton* / 0012652

KUNISAKI *7/2005*, Hachiro Nakai* 1153277

SHIMOKITA *5/2005*, Hachiro Nakai* / 1153278

MINE WARFARE FORCES

2 URAGA CLASS (MINESWEEPER TENDERS) (MSTH/ML)

Name	No	Builders	Launched	Commissioned
URAGA	MST 463	Hitachi, Maizuru	22 May 1996	19 Mar 1997
BUNGO	MST 464	Mitsui, Tamano	24 Apr 1997	23 Mar 1998

Displacement, tons: 5,650 standard; 6,850 full load
Dimensions, feet (metres): 462.6 × 72.2 × 17.7 *(141 × 22 × 5.4)*
Main machinery: 2 Mitsui 12V42MA diesels; 19,500 hp(m) *(14.33 MW)*; 2 shafts
Speed, knots: 22
Complement: 160
Guns: 1 OTO Melara 3 in *(76 mm)*/62 compact; 85 rds/min to 16 km *(8.6 n miles)*; weight of shell 6 kg.
Mines: Laying capability; 4 rails (Type 3). 200 mines.
Radars: Air search: OPS-14C; C-band.
Fire control: Type 2—23; I/J-band.
Navigation: JRC OPS-39C; I-band.
Helicopters: Platform for 1 MH-53E.

Comment: First one authorised 15 February 1994 and laid down 19 May 1995; second authorised in FY95 and laid down 4 July 1996. Capable of laying mines, from four internal rails. Phalanx is planned to be fitted forward of the bridge and on the superstructure aft of the funnel.

URAGA   *5/2005*, Hachiro Nakai* / 1153282

3 YAEYAMA CLASS (MINESWEEPERS — OCEAN) (MSO)

Name	No	Builders	Launched	Commissioned
YAEYAMA	MSO 301	Hitachi Zosen, Kanagawa	29 Aug 1991	16 Mar 1993
TSUSHIMA	MSO 302	Nippon Koukan, Tsurumi	20 Sep 1991	23 Mar 1993
HACHIJYO	MSO 303	Nippon Koukan, Tsurumi	15 Dec 1992	24 Mar 1994

Displacement, tons: 1,000 standard; 1,200 full load
Dimensions, feet (metres): 219.8 × 38.7 × 10.2 *(67 × 11.8 × 3.1)*
Main machinery: 2 Mitsubishi 6NMU-TA1 diesels; 2,400 hp(m) *(1.76 MW)*; 2 shafts; 1 hydrojet bow thruster; 350 hp(m) *(257 kW)*
Speed, knots: 14
Complement: 60
Guns: 1 JM-61 20 mm/76 Sea Vulcan; 3 barrels per mounting; 1,500 rds/min combined to 4 km *(2.2 n miles)*.
Radars: Surface search: Fujitsu OPS-39B; I-band.
Sonars: Raytheon SQQ-32 VDS; high frequency; active.

Comment: First two approved in 1989 estimates, third in 1990. First laid down 30 August 1990, second 20 July 1990 and third 17 May 1991. Wooden hulls. Fitted with S 7 deep sea minehunting system, S 8 (SLQ-48) deep sea moored minesweeping equipment and ADI Dyad sweeps. Appears to be a derivative of the USN Avenger class. An integrated tactical system is fitted. Termination of the programme at three of the class suggests similar problems to US ships of the same class.

YAEYAMA   *5/2005*, Hachiro Nakai* / 1153283

2 NIIJIMA CLASS (DRONE CONTROL SHIPS) (MCSD)

Name	No	Builders	Commissioned
KAMISHIMA	MCL 725 (ex-MSC 664)	Nippon Koukan, Tsurumi	16 Dec 1986
OGISHIMA	MCL 726 (ex-MSC 666)	Hitachi, Kanagawa	19 Dec 1987

Displacement, tons: 440 standard; 510 full load
Dimensions, feet (metres): 180.4 × 30.8 × 8.2 *(55 × 9.4 × 2.5)*
Main machinery: 2 Mitsubishi 12ZC diesels; 1,440 hp(m) *(1.06 MW)*; 2 shafts
Speed, knots: 14
Complement: 28
Guns: 1 GE 20 mm/76 Sea Vulcan 20; 3 barrels per mounting; 1,500 rds/min combined to 4 km *(2.2 n miles)*.
Radars: Surface search: Fujitsu OPS-9B; I-band.

Comment: Both converted to act as Minesweeper Control Ship (MCLs) and equipped to operate SAM remote controlled drones. All minesweeping gear removed. *Ogishima* converted as MCL on 8 February 2006.

NIIJIMA CLASS   *6/2005*, Hachiro Nakai* / 1153284

13 HATSUSHIMA/UWAJIMA CLASS (MINEHUNTERS/SWEEPERS — COASTAL) (MHSC)

Name	No	Builders	Commissioned
YURISHIMA	MSC 668	Nippon Koukan, Tsurumi	15 Dec 1988
HIKOSHIMA	MSC 669	Hitachi, Kanagawa	15 Dec 1988
AWASHIMA	MSC 670	Hitachi, Kanagawa	13 Dec 1989
SAKUSHIMA	MSC 671	Nippon Koukan, Tsurumi	13 Dec 1989
UWAJIMA	MSC 672	Nippon Koukan, Tsurumi	19 Dec 1990
IESHIMA	MSC 673	Hitachi, Kanagawa	19 Dec 1990
TSUKISHIMA	MSC 674	Hitachi, Kanagawa	17 Mar 1993
MAEJIMA	MSC 675	Hitachi, Kanagawa	15 Dec 1993
KUMEJIMA	MSC 676	Nippon Koukan, Tsurumi	12 Dec 1994
MAKISHIMA	MSC 677	Hitachi, Kanagawa	12 Dec 1994
TOBISHIMA	MSC 678	Nippon Koukan, Tsurumi	10 Mar 1995
YUGESHIMA	MSC 679	Hitachi, Kanagawa	11 Dec 1996
NAGASHIMA	MSC 680	Nippon Koukan, Tsurumi	25 Dec 1996

Displacement, tons: 440 (490, MSC 670—680) standard; 520 (550 MSC 670—671) (570 MSC 672—680) full load
Dimensions, feet (metres): 180.4 (190.3, MSC 670 onwards) × 30.8 × 8.2 (9.5) *(55 (58.0) × 9.4 × 2.5 (2.9))*
Main machinery: 2 Mitsubishi 6NMU-TAI diesels; 1,800 hp(m) *(1.3 MW)*; 2 shafts
Speed, knots: 14. **Range, n miles:** 2,500 at 10 kt
Complement: 45; 40 (MSC 675 onwards)

Guns: 1 JM-61 20 mm/76 Sea Vulcan 20; 3 barrels per mounting; 1,500 rds/min combined to 4 km *(2.2 n miles)*.
Radars: Surface search: Fujitsu OPS-9 or OPS-39 (MSC 674 onwards); I-band.
Sonars: Nec/Hitachi ZQS 2B or ZQS 3 (MSC 672 onwards); hull-mounted; minehunting; high frequency.

Programmes: First ordered in 1976. Last two authorised in FY94. Because of the new sonar and mine detonating equipment vessels from MSC 672 onwards are known as the Uwajima class.
Structure: From MSC 670 onwards the hull is lengthened by 2.7 m in order to improve the sleeping accommodation from three tier to two tier bunks. Hulls are made of wood. The last pair have more powerful engines developing 1,800 hp(m) *(1.32 MW)*.
Operational: Fitted with S 4 (S 7 from MSC 672 onwards) mine detonating equipment, a remote-controlled counter-mine charge. Four clearance divers are carried. MSC 668, 669, 670 and 671 formed the Minesweeper Squadron to deploy to the Gulf in 1991. Earlier vessels of the class converted to drone control or paid off at a rate of one or two a year.

YURISHIMA   *5/2005*, Hachiro Nakai* / 1153285

AWASHIMA   *7/2005*, Hachiro Nakai* / 1153287

TOBISHIMA   *7/2005*, Hachiro Nakai* / 1153288

11 + 1 SUGASHIMA CLASS (MINEHUNTER (COASTAL)) (MHC)

Name	No	Builders	Launched	Commissioned
SUGASHIMA	MSC 681	NKK, Tsurumi	25 Aug 1997	16 Mar 1999
NOTOJIMA	MSC 682	Hitachi, Kanagawa	3 Sep 1997	16 Mar 1999
TSUNOSHIMA	MSC 683	Hitachi, Kanagawa	22 Oct 1998	13 Mar 2000
NAOSHIMA	MSC 684	NKK, Tsurumi	7 Oct 1999	16 Mar 2001
TOYOSHIMA	MSC 685	Hitachi, Kanagawa	13 Sep 2000	4 Mar 2002
UKUSHIMA	MSC 686	Universal, Keihin (Tsurumi)	17 Sep 2001	18 Mar 2003
IZUSHIMA	MSC 687	Universal, Keihin (Kanawaga)	31 Oct 2001	18 Mar 2003
AISHIMA	MSC 688	Universal, Keihin (Tsurumi)	8 Oct 2002	16 Feb 2004
AOSHIMA	MSC 689	Universal, Keihin (Kanawaga)	16 Sep 2003	9 Feb 2005
MIYAJIMA	MSC 690	Universal, Keihin (Tsurumi)	10 Oct 2003	9 Feb 2005
SHISHIJIMA	MSC 691	Universal, Keihin (Tsurumi)	29 Sep 2004	8 Feb 2006
KUROSHIMA	MSC 692	Universal, Keihin (Tsurumi)	31 Aug 2005	Feb 2007

Displacement, tons: 510 standard; 590 full load
Dimensions, feet (metres): 177.2 × 30.8 × 9.8 *(54.0 × 9.4 × 3.0)*
Main machinery: 2 Mitsubishi 6 NMU-TAI diesels; 1,800 hp(m) *(1.33 MW)*; 2 shafts; bow thrusters
Speed, knots: 14. **Range, n miles:** 2,500 at 10 kt
Complement: 45
Guns: 1 JM-61 20 mm/76 Sea Vulcan; 3 barrels for mounting; 1,500 rds/min combined to 4 km *(2 n miles).*
Combat data systems: AMS/NEC Nautis-M type MCM control system.
Radars: Surface search: Fujitsu OPS-39B; I-band.
Sonars: THALES Hitachi GEC Type 2093 VDS; high frequency; active.

Comment: First pair authorised in FY95, third in FY96, fourth in FY97, fifth in FY98, sixth and seventh in FY99, eighth in FY00, ninth and tenth in FY01, eleventh in FY02 and twelfth in FY03. Hull is similar to *Uwajima* but the upper deck is extended aft to provide more stowage for mine disposal gear, and there are twin funnels. PAP 104 Mk 5 ROVs are carried and ADI Dyad minesweeping gear fitted.

AOSHIMA   *5/2005*, Hachiro Nakai* / 1153286

0 + 3 570 TON CLASS (MINESWEEPERS — COASTAL) (MSC)

Name	No	Builders	Launched	Commissioned
—	MSC 693	Universal, Keihin (Tsurumi)	Sep 2006	Feb 2008
—	MSC 694	Universal, Keihin (Tsurumi)	2007	Mar 2009

Displacement, tons: 570 standard; 650 full load
Dimensions, feet (metres): 187 × 32.1 × 9.8 *(57.0 × 9.8 × 3.0)*
Main machinery: 2 diesels, 2,200 hp *(1.64 MW)*; 2 shafts
Speed, knots: 14
Complement: 48
Guns: 1 — 20 mm Sea Vulcan.

Comment: First authorised in FY04 budget, second in FY05 budget and third in FY06 budget. To be equipped with S-10 minesweeping and disposal system.

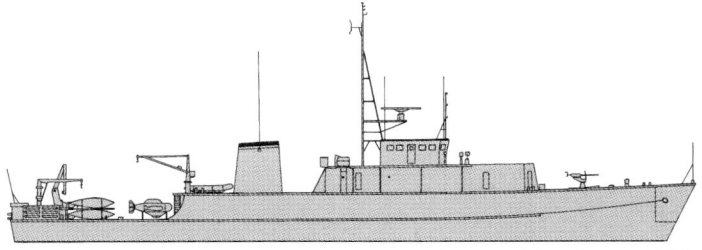

570 TON MSC   *(not to scale), Ian Sturton* / 0569918

6 SAM CLASS (MSD)

SAM 01-06

Displacement, tons: 20 full load
Dimensions, feet (metres): 59.1 × 20 × 5.2 *(18 × 6.1 × 1.6)*
Main machinery: 1 Volvo Penta TAMD 70D diesel; 210 hp(m) *(154 kW)*; 1 Schottel prop
Speed, knots: 8. **Range, n miles:** 330 at 8 kt

Comment: First pair acquired from Karlskronavarvet, Sweden in February 1998 followed by two more in December 1998 and two more in 2000. Remote controlled magnetic and acoustic catamaran sweepers operated by *Kamishima* and *Ogishima.*

SAM 02   *2/2000, Hachiro Nakai* / 0104934

SURVEY AND RESEARCH SHIPS

Notes: (1) The SES trials ship *Merguro II* does not belong to the MSDF.
(2) Survey ships are also included in the Coast Guard section.

2 HIBIKI CLASS (OCEAN SURVEILLANCE SHIPS) (AGOSH)

Name	No	Builders	Launched	Commissioned
HIBIKI	AOS 5201	Mitsui, Tamano	27 July 1990	30 Jan 1991
HARIMA	AOS 5202	Mitsui, Tamano	11 Sep 1991	10 Mar 1992

Displacement, tons: 2,850 standard; 3,000 full load
Dimensions, feet (metres): 219.8 × 98.1 × 24.6 *(67 × 29.9 × 7.5)*
Main machinery: Diesel-electric; 4 Mitsubishi Stu diesels; 3,000 hp(m) *(2.2 MW)*; 4 generators; 2 motors; 3,000 hp(m) *(2.2 MW)*; 2 shafts
Speed, knots: 11 (3 towing)
Range, n miles: 3,800 at 10 kt
Complement: 40
Radars: Surface search: JRC OPS-16; G-band.
Navigation: Koden OPS-9; I-band.
Sonars: UQQ 2 SURTASS; passive surveillance.
Helicopters: Platform only.

Comment: First authorised 24 January 1989, laid down 28 November, second approved in FY90, laid down 26 December 1990. Auxiliary Ocean Surveillance (AOS) ships to a SWATH design similar to USN TAGOS-19 class. A data collection station is based at Yokosuka Bay using WSC-6 satellite data relay to the AOS.

HARIMA   *11/2005*, Hachiro Nakai* / 1153296

1 NICHINAN CLASS (SURVEY SHIP) (AGS)

Name	No	Builders	Launched	Commissioned
NICHINAN	AGS 5105	Mitsubishi, Shimonoseki	11 June 1998	24 Mar 1999

Displacement, tons: 3,300 standard; 4,500 full load
Dimensions, feet (metres): 364.2 × 55.8 × 14.8 *(111 × 17 × 4.5)*
Main machinery: Diesel-electric; 2 Mitsubishi S16U diesel generators; 3 motors; 3,600 hp(m) *(2.7 MW)*; 2 shafts; bow and stern thrusters
Speed, knots: 18
Complement: 90

Comment: Authorisation approved in FY96 to replace *Akashi*. Combination cable repair and hydrographic survey ship. Equipped with one ROV.

NICHINAN   *3/1999, Hachiro Nakai* / 1044425

1 SUMA CLASS (AGS)

Name	No	Builders	Launched	Commissioned
SUMA	AGS 5103	Hitachi, Maizuru	1 Sep 1981	30 Mar 1982

Displacement, tons: 1,180 standard; 1,700 full load
Dimensions, feet (metres): 236.2 × 42 × 11.1 *(72 × 12.8 × 3.4)*
Main machinery: 2 Fuji 6L27.5XF diesels; 3,000 hp(m) *(2.24 MW)*; 2 shafts; cp props; bow thruster
Speed, knots: 15
Complement: 64 plus 5 scientists
Countermeasures: ESM: NOLR-6.
Radars: Navigation: OPS-20; I-band.

Comment: Laid down 24 September 1980. Carries an 11 m launch for surveying work.

SUMA   *2/1999, Hachiro Nakai* / 0080180

2 FUTAMI CLASS (AGS)

Name	No	Builders	Launched	Commissioned
FUTAMI	AGS 5102	Mitsubishi, Shimonoseki	9 Aug 1978	27 Feb 1979
WAKASA	AGS 5104	Hitachi, Maizuru	21 May 1985	25 Feb 1986

Displacement, tons: 2,050 standard; 3,175 full load
Dimensions, feet (metres): 318.2 × 49.2 × 13.8 *(97 × 15 × 4.2)*
Main machinery: 2 Kawasaki-MAN V8V22/30ATL diesels; 4,000 hp(m) *(2.94 MW)* (AGS 5102); 2 Fuji 8L27.5XF diesels; 3,250 hp(m) *(2.39 MW)* (AGS 5104); 2 shafts; cp props; bow thruster
Speed, knots: 16
Complement: 105 (95 AG 5104)
Radars: Navigation: JRC OPS-18-3; G-band.

Comment: AGS 5102 laid down 20 January 1978, AGS 5104 21 August 1984. Built to merchant marine design. Carry an RCV-225 remote-controlled rescue/underwater survey submarine. *Wakasa* has a slightly taller funnel.

FUTAMI   *10/2002, Takeshi Oosaki* / 1044426

1 KURIHAMA CLASS (ASE/AGE)

Name	No	Builders	Launched	Commissioned
KURIHAMA	ASE 6101	Sasebo Heavy Industries	20 Sep 1979	8 Apr 1980

Displacement, tons: 950 standard; 1,100 full load
Dimensions, feet (metres): 223 × 37.9 × 9.8 (screws) *(68 × 11.6 × 3)*
Main machinery: 2 Fuji 6S30B diesels; 2,600 hp(m) *(1.94 MW)*; 2 shafts; 2 cp props; 2 auxiliary electric props; bow thruster
Speed, knots: 15
Complement: 40 plus 12 scientists
Radars: Navigation: Fujitsu OPS-9B; I-band.

Comment: Experimental ship built for the Technical Research and Development Institute and used for testing underwater weapons and sensors.

KURIHAMA   *7/2002, Hachiro Nakai* / 0529049

1 ASUKA CLASS (AGEH)

Name	No	Builders	Launched	Commissioned
ASUKA	ASE 6102	Sumitomo, Uraga	21 June 1994	22 Mar 1995

Displacement, tons: 4,250 standard; 6,200 full load
Dimensions, feet (metres): 495.4 × 56.8 × 16.4 *(151 × 17.3 × 5)*
Main machinery: COGLAG; 2 IHI/GE LM 2500 gas turbines; 43,000 hp *(31.6 MW)*; 2 shafts; cp props
Speed, knots: 27
Complement: 70 plus 100 scientists
Missiles: SAM: 8 cell VLS.
Weapons control: Type 3 FCS.
Radars: Air search: SPY-1D type; E/F-band.
Air/surface search: Melco OPS-14C; D-band.
Surface search: JRC OPS-18-1; G-band.
Fire control: Type 3; I/J-band.
Sonars: Bow-mounted; active search; medium frequency.
Towed passive/active array in due course.
Helicopters: 1 SH-60J Seahawk.

Comment: Included in the FY92 programme and laid down 21 April 1993. For experimental and weapon systems testing which started with the FCS 3 in 1996. The bow sonar dome extends aft to the bridge. The VLS system is on the forecastle. Surveillance and countermeasures systems are also being evaluated.

ASUKA   *7/2005*, Hachiro Nakai* / 1153297

RESCUE VEHICLES

2 RESCUE SUBMARINES (DSRV)

Displacement, tons: 40
Dimensions, feet (metres): 40.7 × 10.5 × 14.1 *(12.4 × 3.2 × 4.6)*
Main machinery: Electric; 30 hp *(22 kW)*; single shaft
Speed, knots: 4
Complement: 2

Comment: Rescue submersibles built by Kawasaki Heavy Industries, Kobe and delivered on 27 August 1999. Space for 12 people. Sonars are fitted on the bow, upper and lower casings for depth sounding and obstacle avoidance. Can be deployed in the submarine rescue ships *Chiyoda* (AS 405) and *Chihaya* (ASR 403).

DSRV   *7/2005*, Hachiro Nakai* / 1153295

TRAINING SHIPS

1 SHIMAYUKI CLASS (TRAINING SHIP) (AXGHM/TV)

Name	No	Builders	Commissioned
SHIMAYUKI	TV 3513 (ex-DD 133)	Mitsubishi, Nagasaki	17 Feb 1987

Displacement, tons: 3,050 standard; 4,200 full load
Dimensions, feet (metres): 426.4 × 44.6 × 14.4 *(130 × 13.6 × 4.4)*
Main machinery: COGOG; 2 Kawasaki-RR Olympus TM3B gas turbines; 45,000 hp *(33.5 MW)* sustained; 2 RR Type RM1C gas turbines; 9,900 hp *(7.4 MW)* sustained; 2 shafts; cp props
Speed, knots: 30; 19 cruise
Complement: 200

Missiles: SSM: 8 McDonnell Douglas Harpoon (2 quad) launchers; active radar homing to 130 km *(70 n miles)* at 0.9 Mach; warhead 227 kg.
SAM: Raytheon Sea Sparrow Mk 29 Type 3A launcher; semi-active radar homing to 14.6 km *(8 n miles)* at 2.5 Mach; warhead 39 kg; 12 missiles.
A/S: Honeywell ASROC Mk 112 octuple launcher; inertial guidance to 1.6 – 10 km *(1 – 5.4 n miles)* at 0.9 Mach; payload Mk 46 Mod 5 Neartip.
Guns: 1 OTO Melara 3 in *(76 mm)*/62 compact; 85 rds/min to 16 km *(8.6 n miles)* anti-surface; 12 km *(6.5 n miles)* anti-aircraft; weight of shell 6 kg.
2 General Electric/General Dynamics 20 mm Phalanx Mk 15 CIWS; 6 barrels per mounting; 3,000 rds/min combined to 1.5 km.
Torpedoes: 6 – 324 mm Type 68 (2 triple) tubes. Honeywell Mk 46 Mod 5 Neartip; anti-submarine; active/passive homing to 11 km *(5.9 n miles)* at 40 kt; warhead 44 kg.
Countermeasures: Decoys: 2 Loral Hycor SRBOC 6-barrelled Mk 36 chaff launchers; range 4 km *(2.2 n miles)*.
ESM: NOLR 6C; intercept.
ECM: Fujitsu OLT 3; jammer.
Combat data systems: OYQ-5 action data automation; Link 14 (receive only). SATCOM.
Radars: Air search: Melco OPS-14B; D-band.
Surface search: JRC OPS-18-1; G-band.
Fire control: Type 2 – 12 A; I/J-band (for SAM).
2 Type 2 – 21/21A; I/J-band (for guns).
Tacan: ORN-6C.
Sonars: Nec OQS 4A (II) (SQS-23 type); bow-mounted; active search and attack; low frequency.
Helicopters: Platform for 1 SH-60J Seahawk.

Comment: Converted to training ship in March 1999. Helicopter hangar converted to lecture rooms.

SHIMAYUKI   *6/2002, Mitsuhiro Kadota* / 0528911

2 ASAGIRI CLASS (TRAINING SHIPS) (AX/TV)

Name	No	Builders	Laid down	Launched	Commissioned
YAMAGIRI	TV 3515 (ex-DD 152)	Mitsui, Tamano	5 Feb 1986	8 Oct 1987	25 Jan 1989
ASAGIRI	TV 3516 (ex-DD 151)	Ishikawajima Harima, Tokyo	13 Feb 1985	19 Sep 1986	17 Mar 1988

Displacement, tons: 3,500 standard; 4,900 full load
Dimensions, feet (metres): 449.4 × 48 × 14.6
  (137 × 14.6 × 4.5)
Main machinery: COGAG; 4 RR Spey SM1A gas turbines;
  53,300 hp *(39.8 MW)* sustained; 2 shafts; cp props
Speed, knots: 30+
Complement: 220

Missiles: SSM: 8 McDonnell Douglas Harpoon (2 quad)
  launchers; active radar homing to 130 km *(70 n miles)* at
  0.9 Mach; warhead 227 kg.
  SAM: Raytheon Sea Sparrow Mk 29 (Type 3/3A) octuple
  launcher; semi-active radar homing to 14.6 km *(8 n miles)*
  at 2.5 Mach; warhead 39 kg; 20 missiles.
  A/S: Honeywell ASROC Mk 112 octuple launcher; inertial
  guidance to 1.6—10 km *(1—5.4 n miles)* at 0.9 Mach;
  payload Mk 46 Mod 5 Neartip. Reload capability.
Guns: 1 Otobreda 3 in *(76 mm)*/62 compact; 85 rds/min
  to 16 km *(8.6 n miles)* anti-surface; 12 km *(6.5 n miles)*
  anti-aircraft; weight of shell 6 kg.
  2 General Electric/General Dynamics 20 mm Phalanx
  Mk 15 CIWS; 6 barrels per mounting; 3,000 rds/min
  combined to 1.5 km.
Torpedoes: 6—324 mm Type 68 (2 triple) HOS 301 tubes.
  Honeywell Mk 46 Mod 5 Neartip; anti-submarine; active/
  passive homing to 11 km *(5.9 n miles)* at 40 kt; warhead
  44 kg.
Countermeasures: Decoys: 2 Loral Hycor SRBOC 6-barrelled
  Mk 36 chaff launchers; range 4 km *(2.2 n miles)*.
  1 SLQ-25 Nixie or Type 4; towed torpedo decoy.

ASAGIRI *4/2005*, Takeshi Oosaki* / 1153299

ESM: Nec NOLR 6C or NOLR 8 (DD 152); intercept.
ECM: Fujitsu OLT-3; jammer.
Combat data systems: OYQ-7B data automation; Link 11/14.
  SATCOM. ORQ-1 helicopter datalink for SH-60J.
Radars: Air search: Melco OPS-14C (DD 151—154); D-band.
  Melco OPS-24 (DD 155—158); 3D; D-band.
  Surface search: JRC OPS-28C; G-band (DD 151, 152, 155—158).
  JRC OPS-28C-Y; G-band (DD 153—154).
  Fire control: Type 2—22 (for guns). Type 2—12E (for SAM)
  (DD 151—154); Type 2—12G (for SAM) (DD 155—158).
  Tacan: ORN-6D (URN 25).

Sonars: Mitsubishi OQS 4A (II); hull-mounted; active search
  and attack; low frequency.
  OQR-1; towed array; passive search; very low frequency.

Helicopters: Platform for 1 SH-60J Seahawk.

Comment: TV 3515 converted to training ship on 18
  March 2004 and TV 3516 on 16 February 2005. Hangars
  converted to lecture rooms.

1 KASHIMA CLASS (TRAINING SHIP) (AXH/TV)

Name	No	Builders	Launched	Commissioned
KASHIMA	TV 3508	Hitachi, Maizuru	23 Feb 1994	26 Jan 1995

Displacement, tons: 4,050 standard; 5,400 full load
Dimensions, feet (metres): 469.2 × 59.1 × 15.1 *(143 × 18 × 4.6)*
Main machinery: CODOG; 2 RR Spey SM1C gas-turbines; 27,000 hp *(20.1 MW)* sustained;
  2 Mitsubishi S16U-MTK diesels; 8,000 hp(m) *(5.88 MW)*; 2 shafts
Speed, knots: 25. **Range, n miles:** 7,000 at 18 kt
Complement: 360 (includes 125 midshipmen)
Guns: 1 OTO Melara 76 mm/62. 2—40 mm saluting guns.
Torpedoes: 6—324 mm (2 triple) tubes.
Radars: Air/surface search: Melco OPS-14C; D-band.
  Surface search: JRC OPS-18-1; D-band.
  Navigation: Fujitsu OPS-20; I-band.
  Fire control: Type 2—23; I/J-band.
Sonars: Hull-mounted; active search and attack; medium frequency. OQS-4.
Helicopters: Platform for 1 medium.

Comment: Approved in FY91 as a dedicated training ship but the project postponed to
  FY92 as a budget saving measure. Laid down 20 April 1993.

KASHIMA *7/2005*, Michael Nitz* / 1153343

1 TENRYU CLASS (TRAINING SUPPORT SHIP) (AVHM/TV)

Name	No	Builders	Launched	Commissioned
TENRYU	ATS 4203	Sumitomo, Uraga	14 Apr 1999	17 Mar 2000

Displacement, tons: 2,450 standard
Dimensions, feet (metres): 347.8 × 54.1 × 13.5 *(106 × 16.5 × 4.1)*
Main machinery: 4 Niigata 8MG28H diesels; 12,800 hp(m) *(9.5 MW)* sustained; 2 shafts
Speed, knots: 22
Complement: 144
Guns: 1 OTO Melara 3 in *(76 mm)*/62 compact; 85 rds/min to 16 km *(8.6 n miles)*; weight
  of shell 6 kg.
Radars: Air/surface search: Melco OPS-14; D-band.
  Surface search: OPS-28D; G/H-band.
  Fire control: Type 2—22; I/J-band.
Helicopters: 1 medium.

Comment: Authorised in 1997 budget as a replacement for *Azuma* and laid down
  19 June 1998. Carries four BQM-34J drones and four Northrop Chukar III drones used
  for evaluating performance of ships SAM systems. Improved 'Kurobe' design.

TENRYU *6/2005*, Hachiro Nakai* / 1153298

1 KUROBE CLASS (TRAINING SUPPORT SHIP) (AVM/TV)

Name	No	Builders	Commissioned
KUROBE	ATS 4202	Nippon Koukan, Tsurumi	23 Mar 1989

Displacement, tons: 2,200 standard; 3,200 full load
Dimensions, feet (metres): 331.4 × 54.1 × 13.1 *(101 × 16.5 × 4)*
Main machinery: 4 Fuji 8L27.5XF diesels; 9,160 hp(m) *(6.8 MW)*; 2 shafts; cp props
Speed, knots: 20
Complement: 143 (17 officers)
Guns: 1 FMC/OTO Melara 3 in *(76 mm)*/62 Mk 75; 85 rds/min to 16 km *(8.6 n miles)* anti-
  surface; 12 km *(6.5 n miles)* anti-aircraft; weight of shell 6 kg.
Radars: Air search: Melco OPS-14C; D-band.
  Surface search: JRC OPS-18-1; G-band.
  Fire control: Type 2—22; I/J-band.

Comment: Approved under 1986 estimates, laid down 31 July 1987, launched 23 May 1988.
  Carries four BQM-34AJ high-speed drones and four Northrop Chukar II drones with two
  stern launchers. Used for training crews in anti-aircraft operations and evaluating the
  effectiveness and capability of ships' anti-aircraft missile systems.

KUROBE *5/2005*, Hachiro Nakai* / 1153300

1 TRAINING TENDER (YXT)

YTE 13

Displacement, tons: 179 standard
Dimensions, feet (metres): 115.0 × 24.2 × 5.6 *(35.3 × 7.4 × 1.72)*
Main machinery: 2 Yanmar 12 LAK ST2 diesels; 2,200 hp(m) *(1.16 MW)*; 2 shafts
Speed, knots: 16

Comment: Approved in FY00 budget and commissioned in 2002. Assigned to 1st Maritime
  Service School for cadet training.

YTE 13 *6/2005*, Hachiro Nakai* / 1153301

AUXILIARIES

2 MASHUU CLASS
(FAST COMBAT SUPPORT SHIPS) (AOE/AORH)

Name	No	Builders	Laid down	Launched	Commissioned
MASHUU	AOE 425	Mitsui, Tamano	21 Jan 2002	5 Feb 2003	15 Mar 2004
OUMI	AOE 426	Universal, Maizuru	7 Feb 2003	19 Feb 2004	3 Mar 2005

Displacement, tons: 13,500 standard; 25,000 full load
Dimensions, feet (metres): 725 × 88.6 × 27,2 *(221 × 27 × 8.3)*
Main machinery: 2 Kawasaki RR Spey SM1C gas turbines; 40,000 hp *(29.8 MW)*; 2 shafts
Speed, knots: 24
Complement: 145
Guns: 2—20 mm CIWS (to be fitted).
Countermeasures: Decoys: 4 SRBOC Mk 36 chaff and IR launchers.

Comment: First ship approved in FY00 and second in FY01. Capacity for 30 containers. Cranes capable of lifting 15 tons. Three replenishment at sea positions on each side.

OUMI   *8/2005*, Hachiro Nakai* / 1153291

6 300 TON CLASS (EOD TENDERS) (YDT)

YDT 01-06

Displacement, tons: 300 standard
Dimensions, feet (metres): 150.9 × 28.2 × 7.2 *(46 × 8.6 × 2.2)*
Main machinery: 2 Niigata 6NSDL diesels; 1,500 hp(m) *(1.1 MW)*; 2 shafts
Speed, knots: 15
Complement: 15 plus 15 divers

Comment: Built by Maehata Zousen. First pair approved in FY98, third in FY99, fourth in FY00 and fifth and sixth in FY01. First two commissioned 24 March 2000, third on 21 March 2001, fourth in December 2001 and last two on 14 March 2003. Used as diving tenders.

YDT 05   *8/2005*, Hachiro Nakai* / 1153289

1 CHIYODA CLASS
(SUBMARINE TENDER DEPOT AND RESCUE SHIP) (AS/ASRH)

Name	No	Builders	Launched	Commissioned
CHIYODA	AS 405	Mitsui, Tamano	7 Dec 1983	27 Mar 1985

Displacement, tons: 3,650 standard; 5,400 full load
Dimensions, feet (metres): 370.6 × 57.7 × 15.1 *(113 × 17.6 × 4.6)*
Main machinery: 2 Mitsui 8L42M diesels; 11,500 hp(m) *(8.6 MW)*; 2 shafts; cp props; bow and stern thrusters
Speed, knots: 17
Complement: 120 plus 80 submarine crew rest facility
Radars: Navigation: JRC OPS-16; G-band.
Sonars: SQS-36D.
Helicopters: Platform for up to MH-53 size.

Comment: Laid down 19 January 1983. Carries a 40 ton Deep Submergence Rescue Vehicle (DSRV), which is lowered and recovered through a centreline moonpool. The DSRV can mate to a decompression chamber. A personnel transfer capsule can also be deployed. Flagship Second Submarine Flotilla based at Yokosuka.

CHIYODA   *7/2005*, Hachiro Nakai* / 1153292

1 CHIHAYA CLASS (SUBMARINE RESCUE SHIP) (ASRH)

Name	No	Builders	Launched	Commissioned
CHIHAYA	ASR 403	Mitsui, Tamano	8 Oct 1998	23 Mar 2000

Displacement, tons: 5,450 standard; 6,900 full load
Dimensions, feet (metres): 419.9 × 65.6 × 16.7 *(128 × 20 × 5.1)*
Main machinery: 2 Mitsui 12V 42M-A diesels; 19,500 hp(m) *(14.33 MW)*; 2 shafts; 2 bow and 2 stern thrusters
Speed, knots: 21
Complement: 125
Radars: Navigation: OPS-20; I-band.
Helicopters: Platform for up to MH-53 size.

Comment: Authorisation approved in the 1996 budget as a replacement for *Fushimi*. Laid down 13 October 1997. Fitted with a search sonar and carries a 40 ton DSRV. Also used as a hospital ship.

CHIHAYA   *6/2004, Hachiro Nakai* / 1044422

3 TOWADA CLASS
(FAST COMBAT SUPPORT SHIPS) (AOE/AORH)

Name	No	Builders	Launched	Commissioned
TOWADA	AOE 422	Hitachi, Maizuru	25 Mar 1986	24 Mar 1987
TOKIWA	AOE 423	Ishikawajima Harima, Tokyo	23 Mar 1989	12 Mar 1990
HAMANA	AOE 424	Hitachi, Maizuru	18 May 1989	29 Mar 1990

Displacement, tons: 8,150 standard; 15,850 full load
Dimensions, feet (metres): 547.8 × 72.2 × 26.9 *(167 × 22 × 8.2)*
Main machinery: 2 Mitsui 16V42MA diesels; 26,000 hp(m) *(19.4 MW)*; 2 shafts
Speed, knots: 22
Range, n miles: 10,500 at 20 kt
Complement: 140
Cargo capacity: 5,700 tons
Countermeasures: Decoys: 2 chaff launchers can be fitted.
Radars: Surface search: JRC OPS-18-1/28C; G-band.
Helicopters: Platform for MH-53 size.

Comment: First approved under 1984 estimates, laid down 17 April 1985. Second and third of class in 1987 estimates. AOE 423 laid down 12 May 1988, and AOE 424 8 July 1988. Three replenishment at sea positions on each side (two fuel only, one stores).

TOKIWA   *11/2004** / 1153344

2 FIREFIGHTING TENDERS (YTR)

YR 01-02

Displacement, tons: 60 standard
Dimensions, feet (metres): 82.0 × 18.0 × 3.6 *(25.0 × 5.5 × 1.1)*
Main machinery: 1 Isuzu Marine UM6WGITCG diesels; 750 hp *(560 kW)*; 2 Isuzu Marine UM6RB diesels; 1,040 hp *(775 kW)*; 3 shafts
Speed, knots: 19
Complement: 10

Comment: Built in Japan by Ishikawajima-Harima Heavy Industries. *YR 01* approved in FY99 budget and commissioned in 2001. *YR 02* approved in FY00 budget and commissioned in 2002. Fitted with three waterjets forward and a crane aft.

YR 01   *9/2002, Takatoshi Okano* / 0570888

34 HARBOUR TANKERS (YO/YW/YG)

Comment: There are: 17 of 490 tons (YO 14, 21—27, 29—31, 33—38); eight of 310 tons (YW 17—24); two of 290 tons (YO 12—13); seven of 270 tons (YO 28, 32 and YG 201—205). A further 490 ton YO and 270 ton YG are to enter service in 2007.

YO 36   *11/2005*, Hachiro Nakai* / 1153293

1 MUROTO CLASS (CABLE REPAIR SHIP) (ARC)

Name	No	Builders	Launched	Commissioned
MUROTO	ARC 482	Mitsubishi, Shimonoseki	25 July 1979	27 Mar 1980

Displacement, tons: 4,500 standard; 6,000 full load
Dimensions, feet (metres): 436.2 × 57.1 × 18.7 *(133 × 17.4 × 5.7)*
Main machinery: 4 Kawasaki-MAN V8V22/30ATL diesels; 8,800 hp(m) *(6.6 MW)*; 2 shafts; bow thruster
Speed, knots: 18
Complement: 135
Radars: Navigation: Fujitsu OPS-9B; I-band.

Comment: Ocean survey capability. Laid down 28 November 1978. Similar vessels in civilian use.

MUROTO   *1/2006*, Hachiro Nakai* / 1154401

1 HASHIDATE CLASS (ASY/YAC)

Name	No	Builders	Launched	Commissioned
HASHIDATE	ASY 91	Hitachi, Kanagawa	26 July 1999	30 Nov 1999

Displacement, tons: 400 standard; 490 full load
Dimensions, feet (metres): 203.4 × 30.8 × 6.6 *(62 × 9.4 × 2.0)*
Main machinery: 2 Niigata 16V 16FX diesels; 5,500 hp(m) *(4.04 MW)*; 2 shafts
Speed, knots: 20
Range, n miles: 1,000 at 12 kt
Complement: 29 plus 130 passengers

Comment: Authorised in FY97 budget. Laid down 28 October 1998. Has replaced *Hiyodori* as a ceremonial yacht. Has facilities for disaster relief. Based at Yokosuka.

HASHIDATE   *10/2004, Hachiro Nakai* / 1044423

3 + 2 HIUCHI CLASS (MULTIPURPOSE SUPPORT SHIPS) (YTT)

Name	No	Builders	Launched	Commissioned
HIUCHI	AMS 4301	NKK, Tsurumi	4 Sep 2001	27 Mar 2002
SUOU	AMS 4302	Universal, Keihin (Tsurumi)	25 Apr 2003	16 Mar 2004
AMAKUSA	AMS 4303	Universal, Keihin (Tsurumi)	6 Aug 2003	16 Mar 2004
—	AMS 4304		2007	2008
—	AMS 4305		2007	2008

Displacement, tons: 980 standard
Dimensions, feet (metres): 213.3 × 39.4 × 11.5 *(65 × 12 × 3.5)*
Main machinery: 2 Daihatsu 6 DKM-28 (L) diesels; 5,000 hp(m) *(3.67 MW)*; 2 shafts
Speed, knots: 15
Complement: 40
Radars: Navigation: OPS-20; I-band.

Comment: First authorised in FY99, two more in FY01 and two further in FY05 budget. Equipped for torpedo launch and recovery. Replaced ASU 81 class. Used as an ocean tug.

HIUCHI   *7/2005*, Hachiro Nakai* / 1153294

ICEBREAKERS

Notes: It is planned to replace *Shirase* with a new Antarctic expedition ship AGB 5003 by 2008. The 146 m ship, which is to be of the order of 12,500 tons displacement, will operate two CH-101 helicopters. It will have diesel-electric propulsion. Construction is expected to start in 2006.

1 SHIRASE CLASS (AGBH)

Name	No	Builders	Launched	Commissioned
SHIRASE	AGB 5002	Nippon Koukan, Tsurumi	11 Dec 1981	12 Nov 1982

Displacement, tons: 11,600 standard; 19,000 full load
Dimensions, feet (metres): 439.5 × 91.8 × 30.2 *(134 × 28 × 9.2)*
Main machinery: Diesel-electric; 6 Mitsui 12V42M diesels; 30,000 hp(m) *(22.4 MW)*; 6 generators; 6 motors; 30,000 hp(m) *(22 MW)*; 3 shafts
Speed, knots: 19
Range, n miles: 25,000 at 15 kt
Complement: 170 (37 officers) plus 60 scientists
Cargo capacity: 1,000 tons
Radars: Surface search: JRC OPS-18-1; G-band.
Navigation: OPS-22; I-band.
Tacan: ORN-6 (URN 25).
Helicopters: 2 Mitsubishi S-61A; 1 Kawasaki OH-6D.

Comment: Laid down 5 March 1981. Fully equipped for marine and atmospheric research. Stabilised. The dome covers a weather radar.

SHIRASE   *9/2005*, Hachiro Nakai* / 1153302

TUGS

21 OCEAN TUGS (ATA/YT)

YT 58	YT 63-74	YT 78-79	YT 81	YT 84	YT 86	YT 89-90

Displacement, tons: 260 standard
Dimensions, feet (metres): 93 × 28 × 8.2 *(28.4 × 8.6 × 2.5)*
Main machinery: 2 Niigata 6L25B diesels; 1,800 hp(m) *(1.32 MW)*; 2 shafts
Speed, knots: 11
Complement: 10

Comment: YT 58 entered service on 31 October 1978, YT 63 on 27 September 1982, YT 64 on 30 September 1983, YT 65 on 20 September 1984, YT 66 on 20 September 1985, YT 67 on 4 September 1986, YT 68 on 9 September 1987, YT 69 on 16 September 1987, YT 70 on 2 September 1988, YT 71 on 28 July 1989, YT 72 on 28 July 1990, YT 73 on 31 July 1991, YT 74 on 30 September 1991, YT 78 in July 1994, YT 79 on 29 September 1994, YT 81 on 8 July 1996, YT 84 on 30 September 1998, YT 86 on 21 March 2000, YT 89 and 90 on 16 March 2001. All built by Yokohama Yacht. Two further 260 ton tugs are to enter service in 2006 and 2007 respectively.

YT 90   *7/2003, Hachiro Nakai* / 0570749

21 COASTAL AND HARBOUR TUGS (YTM/YTB)

YT 51　YT 53-57　YT 59-62　YT 75-77　YT 80　YT 82-83　YT 85　YT 87-88　YT 91

Displacement, tons: 53 standard
Dimensions, feet (metres): 55.8 × 15.8 × 7.8 *(17.0 × 4.8 × 2.4)*
Main machinery: 2 Isuzu UM6SD1TCB diesels; 500 hp (373 kW); 2 shafts
Speed, knots: 8
Complement: 4

Comment: Details given are for 50 ton class (YT 75-77, YT 80, YT 85, YT 87-88 and YT 91). There are also four of 190 tons (YT 53, YT 55-57), two of 35 tons (YT 60-61), one of 30 tons (YT 62) and three of 29 tons (YT 51, YT 54, YT 59). A further 50 ton harbour tug is to enter service in 2006.

YT 75
7/2005*, Hachiro Nakai / 1153303

COAST GUARD

KAIJYOU HOANCHOU

Headquarters Appointments

Commandant of the Coast Guard:
Hiromi Ishikawa

Establishment

The Japan Coast Guard (Maritime Safety Agency before 1 April 2000) was established on 1 May 1948. Its five missions are Maintaining Peace and Security, Ensuring Maritime Traffic Safety, Maritime Search and Rescue, Environmental Protection and Enforcement and Co-operation with other national and international agencies. The HQ is at Tokyo, the Coast Guard Academy is at Kure and the Coast Guard School is at Maizuru.
The main operational branches are the Guard and Rescue, the Hydrographic and the Aids to Navigation Departments. Regional offices control the 11 districts with their location as follows (airbases in brackets): RMS 1-Otaru (Chitose, Hakodate, Kushiro); 2-Shiogama (Sendai); 3-Yokohama (Haneda); 4-Nagoya (Ise); 5-Kobe (Yao); 6-Hiroshima (Hiroshima); 7-Kitakyushu (Fukuoka); 8-Maizuru (Miho); 9-Niigata (Niigata); 10-Kagoshima (Kagoshima); 11-Naha (Naha, Ishigaki). This organisation includes, as well as the RMS HQ, 66 MS offices, 58 MS stations, 14 MS air stations, five district communication centres, seven traffic advisory service centres, four hydrographic observatories, 18 aids to

navigation offices, one Special Rescue station, one Special Security station, one National Strike Team station and one Transnational Organised Crime Strike Force station.

Personnel

2006: 12,258 (2,630 officers)

Strength of the Fleet

Type	Active	Building
GUARD AND RESCUE SERVICE		
Patrol Vessels:		
Large with helicopter (PLH)	13	—
Large (PL)	38	2
Medium (PM)	37	—
Small (PS)	27	—
Firefighting Vessels (FL)	5	—
Patrol Craft:		
Patrol Craft (PC)	61	—
Patrol Craft (CL)	170	—
Firefighting Craft (FM)	4	—
Special Service Craft:		
Monitoring Craft (MS)	3	—
Guard Boats (GS)	2	—
Surveillance Craft (SS)	38	1
Oil Recovery Craft (OR)	5	—
Oil Skimming Craft (OS)	3	—
Oil Boom Craft (OX)	19	—
HYDROGRAPHIC SERVICE		
Surveying Vessels:		
Large (HL)	5	—
Small (HS)	8	—
AIDS TO NAVIGATION SERVICE		
Aids to Navigation Research Vessel (LL)	1	—
Buoy Tenders:		
Large (LL)	3	—
Aids to Navigation Tenders:		
Medium (LM)	10	—
Small (LS)	34	—

DELETIONS

2003	*Kamishima, Yaeyama, Yamagiri, Kotobiki, Nachi, Kurushima* (HS 35), *Kegon, LS 211, LS 149, LS 154, LS 181*
2004	*Fuji, Miyake, Kabashima, Okushiri, SS 25, LS 155, LS 157-158, LS 160, LS 208*
2005	*Yonakuni, Asagumo, Muroto, SS 33, Myojyo, LS 187*
2006	*Iwaki, Rishiri, Choukai, Nojima, Kuma, Tone, Hayagumo, Miyazuki.*

LARGE PATROL VESSELS
1 SHIKISHIMA CLASS (PLH/PSOH)

Name	No	Builders	Laid down	Launched	Commissioned
SHIKISHIMA	PLH 31	Ishikawajima Harima, Tokyo	24 Aug 1990	27 June 1991	8 Apr 1992

Displacement, tons: 6,500 standard; 9,350 full load
Dimensions, feet (metres): 492.1 × 55.8 × 19.7 *(150 × 17 × 6)*
Main machinery: 2 SEMT-Pielstick 16 PC2.5 V 400; 20,800 hp(m) *(15.29 MW)*; 2 shafts; bow thruster
Speed, knots: 25. **Range, n miles:** 20,000 at 18 kt
Complement: 110 plus 30 aircrew
Guns: 4 Oerlikon 35 mm/90 Type GDM-C (2 twin); 1,100 rds/min to 6 km *(3.2 n miles)*; weight of shell 1.55 kg. 2 JM-61 MB 20 mm Gatling.
Radars: Air/surface search: Melco Ops 14; D-band.
Surface search: JMA 1576; I-band.
Navigation: JMA 1596; I-band.
Helo control JMA 3000; I-band.
Tacan: ORN-6 (URN 25).
Helicopters: 2 Bell 212.

Comment: Authorised in the FY89 programme in place of the third Mizuho class. Used to escort the plutonium transport ship. SATCOM fitted.

SHIKISHIMA
5/2005*, Hachiro Nakai / 1153304

---

10 SOYA CLASS (PLH/PSOH)

Name	No	Builders	Commissioned
SOYA	PLH 01	Nippon Kokan, Tsurumi	22 Nov 1978
TSUGARU	PLH 02	IHI, Tokyo	17 Apr 1979
OOSUMI	PLH 03	Mitsui Tamano	18 Oct 1979
HAYATO (ex-*Uraga*)	PLH 04	Hitachi, Maizuru	5 Mar 1980
ZAO	PLH 05	Mitsubishi, Nagasaki	19 Mar 1982
CHIKUZEN	PLH 06	Kawasaki, Kobe	28 Sep 1983
SETTSU	PLH 07	Sumitomo, Oppama	27 Sep 1984
ECHIGO	PLH 08	Mitsui Tamano	28 Feb 1990
RYUKYU	PLH 09	Mitsubishi, Nagasaki	31 Mar 2000
DAISEN	PLH 10	Nippon Kokan, Tsurumi	1 Oct 2001

Displacement, tons: 3,200 normal; 3,744 full load
Dimensions, feet (metres): 323.4 × 51.2 × 17.1 *(98.6 × 15.6 × 5.2)* (PLH 01) 345.8 × 47.9 × 15.7 *(105.4 × 14.6 × 4.8)*
Main machinery: 2 SEMT-Pielstick 12 PC2.5 V 400 diesels; 15,604 hp(m) *(11.47 MW)* sustained; 2 shafts; cp props; bow thruster
Speed, knots: 21 (PLH 01); 22 (others). **Range, n miles:** 5,700 at 18 kt
Complement: 71 (PLH 01—04); 69 (others)
Guns: 1 Bofors 40 mm or Oerlikon 35 mm. 1 Oerlikon 20 mm (PLH 01, 02, 05—07) or 1—20 mm JM61MB Gatling gun.
Radars: Surface search: JMA 1576; I-band.
Navigation: JMA 1596; I-band.
Helo control: JMA 1596; I-band.
Helicopters: 1 Fuji-Bell 212.

Comment: PLH 01 has an icebreaking capability while the other ships are only ice strengthened. Fitted with both fin stabilisers and anti-rolling tanks of 70 tons capacity. The fixed electric hydraulic fins have a lift of 26 tons × 2 at 18 kt which reduces rolling by 90 per cent at that speed. At slow speed the reduction is 50 per cent, using the tanks. PLH 04 name changed on 27 March 1997. PLH 10 laid down 8 March 1999.

TSUGARU
5/2005*, Mitsuhiro Kadota / 1153342

2 MIZUHO CLASS (PLH/PSOH)

Name	No	Builders	Launched	Commissioned
MIZUHO	PLH 21	Mitsubishi, Nagasaki	5 June 1985	19 Mar 1986
YASHIMA	PLH 22	Nippon Koukan, Tsurumi	20 Jan 1988	1 Dec 1988

Displacement, tons: 4,900 standard; 5,204 full load
Dimensions, feet (metres): 426.5 × 50.9 × 17.7 *(130 × 15.5 × 5.4)*
Main machinery: 2 SEMT-Pielstick 14 PC2.5 V 400 diesels; 18,200 hp(m) *(13.38 MW)* sustained; 2 shafts; cp props; bow thruster
Speed, knots: 23. **Range, n miles:** 8,500 at 22 kt
Complement: 100 plus 30 aircrew
Guns: 1 Oerlikon 35 mm/90; 550 rds/min to 6 km *(3.2 n miles)* anti-surface; 5 km *(2.7 n miles)* anti-aircraft; weight of shell 1.55 kg.
1 JM-61 MB 20 mm Gatling.
Radars: Surface search: JMA 8303; I-band.
Navigation: and helo control 2 JMA 3000; I-band.
Helicopters: 2 Fuji-Bell 212.

Comment: PLH 21 ordered under the FY83 programme laid down 27 August 1984. PLH 22 in 1986 estimates, laid down 3 October 1987. Two sets of fixed electric fin stabilisers that have a lift of 26 tons × 2 and reduce rolling by 90 per cent at 18 kt. Employed in search and rescue outside the 200 mile economic zone.

MIZUHO — *5/2005*, Hachiro Nakai* / 1153305

1 IZU CLASS (PL/PSOH)

Name	No	Builders	Launched	Commissioned
IZU	PL 31	Kawasaki, Sakaide	7 Feb 1997	25 Sep 1997

Displacement, tons: 3,500 normal
Dimensions, feet (metres): 360.9 × 49.2 × 17.4 *(110 × 15 × 5.3)*
Main machinery: 2 diesels; 12,000 hp(m) *(8.82 MW)*; 2 shafts; bow thruster
Speed, knots: 20
Guns: 1 Oerlikon 35 mm. 1 JM-61 MB 20 mm Gatling.
Radars: Surface search: I-band.
Navigation: I-band.
Helicopters: Platform for 1 Fuji-Bell 212.

Comment: Authorised in the FY95 programme. Laid down 22 March 1996. Replaced the former *Izu* in 1998, taking the same name and pennant number. Carries two launches.

IZU — *6/2004*, Japan Coast Guard* / 1153306

1 MIURA CLASS (PL/PSOH)

Name	No	Builders	Launched	Commissioned
MIURA	PL 22	Sumitomo, Uraga	11 Mar 1998	28 Oct 1998

Displacement, tons: 3,000 normal
Dimensions, feet (metres): 377.3 × 45.9 × 15.7 *(115 × 14 × 4.8)*
Main machinery: 2 diesels; 8,000 hp(m) *(5.88 MW)*; 2 shafts; cp props
Speed, knots: 18
Complement: 40 plus 10 spare
Guns: 1 Oerlikon 35 mm. 1 — 20 mm JM 61-B Gatling.

Comment: Authorised in FY96 programme. Laid down in October 1996. Has replaced ship of the same name.

MIURA — *5/2003, Hachiro Nakai* / 0570753

1 KOJIMA CLASS (PL/PSOH)

Name	No	Builders	Commissioned
KOJIMA	PL 21	Hitachi, Maizuru	11 Mar 1993

Displacement, tons: 2,650 normal; 2,950 full load
Dimensions, feet (metres): 377.3 × 45.9 × 23.9 *(115 × 14 × 7.3)*
Main machinery: 2 diesels; 8,000 hp(m) *(5.9 MW)*; 2 shafts; cp props
Speed, knots: 18. **Range, n miles:** 7,000 at 15 kt
Complement: 118
Guns: 1 Oerlikon 35 mm/90. 1 — 20 mm JM-61B Gatling. 1 — 12.7 mm MG.
Radars: Navigation: Two JMA 1596; I-band.
Helicopters: Platform for 1 medium.

Comment: Authorised in the FY90 programme and ordered in March 1991. Laid down 7 November 1991, launched 10 September 1992. Training ship which has replaced the old ship of the same name and pennant number. SATCOM fitted.

KOJIMA — *1/2004, Hachiro Nakai* / 1044428

1 NOJIMA CLASS (PL/PSOH)

Name	No	Builders	Commissioned
OKI (ex-*Nojima*)	PL 01	Ishikawajima Harima, Tokyo	21 Sep 1989

Displacement, tons: 1,500 normal
Dimensions, feet (metres): 285.4 × 34.4 × 11.5 *(87 × 10.5 × 3.5)*
Main machinery: 2 Fuji 8S40B diesels; 8,120 hp(m) *(5.97 MW)*; 2 shafts
Speed, knots: 19
Complement: 34
Guns: 1 Oerlikon 35 mm/90. 1 — 20 mm JM-61B Gatling.
Radars: Navigation: 2 JMA 1596; I-band.
Helicopters: Platform for 1 Bell 212.

Comment: Laid down 16 August 1988 and launched 30 May 1989. Equipped as surveillance and rescue command ship. SATCOM fitted. Name changed on 30 November 1997.

OKI — *7/2005*, Hachiro Nakai* / 1153307

7 OJIKA CLASS (PL/PSOH)

Name	No	Builders	Launched	Commissioned
ERIMO (ex-*Ojika*)	PL 02	Mitsui, Tamano	23 Apr 1991	31 Oct 1991
KUDAKA	PL 03	Hakodate Dock	10 May 1994	25 Oct 1994
YAHIKO (ex-*Satsuma*)	PL 04	Sumitomo, Uraga	3 June 1995	26 Oct 1995
HAKATA	PL 05	Ishikawajima, Tokyo	6 July 1998	26 Nov 1998
KURIKOMA (ex-*Dejima*)	PL 06	Mitsui, Tamano	28 June 1999	29 Oct 1999
SATAUMA	PL 07	Kawasaki, Kobe	3 June 1999	29 Oct 1999
MOTOBU	PL 08	Sasebo Heavy Industries	5 June 2000	31 Oct 2000

Displacement, tons: 1,883 normal
Dimensions, feet (metres): 299.9 × 36.1 × 11.5 *(91.4 × 11 × 3.5)*
Main machinery: 2 Fuji 8S40B diesels; 7,000 hp(m) *(5.15 MW)*; 2 shafts; cp props; 2 bow thrusters
Speed, knots: 18. **Range, n miles:** 4,400 at 15 kt
Complement: 38
Guns: 1 Oerlikon 35 mm/90. 1 — 20 mm JM-61B Gatling.
Radars: Navigation: JMA 1596; I-band.
Helicopters: Platform for 1 Bell 212 or Super Puma.

Comment: Equipped as SAR command ships. SATCOM fitted. 30 ton bollard pull. Stern dock for RIB. PL 04 name changed 28 September 1999. PL 02 name changed 1 October 2000. PL 06 name changed 4 January 2005.

ERIMO — *5/2005*, Hachiro Nakai* / 1153308

For details of the latest updates to *Jane's Fighting Ships* online and to discover the additional information available exclusively to online subscribers please visit
jfs.janes.com

22 SHIRETOKO CLASS (PL/PSO)

Name	No	Builders	Commissioned
SHIRETOKO	PL 101	Mitsui Tamano	8 Nov 1978
ESAN	PL 102	Sumitomo	16 Nov 1978
WAKASA	PL 103	Kawasaki, Kobe	29 Nov 1978
KII (ex-*Shimanto*, ex-*Yahiko*)	PL 104	Mitsubishi, Shimonoseki	16 Nov 1978
MATSUSHIMA	PL 107	Tohoku	14 Sep 1979
SHIKINE	PL 109	Usuki	20 Sep 1979
SURUGA	PL 110	Kurushima	28 Sep 1979
REBUN	PL 111	Narasaki	21 Nov 1979
TOSA (ex-*Oki*)	PL 114	Tsuneishi	16 Nov 1979
NOTO	PL 115	Miho	30 Nov 1979
IWAMI (ex-*Kudaka*, ex-*Daisetsu*, ex-*Kurikoma*)	PL 117	Hakodate	31 Jan 1980
SHIMOKITA	PL 118	Ishikawajima, Kakoki	12 Mar 1980
SUZUKA	PL 119	Kanazashi	7 Mar 1980
KUNISAKI	PL 120	Kouyo	29 Feb 1980
AMAGI (ex-*Genkai*)	PL 121	Oshima	31 Jan 1980
GOTO	PL 122	Onomichi	29 Feb 1980
KOSHIKI	PL 123	Kasado	25 Jan 1980
HATERUMA	PL 124	Osaka	12 Mar 1980
KATORI	PL 125	Tohoku	21 Oct 1980
KUNIGAMI	PL 126	Kanda	17 Oct 1980
ETOMO	PL 127	Naikai	17 Mar 1982
YONAKUNI (ex-*Amagi*, ex-*Mashu*)	PL 128	Shiikoku	12 Mar 1982

Displacement, tons: 974 normal; 1,360 full load
Dimensions, feet (metres): 255.8 × 31.5 × 10.5 *(78 × 9.6 × 3.2)*
Main machinery: 2 Fuji 8S40B; 8,120 hp(m) *(5.97 MW)*; or 2 Niigata 8MA40 diesels; 2 shafts; cp props
Speed, knots: 20
Range, n miles: 4,400 at 17 kt
Complement: 41
Guns: 1 Bofors 40 mm or 1 Oerlikon 35 mm or 1 JM-61 20 mm Gatling (PL 101). 1 Oerlikon 20 mm (PL 101 – 105, 127 and 128).
Radars: Surface search: JMA 1576; I-band.
Navigation: JMA 1596; I-band.

Comment: Average time from launch to commissioning was about four to five months. Designed for EEZ patrol duties. PL 117 changed her name on 1 April 1988, again 1 August 1994 and again on 1 October 2000. PL 121 changed her name on 12 February 2005. PL 128 changed 1 April 1997 and again on 12 February 2005, and PL 104 on 28 September 1999 and again on 1 October 2004. PL 105 paid off on 20 October 2000 after being involved in a collision. PL 116 paid off on 12 February 2005, PL 108 and 112 on 12 March 2006 and PL 106 and 113 on 18 March 2006.

AMAGI   *5/2005*, Mitsuhiro Kadota* / 1153341

2 + 1 HIDA CLASS (PL/PSO)

Name	No	Builders	Launched	Commissioned
HIDA	PL 51	Mitsubishi, Shimonoseki	9 Aug 2005	18 Apr 2006
AKAISHI	PL 52	Mitsubishi, Shimonoseki	21 Oct 2005	18 Apr 2006
–	PL 53	IHI Marine United, Yokohama	2006	Mar 2007

Displacement, tons: 1,800 standard
Dimensions, feet (metres): 362.6 × 42.7 × 19.7 *(95.0 × 13.0 × 6.0)*
Main machinery: 4 diesels; waterjet propulsion
Speed, knots: 30
Guns: 1 – 40 mm Bofors Mk 3. 1 – 20 mm JM61 Gatling.
Helicopters: Platform for one medium.

Programme: Two ships authorised in FY03 budget and a third in FY04 budget.

HIDA   *12/2005*, Tetsuya Jin* / 1154400

3 + 1 ASO CLASS (PL/PSO)

Name	No	Builders	Laid down	Launched	Commissioned
ASO	PL 41	Mitsubishi, Shimonoseki	18 Dec 2003	28 Oct 2004	15 Mar 2005
DEWA	PL 42	Universal, Keihin	5 Apr 2004	9 May 2005	12 Apr 2006
HAKUSAN	PL 43	Universal, Keihin	5 Apr 2004	5 Oct 2005	12 Apr 2006
—	PL 44		2005	2006	2007

Displacement, tons: 770 standard
Dimensions, feet (metres): 259.2 × 32.8 × 19.7 *(79.0 × 10.0 × 6.0)*
Main machinery: 4 diesels, waterjet propulsion
Speed, knots: 30
Guns: 1 – 40 mm.

Comment: PL 41 authorised in FY02 budget and *PL 42 – 43* in FY03 budget.

ASO   *5/2005*, Mitsuhiro Kadota* / 1153340

0 + 1 1,300 TON CLASS (PL/PSO)

Displacement, tons: 1,300 standard
Dimensions, feet (metres): 292.0 × ? × ? *(89.0 × ? × ?)*
Main machinery: To be announced
Speed, knots: To be announced
Guns: 1 – 30 mm.

Comment: One authorised in FY05 budget.

SHIPBORNE AIRCRAFT

Numbers/Type: 4 Aerospatiale AS 332L1 Super Puma.
Operational speed: 125 kt *(231 km/h)*.
Service ceiling: 15,090 ft *(4,600 m)*.
Range: 500 n miles *(926 km)*.
Role/Weapon systems: Medium lift, support and SAR. Sensors: Search radar. Weapons: Unarmed.

AS 332L   *5/2005*, Mitsuhiro Kadota* / 1153339

Numbers/Type: 3 Sikorsky S-76C.
Operational speed: 135 kt *(250 km/h)*.
Service ceiling: 11,800 ft *(3,505 m)*.
Range: 607 n miles *(1,125 km)*.
Role/Weapon systems: Utility aircraft acquired in 1994-98. One aircraft lost on 10 January 2005. Up to 20 required to replace Bell 212s. Sensors: Search radar. Weapons: Unarmed.

S-76C   *5/2004, Mitsuhiro Kadota* / 1044437

Numbers/Type: 26/8 Bell 212/412.
Operational speed: 103 kt *(191 km/h).*
Service ceiling: 10,000 ft *(3,048 m).*
Range: 412 n miles *(763 km).*
Role/Weapon systems: Liaison, medium-range support and SAR. Sensors: Search radar.
  Weapons: Unarmed.

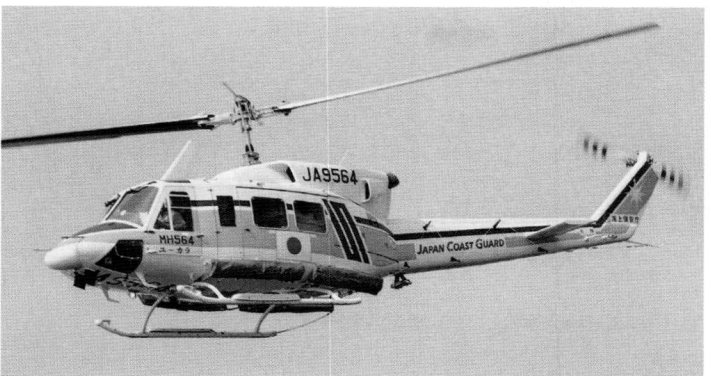

BELL 212   *5/2005*, Hachiro Nakai* / 1153310

BELL 412   *5/2005*, Mitsuhiro Kadota* / 1153338

Numbers/Type: 4 Bell 206B Jet Ranger.
Operational speed: 115 kt *(213 km/h).*
Service ceiling: 13,500 ft *(4,115 m).*
Range: 368 n miles *(682 km).*
Role/Weapon systems: Support helicopter for reconnaissance and SAR.

Bell 206B   *6/2005*, Japan Coast Guard* / 1154399

LAND-BASED MARITIME AIRCRAFT (FRONT LINE)

Notes: There are also a Cessna U-206G.

Numbers/Type: 7/10 Beech Super King Air 200T/350.
Operational speed: 200 kt *(370 km/h).*
Service ceiling: 35,000 ft *(10,670 m).*
Range: 1,460 n miles *(2,703 km).*
Role/Weapon systems: Visual reconnaissance in support of EEZ. Two are trainers.
  Sensors: Weather/search radar. Weapons: Unarmed.

BEECH 350   *5/2005*, Mitsuhiro Kadota* / 1153337

Numbers/Type: 5 NAMCYS-11A.
Operational speed: 230 kt *(425 km/h).*
Service ceiling: 21,600 ft *(6,580 m).*
Range: 1,960 n miles *(3,629 km).*
Role/Weapon systems: Maritime surveillance and associated tasks. Sensors: Weather/
  search radar. Weapons: Unarmed.

YS-11A   *5/2005*, Mitsuhiro Kadota* / 1153336

Numbers/Type: 2 Gulfstream Aerospace G-V.
Operational speed: 510 kt *(945 km/h).*
Service ceiling: 41,000 ft *(12,500 m).*
Range: 6,500 n miles *(12,040 km).*
Role/Weapon systems: Reconnaissance version of long-range business jet ordered on
  14 November 2001 and delivered in 2004. Sensors: Ocean Master radar, FLIR, AMASCOS
  mission system. Can also drop liferafts.

GULFSTREAM G-V   *5/2005*, Hachiro Nakai* / 1153311

Numbers/Type: 2 Dassault Falcon 900.
Operational speed: 428 kt *(792 km/h).*
Service ceiling: 51,000 ft *(15,544 m).*
Range: 4,170 n miles *(7,722 km).*
Role/Weapon systems: Maritime surveillance. Sensors: Weather/search radar. Weapons:
  Unarmed.

FALCON 900   *5/2005*, Mitsuhiro Kadota* / 1153335

Numbers/Type: 2 SAAB 340B.
Operational speed: 250 kt *(463 km/h).*
Service ceiling: 25,000 ft *(7,620 m).*
Range: 570 n miles *(1,056 km).*
Role/Weapon systems: Patrol aircraft procured in 1997. Two SAR variants have been
  ordered for delivery by 2007.

SAAB 340B   *5/2005*, Mitsuhiro Kadota* / 1153334

MEDIUM PATROL VESSELS

14 TESHIO CLASS (PM/PSO)

Name	No	Builders	Commissioned
NATSUI (ex-*Teshio*)	PM 01	Shikoku	30 Sep 1980
KITAKAMI (ex-*Oirose*)	PM 02	Naikai	29 Aug 1980
ECHIZEN	PM 03	Usuki	30 Sep 1980
TOKACHI	PM 04	Narazaki	24 Mar 1981
HITACHI	PM 05	Tohoku	19 Mar 1981
OKITSU	PM 06	Usuki	17 Mar 1981
ISAZU	PM 07	Naikai	18 Feb 1982
CHITOSE	PM 08	Shikoku	15 Mar 1983
KUWANO	PM 09	Naikai	10 Mar 1983
SORACHI	PM 10	Tohoku	30 Aug 1984
YUBARI	PM 11	Usuki	28 Nov 1985
MOTOURA	PM 12	Shikoku	21 Nov 1986
KANO	PM 13	Naikai	13 Nov 1986
SENDAI	PM 14	Shikoku	1 June 1988

Displacement, tons: 630 normal; 670 full load
Dimensions, feet (metres): 222.4 × 25.9 × 6.6 *(67.8 × 7.9 × 2.7)*
Main machinery: 2 Fuji 6S32F or Arakata 6M31E diesels; 3,650 hp(m) *(2.69 MW)*; 2 shafts
Speed, knots: 18. **Range, n miles:** 3,200 at 16 kt
Complement: 33
Guns: 1 JN-61B 20 mm Gatling.
Radars: Navigation: 2 JMA 159B; I-band.

Comment: First three built under FY79 programme and second three under FY80, seventh under FY81, PM 08—09 under FY82, PM 10 under FY83, PM 11 under FY84, PM 12—13 under FY85, PM 14 under FY87. *Isazu* has an additional structure aft of the mainmast which is used as a classroom.

KUWANO   *5/2005*, Mitsuhiro Kadota* / 1153333

2 TAKATORI CLASS (PM/PBO)

Name	No	Builders	Commissioned
TAKATORI	PM 89	Naikai	24 Mar 1978
KUMANO	PM 94	Namura	23 Feb 1979

Displacement, tons: 634 normal
Dimensions, feet (metres): 152.5 × 30.2 × 9.3 *(46.5 × 9.2 × 2.9)*
Main machinery: 2 Niigata 6M31EX diesels; 3,000 hp(m) *(2.21 MW)*; 2 shafts; cp props
Speed, knots: 15. **Range, n miles:** 700 at 14 kt
Complement: 34
Radars: Navigation: JMA 1596 and JMA 1576; I-band.

Comment: SAR vessels equipped for salvage and firefighting.

KUMANO   *5/2005*, Hachiro Nakai* / 1153312

4 AMAMI CLASS (PM/PBO)

Name	No	Builders	Commissioned
AMAMI	PM 95	Hitachi, Kanagawa	28 Sep 1992
KUROKAMI (ex-*Matsuura*)	PM 96	Hitachi, Kanagawa	24 Nov 1995
KUNASHIRI	PM 97	Mitsubishi, Shimonoseki	26 Aug 1998
MINABE	PM 98	Mitsubishi, Shimonoseki	26 Aug 1998

Displacement, tons: 230 normal
Dimensions, feet (metres): 183.7 × 24.6 × 6.6 *(56 × 7.5 × 2)*
Main machinery: 2 Fuji 8S40B diesels; 8,120 hp(m) *(5.97 MW)*; 2 shafts; cp props
Speed, knots: 25
Guns: 1—20 mm JM-61B Gatling.
Radars: Navigation: I-band.

Comment: First one authorised in the FY91 programme; laid down 22 October 1991. Second authorised in FY93 programme; laid down 7 October 1994. Last pair authorised in FY96 programme and both laid down 30 September 1997. Stern ramp for launching RIB. PM 96 changed name 3 April 2000. PM 95 damaged in incident with possible North Korean intelligence collection ship on 22 December 2001.

MINABE   *7/2004, Hachiro Nakai* / 1044443

15 BIHORO CLASS (350-M4 TYPE) (PM/PSO)

Name	No	Builders	Commissioned
BIHORO	PM 73	Tohoku	28 Feb 1974
ISHIKARI	PM 78	Tohoku	13 Mar 1976
ABUKUMA	PM 79	Tohoku	30 Jan 1976
ISUZU	PM 80	Naikai	10 Mar 1976
KIKUCHI	PM 81	Usuki	6 Feb 1976
KUZURYU	PM 82	Usuki	18 Mar 1976
HOROBETSU	PM 83	Tohoku	27 Jan 1977
SHIRAKAMI	PM 84	Tohoku	24 Mar 1977
MATSUURA (ex-*Sagami*)	PM 85	Naikai	30 Nov 1976
MISASA (ex-*Yoshino*)	PM 87	Usuki	28 Jan 1977
NATORI (ex-*Kurobe*)	PM 88	Shikoku	15 Feb 1977
CHIKUGO	PM 90	Naikai	27 Jan 1978
YAMAKUNI	PM 91	Usuki	26 Jan 1978
KATSURA	PM 92	Shikoku	15 Feb 1978
OOYODO (ex-*Shinano*)	PM 93	Tohoku	23 Feb 1978

Displacement, tons: 615 normal; 636 full load
Dimensions, feet (metres): 208 × 25.6 × 8.3 *(63.4 × 7.8 × 2.5)*
Main machinery: 2 Niigata 6M31EX diesels; 3,000 hp(m) *(2.21 MW)*; 2 shafts; cp props
Speed, knots: 18
Range, n miles: 3,200 at 16 kt
Complement: 34
Guns: 1 USN 20 mm/80 Mk 10.
Radars: Navigation: JMA 1596 and JMA 1576; I-band.

Comment: PM 85 and 87 changed names 3 April 2000, PM 93 on 1 April 2001 and PM 88 on 12 March 2006.

YAMAKUNI   *5/2005*, Hachiro Nakai* / 1153313

1 TESHIO CLASS (ICEBREAKER) (PM/AGOB)

Name	No	Builders	Commissioned
TESHIO	PM 15	Nippon Koukan, Tsurumi	19 Oct 1995

Displacement, tons: 550 normal
Dimensions, feet (metres): 180.4 × 34.8 × 12.8 *(55 × 10.6 × 3.9)*
Main machinery: 2 diesels; 3,600 hp(m) *(2.65 MW)*; 2 shafts; bow thruster
Speed, knots: 14.5
Complement: 35
Guns: 1—20 mm JM-61B Gatling.
Radars: Navigation: 2 sets; I-band.

Comment: Authorised in FY93; laid down 7 October 1994, launched 20 April 1995. Has an icebreaker bow.

TESHIO   *6/2002, Japan Coast Guard* / 0570891

3 TOKARA CLASS (PM/PBO)

Name	No	Builders	Commissioned
TOKARA	PM 21	Universal, Keihin (Kanagawa)	12 Mar 2003
FUKUE	PM 22	Mitsubishi, Shimonoseki	12 Mar 2003
OIRASE	PM 23	Mitsui, Tamano	18 Mar 2004

Displacement, tons: 335 standard
Dimensions, feet (metres): 183.8 × 32.4 × 14.4 *(56.0 × 8.5 × 4.4)*
Main machinery: 3 diesels; 3 waterjets
Speed, knots: 30+
Guns: 1—20 mm Gatling gun. 1—12.7 mm MG

Comment: First two authorised in FY01 budget and launched on 4 and 10 December 2002. *Oirase* authorised in FY02 budget.

OIRASE *5/2004, Mitsuhiro Kadota* / 1044442

SMALL PATROL VESSELS

12 MIHASHI AND BANNA CLASS (PS/PBF)

Name	No	Builders	Commissioned
SHINZAN (ex-*Akiyoshi*, ex-*Mihashi*)	PS 01	Mitsubishi, Shimonoseki	9 Sep 1988
SAROMA	PS 02	Hitachi, Kanagawa	24 Nov 1989
INASA	PS 03	Mitsubishi, Shimonoseki	31 Jan 1990
KIRISHIMA	PS 04	Hitachi, Kanagawa	22 Mar 1991
KAMUI	PS 05	Mitsubishi, Shimonoseki	31 Jan 1994
BANNA (ex-*Bizan*)	PS 06	Hitachi, Kanagawa	31 Jan 1994
ASHITAKI	PS 07	Mitsui, Tamano	30 Sep 1994
KARIBA (ex-*Kurama*)	PS 08	Mitsubishi, Shimonoseki	29 Aug 1995
ARASE	PS 09	Mitsubishi, Shimonoseki	29 Jan 1997
SANBE	PS 10	Hitachi, Kanagawa	29 Jan 1997
MIZUKI	PS 11	Mitsui, Tamano	9 June 2000
KOUYA	PS 12	Universal, Keihin	18 Mar 2004

Displacement, tons: 195 normal
Dimensions, feet (metres): 141.1 × 24.6 × 5.6 *(43 × 7.5 × 1.7)*
Main machinery: 2 SEMT-Pielstick 16 PA4 V 200 VGA diesels; 7,072 hp(m) *(5.2 MW)*; 2 shafts
1 SEMT-Pielstick 12 PA4 V 200 VGA diesel; 2,720 hp(m) *(2 MW)*; Kamewa 80 water-jet
Speed, knots: 35. **Range, n miles:** 650 at 34 kt
Complement: 34
Guns: 1—12.7 mm MG or 1—20 mm JM 61 Gatling (PS 01, 03, 08 and 11).
Radars: Navigation: Furuno; I-band.

Comment: Capable of 15 kt on the water-jet alone. PS 01 name changed 28 January 1997 and again on 24 January 2001, PS 06 on 17 April 1999. PS 11 authorised in FY98 programme and PS 12 in FY02 programme. PS 08 name changed on 29 March 2004.

ASHITAKI *5/2005*, *Mitsuhiro Kadota* / 1153331

7 AKAGI CLASS (PS/PB)

Name	No	Builders	Commissioned
AKAGI	PS 101	Sumidagawa	26 Mar 1980
TSUKUBA	PS 102	Sumidagawa	24 Feb 1982
KONGOU	PS 103	Ishihara	16 Mar 1987
KATSURAGI	PS 104	Ishihara	24 Mar 1988
BIZAN (ex-*Hiromine*)	PS 105	Yokohama Yacht Co	24 Mar 1988
SHIZUKI	PS 106	Sumidagawa	24 Mar 1988
TAKACHIHO	PS 107	Sumidagawa	24 Mar 1988

Displacement, tons: 115 full load
Dimensions, feet (metres): 114.8 × 20.7 × 4.3 *(35 × 6.3 × 1.3)*
Main machinery: 2 Pielstick 16 PA4 V 185 diesels; 5,344 hp(m) *(3.93 MW)* sustained; 2 shafts
Speed, knots: 28. **Range, n miles:** 500 at 20 kt
Complement: 22
Guns: 1 Browning 12.7 mm MG.
Radars: Navigation: 1 set; I-band.

Comment: Carry a 25-man inflatable rescue craft. The last four were ordered on 31 August 1987 and commissioned less than seven months later. PS 105 name changed on 1 October 2004.

AKAGI *5/2005*, *Mitsuhiro Kadota* / 1153332

2 TAKATSUKI CLASS (PS/PBF)

Name	No	Builders	Commissioned
TAKATSUKI	PS 108	Mitsubishi, Shimonoseki	23 Mar 1992
NOBARU	PS 109	Hitachi, Kanagawa	22 Mar 1993

Displacement, tons: 115 normal; 180 full load
Dimensions, feet (metres): 114.8 × 22 × 4.3 *(35 × 6.7 × 1.3)*
Main machinery: 2 MTU 16V 396 TB94 diesels; 5,200 hp(m) *(3.82 MW)*; 2 Kamewa 71 water-jets
Speed, knots: 35
Complement: 13
Guns: 1—12.7 mm MG.
Radars: Navigation: I-band.

Comment: First authorised in the FY91 programme, second in FY92. Aluminium hulls.

TAKATSUKI *5/2005*, *Mitsuhiro Kadota* / 1153329

6 TSURUUGI CLASS (PS/PBOF)

Name	No	Builders	Commissioned
TSURUUGI	PS 201	Hitachi, Kanagawa	15 Feb 2001
HOTAKA	PS 202	Mitsubishi, Shimonoseki	16 Mar 2001
NORIKURA	PS 203	Mitsui, Tamano	16 Mar 2001
KAIMON	PS 204	Mitsui, Tamano	21 Apr 2004
ASAMA	PS 205	Mitsui, Tamano	21 Apr 2004
HOUOU	PS 206	Mitsui, Tamano	27 Jan 2005

Displacement, tons: 220 standard
Dimensions, feet (metres): 164.1 × 26.2 × 13.1 *(50.0 × 8.0 × 4.0)*
Main machinery: 3 diesels; 3 waterjets
Speed, knots: 35
Guns: 1—20 mm JM-61 RFS Gatling.

Comment: First three authorised in FY99 budget, fourth and fifth in FY02 budget and sixth in FY03 budget.

KAIMON *5/2005*, *Mitsuhiro Kadota* / 1153330

COASTAL PATROL CRAFT

4 + (1) YODO CLASS (PC/YTR)

Name	No	Builders	Launched	Commissioned
YODO	PC 51	Sumidagawa	2 Oct 2001	29 Mar 2002
KOTOBIKI	PC 52	Sumidagawa	23 Oct 2002	27 Mar 2003
NACHI	PC 53	Ishihara	29 Jan 2003	27 Mar 2003
NUNOBIKI	PC 54	Sumidagawa	4 Dec 2002	27 Mar 2003

Displacement, tons: 125 standard
Dimensions, feet (metres): 121.4 × 22.0 × 11.2 *(37.0 × 6.7 × 3.4)*
Main machinery: 2 diesels; 2 waterjets
Speed, knots: 25

Comment: The first authorised in FY00 budget, three more in FY01 budget and a fifth proposed in FY04 budget. Also equipped for firefighting and replaced firefighting vessel of the same name.

YODO   *5/2005*, Hachiro Nakai* / 1153314

18 MURAKUMO CLASS (PC/PB)

Name	No	Builders	Commissioned
KITAGUMO	PC 202	Hitachi, Kanagawa	17 Mar 1978
YUKIGUMO	PC 203	Hitachi, Kanagawa	27 Sep 1978
AKIGUMO	PC 206	Hitachi, Kanagawa	28 Feb 1979
YAEGUMO	PC 207	Mitsubishi, Shimonoseki	16 Mar 1979
NATSUGUMO	PC 208	Hitachi, Kanagawa	22 Mar 1979
KAWAGIRI	PC 210	Hitachi, Kanagawa	27 July 1979
TOSAGIRI (ex-*Bizan*, ex-*Teruzuki*)	PC 211	Mitsubishi, Shimonoseki	26 June 1979
NATSUZUKI	PC 212	Mitsubishi, Shimonoseki	26 July 1979
NIJIGUMO	PC 214	Mitsubishi, Shimonoseki	29 Jan 1981
TATSUGUMO	PC 215	Mitsubishi, Shimonoseki	19 Mar 1981
ISEYUKI (ex-*Hamayuki*)	PC 216	Hitachi, Kanagawa	27 Feb 1981
ISONAMI	PC 217	Mitsubishi, Shimonoseki	19 Mar 1981
NAGOZUKI	PC 218	Hitachi, Kanagawa	29 Jan 1981
YAEZUKI	PC 219	Hitachi, Kanagawa	19 Mar 1981
HAMAYUKI (ex-*Yamayuki*)	PC 220	Hitachi, Kanagawa	16 Feb 1982
KOMAYUKI	PC 221	Mitsubishi, Shimonoseki	10 Feb 1982
UMIGIRI	PC 222	Hitachi, Kanagawa	17 Feb 1983
ASAGIRI	PC 223	Mitsubishi, Shimonoseki	23 Feb 1983

Displacement, tons: 85 normal
Dimensions, feet (metres): 98.4 × 20.7 × 7.2 *(30 × 6.3 × 2.2)*
Main machinery: 2 Ikegai MTU MB 16V 652 SB70 diesels; 4,400 hp(m) *(3.23 MW)* sustained; 2 shafts
Speed, knots: 30. **Range, n miles:** 350 at 28 kt
Complement: 13
Guns: 1 — 12.7 mm MG.
Radars: Navigation: I-band.

Comment: PC 211 name changed on 17 April 1999 and again on 1 October 2004. P 216 changed name on 22 February 2001 and PC 220 on 18 March 2006.

KAWAGIRI   *5/2004, Mitsuhiro Kadota* / 1044450

UMIGIRI   *9/2002, Mitsuhiro Kadota* / 0528998

3 HAYAGUMO CLASS (PC/PBF)

Name	No	Builders	Commissioned
HAYAGUMO (ex-*Hamayuki*, ex-*Kagayuki*)	PC 105	Mitsubishi, Shimonoseki	24 Dec 1999
MURAKUMO	PC 106	Hitachi, Kanagawa	19 Aug 2002
IZUNAMI	PC 107	Mitsui, Tamano	18 Mar 2003

Displacement, tons: 100 standard
Dimensions, feet (metres): 105.0 × 21.3 × 10.8 *(32.0 × 6.5 × 3.3)*
Main machinery: 2 diesels; 5,200 hp(m) *(3.82 MW)*; 2 waterjets
Speed, knots: 36
Complement: 10
Guns: 1 — 12.7 mm MG.

Comment: Larger version of Asogiri class with waterjet propulsion and higher top speed. PC 105 changed name on 22 February 2001 and again on 18 March 2006. PC 106 authorised in FY01 budget and PC 107 in FY01 extra budget.

MURAKUMO   *5/2005*, Hachiro Nakai* / 1153315

9 AKIZUKI CLASS (PC/SAR)

Name	No	Builders	Commissioned
URAYUKI	PC 72	Mitsubishi, Shimonoseki	31 May 1975
HATAGUMO	PC 75	Mitsubishi, Shimonoseki	21 Feb 1976
MAKIGUMO	PC 76	Mitsubishi, Shimonoseki	19 Mar 1976
HAMAZUKI	PC 77	Mitsubishi, Shimonoseki	29 Nov 1976
ISOZUKI	PC 78	Mitsubishi, Shimonoseki	18 Mar 1977
SHIMANAMI	PC 79	Mitsubishi, Shimonoseki	23 Dec 1977
YUZUKI	PC 80	Mitsubishi, Shimonoseki	22 Mar 1979
TAMANAMI (ex-*Hanayuki*)	PC 81	Mitsubishi, Shimonoseki	27 Mar 1981
AWAGIRI	PC 82	Mitsubishi, Shimonoseki	24 Mar 1983

Displacement, tons: 77 normal
Dimensions, feet (metres): 85.3 × 20.7 × 6.9 *(26 × 6.3 × 2.1)*
Main machinery: 3 Mitsubishi 12DM20MTK diesels; 3,000 hp(m) *(2.21 MW)*; 3 shafts
Speed, knots: 22. **Range, n miles:** 220 at 21.5 kt
Complement: 10
Radars: Navigation: FRA 10 Mk 2; I-band.

Comment: Aluminium hulls. Used mostly for SAR. Being paid off.

AWAGIRI   *7/2005*, Hachiro Nakai* / 1153316

3 SHIMAGIRI CLASS (PC/PB)

Name	No	Builders	Commissioned
SHIMAGIRI	PC 83	Hitachi, Kanagawa	7 Feb 1985
OKINAMI (ex-*Setogiri*)	PC 84	Hitachi, Kanagawa	22 Mar 1985
HAYAGIRI	PC 85	Mitsubishi, Shimonoseki	22 Feb 1985

Displacement, tons: 51 normal
Dimensions, feet (metres): 75.5 × 17.4 × 6.2 *(23 × 5.3 × 1.9)*
Main machinery: 2 Ikegai 12V 175 RTC diesels; 3,000 hp(m) *(2.21 MW)*; 2 shafts
Speed, knots: 30
Complement: 10
Guns: 1 — 12.7 mm MG (not in all).
Radars: Navigation: FRA 10 Mk 2; I-band.

Comment: Aluminium hulls. PC 84 name changed 1 October 2000.

HAYAGIRI   *4/2003, Bob Fildes* / 0570885

1 MATSUNAMI CLASS (PC/PB)

Name	No	Builders	Commissioned
MATSUNAMI	PC 01	Mitsubishi, Shimonoseki	22 Feb 1995

Displacement, tons: 165 normal
Dimensions, feet (metres): 114.8 × 26.2 × 10.8 *(35 × 8 × 3.3)*
Main machinery: 2 diesels; 5,200 hp(m) *(3.82 MW)*; 2 water-jets
Speed, knots: 25
Complement: 30
Radars: Navigation: I-band.

Comment: Has replaced old craft of the same name. Laid down 10 May 1994. Used for patrol and for VIPs.

MATSUNAMI *5/2005*, Hachiro Nakai* / 1153317

1 SHIKINAMI CLASS (PC/PB)

Name	No	Builders	Commissioned
ASOYUKI	PC 74	Hitachi, Kanagawa	16 June 1975

Displacement, tons: 46 normal
Dimensions, feet (metres): 69 × 17.4 × 3.3 *(21 × 5.3 × 1)*
Main machinery: 2 MTU MB 12V 493 TY7 diesels; 2,200 hp(m) *(1.62 MW)* sustained; 2 shafts
Speed, knots: 26
Range, n miles: 230 at 23.8 kt
Complement: 10
Radars: Navigation: MD 806; I-band.

Comment: Built completely of light alloy. PC 69 paid off 8 December 1999 and PC 70 on 19 October 2000.

ASOYUKI *5/2004, Hirotoshi Yamamoto* / 1044454

15 HAYANAMI CLASS (PC/PB/YTR)

Name	No	Builders	Commissioned
HAYANAMI	PC 11	Sumidagawa	25 Mar 1993
SETOGIRI (ex-*Shikinami*)	PC 12	Sumidagawa	24 Mar 1994
MIZUNAMI	PC 13	Ishihara	24 Mar 1994
IYONAMI	PC 14	Sumidagawa	30 June 1994
KURINAMI	PC 15	Sumidagawa	30 Jan 1995
HAMANAMI	PC 16	Sumidagawa	28 Mar 1996
SHINONOME	PC 17	Ishihara	29 Feb 1996
HARUNAMI	PC 18	Ishihara	28 Mar 1996
KIYOZUKI	PC 19	Sumidagawa	23 Feb 1996
AYANAMI	PC 20	Yokohama Yacht	28 Mar 1996
TOKINAMI	PC 21	Yokohama Yacht	28 Mar 1996
HAMAGUMO	PC 22	Sumidagawa	27 Aug 1999
AWANAMI	PC 23	Sumidagawa	27 Aug 1999
URANAMI	PC 24	Sumidagawa	24 Jan 2000
SHIKINAMI	PC 25	Ishihara	24 Oct 2000

Displacement, tons: 110 normal; 190 full load
Dimensions, feet (metres): 114.8 × 20.7 × 7.5 *(35 × 6.3 × 2.3)*
Main machinery: 2 diesels; 4,000 hp(m) *(2.94 MW)*; 2 shafts
Speed, knots: 25
Guns: 1 – 12.7 mm MG.
Radars: Navigation: I-band.

Comment: One more authorised in FY99 budget. From PC 22 onwards these craft are equipped for firefighting. PC 12 changed name 1 October 2000.

HAMAGUMO *5/2005*, Mitsuhiro Kadota* / 1153327

2 NATSUGIRI CLASS (PC/PB)

Name	No	Builders	Commissioned
NATSUGIRI	PC 86	Sumidagawa	29 Jan 1990
SUGANAMI	PC 87	Sumidagawa	29 Jan 1990

Displacement, tons: 68 normal
Dimensions, feet (metres): 88.6 × 18.4 × 3.9 *(27 × 5.6 × 1.2)*
Main machinery: 2 diesels; 3,000 hp(m) *(2.21 MW)*; 2 shafts
Speed, knots: 27
Complement: 10
Radars: Navigation: I-band.

Comment: Built under FY88 programme. Steel hulls.

SUGANAMI *5/2005*, Mitsuhiro Kadota* / 1153328

4 ASOGIRI CLASS (PC/PB)

Name	No	Builders	Commissioned
ASOGIRI	PC 101	Yokohama Yacht	19 Dec 1994
MUROZUKI	PC 102	Ishihara	27 July 1995
WAKAGUMO	PC 103	Ishihara	17 July 1996
KAGAYUKI (ex-*Naozuki*)	PC 104	Sumidagawa	23 Jan 1997

Displacement, tons: 88 normal
Dimensions, feet (metres): 108.3 × 20.7 × 4.6 *(33 × 6.3 × 1.4)*
Main machinery: 2 diesels; 5,200 hp(m) *(3.82 MW)*; 2 shafts
Speed, knots: 30
Complement: 10
Guns: 1 – 12.7 mm MG.

Comment: First pair authorised in FY93 programme, third and fourth in FY95. PC 104 changed names on 1 April 2006.

MUROZUKI *8/2001, Hachiro Nakai* / 0130250

196 COASTAL PATROL and RESCUE CRAFT (CL/PB)

CL 01-04	CL 206-209	CL 213-215	CL 228	CL 237-242	GS 01-02
CL 11-134	CL 211	CL 226	CL 231-235	CL 244-264	SS 51-74

Comment: Some have firefighting capability. Built by Shigi, Ishihara, Sumidagawa, Yokohama Yacht Co and Yamaha. For coastal patrol and rescue duties. Built of high tensile steel. Fourteen CL 11 class authorised in FY01 budget.

CL 240   *5/2005*, Mitsuhiro Kadota* / 1153326

SS 51   *1/2005*, Hachiro Nakai* / 1153318

FIREFIGHTING VESSELS and CRAFT

1 MODIFIED HIRYU CLASS (FL/YTR)

Name	No	Builders	Launched	Commissioned
HIRYU	FL 01	NKK, Tsurumi	5 Sep 1997	24 Dec 1997

Displacement, tons: 280 normal
Dimensions, feet (metres): 114.8 × 40 × 8.9 *(35 × 12.2 × 2.7)*
Main machinery: 2 diesels; 4,000 hp(m) *(2.94 MW)*; 2 shafts
Speed, knots: 14
Complement: 15

Comment: Authorised in FY96 programme. Catamaran design. Replaced ship of the same name and pennant number.

HIRYU   *5/2005*, Hachiro Nakai* / 1153319

4 HIRYU CLASS (FL/YTR)

Name	No	Builders	Commissioned
SHORYU	FL 02	Nippon Kokan, Tsurumi	4 Mar 1970
NANRYU	FL 03	Nippon Kokan, Tsurumi	4 Mar 1971
KAIRYU	FL 04	Nippon Kokan, Tsurumi	18 Mar 1977
SUIRYU	FL 05	Yokohama Yacht Co	24 Mar 1978

Displacement, tons: 215 normal
Dimensions, feet (metres): 90.2 × 34.1 × 7.2 *(27.5 × 10.4 × 2.2)*
Main machinery: 2 Ikegai MTU MB 12V 493 TY7 diesels; 2,200 hp(m) *(1.62 MW)* sustained; 2 shafts
Speed, knots: 13.2
Range, n miles: 300 at 13 kt
Complement: 14

Comment: Catamaran type fire boats designed and built for firefighting services to large tankers.

SHORYU   *9/2005*, Kazumas Watanabe* / 1153320

4 NUNOBIKI CLASS (FM/YTR)

Name	No	Builders	Commissioned
SHIRAITO	FM 04	Yokohama Yacht Co	25 Feb 1975
MINOO	FM 08	Sumidagawa	27 Jan 1978
RYUSEI	FM 09	Yokohama Yacht Co	24 Mar 1980
KIYOTAKI	FM 10	Sumidagawa	25 Mar 1981

Displacement, tons: 89 normal
Dimensions, feet (metres): 75.4 × 19.7 × 5.2 *(23 × 6 × 1.6)*
Main machinery: 1 MTU MB 12V 493 TY7 diesel; 1,100 hp(m) *(810 kW)* sustained; 1 shaft
2 Nissan diesels; 500 hp(m) *(515 kW)*; 3 shafts
Speed, knots: 14
Range, n miles: 180 at 13.5 kt
Complement: 12
Radars: Navigation: FRA 10; I-band.

Comment: Equipped for chemical firefighting. FM 01 paid off 31 October 2000 and FM 02 in 2002. FM 05, FM 06 and FM 07 paid off on 11 March 2003.

KIYOTAKI   *10/2003, Hachiro Nakai* / 0570706

SURVEY SHIPS

1 SHOYO CLASS (AGS)

Name	No	Builders	Launched	Commissioned
SHOYO	HL 01	Mitsui, Tamano	23 June 1997	20 Mar 1998

Displacement, tons: 3,000 normal
Dimensions, feet (metres): 321.5 × 49.9 × 11.8 *(98 × 15.2 × 3.6)*
Main machinery: Diesel-electric; 2 diesels; 8,100 hp(m) *(5.95 MW)*; 2 motors; 5,712 hp(m) *(4.2 MW)*; 2 shafts; cp props
Speed, knots: 17
Complement: 60

Comment: Authorised in FY95 programme. Laid down 4 October 1996. Has replaced former *Shoyo*.

SHOYO *5/2003, Hachiro Nakai* / 0570707

1 TENYO CLASS (AGS)

Name	No	Builders	Commissioned
TENYO	HL 04	Sumitomo, Oppama	27 Nov 1986

Displacement, tons: 770 normal
Dimensions, feet (metres): 183.7 × 32.2 × 9.5 *(56 × 9.8 × 2.9)*
Main machinery: 2 Akasaka diesels; 1,300 hp(m) *(955 kW)*; 2 shafts
Speed, knots: 13. **Range, n miles:** 5,400 at 12 kt
Complement: 43 (18 officers)
Radars: Navigation: 2 JMA 1596; I-band

Comment: Laid down 11 April 1986, launched 5 August 1986. Based at Tokyo.

TENYO *11/2003, Hachiro Nakai* / 0570705

1 TAKUYO CLASS (AGS)

Name	No	Builders	Commissioned
TAKUYO	HL 02	Nippon Kokan, Tsurumi	31 Aug 1983

Displacement, tons: 3,000 normal
Dimensions, feet (metres): 314.9 × 46.6 × 15.1 *(96 × 14.2 × 4.6)*
Main machinery: 2 Fuji 6S40B diesels; 6,090 hp(m) *(4.47 MW)*; 2 shafts; cp props
Speed, knots: 17. **Range, n miles:** 12,000 at 16 kt
Complement: 60 (24 officers)
Radars: Navigation: 2 sets; I-band.

Comment: Laid down on 14 April 1982, launched on 24 March 1983. Based at Tokyo. Side scan sonar fitted. Two survey launches.

TAKUYO *5/2005*, Hachiro Nakai* / 1153321

2 MEIYO CLASS (AGS)

Name	No	Builders	Commissioned
MEIYO	HL 03	Kawasaki, Kobe	24 Oct 1990
KAIYO	HL 05	Mitsubishi, Shimonoseki	7 Oct 1993

Displacement, tons: 550 normal
Dimensions, feet (metres): 196.9 × 34.4 × 10.2 *(60 × 10.5 × 3.1)*
Main machinery: 2 Daihatsu 6 DLM-24 diesels; 3,000 hp(m) *(2.2 MW)*; 2 shafts; bow thruster
Speed, knots: 15
Range, n miles: 5,280 at 11 kt
Complement: 25 + 13 scientists
Radars: Navigation: 2 sets; I-band.

Comment: *Meiyo* laid down 24 July 1989 and launched 29 June 1990; *Kaiyo* laid down 7 July 1992 and launched 26 April 1993. Have anti-roll tanks and resiliently mounted main machinery. Has a 12 kHz bottom contour sonar. A large survey launch is carried on the port side.

KAIYO *5/2005*, Hachiro Nakai* / 1153322

7 HAMASHIO CLASS (YGS)

Name	No	Builders	Commissioned
HAMASHIO	HS 21	Yokohama Yacht	25 Mar 1991
ISOSHI	HS 22	Yokohama Yacht	25 Mar 1993
UZUSHIO	HS 23	Yokohama Yacht	22 Dec 1995
OKISHIO	HS 24	Ishihara	4 Mar 1999
ISESHIO	HS 25	Ishihara	10 Mar 1999
HAYASHIO	HS 26	Ishihara	10 Mar 1999
KURUSHIMA	HS 27	Nissui Marine	26 Mar 2003

Displacement, tons: 42 normal
Dimensions, feet (metres): 66.6 × 14.8 × 3.9 *(20.3 × 4.5 × 1.2)*
Main machinery: 3 diesels; 1,015 hp(m) *(746 kW)*; 3 shafts
Speed, knots: 15
Complement: 10
Radars: Navigation: I-band.

Comment: Survey launches. HS 27 authorised in FY01 extra budget.

UZUSHIO *7/2004, Hachiro Nakai* / 1044460

AIDS TO NAVIGATION SERVICE

1 SUPPLY SHIP (AKSL)

Name	No	Builders	Commissioned
TSUSHIMA	LL 01	Mitsui, Tamano	9 Sep 1977

Displacement, tons: 1,950 normal
Dimensions, feet (metres): 246 × 41 × 13.8 *(75 × 12.5 × 4.2)*
Main machinery: 1 Fuji-Sulzer 8S40C diesel; 4,200 hp(m) *(3.09 MW)*; 1 shaft; cp prop; bow thruster
Speed, knots: 15.5
Range, n miles: 10,000 at 15 kt
Complement: 54

Comment: Lighthouse Supply Ship launched 7 April 1977. Fitted with tank stabilisers. Equipped with modern electronic instruments for carrying out research on electronic aids to navigation.

TSUSHIMA *5/2005*, Mitsuhiro Kadota* / 1153325

3 HOKUTO CLASS (ABU)

Name	No	Builders	Commissioned
HOKUTO	LL 11	Sasebo	29 June 1979
KAIOU	LL 12	Sasebo	11 Mar 1980
GINGA	LL 13	Kawasaki, Kobe	18 Mar 1980

Displacement, tons: 700 normal
Dimensions, feet (metres): 180.4 × 34.8 × 8.7 (55 × 10.6 × 2.7)
Main machinery: 2 Asakasa MH23R diesels; 1,030 hp(m) (757 kW); 2 shafts
Speed, knots: 12. **Range, n miles:** 3,900 at 12 kt
Complement: 31 (9 officers)

Comment: Used as buoy tenders.

HOKUTO　　　　　　*5/2004, Hachiro Nakai* / 1044459

1 SUPPLY SHIP (AKSL)

Name	No	Builders	Commissioned
ZUIUN	LM 101	Usuki	27 July 1983

Displacement, tons: 370 normal
Dimensions, feet (metres): 146.3 × 24.6 × 7.2 (44.6 × 7.5 ×2.2)
Main machinery: 2 Mitsubishi-Asakasa MH23R diesels; 1,030 hp(m) (757 kW); 2 shafts
Speed, knots: 13.5. **Range, n miles:** 1,000 at 13 kt
Complement: 20

Comment: Classed as a medium tender and used to service lighthouses. Can carry 85 tons of stores.

ZUIUN　　　　　　*6/2003, Japan Coast Guard* / 0570701

9 SUPPLY CRAFT (AKSL)

Name	No	Builders	Commissioned
TOKUUN	LM 114	Yokohama Yacht Co	23 Mar 1981
SHOUN	LM 201	Sumidagawa	26 Mar 1986
SEIUN	LM 202	Sumidagawa	22 Feb 1989
SEKIUN	LM 203	Ishihara	12 Mar 1991
HOUUN	LM 204	Ishihara	22 Feb 1991
REIUN	LM 205	Ishihara	28 Feb 1992
GENUN	LM 206	Wakamatsu	19 Mar 1996
AYABANE	LM 207	Ishihara	9 Mar 2000
KOUN	LM 208	Sumidagawa	16 Mar 2001

Displacement, tons: 58 full load
Dimensions, feet (metres): 75.5 × 19.7 × 3.3 (23 × 6 × 1)
Main machinery: 2 GM 12V-71TA diesels; 840 hp (627 kW) sustained; 2 shafts
Speed, knots: 14. **Range, n miles:** 250 at 14 kt
Complement: 9
Radars: Navigation: FRA 10 Mk III; I-band.

KOUN　　　　　　*7/2005*, Hachiro Nakai* / 1153323

34 SMALL TENDERS (YAG)

LS 161	LS 188-195	LS 212-223
LS 164-170	LS 201	LS 231-235

Displacement, tons: 27 full load
Dimensions, feet (metres): 65 × 14.7 × 7.5 (20 × 4.5 × 2.3)
Main machinery: 2 diesels; 1,820 hp(m) (1.34 MW); 2 shafts
Speed, knots: 25
Complement: 8

Comment: Details given are for LS 231-233. Others with varying characteristics.

LS 220　　　　　　*7/2005*, Hachiro Nakai* / 1153324

ENVIRONMENT MONITORING CRAFT

Notes: In addition to those listed there are three oil skimmers OS 01-03.

3 SERVICE CRAFT (YPC)

Name	No	Builders	Commissioned
KINUGASA	MS 01	Ishihara, Takasago	31 Jan 1992
SAIKAI	MS 02	Ishihara, Takasago	4 Feb 1994
KATSUREN	MS 03	Sumidagawa	18 Dec 1997

Displacement, tons: 39 normal
Dimensions, feet (metres): 59.1 × 29.5 × 4.3 (18 × 9 × 1.3)
Main machinery: 2 diesels; 1,000 hp(m) (735 kW); 2 shafts
Speed, knots: 15
Complement: 8

Comment: Details given are for Kinugasa which has a catamaran hull. Saikai and Katsuren are monohulls of 26 tons. Used for monitoring pollution.

KINUGASA　　　　　　*7/2001, Mitsuhiro Kadota* / 0130213

SAIKAI　　　　　　*8/2004, Hachiro Nakai* / 1044464

5 SERVICE CRAFT (YAG)

SHIRASAGI OR 01	**MIZUNANGI** OR 03	**ISOSHIGI** OR 05
SHIRATORI OR 02	**CHIDORI** OR 04	

Displacement, tons: 153 normal
Dimensions, feet (metres): 72.3 × 21 × 2.6 *(22 × 6.4 × 0.9)*
Main machinery: 2 Nissan UD626 diesels; 360 hp(m) *(265 kW)*; 2 shafts
Speed, knots: 6
Range, n miles: 160 at 6 kt
Complement: 7

Comment: Completed by Sumidagawa (OR 01), Shigi (OR 02 and 04) and Ishihara (OR 03 and 05) between 31 January 1977 and 23 March 1979. Used for oil recovery.

SHIRASAGI
5/2004, Hachiro Nakai
1044465

Jordan

Country Overview

The Hashemite Kingdom of Jordan is situated in the Middle East. With an area of 34,445 square miles, it has borders to the north with Syria, to the east with Iraq, to the west with Israel and the West Bank and to the east and south with Saudi Arabia. It has a 14 n mile coastline with the Gulf of Aqaba (in the northern Red Sea) on which Aqaba, the only seaport, is situated. Amman is the capital and largest city. Territorial seas (3 n miles) are claimed but an Exclusive Economic Zone (EEZ) is not claimed.

Headquarters Appointments

Commander Naval Forces:
 Brigadier General Dari al-Zaban
Deputy Commander:
 Lieutenant Colonel Abdelkareem Fdoul

Organisation

The Royal Jordanian Naval Force comes under the Director of Operations at General Headquarters.

Bases

Dead Sea, Aqaba

Personnel

(a) 2006: 500 officers and men
(b) Voluntary service

PATROL FORCES

Notes: In addition to the craft listed, there are also four 17 ft launches and four 14 ft GRP boats used by the Underwater Swimmer unit.

3 AL HUSSEIN (HAWK) CLASS (FAST ATTACK CRAFT—GUN) (PB)

AL HUSSEIN 101	**AL HASSAN** 102	**KING ABDULLAH** 103

Displacement, tons: 124 full load
Dimensions, feet (metres): 100 × 22.5 × 4.9 *(30.5 × 6.9 × 1.5)*
Main machinery: 2 MTU 16V 396 TB94 diesels; 5,800 hp(m) *(4.26 MW)* sustained; 2 shafts
Speed, knots: 32
Range, n miles: 750 at 15 kt; 1,500 at 11 kt
Complement: 16 (3 officers)
Guns: 1 Oerlikon GCM-A03 30 mm. 1 Oerlikon GAM-BO1 20 mm. 2—12.5 mm MGs.
Countermeasures: Decoys: 2 Wallop Stockade chaff launchers.
Combat data systems: Racal Cane 100.
Weapons control: Radamec Series 2000 optronic director for 30 mm gun.
Radars: Surface search: Kelvin Hughes 1007; I-band.

Comment: Ordered from Vosper Thornycroft in December 1987. GRP structure. First one on trials in May 1989 and completed December 1989. Second completed in March 1990 and the third in early 1991. All transported to Aqaba in September 1991.

AL HASSAN
6/2004* / 1130000

4 FAYSAL CLASS (INSHORE PATROL CRAFT) (PB)

FAYSAL	**HUSSEIN** (ex-*Han*)	**HASSAN** (ex-*Hasayu*)	**MUHAMMED**

Displacement, tons: 8 full load
Dimensions, feet (metres): 38 × 13.1 × 1.6 *(11.6 × 4 × 0.5)*
Main machinery: 2 6M 8V715 diesels; 600 hp *(441 kW)*; 2 shafts
Speed, knots: 22
Range, n miles: 240 at 20 kt
Complement: 8
Guns: 1—12.7 mm MG. 1—7.62 mm MG.
Radars: Surface search: Decca; I-band.

Comment: Acquired from Bertram, Miami in 1974. GRP construction. Still operational and no replacements are planned yet.

MUHAMMED
3/2004, Bob Fildes / 0587768

3 HASHIM (ROTORK) CLASS (PB)

HASHIM	**FAISAL**	**HAMZA**

Displacement, tons: 9 full load
Dimensions, feet (metres): 41.7 × 10.5 × 3 *(12.7 × 3.2 × 0.9)*
Main machinery: 2 Deutz diesels; 240 hp *(179 kW)*; 2 shafts
Speed, knots: 28
Complement: 5
Military lift: 30 troops
Guns: 1—12.7 mm MG. 1—7.62 mm MG.
Radars: Surface search: Furuno; I-band.

Comment: Delivered in late 1990 for patrolling the Dead Sea. Due to the annual decrease of water depth, the three craft were moved to Aqaba in 2000.

HAMZA
3/2004, Bob Fildes / 0587769

Kazakhstan

Country Overview

Formerly part of the USSR, the Republic of Kazakhstan declared its independence in 1991. Situated in Central Asia, it has an area of 1,049,155 square miles and is bordered to the north and west with Russia, to the east with China and to the south with Kyrgyzstan, Uzbekistan, and Turkmenistan. It has a 755 n mile coastline with the Caspian Sea on which Aktau, the principal port, is situated. Astana became the capital city in 1995 while Almaty, the former capital, is the largest city. Maritime claims in the Caspian Sea are not clear. The naval Flotilla was inaugurated by President Nazarbayev in June 1998. The plan was to absorb about 30 per cent of the former USSR Caspian Flotilla, but many of these craft are derelict.

Headquarters Appointments

Commander, Navy:
  Rear Admiral Ratmir Komratov

Bases

Aktau (Caspian) (HQ)
Aralsk (Aral Sea), Bautino (Caspian)

Personnel

2006: 3,000

PATROL FORCES

Notes: (1) Plans to expand the Navy were announced by Rear Admiral Komratov in July 2003 although this is likely to take at least ten years, subject to funding. (2) There is also an ex-trawler *Tyulen II* of 39 m with a single diesel of 578 hp(m) *(425 kW)* capable of 10 kt. Acquired in 1997. (3) Six Customs cutters acquired from the UAE in 1998. At least one sunk in transit. (4) Five Guardian class Boston Whalers delivered in November 1995 are unseaworthy. (5) Plans to transfer three Yevgenya class from Russia appear to have been abandoned.

2 TURK (AB 25) CLASS (PB)

Name	No	Builders	Commissioned
— (ex-AB 32)	— (ex-P 132)	Haliç Shipyard	6 June 1969
— (ex-AB 26)	— (ex-P 126)	Haliç Shipyard	6 Feb 1970

Displacement, tons: 170 full load
Dimensions, feet (metres): 132 × 21 × 5.5 *(40.2 × 6.4 × 1.7)*
Main machinery: 4 SACM-AGO V16 CSHR diesels; 9,600 hp(m) *(7.06 MW)*; 2 cruise diesels; 300 hp(m) *(220 kW)*; 2 shafts
Speed, knots: 22
Complement: 31
Guns: 1 Bofors 40 mm/70. 1 Oerlikon 20 mm.
Radars: Surface search: Racal Decca; I-band.

Comment: Presented by the Turkish Navy on 3 July 1999 (AB 32) and 25 July 2001 (AB 26) at Geljuk. May have retained active sonar and ASW rocket launcher but this is unlikely.

TURK CLASS (Turkish colours) *10/2000, Selim San* / 0106636

4 KW 15 (TYPE 369) CLASS (PB)

ALMATY (ex-KW 15) 2013 (ex-201)   **ATYRAU** (ex-KW 17) 2033 (ex-203)
AKTAU (ex-KW 16) 2023 (ex-202)   **SCHAMBYL** (ex-KW 20) 2043 (ex-204)

Displacement, tons: 70 full load
Dimensions, feet (metres): 93.5 × 15.4 × 4.9 *(28.9 × 4.7 × 1.5)*
Main machinery: 2 Mercedes-Benz diesels; 2,000 hp(m) *(1.47 MW)*; 2 shafts
Speed, knots: 25
Complement: 17
Guns: 2 — 20 mm can be fitted.
Radars: Surface search: Kelvin Hughes 14/9; I-band.

Comment: Transferred from Germany at Wilhelmshaven on 23 August 1996. Built in Germany 1952-53 and paid off in 1994, having been used for river patrols and later as range safety craft. Disarmed on transfer. Reported as being non-operational.

ALMATY (old number) *8/1996, Michael Nitz* / 0080219

1 ZHUK (PROJECT 1400) CLASS (PB)

BERKUT

Displacement, tons: 39 full load
Dimensions, feet (metres): 78.7 × 16.4 × 3.9 *(24 × 5 × 1.2)*
Main machinery: 2 Type M401B diesels; 2,200 hp(m) *(1.6 MW)* sustained; 2 shafts
Speed, knots: 30. **Range, n miles:** 1,100 at 15 kt
Complement: 11
Guns: 2 — 14.5 mm (twin); 1 — 12.7 mm MG.
Radars: Surface search: Spin Trough; I-band.

Comment: Built at the Zenith Shipyard, Uralsk, and commissioned 15 July 1998. Reports of a second craft have not been confirmed.

ZHUK (Russian colours) *11/1996, MoD Bonn* / 0019041

1 DAUNTLESS CLASS (PB)

ABAY

Displacement, tons: 11 full load
Dimensions, feet (metres): 42 × 14 × 4.3 *(12.8 × 4.3 × 1.3)*
Main machinery: 2 Detroit 8V-92TA diesels; 1,270 hp *(935 kW)*; 2 shafts
Speed, knots: 35. **Range, n miles:** 600 at 18 kt
Complement: 5
Guns: 1 — 12.7 mm MG. 2 — 7.62 mm MGs.
Radars: Surface search: Furuno; I-band.

Comment: Ordered under US funding in November 1995. Built by SeaArk, Monticello. Used to interdict the smuggling of nuclear materials across the Caspian Sea.

DAUNTLESS *7/1996, SeaArk Marine* / 0080220

2 SAYGAK (PROJECT 1408) CLASS (PB)

Displacement, tons: 13 full load
Dimensions, feet (metres): 46.3 × 11.5 × 3 *(14.1 × 3.5 × 0.9)*
Main machinery: 1 diesel; 980 hp(m) *(720 kW)*; 1 water-jet
Speed, knots: 35. **Range, n miles:** 135 at 35 kt
Complement: 6
Guns: 2 — 7.62 mm MGs.
Radars: Surface search: I-band.

Comment: Russian-built small craft primarily found on the Amur river. Built in 1995 and acquired in early 1996.

SAYGAK (Russian colours) *7/1996, Hartmut Ehlers* / 0052520

Kenya

Country Overview

A former British colony, The Republic of Kenya gained independence in 1963. Located astride the Equator, the country has an area of 224,082 square miles and has borders to the north with Somalia and Ethiopia and to the south with Tanzania. It has a 292 n mile coastline with the Indian Ocean. The country includes almost all of Lake Turkana (Lake Rudolf) and a small portion of Lake Victoria. The capital and largest city is Nairobi and the main seaport is Mombasa. Kisumu is a port on Lake Victoria. Perhaps the first proponent of the Exclusive Economic Zone (EEZ) concept, Kenya claims a 200 n mile EEZ whose limits have been partly defined. Territorial seas (12 n miles) are claimed.

Headquarters Appointments

Commander, Navy:
   Major General Pasteur Awitta
Fleet Commander:
   Colonel Joe Waswa

Personnel

(a)   2006: 1,250 plus 120 marines
(b)   Voluntary service

Bases

Mombasa (Mtongwe port), Manda, Malindi, Lamu, Kisumu (Lake Victoria)

Coast Defence

There are nine Masura coastal radar stations spread along the coast. Each station has 30 ft fast boats to investigate contacts.

Customs/Police

There are some 14 Customs and Police patrol craft of between 12 and 14 m. Mostly built by Cheverton, Performance Workboats and Fassmer in the 1980s. One Cheverton 18 m craft acquired in early 1997.

PATROL FORCES

Notes: (1) There are also five Spanish built inshore patrol craft of 16 m armed with 12.7 mm MGs and driven by twin 538 hp diesels for a speed of 16 kt. Acquired in 1995 and have pennant numbers P 943-947.
(2) Procurement of a new patrol ship was reportedly initiated with a Spanish company in 2003. The ship was expected to be delivered in mid-2005 but, following the return of the standby crew in July 2005, the status of the project is unclear.

2 NYAYO CLASS (FAST ATTACK CRAFT—MISSILE) (PGGF)

Name	No	Builders	Launched	Commissioned
NYAYO	P 3126	Vosper Thornycroft	20 Aug 1986	23 July 1987
UMOJA	P 3127	Vosper Thornycroft	5 Mar 1987	16 Sep 1987

Displacement, tons: 310 light; 430 full load
Dimensions, feet (metres): 186 × 26.9 × 7.9 *(56.7 × 8.2 × 2.4)*
Main machinery: 4 Paxman Valenta 18CM diesels; 15,000 hp *(11.19 MW)* sustained; 4 shafts; 2 motors (slow speed patrol); 100 hp *(74.6 kW)*
Speed, knots: 40. **Range, n miles:** 2,000 at 18 kt
Complement: 40

Missiles: SSM: 4 OTO Melara/Matra Otomat Mk 2 (2 twin); active radar homing to 160 km *(86.4 n miles)* at 0.9 Mach; warhead 210 kg; sea-skimmer for last 4 km *(2.2 n miles)*.
Guns: 1 OTO Melara 3 in *(76 mm)*/62; 85 rds/min to 16 km *(8.7 n miles)* anti-surface; 12 km *(6.5 n miles)* anti-aircraft; weight of shell 6 kg.
2 Oerlikon/BMARC 30 mm GCM-A02 (twin); 650 rds/min to 10 km *(5.4 n miles)* anti-surface; 3 km *(1.6 n miles)* anti-aircraft; weight of shell 0.36 kg.
2 Oerlikon/BMARC 20 mm A41A; 800 rds/min to 2 km; weight of shell 0.24 kg.
Countermeasures: Decoys: 2 Wallop Barricade 18-barrelled launchers; Stockade and Palisade rockets.
ESM: Racal Cutlass; radar warning.
ECM: Racal Cygnus; jammer.
Weapons control: CAAIS 450.
Radars: Surface search: Plessey AWS 4; E/F-band; range 101 km *(55 n miles)*.
Navigation: Decca AC 1226; I-band.
Fire control: Marconi ST802; I-band.

Programmes: Ordered in September 1984. Sailed in company from the UK, arriving at Mombasa 30 August 1988. Similar to Omani Province class.
Operational: First live Otomat firing in February 1989. RIB carried right aft. Form Squadron 86. Both ships awaiting refit.

NYAYO   *2/2001, Sattler/Steele* / 0114357

1 MAMBA CLASS (LARGE PATROL CRAFT) (PB)

Name	No	Builders	Commissioned
MAMBA	P 3100	Brooke Marine, Lowestoft	7 Feb 1974

Displacement, tons: 125 standard; 160 full load
Dimensions, feet (metres): 123 × 22.5 × 5.2 *(37.5 × 6.9 × 1.6)*
Main machinery: 2 Paxman 16YJCM diesels; 4,000 hp *(2.98 MW)* sustained; 2 shafts
Speed, knots: 25. **Range, n miles:** 3,300 at 13 kt
Complement: 25 (3 officers)

Missiles: SSM: 4 IAI Gabriel II.
Guns: 2 Oerlikon/BMARC 30 mm GCM-A02 (twin); 650 rds/min to 10 km *(5.4 n miles)* anti-surface; 3 km *(1.6 n miles)* anti-aircraft; weight of shell 0.36 kg.
Radars: Navigation: Decca AC 1226; I-band.
Fire control: Selenia RTN 10X; I/J-band; range 40 km *(22 n miles)*.

Programmes: Laid down 17 February 1972, launched 6 November 1973.
Modernisation: New missiles, gunnery equipment and optronic director fitted in 1982.
Operational: Refitted at Vosper Thornycroft 1989-90. Although still seagoing, operational capability is limited. Gabriel system non-operational.

MAMBA   *6/2002* / 0533319

2 SHUPAVU CLASS (LARGE PATROL CRAFT) (PBO)

SHUJAA P 3130   **SHUPAVU** P 3131

Displacement, tons: 480 full load
Dimensions, feet (metres): 190.3 × 26.9 × 9.2 *(58 × 8.2 × 2.8)*
Main machinery: 2 diesels; 2 shafts
Speed, knots: 22
Complement: 24
Guns: 1 OTO Melara 3 in *(76 mm)*/62. 1 Mauser 30 mm.
Weapons control: Breda optronic director.
Radars: Surface search: I-band.

Comment: Built to civilian standards at Astilleros Gondan, Castropol and delivered in 1997 when they were taken over by the Navy. Armament fitted in Kenya.

SHUJAA   *2/2001, Michael Nitz* / 0137788

AUXILIARIES

2 GALANA CLASS (LCM)

Name	No	Builders	Commissioned
GALANA	L 38	Astilleros Gondan, Spain	Feb 1994
TANA	L 39	Astilleros Gondan, Spain	Feb 1994

Displacement, tons: 1,400 full load
Dimensions, feet (metres): 208.3 × 43.6 × 7.9 *(63.5 × 13.3 × 2.4)*
Main machinery: 2 MTU/Bazán diesels; 2,700 hp(m) *(1.98 MW)* sustained; 2 shafts; bow thruster
Speed, knots: 12.5
Complement: 30
Radars: Navigation: Racal Decca; I-band.

Comment: Acquired by Galway Ltd for civilian use and taken over by the Navy for logistic support. The 4 m wide ramp is capable of taking 70 ton loads. Guns may be fitted in due course.

TANA   *2/1999* / 0052523

2 TENDERS (LCM)

Dimensions, feet (metres): 60 × 15.7 × 4.9 *(18.3 × 4.8 × 1.5)*
Main machinery: 2 Caterpillar 3306B-DIT diesels; 880 hp(m) *(647 kW)*; 2 shafts
Speed, knots: 10
Range, n miles: 200 at 10 kt
Complement: 2 plus 136 passengers

Comment: Built by Souters, Cowes and delivered in 1998. Personnel tenders.

Kiribati

Country Overview

The Republic of Kiribati, formerly the Gilbert Islands, is a south Pacific island group which gained independence in 1979 after the other part of the former British colony, the Ellice Islands, became independent as Tuvalu the previous year. Straddling the equator some 1,385 n miles southwest of Hawaii, it comprises from west to east Banaba (Ocean Island) and three detached island groups: the 16 Gilbert Islands, including Tarawa, on which the capital, Bairiki, is located, nine Phoenix Islands and eight of the 11 Line Islands. About 20 of the 34 islands are permanently inhabited. An archipelagic state, territorial seas (12 n miles) are claimed. An Exclusive Economic Zone (EEZ) (200 n miles) is also claimed but limits have not been fully defined by boundary agreements.

Headquarters Appointments

Head of Police Maritime Unit:
   Inspector John Mote

Bases

Tarawa

PATROL FORCES

1 PACIFIC CLASS (LARGE PATROL CRAFT) (PB)

Name	No	Builders	Commissioned
TEANOAI	301	Transfield Shipbuilding	22 Jan 1994

Displacement, tons: 165 full load
Dimensions, feet (metres): 103.3 × 26.6 × 6.9 *(31.5 × 8.1 × 2.1)*
Main machinery: 2 Caterpillar 3516TA diesels; 4,400 hp *(3.28 MW)* sustained; 2 shafts
Speed, knots: 18
Range, n miles: 2,500 at 12 kt
Complement: 18 (3 officers)
Guns: Can carry 1—12.7 mm MG but is unarmed.
Radars: Navigation: Furuno 1011; I-band.

Comment: The Pacific Patrol Boat programme was started by Australia in 1987. *Teanoai*, the 16th of the class, was handed over to Kiribati in 1994. The Australian government has announced that the programme will be extended so that all 22 boats will be able to operate for 30 years. *Teanoai* completed a half-life refit at Gladstone in 2001 and will require a life extension refit in 2010.

TEANOAI *6/1998, RAAF* / 0052524

Korea, North
PEOPLE'S DEMOCRATIC REPUBLIC

Country Overview

The Democratic People's Republic of Korea (DPRK) was proclaimed in 1948 and occupies the northern part of the Korean peninsula. Located in north-eastern Asia and with an area of 46,540 square miles, it is bordered to the north by China and Russia and to the south by South Korea. It has a 1,350 n mile coastline with the Sea of Japan and the Yellow Sea. The capital and largest city is Pyóngyang while the principal ports are Nampo and Haeju on the west coast and Chojin and Wónsan on the east coast. Territorial seas (12 n miles) are claimed. A 200 n mile EEZ has also been claimed but the limits have not been defined. A source of tension at sea is the dispute concerning the status of the *Northern Limit Line* and a number of South Korean islands off the south-west coast of DPRK.

The North Korean Navy is principally a coastal force and is the lowest priority military service. Ships are allocated to East or West Fleet Command. The Navy is manpower intensive and most equipment is technologically outdated and incapable of bluewater operations. Nevertheless, considerable emphasis has been placed on high speed infiltration and assault craft and the ability to conduct unconventional operations. Fishing vessels are likely to be converted and/or commandeered for military use.

Headquarters Appointments

Commander of the Navy:
   Admiral Kim Yun-Sim

Commander West Sea Fleet:
   Admiral Kim Yun-Sim
Commander East Sea Fleet:
   Admiral Kwon Sang-Ho

Bases

Naval Commander: Pyongyang.
East Fleet Command (HQ T'oejo-dong (Nagwon-up)).
East coast: T'oejo-dong, Ch'aho (submarines), Munchon-up, Mayang-do, and Najin.
Minor bases: Chakto-dong (Chakto-ri), Hodo-ri, Kosong-up (Changjon-ni), Puam-dong, Sinchang, Sinchang-nodongjagu, Sinpo, Songjin (Kimchaek), Songjon-pando, Wonsan, Yoho-ri, and Yongam-ni.
West Fleet Command: (HQ Nampo).
West coast: Nampo (Chinnampo), Pipa-got (submarines) and Sagon-ni (Sa-got).
Minor bases: Cho-do, Haeju, Kwangyang-ni, Sunwi-do, Tasa-ri and Yongwi-do.

Personnel

(a)   2006: 46,000 officers and other ranks
(b)   5 years' national service

Maritime Security Battalions

In addition to the Navy there is a Coastal and Port Security Police Force which would be subordinate to the Navy in war.

It is reported that the strength of this force is 10-15 Chong-Jin patrol craft and 130 patrol boats of various types.

Coast Defence

Two Regiments (12-15 batteries) with six fixed and several mobile launchers of SSC-2 and SSC-3 missiles. Large numbers of 130 mm and 120 mm guns controlled from radar sites.

Strength of the Fleet

Type	Active
Submarines–Patrol	23
Submarines–Coastal	32
Submarines–Midgets	23
Frigates	3
Corvettes	4
Patrol Forces	400+
Amphibious Craft	129
Hovercraft (LCPA)	135
Minesweepers	24
Depot Ships for Midget Submarines	8
Survey Vessels	4

DELETIONS

Notes: The order of battle and fleet dispositions represent the best estimates that can be made based on incomplete information.

SUBMARINES

Notes: (1) There are four obsolete ex-Soviet Whiskey class based at Pipa-got used for training. Probably restricted to periscope depth when dived.
(2) Reports of a sea-based ballistic missile capability have not been substantiated. A surface-ship based system is considered more likely than a submarine-launched missile which would present considerable technical challenges.

23 ROMEO (PROJECT 033) CLASS (SS)

Displacement, tons: 1,475 surfaced; 1,830 dived
Dimensions, feet (metres): 251.3 × 22 × 17.1
(76.6 × 6.7 × 5.2)
Main machinery: Diesel-electric; 2 Type 37-D diesels; 4,000 hp(m) *(2.94 MW)*; 2 motors; 2,700 hp(m) *(1.98 MW)*; 2 creep motors; 2 shafts
Speed, knots: 15 surfaced; 13 dived
Range, n miles: 9,000 at 9 kt surfaced
Complement: 54 (10 officers)

Torpedoes: 8—21 in *(533 mm)* tubes (6 bow, 2 stern). 14 probably SAET-60; passive homing up to 15 km

(8.1 n miles) at 40 kt; warhead 400 kg. Also some 53—56 may be carried.
Mines: 28 in lieu of torpedoes.
Countermeasures: ESM: China Type 921A Golf Ball (Stop Light); radar warning.
Radars: Surface search: Snoop Plate/Tray; I-band.
Sonars: Pike Jaw; hull-mounted; active.
   Feniks; hull-mounted; passive.

Programmes: Two transferred from China 1973, two in 1974 and three in 1975. First three of class built at Sinpo and Mayang-do shipyards in 1976. Programme ran at about one every 14 months until 1995 when it stopped in favour of the Sang-O class. One reported sunk in February 1985.
Operational: Seventeen are stationed on east coast and have occasionally operated in Sea of Japan. The remainder, including four ex-Chinese units, are based on the west coast. By modern standards these are basic attack submarines with virtually no anti-submarine performance or potential and their operational status is doubtful.

ROMEO (China colours) *3/1995, van Ginderen Collection* / 0080222

32 SANG-O CLASS (SSC)

Displacement, tons: 256 surfaced; 277 dived
Dimensions, feet (metres): 116.5 × 12.5 × 12.1
  (35.5 × 3.8 × 3.7)
Main machinery: 1 Russian diesel generator; 1 North Korean
  motor; 1 shaft; shrouded prop
Speed, knots: 7.6 surfaced; 7.2 snorting; 8.8 dived
Range, n miles: 2,700 at 7 kt
Complement: 19 (2 officers) plus 6 swimmers

Torpedoes: 2 or 4—21 in *(533 mm)* tubes (in some).
  Probably Russian Type 53—56.
Mines: 16 can be carried (in some).
Radars: Surface search: Furuno; I-band.
Sonars: Russian hull-mounted; passive/active search and
  attack.

Programmes: Started building in 1995 at Sinpo accelerating
  up to about four to six a year by 1996. Reported to
  have been building at about three a year from 1997.
  One reported delivered in 2002 and one in 2003 and
  production continues at one or two units per year.
Structure: A variation of a reverse engineered Yugoslav
  design. There are at least two types, one with torpedo
  tubes and one capable of carrying up to six external
  bottom mines. There is a single periscope and a VLF
  radio receiver in the fin. Rocket launchers and a 12.7 mm
  MG can be carried. Diving depth 180 m *(590 ft)*. A longer
  (39 m) variant submarine may replace older boats.
Operational: Used extensively for infiltration operations.
  The submarine can bottom, and swimmer disembarkation
  is reported as being normally exercised from periscope
  depth. One of the class grounded and was captured by
  South Korea on 18 September 1996. Some crew members
  may be replaced by special forces for short operations.
  17 stationed on east coast.

SANG-O   *9/1996* / 0080223

23 (+ 10 RESERVE) YUGO and P-4 CLASS (MIDGET SUBMARINES) (SSW)

Displacement, tons: 90 surfaced; 110 dived
Dimensions, feet (metres): 65.6 × 10.2 × 15.1
  (20 × 3.1 × 4.6)
Main machinery: 2 diesels; 320 hp(m) *(236 kW)*; 1 shaft
Speed, knots: 12 surfaced; 8 dived
Range, n miles: 550 at 10 kt surfaced; 50 at 4 kt dived
Complement: 4 plus 6—7 divers
Torpedoes: 2—406 mm tubes.
Radars: Navigation: I-band.

Comment: Built at Yukdaeso-ri shipyard since early 1960s.
  More than one design. Details given are for the latest
  type, at least one of which has been exported to Iran, and
  have been building since 1987 to a Yugoslavian design.
  Some have two short external torpedo tubes and some
  have a snort mast. The conning tower acts as a wet and
  dry compartment for divers. There is a second and smaller
  propeller for slow speed manoeuvring while dived. Twelve
  of the class are designated P-4s and belong to the KWP.
  This type has two internal torpedo tubes. Operate from
  eight merchant mother ships (see *Auxiliaries*). Some have
  been lost in operations against South Korea, the most
  recent in June 1998. Two exported to Vietnam in June 1997.
  There are also about 50 two-man submersibles of Italian
  design 4.9 × 1.4 m. Overall numbers are approximate due
  to scrapping of older units.

YUGO P-4
6/1998, Ships of the World
0052525

FRIGATES

2 NAJIN CLASS (FFG)

531   591

Displacement, tons: 1,500 full load
Dimensions, feet (metres): 334.6 × 32.8 × 8.9
  (102 × 10 × 2.7)
Main machinery: 3 SEMT-Pielstick Type 16 PA6 280 diesels;
  18,000 hp(m) *(13.2 MW)*; 3 shafts
Speed, knots: 24
Range, n miles: 4,000 at 13 kt
Complement: 180 (16 officers)

Missiles: SSM: 2 CSS-N-1 ❶; active radar or IR homing
  to 46 km *(25 n miles)* at 0.9 Mach; warhead 513 kg HE.
  Replaced torpedo tubes on both ships.
Guns: 2—3.9 in *(100 mm)*/56 ❷; 40° elevation; 15 rds/min to
  16 km *(8.6 n miles)*; weight of shell 13.5 kg.
  4—57 mm/80 (2 twin) ❸; 120 rds/min to 6 km *(3.2 n miles)*;
  weight of shell 2.8 kg.
  12 or 4—30 mm/60 (6 or 2 twin) ❹ (see *Structure*).
  12—25 mm (6 twin) ❺.
A/S mortars: 2 RBU 1200 5-tubed fixed launchers ❻; range
  1,200 m; warhead 34 kg (not in *531*).
Depth charges: 2 projectors; 2 racks. 30 weapons.
Mines: 30 (estimated).
Countermeasures: Decoys: 6 chaff launchers.
ESM: China RW-23 Jug Pair (Watch Dog); intercept.
Weapons control: Optical director ❼.
Radars: Air search: Square Tie ❽; I-band.
Surface search: Pot Head ❾; I-band.
Navigation: Pot Drum; H/I-band.
Fire control: Drum Tilt ❿; H/I-band.
IFF: High Pole. Square Head.
Sonars: Stag Horn; hull-mounted; active search; high
  frequency.

Programmes: Built at Najin and Nampo shipyards. First
  completed 1973, second 1975.

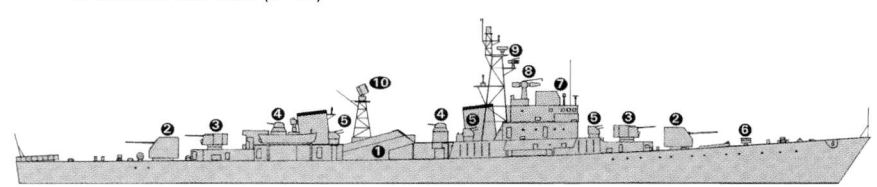

NAJIN   *(Scale 1 : 900), Ian Sturton* / 0506153

NAJIN 531   *5/1993, JMSDF* / 0080224

Structure: There is some resemblance to the ex-Soviet
Kola class, now deleted. The original torpedo tubes were
replaced by CSS-N-1 missile launchers in the mid-1980s
and the RBU 1200 mortars have been removed in at least
one of the class. Gun armaments differ, one having six
twin 30 mm while the other only has one twin 30 mm
and six twin 25 mm.
Operational: One based on each coast but seldom seen
at sea.

1 SOHO CLASS (FFGH)

Name	No	Builders	Laid down	Launched	Commissioned
—	823	Najin Shipyard	June 1980	Nov 1981	May 1982

Displacement, tons: 1,640 full load
Dimensions, feet (metres): 242.1 × 50.9 × 12.5
(73.8 × 15.5 × 3.8)
Main machinery: 2 diesels; 15,000 hp(m) *(11.03 MW)*;
2 shafts
Speed, knots: 23
Complement: 189 (17 officers)

Missiles: SSM: 4 CSS-N-2 ❶; active radar or IR homing to
46 km *(25 n miles)* at 0.9 Mach; warhead 513 kg.
Guns: 1—3.9 in *(100 mm)*/56 ❷; 40° elevation; 15 rds/min to
16 km *(8.6 n miles)*; weight of shell 13.5 kg.
4—37 mm/63 (2 twin) ❸.
4—30 mm/65 (2 twin) ❹. 4—25 mm/60 (2 twin) ❺.
A/S mortars: 2 RBU 1200 5-tubed fixed launchers ❻; range
1,200 m; warhead 34 kg.
Countermeasures: ESM: China RW-23 Jug Pair (Watch
Dog); intercept.
Radars: Surface search: Square Tie ❼; I-band.
Fire control: Drum Tilt ❽; H/I-band.
Navigation: I-band.
Sonars: Stag Horn; hull-mounted; active search and attack;
high frequency.
Helicopters: Platform for 1 medium.

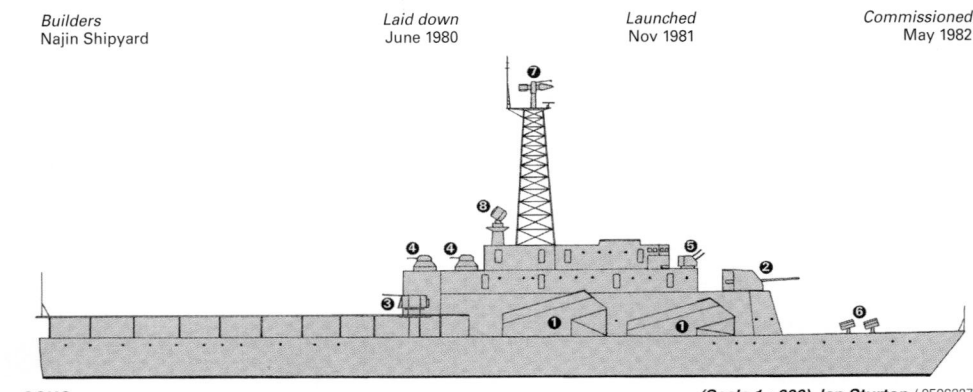

SOHO *(Scale 1 : 600)*, Ian Sturton / 0506237

Programmes: Planned class of six but only one was ordered.
Structure: One of the largest warships built anywhere with
a twin hull design and a helicopter deck aft. Has a large
central superstructure to carry the heavy gun armament.

Operational: Reported operational but is probably very
weather limited like many catamaran designs. Based at
Mugye-po on the east coast.

CORVETTES

4 SARIWON CLASS (FS) and 1 TRAL CLASS (FS)

671 611 612 613 614

Displacement, tons: 650; 580 (Tral); full load
Dimensions, feet (metres): 203.7 × 23.9 × 7.8
(62.1 × 7.3 × 2.4)
Main machinery: 2 diesels; 3,000 hp(m) *(2.21 MW)*;
2 shafts
Speed, knots: 16. **Range, n miles:** 2,700 at 16 kt
Complement: 60 (7 officers)

Guns: 1—85 mm/52 tank turret (Tral) ❶.
4—57 mm/80 (2 twin) (Sariwon).
2 or 4—37 mm/6 (single (Tral) ❷; 2 twin (Sariwon)).
16—14.5 mm ❸; 4 quad.
A/S mortars: 2 RBU 1200 5-tubed fixed launchers
(Sariwon *513*).
Depth charges: 2 rails.
Mines: 30.
Radars: Surface search: Pot Head or Don 2 ❹; I-band.
Navigation: Model 351; I-band.
IFF: Ski Pole.
Sonars: Stag Horn; hull-mounted; active; high frequency.

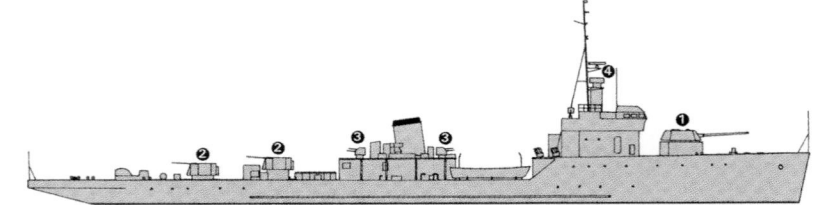

TRAL 671 *(Scale 1 : 600)*, Ian Sturton / 0506198

Programmes: Four Sariwon class built in Korea in the
mid-1960s. The two Tral class were transferred from the
USSR in the mid-1950s, were paid off in the early 1980s
but one returned to service in the early 1990s.
Structure: The Sariwon design is based on the original
USSR Fleet minelayer Tral or Fugas class in service in
the mid-1930s. Minelaying rails are visible along the
whole of upper deck aft of the bridge superstructure.

Sariwon *671* is one of the original Tral class built in
1938 and restored to service. Some variations in gun
armament and one Sariwon is reported as having sonar
and an ASW armament.
Operational: All ships are based on the east coast
(Changjon) and, despite their age, have been reported
as seagoing. Pennant numbers 611—614 have been
reported.

TRAL 671 *5/1993, JMSDF* / 0080225

PATROL FORCES

8 OSA I (PROJECT 205) and 4 HUANGFEN CLASS
(FAST ATTACK CRAFT—MISSILE) (PTFG)

Displacement, tons: 171 standard; 210 full load
Dimensions, feet (metres): 126.6 × 24.9 × 8.9 *(38.6 × 7.6 × 2.7)*
Main machinery: 3 Type M 503A diesels; 8,025 hp(m) *(5.9 MW)* sustained; 3 shafts
Speed, knots: 35. **Range, n miles:** 800 at 30 kt
Complement: 30

Missiles: SSM: 4 SS-N-2A Styx; active radar or IR homing to 46 km *(25 n miles)* at
0.9 Mach; warhead 513 kg.
Guns: 4—30 mm/65 (2 twin) AK 230; 500 rds/min to 5 km *(2.7 n miles)*; weight of shell
0.54 kg.
Countermeasures: ESM: China BM/HZ 8610; intercept (Huangfen class).
Radars: Surface search: Square Tie; I-band.
Fire control: Drum Tilt; H/I-band (Osa I).
IFF: High Pole B. Square Head.

Programmes: Twelve Osa I class transferred from USSR in 1968 and four more in 1972-83.
Eight remain of which four are based on each coast. Four Huangfen class acquired from
China in 1980 and are based on the west coast.

OSA I 0506031

6 KOMAR CLASS and 6 SOHUNG CLASS
(FAST ATTACK CRAFT—MISSILE) (PTFG)

Displacement, tons: 75 standard; 85 full load
Dimensions, feet (metres): 84 × 24 × 5.9 *(25.6 × 7.3 × 1.8)*
Main machinery: 4 Type M 50 diesels; 4,400 hp(m) *(3.3 MW)* sustained; 4 shafts
Speed, knots: 40
Range, n miles: 400 at 30 kt
Complement: 19
Missiles: SSM: 2 SS-N-2A Styx or CSS-N-1; active radar or IR homing to 46 km *(25 n miles)* at 0.9 Mach; warhead 513 kg.
Guns: 2—25 mm/80 (twin); 270 rds/min to 3 km *(1.6 n miles)*; weight of shell 0.34 kg.
2—14.5 mm (twin) MGs.
Radars: Surface search: Square Tie; I-band.
IFF: Square Head.

Programmes: Ten Komar class transferred by USSR, six still in service but with wood hulls replaced by steel. The Sohung class is a North Korean copy of the Komar class, first built in 1980-81 and no longer in production. The 'Komars' and four 'Sohung' are based on the east coast.

KOMAR 0506032

6 HAINAN CLASS (LARGE PATROL CRAFT) (PC)

201-204   **292-293**

Displacement, tons: 375 standard; 392 full load
Dimensions, feet (metres): 192.8 × 23.6 × 6.6 *(58.8 × 7.2 × 2)*
Main machinery: 4 Kolomna/PCR Type 9-D-8 diesels; 4,000 hp(m) *(2.94 MW)*; 4 shafts
Speed, knots: 30.5. **Range, n miles:** 1,300 at 15 kt
Complement: 69
Guns: 4—57 mm/70 (2 twin); 120 rds/min to 8 km *(4.4 n miles)*; weight of shell 2.8 kg.
4—25 mm/80 (2 twin); 270 rds/min to 3 km *(1.6 n miles)*; weight of shell 0.34 kg.
A/S mortars: 4 RBU 1200 5-tubed launchers; range 1,200 m; warhead 34 kg.
Depth charges: 2 projectors; 2 racks for 30 DCs.
Mines: Laying capability for 12.
Countermeasures: Decoys: 2 PK 16 chaff launchers.
ESM: China BM/HZ 8610; intercept.
Radars: Surface search: Pot Head (Model 351); I-band.
Sonars: Stag Ear; hull-mounted; active search and attack; high frequency.

Comment: Transferred from China in 1975 (two), 1976 (two), 1978 (two). All based on the west coast.

HAINAN (China colours) *4/1998* / 0080226

19 SO 1 CLASS (LARGE PATROL CRAFT) (PC)

Displacement, tons: 170 light; 215 normal
Dimensions, feet (metres): 137.8 × 19.7 × 5.9 *(42 × 6 × 1.8)*
Main machinery: 3 Kolomna Type 40-D diesels; 6,600 hp(m) *(4.85 MW)* sustained; 3 shafts
Speed, knots: 28. **Range, n miles:** 1,100 at 13 kt
Complement: 31
Guns: 1—85 mm/52; 18 rds/min to 15 km *(8 n miles)*; weight of shell 9.5 kg.
2—37 mm/63 (twin); 160 rds/min to 9 km *(4.9 n miles)*; weight of shell 0.7 kg.
4 or 6—25 mm/60 (2 or 3 twin); 270 rds/min to 3 km *(1.6 n miles)*; weight of shell 0.34 kg.
4—14.5 mm/93 MGs.
A/S mortars: 4 RBU 1200 5-tubed launchers; range 1,200 m; warhead 34 kg.
Radars: Surface search: Pot Head (Model 351); I-band.
Navigation: Don 2; I-band.
IFF: Ski Pole or Dead Duck.
Sonars: Stag Ear; hull-mounted; active.

Comment: Eight transferred by the USSR in early 1960s, with RBU 1200 ASW rocket launchers and depth charges instead of the 85 mm and 37 mm guns. Remainder built in North Korea to modified design. Twelve are fitted out for ASW with sonar and depth charges; the other seven are used as gunboats. The majority are based on the east coast.

SO 1 (USSR colours) *1988* / 0506030

10 SOJU CLASS (FAST ATTACK CRAFT—MISSILE) (PTG)

Displacement, tons: 265 full load
Dimensions, feet (metres): 139.4 × 24.6 × 5.6 *(42.5 × 7.5 × 1.7)*
Main machinery: 3 Type M 503A diesels; 8,025 hp(m) *(5.9 MW)* sustained; 3 shafts
Speed, knots: 34. **Range, n miles:** 600 at 30 kt
Complement: 32 (4 officers)
Missiles: SSM: 4 SS-N-2 Styx; active radar or IR homing to 46 km *(25 n miles)* at 0.9 Mach; warhead 513 kg.
Guns: 4—30 mm/65 (2 twin) AK 230; 500 rds/min to 5 km *(2.7 n miles)*; weight of shell 0.54 kg.
Countermeasures: ESM: China BM/HZ 8610; intercept.
Radars: Surface search: Square Tie; I-band.
Fire Control: Drum Tilt; H/I-band.

Comment: North Korean built and enlarged version of Osa class. First completed in 1981; built at about one per year at Nampo, Najin and Yongampo shipyards, but the programme terminated in 1996. Six based on the east coast and four on the west.

7 TAECHONG I CLASS and 5 TAECHONG II CLASS
(LARGE PATROL CRAFT) (PC)

Displacement, tons: 385 standard; 410 full load (I); 425 full load (II)
Dimensions, feet (metres): 196.3 (I); 199.5 (II) × 23.6 × 6.6 *(59.8; 60.8 × 7.2 × 2)*
Main machinery: 4 Kolomna Type 40-D diesels; 8,800 hp(m) *(6.4 MW)* sustained; 4 shafts
Speed, knots: 25. **Range, n miles:** 2,000 at 12 kt
Complement: 80
Guns: 1—3.9 in *(100 mm)*/56 (Taechong II); 15 rds/min to 16 km *(8.6 n miles)*; weight of shell 13.5 kg or 1—85 mm/52.
2—57 mm/70 (twin); 120 rds/min to 8 km *(4.4 n miles)*; weight of shell 2.8 kg.
4—30 mm/65 (2 twin) (Taechong II). 2—25 mm/60 (twin) (Taechong I).
16 or 4—14.5 mm MGs (4 quad (Taechong II); 2 twin (Taechong I)).
A/S mortars: 2 RBU 1200 5-tubed fixed launchers; range 1,200 m; warhead 34 kg.
Depth charges: 2 racks.
Radars: Surface search: Pot Head (Model 351); I-band.
Fire control: Drum Tilt; H/I-band.
IFF: High Pole A. Square Head.
Sonars: Stag Ear; hull-mounted; active attack; high frequency.

Comment: North Korean class of mid-1970s design, slightly larger than Hainan class. The first seven are Taechong I class. Taechong II built at about one per year at Najin shipyard up to 1995. They are slightly longer, and are heavily armed for units of this size. Based in both fleets.

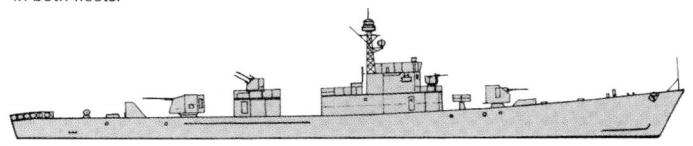

TAECHONG *(not to scale)* / 0506033

TAECHONG II (with *Najin*) *1998* / 0506034

13 SHANGHAI II CLASS (FAST ATTACK CRAFT—GUN) (PBT)

381-388   **391-395**

Displacement, tons: 113 standard; 131 full load
Dimensions, feet (metres): 126.3 × 17.7 × 5.6 *(38.5 × 5.4 × 1.7)*
Main machinery: 2 Type L12-180 diesels; 2,400 hp(m) *(1.76 MW)* (forward)
2 Type 12-D-6 diesels; 1,820 hp(m) *(1.34 MW)* (aft); 4 shafts
Speed, knots: 30. **Range, n miles:** 700 at 16.5 kt
Complement: 34
Guns: 4—37 mm/63 (2 twin); 160 rds/min to 9 km *(4.9 n miles)*; weight of shell 0.7 kg.
4—25 mm/60 (2 twin); 270 rds/min to 3 km *(1.6 n miles)*; weight of shell 0.34 kg.
2—3 in *(76 mm)* recoilless rifles.
Depth charges: 8.
Mines: Rails can be fitted for 10 mines.
Countermeasures: ESM: China BM/HZ 8610; intercept.
Radars: Surface search: Pot Head (Model 351) or Skin Head; I-band.

Comment: Acquired from China since 1967. Based in the west fleet.

SHANGHAI II *1994* / 0080227

6 CHONG-JU CLASS (LARGE PATROL CRAFT) (PC)

Displacement, tons: 205 full load
Dimensions, feet (metres): 138.8 × 23.6 × 6.9 (42.3 × 7.2 × 2.1)
Main machinery: 4 diesels; 4,406 hp(m) (3.24 MW); 4 shafts
Speed, knots: 20. **Range, n miles:** 1,350 at 12 kt
Complement: 48 (7 officers)

Missiles: SSM: 4 CSS-N-1; active radar or IR homing to 46 km (25 n miles) at 0.9 Mach; warhead 513 kg. In three of the class.
Guns: 1—85 mm/52; 18 rds/min to 15 km (8 n miles); weight of shell 9.5 kg.
4—37 mm/63 (2 twin). 4—25 mm/60 (2 twin).
4—14.5 mm/93 (2 twin) MGs.
A/S mortars: 2 RBU 1200; 5-tubed launchers; range 1,200 m; warhead 34 kg.
Radars: Surface search: Pot Head (Model 351); I-band.
Sonars: Stag Ear; hull-mounted; active attack; high frequency.

Comment: Built between 1975 and 1989. At least one has been converted to fire torpedoes and three others have CSS-N-1 missiles and resemble the Soju class. Based in both fleets.

59 CHAHO CLASS (FAST ATTACK CRAFT—GUN) (PTF)

Displacement, tons: 82 full load
Dimensions, feet (metres): 85.3 × 19 × 6.6 (26 × 5.8 × 2)
Main machinery: 4 Type M 50 diesels; 4,400 hp(m) (3.2 MW) sustained; 4 shafts
Speed, knots: 37. **Range, n miles:** 1,300 at 18 kt
Complement: 16 (2 officers)
Guns: 1 BM 21 multiple rocket launcher. 2 USSR 23 mm/87 (twin). 2—14.5 mm (twin) MGs.
Radars: Surface search: Pot Head (Model 351); I-band.

Comment: Building in North Korea since 1974. Based on P 6 hull. Three transferred to Iran in April 1987. Still building and new hulls are replacing the old ones. 35 based in the east and 24 in the west.

CHAHO (Iranian colours)   *4/1998* / 0506035

54 CHONG-JIN CLASS (FAST ATTACK CRAFT—GUN) (PTF/PTK)

Displacement, tons: 80 full load
Dimensions, feet (metres): 85.3 × 19 × 5.9 (26 × 5.8 × 1.8)
Main machinery: 4 Type M 50 diesels; 4,400 hp(m) (3.2 MW) sustained; 4 shafts
Speed, knots: 36. **Range, n miles:** 450 at 30 kt
Complement: 17 (3 officers)
Guns: 1—85 mm/52; 18 rds/min to 15 km (8 n miles); weight of shell 9.5 kg.
4 or 8—14.5 mm (2 or 4 twin) MGs.
Radars: Surface search: Skin Head; I-band.
IFF: High Pole B; Square Head.

Comment: Particulars similar to Chaho class of which this is an improved version. Building began about 1975. About one third reported to be a hydrofoil development. Up to 15 are operated by the Coastal Security Force. Based in both fleets.

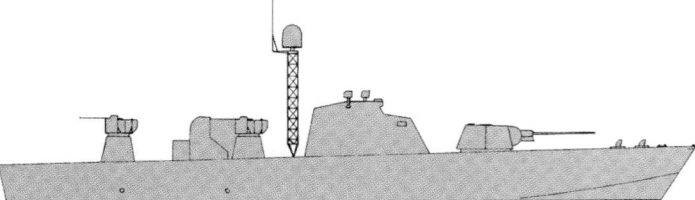

CHONG-JIN   *(not to scale), Ian Sturton* / 0506036

33 SINPO CLASS (FAST ATTACK CRAFT—TORPEDO) (PTF/PTK)

Displacement, tons: 64 standard; 73 full load
Dimensions, feet (metres): 85.3 × 20 × 4.9 (26 × 6.1 × 1.5)
Main machinery: 4 Type M 50 diesels; 4,400 hp(m) (3.2 MW) sustained; 4 shafts
Speed, knots: 45. **Range, n miles:** 450 at 30 kt; 600 at 15 kt
Complement: 15
Guns: 4—25 mm/80 (2 twin) (original). 2—37 mm (others). 6—14.5 mm MGs (Sinpo class).
Torpedoes: 2—21 in (533 mm) tubes (in some). Sinpo class has no tubes.
Depth charges: 8 in some.
Radars: Surface search: Skin Head; I-band (some have Furuno).
IFF: Dead Duck. High Pole.

Comment: Thirteen craft remain of the 27 P 6 class transferred from the USSR and 15 Shantou class transferred from China. Some of the P 6s have hydrofoils and one sank in June 1999. The Sinpo (or Sinnam) class are locally built versions of these craft of which 20 now remain. Based in both fleets.

SINPO   0506038

P 6   0506037

142 KU SONG, SIN HUNG and MOD SIN HUNG CLASSES
(FAST ATTACK CRAFT—TORPEDO) (PTF/PTK)

Displacement, tons: 42 full load
Dimensions, feet (metres): 75.4 × 16.1 × 5.5 (23 × 4.9 × 1.7)
Main machinery: 2 Type M 50 diesels; 2,200 hp(m) (1.6 MW) sustained; 2 shafts
Speed, knots: 40; 50 (Mod Sin Hung)
Range, n miles: 500 at 20 kt
Complement: 20 (3 officers)
Guns: 4—14.5 mm (2 twin) MGs.
Torpedoes: 2—18 in (457 mm) or 2—21 in (533 mm) tubes (not fitted in all).
Radars: Surface search: Skin Head; I-band.
IFF: Dead Duck.

Comment: Ku Song and Sin Hung built in North Korea between mid-1950s and 1970s. Frequently operated on South Korean border. A modified version of Sin Hung with hydrofoils built from 1981-85. Fifty craft, previously thought to have been scrapped, are in various states of repair. Based in both fleets.

SIN HUNG (no torpedo tubes)   *1991* / 0506039

HIGH-SPEED AND SEMI-SUBMERSIBLE INFILTRATION CRAFT
(HSIC/PBF)

Displacement, tons: 5 full load
Dimensions, feet (metres): 30.5 × 8.2 × 3.1 (9.3 × 2.5 × 1)
Main machinery: 1 diesel; 260 hp(m) (191 kW); 1 shaft
Speed, knots: 35
Complement: 2
Guns: 1—7.62 mm MG.
Radars: Navigation: Furuno 701; I-band.

Comment: Up to a hundred built for Agent infiltration and covert operations. These craft have a very low radar cross-section and 'squat' at high speeds. High rate of attrition. A newer version was reported in 1998. This is 12.8 m in length and has a top speed of about 45 kt. It is reported to travel on the surface until submerging to a depth of 3 m using a snort mast. It has a dived speed of 4 kt.

HSIC   *1991, J Bermudez* / 0506041

15 TB 11PA AND 10 TB 40A CLASSES
(INSHORE PATROL CRAFT) (PBF)

Displacement, tons: 8 full load
Dimensions, feet (metres): 36.7 × 8.6 × 3.3 (11.2 × 2.7 × 1)
Main machinery: 2 diesels; 520 hp(m) (382 kW); 2 shafts
Speed, knots: 35
Range, n miles: 200 at 15 kt
Complement: 4
Guns: 1—7.62 mm MG.
Radars: Surface search: Furuno; I-band.

Comment: High-speed patrol boats. Reinforced fibreglass hull. Design closely resembles a number of UK/Western European commercial craft. Larger hull design, known as 'TB 40A' also built. Both classes being operated by the Coastal Security Force.

MODIFIED FISHING VESSELS
(COASTAL PATROL CRAFT) (PB/AGI)

Comment: Approximately 15 fishing vessels have been converted for naval use. Some act as patrol craft, others as AGIs. The vessel sunk by the Japanese Coast Guard on 22 December 2001 carried a 14.5 mm machine-gun, two anti-air missile launchers and numerous small arms. The stern was fitted with outward opening doors.

MFV 801   *7/1991, G Jacobs* / 0506040

Fishing Vessel (being salvaged)   *9/2002, P A News* / 0522267

AMPHIBIOUS FORCES

10 HANTAE CLASS (LSM)

Displacement, tons: 350 full load
Dimensions, feet (metres): 157.5 × 21.3 × 6.6 *(48 × 6.5 × 2)*
Main machinery: 2 diesels; 4,352 hp(m) *(3.2 MW)*; 2 shafts
Speed, knots: 18
Range, n miles: 2,000 at 12 kt
Complement: 36 (4 officers)
Military lift: 350 troops plus 3 MBTs
Guns: 8 — 25 mm/80 (4 twin).

Comment: Built in the early 1980s. Most are based on the east coast.

136 KONGBANG CLASS (HOVERCRAFT) (LCPA)

Comment: Three types: one Type I, 57 Type II and 78 are Type III. Length 25 m (I), 21 m (II) and 18 m (III). A series of high-speed air cushion landing craft first reported in 1987 and building continued until 1996 and then stopped. Use of air cushion technology is an adoption of commercial technology based on the SRN-6. Kongbang II has twin propellers and can carry up to 50 commandos at 50 kt. Kongbang III has a single propeller and can take about 40 troops at 40 kt. All are radar fitted. Some have Styx SSM missiles. Older craft are being replaced continuously in a high priority programme. Divided between both fleets.

96 NAMPO CLASS (LLP)

Displacement, tons: 75 full load
Dimensions, feet (metres): 85.3 × 19 × 5.6 *(26 × 5.8 × 1.7)*
Main machinery: 4 Type M 50 diesels; 4,400 hp(m) *(3.2 MW)* sustained; 4 shafts
Speed, knots: 36
Range, n miles: 450 at 30 kt
Complement: 19
Military lift: 35 troops
Guns: 4 — 14.5 mm (2 twin) MGs.
Radars: Surface search: Skin Head; I-band.

Comment: A class of assault landing craft. Similar to the Chong-Jin class but with a smaller forward gun mounting and with retractable ramp in bows. Building began about 1975. Several have been deleted due to damage. There are 18 of the original class and 73 of a modified version which have a covered-in deck. Most have bow doors welded shut. Four sold to Madagascar in 1979 but now deleted. The Nampo D is the latest version with a multihull design. The first of these entered service in 1997 and four further craft have followed. Based in both fleets.

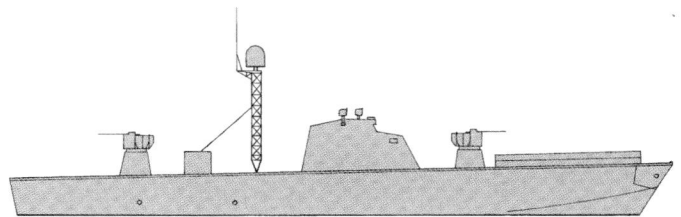

NAMPO   *(not to scale), Ian Sturton* / 0506042

7 HANCHON CLASS (LCM) and 18 HUNGNAM CLASS (LCM)

Displacement, tons: 145 full load
Dimensions, feet (metres): 117.1 × 25.9 × 3.9 *(35.7 × 7.9 × 1.2)*
Main machinery: 2 Type 3-D-12 diesels; 600 hp(m) *(443 kW)* sustained; 2 shafts
Speed, knots: 10
Range, n miles: 600 at 6 kt
Complement: 15 (1 officer)
Military lift: 2 tanks or 300 troops
Guns: 2 — 14.5 mm/93 (twin) MG.
Radars: Surface search: Skin Head; I-band.

Comment: Details given for the Hanchons, built in the 1980s. The Hungnams are older and half the size. Based in both fleets.

MINE WARFARE FORCES

19 YUKTO I CLASS and 5 YUKTO II CLASS
(COASTAL MINESWEEPERS) (MSC)

Displacement, tons: 60 full load (I); 52 full load (II)
Dimensions, feet (metres): 78.7 × 13.1 × 5.6 *(24 × 4 × 1.7)* (Yukto I)
68.9 × 13.1 × 5.6 *(21 × 4 × 1.7)* (Yukto II)
Main machinery: 2 diesels; 2 shafts
Speed, knots: 18
Complement: 22 (4 officers)
Guns: 1 — 37 mm/63 or 2 — 25 mm/80 (twin). 2 — 14.5 mm/93 (twin) MGs.
Mines: 2 rails for 4.
Radars: Surface search: Skin Head; I-band.

Comment: North Korean design built in the 1980s and replaced the obsolete ex-Soviet KN-14 class. Yukto IIs are 3 m shorter overall and have no after gun. Wooden construction. One completed mid-1996 but this may have been of a new design. Based in both fleets.

SURVEY SHIPS

Notes: The Hydrographic Department has four survey ships but also uses a number of converted fishing vessels.

AUXILIARIES

Notes: (1) Trawlers operate as AGIs on the South Korean border where several have been sunk over the years. In addition many ocean-going commercial vessels are used for carrying weapons and ammunition worldwide in support of international terrorism.
(2) There are also eight ocean cargo ships adapted as mother ships for midget submarines. Their names are *Soo Gun-Ho, Dong Geon Ae Gook-Ho, Dong Hae-Ho, Choong Seong-Ho Number One, Choong Seong-Ho Number Two, Choong Seong-Ho Number Three, Hae Gum Gang-Ho* and the *Song Rim-Ho.*

1 KOWAN CLASS (ASR)

Displacement, tons: 2,010 full load
Dimensions, feet (metres): 275.6 × 46.9 × 12.8 *(84 × 14.3 × 3.9)*
Main machinery: 4 diesels; 8,160 hp(m) *(6 MW)*; 2 shafts
Speed, knots: 16
Complement: 150
Guns: 12 — 14.5 mm (6 twin) MGs.
Radars: Navigation: Furuno; I-band.

Comment: Used as a submarine rescue ship. Probable catamaran construction.

Korea, South
REPUBLIC

Country Overview

The Republic of Korea was proclaimed in 1948 and occupies the southern part of the Korean peninsula. Located in northeastern Asia and with an area of 38,375 square miles, it is bordered to the north by North Korea. It has a 1,300 n miles coastline with the Sea of Japan, the Yellow Sea and the Korea Strait, which separates it from Japan. There are numerous offshore islands in the south and west, the largest of which is Cheju. A source of tension at sea is the dispute concerning the status of the *Northern Limit Line* and a number of South Korean islands off the southwest coast of DPRK. The capital and largest city is Seoul. The principal port is Pusan while others include Inchon, the major port on the Yellow Sea, Mokp'o and Kunsan. Territorial seas (12 n miles) are claimed. A 200 n mile EEZ has also been claimed but the limits have not been defined.

Headquarters Appointments

Chief of Naval Operations:
  Admiral Mun Jung Il
Commandant Marine Corps:
  Lieutenant General Kim In Sik
Vice Chief of Naval Operations:
  Vice Admiral Choi Ki Chul
Chief of Maritime Police:
  Commissioner General Lee Seng Jae

Operational Commands

Commander-in-Chief Fleet:
  Vice Admiral Kim, Sung Man
Commander First Fleet:
  Rear Admiral Ahn, Kee Suk
Commander Second Fleet:
  Rear Admiral Sur, Yang Won
Commander Third Fleet:
  Rear Admiral Park, In Young

Diplomatic Representation

Defence Attaché in London:
  Captain K Y Lee

Personnel

(a) 2006: Regulars: 33,000 (Navy) and 24,000 (Marines)
     Conscripts: 17,000 (Navy and Marines)
(b) 2¼ years' national service for conscripts
(c) Reserves: 9,000

Bases

Major: Chinhae (Fleet HQ and 3rd Fleet), Donghae (1st Fleet), Pyongtaek (2nd Fleet)
Minor: Cheju, Mokpo, Mukho, Pohang, Pusan
Aviation: Pohang (MPA base), Chinhae, Cheju
Marines: Pohang, Kimpo, Pengyongdo

A new base, to replace Chinhae as HQ of 3rd Fleet is to be constructed at Nansu, south of Pusan.

Organisation

In 1986 the Navy was reorganised into three Fleets, each commanded by a Rear Admiral, whereas the Marines retained two Divisions and one brigade plus smaller and support units. From October 1973 the RoK Marine Force was placed directly under the RoK Navy command with a Vice Chief of Naval Operations for Marine Affairs replacing the Commandant of Marine Corps. The Marine Corps was re-established as an independent service on 1 November 1987.

1st Fleet: No 11, 12, 13 DD/FF Sqn; No 101, 102 Coastal Defence Sqn; 181, 191, 111, 121 Coastal Defence Units; 121st Minesweeper Sqn.

2nd Fleet: No 21, 22, 23 DD/FF Sqn; No 201, 202 Coastal Defence Sqn; 211, 212 Coastal Defence Units; 522nd Minesweeper Sqn.
3rd Fleet: 301, 302, 303 DD/FF Sqn; 304, 406th Coastal Defence Units.

Coast Defence

Three batteries of Marines with truck-mounted quadruple Harpoon SSM launchers.

Pennant Numbers

Numbers ending in 4 are not used as they are unlucky.

Strength of the Fleet

Type	Active (Reserve)	Building (Proposed)
Submarines (Patrol)	9	3 (6)
Submarines (Midget)	11	—
Destroyers	7	5
Frigates	9	—
Corvettes	28	—
Fast Attack Craft—Missile	5	40
Fast Attack Craft—Patrol	83	—
Minehunters	—	(2)
Minesweepers	3	—
Minelayers	1	—
LPD	—	1
LSTs	8	—
LSMs	—	—
LCU/LCM/LCF	20	—
Logistic Support Ships	3	—

PENNANT LIST

Submarines

061	Chang Bogo
062	Yi Chon
063	Choi Muson
065	Park Wi
066	Lee Jongmu
067	Jung Woon
068	Lee Sunsin
069	Na Daeyong
071	Lee Eokgi

Destroyers

971	Kwanggaeto Daewang
972	Euljimundok
973	Yangmanchun
975	Chungmugong Yi Sun-Shin
976	Moonmu Daewang (bldg)
977	Daejoyoung (bldg)

978	Wang Geon (bldg)
979	Gang Gam Chan (bldg)

Frigates

951	Ulsan
952	Seoul
953	Chung Nam
955	Masan
956	Kyong Buk
957	Chon Nam
958	Che Ju
959	Pusan
961	Chung Ju

Corvettes

751	Dong Hae
752	Su Won
753	Kang Reung
755	An Yang

756	Po Hang
757	Kun San
758	Kyong Ju
759	Mok Po
761	Kim Chon
762	Chung Ju
763	Jin Ju
765	Yo Su
766	Jin Hae
767	Sun Chon
768	Yee Ree
769	Won Ju
771	An Dong
772	Chon An
773	Song Nam
775	Bu Chon
776	Jae Chon
777	Dae Chon
778	Sok Cho
779	Yong Ju
781	Nam Won

782	Kwan Myong
783	Sin Hung
785	Kong Ju

Mine Warfare Forces

560	Won San
561	Kang Kyeong
562	Kang Jin
563	Ko Ryeong
565	Kim Po
566	Ko Chang
567	Kum Wha
571	Yang Yang
572	Ongjin

Amphibious Forces

671	Un Bong
676	Wee Bong

677	Su Yong
678	Buk Han
681	Kojoon Bong
682	Biro Bong
683	Hyangro Bong
685	Seongin Bong

Auxiliaries

21	Cheong Hae Jin
27	Pyong Taek
28	Kwang Yang
57	Chun Jee
58	Dae Chung
59	Hwa Chun
AGS 11	Sunjin

SUBMARINES

Notes: (1) Plans to acquire three Russian Kilo (Project 636) class have been abandoned. (2) The Type 214 programme may be followed by a larger 3,500 ton submarine class of South Korean design. It is planned to develop these submarines (KSS 3 programme) between 2010 and 2022.
(3) Reports of a nuclear submarine programme (SSX) have been officially denied.

0 + 3 (6) KSS-2 (TYPE 214) CLASS (SSK)

Name	No	Builders	Laid down	Launched	Commissioned
—	—	Hyundai, Ulsan	2003	2005	2007
—	—	Hyundai, Ulsan	2004	2006	2008
—	—	Hyundai, Ulsan	2005	2007	2009

Displacement, tons: 1,700 surfaced; 1,860 dived
Dimensions, feet (metres): 213.3 × 20.7 × 19.7 *(65 × 6.3 × 6)*
Main machinery: 1 MTU 16V 396 diesel; 4,243 hp *(3.12 MW)*; 1 Siemens Permasyn motor; 3,875 hp(m) *(2.85 MW)*; 1 shaft; 9 Siemens/HDW PEM fuel cell (AIP) modules; 306 kW; sodium sulphide high-energy batteries
Speed, knots: 20 dived; 12 surfaced
Complement: 27 (5 officers)
Torpedoes: 8—21 in *(533 mm)* bow tubes.
Countermeasures: Decoys: ESM.
Weapons control: STN Atlas.
Radars: Surface search: I-band.
Sonars: Bow, flank and towed arrays.

Programmes: Decision taken in November 2000 to order three HDW designed Air Independent Propulsion (AIP) submarines. The boats are being built by Hyundai Heavy Industries with the German Submarine Corporation, led by HDW, providing construction plans, materials and other equipment. First steel cut for the first of class in November 2002. Following announcements on 4 January 2006, it is planned to build a further six submarines to raise the overall force level to 18. Construction is expected to start in 2012.
Structure: The Type 214 is a synthesis of the proven Type 209 design with AIP from the Type 212. South Korea is the second customer for the Type 214 after Greece. Details given are mainly for the Type 214 as advertised by HDW but changes may have been made. Diving depth 400 m.

TYPE 214   9/2002, *Michael Nitz* / 0529079

2 KSS-1 DOLGORAE CLASS and 9 DOLPHIN (COSMOS) CLASS (MIDGET SUBMARINES)

052-053 (Dolgorae)

Displacement, tons: 150 surfaced; 175 dived (Dolgorae);
70 surfaced; 83 dived (Cosmos)
Dimensions, feet (metres): 82 × 6.9 *(25 × 2.1)* (Cosmos)
Main machinery: Diesel-electric; 1 diesel generator;
1 motor; 1 shaft
Speed, knots: 9 surfaced; 6 dived
Complement: 6 + 8 swimmers
Torpedoes: 2—406 mm tubes (Dolgorae). 2—533 mm tubes
(Cosmos).
Sonars: Atlas Elektronik; hull-mounted; passive search;
high frequency.

Comment: Dolgorae class started entering service in 1983.
Cosmos type used by Marines. Limited endurance, for use
only in coastal waters. Fitted with Pilkington Optronics
periscopes (CK 37 in Dolgorae and CK 41 in Cosmos).
Numbers of each type confirmed but the Dolgorae class
are being replaced by more Cosmos. All are based at
Cheju Island.

DOLGORAE *11/1985, G Jacobs* / 0506044

9 CHANG BOGO (TYPE 209) CLASS (1200) (SSK)

Name	No	Builders	Laid down	Launched	Commissioned
CHANG BOGO	061	HDW, Kiel	1989	18 June 1992	2 June 1993
YI CHON	062	Daewoo, Okpo	1990	14 Oct 1992	30 Apr 1994
CHOI MUSON	063	Daewoo, Okpo	1991	25 Aug 1993	27 Feb 1995
PARK WI	065	Daewoo, Okpo	1992	20 May 1994	3 Feb 1996
LEE JONGMU	066	Daewoo, Okpo	1993	17 Apr 1995	29 Aug 1996
JUNG WOON	067	Daewoo, Okpo	1994	7 May 1996	29 Aug 1997
LEE SUNSIN	068	Daewoo, Okpo	1995	21 May 1998	15 June 1999
NA DAEYONG	069	Daewoo, Okpo	1996	15 June 1999	Nov 2000
LEE EOKGI	071	Daewoo, Okpo	1997	26 May 2000	30 Nov 2001

Displacement, tons: 1,100 surfaced; 1,285 dived
Dimensions, feet (metres): 185.0 × 20.3 × 18
(56.4 × 6.2 × 5.5)
Main machinery: Diesel-electric; 4 MTU 12V 396 SE diesels;
3,800 hp(m) *(2.8 MW)* sustained; 4 alternators; 1 motor;
4,600 hp(m) *(3.38 MW)* sustained; 1 shaft
Speed, knots: 11 surfaced/snorting; 22 dived
Range, n miles: 7,500 at 8 kt surfaced
Complement: 33 (6 officers)

Missiles: SSM: McDonnell Douglas UGM-84B Sub Harpoon;
active radar homing to 130 km *(70 n miles)* at 0.9 Mach;
warhead 227 kg (fitted to at least three boats).
Torpedoes: 8—21 in *(533 mm)* bow tubes. 14 SystemTechnik
Nord (STN) SUT Mod 2; wire-guided; active/passive
homing to 12 km *(6.6 n miles)* at 35 kt or 28 km
(15.1 n miles) at 23 kt; warhead 260 kg. Swim-out discharge.
Mines: 28 in lieu of torpedoes.
Countermeasures: ESM: Argo; radar warning.
Weapons control: Atlas Elektronik ISUS 83 TFCS.
Radars: Navigation: I-band.
Sonars: Atlas Elektronik CSU 83; hull-mounted; passive
search and attack; medium frequency.

Programmes: First three ordered in late 1987, one built at
Kiel by HDW, and two assembled at Okpo by Daewoo
from material packages transported from Germany.
Second three ordered in October 1989 and a further batch
of three in January 1994.
Modernisation: Mid-life upgrade of all nine boats is under
consideration. It is envisaged that AIP propulsion and Sub-
Harpoon SSM may be fitted in stretched hulls and that the
refit programme will be conducted between 2005-10.

NA DAEYONG *6/2002, Ships of the World* / 0529129

Structure: Type 1200 similar to those built for the Turkish
Navy with a heavy dependence on Atlas Elektronik
sensors and STN torpedoes. Diving depth 250 m *(820 ft)*.
A passive towed array may be fitted in due course.

Operational: An indigenous torpedo based on the Honeywell
NP 37 may be available in due course. The class is split
between the three Fleets. Operations conducted off Hawaii
from 1997 to improve operating standards.

CHANG BOGO *7/2004, Michael Nitz* / 1042341

CHANG BOGO *7/2004, Michael Nitz* / 1042342

DESTROYERS

3 + 3 KDX-2 CLASS (DDGHM)

Name	No	Builders	Laid down	Launched	Commissioned
CHUNGMUGONG YI SUN-SHIN	975	Daewoo, Okpo	2001	20 May 2002	Nov 2003
MOONMU DAEWANG	976	Hyundai, Ulsan	2002	11 Apr 2003	30 Sep 2004
DAEJOYOUNG	977	Daewoo, Okpo	2002	12 Nov 2003	June 2005
WANG GEON	978	Hyundai, Ulsan	2003	3 May 2005	2006
GANG GAM CHAN	979	Daewoo, Okpo	2004	16 Mar 2006	2007
CHAE YEON	980	Hyundai, Ulsan	2005	2007	2008

Displacement, tons: 4,800 full load
Dimensions, feet (metres): 506.6 × 55.5 × 14.1
(154.4 × 16.9 × 4.3)
Main machinery: CODOG; 2 GE LM 2500 gas turbines;
58,200 hp *(43.42 MW)* sustained; 2 MTU 20V 956 TB92
diesels; 8,000 hp(m) *(5.88 MW)*; 2 shafts
Speed, knots: 29. **Range, n miles:** 4,000 at 18 kt
Complement: 200 (18 officers)

Missiles: SSM: 8 Harpoon (Block 1C) (2 quad) ❶; active
radar homing to 130 km *(70 n miles)* at 0.9 Mach;
warhead 227 kg
SAM: Mk 41 Mod 2 VLS ❷ 32 cells for GDC Standard
SM-2MR (Block IIIA); command/inertial guidance; semi-
active radar homing to 167 km *(90 n miles)* at 2 Mach.
1 Raytheon RAM Mk 31 systems ❸; 21 rounds per
launcher; passive IR/anti-radiation homing to 9.6 km
(5.2 n miles) at 2 Mach; warhead 9.1 kg.
A/S: ASROCVLS; inertial guidance 1.6—10 km *(1—5.4 n miles)*
at 0.9 Mach; payload Mk 48.
Guns: 1 United Defense 5 in *(127 mm)*/62 Mk 45 Mod 4 ❹;
20 rds/min to 23 km *(12.6 n miles)*; weight of shell 32 kg.
1 Signaal Goalkeeper 30 mm ❺; 7 barrels per mounting;
4,200 rds/min to 1.5 km.
Torpedoes: 6—324 mm Mk 32 (2 triple) tubes ❻; Alliant
techsystems Mk 46 Mod 5; anti-submarine; active/passive
homing to 11 km *(5.9 n miles)* at 40 kt; warhead 44 kg.
Countermeasures: 4 chaff launchers. ESM/ECM.
Combat data systems: BAeSema/Samsung KD COM-2;
Link 11.
Weapons control: Marconi Mk 14 weapons direction system.
Radars: Air search: Raytheon SPS-49(V)5 ❼; C/D-band.
Surface search: Signaal MW08 ❽; G-band.
Navigation: I-band ❾.
Fire control: 2 Signaal STIR 240 ❿; I/J/K-band.
Sonars: DSQS-23; hull-mounted; active search; medium
frequency. Daewoo Telecom towed array; passive low
frequency.

Helicopters: 1 Westland Super Lynx Mk 99 ⓫.

Programmes: Approval for first three given in late 1996
but the final decision was not taken until 1998. Contract
to design and build the first of class won by Daewoo
in November 1999. The first of a second batch of three
was launched at Hyundai in May 2005 and of the second

at Daewoo in March 2006. Work on the sixth ship is
underway at Hyundai.
Operational: Successful SM-2 firings conducted on
the Pacific Missile Range Facility, off Hawaii, in
mid-2004.

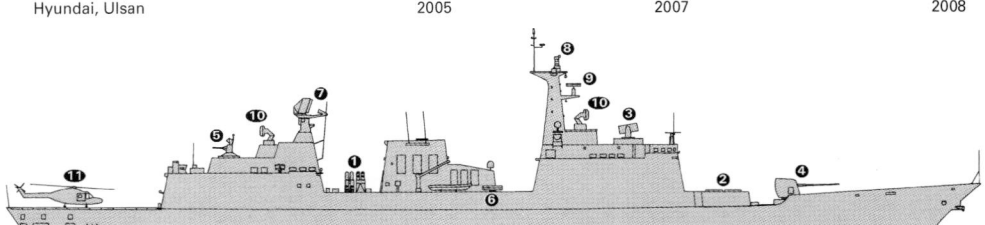

CHUNGMUGONG YI SUN-SHIN   *(Scale 1 : 1,200), Ian Sturton* / 1153009

CHUNGMUGONG YI SUN-SHIN   *7/2005*, Michael Nitz* / 1153440

MOONMU DAEWANG   *8/2005*, Hachiro Nakai* / 1153429

CHUNGMUGONG YI SUN-SHIN   *6/2005*, E & M Laursen* / 1153431

3 KWANGGAETO DAEWANG (KDX-1) CLASS (DDGHM)

Name	No	Builders	Laid down	Launched	Commissioned
KWANGGAETO DAEWANG	971	Daewoo, Okpo	June 1995	28 Oct 1996	24 July 1998
EULJIMUNDOK	972	Daewoo, Okpo	Jan 1996	16 Oct 1997	20 June 1999
YANGMANCHUN	973	Daewoo, Okpo	Aug 1997	19 Oct 1998	29 June 2000

Displacement, tons: 3,855 full load
Dimensions, feet (metres): 444.2 × 46.6 × 13.8
(135.4 × 14.2 × 4.2)
Main machinery: CODOG; 2 GE LM 2500 gas turbines;
58,200 hp *(43.42 MW)* sustained; 2 MTU 20V 956 TB92
diesels; 8,000 hp(m) *(5.88 MW)*; 2 shafts
Speed, knots: 30. **Range, n miles:** 4,000 at 18 kt
Complement: 170 (15 officers)

Missiles: SSM: 8 McDonnell Douglas Harpoon Block 1C
(2 quad) launchers ❶; active radar homing to 130 km
(70 n miles) at 0.9 Mach; warhead 227 kg.
SAM: Raytheon Sea Sparrow; Mk 48 Mod 2 VLS launcher ❷
for 16 cells RIM-7P; semi-active radar homing to 14.6 km
(8 n miles) at 2.5 Mach; warhead 39 kg.
Guns: 1 Otobreda 5 in *(127 mm)*/54 ❸; 45 rds/min to 23 km
(12.4 n miles); weight of shell 32 kg.
2 Signaal 30 mm Goalkeeper ❹; 7 barrels per mounting;
4,200 rds/min combined to 2 km.
Torpedoes: 6—324 mm (2 triple) Mk 32 tubes ❺; Alliant
Techsystems Mk 46 Mod 5; anti-submarine; active/
passive homing to 11 km *(5.9 n miles)* at 40 kt; warhead
44 kg.
Countermeasures: Decoys: 4 CSEE Dagaie Mk 2 chaff
launchers ❻. SLQ-25 Nixie towed torpedo decoy.
ESM/ECM: Argo AR 700/APECS II ❼; intercept and jammer.
Combat data systems: BAeSEMA/Samsung SSCS Mk 7;
Litton NTDS (Link 11). SATCOM ❽.
Radars: Air search: Raytheon SPS-49V5 ❾; C/D-band.
Surface search: Signaal MW08 ❿; G-band.
Fire control: 2 Signaal STIR 180 ⓫; I/J/K-band.
Navigation: Daewoo DTR 92 (SPS 55M) ⓬; I-band.
IFF: UPX-27.
Sonars: Atlas Elektronik DSQS-21BZ; hull-mounted active
search; medium frequency.
Daewoo Telecom towed array; passive low frequency.
Helicopters: 1 Westland Super Lynx ⓭.

Programmes: Project KDX-1. A much delayed programme.
The first keel was to have been laid down at Daewoo in

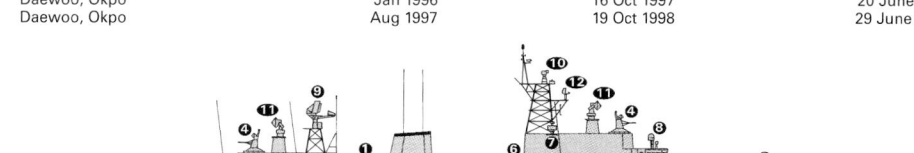

KWANGGAETO DAEWANG *(Scale 1 : 1,200), Ian Sturton* / 0572485

EULJIMUNDOK *7/2004, Michael Nitz* / 1042337

late 1992 for completion in 1996, but definition studies
extended to late 1993, when contracts started to be
signed for the weapon systems. First steel cut at Daewoo
Okpo in April 1994.
Structure: Emphasis is on air defence but the design
has taken so long to reach fulfilment that it has been

overtaken by the KDX-2. McTaggart Scott Trigon 5 helo
handling system.
Operational: The Goalkeepers are also to be used against
close-in surface threats using FAPDS (Frangible Armour
Penetrating Discarding Sabot).

YANGMANCHUN *8/2005*, Hachiro Nakai* / 1153430

YANGMANCHUN *12/2003, Bob Fildes* / 1042335

For details of the latest updates to ***Jane's Fighting Ships*** online and to discover the additional
information available exclusively to online subscribers please visit
jfs.janes.com

0 + 3 KDX-3 CLASS (DDGHM)

Name	No	Builders	Laid down	Launched	Commissioned
SOHN WON-IL	—	Hyundai, Ulsan	12 Nov 2004	2007	2009
—	—	Hyundai, Ulsan	2007	2008	2010
—	—	Hyundai, Ulsan	2009	2010	2012

Displacement, tons: 10,000 standard
Dimensions, feet (metres): 544.3 × 68.9 × ? *(165.9 × 21.0 × ?)*
Main machinery: COGAG; 4 GE LM 2500 gas turbines; 2 shafts
Speed, knots: 30

Missiles: SSM: 8 Harpoon.
SAM: GDC Standard SM-2MR Block IV. 2 Lockheed Martin Mk 41 VLS for Standard and ESSM. 2 magazines; 32 missile tubes forward, 64 aft. 1 RAM system.
Guns: 1—5 in *(127 mm)*.
1 Goalkeeper system.
Torpedoes: To be announced.
Combat data system: Aegis variant.
Weapons control: To be announced.
Radars: Air search: RCA SPY 1D; 3D; F-band.
Air/Surface search: To be announced.
Fire control: Raytheon SPG-62; I/J-band.
Navigation: To be announced.
Sonars: To be announced.

Helicopters: To be announced.

Programmes: A further development of the KDX-2 destroyers but optimised for anti-air warfare. Lockheed

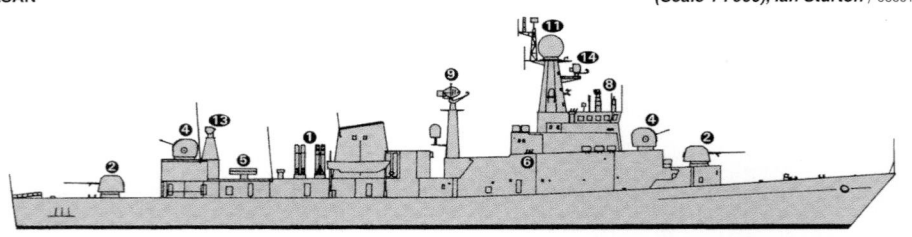

KDX-3   *(not to scale), Ian Sturton* / 0569924

Martin selected on 24 July 2002 to supply the combat data system and multifunction radar. Details are speculative.

FRIGATES

9 ULSAN CLASS (FFG)

Name	No	Builders	Laid down	Launched	Commissioned
ULSAN	951	Hyundai, Ulsan	1979	8 Apr 1980	1 Jan 1981
SEOUL	952	Hyundai, Ulsan	1982	24 Apr 1984	30 June 1985
CHUNG NAM	953	Korean SEC, Pusan	1984	26 Oct 1984	1 June 1986
MASAN	955	Korea Tacoma	1983	26 Oct 1984	20 July 1985
KYONG BUK	956	Daewoo, Okpo	1984	15 Jan 1986	30 May 1986
CHON NAM	957	Hyundai, Ulsan	1986	19 Apr 1988	17 June 1989
CHE JU	958	Daewoo, Okpo	1986	3 May 1988	1 Jan 1990
PUSAN	959	Hyundai, Ulsan	1990	20 Feb 1992	1 Jan 1993
CHUNG JU	961	Daewoo, Okpo	1990	20 Mar 1992	1 June 1993

Displacement, tons: 1,496 light; 2,180 full load (2,300 for FF 957—961)
Dimensions, feet (metres): 334.6 × 37.7 × 11.5 *(102 × 11.5 × 3.5)*
Main machinery: CODOG; 2 GE LM 2500 gas turbines; 53,640 hp *(40 MW)* sustained; 2 MTU 16V 538 TB82 diesels; 5,940 hp(m) *(4.37 MW)* sustained; 2 shafts; cp props
Speed, knots: 34; 18 on diesels. **Range, n miles:** 4,000 at 15 kt
Complement: 150 (16 officers)

Missiles: SSM: 8 McDonnell Douglas Harpoon (4 twin) launchers ❶; active radar homing to 130 km *(70 n miles)* at 0.9 Mach; warhead 227 kg.
Guns: 2—3 in *(76 mm)*/62 OTO Melara compact ❷; 85 rds/min to 16 km *(8.6 n miles)* anti-surface; 12 km *(6.5 n miles)* anti-aircraft; weight of shell 6 kg.
8 Emerson Electric 30 mm (4 twin) (FF 951—955) ❸; 6 Breda 40 mm/70 (3 twin) (FF 956—961) ❹.
Torpedoes: 6—324 mm Mk 32 (2 triple) tubes ❺. Honeywell Mk 46 Mod 1; anti-submarine; active/passive homing to 11 km *(5.9 n miles)* at 40 kt; warhead 44 kg.
Depth charges: 12.
Countermeasures: Decoys: 4 Loral Hycor SRBOC 6-barrelled Mk 36 launchers ❻; range 4 km *(2.2 n miles)*.
SLQ-25 Nixie; towed torpedo decoy.
ESM: ULQ-11K; intercept.
Combat data systems: Samsung/Ferranti WSA 423 action data automation (FF 957—961). Litton systems retrofitted to others. Link 11 in three of the class. WSC-3 SATCOM (F 957).
Weapons control: 1 Signaal Liod optronic director (FF 951—956) ❼; 1 Radamec System 2400 optronic director (FF 957—961) ❽.
Radars: Air/surface search: Signaal DA05 ❾; E/F-band.
Surface search: Signaal ZW06 (FF 951—956) ❿; Marconi S 1810 (FF 957—961) ⓫; I-band.
Fire control: Signaal WM28 (FF 951—956) ⓬; Marconi ST 1802 (FF 957—961) ⓭; I/J-band.
Navigation: Raytheon SPS-10C (FF 957—961) ⓮; I-band.
Tacan: SRN 15.

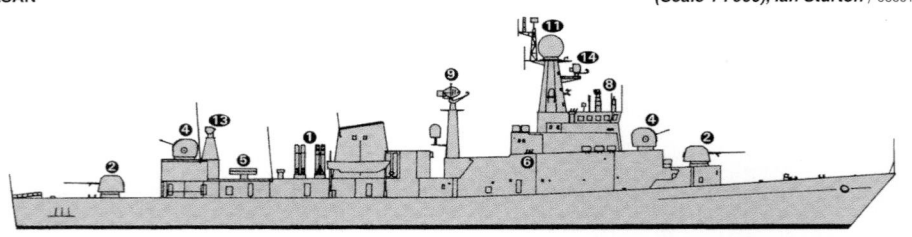

ULSAN   *(Scale 1 : 900), Ian Sturton* / 0506154

CHE JU   *(Scale 1 : 900), Ian Sturton* / 0506155

Sonars: Raytheon DE 1167; hull-mounted; active search and attack; medium frequency.

Modernisation: New sonars fitted. WSC-3 SATCOM fitted in *Chon Nam*.
Structure: Steel hull with aluminium alloy superstructure. There are three versions. The first five ships are the same but *Kyong Buk* has the four Emerson Electric twin 30 mm guns replaced by three Breda twin 40 mm, and the last four of the class have a built-up gun platform aft and a different combination of surface

search, target indication and navigation radars. Weapon systems integration caused earlier concern and a Ferranti combat data system has been installed in the last five; Litton Systems Link 11 fitted in three of the class.
Operational: *Che Ju* and *Chung Nam* conducted the first ever deployment of South Korean warships to Europe during a four month tour from September 1991 to January 1992. Trainees were embarked. Three of the class have a shore datalink and act as local area commanders to control attack craft carrying out coastal protection patrols.

CHE JU   *10/2002, Guy Toremans* / 0528915

CHUNG JU   *2/2001, Ships of the World* / 0130106

CHUNG NAM   *9/2002, Hachiro Nakai* / 0529073

ULSAN   *8/2000, van Ginderen Collection* / 0104996

CHON NAM   *7/2000, Sattler/Steele* / 0104995

CORVETTES

24 PO HANG CLASS (FS/FSG)

Name	No	Builders	Commissioned
PO HANG	756	Korea SEC, Pusan	Dec 1984
KUN SAN	757	Korea Tacoma	Dec 1984
KYONG JU	758	Hyundai, Ulsan	Nov 1986
MOK PO	759	Daewoo, Okpo	Aug 1986
KIM CHON	761	Korea SEC, Pusan	May 1985
CHUNG JU	762	Korea Tacoma	May 1985
JIN JU	763	Hyundai, Ulsan	June 1988
YO SU	765	Daewoo, Okpo	Nov 1988
JIN HAE	766	Korea SEC, Pusan	Feb 1989
SUN CHON	767	Korea Tacoma	June 1989
YEE REE	768	Hyundai, Ulsan	June 1989
WON JU	769	Daewoo, Okpo	Aug 1989
AN DONG	771	Korea SEC, Pusan	Nov 1989
CHON AN	772	Korea Tacoma	Nov 1989
SONG NAM	773	Daewoo, Okpo	May 1989
BU CHON	775	Hyundai, Ulsan	Apr 1989
JAE CHON	776	Korea SEC, Pusan	May 1989
DAE CHON	777	Korea Tacoma	Apr 1989
SOK CHO	778	Korea SEC, Pusan	Feb 1990
YONG JU	779	Hyundai, Ulsan	Mar 1990
NAM WON	781	Daewoo, Okpo	Apr 1990
KWAN MYONG	782	Korea Tacoma	July 1990
SIN HUNG	783	Korea SEC, Pusan	Mar 1993
KONG JU	785	Korea Tacoma	July 1993

Displacement, tons: 1,220 full load
Dimensions, feet (metres): 289.7 × 32.8 × 9.5 *(88.3 × 10 × 2.9)*
Main machinery: CODOG; 1 GE LM 2500 gas turbine; 26,820 hp *(20 MW)* sustained; 2 MTU 12V 956TB82 diesels; 6,260 hp(m) *(4.6 MW)* sustained; 2 shafts; Kamewa cp props
Speed, knots: 32. **Range, n miles:** 4,000 at 15 kt (diesel)
Complement: 95 (10 officers)

Missiles: SSM: 2 Aerospatiale MM 38 Exocet (756–759) ❶; inertial cruise; active radar homing to 42 km *(23 n miles)* at 0.9 Mach; warhead 165 kg; sea-skimmer.
  4 McDonnell Douglas Harpoon (2 twin) launchers ❷; active radar homing to 130 km *(70 n miles)* at 0.9 Mach; warhead 227 kg.
Guns: 1 or 2 OTO Melara 3 in *(76 mm)*/62 compact ❸; 85 rds/min to 16 km *(8.6 n miles)* anti-surface; 12 km *(6.5 n miles)* anti-aircraft; weight of shell 6 kg.
  4 Emerson Electric 30 mm (2 twin) (756–759) ❹; 4 Breda 40 mm/70 (2 twin) (761 onwards) ❺.
Torpedoes: 6–324 mm Mk 32 (2 triple) tubes ❻. Honeywell Mk 46; anti-submarine; active/passive homing to 11 km *(5.9 n miles)* at 40 kt; warhead 44 kg.
Depth charges: 12 (761 onwards).
Countermeasures: Decoys: 4 MEL Protean fixed launchers; 36 grenades.
  2 Loral Hycor SRBOC 6-barrelled Mk 36 launchers (in some); range 4 km *(2.2 n miles)*.
  ESM/ECM: THORN EMI or NobelTech; intercept/jammer.
Combat data systems: Signaal Sewaco ZK (756–759); Ferranti WSA 423 (761 onwards).
Weapons control: Signaal Liod or Radamec 2400 (766 onwards) optronic director ❼.
Radars: Surface search: Marconi 1810 ❽ and/or Raytheon SPS-64 ❾; I-band.
  Fire control: Signaal WM28 ❿; I/J-band; or Marconi 1802 ⓫; I/J-band.
Sonars: Signaal PHS-32; hull-mounted; active search and attack; medium frequency.

Programmes: First laid down early 1983. After early confusion, names, pennant numbers and shipbuilders are now correct. The programme terminated in 1993.
Modernisation: Harpoon has been installed in 769 and may also have been fitted to others.
Structure: The first four are Exocet fitted and have a different weapon systems arrangement. The remainder have an improved combat data system with Ferranti/Radamec/Marconi fire-control systems and radars as in the later versions of the Ulsan class.

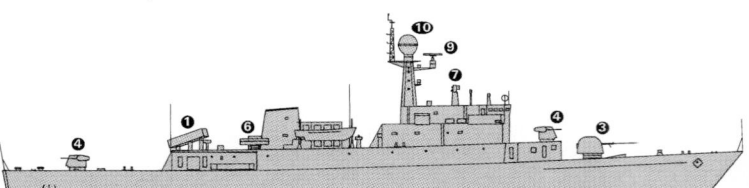

PO HANG   *(Scale 1 : 900), Ian Sturton* / 0572484

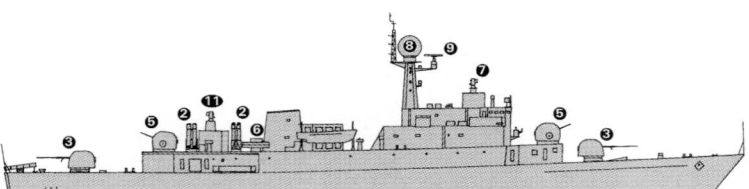

WON JU   *(Scale 1 : 900), Ian Sturton* / 0569920

MOK PO   *10/1998, John Mortimer* / 0052541

4 DONG HAE CLASS (FS)

Name	No	Builders	Commissioned
DONG HAE	751	Korea SEC, Pusan	Aug 1982
SU WON	752	Korea Tacoma	Oct 1983
KANG REUNG	753	Hyundai, Ulsan	Nov 1983
AN YANG	755	Daewoo, Okpo	Dec 1983

Displacement, tons: 1,076 full load
Dimensions, feet (metres): 256.2 × 31.5 × 8.5 *(78.1 × 9.6 × 2.6)*
Main machinery: CODOG; 1 GE LM 2500 gas turbine; 26,820 hp *(20 MW)* sustained; 2 MTU 12V 956TB82 diesels; 6,260 hp(m) *(4.6 MW)* sustained; 2 shafts; Kamewa cp props
Speed, knots: 31. **Range, n miles:** 4,000 at 15 kt (diesel)
Complement: 95 (10 officers)

Guns: 1 OTO Melara 3 in *(76 mm)*/62 compact ❶; 85 rds/min to 16 km *(8.6 n miles)*; weight of shell 6 kg.
  4 Emerson Electric 30 mm (2 twin) ❷. 2 Bofors 40 mm/60 (twin) ❸.
Torpedoes: 6–324 mm Mk 32 (2 triple) tubes ❹. Honeywell Mk 46; anti-submarine; active/passive homing to 11 km *(5.9 n miles)* at 40 kt; warhead 44 kg.
Depth charges: 12.
Countermeasures: Decoys: 4 MEL Protean chaff launchers.
  ESM/ECM: THORN EMI or NobelTech; intercept and jammer.
Combat data systems: Signaal Sewaco ZK.
Weapons control: Signaal Liod optronic director ❺.
Radars: Surface search: Raytheon SPS-64 ❻; I-band.
  Fire control: Signaal WM28 ❼; I/J-band.
Sonars: Signaal PHS-32; hull-mounted; active search and attack; medium frequency.

Programmes: This was the first version of the corvette series, with four being ordered in 1980, one each from the four major warship building yards.
Structure: The design was too small for the variety of different weapons which were intended to be fitted for different types of warfare and was therefore discontinued in favour of the Po Hang class.

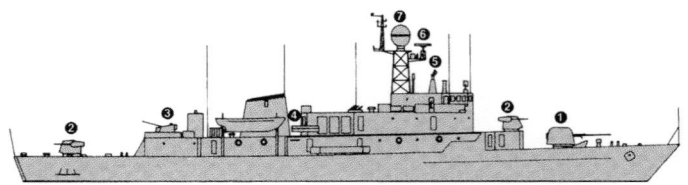

DONG HAE   *(Scale 1 : 900), Ian Sturton* / 0506046

SU WON   *9/2000* / 0104998

WON JU   *7/2002, Chris Sattler* / 0528917

SHIPBORNE AIRCRAFT

Notes: A Request for Proposals for eight mine-hunting helicopters is expected in 2008 with deliveries in 2010-2011.

Numbers/Type: 12/13 Westland Lynx Mk 99/Mk 99A.
Operational speed: 125 kt *(231 km/h)*.
Service ceiling: 12,000 ft *(3,660 m)*.
Range: 320 n miles *(593 km)*.
Role/Weapon systems: 12 Mk 99 helicopters delivered by 1991; 13 Mk 99A ordered in June 1997 and delivered in 1999/2000. Sensors: Ferranti Sea Spray Mk 3 radar and Racal ESM. Bendix AQS 18(V) dipping sonar and ASQ 504(V) MAD in ASW versions. Weapons: 4 BAe Sea Skua missiles. Mk 46 (Mod 5) torpedo (in ASW version). Sea Skua may be replaced in due course.

LYNX MK 99A *1/2001, Mitsuhiro Kadota* / 0130104

Numbers/Type: 5 Aerospatiale SA 316B/SA 319B Alouette III.
Operational speed: 113 kt *(210 km/h)*.
Service ceiling: 10,500 ft *(3,200 m)*.
Range: 290 n miles *(540 km)*.
Role/Weapon systems: Marine support helicopter; operated by RoK Marine Corps. Sensors: None. Weapons: Unarmed.

ALOUETTE III *1990* / 0081162

LAND-BASED MARITIME AIRCRAFT (FRONT LINE)

Notes: (1) F-16 fighters are capable of firing Harpoon ASV missiles.
(2) There are also 10 UH-60 and 10 UH-1 utility helicopters.
(3) Eight Lockheed P-3B Orion are to be reactivated and upgraded. KAI and L-3 Communications selected in December 2004 to undertake the work. The contract is to be completed by 2010.

Numbers/Type: 8 Grumman S-2A/F Tracker.
Operational speed: 130 kt *(241 km/h)*.
Service ceiling: 25,000 ft *(7,620 m)*.
Range: 1,350 n miles *(2,500 km)*.
Role/Weapon systems: Maritime surveillance and limited ASW operations; coastal surveillance and EEZ patrol. Sensors: Search radar, ECM. Weapons: ASW; torpedoes, depth bombs and mines. ASV; underwing 127 mm rockets. HARM missiles may be acquired.

Numbers/Type: 8 Lockheed P-3C Orion Update III.
Operational speed: 411 kt *(761 km/h)*.
Service ceiling: 28,300 ft *(8,625 m)*.
Range: 4,000 n miles *(7,410 km)*.
Role/Weapon systems: Maritime patrol aircraft ordered in December 1990. First pair delivered April 1995, remainder April 1996. Funding constraints have stalled plans for a second squadron of eight aircraft. The Update III version is fitted with ASQ-212 tactical computer. Sensors: APS-134 or 137(V)6 search radar; AAS-36 IR. Weapons: four Harpoon ASM.

Numbers/Type: 5 Rheims-Cessna F 406 Caravan II
Operational speed: 229 kt *(424 km/h)*.
Service ceiling: 30,000 ft *(9,145 m)*.
Range: 1,153 m *(2,135 km)*.
Role/Weapon systems: Maritime surveillance version ordered in 1997 with first one delivered in mid-1999. Sensors: APS 134 radar; Litton FLIR. Weapons: none.

F 406 (Australian colours) *6/1997, Reims Aviation* / 0507595

PATROL FORCES

83 SEA DOLPHIN/WILDCAT CLASS
(FAST ATTACK CRAFT—PATROL) (PBF/PTF)

PKM 212-375 series

Displacement, tons: 148 full load
Dimensions, feet (metres): 121.4 × 22.6 × 5.6 *(37 × 6.9 × 1.7)*
Main machinery: 2 MTU MD 16V 538 TB90 diesels; 6,000 hp(m) *(4.41 MW)* sustained; 2 shafts
Speed, knots: 37
Range, n miles: 600 at 20 kt
Complement: 31 (5 officers)
Guns: 2 Emerson Electric 30 mm (twin) or USN 3 in *(76 mm)*/50 or Bofors 40 mm/60. 2 GE/GD 20 mm Sea Vulcan Gatlings (in most). 2—12.7 mm MGs. Rocket launchers in lieu of after Gatling in some.
Weapons control: Optical director.
Radars: Surface search: Raytheon 1645; I-band.

Comment: Fifty-four Sea Dolphins built by Korea SEC, and 47 Wildcats by Korea Tacoma. First laid down 1978. The class has some gun armament variations and some minor superstructure changes in later ships of the class. These craft form the basis of the coastal patrol effort against incursions by North Korean amphibious units. Five sold to the Philippines in 1995, two transferred to Bangladesh in 2000. Some deleted so far, others are in reserve.

WILDCAT 253 *6/1999* / 0081163

SEA DOLPHIN 279 *6/2004* / 1042332

SEA DOLPHIN 372 (with 40 mm gun) *10/1998, L Stephenson* / 0052551

0 + 40 PKM-X FAST ATTACK CRAFT (PGGF)

Displacement, tons: 300
Dimensions, feet (metres): 183.8 × ? × ? *(56.0 × ? × ?)*
Main machinery: To be announced
Missiles: SSM: 4 Harpoon (2 twin).
Guns: 1—3 in *(76 mm)*.
Radars: Air/Surface search: Thales MW 08; G-band.
Navigation: I-band.

Comment: A new class of patrol craft, to replace existing vessels, is reported to have started construction in 2003. Design and details are speculative but armament is believed to include Harpoon and a 76 mm gun.

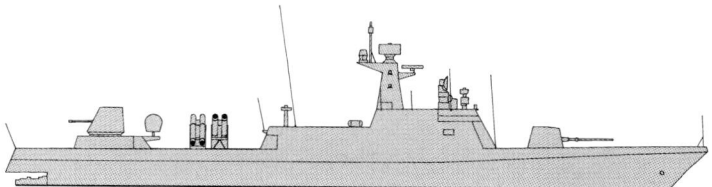

PKM-X (illustrative design) *(Scale 1 : 600), Ian Sturton* / 0569923

AMPHIBIOUS FORCES

0 + 1 (2) AMPHIBIOUS TRANSPORT DOCK (LPD)

Name	No	Builders	Laid down	Launched	Commissioned
DOKDO	611	Hanjin Heavy Industries, Pusan	2003	12 July 2005	June 2007

Displacement, tons: 13,000 standard; 19,000 full load
Dimensions, feet (metres): 656.3 × 105.0 × 21.33 (200.0 × 32.0 × 6.5)
Main machinery: 4 SEMT Pielstick 16PC 2.5 STC diesels; 41,615 hp(m) (30.6 MW) sustained; 2 shafts
Speed, knots: 22
Complement: 400 ship plus 700
Military lift: 700 troops, 10 tanks and two air-cushion landing craft

Missiles: 1 Raytheon RAM system.
Guns: 2 TNNL Goalkeeper systems.
Combat data systems: To be based on Tacticos.
Radars: Air search: Thales SMART L; 3D; D-band.
Surface search: Signaal MW 08; G-band.
Navigation: To be announced.
Helicopters: 10.

Programmes: The contract for an amphibious assault ship was placed with Hanjin Heavy Industries on 28 October 2002. An order for a second ship is expected in 2006 and a third ship may also be under consideration.
Structure: The design includes a well dock.

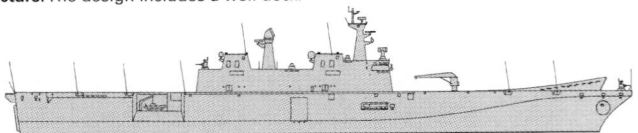

LPX   *(Scale 1 : 2,400), Ian Sturton* / 0569925

DOKDO   *7/2005*, Ships of the World* / 1153432

4 ALLIGATOR CLASS (LSTH)

Name	No	Builders	Launched	Commissioned
KOJOON BONG	681	Korea Tacoma, Masan	Sep 1992	June 1993
BIRO BONG	682	Korea Tacoma, Masan	Dec 1996	Nov 1997
HYANGRO BONG	683	Korea Tacoma, Masan	Oct 1998	Aug 1999
SEONGIN BONG	685	Korea Tacoma, Masan	Feb 1999	Nov 1999

Displacement, tons: 4,278 full load
Dimensions, feet (metres): 369.1 × 50.2 × 9.8 (112.5 × 15.3 × 3)
Main machinery: 2 SEMT-Pielstick 16 PA6 V 280; 12,800 hp(m) (9.41 MW) sustained; 2 shafts; cp props
Speed, knots: 16. **Range, n miles:** 4,500 at 12 kt
Complement: 169
Military lift: 200 troops; 15 MBT; 6—3 ton vehicles; 4 LCVPs.
Guns: 2 Breda 40 mm/70 (LST 683, 685). 2—30 mm (1 twin) (LST 681). 2 Vulcan 20 mm Gatlings.
Countermeasures: Decoys: 1 RBOC chaff launcher.
ESM: radar intercept.
Weapons control: Selenia NA 18. Optronic director. Daeyoung WCS-86.
Radars: Surface search: Raytheon SPS 64; E/F-band.
Navigation: Raytheon SPS 64; I-band.
Tacan: SRN 15.
Helicopters: Platform for 1 UH-60A.

Comment: First one ordered in June 1990 from Korea Tacoma, Masan but delayed by financial problems. Korea Tacoma is now Hanjin Heavy Industries. Design improvements include stern ramp for underway launching of LVTs, helicopter deck, and a lengthened bow ramp. Three more may be added in due course.

KOJOON BONG   *11/1997* / 0081164

KOJOON BONG   *10/1998, John Mortimer* / 0052552

4 LST 512-1152 CLASS (LST)

Name	No	Builders	Commissioned
UN BONG (ex-LST 1010)	671	Bethlehem Steel	25 Apr 1944
WEE BONG (ex-*Johnson County* LST 849)	676	American Bridge	16 Jan 1945
SU YONG (ex-*Kane County* LST 853)	677	Chicago Bridge	11 Dec 1945
BUK HAN (ex-*Lynn County* LST 900)	678	Dravo, Pittsburg	28 Dec 1944

Displacement, tons: 1,653 standard; 2,366 beaching; 4,080 full load
Dimensions, feet (metres): 328 × 50 × 14 (screws) (100 × 15.2 × 4.3)
Main machinery: 2 GM 12-567A diesels; 1,800 hp (1.34 MW); 2 shafts
Speed, knots: 10
Complement: 80
Military lift: 2,100 tons including 20 tanks and 2 LCVPs
Guns: 8 Bofors 40 mm (2 twin, 4 single). 2 Oerlikon 20 mm.

Comment: Former US Navy tank landing ships. Transferred to South Korea between 1955 and 1959. All purchased 15 November 1974. Planned to be replaced by the Alligator class but four reported as still in service.

BUK HAN   *10/1997* / 0081165

1 + 2 TSAPLYA (MURENA E) (PROJECT 12061) CLASS (ACV)

Displacement, tons: 149 full load
Dimensions, feet (metres): 103.7 × 47.6 × 5.2 (31.6 × 14.5 × 1.6)
Main machinery: 2 PR-77 gas turbines for lift and propulsion; 8,000 hp (5.88 MW)
Speed, knots: 50
Range, n miles: 500 at 50 kt
Complement: 11 (3 officers) + 100 troops
Guns: 2—30 mm AK 306M. 2—30 mm grenade launchers. 2—12.7 mm MGs.

Comment: Designed by Almaz, all built at Khabarovsk. First laid down on 26 April 2004 and delivered to Inchon on 11 November 2005. The second and third are to follow in 2006. Capable of carrying one medium tank or 130 troops.

10 LCM 8 CLASS (LCM)

Displacement, tons: 115 full load
Dimensions, feet (metres): 74.5 × 21 × 4.6 (22.7 × 6.4 × 1.4)
Main machinery: 4 GM 6—71 diesels; 696 hp (519 kW) sustained; 2 shafts
Speed, knots: 11
Complement: 11
Military lift: 55 tons

Comment: Previously US Army craft. Transferred in September 1978.

LCM 8   *5/1995, David Jordan* / 0506238

MISCELLANEOUS LANDING CRAFT

Comment: A considerable number of US LCVP type built of GRP in South Korea. In addition there were plans to build up to 20 small hovercraft for special forces; first two reported building in 1994, and one seen on sea trials in May 1995. Also 56 combat support boats of 8 m were ordered from FBM Marine for assembly by Hanjin Heavy Industries.

HOVERCRAFT   *5/1995, David Jordan* / 0081167

MINE WARFARE FORCES

6 SWALLOW CLASS (MINEHUNTERS) (MHSC)

Name	No	Builders	Commissioned
KANG KYEONG	561	Kangnam Corporation	Dec 1986
KANG JIN	562	Kangnam Corporation	May 1991
KO RYEONG	563	Kangnam Corporation	Nov 1991
KIM PO	565	Kangnam Corporation	Apr 1993
KO CHANG	566	Kangnam Corporation	Oct 1993
KUM WHA	567	Kangnam Corporation	Apr 1994

Displacement, tons: 470 standard; 520 full load
Dimensions, feet (metres): 164 × 27.2 × 8.6 *(50 × 8.3 × 2.6)*
Main machinery: 2 MTU diesels; 2,040 hp(m) *(1.5 MW)* sustained; 2 Voith-Schneider props; bow thruster; 102 hp(m) *(75 kW)*
Speed, knots: 15. **Range, n miles:** 2,000 at 10 kt
Complement: 44 (5 officers) plus 4 divers
Guns: 1 Oerlikon 20 mm. 2—7.62 mm MGs.
Countermeasures: MCM: 2 Gaymarine Pluto remote-control submersibles (possibly to be replaced by Double Eagle).
Combat data systems: Racal MAINS 500.
Radars: Navigation: Raytheon SPS 64; I-band.
Sonars: GEC-Marconi 193M Mod 1 or Mod 3; minehunting; high frequency.

Comment: Built to a design developed independently by Kangnam Corporation but similar to the Italian Lerici class. GRP hull. Single sweep gear deployed at 8 kt. Decca/ Racal plotting system. First delivered at the end of 1986 for trials. Two more with some modifications ordered in 1988, three more in 1990.

KANG JIN *1/2000, van Ginderen Collection* / 0104999

1 WON SAN CLASS (MINELAYER) (MLH)

Name	No	Builders	Launched	Commissioned
WON SAN	560	Hyundai, Ulsan	Sep 1996	Sep 1997

Displacement, tons: 3,300 full load
Dimensions, feet (metres): 340.6 × 49.2 × 11.2 *(103.8 × 15 × 3.4)*
Main machinery: CODAD; 4 SEMT-Pielstick 12 PA6 diesels; 17,200 hp(m) *(12.64 MW)*; 2 shafts
Speed, knots: 22. **Range, n miles:** 4,500 at 15 kt
Complement: 160
Guns: 1 OTO Melara 3 in *(76 mm)*/62; 85 rds/min to 16 km *(8.6 n miles)*; weight of shell 6 kg. 2 Breda 40 mm/70.
Torpedoes: 6—324 mm Mk 32 (2 triple) launchers.
Mines: 2 stern launchers. Up to 300.
Countermeasures: Decoys: 2 chaff launchers. ESM/ECM.
Weapons control: Radamec optronic director.
Radars: Air/surface search: E/F-band.
Fire control: Marconi 1802; I/J-band.
Navigation: I-band.
Sonars: Bow-mounted; active search and attack; medium frequency.
Helicopters: Platform only.

Comment: Project design contract ordered October 1991 and completed July 1993 by Hyundai. Order to build given in October 1994.

WON SAN *3/2004, Chris Sattler* / 1042336

3 YANG YANG CLASS (MSC/MHC)

Name	No	Builders	Commissioned
YANG YANG	571	Kangnam Corporation	Dec 1999
ONGJIN	572	Kangnam Corporation	Feb 2004
HAE NAM	573	Kangnam Corporation	Mar 2005

Displacement, tons: 880 full load
Dimensions, feet (metres): 195 × 34.4 × 9.8 *(59.4 × 10.5 × 3.0)*
Main machinery: 2 MTU diesels; 4,000 hp(m) *(2.98 MW)* sustained; 2 Voith-Schneider props; bow thruster; 134 hp(m) *(100 kW)*
Speed, knots: 15. **Range, n miles:** 3,000 at 12 kt
Complement: 56 (7 officers) plus 5 divers
Guns: 1—20 mm Sea Vulcan Gatling. 2—7.62 mm MGs.
Countermeasures: MCM: BAE Systems deep mechanical and combined influence sweep system. 2 Gayrobot Pluto GIGAS ROVs.
Combat data systems: Thomson Marconi TSM 2061 Mk 3.
Radars: Navigation: Raytheon; I-band.
Sonars: Thomson Marconi Type 2093 VDS; minehunting; active multifrequency.

Comment: The first one ordered in late 1995 and a second pair delivered by 2005. Further orders are expected. A large version of the Swallow class built to a design developed by Kangnam Corporation. GRP hull. The integrated navigation and dynamic positioning system developed by Kongsberg Simrad.

ONGJIN *8/2004, John Mortimer* / 1042334

SURVEY SHIPS

17 SURVEY SHIPS (AGOR)

PUSAN 801	**PUSAN** 806	201-204
PUSAN 802	**PUSAN** 810	208-209
PUSAN 803	**CH'UNGNAM** 821	215-216
PUSAN 805	**KANGWON** 831	220

Comment: All ships are painted white with a distinctive yellow coloured crest on the funnel. Most were commissioned in the 1980s. The Hydrographic Service is responsible to the Ministry of Transport.

PUSAN 801 *7/1997, van Ginderen Collection* / 0012709

204 *8/1997* / 0012710

202 *4/2000, M Declerck* / 0105000

TUGS

Notes: In addition to the Edenton class ATS there are a further 10 harbour tugs and numerous port service auxiliaries.

HARBOUR TUG *10/1998, John Mortimer* / 0052559

AUXILIARIES

Notes: The South Korean Navy also operates nine small harbour tugs (designated YTLs). These include one ex-US Navy craft and five ex-US Army craft. There are also approximately 35 small service craft in addition to the YO-type tankers listed and the harbour tugs. These craft include open lighters, floating cranes, diving tenders, dredgers, ferries, non self-propelled fuel barges, pontoon barges, and sludge removal barges; most are former US Navy craft.

1 CHEONG HAE JIN CLASS (ARS)

Name	No	Builders	Launched	Commissioned
CHEONG HAE JIN	21	Daewoo, Okpo	Oct 1995	30 Nov 1996

Displacement, tons: 4,300 full load
Dimensions, feet (metres): 337.3 × 53.8 × 15.1 *(102.8 × 16.4 × 4.6)*
Main machinery: Diesel-electric; 4 MAN Burmeister & Wain 16V 28/32 diesels; 11,800 hp(m) *(8.67 MW)*; 2 motors; 5,440 hp(m) *(4 MW)*; 2 shafts; cp props; 3 bow and 2 stern thrusters
Speed, knots: 18. **Range, n miles**: 9,500 at 15 kt
Complement: 130
Guns: 1 GE/GD 20 mm Vulcan Gatling (can be fitted). 6—12.7 mm MGs.
Radars: Navigation: I-band.
Sonars: Hull-mounted; active search; high frequency.
Helicopters: Platform for 1 light.

Comment: Ordered in 1992. Laid down December 1994. A multipurpose salvage and rescue ship which carries a 300 m ROV as well as two LCVPs on davits plus a diving bell for nine men and a decompression chamber. Two large hydraulic cranes fore and aft and one towing winch. There are also two salvage ships which belong to the Coast Guard.

CHEONG HAE JIN   *9/2003, Hartmut Ehlers* / 0570936

3 CHUN JEE CLASS (LOGISTIC SUPPORT SHIPS) (AORH)

Name	No	Builders	Launched	Commissioned
CHUN JEE	57	Hyundai, Ulsan	May 1990	Dec 1990
DAE CHUNG	58	Hyundai, Ulsan	Jan 1997	Nov 1997
HWA CHUN	59	Hyundai, Ulsan	July 1997	Mar 1998

Displacement, tons: 7,500 full load
Dimensions, feet (metres): 426.5 × 58.4 × 21.3 *(130 × 17.8 × 6.5)*
Main machinery: 2 SEMT-Pielstick 16 PA6 V 280 (AO 57) or 12 PC2.5 diesels; 12,800 hp(m) *(9.4 MW)* sustained; 2 shafts
Speed, knots: 20. **Range, n miles**: 4,500 at 15 kt
Cargo capacity: 4,200 tons liquids; 450 tons solids
Guns: 4 Emerlec 30 mm (2 twin) or 2 Breda 40 mm/70. 2 GE/GD 20 mm Vulcan Gatlings.
Radars: Navigation: 2 Racal Decca; I-band.
Helicopters: Platform for 1 medium.

Comment: *Chun Jee* laid down September 1989. Underway replenishment stations on both sides. Helicopter for Vertrep but no hangar. There are three 6 ton lifts. Possibly based on Italian Stromboli class. Second of class was to have followed on but was eventually ordered together with the third in May 1995, to a slightly different design. More may be built when funds are available.

CHUN JEE   *7/2005*, Michael Nitz* / 1153434

CHUN JEE   *6/2005*, Maritime Photographic* / 1153433

2 EDENTON CLASS (SALVAGE SHIPS) (ATS)

Name	No	Builders	Commissioned
PYONG TAEK (ex-*Beaufort*)	27	Brooke Marine, Lowestoft	22 Jan 1972
KWANG YANG (ex-*Brunswick*)	28	Brooke Marine, Lowestoft	19 Dec 1972

Displacement, tons: 2,929 full load
Dimensions, feet (metres): 282.6 × 50 × 15.1 *(86.1 × 15.2 × 4.6)*
Main machinery: 4 Paxman 12YJCM diesels; 6,000 hp *(4.48 MW)* sustained; 2 shafts; cp props; bow thruster
Speed, knots: 16. **Range, n miles**: 10,000 at 13 kt
Complement: 129 (7 officers)
Guns: 2 Oerlikon 20 mm Mk 68.
Radars: Navigation: Sperry SPS-53; I/J-band.

Comment: Transferred from USA on 29 August 1996. Capable of (1) ocean towing, (2) supporting diver operations to depths of 850 ft, (3) lifting submerged objects weighing as much as 600,000 lb from a depth of 120 ft by static tidal lift or 30,000 lb by dynamic lift, (4) fighting ship fires. Fitted with 10 ton capacity crane forward and 20 ton capacity crane aft. Both recommissioned 28 February 1997.

PYONG TAEK (US colours)   *12/1995, Giorgio Arra* / 0506303

1 TRIALS SUPPORT SHIP (AGE)

Name	No	Builders	Launched	Commissioned
SUNJIN	AGS 11	Hyundai, Ulsan	Nov 1992	Apr 1993

Displacement, tons: 320 full load
Dimensions, feet (metres): 113.2 × 49.2 × 12.1 *(34.5 × 15 × 3.7)*
Main machinery: 1 MTU 16V 396 TE74L diesel; 2,680 hp(m) *(2 MW)*; 1 shaft; cp prop; 2 bow thrusters
Speed, knots: 21. **Range, n miles**: 600 at 16 kt
Complement: 5 plus 20 scientists
Guns: 1—20 mm Gatling.
Radars: Navigation: I-band.

Comment: Experimental design built by Hyundai. Ordered June 1991, laid down June 1992. Aluminium SWATH hull with dynamic positioning system. Fitted with various trials equipment including an integrated navigation system and torpedo tracking pinger system. VDS and towed arrays. Used by the Defence Development Agency and civilian operated.

SUNJIN   *1993, Hyundai* / 0081169

MARITIME POLICE

Notes: (1) The South Korean Maritime Police operates a number of small ships and several hundred craft including tugs and rescue craft, and has taken over the Coast Guard. The overall colour scheme on all units is a medium blue coloured hull with white superstructure and black block style pennant numbers, with the lettering 'POLICE' in both Korean and English on a prominent space on the superstructure. The colour scheme is further distinguished with a black funnel top where appropriate. Immediately below the funnel top is a thin white band separating a thick lightish green band with the Police logo superimposed. This logo is in gold with the blue and red colours of Korea in the centre. Bell 412 helicopters are being acquired.
(2) A 5,000 ton ship, based on *Tae Pung Yang II*, is reported to have been commissioned in 2001.
(3) Six new offshore patrol vessels are to be acquired by 2008. These will include three 3,000 ton helicopter-capable ships and three 1,500 ton ships.

1 DAEWOO TYPE (PSO)

SUMJINKANG PC 1006

Displacement, tons: 1,650 full load
Dimensions, feet (metres): 275.6 × 34.1 × 11.8 *(84 × 10.4 × 3.6)*
Main machinery: 2 Wärtsilä Nohab 16V25 diesels; 10,000 hp(m) *(7.35 MW)* sustained; 2 shafts
Speed, knots: 21. **Range, n miles**: 4,500 at 18 kt
Complement: 57 (7 officers)
Guns: 1—20 mm Sea Vulcan Gatling. 4—12.7 mm MGs.
Radars: Surface search: I-band.

Comment: Ordered in 1997 from Daewoo. Described as a multipurpose patrol ship this is the largest patrol vessel yet built for the Maritime Police. Launched 22 January 1999, and delivered 20 June 1999.

SUMJINKANG   *8/1999, Ships of the World* / 0081173

3 MAZINGER CLASS (PSO)

PC 1001-1003

Displacement, tons: 1,200 full load
Dimensions, feet (metres): 264.1 × 32.2 × 11.5 *(80.5 × 9.8 × 3.2)*
Main machinery: 2 SEMT-Pielstick 12 PA6 V 280 diesels; 9,600 hp(m) *(7.08 MW)* sustained; 2 shafts
Speed, knots: 22
Range, n miles: 7,000 at 18 kt
Complement: 69 (11 officers)
Guns: 1 Bofors 40 mm/70. 4 Oerlikon 20 mm (2 twin).
Radars: Surface search: Raytheon; I-band.

Comment: Ordered 7 November 1980 from Korea Tacoma and Hyundai. *PC 1001* delivered 29 November 1981. *PC 1002* 31 August 1982 and *PC 1003* on 31 August 1983. All-welded mild steel construction. Used for offshore surveillance and general coast guard duties. *PC 1001* is the Coast Guard Command ship. Only three of this class were completed.

MAZINGER (old colours)   *1987, Korea Tacoma* / 0506048

1 HAN KANG CLASS (PG)

HAN KANG PC 1005

Displacement, tons: 1,180 full load
Dimensions, feet (metres): 289.7 × 32.8 × 9.5 *(88.3 × 10 × 2.9)*
Main machinery: CODOG; 1 GE LM 2500 gas turbine; 26,820 hp *(20 MW)* sustained; 2 MTU 12V 956 TB82 diesels; 6,260 hp(m) *(4.6 MW)* sustained; 3 shafts
Speed, knots: 32
Range, n miles: 4,000 at 15 kt
Complement: 72 (11 officers)
Guns: 1 OTO Melara 76/62 compact. 1 Bofors 40 mm/70. 2 GE/GD 20 mm Vulcan Gatlings.
Weapons control: Signaal LIOD optronic director.
Radars: Surface search: Raytheon SPS-64(V); I-band.
Fire control: Signaal WM28; I/J-band.

Comment: Built between May 1984 and December 1985 by Daewoo. Same hull as Po Hang class but much more lightly armed. Only one of the class was completed.

HAN KANG   *9/2000* / 0097740

6 430 TON CLASS (PBO)

300-303   **402-403**

Displacement, tons: 430 full load
Dimensions, feet (metres): 176.2 × 24.3 × 7.9 *(53.7 × 7.4 × 2.4)*
Main machinery: 2 MTU 16V 396 TB83 diesels; 1,990 hp(m) *(1.49 MW)*; 2 shafts; cp props
Speed, knots: 19
Range, n miles: 2,100 at 17 kt
Complement: 14
Guns: 1 or 2 GD/GE 20 mm Vulcan Gatlings. 4—12.7 mm MGs.
Radars: Surface search: Raytheon; I-band.

Comment: All built between 1990 and 1995 by Hyundai except 301 which was built by Daewoo. Multipurpose patrol ships.

300   *3/1996, D Swetnam* / 0081172

301   *8/2000, van Ginderen Collection* / 0097741

6 SEA DRAGON/WHALE CLASS (PBO)

PC 501, 502, 503, 505, 506, 507

Displacement, tons: 640 full load
Dimensions, feet (metres): 199.5 × 26.2 × 8.9 *(60.8 × 8 × 2.7)*
Main machinery: 2 SEMT-Pielstick 12 PA6 V 280 diesels; 9,600 hp(m) *(7.08 MW)* sustained; 2 shafts
Speed, knots: 24. **Range, n miles:** 6,000 at 15 kt
Complement: 40 (7 officers)
Guns: 1 Bofors 40 mm/60. 2 Oerlikon 20 mm. 2 Browning 12.7 mm MGs.
Radars: Navigation: Two sets.

Comment: Delivered 1978-1982 by Hyundai, Korea and Korea Tacoma. Fitted with SATNAV. Welded steel hull. Armament varies between ships, one 76 mm gun can be mounted on the forecastle. Variant of this class built for Bangladesh and delivered in October 1997.

SEA DRAGON 507 (old colours)   *1987, Korea Tacoma* / 0506047

23 SEA WOLF/SHARK CLASS (PBO)

207	255-259	265-269	275-277
251-253	261-263	271-273	

Displacement, tons: 310 full load
Dimensions, feet (metres): 158.1 × 23.3 × 8.2 *(48.2 × 7.1 × 2.5)*
Main machinery: 2 diesels; 7,320 hp(m) *(5.38 MW)*; 2 shafts
Speed, knots: 25. **Range, n miles:** 2,400 at 15 kt
Complement: 35 (3 officers)
Guns: 4 Oerlikon 20 mm (2 twin or 1 twin, 2 single). Some have a twin Bofors 40 mm/70 vice the twin Oerlikon. 2 Browning 12.7 mm MGs.
Radars: Surface search: I-band.

Comment: First four ordered in 1979-80 from Korea SEC (Sea Shark), Hyundai and Korea Tacoma (Sea Wolf). Programme terminated in 1988. Pennant numbers in 200 series up to 277.

SEA WOLF 207   *5/1997, van Ginderen Collection* / 0012711

4 BUKHANSAN CLASS (PBO)

BUKHANSAN 278	CHULMASAN 279	P 281	P 282

Displacement, tons: 380 full load
Dimensions, feet (metres): 174.2 × 24 × 7.2 *(53.1 × 7.3 × 2.2)*
Main machinery: 2 MTU diesels; 8,300 hp(m) *(6.1 MW)* sustained; 2 shafts
Speed, knots: 28. **Range, n miles:** 2,500 at 15 kt
Complement: 35 (3 officers)
Guns: 1 Breda 40 mm/70. 1 GE/GD 20 mm Vulcan Gatling. 2—12.7 mm MGs.
Weapons control: Radamec optronic director.
Radars: Surface search: I-band.

Comment: Follow on to Sea Wolf class developed by Hyundai in 1987. Ordered in 1988 from Hyundai and Daewoo respectively. First pair in service in 1989, and second pair in 1990.

CHULMASAN (old colours)   *1989, Daewoo* / 0506049

5 HYUNDAI TYPE (PB)

| 105 | 113 | 118 | 121 | 125 |

Displacement, tons: 110 full load
Dimensions, feet (metres): 105.6 × 19.7 × 4.6 *(32.2 × 6 × 1.4)*
Main machinery: 2 diesels; 2 shafts
Speed, knots: 25
Complement: 19
Guns: 1 Rheinmetall 20 mm. 2—12.7 mm MGs.
Radars: Surface search: Furuno; I-band.

Comment: Ordered in 1996 and delivered from June 1997.

HYUNDAI 113   *4/2000, M Declerck* / 0097742

INSHORE PATROL CRAFT (PBR)

Displacement, tons: 47 full load
Dimensions, feet (metres): 69.9 × 17.7 × 4.6 *(21.3 × 5.4 × 1.4)*
Main machinery: 2 diesels; 1,800 hp(m) *(1.32 MW)*; 2 shafts
Speed, knots: 22. **Range, n miles:** 400 at 12 kt
Complement: 11
Guns: 1 Rheinmetall 20 mm. 3—12.7 mm MGs.
Radars: Surface search: Furuno; I-band.

Comment: Details are for the largest design of patrol craft. There are numbers of this type of vessel used for inshore patrol work. All Police craft have P pennant numbers. Armaments vary. Customs craft have double numbers.

P 71   *9/2000* / 0097743

CUSTOM 71-810   *6/1996, D Swetnam* / 0506302

1 SALVAGE SHIP (ARSH)

Name	No	Builders	Launched	Commissioned
TAE PUNG YANG I	3001	Hyundai, Ulsan	Oct 1991	18 Feb 1993

Displacement, tons: 3,200 standard; 4,300 full load
Dimensions, feet (metres): 343.5 × 49.2 × 17 *(104.7 × 15 × 5.2)*
Main machinery: 4 Ssangyoung MAN Burmeister & Wain 16V 28/32 diesels; 4,800 hp(m) *(3.53 MW)*; 2 shafts; cp props; bow and stern thrusters
Speed, knots: 21. **Range, n miles:** 8,500 at 15 kt
Complement: 121
Guns: 1 GD/GE 20 mm Vulcan Gatling. 6—12.7 mm MGs.
Radars: Navigation: I-band.
Helicopters: 1 light.

Comment: Laid down February 1991. Has a helicopter deck and hangar, an ROV capable of diving to 300 m and a firefighting capability. Dynamic positioning system. Can be used for cable laying. Operates for the Marine Police.

TAE PUNG YANG 1   *1/2000, van Ginderen Collection* / 0097744

1 SALVAGE SHIP (ARSH)

Name	No	Builders	Commissioned
TAE PUNG YANG II	3002	Hyundai, Ulsan	Nov 1988

Displacement, tons: 3,900 standard
Dimensions, feet (metres): 362.5 × 50.5 × 16.1 *(110.5 × 15.4 × 4.9)*
Main machinery: 2 diesels; 2 shafts
Speed, knots: 18
Complement: 120
Guns: 2—20 mm Vulcan Gatlings. 6—12.7 mm MGs.
Radars: Surface search: I-band.
Helicopters: Platform for 1 large.

Comment: Ordered from Hyundai in mid-1996. Also used for SAR operations.

TAE PUNG YANG II   *8/2000, Ships of the World* / 0097746

1 SALVAGE SHIP (ARSH)

Name	No	Builders	Commissioned
JAEMIN I	1501	Daewoo, Okpo	28 Dec 1992

Displacement, tons: 2,072 full load
Dimensions, feet (metres): 254.6 × 44.3 × 13.8 *(77.6 × 13.5 × 4.2)*
Main machinery: 2 MTU diesels; 8,000 hp(m) *(5.88 MW)*; 2 shafts; cp props
Speed, knots: 18
Range, n miles: 4,500 at 12 kt
Complement: 92
Guns: 1 GD/GE 20 mm Vulcan Gatling.
Radars: Navigation: I-band.

Comment: Ordered in 1990. Fitted with diving equipment and has a four point mooring system. Carries two LCVPs.

JAEMIN I   *8/2000* / 0097745

1 SALVAGE SHIP (ARS)

Name	No	Builders	Launched	Commissioned
JAEMIN II	1502	Hyundai, Ulsan	15 July 1995	Apr 1996

Displacement, tons: 2,500 full load
Dimensions, feet (metres): 288.7 × 47.6 × 15.1 *(88 × 14.5 × 4.6)*
Main machinery: 2 MTU diesels; 12,662 hp(m) *(9.31 MW)*; 2 shafts; Kamewa cp props; bow and stern thrusters
Speed, knots: 20
Range, n miles: 4,500 at 15 kt
Complement: 81
Guns: 1 GE/GD 20 mm Vulcan Gatling.
Radars: Navigation: I-band.

Comment: Ordered in December 1993 for Maritime Police. A general purpose salvage ship capable of towing, firefighting, supply or patrol duties.

JAEMIN II   *8/1999, Ships of the World* / 0081176

1 SALVAGE SHIP (ARSH)

Name	No	Builders	Commissioned
JAEMIN III	1503	Hyundai, Ulsan	Nov 1998

Displacement, tons: 4,200 full load
Dimensions, feet (metres): 362.6 × 50.5 × 16 *(110.5 × 15.4 × 4.9)*
Main machinery: 2 diesels; 2 shafts
Speed, knots: 18
Complement: 120
Guns: 2 GE 20 mm Vulcan Gatlings. 6—12.7 mm MGs.
Radars: Navigation: I-band.

Comment: Ordered in 1996, from Hyundai, Ulsan. Large helicopter deck but no hangar.

1503   *8/2000, van Ginderen Collection* / 0097747

Kuwait

Country Overview

Formerly a British protectorate, the Kingdom of Kuwait gained independence in 1961. Situated on the northwestern coast of the Gulf, it is bordered to the north by Iraq and to the south by Saudi Arabia. The country's total area, including the islands of Bubiyan, Warbah, and Faylakah, is 6,880 square miles. It has a 269 n mile coastline with the Gulf. The capital, largest city and principal port is Kuwait City. The country was annexed by Iraq from August 1990 to February 1991 when the country was liberated. Territorial seas (12 n miles) are claimed. An EEZ has not been claimed.

Headquarters Appointments

Commander of the Navy:
  Major General Ahmed Yousuf Al Mulla
Deputy Commander of the Navy:
  Brigadier Marzouk Hassan al Bader

Personnel

2006: 2,700 (including 500 Coast Guard)

Aviation

The Air Force operates five Eurocopter AS 532C Cougar helicopters armed with Exocet AM 39 ASMs and 40 F/A-18C/D Hornets.

Bases

Navy: Ras Al Qalayah
Coast Guard: Shuwaikh, Umm Al-Hainan, Al-Bida

PATROL FORCES

Notes: (1) There is a requirement for two Fast Missile Strike Craft. This programme has superseded plans to acquire offshore patrol vessels armed with SSMs. The outline requirement calls for craft of 57-72 m.
(2) Acquisition of 12 Mk V class fast interceptor craft is under consideration. Procurement of the craft, which would be similar to those in US service, would be under the US government's FMS programme.

8 UM ALMARADIM (COMBATTANTE I) CLASS (PBM)

Name	No	Builders	Launched	Commissioned
UM ALMARADIM	P 3711	CMN, Cherbourg	27 Feb 1997	31 July 1998
OUHA	P 3713	CMN, Cherbourg	29 May 1997	31 July 1998
FAILAKA	P 3715	CMN, Cherbourg	29 Aug 1997	19 Dec 1998
MASKAN	P 3717	CMN, Cherbourg	6 Jan 1998	19 Dec 1998
AL-AHMADI	P 3719	CMN, Cherbourg	2 Apr 1998	1 July 1999
ALFAHAHEEL	P 3721	CMN, Cherbourg	16 June 1998	1 July 1999
AL-YARMOUK	P 3723	CMN, Cherbourg	3 Mar 1999	7 June 2000
GAROH	P 3725	CMN, Cherbourg	June 1999	7 June 2000

Displacement, tons: 245 full load
Dimensions, feet (metres): 137.8 oa; 121.4 wl × 26.9 × 6.2 *(42; 37 × 8.2 × 1.9)*
Main machinery: 2 MTU 16V 538 TB93 diesels; 4,000 hp(m) *(2.94 MW)*; 2 Kamewa waterjets
Speed, knots: 30
Range, n miles: 1,350 at 14 kt
Complement: 29 (5 officers)

Missiles: SSM: 4 BAe Sea Skua (2 twin). Semi-active radar homing to 15 km *(8.1 n miles)* at 0.9 Mach.
SAM: Sadral sextuple launcher fitted for only.
Guns: 1 Otobreda 40 mm/70; 120 rds/min to 12.5 km *(6.8 n miles)*; weight of shell 0.96 kg.
1 Giat 20 mm M 621. 2—12.7 mm MGs.
Countermeasures: Decoys: 2 Dagaie Mk 2 chaff launchers fitted for only.
ESM: Thomson-CSF DR 3000 S1; intercept.
Combat data systems: Thomson-CSF TAVITAC NT; Link Y.
Weapons control: CS Defence Najir Mk 2 optronic director.
Radars: Air/surface search: Thomson-CSF MRR; 3D; G-band.
Fire control: BAe Seaspray Mk 3; I/J-band (for SSM).
Navigation: Litton Marine 20V90; I-band.

Programmes: Contract signed with CMN Cherbourg on 27 March 1995. First steel cut 9 June 1995. Names are taken from former Kuwaiti patrol craft.
Structure: Late decisions were made on the missile system which has been fitted in the last pair on build and to the remainder from 2000. Provision is also made for Simbad SAM and Dagaie decoy launchers, which may be fitted later. Positions of smaller guns are uncertain.
Operational: Training done in France. The aim is to have 10 crews capable of manning the eight ships. First four arrived in the Gulf in mid-August 1999, second four arrived in mid-2000.

OUHA   *3/2003*, *A Sharma* / 1133078

1 TNC 45 TYPE (FAST ATTACK CRAFT — MISSILE) (PGGF)

Name	No	Builders	Commissioned
AL SANBOUK	P 4505	Lürssen, Vegesack	26 Apr 1984

Displacement, tons: 255 full load
Dimensions, feet (metres): 147.3 × 23 × 7.5 *(44.9 × 7 × 2.3)*
Main machinery: 4 MTU 16V 538 TB92 diesels; 13,640 hp(m) *(10 MW)* sustained; 4 shafts
Speed, knots: 41. **Range, n miles:** 1,800 at 16 kt
Complement: 35 (5 officers)

Missiles: SSM: 4 Aerospatiale MM 40 Exocet; inertial cruise; active radar homing to 70 km *(40 n miles)* at 0.9 Mach; warhead 165 kg; sea-skimmer.
Guns: 1 OTO Melara 3 in *(76 mm)*/62 compact; 85 rds/min to 16 km *(8.6 n miles)* anti-surface; 12 km *(6.5 n miles)* anti-aircraft; weight of shell 6 kg.
2 Breda 40 mm/70 (twin); 300 rds/min to 12.5 km *(6.6 n miles)*; weight of shell 0.96 kg.
Countermeasures: Decoys: CSEE Dagaie; IR flares and chaff; H/J-band.
ESM: Racal Cutlass; intercept.
Weapons control: PEAB 9LV 228 system; Link Y; CSEE Lynx optical sight.
Radars: Air/surface search: Ericsson Sea Giraffe 50HC; G/H-band.
Fire control: Philips 9LV 200; J-band.
Navigation: Decca TM 1226C; I-band.

Programmes: Six ordered from Lürssen in 1980 and delivered in 1983-84.
Operational: *Al Sanbouk* escaped to Bahrain when the Iraqis invaded in August 1990, but the rest of this class was taken over by the Iraqi Navy, and either sunk or severely damaged by Allied forces in February 1991. The ship was refitted by Lürssen in 1995 and again in 2004.

MASKAN   *5/2003*, *A Sharma* / 0559834

AL SANBOUK   *3/2003*, *A Sharma* / 0568872

1 FPB 57 TYPE (FAST ATTACK CRAFT—MISSILE) (PGGF)

Name	No	Builders	Commissioned
ISTIQLAL	P 5702	Lürssen, Vegesack	9 Aug 1983

Displacement, tons: 410 full load
Dimensions, feet (metres): 190.6 × 24.9 × 8.9 *(58.1 × 7.6 × 2.7)*
Main machinery: 4 MTU 16V 956 TB91 diesels; 15,000 hp(m) *(11 MW)* sustained; 4 shafts
Speed, knots: 36. **Range, n miles:** 1,300 at 30 kt
Complement: 40 (5 officers)

Missiles: SSM: 4 Aerospatiale MM 40 Exocet; inertial cruise; active radar homing to 70 km *(40 n miles)* at 0.9 Mach; warhead 165 kg; sea-skimmer.
Guns: 1 OTO Melara 3 in *(76 mm)*/62 compact; 85 rds/min to 16 km *(8.6 n miles)* anti-surface; 12 km *(6.5 n miles)* anti-aircraft; weight of shell 6 kg.
2 Breda 40 mm/70 (twin); 300 rds/min to 12.5 km *(6.6 n miles)*; weight of shell 0.96 kg.
Mines: Fitted for minelaying.
Countermeasures: Decoys: CSEE Dagaie trainable mounting; automatic dispenser; IR flares and chaff; H/J-band.
ESM: Racal Cutlass; radar intercept.
ECM: Racal Cygnus; jammer.
Weapons control: PEAB 9LV 228 system; Link Y; CSEE Lynx optical sight.
Radars: Surface search: Marconi S 810 (after radome); I-band; range 43 km *(25 n miles)*.
Navigation: Decca TM 1226C; I-band.
Fire control: Philips 9LV 200; J-band.

Programmes: Two ordered from Lürssen in 1980.
Operational: *Istiqlal* escaped to Bahrain when the Iraqis invaded in August 1990. The second of this class was captured and sunk in February 1991. Having been laid up since 1997 *Istiqlal* was refitted at Lürssen 2003-2005. In addition to operational roles, it is also used as a training ship.

ISTIQLAL   *4/2005, Michael Nitz* / 1121416

COAST GUARD

Headquarters Appointments

Director of Coast Guard:
  Brigadier Jassim al Failakia

PATROL FORCES

16 VICTORY TEAM P 46 CLASS (PATROL CRAFT) (PBF)

Displacement, tons: 8.5
Dimensions, feet (metres): 45.9 × 10.6 × 2.6 *(14.0 × 3.23 × 0.8)*
Main machinery: 2 Yanmar 6CX diesels; 930 hp *(690 kW)*; 2 Arneson ASD 8 surface drives
Speed, knots: 52
Range, n miles: 200 at 50 kt
Complement: 4
Guns: 2—12.7 mm MGs.
Radars: Navigation.

Comment: Contract for 16 craft signed in April 2004 with delivery of the final vessel expected by mid-2006. The Victory Team of Dubai design is a twin-stepped deep-'vee' monohull developed from its offshore power boats. The hull, deck and internal assembly are built from a sandwich composite comprising a glass fibre, kevlar and carbon mix to provide structural integrity at a minimum weight. The cockpit is protected by 17 mm Dyneema Ballistic panelling.

P 46   *3/2005, Victory Team* / 1127034

4 INTTISAR (OPV 310) CLASS (PB)

Name	No	Builders	Commissioned
INTTISAR	P 301	Australian Shipbuilding Industries	20 Jan 1993
AMAN	P 302	Australian Shipbuilding Industries	20 Jan 1993
MAIMON	P 303	Australian Shipbuilding Industries	7 Aug 1993
MOBARK	P 304	Australian Shipbuilding Industries	7 Aug 1993

Displacement, tons: 150 full load
Dimensions, feet (metres): 103.3 oa; 88.9 wl × 21.3 × 6.6 *(31.5; 27.1 × 6.5 × 2)*
Main machinery: 2 MTU 16V 396 TB94 diesels; 5,800 hp(m) *(4.26 MW)* sustained; 2 shafts; 1 MTU 8V 183 TE62 diesel; 750 hp(m) *(550 kW)* maximum; 1 Hamilton 422 water-jet
Speed, knots: 28. **Range, n miles:** 300 at 28 kt
Complement: 11 (3 officers)
Guns: 1 Oerlikon 20 mm. 1—12.7 mm MG.
Radars: Surface search: 2 Racal Decca; I-band.

Comment: First two ordered from Australian Shipbuilding Industries in 1991. Second pair ordered in July 1992. Steel hulls, aluminium superstructure. The third engine drives a small waterjet to provide a loiter capability. Carries an RIB. Used by the Coast Guard.

AMAN   *1992, Australian Shipbuilding Industries* / 0081178

10 SUBAHI CLASS (PB)

Name	No	Builders	Commissioned
RAYYAN	P 300	OCEA, St Nazaire	23 Aug 2005
SUBAHI	P 308	OCEA, St Nazaire	6 Aug 2003
JABERI	P 309	OCEA, St Nazaire	Dec 2003
SAAD	P 310	OCEA, St Nazaire	Feb 2004
AHMADI	P 311	OCEA, St Nazaire	Mar 2004
NAIF	P 312	OCEA, St Nazaire	May 2004
THAFIR	P 313	OCEA, St Nazaire	July 2004
MARZOUG	P 314	OCEA, St Nazaire	Sep 2004
MASH'NOOR	P 315	OCEA, St Nazaire	Jan 2005
WADAH	P 316	OCEA, St Nazaire	May 2005

Displacement, tons: 116 full load
Dimensions, feet (metres): 115.5 × 22.3 × 4.0 *(35.2 × 6.8 × 1.2)*
Main machinery: 2 MTU 12V 4000 M70 diesels; 4,600 hp *(3.43 MW)*; 2 Kamewa waterjets
Speed, knots: 32. **Range, n miles:** 300 at 28 kt
Complement: 11 (3 officers)
Guns: 1 Oerlikon 20 mm. 2—12.7 mm MGs.
Radars: Sperry Bridgemaster E; I-band.

Comment: Built by OCEA, France based on Al Shaheed class design. Aluminium construction. Operated by the Coast Guard. P 300 is a VIP variant equipped with three cabins.

MARZOUG   *8/2004*, B Prézelin* / 1133080

RAYYAN   *8/2005*, B Prézelin* / 1133079

3 INSHORE PATROL CRAFT (PBR)

KASSIR T 205	**DASTOOR** T 210	**MAHROOS** T 215

Displacement, tons: To be announced
Dimensions, feet (metres): 70.9 × 19.5 × 4.9 *(21.6 × 5.96 × 1.5)*
Main machinery: 2 MTU 12V 183 TE92 diesels; 1,800 hp *(1.45 MW)*; 2 shafts
Speed, knots: 25
Range, n miles: 325 at 25 kt
Complement: 3 + 41 passengers
Radars: Navigation: to be announced.

Comment: Order for three craft for the Coast Guard announced on 7 January 2003. Based on the 22 m craft in service with the New South Wales Police, the vessels were constructed by Austal Ships subsidiary, Image Marine and delivered in June 2004. Aluminium hull.

DASTOOR *6/2004, Austal Ships* / 0587772

3 AL SHAHEED CLASS (PB)

Name	No	Builders	Commissioned
AL SHAHEED	P 305	OCEA, Les Sables d'Olonne	July 1997
BAYAN	P 306	OCEA, Les Sables d'Olonne	Apr 1999
DASMAN	P 307	OCEA, Les Sables d'Olonne	2001

Displacement, tons: 104 full load
Dimensions, feet (metres): 109.3 × 23 × 4 *(33.3 × 7 × 1.2)*
Main machinery: 2 MTU 12V 396 TE94; 4,352 hp(m) *(3.2 MW)* sustained; 2 shafts
Speed, knots: 30
Range, n miles: 360 at 25 kt
Complement: 11 (3 officers)
Guns: 1 Oerlikon 20 mm. 2 — 12.7 mm MGs.
Radars: Surface search: Racal Decca 20V 90 TA; E/F-band.
Navigation: Racal Decca Bridgemaster ARPA; I-band.

Comment: Built by OCEA, France to FPB 100K design. Operated by the Coast Guard.

AL SHAHEED *10/1997, Ships of the World* / 0012718

33 AL-SHAALI TYPE (INSHORE PATROL CRAFT) (PBF)

Comment: Ten 10 m and 23 8.5 m patrol craft built by Al-Shaali Marine, Dubai, and delivered in June 1992. Also used by UAE Coast Guard. More Rapid Intervention patrol craft are to be acquired in due course.

12 MANTA CLASS (INSHORE PATROL CRAFT) (PBF)

1B 1501-1523 series

Displacement, tons: 10 full load
Dimensions, feet (metres): 45.9 × 12.5 × 2.3 *(14 × 3.8 × 0.7)*
Main machinery: 2 Caterpillar 3208 diesels; 810 hp(m) *(595 kW)* sustained; 2 shafts
Speed, knots: 40
Range, n miles: 180 at 35 kt
Complement: 4
Guns: 3 Herstal M2HB 12.7 mm MGs.
Radars: Surface search: Furuno; I-band.

Comment: Original craft ordered in September 1992 from Simonneau Marine and delivered in 1993. Aluminium construction. This version has two inboard engines. Pennant numbers are in odd number sequence. All the class reported to be inoperable due to technical problems. An underlying cause may be that the boats were fitted with inboard engines although designed for outboards.

MANTA 1501 *11/1996* / 0012719

6 COUGAR ENFORCER 40 CLASS
(INSHORE PATROL CRAFT) (PBF)

Displacement, tons: 5.7 full load
Dimensions, feet (metres): 40 × 9 × 2.1 *(12.2 × 2.8 × 0.80)*
Main machinery: 2 Sabre 380 S diesels; 760 hp(m) *(559 kW)*; 2 Arneson ASD 8 surface drives; 2 shafts
Speed, knots: 45
Range, n miles: 250 at 35 kt
Complement: 4
Guns: 1 — 12.7 mm MG.
Radars: Surface search: Koden; I-band.

Comment: First one completed in July 1996 for the Coastguard by Cougar Marine, Warsash. The craft has a V monohull design.

ENFORCER 40 *7/1996, Cougar Marine* / 0081179

17 COUGAR TYPE (INSHORE PATROL CRAFT) (PBF)

Comment: Three Cat 900 (32 ft) and six Predator 1100 (35 ft) all powered by two Yamaha outboards (400 hp(m) *(294 kW)*). Four Type 1200 (38 ft) and four Type 1300 (41 ft) all powered by two Sabre diesels (760 hp(m) *(559 kW)*). All based on the high-performance planing hull developed for racing, and acquired in 1991-92. Most have a 7.62 mm MG and a Kroden I-band radar. Used by the Coast Guard. Most have K numbers on the side.

COUGAR 1200 *1991, Cougar Marine* / 0081180

AUXILIARIES

Notes: (1) There are some unarmed craft with Sawahil numbers which are not naval.
(2) A 95 m ship of about 2,000 tons is required to act as a support ship for patrol vessels. It would also be equipped to undertake a training role. Revised bids were submitted in June 2001 but there have been no further developments.
(3) There is a logistic craft P 140.

P 140 *10/2002* / 0587770

1 LOADMASTER MK 2 (LOGISTIC SUPPORT CRAFT) (LCU)

JALBOUT L 403

Displacement, tons: 420 full load
Dimensions, feet (metres): 108.3 × 33.5 × 5.7 *(33.0 × 10.2 × 1.75)*
Main machinery: 2 Caterpillar V12 diesels; 1,000 hp *(745 kW)*; 2 props
Speed, knots: 10
Complement: 7 (1 officer)
Radars: Navigation: I-band.

Comment: Built by Fairey Marine Cowes, UK and entered service in 1985. Captured by Iraqi forces in 1990 and subsequently recovered and reactivated in 1992.

L 403   *5/2001* / 0525907

2 AL TAHADDY CLASS (LCU)

Name	No	Builders	Commissioned
AL SOUMOOD	L 401	Singapore SBEC	July 1994
AL TAHADDY	L 402	Singapore SBEC	July 1994

Displacement, tons: 215 full load
Dimensions, feet (metres): 141.1 × 32.8 × 6.2 *(43 × 10 × 1.9)*
Main machinery: 2 MTU diesels; 2 shafts
Speed, knots: 13
Complement: 12
Military lift: 80 tons
Radars: Navigation: Racal Decca; I-band.

Comment: Ordered in 1993 and launched on 15 April 1994. Multipurpose supply ships with cargo tanks for fuel, fresh water, refrigerated stores and containers on the main deck. Has 3 ton crane. Capable of beaching. Used by the Coast Guard.

AL TAHADDY   *1/1999, Maritime Photographic* / 0053294

1 SUPPORT SHIP (AGH)

QARUH S 5509

Measurement, tons: 545 dwt
Dimensions, feet (metres): 181.8 × 31.5 × 6.6 *(55.4 × 9.6 × 2)*
Main machinery: 2 diesels; 2,400 hp(m) *(1.76 MW)*; 2 shafts
Speed, knots: 9
Complement: 40
Guns: 2—12.7 mm MGs.
Radars: Navigation: Racal Decca; I-band.

Comment: This is a Sawahil class oil rig replenishment and accommodation ship which was built in South Korea in 1986 and taken on by the Coast Guard in 1990. She escaped to Bahrain during the Iraqi invasion, and is back in service. High-level helicopter platform aft. Used as a utility transport. Refitted in 1996/97.

QARUH   *11/1997, Kuwait Navy* / 0012721

1 LANDING SUPPLY CRAFT (LCU)

Measurement, tons: 300 dwt
Dimensions, feet (metres): 160.8 × ? × ? *(49.0 × ? × ?)*
Main machinery: 2 diesels; 2 shafts
Speed, knots: 12
Complement: 12
Radars: Navigation: I-band.

Comment: Contract for the design and build of a landing craft signed with Singapore Technologies Marine Ltd (ST Marine) on 8 October 2004. The multipurpose vessel is to be used for transport and supply operations as well as law enforcement duties in the Arabian Gulf. In addition to carrying roll-on roll-off goods on the main deck, the vessel is also designed to transport liquid, refrigeration and general cargoes. Delivery of the ship was due in late 2005.

Latvia

LATVIJAS JURAS SPEKI

Country Overview

The Republic of Latvia regained independence in 1991 after 51 years as a Soviet republic. Situated in northeastern Europe, the country has an area of 24,938 square miles and borders to the north with Estonia, east with Russia and to the south with Belarus and Lithuania. It has a 286 n mile coastline with the Baltic Sea. Riga is the capital, largest city and principal port. Territorial seas (12 n miles) are claimed but while it has claimed a 200 n mile Exclusive Economic Zone (EEZ), its limits have not been fully defined by boundary agreements.

Headquarters Appointments

Commander of the Navy:
  Commander Aleksandrs Pavlovičs

Bases

Liepaja, Ventspils, Riga

Personnel

2006: 700 Navy (including Coast Guard)

Coastal Surveillance

Work began in 2002 on a maritime sea surveillance system which includes Swedish PS2-39 radars at Jurmalciens, Ventspils, Ovici and Kolka. The Latvian AIS (Automatic Indentification System) was commissioned in 2005 and is part of the HELCOM network that links other Baltic and Scandinavian navies. The Maritime Search and Rescue Coordination Centre (MRCC) is based at Riga.

Coast Guard

These ships have a diagonal thick white and thin white line on the hull, and have KA numbers. They operate as part of the Navy.

PATROL FORCES

Notes: A programme for replacement of the Storm class patrol craft with new 50 m craft is under consideration.

4 STORM CLASS (PB)

Name	No	Builders	Commissioned
ZIBENS (ex-*Djerv*)	P 01 (ex-P 966)	Westermoen, Mandal	1966
LODE (ex-*Hvass*)	P 02 (ex-P 972)	Westermoen, Mandal	1966
LINGA (ex-*Gnist*)	P 03 (ex-P 979)	Bergens Mek Verksteder	1967
BULTA (ex-*Traust*)	P 04 (ex-P 973)	Bergens Mek Verksteder	1967

Displacement, tons: 135 full load
Dimensions, feet (metres): 120 × 20 × 5 *(36.5 × 6.1 × 1.5)*
Main machinery: 2 MTU MB 872A diesels; 7,200 hp(m) *(5.3 MW)* sustained; 2 shafts
Speed, knots: 32
Complement: 20 (4 officers)
Guns: 1 Bofors 40 mm/60 (P 04). 1 TAK Bofors 76 mm; 1 Bofors 40 mm/70 (P 02 and P 03).
Radars: Surface search: Racal Decca TM 1226; I-band.

Comment: P 04 disarmed and acquired from Norway on 13 December 1994 as a gun patrol craft. Recommissioned 1 February 1995 at Liepaja. 40 mm gun fitted aft in 1998. P 01, P 02 and P 03 transferred from Norway and recommissioned 11 June 2001. Service lives extended to 2010. Other craft given to Lithuania and Estonia.

LODE   *6/2005*, Frank Findler* / 1133084

ZIBENS   *6/2004*, E & M Laursen* / 1133085

MINE WARFARE FORCES

1 LINDAU (TYPE 331) CLASS (MINEHUNTER) (MHC)

Name	No	Builders	Commissioned
NEMEJS (ex-*Völklingen*)	M 03 (ex-M 1087)	Burmester, Bremen	21 May 1960

Displacement, tons: 463 full load
Dimensions, feet (metres): 154.5 × 27.2 × 9.8 (9.2 Troika) *(47.1 × 8.3 × 3) (2.8)*
Main machinery: 2 MTU MD 871 UM/1D diesels; 4,000 hp(m) *(2.94 MW)*; 2 shafts
Speed, knots: 16.5
Range, n miles: 850 at 16.5 kt
Complement: 45 (9 officers)
Guns: 1 Bofors 40 mm/70.
Radars: Navigation: Raytheon, SPS 64; I-band.
Sonars: Plessey 193 m; minehunting; high frequency (100/300 kHz).

Comment: Acquired in June 1999 from Germany. Recommissioned 1 October 1999. Hull is of wooden construction. Converted to minehunter 1979. PAP 105 ROV fitted. Based at Lepaja. *Göttingen* transferred 24 January 2001 for spares.

NEMEJS   *6/2005*, M Declerck* / 1133082

2 KONDOR II (TYPE 89.2) CLASS (MINESWEEPERS) (MSC)

Name	No	Builders	Commissioned
VIESTURS (ex-*Kamenz*)	M 01 (ex-351)	Peenewerft, Wolgast	24 July 1971
IMANTA (ex-*Röbel*)	M 02 (ex-324)	Peenewerft, Wolgast	1 Dec 1971

Displacement, tons: 410 full load
Dimensions, feet (metres): 186 × 24.6 × 7.9 *(56.7 × 7.5 × 2.4)*
Main machinery: 2 Type 40D diesels; 4,408 hp(m) *(3.24 MW)*; 2 shafts; cp props
Speed, knots: 17
Complement: 31 (6 officers)
Guns: 2 Wrobel ZU 23-2MR 23 mm (twin). 2 FK 20 20 mm.
Radars: Surface search: Racal Decca; I-band.
Sonars: Klein 2000 sidescan; 100/500 kHz.

Comment: Former GDR vessels transferred from Germany on 30 August 1993. Weapons and minesweeping equipment were removed on transfer. New guns have been fitted and ex-German Shultz class minesweeping gear was installed in 1997. Both recommissioned in April 1994. Based at Liepaja.

VIESTURS   *6/2004, Harald Carstens* / 0587777

IMANTA   *8/2004, Guy Toremans* / 0587774

0 + 5 ALKMAAR (TRIPARTITE) CLASS (MINEHUNTERS) (MHC)

Name	No	Builders	Launched	Commissioned
— (ex-*Alkmaar*)	— (ex-M 850)	30 Jan 1979	18 May 1982	28 May 1983
— (ex-*Delfzyl*)	— (ex-M 851)	29 May 1980	29 Oct 1982	17 Aug 1983
— (ex-*Dordrecht*)	— (ex-M 852)	5 Jan 1981	26 Feb 1983	16 Nov 1983
— (ex-*Harlingen*)	— (ex-M 854)	30 Nov 1981	9 July 1983	12 Apr 1984
— (ex-*Scheveningen*)	— (ex-M 855)	24 May 1982	2 Dec 1983	18 July 1984

Displacement, tons: 562 standard; 595 full load
Dimensions, feet (metres): 168.9 × 29.2 × 8.5 *(51.5 × 8.9 × 2.6)*
Main machinery: 1 Stork Wärtsilä A-RUB 215X-12 diesel; 1,860 hp(m) *(1.35 MW)* sustained; 1 shaft; LIPS cp props; 2 active rudders; 2 motors; 240 hp(m) *(179 kW)*; 2 bow thrusters
Speed, knots: 15 diesel; 7 electric
Range, n miles: 3,000 at 12 kt
Complement: 29—42 depending on task

Guns: 1 Giat 20 mm.
Countermeasures: MCM: 2 PAP 104 remote-controlled submersibles. OD 3 mechanical minesweeping gear.
Combat data systems: Signaal Sewaco IX. SATCOM.
Radars: Navigation: Racal Decca TM 1229C or Consilium Selesmar MM 950; I-band.
Sonars: Thomson Sintra DUBM 21A; hull-mounted; minehunting; 100 kHz (±10 kHz).

Programmes: Originally procured for the Royal Netherlands Navy, these ships were part of the Netherlands commitment to a tripartite co-operative plan between Netherlands, Belgium and France for GRP hulled minehunters. All five ships built by van der Giessen-de Noord. Ex-*Alkmaar*, *Delfzijl* and *Dordrecht* were withdrawn from RNLN service in 2000 and *Harlingen* and *Scheveningen* in 2003. The ships are to be transferred to Latvia between 2006 and 2008.
Modernisation: The ships are to be overhauled before entering Latvian service and a mid-life upgrade may also be considered.
Structure: A 5 ton container can be shipped, stored for varying tasks-research; patrol; extended diving; drone control.
Operational: Endurance, 15 days. Automatic radar navigation system. Automatic data processing and display. EVEC 20. Decca Hi-fix positioning system. Alcatel dynamic positioning system.

ALKMAAR CLASS   *6/2004*, M Declerck* / 1044158

AUXILIARIES

1 VIDAR CLASS (MCCS/AG)

Name	No	Builders	Launched	Commissioned
VIRSAITIS (ex-*Vale*)	A 53 (ex-N 53)	Mjellem and Karlsen, Bergen	5 Aug 1977	10 Feb 1978

Displacement, tons: 1,500 standard; 1,673 full load
Dimensions, feet (metres): 212.6 × 39.4 × 13.1 *(64.8 × 12 × 4)*
Main machinery: 2 Wichmann 7AX diesels; 4,200 hp(m) *(3.1 MW)*; 2 shafts; auxiliary motor; 425 hp(m) *(312 kW)*; bow thruster
Speed, knots: 15
Complement: 50
Guns: 2 Bofors 40 mm/70; 300 rds/min to 12 km *(6.6 n miles)*; weight of shell 0.96 kg.
Weapons control: TVT optronic director.
Radars: Surface search: 2 Racal Decca TM 1226; I-band.
Sonars: Simrad; hull-mounted; search and attack; medium/high frequency.

Programmes: Decommissioned from Norwegian Navy in 2001 and transferred to Latvia on 27 January 2003.
Operational: Former minelayer modified to undertake mine countermeasures command and support roles. Additional tasks are likely to include training and support of diving operations.

VIRSAITIS   *6/2005*, Per Körnefeldt* / 1133083

1 GOLIAT CLASS (PROJECT 667R) (ATA)

PERKONS A 18 (ex-H 18)

Displacement, tons: 150 full load
Dimensions, feet (metres): 70.2 × 20 × 8.5 *(21.4 × 6.1 × 2.6)*
Main machinery: 1 Buckau-Wolf 8NVD diesel; 300 hp(m) *(221 kW)*; 1 shaft
Speed, knots: 9
Complement: 8 (2 officers)

Comment: Built at Gdynia in the 1960s and transferred from Poland 16 November 1993 at Liepaja.

PERKONS   *4/1995, Hartmut Ehlers* / 0506239

1 NYRYAT 1 CLASS (DIVING TENDER) (YDT)

LIDAKA (ex-*Gefests*) A 51 (ex-A 101)

Displacement, tons: 92 standard; 116 full load
Dimensions, feet (metres): 93.8 × 17.1 × 5.6 *(28.6 × 5.2 × 1.7)*
Main machinery: 1 6CSP 28/3C diesel; 450 hp(m) *(331 kW)*; 1 shaft
Speed, knots: 11
Range, n miles: 1,500 at 10 kt
Complement: 18 (3 officers)
Radars: Navigation: SNN-7; I-band.

Comment: Former SAR vessel acquired in 1992. Based at Liepaja.

LIDAKA   *9/1996, Hartmut Ehlers* / 0506305

1 LOGISTICS VESSEL (AKS/AXL)

Name	No	Builders	Commissioned
VARONIS (ex-*Buyskes*)	A 90 (ex-A 904)	Boele's Scheepswerven	9 Mar 1973

Displacement, tons: 967 standard; 1,033 full load
Dimensions, feet (metres): 196.6 × 36.4 × 12 *(60 × 11.1 × 3.7)*
Main machinery: Diesel-electric; 3 Paxman 12 RPH diesel generators; 2,100 hp *(1.57 MW)*; 1 motor; 1,400 hp(m) *(1.03 MW)*; 1 shaft
Speed, knots: 13.5
Range, n miles: 3,000 at 11.5 kt
Complement: 43 (6 officers)
Radars: Navigation: Racal Decca 1229; I-band.
Sonars: Side scanning and wreck search.

Comment: Originally designed and operated as a hydrographic vessel by the Royal Netherlands Navy from which she was decommissioned in 2003. Donated to Latvia on 8 November 2004 for use as a logistic and training vessel. Hydrographic launches were not transferred and the ship is fitted with an inflatable boat.

VARONIS (Netherlands colours)   *5/2000, van Ginderen Collection* / 0105152

COAST GUARD

1 RIBNADZOR-4 CLASS (WPB)

COMETA KA 03 (ex-KA 103)

Displacement, tons: 160 full load
Dimensions, feet (metres): 114.8 × 22 × 5.6 *(35 × 6.7 × 1.7)*
Main machinery: 1 40 DMM3 diesel; 2,200 hp(m) *(1.62 MW)*; 1 shaft
Speed, knots: 15
Complement: 17 (3 officers)
Guns: 1 — 12.7 mm MG.
Radars: Surface search: MIUS; I-band.

Comment: Ex-fishing vessel built in 1978 and converted in 1992. Recommissioned 5 May 1992 at Bolderaja. Refitted in 1998. Belongs to Coast Guard. Sister ship *Spulga* lost in 2000.

COMETA   *8/1994, E & M Laursen* / 0081182

5 KBV 236 CLASS (WPB)

KRISTAPS KA 01 (ex-KBV 244)	**SAULE** KA 08 (ex-KBV 256)
GAISMA KA 06 (ex-KBV 249)	**KLINTS** KA 09 (ex-KBV 250)
AUSMA KA 07 (ex-KBV 260)	

Displacement, tons: 17 full load
Dimensions, feet (metres): 63 × 13.1 × 4.3 *(19.2 × 4 × 1.3)*
Main machinery: 2 Volvo Penta TMD 100C diesels; 526 hp(m) *(387 kW)*; 2 shafts
Speed, knots: 20
Complement: 3 (1 officer)
Radars: Navigation: Raytheon or Furuno; I-band.

Comment: Former Swedish Coast Guard vessel built in 1964. First one recommissioned 5 March 1993, second pair 9 November 1993 and last pair 27 April 1994. KA 01, 06 and 09 are based at Bolderaja, 07 at Liepaja and 08 at Ventspils. Not all are identical. All belong to Coast Guard.

GAISMA   *8/2004, Guy Toremans* / 0587773

SAULE   *10/2000, van Ginderen Collection* / 0114738

1 LOKKI CLASS (PB)

TIIRA

Displacement, tons: 76 full load
Dimensions, feet (metres): 87.9 × 18 × 6.2 *(26.8 × 5.5 × 1.9)*
Main machinery: 2 MTU 8V 396 TB82 diesels; 1,740 hp(m) *(1.28 MW)* sustained
2 MTU 8V 396 TB84 diesels; 2,100 hp(m) *(1.54 MW)* sustained; 2 shafts
Speed, knots: 25
Complement: 6

Comment: Donated by Finland in 2001. Armament and sonar removed.

LOKKI class (Finnish colours) *6/2001, Finnish Navy* / 0114723

1 PATROL CRAFT (WPB)

ASTRA KA 14

Displacement, tons: 22 full load
Dimensions, feet (metres): 74.8 × 18.4 × 9.2 *(22.8 × 5.6 × 2.8)*
Main machinery: 3 Scania D91 1467M diesels; 1,850 hp *(1.38 MW)*
Speed, knots: 25
Range, n miles: 575 at 25 kt
Complement: 4 (1 officer)
Radars: Navigation: Furuno; I-band.

Comment: Built in Finland in 1996. Commissioned on 12 March 2001.

ASTRA *4/2002, Guy Toremans* / 0524992

3 HARBOUR PATROL CRAFT (WPB)

KA 10   **KA 11**   **GRANATA KA 12**

Displacement, tons: 9.6 full load *(KA 10-11)*; 5.4 full load *(KA 12)*
Dimensions, feet (metres): 41.3 × 10.5 × 2 *(12.6 × 3.2 × 0.6)*
Main machinery: 1 3D6C diesel; 150 hp(m) *(110 kW)*; 1 shaft
Speed, knots: 13
Complement: 2
Radars: Navigation: Furuno; I-band.

Comment: Former USSR craft. *KA 10* and *11* were Sverdlov class cruiser boats. KA 12 is an ex-Border Guard launch of 9 m with a 300 hp(m) *(220 kW)* engine and a speed of 18 kt. All acquired in 1993-94. All belong to Coast Guard.

KA 11 *9/1996, Hartmut Ehlers* / 0506304

1 VALPAS CLASS (OFFSHORE PATROL VESSEL) (WPBO)

VALPAS

Displacement, tons: 545 full load
Dimensions, feet (metres): 159.1 × 27.9 × 12.5 *(48.5 × 8.5 × 3.8)*
Main machinery: 1 Werkspoor diesel; 2,000 hp(m) *(1.47 MW)*; 1 shaft; cp prop
Speed, knots: 15
Complement: 18
Guns: 1 Oerlikon 20 mm.
Sonars: Simrad SS105; active scanning; 14 kHz.

Comment: An improvement on the *Silmä* design. Built by Laivateollisuus, Turku, and commissioned 21 July 1971. Ice strengthened. Donated by Finland on 25 September 2002 and operated by State Border Security Service.

VALPAS *5/2003, J Cíślak* / 0568321

Lebanon

Country Overview

The Lebanese Republic gained independence from France in 1946 but was devastated by civil war between 1975-1991. Situated on the eastern shore of the Mediterranean Sea, it has an area of 4,015 square miles and is bordered to the north and east by Syria and to the south by Israel. It has a 121 n mile coastline with the Mediterranean Sea.

The capital, largest city and principal port is Beirut. Other important ports include Tripoli and Sidon. Territorial seas (12 n miles) are claimed but an EEZ is not claimed.

Headquarters Appointments

Navy Commander:
Major General Georges Chehwan

Personnel

2006: 1,100 (395 officers)

Bases

Beirut (HQ), Jounieh

PATROL FORCES

2 FRENCH EDIC CLASS (LST)

Name	No	Builders	Commissioned
SOUR	21	SFCN, Villeneuve la Garonne	28 Mar 1985
DAMOUR	22	SFCN, Villeneuve la Garonne	28 Mar 1985

Displacement, tons: 670 full load
Dimensions, feet (metres): 193.5 × 39.2 × 4.2 *(59 × 12 × 1.3)*
Main machinery: 2 SACM MGO 175 V12 M1 diesels; 1,200 hp(m) *(882 kW)*; 2 shafts
Speed, knots: 10. **Range, n miles:** 1,800 at 9 kt
Complement: 20 (2 officers)
Military lift: 96 troops; 11 trucks or 8 APCs
Guns: 2 Oerlikon 20 mm. 1 — 81 mm mortar. 2 — 12.7 mm MGs. 1 — 7.62 mm MG.
Radars: Navigation: Decca; I-band.

Comment: Both were damaged in early 1990 but repaired in 1991 and are fully operational. Used by the Marine Regiment formed in 1997.

DAMOUR *2/2000* / 0097755

For details of the latest updates to *Jane's Fighting Ships* online and to discover the additional information available exclusively to online subscribers please visit

jfs.janes.com

2 TRACKER MK 2 CLASS (COASTAL PATROL CRAFT) (PB)

SARAFAND (ex-*Swift*) 307   **BATROUN** (ex-*Safeguard*) 303

Displacement, tons: 31 full load
Dimensions, feet (metres): 63.3 × 16.4 × 4.9 *(19.3 × 5 × 1.5)*
Main machinery: 2 Detroit 12V-71TA diesels; 840 hp *(616 kW)* sustained; 2 shafts
Speed, knots: 25
Range, n miles: 650 at 20 kt
Complement: 13 (1 officer)
Guns: 3 — 12.7 mm MGs.
Radars: Surface search: Racal Decca 1216; I-band.

Comment: Two ex-UK Customs Craft first commissioned in 1979 and acquired by Lebanon in late 1993. Fitted with a twin 23 mm gun after transfer but this may have been replaced by a 12.7 mm MG.

SIDON   *2/2000* / 0097756

BATROUN   *6/1999, Lebanese Navy* / 0081188

5 ATTACKER CLASS (COASTAL PATROL CRAFT) (PB)

TRIPOLI (ex-*Attacker*) 301   **BYBLOS** (ex-*Chaser*) 304   **SIDON** (ex-*Striker*) 306
JOUNIEH (ex-*Fencer*) 302   **BEIRUT** (ex-*HunterII*) 305

Displacement, tons: 38 full load
Dimensions, feet (metres): 65.6 × 17 × 4.9 *(20 × 5.2 × 1.5)*
Main machinery: 2 Detroit 12V-71TA diesels; 840 hp *(616 kW)* sustained; 2 shafts
Speed, knots: 21
Range, n miles: 650 at 14 kt
Complement: 13 (1 officer)
Guns: 3 — 12.7 mm MGs.
Radars: Surface search: Racal Decca 1216; I-band.

Comment: Built at Cowes and Southampton, and commissioned in March 1983. First three transferred from UK 17 July 1992 after serving as patrol craft for the British base in Cyprus. The other two were acquired in 1993. All are operational.

25 INSHORE PATROL CRAFT (PBR)

401   403-418   420-427

Displacement, tons: 6 full load
Dimensions, feet (metres): 26.9 × 8.2 × 2 *(8.2 × 2.5 × 0.6)*
Main machinery: 2 Sabre 212 diesels; 212 hp(m) *(156 kW)*; 2 waterjets
Speed, knots: 22. **Range, n miles:** 154 at 22 kt
Complement: 4
Guns: 3 — 5.56 mm MGs.

Comment: M-boot type used by the US Army on German rivers and 27 were transferred in January 1994. Called Combat Support Boats, there are 20 operational and five laid up. Two were decommissioned in 2002.

CSB   *6/1998, Lebanese Navy* / 0052571

Libya

Country Overview

The Socialist People's Libyan Arab Jamahiriyah is situated in north Africa. With an area of 679,362 square miles, it has a 956 n mile coastline with the Mediterranean Sea and is bordered to the east by Egypt, to the south by Sudan, Chad and Niger and to the west by Algeria and Tunisia. The capital and largest city is Tripoli which, with Benghazi, is a principal port. Territorial seas (12 n miles) are claimed. An EEZ has not been claimed. The status of the Gulf of Sirte, which Libya claims as internal waters, is disputed by numerous states including USA, United Kingdom, France, Italy and Greece.

Headquarters Appointments

Chief of Staff Navy:
Rear Admiral Muhammad al Shaybani Ahmad al Suwaihili

Deputy Chief of Staff Navy:
Captain al-Din Mufti

Personnel

(a) 2006: 8,000 officers and ratings, including Coast Guard
(b) Voluntary service

Bases

Naval HQ at Al Khums.
Operating Ports at Tripoli, Darnah (Derna) and Benghazi.
Naval bases at Al Khums and Tobruq.
Submarine base at Ras Hilal.
Naval air station at Al Girdabiyah.
Naval infantry battalion at Sidi Bilal.

Coast Defence

Batteries of truck-mounted SS-C-3 Styx missiles.

General

Specialist teams in unconventional warfare are a threat and most Libyan vessels can lay mines, but overall operational effectiveness is very low, not least because of poor maintenance and stores support. Sanctions imposed by the UN in April 1992 were reported as 'destroying' the Fleet. The situation improved in late 1995 when mostly Ukrainian technicians were hired on maintenance contracts. Further progress was reported in 1998 and the situation could improve following the lifting of UN sanctions on 12 September 2003. The EU arms embargo was lifted on 11 October 2004 although export licences are still required.

SUBMARINES

2 FOXTROT CLASS (PROJECT 641) (SS)

AL KHYBER 315   **AL HUNAIN** 316

Displacement, tons: 1,950 surfaced; 2,475 dived
Dimensions, feet (metres): 299.5 × 24.6 × 19.7 *(91.3 × 7.5 × 6)*
Main machinery: Diesel-electric; 3 Type 37-D diesels (1 × 2,700 and 2 × 1,350); 6,000 hp(m) *(4.4 MW)*; 3 motors; 5,400 hp(m) *(3.97 MW)*; 3 shafts; 1 auxiliary motor; 140 hp(m) *(103 kW)*
Speed, knots: 16 surfaced; 15 dived
Range, n miles: 20,000 at 8 kt surfaced; 380 at 2 kt dived
Complement: 75 (8 officers)

Torpedoes: 10 — 21 in *(533 mm)* (6 bow, 4 stern) tubes. SAET-60; passive homing to 15 km *(8.1 n miles)* at 40 kt; warhead 400 kg, and SET-65E; active/passive homing to 15 km *(8.1 n miles)* at 40 kt; warhead 205 kg or Type 53-56. Total of 22 torpedoes.
Mines: 44 in place of torpedoes.
Countermeasures: ESM: Stop Light; radar warning.
Radars: Surface search: Snoop Tray; I-band.
Sonars: Herkules; hull-mounted; active; medium frequency.
Feniks; hull-mounted; passive.

Programmes: Six of the class originally transferred from USSR; this last one in April 1982.
Operational: Libyan crews trained in the USSR and much of the maintenance was done by Russian personnel. No routine patrols have been seen since 1984 although both boats have been reported to conduct surface patrols. One submarine was reported to be in dry dock at Tripoli during 2003 but, in view of the poor material state of these submarines, a return to full operational capability remains highly unlikely.

FOXTROT   *6/1992, van Ginderen Collection* / 0081190

FRIGATES

Notes: The *Dat Assawari* F 211 is a training hulk alongside in Tripoli.

2 KONI (PROJECT 1159) CLASS (FFGM)

AL HANI PF 212   **AL QIRDABIYAH** PF 213

Displacement, tons: 1,440 standard; 1,900 full load
Dimensions, feet (metres): 316.3 × 41.3 × 11.5
 (96.4 × 12.6 × 3.5)
Main machinery: CODAG; 1 SGW, Nikolayev, M8B
 gas turbine (centre shaft); 18,000 hp(m) *(13.25 MW)*
 sustained; 2 Russki B-68 diesels; 15,820 hp(m) *(11.63 MW)*
 sustained; 3 shafts
Speed, knots: 27 on gas; 22 on diesel
Range, n miles: 1,800 at 14 kt
Complement: 120

Missiles: SSM: 4 Soviet SS-N-2C Styx (2 twin) launchers ❶;
 active radar/IR homing to 83 km *(45 n miles)* at 0.9 Mach;
 warhead 513 kg; sea-skimmer at end of run.
SAM: SA-N-4 Gecko twin launcher ❷; semi-active radar
 homing to 15 km *(8 n miles)* at 2.5 Mach; altitude
 9.1—3,048 m *(29.5—10,000 ft)*; warhead 50 kg; 20 missiles.
Guns: 4 USSR 3 in *(76 mm)*/60 (2 twin) ❸; 60 rds/min to
 15 km *(8 n miles)* anti-surface; 14 km *(7.6 n miles)* anti-
 aircraft; weight of shell 6.8 kg.
 4 USSR 30 mm/65 (2 twin) automatic ❹; 500 rds/min to
 2 km *(1.1 n miles)*; weight of shell 0.54 kg.
Torpedoes: 4—406 mm (2 twin) tubes amidships ❺. USET-95;
 active/passive homing to 10 km *(5.5 n miles)* at 30 kt;
 warhead 100 kg.
A/S mortars: 1 RBU 6000 12-tubed trainable launcher ❻;
 automatic loading; range 6,000 m; warhead 31 kg.

Depth charges: 2 racks.
Mines: Capacity for 20.
Countermeasures: Decoys: 2—16-barrelled chaff launchers.
 Towed torpedo decoys.
ESM: 2 Watch Dog; radar warning.
Radars: Air search: Strut Curve ❼; F-band; range 110 km
 (60 n miles) for 2 m² target.
Surface search: Plank Shave ❽; E/F-band.
Navigation: Don 2; I-band.
Fire control: Drum Tilt ❾; H/I-band (for 30 mm).
 Hawk Screech ❿; I-band; range 27 km *(15 n miles)* (for
 76 mm).
 Pop Group ⓫; F/H/I-band (for SAM).
IFF: High Pole B. Square Head.
Sonars: Hercules (MG 322); hull-mounted; active search and
 attack; medium frequency.

Programmes: Type III Konis built at Zelenodolsk and
 transferred from the Black Sea. 212 commissioned
 28 June 1986 and 213 on 24 October 1987.
Structure: SSMs mounted either side of small deckhouse
 on forecastle behind gun. A deckhouse amidships
 contains air conditioning machinery. Changes to the
 standard Koni include SSM, four torpedo tubes, only
 one RBU 6000 and Plank Shave surface search and
 target indication radar. Camouflage paint applied in
 1991.
Operational: One of the class fired an exercise Styx missile
 in September 1999. 213 has been reported active but
 212 may be in reserve.

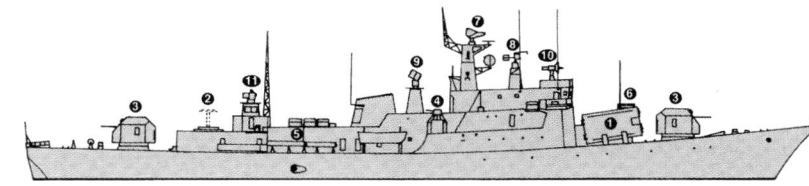

AL HANI   *(Scale 1 : 900), Ian Sturton* / 0506050

AL HANI   *7/1999, van Ginderen Collection* / 0081191

CORVETTES

1 NANUCHKA II (PROJECT 1234) CLASS (MISSILE CORVETTE) (FSGM)

TARIQ IBN ZIYAD (ex-*Ean Mara*) 416

Displacement, tons: 660 full load
Dimensions, feet (metres): 194.5 × 38.7 × 8.5
 (59.3 × 11.8 × 2.6)
Main machinery: 6 M 504 diesels; 26,112 hp(m) *(19.2 MW)*;
 3 shafts
Speed, knots: 33. **Range, n miles:** 2,500 at 12 kt; 900 at 31 kt
Complement: 42 (7 officers)

Missiles: SSM: 4 Soviet SS-N-2C Styx launchers; auto-pilot;
 active radar/IR homing to 83 km *(45 n miles)* at 0.9 Mach;
 warhead 513 kg HE; sea-skimmer at end of run.
SAM: SA-N-4 Gecko twin launcher; semi-active radar homing
 to 15 km *(8 n miles)* at 2.5 Mach; altitude 9.1—3,048 m
 (29.5—10,000 ft); warhead 50 kg HE; 20 missiles.
Guns: 2 USSR 57 mm/80 (twin) automatic; 120 rds/min to
 6 km *(3.2 n miles)*; weight of shell 2.8 kg.
Countermeasures: Decoys: 2 chaff 16-barrelled launchers.
ESM: Bell Tap; radar warning.
Radars: Surface search: Square Tie; I-band (Bandstand
 radome).
Navigation: Don 2; I-band.
Fire control: Muff Cob; G/H-band.
 Pop Group; F/H/I-band (for SAM).

Programmes: First transferred from USSR in October 1981;
 second in February 1983; third in February 1984; fourth in
 September 1985.

TARIQ IBN ZIYAD   *7/1991, van Ginderen Collection* / 0081192

Structure: Camouflage paint applied in 1991 but have been
 reported as having blue hulls since 1993.
Operational: *Ean Zaquit* (419) sunk on 24 March 1986.
 Ean Mara (416) severely damaged on 25 March
 1986 by forces of the US Sixth Fleet; repaired in

Leningrad and returned to Libya in early 1991 as
 the *Tariq Ibn Ziyad*. *Ean Al Gazala* (417) probably in
 reserve as a source of spares and *Ean Zarrah* (418)
 reported non-operational. Reports of refit plans are
 doubtful.

LAND-BASED MARITIME AIRCRAFT

Numbers/Type: 2/5 Aerospatiale SA 321 Frelon/Aerospatiale SA 324 Super Frelon.
Operational speed: 134 kt *(248 km/h)*.
Service ceiling: 10,000 ft *(3,050 m)*.
Range: 440 n miles *(815 km)*.
Role/Weapon systems: Obsolescent helicopter; Air Force manned but used for naval support tasks. Most are non-operational due to lack of spares. Sensors: None. Weapons: Fitted for Exocet AM 39.

Numbers/Type: 5 Aerospatiale SA 316B Alouette III.
Operational speed: 113 kt *(210 km/h)*.
Service ceiling: 10,500 ft *(3,200 m)*.
Range: 290 n miles *(540 km)*.
Role/Weapon systems: Support helicopter. Probably non-operational. Another six are used by the Police. Sensors: None. Weapons: Unarmed.

PATROL FORCES

Notes: (1) More than 50 remote-control explosive craft acquired from Cyprus. Based on Q-Boats with Q-26 GRP hulls and speed of about 30 kt. Also reported that 15 31 ft craft delivered by Storebro, and 60 more built locally are similarly adapted. No reports of recent activity.
(2) There is also a Hamelin 37 m patrol craft *Al Ziffa* 206 based at Tripoli.

6 OSA II (PROJECT 205) CLASS
(FAST ATTACK CRAFT—MISSILE) (PTFG)

AL ZUARA 513	**AL FIKAH** 523	**AL BITAR** 531
AL RUHA 515	**AL MATHUR** 525	**AL SADAD** 533

Displacement, tons: 245 full load
Dimensions, feet (metres): 126.6 × 24.9 × 8.8 *(38.6 × 7.6 × 2.7)*
Main machinery: 3 Type M 504 diesels; 10,800 hp(m) *(7.94 MW)* sustained; 3 shafts
Speed, knots: 37
Range, n miles: 800 at 30 kt; 500 at 35 kt
Complement: 30

Missiles: SSM: 4 Soviet SS-N-2C Styx; active radar or IR homing to 83 km *(45 n miles)* at 0.9 Mach; warhead 513 kg HE; sea-skimmer at end of run.
Guns: 4 USSR 30 mm/65 (2 twin) automatic; 500 rds/min to 5 km *(2.7 n miles)*; weight of shell 0.54 kg.
Radars: Surface search: Square Tie; I-band; range 73 km *(45 n miles)*.
Fire control: Drum tilt; H/I-band.
IFF: 2 Square Head. High Pole.

Programmes: The first craft arrived from USSR in October 1976, four more in August-October 1977, a sixth in July 1978, three in September-October 1979, one in April 1980, one in May 1980 (521) and one in July 1980 (529).
Structure: Some painted with camouflage stripes in 1991 and some were given blue hulls in 1993.
Operational: There have been few sightings of these ships at sea in recent years. One fired an exercise Styx missile in September 1999. Six further craft inactive alongside. *Al Sadad* 533 also reported non-operational. Based at Tobruk.

AL MATHUR *1993* / 0506157

8 COMBATTANTE II G CLASS
(FAST ATTACK CRAFT—MISSILE) (PGGF)

SHARABA (ex-*Beir Grassa*) 518	**SHOULA** (ex-*Beir Ktitat*) 532
SHEHAB (ex-*Beir Gtifa*) 522	**SHAFAK** (ex-*Beir Alkrarim*) 534
WAHAG (ex-*Beir Gzir*) 524	**RAD** (ex-*Beir Alkur*) 538
SHOUAIAI (ex-*Beir Algandula*) 528	**LAHEEB** (ex-*Beir Alkuefat*) 542

Displacement, tons: 311 full load
Dimensions, feet (metres): 160.7 × 23.3 × 6.6 *(49 × 7.1 × 2)*
Main machinery: 4 MTU 20V 538 TB91 diesels; 15,360 hp(m) *(11.29 MW)* sustained; 4 shafts
Speed, knots: 39
Range, n miles: 1,600 at 15 kt
Complement: 27

Missiles: SSM: 4 OTO Melara/Matra Otomat Mk 2 (TG1); active radar homing to 80 km *(43.2 n miles)* at 0.9 Mach; warhead 210 kg.
Guns: 1 OTO Melara 3 in *(76 mm)*/62 compact; 85 rds/min to 16 km *(8.6 n miles)* anti-surface; 12 km *(6.8 n miles)* anti-aircraft; weight of shell 6 kg.
2 Breda 40 mm/70 (twin); 300 or 450 rds/min to 12.5 km *(6.8 n miles)* anti-surface; 4 km *(2.2 n miles)* anti-aircraft; weight of shell 0.96 kg.
Weapons control: CSEE Panda director. Thomson-CSF Vega II system.
Radars: Surface search: Thomson-CSF Triton; G-band; range 33 km *(18 n miles)* for 2 m² target.
Fire control: Thomson-CSF Castor IIB; I-band; range 15 km *(8 n miles)* (associated with Vega fire-control system).

Programmes: Ordered from CMN Cherbourg in May 1977. 518 completed February 1982; 522 3 April 1982; 524 29 May 1982; 528 5 September 1982; 532 29 October 1982; 534 17 December 1982; 542 29 July 1983.
Structure: Steel hull with alloy superstructure.
Operational: *Waheed* (526) sunk on 24 March 1986 and one other severely damaged on 25 March 1986 by forces of the US Sixth Fleet. 524, 534 and 542 visited Malta in late 2001. *Shoula* (532) reported non-operational but continued activity suggests that the remaining craft are at least partly operational.

SHAFAK *1993* / 0506156

AMPHIBIOUS FORCES

Notes: Three Polochny D class landing craft (112, 116 and 118) are in reserve and are unlikely to be restored to operational status.

1 PS 700 CLASS (LSTH)

Name	No	Builders	Commissioned
IBN HARISSA	134	CNI de la Mediterranée	10 Mar 1978

Displacement, tons: 2,800 full load
Dimensions, feet (metres): 326.4 × 51.2 × 7.9 *(99.5 × 15.6 × 2.4)*
Main machinery: 2 SEMT-Pielstick 16 PA4 V 185 diesels; 5,344 hp(m) *(3.93 MW)* sustained; 2 shafts; cp props
Speed, knots: 15.4
Range, n miles: 4,000 at 14 kt
Complement: 35
Military lift: 240 troops; 11 tanks
Guns: 6 Breda 40 mm/70 (3 twin). 1—81 mm mortar.
Weapons control: CSEE Panda director.
Radars: Air search: Thomson-CSF Triton; D-band.
Surface search: Decca 1226; I-band.
Helicopters: 1 Aerospatiale SA 316B Alouette III.

Comment: Laid down 18 April 1977, launched 18 October 1977. Remains active although 40 mm guns appear to have been removed. The status of *Ibn Ouf* 132 is unclear.

IBN HARISSA *5/2004*, Italian Navy* / 1153376

3 TURKISH Ç 107 CLASS (LCT)

IBN AL IDRISI 130	**IBN MARWAN** 131	**EL KOBAYAT** 132

Displacement, tons: 280 standard; 600 full load
Dimensions, feet (metres): 183.7 × 37.8 × 3.6 *(56 × 11.6 × 1.1)*
Main machinery: 3 GM 6-71TI diesels; 930 hp *(694 kW)* maximum; 3 shafts
Speed, knots: 8.5 loaded; 10 max
Range, n miles: 600 at 10 kt
Complement: 15
Military lift: 100 troops; 350 tons including 5 tanks
Guns: 2—30 mm (twin).

Comment: First two transferred 7 December 1979 (ex-Turkish *C130* and *C131*) from Turkish fleet. Third of class reported in 1991. Previously reported numbers were much exaggerated. Not reported at sea in recent years and operational status of all three ships is doubtful.

TURKISH LCT (Turkish colours) *10/1991, Harald Carstens* / 0506053

2 SLINGSBY SAH 2200 (HOVERCRAFT) (UCAC)

Displacement, tons: 5.5 full load
Dimensions, feet (metres): 34.8 × 13.8 *(10.6 × 4.2)*
Main machinery: 1 diesel; 300 hp(m) *(224 kW)*
Speed, knots: 40
Range, n miles: 400 at 30 kt
Complement: 2
Military lift: 2.2 tons
Guns: 1—12.7 mm MG.
Radars: Surface search: I-band.

Comment: Ordered in September 1999 for delivery to Greece in mid-2000 and subsequently to Libya in 2001.

MINE WARFARE FORCES

5 NATYA (PROJECT 266ME) CLASS
(OCEAN MINESWEEPERS) (MSO)

AL TIYAR (ex-*Ras Hadad*) 111	**RAS AL FULAIJAH** 117	**RAS AL HANI** 125
AL ISAR (ex-*Ras El Gelais*) 113	**RAS AL MASSAD** 123	

Displacement, tons: 804 full load
Dimensions, feet (metres): 200.1 × 33.5 × 10.8 *(61 × 10.2 × 3)*
Main machinery: 2 Type M 504 diesels; 5,000 hp(m) *(3.67 MW)* sustained; 2 shafts; cp props
Speed, knots: 16. **Range, n miles:** 3,000 at 12 kt
Complement: 67
Guns: 4 USSR 30 mm/65 (2 twin) automatic; 500 rds/min to 5 km *(2.7 n miles)*; weight of shell 0.54 kg.
   4 USSR 25 mm/60 (2 twin); 270 rds/min to 3 km *(1.6 n miles)*; weight of shell 0.34 kg.
A/S mortars: 2 RBU 1200 5-tubed fixed launchers; elevating; range 1,200 m; warhead 34 kg.
Mines: 10.
Countermeasures: MCM: 1 GKT-2 contact sweep; 1 AT-2 acoustic sweep; 1 TEM-3 magnetic sweep.
Radars: Surface search: Don 2; I-band.
Fire control: Drum Tilt; H/I-band.
IFF: 2 Square Head. 1 High Pole B.
Sonars: Hull-mounted; active search; high frequency.

Comment: Transferred from USSR between 1981 and 1986. At least one of the class painted in green striped camouflage in 1991. Others may have blue hulls. Capable of magnetic, acoustic and mechanical sweeping. Mostly used for coastal patrols and never observed minesweeping. *Ras Al Massad* has been used for training cruises. *Ras Al Hamman* (115), *Ras Al Qula* (119) and *Ras Al Madwar* are inactive.

NATYA   *2/1988* / 0506051

AUXILIARIES

Notes: (1) *Zeltin* 711 is used as an alongside tender for patrol forces but is no longer capable of going to sea.
(2) The Vosper class *Tobruk* is used for alongside training.

10 TRANSPORTS (AG/ML)

GARYOUNIS (ex-*Mashu*)	**EL TEMSAH**	**DERNA**	**GHAT**
GARNATA (ex-*Monte Granada*)	**TOLETELA** (ex-*Monte Toledo*)	**RAHMA** (ex-*Krol*)	**LA GRAZIETTA**
HANNA	**GHARDIA**		

Measurement, tons: 2,412 gross
Dimensions, feet (metres): 546.3 × 80.1 × 21.3 *(166.5 × 24.4 × 6.5)*
Main machinery: 2 SEMT-Pielstick diesels; 20,800 hp(m) *(15.29 MW)*; 2 shafts; bow thruster
Speed, knots: 20

Comment: Details are for *Garyounis*, a converted Ro-Ro passenger/car ferry used as a training vessel in 1989. In addition the 117 m *El Temsah* was refitted and another four of these vessels are of Ro-Ro design. All are in regular civilian service and *Garyounis* is also used by the military. All have minelaying potential.

GARNATA   *8/2004*, Martin Mokrus* / 1153372

1 SPASILAC CLASS (SALVAGE SHIP) (ARS)

AL MUNJED (ex-*Zlatica*) 722

Displacement, tons: 1,590 full load
Dimensions, feet (metres): 182 × 39.4 × 14.1 *(55.5 × 12 × 4.3)*
Main machinery: 2 diesels; 4,340 hp(m) *(3.19 MW)*; 2 shafts; cp props; bow thruster
Speed, knots: 13. **Range, n miles:** 4,000 at 12 kt
Complement: 50
Guns: 4—12.7 mm MGs. Can also be fitted with 8—20 mm (2 quad) and 2—20 mm.
Radars: Surface search: Racal Decca; I-band.

Comment: Transferred from Yugoslavia in 1982. Fitted for firefighting, towing and submarine rescue-carries recompression chamber. Built at Tito SY, Belgrade. Used as the lead vessel for the 1998 training cruise, and is probably not operational.

SPASILAC (Iraqi colours)   *1988, Peter Jones* / 0506054

1 YELVA (PROJECT 535M) CLASS (DIVING TENDER) (YDT)

AL MANOUD PVM 917

Displacement, tons: 300 full load
Dimensions, feet (metres): 134.2 × 26.2 × 6.6 *(40.9 × 8 × 2)*
Main machinery: 2 Type 3-D-12A diesels; 630 hp(m) *(463 kW)* sustained; 2 shafts
Speed, knots: 12.5
Complement: 30
Radars: Navigation: Spin trough; I-band.
IFF: High Pole.

Comment: Built in early 1970s. Transferred from USSR December 1977. Carries two 1.5 ton cranes and has a portable decompression chamber. Based at Tripoli and does not go to sea.

YELVA (Russian colours)   *7/1996, Hartmut Ehlers* / 0506306

2 FLOATING DOCKS

Comment: One of 5,000 tons capacity at Tripoli. One of 3,200 tons capacity acquired in April 1985.

TUGS

7 COASTAL TUGS (YTB)

RAS EL HELAL A 31	**AL KERIAT**	**A 33-35**
AL AHWEIRIF A 32	**AL TABKAH**	

Comment: First four of 34.8 m built in Portugal in 1976-78. Last three of 26.6 m built in the Netherlands in 1979-80. All are in service.

Lithuania

KARINËS JURØ PAJËGOS

Country Overview

The Republic of Lithuania regained independence in 1991 after 51 years as a Soviet republic. Situated in northeastern Europe, the country has an area of 25,175 square miles and borders to the north with Latvia, to the east and south with Belarus, to the southwest with Poland and the Russian exclave of Kaliningrad. It has a 58 n mile coastline with the Baltic Sea. Vilnius is the capital and largest city while Klaipeda is the principal port. Territorial seas (12 n miles) are claimed but while it has claimed a 200 n mile Exclusive Economic Zone (EEZ), its limits have not been fully defined by boundary agreements.

Headquarters Appointments

Commander of the Navy:
   Rear Admiral Kęstutis Macijauskas
Chief of Staff:
   Commander Oleg Marinic

Personnel

2006: 700

Bases

Klaipeda

State Border Police (Pakrančių Apsauga)

Coast Guard Force formed in late 1992. Name changed in 1996 to Border Police. Vessels have one thick and one thin diagonal yellow stripe on the hull.

FRIGATES

2 GRISHA III (ALBATROS) CLASS (PROJECT 1124M) (FFLM)

Name	No	Builders	Commissioned	Recommissioned
ŽEMAITIS	F 11 (ex-MPK 108)	Zelenodolsk Shipyard	1 Oct 1981	6 Nov 1992
AUKŠTAITIS	F 12 (ex-MPK 44)	Kiev Shipyard	15 Aug 1980	6 Nov 1992

Displacement, tons: 950 standard; 1,200 full load
Dimensions, feet (metres): 233.6 × 32.2 × 12.1
(71.2 × 9.8 × 3.7)
Main machinery: CODAG; 1 gas-turbine; 15,000 hp(m)
(11 MW); 2 diesels; 16,000 hp(m) *(11.8 MW)*; 3 shafts
Speed, knots: 30
Range, n miles: 2,500 at 14 kt diesels; 950 at 27 kt
Complement: 67 (9 officers)

Missiles: SAM: SA-N-4 Gecko twin launcher ❶; semi-
active radar homing to 15 km *(8 n miles)* at 2.5 Mach;
warhead 50 kg; altitude 9.1−3,048 m *(30−10,000 ft)*;
20 missiles.
Guns: 2−57 mm/80 (twin) ❷; 120 rds/min to 6 km
(3.3 n miles); weight of shell 2.8 kg.
1−30 mm/65 ❸; 6 barrels; 3,000 rds/min combined to 2 km.
2−12.7 mm MGs.
A/S mortars: 2 RBU 6000 12-tubed trainable ❹; range
6,000 m; warhead 31 kg.
Depth charges: 2 racks (12).
Mines: Capacity for 18 in lieu of depth charges.
Countermeasures: Decoys: 1 PK-16 (F 11) chaff launcher.
ESM: 2 Watch Dog.

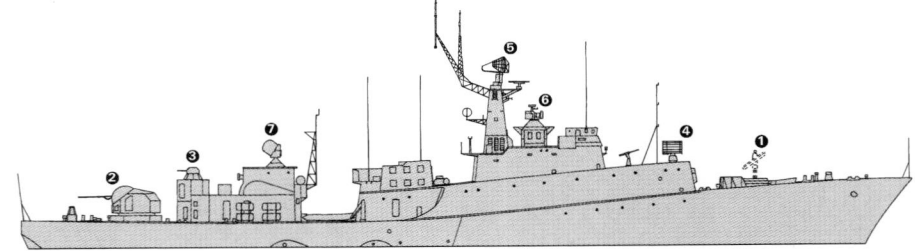

AUKŠTAITIS

(Scale 1 : 600), Ian Sturton / 0587562

Radars: Air/surface search: Strut Curve ❺; F-band.
Navigation: Terma Scanter; I-band.
Fire control: Pop Group ❻; F/H/I-band (for SA-N-4). Bass
Tilt ❼; H/I-band (for guns).
Sonars: Bull Nose; hull-mounted; active search and attack;
high/medium frequency.

Programmes: Transferred from the Russian Baltic Fleet
in 1993.
Modernisation: Torpedo tubes removed from F 12 in 1996
and from F 11 in 1997.
Operational: Expected to remain in service until at
least 2008.

ŽEMAITIS

6/2004, Harald Carstens / 0589759

ŽEMAITIS

6/2005*, Frank Findler / 1133087

PATROL FORCES

Notes: Acquisition of patrol craft is reported to be under consideration. Possibilities include surplus Danish Flyvefisken class that are to be decommissioned by 2009.

3 STORM CLASS (PB)

Name	No	Builders	Commissioned
DZŪKAS (ex-Kjekk)	P 31 (ex-P 965)	Bergens Mek Verksteder	1966
SELIS (ex-Skudd)	P 32 (ex-P 967)	Bergens Mek Verksteder	1966
SKALVIS (ex-Steil)	P 33 (ex-P 969)	Westermoen, Mandal	1967

Displacement, tons: 138 full load
Dimensions, feet (metres): 120 × 20.3 × 5.9 (36.5 × 6.2 × 1.8)
Main machinery: 2 MTU MB 16V 538TB90 diesels; 6,000 hp(m) (4.41 MW) sustained; 2 shafts
Speed, knots: 32. **Range, n miles:** 550 at 32 kt
Complement: 23 (4 officers)
Guns: 1 Bofors 3 in (76 mm)/50; 30° elevation; 30 rds/min to 13 km (7 n miles). Surface fire only; weight of shell 5.9 kg.
    1 Bofors 40 mm/70; 90° elevation; 300 rds/min to 12 km (6.6 n miles); weight of shell 0.96 kg.
Weapons control: TVT 300 optronic tracker.
Radars: Navigation: Furuno; I-band.

Comment: P 31 (ex-Glimt) disarmed and acquired from Norway on 12 December 1994 as a gun patrol craft. Re-armed in 1998. A further craft (ex-Kjekk) transferred in October 2001 and, following refit, commissioned as P 31 in August 2002. Ex-Glimt is laid up at Klaipeda. P 32 and P 33 transferred from Norway in June 2001. Others of the class given to Latvia and Estonia.

SKALVIS   4/2002, Guy Toremans / 0524995

1 COASTAL PATROL CRAFT (PB/YFS)

HK 21 (ex-Vilnele)

Displacement, tons: 88 full load
Dimensions, feet (metres): 75.8 × 19 × 5.9 (23.1 × 5.8 × 1.8)
Main machinery: 2 diesels; 600 hp(m) (441 kW); 2 shafts
Speed, knots: 12
Complement: 5
Guns: 1—12.7 mm MG.

Comment: Acquired in 1992. Former pilot boat and tender to Vetra. Used as a hydrographic vessel.

HK 21   6/2004, Lithuanian Navy / 0589761

MINE WARFARE FORCES

2 LINDAU (TYPE 331) CLASS (MINEHUNTERS) (MHC)

Name	No	Builders	Commissioned
SŪDUVIS (ex-Koblenz)	M 52 (ex-M 1071)	Burmester, Bremen	8 July 1958
KURŠIS (ex-Marburg)	M 51 (ex-M 1080)	Burmester, Bremen	11 June 1959

Displacement, tons: 463 full load
Dimensions, feet (metres): 154.5 × 27.2 × 9.8 (9.2 Troika) (47.1 × 8.3 × 3) (2.8)
Main machinery: 2 MTU MD diesels; 4,000 hp(m) (2.94 MW); 2 shafts
Speed, knots: 16.5. **Range, n miles:** 850 at 16.5 kt
Complement: 42 (5 officers)
Guns: 1 Bofors 40 mm/70. 2—12.7 mm MGs.
Radars: Navigation: Raytheon Mariner Pathfinder; I-band.
Sonars: Plessey 193 m; minehunting; high frequency (100/300 kHz).
    EdgeTech DF-1000 sidescan (M 51); high frequency (100/400 kHz).

Comment: M 52 acquired from Germany in June 1999 and recommissioned 2 December 1999. M 51 transferred in November 2000. Converted to minehunters in 1978. Hulls of wooden construction. Full minehunting equipment including PAP 104 ROVs transferred with the vessels.

KURŠIS   6/2005*, B Sullivan / 1133086

AUXILIARIES

Notes: (1) Victoria 245 is an ex-Swedish Coast Guard vessel now owned by the Fishery Inspection Service.
(2) The former Norwegian minelayer Vidar was transferred on 7 April 2006. She is to replace Vetra.

1 VALERIAN URYVAYEV CLASS (AGOR/AX)

VETRA (ex-Rudolf Samoylovich) A 41

Displacement, tons: 1,050 full load
Dimensions, feet (metres): 180.1 × 31.2 × 13.1 (54.9 × 9.5 × 4)
Main machinery: 1 Deutz diesel; 850 hp(m) (625 kW); 1 shaft
Speed, knots: 12
Complement: 37 (7 officers)
Guns: 2—12.7 mm MGs.
Radars: Navigation: Racal Decca RM 1290; I-band.

Comment: Built at Khabarovsk in early 1980s. Transferred from the Russian Navy in 1992 where she was used as a civilian oceanographic research vessel. Now used as the Flag ship for the Baltic States MCMV unit which includes Olev and Vaindlo (from Estonia) and Viesturs and Imanta (from Latvia). A second of class Vejas works for the Ministry of Environment.

VETRA   6/2004, Marian Wright / 0589760

1 HARBOUR TUG (YTL)

H 22 (ex-A 330)

Displacement, tons: 35
Dimensions, feet (metres): 48 × 14.8 × 8.2 (14.65 × 4.5 × 2.5)
Main machinery: 1 Scania-Vabis DSI 11R82A diesel; 230 hp (171 kW)
Speed, knots: 9
Complement: 4
Radars: Navigation: Racal Decca; I-band.

Comment: Ex-Swedish Atlas transferred in 2000.

H 22   6/2003, Hartmut Ehlers / 0561507

1 KUTTER CLASS (PB)

LOKYS (ex-*Apollo*) H 23

Displacement, tons: 35 full load
Dimensions, feet (metres): 60.4 × 17.1 × 10.5 *(18.4 × 5.2 × 3.2)*
Main machinery: 1 diesel; 165 hp(m) *(121 kW)*; 1 shaft
Speed, knots: 9
Complement: 5
Radars: Surface search: Raytheon RM 1290S; I-band.

Comment: Built in the 1930s and served with the Danish Naval Home Guard. Transferred in July 1997. Manned by naval personnel.

LOKYS *6/2005*, Lithuanian Navy* / 1129992

STATE BORDER SECURITY SERVICE

1 LOKKI CLASS (PB)

KIHU 102 (ex-003)

Displacement, tons: 76 full load
Dimensions, feet (metres): 87.9 × 17 × 6.2 *(26.8 × 5.2 × 1.9)*
Main machinery: 2 MTU 8V 396 TB84 diesels; 2,120 hp(m) *(1.58 MW)* sustained; 2 shafts
Speed, knots: 25
Complement: 6
Radars: Navigation: Furuno FR 2010 and FCR 1411; I-band.

Comment: Armament and sonar removed on transfer. Donated by Finland in 1998.

KIHU *6/2003, Hartmut Ehlers* / 0561506

1 KBV 041 CLASS (PB)

MADELEINE 042 (ex-KBV 041)

Displacement, tons: 69 full load
Dimensions, feet (metres): 73.5 × 17.72 × 5.6 *(22.4 × 5.4 × 1.7)*
Main machinery: 2 diesels; 450 hp(m) *(331 kW)*; 2 shafts
Speed, knots: 10
Complement: 4
Radars: Navigation: Furuno FRS 1000C and FR 1510; I-band.

Comment: Class B sea truck transferred from the Swedish Coast Guard in April 1995. Used for pollution control in Swedish service but now used as patrol craft.

MADELEINE *6/2003, Hartmut Ehlers* / 0561504

1 KBV 101 CLASS (PB)

LILIAN 101 (ex-KBV 101)

Displacement, tons: 69 full load
Dimensions, feet (metres): 82 × 16.4 × 6.5 *(25 × 5 × 2)*
Main machinery: 2 Cummins KTA38-M diesels; 2,120 hp(m) *(1.56 MW)*; 2 shafts
Speed, knots: 18. **Range, n miles:** 1,000 at 15 kt
Complement: 5
Radars: Navigation: Furuno FR 2010 and FCR 1411; I-band.

Comment: Built in Sweden in 1969. Transferred from Swedish Coast Guard on 24 June 1996. Used in Swedish service as a salvage diving vessel and had a high frequency active hull-mounted sonar.

LILIAN *6/2003, Hartmut Ehlers* / 0561503

1 CHRISTINA (GRIFFON 2000 TD) CLASS HOVERCRAFT (UCAC)

CHRISTINA

Displacement, tons: 5 full load
Dimensions, feet (metres): 41.35 × 20 *(12.6 × 6.1)*
Main machinery: 1 Deutz BF8L diesel; 355 hp *(265 kW)*
Speed, knots: 35
Complement: 3
Radars: Furuno 1000C; I-band.

Comment: Built by Griffon UK and delivered in 2000. Similar to crafts supplied to Estonia and Finland.

CHRISTINA *6/2001, Lithuanian Navy* / 0114364

Macedonia, Former Yugoslav Republic of

Country Overview

The Former Yugoslav Republic of Macedonia declared its independence in 1991. A land-locked country with an area of 9,928 square miles, it is situated in south-eastern Europe and is bordered to the north by Serbia, to the east by Bulgaria, to the south by Greece and to the west by Albania. Parts of the borders with Albania and Greece pass through the two principal lakes, Ohrid and Prespa. The capital and largest city is Skopje.

PATROL FORCES

Notes: The Macedonian Lake Service (Ezerska sluzba – EZ) consists of about 400 soldiers and is nominally an independent arm of the Army although in practice it is almost integrated with Land Forces. In addition to the five ex-Yugoslavian Army patrol boats on Lake Ohrid, there are two further small craft on Lake Prespa.

4 BOTICA CLASS (TYPE 16) (RIVER PATROL CRAFT) (PBR)

Displacement, tons: 23 full load
Dimensions, feet (metres): 55.8 × 11.8 × 2.8 *(17.0 × 3.6 × 0.8)*
Main machinery: 2 diesels; 464 hp *(340 kW)*; 2 shafts
Speed, knots: 15
Range, n miles: 340 at 14 kt
Complement: 7
Military lift: 3 tons or 30 troops
Guns: 1 Oerlikon 20 mm. 2 – 7.62 mm MGs.
Radars: Surface search: Decca 110; I-band.

Comment: Former Yugoslavian craft which entered service in the 1970s. One is in Serbian Navy service.

BOTICA CLASS   *6/2003* / 1044466

Madagascar

MALAGASY REPUBLIC MARINE

Country Overview

Formerly a French Protectorate, the Malagasy Republic became self-governing in 1958 and fully independent in 1960. It adopted the name Democratic Republic of Madagascar in 1975. Situated in the Indian Ocean and separated from the southeastern coast of Africa by the Mozambique Channel, it comprises Madagascar Island, the fourth largest island in the world, and several small islands. The country's total area is 226,658 square miles and it has a coastline of 2,608 n miles. Antananarivo is the capital while Toamasina is the principal commercial port. There are further ports at Antsiranana, Mahajanga and Toliara. Territorial seas (12 n miles) are claimed. An Exclusive Economic Zone (EEZ) has been claimed but boundaries have not been agreed.

Headquarters Appointments

Head of Navy:
  Rear Admiral Manny Ranaivonativo

Personnel

2006: 430 officers and men (including Marine Company of 120 men)

Bases

Antsiranana (main), Toamasina, Mahajanga, Toliary, Nosy-Be, Tolagnaro, Manakara.

PATROL FORCES

1 CHAMOIS CLASS (SUPPLY TENDER) (AG/PB)

MATSILO (ex-*Chamois*) (ex-A 767)

Displacement, tons: 495 full load
Dimensions, feet (metres): 136.1 × 24.6 × 10.5 *(41.5 × 7.5 × 3.2)*
Main machinery: 2 SACM AGO 175 V16 diesels; 2,700 hp(m) *(1.98 MW)*; 2 shafts; cp props; bow thruster
Speed, knots: 14
Range, n miles: 6,000 at 12 kt
Complement: 13 plus 7 spare
Cargo capacity: 100 tons cargo; 165 tons of fuel or water
Radars: Navigation: Racal Decca 1226; I-band.

Comment: Built by La Perrière, Lorient and commissioned in the French Navy 24 September 1976. Paid off in 1995 and transferred from France in May 1996. Can act as a tug (bollard pull 25 tons) or for SAR and supply tasks but is mostly used as a patrol craft. There are two 30 ton winches and up to 100 tons of stores can be carried on deck.

6 PATROL CRAFT (PB)

Displacement, tons: 17.7 full load
Dimensions, feet (metres): 44.0 × 12.5 × 3.9 *(13.4 × 3.8 × 1.2)*
Main machinery: 2 General Motors Detroit 6V53 diesels; 2 shafts
Speed, knots: 13
Range, n miles: 200 at 11 kt
Complement: 3
Radars: Surface search: Furuno; I-band.

Comment: Former US Coast Guard lifeboats (MLB) constructed in the 1960s. Formally donated on 12 February 2003 for use as coastal surveillance and SAR vessels. All six craft refitted at Galveston, Texas, before transfer and a further unit was transferred as spares.

MATSILO   *6/1999, Madagascar Navy* / 0081203

MLBs (Seychelles colours)   *9/2003*, Seychelles Coast Guard* / 0568334

AMPHIBIOUS FORCES

1 EDIC CLASS

AINA VAO VAO (ex-L9082)

Displacement, tons: 250 standard; 670 full load
Dimensions, feet (metres): 193.5 × 39.2 × 4.5
  (59 × 12 × 1.3)
Main machinery: 2 SACM MGO diesels; 1,000 hp(m)
  (753 kW); 2 shafts
Speed, knots: 8. **Range, n miles:** 1,800 at 8 kt
Complement: 32 (3 officers)
Military lift: 250 tons
Guns: 2 Giat 20 mm.

Comment: Built in 1964 by Chantier Naval Franco-Belge. Transferred from France 28 September 1985 having been paid off by the French Navy in 1981. Repaired by the French Navy in 1996 and now back in service.

AINA VAO VAO
6/1999, Madagascar Navy
0081202

AUXILIARIES

Notes: (1) There are three Aigrette class harbour tugs, *Tourterelle*, was acquired from France in 1975 and *Engoulevent* and *Martin-Pêcheur* May 1996.
(2) There is also a 400 ton coastal tug *Trozona*.

Malawi

Country Overview

Formerly the British Protectorate of Nyasaland, the Republic of Malawi gained independence in 1964. A landlocked country situated in east Central Africa, it is bordered to the north by Tanzania, to the west by Zambia and to the south and east by Mozambique. The country's total area is 45,747 square miles, nearly a quarter of which is water. The principal lake is Lake Malawi (formerly Lake Nyasa),

with which there is a shoreline of some 475 n miles. The largest city is the former capital Blantyre and the capital, since 1975, is Lilongwe. The naval base at Monkey Bay is situated on a peninsula at the south of the lake.

Headquarters Appointments

Commander of the Malawi Army Marine Unit:
  Lieutenant Colonel G A Ziyabu

Bases

Monkey Bay, Lake Malawi

Personnel

2006: 225

PATROL FORCES

Notes: One survey craft built in France in 1988 is operated on Lake Malawi by Department of Surveys.

1 ANTARES CLASS (PB)

KASUNGU (ex-*Chikala*) P 703

Displacement, tons: 41 full load
Dimensions, feet (metres): 68.9 × 16.1 × 4.9 *(21 × 4.9 × 1.5)*
Main machinery: 2 Poyaud 520 V12 M2 diesels; 1,300 hp(m) *(956 kW)*; 2 shafts
Speed, knots: 22. **Range, n miles:** 650 at 15 kt
Complement: 16
Guns: 1 MG 21 20 mm. 2—7.62 mm MGs.
Radars: Surface search: Decca; I-band.

Comment: Built in prefabricated sections by SFCN Villeneuve-la-Garenne and shipped to Malawi for assembly on 17 December 1984. Commissioned May 1985. Out of service and in need of refit if and when funds become available.

KASUNGU
6/1996, Malawi Navy / 0012737

1 NAMACURRA CLASS (PB)

KANING'A (ex-Y 1520) P 704

Displacement, tons: 5 full load
Dimensions, feet (metres): 29.5 × 9 × 2.8 *(9 × 2.7 × 0.8)*
Main machinery: 2 BMW 3.3 outboards; 380 hp(m) *(279 kW)*
Speed, knots: 32. **Range, n miles:** 180 at 20 kt
Complement: 4
Guns: 1—12.7 mm MG. 2—7.62 mm MGs.
Radars: Surface search: Decca; I-band.

Comment: Donated by South Africa on 29 October 1988.

KANING'A
6/1997, Malawi Navy / 0012736

1 ROTORK CLASS (LCU)

CHIKOKO I L 702

Displacement, tons: 9 full load
Dimensions, feet (metres): 41.5 × 10.5 × 1.5 *(12.7 × 3.2 × 0.5)*
Main machinery: 2 Volvo diesels; 260 hp(m) *(191 kW)*; 2 shafts
Speed, knots: 24. **Range, n miles:** 3,000 at 15 kt
Complement: 8
Guns: 3—7.62 mm MGs.

Comment: Built by Rotork Marine. Needs a refit but no funds are available.

CHIKOKO I
6/1996, Malawi Navy / 0012738

1 + 5 KEDAH (MEKO 100 RMN) CLASS (FSGHM)

Name	No	Builders	Laid down	Launched	Commissioned
KEDAH	171	Blohm + Voss/Penang Shipbuilding	13 Nov 2001	21 Mar 2003	3 Apr 2006
PAHANG	172	Blohm + Voss/Penang Shipbuilding	21 Dec 2001	2 Oct 2003	2006
PERAK	173	Penang Shipbuilding, Lumut	Mar 2002	Mar 2005	2006
TERENGGANU	174	Penang Shipbuilding, Lumut	Aug 2004	Dec 2005	2007
KELANTAN	175	Penang Shipbuilding, Lumut	July 2005	Nov 2006	2007
SELANGOR	176	Penang Shipbuilding, Lumut	July 2006	Sep 2007	2008

Displacement, tons: 1,650 full load
Dimensions, feet (metres): 298.9 × 39.4 × 9.8
(91.1 × 12.0 × 3.0)
Main machinery: 2 Caterpillar 3616 diesels; total of
14,617 hp(m) *(10.9 MW)* sustained; 2 shafts; cp propellors
Speed, knots: 22. **Range, n miles:** 6,050 at 12 kt
Complement: 68 (11 officers)

Missiles: Fitted for SSM (MM40) ❶ and SAM (RAM
CIWS) ❷.
Guns: 1 Otobreda 3 in *(76 mm)*/62 ❸; Super Rapid;
120 rds/min to 16 km *(8.7 n miles)*; weight of shell 6 kg.
1—30 mm Otobreda/Mauser ❹. 2—12.7 mm MGs.
Countermeasures: Decoys: RBOC chaff launcher.
Combat data systems: STN Atlas Cosys 110M1.
Weapons control: Contraves TMEO optronic director ❺.
Radars: Air/surface search: TRS-3D/16ES ❻; G-band.
Sonars: Fitted for.
Helicopters: Platform for medium helicopter.

Programmes: Following a delay of 19 months since initial
signature, the Malaysian government, the Penang

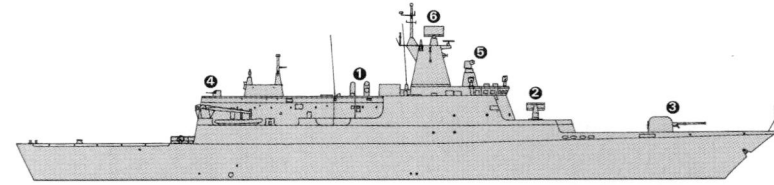

KEDAH

(Scale 1 : 900), Ian Sturton / 1044256

Shipbuilding Corporation and German Naval Group
consortium (led by Blohm + Voss) reached final
agreement in November 2000 for the supply of an
initial batch of six vessels. The first two OPVs were built
in Germany for shipment to Malaysia and assembly
and fitting out at Lumut. The first ship left Hamburg on
1 April 2003 and the second ship on 6 October 2003.
Subsequent ships under construction in Malaysia. The
programme has been delayed by funding issues and
formal handover of the first ship is expected in 2006.

Dates for delivery of subsequent ships have not been
confirmed but completion of the programme by 2008 is
doubtful.
Structure: Design based on Blohm + Voss MEKO 100
including measures to reduce the radar and IR
signatures. Space has been included for future
enhancements which may include SSM, SAM, sonar
and an EW suite.
Operational: Principal tasks are expected to be maritime
surveillance and patrol duties in the Malaysian EEZ.

KEDAH

3/2003, Michael Nitz / 0552763

PAHANG

12/2005*, Chris Sattler / 1153385

SHIPBORNE AIRCRAFT

Notes: Sikorsky S-61A Nuri Army support helicopter can be embarked in two Logistic
Support Ships and two OPVs.

Numbers/Type: 6 GKN Westland Super Lynx.
Operational speed: 120 kt *(222 km/h).*
Service ceiling: 10,000 ft *(3,048 m).*
Range: 320 n miles *(593 km).*
Role/Weapon systems: Ordered on 3 September 1999. All delivered in 2003. Surveillance.
Sensors: Seaspray radar; ESM: Sky Guardian 2500; MST-S FLIR. Weapons: ASW; two
A244S torpedoes. ASV; Sea Skua ASM; 2—12.7 mm MG.

NURI

6/1997 / 0081211

SUPER LYNX

12/2005*, Chris Sattler / 1153387

LAND-BASED MARITIME AIRCRAFT

Notes: The Air Force has eight F/A-18D fighter-bombers with Harpoon ASM, and 15 Hawk fighters with Sea Eagle ASM.

Numbers/Type: 6 Aerospatiale AS 555 Fennec.
Operational speed: 114 kt *(211 km/h).*
Service ceiling: 10,000 ft *(3,050 m).*
Range: 389 n miles *(722 km).*
Role/Weapon systems: Unarmed aircraft ordered late 2001 for delivery in June 2004. Utility, SAR and training roles. Sensors: RDR 1500B radar; EWR 99 Fruit RWR; ARGOS 410-A5 FLIR. Weapons: 7.62 mm MG.

FENNEC *12/2005*, Chris Sattler* / 1153388

Numbers/Type: 4 Beechcraft B 200T Super King.
Operational speed: 282 kt *(523 km/h).*
Service ceiling: 35,000 ft *(10,670 m).*
Range: 2,030 n miles *(3,756 km).*
Role/Weapon systems: Used for maritime surveillance. Acquired in 1994. Air Force operated. Sensors: Search radar. Weapons: Unarmed.

SUPER KING *6/1993* / 0084007

PATROL FORCES

17 COMBATBOAT 90E (PBF)

TANGKIS 1
TEMPUR 11-15, 21-24, 32-34, 41-44

Displacement, tons: 19 full load
Dimensions, feet (metres): 52.2 × 12.5 × 2.6 *(15.9 × 3.8 × 0.8)*
Main machinery: 2 Volvo Penta TAMD 163P diesels; 1,500 hp(m) *(1.1 MW)*; 2 waterjets
Speed, knots: 45
Range, n miles: 240 at 30 kt
Complement: 3
Guns: 1 — 7.62 mm MG.
Radars: Surface search: I-band.

Comment: Ordered from Dockstavarvet in Sweden in April 1997. Have more powerful engines than the boats in Swedish service. Primary role is maritime law enforcement particularly on east coast of Sabah.

TEMPUR 43 *12/2005*, Chris Sattler* / 1153389

4 HANDALAN (SPICA-M) CLASS
(FAST ATTACK CRAFT—MISSILE) (PTFG)

Name	No	Builders	Commissioned
HANDALAN	3511	Karlskrona, Sweden	26 Oct 1979
PERKASA	3512	Karlskrona, Sweden	26 Oct 1979
PENDEKAR	3513	Karlskrona, Sweden	26 Oct 1979
GEMPITA	3514	Karlskrona, Sweden	26 Oct 1979

Displacement, tons: 240 full load
Dimensions, feet (metres): 142.6 × 23.3 × 7.4 (screws) *(43.6 × 7.1 × 2.4)*
Main machinery: 3 MTU 16V 538 TB91 diesels; 9,180 hp(m) *(6.75 MW)* sustained; 3 shafts
Speed, knots: 34.5. **Range, n miles:** 1,850 at 14 kt
Complement: 40 (6 officers)

Missiles: SSM: 4 Aerospatiale MM 38 Exocet; inertial cruise; active radar homing to 42 km *(23 n miles)* at 0.9 Mach; warhead 165 kg; sea-skimmer.
Guns: 1 Bofors 57 mm/70 Mk 1; 200 rds/min to 17 km *(9.2 n miles)*; weight of shell 2.4 kg. Illuminant launchers.
1 Bofors 40 mm/70; 300 rds/min to 12 km *(6.5 n miles)* anti-surface; 4 km *(2.2 n miles)* anti-aircraft; weight of shell 0.96 kg.
Countermeasures: ESM: Thales DR 3000; intercept.
Weapons control: 1 PEAB 9LV212 Mk 2 weapon control system with TV tracking. LME anti-aircraft laser and TV rangefinder.
Radars: Surface search: Philips 9GR 600; I-band (agile frequency).
Navigation: Kelvin Hughes 1007; I-band.
Fire control: Philips 9LV 212; J-band.

Programmes: Ordered 15 October 1976. All named in one ceremony on 11 November 1978, arriving in Port Klang on 26 October 1979.
Modernisation: There are plans to replace the MM 38 with MM 40 or Teseo missiles and to update radar and EW.
Structure: Bridge further forward than in Swedish class to accommodate Exocet. Plans to fit an ASW capability were shelved and the sonar removed.
Operational: Form 2nd Fast Attack Craft Squadron.

HANDALAN *12/2005*, Chris Sattler* / 1153392

4 PERDANA (LA COMBATTANTE II) CLASS
(FAST ATTACK CRAFT—MISSILE) (PTFG)

Name	No	Builders	Launched	Commissioned
PERDANA	3501	CMN, Cherbourg	31 May 1972	21 Dec 1972
SERANG	3502	CMN, Cherbourg	22 Dec 1971	31 Jan 1973
GANAS	3503	CMN, Cherbourg	26 Oct 1972	28 Feb 1973
GANYANG	3504	CMN, Cherbourg	16 Mar 1972	20 Mar 1973

Displacement, tons: 234 standard; 265 full load
Dimensions, feet (metres): 154.2 × 23.1 × 12.8 *(47 × 7 × 3.9)*
Main machinery: 4 MTU MB 870 diesels; 14,000 hp(m) *(10.3 MW)*; 4 shafts
Speed, knots: 36.5. **Range, n miles:** 800 at 25 kt; 1,800 at 15 kt
Complement: 30 (4 officers)

Missiles: SSM: 2 Aerospatiale MM 38 Exocet; inertial cruise; active radar homing to 42 km *(23 n miles)* at 0.9 Mach; warhead 165 kg; sea-skimmer. Not always carried.
Guns: 1 Bofors 57 mm/70; 200 rds/min to 17 km *(9.2 n miles)*; weight of shell 2.4 kg.
1 Bofors 40 mm/70; 300 rds/min to 12 km *(6.5 n miles)* anti-surface; 4 km *(2.2 n miles)* anti-aircraft; weight of shell 0.96 kg.
Countermeasures: Decoys: 4—57 mm chaff/flare launchers.
ESM: Thomson-CSF DR 3000; intercept.
Weapons control: Thomson-CSF Vega optical for guns.
Radars: Air/surface search: Thomson-CSF TH-D 1040 Triton; G-band; range 33 km *(18 n miles)* for 2 m² target.
Navigation: Kelvin Hughes 1007; I-band.
Fire control: Thomson-CSF Pollux; I/J-band; range 31 km *(17 n miles)* for 2 m² target.

Programmes: Left Cherbourg for Malaysia 2 May 1973.
Modernisation: There are plans to replace MM 38 with MM 40 or Teseo SSMs and to update radar and EW.
Structure: All of basic La Combattante II design with steel hulls and aluminium superstructure.
Operational: Form 1st Fast Attack Craft Squadron.

GANYANG *12/2005*, Chris Sattler* / 1153393

6 JERONG CLASS (FAST ATTACK CRAFT—GUN) (PB)

Name	No	Builders	Commissioned
JERONG	3505	Hong Leong-Lürssen, Butterworth	27 Mar 1976
TODAK	3506	Hong Leong-Lürssen, Butterworth	16 June 1976
PAUS	3507	Hong Leong-Lürssen, Butterworth	16 Aug 1976
YU	3508	Hong Leong-Lürssen, Butterworth	15 Nov 1976
BAUNG	3509	Hong Leong-Lürssen, Butterworth	11 Jan 1977
PARI	3510	Hong Leong-Lürssen, Butterworth	23 Mar 1977

Displacement, tons: 244 full load
Dimensions, feet (metres): 147.3 × 23 × 8.3 *(44.9 × 7 × 2.5)*
Main machinery: 3 MTU MB 16V 538 TB90 diesels; 9,000 hp(m) *(6.6 MW)* sustained; 3 shafts
Speed, knots: 32. **Range, n miles:** 2,000 at 14 kt
Complement: 36 (4 officers)
Guns: 1 Bofors 57 mm/70 Mk 1. 200 rds/min to 17 km *(9.2 n miles)*; weight of shell 2.4 kg. 1 Bofors 40 mm/70.
Countermeasures: ESM: Thales DR 3000; intercept.
Radars: Surface search: Kelvin Hughes 1007; I-band.

Comment: Lürssen 45 type. Illuminant launchers on both gun mountings. Design of hull modification is reported to have been contracted. Form 6th Fast Attack Squadron based at Labuan.

PARI
5/1990, John Mortimer / 0081217

MINE WARFARE FORCES

4 MAHAMIRU (LERICI) CLASS (MINEHUNTERS) (MHC)

Name	No	Builders	Launched	Commissioned
MAHAMIRU	11	Intermarine, Italy	23 Feb 1984	11 Dec 1985
JERAI	12	Intermarine, Italy	5 Jan 1984	11 Dec 1985
LEDANG	13	Intermarine, Italy	14 July 1983	11 Dec 1985
KINABALU	14	Intermarine, Italy	19 Mar 1983	11 Dec 1985

Displacement, tons: 610 full load
Dimensions, feet (metres): 167.3 × 32.5 × 9.2 *(51 × 9.9 × 2.8)*
Main machinery: 2 MTU 12V 396TC82 diesels (passage); 2,605 hp(m) *(1.91 MW)* sustained; 2 shafts; Kamewa cp props; 3 Fincantieri Isotta Fraschini ID 36 SS 6V diesels; 1,481 hp(m) *(1.09 MW)* sustained; 2 Riva Calzoni hydraulic thrust jets
Speed, knots: 16 diesels; 7 thrust jet. **Range, n miles:** 2,000 at 12 kt
Complement: 42 (5 officers)
Guns: 1 Bofors 40 mm/70; 300 rds/min to 12.5 km *(6.8 n miles)*; weight of shell 0.96 kg.
Countermeasures: Thomson-CSF IBIS II minehunting system; 2 improved PAP 104 ROVs. Oropesa 'O' MIS-4 mechanical sweep.
Radars: Navigation: Kelvin Hughes 1007; Thomson-CSF Tripartite III; I-band.
Sonars: Thomson Sintra TSM 2022 with Display 2060; minehunting; high frequency.

Comment: Ordered on 20 February 1981. All arrived in Malaysia on 26 March 1986. Heavy GRP construction without frames. Snach active tank stabilisers. Draeger Duocom decompression chamber. Slightly longer than Italian sisters. Endurance, 14 days. Upgrade of tactical data system completed in 2001; Minehunter Technical Display System (MTDS) installed by Altech Defence System, South Africa. Form the 26th Mine Countermeasures Squadron.

JERAI
12/2005*, Chris Sattler / 1153394

SURVEY SHIPS

1 SURVEY VESSEL (AGSH)

Name	No	Builders	Commissioned
MUTIARA	255 (ex-152)	Hong Leong-Lürssen, Butterworth	12 Jan 1978

Displacement, tons: 1,905 full load
Dimensions, feet (metres): 232.9 × 42.6 × 13.1 *(71 × 13 × 4)*
Main machinery: 2 Deutz SBA12M528 diesels; 4,000 hp(m) *(2.94 MW)*; 2 shafts
Speed, knots: 16. **Range, n miles:** 4,500 at 16 kt
Complement: 155 (14 officers)
Guns: 4 Oerlikon 20 mm (2 twin).
Radars: Navigation: 2 Racal Decca 1226/1229; I-band.
Helicopters: Platform only.

Comment: Ordered in early 1975. Carries satellite navigation, auto-data system and computerised fixing system. Davits for six survey launches. Forms part of 36 Squadron.

MUTIARA
12/2005*, Chris Sattler / 1153397

1 SURVEY VESSEL (AGS)

Name	No	Builders	Commissioned
PERANTAU	153	Hong Leong-Lürssen, Butterworth	12 Oct 1998

Displacement, tons: 1,996 full load
Dimensions, feet (metres): 222.4 × 43.6 × 13.1 *(67.8 × 13.3 × 4)*
Main machinery: 2 Deutz/MWM SBV8 M628 diesels; 4,787 hp(m) *(3.52 MW)*; 2 shafts; Berg cp props; Schottel bow thruster
Speed, knots: 16. **Range, n miles:** 6,000 at 10 kt
Complement: 94 (17 officers)
Radars: Navigation: STN Atlas; I-band.

Comment: Ordered from Krogerwerft in 1996. The ship is equipped with two survey launches and four multipurpose boats and has three winches and two cranes, including a hoist for a STN Atlas side scan sonar. Full range of hydrographic and mapping equipment embarked. Forms part of 36 Squadron.

PERANTAU
10/2001, Hartmut Ehlers / 0130737

PERANTAU
12/2005*, Chris Sattler / 1153404

AMPHIBIOUS FORCES

33 LCM/LCP/LCU

LCM 1-5	LCP 1-15	RCP 1-9	LCU 1-4

Displacement, tons: 56 (LCM); 30 (LCU/RCP); 18.5 (LCVP) full load
Main machinery: 2 diesels; 330 hp *(246 kW)* (LCM); 400 hp *(298 kW)* (LCVP); 2 shafts
Speed, knots: 10 (LCM); 16 (LCVP); 17 (LCU/RCP)
Military lift: 30 tons (LCM); 35 troops (LCU/RCP/LCP)

Comment: LCMs and LCPs are Australian built and transferred 1965-70. LCMs have light armour on sides and some have gun turrets. RCPs and LCUs are Malaysian built and in service 1974-84. Transferred to the Army in 1993.

LCM 5 (with gun turret)
6/1995 / 0012753

1 NEWPORT CLASS (LSTH)

Name	No	Builders	Laid down	Launched	Commissioned
SRI INDERAPURA (ex-*Spartanburg County*)	1505 (ex-1192)	National Steel, San Diego	7 Feb 1970	11 Nov 1970	1 Sep 1971

Displacement, tons: 4,975 light; 8,450 full load
Dimensions, feet (metres): 522.3 (hull) × 69.5 × 17.5 (aft)
(159.2 × 21.2 × 5.3)
Main machinery: 6 ALCO 16—251 diesels; 16,500 hp
(12.3 MW) sustained; 2 shafts; cp props; bow thruster
Speed, knots: 20. **Range, n miles:** 14,250 at 14 kt
Complement: 257 (13 officers)
Military lift: 400 troops (20 officers); 500 tons vehicles; 3 LCVPs and 1 LCPL on davits
Guns: 1 General Electric/General Dynamics 20 mm Vulcan Phalanx Mk 15.
Radars: Surface search: Raytheon SPS-67; G-band.
Navigation: Marconi LN66; I/J-band.
Kelvin Hughes 1007; I-band.

Helicopters: Platform only.

Programmes: Transferred by sale from the USN 16 December 1994, arriving in Malaysia in June 1995. Second authorised for transfer by lease in 1998 but this was not confirmed.
Structure: The hull form required to achieve 20 kt would not permit bow doors, thus these ships unload by a 112 ft ramp over their bow. The ramp is supported by twin derrick arms. A ramp just forward of the superstructure connects the lower tank deck with the main deck and a vehicle passage through the superstructure provides access to the parking area amidships. A stern gate to the tank deck permits unloading of amphibious tractors into the water, or unloading of

SRI INDERAPURA *5/1995, Robert Pabst* / 0081219

other vehicles into an LCU or onto a pier. Vehicle stowage covers 19,000 sq ft. Length over derrick arms is 562 ft *(171.3 m)*; full load draught is 11.5 ft forward and 17.5 ft aft.

Operational: 3 in guns removed before transfer. Repeated refits in Johore shipyard between late 1995 and 1998. Damaged by fire on 15 December 2002 at Lumut. Forms 32 Sealift Squadron.

130 DAMEN ASSAULT CRAFT 540

Dimensions, feet (metres): 17.7 × 5.9 × 2
(5.4 × 1.8 × 0.6)
Main machinery: 1 outboard; 40 hp(m) *(29.4 kW)*
Speed, knots: 12
Military lift: 10 troops

Comment: First 65 built by Damen Gorinchem, Netherlands in 1986. Remainder built by Limbungan Timor SY. Army assault craft. Manportable and similar to Singapore craft. Used by the Army. Some have been deleted.

TRAINING SHIPS

1 SAIL TRAINING SHIP (AXS)

Name	No	Builders	Commissioned
TUNAS SAMUDERA	A 13	Brooke Yacht, Lowestoft	16 Oct 1989

Displacement, tons: 239 full load
Dimensions, feet (metres): 114.8 × 25.6 × 13.1 *(35 × 7.8 × 4)*
Main machinery: 2 Perkins diesels; 370 hp *(272 kW)*; 2 shafts
Speed, knots: 9
Complement: 10 plus 26 trainees
Radars: Navigation: Racal Decca; I-band.

Comment: Laid down 1 December 1988 and launched 4 August 1989. Two-masted brig manned by the Navy but used for training all sea services.

TUNAS SAMUDERA *12/2005*, Chris Sattler* / 1153399

1 HANG TUAH (TYPE 41/61) CLASS (FFH/AX)

Name	No	Builders	Commissioned
HANG TUAH (ex-*Mermaid*)	76	Yarrow (Shipbuilders), Glasgow	16 May 1973

Displacement, tons: 2,300 standard; 2,520 full load
Dimensions, feet (metres): 339.3 × 40 × 16 (screws) *(103.5 × 12.2 × 4.9)*
Main machinery: 2 Stork Wärtsilä 12SW28 diesels; 9,928 hp(m) *(7.3 MW)* sustained; 2 shafts; cp props
Speed, knots: 24
Range, n miles: 4,800 at 15 kt
Complement: 210
Guns: 1 Bofors 57 mm/70 Mk 1; 200 rds/min to 17 km *(9.2 n miles)*; weight of shell 2.4 kg. 2 Bofors 40 mm/70; 300 rds/min to 12 km *(6.5 n miles)* anti-surface; 4 km *(2.2 n miles)* anti-aircraft; weight of shell 0.96 kg.
Radars: Navigation: Kelvin Hughes 1007; I-band.
Helicopters: Platform for 1 medium.

Comment: Originally built for Ghana as a display ship for ex-President Nkrumah but put up for sale after his departure. She was launched without ceremony on 29 December 1966 and completed in 1968. Commissioned in Royal Navy 16 May 1973 and transferred to Royal Malaysian Navy May 1977. Refitted in 1991-92 to become a training ship. Main gun and main engines replaced in 1995-96. Sonars removed but Limbo mounting still fitted. There are no plans for further modifications.

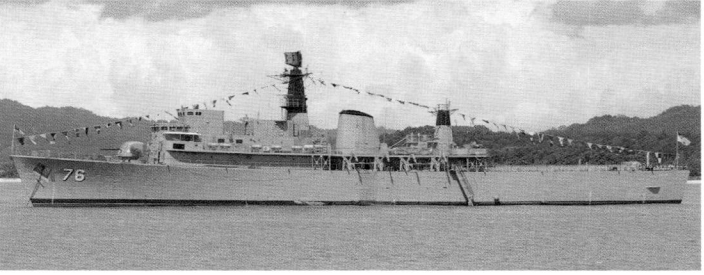

HANG TUAH *12/2005*, Chris Sattler* / 1153398

AUXILIARIES

Notes: (1) There are five miscellaneous personnel launches: *Kempong, Mangkasa, Patak, Selar* and *Tepuruk*.
(2) An ex-tug, *Penyu* (465 tons) is used as a diving tender. Commissioned in 1979, it has a complement of 26.

PENYU *10/2003*, Hartmut Ehlers* / 0567883

2 FAST TROOP VESSELS (AP)

SRI GAYA 331   SRI TIGA 332

Displacement, tons: 116.5 full load
Dimensions, feet (metres): 123.1 × 23.0 × 3.6 *(37.5 × 7.0 × 1.1)*
Main machinery: 4 MAN D2842 LE 408 diesels; 2,080 hp *(1.55 MW)*; 4 water-jets
Speed, knots: 25
Range, n miles: 540
Complement: 8
Military lift: 32 troops + stores
Radars: Navigation: Furuno; I-band.

Comment: Design based on Australian Wave Master fast-ferry monohull. Procured to transport troops and stores particularly in Sabah and Sarawak waters. Built by Naval Dockyard, Lumut and commissioned on 29 May 2001. Based at Labuan.

SRI GAYA *12/2005*, Chris Sattler* / 1153396

2 LOGISTIC SUPPORT SHIPS (AOR/AE/AXH)

Name	No	Builders	Commissioned
SRI INDERA SAKTI	1503	Bremer Vulkan	24 Oct 1980
MAHAWANGSA	1504	Korea Tacoma	16 May 1983

Displacement, tons: 4,300 (1503); 4,900 (1504) full load
Dimensions, feet (metres): 328; 337.9 (1504) × 49.2 × 15.7 *(100; 103 × 15 × 4.8)*
Main machinery: 2 Deutz KHD SBV6M540 diesels; 5,865 hp(m) *(4.31 MW)*; 2 shafts; cp props; bow thruster
Speed, knots: 16.5. **Range, n miles:** 4,000 at 14 kt
Complement: 136 (14 officers) plus 65 spare
Military lift: 17 tanks; 600 troops
Cargo capacity: 1,300 tons dieso; 200 tons fresh water (plus 48 tons/day distillers)

Guns: 2 Bofors 57 mm Mk 1 (1 only fwd in 1503). 2 Oerlikon 20 mm.
Countermeasures: ESM: Thales DR 3000; intercept.
Weapons control: 2 CSEE Naja optronic directors (1 only in 1503).
Radars: Navigation: Kelvin Hughes 1007; I-band.

Helicopters: 1 Sikorsky S-61A Nuri (army support) can be carried.

Programmes: Ordered in October 1979 and 1981 respectively.
Modernisation: 100 mm gun included in original design but used for OPVs.
Structure: Fitted with stabilising system, vehicle deck, embarkation ramps port and starboard, recompression chamber and a stern anchor. Large operations room and a conference room are provided. Transfer stations on either beam and aft, light jackstay on both sides and a 15 ton crane for replenishment at sea. 1504 has additional capacity to transport ammunition and the funnel has been removed to enlarge the flight deck which is also higher in the superstructure.
Operational: Used as training ships for cadets in addition to main roles of long-range support of Patrol Forces and MCM vessels, command and communications and troop or ammunition transport. Form 31 Squadron.

SRI INDERA SAKTI　　　　　*12/2005*, Chris Sattler* / 1153403

MAHAWANGSA　　　　　*12/2005*, Chris Sattler* / 1153395

7 COASTAL SUPPLY SHIPS AND TANKERS (AOTL/AKSL)

LANG TIRAM	ENTERPRISE	KEPAH	LANG SIPUT
MELEBAN	JERNIH	TERIJAH	

Comment: Various auxiliaries mostly acquired in the early 1980s. There are also Sabah supply ships identified by M numbers.

TUGS

10 HARBOUR TUGS (YTM/YTL)

TUNDA SATU 1	TERITUP A 10	SOTONG A 6
TUNDA SATU 2	SIPUT A 9	KUPANG A 7
TUNDA SATU 3	BELANKAS A 11	KEPAH A 8
KETAM A 5		

GOVERNMENT MARITIME FORCES

Notes: The Fire and Rescue Department operates at least eight 10 m rescue craft. Helicopters include Mi-17 and Agusta Westland A 109.

POLICE

6 BROOKE MARINE 29 METRE CLASS (PBF)

SANGITAN PX 28	DUNGUN PX 30	TUMPAT PX 32
SABAHAN PX 29	TIOMAN PX 31	SEGAMA PX 33

Displacement, tons: 114 full load
Dimensions, feet (metres): 95.1 × 19.7 × 5.6 *(29 × 6 × 1.7)*
Main machinery: 2 Paxman Valenta 6CM diesels; 2,250 hp *(1.68 MW)* sustained; 2 shafts
Speed, knots: 36
Range, n miles: 1,200 at 24 kt
Complement: 18 (4 officers)
Guns: 1 Oerlikon 20 mm. 2 — 7.62 mm MGs.

Comment: Ordered 1979 from Penang Shipbuilding Co. First delivery June 1981, last pair completed June 1982. Brooke Marine provided lead yard services.

SANGITAN　　　　　*1991, RM Police* / 0506056

120 INSHORE/RIVER PATROL CRAFT (PBI/PBR)

Comment: Built in several batches and designs since 1964. Some are armed with 7.62 mm MGs. All have PX/PA/PC/PSC/PGR numbers. Included are 23 Simonneau SM 465 type (PC 6-28) built between January 1992 and mid-1993.

PA 3　　　　　*12/2005*, Chris Sattler* / 1153405

PC 6 (SIMONNEAU)　　　　　*4/1997, Maritime Photographic* / 0012763

PSC 6　　　　　*10/2001, Chris Sattler* / 0126267

6 STAN PATROL 1500 CLASS (PBF)

Dimensions, feet (metres): 48.6 × 8.9 × 2.6 *(14.8 × 2.7 × 0.8)*
Main machinery: 4 diesels; 4,500 hp(m) *(33.1 MW)*; 4 shafts; LIPS props
Speed, knots: 55
Complement: 8
Guns: 2 — 12.7 mm MGs.

Comment: Built in Malaysia and completed in 1998/99. Details are not confirmed.

CUSTOMS

Notes: In addition there are about 25 interceptor craft of 9 m, and 30 of 13.7 m and some inflatable chase boats.

HELANG LAUT 4   *12/2005*, Chris Sattler* / 1153406

KB 82   *12/2005*, Chris Sattler* / 1153407

10 PERANTAS FAST INTERCEPT CRAFT (PBF)

KB 71   +9

Displacement, tons: 16.2 full load
Dimensions, feet (metres): 54.1 × 12.8 × ? *(16.5 × 3.9 × ?)*
Main machinery: 2 MTU 12V183 TE94 diesels; 2,600 hp *(1.94 MW)*; 2 Kamewa waterjets
Speed, knots: 45
Range, n miles: 400 at 40 kt
Complement: 8

Comment: Built by Destination Marine Services, Port Klang. GRP hulls.

KB 71   *9/2003, Hartmut Ehlers* / 0567881

4 PEMBANTERAS CLASS (PB)

Displacement, tons: 58 full load
Dimensions, feet (metres): 94.5 × 19.4 × 6.6 *(28.8 × 5.9 × 2)*
Main machinery: 2 Deutz SBA16M816C diesels; 3,140 hp(m) *(2.31 MW)*; 2 shafts
Speed, knots: 20
Complement: 8

Comment: Built at Limbungan Timor shipyard, Terengganu and completed in 1993.

KA 45   *9/2003, Hartmut Ehlers* / 0567886

5 VOSPER 32 METRE (BAHTERA CLASS) PATROL CRAFT (PB)

JUANG K 33	—K 35	**BAYU** K 37	—K 39 —K 42
PULAI K 34	**PERAK** K 36	**HIJAU** K 38	—K 41

Displacement, tons: 143 full load
Dimensions, feet (metres): 106.2 × 23.6 × 5.9 *(32.4 × 7.2 × 1.8)*
Main machinery: 2 Paxman Valenta 16CM diesels; 6,650 hp *(5 MW)* sustained; 2 shafts
    1 Cummins diesel; 575 hp *(423 kW)*; 1 shaft
Speed, knots: 27; 8 on cruise diesel
Range, n miles: 2,000 at 8 kt
Complement: 26
Guns: 1 Oerlikon 20 mm. 2 — 7.62 mm MGs.
Radars: Surface search: Kelvin Hughes; I-band.

Comment: Ordered February 1981 from Malaysia Shipyard and Engineering Company with technical support from Vosper Thornycroft (Private) Ltd, Singapore. Two completed 1982, the remainder in 1983-84. Names are preceded by 'Bahtera'. *Jerai* and four other vessels have been transferred to the new Maritime Enforcement Agency.

BAHTERA CLASS   *10/2003, Hartmut Ehlers* / 0567885

FISHERIES DEPARTMENT

Notes: Patrol craft have distinctive thick blue and thin red diagonal bands on the hull and have been mistaken for a Coast Guard. All have P numbers. There is also a research vessel *K K Senangin II*. Twelve craft are to be transferred to the new Maritime Enforcement Agency.

PL 65   *12/1999, Sattler/Steele* / 0081229

P 204   *12/1999, Sattler/Steele* / 0081228

K K SENANGIN II   *9/2003, Hartmut Ehlers* / 0567880

MARITIME ENFORCEMENT AGENCY

Headquarters Appointments

Director General:
Vice Admiral Dato' Mohammad bin Nik

Establishment

The Malaysian Maritime Enforcement Agency (MMEA) (or Agensi Penguatkuasaan Maritim Malaysia (APMM)) formally came into operational being on 30 November 2005. The MMEA consolidates a number of agencies, including the Royal Malaysian Navy, Royal Malaysian Police, Customs, Fisheries, Marine and Immigration Departments. By July 2006, it is intended to build up to a force of 72 surface patrol craft to form a visible presence in Malaysian waters. Up to six mairitme patrol aircraft and/or helicopters may also be leased. The Agency may be

subsumed within the Malaysian Armed Forces should the security situation dictate.

Principal Missions

Enforcement of law and order under Malaysian federal law
Maritime search and rescue
Air and coastal surveillance
Maintenance of maritime safety and security
Control and prevention of maritime pollution
Prevention and suppression of piracy and illicit traffic in narcotic drugs

Personnel

From an initial baseline of 4,035 seconded from existing agencies, it is planned to build up to a force of about 7,000 personnel.

Organisation

The Malaysian Maritime Zone is divided into five maritime regions which consists of 18 maritime districts.

Bases

MMEA HQ: Seri Kembangan, Selangor
Northern Peninsula: Langkawi (HQ), Bukit Malut, Batu Uban, Lumut
Southern Peninsula: Johore Bahru (HQ), Port Klang, Port Dickson, Tanjung Sedili
Eastern Peninsula: Kuantan (HQ), Kemaman, Tok Bali
Sarawak: Kuching (HQ), Bintulu, Miri
Sabah: Kota Kinabalu (HQ), Labuan, Kudat, Sandakan, Tawau

2 MUSYTARI CLASS (OFFSHORE PATROL VESSELS) (PSOH)

Name	No	Builders	Launched	Commissioned
LANGKAWI (ex-*Musytari*)	7501 (ex-160)	Korea Shipbuilders, Pusan	20 July 1984	19 Dec 1985
— (ex-*Marikh*)	7502 (ex-161)	Malaysia SB and E Co, Johore	21 Jan 1985	9 Apr 1987

Displacement, tons: 1,300 full load
Dimensions, feet (metres): 246 × 35.4 × 12.1 *(75 × 10.8 × 3.7)*
Main machinery: 2 SEMT-Pielstick diesels; 12,720 hp(m) *(9.35 MW)*; 2 shafts
Speed, knots: 22. **Range, n miles:** 5,000 at 15 kt
Complement: 76 (10 officers)

Guns: 1 Creusot-Loire 3.9 in *(100 mm)*/55 Mk 2 compact (161); 20/45/90 rds/min to 17 km *(9.2 n miles)* anti-surface; 6 km *(3.2 n miles)* anti-aircraft; weight of shell 13.5 kg.

1 — 40 mm (160).
2 Emerson Electric 30 mm (twin); 1,200 rds/min combined to 6 km *(3.2 n miles)*; weight of shell 0.35 kg.
Countermeasures: ESM: Thales DR 3000; intercept.
Weapons control: PEAB 9LV 230 optronic system.
Radars: Air/surface search: Signaal DA05; E/F-band; range 137 km *(75 n miles)* for 2 m² target.
Navigation: Kelvin Hughes 1007; I-band.
Fire control: Philips 9LV; J-band.

Helicopters: Platform for 1 medium.

Programmes: Ordered in June 1983.
Structure: Flight deck suitable for Sikorsky S-61A Nuri army support helicopter.
Operational: In naval · service formed 16th Offshore Patrol Vessel Squadron based at Kuantan. These ships were transferred in early 2006 to the new Maritime Enforcement Agency.

LANGKAWI (old number)   *12/2005*, Chris Sattler* / 1153390

7502 (old number)   *12/2005*, Chris Sattler* / 1153391

18 31 METRE PATROL CRAFT (PB)

Name	No	Builders	Commissioned
— (ex-*Sri Sabah*)	— (ex-3144)	Vosper Ltd, Portsmouth	2 Sep 1964
— (ex-*Sri Sarawak*)	— (ex-3145)	Vosper Ltd, Portsmouth	30 Sep 1964
— (ex-*Sri Negri Sembilan*)	— (ex-3146)	Vosper Ltd, Portsmouth	28 Sep 1964
— (ex-*Sri Melaka*)	— (ex-3147)	Vosper Ltd, Portsmouth	2 Nov 1964
— (ex-*Kris*)	— (ex-34)	Vosper Ltd, Portsmouth	1 Jan 1966
— (ex-*Sundang*)	— (ex-36)	Vosper Ltd, Portsmouth	29 Nov 1966
— (ex-*Badek*)	— (ex-37)	Vosper Ltd, Portsmouth	15 Dec 1966
— (ex-*Renchong*)	— (ex-38)	Vosper Ltd, Portsmouth	17 Jan 1967
— (ex-*Tombak*)	— (ex-39)	Vosper Ltd, Portsmouth	2 Mar 1967
— (ex-*Lembing*)	— (ex-40)[1]	Vosper Ltd, Portsmouth	12 Apr 1967
— (ex-*Serampang*)	— (ex-41)	Vosper Ltd, Portsmouth	19 May 1967
KAKUP (ex-*Panah*)	3135 (ex-42)	Vosper Ltd, Portsmouth	27 July 1967
— (ex-*Kerambit*)	— (ex-43)[1]	Vosper Ltd, Portsmouth	28 July 1967
— (ex-*Beladau*)	— (ex-44)[1]	Vosper Ltd, Portsmouth	12 Sep 1967
— (ex-*Kelewang*)	— (ex-45)	Vosper Ltd, Portsmouth	4 Oct 1967
— (ex-*Rentaka*)	— (ex-46)	Vosper Ltd, Portsmouth	22 Sep 1967
— (ex-*Sri Perlis*)	— (ex-47)*	Vosper Ltd, Portsmouth	24 Jan 1968
— (ex-*Sri Johor*)	— (ex-49)*	Vosper Ltd, Portsmouth	14 Feb 1968

* Training

Displacement, tons: 96 standard; 109 full load
Dimensions, feet (metres): 103 × 19.8 × 5.5
(31.4 × 6 × 1.7)
Main machinery: 2 Bristol Siddeley or MTU MD 655/18 diesels; 3,500 hp(m) *(2.57 MW)*; 2 shafts
Speed, knots: 27
Range, n miles: 1,400 (1,660 Sabah class) at 14 kt
Complement: 22 (3 officers)

Guns: 2 Bofors 40 mm/70. 2—7.62 mm MGs.

Radars: Surface search: Racal Decca Bridgemaster ARPA; I-band.

Comment: The four Sabah class were ordered in 1963 for delivery in 1964. The boats of the Kris class were ordered in 1965 for delivery between 1966 and 1968. All are of prefabricated steel construction and are fitted with air conditioning and Vosper roll damping equipment. The differences between the classes are minor, the later ones having improved radar, communications, evaporators and engines of MTU, as opposed to Bristol Siddeley construction. All have been refitted to extend their operational lives. In naval service eight formed the 13th Patrol Craft Squadron, based at Sandakan, eight formed the 14th Patrol Craft Squadron based at Kuantan and two formed the 12th Patrol Craft Squadron based at Lumut. These craft are all transferred to the new Maritime Enforcement Agency. Names and pennant numbers are likely to change. Similar craft in service in Panama.

KAKUP

12/2005*, Chris Sattler / 1153401

14 LANG HITAM CLASS (PBF)

— (ex-*Lang Hitam*) — (ex-PZ 1)	— (ex-*Belian*) — (ex-PZ 6)	— (ex-*Harimau Belang*)
AMANAH (ex-*Lang Malam*)	— (ex-*Kurita*) — (ex-PZ 7)	— (ex-PZ 11)
3906 (ex-PZ 2)	— (ex-*Serangan Batu*)	— (ex-*Harimau Akar*) — (ex-PZ 12)
— (ex-*Lang Lebah*) — (ex-PZ 3)	— (ex-PZ 8)	— (ex-*Perangan*) — (ex-PZ 13)
— (ex-*Lang Kuik*) — (ex-PZ 4)	— (ex-*Harimau Bintang*)	— (ex-*Mersuji*) — (ex-PZ 14)
— (ex-*Balong*) — (ex-PZ 5)	— (ex-PZ 9)	— (ex-*Alu-Alu*) — (ex-PZ 15)

Displacement, tons: 230 full load
Dimensions, feet (metres): 126.3 × 22.9 × 5.9 *(38.5 × 7 × 1.8)*
Main machinery: 2 MTU 20V 538 TB92 diesels; 8,360 hp(m) *(6.14 MW)* sustained; 2 shafts
Speed, knots: 35
Range, n miles: 1,200 at 15 kt
Complement: 38 (4 officers)
Guns: 1 Bofors 40 mm/70 (in a distinctive plastic turret).
1 Oerlikon 20 mm. 2 FN 7.62 mm MGs.
Radars: Navigation: Kelvin Hughes; I-band.

Comment: Ordered from Hong Leong-Lürssen, Butterworth, Malaysia in 1979. First delivered August 1980, last in April 1983. One deleted in 1994. All to be transferred to the new Maritime Enforcement Agency. Names and pennant numbers are likely to change.

AMANAH

12/2005*, Chris Sattler / 1153400

5 VOSPER 32 METRE (BAHTERA CLASS) PATROL CRAFT (PB)

SIANGIN (ex-*Bahtera Jerai*) 3224 (ex-K 40)   **+4**

Displacement, tons: 143 full load
Dimensions, feet (metres): 106.2 × 23.6 × 5.9 *(32.4 × 7.2 × 1.8)*
Main machinery: 2 Paxman Valenta 16CM diesels; 6,650 hp *(5 MW)* sustained; 2 shafts
1 Cummins diesel; 575 hp *(423 kW)*; 1 shaft
Speed, knots: 27; 8 on cruise diesel
Range, n miles: 2,000 at 8 kt
Complement: 26
Guns: 1 Oerlikon 20 mm. 2—7.62 mm MGs.
Radars: Surface search: Kelvin Hughes; I-band.

Comment: Ordered February 1981 from Malaysia Shipyard and Engineering Company with technical support from Vosper Thornycroft (Private) Ltd, Singapore. Two completed 1982, the remainder in 1983-84. Names were preceded by 'Bahtera'. Five are to be transferred to the new Maritime Enforcement Agency and names and numbers are different from those in Customs service.

SIANGIN

12/2005*, Chris Sattler / 1153402

For details of the latest updates to *Jane's Fighting Ships* online and to discover the additional information available exclusively to online subscribers please visit

jfs.janes.com

Maldives

Country Overview

Formerly a British Protectorate, The Maldives gained independence in 1965 and a republic was established in 1968. Situated in the northern Indian Ocean, southwest of the southern tip of India, the country comprises a 468 n mile long chain of nearly 2,000 small coral islands that are grouped together into clusters of atolls. The capital and principal commercial centre is Malé and other populous atolls include Suvadiva and Tiladummati. An archipelagic state, territorial waters (12 n miles) are claimed. A 200 n mile Exclusive Economic Zone (EEZ) has been claimed although the limits have only been partly defined by boundary agreements.

Headquarters Appointments

Director General of Coast Guard:
Colonel Zakariyya Mansoor

Bases

Malé, Kaadeddhoo

Personnel

2006: 400

COAST GUARD

Notes: (1) All pennant numbers add up to seven.
(2) The ex-UK patrol craft *Kingfisher* was acquired by a civilian company in early 1997. It is painted white and is used as a survey ship.
(3) There are also four RIBs in service.
(4) The ex-Indian Navy patrol craft *Tillanchang* was transferred on 16 April 2006.

2 GHAZEE CLASS (PB)

ISKANDHAR 223   **GHAZEE** 214

Displacement, tons: 58 full load
Dimensions, feet (metres): 80.1 × 19.0 × 4.1 *(24.4 × 5.8 × 1.3)*
Main machinery: 2 Paxman diesels; 8,506 hp(m) *(6.26 MW)*; 2 Kamewa waterjets
Speed, knots: 37. **Range, n miles:** 600 at 25 kt
Complement: 18
Guns: 1—20 mm MG. 2—7.62 mm MGs.
Radars: Surface search/navigation: JRC-JMA 2254; I-band.

Comment: Ordered from Colombo Dockyard in 1997. *Ghazee* commissioned on 20 January 1998 and *Iskandhar* on 7 December 1998. Employed on security, fishery protection and SAR tasks.

GHAZEE   *6/2005*, Maldives Coast Guard* / 1133514

3 TRACKER II CLASS (PB)

KAANI 133 (ex-11)   **MIDHILI** 151 (ex-13)   **NIROLHU** 106 (ex-14)

Displacement, tons: 39 full load
Dimensions, feet (metres): 66.3 × 17.1 × 4.9 *(20.2 × 5.2 × 1.5)*
Main machinery: 2 Detroit 12V-71TA diesels; 840 hp *(627 kW)* sustained; 2 shafts
Speed, knots: 25. **Range, n miles:** 450 at 20 kt
Complement: 10
Guns: 1—12.7 mm MG. 1—7.62 mm MG.
Radars: Surface search: JRC-JMA; I-band.

Comment: First one ordered June 1985 from Fairey Marine, UK and commissioned in April 1987. Three more acquired July 1987 ex-UK Customs craft. GRP hulls. Used for fishery protection and security patrols. *Kuredhi* decommissioned in 2002.

NIROLHU   *6/2005*, Maldives Coast Guard* / 1133513

1 CHEVERTON CLASS (PB)

BUREVI 115 (ex-7)

Displacement, tons: 26 full load
Dimensions, feet (metres): 56.7 × 14.4 × 4.3 *(17.3 × 4.4 × 1.3)*
Main machinery: 2 MAN B&W diesels; 850 hp *(634 kW)* sustained; 2 shafts
Speed, knots: 23. **Range, n miles:** 590 at 18 kt
Complement: 10
Guns: 1—12.7 mm MG. 1—7.62 mm MG.
Radars: Surface search: JRC; I-band.

Comment: GRP hull and aluminium superstructure. Originally built by Fairey Marine, UK, for Kiribati and subsequently sold to Maldives and commissioned on 11 September 1981. Used for security and SAR operations.

BUREVI   *6/2005*, Maldives Coast Guard* / 1133512

3 HARBOUR PATROL CRAFT (PB)

HP 1   **HP 2**   **HP 4**

Displacement, tons: 6 full load
Dimensions, feet (metres): 36.1 × 7.5 × 1.6 *(11.0 × 2.3 × 0.5)*
Main machinery: 2 Yamaha outboard engines; 500 hp *(375 kW)*
Speed, knots: 30
Range, n miles: 90 at 25 kt
Complement: 8
Guns: 1—7.62 mm MG.

Comment: Built by Gulf Craft Service based in the Maldives. GRP hull. First craft commissioned 12 December 1999. Used for harbour patrol and SAR duties.

HARBOUR PATROL CRAFT   *6/2005*, Maldives Coast Guard* / 1133510

1 LANDING CRAFT (LCM)

LC 1

Displacement, tons: 38.4
Dimensions, feet (metres): 68.6 × 16.4 × 2.3 *(20.9 × 5.0 × 0.7)*
Main machinery: 2 MAN B&W D 2842 LE 401 diesels; 2 Hamilton waterjets
Speed, knots: 20
Range, n miles: 500 at 18 kt
Complement: 7
Guns: 2—7.62 mm MGs.
Radars: Surface search/Navigation: JRC; I-band.

Comment: Built by Colombo Dockyard and commissioned on 12 December 1999. Aluminium hull and superstructure. Used for carrying troops and supplies.

LC 1   *6/2005*, Maldives Coast Guard* / 1133511

Malta

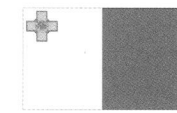

Country Overview

Formerly a British colony, the Republic of Malta gained independence in 1964. Situated 45 n miles south of Sicily, the country comprises the islands of Malta (95 square miles), Gozo (26 square miles), Comino, Kemmunett, and Filfla. It has a 76 n mile coastline with the Mediterranean Sea. The capital, largest town and principal port is Valletta. Territorial seas (12 n miles) are claimed. A fishery conservation zone of 25 n miles is also claimed.

Headquarters Appointments

Officer Commanding Maritime Squadron:
  Major Martin Cauchi Inglott

General

A coastal patrol force of small craft was formed in 1971. It is manned by the 2nd Regiment of the Armed Forces of Malta and primarily employed as a Coast Guard.

Personnel

2006: 220 (9 officers)

PATROL FORCES

2 MARINE PROTECTOR CLASS (PB)

P 51   P 52

Displacement, tons: 91 full load
Dimensions, feet (metres): 86.9 × 19 × 5.2 *(26.5 × 5.8 × 1.6)*
Main machinery: 2 MTU 8V 396TE94 diesels; 2,680 hp(m) *(1.97 MW)* sustained; 2 shafts
Speed, knots: 25. **Range, n miles:** 900 at 8 kt
Complement: 10 (1 officer)
Radars: Navigation: I-band.

Comment: P 51 ordered on 30 July 2001 and delivered on 25 October 2002. P 52 delivered on 7 July 2004. Built by Bollinger Shipyards to US Coast Guard specifications. The vessels are based on the hull of the Damen Stan Patrol 2600 in service with the Hong Kong police. Steel hull with GRP superstructure. A stern ramp is used for launching a 5.5 m RIB.

P 52   *7/2004, Armed Forces of Malta* / 0589762

1 DICIOTTI CLASS (OFFSHORE PATROL VESSEL) (PBO)

P 61

Displacement, tons: 393 full load
Dimensions, feet (metres): 175.2 × 26.6 × 17.7 *(53.4 × 8.1 × 5.4)*
Main machinery: 2 Isotto Fraschini V1716T2 MSD diesels; 6,335 hp *(4.7 MW)*; 2 shafts
Speed, knots: 23. **Range, n miles:** 2,100 at 16 kt
Complement: 25 (4 officers)
Guns: 1 Otobreda 25 mm. 2—12.7 mm MGs.
Radars: Surface search: E/F-band.
Navigation: I-band.
Helicopters: Platform for 1 medium.

Comment: Financed from the 5th Italo-Maltese Protocol, contract signed on 12 March 2004 with Fincantieri, Muggiano, Italy for the construction of one vessel. The ship arrived in Malta on 1 October 2005 and was commissioned on 3 November 2005. The contract included a training and logistic support package. Design based on Diciotti (modified Saettia) class vessels in service with the Italian Coast Guard. Steel hull with helicopter deck and stern ramp for launching a 6.5 m RIB.

P 61   *10/2005*, Air Squadron, AFM* / 1133090

2 BREMSE CLASS (INSHORE PATROL CRAFT) (PBI)

P 32 (ex-G 33/GS 20)   **P 33** (ex-G 22/GS 22)

Displacement, tons: 42 full load
Dimensions, feet (metres): 74.1 × 15.4 × 3.6 *(22.6 × 4.7 × 1.1)*
Main machinery: 2 Iveco diesels; 1,000 hp(m) *(745 kW)*; 2 shafts
Speed, knots: 17
Complement: 9
Guns: 1—12.7 mm MG.
Radars: Surface search: Racal 1290A; I-band.

Comment: Built in 1971-72 for the ex-GDR GBK. Transferred from Germany in mid-1992. Others of the class acquired by Tunisia. P 32 started mid-life upgrade in 2004.

P 33   *11/2000, Lawrence Dalli* / 0114529

2 SUPERVITTORIA 800 CLASS (SAR)

MELITA I   MELITA II

Displacement, tons: 12.5 full load
Dimensions, feet (metres): 37.7 × 16.1 × 2.6 *(11.5 × 4.9 × 0.8)*
Main machinery: 2 Cummins 6CTA 8.3 DIAMONS; 840 hp(m) *(618 kW)*; 2 Kamewa FF310 waterjets
Speed, knots: 34. **Range, n miles:** 160 at 34 kt
Complement: 4
Radars: Surface search: Raytheon Pathfinder SL 70; I-band.

Comment: Built in 1998 by Vittoria Naval Shipyard, Italy, for the Civil Protection Department of Malta. Transferred to the Armed Forces of Malta (AFM) in May 1999 for search and rescue duties. Although still the property of the Civil Protection Department, the Melita I and II are operated and maintained by the Maritime Squadron of the AFM.

MELITA II   *9/2005*, A A de Kruijf* / 1133088

2 SWIFT CLASS (HARBOUR PATROL CRAFT) (YP)

P 23 (ex-C 6823)   **P 24** (ex-C 6824)

Displacement, tons: 22.5 full load
Dimensions, feet (metres): 50 × 13 × 4.9 *(15.6 × 4 × 1.5)*
Main machinery: 2 GM 12V-71 diesels; 680 hp *(507 kW)* sustained; 2 shafts
Speed, knots: 25. **Range, n miles:** 400 at 18 kt
Complement: 6
Guns: 1—12.7 mm MG.
Radars: Surface search: Furuno 1040; I-band.

Comment: Built by Sewart Seacraft Ltd in 1967. Transferred from US in February 1971. Have an operational endurance of about 24 hours. Modernised in Malta in 1998/99.

P 24   *9/2005*, A A de Kruijf* / 1133089

LAND-BASED MARITIME AIRCRAFT

Notes: The Armed Forces of Malta operate two Britten-Norman BN-2B maritime patrol aircraft, five BAe Bulldog T. Mk 1 observation aircraft, two Nardi-MD NH 500HM, five SA.316B/D Alouette III and two AB-47G-2 helicopters.

BN ISLANDER   *2001, Douglas-John Falzon* / 0114534

NH 500   *4/2002, Adolfo Ortigueira Gil* / 0568875

ALOUETTE III   *2001, Pierre Gillard* / 0114533

Marshall Islands

Country Overview

The Republic of the Marshall Islands was a US-administered UN Trust territory from 1947 before becoming a self-governing republic in 1979. In 1986, a Compact of Free Association, delegating to the US the responsibility for defence and foreign affairs, came into effect. The country consists of some 1,200 atolls and reefs in the central Pacific. There are two main island groups: the Ratak and Ralik chains. Majuro is the capital island. Kwajalein is the largest atoll and is leased as a US missile test range. Bikini and Enewetak are former US nuclear test sites. An archipelagic state, territorial seas (12 n miles) are claimed. An Exclusive Economic Zone (EEZ) (200 n miles) is also claimed but limits have not been fully defined.

Headquarters Appointments

Chief of Surveillance:
  Major Thomas Heine

Personnel

2006: 30

Bases

Majuro

PATROL FORCES

1 PACIFIC CLASS (LARGE PATROL CRAFT) (PB)

Name	No	Builders	Commissioned
LOMOR	03	Australian Shipbuilding Industries	29 June 1991

Displacement, tons: 162 full load
Dimensions, feet (metres): 103.3 × 26.6 × 6.9
  (31.5 × 8.1 × 2.1)
Main machinery: 2 Caterpillar 3516TA diesels; 4,400 hp
  (3.3 MW) sustained; 2 shafts
Speed, knots: 20
Range, n miles: 2,500 at 12 kt
Complement: 17 (3 officers)
Guns: 1 — 12.7 mm MG.
Radars: Surface search: Furuno 8111; I-band.

Comment: The 14th craft to be built in this series for a number of Pacific Island coast guards. Ordered in 1989. Following the decision by the Australian government to extend the Pacific Patrol Boat project to a 30-year life for each boat, *Lomor* will undergo a life-extension refit in 2009 having undergone a half-life refit in 1999.

LOMOR
2001, Marshall Islands Sea Patrol Force
0109942

Mauritania

MARINE MAURITANIENNE

Country Overview

A former French colony, The Islamic Republic of Mauritania gained full independence in 1960. With an area of 397,955 square miles, it is situated in northwestern Africa and has borders to the north with western Sahara and Algeria, to the east with Mali and to the south with Senegal. It has a 405 n mile coastline with the Atlantic Ocean. The capital and largest city is Nouakchott while Nouadhibou is the principal port. Territorial seas (12 n miles) are claimed but while it has claimed a 200 n mile Exclusive Economic Zone (EEZ), its limits have not been defined by boundary agreements.

Headquarters Appointments

Commander of Navy:
  Colonel A Ould Yahya

Personnel

(a)   2006: 500 (40 officers) plus 200 marines
(b)   Voluntary service

Bases

Port Etienne, Nouadhibou
Port Friendship, Nouakchott

PATROL FORCES

Notes: An 18 m patrol vessel *Yacoub Ould Rajel* was donated by the European Union. Constructed by Raidco Marine, Lorient, it was delivered in 2000 and is used for fishery protection.

1 OPV 54 CLASS (PBO)

Name	No	Builders	Launched	Commissioned
ABOUBEKR BEN AMER	P 541	Leroux & Lotz, Lorient	17 Dec 1993	7 Apr 1994

Displacement, tons: 374 full load
Dimensions, feet (metres): 177.2 × 32.8 × 9.2 *(54 × 10 × 2.8)*
Main machinery: 2 MTU 16V 396 TE94 diesels; 5,712 hp(m) *(4.2 MW)* sustained; 2 auxiliary motors; 250 hp(m) *(184 kW)*; 2 shafts; cp props
Speed, knots: 23 (8 on motors). **Range, n miles:** 4,500 at 12 kt
Complement: 21 (3 officers)
Guns: 2—12.7 mm MGs.
Radars: Surface search: Racal Decca Bridgemaster 250; I-band.

Comment: Ordered in September 1992. This is the prototype to a Serter design of three similar craft built for the French Navy. Stern ramp for a 30 kt RIB. Option on a second of class not taken up. Refitted at Lorient 2001.

ABOUBEKR BEN AMER *7/2001, Peron/Marsan* / 0137787

1 PATRA CLASS (LARGE PATROL CRAFT) (PB)

Name	No	Builders	Commissioned
ENNASR	P 411	Auroux, Arcachon	14 May 1982
(ex-*Le Dix Juillet*, ex-*Rapière*)			

Displacement, tons: 147.5 full load
Dimensions, feet (metres): 132.5 × 19.4 × 5.2 *(40.4 × 5.9 × 1.6)*
Main machinery: 2 Wärtsilä UD 33 V12 diesels; 4,340 hp(m) *(3.2 MW)* sustained; 2 shafts
Speed, knots: 26.3. **Range, n miles:** 1,750 at 10 kt
Complement: 20 (2 officers)
Guns: 1 Bofors 40 mm/60. 1 Oerlikon 20 mm. 2—12.7 mm MGs.
Radars: Surface search: Racal/Decca 1226; I-band.

Comment: Originally built as a private venture by Auroux. Carried out trials with French crew as *Rapière*. Laid down 15 February 1980, launched 3 June 1981, commissioned for trials 1 November 1981. Transferred to Mauritania in 1982. Re-engined in 1993-94.

ENNASR *4/1998* / 0052598

1 LARGE PATROL CRAFT (PBO)

Name	No	Builders	Commissioned
VOUM-LEGLEITA (ex-*Poseidon*)	B 551 (ex-A 12)	Bazán	8 Aug 1964

Displacement, tons: 1,069 full load
Dimensions, feet (metres): 183.5 × 32.8 × 13.1 *(55.9 × 10 × 4)*
Main machinery: 2 Sulzer diesels; 3,200 hp *(2.53 MW)*; 1 shaft; cp prop
Speed, knots: 15. **Range, n miles:** 4,640 at 14 kt
Complement: 60
Guns: 2 Oerlikon 20 mm.
Radars: Navigation: 2 Decca TM 626; I-band.

Comment: Ocean going tug transferred from Spain in January 2000, about a year later than planned. Used primarily as an OPV and for fishery protection.

VOUM-LEGLEITA *1/2000, Diego Quevedo* / 0081240

1 HUANGPU CLASS (PB)

LIMAM EL HADRAMI P 601

Displacement, tons: 430 full load
Dimensions, feet (metres): 196.8 × 26.9 × 14.8 *(60.0 × 8.2 × 4.5)*
Main machinery: 3 MTU 12V 4000 diesels; 3 shafts
Speed, knots: 20
Guns: 4—37 mm.
Radars: Navigation: I-band.

Comment: Delivered from China on 20 April 2002.

1 ARGUIN CLASS (PBO)

Name	Builders	Commissioned
ARGUIN	Fassmer Werft, Berne/Motzen, Germany	17 July 2000

Measurement, tons: 1,000 dwt
Dimensions, feet (metres): 178.8 × 35.8 × 14.8 *(54.5 × 10.9 × 4.5)*
Main machinery: 2 MaK 6M20 diesels; 2,735 hp *(2.04 MW)*; 1 shaft; cp prop
Speed, knots: 16.5. **Range, n miles:** 15,000 at 12 kt
Complement: 13

Comment: Ordered in 1998. Hull construction at Yantar, Kaliningrad. Steel hull and superstructure. Equipped with interception craft on centreline ramp in mother-daughter configuration.

ARGUIN *7/2000, Fassmer Werft* / 1044268

4 MANDOVI CLASS (INSHORE PATROL CRAFT) (PB)

Displacement, tons: 15 full load
Dimensions, feet (metres): 49.2 × 11.8 × 2.6 *(15 × 3.6 × 0.8)*
Main machinery: 2 Deutz MWM TBD232V12 Marine diesels; 750 hp(m) *(551 kW)*; 2 Hamilton water-jets
Speed, knots: 24. **Range, n miles:** 250 at 14 kt
Complement: 8
Guns: 1—7.62 mm MG.
Radars: Navigation: Furuno FR 8030; I-band.

Comment: Built by Garden Reach, Calcutta and delivered from India in 1990. Some may not be operational.

LAND-BASED MARITIME AIRCRAFT

Numbers/Type: 2 Piper Cheyenne II.
Operational speed: 283 kt *(524 km/h)*.
Service ceiling: 31,600 ft *(9,630 m)*.
Range: 1,510 n miles *(2,796 km)*.
Role/Weapon systems: Coastal surveillance and EEZ protection acquired 1981. Sensors: Bendix 1400 weather radar; cameras. Weapons: Unarmed.

Mauritius

Country Overview

A former British colony, the Republic of Mauritius gained independence in 1968 and became a republic in 1992. Situated in the western Indian Ocean, east of Madagascar, it comprises the islands of Mauritius (720 square miles), Rodrigues (42 square miles), the Agalega islands to the north and the St Brandon Group (also known as the Cargados Carajos Shoals) to the northeast. The capital, largest town and principal port is Port Louis. Territorial seas (12 n miles) are claimed but, while it has declared a 200 n mile Exclusive Economic Zone (EEZ), the claim is complicated by disputes over the sovereignty of Tromelin Island (France) and Diego Garcia (UK).

A maritime security force was established in 1974 with the donation of MNS *Amar* by India. The National Coast Guard, a specialised wing of the Mauritius Police Force, was formed in 1987.

Headquarters Appointments

Commandant National Coast Guard:
  Commander Mahendra V S Negi

Bases

Port Louis (plus 24 manned CG stations)

Personnel

2006: 750 (including officers on deputation)

Maritime Aircraft

2 Dornier 228 (MPCG 1 and 3).
1 Britten-Norman BN-2-T Defender (MPCG 2).

COAST GUARD

Notes: (1) There are approximately 60 inshore craft (RHIBs, glass fibre boats and so on) in addition to those listed.
(2) It was announced on 27 October 2005 that the Coast Guard is to procure an offshore patrol vessel, possibly Sukanya class, and an Advanced Light Helicopter from India.

1 GUARDIAN CLASS (PSOH)

Name	No	Builders	Launched	Commissioned
VIGILANT	21	Talcahuano Yard, Chile	6 Dec 1995	27 June 1996

Displacement, tons: 1,650 full load
Dimensions, feet (metres): 246.1 × 45.9 × 12.8 *(75 × 14 × 3.9)*
Main machinery: 4 Caterpillar 3516 diesels; 11,530 hp *(8.6 MW)*; 2 shafts; cp props; bow thruster; 671 hp *(500 kW)*
Speed, knots: 22
Range, n miles: 6,500 at 19 kt
Complement: 57 (11 officers) plus 20 spare
Guns: 2 Bofors 40 mm/56 (1 twin). 2—12.7 mm MGs.
Radars: Surface search: Kelvin Hughes; I-band.
Helicopters: 1 light.

Comment: Contract signed with the Western Canada Marine Group in March 1994. Keel was laid in April 1994. All-steel construction. The ship can be operated by a crew of 18. Full helicopter facilities are included in the design which is based on a Canadian Fisheries vessel *Leonard J Cowley*. The ship was refitted in India 2003-04.

VIGILANT   *2/2001, Sattler/Steele* / 0114366

1 SDB MK 3 CLASS (PB)

GUARDIAN

Displacement, tons: 210 full load
Dimensions, feet (metres): 124 × 24.6 × 6.2 *(37.8 × 7.5 × 1.9)*
Main machinery: 2 MTU 16V 538 TB92 diesels; 6,820 hp(m) *(5 MW)* sustained; 2 shafts
Speed, knots: 21
Complement: 32
Guns: 1 Bofors 40 mm/60; 120 rds/min to 10 km *(5.5 n miles)*; weight of shell 0.89 kg.
Radars: Surface search: Furuno FK 1505 DA; I-band.

Comment: Transferred from Indian Navy in 1993. Built by Garden Reach, Calcutta in 1984. Undergoing mid-life upgrade at Mumbai 2005-06.

GUARDIAN   *7/2003, Arjun Sarup* / 0568319

2 ZHUK (TYPE 1400M) CLASS (PB)

RESCUER   RETRIEVER

Displacement, tons: 39 full load
Dimensions, feet (metres): 78.7 × 16.4 × 3.9 *(24 × 5 × 1.2)*
Main machinery: 2 M 401B diesels; 2,200 hp(m) *(1.6 MW)* sustained; 2 shafts
Speed, knots: 30
Range, n miles: 1,100 at 15 kt
Complement: 14 (2 officers)
Guns: 4—12.7 mm (2 twin) MGs.
Radars: Surface search: Spin Trough; I-band.

Comment: Acquired from the USSR on 3 December 1989. *Rescuer* machinery systems upgraded in 2004. Similar refit planned for *Retriever*.

RETRIEVER   *7/2003, Arjun Sarup* / 0568318

1 P-2000 CLASS (PB)

OBSERVER (ex-C 39)

Displacement, tons: 40 full load
Dimensions, feet (metres): 68.2 × 19 × 5.9 *(20.8 × 5.8 × 1.8)*
Main machinery: 2 Deutz MWM TBD234 V12 diesels; 1,646 hp(m) *(1.21 MW)* sustained; 1 Deutz MWM TBD234 V8 diesel; 550 hp(m) *(404 kW)* sustained; 3 Hamilton 402 waterjets
Speed, knots: 25
Range, n miles: 600 at 15 kt
Complement: 8 (1 officer)
Guns: 1—7.62 mm MG.
Radars: Navigation: Furuno; I-band.

Comment: Leased from the Indian Coast Guard in 2001. Originally commissioned in 1997, one of ten ordered from Anderson Marine, Goa in September 1990 to a P-2000 design by Amgram, similar to Archer class. GRP hull. Built at Goa.

OBSERVER   *6/2005*, Mauritius Coast Guard* / 1133238

4 HEAVY DUTY BOATS (PBI)

HDB 01-04

Displacement, tons: 5
Dimensions, feet (metres): 29.25 × 11.5 × 1.5 *(8.9 × 3.5 × 0.45)*
Main machinery: 2 Johnson outboard motors; 400 hp
Speed, knots: 45
Range, n miles: 300 at 35 kt
Complement: 4 (plus 14 passengers)

Comment: An initial order of four boats supplied by M/S Praga Marine, India in 2000. Option for six additional boats.

HEAVY DUTY BOAT   *2000, Mauritius Coast Guard* / 0105127

8 KAY MARINE HEAVY DUTY BOATS (PBI)

HDB 5-12

Displacement, tons: 6
Dimensions, feet (metres): 29.0 × 10.5 × 1.5 (8.85 × 3.21 × 0.45)
Main machinery: 2 Suzuki (1 twin) outboard motors; 450 hp
Speed, knots: 40
Complement: 18 including passengers

Comment: Acquired from Kay Marine Malaysia in November 2002. Deep Vee monohull of aluminium construction.

KAY MARINE HDB O5   *8/2003, Arjun Sarup* / 0568316

4 HALMATIC HEAVY DUTY BOATS (PBI)

HDB 13-16

Displacement, tons: 6
Dimensions, feet (metres): 30.2 × 10.2 × 3.3 (9.2 × 3.1 × 1.0)
Main machinery: 2 Yamaha V6 outboard motors; 450 hp
Speed, knots: 35
Complement: 18 including passengers

Comment: Acquired from Halmatic Ltd UK in June 2003.

HALMATIC HDB 16   *7/2003, Arjun Sarup* / 0568315

9 ROVER PATROL BOATS (PBI)

ROVER 1 -9

Displacement, tons: 3.5
Dimensions, feet (metres): 21.3 × 6.5 × 1.6 (6.5 × 2.0 × 0.5)
Main machinery: 1 Mariner outboard motor; 90 hp

Comment: Donated by Australia in 1988-89.

ROVER 2   *4/2003, Arjun Sarup* / 0568314

6 TORNADO VIKING 580 RHIB (PBI)

Displacement, tons: 2
Dimensions, feet (metres): 18.7 × 8.5 × 2.5 (5.7 × 2.6 × 0.75)
Main machinery: 1 Yamaha outboard motor; 90 hp
Speed, knots: 35
Complement: 10 including passengers

Comment: Acquired in 2004.

VIKING 580   *6/2004, Mauritius Coast Guard* / 0589763

Mexico

MARINA NACIONAL

Country Overview

The United Mexican States is a federal republic in North America. A total land area of 756,066 square miles includes a number of offshore islands. Bordered to the north by the United States and to the south by Belize and Guatemala, it has a 1,382 n mile coastline with the Caribbean and Gulf of Mexico and 3,656 n mile coastline with the Pacific Ocean. The capital and largest city is Mexico City while the principal ports are Acapulco (Pacific) and Veracruz (Gulf of Mexico). Territorial seas (12 n miles) are claimed. A 200 n mile EEZ has also been claimed but the limits have not been fully defined by boundary agreements.

Headquarters Appointments

Secretary of the Navy:
  Admiral Marco Antonio Peyrot Gonzalez
Under-Secretary of the Navy:
  Admiral Armando Sanchez Moreno
Inspector General of the Navy:
  Admiral Casimiro Martínez Pretelin
Chief of the Naval Staff:
  Vice Admiral Alberto Castro Rosas

Flag Officers

Commander in Chief, Gulf and Caribbean:
  Admiral Daniel Zamora Contreras
Commander in Chief, Pacific:
  Admiral Mariano Saynez Mendoza

Personnel

(a) 2006: 47,000 officers and men (including 946 Naval Air Force and 11,385 Marines)
(b) Military service

Naval Bases and Commands

The Naval Command is split between the Pacific and Gulf areas each with a Commander-in-Chief with HQs at Manzanillo and Tuxpan respectively. Each area has three naval Regions which are further subdivided into Zones (9), Sectors (11) and Subsectors (7). There is a Central Naval Region that has an HQ in Mexico City.

Gulf Area

First Naval Region (HQ Tampico, Tamaulipas).
  I Naval Zone (HQ Tampico, Tamaulipas).
    Naval Subsector (Matamoros, Tamaulipas).
  III Naval Zone (HQ Veracruz, Veracruz).
    Naval Sector (HQ Tuxpan, Veracruz).
    Naval Sector (HQ Coatzacoalcos, Veracruz).
Third Naval Region (HQ Lerma, Campeche).
  V Naval Zone (HQ Cuidad del Carmen, Campeche).
    Naval Sector (HQ Lerma, Campeche).
      Naval Subsector (HQ Dos Bocas, Tabasco).
      Naval Subsector (HQ Frontera, Tabasco).
Fifth Naval Region (HQ Yukalpeten, Yucatan).
  VII Naval Zone (HQ Isla Mujeres, Quintana Roo).
    Naval Sector (HQ Chetumal, Quintana Roo).
    Naval Sector (HQ Yukalpeten, Yucatan).
      Naval Subsector (HQ Isla Cozumel, Quintana Roo).

Pacific Area

Second Naval Region (HQ Mazatlan, Sinaloa).
  II Naval Zone (HQ Ensenada, Baja California).
  IV Naval Zone (HQ Guaymas, Sonora).
    Naval Sector (HQ Mazatlan, Sinaloa).
    Naval Sector (HQ Topolobampo, Sinaloa).
    Naval Sector (HQ La Paz, Baja California Sur).
      Naval Subsector (HQ Puerto Cortes, Baja California Sur).
      Naval Subsector (HQ Puerto Peñasco, Sonora).
Fourth Naval Region (HQ Manzanillo, Colima).
  VI Naval Zone (HQ Lazaro Cardenas, Michoacán).
    Naval Sector (HQ Puerto Vallarta, Jalisco).
    Naval Sector (HQ Manzanillo, Colima).
      Naval Subsector (HQ San Blas, Nayarit).
Sixth Naval Region (HQ Acapulco, Guerrero).
  VIII Naval Zone (HQ Acapulco, Guerrero).
  X Naval Zone (HQ Salina Cruz, Oaxaca).
    Naval Sector (HQ Puerto Madero, Chiapas).
Central Naval Region (HQ Mexico, DF).

Naval Air Force

Six naval air bases at Mexico City, Veracruz, Campeche, Chetumal, Tapachula and La Paz; there are two Naval Air Stations at Guaymas and Tampico.

Marine Forces

There are two Amphibious Reaction Forces, based at Manzanillo and Tuxpan; one Parachute Battalion, two Infantry Battalions and one Presidential Guards Battalion are based in Mexico City.

Strength of the Fleet

Type	Active	Building
Destroyers	1	—
Frigates	7	—
Gunships	19	2
Large Patrol Craft	26	—
Coast Guard	11	—
Coastal and River Patrol Craft	60	12
Survey Ships	7	—
Support Ships	7	—
Tankers	2	—
Sail Training Ship	1	—

Names and Pennant Numbers

Many of the ship names and pennant numbers were changed in early 1994 and again in 2001. Destroyers and frigates are named after Aztec emperors and forerunners of the Independence War (1810-1825). Gunboats are named after naval and military heroes.

DELETIONS

Patrol Forces

2003   *Andrés Quintana Roo, Manel Ramos Arizpe, José Maria Izazaga, Juan Bautista Morales, José Maria Mata, Pastor Rollaix, Luis Manue Rojas, Ignacio Zaagoza, Campeche, Margarita Maza de Juarez, Leandro Valle, Sebastian Lerdo de Tejada, Ignacio de la Llave, Ignacio Manuel Altamirano, Felipe Xicoténcatl, Juan Aldama*

2004   *Laguna de Tamiahua, Laguna de Lagartos, Lago de Patzcuaro, Benito Juarez*

2005   *Francisco Zarco, Laguna de Cuyutlan, Laguna de Alvarado, Laguna de Catemaco, Lago de Chapala*

Auxiliaries

2004   *Rio Panuco, Vicente Guerrero*

Training Ships

2005   *Aldebarán*

PENNANT LIST

Destroyers

D 102	Netzahualcoyotl

Frigates

F 201	Nicolas Bravo
F 202	Hermengildo Galeana
F 211	Ignacio Allende
F 212	Mariano Abasolo
F 213	Guadaloupe Victoria
F 214	Francisco Javier Mina

Patrol Forces

A 301	Huracán
A 302	Tormenta
PC 202	Cordova
PC 206	Ignacio López Rayón
PC 207	Manuel Crescencio Rejon
PC 208	Juan Antomio de la Fuente
PC 209	Leon Guzman
PC 210	Ignacio Ramirez
PC 211	Ignacio Mariscal
PC 212	Heriberto Jara Corona
PC 214	Colima
PC 215	José Joaquin Fernandez de Lizardi
PC 216	Francisco J Mugica
PC 218	José Maria del Castillo Velasco
PC 220	José Natividad Macias
PC 223	Tamaulipas
PC 224	Yucatan
PC 225	Tabasco
PC 226	Cochimie
PC 228	Puebla
PC 230	Leon Vicario
PC 231	Josefa Ortiz de Dominguez
PC 241	Démocrata
PC 271	Cabo Corrientes
PC 272	Cabo Corzo
PC 273	Cabo Catoche
PC 281	Punta Morro
PC 282	Punta Mastun
PI 1101	Polaris

PI 1102	Sirius
PI 1103	Capella
PI 1104	Canopus
PI 1105	Vega
PI 1106	Achernar
PI 1107	Rigel
PI 1108	Arcturus
PI 1109	Alpheratz
PI 1110	Procyon
PI 1111	Avior
PI 1112	Deneb
PI 1113	Formalhaut
PI 1114	Pollux
PI 1115	Regulus
PI 1116	Acrux
PI 1117	Spica
PI 1118	Hadar
PI 1119	Shaula
PI 1120	Mirfak
PI 1121	Ankaa
PI 1122	Bellatrix
PI 1123	Elnath
PI 1124	Alnilam
PI 1125	Peacock
PI 1126	Betelgeuse
PI 1127	Adhara
PI 1128	Alioth
PI 1129	Rasalhague
PI 1130	Nunki
PI 1131	Hamal
PI 1132	Suhail
PI 1133	Dubhe
PI 1134	Denebola
PI 1135	Alkaid
PI 1136	Alphecca
PI 1137	Eltanin
PI 1138	Kochab
PI 1139	Enif
PI 1140	Schedar
PI 1141	Markab
PI 1142	Megrez
PI 1143	Mizar
PI 1144	Phekda
PI 1145	Acamar
PI 1146	Diphda
PI 1147	Menkar

PI 1148	Sabik
PI 1201	Isla Coronado
PI 1202	Isla Lobos
PI 1203	Isla Guadalupe
PI 1204	Isla Cozumel
PI 1301	Acuario
PI 1302	Aguila
PI 1303	Aries
PI 1304	Auriga
PI 1305	Cancer
PI 1306	Capricorno
PI 1307	Centauro
PI 1308	Geminis
PI 1401	Miaplacidus
PO 102	Juan de la Barrera
PO 103	Mariano Escobedo
PO 104	Manuel Doblado
PO 106	Santos Degollado
PO 108	Juan Alvares
PO 109	Manuel Gutierrez Zamora
PO 110	Valentin Gomez Farias
PO 113	Ignacio Vallarta
PO 114	Jesus Gonzalez Ortega
PO 117	Mariano Matamoros
PO 121	Cadete Virgilio Uribe
PO 122	Teniente José Azueta
PO 123	Capitán de Fragata Pedro Sáinz de Baranda
PO 124	Comodoro Carlos Castillo Bretón
PO 125	Vicealmirante Othón P Blanco
PO 126	Contralmirante Angel Ortiz Monasterio
PO 131	Capitán de Navio Sebastian José Holzinger
PO 132	Capitán de Navio Blas Godinez
PO 133	Brigadier José Mariá de la Vega
PO 134	General Felipe B Berriozábal
PO 141	Justo Sierra Mendez
PO 143	Guillermo Prieto
PO 144	Matias Romero
PO 151	Durango
PO 152	Sonora
PO 153	Guanajuato
PO 154	Veracruz
PO 161	Oaxaca (bldg)
PO 162	Baja California (bldg)

Amphibious Forces

A 402	Manzanillo
A 411	Rio Papaloapan
A 412	Usumacinta

Survey and Research Ships

BI 01	Alejandro de Humboldt
BI 02	Onjuku
BI 03	Altair
BI 04	Antares
BI 05	Rio Suchiate
BI 06	Rio Ondo
BI 07	Moctezuma II
BI 08	Arrecife Alacrán
BI 09	Arrecife Rizo
BI 10	Arrecife Cabezo
BI 11	Arrecife Anegada de Adentro
BI 12	Rio Tuxpan

Auxiliaries

AMP 01	Huasteco
AMP 02	Zapoteco
ARE 01	Otomi
ARE 02	Yaqui
ARE 03	Seri
ARE 04	Cora
ARE 05	Iztaccihuatl
ARE 06	Popocatepetl
ARE 07	Citlaltepl
ARE 08	Xinantecatl
ARE 09	Matlalcueye
ARE 10	Tlaloc
ATQ 01	Aguascalientes
ATQ 02	Tlaxcala
ATR 01	Maya
ATR 03	Tarasco

Training Ships

D 111	Comodoro Manual Azueta
BE 01	Cuauhtemoc

DESTROYERS

1 QUETZALCOATL (GEARING FRAM I) CLASS (DDH)

Name	No	Builders	Laid down	Launched	Commissioned
NETZAHUALCOYOTL (ex-*Steinaker* DD 863)	D 102 (ex-E 11, ex-E 04)	Bethlehem, Staten Island	1 Sep 1944	13 Feb 1945	26 May 1945

Displacement, tons: 3,030 standard; 3,690 full load
Dimensions, feet (metres): 390.2 × 41.9 × 15 *(118.7 × 12.5 × 4.6)*
Main machinery: 4 Babcock & Wilcox boilers; 600 psi *(43.3 kg/cm²)*; 850°F *(454°C)*; 2 GE turbines; 60,000 hp *(45 MW)*; 2 shafts
Speed, knots: 15. **Range, n miles:** 5,800 at 15 kt
Complement: 250

Missiles: A/S: Honeywell Mk 112 octuple launcher ❶.
Guns: 4 USN 5 in *(127 mm)*/38 (2 twin) Mk 38 ❷; 15 rds/min to 17 km *(9.3 n miles)* anti-surface; 11 km *(5.9 n miles)* anti-aircraft; weight of shell 25 kg.
Torpedoes: 6—324 mm Mk 32 (2 triple tubes) ❸.
Countermeasures: ESM; WLR-1; radar warning.
Weapons control: Mk 37 GFCS. Mk 112 TFCS.
Radars: Air search: Lockheed SPS-40; B-band (E 10). Westinghouse SPS-29 ❹; B/C-band (E 11).
Surface search: Kelvin Hughes 17/9 ❺; I-band.
Navigation: Marconi LN66; I-band.
Fire control: Western Electric Mk 12/22 ❻; I/J-band.
Sonars: Sangano SQS 23; hull-mounted; active search and attack; medium frequency.

Helicopters: 1 MBB BO 105 CB ❼.

Programmes: Transferred from US by sale 24 February 1982.
Modernisation: A Bofors 57 mm gun was mounted between the torpedo tubes in B gun position in 1993 but removed in 2002. Flight deck slightly extended in 1996. New topmast and search radar also fitted in 1996. ASROC launchers not removed, as previously reported. Sonar also believed to be fitted.
Structure: The devices on top of the funnel are to reduce IR signature.
Operational: Top speed much reduced from the original 32 kt. Helicopter seldom carried. Pennant number changed in 2001. Based at Manzanillo.

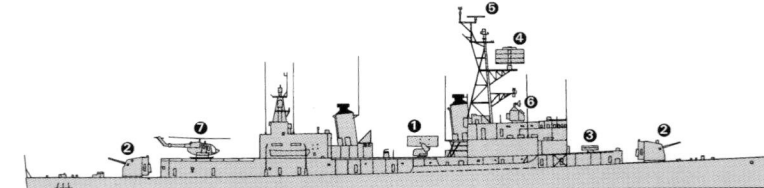

NETZAHUALCOYOTL

(Scale 1 : 1,200), Ian Sturton / 1153490

NETZAHUALCOYOTL

6/2005*, Mexican Navy / 1133543

FRIGATES

4 ALLENDE (KNOX) CLASS (FFHM)

Name	No	Builders	Laid down	Launched	Commissioned
IGNACIO ALLENDE (ex-*Stein*)	F 211 (ex-E 50, ex-FF 1065)	Lockheed	1 June 1970	19 Dec 1970	8 Jan 1972
MARIANO ABASOLO (ex-*Marvin Shields*)	F 212 (ex-E 51, ex-FF 1066)	Todd Shipyards	12 Apr 1968	23 Oct 1969	10 Apr 1971
GUADALOUPE VICTORIA (ex-*Pharris*)	F 213 (ex-E 52, ex-FF 1094)	Avondale Shipyards	11 Feb 1972	16 Dec 1972	26 Jan 1974
FRANCISCO JAVIER MINA (ex-*Whipple*)	F 214 (ex-FF 1062)	Todd Shipyards	24 Apr 1967	12 Apr 1968	22 Aug 1970

Displacement, tons: 3,011 standard; 4,260 full load
Dimensions, feet (metres): 439.6 × 46.8 × 15; 24.8 (sonar)
  (134 × 14.3 × 4.6; 7.8)
Main machinery: 2 Combustion Engineering/Babcock &
  Wilcox boilers; 1,200 psi *(84.4 kg/cm²)*; 950°F *(510°C)*;
  1 Westinghouse turbine; 35,000 hp *(26 MW)*; 1 shaft
Speed, knots: 27. **Range, n miles:** 4,000 at 22 kt on 1 boiler
Complement: 288 (20 officers)

Missiles: SAM: 1 Mk 25 launcher for Sea Sparrow (in F 211)
  ❶ (see *Structure*).
  SA-N-10; IR homing to 5 km *(2.7 n miles)* at 1.7 Mach;
  warhead 1.5 kg.
A/S: Honeywell ASROC Mk 16 octuple launcher with
  reload system (has 2 cells modified to fire Harpoon) **❷**;
  inertial guidance to 1.6 — 10 km *(1—5.4 n miles)*; payload
  Mk 46.
Guns: 1 FMC 5 in *(127 mm)*/54 Mk 42 Mod 9 **❸**; 20-40 rds/
  min to 24 km *(13 n miles)* anti-surface; 14 km *(7.7 n miles)*
  anti-aircraft; weight of shell 32 kg.
  4—12.7 mm MGs (F 214).
Torpedoes: 4—324 mm Mk 32 (2 twin) fixed tubes **❹**.
  22 Honeywell Mk 46; anti-submarine; active/passive
  homing to 11 km *(5.9 n miles)* at 40 kt; warhead 44 kg.
Countermeasures: Decoys: 2 Loral Hycor SRBOC
  6-barrelled fixed Mk 36 **❺**; IR flares and chaff to 4 km
  (2.2 n miles).T Mk-6 Fanfare/SLQ-25 Nixie; torpedo decoy.
  Prairie Masker hull and blade rate noise suppression.
ESM: SLQ-32(V)2 **❻**; intercept.

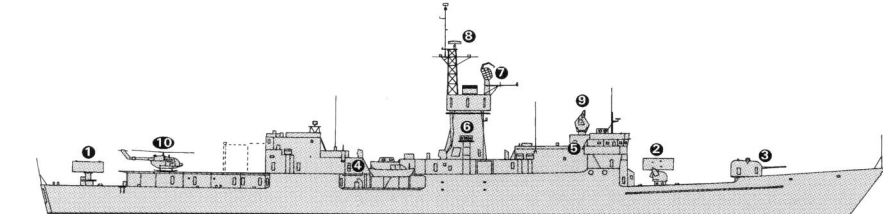

IGNACIO ALLENDE *(Scale 1 : 1,200), Ian Sturton* / 0114668

Weapons control: Mk 68 Mod 3 GFCS. Mk 114 Mod 6 ASW FCS.
  Mk 1 target designation system. MMS target acquisition
  sight (for mines, small craft and low flying aircraft).
Radars: Air search: Lockheed SPS-40B **❼**; B-band.
  Surface search: Raytheon SPS-10 or Norden SPS-67 **❽**; G-band.
  Navigation: Marconi LN66; I-band.
  Fire control: Western Electric SPG-53D/F **❾**; I/J-band.
  Tacan: SRN 15.
Sonars: EDO/General Electric SQS-26CX; bow-mounted;
  active search and attack; medium frequency.

Helicopters: 1 BO 105 CB **❿**.

Programmes: First pair decommissioned from USN in
  1992/93. Both transferred on 29 January 1997 and

arrived in Mexico 16 August 1997. Both then underwent
extensive refits, entering service on 23 November 1998.
Third of class (ex-*Pharris*) transferred 2 February 2000
and recommissioned on 16 March 2000. The fourth
ship (ex-*Whipple*) transferred in August 2001 and
recommissioned on 1 November 2002.
Modernisation: To be fitted with SSM (Harpoon or Gabriel II).
Structure: Four Mk 32 torpedo tubes are fixed in the
midships structure, two to a side, angled out at 45°. The
original Knox class SAM launcher has been put back aft,
in F 211 only.
Operational: In US service these ships had Harpoon SSM,
but it is reported that these weapons are not carried.
Pennant numbers changed in 2001. F 214 based at
Manzanillo, the remainder at Tuxpan.

IGNACIO ALLENDE (old number) *11/1998, Mexican Navy* / 0017679

IGNACIO ALLENDE *6/2005*, Mexican Navy* / 1153500

2 BRAVO (BRONSTEIN) CLASS (FFH)

Name	No	Builders	Laid down	Launched	Commissioned
NICOLAS BRAVO (ex-*McCloy*)	F 201 (ex-E 40, ex-FF 1038)	Avondale Shipyards	15 Sep 1961	9 June 1962	21 Oct 1963
HERMENEGILDO GALEANA (ex-*Bronstein*)	F 202 (ex-E 42, ex-FF 1037)	Avondale Shipyards	16 May 1961	31 Mar 1962	16 June 1963

Displacement, tons: 2,360 standard; 2,650 full load
Dimensions, feet (metres): 371.5 × 40.5 × 13.5; 23 (sonar)
(*113.2 × 12.3 × 4.1; 7*)
Main machinery: 2 Foster-Wheeler boilers; 1 De Laval
geared turbine; 20,000 hp (*14.92 MW*); 1 shaft
Speed, knots: 23.5. **Range, n miles:** 3,924 at 15 kt
Complement: 207 (17 officers)

Missiles: A/S: Honeywell ASROC Mk 112 octuple launcher ❶.
Guns: 2 USN 3 in (*76 mm*)/50 (twin) Mk 33 ❷; 50 rds/min
to 12.8 km (*7 n miles*); weight of shell 6 kg, or 1 Bofors
57 mm/70 Mk 2; 220 rds/min to 17 km (*9.3 n miles*);
weight of shell 2.4 kg.
Torpedoes: 6—324 mm US Mk 32 Mod 7 (2 triple) tubes ❸.
14 Honeywell Mk 46; anti-submarine; active/passive
homing to 11 km (*5.9 n miles*) at 40 kt; warhead 44 kg.
Countermeasures: Decoys: 2 Loral Hycor 6-barrelled fixed
Mk 33; IR flares and chaff to 4 km (*2.2 n miles*).
T-Mk 6 Fanfare; torpedo decoy system.
Weapons control: Mk 56 GFCS. Mk 114 ASW FCS. Mk 1
target designation system. Elsag NA 18 optronic director
may be fitted.
Radars: Air search: Lockheed SPS-40D ❹; B-band; range
320 km (*175 n miles*).
Surface search: Raytheon SPS-10F ❺; G-band.
Navigation: Marconi LN66; I-band.
Fire control: General Electric Mk 35 ❻; I/J-band.

Sonars: EDO/General Electric SQS-26 AXR; bow-mounted;
active search and attack; medium frequency.

Helicopters: Platform and some facilities but no hangar.

Programmes: Transferred from the US to Mexico by sale
12 November 1993 having paid off in December 1990.
Modernisation: Bofors 57 mm SAK may be fitted to replace
the Mk 33 gun, possibly with an Elsag NA 18 optronic
director.

Structure: Position of stem anchor and portside anchor
(just forward of gun mount) necessitated by large
bow sonar dome. As built, a single 3 in (Mk 34) open
mount was aft of the helicopter deck; removed for
installation of towed sonar which has since been
taken out.
Operational: ASROC is non-operational. Pennant numbers
changed in 2001. Both based at Manzanillo.

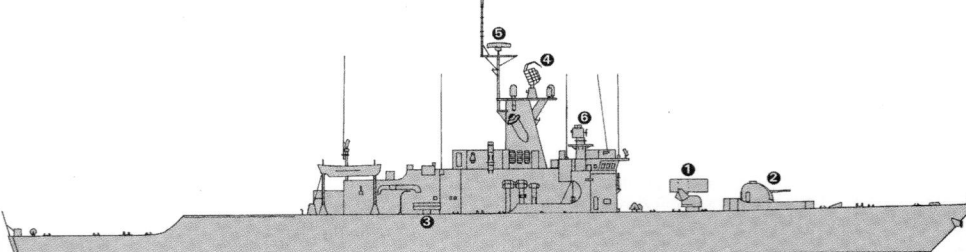

NICOLAS BRAVO (Scale 1 : 900), Ian Sturton / 0506240

HERMENEGILDO GALEANA 6/2004, *Mexican Navy* / 0589777

HERMENEGILDO GALEANA 6/2004, *Mexican Navy* / 0589778

SHIPBORNE AIRCRAFT

Numbers/Type: 6 MD 902 Explorer.
Operational speed: 113 kt (*210 km/h*).
Service ceiling: 9,845 ft (*3,000 m*).
Range: 407 n miles (*754 km*).
Role/Weapon systems: Coastal patrol helicopter acquired 1999-2000 for patrol, fisheries
protection and EEZ protection duties; SAR as secondary role. Sensors: Bendix search
radar. Weapons: MGs or rocket pods.

BO 105CB 9/1994, *Mexican Navy* / 0052606

Numbers/Type: 11 Bolkow BO 105.
Operational speed: 100 kt (*185 km/h*).
Service ceiling: 17,000 ft (*5,180 m*).
Range: 160 n miles (*296 km*).
Role/Weapon systems: Coastal patrol helicopter acquired 1982-86 for patrol, fisheries
protection and EEZ protection duties; SAR as secondary role. A modernisation
programme was announced in October 2003 with the first upgraded aircraft delivered
in 2004. Sensor: Bendix search radar. Weapons: MGs or rocket pods.

BO 105 6/2004*, *Mexican Navy* / 1133542

Numbers/Type: 2 Eurocopter AS 555 AF Fennec.
Operational speed: 121 kt (*225 km/h*).
Service ceiling: 13,120 ft (*4,000 m*).
Range: 389 n miles (*722 km*).
Role/Weapon systems: Patrol helicopter for EEZ protection and SAR. Operated from Oaxaca
class patrol ships. More may be acquired when funds are available. Sensors: Bendix 1500
search radar. Weapons: Can carry up to two torpedoes, rocket pods or an MG.

AS 555 AF 6/2005*, *Mexican Navy* / 1133541

Numbers/Type: 2 Eurocopter AS 565ME Panther.
Operational speed: 165 kt (*305 km/h*).
Service ceiling: 15,223 ft (*4,640 m*).
Range: 200 n miles (*370 km*).
Role/Weapon systems: Transport and reconnaissance helicopter procured in June 2005.
Capable of carrying 8 passengers or 1,000 kg load.

AS 565 ME 6/2005*, *Mexican Navy* / 1133540

LAND-BASED MARITIME AIRCRAFT (FRONT LINE)

Notes: (1) Transport aircraft used include two Rockwell 306 Sabreliners, three Learjets, one Dash 8-200, 18 Mil Mi-17, four Mil Mi-2 Hoplite and four MD 500E.
(2) Training aircraft include seven Aeromacchi M-290TP Redigos, 14 Maule MX-7-180, nine Zlin Z242L, three Beech B55 Baron, one Robinson R22 Mariners and five Lancair.

Mi-2 *6/2005*, Mexican Navy* / 1133539

SABRELINER *6/2005*, Mexican Navy* / 1133538

Mi-17 *6/2005*, Mexican Navy* / 1133537

Numbers/Type: 3 Grumman E-2C Hawkeye.
Operational speed: 323 kt *(598 km/h)*.
Service ceiling: 37,000 ft *(11,278 m)*.
Range: 1,540 n miles *(2,852 km)*.
Role/Weapon systems: Acquired from Israel in 2004 after refurbishment by Israel Aircraft Industries' (IAI's) Bedek Aviation Group. Equipment details are speculative. Sensors: ESM: ALR-73 PDS; Airborne tactical data system with Links 4A and 11; AN/APS-125 radar; Mk XII IFF. Weapons: Unarmed.

E-2C *6/2004, Mexican Navy* / 0589773

Numbers/Type: 8 CASA C-212 Aviocar.
Operational speed: 190 kt *(353 km/h)*.
Service ceiling: 24,000 ft *(7,315 m)*.
Range: 1,650 n miles *(3,055 km)*.
Role/Weapon systems: Acquired from 1987 and used for Maritime Surveillance. Two aircraft upgraded in Spain with EADS/CASA Integrated Tactical System (FITS) in 2003. Two further upgraded in Mexico to be followed by the remainder. Sensors: Search radar; APS 504. Weapons: Unarmed.

C-212 *6/2005*, Mexican Navy* / 1133536

Numbers/Type: 4 Rockwell Turbo Commander.
Operational speed: 250 kt *(463 km/h)*.
Service ceiling: 31,000 ft *(9,450 m)*.
Range: 480 n miles *(890 km)*.
Role/Weapon systems: Acquired in 1992. Used for reconnaissance and transport.

TURBO COMMANDER *6/2004*, Mexican Navy* / 1133544

Numbers/Type: 6 Antonov AN-32B.
Operational speed: 250 kt *(463 km/h)*.
Service ceiling: 26,000 ft *(7,925 m)*.
Range: 750 n miles *(1,390 km)*.
Role/Weapon systems: Acquired 1997-99. Used for transport and reconnaissance. Two aircraft fitted with FLIR.

An-32B *6/2004, Mexican Navy* / 0589775

PATROL FORCES

Notes: Two further missile-armed fast-attack craft are to be acquired.

8 ACUARIO CLASS (COMBATBOAT 90HMN) (PBF)

ACUARIO PI 1301	**CANCER** PI 1305
AGUILA PI 1302	**CAPRICORNO** PI 1306
ARIES PI 1303	**CENTAURO** PI 1307
AURIGA PI 1304	**GEMINIS** PI 1308

Displacement, tons: 19 full load
Dimensions, feet (metres): 52.2 × 12.5 × 2.6 *(15.9 × 3.8 × 0.8)*
Main machinery: 2 CAT 3406E diesels; 1,605 hp(m) *(1.18 MW)*; 2 waterjets
Speed, knots: 47. **Range, n miles:** 240 at 30 kt
Complement: 4
Guns: 1 Oto Melara 12.7 mm MG.
Radars: Surface search: Litton Decca Bridgemaster E; I-band.

Comment: A further development of the Polaris class which are based on the Swedish Combatboat 90 and built by ASTIMAR 3, Coatzacoalcos. 1301 and 1302 commissioned on 1 June 2004 and the remainder on 1 September 2004. All named after stars. P 1307-1308 known as Acuario B class. Based at Puerto Peñasco (1301); El Mezquital (1302, 1303); Frontera (1304); Tampico (1305, 1306); Lázaro (1307, 1308).

AGUILA *6/2005*, Mexican Navy* / 1133523

4 HOLZINGER CLASS (GUNSHIPS) (PSOH)

Name	No	Builders	Laid down	Launched	Commissioned
CAPITÁN DE NAVIO SEBASTIAN JOSÉ HOLZINGER (ex-*Uxmal*)	PO 131 (ex-C 01, ex-GA 01)	ASTIMAR 20, Salina Cruz, Oaxaco	1 June 1985	1 June 1988	1 May 1991
CAPITÁN DE NAVIO BLAS GODINEZ (ex-*Mitla*)	PO 132 (ex-C 02, ex-GA 02)	ASTIMAR 1, Tampico, Tamaulipas	1 July 1985	22 Mar 1988	1 Nov 1991
BRIGADIER JOSÉ MARIÁ DE LA VEGA (ex-*Peten*)	PO 133 (ex-C 03, ex-GA 03)	ASTIMAR 20, Salina Cruz, Oaxaco	22 Sep 1986	1 June 1988	16 Mar 1994
GENERAL FELIPE B BERRIOZÁBAL (ex-*Anahuac*)	PO 134 (ex-C 04, ex-GA 04)	ASTIMAR 1, Tampico, Tamaulipas	9 Mar 1988	21 Apr 1991	16 Mar 1994

Displacement, tons: 1,290 full load
Dimensions, feet (metres): 244.1 × 34.4 × 11.2
(74.4 × 10.5 × 3.4)
Main machinery: 2 MTU 20V 956TB92 diesels; 11,700 hp(m)
(8.6 MW) sustained; 2 shafts
Speed, knots: 22. **Range, n miles:** 3,820 at 16 kt
Complement: 75 (11 officers)

Guns: 2 Bofors 40 mm/60 (1 twin).
Combat data systems: Elsag 2 CSDA-10.
Weapons control: Garfio 1.5 and Garfio 2 optronic
directors.
Radars: Surface search: Raytheon SPS-64(V)6A; I-band.
Navigation: Kelvin Hughes Nucleus; I-band.

Helicopters: 1 MBB BO 105 CB.

Programmes: Originally four were ordered from Tampico
and Veracruz. First laid down November 1983, second
in 1984 but then there were delays caused by financial
problems. Named after military heroes.
Structure: An improved variant of the Bazán Halcon (Uribe)
class with a flight deck extended to the stern. A twin
Bofors 40 mm/60 has replaced the 57 mm gun in PO 134
and is probably now fitted throughout the class.
Operational: Pennant numbers changed in 2001. All based
at Lazaro.

GENERAL FELIPE B BERRIOZÁBAL   *6/2005*, Mexican Navy* / 1133533

3 + 1 SIERRA CLASS (GUNSHIPS) (PSOH)

Name	No	Builders	Laid down	Launched	Commissioned
JUSTO SIERRA MENDEZ	PO 141 (ex-C 2001)	ASTIMAR 1, Tampico, Tamaulipas	19 Jan 1998	1 June 1998	1 June 1998
GUILLERMO PRIETO	PO 143 (ex-C 2003)	ASTIMAR 1, Tampico, Tamaulipas	1 June 1998	18 Sep 1999	18 Sep 1999
MATIAS ROMERO	PO 144 (ex-C 2004)	ASTIMAR 20, Salina Cruz, Oaxaco	23 July 1998	17 Sep 1999	17 Sep 1999

Displacement, tons: 1,344 full load
Dimensions, feet (metres): 231 × 34.4 × 9.3
(70.4 × 10.5 × 2.8)
Main machinery: 2 Caterpillar 3616 V 16 diesels; 6,197 hp(m)
(4.55 MW); 2 shafts
Speed, knots: 18
Complement: 76 (10 officers)

Missiles: SA-N-10 (PO 144); IR homing to 5 km *(2.7 n miles)*
at 1.7 Mach; warhead 1.5 kg.
Guns: 1 Bofors 57 mm/70 Mk 3; 220 rds/min to 17 km
(9.3 n miles); weight of shell 2.4 kg.
Combat data systems: Alenia 2.
Weapons control: Saab EOS 450 optronic director.
Radars: Air/surface search: E/F-band.
Surface search: I-band.
Helicopters: 1 MD 902 Explorer.

Programmes: Follow on to the Holzinger class. Ordered in
1997.
Structure: Derived from the Holzinger class but with a
markedly different superstructure. All ships carry 11 m
interceptor craft capable of 50 kt.
Operational: All based at Lazaro. PO 142 *Benito Juarez*
badly damaged by fire in October 2003 and subsequently
decommissioned. The ship is to be rebuilt with a new
superstructure and systems. Work began in 2005.

JUSTO SIERRA MENDEZ   *6/2005*, Mexican Navy* / 1133535

JUSTO SIERRA MENDEZ   *6/2004, Mexican Navy* / 0589771

4 DURANGO CLASS (GUNSHIPS) (PSOH)

Name	No	Builders	Laid down	Launched	Commissioned
DURANGO	PO 151	ASTIMAR 1, Tampico, Tamaulipas	18 Dec 1999	11 Sep 2000	30 July 2002
SONORA	PO 152	ASTIMAR 20, Salina Cruz, Oaxaco	14 Dec 1999	4 Sep 2000	4 Sep 2000
GUANAJUATO	PO 153	ASTIMAR 1, Tampico, Tamaulipas	2000	13 Dec 2001	13 Dec 2001
VERACRUZ	PO 154	ASTIMAR 20, Salina Cruz, Oaxaco	4 Sep 2000	17 Dec 2001	11 Dec 2003

Displacement, tons: 1,470 full load
Dimensions, feet (metres): 268 × 34.4 × 9.3
  (81.8 × 10.5 × 2.8)
Main machinery: 2 Caterpillar 3616 V16 diesels; 6,197 hp(m)
  (4.55 MW); 2 shafts
Speed, knots: 18
Complement: 76 (10 officers)

Guns: 1 Bofors 57 mm/70 Mk 3; 220 rds/min to 17 km
  (9.3 n miles); weight of shell 2.4 kg.

Combat data systems: Alenia 2.
Weapons control: Saab EOS 450 optronic director.
Radars: Air/surface search: E/F-band.
Surface search: I-band.

Helicopters: 1 MD 902 Explorer.

Programmes: Follow on to the Sierra class. Ordered on
1 June 1998.

Structure: Derived from the Holzinger class but with
a markedly different superstructure. Durango class
slightly larger than the Sierra class. All ships carry 11 m
interceptor craft capable of 50 kt.
Operational: PO 151 and PO 152 based at Tampico and
PO 153 and PO 154 at Coatzacoalcos.

DURANGO　　　　　　　　　　　　　　　　　　　　　　　　　　　　　　*6/2004, Mexican Navy* / 0589770

2 + 4 OAXACA CLASS (GUNSHIPS) (PSOH)

Name	No	Builders	Laid down	Launched	Commissioned
OAXACA	PO 161	ASTIMAR 20, Salina Cruz, Oaxaco	17 Dec 2001	11 Apr 2003	1 May 2003
BAJA CALIFORNIA	PO 162	ASTIMAR 1, Tampico, Tamaulipas	13 Dec 2001	21 May 2003	1 Apr 2003
—	PO 163	ASTIMAR 20, Salina Cruz, Oaxaco	11 Apr 2003	2004	Oct 2006
—	PO 164	ASTIMAR 1, Tampico, Tamaulipas	21 May 2003	2004	Oct 2006
—	PO 165	ASTIMAR 20, Salina Cruz, Oaxaco	2005	2007	2008
—	PO 166	ASTIMAR 1, Tampico, Tamaulipas	2005	2007	2008

Displacement, tons: 1,680
Dimensions, feet (metres): 282.2 × 34.4 × 9.3
  (86.0 × 10.5 × 3.6)
Main machinery: 2 Caterpillar 3916 V16 diesels; 2 shafts
Speed, knots: 20
Complement: 77

Guns: 1 Oto Melara 3 in *(76 mm)*/62 Super Rapid;
  120 rds/min to 16 km *(8.7 n miles)*; weight of shell 6 kg.
  1 Oto Melara 25 mm.
Combat data systems: Alenia.
Radars: Surface search/navigation: Terma Scanter 2001;
  I-band.
Fire control: Alenia NA-25; I-band.

Helicopters: Eurocopter AS 565 Panther.

Structure: A further derivation of the basic Holzinger class
and a slightly longer version of the Durango class.
Capable of operating a helicopter and equipped with
a fast 11 m interception boat capable of 50 kt. PO 161
and PO 162 based at Coatzacoalcos.

BAJA CALIFORNIA　　　　　　　　　　　　　　　　　　　　　　　　*6/2005*, Mexican Navy* / 1133530

6 URIBE CLASS (GUNSHIPS) (PSOH)

Name	No	Builders	Laid down	Launched	Commissioned
CADETE VIRGILIO URIBE	PO 121 (ex-C 11, ex-GH 01)	Bazán, San Fernando	1 July 1981	12 Nov 1981	1 Aug 1982
TENIENTE JOSÉ AZUETA	PO 122 (ex-C 12, ex-GH 02)	Bazán, San Fernando	7 Sep 1981	12 Dec 1981	23 Sep 1982
CAPITÁN de FRAGATA PEDRO SÁINZ de BARANDA	PO 123 (ex-C 13, ex-GH 03)	Bazán, San Fernando	22 Oct 1981	29 Jan 1982	1 May 1983
COMODORO CARLOS CASTILLO BRETÓN	PO 124 (ex-C 14, ex-GH 04)	Bazán, San Fernando	11 Nov 1981	26 Feb 1982	24 May 1983
VICEALMIRANTE OTHÓN P BLANCO	PO 125 (ex-C 15, ex-GH 05)	Bazán, San Fernando	18 Dec 1981	26 Mar 1982	24 Feb 1983
CONTRALMIRANTE ANGEL ORTIZ MONASTERIO	PO 126 (ex-C 16, ex-GH 06)	Bazán, San Fernando	30 Dec 1981	4 May 1982	24 Feb 1983

Displacement, tons: 988 full load
Dimensions, feet (metres): 219.9 × 34.4 × 11.5
(67 × 10.5 × 3.5)
Main machinery: 2 MTU-Bazán 16V 956 TB91 diesels;
7,500 hp(m) *(5.52 MW)* sustained; 2 shafts
Speed, knots: 22
Range, n miles: 5,000 at 13 kt
Complement: 46 (7 officers)

Guns: 1 Bofors 40 mm/70; 300 rds/min to 12.5 km
(6.7 n miles); weight of shell 0.96 kg.
Weapons control: Naja optronic director.
Radars: Surface search: Decca AC 1226; I-band.
Navigation: I-band.
Tacan: SRN 15.

Helicopters: 1 MBB BO 105 CB.

Programmes: Ordered in 1980 to a Halcon class design.
Contracts for a further eight of the class have been
shelved. Pennant numbers changed in 1992. Named after
naval heroes.
Structure: Flight deck extends to the stern. Similar ships
built for Argentina.
Operational: Used for EEZ patrol. Pennant numbers
changed in 2001. All based at Ensenada.

COMODORO CARLOS CASTILLO BRETÓN   *9/2002, B Sullivan* / 0533280

1 + 1 (4) CENTENARIO CLASS (PBO)

Name	No	Builders	Launched	Commissioned
DÉMOCRATA	PC 241 (ex-C 101)	ASTIMAR 6, Varadero, Guaymas	16 Oct 1997	12 Jan 1998
TAMPICO		ASTIMAR 6, Varadero, Guaymas	2006	2007

Displacement, tons: 450 full load
Dimensions, feet (metres): 172.2 × 29.5 × 8.5 *(52.5 × 9 × 2.6)*
Main machinery: 2 MTU 20V 956 TB92 diesels; 6,119 hp(m) *(4.5 MW)*; 2 shafts
Speed, knots: 30
Complement: 36 (13 officers)
Guns: 2 Bofors 40 mm/60 (twin).
Radars: Surface search: Racal Decca; E/F-band.

Comment: Based at Tuxpan. A second unit was under construction in August 2002 but
the building programme has not been confirmed. Further units may be built subject to
funding. A 50 kt Boston Whaler launch is carried at the stern.

DÉMOCRATA   *6/2004, Mexican Navy* / 0589769

3 CAPE (PGM 71) CLASS (LARGE PATROL CRAFT) (PB)

Name	No	Builders	Commissioned
CABO CORRIENTES	PC 271 (ex-P 42)	CG Yard, Curtis Bay	16 Mar 1990
(ex-*Jalisco*, ex-*Cape Carter*)			
CABO CORZO	PC 272 (ex-P 43)	CG Yard, Curtis Bay	21 Apr 1990
(ex-*Nayarit*, ex-*Cape Hedge*)			
CABO CATOCHE (ex-*Cape Hattaras*)	PC 273 (ex-P 44	CG Yard, Curtis Bay	18 Mar 1991

Displacement, tons: 98 standard; 148 full load
Dimensions, feet (metres): 95 × 20.2 × 6.6 *(28.9 × 6.2 × 2)*
Main machinery: 2 GM 16V-149TI diesels; 2,322 hp *(1.73 MW)* sustained; 2 shafts
Speed, knots: 20
Range, n miles: 2,500 at 10 kt
Complement: 14 (1 officer)
Guns: 1—20 mm. 2—12.7 mm MGs.
Radars: Navigation: Raytheon SPS-64; I-band.

Comment: All built in 1953; have been re-engined and extensively modernised.
Transferred under the FMS programme, having paid off from the US Coast Guard.
Pennant numbers changed in 2001. PC 271 and PC 272 based at Puerto Vallarta and
PC 273 at Isla Cozumel.

CABO CORZO   *6/2005*, Mexican Navy* / 1133531

2 POINT CLASS (LARGE PATROL CRAFT) (PB)

Name	No	Builders	Commissioned
PUNTA MORRO	PC 281 (ex-P 60, ex-P 45)	CG Yard, Curtis Bay	19 July 1991
(ex-*Point Verde*)			
PUNTA MASTUN	PC 282 (ex-P 61, ex-P 46)	CG Yard, Curtis Bay	19 July 1991
(ex-*Point Herron*)			

Displacement, tons: 67 full load
Dimensions, feet (metres): 83 × 17.2 × 5.8 *(25.3 × 5.2 × 1.8)*
Main machinery: 2 Caterpillar diesels; 1,600 hp *(1.19 MW)*; 2 shafts
Speed, knots: 12
Range, n miles: 1,500 at 8 kt
Complement: 10
Guns: 2—12.7 mm MGs (can be carried).
Radars: Surface search: Raytheon SPS-64; I-band.

Comment: Ex-US Coast Guard craft built in 1961. Steel hulls and aluminium superstructures.
Speed much reduced from original 23 kt. Pennant numbers changed in 2001. Both based
at Lerma.

PUNTA MASTUN   *6/2005*, Mexican Navy* / 1133529

10 VALLE (AUK) CLASS (COAST GUARD) (PG/PGH)

JUAN DE LA BARRERA (ex-*Guillermo Prieto*, ex-*Symbol* MSF 123) PO 102 (ex-C 71, ex-G-02)
MARIANO ESCOBEDO (ex-*Champion* MSF 314) PO 103 (ex-C 72, ex-G-03)
MANUEL DOBLADO (ex-*Defense* MSF 317) PO 104 (ex-C 73, ex-G-05)
SANTOS DEGOLLADO (ex-*Gladiator* MSF 319) PO 106 (ex-C 75, ex-G-07)
JUAN N ALVARES (ex-*Ardent* MSF 340) PO 108 (ex-C 77, ex-G-09)
MANUEL GUTIERREZ ZAMORA (ex-*Roselle* MSF 379) PO 109 (ex-C 78, ex-G-10)
VALENTIN GOMEZ FARIAS (ex-*Starling* MSF 64) PO 110 (ex-C 79, ex-G-11)
IGNACIO L VALLARTA (ex-*Velocity* MSF 128) PO 113 (ex-C 82, ex-G-14)
JESUS GONZALEZ ORTEGA (ex-*Chief* MSF 315) PO 114 (ex-C 83, ex-G-15)
MARIANO MATAMOROS (ex-*Hermenegildo Galeana*, ex-*Sage* MSF 111) PO 117 (ex-C 86, ex-G-19)

Displacement, tons: 1,065 standard; 1,250 full load
Dimensions, feet (metres): 221.2 × 32.2 × 10.8 *(67.5 × 9.8 × 3.3)*
Main machinery: Diesel-electric; 2 Caterpillar diesels; 2 shafts
Speed, knots: 18. **Range, n miles:** 6,900 at 10 kt
Complement: 73 (9 officers)
Guns: 1 USN 3 in *(76 mm)*/50. 4 Bofors 40 mm/60 (2 twin).
  4—12.7 mm (2 twin) MGs (in some on quarterdeck).
Radars: Surface search: Kelvin Hughes 14/9 (in most); I-band.
Helicopters: Platform for 1 BO 105 (C 72, C 73 and C 79 only).

Comment: Transferred from US, six in February 1973, four in April 1973, nine in September 1973. Eight have since been deleted. Employed on Coast Guard duties. All built during Second World War. Variations are visible in the mid-ships section where some have a bulwark running from the break of the forecastle to the quarterdeck. Minesweeping gear removed. All ships re-engined 1999-2002. Some carry a Pirana 26 kt motor launch armed with 40 mm grenade launchers and 7.62 mm MGs. P 103, P 104 and P 110 have had helicopter flight decks installed aft. Plans to fit flight decks in the others have been shelved. PO 102, 103, 104, 106, 108 and 113 based at Lazaro; PO 109 and 114 based at Tampico; PO 110 and 117 based at Ensenada.

SANTOS DEGOLLADO *6/2005*, Mexican Navy* / 1133532

20 AZTECA CLASS (LARGE PATROL CRAFT) (PB)

Name	No	Builders	Commissioned
MATIAS DE CORDOVA (ex-*Guaycura*)	PC 202 (ex-P 02)	Scott & Sons, Bowling	6 Jan 1974
IGNACIO LÓPEZ RAYÓN (ex-*Tarahumara*)	PC 206 (ex-P 06)	Ailsa Shipbuilding Co Ltd	18 Apr 1975
MANUEL CRESCENCIO REJON (ex-*Tepehuan*)	PC 207 (ex-P 07)	Ailsa Shipbuilding Co Ltd	1 Dec 1975
JUAN ANTONIO DE LA FUENTE (ex-*Mexica*)	PC 208 (ex-P 08)	Ailsa Shipbuilding Co Ltd	28 Dec 1975
LEON GUZMAN (ex-*Zapoteca*)	PC 209 (ex-P 09)	Scott & Sons, Bowling	1 June 1975
IGNACIO RAMIREZ (ex-*Huastela*)	PC 210 (ex-P 10)	Ailsa Shipbuilding Co Ltd	1 June 1975
IGNACIO MARISCAL (ex-*Mazahua*)	PC 211 (ex-P 11)	Ailsa Shipbuilding Co Ltd	25 Dec 1975
HERIBERTO JARA CORONA (ex-*Huichol*)	PC 212 (ex-P 12)	Ailsa Shipbuilding Co Ltd	17 Nov 1975
COLIMA (ex-*Yacqui*)	PC 214 (ex-P 14)	Scott & Sons, Bowling	1 July 1975
JOSE JOAQUIN FERNANDEZ DE LIZARDI (ex-*Tlapaneco*)	PC 215 (ex-P 15)	Ailsa Shipbuilding Co Ltd	1 June 1976
FRANCISCO J MUGICA (ex-*Tarasco*)	PC 216 (ex-P 16)	Ailsa Shipbuilding Co Ltd	1 June 1976
JOSE MARIA DEL CASTILLO VELASCO (ex-*Otomi*)	PC 218 (ex-P 18)	Lamont & Co Ltd	1 Nov 1976
JOSE NATIVIDAD MACIAS (ex-*Pimas*)	PC 220 (ex-P 20)	Lamont & Co Ltd	29 Dec 1976
TAMAULIPAS (ex-*Mazateco*)	PC 223 (ex-P 23)	ASTIMAR 3, Coatzacoalcos	18 May 1977
YUCATAN (ex-*Tolteca*)	PC 224 (ex-P 24)	ASTIMAR 3, Coatzacoalcos	1 May 1975
TABASCO (ex-*Maya*)	PC 225 (ex-P 25)	ASTIMAR 3, Coatzacoalcos	1 Dec 1978
COCHIMIE (ex-*Veracruz*)	PC 226 (ex-P 26)	ASTIMAR 3, Coatzacoalcos	1 Dec 1978
PUEBLA (ex-*Totonaca*)	PC 228 (ex-P 28)	ASTIMAR 3, Coatzacoalcos	1 Aug 1982
LEONA VICARIO (ex-*Olmeca*)	PC 230 (ex-P 30)	ASTIMAR 20, Salina Cruz, Oaxaco	1 May 1977
JOSEFA ORTIZ DE DOMINGUEZ (ex-*Tlahuica*)	PC 231 (ex-P 31)	ASTIMAR 20, Salina Cruz, Oaxaco	1 June 1977

Displacement, tons: 148 full load
Dimensions, feet (metres): 112.7 × 28.3 × 7.2 *(34.4 × 8.7 × 2.2)*
Main machinery: 2 Paxman 12YJCM diesels; 3,000 hp *(2.24 MW)* sustained; 2 shafts
Speed, knots: 24. **Range, n miles:** 1,537 at 14 kt
Complement: 24 (2 officers)
Guns: 1 Bofors 40 mm/60; 300 rds/min to 12 km *(6.5 n miles)* anti-surface; 4 km *(2.2 n miles)* anti-aircraft; weight of shell 2.4 kg.
  1 Oerlikon 20 mm or 1—7.62 mm MG.
Radars: Surface search: Kelvin Hughes; I-band.

Comment: Ordered by Mexico on 27 March 1973 from Associated British Machine Tool Makers Ltd to a design by TT Boat Designs, Bembridge, Isle of Wight. The first 21 were modernised in 1987 in Mexico with spare parts and equipment supplied by ABMTM Marine Division who supervised the work which included engine refurbishment and the fitting of air conditioning. Names and pennant numbers changed in 2001. Based at: Veracruz (PC 202, 207, 223, 228); Yukaltepen (PC 224, 225, 226); Salina Cruz (PC 206, 209); Puerto Chiapas (PC 218, 220); Guaymas (PC 208, 210, 214); Mazatlan (PC 211, 216, 230, 231); Acapulco (PC 212, 215).

JOSE NATIVIDAD MACIAS *6/2005*, Mexican Navy* / 1133528

4 ISLA CLASS (FAST ATTACK CRAFT) (PBF)

Name	No	Builders	Commissioned
ISLA CORONADO	PI 1201 (ex-P 51)	Equitable Shipyards	1 Sep 1993
ISLA LOBOS	PI 1202 (ex-P 52)	Equitable Shipyards	1 Nov 1993
ISLA GUADALUPE	PI 1203 (ex-P 53)	Equitable Shipyards	1 Feb 1994
ISLA COZUMEL	PI 1204 (ex-P 54)	Equitable Shipyards	1 Apr 1994

Displacement, tons: 52 full load
Dimensions, feet (metres): 82 × 17.9 × 4 *(25 × 5.5 × 1.2)*
Main machinery: 3 Detroit diesels; 16,200 hp *(12.9 MW)*; 3 Arneson surface drives
Speed, knots: 50. **Range, n miles:** 1,200 at 30 kt
Complement: 9 (3 officers)
Guns: 1—12.7 mm MG. 2—7.62 mm MGs.
Radars: Surface search: Raytheon SPS 69; I-band.
  Fire control: Thomson-CSF Agrion; J-band.

Comment: Built by the Trinity Marine Group to an XFPB (extra fast patrol boat) design. Deep Vee hulls with FRP/Kevlar construction. Similar craft built for US Navy. May be fitted with MM 15 SSMs in due course and armed with 40 mm or 20 mm guns. Pennant numbers changed 2001. Based at Topolobampo (PI 1201, 1202) and Guaymas (PI 1203, 1204).

ISLA CORONADO *6/2005*, Mexican Navy* / 1133527

48 POLARIS CLASS (COMBATBOAT 90 HMN) (PBF)

POLARIS PI 1101	FOMALHAUT PI 1113	PEACOCK PI 1125	ELTANIN PI 1137
SIRIUS PI 1102	POLLUX PI 1114	BETELGEUSE PI 1126	KOCHAB PI 1138
CAPELLA PI 1103	RÉGULUS PI 1115	ADHARA PI 1127	ENIF PI 1139
CANOPUS PI 1104	ACRUX PI 1116	ALIOTH PI 1128	SCHEDAR PI 1140
VEGA PI 1105	SPICA PI 1117	RASALHAGUE PI 1129	MARKAB PI 1141
ACHERNAR PI 1106	HADAR PI 1118	NUNKI PI 1130	MEGREZ PI 1142
RIGEL PI 1107	SHAULA PI 1119	HAMAL PI 1131	MIZAR PI 1143
ARCTURUS PI 1108	MIRFAK PI 1120	SUHAIL PI 1132	PHEKDA PI 1144
ALPHERATZ PI 1109	ANKAA PI 1121	DUBHE PI 1133	ACAMAR PI 1145
PROCYÓN PI 1110	BELLATRIX PI 1122	DENEBOLA PI 1134	DIPHDA PI 1146
AVIOR PI 1111	ELNATH PI 1123	ALKAID PI 1135	MENKAR PI 1147
DENEB PI 1112	ALNILÁN PI 1124	ALPHECCA PI 1136	SABIK PI 1148

Displacement, tons: 19 full load
Dimensions, feet (metres): 52.2 × 12.5 × 2.6 *(15.9 × 3.8 × 0.8)*
Main machinery: 2 CAT 3406E diesels; 1,605 hp(m) *(1.18 MW)*; 2 waterjets
Speed, knots: 47. **Range, n miles:** 240 at 30 kt
Complement: 4
Guns: 1 Oto Melara 12.7 mm MG.
Radars: Surface search: Litton Decca Bridgemaster E; I-band.

Comment: All named after stars. First 12 ordered from Dockstavarvet, Sweden, on 15 April 1999, second batch of eight on 29 July 1999 and last batch of 20 on 1 February 2000. All delivered by 2001. A further batch of eight constructed at ASTIMAR 3, Coatzacoalcos, and delivered 2004-05. These craft are in service with the Swedish and Norwegian navies and with paramilitary forces in Malaysia and China. Based at Ciudad del Carmen (1103, 1104, 1125, 1140); Cozumel (1105, 1106, 1143, 1144); Yucalpeten (1107, 1108); Isla Mujeres (1109, 1110); Tuxpan (1113, 1114); Chetumel (1101, 1102, 1128, 1129); Veracruz (1131, 1132); Ensenada (1111, 1112); Manzanillo (1115, 1116); Topolobampo (1118); Mazatlan (1121, 1122); Puerto Cortes (1123, 1141); Puerto Vallarta (1124, 1136); Acapulco (1126, 1127); Guaymas (1130, 1139); Puerto Penasco (1138); Isla Socorro (1135); Frontera (1142); Puerto Chiapas (1117, 1120); Los Cabos (1119, 1147); Huatulco (1133, 1134); Isla Maria Nay (1137); San Blas Nay (1145, 1146); La Paz (1148).

RÉGULUS *6/2005*, Mexican Navy* / 1133526

1 + 3 POLARIS II CLASS (COMBATBOAT 90 HMN) (PBF)

MIAPLACIDUS PI 1401

Displacement, tons: 19 full load
Dimensions, feet (metres): 52.2 × 12.5 × 2.6 *(15.9 × 3.8 × 0.8)*
Main machinery: 2 CAT 3406E diesels; 1,605 hp(m) *(1.18 MW)*; 2 waterjets
Speed, knots: 50
Range, n miles: 240 at 30 kt
Complement: 4
Guns: 1 Oto Melara 12.7 mm MG.
Radars: Surface search: Litton Decca Bridgemaster E; I-band.

Comment: A further development of the Polaris and Acuario classes. The first four to be
built at Dockstavarvet, Sweden. Some 60 further craft expected to be built in Mexico.
Based at Coatzacoalcos.

MIAPLACIDUS   *6/2005*, Mexican Navy* / 1133524

61 FAST PATROL CRAFT (PBF)

G 01-36   +25

Dimensions, feet (metres): 22.3 × 7.5 × 1 *(6.8 × 2.3 × 0.3)*
Main machinery: 2 Johnson outboards; 280 hp *(209 kW)*
Speed, knots: 40
Range, n miles: 190 at 40 kt
Complement: 2
Guns: 1 or 2—7.62 mm MGs.

Comment: Details are for the 36 G 01-36 Piraña class. Acquired in 1993/94. A 50 kt
Interceptor class launch is carried in *Démocrata* and modified versions are embarked
in the Sierra, Durango and Oaxaca classes. Ten are in service and more are to be
acquired. There are also ten 29 ft Mako Marine craft, with twin Mercury outboards
acquired in 1995. Five Sea Force 730 RIBs with Hamilton water-jets, also acquired
in 1995-96.

PIRAÑA CLASS   *9/2002, Julio Montes* / 0533285

INTERCEPTOR (old number)   *7/1998, Mexican Navy* / 0052610

INTERCEPTOR (mod)   *6/2004, Mexican Navy* / 0589767

2 ALIYA (SAAR 4.5) CLASS
(FAST ATTACK CRAFT—MISSILE) (PTG)

Name	No	Builders	Launched	Commissioned
HURACAN (ex-*Aliya*)	301	Israel Shipyards, Haifa	11 July 1980	Aug 1980
TORMENTA (ex-*Geoula*)	302	Israel Shipyards, Haifa	Oct 1980	31 Dec 1980

Displacement, tons: 498 full load
Dimensions, feet (metres): 202.4 × 24.9 × 8.2 *(61.7 × 7.6 × 2.5)*
Main machinery: 4 MTU/Bazán 16V 956 TB91 diesels; 15,000 hp(m) *(11.03 MW)* sustained;
4 shafts
Speed, knots: 31
Range, n miles: 3,000 at 17 kt; 1,500 at 30 kt
Complement: 53

Missiles: SSM: 4 IAI Gabriel II; radar or optical guidance; semi-active radar plus anti-
radiation homing to 36 km *(19.4 n miles)* at 0.7 Mach; warhead 75 kg.
Guns: 2 Oerlikon 20 mm; 800 rds/min to 2 km.
1 General Electric/General Dynamics Vulcan Phalanx 6-barrelled 20 mm Mk 15;
3,000 rds/min combined to 1.5 km anti-missile.
4—12.7 mm (twin or quad) MGs.
Countermeasures: Decoys: 1—45-tube, 4—24-tube, 4 single-tube chaff launchers.
ESM/ECM: Elisra NS 9003/5; intercept and jammer.
Combat data systems: IAI Reshet datalink.
Radars: Air/surface search: Thomson-CSF TH-D 1040 Neptune; G-band.
Fire control: Selenia Orion RTN-10X; I/J-band.

Helicopters: To be announced.

Programmes: First two of the original class of five Saar 4.5s, before conversions from Saar
4s were started. Transferred to Mexico in July 2004.
Structure: The CIWS mounted in the eyes of the ship replaced a 40 mm gun.
Operational: Test-firing of a Gabriel missile took place in June 2005.

HURACAN   *7/2004, Diego Quevedo* / 0583999

TORMENTA   *7/2004, Diego Quevedo* / 0584000

AMPHIBIOUS FORCES

2 NEWPORT CLASS (LSTH)

Name	No	Builders	Laid down	Launched	Commissioned	Recommissioned
RIO PAPALOAPAN (ex-*Sonora*, ex-*Newport*)	A 411 (ex-A-04, ex-LST-1179)	Philadelphia Naval Shipyard	1 Nov 1966	3 Feb 1968	7 June 1969	5 June 2001
USUMACINTA (ex-*Frederick*)	A 412 (ex-LST-1184)	National Steel & Shipbuilding Co	13 Apr 1968	8 Mar 1969	11 Apr 1970	1 Dec 2002

Displacement, tons: 4,975 light; 8,450 full load
Dimensions, feet (metres): 522.3 (hull) × 69.5 × 17.5 (aft)
  (159.2 × 21.2 × 5.3)
Main machinery: 6 General Motors 16-645-E5 diesels;
  16,500 hp *(12.3 MW)* sustained; 2 shafts; cp props; bow
  thruster
Speed, knots: 20
Range, n miles: 14,250 at 14 kt
Complement: 257 (13 officers)
Military lift: 400 troops; 500 tons vehicles; 3 LCVPs and
  1 LCPL on davits.
Guns: 4 USN 3 in *(76 mm)*/50 (A 411).
Radars: Surface search: Raytheon SPS-10F; G-band.
Navigation: Raytheon SPS-64; I-band.

Helicopters: Platform only.

Programmes: A-411 sold to Mexico by the US Navy on
  18 January 2001. A-412 sold on 9 December 2002. Both
  ships employed in amphibious role rather than as
  transport ships as previously reported. A 411 based at
  Tampico and A 412 at Manzanillo.

RIO PAPALOAPAN
6/2005*, Mexican Navy
1133522

USUMACINTA
6/2005*, Mexican Navy / 1133521

1 TRANSPORT SHIP (AP)

Name	No	Builders	Commissioned
MANZANILLO (ex-*Clearwater County*)	A 402 (ex-A 02)	Chicago Bridge & Iron Co	31 Mar 1944

Displacement, tons: 4,080 full load
Dimensions, feet (metres): 328 × 50 × 14
  (100 × 15.3 × 4.3)
Main machinery: 2 GM 12-567A diesels; 1,800 hp
  (1.34 MW); 2 shafts
Speed, knots: 11
Range, n miles: 6,000 at 11 kt
Complement: 250
Guns: 8 Bofors 40 mm (2 twin, 4 single).

Comment: Ex-US LST 452 class transferred and
  recommissioned on 1 July 1972. Deployed also as SAR
  and disaster relief ship. Based at Manzanillo.

TRANSPORT SHIP
7/1991, Harald Carstens
0081259

SURVEY AND RESEARCH SHIPS

1 ONJUKU CLASS (SURVEY SHIP) (AGS)

Name	No	Builders	Commissioned
ONJUKU	BI 02 (ex-H 04)	Uchida Shipyard	10 Jan 1980

Displacement, tons: 494 full load
Dimensions, feet (metres): 121 × 26.2 × 11.5
  (36.9 × 8 × 3.5)
Main machinery: 1 Yanmar 6UA-UT diesel; 700 hp(m)
  (515 kW); 1 shaft
Speed, knots: 12
Range, n miles: 5,645 at 10.5 kt
Complement: 20 (4 officers)
Radars: Navigation: Furuno; I-band.
Sonars: Furuno; hull-mounted; high frequency active.

Comment: Launched 9 December 1977 in Japan. Sonar is
  a fish-finder type. New pennant number in 2001. Based
  at Veracruz.

ONJUKU
6/2005*, Mexican Navy
1133520

2 ROBERT D CONRAD CLASS (RESEARCH SHIPS) (AGOR)

Name	No	Builders	Commissioned
ALTAIR (ex-*James M Gilliss*)	BI 03 (ex-H 05, ex-AGOR 4)	Christy Corp, WI	5 Nov 1962
ANTARES (ex-*S P Lee*)	BI 04 (ex-H 06, ex-AG 192)	Defoe, Bay City	2 Dec 1962

Displacement, tons: 1,370 full load
Dimensions, feet (metres): 208.9 × 40 × 15.4 *(63.7 × 12.2 × 4.7)*
Main machinery: Diesel-electric; 2 Caterpillar diesel generators; 1,200 hp *(895 kW)*; 2 motors; 1,000 hp *(746 kW)*; 1 shaft; bow thruster
Speed, knots: 13.5
Range, n miles: 10,500 at 10 kt
Complement: 41 (12 officers) plus 15 scientists
Radars: Navigation: Raytheon 1025; Raytheon R4iY; I-band.

Comment: *Altair* leased from US 14 June 1983. Refitted and modernised in Mexico. Recommissioned 23 November 1984. Primarily used for oceanography. *Antares* served as an AGI with the USN until February 1974 when she transferred on loan to the Geological Survey. Acquired by sale and recommissioned on 1 December 1992. New pennant numbers in 2001. Based at Manzanillo (BI 03) and Tampico (BI 04).

ALTAIR *6/2005*, Mexican Navy* / 1133519

1 SURVEY SHIP (AGS)

Name	No	Builders	Commissioned
RIO HONDO (ex-*Deer Island*)	BI 06 (ex-H 08, ex-A 26, ex-YAG 62)	Halter Marine	May 1962

Displacement, tons: 400 full load
Dimensions, feet (metres): 120.1 × 27.9 × 6.9 *(36.6 × 8.5 × 2.1)*
Main machinery: 2 diesels; 2 shafts
Speed, knots: 10
Range, n miles: 6,000 at 10 kt
Complement: 20

Comment: Acquired from US on 1 August 1996 and adapted for a support ship role in 1997. Converted to Survey Ship in 1999. Used in US service from 1983 as an acoustic research ship to test noise reduction equipment. Started life as an oil rig supply tug. New pennant number in 2001. Based at Coatzacoalcos.

RIO HONDO (old number) *4/1999, M Declerck* / 0081258

4 ARRECIFE (ex-OLMECA II) CLASS (SURVEY CRAFT) (YGS)

ALACRAN BI 08 (ex-PR 301)	**CABEZO** BI 10 (ex-PR 304)
RIZO BI 09 (ex-PR 310)	**ANEGAGADA DE ADENTRO** BI 11 (ex-PR 309)

Displacement, tons: 18 full load
Dimensions, feet (metres): 54.8 × 14.4 × 3.9 *(16.7 × 4.4 × 1.2)*
Main machinery: 2 Detroit 8V-92TA diesels; 700 hp *(562 kW)* sustained; 2 shafts
Speed, knots: 20
Range, n miles: 460 at 10 kt
Complement: 15 (2 officers)
Guns: 1—12.7 mm MG.
Radars: Navigation: Raytheon 1900; I-band.

Comment: Built at Acapulco and completed between 1982 and 1989. GRP hulls. Converted for inshore hydrographic duties in 2003. All have *Arrecife* in front of the names. Based at Manzanillo (BI 08, 09) and Veracruz (BI 10, 11).

ALACRAN *6/2005*, Mexican Navy* / 1133518

1 HUMBOLDT CLASS (RESEARCH SHIP) (AGOR)

Name	No	Builders	Commissioned
ALEJANDRO DE HUMBOLDT	BI 01 (ex-H 03)	JG Hitzler, Elbe	22 June 1987

Displacement, tons: 585 standard; 700 full load
Dimensions, feet (metres): 140.7 × 32 × 13.5 *(42.3 × 9.6 × 4.1)*
Main machinery: 2 diesels; 2 shafts
Speed, knots: 14
Complement: 20 (4 officers)
Radars: Navigation: Kelvin Hughes; I-band.

Comment: Former trawler built in Germany and launched in January 1970. Converted in 1982 to become a hydrographical and acoustic survey ship. Based at Manzanillo. New pennant number in 2001.

ALEJANDRO DE HUMBOLDT (old number) *6/2001, Mexican Navy* / 0114671

1 SURVEY SHIP (AGSC)

MOCTEZUMA II BI 07 (ex-A-09)

Displacement, tons: 150 full load
Dimensions, feet (metres): 108.3 × 20.3 × 13.1 *(33.0 × 6.2 × 4.0)*
Main machinery: 1 Detroit diesel; 1 shaft
Complement: 17

Comment: Two-masted sailing vessel built in 1972 and taken over by the Navy on 6 December 1985. Based at Guaymas.

1 SUPPORT SHIP (AKS)

Name	No	Builders	Commissioned
RIO SUCHIATE (ex-*Monob 1*)	BI 05 (ex-A 27, ex-YAG 61, ex-YW 87)	Zenith Dredge Co	11 Nov 1943

Displacement, tons: 1,390 full load
Dimensions, feet (metres): 191.9 × 33.1 × 15.7 *(58.5 × 10.1 × 4.8)*
Main machinery: 1 Caterpillar D 398 diesel; 850 hp *(634 kW)*; 1 shaft
Speed, knots: 9. **Range, n miles:** 2,500 at 9 kt
Complement: 21

Comment: Acquired from US on 1 August 1996. The ship was converted from a water carrier to an acoustic research role in 1969, and had four laboratories in US service. Adapted to act also in support ship role in 1997. New pennant number in 2001. Based at Guaymas.

RIO SUCHIATE (US colours) *7/1988, Giorgio Arra* / 0506309

1 SURVEY SHIP (AGS)

Name	No	Builders	Commissioned
RIO TUXPAN (ex-*Whiting*)	BI 12	Marietta Manufacturing Company, Mt Pleasant, West Virginia	July 1963

Displacement, tons: 907
Dimensions, feet (metres): 163.0 × 33.0 × 12.2 *(49.7 × 10.1 × 3.7)*
Main machinery: 2 General Motors diesels; 1,600 hp *(1.2 MW)*; 2 cp props
Speed, knots: 12. **Range, n miles:** 5,700 at 11 kt
Complement: 30 (7 officers)
Radars: Surface search: E/F-band.
Navigation: I-band.

Comment: Ex-US NOAA ship designed for hydrographic and bathymetric survey work. Decommissioned in May 2003 and transferred to the Mexican Navy in April 2005. Equipped (in NOAA service) with Intermediate Depth Swath Survey System (IDSSS) (36 kHz), Deep Water Echo Sounder (12 kHz), Shallow Water Echo Sounder (100 kHz), Hydrographic Survey Sounder (24 and 100 kHz), EG&G 270 Side Scan Sonar and Klein T-5000 High Speed/High Resolution Side Scan Sonar.

RIO TUXPAN   *4/2005*, NOAA* / 1133517

AUXILIARIES

Notes: (1) Procurement of up to two Hospital Ships is reported to be under consideration.
(2) Procurement of up to two logistic support vessels, capable of carrying 120 marines and of operating helicopters, is reported to be under consideration.

1 LOGISTIC SUPPORT SHIP (AKS)

Name	No	Builders	Recommissioned
MAYA (ex-*Rio Nautla*)	ATR 01 (ex-A 20, ex-A 23)	Isla Gran Cayman, Ru	1 June 1988

Displacement, tons: 924 full load
Dimensions, feet (metres): 160.1 × 38.7 × 16.1 *(48.8 × 11.8 × 4.9)*
Main machinery: 1 MAN diesel; 1 shaft
Speed, knots: 12
Complement: 15 (8 officers)

Comment: First launched in 1962 and acquired for the Navy in 1988. Unarmed. New name and pennant number in 2001. Based at Mazatlan.

MAYA   *6/2004, Mexican Navy* / 0589766

1 LOGISTIC SUPPORT SHIP (AK)

Name	No	Builders	Recommissioned
TARASCO (ex-*Rio Lerma*, ex-*Sea Point*, ex-*Tricon*, ex-*Marika*, ex-*Arneb*)	ATR 03 (ex-A 22, A 25)	Solvesborg, Sweden	1 Mar 1990

Displacement, tons: 1,970 full load
Dimensions, feet (metres): 282.2 × 40.7 × 16.1 *(86 × 12.4 × 4.9)*
Main machinery: 1 Kloeckner Humboldt Deutz diesel; 2,100 hp(m) *(1.54 MW)*; 1 shaft
Speed, knots: 14
Complement: 35
Cargo capacity: 778 tons

Comment: Built in 1962 as a commercial ship and taken into the Navy in 1990. New name and pennant number in 2001. Based at Tampico.

TARASCO   *6/2005*, Mexican Navy* / 1133516

2 HUASTECO CLASS (APH/AK/AH)

Name	No	Builders	Commissioned
HUASTECO (ex-*Rio Usumacinta*)	AMP 01 (ex-A 10, ex-A 21)	Tampico, Tampa	21 May 1986
ZAPOTECO (ex-*Rio Coatzacoalcos*)	MP 02 (ex-A11, ex-A 22)	Salina Cruz	1 Sep 1986

Displacement, tons: 1,854 standard; 2,650 full load
Dimensions, feet (metres): 227 × 42 × 18.6 *(69.2 × 12.8 × 5.7)*
Main machinery: 1 GM-EMD diesel; 3,600 hp(m) *(2.65 MW)*; 1 shaft
Speed, knots: 14.5
Range, n miles: 5,500 at 14 kt
Complement: 85 plus 300 passengers
Guns: 1 Bofors 40/60 Mk 3.
Radars: Navigation: I-band.
Helicopters: Platform for 1 MBB BO 105C.

Comment: Used in a training role but can also serve as troop transports, supply or hospital ships. New names and pennant numbers in 2001. AMP 01 based at Tampico and AMP 02 at Manzanillo.

HUASTECO   *7/2004, Diego Quevedo* / 0589765

17 DREDGERS (YM)

BANDERAS ADR 01 (ex-D 01)	CHACAGUA ADR 10 (ex-D 24)
MAGDALENA ADR 02 (ex-D 02)	COYUCA ADR 11 (ex-D 25)
KINO ADR 03 (ex-D 03)	FARRALLON ADR 12 (ex-D 26)
YAVAROS ADR 04 (ex-D 04)	CHAIREL ADR 13 (ex-D 27)
CHAMELA ADR 05 (ex-D 05)	SAN ANDRES ADR 14 (ex-D 28)
TEPOCA ADR 06 (ex-D 06)	SAN IGNACIO ADR 15 (ex-D 29)
TODO SANTOS ADR 07 (ex-D 21)	TERMINOS ADR 16 (ex-D 30)
ASUNCION ADR 08 (ex-D 22)	TECULAPA ADR 17 (ex-D 31)
ALMEJAS ADR 09 (ex-D 23)	

Comment: Ships vary in size from 113 m *Kino* to 8 m *Terminos*. Most were taken over by the navy from the Transport Ministry in 1994.

For details of the latest updates to *Jane's Fighting Ships* online and to discover the additional information available exclusively to online subscribers please visit
jfs.janes.com

2 AGUASCALIENTES CLASS (YOG/YO)

Name	No	Builders	Recommissioned
AGUASCALIENTES (ex-*Las Choapas*)	ATQ 01 (ex-A 45, ex-A 03)	Geo H Mathis Co Ltd,	26 Nov 1964
TLAXCALA (ex-*Amatlan*)	ATQ 02 (ex-A 46, ex-A 04)	Geo Lawley & Son, Neponset, MA	26 Nov 1964

Displacement, tons: 895 standard; 1,480 full load
Dimensions, feet (metres): 159.2 × 32.9 × 13.3 *(48.6 × 10 × 4.1)*
Main machinery: 1 Fairbanks-Morse diesel; 500 hp *(373 kW)*; 1 shaft
Speed, knots: 6
Complement: 26 (5 officers)
Cargo capacity: 6,570 barrels
Guns: 1 Oerlikon 20 mm.

Comment: Former US self-propelled fuel oil barges built in 1943. Purchased in August 1964. New names and pennant numbers in 2001. ATQ 01 based at Puerto Cortes and ATQ 02 at Coatzacoalcos.

TLAXCALA   *6/2005*, Mexican Navy* / 1133515

5 FLOATING DOCKS (YOG/YO)

ADI 01 (ex-US ARD 2)	ADI 03 (ex-US AFDL 28)	— (ex-US ARD 31)
ADI 02 (ex-US ARD 15)	ADI 04 (ex-US ARD 11)	

Comment: ARD 2 (150 × 24.7 m) transferred 1963 and ARD 11 (same size) 1974 by sale. Lift 3,550 tons. Two 10 ton cranes and one 100 kW generator. ARD 15 has the same capacity and facilities-transferred 1971 by lease. AFDL 28 built in 1944, transferred 1973. Lift, 1,000 tons. ARD 30 transferred on 20 March 2001 and ARD 31 in 2004.

TRAINING SHIPS

1 SAIL TRAINING SHIP (AXS)

Name	No	Builders	Launched	Commissioned
CUAUHTÉMOC	BE 01 (ex-A 07)	Astilleros Talleres Calaya SA, Bilbao	9 Jan 1982	23 Sep 1982

Displacement, tons: 1,662 full load
Dimensions, feet (metres): 296.9 (bowsprit); 220.5 wl × 39.4 × 17.7 *(90.5; 67.2 × 12 × 5.4)*
Main machinery: 1 Detroit 12V-149T diesel; 1,125 hp *(839 kW)*; 1 shaft
Speed, knots: 17 sail; 7 diesel
Complement: 268 (20 officers, 90 midshipmen)
Guns: 2—65 mm Schneider Model 1902 saluting guns.

Comment: Has 2,368 m² of sail. Similar ships in Ecuador, Colombia and Venezuela. Based at Acapulco.

CUAUHTEMOC   *7/2003, J Cišlak* / 0567900

1 MANUEL AZUETA (EDSALL) CLASS (FF/AX)

Name	No	Builders	Laid down	Launched	Commissioned
COMODORO MANUEL AZUETA (ex-*Hurst* DE 250)	D 111 (ex-E 30, ex-A 06)	Brown SB Co, Houston, TX	27 Jan 1943	14 Apr 1943	30 Aug 1943

Displacement, tons: 1,400 standard; 1,850 full load
Dimensions, feet (metres): 302.7 × 36.6 × 13 *(92.3 × 11.3 × 4)*
Main machinery: 4 Fairbanks-Morse 38D8-1/8-10 diesels; 7,080 hp *(5.3 MW)* sustained; 2 shafts
Speed, knots: 12. **Range, n miles:** 13,000 at 12 kt
Complement: 216 (15 officers)
Guns: 2 USN 3 in *(76 mm)*/50; 20 rds/min to 12 km *(6.6 n miles)*; weight of shell 6 kg.
  8 Bofors 40 mm/60 (1 quad, 2 twin) Mk 2 and Mk 1; 120 rds/min to 10 km *(5.5 n miles)*; weight of shell 0.89 kg.
  2 Oerlikon 20 mm. 2—37 mm saluting guns.
Weapons control: Mk 52 (for 3 in); Mk 51 Mod 2 (for 40 mm).
Radars: Surface search: Kelvin Hughes Type 17; I-band.
  Navigation: Kelvin Hughes Type 14; I-band.

Programmes: Transferred from US 1 October 1973.
Modernisation: OTO Melara 76 mm gun fitted in 1995 but subsequently removed and US 3 in gun restored.
Operational: Employed as training ship and based at Tuxpan. A/S weapons and sensors removed. Speed much reduced. Pennant number changed in 2001.

COMODORO MANUEL AZUETA   *6/2005*, Mexican Navy* / 1133545

TUGS

4 ABNAKI CLASS (ATF)

Name	No	Builders	Commissioned
OTOMI (ex-*Kukulkan*, ex-*Molala* ATF 106)	ARE 01 (ex-A 52, ex-A 17)	United Eng Co, Alameda, CA	29 Sep 1943
YAQUI (ex-*Ehacatl*, ex-*Abnaki* ATF 96)	ARE 02 (ex-A 53, ex-A 18)	Charleston SB and DD Co	15 Nov 1943
SERI (ex-*Tonatiuh*, ex-*Cocopa* ATF 101)	ARE 03 (ex-A 54, ex-A 19)	Charleston SB and DD Co	25 Mar 1944
CORA (ex-*Chac*, ex-*Hitchiti* ATF 103)	ARE 04 (ex-A 55, ex-A 20)	Charleston SB and DD Co	27 May 1944

Displacement, tons: 1,640 full load
Dimensions, feet (metres): 205 × 38.5 × 17 *(62.5 × 11.7 × 5.2)*
Main machinery: Diesel-electric; 4 Busch-Sulzer BS-539 diesels; 6,000 hp *(4.48 MW)*; 4 generators; 1 motor; 3,000 hp(m) *(2.24 MW)*; 1 shaft
Speed, knots: 10. **Range, n miles:** 6,500 at 10 kt
Complement: 75
Guns: 1 US 3 in *(76 mm)*/50 Mk 22.
Radars: Navigation: Marconi LN66; I-band.

Comment: *Otomi* transferred from US 27 September 1978, remainder 1 October 1978. All by sale. Speed reduced. Based at Tampico (ARE 01, ARE 03) and Manzanillo (ARE 02, ARE 04).

SERI   *6/2003, Mexican Navy* / 0567905

6 HARBOUR TUGS (YTL)

IZTACCIHUATL ARE 05 (ex-R-60)	XINANTECATL ARE 08 (ex-R-63)
POPOCATEPTL ARE 06 (ex-R-61)	MATLALCUEYE ARE 09 (ex-R-64)
CITLALTEPL ARE 07 (ex-R-62)	TLALOC ARE 10 (ex-R-65)

Displacement, tons: 140 full load
Dimensions, feet (metres): 73.8 × 22.3 × 9.8 *(22.5 × 6.8 × 3.0)*
Complement: 12

Comment: Details are for ARE 05 built by Seadrec, Ltd, and taken over by the Navy on 1 November 1994. Based at: Tuxpan (ARE 05, ARE 07); Manzanillo (ARE 06); Tampico (ARE 08); Salina Cruz (ARE 09); Coatzacoalcos (ARE 10).

Federated States of Micronesia

Country Overview

The Federated States of Micronesia was a US-administered UN Trust territory from 1947 before becoming a self-governing republic in 1979. In 1986, a Compact of Free Association, delegating to the US the responsibility for defence and foreign affairs, came into effect. Composed of the states of Pohnpei (location of capital, Palikir), Kosrae, Chuuk, and Yap, the country consists of 607 islands in the western Pacific Ocean which extend 1,566 n miles across the Caroline Islands archipelago. Moen Island in Chuuk, is the largest community. Territorial seas (12 n miles) are claimed. An Exclusive Economic Zone (EEZ) (200n miles) is also claimed but limits have not been fully defined.

Headquarters Appointments

Maritime Wing Commander:
   Commander Robert Maluweirang

Personnel

2006: 120

Bases

Kolonia (main base), Kosral, Moen, Takatik.

PATROL FORCES

3 PACIFIC CLASS (LARGE PATROL CRAFT) (PB)

Name	No	Builders	Commissioned
PALIKIR	FSM 01	Australian Shipbuilding Industries	28 Apr 1990
MICRONESIA	FSM 02	Australian Shipbuilding Industries	3 Nov 1990
INDEPENDENCE	FSM 05	Transfield	22 May 1997

Displacement, tons: 162 full load
Dimensions, feet (metres): 103.3 × 26.6 × 6.9
   (31.5 × 8.1 × 2.1)
Main machinery: 2 Caterpillar 3516TA diesels; 4,400 hp
   (3.28 MW) sustained; 2 shafts
Speed, knots: 20
Range, n miles: 2,500 at 12 kt
Complement: 17 (3 officers)
Radars: Surface search: Furuno 1011; I-band.

Comment: First pair ordered in June 1989 from Australian Shipbuilding Industries. Training and support provided by Australia at Port Kolonia. Third of class negotiated with Transfield (former ASI) in 1997. Following the decision by the Australian government to extend the Pacific Patrol Boat programme to enable 30-year boat lives, *Palikir*, *Micronesia* and *Independence*, which underwent half-life refits in 1998, 1999 and 2003, will be due life-extension refits in 2007, 2008 and 2012 respectively.

MICRONESIA
11/1990, Royal Australian Navy
0506060

2 CAPE CLASS (LARGE PATROL CRAFT) (PB)

Name	No	Builders	Commissioned
PALUWLAP (ex-*Cape Cross*)	FSM 03	Coast Guard Yard, Curtis Bay	20 Aug 1958
CONSTITUTION (ex-*Cape Corwin*)	FSM 04	Coast Guard Yard, Curtis Bay	14 Nov 1958

Displacement, tons: 148 full load
Dimensions, feet (metres): 95 × 20.2 × 6.6
   (28.9 × 6.2 × 2)
Main machinery: 2 GM 16V-149TI diesels; 2,070 hp *(1.54 MW)*
   sustained; 2 shafts
Speed, knots: 20
Range, n miles: 2,500 at 10 kt
Complement: 14 (3 officers)
Guns: 2—12.7 mm MGs. 2—40 mm mortars.
Radars: Surface search: Raytheon SPS-64; I-band.

Comment: Two former Coast Guard ships transferred from US on loan in March and September 1991. Re-engined in 1982 and now restricted in speed.

CAPE class (USCG colours)
1990
0506061

Morocco

MARINE ROYALE MAROCAINE

Country Overview

Formerly divided into French and Spanish protectorates, the Kingdom of Morocco gained independence in 1956. Situated in north-western Africa, it has an area of 172,414 square miles and is bordered to the east by Algeria; it occupies 80 per cent of Western Sahara (formerly Spanish Sahara), the country to the south. Two Spanish exclaves, Ceuta and Melilla, are located on the Mediterranean coast. It has coastlines with Atlantic Ocean (756 n miles) and Mediterranean Sea (238 n miles). The capital is Rabat while Casablanca is the largest city and principal port. Other ports are at Tangier, Agadir, Kenitra, Mohammedia, and Safi. Territorial seas (12 n miles) are claimed. An EEZ (200 n mile) has also been claimed but its limits have not been fully defined.

Headquarters Appointments

Inspector of the Navy:
   Captain Muhammad al-Tariqi

Personnel

(a)   2006: 7,800 officers and ratings (including 1,500 Marines)
(b)   18 months' national service

Bases

Casablanca (HQ), Safi, Agadir, Kenitra, Tangier, Dakhla, Al Hoceima

Aviation

The Ministry of Fisheries operates 11 Pilatus Britten-Norman Defender maritime surveillance aircraft.

FRIGATES

1 MODIFIED DESCUBIERTA CLASS (FFGM)

Name	No	Builders	Laid down	Launched	Commissioned
LIEUTENANT COLONEL ERRHAMANI	501	Bazán, Cartagena	20 Mar 1979	26 Feb 1982	28 Mar 1983

Displacement, tons: 1,233 standard; 1,479 full load
Dimensions, feet (metres): 291.3 × 34 × 12.5
  (88.8 × 10.4 × 3.8)
Main machinery: 4 MTU-Bazán 16V 956 TB91 diesels;
  15,000 hp(m) (11 MW) sustained; 2 shafts; cp props
Speed, knots: 25.5. **Range, n miles:** 4,000 at 18 kt (1 engine)
Complement: 100

Missiles: SSM: 4 Aerospatiale MM 38 Exocet ❶; inertial
  cruise; active radar homing to 42 km (23 n miles) at
  0.9 Mach; warhead 165 kg; sea-skimmer. Frequently not
  embarked.
SAM: Selenia/Elsag Albatros octuple launcher ❷;
  24 Aspide; semi-active radar homing to 13 km (8 n miles)
  at 2.5 Mach; height envelope 15–5,000 m (49.2–16,405 ft);
  warhead 30 kg.
Guns: 1 OTO Melara 3 in (76 mm)/62 compact ❸; 85 rds/min
  to 16 km (8.6 n miles) anti-surface; 12 km (6.5 n miles)
  anti-aircraft; weight of shell 6 kg.
  2 Breda Bofors 40 mm/70 ❹; 300 rds/min to 12.5 km
  (6.7 n miles); weight of shell 0.96 kg.
Torpedoes: 6–324 mm Mk 32 (2 triple) tubes ❺. Honeywell
  Mk 46 Mod 1; anti-submarine; active/passive homing to
  11 km (5.9 n miles) at 40 kt; warhead 44 kg.
A/S mortars: 1 Bofors SR 375 mm twin trainable launcher ❻;
  range 3.6 km (1.9 n miles); 24 rockets.

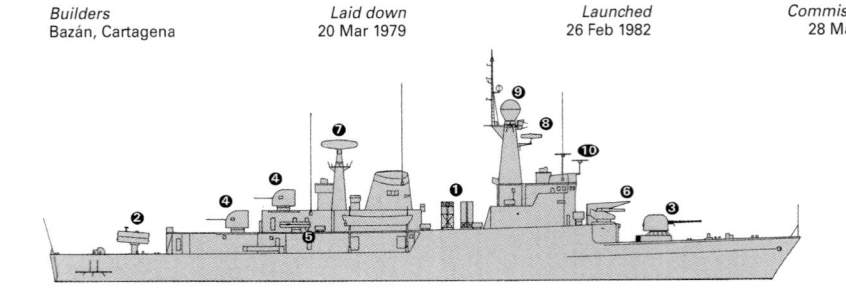

LIEUTENANT COLONEL ERRHAMANI (Scale 1 : 900), Ian Sturton / 1151072

Countermeasures: Decoys: 2 CSEE Dagaie double trainable
  mounting; IR flares and chaff; H/J-band.
ESM/ECM: Elettronica ELT 715; intercept and jammer.
Combat data systems: Signaal SEWACO-MR action data
  automation. SATCOM.
Radars: Air/surface search: Signaal DA05 ❼; E/F-band (see
  Operational).
Surface search: Signaal ZW06 ❽; I-band.
Fire control: Signaal WM25/41 ❾; I/J-band; range 46 km
  (25 n miles).
Navigation: 2 Decca ❿; I-band.

Sonars: Raytheon DE 1160 B; hull-mounted; active/passive;
  medium range; medium frequency.

Programmes: Ordered 7 June 1977.
Modernisation: New 40 mm guns fitted in 1995. Refit in
  Spain in 1996.
Operational: The ship is fitted to carry Exocet but the
  missiles are seldom embarked. The air search radar was
  removed in 1998 but reinstated in 1999.

LIEUTENANT COLONEL ERRHAMANI 7/2005*, B Prézelin / 1133134

LIEUTENANT COLONEL ERRHAMANI 6/2005*, Schaeffer/Marsan / 1151069

2 FLOREAL CLASS (FFGHM)

Name	No	Builders	Laid down	Launched	Commissioned
MOHAMMED V	611	Chantiers de L'Atlantique, St Nazaire	June 1999	9 Mar 2001	12 Mar 2002
HASSAN II	612	Chantiers de L'Atlantique, St Nazaire	Dec 1999	11 Feb 2002	20 Dec 2002

Displacement, tons: 2,950 full load
Dimensions, feet (metres): 306.8 × 45.9 × 14.1
  (93.5 × 14 × 4.3)
Main machinery: CODAD; 4 SEMT-Pielstick 6 PA6 L 280
  diesels; 9,600 hp(m) *(7.06 MW)* sustained; 2 shafts; LIPS
  cp props; bow thruster; 340 hp(m) *(250 kW)*
Speed, knots: 20. **Range, n miles:** 10,000 at 15 kt
Complement: 89 (11 officers)

Missiles: SSM: 2 Aerospatiale MM 38 Exocet ❶.
SAM: 2 Matra Simbad twin launchers ❷ can replace 20 mm
  guns or Dagaie launcher.
Guns: 1 Otobreda 76 mm/62 ❸.
  2 Giat 20 F2 20 mm ❹ (fitted for but not with).
Countermeasures: Decoys: 2 CSEE Dagaie Mk II ❺;
  10-barrelled trainable launchers; chaff and IR flares.
ESM: Thomson-CSF ARBR 17 ❻; radar intercept.
Weapons control: CSEE Najir 2000 optronic director ❼.
Radars: Surface search/Fire control Thales WM28 ❽; I/J-band.
Navigation: 2 Decca Bridgemaster E ❾; I-band (1 for
  helicopter control).

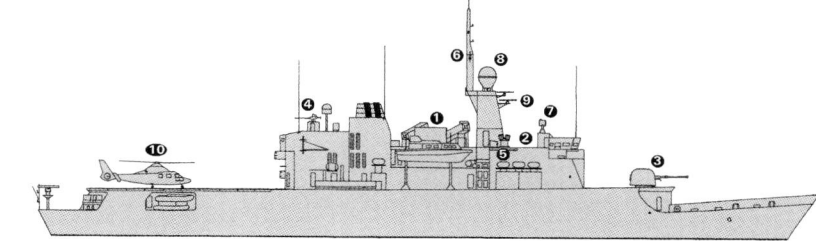

MOHAMMED V *(Scale 1 : 900), Ian Sturton* / 1151071

Helicopters: 1 Aerospatiale AS 565MA Panther ❿.

Programmes: Contract signed with Alstom on 12 July
  1999. 611 delivered on 12 March 2002 and 612 on 20
  December 2002.

Structure: Constructed to DNV standards. Very similar
  to ships in French service with 76 mm in place of
  100 mm gun.

HASSAN II *6/2005*, H M Steele* / 1133135

MOHAMMED V *9/2005*, B Prézelin* / 1151068

SHIPBORNE AIRCRAFT

Numbers/Type: 3 Aerospatiale AS 565MB Panther.
Operational speed: 165 kt *(305 km/h)*.
Service ceiling: 16,700 ft *(5,100 m)*.
Range: 483 n miles *(895 km)*.
Role/Weapon systems: Procured from France for operation from Floréal class. Sensors:
  Thomson-CSF Varan radar. FLIR. Weapons: 7.62 mm MG.

PANTHER (French colours)
9/1998, M Declerck
0052167

PATROL FORCES

2 OKBA (PR 72) CLASS (LARGE PATROL CRAFT) (PG)

Name	No	Builders	Commissioned
OKBA	302	SFCN, Villeneuve la Garenne	16 Dec 1976
TRIKI	303	SFCN, Villeneuve la Garenne	12 July 1977

Displacement, tons: 375 standard; 445 full load
Dimensions, feet (metres): 188.8 × 25 × 7.1 (57.5 × 7.6 × 2.1)
Main machinery: 2 SACM AGO V16 ASHR diesels; 5,520 hp(m) (4.1 MW); 2 shafts
Speed, knots: 20
Range, n miles: 2,500 at 16 kt
Complement: 53 (5 officers)
Guns: 1 OTO Melara 3 in (76 mm)/62 compact; 85 rds/min to 16 km (8.6 n miles) anti-surface; 12 km (6.5 n miles) anti-aircraft; weight of shell 6 kg.
  1 Bofors 40 mm/70; 300 rds/min to 12.5 km (6.7 n miles); weight of shell 0.96 kg.
Weapons control: 2 CSEE Panda optical directors.
Radars: Surface search: Racal Decca 1226; I-band.

Comment: Ordered June 1973. Okba launched 10 October 1975, Triki 1 February 1976. Can be Exocet fitted (with Vega control system). Triki refitted at Lorient 2002-03. Modifications included installation of a funnel and removal of two diesels and two shafts. Speed reduced to 20 kt. Similar refit for Okba completed in early 2005.

TRIKI *6/2003, B Prézelin* / 0589787

4 LAZAGA CLASS (FAST ATTACK CRAFT—MISSILE) (PGG)

Name	No	Builders	Commissioned
EL KHATTABI	304	Bazán, San Fernando	26 July 1981
COMMANDANT BOUTOUBA	305	Bazán, San Fernando	2 Aug 1982
COMMANDANT EL HARTY	306	Bazán, San Fernando	20 Nov 1981
COMMANDANT AZOUGGARH	307	Bazán, San Fernando	25 Feb 1982

Displacement, tons: 425 full load
Dimensions, feet (metres): 190.6 × 24.9 × 8.9 (58.1 × 7.6 × 2.7)
Main machinery: 2 MTU-Bazán 16V 956 TB91 diesels; 7,500 hp(m) (5.51 MW) sustained; 2 shafts
Speed, knots: 30
Range, n miles: 3,000 at 15 kt
Complement: 41
Missiles: SSM: 4 Aerospatiale MM 38 Exocet; inertial cruise; active radar homing to 42 km (23 n miles) at 0.9 Mach; warhead 165 kg; sea-skimmer.
Guns: 1 OTO Melara 3 in (76 mm)/62 compact; 85 rds/min to 16 km (8.6 n miles) anti-surface; 12 km (6.5 n miles) anti-aircraft; weight of shell 6 kg.
  1 Breda Bofors 40 mm/70; 300 rds/min to 12.5 km (6.7 n miles); weight of shell 0.96 kg.
  2 Oerlikon 20 mm/90 GAM-BO1; 800 rds/min to 2 km.
Weapons control: CSEE Panda optical director.
Radars: Surface search: Signaal ZW06; I-band; range 26 km (14 n miles).
Fire control: Signaal WM25; I/J-band; range 46 km (25 n miles).
Navigation: Furuno; I-band.

Comment: Ordered from Bazán, San Fernando (Cadiz), Spain 14 June 1977. New Bofors guns fitted aft in 1996/97. 76 mm gun removed from 305 in 1998.

EL KHATTABI *8/1997, Diego Quevedo* / 0012784

COMMANDANT AZOUGGARH *2/2005*, Marco Ghiglino* / 1133095

4 OSPREY MK II CLASS (LARGE PATROL CRAFT) (PBO)

Name	No	Builders	Commissioned
EL HAHIQ	308	Danyard A/S, Frederickshaven	11 Nov 1987
EL TAWFIQ	309	Danyard A/S, Frederickshaven	31 Jan 1988
EL HAMISS	316	Danyard A/S, Frederickshaven	9 Aug 1990
EL KARIB	317	Danyard A/S, Frederickshaven	23 Sep 1990

Displacement, tons: 475 full load
Dimensions, feet (metres): 179.8 × 34 × 8.5 (54.8 × 10.5 × 2.6)
Main machinery: 2 MAN Burmeister & Wain Alpha 12V23/30-DVO diesels; 4,440 hp(m) (3.23 MW) sustained; 2 water-jets
Speed, knots: 22. **Range, n miles:** 4,500 at 16 kt
Complement: 15 plus 20 spare berths
Guns: 1 Bofors 40 mm/60. 2 Oerlikon 20 mm.
Radars: Surface search; Racal Decca; I-band.
Navigation: Racal Decca; I-band.

Comment: First two ordered in September 1986; two more on 30 January 1989. There is a stern ramp with a hinged cover for launching the inspection boat. Used for Fishery Protection duties.

EL HAHIQ *2/2005*, Marco Ghiglino* / 1133093

6 CORMORAN CLASS (LARGE PATROL CRAFT) (PBO)

Name	No	Builders	Launched	Commissioned
L V RABHI	310	Bázan, San Fernando	23 Sep 1987	16 Sep 1988
ERRACHIQ	311	Bázan, San Fernando	23 Sep 1987	16 Dec 1988
EL AKID	312	Bázan, San Fernando	29 Mar 1988	4 Apr 1989
EL MAHER	313	Bázan, San Fernando	29 Mar 1988	20 June 1989
EL MAJID	314	Bázan, San Fernando	21 Oct 1988	26 Sep 1989
EL BACHIR	315	Bázan, San Fernando	21 Oct 1988	19 Dec 1989

Displacement, tons: 425 full load
Dimensions, feet (metres): 190.6 × 24.9 × 8.9 (58.1 × 7.6 × 2.7)
Main machinery: 2 MTU-Bazán 16V 956 TB82 diesels; 8,340 hp(m) (6.13 MW) sustained; 2 shafts
Speed, knots: 22. **Range, n miles:** 6,100 at 12 kt
Complement: 36 (4 officers) plus 15 spare
Guns: 1 Bofors 40 mm/70. 2 Giat 20 mm.
Weapons control: CSEE Lynx optronic director.
Radars: Surface search: Racal Decca; I-band.

Comment: Three ordered from Bazán, Cadiz in October 1985 as a follow on to the Lazaga class of which these are a slower patrol version with a 10 day endurance. Option on three more taken up. Used for fishery protection.

EL MAHER *2/2005*, Marco Ghiglino* / 1133091

6 EL WACIL (P 32) CLASS (COASTAL PATROL CRAFT) (PB)

Name	No	Builders	Launched	Commissioned
EL WACIL	203	CMN, Cherbourg	12 June 1975	9 Oct 1975
EL JAIL	204	CMN, Cherbourg	10 Oct 1975	3 Dec 1975
EL MIKDAM	205	CMN, Cherbourg	1 Dec 1975	30 Jan 1976
EL KHAFIR	206	CMN, Cherbourg	21 Jan 1976	16 Apr 1976
EL HARIS	207	CMN, Cherbourg	31 Mar 1976	30 June 1976
EL ESSAHIR	208	CMN, Cherbourg	2 June 1976	16 July 1976

Displacement, tons: 74 light; 89 full load
Dimensions, feet (metres): 105 × 17.7 × 4.6 (32 × 5.4 × 1.4)
Main machinery: 2 SACM MGO 12V BZSHR diesels; 2,700 hp(m) (1.98 MW); 2 shafts
Speed, knots: 28. **Range, n miles:** 1,500 at 15 kt
Complement: 17
Guns: 1 Oerlikon 20 mm.
Radars: Surface search: Decca; I-band.

Comment: Ordered in February 1974. In July 1985 a further four of this class were ordered from the same builders but for the Customs Service. Wooden hull sheathed in plastic.

EL JAIL *9/2004, S D Llosá* / 1044135

5 RAÏS BARGACH CLASS (TYPE OPV 64) (PSO)

Name	No	Builders	Launched	Commissioned
RAÏS BARGACH	318	Leroux & Lotz, Lorient	9 Oct 1995	14 Dec 1995
RAÏS BRITEL	319	Leroux & Lotz, Lorient	19 Mar 1996	14 May 1996
RAÏS CHARKAOUI	320	Leroux & Lotz, Lorient	25 Sep 1996	10 Dec 1996
RAÏS MAANINOU	321	Leroux & Lotz, Lorient	7 Mar 1997	21 May 1997
RAÏS AL MOUNASTIRI	322	Leroux & Lotz, Lorient	15 Oct 1997	17 Dec 1997

Displacement, tons: 580 full load
Dimensions, feet (metres): 210 × 37.4 × 9.8 (64 × 11.4 × 3)
Main machinery: 2 Wärtsilä Nohab 25 V16 diesels; 10,000 hp(m) (7.36 MW) sustained; 2 Leroy auxiliary motors; 326 hp(m) (240 kW); 2 shafts; cp props
Speed, knots: 24; 7 (on motors). **Range, n miles:** 4,000 at 12 kt
Complement: 24 (3 officers) + 30 spare
Guns: 1 Bofors 40 mm/60. 1 Oerlikon 20 mm. 4—14.5 mm MGs (2 twin).
Radars: Surface search: Racal Decca Bridgemaster; I-band.

Comment: First pair ordered to a Serter design from Leroux & Lotz, Lorient in December 1993, second pair in October 1994. Option on fifth taken up in 1996. There is a stern door for launching a 7 m RIB, a water gun for firefighting and two passive stabilisation tanks. This version of the OPV 64 does not have a helicopter deck and the armament is fitted after delivery. Manned by the Navy for the Fisheries Department. Based at Agadir.

RAÏS CHARKAOUI *6/2005*, M Declerck* / 1133131

RAÏS AL MOUNASTIRI *7/2004*, M Declerck* / 1133133

AMPHIBIOUS FORCES

1 EDIC CLASS (LCU)

Name	No	Builders	Commissioned
LIEUTENANT MALGHAGH	401	Chantiers Navals Franco-Belges	1965

Displacement, tons: 250 standard; 670 full load
Dimensions, feet (metres): 193.5 × 39.2 × 4.3 (59 × 12 × 1.3)
Main machinery: 2 SACM MGO diesels; 1,000 hp(m) (735 kW); 2 shafts
Speed, knots: 8. **Range, n miles:** 1,800 at 8 kt
Complement: 16 (1 officer)
Military lift: 11 vehicles
Guns: 2 Oerlikon 20 mm. 1—120 mm mortar.
Radars: Navigation: Decca 1226; I-band.

Comment: Ordered early in 1963. Similar to the former French landing craft of the Edic type built at the same yard.

LIEUTENANT MALGHAGH *2/1995, Diego Quevedo* / 0081277

3 BATRAL CLASS (LSMH)

Name	No	Builders	Commissioned
DAOUD BEN AICHA	402	Dubigeon, Normandie	28 May 1977
AHMED ES SAKALI	403	Dubigeon, Normandie	Sep 1977
ABOU ABDALLAH EL AYACHI	404	Dubigeon, Normandie	Mar 1978

Displacement, tons: 750 standard; 1,409 full load
Dimensions, feet (metres): 262.4 × 42.6 × 7.9 (80 × 13 × 2.4)
Main machinery: 2 SACM Type 195 V12 CSHR diesels; 3,600 hp(m) (2.65 MW) sustained; 2 shafts
Speed, knots: 16. **Range, n miles:** 4,500 at 13 kt
Complement: 47 (3 officers)
Military lift: 140 troops; 12 vehicles or 300 tons
Guns: 2 Bofors 40 mm/70. 2—81 mm mortars. 2—12.7 mm MGs.
Radars: Surface search: Thomson-CSF DRBN 32 (Racal Decca 1226); I-band.
Helicopters: Platform only.

Comment: Two ordered on 12 March 1975. Third ordered 19 August 1975. Of same type as the French Champlain. Vehicle-stowage above and below decks. Daoud Ben Aicha was refitted in Lorient by Leroux & Lotz in 1995 and Abou Abdallah el Ayachi in 1997.

DAOUD BEN AICHA *10/2004*, Carlos Pardo Gonzalez* / 1133132

1 NEWPORT CLASS (LSTH)

Name	No	Builders	Commissioned
SIDI MOHAMMED BEN ABDALLAH (ex-Bristol County)	407 (ex-1198)	National Steel, San Diego	5 Aug 1972

Displacement, tons: 4,975 light; 8,450 full load
Dimensions, feet (metres): 522.3 (hull) × 69.5 × 17.5 (aft) (159.2 × 21.2 × 5.3)
Main machinery: 6 ALCO 16-251 diesels; 16,500 hp (12.3 MW) sustained; 2 shafts; cp props; bow thruster
Speed, knots: 20
Range, n miles: 14,250 at 14 kt
Complement: 257 (13 officers)
Military lift: 400 troops (20 officers); 500 tons vehicles; 3 LCVPs and 1 LCPL on davits
Guns: 1 GE/GD 20 mm 6-barrelled Vulcan Phalanx Mk 15.
Radars: Surface search: Raytheon SPS-67; G-band.
Navigation: Marconi LN66; I/J-band.
Helicopters: Platform only.

Comment: Received from the US by grant transfer on 16 August 1994. Has replaced Arrafiq. The ship was non-operational by late 1995 and although back in service, has so far proved to be a poor bargain. The bow ramp is supported by twin derrick arms. A ramp just forward of the superstructure connects the lower tank deck with the main deck and a vehicle passage through the superstructure provides access to the parking area amidships. A stern gate to the tank deck permits unloading of amphibious tractors into the water, or unloading of other vehicles into an LCU or on to a pier. Vehicle stowage covers 19,000 sq ft. Length over derrick arms is 562 ft (171.3 m); full load draught is 11.5 ft forward and 17.5 ft aft. Based at Casablanca.

SIDI MOHAMMED BEN ABDALLAH *11/2004*, Marco Ghiglino* / 1133092

SURVEY AND RESEARCH SHIPS

1 ROBERT D CONRAD CLASS (AGOR)

Name	No	Builders	Commissioned
ABU AL BARAKAT AL BARBARI (ex-Bartlett)	802 (ex-702, ex-T-AGOR 13)	Northwest Marine Iron Works, Portland, OR	31 Mar 1969

Displacement, tons: 1,200 light; 1,370 full load
Dimensions, feet (metres): 208.9 × 40 × 15.3 (63.7 × 12.2 × 4.7)
Main machinery: Diesel-electric; 2 Caterpillar D 378 diesel generators; 1 motor; 1,000 hp (746 kW); 1 shaft; bow thruster
Speed, knots: 13.5
Range, n miles: 12,000 at 12 kt
Complement: 41 (9 officers, 15 scientists)
Radars: Navigation: TM 1660/12S; I-band.

Comment: Leased from the USA on 26 July 1993. Fitted with instrumentation and laboratories to measure gravity and magnetism, water temperature, sound transmission in water, and the profile of the ocean floor. Special features include 10 ton capacity boom and winches for handling over-the-side equipment; bow thruster; 620 hp gas turbine (housed in funnel structure) for providing 'quiet' power when conducting experiments; can propel the ship at 6.5 kt.
Ships of this class are in service with Brazil, Mexico, Chile, Tunisia and Portugal.

ABU EL BARAKAT AL BARBARI *11/2004*, Marco Ghiglino* / 1133094

AUXILIARIES

Notes: (1) There is also a yacht, *Essaouira*, 60 tons, from Italy in 1967, used as a training vessel for watchkeepers.
(2) Bazán delivered a harbour pusher tug, similar to Spanish Y 171 class, in December 1993.
(3) There are two sail training craft *Al Massira* and *Boujdour*.
(4) There is a stern trawler used as a utility and diver support vessel (803 (ex-YFU 14)).

803   *9/2004, S D Llosá* / 1044141

1 LOGISTIC SUPPORT SHIP (AKS)

EL AIGH (ex-*Merc Nordia*) 405

Measurement, tons: 1,500 grt
Dimensions, feet (metres): 252.6 × 40 × 15.4 *(77 × 12.2 × 4.7)*
Main machinery: 1 Burmeister & Wain diesel; 1,250 hp(m) *(919 kW)*; 1 shaft
Speed, knots: 11
Complement: 25
Guns: 2—14.5 mm MGs.

Comment: Logistic support vessel with four 5 ton cranes. Former cargo ship with ice-strengthened bow built by Fredrickshavn Vaerft in 1973 and acquired in 1981.

EL AIGH   *5/1994, M Declerck* / 0506199

1 DAKHLA CLASS (LOGISTIC SUPPORT SHIP) (AKS)

Name	No	Builders	Launched	Commissioned
DAKHLA	408	Leroux & Lotz, Lorient	5 June 1997	1 Aug 1997

Displacement, tons: 2,160 full load
Dimensions, feet (metres): 226.4 × 37.7 × 13.8 *(69 × 11.5 × 4.2)*
Main machinery: 1 Wärtsilä Nohab 8V25 diesel; 2,300 hp(m) *(1.69 MW)* sustained; 1 shaft; cp prop
Speed, knots: 12
Range, n miles: 4,300 at 12 kt
Complement: 24 plus 22 spare
Cargo capacity: 800 tons
Guns: 2—12.7 mm MGs.
Radars: Navigation: 2 Racal Decca Bridgemaster ARPA; I-band.

Comment: Ordered from Leroux & Lotz, Nantes in 1995. Side entry for vehicles. One 15 ton crane. Based at Agadir.

DAKHLA   *8/1997, Leroux & Lotz* / 0012789

CUSTOMS/COAST GUARD/POLICE

Notes: (1) The Coast Guard was created by Royal Decree on 9 September 1997. Responsibility for Search and Rescue conferred on the Ministére des Pêches Maritimes (MPM). Operational control is exercised from the National Rescue Service HQ at Rabat in co-ordination with the Merchant Marine HQ at Casablanca.
(2) There is a 17 m SAR craft *Al Fida* delivered in August 2002.
(3) There are four SAR craft: *Rif, Loukouss, Souss* and *Dghira*.

AL FIDA   *7/2004, S D Llosá* / 1044137

SOUSS   *7/1995, Zamacona* / 1044138

2 SAR CRAFT (SAR)

AL AMANE 2344   **AIT BAÂMRANE** 2345

Displacement, tons: 68 full load
Dimensions, feet (metres): 51.7 × 14.7 × 3.4 *(15.75 × 4.48 × 1.05)*
Main machinery: 2 Volvo D12; 1,300 hp *(970 kW)*; Hamilton waterjets
Speed, knots: 34
Complement: 4

Comment: Constructed by Auxnaval Shipbuilders, Spain and delivered in March 2003. Aluminium hull.

AL AMANE   *7/2003, Auxnaval* / 1044136

3 SAR CRAFT (SAR)

HAOUZ   **ASSA**   **TARIK**

Displacement, tons: 40 full load
Dimensions, feet (metres): 63.6 × 15.7 × 4.3 *(19.4 × 4.8 × 1.3)*
Main machinery: 2 diesels; 1,400 hp(m) *(1.03 MW)*; 2 shafts
Speed, knots: 20
Complement: 6

Comment: Rescue craft built by Schweers, Bardenfleth and delivered in 1991.

2 SAR CRAFT (SAR)

AL WHADA 12-64   SEBOU 12-65

Displacement, tons: 70 full load
Dimensions, feet (metres): 68.0 × 19.2 × 5.9 *(20.7 × 5.8 × 1.8)*
Main machinery: 2 MAN D2842 LE401 diesels; 2,000 hp *(1.49 MW)*; 2 shafts
Speed, knots: 20
Complement: 4

Comment: Constructed by Auxnaval, Asturias, Spain and delivered in 2004.

AL WHADA   *7/2004, Auxnaval* / 1044139

4 ERRAID (P 32) CLASS (COASTAL PATROL CRAFT) (WPB)

Name	No	Builders	Launched	Commissioned
ERRAID	209	CMN, Cherbourg	20 Dec 1987	18 Mar 1988
ERRACED	210	CMN, Cherbourg	21 Jan 1988	15 Apr 1988
EL KACED	211	CMN, Cherbourg	10 Mar 1988	17 May 1988
ESSAID	212	CMN, Cherbourg	19 May 1988	4 July 1988

Displacement, tons: 89 full load
Dimensions, feet (metres): 105 × 17.7 × 4.6 *(32 × 5.4 × 1.4)*
Main machinery: 2 SACM MGO 12V BZSHR diesels; 2,700 hp(m) *(1.98 MW)*; 2 shafts
Speed, knots: 28
Range, n miles: 1,500 at 15 kt
Complement: 17
Guns: 1 Oerlikon 20 mm.
Radars: Navigation: Decca; I-band.

Comment: Similar to the El Wacil class listed under Patrol Forces. Ordered in July 1985.

EL KACED   *6/1999* / 0081279

18 ARCOR 46 CLASS (COASTAL PATROL CRAFT) (WPB)

Displacement, tons: 15 full load
Dimensions, feet (metres): 47.6 × 13.8 × 4.3 *(14.5 × 4.2 × 1.3)*
Main machinery: 2 SACM UD18V8 M5D diesels; 1,010 hp(m) *(742 kW)* sustained; 2 shafts
Speed, knots: 32
Range, n miles: 300 at 20 kt
Complement: 6
Guns: 2 Browning 12.7 mm MGs.
Radars: Surface search: Furuno 701; I-band.

Comment: Ordered from Arcor, La Teste in June 1985. GRP hulls. Delivered in groups of three from April to September 1987. Used for patrolling the Mediterranean coastline.

ARCOR 46 CLASS   *9/2004, S D Llosá* / 1044140

15 ARCOR 53 CLASS (COASTAL PATROL CRAFT) (WPBF)

Displacement, tons: 17 full load
Dimensions, feet (metres): 52.5 × 13 × 3.9 *(16 × 4 × 1.2)*
Main machinery: 2 Saab DSI-14 diesels; 1,250 hp(m) *(919 kW)*; 2 shafts
Speed, knots: 35
Range, n miles: 300 at 20 kt
Complement: 6
Guns: 1 — 12.7 mm MG.
Radars: Surface search: Furuno; I-band.

Comment: Ordered from Arcor, La Teste in 1990 for the Police Force. Delivered at one a month from October 1992.

ARCOR 53 (Police)   *10/1999, M Declerck* / 0105138

Mozambique

MARINHA MOÇAMBIQUE

Country Overview

The Republic of Mozambique gained independence from Portugal in 1975. Situated in south-eastern Africa, it has an area of 308,642 square miles and is bordered to the north by Tanzania, to the south by South Africa and Swaziland and to the west by Zimbabwe, Zambia, and Malawi. It has a 1,334 n mile coastline with the Mozambique Channel of the Indian Ocean. Maputo (formerly Lourenço Marques) is the capital, largest city and principal port. There is another major port at Beira. Territorial Seas (12 n miles) are claimed.

A 200 n mile EEZ has also been claimed but the limits are not fully defined by boundary agreements.

All the Russian built Zhuks and Yevgenyas have sunk alongside or been sold. There are some motorboats operational on Lake Malawi.

Headquarters Appointments

Head of Navy:
  Vice Admiral Pascoal Jose Nhalungo

Personnel

2006: 200

Bases

Maputo (Naval HQ); Nacala; Beira; Pemba (Porto Amelia); Metangula (Lake Malawi); Tete (River Zambesi); Inhambane.

PATROL FORCES

2 NAMACURRA CLASS (INSHORE PATROL CRAFT) (PB)

— (ex-Y 1507)   — (ex-Y 1510)

Displacement, tons: 5 full load
Dimensions, feet (metres): 29.5 × 9 × 2.8 *(9 × 2.7 × 0.8)*
Main machinery: 2 Yamaha outboards; 380 hp(m) *(2.79 kW)*
Speed, knots: 32. **Range, n miles:** 180 at 20 kt
Complement: 4
Guns: 1 — 12.7 mm MG. 2 — 7.62 mm MGs.
Depth charges: 1 rack.
Radars: Surface search: Furuno; I-band.

Comment: Built in South Africa in 1980-81. Can be transported by road. Donated by South Africa in 2004.

NAMACURRA   *8/2001*, van Ginderen Collection* / 0132783

Myanmar
TATMADAW YAY

Country Overview

The Union of Myanmar, also known as the Republic of Burma, gained independence in 1948. Situated in South East Asia, it has an area of 261,218 square miles, is bordered to the north-east by China, to the north-west by India and Bangladesh and to the south-east by Laos and Thailand. It has a 1,042 n mile coastline with the Andaman Sea and the Bay of Bengal. The administrative capital became Pyinmana on 6 November 2005. Rangoon (Yangon) is the commercial capital, largest city and principal port. Some 6,900 n miles of navigable inland waterways are important transport arteries. Territorial waters (12 n miles) are claimed. A 200 n mile EEZ has been claimed although the limits have only been partly defined by boundary agreements.

Headquarters Appointments

Commander in Chief:
 Vice Admiral Soe Thein

Personnel

(a) 2006: 13,000 (this may include 800 naval infantry)
(b) Voluntary service

Bases

There are five regional commands with principal bases as indicated:

Ayeyarwady (Irawaddy): Monkey Point (Navy HQ), Yangon (Rangoon), Thilawa (dockyard), Great Coco Island
Taninthayi (Tenasserim): Myeik (Mergui) (Regional HQ), Zadetgyi Island (Base 58, St Matthew's Island), Kathekyun (Ketthayin), Pale Island, Thetkatan (Kadan Island)
Danyawady: Hainggyi Island (Regional HQ), Pathein
Mawrawady: Mawlamyine (Moulmein) (Regional HQ), Kyaikkami, Dawei (Tavoy)
Panmawady: Kyaukpyu (Regional HQ), Akyab (Base 18, Sittwe), Thandwe
The Headquarters of Training Command is at Thilawa in Rangoon. The main training depot is currently at Syriam

(Thanlyin), but is to be transferred to Seikkyi, near the mouth of the Hlaing (Rangoon) River.
The Pathein base will reportedly be moved to Pyadatgyi Island, where an expanded airfield will permit the basing of air force equipment and personnel as well as navy. The Great Coco Island base has also been expanded through the construction of a large landing jetty to replace the existing small pier. It is also the site of a Chinese surveillance installation.

Organisations

Naval units are usually commanded directly from Rangoon, but operational control is occasionally delegated to regional commands.

Naval Infantry

The existence of 800 naval infantry has been previously reported but not confirmed.

CORVETTES

3 SINMALAIK CLASS (CORVETTES) (FS)

Name	No
ANAWRAHTA	771
—	—
—	—

Builders	Laid down	Launched	Commissioned
Sinmalaik Shipyard, Rangoon	1998	2000	2001
Sinmalaik Shipyard, Rangoon	1998	2001	2002
Sinmalaik Shipyard, Rangoon	1998	2001	2003

Displacement, tons: 1,088 full load
Dimensions, feet (metres): 252.6 × ? × ? *(77.0 × ? × ?)*
Main machinery: To be announced
Speed, knots: To be announced
Complement: 101 (15 officers)

Guns: 1 OTO Breda 3 in *(76 mm)*/62 compact; 85 rds/min to 16 km *(8.7 n miles)* anti-surface; 12 km *(6.5 n miles)* anti-aircraft; weight of shell 6 kg.
 2 Breda 40 mm/70 (twin); 300 rds/min to 12.5 km *(6.8 n miles)*; weight of shell 0.96 kg.
Countermeasures: To be announced.
Radars: Surface search: To be announced.
Navigation: To be announced
Fire control: To be announced
Sonars: To be announced
Helicopters: Platform for 1 medium.

Programmes: The programme to acquire ships to replace the now decommissioned PCE-827 and Admirable class corvettes was probably instituted in the 1990s. As frigates proved to be too expensive, three Chinese hulls are believed to have been acquired in about 1998 for fitting out at Sinmalaik Shipyard. There have been reports that Israeli electronic systems (radars and sonar) have been fitted. The details of the programme are speculative. Further vessels may be under construction.

771 *12/2004* / 0581402

Operational: There has been speculation that these vessels were to be armed with four C-801 anti-ship missiles but is unclear as to whether they have been fitted. The first

ship conducted sea trials in 2001 when the second ship was nearing completion. Three ships were reported in commission by 2004.

PATROL FORCES

6 HOUXIN (TYPE 037/1G) CLASS (FAST ATTACK CRAFT—GUN) (PTG)

MAGA 471	**SAITTRA** 472	**DUWA** 473	**ZEYDA** 474	**475-476**

Displacement, tons: 478 full load
Dimensions, feet (metres): 206 × 23.6 × 7.9 *(62.8 × 7.2 × 2.4)*
Main machinery: 4 PR 230ZC diesels; 4,000 hp(m) *(2.94 MW)*; 4 shafts
Speed, knots: 28. **Range, n miles:** 1,300 at 15 kt
Complement: 71
Missiles: SSM: 4 YJ-1 (C-801) (2 twin); active radar homing to 40 km *(22 n miles)* at 0.9 Mach; warhead 165 kg; sea skimmer. C-802 may be fitted in due course.

Guns: 4—37 mm/63 Type 76A (2 twin); 180 rds/min to 8.5 km *(4.6 n miles)*; weight of shell 1.42 kg.
4—14.5 mm Type 69 (2 twin).
Countermeasures: ESM/ECM: intercept and jammer.
Radars: Surface search: Square Tie; I-band.
Fire control: Rice Lamp; I-band.

Programmes: First pair arrived from China in December 1995, second pair in mid-1996 and last two in late

1997. The first four were wrongly reported as Hainan class.
Structure: Details given are for this class in Chinese service.
Operational: *475* damaged in a collision during sea trials in August 1996. All based at Rangoon.

ZEYDA *6/2001* / 0130747

2 OSPREY CLASS (OFFSHORE PATROL VESSELS) (PBO)

Name	No	Builders	Commissioned
INDAW	FV 55	Frederikshavn Dockyard	30 May 1980
INYA	FV 57	Frederikshavn Dockyard	25 Mar 1982

Displacement, tons: 385 standard; 505 full load
Dimensions, feet (metres): 164 × 34.5 × 9 *(50 × 10.5 × 2.8)*
Main machinery: 2 Burmeister and Wain Alpha diesels; 4,640 hp(m) *(3.4 MW)*; 2 shafts; cp props
Speed, knots: 20
Range, n miles: 4,500 at 16 kt
Complement: 20 (5 officers)
Guns: 1 Bofors 40 mm/60. 2 Oerlikon 20 mm.

Comment: Operated by Burmese Navy for the People's Pearl and Fishery Department. Helicopter deck with hangar in *Indaw*. Carry David Still craft or RIBs capable of 25 kt. *Inya* reported to be in poor condition. Both based at Rangoon. A third of class, *Inma*, reported to have sunk in 1987. A similar ship is in service in Namibia.

INYA *1980* / 0056642

8 MYANMAR CLASS (COASTAL PATROL CRAFT) (PGG)

551-558

Displacement, tons: 213 full load
Dimensions, feet (metres): 147.3 × 23 × 8.2 *(45 × 7 × 2.5)*
Main machinery: 2 Mercedes-Benz diesels; 2 shafts
Speed, knots: 30+
Complement: 34 (7 officers)

Missiles: 4 YJ-1 (Eagle Strike) (C-801) (2 twin) launchers; active radar homing to 40 km *(22 n miles)* at 0.9 Mach; warhead 165 kg.
Guns: 2—37 mm (twin), 2—23 mm (twin), 4—14.5 mm (2 twin) (gun-armed variant). 4—23 mm (2 twin), 4—14.5 mm (missile-armed variant).
Radars: Surface search: I-band.
Fire control: Rice Lamp; I-band.

Comment: First ship under construction at the Naval Engineering Depot, Rangoon in 1991. *551* launched on 2 January 1996 and *552* on 4 January 1996. Four further vessels reported in service by 2004 and a further two in 2005. More may be built. There appear to be two variants of the class. At least two (556 and 558) have missile launchers believed to house C-801. These have a higher mainmast and an additional radar. The remainder have a heavier gun armament.

MYANMAR CLASS 553 *6/2001* / 0130746

MYANMAR CLASS 556 *12/2004* / 0581401

MYANMAR CLASS 556-558 *11/2005** / 1151121

10 HAINAN (TYPE 037) CLASS (COASTAL PATROL CRAFT) (PC)

Name	No
YAN SIT AUNG	441
YAN YE AUNG	445
YAN WIN AUNG	448
YAN MYAT AUNG	442
YAN MIN AUNG	446
YAN AYE AUNG	449
YAN NYEIN AUNG	443
YAN PAING AUNG	447
YAN ZWE AUNG	450
YAN KHWIN AUNG	444

Displacement, tons: 375 standard; 392 full load
Dimensions, feet (metres): 192.8 × 23.6 × 7.2 *(58.8 × 7.2 × 2.2)*
Main machinery: 4 PCR/Kolomna Type 9-D-8 diesels; 4,000 hp(m) *(2.94 MW)* sustained; 4 shafts
Speed, knots: 30.5
Range, n miles: 1,300 at 15 kt
Complement: 69
Guns: 4 China 57 mm/70 (2 twin); 120 rds/min to 12 km *(6.5 n miles)*; weight of shell 6.31 kg.
4 USSR 25 mm/60 (2 twin); 270 rds/min to 3 km *(1.6 n miles)* anti-aircraft; weight of shell 0.34 kg.
A/S mortars: 4 RBU 1200 5-tubed fixed launchers; range 1,200 m; warhead 34 kg.
Depth charges: 2 BMB-2 projectors; 2 racks.
Mines: Rails fitted.
Countermeasures: ESM: Intercept.
Radars: Surface search: Pot Head; I-band.
Navigation: Raytheon Pathfinder; I-band.
IFF: High Pole.
Sonars: Stag Ear; hull-mounted; active search and attack; high frequency.

Comment: First six delivered from China in January 1991, four more in mid-1993. The first six originally had double figure pennant numbers which have been changed to three figures. These ships are the later variant of this class with tripod masts. Based at Rangoon.

YAN WIN AUNG *9/1993* / 0056641

YAN KHWIN AUNG *12/1994, G Toremans* / 0506221

3 PB 90 CLASS (COASTAL PATROL CRAFT) (PB)

424-426

Displacement, tons: 92 full load
Dimensions, feet (metres): 89.9 × 21.5 × 7.2 (27.4 × 6.6 × 2.2)
Main machinery: 3 diesels; 4,290 hp(m) (3.15 MW); 3 shafts
Speed, knots: 32
Range, n miles: 400 at 25 kt
Complement: 17
Guns: 8 — 20 mm M75 (two quad). 2 — 128 mm launchers for illuminants.
Radars: Surface search: Decca 1226; I-band.

Comment: Built by Brodotechnika, Yugoslavia for an African country and completed in 1986-87. Laid up when the sale did not go through and shipped to Burma arriving in October 1990. All are active. Based at Rangoon.

PB 90 (Yugoslav colours)   *1990, Yugoslav FDSP* / 0056643

6 BURMA PGM TYPE (COASTAL PATROL CRAFT) (PB)

PGM 412 -415   **THIHAYARZAR** I and II

Displacement, tons: 168 full load
Dimensions, feet (metres): 110 × 22 × 6.5 (33.5 × 6.7 × 2)
Main machinery: 2 Deutz SBA16MB816 LLKR diesels; 2,720 hp(m) (2 MW); 2 shafts
Speed, knots: 16
Range, n miles: 1,400 at 14 kt
Complement: 17
Guns: 2 Bofors 40 mm/60.

Comment: Built by Burma Naval Dockyard modelled on the US PGM 43 type. First two completed 1983. Two more craft with different superstructure but with identical dimensions and named *Thihayarzar I* and *II* were delivered by Myanma Shipyard to the Customs on 27 June 1993. Both craft may be lightly armed.

PGM 415   *4/1993* / 0056644

THIHAYARZAR CLASS   *11/2005** / 1151118

4 RIVER GUNBOATS (Ex-TRANSPORTS) (PBR)

SAGU   **SEINDA**   **SHWETHIDA**   **SINMIN**

Displacement, tons: 98 full load
Dimensions, feet (metres): 94.5 × 22 × 4.5 (28.8 × 6.7 × 1.4)
Main machinery: 1 Crossley ERL 6-cyl diesel; 160 hp (119 kW); 1 shaft
Speed, knots: 12
Complement: 32
Guns: 1 — 40 mm/60 (Sagu). 1 — 20 mm (3 in Sagu).

Comment: Built in mid-1950s. *Sinmin*, *Seinda* and *Shwethida* have a roofed-in upper deck with a 20 mm gun forward of the funnel. *Sagu* has an open upper deck aft of the funnel and with a 40 mm gun forward and mountings for 20 mm aft on the upper deck and midships either side on the lower deck. Based at Moulmein and at least two are operational. Four other ships of the same type are unarmed and are listed under *Auxiliaries*.

SEINDA   *8/1994* / 0056649

2 IMPROVED Y 301 CLASS (RIVER GUNBOATS) (PBR)

Y 311   **Y 312**

Displacement, tons: 250 full load
Dimensions, feet (metres): 121.4 × 24 × 3.9 (37 × 7.3 × 1.2)
Main machinery: 2 MTU MB diesels; 1,000 hp(m) (735 kW); 2 shafts
Speed, knots: 12
Complement: 37
Guns: 2 Bofors 40 mm/60. 4 Oerlikon 20 mm.
Radars: Surface search: Raytheon; I-band.

Comment: Built at Simmilak in 1969 and based on similar Yugoslav craft which have been scrapped. Based at Sittwe.

Y 311   *11/2005** / 1151120

6 CARPENTARIA CLASS (RIVER PATROL CRAFT) (PBR)

112-117

Displacement, tons: 26 full load
Dimensions, feet (metres): 51.5 × 15.7 × 4.3 (15.7 × 4.8 × 1.3)
Main machinery: 2 MTU 8V 331 TC92 diesels; 1,770 hp(m) (1.3 MW) sustained; 2 shafts
Speed, knots: 29. **Range, n miles:** 950 at 18 kt
Complement: 10
Guns: 1 Oerlikon 20 mm. 1 — 12.7 mm MG.

Comment: Built by De Havilland Marine, Sydney. First two delivered 1979, remainder in 1980. Similar to craft built for Indonesia. Based at Rangoon.

CARPENTARIA 113   *1991* / 0056651

25 MICHAO CLASS (PBR)

001-025

Comment: Small craft, 52 ft (15.8 m) long, acquired from Yugoslavia in 1965. Also used to ferry troops and two are used as VIP launches. 1 to 7 based at Rangoon; 8 to 16 at Moulmein and 17 to 25 at Sittwe.

MICHAO CLASS   *5/1995* / 0056650

2 CGC TYPE (RIVER GUNBOATS) (PBR)

MGB 102   **MGB 110**

Displacement, tons: 49 standard; 66 full load
Dimensions, feet (metres): 83 × 16 × 5.5 *(25.3 × 4.9 × 1.7)*
Main machinery: 4 GM diesels; 800 hp *(596 kW)*; 2 shafts
Speed, knots: 11
Complement: 16
Guns: 1 Bofors 40 mm/60. 1 Oerlikon 20 mm.

Comment: Ex-USCG type cutters with new hulls built in Burma. Completed in 1960. Based at Rangoon but have not been seen recently.

MGB 110   0505966

9 RIVER PATROL CRAFT (PBR)

RPC 11-19

Displacement, tons: 37 full load
Dimensions, feet (metres): 50 × 14 × 3.5 *(15.2 × 4.3 × 1.1)*
Main machinery: 2 Thornycroft RZ 6 diesels; 250 hp *(186 kW)*; 2 shafts
Speed, knots: 10
Range, n miles: 400 at 8 kt
Complement: 8
Guns: 1 Oerlikon 20 mm or 2—12.7 mm MGs (twin). 1—12.7 mm MG.

Comment: Built by the Naval Engineering Depot, Rangoon. First five in mid-1980s; second batch of a modified design in 1990-91. Sometimes used by the Naval Infantry and can carry up to 35 troops. Based at Rangoon.

10 Y 301 CLASS (RIVER GUNBOATS) (PBR)

Y 301-310

Displacement, tons: 120 full load
Dimensions, feet (metres): 104.8 × 24 × 3 *(32 × 7.3 × 0.9)*
Main machinery: 2 MTU MB diesels; 1,000 hp(m) *(735 kW)*; 2 shafts
Speed, knots: 13
Complement: 29
Guns: 2 Bofors 40 mm/60 or 1 Bofors 40 mm/60 and 1 Vickers 2-pdr.

Comment: All of these boats were completed in 1958 at the Uljanik Shipyard, Pula, Yugoslavia. Y 301, 303 and 307 based at Moulmein. The remainder at Rangoon.

Y 309   *11/2005** / 1151119

3 SWIFT TYPE PGM (COASTAL PATROL CRAFT) (PB)

PGM 421-423

Displacement, tons: 128 full load
Dimensions, feet (metres): 103.3 × 23.8 × 6.9 *(31.5 × 7.2 × 3.1)*
Main machinery: 2 MTU 12V 331 TC81 diesels; 2,450 hp(m) *(1.8 MW)* sustained; 2 shafts
Speed, knots: 27
Range, n miles: 1,800 at 18 kt
Complement: 25
Guns: 2 Bofors 40 mm/60. 2 Oerlikon 20 mm. 2—12.7 mm MGs.
Radars: Surface search: Raytheon 1500; I-band.

Comment: Swiftships construction completed between March and September 1979. Acquired 1980 through Vosper, Singapore. *PGM 421* previously reported sunk in 1990s but reported to have been repaired. Based at Rangoon.

PGM   *6/1991* / 0056645

6 PBR Mk II RIVER PATROL CRAFT (PBR)

PBR 211-216

Displacement, tons: 9 full load
Dimensions, feet (metres): 32 × 11 × 2.6 *(9.8 × 3.4 × 0.8)*
Main machinery: 2 GM 6V-53 diesels; 348 hp *(260 kW)* sustained; 2 water-jets
Speed, knots: 25
Range, n miles: 180 at 20 kt
Complement: 4 or 5
Guns: 2—12.7 mm (twin, fwd) MGs. 1—7.9 mm LMG (aft).
Radars: Surface search: Raytheon 1900; I-band.

Comment: Acquired in 1978. Built by Uniflite, Washington. GRP hulls. Based at Moulmein but not reported as active recently.

PBR 211   *1987* / 0505967

6 PGM 43 TYPE (COASTAL PATROL CRAFT) (PB)

PGM 401-406

Displacement, tons: 141 full load
Dimensions, feet (metres): 101 × 21.1 × 7.5 *(30.8 × 6.4 × 2.3)*
Main machinery: 8 GM 6—71 diesels; 1,392 hp *(1.04 MW)* sustained; 2 shafts
Speed, knots: 17
Range, n miles: 1,000 at 15 kt
Complement: 17
Guns: 1 Bofors 40 mm/60. 2 Oerlikon 20 mm (twin). 2—12.7 mm MGs.
Radars: Surface search: Raytheon 1500 (PGM 405-406).
     EDO 320 (PGM 401-404); I/J-band.

Comment: First four built by Marinette Marine in 1959; last pair by Peterson Shipbuilders in 1961. PGM 401-403 based at Moulmein and 404-405 at Rangoon. PGM 406 at Sittwe.

PGM 406   *3/1992* / 0056646

AMPHIBIOUS FORCES

1 LCU

AIYAR LULIN 603

Displacement, tons: 360 full load
Dimensions, feet (metres): 119 × 34 × 6 *(36.3 × 10.4 × 1.8)*
Main machinery: 4 GM diesels; 600 hp *(448 kW)*; 2 shafts
Speed, knots: 10
Range, n miles: 1,200 at 8 kt
Complement: 14
Military lift: 168 tons
Guns: 1—12.7 mm MG.

Comment: Completed in Rangoon in 1966 to the US 1610 design. Based at Rangoon.

AIYAR LULIN   *1990* / 0056654

10 LCM 3 TYPE

LCM 701-710

Displacement, tons: 52 full load
Dimensions, feet (metres): 50 × 14 × 4 *(15.2 × 4.3 × 1.2)*
Main machinery: 2 Gray Marine 64 HN9 diesels; 330 hp *(246 kW)*; 2 shafts
Speed, knots: 9
Complement: 5

Comment: US-built LCM type landing craft. Used as local transports for stores and personnel. Cargo capacity, 30 tons. Guns have been removed. Based at Sittwe.

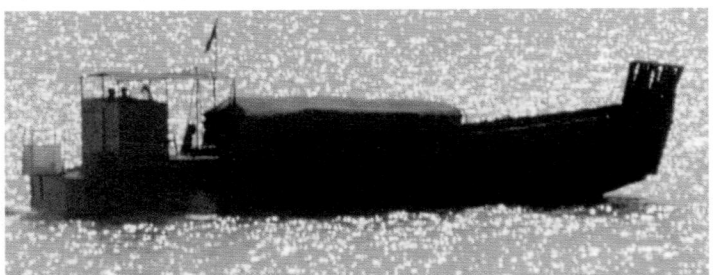

LCM 704   *5/1994* / 0056655

4 ABAMIN CLASS (LCU)

AIYAR MAI 604   **AIYAR MINTHAMEE** 606
AIYAR MAUNG 605   **AIYAR MINTHAR** 607

Displacement, tons: 250 full load
Dimensions, feet (metres): 125.6 × 29.8 × 4.6 *(38.3 × 9.1 × 1.4)*
Main machinery: 2 Kubota diesels; 600 hp(m) *(441 kW)*; 2 shafts
Speed, knots: 10
Complement: 10
Military lift: 100 tons
Guns: 1 — 12.7 mm MG.

Comment: All built by Yokohama Yacht in 1969. Based at Rangoon.

AIYAR MAUNG   *1991* / 0056653

3 LCU

001-003

Comment: Operated by the Army. Dimensions not known.

LANDING CRAFT 003   *7/1992* / 0056652

MINE WARFARE FORCES

Notes: Up to two Chinese-built minesweepers are expected to be acquired when funds are available.

SURVEY SHIPS

Notes: Thu Tay Thi means 'survey vessel'.

1 SURVEY SHIP (AGS)

Name	No	Builders	Commissioned
— (ex-*Changi*)	802	Miho Shipyard, Shimizu	20 June 1973

Displacement, tons: 880 full load
Dimensions, feet (metres): 154.2 × 28.6 × 11.9 *(47 × 8.7 × 3.6)*
Main machinery: 1 Niigata diesel; 1 shaft
Speed, knots: 13
Complement: 45 (5 officers)
Guns: 2 Oerlikon 20 mm.
Radars: Navigation: I-band.

Comment: A fishery research ship of Singapore origin, arrested on 8 April 1974 and taken into service as a survey vessel in about 1981. Stern trawler type. Based at Rangoon.

802   *10/1993* / 0056657

1 SURVEY SHIP (AGS)

Name	No	Builders	Commissioned
—	801	Brodogradiliste Tito, Belgrade, Yugoslavia	1965

Displacement, tons: 1,059 standard
Dimensions, feet (metres): 204 × 36 × 11.8 *(62.2 × 11 × 3.6)*
Main machinery: 2 MTU 12V 493 TY7 diesels; 2,120 hp(m) *(1.62 MW)* sustained; 2 shafts
Speed, knots: 15
Complement: 99 (7 officers)
Guns: 2 Bofors 40 mm/60. 2 Oerlikon 20 mm (twin).
Radars: Navigation: Racal Decca; I-band.

Comment: Has two surveying motor boats. The after gun can be removed to provide a helicopter platform. This ship is sometimes referred to as Thu Tay Thi which means 'survey vessel'. Based at Rangoon.

801   *6/1993* / 0506138

1 SURVEY CRAFT (AGSC)

Name	No	Builders	Commissioned
YAY BO	807	Damen, Netherlands	1958

Displacement, tons: 108 full load
Dimensions, feet (metres): 98.4 × 22.3 × 4.9 *(30 × 6.8 × 1.5)*
Main machinery: 2 diesels; 2 shafts
Speed, knots: 10
Complement: 34 (2 officers)
Guns: 1 — 12.7 mm MG.

Comment: Used for river surveys. Based at Rangoon.

YAY BO   *1990* / 0056656

AUXILIARIES

Notes: As well as the ships listed below there is a small coastal oil tanker, a harbour tug and several harbour launches and personnel carriers.

1 TRANSPORT VESSEL (AK)

AYIDAWAYA

Displacement, tons: 805 full load
Dimensions, feet (metres): 163.4 × 27.6 × 12.1 *(49.8 × 8.4 × 3.7)*
Main machinery: 1 diesel; 600 hp(m) *(441 kW)*; 1 shaft
Speed, knots: 12
Complement: 30

Comment: Built in Norway in 1975. Acquired in 1991 and used as transport for stores and personnel.

AYIDAWAYA *12/1991* / 0056658

1 BUOY TENDER (ABU)

HSAD DAN

Displacement, tons: 706 full load
Dimensions, feet (metres): 130.6 × 37.1 × 8.9 *(39.8 × 11.3 × 2.7)*
Main machinery: 2 Deutz BA8M816 diesels; 1,341 hp(m) *(986 kW)*; 2 shafts
Speed, knots: 10
Complement: 23

Comment: Built by Italthai in 1986. Operated by the Rangoon Port Authority but manned by the Navy.

HSAD DAN *5/1992* / 0056662

8 MFVS

511 **520-523** **901** **905** **906**

Comment: Armed vessels of approximately 200 tons *(901)*, 80 tons *(905, 906)* and 50 tons (remainder) with a 12.7 mm or 6.72 mm MG mounted above the bridge in some. All have navigational radars. Based at Rangoon.

MFV *8/1990* / 0104255

1 TRANSPORT VESSEL (AKL)

PYI DAW AYE

Displacement, tons: 850 full load
Dimensions, feet (metres): 163 × 27 × 11.5 *(49.7 × 8.3 × 3.5)*
Main machinery: 2 diesels; 600 hp *(447 kW)*; 2 shafts
Speed, knots: 11
Complement: 12

Comment: Completed in about 1975. Dimensions are approximate. Naval manned.

PYI DAW AYE *1991* / 0056663

1 DIVING SUPPORT VESSEL (YDT)

YAN LON AUNG 200

Displacement, tons: 536 full load
Dimensions, feet (metres): 179 × 30 × 8 *(54.6 × 9.1 × 2.4)*
Main machinery: 2 diesels; 2 shafts
Speed, knots: 12
Complement: 88
Guns: 1 Bofors 40 mm/60. 2—12.7 mm MGs.

Comment: Support diving ship acquired from Japan in 1967. Based at Rangoon.

YAN LON AUNG *7/1993* / 0056660

4 TRANSPORT VESSELS (AKL)

SABAN **SETHYA** **SHWEPAZUN** **SETYAHAT**

Displacement, tons: 98 full load
Dimensions, feet (metres): 94.5 × 22 × 4.5 *(28.8 × 6.7 × 1.4)*
Main machinery: 1 Crossley ERL 6-cyl diesel; 160 hp *(119 kW)*; 1 shaft
Speed, knots: 12
Complement: 30

Comment: These are sister ships to the armed gunboats shown under *Patrol Forces*. It is possible that a 20 mm gun may be mounted on some occasions. Based at Rangoon.

SHWEPAZUN *1991* / 0056661

1 TANKER (AOT)

608 (ex-*Interbunker*)

Displacement, tons: 2,900 full load
Dimensions, feet (metres): 232 × 36.1 × 16.1 *(70.7 × 11 × 4.9)*
Main machinery: 2 Daihatsu diesels; 1,860 hp(m) *(1.37 MW)*; 1 shaft
Speed, knots: 11. **Range, n miles:** 5,000 at 11 kt
Complement: 15

Comment: Thai owned commercial tanker arrested in October 1991 and taken into the Navy.

608 *12/1991* / 0056659

PRESIDENTIAL YACHT

1 TRANSPORT SHIP (YAC)

YADANABON

Comment: Built in Burma and used for VIP cruises on the Irrawaddy river and in coastal waters. Armed with 2—7.62 mm MGs and manned by the Navy.

PRESIDENT'S YACHT *1990* / 0056665

Namibia

Country Overview

Formerly South West Africa and governed by South Africa, Namibia gained independence in 1990 although South Africa continued to administer an enclave containing the principal seaport, Walvis Bay, until 1994. With an area of 318,252 square miles, it has borders to the north with Angola and to the south with South Africa. It has an 848 n mile coastline with the south Atlantic Ocean. The capital and largest city is Windhoek and there is another port at Lüderitz. Territorial seas (12 n miles) are claimed. It also claims a 200 n mile Exclusive Economic Zone (EEZ)

but its limits have not been fully defined by boundary agreements.

The Maritime Wing became the Navy on 7 October 2004.

Headquarters Appointments

Head of Navy Wing:
Captain Peter Vilho

Bases

Walvis Bay

Personnel

2006: 350

Aviation

Five ex-US Air Force Cessna O-2A observation aircraft operate in a maritime surveillance role.

PATROL FORCES

1 IMPERIAL MARINHEIRO CLASS
(COASTAL PATROL SHIP) (PB)

Name	No	Builders	Commissioned
LIEUTENANT GENERAL DIMO HAMAAMBO (ex-*Purus*)	C 11 (ex-V 23)	Smit, Kinderdijk, Netherlands	17 Apr 1955

Displacement, tons: 911 standard; 1,025 full load
Dimensions, feet (metres): 184 × 30.5 × 11.7 *(56 × 9.3 × 3.6)*
Main machinery: 2 Sulzer 6TD36 diesels; 2,160 hp(m) *(1.59 MW)*; 2 shafts
Speed, knots: 16
Complement: 64 (6 officers)
Guns: 1—3 in *(76 mm)*/50 Mk 33; 50 rds/min to 12.8 km *(6.9 n miles)*; weight of shell 6 kg. 2 or 4 Oerlikon 20 mm.
Radars: Surface search: Racal Decca; I-band.

Comment: Built for Brazilian Navy as fleet tug but subsequently classified as a corvette. Withdrawn from Brazilian service in 2002 and recommissioned into the Namibian Navy on 27 August 2004.

LIEUTENANT GENERAL DIMO HAMAAMBO   *3/2005*, W Clements* / 1129562

0 + 1 GRAJAÚ CLASS (LARGE PATROL CRAFT) (PBO)

Name	No	Builders	Laid down	Launched	Commissioned
BRENDAN SIMBWAYE	—	Inace, Fortalesa	25 Feb 2005	2007	2008

Displacement, tons: 263 full load
Dimensions, feet (metres): 152.6 × 24.6 × 7.5 *(46.5 × 7.5 × 2.3)*
Main machinery: 2 MTU 16V 396TB94 diesels; 5,800 hp(m) *(4.26 MW)* sustained; 2 shafts
Speed, knots: 26. **Range, n miles:** 2,200 at 12 kt
Complement: 29 (4 officers)
Guns: 1 Bofors 40 mm/70. 2 Oerlikon 20 mm.
Radars: Surface search: Racal Decca 1290A; I-band.

Comment: Following an agreement between the governments of Namibia and Brazil in November 2003, the project for a new patrol ship is being conducted by EMGEPRON which contracted Inace for the construction of the vessel. The ship is to be similar to *Guanabara* built for the Brazilian Navy in 1999, and on which details are based.

GRAJAÚ CLASS (Brazilian colours)   *2/2001*, Mario R V Carneiro* / 0130468

0 + 4 TRACKER II CLASS (COASTAL PATROL CRAFT) (PB)

Displacement, tons: 31 standard; 45 full load
Dimensions, feet (metres): 68.6 × 17 × 4.8 *(20.9 × 5.2 × 1.5)*
Main machinery: 2 MTU 8V 396TB83 diesels; 2,100 hp(m) *(1.54 MW)* sustained; 2 shafts
Speed, knots: 25. **Range, n miles:** 600 at 15 kt
Complement: 8 (2 officers)
Guns: 2—12.7 mm MGs.
Radars: Surface search: Racal Decca RM 1070A; I-band.

Comment: Construction of four new craft is to begin once the patrol ship *Brendan Simbwaye* is completed in about 2008.

TRACKER II CLASS (Brazilian colours)   *10/2003*, Gomel/Marsan* / 0569150

1 PATROL SHIP (PBO)

Name	No	Builders	Commissioned
ORYX (ex-S to S)	P 01	Burmeister/Abeking & Rasmussen	May 1975

Displacement, tons: 406 full load
Dimensions, feet (metres): 149.9 × 28.9 × 7.9 *(45.7 × 8.8 × 2.4)*
Main machinery: 2 Deutz RSBA 16M diesels; 2,000 hp(m) *(1.47 MW)*; 1 shaft; cp prop; bow thruster
Speed, knots: 14. **Range, n miles:** 4,100 at 11 kt
Complement: 20 (6 officers)
Guns: 1—12.7 mm MG.
Radars: Surface search: Furuno ARPA FR 1525; I-band.
Navigation: Furuno FR 805D; I-band.

Comment: Built for the Nautical Investment Company, Panama and used as a yacht by the Managing Director of Fiat. Acquired in 1993 by Namibia. Replaced by *Nathanael Maxwilili* in fishery protection role and transferred to the navy as a patrol ship in 2002.

ORYX   *6/1997* / 0081282

2 NAMACURRA CLASS (INSHORE PATROL CRAFT) (PB)

—(ex-Y 1501)   —(ex-Y 1510)

Displacement, tons: 5 full load
Dimensions, feet (metres): 29.5 × 9 × 2.8 *(9 × 2.7 × 0.8)*
Main machinery: 2 Yamaha outboards; 380 hp(m) *(2.79 kW)*
Speed, knots: 32. **Range, n miles:** 180 at 20 kt
Complement: 4
Guns: 1—12.7 mm MG. 2—7.62 mm MGs.
Depth charges: 1 rack.
Radars: Surface search: Furuno; I-band.

Comment: Built in South Africa in 1980-81. Can be transported by road. Donated by South Africa on 29 November 2002.

NAMACURRA   *8/2001, van Ginderen Collection* / 0132783

GOVERNMENT MARITIME FORCES

Notes: There are also four research ships: *Benguela, Welwitschia, Nautilus II* and *Kuiseb.*

1 OSPREY FV 710 CLASS (PBOH)

Name	No	Builders	Commissioned
TOBIAS HAINYEKO	—	Frederikshavn Vaerft	July 1979
(ex-*Havørnen*)			

Displacement, tons: 505 full load
Dimensions, feet (metres): 164 × 34.5 × 9 *(50 × 10.5 × 2.8)*
Main machinery: 2 Burmeister & Wain Alpha 16V23L diesels; 4,640 hp(m) *(3.41 MW)*; 2 shafts; cp props
Speed, knots: 20
Range, n miles: 4,000 at 15 kt
Complement: 15 plus 20 spare
Radars: Surface search: Furuno ARPA FR 1525; I-band.
Navigation: Furuno FRM 64; I-band.

Comment: Donated by Denmark in late 1993, retaining some Danish crew. Recommissioned 15 December 1994. The helicopter deck can handle up to Lynx size aircraft and there is a slipway on the stern for launching an RIB. Similar ships in service in Greece, Morocco and Myanmar.

TOBIAS HAINYEKO *3/2005*, W Clements* / 1129563

1 PATROL SHIP (PBOH)

Name	Builders	Commissioned
NATHANAEL MAXWILILI	Moen Slip AS, Kolvereid, Norway	14 May 2002

Measurement, tons: 380 dwt
Dimensions, feet (metres): 189.0 × 41.0 × 13.8 *(57.6 × 12.5 × 4.2)*
Main machinery: 2 Deutz SBV8M diesel; 4,063 hp *(3.03 MW)*; 2 shafts; Kamewa Ulstein bow thruster
Speed, knots: 17
Radars: Furuno FR-2125; I-band.
Helicopters: Platform only.

Comment: Ordered in 1999. Financed by NORAD (Norwegian Agency for Development Co-Operation). Equipped with inspection craft for fishery protection role.

1 PATROL SHIP (PBO)

Name	Builders	Commissioned
ANNA KAKURUKAZE MUNGUNDA	Freire Shipyards, Vigo	10 Feb 2004

Measurement, tons: 1,400 grt
Dimensions, feet (metres): 193.6 × 41.3 × 13.8 *(59.0 × 12.6 × 4.2)*
Main machinery: 2 Deutz SBV8M 628 diesels; 4,025 hp *(3.0 MW)*; 2 shafts; 1 bow thruster; 385 hp *(285 kW)*
Speed, knots: 17. **Range, n miles:** 8,200 at 16.8 kt
Radars: Navigation: I-band.
Helicopters: Platform for 1 medium.

Comment: Multipurpose fishery protection vessel financed by the Spanish government.

ANNA KAKURUKAZE MUNGUNDA *3/2005*, W Clements* / 1129564

NATO

Overview

The North Atlantic Treaty Organisation (NATO) was formed under Article 9 of the North Atlantic Treaty signed on 4 April 1949. Now comprising 26 members, the original signatories were Belgium, Canada, Denmark, France, Iceland, Italy, Luxembourg, Netherlands, Norway, Portugal, UK and US. Greece and Turkey were admitted to the alliance in 1952, West Germany in 1955, and Spain in 1982. In 1990 the newly unified Germany replaced West Germany. Three former members of the Warsaw Pact, Czech Republic, Hungary and Poland were admitted in 1999. Seven further countries: Bulgaria, Estonia, Latvia, Lithuania, Romania, Slovakia and Slovenia, became members on 29 March 2004. A new NATO-Russia council was inaugurated on 28 May 2002. The 'Council of 20' replaced the 19 + 1 format of the Permanent Joint Council established in 1997.

RESEARCH SHIP

1 RESEARCH SHIP (AGOR)

Name	No	Builders	Launched	Commissioned
ALLIANCE	A 1456	Fincantieri, Muggiano	9 July 1986	6 May 1988

Displacement, tons: 2,466 standard; 3,180 full load
Dimensions, feet (metres): 305.1 × 49.9 × 17.1 *(93 × 15.2 × 5.2)*
Main machinery: Diesel-electric; 2 Fincantieri GMT B 230.12 M diesels; 6,079 hp(m) *(4.47 MW)* sustained; 2 AEG CC 3127 generators; 2 AEG motors; 4,039 hp(m) *(2.97 MW)* sustained; 2 shafts; bow thruster
Speed, knots: 16. **Range, n miles:** 7,200 at 11 kt
Complement: 24 (10 officers) plus 23 scientists
Radars: Navigation: 2 Kelvin Hughes ARPA; E/F- and I-bands.
Sonars: TVDS towed active VDS 200 Hz-4 kHz; medium and low frequency passive towed line arrays.

Comment: Built at La Spezia. NATO's first wholly owned ship is a Public Service vessel of the German Navy with a German, British and Italian crew. Designed for oceanography and acoustic research. Based at La Spezia and operated by SACLANT Undersea Research Centre. Facilities include extensive laboratories, position location systems, silent propulsion, and overside deployment equipment. Can tow a 20 ton load at 12 kt. A Kongsberg gas turbine on 02 deck provides silent propulsion power at 1,945 hp *(1.43 MW)* up to speeds of 12 kt. Atlas hydrosweep side scan echo-sounder fitted in 1993. Qubit KH TRAC integrated navigational system fitted in 1995. Carries two Watercraft R6 RIBs. Similar ships in Taiwan Navy and building for Italy.

ALLIANCE *2/2004, Martin Mokrus* / 0583998

1 COASTAL RESEARCH VESSEL (AGOR(C))

Name	No	Builders	Commissioned
LEONARDO	A 5390	McTay Marine Ltd	6 Sep 2002

Displacement, tons: 393 full load
Dimensions, feet (metres): 93.8 × 29.5 × 8.2 *(28.6 × 9.0 × 2.5)*
Main machinery: Diesel-electric; 1,570 hp *(1,170 kW)*; 2 azimuth thrusters; 1—360° bow thruster
Speed, knots: 11
Range, n miles: 1,500 at 11 kt
Complement: 5 + 7 scientific staff
Radars: Navigation: 2 sets; I-band.
Sonars: Kongsberg Simrad multibeam echo-sounders.

Comment: The order for a coastal underwater research vessel was placed by SACLANT Undersea Research Centre in December 2000. Designed by Corlett and Partners, construction of the hull was undertaken by Remontowa in Poland while the superstructure and final assembly was undertaken by the prime contractor, McTay Marine Ltd. The ship is equipped with a moon pool, oceanographic winches, two cranes and Kongsberg navigation/research suite. A 20 ft container can be embarked to augment the main scientific laboratory. Based at La Spezia, the vessel is the first Italian Public Service vessel.

LEONARDO *1/2004*, Giorgio Ghiglione* / 1133136

Netherlands

Country Overview

The Kingdom of the Netherlands is situated in north-western Europe. With an area of 16,033 square miles, it is bordered to the east by Germany and to the south by Belgium. It has a 244 n mile coastline with the North Sea. The country also includes the self-governing Caribbean territories of Netherlands Antilles and Aruba. The seat of government is at The Hague while Amsterdam is the official capital, largest city and a major port. Rotterdam is one of the world's leading seaports. Both ports are linked both to the North Sea and to a comprehensive system of inland waterways whose total length is some 2,725 n miles. Territorial seas (12 n miles) are claimed. An EEZ and a Fishery Zone (200 n miles) have also been declared.

Headquarters Appointments

Commander, Royal Netherlands Navy:
Vice Admiral J W Kelder
Deputy Commander:
Major General R L Zuiderwijk
Director, Planning and Control:
Brigadier H A van der Til
Director, Operations:
Commodore F J H van den Berg
Director, Operational Support :
Commodore J Snoeks

Commands

Commander Netherlands Maritime Force:
Commodore H Ort
Flag Officer Netherlands Forces Caribbean:
Commodore F Sijtsma

Diplomatic Representation

Defence Attaché in Washington:
Commodore M B Hijmans
Naval Attaché in London and Lisbon:
Captain M C Wouters
Naval Attaché in Madrid and Rabat:
Captain P P Metzelaar
Naval Attaché in Ankara:
Colonel A J Wesselingh
Naval Attaché in Washington:
Captain V C Windt
Naval Attaché in Oslo, Stockholm and Copenhagen:
Captain G F T van der Putten

Diplomatic Representation—*continued*

Naval Attaché in the Gulf:
Commander R J C M van de Rijdt
Naval Attaché in Caracas, Brasilia, Georgetown and Paramaribo:
Commander A Brokke
Naval Attaché in Talinn, Vilnius and Helsinki:
Commander B J Gerrits
Naval Attaché in Berlin:
Commander M F L Walther
Naval Attaché in Budapest and Sofia:
Commander S J Hoekstra Bonnema
Naval Attaché in Kigali, Kinshasa, Kampala and Bujumbura:
Lieutenant Colonel E J van Broekhuizen

Personnel

(a) 2006: 6,550 naval and 3,200 Marines
(b) 1,250 civilians
(c) Voluntary service

Bases

Naval HQ: Den Helder
Main Base: Den Helder
Minor Bases: Flushing, Amsterdam, Rotterdam and Curaçao
NAS De Kooy (helicopters)
R Neth Marines: Rotterdam, Doorn and Texel, Aruba

Naval Air Arm

Squadron	Aircraft	Task
7	Lynx (SH-14)	Utility and Transport/SAR
860	Lynx (SH-14D)	Embarked

Royal Netherlands Marine Corps

Four (one in reserve) Marine battalions; one combat support battalion, one logistic battalion and one amphibious support battalion. Based at Doorn and in the Netherlands Antilles and Aruba.

Prefix to Ships' Names

Hr Ms

Strength of the Fleet

Type	Active	Building (Projected)
Submarines	4	—
Frigates	10	—
Offshore Patrol Vessels	—	(4)
Mine Hunters	10	—
Submarine Support Ship	1	—
Amphibious Transport Ship (LPD)	1	1
Landing Craft	11	—
Survey Ships	2	—
Combat Support Ships	2	(1)
Training Ships	2	—

Fleet Disposition

Operational Control of Belgium and Netherlands surface forces is under Admiral Benelux Command at Den Helder.
(a) Two Task Groups, each with two air defence frigates, three Karel Doormans, one AOR, two SSK, 10 helicopters and five MPA.
(b) One amphibious transport ship.
(c) MCMV of 10 Alkmaar class.
(d) Marine force of two battalions (arctic trained), one battalion for Antilles and Aruba, one battalion in reserve.
(e) Two hydrographic vessels.

DELETIONS

Frigates

2003	*Bloys van Treslong* (to Greece)
2005	*Abraham van der Hulst, Jacob van Heemskerck* (both to Chile)
2006	*Witte de With, Tjerk Hiddes* (both to Chile)

Mine Warfare Forces

| 2003 | *Harlingen, Scheveningen* |

Survey Ships

| 2003 | *Buyskes* |
| 2004 | *Tydeman* |

Auxiliaries

| 2006 | *Pelikaan* (old) |

PENNANT LIST

Submarines

S 802	Walrus
S 803	Zeeleeuw
S 808	Dolfijn
S 810	Bruinvis

Frigates

F 802	De Zeven Provincien
F 803	Tromp
F 804	De Ruyter
F 805	Evertsen
F 827	Karel Doorman
F 828	Van Speijk
F 829	Willem van der Zaan
F 831	Van Amstel
F 833	Van Nes
F 834	Van Galen

Mine Warfare Vessels

M 853	Haarlem
M 856	Maassluis
M 857	Makkum
M 858	Middelburg
M 859	Hellevoetsluis
M 860	Schiedam
M 861	Urk
M 862	Zierikzee
M 863	Vlaardingen
M 864	Willemstad

Amphibious Forces

| L 800 | Rotterdam |
| L 801 | Johan De Witt (bldg) |

Auxiliaries

A 801	Pelikaan
A 802	Snellius
A 803	Luymes
A 832	Zuiderkruis
A 836	Amsterdam
A 851	Cerberus
A 852	Argus
A 853	Nautilus
A 854	Hydra
A 874	Linge
A 875	Regge
A 876	Hunze
A 877	Rotte
A 878	Gouwe
A 887	Thetis
A 900	Mercuur
A 902	Van Kinsbergen
Y 8005	Nieuwediep
Y 8018	Breezand
Y 8019	Balgzand
Y 8050	Urania
Y 8055	Schelde
Y 8056	Wierbalg
Y 8057	Malzwin
Y 8058	Zuidwal
Y 8059	Westwal
Y 8760	Patria

SUBMARINES

WALRUS

4/2004, Derek Fox / 1044164

4 WALRUS CLASS (SSK)

Name	No	Builders	Laid down	Launched	Commissioned
WALRUS	S 802	Rotterdamse Droogdok Mij, Rotterdam	11 Oct 1979	26 Oct 1985 (13 Sep 1989)	25 Mar 1992
ZEELEEUW	S 803	Rotterdamse Droogdok Mij, Rotterdam	24 Sep 1981	20 June 1987	25 Apr 1990
DOLFIJN	S 808	Rotterdamse Droogdok Mij, Rotterdam	12 June 1986	25 Apr 1990	29 Jan 1993
BRUINVIS	S 810	Rotterdamse Droogdok Mij, Rotterdam	14 Apr 1988	25 Apr 1992	5 July 1994

Displacement, tons: 2,465 surfaced; 2,800 dived
Dimensions, feet (metres): 223.1 × 27.6 × 23
 (67.7 × 8.4 × 7)
Main machinery: Diesel-electric; 3 SEMT-Pielstick 12 PA4
 200 VG diesels; 6,300 hp(m) *(4.63 MW)*; 3 alternators;
 2.88 MW; 1 Holec motor; 6,910 hp(m) *(5.1 MW)*; 1 shaft
Speed, knots: 12 surfaced; 20 dived
Range, n miles: 10,000 at 9 kt snorting
Complement: 52 (7 officers)

Missiles: SSM: McDonnell Douglas Sub Harpoon; active
 radar homing to 130 km *(70 n miles)* at 0.9 Mach;
 warhead 227 kg.
Torpedoes: 4—21 in *(533 mm)* tubes. Honeywell Mk 48 Mod 4;
 wire-guided; active/passive homing to 38 km *(20.5 n
 miles)* active at 55 kt; 50 km *(27 n miles)* passive at 40 kt;
 warhead 267 kg; 20 torpedoes or missiles carried. Mk 19
 Turbine ejection pump. Mk 67 water-ram discharge.
Mines: 40 in lieu of torpedoes.
Countermeasures: ESM: ARGOS 700; radar warning.
Weapons control: Signaal SEWACO VIII action data
 automation. Signaal Gipsy data system. GTHW integrated
 Harpoon and Torpedo FCS.
Radars: Surface search: Signaal/Racal ZW07; I-band.
Sonars: Thomson Sintra TSM 2272 Eledone Octopus; hull-
 mounted; passive/active search and attack; medium
 frequency.

GEC Avionics Type 2026; towed array; passive search;
very low frequency.
Thomson Sintra DUUX 5; passive ranging and intercept.

Programmes: Contract for the building of the first was
signed 16 June 1979, the second was on 17 December
1979. In 1981 various changes to the design were made
which resulted in a delay of one to two years. *Dolfijn* and
Bruinvis ordered 16 August 1985; prefabrication started
late 1985. Completion of *Walrus* delayed by serious fire 14
August 1986; hull undamaged but cabling and computers
destroyed. *Walrus* relaunched 13 September 1989.

Modernisation: A snort exhaust diffuser was fitted to *Zeeleeuw*
in 1996. The rest of the class have been similarly modified.
A mid-life upgrade is planned. Modifications are likely to
include modernisation of the sensor, weapon and command
systems and the installation of a mine-avoidance sonar.
Structure: These are improved Zwaardvis class with similar
dimensions and silhouettes except for X stern. Use of
HT steel increases the diving depth by some 50 per cent.
Diving depth, 300 m *(984 ft)*. Pilkington Optronics CK 24
search and CH 74 attack periscopes.
Operational: Weapon systems evaluations completed
1990-93. Sub Harpoon is not carried.

BRUINVIS *7/2004, H M Steele* / 1044146

BRUINVIS *10/2003, Camil Busquets i Vilanova* / 0576320

ZEELEEUW *11/2001, B Sullivan* / 0534110

FRIGATES

6 KAREL DOORMAN CLASS (FFGHM)

Name	No	Builders	Laid down	Launched	Commissioned
KAREL DOORMAN	F 827	Koninklijke Maatschappij De Schelde, Flushing	26 Feb 1985	20 Apr 1988	31 May 1991
WILLEM VAN DER ZAAN	F 829	Koninklijke Maatschappij De Schelde, Flushing	6 Nov 1985	21 Jan 1989	28 Nov 1991
VAN AMSTEL	F 831	Koninklijke Maatschappij De Schelde, Flushing	3 May 1988	19 May 1990	27 May 1993
VAN NES	F 833	Koninklijke Maatschappij De Schelde, Flushing	10 Jan 1990	16 May 1992	2 June 1994
VAN GALEN	F 834	Koninklijke Maatschappij De Schelde, Flushing	7 June 1990	21 Nov 1992	1 Dec 1994
VAN SPEIJK	F 828	Koninklijke Maatschappij De Schelde, Flushing	1 Oct 1991	26 Mar 1994	7 Sep 1995

Displacement, tons: 3,320 full load
Dimensions, feet (metres): 401.2 oa; 374.7 wl × 47.2 × 14.1 *(122.3; 114.2 × 14.4 × 4.3)*
Flight deck, feet (metres): 72.2 × 47.2 *(22 × 14.4)*
Main machinery: CODOG; 2 RR Spey SM1C; 33,800 hp *(25.2 MW)* sustained; 2 Stork-Wärtsilä 12SW280 diesels; 9,790 hp(m) *(7.2 MW)* sustained; 2 shafts; LIPS cp props
Speed, knots: 30 (Speys); 21 (diesels)
Range, n miles: 5,000 at 18 kt
Complement: 156 (16 officers) (accommodation for 163)

Missiles: SSM: 8 McDonnell Douglas Harpoon Block 1C (2 quad) launchers ❶; active radar homing to 130 km *(70 n miles)* at 0.9 Mach; warhead 227 kg.
SAM: Raytheon Sea Sparrow Mk 48 vertical launchers ❷; semi-active radar homing to 14.6 km *(8 n miles)* at 2.5 Mach; warhead 39 kg; 16 missiles. Canisters mounted on port side of hangar.
Guns: 1—3 in *(76 mm)*/62 OTO Melara compact Mk 100 ❸; 100 rds/min to 16 km *(8.6 n miles)* anti-surface; 12 km *(6.5 n miles)* anti-aircraft; weight of shell 6 kg. This is the version with an improved rate of fire.
1 Signaal SGE-30 Goalkeeper with General Electric 30 mm 7-barrelled ❹; 4,200 rds/min combined to 2 km.
2 Oerlikon 20 mm; 800 rds/min to 2 km.
Torpedoes: 4—324 mm US Mk 32 Mod 9 (2 twin) tubes (mounted inside the after superstructure) ❺. Honeywell Mk 46 Mod 5; anti-submarine; active/passive homing to 11 km *(5.9 n miles)* at 40 kt; warhead 44 kg.
Countermeasures: Decoys: 2 Loral Hycor SRBOC 6-tubed fixed Mk 36 quad launchers; IR flares and chaff to 4 km *(2.2 n miles)*.
SLQ-25 Nixie towed torpedo decoy.
ESM/ECM: Argo APECS II (includes AR 700 ESM) ❻; intercept and jammers.
Combat data systems: Signaal SEWACO VIIB action data automation; Link 11. SATCOM ❼. WSC-6 twin aerials.
Weapons control: Signaal IRSCAN infra-red detector (fitted in F 829 for trials and may be retrofitted in all in due course). Signaal VESTA helo transponder.
Radars: Air/surface search: Signaal SMART ❽; 3D; F-band.
Air search: Signaal LW08 ❾; D-band.
Surface search: Signaal Scout ❿; I-band.
Navigation: Racal Decca 1226; I-band.
Fire control: 2 Signaal STIR ⓫; I/J/K-band; range 140 km *(76 n miles)* for 1 m² target.
Sonars: Signaal PHS-36; hull-mounted; active search and attack; medium frequency.
Thomson Sintra Anaconda DSBV 61; towed array; passive low frequency. LFAS may be fitted in due course.

Helicopters: 1 Westland SH-14 Lynx ⓬.

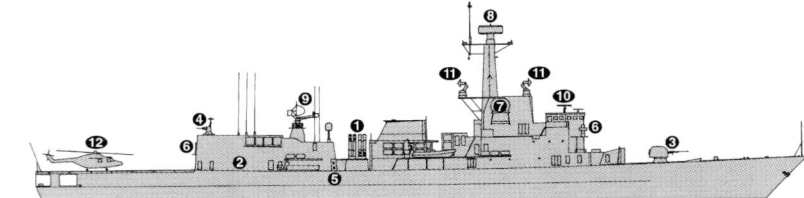

VAN SPEIJK *(Scale 1 : 1,200), Ian Sturton* / 0012800

KAREL DOORMAN *5/2004, Per Körnefeldt* / 1044162

Programmes: Declaration of intent signed on 29 February 1984 although the contract was not signed until 29 June 1985 by which time the design had been completed. A further four ordered 10 April 1986. Names were shuffled to make the new *Van Speijk* the last of the class but she retained her allocated pennant number.
Modernisation: SEWACO VII(A) operational from January 1992 and VII(B) from mid-1994. By 1994 all fitted with APECS II EW system and DSBV 61 towed array. IRSCAN infrared detector fitted on hangar roof in *Willem van der Zaan* for trials in 1993. SHF SATCOM based on the USN WSC-6, with twin aerials providing a 360° coverage even at high latitudes. Scout radar fitted on bridge roof in 1997. Research into the fitting of low frequency active sonar is

being conducted although a system is not expected to be fitted before 2010.
Structure: The VLS SAM is similar to Canadian Halifax and Greek MEKO classes. The ship is designed to reduce radar and IR signatures and has extensive NBCD arrangements. Full automation and roll stabilisation fitted. The APECS jammers are mounted starboard forward of the bridge and port aft corner of the hangar. The SAM launchers have been given added protection and better stealth features with a flat screen in some of the class.
Operational: F 832 and F 830 sold to Chile and transferred in November 2005 and mid-2006 respectively. F 827 and F 829 are to be sold to Belgium in 2007-08 and two further ships are also to be sold.

VAN NES *10/2005*, B Sullivan* / 1151122

VAN AMSTEL *11/2004, John Brodie* / 1044163

WILLEM VAN DER ZAAN *9/2005*, M Declerck* / 1151283

VAN SPEJK *4/2003, M Declerck* / 1044160

VAN NES *6/2004, B Sullivan* / 1044148

4 DE ZEVEN PROVINCIEN CLASS (FFGHM)

Name	No	Builders	Laid down	Launched	Commissioned
DE ZEVEN PROVINCIEN	F 802	Royal Schelde, Vlissingen	1 Sep 1998	8 Apr 2000	26 Apr 2002
TROMP	F 803	Royal Schelde, Vlissingen	3 Sep 1999	7 Apr 2001	14 Mar 2003
DE RUYTER	F 804	Royal Schelde, Vlissingen	1 Sep 2000	13 Apr 2002	22 Apr 2004
EVERTSEN	F 805	Royal Schelde, Vlissingen	6 Sep 2001	19 Apr 2003	10 June 2005

Displacement, tons: 6,048 full load
Dimensions, feet (metres): 473.1 oa; 428.8 wl × 61.7 × 17.1
(144.2; 130.7 × 18.8 × 5.2)
Flight deck, feet (metres): 88.6 × 61.7 *(27 × 18.8)*
Main machinery: CODOG; 2 RR SM1C Spey; 52,300 hp
(39 MW) sustained; 2 Stork-Wärtsilä 16V 26 ST diesels;
13,600 hp(m) *(10 MW)*; 2 shafts; LIPS; cp props
Speed, knots: 28
Range, n miles: 5,000 at 18 kt
Complement: 204 (32 officers) including staff

Missiles: SSM: 8 Harpoon ❶.
SAM: Mk 41 VLS (40 cells) ❷; 32 Standard SM2-MR (Block
IIIA); command/inertial guidance; semi-active radar
homing to 167 km *(90 n miles)* at 2 Mach.
32 Evolved Sea Sparrow (quad pack); semi-active radar
homing to 18 km *(9.7 n miles)* at 3.6 Mach; warhead
39 kg.
Guns: 1 Otobreda 5 in *(127 mm)*/54 ❸; 45 rds/min to 23 km
(12.42 n miles) anti-surface; weight of shell 32 kg.
2 Thales Goalkeeper 30 mm ❹; 4,200 rds/min to 1.5 km.
2 Browning 12.7 mm MGs ❺.
Torpedoes: 4—323 mm (2 twin) Mk 32 Mod 9 fixed
launchers ❻. Mk 46 Mod 5 torpedoes.
Countermeasures: 4 SRBOC Mk 36 chaff launchers; Nixie
torpedo decoy.
ESM/ECM: Racal Sabre ❼; intercept/jammer.
Combat data systems: CAMS Force Vision SEWACO XI;
Link 11/16; SATCOMS ❽.
Weapons control: Thales Sirius IRST optronic director ❾.

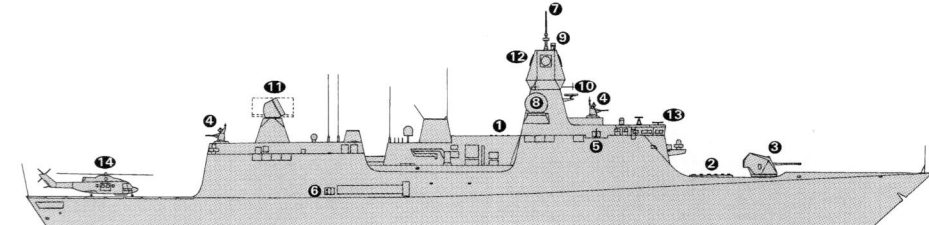

DE ZEVEN PROVINCIEN *(Scale 1 : 1,200), Ian Sturton* / 0569256

Thales Mirador Trainable Electro-Optical Observation
System (TEOOS) ❿.
Radars: Air search: Thales SMART L ⓫; 3D; D-band.
Air/surface search/fire control: Thales APAR ⓬; I/J-band.
Surface search: Thales Scout ⓭; I-band.
IFF: Mk XII.
Sonars: STN Atlas DSQS 24C; bow-mounted; active search
and attack; medium frequency.

Helicopters: 1 NH90 NFH/Lynx ⓮.

Programmes: Project definition awarded to Royal Schelde
on 15 December 1993 with a contract for first two ships
and detailed design following on 30 June 1995. Second
pair ordered 5 February 1997. Shipyards in Germany

(ARGE for Type 124) collaborated to achieve some
commonality of design and equipment.
Modernisation: It is planned to install an additional 8-cell
Mk 41 VLS launcher for Tactical Tomahawk IV from 2008.
Further improvements to achieve a TBMD capability are
under consideration.
Structure: As well as the listed equipment the ship is to have
an electro-optic surveillance system and a navigation
radar. The Scout radar is a Low Probability Intercept
(LPI) set. High standards of stealth and NBC protection
are part of the design. DCN Samahé helicopter handling
system. Space exists to retrofit an additional 8-cell Mk 41
launcher alongside the five already fitted.
Operational: All ships fitted with command facilities. NFH
90 helicopter planned for 2007.

EVERTSEN *10/2004, John Brodie* / 1044161

DE RUYTER *7/2005*, Derek Fox* / 1151131

SHIPBORNE AIRCRAFT

Numbers/Type: 14 NH Industries NH 90 NFH.
Operational speed: 157 kt (291 km/h).
Service ceiling: 13,940 ft (4,250 m).
Range: 621 n miles (1,150 km).
Role/Weapon systems: Up to 14 NFH-90 planned for the RNLN. Six further TTH aircraft for tactical transport. To enter service from 2007. Sensors and weapons to be announced.

NH 90   *3/2004, NHI* / 0062373

Numbers/Type: 21 Westland Lynx Mks 25B/27A/81A.
Operational speed: 125 kt (232 km/h).
Service ceiling: 12,500 ft (3,810 m).
Range: 320 n miles (590 km).
Role/Weapon systems: ASW, SAR and utility helicopter series all converted to SH-14D type. Mk 25B, Mk 27A and Mk 81A can all be embarked for ASW duties in escorts. Sensors: Ferranti Sea Spray radar, Alcatel DUAV-4 dipping sonar, FLIR Model 2000; Ferranti AWARE-3 ESM. Weapons: Two Mk 46 torpedoes or depth bombs.

LYNX   *7/2004, Frank Findler* / 1044159

LAND-BASED MARITIME AIRCRAFT

Notes: The P-3C force was decommissioned on 31 December 2004. Eight modernised aircraft were sold to Germany and a letter of intent has been signed with Portugal for the remaining five aircraft.

PATROL FORCES

Notes: It is planned to procure four 90 m patrol vessels for low-intensity military operations including maritime interdiction, counter-terrorism and humanitarian assistance. Equipped with a flight deck and hangar to support a NH 90 helicopter, the ships are to be capable of operating two super RHIBs capable of 50 kt. Armament is to include a medium calibre gun and machine guns. With a complement of 50, the ships are to have space for 40 extra personnel and evacuees. Further details of the programme are expected in 2006.

AMPHIBIOUS FORCES

5 LCU MK IX (LCU)

L 9525-9529

Displacement, tons: 200 (260 L 9526) full load
Dimensions, feet (metres): 89.6 (118.4 L 9526) × 22.4 × 4.3 (27.3 (36.1) × 6.8 × 1.3)
Main machinery: Diesel-electric; 2 Caterpillar 3412C diesel generators; 1,496 hp(m) (1.1 MW); 2 Alconza D400 motors; 2 Schottel pumpjets; 2 pump jets
Speed, knots: 9. **Range, n miles:** 400 at 8 kt
Complement: 5 plus 2 spare
Military lift: 130 troops or 2 Warriors or 1 BARV or up to 3 trucks
Guns: 1 — 12.7 mm MG; 1 — 7.62 mm MG.
Radars: Navigation: I-band.

Comment: Ordered from Visser Dockyard, Den Helder on 19 July 1996. Steel vessels of which the first commissioned 7 April 1998. The others have been fabricated in Romania and fitted out by Visser in 1999/2000. Embarked in *Rotterdam*. L 9526 lengthened by 8.8 m at Visser dockyard in 2004.

L 9528   *7/2004, Frank Findler* / 1044166

1 ROTTERDAM CLASS (LPD)

Name	No	Builders	Laid down	Launched	Commissioned
ROTTERDAM	L 800	Royal Schelde, Vlissingen	25 Jan 1996	22 Feb 1997	18 Apr 1998

Displacement, tons: 12,750 full load
Dimensions, feet (metres): 544.6 × 82 × 19.3
  (166 × 25 × 5.9)
Flight deck, feet (metres): 183.7 × 82 *(56 × 25)*
Main machinery: Diesel-electric; 4 Stork Wärtsilä 12SW28
  diesel generators; 14.6 MW sustained; 2 Holec motors;
  16,320 hp(m) *(12 MW)*; 2 shafts; bow thruster
Speed, knots: 19. **Range, n miles:** 6,000 at 12 kt
Complement: 113 (13 officers) + 611 (41 officers) Marines
Military lift: 611 troops; 170 APCs or 33 MBTs. 6 LCVP Mk 3
  or 4 LCU Mk 9 or 4 LCM 8

Guns: 2 Signaal Goalkeeper 30 mm ❶. 8–12.7 mm MGs.
Countermeasures: Decoys: 4 SRBOC chaff launchers ❷;
  Nixie torpedo decoy system.
ESM/ECM: Intercept and jammer.
Combat data systems: SATCOM ❸; Link 11. MCCIS.
Weapons control: Signaal IRSCAN infra-red director.
Radars: Air/surface search: Signaal DA08 ❹; E/F-band.
Surface search: Signaal Scout/Kelvin Hughes ARPA ❺; I-band.
Navigation: and CCA: 2 sets; I-band.

Helicopters: 6 NH90 ❻ or 4 Merlin/Sea King.

Programmes: Project definition for a joint design with
  Spain completed in December 1993. Contract signed
  with Royal Schelde 25 April 1994.
Structure: Facilities to transport a fully equipped Marine
  battalion with docking facilities for landing craft and a
  two spot helicopter flight deck with hangar space for six
  NH 90. 25 ton crane for disembarkation. Full hospital
  facilities. Built to commercial standards with military
  command and control and NBCD facilities. Can carry up
  to 30 torpedoes and 300 sonobuoys.
Operational: Alternative employment as an SAR ship for
  environmental and disaster relief tasks.

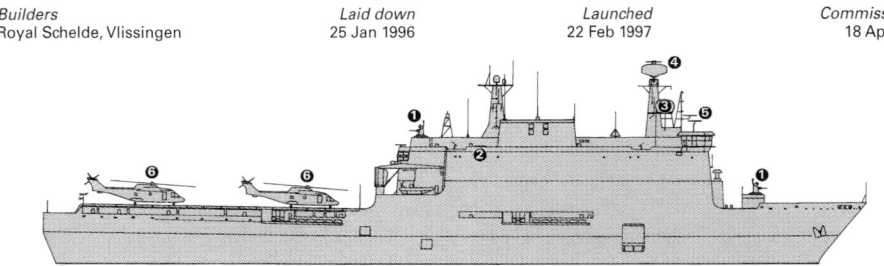

ROTTERDAM   *(Scale 1 : 1,500), Ian Sturton* / 0534086

ROTTERDAM   *6/2005*, John Mortimer* / 1151285

ROTTERDAM   *6/2005*, Michael Nitz* / 1151284

0 + 1 JOHAN DE WITT CLASS (LPD)

Name	No	Builders	Laid down	Launched	Commissioned
JOHAN DE WITT	L 801	Royal Schelde, Vlissingen	18 June 2003	26 Oct 2004	2006

Displacement, tons: 16,680 full load
Dimensions, feet (metres): 577.5 × 95.8 × 19.3
  (176.0 × 29.2 × 5.9)
Flight deck, feet (metres): 183.7 × 82 *(56 × 25)*
Main machinery: Diesel-electric; 4 Wärtsilä 12V26A diesel
  generators; 14.6 MW sustained; 2 Holec motors; 16,320 hp(m)
  12 (MW); 2 Schottel podded propulsors; bow thruster
Speed, knots: 19. **Range, n miles:** 6,000 at 12 kt
Complement: 146 (17 officers) + 555 Marines or 402 CJTF
Military lift: 611 troops; 170 APCs or 33 MBTs. 4 LCVP and
  2 LCU or 2 LCM
Guns: 2 Signaal Goalkeeper 30 mm ❶. 8–12.7 mm MGs.
Countermeasures: Decoys: 4 SRBOC chaff launchers ❷;
  Nixie torpedo decoy system.
ESM/ECM: Intercept and jammer.
Combat data systems: SATCOM ❸; Link 11. MCCIS.
Weapons control: Signaal IRSCAN infra-red director.
Radars: Air/surface search: Thales VARIANT; G/I-band.
Surface search: Signaal Scout/Kelvin Hughes ARPA; I-band.
Navigation and CCA: 2 sets; I-band.

Helicopters: 6 NH90 or 4 Merlin/Sea King.

JOHAN DE WITT   *(Scale 1 : 1,500), Ian Sturton* / 0534121

Programmes: Contract signed with Royal Schelde 3 May
  2002. The hull was constructed at the Damen-owned
  Galati yard in Romania and arrived at the Schelde yard
  on 3 December 2004 for completion. To be fitted with
  command and control facilities for an afloat CJTF-HQ.
Structure: Facilities to transport a fully equipped Marine
  battalion with docking facilities for landing craft and a
  two spot helicopter flight deck with hangar space for

six NH90. 25 ton crane for disembarkation. Full hospital
facilities. Built to commercial standards with military
command and control and NBCD facilities. Can carry
up to 30 torpedoes and 300 sonobuoys. Based on the
L 800 design but larger and wider. The flight deck is also
stronger.
Operational: Alternative employment as an SAR ship for
environmental and disaster relief tasks.

6 LCVP MK III (LCVP)

L 9536-9541

Displacement, tons: 30 full load
Dimensions, feet (metres): 55.4 × 15.7 × 3.6 *(16.9 × 4.8 × 1.1)*
Main machinery: 2 diesels; 750 hp(m) *(551 kW)*; 2 shafts
Speed, knots: 14 (full load); 16.5 (light)
Range, n miles: 200 at 12 kt
Complement: 3
Military lift: 34 troops or 7 tons or 2 Land Rovers or 1 Snowcat
Guns: 1—7.62 mm MG.
Radars: Navigation: Racal Decca 110; I-band.

Comment: Ordered from van der Giessen-de Noord 10 December 1988. First one laid
  down 10 August 1989, commissioned 16 October 1990. Last one commissioned
  19 October 1992.

L 9539
6/2005*, E & M Laursen
1151130

MINE WARFARE FORCES

10 ALKMAAR (TRIPARTITE) CLASS (MINEHUNTERS) (MHC)

Name	No	Builders	Launched	Commissioned
HAARLEM	M 853	16 June 1981	6 May 1983	12 Jan 1984
MAASSLUIS	M 856	7 Nov 1982	5 May 1984	12 Dec 1984
MAKKUM	M 857	25 Feb 1983	27 Sep 1984	13 May 1985
MIDDELBURG	M 858	11 July 1983	23 Feb 1985	10 Dec 1986
HELLEVOETSLUIS	M 859	12 Dec 1983	18 July 1985	20 Feb 1987
SCHIEDAM	M 860	6 May 1984	20 Dec 1985	9 July 1986
URK	M 861	1 Oct 1984	2 May 1986	10 Dec 1986
ZIERIKZEE	M 862	25 Feb 1985	4 Oct 1986	7 May 1987
VLAARDINGEN	M 863	6 May 1986	4 Aug 1988	15 Mar 1989
WILLEMSTAD	M 864	3 Oct 1986	27 Jan 1989	20 Sep 1989

Displacement, tons: 562 standard; 595 full load
Dimensions, feet (metres): 168.9 × 29.2 × 8.5
  (51.5 × 8.9 × 2.6)
Main machinery: 1 Stork Wärtsilä A-RUB 215X-12 diesel; 1,860 hp(m) *(1.35 MW)*
  sustained; 1 shaft; LIPS cp prop; 2 active rudders; 2 motors; 240 hp(m) *(179 kW)*; 2 bow
  thrusters
Speed, knots: 15 diesel; 7 electric
Range, n miles: 3,000 at 12 kt
Complement: 29—42 depending on task

Guns: 1 Giat 20 mm (an additional short-range missile system may be added for patrol
  duties).
Countermeasures: MCM: 2 PAP 104 remote-controlled submersibles. OD 3 mechanical
  minesweeping gear.
Combat data systems: Atlas Elektronic IMCMS. SATCOM.
Radars: Navigation: Racal Decca TM 1229C or Consilium Selesmar MM 950; I-band.
Sonars: Thales TSM 2022 Mk III; hull-mounted; minehunting; 100, 200 and 400 kHz.

Programmes: The two Indonesian ships ordered in 1985 took the place of M 863 and 864
  whose laying down was delayed as a result. This class is the Netherlands' part of a
  tripartite co-operative plan with Belgium and France for GRP hulled minehunters. The
  whole class built by van der Giessen-de Noord. Ships were launched virtually ready
  for trials.
Modernisation: An extensive modernisation programme is underway at Den Helder
  between mid-2003 and 2009 to extend service life to 2020. Upgrades include a
  MCM command and control system, an Integrated Mine Countermeasures System
  (comprising hull-mounted and self-propelled variable-depth sonar (installed in Double
  Eagle Mk III Mod 1 RoV)) and a Mine-Identification and Disposal System (MIDS) based
  on the Atlas Seafox. Linked to the ship by a 3,000 m fibre optic tether, one variant
  (Seafox-C) is used for mine disposal and the other (Seafox-I) is used for identification.
  The equipment was first installed in M 859 after which a 12 month sea acceptance trial
  and operational evaluation programme began in early 2005. M 856 is the second RNLN
  ship to be upgraded and is to become operational in mid-2006. All ten ships are to be
  completed by mid-2009.
Structure: A 5 ton container can be shipped, stored for varying tasks-research; patrol;
  extended diving; drone control.
Operational: Endurance, 15 days. Automatic radar navigation system. Automatic data
  processing and display. EVEC 20. Decca Hi-fix positioning system. Alcatel dynamic
  positioning system. MHCs are sometimes assigned to coast guard operations.
Sales: Two of a modified design to Indonesia, completed March 1988. M 850-852
  decommissioned in 2000. M 854 and M 855 decommissioned in 2003. All five are to be
  sold to Latvia by 2008.

MIDDELBURG *10/2005*, Martin Mokrus* / 1151124

URK *6/2005*, Per Körnefeldt* / 1151123

SURVEY SHIPS

2 SURVEY SHIPS (AGSH)

Name	No	Builders	Launched	Commissioned
SNELLIUS	A 802	Royal Schelde, Vlissingen	30 Apr 2003	11 Dec 2003
LUYMES	A 803	Royal Schelde, Vlissingen	22 Aug 2003	3 June 2004

Displacement, tons: 1,875 full load
Dimensions, feet (metres): 246.1 × 43.0 × 13.1 *(75 × 13.1 × 4)*
Main machinery: Diesel electric; 3 diesel generators; 2,652 hp(m) *(1.95 MW)*; 1 motor;
  1,360 hp(m) *(1 MW)*; 1 shaft; cp prop
Speed, knots: 12
Range, n miles: 4,300 at 12 kt
Complement: 13 plus 5 scientists plus 24 spare
Radars: Navigation: E/F- and I-band.
Sonars: Multi and single beam; high frequency; active

Comment: Designed for military and civil hydrographic surveys. Both laid down on
  25 June 2002.

SNELLIUS *6/2004, Frank Findler* / 0583297

LUYMES *7/2005*, A A de Kruijf* / 1151129

TRAINING SHIPS

Notes: Two Dokkum class minesweepers are used by Sea Cadets.

1 TRAINING SHIP (AXL)

Name	No	Builders	Commissioned
VAN KINSBERGEN	A 902	Damen Shipyards	2 Nov 1999

Displacement, tons: 630 full load
Dimensions, feet (metres): 136.2 × 30.2 × 10.8 *(41.5 × 9.2 × 3.3)*
Main machinery: 2 Caterpillar 3508 BI-TA; 1,572 hp(m) *(1.16 MW)* sustained; 2 shafts; bow
  thruster; 272 hp(m) *(200 kW)*
Speed, knots: 13
Complement: 5 plus 3 instructors and 16 students
Radars: Navigation: Consilium Selesmar; I-band.

Comment: Launched 30 August 1999. Has replaced *Zeefakkel* as the local training ship at
  Den Helder. Carries a 25 kt RIB.

VAN KINSBERGEN *5/2004, Maritime Photographic* / 1044144

1 SAIL TRAINING SHIP (AXS)

Name	No	Builders	Commissioned
URANIA (ex-*Tromp*)	Y 8050	Haarlem	23 Apr 1938

Displacement, tons: 75 full load
Dimensions, feet (metres): 87.9 × 19.8 × 8.5 *(26.8 × 6.05 × 2.6)*
Main machinery: 1 Caterpillar diesel; 235 hp(m) *(186 kW)*; 1 shaft
Speed, knots: 10 diesel; 12 sail
Complement: 3 + 14 trainees

Comment: Schooner used for training in seamanship. Refit 2001-04 included a new hull and aluminium masts.

URANIA 6/2005*, Frank Findler / 1151126

AUXILIARIES

Notes: (1) In addition to the vessels listed there are large numbers of non self-propelled craft with Y pennant numbers, and six harbour launches Y 8200-8205.
(2) An Accommodation Ship *Thetis* (A 887) is based at Den Helder and provides harbour training for divers and underwater swimmers.
(3) The replacement for *Zuiderkruis* is to be a multipurpose logistic support ship, capable of both fleet replenishment and strategic sealift. The ship is to be capable of operating two Chinook-type medium lift helicopters and is to incorporate a hangar and a cargo deck.

1 SUBMARINE SUPPORT SHIP and TORPEDO TENDER (ASL/YTT)

Name	No	Builders	Commissioned
MERCUUR	A 900	Koninklijke Maatschappij de Schelde	21 Aug 1987

Displacement, tons: 1,400 full load
Dimensions, feet (metres): 212.6 × 39.4 × 14.1 *(64.8 × 12 × 4.3)*
Main machinery: 2 Brons 61-20/27 diesels; 1,100 hp(m) *(808 kW)*; 2 shafts; bow thruster
Speed, knots: 14
Complement: 39 (6 officers)
Torpedoes: 3—324 mm (triple) tubes. 1—21 in *(533 mm)* underwater tube.
Mines: Can lay mines.
Radars: Navigation: Racal Decca 1229; I-band.
Sonars: SQR-01; hull-mounted; passive search.

Comment: Replacement for previous ship of same name. Ordered 13 June 1984. Laid down 6 November 1985. Floated out 25 October 1986. Can launch training and research torpedoes above and below the waterline. Services, maintains and recovers torpedoes.

MERCUUR 4/2003, Declerck and Steeghers / 1044150

1 LOGISTIC SUPPORT VESSEL (AP)

Name	No	Builders	Laid down	Launched	Commissioned
PELIKAAN	A 804	Damen Shipyard	25 Aug 2005	2006	2006

Displacement, tons: 1,033 full load
Dimensions, feet (metres): 214.6 × 43.5 × 9.8 *(65.4 × 13.25 × 3.0)*
Main machinery: 2 diesels; 2 shafts
Speed, knots: 14.5
Complement: 14 (2 officers) plus 12 extra plus 45 temporary
Radars: Navigation: I-band.

Comment: In January 2005 a contract was signed between the Royal Netherlands Navy and Damen Shipyards for the design and construction of a Logistic Support Vessel (LSV) to provide sealift for the RNLMC in the Caribbean. The ship is to replace the old vessel of the same name. Following construction of the hull at the Damen-owned Galatz shipyard in Romania, the ship is to be completed at Gorinchem. A large cargo area is located at main deck level and can accommodate six rigid raiding craft, four trucks and a range of support equipment. Loading and unloading is facilitated by a deck crane.

PELIKAAN (artist's impression) 3/2005, Damen Shipyards / 1039148

1 AMSTERDAM CLASS (FAST COMBAT SUPPORT SHIP) (AORH)

Name	No	Builders	Laid down	Launched	Commissioned
AMSTERDAM	A 836	Merwede, Hardinxveld, and Royal Schelde, Vlissingen	25 May 1992	11 Sep 1993	2 Sep 1995

Displacement, tons: 17, 040 full load
Dimensions, feet (metres): 544.6 × 72.2 × 26.2 *(166 × 22 × 8)*
Main machinery: 2 Bazán/Burmeister & Wain 16V 40/45 diesels; 24,000 hp(m) *(176 MW)* sustained; 1 shaft; LIPS cp prop
Speed, knots: 20. **Range, n miles:** 13,440 at 20 kt
Complement: 160 (23 officers) including 24 aircrew plus 20 spare
Cargo capacity: 6,815 tons dieso; 1,660 tons aviation fuel; 290 tons solids

Guns: 2 Oerlikon 20 mm. 1 Signaal Goalkeeper 30 mm CIWS.
Countermeasures: Decoys: 4 SRBOC Mk 36 chaff launchers. Nixie towed torpedo decoy.
ESM: Ferranti AWARE-4; radar warning
Weapons control: Signaal IRSCAN infrared director.
Radars: Surface search and helo control: 2 Kelvin Hughes; F-band.

Helicopters: 3 Lynx or 3 SH-3D or 3 NH90 or 2 EH 101.

Programmes: NP/SP AOR 90 replacement for *Poolster* ordered 14 October 1991. Hull built by Merwede, with fitting out by Royal Schelde from October 1993. A similar ship has been built for the Spanish Navy.
Structure: Close co-operation between Dutch Nevesbu and Spanish Bazán led to this design which has maintenance workshops as well as four abeam and one stern RAS/FAS station, and one Vertrep supply station. Built to merchant ship standards but with military NBC damage control.

AMSTERDAM 6/2001, John Brodie / 0114762

1 MODIFIED POOLSTER CLASS (FAST COMBAT SUPPORT SHIP) (AORH)

Name	No	Builders	Laid down	Launched	Commissioned
ZUIDERKRUIS	A 832	Verolme Shipyards, Alblasserdam	16 July 1973	15 Oct 1974	27 June 1975

Displacement, tons: 16,900 full load
Measurement, tons: 10,000 dwt
Dimensions, feet (metres): 556 × 66.6 × 27.6
  (169.6 × 20.3 × 8.4)
Main machinery: 2 Stork-Werkspoor TM410 diesels;
  21,000 hp(m) *(15.4 MW)*; 1 shaft; LIPS cp props
Speed, knots: 21
Complement: 266 (17 officers)
Cargo capacity: 10,300 tons including 8 – 9,000 tons oil
  fuel

Guns: 1 Signaal Goalkeeper 30 mm CIWS. 5 Oerlikon 20 mm.
Countermeasures: Decoys: 2 Loral Hycor SRBOC Mk 36
  fixed 6-barrelled launchers; IR flares and chaff.
ESM: Ferranti AWARE-4; radar warning
Weapons control: Signaal IRSCAN.
Radars: Air/surface search: Racal Decca 2459; F/I-band.
  Navigation: 2 Racal Decca TM 1226C; Signaal SCOUT;
  I-band

Helicopters: 1 Westland UH-14A Lynx.

Structure: Helicopter deck aft. Funnel heightened by 4.5 m
  (14.8 ft). 20 mm guns, containerised Goalkeeper CIWS
  and SATCOM, fitted for operational deployments.
Operational: Capacity for five helicopters with A/S
  weapons. Two fuelling stations each side for underway
  replenishment. Planned to remain in commission until
  replaced by a multipurpose logistic support ship in
  about 2010.
Sales: *Poolster* sold to Pakistan in June 1994.

ZUIDERKRUIS *8/2003, Harald Carstens* / 1044168

1 TANKER (AOTL)

Name	No	Builders	Commissioned
PATRIA	Y 8760	De Hoop, Schiedam	9 June 1998

Displacement, tons: 681 full load
Dimensions, feet (metres): 145.3 × 22.4 × 8.9 *(44.4 × 6.9 × 2.8)*
Main machinery: 1 Volvo Penta TADM 122A; 381 hp(m) *(280 kW)*; 1 shaft
Speed, knots: 9.5
Complement: 2
Radars: Navigation: Furuno RHRS-2002R; I-band

PATRIA *7/2005*, A A de Kruijf* / 1151128

1 SUPPORT CRAFT (YFL)

Name	No	Builders	Commissioned
NIEUWEDIEP	Y 8005	Akerboom, Leiden	Feb 1972

Displacement, tons: 27 full load
Dimensions, feet (metres): 58.4 × 14.1 × 4.9 *(17.8 × 4.3 × 1.5)*
Main machinery: 2 Volvo Penta diesels; 600 hp(m) *(441 kW)*; 2 shafts
Speed, knots: 10
Complement: 4

Comment: Acquired by the Navy in February 1992 as a passenger craft.

NIEUWEDIEP *7/2004, Frank Findler* / 1044151

4 CERBERUS CLASS (DIVING TENDERS) (YDT)

Name	No	Builders	Commissioned
CERBERUS	A 851	Visser, Den Helder	28 Feb 1992
ARGUS	A 852	Visser, Den Helder	2 June 1992
NAUTILUS	A 853	Visser, Den Helder	18 Sep 1992
HYDRA	A 854	Visser, Den Helder	20 Nov 1992

Displacement, tons: 223 full load
Dimensions, feet (metres): 89.9 × 27.9 × 4.9 *(27.4 × 8.5 × 1.5)*
Main machinery: 2 Volvo Penta TAMD122A diesels; 760 hp(m) *(560 kW)*; 2 shafts
Speed, knots: 12
Range, n miles: 750 at 12 kt
Complement: 8 (2 officers)
Radars: Navigation: Racal Decca; I-band.

Comment: Ordered 29 November 1990. Capable of maintaining 10 kt in Sea State 3. Can
  handle a 2 ton load at 4 m from the ship's side. *Hydra* lengthened by 10.5 m to provide
  more accommodation and recommissioned on 13 March 1998.

NAUTILUS *7/2005*, A A de Kruijf* / 1151127

TUGS

5 COASTAL TUGS (YTM)

Name	No	Builders	Commissioned
LINGE	A 874	Delta SY, Sliedrecht	20 Feb 1987
REGGE	A 875	Delta SY, Sliedrecht	6 May 1987
HUNZE	A 876	Delta SY, Sliedrecht	20 Oct 1987
ROTTE	A 877	Delta SY, Sliedrecht	20 Oct 1987
GOUWE	A 878	Delta SY, Sliedrecht	21 Feb 1997

Displacement, tons: 380 full load
Dimensions, feet (metres): 90.2 × 27.2 × 8.9 *(27.5 × 8.3 × 2.7)*
Main machinery: 2 Stork-Werkspoor or 2 Caterpillar (A 878) diesels; 1,600 hp(m)
  (1.18 MW); 2 Kort nozzle props
Speed, knots: 11
Complement: 7
Radars: Racal Decca; I-band.

Comment: Order for first four placed in 1986. Based at Den Helder. A fifth of class was
  ordered in June 1996 to replace *Westgat*.

HUNZE *7/2005*, A A de Kruijf* / 1151125

7 HARBOUR TUGS (YTL)

BREEZAND Y 8018	**WIERBALG** Y 8056	**ZUIDWAL** Y 8058
BALGZAND Y 8019	**MALZWIN** Y 8057	**WESTWAL** Y 8059
SCHELDE Y 8055		

Comment: *Breezand* completed December 1989, *Balgzand* January 1990. The others are smaller pusher tugs and were completed December 1986 to February 1987. All built by Delta Shipyard.

WESTWAL *5/2004, A A de Kruijf* / 1044153

ARMY

Notes: Seven craft are operated by the Corps of Military Police: RV 160, RV 165-166, RV 168-169, RV 176-177.

1 DIVING VESSEL (YDT)

RV 50

Dimensions, feet (metres): 137.3 × 31.2 × 4.9 *(41.8 × 9.5 × 1.5)*
Main machinery: 2 diesels; 476 hp(m) *(350 kW)*; 2 shafts; 1 bow thruster
Speed, knots: 8
Complement: 21
Radars: Navigation: JRC JMA 606; I-band.

Comment: Built by Vervako as a diving training ship and commissioned 3 November 1989. There is a moonpool aft with a 50 m diving bell, and a decompression chamber.

RV 50 *10/2004, Bram Plokker* / 1047865

COAST GUARD (KUSTWACHT)

Notes: (1) On 26 February 1987, many of the maritime services were merged to form a Coast Guard with its own distinctive colours. Included are assorted craft of the Ministries of Transport and Public Works, Finance, Defence, Justice and Agriculture, Nature Management and Food Quality. Also involved is the Ministry of Home Affairs. From 1 June 1995 the operational command of the Coast Guard has been exercised by the Navy.
(2) The following are the principal ships and craft:

Transport and Public Works: *Arca, Frans Naerebout, Nieuwe Diep, Rotterdam, Schuitengat, Terschelling, Vliestroom, Waddenzee, Waker*

Finance: *Visarend, Zeearend*

Defence: minehunters of the Alkmaar class

Justice: *P 41, P 42, P 44, P 48, P 49, P 96*

Agriculture, Nature Management and Food Quality: *Barend Biesheuvel*

(3) In addition, the Coast Guard can call upon 60 lifeboats in 39 stations from the Royal Netherlands Sea-Rescue Organisation.

WAKER (Transport) *4/2003, Per Körnefeldt* / 0569212

P 49 (Justice) *6/2004, Frank Findler* / 1044154

VISAREND (Finance) *7/2004, Frank Findler* / 1044155

BAREND BIESHEUVEL (Agriculture) *6/2002, Imtech Marine and Offshore* / 0534130

COAST GUARD (ANTILLES and ARUBA)

Notes: (1) Netherlands Antilles and Aruba Coast Guard (NAACG) formed 23 January 1996. Headquarters is co-located with the RNLN at Parera, Curaçao.
(2) Twelve 12 m Super RHIB, capable of 40 kt, have been procured for counter-drug operations. In 2004, two were stationed at Aruba, two at Curacao and one at St Maarten. Four followed in 2005 and the final three are to be delivered in 2006.

SUPER RHIB *3/2005*, RNLN* / 1039147

3 STAN PATROL 4100 CUTTERS (PB)

Name	No	Builders	Commissioned
JAGUAR	P 810	Damen Shipyards	2 Nov 1998
PANTER	P 811	Damen Shipyards	18 Jan 1999
POEMA	P 812	Damen Shipyards	19 Mar 1999

Displacement, tons: 205 full load
Dimensions, feet (metres): 140.4 × 22.3 × 8.2 *(42.8 × 6.8 × 2.5)*
Main machinery: 2 Caterpillar 3516B diesels; 5,685 hp(m) *(4.18 MW)*; 2 shafts; LIPS cp props; bow thruster
Speed, knots: 26. **Range, n miles:** 2,000 at 12 kt
Complement: 11 plus 6 police
Guns: 1 — 12.7 mm MG.
Radars: Surface search: Signaal Scout; I-band.
Navigation: Kelvin Hughes; I-band

Comment: Ordered from Damen shipyards in March 1997 for delivery in late 1998. Equipped with surveillance passive sensors. The cutters have a gas citadel. A 30 kt RIB is launched through a transom door. Based at Willemstad, Curaçao.

POEMA *3/1999, Damen/Flying Focus* / 0081315

New Zealand

Country Overview

New Zealand is an independent island country situated in the south Pacific Ocean with which it has a 8,170 n mile coastline. The British monarch, represented by a governor-general, is head of state. Situated about 865 n miles south-east of Australia, it comprises two main islands, North and South islands, which are separated by the Cook Strait. In addition there are numerous smaller islands including Stewart Island and the Auckland Islands. The overall area is 104,454 square miles. Overseas territories include Ross Dependency (Antarctica) and Tokelau (north of Samoa). In addition, the Cook Islands and Niue are self-governing territories in free association. The capital is Wellington and largest city is Auckland; both are ports located on North Island. Other principal ports are Tauranga, Lyttelton (near Christchurch), and Port Chalmers (Dunedin). Territorial seas (12 n miles) are claimed. An EEZ (200 n mile) is also claimed.

Headquarters Appointments

Chief of Navy:
  Rear Admiral D I Ledson, ONZM
Deputy Chief of Navy:
  Commodore J R Steer, DNZM

Commander Joint Forces:
  Major General L J Gardiner
Maritime Component Commander:
  Commodore D V Anson

Diplomatic Representation

Defence Adviser, Washington:
  Commodore P J Williams
Naval Adviser, London:
  Commander P D Mayer, MZNM
Naval Adviser, Canberra:
  Commander M H M Stumpel
Naval Adviser, Washington:
  Commander A H Keating

Personnel

2006: 1,900 regulars and 400 reserves

Bases

Headquarters Joint Forces New Zealand (established 1 July 2001)
Naval Staff: HMNZS Wakefield (Wellington)

Fleet Support: HMNZS Philomel (Auckland)
Training: RNZN College Tamaki (Auckland)
Ship Repair: HMNZ Dockyard (Auckland)

RNZNVR Divisions

Auckland: HMNZS *Ngapona*
Wellington: HMNZS *Olphert*
Christchurch: HMNZS *Pegasus*
Dunedin: HMNZS *Toroa*

Prefix to Ships' Names

HMNZS

DELETIONS

Frigates

2005 *Canterbury*

FRIGATES

2 ANZAC (MEKO 200) CLASS (FFHM)

Name	No
TE KAHA	F 77
TE MANA	F 111

Builders	Laid down	Launched	Commissioned
Transfield Defence Systems, Williamstown	19 Sep 1994	22 July 1995	22 July 1997
Tenix Defence Systems, Williamstown	28 June 1996	10 May 1997	10 Dec 1999

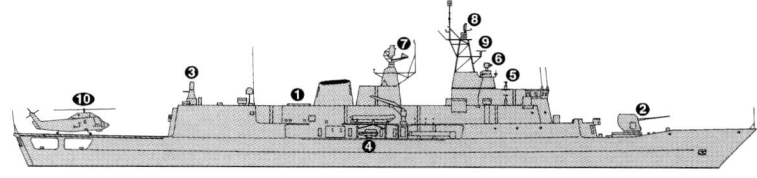

TE KAHA   *(Scale 1 : 1,200), Ian Sturton* / 0081317

Displacement, tons: 3,600 full load
Dimensions, feet (metres): 387.1 oa; 357.6 wl × 48.6 × 14.3 *(118; 109 × 14.8 × 4.4)*
Main machinery: CODOG; 1 GE LM 2500 gas turbine; 30,172 hp *(22.5 MW)* sustained; 2 MTU 12V 1163 TB83 diesels; 8,840 hp(m) *(6.5 MW)* sustained; 2 shafts; cp props
Speed, knots: 27
Range, n miles: 6,000 at 18 kt
Complement: 163

Missiles: SAM: Raytheon Sea Sparrow RIM-7P; Lockheed Martin Marietta Mk 41 Mod 5 octuple cell vertical launcher❶; semi-active radar homing to 14.6 km *(8 n miles)* at 0.9 Mach; warhead 39 kg. ESSM in due course.
Guns: 1 FMC 5 in *(127 mm)*/54 Mk 45 Mod 2 ❷; 20 rds/min to 23 km *(12.6 n miles)*; weight of shell 32 kg.
  1 GE/GD 20 mm Vulcan Phalanx 6 barrelled Mk 15 Block 1 Baseline 2B ❸; 4,500 rds/min combined to 1.5 km.
Torpedoes: 6 — 324 mm US Mk 32 Mod 5 (2 triple) tubes ❹; Mk 46 Mod 2; anti-submarine; active/passive homing to 11 km *(5.9 n miles)* at 40 kt; warhead 44 kg.
Countermeasures: Decoys: 2 Loral Hycor Mk 36 Mod 1 chaff launchers ❺. SLQ-25A torpedo decoy system.
ESM: DASA Maigret; Racal Thorn Sceptre A; intercept (to be replaced by Racal Centaur in 2005).
Combat data systems: CelsiusTech 9LV 453 Mk 3. Link 11; GCCS-M.
Weapons control: CelsiusTech 9LV 453 optronic director ❻. Raytheon CWI Mk 73 Mod 1 (for SAM).
Radars: Air search: Raytheon SPS-49(V)8 ❼; C/D-band.
Air/surface search: CelsiusTech 9LV 453 TIR (Ericsson Tx/Rx) ❽; G-band.
Navigation: Atlas Elektronik 9600 ARPA; I-band.
Fire control: CelsiusTech 9LV 453 ❾; G-band.
IFF: Cossor Mk XII.
Sonars: Thomson Sintra Spherion B Mod 5; hull-mounted; active search and attack; medium frequency.

Helicopters: 1 SH-2G (NZ) Super Seasprite ❿.

Programmes: Contract signed with Amecon consortium on 19 November 1989 to build eight Blohm + Voss designed MEKO 200 ANZ frigates for Australia and two for New

TE MANA   *4/2005*, Chris Sattler* / 1133137

Zealand. Options on a third of class were turned down in November 1998. Modules constructed at Newcastle, Australia and Whangarei, New Zealand, and shipped to Melbourne for final assembly. The two New Zealand ships are the second and fourth of the class. First steel cut on *Te Kaha* on 11 February 1993. *Te Kaha* means Prowess. *Te Mana* means Power.
Modernisation: An upgrade programme is under consideration. Enhancements may include introduction of RIM-162 ESSM, CWI, C2, radar and datalink

improvements, a new torpedo and CIWS upgrade. The programme is likely to be phased between 2008 and 2013.
Structure: The ships include space and weight provision for considerable enhancement including canister-launched SSM, an additional fire-control channel and ECM. Signature suppression features are incorporated in the design. All-steel construction. Fin stabilisers. McTaggert Scott Trigon 3 helicopter traversing system. Two RHIBs are carried.

TE KAHA   *10/2002, Mick Prendergast* / 0567463

SHIPBORNE AIRCRAFT

Numbers/Type: 5 Kaman SH-2G (NZ) Super Seasprite.
Operational speed: 130 kt *(241 km/h).*
Service ceiling: 22,500 ft *(6,860 m).*
Range: 367 n miles *(679 km).*
Role/Weapon systems: Last of five delivered in February 2003. Sensors: Litton ASN 150 C2; Telephonics APS 143 radar; AAQ 32 Safire IRDS; ALR 100 ESM; ALE 47 ECM. Weapons: ASW; 2 Mk 46 torpedoes or Mk 11 depth bomb; ASV; 2 Hughes Maverick AGM 65D (NZ); 1 — 7.62 mm M60 MG.

SUPER SEASPRITE   *5/2003, A Sharma* / 0567466

LAND-BASED MARITIME AIRCRAFT

Numbers/Type: 6 Lockheed P-3K Orion.
Operational speed: 405 kt *(750 km/h).*
Service ceiling: 30,000 ft *(9,146 m).*
Range: 4,000 n miles *(7,410 km).*
Role/Weapon systems: Purchased in 1966. Long-range surveillance and reconnaissance patrol; updated 1984. Modernisation of airframes (Project Kestrel) undertaken 1995-2001 for 20 year extension. Upgrade project in progress to modernise mission avionics, sensors and communication/navigation systems. The upgrade will include an Elta EL/M-2022(V)3 radar and Wescam MX-20 FLIR. Contract signed with L-3 communications on 4 October 2004. The first upgraded aircraft is to be delivered in 2008 and programme is to be completed by 2010. Operated by RNZAF. Sensors: APS-134 radar, ASQ-10 MAD, acoustic processor, AYK 14 computers, IFF, ESM, SSQ 53/62 sonobuoys. Weapons: ASW; eight Mk 46 torpedoes, Mk 80 series depth bombs.

P-3K   *7/2004, Paul Jackson* / 0589788

PATROL FORCES

0 + 2 OFFSHORE PATROL VESSELS (PBO)

Name	No	Builders	Laid down	Launched	Commissioned
OTAGO	P 148	Tenix Defence Systems, Williamstown	2005	2006	May 2007
WELLINGTON	—	Tenix Defence Systems, Williamstown	2005	2006	Nov 2007

Displacement, tons: 1,600
Dimensions, feet (metres): 278.9 × 45.9 × 11.8 *(85.0 × 14.0 × 3.6)*
Main machinery: 2 MAN Burmeister & Wain 12 RK 280 diesels; 2 shafts; cp props
Speed, knots: 22. **Range, n miles:** 6,000 at 15 kt
Complement: 35 plus 44 spare
Guns: 1 MSI DS 25M Autsig 25 mm. 2 — 12.7 mm MGs.
Radars: Navigation: I-band.
Helicopters: 1 SH-2G Super Seasprite.

Programmes: Following selection as 'Project Protector' prime contractor in April 2004, Tenix Defence awarded contract for final design and construction on 28 July 2004. The ships are to meet patrol and surveillance requirements in support of civil agencies in New Zealand's EEZ and the Southern Ocean and to assist South Pacific states to patrol their EEZs. Manufacturing of modules started at Tenix's Whangerai Shipyard in New Zealand in February 2005. Final assembly is to be undertaken at Williamstown, Victoria.
Structure: The design is a lengthened, helicopter-capable variant of a Kvaerner Masa Marine design in service in Ireland and Mauritius. They are to be ice-strengthened.

OPV (computer graphic)   *9/2004, RNZN* / 0589791

0 + 4 INSHORE PATROL VESSELS (PBO)

Name	No	Builders	Laid down	Launched	Commissioned
TAUPO	P 3568	Tenix Defence Systems, Whangerai	2005	2006	Feb 2007
PUKAKI	—	Tenix Defence Systems, Whangerai	2005	2006	June 2007
HAWGA	—	Tenix Defence Systems, Whangerai	2005	2006	Oct 2007
ROTOITI	—	Tenix Defence Systems, Whangerai	2006	2007	Jan 2008

Displacement, tons: 340
Dimensions, feet (metres): 180.4 × 29.5 × 9.5 *(55.0 × 9.0 × 2.9)*
Main machinery: 2 MAN Burmeister & Wain 12VP 185 diesels; 2 shafts; cp props
Speed knots: 25. **Range, n miles:** 3,000 at 15 kt
Complement: 20 plus 16 spare
Guns: 3 — 12.7 mm MGs.
Radars: Navigation: I-band.

Programmes: Following selection as 'Project Protector' prime contractor in April 2004, Tenix Defence awarded contract for final design and construction on 29 July 2004. The ships are to operate in support of civil agencies to meet patrol and surveillance requirements in New Zealand's inshore zone (out to 24 n miles), particularly around North Island, Marlborough Sounds and Tasman Bay. Manufacturing started at Tenix's Whangerai Shipyard in New Zealand in early 2005.
Structure: The Tenix design is based on the 56 m San Juan class built for the Philippines Coast Guard. Capable of operating in up to Sea State 5, they will be able to launch and recover rigid hull inflatable boats in up to Sea State 4.

IPV (computer graphic)   *9/2004, RNZN* / 0589790

4 MOA CLASS (INSHORE PATROL CRAFT) (PB)

Name	No	Builders	Commissioned
MOA	P 3553	Whangarei Engineering and Construction Co Ltd	28 Nov 1983
KIWI	P 3554	Whangarei Engineering and Construction Co Ltd	2 Sep 1984
WAKAKURA	P 3555	Whangarei Engineering and Construction Co Ltd	26 Mar 1985
HINAU	P 3556	Whangarei Engineering and Construction Co Ltd	4 Oct 1985

Displacement, tons: 91.5 standard; 105 full load
Dimensions, feet (metres): 88 × 20 × 7.2 *(26.8 × 6.1 × 2.2)*
Main machinery: 2 Cummins KT-1105M diesels; 710 hp *(530 kW)*; 2 shafts
Speed, knots: 12. **Range, n miles:** 1,000 at 11 kt
Complement: 18 (5 officers (4 training))
Guns: 1 Browning 12.7 mm MG.
Radars: Surface search: Racal Decca Bridgemaster 2000; I-band.
Sonars: Klein 595 Tracpoint; side scan; active high frequency.

Comment: On 11 February 1982 the New Zealand Cabinet approved the construction of four inshore patrol craft. The four IPC are operated by the Reserve Divisions, *Moa* with *Toroa* (Dunedin), *Kiwi* with *Pegasus* (Lyttelton), *Wakakura* with *Olphert* (Wellington), *Hinau* with *Ngapona* (Auckland). Same design as Inshore Survey and Training craft *Kahu* but with a modified internal layout. MCM system fitted in 1993-94. Side scan sonar and MCAIS data system fitted to *Hinau* in 1993; the remainder in 1996. To be replaced by new vessels from 2007.

HINAU   *2002, RNZN* / 0525918

SURVEY AND RESEARCH SHIPS

1 STALWART CLASS (AGS)

Name	No	Builders	Commissioned
RESOLUTION (ex-*Tenacious*)	A 14 (ex-TAGOS 17)	Halter Marine, Moss Point	29 Sep 1989

Displacement, tons: 2,262 full load
Dimensions, feet (metres): 224 × 43 × 18.7 *(68.3 × 13.1 × 5.7)*
Main machinery: Diesel-electric; 4 Caterpillar D 398B diesel generators; 3,200 hp *(2.39 MW)*; 2 motors; 1,600 hp *(1.2 MW)*; 2 shafts; bow thruster; 550 hp *(410 kW)*
Speed, knots: 11. **Range, n miles:** 1,500 at 11 kt
Complement: 26 or 45 (when surveying)
Radars: Navigation: 2 Raytheon; I-band.

Comment: Laid up by USN in 1995 and acquired in September 1996. Reactivated in October 1996 and commissioned into RNZN 13 February 1997 for passage to New Zealand. Conversion commenced mid-1997 to suit the ship for hydrography with secondary role of acoustic research for about three months per year, replacing both *Tui* and *Monowai*. Second stage of conversion to fit Atlas Elektronik MD 2/30 multibeam echo-sounder, completed in January 1999. A fixed dome increased the ship's draught. A DGPS and a towed array fitted for acoustic research. A new survey boat with Atlas Elektronik MD20 multibeam echo sounder was embarked in 2001. The ship has been repainted grey.

RESOLUTION *9/2004, RNZN* / 0587566

AUXILIARIES

Note: In addition to vessels listed below there are three 12 m sail training craft used for seamanship training: *Paea II, Mako II, Manga II* (sail nos 6911-6913).

PAEA *2002, RNZN* / 0525919

0 + 1 MULTIROLE VESSEL (AKRH/AX)

Name	No	Builders	Laid down	Launched	Commissioned
CANTERBURY	L 421	Merwede Shipyard, Netherlands	2005	2006	Dec 2006

Displacement, tons: 8,870
Dimensions, feet (metres): 429.8 × 76.8 × 18.4 *(131.0 × 23.4 × 5.6)*
Main machinery: 2 Wärtsilä 9L32 diesels; 12,000 hp *(9 MW)*; 2 shafts; cp props
Speed, knots: 19. **Range, miles:** 6,000 at 15 kt
Complement: 53 + accommodation for 250 troops and 47 additional
Guns: 1 MSI DS 25M Autsig 25 mm. 2 — 12.7 mm MGs.
Military lift: 1 infantry company including Light Armoured Vehicles and equipment
Radars: Navigation: 2 I-band.
Helicopters: 2 SH-2G Super Seasprites.

Programmes: Following selection as 'Project Protector' prime contractor in April 2004, Tenix Defence awarded contract for final design and construction on 29 July 2004. Manufacturing is to start in early 2005. The ship is to provide a limited tactical sealift capacity for disaster relief, humanitarian relief operations, peace support operations, military support activities and development assistance support. The ship will also be used as the principal sea training platform for the RNZN. After being built in the Netherlands, to be fitted out by Tenix in either Australia or New Zealand.
Structure: With a design based on a commercial roll-on/roll-off vessel, the ship is to be built to comply with Lloyds Register of Shipping rules. To be ice-strengthened for operations in the Southern Ocean and the Ross Sea. Staff facilities to be incorporated.

MRV *9/2004, RNZN* / 0589789

1 REPLENISHMENT TANKER (AORH)

Name	No	Builders	Launched	Commissioned
ENDEAVOUR	A 11	Hyundai, South Korea	14 Aug 1987	6 Apr 1988

Displacement, tons: 12,390 full load
Dimensions, feet (metres): 453.1 × 60 × 23 *(138.1 × 18.4 × 7.3)*
Main machinery: 1 MAN-Burmeister & Wain 12V32/36 diesel; 5,780 hp(m) *(4.25 MW)* sustained; 1 shaft; LIPS cp prop
Speed, knots: 13.5. **Range, n miles:** 8,000 at 13.5 kt
Complement: 49 (10 officers)
Cargo capacity: 7,500 tons dieso; 100 tons Avcat; 20 containers
Radars: Navigation: Racal Decca 1290A/9; ARPA 1690S; I-band.
Helicopters: Platform only.

Comment: Ordered July 1986. Laid down 10 April 1987. Completion delayed by engine problems but arrived in New Zealand in May 1988. Two abeam RAS rigs (one QRC, one Probe) and one astern refuelling rig. Fitted with Inmarsat. Standard merchant design modified on building to provide a relatively inexpensive replenishment tanker.

ENDEAVOUR *4/2004*, Mick Prendergast* / 1133138

1 MOA CLASS (TRAINING SHIP) (AXL)

Name	No	Builders	Commissioned
KAHU (ex-*Manawanui*)	A 04 (ex-A 09)	Whangarei Engineering and Construction Co Ltd	28 May 1979

Displacement, tons: 91.5 standard; 105 full load
Dimensions, feet (metres): 88 × 20 × 7.2 *(26.8 × 6.1 × 2.2)*
Main machinery: 2 Cummins KT-1150M diesels; 710 hp *(530 kW)*; 2 shafts
Speed, knots: 12. **Range, n miles:** 1,000 at 11 kt
Complement: 16
Radars: Navigation: Racal Decca Bridgemaster 2000; I-band.

Comment: Same hull design as Inshore Survey Craft and Patrol Craft. Now used for navigation and seamanship training and as a standby diving tender.

KAHU *6/1999, RNZN* / 0081325

1 DIVING TENDER (YDT)

Name	No	Builders	Commissioned
MANAWANUI (ex-*Star Perseus*)	A 09	Cochrane, Selby	May 1979

Displacement, tons: 911 full load
Dimensions, feet (metres): 143 × 31.2 × 10.5 *(43.6 × 9.5 × 3.2)*
Main machinery: 2 Caterpillar D 379TA diesels; 1,130 hp *(843 kW)*; 2 shafts; cp props; bow thruster
Speed, knots: 10.7
Range, n miles: 5,000 at 10 kt
Complement: 24 (2 officers)
Radars: Surface search: Racal Decca Bridgemaster 2000; I-band.
Sonars: Klein 595 Tracpoint; side scan; active high frequency.

Comment: North Sea Oil Rig Diving support vessel commissioned into the RNZN on 5 April 1988. Completed conversion in December 1988 and has replaced the previous ship of the same name which proved to be too small for the role. Equipment includes two Phantom HDX remote-controlled submersibles, a decompression chamber (to 250 ft), wet diving bell and 13 ton crane. Fitted with Inmarsat. MCAIS data system, side scan sonar and GPS fitted in 1995. More modifications are planned to enable the ship to do some of the work previously undertaken by *Tui*. This includes a stern gantry and general purpose winches for research including MCM. Used to support RAN submarine trials in 1996/97.

MANAWANUI *2002, RNZN* / 0525920

Nicaragua
FUERZA NAVAL-EJERCITO DE NICARAGUA

Country Overview

The Republic of Nicaragua is the largest Central American republic. After many years of civil war, a 1989 peace plan introduced a more stable period of democratic government. With an area of 50,893 square miles, it is situated between Honduras to the north and Costa Rica to the south. It has a 381 n mile coastline with the Caribbean and a 225 n mile coastline with the Pacific Ocean. Lake Nicaragua (Cocibolca), the largest lake in central America, and Lake Managua (Xolotlán) are connected by the river Tipitapa. The capital and largest city is Managua while Corinto, on the Pacific coast, is the principal port. Nicaragua has not claimed an EEZ but is one of a few coastal states which claims a 200 n mile territorial sea.

Headquarters Appointments

Head of Navy:
    Captain Juan Santiago Estrada García

Personnel

2006: 910 officers and men

Bases

Pacific: Corinto (HQ), San Juan del Sur, Puerto Sandino y Potosi
Atlantic: Bluefields (HQ), El Bluff, Puerto Cabezas, Corn Island, San Juan del Norte

---

PATROL FORCES

Notes: A programme to re-engine and return to service one Zhuk (Grif) class has been initiated. Work to renovate two North Korean built Sin Hung class patrol boats may also be funded.

3 DABUR CLASS (PB)

GC 201	GC 203	GC 205

Displacement, tons: 39 full load
Dimensions, feet (metres): 64.9 × 18 × 5.8 *(19.8 × 5.5 × 1.8)*
Main machinery: 2 GM 12V-71TS; 840 hp *(626 kW)* sustained; 2 shafts
Speed, knots: 15
Range, n miles: 450 at 13 kt
Complement: 8
Guns: 2 – 23 mm/80 (twin). 2 – 12.7 mm MGs.
Radars: Surface search: Decca; I-band.

Comment: Two delivered by Israel April 1978 and two more in May 1978. One lost by gunfire in 1985 and three severely damaged in 1988 by a hurricane. The current three were acquired from Israel in May 1996. *GC 201* and *GC 203* overhauled 2000-01 and *GC 205* in 2003-04. All are operational on the Atlantic coast.

EDUARDOÑO class   *1/2000, Julio Montes* / 0109944

GC 201   *5/2001, Julio Montes* / 0109945

PBF   *6/1999, Nicaraguan Navy* / 0081330

19 ASSAULT and RIVER CRAFT (PBF)

Comment: There are 19 Colombian-built Eduardoño class 10 m assault craft, capable of 50 kt and 13 m 'Cigarette' craft and powered by three Yamaha outboards; 400 hp *(298 kW)*.

EDUARDOÑO class   *1/2000, Julio Montes* / 0109943

EDUARDOÑO CLASS   *6/1999, Nicaraguan Navy* / 0081329

Nigeria

Country Overview

Formerly a British protectorate, the Federal Republic of Nigeria gained full independence in 1960. With an area of 356,669 square miles, it is situated in western Africa and is bordered to the north by Niger, to the east by Chad and Cameroon and to the west by Benin. It has a 459 n mile coastline with the Gulf of Guinea. Abuja is the capital while Lagos (the capital until 1991) is the largest city, commercial centre and one of its principal ports. There are other ports at Port Harcourt, Warri, Calabar, Bonny, and Burutu. Territorial Seas (12 n miles) are claimed. An EEZ (200 n miles) has been claimed but the limits have not been defined.

The Navy has suffered from chronic lack of investment over the last ten years but there are signs that a refit programme is attempting to restore a core seagoing capability for operations within the Nigerian EEZ. However, the operational status of weapon systems and sensors remains doubtful.

Headquarters Appointments

Chief of the Naval Staff:
    Vice Admiral Ganiyu Adekeye
Flag Officer Western Command:
    Commodore John Kpokpogri
Flag Officer Eastern Command:
    Commodore Musa Ajadi

Personnel

a)   2006: 5,600 (650 officers) including Coast Guard
b)   Voluntary service

Bases

Apapa-Lagos: Western Naval Command; Naval Base Lagos (NNS *Onaku*), Naval College (NNS *Onura*) and Naval Training (NNS *Quorra*).

Calabar: Eastern Naval Command; Naval Base Calabar (NNS *Anansu*), Naval Base Warri (NNS *Umalokun*) and Naval Base Port Harcourt (NNS *Okemini*). There are plans for further bases at Bonny Island, Rivers State, and at Egwuama, Bayelsa State.

Naval Aviation

The official list includes two Lynx Mk 89, 12 MBB BO 105C, three Fokker F27 and 14 Dornier Do 128-6MPA. These aircraft are believed not to be operational. Four Agusta A 109 have been procured from Italy since 2003 for patrol duties.

Prefix to Ships' Names

NNS

Port Security Police

A separate force of 1,600 officers and men in Lagos.

FRIGATES

1 MEKO TYPE 360 H1 (FFGHM)

Name	No
ARADU (ex-*Republic*)	F 89

Builders	Laid down	Launched	Commissioned
Blohm & Voss, Hamburg	1 Dec 1978	25 Jan 1980	20 Feb 1982

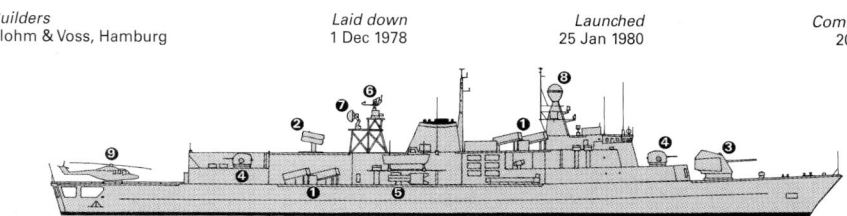

ARADU *(Scale 1 : 1,200), Ian Sturton* / 0081331

Displacement, tons: 3,360 full load
Dimensions, feet (metres): 412 × 49.2 × 19 (screws)
(*125.6 × 15 × 5.8*)
Main machinery: CODOG; 2 RR Olympus TM3B gas
turbines; 50,880 hp *(37.9 MW)* sustained; 2 MTU 20V 956
TB92 diesels; 10,420 hp(m) *(7.71 MW)* sustained; 2 shafts;
2 Kamewa cp props
Speed, knots: 30.5. **Range, n miles:** 6,500 at 15 kt
Complement: 195 (26 officers)

Missiles: SSM: 8 OTO Melara/Matra Otomat Mk 1 ❶;
active radar homing to 80 km *(43.2 n miles)* at 0.9 Mach;
warhead 210 kg.
SAM: Selenia Elsag Albatros octuple launcher ❷; 24
Aspide; semi-active radar homing to 13 km *(7 n miles)* at
2.5 Mach; warhead 30 kg.
Guns: 1 OTO Melara 5 in *(127 mm)*/54 ❸; 45 rds/min to 23 km
(12.4 n miles); weight of shell 32 kg.
8 Breda Bofors 40 mm/70 (4 twin) ❹; 300 rds/min to 12.5 km
(6.8 n miles) anti-surface; weight of shell 0.96 kg.
Torpedoes: 6—324 mm Plessey STWS-1B (2 triple) tubes ❺.
18 Whitehead A244S; anti-submarine; active/passive
homing to 7 km *(3.8 n miles)* at 33 kt; warhead 34 kg
(shaped charge).
Depth charges: 1 rack.

Countermeasures: Decoys: 2 Breda 105 mm SCLAR
20-tubed trainable; chaff to 5 km *(2.7 n miles)*; illuminants
to 12 km *(6.6 n miles)*. ESM: Decca RDL-2; intercept.
ECM: RCM-2; jammer.
Combat data systems: Sewaco-BV action data automation.
Weapons control: M20 series GFCS. Signaal Vesta ASW.
Radars: Air/surface search: Plessey AWS 5 ❻; E/F-band.
Navigation: Racal Decca 1226; I-band.
Fire control: Signaal STIR ❼; I/J/K-band. Signaal WM 25 ❽;
I/J-band.
Sonars: Atlas Elektronik EA80; hull-mounted; active search
and attack; medium frequency.

Helicopters: 1 Lynx Mk 89 ❾.

Modernisation: Refit started at Wilmot Point, Lagos with
Blohm & Voss assistance in 1991 and completed in
February 1994.
Operational: Had two groundings and a major collision in
1987 and ran aground again during post refit trials in early
1994. Assessed as beyond economical repair in 1995 but
managed to go to sea in early 1996, and again in 1997
when she broke down for several months in Monrovia.
Back in Lagos on one engine in 1998 for further repairs.
SSM system reported being refitted in 1999. Following a
refit at Lagos, attended Fleet Review at Portsmouth, UK,
in June 2005.

ARADU *6/2005*, Maritime Photographic* / 1129571

CORVETTES

1 MK 9 VOSPER THORNYCROFT TYPE (FSM)

Name	No	Builders	Commissioned
ENYMIRI	F 84	Vosper Thornycroft	2 May 1980

Displacement, tons: 680 standard; 780 full load
Dimensions, feet (metres): 226 × 31.5 × 9.8 *(69 × 9.6 × 3)*
Main machinery: 4 MTU 20V 956 TB92 diesels; 22,140 hp(m) *(16.27 MW)* sustained;
2 shafts; 2 Kamewa cp props
Speed, knots: 27. **Range, n miles:** 2,200 at 14 kt
Complement: 90 (including Flag Officer)

Missiles: SAM: Short Brothers Seacat triple launcher.
Guns: 1 OTO Melara 3 in *(76 mm)*/62 Mod 6 compact; 85 rds/min to 16 km *(8.7 n miles)*;
weight of shell 6 kg.
1 Breda Bofors 40 mm/70 Type 350; 300 rds/min to 12.5 km *(6.8 n miles)*; weight of shell
0.96 kg.
2 Oerlikon 20 mm.
A/S mortars: 1 Bofors 375 mm twin launcher; range 1,600 or 3,600 m.
Countermeasures: ESM: Decca Cutlass; radar warning.
Weapons control: Signaal WM20 series.
Radars: Air/surface search: Plessey AWS 2; E/F-band.
Navigation: Racal Decca TM 1226; I-band.
Fire control: Signaal WM24; I/J-band; range 46 km *(25 n miles)*.
Sonars: Plessey PMS 26; lightweight; hull-mounted; active search and attack; 10 kHz.

Programmes: Ordered from Vosper Thornycroft 22 April 1975.
Operational: *Enymiri* seriously damaged by fire in 2005 and may not be repaired. Sister
ship *Erinomi* assessed as beyond economical repair in 1996.

ENYMIRI *5/1999* / 0081333

PATROL FORCES

Notes: (1) All the Coastal Patrol Craft belong to the Coast Guard. Some 38 craft were
acquired in the mid-1980s from various shipbuilders including Simonneau, Damen,
Swiftships, Intermarine, Watercraft, Van Mill and Rotork. Few of these vessels have been
reported at sea in recent years although some are visible, laid up ashore, and are still
serviceable.
(2) A Damen 2600 Mk II patrol craft was acquired from South Africa in 2001.
(3) Four 8 m Night Cat 27, capable of 70 kt, were delivered by Intercept Boats in 2003-04.

P 236 (Simonneau) *5/2002* / 0528302

P 240 (Rotork) *5/2002* / 0528301

3 EKPE (LÜRSSEN 57) CLASS (LARGE PATROL CRAFT) (PGF)

Name	No	Builders	Commissioned
EKPE	P 178	Lürssen, Vegesack	Aug 1980
DAMISA	P 179	Lürssen, Vegesack	Apr 1981
AGU	P 180	Lürssen, Vegesack	Apr 1981

Displacement, tons: 444 full load
Dimensions, feet (metres): 190.6 × 24.9 × 10.2 *(58.1 × 7.6 × 3.1)*
Main machinery: 4 MTU 16V 956 TB92 diesels; 17,700 hp(m) *(13 MW)* sustained; 2 shafts
Speed, knots: 42
Range, n miles: 2,000 at 10 kt
Complement: 40
Guns: 1 OTO Melara 3 in *(76 mm)*/62; 60 rds/min to 16 km *(8.7 n miles)*; weight of shell 6 kg.
2 Breda 40 mm/70 (twin); 4 Emerson Electric 30 mm (2 twin).
Radars: Surface search: Racal Decca TM 1226; I-band.
Fire control: Signaal WM28; I/J-band.

Programmes: Ordered in 1977. Major refit in 1984 at Vegesack.
Operational: P 178 refitted at Lagos in 1995 but broke down en route to Sierra Leone in 1997. P 179 believed to be operational but the operational status of the other two is doubtful.

EKPE *3/1998* / 0052656

4 BALSAM CLASS (PBO)

Name	No	Builders	Commissioned
KYANWA	A 501	Marine Iron and Shipbuilding Corp, Duluth,	5 July 1944
(ex-*Sedge*)	(ex-WLB 402)	Minnesota	
OLOGBO	A 502	Marine Iron and Shipbuilding Corp, Duluth,	17 Oct 1942
(ex-*Cowslip*)	(ex-WLB 277)	Minnesota	
NWAMBA	A 503	Marine Iron and Shipbuilding Corp, Duluth,	20 July 1944
(ex-*Firebush*)	(ex-WLB 393)	Minnesota	
OBULA	A 504	Marine Iron and Shipbuilding Corp, Duluth,	23 May 1944
(ex-*Sassafras*)	(ex-WLB 401)	Minnesota	

Displacement, tons: 1,034 full load
Dimensions, feet (metres): 180 × 37 × 12 *(54.9 × 11.3 × 3.8)*
Main machinery: Diesel electric; 2 diesels; 1,402 hp *(1.06 MW)*; 1 motor; 1,200 hp *(895 kW)*; 1 shaft; bow thruster
Speed, knots: 13
Range, n miles: 8,000 at 12 kt
Complement: 53
Guns: 2—12.7 mm MGs.
Radars: Navigation: Raytheon SPS-64(V)1.

Comment: First ship transferred from the US Coast Guard on 30 September 2002, second on 30 December 2002, third on 30 June 2003 and fourth on 30 October 2003. Transfer of a fifth vessel is unlikely.

BALSAM CLASS (USCG colours) *7/1999, USCG* / 0084209

15 DEFENDER CLASS (RESPONSE BOATS) (PBF)

P 313-320 **+7**

Displacement, tons: 2.7 full load
Dimensions, feet (metres): 25.0 × 8.5 × 8.8 *(7.6 × 2.6 × 2.7)*
Main machinery: 2 Honda outboard motors; 450 hp *(335 kW)*
Speed, knots: 46
Range, n miles: 175 at 35 kt
Complement: 4
Guns: 1—12.7mm MG.
Radars: To be announced.

Comment: High-speed inshore patrol craft of aluminium construction and foam collar built by SAFE Boats International, Port Orchard, Washington. An initial order for ten craft, with an option for five further craft, placed in August 2004 through USCG Foreign Military Sales programme. First four delivered on 13 December 2004 and second batch of four on 9 February. The remaining seven had been delivered by mid-2005.

DEFENDER CLASS *10/2003*, Frank Findler* / 0572753

1 COMBATTANTE IIIB CLASS
(FAST ATTACK CRAFT—MISSILE) (PGGF)

Name	No	Builders	Commissioned
AYAM	P 182	CMN, Cherbourg	11 June 1981

Displacement, tons: 385 standard; 430 full load
Dimensions, feet (metres): 184 × 24.9 × 7 *(56.2 × 7.6 × 2.1)*
Main machinery: 4 MTU 16V 956 TB92 diesels; 17,700 hp(m) *(13 MW)* sustained; 2 shafts
Speed, knots: 38. **Range, n miles:** 2,000 at 15 kt
Complement: 42

Missiles: SSM: 4 Aerospatiale MM 38 Exocet; inertial cruise; active radar homing to 42 km *(23 n miles)* at 0.9 Mach; warhead 165 kg; sea-skimmer.
Guns: 1 OTO Melara 3 in *(76 mm)*/62; 60 rds/min to 16 km *(8.7 n miles)*; weight of shell 6 kg.
2 Breda 40 mm/70 (twin); 300 rds/min to 12.5 km *(6.8 n miles)*; weight of shell 0.96 kg.
4 Emerson Electric 30 mm (2 twin); 1,200 rds/min combined to 6 km *(3.3 n miles)*; weight of shell 0.35 kg.
Countermeasures: ESM: Decca RDL; radar intercept.
Weapons control: Thomson-CSF Vega system. 2 CSEE Panda optical directors.
Radars: Air/surface search: Thomson-CSF Triton (TRS 3033); G-band.
Navigation: Racal Decca TM 1226; I-band.
Fire control: Thomson-CSF Castor II (TRS 3203); I/J-band.

Programmes: Ordered in late 1977. Finally handed over in February 1982 after delays caused by financial problems.
Modernisation: Major refit and repairs carried out at Cherbourg from March to December 1991 but the ships were delayed by financial problems.
Operational: *Ayam* believed to be operational but sister ships *Siri* and *Ekun* are almost certainly not.

AYAM (outboard DAMISA) *5/2002* / 0528300

AMPHIBIOUS FORCES

1 FDR TYPE RO-RO 1300 (LST)

Name	No	Builders	Commissioned
AMBE	LST 1312	Howaldtswerke, Hamburg	11 May 1979

Displacement, tons: 1,470 standard; 1,860 full load
Dimensions, feet (metres): 285.4 × 45.9 × 7.5 *(87 × 14 × 2.3)*
Main machinery: 2 MTU 16V 956 TB92 diesels; 8,850 hp(m) *(6.5 MW)* sustained; 2 shafts
Speed, knots: 17. **Range, n miles:** 5,000 at 10 kt
Complement: 56 (6 officers)
Military lift: 460 tons and 220 troops long haul; 540 troops or 1,000 troops seated short haul; can carry 5—40 ton tanks
Guns: 1 Breda 40 mm/70. 2 Oerlikon 20 mm.
Radars: Navigation: Racal Decca 1226; I-band.

Comment: Ordered September 1976. Built to a design prepared for the FGN. Has 19 m bow ramps and a 4 m stern ramp. Reported that bow ramps are welded shut. Second of class beyond repair but *Ambe* reported active in 2004.

AMBE *7/1997* / 0012836

MINE WARFARE FORCES

2 LERICI CLASS (MINEHUNTERS/SWEEPERS) (MHSC)

Name	No	Builders	Commissioned
OHUE	M 371	Intermarine SY, Italy	28 May 1987
BARAMA	M 372	Intermarine SY, Italy	25 Feb 1988

Displacement, tons: 540 full load
Dimensions, feet (metres): 167.3 × 32.5 × 9.2 *(51 × 9.9 × 2.8)*
Main machinery: 2 MTU 12V 396 TB83 diesels; 3,120 hp(m) *(2.3 MW)* sustained; 2 waterjets
Speed, knots: 15.5. **Range, n miles:** 2,500 at 12 kt
Complement: 50 (5 officers)
Guns: 2 Emerson Electric 30 mm (twin); 1,200 rds/min combined to 6 km *(3.3 n miles)*; weight of shell 0.35 kg.
2 Oerlikon 20 mm GAM-BO1.
Countermeasures: MCM: Fitted with 2 Pluto remote-controlled submersibles, Oropesa 'O' Mis 4 and Ibis V control system.
Radars: Navigation: Racal Decca 1226; I-band.
Sonars: Thomson Sintra TSM 2022; hull-mounted; mine detection; high frequency.

Comment: *Ohue* ordered in April 1983 and *Barama* in January 1986. *Ohue* laid down 23 July 1984 and launched 22 November 1985, *Barama* laid down 11 March 1985, launched 6 June 1986. GRP hulls but, unlike Italian and Malaysian versions they do not have separate hydraulic minehunting propulsion. Carry Galeazzi two-man decompression chambers. Both were refitted in 1999, after operations off Liberia. *Barama* reported refitted in late 2004 but the operational effectiveness of both ships in their MCM role is doubtful.

OHUE *7/1987, Marina Fraccaroli* / 0506063

SURVEY SHIPS

1 SURVEY SHIP (AGS)

Name	No	Builders	Launched	Commissioned
LANA	A 498	Brooke Marine, Lowestoft	4 Mar 1976	18 July 1976

Displacement, tons: 1,088 full load
Dimensions, feet (metres): 189 × 37.5 × 12 *(57.8 × 11.4 × 3.7)*
Main machinery: 2 Lister Blackstone diesels; 2,640 hp *(1.97 MW)*; 2 shafts
Speed, knots: 16. **Range, n miles:** 4,500 at 12 kt
Complement: 52 (12 officers)
Radars: Navigation: Decca; I-band.

Comment: Similar to UK Bulldog class. Ordered in 1973. Rarely goes to sea.

LANA *5/1999* / 0081334

TUGS

3 COASTAL TUGS (YTB/YTL)

COMMANDER APAYI JOE A 499   **DOLPHIN MIRA**   **DOLPHIN RIMA**

Comment: A 499 is of 310 tons and was built in 1983. The two Dolphin tugs are under repair.

COMMANDER APAYI JOE *11/1983, Hartmut Ehlers* / 0506064

Norway

Country Overview

The Kingdom of Norway is a constitutional monarchy occupying the northwest part of the Scandinavian Peninsula. With an area of 125,016 square miles, it is bordered to the east by Sweden and to the northeast by Finland and Russia. The coastline of 11,842 n miles with the Atlantic Ocean (Norwegian Sea), Arctic Ocean (Barents Sea), North Sea and Skagerrak Strait contains numerous fjords and offshore islands. External territories in the Arctic Ocean include the Svalbard archipelago and Jan Mayen Island while the uninhabited Bouvet Island lies in the south Atlantic. Territorial claims in Antarctica include the territory known as Queen Maud Land and Peter I Island. The capital, largest city and principal port is Oslo. Other ports include Bergen, Trondheim and Stavanger. Territorial seas (12 n miles) and an EEZ (200 n miles) are claimed.

Headquarters Appointments

Chief of Naval Staff:
Rear Admiral J E Finseth
Deputy Chief of Naval Staff:
Commodore A I Skram
Commander Coast Guard:
Commodore G A Osen
Commander Norwegian Fleet:
Commodore H Tronstad

Diplomatic Representation

Defence Attaché in Ankara:
Colonel O Nordbø
Defence Attaché in Helsinki:
Colonel I L Viddal
Defence Attaché in London:
Colonel J P Ryste
Defence Attaché in Madrid:
Captain S Hauger
Defence Attaché in Moscow:
Brigadier General F S Hauen
Defence Attaché in Paris:
Colonel J E Hynaas
Defence Attaché in Stockholm:
Captain G Heløe
Defence Attaché in Washington:
Major General J F Blom

Diplomatic Representation — *continued*

Defence Attaché in Warsaw:
Colonel L Lindalen
Defence Attaché in Berlin:
Colonel S O Åndal
Defence Attaché in the Hague:
Captain H Smidt
Defence Attaché in the Baltic States:
Colonel L W Strand-Torgersen
Defence Attaché in Rome:
Captain J R Bakke

General

As a result of the Defence Analysis 2000 Plan, which was approved with some changes by the Norwegian parliament, the Royal Norwegian Navy is undergoing a thorough restructuring. This includes a shift of focus from a mainly anti-invasion oriented Navy towards a force capable of international operations as well as operations in national waters.

Personnel

(a) 2006: 4,950 officers and ratings
(b) 9 to 12 months' national service (up to 40 per cent of ships complement)

Coast Artillery

The fixed defence system of nine coastal forts and controlled minefields is in long-term storage. As a result, the Coastal Ranger Command was established in 2001 with a headquarters at Trondenes.

Coast Guard

Founded April 1977 with operational command held by Norwegian Defence Command. Main bases at Sortland (North) and Haakonsvern (South). Tasks include fishery protection, customs, police, SAR and environmental duties at sea.

Bases

Jåtta (Stavanger) Armed Forces HQ.
Reitan (Bodø) Regional Command North HQ.

Haakonsvern (Bergen) – Main base, repair and maintenance
Laksevag (Bergen) – Submarine Repair and Maintenance.
Ramsund-Supply/Repair/Maintenance.

Air Force Squadrons (see *Shipborne* and *Land-based Aircraft*)

Aircraft (Squadron)	Location	Duties
Sea King Mk 43 (330)	Bodø, Banak, Sola, Ørland	SAR
Orion P-3N/C (333)	Andøya	MPA
Lynx (337)	Coast Guard vessels/ Bardufoss	MP
Bell 412 (719, 339 & 720)	Bodø, Rygge, Bardufoss	Army Transport

Prefix to Ships' Names

KNM (Naval)
K/V (Coast Guard)

Strength of the Fleet

Type	Active	Building (Projected)
Submarines — Coastal	6	—
Frigates	3	4
Fast Attack Craft — Missile	15	5
Minelayers	1	—
Minesweepers/Hunters	6	—
Depot Ship	1	—
Auxiliaries	1	—
Naval District Auxiliaries	9	—
Coast Guard Vessels	19	—
Survey Vessels	6	—

DELETIONS

Frigates

2005 *Bergen*

Mine Warfare Forces

2004 *Rauma, Glomma*
2005 *Vidar*

PENNANT LIST

Notes: Naval District Auxiliaries are listed on page 542.

Submarines		Minesweepers/Hunters		P 986	Hauk	A 533	Norge
				P 987	Ørn	A 535	Valkyrien
S 300	Ula	M 340	Oksøy	P 988	Terne		
S 301	Utsira	M 341	Karmøy	P 989	Tjeld	**Coast Guard**	
S 302	Utstein	M 342	Måløy	P 990	Skarv		
S 303	Utvaer	M 343	Hinnøy	P 991	Teist	W 303	Svalbard
S 304	Uthaug	M 350	Alta	P 992	Jo	W 310	Eigun
S 305	Uredd	M 351	Otra	P 993	Lom	W 312	Ålesund
				P 994	Stegg	W 313	Tromsö
Frigates		**Minelayers**		P 995	Falk	W 315	Nordsjøbas
				P 996	Ravn	W 316	Malene Østervold
F 302	Trondheim	N 50	Tyr	P 997	Gribb	W 317	Lafjord
F 304	Narvik			P 998	Geir	W 318	Harstad
F 310	Fridtjof Nansen	**Patrol Forces**		P 999	Erle	W 319	Thorsteinson
F 311	Roald Amundsen (bldg)					W 320	Nordkapp
F 312	Otto Sverdrup (bldg)	P 358	Hessa	**Auxiliaries**		W 321	Senja
F 313	Helge Ingstad (bldg)	P 359	Vigra			W 322	Andenes
F 314	Thor Heyerdahl (bldg)	P 960	Skjold	A 530	Horten		

SUBMARINES

Notes: Norway withdrew from the 'Viking' submarine project on 13 June 2003 at the end of the Project Definition Phase Step 1. It has retained observer status in the project which is being taken forward by Sweden. Following the reduction of submarine forces to the six Ula class, there is no longer a requirement for new submarines before 2020.

6 ULA CLASS (SSK)

Name	No	Builders	Laid down	Launched	Commissioned
ULA	S 300	Thyssen Nordseewerke, Emden	29 Jan 1987	28 July 1988	27 Apr 1989
UREDD	S 305	Thyssen Nordseewerke, Emden	23 June 1988	22 Sep 1989	3 May 1990
UTVAER	S 303	Thyssen Nordseewerke, Emden	8 Dec 1988	19 Apr 1990	8 Nov 1990
UTHAUG	S 304	Thyssen Nordseewerke, Emden	15 June 1989	18 Oct 1990	7 May 1991
UTSTEIN	S 302	Thyssen Nordseewerke, Emden	6 Dec 1989	25 Apr 1991	14 Nov 1991
UTSIRA	S 301	Thyssen Nordseewerke, Emden	15 June 1990	21 Nov 1991	30 Apr 1992

Displacement, tons: 1,040 surfaced; 1,150 dived
Dimensions, feet (metres): 193.6 × 17.7 × 15.1
(59 × 5.4 × 4.6)
Main machinery: Diesel-electric; 2 MTU 16V 396 SB83 diesels; 2,700 hp(m) *(1.98 MW)* sustained; 1 Siemens motor; 6,000 hp(m) *(4.41 MW)*; 1 shaft
Speed, knots: 11 surfaced; 23 dived
Range, n miles: 5,000 at 8 kt
Complement: 21 (5 officers)

Torpedoes: 8 — 21 in *(533 mm)* bow tubes. 14 AEG DM 2A3 Sehecht; dual purpose; wire-guided; active/passive homing to 28 km *(15 n miles)* at 23 kt; 13 km *(7 n miles)* at 35 kt; warhead 260 kg; depth to 460 m.
Countermeasures: ESM: Racal Sealion; radar warning.
Weapons control: Kongsberg MSI-90(U) TFCS.
Radars: Surface search: Kelvin Hughes 1007; I-band.
Sonars: Atlas Elektronik CSU 83; active/passive intercept search and attack; medium frequency.
Thomson Sintra; flank array; passive; low frequency.

Programmes: Contract signed on 30 September 1982. This was a joint West German/Norwegian effort known as Project 210 in Germany. Although final assembly was at Thyssen a number of pressure hull sections were provided by Norway.
Modernisation: MSI-90U being upgraded 2000-2005. A mid-life upgrade of all six boats is under consideration.
Structure: Diving depth, 250 m *(820 ft)*. The basic command and weapon control systems are Norwegian, the attack sonar is German but the flank array, based on piezoelectric polymer antenna technology, was developed in France and substantially reduces flow noise. Calzoni Trident modular system of non-penetrating masts has been installed. Zeiss periscopes.

ULA 8/2004, *Derek Fox* / 1043505

UTVAER 7/2004, *P Froud* / 1043512

FRIGATES

2 OSLO CLASS (FFGM)

Name	No	Builders	Laid down	Launched	Commissioned
TRONDHEIM	F 302	Marinens Hovedverft, Horten	1963	4 Sep 1964	2 June 1966
NARVIK	F 304	Marinens Hovedverft, Horten	1964	8 Jan 1965	30 Nov 1966

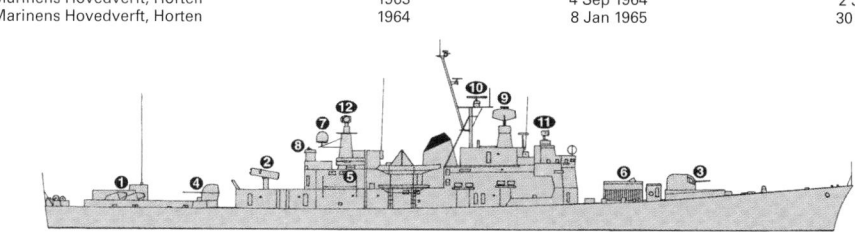

TRONDHEIM
(Scale 1 : 900), Ian Sturton / 0012838

Displacement, tons: 1,650 standard; 1,950 full load
Dimensions, feet (metres): 317 × 36.8 × 18 (screws)
(96.6 × 11.2 × 5.5)
Main machinery: 2 Babcock & Wilcox boilers; 600 psi
(42.18 kg/cm²); 850°F *(454°C)*; 1 set De Laval Ljungstrom
PN20 geared turbines; 20,000 hp(m) *(14.7 MW)*; 1 shaft
Speed, knots: 25+
Range, n miles: 4,500 at 15 kt
Complement: 125 (11 officers)

Missiles: SSM: 4 Kongsberg Penguin Mk 1 ❶; IR homing to
20 km *(10.8 n miles)* at 0.7 Mach; warhead 120 kg.
SAM: Raytheon NATO RIM-7M Sea Sparrow Mk 29 octuple
launcher ❷; semi-active radar homing to 14.6 km *(8 n miles)*
at 2.5 Mach; warhead 39 kg; 24 cell magazine.
Guns: 2 US 3 in *(76 mm)*/50 Mk 33 (twin) ❸; 50 rds/min to
12.8 km *(7 n miles)*; weight of shell 6 kg.
1 Bofors 40 mm/70 ❹; 300 rds/min to 12 km *(6.6 n miles)*;
weight of shell 0.96 kg
2 Rheinmetall 20 mm/20 (not in all); 1,000 rds/min to 2 km.
Torpedoes: 6—324 mm US Mk 32 (2 triple) tubes ❺. Marconi
Stingray; anti-submarine; active/passive homing to 11 km
(5.9 n miles) at 45 kt; warhead 32 kg (shaped charge);
depth to 750 m *(2,460 ft)*.
A/S mortars: Kongsberg Terne III 6-tubed trainable ❻; range
pattern from 400—5,000 m; warhead 70 kg. Automatic
reloading in 40 seconds.
Mines: Laying capability.
Countermeasures: Decoys: 2 chaff launchers.
ESM: Argo AR 700; intercept.

Combat data systems: NFT MSI-3100 (supplemented by
Siemens ODIN) action data automation; Link 11 and 14.
SATCOM ❼.
Weapons control: Mk 91 MFCS. TVT 300 tracker ❽.
Radars: Air search: Siemens/Plessey AWS-9 ❾; 2D; E/F-band.
Surface search: Racal Decca TM 1226 ❿; I-band.
Fire control: NobelTech 9LV 218 Mk 2 ⓫; I-band (includes
search).
Raytheon Mk 95 ⓬, I/J-band (for Sea Sparrow).
Navigation: Decca; I-band.
Sonars: Thomson Sintra/Simrad TSM 2633; combined hull
and VDS; active search and attack; medium frequency.
Simrad Terne III; active attack; high frequency.

Programmes: Built under the five year naval construction
programme approved by the Norwegian Storting
(Parliament) late in 1960. Although all the ships of this class

were constructed in the Norwegian Naval Dockyard, half the
cost was borne by Norway and the other half by the US.
Modernisation: Both ships modernised in 1988. Plessey
AWS-9 radar fitted in 1996-98 together with Link 11
and GPS.
Structure: The hull and propulsion design of these ships is
based on that of the Dealey class destroyer escorts (now
deleted) of the US Navy, but considerably modified to
suit Norwegian requirements. The hulls became stressed
by towing VDS in heavy seas and were strengthened in
1995-96 increasing displacement by over 200 tons.
Operational: The fifth of class *Oslo* sank under tow south
of Bergen in January 1994, after an engine failure had
caused her to run aground in heavy weather. *Stavanger*
laid up in 1999 and later sunk as target for torpedo firings
in 2002. *Bergen* decommissioned in 2005 and *Trondheim*
to be decommissioned in 2006.

NARVIK
6/2005*, E & M Laursen / 1151132

TRONDHEIM
4/2005*, M Declerck / 1151298

TRONDHEIM
6/2005*, E & M Laursen / 1154645

1 + 4 FRIDTJOF NANSEN CLASS (FFGHM)

Name	No	Builders	Laid down	Launched	Commissioned
FRIDTJOF NANSEN	F 310	Navantia, Ferrol	9 Apr 2003	3 June 2004	5 Apr 2006
ROALD AMUNDSEN	F 311	Navantia, Ferrol	3 June 2004	25 May 2005	Dec 2006
OTTO SVERDRUP	F 312	Navantia, Ferrol	25 May 2005	2006	Dec 2007
HELGE INGSTAD	F 313	Navantia, Ferrol	2006	2007	Dec 2008
THOR HEYERDAHL	F 314	Navantia, Ferrol	2007	2008	Dec 2009

Displacement, tons: 5,290 full load
Dimensions, feet (metres): 437.0 × 55.1 × 16.1
 (133.2 × 16.8 × 4.9)
Main machinery: CODAG; 1 GE LM 2500 gas turbine; 26,112 hp
 (19.2 MW); 2 Bazán Bravo 12V diesels; 12,240 hp(m) *(9 MW)*;
 2 shafts; cp props; bow thruster; 1,360 hp(m) *(1 MW)*
Speed, knots: 26
Range, n miles: 4,500 at 16 kt
Complement: 120 plus 26 spare

Missiles: SSM: 8 Kongsberg NSM ❶.
 SAM: Mk 41 VLS (8 cells) ❷; 32 Evolved Sea Sparrow RIM
 162B; semi-active radar homing to 18 km *(9.7 n miles)* at
 3.6 Mach; warhead 39 kg.
Guns: 1 Oto Melara 76 mm/62 Super Rapid ❸. 120 rds/min
 to 15.75 km *(8.5 n miles)* anti-surface; 12 km *(6.5 n miles)*
 anti-aircraft; weight of shell 6 kg.
 4—12.7 mm MGs. Fitted for 1—40 mm/70.
Torpedoes: 4—324 mm (2 double) tubes ❹. Marconi
 Stingray; active/passive homing to 11 km *(5.9 n miles)* at
 45 kt; warhead 35 kg shaped charge.
Countermeasures: Decoys: Terma SKWS chaff, IR. LOKI
 130 mm acoustic decoy.
 ESM: Condor CS-3701; intercept ❺.
Combat data systems: AEGIS with ASW and ASuW
 segments from Kongsberg; Link 11 (fitted for Link 16/22).
Weapons control: Sagem VIGY 20 optronic director ❻.
Radars: Air search: Lockheed Martin SPY-1F ❼; E/F-band.
 Surface search: Litton; E/I-band ❽.
 Fire control: 2 Mk 82 (SPG-62); I/J-band ❾.
 Navigation: 2 Litton; I-band. IFF: Mk XII.
Sonars: Thomson Marconi Spherion MRS 2000 and Mk 2
 ATAS; combined active/passive towed array.

Helicopters: 1 NH90 ❿.

Programmes: Design Definition for a new class of frigates
 started in March 1997. Izar and Lockheed Martin selected
 in March 2000 and contract signed 23 June 2000. Most
 of the construction is being undertaken by Izar. Two
 Norwegian shipyards, Bergen and Kvaerner Kleven,
 are collaborating to build six blocks for the aft section
 and three blocks for the bow section of each ship. These
 blocks are to be shipped to Ferrol where final assembly
 of the first three ships is to take place. The fourth and
 fifth ships may be built in Norway. Lockheed Martin is
 developing the combat system (in conjunction with
 Kongsberg Defence & Aerospace).
Structure: The design is based on the Alvaro de Bazan class.
Operational: Despite being fitted with Lockheed Martin
 SPY-1F radar and an AEGIS-derived combat system the
 primary roles of these ships will be anti-submarine and
 anti-surface warfare.

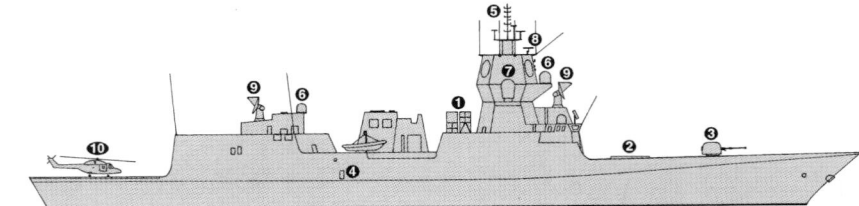

FRIDTJOF NANSEN   *(Scale 1 : 1,200), Ian Sturton* / 0105165

FRIDTJOF NANSEN   *6/2004, Camil Busquets i Vilanova* / 1043493

FRIDTJOF NANSEN
6/2004, Royal Norwegian Navy
1043492

FRIDTJOF NANSEN   *6/2004, Royal Norwegian Navy* / 1043494

SHIPBORNE AIRCRAFT

Numbers/Type: 6 NH Industries NH 90 NFH.
Operational speed: 157 kt *(291 km/h)*.
Service ceiling: 13,940 ft *(4,250 m)*.
Range: 621 n miles *(1,150 km)*.
Role/Weapon systems: Six ASW shipborne aircraft and eight with Coast Guard configuration to start entering service in 2006. Option for further ten SAR aircraft. ASW variant has crew of three. Sensors to be announced.

NH 90   *2001, NH Industries* / 0094462

Numbers/Type: 6 Westland Lynx Mk 86.
Operational speed: 125 kt *(232 km/h)*.
Service ceiling: 12,500 ft *(3,810 m)*.
Range: 320 n miles *(590 km)*.
Role/Weapon systems: Operated by Air Force on behalf of the Coast Guard for fishery protection, offshore oil protection and SAR; embarked in CG vessels and shore-based. Sensors: Search radar, FLIR may be fitted, ESM. Weapons: Generally unarmed.

LYNX   *6/2002, Royal Norwegian Navy* / 0572608

LAND-BASED MARITIME AIRCRAFT

Notes: The Air Force has a total of 56 F-16 Falcons armed with Penguin 3 ASMs.

Numbers/Type: 4 Lockheed P-3C Orion.
Operational speed: 410 kt *(760 km/h)*.
Service ceiling: 28,300 ft *(8,625 m)*.
Range: 4,000 n miles *(7,410 km)*.
Role/Weapon systems: Long-range MR and oceanic surveillance duties in peacetime, with ASW added as a war role. Updated in 1998-99 with new radars and new tactical computers. P-3Ns used by Coast Guard paid off in 1999. Sensors: APS-137(V)5 radar, ASQ-81 MAD, AQS-212 processor and computer, IFF, AAR-36 IR detection; AAR-47 ESM; ALE 47 countermeasures; sonobuoys. Weapons: ASW; 8 MUSL Stingray torpedoes, depth bombs or mines. ASV; Penguin NFT Mk 3 ASM.

P-3C   *6/2001, A Sharma* / 0130100

Numbers/Type: 12 Westland Sea King Mk 43B.
Operational speed: 125 kt *(232 km/h)*.
Service ceiling: 10,500 ft *(3,200 m)*.
Range: 630 n miles *(1,165 km)*.
Role/Weapon systems: SAR, surface search and surveillance helicopter; supplemented by civil helicopters in wartime. Two 43B delivered in May 1996; remainder updated to 43B standard. Sensors: FLIR 2000 and dual Bendix radars RDR 1500 and RDR 1300. Weapons: Generally unarmed.

SEA KING 43B   *2001, GKN Westland* / 0051448

PATROL FORCES

14 HAUK CLASS (FAST ATTACK CRAFT—MISSILE) (PTGM)

Name	No	Builders	Commissioned
HAUK	P 986	Bergens Mek Verksteder	17 Aug 1977
ØRN	P 987	Bergens Mek Verksteder	19 Jan 1979
TERNE	P 988	Bergens Mek Verksteder	13 Mar 1979
TJELD	P 989	Bergens Mek Verksteder	25 May 1979
SKARV	P 990	Bergens Mek Verksteder	17 July 1979
TEIST	P 991	Bergens Mek Verksteder	11 Sep 1979
JO	P 992	Bergens Mek Verksteder	1 Nov 1979
LOM	P 993	Bergens Mek Verksteder	15 Jan 1980
STEGG	P 994	Bergens Mek Verksteder	18 Mar 1980
FALK	P 995	Bergens Mek Verksteder	30 Apr 1980
RAVN	P 996	Westamarin A/S, Alta	20 May 1980
GRIBB	P 997	Westamarin A/S, Alta	10 July 1980
GEIR	P 998	Westamarin A/S, Alta	16 Sep 1980
ERLE	P 999	Westamarin A/S, Alta	10 Dec 1980

Displacement, tons: 120 standard; 160 full load
Dimensions, feet (metres): 120 × 20.3 × 5.9 *(36.5 × 6.2 × 1.8)*
Main machinery: 2 MTU 16V 538 TB92 diesels; 6,820 hp(m) *(5 MW)* sustained; 2 shafts
Speed, knots: 32. **Range, n miles:** 440 at 30 kt
Complement: 24 (6 officers)

Missiles: SSM: Up to 6 Kongsberg Penguin Mk 2 Mod 5; IR homing to 27 km *(14.6 n miles)* at 0.8 Mach; warhead 120 kg.
SAM: Twin Simbad launcher for Matra Sadral; IR homing to 4 km *(2.2 n miles)*; warhead 3 kg.
Guns: 1 Bofors 40 mm/70; 300 rds/min to 12 km *(6.6 n miles)*; weight of shell 0.96 kg.
Torpedoes: 2—21 in *(533 mm)* tubes. FFV Type 613; passive homing to 27 km *(14.5 n miles)* at 45 kt; warhead 240 kg.
Countermeasures: Decoys: Chaff launcher.
ESM: Argo intercept.
Combat data systems: DCN SENIT 2000 (from late 2001). Link 11.
Weapons control: Kongsberg MSI-80S or Sagem VIGY-20 optronic director.
Radars: Surface search/navigation: 2 Litton; I-band.

Programmes: Ordered 12 June 1975.
Modernisation: Simbad twin launchers for SAM fitted from 1994 to replace 20 mm gun. A further upgrade programme has extended the lives of these craft until replaced by the Skjold class or until 2015. 991, 992 and 994 were fitted with the SENIT 2000 combat data system in 2001 with the remainder of the class fitted by late 2003. Other aspects of the upgrade included a new navigation radar, an optronic director and new communications and bridge equipment. Trials on a wave-piercing bow have been conducted in 989 to improve hydrodynamic performance.
Operational: Penguin missiles are not normally embarked.

TJELD   *6/2005*, E & M Laursen* / 1151134

GEIR   *9/2005*, Guy Toremans* / 1151301

1 + 5 SKJOLD CLASS (PTGMF)

Name	No	Builders	Launched	Commissioned
SKJOLD	P 960	Kvaerner Mandal	22 Sep 1998	17 Apr 1999
STORM	P 961	Umoe Mandal	2007	2008
SKUDD	P 962	Umoe Mandal	2007	2008
STEIL	P 963	Umoe Mandal	2007	2008
GLIMT	P 964	Umoe Mandal	2008	2009
GNIST	P 965	Umoe Mandal	2008	2009

Displacement, tons: 260 full load
Dimensions, feet (metres): 153.5 × 44.3 × 7.5; 2.6 on cushion *(46.8 × 13.5 × 2.3; 0.8)*
Main machinery: COGAG: 2 Pratt & Whitney ST 40 gas turbines; 10,730 hp *(8 MW)*; 2 Pratt & Whitney ST 18 gas turbines; 5,365 hp *(4 MW)*
2 MTU 12V 183TE92 diesels (lift); 2,000 hp(m) *(1.47 MW)*
Speed, knots: 57; 44 in Sea State 3. **Range, n miles:** 800 at 40 kt
Complement: 15

Missiles: 8 SSM; 8 Kongsberg NSM.
SAM: Mistral; IR homing to 4 km *(2.2 n miles)* at 2.5 Mach; warhead 3 kg.
Guns: 1 Otobreda 76 mm/62. Super Rapid; 120 rds/min to 16 km *(8.7 n miles)*; weight of shell 6 kg.
Countermeasures: Buck Neue MASS decoys.
ESM: EDO CS 3701; intercept.
Combat data systems: DCN Senit 2000; Link 11/16.
Weapons control: Sagem VIGX-20 optronic director.
Radars: Air/surface search: Thales MRR; 3D-NG; G-band.
Navigation: I-band.
Fire control: CelsiusTech Ceros 2000; I/J-band.

Programmes: Project SMP 6081. A preproduction version (P 960) ordered 30 August 1996. This was tested by the Norwegian Navy from 1999-2001 and was under evaluation by the USN and USCG in 2001-02. The Norwegian parliament decided on 23 October 2003 that five additional vessels were to be built and that the preproduction vessel was to be rebuilt. Contract with Skjold Prime Consortium, comprising Umoe Mandal, Armaris and Kongsberg Defence & Aerospace, was signed 28 November 2003. Ships to be built at Umoe Mandal shipyard for delivery between 2008 and 2009.
Structure: SES hull with advanced stealth technology including anechoic coatings. Building on experience in US trials, a more raked bow has been adopted to improve performance into sea. The foredeck structure is also to be strengthened around the gun mounting. Two quadruple SSM launchers are to be recessed aft of the bridge. These will elevate to fire and then retract.

SKJOLD   *7/2003, Declerck/Steeghers* / 1043502

SKJOLD   *7/2003, Declerck/Steeghers* / 1043503

20 COMBATBOAT 90N (LCP)

TRONDENES KA 1	STANGENES KA 13	BRETTINGEN KA 21
HYSNES KA 2	KJØKØY KA 14	LØKHAUG KA 22
HELLEN KA 3	MØRVIKA KA 15	SØRVIKNES KA 23
TORAAS KA 4	KOPAAS KA 16	OSTERNES KA 31
MØVIK KA 5	TANGEN KA 17	FJELL KA 32
SKROLSVIK KA 11	ODDANE KA 18	LERØY KA 33
KRÅKENES KA 12	MALMØYA KA 19	

Displacement, tons: 19 full load
Dimensions, feet (metres): 52.2 × 12.5 × 2.6 *(15.9 × 3.8 × 0.8)*
Main machinery: 2 SAAB Scania DSI 14 diesels; 1,104 hp(m) *(812 kW)* or 1,251 hp(m) *(920 kW)* (KA 21-43) sustained; 2 FF 450 water-jets or 2 Kamewa FF 410 (KA 21-43)
Speed, knots: 35 or 40; 20 in Sea State 3
Range, n miles: 240 at 20 kt
Complement: 3
Military lift: 2.8 tons or 20 troops
Guns: 1—12.7 mm MG.
Radars: Navigation: I-band.

Comment: Ordered from Dockstavarvet, Sweden. Four Batch 1 units delivered for trials in July and October 1996. Three more of the class delivered in 1997, 13 in 1998. Used to carry mobile light missile units and prime method of transportation for new Coastal Ranger Commando. Similar in most details to the Swedish Coastal Artillery craft. Names are mostly taken from Coastal Fortresses.

BRETTINGEN   *4/2002, P Froud* / 0529076

7 ALUSAFE 1290 CLASS (INSHORE PATROL CRAFT) (PB)

L 4540-4546

Displacement, tons: 7.6
Dimensions, feet (metres): 43.2 × 11.5 × 2.5 *(12.9 × 3.5 × 0.75)*
Main machinery: 2 Volvo Penta TAMD 74 EDC diesels; 900 hp *(670 kW)*; 2 Kamewa K28 waterjets
Speed, knots: 42
Complement: 2 (plus 13 troops)
Guns: 2—12.7 mm MGs.

Comment: Aluminium hull. Built by Maritime Partner, Ålesund and delivered in 2002. Designed for used by the Norwegian Naval Home Guard as multifunction assault and patrol vessels by the coastal rangers. The craft are also available to support police, customs, environmental and fishery authorities.

L 4541   *6/2004, Royal Norwegian Navy* / 1043496

3 ALUSAFE 1300 CLASS (INSHORE PATROL CRAFT) (PB)

SHV 104-106

Displacement, tons: 10
Dimensions, feet (metres): 43.6 × 12.0 × 2.5 *(13.3 × 3.65 × 0.75)*
Main machinery: 2 Volvo Penta TAMD 74EDC diesels; 900 hp *(670 kW)*; 2 Kamewa K28 waterjets
Speed, knots: 40
Complement: 2 (plus 13 troops)
Guns: 2—12.7 mm MGs.

Comment: Aluminium hull. Built by Maritime Partner, Ålesund and delivered in 2003. Based at Stavanger, Bergen and Trondheim. Designed for use by the Norwegian Naval Home Guard as multifunction patrol vessels. The craft are also available to support police, customs, environmental and fishery authorities.

SHV 104   *5/2004, E & M Laursen* / 1043504

MINE WARFARE FORCES

6 OKSØY/ALTA CLASS
(MINEHUNTERS/SWEEPERS) (MHCM/MSCM)

Name	No	Builders	Commissioned
Hunters			
OKSØY	M 340	Kvaerner Mandal	24 Mar 1994
KARMØY	M 341	Kvaerner Mandal	24 Oct 1994
MÅLØY	M 342	Kvaerner Mandal	24 Mar 1995
HINNØY	M 343	Kvaerner Mandal	8 Sep 1995
Sweepers			
ALTA	M 350	Kvaerner Mandal	12 Jan 1996
OTRA	M 351	Kvaerner Mandal	8 Nov 1996

Displacement, tons: 375 full load
Dimensions, feet (metres): 181.1 × 44.6 × 8.2 (2.76 cushion) *(55.2 × 13.6 × 2.5; 0.84)*
Main machinery: 2 MTU 12V 396 TE84 diesels; 3,700 hp(m) *(2.72 MW)* sustained; 2 Kvaerner Eureka water-jets; 2 MTU 8V 396 TE54 diesels; 1,740 hp(m) *(1.28 MW/60 Hz)* sustained; lift engines
Speed, knots: 30. **Range, n miles:** 1,500 at 20 kt
Complement: 38 (12 officers) (minehunters); 32 (10 officers) (minesweepers)

Missiles: SAM: Matra Sadral twin launcher; Mistral; IR homing to 4 km *(2.2 n miles)*; warhead 3 kg.
Guns: 1 or 2 Rheinmetall 20 mm. 2—12.7 mm MGs.
Countermeasures: MCMV: 2 Pluto submersibles (minehunter); mechanical, AGATE (air gun and transducer equipment) acoustic and Elma magnetic sweep (minesweepers). Minesweeper mini torpedoes can be carried.
Radars: Navigation: 2 Racal Decca; I-band.
Sonars: Thomson Sintra/Simrad TSM 2023N; hull-mounted (minehunters); high frequency. Simrad Subsea SA 950; hull-mounted (minesweepers); high frequency.

Programmes: Order placed with Kvaerner on 9 November 1989. Four are minehunters, the remainder minesweepers.
Modernisation: Trials of the Kongsberg Simrad Hugin 1000 Autonomous Underwater Vehicle (AUV) conducted in M 341 2001-05. Designed to conduct route survey and forward mine reconnaissance. A full capability demonstration is planned for 2006. Hugin 1000 can dive to 600 m and has an endurance of 20 hours.
Structure: Design developed by the Navy in Bergen with the Defence Research Institute and Norsk Veritas and uses an air cushion created by the surface effect between two hulls. The hull is built of Fibre Reinforced Plastics (FRP) in sandwich configuration. The ROVs are carried in a large hangar and are launched by two hydraulic cranes. The minesweeper has an A frame aft for the sweep gear. SAM launcher mounted forward of the bridge.
Operational: Simrad Albatross tactical system including mapping; Cast/Del Norte mobile positioning system with GPS. The catamaran design is claimed to give higher transit speeds with lesser installed power than a traditional hull design. Other advantages are lower magnetic and acoustic signatures, clearer water for sonar operations and less susceptibility to shock. *Orkla* M 353 was lost after a catastrophic fire on 19 November 2002. M 352 and M 354 were decommissioned in 2004.

KARMØY *11/2004, Michael Nitz* / 1043497

HINNØY *8/2004, Martin Mokrus* / 1043499

ALTA *6/2005*, E & M Laursen* / 1151133

1 MINELAYER (ML)

Name	No	Builders	Commissioned
TYR (ex-*Standby Master*)	N 50	Alesund Mekaniske Verksted	1981

Displacement, tons: 495 full load
Dimensions, feet (metres): 138.8 × 33.1 × 11.5 *(42.3 × 10.1 × 3.5)*
Main machinery: 2 Deutz SBA12M816 diesels; 1,300 hp(m) *(956 kW)*; 1 shaft; cp prop; 1 MWM diesel; 150 hp(m) *(110 kW)*; bow and stern thrusters
Speed, knots: 12
Complement: 22 (7 officers)
Mines: 2 rails.
Radars: Navigation: Furuno 711 and Furuno 1011; I-band.

Comment: Former oil rig pollution control ship. Acquired in December 1993 and converted by Mjellum & Karlsen, Bergen. Recommissioned 7 March 1995 as a minelayer, and for the maintenance of controlled minefields. Carries a ROV.

TYR *5/2004, Per Körnefeldt* / 1043511

SURVEY AND RESEARCH SHIPS

1 RESEARCH SHIP (AGEH)

Name	Builders	Launched	Commissioned
MARJATA	Tangern Verft A/S	18 Dec 1992	July 1994

Displacement, tons: 7,560 full load
Dimensions, feet (metres): 267.4 × 130.9 × 19.7 *(81.5 × 39.9 × 6)*
Main machinery: Diesel-electric; 2 MTU Siemens 16V 396 TE diesels; 7,072 hp(m) *(5.2 MW)*; 2 Dresser Rand/Siemens gas-turbine generators; 9,792 hp(m) *(7.2 MW)*; 2 Siemens motors; 8,160 hp(m) *(6 MW)*; 2 Schottel 3030 thrusters. 1 Siemens motor; 2,720 hp(m); *(2 MW)*; 1 Schottel thruster (forward)
Speed, knots: 15
Complement: 14 plus 31 scientists

Helicopters: Platform for one medium

Comment: Ordered in February 1992 from Langsten Slip og Batbyggeri to replace the old ship of the same name. Called Project Minerva. Design developed by Ariel A/S, Horten. The three main superstructure-mounted cupolas contain ELINT and SIGINT equipment. Hull-reinforced to allow operations in fringe ice. Equipment includes Sperry radars, Elac sonars, Siemens TV surveillance, and a fully equipped helicopter flight deck. The unconventional hull which gives the ship an extraordinary length to beam ratio of 2:1 is said to give great stability and dynamic qualities. White hull and superstructure.

MARJATA *6/2000, Royal Norwegian Navy* / 0105173

5 SURVEY SHIPS (AGS)

Name	Displacement tons	Launched	Officers	Crew
OLJEVERN 01-04	200	1978	2	6
GEOFJORD	364	1958	2	6

Comment: Under control of Ministry of Environment based at Stavanger. *Oljevern 01* and *03* have red hulls and work for the Pollution Control Authority.

GEOFJORD *5/2002, L-G Nilsson* / 0528972

TRAINING SHIPS

2 TRAINING SHIPS (AXL)

Name	No	Builders	Commissioned
HESSA (ex-*Hitra*, ex-*Marsteinen*)	P 358	Fjellstrand, Omastrand	Jan 1978
VIGRA (ex-*Kvarven*)	P 359	Fjellstrand, Omastrand	July 1978

Displacement, tons: 39 full load
Dimensions, feet (metres): 77 × 16.4 × 3.5 *(23.5 × 5 × 1.1)*
Main machinery: 2 GM 12V-71 diesels; 1,800 hp *(1.34 MW)*; 2 shafts
Speed, knots: 20
Complement: 5 plus 13 trainees
Guns: 1 — 12.7 mm Browning MG.
Radars: Navigation: Racal Decca; I-band.

Comment: The vessels are designed for training students at the Royal Norwegian Naval Academy in navigation, manoeuvring and seamanship. All-welded aluminium hulls. Also equipped with an open bridge and a blind pilotage position below deck. 18 berths.

VIGRA *4/2002, P Froud* / 0529133

AUXILIARIES

Notes: A concept study to explore options for afloat replenishment and logistic support is to report in 2006. Potential conclusions include a multirole Ro-Ro ship and an AOR to support the new frigates. An acquisition programme, as yet unfunded, is unlikely to be initiated before 2008.

1 DEPOT SHIP (ASH/AGP)

Name	No	Builders	Commissioned
HORTEN	A 530	A/S Horten Verft	Apr 1978

Displacement, tons: 2,530 full load
Dimensions, feet (metres): 287 × 42.6 × 16.4 *(87.5 × 13 × 5)*
Main machinery: 2 Wichmann 7AX diesels; 4,200 hp(m) *(3.1 MW)*; 2 shafts; bow thruster
Speed, knots: 16.5
Complement: 86
Guns: 2 Bofors 40 mm/70.
Radars: Navigation: 2 Decca; I-band.
Helicopters: Platform only.

Comment: Contract signed 30 March 1976. Laid down 28 January 1977; launched 12 August 1977. Serves both submarines and fast attack craft. Quarters for 45 extra and can cater for 190 extra.

HORTEN *3/2001, A Sharma* / 0130096

1 SUPPLY AND RESCUE VESSEL

Name	No	Builders	Commissioned
VALKYRIEN	A 535	Ulstein Hatlo	1981

Displacement, tons: 3,000 full load
Dimensions, feet (metres): 223.1 × 47.6 × 16.4 *(68 × 14.5 × 5)*
Main machinery: Diesel-electric; 4 diesels; 10,560 hp(m) *(7.76 MW)* sustained; 2 motors; 3.14 MW; 2 shafts; 2 bow thrusters; 1,600 hp(m) *(1.18 MW)*; 1 stern thruster; 800 hp(m) *(588 kW)*
Speed, knots: 16
Complement: 13
Radars: Navigation: 2 Furuno; H/I-band.

Comment: Tug/supply ship acquired in 1994 for supply and SAR duties. Bollard pull 128 tons. Can carry a 700 ton deck load. Oil recovery equipment is also carried.

VALKYRIEN *6/2005*, E & M Laursen* / 1151139

7 COASTAL VESSELS (YPT/YDT)

Notes: Due to re-organisation of the coastal vessels, the naval districts no longer operate many of the vessels previously assigned. The following remain in service and are prefaced by two letters as follows: HT (torpedo recovery), HM (multirole), HS (tugs), HD (diving), HP (personnel), HR (rescue). *Hitra* (HP 15) is also used for training cruises. All are less than 300 tons displacement.

Name	No	Speed, knots	Commissioned	Role
VIKEN	HD 2	12	1984	Cargo (4 tons)/Passengers (40) Diving vessel
TORPEN	HM 3	12	1977	Cargo (100 tons)/Passengers (15)
KJEØY	HM 7	10	1993	Training ship/Passengers (30)
HITRA	HP 15	—	—	Passengers (30)
KARLSØY	HT 3	10	1978	Torpedo fishing vessel
SLEIPNER	HS 4	11	2002	Tug/Cargo (10 tons)
MJØLNER	HS 5	11	2002	Tug/Cargo (10 tons)

HITRA *6/2005*, E & M Laursen* / 1151138

VIKEN *7/2003, Declerck/Steeghers* / 1043508

ROYAL YACHTS

1 ROYAL YACHT (YAC)

Name	No	Builders	Commissioned
NORGE (ex-*Philante*)	A 533	Camper & Nicholson's Ltd, Southampton	1937

Displacement, tons: 1,786 full load
Dimensions, feet (metres): 263 × 38 × 15.2 *(80.2 × 11.6 × 4.6)*
Main machinery: 2 Bergen KRMB-8 diesels; 4,850 hp(m) *(3.6 MW)* sustained; 2 shafts; bow thruster
Speed, knots: 17
Complement: 50 (18 officers)
Radars: Navigation: 2 Decca; I-band.

Comment: Built to the order of the late T O M Sopwith as an escort and store vessel for the yachts *Endeavour I* and *Endeavour II*. Launched on 17 February 1937. Served in the Royal Navy as an anti-submarine escort during the Second World War, after which she was purchased by the Norwegian people for King Haakon and reconditioned as a Royal Yacht at Southampton. Can accommodate about 50 people in addition to crew. Repaired after serious fire on 7 March 1985 when the ship was fitted with a bow-thruster.

NORGE *6/2005*, E & M Laursen* / 1151137

COAST GUARD (KYSTVAKT)

1 ARCTIC CLASS (WPSOH)

Name	No	Builders	Commissioned
SVALBARD	W 303	Tangen Verft, Krager	5 Jan 2002

Displacement, tons: 6,300 full load
Dimensions, feet (metres): 340.3 × 62.7 × 21.3 *(103.7 × 19.1 × 6.5)*
Main machinery: Diesel electric; 4 diesel generators; 10 MW; 2 azimuth pods
Speed, knots: 17. **Range, n miles:** 10,000 at 13 kt
Complement: 50
Guns: 1 Bofors 57 mm/70.
Helicopters: 1 light.

Comment: Project definition completed in 1997 for an ice-reinforced vessel equipped with a helicopter. Built to Det Norske Veritas standards. Contract placed 15 December 1999 with Langsten Slip and Båtbyggeri A/S, Tomrefjord. Ship launched February 2001. Fitted for firefighting and counter-pollution work. There are two motor cutters and a sea-raider type dinghy. The ship is to be refitted at Fiskerstrand Verft in 2006.

SVALBARD   *7/2003, Freddie Philips* / 0572601

7 CHARTERED SHIPS (WPBO)

Name	No	Tonnage	Completion
EIGUN	W 310	342	1959
ÅLESUND	W 312	1,357	1996
TROMSÖ	W 313	1,970	1997
NORDSJØBAS	W 315	814	1978
MALENE ØSTERVOLD	W 316	1,678	1965
LAFJORD	W 317	814	1978
HARSTAD	W 318	3132	2004

Comment: *Lafjord* and *Nordsjøbas* chartered in 1980 and *Thorsteinson* in 1999. All armed with one 40 mm/60 gun. Two more ships have been built to Coast Guard requirements and leased for 10 years with an option to buy after five. *Tromsö* operates around north Norway while *Ålesund* is based in the south. Some ships are operated with two crews, changing over every three weeks.

EIGUN   *7/2003, Per Körnefeldt* / 0572602

3 NORDKAPP CLASS (WPSOH)

Name	No	Builders	Launched	Commissioned
NORDKAPP	W 320	Bergens Mek Verksteder	2 Apr 1980	25 Apr 1981
SENJA	W 321	Horten Verft	16 Mar 1980	6 Mar 1981
ANDENES	W 322	Haugesund Mek Verksted	21 Mar 1981	30 Jan 1982

Displacement, tons: 3,240 full load
Dimensions, feet (metres): 346 × 47.9 × 16.1 *(105.5 × 14.6 × 4.9)*
Main machinery: 4 Wichmann 9AXAG diesels; 16,163 hp(m) *(11.9 MW)*; 2 shafts
Speed, knots: 23
Range, n miles: 7,500 at 15 kt
Complement: 52 (6 aircrew)

Missiles: SSM: Fitted for 6 Kongsberg Penguin II but not embarked.
Guns: 1 Bofors 57 mm/70; 200 rds/min to 17 km *(9.3 n miles)*; weight of shell 2.4 kg.
  4 Rheinmetall 20 mm/20; 1,000 rds/min to 2 km.
Torpedoes: 6—324 mm US Mk 32 (2 triple) tubes. Honeywell Mk 46; anti-submarine; active/passive homing to 11 km *(5.9 n miles)* at 40 kt; warhead 44 kg. Mountings only in peacetime.
Depth charges: 1 rack.
Countermeasures: Decoys: 2 chaff launchers.
Combat data systems: Navkis or EDO (after modernisation). SATCOM can be carried.
Weapons control: Sagem Vigy 20 optronic director.
Radars: Air/surface search: Plessey AWS 5; E/F-band or DRS Technologies SPS 67(V)3; G-band.
  Navigation: 2 Racal Decca 1226; I-band.
  Fire control: Philips 9LV 218 Mk 2; J-band.
Sonars: Simrad SP 270; hull-mounted; 24—30 kHz.

Helicopters: 1 Westland Lynx Mk 86.

Programmes: In November 1977 the Coast Guard budget was cut resulting in a reduction of the building programme from seven to three ships.
Modernisation: A modernisation programme was conducted 2001-03. Upgrades included an optronic director, new hull-mounted sonar, new air search radar and combat data system. A further refit programme for all three ships is to be conducted by Fiskerstrand Verft from January 2006.
Structure: Ice strengthened. Fitted for firefighting, anti-pollution work, all with two motor cutters and a Gemini-type dinghy. SATCOM fitted for Gulf deployment.
Operational: Bunks for 109. War complement increases to 76.

ANDENES   *6/2005*, E & M Laursen* / 1151136

9 FISHERY PROTECTION SHIPS (WPSOH)

Name	No	Tonnage	Completion
TITRAN	KV 1	184	1992
KONGSØY	KV 2	331	1958
AGDER	KV 5	140	1974
GARSØY	KV 6	195	1988
ÅHAV	KV 7	50	1981
BARENTSHAV	KV 22	318	1957
SJØVEIEN	KV 25	330	1964
NYSLEPPEN	KV 28	343	1967
THORSTEINSON	W 319	272	1960

Comment: An Inshore Patrol Force was established in January 1997. This comprises mostly chartered ships with KV pennant numbers. KV 1-7 are coastal cutters. Five new ships are to replace older ships from 2006.

GARSØY   *6/2005*, Globke Collection* / 1151135

0 + 5 (5) OFFSHORE PATROL VESSELS (PBO)

Name	No	Builders	Commissioned
NORNEN	—	Gryfia Shipyard, Szczecin	2006
FRAM	—	Gryfia Shipyard, Szczecin	2006
HEIMDAL	—	Gryfia Shipyard, Szczecin	2007
NJORD	—	Gryfia Shipyard, Szczecin	2007
TOR	—	Gryfia Shipyard, Szczecin	2007

Displacement, tons: 710 full load
Dimensions, feet (metres): 154.8 × 33.8 × 10.8 *(47.2 × 10.3 × 3.3)*
Main machinery: Diesel-electric; 2 azimuth thrusters
Speed, knots: 16
Complement: 20

Comment: Contract awarded in February 2005 to Remøy Management and Remøy Shipping for the construction of five new vessels with an option for a further five. The vessels are to be owned and managed by the shipping companies and chartered to the Coast Guard for an initial period of 15 years. The design, developed by Skipsteknisk AS, is called ST-610. The ships are to be employed out to 24 n miles from the coast and are to be equipped to conduct towing, counter-pollution operations, fire-fighting and general patrol duties. Two fast rescue craft are to be carried and there is space for 100 m³ of cargo space on deck and 90 m³ in the hold. The ships are to enter service from mid-2006.

ST-610 (artist's impression)   *2/2005, Skipsteknisk AS* / 1043495

Oman

Country Overview

The Sultanate of Oman is an independent Middle-East state extending along the south-east coast of the Arabian Peninsula. It is bordered to the south-west by the Republic of Yemen, to the west by Saudi Arabia and to the north-west by the United Arab Emirates which separates a small exclave on the Musandam peninsula, on the south side of the Strait of Hormuz, from the rest of the country. Masirah island and the Khuriya Muriya Islands lie off the south-east coast. With an area of 82,030 square miles, it has a 1,129 n mile coastline with the Indian Ocean and Gulf of Oman. The capital, largest city and principal port is Muscat while there is a further port at Salalah. Territorial seas (12 n miles) are claimed. An EEZ (200 n miles) has also been claimed but its limits have only been partly defined by boundary agreements.

Headquarters Appointments

Commander Royal Navy of Oman:
   Rear Admiral (Liwaa Rukn Bahry) Salim bin Abdullah bin Rashid al Alawi
Principal Staff Officer:
   Commodore (Ameed) Abdullah Khamis Abdullah Al-Raisi
Director General Operations and Plans:
   Commodore (Ameed) Abdullah Khamis Abdullah Al-Raisi
Commander Coast Guard:
   Captain (Aqeed Bahry) Hamdan bin Marhoon Al Mamary
Commander Royal Yacht Squadron:
   Commodore (Ameed) J M Knapp

Bases

Said bin Sultan, Widam A'Sahil (main base, dockyard and shiplift)
Musandam
Muaskar al Murtafa'a (headquarters)

Personnel

(a)   2006: 4,500 officers and men
(b)   Voluntary service

CORVETTES

2 QAHIR CLASS (FSGMH)

Name	No	Builders	Laid down	Launched	Commissioned
QAHIR AL AMWAJ	C 31	Vosper Thornycroft, Woolston	21 May 1993	21 Sep 1994	3 Sep 1996
AL MUA'ZZAR	C 32	Vosper Thornycroft, Woolston	4 Apr 1994	26 Sep 1995	13 Apr 1997

Displacement, tons: 1,450 full load
Dimensions, feet (metres): 274.6 oa; 249.3 wl × 37.7 × 11.8 *(83.7; 76 × 11.5 × 3.6)*
Main machinery: CODAD; 4 Crossley SEMT-Pielstick 16 PA6V 280 STC; 28,160 hp(m) *(20.7 MW)* sustained; 2 shafts; Kamewa cp props
Speed, knots: 28
Range, n miles: 4,000 at 10 kt
Complement: 76 (14 officers) plus 3 spare

Missiles: SSM: 8 Aerospatiale MM 40 Block 2 Exocet ❶; inertial cruise; active radar homing to 70 km *(40 n miles)* at 0.9 Mach; warhead 165 kg; sea-skimmer. SAM: Thomson-CSF Crotale NG octuple launcher ❷; 16 VT1; command line of sight guidance; radar/IR homing to 13 km *(7 n miles)* at 2.4 Mach; warhead 14 kg.
Guns: 1 OTO Melara 3 in *(76 mm)*/62 Super Rapid ❸; 120 rds/min to 16 km *(8.7 n miles)*; weight of shell 6 kg.
2 Oerlikon/Royal Ordnance 20 mm GAM-BO1 ❹.
2 — 7.62 mm MGs.
Torpedoes: 6 — 324 mm (2 triple) tubes may be fitted in due course.
Countermeasures: Decoys: 2 Barricade 12-barrelled chaff and IR launchers ❺.
ESM: Thomson-CSF DR 3000 ❻; intercept.
Combat data systems: Signaal/Thomson-CSF TACTICOS; Link Y; SATCOM.
Weapons control: Signaal STING optronic and radar tracker ❼; 2 Signaal optical directors.
Radars: Air/surface search: Signaal MW08 ❽; G-band.
Fire control: Signaal STING ❼; I/J-band. Thomson-CSF DRBV 51C ❾; J-band (for Crotale).
Navigation: Kelvin Hughes 1007; I-band.
Sonars: Thomson Sintra/BAeSEMA ATAS; towed array; active search; 3 kHz (may be fitted).

Helicopters: Platform for 1 Super Lynx type ❿.

Programmes: Vosper Thornycroft signed the Muheet Project contract on 5 April 1992. First steel cut 23 September 1992. Q 31 accepted on 27 March 1996, and Q 32 on 26

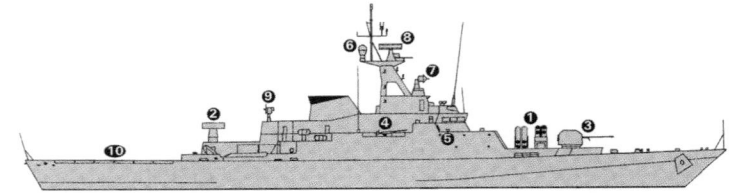

QAHIR AL AMWAJ *(Scale 1 : 900), Ian Sturton* / 0506243

AL MUA'ZZAR *6/2005*, E & M Laursen* / 1151140

November 1996. Commissioned after operational work up in the UK, and on return to Oman. Names mean Conqueror of the Waves, and The Supported.
Structure: The ship is based on the Vigilance class design with enhanced stealth features. It is possible lightweight torpedo tubes may be fitted. The towed array, if fitted, adds another 8 tons on the stern but does not affect the helicopter deck. RAM (Radar Absorbent Material) is widely used on the superstructure.
Operational: The helicopter platform can support a Super Puma sized aircraft.

QAHIR AL AMWAJ *10/2004* / 1151305

1 PATROL SHIP (FSH/AXL/AGS)

Name	No	Builders	Commissioned
AL MABRUKAH (ex-*Al Said*)	Q 30 (ex-A 1)	Brooke Marine, Lowestoft	1971

Displacement, tons: 900 full load
Dimensions, feet (metres): 203.4 × 35.1 × 9.8 *(62 × 10.7 × 3)*
Main machinery: 2 Paxman Valenta 12CM diesels; 5,000 hp *(3.73 MW)* sustained; 2 shafts
Speed, knots: 12
Complement: 39 (7 officers) plus 32 trainees
Guns: 1 Bofors 40 mm/70. 2 Oerlikon 20 mm A41A.
Countermeasures: Decoys: Wallop Barricade 18-barrelled chaff launcher.
ESM: Racal Cutlass; radar warning.
Radars: Surface search: Racal Decca TM 1226; I-band.
Helicopters: Platform only.

Comment: Built by Brooke Marine, Lowestoft. Launched 7 April 1970 as a yacht for the Sultan of Oman. Carried on board is one Rotork landing craft. Converted to training/patrol ship in 1983 with enlarged helicopter deck, additional accommodation and armament. Re-classified as a corvette and pennant number changed in 1997. Fitted with survey equipment in 2000, as an additional role.

AL MABRUKAH   *6/2003, Royal Navy of Oman* / 0589799

SHIPBORNE AIRCRAFT

Numbers/Type: 16 GKN Westland Super Lynx 300.
Operational speed: 120 kt *(222 km/h)*.
Service ceiling: 10,000 ft *(3,048 m)*.
Range: 320 n miles *(593 km)*.
Role/Weapon systems: Contract signed 19 January 2002. First three delivered 24 June 2004. Roles likely to include ASW and ASV. To be operated by Air Force.

SUPER LYNX
7/2004, K Shaw/Jane's
0566685

PATROL FORCES

Notes: 'Project Khareef' calls for the design, construction and support of three OPVs for delivery to the RNO from 2009. VT Shipbuilding selected as preferred bidder on 13 April 2006. A revised statement of requirements issued in 2004 including the capability to operate an embarked helicopter. The length of the ship is likely to be of the order of 100 m. A contract is expected in late 2006.

3 AL BUSHRA CLASS (PBO)

Name	No	Builders	Laid down	Launched	Commissioned
AL BUSHRA	Z 1	CMN, Cherbourg/Wudam Dockyard	10 Nov 1993	3 May 1995	15 June 1995
AL MANSOOR	Z 2	CMN, Cherbourg/Wudam Dockyard	12 Apr 1994	3 May 1995	10 Aug 1995
AL NAJAH	Z 3	CMN, Cherbourg/Wudam Dockyard	27 June 1994	5 Mar 1996	15 Apr 1996

Displacement, tons: 475 full load
Dimensions, feet (metres): 178.6 × 26.2 × 8.9 *(54.5 × 8 × 2.7)*
Main machinery: 2 MTU 16V 538 TB93 diesels; 8,000 hp(m) *(5.88 MW)* sustained; 2 shafts
Speed, knots: 24. **Range, n miles:** 2,400 at 15 kt
Complement: 43 (8 officers)

Guns: 1 OTO Melara 76 mm/62 Compact; 85 rds/min to 16 km *(8.7 n miles)*; weight of shell 6 kg.
2 Oerlikon/Royal Ordnance 20 mm GAM-BO1.
2 — 12.7 mm MGs.

Countermeasures: Decoys: Plessey Barricade chaff launcher.
ESM: Thomson-CSF DR 3000; intercept.
Weapons control: CelsiusTech 9LV 207 Mk 3 command system and optronic director.
Radars: Surface search: Kelvin Hughes 1007 ARPA; I-band.

Programmes: Project Mawj order for three, with an option on five more, on 1 September 1993. The ships have had additional weapon systems fitted in Wudam dockyard.
Structure: Same hull design as the French P 400 class. 20 mm guns, and countermeasures were not fitted at

Cherbourg and are planned to be installed in due course. 76 mm guns were fitted from 1998 from deleted Al Waafi class. The plan to fit torpedoes and sonars has been shelved.
Operational: First pair arrived in Oman on 28 September 1995, last one on 29 June 1996. Pennant numbers have been changed from B to Z.

AL MANSOOR   *6/2003, Royal Navy of Oman* / 0589798

For details of the latest updates to *Jane's Fighting Ships* online and to discover the additional information available exclusively to online subscribers please visit
jfs.janes.com

4 DHOFAR (PROVINCE) CLASS
(FAST ATTACK CRAFT — MISSILE) (PGGF)

Name	No	Builders	Launched	Commissioned
DHOFAR	Z 10	Vosper Thornycroft	14 Oct 1981	7 Aug 1982
AL SHARQIYAH	Z 11	Vosper Thornycroft	2 Dec 1982	5 Dec 1983
AL BAT'NAH	Z 12	Vosper Thornycroft	4 Nov 1982	18 Jan 1984
MUSSANDAM	Z 14	Vosper Thornycroft	19 Mar 1988	31 Mar 1989

Displacement, tons: 311 light; 394 full load
Dimensions, feet (metres): 186 × 26.9 × 7.9 (56.7 × 8.2 × 2.4)
Main machinery: 4 Paxman Valenta 18CM diesels; 15,000 hp (11.2 MW) sustained; 4 shafts; auxiliary propulsion; 2 motors; 200 hp (149 kW)
Speed, knots: 38. **Range, n miles:** 2,000 at 18 kt
Complement: 45 (5 officers) plus 14 trainees

Missiles: SSM: 8 (6 in Z 10) Aerospatiale MM 40 Exocet; inertial cruise; active radar homing to 70 km (40 n miles) at 0.9 Mach; warhead 165 kg; sea-skimmer.
Guns: 1 OTO Melara 3 in (76 mm)/62 compact; 85 rds/min to 16 km (8.7 n miles); weight of shell 6 kg.
2 Breda 40 mm/70 (twin); 300 rds/min to 12.5 km (6.8 n miles); weight of shell 0.96 kg. 2—20 mm.
Countermeasures: Decoys: 2 Wallop Barricade fixed triple barrels; for chaff and IR flares.
ESM: Racal Cutlass; radar warning.
ECM: Scorpion; jammer.
Weapons control: Sperry Sea Archer (B 10). Philips 9LV 307 (remainder).
Radars: Air/surface search: Plessey AWS 4 or AWS 6; E/F-band.
Fire control: Philips 9LV 307; I/J-band.
Navigation: KH 1007 ARPA; I-band.

Programmes: First ordered in 1980, two more in January 1981 and fourth in January 1986.
Structure: Similar to Kenyan Nyayo class. Mast structures are different dependent on radars fitted.
Operational: Pennant numbers have been changed from B to Z.

AL BAT'NAH · *6/2001, Royal Navy of Oman* / 0114772

DHOFAR · *6/2003, Royal Navy of Oman* / 0567467

4 SEEB (VOSPER 25) CLASS (COASTAL PATROL CRAFT) (PB)

Name	No	Builders	Commissioned
SEEB	Z 20	Vosper Private, Singapore	15 Mar 1981
SHINAS	Z 21	Vosper Private, Singapore	15 Mar 1981
SADH	Z 22	Vosper Private, Singapore	15 Mar 1981
KHASSAB	Z 23	Vosper Private, Singapore	15 Mar 1981

Displacement, tons: 74 full load
Dimensions, feet (metres): 82.8 × 19 × 5.2 (25 × 5.8 × 1.6)
Main machinery: 2 MTU 12V 331 TC92 diesels; 2,660 hp(m) (1.96 MW) sustained; 2 shafts
1 Cummins N-855M diesel for slow cruising; 189 hp (141 kW) sustained; 1 shaft
Speed, knots: 25; 8 (Cummins diesel). **Range, n miles:** 750 at 14 kt
Complement: 13
Guns: 1 Oerlikon 20 mm GAM-BO1. 2—7.62 mm MGs.
Radars: Surface search: Racal Decca 1226; I-band.

Comment: Arrived in Oman on 19 May 1981 having been ordered one month earlier. The craft were built on speculation and completed in 1980. Pennant numbers have been changed from B to Z.

SADH · *10/2004* / 1151306

AMPHIBIOUS FORCES

Notes: (1) There are also some French-built Havas Mk 8 two-man SDVs in service.
(2) Following the issue of a restricted request for tender for a multipurpose high-speed sealift vessel, responses closed in March 2003. It is understood that the broad requirement is for a vessel, built to commercial standards, capable of transporting a company group (150 troops) and its equipment. Folding stern and bow ramps are thought to be required but the vessel is not to be fitted with a flight deck. Powered by two diesel engines, the vessel is to have a cruising speed of about 30 kt and a top speed of over 35 kt. With an unrefuelled range of about 500 n miles, the ship would operate in an intra-theatre sealift role. It is expected that the ship will be armed with self-defence weapons and have a complement of 10-12 people. A 40 m catamaran design is a potential contender but the whole project may have been overtaken by the order for an LCT in 2005.

1 LANDING SHIP — LOGISTIC (LSTH)

Name	No	Builders	Commissioned
NASR AL BAHR	A 2	Brooke Marine, Lowestoft	6 Feb 1985

Displacement, tons: 2,500 full load
Dimensions, feet (metres): 305 × 50.8 × 8.5 (93 × 15.5 × 2.6)
Main machinery: 2 Paxman Valenta 18 CM diesels; 7,500 hp (5.6 MW) sustained; 2 shafts; cp props
Speed, knots: 12
Range, n miles: 5,500 at 15 kt
Complement: 104 (13 officers)
Military lift: 7 MBT or 400 tons cargo; 190 troops; 2 LCVPs
Guns: 2 Breda 40 mm/70 (1 twin). 2 Oerlikon 20 mm GAM-BO1. 2—12.7 mm MGs.
Countermeasures: Decoys: Wallop Barricade double layer chaff launchers.
Weapons control: PEAB 9LV 107 GFCS and CSEE Lynx optical sight.
Radars: Surface search/navigation: 2 Racal Decca 1226; I-band.
Helicopters: Platform for Super Puma.

Comment: Ordered 18 May 1982. Launched 16 May 1984. Similar to Algerian LSLs. Carries one 16 ton crane. Bow and stern ramps. Full naval command facilities. The forward ramp is of two sections measuring length 59 ft (when extended) × 16.5 ft breadth (18 × 5 m), and the single section stern ramp measures 14 × 16.5 ft (4.3 × 5 m). Both hatches can support a 60 ton tank. The tank deck side bulkheads extend 7.5 ft (2.25 m) above the upper deck between the forecastle and the forward end of the superstructure, and provides two hatch openings to the tank deck below. Positioned between the hatches is a 2 ton crane with athwartship travel. New engine exhaust system and funnel fitted in 1997. Aft Oerlikon gun removed. Ship is also used as a ratings' training vessel. Pennant number has been changed from L to A.

NASR AL BAHR · *2/2002, A Sharma* / 0533304

3 LCMs (LSTH)

Name	No	Builders	Commissioned
SABA AL BAHR	A 8 (ex-C 8)	Vosper Private, Singapore	17 Sep 1981
AL DOGHAS	A 9 (ex-C 9)	Vosper Private, Singapore	10 Jan 1983
AL TEMSAH	A 10 (ex-C 10)	Vosper Private, Singapore	12 Feb 1983

Displacement, tons: 230 full load
Dimensions, feet (metres): 108.2 (83.6, C 8) × 24.3 × 4.3 (33 (25.5) × 7.4 × 1.3)
Main machinery: 2 Caterpillar 3408TA diesels; 1,880 hp (1.4 MW) sustained; 2 shafts
Speed, knots: 8
Range, n miles: 1,400 at 8 kt
Complement: 11
Military lift: 100 tons
Radars: Navigation: Furuno 701; I-band.

Comment: First one launched 30 June 1981. Second pair of similar but not identical ships, launched 12 November and 15 December 1982. Pennant numbers have been changed from L to A.

AL TEMSAH · *6/2003, Royal Navy of Oman* / 0567468

0 + 1 LANDING CRAFT (LCT)

AL MUNASR

Displacement, tons: 850 approx
Dimensions, feet (metres): 210 × 39.4 × 8.7 *(64.0 × 12.0 × 2.7)*
Main machinery: 2 Caterpillar 3508 diesels; 3,620 hp *(2.7 MW)*; 2 shafts
Speed, knots: 11
Complement: 19 (plus 56 troops)
Military lift: Military vehicles

Comment: The Project Mahmal contract was placed with Abu Dhabi Ship Building on 13 March 2005. The vessel is likely to be similar to those delivered to the UAE in 2004. Details are speculative. Launch of the ship is planned for July 2006 with delivery to follow in September 2006.

1 LCU (LSTH)

Name	No	Builders	Commissioned
AL NEEMRAN	A 7 (ex-C 7)	Lewis Offshore, Stornoway	1979

Measurement, tons: 85 dwt
Dimensions, feet (metres): 84 × 24 × 6 *(25.5 × 7.4 × 1.8)*
Main machinery: 2 diesels; 300 hp *(220 kW)*; 2 shafts
Speed, knots: 7/8
Complement: 6
Radars: Navigation: Furuno; I-band.

Comment: Second of class deleted in 1993. Pennant number has been changed from L to A.

TRAINING SHIPS

1 SAIL TRAINING SHIP (AXS)

Name	No	Builders	Commissioned
SHABAB OMAN (ex-*Captain Scott*)	S 1	Herd and Mackenzie, Buckie, Scotland	1979

Displacement, tons: 386 full load
Dimensions, feet (metres): 144.3 × 27.9 × 15.1 *(44 × 8.5 × 4.6)*
Main machinery: 2 Gardner diesels; 460 hp *(343 kW)*; 2 shafts
Speed, knots: 10 (diesels)
Complement: 20 (5 officers) plus 3 officers and 24 trainees

Comment: Topsail schooner built in 1971 and taken over from Dulverton Trust in 1977 used for sail training. Name means Omani Youth.

SHABAB OMAN *6/2005*, Royal Navy of Oman* / 1151141

AUXILIARIES

Notes: In addition to the listed vessels there are four 12 m Cheverton Work boats (W 41-44) and eight 8 m Work boats (W 4-11).

1 SUPPLY SHIP (AKS)

Name	No	Builders	Launched	Commissioned
AL SULTANA	T 1 (ex-A 2, ex-S 2)	Conoship, Groningen	18 May 1975	4 June 1975

Measurement, tons: 1,380 dwt
Dimensions, feet (metres): 215.6 × 35 × 13.5 *(65.7 × 10.7 × 4.2)*
Main machinery: 1 Mirrlees Blackstone diesel; 1,120 hp(m) *(835 kW)*; 1 shaft
Speed, knots: 11
Complement: 20
Radars: Navigation: Racal Decca TM 1226; I-band.

Comment: Major refit in 1992. Has a 1 ton crane. Pennant number changed in 1997 and again in 2002.

AL SULTANA *4/2002, Schaeffer/Marsan* / 0533305

ROYAL YACHTS

Notes: The Royal Yacht Squadron of Oman is a distinct service that is not part of the Royal Navy of Oman. Based at Muscat, the squadron consists of three major units and a number of smaller craft.

1 ROYAL YACHT (YAC)

Name	No	Builders	Commissioned
AL SAID	—	Picchiotti SpA, Viareggio	July 1982

Displacement, tons: 3,800 full load
Dimensions, feet (metres): 340.5 × 62.4 × 15.4 *(103.8 × 19.0 × 4.7)*
Main machinery: 2 GMT A 420.6 H diesels; 8,400 hp(m) *(6.17 MW)* sustained; 2 shafts; cp props; bow thruster
Speed, knots: 18
Complement: 156 (16 officers)
Radars: Navigation: Decca TM 1226C; ACS 1230C; I-band.

Comment: Fitted with helicopter deck and fin stabilisers. Carries three Puma C service launches and one Rotork beach landing craft. A variety of small arms carried.

AL SAID *4/2002, A Sharma* / 0533307

1 SUPPORT SHIP (AKSH)

Name	No	Builders	Launched	Commissioned
FULK AL SALAMAH (ex-*Ghubat Al Salamah*)	—	Bremer-Vulkan	29 Aug 1986	3 Apr 1987

Measurement, tons: 10,797 grt; 3,239 net
Dimensions, feet (metres): 447.5 × 68.9 × 19.7 *(136.4 × 21 × 6)*
Main machinery: 4 Fincantieri GMT A 420.6 H diesels; 16,800 hp(m) *(12.35 MW)* sustained; 2 shafts; cp props
Speed, knots: 19.5
Military lift: 240 troops
Radars: Navigation: 2 Racal Decca; I-band.
Helicopters: Up to 2 AS 332C Super Pumas.

Comment: Primary role is to support the Royal Yacht on deployments. Secondary roles include government, environmental and training duties. Reported to be fitted with Javelin air-defence missile system.

FULK AL SALAMAH *10/2001, A Sharma* / 0126314

1 ROYAL DHOW (YAC)

Name	No	Builders	Commissioned
ZINAT AL BIHAAR	—	—	1988

Displacement, tons: 510 light
Dimensions, feet (metres): 200.2 × 32.2 × 12.8 (61 × 9.8 × 3.9)
Main machinery: 2 Siemens motors; 965 hp (720 kW); 2 shafts
Speed, knots: 11.5

Comment: Three-masted wooden sailing vessel built in Oman on traditional lines.

ZINAT AL BIHAAR   4/2004, Derek Fox / 0589797

POLICE

Notes: (1) In addition to the vessels listed below there are several harbour craft including a Cheverton 8 m work boat *Zahra 24, Zahra 16* and a fireboat pennant number *10*. There are also two Pilatus aircraft for SAR.
(2) 15 FPBs between 11 and 30 m may be ordered in due course. These could be for the Navy if it takes over Fishery Protection duties from the Police.

ZAHRA 16   6/2003, Hartmut Ehlers / 0567471

3 CG 29 TYPE (COASTAL PATROL CRAFT) (PB)

HARAS 7 H 7   HARAS 9 H 9   HARAS 10 H 10

Displacement, tons: 84 full load
Dimensions, feet (metres): 94.8 × 17.7 × 4.3 (28.9 × 5.4 × 1.3)
Main machinery: 2 MTU 12V 331 TC92 diesels; 2,660 hp(m) (1.96 MW) sustained; 2 shafts
Speed, knots: 25. **Range, n miles:** 600 at 15 kt
Complement: 13
Guns: 2 Oerlikon 20 mm GAM-BO1.
Radars: Navigation: Racal Decca 1226; I-band.

Comment: Built by Karlskrona Varvet. Commissioned in 1981-82. GRP Sandwich hulls.

HARAS 9   12/2000 / 0114776

0 + 3 FAST PATROL CRAFT (PBF)

Displacement, tons: 52 full load
Dimensions, feet (metres): 88.6 × 17.9 × 4 (27 × 5.5 × 1.2)
Main machinery: 3 diesels; 16,200 hp (12.9 MW); 3 surface drives or waterjets
Speed, knots: 50. **Range, n miles:** 1,200 at 30 kt
Complement: 9 (3 officers)
Guns: 1 — 12.7 mm MG. 2 — 7.62 mm MGs.
Radars: Navigation: I-band.

Comment: Order placed on 9 June 2005 with United States Marine, New Orleans, for three craft under the Foreign Military Sales programme. The craft are stretched versions of the Isla class built in the 1990s for the Mexican Navy. These were built to an XFPB (extra fast patrol boat) design with Deep Vee hulls and of FRP/Kevlar construction. The precise details of the Omani craft have not been released but are expected to be similar. The vessels are to be delivered by May 2007 and the contract includes a training and support package.

1 P 1903 TYPE (COASTAL PATROL CRAFT) (PB)

HARAS 8 H 8

Displacement, tons: 32 full load
Dimensions, feet (metres): 63 × 15.7 × 5.2 (19.2 × 4.8 × 1.6)
Main machinery: 2 MTU 8V 331 TC92 diesels; 1,770 hp(m) (1.3 MW); 2 shafts
Speed, knots: 30. **Range, n miles:** 1,650 at 17 kt
Complement: 10
Guns: 2 — 12.7 mm MGs.
Radars: Navigation: Racal Decca 1226; I-band.

Comment: Built by Le Comte, Netherlands. Commissioned August 1981. Type 1903 Mk III.

HARAS 8   10/1992, Hartmut Ehlers / 0506067

1 CG 27 TYPE (COASTAL PATROL CRAFT) (PB)

HARAS 6 H 6

Displacement, tons: 53 full load
Dimensions, feet (metres): 78.7 × 18 × 6.2 (24 × 5.5 × 1.9)
Main machinery: 2 MTU 12V 331 TC92 diesels; 2,660 hp(m) (1.96 MW) sustained; 2 shafts
Speed, knots: 25
Complement: 11
Guns: 1 Oerlikon 20 mm GAM-BO1.
Radars: Navigation: Furuno 701; I-band.

Comment: Completed in 1980 by Karlskrona Varvet. GRP hull.

HARAS 6   10/1992, Hartmut Ehlers / 0506068

14 RODMAN 58 CLASS (PB)

Displacement, tons: 19 full load
Dimensions, feet (metres): 59.0 × 16.0 × 3.9 (18.0 × 4.9 × 1.2)
Main machinery: 2 diesels; 2,000 hp (1.49 MW); 2 waterjets
Speed, knots: 34. **Range, n miles:** 450 at 17 kt
Complement: 5
Radars: Navigation: I-band.

Comment: GRP hull. Built in 2002-03 by Rodman, Vigo.

RODMAN 58   11/2004*, Rodman / 1151307

1 P 2000 TYPE (COASTAL PATROL CRAFT) (PB)

DHEEB AL BAHAR 1 Z 1

Displacement, tons: 80 full load
Dimensions, feet (metres): 68.2 × 19 × 5 *(20.8 × 5.8 × 1.5)*
Main machinery: 2 MTU 12V 396 TB93 diesels; 3,260 hp(m) *(2.4 MW)* sustained; 2 shafts
Speed, knots: 40. **Range, n miles:** 423 at 36 kt; 700 at 18 kt
Guns: 1 — 12.7 mm MG.
Radars: Surface search: Furuno 701; I-band.

Comment: Delivered January 1985 by Watercraft Ltd, Shoreham, UK. GRP hull. Similar to UK Archer class. Carries SATNAV.

DHEEB AL BAHAR 1 6/2003, *Hartmut Ehlers* / 0589794

2 D 59116 TYPE (COASTAL PATROL CRAFT) (PB)

DHEEB AL BAHAR 2 Z 2   **DHEEB AL BAHAR 3** Z 3

Displacement, tons: 65 full load
Dimensions, feet (metres): 75.5 × 17.1 × 3.9 *(23 × 5.2 × 1.2)*
Main machinery: 2 MTU 12V 396 TB93 diesels; 3,260 hp(m) *(2.4 MW)* sustained; 2 shafts
Speed, knots: 36. **Range, n miles:** 420 at 30 kt
Complement: 11
Guns: 1 — 12.7 mm MG.
Radars: Surface search: Furuno 711-2; Furuno 2400; I-band.

Comment: Built by Yokohama Yacht Co, Japan. Commissioned in 1988.

DHEEB AL BAHAR 3 6/2003, *Hartmut Ehlers* / 0567470

5 INSHORE PATROL CRAFT (PBI)

ZAHRA 14 Z 14   **ZAHRA 15** Z 15   **ZAHRA 17** Z 17   **ZAHRA 18** Z 18   **ZAHRA 21** Z 21

Displacement, tons: 16; 18 *(Zahra 18 and 21)* full load
Dimensions, feet (metres): 45.6 × 14.1 × 4.6 *(13.9 × 4.3 × 1.4)*
52.5 × 13.8 × 7.5 *(16 × 4.2 × 2.3)* (Zahra 18 and 21)
Main machinery: 2 Cummins VTA-903M diesels; 643 hp *(480 kW)*; 2 shafts
Speed, knots: 36
Range, n miles: 510 at 22 kt
Complement: 5 — 6
Guns: 1 or 2 — 7.62 mm MGs.
Radars: Navigation: Decca 101; I-band.

Comment: *Zahra 14, 15* and *17* built by Watercraft, Shoreham, UK and completed in 1981. *Zahra 21* completed by Emsworth SB in 1987 to a slightly different design. *Zahra 18* built by Lecomte in 1987.

ZAHRA 17 (alongside Zahra 14) 6/2003, *Hartmut Ehlers* / 0567472

1 DIVING CRAFT (YDT)

ZAHRA 27 Z 27

Displacement, tons: 13 full load
Dimensions, feet (metres): 59 × 12.4 × 3.6 *(18 × 3.8 × 1.1)*
Main machinery: 2 Volvo Penta AQD70D diesels; 430 hp(m) *(316 kW)* sustained; 2 shafts
Speed, knots: 20
Complement: 4
Guns: 2 — 7.62 mm MGs.

Comment: Rotork Type, the last of several logistic support craft, delivered in 1981 and now used as a diving boat. Similar craft used by the Navy.

ZAHRA 27 6/2003, *Hartmut Ehlers* / 0567469

5 VOSPER 75 FT TYPE (COASTAL PATROL CRAFT) (PB)

HARAS 1-5 H 1-5

Displacement, tons: 50 full load
Dimensions, feet (metres): 75 × 20 × 5.9 *(22.9 × 6.1 × 1.8)*
Main machinery: 2 Caterpillar D 348 diesels; 1,450 hp *(1.08 MW)* sustained; 2 shafts
Speed, knots: 24.5. **Range, n miles:** 1,000 at 11 kt
Complement: 11
Guns: 1 Oerlikon 20 mm GAM-BO1.
Radars: Navigation: Decca 101; I-band.

Comment: First four completed 22 December 1975 by Vosper Thornycroft. GRP hulls. *Haras 5* commissioned November 1978.

HARAS 3 3/2004, *Bob Fildes* / 0589795

20 HALMATIC COUGAR ENFORCER 33
(FAST PATROL CRAFT) (PBF)

Displacement, tons: 5.4 full load
Dimensions, feet (metres): 35.7 × 9.3 × 2.5 *(10.88 × 2.84 × 0.75)*
Main machinery: 2 Yanmar diesels; 2 Hamilton waterjets
Speed, knots: 45
Range, n miles: 120 at 45 kt

Comment: Based on Cougar 33 deep Vee hull form, first batch of five craft supplied by Halmatic in March 2003 with further 15 delivered by late 2003. Deployed in coastal patrol and interception role.

ENFORCER 33 3/2004, *Bob Fildes* / 0589796

12 SEASPRAY ASSAULT BOATS (PB)

Displacement, tons: To be announced
Dimensions, feet (metres): 31.2 × 10.2 × 1.6 *(9.5 × 3.1 × 0.5)*
Main machinery: 2 outboards; 500 hp *(375 kW)*
Speed, knots: 50. **Range, n miles:** 450 at 17 kt
Complement: 5
Radars: Navigation: I-band.

Comment: Abu Dhabi Ship Building awarded contract in January 2004. Designed by SeaSpray Aluminium Boats. To be employed in policing, patrol and interception roles by the navy and police.

Pakistan

Country Overview

The Islamic Republic of Pakistan gained independence in 1947. Situated in south Asia, it has an area of 307,293 square miles and is bordered to the west by Iran, to the north by Afghanistan and to the south by India. It has a 567 n mile coastline with the Arabian Sea. The former province of East Pakistan seceded in 1971 and assumed the name Bangladesh. The status of Jammu and Kashmir is disputed with India. The capital is Islamabad while Karachi is the largest city and principal port. There is a further port at Muhammad bin Qasim. Territorial waters (12 n miles) are claimed. A 200 n mile EEZ has been claimed but the limits have not been defined.

Headquarters Appointments

Chief of the Naval Staff:
   Admiral Muhammad Afzal Tahir, HI (M)
Vice Chief of Naval Staff:
   Vice Admiral Mohammad Haroon, HI (M), T Bt
Deputy Chief of Naval Staff (Operations):
   Rear Admiral Muhammad Shafi, SI (M)

Senior Appointments

Commander Pakistan Fleet:
   Rear Admiral Asaf Humayun, SI (M)
Commander Karachi:
   Vice Admiral Sikandar Viqar Naqvi, HI (M)
Flag Officer Sea Training:
   Rear Admiral Bakhtiar Mohsin, SI (M), T Bt
Commander Coast:
   Rear Admiral Iftikar Ahmed, SI (M)
Commander Logistics:
   Rear Admiral Nayyar Iqbal, SI (M)
Commander North:
   Commodore Mumtaz Ali Khan
Director General Maritime Security Agency:
   Rear Admiral Muhammad Atif Sandila

Diplomatic Representation

Naval Adviser in London:
   Commodore Kamran Khan, TI (M)
Naval Attaché in Paris:
   Captain Adnan Nazir
Defence Attaché in Muscat (Oman):
   Captain Wasim Akram, PN
Naval Attaché in Tehran:
   Captain Khalid Saeed
Naval Attaché in Beijing:
   Captain Naveed Rizvi
Naval Attaché in Kuala Lumpur:
   Captain Muhammad Amjad Zaman
Naval Adviser in New Delhi:
   Captain Mateen-ur-Rehman

Personnel

(a)   2006: 25,100 (2,300 officers) including 1,200 Marines and 1,000 (75 officers) seconded to the MSA
(b)   Voluntary service
(c)   Reserves 5,000

Bases

PNS *Haider* (Naval HQ); PNS *Akram* (Gwadar Naval Base); PNS *Iqbal* (Commando Base); PNS *Mehran* (Karachi Naval Air Station); PNS *Qasim* (Marines HQ/Base), Jinnah Naval Base (Port Ormara)

Prefix to Ships' Names

PNS

Maritime Security Agency

Set up in 1986. Main purpose is to patrol the EEZ in co-operation with the Navy and the Army-manned Coast Guard.

Marines

A Marine Commando Unit was formed at PNS *Iqbal*, Karachi in 1991.

Strength of the Fleet

Type	Active	Building
Submarines—Patrol	9	1
Submarines—Midget	3	—
Destroyers/Frigates	7	4 (2)
Fast Attack Craft—Missile	4	1
Large Patrol Craft	2	—
Hovercraft	4	—
Minehunters	3	—
Survey Ship	1	—
Tankers	5	—
Maritime Security Agency		
Destroyers	1	—
Large Patrol Craft	4	—
Fast Attack Craft—Gun	2	—

DELETIONS

Submarines

2005   *Hangor, Shushuk, Mangro, Ghazi*

Frigates

2003   *Shamsher*

Patrol Forces

2003   *Quwwatt*

PENNANT LIST

Submarines						
S 135	Hashmat					
S 136	Hurmat					
S 137	Khalid					
S 138	Saad					
S 139	Hamza (bldg)					

Destroyers/Frigates

D 181	Tariq
D 182	Babur
D 183	Khaibar
D 184	Badr
D 185	Tippu Sultan
D 186	Shahjahan
F 262	Zulfiquar

Mine Warfare Forces

M 163	Muhafiz
M 164	Mujahid
M 166	Munsif

Patrol Forces

P 140	Rajshahi
P 157	Larkana
P 1023	Jurrat
P 1028	Quwwat
P 1029	Jalalat
P 1030	Shujaat

Maritime Security Agency

D 156	Nazim
1060	Barkat
1061	Rehmat
1062	Nusrat
1063	Vehdat
1066	Subqat
1068	Rafaqat

Auxiliaries

A 20	Moawin
A 21	Kalmat
A 40	Attock
A 44	Bholu
A 45	Gama
A 47	Nasr
A 49	Gwadar
—	Janbaz
SV 48	Behr Paima

SUBMARINES

2 + 1 KHALID (AGOSTA 90B) CLASS (SSK)

Name	No	Builders	Laid down	Launched	Commissioned
KHALID	S 137	DCN, Cherbourg	15 July 1995	18 Dec 1998	6 Sep 1999
SAAD	S 138	DCN, Cherbourg/PN Dockyard, Karachi	2 Dec 1999	24 Aug 2002	12 Dec 2003
HAMZA (ex-*Ghazi*)	S 139	PN Dockyard, Karachi	2000	2006	2007

Displacement, tons: 1,510 surfaced; 1,760 dived (1,960 with MESMA)
Dimensions, feet (metres): 221.7; 252.7 (S 139) × 22.3 × 17.7 *(67.6; 77.0 (S 139) × 6.8 × 5.4)*
Main machinery: Diesel-electric; 2 SEMT-Pielstick 16 PA4 V 185 VG diesels; 3,600 hp(m) *(2.65 MW)*; 2 Jeumont Schneider alternators; 1.7 MW; 1 Jeumont motor; 2,992 hp(m) *(2.2 MW)*; 1 cruising motor; 32 hp(m) *(23 kW)*; 1 shaft
Speed, knots: 12 surfaced; 20 dived
Range, n miles: 8,500 at 9 kt snorting; 350 at 3.5 kt dived
Complement: 36 (7 officers)

Missiles: SSM: 4 Aerospatiale Exocet SM 39; inertial cruise; active radar homing to 50 km *(27 n miles)* at 0.9 Mach; warhead 165 kg.
Torpedoes: 4—21 in *(533 mm)* bow tubes. 16 ECAN F17P Mod 2; wire-guided; active/passive homing to 20 km *(10.8 n miles)* at 40 kt; warhead 250 kg. Total of 20 weapons.
Mines: Stonefish.
Countermeasures: ESM: Thomson-CSF DR-3000U; intercept.
Weapons control: Thomson Sintra SUBTICS Mk 2.
Radars: Surface search: KH 1007; I-band.
Sonars: Thomson Sintra TSM 2233 suite; bow cylindrical, passive ranging and intercept, and clip-on towed arrays.

Programmes: A provisional order for a second batch of three more Agostas was reported in September 1992 and this was confirmed on 21 September 1994. First one built in France. Parts for S 138 sent to Pakistan in April 1998 and for S 139 in September 1998.
Structure: The last of the class is to have a 200 kW MESMA liquid oxygen AIP system, thereby extending the hull by 9 m. The MESMA AIP system has a power output of 200 kW which will quadruple dived performance at 4 kt. Testing of the production system started in late 1999. The MESMA system is to be retrofitted in S 137 and

SAAD

S 138 during their next major refits. Hulls also have much improved acoustic quietening and a full integrated sonar suite including flank, intercept and towed arrays. SOPOLEM J 95 search and STS 95 attack periscopes. Sagem integrated navigation system. HLES 80 steel. Diving depth of 320 m *(1,050 ft)*.

9/2003, DCN / 0562934

Operational: *Khalid* completed 29 April 1999 and sailed for Pakistan in November 1999. Assigned to 5th Submarine Squadron. *Saad* completed its deep-dive test on 19 September 2003. The first submarine to be built in Pakistan, it was commissioned by the President.

2 HASHMAT (AGOSTA) CLASS (SSK)

Name	No	Builders	Laid down	Launched	Commissioned
HASHMAT (ex-*Astrant*)	S 135	Dubigeon Normandie, Nantes	15 Sep 1976	14 Dec 1977	17 Feb 1979
HURMAT (ex-*Adventurous*)	S 136	Dubigeon Normandie, Nantes	18 Sep 1977	1 Dec 1978	18 Feb 1980

Displacement, tons: 1,490 surfaced; 1,740 dived
Dimensions, feet (metres): 221.7 × 22.3 × 17.7
 (67.6 × 6.8 × 5.4)
Main machinery: Diesel-electric; 2 SEMT-Pielstick 16 PA4
 V 185 VG diesels; 3,600 hp(m) *(2.65 MW)*; 2 Jeumont
 Schneider alternators; 1.7 MW; 1 motor; 4,600 hp(m)
 (3.4 MW); 1 cruising motor; 32 hp(m) *(23 kW)*; 1 shaft
Speed, knots: 12 surfaced; 20 dived
Range, n miles: 8,500 at 9 kt snorting; 350 at 3.5 kt dived
Complement: 59 (8 officers)

Missiles: SSM: McDonnell Douglas Sub Harpoon; active
 radar homing to 130 km *(70 n miles)* at 0.9 Mach;
 warhead 227 kg.

Torpedoes: 4—21 in *(533 mm)* bow tubes. ECAN F17P;
 wire-guided; active/passive homing to 20 km *(10.8 n miles)*
 at 40 kt; warhead 250 kg; water ram discharge gear.
 E14, E15 and L3 torpedoes are also available. Total of 20
 torpedoes and missiles.
Mines: Stonefish.
Countermeasures: ESM: ARUD; intercept and warning.
Radars: Surface search: Thomson-CSF DRUA 33; I-band.
Sonars: Thomson Sintra TSM 2233D; passive search;
 medium frequency.
 Thomson Sintra DUUA 2B; active/passive search and
 attack; 8 kHz active.
 Thomson Sintra TSM 2933D towed array; passive; very
 low frequency.

Programmes: Purchased from France in mid-1978 after
 United Nations' ban on arms sales to South Africa.
 Hashmat arrived Karachi 31 October 1979, *Hurmat*
 arrived 11 August 1980.
Structure: Diving depth, 300 m *(985 ft)*. Both were modified
 to fire Harpoon in 1985 but may have had to acquire the
 missiles through a third party.
Operational: Assigned to 5th Submarine Squadron.

HURMAT *6/1998* / 0052677

3 MIDGET SUBMARINES (SSW)

X 01-03

Displacement, tons: 118 dived
Dimensions, feet (metres): 91.2 × 18.4 *(27.8 × 5.6)*
Speed, knots: 7 dived
Range, n miles: 2,200 surfaced; 60 dived
Complement: 8 + 8 swimmers
Torpedoes: 2—21 in *(533 mm)* tubes; 2 AEG SUT; wire-
 guided; active homing to 12 km *(6.5 n miles)* at 35 kt;
 passive homing to 28 km *(15 n miles)* at 23 kt; warhead

250 kg plus either two short range active/passive homing
torpedoes or two SDVs
Mines: 12 Mk 414 Limpet type.
Sonars: Hull mounted; active/passive; high frequency.

Comment: MG 110 type built in Pakistan under supervision
by Cosmos. These are enlarged SX 756 of Italian Cosmos
design. Diving depth of 150 m and can carry eight

swimmers with 2 tons of explosives as well as two CF2
FX 60 SDVs (swimmer delivery vehicles). Pilkington
Optronics CK 39 periscopes. Reported as having a
range of 1,000 n miles and an endurance of 20 days.
All have been upgraded since 1995 with improved
sensors and weapons. However, reports that *X 01* has
been equipped with Harpoon are not considered likely.
All are active.

X 03 *5/2003* / 0569226

FRIGATES

Notes: (1) A contract to procure frigates from China was signed on 4 April 2005. Four F-22P frigates, possibly derived from the Jiangwei II class, are to be procured. Construction of three will be undertaken at Karachi. The first ship is to be delivered in 2009 and is likely to have a mix of Chinese and western systems. Six Z-9C helicopters are also to be acquired as part of the package.
(2) Procurement of ex-US Navy destroyer *Fletcher* (DD 992) is under consideration. Subject to agreement, the ship is likely to be transferred in late 2006.

6 TARIQ (AMAZON) CLASS (TYPE 21) (FFHM/FFGH)

Name	No	Builders	Laid down	Launched	Commissioned	Recommissioned
TARIQ (ex-*Ambuscade*)	D 181 (ex-F 172)	Yarrow Shipbuilders, Glasgow	1 Sep 1971	18 Jan 1973	5 Sep 1975	28 July 1993
BABUR (ex-*Amazon*)	D 182 (ex-F 169)	Vosper Thornycroft, Woolston	6 Nov 1969	26 Apr 1971	11 May 1974	30 Sep 1993
KHAIBAR (ex-*Arrow*)	D 183 (ex-F 173)	Yarrow Shipbuilders, Glasgow	28 Sep 1972	5 Feb 1974	29 July 1976	1 Mar 1994
BADR (ex-*Alacrity*)	D 184 (ex-F 174)	Yarrow Shipbuilders, Glasgow	5 Mar 1973	18 Sep 1974	2 July 1977	1 Mar 1994
TIPPU SULTAN (ex-*Avenger*)	D 185 (ex-F 185)	Yarrow Shipbuilders, Glasgow	30 Oct 1974	20 Nov 1975	19 July 1978	23 Sep 1994
SHAHJAHAN (ex-*Active*)	D 186 (ex-F 171)	Vosper Thornycroft, Woolston	23 July 1971	23 Nov 1972	17 June 1977	23 Sep 1994

Displacement, tons: 3,100 standard; 3,700 full load
Dimensions, feet (metres): 384 oa; 360 wl × 41.7 × 19.5 (screws) (*117; 109.7 × 12.7 × 5.9*)
Main machinery: COGOG; 2 RR Olympus TM3B gas turbines; 50,000 hp (*37.3 MW*) sustained; 2 RR Tyne RM1C gas turbines (cruising); 9,900 hp (*7.4 MW*) sustained; 2 shafts; cp props
Speed, knots: 30; 18 on Tynes
Range, n miles: 4,000 at 17 kt; 1,200 at 30 kt
Complement: 175 (13 officers) (accommodation for 192)

Missiles: SSM: 4 McDonnell Douglas Harpoon 1C ❶ fitted in D 186, D 184 and D 182.
SAM: China LY 60N sextuple launchers ❷ semi-active radar homing to 13 km (*7 n miles*) at 2.5 Mach; warhead 33 kg (D 185, D 181 and D 183).
Guns: 1 Vickers 4.5 in (*114 mm*)/55 Mk 8 ❸; 25 rds/min to 22 km (*11.9 n miles*) anti-surface; 6 km (*3.3 n miles*) anti-aircraft; weight of shell 21 kg.
Hughes 20 mm Vulcan Phalanx Mk 15 ❹; 3,000 rds/min to 1.5 km (D 181, D 183, D 184 and D 186).
2 MSI DS 30B 30 mm/75 ❺ (D 182, D 185 and D 186).
4—12.7 mm MGs.
Torpedoes: 6—324 mm Plessey STWS Mk 2 (2 triple) tubes ❼ (D 184 and D 186); others fitted with 2 Bofors Type 43X2 single launchers for Swedish Type 45 torpedoes.
Countermeasures: Decoys: Graseby Type 182; towed torpedo decoy.
2 Vickers Corvus 8-tubed trainable launchers ❽ Mk 36 SRBOC ❾ (D 185, D 181, D 183 and D 182).
ESM: Thomson-CSF DR 3000S; intercept.
Combat data systems: CAAIS combat data system with Ferranti FM 1600B computers (D 186 and D 184). CelsiusTech 9LV Mk 3 including Link Y (in remainder).
Weapons control: Ferranti WSA-4 digital fire-control system. CSEE Najir Mk 2 optronic director ❿ (D 182, D 185 and D 186).
Radars: Air/surface search: Marconi Type 992R ⓫; E/F-band (D 182, D 184 and D 186). Signaal DA08 ⓬; F-band (D 181, D 183 and D 185).
Surface search: Kelvin Hughes Type 1007 ⓭ or Type 1006 (D 184 and D 186); I-band.
Fire control: 1 Selenia Type 912 (RTN 10X) ⓮; I/J-band (D 182, D 184 and D 186).
1 China LL-1 ⓯ (for LY 60N); I/J-band (D 185, D 181 and D 183).
Sonars: Graseby Type 184P; hull-mounted; active search and attack; medium frequency.
Kelvin Hughes Type 162M; hull-mounted; bottom classification; 50 kHz.

Helicopters: 1 Westland Lynx HAS 3 ⓰.

Programmes: Acquired from the UK in 1993-94. *Tariq* arrived in Karachi 1 November 1993 and the last pair in January 1995. These ships replaced the Garcia and Brooke classes and have been classified as destroyers.
Modernisation: Exocet, torpedo tubes and Lynx helicopter facilities were all added in RN service, but torpedo

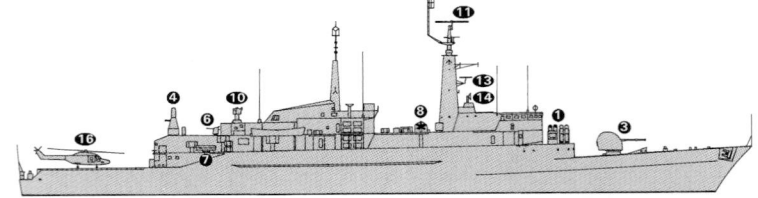
SHAHJAHAN *(Scale 1 : 1,200), Ian Sturton* / 0114784

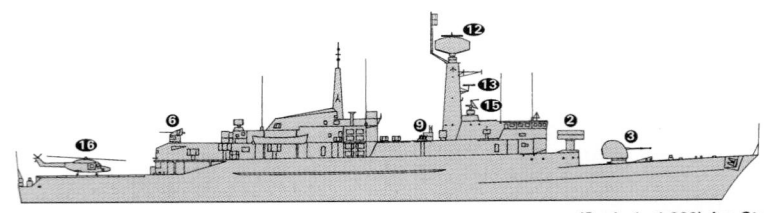
TIPPU SULTAN *(Scale 1 : 1,200), Ian Sturton* / 1133556

SHAHJAHAN *6/2005*, Massimo Annati* / 1153501

tubes were subsequently removed in all but *Badr* and *Shahjahan* and all retrofitted by Pakistan using Swedish equipment. Exocet was not transferred and the obsolete Seacat SAM system was replaced by Phalanx taken from the Gearings. Chinese LY 60N, which is a copy of Aspide, has been fitted in three of the class, Harpoon in three others. New EW equipment has been installed. There are still plans to update the hull sonars but there is no evidence that ATAS sonar has been fitted in D 183 and D 185 as previously reported. Other equipment upgrades include a DA08 search radar in three of the class, an optronic director, new 30 mm and 20 mm guns, SRBOC chaff launchers. An improved combat data system with a datalink to shore HQ is also fitted in four of the class.
Structure: Due to cracking in the upper deck structure large strengthening pieces have been fixed to the ships' side at the top of the steel hull as shown in the illustration. The addition of permanent ballast to improve stability has increased displacement by about 350 tons. Further hull modifications to reduce noise and vibration started in 1988 and completed in all of the class by 1992.
Operational: Form 25th Destroyer Squadron.

BADR *6/2000, Pakistan Navy* / 0105184

KHAIBAR   *6/2000, Pakistan Navy* / 0105186

TARIQ   *6/2000, Pakistan Navy* / 0105185

TIPPU SULTAN   *6/2005*, John Mortimer* / 1133549

1 LEANDER CLASS

Name	No	Builders	Laid down	Launched	Commissioned
ZULFIQUAR (ex-Apollo)	F 262	Yarrows, Glasgow	1 May 1969	15 Oct 1970	28 May 1972

Displacement, tons: 2,500 standard; 2,962 full load
Dimensions, feet (metres): 360 wl; 372 oa × 43 × 14.8 (keel);
18 (screws) *(109.7; 113.4 × 13.1 × 4.5; 5.5)*
Main machinery: 2 Babcock & Wilcox boilers; 550 psi
(38.7 kg/cm²); 850°F *(454°C)*; 2 White/English Electric
turbines; 30,000 hp *(22.4 MW)*; 2 shafts
Speed, knots: 28. **Range, n miles:** 4,000 at 15 kt
Complement: 235 (15 officers)

Guns: 2 Vickers 4.5 in *(114 mm)*/45 Mk 6 (twin) ❶; 20 rds/min
to 19 km *(10.3 n miles)* anti-surface; 6 km *(3.3 n miles)*
anti-aircraft; weight of shell 25 kg.
6—25 mm/60 (3 twin) ❷; 270 rds/min to 3 km
(1.6 n miles); weight of shell 0.34 kg.
A/S mortars: 3-barrelled UK MoD Mortar Mk 10 ❸;
automatic loading; range 1 km; warhead 92 kg.
Countermeasures: Decoys: Graseby Type 182; towed
torpedo decoy.
2 Vickers Corvus 8-barrelled trainable chaff launchers ❹.
ESM: UA-8/9/13; radar warning.
ECM: Type 668; jammer.
Weapons control: MRS 3 system for 114 mm guns.
Radars: Air search: Marconi Type 966 ❺; A-band; AKE-1.

Surface search: Plessey Type 994 ❻; E/F-band.
Navigation: 1 Kelvin Hughes Type 1006 and 1 Kelvin Hughes
Type 1007; I-band.
Fire control: Plessey Type 904 (for 114 mm guns) ❼; I/J-band.
Sonars: Kelvin Hughes Type 162M; hull-mounted; bottom
classification; 50 kHz.
Graseby Type 170B; hull-mounted; active search and
attack; 15 kHz.
Graseby Type 184P; hull-mounted; active search and
attack; 6—9 kHz.

Helicopters: 1 SA 319B Alouette III ❽.

Programmes: Transferred from UK on 14 October 1988.
From the Batch 3B broad-beamed group of this class.
Modernisation: Seacat and 20 mm guns replaced by twin
25 mm mountings. Additional navigation radar mounted
on bridge roof.
Operational: Sailed for Pakistan in December 1988. Extensive
refit carried out 1991-93. Likely to be decommissioned as
new frigates enter service.

LEANDER CLASS *(Scale 1 : 1,200), Ian Sturton* / 0506244

LEANDER CLASS *3/1997* / 0012864

SHIPBORNE AIRCRAFT

Numbers/Type: 3 Westland Lynx HAS 3.
Operational speed: 120 kt *(222 km/h)*.
Service ceiling: 10,000 ft *(3,048 m)*.
Range: 320 n miles *(593 km)*.
Role/Weapon systems: Two delivered August 1994 and one in April 1995. Option on
three more unlikely to be exercised. Sensors: Ferranti Sea Spray radar, Orange Crop
ESM. Weapons: ASW; two Mk 46 torpedoes. ASV; 2—12.7 mm MG pods; possibly Sea
Skua ASM.

Numbers/Type: 6 Westland Sea King Mk 45.
Operational speed: 125 kt *(232 km/h)*.
Service ceiling: 10,500 ft *(3,200 m)*.
Range: 630 n miles *(1,165 km)*.
Role/Weapon systems: Sensors: MEL search radar, Marconi Type 2069 dipping sonar
(two sets), AQS-928G acoustic processors. Weapons: ASW; two Mk 46 torpedoes; Mk 11
depth charges. ASV; one AM 39 Exocet missile.

LYNX HAS 3 *6/2001, Pakistan Navy* / 0114778

SEA KING *6/2003, Pakistan Navy* / 0569229

Numbers/Type: 2/4 Aerospatiale SA 319B/SA 316 Alouette III.
Operational speed: 113 kt *(210 km/h)*
Service ceiling: 10,500 ft *(3,200 m)*
Range: 290 n miles *(540 km)*
Role/Weapon systems: Reconnaissance helicopter. Second four acquired in 1994. Sensors: Weather/search radar MAD (in two). Weapons: ASW; Mk 11 depth charges, one Mk 46 torpedo.

ALOUETTE III   *6/2003, Pakistan Navy* / 0569234

LAND-BASED MARITIME AIRCRAFT

Notes: (1) A provisional contract to procure a reported eight Saab 2000 AEW aircraft was signed on 18 October 2005. The aircraft would be equipped with the Ericsson Erieye radar and would replace the Fokker F 27 fleet.
(2) The Maritime Security Agency operates three Britten-Norman Maritime Defenders. with Bendix RDR 1400C radars.

DEFENDER   *8/1996, MSA* / 0081375

Numbers/Type: 10 Lockheed P-3C Orion (Update II).
Operational speed: 410 kt *(760 km/h).*
Service ceiling: 28,300 ft *(8,625 m).*
Range: 4,000 n miles *(7,410 km).*
Role/Weapon systems: Order of first two completed in 1991 but held up by the Pressler amendment, until delivery in December 1996. May be used for Elint. Eight further aircraft donated by the United States in September 2005. These are all to receive an avionics upgrade. Sensors: APS-115 search radar; up to 100 sonobuoys; ASQ 81 MAD; ESM. Weapons: four Whitehead A 244 torpedoes or Mk 11 depth charges for ASW; Harpoon or Exocet AM 39 or C 802 for ASV.

P-3C   *6/2001, Pakistan Navy* / 0114783

Numbers/Type: 5 Fokker F27-200.
Operational speed: 250 kt *(463 km/h).*
Service ceiling: 29,500 ft *(8,990 m).*
Range: 2,700 n miles *(5,000 km).*
Role/Weapon systems: Acquired in 1994-96 for maritime surveillance. Sensors: APS 504(V)2 radar, Thomson-CSF DR 3000A ESM.

FOKKER F27-200   *6/2001, Pakistan Navy* / 0114780

Numbers/Type: 3 Breguet Atlantic 1.
Operational speed: 355 kt *(658 km/h).*
Service ceiling: 32,800 ft *(10,000 m).*
Range: 4,855 n miles *(8,995 km).*
Role/Weapon systems: Long-range MR/ASW cover for Arabian Sea; ex-French and Dutch stock. Upgraded in 1992-93. Three more acquired in 1994 for spares. An upgrade programme is reported to be planned. Sensors: Thomson-CSF Ocean Master radar, Thomson-CSF DR 3000A ESM, MAD, sonobuoys, Sadang 1C sonobuoy signal processor. Weapons: ASW; nine Mk 46 torpedoes, Mk 11 depth bombs, mines. ASV; AM 39 Exocet missiles.

ATLANTIC 1   *6/2001, Pakistan Navy* / 0114781

Numbers/Type: 12 AMD-BA Mirage III.
Operational speed: 750 kt *(1,390 km/h).*
Service ceiling: 59,055 ft *(18,000 m).*
Range: 740 n miles *(1,370 km).*
Role/Weapon systems: Operated by the Air Force, and all can be used for maritime strike. Sensors: Thomson-CSF radar. Weapons: ASV; two AM 39 Exocet or Harpoon; two 30 mm DEFA.

MIRAGE III   *6/2004, Pakistan Navy* / 1044171

PATROL FORCES

Notes: Eight Mekat type catamarans ordered in late 1997. These may be operated by the Customs.

1 TOWN CLASS (LARGE PATROL CRAFT) (PB)

Name	No	Builders	Commissioned
RAJSHAHI	P 140	Brooke Marine	1965

Displacement, tons: 115 standard; 143 full load
Dimensions, feet (metres): 107 × 20 × 6.9 *(32.6 × 6.1 × 2.1)*
Main machinery: 2 MTU 12V 538 diesels; 3,400 hp(m) *(2.5 MW)*; 2 shafts
Speed, knots: 24
Complement: 19
Guns: 2 Bofors 40 mm/60. 2 — 12.7 mm MGs.
Radars: Surface search: Pot Head; I-band.

Comment: The last survivor in Pakistan of a class of four built by Brooke Marine in 1965. Steel hull and aluminium superstructure. Assigned to 10th Patrol Squadron.

RAJSHAHI   *6/2003, Pakistan Navy* / 0569233

4 JALALAT CLASS (FAST ATTACK CRAFT—MISSILE) (PTG)

Name	No	Builders	Launched	Commissioned
JALALAT	1029 (ex-1022)	PN Dockyard, Karachi	16 Nov 1996	14 Aug 1997
SHUJAAT	1030	PN Dockyard, Karachi	26 Mar 1999	30 Sep 1999
JURRAT	1023	Karachi Shipyards and Engineering Works	9 Sep 2004	24 Feb 2006
QUWWAT	1028	Karachi Shipyards and Engineering Works	13 Sep 2004	24 Feb 2006

Displacement, tons: 185 full load
Dimensions, feet (metres): 128 × 22 × 5.7 *(39 × 6.7 × 1.8)*
Main machinery: 2 MTU diesels; 5,984 hp(m) *(4.4 MW)* sustained; 2 shafts
Speed, knots: 23
Range, n miles: 2,000 at 17 kt
Complement: 31 (3 officers)

Missiles: SSM: 4 China C 802 Saccade (2 twin); active radar homing to 120 km *(66 n miles)* at 0.9 Mach; warhead 165 kg; sea skimmer.
Guns: 2—37 mm/63 (twin); 180 rds/min to 8.5 km *(4.6 n miles)*; weight of shell 1.42 kg.
Countermeasures: Decoys: chaff launcher. ESM.
Radars: Surface search: Kelvin Hughes Type 756; I-band.
Fire control: Type 47G (for gun); Type SR-47 A/R (for SSM); I-band.

Comment: Designed with Chinese assistance to replace deleted Hegu class. Same hull as *Larkana*. Two further similar craft were ordered in September 2002 and have reportedly been developed in cooperation with the Thai company, Marsun.

JALALAT   *6/2000, Pakistan Navy* / 0105187

JURRAT and QUWWAT   *6/2005*, Pakistan Navy* / 1153889

1 LARKANA CLASS (LARGE PATROL CRAFT) (PB)

Name	No	Builders	Commissioned
LARKANA	P 157	PN Dockyard, Karachi	6 June 1994

Displacement, tons: 180 full load
Dimensions, feet (metres): 128 × 22 × 5.4 *(39 × 6.7 × 1.7)*
Main machinery: 2 MTU diesels; 5,984 hp(m) *(4.4 MW)* sustained; 2 shafts
Speed, knots: 23
Range, n miles: 2,000 at 17 kt
Complement: 25 (3 officers)
Guns: 2 Type 76A 37 mm/63 (twin). 4—25 mm/60 (2 twin).
Depth charges: 2 Mk 64 launchers.
Radars: Surface search: Kelvin Hughes Type 756; I-band.

Comment: Ordered in 1991 and started building in October 1992. Has replaced the last of the Hainan class. The missile version on the same hull has taken priority but more may be built. Assigned to 10th Patrol Squadron.

LARKANA   *9/2004*/ 1133552

4 GRIFFON 2000 TDX(M) (HOVERCRAFT) (UCAC)

Displacement, tons: 7.5 full load
Dimensions, feet (metres): 39.0 × 20.0 *(11.9 × 6.1)*
Main machinery: 1 Deutz BF8L513 diesel; 355 hp *(265 kW)* sustained
Speed, knots: 35. **Range, n miles:** 300 at 25 kt
Complement: 2
Military lift: 25 troops or 2 tons
Guns: 2—12.7 mm MGs.
Radars: Navigation: I-band.

Comment: Acquired from Griffon, UK. First craft delivered in April 2004 and the last in July 2005. The first two are of a modular design to enable rapid role-change. The second two have fixed roofs.

GRIFFON 2000   *6/2005*, Griffon Hovercraft* / 1153502

2 KAAN 15 (FAST INTERVENTION CRAFT) (PBF)

P 01   P 02

Displacement, tons: 19 full load
Dimensions, feet (metres): 54.8 × 13.2 × 3.9 *(16.7 × 4.04 × 1.2)*
Main machinery: 2 MTU 12V 183 TE93 diesels; 2,300 hp(m) *(1.69 MW)*; 2 Arneson ASD 12 B1L surface drives
Speed, knots: 54. **Range, n miles:** 350 at 35 kt
Complement: 4 plus 8 mission crew
Guns: 2—12.7 mm MGs.

Comment: Built by Yonca Shipyard, Turkey. Advanced composites structure. The first delivered on 17 August 2004 and the second on 14 October 2004. To be operated by Special Services Group based at PNS Iqbár. Details based on those in Turkish Coast Guard service.

P 01   *7/2004, Selçuk Emre* / 1044173

MINE WARFARE FORCES

3 MUNSIF (ÉRIDAN) CLASS (MINEHUNTERS) (MHSC)

Name	No	Builders	Launched	Commissioned
MUNSIF (ex-*Sagittaire*)	M 166	Lorient Dockyard	9 Nov 1988	27 July 1989
MUHAFIZ	M 163	Lorient Dockyard	8 July 1995	15 May 1996
MUJAHID	M 164	Lorient/PN Dockyard, Karachi	28 Jan 1997	9 July 1998

Displacement, tons: 562 standard; 595 full load
Dimensions, feet (metres): 168.9 × 29.2 × 9.5 *(51.5 × 8.9 × 2.9)*
Main machinery: 1 Stork Wärtsilä A-RUB 215X-12 diesel; 1,860 hp(m) *(1.37 MW)* sustained; 1 shaft; LIPS cp prop; auxiliary propulsion; 2 motors; 240 hp(m) *(179 kW)*; 2 active rudders; 2 bow thrusters
Speed, knots: 15; 7 on auxiliary propulsion. **Range, n miles:** 3,000 at 12 kt
Complement: 46 (5 officers)
Guns: 1 GIAT 20F2 20 mm; 1—12.7 mm MG.
Countermeasures: MCM; 2 PAP 104 Mk 5 systems; mechanical sweep gear. Elesco MKR 400 acoustic sweep; MRK 960 magnetic sweep.
Combat data systems: Thomson-CSF TSM 2061 Mk 2 tactical system in the last pair.
Radars: Navigation: Racal Decca 1229 (M 166) or Kelvin Hughes 1007; I-band.
Sonars: Thomson Sintra DUBM 21B or 21D (163 and 164); hull-mounted; active; high frequency; 100 kHz (±10 kHz).
Thomson Sintra TSM 2054 MCM towed array may be included.

Comment: Contract signed with France 17 January 1992. The first recommissioned into the Pakistan Navy on 24 September 1992 after active service in the Gulf with the French Navy in 1991. Sailed for Pakistan in November 1992. The second was delivered in April 1996. The last one was transferred to Karachi by transporter ship in April 1995 with a final package following in November 1995. Form 21st Mine Countermeasures Squadron.

MUJAHID   *6/2000, Pakistan Navy* / 0105188

SURVEY SHIPS

Notes: Acquisition of a new oceanographic research vessel was reported in November 2002 to have received Presidential approval. It is not clear whether this is to be a specialist or a multipurpose vessel.

1 SURVEY SHIP (AGS/AGOR)

Name	No	Builders	Launched	Commissioned
BEHR PAIMA	SV 48	Ishikawajima, Japan	7 July 1982	17 Dec 1982

Measurement, tons: 1,183 gross
Dimensions, feet (metres): 200.1 × 38.7 × 12.1 (61 × 11.8 × 3.7)
Main machinery: 2 Daihatsu 6DSM-22 diesels; 2,000 hp(m) (1.47 MW); 2 shafts; cp props; bow thruster
Speed, knots: 13.7. **Range, n miles:** 5,400 at 12 kt
Complement: 84 (16 officers)

Comment: Ordered in November 1981. Laid down 16 February 1982. Dynamic positioning system. Has seismic, magnetic and gravity survey equipment. DESO 20 deep echo sounder. There is a second survey ship *Jatli* under civilian control.

BEHR PAIMA   *6/2003, Pakistan Navy* / 0569231

AUXILIARIES

1 FUQING CLASS (AORH)

Name	No	Builders	Commissioned
NASR (ex-X-350)	A 47	Dalian Shipyard	27 Aug 1987

Displacement, tons: 7,500 standard; 21,750 full load
Dimensions, feet (metres): 561 × 71.5 × 30.8 (171 × 21.8 × 9.4)
Main machinery: 1 Sulzer 8RLB66 diesel; 13,000 hp(m) (9.56 MW); 1 shaft
Speed, knots: 18. **Range, n miles:** 18,000 at 14 kt
Complement: 130 (during visit to Australia in October 1988 carried 373 (23 officers) including 100 cadets)
Cargo capacity: 10,550 tons fuel; 1,000 tons dieso; 200 tons feed water; 200 tons drinking water
Guns: 1 GE/GD Vulcan Phalanx CIWS. 4—37 mm (2 twin). 2—12.7 mm MGs.
Countermeasures: Decoys: SRBOC Mk 36 chaff launcher.
Radars: Navigation: 1 Kelvin Hughes 1007; 1 SPS 66; I-band.
Helicopters: 1 SA 319B Alouette III.

Comment: Similar to Chinese ships of the same class. Two replenishment at sea positions on each side for liquids and one for solids. Phalanx fitted on the hangar roof in 1995. Assigned to 42nd Auxiliary Squadron.

NASR   *5/2003* / 0569225

2 COASTAL TANKERS (AOTL)

Name	No	Builders	Commissioned
GWADAR	A 49	Karachi Shipyard	1984
KALMAT	A 21	Karachi Shipyard	29 Aug 1992

Measurement, tons: 831 grt
Dimensions, feet (metres): 206 × 37.1 × 9.8 (62.8 × 11.3 × 3)
Main machinery: 1 Sulzer diesel; 550 hp(m) (404 kW); 1 shaft
Speed, knots: 10
Complement: 25
Cargo capacity: 340 m³ fuel or water
Guns: 2—7.62 mm MGs.

Comment: Assigned to 42nd Auxiliary Squadron.

GWADAR   *6/2003, Pakistan Navy* / 0569230

1 POOLSTER CLASS (AORH)

Name	No	Builders	Launched	Commissioned
MOAWIN (ex-*Poolster*)	A 20 (ex-A 835)	Rotterdamse Droogdok Mij	10 Sep 1964	28 July 1994

Displacement, tons: 16,800 full load
Measurement, tons: 10,000 dwt
Dimensions, feet (metres): 552.2 × 66.6 × 26.9 (168.3 × 20.3 × 8.2)
Main machinery: 2 boilers; 2 turbines; 22,000 hp(m) (16.2 MW); 1 shaft
Speed, knots: 21
Complement: 200 (17 officers)
Cargo capacity: 10,300 tons including 8—9,000 tons oil fuel
Guns: 1 GE/GD 6-barrelled Vulcan Phalanx Mk 15 or 2 Oerlikon 20 mm.
Countermeasures: Decoys: SRBOC Mk 36 chaff launcher.
Radars: Air/surface search: Racal Decca 2459; F/I-band.
Navigation: Racal Decca TM 1229C; I-band.
Sonars: Signaal CWE 10; hull-mounted; active search; medium frequency.
Helicopters: 1 Sea King.

Comment: Acquired from the Netherlands Navy. Helicopter deck aft. Funnel heightened by 4.5 m (14.8 ft). Capacity for five Lynx sized helicopters. Two fuelling stations each side for underway replenishment. Phalanx to be fitted in due course. Assigned to 42nd Auxiliary Squadron.

MOAWIN   *7/2005*, Maritime Photographic* / 1133555

1 TANKER (AOTL)

ATTOCK A 40

Displacement, tons: 1,200 full load
Dimensions, feet (metres): 177.2 × 32.3 × 15.1 (54 × 9.8 × 4.6)
Main machinery: 2 diesels; 800 hp(m) (276 kW); 2 shafts
Speed, knots: 8
Complement: 18
Cargo capacity: 550 tons fuel
Guns: 2 Oerlikon 20 mm.

Comment: Built in Italy in 1957. Assigned to 42nd Auxiliary Squadron.

ATTOCK   *6/2004, Pakistan Navy* / 1044169

TUGS

Notes: *Jandar* and *Jafakash* are two pusher tugs (10 ton bollard pull) built by Karachi Shipyard and commissioned in 2000.

JANDAR and JAFAKASH   *6/2003, Pakistan Navy* / 1044170

4 COASTAL TUGS (YTB)

Name	No	Builders	Commissioned
BHOLU	A 44	Giessendam Shipyard, Netherlands	Apr 1991
GAMA	A 45	Giessendam Shipyard, Netherlands	Apr 1991
JANBAZ	—	Karachi Shipyard	Sep 1990
JOSHILA	—	Karachi Shipyard	Sep 2000

Displacement, tons: 265 full load
Dimensions, feet (metres): 85.3 × 22.3 × 9.5 *(26 × 6.8 × 2.9)*
Main machinery: 2 Cummins KTA38-M diesels; 1,836 hp *(1.26 MW)* sustained; 2 shafts
Speed, knots: 12
Complement: 6

Comment: Details are for *Bholu* and *Gama*, built by Damen Shipyards and which entered service in 1991. *Janbaz* and *Joshila* were built by Karachi Shipyard and delivered in 1990 and 2000 respectively.

JOSHILA　　　　　　　　　　　　　　　　　　*5/2003* / 0569222

MARITIME SECURITY AGENCY

Notes: (1) All ships are painted white with a distinctive diagonal blue and red band and MSA on each side.
(2) One Britten-Norman Maritime Defender acquired in 1993, a second in 1994 and a third in August 2004. Based near Karachi with 93 Squadron.
(3) Plans for new ships and aircraft are under consideration.

1 GEARING (FRAM 1) CLASS (DD)

Name	No	Builders	Commissioned
NAZIM (ex-*Tughril*)	D 156 (ex-D 167)	Todd Pacific	4 Aug 1945

Displacement, tons: 2,425 standard; 3,500 full load
Dimensions, feet (metres): 390.5 × 41.2 × 19 *(119 × 12.6 × 5.8)*
Main machinery: 4 Babcock & Wilcox boilers; 600 psi *(43.3 kg/cm²)*; 850°F *(454°C)*; 2 GE turbines; 60,000 hp *(45 MW)*; 2 shafts
Speed, knots: 32
Range, n miles: 4,500 at 16 kt
Complement: 180 (15 officers)
Guns: 2 US 5 in *(127 mm)*/38 Mk 38 (twin); 15 rds/min to 17 km *(9.3 n miles)* anti-surface; 11 km *(5.9 n miles)*; anti-aircraft; weight of shell 25 kg.
4 — 25 mm (2 twin).
Torpedoes: 6 — 324 mm Mk 32 (2 triple) tubes.
Countermeasures: Decoys: 2 Plessey Shield 6-barrelled fixed launchers; chaff and IR flares in distraction, decoy or centroid modes.
Weapons control: Mk 37 for 5 in guns. OE 2 SATCOM.
Radars: Surface search: Raytheon/Sylvania; SPS-10; G-band.
Navigation: KH 1007; I-band.
Fire control: Western Electric Mk 25; I/J-band.

Comment: Transferred from the US on 30 September 1980 to the Navy. Passed on to the MSA in 1998 and renamed. This is the third Gearing to be renamed *Nazim*, the previous pair having been sunk as targets. All weapon systems removed except the torpedo tubes and main gun. Serves as the MSA Flagship.

NAZIM　　　　　　　　　　　　　　　　　　*5/2003* / 0569224

2 SHANGHAI II CLASS (FAST ATTACK CRAFT — GUN) (PB)

SUBQAT P 1066　　　　**RAFAQAT** P 1068

Displacement, tons: 131 full load
Dimensions, feet (metres): 127.3 × 17.7 × 5.6 *(38.8 × 5.4 × 1.7)*
Main machinery: 2 Type L12-180 diesels; 2,400 hp(m) *(1.76 MW)* (forward); 2 Type 12-D-6 diesels; 1,820 hp(m) *(1.34 MW)* (aft); 4 shafts
Speed, knots: 30
Range, n miles: 700 at 16.5 kt
Complement: 34
Guns: 4 — 37 mm/63 (2 twin). 2 — 25 mm/80 (twin).
Depth charges: 2 projectors; 8 weapons.
Mines: Fitted with mine rails for approx 10 mines.
Radars: Surface search: Anritsu ARC-32A; I-band.

Comment: Four of the class were transferred from the Navy in 1986 and two more in 1998. The last pair were then replaced by naval craft. All were originally acquired from China 1972 — 1976.

SUBQAT　　　　　　　　　　　　　　　　　　*5/2003* / 0569223

4 BARKAT CLASS (PBO)

Name	No	Builders	Commissioned
BARKAT	1060 (ex-P 60)	China Shipbuilding Corp	29 Dec 1989
REHMAT	1061 (ex-P 61)	China Shipbuilding Corp	29 Dec 1989
NUSRAT	1062 (ex-P 62)	China Shipbuilding Corp	13 June 1990
VEHDAT	1063 (ex-P 63)	China Shipbuilding Corp	13 June 1990

Displacement, tons: 435 full load
Dimensions, feet (metres): 190.3 × 24.9 × 7.5 *(58 × 7.6 × 2.3)*
Main machinery: 4 MTU 16V 396 TB93 diesels; 8,720 hp(m) *(6.4 MW)* sustained; 4 shafts
Speed, knots: 27
Range, n miles: 1,500 at 12 kt
Complement: 50 (5 officers)
Guns: 2 — 37 mm/63 (1 twin). 2 — 14.5 mm/60 (twin).
Radars: Surface search: 2 Anritsu ARC-32A; I-band.

Comment: Type P58A patrol craft built in China for the MSA. First two arrived in Karachi at the end of January 1990, second pair in August 1990. Some of this type of ship are in service with Chinese paramilitary forces.

VEHDAT　　　　　　　　　*6/1994, Maritime Security Agency* / 0081380

COAST GUARD

Notes: (1) Unlike the Maritime Security Agency which comes under the Defence Ministry, the official Coast Guard was set up in 1985 and is manned by the Army and answerable to the Ministry of the Interior.
(2) The Customs Service is manned by naval personnel. It operates approximately 18 craft of which most are Crestifalia MV 55.

1 SWALLOW CLASS (PB)

SAIF

Displacement, tons: 52 full load
Dimensions, feet (metres): 65.6 × 15.4 × 4.3 *(20.0 × 4.7 × 1.3)*
Main machinery: 2 GM Detroit 12V71T1 diesels; 2,120 hp *(1.58 MW)*; 2 shafts
Speed, knots: 25
Range, n miles: 500 at 20 kt
Complement: 8
Guns: 2 — 12.7 mm MGs.

Comment: Built by Swallowcraft/Kangnam and delivered in 1986.

4 CRESTITALIA MV 55 CLASS (PBF)

SADD P 551　　　**SHABHAZ** P 552　　　**VAQAR** P 553　　　**BURQ** P 554

Displacement, tons: 23 full load
Dimensions, feet (metres): 54.1 × 17.1 × 2.95 *(16.5 × 5.2 × 0.9)*
Main machinery: 2 MTU diesels; 2,200 hp *(1.64 MW)*; 2 shafts
Speed, knots: 35
Range, n miles: 425 at 25 kt
Complement: 5

Comment: Delivered in 1987.

SHABHAZ　　　　　　　　　　　　　　　　　*5/2003* / 0569228

Palau

Country Overview

The Republic of Palau was a US-administered UN Trust territory from 1947 before becoming independent in 1994 when a Compact of Free Association, delegating to the US the responsibility for defence and foreign affairs, came into effect. Situated in the western Pacific Ocean, the country comprises about 200 of the Caroline Islands archipelago spread in a chain about 350 n miles long. These include Koror (the administrative centre), Babelthuap (the largest island), Arakabesan, Malakal and Peleliu. The capital is currently on Koror, but a new capital is being built in eastern Babelthuap. Territorial seas (3 n miles) are claimed. An extended fisheries zone (200 n miles) is also claimed but limits have not been fully defined.

Headquarters Appointments

Chief of Division of Marine Law Enforcement:
Captain Ellender Ngirameketii

PATROL FORCES

1 PACIFIC CLASS (LARGE PATROL CRAFT) (PB)

Name	No	Builders	Commissioned
PRESIDENT H I REMELIIK	001	Transfield Shipbuilding	May 1996

Displacement, tons: 162 full load
Dimensions, feet (metres): 103.3 × 26.6 × 6.9 *(31.5 × 8.1 × 2.1)*
Main machinery: 2 Caterpillar 3516TA diesels; 4,400 hp *(3.28 MW)* sustained; 2 shafts
Speed, knots: 20
Range, n miles: 2,500 at 12 kt
Complement: 17 (3 officers)
Guns: 2—7.62 mm MGs.
Radars: Surface search: Furuno 1011; I-band.

Comment: Ordered in 1995. This was the 21st hull in the Pacific class programme. Following the decision by the Australian government to extend the Pacific Patrol Boat project, the ship underwent a half-life refit at Gladstone in 2003. A life-extension refit will be required in 2012.

PRESIDENT H I REMELIIK
6/2004, Division of Marine Law Enforcement, Palau
1044175

Panama

Country Overview

The Republic of Panama is an independent state situated on the isthmus linking South America with Central and North America. Bordered to the west by Costa Rica and to the east by Colombia, it has an area of 29,157 square miles and a 664 n mile coastline with the north Pacific Ocean and of 370 n miles with the Caribbean. The country is bisected by the Panama Canal. A new treaty in 1977 ended US operation, maintenance and defence of the canal in 1999. The capital is Panama City while the main ports are Balboa, Cristóbal, Coco Solo, Bahía Las Minas, Vacamonte, Almirante and Puerto Armuelles. Territorial seas (12 n miles) are claimed. An Exclusive Economic Zone (EEZ) (200 n miles) has been defined by boundary agreements. Reform of the security apparatus led to the creation of the Panamanian Public Forces, which includes the National Maritime Service, in 1994.

Headquarters Appointments

Director General National Maritime Service:
Captain Ricardo Traad Porras

Personnel

(a) 2006: 620
(b) Voluntary service

Bases

Isla Flamenco (HQ) (Punta Brujas — HQ designate), Quebrada de Piedra, Largo Remo (under construction), Punta Cocos (air), Kuna Yala (air) (under construction)

PATROL FORCES

Notes: A further patrol craft *Cocle* P 814 has been reported.

1 BALSAM CLASS (PBO)

Name	No	Builders	Commissioned
INDEPENDENCIA	A 401	Marine Iron and Shipbuilding Corp,	20 Nov 1943
(ex-*Sweetgum*)	(ex-WLB 309)	Duluth, Minnesota	

Displacement, tons: 1,034 full load
Dimensions, feet (metres): 180 × 37 × 12 *(54.9 × 11.3 × 3.8)*
Main machinery: Diesel electric; 2 diesels; 1,402 hp *(1.06 MW)*; 1 motor; 1,200 hp *(895 kW)*; 1 shaft; bow thruster
Speed, knots: 13
Range, n miles: 8,000 at 12 kt
Complement: 53
Guns: 2—12.7 mm MGs.
Radars: Navigation: Raytheon SPS-64(V)1.

Comment: Transferred from US Coast Guard on 15 February 2002. Operates as an offshore patrol ship.

2 VOSPER TYPE (COASTAL PATROL CRAFT) (PB)

Name	No	Builders	Commissioned
PANQUIACO	P 301 (ex-GC 10)	Vospers, Portsmouth	July 1971
LIGIA ELENA	P 302 (ex-GC 11)	Vospers, Portsmouth	July 1971

Displacement, tons: 96 standard; 145 full load
Dimensions, feet (metres): 103 × 18.9 × 5.8 *(31.4 × 5.8 × 1.8)*
Main machinery: 2 Detroit diesels; 5,000 hp *(3.73 MW)*; 2 shafts
Speed, knots: 18
Range, n miles: 1,500 at 14 kt
Complement: 17 (3 officers)
Guns: 2—7.62 mm MGs.
Radars: Surface search: Raytheon R-81; I-band.

Comment: *Panquiaco* launched on 22 July 1970, *Ligia Elena* on 25 August 1970. Hull of welded mild steel and upperworks of welded or buck-bolted aluminium alloy. Vosper fin stabiliser equipment. P 302 was sunk in December 1989, but subsequently recovered. Both vessels had major repairs in the Coco Solo shipyard from September 1992. This included new engines, a new radar and replacement guns. Pacific Flotilla. Similar craft in service in Malaysia.

INDEPENDENCIA
1/2004 / 0587788

LIGIA ELENA
6/2003, Panama Maritime Service / 0568905

1 COASTAL PATROL CRAFT (PB)

Name	No	Builders	Commissioned
NAOS (ex-*Erline*)	P 303 (ex-RV 821)	Equitable, NO	Dec 1964

Displacement, tons: 120 full load
Dimensions, feet (metres): 105 × 24.9 × 6.9 *(32 × 7.6 × 2.1)*
Main machinery: 2 Caterpillar diesels; 2 shafts
Speed, knots: 10
Range, n miles: 550 at 8 kt
Complement: 11 (2 officers)
Guns: 2 — 7.62 mm MGs.
Radars: Surface search: Raymarx 2600; I-band.

Comment: Served as a support/research craft at the US Underwater Systems establishment at Bermuda. Transferred from US in July 1992 and recommissioned in December 1992. Refitted in 1997 with new engines. Pacific Flotilla.

NAOS *6/2002, Panama Maritime Service* / 0525006

1 COASTAL PATROL CRAFT (PB)

ESCUDO DE VERAGUAS (ex-*Aun Sin Nombre*, ex-*Kathyuska Kelly*) P 305 (ex-P 206)

Displacement, tons: 158 full load
Dimensions, feet (metres): 90.5 × 24.1 × 6.1 *(27.6 × 7.3 × 1.9)*
Main machinery: 2 Detroit 12V-71 diesels; 840 hp *(627 kW)* sustained; 2 shafts
Speed, knots: 10
Complement: 10 (2 officers)
Guns: 1 — 12.7 mm MG.
Radars: Surface search: Raytheon; I-band

Comment: Confiscated drug runner craft taken into service in 1996. Also used for transport duties. Caribbean Flotilla.

ESCUDO DE VERAGUAS *11/1998, Panama Maritime Service* / 0052687

1 COASTAL PATROL CRAFT (PB)

TABOGA P 306

Comment: Details not confirmed. Possibly a confiscated vessel.

TABOGA *6/2003, Panama Maritime Service* / 0568904

1 NEGRITA CLASS (COASTAL PATROL CRAFT) (PB)

CACIQUE NOME (ex-*Negrita*) P 203

Displacement, tons: 68 full load
Dimensions, feet (metres): 80 × 15 × 6 *(24.4 × 4.6 × 1.8)*
Main machinery: 2 Detroit 12V-71 diesels; 840 hp *(627 kW)*; 2 shafts
Speed, knots: 13
Range, n miles: 250 at 10 kt
Complement: 8 (2 officers)
Guns: 2 — 7.62 mm MGs.
Radars: Surface search: Raytheon 71; I-band.

Comment: Former oilfield crew boat completely rebuilt in the Coco Solo shipyard and recommissioned 5 May 1993. Pacific Flotilla.

CACIQUE NOME *8/1998, Panama Maritime Service* / 0052688

5 POINT CLASS (COASTAL PATROL CRAFT) (PB)

Name	No	Builders	Commissioned
3 DE NOVIEMBRE (ex-*Point Barrow*)	P 204 (ex-82348)	CG Yard, MD	4 Oct 1964
10 DE NOVIEMBRE (ex-*Point Huron*)	P 206 (ex-82357)	CG Yard, MD	17 Feb 1967
28 DE NOVIEMBRE (ex-*Point Frances*)	P 207 (ex-82356)	CG Yard, MD	3 Feb 1967
4 DE NOVIEMBRE (ex-*Point Winslow*)	P 208 (ex-82360)	J M Martinac, Tacoma	3 Mar 1967
5 DE NOVIEMBRE (ex-*Point Hannon*)	P 209 (ex-82355)	J M Martinac, Tacoma	23 Jan 1967

Displacement, tons: 69 full load
Dimensions, feet (metres): 83 × 17.2 × 5.8 *(25.3 × 5.2 × 1.8)*
Main machinery: 2 Cummins V-12-900M diesels; 1,600 hp *(1.18 MW)*; 2 shafts
Speed, knots: 18
Range, n miles: 1,500 at 8 kt
Complement: 10 (2 officers)
Guns: 2 — 7.62 mm MGs.
Radars: Surface search: Raytheon Pathfinder; I-band.

Comment: P 204 transferred from US Coast Guard 7 June 1991 and recommissioned 10 July 1991. P 206 and P 207 transferred 22 April 1999. P 208 transferred 20 September 2000 and P209 on 11 January 2001. Carry a RIB with a 40 hp engine. Caribbean Flotilla.

28 DE NOVIEMBRE *6/2003, Panama Maritime Service* / 0568902

3 COASTAL PATROL CRAFT (PB)

CHIRIQUI P 841   **VERAGUAS** P 842   **BOCAS DEL TORO** P 843

Displacement, tons: 46 full load
Dimensions, feet (metres): 73.8 × 17.3 × 2.9 *(22.5 × 5.3 × 0.9)*
Main machinery: 3 Detroit 12V 71 diesels; 1,260 hp *(940 kW)* sustained; 3 shafts
Speed, knots: 20
Complement: 7 (1 officer)
Guns: 2 — 7.62 mm MGs.
Radars: Surface search: Furuno 1411; I-band.

Comment: Ex-US Sea Spectre PB Mk IV Class transferred as Grant-Aid from the US in March 1998. Used for drug prevention patrols in both Flotillas.

BOCAS DEL TORO *6/2003* / 0568903

2 HARBOUR PATROL CRAFT (PB)

PANAMA P 101   **CALAMAR** P 102 (ex-PC 3602)

Displacement, tons: 11 full load
Dimensions, feet (metres): 36 × 13 × 3 *(11 × 4 × 0.9)*
Main machinery: 1 Detroit 6-71T diesel; 300 hp *(224 kW)*; 1 shaft
Speed, knots: 15. **Range, n miles:** 160 at 12 kt
Complement: 5
Guns: 1 — 7.62 mm MG.

Comment: Ex-US personnel landing craft. P 102 in service from December 1992, P 101 from February 1998. GRP construction. Pacific flotilla.

CALAMAR   *8/1996, Panama Maritime Service* / 0506310

6 FAST PATROL BOATS (PBF)

BPC 2201, 2203, 2206-2209

Dimensions, feet (metres): 22.3 × 7.5 × 2 *(6.8 × 2.3 × 0.6)*
Main machinery: 2 Johnson outboards; 280 hp *(209 kW)*
Speed, knots: 35
Complement: 4
Guns: 1 — 7.62 mm MG.

Comment: *BPC 2201-2205* are Boston Whaler Piraña class acquired between June 1991 and October 1992.

BPC 2203   *11/1998, Panama Maritime Service* / 0052690

11 FAST PATROL BOATS (PBF)

BPC 3201, 3202, 3207-3209, 3214-3215, 3220, 3222-3223, 3225

Dimensions, feet (metres): 33.5 × 7.5 × 2 *(10.2 × 2.3 × 0.6)*
Main machinery: 2 Yamaha outboards; 400 hp(m) *(294 kW)*
Speed, knots: 35
Complement: 4
Guns: 1 — 7.62 mm MG.

Comment: Eduardoño class acquired between June 1995 and October 1998.

BPC 3202   *6/2003, Panama Maritime Service* / 0587789

LAND-BASED MARITIME AIRCRAFT

Numbers/Type: 3 CASA C-212 Aviocar.
Operational speed: 190 kt *(353 km/h)*.
Service ceiling: 24,000 ft *(7,315 m)*.
Range: 1,650 n miles *(3,055 km)*.
Role/Weapon systems: Air Force operated coastal patrol aircraft for EEZ protection and anti-smuggling duties. Sensors: APS-128 radar, limited ESM. Weapons: ASW; two Mk 44/46 torpedoes. ASV; two rocket or machine gun pods.

C-212   *6/2003, Adolfo Ortigueira Gil* / 0587787

Numbers/Type: 1 Pilatus Britten-Norman Islander.
Operational speed: 150 kt *(280 km/h)*.
Service ceiling: 18,900 ft *(5,760 m)*.
Range: 1,500 n miles *(2,775 km)*.
Role/Weapon systems: Air Force operated coastal surveillance duties. Sensors: Search radar. Weapons: Unarmed.

AUXILIARIES

Notes: (1) There are two auxiliary craft *Frailes del Norte* T 06 (ex-US LCM 8 class) and *Frailes del Sur* T 07.
(2) *General Esteban Huertas* (ex-YFU 81) has been reported with pennant number A 402 and may have replaced *Flamenco* in July 2004.

FRAILES DEL NORTE   *6/2003, Panama Maritime Service* / 0568901

1 COASTAL PATROL CRAFT (YO)

FLAMENCO (ex-*Scheherazade*) A 402 (ex-P 304, ex-WB 831)

Displacement, tons: 220 full load
Dimensions, feet (metres): 105 × 25 × 6.9 *(32 × 7.6 × 2.1)*
Main machinery: 2 Caterpillar diesels; 2 shafts
Speed, knots: 10
Complement: 11 (2 officers)
Guns: 2 — 7.62 mm MGs.
Radars: Surface search: Furuno FCR 1411; I-band.

Comment: Built in 1963. Transferred from US 22 July 1992 and commissioned in December 1992. Former US wooden hulled COOP craft. Refitted in Panama in 1994. Now used as a refuelling auxiliary. May have been replaced by ex-YFU 81.

FLAMENCO (old number)   *12/1998, Panama Maritime Service* / 0052686

1 MSB 5 CLASS (YAG)

NOMBRE DE DIOS (ex-MSB 25) L 16

Displacement, tons: 44 full load
Dimensions, feet (metres): 57.2 × 15.5 × 4 *(17.4 × 4.7 × 1.2)*
Main machinery: 2 Detroit diesels; 600 hp *(448 kW)*; 2 shafts
Speed, knots: 12
Complement: 6 (1 officer)
Guns: 1 — 7.62 mm MG.
Radars: Navigation: Raytheon Raystar; I-band.

Comment: Built between 1952 and 1956. Former US minesweeping boat. Served in the canal area until 1992 and transferred from US to Panama in December 1992 after refit. Wooden hull, new engine. Used as logistic craft. Pacific flotilla.

NOMBRE DE DIOS   *6/2003* / 0568899

1 LOGISTIC CRAFT (YAG)

ISLA PARIDAS (ex-*Endeavour*) L 21

Displacement, tons: 120 full load
Dimensions, feet (metres): 75 × 14 × 7 *(22.9 × 4.3 × 2.1)*
Main machinery: 1 Caterpillar diesel; 365 hp *(270 kW)*; 1 shaft
Speed, knots: 12
Complement: 7 (1 officer)
Radars: Navigation: Furuno; I-band.

Comment: Acquired in September 1991. Pacific flotilla.

6 SUPPORT CRAFT (YAG)

DORADO I BA 055	**AGUACERO** BA 057
DORADO II BA 056	**PORTOBELO** BA 058
DORADO III —	**FANTASMA AZUL** BA 059

Comment: *Dorado I* and *II* acquired in February 1998 and are used as 40 kt supply craft. *Aguacero* is a confiscated 50 kt power boat taken into service in November 1998.

DORADO I
12/1998, Panama Maritime Service
0052692

Papua New Guinea

Country Overview

Papua New Guinea lies north of Australia in the eastern half of New Guinea which it shares with the Indonesian province of Irian Jaya. An Australian-administered UN Trust territory from 1949, it became independent in 1975. Its head of state is the British sovereign, who is represented by a Governor-General. Its many island groups include the Bismarck and Louisiade Archipelagos, the Trobriand Islands, the D'Entrecasteaux Islands and Woodlark Island. Amongst other islands are Bougainville (a nine-year separatist conflict ended in 1997) and Buka.

It has a 2,781 n mile coastline. The capital, principal city and port is Port Moresby. An archipelagic state, territorial seas (12 n miles) are claimed. A 200 n mile Exclusive Economic Zone (EEZ) has also been claimed but the limits have not been fully defined by boundary agreements.

Headquarters Appointments

Commander Defence Forces:
   Commodore Peter Ilau, CBE
Director Naval Operations:
   Commander Max S Aleale

Bases

Port Moresby (HQ PNGDF and PNGDF Landing Craft Base); Lombrum (Manus)

Prefix to Ships' Names

HMPNGS

PATROL FORCES

4 PACIFIC CLASS (LARGE PATROL CRAFT) (PB)

Name	No	Builders	Commissioned
TARANGAU	01	Australian Shipbuilding Industries	16 May 1987
DREGER	02	Australian Shipbuilding Industries	31 Oct 1987
SEEADLER	03	Australian Shipbuilding Industries	29 Oct 1988
BASILISK	04	Australian Shipbuilding Industries	1 July 1989

Displacement, tons: 162 full load
Dimensions, feet (metres): 103.3 × 26.6 × 6.9 *(31.5 × 8.1 × 2.1)*
Main machinery: 2 Caterpillar 3516TA diesels; 4,400 hp *(3.3 MW)* sustained; 2 shafts
Speed, knots: 20. **Range, n miles:** 2,500 at 12 kt
Complement: 17 (3 officers)
Guns: 1 Oerlikon GAM-BO1 20 mm. 2—7.62 mm MGs.
Radars: Surface search: Furuno 1011; I-band.

Comment: Contract awarded in 1985 to Australian Shipbuilding Industries (Hamilton Hill, West Australia) under Australian Defence co-operation. These are the first, third, sixth and seventh of the class and some of the few to be armed. All upgraded, during half-life refits in Australia with new radars and navigation support systems in 1997/98. Following the decision by the Australian government to extend the Pacific Patrol Boat project, *Tarangau* underwent a life-extension refit at Gladstone in 2003 and *Dreger* at Townsville in 2004. Similar refits for *Seeadler* and *Basilisk* are due at Townsville in 2005 and 2006 respectively.

TARANGAU
8/2003, John Mortimer
0569236

AUXILIARIES

2 LANDING CRAFT (LSM)

Name	No	Builders	Commissioned
SALAMAUA	31	Walkers Ltd, Maryborough	19 Oct 1973
BUNA	32	Walkers Ltd, Maryborough	7 Dec 1973

Displacement, tons: 310 light; 503 full load
Dimensions, feet (metres): 146 × 33 × 6.5 *(44.5 × 10.1 × 1.9)*
Main machinery: 2 GM diesels; 2 shafts
Speed, knots: 10
Range, n miles: 3,000 at 10 kt
Complement: 15 (2 officers)
Military lift: 160 tons
Guns: 2—12.7 mm MGs.
Radars: Navigation: Racal Decca RM 916; I-band.

Comment: Transferred from Australia in 1975. Underwent extensive refits 1985-86. Both are still active.

SALAMAUA
12/1990, James Goldrick
0081510

Paraguay
ARMADA NACIONAL

Country Overview

The Republic of Paraguay is one of two landlocked countries in South America; Bolivia is the other. With an area of 157,048 square miles, it has borders to the north with Bolivia, to the east with Brazil and to the south with Argentina. There are some 1,800 n miles of internal waterways including the principal rivers, the Pilcomayo, Paraguay and Alto Paraná. Navigable by large ships for much of their length, they link the capital, largest city and principal port, Asunción, with the Rio de la Plata estuary on the Atlantic Ocean. Other ports include Ciudad del Este, Encarnación and Concepción.

Headquarters Appointments

Commander-in-Chief of the Navy:
  Admiral Miguel Angel Zacarias Caballero Della Loggia
Chief of Staff:
  Vice Admiral Rolando Augusto de Barros Barreto
Fleet Commander:
  Rear Admiral Ruben Carmelo Valdez Cuellar

Personnel

2006: 3,600 including 300 Coast Guard, 800 marines and 100 naval air

Bases

Main Base: Puerto Sajonia, Asunción
Minor Bases: Base Naval de Bahia Negra (BNBN) (on upper Paraguay river)
Base Naval de Salto del Guaira (BNSG) (on upper Paraná river)
Base Naval de Ciudad del Este (BNCE) (on Paraná river)
Base Naval de Encarnacion (BNE) (on Paraná river)
Base Naval de Ita-Pirú (BNIP) (on Paraná river)

Training

Specialist training is done with Argentina (Exercise Sirena), Brazil (Exercise Ninfa) and US (Exercise Unitas).

Marine Corps

BIM 1:   Puerto Rosario
BIM 2:   Puerto Vallemi
BIM 3:   Asunción
BIM 5:   Bahia Negra
           Detachments at Pozo Hondo and Ita-Pirú
BIM 8:   Saltos del Guairá
           Detachments at Ciudad del Este and Encarnación

Naval Aviation

Fixed Wing   Asunción International Airport
Helicopters   Puerto Sajonia

Coast Guard

Prefectura General Naval

PATROL FORCES

1 RIVER DEFENCE VESSEL (PGR)

Name	No	Builders	Commissioned
PARAGUAY	C 1	Odero, Genoa	May 1931

Displacement, tons: 636 standard; 865 full load
Dimensions, feet (metres): 231 × 35 × 5.3 *(70 × 10.7 × 1.7)*
Main machinery: 2 boilers; 2 Parsons turbines; 3,800 hp *(2.83 MW)*; 2 shafts
Speed, knots: 17
Range, n miles: 1,700 at 16 kt
Complement: 86
Guns: 4—4.7 in *(120 mm)* (2 twin). 3—3 in *(76 mm)*. 2—40 mm.
Mines: 6.
Radars: Navigation: *(Paraguay)*; I-band.

Comment: Refitted in 1975. Has 0.5 in side armour plating and 0.3 in on deck. Still in restricted operational service with boiler problems. Plans to re-engine with diesels have not yet been implemented and the ship is probably non-operational. Based at Asunción. Gun tubs on either side of bridge can be fitted with single 20 mm guns.

2 BOUCHARD CLASS (PATROL SHIPS) (PBR)

Name	No	Builders	Commissioned
NANAWA (ex-*Bouchard* M 7)	P 02 (ex-P 01, ex-M 1)	Rio Santiago Naval Yard	27 Jan 1937
TENIENTE FARINA (ex-*Py* M 10)	P 04 (ex-P 03, ex-M 3)	Rio Santiago Naval Yard	1 July 1939

Displacement, tons: 450 standard; 620 normal; 650 full load
Dimensions, feet (metres): 197 × 24 × 8.5 *(60 × 7.3 × 2.6)*
Main machinery: 2 sets MAN 2-stroke diesels; 2,000 hp(m) *(1.47 MW)*; 2 shafts
Speed, knots: 16
Range, n miles: 6,000 at 12 kt
Complement: 70
Guns: 4 Bofors 40 mm/60 (2 twin). 2—12.7 mm MGs.
Mines: 1 rail.
Radars: Navigation: I-band.

Comment: Former Argentinian minesweepers of the Bouchard class. Launched on 20 March 1936 and 31 March 1938 respectively. Transferred from the Argentine Navy to the Paraguayan Navy; *Nanawa* recommissioned 14 March 1964; *Teniente Farina* 6 May 1968. Based at Asunción. A third ship, *Capitán Meza*, is used as a barracks ship.

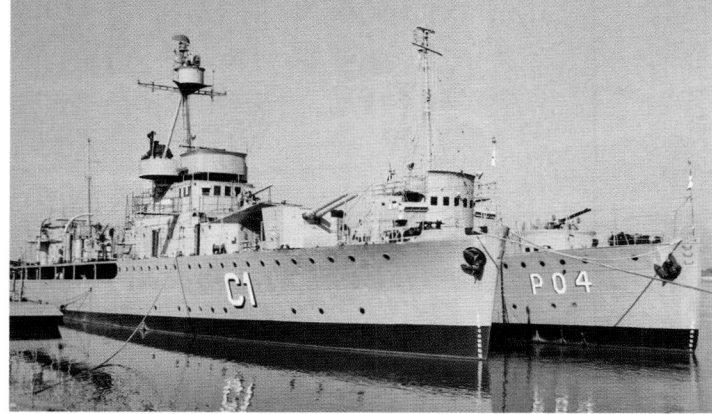

PARAGUAY and TENIENTE FARINA   *4/2003, Hartmut Ehlers* / 0587791

NANAWA   *6/1990, Paraguay Navy* / 0081514

PARAGUAY   *5/2000, Hartmut Ehlers* / 0105192

NANAWA   *5/2000, Hartmut Ehlers* / 0105194

For details of the latest updates to *Jane's Fighting Ships* online and to discover the additional information available exclusively to online subscribers please visit
jfs.janes.com

1 ITAIPÚ CLASS (RIVER DEFENCE VESSEL) (PBR)

Name	No	Builders	Commissioned
ITAIPÚ	P 05 (ex-P 2)	Arsenal de Marinha, Rio de Janeiro	2 Apr 1985

Displacement, tons: 365 full load
Dimensions, feet (metres): 151.9 × 27.9 × 4.6 (46.3 × 8.5 × 1.4)
Main machinery: 2 MAN V6V16/18TL diesels; 1,920 hp(m) (1.41 MW); 2 shafts
Speed, knots: 14. **Range, n miles:** 6,000 at 12 kt
Complement: 40 (9 officers) plus 30 marines
Guns: 1 Bofors 40 mm/60. 2—81 mm mortars. 4—12.7 mm MGs.
Radars: Navigation: I-band.
Helicopters: Platform for 1 HB 350B or equivalent.

Comment: Ordered late 1982. Launched 16 March 1984. Same as Brazilian Roraima class. Has some hospital facilities. Based at Asunción.

ITAIPÚ *4/2003, Hartmut Ehlers* / 0567473

1 RIVER PATROL CRAFT (PBR)

Name	No	Builders	Commissioned
CAPITÁN CABRAL (ex-*Triunfo*)	P 01 (ex-P 04, ex-A 1)	Werf-Conrad, Haarlem	1908

Displacement, tons: 180 standard; 206 full load
Dimensions, feet (metres): 107.2 × 23.5 × 6.7 (32.7 × 7.2 × 2.0)
Main machinery: 1 Caterpillar 3408 diesel; 360 hp (269 kW); 1 shaft
Speed, knots: 9
Complement: 25
Guns: 1 Bofors 40 mm/60. 2 Oerlikon 20 mm. 2—12.7 mm MGs.
Radars: Navigation: I-band.

Comment: Former tug. Launched in 1907. Still in excellent condition. Vickers guns were replaced and a diesel engine fitted by Arsenal de Marina in 1984. Based at Asunción.

CAPITÁN CABRAL *4/2003, Hartmut Ehlers* / 0567474

2 MODIFIED HAI OU CLASS (PBF)

CAPITÁN ORTIZ P 06   TENIENTE ROBLES P 07

Displacement, tons: 47 full load
Dimensions, feet (metres): 70.8 × 18 × 3.3 (21.6 × 5.5 × 1)
Main machinery: 2 MTU 12V 331 TC82 diesels; 2,605 hp(m) (1.92 MW) sustained; 2 shafts
Speed, knots: 36. **Range, n miles:** 700 at 32 kt
Complement: 10
Guns: 1—20 mm Type 75. 3—12.7 mm MGs.
Radars: Surface search: I-band.

Comment: Developed by Taiwan from Dvora class hulls and presented as a gift in 1996. It is possible that one of these craft was one of the two original Dvora hulls acquired by Taiwan.

CAPITÁN ORTIZ *4/2003, Hartmut Ehlers* / 0567475

2 RIVER PATROL CRAFT (PBR)

YHAGUY P 08   TEBICUARY P 09

Displacement, tons: 25
Dimensions, feet (metres): 52.8 × 14.8 × 2.6 (16.1 × 4.5 × 0.8)
Main machinery: Caterpillar diesel; 800 hp (596 kW)
Speed, knots: 40
Radars: Surface search: Furuno; I-band.

Comment: Two former Taiwan coast guard patrol boats transferred 23 June 1999. Capable of 40 kt and armed with two 7.26 mm MGs. Two sister craft transferred to Gambia in 1999.

TEBICUARY *4/2003, Hartmut Ehlers* / 0567476

5 RIVER PATROL CRAFT (PBR)

LP 7-11 (ex-P 7-11)

Displacement, tons: 18 full load
Dimensions, feet (metres): 48.2 × 10.2 × 2.6 (14.7 × 3.1 × 0.8)
Main machinery: 2 GM 6-71 diesels; 340 hp (254 kW); 2 shafts
Speed, knots: 12
Range, n miles: 240 at 12 kt
Complement: 4
Guns: 2—12.7 mm MGs.

Comment: Built by Arsenal de Marina, Paraguay. LP 7 launched March 1989, LP 8-9 in February 1990 and LP 10-11 in October 1991. The programme was then aborted.

LP 10 *4/2003, Hartmut Ehlers* / 0567477

5 TYPE 701 CLASS (PBR)

LP 101   LP 102   LP 103   LP 104   LP 106

Displacement, tons: 15 full load
Dimensions, feet (metres): 42.5 × 12.8 × 3 (13 × 3.9 × 0.9)
Main machinery: 2 diesels; 500 hp (373 kW); 2 shafts
Speed, knots: 20
Complement: 7
Guns: 2—12.7 mm MGs.

Comment: Built by Sewart in 1970. Delivered 1967-71. LP 105 is in reserve.

LP 104 *4/2003, Hartmut Ehlers* / 0567478

LAND-BASED MARITIME AIRCRAFT

Notes: The Naval Aviation inventory includes four fixed wing aircraft (two Cessna 150, two Cessna 310K and one Cessna 401A) in addition to the two Helibras Esquilo. Four further Robinson R44 helicopters have not been ordered, as previously reported.

Numbers/Type: 2 Helibras HB 350B Esquilo.
Operational speed: 125 kt *(232 km/h)*.
Service ceiling: 10,000 ft *(3,050 m)*.
Range: 390 n miles *(720 km)*.
Role/Weapon systems: Support helicopter for riverine patrol craft. Delivered in July 1985.

ESQUILO *5/2000, Hartmut Ehlers* / 0105198

AUXILIARIES

Notes: In addition to the craft listed, there are three LCVPs (EDVP 1-3), two service craft (Arsenal 1 and 2) one utility launch *(Teniente Cabrera)*, one suction dredger *(Teniente Oscar Carreras Saguier)*, one floating crane *(Grua Flotante)* and one floating dry dock *(Dique Flotante* (ex-AFDL 26)).

EDVP-03 *4/2003, Hartmut Ehlers* / 0587790

1 TRAINING SHIP/TRANSPORT (AK/AX)

Name	No	Builders	Commissioned
GUARANI	—	Tomas Ruiz de Velasco, Bilbao	Feb 1968

Measurement, tons: 714 gross; 1,047 dwt
Dimensions, feet (metres): 240.3 × 36.3 × 11.9 *(73.6 × 11.1 × 3.7)*
Main machinery: 1 MWM diesel; 1,300 hp(m) *(956 kW)*; 1 shaft
Speed, knots: 13
Complement: 21
Cargo capacity: 1,000 tons

Comment: Refitted in 1975 after a serious fire in the previous year off the coast of France. Used to spend most of her time acting as a freighter on the Asunción-Europe run, commercially operated for the Paraguayan Navy. Since 1991 she has only been used for river service and for training cruises Asunción-Montevideo. Operational status is doubtful.

GUARANI *4/2003, Hartmut Ehlers* / 0567480

1 RIVER TRANSPORT (AKL)

TENIENTE HERREROS (ex-*Presidente Stroessner*) T 1

Displacement, tons: 420 full load
Dimensions, feet (metres): 124 × 29.5 × 7.2 *(37.8 × 9 × 2.2)*
Main machinery: 2 MWM diesels; 330 hp(m) *(243 kW)*
Speed, knots: 10
Complement: 10
Cargo capacity: 120 tons

Comment: Built by Arsenal de Marina in 1964.

TENIENTE HERREROS *5/1991, Paraguay Navy* / 0081518

1 PRESIDENTIAL YACHT (MYAC)

3 de FEBRERO (ex-*26 de Febrero*)

Displacement, tons: 98.5 full load
Dimensions, feet (metres): 92.2 × 19.7 × 5.2 *(28.1 × 6.0 × 1.6)*
Main machinery: 2 Rolls Royce; 517 hp *(386 kW)*; 2 shafts
Speed, knots: 11
Range, n miles: 1,350 at 11 kt
Complement: 6 + 8 guests

Comment: Built by Naval Arsenal Asunción and launched in 1972. Entered service in 1982.

3 de FEBRERO *4/2003, Hartmut Ehlers* / 0567479

1 HYDROGRAPHIC LAUNCH (YGS)

SUBOFICIAL ROGELIO LESME LH 1

Displacement, tons: 16 full load
Dimensions, feet (metres): 65.5 × 10.2 × 2.6 *(14.7 × 3.1 × 0.8)*
Main machinery: 1 Mercedes-Benz diesel; 100 hp *(74 kW)*; 1 shaft
Speed, knots: 13
Complement: 5

Comment: Built in 1958.

TUGS

3 TUGS (YTM/YTL)

TRIUNFO R 4 (ex-YTL 567)   **ESPERANZA** R 7
ANGOSTURA R 5 (ex-YTL 211)

Displacement, tons: 70 full load
Dimensions, feet (metres): 65 × 16.4 × 7.5 *(19.8 × 5 × 2.3)*
Main machinery: 1 Caterpillar 3408 diesel; 360 hp *(269 kW)*; 1 shaft
Speed, knots: 9
Complement: 5

Comment: Harbour tugs transferred under MAP in the 1960s and 1970s. Details given are for R 4 and R 5. R 7 is a 20 ton vessel.

TRIUNFO *4/2003, Hartmut Ehlers* / 0567481

Peru
ARMADA PERUANA

Country Overview

The Republic of Peru is situated in western South America. With an area of 496,225 square miles it has borders to the north with Ecuador and Colombia, to the east with Brazil and Bolivia and to the south with Chile. It has a coastline of 1,303 n miles with the Pacific Ocean. Lima is capital and largest city and is served by the port of Callao. There are further ports at Salaverry, Paita, Chimbote, Matarani, Ilo and San Juan. Inland, Iquitos is linked to the Atlantic Ocean by the Amazon River. Lake Titicaca is also an important waterway. Peru has not claimed an EEZ but is one of a few coastal states which claims a 200 n mile territorial sea.

Headquarters Appointments

Commander of the Navy:
  Admiral Jorge Ampuero Trabucco
Chief of the Naval Staff:
  Vice Admiral Juan Sierralta Fait
Inspector General:
  Vice Admiral Eduardo Javier Darcourt Adrianzén
Commander Pacific Operations Command (Callao):
  Vice Admiral Jorge Carlos Montoya Manrique
Commander Amazon Operations Command (Iquitos):
  Vice Admiral José Ricardo Rafael Aste Daffós
Commander Marines Force:
  Rear Admiral Jorge Luis Andrade Báscones
Commander, Naval Aviation:
  Rear Admiral Carlos Chanduvi Salazar
Commander, Submarines:
  Rear Admiral Alberto Lozada Frías
Commander Surface Forces:
  Rear Admiral Juan Martinelli Bernos
Commander, Special Operations Force:
  Captain Juan Ampuero Trabucco

Personnel

(a)   2006: 25,000 (2,500 officers)
(b)   2 years' voluntary military service

Organisation and Bases

2 Operational Commands: Pacific (Callao) and Amazon (Iquitos).
5 Naval Zones: 1st (Piura), 2nd (Callao), 3rd (Arequipa), 4th (Pucallpa) and 5th (Iquitos).
Coast Guard General Directorate (Callao).
Callao: Main Naval Base, dockyard with shipbuilding capacity, one dry dock, three floating docks, one floating crane; training schools, Submarine Naval Station. Main Naval Air Base near Jorge Chavez International Airport.
San Lorenzo: Naval Station.
Iquitos: River base for Amazon Flotilla; small building yard, repair, facilities, floating dock.
Pucallpa: River base with logistic facilities.
San Juan de Marcona: Naval Aviation Training School and airfield.
Paita: Naval Station with logistic facilities.
Chimbote: Naval Base, dockyard for small vessels, logistic facilities.
Madre de Dios (river base) at Puerto Maldonado.
La Punta (Naval Academy).
Naval Stations with logistic facilities at El Salto (Tumbes), Mollendo (Arequipa), El Estrecho and Gueppi (Amazon).

Marines

The Peruvian Marines comprise 3,500 men commanded by a Rear Admiral. Headquarters at Ancon. The force includes a Marine Brigade, the Amphibious Support Group and Marine Special Forces. The Marine Brigade has three battalions: First Battalion — Guarnición de Marina; Second Battalion — Guardia Chalaca; Third Battalion (including Fire Support Group armed with 122 mm howitzer and 120 mm mortar and Engineer Support company) — Vencedores de Punta Melpelo. The Amphibious Support Group is composed of the Vehicles and Motor Transport battalions. The Marines Special Forces include a Commando company and anti-terrorist unit. Additionally, the Peruvian Marines have jungle battalions at Iquitos and Pucallpa (BIS 1 and BIS 2).

Special Operations

The Special Operations Command is responsible for the organisation, equipment, training and control of the operations of its subordinate Units; these Units are: the North, Central, South and Northwest Special Operations Groups, the Diving and Salvage Group, the Explosives Ordnance Unit, The Special Operations Station and the Special Operations School.

Prefix to Ships' Names

BAP (Buque Armada Peruana).

Coast Guard

A separate service set up in 1975 with a number of light forces transferred from the Navy.

PENNANT LIST

Submarines			Patrol Forces		Amphibious Forces		Auxiliaries		

Submarines

SS 31	Angamos
SS 32	Antofagasta
SS 33	Pisagua
SS 34	Chipana
SS 35	Islay
SS 36	Arica

Cruisers

CLM 81	Almirante Grau

Frigates

FM 51	Carvajal
FM 52	Villavisencio
FM 53	Montero
FM 54	Mariategui
FM 55	Aguirre
FM 56	Palacios

Patrol Forces

CF 11	Amazonas
CF 12	Loreto
CF 13	Marañón
CF 14	Ucayali
CM 21	Velarde
CM 22	Santillana
CM 23	De los Heros
CM 24	Herrera
CM 25	Larrea
CM 26	Sanchez Carrión

Amphibious Forces

DT 141	Paita
DT 142	Pisco
DT 143	Callao
DT 144	Eten

Survey Ships

AH 171	Carrasco
AH 172	Stiglich
AEH 174	Macha
AEH 175	Carrillo
AEH 176	Melo

Auxiliaries

ABA 332	Barcaza Cisterna de Agua
ABH 302	Morona
ABH 306	Puno
ACA 111	Calayeras
ACP 118	Noguera
ACP 119	Gauden
ARB 120	Mejia
ARB 121	Huertas
ARB 123	Guardian Rios
ARB 126	Dueñas
ARB 128	Olaya
ARB 129	Selendon
ATC 131	Mollendo
ATP 152	Talara
ATP 153	Lobitos
ATP 157	Supe
ART 322	San Lorenzo

SUBMARINES

Notes: Replacement of the current submarine flotilla is under consideration.

6 ANGAMOS/ISLAY CLASS (TYPES 209 and 1200) (SSK)

Name	No	Builders	Laid down	Launched	Commissioned
ANGAMOS (ex-*Casma*)	SS 31	Howaldtswerke, Kiel	15 July 1977	31 Aug 1979	19 Dec 1980
ANTOFAGASTA	SS 32	Howaldtswerke, Kiel	3 Oct 1977	19 Dec 1979	20 Feb 1981
PISAGUA	SS 33	Howaldtswerke, Kiel	15 Aug 1978	19 Oct 1980	12 July 1983
CHIPANA	SS 34	Howaldtswerke, Kiel	1 Nov 1978	19 May 1981	20 Sep 1982
ISLAY	SS 35	Howaldtswerke, Kiel	15 Mar 1971	11 Oct 1973	29 Aug 1974
ARICA	SS 36	Howaldtswerke, Kiel	1 Nov 1971	5 Apr 1974	21 Jan 1975

Displacement, tons: 1,185 surfaced; 1,290 dived
Dimensions, feet (metres): 183.7 × 20.3 × 17.9
  (56 × 6.2 × 5.5)
Main machinery: Diesel-electric; 4 MTU 12V 493 AZ80 GA31L diesels; 2,400 hp(m) *(1.76 MW)* sustained; 4 Siemens alternators; 1.7 MW; 1 Siemens motor; 4,600 hp(m) *(3.38 MW)* sustained; 1 shaft
Speed, knots: 11 surfaced/snorting; 21.5 dived
Range, n miles: 240 at 8 kt
Complement: 35 (5 officers) *(Islay* and *Arica)*; 31 (others)

Torpedoes: 8 — 21 in *(533 mm)* tubes. 14 AEG SST4; wire-guided; active/passive homing to 12/28 km *(6.5/15 n miles)* at 35/23 kt; warhead 260 kg. Swim-out discharge.
Countermeasures: ESM: Radar warning.
Weapons control: Sepa Mk 3 or Signaal Sinbad M8/24 *(Angamos* and *Antofagasta).*
Radars: Surface search: Thomson-CSF Calypso; I-band.
Sonars: Atlas Elektronik CSU 3; active/passive search and attack; medium/high frequency.
  Thomson Sintra DUUX 2C or Atlas Elektronik PRS 3; passive ranging.

Programmes: Two Type 209 (SS 35-36) ordered 1969. Two further Type 209 boats (SS 31-32) ordered 12 August 1976. Two Type 1200 (SS 33-34) ordered 21 March 1977.
Designed by Ingenieurkontor, Lübeck for construction by Howaldtswerke, Kiel and sale by Ferrostaal, Essen all acting as a consortium.

Modernisation: Sepa Mk 3 fire control fitted progressively from 1986. *Angamos* modernised with new batteries, sonar and EW suite.
Structure: A single-hull design with two ballast tanks and forward and after trim tanks. Fitted with snort and remote machinery control. The single screw is slow revving, very high-capacity batteries with GRP lead-acid cells and

PISAGUA
6/2004*, Peruvian Navy / 1127035

battery cooling-by Wilh Hagen and VARTA. Fitted with two periscopes and Omega receiver. Foreplanes retract. Diving depth, 250 m *(820 ft).*
Operational: Endurance, 50 days. Four are in service, two in refit or reserve at any one time. *Angamos* took part in multinational exercises in mid-2004 during which she achieved 156 days at sea.

ISLAY

6/2004, Peruvian Navy / 1121516

CRUISERS

1 DE RUYTER CLASS (CG/CLM)

Name	No	Builders	Laid down	Launched	Commissioned
ALMIRANTE GRAU (ex-*De Ruyter*)	CLM 81	Wilton-Fijenoord, Schiedam	5 Sep 1939	24 Dec 1944	18 Nov 1953

Displacement, tons: 12,165 full load
Dimensions, feet (metres): 624.5 × 56.7 × 22
  (190.3 × 17.3 × 6.7)
Main machinery: 4 Werkspoor-Yarrow boilers; 2 De Schelde-
  Parsons turbines; 85,000 hp *(62.5 MW)*; 2 shafts
Speed, knots: 32
Range, n miles: 7,000 at 12 kt
Complement: 953 (49 officers)

Missiles: SSM: 8 OTO Melara/Matra Otomat Mk 2 (TG 1) ❶;
  active radar homing to 80 km *(43.2 n miles)* at 0.9 Mach;
  warhead 210 kg; sea-skimmer for last 4 km *(2.2 n miles)*.
Guns: 8 Bofors 6 in *(152 mm)*/53 (4 twin) ❷; 15 rds/min to
  26 km *(14 n miles)*; weight of shell 46 kg.
  4 Otobreda 40 mm/70 (2 twin) ❸; 120 rds/min to 12.5 km
  (6.8 n miles); weight of shell 0.96 kg.
  4 Bofors 40 mm/70 ❹; 300 rds/min to 12 km *(6.6 n miles)*;
  weight of shell 0.96 kg.
Countermeasures: Decoys: 2 Dagaie and 1 Sagaie chaff
  launchers.
Combat data systems: Signaal Sewaco PE SATCOM ❺.
Weapons control: 2 Lirod 8 optronic directors ❻.
Radars: Air search: Signaal LW08 ❼; D-band.
  Surface search/target indication: Signaal DA08 ❽; E/F-band.
  Navigation: Racal Decca 1226; I-band.
  Fire control: Signaal WM25 ❾; I/J-band (for 6 in guns);
  range 46 km *(25 n miles)*.
  Signaal STIR ❿; I/J/K-band; range 140 km *(76 n miles)*
  for 1 m² target.

Programmes: Transferred by purchase from Netherlands
  7 March 1973 and commissioned to Peruvian Navy
  23 May 1973.
Modernisation: Taken in hand for a two and a half year
  modernisation at Amsterdam Dry Dock Co in March 1985.
  This was to include reconditioning of mechanical and
  electrical engineering systems, fitting of SSM and SAM,
  replacement of electronics and fitting of one CSEE Sagaie
  and two Dagaie launchers. In 1986 financial constraints
  limited the work but much had been done to update
  sensors and fire-control equipment. Sailed for Peru
  23 January 1988 without her secondary gun armament,
  which was completed at Sima Yard, Callao. Sonar has
  been removed. SATCOM fitted aft.
Operational: Expected to be decommissioned in 2008.

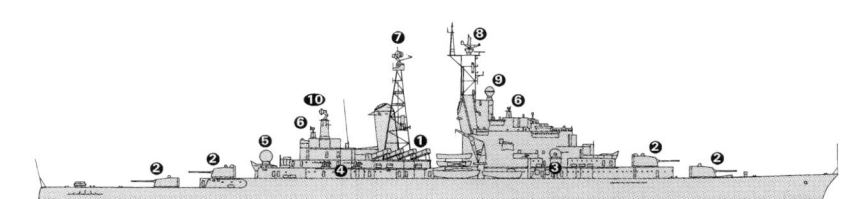

ALMIRANTE GRAU

(Scale 1 : 1,800), Ian Sturton / 0126352

ALMIRANTE GRAU
11/2004*, Globke Collection
1127047

FRIGATES

6 + 2 CARVAJAL (LUPO) CLASS (FFGHM)

Name	No	Builders	Laid down	Launched	Commissioned
CARVAJAL	FM 51	Fincantieri, Riva Trigoso	8 Aug 1974	17 Nov 1976	5 Feb 1979
VILLAVISENCIO	FM 52	Fincantieri, Riva Trigoso	6 Oct 1976	7 Feb 1978	25 June 1979
MONTERO	FM 53	SIMA, Callao	Oct 1978	8 Oct 1982	25 July 1984
MARIATEGUI	FM 54	SIMA, Callao	1979	8 Oct 1984	10 Oct 1987
AGUIRRE (ex-*Orsa*)	FM 55 (ex-F 567)	Fincantieri, Muggiano	1 Aug 1977	1 Mar 1979	1 Mar 1980
PALACIOS (ex-*Lupo*)	FM 56 (ex-F 564)	Fincantieri, Riva Trigoso	11 Oct 1974	29 July 1976	12 Sep 1977
BOLOGNESI (ex-*Sagittario*)	FM 57 (ex-F 565)	Fincantieri, Riva Trigoso	4 Feb 1976	22 June 1977	18 Nov 1978
QUIIÑONES (ex-*Perseo*)	FM 58 (ex-F 566)	Fincantieri, Riva Trigoso	24 Feb 1977	12 July 1978	1 Mar 1980

Displacement, tons: 2,208 standard; 2,500 full load
Dimensions, feet (metres): 371.3 × 37.1 × 12.1
(*113.2 × 11.3 × 3.7*)
Main machinery: CODOG; 2 GE/Fiat LM 2500 gas turbines;
50,000 hp (*37.3 MW*) sustained; 2 GMT A 230.20 M
diesels; 8,000 hp(m) (*5.88 MW*) sustained; 2 shafts; LIPS
cp props
Speed, knots: 35. **Range, n miles:** 3,450 at 20.5 kt
Complement: 185 (20 officers)

Missiles: SSM: 8 OTO Melara/Matra Otomat Mk 2 (TG 1) ❶;
active radar homing to 80 km (*43.2 n miles*) at 0.9 Mach;
warhead 210 kg; sea-skimmer for last 4 km (*2.2 n miles*).
SAM: Selenia Elsag Albatros octuple launcher ❷; 8 Aspide;
semi-active radar homing to 13 km (*7 n miles*) at 2.5
Mach; height envelope 15—5,000 m (*49.2—16,405 ft*);
warhead 30 kg.
An SA-N-10 launcher (MPG-86) may be fitted on the
stern.
Raytheon NATO Sea Sparrow RIM-7M (FM 55-56) Mk 29
octuple launcher; semi-active radar homing to 14.6 km
(*8 n miles*) at 2.5 Mach; warhead 39 kg.
Guns: 1 OTO Melara 5 in (*127 mm*)/54 ❸; 45 rds/min to 16 km
(*8.7 n miles*); weight of shell 32 kg.
4 Breda 40 mm/70 (2 twin) ❹; 300 rds/min to 12.5 km
(*6.8 n miles*); weight of shell 0.96 kg.
2 Oerlikon 20 mm (FM 55-56); fitted for but not with.
Torpedoes: 6—324 mm ILAS or Mk 32 (FM 55-56) (2 triple)
tubes ❺. Whitehead A244; anti-submarine; active/
passive homing to 7 km (*3.8 n miles*) at 33 kt; warhead
34 kg (shaped charge). Honeywell Mk 46 (FM 55-56);
active/passive homing to 11 km (*5.9 n miles*) at 40 kt;
warhead 44 kg.
Countermeasures: Decoys: 2 Breda 105 mm SCLAR
20-barrelled trainable launchers ❻; multipurpose; chaff
to 5 km (*2.7 n miles*); illuminants to 12 km (*6.6 n miles*);
HE bombardment.

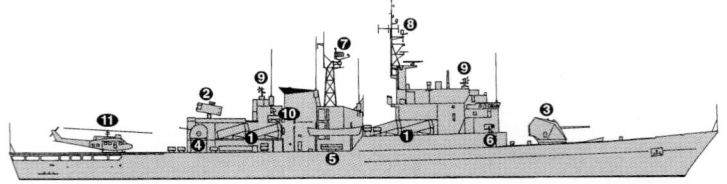

MARIATEGUI (*Scale 1 : 1,200*), Ian Sturton / 0105275

ESM: Elettronica Lambda or SLR-4 (FM 55-56); intercept.
ECM: 2 SLQ-D (FM 55-56); jammer.
Torpedo decoy SLQ-25 Nixie (FM 55-56).
Combat data systems: Selenia IPN-10 or IPN 20 (FM 55-56)
action data automation. Link 11 (FM 55-56).
Weapons control: 2 Elsag Mk 10 Argo with NA-21 directors.
Dardo system for 40 mm.
Radars: Air search: Selenia RAN 10S (FM 52-56) ❼; E/F-band.
Surface search: Selenia RAN 11LX ❽; D/I-band. Signaal LW
08 (FM 51); D-band.
SMA SPQ-2F (FM 55-56); I-band.
SMA SPS-702 (FM 55-56); I-band.
Navigation: SMA 3 RM 20R; I-band.
SMA SPN-748 (FM 55-56); I-band.
Fire control: 2 RTN 10X ❾; I/J-band.
2 RTN 20X ❿; I/J-band (for Dardo).
Sonars: EDO 610E or Raytheon DE 1160B (FM 55-56); hull-
mounted; active search and attack; medium frequency.

Helicopters: 1 Agusta AB 212ASW ⓫. 1 Agusta ASH-3D
Sea King (deck only) (FM 51 and 54).

Programmes: *Montero* and *Mariategui* were the first
major warships to be built on the Pacific Coast of South

America, although some equipment was provided by
Fincantieri. *Palacios* and *Aguirre* formally transferred
from the Italian Navy on 3 November 2004, without
ammunition, torpedoes, SSM and helicopters. Following
eight-month refits at Fincantieri, Muggiano they both
arrived at Callao in mid-2005. A contract for the refit and
transfer of two further decommissioned ships, *Sagittario*
and *Perseo* was signed on 28 October 2005. The ships are
to be refitted at Muggiano before delivery in late 2006.
Modernisation: FM 51 and FM 54 have had flight deck
extensions in order to operate Sea Kings from the deck
although they cannot be stowed in the hangar. SA-N-10
(MPG-86) may be fitted on the sterns of two ships. LW 08
replaced RAN 10S in FM 51 in 2003. A mid-life refit of FM 51-54,
to include propulsion systems and the modernisation of
Aspide, is reported to be under consideration.
Structure: FM 51-54 differ from those built for Italian service by
having a fixed hangar and higher 40 mm mounts. The SAM
system is also different. The ships were commissioned with
a step-down from the flight deck to the stern although this
has been modified in FM 51 and 54.
Operational: Helicopter provides an over-the-horizon
targeting capability for SSM. HIFR facilities fitted in 1989
allow refuelling of Sea King helicopters.

AGUIRRE 4/2005*, Giorgio Ghiglione / 1133140

MONTERO 6/2004*, Peruvian Navy / 1127036

SHIPBORNE AIRCRAFT

Notes: There are also five Bell 206B training helicopters.

BELL 206B *6/2004*, Peruvian Navy* / 1127037

Numbers/Type: 3 Agusta AB 212ASW.
Operational speed: 106 kt *(196 km/h).*
Service ceiling: 14,200 ft *(4,330 m).*
Range: 230 n miles *(425 km).*
Role/Weapon systems: ASW and surface search helicopter for smaller escorts. Sensors: Selenia search radar, Bendix ASQ-18 dipping sonar, ECM. Weapons: ASW; two Mk 46 or 244/S torpedoes or depth bombs.

AB 212 *6/2004*, Peruvian Navy* / 1127038

Numbers/Type: 3 Agusta-Sikorsky ASH-3D Sea King.
Operational speed: 120 kt *(222 km/h).*
Service ceiling: 12,200 ft *(3,720 m).*
Range: 630 n miles *(1,165 km).*
Role/Weapon systems: ASW helicopter; can be operated from two FFGs. Sensors: Selenia search radar, Bendix ASQ-18 dipping sonar, sonobuoys. Weapons: ASW; four Mk 46 or 244/S torpedoes or depth bombs or mines. ASV; two AM 39 Exocet missiles.

ASH-3D *6/2004*, Peruvian Navy* / 1127039

LAND-BASED MARITIME AIRCRAFT (FRONT LINE)

Notes: (1) There are also four Mi-8T transport helicopters.
(2) One Fokker F-27 is used by the Navy and two by the coast Guard for maritime surveillance.
(3) There are two Antonov AN-32 transport aircraft.
(4) Three Beech T-34C are used for training.
(5) One Cessna 206.

Mi-8T *2000, Peruvian Navy* / 0105208

Numbers/Type: 5 Beechcraft Super King Air B200T.
Operational speed: 282 kt *(523 km/h).*
Service ceiling: 35,000 ft *(10,670 m).*
Range: 2,030 n miles *(3,756 km).*
Role/Weapon systems: Coastal surveillance and EEZ patrol duties. Sensors: Search radar, cameras. Weapons: Unarmed.

PATROL FORCES

Notes: (1) Procurement of ten hovercraft for river policing is under consideration.
(2) Three Punta Malpelo class 13 m craft were commissioned in 1996.

6 VERLARDE (PR-72P) CLASS
(FAST ATTACK CRAFT—MISSILE) (CM/PGGFM)

Name	No	Builders	Launched	Commissioned
VELARDE	CM 21	SFCN, France	16 Sep 1978	25 July 1980
SANTILLANA	CM 22	SFCN, France	11 Sep 1978	25 July 1980
DE LOS HEROS	CM 23	SFCN, France	20 May 1979	17 Nov 1980
HERRERA	CM 24	SFCN, France	16 Feb 1979	10 Feb 1981
LARREA	CM 25	SFCN, France	12 May 1979	16 June 1981
SANCHEZ CARRIÓN	CM 26	SFCN, France	28 June 1979	14 Sep 1981

Displacement, tons: 470 standard; 560 full load
Dimensions, feet (metres): 210 × 27.4 × 5.2 *(64 × 8.4 × 2.6)*
Main machinery: 4 SACM AGO 240 V16 M7 or 4 MTU 12V 595 diesels; 22,200 hp(m) *(16.32 MW)* sustained; 4 shafts
Speed, knots: 37
Range, n miles: 2,500 at 16 kt
Complement: 36 plus 10 spare

Missiles: SSM: 4 Aerospatiale MM 38 Exocet; inertial cruise; active radar homing to 42 km *(23 n miles)* at 0.9 Mach; warhead 165 kg; sea-skimmer.
SAM: An SA-N-10 launcher (MPG-86) may be fitted on the stern.
Guns: 1 OTO Melara 3 in *(76 mm)*/62; 85 rds/min to 16 km *(8.7 n miles)*; weight of shell 6 kg.
2 Breda 40 mm/70 (twin); 300 rds/min to 12.5 km *(6.8 n miles)*; weight of shell 0.96 kg.
Countermeasures: ESM: Thomson-CSF DR 2000; intercept.
Weapons control: CSEE Panda director. Vega system.
Radars: Surface search: Thomson-CSF Triton; G-band; range 33 km *(18 n miles)* for 2 m² target.
Navigation: Racal Decca 1226; I-band.
Fire control: Thomson-CSF/Castor II; I/J-band; range 15 km *(8 n miles)* for 1 m² target.
Programmes: Ordered late 1976. Hulls of *Velarde, De los Heros, Larrea* subcontracted to Lorient Naval Yard, the others being built at Villeneuve-la-Garenne. Classified as corvettes.
Modernisation: Three of the class re-engined in 2000. Remainder to follow.

VELARDE *11/2004, Globke Collection* / 1047863

2 LORETO CLASS (RIVER GUNBOATS) (CF/PGR)

Name	No	Builders	Commissioned
AMAZONAS	CF 11 (ex-CF 403)	Electric Boat Co, Groton	1935
LORETO	CF 12 (ex-CF 404)	Electric Boat Co, Groton	1935

Displacement, tons: 250 standard
Dimensions, feet (metres): 145 × 22 × 4 *(44.2 × 6.7 × 1.2)*
Main machinery: 2 diesels; 750 hp(m) *(551 kW)*; 2 shafts
Speed, knots: 15
Range, n miles: 4,000 at 10 kt
Complement: 35 (5 officers)
Guns: 1—3 in *(76 mm).* 3 Bofors 40 mm/60. 2 Oerlikon 20 mm.

Comment: Launched in 1934. In Upper Amazon Flotilla, based at Iquitos. The after 3 in gun has been replaced by a third 40 mm.

LORETO *4/1997, Peruvian Navy* / 0012880

2 MARAÑON CLASS (RIVER GUNBOATS) (CF/PGR)

Name	No	Builders	Commissioned
MARAÑON	CF 13 (ex-CF 401)	John I Thornycroft & Co Ltd	July 1951
UCAYALI	CF 14 (ex-CF 402)	John I Thornycroft & Co Ltd	June 1951

Displacement, tons: 365 full load
Dimensions, feet (metres): 154.8 wl × 32 × 4 *(47.2 × 9.7 × 1.2)*
Main machinery: 2 British Polar M 441 diesels; 800 hp *(597 kW)*; 2 shafts
Speed, knots: 12
Range, n miles: 6,000 at 10 kt
Complement: 40 (4 officers)
Guns: 2—3 in *(76 mm)*/50. 2 Bofors 40 mm/60. 2 Oerlikon 20 mm.

Comment: Ordered early in 1950 and launched 7 March and 23 April 1951 respectively. Employed on police duties in Upper Amazon. Superstructure of aluminium alloy. Based at Iquitos.

MARAÑON *1995, Peruvian Navy* / 0081529

UCAYALI *1993, Peruvian Navy* / 0081530

AMPHIBIOUS FORCES

Notes: There are plans for up to three 300 ft LSLs to be locally built when funds are available.

4 PAITA (TERREBONNE PARISH) CLASS (LSTH)

Name	No	Builders	Commissioned
PAITÁ (ex-*Walworth County* LST 1164)	DT 141	Ingalls SB	26 Oct 1953
PISCO (ex-*Waldo County* LST 1163)	DT 142	Ingalls SB	17 Sep 1953
CALLAO (ex-*Washoe County* LST 1165)	DT 143	Ingalls SB	30 Nov 1953
ETEN (ex-*Traverse County* LST 1160)	DT 144	Bath Iron Works	19 Dec 1953

Displacement, tons: 2,590 standard; 5,800 full load
Dimensions, feet (metres): 384 × 55 × 17 *(117.1 × 16.8 × 5.2)*
Main machinery: 4 GM 16-278A diesels; 6,000 hp *(4.48 MW)*; 2 shafts
Speed, knots: 15
Range, n miles: 15,000 at 9 kt
Complement: 116
Military lift: 2,000 tons; 395 troops
Guns: 5 Bofors 40 mm/60 (2 twin, 1 single).
Radars: Navigation: I-band.

Comment: Four transferred from USA on loan 7 August 1984, recommissioned 4 March 1985. Have small helicopter platform. Original 3 in guns replaced by 40 mm. Lease extended by grant aid in August 1989, again in August 1994, and again in April 1999. All are active.

PAITÁ *11/2004, Globke Collection* / 1047862

SURVEY AND RESEARCH SHIPS

Notes: AH 177 is a 5 ton fast survey craft.

1 INSHORE SURVEY CRAFT (AGSC/EH)

Name	No	Builders	Commissioned
MACHA	AEH 174	SIMA, Chimbote	Apr 1982

Displacement, tons: 53 full load
Dimensions, feet (metres): 64.9 × 17.1 × 3 *(19.8 × 5.2 × 0.9)*
Main machinery: 2 diesels; 2 shafts
Speed, knots: 13
Complement: 8 (2 officers)

Comment: Side scan sonar for plotting bottom contours. EH (Embarcacion Hidrográfica).

MACHA *2000, Peruvian Navy* / 0105213

1 DOKKUM CLASS (AGSC/EH)

Name	No	Builders	Commissioned
CARRASCO (ex-*Abcoude*)	AH 171 (ex-M 810)	Smulders, Schiedam	18 May 1956

Displacement, tons: 373 standard; 453 full load
Dimensions, feet (metres): 152.9 × 28.9 × 7.5 *(46.6 × 8.8 × 2.3)*
Main machinery: 2 Fijenoord MAN V64 diesels; 2,500 hp(m) *(1.84 MW)*; 2 shafts
Speed, knots: 16
Range, n miles: 2,500 at 10 kt
Complement: 27—36
Guns: 2 Oerlikon 20 mm/70 (1 twin).
Radars: Navigation: Racal Decca TM 1229C; I-band.

Comment: Service with the Netherlands Navy as a minesweeper included modernisation in the mid-1970s and a life prolonging refit in the late 1980s. *Carrasco* placed in reserve in 1993 and transferred to Peru 16 July 1994. The ship has been acquired for hydrographic duties. Two more were planned to follow in mid-1996 but the transfer was cancelled.

CARRASCO *6/2004*, Peruvian Navy* / 1127040

2 VAN STRAELEN CLASS (AGSC/EH)

Name	No	Builders	Commissioned
CARRILLO (ex-*van Hamel*)	AEH 175	De Vries, Amsterdam	14 Oct 1960
MELO (ex-*van der Wel*)	AEH 176	De Vries, Amsterdam	6 Oct 1961

Displacement, tons: 169 full load
Dimensions, feet (metres): 108.6 × 18.2 × 5.2 *(33.1 × 5.6 × 1.6)*
Main machinery: 2 GM diesels; 1,100 hp(m) *(808 kW)* sustained; 2 shafts
Speed, knots: 13
Complement: 17 (2 officers)
Guns: 1—20 mm

Comment: Both built as inshore minesweepers. Acquired 23 February 1985 for conversion with new engines and survey equipment.

MELO *2000, Peruvian Navy* / 0105212

2 RIVER VESSELS (AGSC/AH)

Name	No	Builders	Commissioned
MORONA	ABH 302	Sima, Iquitos	1976
STIGLICH	AHI 172	Sima, Iquitos	1981

Displacement, tons: 230 standard; 250 full load
Dimensions, feet (metres): 112.2 × 25.9 × 5.6 *(34.2 × 7.9 × 1.7)*
Main machinery: 2 Detroit 12V-71TA diesels; 840 hp *(616 kW)* sustained; 2 shafts
Speed, knots: 15
Complement: 28 (2 officers)

Comment: *Stiglich* is based at Iquitos for survey work on the Upper Amazon. *Morona* is used as a hospital craft and has a red cross on her superstructure.

STIGLICH   *6/1999, Peruvian Navy* / 0081533

AUXILIARIES

Notes: (1) All auxiliaries may be used for commercial purposes if not required for naval use.
(2) There are three small river hospital craft: *Corrientes* (ABH 303), *Curaray* (ABH 304) and *Pastaza* (ABH 305).
(3) There are four Rio Comaina class 30 m fuel barges (ABP 336-339) and four further fuel barges (ABP 343-346) of about 45 m.
(4) There are two 15 m river cargo barges (ABC 360-361).

1 MOLLENDO CLASS (TRANSPORT) (AOR)

Name	No	Builders	Commissioned
MOLLENDO (ex-*Ilo*)	ATC 131	SIMA, Callao	15 Dec 1971

Displacement, tons: 18,400 full load
Measurement, tons: 13,000 dwt
Dimensions, feet (metres): 507.7 × 67.3 × 27.2 *(154.8 × 20.5 × 8.3)*
Main machinery: 1 Burmeister & Wain 6K47 diesel; 11,600 hp(m) *(8.53 MW)*; 1 shaft
Speed, knots: 15.6
Complement: 60
Cargo capacity: 13,000 tons

Comment: Sister ship *Rimac* has been scrapped.

MOLLENDO   *6/2004*, Peruvian Navy* / 1127041

1 TALARA CLASS (REPLENISHMENT TANKER) (AOT)

Name	No	Builders	Launched	Commissioned
TALARA	ATP 152	SIMA, Callao	9 July 1976	23 Jan 1978

Displacement, tons: 30,000 full load
Measurement, tons: 25,000 dwt
Dimensions, feet (metres): 561.5 × 82 × 31.2 *(171.2 × 25 × 9.5)*
Main machinery: 2 Burmeister & Wain 6K47EF diesels; 12,000 hp(m) *(8.82 MW)*; 1 shaft
Speed, knots: 15.5
Cargo capacity: 35,662 m³

Comment: Capable of underway replenishment at sea from the stern. *Bayovar*, of this class, launched 18 July 1977, having been originally ordered by Petroperu (State Oil Company) and transferred to the Navy while building. Sold back to Petroperu in 1979 and renamed *Pavayacu*. A third, *Trompeteros*, of this class has been built for Petroperu.

TALARA   *2000, Peruvian Navy* / 0105214

1 SEALIFT CLASS (TANKER) (AOT)

Name	No	Builders	Commissioned
LOBITOS (ex-*Sealift Caribbean*)	ATP 153 (ex-ATP 159, ex-TAOT 174)	Bath Iron Works	10 Feb 1975

Displacement, tons: 34,100 full load
Measurement, tons: 27,736 dwt; 15,979 grt
Dimensions, feet (metres): 587 × 84 × 34.6 *(178.9 × 25.6 × 10.6)*
Main machinery: 2 diesels; 1 shaft; cp prop; bow thruster
Speed, knots: 12.5
Range, n miles: 7,500 at 15 kt
Complement: 57
Cargo capacity: 185,000 barrels oil

Comment: Originally built for the US Military Sealift Command. Returned to owners in 1995 and acquired by Peru in 1997. Fitted with RAS gear in 1998.

LOBITOS   *11/2004*, Globke Collection* / 1127046

1 SUPE CLASS TANKER (AOT)

Name	No	Builders	Commissioned
SUPE (ex-*Taxiarchos*)	ATP 157	Voldnes A/S Fosnaveg Noruega	1965

Measurement, tons: 1,138 grt
Dimensions, feet (metres): 219.2 × 31.2 × 12.9 *(66.8 × 9.52 × 3.95)*
Main machinery: Diesel propulsion; 1 shaft
Speed, knots: 11
Complement: 17
Cargo capacity: 7,500 barrels oil

Comment: Acquired from Greece in 1996.

SUPE   *6/2001, Maritime Photographic* / 0126390

4 HARBOUR TANKERS (FUEL/WATER) (YW/YO)

CALAYERAS ACA 111 (ex-YW 128)	**GAUDEN** ACP 119 (ex-YO 171)
NOGUERA ACP 118 (ex-YO 221)	**BARCAZA CISTERNA DE AGUA** ABA 332 (ex-113)

Displacement, tons: 1,235 full load
Dimensions, feet (metres): 174 × 32 × 13.3 *(52.3 × 9.8 × 4.1)*
Main machinery: 1 GM diesel; 560 hp *(418 kW)*; 1 shaft
Speed, knots: 8
Complement: 23
Cargo capacity: 200,000 gallons
Radars: Navigation: Raytheon; I-band.

Comment: Details given are for first three. *YO 221* (fuel) transferred from US to Peru January 1975; *YO 171* (fuel) 20 January 1981; *YW 128* (water) 26 January 1985. *ABA 332* is a water barge built in Peru in 1972, capacity 300 tons.

GAUDEN   *1988, Peruvian Navy* / 0506072

1 TORPEDO RECOVERY VESSEL (YPT)

Name	No	Builders	Commissioned
SAN LORENZO	ART 322	Lürssen/Burmeister	1 Dec 1981

Displacement, tons: 58 standard; 65 full load
Dimensions, feet (metres): 82.7 × 18.4 × 5.6 (25.2 × 5.6 × 1.7)
Main machinery: 2 MTU 8V 396 TC82 diesels; 1,740 hp(m) (1.28 MW) sustained; 2 shafts
Speed, knots: 19
Range, n miles: 500 at 15 kt
Complement: 9

Comment: Can carry four long or eight short torpedoes.

SAN LORENZO   *9/1981, Lürssen Werft* / 0081534

1 LAKE HOSPITAL CRAFT (AH)

Name	No	Builders	Commissioned
PUNO (ex-Yapura)	ABH 306	J Watt Co, Thames Iron Works	18 May 1872

Displacement, tons: 500 full load
Dimensions, feet (metres): 125.1 × 19.7 × 13.1 (38.13 × 6.0 × 4.0)
Main machinery: 1 diesel; 1 shaft
Speed, knots: 14
Complement: 24 (1 officer)

Comment: Stationed on Lake Titicaca. 500 grt and has a diesel engine. The second of the class was finally paid off in 1990.

PUNO   *8/1999, A Campanera i Rovira* / 0081535

1 MARTE CLASS (SAIL TRAINING CRAFT) (AXS)

Name	No	Builders	Commissioned
MARTE (ex-Neptuno, ex-Noah's Ark)	ALY 313	James O Rasborough, Halifax, Canada	1974

Displacement, tons: 49 standard; 55 full load
Dimensions, feet (metres): 66.6 × 17.0 × 6.4 (20.30 × 5.18 × 1.95)
Main machinery: Two Perkins 130C diesels; 260 hp (194 kW); 2 props
Speed, knots: 8
Complement: 26
Radars: Surface search: Furuno; I-band.

Comment: Used for cadet instruction at the Naval Academy.

MARTE   *6/2004*, Peruvian Navy* / 1127042

3 FLOATING DOCKS (AH)

ADF 104   **106-107**

Displacement, tons: 4,500 (104); 1,900 (106); 5,200 (107)

Comment: 106 (ex-US AFDL 33) transferred 1959; 107 (ex-US ARD 8) transferred 1961; 104 built at SIMA, Callao in 1991.

TUGS

Notes: (1) There are three river tugs Tapuina AER 180, Rio Gaudin AER 186 and Rio Zambrano AER 187.
(2) There are also five small harbour tugs Mejia ARB 120, Huertas ARB 121, Dueñas AEB 126, Olaya ARB 128 and Selendón ARB 129.
(3) There is a 43 m salvage tug Unanue (AMB 160), first commissioned in 1944, transferred from the US in 1961.

1 CHEROKEE CLASS (SALVAGE TUG) (ATS)

Name	No	Builders	Commissioned
GUARDIAN RIOS (ex-Pinto ATF 90)	ARB 123	Cramp, Philadelphia, PA	1 Apr 1943

Displacement, tons: 1,640 full load
Dimensions, feet (metres): 205 × 38.5 × 17 (62.5 × 11.7 × 5.2)
Main machinery: Diesel-electric; 4 GM 12-278 diesels; 4,400 hp (3.28 MW); 4 generators; 1 motor; 3,000 hp (2.24 MW); 1 shaft
Speed, knots: 16.5
Range, n miles: 6,500 at 16 kt
Complement: 99

Comment: Transferred from USA on loan in 1960, sold 17 May 1974. Fitted with powerful pumps and other salvage equipment.

GUARDIAN RIOS   *1993, Peruvian Navy* / 0506160

COAST GUARD

Notes: (1) DCB 350-358 are 6 m Cougar 22 class inshore patrol craft. DCB 358 is a one ton harbour patrol launch.
(2) Rio Cañete (PC 231) is a 10 m coastal patrol craft built in Spain and commissioned in 1985.
(3) Rio Santa (PC 232) and Rio Majes (PC 233) are 10 m coastal patrol craft built at Callao and commissioned in 1981-82.
(4) Rio Viru (PC 235) and Rio Lurin (PC 236) are 13 m coastal patrol craft built by Camcraft and commissioned in 1981-82.
(5) PF 250-257 are river patrol craft built at SIMA, Iquitos.
(6) Gamitana 1-3 are three 9 m river patrol craft built at SIMA, Iquitos, which entered service in 2004.

5 RIO CANETE CLASS (LARGE PATROL CRAFT) (WPB)

Name	No	Builders	Commissioned
RIO NEPEÑA	PC 243	SIMA, Chimbote	1 Dec 1981
RIO TAMBO	PC 244	SIMA, Chimbote	1982
RIO OCOÑA	PC 245	SIMA, Chimbote	1983
RIO HUARMEY	PC 246	SIMA, Chimbote	1984
RIO ZAÑA	PC 247	SIMA, Chimbote	12 Feb 1985

Displacement, tons: 476 full load
Dimensions, feet (metres): 167 × 24.8 × 5.6 (50.9 × 7.4 × 1.7)
Main machinery: 4 Bazán MAN V8V diesels; 5,640 hp(m) (4.15 MW); 2 shafts
Speed, knots: 23
Range, n miles: 3,050 at 17 kt
Complement: 24 (5 officers)
Guns: 1 Oerlikon 20 mm. 2—12.7 mm MGs.
Radars: Surface search: Decca 1226; I-band.

Comment: Have aluminium alloy superstructures. The prototype craft was scrapped in 1990. Rio Ocoña completed refit in July 1996 and the rest of the class were refitted at one per year.

RIO OCOÑA   *11/2004, Globke Collection* / 1047861

1 PGM 71 CLASS (LARGE PATROL CRAFT) (PB)

Name	No	Builders	Commissioned
RIO CHIRA	PM 223 (ex-PGM 111)	SIMA, Callao	June 1972

Displacement, tons: 147 full load
Dimensions, feet (metres): 118.2 × 21 × 6 *(36.0 × 6.4 × 1.8)*
Main machinery: 2 Detroit GN-71 diesels; 1,450 hp *(1.08 MW)*; 2 shafts
Speed, knots: 18. **Range, n miles:** 1,500 at 10 kt
Complement: 15
Guns: 1—12.7 mm MG.
Radars: Surface search: Raytheon; I-band.

Comment: Acquired from the Navy in 1975. Paid off in 1994 but back in service again in 1997, with refurbished engines.

RIO CHIRA   *2000, Peruvian Coast Guard* / 0105218

1 RIVER PATROL CRAFT (PBR)

Name	No	Builders	Commissioned
RIO PIURA	PC 242 (ex-P 252)	Viareggio, Italy	5 Sep 1960

Displacement, tons: 55 full load
Dimensions, feet (metres): 65.7 × 17 × 3.2 *(20 × 5.2 × 1)*
Main machinery: 2 GM 8V-71 diesels; 460 hp *(344 kW)* sustained; 2 shafts
Speed, knots: 15. **Range, n miles:** 1,000 at 16 kt
Complement: 9 (2 officers)
Guns: 2—12.7 mm MGs. 1 Oerlikon 20 mm.
Radars: Navigation: Raytheon; I-band.

Comment: Ordered in 1959. Armament changed in 1992. Refitted in 1996.

RIO PIURA   *6/2004*, Peruvian Coast Guard* / 1127043

16 LAKE and RIVER PATROL CRAFT (PBR)

RIO HULLAGA	PF 260	RIO PATAYACU	LIF 271
RIO SANTIAGO	PF 261	RIO ZAPOTE	LIF 272
RIO PUTUMAYO	PF 262	RIO CHAMBIRA	LIF 273
RIO NANAY	PF 263	RIO TAMBOPATA	PF 274
RIO NAPO	LIF 264	RIO RAMIS	PL 290
RIO YAVARI	LIF 265	RIO ILAVE	PL 291
RIO MATADOR	LIF 266	JULI	PL 293
RIO ITAYA	LIF 270	MOHO	PL 294

Displacement, tons: 5 full load
Dimensions, feet (metres): 32.8 × 11.2 × 2.6 *(10 × 3.4 × 0.8)*
Main machinery: 2 Perkins diesels; 480 hp *(358 kW)*; 2 shafts
Speed, knots: 15. **Range, n miles:** 450 at 28 kt
Complement: 3
Guns: 1—12.7 mm MG.
Radars: Surface search: Raytheon 2800; I-band.

Comment: Details given are for PL 290-292. Based at Puno on Lake Titicaca. GRP hulls built in 1982. The remainder are of various types. PF 260-263 are 4-5 ton craft, LIF 264-267 are 2 tons and LIF 270-274 are 2-3 tons. PL 293-294 are 12 ton vessels commissioned in 2003. PL 293 is based on Lake Titicaca.

RIO ILAVE   *2000, Peruvian Coast Guard* / 0105220

RIO NAPO   *2000, Peruvian Coast Guard* / 0105221

5 PORT PATROL CRAFT (PBF/PB)

RIO SUPE PI 210	QUILCA DCB 214
MANCORA DCB 212	PUCUSANA PC 215
HUAURA DCB 213	

Comment: Miscellaneous craft. PI 210 is a Cougar 40 kt fast patrol craft of 2 tons, DCB 212-214 are Cougar 25 (3 ton) and PP 215 of 4 tons. All acquired in 1993.

RIO SUPE   *2000, Peruvian Coast Guard* / 0105223

6 CHICAMA (DAUNTLESS) CLASS (PBR)

CHICAMA PC 216	CHORRILLOS PC 218	CAMANA PC 220
HUANCHACO PC 217	CHANCAY PC 219	CHALA PC 221

Displacement, tons: 14 full load
Dimensions, feet (metres): 40 × 14 × 4.4 *(12.2 × 4.3 × 1.3)*
Main machinery: 2 Caterpillar 3208TA diesels; 870 hp *(650 kW)*; 2 shafts
Speed, knots: 27
Range, n miles: 600 at 18 kt
Complement: 5
Guns: 1—12.7 mm MG. 1—7.62 mm MG.
Radars: Surface search: Furuno 821; I-band.

Comment: Ordered in February 2000 under FMS funding. First pair delivered in August 2000 remainder in November 2000. Formerly river patrol craft, now operational on Pacific Coast.

CHANCAY   *6/2004*, Peruvian Coast Guard* / 1127045

10 ZORRITOS CLASS (RIVER PATROL CRAFT) (PBR)

ZORRITOS PC 222	BARRANCA PC 227	SAN NICOLAS PC 230
PUNTA ARENAS PC 224	COISHCO PC 228	MATARANI PC 234
SANTA ROSA PC 225	INDEPENDENCIA PC 229	SAMA PC 238
PACASMAYO PC 226		

Displacement, tons: 12 full load
Dimensions, feet (metres): 40.0 × 13.8 × 2.3 *(12.2 × 4.2 × 0.7)*
Main machinery: 2 Caterpillar 3126 diesels; 550 hp *(411 kW)*; 2 shafts
Speed, knots: 25
Complement: 5 (1 officer)
Guns: 1—12.7 mm MG.
Radars: Surface search: Furuno; I-band.

Comment: Built by SIMA Chimbote and delivered 2003-04.

SAN NICOLAS   *11/2004*, Globke Collection* / 1133139

Philippines

Country Overview

The Republic of the Philippines was formally proclaimed in 1946. Situated between Taiwan to the north and Indonesia and Malaysia to the south, the country comprises about 7,100 islands with a total coastline of 19,597 n miles with the South China, Philippine and Celebes Seas. Eleven islands, Bohol, Cebu, Leyte, Luzon, Masbate, Mindanao, Mindoro, Negros, Palawan, Panay, and Samar, contain the majority of the population. Most remaining islands are less than 1 square mile in area. The capital, principal city and port is Manila. Other important ports include Davao, Cebu and Zamboanga. An archipelagic state, territorial seas (12 n miles) are claimed. A 200 n mile EEZ has also been claimed but the limits have not been defined.

Headquarters Appointments

Flag Officer-in-Command:
  Vice Admiral Ernesto H De Leon
Commander Fleet:
  Rear Admiral Alfredo Diaz Abueg
Commandant Coast Guard:
  Vice Admiral Arturo Gosingan
Commandant Marines:
  Major General Orlando G Buenaventura

Diplomatic Representation

Defence Attaché in London:
  Colonel C B Boquiren

Personnel

(a) 2006: 20,500 Navy; 8,700 Marines; 3,500 Coast Guard
(b) Reserves: 17,000

Organisation

The Naval Headquarters is at Manila. The fleet is divided into functional units including the Ready Force, Patrol Force, Service Force, Assault Craft Force, Naval Air Group and Naval Special Warfare Group. There are six operational areas of responsibility: Southern Luzon; Northern Luzon; Central; West; Western Mindanao and Eastern Mindanao. The Coast Guard was transferred to the Department of Transport and Communication in 1998. There are eight Coast Guard Districts, 47 stations and 154 Coast Guard Detachment units.

Marine Corps

Marines comprise three tactical brigades composed of 10 tactical battalions, one support regiment, a service group, a guard battalion and a reconnaissance battalion. Headquarters at Ternate, Manila Bay. Deployed in Mindanao and Palawan.

Bases

Main: Cavite.
Operational: San Vicente, Mactan, Ternate.
Stations: Cebu, Davao, Legaspi, Bonifacio, Tacloban, San Miguel, Ulugan, Balabne, Puerto Princesa, Pagasa.

Prefix to Ships' Names

BRP: Barko Republika Pilipinas

Strength of the Fleet

Type	Active	Building
Frigates	(1)	—
Corvettes	13	(2)
Fast Attack Craft	6	—
Large Patrol Craft	5	1 (3)
Coastal Patrol Craft	37	2
LST/LSV Transports	8	—
LCM/LCU/RUC/LCVP	44	—
Repair Ship	1	—
Tankers	4	—
Coast Guard		
Tenders	4	—
Patrol Craft	58	1

PENNANT LIST

Frigates		PG 112	Bienvenido Salting	PG 395	Felix Apolinario	AC 90	Mactan
		PG 114	Salvador Abcede	PG 396	Brigadier Abraham Campo	AD 617	Yakal
PF 11	Rajah Humabon	PG 115	Ramon Aguirre	PG 840	Conrado Yap		
		PG 116	Nicolas Mahusay	PG 842	Tedorico Dominado Jr	**Coast Guard**	
Corvettes		PG 140	Emilo Aguinaldo	PG 843	Cosme Acosta		
		PG 141	Antonio Luna	PG 844	José Artiaga Jr	AE 46	Cape Bojeador
PS 19	Miguel Malvar	PG 370	José Andrada	PG 846	Nicanor Jimenez	PG 61	Agusan
PS 20	Magat Salamat	PG 371	Enrique Jurado	PG 847	Leopoldo Regis	PG 62	Catanduanes
PS 22	Sultan Kudarat	PG 372	Alfredo Peckson	PG 848	Leon Tadina	PG 63	Romblon
PS 23	Datu Marikudo	PG 374	Simeon Castro	PG 849	Loreto Danipog	PG 64	Palawan
PS 28	Cebu	PG 375	Carlos Albert	PG 851	Apollo Tiano	AT 71	Mangyan
PS 29	Negros Occidental	PG 376	Heracleo Alano	PG 853	Sulpicio Hernandez	AU 75	Bessang Pass
PS 31	Pangasinan	PG 377	Liberato Picar			AE 79	Limasawa
PS 32	Iloilo	PG 378	Hilario Ruiz			AG 89	Kalinga
PS 35	Emilio Jacinto	PG 379	Rafael Pargas	**Auxiliaries**		AU 100	Tirad Pass
PS 36	Apolinario Mabini	PG 380	Nestor Reinoso			001	San Juan
PS 37	Artemio Ricarte	PG 381	Dioscoro Papa	LT 86	Zamboanga Del Sur	002	Esda II
PS 38	General Mariano Alvares	PG 383	Ismael Lomibao	LT 87	South Cotabato		
PS 70	Quezon	PG 384	Leovigildo Gantioque	LT 501	Laguna		
PS 74	Rizal	PG 385	Federico Martir	LT 504	Lanao Del Norte		
		PG 386	Filipino Flojo	LT 516	Kalinga Apayao		
Patrol Forces		PG 387	Anastacio Cacayorin	LC 550	Bacolod City		
		PG 388	Manuel Gomez	LC 551	Dagupan City		
PG 101	Kagitingan	PG 389	Testimo Figuracion	AT 25	Ang Pangulo		
PG 102	Bagong Lakas	PG 390	José Loor SR	AW 33	Lake Bulusan		
PG 104	Bagong Silang	PG 392	Juan Magluyan	AW 34	Lake Paoay		
PG 110	Tomas Batilo	PG 393	Florenca Nuno	AF 72	Lake Taal		
PG 111	Bonny Serrano	PG 394	Alberto Navaret	AF 78	Lake Buhi		

FRIGATES

Notes: *Rajah Lakandula*, paid off in 1988, is still afloat as an alongside HQ and depot ship.

1 CANNON CLASS (FF)

Name	No	Builders	Laid down	Launched	Commissioned
RAJAH HUMABON (ex-*Hatsuhi* DE 263, ex-*Atherton* DE 169)	PF 11 (ex-PF 78)	Norfolk Navy Yard, Portsmouth, VA	14 Jan 1943	27 May 1943	29 Aug 1943

Displacement, tons: 1,390 standard; 1,750 full load
Dimensions, feet (metres): 306 × 36.6 × 14
  (93.3 × 11.2 × 4.3)
Main machinery: Diesel-electric; 2 GM EMD 16V-645E7 diesels; 5,800 hp *(4.32 MW)*; 4 generators; 2 motors; 2 shafts
Speed, knots: 18. **Range, n miles:** 6,000 at 14 kt
Complement: 165

Guns: 3 US 3 in *(76 mm)*/50 Mk 22; 20 rds/min to 12 km *(6.6 n miles)*; weight of shell 6 kg.
  6 US/Bofors 40 mm/56 (3 twin). 4 Oerlikon 20 mm/70; 2÷12.7 mm MGs.
Depth charges: 8 K-gun Mk 6 projectors; range 160 m; warhead 150 kg; 1 rack.
Weapons control: Mk 52 GFCS with Mk 41 rangefinder for 3 in guns. 3 Mk 51 Mod 2 GFCS for 40 mm.
Radars: Surface search: Raytheon SPS-5; G/H-band.
  Navigation: RCA/GE Mk 26; I-band.
Sonars: SQS-17B; hull-mounted; active search and attack; medium/high frequency.

Programmes: *Hatsuhi* originally transferred by the US to Japan 14 June 1955 and paid off June 1975 reverting to US Navy. Transferred to Philippines 23 December 1978. Towed to South Korea 1979 for overhaul and modernisation. Recommissioned 27 February 1980. A sister ship *Datu Kalantiaw* lost during Typhoon Clara 20 September 1981.
Modernisation: Upgrade plans have been suspended.
Operational: Hedgehog A/S mortars have been reported.

RAJAH HUMABON   *10/2001, Chris Sattler* / 0126280

CORVETTES

3 JACINTO (PEACOCK) CLASS (FS)

Name	No
EMILIO JACINTO (ex-*Peacock*)	PS 35 (ex-P 239)
APOLINARIO MABINI (ex-*Plover*)	PS 36 (ex-P 240)
ARTEMIO RICARTE (ex-*Starling*)	PS 37 (ex-P 241)

Builders	Laid down	Launched	Commissioned
Hall Russell, Aberdeen	1 Dec 1982	14 July 1984	4 Aug 1997
Hall Russell, Aberdeen	12 Apr 1983	20 July 1984	4 Aug 1997
Hall Russell, Aberdeen	11 Sep 1983	10 Aug 1984	4 Aug 1997

Displacement, tons: 763 full load
Dimensions, feet (metres): 204.1 × 32.8 × 8.9
(62.6 × 10 × 2.7)
Main machinery: 2 Crossley Pielstick 18 PA6 V 280 diesels;
14,000 hp(m) *(10.6 MW)* sustained; 2 shafts; 1 retractable
Schottel prop; 181 hp *(135 kW)*
Speed, knots: 25. **Range, n miles:** 2,500 at 17 kt
Complement: 31 (6 officers) plus 7 spare berths

Guns: 1—3 in *(76 mm)*/62 OTO Melara compact; 85 rds/min
to 16 km *(8.6 n miles)* anti-surface; 12 km *(6.5 n miles)*
anti-aircraft; weight of shell 6 kg. 4 FN 7.62 mm MGs.
Weapons control: BAe Sea Archer GSA-7 for 76 mm gun.
Radars: Navigation: Kelvin Hughes Type 1006; I-band.

Programmes: Letter of Intention to purchase from the UK
signed in November 1996. Transferred 1 August 1997
after sailing from Hong Kong on 1 July 1997. Others of
the class in service with the navy of the Irish Republic.
Modernisation: An upgrade programme was agreed in 2002
and a contract was signed on 6 December 2004 for phase
one of the work which is to include overhaul of the 76 mm
gun, installation of a MSI Defense Systems 25 mm
mounting on the stern, replacement of Sea Archer
fire-control system with a Radamec 1500 optronic director,
replacement of the navigation radar with Sperry Marine
Bridgemaster E and new navigation systems. Phase one
is to be completed by November 2006. Phases two and
three are to involve new propulsion and safety systems.
Structure: Fitted with telescopic cranes, loiter drive and
replenishment at sea equipment. In UK service, two fast
pursuit craft were carried.
Operational: These ships are the workhorses of the fleet.
Based at Cavite.

EMILIO JACINTO   *6/2002* / 0534067

2 AUK CLASS (FS)

Name	No
RIZAL (ex-*Murrelet* MSF 372)	PS 74 (ex-PS 69)
QUEZON (ex-*Vigilance* MSF 324)	PS 70

Builders	Laid down	Launched	Commissioned
Savannah Machine & Foundry Co, GA	24 Aug 1944	29 Dec 1944	21 Aug 1945
Associated Shipbuilders, Seattle, WA	28 Nov 1942	5 Apr 1943	28 Feb 1944

Displacement, tons: 1,090 standard; 1,250 full load
Dimensions, feet (metres): 221.2 × 32.2 × 10.8
(67.4 × 9.8 × 3.3)
Main machinery: Diesel-electric; 2 GM EMD 16V-645E6 diesels;
5,800 hp *(4.32 MW)*; 2 generators; 2 motors; 2 shafts
Speed, knots: 18. **Range, n miles:** 5,000 at 14 kt
Complement: 80 (5 officers)

Guns: 2 US 3 in *(76 mm)*/50 Mk 26; 20 rds/min to 12 km
(6.6 n miles); weight of shell 6 kg.
4 US/Bofors 40 mm/56 (2 twin); 160 rds/min to 11 km
(5.9 n miles); weight of shell 0.9 kg.
2 Oerlikon 20 mm (twin). 2—12.7 mm MGs.
Radars: Surface search: Raytheon SPS-5C; G/H-band.
Navigation: DAS 3; I-band.

Programmes: *Rizal* transferred from the US to the Philippines
on 18 June 1965 and *Quezon* on 19 August 1967.
Modernisation: Upgrade plans have been suspended.
Structure: Upon transfer the minesweeping gear was
removed and a second 3 in gun fitted aft.
Operational: Both ships were to have been deleted in 1994
but have been retained until new class of OPVs is built.
Sonar equipment and depth charges have been removed.

RIZAL   *10/2001, Chris Sattler* / 0534068

8 PCE 827 CLASS (FS)

Name	No	Builders	Commissioned
MIGUEL MALVAR (ex-*Ngoc Hoi*, Ex-*Brattleboro* PCER 852)	PS 19	Pullman Standard Car Co, Chicago	26 May 1944
MAGAT SALAMAT (ex-*Chi Lang II*, ex-*Gayety* MSF 239)	PS 20	Winslow Marine Co, Seattle, WA	14 June 1944
SULTAN KUDARAT (ex-*Dong Da II*, ex-*Crestview* PCER 895)	PS 22	Willamette Iron & Steel Corporation, Portland, OR	30 Oct 1943
DATU MARIKUDO (ex-*Van Kiep II*, ex-*Amherst* PCER 853)	PS 23	Pullman Standard Car Co, Chicago	16 June 1944
CEBU (ex-PCE 881)	PS 28	Albina E and M Works, Portland, OR	31 July 1944
NEGROS OCCIDENTAL (ex-PCE 884)	PS 29	Albina E and M Works, Portland, OR	30 Mar 1944
PANGASINAN (ex-PCE 891)	PS 31	Willamette Iron & Steel Corp, Portland, OR	15 June 1944
ILOILO (ex-PCE 897)	PS 32	Willamette Iron & Steel Corp, Portland, OR	6 Jan 1945

Displacement, tons: 640 standard; 914 full load
Dimensions, feet (metres): 184.5 × 33.1 × 9.5
(56.3 × 10.1 × 2.9)
Main machinery: 2 GM 12-278A diesels; 2,200 hp *(1.64 MW)*;
2 shafts
Speed, knots: 15. **Range, n miles:** 6,600 at 11 kt
Complement: 85 (8 officers)

Guns: 1 US 3 in *(76 mm)*/50; 20 rds/min to 12 km
(6.6 n miles); weight of shell 6 kg.
2 to 6 US/Bofors 40 mm/56 (single or 1—3 twin);
160 rds/min to 11 km *(5.9 n miles)*; weight of shell 0.9 kg.
2 Oerlikon 20 mm/70; 800 rds/min to 2 km.
Radars: Surface search: SPS-50 (PS 23). SPS-21D (PS 19,
28). CRM-NIA-75 (PS 29, 31, 32). SPS-53A (PS 20).
Navigation: RCA SPN-18; I/J-band.

Programmes: Five transferred from the US to the
Philippines in July 1948 (PS 28-32); PS 22 to South Vietnam
from US Navy on 29 November 1961, PS 20 in April 1962,
PS 19 on 11 July 1966, and PS 23 in June 1970. PS 19, 20 and
22 to Philippines November 1975 and PS 23 5 April 1976.
Modernisation: PS 19, 22, 31 and 32 refurbished in 1990-91,
PS 23 and 28 in 1992 and the last pair in 1996/97.
Structure: First three were originally fitted as rescue
ships (PCER). A/S equipment has been removed or is
inoperable. PS 20 has some minor structural differences
having been built as an Admirable class MSF.
Operational: PS 29 is probably not operational.

CEBU   *5/2000, M Declerck* / 0105225

1 CYCLONE CLASS (COASTAL PATROL SHIP) (PB)

Name	No	Builders	Commissioned
GENERAL MARIANO ALVARES	PS 38 (ex-PC 1)	Bollinger, Lockport	7 Aug 1993
(ex-*Cyclone*)			

Displacement, tons: 386 full load
Dimensions, feet (metres): 179 × 25.9 × 7.9 *(54.6 × 7.9 × 2.4)*
Main machinery: 4 Paxman Valenta 16RP200CM diesels; 13,400 hp *(10 MW)* sustained; 4 shafts
Speed, knots: 35. **Range, n miles:** 2,500 at 12 kt
Complement: 28 (4 officers) plus 8
Countermeasures: Decoys: 2 Mk 52 sextuple and/or Wallop Super Barricade Mk 3 chaff launchers.
ESM: Privateer APR-39; radar warning.
Weapons control: Marconi VISTAR IM 405 IR system.
Radars: Surface search: 2 Sperry RASCAR; E/F/I/J-band.
Sonars: Wesmar; hull-mounted; active; high frequency.

Programmes: Transferred from the USN to the Philippines in February 2004 following refit at Bollinger. Recommissioned on 8 March 2004.
Modernisation: All armament was removed before transfer from the USN. New armament is likely to include two 25 mm guns and 12.7 mm machine guns.
Structure: Design based on Vosper Thornycroft Ramadan class modified for USN requirements including 1 in armour on superstructure. The craft has a slow speed loiter capability and has been modified to incorporate a semi-dry well, boat ramp and stern gate to facilitate deployment and recovery of a fully loaded RIB while the ship is making way.

GENERAL MARIANO ALVARES   *3/2004, US Embassy, Manila* / 0563762

LAND-BASED MARITIME AIRCRAFT

Notes: There are two Cessna 177 Cardinal transport aircraft.

Numbers/Type: 7 PADC (Pilatus Britten-Norman) Islander F27MP.
Operational speed: 150 kt *(280 km/h).*
Service ceiling: 18,900 ft *(5,760 m).*
Range: 1,500 n miles *(2,775 km).*
Role/Weapon systems: Short-range MR and SAR aircraft. First purchased in 1989. Three transferred from the Air Force. An upgrade programme, including engines, avionics and communications systems has been completed on five aircraft. The remaining two aircraft are to be similarly modernised. Sensors: Search radar, cameras. Weapons: Unarmed.

F-27MP   *10/2001, Adolfo Ortigueira Gil* / 0567482

Numbers/Type: 5 PADC (MBB) BO 105C.
Operational speed: 145 kt *(270 km/h).*
Service ceiling: 17,000 ft *(5,180 m).*
Range: 355 n miles *(657 km).*
Role/Weapon systems: Sole shipborne helicopter; some shore-based for SAR; some commando support capability. Purchased at the rate of one per year from 1986 to 1992. Upgrade of avionics and communications is planned. Sensors: Some fitted with search radar. Weapons: Unarmed.

PATROL FORCES

Notes: Plans to procure three offshore patrol craft have been suspended although they remain a long-term aspiration.

2 + 1 AGUINALDO CLASS (LARGE PATROL CRAFT) (PBO)

Name	No	Builders	Commissioned
EMILIO AGUINALDO	PG 140	Cavite, Sangley Point	21 Nov 1990
ANTONIO LUNA	PG 141	Cavite, Sangley Point	27 May 1999
—	PG 142	Cavite, Sangley Point	—

Displacement, tons: 236 full load
Dimensions, feet (metres): 144.4 × 24.3 × 5.2 *(44 × 7.4 × 1.6)*
Main machinery: 2 MTU 16V-396TB94 diesels; 3,480 hp *(2.59 MW)* sustained; 2 shafts
Speed, knots: 28. **Range, n miles:** 1,100 at 18 kt
Complement: 58 (6 officers)
Guns: 2 Bofors 40 mm/60. 2 Oerlikon 20 mm. 4—12.7 mm MGs.
Radars: Surface search: Raytheon; I-band.

Comment: Steel hulls of similar design to *Tirad Pass*. First of class launched 23 June 1984 but only completed in 1990. Second laid down 2 December 1990 and launched 23 June 1992. PG 142 laid down on 14 February 1994 and launched in April 2000. While the superstructure is 70 per cent completed, outfitting has been suspended due to budget constraints. For similar reasons, the outlook for completion of the six ship programme looks doubtful as do plans to upgrade existing ships with a SAM system and 76 mm gun.

EMILIO AGUINALDO   *6/1993* / 0081540

2 POINT CLASS (PB)

Name	No	Builders	Commissioned
ALBERTO NAVARET (ex-*Point Evans*)	PG 394 (ex-82354)	CG Yard, Maryland	10 Jan 1967
BRIGADIER ABRAHAM CAMPO	PG 396 (ex-82375)	CG Yard, Maryland	1 June 1970
(ex-*Point Doran*)			

Displacement, tons: 67 full load
Dimensions, feet (metres): 83 × 17.2 × 5.8 *(25.3 × 5.2 × 1.8)*
Main machinery: 2 Caterpillar 3412 diesels; 1,600 hp *(1.19 MW)*; 2 shafts
Speed, knots: 23
Range, n miles: 1,500 at 8 kt
Complement: 10
Guns: 2—12.7 mm MGs.
Radars: Surface search: Furuno; I-band.

Comment: PG 394 transferred from US Coast Guard 16 November 1999. Second transferred 22 March 2001. This class is in service with many other navies.

POINT CLASS (US colours)   *4/1992, van Ginderen Collection* / 0081549

3 KAGITINGAN CLASS (LARGE PATROL CRAFT) (PB)

Name	No	Builders	Commissioned
KAGITINGAN	P 101	Hamelin SY, Germany	9 Feb 1979
BAGONG LAKAS	PG 102 (ex-P 102)	Hamelin SY, Germany	9 Feb 1979
BAGONG SILANG	PG 104 (ex-P 104)	Hamelin SY, Germany	July 1979

Displacement, tons: 150 full load
Dimensions, feet (metres): 121.4 × 20.3 × 5.6 *(37 × 6.2 × 1.7)*
Main machinery: 2 MTU MB 16V-538TB91 diesels; 2,500 hp(m) *(1.86 MW)* sustained; 2 shafts
Speed, knots: 21
Complement: 30 (4 officers)
Guns: 2—30 mm (twin). 4—12.7 mm MGs. 2—7.62 mm MGs.
Radars: Surface search: I-band.

Comment: Based at Cavite. P 103 paid off and used for spares. All still in service.

BAGONG LAKAS   *1993, Philippine Navy* / 0506161

6 TOMAS BATILO (SEA DOLPHIN) CLASS
(FAST ATTACK CRAFT) (PBF)

TOMAS BATILO PG 110	**BIENVENIDO SALTING** PG 112	**RAMON AGUIRRE** PG 115
BONNY SERRANO PG 111	**SALVADOR ABCEDE** PG 114	**NICOLAS MAHUSAY** PG 116

Displacement, tons: 150 full load
Dimensions, feet (metres): 121.4 × 22.6 × 5.6 *(37 × 6.9 × 1.7)*
Main machinery: 2 MTU 20V-538TB91 diesels; 9,000 hp(m) *(6.71 MW)* sustained; 2 shafts
Speed, knots: 38
Range, n miles: 600 at 20 kt
Complement: 31 (5 officers)
Guns: 2 Emerson Electric 30 mm (twin); 1,200 rds/min combined to 6 km *(3.2 n miles)*;
 weight of shell 0.35 kg.
 1 Bofors 40 mm/60. 2 Oerlikon 20 mm.
Weapons control: Optical director.
Radars: Surface search: Raytheon 1645; I-band.

Comment: Transferred from South Korea on 15 June 1995. Part of the PKM 200 series. Different armament to South Korean ships of the same class. Plans to modernise these craft during 2002-03 appear to have been suspended.

BIENVENIDO SALTING *6/1996, Philippine Navy* / 0506311

4 PCF 65 (SWIFT MK 3) CLASS (COASTAL PATROL CRAFT) (PB)

PC 351-354

Displacement, tons: 29 standard; 37 full load
Dimensions, feet (metres): 65 × 16 × 3.4 *(19.8 × 4.9 × 1)*
Main machinery: 3 GM 12V-71TI diesels; 840 hp *(616 kW)* sustained; 3 shafts
Speed, knots: 25
Complement: 8
Guns: 2—12.7 mm MGs.
Radars: Surface search: Koden; I-band.

Comment: Improved Swift type inshore patrol boats built by Peterson and delivered 1975-76. Aluminium construction. Some that were laid up have been returned to service. New radars fitted.

PC 354 *5/1998, John Mortimer* / 0081551

22 JOSÉ ANDRADA CLASS (COASTAL PATROL CRAFT) (PB)

JOSÉ ANDRADA PG 370	**RAFAEL PARGAS** PG 379	**ANASTACIO CACAYORIN** PG 387
ENRIQUE JURADO PG 371	**NESTOR REINOSO** PG 380	**MANUEL GOMEZ** PG 388
ALFREDO PECKSON PG 372	**DIOSCORO PAPA** PG 381	**TESTIMO FIGURACION** PG 389
SIMEON CASTRO PG 374	**ISMAEL LOMIBAO** PG 383	**JOSÉ LOOR SR** PG 390
CARLOS ALBERT PG 375	**LEOVIGILDO GANTIOQUE** PG 384	**JUAN MAGLUYAN** PG 392
HERACLEO ALANO PG 376	**FEDERICO MARTIR** PG 385	**FLORENCA NUNO** PG 393
LIBERATO PICAR PG 377	**FILIPINO FLOJO** PG 386	**FELIX APOLINARIO** PG 395
HILARIO RUIZ PG 378		

Displacement, tons: 56 full load
Dimensions, feet (metres): 78 × 20 × 5.8 *(23.8 × 6.1 × 1.8)*
Main machinery: 2 Detroit 16V-92TA diesels; 1,380 hp *(1.03 MW)* sustained; 2 shafts
Speed, knots: 28
Range, n miles: 1,200 at 12 kt
Complement: 8—12 (1 officer)
Guns: 1 Bushmaster 25 mm or Bofors 40 mm/60.
 4—12.7 mm Mk 26 MGs. 2—7.62 mm M60 MGs.
Radars: Surface search: Raytheon SPS-64(V)2; I-band.

Comment: There are four batches of this class. Batch I (PCF 370-378), Batch II (PCF 379-390), Batch III (PCF 392-393) and Batch IV (PCF 395). The main difference between batches include weapons, electronics and accommodation. First four ordered from Halter Marine in August 1989 under FMS and built at Equitable Shipyards, New Orleans, as were a further four ordered in 1990. Eight more ordered in March 1993 with co-production between Halter Marine and AG&P Shipyard, Batangas. An additional three were ordered in 1995. Built to US Coast Guard standards with an aluminium hull and superstructure. The main gun may be fitted in all after some minor modifications. PG 392 delivered in March 1998, PG 393 in July 1998 and PG 395 on 10 October 2000.

TESTIMO FIGURACION *5/2000, M Declerck* / 0105226

FLORENCA NUNO *5/2000, van Ginderen Collection* / 0105227

10 CONRADO YAP (SEA HAWK/KILLER) CLASS
(COASTAL PATROL CRAFT) (PBF)

CONRADO YAP PG 840	**LEOPOLDO REGIS** PG 847
TEDORICO DOMINADO JR PG 842	**LEON TADINA** PG 848
COSME ACOSTA PG 843	**LORETO DANIPOG** PG 849
JOSÉ ARTIAGA JR PG 844	**APOLLO TIANO** PG 851
NICANOR JIMENEZ PG 846	**SULPICIO FERNANDEZ** PG 853

Displacement, tons: 74.5 full load
Dimensions, feet (metres): 83.7 × 17.7 × 6.2 *(25.5 × 5.4 × 1.9)*
Main machinery: 2 MTU 16V-538TB91 diesels; 5,000 hp(m) *(3.72 MW)*; 2 shafts
Speed, knots: 38. **Range, n miles:** 290 at 20 kt
Complement: 15 (3 officers)
Guns: 1 Bofors 40 mm/60. 2 Oerlikon 20 mm (twin) Mk 16.
Radars: Surface search: Raytheon 1645; I-band.

Comment: Type PK 181 built by Korea Tacoma and Hyundai 1975-78. Twelve craft transferred from South Korea 19 June 1993. Eight were commissioned 23 June 1993 and a further four on 23 June 1994. However PC 845 and PC 852 have not been reactivated and are probably used as spares.

CONRADO YAP CLASS *1993, Philippine Navy* / 0506162

SURVEY AND RESEARCH SHIPS

Notes: (1) Survey ships are operated by Coast and Geodetic Survey of Ministry of National Defence and are not naval.
(2) Two research ships *Fort San Antonio* (AM 700) and *Fort Abad* (AM 701) were acquired in 1993.

AUXILIARIES

Notes: (1) All LSTs, LSVs, LCMs and LCUs are classified as Transports.
(2) Procurement of a new LST and four new LCU is reported to be in progress in order to improve sealift for the marines.

42 LCM/LCU

Comment: Ex-US minor landing craft mostly transferred in the mid-1970s. 11 LCM 6, five LCM 8, eight LCU, 14 RUC and two LCVP. More LCVP are building at Cavite and two LCUs were reported delivered from South Korea in late 1995. More LCMs are planned. Used as transport vessels.

LCU 286 *5/1998, van Ginderen Collection* / 0052706

2 BACOLOD CITY (FRANK S BESSON) CLASS (LSVH)

Name	No	Builders	Commissioned
BACOLOD CITY	LC 550	Moss Point Marine	1 Dec 1993
DAGUPAN CITY	LC 551	Moss Point Marine	5 Apr 1994
(ex-Cagayan De Oro City)			

Displacement, tons: 4,265 full load
Dimensions, feet (metres): 272.8 × 60 × 12 *(83.1 × 18.3 × 3.7)*
Main machinery: 2 GM EMD 16V-645E6 diesels; 5,800 hp *(4.32 MW)* sustained; 2 shafts; bow thruster; 250 hp *(187 kW)*
Speed, knots: 11.6
Range, n miles: 6,000 at 11 kt
Complement: 30 (6 officers)
Military lift: 2,280 tons (900 for amphibious operations) of vehicles, containers or cargo, plus 150 troops; 2 LCVPs on davits
Radars: Navigation: Raytheon SPS-64(V)2; I-band.
Helicopters: Platform for 1 BO 105C.

Comment: Contract announced by Trinity Marine 3 April 1992 for two ships with an option on a third which was not taken up. Ro-ro design with 10,500 sq ft of deck space for cargo. Capable of beaching with 4 ft over the ramp on a 1 : 30 offshore gradient with a 900 ton cargo. Similar to US Army vessels but with only a bow ramp. The stern ramp space is used for accommodation for 150 troops and a helicopter platform is fitted over the stern.

DAGUPAN CITY   *12/1999, Sattler/Steele* / 0081543

DAGUPAN CITY   *12/1999, Sattler/Steele* / 0081544

5 LST 512-1152 CLASS (TRANSPORT SHIPS) (LST)

Name	No	Builders	Commissioned
ZAMBOANGA DEL SUR (ex-Cam Ranh, ex-Marion County LST 975)	LT 86	Bethlehem Steel, Hingham, Mass	3 Feb 1945
SOUTH COTABATO (ex-Cayuga County LST 529)	LT 87	Bethlehem Steel, Hingham, Mass	28 Feb 1944
LAGUNA (ex-T-LST 230)	LT 501	American Bridge, Ambridge, PA	3 Nov 1943
LANAO DEL NORTE (ex-T-LST 566)	LT 504	Missouri Valley Bridge and Iron Co, Evansville, Ind	29 May 1944
KALINGA APAYAO (ex-Can Tho, ex-Garrett County AGP 786, ex-LST 786)	LT 516 (ex-AE 516)	Dravo Corp., Pittsburgh, PA	28 Aug 1944

Displacement, tons: 1,620 standard; 2,472 beaching; 4,080 full load
Dimensions, feet (metres): 328 × 50 × 14 *(100 × 15.2 × 4.3)*
Main machinery: 2 GM 12-567A diesels; 1,800 hp *(1.34 MW)*; 2 shafts
Speed, knots: 10
Complement: Varies-approx 60 — 110 (depending upon employment)
Military lift: 2,100 tons. 16 tanks or 10 tanks plus 200 troops

Guns: 6 US/Bofors 40 mm (2 twin, 2 single) or 4 Oerlikon 20 mm (in refitted ships).
Radars: Navigation: Raytheon SPS-64(V)2; I-band.

Programmes: Transferred from US Navy in 1976 with exception of LT 87 and LT 516 which were used as light craft repair ships in South Vietnam and have retained amphibious capability (transferred to Vietnam 1970 and to Philippines 1976, acquired by purchase 5 April 1976). LT 86 transferred (grant aid) 17 November 1975. LT 501 and 504 commissioned in Philippine Navy 8 August 1978 and LT 507 on 18 October 1978.
Modernisation: Several have had major refits including replacement of frames and plating as well as engines and electrics and provision for four 20 mm guns to replace the 40 mm guns.
Structure: Some of the later ships have tripod masts, others have pole masts.
Operational: All are used for general cargo work in Philippine service. Fourteen were deleted in 1989 and one sank in 1991. Two paid off in 1992 and one in 1993. *South Cotabato* was also paid off in 1993 but brought back in to service in 1994. *Benguet* broke down in the South China Sea in April 1995 and had to be taken in tow. *Benguet* again grounded in the Spratly Islands on 3 November 1999 and after a month on the rocks is probably beyond economical repair. One further ship, *Sierra Madre* is reported to be used as an observation post in the Spratly Islands. Replacements are needed but have not been given priority.

LANAO DEL NORTE   *1993, Philippine Navy* / 0506163

1 ACHELOUS CLASS (REPAIR SHIP) (ARL)

Name	No	Builders	Commissioned
YAKAL (ex-*Satyr* ARL 23, ex-LST 852)	AD 617 (ex-AR 517)	Chicago Bridge & Iron	20 Nov 1944

Displacement, tons: 4,342 full load
Dimensions, feet (metres): 328 × 50 × 14 *(100 × 15.2 × 4.3)*
Main machinery: 2 GM 12-567A diesels; 1,800 hp *(1.34 MW)*; 2 shafts
Speed, knots: 11.6
Complement: 220 approx
Guns: 4 US/Bofors 40 mm (quad). 10 Oerlikon 20 mm (5 twin).

Comment: Transferred from the US to the Philippines on 24 January 1977 by sale. (Originally to South Vietnam 30 September 1971.) Converted during construction. Extensive machine shop, spare parts stowage, and logistic support.

YAKAL   *1994, Philippine Navy* / 0081545

1 ALAMOSA CLASS (SUPPLY SHIP) (AK)

Name	No	Builders	Commissioned
MACTAN (ex-*Kukui*, ex-*Colquith*)	AC 90 (ex-TK 90)	Froemming, Milwaukee	22 Sep 1944

Displacement, tons: 2,500 light; 7,570 full load
Dimensions, feet (metres): 338.5 × 50 × 18 *(103.2 × 15.2 × 5.5)*
Main machinery: 1 Nordberg diesel; 1,700 hp *(1.27 MW)*; 1 shaft
Speed, knots: 11
Complement: 85
Guns: 2 — 12.7 mm MGs.

Comment: Transferred from the US Coast Guard on 1 March 1972. Used to supply military posts and lighthouses in the Philippine archipelago. Was to have been paid off in 1994 but has been kept in service.

MACTAN   *4/1996, Philippine Navy* / 0506312

1 TRANSPORT VESSEL (AP)

Name	No	Builders	Commissioned
ANG PANGULO (ex-*The President*, ex-*Roxas*, ex-*Lapu-Lapu*)	AT 25 (ex-TP 777)	Ishikawajima, Japan	1959

Displacement, tons: 2,239 standard; 2,727 full load
Dimensions, feet (metres): 257.6 × 42.6 × 21 *(78.5 × 13 × 6.4)*
Main machinery: 2 Mitsui DE642/VBF diesels; 5,000 hp(m) *(3.68 MW)*; 2 shafts
Speed, knots: 18. **Range, n miles**: 6,900 at 15 kt
Complement: 81 (8 officers)
Guns: 3 Oerlikon 20 mm/70 Mk 4. 8—7.62 mm MGs.
Radars: Navigation: RCA CRMN-1A-75; I-band.

Comment: Built as war reparation; launched in 1958. Was used as presidential yacht and command ship with accommodation for 50 passengers. Originally named *Lapu-Lapu* after the chief who killed Magellan; renamed *Roxas* on 9 October 1962 after the late Manuel Roxas, the first President of the Philippines Republic. Renamed *The President* in 1967 and *Ang Pangulo* in 1975. In early 1987 was earmarked to transport President Marcos to Hong Kong and exile. The ship is now used as an attack transport, and still as a Presidential Yacht.

2 ANG PANGULO   *5/1998, John Mortimer* / 0081546

2 YW TYPE (WATER TANKERS) (AWT)

Name	No	Builders	Commissioned
LAKE BULUSAN	AW 33 (ex-YW 111)	Marine Iron, Duluth	1 Aug 1945
LAKE PAOAY	AW 34 (ex-YW 130)	Leathem D Smith, Sturgeon Bay	28 Aug 1945

Displacement, tons: 1,237 full load
Dimensions, feet (metres): 174 × 32.7 × 13.2 *(53 × 10 × 4)*
Main machinery: 2 GM 8-278A diesels; 1,500 hp *(1.12 MW)*; 2 shafts
Speed, knots: 7.5
Complement: 29
Cargo capacity: 200,000 gallons
Guns: 1 Bofors 40/60. 1 Oerlikon 20 mm.

Comment: Basically similar to YOG type but adapted to carry fresh water. Transferred from the US to the Philippines on 16 July 1975.

LAKE PAOAY   *5/1998, van Ginderen Collection* / 0052708

2 YOG TYPE (TANKERS) (YO)

Name	No	Builders	Commissioned
LAKE BUHI (ex-YOG 73)	AF 78 (ex-YO 78)	Puget Sound, Bremerton	28 Nov 1944
LAKE TAAL (ex-YOG)	AF 72 (ex-YO 72)	Puget Sound, Bremerton	14 Apr 1945

Displacement, tons: 447 standard; 1,400 full load
Dimensions, feet (metres): 174 × 32.7 × 13.2 *(53 × 10 × 4)*
Main machinery: 2 GM 8-278A diesels; 1,500 hp *(1.12 MW)*; 2 shafts
Speed, knots: 8
Complement: 28
Cargo capacity: 6,570 barrels dieso and gasoline
Guns: 2 Oerlikon 20 mm/70 Mk 4.

Comment: Former US Navy gasoline tankers. Transferred in July 1967 on loan and by purchase 5 March 1980.

LAKE BUHI   *1993, Philippine Navy* / 0506164

4 FLOATING DOCKS (YFD)

YD 200 (ex-AFDL 24)   **YD 204** (ex-AFDL 20)   **YD 205** (ex-AFDL 44)   — (ex-AFDL 40)

Comment: Floating steel dry docks built in the USA; all are former US Navy units with YD 200 transferred in July 1948, YD 204 in October 1961 (sale 1 August 1980), YD 205 in September 1969 and AFDL 40 in 1994.
Capacities: YD 205, 2,800 tons; YD 200 and YD 204, 1,000 tons. In addition there are two floating cranes, YU 206 and YU 207, built in US in 1944 and capable of lifting 30 tons.

TUGS

Notes: A number of harbour tugs have been acquired from the US. The latest type is ex-Army of 390 tons, a speed of 12 kt and a bollard pull of 12 tons.

HARBOUR TUG   *5/1998, John Mortimer* / 0052709

COAST GUARD

Notes: (1) Some of the PCF craft listed are manned by the Navy as is the buoy tender *Mangyan*.
(2) The Coast Guard also operates one LCM 6 (BM 270), one LCVP (BV 182) and a River Utility Craft VU 463.
(3) Ten Rodman 101 and four Rodman 38 were ordered for delivery to the Police by 2005.

4 SAN JUAN CLASS (WPBO)

Name	No	Builders	Commissioned
SAN JUAN	001	Tenix Defence Systems	19 June 2000
EDSA II (ex-*Don Emilio*)	002 (ex-419)	Tenix Defence Systems	14 Dec 2000
PAMPANGA	003	Tenix Defence Systems	30 Jan 2003
BATANGAS	004	Tenix Defence Systems	8 Aug 2003

Displacement, tons: 500 full load
Dimensions, feet (metres): 183.7 × 34.5 × 9.8 *(56 × 10.5 × 3)*
Main machinery: 2 Caterpillar 3612 diesels; 4,800 hp(m) *(3.53 MW)* sustained; 2 shafts; cp props
Speed, knots: 24.5
Range, n miles: 3,000 at 15 kt
Complement: 38
Radars: Navigation: I-band
Helicopters: Platform for one light.

Comment: First reported ordered in mid-1997. Construction of first of class started in February 1999. Steel hull and aluminium superstructure. Primarily used for SAR with facilities for 300 survivors. Fire-fighting and pollution control equipment included. A contract for a further two vessels was finalised in December 2001.

SAN JUAN   *6/2000, Tenix Shipbuilding* / 0105228

1 CORREGIDOR CLASS (BUOY TENDER) (ABU)

Name	No	Builders	Commissioned
CORREGIDOR	AG 891	Niigata Engineering, Japan	2 Mar 1998

Displacement, tons: 1,130 full load
Dimensions, feet (metres): 186.7 × 26.1 × 12.5 *(56.9 × 11.0 × 3.8)*
Main machinery: 2 Niigata diesels; 2 shafts
Speed, knots: 13
Range, n miles: 4,000 at 11 kt
Complement: 37
Radars: Navigation: I-band.

Comment: Lighthouse and buoy tender.

4 + (10) ILOCOS NORTE CLASS (PATROL CRAFT) (PB)

Name	No	Builders	Commissioned
ILOCOS NORTE	3501	Tenix Defence Systems	9 May 2003
NUEVA VIZCAYA	3502	Tenix Defence Systems	8 Aug 2003
ROMBLON	3503	Tenix Defence Systems	20 Oct 2003
DAVAO DEL NORTE	3504	Tenix Defence Systems	16 Jan 2004

Displacement, tons: 115
Dimensions, feet (metres): 114.9 × 24.0 × 7.5 *(35.0 × 7.3 × 2.3)*
Main machinery: 2 diesels; 2 shafts. 1 loiter waterjet
Speed, knots: 23
Range, n miles: 2,000 at 12 kt
Complement: 11
Guns: 2—30 mm (1 twin). 2—12.7 mm MGs.
Radars: Navigation: I-band

Comment: Contract on 9 December 2001 for the construction of four search and rescue vessels with an option for a further ten craft. Based on Bay class design with steel hull and aluminium superstructure.

NUEVA VIZCAYA　　　　　　　　　　　　　*8/2003, Tenix* / 0569803

1 BALSAM CLASS (TENDER) (AKLH)

Name	No	Builders	Commissioned
KALINGA (ex-*Redbud*, WAGL 398, ex-*Redbud*, T-AKL 398)	AG 89	Marine Iron, Duluth	2 May 1944

Displacement, tons: 950 standard; 1,041 full load
Dimensions, feet (metres): 180 × 37 × 13 *(54.8 × 11.3 × 4)*
Main machinery: Diesel-electric; 2 diesels; 1,710 hp *(1.28 MW)*; 2 generators; 1 motor; 1,200 hp *(895 kW)*; 1 shaft
Speed, knots: 12
Range, n miles: 3,500 at 7 kt
Complement: 53
Guns: 2—12.7 mm MGs.
Radars: Navigation: Sperry SPS-53; I/J-band.
Helicopters: Platform for 1 light.

Comment: Originally US Coast Guard buoy tender (WAGL 398). Transferred to US Navy on 25 March 1949 as AG 398 and then to the Philippine Navy 1 March 1972. One 20 ton derrick. New engines fitted.

KALINGA　　　　　　　　　　　　　*1994, Philippine Navy* / 0506201

3 BUOY TENDERS (ABU)

CAPE BOJEADOR (ex-FS 203) AE 46 (ex-TK 46)
LIMASAWA (ex-*Nettle* WAK 129, ex-FS 169) AE 79 (ex-TK 79)
MANGYAN (ex-*Nasami*, ex-FS 408) AT 71 (ex-AE 71, ex-AS 71)

Displacement, tons: 470 standard; 950 full load
Dimensions, feet (metres): 180 × 32 × 10 *(54.9 × 9.8 × 3)*
Main machinery: 2 GM 6-278A diesels; 1,120 hp *(836 kW)*; 2 shafts
Speed, knots: 10
Range, n miles: 4,150 at 10 kt
Complement: 50
Cargo capacity: 400 tons
Guns: 1—12.7 mm MG can be carried.
Radars: Navigation: RCA CRMN 1A 75; I-band.

Comment: Former US Army FS 381 and FS 330 type freight and supply ships built in 1943-44. First two are employed as tenders for buoys and lighthouses. *Mangyan* transferred 24 September 1976 by sale. *Limasawa* acquired by sale 31 August 1978. One 5 ton derrick. *Cape Bojeador* paid off in 1988 but was back in service in 1991 after a major overhaul. *Mangyan* reclassified AT in 1993 and belongs to the Navy. Masts and superstructures have minor variations.

CAPE BOJEADOR　　　　　　　　　　　*1993, Philippine Navy* / 0506165

2 LARGE PATROL CRAFT (PB)

Name	No	Builders	Commissioned
TIRAD PASS	AU 100 (ex-SAR 100)	Sumidagawa, Japan	1974
BESSANG PASS	AU 75 (ex-SAR 99)	Sumidagawa, Japan	1974

Displacement, tons: 279 full load
Dimensions, feet (metres): 144.3 × 24.3 × 4.9 *(44 × 7.4 × 1.5)*
Main machinery: 2 MTU 12V 538 TB82 diesels; 4,050 hp(m) *(2.98 MW)*; 2 shafts
Speed, knots: 27.5. **Range, n miles:** 2,300 at 14 kt
Complement: 32
Guns: 4—12.7 mm (2 twin) MGs.

Comment: Paid for under Japanese war reparations. Similar type as *Emilio Aguinaldo*. *Bessang Pass* grounded in 1983 but was recovered.

TIRAD PASS　　　　　　　　　　　　　*1992, Philippine Navy* / 0081548

4 PGM-39 CLASS (LARGE PATROL CRAFT) (PB)

Name	No	Builders	Commissioned
AGUSAN (ex-PGM 39)	PG 61	Tacoma, WA	Mar 1960
CATANDUANES (ex-PGM 40)	PG 62	Tacoma, WA	Mar 1960
ROMBLON (ex-PGM 41)	PG 63	Peterson Builders, WI	June 1960
PALAWAN (ex-PGM 42)	PG 64	Tacoma, WA	June 1960

Displacement, tons: 124 full load
Dimensions, feet (metres): 100.3 × 18.6 × 6.9 *(30.6 × 5.7 × 2.1)*
Main machinery: 2 MTU MB 12V 493 TY57 diesels; 2,200 hp(m) *(1.6 MW)* sustained; 2 shafts
Speed, knots: 17
Range, n miles: 1,400 at 11 kt
Complement: 26—30
Guns: 2 Oerlikon 20 mm. 2—12.7 mm MGs. 1—81 mm mortar.
Radars: Surface search: Alpelco DFR-12; I/J-band.

Comment: Steel-hulled craft built under US military assistance programmes. Assigned US PGM-series numbers while under construction. Transferred upon completion. These craft are lengthened versions of the US Coast Guard 95 ft Cape class patrol boat design. Operational status is doubtful.

AGUSAN　　　　　　　　　　　　　*1994, Philippine Navy* / 0081550

10 PCF 46 CLASS (COASTAL PATROL CRAFT) (PB)

DB 411	DB 417	DB 422	DB 429	DB 432
DB 413	DB 419	DB 426	DB 431	DB 435

Displacement, tons: 21 full load
Dimensions, feet (metres): 45.9 × 14.5 × 3.3 *(14 × 4.4 × 1)*
Main machinery: 2 Cummins diesels; 740 hp *(552 kW)*; 2 shafts
Speed, knots: 25
Range, n miles: 1,000 at 15 kt
Complement: 8
Guns: 2—12.7 mm (twin) MGs. 1—7.62 mm M60 MG.
Radars: Surface search: Kelvin Hughes 17; I-band.

Comment: Built by Marcelo Yard, Manila and were to have been delivered 1976-78 at the rate of two per month. By the end of 1976, 25 had been completed but a serious fire in the shipyard destroyed 12 new hulls and halted production. Some deleted.

DB 435   *1993, Philippine Navy* / 0506166

12 PCF 50 (SWIFT Mk 1 and Mk 2) CLASS
(COASTAL PATROL CRAFT) (PB)

DF 300-303	DF 305	DF 307-313

Displacement, tons: 22.5 full load
Dimensions, feet (metres): 50 × 13.6 × 4 *(15.2 × 4.1 × 1.2)* (Mk 1) 51.3 × 13.6 × 4 *(15.6 × 4.1 × 1.2)* (Mk 2)
Main machinery: 2 GM 12-71 diesels; 680 hp *(504 kW)* sustained; 2 shafts
Speed, knots: 28
Range, n miles: 685 at 16 kt
Complement: 6
Guns: 2—12.7 mm (twin) MGs. 2 M-79 40 mm grenade launchers.
Radars: Surface search: Decca 202; I-band.

Comment: Most built in the USA. Built for US military assistance programmes and transferred in the late 1960s. Some built in 1970 in the Philippines (ferro-concrete) with enlarged superstructure. *DF 300-303* are Swift Mk 1. *DF 305* and *DF 307-313* are Swift Mk 2.

DF 308   *5/1998, van Ginderen Collection* / 0081552

10 PCF 65 (SWIFT Mk 3) CLASS (COASTAL PATROL CRAFT) (PB)

DF 325-332	DF 334	DF 347

Displacement, tons: 29 standard; 37 full load
Dimensions, feet (metres): 65 × 16 × 3.4 *(19.8 × 4.9 × 1)*
Main machinery: 3 GM 12V-71TI diesels; 840 hp *(616 kW)* sustained; 3 shafts
Speed, knots: 25
Complement: 8
Guns: 2—12.7 mm MGs.
Radars: Surface search: Koden; I-band.

Comment: Improved Swift type inshore patrol boats built by Peterson and delivered 1975-76. Alumnium construction. Some that were laid up have been returned to service. New radars fitted.

DF 347   *5/1998, Sattler & Steele* / 0052711

3 DE HAVILLAND CLASS (PB)

DF 321-323

Displacement, tons: 25 full load
Dimensions, feet (metres): 54.8 × 16.4 × 4.3 *(16.7 × 5 × 1.3)*
Main machinery: 2 diesels; 740 hp *(552 kW)*; 2 shafts
Speed, knots: 25
Range, n miles: 450 at 14 kt
Complement: 8
Guns: 2—12.7 mm MGs.

Comment: Locally built in the mid-1980s. Others of this type have been paid off and numbers are uncertain.

DF 321   *5/1998, van Ginderen Collection* / 0052713

11 CUTTERS (PBR)

CGC 103	CGC 110	CGC 115	CGC 128-130	CGC 132-136

Displacement, tons: 13 full load
Dimensions, feet (metres): 40 × 13.6 × 3 *(12.2 × 4.1 × 0.9)*
Main machinery: 2 Detroit diesels; 560 hp *(418 kW)*; 2 shafts
Speed, knots: 28
Complement: 5
Guns: 1—12.7 mm MG. 1—7.62 mm MG.

Comment: Built at Cavite Yard from 1984. One deleted in 1994. Used for harbour patrols. There are also some small unarmed Police craft.

CGC 130   *1994, Philippine Navy* / 0081553

For details of the latest updates to ***Jane's Fighting Ships*** online and to discover the additional information available exclusively to online subscribers please visit
jfs.janes.com

Poland
MARYNARKA WOJENNA

Country Overview

The modern democratic era of the Republic of Poland began in 1989 after forty-two years of communist rule. Situated in central Europe, the country has an area of 120,725 square miles and is bordered to the north by Russia (Kaliningrad), to the east by Lithuania. Belarus, and Ukraine, to the south by the Czech Republic and Slovakia and to the west by Germany. It has a 265 n mile coastline with the Baltic Sea. Warsaw is the capital and largest city while Gdansk, Szczecin and Gdynia are the principal ports. Territorial seas (12 n miles) are claimed but while it has claimed a 200 n mile EEZ, its limits have not been fully defined by boundary agreements.

Headquarters Appointments

Commander-in-Chief:
  Admiral Roman Krzvzelewski
Deputy Commander-in-Chief:
  Vice Admiral Jedrzej Czajkowski
Chief of Naval Staff:
  Rear Admiral Henryk Solkiewicz
Chief of Naval Logistics:
  Rear Admiral Tomasz Mathea
Chief of Naval Training:
  Rear Admiral Marek Bragoszewski

Diplomatic Representation

Defence and Naval Attaché in London:
  Colonel Tadeusz Jedrzejczak

Personnel

(a) 2006: 14,100
(b) 12 months' national service

Prefix to Ships' Names

ORP, standing for *Okret Rzeczypospolitej Polskiej*

Strength of the Fleet

Type	Active	Building
Submarines — Patrol	5	—
Frigates	2	2 (5)
Corvettes	6	—
Fast Attack Craft — Missile	2	—
Coastal Patrol Craft	4	—
Minehunters — Coastal	20	(14)
LSTs	5	—
LCUs	3	—
Survey and Research Ships	2	—
AGIs	2	—
Training Ships	2	—
Salvage Ships	6	—
Tankers	4	—
Logistic Support Ship	1	—

Sea Department of the Border Guard (MOSG)

A para-naval force, subordinate to the Minister of the Interior.

Bases

Gdynia (3rd Naval Flotilla), Hel (9th Coastal Defence Flotilla), Swinoujscie (8th Coastal Defence Flotilla), Kolobrzeg, Gdansk (Frontier Guard)

Naval Aviation

HQ at Gdynia
1st Wing at Gdynia (MiG-21, W-3, An-28)
2nd Wing at Darlowo (Mi-14, Mi-2, W-3)
3rd Wing at Siemirowice-Cewice (TS-11, B1-R, An-28)

Coast Defence

Two divisions with 24—57 mm guns.

DELETIONS

Submarines

2003 *Wilk, Dzik*

Destroyers

2003 *Warszawa*

Corvettes

2005 *Gornik, Hutnik*

Patrol Forces

2003 *Puck, Darlowo*
2004 *Dziwnów, Grozny, Wytrwaly, Zreczny, Zwinny, Zawziety, Czujny*
2005 *KP 166, KP 169, KP,170, KP 172, KP 173, KP, 175, KP 176*

Mine Warfare Forces

2005 *TR 25, TR 26*

Amphibious Forces

2005 *Grunwald*

Survey and Research Ships

2003 *Zodiak*
2005 *Kopernik*

Training Ships

2003 *Bryza*
2005 *Podchorazy*

Auxiliaries

2005 *RYS*

PENNANT LIST

Submarines

291	Orzeł
294	Sókol
295	Sęp
296	Bielik
297	Kondor

Frigates

272	Generał Kazimierz Pułaski
273	Generał Tadeusz Kościuszko

Corvettes

240	Kaszub
421	Orkan
422	Piorun
423	Grom
436	Metalowiec
437	Rolnik

Patrol Forces

431	Świnoujście
433	Władysławowo

Mine Warfare Forces

621	Flaming
623	Mewa
624	Czajka
630	Goplo
631	Gardno
632	Bukowo
633	Dabie
634	Jamno
635	Mielno
636	Wicko
637	Resko
638	Sarbsko
639	Necko
640	Naklo
641	Druzno
642	Hancza
643	Mamry
644	Wigry
645	Sniardwy
646	Wdzydze

Amphibious Forces

821	Lublin
822	Gniezno
823	Krakow
824	Poznan
825	Torun
851	KD 11
852	KD 12
853	KD 13

Survey Ships and AGIs

262	Nawigator
263	Hydrograf
265	Heweliusz
266	Arctowski

Auxiliaries

251	Wodnik
253	Iskra
281	Piast
282	Lech
511	Kontradmiral X Czernicki
R 11	Gniewko
R 13	Semko
R 14	Zbyszko
R 15	Macko
SD 11	Wrona
SD 13	—
Z 1	Baltyk
Z 3	Krab
Z 8	Meduza
Z 9	Slimak

Maritime Frontier Guard

SG 311	Kaper I
SG 312	Kaper II
SG 323	Zefir
SG 325	Tecza

SUBMARINES

1 KILO CLASS (PROJECT 877EM) (SSK)

Name	No	Builders	Commissioned
ORZEŁ	291	Sudomekh, Leningrad	21 June 1986

Displacement, tons: 2,457 surfaced; 3,076 dived
Dimensions, feet (metres): 243.8 × 32.8 × 21.7
(74.3 × 10 × 6.6)
Main machinery: Diesel-electric; 2 DL 42M diesels; 3,650 hp(m) *(2.68 MW)*; 2 generators; 6 MW; 1 PG 141 motor; 5,900 hp(m) *(4.34 MW)*; 1 shaft; 2 auxiliary motors; 204 hp(m) *(150 kW)*; 1 economic speed motor; 130 hp *(95 kW)*
Speed, knots: 10 surfaced; 17 dived; 9 snorting
Range, n miles: 6,000 at 7 kt snorting; 400 at 3 kt dived
Complement: 60 (16 officers)

Missiles: SAM: 8 SA-N-5 (Strela 2M).
Torpedoes: 6—21 in *(533 mm)* tubes. Combination of 53-65; anti-surface; passive/wake homing to 19 km *(10.3 n miles)* at 45 kt; warhead 300 kg and TEST-71; anti-submarine; active/passive homing to 15 km *(8.1 n miles)* at 40 kt; warhead 205 kg. 53-56 WA and SET 53 M can also be carried. Total of 18 torpedoes.
Mines: 24 in lieu of torpedoes.
Countermeasures: ESM: Brick Group (MRP-25); radar warning; Quad Loop HF D/F.
Weapons control: Murena MWU 110 TFCS.
Radars: Surface search: Racal Decca Bridgemaster; I-band.
Sonars: Shark Teeth (MGK-400); hull-mounted; passive search and attack (some active capability); low/medium frequency.

ORZEŁ

6/2004, J Ciślak / 1044467

Mouse Roar (MG 519); active mine detection; high frequency.

Programmes: This was the second transfer of this class, the first being to India and others have since gone to Romania, Algeria, Iran and China. It was expected that more than one would be acquired as part of an exchange

deal with the USSR for Polish-built amphibious ships, but this class is considered too large for Baltic operations and subsequent transfers were of the Foxtrot class.
Structure: Diving depth, 240 m *(787 ft)*. Has two torpedo tubes modified for wire guided anti-submarine torpedoes.
Operational: Based at Gdynia.

4 SOKÓL (KOBBEN) CLASS (TYPE 207) (SSK)

Name	No	Builders	Laid down	Launched	Commissioned
SOKÓL (ex-*Stord*)	294 (ex-S 308)	Rheinstahl - Nordseewerke, Emden	1 Apr 1966	2 Sep 1966	14 Feb 1967
SĘP (ex-*Skolpen*)	295 (ex-S 306)	Rheinstahl - Nordseewerke, Emden	1 Nov 1965	24 Mar 1966	17 Aug 1966
BIELIK (ex-*Svenner*)	296 (ex-S 309)	Rheinstahl - Nordseewerke, Emden	8 Sep 1966	27 Jan 1967	12 Jun 1967
KONDOR (ex-*Kunna*)	297 (ex-S 319)	Rheinstahl - Nordseewerke, Emden	3 Mar 1964	16 Jul 1964	29 Oct 1964

Displacement, tons: 459 standard; 524 dived
Dimensions, feet (metres): 155.5 × 15 × 14
  (47.4 × 4.6 × 4.3)
Main machinery: Diesel-electric; 2 MTU 12V 493 AZ80
  GA31L diesels; 1,200 hp(m) *(880 kW)* sustained; 1 motor;
  1,800 hp(m) *(1.32 MW)* sustained; 1 shaft
Speed, knots: 12 surfaced; 18 dived
Range, n miles: 5,000 at 8 kt (snorting)
Complement: 21 (5 officers)

Torpedoes: 8—21 in *(533 mm)* bow tubes.
Countermeasures: ESM: Argo radar warning.
Weapons control: Kongsberg MSI-70U TFCS.
Radars: Surface search: Kelvin Hughes 1007; I-band.
Sonars: Atlas Elektronik CSU 83; passive search and attack;
  medium/high frequency.

Programmes: Commissioned into the Norwegian Navy from
  1964, the original building cost was shared between the
  Norwegian and US governments. Decommissioned from
  the Norwegian Navy in 2001. Following announcement on
  18 January 2002 *Sokól* recommissioned on 25 May 2002
  and *Sęp* on 5 August 2002. *Bielik* recommissioned on
  8 September 2003 and *Kondor* on 20 October 2004. The
  ex-*Kobben* has been transferred for spares and as a
  floating training base. The contract also includes provision
  of in-service support. These submarines are understood
  to be a stop-gap measure to maintain a submarine
  capability until about 2012 when these may be replaced.
Modernisation: All modernised at Urivale Shipyard, Bergen
  between 1989-1992.
Structure: A development of the German Type 205 class,
  they have a diving depth of 650 ft *(200 m)*. Pilkington
  optronics CK 30 search periscope.

BIELIK   *7/2004, **B Sullivan*** / 1121522

BIELIK   *2/2005*, **Michael Nitz*** / 1151308

FRIGATES

0 + 2 (5) PROJECT 621 GAWRON II (MEKO A 100) CLASS (FSGHM)

Name	No	Builders	Laid down	Launched	Commissioned
—	—	Naval Shipyard, Gdynia	28 Oct 2001	2007	2009
—	—	Naval Shipyard, Gdynia	2003	2008	2010

Displacement, tons: 2,035 full load
Dimensions, feet (metres): 312.3 × 43.6 × 11.8
  (95.2 × 13.13 × 3.6)
Main machinery: CODAG; 1 gas turbine; 2 diesels; 2 shafts
Speed, knots: 30. **Range, n miles:** 4,000 at 15 kt
Complement: 74

Missiles: SSM: 8 RBS-15 Mk 3 ❶.
SAM: Evolved Sea Sparrow; VLS ❷.
Guns: 1—3 in *(76 mm)*/62 ❸. 2—35 mm. RAM ❹.
A/S mortars: 2 ASW 601 ❺.
Countermeasures: Decoys: 1 — 10 barrelled Jastrzab 122 mm;
  chaff and IR flares.
ESM: Radar warning.
TCM: C310 torpedo decoy system.
Combat data systems: Signaal TACTICOS or Saab Tech 9LV.
Radars: Air/surface search ❻; fire control ❼; navigation.
Sonars: Hull mounted; active; medium frequency.

Helicopters: Platform for 1 medium ❽.

Programmes: Design definition by German Corvette
  Consortium (Blohm + Voss, Lürssen, Thyssen and HDW)
  which is to act as subcontractor to the shipbuilder. There
  are options for a further five vessels. Details of the design
  and of the building programme have not been released
  but, given continuing funding problems, it is unlikely
  that the first of class will enter service before 2009.
Structure: The design is based on the MEKO A 100.

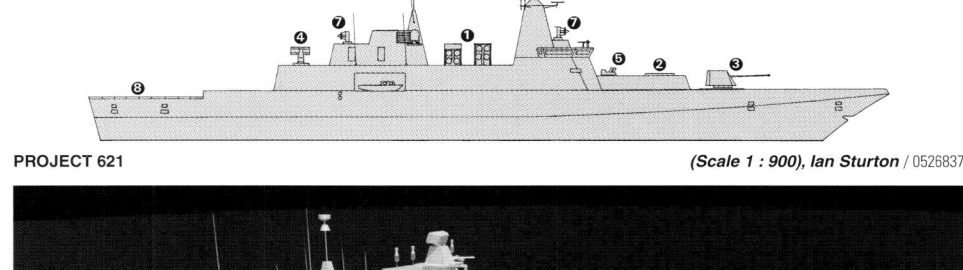

PROJECT 621   *(Scale 1 : 900), **Ian Sturton*** / 0526837

PROJECT 621 *2001, Polish Navy*
0114788

2 OLIVER HAZARD PERRY CLASS (FFGHM)

Name	No	Builders	Laid down	Launched	Commissioned
GENERAŁ KAZIMIERZ PUŁASKI (ex-*Clark*)	272 (ex-FFG 11)	Bath Iron Works	17 July 1978	24 Mar 1979	9 May 1980
GENERAŁ TADEUSZ KOŚCIUSZKO (ex-*Wadsworth*)	273 (ex-FFG 9)	Todd Shipyards, San Pedro	13 July 1977	29 July 1978	28 Feb 1980

Displacement, tons: 2,750 light; 3,638 full load
Dimensions, feet (metres): 445 × 45 × 14.8; 24.5 (sonar)
(*135.6 × 13.7 × 4.5; 7.5*)
Main machinery: 2 GE LM 2500 gas turbines; 41,000 hp
(*30.59 MW*) sustained; 1 shaft; cp prop
2 auxiliary retractable props; 650 hp (*484 kW*)
Speed, knots: 29
Range, n miles: 4,500 at 20 kt
Complement: 200 (15 officers) including 19 aircrew

Missiles: SSM: 4 McDonnell Douglas Harpoon Block 1G;
active radar homing to 130 km (*70 n miles*) at 0.9 Mach;
warhead 227 kg.
SAM: 36 GDC Standard SM-1MR; command guidance;
semi-active radar homing to 46 km (*25 n miles*) at
2 Mach.
1 Mk 13 Mod 4 launcher for both SSM and SAM missiles ❶.
Guns: 1 OTO Melara 3 in (*76 mm*)/62 Mk 75 ❷; 85 rds/min
to 16 km (*8.7 n miles*) anti-surface; 12 km (*6.6 n miles*)
anti-aircraft; weight of shell 6 kg.
1 General Electric/General Dynamics 20 mm/76
6-barrelled Mk 15 Vulcan Phalanx ❸; 3,000 rds/min
combined to 1.5 km.
4—12.7 mm MGs.
Torpedoes: 6—324 mm Mk 32 (2 triple) tubes ❹.
24 Whitehead A244 Mod 3. To be replaced by Mu-90
Impact from 2002.
Countermeasures: Decoys: 2 Loral Hycor SRBOC 6-barrelled
fixed Mk 36 ❺; IR flares and chaff to 4 km (*2.2 n miles*).
T-Mk 6 Fanfare/SLQ-25 Nixie; torpedo decoy.
ESM/ECM: SLQ-32(V)2 ❻; radar warning. Sidekick
modification adds jammer and deception system.
Combat data systems: NTDS with Link 11 and 14. SATCOM
SRR-1, WSC-3 (UHF).
Weapons control: SWG-1 Harpoon LCS. Mk 92 (Mod 2),
WCS with CAS (Combined Antenna System). The Mk 92
is the US version of the Signaal WM28 system. Mk 13
weapon direction system. 2 Mk 24 optical directors.
Radars: Air search: Raytheon SPS-49(V)4 ❼; C/D-band.
Surface search: ISC Cardion SPS-55 ❽; I-band.
Fire control: Lockheed STIR (modified SPG-60) ❾;
I/J-band.
Sperry Mk 92 (Signaal WM28) ❿; I/J-band.

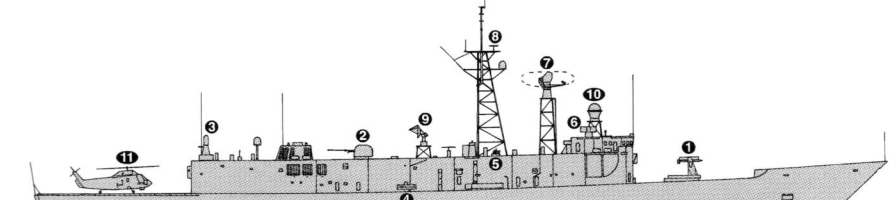

PUŁASKI *(Scale 1 : 1,200), Ian Sturton* / 0105229

PUŁASKI *10/2005*, B Sullivan* / 1151142

Navigation: Furuno; I-band.
Tacan URN 25. IFF Mk XII AIMS UPX-29.
Sonars: SQQ 89(V)2 (Raytheon SQS 56 and Gould SQR 19);
hull-mounted active search and attack; medium frequency
and passive towed array; very low frequency.

Helicopters: 2 Kaman SH-2G Seasprite ⓫.

Programmes: *Pułaski* approved for transfer from US
by grant in 1999. Recommissioned on 8 March 2000.
Kościuszko recommissioned on 12 June 2002.
Structure: Details given are for the ship in service with the
US Navy.
Operational: Based at Gdynia. Seasprite helicopters carried
from 2001.

KOŚCIUSZKO *6/2005*, Maritime Photographic* / 1151309

PUŁASKI *2/2005*, Per Körnefeldt* / 1151144

CORVETTES

1 KASZUB CLASS (PROJECT 620) (FSM)

Name	No
KASZUB	240

Builders	Laid down	Launched	Commissioned
Northern Shipyard, Gdansk	9 June 1984	11 May 1986	3 Mar 1987

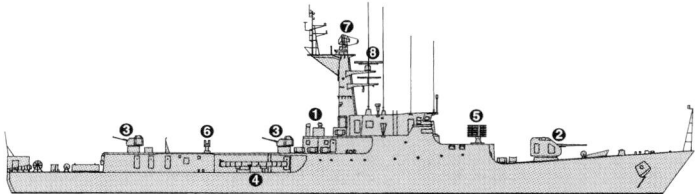

KASZUB *(Scale 1 : 900), Ian Sturton* / 0081558

Displacement, tons: 1,051 standard; 1,183 full load
Dimensions, feet (metres): 270 × 32.8 × 10.2; 16.1 (sonar) *(82.3 × 10 × 3.1; 4.9)*
Main machinery: CODAD; 4 Cegielski-Sulzer AS 16V 25/30 diesels; 16,900 hp(m) *(12.42 MW)*; 2 shafts; cp props
Speed, knots: 27
Range, n miles: 3,500 at 14 kt; 350 at 26 kt
Complement: 82 (10 officers)

Missiles: SAM: 2 SA-N-5 quad launchers ❶; IR homing to 10 km *(5.5 n miles)* at 1.5 Mach. VLS system to replace after 23 mm gun.
Guns: 1 USSR 3 in *(76 mm)*/66 AK 176 ❷; 120 rds/min to 12 km *(6.4 n miles)*; weight of shell 7 kg.
6 ZU-23-2M Wrobel 23 mm/87 (3 twin) ❸; 400 rds/min combined to 2 km.
Torpedoes: 4—21 in *(533 mm)* (2 twin) tubes ❹. SET-53M; passive homing to 15 km *(8.1 n miles)* at 29 kt; warhead 100 kg.
A/S mortars: 2 RBU 6000 12-tubed trainable ❺; range 6,000 m; warhead 31 kg; 120 rockets.
Depth charges: 2 rails. 12 charges.
Countermeasures: Decoys: 1—10 barrelled 122 mm Jastrzab launcher ❻ for chaff.
ESM: Intercept.
Weapons control: Drakon TFCS.
Radars: Air/surface search: Strut Curve (MR 302) ❼; F-band.
Surface search: Racal Bridgemaster C-252 ❽; I-band.
Navigation: Racal Bridgemaster C-341; I-band.
IFF: RAWAR SA-10M2.
Sonars: MG 322T; hull-mounted; active search; medium frequency.
MG 329M; stern-mounted dipping type mounted on the transom; active; high frequency.

Programmes: Second of class cancelled in 1989 and a class of up to ten more ships based on the Kaszub hull and specialised for anti-submarine warfare has been shelved.

Structure: Design based on Grisha class but with many alterations. The 76 mm gun was fitted in late 1991. New decoy system fitted in 1999. There is space for a fire-control director on the bridge roof.

Operational: Finally achieved operational status in 1990. Based at Hel with the Border Guard in 1990 but returned to the Navy in 1991. The ship has to stop to use stern-mounted sonar.

KASZUB *6/2005*, *Frank Findler* / 1151143

KASZUB *6/2004, Harald Carstens* / 1044472

3 ORKAN (SASSNITZ) CLASS (PROJECT 660 (ex-151)) (FSGM)

Name	No	Builders	Launched	Commissioned
ORKAN	421	Peenewerft/Northern Shipyard, Gdansk	29 Sep 1990	18 Sep 1992
PIORUN	422	Peenewerft/Northern Shipyard, Gdansk	19 Oct 1990	11 Mar 1994
GROM (ex-*Huragan*)	423	Peenewerft/Northern Shipyard, Gdansk	11 Dec 1990	28 Mar 1995

Displacement, tons: 331 standard; 326 full load
Dimensions, feet (metres): 163.4 oa; 147.6 wl × 28.5 × 7.2 *(49.8; 45 × 8.7 × 2.2)*
Main machinery: 3 Type M 520T diesels; 16,000 hp(m) *(11.93 MW)* sustained; 3 shafts
Speed, knots: 38. **Range, n miles:** 1,600 at 14 kt
Complement: 36 (4 officers)

Missiles: SSM: 8 (2 quad) launchers; RBS-15 Mk 3; active radar homing to 200 km *(108 n miles)* at 0.9 Mach; warhead 200 kg.
SAM: SA-N-5 Grail quad launcher; manual aiming; IR homing to 6 km *(3.2 n miles)* at 1.5 Mach; warhead 1.5 kg.
Guns: 1 USSR 3 in *(76 mm)*/66 AK 176; 120 rds/min to 12 km *(6.4 n miles)*; weight of shell 7 kg.
1—30 mm/65 AK 630; 6 barrels; 3,000 rds/min combined to 2 km.
Countermeasures: Decoys: 8—9 barrelled Jastrzab 81 mm and 1—10 barrelled Jastrzab 122 mm chaff and IR launchers.
ESM: PIT intercept.
Combat data systems: Signaal TACTICOS.
Weapons control: Thales STING optronic director.
Radars: Surface search: AMB Sea Giraffe; G-band.
Fire control: Bass Tilt MR-123; H/I-band.
Navigation: PIT; I-band.
IFF: Square Head; Salt Pot.

Programmes: Originally six of this former GDR Sassnitz class were to be built at Peenewerft for Poland. Three units were acquired and completed at Gdansk.

PIORUN *6/2005*, *J Cislak* / 1151310

Modernisation: Contract with Thales Naval Nederland (TNNL) as prime contractor for upgrade of all three ships signed 29 June 2001. New equipment includes RBS-15 Mk 3 missiles, TACTICOS combat data system, STING optronic director, AMB Sea Giraffe surveillance radar, PIT navigational radar and ESM equipment, improved communications and Link 11. Refit of *Piorun* was completed by 2003 and the other two ships are to be completed in 2006.

Structure: The prototype vessel had two quadruple SSM launchers with an Exocet type (SS-N-25) of missile and the plan is to fit eight SSM in due course. Plank Shave radar has been replaced by a Polish set. Unlike the German Coast Guard vessels of the same class, these ships have retained three engines.

Operational: Based at Gdynia.

2 GORNIK (TARANTUL I) CLASS (PROJECT 1241RE) (FSGM)

Name	No	Builders	Commissioned
METALOWIEC	436	River Shipyard 341, Rybinsk	13 Feb 1988
ROLNIK	437	River Shipyard 341, Rybinsk	4 Feb 1989

Displacement, tons: 385 standard; 455 full load
Dimensions, feet (metres): 184.1 × 37.7 × 8.2
(56.1 × 11.5 × 2.5)
Main machinery: COGAG; 2 Type M 70 gas turbines;
24,000 hp(m) *(17.65 MW)* sustained; 2 M 75 gas turbines
with reversible gearbox; 8,000 hp(m) *(5.88 MW)* sustained;
2 shafts
Speed, knots: 42. **Range, n miles:** 1,650 at 14 kt
Complement: 45 (6 officers)

Missiles: SSM: 4 SS-N-2C Styx (2 twin) launchers; active
radar or IR homing to 83 km *(45 n miles)* at 0.9 Mach;
warhead 513 kg; sea-skimmer in terminal flight.

SAM: SA-N-5 Grail quad launcher; manual aiming; IR homing
to 6 km *(3.2 n miles)* at 1.5 Mach; warhead 1.5 kg.
Guns: 1—3 in *(76 mm)*/60 AK 176; 120 rds/min to 12 km
(6.4 n miles); weight of shell 7 kg.
2—30 mm/65 AK 630 6-barrelled type; 3,000 rds/min
combined to 2 km.
Countermeasures: Decoys: 2 PK 16 chaff launchers.
Weapons control: Korall-E WFCS; PMK 453 optronic
director.
Radars: Air/surface search: Plank Shave (Garpun E);
E-band.
Navigation: Racal Decca Bridgemaster; I-band.
Fire control: Bass Tilt (MR-123); H/I-band.

IFF: Square Head.
Sonars: Foal Tail; VDS; active; high frequency.

Programmes: Transferred from the USSR.
Modernisation: An upgrade of the two remaining ships is
expected when the 'Orkan' modernisation programme is
completed in 2006.
Structure: Similar to others of the class exported to India,
Yemen, Romania and Vietnam.
Operational: Gornik and Hutnik decommissioned in 2005.
Based at Gdynia.

ROLNIK *5/2005*, J Ciślak* / 1151325

SHIPBORNE AIRCRAFT

Numbers/Type: 4 Kaman SH-2G (P) Seasprite.
Operational speed: 130 kt *(241 km/h).*
Service ceiling: 22,500 ft *(6,860 m).*
Range: 367 n miles *(697 km).*
Role/Weapon systems: First two delivered in 2002. Second pair in August 2003. Sensors:
LN66/HP radar; ALR-66 ESM, ALE-39 ECM, AQS-81(V)2 MAD, AAQ-16 FLIR, ARR 57/84
sonobuoy receivers. Weapons: ASW: two A244S torpedoes (Mu 90 from 2002). ASV:
one 7.62 mm MG.

LAND-BASED MARITIME AIRCRAFT (FRONT LINE)

Notes: In addition there are 6 TS training aircraft.

Numbers/Type: 10/2/1/2 PZL Mielec M-28 B1R/M-28E/M-28RF/M-28TD Bryza.
Operational speed: 181 kt *(335 km/h).*
Service ceiling: 13,770 ft *(4,200 m).*
Range: 736 n miles *(1,365 km).*
Role/Weapon systems: Based on the USSR Cash light transport and used for maritime
patrol and SAR. First one delivered in January 1995. B1R upgrade programme
includes MSC-400 mission system, ARS-400 radar (with SAR/ISAR modes), torpedoes,
sonobuoys, MAD, direction finder and Link 11. Sensors: Search radar ARS 400; ESM.
Weapons: 2 SAB 100 bombs.

SH-2G (P) *7/2005*, J Ciślak* / 1151312

M-28 E *6/2005*, Paul Jackson* / 1151311

Numbers/Type: 10/3 Mil Mi-14PL Haze A/Mil Mi-14PS Haze C.
Operational speed: 120 kt *(222 km/h).*
Service ceiling: 16,000 ft *(4,670 m).*
Range: 500 n miles *(1,100 km).*
Role/Weapon systems: PL for ASW, PS for SAR. PL operates in co-operation with surface units. Adapted for landing and taking off from water. Sensors: I-2ME search radar; APM-60, MAD, sonobuoys, MGM 329M VDS. Weapons: ASW; Whitehead A 244 torpedoes, depth bombs and mines. Arming with Penguin ASM is also under consideration.

Mi-14PL   *7/2005*, J Ciślak* / 1151314

Numbers/Type: 2/7 PZL Świdnik W-3 Sokol/W-3RM Anakonda.
Operational speed: 119 kt *(220 km/h).*
Service ceiling: 19,672 ft *(6,000 m).*
Range: 335 n miles *(620 km).*
Role/Weapon systems: W-3 for transport, W-3RM for SAR. Operates in co-operation with surface units. Adapted for landing and taking off from water. Sensors: RDS-82 VP Meteo, FLIR.

W-3   *7/2005*, J Ciślak* / 1151313

Numbers/Type: 3/1 Mi-2RM Hoplite/Mi-2D.
Operational speed: 100 *(180 km/h).*
Service ceiling: 13,200 ft *(4,000 m).*
Range: 300 n miles *(550 km).*
Role/Weapon systems: Mi-2D is for transport aircraft and Mi-2RM is for SAR.

Mi-2RM   *7/2000, J Ciślak* / 0105237

Numbers/Type: 2 Mi-17 Hip
Operational speed: 124 kt *(230 km/h).*
Service ceiling: 16,400 ft *(5,000 m).*
Range: 324 n miles *(600 km).*
Role/Weapon systems: Transport aircraft. First one delivered in 2001.

Mi-17   *9/2005*, J Ciślak* / 1151315

PATROL FORCES

2 PUCK (OSA I) CLASS (PROJECT 205)
(FAST ATTACK CRAFT—MISSILE) (PTFGM)

Name	No	Builders	Commissioned
ŚWINOUJŚCIE	431	Leningrad	13 Jan 1973
WŁADYSŁAWOWO	433	Leningrad	13 Nov 1975

Displacement, tons: 171 standard; 210 full load
Dimensions, feet (metres): 126.6 × 24.9 × 8.8 *(38.6 × 7.6 × 2.7)*
Main machinery: 3 Type M 503A diesels; 8,025 hp(m) *(5.9 MW)* sustained; 3 shafts
Speed, knots: 35
Range, n miles: 800 at 30 kt
Complement: 30

Missiles: SSM: 4 SS-N-2A Styx; active radar or IR homing to 46 km *(25 n miles)* at 0.9 Mach; warhead 513 kg.
SAM: SA-N-5 quad launcher.
Guns: 4—30 mm/65 (2 twin) AK 230 automatic; 1,000 rds/min to 6.5 km *(3.5 n miles)*; weight of shell 0.54 kg.
Radars: Surface search: Square Tie; I-band.
Fire control: Drum Tilt (MR-104); H/I-band.
Navigation: SRN 207M; I-band.

Modernisation: Retained as training vessels.
Operational: Based at Gdynia. 432 decommissioned in 2004.

WŁADYSŁAWOWO   *5/2005*, J Ciślak* / 1151316

4 PILICA CLASS (PROJECT 918M)
(COASTAL PATROL CRAFT) (PB)

K 167-168   KP 171   KP 174

Displacement, tons: 93 full load
Dimensions, feet (metres): 93.8 × 19 × 4.6 *(28.6 × 5.8 × 1.4)*
Main machinery: 3 M 50-F7 diesels; 3,604 hp(m) *(2.65 MW)*; 3 shafts
Speed, knots: 27
Range, n miles: 1,160 at 12 kt
Complement: 14 (1 officer)
Guns: 2 ZU-23-2M 23 mm/87 (twin); 400 rds/min to 2 km.
Torpedoes: 2—21 in *(533 mm)* tubes; SET 53M; active/passive homing to 14 km *(7.6 n miles)* at 29 kt; warhead 90 kg.
Radars: Surface search: SRN 301; I-band.
Sonars: MG 329M; dipping VDS.

Comment: Built at Naval Shipyard, Gdynia. Original 11 commissioned between 1977 and 1983. Seven vessels decommissioned in 2005. Based at Kolobrzeg. Two similar vessels, without sonars and torpedo tubes, are part of the Border Guard (MOSG).

KP 172   *5/2004, J Ciślak* / 1044475

MINE WARFARE FORCES

0 + (14) KORMORAN CLASS (PROJECT 257)
(MINEHUNTERS—COASTAL MHC)

Displacement, tons: 400 full load
Dimensions, feet (metres): 142.7 × 23.0 × 11.5 *(43.5 × 7.0 × 3.85)*
Main machinery: 2 diesels; 3,700 hp(m) *(2.76 MW)*; 2 shafts. 1 motor; 80 hp (minehunting)
Complement: 36
Missiles: twin 23 mm mount and SA-N-5 (Grail) SAM system.
Sonars: SHL-101/T; hull-mounted.

Comment: Details are speculative. Two batches of six and eight vessels are planned although the construction programme has not been announced. All to be built in a Polish shipyard in conjunction with a foreign partner. The minehunting sonar is under development by Centrum Techniki Morskiej (CTM) and is based on technology from the Thales Underwater Systems TSM 2022 Mk III.

3 KROGULEC CLASS (PROJECT 206FM) (MHCM)

Name	No	Builders	Commissioned
FLAMING	621	Gdynia Shipyard	3 Nov 1966
MEWA	623	Gdynia Shipyard	25 May 1967
CZAJKA	624	Gdynia Shipyard	17 June 1967

Displacement, tons: 550 full load
Dimensions, feet (metres): 190.9 × 25.3 × 6.9 *(58.2 × 7.7 × 2.1)*
Main machinery: 2 Sulzer/Cegielski 6AL 25/30 diesels; 2,203 hp(m) *(1.62 MW)*; 2 shafts; LIPS cp props
Speed, knots: 17. **Range, n miles:** 2,000 at 12 kt
Complement: 52 (6 officers)

Missiles: SAM: 2 Fasta-4M quad launchers. SA-N-5.
2 SA-N-10 (Grom) to be fitted in due course.
Guns: SAM/guns: 2 Wrobel ZU-23-2MR 23 mm (twin) with 2 SA-N-5 missiles.
Depth charges: 2 racks.
Mines: 6—12 depending on type.
Countermeasures: Decoys: 6—9 barrelled Jastrzab 2 launchers for chaff.
ECM: PIT Bren system being fitted.
MCM: 2 Bofors MT2W mechanical, 1 TEM-PE-2MA magnetic and 1 MTA-2 acoustic sweeps. CTM Ukwial ROV with sonar, TV and charges. 10 ZHH 230 sonobuoys.
Combat data systems: CTM Pstrokosz command support system.
Radars: Navigation: Racal Decca Bridgemaster; I-band.
IFF: RAWAR SC-10D2
Sonars: CTM SHL-100MA hull mounted; active minehunting; high frequency; Politechnica Gdansk SHL-200 VDS.

Comment: All taken out of service in 1997. New armament and minehunting equipment installed. Divers recompression chamber carried. *Mewa* returned to service in May 1999, *Czajka* in May 2000 and *Flaming* in 2001. Life extended by ten years.

MEWA *9/2005*, Guy Toremans* / 1151317

13 GOPLO (NOTEC) CLASS (PROJECT 207P/207DM)
(MINESWEEPERS/HUNTERS—COASTAL) (MHC)

Name	No	Builders	Launched	Commissioned
GOPLO	630	Naval Shipyard, Gdynia	16 Apr 1981	13 Mar 1982
GARDNO	631	Naval Shipyard, Gdynia	23 June 1993	31 Mar 1984
BUKOWO	632	Naval Shipyard, Gdynia	19 Sep 1984	23 June 1985
DABIE	633	Naval Shipyard, Gdynia	12 June 1985	11 May 1986
JAMNO	634	Naval Shipyard, Gdynia	11 Feb 1986	11 Oct 1986
MIELNO	635	Naval Shipyard, Gdynia	27 June 1986	9 May 1987
WICKO	636	Naval Shipyard, Gdynia	20 Mar 1987	12 Oct 1987
RESKO	637	Naval Shipyard, Gdynia	1 Oct 1987	26 Mar 1988
SARBSKO	638	Naval Shipyard, Gdynia	10 May 1988	12 Oct 1988
NECKO	639	Naval Shipyard, Gdynia	21 Nov 1988	9 May 1989
NAKLO	640	Naval Shipyard, Gdynia	29 May 1989	2 Mar 1990
DRUZNO	641	Naval Shipyard, Gdynia	29 Nov 1989	17 Sep 1990
HANCZA	642	Naval Shipyard, Gdynia	9 July 1990	1 Mar 1991

Displacement, tons: 216 full load
Dimensions, feet (metres): 126.3 × 24.3 × 5.9 *(38.5 × 7.4 × 1.8)*
Main machinery: 2 M 401A1 diesels; 1,874 hp(m) *(1.38 MW)* sustained; 2 shafts
Speed, knots: 14. **Range, n miles:** 1,100 at 9 kt
Complement: 29 (6 officers)
Guns: 2 ZU-23-2MR 23 mm (twin); 400 rds/min combined to 2 km.
Depth charges: 24
Mines: 6—24
Countermeasures: MCM: MMTK1 mechanical; MTA 1 acoustic and TEM-PE 1 magnetic sweeps.
Radars: Navigation: Bridgemaster; I-band.
Sonars: MG 89 or MG 79; active minehunting; high frequency.

Comment: *Goplo* is an experimental prototype numbered 207D. The 23 mm guns have replaced the original 25 mm. GRP hulls. All are to be upgraded to 207DM for minehunting, and to carry divers. Named after lakes and based at Swinoujscie.

BUKOWO *6/2004, J Ciślak* / 1044476

4 MAMRY (NOTEC II) CLASS (PROJECT 207M)
(MINESWEEPERS/HUNTERS—COASTAL) (MHSCM)

Name	No	Builders	Launched	Commissioned
MAMRY	643	Naval Shipyard, Gdynia	30 Sep 1991	25 Sep 1992
WIGRY	644	Naval Shipyard, Gdynia	28 Nov 1992	14 May 1993
SNIARDWY	645	Naval Shipyard, Gdynia	18 June 1993	28 Jan 1994
WDZYDZE	646	Naval Shipyard, Gdynia	24 June 1994	2 Dec 1994

Displacement, tons: 216 full load
Dimensions, feet (metres): 126.3 × 24.3 × 5.9 *(38.5 × 7.4 × 1.8)*
Main machinery: 2 M 401A diesels; 1,874 hp(m) *(1.38 MW)*; 2 shafts
2 auxiliary motors; 816 hp(m) *(60 kW)*
Speed, knots: 14
Range, n miles: 865 at 14 kt
Complement: 27 (5 officers)
Missiles: SAM/Guns: 2 ZU-23-2MR 23 mm Wrobel II (twin); combination of 2 SA-N-5 missiles; IR homing to 6 km *(3.2 n miles)* at 1.5 Mach; warhead 1.5 kg and guns; 400 rds/min combined to 2 km.
Mines: 6—24 depending on type.
Countermeasures: MCM: MMTK 1m mechanical, MTA 2 acoustic and TEM-PE 1m magnetic sweeps.
Radars: Navigation: SRN 401XTA; I-band.
Sonars: SHL 100/200; hull mounted/VDS; active minehunting; high frequency.

Comment: Modified version of the 207P and equipped to carry divers. Identical hull to the 207P. All based at Hel. An enlarged design, the Type 207 MCMV with a length of 43.5 m, is a longer term project.

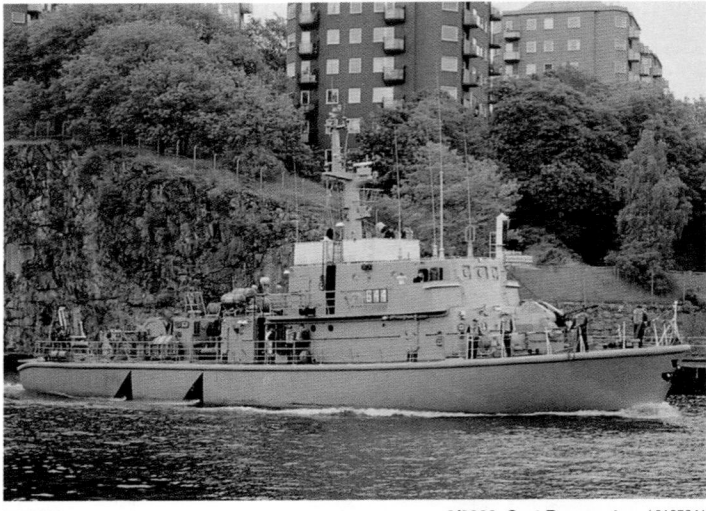

WIGRY *6/2000, Curt Borgenstam* / 0105241

AMPHIBIOUS FORCES

5 LUBLIN CLASS (PROJECT 767)
(LST/MINELAYERS) (LST/ML)

Name	No	Builders	Launched	Commissioned
LUBLIN	821	Northern Shipyard, Gdansk	12 July 1988	12 Oct 1989
GNIEZNO	822	Northern Shipyard, Gdansk	7 Dec 1988	23 Feb 1990
KRAKOW	823	Northern Shipyard, Gdansk	7 Mar 1989	27 June 1990
POZNAN	824	Northern Shipyard, Gdansk	5 Jan 1990	8 Mar 1991
TORUN	825	Northern Shipyard, Gdansk	8 June 1990	24 May 1991

Displacement, tons: 1,350 standard; 1,745 full load
Dimensions, feet (metres): 313 × 35.4 × 6.6 *(95.4 × 10.8 × 2)*
Main machinery: 3 Cegielski 6ATL25D diesels; 5,390 hp(m) *(3.96 MW)* sustained; 3 shafts
Speed, knots: 16
Range, n miles: 1,400 at 16 kt
Complement: 50 (5 officers)
Military lift: 9 Type T-72 tanks or 9 APC or 17 medium or light trucks. 80 troops plus equipment (821-823); 125 troops plus equipment (824); 135 troops and equipment (825).

Missiles: SAM/Guns: 8 ZU-23-2MR 23 mm Wrobel II (4 twin); combination of 2 SA-N-5 missiles; IR homing to 6 km *(3.2 n miles)* at 1.5 Mach; warhead 1.5 kg and guns; 400 rds/min combined.
Depth charges: 9 throwers for counter-mining.
Mines: 50—134.
Countermeasures: Decoys: 2 12-barrelled 70 mm Derkacz chaff launchers (821 and 825). 2 12-barrelled Jastrzab chaff launchers (822-824).
Radars: Navigation: SRN 7453 and SRN 443XTA; I-band.

Comment: Designed with a through deck from bow to stern and can be used as minelayers as well as for amphibious landings. Folding bow and stern ramps and a stern anchor are fitted. The ship has a pressurised citadel for NBC defence and an upper deck washdown system. Mining capabilities upgraded in 1997/98. Based at Swinoujscie.

POZNAN *6/2005*, J Ciślak* / 1151318

3 DEBA CLASS (PROJECT 716) (LCU)

Name	No	Builders	Launched	Commissioned
KD 11	851	Naval Shipyard, Gdynia	13 Nov 1987	7 Aug 1988
KD 12	852	Naval Shipyard, Gdynia	2 July 1990	2 Jan 1991
KD 13	853	Naval Shipyard, Gdynia	26 Oct 1990	3 May 1991

Displacement, tons: 176 full load
Dimensions, feet (metres): 122 × 23.3 × 5.6 *(37.2 × 7.1 × 1.7)*
Main machinery: 3 Type M 401A diesels; 3,000 hp(m) *(2.2 MW)*; 3 shafts
Speed, knots: 20
Range, n miles: 430 at 16 kt
Complement: 12
Military lift: 1 tank or 2 vehicles up to 20 tons and 50 troops
Guns: 2 ZU-23-2M 23 mm (twin).
Radars: Surface search: SRN 207A; I-band.

Comment: The plan was to build 12 but the programme was suspended at three through lack of funds. A similar design has been assembled in Iran. Can carry up to six launchers for strung-out charges. Based at Swinoujscie.

KD 11 *9/2003, J Ciślak* / 0567514

SURVEY AND RESEARCH SHIPS

2 MODIFIED FINIK 2 CLASS (PROJECT 874) (AGS)

Name	No	Builders	Launched	Commissioned
HEWELIUSZ	265	Northern Shipyard, Gdansk	11 Sep 1981	27 Nov 1982
ARCTOWSKI	266	Northern Shipyard, Gdansk	20 Nov 1981	27 Nov 1982

Displacement, tons: 1,135 standard; 1,218 full load
Dimensions, feet (metres): 202.1 × 36.7 × 10.8 *(61.6 × 11.2 × 3.3)*
Main machinery: 2 Cegielski-Sulzer 6AL25/30 diesels; 1,920 hp(m) *(1.4 MW)*; 2 auxiliary motors; 204 hp(m) *(150 kW)*; 2 shafts; cp props; bow thruster
Speed, knots: 13. **Range, n miles:** 5,900 at 11 kt
Complement: 49 (10 officers)
Radars: Navigation: SRN 7453 Nogat; SRN 743X; I-band.

Comment: Sister ships to Russian class which were built in Poland, except that *Heweliusz* and *Arctowski* have been modified and have no buoy handling equipment. Equipment includes Atlas Deso, Atlas Ralog and Atlas Dolog survey. Both ships are based at Gdynia. One sister ship, *Planeta*, is civilian operated and the other, *Zodiak*, was decommissioned in 2003.

ARCTOWSKI *11/2004*, J Ciślak* / 1151319

HEWELIUSZ *6/2004, J Ciślak* / 1044480

2 SURVEY CRAFT (PROJECT 4234) (AGSC)

Name	Builders	Commissioned
K 10	Wisla, Gdansk	6 Feb 1989
K 4	Wisla, Gdansk	25 Sep 1989

Displacement, tons: 45 full load
Dimensions, feet (metres): 62 × 14.4 × 4.9 *(18.9 × 4.4 × 1.5)*
Main machinery: 1 Wola DM 150 diesel; 160 hp(m) *(117 kW)* sustained; 1 shaft
Speed, knots: 9
Complement: 10
Radars: Navigation: SRN 207A; I-band.

Comment: Coastal survey craft based at Gdynia. There are a number of survey launches and buoy tenders listed under *Auxiliaries*.

K 10 *5/2000, J Ciślak* / 0105248

5 SURVEY CRAFT (PROJECT III/C) (AGSC)

M 35   M 37-40

Displacement, tons: 10 full load
Dimensions, feet (metres): 36.1 × 10.5 × 2.3 *(11 × 3.2 × 0.7)*
Main machinery: 1 Puck Rekin SW 400/MZ diesel; 95 hp(m) *(70 kW)*; 1 shaft
Speed, knots: 8
Range, n miles: 184 at 8 kt
Complement: 5
Radars: Navigation: SRN 207A; I-band.

Comment: Based at Gdynia and Swinoujscie (M 35).

M 40 *3/2003, J Ciślak* / 0567515

TRAINING SHIPS

Notes: The three masted sailing ship *Dar Mlodziezy* is civilian owned and operated but also takes naval personnel for training.

1 WODNIK CLASS (PROJECT 888) (AXTH)

Name	No	Builders	Launched	Commissioned
WODNIK	251	Northern Shipyard, Gdansk	19 Nov 1975	28 May 1976

Displacement, tons: 1,697 standard; 1,820 full load
Dimensions, feet (metres): 234.3 × 38.1 × 14.8 *(71.4 × 11.6 × 4.5)*
Main machinery: 2 Zgoda-Sulzer 6TD48 diesels; 2,650 hp(m) *(1.95 MW)* sustained; 2 shafts; cp props
Speed, knots: 16
Range, n miles: 7,200 at 11 kt
Complement: 56 (24 officers) plus 101 midshipmen
Guns: 4 ZU-23-2MR Wrobel 23 mm (2 twin). 2 *(Wodnik)* or 4 *(Gryf)* 30 mm AK 230 (1 or 2 twin).
Radars: Navigation: 2 SRN 7453 Nogat; I-band.
Helicopters: Platform for 1 light.

Comment: Sister to former GDR *Wilhelm Pieck* and two Russian ships. Converted to a hospital ship (150 beds) in 1990 for deployment to the Gulf. Armament removed as part of the conversion but partially restored in 1992. Based at Gdynia. Second of class in reserve from 1999.

WODNIK *10/2003, J Ciślak* / 1044481

1 ISKRA CLASS (PROJECT B79) (SAIL TRAINING SHIP) (AXS)

Name	No	Builders	Launched	Commissioned
ISKRA	253	Gdansk Shipyard	6 Mar 1982	11 Aug 1982

Displacement, tons: 498 full load
Dimensions, feet (metres): 160.8 × 26.6 × 13.1 *(49 × 8.1 × 4.0)*
Main machinery: 1 Wola 75H12 diesel; 310 hp(m) *(228 kW)*; 1 auxiliary shaft; cp prop
Speed, knots: 9 (diesel)
Complement: 14 (6 officers) plus 50 cadets
Radars: Navigation: SRN 206; I-band.

Comment: Barquentine with 1,040 m² of sail. Used by the Naval Academy for training with a secondary survey role. Based at Gdynia.

ISKRA *6/2005*, Michael Nitz* / 1151322

INTELLIGENCE VESSELS

2 MODIFIED MOMA CLASS (PROJECT 863) (AGI)

Name	No	Builders	Commissioned
NAWIGATOR	262	Northern Shipyard, Gdansk	17 Feb 1975
HYDROGRAF	263	Northern Shipyard, Gdansk	8 May 1976

Displacement, tons: 1,677 full load
Dimensions, feet (metres): 240.5 × 35.4 × 12.8 *(73.3 × 10.8 × 3.9)*
Main machinery: 2 Zgoda-Sulzer 6TD48 diesels; 3,300 hp(m) *(2.43 MW)* sustained; 2 shafts
Speed, knots: 17
Range, n miles: 7,200 at 12 kt
Complement: 87 (10 officers)
Missiles: 2 Fasta-4M quad launchers. SA-N-5.
Guns: 4—25 mm (2 twin) (262).
Countermeasures: ESM/ECM intercept and jammer.
Radars: Navigation: 2 SRN 7453 Nogat; I-band.

Comment: Much altered in the upperworks and unrecognisable as Momas. The forecastle in *Hydrograf* is longer than in *Nawigator* and one deck higher. *Hydrograf* fitted for but not with two twin 25 mm gun mountings. Forward radome replaced by a cylindrical type in *Nawigator* and after ones removed on both ships. Based at Gdynia.

NAWIGATOR *2/2005*, J Ciślak* / 1151320

HYDROGRAF *10/2001, J Ciślak* / 0126242

AUXILIARIES

Notes: Procurement of up to four Strategic Support Ships is reported to be under development. The broad requirement is for ships of approximately 10,000 tons with the capability of transporting about 500 troops plus some twenty vehicles and up to six helicopters. Funding is not thought to have been approved.

1 PROJECT 890 CLASS
(LOGISTICS SUPPORT VESSEL) (AKHM/APHM/AGI)

KONTRADMIRAL X CZERNICKI 511

Displacement, tons: 2,250 full load
Dimensions, feet (metres): 239.3 × 45.3 × 13.4 *(72.9 × 13.8 × 4.1)*
Main machinery: 2 Cegielski-Sulzer AL25D diesels; 2,934 hp(m) *(2.16 MW)* sustained; 2 shafts
Speed, knots: 14.1. **Range, n miles:** 7,000 at 12 kt
Complement: 38
Military lift: 140 troops with full individual armament or ten 20 ft containers or four 20 ft containers and six STAR 266 army trucks

Missiles: SAM/Guns: 1 ZU 23-2MR Wrobel I/II mounts: combination of 2 Strela 2M (Grail) missiles and 2—23 mm guns.
Countermeasures: Decoys: 4 WNP81/9 9 barrelled 81 mm Jastrzab chaff launchers.
ESM: PIT intercept.
Radars: Surface search: SRN; E/F-band.
Navigation: SRN; I-band.
Helicopters: Platform for 1 helicopter (up to ten ton).

Comment: Conversion from a Project 130 Degaussing Vessel to Logistic Support Ship in Northern Shipyard, Gdansk, has included new upper and forward hull sections, provision of a helicopter deck and NBC protection. The ship has a 16 ton hydraulic crane and after ramp. The multirole ship is capable of sealift, acting as a forward maintenance unit and maritime surveillance and reconnaissance (using containerised ESM sensors) and replenishment at sea. Commissioned on 1 September 2001.

KONTRADMIRAL X CZERNICKI *4/2003, A Sharma* / 0567505

1 BALTYK CLASS (PROJECT ZP 1200) (TANKER) (AORL)

Name	No	Builders	Commissioned
BALTYK	Z 1	Naval Shipyard, Gdynia	11 Mar 1991

Displacement, tons: 2,937 standard; 3,049 full load
Dimensions, feet (metres): 278.2 × 43 × 15.4 *(84.8 × 13.1 × 4.7)*
Main machinery: 2 Cegielski 8 ASL 25 diesels; 4,025 hp(m) *(2.96 MW)*; 2 shafts; cp props
Speed, knots: 15. **Range, n miles:** 4,250 at 12 kt
Complement: 34 (4 officers)
Cargo capacity: 1,184 tons fuel, 92.7 tons lub oil
Guns: 4 ZU-23-2M Wrobel 23 mm (2 twin).
Radars: Navigation: SRN 7453 and SRN 207A; I-band.

Comment: Beam replenishment stations, one each side. First of a projected class of four, of which the others were cancelled. Based at Gdynia.

BALTYK *2/2005*, J Ciślak* / 1151321

3 MOSKIT CLASS (PROJECT B 199) (TANKER) (AOTL)

Name	No	Builders	Launched	Commissioned
KRAB	Z 3	Rzeczna, Wroclaw Shipyard	22 July 1969	23 Sep 1970
MEDUZA	Z 8	Rzeczna, Wroclaw Shipyard	14 Sep 1969	21 July 1970
SLIMAK	Z 9	Wisla Shipyard, Gdansk	1 Aug 1970	15 May 1971

Displacement, tons: 1,225 full load
Dimensions, feet (metres): 190.3 × 30.5 × 10.8 *(58 × 9.3 × 3.3)*
Main machinery: 1 Magdeburg diesel; 965 hp(m) *(720 kW)*; 1 shaft
Speed, knots: 10. **Range, n miles:** 1,200 at 10 kt
Complement: 21 (3 officers)
Cargo capacity: 656.5 tons
Guns: 4 ZU-23-2M 23 mm (2 twin).
Radars: Navigation: TRN 823; I-band.

Comment: Z 3 and Z 9, previously reported to have been decommissioned in 2002, were back in service in 2005.

MEDUZA *7/2004, J Ciślak* / 1044484

2 KORMORAN CLASS (YPT)

Name	Builders	Launched	Commissioned
K 8	Naval Shipyard, Gdynia	26 Aug 1970	3 July 1971
K 11	Naval Shipyard, Gdynia	23 June 1971	11 Dec 1971

Displacement, tons: 150 full load
Dimensions, feet (metres): 114.8 × 19.7 × 5.2 (35 × 6 × 1.6)
Main machinery: 2 Type M 50F5 diesels; 2,200 hp(m) (1.6 MW); 2 shafts
Speed, knots: 19
Range, n miles: 550 at 15 kt
Complement: 24
Guns: 2 ZU-23-2M Wrobel 23 mm (twin).
Radars: Navigation: SRN 206/301; I-band.

Comment: Armament updated in 1993. Both based at Gdynia.

K 8 *10/2001, J Ciślak* / 0126239

2 MROWKA CLASS (PROJECT B 208)
(DEGAUSSING VESSELS) (YDG)

Name	No	Builders	Commissioned
WRONA	SD 11	Naval Shipyard, Gdynia	10 Oct 1971
—	SD 13	Naval Shipyard, Gdynia	16 Dec 1972

Displacement, tons: 660 full load
Dimensions, feet (metres): 144.4 × 26.6 × 9.5 (44 × 8.1 × 2.9)
Main machinery: 1 6NV D36 diesel; 957 hp(m) (704 kW); 1 shaft
Speed, knots: 9.5
Range, n miles: 2,230 at 9.5 kt
Complement: 37
Guns: 2—25 mm (twin) (SD 11 and 13); 2 ZU-23-2M Wrobel 23 mm (twin) (SD 12).
Radars: Navigation: SRN 206; I-band.

Comment: Names are unofficial. SD 12 decommissioned in 2005. SD 11 and SD 13 based at Gdynia.

RYS *4/2004, Hartmut Ehlers* / 1044483

2 PIAST CLASS (PROJECT 570) (SALVAGE SHIPS) (ARS)

Name	No	Builders	Commissioned
PIAST	281	Northern Shipyard, Gdansk	26 Jan 1974
LECH	282	Northern Shipyard, Gdansk	30 Nov 1974

Displacement, tons: 1,887 full load
Dimensions, feet (metres): 238.5 × 38.1 × 13.1 (72.7 × 11.6 × 4)
Main machinery: 2 Zgoda-Sulzer 6TD48 diesels; 3,300 hp(m) (2.43 MW) sustained; 2 shafts; cp props
Speed, knots: 15
Range, n miles: 3,000 at 12 kt
Complement: 56 (8 officers) plus 12 spare
Missiles: SAM 2 Fasta 4M twin launchers for SA-N-5.
Guns: 4—25 mm (2 twin).
Radars: Navigation: 2 SRN 7453 Nogat; I-band.

Comment: Basically a Moma class hull with towing and firefighting capabilities. Ice-strengthened hulls. Wartime role as hospital ships. Carry three-man diving bells capable of 100 m depth and a decompression chamber. ROV added and other salvage improvements made in 1997/98. Based at Gdynia. Guns may not be carried.

LECH *5/2004, J Ciślak* / 1044485

2 ZBYSZKO CLASS (PROJECT B 823) (SALVAGE SHIPS) (ARS)

Name	No	Builders	Commissioned
ZBYSZKO	R 14	Ustka Shipyard	8 Nov 1991
MACKO	R 15	Ustka Shipyard	20 Mar 1992

Displacement, tons: 380 full load
Dimensions, feet (metres): 114.8 × 26.2 × 9.8 (35 × 8 × 3)
Main machinery: 1 Sulzer 6AL20/24D; 750 hp(m) (551 kW); 1 shaft
Speed, knots: 11
Range, n miles: 3,000 at 10 kt
Complement: 15
Radars: Navigation: SRN 402X; I-band.

Comment: Type B-823 ordered 30 May 1988. Carries a decompression chamber and two divers. Mobile gantry crane on the stern. Based at Kolobrzeg.

MACKO *5/2004, J Ciślak* / 1044486

2 PLUSKWA CLASS (PROJECT R-30) (SALVAGE TUG) (ATS)

Name	No	Builders	Commissioned
GNIEWKO	R 11	Naval Shipyard, Gdynia	29 Sep 1981
SEMKO	R 13	Naval Shipyard, Gdynia	9 May 1987

Displacement, tons: 365 full load
Dimensions, feet (metres): 105 × 29.2 × 10.2 (32 × 8.9 × 3.1)
Main machinery: 1 Cegielski-Sulzer 6AL25/30 diesel; 1,470 hp(m) (1.08 MW); 1 shaft
Speed, knots: 12
Range, n miles: 4,000 at 7 kt
Complement: 18
Radars: Navigation: SRN 443 XEA; I-band.

Comment: Based at Hel. Bollard pull 15 tons.

GNIEWKO *6/2004, J Ciślak* / 1044489

3 TRANSPORT CRAFT (YFB)

M 1	M 3	M 32

Displacement, tons: 74 full load
Dimensions, feet (metres): 94.2 × 19 × 4.3 (28.7 × 5.8 × 1.3)
Main machinery: 3 M50F5 diesels; 3,600 hp(m) (2.65 MW); 3 shafts
Speed, knots: 27
Complement: 7 plus 30
Radars: Navigation: SRN 207A; I-band.

Comment: Details given are for M 1 built at Gdynia. The other two are similar but slower and smaller. All can be used as emergency patrol craft. M 1 based at Gdynia as an Admirals' launch.

M 3 *7/2004, J Ciślak* / 1044490

4 MISCELLANEOUS HARBOUR CRAFT (YFB)

B 3, 7, 9, 11-12, W 2, M 5, M 12, M 21-22, M 37-40

Comment: M numbers are patrol launches; B numbers are freighters and oil lighters; W 2 is a floating workshop.

M 22 *3/2002, J Ciślak* / 0567510

B-12 *7/2004, J Ciślak* / 1044491

TUGS

2 H 960 CLASS (ATA)

H 6   **H 8**

Displacement, tons: 340 full load
Dimensions, feet (metres): 91.2 × 26.2 × 12.1 *(27.8 × 8 × 3.7)*
Main machinery: 1 Sulzer GATL 25 D diesels; 1,306 hp(m) *(960 kW)*; 1 shaft
Speed, knots: 12. **Range, n miles:** 1,150 at 12 kt
Complement: 17 (1 officer)
Radars: Navigation: SRN 401 XTA; I-band.

Comment: Built at Nauta Ship Repair Yard, Gdynia and commissioned 25 September 1992 and 19 March 1993 respectively. Based at Hel (H 6) and Gdynia (H 9).

H 8 *9/2005*, J Ciślak* / 1151324

6 HARBOUR TUGS (PROJECTS H 900, H 800, H 820) (YTB/YTM)

H 3-5 H 7 (Type 900)   **H 9-10** (Type 820)

Displacement, tons: 218 full load
Dimensions, feet (metres): 84 × 22.3 × 11.5 *(25.6 × 6.8 × 3.5)*
Main machinery: 1 Cegielski-Sulzer 6AL20/24H diesel; 935 hp(m) *(687 kW)*; 1 shaft
Speed, knots: 11
Range, n miles: 1,500 at 10 kt
Complement: 17
Radars: Navigation: SRN 206; I-band.

Comment: Details given are for H 3, 4, 5 and 7. Completed 1979-81. Have firefighting capability except H 9-10. H 9-10 completed in 1993.

H 7 *5/2005*, J Ciślak* / 1151323

SEA DETACHMENT OF THE BORDER GUARD (MOSG)

Headquarters Appointments

Commandant MOSG:
  Rear Admiral Konrad Wiśniowski
Deputy Commandant:
  Captain Marek Borkowski
Deputy Commandant:
  Commander Marek Ilnicki

Bases

Gdansk (HQ and Kaszubski Division)
Swinoujscie (Pomorski Division)

General

MOSG (Morski Oddzial Strazy Granicznej) formed on 1 August 1991. Vessels have blue hulls with red and yellow striped insignia. Superstructures are painted white. The use of ships' names was discontinued in 2004. MOSG also operates one Piper PA 34 Seneca II patrol aircraft.

PATROL FORCES

Notes: Four new patrol craft are planned to enter service in 2006.

2 OBLUZE CLASS (PROJECT 912)
(LARGE PATROL CRAFT) (WPB)

No	Builders	Commissioned
SG-323	Naval Shipyard, Gdynia	10 June 1967
SG-325	Naval Shipyard, Gdynia	31 Jan 1968

Displacement, tons: 236 full load
Dimensions, feet (metres): 135.5 × 21.3 × 7 *(41.3 × 6.5 × 2.1)*
Main machinery: 2 40DM diesels; 4,400 hp(m) *(3.24 MW)* sustained; 2 shafts
Speed, knots: 24
Range, n miles: 1,200 at 12 kt
Complement: 19
Guns: 4 AK 230 30 mm (2 twin) (SG 323). 2 AK 230 30 mm (twin) (SG 325).
Depth charges: 2 internal racks.
Radars: Surface search: SRN 207; I-band.
Sonars: Tamir II (MG 11); hull-mounted; active attack; high frequency.

Comment: First of class *Fala* is now a museum ship. Both based at Kolobrzeg.

SG-323 *5/2004, J Ciślak* / 1044492

2 KAPER CLASS (PROJECT SKS-40)
(LARGE PATROL CRAFT) (WPB)

No	Builders	Commissioned
SG-311	Wisla Yard, Gdansk	21 Jan 1991
SG-312	Wisla Yard, Gdansk	3 Apr 1992

Displacement, tons: 470 full load
Dimensions, feet (metres): 139.4 × 27.6 × 9.2 *(42.5 × 8.4 × 2.8)*
Main machinery: 2 Sulzer 8ATL25/30 diesels; 4,720 hp(m) *(3.47 MW)*; 2 shafts; cp props
Speed, knots: 17. **Range, n miles:** 2,800 at 14 kt
Complement: 15
Guns: 2 — 7.62 mm MGs.
Radars: Surface search: SRN 207; I-band.
Navigation: Racal Decca; I-band.

Comment: *Kaper I* completed at Wisla Yard, Gdansk in January 1991, *Kaper II* on 1 October 1994. Have Simrad fish-finding sonars fitted. Used for Fishery Protection. 311 based at Gdansk and 312 at Kolobrzeg.

SG-311   *5/2004, J Ciślak* / 1044493

6 WISLOKA CLASS (PROJECT 90)
(COASTAL PATROL CRAFT) (WPB)

SG-142	SG-144-146	SG-150	SG-152

Displacement, tons: 45 full load
Dimensions, feet (metres): 69.6 × 14.8 × 5.2 *(21.2 × 4.5 × 1.6)*
Main machinery: 2 Wola 31 ANM28 H12A diesels; 1,000 hp(m) *(735 kW)*; 2 shafts
Speed, knots: 18. **Range, n miles:** 300 at 18 kt
Complement: 6
Guns: 2 — 12.7 mm MGs (twin).
Radars: Surface search: SRN 207; I-band.

Comment: Built at Wisla Shipyard, Gdansk and completed between October 1973 and August 1977. Three are based at Gdansk and three at Swinoujscie.

SG-152   *4/2004, Hartmut Ehlers* / 1044494

2 PILICA CLASS (PROJECT 918)
(COASTAL PATROL CRAFT) (WPB)

SG-161	SG-164

Displacement, tons: 93 full load
Dimensions, feet (metres): 93.8 × 19 × 4.6 *(28.6 × 5.8 × 1.4)*
Main machinery: 3 M 50-F6 diesels; 3,604 hp(m) *(2.65 MW)*; 3 shafts
Speed, knots: 27
Range, n miles: 1,160 at 12 kt
Complement: 12
Guns: 2 ZU-23-2M Wrobel 23 mm (twin).
Radars: Surface search: SRN 231; I-band.

Comment: Same as naval craft but without the torpedo tubes and sonar. Built by Naval Shipyard, Gdynia and completed between June 1973 and October 1974. One based at Swinoujscie and one at Gdansk.

SG-161   *3/2002, J Ciślak* / 0567519

1 PATROL LAUNCH (PROJECT M-35) (WYFL)

SG 036

Displacement, tons: 41 full load
Dimensions, feet (metres): 35.3 × 14.4 × 5.2 *(10.7 × 4.4 × 1.6)*
Main machinery: 1 Wola DM 150 diesel; 150 hp *(112 kW)*
Speed, knots: 8
Complement: 4

Comment: Built in 1985. Similar to those in Polish naval service.

SG 036   *5/2003, J Ciślak* / 0567518

4 SPORTIS CLASS (PROJECT 7500)
(FAST INTERCEPT CRAFT) (WPBF)

SG-002-005

Displacement, tons: 2
Dimensions, feet (metres): 24.6 × 9.2 × 1.3 *(7.5 × 2.8 × 0.4)*
Main machinery: Volvo Penta 230 hp (170 kW)
Speed, knots: 42
Complement: 3

Comment: Built in Bojano in 1996.

SG-003   *5/2003, J Ciślak* / 0567484

SG-005   *5/2002, J Ciślak* / 0567485

1 PATROL CRAFT (PROJECT MI-6) (WPB)

SG-008

Displacement, tons: 16
Dimensions, feet (metres): 42.7 × 12.14 × 3.6 *(13.0 × 3.7 × 1.1)*
Main machinery: 1 Wola; 200 hp *(147 kW)*; 1 shaft
Speed, knots: 11
Complement: 4

Comment: Harbour craft built at Wisla Shipyard, Gdansk, 1989.

SG-008   *5/2003, J Ciślak* / 0567483

2 STRAZNIK CLASS (PROJECT SAR-1500) (WPBF)

No	Builders	Commissioned
SG-211	Damen Yard, Gdynia	29 Apr 2000
SG-212	Damen Yard, Gdynia	7 July 2000

Displacement, tons: 26
Dimensions, feet (metres): 49.9 × 17.7 × 2.95 *(15.2 × 5.39 × 0.90)*
Main machinery: 2 MAN D2848 diesels; 1,360 hp *(1,000 kW)*; water jet system
Speed, knots: 35
Range, n miles: 200 at 30 kt
Complement: 4 (1 officer)
Guns: 1 — 7.62 mm MG.
Radars: Surface search: SIMRAD; I-band.

Comment: Contract between MOSG and Damen Shipyard signed 5 October 1999. Based on Dutch SAR 1500 lifeboat. Hull and superstructure of aluminium alloy.

SG 063   *6/2003, MOSG* / 0567506

0 + 2 GRIFFON 2000 TDX CLASS (HOVERCRAFT) (UCAC)

KBV 591-592

Displacement, tons: 3.5 full load
Dimensions, feet (metres): 38.4 × 19.4 *(11.7 × 5.9)*
Main machinery: 1 Deutz BF6M 1015CP diesel; 440 hp *(330 kW)*
Speed, knots: 50
Range, n miles: 450 at 35 kt
Complement: 3
Radars: Navigation: Furuno 7010 D; I-band.

Comment: Order from Griffon Hovercraft, Southampton for delivery in 2006. Aluminium hull. To be employed as patrol ship in shallow waters and rivers.

SG-212   *4/2004, Hartmut Ehlers* / 1044495

6 MODIFIED SPORTIS CLASS (PROJECT S-6100)
(FAST INTERCEPT CRAFT) (WPBF)

SG 061-066

Displacement, tons: 1.9
Dimensions, feet (metres): 20.0 × 7.5 × 1.3 *(6.1 × 2.3 × 0.4)*
Main machinery: 2 Johnson outboard motors; 120 hp *(89.6 kW)*
Speed, knots: 35
Complement: 2

Comment: Built at Bojano in 2001. Located at Border units along the coast.

Griffon 2000 TDX   *6/2003, Swedish Colours* / 0572610

Portugal

MARINHA PORTUGUESA

Country Overview

The Republic of Portugal is situated in south-western Europe in the western portion of the Iberian Peninsula. It is bordered to the north and east by Spain and has a 967 n mile coastline with the Atlantic Ocean. The Azores and Madeira Islands in the Atlantic are integral parts of the republic, the total area of which is 35,553 square miles. Lisbon is the capital, largest city and principal port. There are further ports at Leixões (near Oporto), Setúbal, and Funchal (Madeira). Territorial seas (12 n miles) and an EEZ (200 n miles) are claimed.

Headquarters Appointments

Chief of Naval Staff:
   Admiral Fernando José Ribeiro de Melo Gomes
Deputy Chief of Naval Staff:
   Vice Admiral Victor Manuel Bento e Lopo Cajarabille
Naval Commander:
   Vice Admiral Fernando Manuel de Oliveira Vargas de Matos
Azores Maritime Zone Commander:
   Rear Admiral António Alberto Rodrigues Cabral
Madeira Maritime Zone Commander:
   Captain Raúl Bernardo Mourato Ramos Gouveia
Marine Corps Commander:
   Rear Admiral João da Cruz de Carvalho Abreu

Diplomatic Representation

Defence and Naval Attaché in London, Dublin and The Hague:
   Lieutenant Colonel Jorge Manuel da Costa Ramos
Naval Attaché in Washington and Ottawa:
   Colonel Isidro de Morais Pereira
Defence Attaché in Luanda, Kinshasa, Brazzaville and Windhoek:
   Captain Luís Augusto Loureiro Nunes
Defence Attaché in Maputo, Lillongwe, Harare and Dar-Es-Salam:
   Colonel Armandio Amador Pires Pinelo
Defence Attaché in Madrid, Cairo and Athens:
   Colonel Ulisses Joaquim de Carvaho Nunes de Oliveira

Diplomatic Representation—continued

Defence Attaché in S. Tomé and Libreville:
   Lieutenant Colonel Joaquim Epifânio Santana Santos
Defence Attaché in Bissau, Conakry and Dakar:
   Colonel João Pereira de Araújo
Defence Attaché in Brasilia:
   Colonel Duarte Veríssimo Pires Torrão
Defence Attaché in Berlin, Prague, Copenhagen, Stockholm and Oslo:
   Colonel João Sousa Teles
Defence Attaché in Warsaw, Budapest, Kiev, Bucharest and Bratislava:
   Captain António Maria Mendes Calado
Defence Attaché in Canberra, Dili and Jakarta:
   Commander José António Ruivo
Defence Attaché in Paris, Luxembourg and Brussels:
   Captain José Luís Branco Seabra de Melo
Defence Attaché in Rabat and Tunis:
   Colonel Alberto Jorge Crispim Gomes
Defence Attaché in Praia:
   Captain João Adelino Delduque Pereira Gonçalves
Defence Attaché in Moscow:
   Captain João Alegre Branco
Defence Attaché in Rome, Tel-Aviv and Ankara:
   Commander José Luis Santos Alcobia

Personnel

(a)   2006: 10,560 (1,512 officers) including 1,660 marines
(b)   4 months national service

Marine Corps

2 battalions, 1 special operations detachment, 1 naval police unit

Bases

Main Base: Lisbon — Alfeite
Dockyard: Arsenal do Alfeite
Fleet Support: Porto, Portimão, Funchal, Ponta Delgada, Tróia
Air Base: Montijo (Lisbon)

Naval Air

The helicopter squadron was formally activated on 23 September 1993 at Montijo air force base, Lisbon. Operational and logistic procedures are similar to the air force.

Prefix to Ships' Names

NRP (Navio da República Portuguesa)

Strength of the Fleet

Type	Active (Reserve)	Building (Projected)
Submarines (Patrol)	2	(3)
Frigates	6	(3)
Corvettes	7	—
Patrol Craft	4	(10)
Coastal/River Patrol Craft	12	(5)
LPD	—	(1)
LCTs/LST	1	—
Survey Ships and Craft	7	—
Sail Training Ships	4	—
Replenishment Tanker	1	(1)
Buoy Tenders	2	(2)

DELETIONS

Submarines

2005   *Delfim*

Frigates

2005   *Comandante Hermen Egildo Capelo*

Corvettes

2002   *Oliveira e Carmo, Honorio Barreto*
2004   *Augusto Castilho*

Patrol Forces

2003   *Zambeze, Limpopo, Andorinha*

PENNANT LIST

Submarines			F 476	Jacinto Candido		P 1152	Escorpião		Service Forces	
			F 477	Gen Pereira d'Eça		P 1153	Cassiopeia			
S 164	Barracuda		F 486	Baptista de Andrade		P 1154	Hidra		A 520	Sagres
			F 487	João Roby		P 1155	Centauro		A 521	Schultz Xavier
Frigates			F 488	Afonso Cerqueira		P 1156	Orion		A 522	D. Carlos I
						P 1157	Pégaso		A 523	Almirante Gago Coutinho
F 330	Vasco da Gama					P 1158	Sagitario		A 5201	Vega
F 331	Alvares Cabral		**Patrol Forces**			P 1161	Save		A 5203	Andromeda
F 332	Corte Real					P 1165	Aguia		A 5204	Polar
F 480	Comandante João Belo		P 370	Rio Minho		P 1167	Cisne		A 5205	Auriga
F 483	Comandante Sacadura Cabral		P 1140	Cacine					A 5210	Bérrio
			P 1144	Quanza					UAM 201	Creoula
Corvettes			P 1146	Zaire		**Amphibious Forces**				
			P 1150	Argos						
F 471	Antonio Enes		P 1151	Dragão		LDG 203	Bacamarte			
F 475	João Coutinho									

SUBMARINES

0 + 2 TYPE 209PN CLASS (SSK)

Name	No	Builders	Laid down	Launched	Commissioned
—	—	Howaldtswerke, Kiel	7 March 2005	2007	2009
—	—	Howaldtswerke, Kiel	2006	2008	2010

Displacement, tons: 1,700 (surfaced); 1,970 (dived)
Dimensions, feet (metres): 222.8 × 20.7 × 21.6
(67.9 × 6.3 × 6.6)
Main machinery: 2 MTU 16V 396 diesels; 5,600 hp(m)
(4.17 MW); 1 Siemens Permasyn motor; 1 shaft; 2 HDW
PEM fuel cells; 240 kW
Speed, knots: 20 dived; 12 surfaced
Complement: 32 (5 officers)

Torpedoes: 8—21 in (533 mm) bow tubes. 16 weapons
including torpedoes and SSM.
Countermeasures: To be announced.
Weapons control: To be announced.
Radars: To be announced.
Sonars: Bow, flank and towed arrays.

Programmes: Contract signed on 21 April 2004 with German
Submarine Consortium (GSC) for construction and delivery
of two boats with option for a third. The consortium consists
of Howaldtswerke-Deutsche Werft, Kiel, Nordseewerke,
Emden (NSWE) and Ferrostaal, Essen.
Structure: Very similar to the Type 214 Air-Independent
Propulsion (AIP) submarines under construction for
Greece. Diving depth likely to be about 400 m (1,300 ft).

1 ALBACORA (DAPHNÉ) CLASS (SSK)

Name	No	Builders	Laid down	Launched	Commissioned
BARRACUDA	S 164	Dubigeon-Normandie, Nantes	19 Oct 1965	24 Apr 1967	4 May 1968

Displacement, tons: 869 surfaced; 1,043 dived
Dimensions, feet (metres): 189.6 × 22.3 × 17.1
(57.8 × 6.8 × 5.2)
Main machinery: Diesel-electric; 2 SEMT-Pielstick 12 PA4 V
185 diesels; 2,450 hp(m) (1.8 MW); 2 Jeumont Schneider
alternators; 1.7 MW; 2 motors; 2,600 hp(m) (1.9 MW);
2 shafts
Speed, knots: 13.5 surfaced; 16 dived
Range, n miles: 2,710 at 12.5 kt surfaced; 2,130 at 10 kt
snorting
Complement: 54 (7 officers)

Torpedoes: 12—21.7 in (550 mm) (8 bow, 4 stern) tubes. ECAN
E14; anti-surface; passive homing to 12 km (6.6 n miles)
at 25 kt; warhead 300 kg or ECAN L3; anti-submarine;
active homing to 5.5 km (3 n miles) at 25 kt; warhead
200 kg. No reloads
Countermeasures: ESM: ARUR; radar warning.
Weapons control: DLT D3 torpedo control.
Radars: Surface search: Kelvin Hughes KH 1007; I-band.
Sonars: Thomson Sintra DSUV 2; passive search and attack;
medium frequency.
DUUA 2; active search and attack; 8.4 kHz.

Modernisation: New radar fitted in 1993-94.
Structure: Diving depth, 300 m (984 ft).
Operational: Albacora paid off mid-2000 and cannibalised
for spares. Delfim decommissioned in 2005. Barracuda
expected to remain in service until 2009.

BARRACUDA   *9/2005*, B Prézelin* / 1153409

BARRACUDA   *9/2005*, B Prézelin* / 1153408

FRIGATES

0 + 2 (1) OLIVER HAZARD PERRY CLASS (GUIDED MISSILE FRIGATES) (FFGHM)

Name	No	Builders	Laid down	Launched	Commissioned
— (ex-*George Philip*)	— (ex-FFG 12)	Todd Shipyards, San Pedro	14 Dec 1977	16 Dec 1978	15 Nov 1980
— (ex-*Sides*)	— (ex-FFG 14)	Todd Shipyards, San Pedro	7 Aug 1978	19 May 1979	30 May 1981

Displacement, tons: 2,750 lights; 3,638 full load
Dimensions, feet (metres): 445 × 45 × 14.8; 24.5 (sonar)
  (135.6 × 13.7 × 4.5; 7.5)
Main machinery: 2 GE LM 2500 gas turbines; 41,000 hp
  (30.59 MW) sustained; 1 shaft; cp prop. 2 auxiliary
  retractable props; 650 hp *(484 kW)*
Speed, knots: 29
Range, n miles: 4,500 at 20 kt
Complement: 200 (15 officers) including aircrew

Missiles: SSM: 4 McDonnell Douglas Harpoon; active radar
  homing to 130 km *(70 n miles)* at 0.9 Mach; warhead
  227 kg.
SAM: 36 GDC Standard SM-1MR; command guidance; semi-
  active radar homing to 46 km *(25 n miles)* at 2 Mach.
Guns: 1 OTO Melara 3 in *(76 mm)*/62 Mk 75; 85 rds/min to
  16 km *(8.7 n miles)* anti-surface; 12 km *(6.6 n miles)* anti-
  aircraft; weight of shell 6 kg.
  1 General Electric/General Dynamics 20 mm/76
  6-barrelled Mk 15 Vulcan Phalanx; 3,000 rds/min
  combined to 1.5 km.
  4—12.7 mm MGs.
Torpedoes: 6—324 mm Mk 32 (2 triple) tubes. 24 Honeywell
  Mk 46 Mod 5; anti-submarine; active/passive homing to
  11 km (5.9 n miles) at 40 kt; warhead 44 kg.
Countermeasures: Decoys: 2 Loral Hycor SRBOC 6-barrelled
  fixed Mk 36; IR flares and chaff to 4 km *(2.2 n miles)*.
  T-Mk 6 Fanfare/SLQ-25 Nixie; torpedo decoy.
ESM/ECM: SLQ-32(V)2; radar warning. Sidekick modification
  adds jammer and deception system.
Combat data systems: NTDS with Link 11 and 14.
Weapons control: Mk 92 Mod 4.
Radars: Air Search: Raytheon SPS-49(V)4; C/D-band; range
  457 km *(250 n miles)*.

OLIVER HAZARD PERRY CLASS *10/1999*, Findler & Winter* / 0084111

Surface search: ISC Cardion SPS-55; I-band.
Fire control: Sperry Mk 92 (Signaal WM28); I/J-band.
Navigation: Furuno; I-band.
Tacan: URN 25. IFF Mk XII AIMS UPX-29.
Sonars: SQQ 89 (V)2 (Raytheon SQS 56 and Gould
  SQR 19); hull-mounted active search and attack;
  medium frequency and passive towed array; very low
  frequency.

Helicopters: To be announced.

Programmes: Two ex-US Navy FFG 14 class to replace the
  João Belo class corvettes. Transfer of both ships is scheduled
  for 2006. A third ship may be transferred by 2010.
Structure: The original single hangar was changed to a dual
  hangar configuration, provided with 19 mm Kevlar armour
  protection over vital spaces. 25 mm guns can be fitted.

2 COMANDANTE JOÃO BELO CLASS (FF)

Name	No	Builders	Laid down	Launched	Commissioned
COMANDANTE JOÃO BELO	F 480	At et Ch de Nantes	6 Sep 1965	22 Mar 1966	1 July 1967
COMANDANTE SACADURA CABRAL	F 483	At et Ch de Nantes	18 Aug 1967	15 Mar 1968	25 July 1969

Displacement, tons: 1,750 standard; 2,250 full load
Dimensions, feet (metres): 336.9 × 38.4 × 14.4
  (102.7 × 11.7 × 4.4)
Main machinery: 4 SEMT-Pielstick 12 PC2.2 V 400 diesels;
  16,000 hp(m) *(11.8 MW)* sustained; 2 shafts
Speed, knots: 25
Range, n miles: 7,500 at 15 kt
Complement: 201 (15 officers)
Guns: 2 Creusot-Loire 3.9 in *(100 mm)*/55 Mod 1953 ❶;
  60 rds/min to 17 km *(9 n miles)* anti-surface; 8 km
  (4.4 n miles) anti-aircraft; weight of shell 13.5 kg.
  2 Bofors 40 mm/60 ❷; 300 rds/min to 12 km *(6.6 n miles)*;
  weight of shell 0.89 kg.
Torpedoes: 6—324 mm Mk 32 Mod 5 (2 triple) tubes ❸;
  Honeywell Mk 46 Mod 5; active/passive homing to 11 km
  (5.9 n miles) at 40 kt; warhead 44 kg.
Countermeasures: Decoys: 2 Loral Hycor Mk 36 SRBOC
  6-barrelled chaff launchers.
  SLQ-25 Nixie; towed torpedo decoy.
ESM: AR-700(V2); intercept.
Combat data systems: Link 11.
Weapons control: C T Analogique. Sagem DMA optical
  director.
Radars: Air search: Thomson-CSF DRBV 22A ❹; D-band.
  Surface search: Thomson-CSF DRBV 50 ❺; G-band.

COMANDANTE JOÃO BELO *(Scale 1 : 900), Ian Sturton* / 0121391

Navigation: Kelvin Hughes KH 1007; I-band.
Fire control: Thomson-CSF DRBC 31D ❻; I-band.
Sonars: CDC SQS-510; hull-mounted; active search and
  attack; medium frequency.
  Thomson Sintra DUBA 3A; hull-mounted; active search;
  high frequency.

Modernisation: Modernisation of external communications,
  sensors and electronics completed 1987-90. Chaff
  launchers installed in 1989. Further modernisation started
  in 1993. The hull sonar was replaced, torpedo tubes

updated, the A/S mortar removed, towed torpedo decoy
  installed and ESM equipment changed. F 480 completed
  in 1996 and F 483 in 2000. A combat data system with
  Link 11 has been added, compatible with the Vasco da
  Gama class. The plan to have one or both after guns
  replaced either by flight deck and hangar for helicopter
  or by SSM has been shelved, but X turret is removed.
Operational: Designed for tropical service. A fourth of class
  has been cannibalised for spares. F481 decommissioned
  in 2005 and the remaining two are expected to be deleted
  as two ex-US Navy FFG 7 class enter service in 2006.

COMANDANTE JOÃO BELO *7/2005*, Frank Findler* / 1153411

3 VASCO DA GAMA (MEKO 200 PN) CLASS (FFGHM)

Name	No	Builders	Laid down	Launched	Commissioned
VASCO DA GAMA	F 330	Blohm + Voss, Hamburg	1 Feb 1989	26 June 1989	18 Jan 1991
ALVARES CABRAL	F 331	Howaldtswerke, Kiel	2 June 1989	6 June 1990	24 May 1991
CORTE REAL	F 332	Howaldtswerke, Kiel	24 Nov 1989	6 June 1990	22 Nov 1991

Displacement, tons: 2,700 standard; 3,300 full load
Dimensions, feet (metres): 380.3 oa; 357.6 pp × 48.7 × 20 *(115.9; 109 × 14.8 × 6.1)*
Main machinery: CODOG; 2 GE LM 2500 gas turbines; 53,000 hp *(39.5 MW)* sustained; 2 MTU 12V 1163 TB83 diesels; 8,840 hp(m) *(6.5 MW)*; 2 shafts; cp props
Speed, knots: 32 gas; 20 diesel
Range, n miles: 4,900 at 18 kt; 9,600 at 12 kt
Complement: 182 (23 officers) (including aircrew of 16 (4 officers)) plus 16 Flag Staff

Missiles: SSM: 8 McDonnell Douglas Harpoon (2 quad) launchers ❶; active radar homing to 130 km *(70 n miles)* at 0.9 Mach; warhead 227 kg.
SAM: Raytheon Sea Sparrow Mk 29 Mod 1 octuple launcher ❷; RIM-7M; semi-active radar homing to 14.6 km *(8 n miles)* at 2.5 Mach; warhead 39 kg. Space left for VLS Sea Sparrow ❸.
Guns: 1 Creusot-Loire 3.9 in *(100 mm)*/55 Mod 68 CADAM ❹; 60 rds/min to 17 km *(9 n miles)* anti-surface; 8 km *(4.4 n miles)* anti-aircraft; weight of shell 13.5 kg.
1 General Electric/General Dynamics Vulcan Phalanx 20 mm Mk 15 Mod 11 ❺; 6 barrels per mounting; 3,000 rds/min combined to 1.5 km.
2 Oerlikon 20 mm (on VLS deck) ❻ can be carried.
Torpedoes: 6—324 mm US Mk 32 (2 triple) tubes ❼. Honeywell Mk 46 Mod 5; anti-submarine; active/passive homing to 11 km *(5.9 n miles)* at 40 kt; warhead 44 kg.
Countermeasures: Decoys: 2 Loral Hycor Mk 36 SRBOC 6-barrelled chaff launchers ❽. Sea Gnat.
SLQ-25 Nixie; towed torpedo decoy.
ESM/ECM: APECS II; intercept and jammer.
Combat data systems: Signaal SEWACO action data automation with STACOS tactical command; Link 11 and 14. Matra Marconi SCOT 3 SATCOM ❾ (1 set between 3 ships).
Weapons control: SWG 1A(V) for SSM. Vesta Helo transponder with datalink for OTHT.
Radars: Air search: Signaal MW08 (derived from Smart 3D) ❿; 3D; G-band.
Air/surface search: Signaal DA08 ⓫; F-band.
Navigation: Kelvin Hughes Type 1007; I-band.
Fire control: 2 Signaal STIR ⓬; I/J/K-band; range 140 km *(76 n miles)* for 1 m² target.
IFF: Mk 12 Mod 4.
Sonars: Computing Devices (Canada) SQS-510(V); hull-mounted; active search and attack; medium frequency.

Helicopters: 2 Super Sea Lynx Mk 95 ⓭.

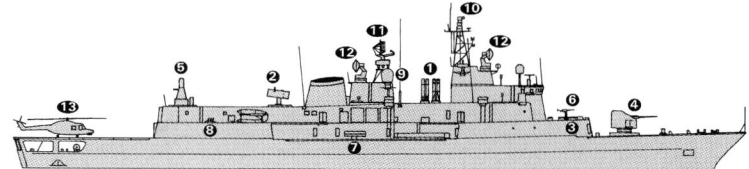

VASCO DA GAMA *(Scale 1 : 1,200), Ian Sturton* / 0567520

CORTE REAL *9/2005*, Martin Mokrus* / 1153412

Programmes: The contract for all three was signed on 25 July 1986. These are Meko 200 type ordered from a consortium of builders. As well as Portugal, which provided 40 per cent of the cost, assistance was given by NATO with some missile, CIWS and torpedo systems being provided by the US.
Modernisation: Full mid-life refits are planned 2009-2014. Upgrades are likely to include CIWS improvements.

Structure: All-steel construction. Stabilisers fitted. Full RAS facilities. Space has been left for a sonar towed array and for VLS Sea Sparrow.
Operational: Designed primarily as ASW ships. SCOT SATCOM rotated between the three ships. 20 mm guns can be mounted on the VLS deck. Three year running cycles include 18 months at full readiness, three months training and six months refit.

ALVARES CABRAL *6/2005*, B Sullivan* / 1153413

CORTE REAL *9/2005*, M Declerck* / 1153428

CORVETTES

3 BAPTISTA DE ANDRADE CLASS (FSH)

Name	No	Builders	Laid down	Launched	Commissioned
BAPTISTA DE ANDRADE	F 486	Empresa Nacional Bazán, Cartagena	1 Sep 1972	13 Mar 1973	19 Nov 1974
JOÃO ROBY	F 487	Empresa Nacional Bazán, Cartagena	1 Dec 1972	3 June 1973	18 Mar 1975
AFONSO CERQUEIRA	F 488	Empresa Nacional Bazán, Cartagena	10 Mar 1973	6 Oct 1973	26 June 1975

Displacement, tons: 1,203 standard; 1,380 full load
Dimensions, feet (metres): 277.5 × 33.8 × 10.2
(84.6 × 10.3 × 3.1)
Main machinery: 2 OEW Pielstick 12 PC2.2 V 400 diesels;
12,000 hp(m) (8.82 MW) sustained; 2 shafts
Speed, knots: 22
Range, n miles: 5,900 at 18 kt
Complement: 71 (7 officers)

Guns: 1 Creusot-Loire 3.9 in (100 mm)/55 Mod 1968;
80 rds/min to 17 km (9 n miles) anti-surface; 8 km (4.4 n
miles) anti-aircraft; weight of shell 13.5 kg.
2 Bofors 40 mm/70; 300 rds/min to 12 km (6.6 n miles);
weight of shell 0.96 kg.
Radars: Navigation: 1 Racal Decca RM 316P and 1 KH 5000
Nucleos 2; I-band.

Helicopters: Platform only.

Programmes: Reclassified as corvettes.
Modernisation: Communications equipment updated
1988-91. Previous modernisation programme was
abandoned in 1998. Between 1999 and 2001 ASW and
weapons control systems removed.
Operational: Class is used for Maritime Law Enforcement/
SAR/Fishery Protection and for Humanitarian Operations.
To be replaced by Viana do Castelo class. F 489
decommissioned in 2002.

JOÃO RUBY

6/2005, Portuguese Navy / 1153426

4 JOÃO COUTINHO CLASS (FSH)

Name	No	Builders	Laid down	Launched	Commissioned
ANTONIO ENES	F 471	Empresa Nacional Bazán, Cartagena	10 Apr 1968	16 Aug 1969	18 June 1971
JOÃO COUTINHO	F 475	Blohm + Voss, Hamburg	24 Dec 1968	2 May 1969	28 Feb 1970
JACINTO CANDIDO	F 476	Blohm + Voss, Hamburg	10 Feb 1969	16 June 1969	29 May 1970
GENERAL PEREIRA D'EÇA	F 477	Blohm + Voss, Hamburg	21 Apr 1969	26 July 1969	10 Oct 1970

Displacement, tons: 1,203 standard; 1,380 full load
Dimensions, feet (metres): 277.5 × 33.8 × 10.8
(84.6 × 10.3 × 3.3)
Main machinery: 2 OEW Pielstick 12 PC2.2 V 400 diesels;
12,000 hp(m) (8.82 MW) sustained; 2 shafts
Speed, knots: 22
Range, n miles: 5,900 at 18 kt
Complement: 70 (7 officers)

Guns: 2 US 3 in (76 mm)/50 (twin) Mk 33; 50 rds/min to
12.8 km (7 n miles); weight of shell 6 kg.
2 Bofors 40 mm/60 (twin); 300 rds/min to 12 km
(6.6 n miles); weight of shell 0.89 kg.
Weapons control: Mk 51 GFCS for 40 mm.
Radars: Air/surface search: Kelvin Hughes 1007; I-band.
Navigation: Racal Decca RM 1226C; I-band.

Helicopters: Platform only.

Programmes: Reclassified as corvettes.
Modernisation: A programme for this class to include
SSM and PDMS has been shelved. In 1989-91 the main

GENERAL PERGIRA D'EÇA

6/2005, Portuguese Navy* / 1153424

radar was updated and SATCOM (INMARSAT) installed.
Also fitted with SIFICAP which is a Fishery Protection
data exchange system by satellite to the main database
ashore.

Operational: A/S equipment no longer operational and
laid apart on shore. Crew reduced as a result. F 484
decommissioned in 2004. To be replaced by Viana do
Castelo class.

SHIPBORNE AIRCRAFT

Notes: Procurement of three further Lynx helicopters is under consideration. Options
include Mk 95 aircraft, Super Lynx 300 (including upgrade of current aircraft) or second-
hand aircraft.

Numbers/Type: 5 Westland Super Navy Lynx Mk 95.
Operational speed: 125 kt (231 km/h).
Service ceiling: 12,000 ft (3,660 m).
Range: 320 n miles (593 km).
Role/Weapon systems: Ordered 2 November 1990 for MEKO 200 frigates; two are updated
HAS 3 and three were new aircraft, all delivered in August and November 1993. Sensors:
Bendix 1500B radar; Bendix AQS-18V dipping sonar; Racal RNS 252 datalink. Weapons:
Mk 46 torpedoes. 1 – 12.7 mm MG.

SUPER LYNX

9/2002, H M Steele / 0534127

LAND-BASED MARITIME AIRCRAFT

Notes: (1) All Air Force manned.
(2) There are 12 EH 101 utility helicopters. Of these, six are in an SAR configuration, four
are outfitted for combat SAR and two are employed on fishery protection.

Numbers/Type: 10 Aerospatiale SA 330c PUMA.
Operational speed: 151 kt (280 km/h).
Service ceiling: 15,090 ft (4,600 m).
Range: 343 n miles (635 km).
Role/Weapon systems: For SAR and surface search. Likely to be retired as EH-101 become
operational. Sensors: Omera search radar. Weapons: Unarmed except for pintle-
mounted 12.7 mm machine guns.

PUMA

6/2002, Adolfo Ortigueira Gil / 0567521

Numbers/Type: 5/2 CASA C-212-200 Aviocar/C-212-300 Aviocar.
Operational speed: 190 kt *(353 km/h).*
Service ceiling: 24,000 ft *(7,315 m).*
Range: 1,650 n miles *(3,055 km).*
Role/Weapon systems: The first five are for short-range SAR support and transport operations. The last pair were ordered in February 1993 for maritime patrol and fisheries surveillance off the Azores and Madeira. Sensors: Search radar and MAD. FLIR and datalink (last pair). Weapons: Unarmed.

CASA 212   *6/2001, Adolfo Ortigueira Gil* / 0529552

Numbers/Type: 5 Lockheed P-3P Orion.
Operational speed: 410 kt *(760 km/h).*
Service ceiling: 28,300 ft *(8,625 m).*
Range: 4,000 n miles *(7,410 km).*
Role/Weapon systems: Long-range surveillance and ASW patrol aircraft; acquired with NATO funding from RAAF update programme and modernised by Lockheed to 3P standard starting in 1987. A further five aircraft to be acquired from the Netherlands by 2006. Sensors: APS-134/137 radar, ASQ-81 MAD, AQS-901 sonobuoy processor, AQS-114 computer, IFF, ALR-66 ECM/ESM. Weapons: ASW; eight Mk 46 torpedoes, depth bombs or mines; ASV; 10 underwing stations for Harpoon. AGM 65 Maverick in due course.

P-3P   *3/2001, Adolfo Ortigueira Gil* / 0567522

PATROL FORCES

1 + 3 (8) VIANA DO CASTELO (NPO 2000) CLASS (PSOH)

Name	No	Builders	Commissioned
VIANA DO CASTELO	P 360	Viana do Castelo Shipyards	Apr 2006
FIGUEIRA DA FOZ	P 361	Viana do Castelo Shipyards	2006
PONTA DELGADA	P 362	Viano do Castelo Shipyards	2007

Displacement, tons: 1,600 full load
Dimensions, feet (metres): 272.6 × 42.5 × 12.1 *(83.1 × 12.95 × 3.69)*
Main machinery: 2 diesels; 10,460 hp *(7.8 MW);* 2 shafts
Speed, knots: 20
Range, n miles: 5,000 at 15 kt
Complement: 35
Guns: 1—40 mm.
Weapons control: Mk 51 GFCS or Optronic director.
Helicopters: Platform for one medium.

Comment: Contract on 15 October 2002 with Viana do Castelo Shipyards for two Offshore Patrol vessels. Construction started in 2003 and the first two ships were floated out on 1 October 2005. These ships are designed for EEZ patrol duties and a further eight are planned to be delivered by 2015 to replace the corvettes. Two further modified vessels, a Buoy Tender and a Pollution Control Ship, were ordered in May 2004 and are to be delivered in 2007.

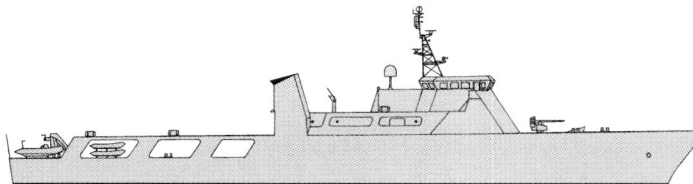

NPO 2000   *(Scale 1 : 900), Ian Sturton* / 0081605

2 ALBATROZ CLASS (RIVER PATROL CRAFT) (PBR)

Name	No	Builders	Commissioned
AGUIA	P 1165	Arsenal do Alfeite	28 Feb 1975
CISNE	P 1167	Arsenal do Alfeite	31 Mar 1976

Displacement, tons: 45 full load
Dimensions, feet (metres): 77.4 × 18.4 × 5.2 *(23.6 × 5.6 × 1.6)*
Main machinery: 2 Cummins diesels; 1,100 hp *(820 kW);* 2 shafts
Speed, knots: 20. **Range, n miles:** 2,500 at 12 kt
Complement: 8 (1 officer)
Guns: 1 Oerlikon 20 mm/65. 2—12.7 mm MGs
Radars: Surface search: Decca RM 316P; I-band

Comment: One other is used for harbour patrol duties. Two transferred to East Timor in 2001. Replacement of these craft is under consideration.

AGUIA   *6/2005*, Portuguese Navy* / 1153421

0 + 5 COASTAL (LFC 2005) PATROL CRAFT (PBO)

Displacement, tons: 660 full load
Dimensions, feet (metres): 196.5 × 32.4 × 8.8 *(59.9 × 9.9 × 2.7)*
Main machinery: 4 diesels; 12,100 hp *(9 MW);* 2 shafts
Speed, knots: 25
Range, n miles: To be announced
Complement: 20 (3 officers)
Guns: 1 Bofors 40 mm/70. 1—12.7 mm MG.
Weapons control: Optronic director.
Radars: To be announced.

Comment: Preliminary contract with Viana do Castelo Shipyard for the construction of five patrol vessels was let on 19 December 2005. Designed for EEZ patrol and fishery protection, the ships are to replace the Cacine class and are to enter service 2008-11.

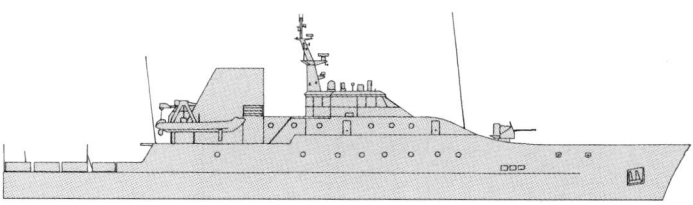

LFC   *(not to scale), Ian Sturton* / 1154415

4 CACINE CLASS (LARGE PATROL CRAFT) (PBO)

Name	No	Builders	Commissioned
CACINE	P 1140	Arsenal do Alfeite	May 1969
QUANZA	P 1144	Estaleiros Navais do Mondego	May 1969
ZAIRE	P 1146	Estaleiros Navais do Mondego	Nov 1970
SAVE	P 1161	Arsenal do Alfeite	May 1973

Displacement, tons: 292.5 standard; 310 full load
Dimensions, feet (metres): 144 × 25.2 × 7.1 *(44 × 7.7 × 2.2)*
Main machinery: 2 MTU 12V 538 TB80 diesels; 3,750 hp(m) *(2.76 MW)* sustained; 2 shafts
Speed, knots: 20
Range, n miles: 4,400 at 12 kt
Complement: 33 (3 officers)
Guns: 1 Bofors 40 mm/60. 1 Oerlikon 20 mm/65.
Radars: Surface search: Kelvin Hughes Type 1007; I/J-band.

Comment: Originally mounted a second Bofors aft but most have been removed as has the 37 mm rocket launcher. Have SIFICAP satellite data handling system for Fishery Protection duties. An RIB is carried. Two of the class are based at Madeira on a two month rotational basis. Re-engined in 1992-94. To be replaced by new coastal patrol craft from 2008.

CACINE   *12/2003, Martin Mokrus* / 1044180

CACINE   *12/2003, Martin Mokrus* / 1044181

5 ARGOS CLASS (RIVER PATROL CRAFT) (PBR)

Name	No	Builders	Commissioned
ARGOS	P 1150	Arsenal do Alfeite	2 July 1991
DRAGÃO	P 1151	Arsenal do Alfeite	18 Oct 1991
ESCORPIÃO	P 1152	Arsenal do Alfeite	26 Nov 1991
CASSIOPEIA	P 1153	Conafi	11 Nov 1991
HIDRA	P 1154	Conafi	18 Dec 1991

Displacement, tons: 94 full load
Dimensions, feet (metres): 89.2 × 19.4 × 4.6 *(27.2 × 5.9 × 1.4)*
Main machinery: 2 MTU 12V 396 TE84 diesels; 3,700 hp(m) *(2.73 MW)* sustained; 2 shafts
Speed, knots: 26
Range, n miles: 1,350 at 15 kt
Complement: 12 (1 officer)
Guns: 2 — 12.7 mm MGs (1150 — 1154).
Radars: Navigation: Furuno 1505 DA or Furuno FR 1411; I-band.

Comment: First five ordered in 1989 and 50 per cent funded by the EC. Of GRP construction, capable of full speed operation up to Sea State 3. Carries a RIB with a 37 hp outboard engine. The boat is recoverable via a stern well at up to 10 kt.

ESCORPIÃO *6/2002* / 0567523

4 CENTAURO CLASS (RIVER PATROL CRAFT) (PBR)

Name	No	Builders	Commissioned
CENTAURO	P 1155	Arsenal do Alfeite	20 Mar 2000
ORION	P 1156	Arsenal do Alfeite	27 Mar 2001
PÉGASO	P 1157	Estaleiros Navais do Mondego	27 Mar 2001
SAGITARIO	P 1158	Estaleiros Navais do Mondego	27 Mar 2001

Displacement, tons: 89 full load
Dimensions, feet (metres): 93.2 × 19.5 × 4.6 *(28.4 × 5.95 × 1.4)*
Main machinery: 2 Cummins KTA-50-M2 diesels; 3,600 hp(m) *(2.64 MW)*; 2 shafts
Speed, knots: 26
Range, n miles: 640 at 20 kt
Complement: 8 (1 officer)
Guns: 1 Oerlikon 20 mm/65.
Radars: 1 Furuno FCR-1411 MK3.

Comment: Similar to Argos class but of aluminium hull. Capable of full speed operation up to Sea State 3. Carries a semi-rigid boat with a 50 hp outboard engine. The boat is recoverable via a stern well at up to 10 kt.

CENTAURO *6/2005*, Portuguese Navy* / 1153420

1 RIO MINHO CLASS (RIVER PATROL CRAFT) (PBR)

Name	No	Builders	Commissioned
RIO MINHO	P 370	Arsenal do Alfeite	1 Aug 1991

Displacement, tons: 72 full load
Dimensions, feet (metres): 73.5 × 19.7 × 2.6 *(22.4 × 6 × 0.8)*
Main machinery: 2 KHD-Deutz diesels; 664 hp(m) *(488 kW)*; 2 Schottel pumpjets
Speed, knots: 9.5
Range, n miles: 420 at 7 kt
Complement: 8 (1 officer)
Guns: 1 — 7.62 mm MG.
Radars: Navigation: Furuno FR 1505DA; I-band.

RIO MINHO *6/2005*, Portuguese Navy* / 1153419

SURVEY SHIPS

2 STALWART CLASS (AGS)

Name	No	Builders	Commissioned
D. CARLOS I (ex-*Audacious*, ex-*Dauntless*)	A 522 (ex-T-AGOS 11)	Tacoma Boat	18 June 1989
ALMIRANTE GAGO COUTINHO (ex-*Assurance*)	A 523 (ex-T-AGOS 5)	Tacoma Boat	1 May 1985

Displacement, tons: 2,285 full load
Dimensions, feet (metres): 224 × 43 × 15.9 *(68.3 × 13.1 × 4.6)*
Main machinery: Diesel-electric; 4 Caterpillar D 398B diesel generators; 3,200 hp *(2.39 MW)*; 2 GE motors; 1,600 hp *(1.2 MW)*; 2 shafts; bow thruster; 550 hp *(410 kW)*
Speed, knots: 11
Range, n miles: 4,000 at 11 kt; 6,450 at 3 kt
Complement: 31 (6 officers) plus 15 scientists
Radars: Navigation: 2 Raytheon; I-band.

Comment: Paid off from USN in November 1995. First one acquired 21 July 1996. Refitted to serve as a hydrographic ship, operating predominantly off the west coast of Africa. Recommissioned 9 December 1996. A second of class acquired by gift 30 September 1999, has been similarly refitted and recommissioned 26 January 2000.

D. CARLOS I *6/2004, Portuguese Navy* / 1044176

2 ANDROMEDA CLASS (AGSC)

Name	No	Builders	Commissioned
ANDROMEDA	A 5203	Arsenal do Alfeite	1 Feb 1987
AURIGA	A 5205	Arsenal do Alfeite	1 July 1987

Displacement, tons: 245 full load
Dimensions, feet (metres): 103.3 × 25.4 × 8.2 *(31.5 × 7.7 × 2.5)*
Main machinery: 1 MTU 12V 396 TC62 diesel; 1,200 hp(m) *(880 kW)* sustained; 1 shaft
Speed, knots: 12
Range, n miles: 1,980 at 10 kt
Complement: 17 (3 officers)
Radars: Navigation: Koden; I-band.

Comment: Both ordered in January 1984. *Auriga* has a research submarine ROV Phantom S2 and a Klein side scan sonar. Mostly used for oceanography.

ANDROMEDA *8/1997, van Ginderen Collection* / 0012932

3 SURVEY CRAFT (YGS)

CORAL UAM 801   **ATLANTA** (ex-*Hidra*) UAM 802   **FISALIA** UAM 805

Comment: Craft are of 36 tons launched in 1980.

FISALIA *3/1992, van Ginderen Collection* / 0081611

AMPHIBIOUS FORCES

Notes: Four new LCMs are to be constructed as part of the LPD (NAVPOL) contract.

0 + 1 ASSAULT SHIP (LPD)

Name	No	Builders	Laid down	Launched	Commissioned
—	—	Viana do Castelo Shipyard	2006	2008	2010

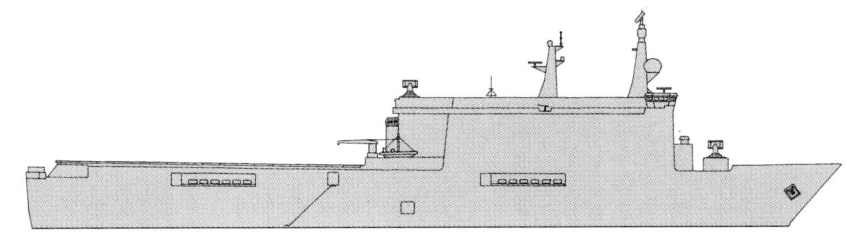

NAVPOL

(Scale 1 : 1,500), Ian Sturton / 1153002

Displacement, tons: 10,500 full load
Dimensions, feet (metres): 531.5 × 82.0 × 17.1
 (162.0 × 25.0 × 5.2)
Flight deck, feet (metres): To be announced
Main machinery: Diesel-electric; 4 diesels; 18,775 hp
 (14 MW); 2 shafts
Speed, knots: 19. **Range, n miles:** 6,000 at 14 kt
Complement: 150
Military lift: 650 troops; 4 LCM, 76 vehicles (including 40 light
 armoured vehicles), 53 light inflatable boats, 3,000 m³
 of storage space

Missiles: SAM 2 RAM 21-cell Mk 49 launchers.
Guns: To be announced.
Countermeasures: To be announced.
Combat data systems: To be announced.
Weapons control: To be announced.
Radars: Air/surface search: 3D radar to be announced.
Surface search: To be announced.
Navigation: To be announced.

Helicopters: Landing spots for 4 EH-101 or 6 Lynx.

Programmes: The Portuguese Ministry of Defence signed
 a contract on 16 February 2005 with ENVC Shipyard for

the design and construction of a Landing Platform Dock
(LPD). The contract is understood to be part of an offset
agreement arising from the contract with the German
Submarine Consortium for two Type 209PN submarines.
The project is known as Navio Polivalente Logístico
(NAVPOL). Construction of LCMs is understood to be
included in the contract.
Structure: The design is very similar to the Schelde Enforcer
 1300 and is to include a dock, flight deck, hangar, vehicle
 garage and hospital.

Operational: Following endorsement of the Portuguese
National Defence Strategic Concept (NDSC) in 2003, the
new LPD is to be the centrepiece of the future Portuguese
Navy and is to be designed to support worldwide joint
operations of national and allied armed forces, including
humanitarian aid and/or disaster relief. The ship is to
be capable of projecting and supporting a battalion of
troops.

1 BOMBARDA CLASS (LCU)

Name	No	Builders	Commissioned
BACAMARTE	LDG 203	Arsenal do Alfeite	Dec 1985

Displacement, tons: 652 full load
Dimensions, feet (metres): 184.3 × 38.7 × 6.2
 (56.2 × 11.8 × 1.9)
Main machinery: 2 MTU MB diesels; 910 hp(m) *(669 kW)*;
 2 shafts
Speed, knots: 9.5. **Range, n miles:** 2,600 at 9 kt
Complement: 21 (3 officers)
Military lift: 350 tons
Guns: 2 Oerlikon 20 mm.
Radars: Navigation: Decca RM 316P; I-band.

Comment: Similar to French EDIC.

BACAMARTE
2000, Portuguese Navy
0105267

TRAINING SHIPS

1 SAIL TRAINING SHIP (AXS)

Name	No	Builders	Commissioned
SAGRES (ex-*Guanabara*, ex-*Albert Leo Schlageter*)	A 520	Blohm + Voss, Hamburg	10 Feb 1938

Displacement, tons: 1,725 standard; 1,940 full load
Dimensions, feet (metres): 231 wl; 295.2 oa × 39.4 × 17 *(70.4; 90 × 12 × 5.2)*
Main machinery: 2 MTU 12V 183 TE92 auxiliary diesels; 1 shaft
Speed, knots: 10.5. **Range, n miles:** 5,450 at 7.5 kt on diesel
Complement: 162 (12 officers)
Radars: Navigation: 1 Racal Decca and 1 KH 1500 Nucleos 2; I-band.

Comment: Former German sail training ship launched 30 October 1937. Sister of US Coast
 Guard training ship *Eagle* (ex-German *Horst Wessel*) and Soviet *Tovarisch* (ex-German
 Gorch Fock). Taken by the USA as a reparation after the Second World War in 1945 and
 sold to Brazil in 1948. Purchased from Brazil and commissioned in the Portuguese Navy
 on 2 February 1962 at Rio de Janeiro and renamed *Sagres*. Sail area, 20,793 sq ft. Height
 of main mast, 142 ft. Phased refits 1987-88 and again in 1991-92 which included new
 engines, improved accommodation, hydraulic crane and updated navigation equipment.

CREOULA

6/2005*, Portuguese Navy / 1153417

2 SAIL TRAINING YACHTS (AXL)

VEGA (ex-*Arreda*) A 5201   **POLAR** (ex-*Anne Linde*) A 5204

Displacement, tons: 70 (60, *Vega*)
Dimensions, feet (metres): 75 × 16 × 8.2 *(22.9 × 4.9 × 2.5) (Polar)*
 65 × 14.1 × 8.2 *(19.8 × 4.3 × 2.5) (Vega)*
Radars: Navigation: Raytheon; I-band.

Comment: Sail numbers are displayed. *Vega* is P-165 and *Polar* is P-551.

SAGRES

6/2005*, Michael Winter / 1153410

1 SAIL TRAINING SHIP (AXS)

Name	No	Builders	Commissioned
CREOULA	UAM 201	Lisbon Shipyard	1937

Displacement, tons: 818 standard; 1,055 full load
Dimensions, feet (metres): 221.1 × 32.5 × 13.8 *(67.4 × 9.9 × 4.2)*
Main machinery: 1 MTU 8V 183 TE92 auxiliary diesel; 665 hp(m) *(490 kW)*; 1 shaft

Comment: Ex-deep sea sail fishing ship used off the coast of Newfoundland for 36 years.
 Bought by Fishing Department in 1976 to turn into a museum ship but because she
 was still seaworthy it was decided to convert her to a training ship. Recommissioned
 in the Navy in 1987. Refit completed in 1992 including a new engine and improved
 accommodation. A life-extension refit is under consideration.

VEGA

8/2004, Diego Quevedo / 1047860

AUXILIARIES

Notes: (1) Two craft are employed on Pollution Control tasks. *Vazante* (UAM 687) is 14 tons and *Enchente* (UAM 688) is 65 tons. *Barrocas* (UAM 854) is an accommodation barge. *Marateca* (UAM 304) and *Meuro* (UAM 305) are fuel lighters.
(2) Studies for the procurement of a new AOR, to enter service in about 2015, are in progress.

1 ROVER CLASS (REPLENISHMENT TANKER) (AORLH)

Name	No	Builders	Launched	Commissioned
BÉRRIO (ex-*Blue Rover*)	A 5210 (ex-A 270)	Swan Hunter	11 Nov 1969	15 July 1970

Displacement, tons: 4,700 light; 11,522 full load
Dimensions, feet (metres): 461 × 63 × 24 *(140.6 × 19.2 × 7.3)*
Main machinery: 2 SEMT-Pielstick 16 PA4 185 diesels; 15,360 hp(m) *(11.46 MW)*; 1 shaft; Kamewa cp prop; bow thruster
Speed, knots: 19
Range, n miles: 15,000 at 15 kt
Complement: 54 (7 officers)
Cargo capacity: 6,600 tons fuel
Guns: 2 Oerlikon 20 mm.
Countermeasures: Decoys: 2 Vickers Corvus launchers. 2 Plessey Shield launchers. 1 Graseby Type 182; towed torpedo decoy.
Radars: Navigation: Kelvin Hughes Type 1006; I-band.
Helicopters: Platform for 1 medium.

Comment: Transferred from UK and recommissioned 31 March 1993. Small fleet tanker designed to replenish oil and aviation fuel, fresh water, limited dry cargo and refrigerated stores under all conditions while under way. Full refit in 1990-91 gave a service life expectancy until 2005 and a further refit is to be undertaken to prolong life beyond 2010. No hangar but helicopter landing platform is served by a stores lift, to enable stores to be transferred at sea by 'vertical lift'. Capable of HIFR. Can pump fuel at 600 m³/h. Others of the class in service in Indonesia and the UK.

BÉRRIO *4/2000, Maritime Photographic* / 0105268

1 BUOY TENDER (ABU)

Name	No	Builders	Commissioned
SCHULTZ XAVIER	A 521	Alfeite Naval Yard	14 July 1972

Displacement, tons: 900 full load
Dimensions, feet (metres): 184 × 33 × 12.5 *(56 × 10 × 3.8)*
Main machinery: 2 diesels; 2,400 hp(m) *(1.76 MW)*; 2 shafts
Speed, knots: 14.5
Range, n miles: 3,000 at 12.5 kt
Complement: 54 (4 officers)

Comment: Used for servicing navigational aids and as an occasional tug. A replacement ship is projected.

SCHULTZ XAVIER *5/1998, Diego Quevedo* / 0052756

1 BUOY TENDER (ABU)

Name	No	Builders	Commissioned
GUIA	UAM 676	S Jacinto, Aveiro	30 Jan 1985

Displacement, tons: 70 full load
Dimensions, feet (metres): 72.2 × 25.9 × 7.2 *(22 × 7.9 × 2.2)*
Main machinery: 1 Deutz MWM SBA6M816 diesel; 465 hp(m) *(342 kW)* sustained; 1 Schottel Navigator prop
Speed, knots: 8.5 (3.5 on auxiliary engine)
Complement: 6

Comment: Belongs to the Lighthouse Service.

GUIA *6/2005*, Portuguese Navy* / 1153416

8 CALMARIA CLASS (HARBOUR PATROL CRAFT) (YP)

CALMARIA UAM 642	MONÇÃO UAM 645	PREIA-MAR UAM 648
CIRRO UAM 643	SUÃO UAM 646	BAIXA-MAR UAM 649
VENDAVAL UAM 644	MACAREU UAM 647	

Displacement, tons: 12 full load
Dimensions, feet (metres): 39 × 12.5 × 2.3 *(11.9 × 3.8 × 0.7)*
Main machinery: 2 Bazán MAN 2866 LXE diesels; 881 hp(m) *(648 kW)*; 2 water-jets
Speed, knots: 32. **Range, n miles:** 275 at 20 kt
Complement: 3
Guns: 1 — 7.62 mm MG.
Radars: Surface search: Furuno 1830; I-band.

Comment: Harbour patrol craft similar to Spanish Guardia Civil del Mar Saetta II craft. Ordered from Bazán, Cadiz on 8 January 1993. First pair completed 30 November 1993, third one on 18 January 1994. Remainder delivered between August and December 1994. GRP hulls.

BAIXA-MAR *3/2004* / 1044182

56 MISCELLANEOUS SERVICE CRAFT (YAG)

UAM 650-652	UAM 685	UAM 851-853
UAM 655-675	UAM 689-696	UAM 901
UAM 677-679	UAM 780	UAM 907-916
UAM 681-682	UAM 831	

Displacement, tons: 14 full load
Dimensions, feet (metres): 45.9 × 12.5 × 3.9 *(14.0 × 3.8 × 1.2)*
Main machinery: 2 diesels; 650 hp *(485 kW)*; 2 waterjets
Speed, knots: 23
Range, n miles: 300 at 15 kt

Comment: Details are for UAM 689-696, Rodman 46 SAR craft commissioned 1997-2000. The remaining craft are personnel and other service craft.

UAM 692 *9/1998, Schaeffer/Marsan* / 0081616

UAM 852 *3/2002, Diego Quevedo* / 0534049

GOVERNMENT MARITIME FORCES
(GUARDIA NACIONAL REPUBLICANA)
POLICE

4 RODMAN 38 CLASS (PB)

Displacement, tons: 10 full load
Dimensions, feet (metres): 36.1 × 12.8 × 2.3 *(11.0 × 3.9 × 0.7)*
Main machinery: 2 diesels; 400 hp *(300 kW)*; 2 waterjets
Speed, knots: 28. **Range, n miles:** 300 at 15 kt
Complement: 4

Comment: GRP hull. Built by Rodman, Vigo in 1985-87.

12 CONAFI 55 CLASS

Displacement, tons: 18 full load
Dimensions, feet (metres): 55.8 × 12.5 × 2.9 *(17.0 × 3.8 × 0.9)*
Main machinery: 2 MTU 12V 183TE93 diesels; 2,400 hp(m) *(1.8 MW)*; 2 waterjets
Speed, knots: 48. **Range, n miles:** 400 at 18 kt
Complement: 5

Comment: Built at Conafi Shipyards with collaboration with Rodman and delivered between 2000 and 2002.

CONAFI 55 *6/2000, Conafi* / 1044183

Qatar

Country Overview

Formerly a British protectorate from 1916, the State of Qatar gained its independence in 1971. Situated on the eastern side of the Arabian Peninsula, it occupies the Qatar Peninsula which has a 304 n mile coastline with the Gulf. With an area of 4,416 square miles, it is bordered to the south by Saudi Arabia and the United Arab Emirates. The dispute with Bahrain over sovereignty of the Hawar islands was settled on 16 March 2001. The capital, largest city and principal port is Doha. Territorial seas (12 n miles) are claimed. An EEZ (200 n miles) has been claimed but the limits are not defined.

Headquarters Appointments

Commander Naval Force:
  Commodore Mohammed Nasir Al-Muhannadi
Commander Coast Guard:
  Colonel Ali al-Mannai

Personnel

2006: 1,800 officers and men (including Marine Police)

Bases

Doha (main); Halul Island (secondary)

Coast Defence

Two truck-mounted batteries of Exocet MM 40 quad launchers.

Prefix to Ships' Names

QENS (Qatar Emiri Navy)

PATROL FORCES

Notes: A requirement for two 49 m patrol craft has been reported.

3 DAMSAH (COMBATTANTE III M) CLASS (FAST ATTACK CRAFT—MISSILE) (PGGF)

Name	No	Builders	Launched	Commissioned
DAMSAH	Q 01	CMN, Cherbourg	17 June 1982	10 Nov 1982
AL GHARIYAH	Q 02	CMN, Cherbourg	23 Sep 1982	10 Feb 1983
RBIGAH	Q 03	CMN, Cherbourg	22 Dec 1982	11 May 1983

Displacement, tons: 345 standard; 395 full load
Dimensions, feet (metres): 183.7 × 26.9 × 7.2
  (56 × 8.2 × 2.2)
Main machinery: 4 MTU 20V 538TB93 diesels; 18,740 hp(m)
  (13.8 MW) sustained; 4 shafts
Speed, knots: 38.5
Range, n miles: 2,000 at 15 kt
Complement: 41 (6 officers)

Missiles: SSM: 8 Aerospatiale MM 40 Exocet; inertial cruise; active radar homing to 70 km *(40 n miles)* at 0.9 Mach; warhead 165 kg; sea-skimmer.
Guns: 1 OTO Melara 3 in *(76 mm)*/62; 60 rds/min to 16 km *(8.7 n miles)*; weight of shell 6 kg.
  2 Breda 40 mm/70 (twin); 300 rds/min to 12.5 km *(6.8 n miles)*; weight of shell 0.96 kg.
  4 Oerlikon 30 mm/75 (2 twin); 650 rds/min to 10 km *(5.5 n miles)*.
Countermeasures: Decoys: CSEE Dagaie trainable single launcher; 6 containers; IR flares and chaff; H/J-band.
ESM/ECM: Racal Cutlass/Cygnus.
Weapons control: Vega system. 2 CSEE Naja optical directors.
Radars: Surface search: Thomson-CSF Triton; G-band.
Navigation: Racal Decca 1226; I-band.
Fire control: Thomson-CSF Castor II; I/J-band; range 15 km *(8 n miles)* for 1 m² target.

Programmes: Ordered in 1980. All arrived at Doha July 1983. All refitted in 1996/98.

AL GHARIYAH *10/2001* / 0121393

RBIGAH
7/2001, Ships of the World
0121396

---

4 BARZAN (VITA) CLASS (PGGFM)

Name	No	Builders	Laid down	Launched	Commissioned
BARZAN	Q04	Vosper Thornycroft	Feb 1994	1 Apr 1995	9 May 1996
HUWAR	Q05	Vosper Thornycroft	Aug 1994	15 July 1995	10 June 1996
AL UDEID	Q06	Vosper Thornycroft	Mar 1995	21 Mar 1996	16 Dec 1996
AL DEEBEL	Q07	Vosper Thornycroft	Aug 1995	31 Aug 1996	3 July 1997

Displacement, tons: 376 full load
Dimensions, feet (metres): 185.7 × 29.5 × 8.2
  (56.3 × 9 × 2.5)
Main machinery: 4 MTU 20V 538TB93 diesels; 18,740 hp(m)
  (13.8 MW) sustained; 4 shafts
Speed, knots: 35
Range, n miles: 1,800 at 12 kt
Complement: 35 (7 officers)

Missiles: SSM: 8 Aerospatiale MM 40 Exocet (Block II) ❶;
  inertial cruise; active radar homing to 70 km *(40 n miles)*
  at 0.9 Mach; warhead 165 kg; sea-skimmer.
  SAM: Matra Sadral sextuple launcher for Mistral ❷;
  IR homing to 4 km *(2.2 n miles)*; warhead 3 kg.
Guns: 1 OTO Melara 76 mm/62 Super Rapid ❸; 120 rds/min
  to 16 km *(8.7 n miles)*; weight of shell 6 kg.
  1 Signaal Goalkeeper 30 mm ❹; 7 barrels; 4,200 rds/min
  combined to 2 km. 2—12.7 mm MGs.
Countermeasures: Decoys: CSEE Dagaie Mk 2 ❺ for chaff
  and IR flares.
  ESM: Thomson-CSF DR 3000S ❻; intercept.
  ECM: Dassault Salamandre ARBB 33 ❼; jammer.
Combat data systems: Signaal SEWACO FD with Thomson-
  CSF TACTICOS; Link Y.
Weapons control: Signaal STING optronic director. Signaal
  IRSCAN electro-optical tracker ❽.
Radars: Air/surface search: Thomson-CSF MRR ❾; G-band.
  Navigation: Kelvin Hughes 1007 ❿; I-band.
  Fire control: Signaal STING ⓫; I/J-band.

Programmes: Order announced on 4 June 1992 by Vosper
  Thornycroft. First steel cut 20 July 1993.
Structure: Vita design derivative based on the hull
  used for Oman and Kenya in the 1980s. Steel hull
  and aluminium superstructure. CSEE Sidewind EW
  management system is installed and a Racal Thorn data
  distribution system is used. Baffles have been added
  around the ECM aerials to prevent mutual interference
  with other sensors. An advanced machinery control and
  surveillance system allows one-man operation of main
  propulsion, electrical generation and auxiliary systems
  from the bridge. The bridge staff are also able to monitor
  the state of all compartments for damage control
  purposes.
Operational: First pair arrived in the Gulf in August 1997,
  second pair in May 1998. All of the class carry 40 kt RIBs
  with twin 60 hp outboards.

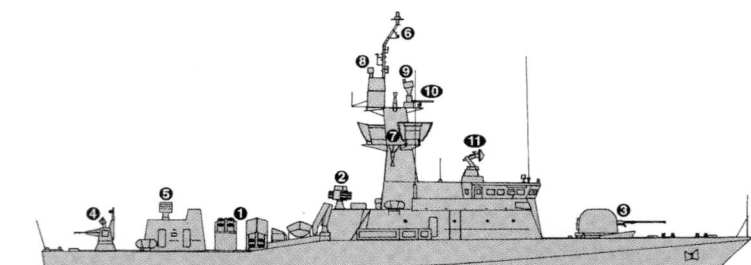

BARZAN

(Scale 1 : 600), Ian Sturton / 0012934

AL DEEBEL
10/2000
0121394

AL DEEBEL

7/2001, Ships of the World / 0121395

3 DAMEN POLYCAT 1450 CLASS
(COASTAL PATROL CRAFT) (PB)

Q 31-36 series

Displacement, tons: 18 full load
Dimensions, feet (metres): 47.6 × 15.4 × 4.9 *(14.5 × 4.7 × 2.1)*
Main machinery: 2 Detroit 12V-71TA diesels; 840 hp *(627 kW)* sustained; 2 shafts
Speed, knots: 26
Complement: 11
Guns: 1 Oerlikon 20 mm
Radars: Navigation: Racal Decca; I-band

Comment: Three remain of six delivered February-May 1980.

Q 33 *3/1980, Damen SY* / 0081617

AUXILIARIES

Notes: There are a number of amphibious craft including an LCT *Rabha* of 160 ft *(48.8 m)* with a capacity for three tanks and 110 troops, acquired in 1986-87. Also four Rotork craft and 30 Sea Jeeps in 1985. It is not clear how many of the smaller craft are for civilian use.

POLICE

Notes: (1) Requirements have been reported for patrol craft, two of 24 m, two of 22 m and 19 of 12 m. Also for two hovercraft.
(2) Two Halmatic 18 m pilot boats (based on Arun class lifeboat hull) delivered in 2000.

4 + (2) DV 15 FAST INTERCEPT CRAFT (HSIC)

Displacement, tons: 12 full load
Dimensions, feet (metres): 50.9 × 9.8 × 2.6 *(15.5 × 3.0 × 0.8)*
Main machinery: 2 diesels; 2 surface drives
Speed, knots: 55
Range, n miles: 400 at 30 kt
Complement: 4. **Guns:** 1 — 12.7 mm MG.
Radars: Surface search: I-band.

Comment: Built by CMN Cherbourg for delivery in 2006 to replace P 1200 class. There is an option for a further two craft. Composite hull construction similar to those in Yemeni service. Roles include coastal protection and security of offshore oil and gas installations.

DV 15 class *2/2003, CMN* / 0531701

3 HALMATIC M 160 CLASS (PB)

Displacement, tons: 20 full load
Dimensions, feet (metres): 52.5 × 15.4 × 4.6 *(16 × 4.7 × 1.4)*
Main machinery: 2 MTU diesels; 520 hp(m) *(388 kW)* sustained; 2 shafts
Speed, knots: 27
Range, n miles: 500 at 17 kt
Complement: 6
Guns: 1 — 7.62 mm MG.
Radars: Surface search: Racal Decca; I-band.

Comment: Order confirmed on 11 October 1995. Delivered to Police in November 1996. Similar to Police craft obtained by Caribbean countries.

M 160 *11/1996, Halmatic* / 0081619

4 CRESTITALIA MV-45 CLASS (PB)

RG 91-94

Displacement, tons: 17 full load
Dimensions, feet (metres): 47.6 × 12.5 × 2.6 *(14.5 × 3.8 × 0.8)*
Main machinery: 2 diesels; 1,270 hp(m) *(933 kW)*; 2 shafts
Speed, knots: 32
Range, n miles: 275 at 29 kt
Complement: 6
Guns: 1 Oerlikon 20 mm. 2 — 7.62 mm MGs.
Radars: Surface search: I-band.

Comment: Built by Crestitalia and delivered in mid-1989. GRP construction.

Romania

Country Overview

Situated in south-eastern Europe, the Republic of Romania has an area of 91,700 square miles and is bordered to the north by Ukraine and Moldova, to the west by Hungary and Serbia, and to the south by Bulgaria. The River Danube forms much of the southern border. Romania has a coastline of 121 n miles with the Black Sea on which Constanta, linked to the Danube port of Cernavodà by canal, is the principal seaport. Prominent river ports include Galati and Bràila on the lower Danube, and Giurgiu, which has pipeline connections to the Ploiesti oil fields. The capital and largest city is Bucharest. Territorial waters (12 n miles) are claimed. An EEZ (299 n miles) is claimed but the limits have not been defined.

Headquarters Appointments

Commander-in-Chief of the Navy:
  Rear Admiral Gheorghe Marin

Personnel

a)   2006: 8,000 Navy
b)   Reserves: 2,700

Organisation

The Navy is composed of the Naval Staff (Bucharest), the Naval Operational Command, Naval Academy, Hydrographic Directorate, Naval Academy, Diving Centre, Electronic Warfare Unit, Logistic Base and one Naval Infantry Battalion.

Bases

Black Sea—Mangalia (Training); Constanta (Naval Operational Command and Naval Logistic Base)
Danube—Bràila

Strength of the Fleet

Type	Active (Reserve)
Frigates	3
Corvettes	7
Patrol craft	21
Minelayer/MCM Support	1
Minesweepers (Coastal and River)	4
Training Ships	2
Survey Ships	2

Border Guard

Responsible for land and sea borders and has four brigades, two of which have sea forces based at Orsova and Constana.

DELETIONS

Corvettes

2004	*Vice Admiral Vasile Scodrea, Vice Admiral Vasile Urseanu*

Patrol Forces

2003	*Virtejul, Trasnetul, Tornada, Soimul, Eretele, Albatrosul*
2004	18 VB 76 river monitors, 6 Huchuan, *Smeul, Vijelia, Vulcanul*

Mine Warfare Forces

2004	*Vice Admiral Ioan Murgescu*

PENNANT LIST

Frigates			264	Contre Admiral Eustatiu Sebastian	Mine Warfare Forces			Training Ships	
111	Marasesti		265	Admiral Horia Macelariu	24	Lieutenant Remus Lepri		288	Mircea
221	Regele Ferdinand				25	Lieutenant Lupu Dunescu		521	Delfinul
222	Regina Maria		**Patrol Forces**		29	Lieutenant Dimitrie Nicolescu			
					30	Sub Lieutenant Alexandru Axente		**Auxiliaries**	
			45	Mikhail Kogalniceanu	274	Vice Admiral Constantin Balescu		281	Constanta
Corvettes			46	I C Bratianu				283	Midia
			47	Lascar Catargiu				296	Electronica
188	Zborul		176	Rahova	**Survey Ships**			298	Magnetica
189	Pescarusul		177	Opanez				500	Grozavu
190	Lastunul		178	Smardan	75	Grigore Antipa		501	Hercules
260	Admiral Petre Barbuneanu		179	Posada	115	Emil Racovita		532	Tulcea
263	Vice Admiral Eugeniu Rosca		180	Rovine					

SUBMARINES

Notes: The Kilo class submarine *Delfinul* 521 is used as a training ship. She has not been to sea in recent years and plans to refit her may be frustrated by lack of funding.

FRIGATES

2 BROADSWORD CLASS (TYPE 22) (FFHM)

Name	No	Builders	Laid down	Launched	Commissioned	Recommissioned
REGINA MARIA (ex-*London*)	222 (ex-F 95)	Yarrow Shipbuilders, Glasgow	7 Feb 1983	27 Oct 1984	5 June 1987	21 Apr 2005
REGELE FERDINAND (ex-*Coventry*)	221 (ex-F 98)	Swan Hunter Shipbuilders, Wallsend-on-Tyne	29 Mar 1984	8 Apr 1986	14 Oct 1988	9 Sep 2004

Displacement, tons: 4,100 standard; 4,800 full load
Dimensions, feet (metres): 480.5 × 48.5 × 21
(146.5 × 14.8 × 6.4)
Main machinery: CODOG: 2 RR Olympus TM3B gas turbines; 50,000 hp *(37.3 MW)* sustained; 2 RR Tyne RM1C gas turbines; 9,900 hp *(7.4 MW)*; 2 shafts; cp props
Speed, knots: 30; 18 on Tynes
Complement: 203

Guns: 1 OTO Melara 3 in *(76 mm)*/62 Super Rapid ❶; 120 rds/min to 16 km *(8.7 n miles)*; weight of shell 6 kg.
Countermeasures: Decoys: 2 Terma 130 mm DL-12 12-barrelled chaff launchers ❷.
Combat data systems: Ferranti CACS 1.
Weapons control: Radamec 2500 optronic director ❸. Nautis 3 fire-control system.
Radars: Air/Surface search: Marconi Type 967/968 ❹; D/E-band.
Navigation: Kelvin-Hughes Type 1007 ❺; I-band.
Sonars: Ferranti/Thomson Sintra Type 2050; hull-mounted search and attack.

Helicopters: Platform for 1 medium.

Programmes: Originally successors to the UK Leander class, these ships entered RN service in 1987 but were withdrawn, half-way through their ships' lives, as a result of the 1998 UK Defence Review. Sale agreement signed on 14 January 2003 included platform overhaul, installation of reconditioned engines and combat system modernisation. Training is also included in the package. Following trials and sea training, *Regele Ferdinand* arrived in Romania on 10 December 2004 and *Regina Maria* in 2005. A 15-year through-life support contract with BAE Systems was signed in October 2005.
Modernisation: BAE Systems was prime contractor and FSL sub-contractor for reactivation and modernisation. CACS command system upgraded and 76 mm gun installed. A second-phase upgrade is to be undertaken in Romania 2008-09. This is expected to include improved command and control, air-defence and anti-ship weapons and an improved EW suite.
Structure: Broadsword Batch 2 ships were stretched versions of Batch 1. The flight decks are capable of embarking medium helicopters.
Opinion: Acquisition of these ships gives Romania its first modern combatants. As well as providing an increase in capability, the ships will enable a higher degree of interoperability with NATO forces.

REGELE FERDINAND *(Scale 1 : 1,200), Ian Sturton* / 1044184

REGELE FERDINAND *11/2004*, B Sullivan* / 1133560

REGELE FERDINAND
11/2004*, John Brodie
1133559

REGINA MARIA *6/2005*, Maritime Photographic* / 1133562

1 MARASESTI CLASS (FFGH)

Name	No	Builders	Laid down	Launched	Commissioned
MARASESTI (ex-*Muntenia*)	111	Mangalia Shipyard	7 Aug 1979	4 June 1981	3 June 1985

Displacement, tons: 5,790 full load
Dimensions, feet (metres): 474.4 × 48.6 × 23
  (144.6 × 14.8 × 7)
Main machinery: 4 diesels; 32,000 hp(m) *(23.5 MW)*;
  4 shafts
Speed, knots: 27
Complement: 270 (25 officers)

Missiles: SSM: 8 SS-N-2C Styx ❶; active radar or IR homing
  to 83 km *(45 n miles)* at 0.9 Mach; warhead 513 kg.
Guns: 4 USSR 3 in *(76 mm)*/60 (2 twin) ❷; 90 rds/min to 15 km
  (8 n miles); weight of shell 6.8 kg.
  4—30 mm/65 ❸; 6 barrels per mounting; 3,000 rds/min
  to 2 km.
Torpedoes: 6—21 in *(533 mm)* (2 triple) tubes ❹. Russian
  53—65; passive/wake homing to 25 km *(13.5 n miles)* at
  50 kt; warhead 300 kg.
A/S mortars: 2 RBU 6000 ❺; 12-tubed trainable; range
  6,000 m; warhead 31 kg.
Countermeasures: Decoys: 2 PK 16 chaff launchers.
ESM/ECM: 2 Watch Dog; intercept. Bell Clout and Bell Slam.
Radars: Air/surface search: Strut Curve ❻; F-band.
Surface search: Plank Shave ❼; E-band.
Fire control: Two Drum Tilt ❽; H/I-band.
  Hawk Screech ❾; I-band.
Navigation: Nayada (MR 212); Racal Decca; I-band.
IFF: High Pole B.
Sonars: Hull-mounted; active search and attack; medium
  frequency.

Helicopters: 2 IAR-316 Alouette III ❿.

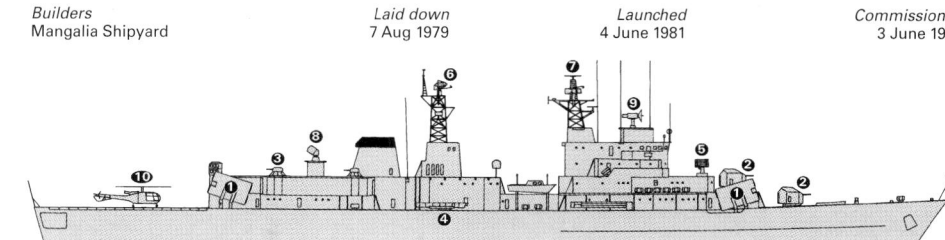

MARASESTI   *(Scale 1 : 1,200), Ian Sturton* / 1044186

MARASESTI   *1/2001, van Ginderen Collection* / 0106855

Modernisation: Attempts have been made to modernise
some of the electronic equipment. Also topweight
problems have been addressed by reducing the height
of the mast structures and lowering the Styx missile
launchers by one deck. Two RBU 6000s have replaced the
RBU 1200. A series of upgrades are planned including
communications, Link 11 and improved weapons and
sensors. Precise details of the package are not known
but implementation is expected by 2006.
Structure: A distinctive Romanian design. Originally
thought to be powered by gas turbines but a diesel
configuration including four shafts is now confirmed.
Operational: Deactivated in June 1988 due to manpower
and fuel shortages but modernisation work was
done from 1990 to 1992 and sea trials started in
mid-1992. Carried out a major naval exercise in
September 1993, which included firing the Styx missile.
Deployed to the Mediterranean in September 1994
for a short cruise, in 1995 on two occasions and
again in March 1998. Reclassified as frigate in 2001.
Based at Constanta.

MARASESTI   *6/2004, C D Yaylali* / 0589801

MARASESTI   *7/1995, Diego Quevedo* / 0052762

CORVETTES

2 TETAL CLASS (FS)

Name	No
ADMIRAL PETRE BARBUNEANU	260
VICE ADMIRAL EUGENIU ROSCA	263

Builders	Launched	Commissioned
Mangalia Shipyard	23 May 1981	4 Feb 1983
Mangalia Shipyard	11 July 1985	23 Apr 1987

Displacement, tons: 1,440 full load
Dimensions, feet (metres): 303.1 × 38.4 × 9.8
  (92.4 × 11.7 × 3)
Main machinery: 4 diesels; 13,000 hp(m) *(9.6 MW)*; 4 shafts
Speed, knots: 24
Complement: 98

Guns: 4 USSR 3 in *(76 mm)*/60 (2 twin) ❶; 90 rds/min to 15 km
  (8 n miles); weight of shell 6.8 kg.
  4 USSR 30 mm/65 (2 twin) ❷; 500 rds/min to 4 km
  (2.2 n miles); weight of shell 0.54 kg.
  2—14.5 mm MGs.
Torpedoes: 4—21 in *(533 mm)* (2 twin) tubes ❸. Russian
  53—65; passive/wake homing to 25 km *(13.5 n miles)* at
  50 kt; warhead 300 kg.
A/S mortars: 2 RBU 2500 16-tubed trainable ❹; range
  2,500 m; warhead 21 kg.
Countermeasures: Decoys: 2 PK 16 chaff launchers.
ESM: 2 Watch Dog; intercept.
Radars: Air/surface search: Strut Curve ❺; F-band.

Fire control: Drum Tilt ❻; H/I-band. Hawk Screech ❼;
  I-band.
Navigation: Nayada; I-band.
IFF: High Pole.
Sonars: Hercules (MG 322); Hull-mounted; active search
  and attack; medium frequency.

Programmes: Building terminated in 1987 in favour of the
  improved design with a helicopter platform.
Structure: A modified Soviet Koni design.
Operational: Both based at Constanta. Two decommissioned
  in 2004.

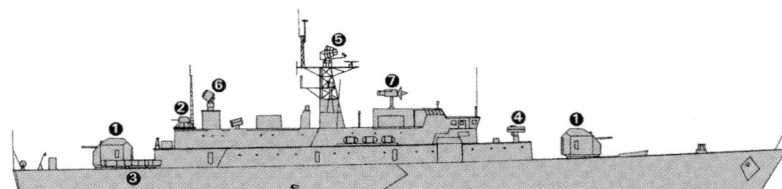

ADMIRAL PETRE BARBUNEANU
(Scale 1 : 900), Ian Sturton / 0506168

ADMIRAL PETRE BARBUNEANU
6/2001 / 0126335

2 IMPROVED TETAL CLASS (FSH)

Name	No
CONTRE ADMIRAL EUSTATIU SEBASTIAN	264
ADMIRAL HORIA MACELARIU	265

Builders	Launched	Commissioned
Mangalia Shipyard	12 Apr 1988	30 Dec 1989
Mangalia Shipyard	15 May 1994	29 Sep 1997

Displacement, tons: 1,500 full load
Dimensions, feet (metres): 303.1 × 38.4 × 10
  (92.4 × 11.7 × 3.1)
Main machinery: 4 diesels; 13,000 hp(m) *(9.6 MW)*; 4 shafts
Speed, knots: 24
Complement: 95

Guns: 1 USSR 3 in *(76 mm/60)* ❶; 120 rds/min to 15 km
  (8 n miles); weight of shell 6.8 kg.
  2—30 mm/65 AK 630 ❷; 6 barrels per mounting;
  3,000 rds/min to 2 km.
  2—30 mm/65 AK 306 ❸; 6 barrels per mounting;
  3,000 rds/min to 2 km.
Torpedoes: 4—21 in *(533 mm)* (2 twin) tubes ❹. Russian
  53—65; passive/wake homing to 25 km *(13.5 n miles)* at
  50 kt; warhead 300 kg.
A/S mortars: 2 RBU 6000 ❺; 12-tubed trainable; range
  6,000 m; warhead 31 kg.
Countermeasures: Decoys: 2 PK 16 chaff launchers ❻.
ESM: 2 Watch Dog; intercept.

Radars: Air/surface search: Strut Curve ❼; F-band.
Fire control: Drum Tilt ❽; H/I-band.
Navigation: Nayada; I-band.
IFF: High Pole.
Sonars: Hull-mounted; active search and attack; medium
  frequency.

Helicopters: 1 IAR-316 Aloutte III ❾.

Programmes: Follow on to Tetal class. Second of class
  was delayed when work stopped for a time in
  1993-94.
Structure: As well as improved armament and a helicopter
  deck, there are superstructure changes from the original
  Tetals, but the hull and propulsion machinery are the
  same.
Operational: Both based at Mangalia.

ADMIRAL HORIA MACELARIU
(Scale 1 : 900), Ian Sturton / 1044187

CONTRE ADMIRAL EUSTATIU SEBASTIAN
9/2003, C D Yaylali / 0589802

ADMIRAL HORIA MACELARIU
4/2005, C D Yaylali* / 1133558

3 ZBORUL (TARANTUL I) CLASS (PROJECT 1241 RE) (FSG)

Name	No	Builders	Commissioned
ZBORUL	188	Petrovsky Shipyard	Dec 1990
PESCARUSUL	189	Petrovsky Shipyard	Feb 1992
LASTUNUL	190	Petrovsky Shipyard	Feb 1992

Displacement, tons: 385 standard; 455 full load
Dimensions, feet (metres): 184.1 × 37.7 × 8.2 *(56.1 × 11.5 × 2.5)*
Main machinery: COGAG; 2 Type DR 77 gas turbines; 16,016 hp(m) *(11.77 MW)* sustained; 2 Nikolayev Type DR 76 gas turbines with reversible gearboxes; 4,993 hp(m) *(3.67 MW)* sustained; 2 shafts
Speed, knots: 36. **Range, n miles:** 2,000 at 20 kt; 400 at 36 kt
Complement: 41 (5 officers)

Missiles: 4 SS-N-2C Styx (2 twin); active radar or IR homing to 83 km *(45 n miles)* at 0.9 Mach; warhead 513 kg.
Guns: 1 USSR 3 in *(76 mm)*/60; 120 rds/min to 15 km *(8 n miles)*; weight of shell 7 kg. 2—30 mm/65 AK 630; 6 barrels per mounting; 3,000 rds/min to 2 km.
Countermeasures: 2 PK 16 chaff launchers.
ESM: 2 Watch Dog; intercept.
Weapons control: Hood Wink optronic director.
Radars: Air/surface search: Plank Shave; E-band.
Fire control: Bass Tilt; H/I-band.
Navigation: Spin Trough; I-band.
IFF: Square Head. High Pole.

Comment: Built in 1985 and later transferred from the USSR. Export version similar to those built for Poland, India and Yemen. Based at Mangalia.

LASTUNUL *6/1998, Valentino Cluru* / 0052766

SHIPBORNE AIRCRAFT

Numbers/Type: 6 IAR-316B Alouette III.
Operational speed: 113 kt *(210 km/h).*
Service ceiling: 10,500 ft *(3,200 m).*
Range: 290 n miles *(540 km).*
Role/Weapon systems: ASW helicopter. Sensors: Nose-mounted search radar. Weapons: ASW; two lightweight torpedoes.

LAND-BASED MARITIME AIRCRAFT

Numbers/Type: 5 Mil Mi-14PL Haze A.
Operational speed: 124 kt *(230 km/h).*
Service ceiling: 15,000 ft *(4,570 m).*
Range: 432 n miles *(800 km).*
Role/Weapon systems: Medium-range ASW helicopter. Sensors: Short Horn search radar, dipping sonar, MAD, sonobuoys. Weapons: ASW; internally stored torpedoes, depth mines and bombs.

HAZE PL (Polish colours) *6/2000* / 0105235

PATROL FORCES

Notes: There is a total of about 20 river patrol boats. These include three 27 ft Boston Whalers presented by the US in March 1993 for Customs/Police patrols on the Danube in support of UN sanctions operations. There is also a hovercraft built at Mangalia in 1998.

1 NEUSTADT CLASS (PB)

GENERAL PARASCHIV VASILESCU (ex-*Bayreuth*) 10 (ex-BG 17)

Displacement, tons: 218 full load
Dimensions, feet (metres): 127.1 × 23 × 5 *(38.5 × 7 × 2.2)*
Main machinery: 2 MTU MD diesels; 6,000 hp(m) *(4.41 MW)*; 1 MWM diesel; 685 hp(m) *(500 kW)*; 3 shafts
Speed, knots: 30. **Range, n miles:** 450 at 27 kt
Complement: 17
Guns: 2—7.62 mm MGs.
Radars: Surface search: Selenia ARP 1645; I-band.
Navigation: Racal Decca Bridgemaster MA 180/4; I-band.

Comment: Built in 1970 by Lürssen, Vegesack. Transferred from German Border Guard on 10 January 2004. Operated by the Romanian Border Guard and based in Constanta.

5 BRUTAR II CLASS (RIVER MONITORS) (PGR)

Name	No	Builders	Commissioned
RAHOVA	176	Mangalia Shipyard	14 Apr 1988
OPANEZ	177	Mangalia Shipyard	24 July 1990
SMARDAN	178	Mangalia Shipyard	24 July 1990
POSADA	179	Mangalia Shipyard	14 May 1992
ROVINE	180	Mangalia Shipyard	30 June 1993

Displacement, tons: 410 full load
Dimensions, feet (metres): 150 × 26.4 × 4.9 *(45.7 × 8 × 1.5)*
Main machinery: 2 diesels; 2,700 hp(m) *(2 MW)*; 2 shafts
Speed, knots: 16
Guns: 1—100 mm (tank turret). 2—30 mm (twin). 10—14.5 mm (2 quad, 2 single) MGs. 2—122 mm BM-21 rocket launchers; 40-tubed trainable.
Radars: Navigation: I-band.

Comment: Operational as patrol craft on the Danube. The first is a Brutar I. The next pair are Brutar IIs based at Tulcea and the last two are Brutar IIs based at Mangalia.

RAHOVA *10/2003, Freddy Philips* / 0567529

OPANEZ *10/2003, Freddy Philips* / 0589804

12 VD 141 CLASS (RIVER PATROL CRAFT) (PBR)

141-165 series

Displacement, tons: 97 full load
Dimensions, feet (metres): 109 × 15.7 × 2.8 *(33.3 × 4.8 × 0.9)*
Main machinery: 2 diesels; 870 hp(m) *(640 kW)*; 2 shafts
Speed, knots: 13
Guns: 4—14.5 mm (2 twin) MGs.
Mines: 6.
Radars: Navigation: Nayada; I-band.

Comment: Built in Romania at Dobreta Severin Shipyard 1976-84. Ex river minesweepers now employed as patrol craft on the Danube.

VD 150 *6/1999, Romanian Navy* / 0081629

3 KOGALNICEANU CLASS (RIVER MONITORS) (PGR)

Name	No	Builders	Commissioned
MIKHAIL KOGALNICEANU	45	Drobeta Santierul, Turnu Severin	19 Dec 1993
I C BRATIANU	46	Drobeta Santierul, Turnu Severin	28 Dec 1994
LASCAR CATARGIU	47	Drobeta Santierul, Turnu Severin	22 Nov 1996

Displacement, tons: 575 full load
Dimensions, feet (metres): 170.6 × 29.5 × 5.6 *(52 × 9 × 1.7)*
Main machinery: 2 24-H-165 RINS diesels; 4,400 hp(m) *(3.3 MW)*; 2 shafts
Speed, knots: 18
Guns: 2—100 mm (tank turrets). 4—30 mm (2 twin). 4—14.5 mm (2 twin). 2—122 mm BM-21 rocket launchers.
Radars: Navigation: I-band.

Comment: Based at Braila.

I C BRATIANU *6/1999, Romanian Navy* / 0081622

MINE WARFARE FORCES

1 CORSAR CLASS
(MINELAYER/MCM SUPPORT SHIP) (ML/MCS)

Name	No	Builders	Commissioned
VICE ADMIRAL CONSTANTIN BALESCU	274	Mangalia Shipyard	16 Nov 1981

Displacement, tons: 1,450 full load
Dimensions, feet (metres): 259.1 × 34.8 × 11.8 *(79 × 10.6 × 3.6)*
Main machinery: 2 diesels; 6,400 hp(m) *(4.7 MW)*; 2 shafts
Speed, knots: 19
Complement: 75
Guns: 1—57 mm/70. 4—30 mm/65 (2 twin) AK 230. 8—14.5 mm (2 quad) MGs.
A/S mortars: 2 RBU 1200 5-tubed fixed; range 1,200 m; warhead 34 kg.
Mines: 200.
Countermeasures: ESM: Watch Dog; intercept.
Radars: Air/surface search: Strut Curve; F-band.
Navigation: Don 2; I-band.
Fire control: Muff Cob; G/H-band. Drum Tilt; H/I-band.
Sonars: Tamir II; hull-mounted; active search; high frequency.

Comment: Has a large crane on the after deck. Similar to survey ship *Grigore Antipa*. Based at Constanta.

VICE ADMIRAL CONSTANTIN BALESCU　　*6/1999, Romanian Navy* / 0081627

4 MUSCA CLASS (MINESWEEPERS—COASTAL) (MSC)

Name	No	Builders	Commissioned
LIEUTENANT REMUS LEPRI	24	Mangalia Shipyard	23 Apr 1987
LIEUTENANT LUPU DUNESCU	25	Mangalia Shipyard	6 Jan 1989
LIEUTENANT DIMITRIE NICOLESCU	29	Mangalia Shipyard	7 Dec 1989
SUB LIEUTENANT ALEXANDRU AXENTE	30	Mangalia Shipyard	7 Dec 1989

Displacement, tons: 790 full load
Dimensions, feet (metres): 194.2 × 31.1 × 9.2 *(59.2 × 9.5 × 2.8)*
Main machinery: 2 diesels; 4,800 hp(m) *(3.5 MW)*; 2 shafts
Speed, knots: 17
Complement: 60
Missiles: SAM: 2 quad SA-N-5 launchers.
Guns: 4—30 mm/65 (2 twin) AK 230.
A/S mortars: 2 RBU 1200 5-tubed fixed; range 1,200 m; warhead 34 kg.
Radars: Surface search: Krivach; I-band.
Fire control: Drum Tilt; H/I-band.
Navigation: Nayada; I-band.
Sonars: Hull-mounted; active search; high frequency.

Comment: Reported as having a secondary mining capability but this is not confirmed. Based at Mangalia.

SUB LIEUTENANT ALEXANDRU AXENTE　　*8/2004** / 1133557

SURVEY AND RESEARCH SHIPS

1 CORSAR CLASS (RESEARCH SHIP) (AGOR)

Name	No	Builders	Commissioned
GRIGORE ANTIPA	75	Mangalia Shipyard	25 May 1980

Displacement, tons: 1,450 full load
Dimensions, feet (metres): 259.1 × 34.8 × 11.8 *(79 × 10.6 × 3.6)*
Main machinery: 2 diesels; 6,400 hp(m) *(4.7 MW)*; 2 shafts
Speed, knots: 19
Complement: 75
Radars: Navigation: Nayada; I-band.

Comment: Large davits aft for launching manned submersible. Same hull as Corsar class. Used as a research ship and for diving support. Based at Constanta.

GRIGORE ANTIPA　　*5/1998, Diego Quevedo* / 0052770

1 RESEARCH SHIP (AGS)

Name	No	Builders	Commissioned
EMIL RACOVITA	115	Drobeta Severin Shipyard	30 Oct 1977

Displacement, tons: 1,900 full load
Dimensions, feet (metres): 229.9 × 32.8 × 12.7 *(70.1 × 10 × 3.9)*
Main machinery: 1 diesel; 3,285 hp(m) *(2.4 MW)*; 1 shaft
Speed, knots: 11
Complement: 80

Comment: Modernised in the mid-1980s. Similar design to *Grigore Antipa*. Used as a hydrographic ship.

EMIL RACOVITA　　*2001, Romanian Navy* / 0114548

TRAINING SHIPS

Notes: (1) *Neptun* belongs to the Merchant Navy.
(2) The Kilo class submarine *Delfinul* is used as an alongside training vessel.

1 SAIL TRAINING SHIP (AXS)

Name	No	Builders	Launched	Commissioned
MIRCEA	288	Blohm + Voss, Hamburg	29 Sep 1938	29 Mar 1939

Displacement, tons: 1,604 full load
Dimensions, feet (metres): 206; 266.4 (with bowsprit) × 39.3 × 16.5 *(62.8; 81.2 × 12 × 5.2)*
Main machinery: 1 MaK 6M 451 auxiliary diesel; 1,000 hp(m) *(735 kW)*; 1 shaft
Speed, knots: 8
Range, n miles: 5,000 at 8 kt
Complement: 83 (5 officers) plus 140 midshipmen
Radars: Navigation: Decca 202; I-band.

Comment: Refitted at Hamburg in 1966. Sail area, 5,739 m² *(18,830 sq ft)*. A smaller version of US Coast Guard cutter *Eagle*, German *Gorch Fock* and Portuguese *Sagres*. Based at Constanta.

MIRCEA　　*6/2005*, M Declerck* / 1133561

AUXILIARIES

2 CROITOR CLASS (LOGISTIC SUPPORT SHIPS) (AETLMH)

Name	No	Builders	Commissioned
CONSTANTA	281	Braila Shipyard	15 Sep 1980
MIDIA	283	Braila Shipyard	26 Feb 1982

Displacement, tons: 2,850 standard; 3,500 full load
Dimensions, feet (metres): 354.3 × 44.3 × 12.5
  (108 × 13.5 × 3.8)
Main machinery: 2 diesels; 6,500 hp(m) *(4.8 MW)*; 2 shafts
Speed, knots: 16
Missiles: SAM: 2 SA-N-5 Grail quad launchers; manual
  aiming; IR homing to 6 km *(3.2 n miles)* at 1.5 Mach;
  warhead 1.5 kg.

Guns: 2—57 mm/70 (twin). 4—30 mm/65 (2 twin). 8—14.5 mm
  (2 quad) MGs.
A/S mortars: 2 RBU 1200 5-tubed fixed; range 1,200 m;
  warhead 34 kg.
Countermeasures: ESM: 2 Watch Dog; intercept.
Radars: Air/surface search: Strut Curve; F-band.
  Navigation: Krivach; I-band.
  Fire control: Muff Cob; G/H-band. Drum Tilt; H/I-band.

Sonars: Tamir II; hull-mounted; active attack; high frequency.

Helicopters: 1 IAR-316 Alouette III type.

Comment: These ships are a scaled down version of Soviet
  Don class. Forward crane for ammunition replenishment.
  Some ASW escort capability. Can carry Styx missiles and
  torpedoes. Based at Constanta.

CONSTANTA   *6/2001, Schaeffer/Marsan* / 0533268

1 TANKER (AOT)

TULCEA 532

Displacement, tons: 2,170 full load
Dimensions, feet (metres): 250.4 × 41 × 16.4 *(76.3 × 12.5 × 5)*
Main machinery: 2 diesels; 4,800 hp(m) *(3.5 MW)*; 2 shafts
Speed, knots: 16
Cargo capacity: 1,200 tons oil
Guns: 2—30 mm/65 (twin). 4—14.5 mm (2 twin) MGs.

Comment: First one built by Tulcea Shipyard and commissioned 24 December 1992.
  Second of class reported in 1997 but not confirmed. Based at Constanta.

TULCEA   *2001, Romanian Navy* / 0114542

2 DEGAUSSING SHIPS (ADG/AGI)

Name	No	Builders	Commissioned
ELECTRONICA	296	Braila Shipyard	6 Aug 1973
MAGNETICA	298	Mangalia Shipyard	18 Dec 1989

Displacement, tons: 299 full load
Dimensions, feet (metres): 134 × 21.6 × 10.7 *(40.8 × 6.6 × 3.2)*
Main machinery: Diesel-electric; 1 diesel generator; 600 kW; 1 shaft
Speed, knots: 12.5
Complement: 18
Guns: 2—14.5 mm (twin) MGs. 2—12.7 mm MGs.

Comment: Built for degaussing ships up to 3,000 tons displacement. Electronica is used
  as an AGI. Based at Tulcea.

MAGNETICA
6/1999, Romanian Navy

0081632

2 COASTAL TANKERS (AOTL)

530 **531**

Displacement, tons: 1,042 full load
Dimensions, feet (metres): 181.2 × 30.9 × 13.4
  (55.2 × 9.4 × 4.1)
Main machinery: 2 diesels; 1,800 hp(m) *(1.3 MW)*; 2 shafts
Speed, knots: 12.5
Cargo capacity: 500 tons oil
Guns: 1—37 mm. 2—12.7 mm MGs.

Comment: Built by Braila Shipyard and both commissioned
  15 June 1971. Based at Constanta.

531
6/1999, Romanian Navy
0081636

1 FLAG OFFICERS BARGE (AOTL)

RINDUNICA

Displacement, tons: 40 full load
Dimensions, feet (metres): 78.7 × 16.4 × 3.6 *(24 × 5 × 1.1)*
Main machinery: 2 diesels; 2,200 hp(m) *(1.6 MW)*; 2 shafts
Speed, knots: 28
Complement: 6

Comment: Used as a barge by the Commander-in-Chief.

RINDUNICA
1/1995
0081637

TUGS

Notes: There are also a number of harbour and river tugs, some of which are armed. These include two Roslavl (101 and 116) at Mangalia.

HARBOUR TUG 570   *12/1994* / 0081638

2 OCEAN TUGS (ATA)

GROZAVU 500   **HERCULES** 501

Displacement, tons: 3,600 full load
Dimensions, feet (metres): 212.6 × 47.9 × 18
  (64.8 × 14.6 × 5.5)
Main machinery: 2 diesels; 5,000 hp(m) *(3.7 MW)*; 2 shafts
Speed, knots: 12
Guns: 2—30 mm (twin). 8—14.5 mm (2 quad) MGs.

Comment: First one built at Oltenitza Shipyard and
  commissioned 29 June 1993. Second of class completed
  in 1995. Based at Constanta.

GROZAVU
2001, Romanian Navy
0114543

Russian Federation
ROSIYSKIY VOENNOMORSKY FLOT

Country Overview

Formerly a constituent republic of the Soviet Union, the Russian Federation was established as an independent state in 1991. The largest country in the world with an area of 6,592,850 square miles, it is bordered to the south by North Korea, China, Mongolia, Kazakhstan, Azerbaijan and Georgia and to the west by Norway, Finland, Latvia, Estonia, Ukraine and Belarus, which with Lithuania separates the Kaliningrad oblast (formerly Königsberg) from the rest of Russia. It has a 20,331 n mile coastline with the Arctic and Pacific Oceans and the Caspian, Baltic and Black Seas. These three seas are inter-connected by an extensive inland waterway system whose main components are the Volga and Don rivers, the Volga-Don canal and the Volga-Baltic Waterway. A canal also links the system to the capital and largest city, Moscow. The Amur River is the most important navigable river in the far east region. Offshore, principal islands in the Arctic Ocean include the Franz Josef Land and Severnaya Zemlya archipelagos, Novaya Zemlya, Vaygach Island, the New Siberian Islands and Wrangel Island. In the Pacific lie the Kuril Islands, which extend from the Kamchatka Peninsula, and Sakhalin Island. Principal seaports include Novorossiysk (Black Sea), St Petersburg and Kaliningrad (Baltic), Nakhodka, Vostochnyy, Vladivostok, and Vanino (Pacific) and Murmansk and Archangel (Arctic). Major river ports include Rybinsk, Nizhniy Novgorod, Samara, Volgograd, Astrakhan and Rostov-on-Don. Territorial waters (12 n miles) are claimed. An EEZ (200 n miles), is also claimed and the limits have been partly defined by boundary agreements.

Headquarters Appointments

Commander-in-Chief:
  Admiral Vladimir Masorin
First Deputy Commander-in-Chief:
  Admiral Mikhail Abramov

Northern Fleet

Commander:
  Vice Admiral Vladimir Vysotskiy

Pacific Fleet

Commander:
  Admiral Victor Fyodorov

Black Sea Fleet

Commander:
  Vice Admiral Alexander Tatarinov

Baltic Fleet

Commander:
  Admiral V Valuyev

Caspian Flotilla

Commander:
  Vice Admiral Yuriy Startsev

Personnel

(a) 2006: 140,000 not including naval aviation and naval infantry. The approximate division is 47,000 in the North, 38,000 in the Pacific, 26,000 in the Baltic, 20,000 in the Black Sea and 9,000 in the Caspian.
(b) Approximately 30 per cent volunteers (officers and senior ratings) – remainder two years' national service (or three years if volunteered)

Associated Navies

The Soviet Union was dissolved in December 1991. In 1992 a Commonwealth of Independent States was formed from the Republics of the former Union, but without the Baltic States. In the Baltic the Russian flotilla had withdrawn from the former East German and Polish ports by 1993 and from the Baltic Republics by the end of 1994. The Caspian flotilla divided with some units going to Azerbaijan, Kazakhstan and Turkmenistan. In the Black Sea the division of the Fleet between Russia and Ukraine was finally implemented in 1997. Facilities are shared in some Crimean ports.

Main Bases

North: Severomorsk (HQ), Polyarny, Gremika, Zapandaya Litsa, Gadzhievo, Vidyayevo
Baltic: Kaliningrad (HQ), St Petersburg, Kronshtadt, Baltiysk
Black Sea: Sevastopol (HQ) (Crimea), Tuapse, Novorssiysk, Feodosiya
Caspian: Astrakhan (HQ), Makhachkala
Pacific: Vladivostok (HQ), Sovetskaya Gavan, Magadan, Petropavlovsk, Komsomolsk, Racovaya

Operational

From 1991 a shortage of funds to pay for dockyard repairs, spare parts and fuel meant that many major surface warships were rarely at sea, and few operated away from their local exercise areas. Activity levels temporarily rose from 1996 but many ships, although technically in commission, remained in harbour. Activity reached a low point in 2002 but, in recent years, improvements in the budgetary situation and the publication of a new naval doctrine have led to a higher operational tempo. A busier pattern of exercises and operations was initiated in 2003 and activity levels were maintained during 2004.

Coast Defence

The Command of Naval Infantry and Coastal Artillery and Missiles includes a Division of Coastal Artillery and three Mechanised Infantry (Coastal Defence Troops) Brigades, an Artillery Self-Propelled Brigade, plus the units of Naval Infantry (five Brigades and one Division) and a number of minor units. The force of Coastal Artillery includes 19 Missile Batallions (SSC-1 Sepal SS-C-3 Styx) and 11 Gun Batallions (130 mm and 152 mm). Many of these units are in reserve. The Naval Infantry were deployed in Chechnya in 2000.

Pennant Numbers

There have been no major changes to pennant numbers since 1993 except when ships transfer fleets. Some submarines have temporary numbers on the side of the fin.

Class and Weapon Systems Names

Most Russian ship class names differ from those allocated by NATO. In such cases the Russian name is placed in brackets after the NATO name. Type or Project numbers are also placed in brackets. Weapon systems retain their NATO names with the Russian name, when known, placed in brackets. Some equipment now has three names – NATO, Russian Navy and Russian export.

Civilian Support Ships

Previously, civilian manned research ships and some icebreakers were effectively under naval control and were therefore included in the former Soviet/Russian section. These ships have been removed as all are now employed solely for commercial purposes.

Strength of the Fleet

Type	Active	Building
Submarines (SSBN)	15	2 (1)
Submarines (SSGN/SSN)	25	3
Submarines (SSK)	19	1
Auxiliary Submarines (SSA(N))	7	—
Aircraft Carriers (CV)	1	—
Battle Cruisers (CGN)	1	—
Cruisers (CG)	4	—
Destroyers (DDG)	19	—
Frigates (FFG)	8	6 (1)
Frigates (FF and FFL)	36	—
Corvettes	44	1 (9)
Patrol Forces	8	2 (4)
Minesweepers—Ocean	13	—
Minesweepers—Coastal	31	—
LPDs	1	—
LSTs	21	1
Hovercraft (Amphib)	9	—
Replenishment Tankers	20	—
Hospital Ships	3	—

Notes: There are large numbers of most classes 'in reserve', and flying an ensign so that skeleton crews may still be paid. The list above reflects only those units assessed as having some realistic operational capability or some prospect of returning to service after refit.

Fleet Disposition (1 January 2006)

Type	Northern	Baltic	Black Sea	Pacific	Caspian
SSBN	11	—	—	4	—
SSGN/SSN	17	—	—	8	—
SSK	6	3	1	9	—
SSA(N)	8	—	—	—	—
CV	1	—	—	—	—
CGN	1	—	—	—	—
CG	1	—	2	1	—
DDG	7	4	1	7	—
FFG	1	3	2	1	1
FF and FFL	10	11	7	8	—
Corvettes	4	12	9	17	2
LPD	1	—	—	—	—
LST	5	5	7	4	—
AOR	7	3	3	7	—

Notes: MCMV are divided evenly between the four main Fleets plus a few in the Caspian Sea.

DELETIONS

Notes: Some of the ships listed are still theoretically 'laid up', and some still fly an ensign so that skeleton crews may be paid.

Submarines

2003 1 Delta I
2004 1 Yankee Notch
2005 1 Yankee Stretch, 1 Yankee SSAN

Cruisers

2003 1 Kynda (*Admiral Golovko*)

Frigates

2004 2 Krivak 1 (*Zharky, Legky*)

PENNANT LIST

Submarines
Ballistic Missile Submarines

Typhoon class
TK 17   Arkhangelsk
TK 29   Severstal
TK 208   Dmitry Donskoy

Delta IV class
K 18   Karelia
K 51   Verchoture
K 84   Ekaterinburg
K 114   Tula
K 117   Briansk
K 407   Novomoskvosk

Delta III class
K 44   Borisoglebsk
K 211   Petropavlosk-Kamchatsky
K 223   Podolsk
K 433   Syvatoy Giorgiy Pobedonosets
K 496   Ryazan
K 506   Zelenograd

Attack Submarines

Oscar II class
K 119   Voronezh
K 139   Belgorod
K 186   Omsk
K 266   Orel

Oscar II class
K 410   Smolensk
K 442   Cheliabinsk
K 456   Vilyachinsk
K 526   Tomsk

Yasen class
K 329   Severodvisnk (bldg)

Akula I and II classes
K 152   Nerpa (bldg)
K 154   Tigr
K 157   Vepr
K 295   Samara
K 317   Pantera
K 328   Leopard
K 322   Kashalot
K 331   Magadan
K 335   Gepard
K 337   Cougar (bldg)
K 419   Kuzbass
K 461   Volk

Sierra I and II classes
K 276   Kostroma
K 336   Pskov
K 534   Nizhny Novgorod

Victor III class
B 138   Obninsk
B 292   Perm
B 388   Snezhnogorsk
B 414   Danil Moskovskiy
B 448   Tambov

Auxiliary Submarines

K 129   —
AS 13   —
AS 16   —
AS 17   —

Patrol Submarines

S 100   Saint Petersburg
B 177   Lipetsk
B 187   —
B 190   —
B 227   Tur
B 229   —
B 260   Razboynik
B 345   —
B 401   Novosibirsk
B 402   Vologda
B 405   —
B 445   —
B 464   UST-Kamshatsk
B 471   Magneto-Gorsk
B 494   Ust-Bolsheretsk
B 800   Kaluga
B 806   —
B 808   Jaroslavl
B 871   Alrosa

Aircraft Carriers

063   Admiral Kuznetsov

Battle Cruisers

099   Pyotr Velikiy

Cruisers

011   Varyag
055   Marshal Ustinov
121   Moskva
713   Kerch

Destroyers

400   Vitse admiral Kulakov
404   Gremyashchy
420   Rastoropny
434   Marshal Ushakov
543   Marshal Shaposhnikov
548   Admiral Panteleyev
564   Admiral Tributs
572   Admiral Vinogradov
605   Admiral Levchenko
610   Nastoychivy
619   Severomorsk
620   Bespokoiny
650   Admiral Chabanenko
678   Admiral Kharlamov
687   Marshal Vasilevsky
715   Bystry
754   Bezboyaznennyy
778   Burny
810   Smetlivy

Frigates

—   Steregushchiy (bldg)
—   Soobrazitelny (bldg)
—   Boiky (bldg)
053   Povorino
054   Eisk
055   Kasimov
059   Akelsandrovets
060   Anadyr (BG)
064   Muromets
103   Kedrov (BG)
113   Menzhinsky (BG)
113   Yunga
138   Naryan-Mar
156   Orel (BG)
158   Dzerzhinksky (BG)
160   Vorovsky (BG)
164   Onega
175   Pskov (BG)
190   Monchegorsk
199   Brest
323   Metel
354   Stelyak
390   Korets
661   Letuchy
691   Tatarstan
702   Pylky
712   Neustrashimy
731   Neukrotimy
801   Ladny
808   Pytlivy
955   Zadorny

Corvettes

409   Moroz
418   Inej
423   Smerch
450   Razliv
520   Rassvet
526   Nakat
533   Tusha
535   Aysberg
551   Liven
555   Geyzer
560   Zyb
570   Passat
590   Meteor
615   Bora
616   Samum
617   Mirazh
620   Shtyl

Mine Warfare Forces

718   MT 265
738   MT 264
762   V Gumavenko
770   Valentin Pikul
—   Vitse admiral Zacharin
806   Motorist
831   Kommendor
855   Kontradmiral Vlasov
901   A Zheleznyakov

Mine Warfare Forces—*continued*

909   Vitse admiral Zhukov
911   N K Golubets
912   Turbinist
913   Kovrovets
919   Snayper

Amphibious Forces

012   Olenegorskiy Gorniak
016   Georgiy Pobedonosets
020   Mitrofan Moskalenko
027   Kondopoga
031   Alexander Otrakovskiy
055   BDK-98
066   Mukhtar Avezov
077   Nikolay Korsakov
081   Nikolay Vilkov
102   Kaliningrad
110   Alexander Shabalin
119   Minsk
127   Minsk
130   Korolev
148   Orsk
150   Saratov
151   Azov
152   Nikolay Filchenkov
156   Yamal
158   Tsesar Kunikov

Auxiliaries

SFP 177 Akademik Isanin
SFP 183 Akademir Seminikhin
200   Perekop
208   Sevan
210   Smolny
212   Yamal
506   Dauriya
SB 921   Paradoks
SB 922   Shakhter

Intelligence Collection Ships

—   Yuri Ivanov
GS 39   Syzran
SSV 080 Pribaltika
SSV 169 Tavriya
SSV 175 Odograf
SSV 201 Priazove
SSV 208 Kurily
SSV 231 Vassily Tatischev
SSV 418 Ekvator
SSV 506 Nakhoda
SSV 512 Kildin
SSV 520 Meridian
SSV 535 Kareliya
SSV 571 Belomore
SSV 824 Liman

SUBMARINES

Notes: Temporary pennant numbers are shown on the fins of some submarines.

NOVOMOSKOVSK

6/2003, B Lemachko / 1121441

Strategic Missile Submarines (SSBN)

Notes: A Borey (Project 955) class submarine *Yuri Dolgoruky* was laid down on 2 November 1996. The plan was to fit a new strategic missile SS-NX-28. When, following three unsuccessful tests, this missile programme was cancelled in 1998, construction of the boat slowed and may have stopped while development of a new missile, a navalised version of the SS-27 Topol-M (known as SS-NX-30 'Bulava')

was undertaken. A full test launch of the missile was made on 27 September 2005 from the Typhoon class SSBN, *Dmitriy Donskoy*. This was an unusual event in that it was not preceded by a land-launch. The first underwater launch was successfully conducted on 21 December 2005. It is also expected that *Yuri Dolgoruky*, the original design of which is likely to have been modified to accommodate 12 of the

smaller 47 tonne 'Bulava', is to be launched in late 2006. The second of class, *Alexander Nevsky*, was laid down at the Sevmash plant in Severodvinsk on 19 March 2004 and is due to be launched in 2007. The third of class, *Vladimir Monomakh* was laid down on 19 March 2006. Overall, a force level of up to 8-10 SSBNs is likely to be maintained after the retirement of the Delta III class.

3 TYPHOON (AKULA) CLASS (PROJECT 941/941U) (SSBN)

Name	No	Builders	Laid down	Launched	Commissioned
DMITRIY DONSKOY	TK 208	Severodvinsk Shipyard	30 June 1976	23 Sep 1979	12 Dec 1981
ARKHANGELSK	TK 17	Severodvinsk Shipyard	24 Feb 1985	Aug 1986	6 Nov 1987
SEVERSTAL	TK 20	Severodvinsk Shipyard	6 Jan 1986	July 1988	4 Sep 1989

Displacement, tons: 18,500 surfaced; 26,500 dived
Dimensions, feet (metres): 562.7 oa; 541.3 wl × 80.7 × 42.7 *(171.5; 165 × 24.6 × 13)*
Main machinery: Nuclear; 2 VM-5 PWR; 380 MW; 2 GT3A turbines; 81,600 hp(m) *(60 MW)*; 2 emergency motors; 517 hp(m) *(380 kW)*; 2 shafts; shrouded props; 2 thrusters (bow and stern); 2,860 hp(m) *(1.5 MW)*
Speed, knots: 25 dived; 12 surfaced
Complement: 175 (55 officers)

Missiles: SLBM: 20 Makeyev SS-N-20 (RSM 52/3M20) Sturgeon; three-stage solid fuel rocket; stellar inertial guidance to 8,300 km *(4,500 n miles)*; warhead nuclear 10 MIRV each of 200 kT; CEP 500 m. 2 missiles can be fired in 15 seconds.
SAM: SA-N-8 SAM capability when surfaced.
A/S: Novator SS-N-15 Starfish; inertial flight to 45 km *(24.3 n miles)*; warhead nuclear 200 kT or Type 40 torpedo.
Torpedoes: 6−21 in *(533 mm)* tubes. Combination of torpedoes (see table at front of section). The weapon load includes a total of 22 torpedoes and A/S missiles.
Mines: Could be carried in lieu of torpedoes.
Countermeasures: Decoys: MG 34/44 tube launched decoys.

ESM: Rim Hat (Nakat M); radar warning. Park Lamp D/F.
Weapons control: 3R65 data control system.
Radars: Surface search: Snoop Pair (Albatros); I/J-band.
Sonars: Shark Gill; hull-mounted; passive/active search and attack; low/medium frequency.
Shark Rib flank array; passive; low frequency.
Mouse Roar; hull-mounted; active attack; high frequency.
Pelamida towed array; passive search; very low frequency.

Modernisation: First of class TK 208 started refit at Severodvinsk in 1994, was relaunched on 26 June 2002 and started sea trials in August 2004. It conducted the first submerged test launch of the Bulava missile on 21 December 2005 and is expected to remain in service as an operational unit. TK 17 and TK 20 may be similarly converted to accommodate the Bulava missile in order to remain in service beyond 2010.
Structure: This is the largest type of submarine ever built. Two separate 7.2 m diameter hulls covered by a single outer free-flood hull with anechoic Cluster Guard tiles plus separate 6 m diameter pressure-tight compartments in the fin and fore-ends. There is a 1.2 m separation

between the outer and inner hulls along the sides. The unique features of Typhoon are her enormous size and the fact that the missile tubes are mounted forward of the fin. The positioning of the launch tubes mean a fully integrated weapons area in the bow section leaving space abaft the fin for the provision of two nuclear reactors, one in each hull. The fin configuration indicates a designed capability to break through ice cover up to 3 m thick; the retractable forward hydroplanes, the rounded hull and the shape of the fin are all related to under-ice operations. Diving depth, 1,000 ft *(300 m)*.
Operational: Strategic targets are within range from anywhere in the world. Two VLF/ELF communication buoys are fitted. VLF navigation system for under-ice operations. Pert Spring SATCOM mast, Cod Eye radiometric sextant and Kremmny 2 IFF. All based in the Northern Fleet at Litsa Guba. Of six boats completed, the second and third, TK 202 and TK 12 have been formally decommissioned while the fourth of class TK 13 is expected to follow. TK 17 was damaged by fire during a missile loading accident in 1991 but was subsequently repaired. Old hulls are being disposed of under the Co-operative Threat Reduction Programme.

SEVERSTAL

1/1997 / 0081639

6 DELTA IV (DELFIN) CLASS (PROJECT 667BDRM) (SSBN)

Name	No	Builders	Laid down	Launched	Commissioned
VERCHOTURE	K 51	Severodvinsk Shipyard	23 Feb 1981	Jan 1984	29 Dec 1984
EKATERINBURG	K 84	Severodvinsk Shipyard	Nov 1983	Dec 1984	Feb 1985
TULA	K 114	Severodvinsk Shipyard	Dec 1985	Sep 1986	Jan 1987
BRIANSK	K 117	Severodvinsk Shipyard	Sep 1986	Sep 1987	Mar 1988
KARELIA	K 18	Severodvinsk Shipyard	Sep 1987	Nov 1988	Sep 1989
NOVOMOSKOVSK	K 407	Severodvinsk Shipyard	Nov 1988	Oct 1989	1991

Displacement, tons: 10,800 surfaced; 13,500 dived
Dimensions, feet (metres): 544.6 oa; 518.4 wl × 39.4 × 28.5 *(166; 158 × 12 × 8.7)*
Main machinery: Nuclear; 2 VM-4 PWR; 180 MW; 2 GT3A-365 turbines; 37,400 hp(m) *(27.5 MW)*; 2 emergency motors; 612 hp(m) *(450 kW)*; 2 shafts
Speed, knots: 24 dived; 14 surfaced
Complement: 130 (40 officers)

Missiles: SLBM: 16 Makeyev SS-N-23 (RSM 54) Skiff (Shtil); 3-stage liquid fuel rocket; stellar inertial guidance to 8,300 km *(4,500 n miles)*; warhead nuclear 4-10 MIRV each of 100 kT; CEP 500 m. Same diameter as SS-N-18 but longer.
A/S: Novator SS-N-15 Starfish; inertial flight to 45 km *(24.3 n miles)*; warhead nuclear 200 kT or Type 40 torpedo.
Torpedoes: 4—21 in *(533 mm)* tubes. Combination of 53 cm torpedoes (see table at front of section). Total of 18 weapons.
Countermeasures: ESM: Brick Pulp/Group; radar warning. Park Lamp D/F.
Radars: Surface search: Snoop Tray; I-band.

Sonars: Shark Gill; hull-mounted; passive/active search and attack; low/medium frequency.
Shark Hide flank array; passive; low frequency.
Mouse Roar; hull-mounted; active attack; high frequency.
Pelamida towed array; passive search; very low frequency.

Programmes: Construction first ordered 10 December 1975. This programme completed in late 1990 and included seven boats.
Modernisation: Tests of the modified SS-N-23 missile, known as Sineva, were conducted from K 84 during 2004. It is expected to be fitted to the later boats of the class.
Structure: A slim fitting is sited on the after fin which is reminiscent of a similar tube in one of the November class in the early 1980s. This is a dispenser for a sonar thin line towed array. The other distinguishing feature, apart from the size being greater than Delta III, is the pressure-tight fitting on the after end of the missile tube housing, which may be a TV camera to monitor communications

buoy and wire retrieval operations. This is not fitted in all of the class. Brick Spit optronic mast. Diving depth, 1,300 ft *(400 m)*. The outer casing has a continuous acoustic coating and fewer free flood holes than the Delta III.
Operational: Two VLF/ELF communication buoys. Navigation systems include SATNAV, SINS, Cod Eye. Pert Spring SATCOM. A modified and more accurate version of SS-N-23 was tested at sea in 1988 bringing the CEP down from 900 to 500 m. These improvements are likely to be incorporated in the 'Sineva' missile, which is planned to be fitted throughout the class. Missile launch is conducted at keel depth 55 m and at a speed of 6 kt.
All operational units based in the Northern Fleet at Saida Guba. Long refits have been completed as follows: K 51 (1999); K 84 (2002); K 114 (2005). K 117 started refit at Severodvinsk in 2002 but is unlikely to be completed until 2007 due to funding difficulties. The refit of K 18 has been similarly delayed and it is possible that K 407 will not now be refitted. K 64 has been paid off, although such a young hull has the potential to be re-roled for other tasks. K 407 launched a German commercial satellite on 7 July 1998 from the Barents Sea.

DELTA IV   *6/2003, B Lemachko* / 1042306

KARELIA and VERCHOTURE   *9/2000, B Lemachko* / 0126226

6 DELTA III (KALMAR) CLASS (PROJECT 667BDR) (SSBN)

Name	No	Builders	Laid down	Launched	Commissioned
BORISOGLEBSK	K 44	Severodvinsk Shipyard	23 Feb 1977	Aug 1977	Apr 1978
RYAZAN	K 496	Severodvinsk Shipyard	May 1978	Sep 1978	Aug 1979
ZELENOGRAD	K 506	Severodvinsk Shipyard	Sep 1978	Mar 1979	Nov 1979
PETROPAVLOSK KAMCHATSKY	K 211	Severodvinsk Shipyard	Apr 1979	Dec 1979	Aug 1980
PODOLSK	K 223	Severodvinsk Shipyard	Nov 1979	Apr 1980	25 Dec 1980
SYVATOY GIORGIY POBEDONOSETS	K 433	Severodvinsk Shipyard	Apr 1980	Nov 1980	Aug 1981

DELTA III
6/1998, S Breyer
0081641

Displacement, tons: 10,550 surfaced; 13,250 dived
Dimensions, feet (metres): 524.9 oa; 498.7 wl × 39.4 × 28.5 *(160; 152 × 12 × 8.7)*
Main machinery: Nuclear; 2 VM-4 PWR; 180 MW; 2 GT3A-635 turbines; 37,400 hp(m) *(27.5 MW)*; 2 emergency motors; 612 hp(m) *(450 kW)*; 2 shafts
Speed, knots: 24 dived; 14 surfaced
Complement: 130 (20 officers)

Missiles: SLBM: 16 Makeyev SS-N-18 (RSM 50) Stingray (Volna); 2-stage liquid fuel rocket with post boost vehicle (PBV); stellar inertial guidance; 3 variants:
Mod 1; range 6,500 km *(3,500 n miles)*; warhead nuclear 3 MIRV each of 200 kT; CEP 900 m.
Mod 2; range 8,000 km *(4,320 n miles)*; warhead nuclear 450 kT; CEP 900 m.
Mod 3; range 6,500 km *(3,500 n miles)*; warhead nuclear 7 MIRV 100 kT; CEP 900 m.
Mods 1 and 3 were the first MIRV SLBMs in Soviet service.
Torpedoes: 4—21 in *(533 mm)* and 2—400 mm tubes. Combination of torpedoes (see table at front of section). Total of 16 weapons.
Countermeasures: ESM: Brick Pulp/Group; radar warning. Park Lamp D/F.
Radars: Surface search: Snoop Tray; I-band.
Sonars: Shark Teeth; hull-mounted; passive/active search and attack; low/medium frequency.
Shark Hide flank array; passive; low frequency.
Mouse Roar; hull-mounted; active attack; high frequency.
Pelamida towed array; passive search; very low frequency.

Modernisation: The dispenser tube on the after fin has been fitted to most of the class. It was planned to retrofit SS-N-23 but this was shelved.
Structure: The missile casing is higher than in Delta I class to accommodate SS-N-18 missiles which are longer than the SS-N-8. The outer casing has a continuous 'acoustic' coating but is less streamlined and has more free flood holes than the Delta IV. Brick Spit optronic mast. Diving depth, 1,050 ft *(320 m)*.
Operational: ELF/VLF communications with floating aerial and buoy; UHF and SHF aerials. Navigation equipment includes Cod Eye radiometric sextant, SATNAV, SINS and Omega. Pert Spring SATCOM. Kremmny 2 IFF. Of the 14 hulls completed, the first of class (K 441) paid of in 1996, three more in 1997 and another two by 1999. Four of these (K 449, K 455, K 487 and K 490) are laid up in fleet bases. The operational state of the remaining six has been variously reported but it must be assumed that they can still fire missiles. K 211 is reported to have test-fired an SS-N-18 on 2 September 2003. K 44 and K 496 are based at Saida Guba in the Northern Fleet and remainder at Tarya Bay in the Pacific. The last hull of the class K 129 converted to a DSRV carrier with missile tubes removed. It is expected that the whole class is likely to have been decommissioned by about 2010.

DELTA III

12/2005*, Ships of the World / 1151151

Attack Submarines (SSN/SSGN)

Notes: (1) Attack submarines are coated with Cluster Guard anechoic tiles. All submarines are capable of laying mines from their torpedo tubes. All SSNs are fitted with non-acoustic environmental sensors for measuring discontinuities caused by the passage of a submarine in deep water.
(2) The cost of recovering the wreck of *Kursk* is estimated to have been of the order of US$100 million.

0 + 1 YASEN CLASS (PROJECT 885) (SSN/SSGN)

Name	No	Builders	Laid down	Launched	Commissioned
SEVERODVINSK	K 329	Severodvinsk Shipyard	21 Dec 1993	2006	2008

Displacement, tons: 5,900 surfaced; 8,600 dived
Dimensions, feet (metres): 364.2 × 39.4 × 27.6 *(111 × 12 × 8.4)*
Main machinery: Nuclear; 1 PWR; 195 MW; 2 GT3A turbines; 43,000 hp(m) *(31.6 MW)*; 1 shaft; pump-jet propulsor; 2 spinners
Speed, knots: 28 dived; 17 surfaced
Complement: 80 (30 officers)

Missiles: SLCM/SSM: Novator Alfa SS-N-27.
8 VLS launchers in after casing. Total of 24 missiles.
A/S: SS-N-15. Fired from torpedo tubes.

Torpedoes: 8—21 in *(533 mm)* tubes. Inclined outwards. Total of about 30 weapons.
Countermeasures: ESM: Radar warning.
Radars: Surface search: I-band.
Sonars: Irtysh Amfora system includes bow-mounted spherical array; passive/active search and attack; low frequency.
Flank and towed arrays; passive; very low frequency.

Programmes: Malakhit design. Confirmed building in 1993. Reported plans were for seven of the class to replace the Victor III class. While it was initially reported that these were to be multipurpose SSNs derived from the Akula II class, delays in the the programme suggest that there has been considerable scope for re-design and/or technical upgrade. The building of a second of class has been reported but not confirmed.
Structure: Some of the details given are speculative. VLS launchers for SSMs, canted torpedo tubes and spherical bow sonars are all new to Russian designs.

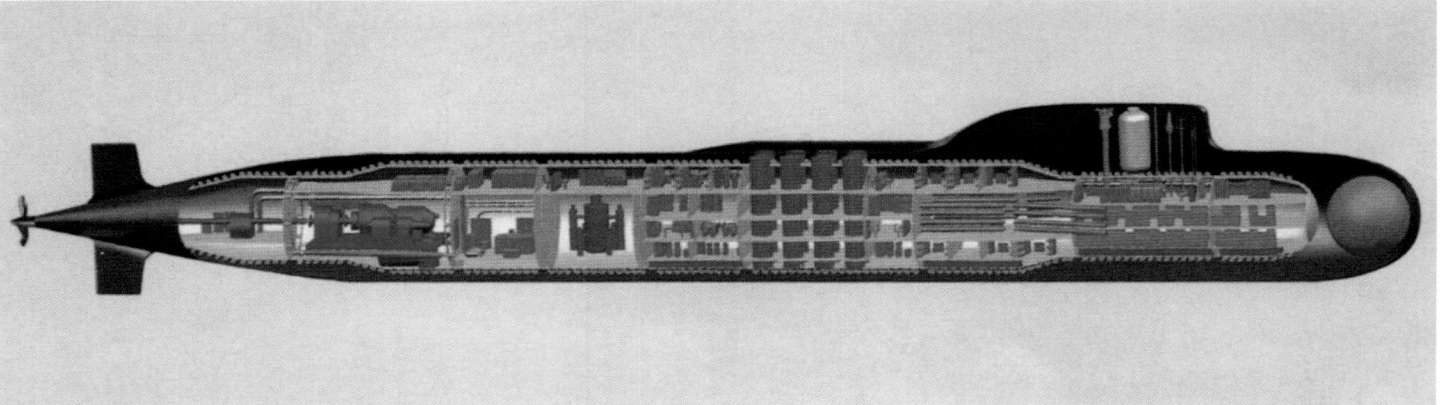

SEVERODVINSK

1996, US Navy / 0019006

2 SIERRA II (KONDOR) CLASS (PROJECT 945B) (SSN)

Name	No	Builders	Laid down	Launched	Commissioned
PSKOV (ex-*Okun*)	K 336	Nizhny Novgorod	May 1990	June 1992	12 Aug 1993
NIZHNY NOVGOROD (ex-*Zubatka*)	K 534	Nizhny Novgorod	June 1986	June 1988	28 Dec 1990

Displacement, tons: 7,600 surfaced; 9,100 dived
Dimensions, feet (metres): 364.2 × 46.6 × 28.9
    (111 × 14.2 × 8.8)
Main machinery: Nuclear; 1 VM-5 PWR; 190 MW; 1 GT3A
    turbine; 47,500 hp(m) *(70 MW)*; 2 emergency motors;
    2,004 hp(m) *(1.5 MW)*; 1 shaft; 2 spinners; 1,006 hp(m)
    (740 kW)
Speed, knots: 32 dived; 10 surfaced
Complement: 61 (31 officers)

Missiles: SLCM: Raduga SS-N-21 Sampson (Granat) fired
    from 21 in *(533 mm)* tubes; land-attack; inertial/terrain-
    following to 3,000 km *(1,620 n miles)* at 0.7 Mach;
    warhead nuclear 200 kT. CEP 150 m. Flies at a height of
    about 200 m.
SAM: SA-N-5/8 Strela portable launcher; 12 missiles.

A/S: Novator SS-N-15 Starfish (Tsakra) fired from 53 cm
    tubes; inertial flight to 45 km *(24.3 n miles)*; warhead
    nuclear 200 kT or Type 40 torpedo.
    Novator SS-N-16 Stallion fired from 65 cm tubes; inertial
    flight to 100 km *(54 n miles)*; payload nuclear 200 kT
    (Vodopad) or Type 40 torpedo (Veder).
Torpedoes: 4—25.6 in *(650 mm)* and 4—21 in *(533 mm)*
    tubes. Combination of 65 and 53 cm torpedoes (see table
    at front of section). Total of 40 weapons.
Mines: 42 in lieu of torpedoes.
Countermeasures: ESM: Rim Hat; intercept. Park Lamp D/F.
Radars: Surface search: Snoop Pair with back-to-back ESM
    aerial.
Sonars: Shark Gill; hull-mounted; passive/active search
    and attack; low/medium frequency.
    Shark Rib flank array; passive; low frequency.

Mouse Roar; hull-mounted; active attack; high frequency.
Skat 3 towed array; passive; very low frequency.

Programmes: A third of class K 536 *Mars,* was scrapped
    before completion in July 1992.
Structure: Titanium hull. The towed communications buoy has
    been recessed. A 10 point environmental sensor is fitted at
    the front end of the fin. The standoff distance between hulls
    is considerable and has obvious advantages for radiated
    noise reduction and damage resistance. Diving depth,
    2,460 ft *(750 m)*. Numbers and sizes of torpedo tubes are
    uncertain with different figures given by Russian sources.
    There are seven watertight compartments.

Operational: Based in the Northern Fleet, at Ara Guba.
    K 534 returned to service in 2003.

SIERRA II   6/1997 / 0019009

SIERRA II   8/1998 / 0050009

PSKOV (with KOSTROMA (Sierra I))   6/2002, B Lemachko / 0570928

5 VICTOR III (SCHUKA) CLASS (PROJECT 671 RTMK) (SSN)

Name	No	Builders	Laid down	Launched	Commissioned
PERM	B 292	Admiralty, Leningrad	15 Apr 1986	29 Apr 1987	27 Nov 1987
SNEZHNOGORSK (ex-*Petrozavodsk*)	B 388	Admiralty, Leningrad	8 Sep 1987	3 June 1988	30 Nov 1988
OBNINSK	B 138	Admiralty, Leningrad	7 Dec 1988	5 Aug 1989	10 May 1990
DANIL MOSKOVSKIY	B 414	Admiralty, Leningrad	1 Dec 1988	31 Aug 1990	30 Dec 1990
TAMBOV	B 448	Admiralty, Leningrad	31 Jan 1991	17 Oct 1991	24 Sep 1992

Displacement, tons: 4,850 surfaced; 6,300 dived
Dimensions, feet (metres): 351.1 × 34.8 × 24.3
  (107 × 10.6 × 7.4)
Main machinery: Nuclear; 2 VM-4 PWR; 150 MW; 2 turbines; 31,000 hp(m) *(22.7 MW)*; 1 shaft; 2 spinners; 1,020 hp(m) *(750 kW)*
Speed, knots: 30 dived; 10 surfaced
Complement: 98 (17 officers)

Missiles: SLCM: Raduga SS-N-21 Sampson (Granat) fired from 21 in *(533 mm)* tubes; land-attack; inertial/terrain-following to 3,000 km *(1,620 n miles)* at 0.7 Mach. CEP 150 m or Novator Alfa SS-N-27 (B 244 only); to 180 km *(97 n miles)*; warhead 200 kg.
A/S: Novator SS-N-15 Starfish (Tsakra) fired from 53 cm tubes; inertial flight to 45 km *(24.3 n miles)*; Type 40 torpedo.
  Novator SS-N-16 Stallion fired from 65 cm tubes; inertial flight to 100 km *(54 n miles)*; payload nuclear 200 kT (Vodopad) or Type 40 torpedo (Veder).

Torpedoes: 4—21 in *(533 mm)* and 2—25.6 in *(650 mm)* tubes. Combination of 53 and 65 cm torpedoes (see table at front of section). Can carry up to 24 weapons. Liners can be used to reduce 650 mm tubes to 533 mm.
Mines: Can carry 36 in lieu of torpedoes.
Countermeasures: ESM: Brick Group (Brick Spit and Brick Pulp); intercept. Park Lamp D/F.
Radars: Surface search: Snoop Tray 2; I-band.
Sonars: Shark Gill; hull-mounted; passive/active search and attack; low/medium frequency.
  Shark Rib flank array; passive; low frequency.
  Mouse Roar; hull-mounted; active attack; high frequency.
  Scat 3 towed array; passive; very low frequency.

Programmes: The first of class was completed at Komsomolsk in 1978. With construction also being carried out at Admiralty Yard, Leningrad, there was a very rapid building programme up to the end of 1984. Construction then continued only at Leningrad and at a rate of about one per year which terminated in 1991.

The last of the class of 26 boats completed sea trials in October 1992. Of these, the first 21 hulls were designated Type 671RTM. The final five hulls were designated Type 671RTMK to reflect modifications to fire cruise missiles. The last four of these are in service and B 292, having been named, is to be re-activated.
Structure: The streamlined pod on the stern fin is a towed sonar array dispenser. Water environment sensors are mounted at the front of the fin and on the forward casing as in the Akula and Sierra classes. Diving depth, 1,300 ft *(400 m)*.
Operational: VLF communications buoy. VHF/UHF aerials. Navigation equipment includes SINS and SATNAV. Pert Spring SATCOM. Kremmny 2 IFF. Much improved acoustic quietening puts the radiated noise levels at the upper limits of the USN Los Angeles class. All remaining operational units are based in the Northern Fleet at Litsa South or Ara Guba although they rarely go to sea. Twenty two have paid off so far although up to nine of these are in reserve and laid up at anchorages in both Fleets.

VICTOR III   *2000, B Lemachko* / 0126230

DANIL MOSKOVSKY   *7/2004* / 1042331

7 + 1 OSCAR II (ANTYEY) (PROJECT 949B) (SSGN)

Name	No	Builders	Laid down	Launched	Commissioned
VORONEZH	K 119	Severodvinsk Shipyard	1984	1986	1988
SMOLENSK	K 410	Severodvinsk Shipyard	1986	1988	1990
CHELIABINSK	K 442	Severodvinsk Shipyard	1987	1989	29 Dec 1990
VILYACHINSK	K 456	Severodvinsk Shipyard	1988	1990	1991
OREL (ex-Severodvinsk)	K 266	Severodvinsk Shipyard	1989	22 May 1992	Dec 1992
OMSK	K 186	Severodvinsk Shipyard	1990	8 May 1993	15 Dec 1993
TOMSK	K 526	Severodvinsk Shipyard	1993	18 July 1996	28 Feb 1997
BELGOROD	K 139	Severodvinsk Shipyard	1994	2006	2008

Displacement, tons: 13,900 surfaced; 18,300 dived
Dimensions, feet (metres): 505.2 × 59.7 × 29.5
    (154 × 18.2 × 9)
Main machinery: Nuclear; 2 VM-5 PWR; 380 MW; 2 GT3A
    turbines; 98,000 hp(m) *(72 MW)*; 2 shafts; 2 spinners
Speed, knots: 28 dived; 15 surfaced
Complement: 107 (48 officers)

Missiles: SSM: 24 Chelomey SS-N-19 Shipwreck (Granit);
    inertial with command update guidance; active radar
    homing to 20—550 km *(10.8—300 n miles)* at 2.5 Mach;
    warhead 750 kg HE or 500 kT nuclear. Novator Alfa SS-N-27
    may be carried in due course.
A/S: Novator SS-N-15 Starfish (Tsakra) fired from 53 cm
    tubes; inertial flight to 45 km *(24.3 n miles)*; warhead
    nuclear 200 kT or Type 40 torpedo.
    Novator SS-N-16 Stallion fired from 65 cm tubes; inertial
    flight to 100 km *(54 n miles)*; payload nuclear 200 kT
    (Vodopad) or Type 40 torpedo (Veder).
Torpedoes: 4—21 in *(533 mm)* and 2—26 in *(650 mm)*
    tubes. Combination of 65 and 53 cm torpedoes (see table
    at front of section). Total of 28 weapons including tube-
    launched A/S missiles.

Mines: 32 can be carried.
Countermeasures: ESM: Rim Hat; intercept.
Weapons control: Punch Bowl for third party targeting.
Radars: Surface search: Snoop Pair or Snoop Half; I-band.
Sonars: Shark Gill; hull-mounted; passive/active search
    and attack; low/medium frequency.
    Shark Rib flank array; passive; low frequency.
    Mouse Roar; hull-mounted; active attack; high
    frequency.
    Pelamida towed array; passive search; very low
    frequency.

Programmes: Building of a class of 14 began in 1978.
    Two Oscar Is and 11 Oscar IIs were completed. Work
    on the 12th Oscar II (K 139, *Belgorod*) was thought
    to have stopped but it was announced by the Defence
    Minister on 16 July 2004 that the boat would be
    completed although funding of the project remains
    problematical.
Modernisation: Replacement of the SS-N-19 missiles is
    reported to be under consideration.
Structure: SSM missile tubes are in banks of 12 either
    side and external to the 8.5 m diameter pressure

hull; they are inclined at 40° with one hatch covering
each pair, the whole resulting in the very large
beam. The position of the missile tubes provides a
large gap of some 4 m between the outer and inner
hulls. Diving depth, 1,000 ft *(300 m)* although
2,000 ft *(600 m)* is claimed. There are 10 watertight
compartments.
Operational: ELF/VLF communications buoy. All have
a tube on the rudder fin as in Delta IV which is
used for dispensing a thin line towed sonar array.
Pert Spring SATCOM. K 119, K 410 and K 266
are based at Litsa South in the Northern Fleet and
K 442, K 186, K 526 and K 456 at Tarya Bay in the
Pacific. In 1999 one Northern Fleet unit deployed
for the first Russian SSGN patrol in the Mediterranean
for ten years. At the same time a Pacific Fleet unit
sailed to the western seaboard of the United States.
The two Oscar Is (K 206 and K 525) are laid up in the
Northern Fleet. K 148, K 173 and K 132 are laid up
awaiting disposal and K 141 *(Kursk)* sunk as the result
of an internal weapon explosion on 12 August 2000.
The submarine was raised in late 2001 and broken
up ashore.

OSCAR II   *11/2001, Ships of the World* / 0528392

OSCAR II   *3/2002, B Lemachko* / 0570930

VORONEZH and DANIL MOSKOVSKIY (VICTOR III)   *6/2002, B Lemachko* / 0570929

OREL   *9/2001, Ships of the World* / 0126366

OSCAR II   *8/2002, Ships of the World* / 0528336

For details of the latest updates to *Jane's Fighting Ships* online and to discover the additional
information available exclusively to online subscribers please visit
jfs.janes.com

10 + 2 AKULA (BARS) CLASS (PROJECT 971/971U/09710) (SSN)

Name	No	Builders	Laid down	Launched	Commissioned
KASHALOT	K 322	Komsomolsk Shipyard	1983	1985	1986
MAGADAN (ex-Narwhal)	K 331	Komsomolsk Shipyard	1984	1986	1990
PANTERA	K 317	Severodvinsk Shipyard	Nov 1986	May 1990	30 Dec 1990
VOLK	K 461	Severodvinsk Shipyard	1986	11 June 1991	30 Dec 1991
KUZBASS (ex-Morzh)	K 419	Komsomolsk Shipyard	1984	1989	1991
LEOPARD	K 328	Severodvinsk Shipyard	Oct 1988	28 July 1992	Dec 1992
TIGR	K 154	Severodvinsk Shipyard	1989	10 June 1993	Dec 1993
SAMARA (ex-Drakon)	K 295	Komsomolsk Shipyard	1985	15 July 1994	29 July 1995
NERPA	K 152	Komsomolsk Shipyard	1986	May 1994	2006
VEPR (II)	K 157	Severodvinsk Shipyard	1991	10 Dec 1994	Dec 1995
GEPARD (II)	K 335	Severodvinsk Shipyard	1991	18 Aug 1999	29 July 2001
COUGAR (II)	K 337	Severodvinsk Shipyard	1993	2006	2007

Displacement, tons: 7,500 surfaced; 9,100 (9,500 Akula II) dived

Dimensions, feet (metres): 360.1 oa; 337.9 wl × 45.9 × 34.1 *(110; 103 × 14 × 10.4)*

Main machinery: Nuclear; 1 VM-5 PWR; 190 MW; 2 GT3A turbines; 47,600 hp(m) *(35 MW)*; 2 emergency propulsion motors; 750 hp(m) *(552 kW)*; 1 shaft; 2 spinners; 1,006 hp(m) *(740 kW)*

Speed, knots: 28 dived; 10 surfaced

Complement: 62 (31 officers)

Missiles: SLCM/SSM: Reduga SS-N-21 Sampson (Granat) fired from 21 in *(533 mm)* tubes; land-attack; inertial/terrain-following to 3,000 km *(1,620 n miles)* at 0.7 Mach; warhead nuclear 200 kT. CEP 150 m. Flies at a height of about 200 m.
Novator Alfa SS-N-27 subsonic flight with supersonic boost for terminal flight; 180 km *(97 mm)*; warhead 200 kg. May be fitted in due course.
SAM: SA-N-5/8 Strela portable launcher. 18 missiles.
A/S: Novator SS-N-15 Starfish (Tsakra) fired from 53 cm tubes; inertial flight to 45 km *(24.3 n miles)*; warhead nuclear 200 kT or Type 40 torpedo.
Novator SS-N-16 Stallion fired from 650 mm tubes; inertial flight to 100 km *(54 n miles)*; payload nuclear 200 kT (Vodopad) or Type 40 torpedo (Veder).

Torpedoes: 4—21 in *(533 mm)* and 4—25.6 in *(650 mm)* tubes. Combination of 53 and 65 cm torpedoes (see table at front of section). Tube liners can be used to reduce the larger diameter tubes to 533 mm. Total of 40 weapons. In addition the Improved Akulas and Akula IIs have six additional 533 mm external tubes in the upper bow area.

Countermeasures: ESM: Rim Hat; intercept.

Radars: Surface search: Snoop Pair or Snoop Half with back-to-back aerials on same mast as ESM.

Sonars: Shark Gill (Skat MGK 503); hull-mounted; passive/active search and attack; low/medium frequency.
Mouse Roar; hull-mounted; active attack; high frequency.
Skat 3 towed array; passive; very low frequency.

Programmes: Malakhit design. From K 461 onwards, the Akula Is were 'improved'. K 157 was the first Akula II to complete. Little is known of K 337; if she is under construction, she may be the last of class before the Yasen class enters service. It is possible she may be leased to the Indian Navy. However it is also possible that construction has been abandoned. Akula I K 152 has been building for 15 years at Komsomolsk but there has been speculation that she may be completed and also that she may be leased to the Indian Navy.

Structure: The very long fin is particularly notable. Has the same broad hull as Sierra and has reduced radiated noise levels by comparison with Victor III of which she is the traditional follow-on design. A number of prominent non-acoustic sensors appear on the fin leading-edge and on the forward casing in the later Akulas. The engineering standards around the bridge and casing are noticeably to a higher quality than other classes. The design has been incrementally improved with reduced noise levels, boundary layer suppression and active noise cancellation reported in the later units. The Improved hulls have an additional six external torpedo tubes and the first two Akula IIs have been lengthened by 3.7 m to incorporate further noise reduction developments. There are six watertight compartments. Operational diving depth, 1,476 ft *(450 m)*.

Operational: Pert Spring SATCOM. Both Akula IIs and the four Severodvinsk built Akula Is serve in the Northern Fleet and are based at Saida Guba and Sevr. The four Komsomolsk built Akula Is serve in the Pacific Fleet and are based at Tarya Bay. These submarines are the core units of the Russian SSN force. *Vepr* visited Brest in September 2004, the first visit by a Russian nuclear submarine to a foreign port.

VEPR   *9/2004, B Prézelin* / 1042292

VEPR (Akula II)   *9/2004, B Prézelin* / 1042291

GEPARD (Akula II)   *6/2002, S Breyer* / 0528327

AKULA II   *6/2003, B Lemachko* / 1042293

1 SIERRA I (BARRACUDA) CLASS (PROJECT 945) (SSN)

Name	No	Builders	Laid down	Launched	Commissioned
KOSTROMA (ex-*Krab*)	K 276	Nizhny Novgorod/Severodvinsk Shipyard	8 May 1982	29 June 1983	21 Sep 1984

Displacement, tons: 7,200 surfaced; 8,100 dived
Dimensions, feet (metres): 351 × 41 × 28.9
  (107 × 12.5 × 8.8)
Main machinery: Nuclear; 1 VM-5 PWR; 190 MW; 1 GT3A
  turbine; 47,500 hp(m) *(70 MW)*; 2 emergency motors;
  2,004 hp(m) *(1.5 MW)*; 1 shaft; 2 spinners; 1,006 hp(m)
  (740 kW)
Speed, knots: 34 dived; 10 surfaced
Complement: 61 (31 officers)

Missiles: SLCM: Raduga SS-N-21 Sampson (Granat) fired
  from 21 in *(533 mm)* tubes; land-attack; inertial/terrain-
  following to 3,000 km *(1,620 n miles)* at 0.7 Mach;
  warhead nuclear 200 kT. CEP 150 m. Probably flies at
  a height of about 200 m.
A/S: Novator SS-N-15 Starfish (Tsakra) fired from 53 cm
  tubes; inertial flight to 45 km *(24.3 n miles)*; warhead
  nuclear 200 kT or Type 40 torpedo.

Novator SS-N-16 Stallion fired from 65 cm tubes; inertial
  flight to 100 km *(54 n miles)*; payload nuclear 200 kT
  (Vodopad) or Type 40 torpedo (Veder).
Torpedoes: 4—25.6 in *(650 mm)* and 4—21 in *(533 mm)*
  tubes. Combination of 65 and 53 cm torpedoes (see table
  at front of section). Total of 40 weapons.
Mines: 42 in lieu of torpedoes.
Countermeasures: ESM: Rim Hat/Bald Head; intercept. Park
  Lamp D/F.
Radars: Surface search: Snoop Pair with back-to-back ESM
  aerial.
Sonars: Shark Gill; hull-mounted; passive/active search
  and attack; low/medium frequency.
  Shark Rib flank array; passive; low frequency.
  Mouse Roar; hull-mounted; active attack; high
  frequency.
  Skat 3 towed array; passive; very low frequency.

Programmes: Launched at Gorky (Nizhny Novgorod) and
  transferred by river/canal to be fitted out at Severodvinsk.
Structure: Based on design experience gained with
  deleted Alfa class, pressure hull constructed of
  titanium alloy, providing deep diving capability.
  Magnetic signature also reduced. Distance between
  hulls increases survivability and reduces radiated
  noise. There are six watertight compartments.
  The pod on the after fin is larger than that in
  'Victor III'. Bulbous casing at the after end of the fin
  is for a towed communications buoy. Diving depth
  2,460 ft *(750 m)*.
Operational: Pert Spring SATCOM. Based in the
  Northern Fleet at Ara Guba. It is believed that
  K 276 was in a collision with USS *Baton Rouge*
  on 11 February 1992. A second of class K 239 *Karp* is
  laid up.

KOSTROMA   *6/2002, B Lemachko* / 0547070

Patrol Submarines (SSK)

Notes: One remaining target submarine of the Bravo class is used for alongside training and one remaining modified Romeo class submarine is used for trials. Both are based in the Black Sea.

1 + 1 LADA CLASS (PROJECT 677) (SSK)

Name	No	Builders	Laid down	Launched	Commissioned
SAINT PETERSBURG	S 100	Admiralty, St Petersburg	26 Dec 1997	28 Oct 2004	2005
—	—	Admiralty, St Petersburg	26 Dec 1997	2006	2007

Displacement, tons: 1,765 surfaced; 2,650 dived
Dimensions, feet (metres): 219.2 × 23.6 × 14.4 *(66.8 × 7.2 × 4.4)*
Main machinery: Diesel-electric; 2 diesel generators; 3,400 hp(m) *(2.5 MW)*; 1 motor; 5,576 hp(m) *(4.1 MW)*; 1 shaft
Speed, knots: 21 dived; 10 surfaced
Range, n miles: 6,000 at 7 kt snorting
Complement: 37

Torpedoes: 6—21 in *(533 mm)* tubes. 18 weapons.
Mines: In lieu of torpedoes.
Countermeasures: ESM: Intercept.

Radars: Surface search: I-band.
Sonars: Hull and flank arrays; active/passive; medium frequency.

Programmes: The national variant of this submarine is known as the Lada class. Work began on the first of class in 1996 and construction started in St Petersburg in 1987. Progress has been slow but further orders are likely. The export version of the submarine is known as the Amur class of which there are six designs based on different surface displacements (550, 750, 950, 1450, 1650 and 1850). The 'Amur 1650' probably has the most export potential and it was possibly in anticipation of an order from India and China that work began on such a submarine at the same time as the similar Lada class. Although work was believed to have been temporarily suspended in 1998, it is expected that the boat will be completed and operated by the Russian Navy as a technology-demonstrator.
Structure: The first Russian single-hulled submarine, built to a Rubin design based on the 'Amur 1650'. A fuel cell plug (for AIP) of about 12 m can be inserted to allow installation of AIP although this is unlikely in the near future. Diving depth: 820 ft *(250 m)*. A non-hull penetrating optronic periscope supplied by Elektropribor, is fitted.
Operational: Sea trials started on 29 November 2005.

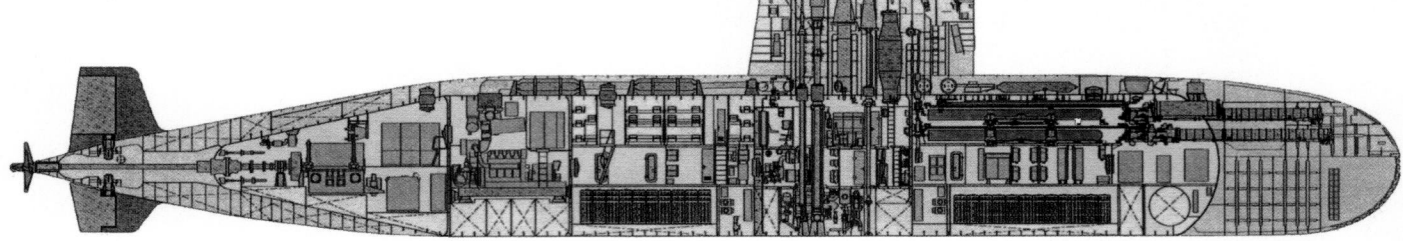

AMUR 1650 *1996, Rubin* / 0019012

SAINT PETERSBURG *6/2005*, A Sheldon-Duplaix* / 1127919

SAINT PETERSBURG *6/2005*, A Sheldon-Duplaix* / 1127920

SAINT PETERSBURG

6/2005*, A Sheldon-Duplaix / 1127918

1 TANGO (SOM) (PROJECT 641B) CLASS (SSK)

B 380

Displacement, tons: 3,100 surfaced; 3,800 dived
Dimensions, feet (metres): 298.6 × 29.9 × 23.6
(91 × 9.1 × 7.2)
Main machinery: Diesel-electric; 3 diesels (2 × 1.4 MW and
1 × 1.8 MW); 6,256 hp(m) *(4.6 MW)*; 3 motors (2 × 1 MW
and 1 × 1.8 MW); 5,168 hp(m) *(3.8 MW)*; 3 shafts
Speed, knots: 16 dived; 13 surfaced
Range, n miles: 500 at 3 kt dived; 14,000 at 7 kt snorting
Complement: 62 (12 officers)

Torpedoes: 6—21 in *(533 mm)* bow tubes. Combination of
24—53 cm torpedoes. There are no stern tubes.
Mines: In lieu of torpedoes.

Countermeasures: ESM: Squid Head or Brick Group; radar
warning. Quad Loop D/F.
Radars: Surface search: Snoop Tray; I-band.
Sonars: Shark Teeth/Shark Fin (MGK-400); hull-mounted;
passive/active search and attack; medium frequency.
Mouse Roar; hull-mounted; active attack; high frequency.

Programmes: This class was first seen at the Sevastopol
Review in July 1973. An improved variant of the Foxtrot
class, eighteen boats of the class were constructed at
Nizhniy Novgorod between 1971 and 1982 when the
programme finished.

Structure: Compared with the Foxtrot, there is a marked
increase in the internal capacity of the hull used to
improve battery capacity and habitability. Diving
depth 820 ft (250 m) normal. The casing and fin have a
continuous acoustic coating. B 437 was modified in 1992
with a towed array stern tube and reel mounted in the
casing forward of the fin. There are no stern torpedo
tubes.
Operational: This last remaining boat of the class was
thought to have been decommissioned but was reported
to be undergoing refit in the floating dock at Sevastopol
in mid-2005.

B 380 with BELUGA

7/2000, Hartmut Ehlers / 0105538

18 KILO CLASS (PROJECT 877K/877M/636) (SSK)

Name	No	Builders	Laid down	Launched	Commissioned
RAZBOYNIK	B 260	Komsomolsk Shipyard	Sep 1980	19 Aug 1981	Dec 1981
TUR	B 227	Komsomolsk Shipyard	Sep 1981	Sep 1982	Dec 1982
—	B 229	Komsomolsk Shipyard	1982	1983	1983
—	B 405	Komsomolsk Shipyard	1983	1984	Dec 1984
VOLOGDA	B 402	Nizhny Novgorod	Feb 1983	1984	27 Dec 1984
—	B 806	Nizhny Novgorod			1986
—	B 445	Komsomolsk Shipyard	1986	1987	Dec 1987
JAROSLAVL	B 808	Nizhny Novogorod			1988
KALUGA	B 800	Nizhny Novgorod			1989
UST-KAMSHATS	B 464	Komsomolsk Shipyard	1988	1988	1989
NOVOSIBIRSK	B 401*	Nizhny Novgorod	June 1988	Aug 1989	4 Jan 1990
MAGNETO-GORSK	B 471	Nizhny Novgorod			1990
UST-BOLSHERETSK	B 494	Komsomolsk Shipyard	1989	1990	1990
ALROSA	B 871	Nizhny Novgorod	May 1998	Aug 1989	Dec 1990
LIPETSK	B 177	Nizhny Novgorod			1991
—	B 187*	Komsomolsk Shipyard	1990	1990	1991
—	B 190*	Komsomolsk Shipyard	8 May 1992	1993	1993
—	B 345	Komsomolsk Shipyard	22 Apr 1993	1993	22 Jan 1994

* indicates Project 636

Displacement, tons: 2,325 surfaced; 3,076 dived
Dimensions, feet (metres): 238.2; 242.1 (Project 636) × 32.5 × 21.7 *(72.6; 73.8 × 9.9 × 6.6)*
Main machinery: Diesel-electric; Type 4-2DL-42M 2 diesels (Type 4-2AA-42M in Project 636); 3,650 hp(m) *(2.68 MW)*; 2 generators; 1 motor; 5,900 hp(m) *(4.34 MW)*; 1 shaft; 2 auxiliary MT-168 motors; 204 hp(m) *(150 kW)*; 1 economic speed motor; 130 hp(m) *(95 kW)*
Speed, knots: 17 dived; 10 surfaced; 9 snorting
Range, n miles: 6,000 at 7 kt snorting; 400 at 3 kt dived
Complement: 52 (13 officers)

Missiles: SSM: Novator Alfa SS-N-27 may be fitted in due course.
SAM: 6-8 SA-N-5/8; IR homing from 600 to 6,000 m at 1.65 Mach; warhead 2 kg; portable launcher stowed in a well in the fin between snort and W/T masts.
Torpedoes: 6—21 in *(533 mm)* tubes. 18 combinations of 53 cm torpedoes (see table at front of section). USET-80 is wire-guided in the 4B version (from 2 tubes).
Mines: 24 in lieu of torpedoes.
Countermeasures: ESM: Squid Head or Brick Pulp; radar warning. Quad Loop D/F.
Weapons control: MVU-110EM or MVU-119EM Murena torpedo fire-control system.
Radars: Surface search: Snoop Tray (MRP-25); I-band.
Sonars: Shark Teeth/Shark Fin (MGK-400); hull-mounted; passive/active search and attack; medium frequency.
Mouse Roar; hull-mounted; active attack; high frequency.

Programmes: Also known as the Vashavyanka class, first launched in 1979 at Komsomolsk and commissioned 12 September 1980. Subsequent construction also at Nizhny Novgorod. A total of 24 were built for Russia of which six were of the improved Project 636 variant.
Structure: Had a better hull form than the now deleted Tango class but was nevertheless considered fairly basic by comparison with contemporary western designs. Diving depth 790 ft *(240 m)* normal. Battery has a 9,700 kW/h capacity. The basic 'Kilo' was the Project 877; 877K has an improved fire-control system and 877M includes wire-guided torpedoes from two tubes. Project 636 is an improved design with uprated diesels, a propulsion motor rotating at half the speed (250 rpm), higher standards of noise reduction and an automated combat information system capable of providing simultaneous fire-control data on five targets. Pressure hull length is 170 ft *(51.8 m)* or 174 ft *(53 m)* for Project 636. Foreplanes on the hull are just forward of the fin. Project 636 can be identified by a vertical cut off to the after casing. B 871 has been fitted with a pump jet propulsor.
Operational: With a reserve of buoyancy of 32 per cent and a heavily compartmented pressure hull, this class is capable of being holed and still surviving. B 401, B 402, B 808, B 471, B 800 and B 177 are based in the Northern

ALROSA   *9/2004, Hartmut Ehlers* / 1042295

TUR   *8/2004, E & M Laursen* / 1042296

Fleet, B 405, B 260, B 445, B 494, B 190, B 345, B 187, B 464 and B 229 are based in the Pacific, B 806 and B 227 in the Baltic and B 871 in the Black Sea. Russian made batteries have been a source of problems in warm water operations.

Sales: Exports of Project 877 have been to Poland (one), Romania (one), India (ten), Algeria (two), Iran (three) and China (two). The only exports of Project 636 have been to China (two). A further eight were ordered by China in 2002. Export versions have the letter E after the project number.

VOLOGDA   *5/2003, Jürg Kürsener* / 0570899

Auxiliary Submarines (SSA(N))

Notes: (1) There are a number of Swimmer Delivery Vessels (SDV) in service including Siren (three-man) and Triton, Sever and Elbrus types.
(2) A new auxiliary submarine (SSAN) was launched at Severodvinsk Shipyard on 6 August 2003. Nicknamed 'Losharik', this is likely to be used for scientific research and there has been speculation that it is similar to the Uniform class. It is known both as Project 210 and as Project 10831. It has a pennant number of AS 12 and is expected to become operational in 2006.

1 DELTA III STRETCH (PROJECT 667 BDR) (SSAN)

Name	No	Builders	Laid down	Launched	Commissioned
—	K 129	Severodvinsk Shipyard	Feb 1979	Mar 1981	5 Nov 1981

Dimensions, feet (metres): 534.9 × 39.4 × 28.5 *(163 × 12 × 8.7)*
Main machinery: Nuclear: 2 VM-4 PWR; 180 MW; 2 GT 3A-635 turbines; 37,400 hp(m) *(27.5 MW)*; 2 emergency motors; 612 hp(m) *(450 kW)*; 2 shafts
Speed, knots: 24 dived 14 surfaced
Complement: 130 (40 officers)

Torpedoes: 4—21 in *(533 mm)* and 2—400 mm tubes.
Countermeasures: ESM: Brick Pulp/Group; radar warning.
Radars: Surface search: Snoop Tray; I-band.
Sonars: Shark Teeth; hull mounted; active/passive search; low/medium frequency.
Shark Hide; flank array; passive low frequency.
Mouse Roar; hull mounted; active high frequency.

Comment: Originally launched in 1981, this former SSBN has been converted by replacing the central section with a 43 m plug, extending the overall hull length by 3 m. The submarine was reported to have returned to service in 2003 and has replaced the Yankee Stretch as the Paltus mother-ship. Both submarines can operate as a mother ship for the Paltus class. Based in the Northern Fleet.

DELTA III (before conversion) *8/1997, JMSDF* / 0019003

3 UNIFORM (KACHALOT) CLASS (PROJECT 1910) (SSAN)

No	Builders	Laid down	Launched	Commissioned
AS 13	Sudomekh, Leningrad	20 Oct 1977	25 Nov 1982	31 Dec 1986
AS 16	Sudomekh, Leningrad	23 Feb 1983	29 Apr 1988	30 Dec 1991
AS 17	Sudomekh, St Petersburg	16 July 1990	26 Aug 1995	Feb 1998

Displacement, tons: 1,340 surfaced; 1,580 dived
Dimensions, feet (metres): 226.4 × 23.0 × 17.0 *(69.0 × 7.0 × 5.2)*
Main machinery: Nuclear; 1 PWR; 15 MW; 2 turbines; 10,000 hp(m) *(7.35 MW)*; 1 shaft; 2 thrusters
Speed, knots: 10 surfaced; 28 dived
Complement: 36

Radars: Navigation: Snoop Slab; I-band.

Comment: Research and development nuclear-powered submarines. Have single hulls and 'wheel' arches either side of the fin which house side thrusters. These are titanium hulled and very deep diving submarines (possibly down to 700 m *(2,300 ft)*), based in the Northern

Fleet at Olenya Guba, and are used mainly for ocean bed operations. Plans to build more of the class were thought to have been shelved. It is not clear whether an auxiliary submarine launched on 6 August 2003 is a fourth 'Uniform' or a different design.

UNIFORM *8/1996* / 0016660

3 PALTUS/X-RAY (PROJECT 1851) CLASS (SSAN/SSA)

AS 23   **AS 35**   **AS 21** (X-Ray)

Displacement, tons: 730 dived
Dimensions, feet (metres): 173.9 × 12.5 × 13.8
(53 × 3.8 × 4.2)
Main machinery: Nuclear; 1 reactor; 10 MW; 1 shaft; ducted
thrusters
Speed, knots: 6 dived
Complement: 14

Comment: Details given are for the two Paltus (Nelhma)
class (A 23, AS 35). The first was launched at Sudomekh,
St Petersburg in April 1991, a second of class in September
1994 and a third was started but not completed. This is
a follow-on to the single 520 ton X-Ray (AS 21) class
which was first seen in 1984 and after a long spell out
of service was back in operation in 1999. Paltus probably

owes much to the USN NR 1. Paltus is associated with
the Delta III Stretch SSAN which acts as a mother ship for
special operations. Titanium hulled and very deep diving
to 1,000 m *(3,280 ft)*. Paltus based in the Northern Fleet
at Olenya Guba, X-Ray at Yagri Island.

PALTUS (artist's impression)   *1994* / 0506318

AIRCRAFT CARRIERS

Notes: (1) Of the former aircraft carriers of the Kiev class, *Kiev* was sold to China for scrap in 2000; *Minsk* and *Novorossiysk* were sold to a South Korean Corporation in 1994. *Minsk*
later became a tourist attraction in Shenzen, China, while *Novorossiysk* was scrapped in India. *Admiral Gorshkov* (ex-*Baku*) and is being refitted is to be sold to the Indian Navy.
(2) The requirement for a new class of four aircraft carriers, to begin construction in 2013-14, was announced in mid-2005. The first of class would enter service in 2017
but it is not known whether this is a funded programme.

1 KUZNETSOV (OREL) CLASS (PROJECT 1143.5/6) (CVGM)

Name	No	Builders	Laid down	Launched	Commissioned
ADMIRAL KUZNETSOV (ex-*Tbilisi*, ex-*Leonid Brezhnev*)	063	Nikolayev South, Ukraine	1 Apr 1982	16 Dec 1985	25 Dec 1990

Displacement, tons: 45,900 standard; 58,500 full load
Dimensions, feet (metres): 999 oa; 918.6 wl × 229.7 oa;
121.4 wl × 34.4 *(304.5; 280 × 70; 37 × 10.5)*
Flight deck, feet (metres): 999 × 229.7 *(304.5 × 70)*
Main machinery: 8 boilers; 4 turbines; 200,000 hp(m)
(147 MW); 4 shafts
Speed, knots: 30. **Range, n miles:** 3,850 at 29 kt; 8,500 at 18 kt
Complement: 1,960 (200 officers) plus 626 aircrew plus
40 Flag staff

Missiles: SSM: 12 Chelomey SS-N-19 Shipwreck (3M-45)
launchers (flush mounted) ❶; inertial guidance with
command update; active radar homing to 20—550 km
(10.8—300 n miles) at 2.5 Mach; warhead 500 kT nuclear
or 750 kg HE.
SAM: 4 Altair SA-N-9 Gauntlet (Klinok) sextuple vertical
launchers (192 missiles) ❷; command guidance and
active radar homing to 12 km *(6.5 n miles)* at 2 Mach;
warhead 15 kg. 24 magazines; 192 missiles; 4 channels
of fire.
SAM/Guns: 8 Altair CADS-N-1 (Kortik/Kashtan) ❸; each has
a twin 30 mm Gatling combined with 8 SA-N-11 (Grisson)
and Hot Flash/Hot Spot fire-control radar/optronic
director. Laser beam-riding guidance for missiles to 8 km
(4.4 n miles); warhead 9 kg; 9,000 rds/min combined to
2 km (for guns).
Guns: 6—30 mm/65 ❹ AK 630; 6 barrels per mounting;
3,000 rds/min combined to 2 km. Probably controlled by
Hot Flash/Hot Spot on CADS-N-1.
A/S mortars: 2 RBU 12,000 ❺; range 12,000 m; warhead
80 kg. UDAV-1M; torpedo countermeasure.

Countermeasures: Decoys: 10 PK 10 and 4 PK 2 chaff
launchers.
ESM/ECM: 8 Foot Ball. 4 Wine Flask (intercept). 4 Flat Track.
10 Ball Shield A and B.
Weapons control: 3 Tin Man optronic trackers. 2 Punch
Bowl SATCOM datalink ❻. 2 Low Ball SATNAV ❼. 2 Bell
Crown and 2 Bell Push datalinks.
Radars: Air search: Sky Watch; four Planar phased
arrays ❽; 3D.
Air/surface search: Top Plate B ❾; D/E-band.
Surface search: 2 Strut Pair ❿; F-band.
Navigation: 3 Palm Frond; I-band.
Fire control: 4 Cross Sword (for SAM) ⓫; K-band. 8 Hot
Flash; J-band.
Aircraft control: 2 Fly Trap B; G/H-band.
Tacan: Cake Stand ⓬.
IFF: 4 Watch Guard.
Sonars: Bull Horn and Horse Jaw; hull-mounted; active
search and attack; medium/low frequency.

Fixed-wing aircraft: 18 Su-33 Flanker D; 4 Su-25 UTG
Frogfoot.
Helicopters: 15 Ka-27 Helix. 2 Ka-31 RLD Helix AEW.

Programmes: This was a logical continuation of the deleted
Kiev class. The full name of *Kuznetsov* is *Admiral Flota
Sovietskogo Sojuza Kuznetsov*. The second of class,
Varyag, was between 70 and 80 per cent complete by
early 1993 at Nikolayev in the Ukraine. Building was then
terminated after an unsuccessful attempt by the Navy
to fund completion. Subsequently the ship was bought

by Chinese interests and, having been towed through
the Bosporus on 2 November 2001, arrived at Dalian in
March 2002.
Structure: The hangar is 183 × 29.4 × 7.5 m and can hold
up to 18 Flanker aircraft. There are two starboard side
lifts, a ski jump of 14° and an angled deck of 7°. There are
four arrester wires. The SSM system is in the centre of
the flight deck forward with flush deck covers. The ship
has some 16.5 m of freeboard. There is no Bass Tilt radar
and the ADG guns are controlled by Kashtan fire-control
system. The ship suffers from severe water distillation
problems.
Operational: AEW, ASW and reconnaissance tasks
undertaken by Helix helicopters. The aircraft complement
listed is based on the number which might be
embarked for normal operations but the Russians claim
a top limit of 60. *Kuznetsov* conducted extensive flight
operations throughout the second half of both 1993
and 1994, and was at sea again by September 1995
after a seven month refit. Deployed to the Mediterranean
for 80 days in early 1996 before returning to the
Northern Fleet. Based alongside at Rosta from
mid-1996 to mid-1998. Sailed for a VIP demonstration
in August 1998 and then continued trials and training
in-area. There were limited local exercises in 2000
but no activity in 2001 and 2002. The ship left the
jetty for Navy Days in 2003. The ship participated
in Northern Fleet exercises in the North Atlantic in
August-September 2005 but her scope operations
remain handicapped by technical problems and financial
constraints.

ADMIRAL KUZNETSOV   *6/2003, B Lemachko* / 1042294

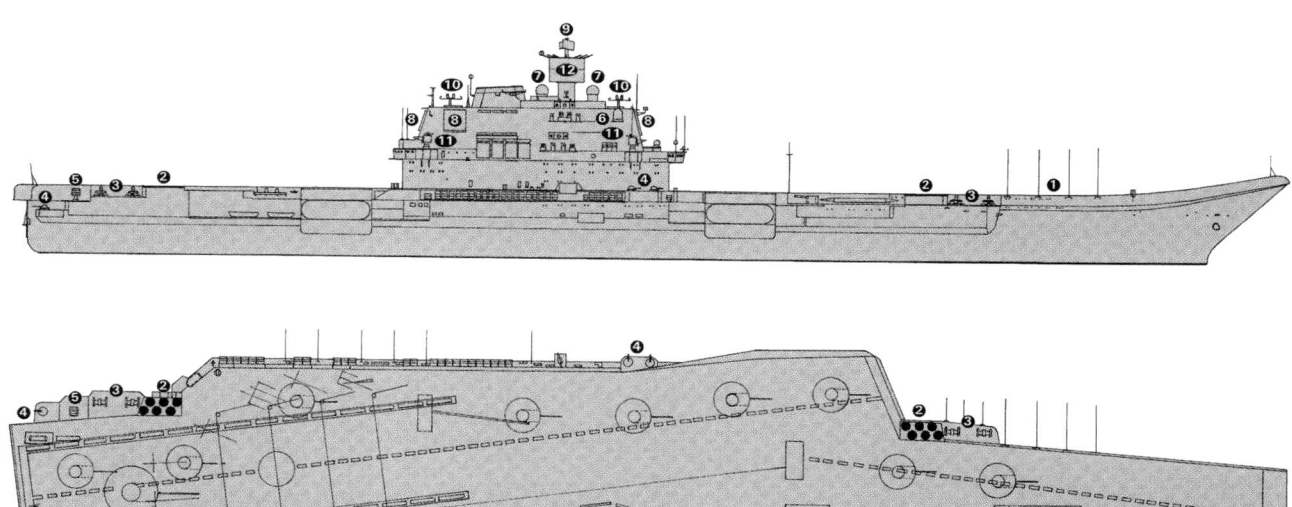

ADMIRAL KUZNETSOV
(Scale 1 : 1,800), Ian Sturton / 0506078

ADMIRAL KUZNETSOV
10/2004, Ships of the World / 1042330

ADMIRAL KUZNETSOV
10/2004* / 1151336

BATTLE CRUISERS

1 KIROV (ORLAN) CLASS (PROJECT 1144.1/1144.2) (CGHMN)

Name	No	Builders	Laid down	Launched	Commissioned
PYOTR VELIKIY (ex-*Yuri Andropov*)	099 (ex-183)	Baltic Yard 189, St Petersburg	11 Mar 1986	29 Apr 1989	9 Apr 1998

Displacement, tons: 19,000 standard; 24,300 full load
Dimensions, feet (metres): 826.8; 754.6 wl × 93.5 × 29.5
(252; 230 × 28.5 × 9.1)
Main machinery: CONAS; 2 KN-3 PWR; 300 MW; 2 oil-fired boilers; 2 GT3A-688 turbines; 140,000 hp(m) *(102.9 MW)*; 2 shafts
Speed, knots: 30
Range, n miles: 14,000 at 30 kt
Complement: 726 (82 officers) plus 18 aircrew

Missiles: SSM: 20 Chelomey SS-N-19 Shipwreck (3M 45) (P-700 Granit) (improved SS-N-12 with lower flight profile) **❶**; inertial guidance with command update; active radar homing to 20—450 km *(10.8—243 n miles)* at 1.6 Mach; warhead 350 kT nuclear or 750 kg HE; no reloads.
SAM: 12 SA-N-6/SA-N-20 Grumble (Fort/Fort M) vertical launchers **❷**; 8 rounds per launcher; command guidance; semi-active radar homing to 100 km *(54 n miles)*; warhead 90 kg (or nuclear?); 96 missiles.
2 SA-N-4 Gecko twin launchers **❸**; semi-active radar homing to 15 km *(8 n miles)* at 2.5 Mach; warhead 50 kg; altitude 9.1—3,048 m *(30—10,000 ft)*; 40 missiles.
2 SA-N-9 Gauntlet (Kinzhal) octuple vertical launchers **❹**; command guidance; active radar homing to 12 km *(6.5 n miles)* at 2 Mach; warhead 15 kg; altitude 3.4—12,192 m *(10—40,000 ft)*; 128 missiles; 4 channels of fire.
SAM/Guns: 6 CADS-N-1 (Kortik/Kashtan) **❺**; each has a twin 30 mm Gatling combined with 8 SA-N-11 (Grisson) and Hot Flash/Hot Spot fire-control radar/optronic director. Laser beam-riding guidance for missiles to 8 km *(4.4 n miles)*; warhead 9 kg; 9,000 rds/min combined to 2 km (for guns).
A/S: Novator SS-N-15 (Starfish); inertial flight to 45 km *(24.3 n miles)*; payload Type 40 torpedo or nuclear warhead; fired from fixed torpedo tubes behind shutters in the superstructure.
Guns: 2—130 mm/70 (twin) AK 130 **❻**; 35/45 rds/min to 29 km *(16 n miles)*; weight of shell 33.4 kg.
Torpedoes: 10—21 in *(533 mm)* (2 quin) tubes. Combination of 53 cm torpedoes (see table at front of section). Mounted in the hull adjacent the RBU 1000s on both quarters. Fixed tubes behind shutters can fire either SS-N-15 (see *Missiles A/S*) or Type 40 torpedoes.
A/S mortars: 1 RBU 12,000 **❼**; 10 tubes per launcher; range 12,000 m; warhead 80 kg.
2 RBU 1000 6-tubed aft **❽**; range 1,000 m; warhead 55 kg. UDAV-1M; torpedo countermeasures.
Countermeasures: Decoys: 2 twin PK 2 150 mm chaff launchers. Towed torpedo decoy.
ESM/ECM: 8 Foot Ball. 4 Wine Flask (intercept). 8 Bell Bash. 4 Bell Nip. Half Cup (laser intercept).
Combat Data Systems: Lesorub-44.
Weapons control: 4 Tin Man optronic trackers **❾**. 2 Punch Bowl C SATCOM **❿**. 4 Low Ball SATNAV. 2 Bell Crown and 2 Bell Push datalinks.
Radars: Air search: Top Pair (Top Sail + Big Net) **⓫**; 3D; C/D-band; range 366 km *(200 n miles)* for bomber, 183 km *(100 n miles)* for 2 m² target.
Air/surface search: Top Plate **⓬**; 3D; D/E-band.
Navigation: 3 Palm Frond; I-band.
Fire control: Cross Sword **⓭**; K-band (for SA-N-9). Top Dome for SA-N-6 **⓮**; Tomb Stone J-band (for Fort M) **⓯**. 2 Pop Group, F/H/I-band (for SA-N-4) **⓰**. Kite Screech **⓱**; H/I/K-band (for main guns). 6 Hot Flash for CADS-N-1; I/J-band.
Aircraft control: Flyscreen B; I-band.
IFF: Salt Pot A and B.
Tacan: 2 Round House B **⓲**.
Sonars: Horse Jaw (Polinom); hull-mounted; active search and attack; low/medium frequency.
Horse Tail; VDS; active search; medium frequency. Depth to 150-200 m *(492.1-656.2 ft)* depending on speed.

Helicopters: 3 Ka-27 Helix **⓳**.

Programmes: Design work started in 1968. Type name is *atomny raketny kreyser* meaning nuclear-powered missile cruiser. A fifth of class was scrapped before being launched in 1989.
Structure: The Kirov class were the first Russian surface warships with nuclear propulsion. In addition to the nuclear plant a unique maritime combination with an auxiliary oil-fuelled system has been installed. This provides a superheat capability, boosting the normal steam output by some 50 per cent. The SS-N-19 tubes are set at an angle of about 45°. CADS-N-1 with a central fire-control radar on six mountings, each of which has two cannon and eight missile launchers. Two are mounted either side of the SS-N-19 forward and four on the after superstructure. Same A/S system as the frigate *Neustrashimy* with fixed torpedo tubes in ports behind shutters in the superstructure for firing SS-N-15 or Type 45 torpedoes. There are reported to be about 500 SAM of different types. *Velikiy*, the only operational ship, has a Tomb Stone fire-control radar instead of a forward Top Dome for SA-N-20 which is a maritime variant of SA-10C.
Operational: Based in the Northern Fleet. Over-the-horizon targeting for SS-N-19 provided by Punch Bowl SATCOM or helicopter. The first ship of the class of four, *Admiral Ushakov*, was formally decommissioned in 2004 and is to be scrapped. The second ship, *Admiral Lazarev* has also been decommissioned and is also likely to be scrapped. Plans to refit the third ship, *Admiral Nakhimov*, laid up since 1999, appear to have been revived but funding continues to be problematical. The scope of the work includes nuclear refuelling and replacement of the SS-N-19 missile system. Work may begin in 2006.

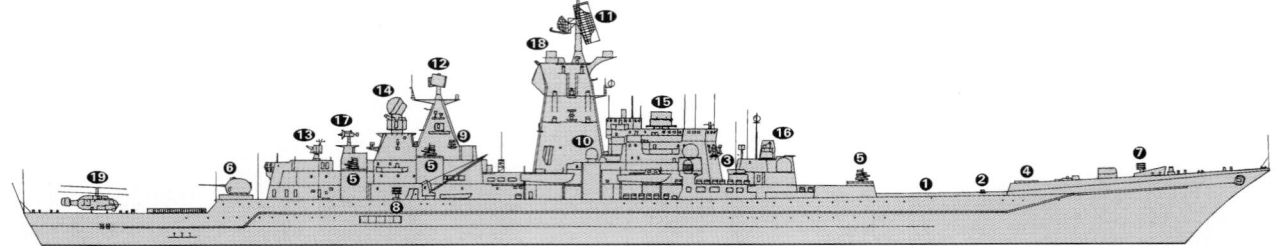

PYOTR VELIKIY   *(Scale 1 : 1,500), Ian Sturton* / 0528401

PYOTR VELIKIY   *6/2001, S Breyer* / 1042309

PYOTR VELIKIY   *10/2004** / 1151339

CRUISERS

3 SLAVA (ATLANT) CLASS (PROJECT 1164) (CGHM)

Name	No	Builders	Laid down	Launched	Commissioned
MOSKVA (ex-*Slava*)	121	Nikolayev North (61 Kommuna), Ukraine	5 Nov 1976	27 July 1979	30 Dec 1982
MARSHAL USTINOV	055	Nikolayev North (61 Kommuna), Ukraine	5 Oct 1978	25 Feb 1982	15 Sep 1986
VARYAG (ex-*Chervona Ukraina*)	011	Nikolayev North (61 Kommuna), Ukraine	31 July 1979	28 Aug 1983	25 Dec 1989

Displacement, tons: 9,380 standard; 11,490 full load
Dimensions, feet (metres): 611.5 × 68.2 × 27.6
(186.4 × 20.8 × 8.4)
Main machinery: COGAG; 4 gas-turbines; 88,000 hp(m)
(64.68 MW); 2 M-70 gas-turbines; 20,000 hp(m) *(14.7 MW)*;
2 shafts
Speed, knots: 32
Range, n miles: 2,200 at 30 kt; 7,500 at 15 kt
Complement: 476 (62 officers)

Missiles: SSM: 16 Chelomey SS-N-12 (8 twin) Sandbox
(Bazalt) launchers ❶; inertial guidance with command
update; active radar homing to 550 km *(300 n miles)* at
1.7 Mach; warhead nuclear 350 kT or HE 1,000 kg.
SAM: 8 SA-N-6 Grumble (Fort) vertical launchers ❷;
8 rounds per launcher; command guidance; semi-active
radar homing to 100 km *(54 n miles)*; warhead 90 kg
(or nuclear?); altitude 27,432 m *(90,000 ft)*. 64 missiles.
2 SA-N-4 Gecko twin retractable launchers ❸; semi-active
radar homing to 15 km *(8 n miles)* at 2.5 Mach; warhead
50 kg; altitude 9.1 – 3,048 m *(30 – 10,000 ft)*; 40 missiles.
Guns: 2 – 130 mm/70 (twin) AK 130 ❹; 35/45 rds/min to
29 km *(16 n miles)*; weight of shell 33.4 kg.
6 – 30 mm/65 AK 650 ❺; 6 barrels per mounting;
3,000 rds/min to 2 km.
Torpedoes: 10 – 21 in *(533 mm)* (2 quin) tubes ❻.
Combination of 53 cm torpedoes (see table at front of
section).
A/S mortars: 2 RBU 6000 12-tubed trainable ❼; range
6,000 m; warhead 31 kg.
Countermeasures: Decoys: 2 PK 2 chaff launchers.
ESM/ECM: 8 Side Globe (jammers). 4 Rum Tub (intercept).
Weapons control: 2 Tee Plinth and 3 Tilt Pot optronic
directors. 2 Punch Bowl satellite data receiving/targeting
systems. 2 Bell Crown and 2 Bell Push datalinks.
Radars: Air search: Top Pair (Top Sail + Big Net) ❽; 3D;
C/D-band; range 366 km *(200 n miles)* for bomber, 183
km *(100 n miles)* for 2 m² target.
Air/surface search: Top Steer ❾ or Top Plate *(Varyag)*; 3D;
D/E-band.
Navigation: 3 Palm Frond; I-band.

MOSKVA   *9/2003, Giorgio Ghiglione* / 0570926

Fire control: Front Door ❿; F-band (for SS-N-12). Top Dome
⓫; J-band (for SA-N-6). 2 Pop Group ⓬; F/H/I-band (for
SA-N-4). 3 Bass Tilt ⓭; H/I-band (for Gatlings). Kite
Screech ⓮; H/I/K-band (for 130 mm).
IFF: Salt Pot A and B. 2 Long Head.
Sonars: Bull Horn and Steer Hide (Platina); hull-mounted;
active search and attack; low/medium frequency.
Helicopters: 1 Ka-27 Helix ⓯.

Programmes: Built at the same yard as the Kara class. This is
a smaller edition of the dual-purpose surface warfare/
ASW *Kirov*, designed as a conventionally powered back-up
for that class. The fourth of class, originally being
completed for Ukraine, was transferred to Russia in
July 1995 but returned to Ukraine in February 1999 for
completion. However, work was not finished due to lack
of funds. Re-sale back to Russia is unlikely. A fifth of class
was started but cancelled in October 1990.
Structure: The notable gap abaft the twin funnels (SA-N-6
area) is traversed by a large crane which stows between
the funnels. The hangar is recessed below the flight deck
with an inclined ramp. The torpedo tubes are behind

shutters in the hull below the Top Dome radar director
aft. Air conditioned citadels for NBCD. There is a bridge
periscope.
Operational: The SA-N-6 system effectiveness is
diminished by having only one radar director. Over-the-
horizon targeting for SS-N-12 provided by helicopter or
Punch Bowl SATCOM. *Moskva* is based in the Black
Sea Fleet at Sevastopol and conducted an Indian
Ocean deployment in 2003. Her nine-year refit was
beset by payment problems. Some funds were
provided by the city of Moscow. *Marshal Ustinov*
deployed to the Northern Fleet in March 1987 and
completed refit at St Petersburg in May 1995 where
she remained until January 1998, when she transferred
back to the Northern Fleet and is based at Severomorsk
and is active. *Varyag* transferred to Petropavlovsk in the
Pacific in October 1990.

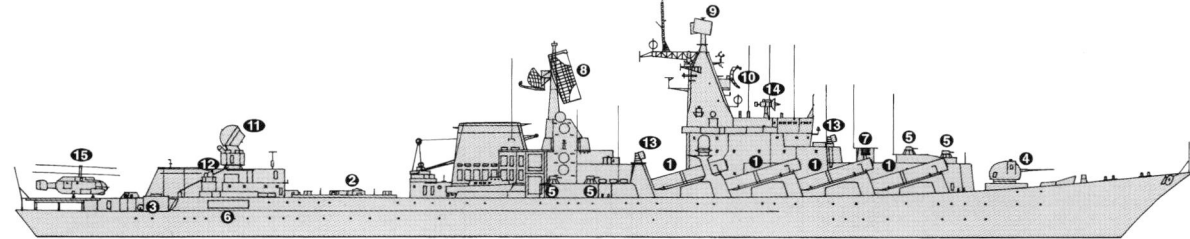

VARYAG   *(Scale 1 : 1,200), Ian Sturton* / 0050017

VARYAG   *12/2005*, Ships of the World* / 1151150

MOSKVA   *9/2004, Selim San* / 1042297

1 KARA (BERKOT-B) CLASS (PROJECT 1134B) (CGHM)

Name	No	Builders	Laid down	Launched	Commissioned
KERCH	713 (ex-711)	Nikolayev North (61 Kommuna), Ukraine	30 Apr 1971	21 July 1972	25 Dec 1974

Displacement, tons: 7,650 standard; 9,900 full load
Dimensions, feet (metres): 568 × 61 × 22
(173.2 × 18.6 × 6.7)
Main machinery: COGAG; 4 gas turbines; 108,800 hp(m)
(80 MW); 2 gas turbines; 13,600 hp(m) *(10 MW)*; 2 shafts
Speed, knots: 32
Range, n miles: 9,000 at 15 kt cruising turbines; 3,000
at 32 kt
Complement: 390 (49 officers)

Missiles: SAM: 2 SA-N-3 Goblet twin launchers ❶; semi-
active radar homing to 55 km *(30 n miles)* at 2.5 Mach;
warhead 80 kg; altitude 91.4-22,860 m *(300-75,000 ft)*; 72
missiles.
2 SA-N-4 Gecko twin launchers (twin either side of
mast) ❷; semi-active radar homing to 15 km *(8 n miles)*
at 2.5 Mach; warhead 50 kg; altitude 9.1-3,048 m
(30-10,000 ft); 40 missiles.
A/S: 2 Raduga SS-N-14 Silex (Rastrub) quad launchers ❸;
command guidance to 55 km *(30 n miles)* at 0.95 Mach;
payload nuclear 5 kT or Type 40 torpedo or E53-72
torpedo. SSM version; range 35 km *(19 n miles)*; warhead
500 kg.
Guns: 4—3 in *(76 mm)*/60 (2 twin) ❹; 90 rds/min to 15 km
(8 n miles); weight of shell 6.8 kg.
4—30 mm/65 ❺; 6 barrels per mounting; 3,000 rds/min
combined to 2 km.
Torpedoes: 10—21 in *(533 mm)* (2 quin) tubes ❻.
Combination of 53 cm torpedoes (see table at front of
section).
A/S mortars: 2 RBU 6000 12-tubed trainable ❼; range
6,000 m; warhead 31 kg.
2 RBU 1000 6-tubed (aft) ❽; range 1,000 m; warhead 55 kg;
torpedo countermeasures.
Countermeasures: Decoys: 2 PK 2 chaff launchers. 1 BAT-1
torpedo decoy.
ESM/ECM: 8 Side Globe (jammers). 2 Bell Slam. 2 Bell
Clout. 4 Rum Tub (intercept) (fitted on mainmast).
Weapons control: 4 Tilt Pot optronic directors. Bell Crown,
Bike Pump and Hat Box datalinks.
Radars: Air search: Flat Screen ❾; E/F-band.
Air/surface search: Head Net C ❿; 3D; E-band; range 128 km
(70 n miles).
Navigation: 2 Don Kay; I-band. Don 2 or Palm Frond; I-band.
Fire control: 2 Head Light B/C ⓫; F/G/H-band (for SA-N-3
and SS-N-14). 2 Pop Group ⓬; F/H/I-band (for SA-N-4).
2 Owl Screech ⓭; G-band (for 76 mm). 2 Bass Tilt ⓮;
H/I-band (for 30 mm).
Tacan: Fly Screen A or Fly Spike.
IFF: High Pole A. High Pole B.
Sonars: Bull Nose (Titan 2-MG 332); hull-mounted; active
search and attack; low/medium frequency.
Mare Tail; VDS (Vega-M 325) ⓯; active search; medium
frequency.

Helicopters: 1 Ka-27 Helix ⓰.

Programmes: Type name is *bolshoy protivolodochny
korabl*, meaning large anti-submarine ship.

KERCH
(Scale 1 : 1,500), Ian Sturton / 0081651

KERCH
7/2000, Hartmut Ehlers / 0105541

Modernisation: The Flat Screen air search radar, replaced
Top Sail.
Structure: The helicopter is raised to flight deck level
by a lift. In addition to the 8 tubes for the SS-N-14
A/S system and the pair of twin launchers for SA-N-3
system with Goblet missiles, Kara class mounts the
SA-N-4 system in 2 silos, either side of the mast. The
SA-N-3 system has only 2 loading doors per launcher
and a larger launching arm.

Operational: Two of the class started refits in July 1987
and have been scrapped by the Ukraine. One more was
scrapped in the Pacific in 1996. *Petropavlovsk* is laid up in
the Pacific and is unlikely to go to sea again. In the Black
Sea, there have been several reports of work being done
on *Ochakov*, most recently in 2005, but these have not
been confirmed. Formally, she remains in service. *Azov*
was cannibalised for spares in 1998. *Kerch* is based in the
Black Sea at Sevastopol and completed a refit in 2005.

DESTROYERS

1 KASHIN (PROJECT 61) CLASS (DDGM)

Name	No	Builders	Laid down	Launched	Commissioned
SMETLIVY	810	Nikolayev North, Ukraine	15 July 1966	26 Aug 1967	25 Sep 1969

Displacement, tons: 4,010 standard; 4,750 full load
Dimensions, feet (metres): 472.4 × 51.8 × 15.4
(144 × 15.8 × 4.7)
Main machinery: COGAG; 4 DE 59 gas turbines; 72,000 hp(m)
(52.9 MW); 2 shafts
Speed, knots: 32
Range, n miles: 4,000 at 18 kt; 1,520 at 32 kt
Complement: 280 (25 officers)

Missiles: SSM: 8 Zvezda SS-N-25 (KH 35 Uran) (2 quad) ❶.
SAM: 2 SA-N-1 Goa twin launchers ❷; command
guidance to 31.5 km *(17 n miles)* at 2 Mach; warhead
72 kg; altitude 91.4—22,860 m *(300—75,000 ft)*;
32 missiles.
Guns: 2—3 in *(76 mm)*/60 (1 or 2 twin) ❸; 90 rds/min to 15 km
(8 n miles); weight of shell 6.8 kg.
Torpedoes: 5—21 in *(533 mm)* (quin) tubes ❹. Combination
of 53 cm torpedoes (see table at front of section).
A/S mortars: 2 RBU 6000 12-tubed trainable ❺; range
6,000 m; warhead 31 kg; 120 rockets.
Countermeasures: Decoys: PK 16 chaff launchers (modified).
2 towed torpedo decoys.
ESM/ECM: 2 Bell Shroud. 2 Watch Dog.
Weapons control: 3 Tee Plinth and 4 Tilt Pot optronic
directors.
Radars: Air/surface search: Head Net C ❻; 3D; E-band.
Big Net ❼; C-band.
Navigation: 2 Don 2/Don Kay/Palm Frond; I-band.
Fire control: 2 Peel Group ❽; H/I-band (for SA-N-1). 1 Owl
Screech ❾; G-band (for guns).
IFF: High Pole B.
Sonars: Bull Nose (MGK 336) or Wolf Paw; hull-mounted;
active search and attack; medium frequency.
Vega; VDS; active search; medium frequency.

Programmes: The first class of warships in the world to rely
entirely on gas-turbine propulsion. Type name is *bolshoy
protivolodochny korabl*, meaning large anti-submarine
ship.

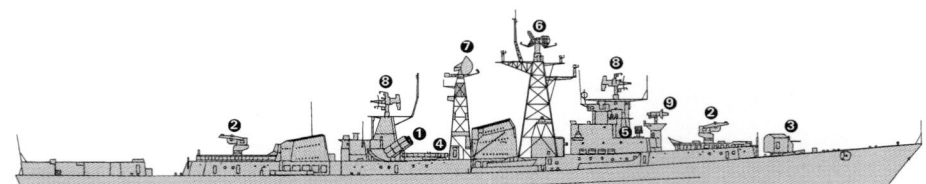

SMETLIVY
(Scale 1 : 1,200), Ian Sturton / 0126351

SMETLIVY
6/2004, Selim San / 1042300

Modernisation: Modernised with a VDS aft, vice the after gun,
and fitted for SS-N-25 in place of the RBU 1000 launchers.
Operational: Based in the Black Sea. Refitted from 1990 to
1996 but back in service in 1997. Deployed to the Indian
Ocean in 2003 and remains active.

Sales: Additional ships of a modified design built for India.
First transferred September 1980, the second in June
1982, the third in 1983, the fourth in August 1986 and
the fifth and last in January 1988. *Smely* transferred to
Poland 9 January 1988.

1 UDALOY II (FREGAT) CLASS (PROJECT 1155.1) (DDGHM)

Name	No	Builders	Laid down	Launched	Commissioned
ADMIRAL CHABANENKO	650 (ex-437)	Yantar, Kaliningrad 820	15 Sep 1988	14 Dec 1992	20 Feb 1999

Displacement, tons: 7,700 standard; 8,900 full load
Dimensions, feet (metres): 536.4 × 63.3 × 24.6
(163.5 × 19.3 × 7.5)
Main machinery: COGAG; 2 gas turbines; 48,600 hp(m)
(35.72 MW); 2 gas turbines; 24,200 hp(m) *(17.79 MW)*;
2 shafts
Speed, knots: 28
Range, n miles: 4,000 at 18 kt
Complement: 249 (29 officers)

Missiles: SSM: 8 Raduga SS-N-22 Sunburn (3M-82 Moskit)
(2 quad) **❶**; active/passive radar homing to 160 km
(87 n miles) at 2.5 Mach (4.5 for attack); warhead nuclear
or HE 300 kg; sea-skimmer.
SAM: 8 SA-N-9 Gauntlet (Klinok) vertical launchers **❷**;
command guidance; active radar homing to 12 km
(6.5 n miles) at 2 Mach; warhead 15 kg. 64 missiles;
4 channels of fire.
SAM/Guns: 2 CADS-N-1 (Kashtan) **❸**; each with twin 30 mm
Gatling; combined with 8 SA-N-11 (Grisson) and Hot
Flash/Hot Spot fire-control radar/optronic director. Laser
beam guidance for missiles to 8 km *(4.4 n miles)*; warhead
9 kg; 9,000 rds/min combined to 1.5 km for guns.
A/S: Novator SS-N-15 (Starfish); inertial flight to 45 km

(24.3 n miles); payload Type 40 torpedo or nuclear, fired
from torpedo tubes.
Guns: 2—130 mm/70 (twin) AK 130 **❹**; 35—45 rds/min to
29.5 km *(16 n miles)*; weight of shell 33.4 kg.
Torpedoes: 8—21 in *(533 mm)* (2 quad tubes) **❺**.
Combination of 53 cm torpedoes (see table at front
of section). The tubes are protected by flaps in the
superstructure.
A/S mortars: 2 RBU 6000 **❻**. 12-tubed trainable; range
6,000 m; warhead 31 kg.
Countermeasures: 8 PK 10 and 2 PK 2 chaff launchers **❼**.
ESM/ECM: 2 Wine Glass (intercept). 2 Bell Shroud. 2 Bell
Squat. 4 Half Cup laser warner. 2 Shot Dome.
Weapons control: M 145 radar and optronic system.
2 Bell Crown datalink. Band Stand **❽** datalink for
SS-N-22; 2 Light Bulb, 2 Round House and 1 Bell Nest
datalinks.
Radars: Air Search: Strut Pair II **❾**; F-band.
Top Plate **❿**; 3D; D/E-band.
Surface Search: 3 Palm Frond **⓫**; I-band.
Fire control: 2 Cross Swords **⓬**; K-band (for SA-N-9). Kite
Screech **⓭**; H/I/K-band (for 100 mm gun).
CCA: Fly Screen B **⓮**.
IFF: Salt Pot B and C.

Sonars: Horse Jaw (Polinom); hull-mounted; active search
and attack; medium/low frequency.
Horse Tail; VDS; active search; medium frequency.

Helicopters: 2 Ka-27 Helix A **⓯**.

Programmes: A single ship follow-on class from the
Udaloys. NATO designator Balcom 12. At least two more
were projected with names *Admiral Basisty* and *Admiral
Kucherov*; *Basisty* was scrapped in March 1994, and
Kucherov was never started.
Structure: Similar size to the Udaloy and has the same
propulsion machinery. Improved combination of weapon
systems owing something to both the Sovremenny
and the Neustrashimy classes. The distribution of
SA-N-9 launchers may be the same as Udaloy class.
The torpedo tubes are protected by a hinged flap in the
superstructure.
Operational: Sea trials started on 14 September 1995
from Baltiysk. Deployed to the Northern Fleet in March
1999 when the pennant number changed. Based at
Severomorsk and is very active.

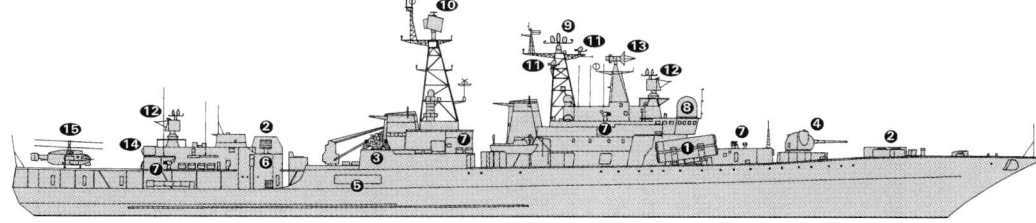

ADMIRAL CHABANENKO

(Scale 1 : 1,200), Ian Sturton / 0569929

ADMIRAL CHABANENKO

9/2004 / 1151344

ADMIRAL CHABANENKO

8/2002 / 0528328

9 UDALOY (FREGAT) CLASS (PROJECT 1155) (DDGHM)

Name	No	Builders	Laid down	Launched	Commissioned
VITSE ADMIRAL KULAKOV	400	Zhdanov Yard, Leningrad 190	7 Nov 1977	16 May 1980	29 Dec 1981
MARSHAL VASILEVSKY	687	Zhdanov Yard, Leningrad 190	22 Apr 1979	29 Dec 1981	8 Dec 1983
ADMIRAL TRIBUTS	564	Zhdanov Yard, Leningrad 190	19 Apr 1980	26 Mar 1983	30 Dec 1985
MARSHAL SHAPOSHNIKOV	543	Yantar, Kaliningrad 820	25 May 1983	27 Dec 1984	30 Dec 1985
SEVEROMORSK (ex-Simferopol, ex-Marshal Budienny)	619	Yantar, Kaliningrad 820	12 June 1984	24 Dec 1985	30 Dec 1987
ADMIRAL LEVCHENKO (ex-Kharbarovsk)	605	Zhdanov Yard, Leningrad 190	27 Jan 1982	21 Feb 1985	30 Sep 1988
ADMIRAL VINOGRADOV	572	Yantar, Kaliningrad 820	5 Feb 1986	4 June 1987	30 Dec 1988
ADMIRAL KHARLAMOV	678	Yantar, Kaliningrad 820	7 Aug 1986	29 June 1988	30 Dec 1989
ADMIRAL PANTELEYEV	548	Yantar, Kaliningrad 820	28 Jan 1988	7 Feb 1990	19 Dec 1991

Displacement, tons: 6,700 standard; 8,500 full load
Dimensions, feet (metres): 536.4 × 63.3 × 24.6
  (163.5 × 19.3 × 7.5)
Flight deck, feet (metres): 65.6 × 59 (20 × 18)
Main machinery: COGAG; 2 gas turbines; 55,500 hp(m)
  (40.8 MW); 2 gas turbines; 13,600 hp(m) (10 MW);
  2 shafts
Speed, knots: 29
Range, n miles: 2,600 at 30 kt; 7,700 at 18 kt
Complement: 249 (29 officers)

Missiles: SAM: 8 SA-N-9 Gauntlet (Klinok) vertical launchers
  ❶; command guidance; active radar homing to 12 km
  (6.5 n miles) at 2 Mach; warhead 15 kg; altitude
  3.4-12,192 m (10-40,000 ft); 64 missiles; four channels
  of fire.
  The launchers are set into the ships' structures with 6 ft
  diameter cover plates-4 on the forecastle, 2 between
  the torpedo tubes and 2 at the forward end of the after
  deckhouse between the RBUs.
A/S: 2 Raduga SS-N-14 Silex (Rastrub) quad launchers ❷;
  command guidance to 55 km (30 n miles) at 0.95 Mach;
  payload nuclear 5 kT or Type 40 torpedo or Type E53-72
  torpedo. SSM version; range 35 km (19 n miles); warhead
  500 kg.
Guns: 2—3.9 in (100 mm)/59 ❸; 60 rds/min to 15 km
  (8.2 n miles); weight of shell 16 kg.
  4—30 mm/65 AK 630 ❹; 6 barrels per mounting;
  3,000 rds/min combined to 2 km.
Torpedoes: 8—21 in (533 mm) (2 quad) tubes ❺. Combination
  of 53 cm torpedoes (see table at front of section).
A/S mortars: 2 RBU 6000 12-tubed trainable ❻; range
  6,000 m; warhead 31 kg.
Mines: Rails for 26 mines.
Countermeasures: Decoys: 2 PK-2 and 8 PK-10 chaff
  launchers. US Masker type noise reduction.
  ESM/ECM: 2 Foot Ball B (Levchenko onwards); 2 Wine Glass
  (intercept). 6 Half Cup laser warner (Levchenko onwards);
  2 Bell Squat (jammers).
Weapons control: MP 145 radar and optronic system. 2 Bell
  Crown and Round House C datalink.
Radars: Air search: Strut Pair ❼; F-band.
  Top Plate ❽; 3D; D/E-band.
  Surface search: 3 Palm Frond ❾; I-band.
  Fire control: 2 Eye Bowl ❿; F-band (for SS-N-14). 2 Cross
  Sword ⓫; K-band (for SA-N-9). Kite Screech ⓬; H/I/K-
  band (for 100 mm guns). 2 Bass Tilt ⓭; H/I/K-band (for
  30 mm guns).
IFF: Salt Pot A and B. Box Bar A and B.
Tacan: 2 Round House.
CCA: Fly Screen B (by starboard hangar) ⓮. 2 Fly Spike B.
Sonars: Horse Jaw (Polinom); hull-mounted; active search
  and attack; low/medium frequency.
  Mouse Tail; VDS; active search; medium frequency.

Helicopters: 2 Ka-27 Helix A ⓯.

Programmes: Design approved in October 1972. Successor
  to Kresta II class but based on Krivak class. Type name
  is bolshoy protivolodochny korabl meaning large anti-
  submarine ship. Programme stopped at 12 in favour of
  Udaloy II class (Type 1155.1).

MARSHAL SHAPOSHNIKOV   10/2005*, Ships of the World / 1151149

ADMIRAL LEVCHENKO   6/2005*, Jurg Kürsener / 1151345

Structure: The two hangars are set side by side with
inclined elevating ramps to the flight deck. Has
pre-wetting NBCD equipment and replenishment
at sea gear. Active stabilisers are fitted. The chaff
launchers are on both sides of the foremast and
inboard of the torpedo tubes. Cage Flask aerials are
mounted on the mainmast spur and on the mast on
top of the hangar. There are indications of a nuclear
release mechanism, or interlock, on the lower tubes of the
SS-N-14 launchers.

Operational: These general purpose ships have good sea-
keeping and endurance and are the backbone of the
fleet. Based as follows: Northern Fleet- Severomorsk,
Kharlamov, Vasilevsky and Levchenko; Pacific Fleet-

Shaposhnikov, Panteleyev, Vinogradov and Tributs.
Baltic Fleet - Kulakov. Vinogradov was in collision in April
2000 but was quickly repaired. Severomorsk deployed to
St Petersburg for refit in June 1998 completing in late 2000,
and Levchenko followed in November 1999 completing
in 2001. The fourth of class, Zakharov was scrapped after
a fire in March 1992. Tributs was in reserve in 1994 and
had a machinery space fire in September 1995, was back
in service in mid-1999. Udaloy and Spiridonov have been
laid up or scrapped. Kulakov started refit in 1990 and
returned to service in 2004. Vasilevsky was in refit during
2001 and completed in 2004.

Opinion: Obvious efforts are being made to keep this class
in service at the expense of the Sovremennys.

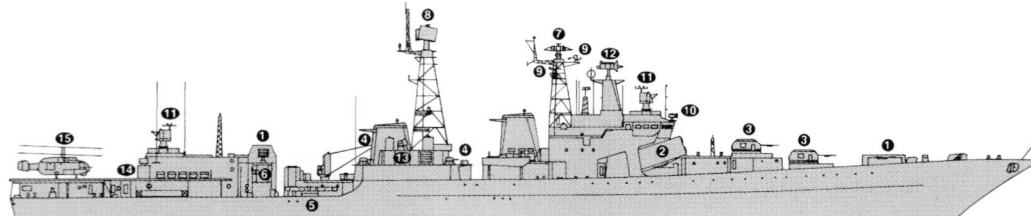

SEVEROMORSK   (Scale 1 : 1,200), Ian Sturton / 0506079

ADMIRAL PANTELEYEV   12/2005*, Ships of the World / 1151148

8 SOVREMENNY (SARYCH) CLASS (PROJECT 956/956A) (DDGHM)

Name	No	Builders	Laid down	Launched	Commissioned
BURNY	778	Zhdanov Yard, Leningrad (190)	4 Nov 1983	30 Dec 1986	30 Sep 1988
GREMYASHCHY	404 (ex-429)	Zhdanov Yard, Leningrad (190)	23 Nov 1984	30 May 1987	14 Jan 1989
BYSTRY	715	Zhdanov Yard, Leningrad (190)	29 Oct 1985	28 Nov 1987	30 Sep 1989
RASTOROPNY	420	Zhdanov Yard, Leningrad (190)	15 Aug 1986	4 June 1988	30 Dec 1989
BEZBOYAZNENNYY	754	Zhdanov Yard, Leningrad (190)	8 Jan 1987	18 Feb 1989	28 Nov 1990
BESPOKOINY	620	Zhdanov Yard, Leningrad (190)	18 Apr 1987	22 Feb 1992	29 Dec 1993
NASTOYCHIVY (ex-Moskowski Komsomolets)	610	Zhdanov Yard, Leningrad (190)	7 Apr 1988	15 Feb 1992	27 Mar 1993
MARSHAL USHAKOV (ex-Besstrashny)	434	Zhdanov Yard, Leningrad (190)	16 Apr 1988	31 Dec 1992	17 Apr 1994

Displacement, tons: 6,500 standard; 7,940 full load
Dimensions, feet (metres): 511.8 × 56.8 × 21.3
(156 × 17.3 × 6.5)
Main machinery: 4 KVN boilers; 2 GTZA-674 turbines;
99,500 hp(m) (73.13 MW) sustained; 2 shafts; bow
thruster
Speed, knots: 32
Range, n miles: 2,400 at 32 kt; 6,500 at 20 kt; 4,000 at 14 kt
Complement: 296 (25 officers) plus 60 spare

Missiles: SSM: 8 Raduga SS-N-22 Sunburn (3M-80 Zubr)
(2 quad) launchers ❶; active/passive radar homing to
110 km (60 n miles) at 2.5 (4.5 for attack) Mach; warhead
nuclear 200 kT or HE 300 kg; sea-skimmer. From
Bespokoiny onwards a modified missile (3M-82 Moskit) with a range of 160 km
(87 n miles).
SAM: 2 SA-N-7 Gadfly 3S 90 (Uragan) ❷; command/semi-
active radar and IR homing to 25 km (13.5 n miles) at
3 Mach; warhead 70 kg; altitude 15—14,020 m
(50—46,000 ft); 44 missiles. Multiple channels of fire.
From Bespokoiny onwards the same launcher is used for
the SA-N-17 Grizzly/SA-N-12 Yezh.
Guns: 4—130 mm/70 (2 twin) AK 130 ❸; 35—45 rds/min to
29.5 km (16 n miles); weight of shell 33.4 kg.
4—30 mm/65 AK 630 ❹; 6 barrels per mounting;
3,000 rds/min combined to 2 km.
Torpedoes: 4—21 in (533 mm) (2 twin) tubes ❺. Combination
of 53 cm torpedoes (see table at front of section).
A/S mortars: 2 RBU 1000 (Smerch 3) 6-barrelled ❻; range
1,000 m; warhead 100 kg; 120 rockets carried. Torpedo
countermeasure.

Mines: Mine rails for up to 22.
Countermeasures: Decoys: 8 PK 10 and 2 PK 2 chaff
launchers.
ESM/ECM: 4 Foot Ball (some variations including 2 Bell
Shroud and 2 Bell Squat). 6 Half Cup laser warner.
Combat data systems: Sapfir-U.
Weapons control: 1 Squeeze Box optronic director
and laser rangefinder ❼. Band Stand ❽ datalink for
SS-N-22. Bell Nest, 2 Light Bulb and 2 Tee Pump
datalinks.
Radars: Air search: Top Plate (MR-750 Fregat) ❾; 3D;
D/E-band.
Surface search: 3 Palm Frond (MR 212/201) ❿; I-band.
Fire control: 6 Front Dome ⓫; G-band (for SA-N-7/17). Kite
Screech (MR-184) ⓬; H/I/K-band (for 130 mm guns).
2 Bass Tilt ⓭; H/I-band (for 30 mm guns).
IFF: Salt Pot A and B. High Pole A and B. Long Head.
Tacan: 2 Light Bulb.
Sonars: Bull Horn (MGK-335 Platina) and Whale Tongue;
hull-mounted; active search and attack; medium
frequency.

Helicopters: 1 Kamov Ka-27 Helix ⓮.

Programmes: Type name is eskadrenny minonosets
meaning destroyer. From Bespokoiny onwards the
class is known as 956A. Total of 17 built for Russia,
two (hulls 18 and 19) for China, and one more
(Bulny) which is unlikely to be completed unless for
export.

Structure: Telescopic hangar. The fully automatic 130 mm
gun was first seen in 1976. Chaff launchers are
fitted on both sides of the foremast and either
side of the after SAM launcher. A longer range
version of SS-N-22 has been introduced in the
Type 956A. This has slightly longer launch tubes.
Also the SAM system has been improved to take
the SA-N-17. There are also some variations in the
EW fit.
Operational: A specialist surface warfare ship
complementing the ASW-capable Udaloy class. Based
as follows: Northern Fleet- Marshal Ushakov and
Gremyashchy. Pacific Fleet- Burny, Bezboyaznennyy
and Bystry. Baltic Fleet- Nastoychivy and Bespokoiny.
So far 9 others have paid off or are non-operational.
Bystry completed refit in 2002 and Bezboyaznennyy
in 2004. 434 renamed Marshal Ushakov in 2004.
Rastoropny was reportedly in refit at Severnaya
Verf in 2004 and is expected to return to service
in 2006. Gremyashchy also reported to have been
re-activated. Steam-plant reliability has been a class
problem.
Sales: Hulls 18 and 19 which were near completion in
1996, were sold to China and sailed in December 1999
and December 2000 respectively, from the Baltic to the
South China Sea. A contract for the procurement of two
new ships was signed by the Chinese government on
3 January 2002.

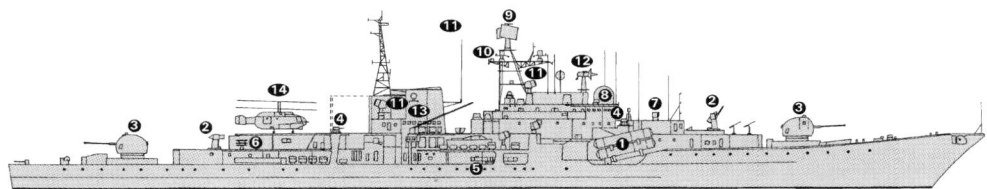

BYSTRY   (Scale 1 : 1,200), Ian Sturton / 1151086

BURNY   10/2005*, Ships of the World / 1151154

NASTOYCHIVY   6/2005*, Michael Winter / 1151152

FRIGATES

Notes: It has been announced that the first of a new class of Project 22350 general-purpose frigates was laid down at Severnaya Verf in February 2006. Up to ten of the class are expected by 2015. The design may be a further development of the Indian Talwar class which were derived from the Russian Krivak III class frigates. The first new major surface units to be laid down for over fifteen years, the ships are expected to be equipped with an A 192 130 mm gun, a medium range SAM system, eight SS-N-26 Oniks/Yakhont anti-ship missile and an ASW weapon system.

0 + 1 GROM CLASS (PROJECT 1244.1) (FFG)

Name	No	Builders	Laid down	Launched	Commissioned
NOVIK	—	Yantar, Kaliningrad	26 July 1997	2001	2005

Displacement, tons: 3,600 full load
Dimensions, feet (metres): 400.3 × 49.2 × 31.2 (sonar) (122.0 × 15.0 × 9.5)
Main machinery: CODAG; 2 gas turbines; 2 diesels; 2 shafts
Speed, knots: 30

Missiles: SSM: Space for eight or 16 Zvezda SS-N-25 (KH 35 Uran) ❶ (2 quad); active radar homing to 130 km (70.2 n miles) at 0.9 Mach; warhead 145 kg; sea skimmer.
SAM: Space for VLS system ❷.
Guns: 1—3 in (76 mm)/60 ❸.
2—30 mm AK 630 ❹.
Radars: Air/surface search: Top Plate (Fregate M) ❺; 3D; D/E-band.
Surface search: Cross Dome; E/F-band ❻.
Fire control: Bass Tilt; H/I-band ❼.
Sonars: Hull mounted and VDS.

Helicopters: 1 Ka-29 Helix.

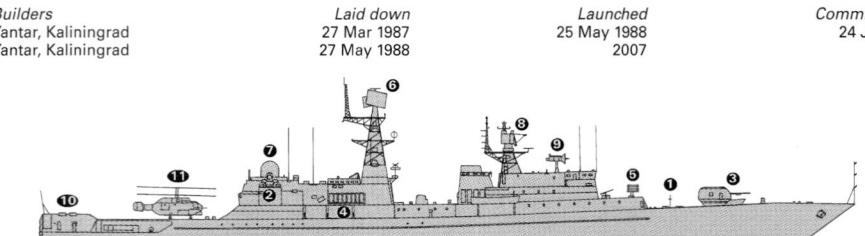

NOVIK

(Scale 1 : 1,200), Ian Sturton / 0019031

Programmes: Designed by Almaz. Considerable publicity when keel laid down in 1997 but the project stalled due to budget cuts. However, building was reported to have been restarted in 2003 and it is speculated that the ship was being modified to act as an unarmed training ship in 2004. The ship may be commissioned in 2006.
Structure: Most details are speculative and are based on the original published export design.
Operational: Likely to be based in the Baltic Fleet.

1 + 1 NEUSTRASHIMY (JASTREB) CLASS (PROJECT 1154) (FFHM)

Name	No	Builders	Laid down	Launched	Commissioned
NEUSTRASHIMY	712	Yantar, Kaliningrad	27 Mar 1987	25 May 1988	24 Jan 1993
YAROSLAV MURDRYY	—	Yantar, Kaliningrad	27 May 1988	2007	2009

Displacement, tons: 3,450 standard; 4,250 full load
Dimensions, feet (metres): 425.3 oa; 403.5 wl × 50.9 × 15.7 (129.6; 123 × 15.5 × 4.8)
Main machinery: COGAG; 2 gas turbines; 48,600 hp(m) (35.72 MW); 2 gas turbines; 24,200 hp(m) (17.79 MW); 2 shafts
Speed, knots: 30
Range, n miles: 4,500 at 16 kt
Complement: 210 (35 officers)

Missiles: SSM: Fitted for but not with 16 SS-N-25 (4 quad). SS-CX-5 Sapless (possibly a version of SS-N-22 (Moskit M)) may be carried (see Torpedoes).
SAM: 4 SA-N-9 Gauntlet (Klinok) octuple vertical launchers ❶; command guidance; active radar homing to 12 km (6.5 n miles) at 2 Mach; warhead 15 kg. 32 missiles.
SAM/Guns: 2 CADS-N-1 (Kortik/Kashtan) (3M87) ❷; each has a twin 30 mm Gatling combined with 8 SA-N-11 (Grisson) and Hot Flash/Hot Spot fire-control radar/optronic director. Laser beam guidance for missiles to 8 km (4.4 n miles); warhead 9 kg; 9,000 rds/min (combined) to 1.5 km (for guns).
A/S: SS-N-15/16; inertial flight to 120 km (65 n miles); payload Type 40 torpedo or nuclear warhead; fired from torpedo tubes.
Guns: 1—3.9 in (100 mm)/59 A 190E ❸; 60 rds/min to 15 km (8.2 n miles); weight of shell 16 kg.
Torpedoes: 6—21 in (533 mm) tubes combined with A/S launcher ❹; can fire SS-N-15/16 missiles with Type 40 anti-submarine torpedoes or 53 cm torpedoes (see table at front of section).
A/S mortars: 1 RBU 12,000 ❺; 10-tubed trainable; range 12,000 m; warhead 80 kg.
Mines: 2 rails.
Countermeasures: Decoys: 8 PK 10 and 2 PK 16 chaff launchers.
ESM/ECM: Intercept and jammers. 2 Foot Ball; 2 Half Hat; 4 Half Cup laser intercept.
Weapons control: 2 Bell Crown datalink.
Radars: Air search: Top Plate ❻; 3D; D/E-band.
Air/Surface search: Cross Dome ❼; E/F-band.
Navigation: 2 Palm Frond; I-band.
Fire control: Cross Sword ❽ (for SAM); K-band. Kite Screech B ❾ (for SSM and guns); I-band.
IFF: 2 Salt Pot; 4 Box Bar.

Sonars: Ox Yoke and Whale Tongue; hull-mounted; active search and attack; medium frequency.
Ox Tail; VDS ❿ or towed sonar array.

Helicopters: 1 Ka-27 Helix ⓫.

Programmes: At least four of the class were planned. The first of the class started sea trials in the Baltic in December 1990. Second of class (Yaroslav Mudryy) was launched in May 1991, but in October 1988 the shipyard stated that the hull would be sold for scrap. However, after several years' inaction, it was reported in 2002 that work had recommenced and it was confirmed in 2005 that the ship is to be completed. The export version of the ship is known as 'Korsar'. The third ship (Tuman) was launched in July 1993 with only the hull completed and work stopped in December 1997 without any work being done. The future of the ship is uncertain.

Structure: Slightly larger than the Krivak and has a helicopter which is a standard part of the armament of modern Western frigates. There are two horizontal launchers at main deck level on each side of the ship, angled at 18° from forward. These double up for A/S missiles of the SS-N-15/16 type using a 'plunge-fly-plunge' launch and flight and normal torpedoes. Similar launchers are behind shutters in the last three of the Kirov class. The helicopter deck extends across the full width of the ship. The after funnel is unusually flush decked but both funnels have been slightly extended after initial sea trials. Attempts have been made to incorporate stealth features. Main propulsion is the same as the Udaloy II class. Reported as having a basic computerised combat data system.
Operational: Based in the Baltic at Baltiysk. Active in 2005.

NEUSTRASHIMY

(Scale 1 : 1,200), Ian Sturton / 0569927

NEUSTRASHIMY

6/2004, Michael Winter / 1042302

NEUSTRASHIMY

9/2005*, Michael Nitz / 1151349

6 KRIVAK (PROJECT 1135/1135M/1135MP) CLASS (FFM)

Name	Type	No	Builders	Laid down	Launched	Commissioned
NEUKROTIMY	II	731	Yantar, Kaliningrad	22 Jan 1976	27 June 1977	30 Dec 1977
LETUCHY	I	661	Zhdanov, Leningrad	9 Mar 1977	19 Mar 1978	10 Aug 1978
PYLKY	I Mod	702	Zhdanov, Leningrad	16 May 1977	20 Aug 1978	28 Dec 1978
ZADORNY	I	955	Zhdanov, Leningrad	10 Nov 1977	25 Mar 1979	15 Sep 1979
LADNY	I	801	Kamish-Burun, Kerch	25 May 1979	7 May 1980	29 Dec 1980
PYTLIVY	II	808	Yantar, Kaliningrad	27 June 1979	16 Apr 1981	30 Nov 1981

Displacement, tons: 3,100 standard; 3,650 full load
Dimensions, feet (metres): 405.2 × 46.9 × 24 (sonar)
(123.5 × 14.3 × 7.3)
Main machinery: COGAG; 2 M8K gas-turbines; 55,500 hp(m)
(40.8 MW); 2 M 62 gas-turbines; 13,600 hp(m) (10 MW);
2 shafts
Speed, knots: 32
Range, n miles: 4,000 at 14 kt; 1,600 at 30 kt
Complement: 194 (18 officers)

Missiles: SSM: 8 Zvezda SS-N-25 (KH 35 Uran) (2 quad) ❶;
(Krivak I after modernisation); fitted for but not with.
SAM: 2 SA-N-4 Gecko (Zif 122) twin launchers ❷; Osa-M
semi-active radar homing to 15 km (8 n miles) at 2.5 Mach;
warhead 50 kg; altitude 9.1–3,048 m (30–10,000 ft);
40 missiles (20 in Krivak III).
A/S: Raduga SS-N-14 Silex quad launcher ❸; command
guidance to 55 km (30 n miles) at 0.95 Mach; payload
nuclear 5 kT or Type 40 torpedo or Type E53-72 torpedo.
SSM version; range 35 km (19 n miles); warhead 500 kg.
Guns: 4—3 in (76 mm)/60 (2 twin) (Krivak I) ❹; 90 rds/min to
15 km (8 n miles); weight of shell 5.9 kg.
2—3.9 in (100 mm)/59 (Krivak II) ❺; 60 rds/min to 15 km
(8.2 n miles); weight of shell 16 kg.
Torpedoes: 8—21 in (533 mm) (2 quad) tubes ❻. Combination
of 53 cm torpedoes (see table at front of section).
A/S mortars: 2 RBU 6000 12-tubed trainable ❼; (not in
modernised Krivak I); range 6,000 m; warhead 31 kg.
Mines: Capacity for 16.
Countermeasures: Decoys: 4 PK 16 or 10 PK 10 chaff
launchers. Towed torpedo decoy.
ESM/ECM: 2 Bell Shroud. 2 Bell Squat. Half Cup laser
warning (in some).
Radars: Air search: Head Net C ❽; 3D; E-band; or Half Plate
(Krivak I mod) ❾.
Surface search: Don Kay or Palm Frond or Don 2 or Spin
Trough ❿; I-band.

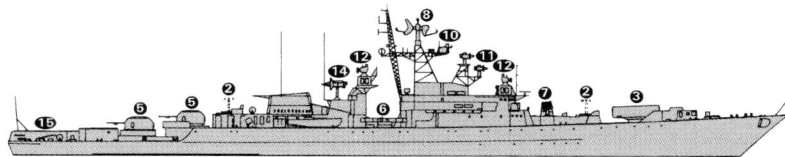

KRIVAK I (mod)   (Scale 1 : 1,200), Ian Sturton / 0506083

KRIVAK II   (Scale 1 : 1,200), Ian Sturton / 0506084

Fire control: 2 Eye Bowl ⓫; F-band (for SS-N-14). 2 Pop
Group (one in Krivak III) ⓬; F/H/I-band (for SA-N-4). Owl
Screech (Krivak I) ⓭; G-band. Kite Screech (Krivak II and
III) ⓮; H/I/K-band. Plank Shave (Harpun B) (for SS-N-25)
not fitted.
IFF: High Pole B.
Sonars: Bull Nose (MGK-335S or MG-332); hull-mounted;
active search and attack; medium frequency.
Mare Tail (MGK-345) or Steer Hide (some Krivak Is after
modernisation); VDS (MG 325) ⓯; active search; medium
frequency.

Programmes: Type name was originally *bolshoy
protivolodochny korabl*, meaning large anti-submarine
ship. Changed in 1977-78 to *storozhevoy korabl*

meaning escort ship. The naval Krivaks I and II are
known as the Burevestnik class and the border
guard ships Krivak III (listed separately) as Nerey
class.
Modernisation: Top Plate radar has replaced Head Net in
some and a more modern VDS is also fitted. SS-N-25
launchers are fitted in *Pylky*. This programme has
stopped and missiles are not embarked. The launchers
replaced the RBU mountings.
Structure: The modified Krivak I class has a larger bow.
Krivak II class has a Y-gun mounted higher than in Krivak I
and the break to the quarterdeck further aft apart from
other variations noted above.
Operational: Northern Fleet: *Zadorny,*. Black Sea: *Ladny,
Pytlivy*. Baltic: *Pylky, Neukrotimy*. Pacific: *Letuchy*.

PYTLIVY (II)   5/2005, C D Yaylali / 1151153

PYLKY   9/2005*, Michael Nitz / 1151350

LADNY (I)   7/2000, Hartmut Ehlers / 0105545

1 + 1 GEPARD (PROJECT 11661) CLASS (FFGM)

Name	No	Builders	Laid down	Launched	Commissioned
TATARSTAN (ex-*Albatros*)	691	Zelenodolsk, Kazan, Tartarstan	15 Sep 1992	July 1993	12 July 2002
DAGESTAN (ex-*Burevestnik*)	—	Zelenodolsk, Kazan, Tartarstan			2007

Displacement, tons: 1,560 standard; 1,930 full load
Dimensions, feet (metres): 334.6 × 44.6 × 14.4
  (102 × 13.6 × 4.4)
Main machinery: CODOG; 2 gas turbines; 30,850 hp(m)
  (23.0 MW); 1 Type 61D diesel; 7,375 hp(m) *(5.5 MW)*;
  2 shafts; cp props
Speed, knots: 26 (18 on diesels)
Range, n miles: 5,000 at 10 kt
Complement: 110 (accommodation for 131)

Missiles: SSM: 8 Zvezda SS-N-25 (KH 35 Uran) (2 quad) ❶;
  IR or radar homing to 130 km *(70.2 n miles)* at 0.9 Mach;
  warhead 145 kg; sea-skimmer.
SAM: 1 SA-N-4 Gecko twin launcher ❷; semi-active radar
  homing to 15 km *(8 n miles)* at 2.5 Mach; warhead 50 kg.
  20 weapons.
Guns: 1—3 in *(76 mm)*/60 AK-176 ❸; 120 rds/min to 15 km
  (8 n miles); weight of shell 5.9 kg.
  2—30 mm/65 AK-630 ❹; 6 barrels per mounting;
  3,000 rds/min combined to 2 km.
Torpedoes: 4—21 in *(533 mm)* (2 twin) tubes ❺ (probably
  not fitted).
A/S mortars: 1 RBU 6000 12-tubed trainable ❻ (probably
  not fitted).
Mines: 2 rails. 48 mines.
Countermeasures: Decoys: 4 PK 16 chaff launchers.
  ESM/ECM: 2 Bell Shroud. 2 Bell Squat. Intercept and
  jammers.
Weapons control: 2 Light Bulb datalink. Hood Wink and
  Odd Box optronic systems. Band Stand ❼ datalink.
Radars: Air/surface search: Cross Dome ❽; E/F-band.
  ESM/ECM: 2 Bell Shroud. 2 Bell Squat. Intercept and
  jammers.
  Fire control: Bass Tilt ❾; H/I-band (for guns). Pop Group ❿.
  F/H/I-band (for SAM). Garpun-B (for SSM); I/J-band.
  Navigation: Nayada; I-band.
  IFF: 2 Square Head. 1 Salt Pot B.
Sonars: Ox Yoke; hull-mounted; active search and attack;
  medium frequency (probably not fitted).
  Ox Tail (probably not fitted); VDS; active search and
  attack; medium frequency.

TATARSTAN *(Scale 1 : 900), Ian Sturton* / 1042094

TATARSTAN *6/2005*, B Lemachko* / 1154646

Programmes: Intended as a successor to the Koni class, the
Gepard family of ships, of which there were some five
variants, was developed with export in mind. The first
of class *Yastreb* was laid down in 1988 but was
later broken up in 1992. The second and third of class
were to have been exported abroad but, following

the completion of *Tatarstan* for the Russian Navy, a
second ship *Dagestan* (ex-*Burevestnik*) is expected to
follow in 2007.
Operational: Flagship of the Caspian Flotilla, the newly
commissioned *Tatarstan* took part in the large Caspian
naval exercise in August 2002.

11 PARCHIM II CLASS (PROJECT 1331) (FFLM)

	No		No		No
MPK 67	301	KAZANETS (ex-MPK 205)	311	MPK 227	243
ZELENODOLSK (ex-MPK 99)	308	MPK 213	222	BASHKORTOSTAN (ex-MPK 228)	244
MPK 105	245	MPK 216	258	KALMYKIA (ex-MPK 229)	232
MPK 192	304	ALEKSIN (ex-MPK 224)	218		

Displacement, tons: 769 standard; 960 full load
Dimensions, feet (metres): 246.7 × 32.2 × 14.4
  (75.2 × 9.8 × 4.4)
Main machinery: 3 Type M 504A diesels; 10,812 hp(m)
  (7.95 MW) sustained; 3 shafts
Speed, knots: 26. **Range, n miles:** 2,500 at 12 kt
Complement: 70 (8 officers)

Missiles: SAM: 2 SA-N-5 Grail quad launchers ❶; manual
  aiming; IR homing to 6 km *(3.2 n miles)* at 1.5 Mach;
  altitude to 2,500 m *(8,000 ft)*; warhead 1.5 kg.
Guns: 1—3 in *(76 mm)*/66 AK 176 ❷; 120 rds/min to 12 km
  (6.4 n miles); weight of shell 5.9 kg.
  1—30 mm/65 AK 630 ❸; 6 barrels; 3,000 rds/min
  combined to 2 km.
Torpedoes: 4—21 in *(533 mm)* (2 twin) tubes ❹. Combination
  of 53 cm torpedoes (see table at front of section).
A/S mortars: 2 RBU 6000 12-tubed trainable ❺; range
  6,000 m; warhead 31 kg. 96 weapons.
Depth charges: 2 racks.
Mines: Rails fitted.
Countermeasures: Decoys: 2 PK 16 chaff launchers.
  ESM: 2 Watch Dog; intercept.
Weapons control: Hood Wink and Odd Box optronic
  systems.
Radars: Air/surface search: Cross Dome ❻; E/F-band.
  Navigation: TSR 333 or Nayala or Kivach III; I-band.

Fire control: Bass Tilt ❼; H/I-band.
IFF: High Pole A.
Sonars: Bull Horn; hull-mounted; active search and attack;
  medium frequency.
  Lamb Tail; helicopter type VDS; high frequency.

Programmes: Built in the GDR at Peenewerft, Wolgast for
the USSR. First one commissioned 19 December 1986
and the last on 6 April 1990.

PARCHIM II *(Scale 1 : 600), Ian Sturton* / 0506204

Structure: Similar design to the ex-GDR Parchim I class now
serving with the Indonesian Navy but some armament
differences.
Operational: All operate in the Baltic and are based at
Baltiysk or Kronshtadt. All of the class refitted at Rostock
in 1994-95. MPK 228 damaged by fire in 1999 but has
been repaired.

KALMYKIA *6/2004, J Ciślak* / 1042323

0 + 3 (1) STEREGUSHCHIY CLASS (PROJECT 20380) (FFGHM)

Name	No	Builders	Laid down	Launched	Commissioned
STEREGUSHCHIY	—	Severnaya, St Petersburg	21 Dec 2001	2006	2008
SOOBRAZITELNY	—	Severnaya, St Petersburg	20 May 2003	2007	2009
BOIKY	—	Severnaya, St Petersburg	27 July 2005	2009	2010

Displacement, tons: 1,900 full load
Dimensions, feet (metres): 366.2 × 45.9 × 12.1
(111.6 × 14.0 × 3.7)
Main machinery: CODOG: 2 gas turbines; 20,000 hp
(14.9 MW); 2 diesels; 7,300 hp *(5.44 MW)*; 2 shafts
Speed, knots: 26. **Range, n miles:** 4,000 at 14 kt

Missiles: SSM: 8 Zvezda SS-N-25 (KH 35 Uran) (2 quad) ❶;
active radar homing to 130 km *(70.2 n miles)* at 0.9 Mach;
warhead 145 kg; sea skimmer. VLS Silo.
SAM: 2 CADS-N-1 (Kashtan) ❷; each with twin 30 mm
Gatling; combined with 8 SA-N-11 (Grisson) and Hot
Flash/Hot Spot fire-control radar/optronic director. Laser
beam guidance for missiles to 8 km *(4.4 n miles)*; warhead
9 kg; 9,000 rds/min combined to 1.5 km for guns.
A/S: Medvedka (SS-N-29); inertial flight to 25 km
(13.5 n miles); payload Type 40 torpedo.
Guns: 1—100 mm A-190 ❸. 2—14.5 mm MGs.
Countermeasures: Decoys/ESM/ECM.
Radars: Air/surface search; 3D ❹; E/F-band.
Fire control: Plank Shave (Granit Harpun B (for SSM)); I-band.
Fire control: Kite Screech; H/I/K-band (for 100 mm gun).

Sonars: Bow fitted.

Helicopters: Platform for 1 Ka-27 Helix ❺.

Programmes: Multipurpose frigate designed to replace
the Grisha class. Variants to be offered for export under

Projects 20382 and 20383. First of class to commission
in 2008 with follow on ships at annual intervals. The first
batch consists of four ships, a reduction from the ten
initially envisaged.
Structure: Not all details are known but measures to reduce
radar cross section are reported.

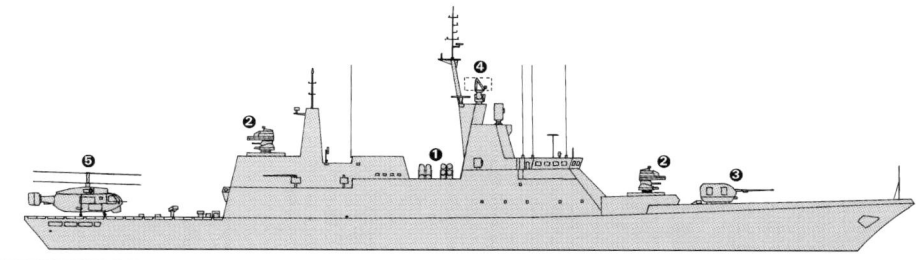

STEREGUSHCHIY
(Scale 1 : 900), Ian Sturton / 0569928

25 GRISHA (ALBATROS) (PROJECT 1124/1124M/1124K/1124EM) CLASS (FFLM)

North
ONEGA (ex-MPK 7) 164
MONCHEGORSK (ex-MPK 14) 190
MPK 56 173
SNEZNOGORSK (ex-MPK 59) 196
MPK 113 171
NARYAN-MAR (ex-MPK 130) 138
MPK 139 129
BREST (ex-MPK 194) 199
MPK 197 117
YUNGA (ex-MPK 203) 113

Pacific
MPK 17 362
METEL (ex-MPK 64) 323
MPK 82 375
MPK 107 332
LENINSKAYA KUZNITSA (ex-MPK 125) 350
MPK 178 (III) 319
MPK 191 (III) 369
STELYAK (ex-MPK 221) 354
KORETS (ex-MPK 222) 390

Black Sea
ALEKSANDROVETS (ex-MPK 49 (III)) 059
SUZDALETS (ex-MPK 118) 071
MPK 127 (III) 078
MUROMETS (ex-MPK 134) 064
KASIMOV (ex-MPK 199) 055
POVORINO (ex-MPK 207) 053
EISK (ex-MPK 217) 054

Displacement, tons: 950 standard; 1,200 full load
Dimensions, feet (metres): 233.6 × 32.2 × 12.1
(71.2 × 9.8 × 3.7)
Main machinery: CODAG; 1 gas-turbine; 15,000 hp(m)
(11 MW); 2 diesels; 16,000 hp(m) *(11.8 MW)*; 3 shafts
Speed, knots: 30
Range, n miles: 2,500 at 14 kt; 1,750 at 20 kt diesels; 950
at 27 kt
Complement: 70 (5 officers) (Grisha III); 60 (Grisha I)

Missiles: SAM: SA-N-4 Gecko twin launcher ❶; semi-active
radar homing to 15 km *(8 n miles)* at 2.5 Mach; warhead
50 kg; altitude 9.1–3,048 m *(30–10,000 ft)*; 20 missiles
(see *Structure* for SA-N-9).
Guns: 2—57 mm/80 (twin) ❷; 120 rds/min to 6 km
(3.3 n miles); weight of shell 2.8 kg.
1—3 in *(76 mm)*/60 (Grisha V) ❸; 120 rds/min to 15 km
(8 n miles); weight of shell 5.9 kg.
1—30 mm/65 (Grisha III and V classes) ❹; 6 barrels;
3,000 rds/min combined to 2 km.
Torpedoes: 4—21 in *(533 mm)* (2 twin) tubes ❺. Combination
of 53 cm torpedoes (see table at front of section).
A/S mortars: 2 RBU 6000 12-tubed trainable ❻; range
6,000 m; warhead 31 kg. (Only 1 in Grisha Vs.)
Depth charges: 2 racks (12).
Mines: Capacity for 18 in lieu of depth charges.
Countermeasures: Decoys: 4 PK 10 or 2 PK 16 chaff
launchers.
ESM: 2 Watch Dog.
Radars: Air/surface search: Strut Curve (Strut Pair in early
Grisha Vs) ❼; F-band; range 110 km *(60 n miles)* for 2 m²
target.
Half Plate Bravo (in later Grisha Vs); E/F-band.
Navigation: Don 2; I-band.
Fire control: Pop Group ❽; F/H/I-band (for SA-N-4). Bass
Tilt (Grisha III and V) ❿; H/I-band (for 57/76 mm and
30 mm).
IFF: High Pole A or B. Square Head. Salt Pot.
Sonars: Bull Nose; hull-mounted; active search and attack;
high/medium frequency.
Elk Tail; VDS ⓫; active search; high frequency. Similar to
Hormone helicopter dipping sonar.

Programmes: Grisha III 1973-85 (three remaining); Grisha V
1982-1996 onwards (22 remaining). All were built at
Kiev, Kharbarovsk and Zelenodolsk. Type name is *maly
protivolodochny korabl* meaning small anti-submarine
ship.
Structure: Grisha III class has Muff Cob radar removed,
Bass Tilt and 30 mm ADG (fitted aft), and Rad-haz screen
removed from abaft funnel as a result of removal of
Muff Cob. Grisha V is similar to Grisha III with the after
twin 57 mm mounting replaced by a single Tarantul type
76 mm gun.
Operational: Ten Grisha Vs are stationed in the Northern
Fleet, one Grisha III and seven Vs in the Pacific and two
IIIs and five Vs in the Black Sea. The modified Grisha III,
known as Grisha IV, has been decommissioned.
Sales: Two Grisha III to Lithuania in November 1992. One
Grisha V in 1994 and four Grisha II in 1996 to Ukraine.

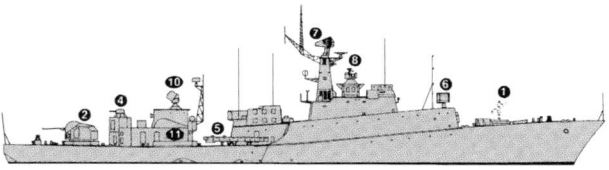

GRISHA III
(Scale 1 : 900), Ian Sturton / 0506081

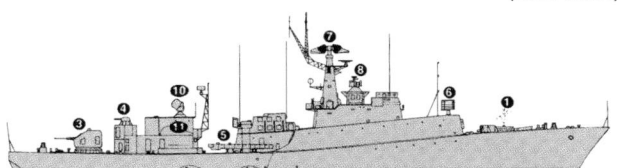

GRISHA V
(Scale 1 : 900), Ian Sturton / 0506082

LENINSKAYA KUZNITSA
12/2005*, Ships of the World / 1151146

SNEZNOGORSK
6/2003, B Lemachko / 1042304

MPK 191
12/2005*, Ships of the World
1151147

CORVETTES

2 DERGACH (SIVUCH) (PROJECT 1239) CLASS (PGGJM)

Name	No	Builders	Launched	Commissioned
BORA (ex-MRK 27)	615	Zelenodolsk, Kazan	1987	20 May 1997
SAMUM (ex-MRK 17)	616 (ex-575, ex-890)	Zelenodolsk, Kazan	1992	31 Dec 1995

Displacement, tons: 1,050 full load
Dimensions, feet (metres): 211.6 × 55.8 × 12.5
 (64.5 × 17 × 3.8)
Main machinery: CODOG; 2 gas turbines; 55,216 hp(m)
 (40.6 MW); 2 diesels; 10,064 hp(m) *(7.4 MW)*; 2 hydroprops;
 2 auxiliary diesels; 2 props on retractable pods
Speed, knots: 53 foil; 12 hullborne
Range, n miles: 600 at 50 kt; 2,500 at 12 kt
Complement: 67 (8 officers)

Missiles: SSM: 8 SS-N-22 (2 quad) Sunburn (3M-82 Moskit)
 launchers ❶; active radar homing to 160 km *(87 n miles)*
 at 2.5 Mach; warhead nuclear or 200 kT or HE 300 kg;
 sea-skimmer.
 SAM: SA-N-4 Gecko twin launcher ❷; semi-active radar
 homing to 15 km *(8 n miles)* at 2.5 Mach; warhead
 50 kg; 20 missiles.
Guns: 1—3 in *(76 mm)*/60 AK 176 ❸; 120 rds/min to 12 km
 (6.4 n miles); weight of shell 7 kg.
 2—30 mm/65 AK 630 ❹; 6 barrels per mounting;
 3,000 rds/min combined to 2 km.
Countermeasures: Decoys: 2 PK 16 and 2 PK 10 chaff
 launchers.
 ESM/ECM: 2 Foot Ball A. 2 Half Hats.
Weapons control: 2 Light Bulb datalink ❺. Band Stand ❻
 datalink for SS-N-22; Bell Nest.
Radars: Air/surface search: Cross Dome ❼; E/F-band.
 Fire control: Bass Tilt ❽; H/I-band (for guns).
 Pop Group ❾; F/H/I-band (for SAM).
 Navigation: SRN-207; I-band.
 IFF: Square Head. Salt Pot.

Programmes: Almaz design approved 24 December 1980.
 Classified as a PGGA (Guided Missile Patrol Air Cushion
 Vessels). Both did trials from 1989 (Bora) and 1993
 (Samum) before being accepted into service.
Structure: Twin-hulled surface effect design. The auxiliary
 diesels are for slow speed operations.
Operational: The design was unreliable but efforts were
 made in 1996/97 to restore both to an operational
 state. Both based at Sevastopol. SS-N-22 missiles
 were test-fired in April 2003. *Bora* has a camouflaged
 hull and is based at Sevastopol but operational status
 is doubtful.

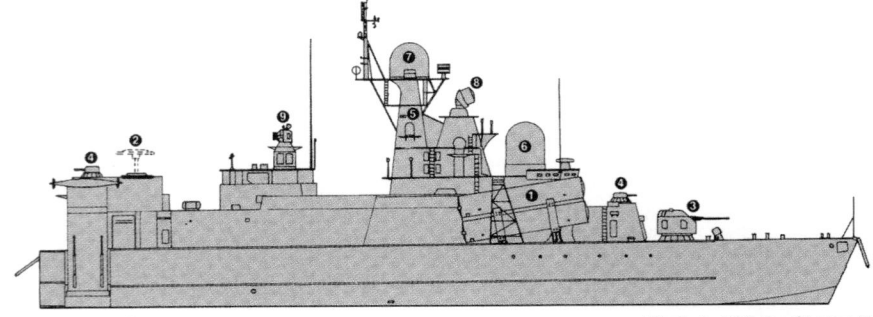

BORA

(Scale 1 : 600), Ian Sturton / 0506086

BORA
6/2003, B Lemachko
0580531

SAMUM

6/2003, B Lemachko / 0580532

15 NANUCHKA III (VETER) (PROJECT 1234.1) CLASS and 1 NANUCHKA IV (NAKAT) (PROJECT 1234.7) CLASS (FSG)

North	Baltic	Pacific	Black Sea
RASSVET 520	**LIVEN** 551	**MOROZ** 409	**SHTYL** 620
TUSHA 533	**GEYZER** 555	**RAZLIV** 450	**MIRAZH** 617
AYSBERG 535	**ZYB** 560	**SMERCH** 423	
NAKAT (IV) 526	**PASSAT** 570	**INEJ** 418	
	METEOR 590		

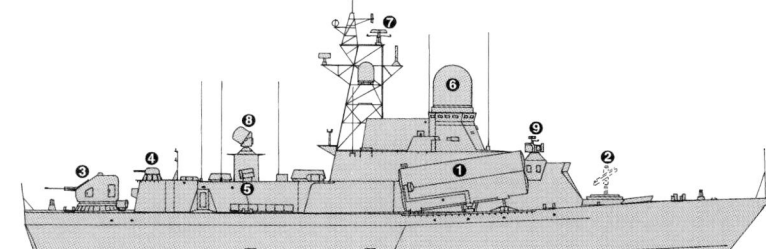

NANUCHKA III *(Scale 1 : 600), Ian Sturton* / 0105552

Displacement, tons: 660 full load
Dimensions, feet (metres): 194.5 × 38.7 × 8.5
(59.3 × 11.8 × 2.6)
Main machinery: 6 M 504 diesels; 26,112 hp(m) (19.2 MW);
3 shafts
Speed, knots: 33. **Range, n miles:** 2,500 at 12 kt; 900 at 31 kt
Complement: 42 (7 officers)

Missiles: SSM: 6 Chelomey SS-N-9 Siren (Malakhit)
(2 triple) launchers ❶; command guidance and IR and
active radar homing to 110 km (60 n miles) at 0.9 Mach;
warhead nuclear 250 kT or HE 500 kg. Nanuchka IV has
2 sextuple launchers for trials of SS-NX-26; radar homing
to 300 km (161.9 n miles) at Mach 2—3.5.
SAM: SA-N-4 Gecko twin launcher ❷; semi-active radar
homing to 15 km (8 n miles) at 2.5 Mach; warhead
50 kg; altitude 9.1—3,048 m (30—10,000 ft); 20 missiles.
Some anti-surface capability.
Guns: 1—3 in (76 mm)/60 ❸; 120 rds/min to 15 km
(8 n miles); weight of shell 7 kg.
1—30 mm/65 ❹; 6 barrels; 3,000 rds/min combined to 2 km.
Countermeasures: Decoys: 4 PK 10 chaff launchers ❺.
ESM: Foot Ball and Half Hat A and B. 4 Half Cup laser
warners.
Weapons control: 2 Bell Nest or Light Bulb (datalinks).
Band Stand ❻ datalink for SS-N-9.
Radars: Air/surface search: Peel Pair ❼; I-band or Plank
Shave; E/F-band.
Fire control: Bass Tilt ❽; H/I-band. Pop Group ❾; F/H/I-band
(for SA-N-4).
Navigation: Nayada; I-band.
IFF: High Pole. Square Head. Spar Stump. Salt Pot A and B.

Programmes: Built from 1969 onwards at Petrovsky,
Leningrad and in the Pacific. Nanuchka III, first seen in
1978. Nanuchka IV completed in 1987 as a trials ship. Type
name is *maly raketny korabl* meaning small missile ship.
Structure: The Nanuchka IV is similar in detail to Nanuchka III
except that she is the trials vehicle for SS-NX-26.
Operational: Intended for deployment in coastal waters
although formerly deployed in the Mediterranean (in
groups of two or three), North Sea and Pacific.

NAKAT (NANUCHKA IV) *8/2002* / 0528321

AYSBERG *6/2003, B Lemachko* / 1042303

0 + 1 (9) SCORPION (PROJECT 12300) CLASS (FSGM)

Displacement, tons: 470 standard
Dimensions, feet (metres): 186.4 × 35.4 × 17.1
(56.8 × 10.8 × 5.2)
Main machinery: CODAG: 1 M-70FR gas turbine; 8,775 hp
(6.54 MW); 2 MTU 16V4000 M 90 diesels; 16,320 hp
(12.2 MW); 2 shafts; 1 hydrojet
Speed, knots: 38
Range, n miles: 1,500 at 12 kt
Complement: 37

Missiles: SSM: 8 NPOMash SS-N-26 (2 quad) 3M55
Oniks/Yakhont launchers ❶; inertial guidance and
active/passive radar homing to 300 km (160 n miles) at
3.5 Mach; warhead 250 kg; sea skimmer (to be
confirmed).
SAM/Guns: 1 CADS-N (Kortik/Kashtan) (3M87) ❷; twin
30 mm Gatling combined with 8 SA-N-11 (Grison) and
Hot Flash/Hot Spot fire-control radar/optronic director.
Laser beam guidance for missiles to 8 km (4.4 n miles);
warhead 9 kg; 9,000 rds/min to 1.5 km (for guns).
Guns: 1—3.9 in (100 mm) A 190 (L 59) ❸ 60 rds/min to 15 km
(8.2 n miles); weight of shell 16 kg.

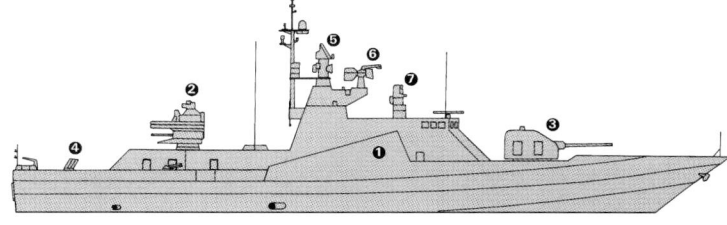

SCORPION *(Scale 1 : 600), Ian Sturton* / 0569930

Countermeasures: Decoys: 4 PK10 chaff launchers ❹. ESM.
Radars: Air/surface search: Positiv M1 ❺; I-band.
Fire control: Plank Shave (Garpun B) ❻; I/J-band.
Ratep 5P-10E Puma ❼; I-band (for 100 mm gun).

Programmes: Designed by ALMAZ, St Petersburg, as
successor to the Tarantul class. First vessel laid down

5 June 2001 at Vympel shipyard, Rybinsk, with delivery
planned for 2005. A class of 10 vessels was envisaged for
the Russian Navy and further sales abroad but the status
of the project is uncertain.
Structure: Designed with stealth features and equipped
with stabilising automatic control system to reduce
rolling.

27 TARANTUL (MOLNYA) (PROJECT 1241.1/ 1241.1M/1241.1MP/1242.1) CLASS (FSGM)

TARANTUL II					
R 101	714	R 29	916	GROZA (ex-R 239)	953
STUPINETS (ex-R 49)	705	R 129	852	IVANOVETS (ex-R 334)	954
		R 271	909	BURYA (ex-R 60)	955
TARANTUL III		R 20	921	R 71	962
R 160	700	R 14	924	R 298	971
R 47	819	R 18	937	R 19	978
DMITROVGRAD (ex-R 291)	825	R 11	940	R 261	991
R 187	855	R 24	946		
R 2	870	R 297	951		
MORSHANSK (ex-R 293)	874	R 109	952		
R 442	907	R 79	995		

Displacement, tons: 385 standard; 455 full load
Dimensions, feet (metres): 184.1 × 37.7 × 8.2 *(56.1 × 11.5 × 2.5)*
Main machinery: COGAG; 2 Nikolayev Type DR 77 gas turbines; 16,016 hp(m) *(11.77 MW)* sustained; 2 Nikolayev Type DR 76 gas turbines with reversible gearboxes; 4,993 hp(m) *(3.67 MW)* sustained; 2 shafts or CODOG with 2 CM 504 diesels; 8,000 hp(m) *(5.88 MW)*, replacing second pair of gas-turbines in Tarantul IIIs
Speed, knots: 36
Range, n miles: 400 at 36 kt; 1,650 at 14 kt
Complement: 34 (5 officers)

Missiles: SSM: 4 Raduga SS-N-2D Styx (2 twin) launchers (Tarantul II); active radar or IR homing to 83 km *(45 n miles)* at 0.9 Mach; warhead 513 kg; sea-skimmer at end of run. 4 Raduga SS-N-22 Sunburn (3M-82 Moskit) (2 twin) launchers (Tarantul III); active radar homing to 160 km *(87 n miles)* at 2.5 Mach; warhead nuclear 200 kT or HE 300 kg; sea-skimmer. Modified version in Type 1242.1.
SAM: SA-N-5 Grail quad launcher; manual aiming; IR homing to 6 km *(3.2 n miles)* at 1.5 Mach; altitude to 2,500 m *(8,000 ft)*; warhead 1.5 kg.
Guns: 1—3 in *(76 mm)*/60; 120 rds/min to 15 km *(8 n miles)*; weight of shell 7 kg.
2—30 mm/65; 6 barrels per mounting; 3,000 rds/min to 2 km.
Countermeasures: Decoys: 2 PK 16 or 4 PK 10 (Tarantul III) chaff launchers.
ESM: 2 Foot Ball, 2 Half Hat (in some).
Weapons control: Hood Wink optronic director. Light Bulb datalink. Band Stand; datalink for SSM; Bell Nest.
Radars: Air/surface search: Plank Shave or Positiv E (Tarantul 874); I-band.
Navigation: Kivach III; I-band.
Fire control: Bass Tilt; H/I-band.
IFF: Square Head. High Pole B.
Sonars: Foal Tail; VDS; active search; high frequency.

Programmes: Tarantul II were built at Kolpino, Petrovsky, Leningrad and in the Pacific in 1980-86. Production of Tarantul IIIs then continued until 1995 although a single experimental Tarantul III with four SS-N-22 had been completed at Petrovsky in 1981. One more was launched in September 1997 at Rybinsk, and a Tarantul III at Kolpino completed in December 1999 for the Baltic Fleet. Type name is *raketny kater* meaning missile cutter.
Modernisation: Tarantul III 874 served as a trials platform for a modified version of SS-N-22 with a longer range; the missile is distinguished by end caps on the launcher doors. Tarantul II 962 (now decommissioned) served as a trials platform for the CADS-N-1 point defence system in the Black Sea.
Structure: Basically same hull as Pauk class, without extension for sonar. The single Type 1242.1 has a Positiv E radar.
Operational: Two Tarantul II (*Stupinets* and R 129) and five IIIs (R 47, R 291, R 187, R 2, R 293) are in the Baltic, five IIIs (R 109, R 239, R 334, R 60, R 71) are in the Black Sea, one II (R 101) and one III (R 160) are in the Caspian and one II (R 79) and 12 IIIs (R 20, R 29, R 14, R 18, R 11, R 24, R 271, R 297, R 298, R 19, R 261 and R 442) are in the Pacific.
Sales: Tarantul I class-one to Poland 28 December 1983, second in April 1984, third in March 1988 and fourth in January 1989. One to India in April 1987, second in January 1988, third in December 1988, fourth in November 1989 and fifth in January 1990. Two to Yemen in November 1990 and January 1991. One to Romania in December 1990, two more in February 1992. One Tarantul II to Bulgaria in March 1990. Two Tarantul Is to Vietnam in 1996 and two more in 1999.

R 18 *10/2002, Hachiro Nakai* / 0528322

R 29 *9/2004, Hachiro Nakai* / 1042313

MOD TARANTUL III *6/1999* / 0081670

SHIPBORNE AIRCRAFT

Notes: (1) A smaller variant of the Kamov Ka-60 is reported to have been offered to the Russian Navy. The Ka-40 anti-submarine helicopter has been under development since 1990. Loosely based on the 'Helix', it is likely to have a similar main rotor and tail-fin configuration.
(2) Haze B helicopters have all been placed in reserve as have all Ka-25 Hormones. The latter remain active and probably have a training role.

Numbers/Type: 18/2 Sukhoi Su-33 Flanker D/Su-33 UB.
Operational speed: 1,345 kt *(2,500 km/h)*.
Service ceiling: 59,000 ft *(18,000 m)*.
Range: 2,160 + n miles *(4,000 km)*.
Role/Weapon systems: Fleet air defence fighter. 20 production aircraft delivered of which 2 have been lost. 10 are believed to be operational. All based in the Northern Fleet. Most training is done from a simulated flight deck ashore. Sensors: Track-while-scan pulse Doppler radar, IR scanner. Weapons: One 30 mm cannon, 10 AAMs (AA-12, AA-11, AA-8).

FLANKER *2/1996* / 0506323

Numbers/Type: 4 Sukhoi Su-25UT Frogfoot UTG.
Operational speed: 526 kt *(975 km/h)*.
Service ceiling: 22,965 ft *(7,000 m)*.
Range: 675 n miles *(1,250 km)*.
Role/Weapon systems: The UTG version is the two seater ground attack aircraft used for deck training in the carrier *Kuznetsov*. About 40 more of these aircraft are Air Force. Sensors: Laser rangefinder, ESM, ECM. Weapons: One 30 mm cannon, AAMs (AA-8), rockets, bombs.

FROGFOOT *2/1996* / 0506324

Numbers/Type: 2 Kamov Ka-31 Helix RLD.
Operational speed: 119 kt *(220 km/h)*.
Service ceiling: 11,480 ft *(3,500 m)*.
Range: 162 n miles *(300 km)*.
Role/Weapon systems: AEW conversions with a solid-state radar under the fuselage. Four sold to India. Sensors: Oko E-801 Surveillance radar, datalinks. Weapons: Unarmed.

HELIX RLD *9/1995* / 0506325

Numbers/Type: 85/30/4 Kamov Ka-27Pl Helix A/Ka-29 Helix B/Ka-32 Helix D.
Operational speed: 135 kt *(250 km/h).*
Service ceiling: 19,685 ft *(6,000 m).*
Range: 432 n miles *(800 km).*
Role/Weapon systems: ASW helicopter; three main versions – 'A' for ASW, 'B' for assault and D for SAR; deployed to surface ships and some shore stations. Sensors: Osminog Splash Drop search radar, VGS-3 dipping sonar, sonobuoys, MAD, ESM. Weapons: ASW; three APR-2 torpedoes, nuclear or conventional S3V depth bombs or mines. Assault type: Two UV-57 rocket pods (2 × 32).

HELIX A *9/2004, Hachiro Nakai* / 1042312

LAND-BASED MARITIME AIRCRAFT (FRONT LINE)

Notes: (1) The MiG-29 Fulcrum D has been abandoned by the Navy and the Ka-34 Hokum is not in production. Yak-41 Freestyle is not being developed but the prototype is for sale. Fitter C/D, Badgers and Bear D aircraft were out of service by 1995, Blinders and Bear G by 1997, and Mail and Haze A/C by 1999 (except for three still active in the Black Sea Fleet). (2) Tu-204P has been proposed as an ASW/reconnaissance aircraft to replace the 'May'. It would be a development of the commercial transport aircraft.

Numbers/Type: 2 Ilyushin Il-20 Coot A.
Operational speed: 364 kt *(675 km/h).*
Service ceiling: 32,800 ft *(10,000 m).*
Range: 3,508 n miles *(6,500 km).*
Role/Weapon systems: Long-range Elint and MR for naval forces' intelligence gathering. Sensors: SLAR, weather radar, cameras, Elint equipment. Weapons: Unarmed.

COOT A *6/1995, Sergey Sergeyev* / 0574163

Numbers/Type: 26 Ilyushin Il-38 May.
Operational speed: 347 kt *(645 km/h).*
Service ceiling: 32,800 ft *(10,000 m).*
Range: 3,887 n miles *(7,200 km).*
Role/Weapon systems: Long-range MR and ASW. 12 in the North, 14 in the Pacific. Test flights of an upgraded version started in 2002 and continued in 2003. Sensors: Wet Eye search/weather radar, MAD, sonobuoys. Weapons: ASW; internal storage for 6 tons weapons.

MAY *6/1999* / 0081667

Numbers/Type: 5 Antonov An-12 Cub ('Cub B/C/D') ('Cub C/D' ECM/ASW).
Operational speed: 419 kt *(777 km/h).*
Service ceiling: 33,500 ft *(10,200 m).*
Range: 3,075 n miles *(5,700 km).*
Role/Weapon systems: Used either for intelligence gathering (B) or electronic warfare (C, D); is versatile with long range. Sensors: Search/weather radar, three EW blisters (B), tail-mounted EW/Elint equipment in addition (C/D). Weapons: Self-defence; two 23 mm cannon (B and D only).

Numbers/Type: 45 Tupolev Tu-22 M Backfire C.
Operational speed: 2.0 Mach.
Service ceiling: 60,000 ft *(18,300 m).*
Range: 2,500 n miles *(4,630 km).*
Role/Weapon systems: Medium-range nuclear/conventional strike and reconnaissance. About 20 are operational. Sensors: Down Beat search/Fan Tail attack radars, EW. Weapons: ASV; 12 tons of 'iron' bombs or standoff missiles AS-4 Kitchen (Kh 22N(A)) and AS-6 Kickback (Kh 15P). Self-defence; two 23 mm cannon.

BACKFIRE *6/2003, Paul Jackson* / 0547316

Numbers/Type: 20/12 Tupolev Tu-142 Bear F/Bear J.
Operational speed: 500 kt *(925 km/h).*
Service ceiling: 60,000 ft *(18,300 m).*
Range: 6,775 n miles *(12,550 km).*
Role/Weapon systems: Multimission long-range aircraft (ASW and communications variants). 36 in the North, remainder Pacific. Sensors: Wet Eye search radar, ESM; search radar, sonobuoys, EW, MAD (F), ELINT systems (J). The Bear J is reported to be equipped with VLF communications for SSBN connectivity. Weapons: ASW; various torpedoes, depth bombs and/or mines (F). Self-defence; some have two 23 mm or more cannon.

BEAR 'J' *6/1994, G Jacobs* / 0564718

Numbers/Type: 40 Sukhoi Su-24 Fencer D/E.
Operational speed: 1.15 Mach.
Service ceiling: 57,400 ft *(17,500 m).*
Range: 950 n miles *(1,755 km).*
Role/Weapon systems: Fitted for maritime reconnaissance (19) and strike (27). Sensors: Radar and EW. Weapons: 30 mm Gatling gun; various ASM missiles and bombs; some have 23 mm cannon.

FENCER E *6/1999, Jane's* / 0048910

PATROL FORCES

0 + 2 (3) BUYAN (PROJECT 21630) CLASS (PG)

ASTRAKHAN   **KASPIYSK**

Displacement, tons: 520 full load
Dimensions, feet (metres): 206.7 × 29.5 × 10.2 *(63.0 × 9.0 × 3.1)*
Main machinery: 2 Zvezda M520 diesels; 9,900 hp *(7.35 MW)*; 2 waterjets
Speed, knots: 25. **Range, n miles:** To be announced
Complement: To be announced

Missiles: SAM: SA-16 Gubka (Strelets); IR homing to 5 km *(2.7 n miles)* at 2.6 Mach; warhead 1.3 kg.
Guns: 1—3.9 in *(100 mm)* A 190; 60 rds/min to 15 km *(8.2 n miles)*; weight of shell 16 kg.
   2—30 mm/65 AK 630; 6 barrels per mounting; 3,000 rds/min to 2 km.
   2—14.5 mm MGs. 3—7.62 mm MGs.
   1—122 mm UMS-73 Grad-M multibarrelled rocket launcher.
Countermeasures: Decoys: 2 KT 216 launchers.
Radars: Air/surface search: Cross Dome (Positiv-E); E/F-band.
Fire control: Bass Tilt (MR-123); I/J-band.
Navigation: I-band.

Comment: Designed by Zelenodolsk Design Bureau and built by Almaz, St Petersburg. *Astrakhan* laid down on 30 January 2004 and launched on 7 October 2005. *Kaspiysk* laid down on 25 February 2005. Heavily armed gunboat designed for littoral operations. The first is likely to become operational in the Caspian Sea in late 2007. At least three further units are expected.

ASTRAKHAN   *10/2005*, Ships of the World* / 1154408

3 SVETLYAK (PROJECT 1041Z) CLASS (PGM)

Displacement, tons: 375 full load
Dimensions, feet (metres): 159.1 × 30.2 × 11.5 *(48.5 × 9.2 × 3.5)*
Main machinery: 3 diesels; 14,400 hp(m) *(10.58 MW)* sustained; 3 shafts
Speed, knots: 31. **Range, n miles:** 2,200 at 13 kt
Complement: 36 (4 officers)

Missiles: SAM: SA-N-5 Grail quad launcher; manual aiming; IR homing to 6 km *(3.2 n miles)* at 1.5 Mach; warhead 1.5 kg.
Guns: 1—3 in *(76 mm)*/60; 120 rds/min to 15 km *(8 n miles)*; weight of shell 7 kg.
   1 or 2—30 mm/65 AK 630; 6 barrels; 3,000 rds/min combined to 2 km.
Torpedoes: 2—16 in *(406 mm)* tubes.
Depth charges: 2 racks; 12 charges.
Countermeasures: Decoys: 2 chaff launchers.
Weapons control: Hook Wink optronic director.
Radars: Air/surface search: Peel cone; E-band.
Fire control: Bass Tilt; H/I-band.
Navigation: Palm Frond B; I-band.
Sonars: Rat Tail; VDS; active search; high frequency.

Comment: Most of this class are in service with the Federal Border Guard but three were reported to have been allocated to the navy and are possibly based in the Caspian.

SVETLYAK 040   *10/2002, B Lemachko* / 0570904

1 MUKHA (SOKOL) (PROJECT 1145) CLASS
(FAST ATTACK CRAFT—PATROL HYDROFOIL) (PGK)

VLADIMIRETS (ex-MPK 220) 060

Displacement, tons: 400 full load
Dimensions, feet (metres): 164 × 27.9 (33.5 over foils) × 13.1 (19.4 foils)
   (50 × 8.5; 10.2 × 4; 5.9)
Main machinery: CODOG; 2 Type NK-12M gas turbines; 23,046 hp(m) *(16.95 MW)* sustained; 2 diesels; 2,400 hp(m) *(1.76 MW)*; 2 shafts
Speed, knots: 40; 12 hullborne
Complement: 45

Guns: 1—3 in *(76 mm)*/60; 120 rds/min to 15 km *(8 n miles)*; weight of shell 7 kg.
   2—30 mm/65 AK 630; 6 barrels per mounting; 3,000 rds/min combined to 2 km
Torpedoes: 8—16 in *(406 mm)* (2 quad) tubes. SAET-40; anti-submarine; active/passive homing to 10 km *(5.4 n miles)* at 30 kt; warhead 100 kg
Countermeasures: Decoys: 2 PK 16 chaff launchers
ESM: Radar warning
Radars: Surface search: Peel Cone; E-band
Navigation: SRN 206; I-band
Fire control: Bass Tilt; H/I-band
Sonars: Foal Tail; VDS; active search; high frequency

Programmes: Built in 1986 at Feodosuja.
Structure: Features include a hydrofoil arrangement with a single fixed foil forward, large gas-turbine exhausts aft, and trainable torpedo mountings.
Operational: The only ship of the class, which was used as a trials platform for the Medveka ASW guided weapon, is based in the Black Sea.

VLADIMIRETS   *9/2004, Hartmut Ehlers* / 1042314

4 MATKA (VEKHR) CLASS (PROJECT 206MP)
(FAST ATTACK CRAFT—MISSILE HYDROFOIL) (PGGK)

BOROVSK (ex-R 30) 702   **R 44** 966
R 25 706   **R 50** —

Displacement, tons: 225 standard; 260 full load
Dimensions, feet (metres): 129.9 × 24.9 (41 over foils) × 6.9 (13.1 over foils)
   (39.6 × 7.6; 12.5 × 2.1; 4)
Main machinery: 3 Type M 504 diesels; 10,800 hp(m) *(7.94 MW)* sustained; 3 shafts
Speed, knots: 40. **Range, n miles:** 600 at 35 kt foilborne; 1,500 at 14 kt hullborne
Complement: 33

Missiles: SSM: 2 SS-N-2C/D Styx; active radar or IR homing to 83 km *(45 n miles)* at 0.9 Mach; warhead 513 kg; sea-skimmer at end of run.
   8 SS-N-25 (in *966*); radar homing to 130 km *(70.2 n miles)* at 0.9 Mach; warhead 145 kg; sea-skimmer.
Guns: 1—3 in *(76 mm)*/60; 120 rds/min to 15 km *(8 n miles)*; weight of shell 7 kg.
   1—30 mm/65 AK 630; 6 barrels per mounting; 3,000 rds/min to 2 km.
Countermeasures: Decoys: 2 PK 16 chaff launchers.
ESM: Clay Brick; intercept.
Weapons control: Hood Wink optronic directors.
Radars: Air/surface search: Plank Shave; E-band.
Navigation: SRN-207; I-band.
Fire control: Bass Tilt; H/I-band.
IFF: High Pole B or Salt Pot B and Square Head.

Programmes: In early 1978 the first of class was seen. Built at Kolpino Yard, Leningrad. Production stopped in 1983 being superseded by Tarantul class. Type name is *raketny kater* meaning missile cutter.
Structure: Similar hull to the deleted Osa class with similar single hydrofoil system to Turya class. The combination has produced a better sea-boat than the Osa class. *R 44* in the Black Sea was the trials craft for the SS-N-25.
Operational: *R 44* is based in the Black Sea and the other three are based in the Caspian. Five units transferred to Ukraine in 1996.

R 44   *6/2003, B Lemachko* / 0570912

AMPHIBIOUS FORCES

Notes: It was announced in mid-2005 that a new large landing ship displacing 8,000—9,000 tons was to be laid down by late 2005. Further details have not been announced.

0 + 1 (5) MODIFIED ALLIGATOR (PROJECT 11711E) CLASS (LSTHM)

Name	No	Builders	Laid down	Launched	Commissioned
IVAN GREN	—	Yantar, Kaliningrad	23 Dec 2004	2006	2007

Displacement, tons: 5,000 full load
Dimensions, feet (metres): 393.7 × 54.1 × 11.8 *(120.0 × 16.5 × 3.6)*
Main machinery: 2 diesels; 10,000 hp(m) *(7.5 MW)*; 2 shafts
Speed, knots: 18. **Range, n miles:** 3,500 at 16 kt
Complement: 100
Military lift: 300 troops; 13—60 ton tanks or 36 armoured personnel carriers
Missiles: 2—140 mm multilaunch rocket system.
Guns: 1—3 in *(76 mm)*/60; AK-176; 120 rds/min to 15 km *(8 n miles)*; weight of shell 7 kg.
   2—30 mm/65 AK-630; 6 barrels per mounting; 3,000 rds/min to 2 km.
Radars: To be announced.

Helicopters: 1 Ka-29 Helix B.

Comment: First of a new class of amphibious ship which, based on the Project number, is likely to be a modified version of the Alligator class landing ships which were built between 1966-76. Up to six ships, to replace the Alligator class, are expected.

1 IVAN ROGOV (YEDNOROG) (PROJECT 1174) CLASS (LPDHM)

Name	No	Builders	Launched	Commissioned
MITROFAN MOSKALENKO	020	Yantar, Kaliningrad	July 1989	Mar 1991

Displacement, tons: 8,260 standard; 14,060 full load
Dimensions, feet (metres): 516.7 × 80.2 × 21.2 (27.8 flooded)
(157.5 × 24.5 × 6.5; 8.5)
Main machinery: 2 M8K gas-turbines; 39,998 hp(m)
(29.4 MW); 2 shafts
Speed, knots: 19
Range, n miles: 7,500 at 14 kt
Complement: 239 (37 officers)
Military lift: 522 troops (battalion); 20 tanks or equivalent weight of APCs and trucks; 3 ACVs or 6 LCM in docking bay

Missiles: SAM: SA-N-4 Gecko twin launcher ❶; semi-active radar homing to 15 km *(8 n miles)* at 2.5 Mach; warhead 50 kg; altitude 9.1—3,048 m *(30—10,000 ft);* 20 missiles.
2 SA-N-5 Grail quad launchers; manual aiming; IR homing to 6 km *(3.2 n miles)* at 1.5 Mach; warhead 1.5 kg.
Guns: 2—3 in *(76 mm)*/60 (twin) ❷; 60 rds/min to 15 km *(8 n miles);* weight of shell 6.8 kg.
1—122 mm UMS-22 Grad-M; 2—40-barrelled rocket launcher; range 20 km *(10.8 n miles).*
4—30 mm/65 AK 630 ❸; 6 barrels per mounting; 3,000 rds/min combined to 2 km.
Countermeasures: Decoys: 16 PK 10 and 4 PK 16 chaff launchers.
ESM: 3 Bell Shroud; intercept.
ECM: 2 Bell Squat; jammers.
Weapons control: 2 Squeeze Box optronic directors ❹.
Radars: Air/surface search: Top Plate A ❺; 3D; E-band.
Navigation: 2 Don Kay or 2 Palm Frond; I-band.
Fire control: Owl Screech ❻; G-band (for 76 mm). 2 Bass Tilt ❼; H/I-band (for 30 mm). Pop Group ❽; F/H/I-band (for SA-N-4).
CCA: Fly Screen ❾ and Fly Spike; I-band.
IFF: Salt Pot B.
Tacan: 2 Round House ❿.
Sonars: Mouse Tail VDS; active search; high frequency.

Helicopters: 4 Ka-29 Helix B ⓫.

MITROFAN MOSKALENKO   *10/1996* / 0019045

Programmes: This was the third of class. Fourth of class was not completed. Type name is *bolshoy desantny korabl* meaning large landing ship.
Structure: Has bow ramp with beaching capability leading from a tank deck 200 ft long and 45 ft wide. Cargo capacity 2,500 tons Stern doors open into a docking bay 250 ft long and 45 ft wide. A helicopter spot forward has a flying-control station and the after helicopter deck and hangar is similarly fitted. Helicopters can enter the hangar from both front and rear. Positions arranged on main superstructure for replenishment of both fuel and solids. Has been reported streaming a VDS from the stern door and has also conducted unidentified missile trials.
Operational: Based in the Northern Fleet at Severomorsk. Two Pacific Fleet units were paid off in 1996 and 1997. The refit and sale of one of these ships to Indonesia was not concluded.

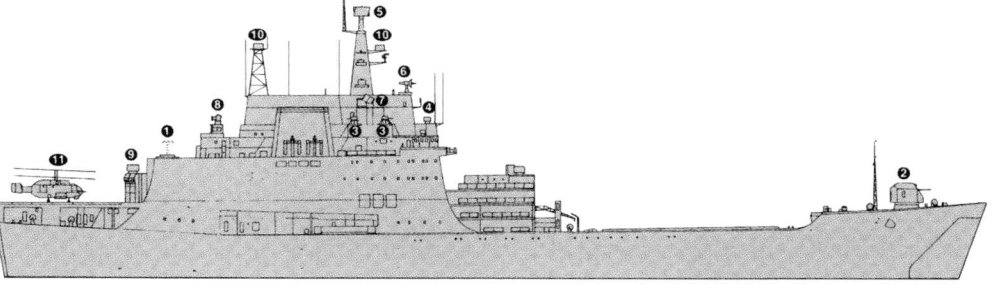

MITROFAN MOSKALENKO   *(Scale 1 : 1,200), Ian Sturton* / 0506088

16 ROPUCHA (PROJECT 775/775M) CLASS (LSTM)

North:	OLENEGORSKIY GORNIAK 012	GEORGIY POBEDONOSETS 016	KONDOPOGA 027	ALEXANDER OTRAKOVSKIY 031	KOTLAS 035
Baltic:	KALININGRAD 102	ALEXANDER SHABALIN 110	MINSK 127	KOROLEV 130 (II)	
Black:	AZOV 151 (II)	YAMAL 156	TSESAR KUNIKOV 158	NOVOCHERKASSK 142	
Pacific:	BDK-98 055	MUKHTAR AVEZOV 066	NIKOLAY KORSAKOV 077 (II)		

Displacement, tons: 4,400 full load
Dimensions, feet (metres): 369.1 × 49.2 × 12.1
(112.5 × 15 × 3.7)
Main machinery: 2 Zgoda-Sulzer 16ZVB40/48 diesels; 19,230 hp(m) *(14.14 MW)* sustained; 2 shafts
Speed, knots: 17.5. **Range, n miles:** 3,500 at 16 kt; 6,000 at 12 kt
Complement: 95 (7 officers)
Military lift: 10 MBT plus 190 troops or 24 AFVs plus 170 troops or mines

Missiles: SAM: 4 SA-N-5 Grail quad launchers (in at least two ships); manual aiming; IR homing to 6 km *(3.2 n miles)* at 1.5 Mach; altitude to 2,500 m *(8,000 ft);* warhead 1.5 kg; 32 missiles.
Guns: 4—57 mm/80 (2 twin) ❶ (Ropucha I); 120 rds/min to 6 km *(3.3 n miles);* weight of shell 2.8 kg.
1—76 mm/60 (Ropucha II); 60 rds/min to 15 km *(8 n miles);* weight of shell 6.8 kg.
2—30 mm/65 AK 630 (Ropucha II).
2—122 mm UMS-73 Grad-M (in some) ❷. 2—40-barrelled rocket launchers; range 9 km *(5 n miles).*
Mines: 92 contact type.
Weapons control: 2 Squeeze Box optronic directors ❸. Hood Wink and Odd Box.
Radars: Air/surface search: Strut Curve ❹ (Ropucha I) or Cross Dome (Ropucha II); F-band.

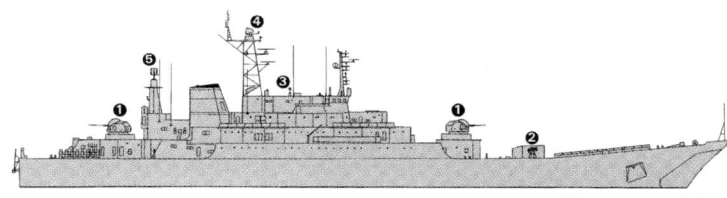

ROPUCHA I   *(Scale 1 : 1,200), Ian Sturton* / 0506247

Navigation: Don 2 or Nayada; I-band.
Fire control: Muff Cob ❺ (Ropucha I); G/H-band.
Bass Tilt (Ropucha II): H/I-band.
IFF: 2 High Pole A or Salt Pot A.
Sonars: Mouse Tail VDS can be carried.

Programmes: Ropucha Is completed at Northern Shipyard, Gdansk, Poland in two spells from 1974-78 (12 ships) and 1980-88. Ropucha IIs started building in 1987 with the first one commissioning in May 1990. The third and last of the class completed in January 1992. Type name is *bolshoy desantny korabl* (BDK) meaning large landing ship.
Structure: A Ro-Ro design with a tank deck running the whole length of the ship. All have very minor differences in appearance. These ships have a higher troop-to-vehicle ratio than the Alligator class. At least five of the class have rocket launchers at the after end of the forecastle. The second type have a 76 mm gun forward in place of one twin 57 mm and an ADG aft instead of the second. Radar and EW suites are also different. The after mast has been replaced by a solid extension to the superstructure.
Operational: Nine more have been deleted so far.
Sales: One to South Yemen in 1979, returned to Russia in late 1991 for refit and was back in Aden in 1993. One to Ukraine in 1996.

KALININGRAD (ROPUCHA I)   *8/2004* / 1042327

NIKOLAY KORSAKOV (ROPUCHA II)
9/2004, Hachiro Nakai
1042311

5 ALLIGATOR (TAPIR) (PROJECT 1171) CLASS (LSTM)

SARATOV (ex-*Voronezhsky Konsomolets*) 150   **MINSK** (ex-*Donetsky Shakhter*) 119   **NIKOLAY FILCHENKOV** 152   **NIKOLAY VILKOV** 081 (IV)   **ORSK** (ex-*Nicolay Obyekov*) 148

Displacement, tons: 3,400 standard; 4,700 full load
Dimensions, feet (metres): 370.7 × 50.8 × 14.7
  (113 × 15.5 × 4.5)
Main machinery: 2 diesels; 9,000 hp(m) *(6.6 MW)*; 2 shafts
Speed, knots: 18. **Range, n miles:** 10,000 at 15 kt
Complement: 100
Military lift: 300 troops; 1,750 tons including about 20 tanks
  and various trucks; 40 AFVs

Missiles: SAM: 2 or 3 SA-N-5 Grail twin launchers;
  manual aiming; IR homing to 6 km *(3.2 n miles)* at
  1.5 Mach; altitude to 2,500 m *(8,000 ft)*; warhead 1.5 kg;
  16 missiles.
Guns: 2—57 mm/70 (twin); 120 rds/min to 8 km
  (4.4 n miles); weight of shell 2.8 kg.
  4—25 mm/80 (2 twin) (Type 4); 270 rds/min to 3 km
  (1.6 n miles); weight of shell 0.34 kg.
  1—122 mm UMS-72 Grad-M; 2—40-barrelled rocket
  launchers (in Types 3 and 4); range 9 km *(5 n miles)*.
Weapons control: 1 Squeeze Box optronic director (Types
  3 and 4).
Radars: Surface search: 2 Don 2; I-band.

Programmes: First ship commissioned in 1966 at
  Kaliningrad. Last of class in service completed in 1976.
  Type name is *bolshoy desantny korabl* meaning large
  landing ship. One more Type 3 in service with Ukraine.
Structure: These ships have ramps on the bow and stern. In
  Type 3 the bridge structure has been raised and a forward
  deck house has been added to accommodate shore
  bombardment rocket launchers. Type 4 is similar to Type 3
  with the addition of two twin 25 mm gun mountings on

SARATOV   *9/2004, Hartmut Ehlers* / 1042316

centreline abaft the bridge superstructure. As well as
a tank deck 300 ft long stretching right across the hull
there are two smaller deck areas and a hold.
Operational: In the 1980s the class operated regularly
  off West Africa, in the Mediterranean and in the
Indian Ocean, usually with Naval Infantry units
embarked. Half the class have been scrapped or laid up.
Of the remainder, *Vilkov* is in the Pacific, *Minsk* in the
Baltic, and the others in the Black Sea.
Sales: One to Ukraine in 1995.

6 POLNOCHNY B CLASS (PROJECT 771) (LSM)

578   +5

Displacement, tons: 760 standard; 834 full load
Dimensions, feet (metres): 246.1 × 31.5 × 7.5 *(75 × 9.6 × 2.3)*
Main machinery: 2 Kolomna Type 40-D diesels; 4,400 hp(m) *(3.2 MW)* sustained; 2 shafts
Speed, knots: 19
Range, n miles: 1,000 at 18 kt
Complement: 40—42
Military lift: 180 troops; 350 tons including 6 tanks
Missiles: SAM: 4 SA-N-5 Grail quad launchers.
Guns: 2 or 4—30 mm (1 or 2 twin).
  2—140 mm WM-18 rocket launchers; 18 barrels.
Weapons control: PED-1 system.
Radars: Surface search: Spin Trough; I-band.
  Fire control: Drum Tilt; H/I-band (for 30 mm guns).
IFF: High Pole A. Square Head.

Comment: Built at Northern Shipyard, Gdansk, Poland in 1970. 578 serves in the Northern
  Fleet as a logistic support ship. Five have been reported active in the Caspian while others
  of the class are in reserve, derelict or scrapped. Tank deck 45.7 × 5.2 m *(150 × 17 ft)*.

POLNOCHNY   *7/1996, van Ginderen Collection* / 0019047

9 ONDATRA (AKULA) (PROJECT 1176) CLASS (LCMS)

701	720	748	DKA 325 799
DKA 286 713	746	751	+2

Displacement, tons: 145 full load
Dimensions, feet (metres): 78.7 × 16.4 × 4.9 *(24 × 5 × 1.5)*
Main machinery: 2 diesels; 300 hp(m) *(220 kW)*; 2 shafts
Speed, knots: 10
Range, n miles: 500 at 5 kt
Complement: 5
Military lift: 1 MBT

Comment: First completed in 1979 and associated with *Ivan Rogov*. 33 deleted so far. Tank
  deck of 45 × 13 ft. Two to Yemen in 1983. Two of unknown pennant number are based in
  the Caspian. The remainder are in the Baltic.

ONDATRA   *7/1996, B Lemachko* / 0570917

3 SERNA CLASS (LCU)

DKA 67 747   +2

Displacement, tons: 105 full load
Dimensions, feet (metres): 86.3 × 19 × 5.2 *(26.3 × 5.8 × 1.6)*
Main machinery: 2 M 503A3 diesels; 5,522 hp(m) *(4.06 MW)*; 2 shafts
Speed, knots: 30. **Range, n miles:** 100 at 30 kt; 600 at 22 kt
Complement: 6
Military lift: 45 tons or 100 troops

Comment: High-speed utility landing craft capable of beaching and in service in
  May 1995. Have an 'air-lubricated' hull. Designed for both military and civilian use by
  the R Alexeyev Central Design Bureau and built at Nizhny Novgorod. Can be armed.
  DKA-67 is operational in the Baltic Fleet and two are reported to be in the Caspian. Three
  others have been sold commercially.

DKA-67   *6/2003, B Lemachko* / 1042315

3 POMORNIK (ZUBR) (PROJECT 1232.2) CLASS (ACVM/LCUJM)

YEVGENIY KOCHESHKOV (ex-MDK-118) 770   **MORDOVIYA** (ex-MDK-94) 782   **MDK-108** 795

Displacement, tons: 550 full load
Dimensions, feet (metres): 189 × 84 *(57.6 × 25.6)*
Main machinery: 5 Type NK-12MV gas-turbines; 2 for lift, 23,672 hp(m) *(17.4 MW)* nominal;
  3 for drive, 35,508 hp(m) *(26.1 MW)* nominal
Speed, knots: 63. **Range, n miles:** 300 at 55 kt
Complement: 31 (4 officers)
Military lift: 3 MBT or 10 APC plus 230 troops (total 130 tons)
Missiles: SAM: 2 SA-N-5 Grail quad launchers; manual aiming; IR homing to 6 km
  (3.2 n miles) at 1.5 Mach; altitude to 2,500 m *(8,000 ft)*; warhead 1.5 kg.
Guns: 2—30 mm/65 AK 630; 6 barrels per mounting; 3,000 rds/min combined to 2 km.
  2—140 mm A-22 Ogon 22-barrelled rocket launchers.
Mines: 2 rails can be carried for 80.
Countermeasures: Decoys: MS227 chaff launcher.
ESM: Tool Box; intercept.
Weapons control: Quad Look (DWU-3) (modified Squeeze Box) optronic director.
Radars: Surface search: Curl Stone; I-band.
  Fire control: Bass Tilt; H/I-band.
IFF: Salt Pot A/B. Square Head.

Comment: First of class delivered 1986, commissioned in 1988. Last of class launched
  December 1994. Produced at St Petersburg and at Feodosiya. Bow and stern ramps for
  ro-ro working. Last survivors are based at Baltiysk and two more are held by Ukraine.
  One (plus two from Ukraine) transferred and one new build for Greece in 2001. These
  are the first Former Soviet Union (FSU) naval platform sales to a NATO country.

YEVGENIY KOCHESHKOV   *6/2003, Guy Toremans* / 0570932

3 AIST (DZHEYRAN) (PROJECT 1232.1) CLASS (ACV/LCUJ)

608	609	610

Displacement, tons: 298 full load
Dimensions, feet (metres): 155.2 × 58.4 *(47.3 × 17.8)*
Main machinery: 2 Type NK-12M gas turbines driving 4 axial lift fans and 4 propeller units for propulsion; 19,200 hp(m) *(14.1 MW)* nominal
Speed, knots: 70. **Range, n miles:** 120 at 50 kt
Complement: 15 (3 officers)
Military lift: 80 tons or 4 light tanks plus 50 troops or 2 medium tanks plus 200 troops or 3 APCs plus 100 troops
Guns: 4—30 mm/65 (2 twin) AK 630; 6 barrels per mounting; 3,000 rds/min combined to 2 km
Countermeasures: Decoys: 2 PK 16 chaff launchers
Radars: Surface search: Kivach; I-band
Fire control: Drum Tilt; H/I-band
IFF: High Pole B. Square Head

Comment: First produced at Leningrad in 1970, subsequent production at rate of about six every four years. The first large hovercraft for naval use. Similar to UK SR. N4. Type name is *maly desantny korabl na vozdushnoy podushke* meaning small ACV. Modifications have been made to the original engines and some units have been reported as carrying two SA-N-5 quadruple SAM systems and chaff launchers. Based in the Caspian. *609* participated in the Caspian Sea exercise in 2002.

MDK 89   *9/2000, J Cislak* / 0105561

3 LEBED (KALMAR) (PROJECT 1206) CLASS (ACV/LCUJ)

533	639	640

Displacement, tons: 87 full load
Dimensions, feet (metres): 80.1 × 36.7 *(24.4 × 11.2)*
Main machinery: 2 Ivchenko AI-20K gas turbines for lift and propulsion; 8,000 hp(m) *(5.88 MW)*
Speed, knots: 50. **Range, n miles:** 100 at 50 kt
Complement: 6 (2 officers)
Military lift: 2 light tanks or 40 tons cargo or 120 troops
Guns: 2—30 mm/65 AK 630; 6 barrels per mounting; 3,000 rds/min combined to 2 km.
Radars: Navigation: Kivach; I-band

Comment: First entered service 1975. Can be carried in Ivan Rogov class. Has a bow ramp with gun on starboard side and the bridge to port. All based in the Caspian. *639* and *640* took part in the Caspian Sea exercise in July 2002.

LEBED CLASS   *4/1995, Eric Grove* / 0081691

70 T-4 CLASS (PROJECT 1785) (LCM)

Displacement, tons: 35 light; 93 full load
Dimensions, feet (metres): 66.9 × 17.7 × 3.9 *(20.4 × 5.4 × 1.2)*
Main machinery: 2 diesels; 2 shafts
Speed, knots: 10
Complement: 2
Military lift: 50 tons cargo

Comment: Numbers are approximate and many may now be employed for civilian use.

T-4 class   *7/2001, B Lemachko* / 0570916

3 GUS (SKAT) (PROJECT 1205) CLASS (ACV/LCMJ)

631	633	634

Displacement, tons: 17 light; 27 full load
Dimensions, feet (metres): 69.9 × 27.5 × 0.6 *(21.3 × 8.4 × 0.2)*
Main machinery: 3 TVD 10 gas turbines for lift and propulsion
Speed, knots: 49. **Range, miles:** 200 at 49 kt
Complement: 7 + 24 troops

Comment: Last survivors of an original class of 32 which entered service 1969-76.

GUS   *6/1992, B Lemachko* / 0583302

MINE WARFARE FORCES

Notes: (1) All remaining Yevgenya (Korond) class MHCs were laid up by 2001, except for two in the Caspian Sea which may still be used as patrol craft.
(2) Some 40 to 50 craft of various dimensions, some with cable reels, some self-propelled and unmanned, some towed and unmanned are reported including the 8 m Kater and Volga unmanned mine clearance craft.

11 NATYA I (AKVAMAREN) (PROJECT 266M) CLASS
(MINESWEEPERS—OCEAN) (MSOM)

North	Pacific	Black
MOTORIST 806	MT 265 718	VALENTIN PIKUL 770
KOMENDOR 831	MT 264 738	VITSEADMIRAL ZHUKOV 909
KONTRADMIRAL VLASOV 855		N K GOLUBETS (ex-*Radist*) 911
		TURBINIST 912
		KOVROVETS 913
		SNAYPER 919

Displacement, tons: 804 full load
Dimensions, feet (metres): 200.1 × 33.5 × 9.8 *(61 × 10.2 × 3)*
Main machinery: 2 Type M 504 diesels; 5,000 hp(m) *(3.67 MW)* sustained; 2 shafts; cp props
Speed, knots: 16. **Range, n miles:** 3,000 at 12 kt
Complement: 67 (8 officers)

Missiles: SAM: 2 SA-N-5/8 Grail quad launchers (in some); manual aiming; IR homing to 6 km *(3.2 n miles)* at 1.5 Mach; altitude to 2,500 m *(8,000 ft)*; warhead 1.5 kg; 18 missiles.
Guns: 4—30 mm/65 (2 twin) AK 230; 500 rds/min to 6.5 km *(3.5 n miles)*; weight of shell 0.54 kg or 2—30 mm/65 AK 306; 6 barrels per mounting; 3,000 rds/min combined to 2 km.
4—25 mm/80 (2 twin); 270 rds/min to 3 km *(1.6 n miles)*; weight of shell 0.34 kg.
A/S mortars: 2 RBU 1200 5-tubed fixed; range 1,200 m; warhead 34 kg.
Depth charges: 62.
Mines: 10.
Countermeasures: MCM: 1 or 2 GKT-2 contact sweeps; 1 AT-2 acoustic sweep; 1 TEM-3 magnetic sweep.
Radars: Surface search: Don 2 or Long Trough; I-band.
Fire control: Drum Tilt; H/I-band (not in all).
IFF: 2 Square Head. High Pole B.
Sonars: MG 79/89; hull-mounted; active minehunting; high frequency.

Programmes: First reported in 1970. Built at Kolpino and Khabarovsk. Type name is *morskoy tralshchik* meaning seagoing minesweeper. MT 264 and MT 265 were a new variant commissioned in 1989 in which the AK 306 mounts replaced the twin AK 230 mounts. Two further units, known as Natya III started construction in 1994. The first, *Valentin Pikul*, left St Petersburg for the Black Sea in July 2002 while the second, *Vitseadmiral Zacharin*, was launched at the Kolpino Yard in June 2002.
Structure: Some have hydraulic gantries aft. Have aluminium/steel alloy hulls. Some have Gatling 30 mm guns and a different radar configuration without Drum Tilt.
Operational: Usually operate in home waters but have deployed to the Mediterranean, Indian Ocean and West Africa. Sweep speed is 14 kt.
Sales: India (two in 1978, two in 1979, two in 1980, one in August 1986, one in 1987, three in 1988). Libya (one in 1981, two in February 1983, one in August 1983, one in January 1984, one in January 1985, one in October 1986). Syria (one in 1985). Yemen (one in 1991). Ethiopia (one in 1991). Some have been deleted.

VALENTIN PIKUL   *6/2003, B Lemachko* / 0570913

TURBINIST   *9/2004, Hartmut Ehlers* / 1042305

2 GORYA (TYPE 12660) CLASS
(MINEHUNTERS—OCEAN) (MHOM)

Name	No	Builders	Laid down	Launched	Commissioned
A ZHELEZNYAKOV	901	Kolpino Yard, Leningrad	28 Feb 1985	17 July 1986	30 Dec 1988
V GUMANENKO	762	Kolpino Yard, Leningrad	15 Sep 1985	4 Mar 1991	9 Jan 1994

Displacement, tons: 1,130 full load
Dimensions, feet (metres): 216.5 × 36.1 × 10.8 *(66.0 × 11.0 × 3.3)*
Main machinery: 2 M 503 diesels; 5,000 hp(m) *(3.7 MW)*; 2 shafts
Speed, knots: 15. **Range, n miles:** 3,000 at 12 kt
Complement: 65 (7 officers)

Missiles: 2 SA-N-5 Grail quad launchers; IR homing to 6 km *(3.2 n miles)* at 1.5 Mach.
Guns: 1—3 in *(76 mm)*/60 AK 176; 120 rds/min to 12 km *(6.4 n miles)*; weight of shell 7 kg.
1—30 mm/65 AK 630; 6 barrels; 3,000 rds/min to 2 km.
Countermeasures: Decoys: 2 PK 16 chaff launchers.
ESM: Cross Loop; Long Fold.
Radars: Surface search: Palm Frond; I-band.
Navigation: Nayada; I-band.
Fire control: Bass Tilt; H/I-band.
IFF: Salt Pot C. 2 Square Head.
Sonars: Hull-mounted; active search; high frequency.

Programmes: A third of class was started but has been scrapped.
Structure: Appears to carry mechanical, magnetic and acoustic sweep gear and may have accurate positional fixing equipment. A remote-controlled submersible is housed behind the sliding doors in the superstructure below the AK 630 mounting. Two 406 mm torpedo tubes are reported as used for mine countermeasures.
Operational: 901 is based in the Black Sea. 762 transferred from the Baltic to the Northern Fleet in 2000.

V GUMANENKO   8/2002 / 0528319

26 SONYA (YAKHONT) (PROJECT 12650/1265M) CLASS
(MINESWEEPERS—HUNTERS/COASTAL) (MHSC/MHSCM)

North		Pacific		Baltic		Caspian		Black	
BT 97	402	BT 232	525	BT 244	501	BT 88	107	BT 40	438
BT 22	411	BT 245	533	—	505			BT 241	426
BT 152	418	BT 114	542	BT 230	510				
BT 226	425	BT 256	560	BT 213	522				
BT 152	443	BT 100	565	BT 115	561				
BT 50	454	BT 325	586	BT 44	563				
BT 111	466	BT 215	593	BT 94	568				
BT 211	469			BT 262	577				

Displacement, tons: 450 full load
Dimensions, feet (metres): 157.4 × 28.9 × 6.6 *(48 × 8.8 × 2)*
Main machinery: 2 Kolomna Type 9-D-8 diesels; 2,000 hp(m) *(1.47 MW)* sustained; 2 shafts
Speed, knots: 15. **Range, n miles:** 3,000 at 10 kt
Complement: 43 (5 officers)
Missiles: SAM: 2 SA-N-5 launchers (in some).
Guns: 2—30 mm/65 AK 630 or 2—30 mm/65 (twin) and 2—25 mm/80 (twin).
Mines: 8.
Radars: Surface search: Don 2 or Kivach or Nayada; I-band.
IFF: 2 Square Head. High Pole B.
Sonars: MG 69/79; hull-mounted; active minehunting; high frequency.

Comment: Wooden hull with GRP sheath. Built at about two a year at Petrozavodsk and at Ulis, Vladivostok (Pacific). First reported 1973 and the last one commissioned in January 1995. Type name is *bazovy tralshchik* meaning base minesweeper. Some have two twin 30 mm Gatling guns, others one 30 mm/65 (twin) plus one 25 mm (twin). In addition there are a further 50 in reserve.
Transfers: Bulgaria, four in 1981-85. Cuba, four in 1980-85. Syria, one in 1986. Vietnam, one in February 1987, one in February 1988, one in July 1989 and one in February 1990. Ethiopia, one in February 1991. Ukraine, two in 1996.

BT 115   6/2003, Guy Toremans / 0570933

5 LIDA (SAPFIR) (PROJECT 10750) CLASS
(MINEHUNTERS—COASTAL) (MHC)

RT 233	219	RT 248	348
RT 57	316	RT 234	372
RT 341	331		

Displacement, tons: 135 full load
Dimensions, feet (metres): 103.3 × 21.3 × 5.2 *(31.5 × 6.5 × 1.6)*
Main machinery: 3 D12MM diesels; 900 hp(m) *(690 kW)*; 3 shafts
Speed, knots: 12. **Range, n miles:** 650 at 10 kt
Complement: 14 (1 officer)
Guns: 1—30 mm/65 AK 630; 6 barrels; 3,000 rds/min to 2 km.
Countermeasures: MCM: AT-6 acoustic, SEMT-1 magnetic and GKT-3M wire sweeps.
Radars: Surface search: Pechora; MR241; I-band.
Sonars: Kabarga I; minehunting; high frequency.

Comment: Type name *Reydnyy Tralshchik* meaning roadstead minesweeper. A follow-on to the Yevgenya class started construction in 1989 at Kolpino Yard, St Petersburg. Similar in appearance to Yevgenya. Building rate was about three a year to 1992 and then slowed to one a year until 1995. Some are painted a blue/grey colour. All are in the Baltic except *RT 233* which is in the Caspian.

LIDA (SAPHIR) CLASS   6/1999, S Breyer / 0528317

SURVEY AND RESEARCH SHIPS

Notes: (1) Civilian research ships are now all used for commercial purposes only or are laid up, and are no longer naval associated, although some can still be leased for short operations. The former section has therefore been deleted since 1998.
(2) A mod-Sorum class AGE GS 31 is based in the Northern fleet.

22 FINIK (PROJECT 872) CLASS (AGS/AGE/AE)

North:	GS 87	GS 260	GS 278	GS 297	GS 392	GS 405	
Pacific:	GS 44	GS 47	GS 84	GS 272	GS 296	GS 397	GS 404
Black:	GS 86	GS 402	VTR 75				
Baltic:	GS 270	GS 301	GS 388	GS 399	GS 400	GS 403	

Displacement, tons: 1,200 full load
Dimensions, feet (metres): 201.1 × 35.4 × 10.8 *(61.3 × 10.8 × 3.3)*
Main machinery: 2 Cegielski-Sulzer 6AL25/30 diesels; 1,920 hp(m) *(1.4 MW)*; auxiliary propulsion; 2 motors; 204 hp(m) *(150 kW)*; 2 shafts; cp props; bow thruster
Speed, knots: 13. **Range, n miles:** 3,000 at 13 kt
Complement: 26 (5 officers) plus 9 scientists
Radars: Navigation: Kivach B; I-band.

Comment: Improved Biya class. Built at Northern Shipyard, Gdansk 1978-83. Fitted with 7 ton crane for buoy handling. Can carry two self-propelled pontoons and a boat on well-deck. Some have been used commercially. Ships of same class serve in the Polish Navy. Three transferred to Ukraine in 1997. Some may be laid up. VTR 75, originally built as a survey ship, was converted for use as an ammunition carrier in 2000.

GS 403   10/2002, B Lemachko / 0570911

VTR 75   5/2003, B Lemachko / 0580533

2 SIBIRIYAKOV (PROJECT 865) CLASS (AGOR)

SIBIRIYAKOV	ROMZUALD MUKLEVITCH

Displacement, tons: 3,422 full load
Dimensions, feet (metres): 281.2 × 49.2 × 16.4 *(85.7 × 15 × 5)*
Main machinery: Diesel-electric; 2 Cegielski-Sulzer 12AS25 diesels; 6,480 hp(m) *(4.44 MW)* sustained; 2 motors; 2 shafts; cp props; bow and stern thrusters
Speed, knots: 14. **Range, n miles:** 11,000 at 14 kt
Complement: 58 plus 12 scientists
Guns: 1—30 mm AK 630 can be carried.
Radars: Navigation: 2 Nayada; I-band.

Comment: Built in Northern Shipyard, Gdansk 1990-92. Has a pressurised citadel for NBC defence, and a degaussing installation. Six separate laboratories for hydrographic and geophysical research. Two submersibles can be embarked. Both ships are very active, *Sibiriyakov* in the Baltic at Kronstadt, and *Muklevitch* in the North.

SIBIRIYAKOV   *5/2000* / 0105564

2 AKADEMIK KRYLOV (PROJECT 852/856) CLASS (AGORH)

LEONID DEMIN	ADMIRAL VLADIMIRSKIY

Displacement, tons: 9,100 full load
Dimensions, feet (metres): 482.3 × 60.7 × 20.3 *(147 × 18.5 × 6.2)*
Main machinery: 4 Sulzer diesels; 14,500 hp(m) *(10.7 MW)*; 2 shafts; bow and stern thrusters
Speed, knots: 20. **Range, n miles:** 36,000 at 15 kt
Complement: 120
Radars: Navigation: Nayada, Palm Frond and Don 2; I-band.
Helicopters: 1 Hormone

Comment: Built in Szczecin 1974-79. Carry two survey launches and have 26 laboratories. Based in the Baltic at Kronstadt. *Akademik Krylov* sold to a Greek company in 1993 and now flies the Cyprus flag. *Admiral Vladimirskiy*, previously inactive at Kronstadt, has been reactivated.

LEONID DEMIN   *5/1994* / 0081696

3 NIKOLAY ZUBOV (PROJECT 850) CLASS (AGOR)

ANDREY VILKITSKY	BORIS DAVIDOV	SEMEN DEZHNEV

Displacement, tons: 2,674 standard; 3,021 full load
Dimensions, feet (metres): 294.2 × 42.7 × 15 *(89.7 × 13 × 4.6)*
Main machinery: 2 Zgoda-Sulzer 8TD48 diesels; 4,400 hp(m) *(3.23 MW)* sustained; 2 shafts
Speed, knots: 16.5. **Range, n miles:** 11,000 at 14 kt
Complement: 50
Radars: Navigation: Palm Frond or Don 2; I-band.

Comment: Oceanographic research ships built at Szczecin Shipyard, Poland in 1964-68. Also employed on navigational, sonar and radar trials. Has nine laboratories and small deck aft for hydromet-balloon work. Carry two to four survey launches. Based in the Northern Fleet. *Bellingsgauzen* to Ukraine in 1995.

BORIS DAVIDOV   *6/1994* / 0081698

8 MOMA (PROJECT 861) CLASS (AGS)

ANTARES	ASKOLD	SEVER (AGE)	ANDROMEDA
ANTARKTYDA	MARS	KRILON	CHELEKEN

Displacement, tons: 1,550 full load
Dimensions, feet (metres): 240.5 × 36.8 × 12.8 *(73.3 × 11.2 × 3.9)*
Main machinery: 2 Zgoda-Sulzer 6TD48 diesels; 3,300 hp(m) *(2.43 MW)* sustained; 2 shafts; cp props
Speed, knots: 17. **Range, n miles:** 9,000 at 11 kt
Complement: 55
Radars: Navigation: Nayada and Don 2; I-band.
IFF: High Pole A.

Comment: Built at Northern Shipyard, Gdansk 1967-72. Some of the class are particularly active in ASW research associated operations. Four laboratories. One survey launch and a 7 ton crane. The AGE is fitted with bow probes. Two in the Northern Fleet, two *(Antarktyda* and *Antares)* in the Pacific, two in the Black and two *(Askold* and *Andromeda)* in the Baltic. One transferred to Ukraine.

ANTARKTYDA   *6/1998, B Lemachko* / 0570919

14 YUG (PROJECT 862) CLASS (AGS/AGI/AGE)

North	Pacific	Baltic	Black
PLUTON	V ADM VORONTSOV	PERSEY	DONUZLAV
STRELETS	(ex-*Briz*)	NIKOLAY MATUSEVICH	STVOR
GORIZONT	PEGAS		
GIDROLOG	MARSHAL GELOVANI		
VIZIR			
SENEZH			
TEMRYUK (ex-*Mangyshlak*)			
SSV 700			

Displacement, tons: 2,500 full load
Dimensions, feet (metres): 270.6 × 44.3 × 13.1 *(82.5 × 13.5 × 4)*
Main machinery: 2 Zgoda-Sulzer Type 6TD48 diesels; 3,300 hp(m) *(2.43 MW)* sustained; 2 auxiliary motors; 272 hp(m) *(200 kW)*; 2 shafts; cp props; bow thruster; 300 hp *(220 kW)*
Speed, knots: 15
Range, n miles: 9,000 at 12 kt
Complement: 46 (8 officers) plus 20 scientists
Guns: 6—25 mm/80 (3 twin) (fitted for but not with).
Radars: Navigation: Palm Frond or Nayada; I-band.

Comment: Built at Northern Shipyard, Gdansk 1977-83. Have 4 ton davits at the stern and two survey craft. Others have minor variations around the stern area. *Pluton* 028 and *Strelets* 025 have been taken over by the Arctic Border Guard. SSV 700 classified as AGE. The Pacific units are understood to be non-operational.

DONUZLAV   *6/2003, B Lemachko* / 1042319

60 GPB-480 (PROJECT 1896) CLASS
(INSHORE SURVEY CRAFT) (YGS)

BGK series

Displacement, tons: 116 full load
Dimensions, feet (metres): 93.8 × 17.1 × 5.6 *(28.6 × 5.2 × 1.7)*
Main machinery: 1 diesel; 300 hp(m) *(223 kW)*; 1 shaft
Speed, knots: 12

Comment: Entered service from 1955. Numbers approximate. Inshore survey craft equipped with two 1.5 ton derricks.

BGK 785   *7/2001, B Lemachko* / 0580537

7 BIYA (PROJECT 870/871) CLASS (AGS)

North	Pacific	Baltic
GS 193	GS 200	GS 204
	GS 210	GS 208
	GS 269	GS 214

Displacement, tons: 766 full load
Dimensions, feet (metres): 180.4 × 32.1 × 8.5 *(55 × 9.8 × 2.6)*
Main machinery: 2 diesels; 1,200 hp(m) *(882 kW)*; 2 shafts; cp props
Speed, knots: 13. **Range, n miles:** 4,700 at 11 kt
Complement: 25
Radars: Navigation: Don 2; I-band.

Comment: Built at Northern Shipyard, Gdansk 1972-76. With laboratory and one survey launch and a 5 ton crane. Two transferred to Ukraine in 1997.

BIYA   *4/1997, Riku Lehtinen* / 0081700

6 KAMENKA (PROJECT 870/871) CLASS (AGS)

GS 66	GS 113	GS 118	GS 199	GS 207	GS 211

Displacement, tons: 760 full load
Dimensions, feet (metres): 175.5 × 29.8 × 8.5 *(53.5 × 9.1 × 2.6)*
Main machinery: 2 Sulzer diesels; 1,800 hp(m) *(1.32 MW)*; 2 shafts; cp props
Speed, knots: 14. **Range, n miles:** 4,000 at 10 kt
Complement: 25
Radars: Navigation: Don 2; I-band.
IFF: High Pole.

Comment: Built at Northern Shipyard, Gdansk 1968-69. A 5 ton crane forward. They do not carry a survey launch but have facilities for handling and stowing buoys. Two in the Baltic and four in the Pacific. One transferred to Vietnam in 1979, one to Estonia in 1996 and one to Ukraine in 1997.

GS 118   *6/2003, B Lemachko* / 0570901

2 ONEGA (PROJECT 1806) CLASS (AGS)

AKADEMIK SEMINIKHIN SFP 183   **AKADEMIK ISANIN** SFP 177

Displacement, tons: 2,150 full load
Dimensions, feet (metres): 265.7 × 36 × 13.7 *(81 × 11 × 4.2)*
Main machinery: 2 gas turbines; 8,000 hp(m) *(5.88 MW)*; 1 shaft
Speed, knots: 20
Complement: 45
Radars: Navigation: Nayada; I-band.

Comment: Built at Zelenodolsk and first seen in September 1973. Helicopter platform but no hangar in earlier ships of the class but in later hulls the space is taken up with more laboratory accommodation. Used as hydroacoustic monitoring ships. *Akademik Seminikhin* was completed in October 1992. One to Ukraine in 1997. *Akademik Seminikhin* based in the Black Sea and *Akademik Isanin* in the Northern Fleet. Others are laid up in each of the four Fleets.

AKADEMIK SEMINIKHIN   *7/2000, Hartmut Ehlers* / 0105566

2 VINOGRAD CLASS (AGOR)

GS 525   GS 526

Displacement, tons: 498 full load
Dimensions, feet (metres): 108.3 × 34.1 × 9.1 *(33 × 10.4 × 2.8)*
Main machinery: Diesel-electric; 2 diesels; 2 motors; 1,200 hp(m) *(882 kW)*; 2 trainable props
Speed, knots: 9
Range, n miles: 1,000 at 6 kt
Complement: 19

Comment: Built by Rauma-Repola, Finland, 1985-87 as hydrographic research ships. *GS 525* commissioned 12 November 1985 and *GS 526* on 17 December 1985. *525* is in the Baltic and *526* in the North. Both have side scan sonars. A similar ship has been reported operating with the Northern Fleet.

GS 525   *6/1998, Hartmut Ehlers* / 0050054

1 MARSHAL NEDELIN (PROJECT 1914) CLASS
(MISSILE RANGE SHIP) (AGMH)

MARSHAL KRYLOV

Displacement, tons: 24,500 full load
Dimensions, feet (metres): 695.5 × 88.9 × 25.3 *(212 × 27.1 × 7.7)*
Main machinery: 2 gas turbines; 54,000 hp(m) *(40 MW)*; 2 shafts
Speed, knots: 20
Range, n miles: 22,000 at 16 kt
Complement: 450
Radars: Air search: Top Plate.
Navigation: 3 Palm Frond; I-band.
Helicopter control: Fly Screen B; I-band.
Space trackers: End Tray (balloons). Quad Leaf. 3 Quad Wedge. 4 smaller aerials.
Tacan: 2 Round House.
Helicopters: 2-4 Ka-32 Helix C.

Comment: Completed at Admiralty Yard, Leningrad 23 February 1990. Fitted with a variety of space and missile associated electronic systems. Fitted for but not with six twin 30 mm/65 ADG guns and three Bass Tilt fire-control radars. Naval subordinated, the task is monitoring missile tests with a wartime role of command ship. The Ship Globe radome is for SATCOM. Based in the Pacific and active. Second of class deleted.

MARSHAL KRYLOV   *10/1995, van Ginderen Collection* / 0506249

INTELLIGENCE VESSELS

Notes: (1) About half the AGIs are fitted with SA-N-5/8 SAM launchers.
(2) SSV in pennant numbers of some AGIs is a contraction of *sudno svyazy* meaning communications vessel.
(3) GS in pennant numbers of some AGIs is a contraction of *gidroficheskoye sudno* meaning survey ship.
(4) Activity reported in all Fleet areas, as well as in the Mediterranean, in 2005.

0 + 2 PROJECT 18280 CLASS (AGI)

Name	Builders	Laid down	Launched	Commissioned
YURI IVANOV	Severnaya, St Petersburg	28 Dec 2004	2007	2008

Displacement, tons: 4,000
Dimensions, feet (metres): 311.7 × 52.5 × 13.1 *(95.0 × 16.0 × 4.0)*
Main machinery: To be announced
Speed, knots: To be announced
Range, n miles: To be announced
Complement: 120
Radars: To be announced.

Comment: A new class of AGI. The first is to be based in the Pacific Fleet and the second in the Northern Fleet.

2 BALZAM (ASIA) (PROJECT 1826) CLASS (AGIM)

Name	No	Builders	Commissioned
PRIBALTIKA	SSV 080	Yantar, Kaliningrad	July 1984
BELOMORE	SSV 571	Yantar, Kaliningrad	Dec 1987

Displacement, tons: 4,500 full load
Dimensions, feet (metres): 344.5 × 50.9 × 16.4 *(105 × 15.5 × 5)*
Main machinery: 2 diesels; 18,000 hp(m) *(13.2 MW)*; 2 shafts
Speed, knots: 20
Range, n miles: 7,000 at 16 kt
Complement: 200
Missiles: SAM: 2 SA-N-5 Grail quad launchers; manual aiming; IR homing to 6 km *(3.2 n miles)* at 1.5 Mach; altitude to 2,500 m *(8,000 ft)*; warhead 1.5 kg; 16 missiles.
Guns: 1 — 30 mm/65 AK 630; 6 barrels per mounting.
Radars: Surface search: Palm Frond and Don Kay; I-band.
Sonars: Lamb Tail/Mouse Tail VDS can be fitted.

Comment: Notable for twin radomes. Full EW and optronic fits. The first class of AGI to be armed. SSV 571 based in the Northern fleet and SSV 080 is based in the Pacific. Capable of underway replenishment.

PRIBALTIKA *7/2004* / 1042324

7 VISHNYA (PROJECT 864) CLASS (AGIM)

Name	No	Builders	Commissioned
TAVRIYA	SSV 169	Northern Shipyard, Gdansk	Dec 1987
ODOGRAF	SSV 175	Northern Shipyard, Gdansk	July 1988
PRIAZOVE	SSV 201	Northern Shipyard, Gdansk	Jan 1987
KURILY	SSV 208	Northern Shipyard, Gdansk	Apr 1987
VASSILY TATISCHEV (ex-*Pelengator*)	SSV 231	Northern Shipyard, Gdansk	Apr 1989
MERIDIAN	SSV 520	Northern Shipyard, Gdansk	July 1986
KARELIYA	SSV 535	Northern Shipyard, Gdansk	July 1987

Displacement, tons: 3,470 full load
Dimensions, feet (metres): 309.7 × 47.9 × 14.8 *(94.4 × 14.6 × 4.5)*
Main machinery: 2 Zgoda 12AV25/30 diesels; 4,406 hp(m) *(3.24 MW)* sustained; 2 auxiliary electric motors; 286 hp(m) *(210 kW)*; 2 shafts; cp props
Speed, knots: 16
Range, n miles: 7,000 at 14 kt
Complement: 146
Missiles: SAM: 2 SA-N-5 Grail quad launchers; manual aiming; IR homing to 6 km *(3.2 n miles)* at 1.5 Mach; altitude to 2,500 m *(8,000 ft)*; warhead 1.5 kg.
Guns: 2 — 30 mm/65 AK 630; 6 barrels per mounting. 2 — 72 mm 4-tubed rocket launchers.
Radars: Surface search: 2 Nayada; I-band.
Sonars: Lamb Tail VDS can be carried.

Comment: SSV 231 and 520 based in the Baltic, SSV 201 in the Black Sea, SSV 169 and SSV 175 in the Northern Fleet and SSV 208 in the Pacific. All have a full EW fit plus optronic systems and datalinks. Punch Bowl is fitted in SSV 231 and possibly in others. Some superstructure differences in all of the class. NBC pressurised citadels. Ice-strengthened hulls. All are comparatively active.

KURILY *10/2004, Ships of the World* / 1042288

ODOGRAF *6/2001* / 0126311

PRIAZOVE *9/2000, B Lemachko* / 0126220

4 MOMA (PROJECT 861M) CLASS (AGI/AGIM)

EKVATOR SSV 418   **LIMAN** SSV 824   **KILDIN** (mod) SSV 512   **NAKHODA** SSV 506

Displacement, tons: 1,240 standard; 1,600 full load
Dimensions, feet (metres): 240.5 × 36.8 × 12.8 *(73.3 × 11.2 × 3.9)*
Main machinery: 2 Zgoda-Sulzer 6TD48 diesels; 3,300 hp(m) *(2.43 MW)* sustained; 2 shafts; cp props
Speed, knots: 17
Range, n miles: 9,000 at 11 kt
Complement: 66 plus 19 scientists
Missiles: SAM: 2 SA-N-5 Grail quad launchers in some.
Radars: Surface search: 2 Don 2; I-band.

Comment: Modernised ships have a foremast in the fore well-deck and a low superstructure before the bridge. Non-modernised ships retain their cranes in the forward well-deck. Similar class operates as survey ships. Built at Gdansk, Poland between 1968-72. Three based in the Black Sea and SSV 506 in the Northern Fleet. One to Ukraine in 1996.

KILDIN *6/2002, Globke Collection* / 0528331

3 ALPINIST (PROJECT 503M/R) CLASS (AGIM)

GS 7   **ZHIGULOVSK** GS 19   **SYZRAN** GS 39

Displacement, tons: 1,260 full load
Dimensions, feet (metres): 177.1 × 34.4 × 13.1 *(54 × 10.5 × 4)*
Main machinery: 1 SKL 8 NVD 48 A2U diesel; 1,320 hp(m) *(970 kW)* sustained; 1 shaft; bow thruster
Speed, knots: 13
Range, n miles: 7,000 at 13 kt
Complement: 50
Missiles: SAM: 1 SA-N-% Grail quad launcher (GS 39).
Countermeasures: ESM: 2 Watch Dog; intercept.
Radars: Surface search: Nayada and Kivach; I-band.
Sonars: Paltus; active; high frequency.

Comment: Similar to Alpinist stern-trawlers which were built at about 10 a year at the Leninskaya Kuznitsa yard at Kiev and at the Volgograd shipyard. These AGIs were built at Kiev. In 1987 and 1988 forecastle was extended further aft and the electronics fit upgraded. GS 7 in the Pacific, the other two in the Baltic. A fourth of class converted for ASW training was laid up in 1997.

SYZRAN *6/2002, Frank Findler* / 0528314

RESCUE AND RESEARCH VEHICLES

2 BESTER CLASS RESCUE SUBMERSIBLES (PROJECT 18270) (DSRV)

AS 36   **+1**

Displacement, tons: 50 dived
Dimensions, feet (metres): 57.4 × 12.8 × 16.7 *(17.5 × 3.9 × 5.1)*
Main machinery: Battery-powered; 1 propeller; 2 vertical thrusters; 2 horizontal thrusters
Speed, knots: 4. **Range, n miles:** 11.5 at 2.5 kt
Complement: 3 + 18 passengers

Comment: Designed by the Lazurit Central Design Bureau and built at the Krasnoye Sormovo Shipyard, Nizhny Novgorod in 1994. Can mate with hulls at angles of 45° to horizontal. Endurance 4 hours. Can be carried onboard rescue ship *Alagez* or the salvage *Mikhail Rudnitsky*. Reported diving depth of over 750 m. Has an underwater manipulation system and four viewing ports. AS 36 based in Northern Fleet.

BESTER   *6/2004*, S Breyer* / 1127289

4 PRIZ CLASS SALVAGE SUBMERSIBLES (PROJECT 1855) (DSRV)

AS 25   **AS 28**   **AS 32**   **AS 35**

Displacement, tons: 58 dived
Dimensions, feet (metres): 44.3 × 12.5 × 12.8 *(13.5 × 3.8 × 3.9)*
Speed, knots: 3.3. **Range, n miles:** 21 at 2.3 kt
Complement: 4 + 20 passengers

Comment: Designed by the Lazurit Central Design Bureau and built in Nizhny Novgorod 1986-89. Can be carried onboard rescue ship *Alagez* or from the salvage ship *Mikhail Rudnitsky*. Has titanium hull and reported diving depth of over 1,000 m. Endurance 2-3 hours submerged. Has an underwater manipulation system. One (possibly AS 32) was involved in the *Kursk* rescue attempt. AS 28 became trapped on the sea-bottom off the Kamchatka peninsula on 5 August 2005. It was later rescued with the help of the British submarine rescue system. AS 25 and AS 32 based in Northern Fleet. AS 28 and AS 35 in Pacific Fleet.

AS 28   *8/2005** / 1151326

4 SALVAGE SUBMERSIBLES (PROJECT 1837) (DSRV)

AS 22   **AS 26**   **+2**

Displacement, tons: 45 dived
Dimensions, feet (metres): 41.7 × 11.5 × 17.7 *(12.7 × 3.5 × 5.4)*
Speed, knots: 3.6. **Range, n miles:** 16 at 2 kt
Complement: 3 + 11 passengers

Comment: Designed and built by Sudomekh, St Petersburg. Can be carried onboard Kashtan class SS 750 rescue ship and Elbrus class *Alagez*. Has steel hull and reported diving depth of 500 m. Has an underwater manipulation system. Twelve reported to have been built of which some were reported to have been decommissioned in the 1990s. Operational numbers are approximate.

AS 22   *8/2004*, E & M Laursen* / 1154409

1 RUS (PROJECT 16810) CLASS (RESEARCH SUBMERSIBLE)

AS 37

Displacement, tons: 25 dived
Dimensions, feet (metres): 26.2 × 12.8 × 12.6 *(8.0 × 3.9 × 3.85)*
Speed, knots: 3
Complement: 3

Comment: Entered naval service in 2000. Designed to perform research and technical underwater work at up to 6,000 m. Titanium spherical hull. Three horizontal propulsion motors, two vertical propulsion motors and one thruster. Based in northern fleet.

2 POISK-2 (PROJECT 1832) CLASS (RESEARCH SUBMERSIBLES)

Displacement, tons: 65 dived
Dimensions, feet (metres): 53.5 × 8.2 × 10.8 *(16.3 × 2.5 × 3.3)*
Speed, knots: 3
Complement: 3

Comment: Entered naval service in 1988 and 1989. Designed to perform research and technical underwater work at up to 2,000 m.

TRAINING SHIPS

Notes: The Mir class sail training ships have no military connections.

2 SMOLNY (PROJECT 887) CLASS

PEREKOP 200   **SMOLNY** 210

Displacement, tons: 9,150 full load
Dimensions, feet (metres): 452.8 × 53.1 × 21.3 *(138 × 16.2 × 6.5)*
Main machinery: 2 Zgoda Sulzer 12ZV 40/48 diesels; 15,000 hp(m) *(11 MW)*; 2 shafts
Speed, knots: 20
Range, n miles: 9,000 at 15 kt
Complement: 137 (12 officers) plus 330 cadets
Guns: 4—3 in *(76 mm)*/60 (2 twin). 4—30 mm/65 (2 twin)
A/S mortars: 2 RBU 2500
Countermeasures: ESM: 2 Watch Dog; radar warning
Radars: Air/surface search: Head Net C; 3D; E-band; range 128 km *(70 n miles)*.
Navigation: 4 Don 2; I-band. Don Kay *(Perekop)*; I-band.
Fire control: Owl Screech; G-band. Drum Tilt; H/I-band.
IFF: 2 High Pole A. Square Head.
Sonars: Mouse Tail VDS; active; high frequency.

Comment: Built at Szczecin, Poland. *Smolny* completed in 1976, *Perekop* in 1977. Have considerable combatant potential. Both are active in the Baltic.

SMOLNY   *7/2002, M Declerck* / 0528296

10 PETRUSHKA (UK-3) CLASS (AXL)

MK 391	**MK 1277**	**MK 1407**	**MK 1409**	**MK 1411**
MK 405	**MK 1303**	**MK 1408**	**MK 1410**	**MK 1556**

Displacement, tons: 335 full load
Dimensions, feet (metres): 129.3 × 27.6 × 7.2 *(39.4 × 8.4 × 2.2)*
Main machinery: 2 Wola H12 diesels; 756 hp(m) *(556 kW)*; 2 shafts
Speed, knots: 11
Range, n miles: 1,000 at 11 kt
Complement: 13 plus 30 cadets

Comment: Training vessels built at Wisla Shipyard, Poland; first one commissioned in 1989. Very similar to the SK 620 class used as ambulance craft. Used for seamanship and navigation training and may be commercially owned.

PETRUSHKA CLASS   *6/2003, E & M Laursen* / 0570909

AUXILIARIES

Notes: (1) Lama class *Voronesh* has been renamed VTR-33 and is an alongside civilian manned support ship in the Black Sea.
(2) Two Belyanka class tankers *Amur* and *Pinega* are used for stowing low level radioactive waste.
(3) A new Project 21300 submarine rescue ship was ordered in 2005. The 100 m vessel is to be of 5,000 tons. Designed by Almaz and constructed at Admiralty Shipyard, St Petersburg, the first of class is expected to enter service in 2010. Up to four vessels may be built.

2 AMGA (PROJECT 1791) CLASS
(MISSILE SUPPORT SHIPS) (AEM)

VETLUGA   **DAUGAVA**

Displacement, tons: 6,100 *(Vetluga)*, 6,350 *(Daugava)* full load
Dimensions, feet (metres): 354.3 × 59 × 14.8 *(108 × 18 × 4.5) (Vetluga)*
Main machinery: 2 diesels; 9,000 hp(m) *(6.6 MW)*; 2 shafts
Speed, knots: 16
Range, n miles: 4,500 at 14 kt
Complement: 210
Guns: 4 — 25 mm/80 (2 twin)
Radars: Surface search: Strut Curve; F-band.
Navigation: Don 2; I-band.
IFF: High Pole B.

Comment: Built at Gorkiy. Ships with similar duties to the Lama class. Fitted with a large 55 ton crane forward and thus capable of handling much larger missiles than their predecessors. Each ship has a different length and type of crane to handle later types of missiles. Designed for servicing submarines. *Vetluga* completed in 1976 and *Daugava* (5 m longer than *Vetluga*) in 1981. Both are in the Pacific Fleet. A third of class is laid up in the North.

DAUGAVA   *3/2003, B Lemachko* / 0573518

1 MALINA (PROJECT 2020) CLASS
(NUCLEAR SUBMARINE SUPPORT SHIP) (AS)

PM 74

Displacement, tons: 10,500 full load
Dimensions, feet (metres): 449.5 × 68.9 × 18.4 *(137 × 21 × 5.6)*
Main machinery: 4 gas turbines; 60,000 hp(m) *(44 MW)*; 2 shafts
Speed, knots: 17
Complement: 260
Radars: Navigation: 2 Palm Frond or 2 Nayada; I-band.

Comment: Built at Nikolayev. First deployed to Pacific in 1986. PM is an abbreviation of Plavuchaya Masterskaya (Floating workshop). A fourth of class *(PM 16)* launched early in 1992, was not completed. Designed to support nuclear-powered submarines and surface ships. Carry two 15 ton cranes. Two others (PM 914 (ex-PM 12) and PM 921 (ex-PM 63)) in the North are inactive and used for storing low level radioactive waste.

PM 74   *7/1996* / 0081704

11 AMUR (PROJECT 304/304M) CLASS (REPAIR SHIPS) (AR)

AMUR I
PM 40, PM 56, PM 64, PM 82, PM 138, PM 140, PM 156
AMUR II
PM 59, PM 69, PM 86, PM 97

Displacement, tons: 5,500 full load
Dimensions, feet (metres): 400.3 × 55.8 × 16.7 *(122 × 17 × 5.1)*
Main machinery: 1 Zgoda 8 TAD-48 diesel; 3,000 hp(m) *(2.2 MW)*; 1 shaft
Speed, knots: 12
Range, n miles: 13,000 at 8 kt
Complement: 145
Radars: Navigation: Kivach or Palm Frond or Nayada; I-band.

Comment: Amur I class general purpose depot and repair ships completed 1968-83 in Szczecin, Poland. Successors to the Oskol class. Carry two 5 ton cranes and have accommodation for 200 from ships alongside. Amur II class has extra deckhouse forward of the funnel. Built at Szczecin 1983-85. Three Amur IIs are based in the Pacific and one in the North. Three are laid up in the Baltic. PM 9 transferred to Ukraine. PM 56, based in the Black Sea, visited Tartous in 2002.

AMUR I PM 138   *9/2002, Globke Collection* / 0528330

AMUR II PM 86   *9/2000, J Cislak* / 0105571

4 VYTEGRALES II (PROJECT 596P) CLASS
(SUPPLY SHIPS) (AKH/AGF)

APSHERON   **DAURIYA**   **SEVAN**   **YAMAL**
(ex-*Vagales*) 204   (ex-*Vyborgles*) 506 (ex-*Siverles*) 208 (ex-*Tosnoles*) 212

Displacement, tons: 6,150 full load
Dimensions, feet (metres): 400.3 × 55.1 × 22.3 *(122.1 × 16.8 × 6.8)*
Main machinery: 1 Burmeister & Wain 950VTBF diesel; 5,200 hp(m) *(3.82 MW)*; 1 shaft
Speed, knots: 15
Complement: 46
Radars: Navigation: Nayada or Palm Frond or Spin Trough; I-band.
CCA: Fly Screen.
Helicopters: 1 Ka-25 Hormone C (not in *Yamal*).

Comment: Standard timber carriers of a class of 27. These ships were modified for naval use in 1966-68 with helicopter flight deck. Built at Zhdanov Yard, Leningrad between 1963 and 1966. *Sevan* fitted as squadron Flagship in support of Indian Ocean detachments. Variations exist between ships of this class; *Dauriya* has a deckhouse over the aft hold. All have two Vee Cone communications aerials. *Yamal* had her flight deck removed in 1995. The first of class, completed in 1962, was originally *Vytegrales*, but this was later changed to *Kosmonaut Pavel Belyayev* and, with three other ships of this class, converted to Space Support Ships. Four others (*Borovichi* and so on) received a different conversion for the same purpose. The civilian-manned ships together with these naval ships are often incorrectly called Vostok or Baskunchak class. *Apsheron* and *Dauriya* are in the Black Sea, *Sevan* and *Yamal* in the Baltic. Two others transferred to Ukraine in 1996.

SEVAN   *6/1998* / 0050059

DAURIYA   *7/2000, Hartmut Ehlers* / 0105572

5 BORIS CHILIKIN (PROJECT 1559V) CLASS (REPLENISHMENT SHIPS) (AOR)

BORIS BUTOMA	IVAN BUBNOV	SEGEY OSIPOV (ex-*Dnestr*)	VLADIMIR KOLECHITSKY	GENRICH GASANOV

Displacement, tons: 23,450 full load
Dimensions, feet (metres): 531.5 × 70.2 × 33.8
  (162.1 × 21.4 × 10.3)
Main machinery: 1 diesel; 9,600 hp(m) *(7 MW)*; 1 shaft
Speed, knots: 17
Range, n miles: 10,000 at 16 kt
Complement: 75 (without armament)
Cargo capacity: 13,000 tons oil fuel and dieso; 400 tons
  ammunition; 400 tons spares; 400 tons victualling stores;
  500 tons fresh water

Guns: 4—57 mm/80 (2 twin). Most are fitted for but not with
  the guns.
Radars: Air/surface search/fire control: Strut Curve (fitted
  for but not with).
  Muff Cob (fitted for but not with).
  Navigation: 2 Nayada or Palm Frond (plus Don 2 in
  V Kolechitsky); I-band.
IFF: High Pole B.

Programmes: Based on the Veliky Oktyabr merchant
  ship tanker design. Built at the Baltic Yard, Leningrad;
  Vladimir Kolechitsky completed in 1972, *Osipov*
  in 1973, *Ivan Bubnov* in 1975, *Genrich Gasanov* in
  1977. Last of class *Boris Butoma* completed
  in 1978.
Structure: This is the only class of purpose-built underway
  fleet replenishment ships for the supply of both liquids

SEGEY OSIPOV   *10/2004*, B Lemachko* / 1151372

and solids. Although most operate in merchant navy
paint schemes, all wear naval ensigns.
Operational: Earlier ships can supply solids on both
  sides forward. Later ships supply solids to starboard,
  liquids to port forward. All can supply liquids either

side aft and astern. *Osipov* and *Gasanov* are based
in the North, *Bubnov* in the Black Sea, *Butoma*
and *Kolechitsky* in the Pacific. Most are used for
commercial purposes. *Boris Chilikin* transferred to
Ukraine in 1997.

VLADIMIR KOLECHITSKY   *3/2001, Ships of the World* / 0126357

30 BOLVA (PROJECT 688/688A) CLASS
(BARRACKS SHIPS) (YPB)

Displacement, tons: 6,500
Dimensions, feet (metres): 560.9 × 45.9 × 9.8 *(110 × 14 × 3)*
Cargo capacity: 350-400 tons

Comment: A total of 59 built by Valmet Oy, Helsinki between 1960 and 1984. Of the
  remaining 30 ships, six are Bolva 1, 16 are Bolva 2 and eight are Bolva 3. Used for
  accommodation of ships' companies during refit and so on. The Bolva 2 and 3 have
  a helicopter pad. Have accommodation facilities for about 400 people. No means of
  propulsion but can be steered. In addition there are several other types of Barracks
  Ships including five ex-Atrek class depot ships as well as converted merchant ships and
  large barges. At least 18 have been scrapped.

IMATRA (at Sevastopol)   *3/2002, Hartmut Ehlers* / 0529803

2 DUBNA CLASS (REPLENISHMENT TANKERS) (AOL/AOT)

DUBNA	PECHENGA

Displacement, tons: 11,500 full load
Dimensions, feet (metres): 426.4 × 65.6 × 23.6 *(130 × 20 × 7.2)*
Main machinery: 1 Russkiy 8DRPH23/230 diesel; 6,000 hp(m) *(4.4 MW)*; 1 shaft
Speed, knots: 16. **Range, n miles:** 7,000 at 16 kt
Complement: 70
Cargo capacity: 7,000 tons fuel; 300 tons fresh water; 1,500 tons stores
Radars: Navigation: 2 Nayada; I-band.

Programmes: Completed 1974 at Rauma-Repola, Finland.
Structure: *Dubna* has 1 ton replenishment stations forward. Normally painted in merchant
  navy colours.
Operational: *Dubna* can refuel on either beam and astern. *Pechenga* has had RAS gear
  removed. Based in North. One of the class transferred to Ukraine in 1997. *Irkut* is
  believed to have been sold commercially in 1999.

DUBNA   *7/1996, van Ginderen Collection* / 0019061

5 MOD ALTAY CLASS (PROJECT 160)
(REPLENISHMENT TANKERS) (AOL)

PRUT	YELNYA	IZHORA	ILIM	YEGORLIK

Displacement, tons: 7,250 full load
Dimensions, feet (metres): 348 × 51 × 22 *(106.2 × 15.5 × 6.7)*
Main machinery: 1 Burmeister & Wain BM550VTBN110 diesel; 3,200 hp(m) *(2.35 MW)*;
  1 shaft
Speed, knots: 14
Range, n miles: 8,600 at 12 kt
Complement: 60
Cargo capacity: 4,400 tons oil fuel; 200 m³ solids
Radars: Navigation: 2 Don 2 or 2 Spin Trough; I-band.

Comment: Built from 1967-72 by Rauma-Repola, Finland. Modified for alongside
  replenishment. This class is part of 38 ships, being the third group of Rauma types built
  in Finland in 1967. *Ilim* and *Yegorlik* transferred to civilian companies in 1996/97 and
  operate in the Pacific with *Izhora*. *Prut* in the North and *Yelnya* in the Baltic.

PECHENGA   *10/2005*, Ships of the World* / 1151156

KOLA   *1/1997, van Ginderen Collection* / 0019062

2 OLEKMA CLASS (PROJECT 92)
(REPLENISHMENT TANKERS) (AORL)

OLEKMA   **IMAN**

Displacement, tons: 7,300 full load
Dimensions, feet (metres): 344.5 × 47.9 × 22 *(105.1 × 14.6 × 6.7)*
Main machinery: 1 Burmeister & Wain diesel; 2,900 hp(m) *(2.13 MW)*; 1 shaft
Speed, knots: 14
Range, n miles: 8,000 at 14 kt
Complement: 40
Cargo capacity: 4,500 tons oil fuel; 180 m³ solids
Radars: Navigation: Don 2 or Nayada and Spin Trough; I-band.

Comment: Built by Rauma-Repola, Finland in 1966. Modified for replenishment with refuelling rig abaft the bridge as well as astern refuelling. *Olekma* based in the Baltic and *Iman* in the Black Sea.

IMAN *3/2002, Hartmut Ehlers* / 0529802

5 UDA CLASS (PROJECT 577D)
(REPLENISHMENT TANKERS) (AOL)

LENA   **TEREK**   **VISHERA**   **KOYDA**   **DUNAY**

Displacement, tons: 5,500 standard; 7,126 full load
Dimensions, feet (metres): 400.3 × 51.8 × 20.3 *(122.1 × 15.8 × 6.2)*
Main machinery: 2 diesels; 9,000 hp(m) *(6.6 MW)*; 2 shafts
Speed, knots: 17. **Range, n miles:** 4,000 at 15 kt
Complement: 85
Cargo capacity: 2,900 tons oil fuel; 100 m³ solids
Radars: Navigation: 2 Don 2 or Nayada/Palm Frond; I-band.
IFF: High Pole A.

Comment: Built between 1962 and 1967 at Vyborg Shipyard. All have a beam replenishment capability. Guns removed. *Vishera* and *Dunay* in the Pacific, *Terek* in the Northern Fleet, *Koyda* in the Black Sea and *Lena* in the Baltic.

LENA *8/2004* / 1042325

2 MANYCH (PROJECT 1549) CLASS (WATER TANKERS) (AWT)

MANYCH   **TAGIL**

Displacement, tons: 7,700 full load
Dimensions, feet (metres): 380.5 × 51.5 × 23.0 *(116.0 × 15.7 × 7.0)*
Main machinery: 2 diesels; 9,000 hp(m) *(6.6 MW)*; 2 shafts
Speed, knots: 18
Range, n miles: 7,500 at 16 kt
Complement: 90
Cargo capacity: 4,400 tons
Radars: Air/surface search: Strut Curve; E/F-band.
Navigation: Don Kay; I-band.

Comment: Distilled water carrier built at Vyborg and completed in 1972. Decommissioned and disarmed in 1996 but returned to service in 1998 after refit in Bulgaria. *Manych* based in the Black Sea.

MANYCH *9/2004, Hartmut Ehlers* / 1042287

1 KALININGRADNEFT CLASS (SUPPORT TANKER) (AORL)

VYAZMA (ex-*Katun*)

Displacement, tons: 8,600 full load
Dimensions, feet (metres): 380.5 × 56 × 21 *(116 × 17 × 6.5)*
Main machinery: 1 Russkiy Burmeister & Wain 5DKRP50/110-2 diesel; 3,850 hp(m) *(2.83 MW)*; 1 shaft
Speed, knots: 14
Range, n miles: 5,000 at 14 kt
Complement: 32
Cargo capacity: 5,400 tons oil fuel and other liquids
Radars: Navigation: Okean; I-band.

Comment: Built by Rauma-Repola, Finland in 1982. Can refuel astern. At least an additional 20 of this class operate with the fishing fleets. Operational in the Northern Fleet.

KALININGRADNEFT *11/1991, G Jacobs* / 0506092

30 TOPLIVO CLASS (PROJECT 1844/1844D) CLASS (YO)

VTN series

Displacement, tons: 1,180 full load
Dimensions, feet (metres): 178.1 × 24.3 × 10.5 *(54.3 × 7.4 × 3.2)*
Main machinery: 1 diesel; 600 hp *(450 kW)*; 1 shaft
Speed, knots: 10. **Range, n miles:** 1,500 at 10 kt
Complement: 20
Radars: Navigation: Don-2; I-band.

Comment: Details given are for the Toplivo-2 class, some of which were built in Egypt but the majority in the USSR. The Toplivo-3 class, built in the USSR, are slightly larger at 1,300 tons full load. Numbers remaining in service are approximate. All the original Toplivo-1 class are believed to have been decommissioned.

VTN-28 (Toplivo-2) *9/2001, B Lemachko* / 1042318

6 KHOBI CLASS (PROJECT 437M) CLASS (YO)

CHEREMSHA   **SHACHA**   **SISOLA**   **SOSHA**   **ORSHA**   **INDIGA** (ex-*Seyma*)

Displacement, tons: 1,520 full load
Dimensions, feet (metres): 221.1 × 33.1 × 11.8 *(67.4 × 10.1 × 3.6)*
Main machinery: 1 diesel; 1,600 hp *(1.2 MW)*; 2 shafts
Speed, knots: 13. **Range, n miles:** 2,000 at 10 kt
Complement: 30
Radars: Navigation: Don-2; I-band.

Comment: *Cheremsha*, *Shacha* and *Sisola* based in the North, *Moksha* in the Pacific, *Sosha* and *Orsha* in the Baltic and *Seyma* in the Black Sea. Used for the transport of all forms of liquids.

INDIGA *9/2004, Hartmut Ehlers* / 1042284

3 OB (PROJECT 320) CLASS (HOSPITAL SHIPS) (AHH)

YENISEI   **SVIR**   **IRTYSH**

Displacement, tons: 11,570 full load
Dimensions, feet (metres): 499.7 × 63.6 × 20.5 *(152.3 × 19.4 × 6.3)*
Main machinery: 2 Zgoda-Sulzer 12ZV40/48; 15,600 hp(m) *(11.47 MW)* sustained; 2 shafts; cp props
Speed, knots: 19. **Range, n miles:** 10,000 at 18 kt
Complement: 124 plus 83 medical staff
Radars: Navigation: 3 Don 2 or 3 Nayada; I-band.
IFF: High Pole A.
Helicopters: 1 Ka-25 Hormone C.

Comment: Built at Szczecin, Poland. *Yenisei* completed 1981 and is based in the Black Sea. *Svir* completed in early 1989 and transferred to the Northern Fleet in September 1989. *Irtysh* completed in June 1990, was stationed in the Gulf in 1990-91 and is now based in the Pacific. A fourth of class is derelict and a fifth was cancelled. Have 100 beds and seven operating theatres. The first purpose-built hospital ships in the Navy, a programme which may have been prompted by the use of several merchant ships off Angola for Cuban casualties in the 'war of liberation.' NBC pressurised citadel. Ship stabilisation system. Decompression chamber. All are in use, mostly as alongside medical facilities.

SVIR *6/2003, B Lemachko* / 1042321

4 KLASMA (PROJECT 1274) CLASS (CABLE SHIPS) (ARC)

DONETS	INGURI	YANA	ZEYA

Displacement, tons: 6,000 standard; 6,900 full load
Measurement, tons: 3,400 dwt; 5,786 gross
Dimensions, feet (metres): 427.8 × 52.5 × 19 *(130.5 × 16 × 5.8)*
Main machinery: Diesel-electric; 5 Wärtsilä Sulzer 624TS diesel generators (4 in *Ingul* and *Yana*); 5,000 hp(m) *(3.68 MW)*; 2 motors; 2,150 hp(m) *(1.58 MW)*; 2 shafts
Speed, knots: 14. **Range, n miles:** 12,000 at 14 kt
Complement: 118
Radars: Navigation: Spin Trough and Nayada; I-band.

Comment: *Yana* built by Wärtsilä, Helsingforsvarvet, Finland in 1962; *Donets* at the Wärtsilä, Åbovarvet in 1968-69; *Zeya* in 1970. *Donets* and *Zeya* are of slightly modified design. *Inguri* completed in 1978. All are ice strengthened and can carry 1,650 miles of cable. *Yana* is distinguished by gantry right aft. *Donets* is in the Baltic, and the other three are in the North. All are active and can be leased for commercial use. One to Ukraine in 1997.

KLASMA *3/1992* / 0081709

4 EMBA (PROJECT 1172/1175) CLASS (CABLE SHIPS) (ARC)

SETUN (I)	NEPRYADAVA (I)	KEM (II)	BIRIUSA (II)

Displacement, tons: 2,050 full load (Group I); 2,400 (Group II)
Dimensions, feet (metres): 249 × 41.3 × 9.8 *(75.9 × 12.6 × 3)* (Group I)
282.4 × 41.3 × 9.9 *(86.1 × 12.6 × 3)* (Group II)
Main machinery: Diesel-electric; 2 Wärtsilä Vasa 6R22 diesel alternators; 2,350 kVA 60 Hz; 2 motors; 1,360 hp(m) *(1 MW)*; 2 shafts (Group I)
2 Wärtsilä Vasa 8R22 diesel alternators; 3,090 kVA 60 Hz; 2 motors; 2,180 hp(m) *(1.6 MW)*; 2 shafts (Group II)
The 2 turnable propulsion units can be inclined to the ship's path giving, with a bow thruster, improved turning movement
Speed, knots: 11
Complement: 40
Radars: Navigation: Kivach and Don 2; I-band.

Comment: Both Emba Is built in 1981. Designed for shallow water cable-laying. Carry 380 tons of cable. Order placed with Wärtsilä in January 1985 for two larger (Group II) ships; *Kem* completed on 23 October 1986. Can lay about 600 tons of cable. Designed for use off Vladivostok but also capable of operations in inland waterways. *Setun* is based in the Black Sea, *Nepryadava* in the Baltic, and *Kem* and *Biriusa* are in the Pacific. Both of the latter two were active in 2005.

SETUN *6/2003, B Lemachko* / 0573515

4 MIKHAIL RUDNITSKY (PROJECT 05360/1) CLASS
(SALVAGE AND MOORING VESSELS) (ARS)

MIKHAIL RUDNITSKY	GEORGY KOZMIN	GEORGY TITOV	SAYANY

Displacement, tons: 10,700 full load
Dimensions, feet (metres): 427.4 × 56.7 × 23.9 *(130.3 × 17.3 × 7.3)*
Main machinery: 1 S5DKRN62/140-3 diesel; 6,100 hp(m) *(4.48 MW)*; 1 shaft
Speed, knots: 16. **Range, n miles:** 12,000 at 15.5 kt
Complement: 72 (10 officers)
Radars: Navigation: Palm Frond; Nayada; I-band.
Sonars: MG 89 *(Sayany)*.

Comment: Built at Vyborg, based on Moskva Pionier class merchant ship hull. First completed 1979, second in 1980, third in 1983 and fourth in 1984. Fly flag of Salvage and Rescue Service. Have two 40 ton and one 20 ton lift with cable fairleads forward and aft. This lift capability is adequate for handling small submersibles, such as Project 1855 Priz, one of which is carried in the centre hold. *Sayany* is also described as a research ship and has a high-frequency sonar. *Rudnitsky* and Project 1837 submersible took part in the *Kursk* rescue attempts in August 2000. *Rudnitsky* and *Titov* in the Northern Fleet and the other two in the Pacific.

MIKHAIL RUDNITSKY *6/2003, B Lemachko* / 0573514

8 KASHTAN (PROJECT 141) CLASS
(BUOY TENDERS) (ABU/AGL/ARS)

ALEXANDR PUSHKIN (ex-KIL 926)	KIL 143	KIL 164	KIL 498
KIL 927	KIL 158 (ex-KIL 140)	SS 750	KIL 168

Displacement, tons: 4,600 full load
Dimensions, feet (metres): 313.3 × 56.4 × 16.4 *(95.5 × 17.2 × 5)*
Main machinery: 4 Wärtsilä diesels; 29,000 hp(m) *(2.31 MW)*; 2 shafts
Speed, knots: 13.5
Complement: 51 plus 20 spare berths
Radars: Navigation: 2 Nayada; I-band.

Comment: Enlarged Sura class built at the Neptun Shipyard, Rostock. Ordered 29 August 1986. *Alexandr Pushkin* handed over in June 1988 and is classified as an AGL in the Baltic; *927* to the Pacific in July 1989; *143* to the North in July 1989; *158* to the Black Sea in November 1989; *164* to the North in January 1990; *498* to the Pacific in November 1990 and *168* to the Pacific in mid-1991. Lifting capacity: one 130 ton lifting frame, one 100 ton derrick, one 12.5 ton crane and one 10 ton derrick. All are civilian operated except *SS 750* in the Baltic which is used to support Project 1837 submersibles AS 22 and AS 26. *158* deployed to Tartous for several months in late 2002.

SS 750 (with mini-sub AS 22) *8/2004, E & M Laursen* / 1042320

4 SURA (PROJECT 145) CLASS (BUOY TENDERS) (ABU)

KIL 22	KIL 27	KIL 29	KIL 31

Displacement, tons: 2,370 standard; 3,150 full load
Dimensions, feet (metres): 285.4 × 48.6 × 16.4 *(87 × 14.8 × 5)*
Main machinery: Diesel-electric; 4 diesel generators; 2 motors; 2,240 hp(m) *(1.65 MW)*; 2 shafts
Speed, knots: 12. **Range, n miles:** 2,000 at 11 kt
Complement: 40
Cargo capacity: 900 tons cargo; 300 tons fuel for transfer
Radars: Navigation: 2 Don 2; I-band.

Comment: Heavy lift ships built as mooring and buoy tenders at Rostock in East Germany between 1965 and 1976. Lifting capacity: one 65 ton derrick and one 65 ton stern cage. Have been seen to carry 12 m DSRVs. *KIL 27* is in the Pacific, *KIL 29* in the Baltic and *KIL 22* and *KIL 31* in the North. Four others are laid up. One to Ukraine in 1997.

KIL 31 *4/1996, van Ginderen Collection* / 0506326

1 ELBRUS (OSIMOL) (PROJECT 537) CLASS
(SUBMARINE RESCUE SHIP) (ASRH)

ALAGEZ

Displacement, tons: 19,000 standard; 22,500 full load
Dimensions, feet (metres): 575.8 × 80.4 × 27.9 *(175.5 × 24.5 × 8.5)*
Main machinery: Diesel-electric; 4 diesel generators; 2 motors; 20,000 hp(m) *(14.7 MW)*; 2 shafts
Speed, knots: 17. **Range, n miles:** 14,500 at 15 kt
Complement: 420
Guns: 4 – 30 mm/65 (2 twin).
Radars: Navigation: 2 Nayada and 2 Palm Frond; I-band.
Helicopters: 1 Ka-25 Hormone C.

Comment: Very large submarine rescue and salvage ship with icebreaking capability, possibly in view of under-ice capability of some SSBNs. Built at Nikolayev, and completed in 1982. Can carry two submersibles in store abaft the funnel which are launched from telescopic gantries. Based in the Pacific. Repairs of the Nepa class ASR *Karpaty* based in the Baltic have been discontinued.

ALAGEZ *6/2004, Ships of the World* / 0583298

24 SHELON I/II (PROJECT 1388/1388M) CLASS (YPT/YAG)

TL and KRH series

Displacement, tons: 270 full load
Dimensions, feet (metres): 150.9 × 19.7 × 6.6 *(46 × 6 × 2)*
Main machinery: 2 diesels; 8,976 hp(m) *(6.6 MW)*; 2 shafts
Speed, knots: 26
Range, n miles: 1,500 at 10 kt
Complement: 14
Radars: Navigation: Spin Trough or Kivach; I-band.

Comment: Type I built 1978-84. Built-in weapon recovery ramp aft. Type II built 1985-87. Type IIs can be used as environmental monitoring ships. One is an Admirals' yacht in the Baltic, and others are used as personnel transports.

SHELON II   *6/2003, B Lemachko* / 0573513

SHELON I   *7/2004* / 1042326

48 FLAMINGO (TANYA) (PROJECT 1415) CLASS (TENDERS) (YDT)

Displacement, tons: 42 full load
Dimensions, feet (metres): 72.8 × 12.8 × 4.6 *(22.2 × 3.9 × 1.4)*
Main machinery: 1 Type 3-D-12 diesel; 300 hp(m) *(220 kW)* sustained; 1 shaft
Speed, knots: 12
Complement: 8

Comment: Successor to Nyryat II. There are some 28 with RVK numbers (diving tenders). There are also about 20 (PSKA numbers) assigned to the Border Guard for harbour patrol duties. These are known as the Kulik class. Other craft have BSK, RK (workboats) PRDKA (counterswimmer cutter) and BGK (inshore survey) numbers.

FLAMINGO (Diving Tender)   *6/2003, A Sheldon-Duplaix* / 0573512

38 POLUCHAT I, II AND III CLASSES (PROJECT 368) (YPT)

TL series

Displacement, tons: 70 standard; 100 full load
Dimensions, feet (metres): 97.1 × 19 × 4.8 *(29.6 × 5.8 × 1.5)*
Main machinery: 2 M 50 diesels; 2,200 hp(m) *(1.6 MW)* sustained; 2 shafts
Speed, knots: 20. **Range, n miles:** 1,500 at 10 kt
Complement: 15
Guns: 2—14.5 mm (twin) MGs (in some).
Radars: Navigation: Spin Trough; I-band.

Comment: Employed as specialised or dual-purpose torpedo recovery vessels and/or patrol boats. They have a stern slipway. Several exported as patrol craft. Some used by the Border Guard.
Transfers: Algeria, Angola, Congo (three), Ethiopia (one), Guinea-Bissau, India, Indonesia (three), Iraq (two), Mozambique, Somalia (six), Syria, Tanzania, Vietnam (five), North Yemen (two), South Yemen. About 13 remain in service.

POLUCHAT I   *11/1991, MoD Bonn* / 0081713

PO 2 (PROJECT 501) AND NYRYAT 2 (PROJECT 1896) CLASSES (TENDERS) (YDT)

Displacement, tons: 56 full load
Dimensions, feet (metres): 70.5 × 11.5 × 3.3 *(21.5 × 3.5 × 1)*
Main machinery: 1 Type 3-D-12 diesel; 300 hp(m) *(220 kW)* sustained; 1 shaft
Speed, knots: 12
Complement: 8
Guns: Some carry 1—12.7 mm MG on the forecastle.

Comment: This 1950s design of hull and machinery has been used for a wide and diverse number of adaptations. Steel hull. Nyryat 2 have the same characteristics but are used as diving tenders (RVK), inshore survey craft (MGK) and workboats (RK).
Transfers: Albania, Bulgaria, Cuba, Guinea, Iraq. Many deleted.

NYRYAT 2   *7/2000, Hartmut Ehlers* / 0105577

30 NYRYAT I (PROJECT 522) CLASS (TENDERS) (YDT)

Displacement, tons: 120 full load
Dimensions, feet (metres): 93 × 18 × 5.5 *(28.4 × 5.5 × 1.7)*
Main machinery: 1 diesel; 450 hp(m) *(331 kW)*; 1 shaft
Speed, knots: 12.5. **Range, n miles:** 1,500 at 10 kt
Complement: 15
Guns: 1—12.7 mm MG (in some).

Comment: Built from 1955. Can operate as patrol craft or diving tenders with recompression chamber. Similar hull and propulsion used for inshore survey craft. Some have BGK, VM or GBP (survey craft) numbers.
Transfers: Albania, Algeria, Cuba, Egypt, Iraq, North Yemen. Many deleted.

NYRYAT I   *7/2000, Hartmut Ehlers* / 0105578

16 SK 620 CLASS (DRAKON) (TENDERS) (YH/YFL)

MK 391	MK 1409	PSK 1411	SN 128
MK 1303	PSK 382	PSK 1518	SN 401
MK 1407	PSK 405	SN 109	SN 1318
MK 1408	PSK 673	SN 126	SN 1520

Displacement, tons: 236 full load
Dimensions, feet (metres): 108.3 × 24.3 × 6.9 *(33 × 7.4 × 2.1)*
Main machinery: 2 56ANM30-H12 diesels; 620 hp(m) *(456 kW)* sustained; 2 shafts
Speed, knots: 12
Range, n miles: 1,000 at 12 kt
Complement: 14 plus 3 spare

Comment: Built at Wisla Shipyard, Poland as a smaller version of the Petrushka class training ship. PSK series serve as harbour ferries. Mostly used as hospital tenders capable of carrying 15 patients.

PSK 405   *7/2001, J Cislak* / 0528310

29 YELVA (KRAB) (PROJECT 535M) CLASS
(DIVING TENDERS) (YDT)

VM 20	VM 263	VM 413-416	VM 807
VM 72	VM 266	VM 420	VM 809
VM 143	VM 268	VM 425	VM 907-910
VM 146	VM 270	VM 429	VM 915
VM 153-154	VM 277	VM 725	VM 919
VM 250	VM 409		

Displacement, tons: 295 full load
Dimensions, feet (metres): 134.2 × 26.2 × 6.6 *(40.9 × 8 × 2)*
Main machinery: 2 Type 3-D-12A diesels; 630 hp(m) *(463 kW)* sustained; 2 shafts
Speed, knots: 12.5. **Range, n miles:** 1,870 at 12 kt
Complement: 30
Radars: Navigation: Spin Trough; I-band.

Comment: Diving tenders built 1971-83. Carry a 1 ton crane and diving bell. Some have submersible recompression chamber. Ice strengthened. One to Cuba 1973, one to Libya 1977. Some have probably been decommissioned.

VM 154   *6/2003, B Lemachko* / 0580535

1 + 2 PROJECT 11980 (DIVING TENDERS) (YDT)

BM 596

Displacement, tons: 330 full load
Dimensions, feet (metres): 121.7 × 25.3 × 8.2 *(37.1 × 7.7 × 2.5)*
Main machinery: 2 diesels
Speed, knots: 12.5
Complement: 29

Comment: A new class of diving vessel designed by Almaz Central Design Bureau and built at Vympel Shipyard, Rybinsk. Construction started in the early 1990s but the building programme was suspended until new funds were assigned in 2002. The ship is designed to support diving and salvage operations down to a depth of 60 m and is equipped with the Falkon remote-controlled underwater equipment, which can work at depths up to 300 m. It also carries hydrological instruments and welding equipment for deep-sea work, a satellite television system and a barochamber. The lead vessel was commissioned in the Northern Fleet on 28 November 2004 and is based at Severomorsk. Two further units are planned.

1 SALVAGE LIFTING SHIP (YS)

Name	Builders	Launched	Commissioned
KOMMUNA (ex-*Volkhov*)	De Schelde, Vlissingen	30 Nov 1913	27 July 1915

Displacement, tons: 2,450 full load
Dimensions, feet (metres): 315.0 × 66.9 × 15.4 *(96.0 × 20.4 × 4.7)*
Main machinery: 2 diesels; 2 shafts
Speed, knots: 10. **Range, n miles:** 1,700 at 6 kt
Complement: 250
Radars: Navigation: I-band.

Comment: Catamaran-hulled vessel fitted with four lifting rigs to enable sunken submarines to be lifted between the hulls. Laid down in 1912, the vessel was thought to have been decommissioned in 1978 but returned to service after a refit from 1980-84. Now based at Sevastopol to support the operation of submersibles.

KOMMUNA   *3/2003, B Lemachko* / 0570910

27 POZHARNY I (PROJECT 364) CLASS
(FIREFIGHTING CRAFT) (YTR)

PZHK 3	PZHK 5	PZHK 17	PZHK 30-32	PZHK 36-37
PZHK 41-47	PZHK 49	PZHK 53-55	PZHK 59	PZHK 64
PZHK 66	PZHK 68	PZHK 79	PZHK 82	PZHK 84
PZHK 86				

Displacement, tons: 180 full load
Dimensions, feet (metres): 114.5 × 20 × 6 *(34.9 × 6.1 × 1.8)*
Main machinery: 2 Type M 50 diesels; 2,200 hp(m) *(1.6 MW)* sustained; 2 shafts
Speed, knots: 12. **Range:** 250 at 12 kt
Complement: 26
Guns: 4 — 12.7 mm (2 twin) MGs (in some).

Comment: Total of 84 built from mid-1950s to mid-1960s. Harbour fire boats but can be used for patrol duties. One transferred to Iraq (now deleted) and two to Ukraine.

POZHARNY I   *8/2000, B Lemachko* / 0126224

15 MORKOV (PROJECT 1461.3) CLASS (YTR)

PZHK 415	PZHK 417	PZHK 900	PZHK 1296	PZHK 1378
PZHK 1514-1515	PZHK 1544-1547	PZHK 1560	PZHK 1680	PZHK 1859	PZHK 2055

Displacement, tons: 320 full load
Dimensions, feet (metres): 119.8 × 25.6 × 7.2 *(36.5 × 7.8 × 2.2)*
Main machinery: 2 diesels; 1,040 hp(m) *(764 kW)*; 2 shafts
Speed, knots: 12.5
Range: 250 at 12 kt
Complement: 20

Comment: Carry four water monitors. Completed in 1984-86 at Rybinsk. Can be used for patrol/towage. Some are under civilian control.

PZHK 2055   *6/2003, B Lemachko* / 0580534

11 PELYM (PROJECT 1799) CLASS (DEGAUSSING SHIPS) (YDG)

SR 26	SR 180	SR 233	SR 334
SR 111	SR 188	SR 267	SR 455
SR 179	SR 203	SR 280	

Displacement, tons: 1,370 full load
Dimensions, feet (metres): 214.8 × 38 × 11.2 *(65.5 × 11.6 × 3.4)*
Main machinery: 1 diesel; 1,536 hp(m) *(1.13 MW)*; 1 shaft
Speed, knots: 14
Range, n miles: 1,000 at 13 kt
Complement: 70
Radars: Navigation: Don 2; I-band.

Comment: Built from 1970 to 1987 at Khabarovsk and Gorokhovets. Earlier ships have stump mast on funnel, later ships a tripod main mast and a platform deck extending to the stern. Type name is *sudno razmagnichivanya* meaning degaussing ship. One to Cuba 1982. Several in reserve.

SR 111   *3/2004, B Lemachko* / 0576441

HARBOUR CRAFT (YFL/YFU)

Comment: There are numerous types of officers' yachts, harbour launches, training cutters and trials vessels in all of the major Fleet bases. Class names include *Bryza* (Project 722), *Nazhimovets* (Project 286), *Admiralets* (Project 371), *Slavyanka* (Project 20150), *Albatros* (Project 183), Project 14670 and Project 360.

BURUN (Project 14670)   *8/2001*, B Lemachko* / 0583299

15 BEREZA (PROJECT 130) CLASS
(DEGAUSSING SHIPS) (YDG)

North	Baltic	Black
SR 74	SR 28	SR 137
SR 216	SR 120	SR 541
SR 478	SR 245	SR 939
SR 548	SR 479	
SR 569	SR 570	
SR 938	SR 936	

Displacement, tons: 1,850 standard; 2,051 full load
Dimensions, feet (metres): 228 × 45.3 × 13.1 *(69.5 × 13.8 × 4)*
Main machinery: 2 Zgoda-Sulzer 8AL25/30 diesels; 2,938 hp(m) *(2.16 MW)* sustained; 2 shafts; cp props
Speed, knots: 13. **Range, n miles:** 1,000 at 13 kt
Complement: 48
Radars: Navigation: Kivach; I-band.

Comment: First completed at Northern Shipyard, Gdansk 1984-1991. One transferred to Bulgaria in 1988. Have NBC citadels and three laboratories. Several in reserve. One to Ukraine in 1997. SR 938 converted to a logistic ship for service in the Polish Navy.

SR 541   *9/2004, Hartmut Ehlers* / 1042283

ICEBREAKERS

Notes: Only military icebreakers are shown in this section. Other icebreakers come under civilian management and are now used predominantly for commercial purposes. Civilian ships include the nuclear powered *Taymyr, Vaygach, Arktika, Rossiya, S Soyuz, Yamal*, all of which are operated by the Murmansk Shipping Company. Diesel powered ships include: 20,000 tons: *Ermak, Admiral Makarov, Krasin*; 14,600 tons: *Kapitan Sorokin, Kapitan Dranitsyn, Kapitan Nikolayev, Kapitan Khlebnikov*; 7,700 tons: *Mudyug*; 6,200 tons: *Magadan, Dikson*; 2,240 tons: *Kapitan Bukayev, Kapitan Chadayev, Kapitan Chechkin, Kapitan Krutov, Kapitan Plakhin, Kapitan Zarubin*; 2,200 tons: *Kapitan Babichev, Kapitan Borodkin, Kapitan Chudinov, Kapitan Demidov, Kapitan Evdokimov, Kapitan Metsayk, Kapitan Moshkin, Kapitan Yevdokimov, Avraamiy Zavenyagin*; 2,100 tons: *Kapitan A Radzhabov, Kapitan Kosolabov, Kapitan M Izmaylov*. The growing demand for oil tanker shipments in the Arctic region means that there is a potential shortage of icebreakers. This may be met by completing *50 Let Pobeda*, a nuclear-powered vessel which has lain unfinished at Baltic Shipyard, St Petersburg since 1989. Construction may be completed by 2006 at which stage *Arktika, Rossiya* and *Taymyr* will require life-extension refits.

ROSSIYA   *3/2005** / 1151374

3 DOBRYNYA NIKITICH (PROJECT 97) CLASS (AGB)

BURAN	PERESVET SADKO

Displacement, tons: 2,995 full load
Measurement, tons: 2,254 gross; 1,118 dwt; 50 net
Dimensions, feet (metres): 222.1 × 59.4 × 20 *(67.7 × 18.1 × 6.1)*
Main machinery: Diesel-electric; 3 Type 13-D-100 or 3 Wärtsilä 6L 26 *(Kruzenshtern)* diesel generators; 3 motors; 5,400 hp(m)*(4 MW)*; 3 shafts (1 fwd, 2 aft)
Speed, knots: 14.5
Range, n miles: 5,500 at 12 kt
Complement: 45
Guns: 2—57 mm/70 (twin). 2—37 mm/63.
Radars: Navigation: 2 Don 2; I-band.

Comment: Built at Admiralty Yard, Leningrad between 1960 and 1971. *Kavraysky* is in the Northern Fleet and *Buran* in the Baltic. Of the 18 others originally built, some have been decommissioned and others (about eight) transferred to civilian service.

BURAN   *6/2004*, Marco Ghiglino* / 1151373

TUGS

Notes: (1) SB means *Spasatelny Buksir* or Salvage Tug. MB means *Morskoy Buksir* or Seagoing Tug.
(2) Two Baklazhan (Project 5757) class tugs are owned by a civilian salvage company.

1 PRUT (PROJECT 527M) CLASS (RESCUE TUG) (ATS)

EPRON

Displacement, tons: 2,120 standard; 2,800 full load
Dimensions, feet (metres): 295.9 × 46.9 × 18.0 *(90.2 × 14.3 × 5.5)*
Main machinery: Diesel-electric; 4 diesel generators; 2 motors; 10,000 hp(m) *(7.35 MW)*; 2 shafts
Speed, knots: 20
Range, n miles: 9,000 at 16 kt
Complement: 140
Radars: Navigation: Don-2; I-band.

Comment: Large rescue tug built at Nikolayev, Ukraine and completed in 1968. Carries two heavy-duty derricks, submersible recompression chambers, rescue chambers and bells. Last survivor of the class which is based in the Black Sea.

EPRON   *9/2004, Hartmut Ehlers* / 1042286

2 NEFTEGAZ (PROJECT B-92) CLASS (ATA)

ILGA   KALAR

Displacement, tons: 4,013 full load
Measurement, tons: 264.8 × 53.5 × 16.4 *(80.3 × 16.3 × 5.0)*
Main machinery: 2 Sulzer diesels; 7,200 hp *(5.3 MW)*; 2 shafts; cp props
Speed, knots: 15. **Range, n miles:** 5,000 at 12 kt
Complement: 23
Radars: Navigation: I-band.

Comment: Large oilfield support tugs built by A Warski SY, Szczecin, Poland. Taken over for naval service; some 40 others are in civilian service. Now employed as ocean-going rescue tugs with heavy towing and firefighting capabilities. *Kalar* also operates in the salvage role. Capacity of 600 tons cargo on deck and 1,000 m³ of liquid cargo. Entered naval service in 1983 *(Ilga)* and 1990 *(Kalar)*. *Ilga* based in the Northern Fleet and *Kalar* in the Pacific.

KALAR   *12/2005*, Ships of the World* / 1151145

3 INGUL (PROJECT 1453) CLASS (SALVAGE TUGS) (ATS)

PAMIR   MASHUK   ALTAY (ex-*Karabakh*)

Displacement, tons: 4,050 full load
Dimensions, feet (metres): 304.4 × 50.5 × 19 *(92.8 × 15.4 × 5.8)*
Main machinery: 2 Type 58-D-4R diesels; 6,000 hp(m) *(4.4 MW)*; 2 shafts; cp props
Speed, knots: 19. **Range, n miles:** 9,000 at 19 kt
Complement: 71 plus salvage party of 18
Radars: Navigation: 2 Palm Frond; I-band.
IFF: High Pole. Square Head.

Comment: Built at Admiralty Yard, Leningrad in 1975-84. NATO class name the same as one of the Klasma class cable-ships. Naval-manned arctic salvage and rescue tugs. Two more, *Yaguar* (Murmansk) and *Bars* (Vladivostok), operate with the merchant fleet. Carry salvage pumps, diving and firefighting gear as well as a high-line for transfer of personnel. Fitted for guns but these are not carried. *Pamir* and *Altay* in the North, *Mashuk* in the Pacific.

ALTAY   *10/2004** / 1151375

3 SLIVA (PROJECT 712) CLASS (SALVAGE TUGS) (ATS)

SB 406   PARADOKS SB 921   SHAKHTER SB 922

Displacement, tons: 3,050 full load
Dimensions, feet (metres): 227 × 50.5 × 16.7 *(69.2 × 15.4 × 5.1)*
Main machinery: 2 Russkiy SEMT-Pielstick 6 PC2.5 L 400 diesels; 7,020 hp(m) *(5.2 MW)* sustained; 2 shafts; cp props; bow thruster
Speed, knots: 16. **Range:** 6,000 at 16 kt
Complement: 43 plus 10 salvage party
Radars: Navigation: 2 Nayada; I-band.

Comment: Built at Rauma-Repola, Finland. Based on Goryn design. *SB 406* completed 20 February 1984. Second pair ordered 1984 *SB 921* completed 5 July 1985 and *SB 922* on 20 December 1985. *SB 922* named *Shakhter* in 1989. A fourth of class, *Iva SB 408*, was sold illegally to a Greek company in March 1993 and now flies the flag of Cyprus but is operated as a 'joint venture' with the Russian Navy. Diving facilities to 60 m. Bollard pull 60 tons. *SB 406* based in the Northern Fleet, *SB 921* in the Baltic and *SB 922* in the Black Sea.

SB 406   *10/2004** / 1151376

6 KATUN I (PROJECT 1893) and 2 KATUN II (PROJECT 1993) CLASSES (SALVAGE TUGS) (ATS)

Katun I: PZHS 98, 123, 124, 273, 279, 282
Katun II: PZHS 92, 95

Displacement, tons: 1,005 (Katun I); 1,220 (Katun II) full load
Dimensions, feet (metres): 205.3 × 33.1 × 11.5 *(62 × 10.1 × 3.5)* (Katun I)
Main machinery: 2 diesels; 5,000 hp(m) *(3.68 MW)*; 2 shafts
Speed, knots: 17. **Range, n miles:** 2,000 at 17 kt
Complement: 32
Radars: Navigation: Spin Trough or Kivach (Katun II); I-band.
IFF: High Pole A.

Comment: Katun I built at Kolpino 1970-78. Equipped for firefighting and rescue. *PZHS 64, 92, 95* and *219*, all Katun II, were completed in 1982 and are 3 m *(9.8 ft)* longer than Katun I with an extra bridge level and lattice masts. *273* and *279* are based in the Caspian Sea, *92, 95, 209* and *219* in the Pacific, *64* and *98* in the North, *96, 551* and *282* in the Baltic and *123* in the Black Sea.

282 (Katun I)   *8/2004* / 1042310

10 GORYN (PROJECT 714) CLASS (ARS/ATA)

MB 15	MB 38	MB 119	SB 521	SB 523
MB 35	MB 105	SB 36	SB 522	SB 931

Displacement, tons: 2,240 standard; 2,600 full load
Dimensions, feet (metres): 208.3 × 46.9 × 16.7 *(63.5 × 14.3 × 5.1)*
Main machinery: 2 Russkiy SEMT-Pielstick 6 PC2.5 L 400 diesels; 7,020 hp(m) *(5.2 MW)* sustained; 2 shafts; cp props; bow thruster
Speed, knots: 15
Complement: 43 plus 16 spare berths
Radars: Navigation: 2 Don 2 or Nayada or Kivach; I-band.

Comment: Built by Rauma-Repola 1977-83. Have sick-bay. First ships have goalpost mast with 10 and 5 ton derricks and bollard pull of 35 tons. Remainder have an A-frame mast with a 15 ton crane and bollard pull of 45 tons. SB number indicates a 'rescue' tug. Three in the North, four in the Pacific, two in the Baltic and one in the Black Sea. One transferred to Ukraine in 1997.

GORYN SB 522   *10/2005*, Ships of the World* / 1151155

12 SORUM (PROJECT 745) CLASS (ATA)

MB 4	MB 37	MB 58	MB 76	MB 100	MB 148
MB 28	MB 56	MB 61	MB 99	MB 110	MB 304

Displacement, tons: 1,660 full load
Dimensions, feet (metres): 190.2 × 41.3 × 15.1 *(58 × 12.6 × 4.6)*
Main machinery: Diesel-electric; 2 Type 5—2-DW2 diesel generators; 2,900 hp(m) *(2.13 MW)*; 1 motor; 2,000 hp(m) *(1.47 MW)*; 1 shaft
Speed, knots: 14. **Range, n miles:** 3,500 at 13 kt
Complement: 35
Guns: 4—30 mm/65 (2 twin) (all fitted for, but only Border Guard ships carry them).
Radars: Navigation: 2 Don 2 or Nayada; I-band.
IFF: High Pole B.

Comment: A class of ocean tugs with firefighting and diving capability. Built in Yaroslavl and Oktyabskoye from 1973 to 1989, design used for Ministry of Fisheries rescue tugs.

MB 99   *10/2005*, Ships of the World* / 1151157

14 OKHTENSKY (PROJECT 733/733S) CLASS (ARS/ATA)

AYANKA SB 3	**MB 162**	**LOKSA** MB 171
MOSHCHNY SB 6	**MB 164**	**MB 172**
MB 21	**SERDITY** MB 165	**MB 174**
MB 23	**MB 166**	**SATURN** MB 178
SPUTNIK MB 52	**POCHETNYY** MB 169	

Displacement, tons: 948 full load
Dimensions, feet (metres): 156.1 × 34 × 13.4 *(47.6 × 10.4 × 4.1)*
Main machinery: Diesel-electric; 2 BM diesel generators; 1 motor; 1,500 hp(m) *(1.1 MW)*; 1 shaft
Speed, knots: 13. **Range, n miles:** 8,000 at 7 kt; 6,000 at 13 kt
Complement: 40
Guns: 2—57 mm/70 (twin) or 2—25 mm/80 (twin) (Border Guard only).
Radars: Navigation: 1 or 2 Don 2 or Spin Trough; I-band.
IFF: High Pole B.

Comment: Ocean-going salvage (MB) and rescue tugs (SB). First of a total of 62 completed 1958. Fitted with powerful pumps and other apparatus for salvage. A number of named ships are operated by the Border Guard and are armed. Two to Ukraine in 1997. Many have been scrapped.

MB 174 *9/2004, Hartmut Ehlers* / 1042285

18 PROMETEY (PROJECT 498/04983/04985) CLASS
(TUGS) (YTB)

RB 1	**RB 98**	**RB 179**	**RB 217**	**RB 265**	**RB 327**
RB 7	**RB 158**	**RB 201**	**RB 239**	**RB 296**	**RB 360**
RB 57	**RB 173**	**RB 202**	**RB 262**	**RB 314**	**RB 362**

Displacement, tons: 360 full load
Dimensions, feet (metres): 96.1 × 27.2 × 10.5 *(29.3 × 8.3 × 3.2)*
Main machinery: 2 diesels; 1,200 hp(m) *(895 kW)*; 2 shafts
Speed, knots: 11

Comment: Entered service 1973-83. Bollard pull 14 tons. Later versions have more powerful engines. Based in the Northern, Pacific, Baltic and Black Sea Fleets.

RB 296 *6/2003, B Lemachko* / 0580540

35 SIDEHOLE I AND II (PROJECT 737 K/M) CLASS (TUGS) (YTB)

BUK 600	**RB 25**	**RB 49**	**RB 194**	**RB 233**	**RB 248**
RB 2	**RB 26**	**RB 51**	**RB 197**	**RB 237**	**RB 250**
RB 5	**RB 29**	**RB 52**	**RB 198**	**RB 240**	**RB 256**
RB 17	**RB 43**	**RB 168**	**RB 199**	**RB 244**	**RB 310**
RB 20	**RB 44**	**RB 192**	**RB 212**	**RB 246**	**RB 311**
RB 23	**RB 46**	**RB 193**	**RB 232**	**RB 247**	

Displacement, tons: 206 full load
Dimensions, feet (metres): 79.4 × 23.0 × 11.1 *(24.2 × 7.0 × 3.4)*
Main machinery: 2 diesels; 900 hp(m) *(670 kW)*; 2 shafts
Speed, knots: 10

Comment: Entered service 1973-83. Bollard pull 10 tons. Based in all fleets.

11 STIVIDOR (PROJECT 192) CLASS (TUGS) (YTB)

RB 22	**RB 108**	**RB 136**	**RB 244**	**RB 280**	**RB 326**
RB 40	**RB 109**	**RB 167**	**RB 247**	**RB 325**	

Displacement, tons: 575 full load
Dimensions, feet (metres): 117.1 × 31.1 × 15.1 *(35.7 × 9.5 × 4.6)*
Main machinery: 2 diesels; 2,400 hp(m) *(1.78 MW)*; 2 shafts; bow-thruster
Speed, knots: 12

Comment: Entered service 1980-90. Bollard pull 35 tons. Equipped with three water cannons. Based in the Northern, Pacific and Black Sea Fleets.

RB 325 *3/2004, B Lemachko* / 0580541

For details of the latest updates to *Jane's Fighting Ships* online and to discover the additional information available exclusively to online subscribers please visit
jfs.janes.com

RUSSIAN FEDERAL BORDER GUARD SERVICE
(EX-MARITIME BORDER GUARD)

General

(1) The Border Guard would be integrated with naval operations in a crisis. Formerly run by the KGB, the force came under the Ministry of Defence in October 1991 and was then given to the Ministry of Interior in December 1993. It merged with the Federal Security Service on 11 March 2003.

(2) From 1993 the Border Guard started to fly its own ensign which is the St Andrews Cross with a white border on a green background. Diagonal stripes are painted on the hull which from 2004 have been painted blue.

(3) Roles include Law Enforcement, Port Security, Counter Intelligence, Counter Terrorism and Fishery Protection.

Personnel

2006: 10,000 approx

FRIGATES

Notes: In addition to the frigates listed, there are believed to be a 'Grisha V' (*Stelyak*), three 'Grisha III' (*Bezuprechniy, Zorkiy* and *Smelyy*), which operate in the Pacific region. However, their operational status is not known. Three 'Grisha II' (*Izumrud, Predaniy* and *Nadezhnyy*) are reported to be based in the Northern region but their operational status is also unknown.

7 KRIVAK III (NEREY) (PROJECT 1135MP) CLASS (FFHM)

Name	No	Builders	Laid down	Launched	Commissioned
MENZHINSKY	113	Kamish-Burun, Kerch	14 Aug 1981	31 Dec 1982	29 Dec 1983
DZERZHINSKY	158 (ex-097)	Kamish-Burun, Kerch	11 Jan 1984	2 Mar 1984	29 Dec 1984
OREL (ex-*Imeni XXVII Sezda KPSS*)	156	Kamish-Burun, Kerch	26 Sep 1983	2 Nov 1985	30 Sep 1986
PSKOV (ex-*Imeni LXX Letiya VCHK-KGB*)	175 (ex-104)	Kamish-Burun, Kerch		1987	30 Dec 1987
ANADYR (ex-*Imeni LXX Letiya Pogranvoysk*)	060	Kamish-Burun, Kerch	22 Oct 1987	28 Mar 1988	16 Aug 1989
KEDROV	103	Kamish-Burun, Kerch	5 Nov 1988	30 Apr 1989	20 Nov 1990
VOROVSKY	160 (ex-052)	Kamish-Burun, Kerch	20 Feb 1990	28 July 1990	29 Dec 1990

Displacement, tons: 3,100 standard; 3,650 full load
Dimensions, feet (metres): 405.2 × 46.9 × 24 (sonar) *(123.5 × 14.3 × 7.3)*
Main machinery: COGAG; 2 M8K gas-turbines; 55,500 hp(m) *(40.8 MW)*; 2 M 62 gas-turbines; 13,600 hp(m) *(10 MW)*; 2 shafts
Speed, knots: 3
Range, n miles: 4,000 at 14 kt; 1,600 at 30 kt
Complement: 194 (18 officers)

Missiles: SAM: 1 SA-N-4 Gecko (Zif 122) twin launchers ❶; Osa-M semi-active radar homing to 15 km *(8 n miles)* at 2.5 Mach; warhead 50 kg; altitude 9.1—3,048 m *(30—10,000 ft)*; 20 missiles.
Guns: 1—3.9 in *(100 mm)*/59 ❷; 60 rds/min to 15 km *(8.2 n miles)*; weight of shell 16 kg.
2—30 mm/65 ❸; 6 barrels per mounting; 3,000 rds/min combined to 2 km.
Torpedoes: 8—21 in *(533 mm)* (2 quad) tubes ❹. Combination of 53 cm torpedoes (see table at front of section).
A/S mortars: 2 RBU 6000 12-tubed trainable ❺; range 6,000 m; warhead 31 kg. MRG-7 55 mm grenade launcher.
Mines: Capacity for 16.

Countermeasures: Decoys: 4 PK 16 or 10 PK 10 chaff launchers. Towed torpedo decoy.
ESM/ECM: 2 Bell Shroud. 2 Bell Squat. Half Cup laser warning (in some).
Radars: Air search: Top Plate ❻; 3D; D/E-band.
Surface search: Peel Cone ❼; I-band.
Fire control: Pop Group ❽; F/H/I-band (for SA-N-4). Kite Screech ❾; H/I/K-band. Bass Tilt ❿; H/I-band.
IFF: High Pole B. Salt Pot.
Sonars: Bull Nose (MGK-335S or MG-332); hull-mounted; active search and attack; medium frequency.

Helicopters: 1 Ka-27 Helix ⓫.

Programmes: Type name was originally *bolshoy protivolodochny korabl*, meaning large anti-submarine ship. Changed in 1977-78 to *storozhevoy korabl* meaning escort ship. The naval Krivaks are known as the Burevestnik class.
Structure: Krivak III class built for the former KGB but now under Border Guard Control. The removal of SS-N-14 and one SA-N-4 mounting compensates for the addition of a hangar and flight deck.
Sales: The Talwar class is an improved version of the Krivak III built for India. Three of the Krivak III class transferred to Ukraine in July 1997.

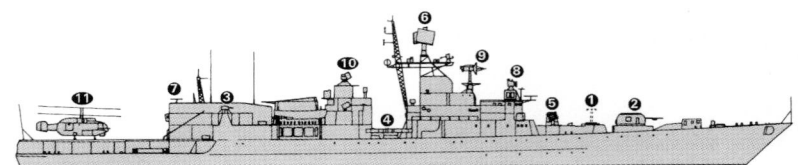

KRIVAK III *(Scale 1 : 1,200), Ian Sturton* / 0506085

VOROVSKY (old number) *10/1991* / 0506321

PATROL FORCES

Notes: In addition to the patrol forces listed, *Pluton* and *Strelets*, two Yug class former research vessels, are operated as patrol craft in Arctic waters.

4 KOMANDOR CLASS (PSO)

KOMANDOR	SHKIPER GYEK	HERLUF BIDSTRUP	MANCHZHUR

Displacement, tons: 2,435 full load
Dimensions, feet (metres): 289.7 × 44.6 × 15.4 *(88.3 × 13.6 × 4.7)*
Main machinery: 2 Russkiy SEMT-Pielstick 6 PC2.5 L400 diesels; 7,020 hp(m) *(5.2 MW)*; 1 shaft; cp prop; bow thruster
Speed, knots: 20
Range, n miles: 7,000 at 19 kt
Complement: 42
Radars: Navigation: Furuno; I-band.
Helicopters: 2 Ka-32 Helix D for SAR.

Comment: Specialist offshore patrol vessels ordered in December 1987 from Danyard, Frederikshaven, Denmark and delivered 1989-1990. The hangar is below the helicopter deck. Transferred from the Ministry of Fisheries to the Federal Border Guard and based in the Pacific.

MANCHZHUR
6/2003, B Lemachko
0580538

8 ALPINIST (PROJECT 503) CLASS (PBO)

ANTIAS   **ARGAL**   **BARS**   **DIANA**   **PALIYA**   **PARELLA**   **+2**

Displacement, tons: 1,150 full load
Dimensions, feet (metres): 176.2 × 34.4 × 13.4 *(53.7 × 10.5 × 4.1)*
Main machinery: 1 diesel; 1 shaft; cp prop
Speed, knots: 12
Range, n miles: 7,000 at 12 kt
Complement: 44

Comment: Trawler design adapted for use as fishery protection role. The named ships were built at Volgograd and at Khabarovsk between 1997 and 2000 while the latest two (unnamed) ships were built at Yarslavl and entered service in late 2001.

1 AKADEMIK FERSMAN CLASS (PSO)

SPASTEL PROCONCHIK (ex-*Akademik Fersman*)

Displacement, tons: 3,250 full load
Dimensions, feet (metres): 268.8 × 48.6 × 16.4 *(81.9 × 14.8 × 5.0)*
Main machinery: 1 Zgoda-Sulzer diesel; 1 shaft; cp prop
Speed, knots: 14. **Range, n miles:** 12,000 at 14 kt
Complement: 30 + 29 spare

Comment: Former seismic research ship which was built at Szczecin, Poland and originally entered service in 1986. Transferred to Russian government service in 1997.

AKADEMIK FERSMAN CLASS   *6/2000* / 0084679

4 IVAN SUSANIN (PROJECT 97P) CLASS (PATROL SHIPS) (PGH)

AISBERG 161   **MURMANSK** (ex-*Dunay*) 018   **NEVA** 170   **VOLGA** 183

Displacement, tons: 3,567 full load
Dimensions, feet (metres): 229.7 × 59.4 × 21 *(70 × 18.1 × 6.4)*
Main machinery: Diesel-electric; 3 Type 13-D-150 diesel generators; 3 motors; 5,400 hp(m) *(4 MW)*; 3 shafts (1 fwd, 2 aft)
Speed, knots: 14.5. **Range, n miles:** 5,500 at 12.5 kt
Complement: 45
Guns: 2—3 in *(76 mm)*/60 (twin). 2—30 mm/65 AK 630 (not in all).
Radars: Surface search: Strut Curve; F-band.
Navigation: 2 Don Kay or Palm Frond; I-band.
Fire control: Hawk Screech; I-band.
Helicopters: Platform only.

Comment: Built at Admiralty Yard, Leningrad between 1974 and 1981. Generally similar to Dobrynya Nikitich class though larger with a tripod mast and different superstructure. Former icebreakers operated primarily as patrol ships. Two in the Pacific and two in the Northern Fleet. Two deleted so far.

MURMANSK   *8/2002* / 0528312

17 SORUM (PROJECT 745P) CLASS (PBO)

ALDAN (ex-*Bug*) 142	**KARELIA** 110	**ZAPOLARYE** 022
AMUR 043	**SAKHALIN** 124	**PRIMORYE** 172
BREST 135	**URAL** 016	**LADOGA** 058
CHUKOTKA 067	**BAYKAL** (ex-*Yan Berzin*) 105	**VICTOR KINGISEPP**
DON 103	**YENISEY** 038	(ex-*Vyatka*) 035
KAMCHATKA 198	**ZABAYKALYE** 196	
GENERAL MATROSOV 101		

Displacement, tons: 1,660 full load
Dimensions, feet (metres): 190.2 × 41.3 × 15.1 *(58 × 12.6 × 4.6)*
Main machinery: Diesel-electric; 2 Type 5-2-DW2 diesel generators; 2,900 hp(m) *(2.13 MW)*; 1 motor; 2,000 hp(m) *(1.47 MW)*; 1 shaft
Speed, knots: 14. **Range, n miles:** 3,500 at 13 kt
Complement: 35
Guns: 4—30 mm/65 (2 twin) (all fitted for, but only Border Guard ships carry them).
Radars: Navigation: 2 Don 2 or Nayada; I-band.
IFF: High Pole B.

Comment: A class of ocean tugs armed for use as patrol vessels in the North, Pacific, Baltic and Caspian. Built in Yaroslavl and Oktyabskoye from 1973 to 1989, design used for Ministry of Fisheries rescue tugs.

PRIMORYE   *9/2002, Hachiro Nakai* / 0528309

0 + 1 (9) SPRUT (PROJECT 6457S) CLASS (PSO)

Displacement, tons: 900 standard
Dimensions, feet (metres): 216.2 × 34.8 × 11.5 *(65.9 × 10.6 × 3.5)*
Main machinery: 1 MTU 16V 1163 diesel; 7,000 hp(m) *(5.2 MW)*; 1 shaft; fixed propeller
Speed, knots: 21.5. **Range, n miles:** 12,000 at 12 kt
Complement: 15 + 10 in temporary accommodation
Radars: Surface search: I-band.
Navigation: I-band.
Helicopters: Platform for 1 light.

Comment: Specialist Fishery Protection vessel based on German Coast Guard Bad Bramstedt design. First of class laid down at Yantar, Kaliningrad on 27 May 2002. Delivery is expected in 2006. Steel hull with aluminium superstructure. Equipped with a high speed RHIB for interception. A class of ten is planned.

SPRUT   *4/2003, Military Parade* / 0570892

2 PAUK II (PROJECT 1241 PE) CLASS (PCM)

NOVOROSSIYSK 043   **KUBAN** 149

Displacement, tons: 495 full load
Dimensions, feet (metres): 191.9 × 33.5 × 11.2 *(58.5 × 10.2 × 3.4)*
Main machinery: 2 Type M 521 diesels; 16,184 hp(m) *(11.9 MW)* sustained; 2 shafts
Speed, knots: 32. **Range, n miles:** 2,400 at 14 kt
Complement: 32

Missiles: SAM: SA-N-5 quad launcher; manual aiming, IR homing to 10 km *(5.4 n miles)* at 1.5 Mach; warhead 1.1 kg.
Guns: 1 USSR 76 mm/60; 120 rds/min to 7 km *(3.8 n miles)*; weight of shell 16 kg.
1—30 mm/65 AK 630; 6 barrels; 3,000 rds/min combined to 2 km.
Torpedoes: 4—21 in *(533 mm)* (2 twin) fixed tubes.
A/S mortars: 2 RBU 1200 5-tubed fixed; range 1,200 m; warhead 34 kg.
Radars: Air/surface search: Cross Dome (Positiv E); E/F-band.
Navigation: Pechora; I-band.
Fire control: Bass Tilt; H/I-band.
Sonars: Rat Tail; VDS (on transom); attack; high frequency.

Comment: Built at Yaroslav Shipyard and entered service in 1997-98 when they were transferred to the Border Guard. Originally intended for Iraq, export Pauk II variant of the type sold to India and Cuba. Has a longer superstructure than the Pauk I with a radome similar to the Parchim II class. The torpedo tubes must be trained out to launch. Both operate in the Black Sea.

3 TERRIER (PROJECT 14170) CLASS (PB)

001-003

Displacement, tons: 8.3 full load
Dimensions, feet (metres): 38.4 × 10.2 × 1.6 *(11.7 × 3.1 × 0.5)*
Main machinery: 2 diesels; 2 waterjets
Speed, knots: 32. **Range, n miles:** 120 at 30 kt
Complement: 6

Comment: Built at Zelenodolsk in 2000.

TERRIER 002   *6/2003, B Lemachko* / 0580539

17 PAUK I (MOLNYA) (PROJECT 12412) CLASS
(FAST ATTACK CRAFT—PATROL) (PCM)

TOLYATTI (ex-PSKR-804)	021
NAKHODKA (ex-PSKR-818)	023
KALININGRAD (ex-PSKR-802)	024
YAROSLAVL (ex-PSKR-810)	031
YASTREB (ex-PSKR-816)	037
SARYCH (ex-PSKR-811)	040
GRIF (ex-PSKR-808)	041
ORLAN (ex-PSKR-814)	042
CHEBOKSARY (ex-PSKR-817)	052
SOKOL (ex-PSKR-812)	063
MINSK (ex-PSKR-806)	065
NIKOLAY KAPLUNOV (ex-PSKR-815)	077
KOBCHIK (ex-PSKR-807)	078
KRECHET (ex-PSKR-809)	099
BERKUT (ex-PSKR-800)	152
KORSHUN (ex-PSKR-805)	161
VORON (ex-PSKR-801)	163

Displacement, tons: 440 full load
Dimensions, feet (metres): 189 × 33.5 × 10.8 *(57.6 × 10.2 × 3.3)*
Main machinery: 2 Type M 521 diesels; 16,184 hp(m) *(11.9 MW)* sustained; 2 shafts
Speed, knots: 32. **Range, n miles:** 2,400 at 14 kt
Complement: 38

Missiles: SAM: SA-N-5 Grail quad launcher; manual aiming; IR homing to 6 km *(3.2 n miles)* at 1.5 Mach; altitude to 2,500 m *(8,000 ft)*; warhead 1.5 kg; 8 missiles.
Guns: 1—3 in *(76 mm)*/60; 120 rds/min to 15 km *(8 n miles)*; weight of shell 7 kg.
  1—30 mm/65 AK 630; 6 barrels; 3,000 rds/min combined to 2 km.
Torpedoes: 4—16 in *(406 mm)* tubes. For torpedo details see table at front of section.
A/S mortars: 2 RBU 1200 5-tubed fixed; range 1,200 m; warhead 34 kg.
Depth charges: 2 racks (12).
Countermeasures: Decoys: 2 PK 16 or 4 PK 10 chaff launchers.
ESM: 3 Brick Plug and 2 Half Hat; radar warning.
Weapons control: Hood Wink optronic director.
Radars: Air/surface search: Peel Cone; E/F-band.
Surface search: Kivach or Pechora or SRN 207; I-band.
Fire control: Bass Tilt; H/I-band.
Sonars: Foal Tail; VDS (mounted on transom); active attack; high frequency.

Programmes: First laid down in 1977 and completed in 1979. In series production at Yaroslavl in the Black Sea and at Vladivostok until 1988 when the Svetlyak class took over. Type name is *maly protivolodochny korabl* meaning small anti-submarine ship. An improved version building at Kharbarovsk in 1995 was not completed.
Structure: An ASW version of the Tarantul class having the same hull form with a 1.8 m extension for dipping sonar. *Berkut*, *Voron* and *Kaliningrad* have a lower bridge than others. A modified version (Pauk II) with a longer superstructure, two twin 533 mm torpedo tubes and a radome similar to the Parchim class built for export.
Operational: Five in the Baltic, two in the Black Sea and the remainder in the Pacific. In addition five naval craft are laid up in the Baltic and one in the Black Sea.
Sales: One to Bulgaria in September 1989 and a second in December 1990. Two to Ukraine in 1996. A variant design built for Vietnam.

MINSK *7/2003, Freddy Philips* / 0570908

3 MURAVEY (ANTARES) (PROJECT 133) CLASS (PCK)

DELFIN	**RYBA**	**TUAPSE**

Displacement, tons: 212 full load
Dimensions, feet (metres): 126.6 × 24.9 × 6.2; 14.4 (foils) *(38.6 × 7.6 × 1.9; 4.4)*
Main machinery: 2 gas turbines; 22,600 hp(m) *(16.6 MW)*; 2 shafts
Speed, knots: 60. **Range, n miles:** 410 at 12 kt
Complement: 30 (5 officers)

Guns: 1—3 in *(76 mm)*/60; 120 rds/min to 15 km *(8 n miles)*; weight of shell 7 kg.
  1—30 mm/65 AK 630; 6 barrels; 3,000 rds/min combined to 2 km.
Weapons control: Hood Wink optronic director.
Radars: Surface search: Peel Cone; E-band.
Fire control: Bass Tilt; H/I-band.
Sonars: Rat Tail; VDS; active attack; high frequency; dipping sonar.

Comment: Thirteen hydrofoil craft built at Feodosiya in the mid-1980s for the USSR Border Guard. Three transferred to Ukraine and the remainder decommissioned.

MURAVEY CLASS *3/1998, Ukraine Coast Guard* / 0050319

1 MUSTANG (PROJECT 18623) CLASS (PBF)

Displacement, tons: 35.5 full load
Dimensions, feet (metres): 65.6 × 14.8 × 3.6 *(20.0 × 4.5 × 1.1)*
Main machinery: 2 Zvezda M-470 diesels; 2,950 hp *(2.2 MW)*; 2 Kamewa waterjets
Speed, knots: 45
Range, n miles: 350 at 40 kt
Complement: 6

Comment: Designed by Redan Bureau, St Petersburg and built at Yaroslavl in 2000.

MUSTANG *6/2005*, A Sheldon-Duplaix* / 1127917

9 + (11) MIRAZH (PROJECT 14310) CLASS (PBF)

PK 500	+8

Displacement, tons: 126 full load
Dimensions, feet (metres): 111.5 × 21.7 × 8.9 *(34.0 × 6.6 × 2.7)*
Main machinery: 2 Zvezda M-521 diesels; 16,184 hp(m) *(11.9 MW)*; 2 shafts
Speed, knots: 48
Range, n miles: 1,500 at 8 kt
Complement: 12 (2 officers)

Guns: 1—30 mm AK 306.
  2—7.62 mm MGs.
Radars: Surface search: I-band.

Comment: Designed by Almaz and built by Vympel Shipbuilding, Rybinsk. Aluminium-magnesium alloy construction. Three vessels authorised for construction in 1993 but only first of class was completed in 1998. It entered service with the Border Guard in 2001 and has been based in the Caspian Sea. Nine craft are believed to be in service and a class of 20 craft is reported to be required.

MIRAZH *6/2003, B Lemachko* / 0570906

MIRAZH *6/2005*, A Sheldon-Duplaix* / 1127916

11 + 2 (3) SOBOL (PROJECT 12200) CLASS (PBF)

BSK 1-11

Displacement, tons: 57 full load
Dimensions, feet (metres): 91.7 × 16.0 × 4.4 *(27.9 × 4.9 × 1.4)*
Main machinery: 2 diesels; 3,600 hp *(2.6 MW)*; 2 shafts
Speed, knots: 47
Range, n miles: 700 at 40 kt
Complement: 6
Missiles: SAM: SA-N-10 (Igla).
Guns: 1—30 mm AK-306. 1—14.5 mm MG.

Comment: Built at Almaz St Petersburg and at Soznovka Zavod, Rybinsk and delivered 2000-03. Two further craft are to be delivered in 2006 and a further three are expected.

SOBOL CLASS (artist's impression)   *6/2004, S Breyer* / 1042412

19 + 2 SVETLYAK (PROJECT 1041Z) CLASS
(FAST ATTACK CRAFT—PATROL) (PGM)

PODOLSK (ex-PSKR-920)	017
NEVELSK (ex-PSKR-915)	023
YUZHNO-SAKHALINSK (ex-PSKR-918)	026
SOCHI (ex-PSKR-906)	028
SIKTIVKAR (ex-PSKR-911)	042
YAMALETS	044
BRIZ (ex-PSKR-908)	065
STOROCHEVIK	076
NEPTUN	077
CHOLMSK (ex-PSKR-903)	088
PTER. ALMAZ	099
STAVROPOL (ex-PSKR-902)	100
KIZLJAR (ex-PSKR-913)	102
DERBENT (ex-PSKR-912)	106
KORSAKOV (ex-PSKR-914)	118
— (ex-PSKR 923)	126
ANATOLY KOPOLEV (ex-PSKR 916)	137
VYBORG (ex-PSKR-909)	141
ALMAZ (ex-PSKR-913)	143

Displacement, tons: 375 full load
Dimensions, feet (metres): 159.1 × 30.2 × 11.5 *(48.5 × 9.2 × 3.5)*
Main machinery: 3 diesels; 14,400 hp(m) *(10.58 MW)*; 3 shafts
Speed, knots: 31
Range, n miles: 2,200 at 13 kt
Complement: 36 (4 officers)

Missiles: SAM: SA-N-5 Grail quad launcher; manual aiming; IR homing to 6 km *(3.2 n miles)* at 1.5 Mach; warhead 1.5 kg.
Guns: 1—3 in *(76 mm)*/60; 120 rds/min to 15 km *(8 n miles)*; weight of shell 7 kg.
  1 or 2—30 mm/65 AK 630; 6 barrels; 3,000 rds/min combined to 2 km; 12 missiles.
Torpedoes: 2—16 in *(406 mm)* tubes; SAET-40; anti-submarine; active/passive homing to 10 km *(5.4 n miles)* at 30 kt; warhead 100 kg.
Depth charges: 2 racks; 12 charges.
Countermeasures: Decoys: 2 PK 16 chaff launchers.
Weapons control: Hood Wink optronic director.
Radars: Air/surface search: Peel Cone; E-band.
Fire control: Bass Tilt (MP 123); H/I-band.
Navigation: Palm Frond B; I-band.
IFF: High Pole B. Square Head.
Sonars: Rat Tail; VDS; active search; high frequency.

Comment: A class of attack craft for the Border Guard built at Vladivostok, St Petersburg and Yaroslavl. Series production after first of class trials in 1989. Although deliveries have been very slow in recent years, the class may still be building with the most recent launch in May 2000. A further two craft are to be delivered in 2006. One has a second AK 630 gun vice the 76 mm and no Bass Tilt radars. Six in the Northern Fleet, three in the Baltic, seven in the Pacific, two in the Caspian and two in the Black Sea are all known to be active. Two have been built for Vietnam. Three additional craft operated by the Navy.

ALMAZ   *6/2003, A Sheldon-Duplaix* / 0570905

15 STENKA (TARANTUL) (PROJECT 205P) CLASS
(FAST ATTACK CRAFT—PATROL) (PTF)

PSKR-714 014		**PSKR-717** 078		**PSKR-641** 133	
PSKR-660 044		**PSKR-712** 132		**PSKR-725** 134	
PSKR-700 047		**PSKR-665** 113		**PSKR-631** 137	
PSKR-715 048		**PSKR-657** 126		**PSKR-659** 139	
PSKR-718 053		**PSKR-690** 129		**PSKR-723** 143	

Displacement, tons: 211 standard; 253 full load
Dimensions, feet (metres): 129.3 × 25.9 × 8.2 *(39.4 × 7.9 × 2.5)*
Main machinery: 3 Type M 517 or M 583 diesels; 14,100 hp(m) *(10.36 MW)*; 3 shafts
Speed, knots: 37. **Range, n miles:** 800 at 24 kt; 500 at 35 kt; 2,300 at 14 kt
Complement: 25 (5 officers)
Guns: 4—30 mm/65 (2 twin) AK 230.
Torpedoes: 4—16 in *(406 mm)* tubes.
Depth charges: 2 racks.
Radars: Surface search: Pot Drum or Peel Cone; H/I- or E-band.
Fire control: Drum Tilt; H/I-band.
Navigation: Palm Frond; I-band.
IFF: High Pole. 2 Square Head.
Sonars: Stag Ear or Foal Tail; VDS; high frequency; Hormone type dipping sonar.

Comment: Based on the hull design of the Osa class. Construction started in 1967 and continued at a rate of about five a year at Petrovsky, Leningrad and Vladivostok for the Border Guard. Programme terminated in 1989 at a total of 133 hulls. Type name is *pogranichny storozhevoy korabl* meaning border patrol ship. Four based in the Baltic, five in the Black Sea, one in the Pacific, and five in the Caspian Sea.
Transfers include: Cuba, two in February 1985 and one in August 1985. Four to Cambodia in October 1985 and November 1987. Five transferred to Azerbaijan control in November 1992 and 10 more to Ukraine.

STENKA   *6/2000* / 0126309

1 + (3) SOKZHOI CLASS (PROJECT 14230) (PBF)

ALBATROS

Displacement, tons: 97.7 full load
Dimensions, feet (metres): 114.8 × 25.7 × 6.6 *(35.0 × 7.85 × 2.0)*
Main machinery: 2 Zvezda M535 diesels; 9,923 hp(m) *(7.4 MW)* sustained; 2 shafts
Speed, knots: 50. **Range, n miles:** 800
Complement: 16
Guns: 2—30 mm AK-306. 1—14.5 mm MG.

Comment: First of a new class of patrol craft launched at Volga Yard, Nizhny Novgorod on 23 June 2000. A feature of the design is that an air-cushion is generated below the hull to produce a planing effect to reduce drag. The machine-gun is mounted in a barbette in the forward part of the craft. Project 14232 is a family of high-speed air-cavern vessels based on a unified platform design developed by the Alekseyev Hydrofoil Design Bureau, Nizhny Novgorod. Other variants of the design have different superstructure configuration, armament and equipment. These include two unarmed vessels of the sister Project 14232 Mercury class *(Petr Matveyev* (TS-100) and *Pavel Vereshchagin* (TS-101)*)* built for the customs service at Yaroslavl between 1996-2000. Two more of this type ship are to be completed in Yaroslavl and Khabarovsk.

SOKZHOI CLASS   *3/2004*, Military Parade* / 1127049

PAVEL VERESHCHAGIN (Customs)   *6/2003, E & M Laursen* / 0570902

12 ZHUK (GRIF) (PROJECT 1400/1400M) CLASS
(COASTAL PATROL CRAFT) (PB)

PSKA series

Displacement, tons: 39 full load
Dimensions, feet (metres): 78.7 × 16.4 × 3.9 *(24 × 5 × 1.2)*
Main machinery: 2 Type M 401B diesels; 2,200 hp(m) *(1.6 MW)* sustained; 2 shafts
Speed, knots: 30
Range, n miles: 1,100 at 15 kt
Complement: 11 (3 officers)
Guns: 2 – 14.5 mm (twin, fwd) MGs. 1 – 12.7 mm (aft) MG.
Radars: Surface search: Spin Trough; I-band.

Comment: Under construction from 1976. Manned by the Border Guard. Export versions
have twin (over/under) 14.5 mm aft. Some have twin guns forward and aft. Ukraine
Border Guard and has received 12 from the Russians. Eight are in the Baltic and four in
the Black Sea. These are the last operational units.
Transfers: Algeria (one in 1981), Angola (one in 1977), Benin (four in 1978-80), Bulgaria
(five in 1977), Cape Verde (one in 1980), Congo (three in 1982), Cuba (40 in 1971-88),
Equatorial Guinea (three in 1974-75), Ethiopia (two in October 1982 and two in June
1990), Guinea (two in July 1987), Iraq (five in 1974-75), Cambodia (three in 1985-87),
Mauritius (two in January 1990), Mozambique (five in 1978-80), Nicaragua (eight in
1982-86), Seychelles (one in 1981, one in October 1982), Somalia (one in 1974), Syria
(six in 1981-84), Vietnam (nine in 1978-88 (at least one passed on to Cambodia), five in
1990 and two in 1995), North Yemen (five in 1978-87), South Yemen (two in 1975). Many
have been deleted.

ZHUK   7/1996, J Ciślak / 0081678

1 + (9) MANGUST (PROJECT 12150) CLASS (PBF)

Displacement, tons: 27 standard
Dimensions, feet (metres): 64.0 × 14.4 × 7.2 *(19.5 × 4.4 × 2.2)*
Main machinery: 2 Zvezda M-470 diesels; 2 Arneson dive props
Speed, knots: 53
Range, n miles: 250 at 40 kt
Complement: 6
Guns: 2 – 14.5 mm MGs.
Radars: Navigation: I-band.

Comment: Prototype TS 300 built by Vympel, Rybinsk for the Customs service and
completed in 1998. GRP construction. First Border Guard unit entered service in 2001.
Further orders are expected.

MANGUST   4/2003, Military Parade / 0570900

RIVER PATROL FORCES

Notes: Attached to Black Sea and Pacific Fleets for operations on the Danube, Amur and
Usuri Rivers, and to the Caspian Flotilla.

2 YAZ (SLEPEN) (PROJECT 1208) CLASS (PGR)

BLAGOVESHCHENSK 066   **SHKVAL** 106

Displacement, tons: 440 full load
Dimensions, feet (metres): 180.4 × 29.5 × 4.9 *(55 × 9 × 1.5)*
Main machinery: 3 diesels; 11,400 hp(m) *(8.39 MW)*; 3 shafts
Speed, knots: 24. **Range, n miles:** 1,000 at 10 kt
Complement: 32 (4 officers)
Guns: 2 – 115 mm tank guns (TB 62) or 100 mm/56.
  2 – 30 mm/65 AK 630; 6 barrels per mounting.
  4 – 12.7 mm MGs (2 twin).
  2 – 40 mm mortars on after deckhouse.
Radars: Surface search: Spin Trough; I-band.
Fire control: Bass Tilt; H/I-band.
IFF: High Pole B. Square Head.

Comment: First entered service in Amur Flotilla 1978. Built at Khabarovsk until 1987. All
but these last two have been placed in reserve.

BLAGOVESHCHENSK   6/1995, B Lemachko / 0570903

15 SHMEL (PROJECT 1204) CLASS (PGR)

AKA 203	**AKA 248**	**AKA 564**
AKA 209	**AKA 384**	**AKA 582**
AKA 211	**AKA 397**	**AKA 583**
AKA 224	**AKA 506**	**AKA 599**
AKA 246	**AKA 563**	**AKA 602**

Displacement, tons: 77 full load
Dimensions, feet (metres): 90.9 × 14.1 × 3.9 *(27.7 × 4.3 × 1.2)*
Main machinery: 2 Type M 50 diesels; 2,200 hp(m) *(1.6 MW)* sustained; 2 shafts
Speed, knots: 25
Range, n miles: 600 at 12 kt
Complement: 12 (4 officers)
Guns: 1 – 3 in *(76 mm)*/48 (tank turret). 1 – 25 mm/70 (later ships). 2 – 14.5 mm (twin) MGs
  (earlier ships). 5 – 7.62 mm MGs. 1 BP 6 rocket launcher; 18 barrels.
Mines: Can lay 9.
Radars: Surface search: Spin Trough; I-band.

Comment: Completed at Kerch and Nikolayev North (61 Kommuna) 1967-74. Some of the
later ships also mount one or two multibarrelled rocket launchers amidships. The 7.62 mm
guns fire through embrasures in the superstructure with one mounted on the 76 mm.
Can be carried on land transport. Type name is *artillerisky kater* meaning artillery cutter.
About 70 have been scrapped or laid up so far including the last naval units. These last
survivors are based on the Amur River and belong to the Border Guard.
Transfers: Four to Cambodia (1984-85) (since decommissioned). Some have been taken
over by Belorussian forces, and others allocated to Ukraine.

SHMEL   6/2000, B Lemachko / 0106875

8 PIYAVKA (PROJECT 1249) CLASS (PBR)

PSKR 52 117	**PSKR 56** 093
PSKR 53 065	**PSKR 57** 058
PSKR 54 146	**PSKR 58** 123
PSKR 55 013	**PSKR 59** 189

Displacement, tons: 229 full load
Dimensions, feet (metres): 136.5 × 20.7 × 2.9 *(41.6 × 6.3 × 0.9)*
Main machinery: 3 diesels; 3,300 hp(m) *(2.42 MW)*; 2 shafts
Speed, knots: 17
Complement: 30 (4 officers)
Guns: 1 – 30 mm/65 AK 630; 6 barrels. 2 – 14.5 mm (twin) MGs.
Radars: Surface search: Spin Trough; I-band.

Comment: Built at Khabarovsk 1979-84. Based in Amur Flotilla mostly for logistic support.

PSKR 58   6/2003, B Lemachko / 0580529

3 OGONEK (PROJECT 12130) CLASS (PBR)

Displacement, tons: 98 full load
Dimensions, feet (metres): 109.6 × 13.8 × 2.6 *(33.4 × 4.2 × 0.8)*
Main machinery: 2 diesels; 2 shafts
Speed, knots: 25
Complement: 17 (2 officers)
Guns: 2—30 mm AK 630.

Comment: A smaller version of the Piyavka class built at Khabarovsk from 1999. Numbers in service are uncertain.

OGONEK   *6/2003, B Lemachko* / 0576442

5 VOSH (MOSKIT) (PROJECT 1248) CLASS (PGR)

PSKR 482-486

Displacement, tons: 229 full load
Dimensions, feet (metres): 140.1 × 20.7 × 3.3 *(42 × 6.3 × 1)*
Main machinery: 3 diesels; 3,300 hp(m) *(2.42 MW)*; 3 shafts
Speed, knots: 17
Complement: 34 (3 officers)
Guns: 1—3 in *(76 mm)*/48 (tank turret). 1—30 mm/65 AK 630. 2—12.7 mm (twin) MGs.
Countermeasures: 1 twin barrel decoy launcher.
Radars: Surface search: Spin Trough; I-band.

Comment: Built at Sretensk on the Shilka river 1980-84. Based on Amur River. Same hull as Piyavka.

VOSH CLASS   *6/2001, B Lemachko* / 0126218

15 SAYGAK (PROJECT 14081/14081M) CLASS (PBF)

Displacement, tons: 11.5 full load
Dimensions, feet (metres): 45.9 × 11.5 × 2.1 *(14.0 × 3.5 × 0.65)*
Main machinery: 1 Zvezda M-401B diesel; 1,000 hp *(746 kW)*; 1 waterjet
Speed, knots: 38. **Range, n miles:** 135 at 35 kt
Complement: 2 plus 8
Radars: Navigation: I-band.

Comment: Built by Kama Zavod, Perm and entered service 1986-2000. Used for riverine and lake patrol. Others are used by the Customs service.

AUXILIARIES

10 NEON ANTONOV (PROJECT 1595) CLASS
(TRANSPORTS) (AK)

VASILIY SUNTZOV 154	**VYACHESLAV DENISOV** 176	**IVAN YEVTEYEV** 105
IVAN LEDNEV 115	**MIKHAIL KONOVALOV** 184	**SERGEY SUDETSKY** 143
NIKOLAY SIPYAGIN 090	**NIKOLAY STARSHINOV** 119	**DVINA**
IRBIT		

Displacement, tons: 6,400 full load
Dimensions, feet (metres): 311.7 × 48.2 × 21.3 *(95 × 14.7 × 6.5)*
Main machinery: 2 diesels; 7,000 hp(m) *(5.15 MW)*; 2 shafts
Speed, knots: 17. **Range, n miles:** 8,500 at 13 kt
Complement: 45
Cargo capacity: 2,500 tons
Missiles: SAM: 2 SA-N-5 Grail twin launchers; manual aiming; IR homing to 6 km *(3.2 n miles)* at 1.5 Mach; altitude to 2,500 m *(8,000 ft)*; warhead 1.5 kg.
Guns: 2—30 mm/65 (twin). 4—14.5 mm (2 twin) MGs. 4—12.7 mm MGs.
Radars: Navigation: Don Kay; Spin Trough or Palm Frond; I-band.

Comment: Ten of the class built at Nikolayev from 1975 to early 1980s. All in the Pacific except *Dvina* and *Irbit* which are operated by the Russian Navy. Have two small landing craft aft. Armament is not normally mounted.

MIKHAIL KONOVALOV   *4/1996* / 0019068

6 KANIN CLASS (PROJECT 16900A) (AKL)

CHANTIJ-MANSISK   JURGA   ARCHANGELSK   KANIN   URENGOY   ANATOLY SHILINSKY

Displacement, tons: 920 full load
Dimensions, feet (metres): 149.6 × 28.9 × 8.2 *(45.6 × 8.8 × 2.5)*
Main machinery: 2 diesels; 800 hp(m) *(558 kW)*; 2 shafts
Speed, knots: 9. **Range, n miles:** 3,500 at 9 kt
Complement: 22

Comment: Built in the Pacific since 1996 for the Border Guard. Others may be building for commercial service. Ice reinforced bows for Arctic service. *Chantij-Mansisk* based in the Black Sea.

KANIN CLASS   *12/2002, S Breyer* / 0576443

AMPHIBIOUS FORCES

4 CZILIM (PROJECT 20910) CLASS (ACV/UCAC)

Displacement, tons: 8.6 full load
Dimensions, feet (metres): 39.4 × 19 *(12 × 5.8)*
Main machinery: 2 Deutz BF 6M 1013 diesels; 435 hp(m) *(320 kW)* sustained; for lift and propulsion
Speed, knots: 40. **Range, n miles:** 300 n miles at 30 kt
Complement: 2 + 6 Border Guard
Guns: 1—7.62 mm MG. 1—40 mm RPG.
Radars: Navigation: I-band.

Comment: Ordered from Jaroslawski Sudostroiteinyj Zawod to an Almaz design for Special Forces of the Border Guard. First one laid down 24 February 1998 and in service in early 2001. Further vessels are expected.

CZILIM   *6/2001, S Breyer* / 0126219

7 TSAPLYA (MURENA) (PROJECT 12061) CLASS (ACV)

DK-143 659	**DK-453** 668	**DK-285** 680	**DK-447** 699
DK-259 665	**DK-323** 670	**DK-458** 688	

Displacement, tons: 149 full load
Dimensions, feet (metres): 103.7 × 47.6 × 5.2 *(31.6 × 14.5 × 1.6)*
Main machinery: 2 MT-70M gas turbines for lift and propulsion; 8,000 hp *(5.88 MW)*
Speed, knots: 50. **Range, n miles:** 500 at 50 kt
Complement: 11 (3 officers) + 100 troops
Guns: 2—300 mm AK 306M. 2—30 mm grenade launchers. 2—12.7 mm MGs.

Comment: Larger version of the Lebed class designed for river patrol. Built at Khabarovsk between 1987 and 1992. Operated on Amur river system.

TSAPLYA   *6/2003, B Lemachko* / 0580542

St Kitts and Nevis

Country Overview

The Federation of St Kitts and Nevis gained independence in 1983; the British monarch, represented by a governor-general, is the head of state. Located at the northern end of the Leeward Islands in the Lesser Antilles chain, the country comprises St Kitts (formerly Saint Christopher) (68 square miles) and, 2 n miles to the southeast, Nevis (36 square miles). The constitution allows for the secession of Nevis from the federation. The capital of St Kitts and of the federation is Basseterre; Charlestown is the capital

and largest town on Nevis. Territorial seas (12 n miles) are claimed. A 200 n mile Exclusive Economic Zone (EEZ) has been claimed but the limits are not defined. The Coast Guard was part of the Police Force until 1997 when it transferred to the Regular Corps of the Defence Force.

Headquarters Appointments

Commanding Officer Coast Guard:
   Major Patrick Wallace

Bases

Basseterre

Personnel

2006: 45

COAST GUARD

Notes: (1) There is a 40 kt RIB number *C 420*.
(2) A 920 Zodiac RHIB was donated by the US government in 2003.

1 SWIFTSHIPS 110 ft CLASS (PB)

STALWART C 253

Displacement, tons: 100 normal
Dimensions, feet (metres): 116.5 × 25 × 7 *(35.5 × 7.6 × 2.1)*
Main machinery: 4 Detroit 12V-71TA diesels; 1,680 hp *(1.25 MW)* sustained; 4 shafts
Speed, knots: 21. **Range, n miles:** 1,800 at 15 kt
Complement: 14
Guns: 2 — 12.7 mm MGs. 2 — 7.62 mm MGs.
Radars: Surface search: Raytheon; I-band.
Navigation: Furuno; I-band.

Comment: Built by Swiftships, Morgan City, and delivered August 1985. Aluminium alloy hull and superstructure.

STALWART   *3/1998* / 0050088

1 DAUNTLESS CLASS (PB)

ARDENT C 421

Displacement, tons: 11 full load
Dimensions, feet (metres): 40 × 14 × 4.3 *(12.2 × 4.3 × 1.3)*
Main machinery: 2 Caterpillar 3208TA diesels; 870 hp *(650 kW)*; 2 shafts
Speed, knots: 27. **Range, n miles:** 600 at 18 kt
Complement: 4
Guns: 1 — 7.62 mm MG.
Radars: Surface search: Raytheon; I-band.

Comment: Built by SeaArk Marine under FMS funding and commissioned 8 August 1995. Aluminium construction.

ARDENT   *8/1996, St Kitts-Nevis Police* / 0081725

1 FAIREY MARINE SPEAR CLASS (PB)

RANGER I

Displacement, tons: 4.3 full load
Dimensions, feet (metres): 29.8 × 9.5 × 2.8 *(9.1 × 2.8 × 0.9)*
Main machinery: 2 Ford Mermaid diesels; 360 hp *(268 kW)*; 2 shafts
Speed, knots: 20
Complement: 2
Guns: Mountings for 2 — 7.62 mm MGs.

Comment: Ordered for the police in June 1974 and delivered 10 September 1974. Refitted 1986. Considerably slower than when new but still in service.

RANGER I   *1992, St Kitts-Nevis Police* / 0081726

2 BOSTON WHALERS (PBF)

ROVER I C 087   **ROVER II** C 088

Displacement, tons: 3 full load
Dimensions, feet (metres): 22 × 7.5 × 2 *(6.7 × 2.3 × 0.6)*
Main machinery: 1 Johnson outboard; 223 hp *(166 kW)*
Speed, knots: 35
Range, n miles: 70 at 35 kt
Complement: 2

Comment: Delivered in May 1988.

ROVER I   *1990, St Kitts-Nevis Police* / 0081727

St Lucia

Country Overview

St Lucia gained independence in 1979; the British monarch, represented by a governor-general, is the head of state. The island (238 square miles) is one of the Windward Islands of the Lesser Antilles chain and is located between Martinique to the north and St Vincent to the south. The capital, main town and principal port is Castries, on the northwestern coast. Territorial seas (12 n miles) are

claimed. Exclusive Economic Zone (EEZ) limits will not be fully defined until outstanding boundary disagreements have been resolved.

Headquarters Appointments

Coast Guard Commander:
   Assistant Superintendent Stephen Mitille

Bases

Castries, Vieux-Fort

Personnel

2006: 49

COAST GUARD

1 POINT CLASS (PB)

ALPHONSE REYNOLDS (ex-*Point Turner*) P 01 (ex-WPB 82365)

Displacement, tons: 66 full load
Dimensions, feet (metres): 83 × 17.2 × 5.8 *(25.3 × 5.2 × 1.8)*
Main machinery: 2 Caterpillar 3412 diesels; 1,600 hp *(1.19 MW)*; 2 shafts
Speed, knots: 23. **Range, n miles:** 1,500 at 8 kt
Complement: 10
Guns: 2 – 12.7 mm MGs.
Radars: Surface search: Raytheon SPS-64(V)1; I-band.

Comment: Ex-US Coast Guard ship transferred on 3 April 1998. Originally built at Curtis Bay and first commissioned 14 April 1967.

ALPHONSE REYNOLDS   *12/2004, Margaret Organ* / 1042343

1 SWIFT 65 ft CLASS (PB)

DEFENDER P 02

Displacement, tons: 42 full load
Dimensions, feet (metres): 64.9 × 18.4 × 6.6 *(19.8 × 5.6 × 2)*
Main machinery: 2 Detroit 12V-71 diesels; 680 hp *(507 kW)* sustained; 2 shafts
Speed, knots: 22. **Range, n miles:** 1,500 at 18 kt
Complement: 7
Radars: Surface search: Furuno; I-band.

Comment: Ordered from Swiftships, Morgan City in November 1983. Commissioned 3 May 1984. Similar to craft supplied to Antigua and Dominica. Painted grey instead of original blue and white.

DEFENDER   *10/1999, St Lucia CG* / 0081729

1 DAUNTLESS CLASS (PB)

PROTECTOR P 04

Displacement, tons: 11 full load
Dimensions, feet (metres): 40 × 14 × 4.3 *(12.2 × 4.3 × 1.3)*
Main machinery: 2 Caterpillar 3208TA diesels; 870 hp *(650 kW)*; 2 shafts
Speed, knots: 27
Range, n miles: 600 at 18 kt
Complement: 4
Radars: Surface search: Raytheon; I-band.

Comment: Ordered October 1994. Built by SeaArk Marine under FMS funding and commissioned 9 October 1995.

PROTECTOR (alongside Defender)   *7/1997, St Lucia CG* / 0019078

4 HARBOUR CRAFT (PB)

P 03   P 05   P 06   P 07

Comment: *P 03* is a 9 m Zodiac 920 RHIB donated by the United States in 2004. *P 05* is a 35 kt Hurricane RIB acquired in June 1993 and *P 06* and *P 07* are 45 kt Mako craft acquired in November 1995.

P 07   *7/1997, St Lucia CG* / 0019080

St Vincent and the Grenadines

Country Overview

St Vincent and the Grenadines gained independence in 1979; the British monarch, represented by a governor-general, is the head of state. Lying between St Lucia to the north and Grenada to the south, they form part of the Windward Islands in the Lesser Antilles chain and comprise the island of St Vincent (133 square miles) and the 32 northernmost islands and cays of the Grenadines group including (north to south): Bequia, Mustique, Canouan, Mayreau, Union Island, Palm (formerly Prune) Island, and Petit St Vincent. The capital, largest town, and principal port is Kingstown, St Vincent. An archipelagic state, territorial seas (12 n miles) are claimed. A 200 n mile Exclusive Economic Zone (EEZ) has been claimed but the limits are not defined.

Headquarters Appointments

Coast Guard Commander:
Lieutenant Commander Marcus Richards

Bases

Calliaqua, Bequia, Union Island

Personnel

2006: 56

COAST GUARD

Notes: A 920 Zodiac RHIB was donated by the US government in 2003.

1 SWIFTSHIPS 120 ft CLASS (PB)

CAPTAIN MULZAC SVG 01

Displacement, tons: 101
Dimensions, feet (metres): 120 × 25 × 7 *(36.6 × 7.6 × 2.1)*
Main machinery: 4 Detroit 12V-71TA diesels; 1,360 hp *(1.01 MW)* sustained; 4 shafts
Speed, knots: 21. **Range, n miles:** 1,800 at 15 kt
Complement: 14 (4 officers)
Guns: 2 – 12.7 mm MGs. 2 – 7.62 mm MGs.
Radars: Surface search: Furuno 1411 Mk II; I/J-band.

Comment: Ordered in August 1986. Built by Swiftships, Morgan City and delivered 13 June 1987. Aluminium construction. Carries a RIB with a 40 hp outboard.

CAPTAIN MULZAC   *6/1994, St Vincent Coast Guard* / 0081730

1 VOSPER THORNYCROFT 75 FT CLASS (PB)

GEORGE McINTOSH SVG 05

Displacement, tons: 70 full load
Dimensions, feet (metres): 75 × 19.5 × 8 *(22.9 × 6 × 2.4)*
Main machinery: 2 Caterpillar D 348 diesels; 1,450 hp *(1.08 MW)* sustained; 2 shafts
Speed, knots: 24.5
Range, n miles: 1,000 at 11 kt; 600 at 20 kt
Complement: 11 (3 officers)
Guns: 1 Oerlikon 20 mm.
Radars: Surface search: Furuno 1411 Mk III; I/J-band.

Comment: Built by Vosper Thornycroft, Portchester. Handed over 23 March 1981. GRP hull.

GEORGE McINTOSH   6/1992, St Vincent Coast Guard / 0081731

2 HARBOUR CRAFT (PB)

SVG 03   CHATHAM BAY SVG 08

Comment: *SVG 03* is a 30 kt Zodiac RIB. *SVG 08* is a 30 kt Boston Whaler acquired in 1994. The Buhler craft *SVG 06* and *SVG 07* are no longer operational.

SVG 03   2001, St Vincent Coast Guard / 0109947

CHATHAM BAY   2001, St Vincent Coast Guard / 0109948

1 DAUNTLESS CLASS (PB)

HAIROUN SVG 04

Displacement, tons: 11 full load
Dimensions, feet (metres): 40 × 14 × 4.3 *(12.2 × 4.3 × 1.3)*
Main machinery: 2 Caterpillar 3208TA diesels; 870 hp *(650 kW)*; 2 shafts
Speed, knots: 27
Range, n miles: 600 at 18 kt
Complement: 4
Guns: 1 — 7.62 mm MG.
Radars: Surface search: Raytheon; I-band.

Comment: Ordered October 1984. Built by SeaArk Marine under FMS funding and commissioned 8 June 1995. Aluminium construction.

HAIROUN   7/1997 / 0019082

Samoa

Country Overview

Samoa was a New Zealand-administered UN Trust territory until it became independent in 1962. At the same time a Treaty of Friendship delegated responsibility to New Zealand for foreign affairs. An island nation, it lies in the south Pacific Ocean, approximately midway between Hawaii and New Zealand, in the western portion of the Samoan archipelago. There are two main islands, Savai'i and Upolu, and several smaller islands, of which only two, Apolima and Manono, are inhabited. The capital and chief port is Apia on Upolu. An archipelagic state, territorial seas (12 n miles) are claimed. An Exclusive Economic Zone (EEZ) (200 n miles) is also claimed but limits have not been fully defined by boundary agreements.

Headquarters Appointments

Head of Maritime Division:
    Commissioner Lorenese Neru
Maritime Surveillance Adviser:
    Commander A Schroder, RAN

Bases

Apia

PATROL FORCES

1 PACIFIC CLASS (LARGE PATROL CRAFT) (PB)

Name	No	Builders	Commissioned
NAFANUA	—	Australian Shipbuilding Industries	5 Mar 1988

Displacement, tons: 165 full load
Dimensions, feet (metres): 103.3 × 26.6 × 6.9 *(31.5 × 8.1 × 2.1)*
Main machinery: 2 Caterpillar 3516TA diesels; 4,400 hp *(3.28 MW)* sustained; 2 shafts
Speed, knots: 20
Range, n miles: 2,500 at 12 kt
Complement: 17 (3 officers)
Guns: 2 — 7.62 mm MGs.
Radars: Surface search: Furuno 1011; I-band.

Comment: Under the Defence Co-operation Programme Australia has provided 22 Pacific class patrol craft to Pacific islands. Training, operational and technical assistance is provided by the Royal Australian Navy. *Nafanua* ordered 3 October 1985. Refitted in 1996. Following the decision by the Australian government to extend the Pacific Patrol Boat programme, a life-extension refit was undertaken at Townsville in 2005.

NAFANUA   6/2005*, Samoa Police / 1127921

Saudi Arabia

Country Overview

The Kingdom of Saudi Arabia occupies most of the Arabian Peninsula and is bordered to the north by Jordan, Iraq, and Kuwait, to the south by Oman and the Republic of Yemen and to the east by Qatar and the United Arab Emirates. With an area of 864,869 square miles, it has coastlines with the Red Sea (972 n miles) and the Gulf (454 n miles). The capital and largest city is Riyadh while the principal ports are Jiddah and Yanbu al Bahr on the Red Sea, and the major oil-exporting ports of Al Jabayl, Ad Dammam, and Ras Tanura on the Gulf. Territorial seas (12 n miles) are claimed. An EEZ has not been claimed.

Headquarters Appointments

Chief of Naval Staff:
  H H Vice Admiral Prince Fahad Bin Abdullah Bin Mohammed
Commander Eastern Fleet:
  Rear Admiral Mohammad Abdul Khalij Al Asseri
Commander Western Fleet:
  Rear Admiral Dakheel Allah Ahmed Al-Wakdani
Director Frontier Force (Coast Guard):
  Lieutenant General Mujib bin Muhammad Al-Qahtani

Personnel

(a) 2006: 15,500 officers and men (including 3,000 marines)
(b) Voluntary service

Bases

Naval HQ: Riyadh
Main bases: Jiddah (HQ Western Fleet), Al Jubail (HQ Eastern Fleet), Aziziah (Coast Guard). Jizan (Red Sea) building from May 1996
Minor bases (Naval and Coast Guard): Ras Tanura, Al Dammam, Yanbo, Ras al-Mishab, Al Wajh, Al Qatif, Haqi, Al Sharmah, Qizan, Duba

General

Funding for the Navy has the lowest defence service priority. New programmes are slow to come forward, and the operational status of existing ships is variable.

Command and Control

The USA provided an update of command and control capabilities during the period 1991-95, including a commercial datalink to improve interoperability.

Coast Defence

Truck-mounted Otomat batteries.

Coast Guard

Part of the Frontier Force under the Minister for Defence and Aviation. 5,500 officers and men. It is not always clear which ships belong to the Navy and which to the Coast Guard.

Strength of the Fleet

Type	Active	Building
Frigates	7	—
Corvettes—Missile	4	—
Fast Attack Craft—Missile	9	—
Patrol Craft	56	—
Minehunters	3	—
Minesweepers—Coastal	4	—
Replenishment Tankers	2	—

SUBMARINES

Notes: (1) Orders for patrol submarines are a low priority although training has been done in France and Pakistan.
(2) Interest has been shown in the acquisition of Midget Submarines.

CORVETTES

4 BADR CLASS

Name	No	Builders	Laid down	Launched	Commissioned
BADR	612	Tacoma Boatbuilding Co, Tacoma	6 Oct 1979	26 Jan 1980	30 Nov 1980
AL YARMOOK	614	Tacoma Boatbuilding Co, Tacoma	3 Jan 1980	13 May 1980	18 May 1981
HITTEEN	616	Tacoma Boatbuilding Co, Tacoma	19 May 1980	5 Sep 1980	3 Oct 1981
TABUK	618	Tacoma Boatbuilding Co, Tacoma	22 Sep 1980	18 June 1981	10 Jan 1983

Displacement, tons: 870 standard; 1,038 full load
Dimensions, feet (metres): 245 × 31.5 × 8.9
  (74.7 × 9.6 × 2.7)
Main machinery: CODOG; 1 GE LM 2500 gas turbine; 23,000 hp *(17.2 MW)* sustained; 2 MTU 12V 652 TB91 diesels; 3,470 hp(m) *(2.55 MW)* sustained; 2 shafts; cp props
Speed, knots: 30 gas; 20 diesels. **Range, n miles:** 4,000 at 20 kt
Complement: 58 (7 officers)

Missiles: SSM: 8 McDonnell Douglas Harpoon (2 quad) launchers ❶; active radar homing to 130 km *(70 n miles)* at 0.9 Mach; warhead 227 kg.
Guns: 1 FMC/OTO Melara 3 in *(76 mm)*/62 Mk 75 Mod 0 ❷; 85 rds/min to 16 km *(8.7 n miles)*; weight of shell 6 kg.
  1 General Electric/General Dynamics 20 mm 6-barrelled Vulcan Phalanx ❸; 3,000 rds/min combined to 2 km.
  2 Oerlikon 20 mm/80 ❹.
  1—81 mm mortar. 2—40 mm Mk 19 grenade launchers.
Torpedoes: 6—324 mm US Mk 32 (2 triple) tubes ❺. Honeywell Mk 46; anti-submarine; active/passive homing to 11 km *(5.9 n miles)* at 40 kt; warhead 44 kg.
Countermeasures: Decoys: 2 Loral Hycor SRBOC 6-barrelled fixed Mk 36 ❻; IR flares and chaff to 4 km *(2.2 n miles)*. ESM: SLQ-32(V)1 ❼; intercept.
Weapons control: Mk 24 optical director ❽. Mk 309 for torpedoes. Mk 92 Mod 5 GFCS. FSI Safire FLIR.

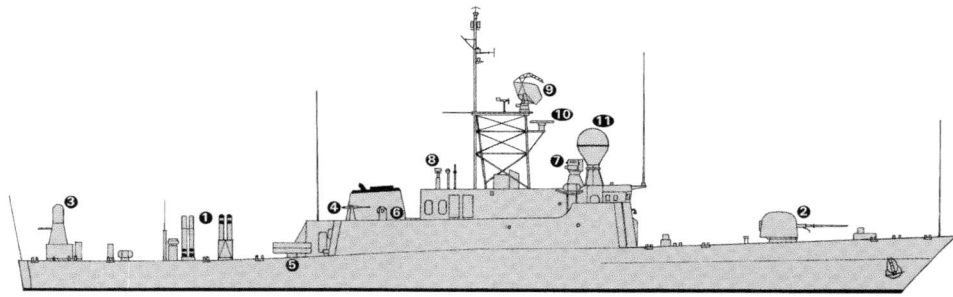

BADR *(Scale 1 : 600), Ian Sturton* / 0506250

Radars: Air search: Lockheed SPS-40B ❾; B-band; range 320 km *(175 n miles)*.
Surface search: ISC Cardion SPS-55 ❿; I/J-band.
Fire control: Sperry Mk 92 ⓫; I/J-band.
Sonars: Raytheon SQS-56 (DE 1164); hull-mounted; active search and attack; medium frequency.

Modernisation: Refitting done in Saudi Arabia with US assistance. FLIR being fitted from 1998.
Structure: Fitted with fin stabilisers.
Operational: All based at Al Jubail on the east coast and spend little time at sea.

AL YARMOOK *2/1997, van Ginderen Collection* / 0019085

FRIGATES

4 MADINA (TYPE F 2000S) CLASS (FFGHM)

Name	No	Builders	Laid down	Launched	Commissioned
MADINA	702	Lorient (DTCN)	15 Oct 1981	23 Apr 1983	4 Jan 1985
HOFOUF	704	CNIM, Seyne-sur-Mer	14 June 1982	24 June 1983	31 Oct 1985
ABHA	706	CNIM, Seyne-sur-Mer	7 Dec 1982	23 Dec 1983	4 Apr 1986
TAIF	708	CNIM, Seyne-sur-Mer	1 Mar 1983	25 May 1984	29 Aug 1986

Displacement, tons: 2,000 standard; 2,870 full load
Dimensions, feet (metres): 377.3 × 41 × 16 (sonar)
  (115 × 12.5 × 4.9)
Main machinery: CODAD; 4 SEMT-Pielstick 16 PA6 280V
  BTC diesels; 38,400 hp(m) *(28 MW)* sustained; 2 shafts
Speed, knots: 30
Range, n miles: 8,000 at 15 kt; 6,500 at 18 kt
Complement: 179 (15 officers)

Missiles: SSM: 8 OTO Melara/Matra Otomat Mk 2
  (2 quad) ❶; active radar homing to 160 km *(86.4 n miles)*
  at 0.9 Mach; warhead 210 kg; sea-skimmer for last 4 km
  (2.2 n miles). ERATO system allows mid-course guidance
  by ship's helicopter.
SAM: Thomson-CSF Crotale Naval octuple launcher ❷;
  command line of sight guidance; radar/IR homing to 13 km
  (7 n miles) at 2.4 Mach; warhead 14 kg; 26 missiles.
Guns: 1 Creusot-Loire 3.9 in *(100 mm)*/55 compact Mk 2 ❸;
  20/45/90 rds/min to 17 km *(9.3 n miles)* weight of shell
  13.5 kg.
  4 Breda 40 mm/70 (2 twin) ❹; 300 rds/min to 12.5 km
  (6.8 n miles); weight of shell 0.96 kg.
Torpedoes: 4—21 in *(533 mm)* tubes ❺. ECAN F17P; anti-
  submarine; wire-guided; active/passive homing to 20 km
  (10.8 n miles) at 40 kt; warhead 250 kg.
Countermeasures: Decoys: CSEE Dagaie double trainable
  mounting ❻; IR flares and chaff; H/J-band.
ESM: Thomson-CSF DR 4000; intercept; HF/DF.
ECM: Thomson-CSF Janet; jammer.

Combat data systems: Thomson-CSF TAVITAC action data
  automation; capability for Link W.
Weapons control: Vega system. 3 CSEE Naja optronic
  directors. Alcatel DLT for torpedoes.
Radars: Air/surface search/IFF: Thomson-CSF Sea Tiger
  (DRBV 15) ❼; E/F-band; range 110 km *(60 n miles)* for
  2 m² target.
Navigation: 2 Racal Decca TM 1226; I-band.
Fire control: Thomson-CSF Castor IIB/C ❽; I/J-band; range
  15 km *(8 n miles)* for 1 m² target.
  Thomson-CSF DRBC 32 ❾; I/J-band (for SAM).
Sonars: Thomson Sintra Diodon TSM 2630; hull-mounted;
  active search and attack with integrated Sorel VDS ❿;
  11, 12 or 13 kHz.

Helicopters: 1 SA 365F Dauphin 2 ⓫.

Programmes: Ordered in 1980, the major part of the Sawari I
  contract. Agreement for France to provide supplies and
  technical help.
Modernisation: The class have been upgraded by DCN
  Toulon, *Madina* completed in April 1997. *Hofouf* in
  mid-1998. *Abha* in late 1999, and *Taif* in March 2000.
  Improvements included updating TAVITAC, Otomat
  missiles, both sonars and fitting a Samahé 110 helo
  handling system.
Structure: Fitted with Snach/Saphir folding fin stabilisers.
Operational: Navigation: CSEE Sylosat. Helicopter can
  provide mid-course guidance for SSM. All based at
  Jiddah. Only a few weeks a year are spent at sea.

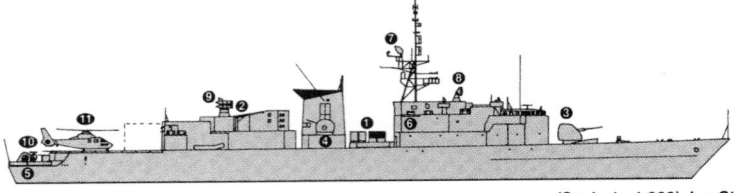

MADINA

(Scale 1 : 1,200), Ian Sturton / 0506097

TAIF

6/2002 / 0526835

HOFOUF

9/2003, Hartmut Ehlers / 0567898

3 AL RIYADH (MODIFIED LA FAYETTE) CLASS (TYPE F-3000S) (FFGHM)

Name	No	Builders	Laid down	Launched	Commissioned
AL RIYADH	812	DCN, Lorient	29 Sep 1999	1 Aug 2000	26 July 2002
MAKKAH	814	DCN, Lorient	25 Aug 2000	20 July 2001	3 Apr 2004
AL DAMMAM	816	DCN, Lorient	26 Aug 2001	7 Sep 2002	23 Oct 2004

Displacement, tons: 4,650 full load
Dimensions, feet (metres): 438.43 × 56.4 × 13.5
 (133.6 × 17.2 × 4.1)
Main machinery: CODAD; 4 SEMT-Pielstick 16 PA6 STC
 diesels; 28,000 hp(m) *(20.58 MW)* sustained; 2 shafts;
 LIPS cp props; bow thruster
Speed, knots: 25. **Range, n miles:** 7,000 at 15 kt
Complement: 181 (25 officers); accommodation for 190

Missiles: SSM: 8 Aerospatiale MM 40 Block II Exocet ❶;
 inertial cruise; active radar homing to 70 km *(40 n miles)*
 at 0.9 Mach; warhead 165 kg; sea-skimmer.
 SAM: Eurosam SAAM ❷; 2 octuple Sylver A43 VLS for
 Aster 15; command guidance active radar homing to
 15 km *(8.1 n miles)* anti-missile, at 30 km *(16.2 n miles)*
 anti-aircraft. 16 missiles.
Guns: 1 OTO Melara 3 in *(76 mm)*/62 Super Rapid ❸;
 120 rds/min to 16 km *(8.7 n miles)*; weight of shell 6 kg.
 2 Giat 15B 20 mm ❹; 800 rds/min to 3 km; weight of shell
 0.1 kg.
 2 — 12.7 mm MGs.
Torpedoes: 4 — 21 in *(533 mm)* tubes; ECAN F17P; anti-
 submarine; wire-guided active/passive homing to 20 km
 (10.8 n miles) at 40 kt; warhead 250 kg.
Countermeasures: Decoys: 2 Matra Dagaie Mk 2 ❺;
 10-barrelled trainable launchers; chaff and IR flares. SLAT
 anti-wake homing torpedoes system (when available).
 RESM: Thomson-CSF (DR 3000-S2) ❻; intercept. Sagem
 Telegon 10.
 CESM: Thales Altesse; intercept.
 ECM: 2 Thales Salamandre; jammers.
Combat data systems: Thales Senit 7.
Weapons control: Thales Castor IIJ radar/EO tracker.
Radars: Air search: Thales DRBV 26C Jupiter II ❼; D-band.
 Surveillance/Fire control: Thomson-CSF Arabel 3D ❽;
 I/J-band.
 Fire control: Thomson-CSF Castor II UJ ❾; J-band; range
 15 km *(8 n miles)* for 1 m² target.
 Navigation: 2 Racal Decca 1226 ❿; I-band. A second set
 fitted for helicopter control.
Sonars: Thomson Marconi CAPTAS 20; active low
 frequency; towed array.

Helicopters: Hangar and platform for NH-90-sized
 helicopter ⓫.

Programmes: A provisional order was made on 11 June
 1989, but this was not finally confirmed until 19 November
 1994 when a contract for two ships was authorised under
 the Sawari II programme. Thomson-CSF was the prime

AL RIYADH   *(Scale 1 : 1,200), Ian Sturton* / 1044496

MAKKAH   *3/2004, B Prézelin* / 1044497

contractor. On 25 May 1997 an order for a third ship
was placed together with a substantial enhancement
of the weapon systems in all three. First steel cut
13 December 1997. Following handover, 812 started an
eight month training programme which concluded in
March 2003. 814 started sea trials on 9 September 2002
and 816 in mid-2003. SAM successfully tested in 816 in
April 2004.
Structure: The design is a development of the French La
Fayette class. Some 10 m longer, space and weight
included for two more octuple SAM launchers or A50

launcher for Aster 30. Provision is made for a larger
NH 90 type helicopter in the future, DCN Samahé helo
handling system. STAF stabilisers. Originally planned to
be fitted with a 100 mm gun, the contract was amended
to incorporate a 76 mm mounting instead.
Operational: OTHT link for helicopters and Air Force F-15s.
Makkah seriously damaged in a grounding incident
80 miles north of Jiddah in December 2004. The ship was
refloated by the Tsavliris Salvage Group in early 2005 and
was towed to Jiddah. A contract for her repair, probably
by DCN, is expected in 2006.

AL DAMMAM   *6/2004, B Prézelin* / 1044498

AL RIYADH   *9/2004, B Prézelin* / 1121520

SHIPBORNE AIRCRAFT

Notes: Procurement of a new shipborne helicopter is under consideration. Up to ten are required for deployment to the Al Riyadh class frigates and for other tasks. The NH Industries NH 90 is reported to be a strong contender.

Numbers/Type: 15/6 Aerospatiale AS 565SA Dauphin 2/Aerospatiale AS 365N Dauphin 2.
Operational speed: 140 kt *(260 km/h)*.
Service ceiling: 15,000 ft *(4,575 m)*.
Range: 410 n miles *(758 km)*.
Role/Weapon systems: AS 565SA is the ASV/ASW helicopter; procured for embarked naval aviation force; surface search/attack is the primary role. Sensors: Thomson-CSF Agrion 15 radar; Crouzet MAD. Weapons: ASV; four AS/15TT missiles. ASW; 2 Mk 46 torpedoes. AS 365N is for SAR and is operated by the Armed Forces Medical Services. Sensors: Omera DRB 32 search radar. Weapons: Unarmed.

Panther   *4/2002*, Aerospatiale* / 0093192

LAND-BASED MARITIME AIRCRAFT

Notes: (1) Six P-3C Orion or CASA CN-235 may be acquired in due course.
(2) Five Boeing E3-A AEW aircraft in service with Air Force.

Numbers/Type: 11 Aerospatiale AS 332SC Super Puma.
Operational speed: 150 kt *(280 km/h)*.
Service ceiling: 15,090 ft *(4,600 m)*.
Range: 335 n miles *(620 km)*.
Role/Weapon systems: First pair delivered in August 1989. Total of 12 by the end of 1990. Shared with the Coast Guard. Sensors: 12 have Omera search radar Safire AAQ-22 FLIR from 1998. Weapons: ASV; six have Giat 20 mm cannon; 12 have AM39 Exocet or Sea Eagle ASM.

AS 532 Cougar   *6/1990*, Paul Jackson* / 0062140

PATROL FORCES

9 AL SIDDIQ CLASS (PGGF)

Name	No	Builders	Launched	Commissioned
AL SIDDIQ	511	Peterson, WI	22 Sep 1979	15 Dec 1980
AL FAROUQ	513	Peterson, WI	17 May 1980	22 June 1981
ABDUL AZIZ	515	Peterson, WI	23 Aug 1980	3 Sep 1981
FAISAL	517	Peterson, WI	15 Nov 1980	23 Nov 1981
KHALID	519	Peterson, WI	23 Mar 1981	11 Jan 1982
AMYR	521	Peterson, WI	13 June 1981	21 June 1982
TARIQ	523	Peterson, WI	23 Sep 1981	11 Aug 1982
OQBAH	525	Peterson, WI	12 Dec 1981	18 Oct 1982
ABU OBAIDAH	527	Peterson, WI	3 Apr 1982	6 Dec 1982

Displacement, tons: 495 full load
Dimensions, feet (metres): 190.5 × 26.5 × 6.6 *(58.1 × 8.1 × 2)*
Main machinery: CODOG; 1 GE LM 2500 gas turbine; 23,000 hp *(17.2 MW)* sustained; 2 MTU 12V 652 TB91 diesels; 3,470 hp(m) *(2.55 MW)* sustained; 2 shafts; cp props
Speed, knots: 38 gas; 25 diesel
Range, n miles: 2,900 at 14 kt
Complement: 38 (5 officers)

Missiles: SSM: 4 McDonnell Douglas Harpoon (2 twin) launchers; active radar homing to 130 km *(70 n miles)* at 0.9 Mach; warhead 227 kg.
Guns: 1 FMC/OTO Melara 3 in *(76 mm)*/62 Mk 75 Mod 0; 85 rds/min to 16 km *(8.7 n miles)*; weight of shell 6 kg.
1 General Electric/General Dynamics 20 mm 6-barrelled Vulcan Phalanx; 3,000 rds/min combined to 2 km.
2 Oerlikon 20 mm/80; 800 rds/min to 2 km anti-aircraft.
2—81 mm mortars. 2—40 mm Mk 19 grenade launchers.

Countermeasures: Decoys: 2 Loral Hycor SRBOC 6-barrelled fixed Mk 36; IR flares and chaff to 4 km *(2.2 n miles)*.
ESM: SLQ-32(V)1; intercept.
Weapons control: Mk 92 mod 5 GFCS. FSI Safire FLIR. Link W.
Radars: Surface search: ISC Cardion SPS-55; I/J-band.
Fire control: Sperry Mk 92; I/J-band.
Modernisation: Safire FLIR and Link W being fitted.
Operational: *Amyr* and *Tariq* operate from Jiddah, the remainder are based at Al Jubail. *Faisal* damaged in the Gulf War in 1991 but was operational again in 1994.

ABU OBAIDAH   *6/2001, Ships of the World* / 0126360

17 HALTER TYPE (COASTAL PATROL CRAFT) (PB)

52-68

Displacement, tons: 56 full load
Dimensions, feet (metres): 78 × 20 × 5.8 *(23.8 × 6.1 × 1.8)*
Main machinery: 2 Detroit 16V-92TA diesels; 1,380 hp *(1.03 MW)* sustained; 2 shafts
Speed, knots: 28. **Range, n miles:** 1,200 at 12 kt
Complement: 8 (2 officers)
Guns: 2 — 25 mm Mk 38. 2 — 7.62 mm MGs.
Radars: Surface search: Raytheon SPS-64; I-band.

Comment: Ordered from Halter Marine 17th February 1991. Aluminium construction. Last delivered in January 1993. Same type for Philippines.

HALTER TYPE *8/1990, Trinity Marine* / 0080563

39 SIMONNEAU 51 TYPE (INSHORE PATROL CRAFT) (PBI)

Displacement, tons: 22 full load
Dimensions, feet (metres): 51.8 × 15.7 × 5.9 *(15.8 × 4.8 × 1.8)*
Main machinery: 4 outboards; 2,400 hp(m) *(1.76 MW)*
Speed, knots: 33. **Range, n miles:** 375 at 25 kt
Guns: 1 — 12.7 mm MG. 2 — 7.62 mm MGs.
Radars: Surface search: Furuno; I-band.

Comment: First 20 ordered from France in June 1988 and delivered in 1989-90. A second batch of 20 ordered in 1991. Aluminium construction. Used by naval commandos. These craft were also reported as Panhards. One deleted so far.

SIMONNEAU TYPE *1989, Simonneau Marine* / 0506098

MINE WARFARE FORCES

4 ADDRIYAH (MSC 322) CLASS
(MINESWEEPERS/HUNTERS — COASTAL) (MHSC)

Name	No	Builders	Launched	Commissioned
ADDRIYAH	MSC 412	Peterson, WI	20 Dec 1976	6 July 1978
AL QUYSUMAH	MSC 414	Peterson, WI	26 May 1977	15 Aug 1978
AL WADEEAH	MSC 416	Peterson, WI	6 Sep 1977	7 Sep 1979
SAFWA	MSC 418	Peterson, WI	7 Dec 1977	2 Oct 1979

Displacement, tons: 320 standard; 407 full load
Dimensions, feet (metres): 153 × 26.9 × 8.2 *(46.6 × 8.2 × 2.5)*
Main machinery: 2 Waukesha L1616 diesels; 1,200 hp *(895 kW)*; 2 shafts
Speed, knots: 13
Complement: 39 (4 officers)
Guns: 1 Oerlikon 20 mm.
Radars: Surface search: ISC Cardion SPS-55; I/J-band.
Sonars: GE SQQ-14; VDS; active minehunting; high frequency.

Comment: Ordered on 30 September 1975 under the International Logistics Programme. Wooden structure. Fitted with fin stabilisers, wire and magnetic sweeps and also for minehunting. *Addriyah* based at Jiddah, the remainder at Al Jubail. Expected to be replaced by arrival of Sandowns but all are still in service mostly as patrol craft.

AL QUYSUMAH *6/1996, van Ginderen Collection* / 0019090

3 AL JAWF (SANDOWN) CLASS
(MINEHUNTERS — COASTAL) (MHC)

Name	No	Builders	Launched	Commissioned
AL JAWF	420	Vosper Thornycroft	2 Aug 1989	12 Dec 1991
SHAQRA	422	Vosper Thornycroft	15 May 1991	7 Feb 1993
AL KHARJ	424	Vosper Thornycroft	8 Feb 1993	7 Aug 1997

Displacement, tons: 450 standard; 480 full load
Dimensions, feet (metres): 172.9 × 34.4 × 6.9 *(52.7 × 10.5 × 2.1)*
Main machinery: 2 Paxman 6RP200E diesels; 1,500 hp *(1.12 MW)* sustained; Voith-Schneider propulsion; 2 shafts; 2 Schöttel bow thrusters
Speed, knots: 13 diesels; 6 electric drive
Range, n miles: 3,000 at 12 kt
Complement: 34 (7 officers) plus 6 spare berths
Guns: 2 Electronics & Space Emerlec 30 mm (twin); 1,200 rds/min combined to 6 km *(3.3 n miles)*; weight of shell 0.35 kg.
Countermeasures: Decoys: 2 Loral Hycor SRBOC Mk 36 Mod 1 6-barrelled chaff launchers.
ESM: Thomson-CSF Shiploc; intercept.
MCM: ECA mine disposal system; 2 PAP 104 Mk 5.
Combat data systems: Plessey Nautis M action data automation.
Weapons control: Contraves TMEO optronic director (Seahawk Mk 2).
Radars: Navigation: Kelvin Hughes Type 1007; I-band.
Sonars: Plessey/MUSL Type 2093; VDS; high frequency.

Comment: Three ordered 2 November 1988 from Vosper Thornycroft. Option for three more appears to have been abandoned. GRP hulls. Combines vectored thrust units with bow thrusters and Remote Controlled Mine Disposal System (RCMDS). *Al Jawf* sailed for Saudi Arabia in November 1995, *Shaqra* in November 1996, and *Al Kharj* in August 1997. All based at Al Jubail.

AL KHARJ *8/1997, Vosper Thornycroft* / 0050091

AUXILIARIES

2 MOD DURANCE CLASS (REPLENISHMENT SHIPS) (AORH)

Name	No	Builders	Launched	Commissioned
BORAIDA	902	La Ciotat, Marseilles	22 Jan 1983	29 Feb 1984
YUNBOU	904	La Ciotat, Marseilles	20 Oct 1984	29 Aug 1985

Displacement, tons: 11,200 full load
Dimensions, feet (metres): 442.9 × 61.3 × 22.9 *(135 × 18.7 × 7)*
Main machinery: 2 SEMT-Pielstick 14 PC2.5 V 400 diesels; 18,200 hp(m) *(13.4 MW)* sustained; 2 shafts; LIPS cp props
Speed, knots: 20.5
Range, n miles: 7,000 at 15 kt
Complement: 129 plus 11 trainees
Cargo capacity: 4,350 tons diesel; 350 tons AVCAT; 140 tons fresh water; 100 tons victuals; 100 tons ammunition; 70 tons spares
Guns: 4 Breda Bofors 40 mm/70 (2 twin); 300 rds/min to 12.5 km *(6.8 n miles)*; weight of shell 0.96 kg.
Weapons control: 2 CSEE Naja optronic directors. 2 CSEE Lynx optical sights.
Radars: Navigation: 2 Decca; I-band.
Helicopters: 2 SA 365F Dauphin or 1 AS 332SC Super Puma.

Comment: Contract signed October 1980 as part of Sawari I programme. Both upgraded by DCN at Toulon; *Boraida* in 1996/97, followed by *Yunbou*, in 1997/98. Refuelling positions: Two alongside, one astern. Also serve as training ships and as depot and maintenance ships. Helicopters can have ASM or ASW armament. Both based at Jiddah.

YUNBOU *1/1998* / 0016635

BORAIDA *9/2003, Hartmut Ehlers* / 0567897

4 LCU 1610 CLASS (TRANSPORTS) (YFU)

AL QIAQ (ex-SA 310) 212	**AL ULA** (ex-SA 312) 216
AL SULAYEL (ex-SA 311) 214	**AFIF** (ex-SA 313) 218

Displacement, tons: 375 full load
Dimensions, feet (metres): 134.9 × 29 × 6.1 *(41.1 × 8.8 × 1.9)*
Main machinery: 4 GM diesels; 1,000 hp *(746 kW)*; 2 Kort nozzles
Speed, knots: 11. **Range, n miles:** 1,200 at 8 kt
Complement: 14 (2 officers)
Military lift: 170 tons; 20 troops
Guns: 2 — 12.7 mm MGs.
Radars: Navigation: Marconi LN66; I-band.

Comment: Built by Newport Shipyard, Rhode Island. Transferred from US June/July 1976. Based at Al Jubail.

LCU 1610 (US colours)   *9/1997, Hachiro Nakai* / 0016483

4 LCM 6 CLASS (TRANSPORTS) (YFU)

DHEBA 220	**UMLUS** 222	**AL LEETH** 224	**AL QUONFETHA** 226

Displacement, tons: 62 full load
Dimensions, feet (metres): 56.2 × 14 × 3.9 *(17.1 × 4.3 × 1.2)*
Main machinery: 2 GM diesels; 450 hp *(336 kW)*; 2 shafts
Speed, knots: 9. **Range, n miles:** 130 at 9 kt
Complement: 5
Military lift: 34 tons or 80 troops
Guns: 2 — 40 mm Mk 19 grenade launchers.

Comment: Four transferred July 1977 and four in July 1980. The first four have been cannibalised for spares. Based at Jiddah.

ROYAL YACHTS

1 ROYAL YACHT (YACH)

Name	No	Builders	Commissioned
AL YAMAMAH	—	Elsinore, Denmark	Feb 1981

Displacement, tons: 1,660 full load
Dimensions, feet (metres): 269 × 42.7 × 10.8 *(82 × 13 × 3.3)*
Main machinery: 2 MTU 12V 1163 TB82 diesels; 6,000 hp(m) *(4.41 MW)*; 2 shafts; cp props; bow thruster; 300 hp(m) *(221 kW)*
Speed, knots: 19
Complement: 42 plus 56 spare
Helicopters: Platform for 1 medium.

Comment: Ordered by Iraq but not delivered because of the war with Iran. Given to Saudi Arabia by Iraq in 1988. Based at Dammam.

1 PEGASUS CLASS (HYDROFOIL) (YAGJ)

AL AZIZIAH

Displacement, tons: 115 full load
Dimensions, feet (metres): 89.9 × 29.9 × 6.2 *(27.4 × 9.1 × 1.9)*
Main machinery: 2 Allison 501-KF20A gas turbines; 8,660 hp *(6.46 MW)* sustained; 2 waterjets (foilborne); 2 Detroit 8V92 diesels; 606 hp *(452 kW)* sustained; 2 shafts (hullborne)
Speed, knots: 46. **Range, n miles:** 890 at 42 kt
Guns: 2 General Electric 20 mm Sea Vulcan.
Weapons control: Kollmorgen GFCS; Mk 35 optronic director.

Comment: Ordered in 1984 from Lockheed and subcontracted to Boeing, Seattle; delivered in August 1985. Mostly used as a tender to the Royal Yacht.

1 ROYAL YACHT (YACH)

Name	No	Builders	Commissioned
ABDUL AZIZ	—	Halsingør Waerft, Denmark	12 June 1984

Displacement, tons: 5,200 full load
Measurement, tons: 1,450 dwt
Dimensions, feet (metres): 482.2 × 59.2 × 16.1 *(147 × 18 × 4.9)*
Main machinery: 2 Lindholmen-Pielstick 12 PC2.5 V diesels; 15,600 hp(m) *(11.47 MW)* sustained; 2 shafts
Speed, knots: 22
Complement: 65 plus 4 Royal berths and 60 spare
Helicopters: 1 Bell 206B JetRanger type.

Comment: Completed March 1983 for subsequent fitting out at Vosper's Ship Repairers, Southampton. Helicopter hangar set in hull forward of bridge-covers extend laterally to form pad. Swimming pool. Stern ramp leading to garage. Based at Jiddah. Operated by the Coast Guard.

ABDUL AZIZ   *5/1994, van Ginderen Collection* / 0506328

TUGS

13 COASTAL TUGS (YTB/YTM)

RADHWA 1-6, 14-15	**TUWAIG** 113	**DAREEN** 111	**RADHWA 12, 16, 17**

Comment: *Radhwa 12, 16* and *17* are 43 m YTMs built in 1982-83. *Tuwaig* and *Dareen* are ex-US YTB transferred in October 1975. These two are used to tow targets for weapons firing exercises and are based at Al Jubail and Damman respectively. The remainder are all of about 35 m built in Singapore and the Netherlands between 1981 and 1983.

YTB TYPE (US colours)   *9/1992, Jürg Kürsener* / 0080564

COAST GUARD

Notes: Three 32 m fireboats *Jubail I, Jubail 2* and *Jubail 3*, entered service in 1982.

2 SEA GUARD CLASS (WPBF)

AL RIYADH 304	**ZULURAB** 305

Displacement, tons: 56 full load
Dimensions, feet (metres): 73.8 × 18.4 × 5.6 *(22.5 × 5.6 × 1.7)*
Main machinery: 2 MTU 12V 331 TC92 diesels; 2,920 hp(m) *(21.46 MW)*; 2 shafts
Speed, knots: 35
Complement: 10
Guns: 2 Giat 20 mm (twin). 2 — 7.62 mm MGs.
Radars: Surface search: Racal Decca; I-band.
Fire control: Thomson-CSF Agrion; J-band.

Comment: Built by Simonneau Marine and delivered by SOFREMA in April 1992. Aluminium construction. Both based at Jiddah. The SSM launcher shown in the picture is not fitted.

ZULURAB   *1992, Simonneau Marine* / 0080565

6 STAN PATROL 2606 CRAFT
(COASTAL PATROL CRAFT) (WPB)

ASSIR 317	**ALDHAHRAN** 318	**ALKAHRJ** 319	**ARAR** 320-322

Displacement, tons: 55 (approx) full load
Dimensions, feet (metres): 87.0 × 20.3 × 6.1 *(26.5 × 6.2 × 1.8)*
Main machinery: 2 MTU 12V 396 TE94 diesels; 4,429 hp *(3.3 MW)*; 2 shafts
Speed, knots: 28

Comment: Built by Damen Shipyards, Gorinchem and delivered 2002-03.

ARAR   *7/2002, A A de Kruijf* / 0533301

4 AL JOUF CLASS (WPBF)

AL JOUF 351	TURAIF 352	HAIL 353	NAJRAN 354

Displacement, tons: 210 full load
Dimensions, feet (metres): 126.6 × 26.2 × 6.2 *(38.6 × 8 × 1.9)*
Main machinery: 3 MTU 16 V 538 TB93 diesels; 11,265 hp(m) *(8.28 MW)* sustained; 3 shafts
Speed, knots: 38. **Range, n miles:** 1,700 at 15 kt
Complement: 20 (4 officers)
Guns: 2 Oerlikon GAM-BO1 20 mm. 2 — 12.7 mm MGs.
Radars: Surface search: Racal S 1690 ARPA; I-band.
Navigation: Racal Decca RM 1290A; I-band.

Comment: Ordered on 18 October 1987 from Blohm + Voss. First two completed 15 June 1989; second pair 20 August 1989. Steel hulls with aluminium superstructure. *Hail* and *Najran* based at Jiddah in the Red Sea and the others at Aziziah.

AL JOUF   *6/1989, Blohm + Voss* / 0080566

2 AL JUBATEL CLASS (WPB)

AL JUBATEL   SALWA

Displacement, tons: 95 full load
Dimensions, feet (metres): 86 × 19 × 6.9 *(26.2 × 5.8 × 2.1)*
Main machinery: 2 MTU 16V 396 TB94 diesels; 5,800 hp(m) *(4.26 MW)* sustained; 2 shafts
Speed, knots: 34
Range, n miles: 1,100 at 25 kt
Complement: 12 (4 officers)
Guns: 1 Oerlikon/GAM-BO1 20 mm. 2 — 12.7 mm MGs.
Radars: Surface search: Racal Decca AC 1290; I-band.

Comment: Built by Abeking & Rasmussen, completed in April 1987. Smaller version of Turkish SAR 33 Type. Steel construction. One based at Jizan and one at Al Wajh.

AL JUBATEL   *1987, Abeking & Rasmussen* / 0080567

3 SLINGSBY SAH 2200 HOVERCRAFT (UCAC)

Dimensions, feet (metres): 34.8 × 13.8 *(10.6 × 4.2)*
Main machinery: 1 Deutz BF6L913C diesel; 192 hp(m) *(141 kW)* sustained; lift and propulsion
Speed, knots: 40
Range, n miles: 500 at 40 kt
Complement: 2
Military lift: 2.2 tons or 16 troops
Guns: 1 — 7.62 mm MG.

Comment: Supplied by Slingsby Amphibious Hovercraft, York in December 1990. Have Kevlar armour. These craft have replaced the SRN type.

SAH 2200   *1990, Slingsby* / 0080568

5 GRIFFON 8000 TD(M) CLASS (HOVERCRAFT) (LCAC)

Displacement, tons: 18.2; 24.6 full load
Dimensions, feet (metres): 69.5 × 36.1 × 1 *(21.15 × 11 × 0.32)*
Main machinery: 2 MTU 12V 183 TB32 V12 diesels; 800 hp *(597 kW)*
Speed, knots: 50
Range, n miles: 400 at 45 kt
Complement: 4 (2 officers) (accommodation for further 16)
Guns: 1 — 12.7 mm MG.
Radars: Raytheon R-80; I-band.

Comment: Five hovercraft ordered from Griffon in 2000 for delivery in 2001. Payload of about 8 tonnes. Similar to those supplied to Indian Coast Guard but with different superstructure. Three based on west coast and two on east coast.

GRIFFON 8000 (Indian colours)   *9/2000, Indian Coast Guard* / 0104592

INSHORE PATROL CRAFT (PBI)

Type	Date	Speed
Rapier 15.2 m	1976	28
Enforcer, USA, 9.4 m	1980s	30
Simonneau SM 331, 9.3 m	1992	40
Boston Whalers, 8.3 m	1980s	30
Catamarans, 6.4 m	1977	30
Task Force Boats, 5.25 m	1976	20
Viper, 5.1 m	1980s	25
Cobra, 3.9 m	1984	40

Comment: About 500 mostly Task Force Boats. Many are based at Jiddah with the rest spread around the other bases. Most are armed with MGs and the larger craft have I-band radars.

SIMONNEAU SM 331   *6/1992, Simonneau Marine* / 0080569

1 TRAINING SHIP (AXL)

TABBOUK

Displacement, tons: 585 full load
Dimensions, feet (metres): 196.8 × 32.8 × 5.8 *(60 × 10 × 1.8)*
Main machinery: 2 MTU MD 16V 538 TB80 diesels; 5,000 hp(m) *(3.68 MW)* sustained; 2 shafts
Speed, knots: 20
Range, n miles: 3,500 at 12 kt
Complement: 26 (6 officers) plus 70 trainees
Guns: 1 Oerlikon GAM-BO1 20 mm.
Radars: Surface search: Racal Decca TM 1226; I-band.
Navigation: Racal Decca 2690BT; I-band.

Comment: Built by Bayerische, Germany and commissioned 1 December 1977. Based at Jiddah.

3 SMALL TANKERS (YO)

AL FORAT	DAJLAH	AL NIL

Displacement, tons: 233 full load
Dimensions, feet (metres): 94.2 × 21.3 × 6.9 *(28.7 × 6.5 × 2.1)*
Main machinery: 2 Caterpillar D343 diesels; 2 shafts
Speed, knots: 12
Range, n miles: 500 at 12 kt
Radars: Navigation: Decca 110; I-band.

Comment: *Al Nil* based at Aziziah, the others at Jiddah.

Senegal
MARINE SÉNÉGALAISE

Country Overview

The Republic of Senegal was a French colony until 1960 when it gained independence. Situated in western Africa, it has an area of 75,750 square miles and is bordered to the north by Mauritania and to the south by Guinea and Guinea-Bissau. Its 286 n mile coastline with the Atlantic Ocean is divided in two by the coast of Gambia with which the country was united to form the confederation of Senegambia between 1981-89. The capital, largest city and principal port is Dakar. Territorial seas (12 n miles) are claimed. A 200 n mile Exclusive Economic Zone (EEZ) has been declared but its limits have only been partially defined by boundary agreements.

Headquarters Appointments

Head of Navy:
  Captain Ousmane Ibrahima Sall

Personnel

(a) 2006: 900 officers and men
(b) 2 years' conscript service

Bases

Dakar, Elinkine (Casamance)

PATROL FORCES

1 IMPROVED OSPREY 55 CLASS (LARGE PATROL CRAFT) (PBO)

Name	No	Builders	Commissioned
FOUTA	—	Danyard A/S, Fredrikshavn	1 June 1987

Displacement, tons: 470 full load
Dimensions, feet (metres): 180.5 × 33.8 × 8.5 *(55 × 10.3 × 2.6)*
Main machinery: 2 MAN Burmeister & Wain Alpha 12V23/30-DVO diesels; 4,400 hp(m) *(3.23 MW)* sustained; 2 shafts; cp props
Speed, knots: 20. **Range, n miles:** 4,000 at 16 kt
Complement: 38 (4 officers) plus 8 spare
Guns: 1 Hispano Suiza 30 mm. 1 Giat 20 mm.
Radars: Surface search: Furuno FR 1411; I-band.
Navigation: Furuno FR 1221; I-band.

Comment: Ordered in 1985. Intended for patrolling the EEZ rather than as a warship, hence the modest armament. A 25 kt rigid inflatable boat can be launched from a stern ramp which has a protective hinged door. Similar vessels built for Morocco.

FOUTA *1/2005*, P Marsan* / 1133233

1 PR 72M CLASS (PBO)

Name	No	Builders	Commissioned
NJAMBUUR	P 773	SFCN, Villeneuve-la-Garenne	Feb 1983

Displacement, tons: 451 full load
Dimensions, feet (metres): 191.0 × 26.9 × 7.2 *(58.2 × 8.2 × 2.2)*
Main machinery: 2 UD 33V16M6D diesels; 5,470 hp *(4.08 MW)* sustained; 2 shafts
Speed, knots: 16. **Range, n miles:** 2,160 at 15 kt
Complement: 46
Guns: 2 OTO Melara 3 in *(76 mm)*/62 compact; 85 rds/min to 16 km *(8.7 n miles)*; weight of shell 6 kg.
2 — 20 mm Oerlikon. 2 — 12.7 mm MGs.
Weapons control: 2 CSEE Naja optical directors.
Radars: Surface search: FR 7112 and FR 2105; I-band.

Comment: Ordered in 1979 and launched 23 December 1980. Completed September 1981 for shipping of armament at Lorient. Underwent overhaul at Lorient 2001-2002.

NJAMBUUR *2/2003*, B Prézelin* / 1129573

2 PR 48 CLASS (LARGE PATROL CRAFT) (PBO)

Name	No	Builders	Launched	Commissioned
POPENGUINE	—	SFCN, Villeneuve-la-Garenne	22 Mar 1974	10 Aug 1974
PODOR	—	SFCN, Villeneuve-la-Garenne	20 July 1976	13 July 1977

Displacement, tons: 250 full load
Dimensions, feet (metres): 156 × 23.3 × 8.1 *(47.5 × 7.1 × 2.5)*
Main machinery: 2 SACM AGO V12 CZSHR diesels; 4,340 hp(m) *(3.2 MW)*; 2 shafts
Speed, knots: 23. **Range, n miles:** 2,000 at 16 kt
Complement: 33 (3 officers)
Guns: 2 Bofors 40 mm/70. 2 — 7.62 mm MGs.
Radars: Surface search: Racal Decca 1226; I-band.

Comment: Ordered in 1973 and 1975. *Saint-Louis* decommissioned in 2003 and the operational status of the remaining two is doubtful.

PR 48 CLASS *6/2000, A Sharma* / 0105589

3 INTERCEPTOR CLASS (COASTAL PATROL CRAFT) (PB)

Name	No	Builders	Commissioned
SÉNÉGAL II	—	Les Bateaux Turbec Ltd, Sainte Catherine, Canada	Feb 1979
SINE-SALOUM II	—	Les Bateaux Turbec Ltd, Sainte Catherine, Canada	16 Nov 1979
CASAMANCE II	—	Les Bateaux Turbec Ltd, Sainte Catherine, Canada	Aug 1979

Displacement, tons: 62 full load
Dimensions, feet (metres): 86.9 × 19.3 × 5.2 *(26.5 × 5.8 × 1.6)*
Main machinery: 2 diesels; 2,700 hp *(2.01 MW)*; 2 shafts
Speed, knots: 32.5
Guns: 1 — 20 mm Giat.
Radars: Surface search: Furuno; I-band.

Comment: Used for EEZ patrol. All still in service with new radars.

SÉNÉGAL II *4/2004* / 0587793

2 PETERSON MK 4 CLASS (PB)

Name	No	Builders	Commissioned
MATELOT ALIOUNE SAMB	—	Peterson Builders Inc	28 Oct 1993
MATELOT OUMAR NDOYE	—	Peterson Builders Inc	4 Nov 1993

Displacement, tons: 22 full load
Dimensions, feet (metres): 51.3 × 14.8 × 4.3 *(15.6 × 4.5 × 1.3)*
Main machinery: 2 Detroit 6V-92TA diesels; 520 hp *(388 kW)*; 2 shafts
Speed, knots: 24. **Range, n miles:** 500 at 20 kt
Complement: 6
Guns: 2 — 12.7 mm (twin) MGs. 2 — 7.62 mm (twin) MGs.
Radars: Surface search: Furuno; I-band.

Comment: Ordered in September 1992. Same type delivered to Cape Verde, Gambia and Guinea-Bissau (since deleted) under FMS. Carries an RIB on the stern.

MATELOT ALIOUNE SAMB *6/1999* / 0080570

LAND-BASED MARITIME AIRCRAFT

Numbers/Type: 1 De Havilland Canada DHC-6 Twin Otter.
Operational speed: 168 kt *(311 km/h).*
Service ceiling: 23,200 ft *(7,070 m).*
Range: 1,460 n miles *(2,705 km).*
Role/Weapon systems: Procured in 1982. Used for coastal surveillance but effectiveness limited. Backed up by a French Navy Breguet Atlantique based at Dakar. Sensors: Search radar. Weapons: Unarmed.

AUXILIARIES

Notes: (1) A modified purse-seiner, *Itaf Deme* is used for fisheries research. Crewed by the Navy.
(2) There is also a harbour tug *Cheik Oumar Fall* (ex-Y 719) on loan from the French Navy since 1990.

AMPHIBIOUS FORCES

1 CTM (LCM)

CTM (ex-CTM 2, ex-CTM 5)

Displacement, tons: 150 full load
Dimensions, feet (metres): 78 × 21 × 4.2
(23.8 × 6.4 × 1.3)
Main machinery: 2 Poyaud 520 V8 diesels; 225 hp(m)
(165 kW); 2 shafts
Speed, knots: 9.5. **Range, n miles:** 350 at 8 kt
Complement: 6
Military lift: 90 tons

Comment: Transferred from French Navy in September 1999. Has a bow ramp.
CTM *12/2001*
0525011

1 CDIC CLASS (LCT)

FALEMÉ II (ex-*Javeline* L 9070)

Displacement, tons: 710 full load
Dimensions, feet (metres): 194.9 × 39 × 5.9
(59.4 × 11.9 × 1.8)
Main machinery: 2 SACM Uni Diesel UD 30 VIZ M1 diesels; 1,200 hp(m) *(882 kW)* sustained; 2 shafts
Speed, knots: 10.5. **Range, n miles:** 1,000 at 10 kt
Complement: 12
Military lift: 336 tons
Guns: Fitted for 2 Giat 20F2 20 mm.
Radars: Navigation: Racal Decca 1229; I-band.

Comment: Acquired vice one Edic class on 7 February 1999.
FALEMÉ II
1/2005*, P Marsan
1133232

1 EDIC 700 CLASS (LCT)

Name	No	Builders	Launched	Commissioned
KARABANE	841	SFCN, Villeneuve-la-Garenne	6 Mar 1986	30 Jan 1987

Displacement, tons: 736 full load
Dimensions, feet (metres): 193.5 × 39 × 5.6
(59 × 11.9 × 1.7)
Main machinery: 2 SACM MGO 175 V12 ASH diesels; 1,200 hp(m) *(882 kW)* sustained; 2 shafts
Speed, knots: 12. **Range, n miles:** 1,800 at 10 kt
Complement: 18 (33 spare billets)
Military lift: 12 trucks; 340 tons equipment
Guns: Fitted for 2 Giat 20 mm.
Radars: Navigation: Racal Decca 1226; I-band.

Comment: Ordered May 1985, delivered 23 June 1986 from France. Second of class from France in 1995 and returned again in 1996.
KARABANE
1/2005*, P Marsan
1133231

Serbia and Montenegro

KORPUS RATNE MORNARIĆE

Country Overview

The Federal Republic of Serbia and Montenegro, known until February 2003 as the Federal Republic of Yugoslavia, was formed in 1992 following the secession of four of the six republics from the former Socialist Federal Republic of Yugoslavia (SFRY). With an area of 39,449 square miles, it is located in south-eastern Europe in the Balkan Peninsula and comprises Serbia (including the provinces of Kosovo and Vojvodina) and Montenegro. It is bordered to the north by Hungary, to the east by Romania and Bulgaria, to the south by Macedonia and Albania and to the west by Croatia and Bosnia and Herzegovina. It has a 107 n mile coastline with the Adriatic Sea on which Bar and Tivat are the principal ports. The capital and largest city is Belgrade. Territorial waters (12 n miles) are claimed but an EEZ has not been claimed.

The status of the union between the two countries is fragile and, funding for the navy will remain low until the future of Montenegro, which may conduct an independence referendum in 2006, has been decided.

Headquarters Appointments

Commander-in-Chief:
  Rear Admiral Dragan Samardzić

Personnel

2006: 1,100

Bases

Headquarters: Bar
Main base: Tivat
Minor base: Bar
River base: Novi Sad

Organisation

The Navy Corps forms part of the Armed Forces of Serbia and Montenegro and is subordinate to the Deputy Chief of General Staff for the Navy.
Flotilla: 88 Submarine Brigade, 18 Missile Boat Brigade, 38 Patrol Brigade and 376 Naval Logistics Command. The Riverine Flotilla (Novi Sad) is subordinate to the Maritime Department of the General Staff.
Coastal Defence Command: 81 Bde Coast Defence (Kumbor), 83 Bde Coast Defence (Bar), 110 Coastal Artillery Brigade and 108 Coastal Missile Brigade. The latter is equipped with 9-12 truck-mounted twin SS-C-3 Styx SSM launchers and a number of Coastal Artillery units with 130 mm, 122 mm and 88 mm guns.

DELETIONS

Submarines

2003 *Drava*

Frigates

2005 *Beograd*

Patrol Forces

2003 PC 303, 11 Type 15
2004 *Ramiz Sadiku, Jordan Nikolov Orč e, Grimeč, Zelengora*

Amphibious Forces

2003 11 Type 11
2004 1 Type 21

Auxiliaries

2003 *Liganj*

SUBMARINES

1 SAVA CLASS (PATROL SUBMARINE) (SSC)

Name	No	Builders	Laid down	Launched	Commissioned
SAVA	831	S and DE Factory, Split	1975	1977	1978

Displacement, tons: 830 surfaced; 960 dived
Dimensions, feet (metres): 182.7 × 23.6 × 16.7
  (55.7 × 7.2 × 5.1)
Main machinery: Diesel-electric; 2 Sulzer diesels; 1,600 hp(m)
  (1.18 MW); 2 generators; 1 MW; 1 motor; 2,040 hp(m)
  (1.5 MW); 1 shaft
Speed, knots: 10 surfaced; 16 dived
Complement: 35

Torpedoes: 6—21 in *(533 mm)* bow tubes. 10 TEST-71ME;
  wire-guided active/passive homing to 15 km *(8.1 n miles)*
  at 40 kt or 20 km *(10.8 n miles)* at 25 kt; warhead 220 kg.
Mines: 20 in lieu of torpedoes.
Countermeasures: ESM: Stop Light; radar warning.
Radars: Surface search: Snoop Group; I-band.
Sonars: Atlas Elektronik PRS-3; hull-mounted; active/passive
  search and attack; medium frequency.

Structure: An improved version of the Heroj class. Diving
  depth, 300 m *(980 ft)*, built with USSR electronic
  equipment and armament. Pressure hull is 42.7 × 5.05 m
  and the casing is made of GRP. Accommodation is poor,
  suggesting the design was intended for only short
  periods at sea.
Operational: Second of class *Drava* was decommissioned
  in 2003. Based at Tivat.

SAVA   *2/1998, Yugoslav Navy* / 0050744

1 HEROJ CLASS (PATROL SUBMARINE) (SSC)

Name	No	Builders	Laid down	Launched	Commissioned
HEROJ	821	Uljanic Shipyard, Pula	1964	1967	1968

Displacement, tons: 615 surfaced; 705 dived
Dimensions, feet (metres): 165.4 × 15.4 × 14.8
  (50.4 × 4.7 × 4.5)
Main machinery: Diesel-electric; 2 Rade Končar diesel
  generators; 1,200 hp(m) *(880 kW)*; 1 motor; 1,560 hp(m)
  (1.15 MW); 1 shaft; auxiliary motor
Speed, knots: 10 surfaced; 15 dived
Range, n miles: 4,100 at 10 kt snorting
Complement: 28

Torpedoes: 4—21 in *(533 mm)* bow tubes. 6 SET-65E; active/
  passive homing to 15 km *(8.1 n miles)* at 40 kt; warhead
  205 kg.
Mines: 12 in lieu of torpedoes.
Countermeasures: ESM: Stop Light; radar warning.
Radars: Surface search: Snoop Group; I-band.
Sonars: Thomson Sintra Eledone; hull-mounted; passive
  ranging; medium frequency.

HEROJ   *1982* / 0506130

Structure: Diving depth 150 m *(500 ft)*.
Operational: *Heroj* was assessed as having been placed
  in reserve in 2000 but was reported officially as being

operational again in 2003. However, its effectiveness is
likely to be mitigated by its age.

3 UNA CLASS (MIDGET SUBMARINES) (SSW)

ZETA 913   **KUPA** 915   **VARDAR** 916

Displacement, tons: 76 surfaced; 88 dived
Dimensions, feet (metres): 61.7 × 9 × 8.2
  (18.8 × 2.7 × 2.5)
Main machinery: 2 motors; 49 hp(m) *(36 kW)*; 1 shaft
Speed, knots: 6 surfaced; 7 dived
Range, n miles: 200 at 4 kt
Complement: 6 plus 4 swimmers
Sonars: Atlas Elektronik; passive/active search; high frequency.

Comment: Building yard, Split. First of class commissioned
  May 1985; last two in 1989. Exit/re-entry capability with
  mining capacity. Can carry six combat swimmers, plus
  four Swimmer Delivery Vehicles (SDV) and limpet mines.
  Diving depth: 120 m *(394 ft)*. Batteries can only be charged
  from shore or from a depot ship. 913 has been refitted and
  the other two are reported operational. All based at Tivat.

VARDAR and ZETA   *6/2005*, Freivogel Collection* / 1151158

2 R-2 MALA CLASS (TWO-MAN SWIMMER DELIVERY VEHICLES) (LDW)

Displacement, tons: 1.4
Dimensions, feet (metres): 16.1 × 4.6 × 4.3
  (4.9 × 1.4 × 1.3)
Main machinery: 1 motor; 4.7 hp(m) *(3.5 kW)*; 1 shaft
Speed, knots: 4.4
Range, n miles: 18 at 4.4 kt; 23 at 3.7 kt
Complement: 2
Mines: 250 kg of limpet mines.

Comment: Free-flood craft with the main motor, battery,
  navigation pod and electronic equipment housed in
  separate watertight cylinders. Instrumentation includes
  aircraft type gyrocompass, magnetic compass, depth
  gauge (with 0—100 m scale), echo-sounder, sonar and two
  searchlights. Constructed of light aluminium and plexiglass,
  it is fitted with fore and after-hydroplanes, the tail being
  a conventional cruciform with a single rudder abaft the
  screw. Large perspex windows give a good all-round view.
  Operating depth 60 m *(196.9 ft)* maximum. Two operated by
  Croatia. Two reported sold to Syria and one to Sweden.

Notes: There are also reported to be four R-1 craft.
  Transportable in submarine torpedo tubes and crewed
  by one man, they are 3.7 m craft, powered by a 1 kW
  electric motor and 24V silver-zinc batteries. Capable of 2.8
  kt, they can dive to 60 m. They have a range of 4 n miles.
  Of a total twelve reported to have been manufactured.
  A further six units have probably been deleted, one unit
  is in Croatia and one was exported to Sweden.

R-2   *6/2003, Serbia and Montenegro Navy* / 0572433

FRIGATES

Notes: The two decommissioned Koni class frigates, *Beograd* and *Podgorica*, may be sold to Egypt or possibly to Sri Lanka.

2 KOTOR CLASS (FFGM)

Name	No	Builders	Launched	Commissioned
KOTOR	33	Tito Shipyard, Kraljevica	21 May 1985	Jan 1987
NOVI SAD (ex-*Pula*)	34	Tito Shipyard, Kraljevica	18 Dec 1986	Nov 1988

Displacement, tons: 1,870 full load
Dimensions, feet (metres): 317.3 × 42 × 13.7
(96.7 × 12.8 × 4.2)
Main machinery: CODAG; 1 SGW Nikolayev gas turbine;
18,000 hp(m) *(13.2 MW)*; 2 SEMT-Pielstick 12 PA6
V 280 diesels; 9,600 hp(m) *(7.1 MW)* sustained;
3 shafts
Speed, knots: 27 gas; 22 diesel
Range, n miles: 1,800 at 14 kt
Complement: 110

Missiles: SSM: 4 SS-N-2C Styx ❶; active radar or IR homing
to 83 km *(45 n miles)* at 0.9 Mach; warhead 513 kg;
sea-skimmer at end of run.
SAM: SA-N-4 Gecko twin launcher ❷; semi-active radar
homing to 15 km *(8 n miles)* at 2.5 Mach; height envelope
9—3,048 m *(29.5— 10,000 ft)*; warhead 50 kg.
Guns: 4 USSR 3 in *(76 mm)*/60 (2 twin) (1 mounting only
in 33 and 34) ❸; 90 rds/min to 15 km *(8 n miles)*; weight
of shell 6.8 kg.
4 USSR 30 mm/65 (2 twin) ❹; 500 rds/min to 5 km
(2.7 n miles); weight of shell 0.54 kg.
A/S mortars: 2 RBU 6000 12-barrelled trainable ❺; range
6,000 m; warhead 31 kg.
Mines: Can lay mines.
Countermeasures: Decoys: 2 Wallop Barricade double layer
chaff launchers.
Radars: Air/surface search: Strut Curve ❻; F-band.
Navigation: Palm Frond; I-band.
Fire control: PEAB 9LV200 ❽; I-band (for 76 mm and SSM).
Drum Tilt ❾; H/I-band (for 30 mm).
Pop Group ❿; F/H/I-band (for SAM).
IFF: High Pole; 2 Square Head.
Sonars: Bull Nose; hull-mounted; active search and attack;
medium frequency.

Programmes: Built under licence. Type name, VPB (Veliki
Patrolni Brod).

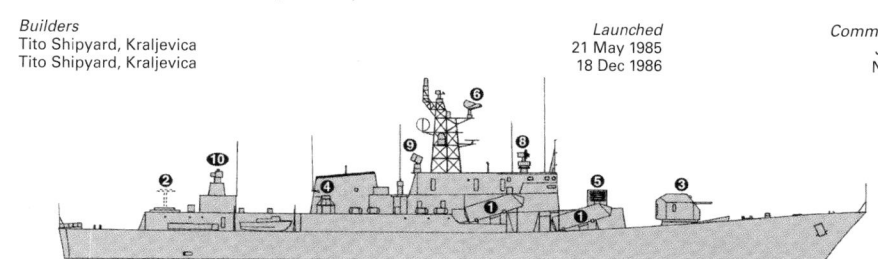

KOTOR   *(Scale 1 : 900), Ian Sturton* / 0506341

KOTOR   *6/1998, Yugoslav Navy* / 0050746

Modernisation: Combat data system fitted in *Novi Sad* in
2000 and may be retrofitted in the other. The intention
is to upgrade the missile system, possibly with Russian
SS-N-25 or Chinese C-802 SSMs.

Structure: The hulls are similar to the Russian Koni class
but are to a Yugoslavian design.
Operational: Based at Tivat.

LAND-BASED MARITIME AIRCRAFT

Notes: There are no operational land-based aircraft.

PATROL FORCES

3 KONČAR CLASS (TYPE 240) (PTFG)

Name	No	Builders	Launched	Commissioned
RADE KONČAR	401	Tito Shipyard, Kraljevica	16 Oct 1976	Apr 1977
HASAN ZAFIROVIĆ-LACA	404	Tito Shipyard, Kraljevica	9 Nov 1978	Dec 1978
ANTE BANINA	406	Tito Shipyard, Kraljevica	23 Nov 1979	Nov 1980

Displacement, tons: 271 full load
Dimensions, feet (metres): 147.6 × 27.6 × 8.5 *(45 × 8.4 × 2.6)*
Main machinery: CODAG; 2 RR Proteus gas turbines; 7,100 hp *(5.29 MW)* sustained; 2 MTU
16V 538 TB91 diesels; 6,000 hp(m) *(4.41 MW)* sustained; 4 shafts; cp props
Speed, knots: 38. **Range, n miles:** 490 at 38 kt; 870 at 23 kt (diesels)
Complement: 30 (5 officers)

Missiles: SSM: 2 SS-N-2B Styx; active radar or IR homing to 46 km *(25 n miles)* at 0.9 Mach;
warhead 513 kg.
Guns: 2 Bofors 57 mm/70; 200 rds/min to 17 km *(9.3 n miles)*; weight of shell 2.4 kg.
2—128 mm rocket launchers for illuminants.
2—30 mm/65 (twin) or 1—30 mm/65 AK 630 may be fitted in place of the after 57 mm.
Countermeasures: 2 Wallop Barricade double layer chaff launchers.
Weapons control: PEAB 9LV 202 GFCS.
Radars: Surface search: Decca 1226; I-band.
Fire control: Philips TAB; I/J-band.

Programmes: Type name, Raketna Topovnjaca.
Structure: Aluminium superstructure. Designed by the Naval Shipping Institute in Zagreb
based on Swedish Spica class with bridge amidships like Malaysian boats. The after
57 mm gun is replaced by a twin 30 mm mounting in at least one of the class.
Operational: 402 was taken by Croatia in 1991 and 401 was badly damaged but has been
repaired. 401, 404 and 406 are reported active. 403 and 405 probably decommissioned.
Three further craft cannibalised for spares. Based at Tivat. Names may no longer be
in use.

ANTE BANINA   *6/2005*, Freivogel Collection* / 1151160

2 MIRNA CLASS (TYPE 140) (PCM)

UČKA 174   KOSMAJ 178

Displacement, tons: 142 full load
Dimensions, feet (metres): 104.9 × 22 × 7.5 *(32 × 6.7 × 2.3)*
Main machinery: 2 SEMT-Pielstick 12 PA4 200 VGDS diesels; 5,292 hp(m) *(3.89 MW)*
sustained; 2 shafts
Speed, knots: 28
Range, n miles: 400 at 20 kt
Complement: 19 (3 officers)

Missiles: SAM: 1 SA-N-5 Grail quad mounting; manual aiming; IR homing to 6 km
(3.2 n miles) at 1.5 Mach; altitude to 2,500 m *(8,000 ft)*; warhead 1.5 kg.
Guns: 1 Bofors 40 mm/70. 4—20 mm (quad). 2—128 mm illuminant launchers.
Depth charges: 8 DCs.
Radars: Surface search: Racal Decca 1216C; I-band.
Sonars: Simrad SQS-3D/3F; active; high frequency.

Comment: Builders, Kraljevica Yard. Launched between June 1981 and December 1983.
An unusual feature of this design is the fitting of an electric outboard motor giving
a speed of up to 6 kt. One sunk possibly by a limpet mine in November 1991. Four held
by Croatia. Others have paid off and been cannibalised and the operational status of the
remaining two is doubtful. Names probably discontinued. Gun armament aft changed
in 1999/2000.

HASAN ZAFIROVIĆ-LACA   *5/2004, Sieche Collection* / 1044500

UČKA   *5/2004, Sieche Collection* / 1044502

4 RTK 401 (RIVER PATROL CRAFT) (PBR)

RTK 404 +3

Displacement, tons: 410 full load
Dimensions, feet (metres): 155.1 × 21.0 × 7.5 *(47.3 × 6.4 × 2.3)*
Main machinery: 3 Gray Marine 64HN8 diesels; 675 hp *(503 kW)*; 3 shafts
Speed, knots: 9
Complement: 15
Guns: 2 — 30 mm grenade launchers. 1 rocket launcher.

Comment: Former river landing ships that have been converted to river patrol boats by the addition of numerous guns and rocket launchers.

RTK 404 *6/2005*, Freivogel Collection* / 1151159

6 TYPE 20 BISCAYA CLASS (RIVER PATROL CRAFT) (PBR)

PC 211-216

Displacement, tons: 55 standard
Dimensions, feet (metres): 71.5 × 17 × 3.9 *(21.8 × 5.3 × 1.2)*
Main machinery: 2 diesels; 1,156 hp(m) *(850 kW)*; 2 shafts
Speed, knots: 16. **Range, n miles:** 200 at 15 kt
Complement: 10
Guns: 2 Oerlikon 20 mm.
Radars: Surface search: Decca 110; I-band.

Comment: Completed in the late 1980s. Steel hull with GRP superstructure. All active with the Riverine Flotilla.

PC 215 *1988, Yugoslav Navy* / 0084261

1 RIVER PATROL BOAT (PBR)

PC 111

Displacement, tons: 29 full load
Dimensions, feet (metres): 79.1 × 13.5 × 2.9 *(24.1 × 4.1 × 0.9)*
Main machinery: 2 diesels; 652 hp(m) *(486 kW)*; 2 shafts
Speed, knots: 17. **Range, n miles:** 720 at 17 kt
Complement: 6
Guns: 2 — 20 mm.

Comment: Built for US Navy's Rhine River patrol and transferred in the 1950s.

PC 111 *6/2001, Vojska* / 0528418

1 BOTICA CLASS (TYPE 16) (RIVER PATROL CRAFT) (PBR)

PC 302

Displacement, tons: 23 full load
Dimensions, feet (metres): 55.8 × 11.8 × 2.8 *(17.0 × 3.6 × 0.8)*
Main machinery: 2 diesels; 464 hp(m) *(340 kW)*; 2 shafts
Speed, knots: 15. **Range, n miles:** 340 at 14 kt
Complement: 7
Guns: 1 Oerlikon 20 mm (fitted for). 2 — 7.62 mm MGs.

Comment: Built in about 1970 and reactivated having been decommissioned in the 1990s. Used for riverine patrols. Can carry up to 30 troops.

PC 302 *5/2004, Sieche Collection* / 0583300

AMPHIBIOUS FORCES

1 SILBA CLASS (LCT/ML)

Name	No	Builders	Commissioned
KRK (ex-*Silba*)	DBM 241	Brodosplit Shipyard, Split	1990

Displacement, tons: 880 full load
Dimensions, feet (metres): 163.1 oa; 144 wl × 33.5 × 8.5 *(49.7; 43.9 × 10.2 × 2.6)*
Main machinery: 2 Burmeister & Wain Alpha 10V23L-VO diesels; 3,100 hp(m) *(2.28 MW)* sustained; 2 shafts; cp props
Speed, knots: 12
Range, n miles: 1,200 at 12 kt
Complement: 33 (3 officers)
Military lift: 460 tons or 6 medium tanks or 7 APCs or 4 — 130 mm guns plus towing vehicles or 300 troops with equipment
Missiles: SAM: 1 SA-N-5 Grail quad mounting.
Guns: 4 — 30 mm/65 (2 twin) AK 230.
4 — 20 mm M75 (quad). 2 — 128 mm illuminant launchers.
Mines: 94 Type SAG-1.
Radars: Surface search: Racal Decca; I-band.

Comment: Ro-ro design with bow and stern ramps. Can be used for minelaying, transporting weapons or equipment and troops. Operational and based at Tivat. Two further craft, launched in 1992 and 1994, are in the Croatian Navy.

KRK *6/1998, MoD Bonn* / 0050751

7 TYPE 22 (LCU)

DJC 627	**DJC 412** (ex-DJC 625)	**DJC 414** (ex-DJC 621)
DJC 628	**DJC 413** (ex-DJC 630)	**DJC 415** (ex-DJC 631)
DJC 411 (ex-DJC 632)		

Displacement, tons: 48 full load
Dimensions, feet (metres): 73.2 × 15.7 × 3.3 *(22.3 × 4.8 × 1)*
Main engines: 2 MTU diesels; 1,740 hp(m) *(1.28 MW)*; 2 water-jets
Speed, knots: 30
Range, n miles: 320 at 22 kt
Complement: 8
Military lift: 40 troops or 15 tons cargo
Guns: 2 — 20 mm M71. 1 — 30 mm grenade launcher.
Radars: Navigation: Decca 101; I-band.

Comment: Built of polyester and glass fibre. Last one completed in 1987. Based in Danube Flotilla.

DJC 412 *6/2003, Serbia and Montenegro Navy* / 0572441

3 TYPE 21 (LCU)

DJC 614	**DJC 616**	**DJC 618**

Displacement, tons: 32 full load
Dimensions, feet (metres): 69.9 × 15.7 × 5.2 *(21.3 × 4.8 × 1.6)*
Main machinery: 1 diesel; 1,450 hp(m) *(1.07 MW)*; 1 shaft
Speed, knots: 23
Range, n miles: 320 at 22 kt
Complement: 6
Military lift: 6 tons
Guns: 1 — 20 mm M71.

Comment: The survivors of a class of 20 built between 1976 and 1979. Four held by Croatia in 1991 of which three have paid off. Others sunk or scrapped. Some of these may be laid up.

DJC 616 *6/2003, Serbia and Montenegro Navy* / 0572440

MINE WARFARE FORCES

2 SIRIUS CLASS (MINESWEEPERS/HUNTERS) (MSC/MHC)

Name	No	Builders	Commissioned
PODGORA (ex-*Smeli*)	M 152 (ex-D 26)	A Normand, France	Sep 1957
BLITVENICA (ex-*Slobodni*)	M 153 (ex-D 27)	A Normand, France	Sep 1957

Displacement, tons: 365 standard; 424 full load
Dimensions, feet (metres): 152 × 28 × 8.2 *(46.4 × 8.6 × 2.5)*
Main machinery: 2 SEMT-Pielstick PA1 175 diesels; 1,620 hp(m) *(1.19 MW)*; 2 shafts
Speed, knots: 15
Range, n miles: 3,000 at 10 kt
Complement: 40
Guns: 2 Oerlikon 20 mm.
Countermeasures: MCMV: PAP 104 (minehunter); remote-controlled submersibles.
Radars: Navigation: Thomson-CSF DRBN 30; I-band.
Sonars: Thomson Sintra TSM 2022 (minehunter); hull-mounted; active minehunting; high frequency.

Comment: Built to a British design as US 'offshore' orders. *Blitvenica* converted to minehunter in 1980-81. Decca Hi-fix. These two are based at Tivat and are both operational.

BLITVENICA *6/2003, Serbia and Montenegro Navy* / 0572435

7 NESTIN CLASS (RIVER MINESWEEPERS) (MSR)

Name	No	Builders	Commissioned
NESTIN	M 331	Brodotehnika, Belgrade	20 Dec 1975
MOTAJICA	M 332	Brodotehnika, Belgrade	18 Dec 1976
BELEGIŠ	M 333	Brodotehnika, Belgrade	1976
BOSUT	M 334	Brodotehnika, Belgrade	1979
VUČEDOL	M 335	Brodotehnika, Belgrade	1979
DJERDAP	M 336	Brodotehnika, Belgrade	1980
NOVI SAD	M 341	Brodotehnika, Belgrade	8 June 1996

Displacement, tons: 65 full load
Dimensions, feet (metres): 88.6 × 21.7 × 5.2 *(27 × 6.3 × 1.6)*
Main machinery: 2 diesels; 520 hp(m) *(382 kW)*; 2 shafts
Speed, knots: 15
Range, n miles: 860 at 11 kt
Complement: 17
Guns: 6 Hispano 20 mm (quad fwd, 2 single aft). Some may still have a 40 mm gun forward.
8 — 20 mm (quad fwd and aft) (M 341).
Mines: 24 can be carried.
Countermeasures: MCMV: Magnetic, acoustic and explosive sweeping gear.
Radars: Surface search: Racal Decca 1226; I-band.

Comment: Some transferred to Hungary and Iraq. One more completed in 1996. The class is based at Novi Sad as part of the Riverine Flotilla. One deleted in 1997. One more building is unlikely to be completed. M 341, which replaced the previously deleted M 337, is to a modified design which includes different armament.

DJERDAP *6/2003, Serbia and Montenegro Navy* / 0572436

AUXILIARIES

Notes: (1) Three 22 m inshore survey vessels BH 11, BH 12 and CH 1 are operated by the Naval Hydrological Institute.
(2) There are seven tenders BM 58, BM 65, BM 66, BM 67, BM 70 and BS 22.
(3) There are five diving tenders BRM 81, BRM 84, BRM 85, BRM 87 and BRM 88.
(4) *Alga* PV 17 is a 44 m water tanker.

1 SAIL TRAINING SHIP (AXS)

JADRAN

Displacement, tons: 737 full load
Dimensions, feet (metres): 196.9 × 29.2 × 13.3 *(60.0 × 8.9 × 4.05)*
Main machinery: 1 Burmeister Alpha diesel; 353 hp *(263 kW)*
Speed, knots: 10.4
Radars: 1 FR 2120 and 1 FR 7061; I-band.

Comment: The contract for a barquentine sail training ship was signed on 4 September 1930 with the German shipbuilding company H C Silken Zon of Hamburg. She was launched on 25 June 1931 and arrived in Tivat on 16 July 1933. During the Second World War, she was used by the Italian Navy under the name of *Marco Polo* before being allowed to fall into disrepair. She returned to Yugoslavia in 1946 and was reconstructed in her original form at Tivat.

JADRAN *6/2005*, John Mortimer* / 1151388

1 KOZARA CLASS (HEADQUARTERS SHIP) (PBR)

KOZARA (ex-*Oregon*, ex-*Kriemhild*) RPB 30

Displacement, tons: 695 full load
Dimensions, feet (metres): 219.8 × 31.2 × 4.6 *(67 × 9.5 × 1.4)*
Main machinery: 2 Deutz RV6M545 diesels; 800 hp(m) *(588 kW)*; 2 shafts
Speed, knots: 12
Guns: 9 Hispano Suiza 20 mm (3 triple).

Comment: Former Presidential Yacht on Danube. Built in Austria in 1940. Acts as Flagship of the Riverine Flotilla. A similar ship served in the Russian Black Sea Fleet before being transferred to Ukraine. Although previously believed to have been decommissioned, continues to be used to accommodate Riverine Flotilla Staff.

KOZARA *6/2003, Serbia and Montenegro Navy* / 0572439

1 LUBIN CLASS (TRANSPORT SHIP) (AKR)

LUBIN PO 91

Displacement, tons: 860 full load
Dimensions, feet (metres): 190.9 × 36.1 × 9.2 *(58.2 × 11.0 × 2.8)*
Main machinery: 2 diesels; 3,500 hp(m) *(2.57 MW)*; 2 shafts; cp props
Speed, knots: 16. **Range, n miles:** 1,500 at 16 kt
Complement: 43
Military lift: 150 troops; 6 tanks
Guns: 1 Bofors 40 mm/70. 4 — 20 mm M75. 128 mm rocket launcher for illuminants.

Comment: Fitted with bow doors and two upper-deck cranes. Ro-Ro cargo ship built in Split in the 1980s and used as an ammunition transport. Based at Tivat. This ship had been assessed decommissioned in the early 1990s but has been officially reported as being in good condition and operational.

LUBIN *5/2004, Sieche Collection* / 1044503

For details of the latest updates to *Jane's Fighting Ships* online and to discover the additional information available exclusively to online subscribers please visit
jfs.janes.com

1 DRINA CLASS (AOTL)

SIPA PN 27

Displacement, tons: 430 full load
Dimensions, feet (metres): 151 × 23.6 × 10.2 (46 × 7.2 × 3.1)
Main machinery: 1 diesel; 300 hp(m) (220 kW); 1 shaft
Speed, knots: 7
Complement: 12
Missiles: SAM: 1 SA-N-5.
Guns: 6 Hispano 20 mm (1 quad, 2 single).

Comment: Built at Kraljevic in mid-1950s. Based at Tivat.

SIPA   6/2003, Serbia and Montenegro Navy / 1044504

1 SABAC CLASS (DEGAUSSING VESSEL) (YDG)

SABAC RSRB 36

Displacement, tons: 110 standard
Dimensions, feet (metres): 105.6 × 23.3 × 3.9 (32.2 × 7.1 × 1.2)
Main machinery: 1 diesel; 528 hp(m) (388 kW); 1 shaft
Speed, knots: 10. **Range, n miles:** 660 at 10 kt
Complement: 20
Guns: 2—20 mm M71.
Radars: Navigation: Decca 101; I-band.

Comment: Built in 1985. Used to degauss River vessels up to a length of 50 m.

SABAC   6/2003, Serbia and Montenegro / 0572437

TUGS

Notes: There are three coastal tugs PR 37, PR 38 and PR 41 (armed with a 20 mm gun) and seven harbour tugs LR 23, LR 72, LR 74, LR 75, LR 77 and LR 80.

Seychelles

Country Overview

A former British colony, the Republic of the Seychelles became independent in 1976. Situated in the western Indian Ocean, northeast of Madagascar, the archipelago consists of some 90 islands, disposed over 13,000 square miles in two groups. The 40 islands of the northern group include the principal islands: Mahé (the largest), Praslin, Silhouette and La Digue. The 50 or so low-lying coral islands in the south are mostly uninhabited. Victoria (Mahé) is the capital, largest town and principal port. Territorial seas (12 n miles) are claimed. A 200 n mile Exclusive Economic Zone (EEZ) has been declared but the limits have not been fully defined by boundary agreements.

Headquarters Appointments

Commander of the Coast Guard:
   Lieutenant Colonel D Gertrude

Bases

Port Victoria, Mahé

Personnel

2006: 300 including 80 air wing and 100 marines

COAST GUARD

1 ZHUK (PROJECT 1400M) CLASS
(COASTAL PATROL CRAFT) (PB)

Name	No	Builders	Commissioned
FORTUNE	604	USSR	6 Nov 1982

Displacement, tons: 39 full load
Dimensions, feet (metres): 78.7 × 16.4 × 3.9 (24 × 5 × 1.2)
Main machinery: 2 Type M 401B diesels; 2,200 hp (1.6 MW) sustained; 2 shafts
Speed, knots: 30
Range, n miles: 1,100 at 15 kt
Complement: 12 (3 officers)
Guns: 4—14.5 mm (2 twin) MGs.
Radars: Surface search: Furuno; I-band.

Comment: Two transferred from USSR. Second of class paid off in 1996 and used for spares.

FORTUNE   6/1998, Seychelles Coast Guard / 0050097

1 TYPE FPB 42 (LARGE PATROL CRAFT) (PB)

Name	No	Builders	Commissioned
ANDROMACHE	605	Picchiotti, Viareggio	10 Jan 1983

Displacement, tons: 268 full load
Dimensions, feet (metres): 137.8 × 26 × 8.2 (41.8 × 8 × 2.5)
Main machinery: 2 Paxman Valenta 16 CM diesels; 6,650 hp (5 MW) sustained; 2 shafts
Speed, knots: 26
Range, n miles: 3,000 at 16 kt
Complement: 22 (3 officers)
Guns: 1 Oerlikon 25 mm. 2—7.62 mm MGs.
Radars: Surface search: 2 Furuno; I-band.

Comment: Ordered from Inma, La Spezia in November 1981. A second of class reported ordered in 1991 but the order was not confirmed.

ANDROMACHE   3/1997 / 0019096

1 COASTAL PATROL CRAFT (PB)

JUNON 602

Displacement, tons: 40 full load
Dimensions, feet (metres): 60.0 × 16.7 × 5.9 *(18.3 × 5.1 × 1.8)*
Speed, knots: 20
Complement: 5
Radars: Surface search: Furuno; I-band.

Comment: Former Port and Marine Services patrol boat reintegrated into the Coast Guard in 2003.

JUNON   *9/2003, Seychelles Coast Guard* / 0568333

5 PATROL CRAFT (PB)

ARIES	VIRGO	LIBRA	TAURUS	PISCES

Displacement, tons: 17.7 full load
Dimensions, feet (metres): 44.0 × 12.5 × 3.9 *(13.4 × 3.8 × 1.2)*
Main machinery: 2 General Motors Detroit 6V53 diesels; 2 shafts
Speed, knots: 13. **Range, n miles:** 200 at 11 kt
Complement: 3
Radars: Surface search: Furuno; I-band.

Comment: Former US Coast Guard lifeboats (MLB) constructed in the 1960s. Three were transported to the Seychelles onboard USS *Anchorage* in October 2000 and a further two onboard USS *Tarawa* in December 2000.

MLBs   *9/2003, Seychelles Coast Guard* / 0568334

1 SDB MK 5 CLASS (LARGE PATROL CRAFT) (PBO)

TOPAZ (ex-*Tarmugli*)

Displacement, tons: 260 full load
Dimensions, feet (metres): 151.0 × 24.6 × 8.2 *(46.0 × 7.5 × 2.5)*
Main machinery: 2 MTU 16V 538 TB92 diesels; 6,820 hp(m) *(5 MW)* sustained; 2 shafts
Speed, knots: 30. **Range, n miles:** 2,000 at 12 kt
Complement: 34 (4 officers)
Guns: 1 Medak 30 mm 2A42.
Radars: Surface search: Bharat 1245; I-band.

Comment: Built at Garden Reach and first commissioned in 2002. Transferred from the Indian Navy and recommissioned on 23 February 2005.

SDB MK 5 CLASS   *5/2002** / 0534083

LAND-BASED MARITIME AIRCRAFT

Numbers/Type: 1 Britten-Norman BN-2A21 Maritime Defender.
Operational speed: 150 kt *(280 km/h).*
Service ceiling: 18,900 ft *(5,760 m).*
Range: 1,500 n miles *(2,775 km).*
Role/Weapon systems: Coastal surveillance and surface search aircraft delivered in 1980. Sensors: Search radar. Weapons: Provision for rockets or guns.

BN2T-4S (Irish Police colours)   *8/1997* / 0016662

Sierra Leone

Country Overview

A former British colony, Sierra Leone became independent in 1961. Located in west Africa, the country has an area of 27,699 square miles, a 217 n mile coastline with the Atlantic Ocean and is bordered to the north by Guinea and to the south by Liberia. The capital, largest city and principal port is Freetown. An EEZ has not been claimed and the country is one of a few that claims 200 n mile territorial seas.

Headquarters Appointments

Senior Officer, Navy:
  Captain A B Sessay

Personnel

(a) 2006: 230 (30 officers)
(b) Voluntary service

Bases

Freetown (HQ), Yeliboya, Sulima and Mania (Turtle Is)

PATROL FORCES

Notes: (1) Two RIBs and five other small craft have been acquired for inshore patrol.
(2) Three patrol craft acquired from the US in 2005.
(3) Replacement fo the Shanghai class is reported to be under consideration by the Chinese government.

1 SHANGHAI III (TYPE 062/1) CLASS (COASTAL PATROL CRAFT) (PB)

ALIMAMY RASSIN PB 103

Displacement, tons: 170 full load
Dimensions, feet (metres): 134.5 × 17.4 × 5.9 *(41 × 5.3 × 1.8)*
Main machinery: 4 Chinese L12-180A diesels; 4,400 hp(m) *(3.22 MW)* sustained; 4 shafts
Speed, knots: 25. **Range, n miles:** 750 at 17 kt
Complement: 43
Guns: 4 China 37 mm/63 (2 twin); 180 rds/min to 8.5 km *(4.6 n miles)*; weight of shell 1.42 kg. 4 China 14.5 mm (2 twin) Type 69 or 4 China 25 mm (2 twin).
Radars: Surface search: Pot Head or Anritsu 726; I-band.

Comment: Transferred from China in 1987. Two further craft laid up. Operational status doubtful.

ALIMAMY RASSIN   *4/2002* / 0528294

Singapore

Country Overview

Formerly under British rule, the Republic of Singapore became self-governing in 1959. It joined Malaysia in 1963, but separated from the Federation in 1965 to become a sovereign state. With an area of 247 square miles and a coastline of 104 n miles, the main island is separated from the southern tip of Malaysia by the narrow Johore Strait. There are 59 small adjacent islets. To the south the Singapore Strait, an important shipping channel linking the Indian Ocean with the South China Sea, separates the island from the Riau archipelago of Indonesia. Territorial seas (3 n miles) are claimed. An EEZ is not claimed.

Headquarters Appointments

Chief of the Navy:
  Rear Admiral Ronnie Tay
Chief of Staff:
  Rear Admiral Sim Gim Guan
Fleet Commander:
  Rear Admiral Chew Men Leong
Commander Police Coast Guard:
  Deputy Assistant Commissioner Jerry See Buck Thye

Personnel

(a) 2006: 4,500 officers and men including 1,800 conscripts
(b) National Service: two and a half years for Corporals and above; two years for the remainder
(c) 5,000 reservists (operationally trained)

Bases

Tuas (Jurong), Changi, Sembawang

Organisation

Five Commands: Fleet, Naval Diving Unit, Coastal, Naval Logistics and Training.
Fleet: First Flotilla (six Victory, six Sea Wolf).
Third Flotilla (three LSTs, Fast Craft at Civil Squadron).
Coastal Command: (11 Fearless, four Bedok, 12 PBs)
Coastal Command operates five unmanned Giraffe 100 air/surface surveillance radar sites at Changi, Pedra Branca, St John's Island, Sultan Shoal Lighthouse and Raffles Lighthouse. Air and surface track data is passed to HQ RSN.

Prefix to Ships' Names

RSS

Police Coast Guard

The Police Coast Guard is a unit of the Singapore Police Force and was first established in 1924. Its role is to maintain coastal security within Singapore territorial waters and to support the Singapore Armed Forces in emergencies. Its four regional commands are Kallang (SE sector), Gul (SW sector), Seletar (NE sector) and Lim Chu Kang (NW sector). The PCG HQ is currently co-located at Kallang but will move to a new site at Brani (near Sentosa) by 2006. The Coastal Patrol Squadron and Special Task Squadron operate under central control. All vessels have Police Coast Guard on the superstructure and a white-red-white diagonal stripe on the hull except for Interceptor craft which have dark blue hulls with grey superstructures. Personnel numbers are about 1,000.

Special Forces

Singapore's special forces include the Naval Diving Unit, Singapore Army Special Operations Force and Singapore Police Special Tactics and Rescue unit.

Strength of the Fleet

Type	Active	Building (Projected)
Submarines	4	2
Frigates	2	4
Missile Corvettes	6	—
Offshore Patrol Vessels	11	—
Fast Attack Craft-Missile	6	—
Inshore Patrol Craft	12	—
Minehunters	4	—
LSL/LPD	4	—
LCMs	4	—

DELETIONS

Patrol Forces

2003   *Courageous*

Amphibious Forces

2002   *Perseverance* (re-roled as submarine rescue ship)

Auxiliaries

2002   *Jupiter* (to Indonesia)

SUBMARINES

0 + 2 VÄSTERGÖTLAND (A 17) CLASS (SSK)

Name	No	Builders	Laid down	Launched	Commissioned
VÄSTERGÖTLAND	—	Kockums, Malmö	10 Jan 1983	17 Sep 1986	27 Nov 1987
HÄLSINGLAND	—	Kockums, Malmö	1 Jan 1984	31 Aug 1987	20 Oct 1988

Displacement, tons: 1,500 surfaced; 1,600 dived
Dimensions, feet (metres): 198.5 × 20 × 18.4
  (60.5 × 6.1 × 5.6)
Main machinery: Diesel-Stirling-electric; 2 Hedemora V12A/15 diesels; 2,200 hp(m) *(1.62 MW)*; 2 Kockums Stirling Mk III AIP; 204 hp *(150 kW)*; 1 Jeumont Schneider motor; 1,800 hp(m) *(1.32 MW)*; 1 shaft; LIPS prop
Speed, knots: 10 surfaced; 20 dived
Complement: 27 (5 officers)

Torpedoes: 6—21 in *(533 mm)* tubes. 12 FFV Type 613; anti-surface; wire-guided; passive homing to 20 km *(10.8 n miles)* at 45 kt; warhead 240 kg. swim-out discharge.
3—15.75 in *(400 mm)* tubes. 6 FFV Type 431/451; anti-submarine; wire-guided; active/passive homing to 20 km *(10.8 n miles)* at 25 kt; warhead 45 kg shaped charge or a small charge anti-intruder version is available
Mines: 12 Type 47 swim-out mines in lieu of torpedoes.
Countermeasures: ESM: Argo AR-700-S5; or Condor CS 3701; intercept.

Weapons control: Ericsson IPS-17 (Sesub 900A) TFCS.
Radars: Navigation: Terma; I-band.
Sonars: Atlas Elektronik CSU 83; hull-mounted; passive search and attack; medium frequency.
Flank array; passive search; low frequency.

Programmes: Original design contract awarded by the Swedish Navy to Kockums, Malmö on 17 April 1978. Contract for construction signed 8 December 1981. Following discussions between the governments of Sweden and Singapore in 2005, both submarines are to be transferred to the Singapore Navy as part of a package that includes modernisation refits to incorporate Air-Independent Propulsion (AIP) systems prior to delivery. On entry into Singapore service in about 2010, the boats are likely to replace two of the Challenger class, also procured from Sweden, that entered service from 2000.
Modernisation: The modernisation package is expected to be similar to those given to the Södermanland class. This included the installation of Air Independent Propulsion

(Stirling Mk 3 AIP) by the insertion of a 12 m plug in the pressure hull. Other work included the installation of a pressurised diver's lock-out in the base of the sail to facilitate special forces operations and a new climate control system. The Thales Optronics CK 038 periscope was upgraded with a thermal imaging camera and an improved image intensifier. A new active sonar suite, Subac, may also be installed.
Structure: Single hulled with an X-type rudder/after hydroplace design. Diving depth 300 m *(984 ft)*. Anechoic coating.
Opinion: The A 14 submarines transferred to Singapore in the mid-1990s under projects Riken I and Riken II and gave the Singapore Navy its first experience of submarine operations. The procurement of *Västergötland* and *Hälsingland* would offer a significant improvement in capability but may again serve as a stepping-stone towards procuring a class of next-generation of submarines. In this respect, further collaboration with Sweden in its A 26 submarine programme is a possibility.

VÄSTERGÖTLAND CLASS

3/2004*, John Brodie / 1043520

4 CHALLENGER (SJÖORMEN) CLASS (SSK)

Name	Builders	Laid down	Launched	Commissioned
CHALLENGER (ex-*Sjöbjörnen*)	Karlskronavarvet	1967	6 Aug 1968	28 Feb 1969
CENTURION (ex-*Sjöörmen*)	Kockums	1965	25 Jan 1967	31 July 1968
CONQUEROR (ex-*Sjölejonet*)	Kockums	1966	29 June 1967	16 Dec 1968
CHIEFTAIN (ex-*Sjohunden*)	Kockums	1966	21 Mar 1968	25 June 1969

Displacement, tons: 1,130 surfaced; 1,210 dived
Dimensions, feet (metres): 167.3 × 20 × 19
 (51 × 6.1 × 5.8)
Main machinery: Diesel-electric; 2 Hedemora-Pielstick
 V12A/A2/15 diesels; 2,200 hp(m) *(1.62 MW)*; 1 ASEA motor;
 1,500 hp(m) *(1.1 MW)*; 1 shaft
Speed, knots: 12 surfaced; 20 dived
Complement: 23 (7 officers)

Torpedoes: 4—21 in *(533 mm)* bow tubes. 10 FFV Type 613;
 anti-surface; wire-guided; passive homing to 15 km
 (8.2 n miles) at 45 kt; warhead 250 kg.
 2—16 in *(400 mm)* tubes: 4 FFV Type 431; anti-submarine;
 wire-guided; active/passive homing to 20 km
 (10.8 n miles) at 25 kt; warhead 45 kg shaped charge.
Mines: Minelaying capability.
Weapons control: UDS SUBTICS.
Radars: Navigation: Terma; I-band.
Sonars: Plessey Hydra; hull-mounted; passive search and
 attack; medium frequency.

Programmes: It was announced on 23 September 1995
 that a submarine would be acquired from Sweden for
 training purposes only. Three more of the same class

CONQUEROR *9/2000, Sattler/Steele* / 0105592

acquired in July 1997 for conversion plus one more for
 spares.
Modernisation: A contract for new periscope systems was
 awarded to Kollmorgen Electro Optical in January 2005.
 Options include Model 76 and Model 90.
Structure: Albacore hull. Twin-decked. Diving depth, 150 m
 (492 ft). Air conditioning added for tropical service,
 together with battery cooling.
Operational: *Challenger* re-launched on 26 September 1997,
 Conqueror and *Centurion* on 28 May 1999 and *Chieftain*

on 22 May 2001. *Conqueror* was recommissioned in
 Singapore on 24 July 2000 and *Chieftain* on 24 August
 2002. *Challenger* and *Centurion* remained in Sweden
 to support training until January 2004 when they were
 transported to Singapore. Ex-*Sjohasten* was also shipped
 as a source of spares. *Centurion* was recommissioned on
 26 June 2004. The four submarines form 171 squadron.
 Based at Changi.

CONQUEROR *3/2000, Per Körnefeldt* / 0084434

CORVETTES

6 VICTORY CLASS (FSGM)

Name	No	Builders	Launched	Commissioned
VICTORY	P 88	Lürssen Werft, Bremen	8 June 1988	18 Aug 1990
VALOUR	P 89	Singapore SB and Marine	10 Dec 1988	18 Aug 1990
VIGILANCE	P 90	Singapore SB and Marine	27 Apr 1989	18 Aug 1990
VALIANT	P 91	Singapore SB and Marine	22 July 1989	25 May 1991
VIGOUR	P 92	Singapore SB and Marine	1 Dec 1989	25 May 1991
VENGEANCE	P 93	Singapore SB and Marine	23 Feb 1990	25 May 1991

Displacement, tons: 595 full load
Dimensions, feet (metres): 204.7 oa; 190.3 wl × 27.9 × 10.2
 (62.4; 58 × 8.5 × 3.1)
Main machinery: 4 MTU 16V 538 TB93 diesels; 15,020 hp(m)
 (11 MW) sustained; 4 shafts
Speed, knots: 35
Range, n miles: 4,000 at 18 kt
Complement: 49 (8 officers)

Missiles: SSM: 8 McDonnell Douglas Harpoon ❶; active
 radar homing to 130 km *(70 n miles)* at 0.9 Mach;
 warhead 227 kg.
 SAM: 2 Octuple IAI/Rafael Barak I ❷ radar or optical
 guidance to 10 km *(5.5 m)* at 2 Mach; warhead 22 kg.
Guns: 1 OTO Melara 3 in *(76 mm)*/62 Super Rapid ❸;
 120 rds/min to 16 km *(8.7 n miles)*; weight of shell 6 kg.
 4 CIS 50 12.7 mm MGs.
Torpedoes: 6—324 mm Whitehead B 515 (2 triple) tubes ❹.
 Whitehead A 244S; anti-submarine; active/passive
 homing to 7 km *(3.8 n miles)* at 33 kt; warhead 34 kg
 (shaped charge).
Countermeasures: Decoys: 2 Plessey Shield 9-barrelled
 chaff launchers ❺. 4 Rafael (2 twin) long-range chaff
 launchers to be fitted below the bridge wings.
ESM: Elisra SEWS ❻; intercept.
ECM: Rafael RAN 1101; ❼ jammer.
Combat data systems: Elbit command system. SATCOM ❽.
Weapons control: Elbit MSIS optronic director ❾.
Radars: Surface search: Ericsson/Radamec Sea Giraffe
 150HC ❿; G/H-band.
 Navigation: Kelvin Hughes 1007; I-band.
 Fire control: 2 Elta EL/M-2221(X) ⓫; I/J/K-band.
Sonars: Thomson Sintra TSM 2064; VDS ⓬; active search
 and attack.

Programmes: Ordered in June 1986 to a Lürssen MGB 62
 design similar to Bahrain and UAE vessels.
Modernisation: Barak launchers fitted on either side of
 the VDS, together with a second fire-control radar on
 the platform aft of the mast and an optronic director
 on the bridge roof. Rudder roll stabilisation retrofitted
 to improve sea-keeping qualities. Unidentified EW
 antennae have been installed below RAN 1101.
Operational: Form 188 Squadron, part of the First Flotilla.
 Designated Missile Corvettes (MCV). First live Barak
 firing in September 1997.

VIGILANCE
3/2004, Bob Fildes
1044507

VICTORY *(Scale 1 : 600), Ian Sturton* / 0114802

VENGEANCE *5/2004, David Boey* / 1044508

FRIGATES

2 + 4 FORMIDABLE (PROJECT DELTA) CLASS (FFGHM)

Name	No	Builders	Laid down	Launched	Commissioned
FORMIDABLE	68	DCN, Lorient	14 Nov 2002	7 Jan 2004	2006
INTREPID	69	Singapore SB and Marine	8 Mar 2003	3 July 2004	2006
STEADFAST	70	Singapore SB and Marine	15 Nov 2003	28 Jan 2005	2006
TENACIOUS	71	Singapore SB and Marine	22 May 2004	15 July 2005	2007
STALWART	72	Singapore SB and Marine	12 Nov 2005	9 Dec 2005	2008
SUPREME	73	Singapore SB and Marine	17 May 2005	2007	2009

Displacement, tons: 3,200 full load
Dimensions, feet (metres): 374.0 × 52.5 × 16.4 *(114 × 16.0 × 5.0)*
Main machinery: CODAD; 4 MTU 20V 8000 M90 diesels; 48,276 hp *(36 kW)*; 2 shafts; cp props; bow thruster
Speed, knots: 27. **Range, n miles:** 4,000 at 15 kt
Complement: 71 + 15 aircrew

Missiles: SSM: 8 Boeing Harpoon ❶; active radar homing to 130 km *(70 n miles)* at 0.9 Mach; warhead 227 kg.
SAM: Eurosam SAAAM; 4 octuple Sylver A 43 VLS ❷ for MBDA Aster 15; command guidance active radar homing to 15 km *(8.1 n miles)* anti-missile and to 30 km *(16.2 n miles)* anti-aircraft. 32 missiles.
Guns: 1 OTO Melara 3 in *(76 mm)*/62 Super rapid ❸; 120 rds/min to 16 km *(8.7 n miles)*; weight of shell 6 kg. 2—20 mm. 2—12.7 mm MGs.
Torpedoes: 6—324 mm (2 triple (recessed)) ❹ tubes. Eurotorp A 244/S Mod 3; anti-submarine; active/passive homing to 7 km *(3.8 n miles)* at 33 kt; warhead 34 kg (shaped charge).
Countermeasures: Decoys: 3 EADS NGDS 12-barrelled chaff ❺, IR and anti-torpedo decoy launchers.
ESM: RAFAEL C-PEARL-M; intercept.
Combat Data Systems: DSTA/ST Electronics system.
Weapons Control: 2 EADS Nagir 2000 optronic directors ❻.
Radars: Air/search: Thales Herakles 3-D radar multifunction ❼; E/F-band.
Surface search/Navigation: 2 Terma Scanter 2001 ❽; I-band.
Sonars: EDO 980 ALOFTS VDS; low frequency (2 kHz).

Helicopters: 1 S-70B Seahawk ❾.

Programmes: Ordered from DCN International on 6 March 2000. First steel cut for hulls two and three on 2 October 2002. Prime Contractor is Singapore's Defence Science and Technology Agency (DSTA) who are also leading combat system integration in partnership with ST Electronics.
Structure: Derived from La Fayette class but there are notable differences to accommodate the weapon and sensor fit.

Operational: *Formidable* arrived in Singapore on 8 July 2005 and joined 185 Squadron. She is to become fully operational in 2007. Based at Changi. All ships to be operational by 2009.

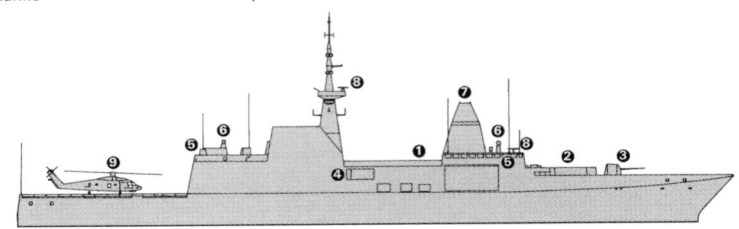

FORMIDABLE   *(Scale 1 : 1,200), Ian Sturton* / 1153492

FORMIDABLE   *5/2005*, B Prézelin* / 1133566

FORMIDABLE   *10/2004, B Prézelin* / 1044522

FORMIDABLE   *10/2004, B Prézelin* / 1044523

SHIPBORNE AIRCRAFT

Numbers/Type: 6 Sikorsky S-70B Seahawk.
Operational speed: 135 kt *(250 km/h)*.
Service ceiling: 10,000 ft *(3,050 m)*.
Range: 600 n miles *(1,110 km)*.
Role/Weapon systems: Contract placed 21 January 2005 for six new helicopters for operation from Formidable class frigates. Delivery between 2008 and 2010. Roles ASW, ASV and surveillance. Weapons and sensors to be announced.

LAND-BASED MARITIME AIRCRAFT

Notes: (1) The Air Force also has 20 A4-SU Skyhawks, 40 F-5 S/T Tiger II and 60 F-16C/D.
(2) There are also 12 CH-47D used for maritime tasks.

Numbers/Type: 4 Grumman E-2C Hawkeye.
Operational speed: 323 kt *(598 km/h)*.
Service ceiling: 30,800 ft *(9,390 m)*.
Range: 1,000 n miles *(1,850 km)*.
Role/Weapon systems: Delivered in 1987 for air control and surveillance of shipping in sea areas around Singapore. Sensors: APS-138 radar; datalink for SSM targeting. Weapons: Unarmed.

HAWKEYE *9/2003, David Boey* / 0567531

Numbers/Type: 5 Fokker F50 Mk 2S Enforcer.
Operational speed: 220 kt *(463 km/h)*.
Service ceiling: 29,500 ft *(8,990 m)*.
Range: 2,700 n miles *(5,000 km)*.
Role/Weapon systems: In service from September 1995. Part of Air Force 121 Squadron but with mixed crews and under naval op con. Sensors: Texas Instruments APS-134(V)7 radar; GEC FLIR; Elta ESM. Jammer fitted under wing-tip. Weapons: Harpoon ASM; mines; A-244S torpedoes.

FOKKER F 50 *9/2003, David Boey* / 0567532

PATROL FORCES

12 INSHORE PATROL CRAFT (PB)

FB 31-42

Displacement, tons: 20 full load
Dimensions, feet (metres): 47.6 × 13.8 × 3.6 *(14.5 × 4.2 × 1.1)*
Main machinery: 2 MAN D2848 LE 401 diesels; 1,341 hp(m) *(1 MW)*; 2 Hamilton 362 water-jets
Speed, knots: 30
Complement: 5
Guns: 1—40 mm grenade launcher. 1—12.7 mm MG. 2—7.62 mm MGs.
Radars: Surface search: Racal Decca; I-band.

Comment: Built by Singapore SBEC and delivered in 1990-91. Based at Tuas. Designated Fast Boats (FB). Some are kept in storage at Tuas. Similar to Police PT 1-19 class.

FB 31 *5/2004, David Boey* / 1044512

11 FEARLESS CLASS (PCM/PGM)

Name	No	Builders	Launched	Commissioned
FEARLESS	94	Singapore STEC	18 Feb 1995	5 Oct 1996
BRAVE	95	Singapore STEC	9 Sep 1995	5 Oct 1996
GALLANT	97	Singapore STEC	27 Apr 1996	3 May 1997
DARING	98	Singapore STEC	27 Apr 1996	3 May 1997
DAUNTLESS	99	Singapore STEC	23 Nov 1996	3 May 1997
RESILIENCE	82	Singapore STEC	23 Nov 1996	7 Feb 1998
UNITY	83	Singapore STEC	19 July 1997	7 Feb 1998
SOVEREIGNTY	84	Singapore STEC	19 July 1997	7 Feb 1998
JUSTICE	85	Singapore STEC	18 Oct 1997	7 Feb 1998
FREEDOM	86	Singapore STEC	18 Oct 1997	22 Aug 1998
INDEPENDENCE	87	Singapore STEC	18 Apr 1998	22 Aug 1998

Displacement, tons: 500 full load
Dimensions, feet (metres): 180.4 × 28.2 × 8.9 *(55 × 8.6 × 2.7)*
Main machinery: 2 MTU 12V 595 TE90 diesels; 8,554 hp(m) *(6.29 MW)* sustained; 2 Kamewa water-jets
Speed, knots: 20
Complement: 32 (5 officers)

Missiles: SAM: Matra Simbad twin launcher; Mistral; IR homing to 4 km *(2.2 n miles)*; warhead 3 kg.
Guns: 1 OTO Melara 3 in *(76 mm)*/62 Super Rapid; 120 rds/min to 16 km *(8.7 n miles)*; weight of shell 6 kg. 4 CIS 50 12.7 mm MGs.
1—25 mm Bushmaster (82).
Torpedoes: 6—324 mm Whitehead B515 (triple) tubes; (94-99) Whitehead A244S; active/passive homing to 7 km *(3.8 m)* at 33 kt; warhead 34 kg (shaped charge).
Countermeasures: Decoys: 2 GEC Marine Shield III 102 mm sextuple fixed chaff launchers.
ESM: Elisra NS-9010C; intercept.
Weapons control: ST 3100 WCS. Elbit MSIS optronic director.
Radars: Surface search and fire control: Elta EL/M-2228(X); I-band.
Navigation: Kelvin Hughes 1007; I-band.
Sonars: Thomson Sintra TSM 2362 Gudgeon; hull-mounted; active attack; medium frequency (94-99 only).
Towed array fitted in *Brave*.

Programmes: Contract awarded on 27 February 1993 for 12 patrol vessels to Singapore Shipbuilding and Engineering.
Structure: First six are ASW specialist ships. All have water-jet propulsion. Second batch were to have been fitted with Gabriel II SSMs but this plan has been shelved. MSIS director being fitted. *Fearless* modified with new EW radome on mainmast. Simbad SAM in *Brave* replaced by towed array and in *Resilience* by 25 mm Bushmaster. *Sovereignty* has deck crane to facilitate special forces operations.
Operational: All serve with Coastal Command. The first five form 189 Squadron and the second six 182 Squadron. *Unity* is to be used as a test bed for new technologies including an Indep 21 combat system. *Courageous* badly damaged in collision on 3 January 2003 and unlikely to be repaired.

SOVEREIGNTY *5/2004, David Boey* / 1044510

BRAVE (with VDS) *3/2004, Bob Fildes* / 1044509

DARING *4/2004*, John Mortimer* / 1133565

6 SEA WOLF CLASS (FAST ATTACK CRAFT—MISSILE) (PTGFM)

Name	No	Builders	Commissioned
SEA WOLF	P 76	Lürssen Werft, Vegesack	1972
SEA LION	P 77	Lürssen Werft, Vegesack	1972
SEA DRAGON	P 78	Singapore SBEC	1974
SEA TIGER	P 79	Singapore SBEC	1974
SEA HAWK	P 80	Singapore SBEC	1975
SEA SCORPION	P 81	Singapore SBEC	29 Feb 1976

Displacement, tons: 226 standard; 254 full load
Dimensions, feet (metres): 147.3 × 23 × 8.2 *(44.9 × 7 × 2.5)*
Main machinery: 4 MTU 16V 538 TB92 diesels; 13,640 hp(m) *(10 MW)* sustained; 4 shafts
Speed, knots: 35
Range, n miles: 950 at 30 kt; 1,800 at 15 kt
Complement: 41 (5 officers)

Missiles: SSM: 4 McDonnell Douglas Harpoon (2 twin); active radar homing to 130 km *(70 n miles)* at 0.9 Mach; warhead 227 kg.
4 IAI Gabriel I launchers; radar or optical guidance; semi-active radar homing to 20 km *(10.8 n miles)* at 0.7 Mach; warhead 75 kg.
SAM: 1 Matra Simbad twin launcher; Mistral; IR homing to 4 km *(2.2 n miles)*; warhead 3 kg.
Guns: 1 Bofors 57 mm/70; 200 rds/min to 17 km *(9.3 n miles)*; weight of shell 2.4 kg.
Countermeasures: Decoys: 2 Hycor Mk 137 sextuple RBOC chaff launchers. 4 Rafael (2 twin) long-range chaff launchers.
ESM/ECM: RQN 3B (INS-3) intercept and jammer. TDF-205 DF.
Weapons control: Elbit MSIS optronic director to be fitted.
Radars: Surface search: Racal Decca; I-band.
Fire control: Signaal WM28/5; I/J-band; range 46 km *(25 n miles)*.

Programmes: Lürssen Werft FPB 45 type. Designated Missile Gunboats (MGB).
Modernisation: *Sea Hawk* was the first to complete refit in January 1988 with two sets of twin Harpoon launchers replacing the triple Gabriel launcher. The remainder were converted by December 1990 with the exception of *Sea Wolf* which finished refit in Spring 1991. ECM equipment has also been fitted on a taller mast. SATCOM and GPS installed. There have also been some superstructure changes. The Bofors 40 mm gun has been replaced with a Matra Simbad SAM launcher. Fitted with four launch pedestals for Gabriel and racks for eight Harpoons, though usual warload will consist of two Gabriel and four harpoons. Retrofitted with MSIS optronic director forward of the mainmast. Expected to pay off as new frigates enter service.
Operational: Form 185 Squadron, part of First Flotilla.

SEA WOLF 5/2004, *David Boey* / 1044511

SEA DRAGON 6/2004, *Singapore Navy* / 1044505

2 RAFAEL PROTECTOR UNMANNED SURFACE VEHICLES (USV)

Displacement, tons: To be announced
Dimensions, feet (metres): 29.5 × ? × ? *(9.0 × ? × ?)*
Main machinery: 1 diesel; 1 waterjet propulsor
Speed, knots: 30+
Guns: 1 Mini-Typhoon stabilised 12.7 mm MG.
Weapons control: Toplite EO sensor pod.

Comment: Developed jointly by Rafael and Aeronautics Defense Systems, Protector was first revealed in June 2003. It is an unmanned patrol craft based on an 9 m Rigid Inflatable Boat (RIB) with composite-materials superstructure that encloses the sensor pod, navigation radar, GPS antenna and gyrostabilised inertial navigation system. Five video channels are used to transmit the outputs from the Toplite and two deck-mounted cameras back to a remote operator. The vessel also carries microphones and loudspeakers, allowing the operator to hail the crew of a suspicious vessel. With an endurance of about eight hours, it can be controlled by line-of-sight communications from ship or shore for various missions such as force protection, anti-terror surveillance and reconnaissance, mine warfare and electronic warfare. An unconfirmed number procured by the Singapore Navy in 2004 to support maritime security and interdiction operations in the Northern Arabian Gulf. They were operated by *RSS Resolution* during a deployment that ended in March 2005. The Singapore Navy also participates in the US Navy's Spartan technology demonstrator programme.

PROTECTOR 5/2005*, *Guy Toremans* / 1127050

AMPHIBIOUS FORCES

Notes: (1) The Tiger 40 hovercraft acquired in 1997 is beyond repair but the design may be used again for a repeat order.
(2) Trials of at least one hovercraft ACVI were reported in early 2005.

ACVI 5/2005*, *Guy Toremans* / 1127051

4 RPL TYPE (LCU)

RPL 60-63

Displacement, tons: 151 standard
Dimensions, feet (metres): 120.4 × 28 × 5.9 *(36.7 × 8.5 × 1.8)*
Main machinery: 2 MAN D2540MLE diesels; 860 hp(m) *(632 kW)*; 2 Schottel props
Speed, knots: 10.7
Complement: 6
Military lift: 2 tanks or 450 troops or 110 tons cargo (fuel or stores)

Comment: First pair built at North Shipyard Point, second pair by Singapore SBEC. First two launched August 1985, next two in October 1985. Cargo deck 86.9 × 21.6 ft *(26.5 × 6.6 m)*. Bow ramp suitable for beaching.

RPL 60 6/2001, *John Mortimer* / 0126301

4 ENDURANCE CLASS (LPDM)

Name	No	Builders	Laid down	Launched	Commissioned
ENDURANCE	207	Singapore Technologies Marine, Banoi	26 Mar 1997	14 Mar 1998	18 Mar 2000
RESOLUTION	208	Singapore Technologies Marine, Banoi	22 Oct 1997	1 Aug 1998	18 Mar 2000
PERSISTENCE	209	Singapore Technologies Marine, Banoi	3 Apr 1998	13 Mar 1999	7 Apr 2001
ENDEAVOUR	210	Singapore Technologies Marine, Banoi	15 Oct 1998	12 Feb 2000	7 Apr 2001

Displacement, tons: 8,500 full load
Dimensions, feet (metres): 462.6 pp × 68.9 × 16.4
  (141 × 21 × 5)
Main machinery: 2 Ruston 16RK 270 diesels; 12,000 hp(m)
  (8.82 MW); 2 shafts; Kamewa cp props; bow thruster
Speed, knots: 15. **Range, n miles:** 10,400 at 12 kt
Complement: 65 (8 officers)
Military lift: 350 troops; 18 tanks; 20 vehicles; 4 LCVP

Missiles: SAM: 2 Matra Simbad twin launchers for Mistral ❶;
  IR homing to 4 km *(2.2 n miles)*; warhead 3 kg. 2 Barak
  octuple launchers may be fitted in due course.
Guns: 1 Otobreda 76 mm/62 Super Rapid ❷; 120 rds/min to
  16 km *(8.7 n miles)*; weight of shell 6 kg.
  1—25 mm Bushmaster (can be fitted).
  5—12.7 mm MGs.
Countermeasures: Decoys: 2 GEC Marine Shield III 102 mm
  sextuple fixed chaff launcher.
ESM/ECM: Rafael RAN 1101; intercept and jammer.
Weapons control: CS Defense NAJIR 2000 optronic
  director ❸.
Radars: Air/surface search: Elta EL/M-2238 ❹; E/F-band.
Navigation: Kelvin Hughes Type 1007; I-band.

Helicopters: 2 Super Pumas.

Programmes: Ordered in September 1994 and confirmed
  in mid-1996.
Structure: US drive through design with bow and stern
  ramps. Single intermediate deck with three hydraulic
  ramps. Helicopter platform aft. Indal ASIST helo handling
  system. Dockwell for four LCUs and davits for four LCVPs.
  Two 25 ton cranes. Four 36 m self-propelled pontoons
  can be secured to winching points on the ships' sides.
  Protector unmanned surface vehicles were operated
  from *Resolution* in 2005.
Operational: *Endurance* completed the RSN's first round-
  the-world deployment in late 2000. *Resolution* deployed
  in November 2004 as part of coalition forces in northern
  Gulf. Based at Changi. Form 191 Squadron.

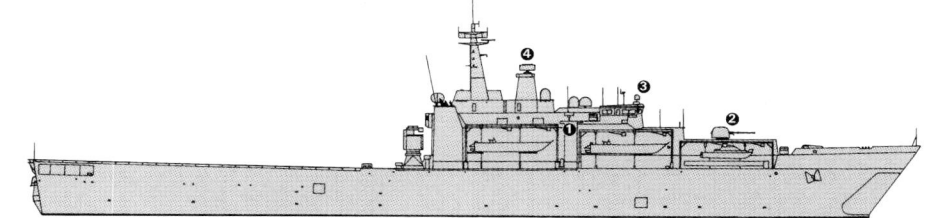
RESOLUTION   *(Scale 1 : 1,200), Ian Sturton* / 1153491

ENDEAVOUR   *5/2004, Chris Sattler* / 1044514

RESOLUTION   *5/2004, David Boey* / 1044513

30 LANDING CRAFT UTILITY (LCU)

300 series

Dimensions, feet (metres): 75.4 × 19.7 × 2.6 *(23 × 6 × 0.8)*
Main machinery: 2 MAN 2842 LZE diesels; 4,400 hp(m) *(3.23 MW)*; 2 Kamewa water-jets
Speed, knots: 20
Range, n miles: 180 at 15 kt
Complement: 4
Military lift: 18 tons
Guns: 2—12.7 mm MGs or 40 mm grenade launchers.

Comment: This is a larger and much faster version of the LCVPs. Being built from 1993.
  Designated Fast Craft Utility (FCU).

LCU 371   *5/2004, John Mortimer* / 1043180

100 LANDING CRAFT (LCVP/FCEP)

Displacement, tons: 4 full load
Dimensions, feet (metres): 44.6 × 12.1 × 2 *(13.6 × 3.7 × 0.6)*
Main machinery: 2 MAN D2866 LE diesels; 816 hp(m) *(600 kW)*; sustained; 2 Hamilton
  362 water-jets
Speed, knots: 20
Range, n miles: 100 at 20 kt
Complement: 3
Military lift: 4 tons or 30 troops

Comment: Fast Craft, Equipment and Personnel (FCEP), built by Singapore SBEC from
  1989 and are used to transport troops around the Singapore archipelago. They have
  a single bow ramp and can carry a rifle platoon. More than 25 are in service and the rest
  in storage. Have numbers in the 500 and 800 series except for those carried in LSTs.

LCVPs   *8/2003, David Boey* / 0567534

10 DIVING SUPPORT CRAFT (YTB)

Comment: Boston Whalers used by the Naval Diving Unit. Armed with 7.62 mm MGs and
  40 mm grenade launchers.

BOSTON WHALER   *8/2000, David Boey* / 0105601

6 FAST INTERCEPT CRAFT (HSIC)

Displacement, tons: 12.5 full load
Dimensions, feet (metres): 47.6 × 9.4 × 4.4 *(14.5 × 2.85 × 1.35)*
Main machinery: Triple Seatek diesels coupled to Trimax drives
Speed, knots: 55+
Guns: 2 CIS 40 mm AGL.
  2 CIS 50 12.7 mm MGs.
  1—7.62 mm GPMG.
Radars: Raytheon SL 72.

Comment: Details are of craft used by Naval Diving Unit. The multistep planing hull design is similar to that in UK service. At least five other planing and wave-piercing craft are reported to be in service with special forces units.

FIC 145   *9/2002, David Boey* / 0554729

450 ASSAULT CRAFT (LCA)

Dimensions, feet (metres): 17.7 × 5.9 × 2.3 *(5.4 × 1.8 × 0.7)*
Main machinery: 1 outboard; 50 hp(m) *(37 kW)*
Speed, knots: 12
Military lift: 12 troops
Guns: 1—7.62 mm MG or 40 mm grenade launcher.

Comment: Built by Singapore SBEC. Man-portable craft which can carry a section of troops in the rivers and creeks surrounding Singapore island. Numbers are approximate.

ASSAULT CRAFT   *9/1995, David Boey* / 0080588

MINE WARFARE FORCES

4 BEDOK (LANDSORT) CLASS (MINEHUNTERS) (MHC)

Name	No	Builders	Launched	Commissioned
BEDOK	M 105	Kockums/Karlskrona	24 June 1993	7 Oct 1995
KALLANG	M 106	Singapore Shipbuilding	29 Jan 1994	7 Oct 1995
KATONG	M 107	Singapore Shipbuilding	8 Apr 1994	7 Oct 1995
PUNGGOL	M 108	Singapore Shipbuilding	16 July 1994	7 Oct 1995

Displacement, tons: 360 full load
Dimensions, feet (metres): 155.8 × 31.5 × 7.5 *(47.5 × 9.6 × 2.3)*
Main machinery: 4 Saab Scania diesels; 1,592 hp(m) *(1.17 MW)*; coupled in pairs to 2 Voith Schneider props
Speed, knots: 15
Range, n miles: 2,000 at 10 kt
Complement: 31 (5 officers)

Guns: 1 Bofors 40 mm/70. 4—12.7 mm MGs.
Mines: 2 rails.
Weapons control: Thomson-CSF TSM 2061 Mk II minehunting and mine disposal system. Signaal WM20 director.
Radars: Navigation: Norcontrol DB 2000; I-band.
Sonars: Thomson-CSF TSM 2022; hull-mounted; minehunting; high frequency.

Programmes: Kockums/Karlskrona design ordered in February 1991. *Bedok* started trials in Sweden in December 1993, and was shipped to Singapore in early 1994 to complete. Prefabrication work done for the other three in Sweden with assembly and fitting out in Singapore at Benoi Basin.
Structure: GRP hulls. Two PAP 104 Mk V ROVs embarked. Racal Precision Navigation system. Two sets of Swedish SAM minesweeping system. Magnavox GPS.
Operational: Form 194 Squadron, based at Tuas.

PUNGGOL   *4/2004*, John Mortimer* / 1133564

BEDOK   *2/2005*, Chris Sattler* / 1133563

AUXILIARIES

Notes: (1) There is one Floating Dock with a lift of 600 tons. *FD 2* at Changi.
(2) A 2,700 ton oil rig supply ship MV *Kendrick*, built in Poland in 1985, is chartered to support submarine rescue operations. Additional roles include acting as a target ship for submarine torpedo firings and torpedo recovery.
(3) MV *Avatar*, a Ro-Ro vessel, is leased to support submarine rescue operations. It has an orange hull and white superstructure.

KENDRICK   *5/2004, David Boey* / 1044517

POLICE COAST GUARD

12 SHARK CLASS (WPB)

HAMMERHEAD SHARK (ex-*Swift Archer*)	PH 50 (ex-P 16)
MAKO SHARK (ex-*Swift Lancer*)	PH 51 (ex-P 12)
WHITE SHARK (ex-*Swift Swordsman*)	PH 52 (ex-P 14)
BLUE SHARK (ex-*Swift Combatant*)	PH 53 (ex-P 18)
TIGER SHARK (ex-*Swift Knight*)	PH 54 (ex-P 11)
BASKING SHARK (ex-*Swift Warrior*)	PH 55 (ex-P 15)
SANDBAR SHARK (ex-*Swift Chieftain*)	PH 56 (ex-P 23)
THRESHER SHARK (ex-*Swift Conqueror*)	PH 57 (ex-P 21)
WHITETIP SHARK (ex-*Swift Warlord*)	PH 58 (ex-P 17)
BLACKTIP SHARK (ex-*Swift Challenger*)	PH 59 (ex-P 19)
GOBLIN SHARK (ex-*Swift Cavalier*)	PH 60 (ex-P 20)
SCHOOL SHARK (ex-*Swift Centurion*)	PH 61 (ex-P 22)

Displacement, tons: 45.7 full load
Dimensions, feet (metres): 74.5 × 20.3 × 5.2 *(22.7 × 6.2 × 1.6)*
Main machinery: 2 Deutz BA16M816 diesels; 2,680 hp(m) *(1.96 MW)* sustained; 2 shafts
Speed, knots: 32
Range, n miles: 550 at 20 kt; 900 at 10 kt
Complement: 15
Guns: 1 Oerlikon 20 mm GAM-BO1. 2 CIS 90 12.7 mm MGs.
Radars: Surface search: Decca 1226; I-band.

Comment: Built by Singapore SBEC and all completed 20 October 1981 for the Navy. First four transferred from the Navy on 15 February 1993, second four on 8 April 1994, last four on 7 November 1996. All to be fitted with ARPA radar in due course. Employed on territorial waters patrol.

HAMMERHEAD SHARK   *4/2004, Bob Fildes* / 1044518

2 COMMAND CRAFT (WPB)

MANTA RAY PT 20   **EAGLE RAY** PT 30

Dimensions, feet (metres): 65.6 × 19.7 × 3.3 *(20.0 × 6.0 × 1.0)*
Main machinery: 2 MTU 16V 2000 M90 diesels; 2 Hamilton 521 water-jets
Speed, knots: 30
Complement: 5
Guns: 2 — 7.62 mm MGs.

Comment: Built by Asia-Pacific Geraldton, Singapore to a Geraldton, Australia design. These command craft are larger versions of the 18 m patrol craft.

MANTA RAY   *4/2002, David Boey* / 0554731

25 PATROL CRAFT (WPB)

PT 21-29   **PT 31-39**   **PT 61-67**

Dimensions, feet (metres): 59.1 × 17.7 × 3 *(18 × 5.4 × 0.9)*
Main machinery: 2 MTU 16V 2000M 90 diesels; 2 Hamilton 521 waterjets
Speed, knots: 40
Complement: 5
Guns: 2 — 7.62 mm MGs.

Comment: 18 patrol craft built by Geraldton Boats, Australia in 1999. A further seven patrol craft delivered late 2000.

PT 39   *3/2004, Bob Fildes* / 1044516

19 PATROL CRAFT (WPB)

PT 1-19

Displacement, tons: 20 full load
Dimensions, feet (metres): 47.6 × 13.8 × 3.9 *(14.5 × 4.2 × 1.2)*
Main machinery: 2 MAN D2542MLE diesels; 1,076 hp(m) *(791 kW)*; or MTU 12V 183 TC91 diesels; 1,200 hp(m) *(882 kW)* maximum; 2 shafts
Speed, knots: 30
Range, n miles: 310 at 22 kt
Complement: 4 plus 8 spare berths
Guns: 1 — 7.62 mm MG.
Radars: Surface search: Furuno or Racal Decca Bridgemaster; I-band.

Comment: First 13 completed by Singapore SBEC between January and August 1984, two more completed February 1987 and eight more (including two Command Boats) in 1989. Of aluminium construction. Four are operated by Customs and Excise. There are differences in the deckhouses between earlier and later vessels. Employed on patrol duties in southern territorial waters.

PT 18   *4/2004, Bob Fildes* / 1044520

11 INTERCEPTOR CRAFT (PBF)

SAILFISH PK 10   **STRIPED MARLIN** PK 23   **BILLFISH** PK 30
SPEARFISH PK 20   **BLACK MARLIN** PK 24   **SWORDFISH** PK 40
WHITE MARLIN PK 21   **BLUE MARLIN** PK 25   **SPIKEFISH** PK 50
SILVER MARLIN PK 22   **JUMPING MARLIN** PK 26

Dimensions, feet (metres): 42 × 10.5 × 1.6 *(12.8 × 3.2 × 0.5)*
Main machinery: 3 Mercuiser 502 Magnum diesels; 3 shafts
Speed, knots: 50
Complement: 5
Guns: 1 — 7.62 mm MG.

Comment: First five built locally and delivered in 1995. Colours have been changed to dark blue hulls and grey superstructures, to make the craft less visible at sea. Six more ordered from Pro Marine/North Shipyard in 1999 to a slightly different design, with twin outboard motors.

SWORDFISH   *4/2002, David Boey* / 0554733

WHITE MARLIN   *1/2000, David Boey* / 0105606

32 FAST RESPONSE CRAFT (PBF)

PC 201- 232

Dimensions, feet (metres): 37.7 × 10.8 × 1.6 *(11.5 × 3.3 × 0.5)*
Main machinery: 3 Mercury outboard motors; 750 hp *(560 kW)*
Speed, knots: 40

Comment: Order placed August 2000 with Asia Pac Geraldton for 20 craft delivered in 2002. A further twelve craft were later added.

PC 209   *4/2002, David Boey* / 0554734

HARBOUR CRAFT

Comment: There are large numbers of harbour craft, many of them armed, with PC numbers. These include four RHIBs with Yamaha 200 hp outboards capable of 43 kt, and with pennant numbers PJ 1-4.

RHIB   *9/2002, David Boey* / 1044506

CUSTOMS

Notes: Customs Craft include CE 1-4 and CE 5-8, the latter being sisters to PT 1 Police Craft.

CE 8
10/2002, Mick Prendergast
0533877

Slovenia

Country Overview

Formerly a constituent republic of Yugoslavia, the Republic of Slovenia proclaimed its independence in 1991. Situated in south-eastern Europe, it is bordered to the north by Austria and Hungary, to the south by Croatia and to the west by Italy. With an area of 7,820 square miles, it has a short 25 n mile coastline with the Adriatic Sea on which the port of Koper is located. The capital and largest city is Ljubljana. Territorial waters (12 n miles) are claimed.

Headquarters Appointments

Chief of General Staff:
  Major General Ladislav Lipič
Chief of Naval Section, Forces Command:
  Lieutenant Ludvik Kožar
Chief of Navy Detachment:
  Commander Ivan Žnidar

General

Navy formed in January 1993.

Personnel

2006: 61

Bases

Ankaran (Slovenski Mornarji)

PATROL FORCES

1 SUPER DVORA MK II (PBF)

Name	No	Builders	Commissioned
ANKARAN	HPL 21	IAI Ramta	Aug 1996

Displacement, tons: 58 full load
Dimensions, feet (metres): 82 × 18.4 × 3.6 *(25 × 5.6 × 1.1)*
Main machinery: 2 MTU 12V 396 TE94 diesels; 4,570 hp(m) *(3.36 MW)*; 2 ASD 15 surface drives
Speed, knots: 45
Range, n miles: 700 at 30 kt
Complement: 10 (5 officers)
Guns: 2 Oerlikon 20 mm; 2 — 7.62 mm MGs.
Weapons control: Elop MSIS optronic director.
Radars: Surface search: Raytheon; I-band.

Comment: First one delivered in August 1996 at Isola base. Plans for a second craft have been cancelled.

ANKARAN
6/1999, Slovenian Navy / 0080597

POLICE

Notes: In addition there is a 40 kt cabin cruiser *Sinji Galeb* (P 101) and two RIBs.

1 HARBOUR PATROL CRAFT (PBF)

Name	No	Builders	Commissioned
LADSE	P 111	Aviotechnica	21 June 1995

Displacement, tons: 44 full load
Dimensions, feet (metres): 65.3 × 16.4 × 3 *(19.9 × 5 × 0.9)*
Main machinery: 2 MTU 8V 396 TE84 diesels; 2,400 hp(m) *(1.76 MW)*; 2 shafts
Speed, knots: 40
Range, n miles: 270 at 38 kt
Complement: 10
Guns: 1 — 7.62 mm MG.
Radars: Surface search: I-band.

Comment: Acquired from Italy in 1995.

LADSE
10/1997 / 0080598

Solomon Islands

Country Overview

Formerly a British protectorate, the Solomon Islands gained independence in 1978. Its head of state is the British sovereign, who is represented by a Governor-General. Situated in the southwest Pacific Ocean, east of New Guinea, the country comprises more than 35 islands and numerous atolls which extend some 650 n miles from east to west and includes most of the Solomon Islands group. The six main islands are: Guadalcanal, Malaita, New Georgia, San Cristobal (now Makira), Santa Isabel and Choiseul. Vella Lavella, Ontong Java, Rennell, Bellona and the Santa Cruz islands are also part of the group, together with the Florida, Russell, Reef and Duff island groups. Honiara, on Guadalcanal, is the capital and principal port.

An archipelagic state, territorial seas (12 n miles) are claimed. An Exclusive Economic Zone (EEZ) (200 n miles) is also claimed but limits have not been fully defined by boundary agreements. Patrol boats are operated by the National Surveillance and Reconnaissance Force (NSRF).

Headquarters Appointments

Director of Maritime forces:
  Chief Superintendent Eddie Tokuru

Bases

Honiara (HQ NSRF)

Personnel

2006: 60 (14 officers)

Prefix to Ships' Names

RSIPV

DELETIONS

2000   *Tulagi*

POLICE

2 PACIFIC CLASS (LARGE PATROL CRAFT) (PB)

Name	No	Builders	Commissioned
LATA	03	Australian Shipbuilding Industries	3 Sep 1988
AUKI	04	Australian Shipbuilding Industries	2 Nov 1991

Displacement, tons: 162 full load
Dimensions, feet (metres): 103.3 × 26.6 × 7.5 *(31.5 × 8.1 × 2.3)*
Main machinery: 2 Caterpillar 3516TA diesels; 4,400 hp *(3.28 MW)* sustained; 2 shafts
Speed, knots: 20. **Range, n miles:** 2,230 at 12 kt
Complement: 14 (1 officer)
Guns: 3—12.7 mm MGs.
Radars: Surface search: Furuno 8100-D; I-band.

Comment: Built under the Australian Defence Co-operation Programme. Training, operational and technical assistance provided by the Royal Australian Navy. Aluminium construction. Nominal endurance of 10 days. The Australian government has extended the Pacific Patrol Boat programme but, following suspension of most of support of the Solomon Islands' craft in 2001, an overdue half-life refit was not completed for *Auki* until 2002. Life-extension refits for *Lata* and *Auki* are due at Townsville in 2005 and 2009 respectively.

AUKI   *8/2004, Chris Sattler* / 0589807

1 INSHORE PATROL CRAFT (PBR)

JACKPOT

Comment: Details are not known.

South Africa

Country Overview

The Republic of South Africa is bordered to the north by Namibia, Botswana, Zimbabwe, Mozambique and Swaziland. With an area of 472,731 square miles, it has a 1,512 n mile coastline with the south Atlantic and Indian Oceans. South Africa also has sovereignty over the Prince Edward Islands which lie some 950 n miles south-east of Port Elizabeth. The independent country of Lesotho forms an enclave in the eastern part of the country. The administrative capital of South Africa is Pretoria and the judicial capital is Bloemfontein. Cape Town is the legislative capital, largest city and a prominent port. There are further ports at Mossel Bay, Port Elizabeth, East London, Durban, Saldanha, and Richards Bay. Territorial seas (12 n miles) are claimed. It also claims a 200 n mile EEZ but its limits have not been fully defined.

Headquarters Appointments

Chief of the Navy:
  Vice Admiral Rifiloe J Mudimu
Chief of Naval Staff:
  Rear Admiral M Magalefa
Flag Officer Fleet:
  Rear Admiral H V E Bester

Diplomatic Representation

Naval Attaché in Washington:
  Captain D J Christian
Defence and Naval Attaché in Paris:
  Captain L O Reeders
Armed Forces Attaché in Buenos Aires:
  Captain L Van Dyk
Defence Attaché in Berlin:
  Captain R R Goveia

Personnel

(a) 2006: 4,728 naval
(b) 2,266 (Public Service Act Personnel)

Prefix to Ships' Names

SAS (South African Ship)

Bases

Simon's Town (main); Durban (naval station).
Saldanha Bay (ratings' training), Gordon's Bay (officer training).

DELETIONS

Submarines

2003   *Umkhonto, Assegaai*

Patrol Forces

2004   *Adam Kok, Job Maseko*

Auxiliaries

2003   *Fleur*, 6 Delta class
2004   *Outeniqua*

SUBMARINES

1 + 2 209 CLASS (TYPE 1400MOD (SA)) (SSK)

Name	No	Builders	Laid down	Launched	Commissioned
MANTHATISI	S 101	Howaldswerke, Kiel	22 May 2001	15 June 2004	3 Nov 2005
—	S 102	Thyssen Nordseewerke, Emden	12 Nov 2003	4 May 2005	Sep 2006
—	—	Thyssen Nordseewerke, Emden	Nov 2004	2006	Sep 2007

Displacement, tons: 1,454 surfaced; 1,594 dived
Dimensions, feet (metres): 201.5 × 24.7 × 18.8
  (62 × 7.6 × 5.8)
Main machinery: Diesel electric: 4 MTU 12V 396 diesels; 3,800 hp(m) *(2.8 MW)*; 4 alternators; 1 Siemens motor; 5,032 hp(m) *(3.7 MW)*; 1 shaft
Speed, knots: 10 surfaced; 21.5 dived
Complement: 30
Torpedoes: 8—21 in *(533 mm)* bow tubes. 14 torpedoes.
Countermeasures: ESM: Grintek Avitronics; intercept.
Weapons control: STN Atlas ISUS 90 TFCS.
Radars: Surface search: I-band.
Sonars: STN Atlas CSU-90; hull mounted and flank arrays.

Programmes: Being acquired from the German Submarine Consortium. Final approval given on 15 September 1999. Contract signed on 7 July 2000. *Manthatisi* arrived at Simon's Town on 7 April 2006. The second and third boats are being built by TNSW and will follow at 12 month intervals.
Structure: Diving depth 250 m *(820 ft)*. Zeiss non-hull penetrating optronic mast.

S 101   *2/2005*, Michael Nitz* / 1127053

MANTHATISI   *2/2005*, Michael Nitz* / 1127052

FRIGATES

1 + 3 VALOUR CLASS (MEKO A-200 SAN) (FFGHM)

Name	No	Builders	Laid down	Launched	Commissioned
AMATOLA	F 145	Blohm + Voss, Hamburg	2 Aug 2001	6 June 2002	25 Sep 2003
ISANDLWANA	F 146	Howaldswerke, Kiel	26 Oct 2001	5 Dec 2002	19 Dec 2003
SPIOENKOP	F 147	Blohm + Voss, Hamburg	28 Feb 2002	6 June 2003	15 Mar 2004
MENDI	F 148	Howaldswerke, Kiel	28 June 2002	15 June 2004	2005

Displacement, tons: 3,590 full load
Dimensions, feet (metres): 397 × 53.8 × 20.3
(121 × 16.4 × 6.2)
Main machinery: CODAG; 1 GE LM 2500 gas turbine
26,820 hp(m) *(20 MW)*; 2 MTU 16V 1163 TB93 diesels
16,102 hp(m) *(11.84 MW)*; 2 shafts; LIPS cp props; 1 LIPS
LJ210E waterjet (centreline)
Speed, knots: 28. **Range, n miles:** 7,700 at 15 kt
Complement: 117 plus 25 spare

Missiles: SSM: 8 Exocet MM 40 Block 2 ❶.
SAM: Denel Umkhonto 32 cell VLS ❷ inertial guidance
with mid-course guidance and IR homing to 12 km
(6.5 n miles) at 2.4 Mach; warhead 23 kg.
Guns: 1 Otobreda 76 mm/62 compact ❸.
2 LIW DPG 35 mm (twin) ❹. 2 Oerlikon 20 mm Mk 1.
Torpedoes: 4—324 mm tubes (2 twin) ❺. 2 Reutech 12.7 mm
MGs.
Countermeasures: Decoys: 2 Super Barricade chaff
launchers ❻.
ESM/ECM: intercept and jammer.
Combat data systems: ADS CMS.
Weapons control: 2 Reutech RTS 6400 optronic trackers.
Radars: Air/surface search: Thales MRR ❼ 3D; G-band.
Fire control: 2 Reutech RTS 6400 ❽; I/J-band.
Navigation/Helicopter control: 2 Racal Bridgemaster E ❾;
I-band.
Sonars: Thomson Marconi 4132 Kingklip; hull mounted,
active search; medium frequency.

Helicopters: 1 Super Lynx ❿ in due course.

Programmes: Contract for four ships, with option for one
further, signed on 3 December 1999 with ESACC which
includes Blohm + Voss, HDW, TRT, African Defence
Systems and Thomson-CSF. Contract effective 28 April
2000. *Amatola* arrived at Simon's Town on 4 November
2003 for weapon systems integration by African Defence
Systems. Sea acceptance trials began in October 2004
and she is expected to become fully operational in early
2006. The others are to follow at six month intervals.
There is an option for a fifth ship.
Modernisation: Exocet MM 40 Block 2 to be replaced by
Block 3 missiles.
Operational: Westland Super Lynx helicopters selected, but
not ordered at the same time as the ships.

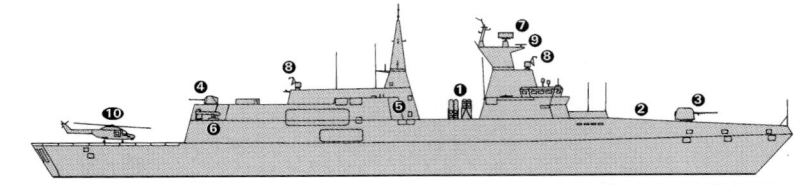

VALOUR CLASS   *(Scale 1 : 1,200), Ian Sturton* / 1044524

SPIOENKOP   *3/2004, Michael Nitz* / 1044526

SPIOENKOP   *5/2004, Robert Pabst* / 1044528

ISANDLWANA   *9/2004, Guy Toremans* / 1044527

PATROL FORCES

Notes: It is planned to replace the current patrol craft inventory with up to ten 60-75 m multipurpose craft.

3 WARRIOR (EX-MINISTER) CLASS (FAST ATTACK CRAFT—MISSILE) (PGG)

Name	No	Builders	Commissioned
ISAAC DYOBHA (ex-*Frans Erasmus*)	P 1565	Sandock Austral, Durban	27 July 1979
GALESHEWE (ex-*Hendrik Mentz*)	P 1567	Sandock Austral, Durban	11 Feb 1983
MAKHANDA (ex-*Magnus Malan*)	P 1569	Sandock Austral, Durban	4 July 1986

Displacement, tons: 430 full load
Dimensions, feet (metres): 204 × 25 × 8
(62.2 × 7.8 × 2.4)
Main machinery: 4 Maybach MTU 16V 965 TB91 diesels; 15,000 hp(m) *(11 MW)* sustained; 4 shafts
Speed, knots: 32
Range, n miles: 1,500 at 30 kt; 3,600+ at economical speed
Complement: 52 (7 officers)

Missiles: SSM: 6 Skerpioen; active radar or optical guidance; semi-active radar homing to 36 km *(19.4 n miles)* at 0.7 Mach; warhead 75 kg. Another pair may be mounted. Skerpioen is an Israeli Gabriel II built under licence in South Africa.
Guns: 1 (P 1567 and 1569) or 2 (P 1565) OTO Melara 3 in *(76 mm)*/62 compact; 85 rds/min to 16 km *(8.7 n miles)*; weight of shell 6 kg; 500 rounds per gun.

2 LIW Vektor 35 mm (twin); 550 rds/min; may replace one 76 mm gun in one craft for trials.
2 LIW Mk 1 20 mm. 2—12.7 mm MGs.
Countermeasures: Decoys: 4 ACDS launchers for chaff.
ESM: Delcon (ADS/Sysdel) EW system.
ECM: Elta Rattler; jammer.
Combat data systems: Air/surface search: ADS Diamant (after upgrade). Mini action data automation with Link.
Radars: Elta EL/M 2208; E/F-band.
Fire control: Selenia RTN 10X; I/J-band.

Programmes: Contract signed with Israel in late 1974 for this class, similar to Saar 4 class. Three built in Haifa and reached South Africa in July 1978. The ninth craft launched late March 1986. Three more improved vessels of this class were ordered but subsequently cancelled.

The last of the class was finally christened in March 1992. Pennant numbers restored to the ships side and stern in 1994.
Modernisation: Ship life extension programme included a new communications refit, improvements to EW sensors, a third-generation target designation assembly, a computer-assisted action information system served by datalinks, improvements to fire control, a complete overhaul of the Skerpioen missiles, and a new engine room monitoring system. P 1565 completed upgrade in April 1999, P 1567 in March 2000 and P 1569 in mid-2000.
Operational: All are based at Simon's Town. Likely to be decommissioned by 2008.

MAKHANDA *9/2004, Guy Toremans* / 1044529

24 NAMACURRA CLASS (INSHORE PATROL CRAFT) (PB)

Y 1502-1505 Y 1508-1509 Y 1511-1519 Y 1521-1529

Displacement, tons: 5 full load
Dimensions, feet (metres): 29.5 × 9 × 2.8 *(9 × 2.7 × 0.8)*
Main machinery: 2 Yamaha outboards; 380 hp(m) *(279 kW)*
Speed, knots: 32
Range, n miles: 180 at 20 kt
Complement: 4
Guns: 1—12.7 mm MG. 2—7.62 mm MGs.
Depth charges: 1 rack.
Radars: Surface search: Furuno; I-band.

Comment: Built in South Africa in 1980-81. Can be transported by road. Y 1520 transferred to Malawi in October 1988 and Y 1506 has sunk at sea. Y 1501 and Y 1510 donated to Namibia on 29 November 2002 and Y 1507 and Y 1530 donated to Mozambique in 2004.

NAMACURRA *8/2001, van Ginderen Collection* / 0132784

3 T CRAFT CLASS (PB)

Name	No	Builders	Commissioned
TOBIE	P 1552	T Craft International, Cape Town	18 July 2003
TERN	P 1553	T Craft International, Cape Town	18 July 2003
TEKWANE	P 1554	T Craft International, Cape Town	22 July 2003

Displacement, tons: 36 full load
Dimensions, feet (metres): 72.2 × 23 × 3 *(22 × 7 × 0.9)*
Main machinery: 2 ADE 444TI 12V diesels; 2,000 hp *(1.5 MW)*; 2 Hamilton waterjets
Speed, knots: 32. **Range, n miles:** 530 at 22 kt
Complement: 16 (1 officer)
Guns: 1—12.7 mm MG.
Weapons control: Hesis optical director.
Radars: Surface search: Racal Decca; I-band.

Comment: Twin hulled catamarans of GRP sandwich construction. Capable of carrying up to 15 people. Originally ordered in mid-1991 but not fully commissioned until 2003. Carries an RIB in the stern well. Three of this type built for Israel in 1997. Two based at Simon's Town and one at Durban.

NAMACURRA *8/2001, van Ginderen Collection* / 0132783

TOBIE *9/2004*, M Declerck* / 1133141

MINE WARFARE FORCES

Notes: Mine countermeasures capability is likely to be replaced by autonomous underwater vehicles rather than by specialist ships.

4 RIVER CLASS (COASTAL MINEHUNTERS) (MHC)

Name	No	Builders	Commissioned
UMKOMAAS (ex-*Navors I*)	M 1499	Abeking & Rasmussen/Sandock Austral	13 Jan 1981
UMGENI (ex-*Navors II*)	M 1213	Abeking & Rasmussen/Sandock Austral	1 Mar 1981
UMZIMKULU (ex-*Navors III*)	M 1142	Sandock Austral	30 Oct 1981
UMHLOTI (ex-*Navors IV*)	M 1212	Sandock Austral	15 Dec 1981

Displacement, tons: 380 full load
Dimensions, feet (metres): 157.5 × 27.9 × 8.2
(48 × 8.5 × 2.5)
Main machinery: 2 MTU 12V 652 TB81 diesels; 4,515 hp(m)
(3.32 MW); 2 Voith Schneider props
Speed, knots: 16. **Range, n miles:** 2,000 at 13 kt
Complement: 40 (7 officers)
Guns: 1 Oerlikon 20 mm GAM-BO1. 2—12.7 mm MGs.
2—7.62 mm MGs.
Countermeasures: MCM: 2 PAP 104 remote-controlled
submersibles.
Radars: Navigation: Decca; I-band.
Sonars: Klein VDS; side scan; high frequency.

Comment: Ordered in 1978 as Research Vessels to be operated by the Navy for the Department of Transport. The lead ship *Navors I* was shipped to Durban from Germany in the heavy lift ship *Uhenfels* in June 1980 for fitting out, shortly followed by the second. The last pair were built in Durban. The vessels were painted blue with white upperworks and formed the First Research Squadron. Painted grey and renamed in 1982 but continued to fly the national flag and not the naval

UMZIMKULU 9/2004, *Guy Toremans* / 1044532

ensign. The prefix RV was only changed to SAS on 3 February 1988 when they were formally accepted as naval ships. Minehunting capability could be enhanced by substituting the diving container on the after deck

with lightweight mechanical and acoustic sweeping gear. Carry an RIB and a decompression chamber. M1499 refitted in 2002 followed by M1213 in 2003. All to continue in service until about 2010.

2 CITY (LINDAU) CLASS (TYPE 351, TROIKA) (MINESWEEPERS—COASTAL) (MSCD)

Name	No	Builders	Commissioned
KAPA (ex-*Düren*)	M1223 (ex-M1079)	Burmester, Bremen	22 Apr 1959
TEKWINI (ex-*Wolfsburg*)	M1225 (ex-M1082)	Burmester, Bremen	8 Oct 1959

Displacement, tons: 465 full load
Dimensions, feet (metres): 154.5 × 27.2 × 9.2
(47.1 × 8.3 × 2.8)
Main machinery: 2 MTU MD 16V 538 TB90 diesels;
5,000 hp(m) *(3.68 MW)* sustained; 2 shafts
Speed, knots: 16.5
Complement: 44 (4 officers)

Guns: 1 Bofors 40 mm/70; 330 rds/min to 12 km
(6.5 n miles); weight of shell 0.96 kg.
2—12.7 mm MGs.
2—7.62 mm MGs (fitted for).
Radars: Navigation: Kelvin Hughes 14/9 or Atlas Electronik TRS N, or Raytheon SPS-64; I-band.
Sonars: Atlas Electronik DSQS-11; minehunting; high frequency.

Programmes: The contract for the acquisition of six German Type 351 minesweepers was finalised on 10 November 2000. After shipment to South Africa in 2001, *Kapa* (ex-*Düren*) and *Tekwini* (ex-*Wolfsburg*) were recommissioned on 5 September 2001 while *Tshwane* (ex-*Schleswig*) and *Mangaung* (ex-*Paderborn*) were placed in reserve. *Konstanz* (M1081) and *Ulm* (M1083) will be used for spares. The ships are based at Simon's Town and are an interim replacement for the four Ton class minesweepers.

KAPA 11/2002, *Robert Pabst* / 0568862

Modernisation: Converted as guidance ships for Troika between 1981 and 1983. Each can guide three of these unmanned minesweeping vehicles as well as maintaining their moored-mine sweeping capabilities.

Structure: The hull is of wooden construction. Laminated with plastic glue. The engines are of non-magnetic materials.
Operational: Likely to be decommissioned in 2006.

SHIPBORNE AIRCRAFT

Numbers/Type: 4 Agusta-Westland Super Lynx 300.
Operational speed: 120 kt *(222 km/h)*.
Service ceiling: 10,000 ft *(3,048 m)*.
Range: 320 n miles *(593 km)*.
Role/Weapon systems: Ordered on 14 August 2003 for delivery in 2007. Surveillance. Sensors: Telephonics APS-143 B(V)3 radar; ESM: Sea Raven 118; Cumulus Leo Mk II FLIR. Weapons: Unarmed (torpedoes and ASM may be fitted in future upgrades)

ORYX 9/2004*, *M Declerck* / 1133145

LAND-BASED MARITIME AIRCRAFT

Notes: There are also some utility Alouette helicopters.

Numbers/Type: 5 Douglas Turbodaks. (INSHORE PATROL CRAFT) (PB)
Operational speed: 161 kt *(298 km/h)*.
Service ceiling: 24,000 ft *(7,315 m)*.
Range: 1,390 n miles *(2,575 km)*.
Role/Weapon systems: A number of Dakotas has been converted for MR/SAR and other tasks. Additional fuel tanks extend the range to 2,620 n miles *(4,800 km)*. Sensors: Elta M-2022 search radar and FLIR; Sysdel ESM; sonobuoy acoustic processor. Weapons: Unarmed.

SUPER LYNX 6/2003 / 0095707

Numbers/Type: 8 Aerospatiale SA 330E/H/J Oryx.
Operational speed: 139 kt *(258 km/h)*.
Service ceiling: 15,750 ft *(4,800 m)*.
Range: 297 n miles *(550 km)*.
Role/Weapon systems: Support helicopter; allocated by SAAF for naval duties and can be embarked in *Drakensberg*, *Outeniqua* and *Agulhas*. Sensors: Doppler navigation with search radar. Weapons: Unarmed but can mount Armscor 30 mm Rattler.

DOUGLAS DC-3 6/2003, *South African Navy* / 0568890

SURVEY AND RESEARCH SHIPS

Notes: (1) As well as *S A Agulhas*, the Department of Environmental Affairs has three research vessels: *Africana* of 2,471 grt, *Algoa* of 760 grt and *Sardinops* of 255 grt. These ships are operated by Smit Pentow Marine. There are also three fishery protection vessels: *Patella*, *Pelagus* and *Jasus*. A contract was signed in 2003 with Damen Shipyards, Gorinchem for the construction of one offshore and three inshore Fishery and Environmental Protection vessels. *Sarah Baartman* is an 83 m offshore patrol vessel whose design is based on the Dutch fishery patrol vessel *Barend Biesheuve*. Built at Damen Shipyards, Okean (Ukraine) and outfitted at Royal Schelde Yard, Vlissingen, delivery was made in June 2004. *Lilian Ngoyi*, *Ruth First* and *Victoria Mxenge* are three 47 m inshore patrol vessels whose design is based on the Damen Stan Patrol 4207 in service with UK Customs. Built by Farocean Marine, Cape Town, deliveries were made in November 2004, February 2005 and May 2005 respectively.
(2) Two survey launches, *Malgas* and *Seemeeu* are carried by *Protea*.
(3) A 50 m trawler, *Eagle Star*, is used as a training ship for the Department of Environmental Affairs.

SARAH BAARTMAN   *1/2005, Robert Pabst* / 1043178

PELAGUS   *3/2005*, W Clements* / 1133142

1 HECLA CLASS (AGSH)

Name	No	Builders	Commissioned
PROTEA	A 324	Yarrow (Shipbuilders) Ltd	23 May 1972

Displacement, tons: 2,733 full load
Dimensions, feet (metres): 260.1 × 49.1 × 15.6 *(79.3 × 15 × 4.7)*
Main machinery: Diesel-electric; 3 MTU diesels; 3,840 hp *(2.68 MW)* sustained; 3 generators; 1 motor; 2,000 hp *(1.49 MW)*; 1 shaft; cp prop; bow thruster
Speed, knots: 14. **Range, n miles:** 12,000 at 11 kt
Complement: 124 (10 officers)
Radars: Navigation: Racal Decca; I-band.
Helicopters: 1 Alouette III.

Comment: Laid down 20 July 1970. Launched 14 July 1971. Equipped for hydrographic survey with limited facilities for the collection of oceanographical data and for this purpose fitted with special communications equipment, Polaris survey system, survey launches *Malgas* and *Seemeeu* and facilities for helicopter operations. Hull strengthened for navigation in ice and fitted with a passive roll stabilisation system. New engines and full overhaul in 1995-96. Carries EGNG sidescan sonar and two survey boats. Fitted for two 20 mm guns.

PROTEA   *5/2004, Robert Pabst* / 1044531

1 ANTARCTIC SURVEY AND SUPPLY VESSEL (AGOBH)

Name	Builders	Launched	Commissioned
S A AGULHAS	Mitsubishi, Shimonoseki	30 Sep 1977	31 Jan 1978

Measurement, tons: 5,353 gross
Dimensions, feet (metres): 358.3 × 59 × 19 *(109.2 × 18 × 5.8)*
Main machinery: 2 Mirrlees-Blackstone K6 major diesels; 6,600 hp *(4.49 MW)*; 1 shaft; bow and stern thrusters
Speed, knots: 14
Range, n miles: 8,200 at 14 kt
Complement: 40 plus 92 spare berths
Radars: Navigation: Racal Decca; I-band.
Helicopters: 2 SA 330J Puma.

Comment: Red hull and white superstructure. A Department of Environmental Affairs vessel, civilian manned and operated by Smit Pentow Marine. Major refit March to October 1992; 25 ton crane moved forward, transverse thrusters and roll damping fitted, improved navigation and communications equipment. A hinged hatch has been fitted at the stern to recover towed equipment.

S A AGULHAS   *8/2001, Robert Pabst* / 0121399

AUXILIARIES

Notes: (1) It is planned to replace *Drakensberg* in about 2017.
(2) It is planned to acquire two landing platforms capable of deploying and supporting joint forces. They would also have a disaster-relief role.

6 LIMA CLASS (LCU)

Displacement, tons: 7.3 full load
Dimensions, feet (metres): 29.8 × 11.6 × 2.3 *(9.1 × 3.55 × 0.7)*
Main machinery: 2 outboards; 400 hp *(298 kW)*
Speed, knots: 38
Range, n miles: 120 at 26 kt
Complement: 3

Comment: Built in 2003 by Stingray Marine, Cape Town. GRP construction. Capable of carrying 24 troops or 2.5 tons of cargo. Two craft can be carried in *Drakensberg*.

L 27
8/2003, Helmoed-Römer Heitman
0530510

For details of the latest updates to *Jane's Fighting Ships* online and to discover the additional information available exclusively to online subscribers please visit
jfs.janes.com

1 FLEET REPLENISHMENT SHIP (AORH)

Name	No	Builders	Launched	Commissioned
DRAKENSBERG	A 301	Sandock Austral, Durban	24 Apr 1986	11 Nov 1987

Displacement, tons: 6,000 light; 12,500 full load
Dimensions, feet (metres): 482.3 × 64 × 25.9
  (147 × 19.5 × 7.9)
Main machinery: 2 diesels; 16,320 hp(m) *(12 MW)*; 1 shaft;
  cp prop; bow thruster
Speed, knots: 20+
Range, n miles: 8,000 at 15 kt
Complement: 96 (10 officers) plus 10 aircrew plus 22 spare
Cargo capacity: 5,500 tons fuel; 750 tons ammunition and
  dry stores; 2 Lima LCUs
Guns: 4 Oerlikon 20 mm GAM-BO1. 8—12.7 mm MGs.
Helicopters: 2 SA 330H/J Oryx.

Comment: The largest ship built in South Africa and the first
  naval vessel to be completely designed in that country.
  In addition to her replenishment role she is employed
  on SAR, patrol and surveillance with a considerable
  potential for disaster relief. As well as LCUs carries
  two diving support boats and two RIBs. Two abeam
  positions and astern fuelling, jackstay and vertrep. Two
  helicopter landing spots, one forward and one astern.
  Main secondary role is the transport of consumables,
  but can also be used to support small craft and transport
  a limited number of troops.

DRAKENSBURG   *2/2004*, *Robert Pabst* / 1133144

DRAKENSBURG   *6/2005*, *Michael Winter* / 1133143

TUGS

Notes: There is also a harbour tug *De Neys*.

1 COASTAL TUG (YTB)

DE MIST

Displacement, tons: 275 full load
Dimensions, feet (metres): 112.5 × 25.6 × 11.1
  (34.3 × 7.8 × 3.4)
Main machinery: 2 Mirlees-Blackstone diesels; 2,440 hp
  (1.82 MW); 2 Voith-Schneider props
Speed, knots: 12
Complement: 11

Comment: Completed by Dorbyl Long, Durban on
  23 December 1978.

DE MIST
9/2004, Guy Toremans
1044534

1 COASTAL TUG (YTB)

UMALUSI (ex-*Golden Energy*)

Displacement, tons: 315 full load
Dimensions, feet (metres): 98.5 × 32.8 × 17.1
  (30 × 10 × 5.2)
Main machinery: 2 Caterpillar V6 diesels
Speed, knots: 10
Complement: 10

Comment: Completed in 1995 by Jaya Holding Ltd. Acquired
  from Taikong Trading Company in January 1997.

UMALUSI
5/2004, Robert Pabst
1044533

Spain
ARMADA ESPAÑOLA

Country Overview

The Kingdom of Spain is a constitutional monarchy that occupies the greater part of the Iberian Peninsula in southwest Europe. It is bordered to the north by France and Andorra and to the west by Portugal. It has a 2,678 n mile coastline with the Atlantic Ocean and Mediterranean Sea. With a total area of 194,897 square miles, the country comprises the mainland, the Balearic Islands in the Mediterranean and the Canary Islands in the Atlantic Ocean. There are also two small exclaves in Morocco, Ceuta and Melilla and three island groups near the Moroccan coast, Peñón de Vélez de la Gomera, the Alhucemas and the Chafarinas. The British dependency of Gibraltar is situated at the southern extremity of Spain. Madrid is the capital and largest city while Barcelona, Algeciras, Valencia and Bilbao are the principal ports. Territorial seas (12 n miles) and an EEZ (200 n miles) are claimed.

Headquarters Appointments

Chief of the Naval Staff:
    Admiral Sebastián Zaragoza Soto
Second Chief of the Naval Staff:
    Admiral Fernando Armada Vadillo
Chief of Fleet Support:
    Admiral Miguel Ángel Beltrán Bengoechea
Chief of Naval Personnel:
    Admiral Rafael Lapique Dobarro

Commands

Commander-in-Chief of the Fleet (ALFLOT):
    Admiral Ángel Manuel Tello Valero
Commander-in-Chief, Maritime Action (ALMART):
    Admiral Mario Rafael Sánchez-Barriga Fernández
Commander, Spanish Maritime Forces (SPMARFOR):
    Vice Admiral José Antonio Martinez Sainz-Rozas
Commander, Logistic Support (Cartagena):
    Vice Admiral Manuel Otero Penelas
Commander, Logistic Support (Cadiz):
    Vice Admiral Francisco Cañete Muñoz
Commander, Logistic Support (Ferrol):
    Vice Admiral Juan Serón Martínez
Commander-in-Chief, Canary Islands Zone:
    Vice Admiral Emilio José Nieto Manso
Marines General Commander:
    Major General Juan García Lizana
Commander, Fleet Task Group (COMGRUFLOT):
    Rear Admiral José Francisco Palomino Ulla
Commander, Northern Forces (ALFNOR):
    Vice Admiral Tomás Bolívar Piñero
Commander, Straits Forces (ALFUEST):
    Rear Admiral Juan José Ollero Marín

Diplomatic Representation

Naval Attaché in Brasilia:
    Captain Francisco Avilés Beriguistain
Naval Attaché in Lisbon:
    Captain Juan Pablo Estrada Madariaga
Naval Attaché in London and Dublin:
    Captain José Joaquín Crespo Páramo
Naval Attaché in Paris:
    Commander Luis Fernando Serrano Huici
Naval Attaché in Rabat:
    Commander Manuel Caridad Villaverde
Naval Attaché in Rome:
    Commander Antonio González Llanos López
Naval Attaché in Santiago, Lima and La Paz:
    Captain Antonio Manuel Pérez Fernández
Naval Attaché in Washington:
    Captain Juan Carlos San Martín Naya
Naval Attaché in Oslo, Stockholm and Helsinki:
    Captain Ricardo Galán Moreno
Naval Attaché in Bangkok, Manila and Singapore:
    Captain José Manuel Verdugo Páez

Diplomatic Representation—*continued*

Naval Attaché in Pretoria:
    Colonel (Marines) Juan Ángel López Díaz
Naval Attaché in Athens:
    Captain Angel Cabrera Juega
Naval Attaché in Kuala Lumpur:
    Captain Felipe Juste Pérez

Personnel

2006: Navy: 20,000 (3,101 officers)
Marines: 4,553 (456 officers)

Bases

Naval Zones are being re-organised into a single Area. Headquarters are to be in Cartagena with subordinate commands in Ferrol, Cádiz and Las Palmas.
Ferrol: Cantabrian Zone HQ-Ferrol arsenal, support centre at La Graña, naval school at Marín, Pontevedra.
Cádiz: Straits Zone HQ-La Carraca arsenal, fleet command HQ and naval air base at Rota, amphibious base at Puntales. Marines Brigade (TEAR) HQ at San Fernando, Cádiz.
Cartagena: Maritime Action, HQ-Cartagena arsenal, underwater weapons and divers school at La Algameca; support base at Mahón, Minorca and at Soller and Porto Pi, Majorca, submarine weapons schools at La Algameca and Porto Pi base, Majorca. Naval Infantry school at Cartagena.
Las Palmas: Canaries Zone HQ-Las Palmas arsenal

Naval Air Service

The Naval Air Arm Flotilla is based at Rota.

Type	Escuadrilla
AB 212	3
Cessna Citation II	4
Sikorsky SH-3D/G Sea King	5
Sikorsky SH-3E Sea King (AEW)	
Hughes 500M (Training)	6
EAV-8B Harrier II/Harrier Plus	9
Sikorsky SH-60B Seahawk	10

Guardia Civil del Mar

Started operations in 1992. For details, see end of section.

Fleet Deployment

(1) Fleet (under Commander-in-Chief, Fleet)

(a) *Principe de Asturias* (based at Rota)
(b) Escuadrillas de Escoltas:
    31st Squadron; 2 Baleares class plus 4 Álvaro de Bazan class (based at Ferrol)
    41st Squadron; 6 Santa María class (based at Rota)
(c) Amphibious Forces: (1 LST and 2 LPD at Rota, small units at Puntales, Cádiz).
    Naval infantry at San Fernando.
(d) Fuerza de Medidas contra Minas: (based at Cartagena) 6 MSCs, 1 MCCS
(e) Flotilla de Submarinos: (based at Cartagena) All submarines

(2) Flotilla de Aeronaves: (based at Rota)

(a) Maritime Action units (under Commander-in-Chief, Maritime Action)
(b) Cantabrian Zone:
    1 Ocean Tug, 8 Tugs, 4 Patrol Ships, 5 Large Patrol Craft, 7 Coastal Patrol Craft, 1 Logistics Support Ship, 4 Sail Training Ships, 5 Training Craft
(c) Straits Zone:
    1 oiler, 6 Oceanographic Ships, 1 Sail Training Ship, 4 Fast Attack Craft, 1 Transport, 1 Ocean Tug, 7 Tugs, 1 Water-boat

Fleet Deployment—*continued*

(d) Mediterranean Zone:
    4 Fast Attack Craft, 4 Patrol Ships, 1 Water-boat, 7 Tugs, 1 Frogman Support Ship
(e) Canaries Zone:
    4 Patrol Ships, 1 Ocean Tug, 2 Tugs, 1 LCT
(f) Minor auxiliaries. Identified by 'Y' pennant numbers and form Tren Naval.

Prefix to Ships' Names

SPS (Spanish Ship)

Strength of the Fleet

Type	Active	Building (Planned)
Submarines—Patrol	4	4 (4)
Aircraft Carriers	1	–
Frigates	12	1 (1)
Offshore Patrol Vessels	13	4 (4)
Coastal Patrol Craft	20	–
Inshore Patrol Craft	3	–
LHD	–	1
LPDs	2	–
LSTs	1	–
Minehunters	6	–
MCM: support ship	1	–
Survey and Research Ships	7	–
Replenishment Tankers	2	1
Tankers	9	–
Transport Ships	5	–
Training Ships	10	–
Ocean Tugs	2	–

DELETIONS

Submarines

2003 *Narval, Delfín*
2005 *Tonina*
2006 *Marsopa*

Frigates

2004 *Cataluña*
2005 *Baleares*
2006 *Andalucia*

Patrol Forces

2004 *Deva*
2005 *Javier Quiroga*

Mine Warfare Forces

2003 *Sil*
2004 *Genil, Odiel, Ebro*

Amphibious Warfare Forces

2004 2 LCT
2006 *Hernán Cortés*

Survey and Research Ships

2003 *Pollux*
2004 *Castor*

Auxiliaries

2003 *Ferrol, Guardiamarina Barrutia*
2004 *Torpedista Hernández*

PENNANT LIST

Submarines

S 71	Galerna
S 72	Siroco
S 73	Mistral
S 74	Tramontana

Aircraft Carriers

R 11	Príncipe de Asturias

Frigates

F 74	Asturias
F 75	Extremadura
F 81	Santa María
F 82	Victoria
F 83	Numancia
F 84	Reina Sofía
F 85	Navarra
F 86	Canarias
F 101	Alvaro de Bazán
F 102	Almirante Don Juan de Borbón
F 103	Blas de Lezo
F 104	Mendez Nuñez

Patrol Forces

F 33	Infanta Elena
P 11	Barceló
P 12	Laya
P 14	Ordóñez
P 15	Acevedo
P 16	Cándido Pérez
P 21	Anaga
P 22	Tagomago
P 23	Marola
P 24	Mouro
P 25	Grosa
P 26	Medas
P 27	Izaro
P 28	Tabarca
P 30	Bergantín
P 31	Conejera
P 32	Dragonera
P 33	Espalmador
P 34	Alcanada
P 61	Chilreu
P 62	Alboran
P 63	Arnomendi
P 64	Tarifa
P 71	Serviola
P 72	Centinela
P 73	Vigía
P 74	Atalaya
P 75	Descubierta
P 76	Infanta Elena
P 77	Infanta Cristina
P 78	Cazadora
P 79	Vencedora
P 201	Cabo Fradera

Amphibious Forces

L 42	Pizarro
L 51	Galicia
L 52	Castilla

Mine Warfare Forces

M 11	Diana
M 31	Segura
M 32	Sella
M 33	Tambre
M 34	Turia
M 35	Duero
M 36	Tajo

Survey Ships

A 23	Antares	A 92	Escandallo	A 14	Patiño	A 75	Sisargas
A 24	Rigel	A 111	Alerta	A 20	Neptuno	A 76	Giralda
A 31	Malaspina			A 51	Mahón	A 77	Sálvora
A 32	Tofiño	**Auxiliaries**		A 53	La Graña	A 82	Guardiamarina Salas
A 33	Hespérides			A 65	Marinero Jarano	A 83	Guardiamarina Godínez
A 52	Las Palmas	A 01	Contramaestre Casado	A 66	Condestable Zaragoza	A 84	Guardiamarina Rull
A 91	Astrolabio	A 04	Martín Posadillo	A 71	Juan Sebastián de Elcano	A 85	Guardiamarina Chereguini
		A 05	El Camino Español	A 72	Arosa	A 101	Mar Caribe
		A 11	Marqués de la Ensenada	A 74	La Graciosa		

SUBMARINES

4 GALERNA (AGOSTA) CLASS (SSK)

Name	No	Builders	Laid down	Launched	Commissioned
GALERNA	S 71	Bazán, Cartagena	5 Sep 1977	5 Dec 1981	22 Jan 1983
SIROCO	S 72	Bazán, Cartagena	27 Nov 1978	13 Nov 1982	5 Dec 1983
MISTRAL	S 73	Bazán, Cartagena	30 May 1980	14 Nov 1983	5 June 1985
TRAMONTANA	S 74	Bazán, Cartagena	10 Dec 1981	30 Nov 1984	27 Jan 1986

Displacement, tons: 1,490 surfaced; 1,740 dived
Dimensions, feet (metres): 221.7 × 22.3 × 17.7
   (67.6 × 6.8 × 5.4)
Main machinery: Diesel-electric; 2 SEMT-Pielstick 16 PA4
   V 185 VG diesels; 3,600 hp(m) *(2.7 MW)*; 2 Jeumont
   Schneider alternators; 1.7 MW; 1 motor, 4,600 hp(m)
   (3.4 MW); 1 cruising motor; 32 hp(m) *(23 kW)*; 1 shaft
Speed, knots: 12 surfaced; 20 dived; 17.5 sustained
Range, n miles: 8,500 snorting at 9 kt; 350 dived on cruising
   motor at 3.5 kt
Complement: 54 (6 officers)

Torpedoes: 4—21 in *(533 mm)* tubes. 20 combination of
   (a) ECAN L5 Mod 3/4; dual purpose; active/passive
   homing to 9.5 km *(5.1 n miles)* at 35 kt; warhead 150 kg;
   depth to 550 m *(1,800 ft)*.

(b) ECAN F17 Mod 2; wire-guided; active/passive homing
   to 20 km *(10.8 n miles)* at 40 kt; warhead 250 kg; depth
   600 m *(1,970 ft)*.
Mines: 19 can be carried if torpedo load is reduced to 9.
Countermeasures: ESM: THORN EMI/Inisel Manta E; radar
   warning.
Weapons control: DLA-2A TFCS.
Radars: Surface search: Thomson-CSF DRUA 33C;
   I-band.
Sonars: Thomson Sintra DSUV 22; passive search and
   attack; medium frequency.
   Thomson Sintra DUUA 2A/2B; active search and attack;
   8 or 8.4 kHz active.
   DUUX 2A/5; passive; rangefinding. Eledone; intercept.
   SAES Solarsub towed passive array; low frequency.

Programmes: First two ordered 9 May 1975 and second pair
   29 June 1977. Built with some French advice. About
   67 per cent of equipment and structure from Spanish
   sources.
Modernisation: Modernised with improved torpedo fire
   control, new ESM and IR enhanced periscopes. New main
   batteries installed with central control monitoring. *Galerna*
   started in April 1993 and completed in late 1994, *Siroco* in
   mid-1995, *Tramontana* in early 1997, and *Mistral* in 2000.
   The plan to fit SSM has been shelved. Solarsub towed
   arrays are being fitted to all of the class during overhauls.
   At least one submarine capable of being fitted with
   Dry Dock Shelter.
Structure: Diving depth, 300 m *(984 ft)*.
Operational: Endurance, 45 days. Based at Cartagena.

GALERNA   *8/2004, Martin Mokrus* / 1044545

GALERNA   *8/2004, E & M Laursen* / 1044546

SIROCO

12/2003, Adolfo Ortigueira Gil / 1044547

0 + 4 (4) S 80A CLASS (SSK)

Name	No	Builders	Laid down	Launched	Commissioned
—	S 81	Navantia, Cartagena	20 Mar 2005	Feb 2010	Oct 2011
—	S 82	Navantia, Cartagena	Jan 2007	Aug 2011	Oct 2012
—	S 83	Navantia, Cartagena	Jan 2008	July 2012	Oct 2013
—	S 84	Navantia, Cartagena	Jan 2009	July 2013	Oct 2014

Displacement, tons: 2,190 surfaced; 2,426 dived
Dimensions, feet (metres): 233.0 × 23.9 × ?
  (71.0 × 7.3 × ?)
Main machinery: Diesel electric; 2 diesels; 3,600 hp
  (2.65 MW); 1 motor; 3,500 hp *(2.6 MW)*; 1 shaft; AIP
  (ethanol reformer fuel cell) system; 300 kW
Speed, knots: 12 surfaced; 20 dived
Complement: 32

Missiles: Boeing Sub-Harpoon.

Torpedoes: 6—21 in *(533 mm)* bow tubes. Atlas Elektronik
  DM2A4 torpedoes.
Countermeasures: To be announced.
Weapons control: To be announced.
Radars: To be announced.
Sonars: SAES Solarsub towed passive array. Active and
  passive arrays.

Programmes: Approval for the procurement of four
  submarines was given by the Spanish Cabinet on

5 September 2003. Contract awarded on 25 March
2004. A land-attack capability, possibly Tomahawk,
is to be fitted. Navantia (55 per cent) and Lockheed
Martin contracted to develop core combat system in
July 2005. This includes the sonar suite and command
and control module. A second batch of four boats may
follow.
Structure: The design includes air-independent propulsion.
  An optronic mast is to be fitted.

S 80

10/2004, Spanish Navy / 1044543

AIRCRAFT CARRIERS

1 PRINCIPE DE ASTURIAS CLASS (CV)

Name	No	Builders	Laid down	Launched	Commissioned
PRÍNCIPE DE ASTURIAS (ex-*Almirante Carrero Blanco*)	R 11	Bazán, Ferrol	8 Oct 1979	22 May 1982	30 May 1988

Displacement, tons: 17,188 full load
Dimensions, feet (metres): 642.7 oa; 615.2 pp × 79.7 × 30.8 *(195.9; 187.5 × 24.3 × 9.4)*
Flight deck, feet (metres): 575.1 × 95.1 *(175.3 × 29)*
Main machinery: 2 GE LM 2500 gas turbines; 46,400 hp *(34.61 MW)* sustained; 1 shaft; LIPS cp prop; 2 motors; 1,600 hp(m) *(1.18 MW)*; retractable prop
Speed, knots: 25 (4.5 on motors)
Range, n miles: 6,500 at 20 kt
Complement: 555 (90 officers) plus 208 (Flag Staff (7 officers) and Air Group)

Guns: 4 Bazán Meroka Mod 2A/2B 12-barrelled 20 mm/120 ❶; 3,600 rds/min combined to 2 km.
2 Rheinmetall 37 mm saluting guns.
Countermeasures: Decoys: 4 Loral Hycor SRBOC 6-barrelled fixed Mk 36; IR flares and chaff to 4 km *(2.2 n miles)*.
SLQ-25 Nixie; towed torpedo decoy.
US Prairie/Masker; hull noise/blade rate suppression.
ESM/ECM: Elettronica Nettunel; intercept and jammers.
Combat data systems: Tritan Digital Command and Control System NTDS; Links 11 and 14. Marconi Matra SCOT 3 Secomsat ❷. SSR-1, WSC-3 (UHF).

Weapons control: 4 Selenia directors (for Meroka). Radamec 2000 series.
Radars: Air search: Hughes SPS-52C/D ❸; 3D; E/F-band; range 439 km *(240 n miles)*.
Surface search: ISC Cardion SPS-55 ❹; I/J-band.
Aircraft control: ITT SPN-35A ❺; J-band.
Fire control: 4 Sperry/Lockheed VPS 2 ❻; I-band (for Meroka).
RTN 11L/X; I/J-band; missile warning.
Selenia RAN 12L (target designation); I/J-band.
Tacan: URN 25.
Fixed-wing aircraft: 6-12 AV-8B Harrier II/Harrier Plus.

Helicopters: 6-10 SH-3 Sea Kings; 2-4 AB 212EW.

Programmes: Ordered on 29 June 1977. Associated US firms were Gibbs and Cox, Dixencast, Bath Iron Works and Sperry SM. Commissioning delays caused by changes to command and control systems and the addition of a Flag Bridge.

Modernisation: After two years' service some modifications were made to the port after side of the island, to improve briefing rooms and provide sheltered parking space for FD vehicles. Also improved accommodation has been added on for six officers and 50 specialist ratings. Mid-life refit planned for 2006-09.
Structure: Based on US Navy Sea Control Ship design. 12° ski-jump of 46.5 m. Two flight deck lifts, one right aft. Two LCVPs carried. Two pairs of fin stabilisers. The hangar is 24,748 sq ft *(2,300 m²)*. The Battle Group Commander occupies the lower bridge. Two saluting guns have been mounted on the port quarter.
Operational: Three Sea Kings have Searchwater AEW radar. Aircraft complement could be increased to 37 (parking on deck) in an emergency but maximum operational number is 29 (17 in hangar, 12 on deck). A typical air wing includes eight/ten AV-8B/AV-8B Plus, five SH-3 (including two AEW) and three/four AB-212. Based at Rota.
Sales: Modified design built for Thailand.

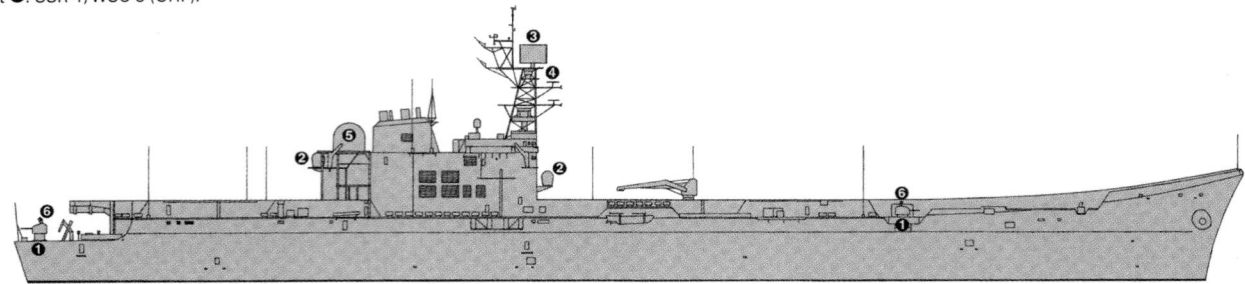

PRÍNCIPE DE ASTURIAS *(Scale 1 : 1,200), Ian Sturton* / 0506330

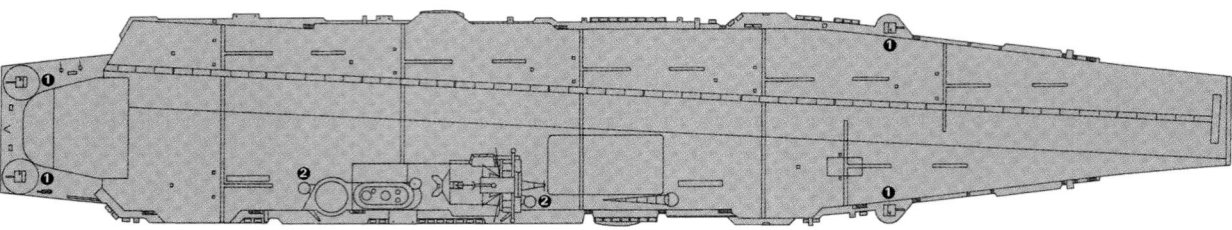

PRÍNCIPE DE ASTURIAS *(Scale 1 : 1,200), Ian Sturton* / 0130391

PRÍNCIPE DE ASTURIAS *6/2005*, Per Körnefeldt* / 1153450

PRÍNCIPE DE ASTURIAS *6/2005*, Maritime Photographic* / 1153474

PRÍNCIPE DE ASTURIAS

6/2003, Spanish Navy / 0570978

FRIGATES

Notes: A new class of frigates, to replace the Santa María class, will be required to enter service from about 2016.

4 + 1 (1) ALVARO DE BAZÁN CLASS (FFGHM)

Name	No	Builders	Laid down	Launched	Commissioned
ALVARO DE BAZÁN	F 101	IZAR, Ferrol	14 June 1999	27 Oct 2000	19 Sep 2002
ALMIRANTE DON JUAN DE BORBÓN	F 102	IZAR, Ferrol	27 Oct 2000	28 Feb 2002	3 Dec 2003
BLAS DE LEZO	F 103	IZAR, Ferrol	28 Feb 2002	16 May 2003	16 Dec 2004
MENDEZ NUÑEZ	F 104	IZAR, Ferrol	16 May 2003	12 Nov 2004	Mar 2006

Displacement, tons: 5,853 full load
Dimensions, feet (metres): 481.3 oa; 437 pp × 61 × 16.1
(146.7; 133.2 × 18.6 × 4.9)
Flight deck, feet (metres): 86.6 × 56 *(26.4 × 17)*
Main machinery: CODOG; 2 GE LM 2500 gas turbines; 47,328 hp(m) *(34.8 MW)* sustained; 2 Bazán/Caterpillar diesels; 12,240 hp(m) *(9 MW)* sustained; 2 shafts; LIPS cp props
Speed, knots: 28. **Range, n miles:** 4,500 at 18 kt
Complement: 250 (35 officers)

Missiles: SSM: 8 Harpoon Block II ❶; active radar homing to 130 km *(70 n miles)* at 0.9 Mach; warhead 227 kg.
SAM: Mk 41 VLS (48 cells) ❷ 32 GDC Standard SM-2MR (Block IIIA); command/inertial guidance; semi-active radar homing to 167 km *(90 n miles)* at 2 Mach. 64 Evolved Sea Sparrow RIM 162B (in quadpacks); semi-active radar homing to 18 km *(9.7 n miles)* at 3.6 Mach; warhead 39 kg.
Guns: 1 FMC 5 in *(127 mm)*/54 Mk 45 Mod 2 ❸ (ex-US); 20 rds/min to 23 km *(12.6 n miles)*; weight of shell 32 kg. 1 Bazán 20 mm/120 Meroka 2B ❹; 3,600 rds/min to 2 km (fitted for but not with) 2 Oerlikon 20 mm.
Torpedoes: 4—323 mm (2 twin) Mk 32 Mod 9 fixed launchers ❺. Honeywell Mk 46 Mod 5; anti-submarine; active/passive homing to 11 km *(5.9 n miles)* at 40 kt; warhead 44 kg.
A/S mortars: 2 ABCAS/SSTDS launchers.
Countermeasures: Decoys: 4 SRBOC Mk 36 Mod 2 chaff launchers ❻. SLQ-25A Nixie torpedo decoy.
ESM: Regulus Mk-9500 ❼ intercept.
ECM: Ceselsa Aldebaran ❽; jammer.
Combat data systems: Lockheed Aegis Baseline 5 Phase III (DANCS); Link 11/16. SCOT 3, SATURN 3S.
Weapons control: Sirius optronic director ❾; FABA Dorna GFCS. Sainsel DLT 309 TFCS. SQR-4 helo datalink.
Radars: Air/surface search: Aegis SPY-1D ❿. E/F-band.
Surface search: DRS SPS-67 (RAN 12S) ⓫. G-band.
Fire control: 2 Raytheon SPG-62 Mk 99 (for SAM) ⓬. I/J-band.
Navigation: 1 Raytheon SPS-73(v) ⓭. I-band.
Sonars: Raytheon DE 1160 LF; hull-mounted; active search and attack; medium frequency. Possible ATAS active towed sonar.

Helicopters: 1 SH-60B Seahawk Lamps III ⓮.

Programmes: Project definition from September 1992 to July 1995, and then extended to July 1996 to incorporate Aegis. Design collaboration with German and Netherlands shipyards started 27 January 1994. Spain withdrew from the APAR air defence radar project in June

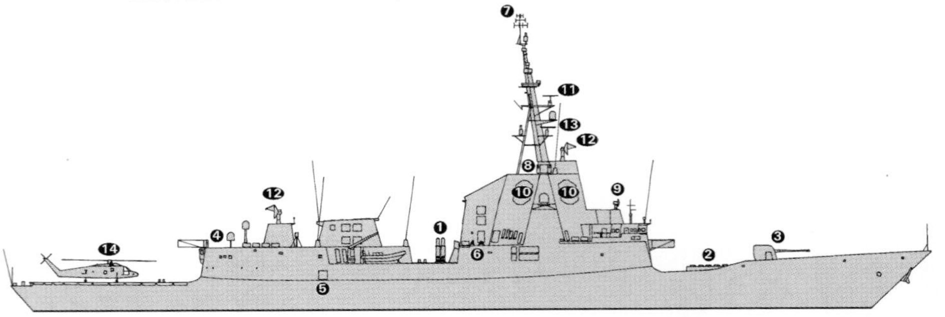

BLAS DE LEZO *(Scale 1 : 1,200), Ian Sturton* / 1153003

BLAS DE LEZO *6/2005*, Maritime Photographic* / 1153475

1995 and decided to incorporate Aegis SPY-1D into the design. Production order for four Flight I ships agreed on 21 October 1996 and building approved 24 January 1997. FSC in November 1997. The acquisition of a fifth ship was authorised by the Spanish government on 27 May 2005 and a contract is expected in 2006. A sixth ship may be procured. These are to be known as Flight II.
Modernisation: Flight I ships are to be upgraded 2007-08. This may include a ballistic missile detect and track capability and possibly land-attack missiles.

Structure: The inclusion of SPY-1D radar increased the original size of the ship and caused major changes to the shape of the superstructure. Stealth technology incorporated. Indal RAST helicopter system. Hangar for one helicopter. 127 mm gun for gunfire support to land forces, taken from USN *Tarawa* class. RAM may be fitted vice Meroka.
Operational: All based at Ferrol as part of the 31st Squadron. F 103 completed the USN Combined Combat Systems Ship Qualifications Trial (CSSQT) 30 September 2005. This included live SM-2 firings.

ALVARO DE BAZÁN *3/2003, Diego Quevedo* / 0570974

2 BALEARES (F 70) CLASS (FFGM)

Name	No	Builders	Laid down	Launched	Commissioned
ASTURIAS	F 74	Bazán, Ferrol	30 Mar 1971	13 May 1972	2 Dec 1975
EXTREMADURA	F 75	Bazán, Ferrol	3 Nov 1971	21 Nov 1972	10 Nov 1976

Displacement, tons: 3,350 standard; 4,177 full load
Dimensions, feet (metres): 438 × 46.9 × 15.4; 25.6 (sonar) (*133.6 × 14.3 × 4.7; 7.8*)
Main machinery: 2 Combustion Engineering V2M boilers; 1,200 psi (*84.4 kg/cm²*); 950°F (*510°C*); 1 Westinghouse turbine; 35,000 hp(m) (*25.7 MW*); 1 shaft
Speed, knots: 28
Range, n miles: 4,500 at 20 kt
Complement: 256 (15 officers)

Missiles: SSM: 8 McDonnell Douglas Harpoon (4 normally carried) ❶; active radar homing to 130 km (*70 n miles*) at 0.9 Mach; warhead 227 kg.
SAM: 16 GDC Pomona Standard SM-1MR; Mk 22 Mod 0 launcher ❷; command guidance; semi-active radar homing to 46 km (*25 n miles*) at 2 Mach.
A/S: Honeywell ASROC Mk 112 octuple launcher ❸ (except F 71); 8 reloads; inertial guidance to 1.6-10 km (*1—5.4 n miles*); payload Mk 46 torpedo.
Guns: 1 FMC 5 in (*127 mm*)/54 Mk 42 Mod 9 ❹; dual purpose; 20-40 rds/min to 24 km (*13 n miles*) anti-surface; 14 km (*7.7 n miles*) anti-aircraft; weight of shell 32 kg; 600 rounds in magazine.
2 Bazán 20 mm/120 12-barrelled Meroka ❺; 3,600 rds/min combined to 2 km. 2—12.7 mm MGs.
Torpedoes: 4—324 mm US Mk 32 fixed tubes (fitted internally and angled at 45° ❻. Honeywell/Alliant Mk 46 Mod 5; anti-submarine; active/passive homing to 11 km (*5.9 n miles*) at 40 kt; warhead 44 kg.
Countermeasures: Decoys: 4 Loral Hycor SRBOC Mk 36 Mod 2 6-barrelled chaff launchers ❼.
ESM: Ceselsa Deneb; or Mk 1600; intercept.
ECM: Ceselsa Canopus; or Mk 1900; jammer.
Combat data systems: Tritan 1 action data automation; Link 11. Saturn SATCOM ❽.
Weapons control: Mk 68 GFCS. Mk 74 missile system with Mk 73 director. Mk 114 torpedo control. Dorna GFCS on trial (F 71).
Radars: Air search: Hughes SPS-52B ❾; 3D; E/F-band; range 439 km (*240 n miles*).
Surface search: Raytheon SPS-10 ❿; G-band
Navigation: Raytheon Marine Pathfinder ⓫; I/J-band.
Fire control: Western Electric SPG-53B ⓬ I/J-band (for Mk 68).
Raytheon SPG-51C ⓭; G/I-band (for Mk 73).
Selenia RAN 12L ⓮; I-band (for Meroka). 2 Sperry VPS 2 ⓯ (for Meroka).
Tacan: SRN 15A ⓰.
Sonars: Raytheon SQS-56 (DE 1160); hull-mounted; active search and attack; medium frequency.
EDO SQS-35V ⓱; VDS; active search and attack; medium frequency.

Programmes: This class resulted from a very close co-operation between Spain and the US. Programme was approved 17 November 1964, technical support agreement with USA being signed 31 March 1966. US Navy supplied weapons and sensors. Major hull sections, turbines and gearboxes made at El Ferrol, superstructures at Alicante, boilers, distilling plants and propellers at Cádiz.
Modernisation: The mid-life update programme was done in two stages; all had completed the first stage by the end of 1987 and *Asturias* was the first to be fully modernised in 1988; *Extremadura* completed in May 1989. Changes included the fitting of two Meroka 20 mm CIWS, Link 11, Tritan data control, Deneb passive EW systems, four Mk 36 SRBOC chaff launchers and replacing SQS-23 with DE 1160 sonar. The stern torpedo tubes have been replaced by VDS.
Structure: Generally similar to US Navy's Knox class although they differ in the missile system and lack of helicopter facilities.
Operational: Both based at Ferrol, forming part of 31st Squadron. F 73 decommissioned in 2004, F 71 in March 2005 and F 72 in 2005. F 74 and F 75 are to remain in service until at least 2009.

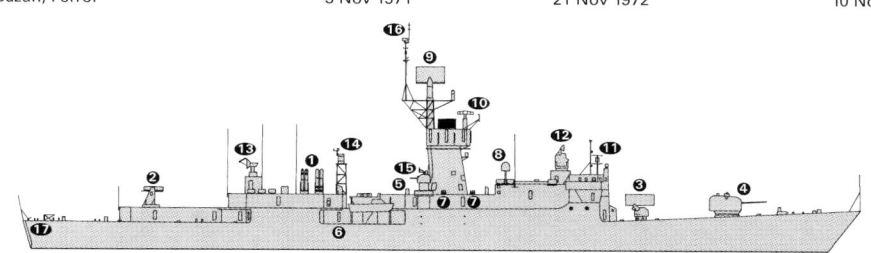

ANDALUCIA — (Scale 1 : 1,200), Ian Sturton / 0529155

EXTREMADURA — 7/2002*, Guy Toremans / 0528922

EXTREMADURA — 1/2004, H M Steele / 1044536

ASTURIAS — 3/2003, B Prézelin / 0570969

6 SANTA MARÍA CLASS (FFGHM)

Name	No	Builders	Laid down	Launched	Commissioned
SANTA MARÍA	F 81	Bazán, Ferrol	23 May 1982	24 Nov 1984	12 Oct 1986
VICTORIA	F 82	Bazán, Ferrol	16 Aug 1983	23 July 1986	11 Nov 1987
NUMANCIA	F 83	Bazán, Ferrol	8 Jan 1986	30 Jan 1987	8 Nov 1988
REINA SOFÍA (ex-*América*)	F 84	Bazán, Ferrol	12 Dec 1987	19 July 1989	18 Oct 1990
NAVARRA	F 85	Bazán, Ferrol	15 Apr 1991	23 Oct 1992	30 May 1994
CANARIAS	F 86	Bazán, Ferrol	15 Apr 1992	21 June 1993	14 Dec 1994

Displacement, tons: 3,610 standard; 3,969 full load
Dimensions, feet (metres): 451.2 × 46.9 × 24.6
 (137.7 × 14.3 × 7.5)
Main machinery: 2 GE LM 2500 gas turbines; 41,000 hp
 (30.59 MW) sustained; 1 shaft; cp prop
 2 auxiliary retractable props; 650 hp *(484 kW)*
Speed, knots: 29.
Range, n miles: 4,500 at 20 kt
Complement: 223 (13 officers)

Missiles: SSM: 8 McDonnell Douglas Harpoon; active radar
 homing to 130 km *(70 n miles)* at 0.9 Mach; warhead
 227 kg.
 SAM: 32 GDC Pomona Standard SM-1MR; Mk 13 Mod 4
 launcher ❶; command guidance; semi-active radar
 homing to 46 km *(25 n miles)* at 2 Mach.
 Both missile systems share a common magazine.
Guns: 1 OTO Melara 3 in *(76 mm)*/62 ❷; 85 rds/min to 16 km
 (8.7 n miles); weight of shell 6 kg.
 1 Bazán 20 mm/120 12-barrelled Meroka Mod 2A or 2B ❸;
 3,600 rds/min combined to 2 km. 2 — 12.7 mm MGs.
Torpedoes: 6 — 324 mm US Mk 32 (2 triple) tubes ❹.
 Honeywell/Alliant Mk 46 Mod 5; anti-submarine; active/
 passive homing to 11 km *(5.9 n miles)* at 40 kt; warhead
 44 kg.
Countermeasures: Decoys: 4 Loral Hycor SRBOC
 6-barrelled fixed Mk 37 Mod 1/2 ❺; IR flares and chaff
 to 4 km *(2.2 n miles)*.
 Prairie/Masker: hull noise/blade rate suppression.
 SLQ-25 Nixie; torpedo decoy.
 ESM/ECM: Elettronica Nettunel or Mk 3000 Neptune
 (F 84—86); intercept and jammer.
Combat data systems: IPN 10 action data automation;
 Link 11. SQQ 28 LAMPS III helo datalink. Saturn and
 SCOT 3 Secomsat ❻ fitted.
Weapons control: Loral Mk 92 Mod 2 (Mod 6 with CORT in
 F 85 and 86). Enosa optronic tracker for Meroka 2B.
Radars: Air search: Raytheon SPS-49(V)4/6 ❼; C/D-band;
 range 457 km *(250 n miles)*.
 Surface search: Raytheon SPS-55 ❽; I-band.
 Navigation: Raytheon 1650/9 ❾; I/J-band.
 Fire control: RCA Mk 92 Mod 4/6 ❿; I/J-band.
 Raytheon STIR ⓫; I/J-band.
 Selenia RAN 12L ⓬; D-band (for Meroka).
 Sperry/Lockheed VPS 2 ⓭; I-band (for Meroka).
 Tacan: URN 25.
Sonars: Raytheon SQS-56 (DE 1160); hull-mounted; active
 search and attack; medium frequency.

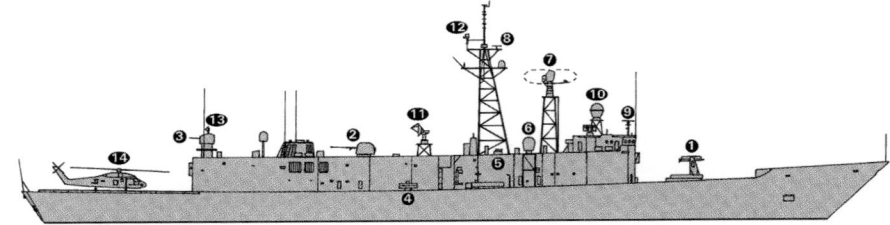

REINA SOFÍA　　　　　　　　*(Scale 1 : 1,200), Ian Sturton* / 0130395

CANARIAS　　　　　　*1/2005*, Camil Busquets i Vilanova* / 1153476

Gould SQR-19(V)2; tactical towed array (TACTASS);
passive; very low frequency.

Helicopters: 2 Sikorsky SH-60B ⓮ (only one normally
 embarked).

Programmes: Three ordered 29 June 1977. The execution of this
 programme was delayed due to the emphasis placed on the
 carrier construction. The fourth ship was ordered on 19 June
 1986, and numbers five and six on 26 December 1989.
Modernisation: F 85 and F 86 are fitted with the improved
 Mod 2B Meroka CIWS which includes an Enosa optronic
 tracker. SCOT SATCOM fitted in F 85 and F 84. Others
 may be similarly fitted. All modernised with RAN 12L

target designator for Meroka but VPS 2 fire control radar
is yet to be replaced by RAN 30X radar. A modernisation
programme started (F 82 and F 83) in 2005. Weapons and
sensors are to be upgraded to improve performance in
the littoral environment. The Batch II (F 84-86) ships are to
receive new ESM/ECM equipment, ESSM and associated
fire-control radar.
Structure: Based on the US FFG 7 Oliver Perry class
although broader in the beam and therefore able to
carry more topweight. Fin stabilisers fitted. RAST
helicopter handling system. *Navarra* and *Canarias* have
an indigenous combat data system thereby increasing
national inputs to 75 per cent.
Operational: All based at Rota as the 41st Squadron.

REINA SOFÍA　　　　　　*10/2005*, Adolfo Ortigueira Gil* / 1153472

SHIPBORNE AIRCRAFT

Notes: An initial purchase of 45 NH-90 helicopters, to replace the SH-3 and AB-212 fleets,
was announced on 20 May 2005. This is likely to include a mixture of naval and transport
versions. Entry into service is expected in 2010.

Numbers/Type: 4/12/1 BAe/McDonnell Douglas EAV-8B (Harrier II)/EAV-8B (Harrier Plus)/
 TAV-8B.
Operational speed: 562 kt *(1,041 km/h)*.
Service ceiling: Not available.
Range: 480 n miles *(889 km)*.
Role/Weapon systems: First batch of nine delivered in 1987-88 and a further eight in
 1996-97. All to be upgraded to AV-8B Harrier Plus standard with APG-65 radar plus FLIR
 by 2004. A further TAV-8B twin seat delivered in September 2000. Sensors: ECM; ALQ
 164. Weapons: Strike; two 25 mm GAU-12/U cannon, two or four AIM-9L Sidewinders,
 two or four AGM-65E Mavericks; up to 16 GP bombs. AMRAAM AIM-120 in updated
 aircraft.

HARRIER PLUS
2/2004, Guy Toremans
1044542

Numbers/Type: 8 Sikorsky SH-3D/G/H Sea King.
Operational speed: 118 kt *(219 km/h)*.
Service ceiling: 14,700 ft *(4,480 m)*.
Range: 542 n miles *(1,005 km)*.
Role/Weapon systems: Former ASW helicopters converted to tactical transport role. ASW equipment fitted for but not with. Can be replaced in 48 hours. Converted to 3H standard in 1996-97. APN-217 Doppler radar and IFF. Sensors: APS-124 search radar, Bendix AQS-18V dipping sonar, sonobuoys. Weapons: ASW; four Mk 46 torpedoes or depth bombs; 1 – 12.7 mm MG.

SH-3D   *10/2005*, Adolfo Ortigueira Gil* / 1153466

Numbers/Type: 3 Sikorsky SH-3D Sea King AEW.
Operational speed: 110 kt *(204 km/h)*.
Service ceiling: 14,700 ft *(4,480 m)*.
Range: 542 n miles *(1,005 km)*.
Role/Weapon systems: Three Sea King helicopters were taken in hand in 1986 for conversion to AEW role to provide organic cover; first entered service August 1987. Radar to be replaced by RACAL 2000. Sensors: THORN EMI Searchwater radar, ESM. Weapons: Unarmed.

SEA KING AEW   *5/2001, Guy Toremans* / 0130130

Numbers/Type: 12 Sikorsky SH-60B Seahawk (LAMPS III).
Operational speed: 135 kt *(249 km/h)*.
Service ceiling: 10,000 ft *(3,050 m)*.
Range: 600 n miles *(1,110 km)*.
Role/Weapon systems: ASW helicopter; delivery in 1988-89 for FFG 7 frigates. Six more Block 1 acquired in 2002 for new frigates, and original six to be upgraded to Block 1 with first three aircraft completed by 2005. Sensors: Search radar, FLIR (Block I), sonobuoys, ECM/ESM. Weapons: ASW; two Mk 46 torpedoes or depth bombs. ASV; AGM-119B Penguin and AGM-114B/K Hellfire.

SH-60B   *10/2005*, Adolfo Ortigueira Gil* / 1153467

Numbers/Type: 8 Agusta AB 212.
Operational speed: 106 kt *(196 km/h)*.
Service ceiling: 14,200 ft *(4,330 m)*.
Range: 230 n miles *(426 km)*.
Role/Weapon systems: Surface search; four are equipped for Fleet ECM support and have a datalink and six for Assault operations with the Amphibious Brigade. All ASW equipment and ASM missiles removed. Sensors: Selenia search radar, Mk 2000 EW system (in four); Elmer ECM. Weapons: 1 – 12.7 mm MG and 70 mm rocket launchers.

AB 212   *10/2005*, Adolfo Ortigueira Gil* / 1153468

Numbers/Type: 10 Hughes 500MD.
Operational speed: 110 kt *(204 km/h)*.
Service ceiling: 10,000 ft *(3,050 m)*.
Range: 203 n miles *(376 km)*.
Role/Weapon systems: Used for training; secondary role is SAR and surface search. ASW role removed. Sensors: Some may have search radar, MAD.

500 MD   *7/2002, Adolfo Ortigueira Gil* / 0528937

LAND-BASED MARITIME AIRCRAFT (FRONT LINE)

Notes: (1) The Air Force F/A-18 Hornet (C.15) and Eurofighter Typhoon (C.16) can be armed with Harpoon ASM. Air Force CN-235 are not used for maritime role.
(2) Three CASA C-212/400 are operated by the Fishery Department and are based at Torrejón (Madrid), Jerez and Alicante. Two Agusta A-109C and two Dauphin N3 helicopters are based at Alicante, Jerez and Santander and Canary Islands.

Numbers/Type: 3 Cessna Citation II (C-550).
Operational speed: 275 kt *(509 km/h)*.
Service ceiling: 27,750 ft *(8,458 m)*.
Range: 2,000 n miles *(3,704 km)*.
Role/Weapon systems: Used for transport, training and reconnaissance.

CESSNA CITATION   *6/2004, Adolfo Ortigueira Gil* / 1044550

Numbers/Type: 14 CASA C-212 Aviocar.
Operational speed: 190 kt *(353 km/h)*.
Service ceiling: 24,000 ft *(7,315 m)*.
Range: 1,650 n miles *(3,055 km)*.
Role/Weapon systems: Operated by Air Force. Primary role SAR, secondary role surveillance. Based at Mallorca, Las Palmas and Madrid. Six are leased by Customs. Sensors: APS-128 radar, MAD, sonobuoys and ESM. Weapons: (not SAR role): ASW; Mk 46 torpedoes or depth bombs. ASV; two rockets or machine gun pods.

C-212   *5/2002, Adolfo Ortigueira Gil* / 0528933

Numbers/Type: 3 Fokker F27 Maritime.
Operational speed: 250 kt *(463 km/h)*.
Service ceiling: 29,500 ft *(8,990 m)*.
Range: 2,700 n miles *(5,000 km)*.
Role/Weapon systems: Canaries and offshore patrol by Air Force. Are to be replaced by CN-235 in due course. Sensors: APS-504 search radar, cameras. Weapons: none.

F-27   *6/2004, Adolfo Ortigueira Gil* / 1044552

Numbers/Type: 2/5 Lockheed P-3A/P-3B Plus Orion.
Operational speed: 410 kt *(760 km/h).*
Service ceiling: 28,300 ft *(8,625 m).*
Range: 4,000 n miles *(7,410 km).*
Role/Weapon systems: Air Force operation for long-range MR/ASW. Original P-3A aircraft supplemented in 1988 by P-3B Orions from Norway after Lockheed modernisation. P-3A aircraft upgraded to P-3A plus in 1995-97. The five P-3Bs are undergoing modernisation programme with improved acoustic signal processor, ALR-66 ESM, FLIR and new radar and communications. Sensors: APS-134 (Searchwater 2000 in due course); FLIR; search radar, AQS-81 MAD, ALR 66 V(3) ECM/ESM, 87 sonobuoys. Weapons: ASW; eight torpedoes or depth bombs internally; 10 underwing stations. ASV; four Harpoon or 127 mm rockets.

Numbers/Type: 10 Eurocopter AS 332 Super Puma.
Operational speed: 130 kt *(240 km/h).*
Service ceiling: 15,090 ft *(4,600 m).*
Range: 672 n miles *(1,245 km).*
Role/Weapon systems: Air Force operated for SAR/CSAR. Based at Mallorca, Las Palmas and Madrid.

P-3B

7/2002, Adolfo Ortigueira Gil / 0528935

AS 332

7/2001, Adolfo Ortigueira Gil / 0528932

PATROL FORCES

6 DESCUBIERTA CLASS (PSOH/MCS/FSGM)

Name	No	Builders	Laid down	Launched	Commissioned
DESCUBIERTA	P 75 (ex-F 31)	Bazán, Cartagena	16 Nov 1974	8 July 1975	18 Nov 1978
DIANA	M 11 (ex-F 32)	Bazán, Cartagena	8 July 1975	26 Jan 1976	30 June 1979
INFANTA ELENA	P 76 (ex-F 33)	Bazán, Cartagena	26 Jan 1976	14 Sep 1976	12 Apr 1980
INFANTA CRISTINA	P 77 (ex-F 34)	Bazán, Cartagena	11 Sep 1976	25 Apr 1977	24 Nov 1980
CAZADORA	P 78 (ex-F 35)	Bazán, Ferrol	14 Dec 1977	17 Oct 1978	20 July 1982
VENCEDORA	P 79 (ex-F 36)	Bazán, Ferrol	1 June 1978	27 Apr 1979	18 Mar 1983

Displacement, tons: 1,233 standard; 1,666 full load
Dimensions, feet (metres): 291.3 × 34 × 12.5
  (88.8 × 10.4 × 3.8)
Main machinery: 4 MTU-Bazán 16V 956 TB91 diesels; 15,000 hp(m) *(11 MW)* sustained; 2 shafts; cp props
Speed, knots: 25
Range, n miles: 4,000 at 18 kt; 7,500 at 12 kt
Complement: 118 (10 officers) plus 30 marines

Guns: 1 OTO Melara 3 in *(76 mm)*/62 compact; 85 rds/min to 16 km *(8.7 n miles)*; weight of shell 6 kg.
  1 or 2 Bofors 40 mm/70 (F 33); 300 rds/min to 12.5 km *(6.8 n miles)*; weight of shell 0.96 kg.
  2 Oerlikon 20 mm.
Countermeasures: ESM: Elsag Mk 1000 (part of Deneb system); or Mk 1600; intercept.
ECM: Ceselsa Canopus; or Mk 1900; jammer.
Combat data systems: Tritan IV. Saturn SATCOM.
Weapons control: Signaal WM25; GM 101.
Radars: Air/surface search: Signaal DA05/2 (not M 11); E/F-band; range 137 km *(75 n miles)* for 2 m² target.
Surface search: Signaal ZW06 (not M 11); I-band.
Navigation: 2 Furuno; I-band.
Fire control: Signaal WM22/41 or WM25 system (not M 11); I/J-band; range 46 km *(25 n miles).*

Programmes: Officially rated as Corvettes. *Diana* (tenth of the name) originates with the galley *Diana* of 1570. *Infanta Elena* and *Infanta Cristina* are named after the daughters of King Juan Carlos. Approval for second four ships given on 21 May 1976. First four ordered 7 December 1973 (83 per cent Spanish ship construction components) and two more from Bazán, Ferrol on 25 May 1976.
Structure: Original Portuguese 'João Coutinho' design by Comodoro de Oliveira PN developed by Blohm + Voss and considerably modified by Bazán including use of Y-shaped funnel. Noise reduction measures include Masker fitted to shafts, auxiliary gas-turbine generator fitted on upper deck, all main and auxiliary diesels sound-mounted. Fully stabilised. Automatic computerised engine and alternator control; two independent engine rooms; normal running on two diesels.
Operational: P 75 completed conversion to an OPV, with capability to act as helicopter platform, in

DIANA

2/2004, Guy Toremans / 1044538

CAZADORA

7/2004, Diego Quevedo / 1044553

2000. Most major weapon systems removed. M 11 completed conversion to MCMV support role in 2000 and based at Cartagena. P 79 converted to OPV role in 2003, P 77 and P 78 in 2004 and P 76 in 2005. P 75,

P 76 and P 77 based at Cartagena and P 78 and P 79 at Las Palmas.
Sales: F 37 and F 38 sold to Egypt prior to completion. One to Morocco in 1983.

INFANTA CRISTINA

11/2005, Adolfo Ortigueira Gil* / 1153469

4 SERVIOLA CLASS (OFFSHORE PATROL VESSELS) (PSOH)

Name	No	Builders	Laid down	Launched	Commissioned
SERVIOLA	P 71	Bazán, Ferrol	17 Oct 1989	10 May 1990	22 Mar 1991
CENTINELA	P 72	Bazán, Ferrol	12 Dec 1989	30 Mar 1990	24 Sep 1991
VIGÍA	P 73	Bazán, Ferrol	30 Oct 1990	12 Apr 1991	24 Mar 1992
ATALAYA	P 74	Bazán, Ferrol	14 Dec 1990	22 Nov 1991	29 June 1992

Displacement, tons: 1,147 full load
Dimensions, feet (metres): 225.4; 206.7 pp × 34 × 11
 (68.7; 63 × 10.4 × 3.4)
Main machinery: 2 MTU-Bazán 16V 956 TB91 diesels;
 7,500 hp(m) *(5.5 MW)* sustained; 2 shafts; LIPS cp props
Speed, knots: 19
Range, n miles: 8,000 at 12 kt
Complement: 42 (8 officers) plus 6 spare berths

Guns: 1 US 3 in *(76 mm)*/50 Mk 27; 20 rds/min to 12 km
 (6.6 n miles); weight of shell 6 kg.
 2—12.7 mm MGs.
Countermeasures: ESM: ULQ-13 (in P 71).
Weapons control: Bazán Alcor or MSP 4000 (P 73) optronic
 director. Hispano mini combat system. SATCOM.
Radars: Surface search: Racal Decca 2459; I-band.
 Navigation: Racal Decca ARPA 2690 BT; I-band.

Helicopters: Platform for 1 AB 212.

Programmes: Project B215 ordered from Bazán, Ferrol in
 late 1988. The larger Milano design was rejected as being
 too expensive.
Modernisation: The guns are old stock refurbished but
 could be replaced by an OTO Melara 76 mm/62 or
 a Bofors 40 mm/70 Model 600 if funds can be found.
 Other equipment fits could include four Harpoon SSM,
 Meroka CIWS, Sea Sparrow SAM or a Bofors 375 mm
 ASW rocket launcher. No plans to carry out any of these
 improvements so far. EW equipment fitted in Serviola for
 training.
Structure: A modified Halcón class design similar to
 ships produced for Argentina and Mexico. Helicopter
 facilities enabling operation in up to Sea State 4
 using non-retractable stabilisers. Three firefighting
 pumps.
Operational: For EEZ patrol. *Vigía* based at Cádiz, *Serviola*
 and *Atalaya* at Ferrol and *Centinela* at Las Palmas.

ATALAYA   *7/2003, Adolfo Ortigueira Gil* / 0570956

ATALAYA
6/2004, Adolfo Ortigueira Gil
1044551

1 PESCALONSO CLASS (OFFSHORE PATROL CRAFT) (PSO)

Name	No	Builders	Commissioned
CHILREU (ex-*Pescalonso 2*)	P 61	Gijon, Asturias	30 Mar 1992

Displacement, tons: 2,101 full load
Dimensions, feet (metres): 222.4 × 36.1 × 15.4 *(67.8 × 11 × 4.7)*
Main machinery: 1 MaK 6M-453K diesel; 2,460 hp(m) *(1.81 MW)* sustained; 1 shaft; cp prop
Speed, knots: 12
Range, n miles: 1,500 at 12 kt
Complement: 35 (7 officers)
Guns: 1—12.7 mm MG.
Radars: Surface search: 2 Consilium Selesmar; E/F/I-band.

Comment: Launched 2 May 1988 and purchased by the Fisheries Department for the
 Navy to use as a Fishery Protection vessel based at Ferrol. Former stern ramp trawler.
 Inmarsat fitted.

CHILREU   *9/2005*, Adolfo Ortigueira Gil* / 1153470

3 ALBORAN CLASS (OFFSHORE PATROL CRAFT) (PSOH)

Name	No	Builders	Commissioned
ALBORAN	P 62	Freire, Vigo	8 Jan 1997
ARNOMENDI	P 63	Freire, Vigo	13 Dec 2000
TARIFA	P 64	Freire, Vigo	14 June 2004

Displacement, tons: 1,963 full load
Dimensions, feet (metres): 218.2 × 36.1 × 14.4 *(66.5 × 11 × 4.4)*
Main machinery: 1 Krupp MaK 6 M 453C diesel; 2,400 hp(m) *(1.76 MW)* sustained (P 62);
 1 Krupp MaK 8M25 diesel; 3,250 hp(m) *(2.39 MW)* sustained (P 63); 1 diesel generator
 and motor for emergency propulsion; 462 hp(m) *(340 kW)*; 1 shaft; bow thruster;
 350 hp(m) *(257 kW)*
Speed, knots: 13 (P 62); 15.8 (P 63) (3.5 on emergency motor)
Range, n miles: 20,000 at 13 kt
Complement: 37 (7 officers) plus 9 spare
Guns: 2—12.7 mm MGs.
Radars: Surface search: Furuno FAR-2825; I-band.
 Navigation: Furuno FR-2130S; I-band.
Helicopters: Platform for 1 light.

Comment: *Alboran* launched in 1991 and purchased by the Fisheries Department to use
 as a Fishery Protection vessel based at Cartagena. *Arnomendi*, with a slightly larger
 bridge and more powerful engine, based at Las Palmas, Canary Islands. *Tarifa* is fitted
 with anti-pollution equipment and is based at Cartagena.

TARIFA   *10/2005*, Adolfo Ortigueira Gil* / 1153471

5 BARCELÓ CLASS (LARGE PATROL CRAFT) (PB)

Name	No	Builders	Commissioned
BARCELÓ	P 11	Lürssen, Vegesack	20 Mar 1976
LAYA	P 12	Bazán, La Carraca	23 Dec 1976
ORDÓÑEZ	P 14	Bazán, La Carraca	7 June 1977
ACEVEDO	P 15	Bazán, La Carraca	14 July 1977
CÁNDIDO PÉREZ	P 16	Bazán, La Carraca	25 Nov 1977

Displacement, tons: 145 full load
Dimensions, feet (metres): 118.7 × 19 × 6.2 *(36.2 × 5.8 × 1.9)*
Main machinery: 2 MTU-Bazán MD 16V 538 TB90 diesels; 6,000 hp(m) *(4.41 MW)*
 sustained; 2 shafts
Speed, knots: 22. **Range, n miles:** 1,200 at 17 kt
Complement: 19 (3 officers)
Guns: 1 Breda 40 mm/70. 1 Oerlikon 20 mm/85. 2—12.7 mm MGs.
Torpedoes: Fitted for 2—21 in *(533 mm)* tubes.
Weapons control: CSEE optical director.
Radars: Surface search: Raytheon 1220/6XB; I/J-band.

Comment: Ordered 5 December 1973. All manned by the Navy although building cost was
 borne by the Ministry of Commerce. Of Lürssen TNC 36 design. Reported as able to take
 two or four surface-to-surface missiles instead of 20 mm gun and torpedo tubes. 40 mm
 gun removed from *Barceló*. Plans to transfer to the Guardia Civil del Mar have been
 shelved. *Javier Quiroga* decommissioned in 2005 and may be transferred to Tunisia.
 Speed much reduced from original 36 kt.

BARCELÓ   *10/2005*, Adolfo Ortigueira Gil* / 1153464

9 ANAGA CLASS (LARGE PATROL CRAFT) (PB)

Name	No	Builders	Commissioned
ANAGA	P 21	Bazán, La Carraca	14 Oct 1980
TAGOMAGO	P 22	Bazán, La Carraca	30 Jan 1981
MAROLA	P 23	Bazán, La Carraca	4 June 1981
MOURO	P 24	Bazán, La Carraca	14 July 1981
GROSA	P 25	Bazán, La Carraca	15 Sep 1981
MEDAS	P 26	Bazán, La Carraca	16 Oct 1981
IZARO	P 27	Bazán, La Carraca	9 Dec 1981
TABARCA	P 28	Bazán, La Carraca	30 Dec 1981
BERGANTÍN	P 30	Bazán, La Carraca	28 July 1982

Displacement, tons: 319 full load
Dimensions, feet (metres): 145.6 × 21.6 × 8.2 *(44.4 × 6.6 × 2.5)*
Main machinery: 1 MTU-Bazán 16V 956 SB90 diesel; 4,000 hp(m) *(2.94 MW)* sustained; 1 shaft; cp prop
Speed, knots: 16
Range, n miles: 4,000 at 13 kt
Complement: 25 (3 officers)
Guns: 1 FMC 3 in *(76 mm)*/50 Mk 22. 1 Oerlikon 20 mm Mk 10. 2 – 7.62 mm MGs.
Radars: Surface search: 1 Racal Decca 1226; I-band.
Navigation: Consilium Selesmar SRL MM 950; F/I-band.

Comment: Ordered from Bazán, Cádiz on 22 July 1978. For fishery and EEZ patrol duties. Rescue and firefighting capability. Speed reduced from original 20 kt.

ANAGA 7/2005*, Marco Ghiglino / 1153477

4 CONEJERA CLASS (COASTAL PATROL CRAFT) (PB)

Name	No	Builders	Commissioned
CONEJERA	P 31	Bazán, Ferrol	31 Dec 1981
DRAGONERA	P 32	Bazán, Ferrol	31 Dec 1981
ESPALMADOR	P 33	Bazán, Ferrol	10 May 1982
ALCANADA	P 34	Bazán, Ferrol	10 May 1982

Displacement, tons: 85 full load
Dimensions, feet (metres): 106.6 × 17.4 × 4.6 *(32.2 × 5.3 × 1.4)*
Main machinery: 2 MTU-Bazán MA 16V 362 SB80 diesels; 2,450 hp(m) *(1.8 MW)*; 2 shafts
Speed, knots: 13
Range, n miles: 1,200 at 13 kt
Complement: 12
Guns: 1 Oerlikon 20 mm/120 Mk 10. 1 – 12.7 mm MG.
Radars: Surface search: Furuno; I-band.

Comment: Ordered in 1978, funded jointly by the Navy and the Ministry of Commerce. Naval manned. Speed reduced from original 25 kt.

ALCANADA 11/2005*, Adolfo Ortigueira Gil / 1153465

2 TORALLA CLASS (COASTAL PATROL CRAFT) (PB)

Name	No	Builders	Commissioned
TORALLA	P 81	Viudes, Barcelona	29 Apr 1987
FORMENTOR	P 82	Viudes, Barcelona	23 June 1988

Displacement, tons: 102 full load
Dimensions, feet (metres): 93.5 × 21.3 × 5.9 *(28.5 × 6.5 × 1.8)*
Main machinery: 2 MTU-Bazán 8V 396 TB93 diesels; 2,100 hp(m) *(1.54 MW)* sustained; 2 shafts
Speed, knots: 19
Range, n miles: 1,000 at 12 kt
Complement: 13
Guns: 1 Browning 12.7 mm MG.
Radars: Surface search: Racal Decca RM 1070; I-band.
Navigation: Racal Decca RM 270; I-band.

Comment: Wooden hull with GRP sheath. Very similar to Customs Alcaravan class. *Formentor* refitted in 1996-97. Based at Cartagena.

TORALLA 6/2004, Diego Quevedo / 1044558

2 P 101 CLASS (PBR)

P 114   P 111

Displacement, tons: 18.5 standard; 20.8 full load
Dimensions, feet (metres): 44.9 × 14.4 × 4.3 *(13.7 × 4.4 × 1.3)*
Main machinery: 2 Baudouin-Interdiesel DNP-350; 768 hp(m) *(564 kW)*; 2 shafts
Speed, knots: 23.3. **Range, n miles:** 430 at 18 kt
Complement: 6
Guns: 1 – 12.7 mm MG.
Radars: Surface search: Decca 110; I-band.

Comment: Ordered under the programme agreed 13 May 1977, funded jointly by the Navy and the Ministry of Commerce. Built to the Aresa LVC 160 design by Aresa, Arenys de Mar, Barcelona. GRP hull. Eight of the class conduct harbour auxiliary duties with Y numbers, the remainder paid off in 1993. P 111 transferred back again to patrol duties in 1996 and is based at Ayamonte (Huelva). P 114 is also used for patrol duties and is based at Ceuta.

P 101 class 6/2000, Adolfo Ortigueira Gil / 0087858

1 INSHORE/RIVER PATROL LAUNCH (PBR)

Name	No	Builders	Commissioned
CABO FRADERA	P 201	Bazán, La Carraca	11 Jan 1963

Displacement, tons: 21 full load
Dimensions, feet (metres): 58.3 × 13.8 × 3 *(17.8 × 4.2 × 0.9)*
Main machinery: 2 diesels; 280 hp(m) *(206 kW)*; 2 shafts
Speed, knots: 11
Complement: 9
Guns: 1 – 7.62 mm MG.
Radars: Surface search: Furuno; I-band.

Comment: Based at Tuy on River Miño for border patrol with Portugal.

CABO FRADERA 4/2003, Camil Busquets i Vilanova / 0570981

0 + 4 (4) OFFSHORE PATROL SHIPS (PSO)

Displacement, tons: 2,500 full load
Dimensions, feet (metres): 306.7 × 46.6 × 11.8 *(93.5 × 14.2 × 3.6)*
Main machinery: Diesel-electric; 2 diesels; 12,000 hp *(9 MW)*; 2 electric motors
Speed, knots: 20. **Range, n miles:** 3,500 at 12 kt
Complement: 35 (5 officers)
Guns: 1 Oto Melara 3 in *(76 mm)*/62. 2 – 30 mm (to be confirmed).
Combat data systems: SCOMBA.
Helicopters: 1 NH-90.

Comment: A programme for the procurement of a new class of up to eight multirole offshore patrol vessels known as Buques de Accion Maritima (BAM) was initiated in 2004. Other variants of the BAM design will be capable of conducting intelligence, hydrographic and diving support tasks. Authorisation for the first batch of four ships was made by the Spanish government on 20 May 2005.

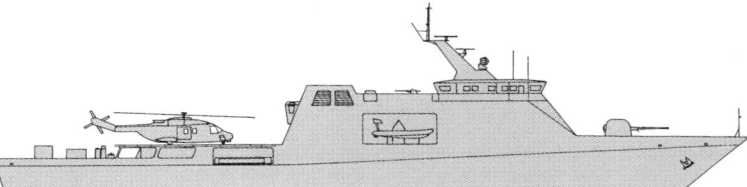

BAM (Scale 1 : 900), Ian Sturton / 1153001

AMPHIBIOUS FORCES

2 GALICIA CLASS (LPD)

Name	No	Builders	Laid down	Launched	Commissioned
GALICIA	L 51	Bazán, Ferrol	31 May 1996	21 July 1997	30 Apr 1998
CASTILLA	L 52	Bazán, Ferrol	11 Dec 1997	14 June 1999	26 June 2000

Displacement, tons: 13,815 full load
Dimensions, feet (metres): 524.9 oa; 465.9 pp × 82 × 19.3 *(160; 142 × 25 × 5.9)*
Flight deck, feet (metres): 196.9 × 82 *(60 × 25)*
Main machinery: 2 Bazán/Caterpillar 3612 diesels; 12,512 hp(m) *(9.2 MW)*; 2 shafts; LIPS cp props; bow thruster 680 hp(m) *(500 kW)*
Speed, knots: 20. **Range, n miles:** 6,000 at 12 kt
Complement: 115 plus 12 spare; 189 (L 52)
Military lift: 543 or 404 (L 52) fully equipped troops and 72 (staff and aircrew)
6 LCVP or 4 LCM or 1 LCU and 1 LCVP. 130 APCs or 33 MBTs.

Guns: 1 Bazán 20 mm/120 12-barrelled Meroka (fitted for) ❶; 3,600 rds/min combined to 2 km. 2 Oerlikon GAM-B01 20 mm.
Countermeasures: Decoys: 4 SRBOC chaff launchers. ESM: Intercept.
Combat data systems: SICOA (L 52); SATCOM; Link 11.
Radars: Surface search: TRS 3D/16 (L 52) ❷; G-band. Surface search: Kelvin Hughes ARPA ❸; I-band. Navigation: and helo control I-band.

Helicopters: 6 AB 212 or 4 SH-3D Sea King ❹ or 4 Eurocopter Tiger.

Programmes: Originally started as a national project by the Netherlands. In 1990 the ATS was seen as a possible solution to fulfil the requirements for a new LPD. Joint project definition study announced in July 1991 and completed in December 1993 and the first ship was authorised on 29 July 1994. The second of class ordered 9 May 1997.
Modernisation: L 52 C² capabilities upgraded in 2002-03 to support Flagship requirements. L 52 embarked the HQ of the Spanish High Readiness Force (Maritime) in November 2003 as part of the NATO Response Force. Both ships are to be fitted with RAM CIWS.
Structure: Able to transport a fully equipped battalion of marines providing a built-in dock for landing craft and a helicopter flight deck for debarkation in offshore conditions. Docking well is 885 m²; vehicle area 1,010 m². Access hatch on the starboard side. Hospital facilities. Built to commercial standards with military command and control and NBCD facilities. *Castilla* has improved command and control facilities with two operations centres, one for amphibious and one for a combat group.
Operational: Alternatively can also be used for a general logistic support for both military and civil operations, including environmental and disaster relief tasks. Based at Rota.

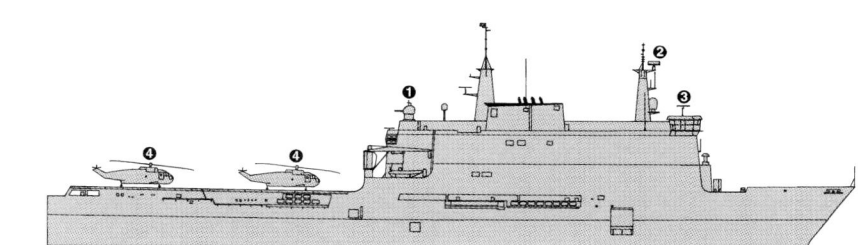
CASTILLA *(Scale 1 : 1,500), Ian Sturton* / 0106549

CASTILLA *4/2005*, Martin Mokrus* / 1153473

CASTILLA *10/2005*, Marco Ghiglino* / 1153479

1 LCU (LSTH)

L 072 (ex-LCU 12, ex-LCU 2, ex-LCU 1491)

Displacement, tons: 360 full load
Dimensions, feet (metres): 119.7 × 31.5 × 5.2 *(36.5 × 9.6 × 1.6)*
Main machinery: 3 Gray Marine 64YTL diesels; 675 hp *(504 kW)*; 3 shafts
Speed, knots: 8
Complement: 14
Military lift: 160 tons
Radars: Navigation: Furuno; I-band.

Comment: Transferred from US June 1972. Purchased August 1976. Refitted 1993-94. Based at Puntales (Cadiz).

LCU *4/1999, Diego Quevedo* / 0080627

7 LCM 8

L 81-86 (ex-LCM 81-86, ex-E 81-86) **L 87**

Displacement, tons: 115—120 full load
Dimensions, feet (metres): 74.5 × 21.7 × 5.9 *(22.7 × 6.6 × 1.8)*
Main machinery: 4 GM 6-71 diesels; 696 hp *(519 kW)* sustained; 2 shafts
Speed, knots: 11
Complement: 5

Comment: First six ordered from Oxnard, California in 1974. Assembled in Spain. Commissioned in June-September 1975. Two more built by Bazán, San Fernando, and completed in April 1989. *L 88* decommissioned 2003. Based at Puntales (Cadiz).

LCM *6/2004, Camil Busquets i Vilanova* / 1043187

0 + 1 STRATEGIC PROJECTION SHIP (LHD)

Builders	Laid down	Launched	Commissioned
Navantia, Ferrol	20 May 2005	Nov 2007	Dec 2008

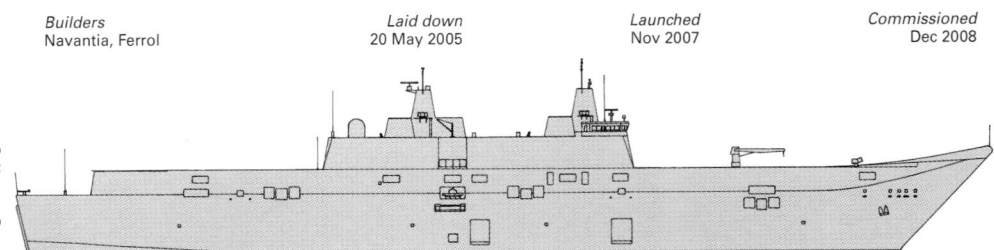

STRATEGIC PROJECTION SHIP
(Scale 1 : 1,800), Ian Sturton / 0569926

Name	No
—	—

Displacement, tons: 27,500 full load
Dimensions, feet (metres): 757.2 × 105.0 × 23.0
(230.8 × 32.0 × 7.0)
Flight deck, feet (metres): 663.9 × 105.0 *(202.3 × 32)*
Main machinery: CODAGE; 1 GE LM 2500 gas turbine; 26,550 hp
(19.8 MW); 2 MAN 324016V; 21,080 hp *(15.7 MW)*;
2 Siemens-Schottel podded propulsors; 29,500 hp *(22 MW)*
Speed, knots: 21. **Range, n miles:** 9,000 at 15 kt
Complement: 243 (plus 1,220 including flag staff, air group
and 900 landing force)

Guns: 4—20 mm. 2—12.7 mm MGs.
Countermeasures: Decoys: Chaff launchers. SLQ-25a Nixie
torpedo decoy.
Combat data systems: Link 11, 16. SATCOM.
Helicopters: 6 landing spots for helicopter or AV-8 operations.

Programmes: Approval for the procurement of a Strategic
Projection Ship was given by the Spanish Cabinet on
5 September 2003. Contract for design and construction
was awarded in March 2004.
Structure: The hangar is 1,000 m². Below the hangar there
is a 2,000 m² garage. Typical transport configurations
include: 46 tanks and 42 Leopard; 70 containers of
20 tons; 32 NH-90 or 19 AV-8 or 12 CH-47 or 12 NH 90 and
11 AV-8. The landing dock (69.3 × 16 m) will be capable
of operating four LCM (1E) landing craft or at least one
landing craft air cushion. Medical facilities will include
operating rooms, intensive care unit and sick bay. There is
space and weight reserved for a point-defence system.
Operational: The principal roles are amphibious, strategic
projection of land forces and disaster relief. The ship will
also be capable of operating the fixed-wing aircraft of
Príncipe de Asturias.

STRATEGIC PROJECTION SHIP (artist's impression)
5/2005*, Navantia / 1039644

1 NEWPORT CLASS (LSTH)

Name	No
PIZARRO (ex-*Harlan County*)	L 42 (ex-L 1196)

Builders	Laid down	Launched	Commissioned
National Steel, San Diego	7 Nov 1970	24 July 1971	8 Apr 1972

Displacement, tons: 4,975 light; 8,550 full load
Dimensions, feet (metres): 522.3 (hull) × 69.5 × 18.2 (aft)
(159.2 × 21.2 × 5.5)
Main machinery: 6 Alco 16-251 diesels; 16,500 hp *(12.3 MW)*
sustained; 2 shafts; cp props; bow thruster
Speed, knots: 20. **Range, n miles:** 14,250 at 14 kt
Complement: 255 (15 officers)
Military lift: 374 troops; (20 officers) 500 tons vehicles;
2 LCVPs and 2 LCPLs on davits
Guns: 1 General Electric/General Dynamics 20 mm Vulcan
Phalanx Mk 15. 2 Oerlikon 20 mm/85. 4—12.7 mm MGs.
Countermeasures: ESM: Celesa Deneb.
Radars: Surface search: Raytheon SPS-10F/67; G-band.
Navigation: Marconi LN66; I-band.

Helicopters: Platform only for 3 AB 212.

Programmes: Transferred from the US on 14 April 1995.
Structure: The 3 in guns removed on transfer. The ramp is
supported by twin derrick arms. A ramp just forward of the
superstructure connects the lower tank deck with the main
deck and a vehicle passage through the superstructure
provides access to the parking area amidships. A stern

PIZARRO
5/2004*, Marco Ghiglino / 1153478

gate to the tank deck permits unloading of amphibious
tractors into the water, or unloading of other vehicles
into an LCU or on to a pier. Vehicle stowage covers
19,000 sq ft. Length over derrick arms is 562 ft *(171.3 m)*;
full load draught is 11.5 ft forward and 17.5 ft aft.
Bow thruster fitted to hold position offshore while

unloading amphibious tractors. SCOT 3 SATCOM fitted
in 1995-96. Can carry four Mexeflotes, two of them
powered.
Operational: Based at Rota. *Hernán Cortés* decommissioned
in 2006 and *Pizarro* to follow as the Strategic Projection
Ship enters service.

2 + 12 LCM (1E)

L 601-602

Displacement, tons: 108 full load
Dimensions, feet (metres): 76.5 × 21 × 3.4 *(23.3 × 6.4 × 1.1)*
Main machinery: 2 MAN-D 2842-LE 402 diesels; 2,200 hp(m)
(1.62 MW); 2 MJP-650 DD waterjets
Speed, knots: 14
Range, n miles: 160 at 12 kt
Complement: 3
Military lift: 100 tons or one main battle tank

Comment: L 601-602 built by IZAR, San Fernando, for LPDs
and delivered in early 2001. Bow and stern ramps. Steel
construction with wheelhouse of composites. Maximum
speed in ballast is 22 kt. Based at Puntales. An order for
a further 12 craft made in November 2004. First three
laid down in 2005. Under construction by Navantia,
San Fernando, and all to be delivered by 2009.

L 601
11/2002, A Campanera i Rovira
0570942

40 LANDING CRAFT

Comment: Apart from those used for divers there are
14 LCM 6 (*L 161-167, L 261-267*), 16 LCVP and 8 LCPL.
All of the LCM 6, eight of the LCVPs and most of
the LCPs were built in Spanish Shipyards 1986-88.
There are also two tug pontoons (mexeflotes)
(L 91-L 92) completed in 1995. Most of these craft are
laid up.

LCM L 162
10/1993, Diego Quevedo
0506170

MINE WARFARE FORCES

6 SEGURA CLASS (MINEHUNTERS) (MHC)

Name	No	Builders	Launched	Commissioned
SEGURA	M 31	Bazán, Cartagena	25 July 1997	27 Apr 1999
SELLA	M 32	Bazán, Cartagena	6 July 1998	28 May 1999
TAMBRE	M 33	Bazán, Cartagena	5 Mar 1999	18 Feb 2000
TURIA	M 34	Bazán, Cartagena	22 Nov 1999	16 Oct 2000
DUERO	M 35	Izar, Cartagena	28 April 2003	5 July 2004
TAJO	M 36	Izar, Cartagena	10 June 2004	10 Jan 2005

Displacement, tons: 530 full load
Dimensions, feet (metres): 177.2 oa; 167.3 wl × 35.1 × 7.2 *(54; 51 × 10.7 × 2.2)*
Main machinery: 2 MTU-Bazán 6V 396 TB83 diesels; 1,523 hp(m) *(1.12 MW)*; 2 motors (for hunting); 200 kW; 2 Voith Schneider props; 2 side thrusters; 150 hp(m) *(110 kW)*
Speed, knots: 14; 7 (hunting)
Range, n miles: 2,000 at 12 kt
Complement: 41 (7 officers)
Guns: 1 Bazán/Oerlikon 20 mm GAM-BO1.
Countermeasures: MCM: FABA/Inisel system. 2 Gayrobot Pluto Plus ROVs.
Combat data systems: FABA/SMYC Nautis.
Radars: Navigation: Kelvin-Hughes 1007; I-band.
Sonars: Raytheon/ENOSA SQQ-32 multifunction VDS mine detection; high frequency.

Comment: On 4 July 1989 a technology transfer contract was signed with Vosper Thornycroft to allow Bazán to design a new MCM vessel based on the Sandown class. The order for four of the class was authorised on 7 May 1993, and an agreement signed on 26 November 1993 between DCN and Bazán provided for training in GRP technology. The first of class laid down 30 May 1995. Two more ordered on 26 January 2001. An option for two further ships is unlikely to be exercised. Sonar includes side scanning, and a towed body tracking and positioning system. M 35 and M 36 are to be fitted with the Minesniper mine disposal system. M 31-34 are to be retrofitted in due course. Form 1st MCM Squadron based at Cartagena.

SEGURA *2/2006*, Antonio Galán Cees* / 1154474

SURVEY AND RESEARCH SHIPS

1 DARSS CLASS (RESEARCH SHIP) (AGI/AGOR)

Name	No	Builders	Commissioned
ALERTA (ex-*Jasmund*)	A 111	Peenewerft, Wolgast	6 Dec 1992

Displacement, tons: 2,292 full load
Dimensions, feet (metres): 250.3 × 39.7 × 13.8 *(76.3 × 12.1 × 4.2)*
Main machinery: 1 Kolomna Type 40-DM diesel; 2,200 hp(m) *(1.6 MW)* sustained; 1 shaft; cp prop
Speed, knots: 11
Range, n miles: 1,000 at 11 kt
Complement: 60
Guns: Fitted for 3 twin 25 mm/70. 2—12.7 mm MGs.
Radars: Navigation: Racal Decca; I-band.

Comment: Former GDR depot ship launched on 27 February 1982 and converted to an AGI, with additional accommodation replacing much of the storage capacity. Was to have transferred to Ecuador in 1991 but the sale was cancelled. Commissioned in the Spanish Navy and sailed from Wilhelmshaven for a refit at Las Palmas prior to being based at Cartagena and used as an AGI and equipment trials ship. Saturn 35 SATCOM.

ALERTA *7/2002*, Diego Quevedo* / 0528951

1 RESEARCH SHIP (AGOBH)

Name	No	Builders	Commissioned
HESPÉRIDES (ex-*Mar Antártico*)	A 33	Bazán, Cartagena	16 May 1991

Displacement, tons: 2,738 full load
Dimensions, feet (metres): 270.7; 255.2 × 46.9 × 14.8 *(82.5; 77.8 × 14.3 × 4.5)*
Main machinery: Diesel-electric; 4 MAN-Bazán 14V20/27 diesels; 6,860 hp(m) *(5 MW)* sustained; 4 generators; 2 AEG motors; 3,800 hp(m) *(2.8 MW)*; 1 shaft; bow and stern thrusters; 350 hp(m) *(257 kW)* each
Speed, knots: 15. **Range, n miles:** 12,000 at 13 kt
Complement: 39 (9 officers) plus 30 scientists
Radars: Surface search: Racal/Hispano ARPA 2690; I-band.
Navigation: Racal 2690 ACS; F-band.
Helicopters: 1 AB 212

Comment: Ordered in July 1988 from Bazán, Cartagena, by the Ministry of Education and Science. Laid down in 1989, launched 12 March 1990. Has 330 sq m of laboratories, Simbad ice sonar. Dome in keel houses several sensors. Ice-strengthened hull capable of breaking first year ice up to 45 cm at 5 kt. Based at Cartagena, the main task is to support the Spanish base at Livingston Island, Antarctica. Manned and operated by the Navy. Has a telescopic hangar. Modifications made to superstructure in 2004 to increase accommodation for scientific staff.

HESPÉRIDES *10/2004*, Diego Quevedo* / 1043175

2 CASTOR CLASS (SURVEY SHIPS) (AGS)

Name	No	Builders	Commissioned
ANTARES	A 23	Bazán, La Carraca	21 Nov 1974
RIGEL	A 24	Bazán, La Carraca	21 Nov 1974

Displacement, tons: 363 full load
Dimensions, feet (metres): 125.9 × 24.9 × 10.2 *(38.4 × 7.6 × 3.1)*
Main machinery: 1 Sulzer 4TD36 diesel; 720 hp(m) *(530 kW)*; 1 shaft
Speed, knots: 11.5. **Range, n miles:** 3,620 at 8 kt
Complement: 36 (4 officers)
Radars: Navigation: Raytheon 1620; I/J-band.

Comment: Fitted with Raydist, Omega and digital presentation of data. Likely to be decommissioned in the near future. Based at Cadiz.

ANTARES *9/2005*, Marco Ghiglino* / 1153480

1 RESEARCH SHIP (AGOB)

Name	No	Builders	Commissioned
LAS PALMAS (ex-*Somiedo*)	A 52	Astilleros Atlántico, Santander	1978

Displacement, tons: 1,450 full load
Dimensions, feet (metres): 134.5 × 38.1 × 18 *(41 × 11.6 × 5.5)*
Main machinery: 2 AESA/Sulzer 16ASV25/30 diesels; 7,744 hp(m) *(5.69 MW)*; 2 shafts
Speed, knots: 13. **Range, n miles:** 27,000 at 12 kt
Complement: 33 (8 officers) plus 45 scientists
Guns: 2—12.7 mm MGs.
Radars: Navigation: 2 Racal Decca; I-band.

Comment: Built as a tug for Compania Hispano Americana de Offshore SA. Commissioned in the Navy 30 July 1981. Converted in 1988 for Polar Research Ship duties in Antarctica with an ice strengthened bow, an enlarged bridge and two containers aft for laboratories. Based at Cartagena.

LAS PALMAS *5/2004*, Diego Quevedo* / 1044561

2 MALASPINA CLASS (SURVEY SHIPS) (AGS)

Name	No	Builders	Commissioned
MALASPINA	A 31	Bazán, La Carraca	21 Feb 1975
TOFIÑO	A 32	Bazán, La Carraca	23 Apr 1975

Displacement, tons: 820 standard; 1,090 full load
Dimensions, feet (metres): 188.9 × 38.4 × 12.8 (57.6 × 11.7 × 3.9)
Main machinery: 2 San Carlos MWM TbRHS-345-61 diesels; 3,600 hp(m) (2.64 MW);
2 shafts; LIPS cp props
Speed, knots: 15
Range, n miles: 4,000 at 12 kt; 3,140 at 14.5 kt
Complement: 63 (9 officers)
Guns: 2 Oerlikon 20 mm.
Radars: Navigation: Raytheon 1220/6XB; I/J-band.

Comment: Ordered mid-1972. Both named after their immediate predecessors. Developed
from British Bulldog class. Fitted with two Atlas DESO-10 AN 1021 (280−1,400 m) echo-
sounders, retractable Burnett 538-2 sonar for deep sounding, Egg Mark B side scan
sonar, Raydist DR-S navigation system, Hewlett Packard 2100A computer inserted into
Magnavox Transit satellite navigation system, active rudder with fixed pitch auxiliary
propeller. *Malaspina* used for a NATO evaluation of a Ship's Laser Inertial Navigation
System (SLINS) produced by British Aerospace. Based at Cadiz.

MALASPINA   *6/2004, Camil Busquets i Vilanova* / 1043186

2 LHT-130 CLASS (SURVEY MOTOR BOATS) (YGS)

Name	No	Builders	Commissioned
ASTROLABIO	A 91	Rodman, Vigo	30 Nov 2001
ESCANDALLO	A 92	Rodman, Vigo	27 Feb 2004

Displacement, tons: 8 full load
Dimensions, feet (metres): 41.3 × 13.8 × 1.6 (12.6 × 4.2 × 0.5)
Main machinery: 2 diesels; 700 hp (522 kW); 2 shafts
Speed, knots: 30

Comment: Support craft of the Hydrographic Flotilla. Based at Puntales and transportable
by road, rail, ship or aircraft.

ESCANDALLO   *10/2004, Diego Quevedo* / 1043174

TRAINING SHIPS

6 SAIL TRAINING SHIPS (AXS)

Name	No	Builders	Commissioned
JUAN SEBASTIÁN DE ELCANO	A 71	Echevarrieta, Cádiz	17 Aug 1928
AROSA	A 72	Inglaterra	1 Apr 1981
LA GRACIOSA (ex-*Dejá Vu*)	A 74	Inglaterra	30 June 1988
GIRALDA (ex-*Southern Cross*)	A 76	Morris & Mortimer, Argyll	26 Aug 1993
SISARGAS	A 75	Novo Glass, Polinya	18 May 1995
SÁLVORA	A 77	—	29 May 2001

Displacement, tons: 3,420 standard; 3,656 full load
Dimensions, feet (metres): 308.5 oa × 43.3 × 24.6 (94.1 × 13.15 × 7.46)
Main machinery: 1 Deutz MWM KHD 6M diesel; 1,950 hp(m) (1.43 MW); 1 shaft
Speed, knots: 9. **Range, n miles:** 10,000 at 9 kt
Complement: 347 (students 120)
Guns: 2−37/80 mm Bazán saluting guns.
Radars: Navigation: 2 Racal Decca; I-band.

Comment: Details are for A 71 (based at La Carraca) which is a four masted top-sail
schooner-near sister of Chilean *Esmeralda*. Named after the first circumnavigator
of the world (1519-22) who succeeded to the command of the expedition led by Magellan
after the latter's death. Laid down 24 November 1925. Launched on 5 March 1927.
Carries 230 tons oil fuel. Engine replaced in 1992. Five further are based at the Naval
School, Marín. A ketch (A 72) (52 tons and 22.84 m in length), a schooner (A 74) (16.8 m
in length), a 90 tons ketch (A 75) launched in 1958 and formerly owned by the
father of King Juan Carlos I and presented to the Naval School in 1993, an ex-yacht
(A 76) and a yacht (A 77).

JUAN SEBASTIÁN DE ELCANO   *3/2002, A Campanera i Rovira* / 0529022

4 TRAINING CRAFT (AXL)

Name	No	Builders	Commissioned
GUARDIAMARINA SALAS	A 82	Cartagena	10 May 1983
GUARDIAMARINA GODÍNEZ	A 83	Cartagena	4 July 1984
GUARDIAMARINA RULL	A 84	Cartagena	11 June 1984
GUARDIAMARINA CHEREGUINI	A 85	Cartagena	11 June 1984

Displacement, tons: 56 full load
Dimensions, feet (metres): 62 × 16.7 × 5.2 (18.9 × 5.1 × 1.6)
Speed, knots: 13
Complement: 15; 22 (A 81)
Radars: Navigation: Halcon 948; I-band.

Comment: Tenders to Naval School. A 81 has been decommissioned.

GUARDIAMARINA CLASS   *2/2002, Diego Quevedo* / 0528943

AUXILIARIES

0 + 1 FLEET REPLENISHMENT SHIP (AORH)

Name	No	Builders	Laid down	Launched	Commissioned
CANTABRIA	—	Navantia, San Fernando	June 2005	2007	2009

Displacement, tons: 19,500 full load
Dimensions, feet (metres): 570.5 × 75.5 × 26.2 (173.9 × 23.0 × 8.0)
Main machinery: 2 diesels; 29,200 hp (21.8 MW); 1 shaft
Speed, knots: 21
Range, n miles: 6,000 at 13 kt
Complement: 112
Cargo capacity: 6,400 tons dieso; 1,600 tons aviation fuel
Guns: To be announced.
Countermeasures: To be announced.
Combat data systems: To be announced.
Radars: To be announced.
Helicopters: 2 SH-3D Sea King or 3 AB 212.

Comment: Similar in design to Patiño class with improved capabilities including
double-hull, container cargo capacity, enhanced sensors and a combat data system. Two
RAS stations on each side and one stern refuelling station. There is to be a small hospital
with ten beds. Contract for construction of the ship signed on 30 December 2004.

REPLENSHMENT SHIP (artist's impression)   *10/2004, Spanish Navy* / 1044544

1 PATIÑO CLASS (FLEET LOGISTIC TANKER) (AORH)

Name	No	Builders	Launched	Commissioned
PATIÑO	A 14	Bazán, Ferrol	22 June 1994	16 June 1995

Displacement, tons: 5,762 light; 17,045 full load
Dimensions, feet (metres): 544.6 × 72.2 × 26.2 *(166 × 22 × 8)*
Main machinery: 2 Bazán/Burmeister & Wain 16V40/45 diesels; 24,000 hp(m) *(17.6 MW)* sustained; 1 shaft; LIPS cp prop
Speed, knots: 20
Range, n miles: 13,440 at 20 kt
Complement: 146 plus 19 aircrew plus 20 spare
Cargo capacity: 6,815 tons dieso; 1,660 tons aviation fuel; 500 tons solids
Guns: 2 Bazán 20 mm/120 Meroka CIWS (fitted for). 2 Oerlikon 20 mm/90.
Countermeasures: Decoys: 4 SRBOC chaff launchers. Nixie torpedo decoy.
ESM/ECM: Aldebaran intercept and jammer.
Radars: 3 navigation/helo control; I-band.
Helicopters: 2 SH-3D Sea King or 3 AB 212.

Comment: The Bazán design AP 21 was rejected in favour of this joint Netherlands/Spain design. Ordered on 26 December 1991. Laid down 1 July 1993. Two supply stations each side for both liquids and solids. Stern refuelling. One Vertrep supply station, and workshops for aircraft maintenance. Medical facilities. Built to merchant ship standards with military NBC. Accommodation for up to 50 female crew members. SCOT 3 SATCOM to be fitted. Based at Ferrol.

PATIÑO   *10/2005*, Marco Ghiglino* / 1153481

1 TRANSPORT SHIP (AKRH)

Name	No	Builders	Commissioned
MARTÍN POSADILLO (ex-*Rivanervión*, ex-*Cala Portals*)	A 04 (ex-ET-02)	Duro Felguera, Gijon	1973

Displacement, tons: 1,920 full load
Dimensions, feet (metres): 246.1 × 42.7 × 14.1 *(75 × 13 × 4.3)*
Main machinery: 1 BMW diesel; 2,400 hp(m) *(1.77 MW)*; 1 shaft
Speed, knots: 10
Complement: 18
Military lift: 42 trucks plus 25 jeeps
Helicopters: Platform for 1 Chinook.

Comment: Ro-Ro ship taken on by the Army in 1990 and transferred to the Navy on 14 February 2000. Based at Cartagena.

MARTÍN POSADILLO   *5/2001, Camil Busquets i Vilanova* / 0130116

1 TRANSPORT SHIP (APH)

Name	No	Builders	Commissioned
CONTRAMAESTRE CASADO (ex-*Thanasis-K*, ex-*Fortuna Reefer*, ex-*Bonzo*, ex-*Bajamar*, ex-*Leeward Islands*)	A 01	Eriksberg-Göteborg, Sweden	15 Dec 1982

Displacement, tons: 4,965 full load
Dimensions, feet (metres): 343.4 × 46.9 × 29.2 *(104.7 × 14.3 × 8.9)*
Main machinery: 1 Burmeister & Wain diesel; 3,600 hp(m) *(2.65 MW)*; 1 shaft
Speed, knots: 14. **Range, n miles:** 8,000 at 14 kt
Complement: 72
Guns: 2 Oerlikon 20 mm.
Radars: Navigation: Racal Decca 1226 and 626; I-band.

Comment: Built in 1953. Impounded as smuggler. Delivered after conversion 6 December 1983. Has a helicopter deck. Since 2001, based at La Carraca (Cadiz).

CONTRAMAESTRE CASADO   *3/2001, Diego Quevedo* / 0132007

7 HARBOUR TANKERS (YO)

No	Displacement, tons	Dimensions metres	Cargo, tons fuel	Commissioned
Y 231	524	34 × 7 × 2.9	300	1981
Y 237	344	34.3 × 6.2 × 2.5	193	1965
Y 251	830	42.8 × 8.4 × 3.1	500	1981
Y 252	337	34.3 × 6.2 × 2.5	193	1965
Y 253	337	34.3 × 6.2 × 2.5	193	1965
Y 254	214.7	24.5 × 5.5 × 2.2	100	1981
Y 255	524	34 × 7 × 2.9	300	1981

Comment: All built by Bazán at Cádiz and Ferrol.

Y 251   *11/2003, Diego Quevedo* / 0570953

1 TRANSPORT SHIP (AKR)

Name	No	Builders	Commissioned
EL CAMINO ESPAÑOL (ex-*Araguary*, ex-*Cyndia*)	A 05 (ex-ET 03)	Maua, Rio de Janeiro	Oct 1984

Displacement, tons: 5,804 full load
Dimensions, feet (metres): 313.6 × 59.8 × 15.2 *(95.5 × 18.3 × 4.6)*
Main machinery: 2 Sulzer diesels; 6,482 hp(m) *(4.76 MW)*; 2 shafts
Speed, knots: 12
Complement: 24 (3 officers) plus 40 Army
Military lift: 24 tanks plus 15 trucks and 102 jeeps
Radars: Navigation: I-band.

Comment: Acquired by the Army in early 1999 but commissioned into the Navy on 21 September 1999. Ro-Ro design converted for military use by Bazán in Cartagena. Used for logistic support of armed forces. Has two 25 ton cranes. Based at Cartagena.

EL CAMINO ESPAÑOL   *7/2004, Diego Quevedo* / 1043184

1 FLEET TANKER (AORLH)

Name	No	Builders	Launched	Commissioned
MARQUÉS DE LA ENSENADA (ex-*Mar del Norte*)	A 11	Bazán, Ferrol	5 Oct 1990	3 June 1991

Displacement, tons: 13,592 full load
Dimensions, feet (metres): 403.9 oa; 377.3 wl × 64 × 25.9 *(123.1; 115 × 19.5 × 7.9)*
Main machinery: 1 MAN-Bazán 18V40/50A; 11,247 hp(m) *(8.27 MW)* sustained; 1 shaft
Speed, knots: 16
Range, n miles: 10,000 at 15 kt
Complement: 80 (11 officers)
Cargo capacity: 7,498 tons dieso; 1,746 tons JP-5; 120 tons deck cargo
Guns: 2—12.7 mm MGs.
Radars: Surface search: Racal Decca 2459; I/F-band.
Navigation: Racal Decca ARPA 2690/9; I-band.
Helicopters: 1 AB 212 or similar.

Comment: Ordered 30 December 1988; laid down 16 November 1989. The deletion of the *Teide* left a serious deficiency in the Fleet's at sea replenishment capability which has been restored by the *Patiño*. In addition, and as a stop gap, this tanker was built at one third of the cost of the larger support ship. Two Vertrep stations and a platform for a Sea King size helicopter. Replenishment stations on both sides and one astern. Provision for Meroka CIWS four chaff launchers as well as ESM. Has a small hospital. Based at Rota.

MARQUÉS DE LA ENSENADA   *5/2001, Giorgio Ghiglione* / 0130115

2 LOGISTIC SUPPORT SHIPS (ATF/AGDS)

Name	No	Builders	Commissioned
MAR CARIBE (ex-*Amatista*)	A 101	Duro Felguera, Gijon	24 Mar 1975
NEPTUNO (ex-*Mar Rojo*, ex-*Amapola*)	A 20 (ex-A 102)	Duro Felguera, Gijon	24 Mar 1975

Displacement, tons: 1,860 full load
Dimensions, feet (metres): 176.4 × 38.8 × 14.8 *(53.8 × 11.8 × 4.5)*
Main machinery: 2 Echevarria-Burmeister & Wain 18V23HU diesels; 4,860 hp(m) *(3.57 MW)*; 2 shafts; bow thruster
Speed, knots: 12
Range, n miles: 6,000 at 10 kt
Complement: 44

Comment: Two offshore oil rig support tugs were acquired and commissioned into the Navy 14 December 1988. Bollard pull, 80 tons. *Neptuno* converted as a diver support vessel. She has a dynamic positioning system and carries a side scan mine detection high-frequency sonar as well as a semi-autonomous remote-controlled DSRV. The control cable restricts operations to within 75 m of an auxiliary diving unit. The DSRV is launched and recovered by a hydraulic arm. *Mar Caribe* works with Amphibious Forces and is based at Cadiz. *Neptuno* based at Cartagena.

MAR CARIBE   5/2004, Diego Quevedo / 1044560

NEPTUNO   11/2002, A Campanera i Rovira / 0570952

1 WATER TANKER (AWT)

Name	No	Builders	Commissioned
MARINERO JARANO	A 65 (ex-AA 31)	Bazán, Cádiz	16 Mar 1981

Displacement, tons: 549 full load
Dimensions, feet (metres): 123 × 23 × 9.8 *(37.5 × 7 × 3)*
Main machinery: 1 diesel; 600 hp(m) *(441 kW)*; 1 shaft
Speed, knots: 10
Complement: 13
Cargo capacity: 300 tons

Comment: Similar to Y 231 and Y 255 (harbour tankers). Based at Cartagena.

MARINERO JARANO   9/2003, Diego Quevedo / 0570951

1 WATER TANKER (AWT)

Name	No	Builders	Commissioned
CONDESTABLE ZARAGOZA	A 66 (ex-AA 41)	Bazán, Cádiz	16 Oct 1981

Displacement, tons: 895 full load
Dimensions, feet (metres): 152.2 × 27.6 × 11.2 *(46.4 × 8.4 × 3.4)*
Main machinery: 1 diesel; 700 hp(m) *(515 kW)*; 1 shaft
Speed, knots: 10
Complement: 16
Cargo capacity: 600 tons

Comment: Based at Puntales (Cadiz).

CONDESTABLE ZARAGOZA   2/1995, Diego Quevedo / 0080637

37 HARBOUR LAUNCHES (YDT/YFL)

Y 502-512	Y 521-527	Y 540	Y 554	Y 583-584
Y 515	Y 529-535	Y 545	Y 556	
Y 519	Y 539	Y 548	Y 579-580	

Comment: Some used as diving tenders, others as harbour ferries. Some are former patrol craft of the P 101 and P 202 class. Y 540 is an Admirals' Yacht.

Y 554   10/2005*, Adolfo Ortigueira Gil / 1153459

Y 526   1/2003, Diego Quevedo / 0570967

47 BARGES (YO/YE)

Comment: Have Y numbers. 11 in 200 series carry fuel, 30 in 300 for ammunition and general stores, six in 400 for anti-pollution. Some floating pontoons have L numbers.

Y 221   10/2005*, Adolfo Ortigueira Gil / 1153458

TUGS

1 OCEAN TUG (ATA)

Name	No	Builders	Commissioned
MAHÓN	A 51	Astilleros Atlántico, Santander	1978
(ex-*Circos*)			

Displacement, tons: 1,450 full load
Dimensions, feet (metres): 134.5 × 38.1 × 18 *(41 × 11.6 × 5.5)*
Main machinery: 2 AESA/Sulzer 16ASV25/30 diesels; 7,744 hp(m) *(5.69 MW)*; 2 shafts
Speed, knots: 13
Range, n miles: 27,000 at 12 kt (A 52)
Complement: 33 (8 officers) plus 45 scientists
Guns: 2 — 12.7 mm MGs.
Radars: Navigation: 2 Racal Decca; I-band.

Comment: Built for Compania Hispano Americana de Offshore SA. Commissioned in the Navy 30 July 1981. Based at Ferrol.

MAHÓN *7/2000, Adolfo Ortigueira Gil* / 0105651

1 OCEAN TUG (ATA)

Name	No	Builders	Commissioned
LA GRAÑA (ex-*Punta Amer*)	A 53 (ex-Y 119)	Astilleros Luzuriaga, San Sebastian	1982

Displacement, tons: 664 full load
Dimensions, feet (metres): 102.4 × 27.6 × 10.5 *(31.2 × 8.4 × 3.2)*
Main machinery: 1 diesel; 3,240 hp(m) *(2.38 MW)*; 1 Voith Schneider prop
Speed, knots: 13
Range, n miles: 1,750 at 12 kt
Complement: 28

Comment: Former civilian tug acquired by Navy on 20 October 1987. Now designated as ocean-going. Based at Cadiz.

LA GRAÑA *4/2005*, B Prézelin* / 1153460

28 COASTAL and HARBOUR TUGS (YTB/YTM/YTL)

No	Displacement tons (full load)	HP/speed	Commissioned
Y 116-117	422	1,500/12	1981
Y 118, Y 121-126	236	1,560/14	1989-91
Y 120 (ex-*Punta Roca*)	260	1,750/12	1973
Y 132, Y 140	70	200/8	1965-67
Y 141-142	229	800/11	1981
Y 143	133	600/10	1961
Y 144-145	195	2,030/11	1983
Y 147-148	87	400/10	1987/1999
Y 171-179	10	440/11	1982/1985

Comment: *Y 143* has a troop carrying capability. *Y 171-176* are pusher tugs for submarines. *Y 118, Y 121-126* have Voith Schneider propulsion.

Y 143 *12/2004*, Diego Quevedo* / 1153461

GOVERNMENT MARITIME FORCES

POLICE (GUARDIA CIVIL — MARITIME SERVICE)

Notes: Created by Royal decree on 22 February 1991 and owned by the Ministry of Interior. Bases at La Coruña, Barcelona, Valencia, Tarragona, Baleares, Cantabria, Almeria, Malaga, Murcia and, Algeciras. Personnel strength 1,000 (35 officers). The force has taken over the anti-terrorist role and some general patrol duties as a peacetime paramilitary organisation coming under the Ministry of Defence in war. In addition to the craft listed there are some 42 smaller craft (under 9 m). 18 BO 105, 8 BK-117 and 31 Eurocopter EC-135 helicopters are used for coastal patrols and are based at Tenerife, Seville, Valencia, Mallorca, Huesca, Logroño, Leon and La Coruña. All vessels are armed.

BK 117 *10/2005*, Adolfo Ortigueira Gil* / 1153462

EC-135 *6/2004, Oris* / 1044563

1 IZAR IVP-22 CLASS (WPB)

SALEMA A 01

Displacement, tons: 52 full load
Dimensions, feet (metres): 80.4 × 19.6 × 5.9 *(24.5 × 5.96 × 1.8)*
Main machinery: 2 MAN diesels; 1,100 hp *(820 kW)*
Speed, knots: 20. **Range, n miles:** 400 at 12 kt
Complement: 8
Guns: 1 — 12.7 mm MG.
Radars: Navigation: I-band.

Comment: Built by Bazán, San Fernando. Steel hull. Commissioned on 24 June 1999 having been procured by Agriculture and Fisheries Ministry for operation by Guardia Civil. Hull lengthened in 2003 to facilitate operation of RIB. Based at Algeciras.

SALEMA *10/2005*, Adolfo Ortigueira Gil* / 1153463

3 RODMAN 82 CLASS (WPB)

RIO GUADIARO (ex-*Seriola*) A 02   **RIO PISUERGA** A 03   **RIO NALON** A 04

Displacement, tons: 93 full load
Dimensions, feet (metres): 85.3 × 19.4 × 4.3 *(26.0 × 5.9 × 1.3)*
Main machinery: 2 diesels; 1,400 hp *(1.04 MW)*; 2 waterjets
Speed, knots: 30
Range, n miles: 720 at 17 kt
Complement: 9
Guns: 1 LAG 40 mm grenade launcher.
Radars: Navigation: I-band.

Comment: Built in 2001 by Rodman, Vigo. A 02 based at Alicante, A 03 at Algeciras and A 04 at Asturias. A 02 purchased by Fisheries department.

RIO GUADIARO   *4/2002, Diego Quevedo* / 0528939

12 RODMAN 101 CLASS (WPB)

RIO PALMA A 05	**RIO GUADALAVIAR** A 10	**RIO DUERO** A 15
RIO ANDARAX A 06	**RIO CABRIEL** A 11	— A 16
RIO GUADALOPE A 07	**RIO CERVANTES** A 12	
RIO ALMANZORA A 08	**RIO ARA** A 13	
RIO NERVION A 09	**RIO ADAJA** A 14	

Displacement, tons: 109 full load
Dimensions, feet (metres): 98.4 × 19.4 × 4.3 *(30.0 × 5.9 × 1.3)*
Main machinery: 2 Caterpillar 3412C diesels; 2,800 hp *(2.06 MW)*; 2 Hamilton waterjets
Speed, knots: 30
Range, n miles: 800 at 12 kt
Complement: 9
Guns: 1 LAG 40 mm grenade launcher.
Radars: Navigation: I-band.

Comment: GRP hull. Built by Rodman, Vigo and delivered in 2002 (A 05), 2003 (A 06-08), 2004 (A 09-13), 2005 (A 14) and 2006 (A 15-16). A 05 A 06 and A 08 purchased by Agriculture and Fisheries Ministry. All operated by Guardia Civil.

RIO CERVANTES   *11/2005*, Marco Ghiglino* / 1153482

13 RODMAN 55M CLASS (WPBF)

M 02-14

Displacement, tons: 15.7 full load
Dimensions, feet (metres): 54.1 × 12.5 × 2.3 *(16.5 × 3.8 × 0.7)*
Main machinery: 2 MAN D2848-LXE diesels; 1,360 hp(m) *(1 MW)* sustained; 2 Hamilton water-jets
Speed, knots: 35
Range, n miles: 500 at 25 kt
Complement: 7
Guns: 1 — 12.7 mm MG.
Radars: Surface search: Ericsson; I-band.

Comment: GRP hulls built by Rodman, Vigo. First five in service in 1992, three in 1993, six more in 1995-96. M 01 sunk in 2002. Known as Baltic class.

M 08   *10/2005*, Adolfo Ortigueira Gil* / 1153451

2 RODMAN 55 CANARIAS CLASS (WPBF)

TINEYCHEIDE M 15   **ALMIRANTE DIAZ PIMIENTA** M 16

Displacement, tons: 18.5
Dimensions, feet (metres): 57.1 × 12.5 × 2.6 *(17.4 × 3.8 × 0.8)*
Main machinery: 2 MAN D2848 LXE406 diesels; 2,300 hp *(1.71 MW)*; 2 Hamilton waterjets
Speed, knots: 48
Range, n miles: 400 at 25 kt
Complement: 5
Guns: 1 — 12.7 mm MG.
Radars: Navigation: I-band.

Comment: GRP hull built by Rodman, Vigo. Purchased in 1999 by Canary Islands Agriculture and Fishery Department. Based at Lanzarote. Same class sold to Cyprus.

TINEYCHEIDE   *8/1999, Rodman* / 0570948

14 RODMAN 55HJ CLASS (PB)

RIO ARBA M 17	**RIO CERVERA** M 24
RIO CAUDAL M 18	**RIO ARAGON** M 25
RIO BERNESGA M 19	**RIO ALFAMBRA** M 26
RIO MARTIN M 20	**RIO ULLA** M 27
RIO GUADALOBON M 21	**RIO JUCAR** M 28
RIO CEDENTA M 22	**RIO SANTA EULALIA** M 29
RIO LADRA M 23	**RIO ULLA** M 30

Displacement, tons: 20 full load
Dimensions, feet (metres): 55.8 × 12.5 × 2.9 *(17.0 × 3.8 × 0.9)*
Main machinery: 2 MAN D2848 LXE406 diesels; 2,300 hp *(1.71 MW)*; 2 Hamilton waterjets
Speed, knots: 52. **Range, n miles:** 400 at 25 kt
Complement: 5
Radars: Navigation: I-band.

Comment: GRP hull built by Rodman, Vigo. Similar to Colimbo class of Spanish Customs. M 17-24 delivered in 2004 and M 25-30 in 2005.

RIO SANTA EULALIA   *10/2005*, Martin Mokrus* / 1154475

11 SAETA-12 CLASS (WPBF)

L 01-02   L 04-12

Displacement, tons: 14 full load
Dimensions, feet (metres): 39 × 12.5 × 2.3 *(11.9 × 3.8 × 0.7)*
Main machinery: 2 MAN D2848-LXE diesels; 1,360 hp(m) *(1 MW)* sustained; 2 Hamilton water-jets
Speed, knots: 38. **Range, n miles:** 300 at 25 kt
Complement: 4
Guns: 1 — 7.62 mm MG.
Radars: Surface search: Ericsson; I-band.

Comment: GRP hulls built by Bazán and delivered in 1993-97. Known as Aegean class. L 03 deleted in 2004 following an accident.

L 02   *11/2005*, Adolfo Ortigueira Gil* / 1153453

CUSTOMS

Notes: Customs service is the responsibility of the Ministry of Treasure. All carry ADUANAS on ships' sides. Some of the larger vessels are armed with machine guns. Ships are based at 17 ports including Ceuta and Melilla in north Africa. There are also three MBB-105, one MBB-117 and one AS 365 Dauphin helicopters. Six CASA C-212 patrol aircraft were transferred to the Air Force in 1997 and are operated by the 37th Air Wing.

CASA C-212   *3/2003, Adolfo Ortigueira Gil* / 0570963

46 PATROL CRAFT (PB)

Name	Displacement tons (full load)	HP/speed	Commissioned
ÁGUILA	80	2,700/29	1974
ALBATROS II and ALBATROS III	85	2,700/29	1964-69
ALCA I and ALCA III	24	2,000/45	1987-88
ALCAUDON II/ALCOTÁN/FENIX	18.5	1,200/55	1997-99
ALCAVARÁN I-V	85	3,920/28	1984-87
COLIMBO II	17	2,400/50	1999-03
CORMORÁN/HJ 1/ COLIMBO III-IV	17	2,400/52	1986-03
FULMAR	623	5,400/21	2006
GAVILÁN II-IV	65	3,200/26	1983-87
ARAO/GERIFALTE I/ DÉCIMO ANIVERSARIO	46	2,366/35	2001/2003
HJA	12	2,200/55	1994
HJ III-X	20	2,300/50	1986-89
HALCÓN II-III	68	3,200/28	1980-83
IMP I-II	5	600/40	1989
IPP I and IPP III	2	200/50	1989
MILANO II	15	2,000/50	1999
PETREL I	1,600	1,200/12	1994
VA II-V	23	1,400/27	1985

Comment: These craft are also listed as auxiliary ships of the Navy. Flagship is *Petrel I* for which replacement is under construction at Astilleros Gondan for delivery in 2006.

PETREL I   *11/2003, Javier Somavilla* / 0570950

GERIFALTE I   *11/2005*, Adolfo Ortigueira Gil* / 1153455

COLIMBO IV   *7/2003, Diego Quevedo* / 1044568

VA II   *9/2004, Adolfo Ortigueira Gil* / 1044569

MARITIME RESCUE, SAFETY AND LOGISTIC SUPPORT

Notes: These roles are discharged by two services: SASEMAR (Sociedad Estatal de Salvamento y Seguridad Marítima) is under the direction of the Merchant Marine but may come under a Coast Guard service in due course. It operates 11 salvage tugs (two UT 740 salvage and pollution control vessels are under construction), 38 small rescue craft, five harbour pollution craft and five Sikorsky S 61 helicopters. All ships are painted red with a white stripe on the hull. A further three helicopters and three CASA/EADS C-235 maritime patrol aircraft are to be acquired by 2009. ISM (Instituto Social de la Marina) operates two specialised medical and logistic ships for support of fishing vessels. *Esperanza del Mar* (5,000 tons) is based at Las Palmas (Canary Islands) Naval Base and *Juan de la Cosa* is based at Santander.

SALVAMAR ALBORAN   *1/2005*, Adolfo Ortigueira Gil* / 1153456

ESPERANZA DEL MAR   *9/2001, Adolfo Ortigueira Gil* / 0130140

V B ANTARTICO   *10/2005*, Adolfo Ortigueira Gil* / 1153457

S 61   *8/2002, Adolfo Ortigueira Gil* / 0528949

RESEARCH SHIPS

Notes: Nine civilian research ships are owned by the Government Science and Technology Ministry and by the Agriculture Fishery and Food Ministry. Those operated by the Instituto Español de Oceanografía (IEO) are *Vizconde de Eza* (1,400 tons), *Cornide de Saavedra* (1,113 tons), *F P Navarro* (178 tons), *Odón de Buen* (64 tons), *Lura* (34 tons), *José Rioja* (32 tons) and *J M Navaz* (30 tons). Two further ships, the first of which is called *Emma Bardán*, are to enter service in 2006. Those operated by CSIC are *Garcia del Cid* (539 tons) and *Mytilus* (170 tons). The ships operate in co-operation with the Spanish Navy ship *Hespérides* and the French research ship *Thalassa*. A new ship is to be delivered to CSIC in 2006.

VIZCONDE DE EZA 6/2005*, Adolfo Ortigueira Gil / 1153454

CORNIDE DE SAAVEDRA 6/2003, Adolfo Ortigueira Gil / 1044566

Sri Lanka

Country Overview

Formerly known as Ceylon, the Democratic Socialist Republic of Sri Lanka gained independence in 1948. Situated off the southeast coast of India, from which it is separated by the Palk Strait and Gulf of Mannar, it has an area of 25,326 square miles and a coastline of 723 n miles with the Indian Ocean. The capital of Sri Lanka is Sri Jayavardhanapura (Kotte) while Colombo is the largest city and principal port. There are further ports at Trincomalee, Kankasanthurai and Galle. Territorial waters (12 n miles) are claimed. A 200 n mile EEZ has been claimed although the limits have only been partly defined by boundary agreements.

Headquarters Appointments

Commander of the Navy:
  Vice Admiral W K J Karannagoda, RSP, USP
Chief of Staff:
  Rear Admiral D S M Wijewickrama, RSP, USP
Deputy Chief of Staff:
  Rear Admiral S P Weerasekara, RWP, USP
Director General, Operations:
  Rear Admiral L D Dharmapriya, RSP, USP

Area Commanders

Commander Western Naval Area:
  Rear Admiral H S Rathnakeerthi, USP
Commander North Central Naval Area:
  Commodore D Samarawickrama, RWP, RSP, USP
Commander Northern Naval Area:
  Rear Admiral T M W K B Thennakoon, RSP, USP
Commander Eastern Naval Area:
  Rear Admiral M R U Siriwardana, USP
Commander Southern Naval Area:
  Rear Admiral J H U Ranaweera, RWP, RSP, USP

Personnel

(a) 2006: 24,897 (1,686 officers) regulars
(b) SLVNF: 3,500 (250 officers)
(c) Reserve force (regular): 77 (8 officers)
(d) Reserve force (volunteer): 71 (6 officers)

Bases

Navy HQ: Colombo.
Western Command HQ: Colombo port (other bases at Welisara and Kalpitiya).
Eastern Command HQ: Trincomalee port (other bases at Nilaweli and Thiriyaya, Naval Academy at Trincomalee).

Southern Command HQ: Galle port (other bases at Tangalle, Boossa training centre and Kirinda harbour).
Northern Command HQ: Kankasanthurai port (other bases at Madagal, Karainagar, Velerni Island, Mandathive Island, Nagadeepa Island and Pungudathive Island).
North Central Command HQ: Medawachchiya (other bases at Punewa training centre, Thalaimannar and Mannar Island).

Pennant Numbers

Pennant numbers were reviewed in 1996 and 2002.

Prefix To Ships Names

SLNS.

DELETIONS

Patrol Forces

2005 *Parakramabahu* (damaged by Tsunami)

Amphibious Forces

2002 *Lihiniya*

PATROL FORCES

1 + (1) SUKANYA CLASS OFFSHORE PATROL VESSEL (PSOH)

Name	No	Builders	Launched	Commissioned
SAYURA (ex-*Saryu*)	P 620 (ex-54)	Hindustan SY, Vishakapatnam	16 Oct 1989	8 Oct 1991

Displacement, tons: 1,890 full load
Dimensions, feet (metres): 331.7 oa; 315 wl × 37.7 × 14.4 *(101.1; 96 × 11.5 × 4.4)*
Main machinery: 2 SEMT-Pielstick 16 PA6 V 280 diesels; 12,800 hp(m) *(9.41 MW)* sustained; 2 shafts
Speed, knots: 21
Range, n miles: 5,800 at 15 kt
Complement: 140 (15 officers)
Guns: 1 Bofors 40 mm/60. 2 China 14.5 mm (twin).
Radars: Surface search: Racal Decca 2459; I-band.
Navigation: Bharat1245; I-band.

Comment: Transferred from India and recommissioned on 9 December 2000. Plans to acquire a second refurbished ship have been reported.

1 RELIANCE CLASS (PSOH)

Name	No	Builders	Commissioned
SAMUDURA (ex-*Courageous*)	P 621 (ex-WMEC 622)	Coast Guard Yard, Baltimore	8 Dec 1967

Displacement, tons: 1,129 full load
Dimensions, feet (metres): 210.5 × 34 × 10.5 *(64.2 × 10.4 × 3.2)*
Main machinery: 2 Alco 16V-251 diesels; 6,480 hp *(4.83 MW)* sustained; 2 shafts; LIPS cp props
Speed, knots: 18. **Range, n miles:** 6,100 at 14 kt; 2,700 at 18 kt
Complement: 75 (12 officers)
Guns: 1 Boeing 25 mm/87 Mk 38 Bushmaster; 200 rds/min to 6.8 km *(3.4 n miles)*. 2 — 12.7 mm MGs.
Radars: Surface search: Hughes/Furuno SPS-73; I-band.

Helicopters: Platform for one medium.

Comment: Transferred to Sri Lanka on 24 June 2004. During 34 years in USCG service, underwent Major Maintenance Availability (MMA) in 1989. The exhausts for main engines, ship service generators and boilers were run in a vertical funnel which reduced flight deck size. Capable of towing ships up to 10,000 tons.

SAYURA 10/2001, Chris Sattler / 0130149

SAMUDURA 6/2005*, Sri Lanka Navy / 1153484

1 JAYASAGARA CLASS (OFFSHORE PATROL VESSEL) (PB)

Name	No	Builders	Launched	Commissioned
JAYASAGARA	P 601	Colombo Dockyard	26 May 1983	9 Dec 1983

Displacement, tons: 330 full load
Dimensions, feet (metres): 130.5 × 23 × 7 *(39.8 × 7 × 2.1)*
Main machinery: 2 MAN 8L20/27 diesels; 2,180 hp(m) *(1.6 MW)* sustained; 2 shafts
Speed, knots: 15
Range, n miles: 3,000 at 11 kt
Complement: 52 (4 officers)
Guns: 2 China 25 mm/80 (twin). 2 China 14.5 mm (twin) MGs. 2—12.7 mm MGs. 2—40 mm AGL. 2—7.62 mm MGs.
Radars: Surface search: Anritsu RA 723; I-band.

Comment: Ordered from Colombo Dockyard on 31 December 1981. Second of class sunk by Tamil forces in September 1994.

JAYASAGARA   *6/2004, Sri Lanka Navy* / 1044193

2 SAAR 4 CLASS (FAST ATTACK CRAFT—MISSILE) (PGG)

Name	No	Builders	Launched	Commissioned
NANDIMITHRA (ex-*Moledt*)	P 701	Israel Shipyard, Haifa	22 Mar 1979	May 1979
SURANIMALA (ex-*Komemiut*)	P 702	Israel Shipyard, Haifa	19 July 1978	Aug 1980

Displacement, tons: 415 standard; 450 full load
Dimensions, feet (metres): 190.6 × 25 × 8 *(58 × 7.8 × 2.4)*
Main machinery: 4 MTU/Bazán 16V 956 TB91 diesels; 15,000 hp(m) *(11.03 MW)* sustained; 4 shafts
Speed, knots: 32
Range, n miles: 1,650 at 30 kt; 4,000 at 17.5 kt
Complement: 75

Missiles: 3 Gabriel II; radar or TV optical guidance; semi-active radar plus anti-radiation homing to 36 km *(20 n miles)* at 0.7 Mach; warhead 75 kg.
Guns: 1 OTO Melara 3 in *(76 mm)*/62 compact; 85 rds/min to 16 km *(8.7 n miles)*; weight of shell 6 kg. Adapated for shore bombardment. 1—40 mm.
2 Rafael Typhoon 20 mm. 2—20 mm. 2—12.7 mm MGs. 2—40 mm AGL.
Radars: Air/surface search: Thomson-CSF TH-D 1040 Neptune; G-band; range 33 km *(18 n miles)* for 2 m² target.
Fire control: Selenia Orion RTN 10X; I-band.

Comment: Transferred from Israel and recommissioned on 9 December 2000.

NANDIMITHRA   *10/2003, Hartmut Ehlers* / 0570991

5 SHANGHAI II (TYPE 062) CLASS
(FAST ATTACK CRAFT—GUN) (PB)

WEERAYA P 311 (ex-P 3141)	ABEETHA II P 316	WICKRAMA II P 318
JAGATHA P 315 (ex-P 3146)	EDITHARA II P 317	

Displacement, tons: 139 full load
Dimensions, feet (metres): 127.3 × 17.7 × 5.2 *(38.8 × 5.4 × 1.6)*
Main machinery: 4 Type L12-180 diesels; 4,800 hp(m) *(3.53 MW)*; 4 shafts
Speed, knots: 28. **Range, n miles:** 750 at 16 kt
Complement: 44
Guns: 4 (2 in P 311, P 315) Royal Ordnance GCM-AO3 30 mm (2 (1 in P 311, P 315) twin).
4—37 mm 2 (twin) (P 311, P 315).
4 China 14.5 mm (2 twin) MG.
2—7.62 mm MGs.
2—40 mm AGL (P 311, P 315).
Radars: Surface search: Koden MD 3220 Mk 2; I-band.
Navigation: Furuno 825 D; I-band.

Comment: Five transferred by China in 1971 of which four since decommissioned and *Weeraya* remains in service. Two further craft transferred in 1980 of which *Jagatha* remains in service. Three further craft (*Abeetha II, Edithara II* and *Wickrama II*) are modified craft with improved habitability but similar specifications. These were built at Qinxin Shipyard and commissioned on 11 June 2000.

WEERAYA   *6/2001, Sri Lanka Navy* / 0130146

EDITHARA II   *6/2003, Sri Lanka Navy* / 0570992

1 MOD SHANGHAI II CLASS
(FAST ATTACK CRAFT—GUN) (PB)

Name	No	Builders	Commissioned
RANARISI	P 322	Guijiang Shipyard	14 July 1992

Displacement, tons: 150 full load
Dimensions, feet (metres): 134.5 × 17.7 × 5.2 *(41 × 5.4 × 1.6)*
Main machinery: 4 diesels; 4,800 hp(m) *(3.53 MW)*; 4 shafts
Speed, knots: 29. **Range, n miles:** 750 at 16 kt
Complement: 44 (4 officers)
Guns: 2 Royal Ordnance GCM-AO3 30 mm (1 twin). 2—25 mm.
4 China 14.5 mm (twin) Type 69. 2—12.7 mm MGs. 2—40 mm AGL.
Radars: Surface search: Racal Decca; I-band.

Comment: Acquired from China in September 1991. Automatic guns and improved habitability. *Ranaviru* and *Ranasuvu* destroyed by Tamil guerrillas.

RANARISI   *6/2003, Sri Lanka Navy* / 0570988

3 HAIZHUI (TYPE 062/1G) CLASS (PB)

Name	No	Builders	Commissioned
RANAJAYA	P 330	Guijiang Shipyard	22 May 1996
RANADEERA	P 331	Guijiang Shipyard	22 May 1996
RANAWICKRAMA	P 332	Guijiang Shipyard	22 May 1996

Displacement, tons: 170 full load
Dimensions, feet (metres): 134.5 × 17.4 × 5.9 *(41 × 5.3 × 1.8)*
Main machinery: 4 Type L12-180A diesels; 4,400 hp(m) *(3.22 MW)* sustained; 4 shafts
Speed, knots: 21
Complement: 44
Guns: 4 China 37 mm/63 (2 twin). 4 China 25 mm/60 (2 twin). 2—12.7 mm MGs. 2—40 mm AGL.
Radars: Surface search: Anritsu 726UA; I-band.

Comment: Transferred from China by lift ship after delivery in 1995.

RANAWICKRAMA   *6/2005*, Sri Lanka Navy* / 1153485

2 MOD HAIZHUI (LUSHUN) (TYPE 062/1G) CLASS
(FAST ATTACK CRAFT—GUN) (PB)

PRATHPA P 340   **UDARA** P 341

Displacement, tons: 212 full load
Dimensions, feet (metres): 149 × 21 × 5.6 (45.5 × 6.4 × 1.7)
Main machinery: 4 Type Z12V 190 BCJ diesels; 4,800 hp(m) (3.53 MW); 4 shafts
Speed, knots: 28. **Range, n miles:** 750 at 16 kt
Complement: 44 (3 officers)
Guns: 4 China 37 mm/63 (2 twin) Type 76.
  2 China 14.5 mm (1 twin) Type 82 MGs.
  2—12.7 mm MGs.
  2—40 mm AGL.
Radars: Surface search: Racal Decca RM 1070A; I-band.

Comment: Built at Lushun Dockyard, Darlin. Commissioned on 2 March 1998. Larger version of Haizhui class.

UDARA   *6/2005*, *Sri Lanka Navy* / 1153483

22 COLOMBO MK I/II/III CLASS
(FAST ATTACK CRAFT—GUN) (PBF)

P 410-424   **P 450-451**   **P 490-492**   **P 494**   **P 497**

Displacement, tons: 56 full load
Dimensions, feet (metres): 81.4 × 19.7 × 3.9 (24.8 × 6 × 1.2)
Main machinery: 2 MTU 12V 396 TE94 diesels; 4,570 hp(m) (3.36 MW); ASD 16 surface drives
Speed, knots: 45. **Range, n miles:** 850 at 16 kt
Complement: 20
Guns: 1 Rafael Typhoon 23 mm. 1 Oerlikon 20 mm. 4—12.7 mm MGs. 8—7.62 mm MGs. 2—40 mm AGL.
Weapons control: Elop MSIS optronic director; Typhoon GFCS.
Radars: Surface search: Furuno FR 8250 or Corden Mk 2; I-band.

Comment: Built by Colombo Dockyard to the Israeli Shaldag design. First deliveries 1997. Mk I (P 450-451); Mk II (P 490-492, P 494, P 497); Mk III (P 410-424). P 493 and P 496 sunk in action in 2000.

Colombo MK II   *11/1999* / 0080695

6 SHALDAG CLASS (FAST ATTACK CRAFT—GUN) (PBF)

P 470 (ex-P 491)   **P 471** (ex-P 492)   **P 472-475**

Displacement, tons: 58 full load
Dimensions, feet (metres): 81.4 × 19.7 × 3.9 (24.8 × 6 × 1.2)
Main machinery: 2 Deutz 620 TB 16V or MTU 396 TE diesels; 5,000 hp(m) (3.68 MW); 2 LIPS or MJP water-jets
Speed, knots: 50. **Range, n miles:** 700 at 32 kt
Complement: 20
Guns: 1 Rafael Typhoon 23 mm. 1—20 mm. 2—12.7 mm MGs. 6—7.62 mm MGs. 2—40 mm AGL.
Weapons control: ELOP compass optronic director. Typhoon GFCS.
Radars: Surface search: MD 3220 Mk II; I-band.

Comment: Originally launched in December 1989, first one acquired from the Israeli Shipyards, Haifa on 24 January 1996, second 20 July 1996 and third on 16 February 2000. Four more followed. Same hull used for the Colombo class. Also in service in Cyprus. P 476 sunk on 7 January 2006.

SHALDAG CLASS   *6/2003*, *Sri Lanka Navy* / 0570989

5 SUPER DVORA MK II CLASS
(FAST ATTACK CRAFT—GUN) (PBF)

P 460 (ex-P 441)   **P 461** (ex-P 496)   **P 462** (ex-P 497)   **P 464-465**

Displacement, tons: 64 full load
Dimensions, feet (metres): 82 × 18.4 × 3.6 (25 × 5.6 × 1.1)
Main machinery: 2 MTU 12V 396 TE94 diesels; 4,570 hp(m) (3.36 MW); ASD16 surface drives
Speed, knots: 50. **Range, n miles:** 700 at 30 kt
Complement: 20 (1 officer)
Guns: 1 Rafael Typhoon 20 mm or 2 Royal Ordnance GCM-AO3 30 mm (twin).
  4—12.7 mm MGs. 6—7.62 mm MGs. 2—40 mm AGL.
Weapons control: Elop MSIS optronic director; Typhoon GFCS.
Radars: Surface search: Koden MD 3220; I-band.

Comment: First four ordered from Israel Aircraft Industries Ramta in early 1995. A slightly larger version of the Mk 1. First one delivered 5 November 1995, second 30 April 1996, third 22 June 1996 and fourth in December 1996. Two more were acquired on 9 June 1999 and 15 September 1999 respectively. The engines are an improved version of those fitted in the Israeli Navy craft. P 463 sunk in action in 2000.

SUPER DVORA Mk II   *11/1999* / 0080697

4 SUPER DVORA MK I CLASS
(FAST ATTACK CRAFT—GUN) (PBF)

P 440-443 (ex-P 465-468)

Displacement, tons: 54 full load
Dimensions, feet (metres): 73.5 × 18 × 5.8 (22.4 × 5.5 × 1.8)
Main machinery: 2 MTU 12V 396 TB93 diesels; 3,260 hp(m) (2.4 MW) sustained; 2 shafts
Speed, knots: 46
Range, n miles: 1,200 at 17 kt
Complement: 20 (1 officer)
Guns: 2 Oerlikon 20 mm. 2—12.7 mm MGs. 4—40 mm AGL.
Radars: Surface search: Decca 926; I-band.

Comment: Ordered from Israel Aircraft Industries in October 1986 and delivered in 1987-88. A more powerful version of the Dvora class. P 464 was destroyed by Tamil guerrillas on 29 August 1993 and P 463 on 29 August 1995. These craft have a deeper draft than the Mk II version with surface drives.

P 443 (ex-P 468)   *1995, Sri Lanka Navy* / 0130147

3 DVORA CLASS (FAST ATTACK CRAFT—GUN) (PBF)

P 401-403 (ex-P 420 (ex-P 453)-P 422 (ex-P 456))

Displacement, tons: 47 full load
Dimensions, feet (metres): 70.8 × 18 × 5.8 (21.6 × 5.5 × 1.8)
Main machinery: 2 MTU 12V 331 TC81 diesels; 2,605 hp(m) (1.91 MW) sustained; 2 shafts
Speed, knots: 36
Range, n miles: 1,200 at 17 kt
Complement: 18
Guns: 2 Oerlikon 20 mm. 2—12.7 mm MGs. 6—7.62 mm MGs. 2—40 mm AGL.
Radars: Surface search: Anritsu 721UA; I-band.

Comment: 'Dvora' class, first pair of which transferred from Israel early 1984, next four in October 1986. Built by Israel Aircraft Industries. One sunk by Tamil forces on 29 August 1995 and second on 30 March 1996. One more deleted in late 1996. Not downgraded to patrol craft as previously reported but speed may have been reduced.

DVORA CLASS   *6/2003, A Sharma* / 0570995

3 SOUTH KOREAN KILLER CLASS
(FAST ATTACK CRAFT—GUN) (PBF)

P 404-406 (ex-P 430 (ex-P 473)-P 432 (ex-P 475))

Displacement, tons: 56 full load
Dimensions, feet (metres): 75.5 × 17.7 × 5.9 *(23 × 5.4 × 1.8)*
Main machinery: 2 MTU 396 TB93 diesels; 3,260 hp(m) *(2.4 MW)* sustained; 2 shafts
Speed, knots: 40
Complement: 18
Guns: 2 Oerlikon 20 mm. 2—12.7 mm MGs. 6—7.62 mm MGs.
Radars: Surface search: Racal Decca 926; I-band.

Comment: 'South Korean Killer' class, built by Korea SB and Eng, Buson. All commissioned February 1988. Not downgraded to patrol craft as previously reported but speed may have been reduced.

KILLER CLASS   *6/2003, A Sharma* / 0570994

5 TRINITY MARINE CLASS (FAST ATTACK CRAFT—GUN) (PBF)

P 480   **P 481**   **P 483-485**

Displacement, tons: 68 full load
Dimensions, feet (metres): 81.7 × 17.7 × 4.9 *(24.9 × 5.4 × 1.5)*
Main machinery: 2 MTU 12V 396 TE94 diesels; 4,570 hp(m) *(3.36 MW)* sustained; 2 water-jets
Speed, knots: 47
Range, n miles: 600 at 17 kt
Complement: 20
Guns: 2 Oerlikon 20 mm. 2—12.7 mm MGs. 2—7.62 mm MGs. 1 Grenade launcher.
Radars: Surface search: Raytheon R 1210; I-band.

Comment: All built at Equitable Shipyard, New Orleans. First three delivered in January 1997; second three in September 1997. All aluminium construction. P 482 sunk in action in 2000.

P 480   *1/1997, Sri Lanka Navy* / 0080701

5 COASTAL PATROL CRAFT (PB)

P 201   **P 211**   **P 214**   **P 215**   **P 233**

Displacement, tons: 21 full load
Dimensions, feet (metres): 46.6 × 12.8 × 3.3 *(14.2 × 3.9 × 1)*
Main machinery: 2 Detroit 8V-71TA diesels; 460 hp *(343 kW)*; 2 shafts
Speed, knots: 20
Range, n miles: 450 at 14 kt
Complement: 15 (1 officer)
Guns: 2—12.7 mm MGs.
Radars: Surface search: Furuno FR 2010; I-band.

Comment: Built by Colombo DY and commissioned in 1982 *(P 201)*, June 1986 *(P 211 and P 214)* and 1993 *(P 215)*. P 241 and P 243 decommissioned in 2001.

P 201   *6/2003, Sri Lanka Navy* / 0570987

4 CHEVERTON CLASS COASTAL PATROL CRAFT (PB)

P 221-224 (ex-P 421-424)

Displacement, tons: 22 full load
Dimensions, feet (metres): 55.9 × 14.8 × 3.9 *(17 × 4.5 × 1.2)*
Main machinery: 2 Detroit 8V-71TA diesels; 460 hp *(343 kW)*; 2 shafts
Speed, knots: 23
Range, n miles: 1,000 at 12 kt
Complement: 15
Guns: 1—12.7 mm MG.
Radars: Surface search: Racal Decca 110; I-band.

Comment: Used for general patrol duties. Built by Cheverton Workboats, UK and commissioned in 1977. One paid off in 1996.

P 222   *6/2004, Sri Lanka Navy* / 1044192

41 INSHORE PATROL CRAFT (PBR)

P 120-131	P 169	P 180-181
P 151-152	P 171-173	P 183-194
P 162-167	P 175	P 196-197

Displacement, tons: 10 full load
Dimensions, feet (metres): 44.3 × 9.8 × 1.6 *(13.5 × 3 × 0.5)*
Main machinery: 2 Cummins 6BTA5. 9-M2; 584 hp *(436 kW)* sustained; 2 water-jets
Speed, knots: 33
Range, n miles: 330 at 25 kt
Complement: 5
Guns: 2—12.7 mm MGs. 2—7.62 mm MGs.
Radars: Surface search: Furuno 1941; I-band.

Comment: First pair (P 151, 152) built by TAOS Yacht Company, Colombo, and delivered in 1991. Next 27 built by Blue Star Marine, Colombo and delivered between 1994 and 1998. There are minor superstructure differences between the first pair and the rest. P 120-131 built by SLN, IPCCP Welisara. More are being built. P 168, P 174 and P 182 sunk in action. P 101 and P 104 decommissioned.

INSHORE PATROL CRAFT   *6/2003, A Sharma* / 0570993

4 INSHORE PATROL CRAFT (TYPE BSM) (PBR)

P 145-147   **P 149**

Displacement, tons: 3.5 full load
Dimensions, feet (metres): 42 × 8 × 1.6 *(12.8 × 2.4 × 0.5)*
Main machinery: 2 outboard motors; 280 hp *(209 kW)*
Speed, knots: 30
Complement: 9
Guns: 1—12.7 mm MG.

Comment: Acquired in 1988 from Blue Star Marine. Similar to *P 111* but with outboard engines. *P 143* (ex-P 150) was mined and sunk in August 1991 and again sunk in 1995.

INSHORE PATROL CRAFT   *6/2004, Sri Lanka Navy* / 1044190

3 SIMONNEAU CLASS (PBF)

P 250 (ex-P 410, ex-P 483)   P 252 (ex-P 412, ex-P 485)   P 253 (ex-P 413, ex-P 486)

Displacement, tons: 28 full load
Dimensions, feet (metres): 56.8 × 16.1 × 4.6 (17.3 × 4.9 × 1.4)
Main machinery: 2 MTU 12V 183 TE93 diesels; 2,300 hp(m) (1.69 MW); 2 Hamilton water-jets
Speed, knots: 42. **Range, n miles:** 500 at 35 kt
Complement: 15
Guns: 1 DCN 20 mm. 2 — 12.7 mm MGs. 2 — 7.62 mm MGs.
Radars: Surface search: Racal Decca; I-band.

Comment: Simonneau Marine Type 508 craft. First pair completed in December 1993 and shipped to Colombo in 1994. Second pair built in Colombo and completed in 1995. The plan to build more was shelved. Downgraded to patrol craft on 1 August 2000. Speed likely to have been reduced. P 251 sunk in 2001.

SIMONNEAU CLASS   6/2004, Sri Lanka Navy / 1044191

4 INSHORE PATROL CRAFT (TYPE CME) (PBR)

P 110-113

Displacement, tons: 5 full load
Dimensions, feet (metres): 44 × 9.8 × 1.6 (13.4 × 3 × 0.5)
Main machinery: 2 Yamaha D 343 diesels; 730 hp(m) (544 kW) sustained; 2 shafts
Speed, knots: 26
Complement: 5
Guns: 1 — 12.7 mm MG. 1 — 7.62 mm MG.
Radars: Surface search: Furuno FR 1941; I-band.

Comment: Built by Consolidated Marine Engineers, Sri Lanka. First nine delivered in 1988; four more in 1992 and two more in 1994. Most of these craft have been destroyed.

P 111   6/2003, Sri Lanka Navy / 0570986

AMPHIBIOUS FORCES

1 YUHAI (WUHU-A) (TYPE 074) CLASS (LSM)

Name	No	Builders	Commissioned
SHAKTHI	L 880	China	22 May 1996

Displacement, tons: 799 full load
Dimensions, feet (metres): 191.6 × 34.1 × 8.9 (58.4 × 10.4 × 2.7)
Main machinery: 2 MAN 8 L 20/27 diesels; 4,900 hp(m) (3.6 MW); 2 shafts
Speed, knots: 14. **Range, n miles:** 1,000 at 12 kt
Complement: 60
Military lift: 150 tons
Guns: 10 — 14.5 mm/93 (5 twin) MGs. 6 — 12.7 mm MGs.
Radars: Navigation: Racal Decca; I-band.

Comment: Transferred by lift ship from China arriving 13 December 1995. A planned second of class was built but not acquired.

SHAKTHI   5/1996, Sri Lanka Navy / 0080710

2 LANDING CRAFT (LCM)

Name	No	Builders	Commissioned
RANAGAJA	L 839	Colombo Dockyard	15 Nov 1991
RANAVIJAYA	L 836	Colombo Dockyard	21 July 1994

Displacement, tons: 268 full load
Dimensions, feet (metres): 108.3 × 26 × 4.9 (33 × 8 × 1.5)
Main machinery: 2 Caterpillar diesels; 1,524 hp (1.14 MW); 2 shafts
Speed, knots: 8
Range, n miles: 1,800 at 8 kt
Complement: 28 (2 officers)
Guns: 4 China 14.5 mm (2 twin) (Ranagaja) or 2 Oerlikon 20 mm. 2 — 12.7 mm MGs.
Radars: Navigation: Furuno FCR 1421; I-band.

Comment: Two built in 1983 and acquired in October 1985. Third of the class taken over by the Navy in September 1991 and a fourth in March 1992. Kandula sank in October 1992 and the hulk was salvaged in mid-December. Pabbatha sank in action in February 1998.

RANAVIJAYA   6/2004, Sri Lanka Navy / 1044189

2 YUNNAN CLASS (TYPE 067)

L 820   L 821

Displacement, tons: 135 full load
Dimensions, feet (metres): 93.8 × 17.7 × 4.9 (28.6 × 5.4 × 1.5)
Main machinery: 2 diesels; 600 hp(m) (441 kW); 2 shafts
Speed, knots: 12
Range, n miles: 500 at 10 kt
Complement: 22 (2 officers)
Military lift: 46 tons
Guns: 4 — 14.5 mm (2 twin) MGs. 2 — 7.62 mm MGs
Radars: Surface search: Fuji; I-band.

Comment: First one acquired from China in May 1991, second in May 1995.

L 820   6/2004, Sri Lanka Navy / 1044188

1 M 10 CLASS HOVERCRAFT (UCAC)

A 530

Displacement, tons: 18 full load
Dimensions, feet (metres): 67.6 × 28.9 (20.6 × 8.8)
Main machinery: 2 Deutz diesels; 1,050 hp(m) (772 kW)
Speed, knots: 40; 7 with cushion deflated
Range, n miles: 600 at 30 kt
Complement: 10
Military lift: 56 troops or 20 troops plus 2 vehicles
Guns: 1 — 12.7 mm MG.
Radars: Navigation: Furuno; I-band.

Comment: Acquired from ABS Hovercraft/Vosper Thornycroft in April 1998 and designated a Utility Craft Air Cushion (UCAC). Has a Kevlar superstructure. More may be ordered in due course.

A 530   4/1998, ABS Hovercraft / 0033561

3 FAST PERSONNEL CARRIERS (LCP)

Name	No	Builders	Commissioned
HANSAYA (ex-*Offshore Pioneer*)	A 540	Sing Koon Seng, Singapore	20 Dec 1987
— (ex-*Lanka Rani*)	A 542	Kvaerner Fielistrand Ltd, Singapore	2000
— (ex-*Lanka Devi*)	A 543	Kvaerner Fielistrand Ltd, Singapore, Singapore	2000

Displacement, tons: 154 full load
Dimensions, feet (metres): 98.4 × 36.8 × 7.7 *(30 × 11.2 × 2.3)*
Main machinery: 2 Paxman Vega 12 diesels; 1,800 hp(m) *(1.32 MW)*; 2 shafts
Speed, knots: 30
Complement: 15 (2 officers)
Military lift: 60 tons; 120 troops
Guns: 1 Oerlikon 20 mm. 2—12.7 mm MGs.
Radars: Navigation: Furuno FR 1012; I-band.

Comment: A 540 acquired in January 1986 from Aluminium Shipbuilders. Catamaran hull built as oil rig tender. Now used as fast transport. A 541 decommissioned in 2002.

HANSAYA   *2001, Sri Lanka Navy* / 0130145

AUXILIARIES

1 CARGO SHIP (AA)

Name	No	Builders	Commissioned
— (ex -*Invincible*)	A520	JJ Sietas, Hamburg	1971

Measurement, tons: 1,188 gross
Dimensions, feet (metres): 242.1 × 35.4 × ? *(73.8 × 10.8 × ?)*
Main machinery: 1 KHW Deutz diesel; 1,320 hp(m) *(970 kW)* sustained; 1 shaft
Speed, knots: 11.5
Complement: 53 (3 officers)
Guns: To be announced.
Radars: Surface search/navigation: FR1932; I-band.

Comment: Formerly owned by Ceyline Shipping and commissioned into the Sri Lanka Navy on 30 March 2005. This may be the same ship that was detained during investigations into a people-smuggling operation in 2003.

1 SUPPORT/TRAINING SHIP (AA/AX)

Name	No	Builders	Commissioned
— (ex-*Simon Keghian*)	A 521	—	1972

Measurement, tons: 1,124 gross
Dimensions, feet (metres): 177.2 × 36.1 × ? *(54.0 × 11.0 × ?)*
Main machinery: 1 KHW Deutz diesel; 1,320 hp(m) *(970 kW)* sustained; 1 shaft
Speed, knots: 10
Complement: 53 (3 officers)
Guns: 6—12.7 mm MGs. 2—40 mm AGLs.
Radars: Surface search/navigation: Furuno FR 2125; I-band.

Comment: Former deep-sea fishing trawler donated by the Lorient-Matara Friendship Foundation of France and commissioned into the Sri Lanka Navy on 26 April 2005. The ship was donated on humanitarian grounds, following the tsunami of 26 December 2004, and it is understood that the vessel is to be used by the navy in support of fishing activities and as a training vessel.

Sudan

Country Overview

The Republic of Sudan is situated in north-eastern Africa. The largest country in Africa, it has an area of 967,500 square miles and is bordered to the north by Egypt, to the east by Eritrea and Ethiopia, to the south by Kenya, Uganda and the Democratic Republic of the Congo and to the west by the Central African Republic, Chad, and Libya. It has a 459 n mile coastline with the Red Sea. Khartoum is the capital and largest city and Port Sudan is the principal port. There are about 2,867 n miles of navigable waterways. Territorial waters (12 n miles) are claimed. An EEZ has not been claimed.

The country has been ravaged by civil war in recent years but a Comprehensive Peace Agreement was finally concluded on 9 January 2005. This allows for the south to become a self-administering region until 2011 by when its future status will be decided by referendum.

Naval Forces are part of the Army and have low budgetary priority.

Headquarters Appointments

Commander, Naval Forces:
  Brigadier Abbas al-Sayyid Uthman

Personnel

(a) 2006: 1,300 officers and men
(b) Voluntary service

Establishment

The Navy was established in 1962 to operate on the Red Sea coast and on the River Nile.

Bases

Port Sudan (HQ). Flamingo Bay (Red Sea), Khartoum (Nile), Kosti (Nile).

PATROL FORCES

4 KURMUK (TYPE 15) CLASS (INSHORE PATROL CRAFT) (PBR)

KURMUK 502	QAYSAN 503	RUMBEK 504	MAYOM 505

Displacement, tons: 19.5 full load
Dimensions, feet (metres): 55.4 × 12.8 × 2.3 *(16.9 × 3.9 × 0.7)*
Main machinery: 2 diesels; 330 hp(m) *(243 kW)*; 2 shafts
Speed, knots: 16
Range, n miles: 160 at 12 kt
Complement: 6
Guns: 1 Oerlikon 20 mm; 2—7.62 mm MGs.

Comment: Delivered by Yugoslavia on 18 May 1989 for operations on the White Nile. All based at Flamingo Bay.

KURMUK   *1989, G Jacobs* / 0506101

4 SEWART CLASS (INSHORE PATROL CRAFT) (PBR)

MAROUB 1161	FIJAB 1162	SALAK 1163	HALOTE 1164

Displacement, tons: 9.1 full load
Dimensions, feet (metres): 40 × 12.1 × 3.3 *(12.2 × 3.7 × 1)*
Main machinery: 2 GM diesels; 348 hp *(260 kW)*; 2 shafts
Speed, knots: 31
Complement: 6
Guns: 1—12.7 mm MG.

Comment: Transferred by Iranian Coast Guard in 1975. All are based at Flamingo Bay but operational status is doubtful.

7 ASHOORA I CLASS (INSHORE PATROL CRAFT) (PBR)

Displacement, tons: 3 full load
Dimensions, feet (metres): 26.6 × 8 × 1.6 *(8.1 × 2.4 × 0.5)*
Main machinery: 2 Yamaha outboards; 400 hp(m) *(294 kW)*
Speed, knots: 42
Complement: 2
Guns: 1—7.62 mm MG.

Comment: Acquired from Iran in 1992-94. Four based at Flamingo Bay and three at Khartoum but operational status is doubtful.

ASHOORA I   *1992, IRI Marine Industries* / 0080715

AUXILIARIES

Notes: (1) In addition there are two small miscellaneous support ships. *Baraka* 21 a water boat, and a Rotork 512 craft. Both restored with Iranian assistance.
(2) Five Type II LCVPs were delivered from Yugoslavia in 1991 and are based at Kosti.

2 SUPPLY SHIPS (AFL)

SOBAT 221	DINDER 222

Displacement, tons: 410 full load
Dimensions, feet (metres): 155.1 × 21 × 7.5 *(47.3 × 6.4 × 2.3)*
Main machinery: 3 Gray Marine diesels; 495 hp *(369 kW)*; 3 shafts
Speed, knots: 9
Complement: 15
Guns: 1 Oerlikon 20 mm. 2—12.7 mm MGs.

Comment: Two Yugoslav MFPD class LCTs transferred in 1969. Used for transporting ammunition, petrol and general supplies.

Suriname

Country Overview

Formerly known as Dutch Guiana, the Republic of Suriname gained full independence in 1975. With an area of 63,037 square miles it has borders to the east with French Guiana, to the west with Guyana and to the south with Brazil; its 208 n mile coastline is on the Atlantic Ocean. The capital, largest city and chief port is Paramaribo. Territorial seas (12 n miles) and a fisheries zone (200 n miles) are claimed.

There are further ports at Nieuw-Nickerie, Moengo, Paranam and Smalkalden. Territorial waters (12 n miles) are claimed. A 200 n mile Exclusive Economic Zone (EEZ) has also been claimed but the limits are not defined.

Personnel

2006: 240 (25 officers)

Bases

Kruktu Tere

Aircraft

Two CASA C-212-400 Aviocar aircraft acquired for maritime patrol in 1998/99.

PATROL FORCES

3 RODMAN 101 CLASS (PB)

JARABAKKA P 01   **SPARI** P 02   **GRAMORGU** P 03

Displacement, tons: 72 full load
Dimensions, feet (metres): 98.4 × 19.4 × 4.3 *(30.0 × 5.9 × 1.3)*
Main machinery: 2 MTU 12V 2000 diesels; 2,900 hp *(2.16 MW)* sustained; 2 Hamilton 571 water-jets
Speed, knots: 26. **Range, n miles:** 800 at 12 kt
Complement: 9
Guns: 1 — 40 mm grenade launcher.
Radars: Surface search: 2 Furuno; I-band.

Comment: Ordered in December 1997, from Rodman, Vigo. First one delivered in February 1999, second and third on 3 July 1999. Carry a RIB with twin outboards. Operational status doubtful.

5 RODMAN 55M CLASS (PBR)

P 04-08

Displacement, tons: 16 full load
Dimensions, feet (metres): 57.1 × 12.8 × 2.3 *(17.4 × 3.9 × 0.7)*
Main machinery: 2 MAN D2848-LXE diesels; 1,360 hp(m) *(1 MW)* sustained; 2 Hamilton water-jets
Speed, knots: 35. **Range, n miles:** 500 at 25 kt
Complement: 7
Guns: 1 — 12.7 mm MG.
Radars: Surface search: Furuno; I-band.

Comment: Ordered in December 1997 from Rodman, Vigo. First one delivered in October 1998, remainder in April 1999. Carry a RIB with a single outboard engine. Operational status doubtful.

SPARI   *9/1999, A Campanera i Rovira* / 0080716

P 06   *4/1999* / 0080717

Sweden

SVENSKA MARINEN

Country Overview

The Kingdom of Sweden is a constitutional monarchy occupying the eastern part of the Scandinavian Peninsula. With an area of 173,730 square miles, it is bordered to the north and west by Norway and to the north-east by Finland. It has a 1,740 n mile coastline with the Gulf of Bothnia, the Baltic Sea, the Öresund, Kattegatt, and Skagerrak. The country comprises the mainland and the islands of Gotland and Öland in the Baltic Sea. The capital and largest city is Stockholm which is also a leading port. Others include Göteborg, Malmö and Norrköping. Territorial seas (12 n miles) and an EEZ (200 n miles) are claimed.

Headquarters Appointments

Inspector General of the Navy:
  Rear Admiral Anders Grenstad

Diplomatic Representation

Defence Attaché in Tokyo:
  Colonel Sven-Åke Asklander
Defence Attaché in Tel Aviv:
  Colonel Stephan Tyrling
Defence Attaché in Beijing:
  Colonel Hans Norman
Defence Attaché in Copenhagen:
  Colonel Lennart Bengtsson
Defence Attaché in Bern and Cairo:
  Colonel Björn Tomtlund
Defence Attaché in Talinn:
  Lieutenant Colonel Lars Ramström
Defence Attaché in London and Dublin:
  Captain Bo Rask
Naval Attaché in Moscow:
  Brigadier Håkan Hedström
Naval Attaché in Washington:
  Captain Bo Wallander
Defence Attaché in Paris:
  Captain Christian Madsen
Defence Attaché in Singapore:
  Captain Bengt Jarvid
Naval Attaché in Berlin:
  Colonel Tommy Bengtsson
Defence Attaché in Sarajevo:
  Colonel Christer Svensson
Defence Attaché in Helsinki:
  Colonel Bengt Nylander
Defence Attaché in Athens and Budapest:
  Colonel Jonny Börjesson

Diplomatic Representation — continued

Defence Attaché in Rome:
  Colonel Thomas Bergqvist
Defence Attaché in Riga:
  Colonel Ulf Persson
Defence Attaché in Warsaw:
  Lieutenant Colonel Tapani Mattus
Defence Attaché in Pretoria:
  Colonel Anders Edquist
Defence Attaché in Ankara:
  Colonel Thomas Hansson
Defence Attaché in Vienna and Bratislava:
  Lieutenant Colonel Leif Küller

Organisation

The Navy consists of the Fleet and the Amphibious Corps (ex-Coastal Artillery). The Navy has one submarine flotilla, two naval warfare flotillas, one amphibious battalion, two naval bases, one naval school and one amphibious school.

Coast Defence

The Amphibious Corps is divided into two amphibious regiments and is the basis for the Amphibious Brigade. The Amphibious Brigade consists of three amphibious battalions with 800 troops divided into two Coast Ranger Companies, one Mortar Company (81 mm) and one Amphibious Company with remote-controlled mines, underwater surveillance systems and short-range land-sea missiles (RBS 17 Hellfire). Each Amphibious Battalion has 35 combat boat 90H, 13 Combat Boat 90E, four small tenders, 26 group landing craft and 19 Klepper collapsible kayaks.

Personnel

(a) 2006: 7,940 including 2,500 officers, 540 civilians, 2,500 reserve officers and 2,600 national servicemen
(b) 10 — 17¼ months' national service

Bases

Muskö (Stockholm), Karlskrona, Göteborg.

Strength of the Fleet

Type	Active	Building (Planned)
Submarines — Patrol	7	—
Missile Corvettes	7	4
Fast Attack Craft — Missile	4	—
Inshore Patrol Craft	13	—
Minelayers/Command Ship	1	—
MCM: Support Ship	1	—
Minelayers — Coastal	4	—
Minelayers-Small	2	—
Minesweepers/Hunters — Coastal	7	—
Minesweepers — Inshore	5	—
Sonobuoy Craft	4	—
LCMs	17	—
Survey Ships	2	—
Electronic Surveillance Ship	1	—
Transport Ships	1	—
Repair and Support Ships	8	—

DELETIONS

Submarines

2005 *Västergötland, Hälsingland*

Patrol Forces

2003 *Väktaren, Snapphanen, Nynäshamn, Piteå, Ekeskär, Skifteskär, Gråskär, Altaskär, Hojskär, Bredskär, Hamnskär*
2004 *Kaparen, Styrbjörn, Starkodder, Tordön*
2005 *Spejaren, Tirfing, Norrköping, Ystad*

Mine Warfare Forces

2004 *Kalmarsund, Barösund,* M 508, M 513, M 515

Amphibious Forces

2004 *Bore, Räfsnäs, Heimdal,* LCU 208, LCU 225, LCU 228

Auxiliaries

2003 26 LCU, *Urd, Hercules*
2005 *Gålö, Skredsvik*

Training Ships

2005 *Nämdö*

PENNANT LIST

Corvettes							
		83	Dristig	M 73	Koster	A 213	Nordanö
K 11	Stockholm	84	Händig	M 74	Kullen	A 214	Belos III
K 12	Malmö	85	Trygg	M 75	Vinga	A 241	Urd
K 21	Göteborg	86	Modig	M 76	Ven	A 247	Pelikanen
K 22	Gävle	87	Hurtig	M 77	Ulvön	A 248	Pingvinen
K 23	Kalmar	88	Rapp	MRF 01	Sökaren	A 251	Achilles
K 24	Sundsvall	89	Stolt	MUL 12	Arkösund	A 253	Hermes
K 31	Visby	90	Ärlig	MUL 13	Kalmarsund	A 265	Visborg
K 32	Helsingborg	91	Munter	MUL 15	Grundsund	A 270	Trossö
K 33	Härnösand (bldg)	92	Orädd	MUL 18	Fårösund	A 322	Heros
K 34	Nyköping (bldg)			MUL 19	Barösund	A 324	Hera
K 35	Karlstad (bldg)	**Mine Warfare Forces**		MUL 20	Furusund	A 343	Sleipner
				B 01	Ejdern	A 344	Loke
		M 04	Carlskrona	B 02	Krickan		
Patrol Forces		M 11	Styrsö	B 03	Svärtan	**Training ships**	
		M 12	Spårö	B 04	Viggen		
R 131	Norrköping	M 13	Skaftö			S 01	Gladan
R 142	Ystad	M 14	Sturkö	**Auxiliaries**		S 02	Falken
77	Huvudskär	M 33	Viksten				
81	Tapper	M 71	Landsort	A 201	Orion		
82	Djärv	M 72	Arholma	A 212	Ägir		

SUBMARINES

Notes: (1) The Swedish requirement for two new submarines is being taken forward via the A 26 (formerly Viking) project. This had been a bilateral programme with Denmark, following the withdrawal of Norway at the end of Project Definition Phase (PDP) Step 1 on 13 June 2003, but in wake of approval of the 2005-09 Defence Plan by the Danish parliament on 10 June 2004, Denmark also decided to end participation. The contract for PDP Step 2, was signed on 6 October 2003, but future progress is likely to be driven by two main factors: the requirement for the boats to enter service in about 2014 and the aspiration to find a partner country to take the project forward. In this latter respect, Singapore is a potential contender.

(2) *Näcken* was decommissioned from the Swedish Navy in 2001. Subsequently, she was leased to the Danish Navy and renamed *Kronborg*. She was returned to Sweden in 2004 and is likely to be sold or scrapped.

3 GOTLAND (A 19) CLASS (SSK)

Name	No	Builders	Laid down	Launched	Commissioned
GOTLAND	—	Kockums, Malmö	20 Nov 1992	2 Feb 1995	2 Sep 1996
UPPLAND	—	Kockums, Malmö	14 Jan 1994	9 Feb 1996	1 May 1997
HALLAND	—	Kockums, Malmö	21 Oct 1994	27 Sep 1996	1 Oct 1997

Displacement, tons: 1,494 surfaced; 1,599 dived
Dimensions, feet (metres): 198.2 × 20.3 × 18.4
  (60.4 × 6.2 × 5.6)
Main machinery: Diesel-stirling-electric; 2 MTU diesels; 2 Kockums V4-275R Stirling AIP; 204 hp(m) (150 kW); 1 Jeumont Schneider motor; 1 shaft; LIPS prop
Speed, knots: 10 surfaced; 20 dived
Complement: 27 (5 officers)

Torpedoes: 4—21 in (533 mm) bow tubes; 12 FFV Type 613/62; anti-surface; wire-guided; passive homing to 20 km (10.8 n miles) at 45 kt; warhead 240 kg or Bofors Type 62 (2000); wire-guided; active/passive homing to 50 km (27 n miles) at 20—50 kt; warhead 250 kg. swim-out discharge.
  2—15.75 in (400 mm) bow tubes; 6 Swedish Ordnance Type 432/451; anti-submarine; wire-guided; active/passive homing to 20 km (10.8 n miles) at 25 kt; warhead 45 kg. Shaped charge or a small charge anti-intruder version.
Mines: 12 Type 47 swim-out mines in lieu of torpedoes.
Countermeasures: ESM: Racal THORN Manta S; radar warning.
Weapons control: CelsiusTech IPS-19 (Sesub 940A); TFCS.
Radars: Navigation: Terma Scanter; I-band.
Sonars: STN/Atlas Elektronik CSU 90-2; hull-mounted; bow, flank and intercept arrays; passive search and attack. Reson Subac; active search (from 2008).

Programmes: In October 1986 a research contract was awarded to Kockums for a design to replace the Sjöormen class. Ordered on 28 March 1990.
Modernisation: A new active sonar suite, Subac, is to be installed by 2008.
Structure: The design has been developed on the basis of the Type A 17 series but this class is the first to be built with Air Independent Propulsion as part of the design. This type of AIP runs on liquid oxygen and diesel in a helium environment. Space has been reserved to fit two more V4-275R engines in due course. Single electro-optic periscope. The periscope is the only hull penetrating mast. Anechoic coatings are being applied. The four 21 in torpedo tubes are mounted over the smaller 15.75 in tubes. The smaller tubes can be tandem-loaded with two torpedoes per tube.
Operational: Reported as being able to patrol at 5 kt for several weeks without snort charging. The Type 47 mine swims out to a predetermined position before laying itself on the bottom. *Gotland* is to participate in exercises with the USN on both the east and west coasts of the USA during 2005. These may be extended to 2007.

UPPLAND   7/2004, E & M Laursen / 1043523

HALLAND   8/2004, L-G Nilsson / 1043522

UPPLAND   6/2003, L-G Nilsson / 0572636

2 SÖDERMANLAND (A 17) CLASS (SSK)

Name	No	Builders	Laid down	Launched	Commissioned
SÖDERMANLAND	—	Kockums, Malmö	2 Feb 1985	12 Apr 1988	21 Apr 1989
ÖSTERGÖTLAND	—	Kockums, Malmö	15 Oct 1985	9 Dec 1988	10 Jan 1990

Displacement, tons: 1,500 surfaced; 1,600 dived
Dimensions, feet (metres): 198.5 × 20 × 18.4
  (60.5 × 6.1 × 5.6)
Main machinery: Diesel-Stirling-electric; 2 Hedemora
  V12A/15 diesels; 2,200 hp(m) *(1.62 MW)*; 2 Kockums
  Stirling Mk III AIP; 204 hp *(150 kW)*; 1 Jeumont Schneider
  motor; 1,800 hp(m) *(1.32 MW)*; 1 shaft; LIPS prop
Speed, knots: 10 surfaced; 20 dived
Complement: 27 (5 officers)

Torpedoes: 6—21 in *(533 mm)* tubes. 12 FFV Type 613;
  anti-surface; wire-guided; passive homing to 20 km
  (10.8 n miles) at 45 kt; warhead 240 kg. swim-out discharge.
  3—15.75 in *(400 mm)* tubes. 6 FFV Type 431/451; anti-
  submarine; wire-guided; active/passive homing to 20 km
  (10.8 n miles) at 25 kt; warhead 45 kg shaped charge or a
  small charge anti-intruder version is available.
Mines: 12 Type 47 swim-out mines in lieu of torpedoes.
Countermeasures: ESM: Argo AR-700-S5; or Condor CS
  3701; intercept.
Weapons control: Ericsson IPS-17 (Sesub 900A) TFCS.
Radars: Navigation: Terma; I-band.
Sonars: Atlas Elektronik CSU 83; hull-mounted; passive
  search and attack; medium frequency.
  Reson Subac; active search (from 2008).
  Flank array; passive search; low frequency.

Programmes: Design contract awarded to Kockums, Malmö
  on 17 April 1978. Contract for construction of these boats
  signed 8 December 1981. Kockums built midship section
  and carried out final assembly while Karlskrona built
  bow and stern sections.
Modernisation: Modernised variants of the Västergötland
  class. Mid-life refit of *Södermanland* began at Kockums in
  late 2000 and included the installation of Air Independent
  Propulsion (Stirling Mk 3 AIP) by the insertion of a 12 m plug
  in the pressure hull. Other work included the installation of a
  pressurised diver's lock-out in the base of the sail to facilitate
  special forces operations. The refit also included a new
  climate control system. Thales Optronics CK 038 periscope
  has been upgraded with a thermal imaging camera and
  an improved image intensifier. Communications may be
  upgraded in the future to improve interoperability. A new
  active sonar suite, Subac, is to be installed by 2008.
Structure: Single hulled with an X type rudder/after hydroplane
  design. Diving depth 300 m *(984 ft)*. Anechoic coating.
Operational: *Södermanland* relaunched on 8 September
  2003 and, after six-months sea trials, returned to
  service in mid-2004, *Östergötland* was relaunched on
  3 September 2004 and returned to service in 2005.

SÖDERMANLAND   *5/2005*, Per Körnefeldt* / 1153893

SÖDERMANLAND   *8/2005*, E & M Laursen* / 1153894

SÖDERMANLAND   *6/2004, Kockums* / 1043513

1 MIDGET SUBMARINE (SSW)

SPIGGEN II

Displacement, tons: 17 dived
Dimensions, feet (metres): 34.8 × 5.6 × 4.6
(10.6 × 1.7 × 1.4)
Main machinery: 1 Volvo Penta diesel; 1 shaft
Speed, knots: 5 dived; 6 surfaced
Complement: 4

Comment: Built by Försvarets Materielverk and
commissioned on 19 June 1990. Has an endurance of
14 days and a diving depth of 100 m *(330 ft)*, and is used
as a target for ASW training. Refitted by Kockums and
back in service in December 1996.

SPIGGEN II
8/1998, Per Körnefeldt
0050201

CORVETTES

2 STOCKHOLM CLASS (FSG)

Name	No	Builders	Laid down	Launched	Commissioned
STOCKHOLM	K 11	Karlskronavarvet	1 Aug 1982	24 Aug 1984	22 Feb 1985
MALMÖ	K 12	Karlskronavarvet	14 Mar 1983	22 Mar 1985	10 May 1985

Displacement, tons: 350 standard; 372 full load
Dimensions, feet (metres): 164 × 24.6 × 10.8
(50 × 7.5 × 3.3)
Main machinery: CODAG; 1 Allied Signal TF50A gas
turbine; 5,440 hp(m) *(4.0 MW)* sustained; 2 MTU 16V
396 TB94 diesels; 5,277 hp(m) *(3.9 MW)* sustained;
3 shafts; Kamewa props
Speed, knots: 32 gas; 20 diesel
Complement: 33 (7 officers)

Missiles: SSM: 8 Saab RBS 15 Mk II (4 twin) launchers ❶;
inertial guidance; active radar homing to 110 km
(54 n miles) at 0.8 Mach; warhead 150 kg.
Guns: 1 Bofors 57 mm/70 Mk 2 ❷; 220 rds/min to 13.5 km
(7.3 n miles); weight of shell 2.4 kg.
Torpedoes: 4 — 15.75 in *(400 mm)* tubes; Swedish Ordnance
Type 43/45; anti-submarine can be fitted.
A/S mortars: 4 Saab 601 ❸ 9-tubed launchers; range 1,200 m;
shaped charge.
Mines: Minelaying capability.
Countermeasures: Decoys: 2 quadruple Bofors 57 mm
rocket launchers for chaff/illumination ❹.
ESM: Condor CS-5460; intercept and warning.
ECM: to be fitted.
Combat data systems: SAAB Tech 9LV Mk 3E Cetris;
datalink.
Weapons control: Philips 9LV 300 GFCS including a 9LV 100
optronic director and laser range-finder.
Radars: Air/surface search: Ericsson Sea Giraffe 50HC ❺;
G-band.
Navigation: Terma Scanter ❻; I-band.
Fire control: Philips 9LV 200 Mk 3 ❼; J-band.
Sonars: Simrad SA 950; hull-mounted; active attack.
Thomson Sintra TSM 2642 Salmon ❽; VDS; search;
medium frequency.

Programmes: Orders placed in September 1981. Developed
from Spica II class.
Modernisation: RBS 15 missile upgraded to Mk II from
1994. Improved A/S mortar fitted in 1998-99. Extensive

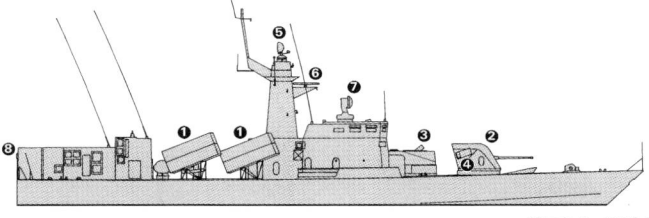

MALMÖ *(Scale 1 : 600), Ian Sturton* / 1153880

MALMÖ *12/2004*, H M Steele* / 1153890

mid-life upgrade carried out 1999-2002. Modernisation
included removal of the 21 in torpedo tubes and
the aft 40 mm mounting and modification of the
superstructure to reduce radar and IR signatures. The
bridge wings have been removed and a pylon mast
has replaced a lattice structure. Upgrades include a

new propulsion system, combat data system and
EW systems. The decoys are situated on either side
of the gun turret. Both ships are to be fitted with CDC
Hydra sonar.
Operational: Both ships are expected to remain in service
until 2015.

STOCKHOLM *6/2005*, B Sullivan* / 1153891

4 + 1 VISBY CLASS (FSGH)

Name	No	Builders	Laid down	Launched	Commissioned
VISBY	K 31	Karlskronavarvet	17 Dec 1996	8 June 2000	May 2006
HELSINGBORG	K 32	Karlskronavarvet	June 1997	27 June 2003	24 Apr 2006
HÄRNÖSAND	K 33	Karlskronavarvet	Dec 1997	16 Dec 2004	May 2006
NYKÖPING	K 34	Karlskronavarvet	June 1998	18 Aug 2005	24 Aug 2006
KARLSTAD	K 35	Karlskronavarvet	Dec 1999	24 Aug 2006	2007

Displacement, tons: 620 full load
Dimensions, feet (metres): 239.5 × 34.1 × 7.9
  (73.0 × 10.4 × 2.4)
Main machinery: CODOG; 4 AlliedSignal TF 50A gas
  turbines; 21,760 hp(m) *(16 MW)*; 2 MTU 16V N90 diesels;
  3,536 hp(m) *(2.6 MW)*; 2 Kamewa 125 water-jets; bow
  thruster
Speed, knots: 35; 15 (diesels)
Complement: 43 (6 officers)

Missiles: SSM: 8 RBS 15 Mk II (Batch 2) inertial guidance;
  active radar homing to 110 km *(54 n miles)* at 0.8 Mach;
  warhead 150 kg.
Guns: 1 Bofors 57 mm/70 SAK Mk 3 ❶. 220 rds/min to 17 km
  (9.3 n miles); weight of shell 2.4 kg.
Torpedoes: 4 fixed 400 mm tubes ❷. Type 43/45 anti-
  submarine.
A/S mortars: Saab Alecto 601 127 mm rocket-powered
  grenades ❸; range 1,200 m.
Mines: Can be carried.
Countermeasures: Decoys: Chaff launcher ❹. Decoys can
  also be fired from the ASW mortar.
  MCMV: STN Atlas Seafox Combat (C) sonar/TV sensor;
  range 500 m at 6 kt; shaped charge.
ESM/ECM: Condor Systems CS 701; intercept and jammer.
Combat data systems: CelsiusTech 9LV Mk 3E CETRIS with
  Link.
Weapons control: Optronic director.
Radars: Air/surface search: Ericsson Sea Giraffe AMB 3D ❺;
  G-band.
  Surface search: CelciusTech Pilot; I-band.
  Fire control: CEROS 200 Mk 3 ❻; I/J-band.
Sonars: Computing Devices Canada (CDC) Hydra; bow
  mounted active high frequency plus passive towed array
  and VDS active.

Helicopters: 1 Agusta A 109M ❼.

Programmes: Order for first two with an option for
  two more on 17 October 1995. Second pair ordered
  17 December 1996 and third pair in mid-1999. However,
  due to cost overruns, order reduced on 9 October 2001
  to five ships.
Structure: Stealth features developed from the trials vessel
  Smyge but without the twin hull design for which this ship
  was considered too large. A hangar for the helicopter is
  included. The hull is of Fibre Reinforced Plastic used in a
  sandwich construction and the superstructure is covered
  with RAM. A Double Eagle ROV with active sonar is

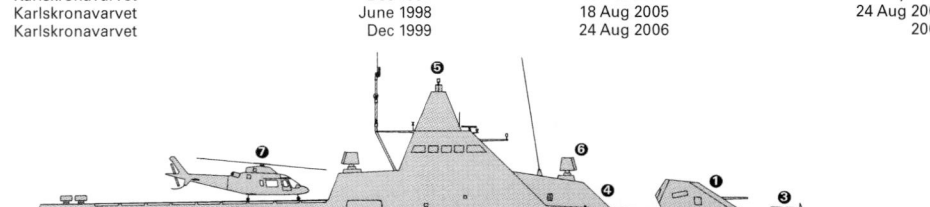

VISBY   *(Scale 1 : 600), Ian Sturton* / 1043484

HÄRNÖSAND   *8/2005*, E & M Laursen* / 1153895

carried in the MCM role as well as expendable mini
torpedoes for mine countermeasures. There is provision
for a SAM system to be installed.
Operational: The first of class, was launched at Karlskrona
shipyard on 8 June 2000 but delays in outfitting schedule
led to 10-month slippage of contractor's sea trials until
7 December 2001. Initially, ships fitted with 57 mm

gun, A/S mortars and torpedo tubes. The combat
system installed from late 2002 followed by trials
from late 2003. None of the ships had been formally
delivered by early 2006. Subject to contract negotiations,
some of the ships are expected to be available for
use in 2006 but the first fully operational unit is unlikely
to enter service before 2008.

NYKÖPING   *8/2005*, L-G Nilsson* / 1153896

HELSINGBORG   *6/2003, L-G Nilsson* / 0576438

4 GÖTEBORG CLASS (FSG)

Name	No	Builders	Laid down	Launched	Commissioned
GÖTEBORG	K 21	Karlskronavarvet	10 Feb 1987	14 Apr 1989	15 Feb 1990
GÄVLE	K 22	Karlskronavarvet	21 Mar 1988	23 Mar 1990	1 Feb 1991
KALMAR	K 23	Karlskronavarvet	21 Nov 1988	1 Nov 1990	1 Sep 1991
SUNDSVALL	K 24	Karlskronavarvet	20 Nov 1989	29 Nov 1991	7 July 1993

Displacement, tons: 300 standard; 399 full load
Dimensions, feet (metres): 187 × 26.2 × 6.6
  (57 × 8 × 2)
Main machinery: 3 MTU 16V 396 TB94 diesels; 8,700 hp(m)
  (6.4 MW) sustained; Kamewa 80562-6 water-jets. Bow
  thruster in K 22
Speed, knots: 30
Complement: 36 (7 officers) plus 4 spare berths

Missiles: SSM: 8 Saab RBS 15 Mark II (4 twin) launchers ❶;
  inertial guidance; active radar homing to 110 km
  (59.4 n miles) at 0.8 Mach; warhead 150 kg.
Guns: 1 Bofors 57 mm/70 Mk 2 ❷; 220 rds/min to 17 km
  (9.3 n miles); weight of shell 2.4 kg.
  1 Bofors 40 mm/70 (stealth dome in K 22) ❸;
  330 rds/min to 12.5 km *(6.8 n miles)*; weight of shell
  0.96 kg.
Torpedoes: 4—15.75 in *(400 mm)* tubes can be fitted ❹.
  Swedish Ordnance Type 43/45; anti-submarine.
A/S mortars: 4 Saab 601 ❺ 9-tubed launchers; range 1,200 m;
  shaped charge.
Depth charges: On mine rails.
Mines: Minelaying capability.
Countermeasures: Decoys: 4 Philips Philax fixed launchers;
  IR flares and chaff grenades. A/S mortars have also been
  adapted to fire IR/chaff decoys.
ESM: Condor; intercept.
Combat data systems: CelsiusTech 9LV Mk 3 SESYM.
  Datalink.
Weapons control: 2 Bofors Electronics 9LV 200 Mk 3 Sea
  Viking or Signaal IRST (K 24) optronic directors. Bofors
  Electronics 9LV 450 GFCS. RC1-400 MFCS. 9AU-300 ASW
  control system with AQS 928G/SM sonobuoy processor.
  Bofors 9EW 400 EW control.
Radars: Air/surface search: Ericsson Sea Giraffe 150 HC ❻;
  G-band.
Navigation: Terma PN 612 ❼; I-band.
Fire control: 2 Bofors Electronics 9GR 400 ❽; I/J-band.
Sonars: Hydra multisonar system (K 22) ❾; bow-mounted
  active high-frequency plus passive towed array and
  active VDS.
  Thomson Sintra TSM 2643 Salmon (K 21, K 23-24); VDS;
  active search; medium frequency.
  Simrad SA 950; hull-mounted; active attack.
  STN Atlas passive towed array; low frequency.

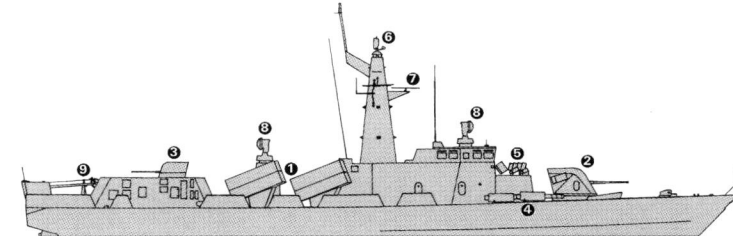

GÄVLE   *(Scale 1 : 600), Ian Sturton* / 1153882

SUNDSVALL   *6/2005*, H M Steele* / 1153892

Programmes: Ordered 1 December 1985 as replacements
  for Spica I class.
Modernisation: *Gävle* refitted to accommodate Hydra
  towed array/VDS aft and 40 mm gun with stealth dome.
  Bridge wings removed and topmast modified. Similar

upgrade expected for rest of class but timetable has not
been confirmed. An IRST director has been fitted aft of
the mast for trials in K 24.
Structure: Efforts have been made to reduce radar and IR
signatures.

GÄVLE   *6/2004, B Sullivan* / 1043546

SHIPBORNE AIRCRAFT

Numbers/Type: 1 Agusta A 109M (HKP-15).
Operational speed: 152 kt (280 km/h).
Service ceiling: 16,500 ft (5,029 m).
Range: 447 n miles (827 km).
Role/Weapon systems: Military version of A 109E with Turbomeca Arrius 2K2 engine. Swedish Armed Forces ordered 20 on 20 June 2001. Of these, eight are to be 'navalised' for operation from Visby class and from shore bases. First delivered on 3 Feb 2006 and the remainder by 2009. ASW and ASV roles.

HKP-15   *6/2005*, Massimo Annati* / 1153908

Numbers/Type: 5 Agusta-Bell 206A JetRanger (HKP-6B).
Operational speed: 115 kt (213 km/h).
Service ceiling: 13,500 ft (4,115 m).
Range: 368 n miles (682 km).
Role/Weapon systems: Operated from shore bases in ASW and surface search roles. To be replaced by A 109M. Weapons: ASW; four Type 11 or depth charges.

HKP-6B   *6/2000, Andreas Karlsson, Swedish Defence image* / 0106563

LAND-BASED MARITIME AIRCRAFT (FRONT LINE)

Notes: (1) In addition 11 AS 332 Super Puma helicopters are used for SAR.
(2) SH-37 Viggen aircraft are Air Force operated and can be used for maritime strike.

Numbers/Type: 7/7 Boeing 107-II-15/Kawasaki KV 107-II.
All to HKP-4C/D standard.
Operational speed: 137 kt (254 km/h).
Service ceiling: 8,500 ft (2,590 m).
Range: 300 n miles (555 km).
Role/Weapon systems: ASW and surface search helicopter; updated with avionics, TM2D engines, radar, sonar, datalink for SSM targeting, MARIL 920 combat information system. The Nordic Standard helicopter is expected to start replacing these aircraft from 2005. Sensors: BEAB Omera radar, Thomson Sintra DUAV-4 dipping sonar. Weapons: ASW; six Type 11/51 depth charges and/or two Type 45 torpedoes.

KV 107   *5/2004, Per Körnefeldt* / 1043525

Numbers/Type: 1 CASA C-212-200 Aviocar.
Operational speed: 190 kt (353 km/h).
Service ceiling: 24,000 ft (7,315 m).
Range: 1,650 n miles (3,055 km).
Role/Weapon systems: For ASW and surface surveillance. Two others belong to the Coast Guard. Sensors: Omera radar, Sonobuoys/Lofar, CDC sonobuoy processor, FLIR, datalink. Weapons: ASW; depth charges.

CASA C-212   *Adolfo Ortigueira Gil* / 0572619

Numbers/Type: 10 NH Industries NH 90.
Operational speed: 157 kt (291 km/h).
Service ceiling: 13,940 ft (4,250 m).
Range: 621 n miles (1,150 km).
Role/Weapon systems: Eighteen aircraft to be procured for tactical troop transport and ASW role. Modular construction is to enable rapid re-roling. There are to be 10 sets of ASW sensors for delivery between 2007 and 2010. Sensors: Telephonics APS-143B(V) ocean eye radar, Galileo Avionica FLIR, Thales FLASH-S dipping sonar. Weapons: To be announced.

NH 90   *5/2004* / 0094463

PATROL FORCES

12 TAPPER CLASS (PBR)

TAPPER 81	**HÄNDIG** 84	**HURTIG** 87	**ÄRLIG** 90
DJÄRV 82	**TRYGG** 85	**RAPP** 88	**MUNTER** 91
DRISTIG 83	**MODIG** 86	**STOLT** 89	**ORÄDD** 92

Displacement, tons: 57 full load
Dimensions, feet (metres): 71.9 × 17.7 × 4.9 (21.9 × 5.4 × 1.5)
Main machinery: 2 MWM TBD234V16 diesels; 1,812 hp(m) (1.33 MW) sustained; 2 shafts
Speed, knots: 25
Complement: 9
Guns: 2 — 12.7 mm MGs.
A/S mortars: 4 Elma/Saab grenade launchers; range 300 m; warhead 4.2 kg shaped charge.
Depth charges: 18.
Mines: 2 rails (in four of the class).
Radars: Surface search: 2 Racal Decca; I-band.
Sonars: Simrad; hull-mounted; active search; high frequency.

Comment: Seven Type 80 ordered from Djupviksvarvet in early 1992, and delivered between February 1993 and December 1995. Five more ordered in 1995 for delivery at six month intervals between December 1996 and January 1999. A Phantom HD-2 ROV is carried. This is equipped with a Tritech ST 525 imaging sonar.

ORÄDD   *6/2005*, E & M Laursen* / 1153900

STOLT   *6/2005*, L G Nilsson* / 1153901

1 TYPE 72 INSHORE PATROL CRAFT (PBR)

HUVUDSKÄR 77

Displacement, tons: 30 full load
Dimensions, feet (metres): 69.2 × 15 × 4.3 *(21.1 × 4.6 × 1.3)*
Main machinery: 3 diesels; 3 shafts
Speed, knots: 22
Guns: 1—20 mm.
Depth charges: Carried in all of the class.
Radars: Surface search: Decca RM 914; I-band.
Sonars: Simrad; hull-mounted; active search; high frequency.

Comment: Last remaining vessel of a class built in 1966-67. Modernised in the 1980s with a tripod mast and radar mounted over the bridge.

TYPE 72   *6/1994, Curt Borgenstam* / 0080731

AMPHIBIOUS FORCES

Notes: Following trials of the mortar fire support concept in a Combatboat 90 craft, development of a new craft, the Mortar Combat Boat 2010, has been initiated. This is likely to be a 20-25 m vessel armed with a Patria Hägglunds SSG 120 AMS. Testing of a prototype is scheduled for 2010.

145 COMBATBOAT 90H/90HS (STRIDSBÅT) (LCPFM)

803-946   **BLÅTUNGA** 947

Displacement, tons: 19 full load
Dimensions, feet (metres): 52.2 × 12.5 × 2.6 *(15.9 × 3.8 × 0.8)*
Main machinery: 2 Saab Scania DSI 14 diesels; 1,250 hp(m) *(935 kW)* (1,350 hp(m) in 90HS *(1,000 kW)*); 2 Kamewa water-jets
Speed, knots: 35-50; 20 (Sea State 3)
Range, n miles: 240 at 30 kt
Complement: 3
Military lift: 20 troops plus equipment or 2.8 tons
Missiles: SSM: Rockwell RBS 17 Hellfire; semi-active laser guidance to 5 km *(3 n miles)* at 1.0 Mach; warhead 8 kg.
Guns: 3—12.7 mm MGs.
Mines: 4 (or 6 depth charges).
Radars: Navigation: Racal Decca; RD 360 or Furuno 8050; I-band.

Comment: The first two prototypes (801-802) ordered in January 1988 are no longer in service. Twelve more (803-814) built in 1991-92. There were 63 (815-877) ordered from Dockstavarvet and Gotlands Varv in mid-January 1992, with an option for 30 more (878-907) which was taken up in 1994. The building period for these completed in mid-1997. A further 40 (908-947) were ordered in August 1996 and delivery was completed in October 2003. Of these, the last 27 (90HS) units were all modified to undertake international peacekeeping operations by the inclusion of armoured protection, an NBC citadel and air conditioning. All have a 20° deadrise and all carry four six-man inflatable rafts. Some of these craft are on loan to the Swedish Police. 947 is equipped as VIP craft and 914 is used as a trials craft and is fitted with a twin 120 mm mortar. There were 22 (90N) of the class delivered to Norway 1999, 40 (90 HEX) to Mexico, 17 (90H) to Malaysia and three (90 HEX) to the Hellenic Coast Guard.

COMBATBOAT 927   *6/2005*, Per Körnefeldt* / 1153904

COMBATBOAT 803   *5/2005*, E & M Laursen* / 1153905

54 COMBATBOAT 90E (STRIDSBÅT) (YH)

101-154

Displacement, tons: 9 full load
Dimensions, feet (metres): 39 × 9.5 × 2.3 *(11.9 × 2.9 × 0.7)*
Main machinery: 1 Scania AB DSI 14 diesel; 398 hp(m) *(293 kW)* sustained; FFJet 410 water-jet
Speed, knots: 40; 37 (laden)
Complement: 2
Military lift: 2 tons or 6-10 troops
Radars: Navigation: Furuno 8050; I-band.

Comment: First batch ordered from Storebro Royal Cruiser AB in 1995 for delivery from August 1995-98. Second batch ordered in 1997 for delivery in 1998-99. These are ambulance boats but may also be used for stores. Two more ordered for Chinese Customs and three for Malaysian Customs in April 1997.

COMBATBOAT 145   *8/2002, E & M Laursen* / 0529915

17 LCMs (TROSSBÅT)

603-612   652-658

Displacement, tons: 55 full load
Dimensions, feet (metres): 68.9 × 19.7 × 4.9 *(21 × 6 × 1.5)*
Main machinery: 2 Saab DSI 11/40 M2 diesels; 340 hp(m) *(250 kW)*; 2 Schottel props
Speed, knots: 10
Military lift: 30 tons
Radars: Navigation: Racal Decca 914C; I-band.

Comment: Completed from 1980-88. Classified as Trossbåt (support boat). Built by Djupviksvarvet.

LCM 609   *5/2004, E & M Laursen* / 1043535

23 LCUs (LCU)

208	234, 235, 237	261, 263, 264
215	241, 244	267-269
223	247, 248	281, 283
230-232	252, 258	

Displacement, tons: 31 full load
Dimensions, feet (metres): 70.2 × 13.8 × 4.2 *(21.4 × 4.2 × 1.3)*
Main machinery: 3 diesels; 600 hp(m) *(441 kW)*; 3 shafts
Speed, knots: 18
Military lift: 40 tons; 40 troops
Guns: 3 to 8—6.5 mm MGs.
Mines: Minelaying capability *(281—283 only)*.

Comment: Built between 1960 and 1987. 35 modernised 1989-93; 12 more 1997-98. Many have been decommissioned and some sold to private buyers.

LCU 281   *6/2002, Per Körnefeldt* / 0529912

2 TRANSPORTBÅT 2000 (AGF/YFLB)

451   452

Displacement, tons: 43 full load
Dimensions, feet (metres): 77.1 × 16.7 × 3.3 *(23.5 × 5.1 × 1)*
Main machinery: 3 Saab Scania DSI 14 diesels or 3 Volvo Penta 163 diesels; 1,194 hp(m) *(878 kW)* sustained; 3 FFJet 450 or 3 Kamewa K40 waterjets
Speed, knots: 25
Complement: 3
Military lift: 45 troops or 10 tons
Guns: 2 — 12.7 mm MGs.
Radars: Navigation: Terma; I-band.

Comment: Two similar prototypes ordered from Djupviks Shipyard in 1997. *452* is configured for troop carrying, and *451* as a command boat. Each has a different propulsion system which are in competition to be fitted in seven more troop carriers and three more command boats. Further orders are not expected.

TRANSPORTBÅT 452   *6/2000, Michael Nitz* / 0106583

1 M 10 CLASS HOVERCRAFT (UCAC)

SVÄV-ARNE

Displacement, tons: 26 full load
Dimensions, feet (metres): 61.8 × 29 *(18.8 × 8.8)*
Main machinery: 2 Scania diesels; 1,224 hp(m) *(900 kW)*
Speed, knots: 40; 7 with cushion deflated
Range, n miles: 600 at 30 kt
Complement: 3
Military lift: 10 tons or 50 troops
Radars: Navigation: I-band.

Comment: ABS design built at Karlskronavarvet under licence and started trials in June 1998 which included ice trials in early 1999. Has a Kevlar superstructure. Three more were planned but there were no further orders.

M 10   *5/2004, E & M Laursen* / 1043536

102 RAIDING CRAFT (GRUPPBÅT) (LCP)

Displacement, tons: 3 full load
Dimensions, feet (metres): 26.2 × 6.9 × 1 *(8 × 2.1 × 0.3)*
Main machinery: 1 Volvo Penta TAMD 42WJ diesel; 230 hp(m) *(169 kW)*; 1 Kamewa 240 waterjet
Speed, knots: 30
Complement: 2
Military lift: 1 ton

Comment: Small raiding craft are used throughout the Archipelago. Some have been replaced.

GRUPPBÅT   *6/2005*, E & M Laursen* / 1153906

0 + 3 GRIFFON 8100TD CLASS HOVERCRAFT (UCAC)

Displacement, tons: 18.2; 24.6 full load
Dimensions, feet (metres): 73.8 × 36.1 × 1 *(22.5 × 11.0 × 0.32)*
Main machinery: 2 Iveco diesels; 2,000 hp *(1.5 MW)*
Speed, knots: 42. **Range, n miles:** 400 at 45 kt
Complement: 13 (2 officers)
Guns: 1 — 12.7 mm MG.
Radars: Raytheon; I-band.

Comment: Three hovercraft ordered in mid-2005 for delivery between October 2006 and March 2007. The aluminium-hulled craft are stretched versions of the Griffon 8000TD. Capable of carrying an 11 ton payload, the craft are to be fitted with ballistic protection and nbc protection.

MINE WARFARE FORCES

Notes: A transportable COOP system was ordered in 1991. The unit can be shifted from one ship to another and comprises a container, processing module and tactical display, an underwater positioning system, sonar, Sea Eagle ROV and mine disposal charge. Optimised for shallow water surveillance and can be used in conjunction with other MCM systems. The primary role is route survey.

1 CARLSKRONA CLASS (MINELAYER) (AXH/MLH)

Name	No	Builders	Launched	Commissioned
CARLSKRONA	M 04	Karlskronavarvet	28 June 1980	11 Jan 1982

Displacement, tons: 3,600 full load
Dimensions, feet (metres): 346.7 × 49.9 × 13.1 *(105.7 × 15.2 × 4)*
Main machinery: 4 Nohab F212 D825 diesels; 10,560 hp(m) *(7.76 MW)*; 2 shafts; cp props
Speed, knots: 20
Complement: 50 plus 136 trainees. Requires 118 as operational minelayer
Guns: 2 Bofors 57 mm/70. 2 Bofors 40 mm/70.
Mines: Can lay 105.
Countermeasures: 2 Philips Philax chaff/IR launchers.
ESM: Argo AR 700; intercept.
Radars: Air/surface search: Ericsson Sea Giraffe 50HC; G/H/I-band.
Surface search: Raytheon; E/F-band.
Fire control: 2 Philips 9LV 200 Mk 2; I/J-band.
Navigation: Terma Scanter 009; I-band.

Helicopters: Platform only.

Comment: Ordered 25 November 1977, laid down in sections late 1979 and launched at the same time as Karlskrona celebrated its tercentenary. Midshipmen's Training Ship as well as a minelayer; also a 'padded' target for exercise torpedoes. Sonar removed. Name is an older form of Karlskrona. Completed a 12-month refit in December 2002.

CARLSKRONA   *5/2003, Diego Quevedo* / 0572622

1 FURUSUND CLASS (COASTAL MINELAYER) (MLC)

Name	No	Builders	Launched	Commissioned
FURUSUND	MUL 20	ASI Verken	16 Dec 1982	10 Oct 1983

Displacement, tons: 225 full load
Dimensions, feet (metres): 106.9 × 26.9 × 7.5 *(32.6 × 8.2 × 2.3)*
Main machinery: Diesel-electric; 2 Scania GAS 1 diesel generators; 2 motors; 416 hp(m) *(306 kW)*; 2 shafts
Speed, knots: 11.5
Complement: 24
Guns: 1 — 12.7 mm MG.
Mines: 22 tons.
Radars: Navigation: Racal Decca 1226; I-band.

Comment: Built for the former Coastal Artillery. Carries a Mantis type ROV.

FURUSUND   *5/2001, Per Körnefeldt* / 0131140

3 ARKÖSUND CLASS (COASTAL MINELAYERS) (MLC)

ARKÖSUND MUL 12   **GRUNDSUND** MUL 15   **FÅRÖSUND** (ex-*Öresund*) MUL 18

Displacement, tons: 200 standard; 245 full load
Dimensions, feet (metres): 102.3 × 24.3 × 10.2 *(31.2 × 7.4 × 3.1)*
Main machinery: Diesel-electric; 2 Nohab/Scania diesel generators; 2 motors; 460 hp(m)
(338 kW); 2 shafts
Speed, knots: 12
Complement: 24
Guns: 4 — 7.62 mm MGs.
Mines: 2 rails; 26 tons.
Radars: Navigation: Racal Decca 1226; I-band.

Comment: All completed by 1954-1957. Former Coastal Artillery craft for laying and
maintaining minefields. One deleted in 1992, one in 1996, *Skramsösund* in 1998 and
Kalmarsund and *Barösund* in 2004. 40 mm guns removed.

ARKÖSUND   *7/2005*, E & M Laursen* / 1153902

2 SMALL MINELAYERS (MLI)

M 502   **M 505**

Displacement, tons: 15 full load
Dimensions, feet (metres): 47.9 × 13.8 × 2.9 *(14.6 × 4.2 × 0.9)*
Main machinery: 2 diesels; 2 shafts
Speed, knots: 14
Complement: 7
Mines: 2 rails; 12.
Radars: Navigation: Racal Decca; I-band.

Comment: Ordered in 1969. Mines are laid from rails or by crane on the stern. Former
Coastal Artillery craft.

SMALL MINELAYER   *5/1995, Curt Borgenstam* / 0080735

5 SAM CLASS (MCM DRONES) (MSD)

SAM 01-02   **SAM 04**   **SAM 06-07**

Displacement, tons: 20 full load
Dimensions, feet (metres): 59.1 × 20 × 5.2 *(18 × 6.1 × 1.6)*
Main machinery: 1 Volvo Penta TAMD70D diesel; 210 hp(m) *(154 kW)*; 1 Schottel prop
Speed, knots: 8
Range, n miles: 330 at 8 kt

Comment: Built by Karlskronavarvet in 1983. *SAM 03* and *05* sold to the USA for Gulf
operation in March 1991 and replaced in 1992/93. Remote-controlled catamaran
magnetic and acoustic sweepers operated by the Landsort and Styrsö classes. Six sold
to Japan.

SAM 07   *4/2003, Per Körnefeldt* / 0572624

7 LANDSORT CLASS (MINEHUNTERS) (MHSCDM)

Name	No	Builders	Launched	Commissioned
LANDSORT	M 71	Karlskronavarvet	2 Nov 1982	19 Apr 1984
ARHOLMA	M 72	Karlskronavarvet	2 Aug 1984	23 Nov 1984
KOSTER	M 73	Karlskronavarvet	16 Jan 1986	30 May 1986
KULLEN	M 74	Karlskronavarvet	15 Aug 1986	28 Nov 1986
VINGA	M 75	Karlskronavarvet	14 Aug 1987	27 Nov 1987
VEN	M 76	Karlskronavarvet	10 Aug 1988	12 Dec 1988
ULVÖN	M 77	Karlskronavarvet	4 Mar 1992	9 Oct 1992

Displacement, tons: 270 standard; 360 full load
Dimensions, feet (metres): 155.8 × 31.5 × 7.3 *(47.5 × 9.6 × 2.2)*
Main machinery: 4 Saab-Scania DSI 14 diesels; 1,592 hp(m) *(1.17 MW)* sustained; coupled
in pairs to 2 Voith Schneider props
Speed, knots: 15. **Range, n miles:** 2,000 at 12 kt
Complement: 29 (12 officers) plus 4 spare

Missiles: SAM: Saab Manpads.
Guns: 1 Bofors 40 mm/70 Mod 48; 240 rds/min to 12.5 km *(6.8 n miles)*; weight of shell
0.96 kg. Bofors Sea Trinity CIWS trial carried out in *Vinga* (fitted in place of 40 mm/70).
2 — 7.62 mm MGs.
A/S mortars: 4 Saab Elma 9-tubed launchers; range 400 m; warhead 4.2 kg shaped charge
or Saab 601 9-tubed launchers; range 1,200 m; shaped charge.
Countermeasures: Decoys: 2 Philips Philax fixed launchers can be carried with 4 magazines
each holding 36 grenades; IR/chaff.
ESM: Matilda; intercept.
MCM: This class is fitted for mechanical sweeps for moored mines as well as magnetic
and acoustic sweeps. In addition it is possible to operate two SAM drones (see separate
entry). Fitted with 2 Sutec Sea Eagle or Double Eagle remote-controlled units with 600 m
tether and capable of 350 m depth.
Weapons control: Philips 9LV 100 optronic director. Philips 9 MJ 400 minehunting
system.
Radars: Navigation: Thomson-CSF Terma; I-band.
Sonars: Thomson-CSF TSM-2022; Racal Decca 'Mains' control system; hull-mounted;
minehunting; high frequency.

Programmes: The first two of this class ordered in early 1981. Second four in 1984 and the
seventh in 1989.
Modernisation: Five of the class are undergoing a two-stage upgrade at Kockums,
Karlskrona. In the first phase, *Kullen* and *Ven* were modernized in 2003 to enable
participation in international operations. The other three ships, *Koster, Vinga* and *Ulvön*,
began a similar first phase modernization period in 2005. This is to be followed by
a second-phase which is a more extensive mid-life modernization. This is to include
installation of a new command system (Atlas Elektronik Integrated Mine Counter
Measure System (IMCMS-S), an integrated mine countermeasures system (comprising
hull-mounted (HMS-12M wideband hull-mounted sonar) and self-propelled variable
depth sonar (installed in Double Eagle Mk III ROV)), and a mine-identification
and -disposal system based on the Atlas SeaFox. The fully upgraded vessels are to enter
service 2008-09.
Structure: The GRP mould for the hull has also been used for the Coast Guard former
KBV 171 class.
Operational: The integrated navigation and action data automation system developed by
Philips and Racal Decca.
Sales: Four built for Singapore.

KULLEN   *9/2004, Per Körnefeldt* / 1043529

ULVÖN   *8/2005*, E & M Laursen* / 1153903

4 EJDERN CLASS (SONOBUOY CRAFT) (MSI)

EJDERN B 01   **KRICKAN** B 02   **SVÄRTAN** B 03   **VIGGEN** B 04

Displacement, tons: 39 full load
Dimensions, feet (metres): 65.6 × 15.7 × 4.3 *(20 × 4.8 × 1.3)*
Main machinery: 2 Volvo Penta TAMD122 diesels; 366 hp(m) *(269 kW)* sustained; 2 shafts
Speed, knots: 15
Complement: 9 (3 officers)
Guns: 1 — 7.62 mm MG.
Radars: Navigation: Terma; I-band.

Comment: Built by Djupviksvarvet and completed in 1991. GRP hulls. Classified as mine
warfare vessels. Used for laying and monitoring sonobuoys to detect intruders in
Swedish territorial waters. Carry an AQS-928 acoustic processor.

VIGGEN   *8/2003, E & M Laursen* / 0572625

1 MSF MK 1 CLASS (MSD)

SÖKAREN MRF 01

Displacement, tons: 128 full load
Dimensions, feet (metres): 86.9 × 23 × 6.9 *(26.5 × 7 × 2.1)*
Main machinery: 2 Scania DSI 14 diesels; 1,000 hp(m) *(736 kW)*; 2 Schottel azimuth thrusters
Speed, knots: 12
Complement: 6
Radars: Navigation: Bridgewater E; I-band.
Sonars: STS 2054 side scan active; high frequency.

Comment: MCMV drone with GRP hull transferred from Denmark in 2001 for evaluation following cancellation of SAM II drone project. Further orders are not expected.

SÖKAREN   *5/2004, E & M Laursen* / 1043531

4 STYRSÖ CLASS
(MINESWEEPERS/HUNTERS—INSHORE)(MHSDI)

Name	No	Builders	Launched	Commissioned
STYRSÖ	M 11	Karlskronavarvet	8 Mar 1996	20 Sep 1996
SPÅRÖ	M 12	Karlskronavarvet	30 Aug 1996	21 Feb 1997
SKAFTÖ	M 13	Karlskronavarvet	20 Jan 1997	13 June 1997
STURKÖ	M 14	Karlskronavarvet	27 June 1997	19 Dec 1997

Displacement, tons: 205 full load
Dimensions, feet (metres): 118.1 × 25.9 × 7.2 *(36 × 7.9 × 2.2)*
Main machinery: 2 Saab Scania DSI 14 diesels; 1,104 hp(m) *(812 kW)*; 2 shafts; bow thruster
Speed, knots: 13
Complement: 17 (9 officers)
Guns: 2—12.7 mm MGs.
Countermeasures: MCM: AK-90 acoustic, EL-90 magnetic, and mechanical sweeps.
2 Sutec Sea Eagle/Double Eagle ROVs equipped with Tritech SE 500 sonar and mine disposal charges.
Combat data systems: Ericsson tactical data system with datalink.
Radars: Navigation: Racal Bridgemaster: I-band.
Sonars: Reson Sea Bat 8100; mine avoidance; active; high frequency.
EG & G side scan; active for route survey; high frequency.

Comment: Contract awarded to KKV and Erisoft AB on 11 February 1994. Capable of operating two SAM drones. These ships are also used for inshore surveillance patrols.

STURKÖ   *5/2001, L-G Nilsson* / 0131148

1 GÅSSTEN CLASS (MINESWEEPER—INSHORE) (MSI)

Name	No	Builders	Commissioned
VIKSTEN	M 33	Karlskronavarvet	15 July 1974

Displacement, tons: 120 standard; 135 full load
Dimensions, feet (metres): 78.7 × 21.3 × 11.5 *(24 × 6.5 × 3.5)*
Main machinery: 1 diesel; 460 hp(m) *(338 kW)*; 1 shaft
Speed, knots: 11
Complement: 9
Guns: 1 Bofors 20 mm.
Radars: Navigation: Terma; I-band.

Comment: Ordered 1972 built of GRP.

VIKSTEN   *4/2004, E & M Laursen* / 1043532

SURVEY SHIPS

Notes: (1) Owned and manned (since 1 January 2002) by the National Maritime Administration.
(2) There is a research ship *Argos*. Civilian manned and owned by the National Board of Fisheries. A second civilian ship *Ocean Surveyor* belongs to the Geological Investigation but has been leased as a Support Ship on occasions.
(3) The Board of Navigation owns two buoy tenders *Scandica* and *Baltica* built in 1982 and two lighthouse tenders *Fyrbyggaren* and *Fyrbjörn*.

SCANDICA   *6/2000, Curt Borgenstam* / 0106585

1 SURVEY SHIP (AGS)

JACOB HÄGG

Displacement, tons: 192 standard
Dimensions, feet (metres): 119.8 × 24.6 × 5.6 *(36.5 × 7.5 × 1.7)*
Main machinery: 4 Saab Scania DSI 14 diesels; 1,592 hp(m) *(1.17 MW)* sustained; 2 shafts
Speed, knots: 16
Complement: 13 (5 officers)

Comment: Laid down April 1982 at Djupviks Shipyard. Launched 12 March 1983. Completed 16 May 1983. Aluminium hull.

JACOB HÄGG   *5/1998, J Ciślak* / 0050199

1 SURVEY SHIP (AGS)

NILS STRÖMCRONA

Displacement, tons: 210 full load
Dimensions, feet (metres): 98.4 × 32.8 × 5.9 *(30 × 10 × 1.8)*
Main machinery: 4 Saab Scania DSI 14 diesels; 1,592 hp(m) *(1.17 MW)* sustained; 2 shafts; bow and stern thrusters
Speed, knots: 12
Complement: 14 (5 officers)

Comment: Completed 28 June 1985. Of catamaran construction-each hull of 3.9 m made of aluminium.

NILS STRÖMCRONA   *9/2001, Per Körnefeldt* / 0131143

INTELLIGENCE VESSELS

1 ELECTRONIC SURVEILLANCE SHIP (AGIH)

Name	No	Builders	Launched	Commissioned
ORION	A 201	Karlskronavarvet	30 Nov 1983	7 June 1984

Displacement, tons: 1,400 full load
Dimensions, feet (metres): 201.1 × 32.8 × 9.8 *(61.3 × 10 × 3)*
Main machinery: 2 Hedemora V8A diesels; 1,800 hp(m) *(1.32 MW)* sustained; 2 shafts; cp props
Speed, knots: 15
Complement: 35
Radars: Navigation: Terma Scanter 009; I-band.
Helicopters: Platform for 1 light.

Comment: Ordered 23 April 1982. Laid down 28 June 1982. The communications aerials are inside the elongated dome.

ORION   *4/2003, Per Körnefeldt* / 0572628

RESCUE VEHICLES

Notes: (1) Kockums is developing S-SRV, a replacement submarine rescue vehicle. A further development of URF, it will be capable of rescuing 35 people in a single mission from a depth of 460 m. With a speed of 4.5 kt, it will be capable of diving to depths of 700 m and mating with the hull of a submarine at angles up to 60°. Rescued personnel will be transferred to a recompression chamber on a surface vessel. Navigational aids will include sonars and underwater cameras. It will be road/air/ship transportable and be capable of operating from another submarine.
(2) Early in 1995 Sweden signed an agreement with Norway to provide submarine rescue.

S-SRV   *6/2004, Kockums* / 1043516

1 RESCUE SUBMERSIBLE (DSRV)

URF

Displacement, tons: 52
Dimensions, feet (metres): 45.6 × 10.5 × 9.2 *(13.9 × 3.2 × 2.8)*
Main machinery: Electric/hydraulic: single shaft
Speed, knots: 3
Complement: 4

Comment: Rescue submersible URF (*Ubåts Räddnings Farkost*) was launched by Kockums on 17 April 1978 and commissioned in 1979. The double-hulled vehicle is capable of operating down to 460 m with an endurance of 85 hours. The URF can mate with the hull of a submarine at angles up to 45° and is equipped with a lockout chamber that can support two divers to 300 m. It has a rescue capacity of 35 per dive and submariners can be transferred directly from the pressurised hull of the submarine to a compression chamber on board the support ship *Belos*. The vehicle is normally based at the Naval Diving Centre at Berga but can be transported by road using a specially designed trailer to a site suitable for loading on to the support ship. URF has recently been refitted and will remain in service until S-SRV enters service in about 2008.

URF   *8/2004, E & M Laursen* / 1043538

TRAINING SHIPS

2 SAIL TRAINING SHIPS (AXS)

Name	No	Builders	Commissioned
GLADAN	S 01	Naval Dockyard, Stockholm	1947
FALKEN	S 02	Naval Dockyard, Stockholm	1947

Displacement, tons: 225 standard
Dimensions, feet (metres): 112.8 × 23.6 × 13.8 *(34.4 × 7.2 × 4.2)*
Main machinery: 1 diesel; 120 hp(m) *(88 kW)*; 1 shaft

Comment: Sail training ships. Two masted schooners. Sail area, 512 sq m. Both had major overhauls in 1986-88 in which all technical systems were replaced.

FALKEN   *5/1997, Marek Twardowski* / 0019218

2 M 15 CLASS (MINESWEEPERS—INSHORE) (MSI/AXL)

M 21   M 22

Displacement, tons: 70 full load
Dimensions, feet (metres): 90.9 × 16.5 × 6.6 *(27.7 × 5 × 2)*
Main machinery: 2 diesels; 320 hp(m) *(235 kW)* sustained; 2 shafts
Speed, knots: 12
Complement: 10
Radars: Navigation: Terma; I-band.

Comment: Launched in 1941 and used for navigation training.

M15 CLASS   *4/2004, Per Körnefeldt* / 1043542

AUXILIARIES

1 TRANSPORT (AKR)

Name	No	Builders	Commissioned
SLEIPNER (ex-*Ardal*)	A 343	Bergen	1980

Displacement, tons: 1,049 full load
Dimensions, feet (metres): 163.1 × 36.1 × 11.5 *(49.7 × 11 × 3.5)*
Main machinery: 1 Normo diesel; 1,300 hp(m) *(956 kW)*; 1 shaft
Speed, knots: 12
Complement: 12
Cargo capacity: 260 tons

Comment: Former Ro-Ro vessel acquired in 1992 from a Norwegian Shipping Company. There is a stern ramp and side door.

SLEIPNER   *7/2003, E & M Laursen* / 0572629

1 TROSSÖ CLASS (SUPPORT SHIP) (AGP)

Name	No	Builders	Commissioned
TROSSÖ (ex-*Arnold Viemer*, ex-*Livonia*)	A 264	Valmet, Finland	1 Jan 1984

Displacement, tons: 2,140 full load
Dimensions, feet (metres): 234.9 × 42 × 14.8 *(71.6 × 12.8 × 4.5)*
Main machinery: 2 Russkiy G74 36/45 diesels; 3,084 hp(m) *(2.27 MW)*; 2 shafts
Speed, knots: 14
Complement: 64

Comment: Built as a survey ship for the USSR and used in the Baltic as an AGOR. Taken on by the Estonian Marine Institute and then transferred to Sweden on 23 September 1996. Converted as a depot ship for corvettes and patrol craft and back in service in 1997. Can act as a Headquarters Ship. A second vessel, *Ornö*, was purchased in 2001 but rebuilding of the ship was abandoned in November 2001 due to its poor material state.

TROSSÖ   *5/2005*, Guy Toremans* / 1153907

1 ÄLVSBORG CLASS (SUPPORT SHIP) (AKH)

Name	No	Builders	Launched	Commissioned
VISBORG	A 265	Karlskronavarvet	25 Jan 1975	6 Feb 1976

Displacement, tons: 2,400 standard; 2,650 full load
Dimensions, feet (metres): 303.1 × 48.2 × 13.2 *(92.4 × 14.7 × 4)*
Main machinery: 2 Nohab-Polar diesels; 4,200 hp(m) *(3.1 MW)*; 1 shaft; cp prop; bow thruster; 350 hp(m) *(257 kW)*
Speed, knots: 16
Complement: 95
Guns: 3 Bofors 40 mm/70 SAK 48.
ESM: Argo 700; intercept.
Radars: Surface search: Raytheon; E/F-band.
Fire control: Philips 9LV 200 Mk 2; I/J-band.
Navigation: Terma Scanter 009; I-band.
Helicopters: Platform only.

Comment: Laid down on 16 October 1973. Formerly a minelayer, now supply ship for second surface flotilla. Sister ship transferred to Chile in 1996.

VISBORG   *8/2003, E & M Laursen* / 0572630

1 DIVER SUPPORT SHIP (YDT/AGF)

ÄGIR (ex-*Bloom Syrveyor*) A 212

Displacement, tons: 117 full load
Dimensions, feet (metres): 82 × 24.9 × 6.6 *(25 × 7.6 × 2)*
Main machinery: 2 GM diesels; 2 shafts
Speed, knots: 11
Complement: 15
Radars: Navigation: Terma; I-band.

Comment: Built in Norway in 1984. Acquired in 1989.

ÄGIR   *7/2003, E & M Laursen* / 0572632

1 DIVER SUPPORT SHIP (YDT)

NORDANÖ (ex-*Sjöjungfrun*) A 213

Displacement, tons: 148 full load
Dimensions, feet (metres): 80.1 × 24.9 × 8.9 *(24.4 × 7.6 × 2.7)*
Main machinery: 2 Volvo Penta TAMD diesels; 767 hp(m) *(564 kW)*; 2 shafts
Speed, knots: 10
Complement: 15

Comment: Launched in 1983 and bought by the Navy in 1992.

NORDANÖ   *6/2002, Swedish Navy* / 0530069

1 SALVAGE SHIP (ARSH)

Name	No	Builders	Commissioned
BELOS III (ex-*Energy Supporter*)	A 214	De Hoop, Netherlands	Nov 1992

Measurement, tons: 5,096 grt
Dimensions, feet (metres): 344.2 × 59.1 × 16.7 *(104.9 × 18 × 5.1)*
Main machinery: 5 MAN 9ASL 25/30 diesel alternators; 8.15 MW; 2 motors; 5,110 hp(m) *(3.76 MW)*; 2 azimuth thrusters and 3 bow thrusters
Speed, knots: 14
Complement: 50 (22 officers)

Comment: Bought from Midland and Scottish Resources in mid-1992 and arrived in Sweden in November 1992. Replaced the previous ship of the same name which paid off in April 1993. Ice-strengthened hull and fitted with a helicopter platform. Acts as the support ship for the rescue submersible URF. Equipped with Dynamic Positioning System MOSHIP. Life-extension refit to be completed in December 2005.

BELOS III   *8/2004, E & M Laursen* / 1043539

1 TORPEDO AND MISSILE RECOVERY VESSEL (YPT)

Name	No	Builders	Commissioned
PELIKANEN	A 247	Djupviksvarvet	26 Sep 1963

Displacement, tons: 144 full load
Dimensions, feet (metres): 108.2 × 19 × 7.2 (33 × 5.8 × 2.2)
Main machinery: 2 MTU MB diesels; 1,040 hp(m) (764 kW); 2 shafts
Speed, knots: 14
Complement: 14
Radars: Navigation: Terma; I-band.

Comment: Torpedo recovery and rocket trials vessel.

PELIKANEN   *5/2005*, E & M Laursen* / 1153897

1 TORPEDO AND MISSILE RECOVERY VESSEL (YPT)

Name	No	Builders	Commissioned
PINGVINEN	A 248	Lunde Varv-och Verstads	20 Mar 1975

Displacement, tons: 191 full load
Dimensions, feet (metres): 109.3 × 20 × 7.2 (33.3 × 6.1 × 2.2)
Main machinery: 2 MTU diesels; 1,140 hp(m) (838 kW); 2 shafts
Speed, knots: 13
Complement: 14
Radars: Navigation: Terma; I-band.

Comment: Recovery vessel for trials firings.

PINGVINEN   *6/2002, Swedish Navy* / 0530068

1 SUPPORT SHIP (AKL)

Name	No	Builders	Commissioned
LOKE	A 344	Oskarsham Shipyard	Sep 1994

Displacement, tons: 455 full load
Dimensions, feet (metres): 117.8 × 29.5 × 8.6 (35.9 × 9 × 2.7)
Main machinery: 2 Scania diesels; 2 shafts
Speed, knots: 12
Complement: 8
Cargo capacity: 50 tons or 50 passengers
Radars: Navigation: Terma; I-band.

Comment: General support craft which can be used as a ferry. Landing craft bow.

LOKE   *4/2004, E & M Laursen* / 1043540

16 SUPPORT VESSEL (TROSSBÅT) (YAG)

662-677

Displacement, tons: 60 full load
Dimensions, feet (metres): 80.1 × 17.7 × 4.6 (24.4 × 5.4 × 1.4)
Main machinery: 3 Saab Scania DSI 14 diesels; 1,194 hp(m) (878 kW) sustained; 3 FFJet 450 water-jets
Speed, knots: 25; 13 (laden)
Complement: 3
Military lift: 22 tons
Guns: 1 — 12.7 mm MG.
Radars: Navigation: Terma; I-band.

Comment: Prototype Trossbåt-built at Holms Shipyard in 1991 and capable of carrying 15 tons of deck cargo and 9 tons internal cargo or 17 troops plus mines. Aluminium hull with a bow ramp. Some ice capability. A second prototype delivered in late 1993, and the first production vessel in 1996. Eight vessels have been modified to undertake international peacekeeping operations by the inclusion of armoured protection, an NBC citadel and air conditioning.

TROSSBÅT 668   *8/2002, E & M Laursen* / 0529906

ICEBREAKERS

Notes: All Icebreakers have been transferred to and are manned by the National Maritime Administration.

1 ODEN CLASS (AGB/ML)

Name	Builders	Launched	Commissioned
ODEN	Gotaverken Arendal, Göteborg	25 Aug 1988	29 Jan 1989

Displacement, tons: 12,900 full load
Dimensions, feet (metres): 352.4 × 102 × 27.9 (107.4 × 31.1 × 8.5)
Main machinery: 4 Sulzer ZAL40S8L diesels; 23,940 hp(m) (17.6 MW) sustained; 2 shafts; cp props
Speed, knots: 17. **Range, n miles:** 30,000 at 13 kt
Complement: 32 plus 17 spare berths
Guns: 4 Bofors 40 mm/70 can be fitted.

Comment: Ordered in February 1987, laid down 19 October 1987. Can break 1.8 m thick ice at 3 kt. Towing winch aft with a pull of 150 tons. Helicopter platform 73.5 × 57.4 ft (22.4 × 17.5 m). The main hull is only 25 m wide but the full width is at the bow. Fitted with water-jet and heeling pump system to assist with ice-breaking operations. Also equipped as a minelayer.

ODEN (with water-jets)   *10/2000, Per Körnefeldt* / 0106584

3 ATLE CLASS (AGBH/ML)

Name	Builders	Launched	Commissioned
ATLE	Wärtsilä, Helsinki	27 Nov 1973	21 Oct 1974
FREJ	Wärtsilä, Helsinki	3 June 1974	30 Sep 1975
YMER	Wärtsilä, Helsinki	3 Sep 1976	25 Oct 1977

Displacement, tons: 7,900 standard; 9,500 full load
Dimensions, feet (metres): 343.1 × 78.1 × 23.9 (104.6 × 23.8 × 7.3)
Main machinery: 5 Wärtsilä-Pielstick diesels; 22,000 hp(m) (16.2 MW); 4 Strömberg motors; 22,000 hp(m) (16.2 MW); 4 shafts (2 fwd, 2 cp aft)
Speed, knots: 19
Complement: 50 (16 officers)
Guns: 4 Bofors 40 mm/70.
Helicopters: 2 light.

Comment: Similar to Finnish Urho class. Also equipped as minelayers.

FREJ   *8/1994, E & M Laursen* / 0080744

1 ALE CLASS (AGB/AGS)

Name	Builders	Launched	Commissioned
ALE	Wärtsilä, Helsinki	1 June 1973	19 Dec 1973

Displacement, tons: 1,550
Dimensions, feet (metres): 154.2 × 42.6 × 16.4 (47 × 13 × 5)
Main machinery: 2 diesels; 4,750 hp(m) (3.49 MW); 2 shafts
Speed, knots: 14
Complement: 32 (8 officers)
Guns: 1 Bofors 40 mm/70 (not embarked).

Comment: Built for operations on Lake Vänern. Is also used as a survey ship.

ALE   *9/2002, E & M Laursen* / 0529911

TUGS

1 OCEAN TUG (ATA/AGB)

ACHILLES A 251

Displacement, tons: 450 full load
Dimensions, feet (metres): 108.2 × 28.9 × 15.1 (33 × 8.8 × 4.6)
Main machinery: 1 diesel; 1,650 hp(m) (1.2 MW); 1 shaft
Speed, knots: 12
Complement: 12
Radars: Navigation: Racal Decca 1226C; I-band.

Comment: Launched in 1962. Icebreaking tug.

ACHILLES   *5/2005*, Per Körnefeldt* / 1153898

3 COASTAL TUGS (YTM)

HERMES A 253	HEROS A 322	HERA A 324

Displacement, tons: 185 standard; 215 full load
Dimensions, feet (metres): 80.5 × 22.6 × 13.1 (24.5 × 6.9 × 4)
Main machinery: 1 diesel; 600 hp(m) (441 kW); 1 shaft
Speed, knots: 11
Complement: 8

Comment: Details given for the first pair launched 1953-57. Third is smaller at 127 tons and was launched in 1969-71. All are icebreaking tugs.

HERA   *6/2000, E & M Laursen* / 0106591

9 COASTAL TUGS (YTL)

A 702-705	A 751	A 753-756

Displacement, tons: 42 full load
Dimensions, feet (metres): 50.9 × 16.4 × 8.9 (15.5 × 5 × 2.7)
Main machinery: 1 diesel; 1 shaft
Speed, knots: 9.5
Complement: 6

Comment: Can carry 40 people. Icebreaking tugs. 702-703 used by Amphibious Corps. All can carry mines.

A 702   *5/2005*, Per Körnefeldt* / 1153899

COAST GUARD (KUSTBEVAKNING)

Establishment: Established in 1638, and for 350 years was a part of the Swedish Customs administration. From 1 July 1988 the Coast Guard became an independent civilian authority with a Board supervised by the Ministry of Defence. Organised in four regions with a central Headquarters.
Duties: Responsible for civilian surveillance of Swedish waters, fishery zone and continental shelf. Supervises and enforces fishing regulations, customs, dumping and pollution regulations, environmental protection and traffic regulations. Also concerned with prevention of drug running and forms part of the Swedish search and rescue organisation.

Headquarters Appointments

Director General:
 Marie Hafstrom

Personnel

2006: 583

Aircraft: Three CASA 212 (to be replaced by Bombardier Dash 8Q ordered in 2005).

Ships: Tv pennant numbers replaced by KBV in 1988 but the KBV is not displayed. Vessels are not normally armed.

0 + 2 (1) KBV 001 CLASS (MULTIPURPOSE VESSELS) (WPSO)

KBV 001-002

Displacement, tons: 3,400
Dimensions, feet (metres): 259.8 × 52.5 × ? (79.2 × 16.0 × ?)
Main machinery: Diesel-electric; 5 generators; azimuth thrusters
Speed, knots: 16
Complement: 41
Radars: To be announced.

Comment: Contract signed on 20 December 2005 with Damen Shipyards for the construction of two multipurpose vessels to be capable of towing, fire-fighting, oil recovery, environmental-control, fishery control, control of territorial waters, rescue operations and diving support. There is an option for a third vessel. The ships are to be built and outfitted at Damen Shipyard, Galati, Romania. Delivery of the vessels is to be in April and October 2008. KBV 001 is to be based at Gothenburg and KBV 002 at Slite, Gotland.

KBV 001 (artist's impression)   *12/2005*, Damen Shipyards* / 1041661

1 KBV 181 CLASS (HIGH ENDURANCE CUTTER) (WHEC/PBO)

KBV 181

Displacement, tons: 991 full load
Dimensions, feet (metres): 183.7 oa; 167.3 wl × 33.5 × 15.1 *(56; 51 × 10.2 × 4.6)*
Main machinery: 2 Wärtsilä Vasa 8R22 diesels; 3,755 hp(m) *(2.76 MW)* sustained; 1 shaft;
    Kamewa cp prop; bow thruster
Speed, knots: 16. **Range, n miles:** 2,800 at 15 kt
Complement: 11
Guns: 1 Oerlikon 20 mm (if required).
Radars: Navigation: Furuno FAR 2830; I-band.
Sonars: Simrad Subsea; active search; high frequency.

Comment: Ordered from Rauma Shipyards in August 1989 and built at Uusikaupunki.
    Commissioned 30 November 1990. Unarmed in peacetime. Equipped as a Command vessel
    for SAR and anti-pollution operations. All-steel construction similar to Finnish *Tursas*.

KBV 181   *6/2000, B Sullivan* / 0106592

2 KBV 101 CLASS
(MEDIUM ENDURANCE CUTTERS) (WMEC/PB)

KBV 104-105

Displacement, tons: 65 full load
Dimensions, feet (metres): 87.6 × 16.4 × 7.2 *(26.7 × 5 × 2.2)*
Main machinery: 2 Cummins KTA38-M diesels; 2,120 hp *(1.56 MW)*; 2 shafts
Speed, knots: 21
Range, n miles: 1,000 at 15 kt
Complement: 5 plus 2 spare
Sonars: Hull-mounted; active search; high frequency.

Comment: Built 1969-73 at Djupviksvarvet. Class A cutters. All-welded aluminium hull and
    upperworks. Equipped for salvage divers. Modernisation with new diesels, a new bridge
    and new electronics completed in 1988. *KBV 101* transferred to Lithuania in 1996.

KBV 101 class   *5/1994, E & M Laursen* / 0080758

2 KBV 201 CLASS (HIGH ENDURANCE CUTTERS) (WHEC/PBO)

KBV 201   **KBV 202**

Displacement, tons: 476 full load
Dimensions, feet (metres): 170.6 × 28.2 × 7.9 *(52 × 8.6 × 2.4)*
Main machinery: 2 MWM 610 diesels; 5,440 hp(m) *(4 MW)*; 2 MWM 616 diesels; 1,904 hp(m)
    (1.4 MW); 2 shafts; Kamewa cp props; 2 bow thruster 424 hp(m) *(312 kW)*
Speed, knots: 21. **Range, n miles:** 1,340 at 16 kt
Complement: 9
Radars: Navigation: E/F- and I-band.

Comment: Ordered from Kockums in January 1999 and built at Karlskrona. First one
    delivered in March 2001 and second in September 2001. Steel hulls. Multirole vessels
    for surveillance and environmental protection. Stern ramp for launching a RIB.

KBV 201   *5/2004, E & M Laursen* / 1043543

6 KBV 281 CLASS
(MEDIUM ENDURANCE CUTTERS) (WMEC/PB)

KBV 281-283   **KBV 285-287**

Displacement, tons: 45 full load
Dimensions, feet (metres): 71.5 × 16.4 × 6.2 *(21.8 × 5 × 1.9)*
Main machinery: 2 Cummins KTA38-M or MWM diesels; 2,120 hp *(1.56 MW)*; 2 shafts
Speed, knots: 27
Complement: 4
Radars: Navigation: Furuno; I-band.

Comment: Built by Djupviksvarvet and delivered at one a year from 1979. Last one
    commissioned in 1990. Aluminium hulls. Some of the class have an upper bridge.

KBV 287   *5/2004, P Marsan* / 1043544

16 KBV 301 CLASS
(MEDIUM ENDURANCE CUTTERS) (WMEC/PB)

KBV 301-316

Displacement, tons: 35 full load
Dimensions, feet (metres): 65.6 × 15.1 × 3.6 *(20 × 4.6 × 1.1)*
Main machinery: 2 MTU 183TE92 diesels; 1,830 hp(m) *(1.35 MW)* sustained; 2 MTP 7500S
    or Kamewa water-jets
Speed, knots: 34. **Range, n miles:** 500 at 25 kt
Complement: 4
Radars: Navigation: 2 Kelvin Hughes 6000; I-band.

Comment: Built at Karlskronavarvet. First one delivered in May 1993 and the remainder
    ordered in December 1993. Three delivered in 1995, four in 1996 and the last three
    in 1997.

KBV 301   *3/2003, Per Körnefeldt* / 0572638

3 KBV 591 (GRIFFON 2000 TDX) CLASS (HOVERCRAFT) (UCAC)

KBV 591-593

Displacement, tons: 3.5 full load
Dimensions, feet (metres): 38.4 × 19.4 *(11.7 × 5.9)*
Main machinery: 1 Deutz BF8L diesel; 350 hp(m) *(235 kW)*
Speed, knots: 50. **Range, n miles:** 450 at 35 kt
Complement: 3
Radars: Navigation: Furuno 7010 D; I-band.

Comment: Built by Griffon Hovercraft, Southampton and delivered in 1992-93. Aluminium
    hulls. Based at Stockholm, Lutea and Umea.

KBV 591   *6/2003, Swedish Coast Guard* / 0572610

For details of the latest updates to *Jane's Fighting Ships* online and to discover the additional
information available exclusively to online subscribers please visit
jfs.janes.com

3 KBV 288 CLASS
(MEDIUM ENDURANCE CUTTERS) (WMEC/PBO)

KBV 288-290

Displacement, tons: 53 full load
Dimensions, feet (metres): 71.5 × 17.7 × 5.9 *(21.8 × 5.4 × 1.8)*
Main machinery: 2 Cummins KTA38-M or MWM diesels; 2,120 hp *(1.56 MW)*; 2 shafts
Speed, knots: 24
Complement: 5
Radars: Navigation: Furuno; I-band.

Comment: An improved design of the KBV 281 class which entered service 1990-93.

KBV 290   *8/2004, Harald Carstens* / 1043545

60 COAST GUARD PATROL CRAFT (SMALL) (PB)

KBV 401-408   +52

Displacement, tons: 2.2 full load
Dimensions, feet (metres): 29.7 × 8.5 × 2.9 *(9.05 × 2.6 × 0.9)*
Main machinery: 2 Yamaha outboard engines; 500 hp *(372 kW)*
Speed, knots: 55. **Range, n miles:** 100 at 35 kt
Complement: 3

Comment: Details are for *KBV 401-408* built in 1994-95. There is a total of some 60 speed boats with Raytheon radars.

KBV 408   *6/2003, Swedish Coast Guard* / 0572612

POLLUTION CONTROL CRAFT (YPC)

Number	Displacement (tons)	Comment
KBV 004	450	Built by Lunde in 1978. Has helipad and carries salvage divers
KBV 005	990	Ice Class 1A built in 1980 and acquired in 1993
KBV 006	450	Built by Lunde in 1985
KBV 010	400	Built by Lunde in 1985. Oil spill clean-up craft
KBV 020	60	Catamaran design built by Djupviks in 1982
KBV 044	100	Class B Sea Trucks built by Djupviks in 1976. Oil spill clean-up craft
KBV 045-049	230	Pollution control craft built by Lunde 1980-83. Have bow ramp
KBV 050-051	340	Enlarged version of KBV 045 class with bow ramp. Built by Lunde in 1983

KBV 047   *6/2003, Per Körnefeldt* / 0572639

KBV 005   *6/2003, Swedish Coast Guard* / 0572611

Switzerland

Country Overview

A landlocked western European country, the Swiss Confederation has an area of 15,940 square miles and is bordered by France, Germany, Austria, Liechtenstein and Italy. The largest city is Zurich and the capital is Bern. The principal lakes are Lake Geneva in the southwest and Lake Constance in the northeast. Others not wholly within Swiss borders are Lake Lugano and Lake Maggiore. The river Rhine, whose source is in the Swiss Alps, is navigable northwards and downstream from the port of Basel. One company of patrol boats, part of the Swiss Army, is available for operations on lakes Constance, Geneva and Maggiore.

Diplomatic Representation

Defence Attaché in London:
  Colonel B Stoll

ARMY

Notes: (1) There are also large numbers of flat bottomed raiding craft powered by single 40 hp outboard engines.
(2) There are a number of 6 m rescue craft equipped with a hydraulic ramp.

11 AQUARIUS CLASS (PATROUILLENBOOT 80) (PBR)

ANTARES	SATURN	PERSEUS	MARS
AQUARIUS	URANUS	SIRIUS	POLLUX
ORION	CASTOR	VENUS	

Displacement, tons: 7 full load
Dimensions, feet (metres): 35.1 × 10.8 × 3.6 *(10.7 × 3.3 × 1.1)*
Main machinery: 2 Volvo KAD 3 diesels; 460 hp(m) *(338 kW)*; 2 shafts
Speed, knots: 35
Complement: 7
Guns: 2 — 12.7 mm MGs.
Radars: Surface search: JFS Electronic 364; I-band.

Comment: Builders Müller AG, Spiez. GRP hulls, wooden superstructure. *Aquarius* commissioned in 1978, *Pollux* in 1984, the remainder in 1981. Re-engined with diesels which have replaced the former petrol engines.

AQUARIUS   *10/1997, Swiss Army* / 0019223

Syria

Country Overview

The Syrian Arab Republic was proclaimed in 1961 following brief federation with Egypt as the United Arab Republic from 1958. Situated in the Middle East, the country has an area of 71,498 square miles and is bordered to the north by Turkey, to the east by Iraq, to the south by Jordan and Israel and to the west by Lebanon. It has a 104 n mile coastline with the Mediterranean Sea. The capital and largest city is Damascus while the principal ports are Latakia and Tartus. It is the only country to claim 35 n mile Territorial seas. An EEZ is not claimed.

Headquarters Appointments

Commander-in-Chief Navy:
  Major General Wael Nasser

Organisation

Naval Forces come under the command of the Chief of General Staff, Commander of Land Forces.

Personnel

(a) 2006: 3,200 officers and men (2,500 reserves)
(b) 18 months' national service

Bases

Latakia, Tartous, Al-Mina-al-Bayda, Baniyas

Coast Defence

Coastal defence has been under naval control since 1984. A missile brigade is equipped with SS-C-1 Sepal and SS-C-3 Styx with sites at Tartous (2), Baniyas and Latakia. Two artillery battalions have a total of 36—130 mm guns and 12—100 mm guns. Coastal observation sites are manned by an Observation Battalion. There are two infantry brigades each of which is assigned to a coastal zone.

DELETIONS

Mine Warfare Forces

2004 Sonya 532

FRIGATES

2 PETYA III (PROJECT 159A) CLASS (FFL)

1-508 (ex-12)   AL HIRASA 2—508 (ex-14)

Displacement, tons: 950 standard; 1,180 full load
Dimensions, feet (metres): 268.3 × 29.9 × 9.5
  (81.8 × 9.1 × 2.9)
Main machinery: CODAG; 2 gas turbines; 30,000 hp(m)
  (22 MW); 1 Type 61V-3 diesel; 5,400 hp(m) *(3.97 MW)*
  sustained (centre shaft); 3 shafts
Speed, knots: 32
Range, n miles: 4,870 at 10 kt; 450 at 29 kt
Complement: 98 (8 officers)

Guns: 4—3 in *(76 mm)*/60 (2 twin) ❶; 90 rds/min to 15 km
  (8 n miles); weight of shell 6.8 kg.
Torpedoes: 3—21 in *(533 mm)* (triple) tubes ❷. SAET-60;
  active/passive homing to 15 km *(8.1 n miles)* at 40 kt;
  warhead 100 kg.
A/S mortars: 4 RBU 2500 16-tubed trainable ❸; range
  2,500 m; warhead 21 kg.
Depth charges: 2 racks.
Mines: Can carry 22.
Radars: Surface search: Slim Net ❹; E/F-band.
Navigation: Don 2; I-band.
Fire control: Hawk Screech ❺; I-band.
IFF: High Pole B. 2 Square Head.
Sonars: Herkules; hull-mounted; active search and attack;
  high frequency.

Programmes: Transferred by the USSR in July 1975 and March 1975.
Operational: Based at Tartous. *2—508* in dock in mid-1998 to 2000 and reported to be sea-going. The operational status of *1—508* is not known.

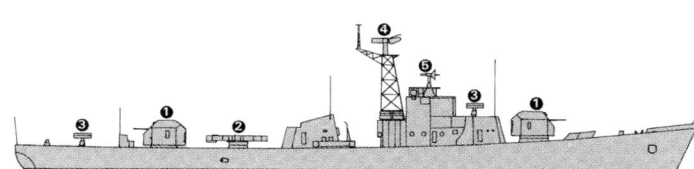

PETYA 1-508   *(Scale 1 : 900), Ian Sturton* / 0506171

AL HIRASA   *6/2001* / 0121400

PATROL FORCES

Notes: Replacement of patrol forces is reported to be under consideration

10 OSA (PROJECT 205) CLASS
(FAST ATTACK CRAFT—MISSILE) (PTFG)

31-32 (OSA I)   33-40 (OSA II)

Displacement, tons: 245 full load
Dimensions, feet (metres): 126.6 × 24.9 × 8.8 *(38.6 × 7.6 × 2.7)*
Main machinery: 3 Type M 504 (Osa II)/M 503 (Osa I) diesels; 8,025/10,800 hp(m)
  (6.0/8.1 MW) sustained; 3 shafts
Speed, knots: 35 (Osa I), 37 (Osa II). **Range, n miles:** 500 at 35 kt
Complement: 25 (3 officers)

Missiles: SSM: 4 SS-N-2C; active radar or IR homing to 83 km *(43 n miles)* at 0.9 Mach;
  warhead 513 kg; sea-skimmer at end of run.
Guns: 4—30 mm/65 (2 twin); 500 rds/min to 5 km *(2.7 n miles)*; weight of shell 0.54 kg.
Countermeasures: Decoys: PK 16 chaff launcher.
Radars: Surface search: Square Tie; I-band.
Fire control: Drum Tilt; H/I-band.
IFF: 2 Square Head. High Pole A or B.

Programmes: Delivered: October 1979 (two), November 1979 (two), August 1982 (one), September 1982 (one) and May 1984 (two). Others have already been deleted.
Structure: Two are modified (Nos 39 and 40).
Operational: OSA II based at Latakia. All are still fully operational and active. Two Osa Is (31 and 32) at Tartous also reported to be operational again. The Osa Is may be fitted with SSN 2A/B.

OSA II 38   *6/1998* / 0050214

8 ZHUK (GRIF) (PROJECT 1400M) CLASS
(COASTAL PATROL CRAFT) (PB)

1-8	2-8	3-8	4-8	5-8	6-8	7-8	8-8

Displacement, tons: 39 full load
Dimensions, feet (metres): 78.7 × 16.4 × 3.9 *(24 × 5 × 1.2)*
Main machinery: 2 Type M 401B diesels; 2,200 hp(m) *(1.6 MW)* sustained; 2 shafts
Speed, knots: 30. **Range, n miles:** 1,100 at 15 kt
Complement: 11 (3 officers)
Guns: 4—14.5 mm (2 twin) MGs.
Radars: Surface search: Spin Trough; I-band.

Comment: Three transferred from USSR in August 1981, three on 25 December 1984 and two more in the late 1980s. All based at Tartous but most are non-operational.

ZHUK 5—8   *6/1998* / 0050215

LAND-BASED MARITIME AIRCRAFT

Numbers/Type: 11/2 Mil Mi-14P Haze A/Haze C.
Operational speed: 124 kt *(230 km/h)*.
Service ceiling: 15,000 ft *(4,570 m)*.
Range: 432 n miles *(800 km)*.
Role/Weapon systems: Medium-range ASW helicopter. Sensors: Short Horn search radar, dipping sonar, MAD, sonobuoys. Weapons: ASW; internally stored torpedoes, depth mines and bombs.

Numbers/Type: 2 Kamov Ka-28 Helix.
Operational speed: 135 kt *(250 km/h)*.
Service ceiling: 19,685 ft *(6,000 m)*.
Range: 432 n miles *(800 km)*.
Role/Weapon systems: ASW helicopter. Delivered in February 1990. Sensors: Splash Drop search radar, dipping sonar, sonobuoys, MAD, ECM. Weapons: ASW; 3 torpedoes, depth bombs, mines.

AMPHIBIOUS FORCES

3 POLNOCHNY B CLASS (PROJECT 771) (LSM)

1-114   **2-114**   **3-114**

Displacement, tons: 760 standard; 834 full load
Dimensions, feet (metres): 246.1 × 31.5 × 7.5 (75 × 9.6 × 2.3)
Main machinery: 2 Kolomna Type 40-D diesels; 4,400 hp(m) (3.2 MW) sustained; 2 shafts
Speed, knots: 19. **Range, n miles:** 1,500 at 15 kt
Complement: 40
Military lift: 180 troops; 350 tons cargo
Guns: 4—30 mm/65 (2 twin); 500 rds/min to 5 km (2.7 n miles); weight of shell 0.54 kg.
  2—140 mm rocket launchers; 18 barrels per launcher; range 9 km (5 n miles).
Radars: Surface search: Spin Trough; I-band.
Fire control: Drum Tilt; H/I-band.

Comment: Built at Northern Shipyard, Gdansk. First transferred from USSR January 1984, two in February 1985 from Black Sea. All based at Tartous and still active.

POLNOCHNY B (Russian colours)   *1988* / 0506104

MINE WARFARE FORCES

1 NATYA (PROJECT 266M) CLASS (MSC/AGORM)

642

Displacement, tons: 804 full load
Dimensions, feet (metres): 200.1 × 33.5 × 10.8 (61 × 10.2 × 3)
Main machinery: 2 Type 504 diesels; 5,000 hp(m) (3.67 MW) sustained; 2 shafts
Speed, knots: 16. **Range, n miles:** 3,000 at 12 kt
Complement: 65
Missiles: SAM: 2 SA-N-5 Grail quad launchers; manual aiming; IR homing to 6 km (3.2 n miles) at 1.5 Mach; altitude to 2,500 m (8,000 ft); warhead 1.5 kg; 16 missiles.
Guns: 4—30 mm/65 (2 twin) can be fitted.
Radars: Surface search: Don 2; I-band.
Fire control: Drum Tilt; H/I-band.

Comment: Arrived in Tartous from USSR in January 1985. Has had sweeping gear and guns removed and converted to serve as an AGOR. Painted white. Based at Latakia in reasonable condition. Reported active.

NATYA 642   *6/1996* / 0080764

3 YEVGENYA (PROJECT 1258) CLASS
(MINESWEEPERS—INSHORE) (MSI/PC)

6-507   **7-507**   **8-507**

Displacement, tons: 77 standard; 90 full load
Dimensions, feet (metres): 80.7 × 18 × 4.9 (24.6 × 5.5 × 1.5)
Main machinery: 2 Type 3-D-12 diesels; 600 hp(m) (444 kW); 2 shafts
Speed, knots: 11. **Range, n miles:** 300 at 10 kt
Complement: 10
Guns: 2—14.5 mm (twin) MGs (first pair). 2—25 mm/80 (twin) (second pair).
Radars: Surface search: Spin Trough; I-band.
IFF: High Pole.
Sonars: MG-7; stern-mounted VDS; active; high frequency.

Comment: First transferred from USSR 1978, two in 1985 and two in 1986. Second pair by Ro-flow from Baltic in February 1985 being new construction with tripod mast. Based at Tartous, at least two are operational. Two others have been deleted.

YEVGENYA (Russian colours)   *1991* / 0506103

TRAINING SHIPS

1 TRAINING SHIP (AX/AKR)

AL ASSAD

Displacement, tons: 3,500 full load
Dimensions, feet (metres): 344.5 × 56.4 × 13.1 (105 × 17.2 × 4)
Main machinery: 2 Zgoda-Sulzer 6ZL40/48 diesels; 8,700 hp(m) (6.4 MW); 2 shafts; bow thruster
Speed, knots: 16. **Range, n miles:** 4,500 at 15 kt
Complement: 56 plus 140 cadets
Radars: Navigation: Decca Seamaster; E/F- and I-band.

Comment: Built in Polnochny Shipyard, Gdansk and launched 18 February 1987. Delivered in late 1988. Ro-ro design used as a naval training ship. Unarmed but has minelaying potential. Based at Latakia and occasionally deploys on cruises.

AL ASSAD   *7/2003, B Prézelin* / 0570996

AL ASSAD   *7/2003, B Prézelin* / 0570997

Taiwan
REPUBLIC OF CHINA

Country Overview

The Republic of China was established in 1949 when the Nationalist government of China withdrew to Taiwan (Formosa) and established its headquarters. Though in practice an autonomous state, Taiwan is still formally a province of China and, as such, is claimed by the People's Republic of China. The country comprises the island of Taiwan (area 13,900 square miles), the Pescadores, or P'eng-hu Islands, the Quemoy Islands off the mainland city of Amoy (Xiamen), and the Matsu group off Fuzhou (Foochow). It has a 783 n mile coastline with East China Sea, Pacific Ocean and South China Sea. The capital and largest city of Taiwan is Taipei while Chi-lung (Keelung), Hualien, Kao-hsiung and T'ai-chung are the principal ports. Territorial seas (12 n miles) are claimed. A 200 n mile EEZ and Fishery Zone have also been claimed.

Headquarters Appointments

Commander-in-Chief:
   General Chen Bon-Chih
Deputy Commander-in-Chief:
   Vice Admiral Shen Fang-Hsiang
Commandant of Marine Corps:
   Lieutenant General Hsu Tai-Shen

Senior Flag Officers

Fleet Commander:
   Vice Admiral Kao Kuan-Chi
Director of Logistics:
   Vice Admiral Gan Ke-Chiang

Personnel

(a)   2006: 31,500 in Navy, 15,000 in Marine Corps
(b)   1 year 4 months conscript service

Bases

Tsoying: HQ First Naval District (Southern Taiwan, Pratas and Spratly). Main Base, HQ of Fleet Command, Naval Aviation Group and Marine Corps. Base of southern patrol and transport squadrons. Officers and ratings training, Naval Academy, Naval shipyard.
Kaohsiung; Naval shipyard.

Bases—*continued*

Makung (Pescadores): HQ Second Naval District (Pescadores, Quemoy and Wu Ch'iu). Base for attack squadrons. Naval shipyard and training facilities.
Keelung: HQ Third Naval District (Northern Taiwan and Matsu group). Base of northern patrol and transport squadrons. Naval shipyard.
Hualien: Naval Aviation Command.
Suao: East Coast Command, submarine depot and shipyard.
Minor bases at Hualien, Tamshui, Hsinchu, Wuchi and Anping.
Building: Taitung.

Organisation

1. Fleet Command:
124th Attack squadron, based at Tsoying
131st Patrol squadron, based at Keelung
146th Attack squadron, based at Pescadores
151st Amphibious squadron, based at Tsoying
168th Patrol squadron, based at Suao
192nd Mine Warfare squadron, based at Tsoying
256th Submarine Unit, based at Tsoying.

2. Naval Aviation Command: There are two Groups. The fixed-wing Group consists of two squadrons (133 and 134) and the helicopter Group of three squadrons (501, 701 and 702). Land bases include Tsoying, Hualien, Hsinchu and Pintung.

Coast Defence

The land-based SSM command has six squadrons equipped with Hsiung-Feng II SSM at Tonying Island of the Matsu Group, Siyu Island of the Pescadores, Shiao Liuchiu off Kaohsiung, north of Keelung harbour, Tsoying naval base and Hualien. The ROCMC deploy eight SAM Platoons, equipped with Chaparral SAM quad-launchers, to the offshore island of Wuchiu, and Pratas islets in the South China Sea. There are also a number of 127 mm guns.

Marine Corps

Increased to three brigades in 2002 supported by one amphibious regiment and one logistics regiment. Equipped

Marine Corps—*continued*

with M-116, M-733, LARC-5, LVTP5 (to be replaced by AAV-7A-IRAM/RS) personnel carriers and LVTH6 armour tractors. Based at Tsoying and in southern Taiwan. Spratly detachment provided by the Coast Guard from 1 January 2000 and Marine Corps detachment withdrawn from Pratas Islands at the same time.

Coast Guard

Formerly the Maritime Security Police but name changed on 1 January 2000. Comes under the Minister of the Interior but its numerous patrol boats are integrated with the Navy for operational purposes.

Strength of the Fleet

Type	Active (Reserve)	Building/ Transfer (Planned)
Submarines	4	(8)
Destroyers	2	2
Frigates	22	—
Corvettes	—	(10)
Fast Attack Craft (Missile)	50	(28)
Large Patrol Craft	20	—
Ocean Minesweepers	4	—
Coastal Minesweepers/Hunters	8	(2)
LSD	2	(1)
Landing Ships (LST and LSM)	14	—
LCUs	18	—
Survey Ships	1	—
Combat Support Ships	1	—
Transports	3	—
Salvage Ships	1	—
Coast Guard	18	—

PENNANT LIST

Submarines

791	Hai Shih
792	Hai Bao
793	Hai Lung
794	Hai Hu

Destroyers

1801	Kee Lung
1802	Suao
1803	Tsoying
1805	Makung

Frigates

932	Chin Yang
933	Fong Yang
934	Feng Yang
935	Lan Yang
936	Hae Yang
937	Hwai Yang
938	Ning Yang
939	Yi Yang
1101	Cheng Kung
1103	Cheng Ho
1105	Chi Kuang
1106	Yueh Fei
1107	Tzu-I
1108	Pan Chao
1109	Chang Chien
1110	Tien Tan (bldg)
1202	Kang Ding
1203	Si Ning
1205	Kun Ming
1206	Di Hua
1207	Wu Chang
1208	Chen Te

Patrol Forces

PCL 1	Ning Hai
PCL 2	An Hai

601	Lung Chiang
602	Sui Chang
603	Jin Chiang
605	Tan Chiang
606	Hsin Chiang
607	Feng Chiang
608	Tseng Chiang
609	Kao Chiang
610	Jing Chiang
611	Hsian Chiang
612	Tsi Chiang
614	Po Chiang
615	Chan Chiang
617	Chu Chiang

Amphibious Forces

191	Chung Cheng
193	Shiu Hai
201	Chung Hai
205	Chung Chien
208	Chung Shun
216	Chung Kuang
217	Chung Chao
218	Chung Chi
221	Chung Chuan
226	Chung Chih
227	Chung Ming
230	Chung Pang
231	Chung Yeh
232	Chung Ho
233	Chung Ping
401	Ho Chi
402	Ho Huei
403	Ho Yao
406	Ho Chao
481	Ho Shun
484	Ho Chung
488	Ho Shan
489	Ho Chuan
490	Ho Seng
491	Ho Meng
492	Ho Mou
493	Ho Shou
494	Ho Chun
495	Ho Yung
LCC1	Kao Hsiung

SB 1	Ho Chie
SB 2	Ho Ten

Mine Warfare Forces

158	Yung Chuan
162	Yung Fu
167	Yung Ren
168	Yung Sui
1301	Yung Feng
1302	Yung Chia
1303	Yung Ting
1305	Yung Shun
1306	Yung Yang
1307	Yung Tzu
1308	Yung Ku
1309	Yung Teh

Auxiliaries and Survey Ships

524	Yuen Feng
525	Wu Kang
526	Hsin Kang
530	Wu Yi
552	Ta Hu
1601	Ta Kuan

Tugs

ATF 551	Ta Wan
ATF 553	Ta Han
ATF 554	Ta Kang
ATF 555	Ta Fung
ATF 563	Ta Tai

SUBMARINES

Notes: Project Kwang Hua 8: Following the announcement in 2001 by the US government that it will support the acquisition of eight diesel submarines, debate has centred on how these will be procured. Northrop Grumman has reportedly offered a modernised version of the Barbel class, which dates from the 1950s. The licence of a design from a third country has proved to be problematic in view of the re-affirmation of earlier decisions by the governments of the Netherlands (1992) and Germany (1993) not to grant export licences for Taiwan. Efforts to sell the Agosta class were similarly discouraged by the French government while Australia has rejected expressions of interest in the Collins class. An indigenous build programme remains a possibility although this would present significant technical and financial challenges. By late 2005, a US-built submarine seemed the most likely solution but the project appeared to have been delayed indefinitely after being blocked in the Legislative Yuan (parliament).

2 HAI LUNG CLASS (SSK)

Name	No	Builders	Laid down	Launched	Commissioned
HAI LUNG	793	Wilton Fijenoord, Netherlands	Dec 1982	6 Oct 1986	9 Oct 1987
HAI HU	794	Wilton Fijenoord, Netherlands	Dec 1982	20 Dec 1986	9 Apr 1988

Displacement, tons: 2,376 surfaced; 2,660 dived
Dimensions, feet (metres): 219.6 × 27.6 × 22
(66.9 × 8.4 × 6.7)
Main machinery: Diesel-electric; 3 Bronswerk D-RUB 215-12 diesels; 4,050 hp(m) *(3 MW)*; 3 alternators; 2.7 MW; 1 Holec motor; 5,100 hp(m) *(3.74 MW)*; 1 shaft
Speed, knots: 12 surfaced; 20 dived
Range, n miles: 10,000 at 9 kt surfaced
Complement: 67 (8 officers)

Missiles: SSM: Sub Harpoon (to be fitted).
Torpedoes: 6—21 in *(533 mm)* bow tubes. 20 AEG SUT; dual purpose; wire-guided; active/passive homing to 12 km *(6.6 n miles)* at 35 kt; warhead 250 kg.
Countermeasures: ESM: Argo AR 700SF and Elbit Timnex 4CH(V)2; intercept.

Weapons control: Sinbads M TFCS.
Radars: Surface search: Signaal ZW06; I-band.
Sonars: Signaal SIASS-Z; hull-mounted; passive/active intercept search and attack; low/medium frequency. Fitted for but not with towed passive array.

Programmes: Order signed with Wilton Fijenoord in September 1981 for these submarines with variations from the standard Netherlands Zwaardvis design. Construction was delayed by the financial difficulties of the builders but was resumed in 1983. Sea trials of *Hai Lung* in March 1987 and *Hai Hu* in January 1988 and both submarines were shipped out on board a heavy dock vessel. The names mean *Sea Dragon* and *Sea Tiger*.
Modernisation: Plans to fit both submarines with McDonnell Douglas UGM-84 Sub Harpoon were announced in September 2005. It is not known whether these are to be Block 2 missiles with a land-attack capability. Harpoon is likely to be a stand-alone system rather than being integrated with the fire-control system.
Structure: The four horns on the forward casing are Signaal sonar intercept transducers. Torpedoes manufactured under licence in Indonesia.
Operational: Hsiung Feng II submerged launch SSMs are planned to be part of the weapons load and a torpedo tube launched version is being developed, although no recent progress has been reported. Belong to 256th Submarine Unit based at Tsoying.

HAI HU and HAI LUNG

*11/2004, **Ships of the World*** / 1044575

2 GUPPY II CLASS (SS)

Name	No	Builders	Laid down	Launched	Commissioned
HAI SHIH (ex-*Cutlass* SS 478)	791 (ex-SS 91)	Portsmouth Navy Yard	22 July 1944	5 Nov 1944	17 Mar 1945
HAI BAO (ex-*Tusk* SS 426)	792 (ex-SS 92)	Federal SB & DD Co, Kearney, New Jersey	23 Aug 1943	8 July 1945	11 Apr 1946

Displacement, tons: 1,870 standard; 2,420 dived
Dimensions, feet (metres): 307.5 × 27.2 × 18
(93.7 × 8.3 × 5.5)
Main machinery: Diesel-electric; 3 Fairbanks-Morse diesels; 4,500 hp *(3.3 MW)*; 2 Elliott motors; 5,400 hp *(4 MW)*; 2 shafts
Speed, knots: 18 surfaced; 15 dived
Range, n miles: 8,000 at 12 kt surfaced
Complement: 75 (7 officers)

Torpedoes: 10—21 in *(533 mm)* (6 fwd, 4 aft) tubes. AEG SUT; active/passive homing to 12 km *(6.5 n miles)* at 35 kt; 28 km *(15 n miles)* at 23 kt; warhead 250 kg.
Countermeasures: ESM: WLR-1/3; radar warning.
Radars: Surface search: US SS 2; I-band.
Sonars: EDO BQR 2B; hull-mounted; passive search and attack; medium frequency.
Raytheon/EDO BQS 4C; adds active capability to BQR 2B.
Thomson Sintra DUUG 1B; passive ranging.

Programmes: Originally fleet-type submarines of the US Navy's Tench class; extensively modernised under the Guppy II programme. *Hai Shih* transferred in April 1973 and *Hai Bao* in October the same year.
Structure: After 56 years in service diving depth is very limited.
Operational: Kept in service because of difficulty in buying replacements, but operational status doubtful. Likely to have an alongside training role only. Belong to the 256th Submarine Unit based at Tsoying.

HAI BAO

*11/2004, **Ships of the World*** / 1044574

DESTROYERS

Notes: (1) Fully operational numbers of destroyers, frigates, corvettes and PGGs are restricted to a total of 48. As a new ship commissions, one of the older ships is paid off.
(2) Acquisition of the Aegis Combat System remains a firm aspiration but, following the decision to procure the Kidd class DDGs as an interim measure, this is unlikely before 2012.

7 GEARING (WU CHIN III CONVERSION) (FRAM I) CLASS (DDGHM)

Name	No	Builders	Laid down	Launched	Commissioned
CHIEN YANG (ex-*James E Kyes*)	912 (ex-DD 787)	Todd Pacific SY, Seattle, WA	27 Dec 1944	4 Aug 1945	8 Feb 1946
LIAO YANG (ex-*Hanson*)	921 (ex-DD 832)	Bath Iron Works Corporation	7 Oct 1944	11 Mar 1945	11 May 1945
SHEN YANG (ex-*Power*)	923 (ex-DD 839)	Bath Iron Works Corporation	26 Feb 1945	30 June 1945	13 Sep 1945
TE YANG (ex-*Sarsfield*)	925 (ex-DD 837)	Bath Iron Works Corporation	15 Jan 1945	27 May 1945	31 July 1945
YUN YANG (ex-*Hamner*)	927 (ex-DD 718)	Federal SB and DD Co	5 Apr 1945	24 Nov 1945	11 July 1946
CHEN YANG (ex-*Johnston*)	928 (ex-DD 821)	Consolidated Steel Corporation	6 May 1945	19 Oct 1945	10 Oct 1946
SHAO YANG (ex-*Hollister*)	929 (ex-DD 788)	Todd Pacific SY, Seattle, WA	18 Jan 1945	9 Oct 1945	26 Mar 1946

Displacement, tons: 2,425 standard; 3,540 full load
Dimensions, feet (metres): 390.5 × 41.2 × 19
(119 × 12.6 × 5.8)
Main machinery: 4 Babcock & Wilcox boilers; 600 psi
(43.3 kg/cm²); 850°F *(454°C)*; 2 GE turbines; 60,000 hp
(45 MW); 2 shafts
Speed, knots: 30. **Range, n miles:** 6,080 at 15 kt
Complement: 275 approx

Missiles: SSM: 4 Hsiung Feng II (quad) ❶; active radar/IR
homing to 80 km *(43.2 n miles)* at 0.85 Mach; warhead
190 kg.
SAM: 10 General Dynamics Standard SM1-MR (2 triple ❷;
2 twin ❸; command guidance; semi-active radar homing
to 46 km *(25 n miles)* at 2 Mach.
A/S: Honeywell ASROC Mk 112 octuple launcher ❹; inertial
guidance to 1.6—10 km *(1—5.4 n miles)*; payload Mk 46
torpedo.
Guns: 1 OTO Melara 3 in *(76 mm)*/62 ❺; 85 rds/min to
16 km *(8.7 n miles)*; weight of shell 6 kg.
1 GE/GD 20 mm Vulcan Phalanx Block 1 6-barrelled Mk 15 ❻;
3,000 rds/min combined to 1.5 km.
2 Bofors 40 mm/70 ❼. 4 or 6—12.7 mm MGs.
Torpedoes: 6—324 mm US Mk 32 (2 triple) tubes ❽.
Honeywell Mk 46; anti-submarine; active/passive homing
to 11 km *(5.9 n miles)* at 40 kt; warhead 44 kg. Some
Mk 44s are still in service.
Countermeasures: Decoys: 4 Kung Fen 6 16-tubed chaff
launchers ❾.
Mk T-6 Fanfare torpedo decoy.
ESM/ECM: Chang Feng III (Hughes SLQ-17/SLQ-31)
intercept and jammers.
Combat data systems: Ta Chen tactical datalink.
Weapons control: Honeywell H 930 MFCS Mk 114 system
(for ASROC). Signaal LIOD Mk 2 optronic director. ❿
Radars: Air search: Signaal DA08 (with DA05 aerial) ⓫;
E/F-band.
Surface search: Raytheon SPS-10 ⓬; G/I-band.
Fire control: Signaal STIR ⓭; I/J-band (for Standard and
76 mm).
Westinghouse W-160 ⓮; I-band (for Bofors).
Navigation: I-band.
Tacan: SRN 15.
Sonars: Raytheon SQS-23H; hull-mounted; active search
and attack; medium frequency.

Helicopters: 1 McDonnell Douglas MD 500 ⓯.

Programmes: *Chien Yang* transferred 18 April 1973; *Liao
Yang*, 18 April 1973; *Te Yang* and *Shen Yang*, 1 October
1977 by sale; *Yun Yang*, December 1980; *Chen Yang*
by sale 27 February 1981; *Shao Yang* by sale 3 March
1983. There has been some confusion over the English
translation of some names. These are now correct.
Modernisation: All ships converted to area air defence
ships under the Wu Chin III programme. This upgrade
involved the installation of the H 930 Modular Combat

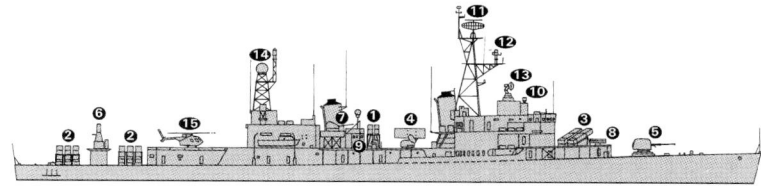

LIAO YANG   *(Scale 1 : 1,200), Ian Sturton* / 0126186

CHEN YANG   *9/2001, Ships of the World* / 0121407

System (MCS) with a Signaal DA08 air search radar
(employing a lightweight DA05 antenna) and a Signaal
STIR missile control radar directing 10 box-launched
Standard SM-1 surface-to-air missiles (two twin in
'B' position, two triple facing either beam aft). The system
can track 24 targets simultaneously and attack four with
an 8 second response time. An OTO Melara 76 mm is
fitted to 'A' position, one Bofors 40 mm/70 is mounted
forward of the seaboat on the starboard side, one abaft
the ASROC magazine on the port side and a Mk 15 Block
1 Phalanx CIWS is aft between two banks of Standard
launchers. A Westinghouse W-160 is mounted on a lattice
mast on the hangar to control the Bofors. The amidships
ASROC launcher is retained, its Mk 114 fire-control system
is integrated with the H 930 MCS via a digital-analogue
interface. The SQS-23 sonar has also been upgraded to

the H standard using a Raytheon solid-state transmitter.
The Chang Feng III EW system was developed jointly by
Taiwan's Chung-Shan Institute of Science and Technology
(CSIST) with the assistance of Hughes. The Chang Feng
III employs phased-array antennas which resemble those
of the Hughes SLQ-17, it is capable of both deception
and noise jamming. An eighth ship, *Lao Yang*, was to
have been given the same conversion but missed the
programme after a grounding incident in 1987 and has
since been deleted. Ta Chen datalink fitted from 1994.
Four Hsiung Feng II SSM launchers (quad) are fitted aft
of the ASROC launcher.
Operational: Having paid off all the other ex-US Second
World War destroyers, these ships are likely to be replaced
by the Kidd class from 2005. Form 131 Squadron. Based
at Keelung.

CHIEN YANG   *9/2001, Ships of the World* / 0121404

Name	No
KEELUNG (ex-*Chi Teh*, ex-*Scott*)	1801 (ex-DD 995)
SUAO (ex-*Wu Teh*, ex-*Callaghan*)	1802 (ex-DD 994)
TSOYING (ex-*Ming Teh*, ex-*Kidd*)	1803 (ex-DD 993)
MAKUNG (ex-*Tong-Teh*, ex-*Chandler*)	1805 (ex-DD 996)

Displacement, tons: 6,950 light; 9,574 full load
Dimensions, feet (metres): 563.3 × 55 × 20
  (171.7 × 16.8 × 6.2)
Main machinery: 4 GE LM 2500 gas turbines; 86,000 hp
  (64.16 MW) sustained; 2 shafts
Speed, knots: 33
Range, n miles: 6,000 at 20 kt
Complement: 363 (31 officers)

Missiles: SSM: 8 McDonnell Douglas RGM 84L Block
  2 Harpoon (2 quad) launchers; active radar homing
  to 130 km *(70 n miles)* at 0.9 Mach; warhead 227 kg.
  SAM: 52 GDC Standard SM-2 Block IIIA; command/inertial
  guidance; semi-active radar homing to 167 km *(90 n miles)*
  at 2 Mach. 2 twin Mk 26 launchers. 37 missiles.
Guns: 2 FMC 5 in *(127 mm)*/54 Mk 45 Mod 0; 20 rds/min to
  23 km *(12.6 n miles)*; weight of shell 32 kg.
  2 General Electric/General Dynamics 20 mm Vulcan Phalanx
  6-barrelled Mk 15; 3,000 rds/min (4,500 in Block 1).
  4—12.7 mm MGs.
Torpedoes: 6—324 mm Mk 32 (2 triple) tubes. Honeywell
  Mk 46 Mod 5; anti-submarine; active/passive
  homing to 11 km *(5.9 n miles)* at 40 kt; warhead
  44 kg. Torpedoes fired from inside the hull under the
  hangar.
Countermeasures: Decoys: 4 Loral Hycor SRBOC
  6-barrelled fixed Mk 36; IR flares and chaff to 4 km
  (2.2 n miles). SLQ-25 Nixie; torpedo decoy.
Combat data systems: ACDS Block 1 Level 1 with
  datalinks.
Weapons control: SWG-1A Harpoon LCS. 2 Mk 74 MFCS.
  Mk 86 Mod 5 GFCS. Mk 116 FCS for ASW. Mk 14 WDS.
  SYS 2(V)2 IADT. 4 SYR 3393 for SAM mid-course
  guidance.

2 + 2 KEELUNG (KIDD) CLASS (DDGHM)

Builders	Laid down	Launched	Commissioned
Ingalls Shipbuilding	12 Feb 1979	1 Mar 1980	24 Oct 1981
Ingalls Shipbuilding	23 Oct 1978	1 Dec 1979	29 Aug 1981
Ingalls Shipbuilding	26 June 1978	11 Aug 1979	27 June 1981
Ingalls Shipbuilding	7 May 1979	24 May 1980	13 Mar 1982

KIDD class (US colours) *4/1997, H M Steele* / 0016364

Radars: Air search: ITT SPS-48E; 3D; E/F-band.
  Raytheon SPS-49(V)5; C/D-band.
  Air/Surface search: ISC Cardion SPS-55; I/J-band.
  Navigation: Raytheon SPS-64; I/J-band.
  Fire control: 2 Raytheon SPG-51D, 1 Lockheed SPG-60,
  1 Lockheed SPQ-9A.
Sonars: General Electric/Hughes SQS-53A; bow-mounted;
  search and attack; medium frequency.
  Gould SQR-19 (TACTAS); passive towed array (may be
  fitted).

Helicopters: 2 Sikorsky S-70C(M) (only 1 embarked).

Programmes: Originally ordered by the Iranian government
  in 1974, the contracts were taken over by the US Navy on

25 July 1979. All paid off from USN service in 1998-99.
Offered to the Taiwan government, intention to buy
confirmed on 2 October 2001.
Modernisation: All received major modernisation from
1988-90. Further package completed prior to transfer.
ASROC has been removed.
Structure: Optimised for general warfare, mainmast
and radar aerials are in different configuration than
Spruance class. Details given are for the ships in USN
service.
Operational: *Keelung* and *Suao* arrived in Taiwan on 8
December 2005 and are to be based initially at Suao port
while a deepwater jetty at Tsoying is completed. *Tsoying*
and *Makung* are to follow in March 2007.

FRIGATES

Notes: The Kuang Hua 7 programme has superseded the former Kuang Hua 5 programme for the procurement of a new class of frigates/corvettes to replace the
Knox class frigates. It is understood that there is a requirement for up to eight new ships of above 2,000 tons with a main armament of Hsiung Feng-II missiles.
It is not clear whether the ships are to be procured abroad (ex-US Spruance class are a possibility) or built locally.

8 KNOX CLASS (FFGH)

Name	No	Builders	Laid down	Launched	Commissioned	Recommissioned
CHIN YANG (ex-*Robert E Peary*)	932 (ex-FF 1073)	Lockheed Shipbuilding	20 Dec 1970	23 June 1971	23 Sep 1972	6 Oct 1993
FONG YANG (ex-*Brewton*)	933 (ex-FF 1086)	Avondale Shipyards	2 Oct 1970	24 July 1971	8 July 1972	6 Oct 1993
FENG YANG (ex-*Kirk*)	934 (ex-FF 1087)	Avondale Shipyards	4 Dec 1970	25 Sep 1971	9 Sep 1972	6 Oct 1993
LAN YANG (ex-*Joseph Hewes*)	935 (ex-FF 1078)	Avondale Shipyards	15 May 1969	7 Mar 1970	22 Apr 1971	4 Aug 1995
HAE YANG (ex-*Cook*)	936 (ex-FF 1083)	Avondale Shipyards	20 Mar 1970	23 Jan 1971	18 Dec 1971	4 Aug 1995
HWAI YANG (ex-*Barbey*)	937 (ex-FF 1088)	Avondale Shipyards	5 Feb 1971	4 Dec 1971	11 Nov 1972	4 Aug 1995
NING YANG (ex-*Aylwin*)	938 (ex-FF 1081)	Avondale Shipyards	13 Nov 1969	29 Aug 1970	18 Sep 1971	18 Oct 1999
YI YANG (ex-*Valdez*)	939 (ex-FF 1096)	Avondale Shipyards	30 June 1972	24 Mar 1973	27 July 1974	18 Oct 1999

Displacement, tons: 3,011 standard; 3,877 (932, 935), 4,260
  (933, 934) full load
Dimensions, feet (metres): 439.6 × 46.8 × 15; 24.8 (sonar)
  (134 × 14.3 × 4.6; 7.8)
Main machinery: 2 Combustion Engineering/Babcock &
  Wilcox boilers; 1,200 psi *(84.4 kg/cm²)*; 950°F *(510°C)*;
  1 turbine; 35,000 hp *(26 MW)*; 1 shaft
Speed, knots: 27
Range, n miles: 4,000 at 22 kt on 1 boiler
Complement: 288 (17 officers) including aircrew

Missiles: SSM: 8 McDonnell Douglas Harpoon; active radar
  homing to 130 km *(70 n miles)* at 0.9 Mach; warhead 227 kg.
  SAM: 10 General Dynamics SM1-MR (2 triple, 2 twin);
  command guidance; semi-active radar homing to 46 km
  (25 n miles) at 2 Mach (to be fitted).
  A/S: Honeywell ASROC Mk 16 octuple launcher with reload
  system (has 2 cells modified to fire Harpoon) **1**; inertial
  guidance from 1.6—10 km *(1—5.4 n miles)*; payload Mk
  46 Mod 5 Neartip.
Guns: 1 FMC 5 in *(127 mm)*/54 Mk 42 Mod 9 **2**; 20—40
  rds/min to 24 km *(13 n miles)* anti-surface; 14 km
  (7.7 n miles) anti-aircraft; weight of shell 32 kg to be
  replaced by 1 OTO Melara 3 in *(76 mm)*/62 Mk 75;
  85 rds/min to 16 km *(8.7 n miles)*; weight of shell 6 kg.
  1 General Electric/General Dynamics 20 mm/76
  6-barrelled Mk 15 Vulcan Phalanx **3**; 3,000 rds/min
  combined to 1.5 km.
  4 Type 75 20 mm.
Torpedoes: 4—324 mm Mk 32 (2 twin) fixed tubes **4**.
  22 Honeywell/Alliant Mk 46 Mod 5; anti-submarine;
  active/passive homing to 11 km *(5.9 n miles)* at 40 kt;
  warhead 44 kg. May be replaced by 2 triple tubes.
Countermeasures: Decoys: 2 Loral Hycor SRBOC
  6-barrelled fixed Mk 36 **5**; IR flares and chaff to 4 km
  (2.2 n miles). T Mk 6 Fanfare/SLQ-25 Nixie; torpedo
  decoy. Prairie Masker hull and blade rate noise
  suppression.
  ESM/ECM: SLQ-32(V)2 **6**; radar warning. Sidekick
  modification adds jammer and deception signals.
Combat data systems: Link 14 receive only. Link W may
  be fitted. FFISTS (Frigate Integrated Shipboard Tactical
  System). RADDS (Radar Displays and Distribution
  System).
Weapons control: SWG-1A Harpoon LCS. Mk 68 GFCS.
  Mk 114 ASW FCS. Mk 1 target designation system. SRQ-4
  for LAMPS I.
Radars: Air search: Lockheed SPS-40B **7**; B-band.
  Surface search: Raytheon SPS-10 or Norden SPS-67 **8**;
  G-band.
  Navigation: Marconi LN66; I-band.
  Fire control: Western Electric SPG-53A/D/F **9**; I/J-band.
  Tacan: SRN 15. IFF: UPX-12.

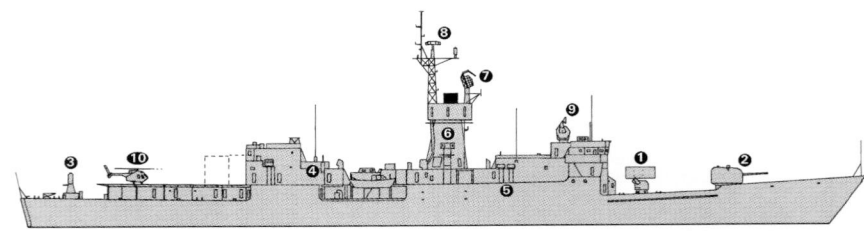

CHIN YANG *(Scale 1 : 1,200), Ian Sturton* / 0121406

FONG YANG *12/2005*, Ships of the World* / 1151164

Sonars: EDO/General Electric SQS-26CX; bow-mounted;
  active search and attack; medium frequency.
  EDO SQR-18A(V)1; passive towed array.

Helicopters: 1 MD 500 **10**.

Programmes: *Fong Yang* leased from the US on 23 July
  1992, *Chin Yang* 7 August 1992 and *Feng Yang* 6 August
  1993. *Hae Yang* leased 31 May 1994. *Hwai Yang* 21 June
  1994 and *Lan Yang* 30 June 1994. The second batch of
  three were overhauled and upgraded by Long Beach
  Shipyard, California. *Ning Yang* and *Yi Yang* transferred
  by sale on 29 April 1998, and refitted at Denton Shipyard,
  South Carolina. The transfer of a third (ex-*Pharris* 1094)
  was declined as were further offers of (ex-*Whipple* (1062)
  and ex-*Downes* (1070) for use as spares.
Modernisation: It is planned to equip all eight ships
  with a limited air-defence capability. Ten standard

SM-1 MR (ex-Gearing class) are to be installed. Two
triple launchers will be located midships, forward
of the hanger, and two twin launchers on the bridge.
The 127 mm gun is to be replaced by the OTO Melara
76 mm/62.
Structure: ASROC-torpedo reloading capability (note
slanting face of bridge structure immediately behind
ASROC). Four Mk 32 torpedo tubes are fixed in
the midships structure, two to a side, angled out
at 45°. The arrangement provides improved loading
capability over exposed triple Mk 32 torpedo tubes.
A 4,000 lb lightweight anchor is fitted on the port
side and an 8,000 lb anchor fits into the after section
of the sonar.
Operational: Seasprite helicopters were planned to be
embarked but this now seems unlikely. All of the class
are assigned to 168 Patrol Squadron at Suao. *Lan Yang*
is the Flagship.

8 CHENG KUNG CLASS (KWANG HUA 1 PROJECT) (FFGHM)

Name	No	Builders	Laid down	Launched	Commissioned
CHENG KUNG	1101	China SB Corporation, Kaohsiung	7 Jan 1990	5 Oct 1991	7 May 1993
CHENG HO	1103	China SB Corporation, Kaohsiung	21 Dec 1990	15 Oct 1992	28 Mar 1994
CHI KUANG	1105	China SB Corporation, Kaohsiung	4 Oct 1991	27 Sep 1993	4 Mar 1995
YUEH FEI	1106	China SB Corporation, Kaohsiung	5 Sep 1992	26 Aug 1994	7 Feb 1996
TZU-I	1107	China SB Corporation, Kaohsiung	7 Aug 1994	13 July 1995	9 Jan 1997
PAN CHAO	1108	China SB Corporation, Kaohsiung	25 July 1995	4 July 1996	16 Dec 1997
CHANG CHIEN	1109	China SB Corporation, Kaohsiung	4 Dec 1995	14 May 1997	1 Dec 1998
TIEN TAN	1110	China SB Corporation, Kaohsiung	21 Feb 2001	15 Oct 2002	11 Mar 2004

Displacement, tons: 2,750 light; 4,105 full load
Dimensions, feet (metres): 453 × 45 × 14.8; 24.5 (sonar)
(138.1 × 13.7 × 4.5; 7.5)
Main machinery: 2 GE LM 2500 gas turbines; 41,000 hp
(30.59 MW) sustained; 1 shaft; cp prop
2 auxiliary retractable props; 650 hp *(484 kW)*
Speed, knots: 29
Range, n miles: 4,500 at 20 kt
Complement: 234 (15 officers) including 19 aircrew

Missiles: SSM: 8 Hsiung Feng II ❶ (2 quad); inertial
guidance; active radar/IR homing to 80 km *(43.2 n miles)*
at 0.85 Mach; warhead 190 kg or Harpoon Block II in due
course.
SAM: 40 GDC Standard SM1-MR; Mk 13 launcher ❷;
command guidance; semi-active radar homing to 46 km
(25 n miles) at 2 Mach.
Guns: 1 OTO Melara 76 mm/62 Mk 75 ❸; 85 rds/min to 16 km
(8.7 n miles); weight of shell 6 kg.
2 Bofors 40 mm/70 ❹. 3—20 mm Type 75 (on hangar roof
when fitted).
1 GE/GD 20 mm/76 Vulcan Phalanx 6-barrelled Mk 15 ❺;
3,000 rds/min combined to 1.5 km.
Torpedoes: 6—324 mm Mk 32 (2 triple) tubes ❻. Honeywell/
Alliant Mk 46 Mod 5; anti-submarine; active/passive
homing to 11 km *(5.9 n miles)* at 40 kt; warhead 44 kg.
Countermeasures: Decoys: 4 Kung Fen 6 chaff launchers
or locally produced version of RBOC (114 mm). SLQ-25A
Nixie; torpedo decoy.
ESM/ECM: Chang Feng IV (locally produced version of
SLQ-32(V)2 with Sidekick); combined radar warning and
jammers.

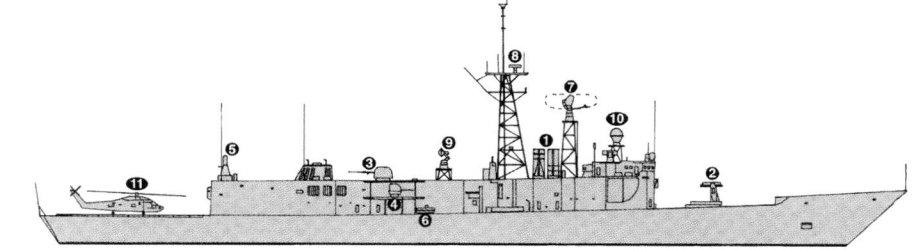

CHENG KUNG   *(Scale 1 : 1,200), Ian Sturton* / 0019226

Combat data systems: Norden SYS-2(V)2 action data
automation with UYK 43 computer. Ta Chen link (from
Chi Kuang onwards and being backfitted).
Weapons control: Loral Mk 92 Mod 6. Mk 13 Mod 4 weapon
direction system. Mk 114 ASW. 2 Mk 24 optical directors.
Mk 309 TFCS.
Radars: Air search: Raytheon SPS-49(V)5 or SPS-49A
(1108—9) ❼; C/D-band.
Surface search: ISC Cardion SPS-55 ❽ or Raytheon Chang
Bai; I/J-band.
Fire control: USN UD 417 STIR ❾; I/J-band.
Unisys Mk 92 Mod 6 ❿; I/J-band.
Sonars: Raytheon SQS-56/DE 1160P; hull-mounted; active
search and attack; medium frequency.
SQR-18A(V)2; passive towed array or BAe/Thomson Sintra
ATAS active towed array (from *Chi Kuang* onwards).

Helicopters: 2 Sikorsky S-70C(M) ⓫ (only 1 embarked).

Programmes: First two ordered 8 May 1989. Named after
Chinese generals and warriors. An eighth of class
was ordered in late July 1999. Originally this ship was
planned to be the first of a Flight II design, which was
scrapped.
Modernisation: It is reported that Harpoon is to replace
Hsiung Feng in due course. A PDMS may be fitted vice
the 40 mm guns. RAM is a possibility.
Structure: Similar to the USS *Ingraham*. RAST helicopter
hauldown. The area between the masts had to be
strengthened to take the Hsiung Feng II missiles. Prairie
Masker hull acoustic suppression system fitted.
Operational: Form the 146th Squadron based at Makung
(Pescadores).

CHENG HO   *10/2001, Chris Sattler* / 0534104

YUEH FEI   *4/2004*, Chris Sattler* / 1044571

6 KANG DING (LA FAYETTE) CLASS (KWANG HUA 2 PROJECT) (FFGHM)

Name	No	Builders	Laid down	Launched	Commissioned
KANG DING	1202	Lorient Dockyard/Kaohsiung Shipyard	26 Aug 1993	12 Mar 1994	24 May 1996
SI NING	1203	Lorient Dockyard/Kaohsiung Shipyard	27 Apr 1994	5 Nov 1994	15 Sep 1996
KUN MING	1205	Lorient Dockyard/Kaohsiung Shipyard	7 Nov 1994	13 May 1995	26 Feb 1997
DI HUA	1206	Lorient Dockyard/Kaohsiung Shipyard	1 July 1995	27 Nov 1995	14 Aug 1997
WU CHANG	1207	Lorient Dockyard/Kaohsiung Shipyard	1 July 1995	27 Nov 1995	16 Dec 1997
CHEN TE	1208	Lorient Dockyard/Kaohsiung Shipyard	27 Dec 1995	2 Aug 1996	16 Jan 1998

Displacement, tons: 3,800 full load
Dimensions, feet (metres): 407.5 × 50.5 × 18 (screws)
(124.2 × 15.4 × 5.5)
Main machinery: CODAD; 4 SEMT-Pielstick 12 PA6 V 280 STC
diesels; 23,228 hp(m) (17.08 MW); 2 shafts; LIPS cp props
Speed, knots: 25. **Range, n miles:** 7,000 at 15 kt
Complement: 134 (15 officers) plus 25 spare

Missiles: SSM: 8 Hsiung Feng II (2 quad) ❶; inertial
guidance; active radar/IR homing to 80 km (43.2 n miles)
at 0.85 Mach; warhead 190 kg.
SAM: 1 Sea Chaparral quad launcher ❷; IR homing to 3 km
(1.6 n miles) supersonic; warhead 5 kg.
Guns: 1 OTO Melara 76 mm/62 Mk 75 ❸; 85 rds/min to
16 km (8.7 n miles); weight of shell 6 kg.
1 Hughes 20 mm/76 Vulcan Phalanx Mk 15 Mod 2 ❹.
2 Bofors 40 mm/70 ❺. 2 CS 20 mm Type 75.
Torpedoes: 6—324 mm Mk 32 (2 triple) tubes ❻; Alliant Mk
46 Mod 5; active/passive homing to 11 km (5.9 n miles) at
40 kt; warhead 44 kg.
Countermeasures: Decoys: 2 CSEE Dagaie chaff launchers ❼.
ESM/ECM: Thomson-CSF DR 3000S; intercept and jammer.
Chang Feng IV (1206); intercept and jammer.
Combat data systems: Thomson-CSF TACTICOS. Link W
(Ta Chen).
Weapons control: CSEE Najir Mk 2 optronic director ❽.
Radars: Air/surface search: Thomson-CSF DRBV-26D
Jupiter II (with LW08 aerial) ❾; D-band.

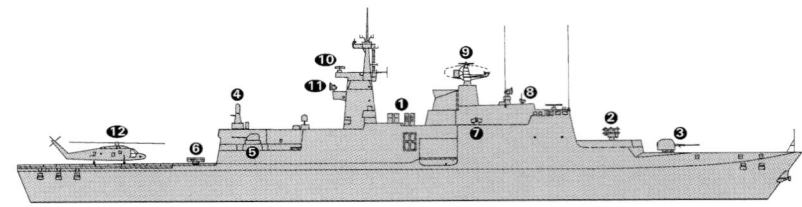

KANG DING *(Scale 1 : 1,200), Ian Sturton* / 0121405

Surface search: Thomson-CSF Triton G ❿; G-band.
Fire control: 2 Thomson-CSF Castor IIC ⓫; I/J-band.
Navigation and helo control: 2 Racal Decca 20V90; I-band.
Sonars: BAe/Thomson Sintra ATAS (V)2; active towed
array.
Thomson Sintra Spherion B; bow-mounted; active
search; medium frequency.

Helicopters: 1 Sikorsky S-70C(M)1 ⓬ Thunderhawk.

Programmes: Sale of up to 16 of the class authorised by
the French government in August 1991. Contract for six
signed with Thomson-CSF in early 1992, manufactured
in France with some weapon assembly by China SB
Corporation at Kaohsiung in Taiwan. First one to Taiwan

in March 1996 and the last in January 1998. Names are
those of Chinese cities. Second batch of 10 to be built by
China SB Corporation was planned but this now seems
unlikely.
Modernisation: There are plans to move Phalanx to the
bridge roof and fit two 10-round RAM launchers on the
hangar.
Structure: There are considerable differences with the
French 'La Fayette' design in both superstructure and
weapon systems. A comprehensive ASW fit has been
added as well as additional gun armament. There is
also no stern hatch for launching RIBs. Some of the
weapons were fitted after arrival in Taiwan. DCN Samahé
helicopter landing gear installed.
Operational: Form 124 Squadron based at Tsoying.

KUN MING *3/2004, Chris Sattler* / 1044572

SI NING *6/2000, Sattler/Steele* / 0106598

SHIPBORNE AIRCRAFT

Notes: Negotiations to acquire SH-2F Seasprite helicopters for the Knox class, conducted for several years, have not been satisfactorily concluded.

Numbers/Type: 21 Sikorsky S-70C(M)1 Thunderhawks.
Operational speed: 145 kt *(269 km/h).*
Service ceiling: 19,000 ft *(5,790 m).*
Range: 324 n miles *(600 km).*
Role/Weapon systems: First delivered in 1991. This is a variant of the SH-60B and became seaborne with the first Cheng Kung and Kang Ding class frigates. 701 and 702 Squadrons. Two modified for EW and Sigint role. Another 14 S-70B/C SAR and assault aircraft belong to the Air Force. Sensors: APS 128 search radar; Litton ALR 606(V)2 ESM; ARR 84 sonobuoy receiver with Litton ASN 150 datalink; Allied AQS 18(V)3 dipping sonar; ASQ 504 MAD. Ta Chen datalink to be fitted. Weapons: ASW; two Hughes Mk 46 Mod 5 torpedoes or two Mk 64 depth bombs. ASV; could carry ASM.

THUNDERHAWK *1/2000, C Chung /* 0106599

Numbers/Type: 9 Hughes MD 500/ASW.
Operational speed: 110 kt *(204 km/h).*
Service ceiling: 16,000 ft *(4,880 m).*
Range: 203 n miles *(376 km).*
Role/Weapon systems: Short-range ASW helicopter with limited surface search capability. 501 ASW Squadron. Sensors: Search radar, Texas Instruments ASQ 81(V)2 MAD. Weapons: ASW; one Mk 46 Mod 5 torpedo or two depth bombs. ASV; could carry machine gun pods.

MD 500 *1/1995, L J Lamb /* 0080778

LAND-BASED MARITIME AIRCRAFT

Notes: (1) Four Grumman E-2T Hawkeye AEW aircraft were acquired by the Air Force in February 1995.
(2) Plans to acquire 12 P-3C maritime patrol aircraft and 12 MH-53E Sea Dragon minehunting helicopters have been delayed indefinitely.

Numbers/Type: 3/21 Grumman S-2E/Grumman S-2T (Turbo) Trackers.
Operational speed: 130 kt *(241 km/h).*
Service ceiling: 25,000 ft *(7,620 m).*
Range: 1,350 n miles *(2,500 km).*
Role/Weapon systems: Patrol and ASW tasks transferred to the Navy in July 1998; 21 aircraft updated with turboprop engines and new sensors. Based at Pintung. To be replaced by P-3C when they enter service. Sensors: APS 504 search radar, ESM, MAD, AAS 40 FLIR, SSQ-41B, SSQ-47B sonobuoys; AQS 902F sonobuoy processor; ASN 150 datalink. Weapons: ASW; four Mk 44 torpedoes, Mk 54 depth charges or Mk 64 depth bombs or mines. ASV; Hsiung Feng II ASM; six 127 mm rockets.

TRACKER *6/2002, Adolfo Ortigueira Gil /* 0569245

PATROL FORCES

Notes: All coastal patrol craft were transferred to the Maritime Police on 8 December 1992. The Maritime Police became the Coast Guard 1 January 2000.

12 + (12) JIN CHIANG CLASS (LARGE PATROL CRAFT) (PCG)

Name	No	Builders	Launched	Commissioned
JIN CHIANG	603	Lien-Ho, Kaohsiung	1 May 1994	1 Dec 1994
TAN CHIANG	605	China SB, Kaohsiung	18 June 1998	7 Sep 1999
HSIN CHIANG	606	China SB, Kaohsiung	14 Aug 1998	7 Sep 1999
FENG CHIANG	607	China SB, Kaohsiung	22 Oct 1998	29 Oct 1999
TSENG CHIANG	608	China SB, Kaohsiung	16 Nov 1998	29 Oct 1999
KAO CHIANG	609	China SB, Kaohsiung	15 Dec 1998	29 Oct 1999
JING CHIANG	610	China SB, Kaohsiung	13 May 1999	15 Feb 2000
HSIAN CHIANG	611	China SB, Kaohsiung	16 July 1999	15 Feb 2000
TSI CHIANG	612	China SB, Kaohsiung	22 Dec 1999	15 Feb 2000
PO CHIANG	614	China SB, Kaohsiung	22 Dec 1999	21 July 2000
CHAN CHIANG	615	China SB, Kaohsiung	21 Jan 2000	21 July 2000
CHU CHIANG	617	China SB, Kaohsiung	25 Feb 2000	21 July 2000

Displacement, tons: 680 full load
Dimensions, feet (metres): 201.4 × 31.2 × 9.5 *(61.4 × 9.5 × 2.9)*
Main machinery: 2 MTU 20V 1163 TB93 diesels; 20,128 hp(m) *(14.79 MW)*; 2 shafts
Speed, knots: 25. **Range, n miles:** 4,150 at 15 kt
Complement: 50 (7 officers)

Missiles: SSM: 4 Hsiung Feng I; radar or optical guidance to 36 km *(19.4 n miles)* at 0.7 Mach; warhead 75 kg.
Guns: 1 Bofors 40 mm/70. 1 CS 20 mm Type 75. 2 — 12.7 mm MGs.
Depth charges: 2 racks.
Mines: 2 rails for Mk 6.
Weapons control: Honeywell H 930 Mod 2 MFCS. Contraves WCS. Rafael Sea Eye FLIR; range out to 3 km.
Radars: Air/surface search: Marconi LN66; I-band.
Fire control: Hughes HR-76C5; I/J-band.
Navigation: Racal Decca Bridgemaster; I-band.
Sonars: Simrad; search and attack; high frequency.

Programmes: Kwang Hua Project 3 design by United Ship Design Centre. First one laid down 25 June 1993. Eleven more ordered 26 June 1997. A further 12 are expected by 2010.

PO CHIANG *12/2005*, Ships of the World /* 1151163

2 LUNG CHIANG CLASS
(FAST ATTACK CRAFT—MISSILE) (PGGF)

Name	No	Builders	Commissioned
LUNG CHIANG	601 (ex-PGG 581)	Tacoma Boatbuilding, WA	15 May 1978
SUI CHIANG	602 (ex-PGG 582)	China SB Corporation, Kaohsiung	31 Dec 1981

Displacement, tons: 270 full load
Dimensions, feet (metres): 164.5 × 23.1 × 9.5 *(50.2 × 7.3 × 2.9)*
Main machinery: CODAG; 3 Avco Lycoming TF-40A gas turbines; 12,000 hp *(8.95 MW)* sustained; 3 Detroit 12V-149TI diesels; 2,736 hp *(2.04 MW)* sustained; 3 shafts; cp props
Speed, knots: 20 kt diesels; 38 kt gas
Range, n miles: 3,100 at 12 kt on 1 diesel; 800 at 36 kt
Complement: 38 (5 officers)

Missiles: SSM: 4 Hsiung Feng I; radar or optical guidance to 36 km *(19.4 n miles)* at 0.7 Mach; warhead 75 kg.
Guns: 1 OTO Melara 3 in *(76 mm)*/62; 60 rds/min to 16 km *(8.7 n miles)*; weight of shell 6 kg.
1 Bofors 40 mm/70. 2 — 12.7 mm MGs.
Countermeasures: Decoys: 4 Israeli AV2 (601) or SMOC-4 (602) chaff launchers.
ESM: WD-2A; intercept.
Combat data systems: IPN 10 action data automation.
Weapons control: NA 10 Mod 0 GFCS. Honeywell H 930 Mod 2 MFCS (602).
Radars: Surface/air search: Selenia RAN 11 L/X; D/I-band.
Fire control: RCA HR 76; I/J-band (for SSM) (602).
Selenia RAN IIL/X; I/J-band for SSM (601).
Navigation: SPS-58(A); I-band.

Programmes: Similar to the US Patrol Ship Multi-Mission Mk 5 (PSMM Mk 5). Second of class was built to an improved design. A much larger number of this class was intended, all to be armed with Harpoon. However at that time the US ban on export of Harpoon to Taiwan coupled with the high cost and doubts about seaworthiness caused the cancellation of this programme.
Structure: Fin stabilisers were fitted to help correct the poor sea-keeping qualities of the design. Both have had engine room fires caused by overheating in GT gearboxes.
Operational: *Lung Chiang* may be non-operational and could be sold.

SUI CHIANG *4/1997, Ships of the World /* 0019231

47 HAI OU CLASS (FAST ATTACK CRAFT—MISSILE) (PTG)

FABG 7-12   **FABG 14-21**   **FABG 23-30**   **FABG 32-39**   **FABG 41-45**
FABG 47-57   **FABG 59**

Displacement, tons: 47 full load
Dimensions, feet (metres): 70.8 × 18 × 3.3 *(21.6 × 5.5 × 1)*
Main machinery: 2 MTU 12V 331 TC82 diesels; 2,605 hp(m) *(1.92 MW)* sustained; 2 shafts
Speed, knots: 30
Range, n miles: 700 at 32 kt
Complement: 10 (2 officers)

Missiles: SSM: 2 Hsiung Feng I; radar or optical guidance to 36 km *(19.4 n miles)* at 0.7 Mach; warhead 75 kg.
Guns: 1 CS 20 mm Type 75. 2—12.7 mm MGs.
Countermeasures: Decoys: 4 Israeli AV2 chaff launchers.
ESM: WD-2A; intercept.
Weapons control: Kollmorgen Mk 35 optical director.
Radars: Surface search: Marconi LN66; I-band.
Fire control: RCA R76 C5; I-band.

Programmes: This design was developed by Sun Yat Sen Scientific Research Institute from the basic Israeli Dvora plans. Built by China SB Corporation (Tsoying SY), Kaohsiung except for the first pair (FABG 5-6) which were the original Dvora class hulls and were commissioned on 31 December 1977.
Structure: Aluminium alloy hulls. The first series had a solid mast and the missiles were nearer the stern. Second series changed to a lattice mast and moved the missiles further forward allowing room for two 12.7 mm MGs right aft. One 20 mm has been added on the stern.
Operational: The prototype reached 45 kt on trials but top speeds are now reported as being much reduced. These craft often carry shoulder-launched SAMs. One task is to provide exercise high-speed targets in shallow waters. From 1997 organised in five divisions based at Makung, Tamsui, Tsoying, Suao and Keelung. Not all are operational and the class is likely to be paid off in the short term.
Sales: Two similar craft to Paraguay in 1996.

FABG 50   *12/2005*, Ships of the World* / 1151162

0 + 1 (28) KWANG HUA 6 CLASS (PTG)

FABG 60

Displacement, tons: 180 standard
Dimensions, feet (metres): 128.0 × 24.9 × 6.2 *(39.0 × 7.6 × 1.9)*
Main machinery: 2 diesels; 2 shafts
Speed, knots: 30. **Range, n miles:** 1,150 at 22 kt
Complement: 14
Missiles: SSM: 4 Hsiung Feng II.
Guns: 1 CS 20 mm Type 75.
Countermeasures: Decoys: Chaff launchers. ESM.
Weapons control: Optronic director.
Radars: Surface search. Fire control.

Comment: Funds allocated for the budget period July 1998 to June 2003 to build these craft in Taiwan to replace the Hai Ou class. First of class laid down in early 2001 and launched on 26 September 2002. Commissioned in October 2003. The construction of the remaining 28 craft has been delayed by contractual difficulties.

FABG 60   *12/2005*, Ships of the World* / 1151161

8 NING HAI CLASS (LARGE PATROL CRAFT) (PCF)

NING HAI PCL 1   **AN HAI** PCL 2   **PCL 3**   **PCL 5-9**

Displacement, tons: 143 full load
Dimensions, feet (metres): 105 × 29.5 × 5.9 *(32 × 9 × 1.8)*
Main machinery: 3 MTU 12V 396 TB93 diesels; 4,890 hp(m) *(3.6 MW)* sustained; 3 shafts
Speed, knots: 40
Complement: 18 (2 officers)
Guns: 1 Bofors 40 mm/60. 1 CS 20 mm Type 75.
Depth charges: 2 racks.
Radars: Surface search: Decca; I-band.
Sonars: Hull-mounted; active search and attack; high frequency.

Comment: Built to Vosper QAF design by China SB Corporation, Kaohsiung in 1987-90. Previously reported numbers had been exaggerated. They are used mainly for harbour defence against midget submarines and frogmen and also for Fishery protection tasks.

PCL 5   *6/2002, Ships of the World* / 0569243

AMPHIBIOUS FORCES

1 ANCHORAGE CLASS (LSDH)

Name	No	Builders	Commissioned
SHIU HAI (ex-*Pensacola*)	LSD 193 (ex-LSD 38)	General Dynamics, Quincy	27 Mar 1971

Displacement, tons: 8,600 light; 13,700 full load
Dimensions, feet (metres): 553.3 × 84 × 20 *(168.6 × 25.6 × 6)*
Main machinery: 2 Foster-Wheeler boilers; 600 psi *(42.3 kg/cm²)*; 870°F *(467°C)*; 2 De Laval turbines; 24,000 hp *(18 MW)*; 2 shafts
Speed, knots: 22. **Range, n miles:** 14,800 at 12 kt
Complement: 374 (24 officers)
Military lift: 366 troops (18 officers); 2 LCU or 18 LCM 6 or 9 LCM 8 or 50 LVT; 1 LCM 6 on deck; 2 LCPL and 1 LCVP on davits. Aviation fuel, 90 tons
Guns: 2 General Electric/General Dynamics 20 mm/76 6-barrelled Vulcan Phalanx Mk 15; 3,000 rds/min combined to 1.5 km.
2—25 mm Mk 38. 6—12.7 mm MGs.
Countermeasures: Decoys: 4 Loral Hycor SRBOC 6-barrelled Mk 36; IR flares and chaff to 4 km *(2.2 n miles)*.
ESM: SLQ-32(V)1; intercept.
Radars: Air search: Lockheed SPS-40B; B-band.
Surface search: Raytheon SPS-10F; G-band.
Navigation: Marconi LN66; I-band.

Helicopters: Platform only.

Comment: First one acquired from US Navy 30 September 1999 and arrived in Taiwan on 2 June 2000. Transfer of ex-*Anchorage* (LSD 36) did not take place as expected in 2004 although procurement of a further amphibious ship remains a requirement. Has a docking well 131.1 × 15.2 m and two 50 ton cranes. Based at Tsoying.

2 NEWPORT CLASS (LSTH)

Name	No	Builders	Commissioned
CHUNG HO (ex-*Manitowic*)	232 (ex-LST 1180)	Philadelphia Shipyard	24 Jan 1970
CHUNG PING (ex-*Sumter*)	233 (ex-LST 1181)	Philadelphia Shipyard	20 June 1970

Displacement, tons: 4,975 light; 8,450 full load
Dimensions, feet (metres): 522.3 × 69.5 × 17.5 *(159.2 × 21.2 × 5.3)*
Main machinery: 6 ALCO 16—251 diesels; 16,500 hp *(12.3 MW)* sustained; 2 shafts; cp props; bow thruster
Speed, knots: 20
Range, n miles: 14,250 at 14 kt
Complement: 257 (13 officers)
Military lift: 400 troops; 500 tons vehicles; 3 LCVPs and 1 LCPL on davits
Guns: 1 General Electric/General Dynamics 20 mm Vulcan Phalanx Mk 15.
4—40 mm/60 (2 twin).
Countermeasures: ESM: WD-2A (233); intercept.
ESM/ECM: Chang Feng III (232); intercept and jammer.
Radars: Surface search: Raytheon SPS-67; G-band.
Navigation: Marconi LN66; I-band.
Helicopters: Platform only.

Comment: First pair transferred from USA by lease confirmed for both ships on 1 July 1995. Refitted at Newport News and recommissioned 8 May 1997, sailing for Taiwan after a short operational work-up. Purchased outright on 29 September 2000. Transfer of further ships is unlikely. These ships unload by a 112 ft ramp over their bow. The ramp is supported by twin derrick arms. A ramp just forward of the superstructure connects the lower tank deck with the main deck and a vehicle passage through the superstructure provides access to the parking area amidships. A stern gate to the tank deck permits unloading of amphibious tractors into the water, or unloading of other vehicles into an LCU or on to a pier. Vehicle stowage covers 19,000 sq ft. Length over derrick arms is 562 ft *(171.3 m)*; full load draught is 11.5 ft forward and 17.5 ft aft. Bow thruster fitted to hold position offshore while unloading amphibious tractors.

CHUNG HO   *6/2000, Sattler/Steele* / 0106602

1 CABILDO CLASS (LSDM)

Name	No	Builders	Commissioned
CHUNG CHENG (ex-*Comstock*)	191 (ex-LSD 19)	Newport News, Virginia	2 July 1945

Displacement, tons: 4,790 standard; 9,375 full load
Dimensions, feet (metres): 475 × 76.2 × 18 *(144.8 × 23.2 × 5.5)*
Main machinery: 2 boilers; 435 psi *(30.6 kg/cm²)*; 740°F *(393°C)*; 2 turbines; 7,000 hp *(5.22 MW)*; 2 shafts
Speed, knots: 15.4. **Range, n miles:** 8,000 at 15 kt
Complement: 316
Military lift: 3 LCUs or 18 LCMs or 32 LVTs in docking well

Missiles: SAM: 1 Sea Chaparral quadruple launcher.
Guns: 12 Bofors 40 mm/56 (2 quad, 2 twin).
Weapons control: US Mk 26 Mod 4.
Radars: Surface search: Raytheon SPS-5; G/H-band.
Navigation: Marconi LN66; I-band.

Comment: Launched 28 April 1945 and transferred to Taiwan on 1 October 1985 having been bought from a ship breaker. SAM system fitted in 1992. Collision with merchant ship on 28 June 2001 resulted in five months repair work. Second of class scrapped in mid-1999.

11 LST 1-510 AND 512-1152 CLASSES (LST)

CHUNG HAI (ex-LST 755) 201 (ex-697)	CHUNG CHIH (ex-*Sagadahoc County* LST 1091) 226 (ex-655)
CHUNG CHIEN (ex-LST 716) 205 (ex-679)	
CHUNG SHUN (ex-LST 732) 208 (ex-624)	CHUNG MING (ex-*Sweetwater County* LST 1152) 227 (ex-681)
CHUNG KUANG (ex-LST 503) 216 (ex-646)	
CHUNG SUO (ex-*Bradley County* LST 400) 217 (ex-667)	CHUNG PANG (ex-LST 578) 230 (ex-629)
CHUNG CHI (ex-*LST 279*) 218	CHUNG YEH (ex-*Sublette County* LST 1144) 231 (ex-699)
CHUNG CHUAN (ex-*LST 1030*) 221 (ex-651)	

Displacement, tons: 1,653 standard; 4,080 (3,640, 1-510 class) full load
Dimensions, feet (metres): 328 × 50 × 14 *(100 × 15.2 × 4.3)*
Main machinery: 2 GM 12-567A diesels; 1,800 hp *(1.34 MW)*; 2 shafts
Speed, knots: 11.6
Range, n miles: 15,000 at 10 kt
Complement: Varies-100-125 in most ships
Guns: Varies-up to 10 Bofors 40 mm/56 (2 twin, 6 single) with some modernised ships rearmed with 2 USN 3 in *(76 mm)*/50 and 6—40 mm (3 twin). Several Oerlikon 20 mm (twin or single).
Radars: Navigation: US SO 1, 2 or 8; I-band.

Comment: Constructed between 1943 and 1945. These ships have been rebuilt in Taiwan. Six transferred from US in 1946; two in 1947; one in 1948; eight in 1958; one in 1959; two in 1960; and one in 1961. Some have davits forward and aft. Pennant numbers have reverted to those used in the 1960s. One deleted in 1990, six more in 1993, one more in 1995 after going aground, and two more in 1997. The midships deck is occasionally used as a helicopter platform. These last 11 may be retained due to the cancellation of the programme for more locally built AKs.

CHUNG SUO *6/2000, DTM* / 0126196

1 LST 512-1152 CLASS (FLAGSHIP) (AGF)

Name	No	Builders	Commissioned
KAO HSIUNG (ex-*Chung Hai*, ex-*Dukes County* LST 735)	LCC 1 (ex-219, ex-663)	Dravo Corporation, Neville Island, Penn	26 Apr 1944

Displacement, tons: 1,653 standard; 3,675 full load
Dimensions, feet (metres): 328 × 50 × 14 *(100 × 15.2 × 4.3)*
Main machinery: 2 GM 12-567A diesels; 1,800 hp *(1.34 MW)*; 2 shafts
Speed, knots: 11.6
Range, n miles: 11,200 at 10 kt
Complement: 195
Guns: 8 Bofors 40 mm/56 (3 twin, 2 single).
Radars: Air search: Raytheon SPS 58; D-band.
Surface search: Raytheon SPS-10; G-band.

Comment: Launched on 11 March 1944. Transferred from US in May 1957 for service as an LST. Converted to a flagship for amphibious operations and renamed and redesignated (AGC) in 1964. Purchased November 1974. Note lattice mast above bridge structure, modified bridge levels, and antenna mountings on main deck. Redesignated as Command and Control Ship LCC 1.

KAO HSIUNG *6/1999* / 0080783

10 LCU 501 CLASS (LCU)

HO CHI (ex-LCU 1212) 401	HO SHUN (ex-LCU 1225) 481	HO YUNG (ex-LCU 1271) 495
HO HUEI (ex-LCU 1218) 402	HO CHUNG (ex-LCU 849) 484	HO CHIE (ex-LCU 700) SB 1
HO YAO (ex-LCU 1244) 403	HO CHUN (ex-LCU 892) 494	HO TEN (ex-LCU 1367) SB 2
HO CHAO (ex-LCU 1429) 406		

Displacement, tons: 158 light; 309 full load
Dimensions, feet (metres): 119 × 32.7 × 5 *(36.3 × 10 × 1.5)*
Main machinery: 3 GM 6-71 diesels; 522 hp *(390 kW)* sustained; 3 shafts
Speed, knots: 10
Complement: 10-25
Guns: 2 Oerlikon 20 mm. Some also may have 2—12.7 mm MGs.

Comment: Built in US in the 1940s and transferred in 1959. *SB 1* and *SB 2* are used as auxiliaries. *Ho Feng* 405 converted for ferry duties in 1998 and serves Matzu island.

HO SHUN *6/2000, DTM* / 0569238

6 LCU 1466 CLASS (LCU)

HO SHAN (ex-LCU 1596) 488	HO SENG (ex-LCU 1598) 490	HO MOU (ex-LCU 1600) 492
HO CHUAN (ex-LCU 1597) 489	HO MENG (ex-LCU 1599) 491	HO SHOU (ex-LCU 1601) 493

Displacement, tons: 180 light; 360 full load
Dimensions, feet (metres): 119 × 34 × 6 *(36.3 × 10.4 × 1.8)*
Main machinery: 3 Gray Marine 64 YTL diesels; 675 hp *(504 kW)*; 3 shafts
Speed, knots: 10
Range, n miles: 800 at 11 kt
Complement: 15-25
Military lift: 167 tons or 300 troops
Guns: 3 Oerlikon 20 mm. Some may also have 2—12.7 mm MGs.

Comment: Built by Ishikawajima Heavy Industries Co, Tokyo, Japan, for transfer to Taiwan; completed in March 1955. All originally numbered in 200 series; subsequently changed to 400 series.

HO CHUAN *1991* / 0506105

2 TAIWAN TYPE LCU (LCU)

HO FONG LCU 497	HO HU LCU 498

Displacement, tons: 190 light; 439 full load
Dimensions, feet (metres): 135.5 × 29.9 × 6.9 *(41.3 × 9.1 × 2.1)*
Main machinery: 4 Detroit diesels; 1,200 hp *(895 kW)*; 2 Kort nozzle props
Speed, knots: 11
Range, n miles: 1,200 at 10 kt
Complement: 16
Military lift: 180 tons or 350 troops
Guns: 2—12.7 mm MGs.

Comment: Locally built versions of US types. Ramps at both ends.

HO FONG *6/2000, DTM* / 0569237

170 LCM 6 CLASS (LCM)

Displacement, tons: 57 full load
Dimensions, feet (metres): 56.4 × 13.8 × 3.9 *(17.2 × 4.2 × 1.2)*
Main machinery: 2 diesels; 450 hp *(336 kW)*; 2 shafts
Speed, knots: 9
Military lift: 34 tons
Guns: 1 — 12.7 mm MG.

Comment: Some built in the US, some in Taiwan. 20 were exchanged for torpedoes with Indonesia. Some 55 have been deleted in the last four years. Form part of 151 Squadron.

LCM 6   *7/2000, C Chung* / 0106603

100 LCVPs and ASSAULT CRAFT

Comment: Some ex-US, and some built in Taiwan. Most are armed with one or two 7.62 mm MGs. Two transferred to Indonesia in 1988. About 20 deleted in the last three years and 30 transferred to Honduras in 1996 for River operations. There are also a number of amphibious reconnaissance boats in the ARP 1000, 2000 and 3000 series. Form part of 151 Squadron.

TYPE 272   *1989, DTM (Raymond Cheung)* / 0506106

MINE WARFARE FORCES

Notes: A new class of minehunters is planned. Tenders may be invited in when funds are available.

4 AGGRESSIVE CLASS (MINESWEEPERS) (MSO)

Name	No	Builders	Commissioned
YUNG YANG (ex-*Implicit*)	1306 (ex-455)	Wilmington Boat	10 Mar 1954
YUNG TZU (ex-*Conquest*)	1307 (ex-488)	Martenac, Tacoma	20 July 1955
YUNG KU (ex-*Gallant*)	1308 (ex-489)	Martenac, Tacoma	14 Sep 1955
YUNG TEH (ex-*Pledge*)	1309 (ex-492)	Martenac, Tacoma	20 Apr 1956

Displacement, tons: 720 standard; 780 full load
Dimensions, feet (metres): 172.5 × 35.1 × 14.1 *(52.6 × 10.7 × 4.3)*
Main machinery: 4 Packard ID-1700 or Waukesha diesels; 2,280 hp *(1.7 MW)*; 2 shafts; cp props
Speed, knots: 14
Range, n miles: 3,000 at 10 kt
Complement: 86 (7 officers)
Guns: 2 — 12.7 mm MGs.
Radars: Navigation: Sperry SPS-53L; I-band.
Sonars: General Electric SQQ-14; VDS; active minehunting; high frequency.

Comment: Transferred by sale to Taiwan from the USN 3 August and 30 September 1994. Delivery was delayed into 1995 while replanking work was carried out in the US. All recommissioned 1 March 1995. Second batch of three planned to transfer but were subsequently scrapped after cannibalisation for spares. All are fitted with SLQ-37 mechanical acoustic and magnetic sweeps and can carry an ROV. The plan is to update the class with a Unisys SYQ-12 minehunting system and Pluto ROVs.

YUNG KU   *6/2000, DTM* / 0569242

4 ADJUTANT and MSC 268 CLASSES
(MINESWEEPERS — COASTAL) (MSC)

YUNG CHUAN (ex-MSC 278) 158	**YUNG REN** (ex-*St Nicholas*, ex-MSC 64) 167
YUNG FU (ex-*Macaw*, ex-MSC 77) 162	**YUNG SUI** (ex-*Disksmude*, ex-MSC 65) 168

Displacement, tons: 375 full load
Dimensions, feet (metres): 144 × 27.9 × 8 *(43.9 × 8.5 × 2.4)*
Main machinery: 2 GM 8-268A diesels; 880 hp *(656 kW)*; 2 shafts
Speed, knots: 13
Range, n miles: 2,500 at 12 kt
Complement: 35
Guns: 1 Oerlikon 20 mm.
Radars: Navigation: Decca 707; I-band.
Sonars: Simrad 950; hull-mounted; minehunting; high frequency.

Comment: Non-magnetic, wood-hulled minesweepers built in the US in the 1950s specifically for transfer to allied navies. All refitted 1984-86. All are in very poor condition. Several deleted so far. Two put back in service in 1996 and one in 1997 to replace three others paid off.

YUNG CHUAN   *6/2000, DTM* / 0569241

4 YUNG FENG (MWV 50) CLASS
(MINEHUNTERS — COASTAL) (MHC)

YUNG FENG 1301	**YUNG CHIA** 1302	**YUNG TING** 1303	**YUNG SHUN** 1305

Displacement, tons: 500 full load
Dimensions, feet (metres): 163.1 × 28.5 × 10.2 *(49.7 × 8.7 × 3.1)*
Main machinery: 2 MTU 8V 396 TB93 diesels; 2,180 hp(m) *(1.6 MW)* sustained; 2 shafts
Speed, knots: 14
Range, n miles: 3,500 at 14 kt
Complement: 45 (5 officers)
Guns: 1 — 20 mm. 2 — 12.7 mm MGs.
Radars: Navigation: I-band.
Sonars: TSM-2022; hull-mounted; active minehunting; high frequency.

Comment: Built for the Chinese Petroleum Corporation by Abeking & Rasmussen at Lemwerder, Germany. First four delivered in 1991 as offshore oil rig support ships and then converted for minehunting in Taiwan. Thomson Sintra IBIS V minehunting system is fitted and two STN Pinguin B3 ROVs are carried. The civilian livery has been abandoned. These ships spend little time at sea.

YUNG FENG   *6/2000, DTM* / 0569240

AUXILIARIES

6 FLOATING DOCKS (YFD)

HAY TAN (ex-AFDL 36) AFDL 1	**FO WU 5** (ex-ARD 9) ARD 5
KIM MEN (ex-AFDL 5) AFDL 2	**FO WU 6** (ex-*Windsor* ARD 22) ARD 6
HAN JIH (ex-AFDL 34) AFDL 3	**FO WU 7** (ex-AFDM 6)

Comment: Former US Navy floating dry docks. *Hay Tan* transferred in March 1947, *Kim Men* in January 1948, *Han Jih* in July 1959, *Fo Wu 5* in June 1971, *Fo Wu 6* in June 1971. *Fo Wu 6* by sale 19 May 1976 and *Fo Wu 5* on 12 January 1977. *Fo Wu 7* transferred by sale in 1999.

1 COMBAT SUPPORT SHIP (AOEHM)

Name	No	Builders	Launched	Commissioned
WU YI	530	China SB Corporation, Keelung	4 Mar 1989	23 June 1990

Displacement, tons: 7,700 light; 17,000 full load
Dimensions, feet (metres): 531.8 × 72.2 × 28 *(162.1 × 22 × 8.6)*
Main machinery: 2 MAN 14-cyl diesels; 25,000 hp(m) *(18.37 MW)*; 2 shafts
Speed, knots: 21. **Range, n miles:** 9,200 at 10 kt
Cargo capacity: 9,300 tons
Missiles: SAM: 1 Sea Chaparral quad launcher.
Guns: 2 Bofors 40 mm/70. 2 Oerlikon 20 mm GAM-BO1. 4 — 12.7 mm MGs.
Countermeasures: Decoys: 2 chaff launchers.
ESM: Radar warning.
Radars: 2 navigation; I-band.

Helicopters: Platform for CH-47 or S-70C(M)1.

Comment: Largest unit built so far for the Taiwanese Navy. Design assisted by the United Shipping Design Center in the US. Beam replenishment rigs on both sides. SAM system on forecastle, 40 mm guns aft of the funnels.

WU YI   *3/2004, Chris Sattler* / 1044573

3 WU KANG CLASS (ATTACK TRANSPORTS) (AKM)

Name	No	Builders	Commissioned
YUEN FENG	524	China SB Corporation, Keelung	10 Sep 1982
WU KANG	525	China SB Corporation, Keelung	9 Oct 1984
HSIN KANG	526	China SB Corporation, Keelung	30 Nov 1988

Displacement, tons: 2,804 standard; 4,845 full load
Dimensions, feet (metres): 334 × 59.1 × 16.4 *(101.8 × 18 × 5)*
Main machinery: 2 diesels; 2 shafts; bow thruster
Speed, knots: 20. **Range, n miles:** 6,500 at 12 kt
Complement: 61 (11 officers)
Military lift: 1,400 troops
Missiles: SAM: 1 Sea Chaparral quad launcher.
Guns: 2 Bofors 40 mm/60. 2 or 4 — 12.7 mm MGs.
Countermeasures: ESM: WD-2A (524 only); intercept.

Comment: First three were built and then the programme stopped. Restarted with the fourth of class laid down in July 1994. The plan was to build at about one a year to a final total of seven, but the programme has been cancelled without the fourth ship being completed. With a helicopter platform, stern docking facility and davits for four LCVP, the design resembles an LPD. Used mostly for supplying garrisons in offshore islands, and on the Spratley and Pratas islands in the South China Sea. SAM launcher is mounted aft of the foremast. Accommodation is air conditioned. *Hsin Kang* was badly damaged in harbour in collision with a merchant ship in March 1996, but was back in service by mid-1999.

HSIN KANG   *6/2002, Ships of the World* / 0569239

1 SALVAGE SHIP (ARS)

Name	No	Builders	Commissioned
TA HU (ex-*Grapple*)	552 (ex-ARS 7)	Basalt Rock, USA	16 Dec 1943

Displacement, tons: 1,557 standard; 1,745 full load
Dimensions, feet (metres): 213.5 × 39 × 15 *(65.1 × 11.9 × 4.6)*
Main machinery: Diesel-electric; 4 Cooper Bessemer GSB-8 diesels; 3,420 hp *(2.55 MW)*; 2 generators; 2 motors; 2 shafts
Speed, knots: 14. **Range, n miles:** 8,500 at 13 kt
Complement: 85
Guns: 2 Oerlikon 20 mm.
Radars: Navigation: SPS-53; I-band.

Comment: Fitted for salvage, towing and compressed-air diving. *Ta Hu* transferred from US 1 December 1977 by sale. The reported transfer from the US of ex-*Conserver* did not take place.

TA HU   *6/2005*, C Chung* / 1151389

SURVEY AND RESEARCH SHIPS

1 ALLIANCE CLASS (AGOR)

Name	No	Builders	Launched	Commissioned
TA KUAN	1601	Fincantieri, Muggiano	17 Dec 1994	27 Sep 1995

Displacement, tons: 2,466 standard; 3,180 full load
Dimensions, feet (metres): 305.1 × 49.9 × 16.7 *(93 × 15.2 × 5.1)*
Main machinery: Diesel-electric; 3 MTU/AEG diesel generators; 5,712 hp(m) *(4.2 MW)*; 2 AEG motors; 5,100 hp(m) *(3.75 MW)*; 2 shafts; bow thruster; stern trainable and retractable thruster
Speed, knots: 15. **Range, n miles:** 12,000 at 12 kt
Complement: 82
Guns: 2 — 12.7 mm MGs.
Radars: Navigation: H/I-band.

Comment: Ordered in June 1993 and laid down 8 April 1994. Almost identical to the NATO vessel. Designed for oceanography and hydrographic research. Facilities include laboratories, position location systems, and overside deployment equipment. Equipment includes a Simrad side scan sonar EM 1200, deep and shallow echo-sounders, two radars, Navsat and Satcom, an ROV for remote inspection, and a dynamic positioning system with bow thruster and stern positioning propeller.

TA KUAN   *8/1997, C Chung* / 0019239

TUGS

5 CHEROKEE CLASS (ATF/ARS)

TA WAN (ex-*Apache*) ATF 551   TA FUNG (ex-*Narragansett*) ATF 555
TA HAN (ex-*Tawakoni*) ATF 553   TA TAI (ex-*Shakori*) ATF 563
TA KANG (ex-*Achomawi*) ATF 554

Displacement, tons: 1,235 standard; 1,731 full load
Dimensions, feet (metres): 205 × 38.5 × 17 *(62.5 × 11.7 × 5.2)*
Main machinery: Diesel-electric; 4 GM 12-278 diesels; 4,400 hp *(3.28 MW)*; 4 generators; 1 motor; 3,000 hp *(2.24 MW)*; 1 shaft
Speed, knots: 15. **Range, n miles:** 6,000 at 14 kt
Complement: 85
Guns: 1 Bofors 40 mm/60. Several 12.7 mm MGs.

Comment: All built between 1943 and 1945. *Ta Wan* transferred from US in June 1974; *Ta Han* in June 1978; and the last three in June 1991 together with two more which were cannibalised for spares.

TA HAN   *4/1995* / 0080790

19 LARGE HARBOUR TUGS (YTB)

YTB 37-39   YTB 41-43   YTB 45-49   YTB 150-157

Comment: Various types of about 30 m length.

11 HARBOUR TUGS (YTL)

YTL 16-17   YTL 27-30   YTL 32-36

Comment: Replacements for the old US Army type which were scrapped in 1990/91. Some are used for fire fighting.

YTL 36   *5/1997, van Ginderen Collection* / 0019242

COAST GUARD

Headquarters Appointments

Director General of the Coast Guard:
  Hsu Hui-Yio
Deputy Director General (Law Enforcement):
  You Chian-Tshiz
Deputy Administrator (Coastal Patrol):
  Lieutenant General Heh Shiang-Tai
Deputy Administrator (Oceanic Patrol):
  Chen Chang-Hsiung
Director, General Customs:
  Chung Huo-Cheng

Notes: The Coast Guard Agency was restructured on 28 January 2001 by merging the former agencies of Maritime Police, Customs and Coastal Defence Command. It is responsible for coastal and harbour security, maritime law enforcement, anti-smuggling, anti-terrorism, SAR, fishery protection, and pollution control. It consists of two major wings. The Oceanic Patrol wing has 2,500 personnel in 20 patrol detachments around the coast. The Coastal Patrol wing has 14,701 personnel in 24 battalions. In times of crisis, the Oceanic and Coastal patrol wings would be integrated into the Navy and Army respectively. There are four regional commands: Taipei, Taichung, Kaohisung and Taitung.

Bases

HQ: Tamsui

2 HO HSING CLASS (LARGE PATROL CRAFT) (WPSO)

HO HSING 101   **WEI HSING** 102

Displacement, tons: 1,823 full load
Dimensions, feet (metres): 270 × 38.1 × 13.5 *(82.3 × 11.6 × 4.1)*
Main machinery: 2 MTU 16V 1163 TB93 diesels; 13,310 hp(m) *(9.78 MW)* sustained; 2 shafts; cp props; bow thruster
Speed, knots: 22. **Range, n miles:** 7,000 at 16 kt
Complement: 80 (18 officers)
Guns: 2 — 12.7 mm MGs.
Radars: Surface search: Racal Decca; I-band.

Comment: Built by the China SB Corporation, Keelung, to a Tacoma design and both delivered 26 December 1991. Four high-speed interceptor boats are carried on individual davits. This is a variant of the US Coast Guard Bear class.

WEI HSING   *4/2004*, C Chung* / 1151404

5 + (4) OFFSHORE PATROL VESSELS (WPBO)

Name	Tonnage	Length	SP	Commissioned
SHUN HU 1	800	60 m	12	1992
SHUN HU 2	400	51 m	16	1992
SHUN HU 3	400	51 m	16	1992
SHUN HU 5	100	31 m	—	1992
SHUN HU 6	200	38 m	—	1993

Comment: Five former Ministry of Agriculture vessels conduct fishery protection duties. Ocean operations are conducted by: *Shun Hu 1* and *Shun Hu 2-3*; Coastal operations are conducted by: *Shun Hu 5* and *Shun Hu 6*. There are plans to replace the four larger vessels but a contract has not been confirmed.

SHUN HU 1   *6/2001, Mitsuhiro Kadota* / 0121409

SHUN HU 2   *6/2001, Ships of the World* / 0121410

SHUN HU 5   *6/2001, C Chung* / 0126199

1 YUN HSING CLASS (COASTAL PATROL CRAFT) (ABU)

YUN HSING

Displacement, tons: 964 full load
Dimensions, feet (metres): 213.3 × 32.8 × 9.5 *(65 × 10 × 2.9)*
Main machinery: 2 MAN 12V 25/30 diesels; 7,183 hp(m) *(5.28 MW)*; 2 shafts
Speed, knots: 18
Complement: 67
Guns: 2 — 12.7 mm MGs.
Radars: Surface search: JRC; I-band.

Comment: Built by China SB Corporation and delivered 28 December 1987. Operated by Customs as a light-house tender.

YUN HSING   *1/2000, C Chung* / 0106606

1 OFFSHORE PATROL VESSEL (WPSO)

TAIPEI 116

Displacement, tons: 680 full load
Dimensions, feet (metres): 201.4 × 31.2 × 9.2 *(61.4 × 9.5 × 2.8)*
Main machinery: 2 MTU 20V 1163 TB93 diesels; 20,128 hp(m) *(14.79 MW)*; 2 shafts
Speed, knots: 25
Range, n miles: 4,150 at 15 kt
Complement: 40
Guns: 2 — 20 mm T75. 3 — 12.7 mm MGs.
Radars: Navigation: I-band.

Comment: Based on the naval Jin Chiang class, ship built by Chung-Hsin Ship Building Corporation, launched in November 1999 and commissioned on 20 March 2000.

TAIPEI   *6/2005*, C Chung* / 1151405

4 OFFSHORE PATROL CRAFT (WPSO)

TAICHUNG 117   **KEELUNG** 118   **HUALIEN** 119   **PENHU** 120

Displacement, tons: 630 full load
Dimensions, feet (metres): 208.3 × 30.4 × 8.9 *(63.5 × 9.28 × 2.7)*
Main machinery: 2 MTU 1163 TB93 diesels; 15,608 hp(m) *(11.48 MW)* sustained; 2 shafts
Speed, knots: 30
Range, n miles: 2,400 at 18 kt
Complement: 46 (9 officers)
Guns: 1 — 20 mm T 75.
Radars: Surface search: JRC E/F- and I-bands.

Comment: Built by Ching-Fu SB Corporation in Kaohsiung, to Lürssen Asia design. Delivered 28 June 2001. Two high-speed interceptor boats are carried on individual davits.

PENHU   *10/2001, C Chung* / 0126201

3 PAO HSING CLASS (COASTAL PATROL CRAFT) (WPBO)

PAO HSING 107	CHIN HSING 108	TEH HSING 109

Displacement, tons: 550 full load
Dimensions, feet (metres): 189.6 × 25.6 × 6.9 *(57.8 × 7.8 × 2.1)*
Main machinery: 2 MAN 12V25/30 diesels; 7,183 hp(m) *(5.28 MW)* sustained; 2 shafts
Speed, knots: 20
Complement: 40
Guns: 2 — 12.7 mm MGs.
Radars: Surface search: JRC; I-band.

Comment: First delivered 20 May 1980; second 23 May 1985. Built by Keelung yard of China SB Corporation.

PAO HSING (Customs colours)　　　　　*1994, Taiwan Customs* / 0080793

2 COASTAL PATROL CRAFT (WPSO)

MOU HSING 105	FU HSING 106

Displacement, tons: 917 full load
Dimensions, feet (metres): 214.6 × 31.5 × 10.5 *(65.4 × 9.6 × 3.2)*
Main machinery: 2 MTU 16V 1163 TB93 diesels; 13,310 hp(m) *(9.78 MW)* sustained; 2 shafts
Speed, knots: 28. **Range, n miles:** 4,500 at 12 kt
Complement: 54
Guns: 2 — 12.7 mm MGs.
Radars: Surface search: Racal Decca; I-band.

Comment: Ordered from Wilton Fijenoord in September 1986, and commissioned 14 June 1988.

FU HSING　　　　　*9/2002, C Chung* / 0534122

13 COASTAL PATROL CRAFT (WPBF)

PP 6001-6003	6005-6007	6009-6012	6014-6016

Displacement, tons: 91 full load
Dimensions, feet (metres): 91.9 × 20.3 × 7.9 *(28 × 6.2 × 2.4)*
Main machinery: 2 Paxman 12V P185 diesels; 6,645 hp(m) *(4.89 MW)* sustained; 2 shafts; cp props
Speed, knots: 40
Range, n miles: 600 at 25 kt
Complement: 12
Guns: 2 — 12.7 mm MGs.
Radars: Surface search: 2 Racal Decca; I-band.

Comment: Built by Lung Teh Shipyard, Taiwan from March 1996. First six delivered in 1997 and following seven in 2001. GRP hulls with some Kevlar protection. Can carry a 6.5 m RIB. May be given new pennant numbers.

PP 6002　　　　　*10/2001, C Chung* / 0126203

11 LARGE PATROL CRAFT (WPB)

PP 10001-10002	10005-10010	10017-10019

Displacement, tons: 140 full load
Dimensions, feet (metres): 90 × 28.6 × 6 *(27.4 × 8.7 × 1.8)*
Main machinery: 2 MTU diesels; 6,000 hp(m) *(4.4 MW)*; 2 shafts
Speed, knots: 30
Guns: 2 — 12.7 mm MGs (aft).
Radars: Surface search: Decca; I-band.

Comment: The first pair were former naval craft transferred 8 December 1992. Two more completed in October 1994, three more by February 1995. The construction programme continues.

PP 10017　　　　　*10/2001, C Chung* / 0126205

4 HAI YING CLASS (INSHORE PATROL CRAFT) (WPB)

HAI YING	HAI TUNG	HAI KO	HAI TA

Displacement, tons: 99.43 full load
Dimensions, feet (metres): 82.8 × 19.0 × 10.7 *(25.25 × 5.8 × 3.3)*
Main machinery: 2 Deutz MWM TBD 620 V12 diesels; 4,314 bhp *(2,646 kW)*; 2 shafts
Speed, knots: 32.6
Complement: 7
Guns: 2 — 9 mm T75.
Radars: Surface search: Furuno; I-band.

Comment: Transferred to Customs on 28 December 2000.

HAI YING CLASS　　　　　*12/2000, Taiwan Customs* / 0114555

4 HAI CHENG CLASS (INSHORE PATROL CRAFT) (WPB)

HAI CHENG	HAI EN	HAI LIANG	HAI CHING

Displacement, tons: 147 full load
Dimensions, feet (metres): 100 × 22.3 × 11.6 *(30.5 × 6.8 × 3.6)*
Main machinery: 2 MTU diesels; 6,000 hp(m) *(4.4 MW)*; 2 shafts
Speed, knots: 30
Complement: 8
Guns: 2 — 9 mm T75.
Radars: Surface search: Decca; I-band.

Comments: Transferred to Customs on 26 December 2000.

HAI CHENG CLASS　　　　　*12/2000, Taiwan Customs* / 0114556

54 COASTAL PATROL CRAFT (WPB)

No/Type	Displacement, tons	Speed, knots	Pennant Numbers series
15 PP 5000	50	32	PP 5001-5003, 5005-5008, 5010-5013, 5015-5016, 5022-5023, 5025-5026, 5028-5032
9 PP 3550	35		PP 3550, 3552-3553, 3555-3559, 3561
16 PP 3500	35	28	PP 3516-3522, 3525, 3527, 3530-3531, 3535-3539
14 PP 3000	30	45	PP 3002-3003, 3005-3009, 3011-3012, 3015-3019

Comment: These are all armed with 12.7 mm MGs and capable of speeds up to 35 kt. The pennant numbers are not consecutive, as some have been deleted.

PP 5025   10/2001, *C Chung* / 0126207

PP 3005   10/2001, *C Chung* / 0126204

PP 3539   10/2001, *C Chung* / 0126208

Tanzania

Country Overview

The United Republic of Tanzania was formed by the federation of the former British protectorates of Tanganyika and Zanzibar in 1964. It also includes Pemba, Mafia and other offshore islands. Situated in south-eastern Africa, it has a total area of 364,900 square miles and is bordered to the north by Uganda and Kenya, to the west by Rwanda, Burundi, Democratic Republic of Congo and Zambia and to the south by Mozambique and Malawi. It has a 767 n mile coastline with the Indian Ocean. The country also includes parts of Lake Tanganyika, Lake Victoria and Lake Malawi. Dodoma is the capital while the former capital, Dar es Salaam, is the largest city and principal port. Territorial seas (12 n miles) are claimed. A 200 n mile EEZ has also been claimed but the limits are not fully defined by boundary agreements.

General

The Tanzanian People's Defence Force includes the Army, Air Defence Command and a naval wing.

There is a small Coastguard Service (KMKM), based on Zanzibar, which uses small boats for anti-smuggling patrols.

Personnel

(a)   2006: 1,050 (including Zanzibar)
(b)   Voluntary service

Coast Defence

85 mm mobile gun battery.

Bases

Dar Es Salaam, Zanzibar, Mtwara. Kigoma (Lake Tanganyika) and Mwanza (Lake Victoria).

PATROL FORCES

Notes: The Police have four Yulin class patrol boats which are probably non-operational.

2 HUCHUAN CLASS (FAST ATTACK CRAFT — TORPEDO) (PTK)

P 43	P 44

Displacement, tons: 39 standard; 45.8 full load
Dimensions, feet (metres): 71.5 × 20.7 oa × 11.8 (hullborne) *(21.8 × 6.3 × 3.6)*
Main machinery: 3 Type M 50 diesels; 3,300 hp(m) *(2.4 MW)* sustained; 3 shafts
Speed, knots: 50
Range, n miles: 500 at 30 kt
Complement: 16
Guns: 4 — 14.5 mm (2 twin) MGs.
Torpedoes: 2 — 21 in *(533 mm)* tubes.
Radars: Surface search: Skin Head; E/F-band.

Comment: Four transferred from the People's Republic of China 1975. After a major effort in 1992, were all operational and reported to be in good condition but by 1998 two had been laid up. Present operational status is unclear but one at least appears to have had torpedo tubes removed.

HUCHUAN   6/2003 / 0587794

2 VOSPER THORNYCROFT 75 ft TYPE
(COASTAL PATROL CRAFT) (PB)

Displacement, tons: 70 full load
Dimensions, feet (metres): 75 × 19.5 × 8 *(22.9 × 6 × 2.4)*
Main machinery: 2 Caterpillar D 348 diesels; 1,450 hp *(1.08 MW)* sustained; 2 shafts
Speed, knots: 24.5
Range, n miles: 800 at 20 kt
Complement: 11
Guns: 2 Oerlikon 20 mm GAM-BO1.
Radars: Surface search: Furuno; I-band.

Comment: First pair delivered 6 July 1973, second pair 1974. Used for anti-smuggling patrols off Zanzibar. Two still operational.

VOSPER 75 ft (Omani colours)   1984, *N Overington* / 0506066

1 PROTECTOR CLASS (PATROL CRAFT) (PB)

NGUNGURI (ex-*Vincent*) P 19

Displacement, tons: 100 full load
Dimensions, feet (metres): 84.3 × 20.3 × 5.6 *(25.7 × 6.2 × 1.7)*
Main machinery: 2 Paxman diesels; 2,880 hp *(2.15 MW)*; 2 shafts. 1 Perkins diesel;
  200 hp *(150 kW)*; 1 waterjet
Speed, knots: 25
Complement: 4
Radars: Navigation: 2 Decca; I-band.

Comment: Built for UK Customs by Babcock, Rosyth, in 1993. Subsequently sold to
  Damen Shipyards, Netherlands, in September 2004. Following refit, entered Tanzanian
  service in 2005.

MZIZI   *11/2005*, Rob Cabo* / 1151073

NGUNGURI   *11/2005*, Rob Cabo* / 1151081

2 SHANGHAI II CLASS (FAST ATTACK CRAFT—GUN) (PB)

MZIZI P 67   MZIA P 68

Displacement, tons: 134 full load
Dimensions, feet (metres): 127.3 × 17.7 × 5.6 *(38.8 × 5.4 × 1.7)*
Main machinery: 2 Type L12-180 diesels; 2,400 hp(m) *(1.76 MW)* (forward); 2 Type 12-D-6
  diesels; 1,820 hp(m) *(1.34 MW)* (aft); 4 shafts
Speed, knots: 30
Range, n miles: 700 at 16.5 kt
Complement: 38
Guns: 4 — 37 mm/63 (2 twin). 4 — 25 mm/80 (2 twin).
Radars: Surface search: Skin Head; E/F-band.

Comment: Six transferred by the People's Republic of China in 1971-72, two more in
  June 1992.

AUXILIARIES

2 YUCH'IN (TYPE 069) CLASS (LCU)

PONO L 08   KIBUA L 09

Displacement, tons: 85 full load
Dimensions, feet (metres): 81.2 × 17.1 × 4.3 *(24.8 × 5.2 × 1.3)*
Main machinery: 2 diesels; 600 hp(m) *(441 kW)*; 2 shafts
Speed, knots: 12. **Range, n miles:** 450 at 11.5 kt
Complement: 12
Military lift: 46 tons
Guns: 4 — 14.5 mm (2 twin) MGs.
Radars: Navigation: Fuji; I-band.

Comment: Transferred from China in 1995 probably to replace the Police Yuchai transport
  craft. Based at Dar-es-Salaam. *Pono* reported to be operational.

PONO   *1/2001* / 0109946

Thailand

Country Overview

The Kingdom of Thailand (formerly Siam) is a constitutional
monarchy in South East Asia. With an area of 198,114 square
miles, it is bordered to the west by Burma, to the east by
Laos and Cambodia and to the south by Malaysia. It has a
1,739 n mile coastline with the Gulf of Thailand and with
the Andaman Sea. The capital, largest city and principal
port (which also serves neighbouring Laos) is Bangkok.
Territorial seas (12 n miles). An EEZ (200 n miles) is claimed
and the limits have been partly defined by boundary
agreements.

Headquarters Appointments

Commander-in-Chief of the Navy:
  Admiral Satirapan Keyanon
Deputy Commander-in-Chief:
  Admiral Vichai Yuwananggoon
Assistant Commander-in-Chief:
  Admiral Suchart Yanotai
Chief of Staff:
  Admiral Veeraphon Waranont
Deputy Chiefs of Staff:
  Vice Admiral Nibhon Chaksudul
  Vice Admiral Wallop Kerd-phol

Senior Appointments

Commander-in-Chief, Fleet:
  Admiral Nopporn Ajavakhom
Deputy Commanders-in-Chief, Fleet:
  Vice Admiral Pravit Srisookwattana
  Vice Admiral Verawatch Wongdontri
Chief of Staff, Fleet:
  Vice Admiral Somded Tongpiam

Diplomatic Representation

Naval Attaché in London:
  Captain P Rujites
Naval Attaché in Washington:
  Captain Chonlathis Navanugraha
Naval Attaché in Paris:
  Captain Chartchai Thongsa-ard
Naval Attaché in Canberra:
  Captain Adoong Pan-lam

Diplomatic Representation — *continued*

Naval Attaché in Madrid:
  Captain Chatchai Srivorakan
Naval Attaché in New Delhi:
  Captain Graivut Vattanatham
Naval Attaché in Singapore:
  Captain Pallop Tami-sanont
Naval Attaché in Kuala Lumpur:
  Captain Nuttapol Diewvanich
Naval Attaché in Beijing:
  Captain Ranat Debavalya
Naval Attaché in Rome:
  Captain Banjerd Sripraram

Personnel

(a) 2006: Navy, 74,000 (including 2,000 Naval Air Arm,
     11,000 Marines and Coastal Defense Command)
(b) 2 years' national service (28,000 conscripts)

Organisation

First naval area command (Upper Thai Gulf)
Second naval command (Lower Thai Gulf)
Third naval command (Andaman Sea)

Bases

Bangkok, Sattahip, Songkhla, Phang-Nga (west coast)

Naval Aviation

First air wing (U-Tapao)
Second air wing (Songkhla)
101 Sqdn   MPA/ASW
102 Sqdn   MPA/ASuW
103 Sqdn   Utility
104 Sqdn   Maritime Strike
105 Sqdn   Matador
201 Sqdn   Central Patrol
202 Bell Helos
203 Sikorsky Helos

Pennant Numbers

Ships over 150 tons displacement which had single digit
numbers, had new numbers allocated in 1994-95.

Prefix to Ships' Names

HTMS

Strength of the Fleet

Type	Active	Building (Projected)
Aircraft Carrier	1	—
Frigates	8	—
Corvettes	7	—
Fast Attack Craft (Missile)	6	—
Fast Attack Craft (Gun)	3	—
Offshore Patrol Craft	9	2
Coastal Patrol Craft	52	—
MCM Support Ship	1	—
Minehunters	4	—
Coastal Minesweepers	2	—
MSBs	12	—
LSTs	6	—
LSM	1	—
Hovercraft	3	—
Survey Vessels	5	—
Replenishment Ship	1	—
MCMV Depot Ship	1	—
Tankers/Transports	8	—
Training Ships	3	(1)

Coast Defence

Coastal Defence Command was rapidly expanded to
the 1992 two Division level after the government
charged the RTN with the responsibility of defending
the entire Eastern Seaboard. Ships and aircraft are rotated
monthly from the Navy. Equipment includes 10 batteries
of truck-mounted Exocet MM 40, 155 and 130 mm guns
for coastal defence, 76, 40, 37, 20 mm guns and PL-9B SAM
for air defence.

Marine Police

Acts as a Coast Guard in inshore waters with some
60 armed patrol craft and another 65 equipped with small
arms only.

PENNANT LIST

Aircraft Carriers			**Patrol Forces**			632	Nongsarai	**Training Ships**	
						633	Lat Ya		
911	Chakri Naruebet		311	Prabparapak		634	Tha Din Daeng	413	Pin Klao
			312	Hanhak Sattru				611	Phosamton
Frigates			313	Suphairin		**Amphibious Forces**			
			321	Ratcharit				**Survey and Research Ships**	
421	Naresuan		322	Witthayakhom		712	Chang		
422	Taksin		323	Udomdet		713	Pangan	811	Chanthara
433	Makut Rajakumarn		331	Chon Buri		714	Lanta	812	Suk
455	Chao Phraya		332	Songkhla		715	Prathong		
456	Bangpakong		333	Phuket		721	Sichang	**Auxiliaries**	
457	Kraburi		521	Sattahip		722	Surin		
458	Saiburi		522	Klongyai		731	Kut	821	Suriya
461	Phuttha Yotfa Chulalok		523	Takbai		741	Prab	831	Chula
462	Phuttha Loetla Naphalai		524	Kantang		742	Satakut	832	Samui
			525	Thepha		761	Mataphon	833	Prong
			526	Taimuang		762	Rawi	834	Proet
Corvettes			541	Hua Hin		763	Adang	835	Samed
			542	Klaeng		764	Phetra	841	Chuang
431	Tapi		543	Si Racha		765	Kolam	842	Chik
432	Khirirat					766	Talibong	851	Klueng Badaan
441	Rattanakosin					771	Thong Kaeo	852	Marn Vichai
442	Sukothai		**Mine Warfare Forces**			772	Thong Lang	853	Rin
511	Pattani					773	Wang Nok	854	Rang
512	Narathiwat		612	Bangkeo		774	Wang Nai	855	Samaesan
531	Khamronsin		613	Donchedi		781	Man Nok	856	Raet
532	Thayanchon		621	Thalang		782	Man Klang	861	Kled Keo
533	Longlom		631	Bang Rachan		783	Man Nai	871	Similan

SUBMARINES

Notes: Acquisition of a submarine force remains a high priority but funding difficulties continue to frustrate plans.

AIRCRAFT CARRIERS

1 CHAKRI NARUEBET CLASS (CVM)

Name	No	Builders	Laid down	Launched	Commissioned
CHAKRI NARUEBET	911	Bazán, Ferrol	12 July 1994	20 Jan 1996	27 Mar 1997

Displacement, tons: 11,485 full load
Dimensions, feet (metres): 599.1 oa; 538.4 wl × 100.1 oa; 73.8 wl × 20.3 *(182.6; 164.1 × 30.5; 22.5 × 6.2)*
Flight deck, feet (metres): 572.8 × 90.2 *(174.6 × 27.5)*
Main machinery: CODOG; 2 GE LM 2500 gas turbines; 44,250 hp *(33 MW)* sustained; 2 MTU 16V 1163 TB83 diesels; 11,780 hp(m) *(8.67 MW)*; 2 shafts; LIPS cp props
Speed, knots: 26; 16 (diesels). **Range, n miles:** 10,000 at 12 kt
Complement: 455 (62 officers) plus 146 aircrew plus 4 (Royal family)

Missiles: SAM: 1 Mk 41 LCHR 8 cell VLS launcher (fitted for but not with) **❶**.
3 Matra Sadral sextuple launchers for Mistral **❷**; IR homing to 4 km *(2.2 n miles)*; warhead 3 kg.
Guns: 2—30 mm. To be fitted.
Combat data systems: Tritan derivative with Unisys UYK-3 and 20 computers.
Radars: Air search: Hughes SPS-52C **❸**; E/F-band.

Surface search: SPS-64 **❹**; I-band. To be fitted.
Fire control: to be fitted.
Navigation: Kelvin Hughes; I-band.
Aircraft control: Kelvin Hughes; E/F-band.
Tacan: URN 25.

Fixed-wing aircraft: 6 AV-8S Matador (Harrier).
Helicopters: 6 S-70B-7 Seahawk; Chinook capable.

Programmes: An initial contract for a 7,800 ton vessel with Bremer Vulcan was cancelled on 22 July 1991 and replaced on 27 March 1992 with a government to government contract for a larger ship to be built by Bazán. Fabrication started in October 1993. Sea trials conducted

from November 1996 to January 1997 followed by an aviation work-up at Rota from April 1997. The ship arrived in Thailand on 10 August 1997.
Structure: Similar to Spanish *Príncipe de Asturias*. 12° ski jump and two 20 ton aircraft lifts. Provision made to fit a Mk 41 VLS launcher, a surface search radar, EW systems, a hull mounted sonar and CIWS. Matra Sadral fitted in 2001. Hangar can take up 10 Sea Harrier or Seahawk aircraft.
Operational: Main tasks are SAR co-ordination and EEZ surveillance. Secondary role is air support for all maritime operations. Due to funding shortages, the ship rarely goes to sea and fixed-wing flying has been conducted from shore bases.

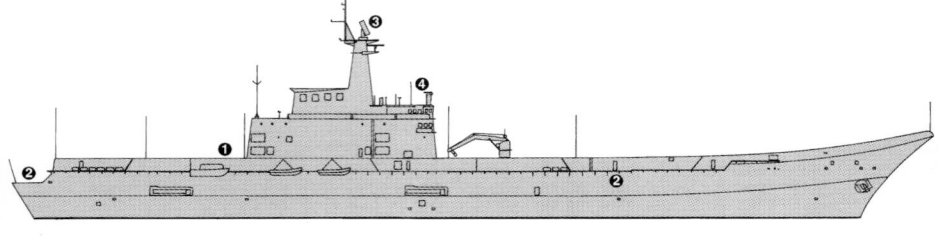

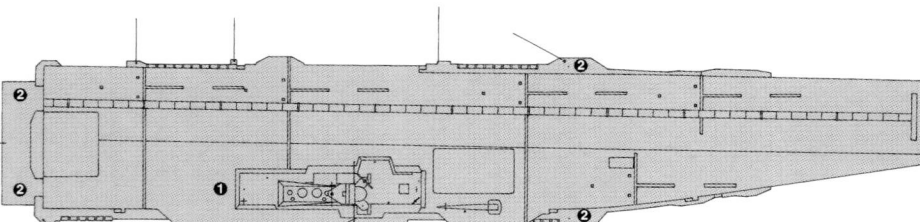

CHAKRI NARUEBET   *(Scale 1 : 1,500), Ian Sturton* / 0080799

CHAKRI NARUEBET   *5/1997, S G Gaya* / 0019250

CHAKRI NARUEBET   *1/2004, Thai Navy League* / 0589817   **CHAKRI NARUEBET**   *1/2004, Thai Navy League* / 0589816

FRIGATES

Notes: It was announced on 22 July 2003 that two frigates were to be procured from the UK. These were likely to be based on the design of those acquired by the Royal Malaysian Navy. However, a contract had not been signed by early 2006 and, despite alternative solutions promoted by other companies, plans are probably being frustrated by funding difficulties.

2 NARESUAN CLASS (TYPE 25T) (FFGHM)

Name	No	Builders	Laid down	Launched	Commissioned
NARESUAN	421 (ex-621)	Zhonghua SY, Shanghai	Feb 1992	24 July 1993	15 Dec 1994
TAKSIN	422 (ex-622)	Zhonghua SY, Shanghai	Nov 1992	14 May 1994	28 Sep 1995

Displacement, tons: 2,500 standard; 2,980 full load
Dimensions, feet (metres): 393.7 × 42.7 × 12.5
(120 × 13 × 3.8)
Main machinery: CODOG; 2 GE LM 2500 gas turbines; 44,250 hp *(33 MW)* sustained; 2 MTU 20 V 1163 TB83 diesels; 11,780 hp(m) *(8.67 MW)* sustained; 2 shafts; LIPS cp props
Speed, knots: 32. **Range, n miles:** 4,000 at 18 kt
Complement: 150

Missiles: SSM: 8 McDonnell Douglas Harpoon (2 quad) launchers ❶; active radar homing to 130 km *(70 n miles)* at 0.9 Mach; warhead 227 kg.
SAM: Mk 41 LCHR 8 cell VLS launcher ❷ Sea Sparrow; semi-active radar homing to 14.6 km *(8 n miles)* at 2.5 Mach; warhead 39 kg (fitted for but not with).
Guns: 1 FMC 5 in *(127 mm)*/54 Mk 45 Mod 2 ❸; 20 rds/min to 23 km *(12.6 n miles)*; weight of shell 32 kg.
4 China 37 mm/76 (2 twin) H/PJ 76 A ❹; 180 rds/min to 8.5 km *(4.6 n miles)* anti-aircraft; weight of shell 1.42 kg.
Torpedoes: 6—324 mm Mk 32 Mod 5 (2 triple) tubes ❺. Honeywell Mk 46; active/passive homing to 11 km *(5.9 n miles)* at 40 kt; warhead 44 kg.
Countermeasures: Decoys: 4 China Type 945 GPJ 26-barrelled launchers ❻; chaff and IR.
ESM/ECM: Elettronica Newton Beta EW System; intercept and jammer.
Weapons control: 1 JM-83H Optical Director ❼.
Radars: Air search: Signaal LW08 ❽; D-band.
Surface search: China Type 360 ❾; E/F-band.
Navigation: 2 Raytheon SPS-64(V)5; I-band.
Fire control: 2 Signaal STIR ❿; I/J/K-band (for SSM and 127 mm). After one to be fitted.
China 374 G ⓫ (for 37 mm).
Sonars: China SJD-7; hull-mounted; active search and attack; medium frequency.

Helicopters: 1 Super Lynx ⓬ in due course or 1 Sikorsky S-70B-7 Seahawk.

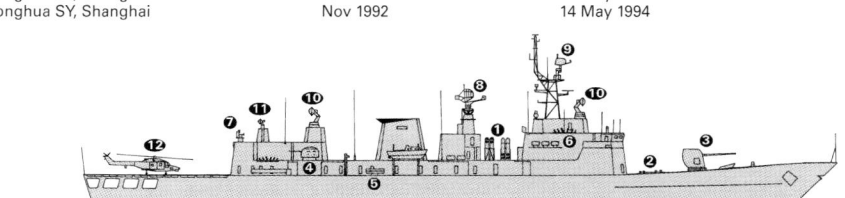

NARESUAN *(Scale 1 : 1,200), Ian Sturton* / 0543398

TAKSIN *8/2005*, Chris Sattler* / 1153916

Programmes: Contract signed 21 September 1989 for construction of two ships by the China State SB Corporation (CSSC) with delivery in 1994. US and European weapon systems were fitted as funds became available. The first ship sailed for Bangkok without most weapon systems in January 1995 with the second following in October 1995.
Structure: Jointly designed by the Royal Thai Navy and China State Shipbuilding Corporation (CSSC). This is a design incorporating much Western machinery and

equipment and provides enhanced capabilities by comparison with the four Type 053 class. The anti-aircraft guns are Breda 40 mm types with 37 mm ammunition and they are controlled by a Chinese RTN-20 Dardo tracker.
Operational: *Naresuan* acted as one of the escorts for the aircraft carrier during her aviation work-up in Spanish waters in 1997.

TAKSIN *8/2005*, Chris Sattler* / 1153917

NARESUAN *10/2002, Hachiro Nakai* / 0530029

For details of the latest updates to ***Jane's Fighting Ships*** online and to discover the additional information available exclusively to online subscribers please visit
jfs.janes.com

4 CHAO PHRAYA CLASS (TYPES 053 HT and 053 HT (H)) (FFG/FFGH)

Name	No	Builders	Laid down	Launched	Commissioned
CHAO PHRAYA	455	Hudong SY, Shanghai	1989	24 June 1990	5 Apr 1991
BANGPAKONG	456	Hudong SY, Shanghai	1989	25 July 1990	20 July 1991
KRABURI	457	Hudong SY, Shanghai	1990	28 Dec 1990	16 Jan 1992
SAIBURI	458	Hudong SY, Shanghai	1990	27 Aug 1991	4 Aug 1992

Displacement, tons: 1,676 standard; 1,924 full load
Dimensions, feet (metres): 338.5 × 37.1 × 10.2
(103.2 × 11.3 × 3.1)
Main machinery: 4 MTU 20V 1163 TB83 diesels; 29,440 hp(m)
(21.6 MW) sustained; 2 shafts; LIPS cp props
Speed, knots: 30
Range, n miles: 3,500 at 18 kt
Complement: 168 (22 officers)

Missiles: SSM: 8 Ying Ji (Eagle Strike) (C-801) ❶; active
radar/IR homing to 85 km *(45.9 n miles)* at 0.9 Mach;
warhead 165 kg; sea-skimmer. This is the extended range
version.
SAM: 1 HQ-61 launcher for PL-9 or Matra Sadral for Mistral
to be fitted.
Guns: 2 (457 and 458) or 4 China 100 mm/56 (1 or 2 twin) ❷;
25 rds/min to 22 km *(12 n miles)*; weight of shell 15.9 kg.
8 China 37 mm/76 (4 twin) H/PJ 76 A ❸; 180 rds/min to
8.5 km *(4.6 n miles)* anti-aircraft; weight of shell 1.42 kg.
A/S mortars: 2 RBU 1200 (China Type 86) 5-tubed fixed
launchers ❹; range 1,200 m.
Depth charges: 2 BMB racks.
Countermeasures: Decoys: 2 China Type 945 GPJ
26-barrelled chaff launchers.
ESM: China Type 923(1); intercept.
ECM: China Type 981(3); jammer.
Combat data systems: China Type ZKJ-3 or STN Atlas mini
COSYS action data automation being fitted.
Radars: Air/surface search: China Type 354 Eye Shield ❺;
G-band.
Surface search/fire control: China Type 352C Square Tie ❻;
I-band (for SSM).
Fire control: China Type 343 Sun Visor ❼; I-band (for 100 mm).
China Type 341 Rice Lamp ❽; I-band (for 37 mm).
Navigation: Racal Decca 1290 A/D ARPA and Anritsu
RA 71CA ❾; I-band.
IFF: Type 651.
Sonars: China Type SJD-5A; hull-mounted; active search
and attack; medium frequency.

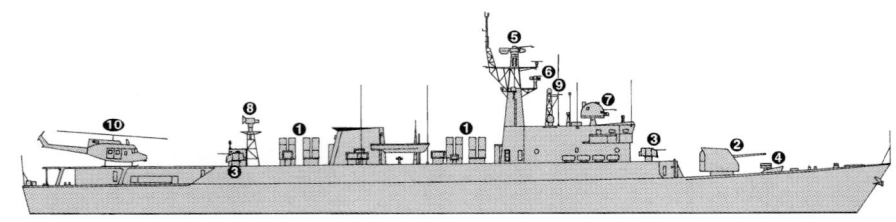

CHAO PHRAYA *(Scale 1 : 900), Ian Sturton* / 0080802

KRABURI *(Scale 1 : 900), Ian Sturton* / 0080803

Helicopters: Platform for 1 Bell 212 (457 and 458) ❿.

Programmes: Contract signed 18 July 1988 for four
modified Jianghu class ships to be built by the China
State SB Corporation (CSSC).
Modernisation: A mini COSYS system was acquired for
two of the class in 1999.
Structure: Thailand would have preferred only the hulls
but China insisted on full armament. Two of the ships are
the Type III variant with 100 mm guns, fore and aft, and
the other two are a variation with a helicopter platform

replacing the after 100 mm gun. German communication
equipment fitted. The EW fit is Italian designed.
Operational: On arrival in Thailand each ship was docked
to make good poor shipbuilding standards and improve
damage control capabilities. The ships are mostly
used for rotating monthly to the Coast Guard, and
for training, although *Kraburi* was part of the escort
force for the aircraft carrier in Spanish waters in 1997.
Kraburi damaged by the tsunami on 26 December 2004
but had been restored to operational service by
February 2005.

KRABURI *5/1998, Ships of the World* / 0050235

BANGPAKONG *10/2002, John Mortimer* / 0529998

2 KNOX CLASS (FFGHM)

Name	No	Builders	Laid down	Launched	Commissioned
PHUTTHA YOTFA CHULALOK (ex-*Truett*)	461 (ex-FF 1095)	Avondale Shipyards	27 Apr 1972	3 Feb 1973	1 June 1974
PHUTTHA LOETLA NAPHALAI (ex-*Ouellet*)	462 (ex-FF 1077)	Avondale Shipyards	15 Jan 1969	17 Jan 1970	12 Dec 1970

Displacement, tons: 3,011 standard; 4,260 full load
Dimensions, feet (metres): 439.6 × 46.8 × 15; 24.8 (sonar)
(134 × 14.3 × 4.6; 7.8)
Main machinery: 2 Combustion Engineering/Babcock &
Wilcox boilers; 1,200 psi *(84.4 kg/cm²)*; 950°F *(510°C)*;
1 turbine; 35,000 hp *(26 MW)*; 1 shaft
Speed, knots: 27. **Range, n miles:** 4,000 at 22 kt on 1 boiler
Complement: 288 (17 officers)

Missiles: SSM: 8 McDonnell Douglas Harpoon; active radar
homing to 130 km *(70 n miles)* at 0.9 Mach; warhead
227 kg.
A/S: Honeywell ASROC Mk 16 octuple launcher with reload
system (has 2 starboard cells modified to fire Harpoon) ❶;
inertial guidance to 1.6-10 km *(1—5.4 n miles)*; payload
Mk 46.
Guns: 1 FMC 5 in *(127 mm)*/54 Mk 42 Mod 9 ❷; 20—40 rds/
min to 24 km *(13 miles)* anti-surface; 14 km *(7.7 n miles)*
anti-aircraft; weight of shell 32 kg.
1 General Electric/General Dynamics 20 mm/76
6-barrelled Mk 15 Vulcan Phalanx ❸; 3,000 rds/min
combined to 1.5 km.
Torpedoes: 4—324 mm Mk 32 (2 twin) fixed tubes ❹.
22 Honeywell Mk 46; anti-submarine; active/passive
homing to 11 km *(5.9 n miles)* at 40 kt; warhead 44 kg.
Countermeasures: Decoys: 2 Loral Hycor SRBOC
6-barrelled fixed Mk 36 ❺; IR flares and chaff to 4 km *(2.2 n
miles)*. T Mk-6 Fanfare/SLQ-25 Nixie; torpedo decoy.
Prairie Masker hull and blade rate noise suppression.
ESM/ECM: SLQ-32(V)2 ❻; radar warning. Sidekick
modification adds jammer and deception system.
Combat data systems: Link 14 receive only.
Weapons control: SWG-1A Harpoon LCS. Mk 68 GFCS.
Mk 114 ASW FCS. Mk 1 target designation system.
MMS target acquisition sight (for mines, small craft and
low-flying aircraft).
Radars: Air search: Lockheed SPS-40B ❼; B-band; range
320 km *(175 n miles)*.
Surface search: Raytheon SPS-10 or Norden SPS-67 ❽;
G-band.
Navigation: Marconi LN66; I-band.
Fire control: Western Electric SPG-53A/D/F ❾; I/J-band.
Tacan: SRN 15. IFF: UPX-12.

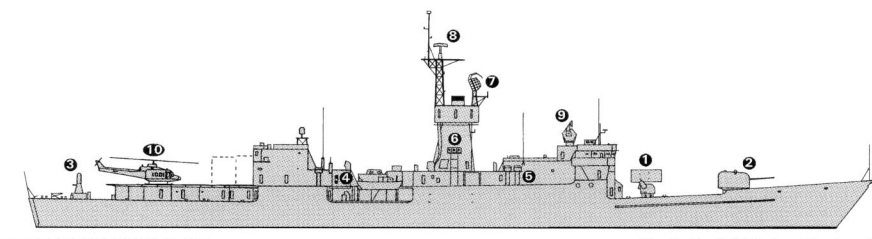

PHUTTHA YOTFA CHULALOK (Scale 1 : 1,200), *Ian Sturton* / 0543397

PHUTTHA LOETLA NAPHALAI *1/2001, Thai Navy League* / 0105841

Sonars: EDO/General Electric SQS-26CX; bow-mounted;
active search and attack; medium frequency.
EDO SQR-18(V) TACTASS; passive; low frequency.

Helicopters: 1 Bell 212 ❿.

Programmes: The first ship transferred on five year
lease from the USA on 30 July 1994. This was
renewed by grant in 1999. The second transferred on
lease 27 November 1996 and arrived in Thailand in
November 1998.
Structure: Four Mk 32 torpedo tubes are fixed in the
midships structure, two to a side, angled out at 45°.
The arrangement provides improved loading capability
over exposed triple Mk 32 torpedo tubes. A 4,000 lb
lightweight anchor is fitted on the port side and an
8,000 lb anchor fits into the after section of the sonar
dome.

1 YARROW TYPE (FFH)

Name	No	Builders	Laid down	Launched	Commissioned
MAKUT RAJAKUMARN	433 (ex-7)	Yarrow Shipbuilders	11 Jan 1970	18 Nov 1971	7 May 1973

Displacement, tons: 1,650 standard; 1,900 full load
Dimensions, feet (metres): 320 × 36 × 18.1
(97.6 × 11 × 5.5)
Main machinery: CODOG; 1 RR Olympus TM3B gas turbine;
22,500 hp *(16.8 MW)* sustained; 1 Crossley-SEMT-Pielstick
12 PC2.2 V 400 diesel; 6,000 hp(m) *(4.4 MW)* sustained;
2 shafts
Speed, knots: 26 gas; 18 diesel
Range, n miles: 5,000 at 18 kt; 1,200 at 26 kt
Complement: 140 (16 officers)

Guns: 2 Vickers 4.5 in *(114 mm)*/55 Mk 8 ❶; 25 rds/min to
22 km *(12 n miles)* anti-surface; 6 km *(3.3 n miles)* anti-
aircraft; weight of shell 21 kg.
2 Breda 40 mm/70 (twin) ❷; 300 rds/min to 12.5 km
(6.8 n miles); weight of shell 0.96 kg.
2 Oerlikon 20 mm.
Torpedoes: 6 Plessey PMW 49A tubes ❸ Mk 46; active/
passive homing to 11 km *(5.9 n miles)* at 40 kt; warhead
44 kg.
A/S mortars: 1 Limbo 3-tubed Mk 10 ❹.
Depth charges: 1 rack.
Countermeasures: Decoys: 2 Loral Mk 135 chaff launchers
ESM/ECM: Elettronica Newton ❺; intercept and jammer.
WLR-1; radar warning.
Combat data systems: Signaal Sewaco TH.
Radars: Air/surface search: Signaal DA05 ❻; E/F-band;
range 137 km *(75 n miles)* for 2 m² target.
Surface search: Signaal ZW06 ❼; I-band.

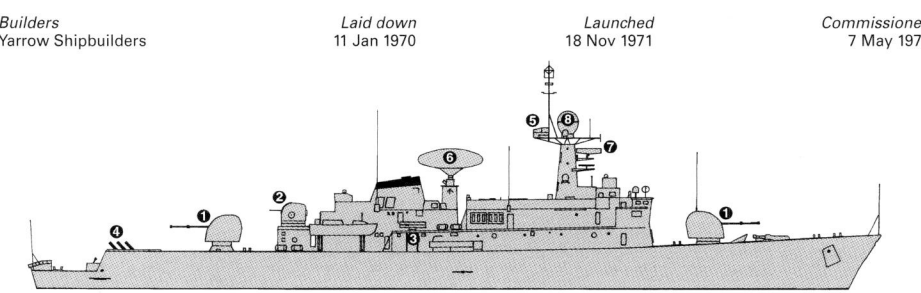

MAKUT RAJAKUMARN (Scale 1 : 900), *Ian Sturton* / 0080806

Fire control: Signaal WM22/61 ❽; I/J-band; range 46 km
(25 n miles).
Navigation: Racal Decca; I-band.
Sonars: Atlas Elektronik DSQS-21C; hull-mounted; active
search and attack; medium frequency.

Helicopters: A small helicopter can land when the Mortar
Mk 10 well is closed.

Programmes: Ordered on 21 August 1969.
Modernisation: A severe fire in February 1984 resulted
in extensive work including replacement of the
Olympus gas turbine, a new ER control room and
central electric switchboard. Further modifications
included the removal of Seacat SAM system and the
installation of new EW equipment in 1993. In 1997
two Bofors 40 mm were fitted on the old Seacat
mounting, and torpedo tubes replaced the old Bofors
abreast the funnel.
Operational: The ship is largely automated with a
consequent saving in complement, and has been most
successful in service. Has lost its Flagship role to one of
the Chinese-built frigates and is employed on general
duties rather than as a training ship as previously
reported.

MAKUT RAJAKUMARN *2/2004, Bob Fildes* / 0589813

CORVETTES

2 + (2) OFFSHORE PATROL VESSELS (PBOH)

Name	No	Builders	Laid down	Launched	Commissioned
PATTANI	511	Hudong Shipyard, Shanghai	2003	19 Sep 2004	16 Dec 2005
NARATHIWAT	512	Hudong Shipyard, Shanghai	2004	Mar 2005	2006

Displacement, tons: 1,300; 1,440 full load
Dimensions, feet (metres): 313.3 × 38.0 × 10.2
  (95.5 × 11.6 × 3.1)
Main machinery: 2 Ruston diesels; 15,660 hp *(11.7 MW)*;
  2 shafts; cp props
Speed, knots: 25. **Range, n miles:** 3.500 at 15 kt
Complement: 78 (18 officers)
Guns: 1 OTO Melara 3 in *(76 mm)*/62; 85 rds/min to 16 km
  (8.6 n miles). 2—200 mm.
Combat data systems: COSYS.
Weapons control: Optronic director combined with TMX.
Radars: Surface search: Alenia Marconi RAN 30X; I-band.
Fire control: Oerlikon/Contraves TMX; I/J-band.
Navigation: I-band.

Helicopters: Platform for one medium.

Programmes: The contract for two Offshore Patrol Vessels
  was signed with China Shipbuilding Trading Company on
  20 December 2002. A further two vessels are projected.
Structure: Space and weight provision for the addition of
  eight SSM, CIWS and ASW capabilities at a late date.
Operational: *Pattani* arrived at Sattahip on 16 December
  2005. *Narathiwat* is to follow in 2006.

PATTANI — *12/2005*, Thai Navy League* / 1153915

PATTANI — *12/2005*, Thai Navy League* / 1153914

2 RATTANAKOSIN CLASS (FSGM)

Name	No	Builders	Laid down	Launched	Commissioned
RATTANAKOSIN	441 (ex-1)	Tacoma Boatbuilders, WA	6 Feb 1984	11 Mar 1986	26 Sep 1986
SUKHOTHAI	442 (ex-2)	Tacoma Boatbuilders, WA	26 Mar 1984	20 July 1986	10 June 1987

Displacement, tons: 960 full load
Dimensions, feet (metres): 252 × 31.5 × 8
  (76.8 × 9.6 × 2.4)
Main machinery: 2 MTU 20V 1163 TB83 diesels; 14,730 hp(m)
  (10.83 MW) sustained; 2 shafts; Kamewa cp props
Speed, knots: 26. **Range, n miles:** 3,000 at 16 kt
Complement: 87 (15 officers) plus Flag Staff

Missiles: SSM: 8 McDonnell Douglas Harpoon (2 quad)
  launchers ❶; active radar homing to 130 km *(70 n miles)*
  at 0.9 Mach; warhead 227 kg (84A) or 258 kg (84B/C).
SAM: Selenia Elsag Albatros octuple launcher ❷; 24
  Aspide; semi-active radar homing to 13 km *(7 n miles)*
  at 2.5 Mach; height envelope 15-5,000 m *(49.2—16,405 ft)*;
  warhead 30 kg.
Guns: 1 OTO Melara 3 in *(76 mm)*/62 ❸; 60 rds/min to 16 km
  (8.7 n miles); weight of shell 6 kg.
  2 Breda 40 mm/70 (twin) ❹; 300 rds/min to 12.5 km
  (6.8 n miles); weight of shell 0.96 kg.
  2 Rheinmetall 20 mm ❺.
Torpedoes: 6—324 mm US Mk 32 (2 triple) tubes ❻. MUSL
  Stingray; active/passive homing to 11 km *(5.9 n miles)*
  at 45 kt; warhead 35 kg (shaped charge); depth to 750 m
  (2,460 ft).
Countermeasures: Decoys: CSEE Dagaie 6- or 10-tubed
  trainable; IR flares and chaff; H- to J-band.
ESM: Elettronica; intercept.
Weapons control: Signaal Sewaco TH action data
  automation. Lirod 8 optronic director ❼.
Radars: Air/surface search: Signaal DA05 ❽; E/F-band;
  range 137 km *(75 n miles)* for 2 m² target.
Surface search: Signaal ZW06 ❾; I-band.
Navigation: Decca 1226; I-band.
Fire control: Signaal WM25/41 ❿; I/J-band; range 46 km
  (25 n miles).
Sonars: Atlas Elektronik DSQS-21C; hull-mounted; active
  search and attack; medium frequency.

Programmes: Contract signed with Tacoma on 9 May 1983.
  Intentions to build a third were overtaken by the Vosper
  corvettes.
Structure: There are some similarities with the missile
  corvettes built for Saudi Arabia five years earlier. Space
  for Phalanx aft of the Harpoon launchers, but there are no
  plans to fit.

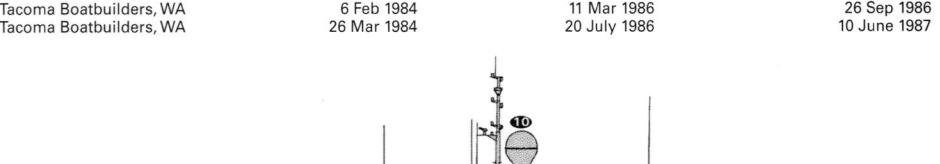
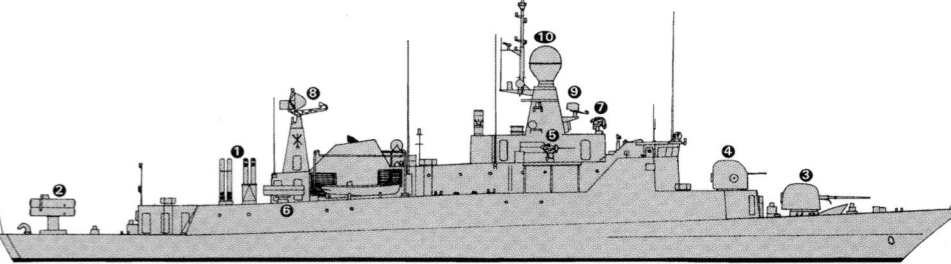

RATTANAKOSIN — *(Scale 1 : 600), Ian Sturton* / 0506173

SUKHOTHAI
6/2001, Royal Thai Navy
0130170

3 KHAMRONSIN CLASS (FS)

Name	No	Builders	Laid down	Launched	Commissioned
KHAMRONSIN	531 (ex-1)	Ital Thai Marine, Bangkok	15 Mar 1988	15 Aug 1989	29 July 1992
THAYANCHON	532 (ex-2)	Ital Thai Marine, Bangkok	20 Apr 1988	7 Dec 1989	5 Sep 1992
LONGLOM	533 (ex-3)	Bangkok Naval Dockyard	15 Mar 1988	8 Aug 1989	2 Oct 1992

Displacement, tons: 630 full load
Dimensions, feet (metres): 203.4 oa; 186 wl × 26.9 × 8.2
  (62; 56.7 × 8.2 × 2.5)
Main machinery: 2 MTU 12V 1163 TB93; 9,980 hp(m) *(7.34 MW)*
  sustained; 2 Kamewa cp props
Speed, knots: 25. **Range, n miles:** 2,500 at 15 kt
Complement: 57 (6 officers)

Guns: 1 OTO Melara 76 mm/62 Mod 7 ❶; 60 rds/min to 16 km
  (8.7 n miles); weight of shell 6 kg.
  2 Breda 30 mm/70 (twin) ❷; 800 rds/min to 12.5 km
  (6.8 n miles); weight of shell 0.37 kg.
  2—12.7 mm MGs.
Torpedoes: 6 Plessey PMW 49A (2 triple) launchers ❸; MUSL
  Stingray; active/passive homing to 11 km *(5.9 n miles)*
  at 45 kt; warhead 35 kg shaped charge.
Combat data systems: Plessey Nautis P action data
  automation.
Weapons control: British Aerospace Sea Archer 1A Mod 2
  optronic GFCS ❹.
Radars: Air/surface search: Plessey AWS 4 ❺; E/F-band.
  Navigation: Racal Decca 1226; I-band.

KHAMRONSIN *(Scale 1 : 600), Ian Sturton* / 0572649

Sonars: Atlas Elektronik DSQS-21C; hull-mounted; active
  search and attack; medium frequency.

Programmes: Contract signed on 29 September 1987
  with Ital Thai Marine of Bangkok for the construction
  of two ASW corvettes and for technical assistance
  with a third to be built in Bangkok Naval Dockyard.

A fourth of the class with a different superstructure
and less armament was ordered by the Police in
September 1989.
Structure: The vessels are based on a Vosper Thornycroft
Province class 56 m design stretched by increasing the
frame spacing along the whole length of the hull. Depth
charge racks and mine rails may be added.

LONGLOM *9/2003, Hartmut Ehlers* / 0572641

2 TAPI (PF 103) CLASS (FS)

Name	No	Builders	Laid down	Launched	Commissioned
TAPI	431 (ex-5)	American SB Co, Toledo, OH	1 July 1970	17 Oct 1970	19 Nov 1971
KHIRIRAT	432 (ex-6)	Norfolk SB & DD Co	18 Feb 1972	2 June 1973	10 Aug 1974

Displacement, tons: 885 standard; 1,172 full load
Dimensions, feet (metres): 275 × 33 × 10; 14.1 (sonar)
  (83.8 × 10 × 3; 4.3)
Main machinery: 2 Fairbanks-Morse 38TD8-1/8-9 diesels;
  5,250 hp *(3.9 MW)* sustained; 2 shafts
Speed, knots: 20
Range, n miles: 2,400 at 18 kt
Complement: 135 (15 officers)

Guns: 1 OTO Melara 3 in *(76 mm)*/62 compact ❶; 85 rds/min
  to 16 km *(8.7 n miles)* anti-surface; 12 km *(6.6 n miles)*
  anti-aircraft; weight of shell 6 kg.
  1 Bofors 40 mm/70 ❷; 300 rds/min to 12.5 km
  (6.8 n miles); weight of shell 0.96 kg.
  2 Oerlikon 20 mm ❸. 2—12.7 mm MGs.
Torpedoes: 6—324 mm US Mk 32 (2 triple) tubes ❹.
  Honeywell Mk 46; anti-submarine; active/passive homing
  to 11 km *(5.9 n miles)* at 40 kt; warhead 44 kg.
Depth charges: 1 rack.
Combat data systems: Signaal Sewaco TH.
Radars: Air/surface search: Signaal LW04 ❺; D-band; range
  137 km *(75 n miles)* for 2 m² target.
  Surface search: Raytheon SPS-53E ❻; I-band.
  Fire control: Signaal WM22-61 ❼; I/J-band; range 46 km
  (25 n miles).
  IFF: UPX-23.
Sonars: Atlas Elektronik DSQS-21C; hull-mounted; active
  search and attack; medium frequency.

Programmes: *Tapi* was ordered on 27 June 1969. *Khirirat*
  was ordered on 25 June 1971.
Modernisation: *Tapi* completed 1983 and *Khirirat* in 1987.
  This included new gunnery and radars and a slight
  heightening of the funnel. Further modernisation in 1988-89
  mainly to external and internal communications.
Structure: Of similar design to the Iranian ships of the
  Bayandor class.
Operational: Used for EEZ patrols.

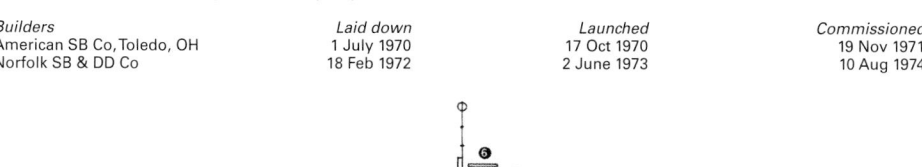
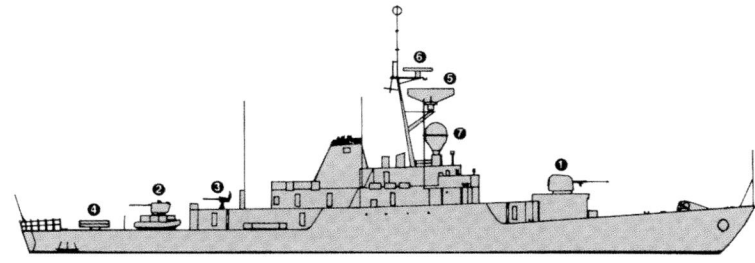

TAPI *(Scale 1 : 900), Ian Sturton* / 0506109

TAPI
6/2001, Royal Thai Navy
0130171

SHIPBORNE AIRCRAFT

Numbers/Type: 4 Bell 214 ST.
Operational speed: 120 kt *(228 km/h)*.
Service ceiling: 13,200 ft *(4,025 m)*.
Range: 400 n miles *(740 km)*.
Role/Weapon systems: Procured in 1987 for maritime surveillance and utility roles.

BELL 214   *6/2004, Royal Thai Navy* / 1044195

Numbers/Type: 2 AgustaWestland Super Lynx 300.
Operational speed: 125 kt *(231 km/h)*.
Service ceiling: 12,000 ft *(3,660 m)*.
Range: 340 n miles *(630 km)*.
Role/Weapon systems: Two helicopters ordered 7 August 2001 for ASW, ASV and surveillance roles. Delivered in 2005.

SUPER LYNX   *9/2004, AgustaWestland* / 0566704

Numbers/Type: 7/2 BAe/McDonnell Douglas AV-8A (Harrier)/TAV-8A (Harrier).
Operational speed: 640 kt *(1,186 km/h)*.
Service ceiling: 51,200 ft *(15,600 m)*.
Range: 800 n miles *(1,480 km)*.
Role/Weapon systems: AV-8S supplied via USA to Spain and transferred in 1996. Sensors: None. Weapons: Strike; two 30 mm Aden cannon, two AIM-9 Sidewinder or 20 mm/127 mm rockets and 'iron' bombs.

HARRIER   *1/2001, Thai Navy League* / 0130153

Numbers/Type: 6 Sikorsky S-70B7 Seahawk.
Operational speed: 135 kt *(250 km/h)*.
Service ceiling: 10,000 ft *(3,050 m)*.
Range: 600 n miles *(1,110 km)*.
Role/Weapon systems: Multimission helicopters delivered by June 1997. Plans to acquire ASW equipment have been abandoned. Sensors: Telephonics APS-143(V)3 radar; ASN 150 databus; provision for sonobuoys and dipping sonar; ALR 606(V)2 ESM. Weapons: Provision for ASM and MUSL Stingray torpedoes.

SEAHAWK   *7/2005*, Thai Navy League* / 1153913

Numbers/Type: 4 Bell 212.
Operational speed: 100 kt *(185 km/h)*.
Service ceiling: 13,200 ft *(4,025 m)*.
Range: 200 n miles *(370 km)*.
Role/Weapon systems: Commando assault and general support. At least two transferred from Army. May be sold to help pay for new shipborne helicopter. Mostly based ashore but operate from Normed class and frigates. Weapons: Pintle-mounted M60 machine guns.

BELL 212   *6/2000, Thai Navy League* / 0105842

LAND-BASED MARITIME AIRCRAFT (FRONT LINE)

Notes: There are also five Cessna Bird Dog light reconnaissance aircraft, 9 Cessna Skywagon and two UH-1H helicopters.

Numbers/Type: 4 Sikorsky S-76B.
Operational speed: 145 kt *(269 km/h)*.
Service ceiling: 6,500 ft *(1,980 m)*.
Range: 357 n miles *(661 km)*.
Role/Weapon systems: Six originally acquired in 1996 for maritime surveillance and utility purposes. Sensors: Weather radar. Weapons: Unarmed.

S-76   *8/1996, Royal Thai Navy* / 0050241

Numbers/Type: 2/1 Lockheed P-3T Orion/UP-3T Orion.
Operational speed: 411 kt *(761 km/h)*.
Service ceiling: 28,300 ft *(8,625 m)*.
Range: 4,000 n miles *(7,410 km)*.
Role/Weapon systems: Delivered in 1996. Two for ASW and one utility. Two more are required. Sensors: APS-115 radar, ECM/ESM. Weapons: ASW; Mk 46 or Stingray torpedoes. ASV; four Harpoon.

ORION   *8/1997, Royal Thai Navy* / 0019261

Numbers/Type: 14/4 A-7E Corsair II/TA-7E Corsair II.
Operational speed: 600 kt *(1,112 km/h)*.
Service ceiling: 50,000 ft *(15,240 m)*.
Range: 2,000 n miles *(3,705 km)*.
Role/Weapon systems: Delivered in 1996-97 from the US. Reconditioning programme in progress 2004. Weapons: AIM-9L Sidewinder; 1 — 20 mm cannon.

CORSAIR II   *8/1996, Royal Thai Navy* / 0053451

Numbers/Type: 3/2 Fokker F27 Maritime 200ME/400M.
Operational speed: 250 kt *(463 km/h)*.
Service ceiling: 25,000 ft *(7,620 m)*.
Range: 2,700 n miles *(5,000 km)*.
Role/Weapon systems: Increased coastal surveillance and response is provided, including ASW and ASV action by 200ME. 400M is for transport. Sensors: APS-504 search radar, Bendix weather radar, ESM and MAD equipment. Weapons: ASW; four Mk 46 or Stingray torpedoes or depth bombs or mines. ASV; two Harpoon ASM.

FOKKER 400   *1994, Royal Thai Navy* / 0053452

Numbers/Type: 5 GAF N24A Searchmaster B (Nomad).
Operational speed: 168 kt *(311 km/h)*.
Service ceiling: 21,000 ft *(6,400 m)*.
Range: 730 n miles *(1,352 km)*.
Role/Weapon systems: Short-range MR for EEZ protection and anti-smuggling operations. Sensors: Search radar, cameras. Weapons: Unarmed.

NOMAD (US colours)   *2/2004, ASTA* / 0010107

Numbers/Type: 7/2 Summit T-337SP/T-337G.
Operational speed: 200 kt *(364 km/h)*.
Service ceiling: 20,000 ft *(6,100 m)*.
Range: 900 n miles *(1,650 km)*.
Role/Weapon systems: Maritime surveillance and targeting. Weapons: LAU-32 and 59A rocket launchers, CBU-14 bomblets and 12.7 mm MG.

Numbers/Type: 6 Dornier 228.
Operational speed: 200 kt *(370 km/h)*.
Service ceiling: 28,000 ft *(8,535 m)*.
Range: 940 n miles *(1,740 km)*.
Role/Weapon systems: Coastal surveillance and EEZ protection. Three acquired in 1991, three more in 1996. Sensors: APS-128/504 search radar.

DORNIER 228   *6/1996, Royal Thai Navy* / 0019262

Numbers/Type: 2 Canadair CL-215.
Operational speed: 206 kt *(382 km/h)*.
Service ceiling: 10,000 ft *(3,050 m)*.
Range: 1,125 n miles *(2,085 km)*.
Role/Weapon systems: Used for general purpose transport, SAR and fire-fighting.

CL-215   *1993, Royal Thai Navy* / 0053453

PATROL FORCES

3 HUA HIN CLASS (PSO)

Name	No	Builders	Laid down	Launched	Commissioned
HUA HIN	541	Asimar, Samut Prakarn	Mar 1997	3 Mar 1999	25 Mar 2000
KLAENG	542	Asimar, Samut Prakarn	May 1997	19 Apr 1999	17 Jan 2001
SI RACHA	543	Bangkok Naval Dockyard	Dec 1997	6 Sep 1999	17 Jan 2001

Displacement, tons: 645 full load
Dimensions, feet (metres): 203.4 × 29.2 × 8.9
(62 × 8.9 × 2.7)
Main machinery: 3 Paxman 12VP 185 diesels; 10,372 hp(m)
(7.63 MW) sustained; 3 shafts; 1 LIPS cp prop (centreline)
Speed, knots: 25
Range, n miles: 2,500 at 15 kt
Complement: 45 (11 officers)

Guns: 1—3 in *(76 mm)*/50 Mk 22 ❶; 50 rds/min to 12 km *(6.5 n miles)*; weight of shell 6 kg.
1 Bofors 40 mm/60 ❷; 2 Oerlikon 20 mm GAM-BO1 ❸.
2—12.7 mm MGs.
Weapons control: Optronic director ❹.
Radars: Surface search: Sperry Rascar ❺; E/F-band.
Navigation: Sperry Apar; I-band.

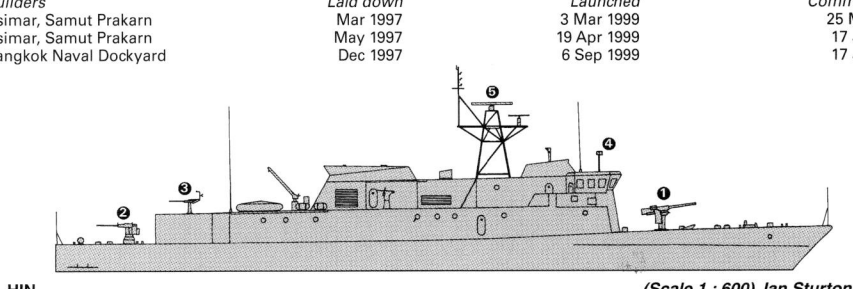

HUA HIN   *(Scale 1 : 600), Ian Sturton* / 0587563

Programmes: Ordered in September 1996 from Asian Marine. Delayed and reported cancelled by the Thai Navy in late 1997 but, despite being beset by building delays, all three ships had entered service by 2001.

Structure: Derived from the Khamronsin design.
Operational: Due to budgetary constraints, older weapon systems have been installed as a temporary measure.

KLAENG   *6/2001, Royal Thai Navy* / 0130174

3 RATCHARIT CLASS (FAST ATTACK CRAFT—MISSILE) (PGGF)

Name	No	Builders	Commissioned
RATCHARIT	321 (ex-4)	CN Breda (Venezia)	10 Aug 1979
WITTHAYAKHOM	322 (ex-5)	CN Breda (Venezia)	12 Nov 1979
UDOMDET	323 (ex-6)	CN Breda (Venezia)	21 Feb 1980

Displacement, tons: 235 standard; 270 full load
Dimensions, feet (metres): 163.4 × 24.6 × 7.5 *(49.8 × 7.5 × 2.3)*
Main machinery: 3 MTU MD 20V 538 TB91 diesels; 11,520 hp(m) *(8.47 MW)* sustained; 3 shafts; Kamewa cp props
Speed, knots: 37. **Range, n miles:** 2,000 at 15 kt
Complement: 45 (7 officers)

Missiles: SSM: 4 Aerospatiale MM 38 Exocet; inertial cruise; active radar homing to 42 km *(23 n miles)* at 0.9 Mach; warhead 165 kg; sea-skimmer.
Guns: 1 OTO Melara 3 in *(76 mm)*/62 compact; 85 rds/min to 16 km *(8.7 n miles)* anti-surface; 12 km *(6.6 n miles)* anti-aircraft; weight of shell 6 kg.
1 Bofors 40 mm/70; 300 rds/min to 12.5 km *(6.8 n miles)*; weight of shell 0.96 kg.
2—12.7 mm MGs.
Countermeasures: ESM: Racal RDL-2; intercept.
Radars: Surface search: Decca; I-band.
Fire control: Signaal WM25; I/J-band; range 46 km *(25 n miles)*.

Programmes: Ordered June 1976. *Ratcharit* launched 30 July 1978, *Witthayakhom* 2 September 1978 and *Udomdet* 28 September 1978.
Structure: Standard Breda BMB 230 design.

UDOMDET   *3/2004, Bob Fildes* / 0589809

3 PRABPARAPAK CLASS
(FAST ATTACK CRAFT—MISSILE) (PTFG)

Name	No	Builders	Commissioned
PRABPARAPAK	311 (ex-1)	Singapore SBEC	28 July 1976
HANHAK SATTRU	312 (ex-2)	Singapore SBEC	6 Nov 1976
SUPHAIRIN	313 (ex-3)	Singapore SBEC	1 Feb 1977

Displacement, tons: 224 standard; 268 full load
Dimensions, feet (metres): 149 × 24.3 × 7.5 *(45.4 × 7.4 × 2.3)*
Main machinery: 4 MTU 16V 538 TB92 diesels; 13,640 hp(m) *(10 MW)* sustained; 4 shafts
Speed, knots: 40. **Range, n miles:** 2,000 at 15 kt; 750 at 37 kt
Complement: 41 (5 officers)

Missiles: SSM: 5 IAI Gabriel I (1 triple, 2 single) launchers; radar or optical guidance; semi-active radar homing to 20 km *(10.8 n miles)* at 0.7 Mach; warhead 75 kg.
Guns: 1 Bofors 57 mm/70; 200 rds/min to 17 km *(9.3 n miles)*; weight of shell 2.4 kg.
8 rocket illuminant launchers on either side of 57 mm gun.
1 Bofors 40 mm/70; 300 rds/min to 12 km *(6.6 n miles)*; weight of shell 0.96 kg.
Countermeasures: ESM: Racal RDL-2; intercept.
Radars: Surface search: Kelvin Hughes Type 17; I-band.
Fire control: Signaal WM28/5 series; I/J-band.

Programmes: Ordered June 1973. Built under licence from Lürssen. Launch dates- *Prabparapak* 29 July 1975, *Hanhak Sattru* 28 October 1975, *Suphairin* 20 February 1976.
Modernisation: There are plans to replace Gabriel possibly by RBS 15.
Structure: Same design as Lürssen standard 45 m class built for Singapore. Normally only three Gabriel SSM are carried.

PRABPARAPAK   *6/2001, Royal Thai Navy* / 0130172

3 T 81 CLASS (COASTAL PATROL CRAFT) (PB)

T 81   T 82   T 83

Displacement, tons: 120 full load
Dimensions, feet (metres): 98.8 × 20.7 × 5.6 *(30.1 × 6.3 × 1.7)*
Main machinery: 2 MTU 16V 2000 TE90 diesels; 3,600 hp(m) *(2.56 MW)*; 2 shafts
Speed, knots: 25
Range, n miles: 1,300 at 15 kt
Complement: 28 (3 officers)
Guns: 1 Bofors 40 mm/70. 1 Oerlikon 20 mm. 2—12.7 mm MGs.
Radars: Surface search: Sperry SM 5000; I-band.

Comment: Ordered in October 1996 from ASC Silkline in Pranburi. First one commissioned 5 August 1999, second 9 December 1999 and the third in 2000. Plans for seven more have been shelved.

T 83   *3/2004, Bob Fildes* / 0589810

3 CHON BURI CLASS (FAST ATTACK CRAFT—GUN) (PG)

Name	No	Builders	Commissioned
CHON BURI	331 (ex-1)	CN Breda (Venezia) Mestre	22 Feb 1983
SONGKHLA	332 (ex-2)	CN Breda (Venezia) Mestre	15 July 1983
PHUKET	333 (ex-3)	CN Breda (Venezia) Mestre	13 Jan 1984

Displacement, tons: 450 full load
Dimensions, feet (metres): 198 × 29 × 15 *(60.4 × 8.8 × 4.5)*
Main machinery: 3 MTU 20V 538 TB92 diesels; 12,795 hp(m) *(9.4 MW)* sustained; 3 shafts; cp props
Speed, knots: 30. **Range, n miles:** 2,500 at 18 kt; 900 at 30 kt
Complement: 41 (6 officers)
Guns: 2 OTO Melara 3 in *(76 mm)*/62; 85 rds/min to 16 km *(8.7 n miles)*; weight of shell 6 kg.
2 Breda 40 mm/70 (twin).
Countermeasures: Decoys: 4 Hycor Mk 135 chaff launchers.
ESM: Elettronica Newton; intercept.
Weapons control: Signaal Lirod 8 optronic director.
Radars: Surface search: Signaal ZW06; I-band.
Fire control: Signaal WM22/61; I/J-band; range 46 km *(25 n miles)*.

Comment: Ordered in 1979 (first pair) and 1981. Laid down — *Chon Buri* 15 August 1981 (launched 29 November 1982), *Songkhla* 15 September 1981 (launched 6 September 1982), *Phuket* 15 December 1981 (launched 3 February 1983). Steel hulls, alloy superstructure. Can be adapted to carry SSMs.

PHUKET   *10/2001, Chris Sattler* / 0130157

CHON BURI   *9/2003, Hartmut Ehlers* / 0572642

6 SATTAHIP (PSMM MK 5) CLASS (LARGE PATROL CRAFT) (PG)

Name	No	Builders	Commissioned
SATTAHIP	521 (ex-4)	Ital Thai (Samutprakarn) Ltd	16 Sep 1983
KLONGYAI	522 (ex-5)	Ital Thai (Samutprakarn) Ltd	7 May 1984
TAKBAI	523 (ex-6)	Ital Thai (Samutprakarn) Ltd	18 July 1984
KANTANG	524 (ex-7)	Ital Thai (Samutprakarn) Ltd	14 Oct 1985
THEPHA	525 (ex-8)	Ital Thai (Samutprakarn) Ltd	17 Apr 1986
TAIMUANG	526 (ex-9)	Ital Thai (Samutprakarn) Ltd	17 Apr 1986

Displacement, tons: 270 standard; 300 full load
Dimensions, feet (metres): 164.5 × 23.9 × 5.9 *(50.1 × 7.3 × 1.8)*
Main machinery: 2 MTU 16V 538 TB92 diesels; 6,820 hp(m) *(5 MW)* sustained; 2 shafts
Speed, knots: 22. **Range, n miles:** 2,500 at 15 kt
Complement: 56
Guns: 1 OTO Melara 3 in *(76 mm)*/62 (in 521-523). 1 USN 3 in *(76 mm)*/50 Mk 26 (in 524-526). 1 Bofors 40 mm/70 or 40 mm/60. 2 Oerlikon 20 mm GAM-BO1. 2—12.7 mm MGs.
Weapons control: NA 18 optronic director (in 521-523).
Radars: Surface search: Decca; I-band.

Comment: First four ordered 9 September 1981, *Thepha* on 27 December 1983 and *Taimuang* on 31 August 1984.

TAKBAI   *10/1999, Royal Thai Navy* / 0080815

10 PGM 71 CLASS (COASTAL PATROL CRAFT) (PB)

T 11-19   T 110

Displacement, tons: 130 standard; 147 full load
Dimensions, feet (metres): 101 × 21 × 6 *(30.8 × 6.4 × 1.9)*
Main machinery: 2 GM diesels; 1,800 hp *(1.34 MW)*; 2 shafts
Speed, knots: 18.5. **Range, n miles:** 1,500 at 10 kt
Complement: 30
Guns: 1 Bofors 40 mm/60. 1 Oerlikon 20 mm. 2—12.7 mm MGs.
   In some craft the 20 mm gun has been replaced by an 81 mm mortar/12.7 mm combined
   mounting aft.
Radars: Surface search: Decca 303 *(T 11* and *12)* or Decca 202 (remainder); I-band.

Comment: Built by Peterson Inc between 1966 and 1970. Transferred from US. Some likely
   to be retained in service in view of curtailment of T 81 building programme.

T 16   *10/1999, Royal Thai Navy* / 0080816

9 T 91 CLASS (COASTAL PATROL CRAFT) (PB)

T 91-99

Displacement, tons: 87.5 *(T 91-92)*, 117 (remainder) standard
Dimensions, feet (metres): 103.4 × 17.6 × 4.9 *(31.5 × 5.4 × 1.5) (T 91-92)*
   111.6 × 18.7 × 4.9 *(34.0 × 5.7 × 1.5)* (remainder)
Main machinery: 2 MTU 12V 538 TB81/82 diesels; 3,300 hp(m) *(2.43 MW)*/4,430 hp(m)
   (3.26 MW) sustained; 2 shafts
Speed, knots: 25. **Range, n miles:** 700 at 21 kt
Complement: 21 *(T 91-92)*; 25 (remainder)
Guns: 2 or 1 Bofors 40 mm/60 *(T 91* and *T 99)*. 1 Oerlikon 20 mm GAM-BO1 *(T 91* and *T 99)*.
   2—12.7 mm MGs *(T 93-99)*.
Weapons control: Sea Archer 1A optronic director *(T 99* only).
Radars: Surface search: Raytheon SPS-35 (1500B); I-band.

Comment: Built by Royal Thai Naval Dockyard, Bangkok. *T 91* commissioned in 1965;
   T 92-93 in 1973; *T 94-98* between 1981 and 1984; *T 99* in 1987. *T 91* has an extended
   upperworks and a 20 mm gun in place of the after 40 mm. *T 99* has a single Bofors 40/70, one
   Oerlikon 20 mm and two MGs. Major refits from 1983-86 for earlier vessels of the class.

T 96   *10/2001, Chris Sattler* / 0130457

0 + 3 MODIFIED T 91 CLASS (COASTAL PATROL CRAFT) (PB)

991-993

Displacement, tons: 186 full load
Dimensions, feet (metres): 127.0 × 24.6 × 5.9 *(38.7 × 7.5 × 1.8)*
Main machinery: To be announced
Speed, knots: 25
Complement: To be announced
Guns: 2—30 mm. 2—12.7 mm MGs.
Weapons control: To be announced.
Radars: Surface search: To be announced.
Navigation: To be announced.

Comment: Modified versions of the T 91 class. First vessel laid down at Naval Dockyard
   on 9 September 2005. The second two are to be built by a commercial shipbuilder.
   All three boats to be delivered by December 2007.

MODIFIED T 91 CLASS   *9/2005*, Thai Navy League* / 1153912

3 SEA SPECTRE MK III CLASS (PB)

T 210-212

Displacement, tons: 28; 37 full load
Dimensions, feet (metres): 65.0 × 18.0 × 5.9 *(19.8 × 5.5 × 1.8)*
Main machinery: 3 Detroit diesels; 1,800 hp *(1.34 MW)*; 3 shafts
Speed, knots: 30
Range, n miles: 450 at 20 kt
Complement: 9 (1 officer)
Guns: 2 Oerlikon 20 mm. 1—12.7 MG.
Radars: Surface search: Raytheon; I-band.

Comment: Aluminium hulled craft built by Peterson. Transferred from the US in 1975.

9 SWIFT CLASS (COASTAL PATROL CRAFT) (PB)

T 21-29

Displacement, tons: 22 full load
Dimensions, feet (metres): 50 × 13 × 3.5 *(15.2 × 4 × 1.1)*
Main machinery: 2 Detroit diesels; 480 hp *(358 kW)*; 2 shafts
Speed, knots: 25
Range, n miles: 400 at 25 kt
Complement: 8 (1 officer)
Guns: 1—81 mm mortar. 2—12.7 mm MGs.
Radars: Surface search: Raytheon Pathfinder; I-band.

Comment: Transferred from US Navy from 1967-75.

T 26   *8/1998, P Marsan* / 0080818

13 T 213 CLASS (COASTAL PATROL CRAFT) (PB)

T 213-214   T 216-226

Displacement, tons: 35 standard
Dimensions, feet (metres): 64 × 17.5 × 5 *(19.5 × 5.3 × 1.5)*
Main machinery: 2 MTU diesels; 715 hp(m) *(526 kW)*; 2 shafts
Speed, knots: 25
Complement: 8 (1 officer)
Guns: 1 Oerlikon 20 mm. 1—81 mm mortar with 12.7 mm MG.
Radars: Surface search: Racal Decca 110; I-band.

Comment: Built by Ital Thai Marine Ltd. Commissioned-*T 213-214*, 29 August 1980;
   T 216-218, 26 March 1981; *T 219-223*, 16 September 1981; *T 224*, 19 November 1982; *T 225*
   and *T 226*, 28 March 1984. Construction of *T 227-230* is not to have been completed. Of
   alloy construction. Used for fishery patrol and coastal control duties. T 215 damaged
   beyond repair by tsunami on 26 December 2004.

T 219   *9/2003, Hartmut Ehlers* / 0572643

3 SEAL ASSAULT CRAFT (LCP)

Comment: Locally built for special forces operations. Details are not known but reported
   to be larger and faster than PBR Mk II craft. Equipped with stern ramp.

T 242 (SEAL)   *5/1997, A Sharma* / 0050242

13 PBR MK II (RIVER PATROL CRAFT) (PBR)

Displacement, tons: 8 full load
Dimensions, feet (metres): 32.1 × 11.5 × 2.3 *(9.8 × 3.5 × 0.7)*
Main machinery: 2 Detroit diesels; 430 hp *(321 kW)*; 2 Jacuzzi water-jets
Speed, knots: 25. **Range, n miles:** 150 at 23 kt
Complement: 4
Guns: 2 — 7.62 mm MGs. 1 — 60 mm mortar.
Radars: Surface search: Raytheon SPS-66; I-band.

Comment: Transferred from US from 1967-73. Employed on Mekong River. Reported to be getting old, numbers are reducing and maximum speed has been virtually halved. All belong to the Riverine and SEAL Squadron.

PBR MK II   *6/2002, Thai Navy League* / 0543390

90 ASSAULT BOATS (LCP)

Displacement, tons: 0.4 full load
Dimensions, feet (metres): 16.4 × 6.2 × 1.3 *(5 × 1.9 × 0.4)*
Main machinery: 1 outboard; 150 hp *(110 kW)*
Speed, knots: 24
Complement: 2
Guns: 1 — 7.62 mm MG.

Comment: Part of the Riverine Squadron with the PBRs and two PCFs. Can carry six people. Numbers uncertain.

ASSAULT BOAT   *6/2002, Thai Navy League* / 0530060

AMPHIBIOUS FORCES

Note: There are approximately 24 landing craft of about 100 tons operated by the Army.

2 NORMED CLASS (LSTH)

Name	No	Builders	Launched	Commissioned
SICHANG	721 (ex-LST 6)	Ital Thai	14 Apr 1987	9 Oct 1987
SURIN	722 (ex-LST 7)	Bangkok Dock Co Ltd	12 Apr 1988	16 Dec 1988

Displacement, tons: 3,540 standard; 4,235 full load
Dimensions, feet (metres): 337.8; 357.6 *(722)* × 51.5 × 11.5 *(103; 109 × 15.7 × 3.5)*
Main machinery: 2 MTU 20V 1163 TB82 diesels; 11,000 hp(m) *(8.1 MW)* sustained; 2 shafts; cp props
Speed, knots: 16. **Range, n miles:** 7,000 at 12 kt
Complement: 53
Military lift: 348 troops; 14 tanks or 12 APCs or 850 tons cargo; 3 LCVP; 1 LCPL
Guns: 2 Bofors 40 mm/70. 2 Oerlikon GAM-CO1 20 mm. 2 — 12.7 mm MGs. 1 — 81 mm mortar.
Weapons control: 2 BAe Sea Archer Mk 1A optronic directors.
Radars: Navigation: Racal Decca 1226; I-band.
Helicopters: Platform for 2 Bell 212.

Comment: First ordered 31 August 1984 to a Chantier du Nord (Normed) design. Second ordered to a modified design and lengthened to accommodate a battalion. The largest naval ships yet built in Thailand. Have bow doors and a 17 m ramp.

SURIN   *11/2001, Maritime Photographic* / 0130163

SICHANG   *2/2004, Bob Fildes* / 0589812

4 LST 512-1152 CLASS (LST)

Name	No	Builders	Commissioned
CHANG (ex-*Lincoln County* LST 898)	712 (ex-LST 2)	Dravo Corporation	29 Dec 1944
PANGAN (ex-*Stark County* LST 1134)	713 (ex-LST 3)	Chicago Bridge and Iron Co, ILL	7 Apr 1945
LANTA (ex-*Stone County* LST 1141)	714 (ex-LST 4)	Chicago Bridge and Iron Co, ILL	9 May 1945
PRATHONG (ex-*Dodge County* LST 722)	715 (ex-LST 5)	Jefferson B & M Co, Ind	13 Sep 1944

Displacement, tons: 1,650 standard; 3,640/4,145 full load
Dimensions, feet (metres): 328 × 50 × 14 *(100 × 15.2 × 4.4)*
Main machinery: 2 GM 12-567A diesels; 1,800 hp *(1.34 MW)*; 2 shafts
Speed, knots: 11.5. **Range, n miles:** 9,500 at 9 kt
Complement: 80; 157 (war)
Military lift: 1,230 tons max; 815 tons beaching
Guns: 1 — 3 in (76 mm).
  8 Bofors 40 mm/60 (2 twin, 4 single) (can be carried).
  2 — 12.7 mm MGs *(Chang)*. 2 Oerlikon 20 mm (others).
Weapons control: 2 Mk 51 GFCS. 2 optical systems.
Radars: Navigation: Racal Decca 1229; I/J-band.

Comment: *Chang* transferred from USA in August 1962. *Pangan* 16 May 1966, *Lanta* on 15 August 1973 (by sale 1 March 1979) and *Prathong* on 17 December 1975. *Chang* has a reinforced bow and waterline. *Lanta, Prathong* and *Chang* have mobile crane on the well-deck. All have tripod mast.

LANTA   *5/2002, Mick Prendergast* / 0530001

1 LSM 1 CLASS (LSM)

Name	No	Builders	Commissioned
KUT (ex-LSM 338)	731 (ex-LSM 1)	Pullman Std Car Co, Chicago	10 Jan 1945

Displacement, tons: 743 standard; 1,107 full load
Dimensions, feet (metres): 203.5 × 34.5 × 9.9 *(62 × 10.5 × 3)*
Main machinery: 2 Fairbanks-Morse 38D8-1/8-10 diesels; 3,540 hp *(2.64 MW)* sustained; 2 shafts
Speed, knots: 12.5. **Range, n miles:** 4,500 at 12.5 kt
Complement: 91 (6 officers)
Military lift: 452 tons beaching; 50 troops with vehicles
Guns: 2 Bofors 40 mm/60 Mk 3 (twin). 4 Oerlikon 20 mm/70.
Weapons control: Mk 51 Mod 2 optical director *(Kram)*.
Radars: Surface search: Raytheon SPS-5 *(Kram)*; G/H-band.
Navigation: Raytheon 1500 B; I-band.

Comment: Former US landing ship of the LCM, later LSM (Medium Landing Ship) type. Transferred in 1946. *Kram* reported sunk as a target in February 2003.

KUT   *6/1998, Royal Thai Navy* / 0050244

3 MAN NOK CLASS (LCU)

Name	No	Builders	Launched	Commissioned
MAN NOK	781	Sahai Sant, Pratum Thani	1 May 2001	6 Dec 2001
MAN KLANG	782	Sahai Sant, Pratum Thani	1 May 2001	14 Nov 2001
MAN NAI	783	Sahai Sant, Pratum Thani	1 May 2001	6 Dec 2001

Displacement, tons: 170 light; 550 full load
Dimensions, feet (metres): 172 × 36.7 × 5.9 *(52.4 × 11.2 × 1.8)*
Main machinery: 2 Caterpillar 3432 DITA diesels; 700 hp(m) *(515 kW)*; 2 shafts
Speed, knots: 12. **Range, n miles:** 1,500 at 10 kt
Complement: 30 (3 officers)
Military lift: 2 M60 tanks or 25 tons vehicles
Guns: 2 Oerlikon 20 mm.
Radars: Navigation: I-band.

Comment: Ordered from Silkline ASC in 1997. All three craft launched 1 May 2000.

MAN NAI   *5/2002, Mick Prendergast* / 0530000

2 LSIL 351 CLASS

PRAB 741 (ex-LSIL 1)   **SATAKUT** 742 (ex-LSIL 2)

Displacement, tons: 230 standard; 399 full load
Dimensions, feet (metres): 157 × 23 × 6 *(47.9 × 7 × 1.8)*
Main machinery: 4 GM diesels; 2,320 bhp *(1.73 MW)*; 2 shafts
Speed, knots: 15
Range, n miles: 5,600 at 12.5 kt
Complement: 49 (7 officers)
Military lift: 101 tons or 76 troops
Guns: 1 US 3 in *(76 mm)*/50. 1 Bofors 40 mm/60. 2 Oerlikon 20 mm/70.
Radars: Surface search: Raytheon SPS-35 (1500B); I-band.

Comment: *Prab* transferred to Thailand in October 1946. *Satakut* was refitted in the mid-1990s.

PRAB   *6/2005*, Thai Navy League* / 1153910

4 THONG KAEO CLASS (LCU)

Name	No	Builders	Commissioned
THONG KAEO	771 (ex-7)	Bangkok Dock Co Ltd	23 Dec 1982
THONG LANG	772 (ex-8)	Bangkok Dock Co Ltd	19 Apr 1983
WANG NOK	773 (ex-9)	Bangkok Dock Co Ltd	16 Sep 1983
WANG NAI	774 (ex-10)	Bangkok Dock Co Ltd	11 Nov 1983

Displacement, tons: 193 standard; 396 full load
Dimensions, feet (metres): 134.5 × 29.5 × 6.9 *(41 × 9 × 2.1)*
Main machinery: 2 GM 16V-71 diesels; 1,400 hp *(1.04 MW)*; 2 shafts
Speed, knots: 10
Range, n miles: 1,200 at 10 kt
Complement: 31 (3 officers)
Military lift: 3 lorries; 150 tons equipment
Guns: 2 Oerlikon 20 mm. 2—7.62 mm MGs.

Comment: Ordered in 1980.

WANG NAI   *5/1997, Maritime Photographic* / 0019276

6 MATAPHON CLASS (LCM/LCVP/LCP)

MATAPHON 761 (ex-LCU 1260)   **ADANG** 763 (ex-LCU 861)   **KOLAM** 765 (ex-LCU 904)
RAWI 762 (ex-LCU 800)   **PHETRA** 764 (ex-LCU 1089)   **TALIBONG** 766 (ex-LCU 753)

Displacement, tons: 145 standard; 330 full load
Dimensions, feet (metres): 120.4 × 32 × 4 *(36.7 × 9.8 × 1.2)*
Main machinery: 3 Gray Marine 65 diesels; 675 hp *(503 kW)*; 3 shafts
Speed, knots: 10
Range, n miles: 650 at 8 kt
Complement: 13
Military lift: 150 tons or 3-4 tanks or 250 troops
Guns: 4 Oerlikon 20 mm (2 twin).
Radars: Navigation: Raytheon Pathfinder; I-band.

Comment: Transferred from US 1946-47. Employed as transport ferries.

TALIBONG   *11/2001, Maritime Photographic* / 0130160

40 LANDING CRAFT (LCM/LCVP/LCA)

Displacement, tons: 56 full load
Dimensions, feet (metres): 56.1 × 14.1 × 3.9 *(17.1 × 4.3 × 1.2)*
Main machinery: 2 Gray Marine 64 HN9 diesels; 330 hp *(264 kW)*; 2 shafts
Speed, knots: 9
Range, n miles: 135 at 9 kt
Complement: 5
Military lift: 34 tons

Comment: Details given are for the 24 ex-US LCMs delivered in 1965-69. The 12 ex-US LCVPs can lift 40 troops and are of 1960s vintage. The four LCAs can lift 35 troops and were built in 1984 in Bangkok.

LCM 208   *11/1998, Thai Navy League* / 0050247

3 GRIFFON 1000 TD HOVERCRAFT (UCAC)

401-403

Dimensions, feet (metres): 27.6 × 12.5 *(8.4 × 3.8)*
Main machinery: 1 Deutz BF6L913C diesel; 190 hp(m) *(140 kW)*
Speed, knots: 33
Range, n miles: 200 at 27 kt
Complement: 2
Cargo capacity: 1,000 kg plus 9 troops
Radars: Navigation: Raytheon; I-band.

Comment: Acquired in mid-1990 from Griffon Hovercraft. Although having an obvious amphibious capability they are also used for rescue and flood control.

GRIFFON 401   *6/1999, Royal Thai Navy* / 0084413

MINE WARFARE FORCES

2 LAT YA (GAETA) CLASS
(MINEHUNTERS/SWEEPERS) (MHSC)

Name	No	Builders	Launched	Commissioned
LAT YA	633	Intermarine, Sarzana	30 Mar 1998	18 June 1999
THA DIN DAENG	634	Intermarine, Sarzana	31 Oct 1998	18 Dec 1999

Displacement, tons: 680 full load
Dimensions, feet (metres): 172.1 × 32.4 × 9.4 *(52.5 × 9.9 × 2.9)*
Main machinery: 2 MTU 8V 396 TE74K diesels; 1,600 hp(m) *(1.18 MW)* sustained; 2 Voith Schneider props; auxiliary propulsion; 2 hydraulic motors
Speed, knots: 14
Range, n miles: 2,000 at 12 kt
Complement: 50 (8 officers)
Guns: 1 MSI 30 mm.
Countermeasures: MCM: Atlas MWS 80-6 minehunting system. Magnetic, acoustic and mechanical sweeps; ADI Mini Dyad, Noise Maker, Bofors MS 106, 2 Pluto Plus ROVs.
Radars: Navigation: Atlas Elektronik 9600M (ARPA); I-band.
Sonars: Atlas Elektronik DSQS-11M; hull-mounted; active; high frequency.

Comment: Invitations to tender lodged by 3 April 1996. Ordered 19 September 1996. Specifications include hunting at up to 6 kt and sweeping at 10 kt. No further ships are planned.

THA DIN DAENG   *4/2004*, John Mortimer* / 1153909

1 MCM SUPPORT SHIP (MCS)

Name	No	Builders	Commissioned
THALANG	621 (ex-1)	Bangkok Dock Co Ltd	4 Aug 1980

Displacement, tons: 1,000 standard
Dimensions, feet (metres): 185.5 × 33 × 10 *(55.7 × 10 × 3.1)*
Main machinery: 2 MTU diesels; 1,310 hp(m) *(963 kW)*; 2 shafts
Speed, knots: 12
Complement: 77
Guns: 1 Bofors 40 mm/60. 2 Oerlikon 20 mm. 2 – 12.7 mm MGs.
Radars: Surface search: Racal Decca 1226; I-band.

Comment: Has minesweeping capability. Two 3 ton cranes provided for change of minesweeping gear in MSCs-four sets carried. Design by Ferrostaal, Essen. Has dormant minelaying capability.

THALANG *11/2001, Maritime Photographic* / 0130165

2 BANG RACHAN CLASS
(MINEHUNTERS/SWEEPERS) (MHSC)

Name	No	Builders	Commissioned
BANG RACHAN	631 (ex-2)	Lürssen Vegesack	29 Apr 1987
NONGSARAI	632 (ex-3)	Lürssen Vegesack	17 Nov 1987

Displacement, tons: 444 full load
Dimensions, feet (metres): 161.1 × 30.5 × 8.2 *(49.1 × 9.3 × 2.5)*
Main machinery: 2 MTU 12V 396 TB83 diesels; 3,120 hp(m) *(2.3 MW)* sustained; 2 shafts; Kamewa cp props; auxiliary propulsion; 1 motor
Speed, knots: 17; 7 (electric motor). **Range, n miles:** 3,100 at 12 kt
Complement: 33 (7 officers)
Guns: 3 Oerlikon GAM-BO1 20 mm.
Countermeasures: MCM: MWS 80R minehunting system. Acoustic, magnetic and mechanical sweeps. 2 Gaymarine Pluto 15 remote-controlled submersibles.
Radars: Navigation: 2 Atlas Elektronik 8600 ARPA; I-band.
Sonars: Atlas Elektronik DSQS-11H; hull-mounted; minehunting; high frequency.

Comment: First ordered from Lürssen late 1984, arrived Bangkok 22 October 1987. Second ordered 5 August 1985 and arrived in Bangkok May 1988. Amagnetic steel frames and deckhouses, wooden hull. Motorola Miniranger MRS III precise navigation system. Draeger decompression chamber. Plans to upgrade the sonar have not been confirmed.

NONGSARAI *2/2005*, Chris Sattler* / 1153911

2 BLUEBIRD CLASS (MINESWEEPERS — COASTAL) (MSC)

Name	No	Builders	Commissioned
BANGKEO (ex-MSC 303)	612 (ex-6)	Dorchester SB Corporation, Camden	9 July 1965
DONCHEDI (ex-MSC 313)	613 (ex-8)	Peterson Builders Inc, Sturgeon Bay, WI	17 Sep 1965

Displacement, tons: 317 standard; 384 full load
Dimensions, feet (metres): 145.3 × 27 × 8.5 *(44.3 × 8.2 × 2.6)*
Main machinery: 2 GM 8-268 diesels; 880 hp *(656 kW)*; 2 shafts
Speed, knots: 13. **Range, n miles:** 2,750 at 12 kt
Complement: 43 (7 officers)
Guns: 2 Oerlikon 20 mm/80 (twin).
Countermeasures: MCM: US Mk 4 (V). Mk 6. US Type Q2 magnetic.
Radars: Navigation: Decca TM 707; I-band.
Sonars: UQS-1; hull-mounted; minehunting; high frequency.

Comment: Constructed for Thailand. One paid off in 1992, one in 1995 and the last two are in limited operational service.

DONCHEDI *11/2001, Maritime Photographic* / 0130164

12 MSBs (MSR)

MLM 6-10	MSB 11-17

Displacement, tons: 25 full load
Dimensions, feet (metres): 50.2 × 13.1 × 3 *(15.3 × 4 × 0.9)*
Main machinery: 1 Gray Marine 64 HN9 diesel; 165 hp *(123 kW)*; 1 shaft
Speed, knots: 8
Complement: 10
Guns: 2 – 7.62 mm MGs.

Comment: Three transferred from USA in October 1963 and two in 1964. More were built locally from 1994. Wooden hulled, converted from small motor launches. Operated on Chao Phraya river.

MSB 11 *10/1995, Royal Thai Navy* / 0080822

SURVEY AND RESEARCH SHIPS

Notes: There is also a civilian research vessel *Chulab Horn* which completed in 1986.

0 + 1 SURVEY SHIP (AGSH)

Name	No	Builders	Laid down	Launched	Commissioned
—	—	Unithai Shipyard and Engineering, Laem Chambang	2006	2007	2008

Displacement, tons: To be announced
Dimensions, feet (metres): 217.5 × 50.2 × 10.2 *(66.3 × 13.2 × 3.1)*
Main machinery: Diesel-electric; 3 diesel generators; 2,652 hp(m) *(1.95 MW)*; 1 motor; 1,073 hp(m) *(800 kW)*; 2 azimuth thrusters; 1 bow thruster
Speed, knots: 12
Range, n miles: 3,000 at 12 kt
Complement: 13 (accommodation for 71)
Radars: Navigation: E/F- and I-band.
Sonars: Multi- and single-beam; high frequency; active.

Comment: Multipurpose hydrographic and oceanographic survey, training and mine countermeasures vessel ordered 22 December 2005 from a consortium comprising Schelde Naval Shipbuilding, Flushing, and Unithai Shipyard and Engineering, Thailand. The ship is to be a derivative of the Snellius class vessels built for the RNLN. The ships are to be built in Thailand. Hydrographic equipment is to include an exploration computer system; multibeam echosounder; single-beam echosounder; side-scan sonar; Ultra-Short BaseLine (USBL); Motion and Reference Unit (MRU); draught indication system; tidal measurement system; seawater collection system; seawater measurement system; expendable bathythermograph/sound velocity meter; current flow measurement system; current meter system; sediment collection system; and oceanography equipment.

1 OCEANOGRAPHIC SHIP (AGOR)

Name	No	Builders	Commissioned
SUK	812	Bangkok Dock Co Ltd	3 Mar 1982

Displacement, tons: 1,450 standard; 1,526 full load
Dimensions, feet (metres): 206.3 × 36.1 × 13.4 *(62.9 × 11 × 4.1)*
Main machinery: 2 MTU diesels; 2,400 hp(m) *(1.76 MW)*; 2 shafts
Speed, knots: 15
Complement: 86 (20 officers)
Guns: 2 Oerlikon 20 mm. 2 – 7.62 mm MGs.
Radars: Navigation: Racal Decca 1226; I-band.

Comment: Laid down 27 August 1979, launched 8 September 1981. Designed for oceanographic and survey duties.

SUK *5/1999, van Ginderen Collection* / 0080828

1 SURVEY SHIP (AGS)

Name	No	Builders	Commissioned
CHANTHARA	811 (ex-AGS 11)	Lürssen Werft	30 May 1961

Displacement, tons: 870 standard; 996 full load
Dimensions, feet (metres): 229.2 × 34.5 × 10
  (69.9 × 10.5 × 3)
Main machinery: 2 KHD diesels; 1,090 hp(m) *(801 kW)*; 2 shafts
Speed, knots: 13.25
Range, n miles: 10,000 at 10 kt
Complement: 68 (8 officers)
Guns: 2 Bofors 40 mm/60.

Comment: Laid down on 27 September 1960. Launched on
  17 December 1960. Has served as a Royal Yacht.

CHANTHARA
12/2001, Thai Navy League
0130158

TRAINING SHIPS

1 CANNON CLASS (FFT)

Name	No	Builders	Laid down	Launched	Commissioned
PIN KLAO (ex-*Hemminger* DE 746)	413 (ex-3, ex-1)	Western Pipe & Steel Co	1943	12 Sep 1943	30 May 1944

Displacement, tons: 1,240 standard; 1,930 full load
Dimensions, feet (metres): 306 × 36.7 × 14
  (93.3 × 11.2 × 4.3)
Main machinery: Diesel-electric; 4 GM 16-278A diesels;
  6,000 hp *(4.5 MW)*; 4 generators; 2 motors; 2 shafts
Speed, knots: 20
Range, n miles: 10,800 at 12 kt; 6,700 at 19 kt
Complement: 192 (14 officers)

Guns: 3 USN 3 in *(76 mm)*/50 Mk 22; 20 rds/min to 12 km
  (6.6 n miles); weight of shell 6 kg.
  6 Bofors 40 mm/60 (3 twin); 120 rds/min to 10 km
  (5.5 n miles); weight of shell 0.89 kg.

Torpedoes: 6—324 mm US Mk 32 (2 triple) tubes; anti-
  submarine.
A/S mortars: 1 Hedgehog Mk 10 multibarrelled fixed; range
  250 m; warhead 13.6 kg; 24 rockets.
Depth charges: 8 projectors; 2 racks.
Countermeasures: ESM: WLR-1; radar warning.
Weapons control: Mk 52 radar GFCS for 3 in guns. Mk 63
  radar GFCS for aft gun only. 2 Mk 51 optical GFCS for
  40 mm.
Radars: Air/surface search: Raytheon SPS-5; G/H-band
  Navigation: Raytheon SPS-21; G/H-band
  Fire control: Western Electric Mk 34; I/J-band
    RCA/General Electric Mk 26; I/J-band

IFF: SLR 1.
Sonars: SQS-11; hull-mounted; active attack; high frequency.

Programmes: Transferred from US Navy at New York
  Navy Shipyard in July 1959 under MDAP and by sale
  6 June 1975.
Modernisation: The three 21 in torpedo tubes were removed
  and the 20 mm guns were replaced by 40 mm. The six
  A/S torpedo tubes were fitted in 1966.
Operational: Used mostly as a training ship.

PIN KLAO   *6/1997, Royal Thai Navy* / 0019254

1 ALGERINE CLASS (AXL)

Name	No	Builders	Commissioned
PHOSAMTON (ex-*Minstrel*)	611 (ex-415, ex-MSF 1)	Redfern Construction Co	9 June 1945

Displacement, tons: 1,040 standard; 1,335 full load
Dimensions, feet (metres): 225 × 35.5 × 11.5 *(68.6 × 10.8 × 3.5)*
Main machinery: 2 boilers; 2 reciprocating engines; 2,000 ihp
  (1.49 MW); 2 shafts
Speed, knots: 16
Range, n miles: 4,000 at 10 kt
Complement: 103
Guns: 1 USN 3 in *(76 mm)*/50. 1 Bofors 40 mm/60.
  4 Oerlikon 20 mm.
Radars: Navigation: Raytheon Pathfinder; I-band.

Comment: Transferred from UK in April 1947. Received
  engineering overhaul in 1984. Minesweeping gear
  replaced by a deckhouse to increase training space.
  Vickers 4 in gun replaced.

PHOSAMTON
8/2002, John Mortimer
0529999

AUXILIARIES

1 SIMILAN (HUDONG) CLASS (TYPE R22T)
(REPLENISHMENT SHIP) (AORH)

Name	No	Builders	Launched	Commissioned
SIMILAN	871	Hudong Shipyard, Shanghai	9 Nov 1995	12 Sep 1996

Displacement, tons: 23,000 full load
Dimensions, feet (metres): 562.3 × 80.7 × 29.5 *(171.4 × 24.6 × 9)*
Main machinery: 2 HD-SEMT-Pielstick 16 PC2 6V400; 24,000 hp(m) *(17.64 MW)*; 2 shafts; Kamewa cp props
Speed, knots: 19
Range, n miles: 10,000 at 15 kt
Complement: 157 (19 officers) plus 26
Cargo capacity: 9,000 tons fuel, water, ammunition and stores
Radars: Air/surface search: Eye Shield (Type 354); E/F-band.
Navigation: Racal Decca 1290 ARPA; I-band.
Helicopters: 1 Seahawk type.

Comment: Contract signed with China State Shipbuilding Corporation on 29 September 1993. Fabrication started in December 1994. Two replenishment at sea positions each side and facilities for Vertrep. This ship complements the carrier and the new frigates to give the Navy a full deployment capability. Four twin 37 mm guns (Type 354) and associated Rice Lamp FC radar were not fitted.

SIMILAN   *10/1998, Thai Navy League* / 0050248

1 REPLENISHMENT TANKER (AORL)

Name	No	Builders	Commissioned
CHULA	831 (ex-2)	Singapore SEC	24 Sep 1980

Displacement, tons: 2,000 full load
Measurement, tons: 960 dwt
Dimensions, feet (metres): 219.8 × 31.2 × 14.4 *(67 × 9.5 × 4.4)*
Main machinery: 2 MTU 12V 396 TC62 diesels; 2,400 hp(m) *(1.76 MW)* sustained; 2 shafts
Speed, knots: 14
Complement: 39 (7 officers)
Cargo capacity: 800 tons oil fuel
Guns: 2 Oerlikon 20 mm.
Radars: Navigation: Racal Decca 1226; I-band.

Comment: Replenishment is done by a hose handling crane boom.

CHULA   *6/1998, Royal Thai Navy* / 0050249

4 HARBOUR TANKERS (YO)

PRONG 833 (ex-YO 5) **PROET** 834 (ex-YO 9) **SAMED** 835 (ex-YO 10) **CHIK** 842 (ex-YO 11)

Displacement, tons: 360 standard; 485 full load
Dimensions, feet (metres): 122.7 × 19.7 × 8.7 *(37.4 × 6 × 2.7)*
Main machinery: 1 GM 8-268A diesel; 500 hp(m) *(368 kW)*; 1 shaft
Speed, knots: 9
Cargo capacity: 210 tons

Comment: Details are for 834, 835 and 842. Built by Bangkok Naval Dockyard. 834 commissioned 27 January 1967, remainder the same year. Details of 833 not known but reported to be approximately 180 tons.

SAMED   *5/1999* / 0080829

1 HARBOUR TANKER (YO)

SAMUI 832 (ex-YOG 60, ex-YO 4)

Displacement, tons: 1,420 full load
Dimensions, feet (metres): 174.5 × 32 × 15 *(53.2 × 9.7 × 4.6)*
Main machinery: 1 Union diesel; 600 hp *(448 kW)*; 1 shaft
Speed, knots: 8
Complement: 29
Cargo capacity: 985 tons fuel
Guns: 2 Oerlikon 20 mm can be carried.
Radars: Navigation: Raytheon Pathfinder; I-band

SAMUI   *12/1995* / 0506255

1 WATER TANKER (YW)

Name	No	Builders	Commissioned
CHUANG	841 (ex-YW 5)	Royal Thai Naval Dockyard, Bangkok	1965

Displacement, tons: 305 standard; 485 full load
Dimensions, feet (metres): 136 × 24.6 × 10 *(42 × 7.5 × 3.1)*
Main machinery: 1 GM diesel; 500 hp *(373 kW)*; 1 shaft
Speed, knots: 11
Complement: 29
Guns: 1 Oerlikon 20 mm.

Comment: Launched on 14 January 1965.

CHUANG (alongside Proet)   *5/1997, Maritime Photographic* / 0019284

1 TRANSPORT SHIP (AKS)

Name	No	Builders	Commissioned
KLED KEO	861 (ex-AF-7)	Norfjord, Norway	1948

Displacement, tons: 450 full load
Dimensions, feet (metres): 150.1 × 24.9 × 14 *(46 × 7.6 × 4.3)*
Main machinery: 1 CAT diesel; 900 hp(m) *(662 kW)*; 1 shaft
Speed, knots: 12
Complement: 54 (7 officers)
Guns: 3 Oerlikon 20 mm.

Comment: Former Norwegian transport acquired in 1956. Paid off in 1990 but back in service in 1997. Operates with the patrol boat squadron.

KLED KEO   *6/1998, Royal Thai Navy* / 0050250

1 BUOY TENDER (ABU)

Name	No	Builders	Commissioned
SURIYA	821	Bangkok Dock Co Ltd	15 Mar 1979

Displacement, tons: 690 full load
Dimensions, feet (metres): 177.8 × 33.5 × 10.2 *(54.2 × 10.2 × 3.1)*
Main machinery: 2 MTU diesels; 1,310 hp(m) *(963 kW)*; 2 shafts; bow thruster; 135 hp(m) *(99 kW)*
Speed, knots: 12
Complement: 60 (12 officers)
Radars: Navigation: Racal Decca; I-band.

Comment: Can carry 20 mm guns.

SURIYA *11/2001, Maritime Photographic* / 0130167

TUGS

2 COASTAL TUGS (YTB)

RIN 853 (ex-ATA 5)   RANG 854 (ex-ATA 6)

Displacement, tons: 350 standard
Dimensions, feet (metres): 106 × 29.7 × 15.2 *(32.3 × 9 × 4.6)*
Main machinery: 1 MWM TBD441V/12K diesel; 2,100 hp(m) *(1.54 MW)*; 1 shaft
Speed, knots: 12. **Range, n miles:** 1,000 at 10 kt
Complement: 19

Comment: Launched 12 and 14 June 1980 at Singapore Marine Shipyard. Both commissioned 5 March 1981. Bollard pull 22 tons.

RANG *1992, Royal Thai Navy* / 0080830

2 SAMAESAN CLASS (COASTAL TUGS) (YTR)

SAMAESAN 855   RAET 856

Displacement, tons: 300 standard
Dimensions, feet (metres): 82 × 27.9 × 7.9 *(25 × 8.5 × 2.4)*
Main machinery: 2 Caterpillar 3512TA diesels; 2,350 hp(m) *(1.75 MW)* sustained; 2 Aquamaster US 901 props
Speed, knots: 10
Complement: 6

Comment: Contract signed 23 September 1992 for local construction at Thonburi Naval dockyard. Completed in December 1993. Equipped for firefighting.

RAET *5/1997, A Sharma* / 0050251

2 YTL 422 CLASS (YTL)

KLUENG BADAAN 851 (ex-YTL 2)   MARN VICHAI 852 (ex-YTL 3)

Displacement, tons: 63 standard
Dimensions, feet (metres): 64.7 × 16.5 × 6 *(19.7 × 5 × 1.8)*
Main machinery: 1 diesel; 240 hp *(179 kW)*; 1 shaft
Speed, knots: 8

Comment: Built by Central Bridge Co, Trenton and bought from Canada 1953.

KLUENG BADAAN *11/2001, Maritime Photographic* / 0130166

POLICE

Notes: (1) There is also a Customs service, subordinate to the Marine Police, which operates unarmed patrol craft with CUSTOMS on the hull, and a Fishery Patrol Service also unarmed but vessels are painted blue with broad white and narrow gold diagonal stripes on the hull. Two Hydrofoil craft are on loan from the Police to the Customs service.
(2) There are large numbers of RIBs in service.

1 VOSPER THORNYCROFT TYPE (LARGE PATROL CRAFT) (PSO)

SRINAKARIN 1804

Displacement, tons: 630 full load
Dimensions, feet (metres): 203.4 × 26.9 × 8.2 *(62 × 8.2 × 2.5)*
Main machinery: 2 Deutz MWM BV16M628 diesels; 9,524 hp(m) *(7 MW)* sustained; 2 shafts; Kamewa cp props
Speed, knots: 25
Range, n miles: 2,500 at 15 kt
Complement: 45
Guns: 4—30 mm (2 twin).
Radars: Surface search: Racal Decca 1226; I-band.

Comment: Ordered in September 1989 from ItalThai Marine. Same hull as the Khamronsin class corvettes for the Navy but much more lightly armed. Delivered in April 1992.

SRINAKARIN *6/2003, Royal Thai Navy* / 0572648

2 HAMELN TYPE (LARGE PATROL CRAFT) (PBO)

DAMRONG RACHANUPHAP 1802   LOPBURI RAMES 1803

Displacement, tons: 430 full load
Dimensions, feet (metres): 186 × 26.6 × 8 *(56.7 × 8.1 × 2.4)*
Main machinery: 4 MTU diesels; 4,400 hp(m) *(3.23 MW)*; 2 shafts
Speed, knots: 23
Complement: 45
Guns: 2 Oerlikon 30 mm/75 (twin). 2 Oerlikon 20 mm.
Radars: Surface search: Racal Decca 1226; I-band.

Comment: Delivered by Schiffwerft Hameln, Germany, on 3 January 1969 and 10 December 1972 respectively.

LOPBURI RAMES *6/2003, Royal Thai Navy* / 0572647

2 SUMIDAGAWA TYPE (COASTAL PATROL CRAFT) (PB)

CHASANYABADEE 1101   PHROMYOTHEE 1103

Displacement, tons: 130 full load
Dimensions, feet (metres): 111.5 × 19 × 9.1 *(34 × 5.8 × 2.8)*
Main machinery: 3 Ikegai diesels; 4,050 hp(m) *(2.98 MW)*; 3 shafts
Speed, knots: 32
Complement: 23
Guns: 2—12.7 mm MGs.
Radars: Surface search: Racal Decca; I-band.

Comment: Commissioned in August 1972 and May 1973 respectively.

PHROMYOTHEE   *1990, Marine Police* / 0080833

1 YOKOHAMA TYPE (COASTAL PATROL CRAFT) (PB)

CHAWENGSAK SONGKRAM 1102

Displacement, tons: 190 full load
Dimensions, feet (metres): 116.5 × 23 × 11.5 *(35.5 × 7 × 3.5)*
Main machinery: 4 Ikegai diesels; 5,400 hp(m) *(3.79 MW)*; 2 shafts
Speed, knots: 32
Complement: 18
Guns: 2 Oerlikon 20 mm.

Comment: Commissioned 13 April 1973. A second of class operates for the Customs with the number 1201.

CHAWENGSAK SONGKRAM   *1990, Marine Police* / 0080834

1 ITAL THAI MARINE TYPE (COASTAL PATROL CRAFT) (PB)

SRIYANONT 901

Displacement, tons: 52 full load
Dimensions, feet (metres): 90 × 16 × 6.5 *(27.4 × 4.9 × 2)*
Main machinery: 2 Deutz BA16M816 diesels; 2,680 hp(m) *(1.97 MW)* sustained; 2 shafts
Speed, knots: 23
Complement: 14
Guns: 1 Oerlikon 20 mm. 2—7.62 mm MGs.
Radars: Surface search: Racal Decca; I-band.

Comment: Commissioned 12 June 1986.

SRIYANONT   *12/2001, Thai Navy League* / 0130155

1 BURESPADOONGKIT CLASS (COASTAL PATROL CRAFT) (PB)

BURESPADOONGKIT 813

Displacement, tons: 65 full load
Dimensions, feet (metres): 80.5 × 19.4 × 6 *(24.5 × 5.9 × 1.8)*
Main machinery: 2 SACM UD 23 V12 M5D diesels; 2,534 hp(m) *(1.86 MW)* sustained; 2 shafts
Speed, knots: 28. **Range, n miles:** 650 at 20 kt
Complement: 14
Guns: 1 Oerlikon GAM-CO1 20 mm; 2—7.62 mm MGs.

Comment: Built by Matsun, Thailand and commissioned 9 August 1995. Badly damaged in the Tsunami of 26 December 2004.

BURESPADOONGKIT   *6/1999, Marine Police* / 0080835

3 CUTLASS CLASS (COASTAL PATROL CRAFT) (PB)

PHRAONGKAMROP 807   PICHARNPHOLAKIT 808   RAMINTHRA 809

Displacement, tons: 34 full load
Dimensions, feet (metres): 65 × 17 × 8.3 *(19.8 × 5.2 × 2.5)*
Main machinery: 3 Detroit 12V-71TA diesels; 1,020 hp(m) *(761 kW)* sustained; 3 shafts
Speed, knots: 25
Complement: 14
Guns: 1 Oerlikon 20 mm. 2—7.62 mm MGs.

Comment: Delivered by Halter Marine, New Orleans, and all commissioned on 9 March 1969. Aluminium hulls.

PICHARNPHOLAKIT   *6/1999* / 0080836

3 TECHNAUTIC TYPE (COASTAL PATROL CRAFT) (PB)

810-812

Displacement, tons: 50 full load
Dimensions, feet (metres): 88.6 × 19.4 × 6.2 *(27 × 5.9 × 1.9)*
Main machinery: 3 Isotta Fraschini diesels; 2,500 hp(m) *(1.84 MW)*; 3 Castoldi hydrojets
Speed, knots: 27
Complement: 14
Guns: 1 Oerlikon 20 mm GAM-BO1. 2—7.62 mm MGs.

Comment: Delivered by Technautic, Bangkok in 1984.

812   *1990, Marine Police* / 0080837

5 ITAL THAI MARINE TYPE (COASTAL PATROL CRAFT) (PB)

625-629

Displacement, tons: 42 full load
Dimensions, feet (metres): 64 × 17.5 × 5 *(19.5 × 5.3 × 1.5)*
Main machinery: 2 MAN D2842LE diesels; 1,350 hp(m) *(992 kW)* sustained; 2 shafts
Speed, knots: 27
Complement: 14
Guns: 1—12.7 mm MG.

Comment: Built in Bangkok 1987-90. Aluminium hulls. More of the class operated by the Fishery Patrol Service.

ITAL THAI 626   *3/2004, Bob Fildes* / 0589814

8 MARSUN TYPE (COASTAL PATROL CRAFT) (PB)

630-637

Displacement, tons: 38 full load
Dimensions, feet (metres): 65.6 × 18.2 × 5 *(20 × 5.6 × 1.5)*
Main machinery: 2 MAN D2840LXE diesels; 1,640 hp(m) *(1.2 MW)* sustained; 2 shafts
Speed, knots: 25
Complement: 11
Guns: 1 — 12.7 mm MG.

Comment: Built by Marsun, Thailand and commissioned from 2 August 1994.

MARSUN 634   *3/2004, Bob Fildes* / 0589815

17 TECHNAUTIC TYPE (COASTAL PATROL CRAFT) (PB)

608-624

Displacement, tons: 30 full load
Dimensions, feet (metres): 60 × 16 × 2.9 *(18.3 × 4.9 × 0.9)*
Main machinery: 2 Isotta Fraschini ID 36 SS 8V diesels; 1,760 hp(m) *(1.29 MW)* sustained; 2 Castoldi hydrojets
Speed, knots: 27
Complement: 11
Guns: 1 — 12.7 mm MG.

Comment: Built from 1983 — 87 in Bangkok. Operational status of some of these craft doubtful.

TECHNAUTIC 609   *11/2001, Maritime Photographic* / 0130168

2 MARSUN TYPE (PB)

539-540

Displacement, tons: 30 full load
Dimensions, feet (metres): 57 × 16 × 3 *(17.4 × 4.9 × 0.9)*
Main machinery: 2 Detroit 12V-71TA diesels; 840 hp *(627 kW)* sustained; 2 shafts
Speed, knots: 25
Complement: 8
Guns: 1 — 12.7 mm MG.

Comment: Built in Thailand. Both commissioned 26 March 1986.

MARSUN 539   *11/2001, Maritime Photographic* / 0130169

38 RIVER PATROL BOATS (PBR)

301-338

Displacement, tons: 5 full load
Dimensions, feet (metres): 37.1 × 11.1 × 2.3 *(11.3 × 3.4 × 0.7)*
Main machinery: 2 diesels; 2 shafts
Speed, knots: 25

26 SUMIDAGAWA TYPE (RIVER PATROL CRAFT) (PBR)

513-538

Displacement, tons: 18 full load
Dimensions, feet (metres): 54.1 × 12.5 × 2.3 *(16.5 × 3.8 × 0.7)*
Main machinery: 2 Cummins diesels; 800 hp *(597 kW)*; 2 shafts
Speed, knots: 23
Complement: 6
Guns: 1 — 12.7 mm MG.

Comment: First 21 built by Sumidagawa, last five by Captain Co, Thailand 1978-79.

SUMIDAGAWA 529   *6/1999, Marine Police* / 0080841

SUMIDAGAWA 526   *6/2003, Royal Thai Navy* / 0572646

20 CAMCRAFT TYPE (RIVER PATROL CRAFT) (PBR)

415-440 series

Displacement, tons: 13 full load
Dimensions, feet (metres): 40 × 12 × 3.2 *(12.2 × 3.7 × 1)*
Main machinery: 2 Detroit diesels; 540 hp *(403 kW)*; 2 shafts
Speed, knots: 25
Complement: 6

Comment: Delivered by Camcraft, Louisiana. Aluminium hulls. Numbers uncertain.

CAMCRAFT 435   *6/1999, Marine Police* / 0080842

1 RIVER PATROL CRAFT (PBR)

339

Displacement, tons: 5 full load
Dimensions, feet (metres): 37 × 11 × 6 *(11.3 × 3.4 × 1.8)*
Main machinery: 2 diesels; 2 shafts
Speed, knots: 25
Complement: 4

Comment: Built in 1990.

RIVER PATROL CRAFT 339 (alongside Technautic 609)   *7/2000* / 0106613

Togo

Country Overview

Formerly French Togoland, the Togolese Republic gained full independence in 1960 having rejected proposals to be united with Ghana. Situated in west Africa, it has an area of 21,925 square miles and borders to the east with Benin and to the west with Ghana. Togo has a short coastline of 30 n miles with the Gulf of Guinea. Lomé is the capital, largest town and principal port. Togo is the only coastal state to claim territorial seas of 30 n miles. A 200 n mile Exclusive Economic Zone (EEZ) is also claimed but this has not been defined by boundary agreements.

Headquarters Appointments

Commanding Officer, Navy:
Commander Lucien Laval

Personnel

(a)   2006: 120
(b)   Conscription (2 years)

Bases

Lomé

PATROL FORCES

2 COASTAL PATROL CRAFT (PB)

Name	No	Builders	Commissioned
KARA	P 761	Chantiers Navals de l'Esterel, Cannes	18 May 1976
MONO	P 762	Chantiers Navals de l'Esterel, Cannes	16 June 1976

Displacement, tons: 80 full load
Dimensions, feet (metres): 105 × 19 × 5.3 *(32 × 5.8 × 1.6)*
Main machinery: 2 MTU MB 12V 493 TY60 diesels; 2,000 hp(m) *(1.47 MW)* sustained; 2 shafts
Speed, knots: 30. **Range, n miles:** 1,500 at 15 kt
Complement: 17 (1 officer)
Missiles: SSM: Aerospatiale SS 12M; wire-guided to 5 km *(3 n miles)* subsonic; warhead 30 kg.
Guns: 1 Bofors 40 mm/70. 1 Oerlikon 20 mm.
Radars: Surface search: Decca 916; I-band.

Comment: Both craft operational.

MONO   *6/1998* / 0050252

Tonga

Country Overview

A former British protectorate, the Kingdom of Tonga became a sovereign state in 1970. Situated in the southwestern Pacific Ocean some 1,080 n miles northeast of New Zealand, the country consists of more than 170 islands and islets running generally north-south. There are three main groups, Tongatapu, Ha'apai and Vava'u, and several outlying islands. Nuku'alofa, on Tongatapu Island, is the capital, largest town and principal port. Territorial seas (12 n miles) are claimed. An Exclusive Economic Zone (EEZ) (200 n miles) is claimed but limits have not been fully defined by boundary agreements.

Headquarters Appointments

Commanding Officer, Navy:
Lieutenant Commander Sione Fifita

Personnel

2006: 115

Bases

Touliki Base, Nuku'alofa (HMNB *Masefield*)

Prefix to Ships' Names

VOEA (Vaka O Ene Afio)

PATROL FORCES

Notes: A Beech 18 aircraft was acquired in May 1995 for maritime surveillance.

3 PACIFIC CLASS (LARGE PATROL CRAFT) (PB)

Name	No	Builders	Commissioned
NEIAFU	P 201	Australian Shipbuilding Industries	28 Oct 1989
PANGAI	P 202	Australian Shipbuilding Industries	30 June 1990
SAVEA	P 203	Australian Shipbuilding Industries	23 Mar 1991

Displacement, tons: 162 full load
Dimensions, feet (metres): 103.3 × 26.6 × 6.9 *(31.5 × 8.1 × 2.1)*
Main machinery: 2 Caterpillar 3516TA diesels; 2,820 hp *(2.1 MW)* sustained; 2 shafts
Speed, knots: 20
Range, n miles: 2,500 at 12 kt
Complement: 17 (3 officers)
Guns: 2 – 12.7 mm MGs.
Radars: Surface search: Furuno 1101; I-band.

Comment: Part of the Pacific Forum Australia Defence co-operation. First laid down 30 January 1989, second 2 October 1989, third February 1990. *Savea* has a hydrographic survey capability. Following half-life refits 1998-99 and the decision of the Australian government to extend the Pacific Patrol Boat programme, *Neiafu, Pangai* and *Savea* will be due life-extension refits in 2007, 2008 and 2008 respectively.

PANGAI   *2/2003, Chris Sattler* / 0558665

AUXILIARIES

1 LCM

Name	No	Builders	Commissioned
LATE (ex-1057)	C 315	North Queensland, Cairns	1 Sep 1982

Displacement, tons: 116 full load
Dimensions, feet (metres): 73.5 × 21 × 3.3 *(22.4 × 6.4 × 1)*
Main machinery: 2 Detroit 12V-71 diesels; 680 hp *(507 kW)* sustained; 2 shafts
Speed, knots: 10
Range, n miles: 480 at 10 kt
Complement: 5
Cargo capacity: 54 tons
Guns: 1 – 7.62 mm MG can be carried.
Radars: Surface search: Koden MD 305; I-band.

Comment: Acquired from the Australian Army for inter-island transport.

LATE
6/1999, Tongan Navy
0084414

Trinidad and Tobago

Country Overview

Trinidad and Tobago gained independence in 1962 and became a republic in 1976. The country lies at the southern end of the Lesser Antilles chain and comprises the main islands of Trinidad (1,864 square miles), Tobago (116 square miles) and 21 minor islands and rocks. Trinidad is close to the northeastern coast of Venezuela and the mouth of the Orinoco River. The capital, largest town, and principal port is Port-of-Spain, Trinidad. An archipelagic state, territorial seas (12 n miles) are claimed.

While a 200 n mile Exclusive Economic Zone (EEZ) has been claimed, the limits have only been partly defined by boundary agreements.

Headquarters Appointments

Commanding Officer, Coast Guard:
Captain Garnet Best

Aircraft

The Coast Guard operates three Cessna (Types 172, 402B and 310R) for surveillance and two C26B acquired in 1999. These aircraft can be backed by Air Division Gazelle and Sikorsky S-76 helicopters when necessary.

Personnel

(a) 2006: 650 (55 officers)
(b) Voluntary service

Bases

Staubles Bay (HQ)
Hart's Cut, Tobago, Point Fortin (all from 1989)

Piarco (Air station), Cedros (from 1992)
Galeota (from 1995)

Coast Defence

There are plans to install a coastal radar system.

Prefix to Ships' Names

TTS

COAST GUARD

Notes: The 2003 Budget first announced plans to acquire new offshore patrol vessels. Following a request for proposals in December 2004, bids for the design, build and support of three new 80 m offshore patrol vessels were submitted in March 2005. The new ships are to be capable of operating a helicopter and of embarking a 10 m fast intercept craft for interdiction operations. The rival bids are believed to include a derivative of the MEKO 100 OPV design (Blohm+Voss), a derivative of the Cigala Fulgosi class (Fincantieri) and a variant of the River class (VT Shipbuilding). The ships are expected to enter service from 2008.

1 ISLAND CLASS (PBO)

Name	No	Builders	Commissioned
NELSON (ex-*Orkney*)	CG 20 (ex-P 299)	Hall Russell	25 Feb 1977

Displacement, tons: 925 standard; 1,260 full load
Dimensions, feet (metres): 176 wl; 195.3 oa × 36 × 15 *(53.7; 59.5 × 11 × 4.5)*
Main machinery: 2 Ruston 12RKC diesels; 5,640 hp *(4.21 MW)* sustained; 1 shaft; cp prop
Speed, knots: 16.5. **Range, n miles:** 7,000 at 12 kt
Complement: 35 (5 officers)
Guns: 2—7.62 mm MGs can be carried.
Radars: Navigation: Kelvin Hughes Type 1006; I-band.

Comment: Transferred from the UK Navy on 18 December 2000 and recommissioned on 22 February 2001. Based at Port of Spain.

NELSON *1/2001, H M Steele* / 0106616

2 TYPE CG 40 (LARGE PATROL CRAFT) (PB)

Name	No	Builders	Commissioned
BARRACUDA	CG 5	Karlskronavarvet	15 June 1980
CASCADURA	CG 6	Karlskronavarvet	15 June 1980

Displacement, tons: 210 full load
Dimensions, feet (metres): 133.2 × 21.9 × 5.2 *(40.6 × 6.7 × 1.6)*
Main machinery: 2 Paxman Valenta 16CM diesels; 6,700 hp *(5 MW)* sustained; 2 shafts
Speed, knots: 30
Range, n miles: 3,000 at 15 kt
Complement: 25
Guns: 1 Bofors 40 mm/70. 1 Oerlikon 20 mm.
Weapons control: Optronic GFCS.
Radars: Surface search: Racal Decca 1226; I-band.

Comment: Ordered in Sweden mid-1978. Laid down early 1979. Fitted with foam-cannon oil pollution equipment and for oceanographic and hydrographic work. Nine spare berths. The hull is similar to Swedish Spica class but with the bridge amidships. One refitted in 1988, the other in 1989. *Cascadura* refitted again in 1998/99.

CASCADURA *1/1994, Maritime Photographic* / 0506207

4 POINT CLASS (COASTAL PATROL CRAFT) (PB)

Name	No	Builders	Commissioned
COROZAL POINT (ex-*Point Heyer*)	CG 7 (ex-82369)	J Martinac, Tacoma	3 Aug 1967
CROWN POINT (ex-*Point Bennett*)	CG 8 (ex-82351)	Coast Guard Yard, Curtis Bay	19 Dec 1966
GALERA POINT (ex-*Point Bonita*)	CG 9 (ex-82347)	J Martinac, Tacoma	12 Sep 1966
BARCOLET POINT (ex-*Point Highland*)	CG 10 (ex-82333)	Coast Guard Yard, Curtis Bay	27 June 1962

Displacement, tons: 66 full load
Dimensions, feet (metres): 83 × 17.2 × 5.8 *(25.3 × 5.2 × 1.8)*
Main machinery: 2 Caterpillar 3412 diesels; 1,600 hp *(1.19 MW)*; 2 shafts
Speed, knots: 23
Range, n miles: 1,500 at 8 kt
Complement: 10
Guns: 2—7.62 mm MGs.
Radars: Surface search: Raytheon SPS-64(V)I and Raytheon SPS 69AN; I-band.

Comment: CG 7 and CG 8 transferred from US Coast Guard 12 February 1999 and CG 9 on 14 November 2000. CG 10 transferred on 24 July 2001.

CROWN POINT *6/1999, Trinidad and Tobago Coast Guard* / 0080846

4 SOUTER WASP 17 METRE CLASS (COASTAL PATROL CRAFT) (PB)

Name	No	Builders	Commissioned
PLYMOUTH	CG 27	WA Souter, Cowes	27 Aug 1982
CARONI	CG 28	WA Souter, Cowes	27 Aug 1982
GALEOTA	CG 29	WA Souter, Cowes	27 Aug 1982
MORUGA	CG 30	WA Souter, Cowes	27 Aug 1982

Displacement, tons: 20 full load
Dimensions, feet (metres): 55.1 × 13.8 × 4.6 *(16.8 × 4.2 × 1.4)*
Main machinery: 2 MANN 8V diesels; 1,470 hp *(1.1 MW)*; 2 shafts
Speed, knots: 32
Range, n miles: 500 at 18 kt
Complement: 7 (2 officers)
Guns: 1—7.62 mm MG.
Radars: Surface search: Raytheon SPS 69AN; I-band.

Comment: GRP hulls. All refitted from September 1997 with new engines.

MORUGA *6/1996, Trinidad and Tobago Coast Guard* / 0506333

2 WASP 20 METRE CLASS (COASTAL PATROL CRAFT) (PB)

Name	No	Builders	Commissioned
KAIRI (ex-*Sea Bird*)	CG 31	WA Souter, Cowes	Dec 1982
MORIAH (ex-*Sea Dog*)	CG 32	WA Souter, Cowes	Dec 1982

Displacement, tons: 32 full load
Dimensions, feet (metres): 65.8 × 16.5 × 5 *(20.1 × 5 × 1.5)*
Main machinery: 2 MANN 12V diesels; 2,400 hp *(1.79 MW)*; 2 shafts
Speed, knots: 30. **Range, n miles:** 450 at 30 kt
Complement: 6 (2 officers)
Guns: 2 — 7.62 mm MGs.
Radars: Surface search: Decca 150; I-band.

Comment: Ordered 30 September 1981. Aluminium alloy hull. Transferred from the Police in June 1989. New engines in 1999.

KAIRI *7/2001, Margaret Organ* / 0114370

1 SWORD CLASS (COASTAL PATROL CRAFT) (PB)

Name	No	Builders	Commissioned
MATELOT (ex-*Sea Skorpion*)	CG 33	SeaArk Marine	May 1979

Displacement, tons: 15.5 full load
Dimensions, feet (metres): 44.9 × 13.4 × 4.3 *(13.7 × 4.1 × 1.3)*
Main machinery: 2 GM diesels; 850 hp *(634 kW)*; 2 shafts
Speed, knots: 28. **Range, n miles:** 500 at 20 kt
Complement: 6
Guns: 1 — 7.62 mm MG.
Radars: Surface search: Decca 150; I-band.

Comment: Two transferred from the Police 30 June 1989, one scrapped in 1990. Refitted in 1998.

MATELOT *1/1994, Maritime Photographic* / 0506174

3 DAUNTLESS CLASS (PB)

Name	No	Builders	Commissioned
SOLDADO	CG 38	SeaArk Marine, Monticello	14 June 1995
ROXBOROUGH	CG 39	SeaArk Marine, Monticello	14 June 1995
MAYARO	CG 40	SeaArk Marine, Monticello	14 June 1995

Displacement, tons: 11 full load
Dimensions, feet (metres): 40 × 14 × 4.3 *(12.2 × 4.3 × 1.3)*
Main machinery: 2 Caterpillar 3208TA diesels; 870 hp *(650 kW)* sustained; 2 shafts
Speed, knots: 27. **Range, n miles:** 600 at 18 kt
Complement: 4
Guns: 1 — 7.62 mm MG.
Radars: Surface search: Raytheon R40; I-band.

Comment: Several of these craft provided to Caribbean navies through FMS funding. Used as utility boats.

SOLDADO *6/1995, SeaArk Marine* / 0080848

2 BOWEN CLASS and 3 RHIB (FAST INTERCEPTOR CRAFT) (PBF)

CG 001   CG 002   CG 003-005

Comment: The first pair are 31 ft fast patrol boats acquired in May 1991. Capable of 40 kt. The last three are 25 ft RHIBs with twin Johnson outboards acquired from the US in 1993. Capable of 45 kt.

CG 001 *1991, Trinidad and Tobago Coast Guard* / 0080849

2 AUXILIARY VESSELS

NAPARIMA (ex-*CG 26*) A 01   **REFORM** A 04

Comment: Used for Port Services and other support functions.

CUSTOMS

Notes: Among other craft, the Customs service operate a High Speed Interception craft *Kenneth Mohammed*.

KENNETH MOHAMMED *2/2001, van Ginderen Collection* / 0114369

Tunisia

Country Overview

Formerly a French protectorate, the Tunisian Republic gained independence in 1957. Situated in northern Africa, it has an area of 63,170 square miles and is bordered to the west by Algeria and to the south by Libya. It has a 619 n mile coastline with the Mediterranean Sea. The capital and largest city is the seaport of Tunis. There are further ports at Bizerta, Sousse, Sfax and Gabès while

as-Sukhayrah, specialises in petroleum bunkering. Territorial seas (12 n miles) are claimed. An EEZ has not been claimed.

Headquarters Appointments

Naval Chief of Staff:
  Commodore Tarek Faouzi El Arbi

Personnel

(a) 2006: 4,800 officers and men (including 800 conscripts)
(b) 1 year's national service

Bases

Bizerte, Sfax, La Goulette, Kelibia

PATROL FORCES

3 COMBATTANTE III M CLASS
(FAST ATTACK CRAFT—MISSILE) (PGGF)

Name	No	Builders	Launched	Commissioned
LA GALITÉ	501	CMN, Cherbourg	16 June 1983	27 Feb 1985
TUNIS	502	CMN, Cherbourg	27 Oct 1983	27 Mar 1985
CARTHAGE	503	CMN, Cherbourg	24 Jan 1984	29 Apr 1985

Displacement, tons: 345 standard; 425 full load
Dimensions, feet (metres): 183.7 × 26.9 × 7.2 *(56 × 8.2 × 2.2)*
Main machinery: 4 MTU 20V 538 TB93 diesels; 18,740 hp(m) *(13.8 MW)* sustained; 4 shafts
Speed, knots: 38.5. **Range, n miles:** 700 at 33 kt; 2,800 at 10 kt
Complement: 35

Missiles: SSM: 8 Aerospatiale MM 40 Exocet (2 quad) launchers; inertial cruise; active radar homing to 70 km *(40 n miles)* at 0.9 Mach; warhead 165 kg; sea-skimmer.
Guns: 1 OTO Melara 3 in *(76 mm)*/62; 55-65 rds/min to 16 km *(8.7 n miles)*; weight of shell 6 kg.
2 Breda 40 mm/70 (twin); 300 rds/min to 12.5 km *(6.8 n miles)*; weight of shell 0.96 kg.
4 Oerlikon 30 mm/75 (2 twin); 650 rds/min to 10 km *(5.5 n miles)*; weight of shell 1 kg or 0.36 kg.
Countermeasures: Decoys: 1 CSEE Dagaie trainable launcher; IR flares and chaff.
ESM: Thomson-CSF; DR 2000; intercept.
Combat data systems: Tavitac action data automation.
Weapons control: 2 CSEE Naja optronic directors for 30 mm. Thomson-CSF Vega II for SSM, 76 mm and 40 mm.
Radars: Air/surface search: Thomson-CSF Triton S; G-band; range 33 km *(18 n miles)* for 2 m² target.
Fire control: Thomson-CSF Castor II; I/J-band; range 31 km *(17 n miles)* for 2 m² target.

Programmes: Ordered 27 June 1981.
Operational: CSEE Sylosat navigation system. All three ships operating but reported in need of refits.

CARTHAGE   *8/2004, Schaeffer/Marsan* / 1044197

CARTHAGE   *8/2004, B Prézelin* / 1044198

3 MODIFIED HAIZHUI CLASS (LARGE PATROL CRAFT) (PB)

UTIQUE P 207   JERBA P 208   KURIAT P 209

Displacement, tons: 120 full load
Dimensions, feet (metres): 114.8 × 17.7 × 5.9 *(35 × 5.4 × 1.8)*
Main machinery: 4 MWM TB 604 BV12 diesels; 4,400 hp(m) *(3.22 MW)* sustained; 4 shafts
Speed, knots: 28. **Range, n miles:** 750 at 17 kt
Complement: 39
Guns: 4 China 25 mm/80 (2 twin).
Radars: Surface search: Pot Head; I-band.

Comment: Delivered from China in March 1994. These craft resemble a smaller version of the Haizhui class in service with the Chinese Navy but with a different armament and some superstructure changes. Built to Tunisian specifications.

KURIAT   *4/1995* / 0080852

3 BIZERTE CLASS (TYPE PR 48) (LARGE PATROL CRAFT) (PBOM)

Name	No	Builders	Commissioned
BIZERTE	P 301	SFCN, Villeneuve-la-Garenne	10 July 1970
HORRIA (ex-*Liberté*)	P 302	SFCN, Villeneuve-la-Garenne	Oct 1970
MONASTIR	P 304	SFCN, Villeneuve-la-Garenne	25 Mar 1975

Displacement, tons: 250 full load
Dimensions, feet (metres): 157.5 × 23.3 × 7.5 *(48 × 7.1 × 2.3)*
Main machinery: 2 MTU 16V 652 TB81 diesels; 4,600 hp(m) *(3.4 MW)* sustained; 2 shafts
Speed, knots: 20. **Range, n miles:** 2,000 at 16 kt
Complement: 34 (4 officers)

Missiles: SSM: 8 Aerospatiale SS 12M; wire-guided to 5.5 km *(3 n miles)* subsonic; warhead 30 kg.
Guns: 4—37 mm/63 (2 twin). 2—14.5 mm MGs.
Radars: Surface search: Thomson-CSF DRBN 31; I-band.

Comment: First pair ordered in 1968, third in August 1973. Guns changed in 1994. All are active.

BIZERTE   *3/2002, van Ginderen Collection* / 0141859

HORRIA   *10/2001* / 0533311

4 COASTAL PATROL CRAFT (PB)

Name	No	Builders	Commissioned
ISTIKLAL (ex-VC 11, P 761)	P 201	Ch Navals de l'Esterel	Apr 1957
JOUMHOURIA	P 202	Ch Navals de l'Esterel	Jan 1961
AL JALA	P 203	Ch Navals de l'Esterel	Nov 1963
REMADA	P 204	Ch Navals de l'Esterel	July 1967

Displacement, tons: 60 standard; 80 full load
Dimensions, feet (metres): 104 × 19 × 5.3 *(31.5 × 5.8 × 1.6)*
Main machinery: 2 MTU MB 12V 493 TY70 diesels; 2,200 hp(m) *(1.62 MW)* sustained; 2 shafts
Speed, knots: 30. **Range, n miles:** 1,500 at 15 kt
Complement: 17 (3 officers)
Guns: 2 Oerlikon 20 mm.
Radars: Surface search: Racal Decca 1226; I-band.

Comment: *Istiklal* transferred from France March 1959. Wooden hulls. At least one may belong to the Coast Guard.

REMADA   *4/1997* / 0019295

6 COASTAL PATROL CRAFT (PB)

V 101-106

Displacement, tons: 38 full load
Dimensions, feet (metres): 83 × 15.6 × 4.2 *(25 × 4.8 × 1.3)*
Main machinery: 2 Detroit 12V-71TA diesels; 840 hp *(627 kW)* sustained; 2 shafts; LIPS cp props
Speed, knots: 23. **Range, n miles:** 900 at 15 kt
Complement: 11
Guns: 1 Oerlikon 20 mm.
Radars: Surface search: Racal Decca 1226; I-band.

Comment: Built by Chantiers Navals de l'Esterel and commissioned in 1961-63. Two further craft of the same design (*Sabaq el Bahr* T 2 and *Jaouel el Bahr* T 1) but unarmed were transferred to the Fisheries Administration in 1971-same builders. Refitted in 1997/98. *V 102* is Coast Guard.

V 106   *4/2005*, B Prézelin* / 1133151

6 ALBATROS CLASS (TYPE 143B) (PG)

Name	No	Builders	Commissioned
HAMILCAR (ex-*Sperber*)	505 (ex-P 6115)	Kroger, Rendsburg	27 Sep 1976
HANNON (ex-*Greif*)	506 (ex-P 6116)	Lurssen, Vegesack	25 Nov 1976
HIMILCON (ex-*Geier*)	507 (ex-P 6113)	Lurssen, Vegesack	2 June 1976
HANNIBAL (ex-*Seeadler*)	508 (ex-P 6118)	Lurssen, Vegesack	28 Mar 1977
HASDRUBAL (ex-*Habicht*)	509 (ex-P 6119)	Kroger, Rendsburg	23 Dec 1977
GISCON (ex-*Kormoran*)	510 (ex-P 6120)	Lurssen, Vegesack	29 July 1977

Displacement, tons: 398 full load
Dimensions, feet (metres): 189 × 25.6 × 8.5 *(57.6 × 7.8 × 2.6)*
Main machinery: 4 MTU 16V 956 TB91 diesels; 17,700 hp(m) *(13 MW)* sustained; 4 shafts
Speed, knots: 40. **Range, n miles:** 1,300 at 30 kt
Complement: 40 (4 officers)

Guns: 2 OTO Melara 3 in *(76 mm)*/62 compact; 85 rds/min to 16 km *(8.6 n miles)* anti-surface; 12 km *(6.5 n miles)* anti-aircraft; weight of shell 6 kg.
2—12.7 mm MGs (may be fitted).
Torpedoes: 2—21 in *(533 mm)* aft tubes. AEG Seeal; wire-guided; active homing to 13 km *(7 n miles)* at 35 kt; passive homing to 28 km *(15 n miles)* at 23 kt; warhead 260 kg.
Countermeasures: Decoys: Buck-Wegmann Hot Dog/Silver Dog; IR/chaff dispenser.
ESM/ECM: Racal Octopus (Cutlass intercept, Scorpion jammer).
Combat data systems: AEG/Signaal command and fire-control system; Link 11.
Weapons control: ORG7/3 optronics GFCS. STN Atlas WBA optronic sensor to be fitted.
Radars: Surface search/fire control: Signaal WM27; I/J-band.
Navigation: SMA 3 RM 20; I-band.

Programmes: Sold to Tunisia on being decommissioned from the German Navy in 2005.
Structure: Wooden hulled craft.
Operational: 505 and 506 transferred on 4 July 2005, 507 and 508 in September 2005 and 509 and 510 on 13 December 2005. Exocet missiles were not transferred although the containers remain on board for structural reasons.

HANNON *7/2005*, B Prézelin* / 1133150

HAMILCAR *7/2005*, B Prézelin* / 1133152

TRAINING/SURVEY SHIPS

Notes: *Degga* A 707 and *El Jem* A 708 are converted fishing vessels used for divers' training.

EL JEM *7/2002, Schaeffer/Marsan* / 0533312

1 WILKES CLASS (AGS)

Name	No	Builders	Launched	Commissioned
KHAIREDDINE (ex-*Wilkes*)	A 700 (ex-T-AGS 33)	Defoe SB Co, Bay City, MI	31 July 1969	28 June 1971

Displacement, tons: 2,843 full load
Dimensions, feet (metres): 285.3 × 48 × 15.1 *(87 × 14.6 × 4.6)*
Main machinery: Diesel-electric; 2 Alco diesel generators; 1 Westinghouse/GE motor; 3,600 hp *(2.69 MW)*; 1 shaft; bow thruster; 350 hp *(261 kW)*
Speed, knots: 15
Range, n miles: 8,000 at 13 kt
Complement: 37
Radars: Navigation: RM 1650/9X; I-band.

Comment: Decommissioned on 29 August 1995 and transferred from the USA by grant aid on 29 September 1995. Designed specifically for surveying operations. Bow propulsion unit for precise manoeuvrability and station keeping. Second of class planned for transfer but not confirmed.

KHAIREDDINE *7/2001, Diego Quevedo* / 0126191

1 ROBERT D CONRAD CLASS (AGOR/AX)

Name	No	Builders	Launched	Commissioned
N N O SALAMMBO (ex-*De Steiguer*)	A 701 (ex-T-AGOR 12)	Northwest Iron Works, Portland	13 June 1966	28 Feb 1969

Displacement, tons: 1,370 full load
Dimensions, feet (metres): 208.9 × 40 × 15.3 *(63.7 × 12.2 × 4.7)*
Main machinery: Diesel-electric; 2 Cummins diesel generators; 1 motor; 1,000 hp *(746 kW)*; 1 shaft; bow thruster; 350 hp *(257 kW)*
Speed, knots: 13
Range, n miles: 12,000 at 12 kt
Complement: 40
Radars: Navigation: Raytheon 1650/6X; I-band.

Comment: Transferred from USA on 2 November 1992 and recommissioned on 11 February 1993. Built as an oceanographic research ship. Special features include a 10 ton boom, and a gas turbine for quiet propulsion up to 6 kt. Used primarily for training having replaced the frigate *Inkadh*, which is now an accommodation hulk.

N N O SALAMMBO *7/1997, Camil Busquets i Vilanova* / 0019296

AUXILIARIES

Notes: *Sidi Bou Said* A 802 is a 38 m buoy tender. Procured from Damen in 1998.

2 WHITE SUMAC CLASS (BUOY TENDERS) (ABU)

Name	No	Launched	Commissioned
TABARKA (ex-*White Heath*)	A 804 (ex-WLM 545)	21 July 1943	31 Mar 1998
TAGUERMESS (ex-*White Lupine*)	A 805 (ex-WLM 546)	28 July 1943	31 Mar 1998

Displacement, tons: 485 full load
Dimensions, feet (metres): 133 × 31 × 9 *(40.5 × 9.5 × 2.7)*
Main machinery: 2 Caterpillar diesels; 600 hp *(448 kW)*; 2 shafts
Speed, knots: 9
Complement: 24
Radars: Navigation: Raytheon; I-band.

Comment: Former US Coast Guard vessels transferred by gift on 10 June 1998. Arrived in Tunisia one month later.

TAGUERMESS (US colours) *9/1997, Harald Carstens* / 0012986

1 COASTAL TUG (YTB)

SIDI DAOUD (ex-*Porto D'Ischia*) — (ex-Y436)

Displacement, tons: 412 full load
Measurement, tons: 122 dwt
Dimensions, feet (metres): 106.3 × 27.9 × 12.8 *(32.4 × 8.5 × 3.9)*
Main machinery: 1 GMT B 230.8 M diesels; 1,600 hp(m) *(1.18 MW)* sustained; 1 shaft; cp prop
Speed, knots: 12.7
Range, n miles: 4,000 at 12 kt
Complement: 13
Radars: Navigation: GEM BX 132; I-band.

Comment: Built in 1970. Transferred from Italy in November 2002.

COASTAL TUG (Italian colours) *5/2001, Giorgio Ghiglione* / 0130337

1 SIMETO CLASS (WATER TANKER) (AWT)

AIN ZAGHOUAN (ex-*Simeto*) — (ex-A 5375)

Displacement, tons: 1,858 full load
Dimensions, feet (metres): 229 × 33.1 × 14.4 *(69.8 × 10.1 × 4.1)*
Main machinery: 2 GMT B 230.6 BL diesels; 2,530 hp(m) *(1.86 MW)* sustained; 2 shafts; cp props; bow thruster; 300 hp(m) *(220 kW)*
Speed, knots: 13
Range, n miles: 1,800 at 12 kt
Complement: 36 (3 officers)
Cargo capacity: 1,130 tons
Guns: 1 — 20 mm/70. 2 — 7.62 mm MGs can be carried.
Radars: Navigation: 2 SPN-753B(V); I-band.

Comment: Built by Cinet, Molfetta and originally commissioned on 9 July 1988. Transferred from Italy on 30 June 2003.

SIMETO CLASS (Italian colours) *2/2000, van Ginderen Collection* / 0104888

NATIONAL GUARD

Notes: (1) *Tazarke* P 205 and *Menzel Bourguiba* P 206 may have transferred from the Navy to the National Guard but this is not confirmed.
(2) There are at least nine further patrol craft; GN 1602, GN 1701, GN 1704, GN 1705, GN 1105, GN 1401, GN 1402, GN 1403, GN 2004, GN 2005 and GN 907.

GN 1602 *6/2005*, Marco Ghiglino* / 1133147

GN 1701 *6/2004*, Marco Ghiglino* / 1133146

6 KONDOR I CLASS (PBO)

RAS EL BLAIS (ex-*Demmin*) 601
RAS AJDIR (ex-*Malchin*) 602
RAS EL EDRAK (ex-*Altentreptow*) 603
RAS EL MANOURA (ex-*Templin*) 604
RAS ENGHELA (ex-*Ahrenshoop*) 605
RAS IFRIKIA (ex-*Warnemunde*) 606

Displacement, tons: 377 full load
Dimensions, feet (metres): 170.3 × 23.3 × 7.2 *(51.9 × 7.1 × 2.2)*
Main machinery: 2 Russki/Kolomna 40-DM; 4,408 hp(m) *(3.24 MW)* sustained; 2 shafts; cp props
Speed, knots: 20. **Range, n miles:** 1,800 at 15 kt
Complement: 24
Guns: 2 — 25 mm (twin) can be carried.
Radars: Navigation: TSR 333 or Racal Decca 360; I-band.

Comment: Former GDR minesweepers built at Peenewerft, Wolgast in 1969. First four transferred in May 1992, one in August 1997 and the last one in May 2000. In German service they were fitted with a twin 25 mm gun and a hull-mounted sonar. *Ras Ifrikia* which was used as a fishery protection and research vessel in East German and, later, German service has a more extensive superstructure. These ships may belong to the Navy. Ships of the same class acquired by Cape Verde. Reported operational.

RAS ENGHELA *8/1997, Diego Quevedo* / 0050258

RAS IFRIKIA *5/2000, Kristian Lundgren* / 0567538

5 BREMSE CLASS (PB)

SBEITLA (ex-G 32)
BULLARIJIA (ex-G 36)
UTIQUE GN 2301 (ex-G 37)
UERKOUANE (ex-G 38)
SELEUTA (ex-G 39)

Displacement, tons: 42 full load
Dimensions, feet (metres): 74.1 × 15.4 × 3.6 *(22.6 × 4.7 × 1.1)*
Main machinery: 2 SKL 6VD 18/5 AL-1 diesels; 944 hp(m) *(694 kW)* sustained; 2 shafts
Speed, knots: 14
Complement: 6
Guns: 2 — 14.5 mm (twin) MGs can be carried.
Radars: Navigation: TSR 333; I-band.

Comment: Built in 1971-72 for the ex-GDR GBK. Transferred from Germany in May 1992. Others of the class sold to Malta and Cyprus.

UTIQUE *6/2005*, Marco Ghiglino* / 1133148

For details of the latest updates to *Jane's Fighting Ships* online and to discover the additional information available exclusively to online subscribers please visit
jfs.janes.com

2 SOCOMENA (PATROL CRAFT) (PB)

ASSAD BIN FOURAT **MOHAMMED BRAHIM REJEB**

Displacement, tons: 32 full load
Dimensions, feet (metres): 67.3 × 15.4 × 4.3 *(20.5 × 4.7 × 1.3)*
Main machinery: 2 diesels; 1,000 hp(m) *(735 kW)*; 2 shafts
Speed, knots: 28. **Range, n miles:** 500 at 20 kt
Complement: 8
Guns: 1 — 12.7 mm MG.

Comment: Built by Socomena Bizerte, with assistance from South Korea, and completed 2 March 1986.

SOCOMENA CRAFT (inboard) *3/2002, van Ginderen Collection* / 0141833

4 GABES CLASS (PB)

GABES **JERBA** **KELIBIA** **TABARK**

Displacement, tons: 18 full load
Dimensions, feet (metres): 42.3 × 12.5 × 3 *(12.9 × 3.8 × 0.9)*
Main machinery: 2 diesels; 800 hp(m) *(588 kW)*; 2 shafts
Speed, knots: 38. **Range, n miles:** 250 at 15 kt
Complement: 6
Guns: 2 — 12.7 mm MGs.

Comment: Built by SBCN, Loctudy in 1988-89.

GABES *1/1995* / 0080857

4 RODMAN 38 CLASS (PB)

Displacement, tons: 11.2 full load
Dimensions, feet (metres): 38.7 × 12.8 × 2.82 *(11.6 × 3.9 × 0.86)*
Main machinery: 2 diesels; 2 shafts
Speed, knots: 28. **Range, n miles:** 300 at 28 kt
Complement: 4
Radars: Navigation: I-band.

Comment: GRP hull. Two supplied in 2000 and two in 2002. Built by Rodman, Vigo for Customs Service.

RODMAN 38 *6/2004** / 1133149

Turkey

TÜRK DENIZ KUVVETLERI

Country Overview

The modern Republic of Turkey was founded in 1923. Situated in south-east Europe and south-west Asia, the country has an area of 300,948 square miles and is bordered to the north-west by Bulgaria and Greece, to the north-east by Georgia and Armenia, to the east by Iran and to the south with Iraq and Syria. It has a 739 n mile coastline with the Black Sea and 3,149 n mile coastline with the Aegean and Mediterranean Seas. The capital is Ankara, while the leading ports are Istanbul (largest city) and Izmir. In addition, Black Sea ports include Trabzon, Giresun, Samsun, and Zonguldak while Iskenderun and Mersin lie on the Mediterranean. Territorial waters for Black Sea and Mediterranean (12 n miles) are claimed and for Aegean (6 n miles). An EEZ (200 n miles) is claimed in the Black Sea only.

Headquarters Appointments

Commander-in-Chief, Turkish Naval Forces:
  Admiral Yener Karahanoğlu
Chief of Naval Staff:
  Vice Admiral Feyyaz Öğütçü
Chief of Coast Guard:
  Rear Admiral Can Erenoğlu

Flag Officers

Comturfleet (Gölcük):
  Admiral Metin Ataç
Comtursarnorth (Istanbul):
  Vice Admiral Uğur Yiğit
Comtursarsouth (Izmir):
  Vice Admiral Alev Gümüşoğlu
Comturnavtrain (Istanbul):
  Vice Admiral Murat Bilgel
Comturampgroup (Foça):
  Rear Admiral M Tayfun Uraz
Comtursuracgroup (Gölcük):
  Rear Admiral Nusret Güner
Comturfastgroup (Gölcük):
  Rear Admiral Ergun Mengi
Comturcoguard (Ankara):
  Rear Admiral Can Erenoğlu
Comturminegroup (Erdek):
  Rear Admiral Mehmet Otuzbiroğlu
Comtursubgroup (Gölcük):
  Rear Admiral Izzet Artunç
Comturespatgroup (Izmir):
  Rear Admiral Levent Temel
Comiststrait (Istanbul):
  Rear Admiral Ömer Akdağli
Comcanstrait (Çanakkale):
  Rear Admiral Veysel Kösele
Comturageanzone (Izmir):
  Rear Admiral Hüseyin Çiftçi
Comturmedzone (Mersin):
  Rear Admiral Serdar Akinsel
Comtursouthtskgrp (Aksaz):
  Rear Admiral Deniz Cora
Comturnavgolbase (Gölcük):
  Rear Admiral Atilla Kezek

Flag Officers — *continued*

Comturnavaksbase (Aksaz):
  Rear Admiral Engin Baykal
Comturmairbase (Topel):
  Rear Admiral Deniz Dağlilar
Comturblackzone (Ereğli):
  Rear Admiral Ibrahim Akin

Diplomatic Representation

Defence and Naval Attaché in London:
  Captain A Kenanoglu

Personnel

(a) 2006: 55,000 (5,500 officers) including 31,000 conscripts, 3,000 Marines and 900 Air Arm (reserves 70,000)
(b) 15 months' national service

Organisation

Fleet HQ (Ankara), Fleet Command (Gölcük), Northern Area Command (Black Sea and Marmara), Southern Area Command (Aegean and Mediterranean), Naval Training Command (Istanbul).

Bases

Headquarters: Ankara
Black Sea: Ereğli, Bartin, Samsun, Trabzon
Marmara: Istanbul, Erdek, Çanakkale, Gölcük
Mediterranean: Izmir, Foça, Antalya, Mersin, Iskenderun, Aksaz
Dockyards: Gölcük, Pendik (Istanbul), Izmir

Prefix to Ships' Names

TCG (Turkish Republic Ship)
TCSG (Turkish Republic Coast Guard)

Strength of the Fleet (including Coast Guard)

Type	Active	Building (Planned)
Submarines — Patrol	12	2
Frigates	19	—
Corvettes	6	—
Fast Attack Craft — Missile	23	4
Large Patrol Craft	15	—
Minesweepers/Hunters — Coastal	14	5
Minesweepers — Inshore	4	—
LSTs/Minelayers	5	—
LCTs	24	—
Survey Vessels	3	—
Training Ships	10	—
Fleet Support Ships	2	—
Tankers	4	—
Transports — Large and small	22	—
Salvage Ships	3	—
Boom Defence Vessels	2	—

Pennant Numbers

From mid-1997 all pennant numbers have been repainted in non-reflective paint.

Marines

Total: 3,000
One brigade of HQ company, three infantry battalions, one artillery battalion, support units.

Coast Guard (Sahil Güvenlik)

Formed in July 1982 from the naval wing of the Jandarma. Prefix J replaced by SG and paint scheme is very light grey with a diagonal stripe forward. About 1,700 officers and men.

DELETIONS

Submarines

2004 *Hizirreis, Pirireis*

Frigates

2003 *Trakya*
2005 *Ege*

Mine Warfare Forces

2004 *Sinop, Sürmene*

Patrol Forces

2003 *Bora*
2005 *Yarhisar, AB 33*

Amphibious Forces

2003 *Bayraktar, Ç 113, Ç 117, Ç 122, Ç 124, Ç 302, Ç 303, Ç 309*
2005 *Ç 129*

Auxiliaries

2005 *Samsun*

PENNANT LIST

Submarines		Mine Warfare Forces (Sweepers/Hunters)		P 128	AB 28	A 572	Yuzbasi Ihsan Tolunay
				P 129	AB 29	A 573	Binbaşi Sadettin Gürcan
S 347	Atilay	M 260	Edincik	P 131	AB 31	A 576	Değirmendere
S 348	Saldiray	M 261	Edremit	P 135	AB 35	A 577	Sokullu Mehmet Paşa
S 349	Batiray	M 262	Enez	P 136	AB 36	A 578	Darica
S 350	Yildiray	M 263	Erdek	P 301	Kozlu	A 579	Cezayirli Gazi Hasan Paşa
S 351	Doğanay	M 264	Erdemli	P 302	Kuşadasi	A 580	Akar
S 352	Dolunay	M 265	Alanya	P 321	Denizkuşu	A 581	Çinar
S 353	Preveze	M 266	Amasra	P 322	Atmaca	A 582	Kemer
S 354	Sakarya	M 267	Ayvalik (bldg)	P 323	Şahin	A 583	Aksaz
S 355	18 Mart	M 268	Akçakoca	P 324	Kartal	A 585	Akin
S 356	Anafartalar	M 269	Anamur	P 326	Pelikan	A 586	Akbas
S 357	Gür	M 270	Akçay	P 327	Albatros	A 587	Gazal
S 358	Çanakkale	M 500	Foça	P 328	Şimşek	A 588	Çandarli
S 359	Burakreis	M 501	Fethiye	P 329	Kasirga	A 589	Işin
S 360	Birinci Inönü (bldg)	M 502	Fatsa	P 330	Kiliç	A 592	Karadeniz Ereğlisi
		M 503	Finike	P 331	Kalkan	A 593	Eceabat
Frigates		M 514	Silifke	P 332	Mizrak	A 594	Çubuklu
		M 515	Saros	P 333	Tufan	A 595	Yarbay Kudret Güngör
F 240	Yavuz	M 516	Sigacik	P 334	Meltem	A 596	Ulubat
F 241	Turgutreis	M 517	Sapanca	P 335	Imbat (bldg)	A 597	Van
F 242	Fatih	M 518	Sariyer	P 336	Zipkin (bldg)	A 598	Sögüt
F 243	Yildirim	M 520	Karamürsel	P 337	Atak (bldg)	A 599	Çeşme
F 244	Barbaros	M 521	Kerempe	P 338	Bora (bldg)	A 600	Kavak
F 245	Orucreis	M 522	Kilimli	P 340	Doğan	A 1531	E 1
F 246	Salihreis	P 313-314	MTB 3-4	P 341	Marti	A 1532	E 2
F 247	Kemalreis	P 316-319	MTB 6-9	P 342	Tayfun	A 1533	E 3
F 250	Muavenet			P 343	Volkan	A 1534	E 4
F 253	Zafer	**Amphibious Forces**		P 344	Rüzgar	A 1535	E 5
F 255	Karadeniz			P 345	Poyraz	A 1536	E 6
F 490	Gaziantep	L 401	Ertuğrul	P 346	Gurbet	A 1537	E 7
F 491	Giresun	L 402	Serdar	P 347	Firtina	A 1538	E 8
F 492	Gemlik	NL 123	Sarucabey	P 348	Yildiz	A 1542	Söndüren 2
F 493	Gelibolu	NL 124	Karamürselbey	P 349	Karayel	A 1543	Söndüren 3
F 494	Gökçeada	NL 125	Osman Gazi	P 530	Trabzon	A 1544	Söndüren 4
F 495	Gediz			P 531	Terme	A 1600	Iskenderun
F 496	Gökova	**Patrol Forces**				Y 50	Gölcük
F 497	Göksu					Y 95	Torpido Tenderi
F 500	Bozcaada	P 114	Akhisar	**Auxiliaries**		Y 98	Takip 1
F 501	Bodrum	P 121	AB 21			Y 99	Takip 2
F 502	Bandirma	P 122	AB 22	P 305	AG 5	Y 107	Layter-7
F 503	Beykoz	P 123	AB 23	P 306	AG 6	Y 111-116	Pinar 1-6
F 504	Bartin	P 124	AB 24	A 570	Taşkizak	Y 139	Yakit
F 505	Bafra	P 127	AB 27	A 571	Albay Hakki Burak	Y 140-142	H 500-502

SUBMARINES

6 ATILAY (209) CLASS (TYPE 1200) (SSK)

Name	No	Builders	Laid down	Launched	Commissioned
ATILAY	S 347	Howaldtswerke, Kiel	1 Dec 1972	23 Oct 1974	12 Mar 1976
SALDIRAY	S 348	Howaldtswerke, Kiel	2 Jan 1973	14 Feb 1975	15 Jan 1977
BATIRAY	S 349	Howaldtswerke, Kiel	1 June 1975	24 Oct 1977	7 Nov 1978
YILDIRAY	S 350	Gölcük, Izmit	1 May 1976	20 July 1979	20 July 1981
DOĞANAY	S 351	Gölcük, Izmit	21 Mar 1980	16 Nov 1983	16 Nov 1984
DOLUNAY	S 352	Gölcük, Izmit	9 Mar 1981	22 July 1988	29 June 1990

Displacement, tons: 980 surfaced; 1,185 dived
Dimensions, feet (metres): 200.8 × 20.3 × 17.9
(61.2 × 6.2 × 5.5)
Main machinery: Diesel-electric; 4 MTU 12V 493 TY60
diesels; 2,400 hp(m) *(1.76 MW)* sustained; 4 alternators;
1.7 MW; 1 Siemens motor; 4,600 hp(m) *(3.38 MW)*
sustained; 1 shaft
Speed, knots: 11 surfaced; 22 dived
Range, n miles: 7,500 at 8 kt surfaced
Complement: 38 (9 officers)

Torpedoes: 8—21 in *(533 mm)* tubes. 14 AEG SST 4; wire-
guided; active/passive homing to 28 km *(15.3 n miles)*
at 23 kt; 12 km *(6.6 n miles)* at 35 kt; warhead 260 kg.
Swim-out discharge.
Countermeasures: ESM: Thomson-CSF DR 2000 or Racal
Sealion (UAP) or Racal Porpoise; intercept
Weapons control: Signaal M8 (S 347-348). Signaal Sinbads
(remainder). Link 11 receive.
Radars: Surface search: S 63B; I-band.
Sonars: Atlas Elektronik CSU 3; hull-mounted; passive/
active search and attack; medium/high frequency.

Programmes: Designed by Ingenieurkontor, Lübeck
for construction by Howaldtswerke, Kiel and sale by
Ferrostaal, Essen, all acting as a consortium. Last three
built in Turkey with assistance given by HDW.
Modernisation: Mid-life upgrades are planned, for the
last four boats. The programme, which may include

BATIRAY *12/2001, M Declerck* / 0533242

command system and weapon system upgrades may
begin in 2006 although details have not been confirmed.
Structure: A single-hull design with two ballast tanks and
forward and after trim tanks. Fitted with snort and remote
machinery control. The single screw is slow revving. Very
high-capacity batteries with GRP lead-acid cells and
battery cooling-by Wilh Hagen. Active and passive sonar,

sonar detection equipment, sound ranging gear and
underwater telephone. Fitted with two periscopes, radar
and Omega receiver. Fore-planes retract. Diving depth,
250 m *(820 ft)*.
Operational: Endurance, 50 days. Some US Mk 37
torpedoes may also be carried. S 347 and S 348 are to
be decommissioned.

YILDIRAY *1/2002, M Declerck* / 0132790

7 + 1 PREVEZE (209) CLASS (TYPE 1400) (SSK)

Name	No	Builders	Laid down	Launched	Commissioned
PREVEZE	S 353	Gölcük, Kocaeli	12 Sep 1989	22 Oct 1993	22 Mar 1994
SAKARYA	S 354	Gölcük, Kocaeli	1 Feb 1990	28 July 1994	6 Jan 1995
18 MART	S 355	Gölcük, Kocaeli	28 July 1994	25 Aug 1997	27 Aug 1997
ANAFARTALAR	S 356	Gölcük, Kocaeli	1 Aug 1995	1 Sep 1998	12 Oct 1998
GÜR	S 357	Gölcük, Kocaeli	24 July 1998	25 July 2001	24 July 2003
ÇANAKKALE	S 358	Gölcük, Kocaeli	22 July 1999	Aug 2002	26 July 2005
BURAKREIS	S 359	Gölcük, Kocaeli	19 Dec 2001	5 Sep 2005	15 Jan 2006
BIRINCI INÖNÜ	S 360	Gölcük, Kocaeli	19 Oct 2002	2006	2007

Displacement, tons: 1,454 surfaced; 1,586 dived
Dimensions, feet (metres): 203.4 × 20.3 × 18
  (62 × 6.2 × 5.5)
Main machinery: Diesel-electric; 4 MTU 12V 396 SB83
  diesels; 3,800 hp(m) *(2.8 MW)* sustained; 4 alternators;
  1 Siemens motor; 4,000 hp(m) *(3.38 MW)* sustained;
  1 shaft
Speed, knots: 10 surfaced/snorting; 21.5 dived
Range, n miles: 8,200 at 8 kt surfaced; 400 at 4 kt dived
Complement: 30 (8 officers)

Missiles: SSM: McDonnell Douglas Sub Harpoon; active
  radar homing to 130 km *(70 n miles)* at 0.9 Mach;
  warhead 227 kg.
Torpedoes: 8—21 in *(533 mm)* bow tubes. GEC-Marconi
  Tigerfish Mk 24 Mod 2; wire-guided; active/passive
  homing to 13 km *(7 n miles)* at 35 kt active; 29 km
  (15.7 n miles) at 24 kt passive; warhead 134 kg or STN
  Atlas DM 2A4 (S 357 onwards). Total of 14 torpedoes
  and missiles.
Mines: In lieu of torpedoes.
Countermeasures: ESM: Racal Porpoise or Racal Sealion
  (UAP) (S 357 onwards); intercept.
Weapons control: Atlas Elektronik ISUS 83-2 TFCS. Link 11
  receive only.
Radars: Surface search; I-band.
Sonars: Atlas Elektronik CSU 83; passive/active search and
  attack; medium/high frequency.
  Atlas Elektronik TAS-3; towed array; passive low
  frequency.
  STN Atlas flank array; passive low frequency.

Programmes: Order for first two signed in Ankara on
  17 November 1987 with option on two more taken up
  in 1993. Four more ordered 22 July 1998. All built with
  HDW prefabrication and assembly at Gölcük. The last
  four are to complete at one a year from 2004 and are
  called the Gür class. Despite the earthquake damage to
  Gölcük in 1999, the building programme is reported to be
  keeping to schedule. The first four names commemorate
  Turkish victories. 18 March 1915 marks a victory in the
  Dardanelles and *Anafartalar* is a hill in Gallipoli.
Structure: Single hull design. Diving depth, 280 m *(820 ft)*.
  Kollmorgen masts. Four torpedo tubes can be used for
  SSM. STN Atlas flank arrays fitted in 1998/99 to the first
  four.
Operational: Endurance, 50 days.

ÇANAKKALE   9/2005*, Selçuk Emre / 1133567

18 MART
7/2000, Michael Nitz
0106618

PREVEZE   10/2003, C D Yaylali / 0567543

ANAFARTALAR   4/2001, Selçuk Emre / 0132789

FRIGATES

Notes: (1) The Turkish Frigate 2000 (TF 2000) project has been delayed due to economic difficulties. Three batches of two ships are envisaged with a mix of in-country and foreign construction. TF 2000 is to meet the requirement for an area air defence capability.
(2) Approval for the transfer of two ex-USN Spruance class destroyers (*Cushing* and *O'Bannon*) was made in the US Congress in 2005. A decision on whether to accept the ships is expected in 2006.

4 YAVUZ CLASS (MEKO 200 TN) (FFGHM)

Name	No	Builders	Laid down	Launched	Commissioned
YAVUZ	F 240	Blohm + Voss, Hamburg	30 May 1985	7 Nov 1985	17 July 1987
TURGUTREIS (ex-*Turgut*)	F 241	Howaldtswerke, Kiel	20 May 1985	30 May 1986	4 Feb 1988
FATIH	F 242	Gölcük, Izmit	1 Jan 1986	24 Apr 1987	28 Aug 1988
YILDIRIM	F 243	Gölcük, Izmit	24 Apr 1987	22 July 1988	17 Nov 1989

Displacement, tons: 2,414 standard; 2,919 full load
Dimensions, feet (metres): 378.9 × 46.6 × 13.5
  (115.5 × 14.2 × 4.1)
Main machinery: CODAD; 4 MTU 20V 1163 TB93 diesels; 29,940 hp(m) *(22 MW)* sustained; 2 shafts; cp props
Speed, knots: 27. **Range, n miles:** 4,100 at 18 kt
Complement: 180 (24 officers)

Missiles: SSM: 8 McDonnell Douglas Harpoon (2 quad) launchers ❶; active radar homing to 130 km *(70 n miles)* at 0.9 Mach; warhead 227 kg.
SAM: Raytheon Sea Sparrow RIM-7M Mk 29 Mod 1 octuple launcher ❷; 24 Selenia Elsag Aspide; semi-active radar homing to 13 km *(7 n miles)* at 2.5 Mach; warhead 39 kg.
Guns: 1 FMC 5 in *(127 mm)*/54 Mk 45 Mod 1 ❸; 20 rds/min to 23 km *(12.6 n miles)* anti-surface; 15 km *(8.2 n miles)* anti-aircraft; weight of shell 32 kg.
3 Oerlikon-Contraves 25 mm Sea Zenith ❹; 4 barrels per mounting; 3,400 rds/min combined to 2 km.
Torpedoes: 6—324 mm Mk 32 (2 triple) tubes ❺. Honeywell Mk 46 Mod 5; anti-submarine; active/passive homing to 11 km *(5.9 n miles)* at 40 kt; warhead 44 kg.
Countermeasures: Decoys: 2 Loral Hycor 6-tubed fixed Mk 36 Mod 1 SRBOC ❻; IR flares and chaff to 4 km *(2.2 n miles)*.
Nixie SLQ-25; towed torpedo decoy.
ESM/ECM: Signaal Rapids/Ramses; intercept and jammer.
Combat data systems: Signaal STACOS-TU; action data automation; Link 11. WSC 3V(7) SATCOMs. Marisat.
Weapons control: 2 Siemens Albis optronic directors (for Sea Zenith). SWG-1A for Harpoon.
Radars: Air search: Signaal DA08 ❼; F-band.
Air/surface search: Plessey AWS 6 Dolphin ❽; G-band.
Fire control: Signaal STIR ❾; I/J/K-band (for SAM); range 140 km *(76 n miles)* for 1 m² target.
Signaal WM25 ❿; I/J-band (for SSM and 127 mm).
2 Contraves Seaguard ⓫; I/J-band (for 25 mm).

Navigation: Racal Decca TM 1226; I-band.
Tacan: URN 25. IFF Mk XII.
Sonars: Raytheon SQS-56 (DE 1160); hull-mounted; active search and attack; medium frequency.

Helicopters: 1 AB 212ASW ⓬.

Programmes: Ordered 29 December 1982 with builders and Thyssen Rheinstahl Technik of Dusseldorf. Meko 200 type similar to Portuguese frigates. *Turgutreis* was renamed on 14 February 1988.
Operational: Helicopter has Sea Skua anti-ship missiles.

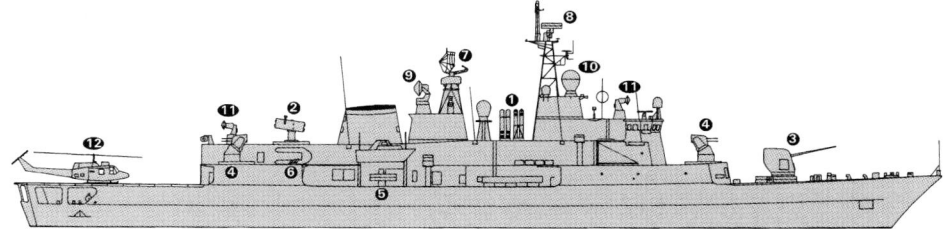

YAVUZ *(Scale 1 : 900), Ian Sturton* / 1153493

FATIH *7/2005*, C D Yaylali* / 1133597

YILDIRIM *6/2004*, E & M Laursen* / 1133598

YAVUZ *9/2005*, C D Yaylali* / 1133596

4 BARBAROS CLASS (MEKO 200 TN II-A/B) (FFGHM)

Name	No	Builders	Laid down	Launched	Commissioned
BARBAROS	F 244	Blohm + Voss, Hamburg	18 Mar 1993	29 Sep 1993	16 Mar 1995
ORUCREIS	F 245	Gölcük, Kocaeli	15 Sep 1993	28 July 1994	10 May 1996
SALIHREIS	F 246	Blohm + Voss, Hamburg	24 July 1995	26 Sep 1997	17 Dec 1998
KEMALREIS	F 247	Gölcük, Kocaeli	4 Apr 1997	24 July 1998	8 June 2000

Displacement, tons: 3,380 full load
Dimensions, feet (metres): 387.1 × 48.6 × 14.1; 21 (sonar)
(118 × 14.8 × 4.3; 6.4)
Main machinery: CODOG; 2 GE LM 2500 gas turbines;
60,000 hp *(44.76 MW)* sustained; 2 MTU 16V 1163 TB83
diesels; 11,780 hp(m) *(8.67 MW)* sustained; 2 shafts;
Escher Wyss; cp props
Speed, knots: 32
Range, n miles: 4,100 at 18 kt
Complement: 187 (22 officers) plus 9 aircrew plus 8 spare

Missiles: SSM: 8 McDonnell Douglas Harpoon (2 quad)
launchers ❶; active radar homing to 130 km *(70 n miles)* at
0.9 Mach; warhead 227 kg.
SAM: Raytheon Sea Sparrow RIM-7M Mk 29 Mod 1 octuple
launcher ❷ (F 244 and F 245) and VLS Mk 41 Mod 8 ❸
(F 246 and F 247); 24 Selenia Elsag Aspide; semi-active
radar homing to 13 km *(7 n miles)* at 2.5 Mach; warhead
39 kg. Evolved Sea Sparrow (ESSM) in due course.
Guns: 1 FMC 5 in *(127 mm)*/54 Mk 45 Mod 1/2 ❹; 20 rds/min
to 23 km *(12.6 n miles)* anti-surface; 15 km *(8.2 n miles)*
anti-aircraft; weight of shell 32 kg.
3 Oerlikon-Contraves 25 mm Sea Zenith ❺; 4 barrels per
mounting; 3,400 rds/min combined to 2 km.
Torpedoes: 6—324 mm Mk 32 Mod 5 (2 triple) tubes ❻.
Honeywell Mk 46 Mod 5; anti-submarine; active/passive
homing to 11 km *(5.9 n miles)* at 40 kt; warhead 44 kg.
Countermeasures: Decoys: 2 Loral Hycor 6-tubed fixed
Mk 36 Mod 1 SRBOC ❼; IR flares and chaff to 4 km
(2.2 n miles).
Nixie SLQ-25; towed torpedo decoy.
ESM/ECM: Racal Cutlass/Scorpion; intercept and jammer.
Combat data systems: Thomson-CSF/Signaal STACOS
Mod 3; Link 11. WSC 3V(7) SATCOMs. Marisat.
Weapons control: 2 Siemens Albis optronic directors ❽.
SWG-1A for Harpoon.
Radars: Air search: Siemens/Plessey AWS 9 (Type 996) ❾;
3D; E/F-band.
Air/surface search: Plessey/BAe AWS 6 Dolphin ❿; G-band.
Fire control: 1 or 2 (F 246-247) Signaal STIR ⓫; I/J/K-band
(for SAM); range 140 km *(76 n miles)* for 1 m² target.
Contraves TMKu (F 244-245) ⓬; I/J-band (for SSM and
127 mm).
2 Contraves Seaguard ⓭; I/J-band (for 25 mm).
Navigation: Racal Decca 2690 BT ARPA; I-band.
Tacan: URN 25. IFF Mk XII Mod 4.
Sonars: Raytheon SQS-56 (DE 1160); hull-mounted; active
search and attack; medium frequency.

Helicopters: 1 AB 212ASW ⓮ or S-70B Seahawk.

Programmes: First pair ordered 19 January 1990, second
pair authorised 14 December 1992. Programme started
5 November 1991 with construction commencing in June
1992 in Germany. Completion of the last one delayed by
the Gölcük earthquake in 1999.
Structure: An improvement on the Yavuz class. Mk 29
Sea Sparrow launchers fitted in the first two, while the
second pair have Mk 41 VLS aft of the funnel, which will
be retrofitted in the first two in due course. The ships
have CODOG propulsion for a higher top speed. Other

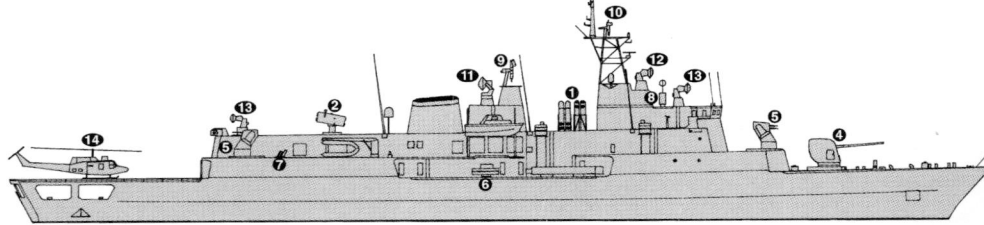

BARBAROS *(Scale 1 : 900), Ian Sturton* / 0019315

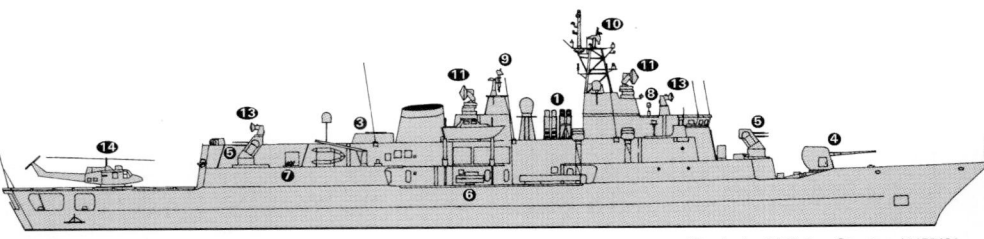

SALIHREIS *(Scale 1 : 900), Ian Sturton* / 1153494

BARBAROS *8/2005*, Derek Fox* / 1133594

differences with *Yavuz* include a full command system,
improved radars and a citadel for NBCD protection.
A bow bulwark has been added in the second pair.

Operational: Helicopter has Sea Skua anti-ship missiles. All
can be used as Flagships.

SALIHREIS *7/2005*, C D Yaylali* / 1133595

ORUCREIS *5/2005*, John Brodie* / 1133593

8 GAZIANTEP (OLIVER HAZARD PERRY) CLASS (FFGHM)

Name	No	Builders	Laid down	Launched	Commissioned	Recommissioned
GAZIANTEP (ex-*Clifton Sprague*)	F 490 (ex-FFG 16)	Bath Iron Works	30 Sep 1979	16 Feb 1980	21 Mar 1981	24 July 1998
GIRESUN (ex-*Antrim*)	F 491 (ex-FFG 20)	Todd Shipyards, Seattle	21 June 1978	27 Mar 1979	26 Sep 1981	24 July 1998
GEMLIK (ex-*Flatley*)	F 492 (ex-FFG 21)	Bath Iron Works	13 Nov 1979	15 May 1980	20 June 1981	24 July 1998
GELIBOLU (ex-*Reid*)	F 493 (ex-FFG 30)	Todd Shipyards, San Pedro	8 Oct 1980	27 June 1981	19 Feb 1983	22 July 1999
GÖKÇEADA (ex-*Mahlon S Tisdale*)	F 494 (ex-FFG 27)	Todd Shipyards, San Pedro	19 Mar 1980	7 Feb 1981	27 Nov 1982	8 June 2000
GEDIZ (ex-*John A Moore*)	F 495 (ex-FFG 19)	Todd Shipyards, San Pedro	19 Dec 1978	20 Oct 1979	14 Nov 1981	25 July 2000
GOKOVA (ex-*Samuel Eliot Morison*)	F 496 (ex-FFG 13)	Bath Iron Works	4 Aug 1978	14 July 1979	11 Oct 1980	11 Apr 2002
GÖKSU (ex-*Estocin*)	F 497 (ex-FFG 15)	Bath Iron Works	2 Apr 1979	3 Nov 1979	10 Jan 1981	4 Apr 2003

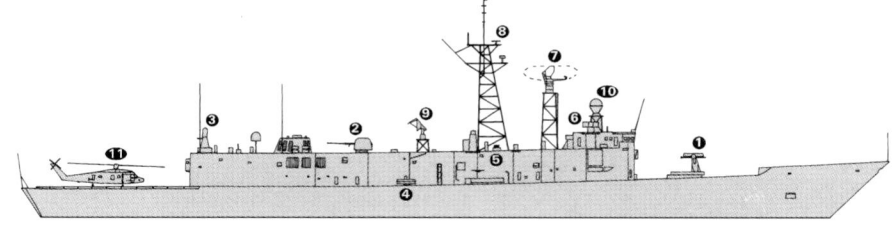

GÖKÇEADA *(Scale 1 : 1,200), Ian Sturton* / 0587565

Displacement, tons: 2,750 light, 3,638 full load
Dimensions, feet (metres): 453 × 45 × 14.8; 24.5 (sonar) *(138.1 × 13.7 × 4.5; 7.5)*
Main machinery: 2 GE LM 2500 gas turbines; 41,000 hp *(30.59 MW)* sustained; 1 shaft; cp prop. 2 auxiliary retractable props; 650 hp *(484 kW)*
Speed, knots: 29. **Range, n miles:** 4,500 at 20 kt
Complement: 206 (13 officers) including 19 aircrew

Missiles: SSM: 4 McDonnell Douglas Harpoon; active radar homing to 130 km *(70 n miles)* at 0.9 Mach; warhead 227 kg.
SAM: 36 GDC Standard SM-1MR; command guidance; semi-active radar homing to 46 km *(25 n miles)* at 2 Mach. 1 Mk 13 Mod 4 launcher for both SSM and SAM missiles ❶.
Guns: 1 OTO Melara 3 in *(76 mm)*/62 Mk 75 ❷; 85 rds/min to 16 km *(8.7 n miles)* anti-surface; 12 km *(6.6 n miles)* anti-aircraft; weight of shell 6 kg.
1 General Electric/General Dynamics 20 mm/76 6-barrelled Mk 15 Vulcan Phalanx ❸; 3,000 rds/min combined to 1.5 km.
4—12.7 mm MGs.
Torpedoes: 6—324 mm Mk 32 (2 triple) tubes ❹. 24 Honeywell Mk 46 Mod 5; anti-submarine; active/passive homing to 11 km *(5.9 n miles)* at 40 kt; warhead 44 kg.
Countermeasures: Decoys: 2 Loral Hycor SRBOC 6-barrelled fixed Mk 36 ❺; IR flares and chaff to 4 km *(2.2 n miles)*. T-Mk-6 Fanfare/SLQ-25 Nixie; torpedo decoy.
ESM/ECM: SLQ-32(V)2 ❻; radar warning. Sidekick modification adds jammer and deception system.

Combat data systems: NTDS with Link 11 and 14. SATCOM.
Weapons control: SWG-1 Harpoon LCS. Mk 92 Mod 4 WCS with CAS (Combined Antenna System). The Mk 92 is the US version of the Signaal WM28 system. Mk 13 weapon direction system. 2 Mk 24 optical directors.
Radars: Air search: Raytheon SPS-49(V)4 ❼; C/D-band.
Surface search: ISC Cardion SPS-55 ❽; I-band.
Fire control: Lockheed STIR (modified SPG-60) ❾; I/J-band.
Sperry Mk 92 (Signaal WM28) ❿; I/J-band.
Navigation: Furuno; I-band.
Tacan: URN 25.
Sonars: Raytheon SQS-56; hull-mounted; active search and attack; medium frequency.

Helicopters: 1 S-70B Seahawk ⓫.

Programmes: Three approved for transfer by grant aid. Transfer delayed by Greek objections, and Turkish sailors were sent home from the US in mid-1996. Congress authorised the go-ahead again on 27 August 1997. Two more approved for transfer by sale 30 September 1998, one in February 2000, one in April 2002 and one in April 2003. At least one other *Duncan* FFG 10 for spares.
Modernisation: Project 'Genesis' includes plans to upgrade the combat data system.
Structure: A flight deck extension programme, to enable S-70 helicopters has been completed. The work involved angling the transom as in later USN ships of the class.
Operational: Sonar towed arrays were not transferred.

GIRESUN *4/2004*, C D Yaylali* / 1133585

GEMLIK *1/2005*, Camil Busquets i Vilanova* / 1133586

3 TEPE (KNOX) CLASS (FFGH)

Name	No	Builders	Laid down	Launched	Commissioned	Recommissioned
MUAVENET (ex-*Capodanno*)	F 250 (ex-1093)	Avondale Shipyards	12 Oct 1971	21 Oct 1972	17 Nov 1973	12 Sep 1993
ZAFER (ex-*Thomas C Hart*)	F 253 (ex-1092)	Avondale Shipyards	8 Oct 1971	12 Aug 1972	28 July 1973	30 Aug 1993
KARADENIZ (ex-*Donald B Beary*)	F 255 (ex-1085)	Avondale Shipyards	24 July 1970	22 May 1971	22 July 1972	20 May 1994

Displacement, tons: 3,011 standard; 4,260 full load
Dimensions, feet (metres): 439.6 × 46.8 × 15; 24.8 (sonar)
(*134 × 14.3 × 4.6; 7.8*)
Main machinery: 2 Combustion Engineering/Babcock &
Wilcox boilers; 1,200 psi (*84.4 kg/cm²*); 950°F (*510°C*);
1 Westinghouse turbine; 35,000 hp (*26 MW*); 1 shaft
Speed, knots: 27
Range, n miles: 4,000 at 22 kt on 1 boiler
Complement: 288 (20 officers)

Missiles: SSM: 8 McDonnell Douglas Harpoon; active radar
homing to 130 km (*70 n miles*) at 0.9 Mach; warhead
227 kg.
A/S: Honeywell ASROC Mk 16 octuple launcher with reload
system (has 2 cells modified to fire Harpoon) **1**; inertial
guidance to 1.6 — 10 km (*1 — 5.4 n miles*); payload Mk 46
Mod 5 Neartip.
Guns: 1 FMC 5 in (*127 mm*)/54 Mk 42 Mod 9 **2**; 20 — 40 rds/
min to 24 km (*13 n miles*) anti-surface; 14 km (*7.7 n miles*)
anti-aircraft; weight of shell 32 kg.
1 General Electric/General Dynamics 20 mm/76
6-barrelled Mk 15 Vulcan Phalanx **3**; 3,000 rds/min
combined to 1.5 km.
Torpedoes: 4 — 324 mm Mk 32 (2 twin) fixed tubes **4**.
22 Honeywell Mk 46 Mod 5; anti-submarine; active/passive
homing to 11 km (*5.9 n miles*) at 40 kt; warhead 44 kg.
Countermeasures: Decoys: 2 Loral Hycor SRBOC
6-barrelled fixed Mk 36 **5**; IR flares and chaff to 4 km
(*2.2 n miles*). T Mk-6 Fanfare/SLQ-25 Nixie; torpedo decoy.
Prairie Masker hull and blade rate noise suppression.
ESM: SLQ-32(V)2 **6**; intercept.
Combat data systems: Signaal Sigma K5 with Link 11.
Weapons control: SWG-1A Harpoon LCS. Mk 68 Mod 3
GFCS. Mk 114 Mod 6 ASW FCS. Mk 1 target designation

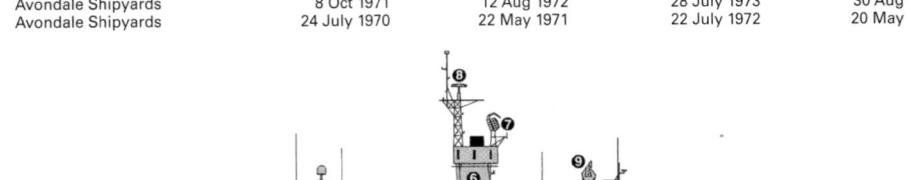

MUAVENET

(Scale 1 : 1,200), Ian Sturton / 0506334

system. MMS target acquisition sight (for mines, small
craft and low-flying aircraft).
Radars: Air search: Lockheed SPS-40B **7**; B-band.
Surface search: Raytheon SPS-10 or Norden SPS-67 **8**;
G-band.
Navigation: Marconi LN66; I-band.
Fire control: Western Electric SPG-53D/F **9**; I/J-band.
Tacan: SRN 15.
Sonars: EDO/General Electric SQS-26CX; bow-mounted;
active search and attack; medium frequency.

Helicopters: 1 AB 212ASW **10**.

Programmes: In late 1992 the US offered Turkey four of the
class. A proposal was put to Congress in June 1993 and
four approved for transfer on a five year lease, plus one
more, *Elmer Montgomery* for spares, on a grant basis
under the Foreign Assistance Act. The latter replaced the
former destroyer *Muavenet* which was scrapped after

being hit by a Sea Sparrow missile. The second batch of
four transferred in 1994. All eight purchased outright in
1999. F 251 decommissioned in 2000, F 257 in 2001, F 252
in 2002, F 254 in 2003 and F 256 in 2005.
Modernisation: Hangar and flight deck enlarged. In 1979
a programme was initiated to fit 3.5 ft bow bulwarks
and spray strakes adding 9.1 tons to a displacement.
Sea Sparrow SAM replaced by Phalanx 1982-88. Link
11 fitted after transfer. Project 'Kalyon-5' integrated new
multipurpose consoles into the combat data system.
Structure: Improved ASROC torpedo reloading capability
(note slanting face of bridge structure immediately
behind ASROC). Four Mk 32 torpedo tubes are fixed
in the midships structure, two to a side, angled out
at 45°. The arrangement provides improved loading
capability over exposed triple Mk 32 torpedo tubes.
A 4,000 lb lightweight anchor is fitted on the port side
and an 8,000 lb anchor fits into the after section of the
sonar dome.

MUAVENET

5/2005, C D Yaylali* / 1133584

ZAFER

1/2002, M Declerck / 0533245

6 BURAK (TYPE A 69) CLASS (FFGM)

Name	No	Builders	Laid down	Launched	Commissioned	Recommissioned
BOZCAADA (ex-*Commandant de Pimodan*)	F 500 (ex-F 787)	Lorient Naval Dockyard	15 July 1975	7 Aug 1976	20 May 1978	22 June 2001
BODRUM (ex-*Drogou*)	F 501 (ex-F 783)	Lorient Naval Dockyard	16 Oct 1973	30 Nov 1974	1 Oct 1976	18 Oct 2001
BANDIRMA (ex-*Quartier Maitre Anquetil*)	F 502 (ex-F 786)	Lorient Naval Dockyard	1 Aug 1975	7 Aug 1976	4 Feb 1978	15 Oct 2001
BEYKOZ (ex-*d'Estienne d'Orves*)	F 503 (ex-F 781)	Lorient Naval Dockyard	1 Sep 1972	1 June 1973	10 Sep 1976	18 Mar 2002
BARTIN (ex-*Amyot d'Inville*)	F 504 (ex-F 782)	Lorient Naval Dockyard	2 July 1973	30 Nov 1974	13 Oct 1976	3 June 2002
BAFRA (ex-*Second Maitre Le Bihan*)	F 505 (ex-F 788)	Lorient Naval Dockyard	1 Nov 1976	13 Aug 1977	7 July 1979	26 June 2002

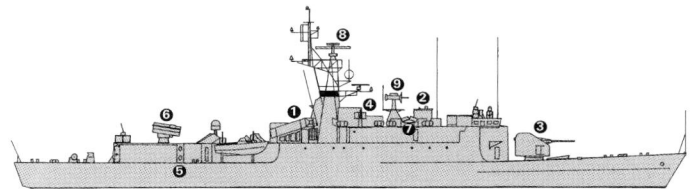

Displacement, tons: 1,175 standard; 1,250 (1,330 later ships) full load
Dimensions, feet (metres): 264.1 × 33.8 × 18 (sonar) (80.5 × 10.3 × 5.5)
Main machinery: 2 SEMT-Pielstick 12 PC2 V 400 diesels; 12,000 hp(m) (8.82 MW); 2 shafts; LIPS cp props
Speed, knots: 23
Range, n miles: 4,500 at 15 kt
Complement: 104 (10 officers)

Missiles: SSM: 2 Aerospatiale MM 38 Exocet ❶; inertial cruise; active radar homing to 70 km (40 n miles) or 42 km (23 n miles) at 0.9 Mach; warhead 165 kg; sea-skimmer.
SAM: Matra Simbad twin launcher for Mistral ❷; IR homing to 4 km (2.2 n miles); warhead 3 kg. This may be replaced by Stinger.
Guns: 1 DCN/Creusot-Loire 3.9 in (100 mm)/55 Mod 68 CADAM automatic ❸; 80 rds/min to 17 km (9 n miles) anti-surface; 8 km (4.4 n miles) anti-aircraft; weight of shell 13.5 kg.
2 Giat 20 mm ❹; 720 rds/min to 10 km (5.5 n miles).
4—12.7 mm MGs.
Torpedoes: 4 fixed tubes ❺. ECAN L5; dual purpose; active/passive homing to 9.5 km (5.1 n miles) at 35 kt; warhead 150 kg; depth to 550 m (1,800 ft).
A/S mortars: 1 Creusot-Loire 375 mm Mk 54 6-tubed trainable launcher ❻; range 1,600 m; warhead 107 kg.
Countermeasures: Decoys: 2 CSEE Dagaie 10-barrelled trainable launchers ❼; chaff and IR flares; H- to J-band. Nixie torpedo decoy.
ESM: ARBR 16; radar warning.
Weapons control: Thomson-CSF Vega system; CSEE Panda optical secondary director.
Radars: Air/surface search: Thomson-CSF DRBV 51A ❽; G-band.
Navigation: Racal Decca 1226; I-band.
Fire control: Thomson-CSF DRBC 32E ❾; I-band.

BOZCAADA — *(Scale 1 : 900), Ian Sturton* / 0114803

BANDIRMA — *4/2005*, C D Yaylali* / 1133583

Sonars: Thomson Sintra DUBA 25; hull-mounted; search and attack; medium frequency.

Comment: Six Type A 69 class bought second-hand from France in October 2000. All, except *Bafra*, refitted at Brest.

Work done on propulsion and weapons systems. Exocet MM 38 SSMs procured under separate contract. Operational use is coastal patrol duties, for which they were designed, in order to release more capable ships for front-line service.

CORVETTES

0 + 1 (11) MILGEM CLASS (FSG)

Name	No	Builders	Laid down	Launched	Commissioned
HEYBELIADA	—	Istanbul Naval Shipyard	26 July 2005	2007	2010

Displacement, tons: 1,500 standard; 2,000 full load
Dimensions, feet (metres): 324.8 × 45.9 × 12.3 (99.0 × 14.0 × 3.75)
Main machinery: 2 diesels; 1 gas turbine; 2 shafts; cp props
Speed, knots: 29
Range, n miles: To be announced
Complement: To be announced

Missiles: SSM: 8 McDonnell Douglas Harpoon (2 quadruple); active radar homing to 130 km (70 n miles) at 0.9 Mach; warhead 227 kg.
SAM: 1 RAM 21-cell Mk 49 launcher.
Guns: 1—3 in (76 mm). 2—12.7 mm MGs.
Torpedoes: 4—324 mm (2 twin) tubes.
Countermeasures: Decoys: To be announced.
ESM/ECM: To be announced.
Torpedo decoy system: To be announced.
Combat data systems: To be announced.
Weapons control: E/O system to be announced.
Radars: Air/surface search: 3D to be announced.
Fire control: To be announced.
Navigation: To be announced.
Sonars: To be announced.

HEYBELIADA (model) — *8/2005*, C D Yaylali* / 1133234

Helicopters: To be announced.

Programmes: The MILGEM project was launched in 1996 for the in-country design and construction of up to

12 anti-submarine warfare and offshore patrol vessels. The first of class is under construction in Istanbul and construction of follow-on ships is likely to be shared between several shipyards.

SHIPBORNE AIRCRAFT

Note: There are three AB 204 utility aircraft.

Numbers/Type: 9 Agusta AB 212ASW.
Operational speed: 106 kt (196 km/h).
Service ceiling: 14,200 ft (4,330 m).
Range: 230 n miles (426 km).
Role/Weapon systems: ASV/ASW helicopter with updated systems. Sensors: BAe Ferranti Sea Spray Mk 3 radar, ECM/ESM, MAD, Bendix ASQ-18 dipping sonar. Weapons: ASW; two Mk 46 or 244/S torpedoes. AVS; two Sea Skua missiles.

Numbers/Type: 7 Sikorsky S-70B Seahawk.
Operational speed: 135 kt (250 km/h).
Service ceiling: 10,000 ft (3,050 m).
Range: 600 n miles (1,110 km).
Role/Weapon systems: Contracts placed 3 June 1998 for first four. Second contract for four further aircraft on 31 December 1998. First three delivered 26 April 2002 and second four on 24 July 2003. One aircraft lost in accident. An order for a further 12 aircraft (with options for a further five) was placed on 24 June 2005. Deliveries to be made from 2008. Helras ASW weapon systems ordered. Sensors: APS-124 search radar; Helras dipping sonar. Weapons: ASW: 2 Mk 46 torpedoes; AGM-114B Hellfire II ASM.

AB 212 — *1/2002, M Declerck* / 0533250

SEAHAWK S-70B — *6/2002, Selçuk Emre* / 0533251

LAND-BASED MARITIME AIRCRAFT

Notes: Three Agusta AB 212EW helicopters are reported to be based at Topel.

Numbers/Type: 6 CASA CN-235 D/K MPA.
Operational speed: 240 kt *(445 km/h).*
Service ceiling: 26,600 ft *(8,110 m).*
Range: 669 n miles *(1,240 km).*
Role/Weapon systems: Initial batch of four delivered 25 July 2002 and a further two on 24 July 2003. Thales AMACOS mission control system. Long-range maritime patrol for surface surveillance and ASW. Sensors: Ocean Master radar (SAR, ISAR, MTI and air-to-air modes); FLIR; AAR-60 missile warning; DR 3000 A ESM; MAD; Link 11. Weapons: 2 Mk-46 torpedoes.

CN-235MPA   *1997, Paul Jackson* / 0056630

Numbers/Type: 10 Alenia ATR-72 ASW.
Operational speed: 255 kt *(472 km/h).*
Service ceiling: 22,000 ft *(6,705 m).*
Range: 1,200 n miles *(2,200 km).*
Role/Weapon systems: Project Meltem-3. Contract signed on 20 July 2005 for ten maritime patrol aircraft which are to receive a modified Thales Airborne Systems Amascos mission and sensor suite. Alenia will conduct platform modifications and perform systems integration on the first aircraft with the assistance of Turkish companies. First flight planned for 2008 and deliveries to take place between December 2009 and November 2011. Full details of weapons and sensors to be announced. The ATR72-ASW is based on the ATR72-500 which is a stretched version of the ATR42.

ATR-72 (model)   *9/2005*, C D Yaylali* / 1133582

PATROL FORCES

Notes: (1) *Kozlu* P 301 and *Kuşadasi* P 302 are listed under Vegesack class in Mine Warfare section.
(2) Request for Proposals for 16 new patrol craft was issued on 1 August 2005. A 400 ton vessel, capable of 25 kt, is required to replace the Turk, Trabzon and PGM 71 classes.

5 + 4 KILIÇ CLASS (FAST ATTACK CRAFT—MISSILE) (PGGF)

Name	No	Builders	Launched	Commissioned
KILIÇ	P 330	Lürssen, Vegesack	15 July 1997	17 Mar 1998
KALKAN	P 331	Taşkizak, Istanbul	22 Sep 1998	22 July 1999
MIZRAK	P 332	Taşkizak, Istanbul	5 Apr 1999	8 June 2000
TUFAN	P 333	Lürssen, Vegesack	25 July 2001	26 July 2005
MELTEM	P 334	Istanbul Naval Shipyard	1 Sep 2004	26 July 2005
IMBAT	P 335	Istanbul Naval Shipyard	26 July 2005	2006
ZIPKIN	P 336	Istanbul Naval Shipyard	2005	2007
ATAK	P 337	Istanbul Naval Shipyard	2006	2008
BORA	P 338	Istanbul Naval Shipyard	2007	2009

Displacement, tons: 550 full load
Dimensions, feet (metres): 204.6 × 27.2 × 8.5 *(62.4 × 8.3 × 2.6)*
Main machinery: 4 MTU 16V 956 TB91 diesels; 15,120 hp(m) *(11.1 MW)* sustained; 4 shafts
Speed, knots: 38
Range, n miles: 1,050 at 30 kt
Complement: 46 (12 officers)

Missiles: SSM: 8 McDonnell Douglas Harpoon (2 quad) launchers; active radar homing to 130 km *(70 n miles)* at 0.9 Mach; warhead 227 kg.
Guns: 1 Otobreda 3 in *(76 mm)*/62 compact; 85 rds/min to 16 km *(8.7 n miles)* anti-surface; 12 km *(6.6 n miles)* anti-aircraft; weight of shell 6 kg.
2 Otobreda 40 mm/70 (twin); 300 rds/min to 12 km *(6.6 n miles)*; weight of shell 0.96 kg.
Countermeasures: Decoys: 2 Mk 36 SRBOC chaff launchers.
ESM: Racal Cutlass; intercept.
Combat data systems: Signaal/Thomson-CSF STACOS.
Weapons control: LIROD Mk 2 optronic director; Vesta helo datalink/transponder.
Radars: Surface search: Signaal MW08; G-band.
Fire control: Signaal STING; I/J-band.
Navigation: KH 1007; I-band.

Programmes: Contract for first three signed in May 1993 but there was a delay in confirming it. Further four ordered 19 June 2000 since when a further two craft have been ordered.
Structure: A development of the Yildiz class but with reduced radar cross-section mast and a redesigned bow to improve sea-keeping. The after gun and radars are also different to *Yildiz.*
Operational: First of class arrived in Turkey in April 1998.

TUFAN   *6/2005*, Michael Nitz* / 1127054

KALKAN   *7/2005*, C D Yaylali* / 1133581

1 HISAR (PC 1638) CLASS (LARGE PATROL CRAFT) (PBO)

Name	No	Builders	Commissioned
AKHISAR (ex-PC 1641)	P 114	Gunderson, Portland	Dec 1964

Displacement, tons: 325 standard; 477 full load
Dimensions, feet (metres): 173.7 × 23 × 10.2 *(53 × 7 × 3.1)*
Main machinery: 2 Fairbanks-Morse diesels; 2,800 hp *(2.09 MW)*; 2 shafts
Speed, knots: 19
Range, n miles: 6,000 at 10 kt
Complement: 31 (3 officers)
Guns: 2 Bofors 40 mm/60.
Depth charges: 4 projectors; 1 rack (9).
Radars: Surface search: Decca 707; I-band.

Comment: Transferred from the US on build. ASW equipment removed. Three paid off in 2000. One in 2002 and one in 2005. P 114 expected to decommission as Kiliç class enter service.

HISAR CLASS   *6/2002, C D Yaylali* / 0533253

2 TRABZON CLASS (LARGE PATROL CRAFT) (PBO/AGI)

TRABZON (ex-*Gaspe*) P 530 (ex-M 530)   TERME (ex-*Trinity*) P 531 (ex-M 531)

Displacement, tons: 370 standard; 470 full load
Dimensions, feet (metres): 164 × 30.2 × 9.2 *(50 × 9.2 × 2.8)*
Main machinery: 2 GM 12-278A diesels; 2,200 hp *(1.64 MW)*; 2 shafts
Speed, knots: 15
Range, n miles: 4,500 at 11 kt
Complement: 35 (4 officers)
Guns: 1 Bofors 40 mm/60. 2 — 12.7 mm MGs.
Radars: Surface search: Racal Decca 1226; I-band.

Comment: All transferred from Canada and recommissioned 31 March 1958. Built by Davie SB Co 1951-53. Of similar type to British Ton class. Pennant numbers changed in 1991 reflecting use as patrol ships with all minesweeping gear removed.

TRABZON CLASS   *6/1999, Selim San* / 0080879

8 DOĞAN CLASS (FAST ATTACK CRAFT—MISSILE) (PGGF)

Name	No	Builders	Commissioned
DOĞAN	P 340	Lürssen, Vegesack	23 Dec 1977
MARTI	P 341	Taşkizak Yard, Istanbul	1 Aug 1978
TAYFUN	P 342	Taşkizak Yard, Istanbul	9 Aug 1979
VOLKAN	P 343	Taşkizak Yard, Istanbul	25 July 1980
RÜZGAR	P 344	Taşkizak Yard, Istanbul	24 May 1985
POYRAZ	P 345	Taşkizak Yard, Istanbul	28 Aug 1986
GURBET	P 346	Taşkizak Yard, Istanbul	24 July 1988
FIRTINA	P 347	Taşkizak Yard, Istanbul	14 Oct 1988

Displacement, tons: 436 full load
Dimensions, feet (metres): 190.6 × 25 × 8.8 *(58.1 × 7.6 × 2.7)*
Main machinery: 4 MTU 16V 956TB92 diesels; 17,700 hp(m) *(13 MW)* sustained; 4 shafts
Speed, knots: 38
Range, n miles: 1,050 at 30 kt
Complement: 40 (5 officers)

Missiles: SSM: 8 McDonnell Douglas Harpoon (2 quad) launchers; active radar homing to 130 km *(70 n miles)* at 0.9 Mach; warhead 227 kg.
Guns: 1 OTO Melara 3 in *(76 mm)*/62 compact; 85 rds/min to 16 km *(8.7 n miles)* anti-surface; 12 km *(6.6 n miles)* anti-aircraft; weight of shell 6 kg.
2 Oerlikon 35 mm/90 (twin); 550 rds/min to 6 km *(3.3 n miles)*; weight of shell 1.55 kg.
Countermeasures: Decoys: 2 Mk 36 SRBOC chaff launchers.
ESM: MEL Susie (344—347); intercept.
Combat data systems: Signaal miniTACTICOS (344—347).
Weapons control: LIOD Mk 2 optronic director.
Radars: Surface search: Racal Decca 1226; I-band.
Fire control: Signaal WM28/41; I/J-band.

Programmes: First ordered 3 August 1973 to a Lürssen FPB 57 design.
Modernisation: A mid-life programme includes upgrade to the combat data system, communications and ESM. Work on the first four was completed in 2002 while work on the second four is to start in 2004.
Structure: Aluminium superstructure; steel hulls. The last pair were built with optronic directors which are being retrofitted in all, together with an improved Signaal combat data system.

DOĞAN *7/2005*, C D Yaylali* / 1133580

VOLKAN *11/2005*, Manuel Declerck* / 1153503

2 YILDIZ CLASS (FAST ATTACK CRAFT—MISSILE) (PGGF)

Name	No	Builders	Commissioned
YILDIZ	P 348	Taşkizak Yard, Istanbul	3 June 1996
KARAYEL	P 349	Taşkizak Yard, Istanbul	19 Sep 1996

Displacement, tons: 433 full load
Dimensions, feet (metres): 189.6 oa; 178.5 wl × 25 × 8.8 *(57.8; 54.4 × 7.6 × 2.7)*
Main machinery: 4 MTU 16V 956 TB91 diesels; 15,120 hp(m) *(11.1 MW)* sustained; 4 shafts
Speed, knots: 38
Range, n miles: 1,050 at 30 kt
Complement: 45 (6 officers)

Missiles: SSM: 8 McDonnell Douglas Harpoon (2 quad) launchers; active radar homing to 130 km *(70 n miles)* at 0.9 Mach; warhead 227 kg.
Guns: 1 OTO Melara 3 in *(76 mm)*/62 compact; 85 rds/min to 16 km *(8.7 n miles)* anti-surface; 12 km *(6.6 n miles)* anti-aircraft; weight of shell 6 kg.
2 Oerlikon 35 mm/90 (twin); 550 rds/min to 6 km *(3.3 n miles)*; weight of shell 1.55 kg.
Countermeasures: Decoys: 2 Mk 36 SRBOC chaff launchers.
ESM: Racal Cutlass; intercept.
Combat data systems: Signaal/Thomson-CSFTACTICOS.
Weapons control: LIOD Mk 2 optronic director; Vesta helo datalink/transponder.
Radars: Surface search: Siemens/Plessey AW 6 Dolphin; G-band.
Fire control: Oerlikon/Contraves TMX; I/J-band.
Navigation: Racal DeccaTM 1226; I-band.

Programmes: Ordered in June 1991. *Karayel* launched 20 June 1995.
Structure: Doğan class hull with much improved weapon systems. A second batch is sufficiently different to merit a separate entry.

YILDIZ *10/2003, C D Yaylali* / 0567552

8 KARTAL CLASS (FAST ATTACK CRAFT—MISSILE) (PTGF)

Name	No	Builders	Commissioned
DENIZKUŞU	P 321 (ex-P 336)	Lürssen, Vegesack	9 Mar 1967
ATMACA	P 322 (ex-P 335)	Lürssen, Vegesack	9 Mar 1967
ŞAHIN	P 323 (ex-P 334)	Lürssen, Vegesack	3 Nov 1966
KARTAL	P 324 (ex-P 333)	Lürssen, Vegesack	3 Nov 1966
PELIKAN	P 326	Lürssen, Vegesack	11 Feb 1970
ALBATROS	P 327 (ex-P 325)	Lürssen, Vegesack	18 Mar 1970
ŞIMŞEK	P 328 (ex-P 332)	Lürssen, Vegesack	6 Nov 1969
KASIRGA	P 329 (ex-P 338)	Lürssen, Vegesack	25 Nov 1967

Displacement, tons: 160 standard; 190 full load
Dimensions, feet (metres): 139.4 × 23 × 7.9 *(42.5 × 7 × 2.4)*
Main machinery: 4 MTU MD 16V 538TB90 diesels; 12,000 hp(m) *(8.82 MW)* sustained; 4 shafts
Speed, knots: 42. **Range, n miles:** 500 at 40 kt
Complement: 39 (4 officers)

Missiles: SSM: 2 or 4 Kongsberg Penguin Mk 2; IR homing to 27 km *(14.6 n miles)* at 0.8 Mach; warhead 120 kg.
Guns: 2 Bofors 40 mm/70; 300 rds/min to 12 km *(6.6 n miles)*; weight of shell 0.96 kg.
Torpedoes: 2—21 in *(533 mm)* tubes; anti-surface.
Mines: Can carry 4.
Radars: Surface search: Racal Decca 1226; I-band.

Operational: *Meltem* sunk in collision with Soviet naval training ship *Khasan* in Bosphorus in 1985. Subsequently salvaged but beyond repair. Although these craft are getting old, there are no plans to decommission them in the short term.

ŞIMŞEK *4/2004*, Marco Ghiglino* / 1133592

6 TURK CLASS (LARGE PATROL CRAFT) (PC)

Name	No	Builders	Commissioned
AB 27	P 127 (ex-P 1227)	Haliç Shipyard	27 June 1969
AB 28	P 128 (ex-P 1228)	Haliç Shipyard	Apr 1969
AB 29	P 129 (ex-P 1229)	Haliç Shipyard	21 Feb 1969
AB 31	P 131 (ex-P 1231)	Haliç Shipyard	17 Nov 1971
AB 35	P 135 (ex-P 1235)	Taşkizak Shipyard	13 Apr 1976
AB 36	P 136 (ex-P 1236)	Taşkizak Shipyard	13 Apr 1976

Displacement, tons: 170 full load
Dimensions, feet (metres): 132 × 21 × 5.5 *(40.2 × 6.4 × 1.7)*
Main machinery: 4 SACM-AGO V16CSHR diesels; 9,600 hp(m) *(7.06 MW)*
2 cruise diesels; 300 hp(m) *(220 kW)*; 2 shafts
Speed, knots: 22
Complement: 31 (3 officers)
Guns: 1 or 2 Bofors 40 mm/70.
1 Oerlikon 20 mm (in those with 1—40 mm). 2—12.7 mm MGs.
A/S mortars: 1 Mk 20 Mousetrap 4 rocket launcher; range 200 m; warhead 50 kg.
Depth charges: 1 rack.
Radars: Surface search: Racal Decca; I-band.
Sonars: Plessey PMS 26; hull-mounted; active search and attack; high frequency.

Comment: Pennant numbers changed in 1991. Similar to *SG 21* Coast Guard class. One to Georgia *(AB 30)* in December 1998, one to Azerbaijan *(AB 34)* in July 2000 and one to Kazakhstan *(AB 26)* in July 2001. *AB 33* decommissioned in 2005.

AB 31 *5/2005*, Martin Mokrus* / 1133571

4 PGM 71 CLASS (LARGE PATROL CRAFT) (PC)

AB 21-24 (ex-PGM 104-107) P121-124 (ex-P1221-1224)

Displacement, tons: 130 standard; 147 full load
Dimensions, feet (metres): 101 × 21 × 7 *(30.8 × 6.4 × 2.1)*
Main machinery: 8 GM diesels 2,040 hp *(1.52 MW)*; 2 shafts
Speed, knots: 18.5. **Range, n miles:** 1,500 at 10 kt
Complement: 31 (3 officers)
Guns: 1 Bofors 40 mm/60. 4 Oerlikon 20 mm (2 twin). 1—7.62 mm MG.
A/S mortars: 2 Mk 22 Mousetrap 8 rocket launchers; range 200 m; warhead 50 kg.
Depth charges: 2 racks (4).
Radars: Surface search: Raytheon 1500B; I-band.
Sonars: EDO SQS-17A; hull-mounted; active attack; high frequency.

Comment: Built by Peterson, Sturgeon Bay and commissioned 1967-68. Transferred from US almost immediately after completion. Pennant numbers changed in 1991.

AB 24 *11/2005*, Manuel Declerck* / 1153506

AMPHIBIOUS FORCES

Notes: (1) The prefix 'Ç' for smaller amphibious vessels stands for 'Çikartma Gemisi' (landing vessel) and indicates that the craft are earmarked for national rather than NATO control.

(2) There are plans to procure a landing platform dock capable of both military and humanitarian assistance operations. The ship is expected to be of the order of 12-15,000 tons and to be capable of carrying 600 troops. Entry into service is planned to be 2012 although this may be delayed by funding constraints.

1 OSMAN GAZI CLASS (LSTH/ML)

Name	No	Builders	Launched	Commissioned
OSMAN GAZI	NL 125	Taşkizak Yard, Istanbul	20 July 1990	27 July 1994

Displacement, tons: 3,773 full load
Dimensions, feet (metres): 344.5 × 52.8 × 15.7 *(105 × 16.1 × 4.8)*
Main machinery: 2 MTU 12V 1163 TB73 diesels; 8,800 hp(m) *(6.47 MW)*; 2 shafts
Speed, knots: 17
Range, n miles: 4,000 at 15 kt
Military lift: 900 troops; 15 tanks; 4 LCVPs
Guns: 2 Oerlikon 35 mm/90 (twin). 4 Bofors 40 mm/70 (2 twin). 2 Oerlikon 20 mm.
Radars: Navigation: Racal Decca; I-band.
Helicopters: Platform for 1 large.

Comment: Laid down 7 July 1989. Full NBCD protection. Equipped with a support weapons co-ordination centre to control amphibious operations. The ship has about a 50 per cent increase in military lift capacity compared with the Sarucabey class. Secondary role as minelayer. Second of class cancelled in 1991 and *Osman Gazi* took a long time to complete. Marisat fitted.

OSMAN GAZI *7/2004**, Schaeffer/Marsan / 1133579

OSMAN GAZI *6/2004**, Camil Busquets i Vilanova / 1133590

2 ERTUĞRUL (TERREBONNE PARISH) CLASS (LSTH/ML)

Name	No	Builders	Commissioned
ERTUĞRUL (ex-*Windham County* LST 1170)	L 401	Christy Corporation	15 Dec 1954
SERDAR (ex-*Westchester County* LST 1167)	L 402	Christy Corporation	10 Mar 1954

Displacement, tons: 2,590 light; 5,800 full load
Dimensions, feet (metres): 384 × 55 × 17 *(117.1 × 16.8 × 5.2)*
Main machinery: 4 GM 16-278A diesels; 6,000 hp *(4.48 MW)*; 2 shafts; cp props
Speed, knots: 15
Complement: 163 (14 officers)
Military lift: 395 troops; 2,200 tons cargo; 4 LCVPs
Guns: 6 USN 3 in *(76 mm)*/50 (3 twin).
Weapons control: 2 Mk 63 GFCS.
Radars: Surface search: Racal Decca 1226; I-band.
Fire control: 2 Western Electric Mk 34; I/J-band.

Comment: Transferred by US and recommissioned 3 October 1973 and 24 February 1975 respectively. Purchased outright 6 August 1987. Marisat fitted.

ERTUĞRUL *11/2004**, M Declerck / 1133577

2 SARUCABEY CLASS (LSTH/ML)

Name	No	Builders	Launched	Commissioned
SARUCABEY	NL 123	Taşkizak Naval Yard	30 July 1981	17 July 1984
KARAMÜRSELBEY	NL 124	Taşkizak Naval Yard	26 July 1984	19 June 1987

Displacement, tons: 2,600 full load
Dimensions, feet (metres): 301.8 × 45.9 × 7.5 *(92 × 14 × 2.3)*
Main machinery: 3 diesels; 4,320 hp *(3.2 MW)*; 3 shafts
Speed, knots: 14
Military lift: 600 troops; 11 tanks; 12 jeeps; 2 LCVPs
Guns: 3 Bofors 40 mm/70. 4 Oerlikon 20 mm (2 twin).
Mines: 150 in lieu of amphibious lift.
Radars: Navigation: Racal Decca 1226; I-band.
Helicopters: Platform only.

Comment: *Sarucabey* is an enlarged Çakabey design more suitable for naval requirements. Dual-purpose minelayers. NL 124 has superstructure one deck lower.

KARAMÜRSELBEY *2/2004**, Selim San / 1133578

1 EDIC TYPE (LCT)

120

Displacement, tons: 580 full load
Dimensions, feet (metres): 186.9 × 39.4 × 4.6 *(57 × 12 × 1.4)*
Main machinery: 3 GM 6-71 diesels; 522 hp *(390 kW)* sustained; 3 shafts
Speed, knots: 8.5
Range, n miles: 600 at 10 kt
Complement: 15
Military lift: 100 troops; up to 5 tanks
Guns: 2 Oerlikon 20 mm. 2—12.7 mm MGs.
Radars: Navigation: Racal Decca; I-band.

Comment: Vessel built at Gölcük Naval Shipyard in 1973. French EDIC type.

EDIC TYPE *2/1996, C D Yaylali / 0080888*

23 LCT

Ç 123, Ç 125-128, Ç 132-135, Ç 137-150

Displacement, tons: 600 standard
Dimensions, feet (metres): 195.5 × 38 × 10.5 *(59.6 × 11.6 × 3.2)*
Main machinery: 3 GM 6—71 diesels; 522 hp *(390 kW)* sustained; 3 shafts *(119— 138)* or 3 MTU diesels; 900 hp(m) *(662 kW)*; 3 shafts *(139— 150)*
Speed, knots: 8.5
Range, n miles: 600 at 8 kt
Complement: 17 (1 officer)
Military lift: 100 troops; 5 tanks
Guns: 2 Oerlikon 20 mm. 2—12.7 mm MGs.
Radars: Navigation: Racal Decca; I-band.

Comment: Follow-on to the Ç 107 type started building in 1977. Ç 130 and Ç 131 transferred to Libya January 1980 and Ç 136 sunk in 1985. The delivery rate was about two per year from the Taşkizak and Gölcük yards until 1987. Then two launched in July 1987 and commissioned in 1991. Last three completed in 1992. Dimensions given are for Ç 139 onwards, earlier craft are 3.6 m shorter and have less freeboard.

LCT *8/1995, Selçuk Emre / 0080889*

17 LCM 8 TYPE

Ç 305, Ç 308, Ç 312-314, Ç 316, Ç 319, Ç 321-327, Ç 329-331

Displacement, tons: 58 light; 113 full load
Dimensions, feet (metres): 72 × 20.5 × 4.8 *(22 × 6.3 × 1.4)*
Main machinery: 4 GM 6-71 diesels; 696 hp *(520 kW)* sustained; 2 shafts
Speed, knots: 9.5
Complement: 9
Military lift: 60 tons or 140 troops
Guns: 2—12.7 mm MGs.

Comment: Up to Ç 319 built by Taşkizak and Haliç in 1965-66. Ç 321-331 built by Taşkizak and Naldöken in 1987-89.

Ç 308 *6/2003, Turkish Navy / 0567540*

2 FAST INTERVENTION CRAFT (HSIC)

Displacement, tons: 18 full load
Dimensions, feet (metres): 55.1 × 13.2 × 3.2 *(16.8 × 4.04 × 1.0)*
Main machinery: 2 MTU 12V 183 TE94 diesels; 2,588 hp(m) *(1.93 MW)*; 2 Arneson ASD 12 B1L surface drives
Speed, knots: 50+
Complement: 2 plus 10 mission crew

Comment: Capable of carrying a RIB and used by Special Forces. Details are speculative.

FAST INTERVENTION CRAFT   *10/2000* / 0106641

MINE WARFARE FORCES

Notes: Minelayers: see *Sarucabey, Karamürselbey* and *Osmangazi* under Amphibious Forces.

2 + 4 AYDIN CLASS (TYPE MHV 54-014) (MHSC)

Name	No	Builders	Commissioned
ALANYA	M 265	Abeking & Rasmussen	26 July 2005
AMASRA	M 266	Instanbul Naval Shipyard	26 July 2005
AYVALIK	M 267	Instanbul Naval Shipyard	2006
AKÇAKOCA	M 268	Instanbul Naval Shipyard	2007
ANAMUR	M 269	Instanbul Naval Shipyard	2007
AKÇAY	M 270	Instanbul Naval Shipyard	2008

Displacement, tons: 715 full load
Dimensions, feet (metres): 178.8 × 31.8 × 8.5 *(54.5 × 9.7 × 2.6)*
Main machinery: 2 MTU 8V 396 TB84 diesels; 2 Voith-Schneider props; 2 Schottel bow thrusters
Speed, knots: 14
Complement: 53 (6 officers)
Guns: 1 Otobreda 30 mm. 2—12.7 mm MGs.
Countermeasures: MCM: 2 ECA PAP 104 Mk 5. 1 Oropesa mechanical sweep.
Combat data systems: Alenia Marconi Nautis-M.
Radars: Navigation: KH 1007; I-band.
Sonars: Thomson Marconi Type 2093; VDS; active high frequency.

Comment: Ordered from Abeking & Rasmussen and Lürssen on 30 July 1999. First one built in Bremen, remainder in Turkey. The design is based on the German Type 332 but with different propulsion and mine countermeasures equipment. Non-magnetic steel hull. First of class laid down 6 November 2000, second on 25 July 2001, third on 25 July 2002 and fourth on 24 July 2003, the fifth on 27 July 2004 and sixth on 26 July 2005. All to complete by 2007.

ALANYA   *5/2004, Frank Findler* / 0589819

ALANYA   *6/2003, Martin Mokrus* / 0567555

2 MINELAYER TENDERS (MLI)

ŞAMANDIRA MOTORU-1 Y 91   ŞAMANDIRA MOTORU-2 Y 92
(ex-Y 132, ex-Y 1149)   (ex-Y 1150)

Displacement, tons: 72 full load
Dimensions, feet (metres): 64.3 × 18.7 × 5.9 *(19.6 × 5.7 × 1.8)*
Main machinery: 1 Gray Marine 64 HN9 diesel; 225 hp *(168 kW)*; 1 shaft
Speed, knots: 10
Complement: 8

Comment: Acquired in 1959. Used for laying and recovering mine distribution boxes.

ŞAMANDIRA MOTORU-1   *6/2004, Turkish Navy* / 0589830

5 EDINCIK (CIRCÉ) CLASS (MINEHUNTERS) (MHC)

Name	No	Builders	Launched	Commissioned
EDINCIK (ex-*Cybèle*)	M 260 (ex-M 712)	CMN, Cherbourg	28 Sep 1972	24 July 1998
EDREMIT (ex-*Calliope*)	M 261 (ex-M 713)	CMN, Cherbourg	28 Sep 1972	28 Aug 1998
ENEZ (ex-*Cérès*)	M 262 (ex-M 716)	CMN, Cherbourg	7 Mar 1973	30 Oct 1998
ERDEK (ex-*Circé*)	M 263 (ex-M 715)	CMN, Cherbourg	18 May 1972	4 Dec 1998
ERDEMLI (ex-*Clio*)	M 264 (ex-M 714)	CMN, Cherbourg	18 May 1972	15 Jan 1999

Displacement, tons: 460 standard; 495 normal; 510 full load
Dimensions, feet (metres): 167 × 29.2 × 11.2 *(50.9 × 8.9 × 3.4)*
Main machinery: 1 MTU diesel; 1,800 hp(m) *(1.32 MW)*; 2 active rudders; 1 shaft
Speed, knots: 15
Range, n miles: 3,000 at 12 kt
Complement: 48 (5 officers)
Guns: 1 Oerlikon 20 mm.
Countermeasures: MCM: DCN Mintac minehunting system with PAP Plus ROV.
Radars: Navigation: Racal Decca 1229; I-band.
Sonars: Thomson Sintra DUBM 20B; hull-mounted; active search; high frequency.

Comment: Acquired from France on 24 September 1997. Full refits included installation of Mintac system before being handed over.

ENEZ   *1/2004, Giorgio Ghiglione* / 0589820

6 VEGESACK CLASS (MSC/AGS/PBO)

Name	No	Builders	Commissioned
KARAMÜRSEL (ex-*Worms* M 1253)	M 520	Amiot, Cherbourg	30 Apr 1960
KEREMPE (ex-*Detmold* M 1252)	M 521	Amiot, Cherbourg	20 Feb 1960
KILIMLI (ex-*Siegen* M 1254)	M 522	Amiot, Cherbourg	9 July 1960
KOZLU (ex-*Hameln* M 1251)	P 301 (ex-M 523)	Amiot, Cherbourg	15 Oct 1959
KUŞADASI (ex-*Vegesack* M 1250)	P 302 (ex-M 524)	Amiot, Cherbourg	19 Sep 1959
KEMER (ex-*Passau* M 1255)	A 582 (ex-M 525)	Amiot, Cherbourg	15 Oct 1960

Displacement, tons: 362 standard; 378 full load
Dimensions, feet (metres): 155.1 × 28.2 × 9.5 *(47.3 × 8.6 × 2.9)*
Main machinery: 2 MTU MB diesels; 1,500 hp(m) *(1.1 MW)*; 2 shafts; cp props
Speed, knots: 15
Complement: 33 (2 officers)
Guns: 2 Oerlikon 20 mm (twin).
Radars: Navigation: Decca 707; I-band.
Sonars: Simrad; active mine detection; high frequency.

Comment: Transferred by West Germany and recommissioned in the mid-1970s. Sonars were fitted from 1989. *Kemer* paid off in 1998 but returned as a survey ship in 1999. *Kozlu* and *Kuşadasi* similarly refitted as patrol ships in 1999.

KEMER   *4/2005*, Selim San* / 1133591

5 MSC 289 CLASS (MINESWEEPERS—COASTAL) (MSC)

SILIFKE (ex-MSC 304) M 514   **SAPANCA** (ex-MSC 312) M 517
SAROS (ex-MSC 305) M 515   **SARIYER** (ex-MSC 315) M 518
SIGACIK (ex-MSC 311) M 516

Displacement, tons: 320 standard; 370 full load
Dimensions, feet (metres): 141 × 26 × 8.3 *(43 × 8 × 2.6)*
Main machinery: 4 GM 6—71 diesels; 696 hp *(519 kW)* sustained; 2 shafts (M 510—M 513)
  2 Waukesha L 1616 diesels; 1,200 hp *(895 kW)*; 2 shafts (M 514—M 518)
Speed, knots: 14. **Range, n miles:** 2,500 at 10 kt
Complement: 35 (2 officers)
Guns: 2 Oerlikon 20 mm (twin).
Radars: Navigation: Racal Decca 1226; I-band.
Sonars: UQS-1D; hull-mounted mine search; high frequency.

Comment: Built 1965-67. Transferred from US. Commissioning dates in the Turkish Navy
were respectively: 21 March 1966, 25 October 1966, 20 December 1965, 20 December 1965
and 7 December 1967.

SAPANCA   *10/2003, C D Yaylali* / 0567556

SARIYER   *10/2003, C D Yaylali* / 0567557

4 COVE CLASS (MINESWEEPERS—INSHORE) (MSI)

Name	No	Builders	Commissioned
FOÇA (ex-MSI 15)	M 500	Peterson, WI	19 Apr 1968
FETHIYE (ex-MSI 16)	M 501	Peterson, WI	24 Apr 1968
FATSA (ex-MSI 17)	M 502	Peterson, WI	21 Mar 1968
FINIKE (ex-MSI 18)	M 503	Peterson, WI	26 Apr 1968

Displacement, tons: 180 standard; 235 full load
Dimensions, feet (metres): 111.9 × 23.5 × 7.9 *(34 × 7.1 × 2.4)*
Main machinery: 4 GM 6-71 diesels; 696 hp *(520 kW)* sustained; 2 shafts
Speed, knots: 13
Range, n miles: 900 at 11 kt
Complement: 25 (3 officers)
Guns: 1—12.7 mm MG.
Radars: Navigation: I-band.

Comment: Built in US and transferred under MAP at Boston, Massachusetts, August-
December 1967.

FINIKE   *5/2001, Selim San* / 0114808

6 MINEHUNTING TENDERS (YAG/YDT)

MTB 3 P 313   **MTB 6** P 316   **MTB 8** P 318
MTB 4 P 314   **MTB 7** P 317   **MTB 9** P 319

Displacement, tons: 70 standard
Dimensions, feet (metres): 71.5 × 13.8 × 8.5 *(21.8 × 4.2 × 2.6)*
Main machinery: 2 diesels; 2,000 hp(m) *(1.47 MW)*; 2 shafts
Speed, knots: 20
Guns: 1 Oerlikon 20 mm or 1—12.7 mm MG (aft) (in some).

Comment: All launched in 1942. Now employed as minehunting base ships.

MTB 6   *7/1995, van Ginderen Collection* / 0080886

SURVEY SHIPS

Notes: *Kemer* A 582 (ex-M 525) is listed under Vegesack class in Mine Warfare Forces.

2 SILAS BENT CLASS (AGS)

Name	No	Builders	Commissioned
ÇESME (ex-*Silas Bent*)	A 599 (ex-TAGS 26)	American SB Co, Lorain	23 July 1965
ÇANDARLI (ex-*Kane*)	A 588 (ex-TAGS 27)	Christy Corp, Sturgeon Bay	19 May 1967

Displacement, tons: 2,843 full load
Dimensions, feet (metres): 285.3 × 48 × 15.1 *(87 × 14.6 × 4.6)*
Main machinery: Diesel-electric; 2 Alco diesel generators; 1 Westinghouse/GE motor;
  3,600 hp *(2.69 MW)*; 1 shaft; cp prop; bow thruster 350 hp *(261 kW)*
Speed, knots: 15. **Range, n miles:** 12,000 at 14 kt
Complement: 31 plus 28 spare
Radars: Navigation: RM 1650/9X; I-band.

Comment: *Çesme* transferred from US on 28 October 1999 and *Çanadarli* on 14 March 2001.

ÇANDARLI   *11/2005*, Manuel Declerck* / 1153505

1 SURVEY SHIP (AGS)

Name	No	Builders	Launched	Commissioned
ÇUBUKLU (ex-Y 1251)	A 594	Gölcük	17 Nov 1983	24 June 1987

Displacement, tons: 680 full load
Dimensions, feet (metres): 132.8 × 31.5 × 10.5 *(40.5 × 9.6 × 3.2)*
Main machinery: 1 MWM diesel; 820 hp(m) *(603 kW)*; 1 shaft; cp prop
Speed, knots: 11
Complement: 37 (6 officers)
Guns: 2 Oerlikon 20 mm.
Radars: Navigation: Racal Decca; I-band.

Comment: Qubit advanced integrated navigation and data processing system fitted in 1991.

ÇUBUKLU   *6/1997, Turkish Navy* / 0050296

2 SURVEY CRAFT (AGSC)

MESAHA 1 Y 35   **MESAHA 2** Y 36

Displacement, tons: 38 full load
Dimensions, feet (metres): 52.2 × 14.8 × 4.3 *(15.9 × 4.5 × 1.3)*
Main machinery: 2 GM 6—71 diesels; 348 hp *(260 kW)* sustained; 2 shafts
Speed, knots: 10. **Range, n miles:** 600 at 10 kt
Complement: 9

Comment: Completed in 1994 and took the names and pennant numbers of their deleted
predecessors.

MESAHA 2   *9/1994, C D Yaylali* / 0080890

TRAINING SHIPS

Notes: *Samsun* decommissioned in 2005.

2 RHEIN CLASS (AG/AX)

Name	No	Builders	Commissioned
CEZAYIRLI GAZI HASAN PAŞA (ex-*Elbe*)	A 579	Schliekerwerft, Hamburg	17 Apr 1962
SOKULLU MEHMET PAŞA (ex-*Donau*)	A 577	Schlichting, Travemünde	23 May 1964

Displacement, tons: 2,370 standard; 2,940 full load
Dimensions, feet (metres): 322.1 × 38.8 × 14.4 *(98.2 × 11.8 × 4.4)*
Main machinery: Diesel-electric; 6 MTU MD diesels; 14,400 hp(m) *(10.58 MW)*; 2 Siemens motors; 11,400 hp(m) *(8.38 MW)*; 2 shafts
Speed, knots: 20.5. **Range, n miles:** 1,625 at 15 kt
Complement: 188 (15 officers)
Guns: 2 Creusot-Loire 3.9 in *(100 mm)*/55. 4 Bofors 40 mm/60.
Radars: Surface search: Signaal DA02; E/F-band.
Fire control: 2 Signaal M 45; I/J-band.

Comment: *Elbe* transferred from Germany on 15 March 1993, taking over the same name and pennant number as the former *Ruhr*. *Donau* transferred 13 March 1995 taking the same name and pennant number as the deleted *Isar*.

SOKOLLU MEHMET PAŞA   *5/2005*, Martin Mokrus* / 1133576

8 TRAINING CRAFT (AXL)

Name	No	Builders	Commissioned
E 1	A 1531	Bora-Duzgit	22 July 1999
E 2	A 1532	Bora-Duzgit	22 July 1999
E 3	A 1533	Bora-Duzgit	8 June 2000
E 4	A 1534	Bora-Duzgit	8 June 2000
E 5	A 1535	Bora-Duzgit	8 June 2000
E 6	A 1536	Bora-Duzgit	8 June 2000
E 7	A 1537	Bora-Duzgit	8 June 2000
E 8	A 1538	Bora-Duzgit	8 June 2000

Displacement, tons: 94 full load
Dimensions, feet (metres): 94.5 × 19.7 × 6.2 *(28.8 × 6 × 1.9)*
Main machinery: 1 MTU diesel; 1 shaft
Speed, knots: 12. **Range, n miles:** 240 at 12 kt
Complement: 15

Comment: Naval Academy training craft ordered in 1998.

E 1   *7/1999, Selçuk Emre* / 0080892

AUXILIARIES

1 TRANSPORT SHIP (AK)

Name	No	Builders	Commissioned	Recommissioned
ISKENDERUN	A 1600	Camialti Shipyard, Istanbul	25 July 2002	1991

Measurement, tons: 10,583 gross; 3,872 net
Dimensions, feet (metres): 418.4 × 64.0 × 17.7 *(127.5 × 19.5 × 5.4)*
Main machinery: 4 Skoda and Sulzer diesels; 16,800 hp *(12.52 MW)*; 2 shafts
Speed, knots: 15.5
Complement: 129 (11 officers)

Comment: Car ferry (214 cars and passengers) built to Polish design. Commissioned in Turkish Navy on 25 July 2002.

ISKENDERUN   *3/2004, Selim San* / 0587559

2 FLEET SUPPORT SHIPS (AORH)

Name	No	Builders	Laid down	Launched	Commissioned
AKAR	A 580	Gölcük Naval Dockyard	5 Aug 1982	17 Nov 1983	9 Sep 1987
YARBAY KUDRET GÜNGÖR	A 595	Sedef Shipyard, Istanbul	5 Nov 1993	15 Nov 1994	24 Oct 1995

Displacement, tons: 19,350 full load
Dimensions, feet (metres): 475.9 × 74.8 × 27.6 *(145.1 × 22.8 × 8.4)*
Main machinery: 1 diesel; 6,500 hp(m) *(4.78 MW)*; 1 shaft
Speed, knots: 16
Range, n miles: 6,000 at 14 kt
Complement: 203 (14 officers)
Cargo capacity: 16,000 tons oil fuel (A 580); 9,980 tons oil fuel (A 595); 2,700 tons water (A 595); 80 tons hub oil (A 595); 500 m³ stores (A 595)
Guns: 2—3 in *(76 mm)*/50 (twin) Mk 34 (A 580). 1—20 mm/76 Mk 15 Vulcan Phalanx (A 595). 2 Bofors 40 mm/70.
Weapons control: Mk 63 GFCS (A 580).
Radars: Fire control: SPG-34; I-band (A 580).
Navigation: Racal Decca 1226; I-band.
Helicopters: Platform for 1 medium.

Comment: Helicopter flight deck aft. *Akar* is primarily a tanker whereas the second ship of the same type is classified as logistic support vessel. *Güngör* was the first naval ship to be built at a civilian yard in Turkey.

AKAR   *6/2003, Selçuk Emre* / 0589821

1 SUPPORT TANKER (AOTL)

Name	No	Builders	Launched	Commissioned
TAŞKIZAK	A 570	Taşkizak Naval DY, Istanbul	28 July 1983	14 Aug 1985

Displacement, tons: 1,440 full load
Dimensions, feet (metres): 211.9 × 30.8 × 11.5 *(64.6 × 9.4 × 3.5)*
Main machinery: 1 diesel; 1,400 hp(m) *(1.03 MW)*; 1 shaft
Speed, knots: 13
Complement: 57
Cargo capacity: 800 tons
Guns: 1 Bofors 40 mm/60. 2 Oerlikon 20 mm.
Radars: Navigation: Racal Decca 1226; I-band.

Comment: Laid down 20 July 1983.

TAŞKIZAK (Doğan class in background)   *5/1990, A Sheldon Duplaix* / 0080893

2 SUPPORT TANKERS (AOT)

Name	No	Builders	Commissioned
ALBAY HAKKI BURAK	A 571	RMK Tuzla, Istanbul	21 Nov 1999
YUZBASI IHSAN TOLUNAY	A 572	RMK Tuzla, Istanbul	8 June 2000

Displacement, tons: 3,300 full load
Dimensions, feet (metres): 267.1 × 40 × 16.4 *(81.4 × 12.2 × 5)*
Main machinery: 2 Caterpillar 3606TA diesels; 5,522 hp(m) *(4.06 MW)*; 2 shafts
Speed, knots: 15
Complement: 50
Cargo capacity: 2,355 m³ dieso

Comment: Ordered in 1998.

ALBAY HAKKI BURAK   *6/2002, Selçuk Emre* / 0533258

1 SUPPORT TANKER (AORL)

Name	No	Builders	Commissioned
BINBAŞI SADETTIN GÜRCAN	A 573	Taşkizak Naval DY, Istanbul	4 Sep 1970

Displacement, tons: 1,505 standard; 4,460 full load
Dimensions, feet (metres): 294.2 × 38.7 × 17.7 *(89.7 × 11.8 × 5.4)*
Main machinery: Diesel-electric; 4 GM 16-567A diesels; 5,600 hp *(4.12 MW)*; 4 generators; 2 motors; 4,400 hp *(3.28 MW)*; 2 shafts
Speed, knots: 16
Complement: 63
Guns: 2 Oerlikon 20 mm.
Radars: Navigation: E/F-band.

Comment: Main armament removed. Can be used for replenishment at sea.

BINBAŞI SADETTIN GÜRCAN   *6/1995, Turkish Navy* / 0080895

3 WATER TANKERS (AWT)

SÖGÜT (ex-FW 2) A 598 (ex-Y 1217)   **KAVAK** (ex-FW 4) A 600   **ÇINAR** (ex-FW 1) A 581

Displacement, tons: 626 full load
Dimensions, feet (metres): 144.4 × 25.6 × 8.2 *(44.1 × 7.8 × 2.5)*
Main machinery: 1 MWM diesel; 230 hp(m) *(169 kW)*; 1 shaft
Speed, knots: 9.5
Range, n miles: 2,150 at 9 kt
Complement: 12
Cargo capacity: 340 tons

Comment: *Sögüt* acquired from West Germany and commissioned 12 March 1976. Pennant number changed in 1991. *Kavak* transferred from Germany 12 April 1991 and *Çinar* in early 1996.

ÇINAR   *4/2005*, Selim San* / 1133589

2 WATER TANKERS (AWT)

Name	No	Builders	Commissioned
VAN	A 597 (ex-Y 1208)	Camialti Shipyard	12 Aug 1968
ULUBAT	A 596 (ex-Y 1209)	Camialti Shipyard	3 July 1969

Displacement, tons: 1,250 full load
Dimensions, feet (metres): 174.2 × 29.5 × 9.8 *(53.1 × 9 × 3)*
Main machinery: 1 diesel; 650 hp(m) *(478 kW)*; 1 shaft
Speed, knots: 14
Complement: 39 (3 officers)
Cargo capacity: 700 tons
Guns: 1 Oerlikon 20 mm.
Radars: Racal Decca 707; I-band.

Comment: Pennant numbers changed in 1991.

VAN   *6/2003, Turkish Navy* / 0567542

6 WATER TANKERS (YW)

PINAR 1-6 Y 111-116 (ex-Y 1211-1216)

Displacement, tons: 300 full load
Dimensions, feet (metres): 110.2 × 27.9 × 5.9 *(33.6 × 8.5 × 1.8)*
Main machinery: 1 GM diesel; 225 hp *(168 kW)*; 1 shaft
Speed, knots: 11
Complement: 12
Cargo capacity: 150 tons

Comment: Built by Taşkizak Naval Yard. Details given for last four, sisters to harbour tankers H 500—502. First pair differ from these particulars and are individually different. *Pinar 1* (launched 1938) of 490 tons displacement with one 240 hp *(179 kW)* diesel, and *Pinar 2* built in 1958 of 1,300 tons full load, 167.3 × 27.9 ft *(51 × 8.5 m)*.

PINAR 6   *12/2000, Selim San* / 0106643

3 HARBOUR TANKERS (YW)

H 500-502 Y 140-142 (ex-Y 1231-1233)

Displacement, tons: 300 full load
Dimensions, feet (metres): 110.2 × 27.9 × 5.9 *(33.6 × 8.5 × 1.8)*
Main machinery: 1 GM diesel; 225 hp(m) *(165 kW)*; 1 shaft
Speed, knots: 11
Complement: 12
Cargo capacity: 150 tons

Comment: Sisters of water tankers of Pinar series. Built at Taşkizak in early 1970s.

H 500   *11/2005*, Manuel Declerck* / 1153504

1 HARBOUR TANKER (YO)

GÖLCÜK Y 50

Displacement, tons: 310 full load
Dimensions, feet (metres): 108.8 × 19.2 × 9.2 *(33.2 × 5.8 × 2.8)*
Main machinery: 1 diesel; 550 hp(m) *(404 kW)*; 1 shaft
Speed, knots: 12
Complement: 12

GÖLCÜK   *7/1992, Selçuk Emre* / 0080898

2 BARRACK SHIPS (YPB)

YÜZBAŞI NAŞIT ÖNGÖREN (ex-US APL 47) Y 38 (ex-Y 1204)
BINBAŞI METIN SÜLÜŞ (ex-US APL 53) Y 39 (ex-Y 1205)

Comment: Ex-US barrack ships transferred on lease: Y 1204 in October 1972 and Y 1205 on 6 December 1974. Y 1204 based at Ereğli and Y 1205 at Gölcük. Purchased outright June 1987. Pennant numbers changed in 1991.

16 SMALL TRANSPORTS (YFB/YE)

ŞALOPA 11-12, 15, 18, 22-24, 27, 30-35
LAYTER 7 Y 107
PONTON 7 Y 137
YAKIT Y 139
PONTON 1 Y 101

Comment: Of varying size and appearance. Pennant numbers changed in 1991.

1 DIVER CLASS (SALVAGE SHIP) (ARS)

Name	No	Builders	Launched	Commissioned
IŞIN (ex-*Safeguard* ARS 25)	A 589	Basalt Rock, Napa	20 Nov 1943	31 Oct 1944

Displacement, tons: 1,530 standard; 1,970 full load
Dimensions, feet (metres): 213.5 × 41 × 13 *(65.1 × 12.5 × 4)*
Main machinery: Diesel-electric; 4 Cooper-Bessemer GSB-8 diesels; 3,420 hp *(2.55 MW)*; 4 generators; 2 motors; 2 shafts
Speed, knots: 14.8
Complement: 110
Guns: 2 Oerlikon 20 mm.

Comment: Transferred from US 28 September 1979 and purchased outright 6 August 1987.

IŞIN *4/2005*, C D Yaylali* / 1133575

1 CHANTICLEER CLASS (SUBMARINE RESCUE SHIP) (ASR)

Name	No	Builders	Launched	Commissioned
AKIN (ex-*Greenlet* ASR 10)	A 585	Moore SB & DD Co	12 July 1942	29 May 1943

Displacement, tons: 1,653 standard; 2,321 full load
Dimensions, feet (metres): 251.5 × 44 × 16 *(76.7 × 13.4 × 4.9)*
Main machinery: Diesel-electric; 4 Alco 539 diesels; 3,532 hp *(2.63 MW)*; 4 generators; 1 motor; 1 shaft
Speed, knots: 15
Complement: 111 (9 officers)
Guns: 1 Bofors 40 mm/60. 4 Oerlikon 20 mm (2 twin).
Radars: Navigation: Racal Decca 1226; I-band.

Comment: Transferred from US, recommissioned 23 December 1970 and purchased 15 February 1973. Carries a Diving Bell.

AKIN *4/1996, van Ginderen Collection* / 0080902

2 TRANSPORTS (AKS/AWT)

Name	No	Builders	Commissioned
KARADENIZ EREĞLISI	A 592 (ex-Y 1157)	Erdem	30 Aug 1982
ECEABAT	A 593 (ex-Y 1165)	Taşkazik	4 Nov 1968

Displacement, tons: 820 full load
Dimensions, feet (metres): 166.3 × 26.2 × 9.2 *(50.7 × 8 × 2.8)*
Main machinery: 1 diesel; 1,440 hp *(1.06 MW)*; 1 shaft
Speed, knots: 10
Complement: 23 (3 officers)
Cargo capacity: 300 tons
Guns: 1 Oerlikon 20 mm.

Comment: Funnel-aft coaster type. Pennant numbers changed in 1991. *Karadeniz Ereğlisi* is a stores ship, *Eceabat* is a water carrier.

ECEABAT *11/1999, Selim San* / 0084417

1 BOOM DEFENCE VESSEL (ABU)

Name	No	Builders	Commissioned
AG 6 (ex-AN 93, ex-Netherlands *Cerberus* A 895)	P 306	Bethlehem Steel Corporation, Staten Island, NY	10 Nov 1952

Displacement, tons: 780 standard; 855 full load
Dimensions, feet (metres): 165 × 33 × 10 *(50.3 × 10.1 × 3)*
Main machinery: Diesel-electric; 2 GM 8-268A diesels; 880 hp *(656 kW)*; 2 generators; 1 motor; 1 shaft
Speed, knots: 12.8
Range, n miles: 5,200 at 12 kt
Complement: 32 (3 officers)
Guns: 1 USN 3 in *(76 mm)*/50. 4 Oerlikon 20 mm.
Radars: Navigation: Racal Decca 1226; I-band.

Comment: Netlayer. Transferred from US to Netherlands in December 1952. Used first as a boom defence vessel and latterly as salvage and diving tender since 1961 but retained her netlaying capacity. Handed back to US Navy on 17 September 1970 but immediately turned over to the Turkish Navy under grant aid.

AG 6 *7/1995, Frank Behling* / 0080906

1 BOOM DEFENCE VESSEL (ABU)

Name	No	Builders	Commissioned
AG 5 (ex-AN 104)	P 305	Kröger, Rendsburg	25 Feb 1962

Displacement, tons: 960 full load
Dimensions, feet (metres): 173.8 × 35 × 13.5 *(53 × 10.7 × 4.1)*
Main machinery: Diesel-electric; 1 MAN G7V40/60 diesel generator; 1 motor; 1,470 hp(m) *(1.08 MW)*; 1 shaft
Speed, knots: 12
Range, n miles: 6,500 at 11 kt
Complement: 32 (3 officers)
Guns: 1 Bofors 40 mm/60. 3 Oerlikon 20 mm.
Radars: Navigation: Racal Decca 1226; I-band.

Comment: Netlayer P 305 built in US offshore programme for Turkey.

AG 5 *6/2003, Selçuk Emre* / 0589823

3 TORPEDO RETRIEVERS (YPT)

TORPIDO TENDERI Y 95 (ex-Y 1051)   **TAKIP 1** Y 98 (ex-Y 1052)   **TAKIP 2** Y 99

Comment: Of different types.

Y 44 *9/1998, C D Yaylali* / 0050297

2 OFFICERS' YACHTS (YAC)

GÜL   NEVCIHAN

Comment: Pennant numbers not displayed.

GÜL   *6/2003, Turkish Navy* / 0567541

NEVCIHAN   *10/2003, C D Yaylali* / 0567559

15 FLOATING DOCKS/CRANES (YAC)

Name	Lift	Name	Lift
LEVENT Y 59 (ex-Y 1022)	—	HAVUZ 5 Y 125 (ex-Y 1085)	400 tons
ALGARNA 1 Y 58		HAVUZ 6 Y 126 (ex-Y 1086)	3,000 tons
ALGARNA 3 Y 60	—	HAVUZ 8 Y 128 (ex-Y-1088)	700 tons
(ex-Y 1021)		HAVUZ 9 Y 129 (ex-Y-1089)	4,500 tons
HAVUZ 1 Y 121 (ex-Y 1081)	16,000 tons	HAVUZ 10 Y 130 (ex-Y-1090)	3,500 tons
HAVUZ 2 Y 122 (ex-Y 1082)	12,000 tons	HAVUZ 11 Y 134	14,500 tons
HAVUZ 3 Y 123 (ex-Y 1083)	2,500 tons	HAVUZ 12 Y 135	5,000 tons
(ex-US AFDL)		HAVUZ 13 Y 136	7,500 tons
HAVUZ 4 Y 124 (ex-Y 1084)	4,500 tons		

Comment: Algarna and *Levent* are ex-US floating cranes.

TUGS

1 CHEROKEE CLASS (ATF)

GAZAL (ex-*Sioux* ATF 75) A 587

Displacement, tons: 1,235 standard; 1,675 full load
Dimensions, feet (metres): 205 × 38.5 × 17 *(62.5 × 11.7 × 5.2)*
Main machinery: Diesel-electric; 4 GM 12-278 diesels; 4,400 hp *(3.28 MW)*; 4 generators; 1 motor; 3,000 hp *(2.24 MW)*; 1 shaft
Speed, knots: 16
Range, n miles: 15,000 at 8 kt
Complement: 85
Guns: 1 USN 3 in *(76 mm)*/50. 2 Oerlikon 20 mm.
Radars: Navigation: Racal Decca; I-band.

Comment: Originally completed on 6 December 1942. Transferred from US and commissioned 9 March 1973. Purchased 15 August 1973. Can be used for salvage. 3 in gun removed in 1987 but has since been restored.

GAZAL   *6/1995, Turkish Navy* / 0080908

1 TENACE CLASS (ATA)

Name	No	Builders	Commissioned
DEĞIRMENDERE (ex-*Centaure*)	A 576 (ex-A 674)	Chantiers de la Rochelle	14 May 1974

Displacement, tons: 1,454 full load
Dimensions, feet (metres): 167.3 × 37.8 × 18.6 *(51 × 11.5 × 5.7)*
Main machinery: 2 SACM AGO 240 V12 diesels; 4,600 hp(m) *(3.38 MW)*; 1 shaft; Kort nozzle
Speed, knots: 13
Range, n miles: 9,500 at 13 kt
Complement: 37 (3 officers)
Radars: Navigation: Racal Decca RM 1226 and Racal Decca 060; I-band.

Comment: Transferred from French Navy 16 March 1999. Recommissioned after refit 22 July 1999. Bollard pull 60 tons.

DEĞIRMENDERE   *1/2002, M Declerck* / 0533259

16 COASTAL/HARBOUR TUGS (YTB/YTM/YTL)

Name	No	Displacement, tons/ Speed, knots	Commissioned
AKBAŞ	A 586	1660/14	1978
SÖNDÜREN 2	A 1542	385/12	1999/2000
SÖNDÜREN 3-4	A 1543-1544	128/12	1954
SÖNDÜREN 1	Y 51 (ex-Y 1117)	128/12	1954
KUVVET	Y 53 (ex-Y 1122)	390/10	1962
DOĞANARSLAN	Y 52 (ex-Y 1123)	500/12	1985
ATIL	Y 55 (ex-Y 1132)	300/10	1962
PENDIK	Y 56	238/10	2000
ERSEV BAYRAK	Y 64 (ex-Y 1134)	30/9	1946
AKSAZ (ex-*Koos*)	(ex-Y 1651, ex-A 08)	320/11	1962
ÖNDER	Y 160	230/12	1998
ÖNCÜ	Y 161	230/12	1998
ÖZGEN	Y 162	230/12	1999
ÖDEV	Y 163	230/12	1999
ÖZGÜR	Y 164	230/12	2000

Comment: In addition there are 47 Katir pusher berthing tugs. *Koos* was transferred from Germany on 7 October 1996.

ÖZGEN   *5/2005*, C D Yaylali* / 1133574

SÖNDÜREN 2   *4/2005*, Selim San* / 1133588

1 OCEAN TUG (ATR)

DARICA A 578 (ex-Y 1125)

Displacement, tons: 750 full load
Dimensions, feet (metres): 134.2 × 32.2 × 12.8 *(40.9 × 9.8 × 3.9)*
Main machinery: 2 ABC diesels; 4,000 hp *(2.94 MW)*; 2 shafts
Speed, knots: 14. **Range, n miles:** 2,500 at 14 kt

Comment: Built at Taşkizak Naval Yard and commissioned 13 June 1991. Equipped for firefighting and as a torpedo tender. Pennant number changed in 1991.

DARICA   *11/1994, van Ginderen Collection* / 0080910

COAST GUARD (SAHIL GÜVENLIK)

Notes: (1) Patrol craft based in North Cyprus include KKTCSG 101 *(Raif Denktas)* KKTCSG 01, KKTCSG 02, 2 Kaan 15 class, KKTCSG 11 and 12 and a converted cabin cruiser KKTCSG 104.
(2) Four Vigilante class Boston Whalers were acquired by the Police in September 1999.
(3) There are a number of inshore patrol craft of various designs.

KKTCSG 104   *6/2004*, Selçuk Emre / 1133570

SG 23 INSHORE PATROL CRAFT   *5/2005*, C D Yaylali / 1133568

12 LARGE PATROL CRAFT (WPB)

SG 80-91

Displacement, tons: 195 full load
Dimensions, feet (metres): 133.5 × 23.3 × 7.2 *(40.7 × 7.1 × 2.2)*
Main machinery: 2 diesels; 5,700 hp(m) *(4.19 MW)*; 2 shafts
Speed, knots: 27
Complement: 25
Guns: 1 Breda 40 mm/70. 2 — 12.7 mm MGs.
Radars: Surface search: Racal Decca; I-band.

Comment: All built at Taşkizak Shipyard except SG 89 which was built at Istanbul Shipyard. SG 80 — 82 commissioned in 1996, 83 — 84 in 1997, 85 in 1998, 86 — 87 in 2000, 89 — 90 in 2001, 88 in 2002 and 91 in 2004. Two based in northern Cyprus with pennant numbers KKTCSG 01-02.

SG 90   *10/2003, C D Yaylali* / 0567560

KKTCSG 02   *6/2004, Selçuk Emre* / 1044200

14 LARGE PATROL CRAFT (WPB)

SG 121-134

Displacement, tons: 180 full load
Dimensions, feet (metres): 132 × 21 × 5.5 *(40.2 × 6.4 × 1.7)*
  131.2 × 21.3 × 4.9 *(40 × 6.5 × 1.5)* (SG 130 — 134)
Main machinery: 2 SACM AGO 195 V16 CSHR diesels; 4,800 hp(m) *(3.53 MW)* sustained
  2 cruise diesels; 300 hp(m) *(220 kW)*; 2 shafts
Speed, knots: 22
Complement: 25
Guns: 1 or 2 Bofors 40 mm/60. 2 — 12.7 mm MGs.
Radars: Surface search: Racal Decca 1226; I-band.

Comment: *SG 121* and *122* built by Gölcük Naval Yard, remainder by Taşkizak Naval Yard. *SG 134* commissioned in 1977, remainder 1968-71. *SG 130-134* have minor modifications-knuckle at bow, radar stirrup on bridge and MG on superstructure sponsons. These are similar craft to the Turk class listed under *Patrol Forces* for the Navy.

SG 134   *6/2004, C D Yaylali* / 0589825

10 SAR 33 TYPE (LARGE PATROL CRAFT) (WPB)

SG 61-70

Displacement, tons: 180 full load
Dimensions, feet (metres): 113.5 × 28.3 × 9.7 *(34.6 × 8.6 × 3)*
Main machinery: 3 SACM AGO 195 V16 CSHR diesels; 7,200 hp(m) *(5.29 MW)* sustained; 3 shafts; cp props
Speed, knots: 33. **Range, n miles:** 450 at 24 kt; 550 at 18 kt
Complement: 24
Guns: 1 Bofors 40 mm/60. 2 — 12.7 mm MGs.
Radars: Surface search: Racal Decca; I-band.

Comment: Prototype Serter design ordered from Abeking & Rasmussen, Lemwerder in May 1976. The remainder were built at Taşkizak Naval Yard, Istanbul between 1979 and 1981. Fourteen of this class were to have been transferred to Libya but the order was cancelled. Two delivered to Saudi Arabia. The engines have been governed back and the top speed correspondingly reduced from the original 12,000 hp and 40 kt.

SG 67   *5/2004, Martin Mokrus* / 0589828

4 SAR 35 TYPE (LARGE PATROL CRAFT) (WPB)

SG 71-74

Displacement, tons: 210 full load
Dimensions, feet (metres): 120 × 28.3 × 6.2 *(36.6 × 8.6 × 1.9)*
Main machinery: 3 SACM AGO 195 V16 CSHR diesels; 7,200 hp(m) *(5.29 MW)* sustained; 3 shafts; cp props
Speed, knots: 33. **Range, n miles:** 450 at 24 kt; 550 at 18 kt
Complement: 24
Guns: 1 Bofors 40 mm/60. 2 — 12.7 mm MGs.
Radars: Surface search: Racal Decca 1226; I-band.

Comment: A slightly enlarged version of the Serter designed SAR 33 Type built by Taşkizak Shipyard between 1985 and 1987. Restricted to less than designed speed.

SG 71   *8/2000, C D Yaylali* / 0106645

9 KAAN 29 CLASS (LARGE PATROL CRAFT) (WPBF)

SG 101-109

Displacement, tons: 98 full load
Dimensions, feet (metres): 104.0 × 22.0 × 4.6 *(31.7 × 6.7 × 1.4)*
Main machinery: 2 MTU 16V 400 M90 diesels; 7,398 hp(m) *(5.44 MW)*; 2 MJP 753DD waterjets
Speed, knots: 49
Range, n miles: 750 at 20 kt
Complement: 13 (2 officers)
Guns: 4—12.7 mm MGs.
Radars: Surface search/navigation: Raytheon; I-band.

Comment: All built at Yonca Shipyard. Onuk MRTP 29 design. Advanced composites structure. TCSG 101—103 commissioned 25 July 2001, TCSG 104—105 on 25 July 2002, TCSG 106—108 in 2003 and TCSG 109 in February 2004.

SG 107   *5/2005*, Martin Mokrus* / 1133573

3 + 9 KAAN 33 CLASS (LARGE PATROL CRAFT) (WPBF)

SG 301-303

Displacement, tons: 120 full load
Dimensions, feet (metres): 116.8 × 22.0 × 4.7 *(35.6 × 6.7 × 1.4)*
Main machinery: 2 MTU 16V 4000 M90 diesels; 7,396 hp(m) *(5.44 MW)*; 2 MJP 753DD waterjets
Speed, knots: 47
Range, n miles: 650 at 20 kt
Complement: 18 (2 officers)
Guns: 4—12.7 mm MGs.
Radars: Navigation: Raytheon; I-band.

Comment: All built at Yonca Shipyard. Onuk MRTP 33 design. Advanced composites structure. TCSG 301 commissioned in July 2004, TCSG 302 in July 2005 and TCSG 303 in September 2005. Nine further craft are expected.

SG 301   *6/2005*, Yonca-Onuk* / 1133587

7 KW 15 CLASS (LARGE PATROL CRAFT) (WPB)

SG 113-116, SG 118-120

Displacement, tons: 70 full load
Dimensions, feet (metres): 94.8 × 15.4 × 4.6 *(28.9 × 4.7 × 1.4)*
Main machinery: 2 MTU diesels; 2,700 hp(m) *(1.98 MW)*; 2 shafts
Speed, knots: 20
Range, n miles: 550 at 16 kt
Complement: 16
Guns: 1 Bofors 40 mm/60. 2 Oerlikon 20 mm.
Radars: Surface search: Racal Decca; I-band.

Comment: Built by Schweers, Bardenfleth. Commissioned 1961-62.

SG 119   *9/2002, Selim San* / 0533264

18 KAAN 15 CLASS (FAST INTERVENTION CRAFT) (WPBF)

SG 1-18

Displacement, tons: 19 full load
Dimensions, feet (metres): 54.8 × 13.2 × 3.9 *(16.7 × 4.04 × 1.2)*
Main machinery: 2 MTU 12V 183TE93 diesels; 2,300 hp(m) *(1.69 MW)*; 2 Arneson ASD 12 B1L surface drives
Speed, knots: 54. **Range, n miles:** 350 at 35 kt
Complement: 4 plus 8 mission crew
Guns: 2—12.7 mm MGs.
Radars: Surface search: Raytheon; I-band.

Comment: Contract for first six with Yonca Technical Investment signed in May 1997, second order for six more in February 1999, and third for 6 more in August 2000. All built atTuzla-Istanbul shipyard.Three delivered in 1998, seven in 1999, two in April 2000, four in July 2001 and two in July 2002. Onuk MRTP 15 design. Advanced composites structure. SG 11 and SG 12 are based in northern Cyprus.

SG 12   *8/2005*, C D Yaylali* / 1133572

KKTCSG 11 (North Cyprus)   *6/2004, Selçuk Emre* / 1044202

12 COASTAL PATROL CRAFT (WPB)

SG 50-59   SG 102-103

Displacement, tons: 29 full load
Dimensions, feet (metres): 47.9 × 13.7 × 3.6 *(14.6 × 4.2 × 1.1)*
Main machinery: 2 diesels; 700 hp(m) *(514 kW)*; 2 shafts
Speed, knots: 15
Complement: 7
Guns: 1—12.7 mm MG or 1 Oerlikon 20 mm *(SG 102—103)*.
Radars: Surface search: Raytheon; I-band.

Comment: SG 102 and 103 were built for North Cyprus and have been based there since August 1990 and July 1991 respectively. Both these craft were given a heavier gun in 1992. Second batch of three completed by Taşkizak in October 1992, three more in June 1993, four more in December 1993.

SG 55   *9/2004, Selim San* / 0587558

1 COASTAL PATROL CRAFT (WPB)

SG 43

Displacement, tons: 45 full load
Dimensions, feet (metres): 55.1 × 13.9 × 3.6 *(16.8 × 4.2 × 1.1)*
Main machinery: 2 Gray Marine 64HN9 diesels; 450 hp *(335 kW)*; 2 shafts
Speed, knots: 12. **Range, n miles:** 200 at 12 kt
Complement: 7
Guns: 1—12.7 mm MG.

Comment: Former US Mk 5 craft built in Second World War. SG 45 and 46 transferred to north Cyprus in August 1993.

COASTAL PATROL CRAFT   *3/2001, Selim San* / 0114805

1 INSHORE PATROL CRAFT (WPBI)

RAIF DENKTAŞ 101 (ex-74)

Displacement, tons: 10 full load
Dimensions, feet (metres): 38 × 11.5 × 2.4 *(11.6 × 3.5 × 0.7)*
Main machinery: 2 Volvo Aquamatic AQ200F petrol engines; 400 hp(m) *(294 kW)*; 2 shafts
Speed, knots: 28. **Range, n miles:** 250 at 25 kt
Complement: 6
Guns: 1—12.7 mm MG.
Radars: Surface search: Raytheon; I-band.

Comment: Built by Protekson, Istanbul. Transferred to North Cyprus 23 September 1988. Can be equipped with a rocket launcher.

RAIF DENKTAŞ *6/2004, Selçuk Emre* / 1044201

1 HARBOUR PATROL CRAFT (WPBI)

SG 41

Displacement, tons: 35
Dimensions, feet (metres): 55.8 × 16.4 × 3.3 *(17 × 5 × 1)*
Main machinery: 2 diesels; 1,050 hp(m) *(771 kW)*
Speed, knots: 20
Complement: 7
Radars: Surface search: I-band.

Comment: Used for anti-smuggling duties. Probably confiscated drug smuggling craft.

SG 41 *6/2004, Selim San* / 0587557

LAND-BASED MARITIME AIRCRAFT

Numbers/Type: 8 Agusta AB 412 EP.
Operational speed: 122 kt *(226 km/h)*.
Service ceiling: 17,000 ft *(5,180 m)*.
Range: 374 n miles *(656 km)*.
Role/Weapon systems: Nine aircraft ordered 15 April 1999. A further five ordered in early 2005. Operated by Coast Guard/Frontier Force for patrol SAR. Sensors: Radar and FLIR. Weapons: Unarmed.

AB 412 *10/2003, C D Yaylali* / 0567563

Numbers/Type: 3 Casa CN-235.
Operational speed: 240 kt *(445 km/h)*.
Service ceiling: 26,600 ft *(8,110 m)*.
Range: 669 n miles *(1,240 km)*.
Role/Weapon systems: Three delivered in July 2002. Long range maritime patrol for surveillance.

CN-235 *2/2003, CASA* / 0531695

Turkmenistan

Country Overview

Formerly part of the USSR, the Republic of Turkmenistan declared its independence in 1991. Situated in Central Asia, it has an area of 188,460 square miles and is bordered to the north by Kazakhstan, to the east by Uzbekistan and Afghanistan and to the south by Iran. It has a 954 n mile coastline with the Caspian Sea. Türkmenbashi, the principal port, is linked by rail to Ashgabat, the capital and largest city. Maritime claims in the Caspian Sea are yet to be resolved. The Navy acts under the operational control of the Border Guard but is the weakest component of the Turkmen armed forces.

Personnel

2006: 700

Base

Türkmenbashi (formerly Krasnovodsk)

PATROL FORCES

1 POINT CLASS (WPB)

Name	No	Builders	Commissioned
MERJEN (ex-*Point Jackson*)	PB-129 (ex-82378)	USCG Yard Curtis Bay	3 Aug 1970

Displacement, tons: 66; 69 full load
Dimensions, feet (metres): 83 × 17.2 × 5.8 *(25.3 × 5.2 × 1.8)*
Main machinery: 2 Caterpillar 3412 diesels; 1,600 hp *(1.19 MW)*; 2 shafts
Speed, knots: 23.5. **Range, n miles:** 1,200 at 8 kt
Complement: 10 (1 officer)
Guns: 2—12.7 mm MGs.
Radars: Surface search: Hughes/Furuno SPS-73; I-band.

Comment: Steel hulled craft with aluminium superstructure. Transferred from United States on 30 May 2000.

MERJEN (inboard ship)
11/2000, Selim San
0104495

For details of the latest updates to *Jane's Fighting Ships* online and to discover the additional information available exclusively to online subscribers please visit

jfs.janes.com

5 KALKAN (PROJECT 50030) M CLASS
(INSHORE PATROL CRAFT) (PBI)

Displacement, tons: 8.5 full load
Dimensions, feet (metres): 38.1 × 10.8 × 2.0 *(11.6 × 3.3 × 0.6)*
Main machinery: 1 Type 475K diesel; 496 hp *(370 kW)*; 1 waterjet
Speed, knots: 34
Complement: 2
Guns: 1 — 12.7 mm MG.

Comment: Five craft delivered during 2002. Further craft were expected but reportedly not delivered. Built by Morye Feodosiya (Ukraine) and constructed with aluminium hulls and GRP superstructure. Can be armed with 7.62 mm or 12.7 mm MGs.

KALKAN
6/2003, Morye
0573698

Tuvalu

Country Overview

Tuvalu, formerly the Ellice Islands, is a south Pacific island group which gained independence in 1978; the other part of the former British colony, the Gilbert Islands, became independent as Kiribati the following year. Situated some 1,600 n miles east of Papua New Guinea, the country comprises nine atolls of which Funafuti is the location of the capital, Fongafale, and home to more than 30 per cent of the population. An archipelagic state, territorial seas (12 n miles) are claimed. An Exclusive Economic Zone (EEZ) (200 n miles) is also claimed but limits have not been fully defined by boundary agreements.

Headquarters Appointments

Commander Maritime Wing:
Inspector Sele Fusi

Bases

Funafuti

PATROL FORCES

1 PACIFIC CLASS (LARGE PATROL CRAFT) (PB)

Name	No	Builders	Commissioned
TE MATAILI	801	Transfield Shipbuilding, WA	8 Oct 1994

Displacement, tons: 165 full load
Dimensions, feet (metres): 103.3 × 26.6 × 6.9 *(31.5 × 8.1 × 2.1)*
Main machinery: 2 Caterpillar 3516TA diesels; 4,400 hp *(3.28 MW)* sustained; 2 shafts
Speed, knots: 18. **Range, n miles:** 2,500 at 12 kt
Complement: 18 (3 officers)
Guns: Can carry 1 — 12.7 mm MG but is unarmed.
Radars: Navigation: Furuno 1011; I-band.

Comment: This is the 18th of the class to be built by the Australian Government for Exclusive Economic Zone (EEZ) patrols in the Pacific islands. The programme originally terminated at 15 but was re-opened on 19 February 1993 to include construction of five more craft for Fiji, Kiribati and Tuvalu. Training and support assistance is given by the Australian Navy. Half-life refit completed at Gladstone in 2001. Following the decision by the Australian government to extend the Pacific Patrol Boat programme, *Te Mataili* will require a life-extension refit in 2011 in order to achieve a 30-year ship life.

TE MATAILI
2000, RAN*
0106647

Ukraine

Country Overview

Formerly part of the USSR, Ukraine declared its independence in 1991. Situated in eastern Europe, it has an area of 233,090 square miles and is bordered to the north by Belarus, to the east by Russia, to the south-west by Romania and Moldova and to the west by Hungary, Slovakia and Poland. It has a 1,501 n mile coastline with the Black Sea and the Sea of Azov. Kiev is the capital and largest city while Sevastopol, Odessa, Kerch, and Mariupol are the principal ports. Territorial Seas (12 n miles) have been claimed. An EEZ (200 n miles) has been claimed but the limits have not been defined.

Division of the former Soviet Black Sea Fleet between Russia and Ukraine had been achieved by 1997.

Headquarters Appointments

Commander of the Navy:
Vice Admiral Igor Knyaz
First Deputy Commander of the Navy and Chief of Staff:
Rear Admiral Mykola Kostrov

Headquarters Appointments — *continued*

Commander Western Naval District:
Rear Admiral Dmytro Ukrainets
Commander Southern Naval District:
Rear Admiral Borys Rekuts

Bases

Sevastopol (HQ), Donuzlav (Southern Region), Odessa (Western Region), Mikolaiv, Feodosiya, Izmail, Balaklava, Kerch

Personnel

2006: 13,000 navy

Border Guard

The Maritime Border Guard is an independent subdivision of the State Committee for Border Guards, and is not part of the Navy. It has three cutter brigades, based in Kerch, Odessa and Balaklava, to patrol the 827 mile coastline and two river brigades, which include a gunship squadron, a minesweeping squadron, an auxiliary ship group and a training division. Pennant numbers changed in July 1999.

DELETIONS

Notes: Some of these ships are laid up and may return to service, but this is unlikely.

Patrol Forces

2003 *Kremenchuk*

Mine Warfare Forces

2003 *Mariupol*

PENNANT LIST

Submarines		Patrol Forces		U 330	Melitopol	Auxiliaries	
				U 360	Genichesk		
U 01	Zaporizya	U 120	Skadovsk			U 240	Feodisiya
		U 153	Priluki	**Amphibious Forces**		U 510	Slavutich
		U 154	Kahovka			U 540	Chigirin
Frigates		U 155	Nikopol	U 400	Rivne	U 541	Smila
		U 208	Khmelnitsky	U 410	Kirovograd	U 542	Darnicha
U 130	Hetman Sagaidachny			U 402	Konstantin Olshansky	U 635	Skvyra
U 200	Lutsk	**Mine Warfare Forces**		U 420	Donetsk	U 700	Netisin
U 205	Chernigiv			U 424	Artemivsk	U 705	Kremenets
U 206	Vinnitsa	U 310	Zhovti Vody	U 862	Korosten	U 706	Izyaslav
U 209	Ternopil	U 311	Cherkasy	U 904	Bilyaïvka	U 707	Brodi

PENNANT LIST

Auxiliaries—continued							Survey Ships	
		U 756	Sudak	U 830	Korets		U 511	Simferopol
		U 757	Makivka	U 831	Kovel		U 512	Pereyaslav
U 721	V Volnidsky	U 759	Bahmach	U 852	Shostka		U 601	Alchevsk
U 722	Borshev	U 760	Fastiv	U 860	Kamyankha		U 754	Dzhankoi
U 728	Evpatoriya	U 782	Sokal	U 890	Malin			
U 731	Mirgood	U 783	Illichivsk	U 891	Kherson			
U 733	Tokmak	U 803	Krasnodon	U 947	Krasnoperekovsk			
U 753	Kriviy Rig	U 811	Balta	U 953	Dubno			

SUBMARINES

1 FOXTROT CLASS (PROJECT 641) (SS)

Name	No	Builders	Laid down	Launched	Commissioned
ZAPORIZYA (ex-B 435)	U 01	Sudomekh, Leningrad	24 Mar 1970	29 May 1970	6 Nov 1970

Displacement, tons: 1,952 surfaced; 2,475 dived
Dimensions, feet (metres): 299.5 × 24.6 × 19.7 *(91.3 × 7.5 × 6)*
Main machinery: Diesel-electric; 3 Type 37-D diesels; 6,000hp(m)*(4.4MW)*;3motors(1×2,700and2×1,350);5,400 hp(m) *(3.97 MW)*; 3 shafts; 1 auxiliary motor; 140 hp(m) *(103 kW)*
Speed, knots: 16 surfaced; 15 dived; 9 snorting
Range, n miles: 20,000 at 8 kt surfaced; 380 at 2 kt dived
Complement: 75

Torpedoes: 10—21 in *(533 mm)* (6 bow, 4 stern) tubes. Combination of 22—53 cm torpedoes.
Mines: 44 in lieu of torpedoes.
Countermeasures: ESM: Stop Light; radar warning.
Radars: Surface search: Snoop Tray; I-band.
Sonars: Pike Jaw; hull-mounted; passive/active search and attack; high frequency.

Programmes: Transferred from Russia in August 1997 with three others of the class.

Operational: Based at Balaklava and, following a three year refit which completed in 2000, further work is required to restore hydraulic systems and replace batteries. The boat was expected to return to operational service in 2004 but there have been no reports of activity and the boat has probably been relegated to a training role.

ZAPORIZYA   *8/2000, Hartmut Ehlers* / 0106649

FRIGATES

1 KRIVAK III (NEREY) CLASS (PROJECT 1135.1) (FFHM)

Name	No	Builders	Laid down	Launched	Commissioned
HETMAN SAGAIDACHNY (ex-Kirov)	U 130 (ex-201)	Kamysh-Burun, Kerch	5 Oct 1990	29 Mar 1992	5 July 1993

Displacement, tons: 3,100 standard; 3,650 full load
Dimensions, feet (metres): 405.2 × 46.9 × 16.4 *(123.5 × 14.3 × 5)*
Main machinery: COGAG; 2 gas turbines; 55,500 hp(m) *(40.8 MW)*; 2 gas turbines; 13,600 hp(m) *(10 MW)*; 2 shafts
Speed, knots: 32
Range, n miles: 4,600 at 20 kt; 1,600 at 30 kt
Complement: 180 (18 officers)

Missiles: SAM: 1 SA-N-4 Gecko twin launcher ❶; semi-active radar homing to 15 km *(8.1 n miles)* at 2.5 Mach; warhead 50 kg; altitude 9.1—3,048 m *(30—10,000 ft)*; 20 missiles. The launcher retracts into the mounting for stowage and protection, rising to fire and retracting to reload. The two mountings are forward of the bridge and abaft the funnel.
Guns: 1—3.9 in *(100 mm)*/59 ❷; 60 rds/min to 15 km *(8.1 n miles)*; weight of shell 16 kg. 2—30 mm/65 ❸; 6 barrels per mounting; 3,000 rds/min combined to 2 km.
Torpedoes: 8—21 in *(533 mm)* (2 quad) tubes ❹. Combination of Russian 53 cm torpedoes.
A/S mortars: 2 RBU 6000 12-tubed trainable ❺; range 6,000 m; warhead 31 kg.

HETMAN SAGAIDACHNY   *(Scale 1 : 1,200), Ian Sturton* / 0506208

Countermeasures: Decoys: 4 PK 16 chaff launchers. Towed torpedo decoy.
ESM: 2 Bell Shroud; intercept.
ECM: 2 Bell Squat; jammers.
Radars: Air search: Top Plate ❻; 3D; D/E-band.
Surface search: Spin Trough ❼; I-band. Peel Cone ❽; E-band.
Fire control: Pop Group ❾; F/H/I-band (for SA-N-4). Kite Screech ❿; H/I/K-band. Bass Tilt (Krivak III) ⓫; H/I-band.
Navigation: Kivach; I-band.
IFF: Salt Pot (Krivak III).
Sonars: Bull Nose (MGK 335MS); hull-mounted; active search and attack; medium frequency.

Helicopters: 1 Ka-27 Helix ⓬.

Programmes: This is the last of the 'Krivak IIIs' originally designed for the USSR Border Guard. The seven others are based in the Russian Pacific Fleet. A ninth of class was not completed.
Operational: *Sagaidachny* has so far not been sighted with a helicopter embarked. Deployed to the Mediterranean in 1994 and late 1995, to the Indian Ocean in early 1995 and to the US in late 1996. 'Krivak II' *Sevastopol* (U 132) is probably being used for spares while 'Krivak I' *Mikolaiv* is to be scrapped. *Dnipropetrovsk* is reported to have sunk in the Black Sea in 2005.

HETMAN SAGAIDACHNY   *6/2003, Ships of the World* / 0572651

4 GRISHA CLASS (PROJECT 1124EM/P) (FFLM)

Name	No	Builders	Laid down	Launched	Commissioned
LUTSK	U 200	Leninskaya Kuznitsa, Kiev	—	12 May 1993	12 Feb 1994
TERNOPIL	U 202	Leninskaya Kuznitsa, Kiev	—	20 Mar 2002	16 Feb 2006
CHERNIGIV (ex-*Izmail*)	U 205	Zrelenodolsk	12 Sep 1978	22 June 1980	28 Dec 1980
VINNITSA (ex-*Dnepr*)	U 206	Zrelenodolsk	23 Dec 1975	12 Sep 1976	31 Dec 1976

Displacement, tons: 950 standard; 1,150 full load
Dimensions, feet (metres): 233.6 × 32.2 × 12.1
(71.2 × 9.8 × 3.7)
Main machinery: CODAG; 1 gas turbine; 15,000 hp(m)
(11 MW); 2 diesels; 16,000 hp(m) (11.8 MW); 3 shafts
Speed, knots: 30
Range, n miles: 2,500 at 14 kt; 1,750 at 20 kt diesels;
950 at 27 kt
Complement: 70 (5 officers)

Missiles: SAM: SA-N-4 Gecko twin launcher ❶ (*Lutsk*);
semi-active radar homing to 15 km (8 n miles) at 2.5 Mach;
warhead 50 kg; altitude 9.1–3,048 m (30–10,000 ft);
20 missiles.
Guns: 1–3 in (76 mm)/60 ❷; (*Lutsk*); 120 rds/min to 15 km
(8 n miles); weight of shell 7 kg.
4–57 mm/80 (twin); 120 rds/min to 6 km (3.3 n miles);
weight of shell 2.8 kg.
1–30 mm/65 ❸; (*Lutsk*); 6 barrels; 3,000 rds/min
combined to 2 km.
Torpedoes: 4–21 in (533 mm) (2 twin) tubes ❹. SAET-60;
passive homing to 15 km (8.1 n miles) at 40 kt; warhead
400 kg.
A/S mortars: 1 or 2 RBU 6000 12-tubed trainable ❺; range
6,000 m; warhead 31 kg.

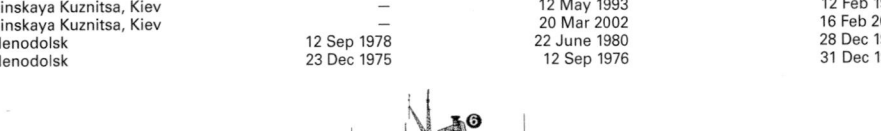
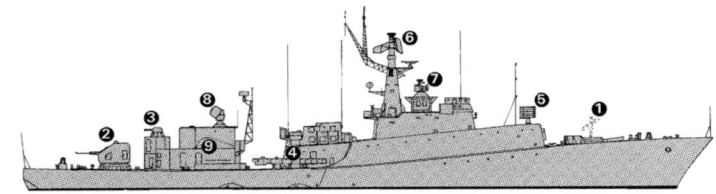

LUTSK *(Scale 1 : 900), Ian Sturton* / 0506209

Depth charges: 2 racks (12).
Mines: Capacity for 18 in lieu of depth charges.
Countermeasures: ESM: 2 Watch Dog. 2 PK 16 chaff
launchers.
Radars: Air/surface search: Half Plate B ❻; (*Lutsk*);
E/F-band.
Strut Curve (remainder); F-band.
Navigation: Don 2; I-band.
Fire control: Pop Group ❼; (*Lutsk*); F/H/I-band (for SA-N-4).
Bass Tilt ❽; (*Lutsk*); H/I-band (for 76 mm and 30 mm).
Muff Cobb (remainder); G/H-band.
IFF: High Pole A or B. Square Head. Salt Pot.

Sonars: Bull Nose (MGK 335MS); hull-mounted; active
search and attack; high/medium frequency.
Elk Tail VDS ❾; active search; high frequency.

Programmes: *Lutsk* is a 'Grisha V' (Type 1124EM) launched
12 May 1993 and completed 27 November 1993. *Ternopil*
was the first new ship to join the fleet since 1992 when it
commissioned in 2005. *Chernigiv* and *Vinnitsa* are both
'Grisha II' (Type 1124P) ex-Russian Border Guard ships
transferred in 1996. Two 'Grisha I' were also transferred
but have been deleted.
Operational: All are active.

VINNITSA *7/2000, Hartmut Ehlers* / 0106652

LUTSK *8/2003, Guy Toremans* / 0572654

TERNOPIL *12/2005*, B Lemachko* / 0581616

LAND-BASED MARITIME AIRCRAFT

Notes: The Naval Aviation Force is based at Sevastopol. It comprises 4 Ka-29 Helix B assault helicopters, 17 Ka-25 Hormone ASW helicopters, 12 Ka-27 Helix A ASW helicopter, 5 Mi-14 Haze, 1 An-12 Cub, 1 An-26 Curl and 8 Mi-8 Hip transport helicopters. The Air Force inventory includes 26 Tu-22 Backfire and 120 Su-24 Fencer.

PATROL FORCES

1 PAUK I (MOLNYA) (PROJECT 1241P) CLASS (PCM)

KHMELNITSKY (ex-MPK 116) U 208

Displacement, tons: 440 full load
Dimensions, feet (metres): 189 × 33.5 × 10.8 *(57.6 × 10.2 × 3.3)*
Main machinery: 2 Type M 521 diesels; 16,184 hp(m) *(11.9 MW)* sustained; 2 shafts
Speed, knots: 32
Range, n miles: 2,400 at 14 kt
Complement: 32

Missiles: SAM: SA-N-5 Grail quad launcher; manual aiming; IR homing to 6 km *(3.2 n miles)* at 1.5 Mach; altitude to 2,500 m *(8,000 ft)*; warhead 1.5 kg; 8 missiles.
Guns: 1—3 in *(76 mm)*/60; 120 rds/min to 15 km *(8 n miles)*; weight of shell 7 kg.
1—30 mm/65 AK 630; 6 barrels; 3,000 rds/min combined to 2 km.
Torpedoes: 4 16 in *(406 mm)*.
A/S mortars: 2 RBU 1200 5-tubed fixed; range 1,200 m; warhead 34 kg.
Depth charges: 2 racks (12).
Countermeasures: Decoys: 2 PK 16 or 4 PK 10 chaff launchers.
ESM: 3 Brick Plug and 2 Half Hat; radar warning.
Weapons control: Hood Wink optronic director.
Radars: Air/surface search: Peel Cone; E/F-band.
Surface search: Kivach or Pechora; I-band.
Fire control: Bass Tilt; H/I-band.
Sonars: Foal Tail; VDS (mounted on transom); active attack; high frequency.

Programmes: Built at Yaroslavl in 1985. Transferred from Black Sea Fleet Border Guard in 1996. Others of this class are in the Ukraine Border Guard.
Structure: ASW version of the Russian Tarantul class.
Operational: A second of class (*Uzhgorod* (ex-MPK 93) U 207) is reported to be laid up.

KHMELNITSKY *7/2000, Hartmut Ehlers* / 0106653

1 TARANTUL II (MOLNYA) (PROJECT 1241.1/2) CLASS (FSGM)

PRIDNEPROVYE (ex-*Nikopol*, ex-R-54) U 155

Displacement, tons: 385 standard; 455 full load
Dimensions, feet (metres): 184.1 × 37.7 × 8.2 *(56.1 × 11.5 × 2.5)*
Main machinery: COGAG: 2 Nikolayev Type DR 77 gas turbines; 16,016 hp(m) *(11.77 MW)*; 2 Nikolayev DR 76 gas turbines with reversible gearboxes; 4,993 hp(m) *(3.67 MW)* sustained 2 shafts; cp props
Speed, knots: 36
Range, n miles: 1,650 at 14 kt
Complement: 34 (5 officers)

Missiles: SSM: 4 Raduga SS-N-2D Styx (2 twin); active radar or IR homing to 83 km *(45 n miles)* at 0.9 Mach; warhead 513 kg; sea skimmer at end of run
SAM: 1 SA-N-5 Grail quad launcher; manual aiming; IR homing to 6 km *(3.2 n miles)* at 1.5 Mach; warhead 1.5 kg.
Guns: 1—3 in *(76 mm)*/60; AK-176; 120 rds/min to 15 km *(8 n miles)*; weight of shell 7 kg.
2—30 mm/65 AK-630; 6 barrels per mounting; 3,000 rds/min to 2 km.
Countermeasures: Decoys: 4 PK 16 chaff launchers.
Weapons control: Hood Wink optronic director. Light bulb datalink. Band Stand for SSM.
Radars: Air/surface search: Plank Shave; I-band.
Fire control: Bass Tilt; H/I-band (for guns).
Navigation: Kivach III; I-band.
IFF: High Pole B.

Programmes: Built at Kolpino and originally commissioned in 1983. Transferred in 1997 and recommissioned in 2002 following a refit.

PRIDNEPROVYE *3/2002, Hartmut Ehlers* / 0529997

2 MATKA (VEKHR) CLASS (PROJECT 206MP)
(FAST ATTACK CRAFT—MISSILE HYDROFOIL) (PGGK)

PRILUKI (ex-R-262) U 153   **KAHOVKA** (ex-R-265) U 154

Displacement, tons: 225 standard; 260 full load
Dimensions, feet (metres): 129.9 × 24.9 (41 over foils) × 6.9 (13.1 over foils)
   (39.6 × 7.6; 12.5 × 2.1; 4)
Main machinery: 3 Type M 504 diesels; 10,800 hp(m) *(7.94 MW)* sustained; 3 shafts
Speed, knots: 40. **Range, n miles:** 600 at 35 kt foilborne; 1,500 at 14 kt hullborne
Complement: 33
Missiles: SSM: 2 SS-N-2C/D Styx; active radar or IR homing to 83 km *(45 n miles)*
   at 0.9 Mach; warhead 513 kg; sea-skimmer at end of run.
Guns: 1—3 in *(76 mm)*/60; 120 rds/min to 15 km *(8 n miles)*; weight of shell 7 kg.
   1—30 mm/65 AK 630; 6 barrels per mounting; 3,000 rds/min to 2 km.
Countermeasures: Decoys: 2 PK 16 chaff launchers.
ESM: Clay Brick; intercept.
Weapons control: Hood Wink optronic directors.
Radars: Air/surface search: Plank Shave; E-band.
Navigation: SRN-207; I-band.
Fire control: Bass Tilt; H/I-band.
IFF: High Pole B or Salt Pot B and Square Head.

Comment: Five Russian Black Sea Fleet units transferred in 1996. Built between 1978 and
   1983 with similar hulls to the Osa class. One was transferred to Georgia in 1999 and two
   others (*Uman* and *Tsurupinsk*) have been cannibalised for spares.

PRILUKI   *7/2000* / 0106654

1 ZHUK (GRIF) CLASS (PROJECT 1400M) (PB)

SKADOVSK (ex-AK 327) U 120

Displacement, tons: 39 full load
Dimensions, feet (metres): 78.7 × 16.4 × 3.9 *(24 × 5 × 1.2)*
Main machinery: 2 Type M 401B diesels; 2,200 hp(m) *(1.6 MW)* sustained; 2 shafts
Speed, knots: 30. **Range, n miles:** 1,100 at 15 kt
Complement: 13
Guns: 2—14.5 mm (twin). 1—12.7 mm MG.
Radars: Surface search: Spin Trough; I-band.

Comment: Transferred from Russia in 1997 and became operational in 2000. Others of
   the class are in service with the Border Guard.

SKADOVSK   *7/2000, Hartmut Ehlers* / 0106655

AMPHIBIOUS FORCES

Notes: Two Vydra class LCUs, *Korosten* U 862 and *Bilyaïvka* U 904, are used as trials and
transport craft. There are also two Ondatra class LCM, *Svatove* U 430 and *Vil* U 537 and a
T-4 LCM *Tarpan* U 538 which are laid up.

1 ROPUCHA I (PROJECT 775) CLASS (LST)

KONSTANTIN OLSHANSKY (ex-BDK 56) U 402

Displacement, tons: 4,400 full load
Dimensions, feet (metres): 370.7 × 47.6 × 11.5 *(113 × 14.5 × 3.6)*
Main machinery: 2 Zgoda-Sulzer 16ZVB40/48 diesels; 19,230 hp(m) *(14.14 MW)* sustained;
   2 shafts
Speed, knots: 17.5
Range, n miles: 3,500 at 16 kt
Complement: 95 (7 officers)
Military lift: 10 MBT plus 190 troops or 24 AFVs plus 170 troops
Missiles: SAM: 4 SA-N-5 Grail quad launchers.
Guns: 4—57 mm/80 (2 twin); 120 rds/min to 6 km *(3.3 n miles)*; weight of shell 2.8 kg.
Weapons control: 2 Squeeze Box optronic directors.
Radars: Air/surface search: Strut Curve; F-band.
Navigation: Don 2; I-band.
Fire control: Muff Cob; G/H-band.
IFF: High Pole B.

Comment: Built at Gdansk, Poland in 1978 and transferred from Russia in 1996. Can be
   used to carry mines. Ro-Ro design with 540 m² of parking space between the stern gate
   and the bow doors.

KONSTANTIN OLSHANSKY   *8/2000, B Lemachko* / 0131165

1 POLNOCHNY C (PROJECT 773 I) CLASS (LSM)

KIROVOGRAD (ex-SDK 123) U 401

Displacement, tons: 1,120 standard; 1,150 full load
Dimensions, feet (metres): 266.7 × 31.8 × 7.9 *(81.3 × 9.7 × 2.4)*
Main machinery: 2 Kolomna Type 40-D diesels; 4,400 hp(m) *(3.2 MW)* sustained; 2 shafts
Speed, knots: 18
Range, n miles: 2,000 at 12 kt
Complement: 40—42
Military lift: 350 tons including 6 tanks; 180 troops
Missiles: 4 SA-N-5 Grail quad launchers; manual aiming; IR homing to 6 km *(3.2 n miles)*
   at 1.5 Mach; warhead 1.5 kg; 32 missiles.
Guns: 4—30 mm/65 (2 twin); 2—140 mm 18-tubed rocket launchers.
Radars: Surface search: Spin Trough; I-band.
Fire control: Drum Tilt; H/I-band (for 30 mm guns).

Comment: Built in 1970s and transferred from Russian Fleet in 1994. Reported operational
   again in 2001 following refit.

KIROVOGRAD   *6/2003, Ships of the World* / 0572650

1 ALLIGATOR (PROJECT 1171) CLASS (LST)

RIVNE (ex-BDK 104) U 400

Displacement, tons: 4,700 full load
Measurement, tons: 370.7 × 50.8 × 14.7 *(113 × 15.5 × 4.5)*
Main machinery: 2 diesels; 9,000 hp(m) *(6.6 MW)*; 2 shafts
Speed, knots: 18
Range, n miles: 10,000 at 15 kt
Complement: 100
Military lift: 300 troops; 1,700 tons including about 20 tanks and various trucks; 40 AFVs
Radars: Surface search: 2 Don 2; I-band.

Comment: Launched in 1971 and transferred from Russian Fleet in 1994. This is the Type 2
   variant of this class. Disarmed in 1997, refitted in 1999 and reported undergoing repairs
   in dock in 2004.

RIVNE   *4/1997, Ukraine Navy* / 0019345

2 POMORNIK (ZUBR) (PROJECT 1232.2) CLASS (ACV/LCUJM)

DONETSK U 420   **ARTEMIVSK** (ex-MDK-93) U 424

Displacement, tons: 550 full load
Dimensions, feet (metres): 189 × 70.5 (57.6 × 21.5)
Main machinery: 5 Type NK-12MV gas turbines; 2 for lift, 23,672 hp(m) (17.4 MW) nominal; 3 for drive, 35,508 hp(m) (26.1 MW) nominal
Speed, knots: 60
Range, n miles: 300 at 55 kt
Complement: 31 (4 officers)
Military lift: 3 MBT or 10 APC plus 230 troops (total 170 tons)
Missiles: SAM: 2 SA-N-5 Grail quad launchers; manual aiming; IR homing to 6 km (3.2 n miles) at 1.5 Mach; altitude to 2,500 m (8,000 ft); warhead 1.5 kg.
Guns: 2—30 mm/65 AK 630; 6 barrels per mounting; 3,000 rds/min combined to 2 km. 2 retractable 122 mm rocket launchers.
Mines: 80.
Countermeasures: Decoys: TSP 41 chaff.
ESM: Tool Box; intercept.
Weapons control: Quad Look (modified Squeeze Box) (DWU 3) optronic director.
Radars: Air/surface search: Cross Dome (Ekran); I-band.
Fire control: Bass Tilt MR 123; H/I-band.
IFF: Salt Pot A/B. Square Head.

Comment: *Donetsk* was completed by Morye, Feodosiya on 20 July 1993. Sister *U 421* was incomplete in 1999 when procured by Greece, delivery being made in 2001. Three further craft were transferred from Russia in 1996. Of these, *U 423* (ex-MDK 123) was also sold to Greece, *U 422* (ex-MDK 57) is not operational and U 424 remains in service.

DONETSK   *8/2000, B Lemachko* / 0131164

MINE WARFARE FORCES

2 NATYA I CLASS (PROJECT 266M) (MSO)

ZHOVTI VODY (ex-*Zenitchik*) U 310   **CHERKASY** (ex-*Razvedchik*) U 311

Displacement, tons: 804 full load
Dimensions, feet (metres): 200.1 × 33.5 × 9.8 (61 × 10.2 × 3)
Main machinery: 2 Type M 504 diesels; 5,000 hp(m) (3.67 MW) sustained; 2 shafts; cp props
Speed, knots: 16
Range, n miles: 3,000 at 12 kt
Complement: 67 (8 officers)

Guns: 4—30 mm/65 (2 twin) AK 306 or 2—30 mm/65 AK 630; 4—25 mm/80 (2 twin).
A/S mortars: 2 RBU 1200 5-tubed fixed.
Depth charges: 62.
Mines: 10.
Countermeasures: MCM: 1 or 2 GKT-2 contact sweeps; 1 AT-2 acoustic sweep. 1 TEM-3 magnetic sweep
Radars: Surface search: Long Trough; E-band.
Fire control: Drum Tilt; H/I-band.
IFF: 2 Square Head. High Pole B.
Sonars: MG 79/89; hull-mounted; active minehunting; high frequency.

Comment: Built in the mid-1970s. Transferred from Russia in 1996. Both are operational.

ZHOVTI VODY   *9/2002, C D Yaylali* / 0530030

1 SONYA (YAKHONT) (PROJECT 1265) CLASS (MHSC)

MELITOPOL (ex-BT 79) U 330

Displacement, tons: 460 full load
Dimensions, feet (metres): 157.4 × 28.9 × 6.6 (48 × 8.8 × 2)
Main machinery: 2 Kolomna diesels; 2,000 hp(m) (1.47 MW) sustained; 2 shafts
Speed, knots: 15
Range, n miles: 3,000 at 10 kt
Complement: 43
Guns: 2—30 mm/65 (twin). 2—25 mm/80 (twin).
Mines: 8.
Radars: Surface search: Don 2; I-band.
IFF: Two Square Head.
Sonars: MG 69/79; hull-mounted; active; high frequency.

Comment: Built in 1978. Transferred from Russia in 1996. Wooden hull.

MELITOPOL   *6/2003, B Lemachko* / 0572653

1 YEVGENYA (KOROND) (PROJECT 1258) CLASS (MHC)

GENICHESK (ex-RT 214) U 360

Displacement, tons: 77 standard; 90 full load
Dimensions, feet (metres): 80.7 × 18 × 4.9 (24.6 × 5.5 × 1.5)
Main machinery: 2 Type 3-D-12 diesels; 600 hp(m) (440 kW) sustained; 2 shafts
Speed, knots: 11
Range, n miles: 300 at 10 kt
Complement: 10
Guns: 2—14.5 mm (twin) MGs.
Mines: 8 racks.
Radars: Surface search: Spin Trough or Mius; I-band.
IFF: Salt Pot.
Sonars: A small MG-7 sonar is lifted over stern on crane; a TV system may also be used.

Comment: Transferred from Russia in 1996. Reported as being operational.

GENICHESK   *6/2003, Ships of the World* / 0572652

SURVEY SHIPS

Notes: (1) Also transferred in 1997 were two Muna class AGIs, *Pereyaslav* U 512 and *Dzhankoi* U 754. Both are used as transports, mostly for commercial goods.
(2) Ten former Russian civilian research ships were transferred in 1996/97. All are now in commercial service.

2 MOMA (PROJECT 861M) CLASS (AGS)

SIMFEROPOL (ex-*Jupiter*) U 511   — (ex-*Berezan*) U 602

Displacement, tons: 1,600 full load
Dimensions, feet (metres): 240.5 × 36.8 × 12.8 (73.3 × 11.2 × 3.9)
Main machinery: 2 Zgoda-Sulzer diesels; 3,300 hp(m) (2.43 MW) sustained; 2 shafts; cp props
Speed, knots: 17
Range, n miles: 9,000 at 11 kt
Complement: 56
Radars: Navigation: Don 2; I-band.

Comment: U 511 transferred from Russia in February 1996 and is active. A second of class U 602 has also been reported as active.

SIMFEROPOL   *7/2000, Hartmut Ehlers* / 0106669

2 BIYA (PROJECT 870) CLASS (AGS)

ALCHEVSK U 601 (ex-GS 212)   **U 603** (ex-GS 273)

Displacement, tons: 766 full load
Dimensions, feet (metres): 180.4 × 32.1 × 8.5 *(55 × 9.8 × 2.6)*
Main machinery: 2 diesels; 1,200 hp(m) *(882 kW)*; 2 shafts; cp props
Speed, knots: 13. **Range, n miles:** 4,700 at 11 kt
Complement: 25
Radars: Navigation: Don 2; I-band.

Comment: Built at Northern Shipyard, Gdansk 1972-76. Transferred from Russia in 1997. Laboratory and one survey launch, and a 5 ton crane.

ALCHEVSK   *8/1997, W Globke* / 0019356

TRAINING SHIPS

Note: In addition there are two Bryza class training cutters *U 543* and *U 544*.

3 PETRUSHKA (UK-3) CLASS (AXL)

CHIGIRIN U 540   **SMILA** U 541   **DARNICHA** U 542

Displacement, tons: 335 full load
Dimensions, feet (metres): 129.3 × 27.6 × 7.2 *(39.4 × 8.4 × 2.2)*
Main machinery: 2 Wola H12 diesels; 756 hp(m) *(556 kW)*; 2 shafts
Speed, knots: 11. **Range, n miles:** 1,000 at 11 kt
Complement: 13 plus 30 cadets

Comment: Training vessels built at Wisla Shiyard, Poland in 1989. Transferred from Russia in 1997. Used for seamanship and navigation training.

SMILA   *4/2001, B Lemachko* / 0131162

1 MIR CLASS (SAIL TRAINING SHIP) (AXS)

Name	No	Builders	Commissioned
KHERSONES	—	Northern Shipyard, Gdansk	10 June 1988

Measurement, tons: 2,996 grt
Dimensions, feet (metres): 346.1 × 45.9 × 19.7 *(105.5 × 14 × 6)*
Main machinery: 1 Sulzer 8AL20/24 diesels; 1,500 hp(m) *(1.1 MW)*; 1 shaft
Speed, knots: 17
Complement: 55 plus 144 trainees

Comment: One of five of a class ordered in July 1985. Civilian manned.

KHERSONES   *6/2003, Martin Mokrus* / 1043549

AUXILIARIES

Notes: Other ships transferred from Russia in 1997, and possibly still in limited service, are a Keyla II class tanker, *Kriviy Rig* U 753, two Toplivo class tankers, *Fastiv* U 760 and *Bahmach* U 759, two Pozharny class, ATR *Borshev* U 722 and *Evpatoriya* U 728 and a Shalanda class trials craft *Kamyankha* U 860.

KAMYANKHA   *6/2003, B Lemachko* / 1043552

1 AMUR (PROJECT 304) CLASS SUPPORT SHIP (AGF/AR)

DONBAS (ex-*Krasnodon*) U 500 (ex-U 803)

Displacement, tons: 5,500 full load
Dimensions, feet (metres): 400.3 × 55.8 × 16.7 *(122 × 17 × 5.1)*
Main machinery: 1 Zgoda 8TAD-48 diesel; 3,000 hp(m) *(2.2 MW)*; 1 shaft
Speed, knots: 12. **Range, n miles:** 13,000 at 8 kt
Complement: 145
Radars: Navigation: Don 2; I-band.

Comment: Transferred in 1977. Completed refit in 2001 to serve as command ship and support ships for surface ships and submarines based at Sevastopol. Has two 3-ton cranes and one 1.5-ton crane.

DONBAS   *7/2003, B Lemachko* / 0576461

1 VODA (PROJECT 561) CLASS WATER TANKER (AWT)

SUDAK (ex-*Sura*) U 756

Displacement, tons: 982 standard; 2,250 full load
Dimensions, feet (metres): 266.8 × 37.4 × 11.3 *(81.3 × 11.4 × 3.44)*
Main machinery: 2 diesels; 2 shafts
Speed, knots: 12. **Range, n miles:** 2,900 at 10 kt
Complement: 22
Radars: Navigation: Don 2; I-band.

Comment: Transferred in 1977. Has a three ton derrick.

SUDAK   *3/2002, Hartmut Ehlers* / 0529996

1 BEREZA CLASS (PROJECT 18061) (ADG)

BALTA U 811 (ex-SR 568)

Displacement, tons: 1,850 standard; 2,051 full load
Dimensions, feet (metres): 228 × 45.3 × 13.1 *(69.5 × 13.8 × 4)*
Main machinery: 2 Zgoda-Sulzer 8AL25/30 diesels; 2,938 hp(m) *(2.16 MW)* sustained; 2 shafts
Speed, knots: 14
Range, n miles: 1,000 at 14 kt
Complement: 88
Radars: Navigation: Kivach; I-band.

Comment: Built at Northern Shipyard, Gdansk in 1987. Transferred from Russia in 1997. Degaussing vessel with an NBC citadel and three laboratories. Not seen at sea since being transferred but may be in use.

BALTA   *5/2005*, C D Yaylali* / 1153919

1 BAMBUK (PROJECT 12884) CLASS (AGFHM)

Name	No	Builders	Launched	Commissioned
SLAVUTICH	U 510 (ex-800, ex-SSV 189)	Nikolayev	12 Oct 1990	28 July 1992

Displacement, tons: 5,403 full load
Dimensions, feet (metres): 350.1 × 52.5 × 19.7 *(106.7 × 16 × 6)*
Main machinery: 2 Skoda 6L2511 diesels; 6,100 hp(m) *(4.5 MW)*; 2 shafts
Speed, knots: 16
Range, n miles: 8,000 at 12 kt
Complement: 178
Missiles: SAM: 2 SA-N-5/8 Grail quad launchers; manual aiming; IR homing to 6 km *(3.2 n miles)* at 1.5 Mach; altitude to 2,500 m *(8,000 ft)*; warhead 1.5 kg.
Guns: 2—30 mm/65 AK 630; 6 barrels per mounting.
Countermeasures: Decoys: 2 PK 16 chaff launchers.
Radars: Navigation: 3 Palm Frond; I-band.
CCA: Fly Screen; I-band.
Tacan: 2 Round House.

Comment: Laid down on 20 March 1988. Second of a class built for acoustic research but taken over before completion and used as a command ship by the Ukrainian Navy. The ship is not capable of helicopter operations as previously reported.

SLAVUTICH *4/2005*, C D Yaylali* / 1153918

1 SURA (PROJECT 145) CLASS (ABU)

SHOSTKA (ex-Kil 33) U 852

Displacement, tons: 2,370 standard; 3,150 full load
Dimensions, feet (metres): 285.4 × 48.6 × 16.4 *(87 × 14.8 × 5)*
Main machinery: Diesel-electric; 4 diesel generators; 2 motors; 2,240 hp(m) *(1.65 MW)*; 2 shafts
Speed, knots: 12
Range, n miles: 2,000 at 11 kt
Complement: 40
Cargo capacity: 900 tons cargo; 300 tons fuel for transfer
Radars: Navigation: 2 Don 2; I-band.

Comment: Transferred from Russia in 1997. Heavy lift ship built at Rostock in 1973. Lifting capacity includes one 65 ton derrick and one 65 ton stern cage. Can carry a 12 m DSRV, although this has not been seen in Ukrainian service.

SHOSTKA *8/2000, Hartmut Ehlers* / 0106666

1 YELVA (PROJECT 535M) CLASS (DIVING TENDER) (YDT)

NETISIN (ex-VM 114) U 700

Displacement, tons: 295 full load
Dimensions, feet (metres): 134.2 × 26.2 × 6.6 *(40.9 × 8 × 2)*
Main machinery: 2 Type 3-D-12A diesels; 630 hp(m) *(463 kW)* sustained; 2 shafts
Speed, knots: 12.5
Range, n miles: 1,870 at 12 kt
Complement: 30
Radars: Navigation: Spin Trough; I-band.

Comment: Diving tender built in mid-1970s. Transferred from Russia in 1997. Carries a 1 ton crane and diving bell. Operational.

YELVA CLASS (to left) *6/1998, van Ginderen Collection* / 0050315

20 HARBOUR CRAFT (YDT/YFL/YPT)

FEODOSIYA U 240	V VOLNIDSKY U 721	SHULYAVKA U 853
U 241	MIRGOOD U 731	MALIN U 890
U 631-634	U 732	KHERSON (ex-*Monastirishze*) U 891
SKVYRA U 635	TOKMAK U 733	U 926
BRODI U 707	ILLICHIVSK U 783	+3

Displacement, tons: 42 full load
Dimensions, feet (metres): 72.8 × 12.8 × 4.6 *(22.2 × 3.9 × 1.4)*
Main machinery: 1 diesel; 300 hp(m) *(220 kW)* sustained; 1 shaft
Speed, knots: 12
Complement: 8

Comment: Details given are for the Flamingo class harbour patrol craft of which there are five (U 240, U 634, U 721, U 732, U 733). There are also five 'Nyryat 1' diving tenders and inshore survey craft (U 631, U 632, U 633, U 635, U 707) and six PO 2 class tenders (U 731, U 926 plus four). There are also two Shelon class YPTs (U 890, U 891), an ambulance craft U 783 and a flag officers' yacht U 853.

ILLICHIVSK *7/2003, B Lemachko* / 1043554

KHERSON *9/2004, Hartmut Ehlers* / 1043553

1 SK 620 CLASS (DRAKON) (YH/TFL)

SOKAL U 782

Displacement, tons: 236 full load
Dimensions, feet (metres): 108.3 × 24.3 × 6.9 *(33 × 7.4 × 2.1)*
Main machinery: 2 56ANM30-H12 diesels; 620 hp(m) *(456 kW)* systained; 2 shafts
Speed, knots: 12
Range, n miles: 1,000 at 12 kt
Complement: 14 plus 3 spare

Comment: Built at Wisla Shipyard, Poland as a smaller version of the Petrushka class training ship. Transferred from Russia in 1997. Used as a general purpose craft. The status of two other craft, *Akar* and *Suvar* is not known.

TUGS

6 TUGS (ATA/YTM)

KREMENETS U 705	KOVEL U 831
IZYASLAV U 706	KRASNOPEREKOPSK U 947
KORETS U 830	DUBNO U 953

Comment: All transferred from Russia in 1997. U 706 and U 831 are Okhtensky class coastal tugs built in 1958. U 705 is a Goryn class ocean going tug with a bollard pull of 45 tons, U 830 is a Sorum class and U 947 a Prometey class large tug. U 953 is a Sidehole II class harbour tug.

KORETS *6/2003, B Lemachko* / 1043550

BORDER GUARD (MORSKA OKHORONA)

Notes: (1) There are plans to build new patrol cutters of the 'Kordon' (47 m) and 'Afalina' (44 m) classes, and new patrol boats of the 'Scif' (26 m) class. These new designs are also on offer for export by the Feodosiya Shipbuilding Association Morye. A 67 m OPV design, by Nikolayev 61 Kommuna shipyard, is also in the export market.
(2) The river brigades also include four minesweeping boats, and 16 training craft. Not all of these are operational.
(3) Border Guard vessels are painted dark grey with a thick yellow and thin blue diagonal line on the hull. From July 1999, pennant numbers were changed and are preceded by the letters BG.

3 PAUK I (MOLNYA) CLASS (PROJECT 1241) (PC)

GRIGORY KUROPIATNIKOV BG 50 (ex-PSKR 817)   POLTAVA BG 51 (ex-PSKR 813)
GRIGORY GNATENKO BG 52 (ex-PSKR 815)

Displacement, tons: 475 full load
Dimensions, feet (metres): 189 × 33.5 × 10.8 *(57.6 × 10.2 × 3.3)*
Main machinery: 2 Type M 521 diesels; 16,184 hp(m) *(11.9 MW)* sustained; 2 shafts
Speed, knots: 32
Range, n miles: 1,260 at 14 kt
Complement: 44 (7 officers)

Guns: 1—3 in *(76 mm)*/60; 120 rds/min to 15 km *(8 n miles)*; weight of shell 7 kg.
1—30 mm/65 AK 630; 6 barrels; 3,000 rds/min combined to 2 km.
Torpedoes: 4—16 in *(406 mm)* tubes. SAET-40; anti-submarine; active/passive homing to 10 km *(5.4 n miles)* at 30 kt; warhead 100 kg.
A/S mortars: 2 RBU 1200 5-tubed fixed; range 1,200 m; warhead 34 kg.
Depth charges: 2 racks (12).
Countermeasures: Decoys: 2 PK 16 or 4 PK 10.
ESM: Brick Plug and Half Hat; radar warning.
Weapons control: Hood Wink optronic director.
Radars: Air/surface search: Peel Cone; E/F-band.
Surface search: Kivach or Pechora or SRN 207; I-band.
Fire control: Bass Tilt; H/I-band.
Sonars: Foal Tail; VDS (mounted on transom); active attack; high frequency.

Comment: Built at Yaroslavl in the early 1980s and transferred from Russian Black Sea Fleet. Pennant numbers changed from July 1999. All are based at Balaklava.

POLTAVA   *9/2004, Hartmut Ehlers* / 1043548

GRIGORY GNATENKO   *6/2003, B Lemachko* / 0576460

10 STENKA (TARANTUL) CLASS (PROJECT 205P) (PCF)

PEREKOP BG 30	ZAKARPATTIYA	BUKOVINA BG 31
DONBAS BG 32	(ex-031, ex-PSKR 648)	(ex-034, ex-PSKR 702)
(ex-PSKR 705)	ZAPORIZKAYA SEC	PODILLIYA BG 62
MIKOLAIV BG 57	(ex-032, ex-PSKR 650)	(ex-036, ex-PSKR 709)
(ex-PSKR 722)	ODESSA BG 61	PAVEL DERZHAVIN BG 63
VOLIN (ex-020, ex-PSKR 637)	(ex-033, ex-PSKR 652)	(ex-037, ex-PSKR 720)

Displacement, tons: 253 full load
Dimensions, feet (metres): 129.3 × 25.9 × 8.2 *(39.4 × 7.9 × 2.5)*
Main machinery: 3 Type M 517 or M 583 diesels; 14,100 hp(m) *(10.36 MW)*; 3 shafts
Speed, knots: 37
Range, n miles: 500 at 35 kt; 1,540 at 14 kt
Complement: 30 (5 officers)
Guns: 4—30 mm/65 (2 twin) AK 230.
Torpedoes: 4—16 in *(406 mm)* tubes.
Depth charges: 2 racks (12).
Radars: Surface search: Pot Drum or Peel Cone; H/I- or E-band.
Fire control: Drum Tilt; H/I-band.
Navigation: Palm Frond; I-band.
IFF: High Pole. 2 Square Head.
Sonars: Stag Ear or Foal Tail; VDS; high frequency; Hormone type dipping sonar.

Comment: Similar hull to the Osa class. Built in the 1970s and 1980s. Transferred from Russia. Others have been cannibalised for spares. Based at Kerch, Odessa and Balaklava.

ODESSA   *6/2001, B Lemachko* / 0131160

1 SSV-10 CLASS (SUPPORT SHIP) (AGF)

DUNAI BG 80 (ex-500)

Displacement, tons: 340 full load
Dimensions, feet (metres): 129.3 × 23 × 3.9 *(39.4 × 7 × 1.2)*
Main machinery: 2 diesels; 2 shafts
Speed, knots: 12
Complement: 20 (4 officers)

Comment: Headquarters ship built in 1940. Taken over from the Russian Danube Flotilla and now acts as the command ship for the river brigades. Based at Odessa.

DUNAI (old number)   *4/1998, Ukraine Coast Guard* / 0050322

3 MURAVEY (ANTARES) CLASS (PROJECT 133) (PCK)

BG 53 (ex-PSKR 105)   BG 54 (ex-PSKR 108)   GALICHINA BG 55 (ex-PSKR 115)

Displacement, tons: 212 full load
Dimensions, feet (metres): 126.6 × 24.9 × 6.2; 14.4 (foils) *(38.6 × 7.6 × 1.9; 4.4)*
Main machinery: 2 gas turbines; 22,600 hp(m) *(16.6 MW)*; 2 shafts
Speed, knots: 60. **Range, n miles:** 410 at 12 kt
Complement: 30 (5 officers)

Guns: 1—3 in *(76 mm)*/60; 120 rds/min to 15 km *(8 n miles)*; weight of shell 7 kg.
1—30 mm/65 AK 630; 6 barrels; 3,000 rds/min combined to 2 km.
Torpedoes: 2—16 in *(406 mm)* tubes; SAET-40; anti-submarine; active/passive homing to 10 km *(5.4 n miles)* at 30 kt; warhead 100 kg.
Depth charges: 6.
Weapons control: Hood Wink optronic director.
Radars: Surface search: Peel Cone; E-band.
Fire control: Bass Tilt; H/I-band.
Sonars: Rat Tail; VDS; active attack; high frequency; dipping sonar.

Comment: Built at Feodosiya in the mid-1980s for the USSR Border Guard. High speed hydrofoil craft. All based at Balaklava. Pennant numbers changed from July 1999.

BG 53 (old number)   *3/1998, Ukraine Coast Guard* / 0050319

1 PO2 CLASS (COASTAL PATROL CRAFT) (PB)

BG 501

Displacement, tons: 56 full load
Dimensions, feet (metres): 70.5 × 11.5 × 3.3 *(21.5 × 3.5 × 1)*
Main machinery: 1 Type 3-D-12 diesel; 150 hp(m) *(110 kW)* sustained; 1 shaft
Speed, knots: 12
Complement: 8

Comment: Based at Balaclava.

6 PROJECT 1398B (AIST) CLASS
(INSHORE PATROL CRAFT) (PBR)

BG 316	BG 329	BG 812
BG 318	BG 349	BG 814

Displacement, tons: 5 full load
Dimensions, feet (metres): To be announced
Main machinery: To be announced
Speed, knots: To be announced
Complement: To be announced

Comment: Inshore patrol craft originally designed in the 1960s by the Redan boat building yard in St Petersburg.

16 ZHUK (GRIF) CLASS (PROJECT 1400M) (PB)

BG 100-107   BG 109-111   BG 115-119

Displacement, tons: 39 full load
Dimensions, feet (metres): 78.7 × 16.4 × 3.9 *(24 × 5 × 1.2)*
Main machinery: 2 Type M 401B diesels; 2,200 hp(m) *(1.6 MW)* sustained; 2 shafts
Speed, knots: 30
Range, n miles: 1,100 at 15 kt
Complement: 13 (1 officer)
Guns: 2 — 14.5 mm (twin, fwd) MGs. 1 — 12.7 mm (aft) MG.
Radars: Surface search: Spin Trough; I-band.

Comment: Russian Border Guard vessels built in the 1980s and transferred in 1996. Pennant numbers changed from the 600 series in mid-1999.

LUBNY (old number)   *4/1998, Ukraine Coast Guard* / 0050323

BG 119   *9/2004, Hartmut Ehlers* / 1043547

4 SHMEL CLASS (PROJECT 1204) (PGR)

LUBNY BG 81 (ex-171)   **KANIV** BG 82 (ex-173)   **NIZYN** BG 83 (ex-172)   **IZMAYL** BG 84 (ex-174)

Displacement, tons: 77 full load
Dimensions, feet (metres): 90.9 × 14.1 × 3.9 *(27.7 × 4.3 × 1.2)*
Main machinery: 2 Type M 50 diesels; 2,200 hp(m) *(1.6 MW)* sustained; 2 shafts
Speed, knots: 25
Range, n miles: 600 at 12 kt
Complement: 12 (4 officers)
Guns: 1 — 3 in *(76 mm)*/48 (tank turret). 2 — 14.5 mm (twin) MGs. 5 — 7.62 mm MGs. 1 BP 6 rocket launcher; 18 barrels.
Mines: Can lay 9.
Radars: Surface search: Spint Trough; I-band.

Comment: Built at Kerch from 1967-74. Now part of the river brigade having been transferred from the Russian Danube flotilla. New pennant numbers are unconfirmed and there is doubt about the operational status of this class.

7 KALKAN (PROJECT 50030) M CLASS
(INSHORE PATROL CRAFT) (PBR)

BG 303-304   BG 503-504   MATROS MIKOLA MUSHNIROV
BG 310   BG 604

Displacement, tons: 8.5 full load
Dimensions, feet (metres): 38.1 × 10.8 × 2.0 *(11.6 × 3.3 × 0.6)*
Main machinery: 1 Type 475K diesel; 496 hp *(370 kW)*; 1 waterjet
Speed, knots: 34
Complement: 2

Comment: Built by Morye Feodosiya and entered service from 1996. Aluminium hulls and GRP superstructure. Can be armed with 7.62 mm or 12.7 mm MGs and 'Strela' shoulder launched missile.

KALKAN class   *6/2003, Morye* / 0572655

United Arab Emirates

Country Overview

The United Arab Emirates was formed on 2 December 1971 by the federation of seven states (formerly the Trucial States) lying along the east-coast of the Arabian Peninsula. With an area of 30,000 square miles, the country includes Abu Dhabi, Ajman, Dubai, al-Fujairah, Ras al Khaimah, Sharjah and Umm al-Qaiwain. It is bordered to the north by Qatar and to the south by Saudi Arabia. To the east lies Oman which is separated from its small exclave on the Musandam peninsula. There is a coastline of 713 n miles with the Gulf and with the Gulf of Oman. The city of Abu Dhabi is the capital and largest city while Dubai is the principal port and commercial centre. Territorial Seas (12 n miles) are claimed. An EEZ (200 n miles) has also been claimed but its limits have not been defined.

Following a decision of the UAE Supreme Defence Council on 6 May 1976 the armed forces of the member states were unified and the organisation of the UAE armed forces was furthered by decisions taken on 1 February 1978.

Headquarters Appointments

Commander, Naval Forces:
 Rear Admiral Suhail Mohammed Khalifa Al Marrar
Deputy Commander, Naval Forces:
 Brigadier Mohammed Mahmoud Al Madini
Director General, Coast Guard:
 Colonel Mohammed Rashid Al Raumaithy

Personnel

(a) 2006: 2,400 (200 officers) Navy. 1,200 (110 officers) Coast Guard
(b) Voluntary service

Bases

Abu Dhabi (main base).
Mina Rashid and Mina Jebel Ali (Dubai),
Mina Saqr (Ras al Khaimah), Mina Sultan (Sharjah),
Khor Fakkan (Sharjah-East Coast).

SUBMARINES

Notes: Submarine training has been conducted in the past but acquisition of submarines is understood to be a long-term aspiration.

10 SWIMMER DELIVERY VEHICLES (SDV)

Comment: Two classes of indigenously built Long Range Submersible Carriers (LRSC) have been developed by Emirates Marine Technologies. The 7.35 × 0.95 m Class 4 variant, of which approximately ten are believed to have been in service with UAE Special Forces since 1998, is capable of deploying a 200 kg payload. These are likely to be augmented by the larger 9.1 × 1.15 m Class 5 variant which can deliver 450 kg. Constructed of glass and carbon fibres, both variants are manned by two people, have a top speed of 7 kt, a range of 60 n miles at 6 kt and an operational depth of 30 m. They are equipped with depth-sounder, sonar and built-in breathing system.

CLASS 5 LRSC
2001, Emirates Marine Technologies
0095256

FRIGATES

2 KORTENAER CLASS (FFGHM)

Name	No	Builders	Laid down	Launched	Commissioned
ABU DHABI (ex-*Abraham Crijnssen*)	F 01 (ex-F 816)	Koninklijke Maatschappij De Schelde, Flushing	25 Oct 1978	16 May 1981	27 Jan 1983
AL EMIRAT (ex-*Piet Heyn*)	F 02 (ex-F 811)	Koninklijke Maatschappij De Schelde, Flushing	28 Apr 1977	3 June 1978	14 Apr 1981

Displacement, tons: 3,050 standard; 3,630 full load
Dimensions, feet (metres): 428 × 47.9 × 14.1; 20.3 (screws)
(130.5 × 14.6 × 4.3; 6.2)
Main machinery: GOGOG; 2 RR Olympus TM3B gas
turbines; 50,880 hp (37.9 MW) sustained
2 RR Tyne RM1C gas turbines; 9,900 hp (7.4 MW)
sustained; 2 shafts; cp props
Speed, knots: 30
Range, n miles: 4,700 at 16 kt on Tynes
Complement: 176 (18 officers) plus 24 spare berths

Missiles: SSM: 8 McDonnell Douglas Harpoon (2 quad)
launchers ❶; active radar homing to 130 km (70 n miles)
at 0.9 Mach; warhead 227 kg.
SAM: Raytheon Sea Sparrow Mk 29 octuple launcher ❷;
semi-active radar homing to 14.6 km (8 n miles) at
2.5 Mach; warhead 39 kg; 24 missiles.
Guns: 1 OTO Melara 3 in (76 mm)/62 compact ❸;
85 rds/min to 16 km (8.6 n miles) anti-surface; 12 km
(6.5 n miles) anti-aircraft; weight of shell 6 kg.
1 Signaal SGE-30 Goalkeeper with General Electric
30 mm ❹; 7-barrelled; 4,200 rds/min combined to 2 km.
2 Oerlikon 20 mm.
Torpedoes: 4—324 mm US Mk 32 (2 twin) tubes ❺.
Honeywell Mk 46 or Whitehead A-244S Mod 1.
Countermeasures: Decoys: 2 Loral Hycor SRBOC Mk 36
6-tubed launchers ❻; chaff distraction or centroid modes.
ESM/ECM: Ramses ❼; intercept and jammer.
Combat data systems: Signaal SEWACO II action data
automation; Link 11.
Radars: Air search: Signaal LW08 ❽; D-band; range 264 km
(145 n miles) for 2 m² target.
Surface search: Signaal Scout ❾; I-band.
Fire control: Signaal STIR ❿; I/J-band; range 140 km
(76 n miles) for 1 m² target.
Signaal WM25 ⓫; I/J-band; range 46 km (25 n miles).
Sonars: Westinghouse SQS-505; bow-mounted; active
search and attack; medium frequency.

Helicopters: 2 Eurocopter AS 565 Panther ⓬.

Programmes: Contract signed on 2 April 1996 to transfer
two Netherlands frigates, after refits by Royal Schelde.
First one recommissioned in December 1997, second one
in May 1998. Further transfers are unlikely.
Structure: Harpoon SSM and Goalkeeper CIWS has
been purchased separately, as have the Scout radars.
Additional air conditioning has been fitted.
Operational: Crew training takes place in the Netherlands.
Both based at Jebel Ali.

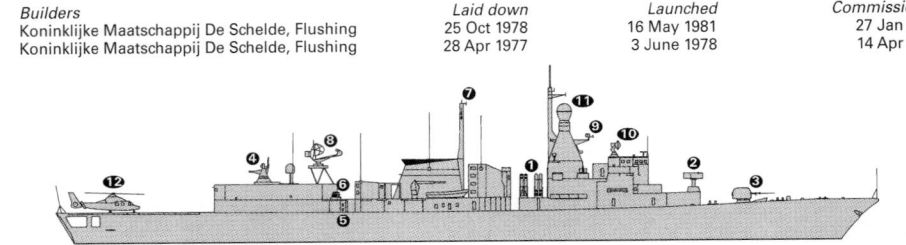

ABU DHABI (Scale 1 : 1,200), Ian Sturton / 0121417

ABU DHABI 3/2005*, Ships of the World / 1127290

ABU DHABI
1/2002, A Sharma
0534062

CORVETTES

Notes: Project Fallah (LEWA 2) is for 90 m multirole corvettes.

0 + 6 BAYNUNAH CLASS (FAST ATTACK CRAFT—MISSILE) (PGGMH)

Name	No	Builders	Commissioned
–	–	CMN, Cherbourg	2008
–	–	Abu Dhabi Shipbuilding	2010
–	–	Abu Dhabi Shipbuilding	2011
–	–	Abu Dhabi Shipbuilding	2012

Displacement, tons: 630 full load
Dimensions, feet (metres): 229.6 × 36.1 × 9.2
(70.0 × 11.0 × 2.8)
Main machinery: 4 MTU 12V 595 TE 90 diesels; 22,500 hp
(16.8 MW); 3 (2-112 SII; 1-125 BII) Kamewa waterjets
Speed, knots: 32. **Range, n miles:** 2,400 at 15 kt
Complement: 37 (accommodation for 45)

Missiles: SSM: 8 MBDA MM 40 Block III.
SAM: Raytheon Evolved Sea Sparrow RIM-162; Mk 56 VLS
(8 missiles).
Guns: 1 OTO Melara 3 in (76 mm)/62 Super Rapid.
2—30 mm.
Countermeasures: Decoys: 2 Rheinmetall MASS launchers.
RESM: Elettronica.
Combat data systems: Alenia Marconi Systems IPN-S. Link
11 and LinkY Mk 2.
Weapons control: Sagem-EOMS optronic director.
Radars: Air/surface search: Ericsson Sea Giraffe; G/H-band.
Surface search: Terma Scanter 2001; I-band.
Fire control: 2 Alenia Marconi NA-25/XM; I-band.

Helicopters: 1 Eurocopter AS 565 Panther.

Comment: Project Baynunah succeeded Project LEWA 1
for the procurement of patrol boats and is a joint
venture between Abu Dhabi Shipbuilding (ADSB) (Prime
Contractor) and CMN of France. Systems integration is
being undertaken by Abu Dhabi Systems Integration, a
joint venture between ADSB and Selex Sistemi Integrati.
Contract signed 28 December 2003 for four ships and
option for a further two exercised in 2005. Based on a
CMN BR67 design, it has a steel hull and aluminium
superstructure. The first of class was laid down at
Cherbourg on 8 September 2005 for launch in 2006.

CMN is to provide materials for follow-on vessels to be
built by ADSB.

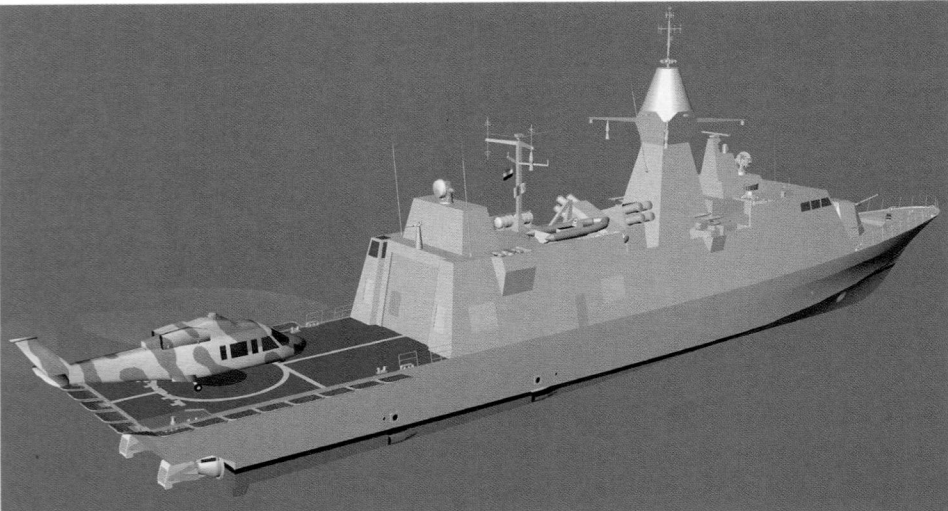

BAYNUNAH PATROL CRAFT 7/2005*, CMN / 1116361

2 MURAY JIB (MGB 62) CLASS (FSGHM)

Name	No	Builders	Launched	Commissioned
MURAY JIB	P 161 (ex-CM 01, ex-P 6501)	Lürssen, Bremen	Mar 1989	Nov 1990
DAS	P 162 (ex-CM 02, ex-P 6502)	Lürssen, Bremen	May 1989	Jan 1991

Displacement, tons: 630 full load
Dimensions, feet (metres): 206.7 × 30.5 × 8.2
(63 × 9.3 × 2.5)
Main machinery: 4 MTU 16V 538TB92 diesels; 13,640 hp(m)
(10 MW) sustained; 4 shafts
Speed, knots: 32
Range, n miles: 4,000 at 16 kt
Complement: 43

Missiles: SSM: 8 Aerospatiale MM 40 Exocet
(Block II) ❶; inertial cruise; active radar homing to
70 km *(40 n miles)* at 0.9 Mach; warhead 165 kg;
sea-skimmer.
SAM: Thomson-CSF modified Crotale Navale octuple
launcher ❷; radar guidance; IR homing to 13 km
(7 n miles) at 2.4 Mach; warhead 14 kg.
Guns: 1 OTO Melara 3 in *(76 mm)*/62 Super Rapid ❸; 120
rds/min to 16 km *(8.7 n miles);* weight of shell 6 kg.
1 Signaal Goalkeeper with GE 30 mm 7-barrelled ❹;
4,200 rds/min combined to 2 km.
2 – 12.7 mm MGs.
Countermeasures: Decoys: 2 Dagaie launchers ❺; IR flares
and chaff.
ESM/ECM: Racal Cutlass/Cygnus ❻; intercept/jammer.
Weapons control: CSSE Najir optronic director ❼.

Radars: Air/surface search: Bofors Ericsson Sea Giraffe
50HC ❽; G-band.
Navigation: Racal Decca 1226; I-band.
Fire control: Bofors Electronic 9LV 223 ❾; J-band (for gun
and SSM).
Thomson-CSF DRBV 51C ❿; J-band (for Crotale).

Helicopters: 1 Aerospatiale Alouette SA 316 ⓫.

Programmes: Ordered in late 1986. Similar vessels to
Bahrain craft. Delivery in October 1991.
Structure: Lürssen design adapted for the particular
conditions of the Gulf. This class has good air defence
and a considerable anti-ship capability. The helicopter
hangar is reached by flight deck lift.
Operational: Pennant numbers changed in 2002.

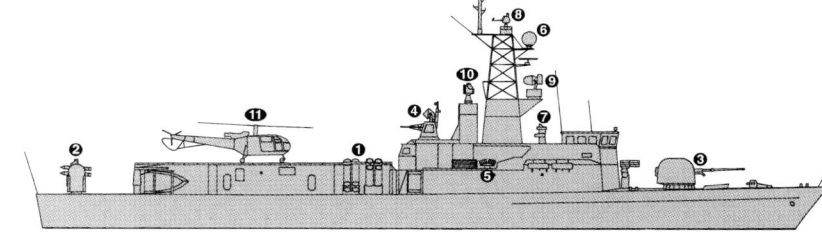

MURAY JIB
(Scale 1 : 600), Ian Sturton / 0080921

MURAY JIB
5/2003, A Sharma / 0567564

MURAY JIB
3/2005, Ships of the World* / 1127284

SHIPBORNE AIRCRAFT

Numbers/Type: 4 Aerospatiale SA 316/319S Alouette.
Operational speed: 113 kt *(210 km/h)*.
Service ceiling: 10,500 ft *(3,200 m)*.
Range: 290 n miles *(540 km)*.
Role/Weapon systems: Reconnaissance and general purpose helicopters. Sensors: radar. Weapons: Unarmed.

Numbers/Type: 7 Eurocopter AS 565 Panther.
Operational speed: 165 kt *(305 km/h)*.
Service ceiling: 16,700 ft *(5,100 m)*.
Range: 483 n miles *(895 km)*.
Role/Weapon systems: Ordered in March 1995 and delivered from 1998. Sensors: Thomson-CSF Agrion radar. Weapons: ASV; Aerospatiale AS 15TT ASM.

AS 565   *10/2002*, Eurocopter/Patrick Penna* / 0526393

LAND-BASED MARITIME AIRCRAFT

Notes: Procurement of five refurbished E-2C Hawkeye aircraft from the USA, under FMS funding arrangements, is under consideration.

Numbers/Type: 4 EADS CASA C-295M.
Operational speed: 256 kt *(474 km/h)*.
Service ceiling: 13,540 ft *(4,125 m)*.
Range: 2,250 n miles *(4,167 km)*.
Role/Weapon systems: Stretched version of CN-235M for maritime patrol and reconnaissance. Order announced in March 2001. Delivery dates not confirmed. Fitted with EADS Fully Integrated Tactical System (FITS), sensors and weapons to be selected.

C-295M   *2001, EADS CASA* / 0094291

Numbers/Type: 7 Aerospatiale AS 535 Cougar/Super Puma.
Operational speed: 150 kt *(280 km/h)*.
Service ceiling: 15,090 ft *(4,600 m)*.
Range: 335 n miles *(620 km)*.
Role/Weapon systems: Former transport helicopters. Five updated from 1995 with ASW equipment. Two used as VIP transports. Sensors: Omera ORB 30 radar; Thomson Marconi HS 312 dipping sonar. Weapons: ASV; one AM 39 Exocet ASM. ASW; A 244S torpedoes and mines.

COUGAR   *6/1994* / 0080927

Numbers/Type: 2 Pilatus Britten-Norman Maritime Defender.
Operational speed: 150 kt *(280 km/h)*.
Service ceiling: 18,900 ft *(5,760 m)*.
Range: 1,500 n miles *(2,775 km)*.
Role/Weapon systems: Coastal patrol and surveillance aircraft although seldom used in this role. Sensors: Nose-mounted search radar, underwing searchlight. Weapons: Underwing rocket and gun pods.

PATROL FORCES

Notes: Three Fast Intercept Craft are reported to be in service.

6 BAN YAS (TNC 45) CLASS
(FAST ATTACK CRAFT—MISSILE) (PGGF)

Name	No	Builders	Commissioned
BAN YAS	P 151 (ex-P 4501)	Lürssen Vegesack	Nov 1980
MARBAN	P 152 (ex-P 4502)	Lürssen Vegesack	Nov 1980
RODQM	P 153 (ex-P 4503)	Lürssen Vegesack	July 1981
SHAHEEN	P 154 (ex-P 4504)	Lürssen Vegesack	July 1981
SAGAR	P 155 (ex-P 4505)	Lürssen Vegesack	Sep 1981
TARIF	P 156 (ex-P 4506)	Lürssen Vegesack	Sep 1981

Displacement, tons: 260 full load
Dimensions, feet (metres): 147.3 × 23 × 8.2 *(44.9 × 7 × 2.5)*
Main machinery: 4 MTU 16V 538 TB92 diesels; 13,640 hp(m) *(10 MW)* sustained; 4 shafts
Speed, knots: 40
Range, n miles: 500 at 38 kt
Complement: 40 (5 officers)

Missiles: SSM: 4 Aerospatiale MM 40 Exocet; inertial cruise; active radar homing to 70 km *(40 n miles)* at 0.9 Mach; warhead 165 kg; sea-skimmer.
Guns: 1 OTO Melara 3 in *(76 mm)*/62; 60 rds/min to 16 km *(8.7 n miles)*; weight of shell 6 kg. 2 Breda 40 mm/70 (twin); 300 rds/min to 12.5 km *(6.8 n miles)*; weight of shell 0.96 kg. 2 —7.62 mm MGs.
Countermeasures: Decoys: 1 CSEE trainable Dagaie; IR flares and chaff.
ESM: Racal Cutlass; intercept.
Combat data systems: CelsiusTech 9LV Mk 3E CETRIS.
Weapons control: 1 CSEE Panda director for 40 mm. PEAB low-light USFA IR and TV tracker.
Radars: Surface search: Bofors Ericsson Sea Giraffe 50HC; G-band.
Navigation: Signaal Scout; I-band.
Fire control: Philips 9LV 200 Mk 2/3; J-band.

Programmes: Ordered in late 1977. First two shipped in September 1980 and four more in Summer 1981. This class was the first to be fitted with MM 40.
Modernisation: Upgrade contract for ship and propulsion systems given to Newport News. Work done by Abu Dhabi Shipbuilding Company. First pair completed in late 1998, second pair in mid-1999 and the third pair in mid-2000. Further modernisation to be undertaken at ADSB under Project Tarif-45. This includes replacement of the combat data system, fire-control systems and improvement of Exocet to Block III configuration. The programme began in February 2004; two craft per year are to undergo the nine-month upgrades.

MARBAN   *3/2005*, Ships of the World* / 1127294

8 ARCTIC 28 RIBs and 12 AL-SHAALI TYPE (PBF)

Displacement, tons: 4 full load
Dimensions, feet (metres): 27.9 × 9.7 × 2 *(8.5 × 3 × 0.6)*
Main machinery: 2 outboards; 450 hp *(336 kW)*
Speed, knots: 38
Complement: 1 plus 11 troops

Comment: RIBs ordered from Halmatic, Southampton in June 1992 and delivered in mid-1993. GRP hulls. Speed given is fully laden. Used by Special Forces. The Al-Shaali type were ordered in 1994 and built in Dubai.

ARCTIC   *3/1995, H M Steele* / 0080926

2 MUBARRAZ CLASS
(FAST ATTACK CRAFT—MISSILE) (PGGFM)

Name	No	Builders	Commissioned
MUBARRAZ	P 141 (ex-P 4401)	Lürssen, Bremen	Aug 1990
MAKASIB	P 142 (ex-P 4402)	Lürssen, Bremen	Aug 1990

Displacement, tons: 260 full load
Dimensions, feet (metres): 147.3 × 23 × 7.2 *(44.9 × 7 × 2.2)*
Main machinery: 2 MTU 20V 538 TB93 diesels; 9,370 hp(m) *(6.9 MW)* sustained; 2 shafts
Speed, knots: 40. **Range, n miles:** 500 at 38 kt
Complement: 40 (5 officers)

Missiles: SSM: 4 Aerospatiale MM 40 Exocet; inertial cruise; active radar homing to 70 km *(40 n miles)* at 0.9 Mach; warhead 165 kg; sea-skimmer.
SAM: 1 Matra Sadral sextuple launcher; Mistral; IR homing to 4 km *(2.2 n miles)*; warhead 3 kg.
Guns: 1 OTO Melara 3 in *(76 mm)*/62 Super Rapid; 120 rds/min to 16 km *(8.7 n miles)*; weight of shell 6 kg.
2 Rheinmetall 20 mm.
Countermeasures: Decoys: 2 Dagaie launchers; IR flares and chaff.
ESM/ECM: Racal Cutlass/Cygnus; intercept/jammer.
Weapons control: CSEE Najir optronic director (for SAM).
Radars: Air/surface search: Bofors Ericsson Sea Giraffe 50HC; G-band.
Navigation: Racal Decca 1226; I-band.
Fire control: Bofors Electronic 9LV 223; J-band (for gun and SSM).

Programmes: Ordered in late 1986 from Lürssen Werft at the same time as the two Type 62 vessels. Delivered in February 1991.
Modernisation: Mid-life refits for both vessels to be undertaken by Abu Dhabi Shipbuilding from 2004.
Structure: This is a modified TNC 38 design, with the first export version of Matra Sadral. The radome houses the jammer. The 20 mm guns are mounted on the bridge deck aft of the mast.

MAKASIB *2/2002, A Sharma* / 0534063

MUBARRAZ *9/2000* / 0121415

6 ARDHANA CLASS (LARGE PATROL CRAFT) (PB)

Name	No	Builders	Commissioned
ARDHANA	P 3301 (ex-P 1101)	Vosper Thornycroft	24 June 1975
ZURARA	P 3302 (ex-P 1102)	Vosper Thornycroft	14 Aug 1975
MURBAN	P 3303 (ex-P 1103)	Vosper Thornycroft	16 Sep 1975
AL GHULLAN	P 3304 (ex-P 1104)	Vosper Thornycroft	16 Sep 1975
RADOOM	P 3305 (ex-P 1105)	Vosper Thornycroft	1 July 1976
GHANADHAH	P 3306 (ex-P 1106)	Vosper Thornycroft	1 July 1976

Displacement, tons: 110 standard; 175 full load
Dimensions, feet (metres): 110 × 21 × 6.6 *(33.5 × 6.4 × 2)*
Main machinery: 2 Paxman 12CM diesels; 5,000 hp *(3.73 MW)* sustained; 2 shafts
Speed, knots: 30. **Range, n miles:** 1,800 at 14 kt
Complement: 26
Guns: 2 Oerlikon/BMARC 30 mm/75 A32 (twin); 650 rds/min to 10 km *(5.5 n miles)*; weight of shell 1 kg or 0.36 kg.
1 Oerlikon/BMARC 20 mm/80 A41A; 800 rds/min to 2 km.
2—51 mm projectors for illuminants.
Radars: Surface search: Racal Decca TM 1626; I-band.

Comment: A class of round bilge steel hull craft. Originally operated by Abu Dhabi. New pennant numbers in 1996. To be replaced by the Project Baynunah craft from approximately 2004.

AL GHULLAN *2/1997, A Sharma* / 0567566

AUXILIARIES

1 DIVING TENDER (YDT)

AL GAFFA D 1051

Displacement, tons: 100 full load
Dimensions, feet (metres): 103 × 22.6 × 3.6 *(31.4 × 6.9 × 1.1)*
Main machinery: 2 MTU 12V 396 TB93 diesels; 3,260 hp(m) *(2.4 MW)* sustained; 2 water-jets
Speed, knots: 26
Range, n miles: 390 at 24 kt
Complement: 6

Comment: Ordered from Crestitalia in December 1985 for Abu Dhabi and delivered in July 1987. GRP hull. Used primarily for mine clearance but also for diving training, salvage and SAR. Fitted with a decompression chamber and diving bell. Lengthened version of Italian *Alcide Pedretti*.

AL GAFFA *3/1997* / 0019363

1 COASTAL TUG (YTB)

ANNAD A 3501

Displacement, tons: 795 full load
Dimensions, feet (metres): 114.8 × 32.2 × 13.8 *(35 × 9.8 × 4.2)*
Main machinery: 2 Caterpillar 3606TA diesels; 4,180 hp *(3.12 MW)* sustained; 2 shafts; cp props; bow thruster; 362 hp *(266 kW)*
Speed, knots: 14
Range, n miles: 2,500 at 14 kt
Complement: 14 (3 officers)
Radars: Navigation: Racal Decca 2070; I-band.

Comment: Built by Dunston, Hessle, and completed in April 1989. Bollard pull, 55 tons. Equipped for SAR and is also used for logistic support.

ANNAD *6/1994* / 0080930

2 HARBOUR TUGS (YTM)

TEMSAH A 51   **UGAAB** A 52

Displacement, tons: 90 full load
Dimensions, feet (metres): 54.1 × 16.4 × 5.9 *(16.5 × 5.0 × 1.8)*
Main machinery: 2 Volvo Penta TAMD-122A diesels; 760 hp *(560 kW)*; 2 shafts

Comment: Ordered from Damen shipyard, Gorinchem in 1996 and entered service in 1998. Main role to attend Kortenaer class frigates. Equipped with fire-fighting platform abaft the mainmast.

UGAAB *1/2002, A Sharma* / 0534119

AMPHIBIOUS FORCES

Notes: (1) There are also four civilian LCM ships, *El Nasirah 2, Baava 1, Makasib* and *Ghagha II.* Two Serna class LCUs are also civilian owned.
(2) A 42 m LCU was reportedly delivered by Abu Dhabi Shipbuilding in mid-2004 when a second unit was ordered.

4 LCT

L 64 (ex-6401)   **L 65** (ex-6402)   **L 66** (ex-6403)   **L 67** (ex-6404)

Displacement, tons: 850 approx
Dimensions, feet (metres): 210 × 39.4 × 8.7 *(64.0 × 12.0 × 2.7)*
Main machinery: 2 Caterpillar diesels; 3,620 hp *(2.7 MW)*; 2 shafts
Speed, knots: 12
Guns: 2 — 12.7 mm MGs.

Comment: Built at Abu Dhabi Naval Base and completed in 1996-99. Details are incomplete. Pennant numbers changed in 2001.

L 65   *3/2005*, Ships of the World* / 1127293

3 LANDING CRAFT (LCT)

L 62   **+ 2**

Displacement, tons: 850 approx
Dimensions, feet (metres): 210 × 39.4 × 8.7 *(64.0 × 12.0 × 2.7)*
Main machinery: 2 Caterpillar 3508 diesels; 3,620 hp *(2.7 MW)*; 2 shafts
Speed, knots: 11
Complement: 19 (plus 56 troops)
Military lift: military vehicles

Comment: Fully designed in the UAE, the vessels were ordered from ADSB in November 2001 and laid down in early 2002 and delivery reportedly started in 2004. Details are speculative and based on those already in service. Weapons are expected to include medium calibre machine guns.

L 62   *3/2005*, Ships of the World* / 1127292

3 AL FEYI CLASS (LCU)

AL FEYI L 51 (ex-5401)   **DAYYINAH** L 52 (ex-5402)   **JANANAH** L 53 (ex-5403)

Displacement, tons: 650 full load
Dimensions, feet (metres): 164 × 36.1 × 9.2 *(50 × 11 × 2.8)*
Main machinery: 2 diesels; 1,248 hp *(931 kW)*; 2 shafts
Speed, knots: 11
Range, n miles: 1,800 at 11 kt
Complement: 10
Military lift: 4 vehicles
Guns: 2 — 12.7 mm MGs.

Comment: *Al Feyi* built by Siong Huat, Singapore; completed 4 August 1987. The other pair built by Argos Shipyard, Singapore to a similar design and completed in December 1988. Used mostly as transport ships. Pennant numbers changed in 2001.

DAYYINAH (old number)   *6/1996* / 0080929

12 + 4 TRANSPORTBÅT 2000 (LCP)

P 201-212

Displacement, tons: 43 full load
Dimensions, feet (metres): 77.1 × 16.7 × 3.3 *(23.5 × 5.1 × 1)*
Main machinery: 2 MTU 12V 2000 diesels; 2 Kamewa FF 550 waterjets
Speed, knots: 33
Complement: 3
Military lift: 42 troops or 10 tons
Guns: 2 — 12.7 mm MGs.
Radars: Navigation: Terma; I-band.

Comment: Project 'Ghannatha' was for 12 amphibious transport craft based on the Transportbåt 2000 craft in service with the Royal Swedish Navy. Three craft were constructed at the Djupviks yard in Sweden while ADSB built the other nine. Details of the aluminium craft are based on those in Swedish service and have not been confirmed. Delivery was completed in 2004. A contract for a further four vessels was made with ADSB on 27 June 2004.

TRANSPORTBÅT 208   *3/2005*, Ships of the World* / 1127291

COAST GUARD

Notes: Under control of Minister of Interior. In addition to the vessels listed below there is a number of Customs and Police launches including Barracuda craft, three Swedish Boghammar 13 m craft of the same type used by Iran and delivered in 1985, two Baglietto police launches acquired in 1988, about 10 elderly Dhafeer and Spear class of 12 and 9 m respectively, and two Halmatic Arun class Pilot craft delivered in 1990-91; some of these launches carry light machine guns.

POLICE BARRACUDA   *1/2002, A Sharma* / 0534111

35 HARBOUR PATROL CRAFT (PB/YDT)

Comment: The latest are 11 Shark 33 built by Shaali Marine, Dubai and delivered in 1993-94. The remainder are a mixture of Barracuda 30 ft and FPB 22 ft classes. All are powered by twin outboard engines and most carry a 7.62 mm MG and have a Norden radar. There are also two Rotork craft used as diving tenders. Customs boats are operated separately by each of the UAE states. Some have been built for Kuwait.

BARRACUDA 271   *12/2001, A Sharma* / 0534117

aaa:

aa:

2 PROTECTOR CLASS (WPB)

1101 1102

Displacement, tons: 180 full load
Dimensions, feet (metres): 108.3 × 22 × 6.9 *(33 × 6.7 × 2.1)*
Main machinery: 2 MTU 16V 396 TE94 diesels; 5,911 hp(m) *(4.35 MW)* sustained; 2 shafts; LIPS props
Speed, knots: 33
Complement: 14
Guns: 1 Mauser 20 mm. 2—12.7 mm MGs.
Weapons control: 1 SAGEM optronic director.
Radars: Surface search: I-band.

Comment: Ordered from FBM Marine, Cowes in 1998. Aluminium hulls. First one laid down 15 June 1998. Both delivered in late 1999. More may be built by Abu Dhabi Shipbuilders. Similar to Bahamas and Chilean naval craft.

PROTECTOR 1101 *11/1999, UAE Coast Guard* / 0106675

5 CAMCRAFT 77 ft (COASTAL PATROL CRAFT) (WPB)

753-757

Displacement, tons: 70 full load
Dimensions, feet (metres): 76.8 × 18 × 4.9 *(23.4 × 5.5 × 1.5)*
Main machinery: 2 GM 12V-71TA diesels; 840 hp *(627 kW)* sustained; 2 shafts
Speed, knots: 25
Complement: 8
Guns: 2 Lawrence Scott 20 mm (not always embarked).
Radars: Surface search: Racal Decca; I-band.

Comment: Completed 1975 by Camcraft, New Orleans. Not always armed.

CAMCRAFT 755 *6/1997* / 0019364

16 CAMCRAFT 65 ft (COASTAL PATROL CRAFT) (WPB)

650-665

Displacement, tons: 50 full load
Dimensions, feet (metres): 65 × 18 × 5 *(19.8 × 5.5 × 1.5)*
Main machinery: 2 MTU 6V 396TB93 diesels; 1,630 hp(m) *(1.2 MW)* sustained; 2 shafts (in 14)
 2 Detroit 8V-92TA diesels; 700 hp *(522 kW)* sustained; 2 shafts (in 2)
Speed, knots: 25
Complement: 8
Guns: 1 Oerlikon 20 mm GAM-BO1.
Radars: Surface search: Racal Decca; I-band.

Comment: Built by Camcraft, New Orleans and delivered by September 1978.

CAMCRAFT 655 *12/2001, A Sharma* / 0534118

6 BAGLIETTO GC 23 TYPE (COASTAL PATROL CRAFT) (WPBF)

758-763

Displacement, tons: 50.7 full load
Dimensions, feet (metres): 78.7 × 18 × 3 *(24 × 5.5 × 0.9)*
Main machinery: 2 MTU 12V 396TB93 diesels; 3,260 hp(m) *(2.4 MW)* sustained; 2 Kamewa water-jets
Speed, knots: 43. **Range, n miles:** 700 at 20 kt
Complement: 9
Guns: 1 Oerlikon 20 mm. 2—7.62 mm MGs.
Radars: Surface search: I-band.

Comment: Built by Baglietto, Varazze. First two completed in March and May 1986, second pair in July 1987 and two more in 1988. All were delivered to UAE Coast Guard in Dubai.

BAGLIETTO 758 *1987, UAE Coast Guard* / 0080934

3 BAGLIETTO 59 ft (COASTAL PATROL CRAFT) (WPBF)

501-503

Displacement, tons: 22 full load
Dimensions, feet (metres): 59.4 × 13.9 × 2.3 *(18.1 × 4.3 × 0.7)*
Main machinery: 2 MTU 12V 183 TE92 diesels; 2 shafts
Speed, knots: 40
Complement: 6
Guns: 2—7.62 mm MGs.
Radars: Surface search: Racal Decca; I-band.

Comment: Ordered in 1992 and delivered in late 1993.

BAGLIETTO 503 *10/1993, UAE Coast Guard* / 0080935

6 WATERCRAFT 45 ft (COASTAL PATROL CRAFT) (PB)

Displacement, tons: 25 full load
Dimensions, feet (metres): 45 × 14.1 × 4.6 *(13.7 × 4.3 × 1.4)*
Main machinery: 2 MAN D2542 diesels; 1,300 hp(m) *(956 kW)*; 2 shafts
Speed, knots: 26. **Range, n miles:** 380 at 18 kt
Complement: 5
Guns: Mounts for 2—7.62 mm MGs.
Radars: Surface search: Racal Decca; I-band.

Comment: Ordered from Watercraft, UK in February 1982. Delivery in early 1983. Four deleted. Two similar craft built by Halmatic were delivered to the Dubai Port Authority in October 1997.

WATERCRAFT 45 ft *1984, UAE Coast Guard* / 0506115

24 + 30 SEASPRAY ASSAULT BOATS (PB)

Displacement, tons: To be announced
Dimensions, feet (metres): 31.2 × 10.2 × 1.6 *(9.5 × 3.1 × 0.5)*
Main machinery: 2 outboards; 500 hp *(375 kW)*
Speed, knots: 50. **Range, n miles:** 450 at 17 kt
Complement: 5
Radars: Navigation: I-band.

Comment: Initial batch of 24 craft delivered in September 2003. A further thirty were ordered in early 2004. Designed by Sea Spray Aluminium Boats.

SEASPRAY *2/2004, ADSB* / 0563487

United Kingdom

Country Overview

The United Kingdom of Great Britain and Northern Ireland is situated in north-western Europe. It has a coastline of 6,700 n miles with the English Channel, the North Sea, the Irish Sea and the Atlantic Ocean. With an area of 93,341 square miles, it comprises the island of Great Britain (England, Scotland and Wales) and the six counties of Ulster that remained a constituent part of UK after Irish independence in 1922. It also includes the Isle of Wight, Anglesey, the Scilly, Orkney, Shetland, and Hebridean archipelagos and numerous smaller islands. The Isle of Man and the Channel Islands are direct dependencies but are not part of the UK. Other dependent territories are: Anguilla; Bermuda; British Antarctic Territory; British Indian Ocean Territory (BIOT); British Virgin Islands; Cayman Islands; Cyprus Sovereign Base Areas; Falkland Islands; Gibraltar; Montserrat; Ducie, Henderson and Oeno; St Helena and Dependencies (Ascension and Tristan da Cunha); South Georgia and South Sandwich Islands and the Turks and Caicos Islands. London is the capital, largest city and a major port. Major oil ports are at Forth, Sullom Voe and Milford Haven and non-oil ports at Tees and Hartlepool, Grimsby and Immingham, Southampton, Liverpool, Felixstowe, Medway, and Dover. Territorial seas of 12 n miles are claimed around the UK mainland and many dependencies. An EEZ (200 n miles) is claimed for Bermuda, South Georgia and South Sandwich Islands and Pitcairn. A Fishery Zone (200 n miles) is claimed for the mainland and some dependencies.

Headquarters Appointments

Chief of the Naval Staff and First Sea Lord:
  Admiral Sir Jonathon Band, KCB, ADC
Commander-in-Chief, Fleet:
  Admiral Sir James Burnell-Nugent, KCB, CBE
Chief of Naval Personnel and Commander-in-Chief, Naval Home Command and Admiral Fleet Air Arm:
  Vice Admiral A J Johns, CBE, ADC
Director General Logistics Fleet:
  Rear Admiral R P Boissier
Controller of the Navy:
  Rear Admiral A D H Matthews
Assistant Chief of the Naval Staff:
  Rear Admiral A M Massey, CBE

Flag Officers, Operational and National Commanders

Chief of Joint Operations:
  Lieutenant General N Houghton, CBE
Deputy Commander-in-Chief, Fleet:
  Vice Admiral T P McClement, OBE
Chief of Staff (Warfare) (Rear Admiral Surface Ships):
  Rear Admiral D G Snelson, CB
Commander, Operations (Rear Admiral Submarines):
  Rear Admiral D J Cooke
Commander, UK Maritime Forces:
  Rear Admiral N Morisetti
Chief of Staff (Personnel & Support):
  Rear Admiral M Kimmons
Flag Officer, Sea Training:
  Rear Admiral A J Rix
Commander, UK Amphibious Forces and Commandant General Royal Marines:
  Major General G S Robison
Flag Officer, Scotland, Northern England and Northern Ireland:
  Rear Admiral P L Wilcocks, DSC
Commander, British Forces Cyprus:
  Major General P T C Pearson, CBE
Commander United Kingdom Task Group:
  Commodore B N B Williams, OBE
Commander, UK Maritime Component:
  Commodore S T Williams, OBE
Commander Amphibious Task Group:
  Commodore G M Zambellas
Commander, 3 Commando Brigade:
  Brigadier J H Thomas

Flag Officers, Operational and National Commanders —continued

Commander, British Forces Gibraltar:
  Commodore A A S Adair
Commander, British Forces South Atlantic Islands:
  Commodore I Moncrieff
Commodore Royal Fleet Auxiliary:
  Commodore R C Thornton
Commodore Portsmouth Flotilla:
  Commodore A J B Cameron
Commodore Devonport Flotilla:
  Commodore P K Walpole
Captain Faslane Flotilla:
  Captain S C Ramm
Hydrographer to the Navy:
  Captain I Turner OBE

Diplomatic Representation

Naval Attaché in Ankara:
  Wing Commander R Snook, RAF
Naval Attaché in Athens:
  Captain J R Wills
Naval Attaché in Beijing:
  Group Captain K J Parke, MBE, RAF
Naval Attaché in Berlin:
  Captain S R Gosden
Naval Attaché in Brasilia:
  to be announced
Defence Adviser in Bridgetown:
  Captain S J Wilson
Defence Adviser in Brunei:
  Captain R Thoburn
Naval Attaché in Buenos Aires:
  Captain C J Hyldon
Naval Attaché in Cairo:
  Commander M J Lovett
Defence Adviser in Canberra:
  Commodore R T Love
Defence Attaché in Copenhagen:
  Commander C Wilson, OBE
Naval Attaché in The Hague:
  Captain A R Davies
Naval Adviser in Islamabad:
  Colonel M W Bibbey RM
Defence Attaché in Kiev:
  Captain S E Airey
Assistant Defence Adviser in Kuala Lumpur:
  Lieutenant Commander M P Davies
Defence Attaché in Lisbon:
  Commander N Sibbit
Naval Attaché in Madrid:
  Captain D E Wolfe
Defence Attaché in Manama:
  Commander C Spicer
Defence Attaché in Manila:
  Group Captain R M Bailey
Naval Attaché in Moscow:
  Captain R E Drewett
Naval Adviser in Ottawa:
  Group Captain G W A Wallace
Naval Attaché in Paris:
  Captain N A M Butler
Naval Adviser in Pretoria:
  Commander P Lankester
Defence Attaché in Riyadh:
  Bridadier J G Askew, OBE
Naval Attaché in Rome:
  Commander S Steeds
Defence Attaché in Santiago:
  Colonel I Campbell
Naval Attaché in Seoul:
  Captain T N E Williams
Naval Adviser in Singapore:
  Commander N Race
Defence Attaché in Stockholm:
  Wing Commander N Phillips
Naval Attaché in Tokyo:
  Captain S Chelton

Diplomatic Representation —continued

Naval Attaché in Warsaw:
  Lieutenant Colonel S Croft
Naval Attaché in Washington:
  Commodore C J Gass

Royal Marines Operational Units

HQ 3 Commando Brigade RM; 40 Commando RM; 42 Commando RM; 45 Commando Group (RM/Army); Commando Logistic Regiment RM (RN/RM/Army); 3 Commando Brigade Command Support Group, EW Troop RM, Tactical Air Command Posts RM (3 regular, 1 reserve); 539 Assault Squadron RM (hovercraft, landing craft and raiding craft); Brigade Patrol Troop (reconnaissance); Special Boat Service RM; Fleet Royal Marines Protection Group (FRMPG); T Company RMR; 29 Commando Regiment RA (Army); 59 Independent Commando Squadron RE (Army); 20 Commando Battery RA; 131 Independent Squadron RE (Volunteers).

Bases

Northwood: C-in-C Fleet; CJO; Commander Operations
Portsmouth: C-in-C Navhome; DC-in-C Fleet; COS Warfare; COS Support; COMUKMARFOR; COMUKAMPHIBFOR; Com Portsmouth Flotilla; COMUKTG
Devonport: FOST; Com Devonport Flotilla; COMATG
Faslane: FOSNNI; Captain Faslane Flotilla

Prefix to Ships' Names

HMS (Her Majesty's Ship)

Personnel

2006:
(a)   Regulars: RN and RM 39, 430 (7,680 officers)
(b)   Volunteer Reserves: RN 988 (198 officers)

Fleet Disposition

Portsmouth: 3 CV; 8 Type 42 DDG, 7 Type 23 FFG, 1st MCM Squadron; 2nd MCM Squadron; Fishery Protection Squadron; Antarctic Patrol Ship; 1st Patrol Boat Squadron; Fleet Diving Squadron
Devonport: 1 LPH; 2 LPD; 4 Type 22 FFG; 7 Type 23 FFG; 7 Trafalgar Class SSN; Surveying Squadron; Gibralter Squadron; Cyprus Squadron
Faslane: 4 SSBN; 4 Swiftsure Class SSN; 3rd MCM Squadron

Strength of the Fleet

Type	Active (Reserve)	Building (Projected)
SSBNs	4	—
Submarines—Attack	10	3 (3)
Aircraft Carriers	2 (1)	(2)
Destroyers	8	6 (2)
Frigates	17	—
Assault Ships (LPD)	2	—
Helicopter Carriers (LPH)	1	—
LSD/LSL (RFA)	3	3
Offshore Patrol Vessels	4	—
Patrol/Training Craft	18	—
Minehunters	16	—
Repair/Maintenance Ships (RFA)	1	—
Survey Ships	5	—
Antarctic Patrol Ships	1	—
Large Fleet Tankers (RFA)	2	—
Support Tankers (RFA)	4	—
Small Fleet Tankers (RFA)	2	—
Aviation Training Ships (RFA)	1	—
Fleet Replenishment Ships (RFA)	4	—
Transport Ro-Ro (RFR)	6	—

Principal Fleet Air Arm Squadrons (see *Shipborne Aircraft* section) on 1 January 2006
HMA = Helicopter Maritime Attack.

F/W	Aircraft	Role	Deployment	Squadron no	F/W	Aircraft	Role	Deployment	Squadron no
7	Harrier	GR 7A/GR 9	RAF Cottesmore	800	5	Grob	Aircrew Training	Roborough	727
13	Jetstream	Aircrew Training	Culdrose, *Seahawk*	750					

Helicopters		Role	Deployment	Squadron no	Helicopters		Role	Deployment	Squadron no
2	Merlin HM Mk 1	OEU	Culdrose, *Seahawk*	700M	8	Sea King HU Mk 5	SAR/Training	Culdrose, *Seahawk*	771
6	Merlin HM Mk 1	ASW/ASUW	Culdrose, *Seahawk*	814	3	Sea King HAS Mk 6	SAR/Utility	Culdrose, *Seahawk*	771
4	Merlin HM Mk 1	ASW/ASUW	Culdrose, *Seahawk*	820	10	Sea King HC 4	Commando Assault	Yeovilton, *Heron*	845
8	Merlin HM Mk 1	ASW/ASUW	Culdrose, *Seahawk*	824	10	Sea King HC 4	Commando Assault	Yeovilton, *Heron*	846
8	Merlin HM Mk 1	ASW/ASUW	Culdrose, *Seahawk*	829	9	Sea King HC 4	Commando Assault	Yeovilton, *Heron*	848
13	Sea King ASAC Mk 7	AEW	Culdrose, *Seahawk*	849 HQ	35	Lynx HMA. Mk 3/8	ASUW/ASW	Yeovilton, *Heron*	815
	Sea King ASAC Mk 7	AEW	Culdrose, *Seahawk*	849 A flight	13	Lynx HAS. Mk 3/8	Aircrew Training	Yeovilton, *Heron*	702
	Sea King ASAC Mk 7	AEW	Culdrose, *Seahawk*	849 B flight	6	Lynx Mk 7	Commando Support	Yeovilton, *Heron*	847
3	Sea King HU Mk 5	SAR	Prestwick, *Gannet*	Prestwick, SAR flight					

Notes: (1) Joint Force Harrier (JFH) formed on 1 April 2000. RAF GR. 7A/9As form 3 Group whose Headquarters are at RAF High Wycombe. Following the withdrawal of the Sea Harrier from service in 2006, JFH continues to be complemented by RN and RAF pilots.   (2) 801 Squadron disbanded on 31 March 2006 and is to rededicate in October 2006 with GR9A at RAF Cottesmore.   (3) 899 Squadron disbanded on 31 March 2005 and joined Joint OCU 20 Squadron at RAF Wittering.   (4) The Joint Helicopter Command (JHC) became operational on 1 April 2000 and brought all battlefield helicopters from all three services under one command at HQ Land, Wilton. Total helicopter assets number some 450. The command includes the Commando Helicopter Force (CHF), a group of four RN/RM squadrons, based at Yeovilton, which specialises in amphibious warfare and whose prime task is to support 3 Cdo Brigade.   (5) Mirach 100/5 subsonic drones are operated by 792 Squadron at Culdrose.   (6) The Royal Navy SAR force comprises 771 Squadron (Culdose) and the Gannet SAR flight (Prestwick). 771 Squadron covers the SW approaches and the Gannet SAR flight the NW approaches and northern Irish Sea.

DELETIONS

Submarines

2003 *Splendid*
2006 *Spartan*

Destroyers

2005 *Newcastle, Glasgow, Cardiff*

Frigates

2003 *London* (to Romania)
2005 *Norfolk, Marlborough* (both to Chile)
2006 *Grafton* (to Chile)

Amphibious Forces

2004 *Sir Geraint, Sir Percivale*

Mine Warfare Forces

2004 *Bridport*
2005 *Sandown, Inverness, Brecon, Cottesmore, Dulverton*

Patrol Forces

2003 *Anglesey, Guernsey* (both to Bangladesh)
2004 *Lindisfarne* (to Bangladesh)
2005 *Leeds Castle*

Auxiliaries

2003 *Dalmatian, Joan, Norah, Seagull*
2004 *Cameron, Kinterbury*
2005 *Ladybird, Setter*
2006 *Grey Rover, Sir Tristram*

PENNANT LIST

Notes: Numbers are not displayed on Submarines.

Submarines

Ballistic Missile Submarines

S 28	Vanguard
S 29	Victorious
S 30	Vigilant
S 31	Vengeance

Attack Submarines

S 20	Astute (bldg)
S 21	Artful (bldg)
S 22	Ambush (bldg)
S 87	Turbulent
S 88	Tireless
S 90	Torbay
S 91	Trenchant
S 92	Talent
S 93	Triumph
S 104	Sceptre
S 107	Trafalgar
S 108	Sovereign
S 109	Superb

Aircraft Carriers

R 05	Invincible
R 06	Illustrious
R 07	Ark Royal

Destroyers

D 32	Daring (bldg)
D 33	Dauntless (bldg)
D 34	Diamond (bldg)
D 35	Defender (bldg)
D 36	Dragon (bldg)
D 37	Duncan (bldg)
D 89	Exeter
D 90	Southampton
D 91	Nottingham
D 92	Liverpool
D 95	Manchester
D 96	Gloucester
D 97	Edinburgh
D 98	York

Frigates

F 78	Kent
F 79	Portland

F 81	Sutherland
F 82	Somerset
F 83	St Albans
F 85	Cumberland
F 86	Campbeltown
F 87	Chatham
F 99	Cornwall
F 229	Lancaster
F 231	Argyll
F 234	Iron Duke
F 235	Monmouth
F 236	Montrose
F 237	Westminster
F 238	Northumberland
F 239	Richmond

Amphibious Warfare Forces

L 12	Ocean
L 14	Albion
L 15	Bulwark
L 105	Arromanches
L 107	Andalsnes
L 109	Akyab
L 110	Aachen
L 111	Arezzo
L 113	Audemer
L 3004	Sir Bedivere
L 3005	Sir Galahad
L 3006	Largs Bay (bldg)
L 3007	Lyme Bay (bldg)
L 3008	Mounts Bay
L 3009	Cardigan Bay (bldg)

Mine Warfare Forces

M 30	Ledbury
M 31	Cattistock
M 33	Brocklesby
M 34	Middleton
M 37	Chiddingfold
M 38	Atherstone
M 39	Hurworth
M 41	Quorn
M 104	Walney
M 106	Penzance
M 107	Pembroke
M 108	Grimsby
M 109	Bangor
M 110	Ramsey

M 111	Blyth
M 112	Shoreham

Patrol Forces

P 163	Express
P 164	Explorer
P 165	Example
P 167	Exploit
P 257	Clyde
P 264	Archer
P 265	Dumbarton Castle
P 270	Biter
P 272	Smiter
P 273	Pursuer
P 274	Tracker
P 275	Raider
P 279	Blazer
P 280	Dasher
P 281	Tyne
P 282	Severn
P 283	Mersey
P 284	Scimitar
P 285	Sabre
P 291	Puncher
P 292	Charger
P 293	Ranger
P 294	Trumpeter

Survey Ships

H 86	Gleaner
H 87	Echo
H 88	Enterprise
H 130	Roebuck
H 131	Scott

Auxiliaries

A 81	Brambleleaf
A 83	Melton
A 84	Menai
A 87	Meon
A 96	Sea Crusader
A 98	Sea Centurion
A 109	Bayleaf
A 110	Orangeleaf
A 111	Oakleaf
A 132	Diligence
A 135	Argus
A 140	Tornado
A 142	Tormentor

A 146	Waterman
A 147	Frances
A 149	Florence
A 150	Genevieve
A 170	Kitty
A 171	Endurance
A 172	Lesley
A 178	Husky
A 182	Saluki
A 185	Salmoor
A 187	Salmaid
A 191	Bovisand
A 192	Cawsand
A 198	Helen
A 199	Myrtle
A 201	Spaniel
A 221	Forceful
A 222	Nimble
A 223	Powerful
A 224	Adept
A 225	Bustler
A 226	Capable
A 227	Careful
A 228	Faithful
A 229	Colonel Templer
A 231	Dexterous
A 232	Adamant
A 250	Sheepdog
A 271	Gold Rover
A 273	Black Rover
A 280	Newhaven
A 281	Nutbourne
A 282	Netley
A 283	Oban
A 284	Oronsay
A 285	Omagh
A 286	Padstow
A 308	Ilchester
A 309	Instow
A 344	Impulse
A 345	Impetus
A 367	Newton
A 368	Warden
A 385	Fort Rosalie
A 386	Fort Austin
A 387	Fort Victoria
A 388	Fort George
A 389	Wave Knight
A 390	Wave Ruler
Y 21	Oilpress
Y 32	Moorhen
Y 33	Moorfowl

SUBMARINES

Notes: Three 6.7 m US-made Mk VIII Mod 1 Swimmer Delivery Vehicles were acquired in 1999. Battery-powered, they can transport six combat swimmers and have a radius of 67 km *(36 n miles)*.

SDV Mk VIII   *1/2002, M Declerck* / 0132551

Strategic Missile Submarines (SSBN)

Notes: Decisions on the future of the UK nuclear deterrent are expected in about 2008.

4 VANGUARD CLASS (SSBN)

Name	No	Builders	Laid down	Launched	Commissioned
VANGUARD	S 28	Vickers Shipbuilding & Engineering, Barrow-in-Furness	3 Sep 1986	4 Mar 1992	14 Aug 1993
VICTORIOUS	S 29	Vickers Shipbuilding & Engineering, Barrow-in-Furness	3 Dec 1987	29 Sep 1993	7 Jan 1995
VIGILANT	S 30	Vickers Shipbuilding & Engineering, Barrow-in-Furness	16 Feb 1991	14 Oct 1995	2 Nov 1996
VENGEANCE	S 31	Vickers Shipbuilding & Engineering, Barrow-in-Furness	1 Feb 1993	19 Sep 1998	27 Nov 1999

Displacement, tons: 15,980 dived
Dimensions, feet (metres): 491.8 × 42 × 39.4
(149.9 × 12.8 × 12)
Main machinery: Nuclear; 1 RR PWR 2; 2 GEC turbines; 27,500 hp *(20.5 MW)*; 1 shaft; pump jet propulsor; 2 auxiliary retractable propulsion motors; 2 WH Allen turbo generators; 6 MW; 2 Paxman diesel alternators; 2,700 hp *(2 MW)*
Speed, knots: 25 dived
Complement: 135 (14 officers)

Missiles: SLBM: 16 Lockheed Trident 2 (D5) 3-stage solid fuel rocket; stellar inertial guidance to 12,000 km *(6,500 n miles)*; thermonuclear warhead of up to 8 MIRV of 100–120 kT; cep 90 m. The D5 can carry up to 12 MIRV but under plans announced in November 1993 each submarine carried a maximum of 96 warheads (of UK manufacture). This reduced to 48 in 1999. Substrategic low yield nuclear warheads introduced in 1996.
Torpedoes: 4–21 in *(533 mm)* tubes. Marconi Spearfish; dual purpose; wire-guided; active/passive homing to 26 km *(14 n miles)* at 65 kt; or 31.5 km *(17 n miles)* at 50 kt; attack speed 55 kt; warhead 300 kg directed charge.
Countermeasures: Decoys: 2 SSE Mk 10 launchers for Submarine Countermeasures Acoustic Device (SCAD) Types 101, 102 and 200.

ESM: Racal UAP 3; intercept.
Combat data systems: Alenia Marconi Systems SMCS.
Weapons control: Ultra Electronics Outfit DCM 4.
Radars: Navigation: Kelvin Hughes Type 1007; I-band.
Sonars: TMSL Type 2054 composite multifunctioned sonar suite includes towed array, hull-mounted active/passive search and passive intercept and ranging. Type 2081 Environmental Sensor System.

Programmes: On 15 July 1980 the decision was made to buy the US Trident I (C4) weapon system. On 11 March 1982 it was announced that the government had opted for the improved Trident II weapon system, with the D5 missile, to be deployed in a force of four submarines. *Vanguard* ordered 30 April 1986; *Victorious* 6 October 1987; *Vigilant* 13 November 1990 and *Vengeance* 7 July 1992.
Modernisation: *Vanguard* underwent LOP(R) at Devonport February 2002 to June 2004. *Victorious* started LOP(R) in April 2005 and is to complete in 2008. Invitations for tender for the upgrade of the inboard signal, data and display processing systems of sonar Type 2054 were released in April 2005. A contract is expected in 2006. There are no plans to deploy conventional warheads on Trident or to modify launch tubes to accommodate cruise missiles.

Structure: A new reactor core, Core H, has been fitted to *Vanguard* and is to be installed in the other three boats at their Long Overhaul Period (LOP(R)). No further reactor fuelling will be required during their service lives. The outer surface of the submarine is covered with conformal anechoic noise reduction coatings. The limits placed on warhead numbers leaves spare capacity within the Trident system. This capacity is used for a non-strategic warhead variant which has been available since 1996. Fitted with Pilkington Optronics CK 51 search and CH 91 attack periscopes.
Operational: Three successful submerged launched firings of the D5 missile from USS *Tennessee* in December 1989 and the US missile was first deployed operationally in March 1990. *Vanguard* started sea trials in October 1992; the first UK missile firing was on 26 May 1994 and the first operational patrol in early 1995. The eight successful firing of a D5 missile was made by *Vanguard* on 10 October 2005. At least one SSBN has been at immediate readiness to fire ballistic missiles since 1969, but as a result of the Strategic Defence Review in 1998, readiness to fire has been relaxed 'to days rather than minutes'. There are no plans to phase out the two crew system. Submarines on patrol can be given secondary tasks without compromising security. Based at Faslane.

VIGILANT   *7/2005*, H M Steele* / 1153921

VENGEANCE   *6/2000* / 0106676

VENGEANCE *6/2000* / 0106677

VENGEANCE *11/2004, H M Steele* / 1043570

For details of the latest updates to *Jane's Fighting Ships* online and to discover the additional
information available exclusively to online subscribers please visit
jfs.janes.com

Attack Submarines (SSN)

Notes: Future submarine requirements are being taken forward in a twin-track approach. In the short-term, technology advances to an extended Astute class are under consideration. Conceptual studies are also investigating requirements for a 'Maritime Underwater Future Capability' (MUFC) post 2020. Decisions on the future of the Strategic Deterrent will also be a major factor.

7 TRAFALGAR CLASS (SSN)

Name	No	Builders	Laid down	Launched	Commissioned
TRAFALGAR	S 107	Vickers Shipbuilding & Engineering, Barrow-in-Furness	25 Apr 1979	1 July 1981	27 May 1983
TURBULENT	S 87	Vickers Shipbuilding & Engineering, Barrow-in-Furness	8 May 1980	1 Dec 1982	28 Apr 1984
TIRELESS	S 88	Vickers Shipbuilding & Engineering, Barrow-in-Furness	6 June 1981	17 Mar 1984	5 Oct 1985
TORBAY	S 90	Vickers Shipbuilding & Engineering, Barrow-in-Furness	3 Dec 1982	8 Mar 1985	7 Feb 1987
TRENCHANT	S 91	Vickers Shipbuilding & Engineering, Barrow-in-Furness	28 Oct 1985	3 Nov 1986	14 Jan 1989
TALENT	S 92	Vickers Shipbuilding & Engineering, Barrow-in-Furness	13 May 1986	15 Apr 1988	12 May 1990
TRIUMPH	S 93	Vickers Shipbuilding & Engineering, Barrow-in-Furness	2 Feb 1987	16 Feb 1991	12 Oct 1991

Displacement, tons: 4,740 surfaced; 5,208 dived
Dimensions, feet (metres): 280.1 × 32.1 × 31.2
   (85.4 × 9.8 × 9.5)
Main machinery: Nuclear; 1 RR PWR 1; 2 GEC turbines; 15,000 hp *(11.2 MW)*; 1 shaft; pump jet propulsor; 2 WH Allen turbo generators; 3.2 MW; 2 Paxman diesel alternators; 2,800 hp *(2.09 MW)*; 1 motor for emergency drive; 1 auxiliary retractable prop
Speed, knots: 32 dived
Complement: 130 (18 officers)

Missiles: SLCM: Raytheon Tomahawk Block IV; Tercom and GPS aided inertial navigation system with DSMAC to 1,500 km *(810 n miles)* at 0.7 Mach; warhead 318 kg shaped charge or submunitions. Being fitted to all from 2005.
Torpedoes: 5–21 in *(533 mm)* bow tubes. Marconi Spearfish; wire-guided; active/passive homing to 26 km *(14 n miles)* at 65 kt; or 31.5 km *(17 n miles)* at 50 kt; attack speed 55 kt; warhead 300 kg directed charge; 20 reloads.
Mines: Can be carried in lieu of torpedoes.
Countermeasures: Decoys: SAWCS from 2002. 2 SSE Mk 8 launchers. Type 2066 torpedo decoys.
RESM: Racal UAP; passive intercept.
CESM: Eddystone.
Combat data systems: BAE Systems SMCS tactical data handling system.
Weapons control: BAE Systems SMCS.
Radars: Navigation: Kelvin Hughes Type 1007; I-band.

Sonars: TUSL 2074 LRE; hull-mounted; passive/active, search and attack; low frequency.
TUSL 2046; towed array, passive search, very low fequency.
Ultra Electonics 2082; achive intercept and ranging or TUSL 2076 integrated sonar suite comprising flank array, towed array, conformal bow array, mine avoidance array.
TUSL 2077; ice navigation.

Programmes: *Trafalgar* ordered 7 April 1977; *Turbulent* 28 July 1978; *Tireless* 5 July 1979; *Torbay* 26 June 1981; *Trenchant* 22 March 1983; *Talent* 10 September 1984; *Triumph* 3 January 1986.
Modernisation: *Trafalgar* completed refuel in December 1995 and was fitted with SMCS and Spearfish torpedoes. *Turbulent* refuelled by mid-1997 and was refitted with sonar 2074, SMCS and Spearfish. *Tireless* completed similar modernisation and refuelling in January 1999. Refuel periods for the last four boats are being undertaken in parallel with a major tactical modernisation programme, the main feature of which is installation of the sonar 2076 integrated sonar suite to replace the 2074 bow array and 2046 towed array. Other upgrades include enhancements to SMCS, a new command console and improved signature reduction measures. *Torbay* and *Trenchant* were the first and second boats to complete a 2076 refit and refuel in 2003 and 2004 respectively. *Talent* is expected to complete

her three-year refit in 2006 and *Triumph* is expected to complete her refit in 2009. Meanwhile, an ongoing programme of software replacement will continue to realise capability improvements in the last four boats. As a parallel programme, SMCS is being upgraded to SMCS NG and Tomahawk cruise missiles are being fitted to the whole class. *Triumph* and *Trafalgar* were completed by mid-2001, *Turbulent* by the end of 2002 and *Trenchant* in 2004. *Tireless* and *Talent* are to be fitted in 2006 and *Torbay* in 2007. Following successful US/UK development of an encapsulated torpedo-tube launch system for Block IV Tactical Tomahawk, Block III missiles are to be replaced. The Tactical Tomahawk Weapons Control (TTWC) and Tomahawk Strike Network (TSN) systems were installed in *Trafalgar* in 2004. *Turbulent* is to be the next to receive both systems. Replacement of the CESM system was initiated in 2002.
Structure: The pressure hull and outer surfaces are covered with conformal anechoic noise reduction coatings. Retractable forward hydroplanes and strengthened fins for under ice operations. Diving depth in excess of 300 m *(985 ft)*. Fitted with Pilkington Optronics CK 34 search and CH 84 attack periscopes.
Operational: *Trafalgar* conducted test-firings of Tomahawk Block IV in May 2005. *Torbay* is to conduct final 2076 software trials in 2006. All of the class based at Devonport. The class is planned to pay off as follows: *Trafalgar* 2008; *Turbulent* 2011; *Tireless* 2013 and the remainder of the class by 2022.

TRENCHANT

TRAFALGAR

6/2005*, Per Körnefeldt / 1153922

TRENCHANT

6/2005*, Maritime Photographic / 1153968

TRAFALGAR

6/2005*, B Sullivan / 1153920

3 SWIFTSURE CLASS (SSN)

Name	No	Builders	Laid down	Launched	Commissioned
SOVEREIGN	S 108	Vickers Shipbuilding & Engineering, Barrow-in-Furness	18 Sep 1970	17 Feb 1973	11 July 1974
SUPERB	S 109	Vickers Shipbuilding & Engineering, Barrow-in-Furness	16 Mar 1972	30 Nov 1974	13 Nov 1976
SCEPTRE	S 104	Vickers Shipbuilding & Engineering, Barrow-in-Furness	19 Feb 1974	20 Nov 1976	14 Feb 1978

Displacement, tons: 4,000 light; 4,400 standard; 4,900 dived
Dimensions, feet (metres): 272 × 32.3 × 28
(82.9 × 9.8 × 8.5)
Main machinery: Nuclear; 1 RR PWR 1; 2 GEC turbines;
15,000 hp (11.2 MW); 1 shaft; pump jet propulsor; 2 WH
Allen turbo generators; 3.6 MW; 1 Paxman diesel
alternator; 1,900 hp (1.42 MW); 1 motor for emergency
drive; 1 auxiliary retractable prop
Speed, knots: 30+ dived
Complement: 116 (13 officers)

Missiles: SLCM: Hughes Tomahawk Block IV; Tercom and GPS
aided inertial navigation system with DSMAC to 1,500 km
(810 n miles) at 0.7 Mach; warhead 318 kg shaped charge
or submunitions. To be fitted in S 104 only.
Torpedoes: 5–21 in (533 mm) bow tubes. Marconi
Spearfish; wire-guided; active/passive homing to 26 km
(14 n miles) at 65 kt; or 31.5 km (17 n miles) at 50 kt; attack
speed 55 kt; warhead 300 kg directed charge; 20 reloads.
Mines: Can be carried in lieu of torpedoes.
Countermeasures: Decoys: SAWCS from 2002. 2 SSE Mk 6
launchers. Type 2066 torpedo decoys.
ESM: Racal UAP; passive intercept.
Combat data systems: Dowty Sema SMCS tactical data
handling system. Link 11 can be fitted.
Radars: Navigation: Kelvin Hughes Type 1007; I-band.
Sonars: TUSL Type 2074 LRE; hull-mounted; active/passive
search and attack; low frequency.
TUSL Type 2046; towed array; passive search; very low
frequency.
Ultra Electronics 2082; active intercept and ranging.
Marconi Type 2077; ice navigation; active; high frequency.

Programmes: Sovereign ordered 16 May 1969; Superb,
20 May 1970; Sceptre, 1 November 1971; Spartan,
7 February 1973; Splendid, 26 May 1976.
Modernisation: Each boat fitted with a PWR 1 Core Z
during major refits to give a 8 to 10 year refit cycle
(12 year life). Sovereign completed her first refit in 1984
and her second, with full tactical weapons system upgrade
and Spearfish, in 1997. Similarly, Superb completed refits
in 1986 and 1998 and Sceptre in 1987 and 2001. Other
improvements to the class included acoustic elastomeric
tiles, sonar processing equipment and improved
decoys. Sceptre to be equipped with Tactical Tomahawk
in 2006.
Structure: The pressure hull in the Swiftsure class maintains
its diameter for much greater length than previous

SUPERB   1/2002*, Ships of the World / 0131254

SUPERB   9/2001*, Lockheed Martin / 0131248

classes. Control gear by MacTaggart, Scott & Co Ltd
for: attack and search periscopes, snort induction and
exhaust, radar and ESM masts. The forward hydroplanes
house within the casing. Fitted with Pilkington
Optronics CK 33 search and CH 83 attack electro-optic
periscopes.
Operational: All based at Faslane. As a result of budget
cuts Swiftsure paid off in 1992 after less than 20 years'

service. Splendid decommissioned in 2003 and Spartan
in early 2006. Sovereign is to decommission in late 2006,
Superb in 2008 and Sceptre in 2010. The Dry Deck Hangar
fitted to Spartan 2004-06 is not to be fitted in another
boat and there will be a gap in capability until the Astute
class enter service.

SOVEREIGN   5/2003, B Prézelin / 0572689

0 + 3 (4) ASTUTE CLASS (SSN)

Name	No	Builders	Laid down	Launched	Commissioned
ASTUTE	S 20	BAE Systems, Barrow	31 Jan 2001	Aug 2007	2009
AMBUSH	S 21	BAE Systems, Barrow	22 Oct 2003	Feb 2009	2010
ARTFUL	S 22	BAE Systems, Barrow	11 Mar 2005	Aug 2010	2012

Displacement, tons: 6,500 surfaced; 7,800 dived
Dimensions, feet (metres): 318.2 × 37.0 × 32.8
(97 × 11.27 × 10)
Main machinery: Nuclear; 1 RR PWR 2; 2 Alsthom turbines;
27,500 hp (20.5 MW); 1 shaft; pump jet propulsor; 2 turbo
generators; 2 diesel alternators; 2 motors for emergency
drive; 1 auxiliary retractable prop
Speed, knots: 29 dived
Complement: 84 (12 officers) plus 14 spare

Missiles: SLCM: Tomahawk. Block IV (Tactical Tomahawk).
SSM: Sub Harpoon.
Torpedoes: 6–21 in (533 mm) tubes for Tomahawk, Sub
Harpoon and Spearfish torpedoes. Total of 38 weapons.
Mines: In lieu of torpedoes.
Countermeasures: Decoys. ESM: Racal UAP 4; intercept.
Combat data systems: BAE Systems ACMS tactical data
handling system. Links 11/16.
Radars: Navigation: I-band.
Sonars: Thomson Marconi 2076 integrated suite (bow,
flank, fin and towed arrays).

Programmes: Invitations to tender issued on 14 July 1994
to build three of the class with an option for two more.
GEC-Marconi selected as prime contractor in December
1995. Contract to start building the first three placed on 17
March 1997. First steel cut late 1999 but although formal
keel-laying took place in 2001, design, engineering and
programme management difficulties led to a three-year
delay to the first of class. There were similar delays to

ASTUTE (computer graphic)   2001, BAE Systems / 0131260

the second and third of class. Following the future force-
structure announcements on 21 July 2004, a decision on
the scope of Batch 2 remains under consideration. Based
on published decommissioning plans, a fourth Astute
class is required in about 2013 to maintain an eight-
strong SSN force. Thereafter, replacements for the last
four Trafalgar class will be required between about 2015
and 2022. A proposal for the construction of the fourth of
class is expected in June 2006 but unsolicited proposals
for a batch order (up to four boats) may also be made at
the same time.

Structure: An evolution of the Trafalgar design with
increased weapon load and reduced radiated noise but
with overall performance similar to Trafalgar after full
modernisation. The fin is slightly longer and there are
two Pilkington Optronics CM010 non-hull-penetrating
periscopes. The boats are to have a dry dock hangar
capability (Project Chalfont).
Operational: Fitted with Core H, nuclear refuelling will
not be necessary in the lifetime of the submarine. To be
based at Faslane.

AIRCRAFT CARRIERS

0 + (2) QUEEN ELIZABETH CLASS (CV)

Name	No	Builders	Laid down	Launched	Commissioned
QUEEN ELIZABETH	–	–	2007	2010	2013
PRINCE OF WALES	–	–	2010	2013	2016

Displacement, tons: 65,000 full load
Dimensions, feet (metres): 931.7 × 127.9 × 29.5
   (284 × 39.0 × 9.0)
Flight deck, feet (metres): to be announced
Main machinery: Integrated Full Electric Propulsion; 2 Rolls-Royce MT 30 gas turbine alternators; 96,500 hp *(72 MW)*; 4 diesel generators; 53,640 hp *(40 MW)*; 2 induction motors; 53,640 hp *(40 MW)*; 2 shafts
Speed, knots: 26+
Range, n miles: to be announced
Complement: 1,500 (including aircrew)

Guns: to be announced.
Countermeasures: to be announced.
Combat data systems: to be announced.
Weapons control: to be announced.
Radars: Air search: to be announced.
Surface search: to be announced.
Navigation: to be announced.
Fire control: to be announced.
Tacan: to be announced.

Fixed-wing aircraft: Approximately 40: typically a mix of 30 F35 combat aircraft, six Merlin anti-submarine aircraft and four Maritime Airborne Surveillance & Control aircraft.

Programmes: An alliance approach, initially involving BAE Systems, Thales UK and the UK MoD, for the procurement of new aircraft carriers, was announced on 30 January 2003. Kellogg, Brown & Root was later appointed on 7 February 2005 as 'physical integrator' to oversee the construction programme of the two ships. The Assessment Phase, which had begun on 5 September 2003, was formally concluded on 14th December 2005 when it was announced that Main Gate approval for Demonstration and Manufacture, was to be split into two incremental steps. The Demonstration Phase, to which GBP300 million is to be committed for detailed design and production engineering activities is to be undertaken first. This is to lead to the Manufacturing Phase which is expected to be launched by early 2007. It was also announced that VT Group and Babcock were to be added to the Aircraft Carrier Alliance (ACA) which would be charged with building the two ships. An Alliance Management Board, chaired by the UK MOD, is to lead and collectively manage the project; BAE Systems is to be responsible for integration of design, build, commissioning and acceptance of the ships; lead the

CVF
9/2005*, Thales / 1123122

engineering team; and have responsibility for mission systems design. Thales is to lead design of platform, power and propulsion and take responsibility for the aviation interface; KBR is to provide project management services. Construction and assembly of the ships is to be as follows: Block 4 at BAES Govan; Block 3 at BAES Barrow; Block 2 at VT Group Portsmouth; Block 1 (bow) and final assembly at Babcock Roysth. The remaining forty per cent of the ship (super structure) is to be competed for by other UK shipyards and manufacturing facilities.

Structure: The final 280 m 'Delta' design retains some of the original 292 m 'Alpha' design features including a two-island arrangement, with flight control from the after island, and two deck-edge aircraft lifts. It is to have

the capability to operate up to 40 aircraft. While fitted with a ski-jump to operate short take off and vertical landing (STOVL) aircraft on build, the design is adaptable and 'future-proofed' in that it allows for the retrofit of catapults and arrestor gear at a later date if required. Planning assumptions are that CVF is to operate the F-35B STOVL variant of the Joint Strike Fighter, the preferred choice to meet the UK Joint Combat Aircraft (JCA) requirement. A final choice between this aircraft and the F-35C CV variant is expected by late 2006. Studies to examine the feasibility of fitting the electromagnetic aircraft launcher system (EMALS), being developed for the US Navy's CVN-21 class, have been conducted. The hangar has the capability to stow 20 JCA.

Operational: To be based at Portsmouth.

CVF
9/2005*, Aircraft Carrier Alliance / 0590143

3 INVINCIBLE CLASS (CV)

Name	No	Builders	Laid down	Launched	Commissioned
INVINCIBLE	R 05	Vickers Shipbuilding & Engineering, Barrow-in-Furness	20 July 1973	3 May 1977	11 July 1980
ILLUSTRIOUS	R 06	Swan Hunter Shipbuilders, Wallsend	7 Oct 1976	1 Dec 1978	20 June 1982
ARK ROYAL	R 07	Swan Hunter Shipbuilders, Wallsend	14 Dec 1978	2 June 1981	1 Nov 1985

Displacement, tons: 20,600 full load
Dimensions, feet (metres): 685.8 oa; 632 wl × 118 oa; 90 wl × 26 (screws) (209.1; 192.6 × 36; 27.5 × 8)
Flight deck, feet (metres): 550 × 44.3 (167.8 × 13.5)
Main machinery: COGAG; 4 RR Olympus TM3B gas turbines; 97,200 hp (72.5 MW) sustained; 2 shafts
Speed, knots: 28. **Range, n miles:** 7,000 at 19 kt
Complement: 685 (60 officers) plus 366 (80 officers) aircrew plus up to 600 marines

Guns: 3 Signaal/General Electric 30 mm 7-barrelled Gatling Goalkeeper (R 06) ❶; 4,200 rds/min to 1.5 km.
3 General Dynamics 20 mm Phalanx Mk 15 (R 07); 6 barrels/launcher; 4,500 rds/min to 1.5 km.
2 Oerlikon/BMARC 20 mm GAM-BO1 ❷.
4 M 323 Mk 44 7.62 mm Miniguns.
Countermeasures: Decoys: Outfit DLH; 8 Sea Gnat 6-barrelled 130 mm/102 mm dispensers ❸. Prairie Masker noise suppression system.
ESM: Racal UAT ❹; intercept.
Combat data systems: ADAWS 20 Ed 3.0+; Link 11 and Siemens Plessey JTIDS Link 16. JMCIS. SCOT 5 SATCOM ❺. WECDIS. AIS. CSS.
Weapons control: Rademec optronic director.
Radars: Air search: Marconi/Signaal Type 1022 ❻; D-band.
Air/Surface search: AMS Type 996 ❼; E/F-band.
Navigation: 2 Kelvin Hughes Type 1007 ❽; I-band.
1 Racal Decca 1008; E/F-band.
CCA: Finmeccanica SPN 720 (V)5; I-band
Tacan: TRN 26(M)
Fixed-wing aircraft: Tailored air group of up to 24 aircraft including: BAE Harrier GR 7A/9A ❾.

Helicopters: Westland Merlin HM.Mk 1 ❿; Westland Sea King ASAC Mk 7. Chinook HC2. Apache AH1.

Programmes: The first of class, the result of many compromises, was ordered from Vickers on 17 April 1973. The order for the second ship was placed on 14 May 1976, the third in December 1978.
Modernisation: In January 1989 R 05 completed modernisation which included a 12° ski ramp, space and support facilities for at least 21 aircraft, three Goalkeeper systems, Sea Gnat decoys, 996 radar, Flag and Command facilities and accommodation for an additional 120 aircrew and Flag Staff. In February 1994 R 06 completed a similar modernisation to bring her to the same standard, but with additional command and weapon system improvements. Ski ramp has been increased to 13°. Modifications to operate Harrier GR.7 have been completed in all three ships (R 06 – 1998, R 05 – 2000 and R 07 – 2001). This included the removal of Sea Dart, increasing the flight deck area by 7 per cent (23 × 18 m) and fitting GR.7 support facilities.
Structure: In 1976-77 an amendment was incorporated to allow for the transport and landing of an RM Commando. The forward end of the flight deck (ski ramp) allows STOVL aircraft of greater all-up weight to operate more efficiently. *Illustrious* fitted with a composite third mast at the after end of the island structure to provide mountings for additional communications. She has also had substantial internal changes to accommodate troops in the LPH role. *Ark Royal* is to receive a third advanced technology mast in 2006.
Operational: The primary role of this class is to operate STOVL aircraft and helicopters. Sea Harriers were phased out in 2006 and the embarked fixed-wing air-group has migrated to an all Harrier GR. Mk 7A/9A ground-attack force. Changes to weapon magazines to accommodate Smart weapons incorporated. *Ark Royal* deployed the first front-line Merlin helicopter squadron. *Illustrious* completed a two-year refit in late 2004 when she relieved *Ark Royal* (including the standby LPH role). Following a restorative docking in 2006, *Ark Royal* is to return to service in 2007. *Invincible* reverted to extended readiness in 2005. Reactivation could be achieved in about eighteen months. The transition between the retirement of *Illustrious* and *Ark Royal* and the entry into service of CVF is to be managed by the Aircraft Carrier Alliance to ensure continuity of capability.

ILLUSTRIOUS　　　　　*11/2005*, S Russell-Stevenson, RN* / 1153967

ILLUSTRIOUS　　　　　*11/2005*, S Russell-Stevenson RN* / 1153966

ILLUSTRIOUS　　　　　*(Scale 1 : 1,200), Ian Sturton* / 1153886

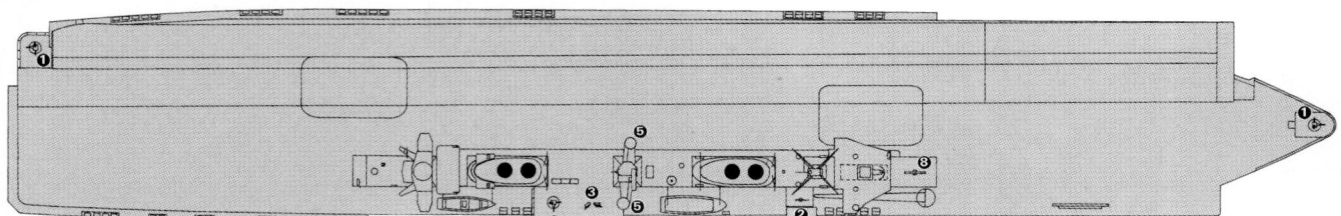

ILLUSTRIOUS　　　　　*(Scale 1 : 1,200), Ian Sturton* / 1153887

ILLUSTRIOUS

11/2005*, S Russell-Stevenson, RN / 1153964

ILLUSTRIOUS

11/2005*, S Russell-Stevenson. RN / 1153965

DESTROYERS

Notes: *Bristol* (D 23) is an immobile tender used for training in Portsmouth Harbour.

4 TYPE 42 CLASS (BATCH 2) (DDGH)

Name	No	Builders	Laid down	Launched	Commissioned
EXETER	D 89	Swan Hunter Shipbuilders, Wallsend-on-Tyne	22 July 1976	25 Apr 1978	19 Sep 1980
SOUTHAMPTON	D 90	Vosper Thornycroft, Woolston	21 Oct 1976	29 Jan 1979	31 Oct 1981
NOTTINGHAM	D 91	Vosper Thornycroft, Woolston	6 Feb 1978	18 Feb 1980	14 Apr 1983
LIVERPOOL	D 92	Cammell Laird, Birkenhead	5 July 1978	25 Sep 1980	1 July 1982

Displacement, tons: 4,500 standard; 4,800 full load
Dimensions, feet (metres): 412 oa; 392 wl × 47 × 19 (screws) *(125; 119.5 × 14.3 × 5.8)*
Main machinery: COGOG; 2 RR Olympus TM3B gas turbines; 50,000 hp *(37.3 MW)* sustained; 2 RR Tyne RM1C gas turbines (cruising); 9,900 hp *(7.4 MW)* sustained; 2 shafts; cp props
Speed, knots: 29. **Range, n miles:** 4,000 at 18 kt
Complement: 287 (24 officers) (accommodation for 312)

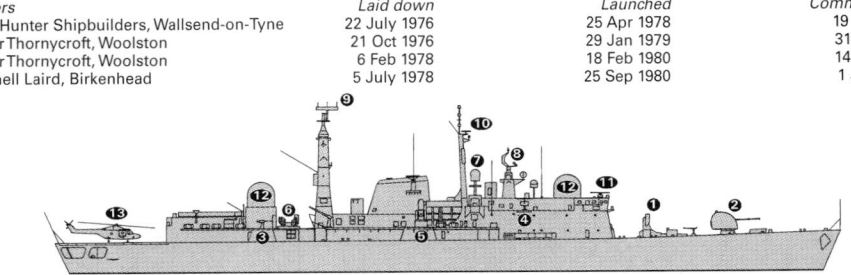

SOUTHAMPTON

(Scale 1 : 1,200), Ian Sturton / 0572736

Missiles: SAM: BAE Systems Sea Dart twin launcher ❶; semi-active radar guidance to 40 km *(21.5 n miles)* at 2 Mach; height envelope 100—18,300 m *(328—60,042 ft)*; 22 missiles; limited anti-ship capability.
Guns: 1 Vickers 4.5 in *(114 mm)*/55 Mk 8 ❷; 25 rds/min to 27 km *(14.6 n miles)* anti-surface; weight of shell 21 kg.
2 BEMARC 20 mm GAM-BO1 ❸ or ❹; 1,000 rds/min to 2 km.
2 General Dynamics 20 mm Phalanx Mk 15 Mod 1b ❺; 6 barrels per launcher; 4,500 rds/min combined to 1.5 km.
2 M 323 Mk 44 7.62 mm Miniguns
Countermeasures: Decoys: Outfit DLH; 4 Sea Gnat 130 mm/102 mm 6-barrelled launchers ❻. Irvin DLF 3 offboard decoys.
Type 2170 (SLQ-25A); towed torpedo decoy.
ESM: Racal UAT 1; intercept.

Combat data systems: ADAWS 20 Ed 3.0. 2 SCOT 1C (to be replaced by SCOT 1A and SCOT 5 (D 91 only) SATCOMs ❼; Link 11. JTIDS. Link 16. WECDIS. AIS. CSS.
Weapons control: GWS 30 Mod 2; GSA 1 secondary system.
2 Radamec 2100 series optronic surveillance directors.
Radars: Air search: Marconi/Signaal Type 1022 ❽; D-band.
Air/surface search: AMS Type 996 ❾; E/F-band.
Navigation: Kelvin Hughes Type 1007 ❿; I-band and Racal Decca Type 1008 ⓫; E/F-band.
Fire control: 2 Marconi Type 909 ⓬; I/J-band.
Sonars: Ferranti/Thomson Type 2050 or Plessey Type 2016; hull-mounted; active search and attack; medium frequency.

Helicopters: 1 Westland Lynx HAS 3/8 ⓭.

Programmes: Batch 1 ships decommissioned. All remaining ships Batch 2.
Modernisation: Phalanx replaced 30 mm guns in 1987-89. Batch 2 have had a command system update JTIDS (Link 16) improved ammunition.
Structure: Torpedo tubes removed.
Operational: First of class paid off in 1999. *Newcastle* and *Glasgow* in January 2005 and *Cardiff* in August 2005. Decommissioning plans: *Exeter* 2009; *Liverpool* 2009; *Southampton* 2010; *Nottingham* 2012.

EXETER

10/2005*, Maritime Photographic / 1154004

SOUTHAMPTON

6/2005*, M Declerck / 1154005

NOTTINGHAM

9/2005*, Derek Fox / 1153956

4 TYPE 42 CLASS (BATCH 3) (DDGH)

Name	No	Builders	Laid down	Launched	Commissioned
MANCHESTER	D 95	Vickers Shipbuilding & Engineering, Barrow-in-Furness	19 May 1978	24 Nov 1980	16 Dec 1982
GLOUCESTER	D 96	Vosper Thornycroft, Woolston	29 Oct 1979	2 Nov 1982	11 Sep 1985
EDINBURGH	D 97	Cammell Laird, Birkenhead	8 Sep 1980	14 Apr 1983	17 Dec 1985
YORK	D 98	Swan Hunter Shipbuilders, Wallsend-on-Tyne	18 Jan 1980	21 June 1982	9 Aug 1985

Displacement, tons: 4,500 standard; 5,200 full load
Dimensions, feet (metres): 462.8 oa; 434 wl × 49.9 × 19 (screws) *(141.1; 132.3 × 15.2 × 5.8)*
Main machinery: COGOG; 2 RR Olympus TM3B gas turbines; 50,000 hp *(37.3 MW)* sustained; 2 RR Tyne RM1C gas turbines (cruising); 10,680 hp *(8 MW)* sustained; 2 shafts; cp props
Speed, knots: 30+
Range, n miles: 4,000 at 18 kt
Complement: 287 (26 officers)

Missiles: SAM: BAE Systems Sea Dart twin launcher ❶; semi-active radar guidance to 40 km *(21 n miles)*; warhead HE; 22 missiles; limited anti-ship capability.
Guns: 1 Vickers 4.5 in *(114 mm)*/55 Mk 8 ❷; 25 rds/min to 27 km *(14.6 n miles)* anti-surface; weight of shell 21 kg. Mod 1 (range 33.5 km *(18.1 n miles)*) in D 97 and D 98.
2 BEMARC 20 mm GAM-BO1 ❸; 1,000 rds/min to 2 km.
2 General Dynamics 20 mm Phalanx Mk 15 Mod 1b ❹; 6 barrels per launcher; 4,500 rds/min combined to 1.5 km.
2 M 323 Mk 44 7.62 mm Miniguns
Countermeasures: Outfit DLH; 4 Sea Gnat 130 mm/102 mm 6-barrelled launchers ❺. DLF-3 offboard decoys. Type 2170 (SLQ-25A); towed torpedo decoy.
ESM: Racal UAT; intercept.
Combat data systems: ADAWS 20 Ed 3.0 action data automation. SCOT 5 SATCOM ❻; Link 11. JTIDS. Link 16. WECDIS.AIS.CSS.

Weapons control: GWS 30 Mod 2 (for SAM); GSA 1 secondary system. 2 Radamec 2100 series optronic surveillance directors.
Radars: Air search: Marconi/Signaal Type 1022 ❼; D-band.
Air/surface search: AMS Type 996 ❽; E/F-band.
Navigation: Kelvin Hughes Type 1007 ❾; I-band and Racal Decca Type 1008 ❿; E/F-band.
Fire control: 2 Marconi Type 909 Mod 1 ⓫; I/J-band.
Sonars: Ferranti/Thomson Type 2050 or Plessey Type 2016; hull-mounted; active search and attack.

Helicopters: 1 Westland Lynx HAS.Mk 3/8 ⓬.

Programmes: The completion of the last three ships was delayed to allow for some modifications resulting from experience in the Falklands' campaign (1982).

Modernisation: Vulcan Phalanx replaced 30 mm guns 1987-89. D 97 had a partial conversion in 1990 with the Phalanx moved forward and a protective visor fitted around the bow of the ship but reverted to the standard armament in 1994. All have had a command system update. Sea Gnat decoy launchers can fire a variety of devices.
Structure: A strengthening beam has been fitted on each side which increased displacement by 50 tons and beam by 2 ft. Torpedo tubes removed. Transom flaps, to improve fuel efficiency, to be fitted in D 95 in 2006.
Operational: The helicopter carries the Sea Skua air-to-surface weapon for use against lightly defended surface ship targets. Decommissioning plans: *Manchester* 2011; *Gloucester* 2011; *York* 2012; *Edinburgh* 2013. Based at Portsmouth.

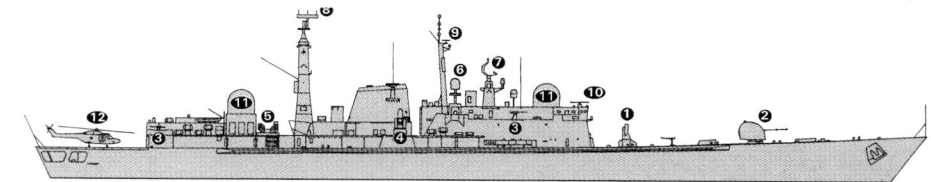

MANCHESTER
(Scale 1 : 1,200), Ian Sturton / 0572735

MANCHESTER
7/2005*, H M Steele / 1153962

GLOUCESTER
6/2005*, Michael Nitz / 1154003

EDINBURGH
10/2004*, Marion Ferrette / 1043595

0 + 6 (2) DARING CLASS (TYPE 45) (DDGHM)

Name	No	Builders	Laid down	Launched	Commissioned
DARING	D 32	BAE Systems Marine/Vosper Thornycroft	28 Mar 2003	1 Feb 2006	May 2009
DAUNTLESS	D 33	BAE Systems Marine/Vosper Thornycroft	26 Aug 2004	2007	2010
DIAMOND	D 34	BAE Systems Marine/Vosper Thornycroft	25 Feb 2005	2008	2010
DRAGON	D 35	BAE Systems Marine/Vosper Thornycroft	19 Dec 2005	2008	2011
DEFENDER	D 36	BAE Systems Marine/Vosper Thornycroft	2006	2008	2012
DUNCAN	D 37	BAE Systems Marine/Vosper Thornycroft	2006	2009	2013

Displacement, tons: 5,800 standard; 7,350 full load
Dimensions, feet (metres): 500.1 oa; 462.9 wl × 69.6 × 17.4 *(152.4; 141.1 × 21.2 × 5.3)*
Main machinery: Integrated Electric Propulsion; 2 RR WR-21 gas turbine alternators; 42 MW; 2 Wärtsilä diesel generators; 4 MW; 2 motors; 40 MW; 2 shafts; fixed props
Speed, knots: 29
Range, n miles: 7,000 at 18 kt
Complement: 187 plus 38 spare

Missiles: SSM: Space for 8 Harpoon (2 quad) ❶.
SAM: 6 DCN Sylver A 50 48 cell VLS ❷ PAAMS (principal anti-air missile system); typical mix of 32 Aster 30; active pulse doppler radar homing to 80 km *(43.2 n miles)* at 4.0 Mach; warhead 15 kg and 16 Aster 15; active pulse doppler radar homing to 30 km *(16 n miles)* at 3.0 Mach.
Guns: 1 Vickers 4.5 in *(114 mm)*/55 Mk 8 Mod 1 ❸. 25 rds/min to 33.5 km (18.1 n miles); weight of shell 21 kg.
2—20 mm Vulcan Phalanx Mk 15 Mod 1b (fitted for both not with) ❹. 2 DES/MSI 30 mm/75; 650 rds/min to 10 km *(5.4 n miles)*; weight of shell 0.36 kg ❺.
Countermeasures: Decoys: 4 DLH (chaff, IR); DLF offboard decoys; ❻. Type 2170 torpedo defence system.
ECM: to be decided.
RESM: Thales Type UAT (mod) ❼; intercept.
CESM: to be decided.
Combat data systems: CMS-1 (based on DNA SSCS with additional AAW functions); Links 11, 16 STDL and 22. SATCOM ❽. CEC to be fitted.
Weapons control: 2 EOGCS (based on Radamec 2500).
Radars: Air/surface search: Signaal/Marconi S1850M ❾; D-band.
Surveillance/fire control: BAE Systems Sampson ❿; E/F-band; multifunction.
Surface search: ⓫. E/F-band.
Navigation: E/F- and I-band.
Sonars: EDO/ULTRA MFS-7000; bow mounted; medium frequency.

Helicopters: Lynx Mk HMA 8 (first batch) or Merlin HM.Mk 1 ⓬.

Programmes: This project has gone through many stages, the result of which has been slippage of the originally envisaged in-service date of 2000 to 2009 and the concomitant extension of the ship-lives of the ageing Type 42s. Starting life as NFR 90 in the 1980s, it was taken forward via the Anglo-French Future Frigate, the tri-nation Common New Generation Frigate (Horizon) and finally, when UK withdrew from the collaborative ship programme on 25 April 1999, a national Type 45 ship project. The contract for the design and build of the first three ships (Batch 1) was placed with the prime contractor, BAE Systems, on 20 December 2000. This was amended in late 2001 to reflect a new procurement strategy in which commitment was made to the first six ships. The second three ships comprise Batch 2. Vosper Thornycroft is building and outfitting the forward section of each ship together with the masts and funnel. The remainder of the ship is being built by BAE Marine. Final assembly of D 32 is at Scotstown and assembly of follow-on ships is to be at Govan. Stage I trials are to be conducted by the final assembly shipyard and Stage II trials by BAE Systems. Procurement of the missile system is being pursued separately and a contract for full development and initial production of PAAMS was placed with the tri-national consortium, EUROPAAMS, in August 1999. Test firings are to be conducted from the trials barge *Longbow* from 2006. It was announced on 21 July 2004 that a class of eight ships is to be built. The decision on order for Batch 3 (2 ships) is expected in Autumn 2006.

Structure: Built to Lloyd's Naval Ship Rules. Provision for future installation of 155 mm gun or a 16-cell VLS silo, SSM, CIWS and magazine-launched torpedoes. An integrated technology mast is another potential modification. The ships are designed to support and deploy at least 30 troops. OTC facilities are to be included. The suitability of the Type 45 as a BMD platform is being studied.

Operational: Stage 1 sea trials of *Daring* are to start in July 2007. A series of trials will follow before contract acceptance in May 2009.

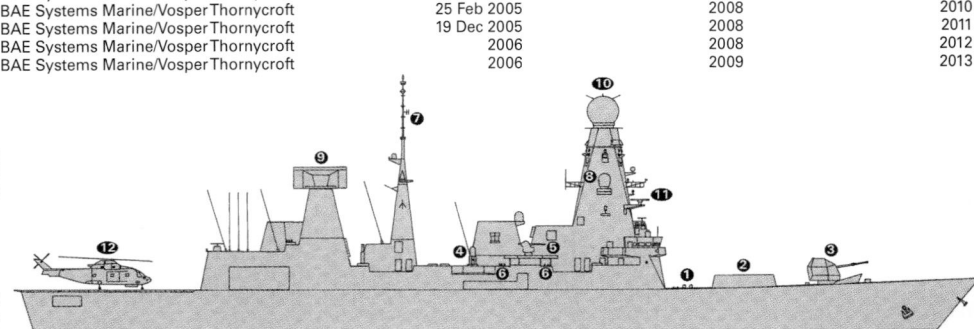

DARING   *(Scale 1 : 1,200), Ian Sturton* / 0131365

DARING   *2/2006*, Richard Scott* / 1130823

DARING (computer graphic)   *9/2002, BAE Systems* / 0523834

FRIGATES

Notes: Following the decision in 2004 to discontinued the Future Surface Combatant (FSC) programme, the structure of the future surface fleet is under consideration. The long-term aim is to achieve a single surface combatant force of multirole and interrelated ships that field the capabilities of destroyers, frigates and mine-countermeasures vessels. Options under consideration include life-extension of the Type 23 frigate class, replacement of the four Type 22 Batch 3 frigates by a class of off-the-shelf Medium Vessel Derivative (MV(D)) (contenders include a Type 45 derivative or the Franco-Italian FREMM) from around 2016 and a future Versatile Surface Combatant (VSC) to enter service from about 2023.

4 BROADSWORD CLASS (TYPE 22 BATCH 3) (FFGHM)

Name	No	Builders	Laid down	Launched	Commissioned
CORNWALL	F 99	Yarrow Shipbuilders, Glasgow	14 Dec 1983	14 Oct 1985	23 Apr 1988
CUMBERLAND	F 85	Yarrow Shipbuilders, Glasgow	12 Oct 1984	21 June 1986	10 June 1989
CAMPBELTOWN	F 86	Cammell Laird, Birkenhead	4 Dec 1985	7 Oct 1987	27 May 1989
CHATHAM	F 87	Swan Hunter Shipbuilders, Wallsend-on-Tyne	12 May 1986	20 Jan 1988	4 May 1990

Displacement, tons: 4,200 standard; 4,900 full load
Dimensions, feet (metres): 485.9 × 48.5 × 21
  (148.1 × 14.8 × 6.4)
Main machinery: COGOG; 2 RR Spey SM1A gas turbines; 29,500 hp *(22 MW)* sustained; 2 RR Tyne RM3C gas turbines; 10,680 hp *(8 MW)* sustained; 2 shafts; LIPS; cp props
Speed, knots: 30; 18 on Tynes
Range, n miles: 4,500 at 18 kt on Tynes
Complement: 250 (31 officers) (accommodation for 301)

Missiles: SSM: 8 McDonnell Douglas Harpoon Block 1C (2 quad) launchers ❶; preprogrammed; active radar homing to 130 km *(70 n miles)* at 0.9 Mach; warhead 227 kg.
SAM: 2 British Aerospace Seawolf GWS 25 Mod 3 ❷; command line of sight (CLOS) with 2 channel radar tracking to 5 km *(2.7 n miles)* at 2+ Mach; warhead 14 kg.
Guns: 1 Vickers 4.5 in *(114 mm)*/55 Mk 8 ❸; 25 rds/min to 22 km *(11.9 n miles)*; 27.5 km *(14.8 n miles)* Mod 1 anti-surface; weight of shell 21 kg.
1 Signaal/General Electric 30 mm 7-barrelled Goalkeeper ❹; 4,200 rds/min combined to 1.5 km.
2 GAM-BO1-1 20 mm ❺; 700-900 rds/min to 1 km.
Countermeasures: Decoys: Outfit DLH; 4 Sea Gnat 6-barrelled 130 mm/102 mm fixed launchers ❻. DLF offboard decoys.
Type 2170 torpedo defence system.
RESM: Racal UAT; intercept.
CESM: CoBLU; intercept.
Combat data systems: CACS 5 action data automation; Link 11. 2 Matra Marconi SCOT 1C (being replaced by SCOT 5) SATCOMs ❼. ICS-3 integrated comms. INMARSAT.
Weapons control: 2 BAe GSA 8B GPEOD Sea Archer optronic directors with TV and IR imaging and laser rangefinders ❽. GWS 25 Mod 3 (for SAM). GWS 60.
Radars: Air/surface search: Marconi Type 967/968 ❾; D/E-band.
Navigation: Kelvin Hughes Type 1007; I-band.
Fire control: 2 Marconi Type 911 ❿; I/Ku-band (for Seawolf).
Sonars: Ferranti/Thomson Sintra Type 2050; hull-mounted; active search and attack.

Helicopters: 2 Westland Lynx HMA. Mk 3/8 ⓫.

Modernisation: Sonar 2016 replaced by Sonar 2050. EW fit updated and Sea Gnat is the standard launcher for a variety of distraction and seduction decoys. EDS Command Support System fitted. A major upgrade to the Seawolf system to be implemented from 2008; a rolling installation programme is planned to be completed by 2011. Enhancements include an improved I-band radar, an additional optronic tracker to improve low level performance and improved software. In a separate contract, the Mk 4 SWELL (Seawolf Enhanced Low Level) fuze is being incorporated into existing rounds and in Block 2 missiles from 2005. Mk 8 Mod 1 gun fitted in F 85 and is being progressively fitted to the rest of the class.

Structure: Batch 3 are stretched versions of original Batch 1. Flight decks enlarged to operate Sea King helicopters.
Operational: This class is primarily designed for ASW operations and is capable of acting as OTC. All have facilities for Flag and staff. One Lynx normally embarked. All are based at Devonport.
Sales: All Batch 1 to Brazil. Batch 2 ships *London* and *Coventry* to Romania and *Sheffield* to Chile.

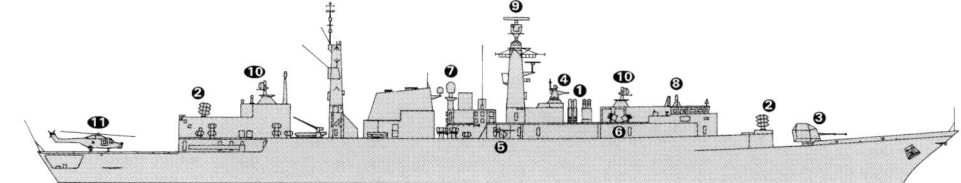

CORNWALL   *(Scale 1 : 1,200), Ian Sturton* / 0572734

CORNWALL   *3/2002, John Brodie* / 0530028

CUMBERLAND   *6/2005*, Michael Nitz* / 1154002

CHATHAM   *6/2005*, B Sullivan* / 1153963

13 DUKE CLASS (TYPE 23) (FFGHM)

Name	No	Builders	Laid down	Launched	Commissioned
ARGYLL	F 231	Yarrow Shipbuilders, Glasgow	20 Mar 1987	8 Apr 1989	31 May 1991
LANCASTER	F 229 (ex-F 232)	Yarrow Shipbuilders, Glasgow	18 Dec 1987	24 May 1990	1 May 1992
IRON DUKE	F 234	Yarrow Shipbuilders, Glasgow	12 Dec 1988	2 Mar 1991	20 May 1993
MONMOUTH	F 235	Yarrow Shipbuilders, Glasgow	1 June 1989	23 Nov 1991	24 Sep 1993
MONTROSE	F 236	Yarrow Shipbuilders, Glasgow	1 Nov 1989	31 July 1992	2 June 1994
WESTMINSTER	F 237	Swan Hunter Shipbuilders, Wallsend-on-Tyne	18 Jan 1991	4 Feb 1992	13 May 1994
NORTHUMBERLAND	F 238	Swan Hunter Shipbuilders, Wallsend-on-Tyne	4 Apr 1991	4 Apr 1992	29 Nov 1994
RICHMOND	F 239	Swan Hunter Shipbuilders, Wallsend-on-Tyne	16 Feb 1992	6 Apr 1993	22 June 1995
SOMERSET	F 82	Yarrow Shipbuilders, Glasgow	12 Oct 1992	25 June 1994	20 Sep 1996
SUTHERLAND	F 81	Yarrow Shipbuilders, Glasgow	14 Oct 1993	9 Mar 1996	4 July 1997
KENT	F 78	Yarrow Shipbuilders, Glasgow	16 Apr 1997	27 May 1998	8 June 2000
PORTLAND	F 79	Yarrow Shipbuilders, Glasgow	14 Jan 1998	15 May 1999	3 May 2001
ST ALBANS	F 83	Yarrow Shipbuilders, Glasgow	18 Apr 1999	6 May 2000	6 June 2002

Displacement, tons: 3,500 standard; 4,200 full load
Dimensions, feet (metres): 436.2 × 52.8 × 18 (screws);
24 (sonar) *(133 × 16.1 × 5.5; 7.3)*
Main machinery: CODLAG; 2 RR Spey SM1A (F 229-F 236) or
SM1C (F 237 onwards) gas turbines (see *Structure*); 31,100 hp
(23.2 MW) sustained; 4 Paxman 12CM diesels; 8,100 hp
(6 MW); 2 GEC motors; 4,000 hp *(3 MW)*; 2 shafts
Speed, knots: 28; 15 on diesel-electric
Range, n miles: 7,800 miles at 15 kt
Complement: 181 (13 officers)

Missiles: SSM: 8 McDonnell Douglas Harpoon (2 quad)
launchers ❶; active radar homing to 130 km *(70 n miles)*
at 0.9 Mach; warhead 227 kg *(84C)*. 4 normally carried.
SAM: British Aerospace Seawolf GWS 26 Mod 1 VLS ❷;
command line of sight (CLOS) radar/TV tracking to 6 km
(3.3 n miles) at 2.5 Mach; warhead 14 kg; 32 canisters.
Guns: 1 Vickers 4.5 in *(114 mm)*/55 Mk 8 ❸; 25 rds/min
to 22 km *(11.9 n miles)*; 27.5 km *(14.8 n miles)* Mod 1
anti-surface; weight of shell 21 kg. Mk 8 Mod 1 being
progressively fitted.
2 DES/MSI DS 30B 30 mm/75 ❹; 650 rds/min to 10 km
(5.4 n miles) anti-surface; 3 km *(1.6 n miles)* anti-aircraft;
weight of shell 0.36 kg.
Torpedoes: 4 Cray Marine 324 mm fixed (2 twin) tubes ❺.
Marconi Stingray; active/passive homing to 11 km *(5.9 n
miles)* at 45 kt; warhead 35 kg (shaped charge); depth to
750 m *(2,460 ft)*. Reload in 9 minutes.
Countermeasures: Decoys: Outfit DLH; 4 Sea Gnat
6-barrelled 130 mm/102 mm launchers ❻. DLF 2/3 offboard
decoys.
Type 2170 torpedo defence system.
ESM: Racal UAT ❼; intercept.
Combat data systems: Insyte Surface Ship Command
System (DNA); Links 11 and JTIDS 16 in due course.
2 Matra Marconi SCOT 1D SATCOMs (being replaced by
SCOT 5) ❽.
Weapons control: BAe GSA 8B/GPEOD optronic director ❾.
GWS 60 (for SSM). GWS 26 (for SAM).
Radars: Air/surface search: Plessey Type 996(I) ❿; 3D;
E/F-band.

Surface search: Racal Decca Type 1008 ⓫; E/F-band.
Navigation: Kelvin Hughes Type 1007; I-band.
Fire control: 2 Marconi Type 911 ⓬; I/Ku-band.
IFF: 1010/1011 or 1018/1019.
Sonars: Ferranti/Thomson Sintra Type 2050; bow-mounted;
active search and attack.
Dowty Type 2031Z (F 229, 231, 234-236, 238-239); towed
array; passive search; very low frequency.
Thales Type 2087 (F 237); active low-frequency (500 Hz)
towed body with passive array (100 Hz).

Helicopters: 1 Westland Lynx HMA 3/8 or 1 Merlin HM 1 (F 229,
F 235 and F 237) ⓭.

Programmes: The first of this class was ordered from
Yarrows on 29 October 1984. Further batches of three
ordered in September 1986, July 1988, December 1989,
January 1992 and February 1996. Further orders are
unlikely. F 229 pennant number changed, because 232
was considered unlucky, as it is the RN report form
number used for collisions and groundings.
Modernisation: Major improvement programmes are
planned. The Command System has been upgraded
to Phase 5 with DNA(2) programmed to commence in
2008. The Mk 8 Mod 1 gun is to be installed in the whole
class. Modifications to improve the performance of
Type 966 radar are being made. The Seawolf system is
to be upgraded from 2007-2011; enhancements include
improved I-band radar, an additional optronic tracker to

improve low level performance and improved software.
In a separate contract the Mk 4 SWELL (Seawolf Enhanced
Low Level) fuze is being incorporated into existing rounds
and in Block 2 missiles from 2005. Surface Ship Torpedo
Defence, a development of Sonar 2070, is being fitted.
Low Frequency Active Sonar (Type 2087) is replacing
Type 2031 in eight ships. F 237 and F 238 have been fitted
and installation in F 239 is in progress. Future outfitting
plans are: F 82 2006; F 83 2007; F 81 2007; F 78 2010
and F 79 2010. Following trials in F 229, Merlin HM1 is
to be embarked in Type 2087 fitted ships. Plans to instal
Co-operative Engagement Capability have been
postponed. Trial launch and recovery of a Scan Eagle
UAV were conducted in March 2006.
Structure: Incorporates stealth technology to minimise
acoustic, magnetic, radar and IR signatures. The design
includes a 7° slope to all vertical surfaces, rounded
edges, reduction of IR emissions and a hull bubble
system to reduce radiated noise. The combined diesel
electric and GT propulsion system provides quiet
motive power during towed sonar operations. The SM1C
engines although capable of 41 MW of power combined
are constrained by output into the gearbox. MacTaggart
Scott Helios helo landing system.
Operational: F 78, F 83, F 229, F 234, F 237 and F 239 are
based at Portsmouth and the remainder, at Devonport.
Following announcements on 21 July 2004, *Norfolk* and
Marlborough decommissioned in 2005 and *Grafton* in
March 2006. All three ships have been sold to Chile.

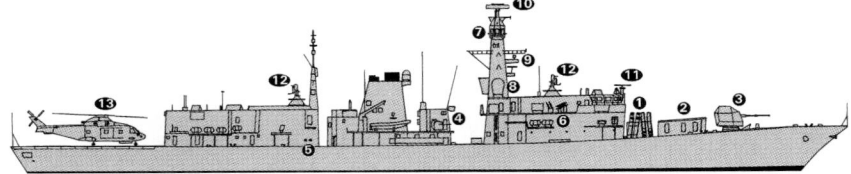

MARLBOROUGH

(Scale 1 : 1,200), Ian Sturton / 0530055

ST ALBANS

6/2005*, Frank Findler / 1153953

MONMOUTH

1/2005*, Camil Busquets i Vilanova / 1154001

LANCASTER

6/2005*, Derek Fox / 1153954

WESTMINISTER

5/2005*, John Brodie / 1153955

SUTHERLAND

6/2005*, Frank Findler / 1153950

IRON DUKE

6/2005*, Maritime Photographic / 1154000

SHIPBORNE AIRCRAFT

Notes: (1) The STOVL (short take-off and landing) variant of the Lockheed Martin F-35 Joint Strike Fighter selected on 30 September 2002 to fulfil the Joint Combat Aircraft (JCA) requirement. The aircraft is to replace the RAF/RN aircraft operated by the Joint Force Harrier for operation both from the future carriers and from land bases. There are 150 aircraft planned, first delivery of which is expected to meet an in-service date of 2014. The Main Gate decision for JCA is expected by early 2007.
(2) Following the withdrawal from service of Sea Harrier, the Harrier force has migrated to an all GR force. 30 GR.7 aircraft upgraded to GR.7A standard (re-engined with Pegasus Mk.107) for carrier operations by 2005. In parallel, 60 GR.7 and GR.7A and 10 T.10 aircraft to receive an avionics and weapons upgrade to GR.9/GR.9A/T.12 standard by 2008.
(3) A programme to replace the current organic airborne early-warning capability in 2012 is in progress. Initial Gate for The Maritime Airborne Surveillance and Control (MASC) programme was passed in July 2005 with Main Gate decisions to follow in December 2008. Potential solutions are likely to be based on rotary-wing platforms and UAVs. The V-22 Osprey is a futher option.
(4) AgustaWestland Future Lynx selected on 27 March 2005 as preferred option to meet the requirement for the Maritime (Surface) Attack Helicopter. Entry into service is expected in 2013/14. Overall numbers have not been decided.
(5) Dauphin 2 helicopters with Royal Naval markings are leased by FOST for staff transfers. Painted red.
(6) Proposals for a maritime version of the Chinook medium-lift helicopter were formalised in September 2004 with the launch of a three-year assessment phase.

DAUPHIN 2   *7/2004, B Sullivan* / 1043559

Numbers/Type: 30 British Aerospace Harrier GR.7A/GR.9A.
Operational speed: 575 kt *(1,065 km/h)*.
Service ceiling: 45,000 ft *(13,716 m)*.
Range: 594 n miles *(1,101 km)*.
Role/Weapon systems: RAF all weather single-seat close support, battlefield interdiction night attack and reconnaissance aircraft, first operated from HMS *Illustrious* in 1994. All are being upgraded to GR.9A standard by 2008. Sensors: FLIR, TIALD, VICON recce pod, ESM, ECM and chaff dispensers. Weapons: AAM; 2 or 4 AIM-9L Sidewinder. Ground attack: 'iron' bombs, Paveway II LGB, Paveway III LGB, Paveway IV Precision guided bomb, Maverick IR and TV, Brimstone advanced anti-armour weapon system.

HARRIER GR. 7A   *6/2004, Royal Navy* / 1043610

Numbers/Type: 42 Westland/Agusta Merlin HM Mk 1.
Operational speed: 150 kt *(277 km/h)*.
Service ceiling: 10,000 ft *(3,048 m)*.
Range: 550 n miles *(1,019 km)*.
Role/Weapon systems: Primary anti-submarine role with secondary anti-surface and troop-carrying capabilities. Contract for 44 signed 9 October 1991. In service with 700, 814, 820, 824 and 829 Squadrons. A full system upgrade is planned to start in 2013. Sensors: GEC-Marconi Blue Kestrel 5000 radar, Thales Flash AQS 950 dipping sonar, GEC-Marconi sonobuoy acoustic processor AQS-903A, Thales Orange Reaper ESM, ECM. Link 11. Weapons: ASW; four Stingray torpedoes or Mk 11 Mod 3 depth bombs. ASV; OTHT for ship-launched SSM.

MERLIN HM Mk 1   *10/2003, B Sullivan* / 0572694

Numbers/Type: 22 Westland/Agusta Merlin HC Mk 3.
Operational speed: 150 kt *(296 km/h)*.
Service ceiling: 13,125 ft *(4,000 m)*.
Range: 550 n miles *(1,019 km)*.
Role/Weapon systems: Operated by RAF. Roles include cargo and troop transport and combat SAR. Military lift is 24 troops and up to four tonnes underslung. Sensors: integrated defensive aids including Raytheon laser detection, BAE Systems Sky Guardian 2000 RWR, Doppler-based MAWS, Northrop Grumman AN/AAQ-24 Nemesis DIRCM and BAE Systems North America AN/ALE-47 chaff/flare dispensers. Weapons: machine guns.

MERLIN Mk 3   *6/2003, Paul Jackson* / 0572697

Numbers/Type: 11/3 Westland Sea King HU Mk 5/HAS Mk 6.
Operational speed: 112 kt *(207 km/h)*.
Service ceiling: 10,000 ft *(3,050 m)*.
Range: 400 n miles *(740 km)*.
Role/Weapon systems: ASW capability of Sea King HAS Mk 6 variants removed. Remaining aircraft provide SAR/utility cover for CVS and also have force protection role. Sea King HU Mk 5 is primary SAR platform and utilises night vision goggles for overland and oversea operations. Sensors: Sea Searcher radar, Orange Crop ESM (Mk 6 only). Weapons: Both the Mk 5 and 6 can be fitted with the 7.62 mm MGs.

SEA KING HU Mk 5   *7/2005*, Michael Winter* / 1153951

Numbers/Type: 27 (+21 reserve) Westland Lynx HAS 3/HMA 8.
Operational speed: 120 kt *(222 km/h)*.
Service ceiling: 10,000 ft *(3,048 m)*.
Range: 320 n miles *(593 km)*.
Role/Weapon systems: Primarily anti-surface helicopter with short-range ASW capability; embarked in all modern RN escorts. Contract in 2001 for new Thales tactical situation displays to be fitted in all. 19 aircraft fitted with night vision goggles; all may be fitted in due course. All aircraft receiving a Saturn radio upgrade from 2006. Sensors: Ferranti Sea Spray Mk 1 radar, 'Orange Crop' ESM, chaff and flare dispenser. Weapons: ASW; two Stingray torpedoes or Mk 11 Mod 3 depth bombs. ASV; four Sea Skua missiles; two 12.7 mm MG pods.

LYNX HMA 8   *4/2005*, Martin Mokrus* / 1153952

LYNX HAS 3   *6/2005*, Paul Jackson* / 1153999

Numbers/Type: 13 Westland Sea King ASAC Mk 7.
Operational speed: 112 kt *(207 km/h)*.
Service ceiling: 10,000 ft *(3,050 m)*.
Range: 400 n miles *(740 km)*.
Role/Weapon systems: Primary role Airborne Surveillance and Control (ASaC) for maritime strike, littoral manoeuvre end force protection operations. Conversion contract awarded in October 1996 to upgrade AEW Mk 2 Fleet to ASAC Mk 7. Programme completed mid-2004. Two aircraft lost in Iraq conflict to be replaced by 2007. Sensors: Thales Searchwater 2000, Racal MIR-2 'Orange Crop' ESM, IFF Mk XII, Litton 100g navigation system and JTIDS/Link 16. Weapons: None.

SEA KING ASAC MK 7   *6/2004, Royal Navy* / 1043607

Numbers/Type: 29 Westland Sea King HC Mk 4.
Operational speed: 112 kt *(208 km/h)*.
Service ceiling: 10,000 ft *(3,050 m)*.
Range: 664 n miles *(1,230 km)*.
Role/Weapon systems: 24 commando support and five training/special task helicopters; capable of carrying most Commando Force equipment underslung. Expected to remain in service to 2010. Engines of 10 aircraft upgraded in 2003 to improve hot weather performance. Six HAS 6 ASW aircraft undergoing conversion to Mk 6C commando assault configuration. Sensors: Prophet 2 plus AAR-47 ESM; jammer, chaff and IR flares ECM. Weapons: Can fit 7.62 mm GPMG or similar.

SEA KING HC MK 4   *8/2004, B Sullivan* / 1043561

Numbers/Type: 35/6/8 Boeing Chinook HC Mk 2/HC Mk 2A/HC Mk 3.
Operational speed: 140 kt *(259 km/h)*.
Service ceiling: 10,140 ft *(3,090 m)*.
Range: 651 n miles *(1,207 km)*.
Role/Weapon systems: All-weather medium-lift helicopter equivalent to CH-47D and operated by RAF. Operable from surface ships (CVS/LPH/LPD/LSL). Mk 2/2A capable of carrying 44 troops and up to ten tonnes cargo. Mk 3 is Special Forces version. Sensors: defensive aids suite including missile approach warning, IR jammers and chaff/flare dispensers. Weapons: machine guns.

CHINOOK   *6/2004, Royal Navy* / 1043609

Numbers/Type: 67 Westland/Boeing WAH-64D AH Mk 1.
Operational speed: 150 kt *(278 km/h)*.
Service ceiling: 21,000 ft *(6,400 m)*.
Range: 260 n miles *(480 km)*.
Role/Weapon systems: Westland selected on 13 July 1995 to build McDonnell Douglas (now Boeing) Apache. Total 67 ordered. All-weather attack helicopter with day and night capability. One squadron to be earmarked for amphibious operations. To be operable from surface ships (CVS/LPH/LPD/LSL). First embarkation in *Ocean* in 2004 followed by two embarkations in 2005. Initial operational capability achieved in late 2005. Sensors: Lockheed Martin/Northrop Grumman AN/APG-78 Longbow radar, Lockheed Martin target acquisition and designation sight (TV and direct view) and AN/AAQ-11 pilot's night vision FLIR sensor (TADS/PNVS), BAE Systems HIDAS helicopter integrated defensive aids system, including Sky Guardian 2000 RWR, Type 1223 Laser warning receiver, Thales (Vinten) Vicon 78 Srs 455 chaff/flare dispenser, BAE Systems AN/AAR-57(V) common missile warning system (CMWS) and Lockheed Martin AN/APR-48A radar frequency interferometer. Weapons: 16 Hellfire missiles or 76 CRV-7 70 mm rockets. 1—30 mm chain gun.

APACHE AH MK 1   *3/2004*, *Royal Navy* / 1153998

Numbers/Type: 6 Westland Lynx AH Mk 7.
Operational speed: 140 kt *(259 km/h)*.
Service ceiling: 10,600 ft *(3,230 m)*.
Range: 340 n miles *(630 km)*.
Role/Weapon systems: Military general purpose and anti-tank with 847 Squadron. Sensors: Day/thermal imaging sight. Weapons: Up to eight Hughes TOW anti-tank missiles.

LYNX AH MK 7   *7/2005*, *Maritime Photographic* / 1153996

LAND-BASED MARITIME AIRCRAFT (FRONT LINE)

Notes: Training and Liaison aircraft not listed include four Jetstream, Falcon 20 (under contract) and 16 Hawk (FRADU).

FALCON 20   *6/2005*, *Paul Jackson* / 1153997

Numbers/Type: 16 Hawker Siddeley Nimrod MR 2/2P/4.
Operational speed: 500 kt *(926 km/h)*.
Service ceiling: 42,000 ft *(12,800 m)*.
Range: 5,000 n miles *(9,265 km)*.
Role/Weapon systems: ASW but with ASV, OTHT and control potential at long range from shore bases; duties include SAR, maritime surveillance. Contract in July 1996 to convert and upgrade 21 (reduced to 12 in 2004) aircraft to MRA.4 standard. First development aircraft flew in August 2004. To enter service in 2009. MRA 4 equipment includes Thales Searchwater 2000MR radar, Elta EL-8300 and ALR-56M ESM. Sensors: Thales Searchwater radar, ECM, Yellowgate ESM, cameras, CAE MAD, Ultra sonobuoys, Ultra/GDC AQS 971 acoustics suite, WESCAM EO system, cameras. Weapons: ASW; 6.1 tons of Stingray torpedoes or depth bombs or mines. ASV; four Harpoon missiles. Self-defence; four AIM-9L Sidewinder.

NIMROD MR 2   *6/2005*, *Michael Winter* / 1153949

NIMROD MRA 4   *8/2004, BAE Systems* / 0577851

Numbers/Type: 7 Boeing E-3D Sentry AEW Mk 1.
Operational speed: 460 kt *(853 km/h)*.
Service ceiling: 36,000 ft *(10,973 m)*.
Range: 870 n miles *(1,610 km)*.
Role/Weapon systems: Air defence early warning aircraft with secondary role to provide coastal AEW for the Fleet; 6 hours endurance at the range given above. Sensors: Westinghouse APY-2 surveillance radar, Bendix weather radar, Mk XII IFF, Yellow Gate, ESM, ECM. Weapons: Unarmed.

E-3D   *10/2001, Ships of the World* / 0131206

PATROL FORCES

1 ANTARCTIC PATROL SHIP (AGOBH)

Name	No	Builders	Commissioned
ENDURANCE (ex-*Polar Circle*)	A 171 (ex-A 176)	Ulstein Hatlo, Norway	21 Nov 1991

Displacement, tons: 6,500 full load
Dimensions, feet (metres): 298.6 × 57.4 × 27.9 *(91 × 17.9 × 8.5)*
Main machinery: 2 Bergen BRM8 diesels, 8,160 hp(m) *(6 MW)* sustained; 1 shaft; cp prop; bow and stern thrusters
Speed, knots: 15. **Range, n miles:** 6,500 at 12 kt
Complement: 112 (15 officers) plus 14 Royal Marines
Radars: Surface search: Raytheon R 84 and M 34 ARG; E/F- and I-bands
Navigation: Kelvin Hughes Type 1007; I-band.
IFF: Type 1011.
Helicopters: 2 Westland Lynx HAS.Mk 3.

Comment: Leased initially in late 1991 and then bought outright in early 1992 as support ship and guard vessel for the British Antarctic Survey. Hull is painted red. Inmarsat fitted. Main machinery is resiliently mounted. Ice-strengthened hull capable of breaking 1 m thick ice at 3 kt. Helicopter hangar is reached by lift from the flight deck. Accommodation is to high standards. Name and pennant number changed during refit in mid-1992. Sonars 2053, 2090 and 60–88. Based at Portsmouth.

ENDURANCE   6/2005*, Maritime Photographic / 1153985

1 CASTLE CLASS (OFFSHORE PATROL VESSEL MK 2) (PSOH)

Name	No	Builders	Launched	Commissioned
DUMBARTON CASTLE	P 265	Hall Russell, Aberdeen	3 June 1981	26 Mar 1982

Displacement, tons: 1,427 full load
Dimensions, feet (metres): 265.7 × 37.7 × 11.8 *(81 × 11.5 × 3.6)*
Main machinery: 2 Ruston 12RKC diesels; 5,640 hp *(4.21 MW)* sustained; 2 shafts; cp props
Speed, knots: 19.5
Range, n miles: 10,000 at 12 kt
Complement: 45 (6 officers) plus austerity accommodation for 25 Royal Marines
Guns: 1 DES/MSI DS 30B 30 mm/75; 650 rds/min to 10 km *(5.4 n miles)*; weight of shell 0.36 kg.
Mines: Can lay mines.
Countermeasures: Decoys: Outfit DLE; 2 or 4 Plessey Shield 102 mm 6-tubed launchers. ESM: 'Orange Crop'; intercept.
Combat data systems: Racal CANE DEA-3 action data automation; SATCOM.
Weapons control: Radamec 2000 series optronic director.
Radars: Surface search: Plessey Type 994; E/F-band.
Navigation: Kelvin Hughes Type 1006; I-band.
Helicopters: Platform for operating Sea King or Lynx.

Comment: Started as a private venture. Ordered 8 August 1980. Design includes an ability to lay mines. Inmarsat commercial terminals fitted. Two Avon Sea Rider high-speed craft are embarked. P 265 based in the Falklands. The 76 mm (never fitted) gunbay has been converted to an operations room. Fitted with two cranes to facilitate launch/recovery of RIBs, during refit which completed in mid-2004. To be decommissioned in October 2007.

DUMBARTON CASTLE   5/2004, Maritime Photographic / 1043616

2 FAST PATROL CRAFT (PBF)

SCIMITAR (ex-*Grey Fox*) P 284   SABRE (ex-*Grey Wolf*) P 285

Displacement, tons: 26 full load
Dimensions, feet (metres): 52.5 × 14.43 × 3.9 *(16 × 4.4 × 1.2)*
Main machinery: 2 MAN V10 diesels; 740 hp *(603 kW)*; 2 shafts
Speed, knots: 32
Range, n miles: 260 at 19 kt
Complement: 5
Guns: 2–7.62 mm MGs.
Radars: Racal Decca Bridgemaster 360; I-band.

Comment: Halmatic M160 craft operated in Northern Ireland from 1988 but transferred to Gibraltar in September 2002 to augment the Gibraltar squadron. Both vessels renamed and commissioned on 31 January 2003. After mid-life refit and design modifications, the vessels replaced *Trumpeter* and *Ranger* as Gibraltar guard ships in 2004.

SABRE   11/2003, W Sartori / 0573697

3 RIVER CLASS (OFFSHORE PATROL VESSELS) (PSO)

Name	No	Builders	Commissioned
TYNE	P 281	Vosper Thornycroft, Woolston	4 July 2003
SEVERN	P 282	Vosper Thornycroft, Woolston	31 July 2003
MERSEY	P 283	Vosper Thornycroft, Woolston	26 Mar 2004

Displacement, tons: 1,700 full load
Dimensions, feet (metres): 261.7 × 44.6 × 12.5 *(79.75 × 13.6 × 3.8)*
Main machinery: 2 MAN 12RK 270 diesels; 11,063 hp *(8.25 MW)*; 2 shafts; bow thruster; 375 hp *(280 kW)*
Speed, knots: 20. **Range, n miles:** 5,500 at 15 kt
Complement: 30 (plus 18 boarding party)
Guns: 1–20 mm Oerlikon/BMARC. 2–7.62 mm MGs.
Radars: Surface search: Kelvin Hughes Nucleus; E/F-band.
Navigation: Kelvin Hughes Nucleus; I-band.
Helicopters: Vertrep only.

Programmes: In the first agreement of its kind, Vosper Thornycroft contracted on 8 May 2001 for the construction, lease and support of three vessels over initial five-year period to replace five ships of Island class.
Structure: Based on Vosper Thornycroft EEZ Management Vessel concept design. The ships are capable of operating two RIBs. Fitted with a 3 tonne crane.
Operational: Part of Fishery Protection Squadron based at Portsmouth.

TYNE   6/2005*, Derek Fox / 1153942

0 + 1 MODIFIED RIVER CLASS (OFFSHORE PATROL VESSEL) (PSO)

Name	No	Builders	Commissioned
CLYDE	P 257	VT Shipbuilding, Portsmouth	Oct 2006

Displacement, tons: 1,865 full load
Dimensions, feet (metres): 267.4 × 44.6 × 12.5 *(81.5 × 13.6 × 3.8)*
Main machinery: 2 MAN 12RK diesels; 11,063 hp *(8.25 MW)*; 2 shafts; bow thruster; 375 hp *(280 kW)*; stern thruster; 248 hp *(185 kW)*
Speed, knots: 21. **Range, n miles:** 5,500 at 15 kt
Complement: 35 (plus 18 boarding party). Accommodation for 59
Guns: 1 DES/MSI DS 30B 30 mm; 650 rds/min to 10 km *(5.4 n miles)*; weight of shell 0.36 kg. 2 M323 Mk 44 7.62 mm Miniguns. 4–12.7 mm MGs.
Combat data systems: BAE Insyte CMS-1.
Radars: Surface search and navigation: Terma Scanter 4100; E/F/I-bands.
Helicopters: Platform for one Merlin-sized.

Comment: Contract let with VT Shipbuilding on the 28 February 2005 to build a modified River class to undertake Falkland Islands patrol duties from 2007. The ship is to be leased to the MoD with a Contractor Logistic Support (CLS) arrangement until 2012. The ship is to be built to commercial standards with some military features. The ship is to be operated and manned by the Fishery Protection Squadron based at Portsmouth. Launch is due in June 2006.

CLYDE (artist's impression)   12/2004*, VT Shipbuilding / 0585955

AMPHIBIOUS FORCES

Notes: Further amphibious ships and craft covered in RFA and Army sections. These include a Helicopter Support Ship, four LSD, two LSLs, and six LCLs.

2 ALBION CLASS (ASSAULT SHIPS) (LPD)

Name	No	Builders	Laid down	Launched	Commissioned
ALBION	L 14	BAE Systems, Barrow	22 May 1998	9 Mar 2001	19 June 2003
BULWARK	L 15	BAE Systems, Barrow	27 Jan 2000	15 Nov 2001	28 Apr 2005

Displacement, tons: 14,600 standard; 18,500 full load
Dimensions, feet (metres): 577.4 × 94.8 × 23.3
   (176 × 28.9 × 7.1)
Main machinery: Diesel-electric; 2 Wärtsilä Vasa 16V 32E diesel generators; 17,000 hp(m) *(12.5 MW)*; 2 Wärtsilä Vasa 4R 32LNE diesel generators; 4,216 hp(m) *(3.1 MW)*; 2 motors; 2 shafts; LIPS props; 1 bow thruster; 1,176 hp(m) *(865 kW)*
Speed, knots: 18
Range, n miles: 8,000 at 15 kt
Complement: 325
Military lift: 305 troops; 710 troops (including overload); 67 support vehicles; 4 LCU Mk 10 or 2 LCAC (dock); 4 LCVP Mk 5 (davits)

Guns: 2—20 mm ❶. 2 Signaal/General Dynamics 30 mm 7-barrelled Goalkeeper; 4,200 rds/min to 1.5 km ❷.
Countermeasures: Decoys: Outfit DLJ; 8 Sea Gnat launchers ❸ and DLH offboard decoys.
ESM/ECM: Racal Thorn UAT 1/4.
Combat data systems: ADAWS 2000. Thomson-CSF/Redifon/BAeSEMA/CS comms system. Marconi Matra SCOT 2D SATCOM ❹.
Radars: Air/surface search: Siemens Plessey Type 996 ❺; E/F-band.
Surface search: Racal Decca 1008; E/F-band.
Navigation/aircraft control: 2 Racal Marine Type 1007 ❻; I-band.
IFF: Type 1016/1017.

Helicopters: Platform for 3 Sea King Mk 4 ❼. Chinook capable.

Programmes: A decision was taken in mid-1991 to replace both existing LPDs. Project definition studies by YARD completed in February 1994. Invitations to tender for design and build of two ships were issued to VSEL and Yarrow on 18 August 1994 with an additional tender package to Vosper Thornycroft in November 1994. In March 1995 it was announced that only VSEL would bid,

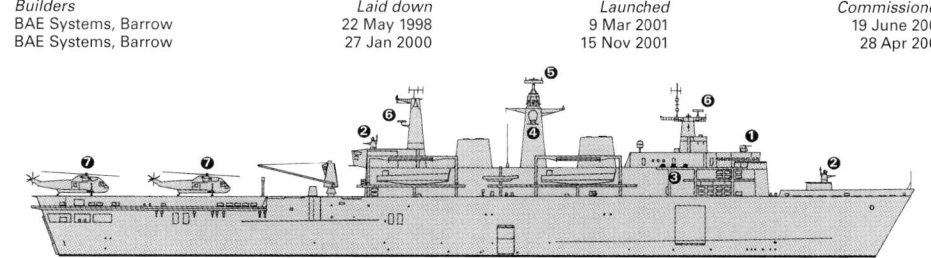

ALBION   *(Scale 1 : 1,500), Ian Sturton* / 0572733

BULWARK   *6/2005*, John Brodie* / 1153944

conforming to the rules governing non-competitive tenders. The contract to build the ships was awarded on 18 July 1996. First steel cut 17 November 1997.
Structure: The design includes a floodable well dock, garage (with capacity for six Challenger tanks), stern gate and side ramp access. The Flight Deck has two helicopter landing spots. A large joint operations room contains substantial command and control facilities. The ships are built to military damage control standards.
Operational: Based at Devonport.

ALBION   *6/2005*, Camil Busquets i Vilanova* / 1153991

ALBION   *6/2005*, John Brodie* / 1153945

1 HELICOPTER CARRIER (LPH)

Name	No	Builders	Laid down	Launched	Commissioned
OCEAN	L 12	Vickers Shipbuilding/Kvaerner Govan	30 May 1994	11 Oct 1995	30 Sep 1998

Displacement, tons: 21,758 full load
Dimensions, feet (metres): 667.3 oa; 652.2 pp × 112.9 × 21.3
(203.4; 198.8 × 34.4 × 6.6)
Flight deck, feet (metres): 557.7 × 104 (170 × 31.7)
Main machinery: 2 Crossley Pielstick 12 PC2.6 V 400 diesels;
18,360 hp(m) (13.5 MW) sustained; 2 shafts; Kamewa fp
props; bow thruster; 612 hp (450 kW)
Speed, knots: 19
Range, n miles: 8,000 at 15 kt
Complement: 285 plus 206 aircrew plus up to 830 Marines
Military lift: 4 LCVP Mk 5 (on davits); 2 Griffon hovercraft;
40 vehicles and equipment for most of a marine
commando unit

Guns: 8 BEMARC 20 mm GAM-B03 (4 twin) ❶. 650 rds/min
to 10 km (5.4 n miles) anti-surface; 3 km (1.6 n miles) anti-
aircraft; weight of shell 0.36 kg.
3 General Dynamics 20 mm Phalanx Mk 15 ❷. 6 barrels
per launcher; 4,500 rds/min combined to 1.5 km.
Countermeasures: Decoys: Outfit DLH; 8 Sea Gnat 130 mm/
102 mm launchers ❸.
ESM: Racal UAT; intercept.
Combat data systems: Ferranti ADAWS 2000 Mod 1; Link 11,
Link 16; Marconi Matra SCOT SATCOM 1D ❹.
Radars: Air/surface search: AMS Type 996 ❺; E/F-band.
Surface search: Racal Decca 1008 ❻; E/F-band.
Surface search/aircraft control: 2 Kelvin Hughes Type 1007
❼; I-band.
IFF: Type 1016/1017.

Helicopters: 12 Sea King HC.Mk 4/Merlin plus 6 Lynx
(or WAH-64 Apache by 2005).

Programmes: Initial invitations to tender were issued in
1987. Tenders submitted in July 1989 were allowed to
lapse and it was not until 11 May 1993 that a contract
was placed. The hull was built on the Clyde by Kvaerner
Govan and sailed under its own power to Vickers at
Barrow in November 1996 for the installation of military
equipment.
Modernisation: Command and control facilities upgraded
in 2002 to facilitate UKMCC role. Attack helicopter
infrastructure fitted 2004-05.
Structure: The hull form is based on the Invincible class
with a modified superstructure. The deck is strong
enough to take Chinook helicopters. Six landing and
six parking spots for the aircraft. Accommodation for
972 plus 303 bunk overload. A garage is situated at

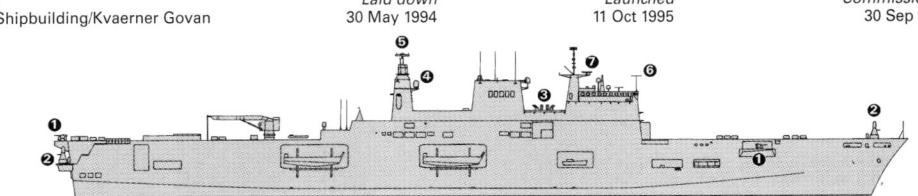

OCEAN   (Scale 1 : 1,800), Ian Sturton / 1043485

OCEAN   10/2005*, B Sullivan / 1153961

the after end of the hangar. This is accessible from the
after aircraft lift and via ramps through the ship's stern. Hull
'blisters' were fitted at waterline level port and starboard
during 2002 to improve deployment and recovery
of LCVPs.
Operational: The LPH provides a helicopter lift and assault
capability. The prime role of the vessel is embarking,

supporting and operating a squadron of helicopters and
carrying a Royal Marine Commando including vehicles,
arms and ammunition. Up to 20 Sea Harriers can be
carried but not supported. Operational sea trials started in
June 1998 and completed in February 1999. Twin 20 mm
guns are not always carried and may be replaced by
single 20 mm. Based at Devonport.

OCEAN   6/2005*, Michael Nitz / 1153993

OCEAN   6/2005*, Maritime Photographic / 1153992

10 LCU MK 10

L 1001-1010

Displacement, tons: 170 light; 240 full load
Dimensions, feet (metres): 97.8 × 24.3 × 5.6 *(29.8 × 7.4 × 1.7)*
Main machinery: 2 MAN diesels; 2 Schottel propulsors; bow thruster
Speed, knots: 10. **Range, n miles:** 600 at 12 kt
Complement: 7
Military lift: 1 MBT or 4 vehicles or 120 troops
Radars: Navigation: I-band.

Comment: Ordered in 1998 from Ailsa Troon Yard. First pair delivered in November 1999 and, following extensive trials, modifications made to ballast tanks to improve beach landing capabilities. This work carried out by BAE Systems Marine, Govan, from whom a further eight craft were ordered for delivery by mid-2003. Fitted with interlocking bow and stern ramps, they operate from the Albion class LPDs.

LCU MK 10   *6/2005*, E & M Laursen* / 1153946

3 LCU MK 9S

L 705   **L 709**   **L 711**

Displacement, tons: 115 light; 175 full load
Dimensions, feet (metres): 90.2 × 21.5 × 5 *(27.5 × 6.8 × 1.6)*
Main machinery: 2 Paxman or Dorman diesels; 474 hp *(354 kW)* sustained; Kort nozzles or Schottel propulsors
Speed, knots: 10. **Range, n miles:** 300 at 9 kt
Complement: 7
Military lift: 1 MBT or 60 tons of vehicles/stores or 90 troops
Radars: Navigation: Raytheon; I-band.

Comment: Last remaining craft of class of 14. Built in the mid-1960s and originally designated Mk 9M. Upgraded with Schottel propulsors in the 1990s and redesignated Mk 9S.

LCU Mk 9   *3/2003, A Sharma* / 0572671

4 GRIFFON 2000 TDX(M) (LCAC(L))

C 21-24

Displacement, tons: 6.8 full load
Dimensions, feet (metres): 36.1 × 15.1 *(11 × 4.6)*
Main machinery: 1 Deutz BF8L513 diesel; 320 hp *(239 kW)* sustained
Speed, knots: 33. **Range, n miles:** 300 at 25 kt
Complement: 2
Military lift: 16 troops plus equipment or 2 tons
Guns: 1 — 7.62 mm MG.
Radars: Navigation: Raytheon; I-band.

Comment: Ordered 26 April 1993. Design based on 2000 TDX(M) hovercraft. Aluminium hulls. Speed indicated is at Sea State 3 with a full load.

C 23   *6/2005*, Maritime Photographic* / 1153990

11 LCVP MK 4

8401	**8407**	**8411-8413**
8402	**8409**	**8619-8622**

Displacement, tons: 10.5 light; 16 full load
Dimensions, feet (metres): 43.8 × 10.9 × 2.8 *(13.4 × 3.3 × 0.8)*
Main machinery: 2 Perkins T6.3544 diesels; 290 hp *(216 kW)*; 2 shafts
Speed, knots: 15. **Range, n miles:** 150 at 14 kt
Complement: 3
Military lift: 20 Arctic equipped troops or 5.5 tons

Comment: Built by Souters and McTays. Introduced into service in 1986. Fitted with removable arctic canopies across well-deck. Some Royal Marines' craft replaced by LCVP Mk 5. Six craft operated by Royal Logistics Corps. These serve in rotation between the Falklands and UK.

LCVP MK 4   *6/2005*, Maritime Photographic* / 1153989

23 LCVP MK 5

LCVP 9473	**9673-9692**	**9707**	**9708**

Displacement, tons: 25 full load
Dimensions, feet (metres): 50.9 × 13.8 × 3 *(15.5 × 4.2 × 0.9)*
Main machinery: 2 Volvo Penta TAMD 72 WJ diesels; 2 PP 170 water-jets
Speed, knots: 25. **Range, n miles:** 210 at 18 kt
Complement: 3
Military lift: 35 troops plus 2 tons equipment or 8 tons vehicles and stores
Radars: Navigation: Raytheon 40; I-band.

Comment: Contract placed with Vosper Thornycroft on 31 January 1995 for one craft which was handed over on 17 January 1996. Four more ordered on 23 October 1996 for *Ocean* were delivered 6 December 1997; and two more for RM Poole in October 1998. Sixteen more ordered from FBM Babcock Marine in August 2001. Can beach fully laden on a 1 : 120 gradient. Speed 18 kt at full load.

LCVP MK 5   *6/2005*, Maritime Photographic* / 1153988

FAST INTERCEPT CRAFT (HSIC)

Comment: Two main types in service. Both around 15 m in length and powered by two or three 660 hp diesels to give speeds up to 55 kt. One has a VSV wave piercing hull which can maintain fast speeds in high sea states. Both types can be transported by air.

VSV   *10/2003, Derek Fox* / 0572670

RRC and RIB

Comment: (1) 36 RRC Mk 3: 2.6 tons and 7.4 m *(24.2 ft)* powered by single Yamaha 220 hp *(162 kW)* diesel; 36 kt fully laden (40 light); carry 8 troops. Some used by the Army. In service 1996-98.
(2) RIBs: Halmatic Arctic 22/Pacific 22/Arctic 28/Pacific 28. Rolling contract for all four types. Capable of carrying 10 to 15 fully laden troops at speeds of 26 to 35 kt.

For details of the latest updates to *Jane's Fighting Ships* online and to discover the additional information available exclusively to online subscribers please visit
jfs.janes.com

1/2006*, Derek Fox / 1153948

MINE WARFARE FORCES

Notes: (1) The long-term future of the mine-countermeasures (MCM) force is under consideration. The future capability is likely to be based on the requirement to conduct MCM in support of joint expeditionary operations in littoral waters. Speed of deployment is an important consideration. Future capability is likely to be delivered by a combination of:

(a) a portable, modular, self-contained system that could be delivered rapidly into theatre

(b) an organic mine reconnaissance capability, deployed from future classes of surface combatants

(c) a dedicated capability involving unmanned underwater vehicles deployed from auxiliary surface craft.

(2) Replacement of the Combined Influence Sweep (CIS), removed from the Hunt class (and placed at 30 days notice) in 2005, is under consideration. Plans to replace CIS with a new Remote Influence Minesweeping System (RIMS) were cancelled in 2002. The Shallow Water Influence Minesweeping System (SWIMS), brought into service during operations in Iraq during 2003, has not been maintained. Future options under examination include an influence sweep system deployable from an Unmanned Surface Vehicle (USV). A collaborative venture with the US Navy is also being explored.

(3) The Remote Control Mine Disposal Systems Mk 1 (PAP Mk 3) and 2 (PAP Mk 5) are to be replaced by the Atlas Electronik Seafox C expendable mine destructor. Stowage for 24 warshots and four surveillance vehicles is to be provided on each MCM platform.

(4) Mine reconnaissance in very shallow waters (less than 30 m) is to be met by the Hydroid Remus Unmanned Underwater Vehicle (UUV). GPS-enabled, it is equipped with a high-frequency side-scan sonar. Eight systems are to enter service by mid-2006.

(5) The capability to conduct Rapid Environmental Assessment (REA) using a UUV in water depths up to 200 m is under investigation. This may be filled by commercially available vehicles. Introduction into service is planned for 2008-09.

8 HUNT CLASS
(MINESWEEPERS/MINEHUNTERS—COASTAL) (MHSC/PP)

Name	No	Builders	Launched	Commissioned
LEDBURY	M 30	Vosper Thornycroft, Woolston	5 Dec 1979	11 June 1981
CATTISTOCK	M 31	Vosper Thornycroft, Woolston	22 Jan 1981	16 June 1982
BROCKLESBY	M 33	Vosper Thornycroft, Woolston	12 Jan 1982	3 Feb 1983
MIDDLETON	M 34	Yarrow Shipbuilders, Glasgow	27 Apr 1983	15 Aug 1984
CHIDDINGFOLD	M 37	Vosper Thornycroft, Woolston	6 Oct 1983	10 Aug 1984
ATHERSTONE	M 38	Vosper Thornycroft, Woolston	1 Mar 1986	30 Jan 1987
HURWORTH	M 39	Vosper Thornycroft, Woolston	25 Sep 1984	2 July 1985
QUORN	M 41	Vosper Thornycroft, Woolston	23 Jan 1988	21 Apr 1989

Displacement, tons: 615 light; 750 full load

Dimensions, feet (metres): 187 wl; 197 oa × 32.8 × 9.5 (keel); 11.2 (screws) *(57; 60 × 10 × 2.9; 3.4)*

Main machinery: 2 Ruston-Paxman 9-59K Deltic diesels; 1,900 hp *(1.42 MW)*; 1 Deltic Type 9-55B diesel for pulse generator and auxiliary drive; 780 hp *(582 kW)*; 2 shafts; bow thruster

Speed, knots: 15 diesels; 8 hydraulic drive. **Range, n miles:** 1,500 at 12 kt

Complement: 45 (5 officers)

Guns: 1 DES/MSI DS 30B 30 mm/75; 650 rds/min to 10 km *(5.4 n miles)* anti-surface; 3 km *(1.6 n miles)* anti-aircraft; weight of shell 0.36 kg.

2 Oerlikon/BMARC 20 mm GAM-CO1 (enhancement); 900 rds/min to 2 km.

Dillon Aero M 134 7.62 mm Minigun; 6 barrels; 3,000 rds/min.

Countermeasures: MCM: 2 PAP 104 Mk 3/105 (RCMDS 1) remotely controlled submersibles, (to be replaced by Seafox C expendable mine-disposal system).

Combat data systems: BAE Insyte Nautis 3.

Radars: Navigation: Kelvin Hughes Type 1007; I-band.

Sonars: Thales 2193; hull-mounted; minehunting; 100/300 kHz.

Hull-mounted; active; high frequency.

Type 2059 to track PAP 104/105.

Programmes: A class of MCM Vessels combining both hunting and sweeping (at 30 days notice) capabilities.

Modernisation: RCMDS is being replaced by Seafox C. 30 mm gun has replaced the Bofors 40 mm. Drumgrange Precise Fixing System fitted 2003-04. A new minehunting sonar (Sonar 2193) and NAUTIS III command system have been fitted in all eight ships 2004-05. M 134 Minigun CIWS fitted in 2005. The influence sweeping system has been removed and is at 30 days notice.

Structure: GRP hull. Combines conventional propellers with bow thrusters. Fitted with an improved two-man decompression chamber by 2004/05.

Operational: For operational deployments fitted with enhanced weapons systems. *Brecon*, *Cottesmore* and *Dulverton* were decommissioned in 2005. All eight ships to be based at Portsmouth from mid-2006.

Sales: *Bicester* and *Berkeley* to Greece in July 2000 and February 2001 respectively.

ATHERSTONE *6/2005*, Maritime Photographic* / 1153995

LEDBURY *6/2005*, Frank Findler* / 1153947

8 SANDOWN CLASS (MINEHUNTERS) (MHC/SRMH)

Name	No	Builders	Launched	Commissioned
WALNEY	M 104	Vosper Thornycroft, Woolston	25 Nov 1991	20 Feb 1993
PENZANCE	M 106	Vosper Thornycroft, Woolston	11 Mar 1997	14 May 1998
PEMBROKE	M 107	Vosper Thornycroft, Woolston	15 Dec 1997	6 Oct 1998
GRIMSBY	M 108	Vosper Thornycroft, Woolston	10 Aug 1998	25 Sep 1999
BANGOR	M 109	Vosper Thornycroft, Woolston	16 Apr 1999	26 July 2000
RAMSEY	M 110	Vosper Thornycroft, Woolston	25 Nov 1999	22 June 2001
BLYTH	M 111	Vosper Thornycroft, Woolston	4 July 2000	20 July 2001
SHOREHAM	M 112	Vosper Thornycroft, Woolston	9 Apr 2001	2 Sep 2002

Displacement, tons: 450 standard; 484 full load

Dimensions, feet (metres): 172.2 × 34.4 × 7.5 *(52.5 × 10.5 × 2.3)*

Main machinery: 2 Paxman Valenta 6RP200E/M diesels; 1,523 hp *(1.14 MW)* sustained; Voith-Schneider propulsion; 2 Schottel bow thrusters

Speed, knots: 13 diesels; 6.5 electric drive

Range, n miles: 2,500 at 12 kt

Complement: 34 (5 officers) plus 6 spare berths

Guns: 1 DES/MSI DS 30B 30 mm/75; 650 rds/min to 10 km *(5.4 n miles)* anti-surface; 3 km *(1.6 n miles)* anti-aircraft; weight of shell 0.36 kg.

Dillon Aero M 134 7.62 mm Minigun; 6 barrels; 3,000 rds/min.

Countermeasures: MCM: ECA mine disposal system, 2 PAP 104 Mk 5 (RCMDS 2). These craft can carry 2 mine wire cutters, a charge of 100 kg and a manipulator with TV/projector. Control cables are 2,000 m. To be replaced by Seafox C expendable mine-disposal system.

Combat data systems: BAE Insyte Nautis 3.

Radars: Navigation: Kelvin Hughes Type 1007; I-band.

Sonars: Marconi Type 2093; VDS; VLF-VHF multifunction with 5 arrays; mine search and classification.

Programmes: A class designed for hunting and destroying mines and for operating in deep and exposed waters. Single role minehunter (SRMH) complements the Hunt class. On 9 January 1984 the Vosper Thornycroft design for this class was approved. First one ordered August 1985, four more on 23 July 1987. A contract was to have been placed for a second batch in 1990 but this was deferred twice, until an order for seven more (M 106-112) was placed in July 1994.

Modernisation: RCMDS 2 to be replaced with Seafox C. Drumgrange Precise Fixing System fitted in 2004. Nautis M combat system replaced by Nautis 3. M 134 Minigun CIWS fitted in 2005.

Structure: GRP hull. Combines vectored thrust units with bow thrusters and Remote-Control Mine Disposal System (RCMDS). The sonar is deployed from a well in the hull. Batch 2 have larger diameter (1.8 m) Voith-Schneider props and an improved two-man decompression chamber.

Operational: All based at Faslane from mid-2006.

Sales: Three to Saudi Arabia. *Bridport*, *Sandown* and *Inverness* to Estonia 2007-08.

RAMSEY *7/2005*, H M Steele* / 1153960

SHOREHAM *6/2005*, Maritime Photographic* / 1153994

SURVEY SHIPS

Notes: In addition to the ships listed below, further survey work is undertaken by Naval Party 1016 embarked in a chartered vessel, *MV Confidante*. Naval Party 1008 was disbanded in December 2003.

1 SCOTT CLASS (AGSH)

Name	No	Builders	Launched	Commissioned
SCOTT	H 131	Appledore Shipbuilders, Bideford	13 Oct 1996	30 June 1997

Displacement, tons: 13,500 full load
Dimensions, feet (metres): 430.1 × 70.5 × 29.5 *(131.1 × 21.5 × 9)*
Main machinery: 2 Krupp MaK 9M32 9-cyl diesels; 10,800 hp(m) *(7.94 MW)*; 1 shaft; LIPS cp prop; retractable bow thruster
Speed, knots: 17.5
Complement: 62 (12 officers) (see *Comment*)
Radars: Navigation: Kelvin Hughes ARPA 1626; I-band.
Helicopters: Platform for 1 light.

Comment: Designed by BAeSEMA/YARD and ordered 20 January 1995 to replace *Hecla*. Ice-strengthened bow. Foredeck strengthened for helicopter operations. The centre of the OSV surveying operations consists of an integrated navigation suite, the Sonar Array Sounding System (SASS) and data processing equipment. Additional sensors include gravimeters, a towed proton magnetometer and the Sonar 2090 ocean environment sensor. The SASS IV multibeam depth-sounder is capable of gathering 121 individual depth samples concurrently over a 120° swathe, producing a three-dimensional image of the seabed. 8,000 tons of seawater ballast can be used to achieve a sonar trim. The ship is at sea for 300 days a year with a crew of 42 embarked, rotating with the other 20 ashore. Can be used as an MCMV support ship. *Scott* undertook a survey of the Indian Ocean tsunami epicentre in early 2005. Based at Devonport.

SCOTT *6/2005*, Michael Winter* / 1153941

2 ECHO CLASS (AGSH)

Name	No	Builders	Launched	Commissioned
ECHO	H 87	Appledore, Bideford	4 Mar 2002	7 Mar 2003
ENTERPRISE	H 88	Appledore, Bideford	2 May 2002	17 Oct 2003

Displacement, tons: 3,470 full load
Dimensions, feet (metres): 295.3 × 55.1 × 18 *(90 × 16.8 × 5.5)*
Main machinery: Diesel electric; 4.8 MW; 2 azimuth thrusters; 1 bow thruster
Speed, knots: 15
Range, n miles: 9,000 at 12 kt
Complement: 49 with accommodation for 81
Guns: 2—20 mm. 4—7.62 mm MGs.
Radars: Navigation: 2 sets; I-band.
Helicopters: Platform for 1 medium.

Comment: The order for two multirole Hydrographic and Oceanographic Survey Vessels was placed with the prime contractor, Vosper Thornycroft Ltd, on 19 June 2000. The ships were built by Appledore Shipbuilders in Devon. The contract covers the design, build and through-life support of the ships over their 25 year service. In addition to specialist surveying tasks, the ships' operational roles include Rapid Environmental Assessment, Amphibious Warfare surveys and Mine Countermeasures Tasking Support. The survey suite consists of hull mounted multibeam sonar, towed side scan sonar, towed undulating sensors, an adaptive survey planning system and a Survey Motor Launch. Both based at Devonport.

ENTERPRISE *6/2005*, Maritime Photographic* / 1153983

1 ROEBUCK CLASS (AGS)

Name	No	Builders	Launched	Commissioned
ROEBUCK	H 130	Brooke Marine, Lowestoft	14 Nov 1985	3 Oct 1986

Displacement, tons: 1,477 full load
Dimensions, feet (metres): 210 × 42.6 × 13 *(63.9 × 13 × 4)*
Main machinery: 4 Mirrlees Blackstone ESL8 Mk 1 diesels; 3,040 hp *(2.27 MW)*; 2 shafts; cp props
Speed, knots: 14
Range, n miles: 4,000 at 10 kt
Complement: 46 (6 officers)
Guns: 1—20 mm.
Radars: Navigation: Kelvin Hughes Nucleus 2—6000; I-band.

Comment: Designed for hydrographic surveys to full modern standards on UK continental shelf. Air conditioned. Carries a 9 m surveying motor boat and one 4.5 m RIB. The decision to decommission in 2003 was cancelled and a Ship Life Extension Programme started in September 2004 and was completed in mid-2005. The upgrade included refurbishment and renewal of engineering systems and habitability improvements. A 20 mm gun system has been installed. Roles include Rapid Environmental Assessment and Amphibious Warfare survey. The new survey suite consists of a hull-mounted multibeam sonar, towed side-scan sonar and adaptive planning system.

ROEBUCK *6/2005*, Maritime Photographic* / 1153982

1 GLEANER CLASS (YGS)

Name	No	Builders	Launched	Commissioned
GLEANER	H 86	Emsworth Shipyard	18 Oct 1983	5 Dec 1983

Displacement, tons: 26 full load
Dimensions, feet (metres): 48.6 × 15.4 × 5.2 *(14.8 × 4.7 × 1.6)*
Main machinery: 2 Volvo Penta TMD 112; 524 hp(m) *(391 kW)*; 2 shafts
Speed, knots: 14 diesels; 7 centre shaft only
Complement: 5 plus 1 spare bunk
Radars: Navigation: Raytheon R40SX; I-band.

Comment: This craft is prefixed HMSML-HM Survey Motor Launch. Sonar 2094 and Kongsberg Simrad dual head multibeam echo sounder.

GLEANER *6/2005*, Camil Busquets i Vilanova* / 1153981

4 NESBITT CLASS (YGS)

NESBITT 9423   **PAT BARTON** 9424   **COOK** 9425   **OWEN** 9426

Displacement, tons: 11 full load
Dimensions, feet (metres): 34.8 × 9.4 × 3.3 *(10.6 × 2.9 × 1)*
Main machinery: 2 Perkins Sabre 185C diesels; 430 hp(m) *(316 kW)* sustained; 2 shafts
Speed, knots: 15
Range, n miles: 300 at 8 kt
Complement: 2 plus 10 spare

Comment: Delivered by Halmatic, Southampton by September 1996. Fitted with GPS, Ultra 3000 Side scan sonar and Qubit SIPS. In service at the Hydrographic School and can be carried in Echo class survey vessels.

NESBITT *11/1998, John Brodie* / 0053244

RESCUE VEHICLES

0 + 1 NATO SUBMARINE RESCUE SYSTEM (DSRV)

Displacement, tons: 28 full load
Dimensions, feet (metres): 28.5 × 11.1 × 11.5 *(8.7 × 3.4 × 3.5)*
Main machinery: 2 external ZEBRA rechargeable sodium nickel chloride battery pods
Speed, knots: 3.8
Complement: 3

Comment: Project definition of a NATO Submarine Rescue System (NSRS) was completed by W S Atkins Ltd in late 2001. The three partner nations are UK, Norway and France with the UK Defence Procurement Agency acting as contracting authority and host nation for project management. Following Invitations to Tender, award of the contract for the Design and Manufacture Phase was made in June 2004 to a team led by Rolls-Royce Naval Marine. The core of the service is to be a new free-swimming Submarine Rescue Vehicle (SRV), the Perry Slingsby SR1, which will be capable of accommodating up to 15 rescued submariners from a submarine at an angle of up to 60°. Capable of reaching depths down to 600 m, the SRV will be launched and recovered from suitable commercial or military 'motherships' equipped with a portable launch-and-recovery installation. It has an endurance of 12 hours. In addition, the contract provides for an unmanned Intervention Remotely-Operated Vehicle (IROV), the Perry Slingsby Super Spartan, which will be used to locate the stricken submarine to a depth of 1,000 m. Other facilities include decompression chambers; medical facilities and support equipment. Achievement of an Initial Operating Capability is planned for December 2006 with a full operational capability following in the second quarter of 2007. The system is expected to remain in service for 25 years. It will be permanently maintained at HM Naval Base Clyde at 12 hours notice to meed a Time to First Rescue of no more than 72 hours worldwide. NSRS will complement other submarine rescue systems operated by Australia, Italy, Sweden and US.

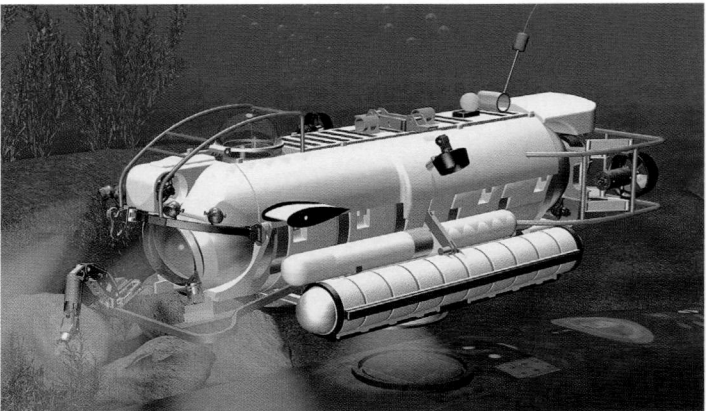

SR1   *6/2004, Rolls-Royce* / 0566635

1 RESCUE SUBMERSIBLE (DSRV)

LR 5

Displacement, tons: 21.5
Dimensions, feet (metres): 30.2 × 9.8 × 11.5 *(9.2 × 3.0 × 3.5)*
Main machinery: 2 electric motors; 16 hp *(12 kW)*; 2 hydraulic transverse thrusters; 9 hp *(6.7 kW)*; 2 hydraulic tiltable side thrusters; 9 hp *(6.7 kW)*
Speed, knots: 2.5 dived
Complement: 2 pilots and 1 rescue chamber operator

Comment: LR 5 is the Rescue submersible that is part of the UK Submarine Rescue System (UKSRS). Manufactured in 1978 by Slingsby Ltd for North Sea commercial operations and subsequently purchased by the Royal Navy for whom it is managed, maintained (at 12 hours notice) and operated by James Fisher Rumic Ltd. Capable of operating down to 400 m depth, it can be deployed anywhere in the world and operated from the deck of any suitable mother ship. Its role is to rescue up to 16 survivors at a time from a disabled submarine on the seabed and bring them back to the surface. This can be done at normal atmospheric pressure and at increased pressure up to 5 bar. Mating with the disabled submarine can be achieved at up to 10° heel on LR 5 or at up to 60° bow up. LR 5 is complemented by an ROV, Scorpio 45, which is attached to a 1,000 m umbilical. This is used to locate the disabled submarine, clear obstructions from the escape hatches and replenish life support stores. LR 5 was refitted in 2005 and is due to be replaced by the NATO Submarine Rescue System (NSRS) in mid-2007.

LR 5   *6/2004, Royal Navy* / 1043614

TRAINING SHIPS

16 ARCHER CLASS (TRAINING and PATROL CRAFT) (PB/AXL)

EXPRESS P 163 (ex-A 163)	**ARCHER** P 264	**PURSUER** P 273	**BLAZER** P 279	**CHARGER** P 292
EXPLORER P 164 (ex-A 154)	**BITER** P 270	**TRACKER** P 274	**DASHER** P 280	**RANGER** P 293
EXAMPLE P 165 (ex-A 153)	**SMITER** P 272	**RAIDER** P 275	**PUNCHER** P 291	**TRUMPETER** P 294
EXPLOIT P 167 (ex-A 167)				

Displacement, tons: 54 full load
Dimensions, feet (metres): 68.2 × 19 × 5.9 *(20.8 × 5.8 × 1.8)*
Main machinery: 2 RR CV 12 M800T diesels; 1,590 hp *(1.19 MW)*; or 2 MTU diesels; 2,000 hp(m) *(1.47 MW)* (P 274-275); 2 shafts
Speed, knots: 22 or 25 (P 274-275)
Range, n miles: 550 at 15 kt
Complement: 11 (3 officers)
Guns: 1 Oerlikon 20 mm (can be fitted). 2 – 7.62 mm MGs (P 293, P 294).
Radars: Navigation: Racal Decca 1216; I-band.

Comment: First 14 ordered from Watercraft Ltd, Shoreham. Commissioning dates: *Archer*, August 1985; *Example*, September 1985; *Explorer*, January 1986; *Biter* and *Smiter*, February 1986. The remaining nine were incomplete when Watercraft went into liquidation in 1986 and were towed to Portsmouth for completion in 1988 by Vosper Thornycroft. Initially allocated for RNR training but underused in that role and now employed as University Naval Units (URNU)– *Ranger* (Sussex), *Trumpeter* (Bristol), *Puncher* (London), *Blazer* (Southampton), *Smiter* (Glasgow), *Charger* (Liverpool), *Archer* (Aberdeen), *Biter* (Manchester and Salford), *Exploit* (Birmingham), *Express* (Wales), *Example* (Northumbria) and *Explorer* (Hull). The four ex-RNXS ships (P 163-P 167) are also part of the Inshore Training Squadron and are based at Gosport, Ipswich and Penarth. *Dasher* and *Pursuer* are based at Cyprus. Similar craft built for the Indian and Omani Coast Guards. Two more ordered from BMT in early 1997 to a modified design and built at Ailsa, Troon. *Tracker* and *Raider* commissioned January 1998 for Oxford and Cambridge University respectively.

BLAZER   *6/2005*, *John Mortimer* / 1153984

RANGER
3/2005, *Derek Fox*
1153940

ROYAL FLEET AUXILIARY SERVICE

Personnel

1 January 2006: 2,274 (891 officers)

General

The Royal Fleet Auxiliary Service is a civilian-manned fleet under the command of the Commander in Chief Fleet from 1 April 1993. Its main task is to supply warships at sea with fuel, food, stores and ammunition. It also provides aviation platforms, amphibious support for the Navy and Marines and sea transport for Army units. All ships take part in operational sea training. An order in council on 30 November 1989 changed the status of the RFA service to government-owned vessels on non-commercial service.

Ships taken up from Trade

The following ships taken up from trade: *Confidante* operates in home waters under the Hydrographer. *Seabulk*

Condor (supply), *St Brandan* (ferry), *Indomitable* (tug), all operate in the Falkland Islands.

New Construction

(1) The Joint Casualty Treatment Ship (JCTS), formerly known as the Joint Casualty Receiving Ship (JCRS) is due to enter service after 2010. The requirement for such a ship was identified in the 1998 Strategic Defence Review. The aviation support ship *Argus* was configured as a PCRS during the 1990-91 Gulf War and the 2003 Iraq War. The contract for the Assessment Phase was awarded to BMT Ltd in February 2002 since when the key drivers have been identified as a need for eight operating tables and a 150-200 bed hospital. A two-spot flight deck and the ability to embark personnel by sea or land are also needed. Development of the Systems Requirement Document (SRD) by Atkins Aviation and Defence Systems

has been completed and following the down-selection of two consortia in 2006, it is planned to select a single consortium in mid-2008 for demonstration and manufacture. Potential solutions range from a bespoke vessel to conversion/modification of an existing military or merchant hull. The ship will be manned by RFA personnel. The requirement for a second ship at 12 months notice is to be met by chartering a commercial hull.

(2) The future afloat support capability is being taken forward through the Military Afloat Reach and Sustainability programme (MARS). The Concept Phase formally ended at Initial Gate in mid-2005 when the Assessment phase began. Three potential integrators (Amec, KBR and Raytheon) selected on 14 February 2006 to take part in this phase. From these a single integrator will be selected when the Demonstration and Manufacture phase starts in 2008. A total of 11 ships are to be acquired; five fleet tankers (2011-15); three joint sea-based logistic vessels (2016-20); two fleet support ships (2017-20) and a fleet tanker (carrier strike) (2021).

2 WAVE CLASS (LARGE FLEET TANKERS) (AORH)

Name	No	Builders	Laid down	Launched	Commissioned
WAVE KNIGHT	A 389	BAE Systems, Barrow	22 Oct 1998	29 Sep 2000	8 Apr 2003
WAVE RULER	A 390	BAE Systems, Govan	10 Feb 2000	9 Feb 2001	27 Apr 2003

Displacement, tons: 31,500 full load
Measurement, tons: 18,200 dwt
Dimensions, feet (metres): 643.2 × 91.2 × 32.8 *(196.0 × 27.8 × 10.0)*
Main machinery: Diesel-electric: 4 Wärtsilä 12V 32E/GECLM diesel generators; 25,514 hp(m) *(18.76 MW)*; 2 GECLM motors; 19,040 hp(m) *(14 MW)*; 1 shaft; Kamewa bow and stern thrusters
Speed, knots: 18. **Range, n miles:** 10,000 at 15 kt

Complement: 80 plus 22 aircrew
Cargo capacity: 16,000 m³ total liquids including 3,000 m³ aviation fuel; 8-20 ft refrigerated containers plus 500 m³ solids
Guns: 2 Vulcan Phalanx CIWS; fitted for but not with. 2—30 mm. 4—7.62 mm MGs.
Countermeasures: Decoys: Outfit DLJ.
Radars: Navigation: KH 1007; E/F/I-band. IFF: Type 1017.

Helicopters: 1 Merlin HM.Mk 1.

Comment: Feasibility studies by BAeSEMA/YARD completed in early 1995. Draft invitation to tender issued 10 October 1995 followed by full tender on 26 June 1996. Contracts to build placed with VSEL (BAE Systems) on 12 March 1997. One spot flight deck with full hangar facilities for one Merlin. Enclosed bridge including bridge wings. Double hull construction. Inclined RAS gear with three rigs and two cranes.

WAVE RULER
6/2005*, Maritime Photographic / 1153980

1 OAKLEAF CLASS (SUPPORT TANKER) (AOR)

Name	No	Builders	Commissioned	Recommissioned
OAKLEAF (ex-*Oktania*)	A 111	Uddevalla, Sweden	1981	14 Aug 1986

Displacement, tons: 49,648 full load
Measurement, tons: 37,328 dwt
Dimensions, feet (metres): 570 × 105.6 × 36.7 *(173.7 × 32.2 × 11.2)*
Main machinery: 1 Burmeister & Wain 4L80MCE diesel; 10,800 hp(m) *(7.96 MW)* sustained; 1 shaft; cp prop; bow and stern thrusters
Speed, knots: 14

Complement: 35 (14 officers)
Cargo capacity: 22,000 m³ fuel

Guns: 2—7.62 mm MGs.
Countermeasures: Decoys: 2 Plessey Shield chaff launchers can be fitted.
Radars: Navigation: Racal Decca 1226 and 1229; I-band.

Comment: Acquired in July 1985 and converted by Falmouth Ship Repairers to include full RAS rig and extra accommodation. Handed over on completion and renamed. Single hulled, ice strengthened. Marisat fitted. Major refit in 1994-95. Purchased by MoD in 2004 and to continue in service until 2010.

OAKLEAF
8/2004, B Prézelin / 1043587

3 APPLELEAF CLASS (SUPPORT TANKERS) (AOR)

Name	No	Builders	Launched	Commissioned
BRAMBLELEAF (ex-*Hudson Deep*)	A 81	Cammell Laird, Birkenhead	22 Jan 1976	3 Mar 1980
BAYLEAF	A 109	Cammell Laird, Birkenhead	27 Oct 1981	26 Mar 1982
ORANGELEAF (ex-*Balder London*, ex-*Hudson Progress*)	A 110	Cammell Laird, Birkenhead	—	2 May 1984

Displacement, tons: 37,747 full load (A 109—110); 40,870 (A 81)
Measurement, tons: 20,761 gross; 11,573 net; 29,999 dwt
Dimensions, feet (metres): 560 × 85 × 36.1
 (170.7 × 25.9 × 11)
Main machinery: 2 Pielstick 14 PC2.2 V 400 diesels; 14,000 hp(m) *(10.29 MW)* sustained; 1 shaft
Speed, knots: 15.5; 16.3 (A 109)
Complement: 56 (19 officers)
Cargo capacity: 22,000 m³ dieso; 3,800 m³ Avcat

Guns: 2 Oerlikon 20 mm. 4—7.62 mm MGs.
Countermeasures: Decoys: 2 Corvus or 2 Plessey Shield launchers.
Radars: Navigation: Racal Decca 1226 and 1229; I-band.

Comment: *Brambleleaf* chartered in 1979-80 and converted, completing Autumn 1979. Part of a four-ship order cancelled by Hudson Fuel and Shipping Co, but completed by the shipbuilders, being the only mercantile order then in hand. *Bayleaf* built under

BRAMBLELEAF

4/2004, Marian Ferrette / 1043586

commercial contract to be chartered by MoD and expected to be purchased in 2006. *Orangeleaf* major refit September 1985 to fit full RAS capability and extra accommodation. Single-hull construction. *Appleleaf* sold to Australia in September 1989. Decommissioning dates: *Brambleleaf* 2011; *Bayleaf* 2014 and *Orangeleaf* 2015.

2 ROVER CLASS (SMALL FLEET TANKERS) (AORLH)

Name	No	Builders	Launched	Commissioned
GOLD ROVER	A 271	Swan Hunter Shipbuilders, Wallsend-on-Tyne	7 Mar 1973	22 Mar 1974
BLACK ROVER	A 273	Swan Hunter Shipbuilders, Wallsend-on-Tyne	30 Oct 1973	23 Aug 1974

Displacement, tons: 4,700 light; 11,522 full load
Measurement, tons: 6,692 (A 271, 273), 6,822 (A 269) dwt; 7,510 gross; 3,185 net
Dimensions, feet (metres): 461 × 63 × 24
 (140.6 × 19.2 × 7.3)
Main machinery: 2 SEMT-Pielstick 16 PA4 185 diesels; 15,360 hp(m) *(11.46 MW)*; 1 shaft; Kamewa cp prop; bow thruster
Speed, knots: 19. **Range, n miles:** 15,000 at 15 kt
Complement: 48 (17 officers) (A 269); 55 (18 officers) (A 271, 273)
Cargo capacity: 3,000 m³ fuel

Guns: 2 Oerlikon 20 mm. 2—7.62 mm MGs.
Countermeasures: Decoys: 2 Corvus and 2 Plessey Shield launchers. 1 Graseby Type 182; towed torpedo decoy.
Radars: Navigation: Racal Decca 52690 ARPA; Racal Decca 1690; I-band.

Helicopters: Platform for Westland Sea King HAS. Mk 5 or HC.Mk 4.

Comment: Single-hull construction. Small fleet tankers designed to replenish HM ships at sea with fuel, fresh water, limited dry cargo and refrigerated stores under all

BLACK ROVER

12/2005, R G Sharpe* / 1153939

conditions while under way. No hangar but helicopter landing platform is served by a stores lift, to enable stores to be transferred at sea by 'vertical lift'. Capable of HIFR. Siting of SATCOM aerial varies. *Green Rover* sold in September 1992 to Indonesia. *Blue Rover* to Portugal in March 1993. *Grey Rover* decommissioned in 2006. The remaining two are expected to be decommissioned by 2013.

2 FORT VICTORIA CLASS (FLEET REPLENISHMENT SHIPS) (AORH)

Name	No	Builders	Laid down	Launched	Commissioned
FORT VICTORIA	A 387	Harland & Wolff/Cammell Laird	4 Apr 1988	12 June 1990	24 June 1994
FORT GEORGE	A 388	Swan Hunter Shipbuilders, Wallsend-on-Tyne	9 Mar 1989	1 Mar 1991	16 July 1993

Displacement, tons: 36,580 full load
Dimensions, feet (metres): 667.7 oa; 607 wl × 99.7 × 32
 (203.5; 185 × 30.4 × 9.8)
Main machinery: 2 Crossley SEMT-Pielstick 16 PC2.6 V 400 diesels; 23,904 hp(m) *(17.57 MW)* sustained; 2 shafts
Speed, knots: 20
Complement: 134 (95 RFA plus 15 RN plus 24 civilian stores staff) plus 154 (28 officers) aircrew
Cargo capacity: 12,505 m³ liquids; 3,000 m³ solids

Guns: 2 DES/MSI DS 30B 30 mm/75.
 2 Vulcan Phalanx 20 mm Mk 15.
Countermeasures: Decoys: 4 Plessey Shield or 4 Sea Gnat 6-barrelled 130 mm/102 mm launchers. Graseby Type 182; towed torpedo decoy.

ESM: Marconi Racal Thorn UAT; intercept.
Combat data systems: Marconi Matra SCOT 1D SATCOM.
Radars: Air search: Plessey Type 996; 3D; E/F-band (can be fitted).
 Navigation: Kelvin Hughes Type 1007; I-band.
 Aircraft control: Kelvin Hughes NUCLEUS; E/F-band.

Helicopters: 5 Westland Sea King/Merlin helicopters.

Programmes: The requirement for these ships is to provide fuel and stores support to the Fleet at sea. *Fort Victoria* ordered 23 April 1986 and *Fort George* on 18 December 1987. *Fort Victoria* delayed by damage during building and entered Cammell Laird Shipyard for post sea trials completion in July 1992. The original plan for six of this

class was progressively eroded and no more of this type will be built.
Structure: Single-hull construction. Four dual-purpose abeam replenishment rigs for simultaneous transfer of liquids and solids. Stern refuelling. Repair facilities for Merlin helicopters. The plan to fit Seawolf GWS 26 VLS has been abandoned in favour of Phalanx CIWS fitted in 1998/99 to both ships.
Operational: Two helicopter spots. There is a requirement to provide an emergency landing facility for Harriers. To remain in service until 2019.

FORT GEORGE

6/2005, Maritime Photographic* / 1153979

2 FORT GRANGE CLASS (FLEET REPLENISHMENT SHIPS) (AFSH)

Name	No	Builders	Laid down	Launched	Commissioned
FORT ROSALIE (ex-Fort Grange)	A 385	Scott-Lithgow, Greenock	9 Nov 1973	9 Dec 1976	6 Apr 1978
FORT AUSTIN	A 386	Scott-Lithgow, Greenock	9 Dec 1975	9 Mar 1978	11 May 1979

Displacement, tons: 23,384 full load
Measurement, tons: 8,300 dwt
Dimensions, feet (metres): 607.4 × 79 × 28.2
(185.1 × 24.1 × 8.6)
Main machinery: 1 Sulzer RND90 diesel; 23,200 hp(m)
(17.05 MW); 1 shaft; 2 bow thrusters
Speed, knots: 22. **Range, n miles:** 10,000 at 20 kt
Complement: 114 (31 officers) plus 36 RNSTS (civilian supply staff) plus 45 RN aircrew
Cargo capacity: 3,500 tons armament, naval and victualling stores in 4 holds of 12,800 m³

Guns: 2 Oerlikon 20 mm. 4—7.62 mm MGs.
Countermeasures: Decoys: 2 Corvus or 2 Plessey Shield launchers (upper bridge).
Radars: Navigation: Kelvin Hughes Type 1007; I-band.
Helicopters: 4 Westland Sea King.

Comment: Ordered in November 1971. Fitted for SCOT SATCOMs but carry Marisat. Normally only one helicopter is embarked. ASW stores for helicopters carried on board. Emergency flight deck on the hangar roof. There are six cranes, three of 10 tons lift and three of 5 tons. To remain in service until at least 2013.

FORT AUSTIN   *10/2004, B Sullivan* / 1043556

1 STENA TYPE (FORWARD REPAIR SHIP) (ARH)

Name	No	Builders	Commissioned	Recommissioned
DILIGENCE (ex-Stena Inspector)	A 132	Oresundsvarvet AB, Landskrona, Sweden	1981	12 Mar 1984

Displacement, tons: 10,765 full load
Measurement, tons: 6,550 gross; 4,939 dwt
Dimensions, feet (metres): 367.5 × 67.3 × 22.3
(112 × 20.5 × 6.8)
Flight deck, feet (metres): 83 × 83 (25.4 × 25.4)
Main machinery: Diesel-electric; 5 V16 Nohab-Polar diesel generators; 2,650 kW; 4 NEBB motors; 6,000 hp(m) (4.41 MW); 1 shaft; Kamewa cp prop; 2 Kamewa bow tunnel thrusters; 3,000 hp(m) (2.2 MW); 2 azimuth thrusters (aft); 3,000 hp(m) (2.2 MW)
Speed, knots: 12
Range, n miles: 5,000 at 12 kt
Complement: 38 (15 officers) plus accommodation for 147 plus 55 temporary
Cargo capacity: Long-jib crane SWL 5 tons; maximum lift, 40 tons

Guns: 4 Oerlikon 20 mm. 3—7.62 mm MGs.
Countermeasures: Decoys: Outfit DLE; 4 Plessey Shield 102 mm 6-tubed launchers.

Helicopters: Facilities for up to Boeing Chinook HC. Mk 1 (medium lift) size.

Programmes: Stena Inspector was designed originally as a Multipurpose Support Vessel for North Sea oil operations, and completed in January 1981. Chartered on 25 May 1982 for use as a fleet repair ship during the Falklands War. Purchased from Stena (UK) Line in October 1983, and converted for use as Forward Repair Ship in the South Atlantic (Falkland Islands). Conversion by Clyde Dock Engineering Ltd, Govan from 12 November 1983 to 29 February 1984.
Modernisation: Following items added during conversion: large workshop for hull and machinery repairs (in well-deck); accommodation for naval Junior Rates (new accommodation block); accommodation for crew of conventional submarine (in place of Saturation Diving System); extensive craneage facilities; overside supply of electrical power, water, fuel, steam, air, to ships alongside; large naval store (in place of cement tanks); armament and magazines; Naval Communications System; decompression chamber.
Structure: Four 5 ton anchors for four-point mooring system. Strengthened for operations in ice (Ice Class 1A).

DILIGENCE   *9/2004*, *Royal Navy* / 1153978

Kongsberg Albatross Positioning System has been retained in full. Uses bow and stern thrusters and main propeller to maintain a selected position to within a few metres, up to Beaufort Force 9. Controlled by Kongsberg KS 500 computers.

Operational: Falkland Islands support team (Naval Party 2010) embarked when the ship is in the South Atlantic. Has also been used as MCMV support ship in the Gulf and is capable of SSN support. Likely to remain in service until 2018.

1 AVIATION TRAINING SHIP (HSS/APCR)

Name	No	Builders	Commissioned	Recommissioned
ARGUS (ex-Contender Bezant)	A 135	CNR Breda, Venice	1981	1 June 1988

Displacement, tons: 18,280 standard; 26,421 full load
Measurement, tons: 9,965 dwt
Dimensions, feet (metres): 574.5 × 99.7 × 27
(175.1 × 30.4 × 8.2)
Main machinery: 2 Lindholmen SEMT-Pielstick 18 PC2.5 V 400 diesels; 23,400 hp(m) (17.2 MW) sustained; 2 shafts
Speed, knots: 18
Range, n miles: 20,000 at 19 kt
Complement: 80 (22 officers) plus 35 permanent RN plus 137 RN aircrew
Military lift: 3,300 tons dieso; 1,100 tons aviation fuel; 138 4 ton vehicles in lieu of aircraft

Guns: 4 BMARC 30 mm Mk 1. 4—7.62 mm MGs.
Countermeasures: Decoys: Outfit DLB; 4 Sea Gnat 130 mm/102 mm launchers. Graseby Type 182; torpedo decoy.
ESM: THORN EMI Guardian; radar warning.
Combat data systems: Racal CANE DEB-1 data automation. Inmarsat SATCOM communications. Marisat.
Radars: Air search: Type 994 MTI; E/F-band.
Air/surface search: Kelvin Hughes Type 1006; I-band.
Navigation: Racal Decca Type 994; I-band.
Fixed-wing aircraft: Provision to transport 12 BAe Sea Harrier FA-2.

Helicopters: 6 Westland Sea King HAS.Mk 5/6 or similar.

ARGUS   *12/2005*, *Piet Cornelis* / 1153977

Programmes: Ro-Ro container ship whose conversion for her new task was begun by Harland and Wolff in March 1984 and completed on 3 March 1988.
Structure: Uses former ro-ro deck as hangar with four sliding WT doors able to operate at a speed of 10 m/min. Can replenish other ships underway. One lift port midships, one abaft funnel. Domestic facilities are very limited if she is to be used in the Command support role. Flight deck is 372.4 ft (113.5 m) long and has a 5 ft thick concrete layer on its lower side. First RFA to be fitted with a command system. Ability to conduct subsidiary role as Primary Casualty Receiving Ship improved significantly following upgrade period completed late 2001. This included conversion of three decks into permanent 100-bed hospital with three operating theatres.
Operational: Decommissioning date is under consideration.

6 TRANSPORT SHIPS (AKR)

Name	No	Builders	Commissioned
HURST POINT	—	Flensburger Schiffbau	16 Aug 2002
HARTLAND POINT	—	Harland & Wolff, Belfast	11 Dec 2002
EDDYSTONE	—	Flensburger Schiffbau	28 Nov 2002
ANVIL POINT	—	Harland & Wolff, Belfast	17 Jan 2003
LONGSTONE	—	Flensburger Schiffbau	24 Apr 2003
BEACHY HEAD	—	Flensburger Schiffbau	17 Apr 2003

Displacement, tons: 20,000 full load
Measurement, tons: 14,200 dwt
Dimensions, feet (metres): 633.4 × 85.3 × 24.3
  (193.0 × 26.0 × 7.4)
Main machinery: 2 MaK 9M43 diesels; 21,700 hp *(16.2 MW)*; 2 cp props; bow thruster
Speed, knots: 21.5
Range, n miles: 9,200 at 21.5 kt
Complement: 18
Military lift: 2,650 linear metres of space for vehicles equating to 130 armoured vehicles plus 60 trucks and ammunition
Radars: Navigation: I-band.

HURST POINT   *6/2005*, E & M Laursen* / 1153938

Comment: On 26 October 2000, it was announced that AWSR Ltd had been awarded the contract to provide a strategic sealift service in support of the Joint Rapid Reaction Force (JRRF) until late 2024. A key feature of the contract is that four Ro-Ro are in constant MoD use while the remaining ships are available for use by AWSR for the generation of commercial revenue. These can be called upon to support major operations and exercises.

1 + 3 BAY CLASS LANDING SHIPS DOCK (AUXILIARY) (LSD)

Name	No	Builders	Laid down	Launched	Commissioned
LARGS BAY	L 3006	Swan Hunter (Tyneside) Ltd	1 Oct 2001	18 July 2003	2007
LYME BAY	L 3007	Swan Hunter (Tyneside) Ltd	2003	27 Aug 2005	2007
MOUNTS BAY	L 3008	BAE Systems Govan	24 Feb 2003	9 Apr 2004	2006
CARDIGAN BAY	L 3009	BAE Systems Govan	Apr 2004	8 Apr 2005	2007

Displacement, tons: 16,160 full load
Dimensions, feet (metres): 577.6 × 86.6 × 19
  (176 × 26.4 × 5.8)
Main machinery: Diesel-electric; 2 steerable propulsors
Speed, knots: 18. **Range, n miles:** 8,000 at 15 kt
Complement: 60 (plus 356 troops)
Military lift: 1,150 linear metres of space for vehicles equating to 36 Challenger MBTs or 150 light trucks plus 200 tons ammunition
Radars: Navigation: I-band.

Helicopters: Platform capable of operating Chinook.

Programmes: Two ships ordered from Swan Hunter on 18 December 2000 to enter Royal Fleet Auxiliary service to replace RFAs *Sir Percivale* and *Sir Geraint*. Contract for two further ships of the class, to replace RFAs *Sir Galahad* and *Sir Tristram* placed on 19 November 2001 with BAE Systems (Marine) at Govan. The programme has been badly affected by escalating costs and delays.
Structure: Based on the Dutch LPD *Rotterdam*, the LSD(A)s are designed to transport troops, vehicles, ammunition and stores in support of amphibious operations. Offload

MOUNTS BAY   *10/2005*, H M Steele* / 1153959

is enabled by a flight deck capable of operating heavy helicopters, an amphibious dock capable of operating one LCU and mexeflotes which can be hung on the ships' sides. There is no beaching capability. Davit-launched infantry landing craft (LCVPs) are not fitted but two can be carried in the dock.
Operational: *Mounts Bay* began sea trials on 8 September 2005 and is to be the first of the class to enter service.

1 SIR BEDIVERE CLASS (LANDING SHIP LOGISTIC) (LSLH)

Name	No	Builders	Laid down	Launched	Commissioned
SIR BEDIVERE	L 3004	Hawthorn Leslie, Hebburn-on-Tyne	Oct 1965	20 July 1966	18 May 1967

Displacement, tons: 3,270 light; 6,700 full load
Dimensions, feet (metres): 441.1 × 59.8 × 13
  (134.4 × 18.2 × 4)
Main machinery: 2 Mirrlees 10-ALSSDM diesels; 9,400 hp *(7.01 MW)* or 2 Wärtsilä 280 V12 diesels; 9,928 hp(m) *(7.3 MW)* sustained (SLEP); 2 shafts; bow thruster 980 hp(m) *(720 kW)* (SLEP)
Speed, knots: 17. **Range, n miles:** 8,000 at 15 kt
Complement: 51 (18 officers); 49 (15 officers) (SLEP)
Military lift: 340 troops (534 hard lying); 18 MBTs; 34 mixed vehicles; 120 tons POL; 30 tons ammunition; 1—25 ton crane; 2—4.5 ton cranes. Capacity for 20 helicopters (11 tank deck and 9 vehicle deck)

Guns: 2 or 4 Oerlikon 20 mm. 4—7.62 mm MGs.
Countermeasures: Decoys: 2 Plessey Shield chaff launchers.
Radars: Navigation: Kelvin Hughes Type 1006 or Racal Decca 2690; I-band.
Aircraft control: Kelvin Hughes Type 1007; I-band (SLEP).

Helicopters: Platform to operate Lynx, Chinook or Sea King.

Comment: Fitted for bow and stern loading with drive-through facilities and deck-to-deck ramps. Facilities provided for onboard maintenance of vehicles and for

SIR BEDIVERE   *3/2005*, R G Sharpe* / 1153934

laying out pontoon equipment. Mexeflote self-propelled floating platforms can be strapped one on each side. *Sir Bedivere* had a SLEP in Rosyth from December 1994 to January 1998. This included lengthening by 29 ft an enlarged flight deck, new main engines and a new bridge. The helicopter platform was lowered by one deck, which has reduced the size of the stern ramp. Due to be decommissioned in 2011. Based at Southampton.

1 SIR GALAHAD CLASS (LSLH)

Name	No	Builders	Laid down	Launched	Commissioned
SIR GALAHAD	L 3005	Swan Hunter Shipbuilders, Wallsend-on-Tyne	12 May 1985	13 Dec 1986	25 Nov 1987

Displacement, tons: 8,585 full load
Dimensions, feet (metres): 461 × 64 × 14.1
  (140.5 × 19.5 × 4.3)
Main machinery: 2 Mirrlees-Blackstone diesels; 13,320 hp *(9.94 MW)*; 2 shafts; cp props
Speed, knots: 18
Range, n miles: 13,000 at 15 kt
Complement: 49 (15 officers)
Military lift: 343 troops (537 hard-lying); 18 MBT; 20 mixed vehicles; ammunition, fuel and stores

Guns: 2 Oerlikon 20 mm GAM-BO3. 2—12.7 mm MGs.
Countermeasures: Decoys: 4 Plessey Shield 102 mm 6-tubed launchers.
Combat data systems: Racal CANE data automation.
Radars: Navigation: Kelvin Hughes Type 1007; I-band.

Helicopters: 1 Westland Sea King HC.Mk 4.

Comment: Ordered on 6 September 1984 as a replacement for *Sir Galahad*, sunk as a war grave after air attack at

SIR GALAHAD   *6/2005*, B Prézelin* / 1153935

Bluff Cove, Falkland Islands on 8 June 1982. Has bow and stern ramps with a visor bow gate. One 25 ton and three 8.6 ton cranes. Up to four (total) Mexeflote pontoons can be attached on both sides of the hull superstructure. To be replaced by *Mounts Bay* in Autumn 2006. Based at Southampton.

ROYAL MARITIME AUXILIARY AND GOVERNMENT AGENCY SERVICES

Notes: (1) As of May 2006, the following ships were operated by the RMAS or SERCo Denholm as part of the In Ports and Out of Ports contracts. These contracts are to be re-let as one Future Provisions of Marine Services (FPMS) contract (SERCO Denholm selected as preferred bidder on 6 February 2006) that is due to start in early 2007 and run for 15 years. It is expected that most current assets will be taken into the new contract until replacements are found or built.

(2) *Longbow* is a 12,000 ton trials barge whose conversion 2003-04 by FSL Portsmouth includes a mast, missile silo and firing system to facilitate PAAMS development trials.

(3) The research vessel *Triton*, used to prove the concept of trimaran design, was sold by QinetiQ to Gardline in January 2005. The ship is used for civilian hydrographic survey work.

LONGBOW   *5/2004, Derek Fox* / 1043579

2 SAL CLASS (MOORING SHIPS) (ARSD)

Name	No	Builders	Commissioned
SALMOOR	A 185	Hall Russell, Aberdeen	12 Nov 1985
SALMAID	A 187	Hall Russell, Aberdeen	28 Oct 1986

Displacement, tons: 1,605 light; 2,225 full load
Dimensions, feet (metres): 253 × 48.9 × 12.5 *(77 × 14.9 × 3.8)*
Main machinery: 2 Ruston 8RKC diesels; 4,000 hp *(2.98 MW)* sustained; 1 shaft; cp prop
Speed, knots: 15
Complement: 17 (4 officers) plus 27 spare billets
Radars: Navigation: Racal Decca; I-band.

Comment: Ordered on 23 January 1984. *Salmoor* on the Clyde and *Salmaid* at Devonport. Lift, 400 tons; 200 tons on horns. Can carry submersibles including LR 5. Both operated by RMAS.

SALMOOR   *3/2005*, Derek Fox* / 1153936

1 SUPPORT SHIP (AG)

Name	No	Builders	Commissioned
NEWTON	A 367	Scott-Lithgow, Greenock	17 June 1976

Displacement, tons: 3,140 light; 4,652 full load
Dimensions, feet (metres): 323.5 × 53 × 18.5 *(98.6 × 16 × 5.7)*
Main machinery: Diesel-electric; 3 Ruston 8 RK-215 diesels; 5,520 hp *(4.06 MW)*; 1 GEC motor; 2,040 hp *(1.52 MW)*; Kort nozzle; bow thruster
Speed, knots: 14
Range, n miles: 5,000 at 14 kt
Complement: 24
Radars: Navigation: Kelvin Hughes 1006; I-band.

Comment: Primarily used in support of RN training exercises. Limited support provided to trials. Refitted in 2001. Operated by the RMAS.

NEWTON   *7/2003, B Sullivan* / 0572707

2 MOORHEN CLASS (MOORING SHIPS) (ARS)

Name	No	Builders	Commissioned
MOORHEN	Y 32	McTay, Bromborough	26 Apr 1989
MOORFOWL	Y 33	McTay, Bromborough	30 June 1989

Displacement, tons: 530 full load
Dimensions, feet (metres): 106 × 37.7 × 6.6 *(32.3 × 11.5 × 2)*
Main machinery: 2 Cummins KT19-M diesels; 730 hp *(545 kW)* sustained; 2 Aquamasters; bow thruster
Speed, knots: 8
Complement: 10 (2 officers) plus 2 divers

Comment: Classified as powered mooring lighters. The whole ship can be worked from a 'flying bridge' which is constructed over a through deck. Day mess for five divers. *Moorhen* at Portsmouth, *Moorfowl* at Devonport are RMAS vessels. *Cameron* sold to Briggs Marine in 2004.

MOORFOWL   *11/2005*, W Sartori* / 1153937

1 OILPRESS CLASS (COASTAL TANKER) (AOTL)

Name	No	Builders	Commissioned
OILPRESS	Y 21	Appledore Ferguson	29 Aug 1968

Displacement, tons: 280 standard; 530 full load
Dimensions, feet (metres): 139.5 × 30 × 8.3 *(42.5 × 9 × 2.5)*
Main machinery: 1 Lister-Blackstone ES6 diesel; 405 hp *(302 kW)*; 1 shaft
Speed, knots: 9
Complement: 4
Cargo capacity: 250 tons dieso

Comment: Ordered on 10 May 1967. GS ship on the Clyde.

OILPRESS   *10/1998, M Declerck* / 0053258

1 RESEARCH SHIP (AGOR)

Name	No	Builders	Commissioned
COLONEL TEMPLER (ex-*Criscilla*)	A 229	Hall Russell, Aberdeen	1966

Displacement, tons: 1,300 full load
Dimensions, feet (metres): 185.4 × 36 × 18.4 *(56.5 × 11 × 5.6)*
Main machinery: Diesel-electric; 2 Cummins KTA-38G4M diesels; 2,557 hp(m) *(1.88 MW)* sustained; 2 Newage HC M734E1 generators; 1 Amsaldo DH 560S motor; 2,312 hp(m) *(1.7 MW)*; 1 Aquamaster azimuth thruster with contra rotating props
Speed, knots: 13.5
Complement: 14 plus 12 scientists
Radars: Navigation: Racal Decca 2690 ARPA; I-band.

Comment: Built as a stern trawler. Converted in 1980 for use at RAE Farnborough as an acoustic research ship. Major rebuild in 1992. Re-engined in early 1997 with a raft mounted diesel-electric plant to reduce noise and vibration. Carries a 9 m workboat *Quest* Q 26. Well equipped laboratories. Capable of deploying and recovering up to 5 tons of equipment from deck winches and a 5 ton hydraulic A frame. The ship is also used to support diving operations. GS vessel operated on the Clyde by SERCo Denholm.

COLONEL TEMPLER   *7/2002, H M Steele* / 0530049

2 TORNADO CLASS
(TORPEDO RECOVERY VESSELS) (YDT/YPT)

Name	No	Builders	Commissioned
TORNADO	A 140	Hall Russell, Aberdeen	15 Nov 1979
TORMENTOR	A 142	Hall Russell, Aberdeen	29 Apr 1980

Displacement, tons: 698 full load
Dimensions, feet (metres): 154.5 × 26.2 × 11.3 *(47.1 × 8.0 × 3.4)*
Main machinery: 2 Mirrlees-Blackstone ESL8 MCR diesels; 2,200 hp *(1.64 MW)*; 2 shafts
Speed, knots: 14
Range, n miles: 3,000 at 14 kt
Complement: 12
Radars: Navigation: Kelvin Hughes 1006; I-band.

Comment: Ordered on 1 July 1977. GS vessels on the Clyde. Both ships converted to support diving operations.

TORNADO   *12/1999, W Sartori* / 0075841

1 WATERMAN CLASS (COASTAL TANKER) (AWT)

Name	No	Builders	Commissioned
WATERMAN	A 146	Dunston, Hessle	1978

Displacement, tons: 220 standard; 470 full load
Dimensions, feet (metres): 131.2 × 25.9 × 11.1 *(40.0 × 7.9 × 3.4)*
Main machinery: 1 Mirrlees Blackstone ERS8 diesel; 360 hp *(268 kW)*; 1 shaft
Speed, knots: 11
Range, n miles: 1,500 at 10 kt
Complement: 4
Cargo capacity: 250 tons fresh water

Comment: GS ship on the Clyde.

WATERMAN   *6/2005*, John Mortimer* / 1153976

9 ADEPT CLASS (COASTAL TUGS) (YTB)

FORCEFUL A 221	**ADEPT** A 224	**CAREFUL** A 227
NIMBLE A 222	**BUSTLER** A 225	**FAITHFUL** A 228
POWERFUL A 223	**CAPABLE** A 226	**DEXTEROUS** A 231

Displacement, tons: 450
Dimensions, feet (metres): 127.3 × 30.8 × 11.2 *(38.8 × 9.4 × 3.4)*
Main machinery: 2 Ruston 6RKC diesels; 3,000 hp *(2.24 MW)* sustained; 2 Voith-Schneider props
Speed, knots: 12
Complement: 5

Comment: 'Twin unit tractor tugs' (TUTT). First four ordered from Richard Dunston (Hessle) on 22 February 1979 and next five on 8 February 1984. Primarily for harbour work with coastal towing capability. Nominal bollard pull, 27.5 tons. *Adept* accepted 28 October 1980, *Bustler* 15 April 1981, *Capable* 11 September 1981, *Careful* 12 March 1982, *Forceful* 18 March 1985, *Nimble* 25 June 1985, *Powerful* 30 October 1985, *Faithful* 21 December 1985, *Dexterous* 23 April 1986. *Powerful* and *Bustler* at Portsmouth, *Forceful, Faithful, Adept* and *Careful* at Devonport, *Nimble* and *Dexterous* on the Clyde. All are GS vessels except *Capable* at Gibraltar.

FAITHFUL   *6/2005*, W Sartori* / 1153929

1 ATLAS CLASS (YTM)

ATLAS

Measurement, tons: 88 grt
Dimensions, feet (metres): 72.2 × 25.7 × 10.8 *(22.0 × 7.82 × 3.3)*
Main machinery: 2 Caterpillar diesels; 2,100 hp *(1.6 MW)*; 2 shafts
Speed, knots: To be announced
Complement: 3 plus 12 passengers

Comment: Brought into service by SERCo in 2005 as an interim measure until the new FPMS contract is awarded. Built in Istanbul in 1999 and on charter from a Turkish company. It is British registered. Based at Portsmouth.

ATLAS   *9/2005*, Derek Fox* / 1153923

4 DOG CLASS (YTM)

HUSKY A 178	**SPANIEL** A 201
SALUKI A 182	**SHEEPDOG** A 250

Displacement, tons: 248 full load
Dimensions, feet (metres): 94 × 24.5 × 12 *(28.7 × 7.5 × 3.7)*
Main machinery: 2 Lister-Blackstone ERS8 MCR diesels; 1,320 hp *(985 kW)*; 2 shafts
Speed, knots: 10
Range, n miles: 2,236 at 10 kt
Complement: 7

Comment: Harbour berthing tugs. Nominal bollard pull, 17.5 tons. Completed 1962-72. GS vessels serving at Portsmouth, Devonport and on the Clyde. Appearance varies considerably, some with mast, some with curved upper-bridge work, some with flat monkey-island.

SHEEPDOG   *6/2004, Maritime Photographic* / 1043619

3 TRITON CLASS (YTL)

KITTY A 170	**LESLEY** A 172	**MYRTLE** A 199

Displacement, tons: 107.5 standard
Dimensions, feet (metres): 57.7 × 18 × 7.9 *(17.6 × 5.5 × 2.4)*
Main machinery: 1 Lister Blackstone ARS4M diesel; 330 hp *(264 kW)*; 1 shaft
Speed, knots: 7.5
Complement: 2

Comment: All completed by August 1974 by Dunstons. 'Water-tractors' with small wheelhouse and adjoining funnel. Later vessels have masts stepped abaft wheelhouse. Voith-Schneider vertical axis propellers. Nominal bollard pull, 3 tons. All are GS vessels divided between Devonport and Portsmouth.

TRITON CLASS   *6/2001, A Sharma* / 0131181

4 FELICITY CLASS (YTL)

FRANCES A 147 **FLORENCE** A 149 **GENEVIEVE** A 150 **HELEN** A 198

Displacement, tons: 144 full load
Dimensions, feet (metres): 70 × 21 × 9.8 (21.5 × 6.4 × 3)
Main machinery: 1 Mirrlees-Blackstone ESM8 diesel; 615 hp (459 kW); 1 Voith-Schneider cp prop
Speed, knots: 10
Complement: 4
Radars: Navigation: Raytheon; I-band.

Comment: Four completed 1973 by Hancocks. A 147, 149 and 150 ordered early 1979 from Richard Dunston (Thorne) and completed by end 1980. Nominal bollard pull, 5.7 tons. All are GS vessels divided between Devonport and Portsmouth.

GENEVIEVE   6/2005*, Per Körnefeldt / 1153930

1 RANGE SUPPORT VESSEL (YFRT)

WARDEN A 368

Displacement, tons: 900 full load
Dimensions, feet (metres): 159.4 × 34.4 × 8.2 (48.6 × 10.5 × 2.5)
Main machinery: 2 Ruston 8RKC diesels; 4,000 hp (2.98 MW) sustained; 1 shaft; cp prop
Speed, knots: 15
Complement: 6
Radars: Navigation: Racal Decca RM 1250; I-band.
Sonars: Dowty 2053; high frequency.

Comment: Built by Richards, Lowestoft and completed 20 November 1989. Reverted in 1998 to being an RMAS ship at Kyle of Lochalsh in support of BUTEC. Modified in 1998 to act, at BUTEC, as a ROV host ship and weapons launch and recovery platform.

WARDEN   5/1997, B Sullivan / 0075845

2 RANGE SAFETY CRAFT (YFRT)

RSC 7713 (ex-Samuel Morley VC) **SIR WILLIAM ROE** 8127

Displacement, tons: 20.2 full load
Dimensions, feet (metres): 48.2 × 11.5 × 4.3 (14.7 × 3.5 × 1.3)
Main machinery: 2 RR C8M 410 or Volvo Penta TAMD-122A diesels; 820 hp (612 kW); 2 shafts
Speed, knots: 22. **Range, n miles:** 300 at 20 kt
Complement: 3
Radars: Navigation: Furuno; I-band.

Comment: Range Safety Craft of the Honours and Sirs classes, built by Fairey Marine, A R P Whitstable and Halmatic. Completed 1982-86. Transferred from the RCT on 30 September 1988. RSC 7713 operates at Kyle of Loch Alsh as RMAS Range trials vessel. Sir William Roe is based in Cyprus and has remained with the Royal Logistic Corps. New engines fitted from 1993.

RSC craft   10/2003, Maritime Photographic / 0572713

2 SUBMARINE BERTHING TUGS (YTL)

Name	No	Builders	Commissioned
IMPULSE	A 344	Dunston, Hessle	11 Mar 1993
IMPETUS	A 345	Dunston, Hessle	28 May 1993

Displacement, tons: 530 full load
Dimensions, feet (metres): 106.7 × 34.2 × 11.5 (32.5 × 10.4 × 3.5)
Main machinery: 2 WH Allen 8S12 diesels; 3,400 hp (2.54 MW) sustained; 2 Aquamaster Azimuth thrusters; 1 Jastrom bow thruster
Speed, knots: 12
Complement: 5

Comment: Ordered 28 January 1992 for submarine berthing duties. There are two 10 ton hydraulic winches forward and aft with break capacities of 110 tons. Bollard pull 38.6 tons ahead, 36 tons astern. Fitted with firefighting and oil pollution equipment. Designed for one-man control from the bridge with all round vision and a comprehensive Navaids fit. Impulse launched 10 December 1992; Impetus 9 February 1993. GS vessels based on the Clyde.

IMPETUS   10/2004, Maritime Photographic / 1043618

4 TOWED ARRAY TENDERS (YAG)

TARV 8611 **OHMS LAW** 8612 —8613 **SAPPER** 8614

Dimensions, feet (metres): 65.9 × 19.7 × 7.9 (20.1 × 6 × 2.4)
Main machinery: 2 Perkins diesels; 400 hp (298 kW); 2 Kort nozzles
Speed, knots: 12
Complement: 8
Radars: Navigation: Racal Decca; I-band

Comment: First three built by McTay Marine, Bromborough in 1986. Sapper completed in February 1999. Used for transporting clip-on towed arrays from submarine bases, Faslane and Devonport. Also used as divers' support craft. Naval manned.

SAPPER   6/2005*, E & M Laursen / 1153931

9 RANGE SAFETY CRAFT (YFRT)

SMIT STOUR **SMIT ROTHER** **SMIT ROMNEY** **SMIT CERNE** **SMIT WEY**
SMIT FROME **SMIT MERRION** **SMIT PENALLY** **SMIT NEYLAND**

Displacement, tons: 6.1 full load
Dimensions, feet (metres): 37.1 × 11.2 × 3.9 (11.3 × 3.4 × 1.2)
Main machinery: 2 Volvo Penta KAD 42P diesels; 680 hp (507 kW); 2 × Hamilton waterjets
Speed, knots: 35. **Range, n miles:** 160 at 21 kt
Complement: 2

Comment: MP-1111 class of vessels designed (based on a fast rescue boat) and built at Maritime Partners Ltd (Norway). Aluminium alloy hull and GRP superstructure. The order for the craft followed a contract awarded to Smit International (Scotland) Ltd for the provision of Range Clearance and Safety duties in and around the various sea danger areas of UK military ranges. Three based at Dover, Portland and Pembroke Dock.

SMIT STOUR   6/2004, Royal Navy / 1043617

8 AIRCREW TRAINING CRAFT (YXT)

SMIT DEE	**SMIT YARE**	**SMIT SPEY**	**SMIT TAMAR**
SMIT DON	**SMIT TOWY**	**SMIT DART**	**SMIT CYMYRAN**

Displacement, tons: 55 full load
Dimensions, feet (metres): 90.5 × 21.6 × 4.9 *(27.6 × 6.6 × 1.5)*
Main machinery: 2 Cummins KTA 19M4 diesels; 1,400 hp *(1.04 MW)*; 2 shafts
1 Ultrajet 305 centreline waterjet; 305 hp *(227 kW)*
Speed, knots: 21. **Range, n miles:** 650 at 21 kt
Complement: 6
Radars: Furuno FR-2115 EPA; I-band.

Comment: Vessels built at Babcock Engineering Services, Rosyth, and FBMA Babcock Marine, Cebu, Philippines *(Yare, Towy* and *Spey)*. All delivered on 11 July 2003. Of aluminium alloy construction, the design is an adaptation of FBM Babcock Marine's Protector class patrol vessel. The order for the craft followed a contract awarded to MoD and to Smit International for provision of marine support to aircrew training, high speed marine target towing and recovery of air-sea rescue apparatus. The craft have an after docking well for a daughter craft. Based at Buckie *(Dee)*, Blyth *(Don)*, Great Yarmouth *(Yare)*, Pembroke Dock *(Towy)* and Plymouth *(Spey* and *Dart)*. *Smit Dart* is employed as a passenger craft. *Tamar* (Plymouth) and *Cymyran* (Holyhead) are similar second-hand craft used for passengers.

SMIT DART *6/2005*, Per Körnefeldt* / 1153932

1 SUBMARINE TENDER (YFB)

Name	No	Builders	Commissioned
ADAMANT	A 232	FBM, Cowes	18 Jan 1993

Displacement, tons: 170 full load
Dimensions, feet (metres): 101 × 25.6 × 3.6 *(30.8 × 7.8 × 1.1)*
Main machinery: 2 Cummins KTA-19M2 diesels; 970 hp *(724 kW)* sustained; 2 water-jets
Speed, knots: 23. **Range, n miles:** 250 at 22 kt
Complement: 5 plus 36 passengers plus 1 ton stores

Comment: Twin-hulled support ship ordered in 1991 and launched 8 October 1992. A GS vessel used for personnel and stores transfers in the Firth of Clyde. In addition to the passengers, half a ton of cargo can be carried. Capable of top speed up to Sea State 3 and able to transit safely up to Sea State 6.

ADAMANT *10/1998, M Verschaeve* / 0053268

2 STORM CLASS (YFB)

Name	No	Builders	Commissioned
CAWSAND	A 192	FBM Marine, Cowes	July 1997
BOVISAND	A 191	FBM Marine, Cowes	Sep 1997

Displacement, tons: 97
Dimensions, feet (metres): 78.4 × 36.4 × 7.5 *(23.9 × 11.1 × 2.3)*
Main machinery: 2 Caterpillar 3408TA diesels; 1,224 hp(m) *(900 kW)*; 2 shafts
Speed, knots: 14
Complement: 5 plus 75 passengers

Comment: GS vessels for the use of FOST staff at Devonport. Swath design with hydraulically operated telescopic gangways. Have replaced *Fionan of Skellig*.

CAWSAND *5/2002, John Brodie* / 0530050

3 OBAN CLASS (YFL)

OBAN A 283	**ORONSAY** A 284	**OMAGH** A 285

Displacement, tons: 230 full load
Dimensions, feet (metres): 90.9 × 24 × 12.3 *(27.7 × 7.3 × 3.8)*
Main machinery: 2 Cummins N14M diesels; 1,017 hp(m) *(748 kW)*; 2 Kort-Nozzles
Speed, knots: 10
Complement: 5

Comment: Built by McTay Marine and completed January to July 2000. Capable of carrying 60 passengers. *Oban* based at Devonport and the other two on the Clyde.

ORONSAY *6/2005*, Martin Mokrus* / 1153933

4 PADSTOW AND NEWHAVEN CLASSES (YFL)

PADSTOW A 286	**NEWHAVEN** A 280	**NUTBOURNE** A 281	**NETLEY** A 282

Displacement, tons: 125 full load
Dimensions, feet (metres): 60 × 22.3 × 6.2 *(18.3 × 6.8 × 1.9)*
Main machinery: 2 Cummins 6 CTA diesels; 710 hp(m) *(522 kW)*; 2 shafts
Speed, knots: 10
Complement: 4

Comment: Built by Aluminium Shipbuilders at Fishbourne, Isle of Wight and completed May to November 2000. Capable of carrying 60 passengers and based at Devonport (A 286) and Portsmouth. Catamaran hulls.

NEWHAVEN *7/2005*, Guy Toremans* / 1153975

3 MANLY CLASS (YAG)

MELTON A 83	**MENAI** A 84	**MEON** A 87

Displacement, tons: 143 full load
Dimensions, feet (metres): 80 × 21 × 6.6 *(24.4 × 6.4 × 2)*
Main machinery: 1 Lister-Blackstone ESR4 MCR diesel; 320 hp *(239 kW)*; 1 shaft
Speed, knots: 10. **Range, n miles:** 600 at 10 kt
Complement: 6 (1 officer)

Comment: All built by Richard Dunston, Hessle. All completed by early 1983. *Melton* is an RMAS vessel at Kyle of Loch Alsh, the other two are GS ships at Falmouth.

MANLY CLASS *6/1999, A Sharma* / 0075851

1 FBM CATAMARAN CLASS (YFL)

8837

Displacement, tons: 21 full load
Dimensions, feet (metres): 51.8 × 18 × 4.9 (15.8 × 5.5 × 1.5)
Main machinery: 2 Mermaid Turbo 4 diesels; 280 hp (209 kW); 2 shafts
Speed, knots: 13
Range, n miles: 400 at 10 kt
Complement: 2

Comment: Built by FBM Marine in 1989. Can carry 30 passengers or 2 tons stores. A catamaran type designed to replace some of the older harbour launches but no more have been ordered. GS vessel.

8837 — *3/2005*, W Sartori* / 1153925

ARMY (ROYAL LOGISTIC CORPS)

Notes: (1) Six Mk 4 LCVPs are listed in the RN section. One is based in the Falklands.
(2) One Range Safety Craft is listed in RMAS section.
(3) 32 new Combat Support Boats delivered by 2002. These are 8.2 m craft, road transportable and with a top speed of 30 kt.
(4) The RLC is based at Marchwood, Southampton.

6 RAMPED CRAFT, LOGISTIC (RCL)

Name	No	Builders	Commissioned
ANDALSNES	L 107	James and Stone, Brightlingsea	22 May 1984
AKYAB	L 109	James and Stone, Brightlingsea	15 Dec 1984
AACHEN	L 110	James and Stone, Brightlingsea	12 Feb 1987
AREZZO	L 111	James and Stone, Brightlingsea	26 Mar 1987
ARROMANCHES (ex-Agheila)	L 105 (ex-L 112)	James and Stone, Brightlingsea	12 June 1987
AUDEMER	L 113	James and Stone, Brightlingsea	21 Aug 1987

Displacement, tons: 290 full load
Dimensions, feet (metres): 109.2 × 27.2 × 4.9 (33.3 × 8.3 × 1.5)
Main machinery: 2 Dorman 8JTCWM diesels; 504 hp (376 kW) sustained; 2 shafts
Speed, knots: 10
Range, n miles: 900 at 10 kt
Complement: 6 (2 NCOs)
Military lift: 96 tons
Radars: Navigation: Racal Decca; I-band.

Comment: Andalsnes and Akyab based in Cyprus, remainder at Southampton.

AACHEN — *9/2005*, R G Sharpe* / 1153926

AUDEMER — *6/2005*, Michael Winter* / 1153927

4 WORK BOATS (YAG)

BREAM WB 03   **ROACH** WB 05   **PERCH** WB 06   **MILL REEF** WB 08

Displacement, tons: 27 full load
Dimensions, feet (metres): 48.6 × 14.1 × 4.2 (14.8 × 4.3 × 1.3)
Main machinery: 2 Gardner diesels; 640 hp (460 kW); 2 shafts
Speed, knots: 10
Range, n miles: 500 at 10 kt
Complement: 4
Radars: Navigation: Raytheon; I-band.

Comment: First three built 1966-71; fourth one built in 1987.

ROACH — *6/2005*, Per Körnefeldt* / 1153928

SCOTTISH FISHERIES PROTECTION AGENCY

Notes: (1) The Agency is responsible for the enforcement of sea fisheries regulations around the Scottish coast to a distance of 200 n miles. It has a complement of 275.
(2) There are two Cessna F-406 Caravan II aircraft with Bendix 1500 radars.

1 + 1 JURA CLASS (PSO)

JURA

Measurement, tons: 2,200 grt
Dimensions, feet (metres): 275.6 × 42.6 × 14.7 (84.0 × 13.0 × 4.5)
Main machinery: Diesel-electric; 2 Wärtsilä Gensets; 6,200 hp (4.6 MW); 1 shaft
Speed, knots: 18
Complement: 15 (6 officers)

Comment: Jura built by Ferguson Shipbuilders, Port Glasgow. Launched on 28 April 2005 and entered service in early 2006 to replace Sulisker. A second ship was ordered in early 2006 for delivery in late 2007 to replace Vigilant.

2 SULISKER CLASS (PSO)

VIGILANT   **NORNA**

Displacement, tons: 1,566 (1,586 Norna) full load
Dimensions, feet (metres): 234.3 × 38 × 17.6 (71.4 × 11.6 × 5.4)
Main machinery: 2 Ruston 6AT350 diesels; 6,000 hp (4.48 MW) sustained (Norna); 2 Ruston 12 RK 3 diesels; 5,600 hp (4.18 MW) sustained; 2 shafts; cp props; bow thruster; 450 hp (336 kW)
Speed, knots: 18
Range, n miles: 7,000 at 13 kt
Complement: 16 (7 officers) plus 6 spare bunks
Radars: Navigation: 2 Racal Decca Bridgemaster; I-band.

Comment: Vigilant built by Ferguson Shipbuilders, Port Glasgow and completed June 1982. Norna built by Richards, Lowestoft and completed in June 1988. There are some structural differences in Norna including an A frame aft. Sulisker was decommissioned in early 2006 and Vigilant is to be replaced in late 2007.

NORNA — *6/2005*, Maritime Photographic* / 1153974

VIGILANT — *9/2004** / 1153973

1 + 1 MINNA CLASS (PBO)

MINNA

Displacement, tons: 855 full load
Dimensions, feet (metres): 156.5 × 32.8 × 14.8 *(47.7 × 10.0 × 4.5)*
Main machinery: 2 Wärtsilä Gensets; 2,896 hp *(2.16 MW)*; 2 Indar propulsion motors; 2,145 hp *(1.6 MW)*; 2 shafts; 1 Kamewa transverse thruster *(150 kW)*
Speed, knots: 14
Complement: 15 (6 officers)

Comment: Built by Ferguson Shipbuilders, Port Glasgow. Launched in February 2003 and accepted by SFPA on 31 July 2003 as replacement for *Westra*. Expressions of interest for the construction of a second vessel were sought from shipbuilders in 2005.

MINNA   6/2003, *SFPA* / 0561556

CUSTOMS

Notes: HM Revenue and Customs Maritime Branch operates five offshore patrol vessels. The fleet comprises four Damen 42 m craft *(Seeker, Searcher, Vigilant, Valiant)*, one Vosper Thornycroft 36 m craft *(Sentinel)*.

SEARCHER   7/2005*, *Derek Fox* / 1153924

SENTINEL   5/2001, *A Sharma* / 0131218

TRINITY HOUSE

Notes: The Corporation of Trinity House is the General Lighthouse Authority for England, Wales and the Channel Islands. The Deep Sea Pilotage Authority for UK, it is a self-endowed charity which supports the education, welfare and training of mariners. The Trinity House Lighthouse Service (THLS) provides nearly 600 Aids to Navigation (AtoN) including lighthouses, buoys, beacons and a differential global positioning service. THLS is funded by dues levied on commercial shipping calling at UK ports. The majority of its operations are controlled from a new (2005) centre at Harwich while a depot at Swansea serves the west coast.

PATRICIA

Displacement, tons: 3,139 full load
Dimensions, feet (metres): 284.0 × 46.0 × 14.0 *(86.3 × 13.8 × 4.3)*
Main machinery: 4 Ruston Oil diesels; 4,285 bhp *(3.2 MW)*; connected via 4 generators to 2 motors; 3,452 hp *(2.54 MW)*; 2 shafts
Speed, knots: 14
Range, n miles: 10,000 at 12 kt
Complement: 25 (8 officers)

Comment: Built by Henry Robb Ltd, Leith. Commissioned in May 1982.

PATRICIA   6/2005*, *Maritime Photographic* / 1153972

MERMAID

Displacement, tons: 3,031 full load
Dimensions, feet (metres): 264.0 × 48.0 × 13.0 *(80.3 × 14.5 × 4.0)*
Main machinery: 4 Ruston Oil diesels; 5,329 bhp *(3.9 MW)*; connected via 4 generators to 2 motors; 2,338 hp *(1.72 MW)*; 2 shafts
Speed, knots: 13. **Range, n miles:** 10,000 at 12 kt
Complement: 25 (8 officers)

Comment: Built by Hyundai Heavy Industries, South Korea. Commissioned in March 1987.

MERMAID   6/2005*, *Alvey & Towers* / 1153971

GALATEA

Displacement, tons: 3,960 full load
Dimensions, feet (metres): 275.5 × 54.1 × 14.8 *(84.0 × 16.5 × 4.25)*
Main machinery: 3 Wärtsilä 8L20 diesels; 2 shafts
Speed, knots: 13. **Range, n miles:** 5,250 at 12 kt
Complement: 18

Comment: New multifunction tender built by Stocznia Remontowa SA shipbuilders at Gdansk, Poland. First steel cut on 11 October 2005 and delivery is scheduled for early 2007.

GALATEA (artist's impression)   10/2005*, *Trinity House* / 1153970

ALERT

Displacement, tons: 325 full load
Dimensions, feet (metres): 128.9 × 26.2 × 7.8 *(39.3 × 8.0 × 2.4)*
Main machinery: 2 Caterpillar 3512 diesels; 4,023 hp *(3 MW)*; 2 shafts; cp props; bow thruster
Speed, knots: 16. **Range, n miles:** 400 at 12 kt
Complement: 5

Comment: New rapid intervention vessel built by Stocznia Remontowa SA shipbuilders at Gdansk, Poland. Launched on 11 October 2005, delivery is scheduled for 2006. In addition to maintaining aids to navigation, the vessel is to provide a fast response capability and the means to carry out emergency wreck marking and hydrographic survey services. Her primary areas of operation are the Dover Strait, English Channel and Southern North Sea. The ship is equipped with a dynamic positioning system.

ALERT   10/2005*, *Trinity House* / 1153969

MARITIME & COASTGUARD AGENCY

Notes: The Maritime & Coastguard Agency is responsible for the development, promotion and enforcement of high standards of marine safety, response to maritime emergencies 24 hours a day, reduction of the risk of pollution of the marine environment from ships and, where pollution occurs, minimisation of its impact on the United Kingdom.

Response to maritime emergencies within the UK SAR region is undertaken by HM Coastguard and the MCA's Counter-pollution and Salvage Branch. SAR is co-ordinated through a network of 18 Maritime Rescue Co-ordination Centres (MRCCs). Each MRCC provides continuous emergency telephone, radio and satellite communications distress watch plus safety information and radio medical advice services. The counter-pollution branch provides response to marine pollution and provides scientific and technical advice on shoreline clean up. The MCA has recently introduced a new fleet of patrol vessels for ship inspection, surveillance and accident prevention.

The MCA provides four civilian SAR helicopters (Sikorsky S-61N) under contract from Bristow Helicopters. They are based at Sumburgh, Stornoway, Lee-on-Solent and Portland. A new contract with CHC Scotia is to take effect on 1 July 2007. Fixed-wing aircraft include a BN Islander which conducts surveillance patrols over the Dover Strait and forms part of the Channel Navigation Information Service while, for counter-pollution, a Cessna 404 and Cessna 406 are operated by Atlantic Reconnaissance of Coventry. Fitted with radar, IR and UV detection equipment. Additionally a Cessna 406 and two Lockheed Electra aircraft are available for dispersant spraying. Four emergency towing vessels for SAR, counter-pollution and salvage are under contract from Klyne Tugs Ltd: *Anglian Prince* (1,598 tons gwt), *Anglian Princess* and *Anglian Sovereign* (2,270 tons gwt) and *Anglian Monarch* (1,480 tons gwt). These are stationed in the Fair Isle, Minches, SW Approaches and Dover Strait areas. The MCA also operates a fleet of patrol boats and inshore rescue craft.

HM Coastguard has its own corps of 3,500 volunteer Auxiliary Coastguards divided into 401 Coastguard Rescue Teams around the coast of UK. HM Coastguard also make significant use of Royal National Lifeboat Institution all-weather and inshore lifeboats and military SAR helicopters.

The MCA is also responsible for inspections and surveys of UK vessels, port state control inspections of non UK ships, the enforcement of merchant shipping legislation, the setting of ship and seafarer standards and maritime security.

ANGLIAN PRINCESS   *7/2004, B Sullivan* / 1043562

S-61N
6/2005, Michael Winter*
1153958

ANGLIAN PRINCE   *10/2004, Maritime Photographic* / 1043623

NORTHERN LIGHTHOUSE BOARD

Notes: The Northern Lighthouse Board (NLB) is the General Lighthouse Authority for Scotland and the Isle of Man. The Board provides (AtoN) including lighthouses, buoys and beacons and radio navigation aids. NLB is funded from the General Lighthouse Fund, which draws most of its income from the levy of light dues on commercial and fishing vessels calling at UK and Republic of Ireland ports. Operations are directed from its headquarters in Edinburgh. The board has two ships *Pharos* (1,986 gross tons, commissioned 1993) and *Pole Star* (1,174 gross tons, commissioned 2000). Both are based at Oban.

PHAROS   *6/2005*, Michael Winter* / 1153957

United States

Country Overview

The United States of America is a federal republic which comprises 48 contiguous states (bounded to the north by Canada and to the south by Mexico) and the states of Alaska and Hawaii. External territories include Puerto Rico, American Samoa, Guam and the US Virgin Islands. With an area of 3,717,800 square miles, it occupies much of North America and has a coastline of 10,762 n miles with the Atlantic and Pacific Oceans and with the Gulf of Mexico. Washington, DC is the capital while New York, New York, is the largest city and a leading seaport. Other principal ports include New Orleans, Louisiana; Houston, Texas; Valdez, Alaska; Baton Rouge, Louisiana; Corpus Christi, Texas; Long Beach, California; Norfolk, Virginia; Tampa, Florida; Los Angeles, California; St Louis, Missouri; and Duluth, Wisconsin. There is an extensive inland waterway network, the three main components of which are the Mississippi river system (13,000 n miles long), the Great Lakes (ocean-going vessels can sail between the Great Lakes and the Atlantic Ocean via the St Lawrence Seaway (opened 1959)) and coastal waterways. Territorial seas (12 n miles) are claimed. A 200 n mile EEZ has been claimed but the limits have only been partly defined by boundary agreements.

Headquarters Appointments

Chief of Naval Operations:
Admiral Michael G Mullen
Vice Chief of Naval Operations:
Admiral Robert F Willard
Director, Naval Nuclear Propulsion:
Admiral Kirkland H Donald
Chief of Naval Personnel:
Vice Admiral John C Harvey, Jr
Commander, Naval Sea Systems Command:
Vice Admiral Paul E Sullivan
Commander, Naval Air Systems Command:
Vice Admiral Walter B Massenburg
Commander, Space and Naval Warfare Systems Command:
Rear Admiral Michael C Bachman

Unified Combatant Commanders

Commander, US Strategic Command:
General James E Cartwright
Commander, US Pacific Command:
Admiral William J Fallon

Unified Combatant Commanders—*continued*

Commander, US Joint Forces Command:
General Lance L Smith
Commander, US European Command:
General James L Jones
Commander, US Northern Command:
Admiral Timothy J Keating
Commander, US Southern Command:
General Bantz J Craddock
Commander, US Central Command:
General John Abizaid

Fleet Commanders

Commander, US Fleet Forces Command:
Admiral John B Nathman
Commander, US Pacific Fleet:
Admiral Gary Roughead
Commander, Allied Joint Forces Command, Naples, and US Naval Forces Europe:
Admiral Henry G Ulrich III
Commander, Military Sealift Command:
Vice Admiral Robert D Reilly, Jr

Flag Officers (Atlantic Area)

Commander, Second Fleet:
Vice Admiral Mark P Fitzgerald
Commander, Surface Force, Atlantic Fleet:
Rear Admiral Michael P Nowakowski
Commander, Sixth Fleet, Joint Command Lisbon and Striking and Support Forces NATO:
Vice Admiral John D Stufflebeem
Commander, Naval Submarine Forces and Submarine Allied Command, Atlantic:
Vice Admiral Charles L Munns
Commander, Naval Air Force, Atlantic Fleet:
Rear Admiral Harold D Starling II
Commander, Maritime Air Forces, Mediterranean:
Rear Admiral Noel G Preston
Commander, Mine Warfare Command:
Rear Admiral Deborah A Loewer

Flag Officers (Pacific Area)

Commander, Seventh Fleet:
Vice Admiral Jonathan W Greenert
Commander, Naval Surface Force, Pacific Fleet:
Vice Admiral Terrance T Etnyre

Flag Officers (Pacific Area)—*continued*

Commander, Third Fleet:
Vice Admiral Barry M Costello
Commander, Naval Air Force, Pacific Fleet:
Vice Admiral James M Zortman
Commander, US Naval Forces, Japan:
Rear Admiral James D Kelly
Commander, Submarine Force, Pacific Fleet:
Rear Admiral Jeffrey B Cassias
Commander, US Naval Forces, Korea:
Rear Admiral James P Wisecup
Commander, US Naval Forces, Marianas:
Rear Admiral Charles J Leidig
Commander, Fleet Anti-Submarine Warfare Command:
Rear Admiral John J Waickwicz

Flag Officer (Central Area)

Commander, US Naval Forces, Central Command, and Fifth Fleet:
Vice Admiral Patrick M Walsh

Marine Corps

Commandant:
General Michael W Hagee
Assistant Commandant:
General Robert Magnus
Commander, Fleet Marine Force, Atlantic:
Lieutenant General Robert R Blackman, Jr
Commander, Fleet Marine Force, Pacific:
Lieutenant General John F Goodman

Prefix to Ships' Names

USS (United States Ship) Warships
USNS (United States Naval Ship) Military Sealift Command

Personnel

	1 Jan 2004	1 Jan 2005	1 Jan 2006
Navy			
Officers	55,036	53,925	52,539
Enlisted	320,132	313,186	301,693
Marine Corps			
Officers	18,431	18,847	18,933
Enlisted	156,473	158,674	159,771

Strength of the Fleet (1 January 2006)

Type	Active (NRF) (Reserve)	Building (Projected) + Conversion/SLEP
SHIPS OF THE FLEET		
Strategic Missile Submarines		
SSBN (Ballistic Missile Submarines) (nuclear-powered)	14	—
Cruise Missile Submarines (SSGN) (nuclear-powered)	1	3
Attack Submarines		
SSN Submarines (nuclear-powered)	54	5 (3)
Aircraft Carriers		
CVN Multipurpose Aircraft Carriers (nuclear-powered)	10	1 (2)
CV Multipurpose Aircraft Carriers (conventionally powered)	2	—
Cruisers		
CG Guided Missile Cruisers	22	—
Destroyers		
DDX	—	2 (5)
DDG Guided Missile Destroyers	50	12
Frigates		
FFG Guided Missile Frigates	21 (9)	2 (2)
Patrol Forces		
PC Coastal Defense Ships	8	—
Command Ships		
LCC Command Ships	2	—
AGF Command Ships	1	—
Amphibious Warfare Forces		
LHA Amphibious Assault Ships (general purpose)	4	—
LHD Amphibious Assault Ships (multipurpose)	7	1
LPD Amphibious Transport Docks	12	3 (4)
LSD Dock Landing Ships	12	—
LSV Logistic Support Vessels	7	1 (1)
Mine Warfare Forces		
MCM Mine Countermeasures Ships	14	—
MHC Minehunters (Coastal)	12	—

Type	Active (NRF) (Reserve)	Building (Projected) + Conversion/SLEP
Auxiliaries		
AGSS Auxiliary Research Submarine	1	—
ARS Salvage Ships	2	—
AS Submarine Tenders	2	—
Research		
AGE Research	2	—
HSV High Speed Vessels	2	—
AGOR Oceanographic	6	—
MILITARY SEALIFT COMMAND INVENTORY		
Naval Fleet Auxiliary Force		
T-AOE Fast Combat Support	4	—
T-AKE Auxiliary Cargo and Ammunition	—	9 (2)
T-AE Ammunition	5	—
T-AFS Combat Stores	5	—
T-AH Hospital	2	—
T-AO Oilers	15	—
T-ARS Salvage	2	2
T-ATF Fleet Ocean Tugs	4	—
Special Mission Ships		
T-AG/T-AGM Miscellaneous	4	—
T-AGOS Surveillance/Patrol	4	—
T-AGS Surveying	7	—
T-ARC Cable Repair	1	—
HSV Logistic Support	1	—
Strategic Sealift Force		
T-AKR Fast Sealift	19	—
T-AOT Tankers	4	—
Prepositioning Programme		
HSV Theatre Support	1	—
T-AK Container Ro-Ro	4	—
T-AK Container	5	—
T-AK Vehicle Cargo	13	—
T-AKR Large, Medium-Speed, Ro-Ro	8	1
T-AVB Aviation Logistic	2	—
Ready Reserve Force		
T-ACS Crane Ships	10	—
T-AK Break Bulk	3	—
T-AKR Ro-ro	31	—
T-AOT/T-AOG Product Tankers	6	—
T-AK/T-AP Miscellaneous	6	—

Special Notes

To provide similar information to that included in other major navies' Deployment Tables the fleet assignment (abbreviated 'F/S') status of each ship in the US Navy has been included. The assignment appears in a column immediately to the right of the commissioning date. In the case of the Floating Dry Dock section this system is not used. The following abbreviations are used to indicate fleet assignments:

AA	active Atlantic Fleet
Active	active under charter with MSC
AR	in reserve Out of Commission, Atlantic Fleet
ASA	active In Service, Atlantic Fleet
ASR	in reserve Out of Service, Atlantic Fleet
Bldg	Building
CONV	ship undergoing conversion
LOAN	ship or craft loaned to another government, or non-government agency, but US Navy retains title and the ship or craft is on the NVR
MAR	in reserve Out of Commission, Atlantic Fleet and laid up in the temporary custody of the Maritime Administration
MPR	same as 'MAR', but applies to the Pacific Fleet
NRF	assigned to the Naval Reserve Force (ships so assigned are listed in a special table for major warships and amphibious ships)
Ord	the contract for the construction of the ship has been let, but actual construction has not yet begun
PA	active Pacific Fleet
PR	in reserve Out of Commission, Pacific Fleet
Proj	the ship is scheduled for construction at some time in the immediate future
PSA	active In Service, Pacific Fleet
PSR	in reserve Out of Service, Pacific Fleet
ROS	reduced Operating Status
TAA	active Military Sealift Command, Atlantic Fleet
TAR	in Ready Reserve, Military Sealift Command, Atlantic Fleet
TPA	active Military Sealift Command, Pacific Fleet
TPR	in Ready Reserve, Military Sealift Command, Pacific Fleet
TWWR	active Military Sealift Command, Worldwide Routes

Ship Status Definitions

In Commission: as a rule any ship, except a Service Craft, that is active, is in commission. The ship has a Commanding Officer and flies a commissioning pennant. 'Commissioning date' as used in this section means the date of being 'in commission' rather than 'completion' or 'acceptance into service' as used in some other navies.
In Service: all service craft (dry docks and with classifications that start with 'Y'), with the exception of *Constitution*, that are active, are 'in service'. The ship has an Officer-in-Charge and does not fly a commissioning pennant.
Ships 'in reserve, out of commission' or 'in reserve, out of service' are put in a state of preservation for future service. Depending on the size of the ship or craft, a ship in 'mothballs' usually takes from 30 days to nearly a year to restore to full operational service.
The above status definitions do not apply to the Military Sealift Command.

Approved Fiscal Year 2006 Programme

	Appropriations (US dollars millions)
CVN 21 (Advance procurement)	619
SSGN conversion (Advance procurement)	283
SSN Virginia class (SSN 780)	2,368
DD(X) Destroyer (Advance procurement)	706
San Antonio class (LPD 19)	1,326
3 Littoral Combat Ships (1 funded with R & D)	440

Proposed Fiscal Year 2007 Programme

	Appropriations (US dollars millions)
CVN 21 (R & D, Advance procurement)	784
Virginia class (SSN 781)	2,452
2 DD(X) Destroyers	2,568
2 Littoral Combat Ships	521
1 LHA (R)	1,136

Naval Aviation

Naval Aviation had an active inventory of 3,822 aircraft as of 1 January 2006, with approximately 33 per cent of those being operated by the US Marine Corps. The principal aviation organisations are 10 active carrier air wings and one reserve, 12 active maritime patrol squadrons and seven reserve, and three Marine aircraft wings and one reserve. Reserve squadrons fly and maintain their own aircraft. Fleet Replacement Squadrons (FRS) train winged aviators in the aircraft they will fly in fleet.

Fighter Attack: 19 Navy active squadrons, three Navy reserve and one Navy FRS with F/A-18 Hornets. 14 Marine active squadrons, three reserve and one FRS with F/A-18 Hornets. 14 Navy active squadrons and one Navy Reserve with F/A-18 Super Hornets and two Navy squadrons with F-14 Tomcats.
Attack: Seven Marine squadrons with AV-8B Harriers, one FRS.
Airborne Early Warning: 10 Navy active squadrons, one reserve and one FRS with E-2C Hawkeyes
Electronic Warfare: 13 Navy active, one reserve, 1 FRS and four Marine squadrons with EA-6B Prowlers.
Communication Relay: Two Navy squadrons of EA-6B Mercurys.

Anti-Submarine Warfare: Six Navy squadrons with S-3B Vikings.
Maritime Patrol: 12 active, three reserve and one FRS Navy squadrons with P-3C Orions.
Electronic Reconnaissance: Two Navy squadrons, one FRS with EP-3E Orions (Aries II).
Helicopter Anti-Submarine: 10 Navy active, one reserve and one FRS squadrons with SH/HH-60 Seahawks.
Helicopter Mine Countermeasures: Two Navy squadrons with MH-53E Sea Dragons.
Helicopter Combat Support: Four Navy active squadrons and two FRS of MH-60S Knighthawks, one Navy active squadron of MH-53E Sea Dragons and one reserve Navy squadron of UH-3H Sea Kings.
Helicopter Combat Support/Gunship: Six Marine squadrons with AH-1W Super Cobras and UH-1N Hueys, three reserve and one FRS.
Helicopter Transport: 12 Marine squadrons of CH-46E Sea Knights, two reserve and one FRS; three with CH-53D Sea Stallions and six with CH-53E Super Stallions, two reserve and one FRS.
Special or Composite: Two Navy special squadrons of HH-60H Seahawks.

Aircraft Procurement Plan FY2006-2008

	06	07	08
Joint Strike Fighter	—	—	8
F/A-18E/F Super Hornet	38	30	24
EA-18G Growler	4	12	18
MV-22 Osprey	9	14	19
AH-1Z/UH-1Y Super Cobra/Huey	10	18	19
MH-60S Seahawk	26	18	20
MH-60R Seahawk	12	25	25
E-2C Hawkeye	2	2	—
E-2D Advanced Hawkeye	—	—	4
P-8A MMA	—	—	4
T-45 Goshawk	6	12	—
T-6A JPATS	3	21	48
KC-130J Tanker	5	4	4
VH-71 (VXX) Kestrel	5	—	3
RA-8A VTUAV	5	4	7
F-5N Adversary aircraft	9	5	—

Naval Special Warfare (NSW)

The Naval Special Warfare Command was commissioned 16 April 1987.
SEAL (Sea Air Land) teams are manned at a nominal 6 platoons per team, with 24 platoons on each coast based at Coronado, California (Group 1) and Little Creek, Virginia (Group 2). Platoons are allocated to theatre commanders during operational deployments. The naval special warfare community has approximately 5,700 personnel including 2,400 SEALs and 600 Special Warfare Combatant-craft Crewmen (SWCC) operators. The remainder are support personnel for the NSW mission.

Bases

Naval Air Stations and Air Facilities

Naval Air Weapons Station (NAWS) China Lake, CA; Naval Air Facility (NAF) El Centro, CA; Naval Air Station (NAS) Lemoore, CA; NAF Washington, DC; NAS Jacksonville, FL; NAF Key West, FL; NAS Whiting Field (Milton), FL; NAS Pensacola, FL; NAS Atlanta (Marietta), GA; PMRF Barking Sands, HI; NAS Joint Reserve Base, New Orleans, LA; NAS Brunswick, ME; NAS Patuxent River, MD; NAS Meridian, MS; NAS Fallon, NV; Naval Air Engineering Station (NAES) Lakehurst, NJ; NAS Joint Reserve Base, Willow Grove, PA; NAS, Corpus Christi, TX; NAS Joint Reserve Base Fort Worth, TX; NAS Kingsville, TX; NAS Oceana, VA; NAS Whidbey Island (Oak Harbor), WA; NAS Keflavik, Iceland; NAS Sigonella, Italy; NAF Atsugi, Japan; NAF Misawa, Japan; NAF Mildenhall, UK.

Naval Stations and Naval Bases

Naval Station San Diego, CA; NB Coronado, CA; NB Ventura County, CA; NB Point Loma (San Diego), CA; NS Mayport, FL; Naval Station (NS) Pearl Harbor, HI; NS Great Lakes, ILL; NS Annapolis, MD; NS Pascagoula, MS; NS Ingleside, TX; NS Newport, RI; Naval Amphibious Base (NAB) (Amphibious) Little Creek, VA; NS Norfolk, VA; NB Kitsap, WA; NS Everett, WA; NS Guantanamo Bay, Cuba; Fleet Activities (FA) Okinawa, Japan; CFA Sasebo, Japan; CFA Chinhae, Korea; CFA Yokosuka, Japan; NS Rota, Spain; CBC Gulfport.

Naval Support Facilities

Naval Post Graduate School Monterey, CA; NSA Washington, DC; NSA New Orleans, LA; NSA Mechanicsburg, PA; NSA Mid-South (Millington), TN; NSA Norfolk, VA.
NSF Diego Garcia, BIOT; Naval Forces Marianas Support Activity, Guam; NSA Souda Bay, Greece; NSA Gaeta, Italy; NSA La Maddalena, Italy; NSA Naples, Italy; Naval Activities (NA) United Kingdom (London), UK; NSA Bahrain; NAVREGCONTCTR Singapore; NCTAMS EASTPAC (Hawaii); NSGA Kunia; NUWC Keyport (WA); NAVMAG Indian Island (WA); NAVWPNSTA Seal Beach (CA); NSA Corona (CA); NSA Crane (IN); NAVWPNSTA Earle (NJ); NSU Saratoga Springs (NY); JMF St Mawgans (UK); NA Puerto Rico (PR); NSA Indian Head (MD); NSA Carderock (MD); NSF Thurmont (MD); NSA Dahlgren (VA); NAVWPNSTA Yorktown; NSWC Philadelphia; NSA Wallops Island; NSGA Sugar Grove; NAVWPNSTA Charleston; NSA Panama City; NAVSCSCOL Athens (GA); NSA Orlando; NUWC Bahamas (Andros Is).

Strategic Missile Submarine Bases

SUBASE Kings Bay, GA (East Coast); SUBASE New London, CT (East Coast).

Naval Shipyards

NSY/IMF Pearl Harbor, HI; Puget Sound NSY/IMF, Bremerton, WA; NSY Norfolk, VA; NSY Portsmouth, NH (located in Kittery, ME).

Marine Corps Air Stations and Helicopter Facilities

MCAS: Beaufort, SC; Yuma, AZ; Kaneohe Bay, Oahu, HI; Quantico, VA; Cherry Point, NC; Iwakuni, Honshu, Japan; New River (Jacksonville), NC. Futema, Okinawa, Miramar (San Diego), CA.

Marine Corps Bases

Camp Pendleton, CA; Twentynine Palms, CA; Camp H M Smith (Oahu), HI; Camp Lejeune, NC; Camp Smedley D Butler (Kawasaki), Okinawa, Japan.

Command and control of US naval forces

Strategic and Operational Command

All US Military Forces operate under Title 10 of US Code and subsidiary Joint Force Doctrine publications. The President of the United States is the Commander-in-Chief of all US forces and exercises authority for the application of military force through the Secretary of Defense who is advised by the Chairman of the Joint Chiefs of Staff. The Unified Combatant Commanders are four-star officers who have broad geographic area of functional responsibilities. Exercising Combatant Command (COCOM), they have authority to employ forces as necessary to accomplish assigned military missions and are as follows:

Commander US European Command (Stuttgart-Vaihingen, Germany)
Commander US Northern Command (Peterson AFB, Colorado)

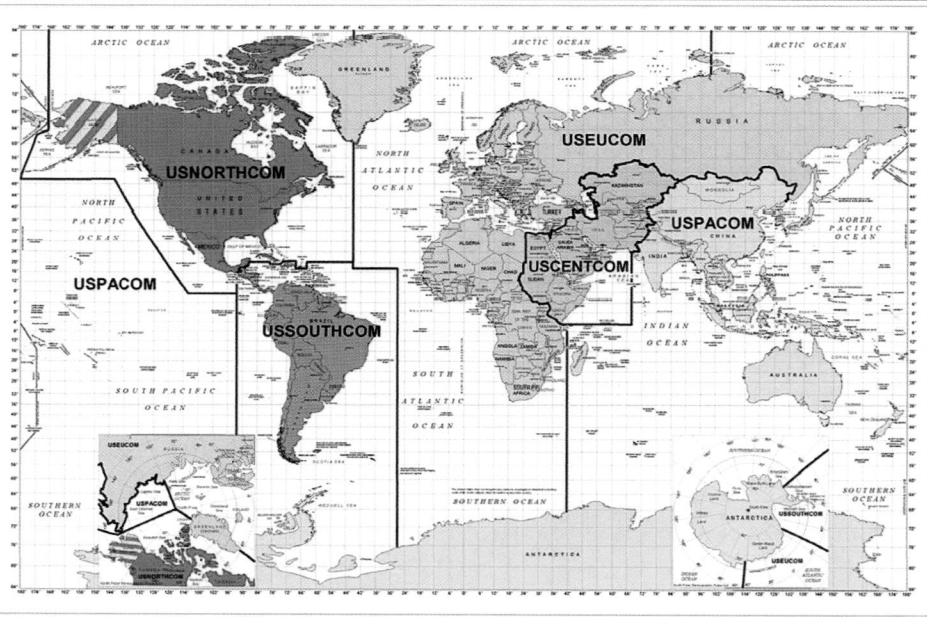

THE WORLD 1:135,000,000 **THE WORLD WITH COMMANDERS' AREAS OF RESPONSIBILITY** EDITION 5-NIMA SERIES 1107 Based on Unified Command Plan February 2002

AREAS OF RESPONSIBILITY *4/2002, US DoD* / 0127116

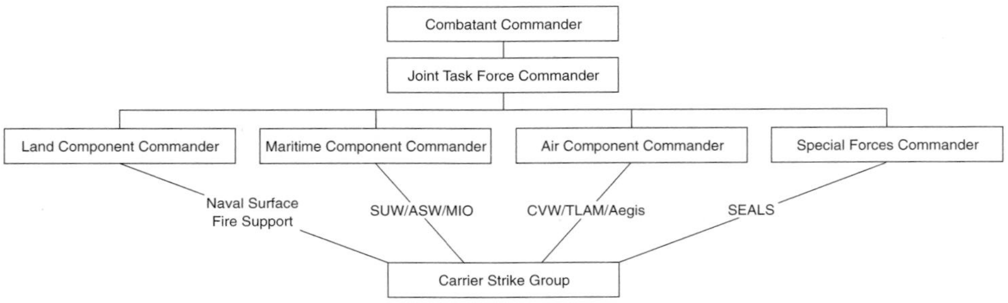
Combatant Commander
Joint Task Force Commander
Land Component Commander
Maritime Component Commander
Air Component Commander
Special Forces Commander
Naval Surface Fire Support
SUW/ASW/MIO
CVW/TLAM/Aegis
SEALS
Carrier Strike Group

0531964

CHAIN OF COMMAND

Commander US Pacific Command (Honolulu, Hawaii)
Commander US Southern Command (Miami, Florida)
Commander US Central Command (MacDill AFB, Florida)
Commander US Joint Forces Command (Norfolk, Virginia)
Commander US Special Operations Command (MacDill AFB, Florida)
Commander US Transportation Command (Scott AFB, Illinois)
Commander US Strategic Command (Offutt AFB, Nebraska)

The Unified Combatant Commanders may decide to exercise Operational (OPCON) command of naval forces directly. Alternatively, they may delegate such powers to another officer who might be a subordinate Unified Commander (for example Commander, US Forces Korea), a service component commander (Army, Navy, Air Force, Marine Corps and so on), a functional component commander (air, maritime, land, special forces), a joint task force commander or a single service force commander.
Navy force commanders have a dual chain of command. They report to the Chief of Naval Operations for administrative matters such as training and equipping of forces and are also responsible to the combatant commanders for providing forces to accomplish missions. They include the following:

Commander US Fleet Forces Command
Commander Pacific Fleet
Commander US Naval Forces Europe
Commander US Naval Forces Central Command
Commander Naval Reserve Force
Commander Military Sealift Command

Once deployed in theatre, naval forces are operationally assigned to three-star numbered fleet commanders:

Commander Second Fleet (Atlantic)
Commander Third Fleet (Eastern Pacific)
Commander Fifth Fleet (Arabian Gulf and Indian Ocean)
Commander Sixth Fleet (Mediterranean)
Commander Seventh Fleet (Western Pacific)

These arrangements are intended to provide a framework that provides a clear chain of command while retaining the flexibility to be adapted to the operational circumstances. For example, it is feasible for a multimission naval task group, such as a carrier strike group (CSG) (baseline composition: 1 CVN/CV, 2 CG/DDG, 1 DD/FFG, 1 SSN and 1 logistic support ship) or an expeditionary strike group (ESG) (baseline composition: 3 amphibious ships (LHD/LHA, LPD and LSD), 2 CG/DDG, 1 DD/FFG and 1 SSN) to support service, component, and other superior commanders simultaneously.

Tactical Command and Composite Warfare Commander

US naval task groups and forces operate under Composite Warfare Commander (CWC) doctrine. The officer in tactical command (OTC) is responsible for accomplishing the missions of his assigned forces. The CWC directs the force and controls warfare functions. The OTC may designate a subordinate commander as CWC but, in general practice, the roles are combined. The OTC/CWC is supported by Principal Warfare Commanders (PWC), Functional Warfare Commanders (FWC) and Coordinators.

PWCs include the Air Defense Commander (ADC), Strike Warfare Commander (STWC), Information Warfare Commander (IWC), Anti-submarine Warfare Commander (ASWC), and Surface Warfare Commander (SUWC). ASW and SUW areas can be combined under a Sea Combat Commander (SCC). PWCs collect and distribute information pertinent to their warfare areas and can be delegated authority to respond to threats with assigned assets.

FWCs perform duties of a scope or duration more limited than that of a PWCs. Typical FWCs include Maritime Interception Operations Commander (MIOC), Mine Warfare Commander (MIWC), Operational Deception Group Commander, Screen Commander (SC) and Underway Replenishment Group (URG) Commander.

Coordinators are responsible to the OTC/CWC for managing assets and resources. Among assigned Coordinators are the Air Resource Element Coordinator (AREC), Air Control Authority (ACA), Cryptologic Resource Coordinator (CRC), Force Over-the-horizon Track Coordinator (FOTC), Force Track Coordinator (FTC), Helicopter Element Coordinator (HEC), Submarine Operations Coordinating Authority (SOCA), TLAM Launch Area Coordinator (LAC) and TLAM Strike Coordinator (TSC).

The OTC/CWC may activate any or all of these warfare commanders and coordinators as necessary. The guiding principle of CWC doctrine is flexibility to meet operational requirements.

Multinational Operations

US naval forces regularly participate in peacetime and wartime multinational operations. Although the President always retains command authority over US forces, he may place them under control of a foreign commander as required to achieve specific military objectives. Multinational operations may be conducted under the structure of a formal alliance (such as NATO) or of an ad hoc coalition (Operation Desert Shield/Desert Storm).

Complex Naval Task Forces

Complex Task Forces usually consist of multiple CSGs and/or ESGs and may also include naval assets of allied nations. Such forces may operate together under three generic command and control structures.

In Situation A, the forces integrate, the senior officer present becomes the overall OTC/CWC and a new single CWC organisation is established.

In Situation B, task groups do not integrate. The senior OTC/CWC coordinates the tactical operations of all naval forces and delegates responsibilities and TACON of specific forces to junior commanders as appropriate. The senior OTC/CWC may also designate junior commanders as sector OTC/CWCs.

In Situation C, each group retains its own OTC/CWC and its own set of warfare commanders and coordinators. The OTC/CWC of the supported force (or a common superior) draws on the assets of the entire force to achieve joint and combined force objectives.

Amphibious Operations

'Commander Amphibious Task Force' (CATF) and 'Commander Landing Force' (CLF) are historic naval command terms whose functional responsibilities are recognised by Joint Doctrine. The common superior establishes command relationships between CATF and CLF who are considered coequal in planning. CATF is responsible for operations at sea while CLF dictates landing force objectives and landing and drop zones.

US Marine Corps Organisation

Marine Corps Structure

Title 10 directs that the Marine Corps is to consist of three divisions and three air wings with their necessary logistics support and that there is to be a similar organisation in the reserves consisting of one division, one air wing, and their respective logistical support groups. MEFs I (Camp Pendleton, CA), II (Camp Lejeune, NC) and III (Okinawa, Japan) are the three standing Marine Expeditionary Forces (MEFs).

The MEF is the USMC's principle war-fighting organisation. Commanded by a lieutenant general, it consists of 50-60,000 personnel and includes, typically, a division, air wing, FSSG and headquarters group. MEFs can conduct a broad scope of missions in any environment for sixty days and are supported by amphibious shipping and/or Maritime Prepositioning Squadrons (MPS). Because of its size, the MEF is normally committed sequentially, building on a smaller operational unit such as a Marine Expeditionary Brigade (MEB) or Marine Expeditionary Unit (MEU).

The MEB is designed as the lead element for a MEF or for small-scale contingencies. Command by a major general or brigadier, it consists of 14—18,000 Marine and Navy personnel and has thirty days sustainability. The ground combat element consists of an infantry regiment reinforced by artillery, some armour, light armoured vehicles, assault amphibian vehicles, and combat engineers. These assets can be divided into four battalion-size manoeuvre elements, supported by three to six fixed- and rotary-wing aircraft squadrons.

MEUs routinely forward deploy on Amphibious Ready Groups (ARGs). Commanded by a colonel, they contain approximately 2,200 Marine and Navy personnel and can sustain operations for fifteen days. MEUs normally consist of a reinforced infantry Battalion Landing Team (BLT), a composite helicopter squadron (with air command and control and six Harriers), and a MEU service support group (MSSG). Typically, such a force can act as the lead element for a larger force and/or provide shaping/engagement activities, deterrence, and limited power projection. It has the capability to conduct company to battalion-sized raids to the range limits of assigned helicopters, roughly 70—100 miles from the ARG. An ARG typically consists of 1 LHD/LHA, 1 LPD and 1 LSD.

Marine Corps Operations

Operations are conducted by Marine Air Ground Task Forces (MAGTFs) whose size and composition will be dictated by operational circumstances. A MAGTF can be established by drawing ground, aviation, and combat service support assets from divisions, air wings, and their support groups. At the lower end of the scale, MEUs are available as immediately responsive, sea-based MAGTFs while, on a much greater scale, a full MEF might be required. This might be based on one of the standing MEFs or, as in Operation Desert Shield/Desert Storm, drawn from all three standing MEFs. A MAGTF always consists of a Command Element (CE), Ground Combat Element (GCE), Aviation Combat Element (ACE) and a Combat Service Support Element (CSSE).

Expeditionary Strike Group (ESG)

These are designed to give the Unified Combatant Commanders greater combat power and flexibility. A pilot deployment was conducted in early 2003. Under the ESG concept, an Amphibious Ready Group (LHA/LHD, LPD and LSD) and embarked MEU will be augmented by a cruiser, a destroyer, a frigate, and an attack submarine, together with a P-3 Orion ASW/Recce aircraft. Ultimately, the Navy plans to maintain 12 ESGs and 12 CVBGs.

Embarked MEU

Marine Corps amphibious forces embarked on ARGs come under the OPCON of the naval or maritime component commander. They remain under the naval or maritime component commander throughout an amphibious operation if they will re-embark. If they transition to sustained operations ashore, they chop to either the Marine component commander or the land component commander. A Marine Corps component commander may be designated as the joint force maritime, land, or air component commander.

Communications and Data Systems

Advanced Combat Direction System (ACDS)

ACDS is a centralised, automated command and control system. An upgrade from the Naval Tactical Data System (NTDS) for aircraft carriers and large-deck amphibious ships, it provides the capability to identify and classify

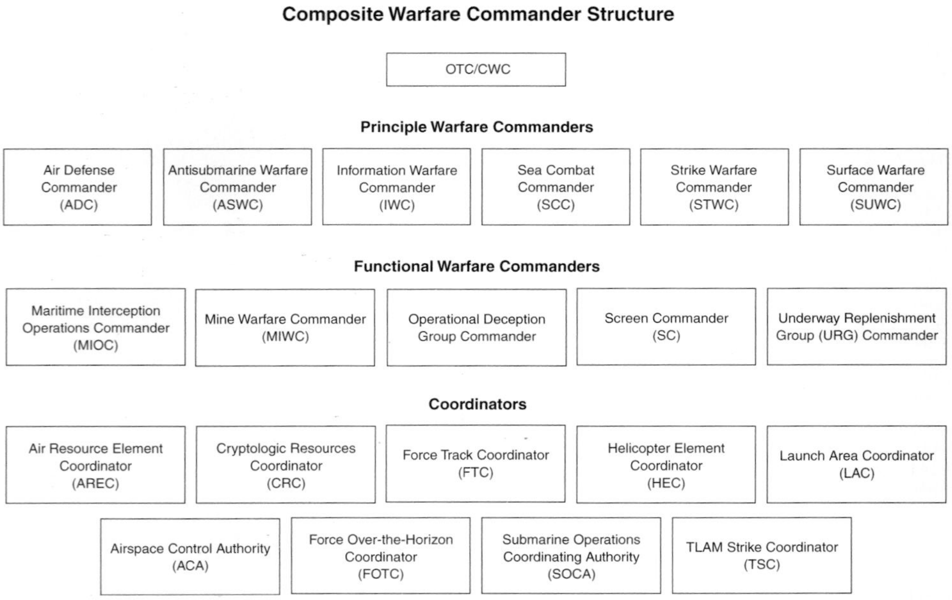
Composite Warfare Commander Structure
OTC/CWC
Principle Warfare Commanders
Air Defense Commander (ADC)
Antisubmarine Warfare Commander (ASWC)
Information Warfare Commander (IWC)
Sea Combat Commander (SCC)
Strike Warfare Commander (STWC)
Surface Warfare Commander (SUWC)
Functional Warfare Commanders
Maritime Interception Operations Commander (MIOC)
Mine Warfare Commander (MIWC)
Operational Deception Group Commander
Screen Commander (SC)
Underway Replenishment Group (URG) Commander
Coordinators
Air Resource Element Coordinator (AREC)
Cryptologic Resources Coordinator (CRC)
Force Track Coordinator (FTC)
Helicopter Element Coordinator (HEC)
Launch Area Coordinator (LAC)
Airspace Control Authority (ACA)
Force Over-the-Horizon Coordinator (FOTC)
Submarine Operations Coordinating Authority (SOCA)
TLAM Strike Coordinator (TSC)

CWC STRUCTURE 0531963

targets, prioritise and conduct engagements, and exchange targeting information and engagement orders within the battle group and among different service components in the joint theatre of operations. ACDS is a core Sea Shield component of non-Aegis/non-SSDS combat systems.

ACDS consists of two variants. The ACDS Block 0 system replaces obsolete NTDS computers and display consoles and incorporates new software. ACDS Block 0 is deployed on nine aircraft carriers, five Wasp (LHD-1) class amphibious assault ships, and all five Tarawa (LHA-1) class amphibious assault ships. ACDS Block 1 has been installed in five ships from 1996: *Eisenhower* (CVN 69), *John F Kennedy* (CV 67), *Nimitz* (CVN-68), *Wasp* and *Iwo Jima* (LHD-7). Following the OPEVAL failure of ACDS Block 1, it is to be replaced by the Ship Self Defense System (SSDS). Installation in *Nimitz* and *Eisenhower* is in progress and *John F Kennedy* and *Iwo Jima* are to be fitted in 2006 and 2007 respectively.

AEGIS Combat System

The AEGIS system is designed as a total weapon system, from detection to kill in the air, surface and sub-surface domains.

The SPY-1 radar system is the primary air and surface radar for the Aegis Combat System installed in the *Ticonderoga* (CG-47) and Arleigh Burke (DDG-51) class warships. It is a multifunction, phased-array radar capable of search, automatic detection, transition to track, tracking of air and surface targets, and missile engagement support. The third variant of this radar, SPY-1D(V), the Littoral Warfare Radar, improves the radar's capability against low-altitude, reduced radar cross-section targets in heavy clutter environments, and in the presence of intense electronic countermeasures. The SPY-1 Series radars also demonstrated the capability to detect and track theatre ballistic missiles. AEGIS equipped platforms include Spanish F-100 and Japanese DDG ship classes.

Automated Digital Network System (ADNS)

The Automated Digital Network System is responsible for the transport of all Wide Area Network (WAN) Internet Protocol (IP) services which connect afloat units to various global shore sites. It provides ship and shore IP connectivity and promotes efficient use of available satellite and line of sight communications bandwidth. ADNS converges all voice, video, and data communications between ship and shore to an IP medium and takes advantage of all shipborne RF to transmit data efficiently. Specifically, it automates routing and switching of tactical and strategic C4I data via Transmission Control Protocol/Internet Protocol (TCP/IP) networks linking deployed battle group units with each other and with the Defense Information Systems Network (DISN) ashore. ADNS uses Commercial Off-the-Shelf (COTS) and Non-Developmental Item (NDI) Joint Tactical Architecture (JTA) – compliant hardware (routers, processors and switches), and commercial-compliant software in a standardised, scalable, shock-qualified rack design.

Challenge Athena (WSC-8)

Challenge Athena is part of the Navy commercial wideband satellite program (CWSP). It is a full-duplex, high data-rate communications link that operates in the C-band spectrum up to 2.048 Mbps. The Challenge Athena terminal (AN/WSC-8(V)1,2) with modifications by the developer/manufacturer is also capable of operating in the Ku-band spectrum. Because of open ocean limitations, there are currently no plans to enhance Navy's commercial satellite terminal to include Ku coverage. CWSP provides access to voice, video, data and imagery circuit requirements. It supports fleet commander flagships (LCC/AGF), aircraft carriers (CV/CVN), amphibious ships (LHA/LHD/LPD) and other selected ships, including hospital ships (T-AH) and submarine tenders (AS). Terminals are also installed at training locations in San Diego, California, and Norfolk, Virginia. Examples of communications circuits that are provided include: Joint Service Imagery Processing System-Navy/Concentrator Architecture (JSIPS-N/JCA), Naval and Joint Fires Network (NFN), VideoTele-Conferencing (VTC), Video Information Exchange system (VIXS), Video Tele-Medicine (VTM), Video Tele-Training (VTT), Afloat Personal Telephone Service (APTS), Automated Digital Network System (ADNS), Integrated Digital Switching Network (IDSN) for voice/telephone, Secret/Unclassified Internet Protocol Router Networks (SIPRNET/NIPRNET), and Joint Worldwide Intelligence Communications System (JWICS). The CWSP terminal uses commercial satellite connectivity and COTS/NDI Equipment. In recent years, it has become an integral part of Navy's SATCOM architecture because of the overburdened military satellite communications systems.

Common Data Link – Navy (USQ-123 CDL-N)

This programme provides a common data terminal for the receipt of signal and imagery intelligence data from remote sensors and transmission of link and sensor control data to airborne platforms. CDL-N interfaces with shipboard processors of the Joint Services Imagery Processing System – Navy (JSIPS-N) and the Battle Group Passive Horizon Extension System Terminal (BGPHES), and links with BGPHES via CDL airborne terminal to airborne sensor systems. CDL-N is in production and the first ten systems are installed in Carriers. Future installations are planned for the remaining carriers, amphibious ships and command ships. The Shared Reconnaissance Pod (SHARP), which replaces the F-14 Tactical Airborne Reconnaissance Pod System (TARPS) and will be carried on the F/A-18F, supports strike warfare, amphibious warfare, and anti-surface warfare decision – making and utilises CDL-N for real time connectivity.

Co-operative Engagement Capability (CEC)

Co-operative Engagement Capability (CEC) improves battle force air-defense capabilities by integrating the sensor data of each co-operating ship and aircraft into a single, real-time, fire-control-quality composite track picture. CEC also interfaces the weapons capabilities of each CEC-equipped ship in the battle group to integrate engagement capability. By simultaneously distributing sensor data on airborne threats to each ship within a battle group, CEC extends the range at which a ship can engage hostile missiles to well beyond the radar horizon, thereby improving area, local, and self-defense capabilities. Operating under the direction of a designated commander, CEC enables a battle group or joint task force to act as a single, geographically dispersed combat system to confront the evolving threat of anti-ship cruise missiles and theatre ballistic missiles. As of 2006, CEC is installed on five aircraft carriers, *John F Kennedy, Nimitz, Eisenhower, John C Stennis* and *Ronald Reagan*; six Aegis cruisers, *Princeton, Chosin, Hue City, Anzio, Vicksburg* and *Cape St George*; 13 new construction destroyers, including *McCampbell, Shoup, Mason, Mustin, Prebel, Chaffee, Pinckney, Momsen, Chung Hoon, Nitze* and *James E Williams*; six amphibious ships including *Wasp* and *San Antonio*; and four E-2C Hawkeye 2000 air squadrons. It is planned to install CEC in all CV/CVN, LHD 7 and 8, CG 47, DDG 51, LHD, LPD 17, DD(X) and LCS class ships, in one more E-2C squadron and follow-on E-2D aircraft.

Global Broadcast Service (GBS)

The Global Broadcast Service augments and interfaces with other systems to provide virtual two-way Internet Protocol (IP) networked communications to deliver a continuous, high-speed, one-way flow of high-volume information broadcast to support: routine operations, training and military exercises, special activities, crisis, situational awareness, weapons targeting, intelligence, and the transition to and conduct of operations short of nuclear war. Homeland defensive operations are supported by a requirement for continental US coverage, which also provides exercise support, training and work-ups for deployment. GBS also supports military operations with US allies or coalition forces. GBS is an information technologies, mission-essential, national security system providing network-centric warfare communications, but does not incorporate nuclear survivability and hardening features. GBS provides a limited anti-jam capability and this may become a required capability in future. GBS will provide the capability to disseminate quickly large information products to various joint and small user platforms. With increased capacity, faster delivery of data, and near real-time receipt of imagery and data to the warfighter, it will reduced reliance on current MILSATCOM systems.

Global Command and Control System (GCCS)

GCCS is a comprehensive, worldwide network-centric system which provides the National Command Authority (NCA), Joint Chiefs of Staff, combatant and functional unified commands, Services, Defense Agencies, Joint Task Forces and their Service components, and others with information processing and dissemination capabilities necessary to conduct Command and Control (C^2) of forces. GCCS is a means to implement the Command, Control, Communications, Computers, and Intelligence for the Warrior (C^4IFTW) concept. GCCS provides the operational commanders with a near-realtime Common Operational Picture, intelligence information, collaborative joint operational planning and execution tools, and other information necessary for the execution of joint operations.

Global Command and Control System (Maritime) (GCCS-M) (ex-JMCIS)

GCCS-Maritime (GCCS-M) (formerly the Joint Maritime Command Information System (JMCIS)) is the designated command and control (C2) migration system for the Navy and is the naval implementation of the Global Command and Control System (GCCS). The evolutionary integration of previous C2 and intelligence systems, GCCS-M supports multiple warfighting and intelligence missions for commanders at every echelon, in all afloat, ashore, and tactical naval environments, and for joint, coalition, and allied forces. GCCS-M meets the joint and service requirements for a single, integrated, scalable Command and Control (C2) system that receives, displays, correlates, fuses, and maintains geo-locational track information on friendly, hostile, and neutral land, sea, and air forces and integrates it with available intelligence and environmental information.

- GCCS-M supports evolving concepts for Network-Centric Operations by receiving, displaying, correlating, fusing, and integrating all available track, intelligence and imagery information for the warfighter. In early 2004, more than 56 joint and Naval systems interfaced with GCCS-M to exchange data and support warfighter capabilities in 14 mission areas. Key capabilities include: Multisource information management
- Display and dissemination through extensive communications interfaces
- Multisource data fusion and analysis/decision making tools
- Force co-ordination.

GCCS-M is implemented afloat (formerly referred to as Navy Tactical Command System-Afloat (NTCS-A) and Joint Maritime Command Information System (JMCIS) Afloat), at ashore fixed command centers (formerly referred to as Operational Support System (OSS) and JMCIS Ashore), and as the command and control (C^2) portion of mobile command centers (formerly known as Tactical Support Center (TSC) and JMCIS Tactical-Mobile). GCCS-M now refers to all three GCCS-M implementations.

Integrated Broadcast Service/Joint Tactical Terminal (IBS/JTT)

The Integrated Broadcast Service (IBS) is a system-of-systems that will migrate the Tactical Receive Equipment and Related Applications Data Dissemination System (TDDS), Tactical Information Broadcast Service (TIBS), Tactical Reconnaissance Intelligence Exchange System (TRIXS), and Near Real-Time Dissemination (NRTD) system into an integrated service with a common format. The IBS will send data via communications paths, such as UHF, SHF, EHF, GBS, and via networks. This program supports Indications Warning (I&W), surveillance, and targeting data requirements of tactical and operational commanders and targeting staffs across all warfare areas. It comprises broadcast-generation and transceiver equipment that provides intelligence data to tactical users. The Joint Tactical Terminal (JTT) will receive, decrypt, process, format, distribute, and transmit tactical data according to preset user-defined criteria across open-architecture equipment. JTT will be modular and will have the capability to receive all current tactical intelligence broadcasts (TDDS, TADIXS-B, TIBS, and TRIXS). JTT will also be interoperable with the follow-on IBS UHF broadcasts. However, the current JTT form factor does not meet space and weight constraints for a majority of the Navy and Air Force airborne platforms. Therefore, to ensure joint interoperability, the Navy and Air Force will continue to support the current Multimission Airborne Tactical Terminal (MATT) through a low cost Pre-Planned Product Improvement (P3I) program until the transition to an IBS capable JTRS airborne variant starting in FY 2007.

The US Army-procured Joint Tactical Terminal will receive, decrypt, process, format and distribute tactical data according to preset user-defined criteria across open-architecture equipment.

Integrated Radar Optical Surveillance and Sighting System (IROS3)

IROS3 is the Situational Awareness component of the Shipboard Protection System (SPS) Increment one. It employs COTS-based/Open Architecture products, and its key components include SPS-73 or equivalent surface search radar, electro-optical/infra-red devices, an integrated surveillance system, spotlights, long range acoustic devices, and remotely operated stabilised small arms mounts. SPS Increment I is designed to detect, classify and engage real-time asymmetric threats at close-range to ships in port, at anchor and while transiting choke points or operating in restricted waters. The system provides 360° Situational Awareness (SA) and employs COTS integration to support incremental modifications as needed to tailor the system to the mission. The system has undergone extensive testing in the laboratory and a prototype is being tested at sea in *Ramage*. The system is scheduled to be installed in most ship classes, including surface combatants, patrol boats, amphibious and auxiliary ships, and Coast Guard cutters from FY05.

Joint Service Imagery Processing System (JSIPS)

JSIPS-N is the component of the joint programme to receive and exploit infra-red and electro-optical imagery from tactical airborne reconnaissance systems. It is proposed to install the system in all aircraft carriers, amphibious assault ships and possibly in command ships. JSIPS will also provide the USMC with an afloat/ashore processing facility that can be deployed as an integral element of Marine Air-Ground Task Forces (MAGTFs). JSIPS upgrades under consideration include a common radar processor for both tactical and theatre-level radars, and an automated capability to insert and process mapping, charting and geodesy products.

Joint Surveillance Target Attack Radar System (JSTARS)

JSTARS is described as a 'bulletproof anti-jam datalink', utilising omnidirectional broadcast on UHF SATCOM. It receives and transmits real time MTI/FTI/SAR data via a secure uplink and downlink. It is used to demonstrate 'sensor to shooter' technology.

Joint Tactical Information Distribution System (JTIDS)

A joint program directed by the Office of the Secretary of Defense, JTIDS is a digital information-distribution system which provides rapid, crypto-secure, jam-resistant (frequency-hopping), and low-probability-of-exploitation tactical data and voice communication at a high data rate to Navy tactical aircraft and ships and Marine Corps units. JTIDS also provides capabilities for common-grid navigation and automatic communications relay. It has been integrated into numerous platforms and systems, including US Navy aircraft carriers, surface warships, amphibious assault ships, and E-2C Hawkeye aircraft; US Air Force Airborne Warning and Command System (AWACS) aircraft; and Marine Corps Tactical Air Operations Centers (TAOCs) and Tactical Air Command Centers (TACCs). Other service and foreign country participants include the US Army, UK and Canada. Additionally, JTIDS has been identified as the preferred communications link for Theatre Ballistic Missile Defense programs. JTIDS is the first implementation of the Link-16 Joint Message Standard (J-series) and provides the single, near real-time, joint datalink network for information exchange among joint and combined forces for command and control of tactical operations.

Land Attack Warfare System (LAWS)

This prototype system networks all shooters (tactical air, shore artillery and seaborne fire support) into a Battle Local Area Network (Battle LAN) known as the 'Ring of Fire'. This automatically assigns fire missions to the most capable unit in the Battle LAN. LAWS controls preplanned missions, including Tomahawk, as well as time critical calls for fire from land forces. Fleet Battle Experiment ALFA was the initial test of this system.

Link Eleven Improvement Program (LEIP)

This programme improves Link 11 connectivity and reliability and supports NILE (NATO Improved Link 11 and Link 22). Link 11 will be the common datalink for all US Navy and allied ships (seven NATO navies) not equipped with JTIDS/Link 16. NILE/Link 22 is an element of the TADIL-J family. LEIP thus provides improvements in fleet support, training, commonality and interoperability. In addition to NILE, the programme comprises the Common Shipboard Data Terminal Set (CSDTS), Mobile Universal Link Translator System (MULTS), and Multiple Unit Link 11 Test and Operational Training System (MULTOTS). Some 190 CSDTS installations are planned.

Miniature Demand Assigned Multiple Access (Mini-DAMA)

Mini-DAMA is a communications system that supports the exchange of secure and non-secure Battle Group coordination data, tactical data and voice between base band processing equipment over UHF SATCOM, 25/5 kHz DAMA, 25/5 kHz Non-DAMA, and UHF LOS. In 2000, the Navy completed installations for submarines AV(2) and mine warfare ships V(2). Aircraft installations V(3) continue. These Mini-DAMA radio installations provide the channel utilisation efficiencies by employing Time Division Multiple Access (TDMA) methods that have been achieved for surface warfare ships and shore stations equipped with the larger version TD-1271 DAMA multiplexer.

Mission Data System (MDS)

This system allows planners to view Tomahawk Land Attack Missile information. MDS receives via TADIXS A or OTCIXS I digital Mission Data Updates (MDUs) from the Cruise Missile Support Activity (CMSA) and stores preplanned TLAM strike plans. Initial TLAM mission data fill is distributed via magnetic tape media provided by the CMSA.

Multifunctional Information Distribution – Low Volume Terminal (MIDS-LVT)

MIDS-LVT is a multinational co-operative development program to design, develop, and produce a tactical information distribution system equivalent in capability to Joint Tactical Information Distribution System (JTIDS), but in a low-volume, lightweight, compact terminal designed for fighter aircraft with applications in helicopters, ships, and ground sites. US Navy procurement, limited by available resources, is planned for F/A-18 Hornet aircraft as the lead aviation platform and surface craft. As a P3I of the JTIDS Class 2 Terminal, MIDS-LVT will employ the Link-16 (TADIL-J) message standard of US Navy/NATO publications. MIDS-LVT is fully interoperable with JTIDS and was designed in response to current aircraft, surface

ship, submarine, and ground host volume and weight constraints. The solution variants-MIDS-LVT (1), MIDS-LVT (2), and MIDS-LVT (3)-support US Navy, Marine Corps, and Air Force aircraft; US Navy ships; US Army Patriot, THAAD, MEADS and ground-based defense systems; USAF and USMC ground-based Command and Control platforms; and potentially other tactical aircraft and ground-based systems. MIDS-LVT is an international project involving the United States, Germany, Spain, Italy, and France.

Trusted Information Systems (TIS)

The Multi-Level Security (MLS) capabilities of the Navy's Ocean Surveillance Information System (OSIS) and Radiant Mercury are complementary systems which have been combined into a single TIS programme. The aim is to facilitate development and expansion of a Commander's capability automatically to exchange critical intelligence and operational information with all forces whether US, allied, or coalition.

The OSIS Evolutionary Development (OED) system is DoD's only PL-4 accredited C4I processing and dissemination system. It serves as the backbone automated information system supporting the Common Operational Picture (COP) at US and allied Joint Intelligence Centers (JICs). OED receives, processes, and disseminates timely all-source surveillance information on fixed and mobile targets of interest, both afloat and ashore, within an MLS environment. OED permits operators to collaborate in multiple domains, monitor, analyse, and support multiple views of the battle space corresponding to multiple security classification levels. Its robust correlation and communications subsystems ensure extremely rapid delivery of both record message traffic and intelligence broadcasts in support of the Unified Combatant Commanders, Joint Task Force commanders, individual units, and allies. The MLS capabilities in OED are certified and accredited to support compartmented multilevel networks at the SCI level and are envisioned to serve as the core technology upon which future Navy networks and databases running at multiple classification levels can be effectively combined to allow appropriately cleared operators access to information from a single workstation.

Radiant Mercury (RM) provides the accredited capability to automatically sanitise, transliterate, and downgrade classified, formatted information to users at lower classification levels. RM helps ensure critical Indications and Warning intelligence is provided quickly to operational decision makers at various security and releasability levels.

RM is currently fielded on Force Level ships bridging data transfer between SCI GCCS-M and GENSER GCCS-M. RM also serves as a sanitiser within OED. Radiant Mercury Imagery Guard (RMIG) combines a digital signature process with RM allowing the networked transfer of imagery between security domains.

Ship Self-Defense System (SSDS) Mk 1 and 2

SSDS provides the integrated combat system for aircraft carriers and amphibious ships, enabling them to keep pace with the anti-ship cruise missile (ASCM) threat. Moving toward an open-architecture distributed-processing system, SSDS integrates the detection and engagement elements of the combat system. With automated weapons control doctrine, Cooperative Engagement Capability (CEC), and enhanced battlespace awareness, SSDS provides these ships with a robust self-defense capability in support of Sea Shield.

SSDS Mk 1 provides doctrine-based, Quick Reaction Combat Capability (QRCC), plus automated detect through multithreat engagement capability. It enhances capabilities for Force Protection using own-ship and remote data in support of AAW capstone requirements.

SSDS Mk 2 integrates with Co-operative Engagement Capability (CEC) and provides the QRCC of SSDS Mk 1 and selected features of the Advanced Combat Direction System (ACDS) to support multiwarfare area capability, improve joint interoperability and provide an integrated, coherent real-time command and control system for CV/CVN, LPD and LHD class ships. SSDS Mk 1 has been installed in 12 LSDs; and SSDS Mk 2 in three CVNs (CVN 68, CVN 76, CVN 69) and one LPD (LPD 17). Mk 2 is also to be fitted in LHD 8. An open-architecture version of Mk 2 is expected to be deployed by 2008 and SSDS is expected to be integral to future combat systems such as DD(X).

Theatre Battle Management Core System (TBMCS)

TBMCS replaces the Contingency Theatre Automated Planning System (CTAPS) as the only command and control system authorised to produce the Air Tasking Order (ATO). TBMCS has the capability to plan and execute air operations in any theatre of operations and is considered the core system for the Air Force's Air Operation Center (AOC). All services use TBMCS and, within the USN, it is installed in carriers, command ships and large-deck amphibious ships (LHA/LHD).

Major commercial shipyards

Shipbuilders

General Dynamics Corporation, Bath Iron Works, Bath, Maine.
General Dynamics Corporation, Electric Boat Division, Groton, Connecticut.
General Dynamics Corporation, National Steel and Shipbuilding Company, San Diego, California.
Northrop Grumman, Ship Systems Sector, Avondale Operation, New Orleans, Louisiana.
Northrop Grumman, Ship Systems Sector, Ingalls Operation, Pascagoula, Mississippi.
Northrop Grumman, Newport News Shipbuilding, Newport News, Virginia.

Ship Repairers

Al Larson Boat Shop, Long Beach, California.
American Shipyard Co. L.L.C. Newport, Rhode Island.

Atlantic Drydock Corp., Jacksonville, Florida.
Atlantic Marine, Inc, Jacksonville, Florida.
Atlantic Marine, Inc, Mobile, Alabama.
Bay Ship & Yacht Co., San Francisco, California.
Bender Shipbuilding & Repair Co., Inc, Mobile, Alabama.
Cascade General Inc, Portland, Oregon.
Colonna's Shipyard, Inc, Norfolk, Virginia.
Continental Maritime of San Diego, San Diego, California.
Detyens Shipyards, Inc, Charleston, South Carolina.
Earl Industries, L.L.C., Norfolk, Virginia.
Halter Marine Inc, Gulfport, Mississippi.
Intermarine USA (Montedison Spa/Hercules, Inc.), Savannah, Georgia.
Lake Union Drydock Co., Seattle, Washington.
Marine Hydraulics International Inc, Norfolk, Virginia.
Metal Trades, Inc, Charleston, South Carolina.
Metro Machine Corp., Norfolk, Virginia.
Moon Engineering Co. Inc, Norfolk, Virginia.
Norfolk Shipbuilding & Drydock Corp., Norfolk, Virginia.

Norfolk Ship Repair & Drydock Co., Inc, Norfolk, Virginia.
North Florida Shipyards, Inc, Jacksonville, Florida.
Pacific Ship Repair & Fabrication, San Diego, California.
San Francisco Drydock, Inc, San Francisco, California.
Southwest Marine, Inc, San Diego, California.
Southwest Marine, Inc, (San Pedro Div) Long Beach, California.
Tampa Bay Shipbuilding & Repair Co., Tampa, Florida.
Tecnico Corporation, Norfolk, Virginia.
Todd Pacific Shipyards Corp., Seattle, Washington.

Notes: All the yards mentioned have been involved in naval shipbuilding, overhaul, or modernisation. General Dynamics/Electric Boat yard is engaged only in submarine work and Newport News is the only US shipyard capable of building nuclear-powered aircraft carriers.

Major Warships Taken Out of Service 2003 to mid-2006

Submarines

2004 *Parche, Portsmouth*
2005 *Salt Lake City*

Aircraft Carriers

2003 *Constellation*

Cruisers

2004 *Ticonderoga, Yorktown, Valley Forge*
2005 *Vincennes, Thomas S Gates*

Destroyers

2003 *Kinkaid, Fife, Paul F Foster, Arthur W Radford, Hayler, Oldendorf, Briscoe, Deyo, Elliot*
2004 *O'Brien, Stump, Thorn, Fletcher*
2005 *Spruance, Cushing, O'Bannon*

Frigates

2003 *Sides, George Philip, Estocin* (to Turkey)

Command Ships

2005 *La Salle*

Amphibious Forces

2003 *Mount Vernon, Portland, Anchorage*
2005 *Belleau Wood, Duluth*

Auxiliaries

2005 *Sacramento, Seattle, Detroit*
2006 *Camden*

Special Mission Ships

2004 *Capable*

HULL NUMBERS

Notes: Ships in reserve not included.

SUBMARINES

Ballistic Missile Submarines

Ohio class
SSBN 730	Henry M Jackson
SSBN 731	Alabama
SSBN 732	Alaska
SSBN 733	Nevada
SSBN 734	Tennessee
SSBN 735	Pennsylvania
SSBN 736	West Virginia
SSBN 737	Kentucky
SSBN 738	Maryland
SSBN 739	Nebraska
SSBN 740	Rhode Island
SSBN 741	Maine
SSBN 742	Wyoming
SSBN 743	Louisiana

Cruise Missile Submarines

Ohio class
SSGN 726	Ohio
SSGN 727	Michigan (conversion)
SSGN 728	Florida (conversion)
SSGN 729	Georgia (conversion)

Attack Submarines

Seawolf class
SSN 21	Seawolf
SSN 22	Connecticut
SSN 23	Jimmy Carter

Los Angeles class
SSN 688	Los Angeles
SSN 690	Philadelphia
SSN 691	Memphis
SSN 698	Bremerton
SSN 699	Jacksonville

Attack Submarines—*continued*

SSN 700	Dallas
SSN 701	La Jolla
SSN 705	City of Corpus Christi
SSN 706	Albuquerque
SSN 708	Minneapolis-Saint Paul
SSN 709	Hyman G Rickover
SSN 710	Augusta
SSN 711	San Francisco
SSN 713	Houston
SSN 714	Norfolk
SSN 715	Buffalo
SSN 717	Olympia
SSN 718	Honolulu
SSN 719	Providence
SSN 720	Pittsburgh
SSN 721	Chicago
SSN 722	Key West
SSN 723	Oklahoma City
SSN 724	Louisville
SSN 725	Helena
SSN 750	Newport News
SSN 751	San Juan
SSN 752	Pasadena
SSN 753	Albany
SSN 754	Topeka
SSN 755	Miami
SSN 756	Scranton
SSN 757	Alexandria
SSN 758	Asheville
SSN 759	Jefferson City
SSN 760	Annapolis
SSN 761	Springfield
SSN 762	Columbus
SSN 763	Santa Fe
SSN 764	Boise
SSN 765	Montpelier
SSN 766	Charlotte
SSN 767	Hampton
SSN 768	Hartford
SSN 769	Toledo
SSN 770	Tucson
SSN 771	Columbia
SSN 772	Greeneville
SSN 773	Cheyenne

Virginia class

SSN 774	Virginia
SSN 775	Texas
SSN 776	Hawaii (bldg)
SSN 777	North Carolina (bldg)
SSN 778	New Hampshire (bldg)
SSN 779	New Mexico (bldg)

SURFACE COMBATANTS

Aircraft Carriers

Kitty Hawk class

CV 63	Kitty Hawk

John F Kennedy class

CV 67	John F Kennedy

Enterprise class

CVN 65	Enterprise

Nimitz class

CVN 68	Nimitz
CVN 69	Dwight D Eisenhower
CVN 70	Carl Vinson
CVN 71	Theodore Roosevelt
CVN 72	Abraham Lincoln
CVN 73	George Washington
CVN 74	John C Stennis
CVN 75	Harry S Truman
CVN 76	Ronald Reagan
CVN 77	George H W Bush (bldg)

Cruisers

Ticonderoga class

CG 52	Bunker Hill
CG 53	Mobile Bay
CG 54	Antietam
CG 55	Leyte Gulf
CG 56	San Jacinto
CG 57	Lake Champlain
CG 58	Philippine Sea
CG 59	Princeton
CG 60	Normandy
CG 61	Monterey
CG 62	Chancellorsville
CG 63	Cowpens
CG 64	Gettysburg
CG 65	Chosin
CG 66	Hue City
CG 67	Shiloh
CG 68	Anzio
CG 69	Vicksburg
CG 70	Lake Erie
CG 71	Cape St George
CG 72	Vella Gulf
CG 73	Port Royal

Destroyers

Arleigh Burke class

DDG 51	Arleigh Burke
DDG 52	Barry
DDG 53	John Paul Jones
DDG 54	Curtis Wilbur
DDG 55	Stout
DDG 56	John S McCain
DDG 57	Mitscher

Destroyers—*continued*

DDG 58	Laboon
DDG 59	Russell
DDG 60	Paul Hamilton
DDG 61	Ramage
DDG 62	Fitzgerald
DDG 63	Stethem
DDG 64	Carney
DDG 65	Benfold
DDG 66	Gonzalez
DDG 67	Cole
DDG 68	The Sullivans
DDG 69	Milius
DDG 70	Hopper
DDG 71	Ross
DDG 72	Mahan
DDG 73	Decatur
DDG 74	McFaul
DDG 75	Donald Cook
DDG 76	Higgins
DDG 77	O'Kane
DDG 78	Porter
DDG 79	Oscar Austin
DDG 80	Roosevelt
DDG 81	Winston S Churchill
DDG 82	Lassen
DDG 83	Howard
DDG 84	Bulkeley
DDG 85	McCampbell
DDG 86	Shoup
DDG 87	Mason
DDG 88	Preble
DDG 89	Mustin
DDG 90	Chaffee
DDG 91	Pinckney
DDG 92	Momsen
DDG 93	Chung-Hoon
DDG 94	Nitze
DDG 95	James E Williams
DDG 96	Bainbridge
DDG 97	Halsey
DDG 98	Forrest Sherman
DDG 99	Farragut (bldg)
DDG 100	Kidd (bldg)
DDG 101	Gridley (bldg)
DDG 102	Sampson (bldg)
DDG 103	Truxtun (bldg)
DDG 104	Sterett (bldg)
DDG 105	Dewey (bldg)
DDG 106	Stockdale (ord)

Frigates

Oliver Hazard Perry class

FFG 8	McInerney
FFG 28	Boone (NRF)
FFG 29	Stephen W Groves (NRF)
FFG 32	John L Hall
FFG 33	Jarrett
FFG 36	Underwood
FFG 37	Crommelin (NRF)
FFG 38	Curts (NRF)
FFG 39	Doyle (NRF)
FFG 40	Halyburton
FFG 41	McClusky (NRF)
FFG 42	Klakring (NRF)
FFG 43	Thach
FFG 45	De Wert
FFG 46	Rentz
FFG 47	Nicholas
FFG 48	Vandegrift
FFG 49	Robert G Bradley
FFG 50	Taylor
FFG 51	Gary
FFG 52	Carr
FFG 53	Hawes
FFG 54	Ford
FFG 55	Elrod
FFG 56	Simpson (NRF)
FFG 57	Reuben James
FFG 58	Samuel B Roberts
FFG 59	Kauffman
FFG 60	Rodney M Davis (NRF)
FFG 61	Ingraham

Coastal Patrol Craft

Cyclone class

PC 3	Hurricane
PC 5	Typhoon
PC 6	Sirocco
PC 7	Squall
PC 9	Chinook
PC 10	Firebolt
PC 11	Whirlwind
PC 12	Thunderbolt

COMMAND SHIPS

Blue Ridge class

LCC 19	Blue Ridge
LCC 20	Mount Whitney

Raleigh and Austin class

AGF 11	Coronado

AMPHIBIOUS FORCES

Amphibious Assault Ships

Wasp class

LHD 1	Wasp
LHD 2	Essex
LHD 3	Kearsarge

Amphibious Assault Ships—*continued*

LHD 4	Boxer
LHD 5	Bataan
LHD 6	Bonhomme Richard
LHD 7	Iwo Jima
LHD 8	Makin Island (bldg)

Tarawa class

LHA 1	Tarawa
LHA 2	Saipan
LHA 4	Nassau
LHA 5	Peleliu

Amphibious Transport Docks

Austin class

LPD 4	Austin
LPD 5	Ogden
LPD 7	Cleveland
LPD 8	Dubuque
LPD 9	Denver
LPD 10	Juneau
LPD 12	Shreveport
LPD 13	Nashville
LPD 14	Trenton
LPD 15	Ponce

San Antonio class

LPD 17	San Antonio
LPD 18	New Orleans
LPD 19	Mesa Verde (bldg)
LPD 20	Green Bay (bldg)
LPD 21	New York (bldg)
LPD 22	San Diego (ord)
LPD 23	Anchorage (ord)
LPD 24	Arlington (ord)
LPD 25	Somerset (ord)

Amphibious Cargo Ships

Whidbey Island class

LSD 41	Whidbey Island
LSD 42	Germantown
LSD 43	Fort McHenry
LSD 44	Gunston Hall
LSD 45	Comstock
LSD 46	Tortuga
LSD 47	Rushmore
LSD 48	Ashland

Harpers Ferry class

LSD 49	Harpers Ferry
LSD 50	Carter Hall
LSD 51	Oak Hill
LSD 52	Pearl Harbor

MINE WARFARE FORCES

Mine Countermeasures Ships

Avenger class

MCM 1	Avenger (NRF)
MCM 2	Defender (NRF)
MCM 3	Sentry (NRF)
MCM 4	Champion (NRF)
MCM 5	Guardian
MCM 6	Devastator
MCM 7	Patriot
MCM 8	Scout
MCM 9	Pioneer
MCM 10	Warrior
MCM 11	Gladiator (NRF)
MCM 12	Ardent
MCM 13	Dextrous
MCM 14	Chief

Osprey class

MHC 51	Osprey (NRF)
MHC 52	Heron (NRF)
MHC 53	Pelican (NRF)
MHC 54	Robin (NRF)
MHC 55	Oriole (NRF)
MHC 56	Kingfisher (NRF)
MHC 57	Cormorant (NRF)
MHC 58	Black Hawk (NRF)
MHC 59	Falcon (NRF)
MHC 60	Cardinal
MHC 61	Raven
MHC 62	Shrike (NRF)

MATERIAL SUPPORT SHIPS

Submarine Tenders

Emory S Land class

AS 39	Emory S Land
AS 40	Frank Cable

Salvage Ships

Safeguard class

ARS 50	Safeguard
ARS 52	Salvor

MISCELLANEOUS

Auxiliary Research Submarine

Dolphin class

AGSS 555	Dolphin

High Speed Vessels

HSV-1X	Joint Venture
TSV-1X	Spearhead

Oceanographic Research Ships

AGOR 14	Melville
AGOR 15	Knorr
AGOR 23	Thomas G Thompson
AGOR 24	Roger Revelle
AGOR 25	Atlantis
AGOR 26	Kilo Moana

MILITARY SEALIFT COMMAND

NAVAL FLEET AUXILIARY FORCE

Fast Combat Support Ships

T-AOE 6	Supply
T-AOE 7	Rainier
T-AOE 8	Arctic
T-AOE 10	Bridge

Ammunition Ships

T-AE 26	Kilauea
T-AE 32	Flint
T-AE 33	Shasta
T-AE 34	Mount Baker
T-AE 35	Kiska

Cargo and Ammunition Ships

T-AKE 1	Lewis and Clark (bldg)
T-AKE 2	Sacagawea (bldg)
T-AKE 3	Alan Shepard (bldg)

Combat Stores Ships

T-AFS 3	Niagara Falls
T-AFS 5	Concord
T-AFS 7	San Jose
T-AFS 9	Spica
T-AFS 10	Saturn

Hospital Ships

T-AH 19	Mercy
T-AH 20	Comfort

Oilers

Henry J Kaiser class

T-AO 187	Henry J Kaiser (PREPO)
T-AO 188	Joshua Humphries
T-AO 189	John Lenthall
T-AO 193	Walter S Diehl
T-AO 194	John Ericsson
T-AO 195	Leroy Grumman
T-AO 196	Kanawha
T-AO 197	Pecos
T-AO 198	Big Horn
T-AO 199	Tippecanoe
T-AO 200	Guadalupe
T-AO 201	Patuxent
T-AO 202	Yukon
T-AO 203	Laramie
T-AO 204	Rappahannock

Salvage Ships

T-ARS 50	Grasp
—	Grapple

Fleet Ocean Tugs

Powhatan class

T-ATF 168	Catawba
T-ATF 169	Navajo
T-ATF 171	Sioux
T-ATF 172	Apache

SPECIAL MISSION SHIPS

Acoustic Survey Ship

T-AG 195	Hayes

Cable Repair Ship

T-ARC 7	Zeus

High Speed Vessel

HSV-2	Swift

Missile Range Instrumentation Ships

T-AGM 23	Observation Island
T-AGM 24	Invincible

Navigation Test/Launch Area Support Ship

T-AG 45	Waters

Surveying Ships/Oceanographic Ships

T-AGS 51	John McDonnell
T-AGS 60	Pathfinder
T-AGS 61	Sumner
T-AGS 62	Bowditch
T-AGS 63	Henson
T-AGS 64	Bruce C Heezen
T-AGS 65	Mary Sears

Ocean/Air Surveillance Ships

T-AGOS 19	Victorious
T-AGOS 21	Effective
T-AGOS 22	Loyal
T-AGOS 23	Impeccable

STRATEGIC SEALIFT FORCE

Fast Sealift Ships

T-AKR 287	Algol
T-AKR 288	Bellatrix
T-AKR 289	Denebola
T-AKR 290	Pollux
T-AKR 291	Altair
T-AKR 292	Regulus
T-AKR 293	Capella
T-AKR 294	Antares

Large, Medium-speed Ro-Ro

T-AKR 295	Shughart
T-AKR 296	Gordon
T-AKR 297	Yano

Large, Medium-speed Ro-Ro — *continued*

T-AKR 298	Gilliland
T-AKR 300	Bob Hope
T-AKR 301	Fisher
T-AKR 302	Seay
T-AKR 303	Mendonca
T-AKR 304	Pililaau
T-AKR 305	Brittin
T-AKR 306	Benavidez

Tankers

T-AOT 1122	Paul Buck
T-AOT 1123	Samuel L Cobb
T-AOT 1124	Richard G Matthiesen
T-AOT 1125	Lawrence H Gianella

PREPOSITIONING PROGRAMME

Container Ships

T-AK 4296	Capt Steven L Bennett
T-AK 4396	Maj Bernard F Fisher
T-AK 4543	Lt Col John U D Page
T-AK 4544	SSGT Edward A Carter Jr
T-AK 4638	A1C William H Pitsenbarger
T-AK 323	MV TSGT John A Chapman

Large, Medium-Speed, Ro-Ro

T-AKR 310	Watson
T-AKR 311	Sisler
T-AKR 312	Dahl
T-AKR 313	Red Cloud
T-AKR 314	Charlton
T-AKR 315	Watkins
T-AKR 316	Pomeroy
T-AKR 317	Soderman

Aviation Logistic Ships

T-AVB 3	Wright
T-AVB 4	Curtiss

Maritime Prepositioning Ships

T-AK 3000	CPL Louis J Hauge, Jr
T-AK 3001	PFC William B Baugh
T-AK 3002	PFC James Anderson, Jr
T-AK 3003	1st Lt Alex Bonnyman
T-AK 3004	PVT Franklin J Phillips
T-AK 3005	SGT Matej Kocak
T-AK 3006	PFC Eugene A Obregon
T-AK 3007	MAJ Stephen W Pless
T-AK 3008	2nd Lt John P Bobo
T-AK 3009	PFC Dewayne T Williams
T-AK 3010	1st Lt Baldomero Lopez
T-AK 3011	1st Lt Jack Lummus
T-AK 3012	SGT William R Button
T-AK 3015	1st Lt Harry L Martin
T-AK 3016	L/Cpl Roy M Wheat
T-AK 3017	GYSGT Fred W Stockham

Heavy Lift Vessel

HSV	Westpac Express

READY RESERVE FORCE
(see page 917-918)

(see page 917-918)

SUBMARINES

Notes: (1) **Deep submergence vehicles:** The Deep Submergence Vehicles (DSV), including the nuclear-propelled *NR-1*, are listed following the 'Research Ships' section.

(2) **Seal Delivery Vehicles (SDVs):** There are 10 Mk VIII Mod 1 six-man mini wet submersibles in service for naval commando units. These SDVs can be carried by suitably modified SSNs. Range 35 n miles at up to 150 ft. All have been SLEPed from 1995 to improve performance. A new design ASDS (Advanced SEAL Delivery System) is a dry submersible (65 × 10 ft) with electrical propulsion and a crew of two. Designed to operate from a mother submarine, it can carry SEALs and combat gear clandestinely to and from hostile shores. Range is greater than 125 n miles. Optical and communications periscopes and a small sonar are fitted. A prototype was ordered from Northrop Grumman in September 1994 and contractor trials were completed in 2000. Final trials were successfully completed in September 2002. These included launch and recovery of ASDS from a host submarine SSN 722 *Greeneville* over several days to validate its underwater capability. Operational evaluation followed in mid-2003. SSN 776 *Charlotte* is also configured to host ASDS. As of early 2006, the first of a planned six ASDS was awaiting evaluation pending resolution of a number of reported problems. Procurement of the second craft, scheduled for 2008, may therefore be delayed. It is anticipated that two will be carried by the Ohio class SSGNs in due course. The craft can also be air-transported.

(3) **Unmanned Undersea Vehicles (UUVs):** Torpedo-sized and larger unmanned undersea vehicles are under development. Potential applications include underwater surveillance, mine-countermeasures and anti-submarine warfare. Early experience was gained with the Mine Search System (MSS), operational testing of which was completed in 1993. The 35 ft long vehicle had a titanium hull and demonstrated the performance of mine detection sonars and the ability of a UUV to survey designated areas with precise navigation. Further proof-of-concept experience was gained with the Long-Term Mine Reconnaissance System (LMRS) which was designed to be launched from the 21 in torpedo tubes of an SSN. An engineering development system was delivered in 2002 but the programme was discontinued in favour of development of a modular UUV in which payloads can be swapped. This concept is to be demonstrated in the experimental Advanced Development UUV (ADUUV) which should lead to the Mission-Reconfigurable UUV (MRUUV) which is scheduled to enter service in 2011. Further ahead, MRUUVs of larger size and longer endurance (perhaps two weeks) might be developed for launch from submarines and surface ships. Surface ship near-term programmes include the Battlespace Preparation Autonomous Underwater Vehicle, to be deployed in the Littoral Combat Ship, and the Surface Mine Countermeasures UUV.

SDV Mk VIII   *10/1997, A McKaskle, USN* / 0053312

ASDS   *6/2003, US Navy* / 0572767

Strategic Missile Submarines (SSBN)

Notes: The Trident missile fitted SSBN force provides the principal US strategic deterrent under the control of US Strategic Command at Offut Air Force Base, Nebraska. The Strategic Arms Reduction Treaty (START), implemented in December 2001, limits the combined number of SLBM and ICBM re-entry bodies (RBs) to 4,900.

Although there may be further bi-lateral agreements with Russia to update verification regimes, the Bush administration has decided to pursue long-term strategic nuclear force reductions without further detailed arms control negotiations. The START II treaty has thus been overtaken. As part of the reduction, the first four Ohio class

submarines are no longer required for strategic service. These boats are being converted into conventionally-armed guided missile SSGNs, capable also of deploying Special Forces. Although the missile tubes on SSGNs will not contain SLBMs, they will continue to count against START treaty limits.

14 OHIO CLASS (SSBN)

Name	No	Builders	Launched	Commissioned	F/S
HENRY M JACKSON	SSBN 730	General Dynamics (Electric Boat Div)	15 Oct 1983	6 Oct 1984	PA
ALABAMA	SSBN 731	General Dynamics (Electric Boat Div)	19 May 1984	25 May 1985	PA
ALASKA	SSBN 732	General Dynamics (Electric Boat Div)	12 Jan 1985	25 Jan 1986	PA
NEVADA	SSBN 733	General Dynamics (Electric Boat Div)	14 Sep 1985	16 Aug 1986	PA
TENNESSEE	SSBN 734	General Dynamics (Electric Boat Div)	13 Dec 1986	17 Dec 1988	AA
PENNSYLVANIA	SSBN 735	General Dynamics (Electric Boat Div)	23 Apr 1988	9 Sep 1989	PA
WEST VIRGINIA	SSBN 736	General Dynamics (Electric Boat Div)	14 Oct 1989	20 Oct 1990	AA
KENTUCKY	SSBN 737	General Dynamics (Electric Boat Div)	11 Aug 1990	13 July 1991	PA
MARYLAND	SSBN 738	General Dynamics (Electric Boat Div)	10 Aug 1991	13 June 1992	AA
NEBRASKA	SSBN 739	General Dynamics (Electric Boat Div)	15 Aug 1992	10 July 1993	PA
RHODE ISLAND	SSBN 740	General Dynamics (Electric Boat Div)	17 July 1993	9 July 1994	AA
MAINE	SSBN 741	General Dynamics (Electric Boat Div)	16 July 1994	29 July 1995	PA
WYOMING	SSBN 742	General Dynamics (Electric Boat Div)	15 July 1995	13 July 1996	AA
LOUISIANA	SSBN 743	General Dynamics (Electric Boat Div)	27 July 1996	6 Sep 1997	PA

Displacement, tons: 16,600 surfaced; 18,750 dived
Dimensions, feet (metres): 560 × 42 × 36.4
  (170.7 × 12.8 × 11.1)
Main machinery: Nuclear; 1 GE PWR S8G; 2 turbines; 60,000 hp *(44.8 MW)*; 1 shaft; 1 Magnetek auxiliary prop motor; 325 hp *(242 kW)*
Speed, knots: 24 dived
Complement: 155 (15 officers)

Missiles: SLBM: 24 Lockheed Trident C4 (730, 731); stellar inertial guidance to 7,400 km *(4,000 n miles)*; thermonuclear warhead of up to 8 MIRV Mk 4 with W76 warhead of 100 kT; CEP 450 m. Trident C4 is to be fully replaced by Trident D5 in 730-733 by 2008.
  24 Lockheed Trident D5 (732-743); stellar inertial guidance to 12,000 km *(6,500 n miles)*; thermonuclear warheads of up to 12 MIRVs of either Mk 4 with W76 of 100 kT each, or Mk 5 with W88 of 300-475 kT each; CEP 90 m. A limit of 8 RVs was set in 1991 under the START counting rules.
Torpedoes: 4—21 in *(533 mm)* Mk 68 bow tubes. Gould/Westinghouse Mk 48; ADCAP; wire-guided (option); active/passive homing to 50 km *(27 n miles)*/38 km

(21 n miles) at 40/55 kt; warhead 267 kg; depth to 900 m *(2,950 ft)*.
Countermeasures: Decoys: 8 launchers for Emerson Electric Mk 2; torpedo decoy.
  ESM: WLR-8(V)5; intercept. WLR-10; radar warning.
Combat data systems: DWS-118 and CCS Mk 2 Mod 3 with UYK 43/UYK 44 computers.
Weapons control: Mk 98 fire-control system.
Radars: Surface search/navigation/fire control: BPS 15A/H; I/J-band.
Sonars: IBM BQQ 6; passive search.
  Raytheon BQS 13; spherical array for BQQ 6.
  Ametek BQS 15; active/passive for close contacts; high frequency.
  Western Electric BQR 15 (with BQQ 9 signal processor); passive towed array. TB 23 thin line array.
  Raytheon BQR 19; active for navigation; high frequency.

Programmes: The size of the SSBN forces has been reduced to 14 hulls. *Ohio* completed conversion to SSGN in 2005 and conversion continues in *Michigan, Florida* and *Georgia*.

Modernisation: *Alaska* and *Nevada* have been upgraded to deploy Trident D5 missiles. *Jackson* is to complete conversion in 2007 and *Alabama* in 2008. Ohio class SSBNs are being upgraded with ARCI (Acoustic Rapid COTS Insertion) sonar and CCS Mk 2 Block 1 fire-control systems. Installation in *Alaska, Nevada, Pennsylvania* and *Kentucky* is complete and is to be undertaken in *West Virginia* in 2006.
Structure: The size of the Trident submarine is dictated primarily by the 24 vertically launched Trident missiles and the reactor plant to drive the ship. The reactor has a nuclear core life of about 20 years between refuellings. Diving depth is 244 m *(800 ft)*. Kollmorgen Type 152 and Type 82 periscopes. Mk 19 Air Turbine Pump for torpedo discharge.
Operational: Pacific Fleet units are based at Bangor, Washington, while the Atlantic Fleet units are based at King's Bay, Georgia. SSBNs 741 and 743 transferred to Bangor on 1 October 2005. In the current state of worldwide tensions, a modified alert status has been implemented. Single crews were considered but rejected. Hull life of the class is extended to 42 years.

PENNSYLVANIA   *12/2005*, Ships of the World* / 1154028

ALABAMA   *4/2004, Ships of the World* / 1043704

Cruise Missile Submarines (SSGN)

1 + 3 OHIO CLASS (SSGN)

Name	No	Builders	Launched	Commissioned	F/S
OHIO	SSGN 726 (ex-SSBN 726)	General Dynamics (Electric Boat Div)	7 Apr 1979	11 Nov 1981	PA
MICHIGAN	SSGN 727 (ex-SSBN 727)	General Dynamcis (Electric Boat Div)	26 Apr 1980	11 Sep 1982	Conv/PA
FLORIDA	SSGN 728 (ex-SSBN 728)	General Dynamics (Electric Boat Div)	14 Nov 1981	18 June 1983	Conv/AA
GEORGIA	SSGN 729 (ex-SSBN 729)	General Dynamics (Electric Boat Div)	6 Nov 1982	11 Feb 1984	Conv/AA

Displacement, tons: 16,764 surfaced; 18,750 dived
Dimensions, feet (metres): 560 × 42 × 36.4
(170.7 × 12.8 × 11.1)
Main machinery: Nuclear; 1 GE PWR S8G; 2 turbines; 60,000 hp *(44.8 MW)*; 1 shaft; 1 Magnetek auxiliary prop motor; 325 hp *(242 kW)*
Speed, knots: 24 dived
Complement: 155 (15 officers)

Missiles: SLCM: up to 154 Tomahawk and Tactical Tomahawk.
Torpedoes: 4—21 in *(533 mm)* Mk 68 bow tubes. Gould/Westinghouse Mk 48; ADCAP; wire-guided (option); active/passive homing to 50 km *(27 n miles)*/38 km *(21 n miles)* at 40/55 kt; warhead 267 kg; depth to 900 m *(2,950 ft)*.
Countermeasures: Decoys: 8 launchers for Countermeasures Set Acoustic (CSA).
ESM: BLQ-10; radar and comms intercept and analysis.
Combat data systems: AN/BYG-1 Combat Control System.
Weapons control: AN/BYG-1.
Radars: Surface search/navigation/fire control: BPS 15J; I/J-band.

Sonars: Lockheed Martin AN/BQQ-10 suite.
AN/BQQ-6; passive search (spherical array).
TB 23; passive towed array (thin line).
TB 16; passive towed array (fat line).

Programmes: The 1994 nuclear posture review recommended a 14-strong SSBN force and that the remaining four Ohio class be converted to SSGN role. The SSGN would include land attack, special forces insertion and support and ISR roles. Conversion contract with General Dynamics Electric Boat in October 2002. *Ohio* started mid-life refuelling on 15 November 2002 and conversion work (at Puget Sound Naval Shipyard) on 19 November 2003. She completed conversion in November 2005. *Florida* started mid-life refuelling in August 2003 and conversion work (at Norfolk Naval Shipyard) in April 2004. *Michigan* started refuelling in March 2004 and conversion work (at Puget Sound) in January 2005. *Georgia* started refuelling in March 2005 and started conversion (at Norfolk) in October 2005.
Modernisation: Conversion work will allow SSGN to carry up to 154 Tomahawk or Tactical Tomahawk missiles by enabling seven cruise missiles to be fired from each

of 22 of the current 24 Trident missile tubes. Eight of these tubes are likely to be interchangeable with Special Forces stowage canisters. The remaining two tubes will be permanently configured for wet/dry launch of up to 66 special operations forces. The combat system is also to be upgraded and future payloads are being developed to augment the baseline configuration.
Structure: The size of the submarine was dictated primarily by the 24 missile tubes and the reactor plant to drive the ship. The reactor has a nuclear core life of about 20 years between refuellings. Diving depth is 244 m *(800 ft)*. Type 8J periscope and Integrated Submarine Imaging System (ISIS). Mk 19 Air Turbine Pump for torpedo discharge.
Operational: *Georgia* played the part of an SSGN during Exercise 'Silent Hammer' in mid-2004. This tested procedures for strikes against time-critical targets and use of special operations forces. An onboard battle-centre tested communications and networking required to support them. All boats will return to the fleet by 2007. *Ohio* is based at Bangor, WA, and *Florida* is to be based at King's Bay, GA. Homeporting for the other boats is yet to be confirmed and may include Guam.

OHIO   *12/2005*, Scott Gourley* / 1130483

Attack Submarines (SSN)

JIMMY CARTER   *2/2005*, Ships of the World* / 1127056

3 SEAWOLF CLASS (SSN)

Name	No	Builders	Start date	Launched	Commissioned	F/S
SEAWOLF	SSN 21	General Dynamics (Electric Boat)	25 Oct 1989	24 June 1995	19 July 1997	AA
CONNECTICUT	SSN 22	General Dynamics (Electric Boat)	14 Sep 1992	1 Sep 1997	11 Dec 1998	AA
JIMMY CARTER	SSN 23	General Dynamics (Electric Boat)	12 Dec 1995	5 June 2004	19 Feb 2005	PA

Displacement, tons: 8,060 surfaced; 9,142; 12,139 (SSN 23) dived

Dimensions, feet (metres): 353; 453.2 (SSN 23) × 42.3 × 35.8 *(107.6; 138.1 × 12.9 × 10.9)* (see *Modernisation*)

Main machinery: Nuclear; 1 Westinghouse PWR S6W; 2 turbines; 45,000 hp *(33.57 MW)*; 1 shaft; pumpjet propulsor; 1 (4 in SSN 23) Westinghouse secondary propulsion submerged motor(s)

Speed, knots: 39 dived

Complement: 134 (14 officers)

Missiles: SLCM: Hughes Tomahawk (TLAM-N); land attack; Tercom Aided Inertial Navigation System (TAINS) to 2,500 km *(1,400 n miles)* at 0.7 Mach; altitude 15 — 100 m; nuclear warhead 200 kT; CEP 80 m. There are also 2 versions (TLAM-C/D) with either a single 454 kg HE warhead or a single warhead with submunitions; range 900 km *(485 n miles)*; CEP 10 m.
Nuclear warheads are not normally carried. Block III missiles increase TLAM-C range to 1,700 km *(918 n miles)*, add GPS back-up to TAINS and substitute a 318 kg shaped charge warhead.

Torpedoes: 8 — 26 in *(660 mm)* tubes (external measurement is 30 in *(762 mm)*); Gould Mk 48 ADCAP; wire-guided (option); active/passive homing to 50 km *(27 n miles)*/38 km *(21 n miles)* at 40/55 kt; warhead 267 kg; depth to 900 m *(2,950 ft)*. Air turbine discharge. Total of 50 tube-launched missiles and torpedoes, and UUVs in due course.

Mines: 100 in lieu of torpedoes.

Countermeasures: Decoys: torpedo decoys. WLY-1 system in due course.
ESM: WLQ-4(V)1; BLD-1; intercept.

Combat data systems: General Electric BSY-2 system. USC-38 EHF. JMCIS.

Weapons control: Raytheon Mk 2 FCS.

Radars: Navigation: BPS 16; I-band.

Sonars: BSY-2 suite with bow spherical active/passive array and wide aperture passive flank arrays; TB 16 and TB 29 surveillance and tactical towed arrays.

Programmes: First of class ordered on 9 January 1989; second of class on 3 May 1991 and third on 30 April 1996. Design changes to *Carter* contracted in late 1999 delayed the launch by four years.

Modernisation: The hull of SSN 23 is about 30 m longer to accommodate an hour-glass shaped Ocean Interface section with larger payload apertures to the sea. Modular architecture allows configuration for specific missions. Payloads could include standoff vehicles, distributed sensors and leave-behind weapons that would be activated after the submarine has left the area. It also supports Special Operations Forces including Dry Deck Shelter (DDS) and the Advanced SEAL Delivery System (ASDS). *Carter* retains all of the Seawolf class's original war-fighting capability.

Structure: The modular design has more weapons, a higher tactical speed, better sonars and an ASW mission

effectiveness 'three times better than the improved Los Angeles class' according to the Navy. It is estimated that over a billion dollars has been allocated for research and development including the S6W reactor system. Full acoustic cladding fitted. Panels around wide aperture sonar array and torpedo tube doors were redesigned and refitted following sea-trials of SSN 21. Mk 21 Air turbine torpedo discharge pump. There are no external weapons. Emphasis has been put on sub-ice capabilities including retractable bow planes. SSN 23 equipped with a range of photonic masts and an advanced communications mast for covert operations. Test depth 1,950 ft *(594 m)*.

Operational: A quoted 'silent' speed of 20 kt. Other operational advantages include greater manoeuvrability and space for subsequent weapon systems development.

Opinion: This submarine was intended to restore the level of acoustic advantage (in the one to one nuclear submarine engagement against the Russians) which the USN had enjoyed for three decades. At the same time the larger capacity of the magazine enhances overall effectiveness in a number of other roles. The decision to discontinue building this very expensive design was the result of falling defence budgets at the end of the Cold War and technical problems.

SEAWOLF   *4/2004, Ships of the World* / 1043702

JIMMY CARTER   *2/2005*, Ships of the World* / 1127057

49 LOS ANGELES CLASS (SSN)

Name	No	Builders	Laid down	Launched	Commissioned	F/S
LOS ANGELES	SSN 688	Newport News Shipbuilding	8 Jan 1972	6 Apr 1974	13 Nov 1976	PA
PHILADELPHIA	SSN 690	General Dynamics (Electric Boat Div)	12 Aug 1972	19 Oct 1974	25 June 1977	AA
MEMPHIS	SSN 691	Newport News Shipbuilding	23 June 1973	3 Apr 1976	17 Dec 1977	AA
BREMERTON	SSN 698	General Dynamics (Electric Boat Div)	8 May 1976	22 July 1978	28 Mar 1981	PA
JACKSONVILLE	SSN 699	General Dynamics (Electric Boat Div)	21 Feb 1976	18 Nov 1978	16 May 1981	AA
DALLAS	SSN 700	General Dynamics (Electric Boat Div)	9 Oct 1976	28 Apr 1979	18 July 1981	AA
LA JOLLA	SSN 701	General Dynamics (Electric Boat Div)	16 Oct 1976	11 Aug 1979	24 Oct 1981	PA
CITY OF CORPUS CHRISTI	SSN 705	General Dynamics (Electric Boat Div)	4 Sep 1979	25 Apr 1981	8 Jan 1983	AA
ALBUQUERQUE	SSN 706	General Dynamics (Electric Boat Div)	27 Dec 1979	13 Mar 1982	21 May 1983	AA
MINNEAPOLIS-SAINT PAUL	SSN 708	General Dynamics (Electric Boat Div)	30 Jan 1981	19 Mar 1983	10 Mar 1984	AA
HYMAN G RICKOVER	SSN 709	General Dynamics (Electric Boat Div)	24 July 1981	27 Aug 1983	21 July 1984	AA
AUGUSTA	SSN 710	General Dynamics (Electric Boat Div)	1 Apr 1982	21 Jan 1984	19 Jan 1985	AA
SAN FRANCISCO	SSN 711	Newport News Shipbuilding	26 May 1977	27 Oct 1979	24 Apr 1981	PA
HOUSTON	SSN 713	Newport News Shipbuilding	29 Jan 1979	21 Mar 1981	25 Sep 1982	PA
NORFOLK	SSN 714	Newport News Shipbuilding	1 Aug 1979	31 Oct 1981	21 May 1983	PA
BUFFALO	SSN 715	Newport News Shipbuilding	25 Jan 1980	8 May 1982	5 Nov 1983	PA
OLYMPIA	SSN 717	Newport News Shipbuilding	31 Mar 1981	30 Apr 1983	17 Nov 1983	PA
HONOLULU	SSN 718	Newport News Shipbuilding	10 Nov 1981	24 Sep 1983	6 July 1985	PA
PROVIDENCE	SSN 719	General Dynamics (Electric Boat Div)	14 Oct 1982	4 Aug 1984	27 July 1985	AA
PITTSBURGH	SSN 720	General Dynamics (Electric Boat Div)	15 Apr 1983	8 Dec 1984	23 Nov 1985	AA
CHICAGO	SSN 721	Newport News Shipbuilding	5 Jan 1983	13 Oct 1984	27 Sep 1986	PA
KEY WEST	SSN 722	Newport News Shipbuilding	6 July 1983	20 July 1985	12 Sep 1987	PA
OKLAHOMA CITY	SSN 723	General Dynamics (Electric Boat Div)	4 Jan 1984	2 Nov 1985	9 July 1988	AA
LOUISVILLE	SSN 724	General Dynamics (Electric Boat Div)	16 Sep 1984	14 Dec 1985	8 Nov 1986	PA
HELENA	SSN 725	General Dynamics (Electric Boat Div)	28 Mar 1985	28 June 1986	11 July 1987	PA
NEWPORT NEWS	SSN 750	Newport News Shipbuilding	3 Mar 1984	15 Mar 1986	3 June 1989	AA
SAN JUAN	SSN 751	General Dynamics (Electric Boat Div)	16 Aug 1985	6 Dec 1986	6 Aug 1988	AA
PASADENA	SSN 752	General Dynamics (Electric Boat Div)	20 Dec 1985	12 Sep 1987	11 Feb 1989	PA
ALBANY	SSN 753	Newport News Shipbuilding	22 Apr 1985	13 June 1987	7 Apr 1990	AA
TOPEKA	SSN 754	General Dynamics (Electric Boat Div)	13 May 1986	23 Jan 1988	21 Oct 1989	PA
MIAMI	SSN 755	General Dynamics (Electric Boat Div)	24 Oct 1986	12 Nov 1988	30 June 1990	AA
SCRANTON	SSN 756	Newport News Shipbuilding	29 June 1986	3 July 1989	26 Jan 1991	AA
ALEXANDRIA	SSN 757	General Dynamics (Electric Boat Div)	19 June 1987	23 June 1990	29 June 1991	AA
ASHEVILLE	SSN 758	Newport News Shipbuilding	1 Jan 1987	28 Oct 1989	28 Sep 1991	PA
JEFFERSON CITY	SSN 759	Newport News Shipbuilding	21 Sep 1987	24 Mar 1990	29 Feb 1992	PA
ANNAPOLIS	SSN 760	General Dynamics (Electric Boat Div)	15 June 1988	18 May 1991	11 Apr 1992	AA
SPRINGFIELD	SSN 761	General Dynamics (Electric Boat Div)	29 Jan 1990	4 Jan 1992	9 Jan 1993	AA
COLUMBUS	SSN 762	General Dynamics (Electric Boat Div)	7 Jan 1991	1 Aug 1992	24 July 1993	PA
SANTA FE	SSN 763	General Dynamics (Electric Boat Div)	9 July 1991	12 Dec 1992	8 Jan 1994	PA
BOISE	SSN 764	Newport News Shipbuilding	25 Aug 1988	20 Oct 1990	7 Nov 1992	AA
MONTPELIER	SSN 765	Newport News Shipbuilding	19 May 1989	6 Apr 1991	13 Mar 1993	AA
CHARLOTTE	SSN 766	Newport News Shipbuilding	17 Aug 1990	3 Oct 1992	16 Sep 1994	PA
HAMPTON	SSN 767	Newport News Shipbuilding	2 Mar 1990	28 Sep 1991	6 Nov 1993	PA
HARTFORD	SSN 768	General Dynamics (Electric Boat Div)	27 Apr 1992	4 Dec 1993	10 Dec 1994	AA
TOLEDO	SSN 769	Newport News Shipbuilding	6 May 1991	28 Aug 1993	24 Feb 1995	AA
TUCSON	SSN 770	Newport News Shipbuilding	15 Aug 1991	19 Mar 1994	9 Sep 1995	PA
COLUMBIA	SSN 771	General Dynamics (Electric Boat Div)	24 Apr 1993	24 Sep 1994	9 Oct 1995	PA
GREENEVILLE	SSN 772	Newport News Shipbuilding	28 Feb 1992	17 Sep 1994	16 Feb 1996	PA
CHEYENNE	SSN 773	Newport News Shipbuilding	6 July 1992	4 Apr 1995	13 Sep 1996	PA

Displacement, tons: 6,082 standard; 6,927 dived
Dimensions, feet (metres): 362 × 33 × 32.3
(110.3 × 10.1 × 9.9)
Main machinery: Nuclear; 1 GE PWR S6G; 2 turbines; 35,000 hp *(26 MW)*; 1 shaft; 1 Magnetek auxiliary prop motor; 325 hp *(242 kW)*
Speed, knots: 33 dived
Complement: 133 (13 officers)

Missiles: SLCM: GDC/Hughes Tomahawk (TLAM-N); land attack; Tercom aided inertial navigation system (TAINS) to 2,500 km *(1,400 n miles)* at 0.7 Mach; altitude 15-100 m; nuclear warhead 200 kT; CEP 80 m. There are also 2 versions (TLAM-C/D) with either a single 454 kg HE warhead or a single warhead with submunitions; range 900 km *(485 n miles)*; CEP 10 m. Nuclear warheads are not normally carried. Block III missiles, installed from 1994, increase TLAM-C range to 1,700 km *(918 n miles)*, add GPS back-up to TAINS and substitute a 318 kg shaped charge warhead.
From SSN 719 onwards all are equipped with the Vertical Launch System, which places 12 launch tubes external to the pressure hull behind the BQQ 5 spherical array forward.
Torpedoes: 4 — 21 in *(533 mm)* tubes midships. Gould Mk 48; ADCAP Mod 5/6; wire-guided (option); active/passive homing to 50 km *(27 n miles)*/38 km *(21 n miles)* at 40/55 kt; warhead 267 kg; depth to 900 m *(2,950 ft)*. Air turbine pump discharge.
Total of 26 weapons can be tube-launched, for example - 12 Tomahawk, 14 torpedoes.
Mines: Can lay Mk 67 Mobile and Mk 60 Captor mines.
Countermeasures: Decoys: Emerson Electric Mk 2; torpedo decoy.
ESM: BRD-7; direction finding. WLR-1H (in 771-773). WLR-8(V)2/6; intercept. WSQ-5 (periscope) and WLR-10; radar warning. BLQ-10 being fitted in some.
Combat data systems: CCS Mk 2 (688-750) with UYK 7 computers; IBM BSY-1 (751-773) with UYK 43/UYK 44 computers. JOTS, BGIXS and TADIX-A can be fitted. USC-38 EHF (in some). Link 11; Link 16 being fitted.
Radars: Surface search/navigation/fire control: Sperry BPS 15 H/16; I/J-band.
Sonars: IBM BQQ 5D/E; passive/active search and attack; low frequency. BSY-1 (SSN 751 onwards).
BQG 5D wide aperture flank array (SSN 710 and SSN 773). TB 23/29 thin line array and TB 16; passive towed array.

JEFFERSON CITY   *6/2002, Royal Australian Navy* / 0530095

Ametek BQS 15; active close range including ice detection; high frequency.
MIDAS (mine and ice detection avoidance system) (SSN 751 onwards); active high frequency.

Programmes: Various major improvement programmes and updating design changes caused programme delays in the late 1980s. From SSN 751 onwards the class is prefixed by an 'I' for 'improved'. Programme terminated at 62 hulls. Eleven paid off by mid-1999. Plans to refuel the majority of the class have delayed de-activations but these have continued with the decommissioning of SSN 716 in October 2005.
Modernisation: Mk 117 TFCS backfitted in earlier submarines of the class. EHF communications and Link 16 are being fitted. Prototype HDR antenna fitted in SSN 719. Production versions being installed from 2002. BQQ 10 and TB 29 fitted in all. An ARCI (Acoustic Rapid COTS Insertion) AN/BQQ-10 programme from 1997 to 2002 to backfit BQQ 5 sonars with open system architecture. Five of the class are fitted with DDS (SSN 688, 690, 700, 701 and 715). Two others are fitted to operate ASDS (SSN 772, 766). C-303 acoustic jammer in one of the class for trials in 1998. 25 mm guns may be fitted in the future.
Structure: Every effort has been made to improve sound quieting and from SSN 751 onwards the class has acoustic tile cladding to augment the 'mammalian' skin which up to then had been the standard USN outer casing coating. Also from SSN 751 the forward hydro planes are fitted forward instead of on the fin. The planes are retractable mainly for surfacing through ice. The S6G reactor is a modified version of the D2G type. The towed sonar array is stowed in a blister on the side of the casing. A single refuelling is required during the life of the boat. Diving

depth is 450 m *(1,475 ft)*. *Miami* was withdrawn from active service in late 1989 to become an interim research platform for advanced submarine technology. Early trials did not involve major changes to the submarine but tests started in September 1990 for optronic non-hull-penetrating masts and a major overhaul included installation of a large diameter tube for testing UUVs and large torpedoes. An after casing hangar is fitted for housing larger UUVs and towed arrays. Many other ideas are being evaluated with the main aim of allowing contractors easy access for trials at sea of new equipment. *Augusta* was the trials platform for the BQQ-5D wide aperture array passive sonar system. Various staged design improvements have added some 220 tons to the class displacement between 688 and 773.
Operational: The Los Angeles class is the mainstay of the attack submarine force. The land-attack mission has been a notable feature of operations in Iraq, Kosovo and Afghanistan (SSN 719). Under-ice operations are still a priority and SSN 767 surfaced at the North Pole in 2004. Special forces and intelligence gathering missions are also conducted. Normally 12 Tomahawk missiles are carried internally (in addition to the external tubes in 719 onwards) but this load can be increased depending on the mission. Neither TASM nor Harpoon are now deployed. Subroc phased out in 1990. Nuclear weapons disembarked but still available. Predator and Sea Ferret UAV trials done in two of the class in 1996-97 and may become available for launching from a sub-Harpoon canister in due course. ASDS trials in SSN 772 during 2002. SSN 711 seriously damaged in collision with an undersea mountain south of Guam on 8 January 2005. SSN 690 damaged in collision with Turkish freighter in the Gulf on 5 September 2005.

PHILADELPHIA (with DDS)   *5/2001, H M Steele* / 0131330

OLYMPIA 7/2004, *Michael Nitz* / 1043662

LA JOLLA (with DSRV-1) 4/2002, *Hachiro Nakai* / 0530031

LOUISVILLE 6/2004, *US Navy* / 1043663

AUGUSTA 6/2005*, *B Sullivan* / 1154031

For details of the latest updates to *Jane's Fighting Ships* online and to discover the additional information available exclusively to online subscribers please visit

jfs.janes.com

2 + 5 (3) VIRGINIA CLASS (SSN)

Name	No	Builders	Start date	Launched	Commissioned	F/S
VIRGINIA	SSN 774	General Dynamics (Electric Boat)	30 Sep 1998	16 Aug 2003	23 Oct 2004	AA
TEXAS	SSN 775	Northrop Grumman, Newport News Shipbuilding	7 Dec 1998	31 July 2004	2006	Bldg
HAWAII	SSN 776	General Dynamics (Electric Boat)	13 Nov 2000	2006	2007	Bldg
NORTH CAROLINA	SSN 777	Northrop Grumman, Newport News Shipbuilding	29 Jan 2002	2007	2008	Bldg
NEW HAMPSHIRE	SSN 778	General Dynamics (Electric Boat)	14 Aug 2003	2008	2009	Bldg
NEW MEXICO	SSN 779	Northrop Grumman, Newport News Shipbuilding	29 Jan 2004	2009	2010	Bldg
—	SSN 780	General Dynamics (Electric Boat)	29 Dec 2004	2010	2011	Bldg
—	SSN 781	Northrop Grumman, Newport News Shipbuilding	2006	2011	2012	
—	SSN 782	General Dynamics (Electric Boat)	2007	2012	2013	
—	SSN 783	Northrop Grumman, Newport News Shipbuilding	2008	2013	2014	

Displacement, tons: 7,800 dived
Dimensions, feet (metres): 377 × 34 × 30.5
(114.9 × 10.4 × 9.3)
Main machinery: Nuclear; 1 GE PWR S9G; 2 turbines; 40,000 hp *(29.84 MW)*; 1 shaft; pump jet propulsor; 1 secondary propulsion submerged motor
Speed, knots: 34 dived
Complement: 134 (14 officers)

Missiles: SLCM: GDC/Hughes Tomahawk (TLAM-N); land attack; Tercom Aided Inertial Navigation System (TAINS) to 2,500 km *(1,400 n miles)* at 0.7 Mach; altitude 15–100 m; nuclear warhead 200 kT; CEP 80 m. There are also two versions (TLAM-C/D) with either a single 454 kg HE warhead or a single warhead with submunitions; range 900 km *(485 n miles)*; CEP 10 m. Nuclear warheads are not normally carried. Block III missiles increase TLAM-C range to 1,700 km *(918 n miles)*, add GPS back-up to TAINS and substitute a 318 kg shaped charge warhead. 12 VLS tubes external to the pressure hull.
Torpedoes: 4—21 in *(533 mm)* tubes midships. Gould Mk 48; ADCAP Mod 6; wire-guided (option); active/passive homing to 50 km *(27 n miles)*/38 *(21 n miles)* at 40/55 kt; warhead 267 kg; depth to 900 m *(2,950 ft)*. Air turbine pump discharge. Total of 38 including SLCM, torpedoes and UUVs.
Mines: Can lay Mk 67 Mobile and Mk 60 Captor mines (until new mines are available).
Countermeasures: Decoys: 14 external and 1 internal (reloadable). Anti-torpedo decoy.
ESM: AN/BLQ-10; radar and comms intercept and analysis.
Combat data systems: AN/BYG-1.
Radars: Surface search/navigation/fire control: Sperry BPS 16(V)4; I/J-band.
Sonars: Lockheed Martin BQQ-10 sonar suite including bow spherical active/passive array; BQG-5A wide aperture flank passive arrays; high-frequency active keel and fin arrays; TB 16 and TB 29(A) towed arrays; WLY-1 acoustic intercept.

Programmes: In February 1997, a teaming agreement was reached between Electric Boat Division of General Dynamics Corporation and Newport News Shipbuilding (now Northrop Grumman Newport News) to build jointly the Virginia class. Electric Boat is the lead design yard and prime contractor and delivers the even numbered hulls. Newport News delivers the odd numbered hulls.

VIRGINIA   *7/2004, US Navy* / 1043661

Construction of sub-assemblies is undertaken at the Electric Boat facilities in Groton, CT, at Quonset Point RI and at Northrop Grumman Newport News. Components are then shipped either to the Groton shipyard or to Newport News for final assembly and delivery. This division of construction responsibility takes advantage of modular design and construction and provides the most affordable approach to submarine construction at the two shipyards. Advanced funding for first of class in FY96 and this continued to FY98. Second of class funding in FY99, third in FY01 and fourth in FY02. A follow-on block buy procurement contract, signed in August 2003 for six submarines, maintained the Electric Boat and Northrop Grumman Newport News Teaming arrangement. This contract was modified in January 2004 to a multi-year procurement contract for five (second through sixth) boats. This modification includes provisions to provide early funding, allowing the bulk purchase of materials for more than one submarine at a significant overall cost saving. A program of 30 hulls is planned.

Structure: Seawolf level quietening. Acoustic hull cladding. Reactor core will last the life of the ship. Automated steering and diving control, using fly-by-wire technology, and automated hovering system. Host ship for Advanced SEAL Delivery System (ASDS) mini-submarine or dry deck shelter. Integral lockout chamber and reconfigurable torpedo room to accommodate approximately 40 Special Operations Forces and equipment. Fibre-optic photonics masts replace conventional periscopes for imaging. High frequency sonar for mine and obstacle detection. Twelve Vertical Launch System (VLS) tubes. Test depth 488 m *(1,600 ft)*. A scale version (0.294) *Cutthroat* LSV-2 is listed under Deep Submergence Vehicles.
Operational: Optimised for coastal operations without sacrificing traditional deep-water capabilities. Designed for flexibility to change missions and perform across a variety of mission areas: anti-submarine warfare, anti-surface warfare, covert intelligence/surveillance and reconnaissance, covert mine warfare, battle group support, covert support of Special Operations Forces, and power projection/strike.

VIRGINIA   *7/2004, US Navy* / 1043660

AIRCRAFT CARRIERS

9 + 1 NIMITZ CLASS (CVNM)

Name	No	Builders	Laid down	Launched	Commissioned	F/S
NIMITZ	CVN 68	Newport News Shipbuilding	22 June 1968	13 May 1972	3 May 1975	PA
DWIGHT D EISENHOWER	CVN 69	Newport News Shipbuilding	15 Aug 1970	11 Oct 1975	18 Oct 1977	AA
CARL VINSON	CVN 70	Newport News Shipbuilding	11 Oct 1975	15 Mar 1980	13 Mar 1982	PA
THEODORE ROOSEVELT	CVN 71	Newport News Shipbuilding	13 Oct 1981	27 Oct 1984	25 Oct 1986	AA
ABRAHAM LINCOLN	CVN 72	Newport News Shipbuilding	3 Nov 1984	13 Feb 1988	11 Nov 1989	PA
GEORGE WASHINGTON	CVN 73	Newport News Shipbuilding	25 Aug 1986	21 July 1990	4 July 1992	AA
JOHN C STENNIS	CVN 74	Newport News Shipbuilding	13 Mar 1991	13 Nov 1993	9 Dec 1995	PA
HARRY S TRUMAN	CVN 75	Newport News Shipbuilding	29 Nov 1993	14 Sep 1996	25 July 1998	AA
RONALD REAGAN	CVN 76	Newport News Shipbuilding	12 Feb 1998	4 Mar 2001	12 July 2003	PA
GEORGE H W BUSH	CVN 77	Newport News Shipbuilding	6 Sep 2003	2006	Apr 2008	Bldg

Displacement, tons: 72,916 (CVN 68-70), 73,973 (CVN 71) light; 91,487 (CVN 68-70), 96,386 (CVN 71), 102,000 (CVN 72-77) full load

Dimensions, feet (metres): 1,040 pp; 1,092 oa × 134 wl × 37 (CVN 68-70); 38.7 (CVN 71); 39 (CVN 72-76); 39.8 (CVN 77) *(317;332.9 × 40.8 × 11.3;11.8;11.9;12.1)*

Flight deck, feet (metres): 1,092; 779.8 (angled) × 252 *(332.9; 237.7 × 76.8)*

Main machinery: Nuclear; 2 Westinghouse/GE PWR A4W/A1G; 4 turbines; 280,000 hp *(209 MW)*; 4 emergency diesels; 10,720 hp *(8 MW)*; 4 shafts

Speed, knots: 30+

Complement: 3,200 (160 officers); 2,480 aircrew (320 officers); Flag 70 (25 officers)

Missiles: SAM: 2 Raytheon GMLS Mk 29 octuple launchers ❶; NATO Sea Sparrow RIM-7; semi-active radar homing to 14.6 km *(8 n miles)* at 2.5 Mach; warhead 39 kg. ESSM in due course.
2 GMLS Mk 49 RAM RIM-116 launchers ❷ (CVN 68, 69, 70, 72, 73, 74, 76 and 77); passive IR/anti-radiation homing to 9.6 km *(5.2 n miles)* at 2 Mach; warhead 9.1 kg.

Guns: 2 (CVN 70, 77), 3 (CVN 71, 73, 74) or 4 (CVN 72, 75) General Electric/General Dynamics 20 mm Vulcan Phalanx 6-barrelled Mk 15 (CVN 70-75, 77); 4,500 rds/min combined to 1.5 km.

Countermeasures: Decoys: SLQ 25 Torpedo Countermeasures Transmitting Set (Nixie).
ESM/ECM: SLQ-32(V)4 intercept and jammers. WLR-1H is being removed.

Combat data systems: ACDS Block 0 (CVN 71-73, 75) or 1 (CVN 68) naval tactical and advanced combat direction systems; Links 4A, 11, 16 and Satellite Tadil J. GCCS (M) SATCOMS; SSR-1, WCS-3A (UHF DAMA), WSC-6 (SHF), WSC-8 (SHF), USC-38 (EHF), SSR-2A (GBS) (see Data Systems at front of section). SSDS Mk 2 (CVN 68, 69, 70, 74, 76, 77). To be back-fitted in all as part of the CAPSTONE combat system upgrade.

Weapons control: 3 Mk 91 Mod 1 MFCS directors (part of the NSSMS Mk 57 SAM system).

Radars: Air search: ITT SPS-48E ❸; 3D; E/F-band.
Raytheon SPS-49(V)5 (CVN 71, 72, 73, 75) or SPS-49(V)1 (CVN 68, 69, 70, 74, 76, 77) ❹; C/D-band.
Hughes Mk 23 TAS (CVN 71-73, 75) ❺; D-band or SPQ-9B (CVN 68-70, 74, 76, 77).
Surface search: Norden SPS-67(V)1; G-band.
CCA: SPN-41, SPN-43C, 2 SPN-46; J/F/J/K-band.
TPX-42A Direct Altitude and Identity Readout (DAIR).
Navigation: Raytheon SPS-64(V)9 (CVN 71, 73, 75) or SPS-73(V)12 (CVN 68, 70, 72, 74) or SPS-73(V)17 (CVN 69, 76, 77); Furuno 900; I/J-band.
Fire control: 4 Mk 95; I/J-band (2 per GMLS Mk 29 launcher).
Tacan: URN 25.

Fixed-wing aircraft: Composition of air-wing depends on mission and typically includes: 12 F/A-18F Hornet; 36 F/A-18A/C/E Hornet; 4 EA-6B Prowler; 4 E-2C Hawkeye.

Helicopters: 4 SH-60F and 2 HH-60H Seahawk and up to 9 SH-60B Seahawk.

Programmes: *Nimitz* was authorised in FY67, *Dwight D Eisenhower* in FY70, *Carl Vinson* in FY74, *Theodore Roosevelt* in FY80 and *Abraham Lincoln* and *George Washington* in FY83. Construction contracts for *John C Stennis* and *Harry S Truman* were awarded in June 1988 and for *Ronald Reagan* in December 1994. Authorised in FY99, construction contract for *George H W Bush* awarded in January 2001.

Modernisation: CVN 68 completed a three-year Refuelling and Complex Overhaul (RCOH) in 2001. RCOH of CVN 69 started in 2001 and completed in January 2005. RCOH of CVN 70 is to start in 2006 and complete in March 2009. SSDS Mk 2 Mod 0 installed in CVN 68 (to be upgraded to Mk 2 Mod 1 in due course). This includes fitting two RAM systems and SPQ-9B radar vice Mk 23 TAS. SSDS Mk 2 Mod 1 fitted to CVN 69, CVN 76 and 77. RAM systems replace one Mk 29 and all Phalanx launchers on CVN 68 and 69. CVN 74 similarly refitted during 2005 docking but will retain upgraded CIWS (Phalanx) mounts as well. The

SSDS upgrade package in CVN 74 is known as the CAPSTONE combat system upgrade. CAPSTONE will be installed in CVN 70 during RCOH and will be scheduled for CVN 71-75 in due course.

Structure: Damage control measures include sides with system of full and empty compartments (full compartments can contain aviation fuel), approximately 2.5 in Kevlar plating over certain areas of side shell, box protection over magazine and machinery spaces. Aviation facilities include four lifts, two at the forward end of the flight deck, one to starboard abaft the island and one to port at the stern. There are four steam catapults (C13-1 (CVN 68-71), C13-2 (CVN 72-77)) and four (or three on CVN 76 and 77) Mk 7 Mod 3 arrester wires. Launch rate is one every 20 seconds. The hangar can hold less than half the full aircraft complement, deckhead is 25.6 ft. Aviation fuel, 8,500 tons. Tactical Flag Command Centre for Flagship role. During RCOH, CVN 68 and 69 fitted with reshaped island (the mainmast has three yardarms to support more antennas). Major structural differences in CVN 76 (also to be incorporated in CVN 77) include: a stretched island which includes a bigger bridge and a three yardarm mainmast and which incorporates the after mast (separate in previous ships) and the internal bomb elevator. Other changes include a bulbous bow to reduce drag and a modified flight deck (angled deck increased by 0.1 degrees) to allow the use of two catapults while aircraft land.

Operational: Multimission role of 'strike/ASW'. From CVN 70 onwards ships have an A/S control centre and A/S facilities; CVN 68 and 69 are backfitted. Endurance of 16 days for aviation fuel (steady flying) with greater than 1 million miles between refuelling. Only one refuelling is required in the life of the ship. Ships' complements and air wings can be changed depending on the operational task. CVN 73 is to replace CV 63 as forward-deployed carrier in western Pacific, based at Yokosuka, Japan, in 2008. Until then CVN 73 based at Norfolk, VA, as are CVNs 69, 70, 71 and 75. CVNs 68 and 76 based at San Diego, CA, CVN 74 at Bremerton, WA, and CVN 72 at Everett, WA.

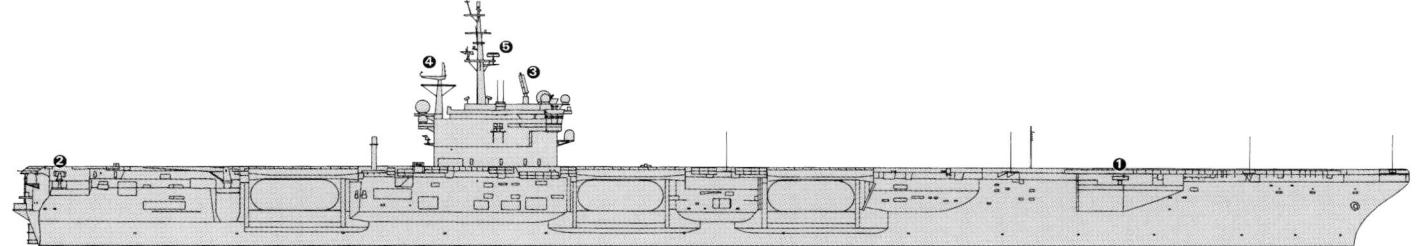

RONALD REAGAN

(Scale 1 : 1,800), Ian Sturton / 1043489

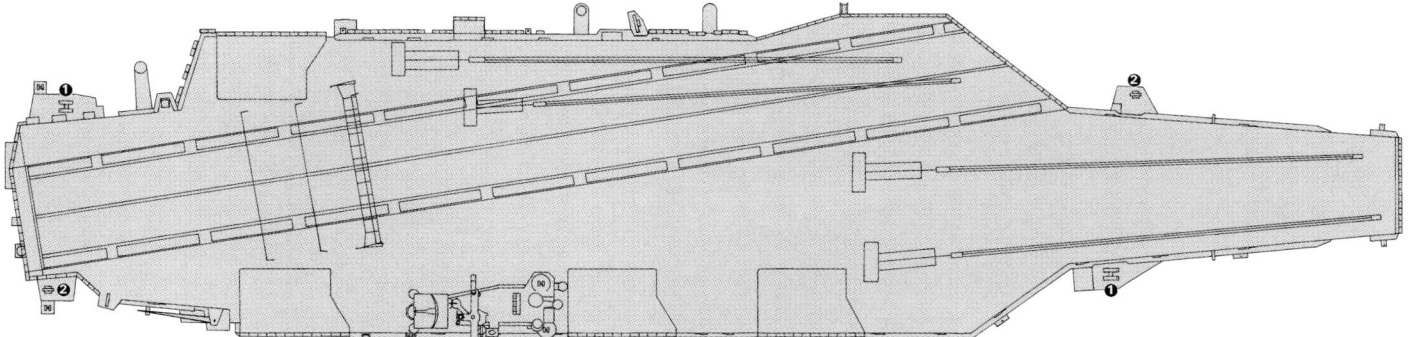

RONALD REAGAN

(Scale 1 : 1,800), Ian Sturton / 1043490

RONALD REAGAN

7/2004, US Navy / 1043664

NIMITZ *9/2003, US Navy* / 1043665

HARRY S TRUMAN *6/2004, Ships of the World* / 1043700

THEODORE ROOSEVELT *10/2005*, **US Navy*** / 1154033

GEORGE H W BUSH (computer graphic) *3/2003, **Ships of the World*** / 0572799

JOHN C STENNIS *8/2004, **Hachiro Nakai*** / 1043694

2 KITTY HAWK AND JOHN F KENNEDY CLASSES (CVM)

Name	No	Builders	Laid down	Launched	Commissioned	F/S
KITTY HAWK	CV 63	New York Shipbuilding	27 Dec 1956	21 May 1960	29 Apr 1961	PA
JOHN F KENNEDY	CV 67	Newport News Shipbuilding	22 Oct 1964	27 May 1967	7 Sep 1968	AA

Displacement, tons: 83,960 full load (CV 63); 81,430 full load (CV 67)

Dimensions, feet (metres): 1,062.5 (CV 63); 1,052 (CV 67) × 130 × 37.4
(323.8; 320.6 × 39.6 × 11.4)

Flight deck, feet (metres): 1,046 × 252 *(318.8 × 76.8)*

Main machinery: 8 Foster-Wheeler boilers; 1,200 psi *(83.4 kg/cm²)*; 950°F *(510°C)*; 4 Westinghouse turbines; 280,000 hp *(209 MW)*; 4 shafts

Speed, knots: 32

Range, n miles: 4,000 at 30 kt; 12,000 at 20 kt

Complement: 2,930 (155 officers); aircrew 2,480 (320 officers); Flag 70 (25 officers)

Missiles: SAM: 2 Raytheon GMLS Mk 29 octuple launchers ❶; NATO Sea Sparrow RIM-7; semi-active radar homing to 14.6 km *(8 n miles)* at 2.5 Mach; warhead 39 kg. ESSM in due course.
2 GMLS Mk 49 RAM RIM-116 ❷; 21 rds/launcher; passive IR/anti-radiation homing to 9.6 km *(5.2 n miles)* at 2 Mach; warhead 9.1 kg.

Guns: 2 General Electric/General Dynamics 20 mm Vulcan Phalanx 6-barrelled Mk 15/14 Block I (CV 63), Mk 15/13 Block I (CV 67) ❸; 3,000 rds/min (or 4,500 in Block 1) combined to 1.5 km.

Countermeasures: Decoys: SLQ-25 Torpedo Countermeasures Transmitting Set (Nixie).
ESM/ECM: SLQ-32(V)4 intercept and jammers.

Combat data systems: ACDS Block 0 (Block 1 Level 1 in CV 67) naval tactical and advanced combat direction systems Links 4A, 11, 14, 16 and Satellite Tadil J. GCCS (M) SATCOMS; SSR-1, WSC-3A (UHF DAMA), WSC-6 (SHF), WSC-8 (SHF), USC-38 (EHF), SSR-2A (GBS) (see Data Systems at front of section).

Weapons control: 2 Mk 91 MFCS directors (part of NSSMS Mk 57 SAM system).

Radars: Air search: ITT SPS-48E ❹; 3D; E/F-band.
Raytheon SPS-49(V)5, ❺; C/D-band.
Hughes Mk 23/7 TAS ❻; D-band.
Surface search: Norden SPS-67; G-band.

CCA: SPN-41, SPN-43A; 2 SPN-46; J/K/F-band.
Navigation: Furuno 900; I-band.
Fire control: 4 Mk 95; I/J-band (for SAM).
Tacan: URN 25.

Fixed-wing aircraft: Composition of air-wing depends on mission and typically includes: 44 F/A-18A/C/E/F Hornet; 4 EA-6B Prowler; 4 E-2C Hawkeye.

Helicopters: 4 SH-60F, 3 HH-60H Seahawk. Up to 9 SH-60B Seahawk dispersed among carrier group.

Programmes: *Kitty Hawk* was authorised in FY56 and *John F Kennedy* in FY63.

Modernisation: Service Life Extension Programme (SLEP): *Kitty Hawk* completed in February 1991. A 'complex overhaul' of *Kennedy* completed in September 1995 but a second 15-month complete overhaul scheduled to begin in 2005 has been cancelled. ACDS Block 1 trials done in *Kennedy* in 1998. SSDS Mk 2 Mod 1 to be fitted in CV 67 in due course including SPQ-9B radar. *Kennedy* strike group conducted successful CEC operational evaluation in 2001. *Kennedy* completed nine month maintenance period at Mayport, FL, in November 2003.

Structure: These ships were built to an improved Forrestal design. They have two deck-edge lifts forward of the superstructure, a third lift aft of the structure, and the port-side lift on the after quarter. Four C13 steam catapults (with one C13-1 in *Kennedy*) and four arrester wires. Aviation fuel of 5,882 tons carried.

Operational: Air wings are changed depending on the operational role. CV 63 was used as Special Forces base during operations off Afghanistan in 2001. CV 63 based in Yokosuka from July 1998 and expected to remain in service until 2008 when it will be replaced in the force structure by CVN 77. It will be replaced at Yokosuka by CVN 73. The future of CV 67 is uncertain. The US Navy decision to decommission the ship by 2008, rather than 2018, was blocked, at least temporarily, by Congress. CV 67 based at Mayport, FL.

JOHN F KENNEDY *7/2000, Hachiro Nakai* / 0106751

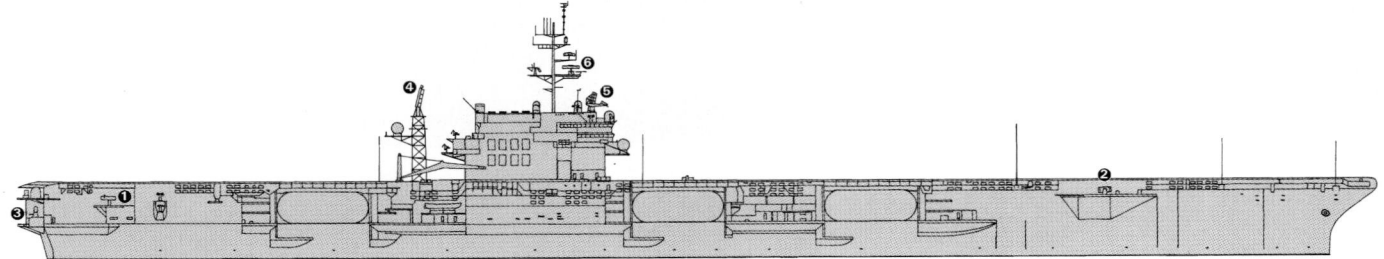

KITTY HAWK *(Scale 1 : 1,800), Ian Sturton* / 0573701

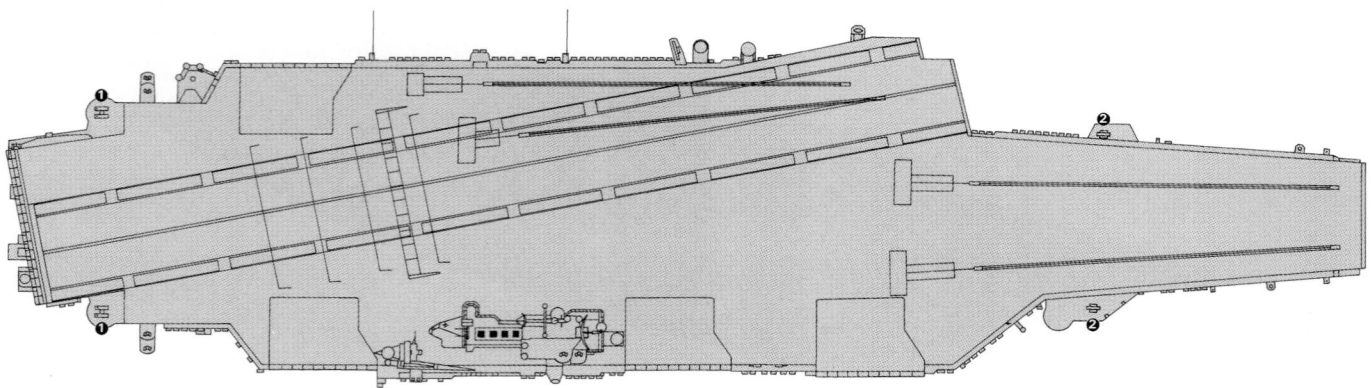

KITTY HAWK *(Scale 1 : 1,800), Ian Sturton* / 0573700

KITTY HAWK *8/2004, US Navy* / 1043670

JOHN F KENNEDY *8/2005*, Ships of the World* / 1154032

KITTY HAWK *11/2005*, US Navy* / 1154035

0 + 1 (1) FUTURE CARRIER (CVN 21) (CVN)

Name	No	Builders	Laid down	Launched	Commissioned
—	CVN 78	Northrop Grumman Newport News	2008	2012	2015
—	CVN 79	Northrop Grumman Newport News	2012	2016	2019

Displacement, tons: 100,000 approx
Dimensions, feet (metres): 1,091.8 × 134.0 × 40.8
  (332.8 × 40.8 × 12.4)
Flight deck, feet (metres): 109.8 × 256 *(332.8 × 78.0)*
Main machinery: Nuclear; 2 reactors; 4 shafts
Speed, knots: 30+
Complement: 4,660 ship and aircrew

Missiles: SAM: 2 VLS launchers for Raytheon Evolved Sea
  Sparrow.
  2 RAM launchers.
Countermeasures: Decoys: ESM; ECM; torpedo defence.
Combat data systems: To be announced.
Weapons control: To be announced.
Radars: Air search: Dual Band Radar (DBR); Raytheon SPY-3;
  3D; E/F/I-bands.
Navigation: To be announced.
Fire control: To be announced.
Tacan: To be announced.

Fixed-wing aircraft: Composition will depend on mission
  but will comprise 75+ aircraft (JSF, F/A-18E/F, EA-18G,
  E-2D, MH-60R/S, J-UCAS).

Programmes: Northrop Grumman Newport News awarded a
  construction preparation contract in May 2004 for detailed
  design, component development, long-lead procurement
  and advanced construction. First steel cut for CVN 78 on
  11 August 2005. The second ship is to be laid down in 2012
  with follow-on ships at four year intervals.
Structure: The Nimitz class flight deck has been re-arranged
  to increase sortie rates and improve weapons movement.
  This is to be accomplished with a new island design,
  three rather than four aircraft lifts and an advanced
  weapons elevator (AWE). Other features include four
  electromagnetic catapults, advanced arresting gear, new
  integrated warfare system (IWS) and new nuclear power
  plant, and a flexible ship architecture to support the rapid

CVN 21 *6/2004, Northrop Grumman Newport News* / 1043671

insertion of future warfighting technologies. Electrical
generating capacity is to be at least 2½ times that of the
Nimitz class. Significant habitability improvements are
to be included.
Operational: CVN 21 is to require 500-900 fewer complement
  than the Nimitz class. Increased sortie rates (by 25 per cent)

and reduced depot maintenance requirements to increase
operational availability. New command centre to combine
force networking with flexible, open system architecture
to support simultaneous multiple missions, including
integrated strike planning, joint/coalition operations and
special warfare missions. Service life 50 years.

1 ENTERPRISE CLASS (CVNM)

Name	No	Builders	Laid down	Launched	Commissioned	F/S
ENTERPRISE	CVN 65	Newport News Shipbuilding	4 Feb 1958	24 Sep 1960	25 Nov 1961	AA

Displacement, tons: 73,502 light; 75,700 standard; 89,600 full load

Dimensions, feet (metres): 1,123 × 133 × 39 (342.3 × 40.5 × 11.9)

Flight deck, feet (metres): 1,088 × 252 (331.6 × 76.8)

Main machinery: Nuclear; 8 Westinghouse PWR A2W; 4 Westinghouse turbines; 280,000 hp (209 MW); 4 emergency diesels; 10,720 hp (8 MW); 4 shafts

Speed, knots: 33

Complement: 3,350 (171 officers); 2,480 aircrew (225 officers); Flag staff 70 (25 officers)

Missiles: SAM: 2 Raytheon GMLS Mk 29 octuple launchers ❶; NATO Sea Sparrow RIM-7; semi-active radar homing to 14.6 km (8 n miles) at 2.5 Mach; warhead 39 kg. 2 GMLS Mk 49 RAM RIM-116 ❷; 21 rds/launcher; passive IR/anti-radiation homing to 9.6 km (5.2 n miles) at 2 Mach; warhead 9.1 kg.

Guns: 2 General Electric/General Dynamics 20 mm Vulcan Phalanx 6-barrelled Mk 15 ❸; 3,000 rds/min (or 4,500 in Block 1) combined to 1.5 km.

Countermeasures: Decoys: SLQ-25 Torpedo Countermeasures Transmitting Set (Nixie). ESM/ECM: SLQ-32(V)4; intercept and jammers.

Combat data systems: ACDS Block 0 naval tactical and advanced combat direction systems; Links 4A, 11, 14, 16 and Satellite Tadil J. GCCS(M) SATCOMS; SSR-1, WSC-3 (UHF DAMA), WSC-6 (SHF), WSC-8 (SHF), USC-38 (EHF), SSR-2A (GBS) (see Data Systems at front of section).

Weapons control: 2 Mk 91 Mod 1 MFCS directors (part of NSSMS Mk 57 SAM system).

Radars: Air search: ITT SPS-48E ❹; 3D; E/F-band. Raytheon SPS-49(V)5 ❺; C/D-band. Hughes Mk 23 TAS ❻; D-band. SPQ-9B in due course.

Surface search: Norden SPS-67; G-band.

CCA: SPN-41, SPN-43C; 2 SPN-46; J/F/K-band.

Navigation: Raytheon SPS-64(V)9; Furuno 900; I/J-band.

Fire control: 4 Mk 95; I/J-band (for SAM).

Tacan: URN 25.

Fixed-wing aircraft: Composition of air-wing depends on mission and typically includes: 44 F/A-18A/C/E/F Hornet; 4 EA-6B Prowler; 4 E-2C Hawkeye.

Helicopters: 4 SH-60F, 2 HH-60H Seahawk. Up to 9 SH-60B Seahawk are dispersed among carrier strike group.

Programmes: Authorised in FY58. Underwent a refit/overhaul at Puget Sound Naval SY, Bremerton, Washington from January 1979 to March 1982. Latest complex overhaul including refuelling started at Newport News in early 1991 and completed 27 September 1994. Minor refit in 1997 and again in 2002.

Modernisation: Mk 25 Sea Sparrow was installed in late 1967 and this has been replaced by two Mk 29 and supplemented with three 20 mm Mk 15 CIWS. A reshaping of the island took place in her 1979-82 refit. This included a replacement mast similar to the Nimitz class with SPS-48C and 49 radars. Improvements during latest overhaul included SPS-48E and Mk 23 TAS air search radars, SPN-46 precision approach and landing radar and C³ and EW systems. RAM was fitted in 2004.

Structure: Built to a modified Forrestal class design. Enterprise was the world's second nuclear-powered surface warship (the cruiser Long Beach was completed a few months earlier). Aviation facilities include four deck edge lifts, two forward and one each side abaft the island. There are four 295 ft C 13 Mod 1 catapults. Hangars cover 216,000 sq ft with 25 ft deck head. Aviation fuel, 8,500 tons.

Operational: 12 days' aviation fuel for intensive flying. Expected to remain in service until 2013 when it will be replaced in the force structure by CVN 78. Based at Norfolk, VA.

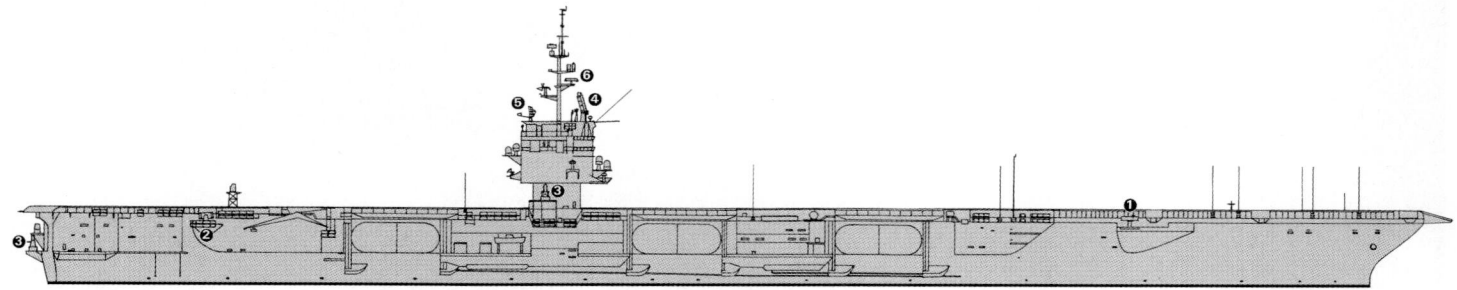

ENTERPRISE

(Scale 1 : 1,800), Ian Sturton / 0573702

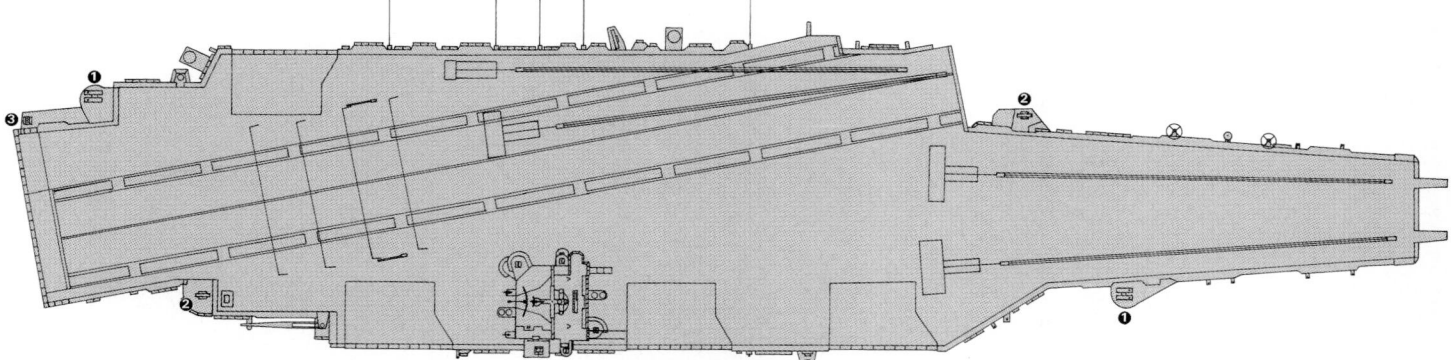

ENTERPRISE

(Scale 1 : 1,800), Ian Sturton / 0573703

ENTERPRISE

11/2005*, US Navy / 1154034

CRUISERS

Notes: (1) **Integrated Ship Controls.** Formerly known as Smart Ship, Integrated Ship Controls (ISC) began as Naval Research Advisory Committee recommendation in 1996 to reduce manning through technology. *Yorktown* (CG 48) was selected as first Smart Ship with implementation of 47 workload-reduction initiatives tested and evaluated during a five-month deployment completed in June 1997. Fourteen more initiatives were installed in July 1997. Core systems included: Integrated Bridge System (IBS), Integrated Condition Assessment System (ICAS), Machinery Control System (MCS), Damaged Control System (DCS), Fuel Control System (FCS), fibre optic Local Area Network (LAN) and Wireless Internal Communication System (WICS). *Yorktown's* experience validated these technologies, combined with changes in policies, procedures and new watch routines, to generate substantial reductions in workload. The first installation of ISC in *Ticonderoga* (CG 47) was very challenging and more costly than originally anticipated. All subsequent ISC installations have been completed successfully and within budget during 20-week installation periods: *Monterey* (CG 61) was fitted in 2000; *Valley Forge* (CG 50) and *Mobile Bay* (CG 53) in 2001; *Antietam* (CG 54) in 2002; *Hue City* (CG 66) in 2003; *Cape St George* (CG 71) in 2004. *San Jacinto* (CG 56) is scheduled for 2006. Remaining ships of class will receive ISC either as a stand-alone upgrade or during the Cruiser Modernisation Programme.

(2) CG(X) is the proposed replacement for the Ticonderoga (CG 47) class cruisers. It is expected to be a follow-on variant of the DD(X), incorporating an integrated power system and using a similar hull-form, but with enhanced missile-defence and air warfare capability. Entry into service is expected in about 2017.

22 TICONDEROGA CLASS: GUIDED MISSILE CRUISERS (AEGIS) (CGHM)

Name	No	Builders	Laid down	Launched	Commissioned	F/S
BUNKER HILL	CG 52	Ingalls Shipbuilding	11 Jan 1984	11 Mar 1985	20 Sep 1986	PA
MOBILE BAY	CG 53	Ingalls Shipbuilding	6 June 1984	22 Aug 1985	21 Feb 1987	PA
ANTIETAM	CG 54	Ingalls Shipbuilding	15 Nov 1984	14 Feb 1986	6 June 1987	PA
LEYTE GULF	CG 55	Ingalls Shipbuilding	18 Mar 1985	20 June 1986	26 Sep 1987	AA
SAN JACINTO	CG 56	Ingalls Shipbuilding	24 July 1985	14 Nov 1986	23 Jan 1988	AA
LAKE CHAMPLAIN	CG 57	Ingalls Shipbuilding	3 Mar 1986	3 Apr 1987	12 Aug 1988	PA
PHILIPPINE SEA	CG 58	Bath Iron Works	8 May 1986	12 July 1987	18 Mar 1989	AA
PRINCETON	CG 59	Bath Iron Works	15 Oct 1986	2 Oct 1987	11 Feb 1989	PA
NORMANDY	CG 60	Bath Iron Works	7 Apr 1987	19 Mar 1988	9 Dec 1989	AA
MONTEREY	CG 61	Bath Iron Works	19 Aug 1987	23 Oct 1988	16 June 1990	AA
CHANCELLORSVILLE	CG 62	Ingalls Shipbuilding	24 June 1987	15 July 1988	4 Nov 1989	PA
COWPENS	CG 63	Bath Iron Works	23 Dec 1987	11 Mar 1989	9 Mar 1991	PA
GETTYSBURG	CG 64	Bath Iron Works	17 Aug 1988	22 July 1989	22 June 1991	AA
CHOSIN	CG 65	Ingalls Shipbuilding	22 July 1988	1 Sep 1989	12 Jan 1991	PA
HUE CITY	CG 66	Ingalls Shipbuilding	20 Feb 1989	1 June 1990	14 Sep 1991	AA
SHILOH	CG 67	Bath Iron Works	1 Aug 1989	8 Sep 1990	2 July 1992	PA
ANZIO	CG 68	Ingalls Shipbuilding	21 Aug 1989	2 Nov 1990	2 May 1992	AA
VICKSBURG	CG 69	Ingalls Shipbuilding	30 May 1990	2 Aug 1991	14 Nov 1992	AA
LAKE ERIE	CG 70	Bath Iron Works	6 Mar 1990	13 July 1991	24 July 1993	PA
CAPE ST GEORGE	CG 71	Ingalls Shipbuilding	19 Nov 1990	10 Jan 1992	12 June 1993	AA
VELLA GULF	CG 72	Ingalls Shipbuilding	22 Apr 1991	13 June 1992	18 Sep 1993	AA
PORT ROYAL	CG 73	Ingalls Shipbuilding	18 Oct 1991	20 Nov 1992	9 July 1994	PA

Displacement, tons: 9,957 full load
Dimensions, feet (metres): 567 × 55 × 31 (sonar)
(172.8 × 16.8 × 9.5)
Main machinery: 4 GE LM 2500 gas turbines; 86,000 hp *(64.16 MW)* sustained; 2 shafts; cp props
Speed, knots: 30+. **Range, n miles:** 6,000 at 20 kt
Complement: 358 (24 officers); accommodation for 405 total

Missiles: SLCM: GDC Tomahawk; Tercom aided guidance to 1,300 km *(700 n miles)* (TLAM-C and D) or 1,853 km *(1,000 n miles)* (TLAM-C Block III) at 0.7 Mach; warhead 454 kg (TLAM-C) or 347 kg shaped charge (TLAM-C Blocks II and III) or submunitions (TLAM-D). TLAM-C has GPS back-up to Tercom and a CEP of 10 m.
SSM: 8 McDonnell Douglas Harpoon (2 quad) ❶; active radar homing to 130 km *(70 n miles)* at 0.9 Mach; warhead 227 kg. Extended range SLAM can be fired from modified Harpoon canisters.
SAM: 122 GDC Standard SM-2MR; command/inertial guidance; semi-active radar homing to 167 km *(90 n miles)* at 2 Mach. SM-2 Block IIIB uses an IR seeker. SAM and ASROC missiles are fired from 2 Mk 41 Mod 0 vertical launchers ❸ (61 missiles per launcher).
A/S: Loral ASROC VLA which has a range of 16.6 km *(9 n miles)*; inertial guidance of 1.6 – 10 km *(1 – 5.4 n miles)*; payload Mk 46 Mod 5 Neartip or Mk 50.
Guns: 2 FMC 5 in *(127 mm)*/54 Mk 45 Mod 1 ❹; 20 rds/min to 23 km *(12.6 n miles)* anti-surface; weight of shell 32 kg.
2 General Electric/General Dynamics 20 mm/76 Vulcan Phalanx 6-barrelled Mk 15 Mod 2 ❺; 3,000 rds/min (4,500 in Block 1) combined to 1.5 km. To be fitted with high-definition thermal imagers (HDTI) for tracking small craft.
2 McDonnell Douglas 25 mm. 4 – 12.7 mm MGs.
Torpedoes: 6 – 324 mm Mk 32 (2 triple) Mod 14 tubes (fitted in the ship's side aft) ❻. 36 Honeywell Mk 46 Mod 5; anti-submarine; active/passive homing to 11 km *(5.9 n miles)* at 40 kt; warhead 44 kg or Alliant/Westinghouse Mk 50; active/passive homing to 15 km *(8.1 n miles)* at 50 kt; warhead 45 kg shaped charge.
Countermeasures: Decoys: Up to 8 Loral Hycor SRBOC 6-barrelled fixed Mk 36 Mod 2 ❼; IR flares and chaff. Nulka being acquired. SLQ-25 Nixie; towed torpedo decoy.
ESM/ECM: Raytheon SLQ-32V(3)/SLY-2 ❽; intercept, jammers.
Combat data systems: CEC being fitted 1996-2007 starting with CG 66 and 69. NTDS with Links 4A, 11, 14. GCCS (M) and Link 16 being fitted. Link 22 in due course. SATCOM WRN-5, WSC-3 (UHF), USC-38 (EHF). UYK 7 and 20 computers (CG 52-58); UYK 43/44 (CG 59 onwards and being backfitted to CG 56-58). SQQ-28 for LAMPS sonobuoy datalink ❾ (see Data Systems at front of section).
Weapons control: SWG-3 Tomahawk WCS. SWG-1A Harpoon LCS. Aegis Mk 7 Mod 4 multitarget tracking with Mk 99 MFCS (includes 4 Mk 80 illuminator directors); has at least 12 channels of fire. Singer Librascope Mk 116 Mod 6 (53B) or Mod 7 (53C) FCS for ASW. Lockheed Mk 86 Mod 9 GFCS (to be replaced by Mk-160 Mod 11 from 2008).
Radars: Air search/fire control: RCA SPY-1A phased arrays ❿; 3D; E/F-band (CG 52-58).
Raytheon SPY-1B phased arrays ⓫; 3D; E/F-band (CG 59 on).
Air search: Raytheon SPS-49(V)7 or 8 ⓬; C/D-band; range 457 km *(250 n miles)*.
Surface search: ISC Cardion SPS-55 ⓭; I/J-band.
Navigation: Raytheon SPS-64(V)9; I-band.
Fire control: Lockheed SPQ-9A/B ⓮; I/J-band.
Four Raytheon SPG-62 ⓯; I/J-band.
Tacan: URN 25. IFF Mk XII AIMS UPX-29.
Sonars: Gould/Raytheon SQQ-89(V)3 (CG 52 onwards); combines hull-mounted active SQS-53B (CG 52-67) or SQS-53C (CG 68-73) and passive towed array SQR-19.

Helicopters: 2 SH-60B Seahawk LAMPS III ⓰; 2 SH-2F LAMPS I (CG 47-48) ⓱. UAV in due course.

Modernisation: Four major combat system Baselines define the broad capability categories of this class. Baseline 1 ships (decommissioned) were fitted with SPY-1A radar, LAMPS I/III helicopter, Mk 26 missile launchers, Standard SM-2 MR Block I/II missiles, ASROC and the UYK-7 computing system. In the Baseline 2 ships (CG 52-58), Mk 26 launchers were replaced by Mk 41 Mod 0 Vertical Launch System (VLS) and Tomahawk was fitted. ASW improvements included SQR-19 in CG 54-55 and SQQ-89(V)3 integrated ASW suite with ASROC VLA in 1998. Baseline 3 ships (CG 59-64) incorporated the lighter SPY-1B radar, UYK-21 displays and UYK-43/44 computers in place of UYK-7s. Baseline 4 ships (CG 65-73) were fitted with SPY-1B(V) radar. While the basic hardware configurations have remained constant, the primary combat system computer has been progressively upgraded. Computer programmes currently in service are: Baseline 2 (2.10 which includes COTS Shipboard Advanced Radar Target Identification System (SARTIS)); Baselines 3 and 4 (5 phase 3). Link 16 was also added to the Baseline 3 and 4 ships as part of the computer system upgrade. The Cruiser Modernisation Programme (formerly the Cruiser Conversion Programme) is an extensive upgrade that will be applied to CG 52-73 (Baselines 2, 3 and 4). The core components of the programme include modification of the Mk 41 VLS launchers to fire ESSM, Integrated Ship Controls (ISC), replacement of SPQ-9A with SPQ-9B fire-control radar, installation of the SQQ-89A(V)15 sonar suite, fitting of the 62 calibre 127 mm gun, upgrade of Vulcan Phalanx to Block 1B, upgrade of the Aegis computer to 7PH1C with open architecture, display upgrades, COTS SARTIS and further platform and habitability upgrades to prolong service life. Modernisation will occur in two primary phases. Phase one will involve upgrades of Hull, Mechanical and Electrical (HM&E) upgrades, including ISC and All-Electric, as well as stand-alone combat system upgrades. Phase one upgrades, beginning in FY06 with the CG56, are expected to take less than six months and are to be accomplished while the ship is in homeport. Phase two is to start in FY08. The upgrades, which will take over six months to complete, is to consist of an Integrated Combat Systems package.

Structure: The Ticonderoga class design is a modification of the Spruance class. The same basic hull is used, with the same gas-turbine propulsion plant although the overall length is slightly increased. The design includes Kevlar armour to protect vital spaces. No stabilisers. Later ships have a lighter tripod mainmast vice the square quadruped of the first two.

Operational: The continuing development of the sea-based element of the Ballistic Missile Defense Programme is known as Aegis BMD. Test firings of the experimental Standard SM-3 missile were made by CG 67 on 24 September 1999. Since then CG 70 has successfully fired an SM-3 missile with a Lightweight Exo-Atmospheric Projectile (LEAP) to intercept an 'Aries' missile target on four occasions: during FM-2 (Flight Mission-2) on 25 January 2002, FM-3 on 13 June 2002, FM-4 on 21 November 2002, FM-6 on 11 December 2003. Further testings are planned. Baseline 1 ships (CG 47-51) paid off in 2004-05.

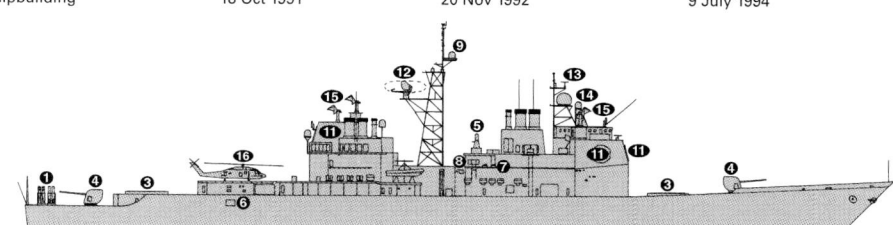

BUNKER HILL *(Scale 1 : 1,500), Ian Sturton* / 0016356

COWPENS *7/2005*, **Bob Fildes** / 1154006

PORT ROYAL *11/2003, US Navy* / 1043641

MOBILE BAY *10/2004*, Frank Findler* / 1154007

SAN JACINTO *6/2004, Frank Findler* / 1121519

ANZIO
7/2005*, H M Steele / 1154030

GETTYSBURG
7/2004, US Navy / 1043640

For details of the latest updates to *Jane's Fighting Ships* online and to discover the additional
information available exclusively to online subscribers please visit
jfs.janes.com

DESTROYERS

28 ARLEIGH BURKE CLASS (FLIGHTS I and II): GUIDED MISSILE DESTROYERS (AEGIS) (DDGHM)

Name	No	Builders	Laid down	Launched	Commissioned	F/S
ARLEIGH BURKE	DDG 51	Bath Iron Works	6 Dec 1988	16 Sep 1989	4 July 1991	AA
BARRY (ex-John Barry)	DDG 52	Ingalls Shipbuilding	26 Feb 1990	10 May 1991	12 Dec 1992	AA
JOHN PAUL JONES	DDG 53	Bath Iron Works	8 Aug 1990	26 Oct 1991	18 Dec 1993	PA
CURTIS WILBUR	DDG 54	Bath Iron Works	12 Mar 1992	16 May 1991	4 Apr 1994	PA
STOUT	DDG 55	Ingalls Shipbuilding	8 Aug 1991	16 Oct 1992	13 Aug 1994	AA
JOHN S McCAIN	DDG 56	Bath Iron Works	3 Sep 1991	26 Sep 1992	2 July 1994	PA
MITSCHER	DDG 57	Ingalls Shipbuilding	12 Feb 1992	7 May 1993	10 Dec 1994	AA
LABOON	DDG 58	Bath Iron Works	23 Mar 1992	20 Feb 1993	18 Mar 1995	AA
RUSSELL	DDG 59	Ingalls Shipbuilding	24 July 1992	20 Oct 1993	20 May 1995	PA
PAUL HAMILTON	DDG 60	Bath Iron Works	24 Aug 1992	24 July 1993	27 May 1995	PA
RAMAGE	DDG 61	Ingalls Shipbuilding	4 Jan 1993	11 Feb 1994	22 July 1995	AA
FITZGERALD	DDG 62	Bath Iron Works	9 Feb 1993	29 Jan 1994	14 Oct 1995	PA
STETHEM	DDG 63	Ingalls Shipbuilding	11 May 1993	17 June 1994	21 Oct 1995	AA
CARNEY	DDG 64	Bath Iron Works	3 Aug 1993	23 July 1994	13 Apr 1996	AA
BENFOLD	DDG 65	Ingalls Shipbuilding	27 Sep 1993	9 Nov 1994	30 Mar 1996	PA
GONZALEZ	DDG 66	Bath Iron Works	3 Feb 1994	18 Feb 1995	12 Oct 1996	AA
COLE	DDG 67	Ingalls Shipbuilding	28 Feb 1994	10 Feb 1995	8 June 1996	AA
THE SULLIVANS	DDG 68	Bath Iron Works	27 July 1994	12 Aug 1995	19 Apr 1997	AA
MILIUS	DDG 69	Ingalls Shipbuilding	8 Aug 1994	1 Aug 1995	23 Nov 1996	PA
HOPPER	DDG 70	Bath Iron Works	23 Feb 1995	6 Jan 1996	6 Sep 1997	PA
ROSS	DDG 71	Ingalls Shipbuilding	10 Apr 1995	23 Mar 1996	28 June 1997	AA
MAHAN	DDG 72	Bath Iron Works	17 Aug 1995	29 June 1996	14 Feb 1998	AA
DECATUR	DDG 73	Bath Iron Works	11 Jan 1996	10 Nov 1996	29 Aug 1998	PA
McFAUL	DDG 74	Ingalls Shipbuilding	26 Jan 1996	18 Jan 1997	25 Apr 1998	AA
DONALD COOK	DDG 75	Bath Iron Works	9 July 1996	3 May 1997	4 Dec 1998	AA
HIGGINS	DDG 76	Bath Iron Works	14 Nov 1996	4 Oct 1997	24 Apr 1999	PA
O'KANE	DDG 77	Bath Iron Works	5 May 1997	28 Mar 1998	23 Oct 1999	PA
PORTER	DDG 78	Ingalls Shipbuilding	2 Dec 1996	12 Nov 1997	20 Mar 1999	AA

Displacement, tons: 8,950 (DDG 51-71); 8,946 (DDG 72-78)

Dimensions, feet (metres): 504.5 oa; 466 wl × 66.9 × 20.7; 32.7 (sonar) *(153.8; 142 × 20.4 × 6.3; 9.9)*

Main machinery: 4 GE LM 2500 gas turbines; 105,000 hp *(78.33 MW)* sustained; 2 shafts; cp props

Speed, knots: 32. **Range, n miles:** 4,400 at 20 kt

Complement: 346 (DDG 51-71); 352 (DDG 72-78) (22 officers)

Missiles: SLCM: 56 GDC/Hughes Tomahawk; Tercom aided guidance to 1,300 km *(700 n miles)* (TLAM-C and D) or 1,853 km *(1,000 n miles)* (TLAM-C Block III) at 0.7 Mach; warhead 454 kg (TLAM-C) or 347 kg shaped charge (TLAM-C Blocks II and III) or submunitions (TLAM-D). TLAM-C has GPS back-up to Tercom and a CEP of 10 m.
SSM: 8 McDonnell Douglas Harpoon (2 quad) ❶; active radar homing to 130 km *(70 n miles)* at 0.9 Mach; warhead 227 kg.
SAM: GDC Standard SM-2MR Block IV; command/inertial guidance; semi-active radar homing to 167 km *(90 n miles)* at 2 Mach. SM-2ER extended range to 137 km *(74 n miles)* from DDG 72 onwards. 2 Martin Marietta Mk 41 (Mod 0 forward, Mod 1 aft) Vertical Launch Systems (VLS) for Tomahawk, Standard and ASROC VLA ❷; 2 magazines; 29 missiles forward, 61 aft. Mod 2 from DDG 59 onwards.
A/S: Loral ASROC VLA; inertial guidance to 1.6—16.6 km *(1—9 n miles)*; payload Mk 46 Mod 5 Neartip.

Guns: 1 FMC/UDLP 5 in *(127 mm)*/54 Mk 45 Mod 1 or 2 ❸; 20 rds/min to 23 km *(12.6 n miles)*; weight of shell 32 kg. 2 General Electric/General Dynamics 20 mm Vulcan Phalanx 6-barrelled Mk 15 ❹; 3,000 rds/min (4,500 in Block 1) combined to 1.5 km. Being fitted with IR detectors for tracking small craft. To be replaced by RAM from 2004.

Torpedoes: 6—324 mm Mk 32 Mod 14 (2 triple) tubes ❺. Alliant Mk 46 Mod 5; anti-submarine; active/passive homing to 11 km *(5.9 n miles)* at 40 kt; warhead 44 kg or Alliant/Westinghouse Mk 50; active/passive homing to 15 km *(8.1 n miles)* at 50 kt; warhead 45 kg shaped charge.

Countermeasures: Decoys: 2 Loral Hycor SRBOC 6-barrelled fixed Mk 36 Mod 12 ❻; IR flares and chaff to 4 km *(2.2 n miles)*. SLQ-25 Nixie; torpedo decoy. NATO Sea Gnat. SLQ-95 AEB. SLQ-39 chaff buoy. Nulka being acquired.
ESM/ECM: Raytheon SLQ-32(V)2 ❼ or SLQ-32(V)3/SLY-2 (from DDG 72 and being backfitted); radar warning.

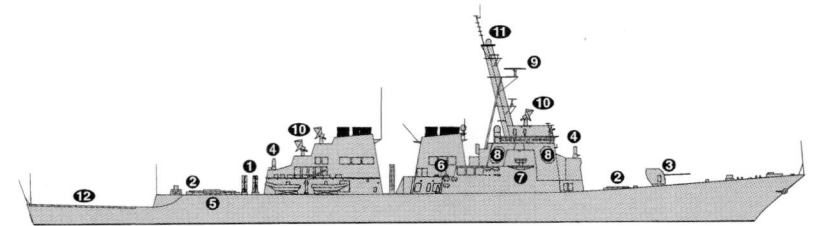

ARLEIGH BURKE *(Scale 1 : 1,500), Ian Sturton* / 0053331

Sidekick modification adds jammer and deception system to (V)2. SRS-1 DF (from DDG 72).

Combat data systems: CEC being fitted. NTDS Mod 5 with Links 4A, 11, 14 and 16 (from DDG 72) and being back fitted. SATCOM SRR-1, WSC-3 (UHF), USC-38 (EHF). SQQ-28 for LAMPS processor datalink. TADIX B Tactical Information Exchange System (from DDG 72). Link 22 in due course (see Data Systems at front of section).

Weapons control: SWG-3 Mk 37 Tomahawk WCS. SWG-1A Harpoon LCS. Aegis multitarget tracking with Mk 99 Mod 3 MFCS and three Mk 80 illuminators. Mk 34 GWS (includes Mk 160 computing system and Kollmorgen Mk 46 Mod 0/1 optronic sight). Singer Librascope Mk 116 Mod 7 FCS for ASW.

Radars: Air search/fire control: RCA SPY-1D phased arrays ❽; 3D; E/F-band.
Surface search: Norden/DRS SPS-67(V)3 ❾; G-band.
Navigation: Raytheon SPS-64(V)9; I-band.
Fire control: Three Raytheon/RCA SPG-62 ❿; I/J-band.
Tacan: URN 25 ⓫. IFF Mk XII AIMS UPX-29.

Sonars: Gould/Raytheon/GE SQQ-89(V)6; combines SQS-53C; bow-mounted; active search and attack with SQR-19B passive towed array (TACTAS) low frequency.

Helicopters: Platform and facilities to fuel and rearm LAMPS III SH-60B/F helicopters ⓬. UAV in due course.

Programmes: First ship authorised in FY85, last pair in FY94. The first 21 are Flight I and the next seven are Flight II.

Modernisation: A modernisation programme is under development. There are likely to be two phases: the first

to improve machinery, navigation and damage-control systems and the second to upgrade combat systems.

Structure: The ship, except for the aluminium mast, is constructed of steel. 70 tons of armour provided to protect vital spaces. This is the first class of US Navy warship designed with a 'collective protection system for defense against the fallout associated with NBC warfare'. The ship's crew are protected by double air-locked hatches, fewer accesses to the weatherdecks and positive pressurisation of the interior of the ship to keep out contaminants. All incoming air is filtered and more reliance placed on recirculating air inside the ship. All accommodation compartments have sprinkler systems. Stealth technology includes angled surfaces and rounded edges to reduce radar signature and IR signature suppression plus Prairie Masker hull/blade rate suppression. The CIC room is below the waterline and electronics are EMP hardened. The original upright mast design has been changed to increase separation between electronic systems and the forward funnel. Differences in Flight II starting with DDG 72 include Link 16, SLQ-32(V)3 EW suite, extended-range SAM missiles and improved tactical information exchange systems. The topmast is vertical to take the SRS-1. There is also an increase in displacement caused by using more space to carry fuel.

Operational: Two of the class are based at Yokosuka in Japan. Repairs to *Cole*, damaged by a terrorist attack at Aden on 12 October 2000, began in January 2001 at Ingalls and completed on 19 April 2002 when she returned to the fleet. *Curtis Wilbur* began missile-defence patrols in the Sea of Japan in October 2004.

JOHN PAUL JONES *5/2005*, Hachiro Nakai* / 1154025

ROSS

12/2005*, Ships of the World / 1154027

RUSSELL

9/2005*, Frank Findler / 1154026

HOPPER

9/2005*, Nicola Mazumdar / 1154037

22 + 12 ARLEIGH BURKE CLASS (FLIGHT IIA): GUIDED MISSILE DESTROYERS

Name	No	Builders	Laid down	Launched	Commissioned	F/S
OSCAR AUSTIN	DDG 79	Bath Iron Works	9 Oct 1997	7 Nov 1998	19 Aug 2000	AA
ROOSEVELT	DDG 80	Ingalls Shipbuilding	15 Dec 1997	10 Jan 1999	14 Oct 2000	AA
WINSTON S CHURCHILL	DDG 81	Bath Iron Works	7 May 1998	17 Apr 1999	10 Mar 2001	AA
LASSEN	DDG 82	Ingalls Shipbuilding	24 Aug 1998	16 Oct 1999	21 Apr 2001	PA
HOWARD	DDG 83	Bath Iron Works	9 Dec 1998	20 Nov 1999	20 Oct 2001	PA
BULKELEY	DDG 84	Ingalls Shipbuilding	10 May 1999	21 June 2000	8 Dec 2001	AA
McCAMPBELL	DDG 85	Bath Iron Works	15 July 1999	2 July 2000	17 Aug 2002	PA
SHOUP	DDG 86	Ingalls Shipbuilding	13 Dec 1999	22 Nov 2000	22 June 2002	PA
MASON	DDG 87	Bath Iron Works	20 Jan 2000	23 June 2001	12 Apr 2003	AA
PREBLE	DDG 88	Ingalls Shipbuilding	22 June 2000	1 June 2001	9 Nov 2002	PA
MUSTIN	DDG 89	Ingalls Shipbuilding	15 Jan 2001	12 Dec 2001	26 July 2003	PA
CHAFFEE	DDG 90	Bath Iron Works	12 Apr 2001	2 Nov 2002	20 Sep 2003	PA
PINCKNEY	DDG 91	Ingalls Shipbuilding	16 July 2001	29 June 2002	29 May 2004	PA
MOMSEN	DDG 92	Bath Iron Works	15 Oct 2001	9 Aug 2003	28 Aug 2004	PA
CHUNG-HOON	DDG 93	Ingalls, Shipbuilding	14 Jan 2002	11 Jan 2003	18 Sep 2004	PA
NITZE	DDG 94	Bath Iron Works	11 Aug 2002	17 Apr 2004	5 Mar 2005	AA
JAMES E WILLIAMS	DDG 95	Ingalls Shipbuilding	15 July 2002	28 June 2003	11 Dec 2004	AA
BAINBRIDGE	DDG 96	Bath Iron Works	16 Mar 2003	13 Nov 2004	12 Nov 2005	AA
HALSEY	DDG 97	Ingalls Shipbuilding	13 Jan 2003	17 Jan 2004	30 July 2005	PA
FORREST SHERMAN	DDG 98	Ingalls Shipbuilding	21 July 2003	2 Oct 2004	28 Jan 2006	AA
FARRAGUT	DDG 99	Bath Iron Works	23 Nov 2003	9 July 2005	June 2006	Bldg/AA
KIDD	DDG 100	Ingalls Shipbuilding	1 Mar 2004	22 Jan 2005	Feb 2006	Bldg/PA
GRIDLEY	DDG 101	Bath Iron Works	7 July 2004	11 Feb 2006	Sep 2006	Bldg/PA
SAMPSON	DDG 102	Bath Iron Works	19 Mar 2005	July 2006	2007	Bldg
TRUXTUN	DDG 103	Northrop Grumman Ship Systems	28 Mar 2005	Mar 2006	2007	Bldg
STERETT	DDG 104	Bath Iron Works	19 Nov 2005	Apr 2007	2008	Bldg
DEWEY	DDG 105	Northrop Grumman Ship Systems	Apr 2006	Feb 2007	2008	Bldg
STOCKDALE	DDG 106	Bath Iron Works	July 2006	Nov 2007	2009	Ord
—	DDG 107	Northrop Grumman Ship Systems	Mar 2007	Feb 2008	2009	Ord
—	DDG 108	Bath Iron Works	Feb 2007	Jun 2008	2009	Ord
—	DDG 109	Bath Iron Works	Oct 2007	Feb 2009	2010	Ord
—	DDG 110	Northrop Grumman Ship Systems	Mar 2007	Feb 2009	2010	Ord
—	DDG 111	Bath Iron Works	May 2008	Sep 2009	2011	Ord
—	DDG 112	Bath Iron Works	Dec 2008	May 2010	2011	Ord

Displacement, tons: 9,188 full load
Dimensions, feet (metres): 509.5 oa; 471 wl × 66.9 × 20.7; 32.7 (sonar) *(155.3; 143.6 × 20.4 × 6.3; 9.9)*
Main machinery: 4 GE LM 2500-30 gas turbines; 100,000 hp *(74.6 MW)* sustained; 2 shafts; cp props
Speed, knots: 31. **Range, n miles:** 4,400 at 20 kt
Complement: 292 (24 officers)

Missiles: SLCM: GCD/Hughes Tomahawk; Tercom aided guidance to 1,300 km *(700 n miles)* (TLAM-C and D) or 1,853 km *(1,000 n miles)* (TLAM-C Block III) at 0.7 Mach; warhead 454 kg (TLAM-C) or 347 kg shaped charge (TLAM-C Blocks II and III) or submunitions (TLAM-D). TLAM-C has GPS back-up to Tercom and a CEP of 10 m. Tactical Tomahawk from 2004.
SAM: GDC Standard SM-2MR Block IV; command/inertial guidance; semi-active radar homing to 167 km *(90 n miles)* at 2 Mach. 2 Lockheed Martin Mk 41 Vertical Launch Systems (VLS) for Tomahawk, Standard and ASROC VLS ❶; 2 magazines; 32 missile tubes forward, 64 aft. 32 Raytheon RIM-162 ESSM (4 quad forward, 4 quad aft) (DDG 85 onwards); semi-active radar homing to 18.5 km *(10 n miles)* at 3.6 Mach. ESSM retro-fitted to DDG 79-84 (2004-06).
A/S: Loral ASROC VLA; inertial guidance to 1.6—16.6 km *(1—9 n miles)*; payload Mk 46 Mod 5 Neartip.
Guns: 1 United Defense 5 in *(127 mm)*/54 Mk 45 Mod 2 (DDG 79-80) ❷; 20 rds/min to 23 km *(12.6 n miles)*; weight of shell 32 kg.
United Defense 5 in *(127 mm)*/62 (DDG 81 onwards); 20 or 10 (ERGM) rds/min; GPS guidance to 116.7 km *(63 n miles)*; warhead 72 bomblets; cep 10 m.
Torpedoes: 6—324 mm Mk 32 Mod 14 (2 triple) tubes ❸. Alliant Mk 46 Mod 5; anti-submarine; active/passive homing to 11 km *(5.9 n miles)* at 40 kt; warhead 44 kg or Alliant/Westinghouse Mk 50; active/passive homing to 15 km *(8.1 n miles)* at 50 kt; warhead 45 kg shaped charge.
Countermeasures: Decoys: 2 Loral Hycor SRBOC 6-barrelled fixed Mk 36 Mod 12 ❹; Nulka decoy (DDG 91 onwards); IR flares and chaff to 4 km *(2.2 n miles)*. SLQ-25 Nixie; torpedo decoy. NATO Sea Gnat. SLQ-95 AEB. SLQ-39 chaff buoy.
ESM/ECM: Raytheon SLQ-32(V)3/SLY-2 ❺; intercept and jammer.

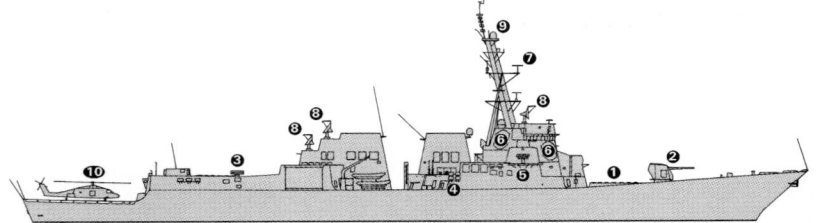

MOMSEN *(Scale 1 : 1,500), Ian Sturton* / 1153884

Combat data systems: TADIX-B and TADIL-J. CEC. Links 4A, 11 and 16. (See Data Systems at front of section.) Link 22 in due course. CDS upgrade for DDG 91.
Weapons control: SWG-3 Mk 37 Tomahawk WCS. Aegis multitarget tracking with Mk 99 Mod 3 MFCS and three Mk 80 illuminators. Mk 34 GWS (consisting of Mk 160 computing system and Kollmorgen Mk 46 optronic sight). Singer Librascope Mk 116 FCS for ASW.
Radars: Air search/fire control: Lockheed Martin SPY-1D (SPY-1D(V) DDG 91 onwards) phased arrays ❻; 3D; E/F-band.
Surface search: DRS SPS-67(V)3 ❼; G-band.
Navigation: Raytheon SPS-64(V)9 (DDG 79-86, 88); Sperry-Marine BME 740 (DDG 87, 89-112); I-band.
Fire control: Three Raytheon AN/SPG-62 ❽; I/J-band.
Tacan: AN/URN 25 ❾. IFF AIMS Mk XII with AN/UPX-29.
Sonars: Lockheed Martin SQQ-89(V)10; underwater combat system with SQS-53C; bow-mounted; active search and attack. Kingfisher; mine detection; active; high frequency.
Remote Minehunting System (DDG 91-96).

Helicopters: 2 LAMPS III SH-60B/F helicopters ❿.

Programmes: DDG 79 was authorised in the FY94 budget. Funding for DDG 80-82 provided in FY95 and DDG 83-84 in FY96 plus partial funding for a third. Balance for DDG 85 plus DDG 86-88 in FY97 and DDG 89-101 in FY98. On 6 March 1998, multi-year contract for six ships and

one option (DDG 89) awarded to Ingalls Shipbuilding and contract for six ships awarded to Bath Iron Works. On 1 August 2002, contract awarded to Bath Iron Works for the construction of DDG 102 and on 13 September 2002 a fixed-price multi-year contract awarded to Bath Iron Works (DDGs 104, 106, 108, 109, 111 and 112) and Northrop Grumman Ship Systems (DDGs 103, 105, 107, 110) for the construction of ten ships. Further orders are not expected.
Modernisation: Future planned upgrades include Aegis Baseline 7.1, SPY 1D(V) radar, CEC, Nulka decoys, Remote Minehunting System, Integrated Bridge System and Tactical Tomahawk.
Structure: The upgrade from Flight II includes two hangars for embarked helicopters and an extended transom to increase the size of a dual RAST fitted flight deck at the expense of SQR-19 TACTAS. Vertical launchers are increased at each end by three cells. Other changes include the Kingfisher minehunting sonar, a reaeconfiguration of the SPY-1D arrays and the inclusion of a Track Initiation Processor in the Aegis radar system. Use of fibre optic technology should reduce weight and improve reliability.
Operational: The helicopter carries Penguin and Hellfire missiles. ESSM fired from DDG 86 on 24 July 2002, the first to be fired from a USN ship.

CHAFFEE *12/2005*, Ships of the World* / 1154029

BULKELEY   *4/2004, US Navy* / 1043644

HOWARD   *7/2004, Michael Nitz* / 1043642

OSCAR AUSTIN   *6/2004, Harald Carstens* / 1043684

0 + 2 (5) ZUMWALT CLASS DESTROYER (DD(X)) (DDGH)

Name	No	Builders	Laid down	Launched	Commissioned
ZUMWALT	DDG 1000	Northrop Grumman Ship Systems	2007	2010	2012
		General Dynamics Bath Iron Works	2007	2010	2012

Displacement, tons: 14,564
Dimensions, feet (metres): 600.0 × 79.0 × 28.0
 (182.8 × 24.1 × 8.5)
Main machinery: Integrated Power System (IPS); 2 Main Turbine Generators (MTG); 2 Auxiliary Turbine Generators (ATG); 2 propulsion motors; 97,625 hp (72.8 MW); 2 shafts
Speed, knots: 30. **Range, n miles:** To be announced
Complement: 142

Missiles: 80 VLS cells.
SLCM: Tactical Tomahawk.
SAM: Standard SM-2 and Evolved Sea Sparrow.
A/S: Vertical launched ASROC.
Guns: 2—155 mm advanced gun systems capable of firing Long Range Land Attack Projectiles (LRLAP) at ranges up to 83 n miles. 2—57 mm close-in guns.
Torpedoes: To be announced.
Countermeasures: To be announced.
Combat data systems: To be announced.
Weapons control: To be announced.
Radars: Air/surface search: Dual Band Radar (DBR); Raytheon SPY-3; phased arrays; 3D; E/F/I-band.
Navigation: To be announced.
Sonars: Hull mounted and towed arrays.

Helicopters: 1 MH-60R and 3 UAVs.

Programmes: DD(X) programme instituted on November 2001. Principal roles of DD(X) are sustained operations in the littorals and land-attack. Ten Engineering Development Models (EDMs) have passed Critical Design Review (CDR). Ship design completed CDR in September 2005 and received approval to proceed with Milestone B in November 2005. This authorises commencement of detailed design and construction of the DD(X) class. Initially, the acquisition strategy calls for two lead ships to be built, one by Northrop Grumman Ship Systems and the other by General Dynamics Bath Iron Works. Raytheon is the Combat Systems Integrator. Construction contract award is expected in 2007 and delivery of the first two

DD(X)   *12/2005*, **US Navy** / 1154036

ships is scheduled for 2012. The acquisition strategy for further ships has yet to be decided. The overall size of the class is also under review but the shipbuilding plan declared to Congress includes seven ships.
Structure: Features of the ship include a forward-swept, wave-piercing 'tumblehome' hull, designed to reduce radar signatures and provide stability in high sea states. Hull structure and missile cells spread impacts outward to increase survivability and reduce risk of single-hit ship loss. Integrated deckhouse and composite superstructure encloses masts, sensors and antennas, bridge and

exhaust silos. There are two shielded 155 mm Advanced Gun Systems (AGS) and an 80-cell Peripheral (port and starboard) Vertical Launch System for both land attack and air defense missiles. EDMs for key systems include an Integrated Power System (IPS), AGS, Integrated Undersea Warfare Suite (IUWS) and an open architecture Total Ship Computing Environment (TSCE). IPS reduces number of prime movers from seven to four and enables power to be distributed to any system as the tactical situation demands. IPS designed to create sufficient reserve energy to power energy weapons in the future.

FRIGATES

FREEDOM (artist's impression)   *4/2004*, **Lockheed Martin** / 0566824

0 + 2 FREEDOM CLASS LITTORAL COMBAT SHIP FLIGHT 0

Name	No	Builders	Laid down	Launched	Commissioned	F/S
FREEDOM	LCS 1	Marinette Marine, Wisconsin	2 June 2005	Sep 2006	2007	Bldg/PA
—	LCS 3		2006	2008	2008	Bldg/PA

Displacement, tons: 3,089 full load
Dimensions, feet (metres): 379.0 × 43.0 × 12.8
  (115.5 × 13.1 × 3.9)
Main machinery: CODAG: 2 Rolls Royce MT-30 gas turbines;
  96,550 hp *(72 MW)*; 2 Fairbanks Morse Colt-Pielstick
  16PA6B diesels; 17,160 hp *(12.8 MW)*; 4 Rolls Royce
  Kamewa 153SII waterjets
Speed, knots: 45. **Range, n miles:** 3,500 at 18 kt
Complement: 50

Missiles: 1 Raytheon RAM.
Guns: 1 United Defence 57 mm/70 Mk 2; 220 rds/min to
  17 km (9 n miles); weight of shell 2.4 kg. 4—12.7 mm MGs.
Countermeasures: 2 SKWS/SRBOC decoy launching
  systems. ESM/ECM.
Combat data systems: COMBATSS-21.
Weapons control: To be announced.
Radars: Air/surface search: EADS TRS-3D; C-band.
Navigation: To be announced.
Fire control: To be announced.
Sonars: To be announced.

Helicopters: 2 MH-60 R/S helicopters or 1 MH-60 R/S and
  3 Firescout VTUAVs.

Programmes: Three winning LCS designs selected on
  17 July 2003 to proceed to the Flight 0 preliminary design

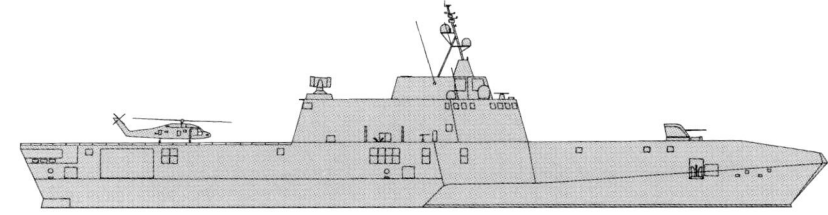

FREEDOM *(Scale 1 : 1,200), Ian Sturton* / 1153883

stage. Thereafter, General Dynamics and Lockheed Martin won competition on 27 May 2004 to build first four Flight 0 ships (two of each design). Contract to build first ship awarded to Lockheed Martin on 15 December 2004 for delivery in 2007. First steel cut February 2005. This is to be followed by an order for a second ship for delivery in 2008. Following evaluation of both (General Dynamics and Lockheed Martin) Flight 0 variants, construction of three Flight I ships to begin in 2008 and of six further ships in 2009. Seven mission modules (three mine warfare; two ASW and two ASUW) are budgeted from FY05-07. Up to 60 ships of the class may ultimately be required.

Structure: Semi-planing steel monohull design. Steel hull and aluminium superstructure. The design incorporates

a large reconfigurable seaframe to allow rapidly interchangeable mission modules, a flight deck with integrated helicopter launch, recovery and handling system and the capability to launch and recover boats from both the stern and side.

Operational: Concept of operations for LCS includes deployment of two or three-ship team to operate near shore in support of surface strike groups. Role in homeland defense also likely. Principal capabilities to include shallow-water ASW, mine countermeasures and defence against attacking small boats. LCS ships are to be networked to share tactical information with other units.

0 + 2 INDEPENDENCE CLASS LITTORAL COMBAT SHIP (GENERAL DYNAMICS) FLIGHT 0

Name	No	Builders	Laid down	Launched	Commissioned	F/S
INDEPENDENCE	LCS 2	Austal USA, Mobile, Alabama	19 Jan 2006	2008	2008	Bldg/PA
—	LCS 4		2006	2008	2008	Bldg/PA

Displacement, tons: 2,790 full load
Dimensions, feet (metres): 417.3 × 99.7 × 14.8
  (127.2 × 30.4 × 4.5)
Main machinery: CODAG: 2 gas turbines, 2 diesels;
  4 steerable waterjets; 1 steerable thruster
Speed, knots: 45. **Range, n miles:** 4,300 at 18 kt
Complement: 40

Missiles: Raytheon RAM.
Guns: 1 United Defence 57 mm/70 Mk 2; 220 rds/min to
  17 km (9 n miles); weight of shell 2.4 kg. 4—12.7mm MGs.
Countermeasures: Decoys: ESM/ECM.
Combat data systems: Northrop Grumman Electronic
  Systems Integrated Combat Management System
  (ICMS).
Weapons control: To be announced.
Radars: Air/surface search: Ericson Sea Giraffe; G/H-band.
Navigation: To be announced.
Fire control: To be announced.
Sonars: To be announced.

Helicopters: 2 H-60 helicopters; multiple UAVs/VTUAVs;
  large flight deck area can accommodate CH-53.

Programmes: Three winning LCS designs selected on
  17 July 2003 to proceed to the Flight 0 preliminary design

LCS 2 *(Scale 1 : 1,200), Ian Sturton* / 1153881

stage. Thereafter, General Dynamics and Lockheed Martin won competition on 27 May 2004 to build first four Flight 0 ships (two of each design). Contract for first General Dynamics ship awarded in October 2005 for delivery in early 2008. This is to be followed by a second ship for delivery in 2008. Following evaluation of both (General Dynamics and Lockheed Martin) Flight 0 variants, construction of three Flight I ships to begin in 2008 and of four further ships in 2009. Seven mission modules (three mine warfare; two ASW and two ASUW) are budgeted from FY05-07. Up to 60 ships of the class may ultimately be required.

Structure: Trimaran hullform based on fast commercial ferry design for Fred Olsen Line. Aluminium construction. Large flight deck capable of operating Sea Stallion heavy-lift helicopter. Stern launch of boats. Side-ramp Ro-Ro capability. Reconfigurable seaframe to allow rapidly interchangeable mission modules.

Operational: Concept of operations for LCS includes deployment of two or three-ship team to operate near shore in support of surface strike groups. Role in homeland defense also likely. Principal capabilities to include shallow-water ASW, mine countermeasures and defence against attacking small boats.

INDEPENDENCE (artist's impression) *1/2005, General Dynamics* / 1043677

30 OLIVER HAZARD PERRY CLASS: GUIDED MISSILE FRIGATES (FFGHM)

Name	No	Builders	Laid down	Launched	Commissioned	F/S
McINERNEY	FFG 8	Bath Iron Works	7 Nov 1977	4 Nov 1978	15 Dec 1979	AA
BOONE	FFG 28	Todd Shipyards, Seattle	27 Mar 1979	16 Jan 1980	15 May 1982	NRF
STEPHEN W GROVES	FFG 29	Bath Iron Works	16 Sep 1980	4 Apr 1981	17 Apr 1982	NRF
JOHN L HALL	FFG 32	Bath Iron Works	5 Jan 1981	24 July 1981	26 June 1982	AA
JARRETT	FFG 33	Todd Shipyards, San Pedro	11 Feb 1981	17 Oct 1981	2 July 1983	PA
UNDERWOOD	FFG 36	Bath Iron Works	3 Aug 1981	6 Feb 1982	29 Jan 1983	AA
CROMMELIN	FFG 37	Todd Shipyards, Seattle	30 May 1980	1 July 1981	18 June 1983	NRF
CURTS	FFG 38	Todd Shipyards, San Pedro	1 July 1981	6 Mar 1982	8 Oct 1983	NRF
DOYLE	FFG 39	Bath Iron Works	16 Nov 1981	22 May 1982	21 May 1983	NRF
HALYBURTON	FFG 40	Todd Shipyards, Seattle	26 Sep 1980	15 Oct 1981	7 Jan 1984	AA
McCLUSKY	FFG 41	Todd Shipyards, San Pedro	21 Oct 1981	18 Sep 1982	10 Dec 1983	NRF
KLAKRING	FFG 42	Bath Iron Works	19 Feb 1982	18 Sep 1982	20 Aug 1983	NRF
THACH	FFG 43	Todd Shipyards, San Pedro	10 Mar 1982	18 Dec 1982	17 Mar 1984	PA
De WERT	FFG 45	Bath Iron Works	14 June 1982	18 Dec 1982	19 Nov 1983	AA
RENTZ	FFG 46	Todd Shipyards, San Pedro	18 Sep 1982	16 July 1983	30 June 1984	PA
NICHOLAS	FFG 47	Bath Iron Works	27 Sep 1982	23 Apr 1983	10 Mar 1984	AA
VANDEGRIFT	FFG 48	Todd Shipyards, Seattle	13 Oct 1981	15 Oct 1982	24 Nov 1984	PA
ROBERT G BRADLEY	FFG 49	Bath Iron Works	28 Dec 1982	13 Aug 1983	11 Aug 1984	AA
TAYLOR	FFG 50	Bath Iron Works	5 May 1983	5 Nov 1983	1 Dec 1984	AA
GARY	FFG 51	Todd Shipyards, San Pedro	18 Dec 1982	19 Nov 1983	17 Nov 1984	PA
CARR	FFG 52	Todd Shipyards, Seattle	26 Mar 1982	26 Feb 1983	27 July 1985	AA
HAWES	FFG 53	Bath Iron Works	22 Aug 1983	18 Feb 1984	9 Feb 1985	AA
FORD	FFG 54	Todd Shipyards, San Pedro	16 July 1983	23 June 1984	29 June 1985	PA
ELROD	FFG 55	Bath Iron Works	21 Nov 1983	12 May 1984	6 June 1985	AA
SIMPSON	FFG 56	Bath Iron Works	27 Feb 1984	21 Aug 1984	9 Nov 1985	NRF
REUBEN JAMES	FFG 57	Todd Shipyards, San Pedro	19 Nov 1983	8 Feb 1985	22 Mar 1986	PA
SAMUEL B ROBERTS	FFG 58	Bath Iron Works	21 May 1984	8 Dec 1984	12 Apr 1986	AA
KAUFFMAN	FFG 59	Bath Iron Works	8 Apr 1985	29 Mar 1986	21 Feb 1987	AA
RODNEY M DAVIS	FFG 60	Todd Shipyards, San Pedro	8 Feb 1985	11 Jan 1986	9 May 1987	NRF
INGRAHAM	FFG 61	Todd Shipyards, San Pedro	30 Mar 1987	25 June 1988	5 Aug 1989	PA

Displacement, tons: 2,750 light; 3,638 (FFG 33); 4,100 full load
Dimensions, feet (metres): 445 (FFG 33); 453 × 45 × 14.8;
  24.5 (sonar)
  (135.6; 138.1 × 13.7 × 4.5; 7.5)
Main machinery: 2 GE LM 2500 gas turbines; 41,000 hp
  (30.59 MW) sustained; 1 shaft; cp prop
  2 auxiliary retractable props; 650 hp *(484 kW)*
Speed, knots: 29
Range, n miles: 4,500 at 20 kt
Complement: 200 (15 officers) including 19 aircrew

Guns: 1 OTO Melara 3 in *(76 mm)*/62 Mk 75 ❶; 85 rds/min
  to 16 km *(8.7 n miles)* anti-surface; 12 km *(6.6 n miles)*
  anti-aircraft; weight of shell 6 kg.
  1 General Electric/General Dynamics 20 mm/76
  6-barrelled Mk 15 Block 1B Vulcan Phalanx ❷; 4,500 rds/min
  combined to 1.5 km.
  2 Boeing 25 mm Mk 38 guns can be fitted amidships.
  4—12.7 mm MGs.
Torpedoes: 6—324 mm Mk 32 (2 triple) tubes ❸. 24
  Honeywell Mk 46 Mod 5; anti-submarine; active/passive
  homing to 11 km *(5.9 n miles)* at 40 kt; warhead 44 kg or
  Alliant/Westinghouse Mk 50; active/passive homing to
  15 km *(8.1 n miles)* at 50 kt; warhead 45 kg shaped charge.
Countermeasures: Decoys: 2 Loral Hycor SRBOC
  6-barrelled fixed Mk 36 ❹; IR flares and chaff to 4 km
  (2.2 n miles). Mk 34 launcher for Mk 53 Nulka decoys.
  T-Mk 6 Fanfare/SLQ-25 Nixie; torpedo decoy.
ESM/ECM: SLQ-32(V)2 ❺; radar warning. Sidekick
  modification adds jammer and deception system.
Combat data systems: NTDS with Link 11 and 14. Link 14
  only (NRF ships). SATCOM ❻ SRR-1, WSC-3 (UHF).
  SQQ-28 for LAMPS III datalink.
Weapons control: Mk 92 (Mod 4 or Mod 6 (FFG 61 and
  during modernisation in 11 others of the class)), WCS
  with CAS (Combined Antenna System). The Mk 92 is the
  US version of the Signaal WM28 system. SYS 2(V)2 IADT
  (FFG 61 and in 11 others of the class-see *Modernisation*).
  SRQ-4 for LAMPS III, SKR-4A for LAMPS I.
Radars: Air search: Raytheon SPS-49(V)4 or 5 (FFG 61 and
  during modernisation of others) ❼; C/D-band; range
  457 km *(250 n miles)*.
  Surface search: ISC Cardion SPS-55 ❽; I-band.
  Fire control: Sperry Mk 92 (Signaal WM28) ❾; I/J-band.

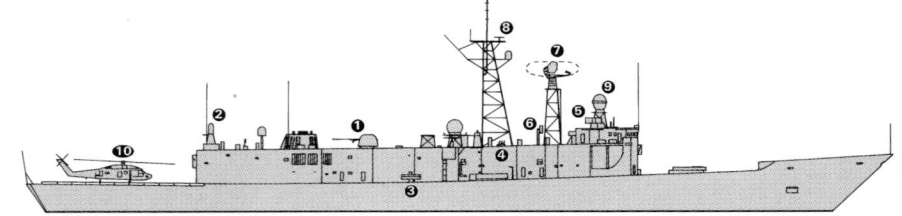

RENTZ   *(Scale 1 : 1,200), Ian Sturton* / 0572737

Navigation: Furuno; I-band.
Tacan: URN 25. IFF Mk XII AIMS UPX-29.
Sonars: SQQ 89(V)2 (Raytheon SQS 56 and Gould SQR
  19); hull-mounted active search and attack; medium
  frequency and passive towed array; very low frequency.

Helicopters: 2 SH-60B LAMPS III ❿ in Flight III/IV and
  certified ships.

Programmes: The lead ship was authorised in FY73.
Modernisation: To accommodate the helicopter landing
  system (RAST), the overall length of the ship was
  increased by 8 ft *(2.4 m)* by increasing the angle of
  the ship's transom, between the waterline and the
  fantail, from virtually straight up to a 45° angle outwards.
  LAMPS III support facilities and RAST were fitted in
  all ships authorised from FFG 36 onwards, during
  construction and have been backfitted to all. The remainder
  can operate this aircraft without landing facilities. FFG 61
  has much improved Combat Data and Fire-Control
  equipment which has been retrofitted in FFG 36, 47, 48,
  50-55, 57 and 59. SQS-56 is modified for mine detection.
  Block 1B Phalanx fitted first in FFG 36 in October 1999.
  This has a capability against high speed surface craft at
  short range. Engineering and platform improvements
  programme initiated in 2003. Upgrades include new
  diesel generators, the addition of reverse osmosis
  plants, COTS slewing arm davits, and self-contained
  breathing apparatus. Mk 13 launchers for Standard

SM-1 and Harpoon missiles are being removed. Combat
system improvements include the installation of Mk 53
Nulka decoys and Mk 15 Block 1B gun with surface mode
capability.
Structure: The original single hangar has been changed
  to two adjacent hangars. Provided with 19 mm Kevlar
  armour protection over vital spaces. 25 mm guns can be
  fitted for some operational deployments.
Operational: Ships of this class were the first Navy
  experience in implementing a design-to-cost acquisition
  concept. Many of their limitations were manifest during
  the intense fires which resulted from *Stark* (FFG 31) being
  struck by two Exocet missiles in the Persian Gulf 17 May
  1987. Since then there have been many improvements in
  firefighting and damage control doctrine and procedures
  and equipment to deal with residual missile propellant-
  induced fires. On 14 April 1988, *Samuel B Roberts*
  (FFG 58), was mined in the Gulf. Penguin SSM can be
  carried in some LAMPS III helicopters. Two of the class
  are based at Yokosuka. Nine ships are assigned to the
  Combatant Naval Reserve Force. FFGs 28, 29 and 38 are
  commanded by full-time reserve officers. SAM and
  SSM systems removed by the end of FY04.
Sales: Australia bought four of the class and has built two
  more. Spain has six and Taiwan eight. Transfers include
  six to Turkey plus one for spares, four to Egypt, one to
  Bahrain and one to Poland. In 2002, one sold to Turkey
  and one transferred to Poland. FFG 15 to Turkey in
  April 2003. Further transfers are likely.

FORD   *7/2004, Michael Nitz* / 1043651

McINERNEY *4/2005*, E & M Laursen* / 1154023

KLAKRING *9/2005*, Martin Mokrus* / 1154024

CROMMELIN *5/2004, US Navy* / 1043650

SHIPBORNE AIRCRAFT (FRONT LINE)

Notes: (1) Numbers given are for 1 January 2006.

(2) **Joint Strike Fighter:** The Joint Strike Fighter programme is a family of aircraft to replace platforms in the US Navy, Air Force and Marine Corps. Known as F-35, the conventional (angled deck) take off and landing (CTOL) variant (F-35B) is to complement the US Navy's F/A-18E/F and replace the A6 Intruder. The Short Take Off and Vertical Landing (STOVL) variant (F-35C) is to replace the Marine Corps' AV-8B and F/A-18A/C/D. The US government awarded the USD19 billion contract for the Systems Development and Demonstration phase on 26 October 2001 to the industry team of Lockheed Martin, Northrop Grumman and BAE Systems. First delivery of operational aircraft is expected in 2008. Pratt and Whitney was awarded a USD4 billion contract to develop an engine to compete in production with that developed by General Electric and Rolls Royce.

(3) **Electronic Warfare:** Navy EA-6B Prowlers are to be replaced by the EA-18G Growler from 2009. A replacement for USMC EA-6Bs has not been decided but an EW variant of the F-35 is being studied.

(4) **Unmanned Aircraft:** The UAV strategy has been given significantly increased impetus since operations in Afghanistan in 2001. It is envisaged that a family of UAVs will be required to meet three principal capability requirements:

(a) Tactical Surveillance and Targeting: provided by the RQ-2B Pioneer system, which originally was a joint US Navy and US Marine Corps program but is now operated by the Marine Unmanned Aircraft Squadrons VMU-1 and VMU-2. Replacement will be the Vertical Unmanned Aircraft System (VUAS), with a planned fielding date circa 2015.

(b) Long Dwell/Stand-off Intelligence Surveillance and Reconnaissance (ISR). Current development work on Unmanned Combat Air Vehicles (UCAV) is expected to be taken forward into a full acquisition programme with an ISR capability expected in about 2015.

(c) Penetrating Surveillance/Suppression of Enemy Air Defences (SEAD): Initial Operational Capability for a full weapons capability is not expected until 2020.

(5) **Tacair Integration:** Navy/Marine Corps Tactical Aviation Integration (TAI) plan was approved in 2002 to optimize combat capability and efficiencies by relying on fewer but more capable aircraft. As part of the Navy's Fleet Response Plan, the Navy/Marine Corps in 2004 began integrating Marine Corps squadrons into carrier air wings and Navy squadrons into the Marine Corps' Unit Deployment Plan (UDP). Through 2005, one Navy active VFA squadron, one reserve VFA squadron and one Marine VMFA squadron were deactivated. TACAIR Integration to reduce Navy and Marine Corps force structure by five squadrons from 64 to 59. As a result, new aircraft procurement through FY11 is to fall by 487, from 1,637 to 1,150.

(6) **Capabilities Based Scheduling (CBS):** This scheduling mechanism is designed to source tactical aviation (TACAIR) requirements while promoting goals of TAI. Under CBS, all Department of the Navy (DON) TACAIR squadrons are available to fill land or sea-based requirements. Objective is to fill all operational and training requirements with the most appropriate unit while balancing operational tempo across force. CBS furthers integration to a fully interdependent DON TACAIR force in which VMFA and VFA squadrons routinely deploy as part of carrier wings and land-based expeditionary operations. CBS flexes TACAIR response to global sourcing requirements.

(7) **Advanced Hawkeye:** A contract was awarded Northrop Grumman Corporation in August 2003 for the Systems Development and Demonstration (SD&D) phase of the Advanced Hawkeye (AHE) programme. This began in 2003 and is to continue until 2013. The first developmental AHE aircraft is scheduled for delivery in 2007, followed by Initial Operating Capability (IOC) in FY11. AHE will use the Northrop Grumman-built E-2C Hawkeye 2000 configuration as a baseline but the existing AN/APS-145 radar system will be replaced along with other aircraft systems components that enable the radar upgrade.

Numbers/Type: 10/4/22 Grumman F-14A/B/D Tomcat.
Operational speed: 1,342 kt (2,485 km/h).
Service ceiling: 60,000 ft (18,283 m).
Range: 2,000 n miles (3,704 km).
Role/Weapon systems: Fleet strike fighter aircraft for long range air defense, precision strike and reconnaissance roles. All remaining aircraft are to have been taken out of service by late 2006. Sensors: AWG-9 (A/B) or APG-71 (D). ALQ-126 jammer (A/B) or ALQ-165 (D). ASN-92 nav (A) embedded GPS-INS (B) or ASN-139/MAGR (D), LANTIRN (all models); ALR-67 (all models); IRST and JTIDS(D). Weapons: two AIM-9, one AIM-7, two GBU, 20 mm (strike). Two AIM-7, two AIM-9, 20 mm (OCA/DCA). Two AIM-7, two AIM-9, 20 mm (recce).

F-14D *11/2005*, USAF* / 1154038

Numbers/Type: 123/28/388/137 McDonnell Douglas F/A-18A/F/A-18B/F/A-18C/F/A-18D Hornet.
Operational speed: 1,032 kt (1,910 km/h).
Service ceiling: 50,000 ft (15,240 m).
Range: 1,000 n miles (1,850 km).
Role/Weapon systems: Strike interdictor (VFA) for USN/USMC air groups. Some are used for EW support with ALQ-167 jammers. Sensors: ESM: Litton ALR 67(V)2, ALQ 165 ASPJ jammer (18C/D), ALQ-126B jammer, APG-65 or APG-73 radar, AAS-38 FLIR, AAR-50 Nav FLIR, ASQ-173 tracker. Weapons: ASV; four Harpoon or SLAM (18D) or AGM-88 HARM (18D) missiles. Strike; up to 7.7 tons of bombs (or LGM). AD; one 20 mm Vulcan cannon, nine AIM-7/AIM-9 missiles. Typical ASV load might include 20 mm gun, 7.7 ton bombs including AGM 154A JSOW, two AIM-9 missiles. Typical AAW load might include 20 mm gun, four AIM-7, two AIM-9 missiles. 18C/D includes AIM-120 AMRAAM and AGM-65 Maverick or AGM 62 Walleye capability.

F/A-18D *10/2005*, US Navy* / 1154039

Numbers/Type: 109/137 Boeing F/A-18E/F/A-18F Super Hornet.
Operational speed: 930 kt (1,721 km/h).
Service ceiling: 50,000 ft (15,240 m).
Range: 1,320 n miles (2,376 km).
Role/Weapon systems: Strike interdictor for USN. First one rolled out in September 1995. First 12 production aircraft ordered in FY97. First sea trials January 1997. Entered operational service November 1999. Initial deployment to CVN 72 in July 2002. 200th aircraft delivered in August 2004. A further 210 aircraft to be delivered by 2009. Sensors: APG-73 radar, ALR-67(V)3 RWR. ECM: ALQ-165 ASPJ, ALQ-214 RFCM, towed decoys. Weapons: 11 wing stations for 8,680 kg of weapons (same armament as C/D) plus 20 mm guns.

F/A-18F *9/2005*, USAF* / 1154040

Numbers/Type: 40/94/17 Boeing/British Aerospace AV-8B/AV-8B II Plus/TAV-8B Harrier II.
Operational speed: 585 kt (1,083 km/h).
Service ceiling: 50,000 ft (15,240 m).
Range: 800 n miles (1,480 km).
Role/Weapon systems: Attack and destroy surface and air targets in support of USMC. Operational since 1985, a total of 94 AV-8B II Plus conversions completed in 2003. Sensors: Litening II targeting pod, Navigation FLIR, moving map, AN/AVS-9 night vision goggles, laser spot tracker and ECM; Litton ALR-67 ESM; APG-65 radar (AV-8B II Plus). Weapons: Strike; 500 and 1,000 lb general purpose bombs, Paveway II LGM, Joint Direct Attack Munition, AGM-65 Maverick, Cluster Bomb Units, 300—25 mm rounds, 2.75 in and 5.00 in rockets. Self-defence: one GAU-12/U 25 mm cannon and four AIM-9M Sidewinder.

AV-8B *4/2005*, US Navy* / 1154041

Numbers/Type: 113 Grumman EA-6B Prowler.
Operational speed: 566 kt (1,048 km/h).
Service ceiling: 41,200 ft (12,550 m).
Range: 955 n miles (1,769 km).
Role/Weapon systems: EW and jamming aircraft (VAQ) to accompany strikes and armed reconnaissance. Block 89A avionics/computer upgrades first delivered 2001 and continuing. All aircraft to be modernised. Further update (ICAP III) planned with first in service in 2005. Sensors: APS-130 radar; ALQ-99, USQ-113 jammers. Weapons: AGM-88 HARM anti-radiation missile capable.

EA-6B *10/2005*, US Navy* / 1154043

Numbers/Type: 58 Lockheed S-3B Viking/Shadow.
Operational speed: 450 kt *(834 km/h).*
Service ceiling: 40,000 ft *(12,192 m).*
Range: 1,800 n miles *(3,333 km).*
Role/Weapon systems: Originally configured as carrier-borne ASW aircraft. ASW capability removed since 1998 and primary roles are reconnaissance and in-flight refuelling. All aircraft are to leave service by 2009. Sensors: APS-137(V)1 ISAR radar; FLIR, OR-263AA, ESM: ALR-76; ECM; ALE 39 chaff. Weapons: SLAM-ER, Maverick and Harpoon missiles; GP and cluster bombs; 2.75 and 3 in rockets.

S-3B   *3/2005*, US Navy* / 1154042

Numbers/Type: 68 Grumman E-2C Hawkeye.
Operational speed: 323 kt *(598 km/h).*
Service ceiling: 37,000 ft *(11,278 m).*
Range: 1,540 n miles *(2,852 km).*
Role/Weapon systems: Used for direction of AD and strike operations; (VAW); 16 Group II upgrades from 1995-2000 included APS 145 radar and Link 16. Sensors: ESM: ALR-73 PDS; Airborne tactical data system with Links 4A, 11 or 16; CEC from 2000. APS-125/138/145 radar; Mk XII IFF. Weapons: Unarmed.

E-2C   *4/2005*, Hachiro Nakai* / 1154022

Numbers/Type: 36/5 Boeing MV-22/CV-22 Osprey.
Operational speed: 255 kt *(472 km/h).*
Service ceiling: 25,000 ft *(7,620 m).*
Range: 2,108 n miles *(2,110 km).*
Role/Weapon systems: Replacement for legacy assault/support helicopters (CH-46E, CH-53D) for Marines (MV), strike rescue for the Navy (Navy MV), and special ops for SOCOM (CV). Five CV-22s conducting developmental and operational test at Edwards AFB; 7 MV-22s conducting developmental test at NAS Patuxent River (2 EMD, 4 LRIP, and 1 Block A); four Block A/B MV-22s conducting operational test with Marine Tiltrotor Test and Evaluation Squadron-22 (VMX-22) Marine Corps Air Station New River, NC. 25 Block A MV-22s conducting maintenance and aircrew training for transition of the CH-46E Fleet Marine Force with Marine Tiltrotor Training Squadron 204 (VMMT-204) also at New River. Final operational evaluation led to full rate production decision in September 2005. Eleven aircraft procured in FY05. Annual production expected to increase to 48. MV-22 10C in late 2007. CV-22 10C in 2009. Full fleet of 360 MV, 50 CV and 48 Navy MV projected. Sensors: AAR-47 ESM; AN/ALQ-211 Suite of Integrated RF CounterMeasures (SIRFC), AN/AAQ-24(V) Nemesis Directional Infra-Red CounterMeasures (DIRCM); AN/AAQ-27 FLIR; APR 39A(V)2. Weapons: 12.7 mm MG or self-defence gun.

MV-22   *11/2005*, US Navy* / 1154048

Numbers/Type: 148 Sikorsky SH-60B Seahawk (LAMPS Mk III).
Operational speed: 145 kt *(268 km/h).*
Service ceiling: 10,000 ft *(3,050 m).*
Range: 450 n miles *(833 km).*
Role/Weapon systems: LAMPS Mk III is airborne platform for ASW and ASUW: operated from cruisers, destroyers and frigates. First deployed in 1984. To be replaced by MH-60R. Sensors: APS-124 search radar, AAS-44 FLIR with laser designator, ASQ-81(V) MAD, 25 sonobuoys, ALQ-142 ESM, AAR-47 MWR, ALQ-144 IRCM suppressor and ALE-39 CMDS. UYS-1 Acoustic processor. Weapons: ASW; three Mk 46 or Mk 50 torpedoes. ASUW; one Penguin Mk 2 Mod 7 AGM-119B missile, one 7.62 mm MG M60 or 12.7 mm MG, AGM-114B/K Hellfire missile.

SH-60B   *1/2001, Darren Yates, RAN* / 0131323

Numbers/Type: 9 Sikorsky MH-60R Seahawk.
Operational speed: 145 kt *(268 km/h).*
Service ceiling: 10,000 ft *(3,050 m).*
Range: 450 n miles *(833 km).*
Role/Weapon systems: The plan is to replace the SH-60B/F fleet with the MH-60R which is to be the future tactical helicopter operated from carriers, cruisers, destroyers and frigates to enter front-line service in 2006. The first production aircraft was flown on 28 July 2005. Sensors: APS-147 long-range search radar with ISAR, ALQ-210 ESM, AQS-22 ALFS sonar, acoustic processor, Raytheon AAS-44 FLIR with laser designator, Hawklink sensor datalink, Link 16, AAR-47 MWR, ALE-47 CMDS, and ALQ-144 IRCM. Weapons: ASW: three Mk 46/50 torpedoes. ASUW: four AGM-114B/K Hellfire missiles, one 7.62 mm MG M60 or 12.7 mm MG. Block One, which is scheduled to be fielded incrementally from 2006 to 2009, will upgrade the aircraft with the AAS-44A 3rd Gen FLIR, including Low Light Camera, CDL-N Ku-band sensor datalink, Link 16, and Mk 54 torpedoes.

MH-60R   *7/2005*, Sikorsky* / 1123282

Numbers/Type: 72 Sikorsky SH-60F Seahawk (CV).
Operational speed: 145 kt *(268 km/h).*
Service ceiling: 10,000 ft *(3,050 m).*
Range: 600 n miles *(1,111 km).*
Role/Weapon systems: Derivation of SH-60B that replaced SH-3H Sea King to provide close-in ASW protection to Carrier Battle Groups. First deployed in *Nimitz* 1991. To be replaced by MH-60R. Sonar: AQS-13F dipping sonar; ASQ-81 (V) MAD; UYS-2 acoustic processor; 14 sonobuoys. Weapons: ASW: three Mk 46/54 torpedoes. ASUW: One GAU 12.7 mm MG or one 7.62 mm MG.

SH-60F   *11/2005*, US Navy* / 1154047

Numbers/Type: 38 Sikorsky HH-60H Seahawk.
Operational speed: 147 kt *(272 km/h).*
Service ceiling: 10,000 ft *(3,050 m).*
Range: 500 n miles *(926 km).*
Role/Weapon systems: Strike, special warfare support and SAR derivative (HCS) of the SH-60F. To be replaced by MH-60S. Sensors: AAS-44 FLIR with laser designator, APR-39A RWR, AVR-2 LWR and AAR 47 MWR, ALE-47 CMDS, ALQ-144 IRCM. Weapons: ASV; Hellfire AGM-114B/K; one GAU-16 12.7 mm MG or one M-240 7.62 mm MG. Can deploy eight SEAL to a range of 200 n miles.

HH-60H   *10/2003, US Navy* / 1043656

Numbers/Type: 85 Sikorsky MH-60S Seahawk.
Operational speed: 154 kt *(284 km/h)*.
Service ceiling: 10,000 ft *(3,050 m)*.
Range: 420 n miles *(777 km)*.
Role/Weapon systems: The MH-60S replaced the CH-46D in the Combat Support (HC) mission. Mission areas include vertical replenishment, vertical onboard delivery, day/night amphibious search and rescue, and over-water special warfare support. Sensors (from September 2006): AAS-44 FLIR with laser designator, AAR-47 MWR, APR-39 RWR, ALE-47 CMDS, and ALQ-144 IRCM. Weapons (from September 2006): eight AGM-114B/K Hellfire missiles, two 7.62 mm or two 12.7 mm MGs. Organic Airborne Mine Countermeasures capabilities are scheduled for introduction by September 2007. Sensors: AN/AQS-20A Sonar Mine Detection Set, AN/AES-1 Airborne Laser Mine Detection System. Mine Neutralization Systems: Airborne Mine Neutralization System, AN/ALQ-220 Organic & Surface Influence Sweep, and AN/AWS-2 Rapid Airborne Mine Clearance System.

MH-60S *11/2005*, US Navy* / 1154046

Numbers/Type: 19 Sikorsky UH-3H Sea King.
Operational speed: 144 kt *(267 km/h)*.
Service ceiling: 10,000 ft *(3,050 m)*.
Range: 630 n miles *(1,166 km)*.
Role/Weapon systems: Used for liaison and SAR tasks having been replaced in CV service by SH-60F. Most are in reserve. Sensors: ALR 606B ESM.

UH-3H *3/2002, Michael Nitz* / 0530016

Numbers/Type: 4/224 Boeing HH-46D/CH-46E Sea Knight.
Operational speed: 137 kt *(254 km/h)*.
Service ceiling: 8,500 ft *(2,590 m)*.
Range: 180 n miles *(338 km)*.
Role/Weapon systems: Support/assault (HMM) for 18 Marines and resupply (USN) helicopter. To be replaced by V-22 in due course. Can lift 1.3 or 4.5 tons in a cargo net or sling. Sensors: None. Weapons: Unarmed.

CH-46E *9/2002, Paul Jackson* / 0069856

Numbers/Type: 37 Sikorsky CH-53D Sea Stallion.
Operational speed: 160 kt *(294 km/h)*.
Service ceiling: 10,000 ft *(3,048 m)*.
Range: 578 n miles *(1,070 km)*.
Role/Weapon systems: Assault, support and transport helicopters (MMH); can carry 37 Marines. Sensors: None. Weapons: Up to three 12.7 mm machine guns.

CH-53D *7/2004, US Navy* / 1043654

Numbers/Type: 150 Sikorsky CH-53E Super Stallion.
Operational speed: 170 kt *(315 km/h)*.
Service ceiling: 10,000 ft *(3,048 m)*.
Range: 580 n miles *(1,074 km)*.
Role/Weapon systems: Uprated, three-engined version of Sea Stallion (MMH) with heavy lift (USN) and logistics (USMC) roles. Carries 55 Marines. Sensors: None. Weapons: Up to three 12.7 mm machine guns.

CH-53E *9/2005*, US Navy* / 1154045

Numbers/Type: 32 Sikorsky MH-53E Sea Dragon.
Operational speed: 170 kt *(315 km/h)*.
Service ceiling: 10,000 ft *(3,048 m)*.
Range: 1,000 n miles *(1,850 km)*.
Role/Weapon systems: Three-engined AMCM helicopter (HM) similar to Super Stallion; tows ALQ-166 Mod 4 MCM sweep equipment; self-deployed if necessary. Sensors: Northrop Grumman AQS-14A or AQS-20 (in due course) dipping sonar. Weapons: Two 12.7 mm guns for self-defence.

MH-53E *7/2005*, US Navy* / 1154044

Numbers/Type: 177/3 Bell AH-1W/AH-1Z Super Cobra.
Operational speed: 149 kt *(277 km/h)*.
Service ceiling: 10,000 ft *(3,048 m)*.
Range: 317 n miles *(587 km)*.
Role/Weapon systems: Close support helicopter (HMLA) with own air-to-air capability. In 2005, USMC accepted first AH-1Z and UH-1Y helicopters for operational evaluation at NAS Patuxent, Maryland, as part of AH-1W upgrade programme. AH-1Z is four-bladed rotor upgrade to improve speed, range and lift. Remanufacture of AH-1W features composite blades, new engines and gearboxes. To enter service in 2011. Sensors: NTS (laser and FLIR nightsight). Weapons: Strike/assault; one triple 20 mm cannon, eight TOW or Hellfire missiles and gun. AAW; two AIM-9L Sidewinder missiles.

AH-1W *8/2005*, US Navy* / 1154053

Numbers/Type: 21/87/3 Bell HH-1N/UH-1N/UH-1Y Twin Huey.
Operational speed: 110 kt *(204 km/h)*.
Service ceiling: 10,000 ft *(3,048 m)*.
Range: 230 n miles *(426 km)*.
Role/Weapon systems: HH-1N is SAR, training, support and logistics helicopter for USN/USMC operations ashore. Can carry eight Marines. UH-1N is USMC Light Utility platform for all-weather assault, transport, airborne command and control, armed reconnaissance and SAR. Can carry eight marines. Four-bladed upgrade being fitted from 2004 to improve speed, range and lift. Can carry eight marines. UH-1Y is remanufacture of UH-1N featuring composite blades and new engines gearboxes. Service entry expected in 2009. Sensors: BRITE Star FLIR. Weapons: Can be armed with 12.7 mm or 7.62 mm machine guns and 2.75 in rockets.

UH-1N *5/1999, A Sharma* / 0084120

LAND-BASED MARITIME AIRCRAFT (FRONT LINE)

Notes: There are also 32/12 Lockheed KC-130F/R Hercules tankers.

Numbers/Type: 13 Lockheed EP-3E Aries.
Operational speed: 411 kt *(761 km/h)*.
Service ceiling: 28,300 ft *(8,625 m)*.
Range: 2,380 n miles *(4,407 km)*.
Role/Weapon systems: Electronic warfare and intelligence gathering aircraft (VQ). Sensors: EW equipment including AN/ALR-60, AN/ALQ-76, AN/ALQ-78, AN/ALQ-108 and AN/ASQ-114. Weapons: Unarmed.

EP-3E   *10/2003, Paul Jackson* / 0110197

Numbers/Type: 173/1 Lockheed P-3C/P-3B Orion.
Operational speed: 411 kt *(761 km/h)*.
Service ceiling: 28,300 ft *(8,625 m)*.
Range: 2,380 n miles *(4,407 km)*.
Role/Weapon systems: 136 in active (28 in reserve) operational squadrons (VP) deployed worldwide; primary ASW/ASUW; mission aircraft include Update III, Block Mod Upgrade (BMUP) and ASuW Improvement Program (AIP) configurations. Sensors (Update III/BMUP): APS-115 radar, ASQ-81 MAD, USQ-78/USQ-78B acoustic suite, 84 sonobuoys, AAS-36 FLIR and ALR-66B ESM. ASUW Improvement Program (AIP) aircraft employ the APS-137D(V)5 ISAR/SAR radar, ASQ-81 MAD, ASX-4 Electro-Optics, ALR-95 ESM, USQ-78/78A/78B acoustic suite, OASIS III/OTCIXS communications suite, SATCOM and AAR 47 and ALE 47 chaff/IR dispenser. Weapons: ASW; Mk 46/50 torpedoes or depth bombs. ASUW; AGM-84C Harpoon, AGM-65F Maverick, AGM-84E SLAM-ER, Mk 52/56/62/63/65 mines, Mk 82 series bombs, and Mk 20 Rockeye. Counter-Drug Upgrade (CDU) aircraft employ APG-66 air-to-air radar and AVX-1 Electro-Optics.

P-3C   *7/2002, Hachiro Nakai* / 0530043

Numbers/Type: Boeing P-8A Multimission Maritime Aircraft.
Operational speed: 490 kt *(907 km/h)*.
Service ceiling: 41,000 ft *(12,500 m)*.
Range: 1,380 n miles *(2,555 km)*.
Role/Weapon systems: Contract for MMA System Development and Demonstration (SDD) awarded 14 June 2004. To replace fleet of P-3C aircraft. Design based on Boeing 737-800ERX. Crew of nine. First delivery in April 2009. To enter operational service in 2013. A total of 108 aircraft is planned. Sensors: To be equipped with modern ASW, ASUW and intelligence, surveillance and reconnaissance (ISR) sensors. Weapons: To be announced.

BOEING P-8A MMA   *6/2004, US Navy* / 1043653

Numbers/Type: 16 Boeing E-6B Mercury/TACAMO/ABNCP.
Operational speed: 455 kt *(842 km/h)*.
Service ceiling: 42,000 ft *(12,800 m)*.
Range: 6,350 n miles *(11,760 km)*.
Role/Weapon systems: Provides survivable command, control and communications to US strategic and non-strategic nuclear forces, including support in the submarine communications role, known as TACAMO, and Airborne National Command Post (ABNCP) capability for US Strategic Command. First flown in E-6A configuration in 1990(VQ). E-6B first flown in TACAMO/ABNCP configuration in 1997 and assumed ABNCP role in 1998. Sensors: Radar Bendix APS-133; ALR-68(V)4 ESM; supports Trident Fleet radio communications with up to 28,000 ft of VLF trailing wire antenna. Weapons: Unarmed.

E-6B   *6/2005*, Paul Jackson* / 1154051

UNMANNED AIR VEHICLES

Notes: The US Navy has transferred its UAV program to the US Marine Corps. Marines were the first US service to use unmanned air vehicles in combat, during Operation Desert Storm, in 1991. The US Navy also flew UAVs in that war. Of current systems, two Pioneer UAV systems are maintained, one for test and evaluation and the other for training. Fire Scout is to provide organic UAV capability for Littoral Combat Ship (LCS) in 2008. The US Navy also operates a Predator system for US Joint Forces Command's Joint Operational Test Bed System (JOTBS) to examine UAV interoperability and to test warfighting concepts. For the future, a Broad Area Maritime Surveillance (BAMS) UAV is sought for worldwide access and persistent maritime Intelligence, Surveillance and Reconnaissance (ISR) by 2013. For maritime demonstration, the navy took delivery of the first of two Global Hawk UAVs in 2005.

Numbers/Type: 35 RQ-2 Pioneer UAV.
Operational speed: 65 kt *(120 km/h)*.
Service ceiling: 15,000 ft *(4,570 m)*.
Range: 100 n miles+ *(185 km+)*.
Role/Weapon systems: Two systems in service with USMC UAV squadrons. One in service for training. Sensors: Optronic surveillance with Link terminal. This provides tactical commanders with day and night, battlefield and maritime intelligence, reconnaissance, surveillance and target acquisition. The Pioneer programme uses major subsystems from the US Army's Shadow 200 and Hunter UAV systems. Used extensively in support of Operation Iraqi Freedom.

RQ-2   0106054

Numbers/Type: 6 Northrop Grumman RQ-8A Fire Scout UAV.
Operational speed: 115 kt *(213 km/h)*.
Service ceiling: 20,000 ft *(6,094 m)*.
Range: 110 n miles *(205 km)*.
Role/Weapon systems: A vertical take-off and landing tactical UAV, Fire Scout selected in February 2000 as the next generation UAV and development continues to achieve the capability to operate from all air-capable ships, carry modular mission payloads, and operate using the Tactical Control System (TCS) and Tactical Common Data Link (TCDL). With over six hours endurance, will provide day/night real time Intelligence, Surveillance and Reconnaissance (ISR) and targeting, communications-relay and battlefield management capabilities to support Littoral Combat Ship (LCS) mission areas of ASW, MIW and ASUW. The six currently in service include one prototype, two in EMD and three in LRIP. An upgraded version, which will be fielded with LCS Flight 0, is to be equipped with a four-bladed rotor and increased payload capacity. It is intended that the Army and Navy sign agreement for joint acquisition of Fire Scout airframes but separate contracts for selected subsystems.

RQ-8A   *1/2006*, Northrop Grumman* / 1154052

PATROL FORCES

Notes: 'Spartan' is a technology demonstrator programme to prove utility of unmanned surface craft. It is envisaged that such craft will be capable of conducting mine warfare, force protection (including surveillance and reconnaissance) and anti-surface warfare. A prototype, a 7 m RHIB installed with navigation, communications and remote control equipment, underwent sea trials in 2003 which included embarkation in USS *Gettysburg* as part of the *Enterprise* carrier strike group.

8 CYCLONE CLASS (PATROL COASTAL SHIPS) (PBFM)

Name	No	Builders	Commissioned	F/S
HURRICANE	PC 3	Bollinger, Lockport	15 Oct 1993	PA
TYPHOON	PC 5	Bollinger, Lockport	12 Feb 1994	AA
SIROCCO	PC 6	Bollinger, Lockport	11 June 1994	AA
SQUALL	PC 7	Bollinger, Lockport	4 July 1994	PA
CHINOOK	PC 9	Bollinger, Lockport	28 Jan 1995	AA
FIREBOLT	PC 10	Bollinger, Lockport	10 June 1995	AA
WHIRLWIND	PC 11	Bollinger, Lockport	1 July 1995	AA
THUNDERBOLT	PC 12	Bollinger, Lockport	7 Oct 1995	AA

Displacement, tons: 354 full load
Dimensions, feet (metres): 170.3 × 25.9 × 7.9 *(51.9 × 7.9 × 2.4)*
Main machinery: 4 Paxman Valenta 16RP200CM diesels; 13,400 hp *(10 MW)* sustained; 4 shafts
Speed, knots: 35. **Range, n miles:** 2,500 at 12 kt
Complement: 39 (4 officers) plus 9 SEALs or law enforcement detachment
Missiles: SAM: 1 Stinger MANPAD system (6 missiles).
Guns: 1 Bushmaster 25 mm Mk 38. 1 Bushmaster 25 mm Mk 96 (aft). 2—12.7 mm MGs. 2—7.62 mm MGs. 2—40 mm Mk 19 grenade launchers (MGs and grenade launchers are interchangeable).
Countermeasures: Decoys: 2 Mk 52 sextuple.
ESM: Privateer APR-39; radar warning. Sensytech Bobcat.
Weapons control: FLIR systems AN/KAX-1 Marflir.
Radars: Surface search: 2 Sperry RASCAR; E/F/I/J-band.
Sonars: Wesmar; hull-mounted; active scanning sonar; high frequency.

Programmes: Contract awarded for eight in August 1990, five in July 1991 and one in August 1997.
Structure: Design based on Vosper Thornycroft Ramadan class modified for USN requirements including ballistic plating to protect electronics, communications and the pilot house. The craft have a slow speed loiter capability. Swimmers can be launched from a platform at the stern. Two SEAL raiding craft and one RIB are carried.
Modernisation: The ships have been modernised to incorporate advanced ESM, an integrated bridge system, a Mk 96 stabilised weapon platform and improved communications.
Operational: The ships perform maritime interdiction, homeland security, law enforcement and SAR missions. Can be operated in pairs with a maintenance team in two vans ashore. Operational control transferred from Special Operations Command to the Atlantic and Pacific Fleets on 1 October 2002. Five ships (PC 2, PC 4, PC 8, PC 13 and PC 14) were transferred to the USCG 2004-05 and are expected to be returned in 2008. Remaining ships are to be retained by the USN until at least 2008.
Sales: PC1 (*Cyclone*) transferred to the Philippines Navy for counter-terrorism duties.

CHINOOK *3/2003, US Navy* / 1043629

SQUALL *10/2002, M Mazumdar* / 0529973

20 MK V CLASS (HSIC)

Displacement, tons: 54 full load
Dimensions, feet (metres): 81.2 × 17.5 × 4.3 *(24.7 × 5.3 × 1.3)*
Main machinery: 2 MTU 12V 396 TE94 diesels; 4,506 hp *(3.36 MW)* sustained; 2 Kamewa water-jets
Speed, knots: 45. **Range, n miles:** 515 at 35 kt
Complement: 5
Military lift: 16 fully equipped troops
Guns: 5 Mk 46 Mod 4 mountings for twin 12.7 mm or 7.6 mm MGs, 1 Mk 19 40 mm grenade launcher.
Countermeasures: ESM: Sensytech Bobcat; radar intercept.
Radars: Navigation: Furuno; I-band.
IFF: APX-100(V).

Comment: This was the winning design of a competition held in 1994 to find a high-speed craft to insert and withdraw Navy SEAL teams and other special operations forces personnel. Fourteen delivered by mid-1998 and six more by mid-1999. All built at the Halter Marine Equitable Shipyard in New Orleans. The craft has an aluminium hull and is transportable by C-5 aircraft. Stinger missiles may be carried and gun armaments can be varied. A variant with three engines is in service with the Mexican Navy.

MK V *4/2003, A Sharma* / 0572743

20 SPECIAL OPERATIONS CRAFT RIVERINE (SOCR)

Displacement, tons: 9.1 full load
Dimensions, feet (metres): 33.0 × 9.0 × 2.0 *(10.1 × 2.7 × 0.6)*
Main machinery: 2 Yanmar 6LY2M-STE diesels; 440 hp *(328 kW)*; 2 Hamilton HJ292 waterjets
Speed, knots: 40+. **Range, n miles:** 195
Complement: 4
Military lift: 8 fully equipped troops
Guns: Combination of Mk 19 40 mm, 12.7 mm MG, 7.62 mm/M60, M240, GAU17 at 5 stations.

Comment: Built by United States Marine, Inc. Aluminium hull.

SOCR *2/2005, US Navy* / 1043672

72 RIBS (RIGID INFLATABLE BOATS) (PBF)

Displacement, tons: 9 full load
Dimensions, feet (metres): 36.1 × 10.5 × 3 *(11 × 3.2 × 0.9)*
Main machinery: 2 Caterpillar 3126 diesels; 940 hp *(700 kW)*; 2 Kamewa FF 280 water-jets
Speed, knots: 35
Range, n miles: 200 at 33 kt
Complement: 4 plus 9 SEALs
Guns: 1—12.7 mm MG, 1—7.62 mm MG or Mk 19 Mod 3 grenade launcher.

Comment: Capable of carrying nine SEALS at 35 kt. Details given are for the latest type being built by USMI, New Orleans. Entered service from 1998 to 2002.

RIB *1/2002, M Declerck* / 0529972

RIB *1/1998, US Navy* / 0016492

116 LIGHT PATROL BOATS (PBF)

Displacement, tons: 1.2 full load
Dimensions, feet (metres): 22.3 × 8.6 × 1.5 *(6.8 × 2.6 × 0.5)*
Main machinery: 2 OMC outboards; 300 hp *(224 kW)*
Speed, knots: 35
Complement: 3
Guns: 3—12.7 mm MGs. 1—7.62 mm MG.
Radars: Surface search: Furuno 1731; I-band

Comment: Built by Boston Whaler in 1988 for US Special Operations Command. Air transportable. Glass fibre hulls. Replacement began in 2001.

PBL-CD
1996, Boston Whaler
0084150

COMMAND SHIPS

Notes: Options for replacement of the three in-service command ships remain under consideration.
They include new construction ships, service-life extensions of current ships and/or a mix of sea and land-based facilities.

2 BLUE RIDGE CLASS: COMMAND SHIPS (LCCH/AGFH)

Name	No	Builders	Laid down	Launched	Commissioned	F/S
BLUE RIDGE	LCC 19	Philadelphia Naval Shipyard	27 Feb 1967	4 Jan 1969	14 Nov 1970	PA
MOUNT WHITNEY	LCC 20	Newport News Shipbuilding	8 Jan 1969	8 Jan 1970	16 Jan 1971	AA

Displacement, tons: 13,077 light; 19,648 full load *(Blue Ridge)* 12,435 light; 17,485 full load *(Mount Whitney)*
Dimensions, feet (metres): 634.0 × 107.9 × 24.8 *(193.2 × 32.9 × 7.6)*
Main machinery: 2 Foster-Wheeler boilers; 600 psi *(42.3 kg/cm²)*; 870°F *(467°C)*; 1 GE turbine; 22,000 hp *(16.4 MW)*; 1 shaft
Speed, knots: 23
Range, n miles: 13,000 at 16 kt
Complement: 786: 637 Flag staff (LCC 19). 303 (157 military, 146 civilian): 562 Flag staff (LCC 20)
Military lift: 700 troops; 3 LCPs; 2 LCVPs; 2—7 m RHIBs

Guns: 2 General Electric/General Dynamics 20 mm/76 6-barrelled Vulcan Phalanx Mk 15; 3,000 rds/min (4,500 in Block 1) combined to 1.5 km.
2—25 mm Mk 38.
Countermeasures: Decoys: 4 Loral Hycor SRBOC 6-barrelled fixed Mk 36; IR flares and chaff to 4 km *(2.2 n miles)*. SLQ-25 Nixie; torpedo decoy.
ESM/ECM: SLQ-32(V)3; combined radar intercept, jammer and deception system.
Combat data systems: GCCS (M) Link 4A, Link 11, Link 14 and JTIDS. Theatre Battle Management Core Systems (TBMCS). Wide band commercial SATCOM, USC-38 SATCOM, WSC-3 EHF SATCOM, WSC-6(V)1 and 5, and WSC-6A(V)4 SHF SATCOM. High Frequency Radio Group (HFRG). Mission Display System (MDS). Demand Assigned Multiple Access (DAMA QUAD). Area Air Defense Commander, Naval Fires Network, Joint Service Imagery Processing System (JSIPS-N), Common High Bandwidth Data Link, Shipboard Terminal (CHBDL-ST), Ring Laser Gyro Network (RLGN), NITES 2000, Joint Tactical Information Distribution System (JTIDS), Navigational Sensor System Interface (NAVSSI). (See Data Systems at front of section.)
Radars: Air search: Lockheed SPS-40E; B-band.
Surface search: Lockheed SPS-10B; G-band.
Navigation: Marconi LN66; Raytheon SPS-64(V)9; I-band.
Tacan: URN 25. IFF: Mk XII AIMS UPX-29.

Helicopters: 1 Sikorsky SH-3H Sea King.

Programmes: Authorised in FY65 and 1966. Originally designated Amphibious Force Flagships (AGC); redesignated Command Ships (LCC) on 1 January 1969.
Modernisation: Modernisation completed FY87. 3 in guns removed in 1996/97 and Sea Sparrow missile launchers

MOUNT WHITNEY
10/2005*, US Navy / 1154050

have been disembarked. Mk 23 TAS and RAM are not now to be fitted.
Structure: General hull design and machinery arrangement are similar to the Iwo Jima class assault ships. Accommodation for 250 officers and 1,300 enlisted men.
Operational: These are large force command ships of post-Second World War design. They can provide integrated command and control facilities for sea, air and land commanders in all types of operations. *Blue Ridge* is the

Seventh Fleet flagship, based at Yokosuka, Japan. *Mount Whitney* served since January 1981 as flagship Second Fleet, based at Norfolk, Virginia except during the period June to November 1999 when she served as Sixth Fleet flagship. In March 2005, *Mount Whitney* became part of MSC Special Mission programme and replaced *La Salle* as flagship Sixth Fleet, based at Gaeta, Italy. *Mount Whitney* retains US Navy status but with a 'hybrid military/civilian crew.

BLUE RIDGE
6/2005*, Bob Fildes / 1154021

1 CONVERTED AUSTIN CLASS: COMMAND SHIP (AGFH)

Name	No	Builders	Laid down	Launched	Commissioned	F/S
CORONADO	AGF 11 (ex-LPD 11)	Lockheed SB & Construction Co	3 May 1965	30 July 1966	23 May 1970	PA

Displacement, tons: 11,482 light; 16,430 full load
Dimensions, feet (metres): 570 × 100 (84 hull) × 23
(173.8 × 30.5; 25.6 × 7)
Main machinery: 2 Foster-Wheeler boilers; 600 psi *(42.2 kg/cm²)*; 870°F *(467°C)*; 2 De Laval turbines; 24,000 hp *(17.9 MW)*; 2 shafts
Speed, knots: 21
Range, n miles: 7,700 at 20 kt
Complement: 243 (117 USN + 126 civilian) + 491 Flag staff

Guns: 2 General Electric/General Dynamics 20 mm Vulcan Phalanx Mk 15. 2 – 12.7 mm MGs.
Countermeasures: Decoys: 4 Loral Hycor SRBOC 6-barrelled Mk 36; IR flares and chaff.
ESM: SLQ-32V(2).
Combat data systems: GCCS (M) Link 11 and Link 16 (receive only). Theatre Battle Management Core Systems (TBMCS). Land Attack Warfare System (LAWS). Wide band commercial SATCOM, USC-38 SATCOM, WSC-3 EHF

SATCOM, WSC-6 SHF SATCOM. High Frequency Radio Group (HFRG). Single Channel Ground Air Radio System, Joint Service Imagery Processing System (JSIPS-N), Common High Bandwidth Data Link, Shipboard Terminal (CHBDL-ST), Naval Fires Network (NFN), Secure Voice System, TBMCS Host 1.1, COWAN, TVDTS, SCI ADNS, EHF MDR, Tactical Switching System, Ring Laser Gyro Network (RLGN), Navigational Sensor System Interface (NAVSSI). (See Data Systems at front of section.)
Radars: Surface search: AN/SPS 67V(1); G-band.
Navigation: 2 Raytheon SPS-73(V); I-band.
Tacan: URN 25.

Helicopters: 2 light.

Programmes: A former LPD of the Austin class. Authorised in FY64.
Structure: The well deck was converted in 1997 to offices, with a three deck command facility and additional

accommodation for up to four Flag Officers with a combined staff of 259. The stern gate has been removed and sealed. 3 in guns removed.
Operational: Converted in late 1980 as a temporary replacement for *La Salle* (AGF 3), as flagship, Middle East Force and continued in flagship role thereafter. Served as Sixth Fleet flagship for three years until relieved by *Belknap* in July 1986. Then served as Third Fleet flagship in Hawaii and subsequently San Diego. In 1998, major modifications to install network technology were undertaken. In 2000 *Coronado* was designated as the US Navy's sea-based Battle-Lab to act as a testbed for new IT systems. In 2002, acted as hub for major joint exercises including 'Millenium Challenge', 'Rimpac 2002' and 'Fleet Battle Experiment 2002'. In 2003 underwent MSC conversion and became largely civilian manned under USN command. To be decommissioned in FY06.

CORONADO   *4/2004, US Navy* / 1043652

AMPHIBIOUS FORCES

Notes: (1) Additional capacity is provided by the maritime pre-positioning ships (see listing under *Military Sealift Command* (MSC) section) which are either new construction or conversions of commercial ships. One squadron is maintained on station in the Mediterranean, a second at Guam, and a third at Diego Garcia. Each squadron carries equipment to support a Marine Expeditionary Brigade.
(2) **Minesweeping:** Several of the larger amphibious ships have been used as operating bases for minesweeping helicopters.
(3) Five decommissioned LKAs and four LSTs are kept in an inactive reduced maintenance status (ROS). These are *Fresno* (LST 1182), *Tuscaloosa* (LST 1187), *Boulder* (LST 1190), *Racine* (LST 1191), *Charleston* (LKA 113), *Durham* (LKA 114), *Mobile* (LKA 115), *St Louis* (LKA 116) and *El Paso* (LKA 117).

0 + 1 LHA 6 CLASS (AMPHIBIOUS ASSAULT SHIP) (LHA)

Name	No	Builders	Laid down	Launched	Commissioned
—	—	Northrop Grumman Ship Systems, Pascagoula, MS	2007	2010	2012

Displacement, tons: 44,850 full load
Dimensions, feet (metres): 844 oa; 778 wl × 194 oa; 106 wl × 28.7
(257.3; 237.1 × 59.1; 32.3 × 8.7)
Flight deck, feet (metres): 819 × 118 *(249.6 × 36.0)*
Main machinery: COGES: 2 GE LM 2500+ gas turbines; 70,000 hp *(52.2 MW)*; 2 auxiliary propulsion motors; 10,000 hp *(7.46 MW)*; 2 shafts
Speed, knots: 22
Range, n miles: 9,000 at 12 kt
Complement: 1,059 (65 officers)
Military lift: 1,686 troops

Missiles: SAM: 2 Raytheon GMLS Mk 29 octuple launchers; 16 Evolved Sea Sparrow RIM-162D.
Guns: 2 General Electric/General Dynamics 20 mm 6-barrelled Vulcan Phalanx Mk 15.
Countermeasures: Mk 53 Mod 3 NULKA DLS; SLQ-25 Nixie; acoustic torpedo decoy system.
ESM/ECM: SLQ-32(V)2.
Combat data systems: SSDS Mk 2 Mod 4B, Links 4A, 11 (modified), 16 and 22. SATCOMS: SSR-1, SRC-XX (UHF), USC-38 (EHF), URC-131(H)(HF), URC-139 (VHF) and 2 WSC-6C(V)9 (SHF). SMQ-11 Metsa. Advanced Field Artillery TDS.
Weapons control: 2 Mk 9 MFCS.
Radars: Air search: ITT SPS-48E(V)10; 3D; E/F-band; Raytheon SPS-49A(V)1; SPQ-9B.
Surface search/Navigation: 2 SPS-73; I-band.
CCA: SPN-35C and SPN-43C.
Tacan: URN 25. IFF: CIS UPX-29.

Fixed-wing aircraft: Similar to Wasp class with improved facilities to operate and support MV-22 Osprey and up to 23 F-35B Joint Strike Fighter (JSF).

Programmes: It was announced on 6 April 2004 that the LHA Replacement design was to be a modified version of the LHD 8 design. The detailed design and construction phase started in January 2006 following ship design approval to proceed with Milestone B. A contract for the construction of the first ship is expected in 2007 to achieve an in-service date of 2012.

LHA (R)   *6/2005*, Northrop Grumman* / 1154062

Structure: LHA Replacement is optimised for aviation operations and is to have additional cargo/magazine capacity in lieu of a traditional well deck. The flight deck has nine helicopter landing spots and is to be equipped with two aircraft elevators, one to starboard and aft of the island and one to port amidships; the folding capability has been removed. Cargo capacity is 160,000 cu ft total with an additional 12,000 sq ft to accommodate vehicle stowage. The ship is to be fitted with a 24 bed capacity hospital and two operating rooms. The bridge is two decks lower than that of an LHA 1; the command, control and communications spaces having been moved inside the hull. The ship has gas turbine propulsion and all electric auxiliaries.
Operational: Homeport is yet to be announced.

4 TARAWA CLASS: AMPHIBIOUS ASSAULT SHIPS (LHAM)

Name	No	Builders	Laid down	Launched	Commissioned	F/S
TARAWA	LHA 1	Ingalls Shipbuilding	15 Nov 1971	1 Dec 1973	29 May 1976	PA
SAIPAN	LHA 2	Ingalls Shipbuilding	21 July 1972	18 July 1974	15 Oct 1977	AA
NASSAU	LHA 4	Ingalls Shipbuilding	13 Aug 1973	21 Jan 1978	28 July 1979	AA
PELELIU (ex-*Da Nang*)	LHA 5	Ingalls Shipbuilding	12 Nov 1976	25 Nov 1978	3 May 1980	PA

Displacement, tons: 39,967 full load
Dimensions, feet (metres): 834 × 131.9 × 25.9
(254.2 × 40.2 × 7.9)
Flight deck, feet (metres): 820 × 118.1 *(250 × 36)*
Main machinery: 2 Combustion Engineering boilers;
600 psi *(42.3 kg/cm²)*; 900°F *(482°C)*; 2 Westinghouse
turbines; 70,000 hp *(52.2 MW)*; 2 shafts; bow thruster;
900 hp *(670 kW)*
Speed, knots: 24. **Range, n miles:** 10,000 at 20 kt
Complement: 964 (56 officers)
Military lift: 1,703 troops; 4 LCU 1610 type or 2 LCU and
2 LCM 8 or 17 LCM 6 or 45 Assault Amphibious Vehicles;
1,200 tons aviation fuel. 1 LCAC may be embarked.
4 LCPL

Missiles: SAM: 2 GDC Mk 49 RAM ❶; 21 rounds per
launcher; passive IR/anti-radiation homing to 9.6 km
(5.2 n miles) at 2 Mach; warhead 9.1 kg.
Guns: 2 General Electric/General Dynamics 20 mm/76
6-barrelled Vulcan Phalanx Mk 15 ❷; 3,000 rds/min (4,500
in Block 1) combined to 1.5 km.
6 Mk 242 25 mm automatic cannons. 8 – 12.7 mm MGs.
Countermeasures: Decoys: 4 Loral Hycor SRBOC 6-barrelled
fixed Mk 36; IR flares and chaff to 4 km *(2.2 n miles)*.
SLQ-25 Nixie; acoustic torpedo decoy system. NATO Sea
Gnat. SLQ-49 chaff buoys. AEB SSQ-95.
ESM/ECM: SLQ-32V(3); intercept and jammers.
Combat data systems: ACDS Block 0. Advanced Combat
Direction System to provide computerised support in
control of helicopters and aircraft, shipboard weapons
and sensors, navigation, landing craft control and
electronic warfare. Links 4A, 11 and 16. SATCOM SRR-1,
WSC-3 (UHF), USC-38 (EHF). SMQ-11 Metsat (see Data
Systems at front of section).
Radars: Air search: ITT SPS-48E ❸; E/F-band.
Lockheed SPS-40E ❹; B-band.
Hughes Mk 23 TAS ❺; D-band.
Surface search: Raytheon SPS-67(V)3 ❻; G-band.
Navigation: Raytheon SPS-73; I-band.
CCA: SPN-35A; SPN-43B.
Tacan: URN 25. IFF: CIS Mk XV/UPX-36.

Fixed-wing aircraft: Harrier AV-8B VSTOL aircraft in place of
some helicopters as required. V22 Osprey in due course.
Helicopters: 19 CH-53D Sea Stallion or 26 CH-46D/E Sea
Knight UAV in due course.

SAIPAN   *6/2005*, Michael Nitz / 1154054*

Programmes: Originally intended to be a class of nine
ships. LHA 1 was authorised in FY69, LHA 2 in FY70 and
LHA 4 and LHA 5 in FY71.
Modernisation: Two Vulcan Phalanx CIWS replaced the
GMLS Mk 25 Sea Sparrow launchers. Programme
completed in early 1991. RAM launchers fitted to all
of the class 1993-95. One launcher is above the bridge
offset to port, and the other on the starboard side at
the after end of the flight deck. Mk 23 TAS target
acquisition radar fitted in LHA 5 in 1992, LHA 4 in 1993
and the last pair in 1994. SPS-48E started replacing
SPS-52D in 1994 to improve low altitude detection of
missiles and aircraft. ACDS Block 0 in 1996. 5 in guns
removed in 1997/98. Plans to fit SSDS have been shelved.
Collective Protection Systems upgrade in progress.
Fuel oil compensation system has been installed to
improve damaged stability.
Structure: There are two lifts, one on the port side aft and
one at the stern. Beneath the after elevator is a floodable

docking well measuring 268 ft in length and 78 ft in width
which is capable of accommodating four LCU 1610 type
landing craft. Also included is a large garage for trucks
and AFVs and troop berthing for a reinforced battalion.
33,730 sq ft available for vehicles and 116,900 cu ft for
palletted stores. Extensive medical facilities including
operating rooms, X-ray room, hospital ward, isolation
ward, laboratories, pharmacy, dental operating room
and medical store rooms.
Operational: The flight deck can operate a maximum of
nine CH-53D Sea Stallion or 12 CH-46D/E Sea Knight
helicopters or a mix of these and other helicopters at
any one time. With some additional modifications, ships
of this class can effectively operate AV-8B aircraft. The
normal mix of aircraft allows for six AV-8Bs. The optimum
aircraft configuration is dependent upon assigned
missions. Unmanned Reconnaissance Vehicles (URVs)
can be operated. LHA 3 decommissioned 28 October
2005 and LHA 2 to be paid off in FY07.

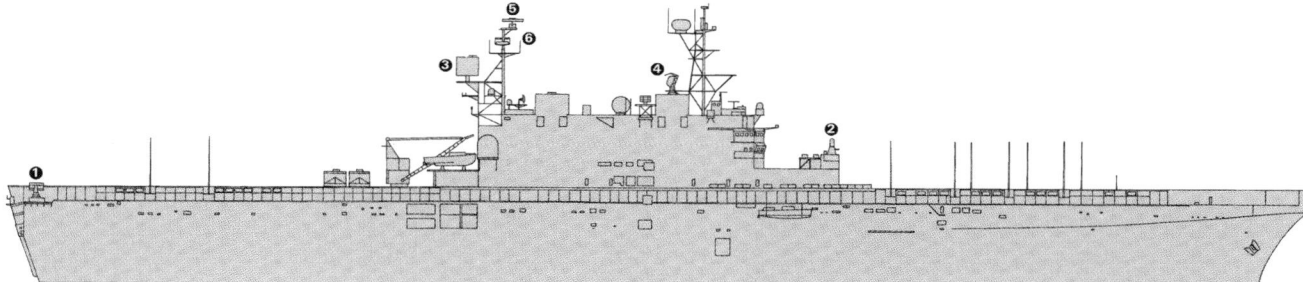

PELELIU   *(Scale 1 : 1,500), Ian Sturton / 0131369*

NASSAU   *7/2004, US Navy / 1043625*

7 + 1 WASP CLASS: AMPHIBIOUS ASSAULT SHIPS (LHDM/MCSM)

Name	No	Builders	Laid down	Launched	Commissioned	F/S
WASP	LHD 1	Ingalls Shipbuilding	30 May 1985	4 Aug 1987	29 July 1989	AA
ESSEX	LHD 2	Ingalls Shipbuilding	16 Feb 1989	4 Jan 1991	17 Oct 1992	PA
KEARSARGE	LHD 3	Ingalls Shipbuilding	6 Feb 1990	26 Mar 1992	16 Oct 1993	AA
BOXER	LHD 4	Ingalls Shipbuilding	26 Mar 1991	13 Aug 1993	11 Feb 1995	PA
BATAAN	LHD 5	Ingalls Shipbuilding	16 Mar 1994	15 Mar 1996	20 Sep 1997	AA
BONHOMME RICHARD	LHD 6	Ingalls Shipbuilding	29 Mar 1995	14 Mar 1997	15 Aug 1998	PA
IWO JIMA	LHD 7	Ingalls Shipbuilding	12 Dec 1997	4 Feb 2000	30 June 2001	AA
MAKIN ISLAND	LHD 8	Northrop Grumman Ship Systems (Ingalls)	14 Feb 2004	21 July 2006	2008	Bldg/PA

Displacement, tons: 40,650 (LHD 1-4); 40,358 (LHD 5-7); 41,661 (LHD 8) full load
Dimensions, feet (metres): 847 oa; 788 wl × 140.1 oa; 106 wl × 26.6 *(258.2; 240.2 × 42.7; 32.3 × 8.1)*
Flight deck, feet (metres): 819 × 118 *(249.6 × 36.0)*
Main machinery: 2 Combustion Engineering boilers; 600 psi *(42.3 kg/cm²)*; 900°F *(482°C)*; 2 Westinghouse turbines; 70,000 hp *(52.2 MW)*; 2 shafts
2 GE LM 2500+ gas turbines; 70,000 hp *(52.2 MW)*; 2 Alstom variable speed electric motors; 10,000 hp *(7.5 MW)* (LHD 8)
Speed, knots: 22. **Range, n miles:** 9,500 at 20 kt
Complement: 1,123 (65 officers)
Military lift: 1,800 troops; 12 LCM 6s or 3 LCACs; 1,232 tons aviation fuel (LHD 1-4); 1,960 tons (LHD 5-8); 4 LCPL

Missiles: SAM: 2 Raytheon GMLS Mk 29 octuple launchers ❶; 16 Sea Sparrow; semi-active radar homing to 14.6 km *(8 n miles)* at 2.5 Mach; warhead 39 kg. ESSM in due course.
2 GDC Mk 49 RAM; 21 rounds per launcher ❷; passive IR/anti-radiation homing to 9.6 km *(5.2 n miles)* at 2 Mach; warhead 9.1 kg.
Guns: 2 General Electric/General Dynamics 20 mm 6-barrelled Vulcan Phalanx Mk 15 ❸; 3,000 rds/min (4,500 in Batch 1) combined to 1.5 km.
3 Boeing Bushmaster 25 mm Mk 38. 4 – 12.7 mm MGs.
Countermeasures: Decoys: 4 or 6 Loral Hycor SRBOC 6-barrelled fixed Mk 36; IR flares and chaff to 4 km *(2.2 n miles)*.
SLQ-25 Nixie; acoustic torpedo decoy system. NATO Sea Gnat. SLQ-49 chaff buoys. AEB SSQ-95.
ESM/ECM: SLQ-32(V)3/SLY-2; intercept and jammers. Raytheon ULQ-20.

Combat data systems: ACDS Block 1 level 2 (LHD 1 and 7) and Block 0 (LHD 2-6). SSDS Mk 2 (LHD 8 on build and LHD 1 and 7 in 2007). Integrated Tactical Amphibious Warfare Data System (ITAWDS) and Marine Tactical Amphibious C² System (MTACCS). Links 4A, 11 (modified), 14 and 16. SATCOMS ❹ SSR-1, WSC-3 (UHF), USC-38 (EHF). SMQ-11 Metsat (see Data Systems at front of section). Advanced Field Artillery TDS (LHD 6-8).
Weapons control: 2 Mk 91 MFCS (LHD 1-6). 2 Mk 9 MFCS (LHD 7-8).
Radars: Air search: ITT SPS-48E ❺; 3D; E/F-band.
Raytheon SPS-49(V)9 ❻; C/D-band.
Hughes Mk 23 TAS ❼; D-band. SPQ-9B (LHD 8).
Surface search: Norden SPS-67 ❽; G-band.
Navigation: SPS-73; I-band.
CCA: SPN-35B and SPN-43C.
Fire control: 2 Mk 95; I/J-band. SPQ-9B to be fitted.
Tacan: URN 25. IFF: CIS Mk XV UPX-29.

Fixed-wing aircraft: 6-8 AV-8B Harriers or up to 20 in secondary role. MV-22 Osprey and Joint Strike Fighter in due course.
Helicopters: Capacity for 42 CH-46E Sea Knight but has the capability to support: AH-1W Super Cobra, CH-53E Super Stallion, CH-53D Sea Stallion, UH-1N Twin Huey, AH-1T Sea Cobra, and SH-60B Seahawk helicopters. UAV in due course.

Programmes: LHD 8 being funded incrementally by Congress from FY99-FY06.
Modernisation: RAM launchers retrofitted in all.
Structure: Two aircraft elevators, one to starboard and aft of the 'island' and one to port amidships; both fold

for Panama canal transits. The well-deck is 267 × 50 ft and can accommodate up to three LCACs. The flight deck has nine helicopter landing spots. Cargo capacity is 125,000 cu ft total with an additional 20,000 sq ft to accommodate vehicles. Vehicle storage is available for five M1 tanks, 25 LAVs, eight M 198 guns, 68 trucks, 10 logistic vehicles and several service vehicles. The bridge is two decks lower than that of an LHA, command, control and communication spaces having been moved inside the hull to avoid 'cheap kill' damage. Fitted with a 64 bed capacity hospital and six operating rooms. HY-100 steel covers the flight deck. Three 32 ft monorail trains each carrying 6,000 lbs, deliver material to the well-deck at 6.8 mph. *Iwo Jima* is likely to be the last oil-fired steam turbine ship in the USN. LHD 8 is to be fitted with gas turbine propulsion and electric drive. Other features include watermist fire suppression system, fibre-optic machinery control system, SPQ-9B radar and CEC. LHD-3 upgraded in 2006 to accommodate/operate MV-22 Osprey.

Operational: A typical complement of aircraft is a mix of 25 helicopters and six to eight Harriers (AV-8B). In the secondary role as a sea control ship the most likely mix is 20 AV-8B Harriers and four to six SH-60B Seahawk helicopters. LHD 3 modified to provide interim Mine Countermeasures Command (MCS) capability following decommissioning of *Inchon* in June 2002. In 2003, LHA 5 deployed as the centrepiece of the first Expeditionary Strike Group (ESG). LHD 6 first amphibious ship to deploy with MH-60S helicopter. LHDs 1, 3, 5 and 7 based at Norfolk, Virginia, and LHDs 4 and 6 at San Diego, California where LHD 8 is also to be based. LHD 2 is based at Sasebo, Japan.

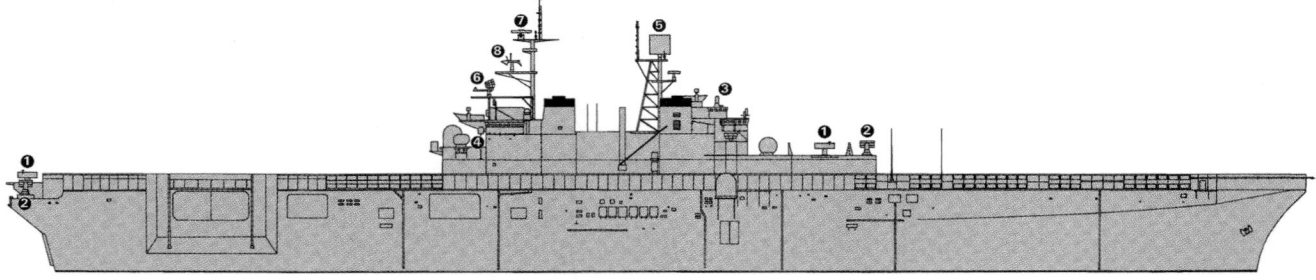

ESSEX　　　　　　　　　　　　　　　　　　　　　　*(Scale 1 : 1,500), Ian Sturton* / 0131367

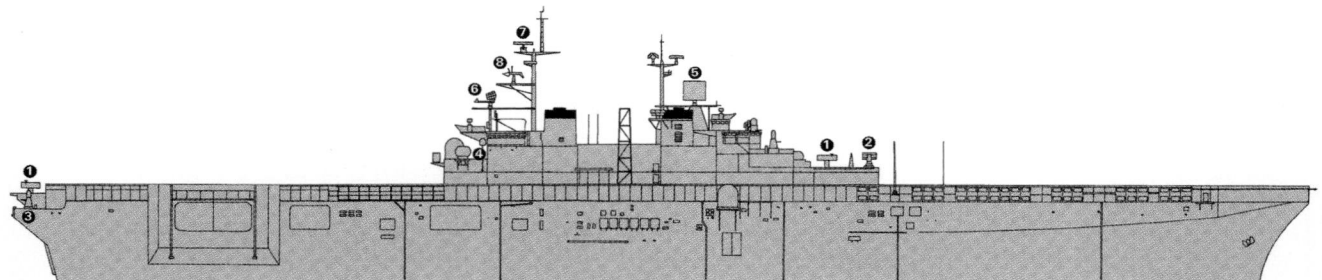

BONHOMME RICHARD　　　　　　　　　　　　　　*(Scale 1 : 1,500), Ian Sturton* / 0131368

KEARSARGE　　　　　　　　　　　　　　　　　　*4/2003, A Sharma* / 0572779

BONHOMME RICHARD *12/2004, US Navy* / 1043627

BOXER *5/2005*, Hachiro Nakai* / 1154020

BATAAN *9/2005*, US Navy* / 1154049

10 AUSTIN CLASS: AMPHIBIOUS TRANSPORT DOCKS (LPD)

Name	No	Builders	Laid down	Launched	Commissioned	F/S
AUSTIN	LPD 4	New York Naval Shipyard	4 Feb 1963	27 June 1964	6 Feb 1965	AA
OGDEN	LPD 5	New York Naval Shipyard	4 Feb 1963	27 June 1964	19 June 1965	PA
CLEVELAND	LPD 7	Ingalls Shipbuilding	30 Nov 1964	7 May 1966	21 Apr 1967	PA
DUBUQUE	LPD 8	Ingalls Shipbuilding	25 Jan 1965	6 Aug 1966	1 Sep 1967	PA
DENVER	LPD 9	Lockheed SB & Construction Co	7 Feb 1964	23 Jan 1965	26 Oct 1968	PA
JUNEAU	LPD 10	Lockheed SB & Construction Co	23 Jan 1965	12 Feb 1966	12 July 1969	PA
SHREVEPORT	LPD 12	Lockheed SB & Construction Co	27 Dec 1965	25 Oct 1966	12 Dec 1970	AA
NASHVILLE	LPD 13	Lockheed SB & Construction Co	14 Mar 1966	7 Oct 1967	14 Feb 1970	AA
TRENTON	LPD 14	Lockheed SB & Construction Co	8 Aug 1966	3 Aug 1968	6 Mar 1971	AA
PONCE	LPD 15	Lockheed SB & Construction Co	31 Oct 1966	20 May 1970	10 July 1971	AA

Displacement, tons: 9,130 light; 16,500—17,244 full load
Dimensions, feet (metres): 570 × 100 (84 hull) × 23
(173.8 × 30.5; 25.6 × 7)
Main machinery: 2 Foster-Wheeler boilers (Babcock & Wilcox in LPD 5 and LPD 12); 600 psi (42.3 kg/cm²); 870°F (467°C); 2 De Laval (General Electric in LPD 9 and LPD 10) turbines, 24,000 hp (18 MW); 2 shafts
Speed, knots: 21. **Range, n miles:** 7,700 at 20 kt
Complement: 420 (24 officers); Flag 90 (in LPD 7-13)
Military lift: 930 troops (840 only in LPD 7-13); 9 LCM 6s or 4 LCM 8s or 2 LCAC or 20 LVTs. 4 LCPL/LCVP

Guns: 2 General Electric/General Dynamics 20 mm/76 6-barrelled Vulcan Phalanx Mk 15 ❶; 3,000 rds/min (4,500 in Block 1) combined to 1.5 km.
2—25 mm Mk 38. 8—12.7 mm MGs.
Countermeasures: Decoys: 4 Loral Hycor SRBOC 6-barrelled Mk 36; IR flares and chaff to 4 km (2.2 n miles).
ESM: SLQ-32(V)1; intercept.
Combat data systems: SATCOM ❷, WSC-3 (UHF), WSC-6 (SHF) (see Data Systems at front of section).
Radars: Air search: Lockheed SPS-40E ❸; B-band.
Surface search: Norden SPS-67 ❹; G-band.
Navigation: Raytheon SPS-73(V)12; I-band.
Tacan: URN 25. IFF: Mk XII UPX-36.

Helicopters: Up to 6 CH-46D/E Sea Knight can be carried. Hangar for only 1 light (not in LPD 4).

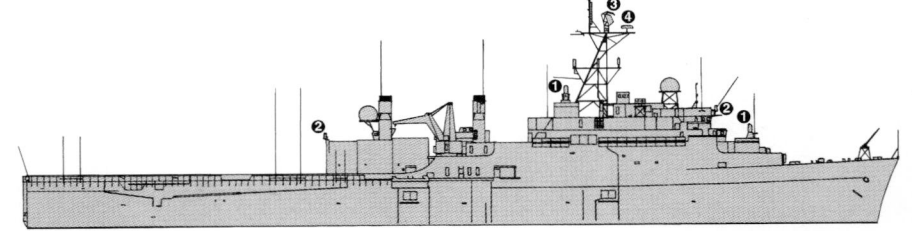

DENVER   (Scale 1 : 1,500), Ian Sturton / 0016471

Programmes: LPD 4-5 were authorised in the FY62 new construction programme, LPD 7—10 in FY63, LPD 12 and 13 in FY64, LPD 14 and LPD 15 in FY65.
Modernisation: Modernisation carried out in normal maintenance periods from FY87. This included fitting two Phalanx, SPS-67 radar replacing SPS-10 and updating EW capability. 3 in guns have been removed. Five ships have received machinery, electrical and habitability upgrades to extend service lives.
Structure: LPD 7-13 have an additional bridge and are fitted as flagships. One small telescopic hangar. There are structural variations in the positions of guns and electronic equipment in different ships of the class.

Flight deck is 168 ft (51.2 m) in length. Well-deck 394 × 50 ft (120.1 × 15.2 m). Communications domes are not uniformly fitted.
Operational: A typical operational load might include one Seahawk, two Sea Knight, two Twin Huey, four Sea Cobra helicopters and one Cyclone patrol craft. LPD 10 based at Sasebo, Japan. LPDs 5, 7-9 at San Diego and LPDs 4 and 12-15 at Norfolk. LPD 6 decommissioned in 2005, LPD 4 is to decommission in 2006 and LPDs 5 and 14 in 2007.

JUNEAU   8/2005*, Hachiro Nakai / 1154019

CLEVELAND   8/2005*, John Mortimer / 1154055

8 WHIDBEY ISLAND CLASS and 4 HARPERS FERRY CLASS (DOCK LANDING SHIPS) (LSDHM and LSD-CV)

Name	No	Builders	Laid down	Launched	Commissioned	F/S
WHIDBEY ISLAND	LSD 41	Lockheed SB & Construction Co	4 Aug 1981	10 June 1983	9 Feb 1985	AA
GERMANTOWN	LSD 42	Lockheed SB & Construction Co	5 Aug 1982	29 June 1984	8 Feb 1986	PA
FORT McHENRY	LSD 43	Lockheed SB & Construction Co	10 June 1983	1 Feb 1986	8 Aug 1987	PA
GUNSTON HALL	LSD 44	Avondale Industries	26 May 1986	27 June 1987	22 Apr 1989	AA
COMSTOCK	LSD 45	Avondale Industries	27 Oct 1986	16 Jan 1988	3 Feb 1990	PA
TORTUGA	LSD 46	Avondale Industries	23 Mar 1987	15 Sep 1988	17 Nov 1990	AA
RUSHMORE	LSD 47	Avondale Industries	9 Nov 1987	6 May 1989	1 June 1991	PA
ASHLAND	LSD 48	Avondale Industries	4 Apr 1988	11 Nov 1989	9 May 1992	AA
HARPERS FERRY	LSD 49	Avondale Industries	15 Apr 1991	16 Jan 1993	7 Jan 1995	PA
CARTER HALL	LSD 50	Avondale Industries	11 Nov 1991	2 Oct 1993	30 Sep 1995	AA
OAK HILL	LSD 51	Avondale Industries	21 Sep 1992	11 June 1994	8 June 1996	AA
PEARL HARBOR	LSD 52	Avondale Industries	27 Jan 1995	24 Feb 1996	30 May 1998	PA

Displacement, tons: 11,125 light; 15,939 (LSD 41-48), 16,740 (LSD 49 onwards) full load

Dimensions, feet (metres): 609.5 × 84 × 20.5 *(185.8 × 25.6 × 6.3)*

Main machinery: 4 Colt SEMT-Pielstick 16 PC2.5 V 400 diesels; 33,000 hp(m) *(24.6 MW)* sustained; 2 shafts; cp props

Speed, knots: 22. **Range, n miles:** 8,000 at 18 kt

Complement: 413 (21 officers)

Military lift: 402 (+102 surge) troops; 2 (CV) or 4 LCACs, or 9 (CV) or 21 LCM 6, or 1 (CV) or 3 LCUs, or 64 LVTs. 2 LCPL

Cargo capacity: 5,000 cu ft for marine cargo, 12,500 sq ft for vehicles (including four preloaded LCACs in the well-deck). The cargo version' has 67,600 cu ft for marine cargo, 20,200 sq ft for vehicles but only two LCACs. Aviation fuel, 90 tons.

Missiles: 2 GDC/Hughes Mk 49 RAM ❶; passive IR/anti-radiation homing to 9.6 km *(5.2 n miles)* at 2 Mach; warhead 9.1 kg. Being fitted in all.

Guns: 2 General Electric/General Dynamics 20 mm/76 6-barrelled Vulcan Phalanx Mk 15 ❷; 3,000 rds/min (4,500 in Block 1) combined to 1.5 km. 2—25 mm Mk 38. 6—12.7 mm MGs.

Countermeasures: Decoys: 4 Loral Hycor SRBOC 6-barrelled Mk 36 and Mk 50; IR flares and chaff. SLQ-25 Nixie. ESM: SLQ-32(V)1; intercept. SLQ-49.

Combat data systems: SATCOM SRR-1, WSC-3 (UHF) (see Data Systems at front of section). SSDS Mk 1.

Radars: Air search: Raytheon SPS-49(V)1 ❸; C-band. Surface search: Norden SPS-67V ❹; G-band. Navigation: Raytheon SPS-64(V)9 or SPS-73(V)12; I/J-band. Tacan: URN 25. IFF: Mk XII UPX-29/UPX-36.

Helicopters: Platform only for 2 CH-53 Sea Stallion.

Programmes: Originally it was planned to construct six ships of this class as replacements for the Thomaston class LSDs. Eventually, the level of Whidbey Island class ships was established at eight, with four additional cargo-carrying variants of that class to provide increased cargo-carrying capability. The first cargo variant, LSD 49, was authorised and funded in the FY88 budget; LSD 50 in FY89 and LSD 51 in FY91. The fourth was authorised in FY92 but not ordered until 12 October 1993.

Modernisation: A Quick Reaction Combat Capability (QRCC)/Ship Self-Defense System (SSDS) was installed and successfully demonstrated in LSD 41 in 1993. During the QRCC demonstrations, the ship's SPS-49, SLQ-32, RAM and Phalanx were successfully integrated via SSDS. All ships of the class fitted with SSDS Mk 1. A mid-life upgrade package, to extend service life to 40 years, is under development.

Structure: Based on the earlier Anchorage class. One 60 and one 20 ton crane. Well-deck measures 440 × 50 ft *(134.1 × 15.2 m)* in the LSD but is shorter in the Cargo

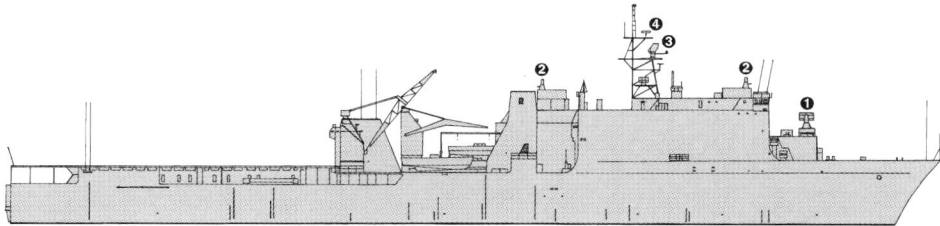

ASHLAND *(Scale 1 : 1,500), Ian Sturton* / 0053362

TORTUGA *6/2005*, John Brodie* / 1154018

PEARL HARBOR *6/2003, Mick Prendergast* / 0572788

Variant (CV). The cargo version is a minimum modification to the LSD 41 design. Changes in that design include additional troop magazines, air conditioning, piping and hull structure; the forward Phalanx is forward of the bridge, RAM is on the bridge roof, and there is only one crane. There is approximately 90 per cent commonality between the two classes.

Operational: LSDs 41, 44, 46, 48, 50 and 51 are based at Little Creek, VA. LSDs 42, 45, 47 and 52 are based at San Diego, CA. LSDs 43 and 49 are based at Sasebo, Japan.

ASHLAND *9/2005*, US Navy* / 1154057

1 + 4 (4) SAN ANTONIO CLASS: AMPHIBIOUS TRANSPORT DOCKS (LPDM)

Name	No	Builders	Laid down	Launched	Commissioned	F/S
SAN ANTONIO	LPD 17	Northrop Grumman Ship Systems (Avondale)	9 Dec 2000	19 July 2003	14 Jan 2006	AA
NEW ORLEANS	LPD 18	Northrop Grumman Ship Systems (Avondale)	14 Oct 2002	20 Dec 2004	10 Mar 2007	PA
MESA VERDE	LPD 19	Northrop Grumman Ship Systems (Ingalls)	25 Feb 2003	15 Jan 2005	2007	Bldg/AA
GREEN BAY	LPD 20	Northrop Grumman Ship Systems (Avondale)	26 Aug 2003	2006	2007	Bldg/PA
NEW YORK	LPD 21	Northrop Grumman Ship Systems (Avondale)	10 Sep 2004	2006	2008	Bldg/PA
SAN DIEGO	LPD 22	Northrop Grumman Ship Systems (Avondale)	2006	2008	2009	Ord/PA
ANCHORAGE	LPD 23	Northrop Grumman Ship Systems (Avondale)	2007	2009	2010	Ord/PA
ARLINGTON	LPD 24	Northrop Grumman Ship Systems (Avondale)	2008	2010	2011	Ord/PA
SOMERSET	LPD 25	Northrop Grumman Ship Systems (Avondale)	2009	2012	2014	Ord/AA

Displacement, tons: 25,885 full load
Dimensions, feet (metres): 683.7 × 104.7 × 23
(208.4 × 31.9 × 7)
Main machinery: 4 Colt Pielstick PC 2.5 diesels; 40,000 hp
(29.84 MW); 2 shafts; cp props
Speed, knots: 22
Complement: 360 (28 officers) plus 34 spare
Military lift: 720 troops; 2 LCACs, 14 AAAVs

Missiles: SAM: Mk 41 VLS for 2 octuple cell Evolved Sea
Sparrow ❶. 64 missiles. May be fitted later.
2 Mk 31 Mod 1 RAM launchers ❷.
Guns: 2—30 mm Mk 46 ❸. 4—12.7 mm MGs.
Countermeasures: Decoys: 6 Mk 53 Mod 4 Nulka and chaff
launcher ❹. SLQ-25A Nixie towed torpedo decoy.
ESM/ECM: SLQ-32A(V)2 ❺; intercept and jammer.
Combat data systems: SSDS Mk 2; GCCS (M), CEC, JTIDS
(Link 16), AADS (see Data Systems at front of section).
Radars: Air search: ITT SPS-48E ❻; 3D; E/F-band.
Surface search/navigation: Raytheon SPS-73(V)13 ❼;
I-band.
Fire control: Lockheed SPQ-9B ❽; I-band.

Helicopters: 1 CH-53E Sea Stallion or 2 CH-46E Sea Knight
or 1 MV-22 Osprey.

Programmes: The LPD 17 (ex-LX) programme was
first approved by the Defense Acquisition Board on
11 January 1993. It will replace four classes of amphibious
ships: LPD 4s, LSTs, LKAs and LSD 36s. Contract for first
ship, with an option on two more, awarded to Avondale
on 17 December 1996. A protest about the award delayed
the effective contract date to April 1997. The lead ship

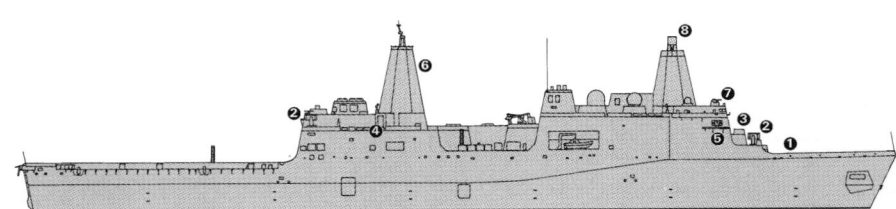

SAN ANTONIO   *(Scale 1 : 1,800), Ian Sturton* / 1153885

contract options for FY99 and FY00 on LPD 18 and
LPD 19 respectively were exercised in December 1998 and February
2000 respectively. A negotiated modification added the
second FY00 ship, LPD 20, to the lead ship contract in
May 2000. Contract awarded for LPD 21 in November
2003 and for LPD 22 and 23 long-lead items in 2004.
Full award for LPD 22 and 23 expected in 2006. Under
agreement reached in June 2002, NGSS is to build all
ships. Difficulties in design phase led to two-year delay
to delivery date of lead ship. Launch and commissioning
dates for LPD 18-20 delayed due to shipyard damage
caused by Hurricane Katrina in 2005. Delivery of final
ship is planned for 2014.
Structure: Panama Canal-capable ships able to control and
support landing forces disembarking either via surface
craft such as LCACs or by VTOL aircraft, principally
helicopters. The design supports a lift capability of
24,000 sq ft of deck space for vehicles, 34,000 cu ft of
cargo below decks and 720 embarked Marines with

surge lift capacity to 800 troops. The well-deck and stern
gate arrangements are similar to those of the Wasp
class; the well-deck can carry two LCACs or one LCU, or
14 Expeditionary Fighting Vehicles. The Flight deck can
land/launch four CH-46s or two CH-53s or two MV-22s.
The hangar will accommodate two CH-46s or one CH-53
or one MV-22. There is a 24-bed medical facility. Although
with similar capabilities as the classes they are to
replace, the ships are not equipped with the flag facilities
of some Austin class LPDs, the heavy over-the-side lift
capability of LKAs or the ability of LSTs to beach. There is
a crane for support of boat operations and an Advanced
Enclosed Mast System, trialled in DD 968, is being fitted
in all. On 9 September 2003, salvaged steel from the
World Trade Centre was cast into the bow section of USS
New York.
Operational: Sea trials for LPD 17 began in December
2005. First deployment is planned for 2007. Based at
Norfolk, VA.

SAN ANTONIO   *4/2005, Northrop Grumman* / 1121524

39 MECHANISED LANDING CRAFT: LCM 6 TYPE

Displacement, tons: 64 full load
Dimensions, feet (metres): 56.2 × 14 × 3.9 *(17.1 × 4.3 × 1.2)*
Main machinery: 2 Detroit 6V-71 diesels; 348 hp *(260 kW)* sustained or 2 Detroit 8V-71
diesels; 460 hp *(344 kW)* sustained; 2 shafts
Speed, knots: 9
Range, n miles: 130 at 9 kt
Complement: 5
Military lift: 34 tons or 80 troops

Comment: Welded steel construction. All used for various utility tasks, none as
landing craft.

LCM 6
6/1997, J W Currie
0016482

74 LANDING CRAFT AIR CUSHION (LCAC)

Displacement, tons: 87.2 light; 170—182 full load
Dimensions, feet (metres): 88 oa (on-cushion) (81 between hard structures) × 47 beam (on-cushion) (43 beam hard structure) × 2.9 draught (off-cushion) *(26.8 (24.7) × 14.3 (13.1) × 0.9)*
Main machinery: 4 Allied-Signal TF40B marine gas turbines for propulsion and lift; 16,000 hp *(11.9 MW)* sustained; 2 shrouded reversible-pitch airscrews (propulsion); 4 double-entry fans, centrifugal or mixed-flow (lift). SLEP configuration, 4 Vericor Power Systems ETF40B marine gas turbines with Full Authority Digital Engine Control (FADEC) for propulsion and lift; 19,000 hp *(1.41 MW)* sustained; 2 shrouded reversible-pitch airscrews (propulsion); 4 double-entry fans, centrifugal or mixed-flow (lift)
Speed, knots: 40 (loaded). **Range, n miles:** 300 at 35 kt; 200 at 40 kt
Complement: 5
Military lift: 23 troops; 1 Main Battle Tank or 60—75 tons
Radars: Navigation: Marconi LN66 or Decca Bridgemaster E; I-band.

Programmes: Built by Textron Marine and Land Systems and Avondale Gulfport. A total of 90 craft delivered 1984-1997. The final craft LCAC 91 delivered in 2001 in SLEP configuration.
Modernisation: 72 in-service craft to receive Ship Life Extension Programme (SLEP) from 2002-2016. The programme includes the installation of more powerful engines to provide greater lift capacity, an improved deep skirt for better handling in heavier sea states and an integrated navigation suite for precise navigation, and advanced Multimode Integrated Communications System in either normal, secure modes. Four craft were upgraded in FY04, five in FY05, six in FY06 and planned for subsequent years.
Structure: Incorporates the best attributes of the JEFF(A) and JEFF(B) learned from over five years of testing the two prototypes. Bow ramp 28.8 ft, stern ramp 15 ft. Cargo space capacity is 1,809 sq ft. Noise and dust levels are high and if disabled the craft is not easy to tow. 30 mm Gatling guns can be fitted.
Operational: Ship classes capable of carrying the LCAC are Wasp (three), Tarawa (one), Austin (one), Whidbey Island (four), Harpers Ferry (two) and San Antonio (two). A portable transport module can be carried on the cargo deck to transport up to 180 troops. It is claimed that LCACs are capable of accessing 70 per cent of the world's coastlines compared to 17 per cent for conventional landing craft. Some limitations in very rough seas. Shore bases on each coast at Little Creek, VA and Camp Pendleton, CA.
Sales: Six to Japan. One of a similar type built by South Korea.

LCAC 53 *9/2002, Winter & Findler* / 0529980

LCAC 86 *6/2005*, J Cislak* / 1154056

7 + 1 (1) FRANK S BESSON CLASS: LOGISTIC SUPPORT VESSELS (LSV-ARMY)

Name	No	Builders	Commissioned
GEN FRANK S BESSON JR	LSV 1	Moss Point Marine, MS	18 Dec 1987
CW 3 HAROLD C CLINGER	LSV 2	Moss Point Marine, MS	20 Feb 1988
GEN BREHON B SOMERVELL	LSV 3	Moss Point Marine, MS	2 Apr 1988
LTG WILLIAM B BUNKER	LSV 4	Moss Point Marine, MS	18 May 1988
MG CHARLES P GROSS	LSV 5	Moss Point Marine, MS	30 Apr 1991
SP/4 JAMES A LOUX	LSV 6	Moss Point Marine, MS	16 Dec 1994
SSGT ROBERT T KURODA	LSV 7	VT Halter Marine	June 2006
MG ROBERT SMAILS	LSV 8	VT Halter Marine	Aug 2006

Displacement, tons: 4,265 full load
Dimensions, feet (metres): 272.8 × 60 × 12 *(83.1 × 18.3 × 3.7)*
314 (LSV 7) × 60.0 × 12.0 *(95.7 × 18.3 × 36.6)*
Main machinery: 2 GM EMD 16-645E2 diesels; 3,900 hp *(2.9 MW)* sustained; 2 shafts; Schottel bow thruster; 650 hp *(485 kW)*
Speed, knots: 11.6. **Range, n miles:** 8,300 at 11 kt
Complement: 30 (6 officers)
Military lift: 2,280 tons of vehicles including 26 M-1 tanks, containers or general cargo
Radars: Navigation: 2 Raytheon; E/F-band; I-band.

Comment: First one approved in FY85, second in FY87, remainder from Army reserve funds. Army owned ro-ro design with 10,500 sq ft of deck space for cargo. Capable of beaching with 4 ft over the ramp on a 1:30 offshore gradient with a payload of 900 tons of cargo. LSV 1 is based at Fort Eustis, Virginia, LSVs 2 and 5 are based at Pearl Harbour, HI, and are to be joined by LSV 7. LSV 3 is with the National Guard and based at Tacoma, WA. LSVs 4 and 6 are based in Kuwait. LSV 8 is to be based at Baltimore, MD. Delivery of LSVs 7 and 8 delayed by Hurricane Katrina. Two modified ships of the class built for the Philippines Navy in 1993-94.

CW 3 HAROLD C CLINGER *7/2002, Chris Sattler* / 0529979

35 LCU 2000 CLASS: UTILITY LANDING CRAFT (LCU-ARMY)

LCU 2001-2035

Displacement, tons: 1,102 full load
Dimensions, feet (metres): 173.8 × 42 × 8.5 *(53 × 12.8 × 2.6)*
Main machinery: 2 Cummins KTA50-M diesels; 2,500 hp *(1.87 MW)* sustained; 2 shafts; bow thruster
Speed, knots: 11.5. **Range, n miles:** 4,500 at 11.5 kt
Complement: 13 (2 officers)
Military lift: 350 tons
Radars: Navigation: 2 Raytheon; E/F-band; I-band.

Comment: Order placed with Lockheed by US Army 11 June 1986. First one completed 21 February 1990 by Moss Point Marine. The 2000 series have names, some of which duplicate naval ships. These are the first LCUs to have been built to an Army specification. 14 are active, 12 in reserve, eight prepositioned and one used for training.

LCU 2024 *7/2003, A Sharma* / 0572813

LCU 2029 *6/2003, A Sharma* / 0572815

0 + 10 LANDING CRAFT (MPF TYPE)

Displacement, tons: To be announced
Dimensions, feet (metres): 40.0 × 14.0 ×? *(12.2 × 4.3 × ?)*
Main machinery: 2 Cummins QSM11 diesels; 660 hp *(492 kW)*; 2 Hamilton 364 waterjets
Speed, knots: 30 (light); 25 (full load)
Complement: To be announced
Guns: 2 — 12.7 mm MGs.
Radars: Navigation: To be announced.

Comment: Contract for the construction of ten MPF utility craft awarded to Kvichak Marine Industries, Seattle, WA, in August 2005. The craft are to replace the LCM-8 craft as part of the lighterage system in support of prepositioned Marine amphibious assault missions. The craft is of aluminium construction and has an articulated bow-door for beach deployment. Delivery of all ten craft is expected by December 2006. Two are to be stationed at San Diego, CA, two at Norfolk, VA, and six onboard prepositioned MSC ships.

45 MECHANISED LANDING CRAFT: LCM 8 TYPE

Displacement, tons: 65.6 light; 127 full load
Dimensions, feet (metres): 73.7 × 21 × 5.2 *(22.5 × 6.4 × 1.6)*
Main machinery: 2 Detroit 12V-71 diesels; 400 hp *(298 kW)* sustained; 2 shafts; Kort nozzles
Speed, knots: 12
Range, n miles: 190 at 9 kt full load
Complement: 4
Military lift: 67.5 tons or 1 M48/1 M60 tank or 110 fully equipped troops or 200 non-combat troops

Comment: Naval craft are for use in amphibious ships. 21 are currently employed as landing craft, the remainder as work boats. The last 12 were built in 1993-94. 22 similar craft are used by the Army.

LCM 8 *5/2003, A Sharma* / 0572786

37 LCU 1600 CLASS: UTILITY LANDING CRAFT
(LCU-ARMY (2) and NAVY (35))

Displacement, tons: 200 light; 375 full load
Dimensions, feet (metres): 134.9 × 29 × 6.1 *(41.1 × 8.8 × 1.9)*
Main machinery: 4 Detroit 6-71 diesels; 696 hp *(519 kW)* sustained; 2 shafts; Kort nozzles
  2 Detroit 12V-71 diesels (LCU 1680-1681); 680 hp *(508 kW)* sustained; 2 shafts; Kort nozzles
Speed, knots: 11. **Range, n miles:** 1,200 at 8 kt
Complement: 14 (2 officers)
Military lift: 134 tons; 3 M103 (64 tons) or 2 M1A1 tanks or 350 troops
Guns: 2 — 12.7 mm MGs.
Radars: Navigation: Furuno; I-band.

Comment: Steel hulled construction. Versatile craft used for a variety of tasks. Most were built between the mid-1960s and mid-1980s. There are no plans for more of this type and a replacement craft is under consideration. Three converted to Diver Support Craft (ASDV). LCU 1667 and 1675 operated by the US Army. Two USN craft are in reserve. It is planned to reduce US Navy inventory to 28.

LCU 1651   *8/2004, Hachiro Nakai* / 1043687

145 LANDING CRAFT PERSONNEL (LCPL)

Displacement, tons: 11 full load
Dimensions, feet (metres): 36 × 12.1 × 3.8 *(11 × 3.7 × 1.2)*
Main machinery: 1 GM 8V-71TI diesel; 425 hp *(317 kW)* sustained; 1 shaft
Speed, knots: 20. **Range, n miles:** 150 at 20 kt
Complement: 3
Military lift: 17 troops
Radars: Navigation: Marconi LN66; I-band.

Comment: There are 13 Mk 11, 105 Mk 12, 15 Mk 13 and 12 11 m LCPLs. Details given are for Mk 12 and 13. For use as control craft and carried aboard LHA, LPD and LSD classes. 33 are active.

LCU 1600 class (Army)   *2/2001, M Declerck* / 0529975

LCPL Mk 13   *4/1991, Bollinger* / 0084143

MINE WARFARE FORCES

Notes: (1) There are no surface minelayers. Mining is done by carrier-based aircraft, land-based aircraft and submarines. The mine inventory includes Mk 56 moored influence mines, the Mk 67 submarine launched mobile mine (SLMM) and the Quickstrike series of bottom mines. Mk 56 is being phased out.
(2) NRF ships are manned by active and reserve crews.
(3) MH-53E Sea Stallion helicopters can be deployed in LHDs or transported by C-5 aircraft for mine countermeasures.
(4) The Long-term Mine Reconnaissance System (LMRS), developed by Boeing, is being used as a risk reduction vehicle for the US Navy's 21 in Mission Reconfigurable Unmanned Undersea Vehicle System (MRUUV). This programme is to develop and procure a modular UUV

capable of supporting multiple payloads, reconfigurable for mine countermeasures; intelligence, surveillance and reconnaissance; and other missions.
(5) Marine Mammal Systems (MMS) uses trained dolphins and sea lions for mine detection, detection of unauthorised swimmers, protection of fleet assets in port and critical infrastructure, and recovery of exercise mines and torpedoes. The dolphins can be transported by C-5 aircraft or amphibious ships. MMS is the only operational method of detecting and neutralising buried mines.
(6) The AN/WLD1 Remote Minehunting System (RMS) is comprised of a 14,500 lb diesel-powered semi-submersible (the Remote Minehunting Vehicle) combined with the towed AN/AQS-20A Sonar Mine Detecting Set.

RMS is being developed for deployment from the US's Flight IIA Arleigh Burke class DDGs as well as from the new Littoral Combat Ship (LCS) seaframes (where RMS forms part of the LCS Mine Interdiction Warfare Mission Package).
(7) Rapid Airborne Mine Clearance System (RAMICS) is under development. RAMICS is to be operated from a MH-60S helicopter and consists of an electro-optic detection and ranging system and a 30 mm gun system to destroy near-surface and floating moored mines.
(8) Organic Airborne and Surface Influence Sweep (OASIS) is being developed for deployment from MH-53 and MH-60S helicopters, and selected surface craft. OASIS will provide organic, high-speed magnetic and acoustic influence minesweeping capability.

14 AVENGER CLASS: MINE COUNTERMEASURES VESSELS (MCM/MHSO)

Name	No	Builders	Laid down	Launched	Commissioned	F/S
AVENGER	MCM 1	Peterson Builders Inc	3 June 1983	15 June 1985	12 Sep 1987	NRF
DEFENDER	MCM 2	Marinette Marine Corp	1 Dec 1983	4 Apr 1987	30 Sep 1989	NRF
SENTRY	MCM 3	Peterson Builders Inc	8 Oct 1984	20 Sep 1986	2 Sep 1989	NRF
CHAMPION	MCM 4	Marinette Marine Corp	28 June 1984	15 Apr 1989	27 July 1991	NRF
GUARDIAN	MCM 5	Peterson Builders Inc	8 May 1985	20 June 1987	16 Dec 1989	PA
DEVASTATOR	MCM 6	Peterson Builders Inc	9 Feb 1987	11 June 1988	6 Oct 1990	AA
PATRIOT	MCM 7	Marinette Marine Corp	31 Mar 1987	15 May 1990	18 Oct 1991	PA
SCOUT	MCM 8	Peterson Builders Inc	8 June 1987	20 May 1989	15 Dec 1990	AA
PIONEER	MCM 9	Peterson Builders Inc	5 June 1989	25 Aug 1990	7 Dec 1992	AA
WARRIOR	MCM 10	Peterson Builders Inc	25 Sep 1989	8 Dec 1990	3 Apr 1993	AA
GLADIATOR	MCM 11	Peterson Builders Inc	7 July 1990	29 June 1991	18 Sep 1993	NRF
ARDENT	MCM 12	Peterson Builders Inc	22 Oct 1990	16 Nov 1991	18 Feb 1994	AE
DEXTROUS	MCM 13	Peterson Builders Inc	11 Mar 1991	20 June 1992	9 July 1994	AE
CHIEF	MCM 14	Peterson Builders Inc	19 Aug 1991	12 June 1993	5 Nov 1994	AA

Displacement, tons: 1,379 full load
Dimensions, feet (metres): 224.3 × 38.9 × 12.2 *(68.4 × 11.9 × 3.7)*
Main machinery: 4 Waukesha L-1616 diesels (MCM 1-2); 2,600 hp(m) *(1.91 MW)* or 4 Isotta Fraschini ID 36 SS 6V AM diesels (MCM 3 onwards); 2,280 hp(m) *(1.68 MW)* sustained; 2 Hansome Electric motors; 400 hp(m) *(294 kW)* for hovering; 2 shafts; cp props; 1 Omnithruster hydrojet; 350 hp *(257 kW)*
Speed, knots: 13.5. **Range, n miles:** 2,500 at 10 kt
Complement: 84 (8 officers)

Guns: 2 — 12.7 mm MGs.
Countermeasures: MCM: 2 SLQ-48; includes Honeywell/Hughes ROV mine neutralisation system, capable of 6 kt (1,500 m cable with cutter (MP1), and countermining charge) (MP 2). SLQ-37(V)3; magnetic/acoustic influence sweep equipment. Oropesa SLQ-38 Type 0 Size 1; mechanical sweep.
Combat data systems: SATCOM SRR-1; WSC-3 (UHF). GEC/Marconi Nautis M in last two ships includes SSN 2 PINS command system and control. USQ-119E(V), UHF Dama and OTCIXS provide JMCIS connectivity.
Radars: Surface search: ISC Cardion SPS-55; I/J-band.
Navigation: ARPA 2525 or LN66; I-band. Both to be replaced by SPS-73.
Sonars: Raytheon/Thomson Sintra SQQ-32(V)3; VDS; active minehunting; high frequency.

Programmes: The contract for the prototype MCM was awarded in June 1982. The last three were funded in FY90.
Modernisation: Integrated Ship Control System (ISCS) installed in all hulls.
Structure: The hull is constructed of oak, Douglas fir and Alaskan cedar, with a thin coating of fibreglass on the outside, to permit taking advantage of wood's low

AVENGER   *4/2004, US Navy* / 1043631

magnetic signature. A problem of engine rotation on the Waukesha diesels in MCM 1-2 was resolved; however, those engines have been replaced in the rest of the class by low magnetic engines manufactured by Isotta-Fraschini of Milan, Italy. Fitted with SSN2(V) Precise Integrated Navigation System (PINS).

Operational: *Avenger* fitted with the SQQ-32 for Gulf operations in 1991 and all of the class have been retrofitted. Two transferred to NRF in 1995, two more in 1996. *Ardent* and *Dextrous* permanently stationed in Bahrain from March 1996, and *Guardian* and *Patriot* are at Sasebo, Japan. The remainder are based at Ingleside, Texas.

12 OSPREY CLASS (MINEHUNTERS COASTAL) (MHC)

Name	No	Builders	Launched	Commissioned	F/S
OSPREY	MHC 51	Intermarine, Savannah	23 Mar 1991	20 Nov 1993	NRF
HERON	MHC 52	Intermarine, Savannah	21 Mar 1992	6 Aug 1994	NRF
PELICAN	MHC 53	Avondale Industries	27 Feb 1993	18 Nov 1995	NRF
ROBIN	MHC 54	Avondale Industries	11 Sep 1993	11 May 1996	NRF
ORIOLE	MHC 55	Intermarine, Savannah	22 May 1993	16 Sep 1995	NRF
KINGFISHER	MHC 56	Avondale Industries	18 June 1994	26 Oct 1996	NRF
CORMORANT	MHC 57	Avondale Industries	21 Oct 1995	12 Apr 1997	NRF
BLACK HAWK	MHC 58	Intermarine, Savannah	27 Aug 1994	11 May 1996	NRF
FALCON	MHC 59	Intermarine, Savannah	3 June 1995	26 Oct 1997	NRF
CARDINAL	MHC 60	Intermarine, Savannah	9 Mar 1996	18 Oct 1997	AE
RAVEN	MHC 61	Intermarine, Savannah	28 Sep 1996	5 Sep 1998	AE
SHRIKE	MHC 62	Intermarine, Savannah	24 May 1997	31 May 1999	NRF

Displacement, tons: 930 full load
Dimensions, feet (metres): 187.8 × 35.9 × 9.5
(57.2 × 11 × 2.9)
Main machinery: 2 Isotta Fraschini ID 36 SS 8V AM diesels;
1,600 hp(m) *(1.18 MW)* sustained; 2 Voith-Schneider
props; 3 Isotta Fraschini ID 36 diesel generators; 984 kW
Speed, knots: 10
Range, n miles: 1,500 at 10 kt
Complement: 51 (5 officers)

Guns: 2 — 12.7 mm MGs.
Countermeasures: MCM: Alliant SLQ-48 mine neutralisation
system ROV (with 1,070 m cable). Degaussing DGM-4.

Combat data systems: Unisys SYQ 13 and SYQ 109; integrated
combat and machinery control system. USQ-119E(V), UHF
Dama, and OTCIXS provide GCCS connectivity.
Radars: Surface search: Raytheon SPS-64(V)9; I-band.
Navigation: R41XX; I-band.
Sonars: Raytheon/Thomson Sintra SQQ-32(V)3; VDS; active
minehunting; high frequency.

Programmes: A design contract for Lerici class mine hunters
was awarded in August 1986 followed by a construction
contract with Intermarine USA in May 1987 for eight of
the 12 ships of the class. On 2 October 1989 Avondale,
Gulfport was named as the second construction source.

Contracts were awarded for four ships which were
delivered between 1995 and 1997.
Structure: Construction is of monocoque GRP throughout
hull, with frames eliminated. Main machinery is mounted
on GRP cradles and provided with acoustic enclosures.
SQQ-32 is deployed from a central well forward. Fitted
with Voith cycloidal propellers which eliminate need for
forward thrusters during station keeping.
Operational: All but two are NRF based at Ingleside, Texas.
MHC-60 and MHC-61 are based at Bahrain. It is planned
to decommission the whole class as follows: 2006 (MHCs
51, 54, 55 and 59); 2007 (MHCs 60 and 61); 2008 (MHCs
52, 53, 56, 57, 58 and 62).

RAVEN   *4/2004, US Navy* / 1043630

RESEARCH SHIPS

Notes: There are many naval associated research vessels which are civilian manned and
not carried on the US Naval Vessel Register. In addition civilian ships are leased for short
periods to support a particular research project or trial. Some of those employed include
RSB-1 (missile booster recovery), *Acoustic Pioneer* and *Acoustic Explorer* (acoustic
research).

1 RESEARCH SHIP (AGE)

SEA SHADOW

Displacement, tons: 560 full load
Dimensions, feet (metres): 164.0 × 68.0 × 14.5 *(50.0 × 20.7 × 4.4)*
Main machinery: Diesel-electric; 2 Detroit 12V-149TI diesels; 2 shafts
Speed, knots: 10
Range, n miles: 2,250 at 9 kt
Complement: 12

Comment: Built by Lockheed in 1983-84. Testing started in 1985 but the ship was then laid
up until April 1993 when testing resumed off Santa Cruz island, southern California. This
is a stealth ship prototype of SWATH design with sides angled at 45° to minimise the
radar cross-section. Operated by Lockheed for testing all aspects of stealth technology
and reactivated for a six year programme at San Diego in early 1999.

ACOUSTIC PIONEER   *3/1996, W H Clements* / 0085302

SEA SHADOW   *9/1999, van Ginderen Collection* / 0084164

---

1 EXPERIMENTAL CATAMARAN (X-CRAFT) (AGE)

SEA FIGHTER FSF-1

Displacement, tons: 1,150 full load
Dimensions, feet (metres): 262.0 × 72.2 × 11.5 *(79.9 × 22.0 × 3.5)*
Main machinery: CODOG; 2 GE LM 2500 gas turbines; 2 MTU 16V595 diesels; four
Rolls-Royce Kamewa 125 SII waterjets
Speed, knots: 50. **Range, n miles:** 4,000 at 20 kt
Complement: 26 (5 officers)
Radars: Navigation: to be announced.
Helicopters: Platform for 2 SH-60R.

Comment: Titan Corporation of San Diego, California and Nigel Gee and Associates Ltd of
Southampton, UK (later acquired by BMT) selected in September 2002 by the Office of
Naval Research (ONR) to design an experimental vessel known as X-Craft. Contract for
development and build awarded to Titan on 25 February 2003. Laid down 5 June 2003
and launched 5 February 2005 at Nichols Brothers Boat Builders, Whidbey Island, WA.
For completion in 2005. The ship is based at San Diego and is to be used by ONR for
hydrodynamic experimentation and operational concept development for high speed
craft. Catamaran design of aluminium construction. A flush upper deck has a landing
area for two helicopters. Access is via a large lift from the flight deck or over folding
ramps at the stern. Propulsion is by waterjets driven by gas turbines for high speed
operation and diesel engines for lower speed loitering and transit.

SEAFIGHTER   *10/2005*, US Navy* / 1123764

3 ASHEVILLE CLASS (YFRT)

ATHENA (ex-*Chehalis*)   **ATHENA II** (ex-*Grand Rapids*)   **LAUREN** (ex-*Douglas*)

Displacement, tons: 245 full load
Dimensions, feet (metres): 164.5 × 23.8 × 9.5 *(50.1 × 7.3 × 2.9)*
Main machinery: CODOG; 1 GE LM 1500 gas-turbine; 12,500 hp *(9.3 MW)*; 2 Cummins
VT12-875 diesels; 1,450 hp *(1.07 MW)*; 2 shafts; cp props
Speed, knots: 16
Range, n miles: 1,700 at 16 kt
Complement: 22

Comment: All built 1969-71. Work for the Naval Surface Warfare Center, at Panama City,
Florida. Disarmed except *Lauren* which has maintained its military appearance.

ATHENA II   *6/1993, Giorgio Arra* / 0506179

RESEARCH OCEANOGRAPHIC SHIPS

2 MELVILLE CLASS (AGOR)

Name	No	Builders	Commissioned	F/S
MELVILLE	AGOR 14	Defoe SB Co, Bay City, MI	27 Aug 1969	Loan
KNORR	AGOR 15	Defoe SB Co, Bay City, MI	14 Jan 1970	Loan

Displacement, tons: 2,944 full load
Dimensions, feet (metres): 278.9 × 46.3 × 16.5 *(85 × 14.1 × 5.0)*
Main machinery: Diesel-electric; 3 Caterpillar 3516 diesel generators; 1 Caterpillar 3508
diesel generator; 2 motors; 1,385 hp *(1 MW)*; 3 shafts (2 aft, 1 fwd)
Speed, knots: 14
Range, n miles: 10,060 at 11.7 kt
Complement: 23 (9 officers) plus 38 scientists

Comment: *Melville* operated by Scripps Institution of Oceanography and *Knorr* by Woods
Hole Oceanography Institution for the Office of Naval Research, under technical control
of the Oceanographer of the Navy. Fitted with internal wells for lowering equipment,
underwater lights and observation ports. Problems with the propulsion system have
led to major modifications including electric drive (vice the original mechanical) and
the insertion of a 34 ft central section increasing the displacement from the original
1,915 tons and allowing better accommodation and improved laboratory spaces. The
forward propeller is retractable. These ships are highly manoeuvrable for precise
position keeping.

MELVILLE   *3/2003, Robert Pabst* / 0572738

1 AGOR-26 CLASS (AGOR)

Name	No	Builders	Commissioned
KILO MOANA	AGOR 26	Atlantic Marine, Jacksonville	3 Sep 2002

Displacement, tons: 2,542 full load
Dimensions, feet (metres): 186 × 88 × 25 *(56.7 × 26.8 × 7.6)*
Main machinery: Diesel-electric; 4 Caterpillar 3508B diesel generators; 2 Westinghouse
motors; 4,025 hp *(3 MW)*; 1 bow thruster 1,100 hp *(820 kW)*
Speed, knots: 15. **Range, n miles:** 10,000 at 11 kt
Complement: 48 (31 scientists)

Comment: Replacement for R/V *Moana Wave*. Designed to commercial standards and
constructed by Atlantic Marine, Jacksonville. Launched on 17 November 2001. The
ship is a small waterplane area, twin hull (SWATH) oceanographic vessel capable of
performing general purpose oceanographic research in coastal and deep ocean areas.
The University of Hawaii School of Ocean and Earth Science and Technology operates
the ship under a charter agreement with the Office of Naval Research (ONR). The survey
suite consists of a Simrad EM 120 multibeam echosounder (12 kHz), a Simrad EM 1002
shallow water echo sounder (95 kHz), a Sontek current profiler and Simrad HPR-418
acoustic positioning system.

KILO MOANA   *6/2004, University of Hawaii Marine Center* / 1043633

3 THOMAS G THOMPSON CLASS (AGOR)

Name	No	Builders	Launched	Commissioned	F/S
THOMAS G THOMPSON	AGOR-23	Halter Marine	27 July 1990	8 July 1991	Loan
ROGER REVELLE	AGOR-24	Halter Marine	20 Apr 1995	11 June 1996	Loan
ATLANTIS	AGOR-25	Halter Marine	1 Feb 1996	3 Mar 1997	Loan

Displacement, tons: 3,400 full load
Dimensions, feet (metres): 274 oa; 246.8 wl × 52.5 × 19 *(83.5; 75.2 × 16 × 5.6)*
Main machinery: Diesel-electric; 6 Caterpillar diesel generators; 6.65 MW (3-1.5 MW and
3-715 kW); 2 motors; 6,000 hp *(4.48 MW)*; 2 shafts; bow thruster; 1,140 hp *(850 kW)*
Speed, knots: 15. **Range, n miles:** 15,000 at 12 kt
Complement: 22 plus 37 scientists
Sonars: Simrad EM 120; Seabeam 2112

Comment: *Thomas G Thompson* was the first of a class of oceanographic research vessels
capable of operating worldwide in all seasons and suitable for use by navy laboratories,
contractors and academic institutions. Dynamic positioning system enables station to
be held within 300 ft of a point. 4,000 sq ft of laboratories. AGORs 23, 24 and 25 are
operated by academic institutions for the Office of Naval Research through charter
party agreements (AGOR 23-University of Washington; AGOR 24-Scripps Institution of
Oceanography; AGOR 25-Woods Hole Oceanographic Institution). Ships in this series are
able to meet changing oceanographic requirements for general, year-round, worldwide
research. This includes launching, towing and recovering a variety of equipment. The
ships are also involved in hydrographic data collection. *Roger Revelle* was authorised in
FY92, ordered 11 January 1993. *Atlantis* can carry *Alvin* DSV 2.

THOMAS G THOMPSON   *6/2004, Mitsuhiro Kadota* / 1043632

HIGH SPEED VESSELS

Notes: The Joint High Speed Vessel (JHSV) Program is to procure eight vessels by FY11. This is a joint service program which was initiated following signature of a Memorandum of Agreement (MOA) by the US Army and US Navy to procure a high speed, medium load platform. It marries the Army's Theater Support Vessel (TSV) program with the Navy's High Speed Connector (HSC) program. Acquisition for JHSV is under the auspices of the Navy's Program Executive Office, Ships, but each service is to fund procurement and life-cycle costs of its own ships. An Analysis of Alternatives (AoA), by a private contractor, is to determine a preferred system concept for the joint platform. The analysis is to draw on data from the four high-speed catamarans currently operated by the US military.

1 HIGH SPEED VESSEL (HSVH)

JOINT VENTURE HSV-X1

Displacement, tons: 1,932
Dimensions, feet (metres): 314.9 × 87.2 × 13.1 *(96.0 × 26.6 × 4.0)*
Main machinery: 4 CAT 3618 diesels; 38,620 hp *(28.8 MW)*; 4 LIPS 150D waterjets
Speed, knots: 35
Range, n miles: 2,400 at 35 kt
Military lift: 150 passengers
Helicopters: Platform for SH-60 and CH-46.

Comment: Originally built by Incat in Tasmania, Australia and based on the shipbuilder's design of high-speed wave-piercing catamaran ferries. It is being leased by US Army Tank-Automotive and Armaments Command in support of US Special Operations Command. The lease is to support detailed analysis of the military utility of this type of platform to support special operations worldwide. Of aluminium construction, modifications to the commercial design include deck strengthening, a 472 m² helicopter deck suitable for SH-60 and CH-46, and a two-part hydraulically operated vehicle ramp to facilitate rapid loading/unloading from stern or alongside. Military communications have also been fitted. Manned by a joint Army/Navy crew, the ship has been used by both services in a series of exercises and trials. Typical roles being examined include: Mine Warfare Command and Control, Mine Countermeasures, Naval Special Warfare, Ship to Objective Manoeuvre and intra-theatre lift of an interim Brigade Combat Team. Trials in 2003 included exploration of Littoral Combat Ship concepts. Based at Norfolk, Virginia.

JOINT VENTURE *3/2003, A Sharma /* 0572741

1 HIGH SPEED VESSEL (HSV)

SPEARHEAD TSV-1X

Displacement, tons: 1,980
Dimensions, feet (metres): 318.9 × 87.3 × 11.2 *(97.2 × 26.6 × 3.43)*
Main machinery: 4 MAN B&W 20 RK 270 diesels; 37,950 hp *(28.3 MW)*; 4 LIPS 150D waterjets
Speed, knots: 48 (light); 38 (full load)
Range, n miles: 2,400 at 30 kt
Military lift: 680 tons of vehicles and equipment

Comment: A high-speed, wave-piercing catamaran, TSV-1X is being chartered under a two-year contract with three one-year options by US Army Tank-Automotive and Armament Command (TACOM) and Bollinger/Incat USA. Design is similar to HSV-2 but with no helicopter deck. Army will test its ability to perform specific missions such as transport of combat ready units, with en route mission planning, and service as state-of-the-art battle command centre. *Spearhead* successfully has completed self-protection demonstrations using existing, low-cost electronic warfare and anti-terrorist systems. In 2005, *Spearhead* participated in Foal Eagle, Cobra Gold and Talisman Sabre 05 Joint exercises with coalition forces and demonstrated C4ISR interoperability capabilities.

SPEARHEAD *6/2005*, Mick Prendergast /* 1154017

DEEP SUBMERGENCE VEHICLES

(Included in US Naval Vessel Register)
Notes: (1) Deep submergence vehicles and other craft and support ships are operated by Submarine Development Squadron Five at San Diego, California. The Squadron is a major operational command that includes advanced diving equipment; divers trained in 'saturation' techniques; DSRV-1; the submarine *Dolphin* (AGSS 555). DSRV-2 is inactive in lay-up condition. Two unmanned vessels CURV (Cable Controlled Underwater Remote Vehicle) Super Scorpios made test dives to 5,000 ft *(1,524 m)*.
(2) The Submarine Rescue, Diving and Recompression System (SRDRS) will replace the current DSRVs in 2007. A Remotely Operated Vehicle (ROV), launchable from a craft of opportunity in up to Sea State 4, will be based on the Australian 'Remora' system. Capable of rescuing up to 16 submariners at a time from depths up to 600 m, the ROV will be able to mate with decompression chambers. All components will fit into an ISO container to facilitate worldwide deployment.
(3) There are also four naval ROVs operated by the Supervisor of Salvage and Diving. These are air-transportable and can be operated from many warships and commercial vessels.

1 DOLPHIN CLASS (DSV)

Name	No	Builders	Launched	Commissioned	F/S
DOLPHIN	AGSS 555	Portsmouth Naval Shipyard, NH	8 June 1968	17 Aug 1968	PA

Displacement, tons: 860 standard; 948 full load
Dimensions, feet (metres): 165 × 19.3 × 18 *(50.3 × 5.9 × 5.5)*
Main machinery: Diesel-electric; 2 Detroit 12V42S diesels; 840 hp *(616 kW)* sustained; 2 generators; 1 motor; 1 shaft
Fitted with 246 cell VRLA battery
Speed, knots: 10 dived; 5 surfaced
Complement: 29 (3 officers) plus 4-7 scientists
Radars: Surface search: BPS-15; I/J-band.
Navigation: Furuno; I-band.
Sonars: Ametek BQS 15; active close-range detection; high frequency.
EDO BQR 2; passive search; low frequency; obstacle avoidance.

Comment: Authorised in FY61. Has a constant diameter cylindrical pressure hull approximately 15 ft in outer diameter closed at both ends with hemispherical heads. Pressure hull fabricated of HY-80 steel with aluminium and fibreglass used in secondary structures to reduce weight. No conventional hydroplanes are mounted, improved rudder design and other features provide manoeuvring control and hovering capability. Fitted for deep-ocean sonar and oceanographic research. There are several research stations for scientists and she is fitted to take water samples down to her operating depth. Assigned to Submarine Development Squadron Five at San Diego. Designed for deep diving operations and fitted with Helios seafloor imaging system, Draper Labs integrated navigation system and integrated science suite. Submerged endurance is approximately 24 hours with an at-sea endurance of 14 days. Refitted in 1993. Based at San Diego. Damaged by flooding in June 2002.

DOLPHIN *5/2002, Ships of the World /* 0530087

1 CUTTHROAT CLASS (DSV)

Name	No	Builders	Commissioned
CUTTHROAT	LSV-2	Newport News Shipbuilding and General Dynamics Electric Boat Division	Apr 2001

Displacement, tons: 205
Dimensions, feet (metres): 111 × 10 × 9 *(33.8 × 3.1 × 2.7)*
Main machinery: Permanent Magnet electric motor; 3,000 hp(m) *(2.23 MW)*
Speed, knots: 34 dived

Comment: The contract was placed with Newport News and Electric Boat in January 1999 to build *Cutthroat* LSV-2. The largest autonomous unmanned submarine in the world, it is a 1 : 3.4 scaled-down model of the Virginia class submarine and is to be used to test advanced submarine technologies, including hydroacoustics, hydrodynamics and manoeuvring. Its diving depth matches that of the Virginia class. The forward compartment contains 1,680 lead acid batteries and the after compartment contains the propulsion and auxiliary systems together with data recording and control systems. All appendages, including control surfaces and simulated sonar fairing, can be removed or relocated. LSV-2 is operated by the Acoustic Research Department at the instrumented range at Lake Pend Oreille in Bayview, Idaho. It is named after a species of trout indigenous to the lake.

CUTTHROAT *2000, Newport News /* 0105821

1 DEEP SUBMERGENCE RESCUE VEHICLE (DSRV)

Name	No	Builders	In service	F/S
MYSTIC	DSRV 1	Lockheed Missiles and Space Co,	7 Aug 1971	PSA

Displacement, tons: 30 surfaced; 38 dived
Dimensions, feet (metres): 49.2 × 8 *(15 × 2.4)*
Main machinery: Electric motors; silver/zinc batteries; 1 prop (movable control shroud);
   4 ducted thrusters (2 fwd, 2 aft)
Speed, knots: 4
Range, n miles: 24 at 3 kt
Complement: 4 (pilot, co-pilot, 2 rescue sphere operators) plus 24 rescued men
Sonars: Search and navigational sonar, obstacle avoidance sonar and closed-circuit
   television (supplemented by optical devices) are installed in the DSRV to determine
   the exact location of a disabled submarine within a given area and for pinpointing the
   submarine's escape hatches. Side-looking sonar can be fitted for search missions

Comment: The DSRV is intended to provide a quick-reaction worldwide, all-weather
capability for the rescue of survivors in a disabled submarine. Transportable by road,
aircraft (in C-141 and C-5 jet cargo aircraft), specially designed surface ship, and specially
modified mother ships (MOSUBs).
   The carrying submarine will launch and recover the DSRV while submerged and, if
necessary, while under ice. A total of six DSRVs were planned, but only two were
funded. DSRV 2 is now inactive.
   The outer hull is constructed of formed fibreglass. Within this outer hull are three
interconnected spheres which form the main pressure capsule. Each sphere is 7.5 ft in
diameter and is constructed of HY-140 steel. The forward sphere contains the vehicle's
control equipment and is manned by the pilot and co-pilot, the centre and after spheres
accommodate 24 passengers and two additional life-support technicians. Under the
DSRV's centre sphere is a hemispherical protrusion or 'skirt' which seals over the disabled
submarine's hatch. During the mating operation the skirt is pumped dry to enable
personnel to transfer. Operating depth, 1,525 m *(5,000 ft)*. Rescue depth limit 610 m
(2,000 ft). Name is not 'official'. Upgraded with modern electronics and navigation
systems. In 2001, deployed from UK SSBN *Vanguard* to conduct simulated rescue from
Swedish Submarine *Gotland* at 135 m in Raasay Sound, Scotland. To be replaced in
2006 by SRDRS.

MYSTIC *4/2002, Hachiro Nakai* / 0530003

1 DEEP SUBMERGENCE VEHICLE: ALVIN TYPE (DSV)

Name	No	Builders	F/S
— (ex-*Alvin*)	DSV 2	General Mills Inc, Minneapolis	PSA

Displacement, tons: 18 full load
Dimensions, feet (metres): 26.5 × 8.5 *(8.1 × 2.6)*
Main machinery: 6 brushless DC motors; 6 thrusters; 2 vertical-motion thrusters (located
   near the centre of gravity); 2 horizontally (near stern) (1 directed athwartships, 1 directed
   longitudinally); 2 on rotatable shaft near stern for vertical or longitudinal motion
Speed, knots: 2
Range, n miles: 3 at 0.5 kt
Complement: 3 (1 pilot, 2 observers)

Comment: Ex-*Alvin* built for operation by the Woods Hole Oceanographic Institution
for the Office of Naval Research. Original configuration had an operating depth of
6,000 ft. Named for Allyn C Vine of Woods Hole Oceanographic Institution. The vehicle
accidentally sank in 5,051 ft of water on 16 October 1968; subsequently raised in August
1969; refurbished 1970-71 in original configuration. Placed in service on Navy List 1 June
1971. Subsequently refitted with titanium pressure sphere to provide increased depth
capability and again operational in November 1973. She has two banks of lead acid
batteries, 120 V DC system with 47 kW/h capacity. Operating depth, 4,500 m *(14,764 ft)*.
Available to the navy for emergency use until 2010 but submersible is in continuous
operation in support of US science programmes. Conducted dive number 4,162 in
October 2005 before undergoing overhaul. The National Science Foundation is funding
a replacement, capable of depths of 6,500 m. This is expected to become operational
in 2010. Two other DSVs were placed out of service in 1997/98, one transferred to the
Woods Hole Institute.

DSV 2 *10/2003, Rod Catanach, Woods Hole Oceanographic Institution* / 0009310

1 NUCLEAR-POWERED OCEAN ENGINEERING AND RESEARCH VEHICLE (DSVN)

Name	Builders	In service	F/S
NR 1	General Dynamics (Electric Boat Div)	27 Oct 1969	ASA

Displacement, tons: 380 surfaced; 700 dived
Dimensions, feet (metres): 145.7 × 12.5 × 15.09 *(44.4 × 3.8 × 4.6)*
Main machinery: Nuclear; 1 PWR; 1 turbo-alternator; 2 motors (external to the hull);
   2 props; 4 ducted thrusters (2 vertical, 2 horizontal)
Speed, knots: 3.5 dived
Complement: 13 (3 officers, 2 scientists)

Comment: NR 1 was built primarily to serve as a test platform for a small nuclear propulsion
plant; however, the craft additionally provides an advanced deep submergence ocean
engineering and research capability. She was the only Naval deep submergence vehicle
to be used in the recovery of the wreckage of the space shuttle *Challenger* January to
April 1986. Laid down on 10 June 1967; launched on 25 January 1969. Commanded
by an officer-in-charge vice commanding officer. First nuclear-propelled service craft.
Overhauled and refuelled in 1993. Refitted with a new bow which extended her length
by 9.6 ft, and new sonars and cameras. In 1995 and again in 1997 she was used for an
archaeological survey of the Carthage-Ostia trade route. In 2002, conducted deep water
operations in Gulf of Mexico including study of *Mississippi Canyon* shipwreck site.
   The NR 1 has wheels beneath the hull to permit 'bottom crawling' and she is fitted
with external lights, external television cameras, a remote-controlled manipulator,
and various recovery devices. No periscopes, but fixed television mast. Diving depth,
3,000 ft *(914 m)*. A surface 'mother' ship is required to support her. Based at Groton,
Connecticut.

NR 1 *7/2000, H M Steele* / 0106816

AUXILIARIES

Notes: (1) The current plan is to be able to provide support in two regional crises
simultaneously. This plan is based on the availability of some storage depots on foreign
territory, and the use of Military Sealift Ships to carry fuels, munitions and the stores
from the USA or overseas sources for transfer to UNREP (Underway Replenishment)
ships in overseas areas. Some 16 to 18 UNREP ships are normally forward deployed in
the Mediterranean, Western Pacific and Indian Ocean areas in support of the 5th, 6th and
7th Fleets, respectively.
   Fleet support ships provide primarily maintenance and related towing and salvage
services at advanced bases and at ports in the USA. These ships normally do not provide
fuel, munitions, or other supplies except when ships are alongside for maintenance. Most
fleet support ships operate from bases in the USA.
   (2) A few underway replenishment ships and fleet support ships are Navy manned and
armed, but most are operated by the Military Sealift Command (MSC) with civilian crews
and are unarmed. The latter ships have T-prefix before their designations and are listed in
the MSC section.

2 SAFEGUARD CLASS: SALVAGE SHIPS (ARS)

Name	No	Builders	Commissioned	F/S
SAFEGUARD	ARS 50	Peterson Builders	16 Aug 1985	PA
SALVOR	ARS 52	Peterson Builders	14 June 1986	PA

Displacement, tons: 3,200 full load
Dimensions, feet (metres): 255 × 51 × 17 *(77.7 × 15.5 × 5.2)*
Main machinery: 4 Caterpillar diesels; 4,200 hp *(3.13 MW)*; 2 shafts; cp Kort nozzle props;
   bow thruster; 500 hp *(373 kW)*
Speed, knots: 14
Range, n miles: 8,000 at 12 kt
Complement: 99 (7 officers)
Guns: 2 — 25 mm Mk 38.
Radars: Navigation: SPS-64(V)9; I-band.

Comment: Prototype approved in FY81, two in FY82 and one in FY83. The procurement
of the fifth ARS was dropped on instructions from Congress. The design
follows conventional commercial and Navy criteria. Can support surface-supplied
diving operations to a depth of 58 m. Equipped with recompression chamber. Bollard
pull, 65.5 tons. Using beach extraction equipment the pull increases to 360 tons.
150 ton deadlift. ARS 51 transferred to the MSC on 19 January 2006 and ARS 53 in
July 2006. ARS 52 and 50 are scheduled to transfer in January and September 2007
respectively.

SALVOR *6/2004, Chris Sattler* / 1043628

2 EMORY S LAND CLASS: SUBMARINE TENDERS (ASH)

Name	No	Builders	Laid down	Launched	Commissioned	F/S
EMORY S LAND	AS 39	Lockheed SB & Construction Co, Seattle	2 Mar 1976	4 May 1977	7 July 1979	AA
FRANK CABLE	AS 40	Lockheed SB & Construction Co, Seattle	2 Mar 1976	14 Jan 1978	29 Oct 1979	PA

Displacement, tons: 13,911 standard; 22,978 full load
Dimensions, feet (metres): 643.8 × 85 × 28.5
 (196.2 × 25.9 × 8.7)
Main machinery: 2 Combustion Engineering boilers;
 620 psi *(43.6 kg/cm²)*; 860°F *(462°C)*; 1 De Laval turbine;
 20,000 hp *(14.9 MW)*; 1 shaft
Speed, knots: 20. **Range, n miles:** 10,000 at 12 kt
Complement: AS 39: 1,363 (97 officers); AS 40: 1,341
 (81 officers)
Guns: 4 Oerlikon 20 mm Mk 67
Radars: Navigation: ISC Cardion SPS-55; I/J-band
Helicopters: Platform only

Comment: The first US submarine tenders designed
 specifically for servicing nuclear-propelled attack
 submarines. Each ship can simultaneously provide
 services to four submarines moored alongside. Carry
 one 30 ton crane and two 5 ton mobile cranes. Have
 a 23 bed sick bay. *Frank Cable* is based at Guam and
 Emory S Land in the Mediterranean.

EMORY S LAND　　　　　　　　　　　　　　　　*4/1999, Jürg Kürsener* / 0084155

MINOR AUXILIARIES

Notes: As of January 2006, the US Navy had about 499 active and 9 inactive service
craft, primarily small craft, on the US Naval Vessel Register. A majority of these vessels
provide services to the fleet in various harbours and ports. Others are ocean-going
ships that provide services to the fleet for research purposes. Most of the service craft
are rated as 'active, in service', while others are rated as 'in commission' and some are
accommodation ships.

2 DIVING TENDERS (YDT)

YDT 17　　　　　　　　　　**YDT 18**

Displacement, tons: 275 full load
Dimensions, feet (metres): 132 × 27 × 6.0 *(40.2 × 8.2 × 1.8)*
Main machinery: 2 Caterpillar diesels; 2,600 hp *(1.91 MW)*; 2 Hamilton waterjets
Speed, knots: 20
Complement: 8 plus 7 divers

Comment: Tenders used to support shallow-water diving operations and are based at
Panama City, FL. Ordered from Swiftships in July 1997 and delivered in April 1999.

YDT 17　　　　　　　　　　　　　　　*8/1999, US Navy* / 0084159

23 PATROL CRAFT (YP)

YP 663	YP 665	YP 680-692	YP 694-698	YP 700-702

Displacement, tons: 167 full load
Dimensions, feet (metres): 108 × 24 × 8 *(32.9 × 7.3 × 2.4)*
Main machinery: 2 Detroit 12V-71 diesels; 680 hp *(507 kW)* sustained; 2 shafts
Speed, knots: 13.3
Range, n miles: 1,500 at 12 kt
Complement: 6 (2 officers) plus 24 midshipmen
Radars: Navigation: I-band.

Comment: Built in the 1980s by Peterson Builders and Marinette Marine, both in Wisconsin.
Twenty-one are based at the Naval Academy, Annapolis and two at Naval Underwater
Warfare Centre, Keyport, WA.

YP 683　　　　　　　　　　　　　*7/2000, Hachiro Nakai* / 0106812

2 CAPE FLATTERY CLASS (TORPEDO TRIALS CRAFT) (YTT)

BATTLE POINT YTT 10　　　　　　**DISCOVERY BAY** YTT 11

Displacement, tons: 1,168 full load
Dimensions, feet (metres): 186.5 × 40 × 10.5 *(56.9 × 12.2 × 3.2)*
Main machinery: 1 Cummins KTA50-M diesel; 1,250 hp *(932 kW)* sustained; 1 shaft; 1 bow
 thruster; 400 hp *(298 kW)*; 2 stern thrusters; 600 hp *(448 kW)*
Speed, knots: 11
Range, n miles: 1,000 at 10 kt
Complement: 31 plus 9 spare berths

Comment: Built by McDermott Shipyard, Morgan City, and delivered in 1991-92. Fitted
with two 21 in Mk 59 and three (one triple) 12.75 in Mk 32 Mod 5 torpedo tubes. Used
for torpedo trials and development at Keyport, Washington. A battery is fitted for limited
duration operations with the diesel shutdown. Both based at Naval Underwater Warfare
Centre, Keyport, WA.

YTT　　　　　　　　　　　*9/1999, van Ginderen Collection* / 0084162

14 TORPEDO RETRIEVERS (YPT)

Comment: Five different types spread around the Fleet bases and at AUTEC. There are
2 TRs × 65 ft (aluminium), 2 TRBs × 72 ft (wood), 4 TWRs × 85 ft (aluminium), 1 TWR × 82 ft
(aluminium) and 5 TWRs × 120 ft (steel).

TR 6　　　　　　　　　　　*7/2000, Sattler/Steele* / 0106813

FLOATING DRY DOCKS

Notes: The US Navy operates a limited number of floating dry docks to supplement dry
dock facilities at major naval activities. The larger floating dry docks are made sectional to
facilitate movement and to render them self-docking. Some of the ARD-type docks have
the forward end of their docking well closed by a structure resembling the bow of a ship
to facilitate towing. Berthing facilities, repair shops and machinery are housed in sides of
larger docks. None is self-propelled.

1 MEDIUM AUXILIARY FLOATING DRY DOCK (AFDM)

Name/No	Commissioned	Capacity (tons)	Construction	Status
AFDM 7	1945	13,500	Steel (3)	Active, Jacksonville, FL

Sales: AFDM 2 at Marad Reserve Fleet, Beaumont, Texas. To be donated or transferred
to Federal or State government or non-profit making organisation. AFDM 3 sold to
Bender Shipbuilding and Repair, Mobile, AL in 2002. AFDM 10 deactivated in Norfolk in
May 2004. AFDM 10 leased to Todd Shipyard, Seattle, WA in July 2005.

SMALL AUXILIARY FLOATING DRY DOCKS (AFDL)

Name/No	Completed	Capacity (tons)	Construction	Status
DYNAMIC (AFDL 6)	1944	950	Steel	Active, Norfolk, VA
ADEPT (AFDL 23)	1944	1,770	Steel	Commercial lease, Ingleside, TX
RELIANCE (AFDL 47)	1946	7,000	Steel	Commercial lease, Charleston, SC

Sales: AFDL 1 to Dominican Republic; 4, Brazil; 5, Taiwan; 11, Kampuchea; 20, Philippines; 22, Vietnam; 24, Philippines; 26, Paraguay; 28, Mexico; 33, Peru; 34 and 36, Taiwan; 39, Brazil; 40 and 44, Philippines.

DYNAMIC   *6/1986, Giorgio Arra* / 0506118

AUXILIARY REPAIR DRY DOCKS and MEDIUM AUXILIARY REPAIR DRY DOCKS (ARDM)

Name/No	Commissioned	Capacity (tons)	Construction	Status
SHIPPINGPORT (ARDM 4)	1979	7,800	Steel	Active, New London, CT
ARCO (ARDM 5)	1986	7,800	Steel	Active, San Diego, CA

Sales: ARD 2 to Mexico; 5, Chile; 6, Pakistan; 8, Peru; 9, Taiwan; 11, Mexico; 12, Turkey; 13, Venezuela; 14, Brazil; 15, Mexico; 17, Ecuador; 22 *(Windsor)*, Taiwan; 23, Argentina; 24, Ecuador; 25, Chile; 28, Colombia; 29, Iran; 32, Chile. ARDM 1 (ex-ARD 19) awaiting disposal decision.

ARCO   *8/2002, Hachiro Nakai* / 0530009

YARD FLOATING DRY DOCKS (YFD)

Name/No	Completed	Capacity (tons)	Construction	Status
YFD 70	1945	15,000	Steel (3)	Commercial lease, Seattle, WA
YFD 83 (ex-AFDL 31)	1943	1,000	Steel	Loan, US Coast Guard

UNCLASSIFIED MISCELLANEOUS (IX)

Notes: (1) In addition to the vessels listed below, one of the ex-Forrest Sherman class, *Decatur*, completed conversion on 21 October 1994 as a Self-Defence testing-ship, including high-energy laser trials. Tests with HFSWR (high-frequency surface wave radar) started mid-1997.
(2) *Mercer* APL 39 (ex-IX 502) and *Nueces* APL 40 (ex-IX 503) are barrack ships of mid-1940s vintage.
(3) IX 516 is a decommissioned SSBN used for propulsion plant training.
(4) IX 517 is a submarine sea trials escort vessel *(Gosport)*.
(5) IX 523 is used for security training, both at Norfolk, VA.
(6) IX 310 is an accommodation barge at Naval Undersea Warfare Center, Dresden, NJ.
(7) IX 521, IX 522 and IX 525 are individual drydock sections.
(8) IX 527 and IX 528 are submarine test platforms, IX 529 is a surface ship test platform and IX 531 a test platform for HM&E.
(9) IX 530 (ex-YFND 5) is a berthing barge.

IX 517   *7/2003, Declerck/Steeghers* / 1043688

1 CONSTITUTION CLASS (AXS)

Name	Builders	Launched	Under Way	F/S
CONSTITUTION	Edmund Hartt's Shipyard, Boston	21 Oct 1797	22 July 1798	AA

Displacement, tons: 2,250
Dimensions, feet (metres): 204 oa; 175 wl × 43.5 × 22.5 *(62.2; 53.3 × 13.2 × 6.8)*
Speed, knots: 13 under sail
Complement: 75 (4 officers)

Comment: The oldest ship remaining on the Navy List. One of six frigates authorised 27 March 1794. Best remembered for her service in the war of 1812, in which she earned the nickname 'Old Ironsides'. Following extensive restoration (1927-30), went on a three year goodwill tour around the United States (1931-34), travelling over 22,000 miles and receiving over 4 million visitors. Open to the public in her homeport of Boston, the ship receives over 400,000 visitors a year. The most recent overhaul was conducted at the Charlestown Navy Yard, Boston from 1992-96. Under fighting sails (jibs, topsails and spanker) *Constitution* sailed for the first time in 116 years on 21 July 1997 as part of her bicentennial celebration. Armament is 32 × 24 pounder guns, 20 × 32 pounder carronades and 2-24 pounder bow-chasers. Sail area 42,710 sq ft *(13,018 m²)*.

CONSTITUTION   *7/1997, Todd Stevens, US Navy* / 0016501

1 RESEARCH SHIP (YAGK)

Name	Builders	Commissioned
IX 515 (SES-200) (ex-USCG *Dorado*)	Bell Halter, New Orleans	Feb 1979

Displacement, tons: 205 full load
Dimensions, feet (metres): 159.1 × 39.0 × 9; 3 on cushion *(48.5 × 11.9 × 2.7; 0.9)*
Main machinery: 2 MTU 16V 396 TB94 diesels (propulsion); 5,800 hp(m) *(4.26 MW)* sustained; 2 Kamewa 71 water-jets
2 MTU 6V 396 TB83 diesels (lift); 1,560 hp(m) *(1.15 MW)* sustained
Speed, knots: 45
Range, n miles: 2,950 at 30 kt
Complement: 22 (2 officers)

Comment: The *IX 515* is a waterborne, air-supported craft with catamaran-style rigid sidewalls. It uses a cushion of air trapped between the sidewalls and flexible bow and stern seals to lift a large part of the hull clear of the water to reduce drag. A portion of the sidewall remains in the water to aid in stability and manoeuvrability. Modifications to the advanced ride control system were made in 1989. Serves as a high-performance test platform for weapon system development programmes, and as operational demonstrator for an advanced naval vehicle hullform. Trials of ALISS (Advanced Lightweight Influence Sweep System) in 1996-97. Based at Office of Naval Research, Arlington, VA.

IX 515   *9/1998, Findler & Winter* / 0053382

1 TRAINING SHIP (AXT)

Name	Builders	Commissioned
IX 514 (ex-YFU 79)	Pacific Coast Eng, Alameda	1968

Displacement, tons: 380 full load
Dimensions, feet (metres): 125 × 36 × 8.0 *(38.1 × 10.9 × 2.4)*
Main machinery: 4 GM 6-71 diesels; 696 hp *(519 kW)* sustained; 2 shafts
Speed, knots: 8
Radars: Navigation: Racal Decca; I-band.

Comment: Harbour utility craft converted in 1986 with a flight deck covering two thirds of the vessel and a new bridge and flight control position at the forward end. Used for basic helicopter flight training at Pensacola, Florida. Similar craft *IX 501* deleted.

IX 514 *12/1994, van Ginderen Collection* / 0506212

1 RESEARCH SHIP (AGE)

SLICE

Displacement, tons: 180 full load
Dimensions, feet (metres): 105 × 55.5 × 14 *(32 × 16.9 × 4.3)*
Main machinery: 2 MTU 16V 396 TB94 diesels; 13,700 hp(m) *(10.07 MW)*; 2 shafts; LIPS cp props
Speed, knots: 30
Complement: 12

Comment: Technology demonstrator built by Pacific Marine and owned by Lockheed Martin. Participated as a littoral warfare combatant in Fleet Battle Experiment Juliet (FBE-J) (part of Millennium Challenge 2002) accompanied by *Joint Venture* (HSV-X1). Modular capability packages, carried to simulate Littoral Combat Ship (LCS), included Mine Countermeasures (MCM), Antisubmarine Warfare (ASW), Force Protection and Time Critical Targeting. Weapons tested during FBE-J included the Lockheed Martin/Oerlikon Contraves 35 mm Millennium Gun and the NetFires System and launcher.

SLICE *10/2002, US Navy* / 0572739

TUGS

21 LARGE HARBOUR TUGS (YTB)

MUSKEGON	YTB 763	NEODESHA	YTB 815
KEOKUK	YTB 771	WANAMASSA	YTB 820
NIANTIC	YTB 781	CANONCHET	YTB 823
MANISTEE	YTB 782	SANTAQUIN	YTB 824
KITTANNING	YTB 787	CATAHECASSA	YTB 828
TUSKEGEE	YTB 806	DEKANAWIDA	YTB 831
MASSAPEQUA	YTB 807	PETALESHARO	YTB 832
WENATCHEE	YTB 808	NEWGAGON	YTB 834
ACCONAC	YTB 812	SKENANDOA	YTB 835
POUGHKEEPSIE	YTB 813	POKAGON	YTB 836
WAXAHACHIE	YTB 814		

Displacement, tons: 356 full load
Dimensions, feet (metres): 109 × 30 × 13.8 *(33.2 × 9.1 × 4.2)*
Main machinery: 1 Fairbanks-Morse 38D8-1/8 diesel; 2,000 hp *(1.49 MW)* sustained; 1 shaft
Speed, knots: 12
Range, n miles: 2,000 at 12 kt
Complement: 10–12
Radars: Navigation: Marconi LN66; I-band.

Comment: Built between 1959 and 1975. Two transferred to Saudi Arabia in 1975. Being withdrawn from service and tugs are being provided by MSC charter.

HARBOUR TUG *7/2004, US Navy* / 1043634

MILITARY SEALIFT COMMAND (MSC)

Notes: (1) The Military Sealift Command consists of the Naval Fleet Auxiliary Force, Special Missions Ships, Strategic Sealift Force and Prepositioning Programme.
(2) Headquarters are in the Washington Navy Yard, Washington DC. The organisation is commanded by a Vice Admiral, and its five principal area commands (Atlantic, Pacific, Europe, Far East, Central) by Navy Captains.
(3) MSC ships are assigned standard hull designations with the added prefix 'T'. All are unarmed and crewed by civilians. Ships' funnels have black, grey, blue and gold horizontal bands.

NAVAL FLEET AUXILIARY FORCE

15 HENRY J KAISER CLASS: OILERS (AOH)

Name	No	Builders	Laid down	Commissioned	F/S
HENRY J KAISER	T-AO 187	Avondale	22 Aug 1984	19 Dec 1986	TPA/ROS
JOSHUA HUMPHRIES	T-AO 188	Avondale	17 Dec 1984	3 Apr 1987	TAA/ROS
JOHN LENTHALL	T-AO 189	Avondale	15 July 1985	2 June 1987	TAA
WALTER S DIEHL	T-AO 193	Avondale	8 July 1986	13 Sep 1988	TPA
JOHN ERICSSON	T-AO 194	Avondale	15 Mar 1989	18 Mar 1991	TPA
LEROY GRUMMAN	T-AO 195	Avondale	7 June 1987	2 Aug 1989	TAA
KANAWHA	T-AO 196	Avondale	13 July 1989	6 Dec 1991	TAA
PECOS	T-AO 197	Avondale	17 Feb 1988	6 July 1990	TPA
BIG HORN	T-AO 198	Avondale	9 Oct 1989	31 July 1992	TAA
TIPPECANOE	T-AO 199	Avondale	19 Nov 1990	26 Mar 1993	TPA
GUADALUPE	T-AO 200	Avondale	9 July 1990	26 Oct 1992	TPA
PATUXENT	T-AO 201	Avondale	16 Oct 1991	21 June 1995	TAA
YUKON	T-AO 202	Avondale	13 May 1991	11 Dec 1993	TPA
LARAMIE	T-AO 203	Avondale	1 Oct 1994	24 May 1996	TAA
RAPPAHANNOCK	T-AO 204	Avondale	29 June 1992	7 Nov 1995	TPA

Displacement, tons: 40,700; 42,000 (T-AO 201, 203-204) full load
Dimensions, feet (metres): 677.5 × 97.5 × 36 *(206.5 × 29.7 × 10.9)*
Main machinery: 2 Colt-Pielstick 10 PC4.2 V 570 diesels; 34,422 hp(m) *(24.3 MW)* sustained; 2 shafts; cp props
Speed, knots: 20. **Range, n miles:** 6,000 at 18 kt
Complement: 81 civilian (18 officers); 23 naval (1 officer) plus 22 spare
Cargo capacity: 180,000; 159,500 (T-AO 201, 203-204) barrels of fuel oil or aviation fuel
Countermeasures: Decoys: SLQ-25 Nixie; towed torpedo decoy
Radars: Navigation: 2 Raytheon; I-band.
Helicopters: Platform only.

Comment: Construction was delayed initially by design difficulties, by excessive vibration at high speeds and other problems encountered in the first ship of the class. There are stations on both sides for underway replenishment of fuel and solids. Fitted with integrated electrical auxiliary propulsion. T-AOs 201, 203 and 204 were delayed by the decision to fit double hulls to meet the requirements of the Oil Pollution Act of 1990. This modification increased construction time from 32 to 42 months and reduced cargo capacity by 17 per cent although this can be restored in an emergency. Hull separation is 1.83 m at the sides and 1.98 m on the bottom. T-AOs 191 and 192 were transferred from Penn Ship (when the yard became bankrupt) to Tampa. Tampa's contract was also cancelled on 25 August 1993. Neither ship was completed. T-AO 187 is kept in reduced operating status on the west coast. T-AO 188 and 190 were laid up in mid-1996 and T-AO 189 in September 1997, but returned to service in January 1999. T-AO 188 returned to reduced operating status in April 2005.

JOHN LENTHALL *9/2003, Jürg Kürsener* / 0572793

GUADALUPE *3/2005*, Mick Prendergast* / 1154009

4 SUPPLY CLASS (FAST COMBAT SUPPORT SHIPS) (AOEH)

Name	No	Builder	Laid down	Launched	Commissioned	F/S
SUPPLY	T-AOE 6	National Steel & Shipbuilding Co	24 Feb 1989	6 Oct 1990	26 Feb 1994	AA
RAINIER	T-AOE 7	National Steel & Shipbuilding Co	31 May 1990	28 Sep 1991	21 Jan 1995	PA
ARCTIC	T-AOE 8	National Steel & Shipbuilding Co	2 Dec 1991	30 Oct 1993	16 Sep 1995	AA
BRIDGE	T-AOE 10	National Steel & Shipbuilding Co	16 Sep 1993	25 Aug 1996	5 Aug 1998	PA

Displacement, tons: 19,700 light; 49,000 full load
Dimensions, feet (metres): 753.7 × 107 × 38 (229.7 × 32.6 × 11.6)
Main machinery: 4 GE LM 2500 gas turbines; 105,000 hp (78.33 MW) sustained; 2 shafts
Speed, knots: 30. **Range, n miles:** 6,000 at 22 kt
Complement: 160 civilian; 28 military
Cargo capacity: 156,000 barrels of fuel; 1,800 tons ammunition; 400 tons refrigerated cargo; 250 tons general cargo; 20,000 gallons water
Helicopters: 2 MH-60

Comment: Construction started in June 1988. *Supply* decommissioned and transferred to MSC in July 2001, *Arctic* in June 2002, *Rainier* in August 2003 and *Bridge* in June 2004.

RAINIER   *8/2004, Hachiro Nakai* / 1043691

0 + 9 (3) LEWIS AND CLARK CLASS
(DRY CARGO/AMMUNITION SHIPS) (AKEH)

Name	No	Builders	Launched	Commissioned
LEWIS AND CLARK	T-AKE 1	National Steel & Shipbuilding Co	21 May 2005	2006
SACAGAWEA	T-AKE 2	National Steel & Shipbuilding Co	2006	2006
ALAN SHEPARD	T-AKE 3	National Steel & Shipbuilding Co	2006	2007
—	T-AKE 4	National Steel & Shipbuilding Co	2007	2007
—	T-AKE 5	National Steel & Shipbuilding Co	2008	2007
—	T-AKE 6	National Steel & Shipbuilding Co	2008	2008
—	T-AKE 7	National Steel & Shipbuilding Co	2008	2009
—	T-AKE 8	National Steel & Shipbuilding Co	2008	2009
—	T-AKE 9	National Steel & Shipbuilding Co	2008	2009

Displacement, tons: 24,833 light; 41,592 full load
Dimensions, feet (metres): 689.0 × 107.9 × 29.8 (210.0 × 32.2 × 9.1)
Main machinery: Integrated electric propulsion; 4 FM/MAN B&W 9L and 8L 48/60 diesel generators (35.7 MW); 2 Alstom motors; 1 shaft; fixed pitch prop; bow thruster
Speed, knots: 20. **Range, n miles:** 14,000 at 20 kt
Complement: 197 (49 officers)
Cargo capacity: 3,442 tons fuel; 200 tons potable water; 6,675 dry cargo; 1,716 tons refrigerated stores
Countermeasures: AN/SLQ-25 towed torpedo decoy.
Radars: Decca BridgeMaster; I-band.
Helicopters: 2 UH-46D/MH-60.

Comment: Design and construction contract placed on 18 October 2001 for delivery of first and second vessels in 2005. Contract for construction of the third of class in July 2002 and for the fourth in July 2003. A further two were ordered in January 2004 and two more on 11 January 2005. A ninth ship was ordered on 30 January 2006. The ships are being built to commercial standards to replace existing AE and AFS. Three RAS stations are to be fitted each side.

LEWIS AND CLARK   *11/2005*, Brian Gauvin* / 1154058

3 MARS CLASS: COMBAT STORE SHIPS (AFSH)

Name	No	Builders	Commissioned	F/S
NIAGARA FALLS	T-AFS 3	National Steel & Shipbuilding Co	29 Apr 1967	TPA
CONCORD	T-AFS 5	National Steel & Shipbuilding Co	27 Nov 1968	TPA
SAN JOSE	T-AFS 7	National Steel & Shipbuilding Co	23 Oct 1970	TPA

Displacement, tons: 9,200 light; 15,900 – 18,663 full load
Dimensions, feet (metres): 581 × 79 × 26 (177.1 × 24.1 × 7.9)
Main machinery: 3 Babcock & Wilcox boilers; 580 psi (40.8 kg/cm²); 825°F (440°C); 1 De Laval turbine (Westinghouse in AFS 6); 22,000 hp (16.4 MW); 1 shaft
Speed, knots: 20. **Range, n miles:** 10,000 at 18 kt
Complement: 123-134 civilians plus 29-49 naval
Cargo capacity: 2,625 tons dry stores; 1,300 tons refrigerated stores (varies with specific loadings)
Radars: Navigation: 2 Raytheon; I-band.
Tacan: URN 25.
Helicopters: 2 MH-60.

Comment: *Concord* transferred to MSC on 15 October 1992 after disarming and conversion to a civilian crew. *San Jose* followed on 2 November 1993 and *Niagara Falls* on 23 September 1994. All have accommodation improvements and stores lifts installed. These ships carry comprehensive inventories of aviation spare parts as well as the cargo listed above. Two others of the class de-activated in 1997.

SAN JOSE   *4/2001, Mick Prendergast* / 0131281

5 KILAUEA CLASS: AMMUNITION SHIPS (AEH)

Name	No	Builders	Commissioned	F/S
KILAUEA	T-AE 26	General Dynamics, Quincy	10 Aug 1968	TAA/ROS
FLINT	T-AE 32	Ingalls Shipbuilding	20 Nov 1971	TPA
SHASTA	T-AE 33	Ingalls Shipbuilding	26 Feb 1972	TPA
MOUNT BAKER	T-AE 34	Ingalls Shipbuilding	22 July 1972	TAA
KISKA	T-AE 35	Ingalls Shipbuilding	16 Dec 1972	TPA

Displacement, tons: 9,340 light; 19,940 full load
Dimensions, feet (metres): 564 × 81 × 28 (171.9 × 24.7 × 8.5)
Main machinery: 3 Foster-Wheeler boilers; 600 psi (42.3 kg/cm²); 870°F (467°C); 1 GE turbine; 22,000 hp (16.4 MW); 1 shaft
Speed, knots: 20
Range, n miles: 10,000 at 18 kt
Complement: 133 civilians
Radars: Navigation: 2 Raytheon; I-band.
Tacan: URN 25.
Helicopters: 2 CH-46E Sea Knight (cargo normally embarked).

Comment: *Kilauea* transferred to MSC 1 October 1980, *Flint* in August 1995, *Kiska* in August 1996, *Mount Baker* in December 1996, *Shasta* in October 1997 and *Santa Barbara* in September 1998. An eighth of class was to have transferred in 1999, but has been decommissioned. *Butte* decommissioned in 2002 and *Santa Barbara* in 2005. Ships underwent a civilian modification overhaul during which accommodation was improved. Main armament taken out. Seven UNREP stations operational: four port, three starboard. *Kilauea* (Port Hueneme, CA) is kept in reduced operating status.

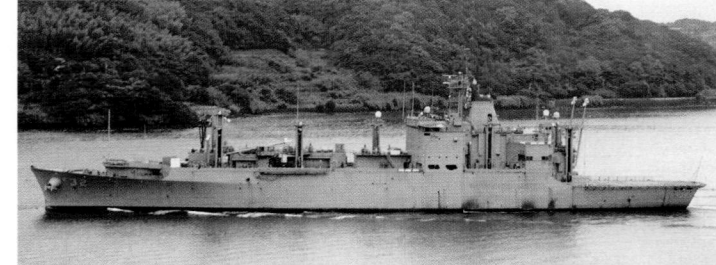

FLINT   *8/2005*, Hachiro Nakai* / 1154008

2 SIRIUS (LYNESS) CLASS: COMBAT STORES SHIP (AFSH)

Name	No	Builders	Commissioned	F/S
SPICA (ex-*Tarbatness*)	T-AFS 9	Swan Hunter & Wigham Richardson Ltd, Wallsend-on-Tyne	21 Mar 1967	TAA
SATURN (ex-*Stromness*)	T-AFS 10	Swan Hunter & Wigham Richardson Ltd, Wallsend-on-Tyne	10 Aug 1967	TAA

Displacement, tons: 9,010 light; 16,792 full load
Measurement, tons: 7,782 dwt; 12,359 gross; 4,744 net
Dimensions, feet (metres): 524 × 72 × 22 (159.7 × 22 × 6.7)
Main machinery: 1 Wallsend-Sulzer 8RD76 diesel; 11,520 hp (8.59 MW); 1 shaft
Speed, knots: 18
Range, n miles: 12,000 at 16 kt
Complement: 108-119 civilians plus 29-49 naval
Cargo capacity: 8,313 m³ dry; 3,921 m³ frozen
Radars: Navigation: 2 Raytheon; I-band.
Tacan: URN 25.
Helicopters: 2 MH-60.

Comment: *Spica* purchased from the UK on 30 September 1982 and *Saturn* on 1 October 1983. Refitted from August 1992-96 to improve communications, RAS facilities and cargo handling equipment. *Sirius* decommissioned in 2005.

SIRIUS CLASS   *7/2002, John Chaney* / 0529970

1 HIGH SPEED LOGISTIC SUPPORT VESSEL (HSV/MCS)

SWIFT HSV-2

Displacement, tons: 1,800
Dimensions, feet (metres): 321.5 × 87.3 × 10.8 *(98.0 × 26.6 × 3.3)*
Main machinery: 4 CAT 3618 diesels; 38,620 hp *(28.8 MW)*; 4 LIPS 150D waterjets
Speed, knots: 48 (light); 38 (full load)
Range, n miles: 2,400 at 35 kt
Complement: 42
Military lift: 680 tons cargo and 250 personnel
Guns: 1 Mk 96 25 mm.
Helicopters: Platform for AH-1, MH/SH-60, UH-1 or CH-46.

Comment: Built as *Incat 61* (Incat Evolution 10B) of aluminium construction and leased for one year (with option to extend until 2008) by Military Sealift Command from Bollinger/Incat of Lockport, Louisiana from June 2003. The ship is utilised as a platform to conduct trials and exercises required by the Navy Warfare Development Command. A stern ramp, loading directly astern or to the starboard quarter, is to be fitted. It will be capable of loading/unloading vehicles up to and including main battle tanks. The ramp will also be capable of launch and recovery of assault vehicles. A protected area for the storage and maintenance of two MH-60S helicopters will also be provided. *Swift* was involved in tsunami and hurricane Katrina relief operations and has participated in numerous exercises.

SWIFT   *2/2004, US Navy* / 1043637

3 VICTORIOUS CLASS: OCEAN SURVEILLANCE SHIPS (AGOS)

Name	No	Builders	Commissioned	F/S
VICTORIOUS	T-AGOS 19	McDermott Marine	5 Sep 1991	TPA
EFFECTIVE	T-AGOS 21	McDermott Marine	27 Jan 1993	TPA
LOYAL	T-AGOS 22	McDermott Marine	1 July 1993	TAA

Displacement, tons: 3,396 full load
Dimensions, feet (metres): 234.5 × 93.6 × 24.8 *(71.5 × 28.5 × 7.6)*
Main machinery: Diesel-electric; 4 Caterpillar 3512TA diesels; 5,440 hp *(4 MW)* sustained; 2 GE motors; 3,200 hp *(2.39 MW)*; 2 shafts; 2 bow thrusters; 2,400 hp *(1.79 MW)*
Speed, knots: 16; 3 when towing
Complement: 22 civilian plus 5 Navy
Radars: Navigation: 2 Raytheon; I-band.
Sonars: SURTASS and LFA; towed array; passive/active surveillance.

Comment: All of SWATH design because of its greater stability at slow speeds in high latitudes under adverse weather conditions. A contract for the first SWATH ship, T-AGOS 19, was awarded in November 1986, and options for a further three were exercised in October 1988. T-AGOS 20 deactivated in July 2003.

EFFECTIVE   *7/2004, Michael Nitz* / 1043635

1 JOHN McDONNELL CLASS: SURVEYING SHIP (AGS)

Name	No	Builders	Commissioned	F/S
JOHN McDONNELL	T-AGS 51	Halter Marine	16 Dec 1991	TPA

Displacement, tons: 2,054 full load
Dimensions, feet (metres): 208 × 45 × 14 *(63.4 × 13.7 × 4.3)*
Main machinery: 1 GM EMD 12-645E6 diesel; 2,550 hp *(1.9 MW)* sustained; 1 auxiliary diesel; 230 hp *(172 kW)*; 1 shaft
Speed, knots: 12
Range, n miles: 13,800 at 12 kt
Complement: 22 civilians plus 11 scientists

Comment: Laid down on 3 August 1989 and launched on 15 August 1990. Carry 34 ft survey launches for data collection in coastal regions with depths between 10 and 600 m and in deep water to 4,000 m. A small diesel is used for propulsion at towing speeds of up to 6 kt. Simrad high-frequency active hull-mounted and side scan sonars are carried. *Littlehales* was deactivated in March 2003 and transferred to NOAA.

JOHN McDONNELL   *8/2004, Hachiro Nakai* / 1043695

6 PATHFINDER CLASS: SURVEYING SHIPS (AGS)

Name	No	Builders	Launched	Commissioned	F/S
PATHFINDER	T-AGS 60	Halter Marine	7 Oct 1993	5 Dec 1994	TAA
SUMNER	T-AGS 61	Halter Marine	19 May 1994	30 May 1995	TPA
BOWDITCH	T-AGS 62	Halter Marine	15 Oct 1994	30 Dec 1995	TPA
HENSON	T-AGS 63	Halter Marine	21 Oct 1996	20 Feb 1998	TAA
BRUCE C HEEZEN	T-AGS 64	Halter Marine	17 Dec 1998	13 Jan 2000	TAA
MARY SEARS	T-AGS 65	Halter Marine	19 Oct 2000	17 Dec 2001	TAA

Displacement, tons: 4,762 full load
Dimensions, feet (metres): 328.5 × 58 × 19 *(100.1 × 17.7 × 5.8)*
Main machinery: Diesel-electric; 4 EMD/Baylor diesel generators; 11,425 hp *(8.52 MW)*; 2 GE CDF 1944 motors; 8,000 hp *(5.97 MW)* sustained; 6,000 hp *(4.48 MW)*; 2 LIPS Z drives; bow thruster; 1,500 hp *(1.19 MW)*
Speed, knots: 16. **Range, n miles:** 12,000 at 12 kt
Complement: 24 civilians plus 27 oceanographers

Comment: Contract awarded in January 1991 for two ships with an option for a third which was taken up on 29 May 1992. A fourth ship was ordered in October 1994 with an option for two more. Fifth ordered 15 January 1997 and sixth on 6 January 1999. There are three multipurpose cranes and five winches plus a variety of oceanographic equipment including multibeam echo-sounders, towed sonars and expendable sensors. ROVs may be carried.

BRUCE C HEEZEN   *8/2004, Hachiro Nakai* / 1043693

HENSON   *8/2002, John Brodie* / 0530035

STRATEGIC SEALIFT FORCE

Notes: These ships provide ocean transportation for Defense and other government agencies. As well as those listed below, MSC also contracts additional tankers and dry cargo ships as needed. As a result these numbers vary with the operational requirement.

2 SHUGHART CLASS:
LARGE, MEDIUM-SPEED, RO-RO (LMSR) SHIPS (AKR)

Name	No	Commissioned	F/S
SHUGHART (ex-*Laura Maersk*)	T-AKR 295	7 May 1996	TWWR
YANO (ex-*Leise Maersk*)	T-AKR 297	8 Feb 1997	TWWR

Measurement, tons: 54,298 grt
Dimensions, feet (metres): 906.8 × 105.5 × 34.4 *(276.4 × 32.2 × 10.5)*
Main machinery: 1 Burmeister & Wain 12L90 GFCA diesel; 46,653 hp(m) *(34.29 MW)*; 1 shaft; bow and stern thrusters
Speed, knots: 24. **Range, n miles:** 12,000 at 24 kt
Complement: 21-44 civilian; up to 50 Navy
Cargo capacity: 255,064 sq ft plus 47,023 sq ft deck cargo
Radars: Navigation: 2 Sperry ARPA; I-band.

Comment: Both were container ships built in Denmark in 1981 and lengthened by Hyundai in 1987. Conversion contract awarded to National Steel and Shipbuilding in July 1993. Both fitted with a stern slewing ramp, side accesses and cranes for both roll-on/roll-off and lift-on/lift-off capabilities. Two twin 57 ton cranes. Conversion for *Shughart* started in June 1994; *Yano* in May 1995; *Soderman* underwent conversion to maritime prepositioning ship and renamed *Stockham*.

YANO   *11/2004, Frank Findler* / 1043692

8 ALGOL CLASS: FAST SEALIFT SHIPS (AKRH)

Name	No	Builders	Delivered
ALGOL	T-AKR 287	Rotterdamsche DD Mij NV, Rotterdam	7 May 1973
(ex-SS *Sea-Land Exchange*)			
BELLATRIX	T-AKR 288	Rheinstahl Nordseewerke, Emden, West Germany	6 Apr 1973
(ex-SS *Sea-Land Trade*)			
DENEBOLA	T-AKR 289	Rotterdamsche DD Mij NV, Rotterdam	4 Dec 1973
(ex-SS *Sea-Land Resource*)			
POLLUX	T-AKR 290	A G Weser, Bremen, West Germany	20 Sep 1973
(ex-SS *Sea-Land Market*)			
ALTAIR	T-AKR 291	Rheinstahl Nordseewerke, Emden, West Germany	17 Sep 1973
(ex-SS *Sea-Land Finance*)			
REGULUS	T-AKR 292	A G Weser, Bremen, West Germany	30 Mar 1973
(ex-SS *Sea-Land Commerce*)			
CAPELLA	T-AKR 293	Rotterdamsche DD Mij NV, Rotterdam	4 Oct 1972
(ex-SS *Sea-Land McLean*)			
ANTARES	T-AKR 294	A G Weser, Bremen, West Germany	27 Sep 1972
(ex-SS *Sea-Land Galloway*)			

Displacement, tons: 55,355 full load
Measurement, tons: 25,389 net; 27,051-28,095 dwt
Dimensions, feet (metres): 946.2 × 105.6 × 36.8 *(288.4 × 32.2 × 11.2)*
Main machinery: 2 Foster-Wheeler boilers; 875 psi *(61.6 kg/cm²)*; 950°F *(510°C)*; 2 GE MST-19 steam turbines; 120,000 hp *(89.5 MW)*; 2 shafts
Speed, knots: 33. **Range, n miles:** 12,200 at 27 kt
Complement: 43 (as merchant ship); 29 (minimum); 15 (ROS)
Helicopters: Platform only.

Comment: All were originally built as container ships for Sea-Land Services, Port Elizabeth, NJ, but used too much fuel to be cost-effective as merchant ships. Six ships of this class were approved for acquisition in FY81 and the remaining two in FY82. The purchase price included 4,000 containers and 800 container chassis for use in container ship configuration. All eight were converted to Fast Sealift Ships, which are vehicle cargo ships. Conversion included the addition of roll-on/roll-off features. The area between the forward and after superstructures allows for a helicopter flight deck. Capacities are as follows: (sq ft) 150,016 to 166,843 ro-ro; 43,407 lift-on/lift-off; and either 44 or 46 20 ft containers. In addition to one ro-ro ramp port and starboard, twin 35 ton pedestal cranes are installed between the deckhouses and twin 50 ton cranes are installed aft. Ninety-three per cent of a US Army mechanised division can be lifted using all eight ships. Seven of the class moved nearly 11 per cent of all the cargo transported between the US and Saudi Arabia during and after the Gulf War. Six were activated for the Somalian operation in December 1992 and all have been used in various operations and exercises since then. All based in Atlantic and Gulf of Mexico ports.

DENEBOLA   *2/2005*, Robert Pabst* / 1154010

7 BOB HOPE CLASS:
LARGE, MEDIUM-SPEED, RO-RO (LMSR) SHIPS (AKR)

Name	No	Builders	Launched	Commissioned	F/S
BOB HOPE	T-AKR 300	Avondale	27 Mar 1997	18 Nov 1998	TWWR
FISHER	T-AKR 301	Avondale	21 Oct 1997	4 Aug 1999	TWWR
SEAY	T-AKR 302	Avondale	25 June 1998	30 Mar 2000	TWWR
MENDONCA	T-AKR 303	Avondale	25 May 1999	30 Jan 2001	TWWR
PILILAAU	T-AKR 304	Avondale	18 Jan 2000	24 July 2001	TWWR
BRITTIN	T-AKR 305	Avondale	21 Oct 2000	11 July 2002	TWWR
BENAVIDEZ	T-AKR 306	Avondale	11 Aug 2001	10 Sep 2003	TWWR

Displacement, tons: 61,680 full load
Dimensions, feet (metres): 948.9 × 106 × 35 *(289.1 × 32.3 × 11)*
Main machinery: 4 Colt Pielstick 10 PC4.2 V diesels; 65,160 hp(m) *(47.89 MW)*; 2 shafts; cp props
Speed, knots: 24. **Range, n miles:** 12,000 at 24 kt
Complement: 26-45 civilian; up to 50 Navy
Cargo capacity: 317,510 sq ft plus 70,152 sq ft deck cargo

Comment: Contract awarded in 1993; options for additional ships exercised in 1994, 1995, 1996 and 1997. All fitted with a stern slewing ramp, side accesses and cranes for both roll-on/roll-off and lift-on/lift-off capabilities. Ramps extend to 130 ft *(40 m)* and two twin 55 ton cranes are installed.

SEAY   *3/2005*, Robert Pabst* / 1154011

2 GORDON CLASS:
LARGE, MEDIUM-SPEED, RO-RO (LMSR) SHIPS (AKR)

Name	No	Commissioned	F/S
GORDON (ex-*Selandia*)	T-AKR 296	23 Aug 1996	TWWR
GILLILAND (ex-*Jutlandia*)	T-AKR 298	24 May 1997	TWWR

Measurement, tons: 55,422 grt
Dimensions, feet (metres): 956 × 105.8 × 36.3 *(291.4 × 32.2 × 11.9)*
Main machinery: 1 Burmeister & Wain 12K84EF diesel; 26,000 hp(m) *(19.11 MW)*; 2 Burmeister & Wain 9K84EF diesels; 39,000 hp(m) *(28.66 MW)*; 3 shafts (centre cp prop); bow thruster
Speed, knots: 24. **Range, n miles:** 12,000 at 24 kt
Complement: 21 civilian; 50 Navy
Cargo capacity: 276,109 sq ft plus 45,722 sq ft deck cargo
Radars: Navigation: 2 Sperry ARPA; I-band.

Comment: Built in Denmark in 1972 and lengthened by Hyundai in 1984. Conversion contract given to Newport News Shipbuilding on 30 July 1993. Both fitted with a stern slewing ramp, side accesses and improved craneage. Conversion started for both ships on 15 October 1993.

GILLILAND   *2/2000, A Sharma* / 0085304

4 CHAMPION CLASS (TANKERS) (AOT/AOR)

Name	No	Builders	Commissioned
PAUL BUCK	T-AOT 1122	American SB Co, Tampa, FL	7 June 1985
SAMUEL L COBB	T-AOT 1123	American SB Co, Tampa, FL	15 Nov 1985
RICHARD G MATTHIESEN	T-AOT 1124	American SB Co, Tampa, FL	18 Feb 1986
LAWRENCE H GIANELLA	T-AOT 1125	American SB Co, Tampa, FL	22 Apr 1986

Displacement, tons: 39,624 full load
Dimensions, feet (metres): 615 × 90 × 36 *(187.5 × 27.4 × 10.8)*
Main machinery: 1 Sulzer 5RTA76 diesel; 18,400 hp(m) *(13.52 MW)* sustained; 1 shaft
Speed, knots: 16
Range, n miles: 12,000 at 16 kt
Complement: 23 (9 officers)
Cargo capacity: 238,400 barrels of oil fuel

Comment: Built for Ocean Carriers Inc, Houston, Texas specifically for long-term time charter to the Military Sealift Command (20 years) as Point-to-Point fuel tankers. Purchased by the US Navy in 2003 and designated USNS. The last two are equipped with a modular fuel delivery system to allow them to rig underway replenishment gear.

LAWRENCE H GIANELLA   *1/2002, A Sharma* / 0530036

PREPOSITIONING PROGRAMME

Notes: (1) Military Sealift Command's Afloat Prepositioning Force (APF) improves US capabilities to deploy forces rapidly to any area of conflict. The force includes long-term chartered commercial vessels, activated Ready Reserve Force ships and government ships and includes vehicle/cargo carriers, container ships, aviation logistics ships and Large, Medium-Speed, Roll-on/roll-off (LMSR) ships. Together these ships preposition equipment and supplies for the Marine Corps, Navy, Army, Air Force and the Defense Logistics Agency. The APF comprises: the Maritime Prepositioning Force (MPF), Logistics Prepositioning Ships (LPS) and Combat Prepositioning Ships (CPS).
(2) The MPF operate in forward-deployed squadrons: Squadron One is located in the Mediterranean, Squadron Two at Diego Garcia and Squadron Three in the Western Pacific. 16 ships are loaded with equipment and supplies for the US Marine Corps.
(3) Nine LPS are loaded with US Air Force and Navy ammunition and Defense Logistics Agency Petroleum products, while two are aviation logistic ships serving as USMC intermediate maintenance facilities.
(4) The 10 CPS preposition equipment and supplies for a US Army heavy brigade and combat support/combat service support elements.
(5) Maritime Prepositioning Force (Future): the US Navy's Seabasing initiative, in which manoeuvre forces are supported by logistics and combat fire support in staging bases in or near the theatre of operations, is under development. This is likely to require a variety of platforms that can assemble offshore and redeploy quickly. It is envisaged that a seabase would comprise an Expeditionary Strike Group (ESG), a Carrier Strike Group (CSG), and a Maritime Prepositioning Group (MPG) supported by a Combat Logistics Force. Various classes of Maritime Prepositioning Force (Future) ships are to be capable of selectively offloading containerised loads and other equipment. Large deck areas suitable for flight operations are also necessary. MPF(F) could additionally assume some of the roles planned for the JCC(X) future command and control ship. Other potential applications of the MPF(F) include acting as intra-theatre shuttles, afloat medical care and mine-countermeasures support. Some 18 vessels are required and construction of the first ship could begin in FY12.
(6) Army Strategic Flotillas (ASF): The updated US Army prepositioning plan calls for the deployment of five ASFs. Three ASFs would be composed of LMSRs carrying a heavy brigade combat team and the remaining two would each contain LMSRs carrying sustainment supplies plus an ammunition ship and a warehouse ship. ASFs will be based around Guam and Saipan in the Pacific Ocean, Diego Garcia in the Indian Ocean and in the Mediterranean.

1 HEAVY LIFT VESSEL (HSV)

WESTPAC EXPRESS

Measurement, tons: 750 dwt
Dimensions, feet (metres): 331.4 × 87.4 × 13.8 *(101.0 × 26.65 × 4.2)*
Main machinery: 4 Caterpillar 3618 diesels; 38,620 hp *(28.8 MW)*; 4 Kamewa waterjets
Speed, knots: 40. **Range, n miles:** 1,100 at 35 kt
Military lift: 550 tonnes of equipment and 970 personnel

Comment: Following trials which started in July 2001, chartered by Military Sealift Command from Austal Ships, West Australia. The current charter expires on 14 February 2007. Aluminium construction. Employed by US Marine Corps Third Expeditionary Force (III MEF) to transport equipment and troops from Okinawa for training exercises in Yokohama, Guam and other regional destinations. The benefits include reduced dependence on and cost of airlift. The vessel will retain commercial livery and markings. Based at Okinawa.

WESTPAC EXPRESS   *8/2001, Mitsuhiro Kadota* / 0131282

1 CONTAINER SHIP (AK)

Name	No	Builders	Commissioned	F/S
A1C WILLIAM H PITSENBARGER	T-AK 4638	Chantiers de l'Atlantique, St Nazaire	28 Nov 2001	PREPO

Displacement, tons: 31,986 full load
Dimensions, feet (metres): 621.3 × 105.6 × 37.5 *(189.3 × 32.2 × 11.4)*
Main machinery: 1 Sulzer 7RLB 66 reversible diesel; one shaft
Speed, knots: 17.5. **Range, n miles:** 16,800 at 13 kt
Complement: 17
Cargo capacity: 1,670 TEU (808 under deck)

Comment: Completed in 1984. Chartered by MSC in October 2001 as an LPS ship to carry Air Force munitions in Guam/Saipan. Reflagged and renamed. Owned by RR and VO LCC and operated by Red River Shipping Corporation.

A1C WILLIAM H PITSENBARGER   *6/2003, US Navy* / 0572807

1 RO-RO CONTAINER: CARGO SHIP (AK)

Name	No	Builders	Commissioned	F/S
TSGT JOHN A CHAPMAN (ex-*Merlin*)	AK 323	Chantiers, France	1978	PREPO

Displacement, tons: 26,378 full load
Dimensions, feet (metres): 669.8 × 86.9 × 34.5 *(204.1 × 26.5 × 10.5)*
Main machinery: Pielstick medium speed diesel; 1 shaft
Speed, knots: 16. **Range, n miles:** 23,200 at 13 kt
Complement: 19
Cargo capacity: 1,066 TEU

Comment: The ship is owned and operated by Sealift, Inc and is under charter to Military Sealift Command. Acquired in 2002. The ship can carry more than 1,000 20 ft container equivalents of aviation munitions and serves as an LPS ship.

TSGT JOHN A CHAPMAN   *6/2003, US Navy* / 0572808

8 WATSON CLASS:
LARGE, MEDIUM-SPEED, RO-RO (LMSR) SHIPS (AKR)

Name	No	Builders	Launched	Commissioned	F/S
WATSON	T-AKR 310	NASSCO	26 July 1997	23 June 1998	PREPO
SISLER	T-AKR 311	NASSCO	28 Feb 1998	1 Dec 1998	PREPO
DAHL	T-AKR 312	NASSCO	2 Oct 1998	13 July 1999	PREPO
RED CLOUD	T-AKR 313	NASSCO	7 Aug 1999	18 Jan 2000	PREPO
CHARLTON	T-AKR 314	NASSCO	11 Dec 1999	23 May 2000	PREPO
WATKINS	T-AKR 315	NASSCO	28 July 2000	5 Dec 2000	PREPO
POMEROY	T-AKR 316	NASSCO	10 Mar 2001	14 Aug 2001	PREPO
SODERMAN	T-AKR 317	NASSCO	26 Apr 2002	25 Sep 2002	PREPO

Displacement, tons: 62,968 full load
Dimensions, feet (metres): 951.4 × 106 × 35 *(290 × 32.3 × 11)*
Main machinery: 2 GE Marine LM gas turbines; 64,000 hp *(47.7 MW)*; 2 shafts; cp props
Speed, knots: 24. **Range, n miles:** 12,000 at 22 kt
Complement: 26-45 civilian; up to 50 Navy
Cargo capacity: 394,673 sq ft. 13,000 tons

Comment: Contract awarded in 1993; options for additional ships exercised at one a year to 2002. All are fitted with a stern slewing ramp, side accesses and cranes for both roll-on/roll-off and lift-on/lift-off capabilities. Ramps extend to 130 ft *(40 m)*, and two twin 55 ton cranes are installed. Serve as Combat Prepositioning Ships.

SODERMAN   *5/2003, A Sharma* / 0572811

2 T-AVB 3 CLASS: AVIATION LOGISTIC SHIPS (AVB)

Name	No	Builders	Commissioned	F/S
WRIGHT (ex-SS *Young America*)	T-AVB 3	Ingalls Shipbuilding	1970	PREPO/ROS
CURTISS (ex-SS *Great Republic*)	T-AVB 4	Ingalls Shipbuilding	1969	PREPO/ROS

Displacement, tons: 23,872 full load
Measurement, tons: 11,757 gross; 6,850 net; 15,946 dwt
Dimensions, feet (metres): 602 × 90.2 × 29.8 *(183.5 × 27.5 × 9.1)*
Main machinery: 2 Combustion Engineering boilers; 2 GE turbines; 30,000 hp *(22.4 MW)*; 1 shaft
Speed, knots: 20. **Range, n miles:** 11,000 at 20 kt
Complement: 38 crew and 1 Aircraft Maintenance Detachment totalling 363 men

Comment: To reinforce the capabilities of the Maritime Prepositioning Ship programme, conversion of two ro-ro ships into maintenance aviation support ships was approved in FY85 and FY86. *Wright* was completed 14 May 1986, *Curtiss* 18 August 1987. Both conversions took place at Todd Shipyards, Galveston, Texas. Each ship has side ports and three decks aft of the bridge superstructure and has the capability to load the vans and equipment of a Marine Aviation Intermediate Maintenance Activity. The ships' mission is to service aircraft from an afloat platform. They can then revert to a standard sealift role if required. Maritime Administration hull design is C5-S-78a. These Logistics Prepositioning Ships are operated by Crowley Liner Services and maintained in a reduced operating status.

WRIGHT   *4/2003, A Sharma* / 0572752

1 CONTAINER SHIP (AK)

Name	No	Builders	Commissioned	F/S
MAJ BERNARD F FISHER (ex-*Sea Fox*)	T-AK 4396	Odense	1985	PREPO

Displacement, tons: 48,012 full load
Dimensions, feet (metres): 652.2 × 105.6 × 36.1 *(198.1 × 32.2 × 11)*
Main machinery: 1 BMW diesel; 1 shaft
Speed, knots: 19
Complement: 24
Cargo capacity: 1,466 TEUs with 10,227 sq ft garage space for ro-ro cargo

Comment: An LPS ship owned and operated by Sealift, Inc. Acquired in 1998, it is used to preposition US Air Force war stocks at sea.

MAJ BERNARD F FISHER   *6/1999, US Navy* / 0084185

2 CONTAINER SHIPS (AK)

Name	No	Builders	Commissioned	F/S
LTC JOHN U D PAGE (ex-*Newark Bay*)	T-AK 4543	Daewoo Shipbuilding	1985	PREPO
SSGT EDWARD A CARTER (ex-*OOCL Innovation*)	T-AK 4544	Daewoo Shipbuilding	1984	PREPO

Displacement, tons: 81,284 full load
Dimensions, feet (metres): 950 × 106 × 38 *(289.5 × 32.3 × 11.6)*
Main machinery: 1 Sulzer RLB 90 diesel; 1 shaft
Speed, knots: 18
Complement: 20
Cargo capacity: 2,500 TEU

Comment: *LTC John U D Page* delivered to MSC in February 2001 and *SSGT Edward A Carter* in June 2001. Both operated by Maersk Sealand and are CPS ships for army prepositioning in the Indian Ocean. Both ships re-chartered in December 2005.

SSGT EDWARD A CARTER   *2/2003, A Sharma* / 0572750

1 CONTAINER SHIP (AK)

Name	No	Builders	Commissioned	F/S
CAPT STEVEN L BENNETT (ex-*Sea Pride*)	T-AK 4296	Samsung Shipbuilding	1984	PREPO

Displacement, tons: 52,878 full load
Dimensions, feet (metres): 687 × 99.8 × 49.9 *(209.4 × 30.4 × 15.2)*
Main machinery: 1 diesel; 1 shaft
Speed, knots: 16.5
Complement: 21 civilian
Cargo capacity: 520 TEU (on deck within cocoons); 1,006 TEU (under deck); 422 TEU (reefer)

Comment: The ship is owned and operated by Sealift Inc, under charter to Military Sealift Command. When fully loaded, *Bennett* carries over 1,500 20 ft containers of various aviation munitions intended to resupply forward-deployed fighter and attack squadrons. The ship is fitted with an extensive cocoon system enabling it to maintain deck-loaded munitions in an environmentally controlled atmosphere. While lightweight and easy to maintain, the fabric cocoon system is able to withstand gusts of up to 90 kt. *Bennett* is an LPS ship.

CAPT STEVEN L BENNETT   *6/1999, US Navy* / 0016575

1 RO-RO CONTAINER: CARGO SHIP (AKR)

Name	No	Builders	Commissioned	F/S
1st LT HARRY L MARTIN (ex-*Tarago*)	T-AK 3015	Tarago Shipyard	20 Apr 2000	Sqn 3

Displacement, tons: 47,777 full load
Dimensions, feet (metres): 754.3 × 106 × 36.1 *(229.9 × 32.3 × 11)*
Main machinery: 1 MAN K7-SZ-90/160 diesel; 25,690 hp(m) *(18.88 MW)*; 1 shaft
Speed, knots: 18
Range, n miles: 17,000 at 17 kt
Complement: 23 plus 100 marines
Cargo capacity: 168,547 sq ft. 735 TEU

Comment: Acquired in February 1997 for conversion at Atlantic Drydock, Jacksonville. Carries USMC expeditionary airfield, fleet hospital package and construction equipment.

1st LT HARRY L MARTIN   *7/2003, Frank Findler* / 0572751

1 RO-RO CONTAINER: CARGO SHIP (AKR)

Name	No	Builders	Commissioned	F/S
L/CPL ROY M WHEAT (ex-*Bazaliya*)	T-AK 3016	Bender Shipbuilding	Oct 2001	Sqn 1

Displacement, tons: 50,101 full load
Dimensions, feet (metres): 863.8 × 98.4 × 34.8 *(263.3 × 30 × 10.6)*
Main machinery: 2 gas turbines; 47,020 hp(m) *(34.56 MW)*; 2 shafts
Speed, knots: 20. **Range, n miles:** 12,000 at 20 kt
Complement: 30 plus 100 marines
Cargo capacity: 109,170 sq ft. 846 TEU

Comment: Acquired in March 1997 for conversion for Maritime Prepositioning Force by Bender Shipbuilding, Mobile. The ship has been lengthened by 117 ft. Carries USMC expeditionary airfield, fleet hospital package and construction equipment.

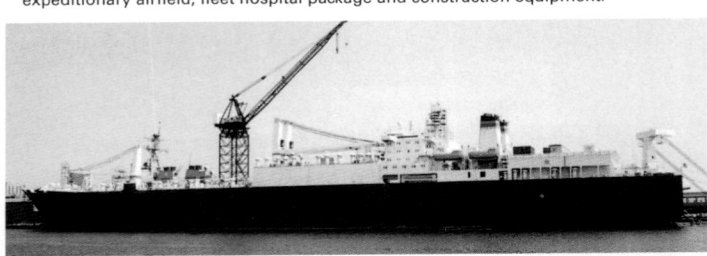

L/CPL ROY M WHEAT   *9/2002, Winter & Findler* / 0529989

1 RO-RO CONTAINER: CARGO SHIP (AKR)

Name	No	Builders	Commissioned	F/S
GYSGT FRED W STOCKHAM (ex-*Soderman*)	T-AK 3017	National Steel and Shipbuilding	July 2001	Sqn 2

Displacement, tons: 55,123 full load
Dimensions, feet (metres): 907 × 106 × 36 *(276.4 × 32.2 × 10.9)*
Main machinery: 1 Burmeister & Wain 12L90 GFCA diesel; 46,653 hp(m) *(34.29 MW)*; 1 shaft; bow and stern thrusters
Speed, knots: 24. **Range, n miles:** 12,000 at 24 kt
Complement: 28 crew, 12 cargo maintenance, 83 opp
Cargo capacity: 94,337 sq ft. 1,126 TEU

Comment: Ex-USNS *Soderman* joined the Maritime Prepositioning Force in July 2001 and is assigned to MPSRON Two. Carries USMC expeditionary airfield, fleet hospital package and construction equipment.

GYSGT FRED W STOCKHAM   *8/2001, van Ginderen Collection* / 0131276

5 CPL LOUIS J HAUGE, JR CLASS: VEHICLE CARGO SHIPS (AKRH)

Name	No	Builders	Commissioned	F/S
CPL LOUIS J HAUGE, JR (ex-MV *Estelle Maersk*)	T-AK 3000	Odense Staalskibsvaerft A/S, Lindo	Oct 1979	Sqn 3
PFC WILLIAM B BAUGH (ex-MV *Eleo Maersk*)	T-AK 3001	Odense Staalskibsvaerft A/S, Lindo	Apr 1979	Sqn 1
PFC JAMES ANDERSON, JR (ex-MV *Emma Maersk*)	T-AK 3002	Odense Staalskibsvaerft A/S, Lindo	July 1979	Sqn 3
1st LT ALEX BONNYMAN (ex-MV *Emilie Maersk*)	T-AK 3003	Odense Staalskibsvaerft A/S, Lindo	Jan 1980	Sqn 3
PVT FRANKLIN J PHILLIPS (ex-*Pvt Harry Fisher*, ex-MV *Evelyn Maersk*)	T-AK 3004	Odense Staalskibsvaerft A/S, Lindo	Apr 1980	Sqn 2

Displacement, tons: 46,552 full load
Dimensions, feet (metres): 755 × 90 × 37.1 *(230 × 27.4 × 11.3)*
Main machinery: 1 Sulzer 7RND76M diesel; 16,800 hp(m) *(12.35 MW)*; 1 shaft; bow thruster
Speed, knots: 16.4. **Range, n miles:** 10,800 at 16 kt
Complement: 27 plus 10 technicians
Cargo capacity: Containers, 383; Ro-Ro, 121,595 sq ft; JP-5 bbls, 17,128; DF-2 bbls, 10,642; Mogas bbls, 3,865; stable water, 2,022; cranes, 3 twin 30 ton; 92,831 cu ft breakbulk
Helicopters: Platform only.

Comment: Converted from five Maersk Line ships by Bethlehem Steel, Sparrow Point, MD. Conversion work included the addition of 157 ft *(47.9 m)* amidships. All operated by Maersk Line Ltd.

CPL LOUIS J HAUGE JR   *3/1998, A Sharma* / 0053410

3 SGT MATEJ KOCAK CLASS: VEHICLE CARGO SHIPS (AKRH)

Name	No	Builders	Commissioned	F/S
SGT MATEJ KOCAK (ex-SS *John B Waterman*)	T-AK 3005	Pennsylvania SB Co, Chester, PA	14 Mar 1981	Sqn 2
PFC EUGENE A OBREGON (ex-SS *Thomas Heywood*)	T-AK 3006	Pennsylvania SB Co, Chester, PA	1 Nov 1982	Sqn 1
MAJ STEPHEN W PLESS (ex-SS *Charles Carroll*)	T-AK 3007	General Dynamics Corp, Quincy, MA	14 Mar 1983	Sqn 3

Displacement, tons: 48,754 full load
Dimensions, feet (metres): 821 × 105.6 × 32.3 *(250.2 × 32.2 × 9.8)*
Main machinery: 2 boilers; 2 GE turbines; 30,000 hp *(22.4 MW)*; 1 shaft
Speed, knots: 20
Range, n miles: 13,000 at 20 kt
Complement: 29 plus 10 technicians
Cargo capacity: Containers, 562; Ro-Ro, 152,236 sq ft; JP-5 bbls, 20,290; DF-2 bbls, 12,355; Mogas bbls, 3,717; stable water, 2,189; cranes, 2 twin 50 ton and 1 — 30 ton gantry
Helicopters: Platform only.

Comment: Converted from three Waterman Line ships by National Steel and Shipbuilding, San Diego. Delivery dates T-AK 3005, 1 October 1984; T-AK 3006, 16 January 1985; T-AK 3007, 15 May 1985. Conversion work included the addition of 157 ft *(47.9 m)* amidships. All operated by Waterman SS Corp.

SGT MATEJ KOJAK *10/2002, H M Steele* / 0530097

5 2nd LT JOHN P BOBO CLASS: VEHICLE CARGO SHIPS (AKRH)

Name	No	Builders	Commissioned	F/S
2nd LT JOHN P BOBO	T-AK 3008	General Dynamics, Quincy	14 Feb 1985	Sqn 1
PFC DEWAYNE T WILLIAMS	T-AK 3009	General Dynamics, Quincy	6 June 1985	Sqn 1
1st LT BALDOMERO LOPEZ	T-AK 3010	General Dynamics, Quincy	20 Nov 1985	Sqn 2
1st LT JACK LUMMUS	T-AK 3011	General Dynamics, Quincy	6 Mar 1986	Sqn 3
SGT WILLIAM R BUTTON	T-AK 3012	General Dynamics, Quincy	27 May 1986	Sqn 2

Displacement, tons: 44,330 full load
Dimensions, feet (metres): 675.2 × 105.5 × 29.6 *(205.8 × 32.2 × 9)*
Main machinery: 2 Stork-Wärtsilä Werkspoor 16TM410 diesels; 27,000 hp(m) *(19.84 MW)* sustained; 1 shaft; bow thruster; 1,000 hp *(746 kW)*
Speed, knots: 17.7
Range, n miles: 12,840 at 18 kt
Complement: 30 plus 10 technicians
Cargo capacity: Containers, 578; Ro-Ro, 156,153 sq ft; JP-5 bbls, 20,776; DF-2 bbls, 13,334; Mogas bbls, 4,880; stable water, 2,357; cranes, 1 single and 2 twin 39 ton
Helicopters: Platform only.

Comment: Built for MPS operations. Owned and operated by American Overseas Marine.

PFC DEWAYNE T WILLIAMS *3/2005*, W Clements* / 1154012

READY RESERVE FORCE (RRF)

Notes: (1) The Ready Reserve Force was created in 1976, to support military sea transportation needs. Composed of merchant ships that are no longer commercially useful, the RRF is designed to be made available quickly for military sealift operations. Its functions have been widened to include humanitarian and domestic security issues.
(2) On 1 January 2006 the RRF consisted of 56 ships, including Ro-Ro, breakbulk, auxiliary crane, heavy lift barge carriers, special mission tankers and aviation logistic support ships. These are maintained in various stages of readiness and able to get underway in four, five, 10 or 20 days. They are located in various ports along the US East, West and Gulf Coasts and in Japan.
(3) The Department of Transportation's Maritime Administration (MARAD) is responsible for the maintenance and administration of the ships when they are not operating. Military Sealift Command assumes operational control once the ships are activated for military missions.
(4) RRF ships have red, white and blue funnel stripes.

6 PRODUCT TANKERS (AOT)

NODAWAY T-AOG 78
ALATNA T-AOG 81
CHATTAHOOCHEE T-AOG 82

POTOMAC T-AOT 181
CHESAPEAKE T-AOT 5084
PETERSBURG T-AOT 9109

Comment: *Chesapeake* and *Petersburg* are operational as APS ships.

POTOMAC *6/2000, Bob Fildes* / 0106835

10 AUXILIARY CRANE SHIPS (AK)

Name	No	Builders	Conversion Commissioned
KEYSTONE STATE (ex-SS *President Harrison*)	T-ACS 1	Defoe SB Co, Bay City	1984
GEM STATE (ex-SS *President Monroe*)	T-ACS 2	Defoe SB Co, Bay City	1985
GRAND CANYON STATE (ex-SS *President Polk*)	T-ACS 3	Dillingham SR, Portland	1986
GOPHER STATE (ex-*Export Leader*)	T-ACS 4	Norshipco, Norfolk	Oct 1987
FLICKERTAIL STATE (ex-*Export Lightning*)	T-ACS 5	Norshipco, Norfolk	Dec 1987
CORNHUSKER STATE (ex-*Staghound*)	T-ACS 6	Norshipco, Norfolk	Mar 1988
DIAMOND STATE (ex-*President Truman*)	T-ACS 7	Tampa SY	Jan 1989
EQUALITY STATE (ex-*American Banker*)	T-ACS 8	Tampa SY	May 1989
GREEN MOUNTAIN STATE (ex-*American Altair*)	T-ACS 9	Norshipco, Norfolk	Sep 1990
BEAVER STATE (ex-*American Draco*)	T-ACS 10	Kreith Ship Repair, New Orleans	4 May 1997

Displacement, tons: 31,500 full load
Dimensions, feet (metres): 668.6 × 76.1 × 33.5 *(203.8 × 23.2 × 10.2)*
Main machinery: 2 boilers; 2 GE turbines; 19,250 hp *(14.4 MW)*; 1 shaft
Speed, knots: 20. **Range, n miles:** 13,000 at 20 kt
Complement: 89
Cargo capacity: 300+ standard containers

Comment: Auxiliary crane ships are container ships to which have been added up to three twin boom pedestal cranes which will lift containerised or other cargo from itself or adjacent vessels and deposit it on a pier or into lighterage. There are dimensional differences between some of the class.

GOPHER STATE *7/2003, W Sartori* / 0572766

3 BREAK BULK SHIPS (AK/AKR/AE)

CAPE JACOB T-AK 5029 **CAPE GIRARDEAU** T-AK 2039 **CAPE GIBSON** T-AK 5051

Comment: *Cape Jacob* is operational as an APS ship.

BREAK BULK SHIP *8/2002, Royal Australian Navy* / 0572796

6 MISCELLANEOUS HEAVY LIFT SHIPS (AK/AP/AKR)

Lash ships
CAPE FEAR T-AK 5061
CAPE FLATTERY T-AK 5070
CAPE FLORIDA T-AK 5071
CAPE FAREWELL T-AK 5073

Heavy lift ships
CAPE MAY T-AKR 5063
CAPE MOHICAN T-AKR 5065

CAPE MOHICAN *3/1999, van Ginderen Collection* / 0084193

31 RO-RO SHIPS (AKR)

COMET T-AKR 7	**CAPE HENRY** T-AKR 5067
METEOR T-AKR 9	**CAPE HORN** T-AKR 5068
CAPE ISLAND (ex-*Mercury*) T-AKR 10	**CAPE EDMONT** T-AKR 5069
CAPE INTREPID (ex-*Lyra*) T-AKR 11	**CAPE INSCRIPTION** T-AKR 5076
CAPE TEXAS T-AKR 112	**CAPE LAMBERT** T-AKR 5077
CAPE TAYLOR (ex-*Cygnus*) T-AKR 113	**CAPE LOBOS** T-AKR 5078
ADM WM H CALLAGHAN T-AKR 1001	**CAPE KNOX** T-AKR 5082
CAPE ORLANDO (ex-*American Eagle*)	**CAPE KENNEDY** T-AKR 5083
T-AKR 2044	**CAPE VINCENT** (ex-*Taabo Italia*) T-AKR 9666
CAPE DUCATO T-AKR 5051	**CAPE RISE** (ex-*Saudi Riyadh*) T-AKR 9678
CAPE DOUGLAS T-AKR 5052	**CAPE RAY** (ex-*Saudi Makkah*) T-AKR 9679
CAPE DOMINGO T-AKR 5053	**CAPE VICTORY** (ex-*Merzario Britania*) T-AKR 9701
CAPE DECISION T-AKR 5054	**CAPE TRINITY** (ex-*Santos*) T-AKR 9711
CAPE DIAMOND T-AKR 5055	**CAPE RACE** (ex-*G&C Admiral*) T-AKR 9960
CAPE ISABEL T-AKR 5062	**CAPE WASHINGTON** (ex-*Hual Transporter*) T-AKR 9961
CAPE HUDSON T-AKR 5066	**CAPE WRATH** (ex-*Hual Trader*) T-AKR 9962

CAPE DOUGLAS

8/2005, Robert Pabst* / 1154013

COAST GUARD

Headquarters Appointments

Commandant:
Admiral Thomas Collins
Vice Commandant:
Vice Admiral Terry M Cross
Commander, Atlantic Area:
Vice Admiral Vivien S Crea
Commander, Pacific Area:
Vice Admiral Harvey E Johnson Jr

Establishment

The United States Coast Guard was established by an Act of Congress approved 28 January 1915, which consolidated the Revenue Cutter Service (founded in 1790) and the Life Saving Service (founded in 1848). The act of establishment stated the Coast Guard 'shall be a military service and a branch of the armed forces of the USA at all times. The Coast Guard shall be a service in the Treasury Department except when operating as a service in the Navy'.

Congress further legislated that in time of national emergency or when the President so directs, the Coast Guard operates as a part of the Navy. The Coast Guard did operate as a part of the Navy during the First and Second World Wars.

The Lighthouse Service (founded in 1789) was transferred to the Coast Guard on 1 July 1939 and the Bureau of Navigation and Steamboat Inspection on 28 February 1942.

The Coast Guard was transferred from the Department of Transportation to the Department of Homeland Security on 1 March 2003.

Missions

The Coast Guard has five strategic aims:
Safety: Prevent deaths, injuries, and property damage associated with maritime transportation, fishing and recreational boating
National Defense: Defend the nation as one of the five US Armed Services. Enhance regional stability in support of the National Security Strategy specifically maritime homeland security
Maritime Security: Protect maritime borders from all intrusions by (a) halting the flow of illegal drugs, aliens, and contraband into the United States through maritime routes; (b) preventing illegal fishing; and (c) suppressing violations of federal law in the maritime arena

Mobility: Facilitate maritime commerce and eliminate interruptions and impediments to the economical movement of goods and people, while maximizing recreational access and enjoyment of the water
Protection of Natural Resources: Prevent environmental damage and natural resource degradation associated with maritime transportation, fishing, and recreational boating

Personnel

2006: 6,346 officers, 1,536 warrant officers, 31,879 enlisted, 8,062 reserves

Integrated Deepwater System (IDS)

IDS is a progressive 25-year programme to modernise, convert and replace USCG ships and aircraft and to improve command and control and logistics systems. The first contract for the programme, was awarded in June 2002 to Integrated Coast Guard Systems (ICGS), a partnership of Lockheed Martin and Northrop Grumman. Northrop Grumman Ship Systems will conduct the design and build three classes of new cutters and associated small boats. Up to 91 vessels are planned. Lockheed Martin is responsible for the C4ISR and system integration aspects of the programme and for aircraft procurement. Following a 2005 assessment of post-11 September 2001 (9/11) operational requirements, the Deepwater programme has been revised to incorporate more robust capabilities.

Cutter Strength

All Coast Guard vessels over 65 ft in length and that have adequate crew accommodation are referred to as 'cutters'. All names are preceded by USCG. The first two digits of the hull number for all Coast Guard vessels under 100 ft in length indicates the approximate length overall.
Approximately 2,000 standard and non-standard boats are in service ranging in size from 11 ft skiffs to 55 ft aids-to-navigation craft.

Category/Classification		Active	Building (Projected)
Cutters			
WHEC	High Endurance Cutters	12	—
WMEC	Medium Endurance		
Cutters	30		—
WMSL	National Security Cutters	—	2 (6)
WMSM	Offshore Patrol Cutters	—	(25)

Category/Classification		Active	Building (Projected)
Icebreakers			
WAGB	Icebreakers	3	—
WLBB	Icebreaker	1	—
WTGB	Icebreaking Tugs	9	—
Patrol Forces			
WPC	Patrol Coastal	5	(58)
WPB	Patrol Craft	114	—
Training Cutters			
WIX	Training Cutters	2	—
Buoy Tenders			
WLB	Buoy Tenders, Seagoing	17	—
WLM	Buoy Tenders, Coastal	14	—
WLI	Buoy Tenders, Inland	5	—
WLR	Buoy Tenders, River	18	—
Construction Tenders			
WLIC	Construction Tenders, Inland	13	—
Harbour Tugs			
WYTL	Harbour Tugs, Small	11	—

DELETIONS

Tenders and Tugs

2003	*Bramble, Firebush* and *Sassafras* (both to Nigeria)
2004	*Sundew*

HIGH ENDURANCE CUTTERS

0 + 2 (6) LEGEND CLASS (NATIONAL SECURITY CUTTERS) (PSOH/WMSL)

Name	No	Builders	Laid down	Launched	Commissioned
BERTHOLF	WMSL 750	Northrop Grumman Ingalls Shipbuilding	29 Mar 2005	Aug 2006	2007
—	WMSL 751	Northrop Grumman Ingalls Shipbuilding	2006	2006	2008

Displacement, tons: 3,206 standard; 4,112 full load
Dimensions, feet (metres): 418 × 54.0 × 21.0
(127.4 × 16.5 × 6.4)
Main machinery: CODAG; 1 GE LM2500 gas turbine; 29,500 hp *(22.0 MW)*; 2 MTU20V 1163 diesels; 19,310 hp *(14.4 MW)*; bow thruster; 2 shafts; cp props
Speed, knots: 28. **Range, n miles:** 12,000 at 9 kt
Complement: 106 (19 officers)
Guns: 1 Bofors 57 mm/70 Mk 3; 220 rds/min to 17 km *(9.3 n miles)*; weight of shell 2.4 kg.
1 General Dynamics 20 mm Phalanx Mk 15 CIWS.
4—12.7 mm MGs.
Countermeasures: Decoys: 6 Mk 53 Nulka.
ESM/ECM: SLQ 32.
Combat data systems: To be announced.
Weapons control: Kollmorgen Mk 46 optronic sight.
Radars: Surface search: TRS 3D/16; E/F-band.
Navigation: SPS 73; I-band.
Fire control: SPQ-9B; I/J-band.
Tacan: AN/URN 25.
Helicopters: 1 MCH and two Eagle Eye VUAV or 2 MCH.

Programmes: Contracts awarded to Northrop Grumman Ship Systems on 2 April 2003 for the design and long lead material procurement of the first of a class of eight Maritime (formerly National) Security Cutters to replace High Endurance Cutters. Lockheed Martin providing command/control/communications and intelligence integration and hardware. Contract for production and delivery of first ship on 28 June 2004 and for second on 18 January 2005. Four are expected to be delivered by 2010.
Structure: Can carry up to 11 m interceptor craft; stern ramps for rapid launch and recovery. Two helicopter hangars.

NATIONAL SECURITY CUTTER

1/2005, USCG / 1043676

Operational: Although designed to deploy 230 days per year, deployments are likely to be of the order of 185 days away from homeport through an augmented crew concept.

12 HAMILTON and HERO CLASSES (PSOH/WHEC)

Name	No	Builders	Laid down	Launched	Commissioned	F/S	Home Port
HAMILTON	WHEC 715	Avondale Shipyards	Jan 1965	18 Dec 1965	20 Feb 1967	PA	San Diego, CA
DALLAS	WHEC 716	Avondale Shipyards	7 Feb 1966	1 Oct 1966	1 Oct 1967	AA	Charleston, SC
MELLON	WHEC 717	Avondale Shipyards	25 July 1966	11 Feb 1967	22 Dec 1967	PA	Seattle, WA
CHASE	WHEC 718	Avondale Shipyards	27 Oct 1966	20 May 1967	1 Mar 1968	PA	San Diego, CA
BOUTWELL	WHEC 719	Avondale Shipyards	5 Dec 1966	17 June 1967	14 June 1968	PA	Alameda, CA
SHERMAN	WHEC 720	Avondale Shipyards	23 Jan 1967	23 Sep 1967	23 Aug 1968	PA	Alameda, CA
GALLATIN	WHEC 721	Avondale Shipyards	27 Feb 1967	18 Nov 1967	20 Dec 1968	AA	Charleston, SC
MORGENTHAU	WHEC 722	Avondale Shipyards	17 July 1967	10 Feb 1968	14 Feb 1969	PA	Alameda, CA
RUSH	WHEC 723	Avondale Shipyards	23 Oct 1967	16 Nov 1968	3 July 1969	PA	Honolulu, HI
MUNRO	WHEC 724	Avondale Shipyards	18 Feb 1970	5 Dec 1970	10 Sep 1971	PA	Alameda, CA
JARVIS	WHEC 725	Avondale Shipyards	9 Sep 1970	24 Apr 1971	30 Dec 1971	PA	Honolulu, HI
MIDGETT	WHEC 726	Avondale Shipyards	5 Apr 1971	4 Sep 1971	17 Mar 1972	PA	Seattle, WA

Displacement, tons: 3,300 full load
Dimensions, feet (metres): 378 × 42.8 × 20
(115.2 × 13.1 × 6.1)
Flight deck, feet (metres): 88 × 40 *(26.8 × 12.2)*
Main machinery: CODOG; 2 Pratt & Whitney FT4A-6 gas
turbines; 36,000 hp *(26.86 MW)*; 2 Fairbanks-Morse 38TD8-
1/8-12 diesels; 7,000 hp *(5.22 MW)* sustained; 2 shafts;
cp props; retractable bow propulsor; 350 hp *(261 kW)*
Speed, knots: 29. **Range, n miles:** 9,600 at 15 kt
Complement: 167 (19 officers)

Guns: 1 OTO Melara 3 in *(76 mm)*/62 Mk 75 Compact;
85 rds/min to 16 km *(8.7 n miles)* anti-surface; 12 km
(6.6 n miles) anti-aircraft; weight of shell 6 kg.
2 Boeing 25 mm/87 Mk 38 Bushmaster.
1 GE/GD 20 mm Vulcan Phalanx 6-barrelled Mk 15; 3,000
rds/min combined to 1.5 km. 4 — 12.7 mm MGs.
Countermeasures: Decoys: 2 Loral Hycor SRBOC
6-barrelled fixed Mk 36; IR flares and chaff.
ESM: WLR-1C, WLR-3; intercept.
Combat data systems: SCCS 378 includes OTCIXS satellite
link.
Weapons control: Mk 92 Mod 1 GFCS.
Radars: Air search: Lockheed SPS-40B; B-band.
Surface search: Hughes/Furuno SPS-73; E/F- and I-bands.
Fire control: Sperry Mk 92; I/J-band.
Tacan: URN 25.

Helicopters: 1 HH-65A or 1 HH-60J or 1 MH-68A.

Programmes: Twelve built of a total of 36 originally planned.
Modernisation: FRAM programme for all 12 ships in this
class from October 1985 to October 1992. Work included
standardising the engineering plants, improving the

JARVIS

5/2005*, Hachiro Nakai / 1154014

clutching systems, replacing SPS-29 air search radar
with SPS-40 radar and replacing the Mk 56 fire-control
system and 5 in/38 gun mount with the Mk 92 system
and a single 76 mm OTO Melara Compact gun. In
addition Harpoon and Phalanx CIWS fitted to five of
the class by 1992 and CIWS to all by late 1993. The flight
deck and other aircraft facilities upgraded to handle
a Jay Hawk helicopter including a telescopic hangar.
URN 25 Tacan added along with the SQR-4 and SQR-17
sonobuoy receiving set and passive acoustic analysis
systems. SRBOC chaff launchers were also fitted but not
improved ESM which has been shelved. All missiles,
torpedo tubes, sonar and ASW equipment removed in
1993-94. 25 mm Mk 38 guns replaced the 20 mm Mk 67.
Shipboard Command and Control System (SCCS) fitted

to all of the class by 1996. Surface search radar replaced
1997-99. First phase of C4ISR upgrades, including access
to SIPRNET and classified networks, completed in 2004.
Structure: These ships have clipper bows, twin funnels
enclosing a helicopter hangar, helicopter platform aft.
All are fitted with elaborate communications equipment.
Superstructure is largely of aluminium construction.
Bridge control of manoeuvring is by aircraft-type joystick
rather than wheel.
Operational: Ten of the class are based in the Pacific,
leaving only two on the East Coast. The removal of SSMs
and all ASW equipment sensibly refocuses on Coast
Guard roles. *Munro* to change homeport to Kodiak, AK,
in 2007. Decommissioning of the class is expected to
begin in 2010.

MEDIUM ENDURANCE CUTTERS

13 FAMOUS CUTTER CLASS (PSOH/WMEC)

Name	No	Builders	Laid down	Launched	Commissioned	F/S	Home Port
BEAR	WMEC 901	Tacoma Boatbuilding Co	23 Aug 1979	25 Sep 1980	4 Feb 1983	AA	Portsmouth, VA
TAMPA	WMEC 902	Tacoma Boatbuilding Co	3 Apr 1980	19 Mar 1981	16 Mar 1984	AA	Portsmouth, VA
HARRIET LANE	WMEC 903	Tacoma Boatbuilding Co	15 Oct 1980	6 Feb 1982	20 Sep 1984	AA	Portsmouth, VA
NORTHLAND	WMEC 904	Tacoma Boatbuilding Co	9 Apr 1981	7 May 1982	17 Dec 1984	AA	Portsmouth, VA
SPENCER	WMEC 905	Robert E Derecktor Corp	26 June 1982	17 Apr 1984	28 June 1986	AA	Boston, MA
SENECA	WMEC 906	Robert E Derecktor Corp	16 Sep 1982	17 Apr 1984	4 May 1987	AA	Boston, MA
ESCANABA	WMEC 907	Robert E Derecktor Corp	1 Apr 1983	6 Feb 1985	27 Aug 1987	AA	Boston, MA
TAHOMA	WMEC 908	Robert E Derecktor Corp	28 June 1983	6 Feb 1985	6 Apr 1988	AA	Kittery, ME
CAMPBELL	WMEC 909	Robert E Derecktor Corp	10 Aug 1984	29 Apr 1986	19 Aug 1988	AA	Kittery, ME
THETIS	WMEC 910	Robert E Derecktor Corp	24 Aug 1984	29 Apr 1986	30 June 1989	AA	Key West, FL
FORWARD	WMEC 911	Robert E Derecktor Corp	11 July 1986	22 Aug 1987	4 Aug 1990	AA	Portsmouth, VA
LEGARE	WMEC 912	Robert E Derecktor Corp	11 July 1986	22 Aug 1987	4 Aug 1990	AA	Portsmouth, VA
MOHAWK	WMEC 913	Robert E Derecktor Corp	15 Mar 1987	5 May 1988	20 Mar 1991	AA	Key West, FL

Displacement, tons: 1,820 full load
Dimensions, feet (metres): 270 × 38 × 13.9
(82.3 × 11.6 × 4.2)
Main machinery: 2 Alco 18V-251 diesels; 7,290 hp *(5.44 MW)*
sustained; 2 shafts; cp props
Speed, knots: 19.5. **Range, n miles:** 12,700 at 15 kt
Complement: 100 (14 officers) plus 5 aircrew

Guns: 1 OTO Melara 3 in *(76 mm)*/62 Mk 75; 85 rds/min to
16 km *(8.7 n miles)* anti-surface; 12 km *(6.6 n miles)* anti-
aircraft; weight of shell 6 kg.
2 — 12.7 mm MGs or 2 — 40 mm Mk 19 grenade launchers.
Countermeasures: Decoys: 2 Loral Hycor SRBOC
6-barrelled fixed Mk 36; IR flares and chaff.
ESM/ECM: SLQ-32(V)2; radar intercept.

Combat data systems: SCCS-270; OTCIXS satellite link.
Radars: Surface search: Hughes/Furuno SPS-73; I-band.
Fire control: Sperry Mk 92 Mod 1; I/J-band.
Tacan: URN 25.

Helicopters: 1 HH-65A or HH-60J or MH-68A or SH-60B.

Programmes: The contract for construction of WMEC
905-913 was originally awarded to Tacoma Boatbuilding
Co on 29 August 1980. However, under lawsuit from the
Robert E Derecktor Corp, Middletown, Rhode Island, the
contract to Tacoma was determined by a US District Court
to be invalid and was awarded to Robert E Derecktor
Corp on 15 January 1981.

Modernisation: OTCIXS satellite link fitted from 1992. C4ISR
upgrades completed in 2004. *Tampa* refitted 2005-06 as
part of the Mission Effectiveness Project to extend service
lives. The work includes engineering and habitability
measures. All of the class are to be similarly refitted.
Structure: They are the only medium endurance cutters
with a helicopter hangar (which is telescopic) and the first
cutters with automated command and control centre. Fin
stabilisers fitted. Plans to fit SSM and/or CIWS have been
abandoned as has towed array sonar and sonobuoy
datalinks. New radars fitted 1997-99.
Operational: Very lively in heavy seas because the length
to beam ratio is unusually small for ships required to
operate in Atlantic conditions.

TAHOMA

4/2003, Declerck/Steeghers / 1043681

14 RELIANCE CLASS (PSOH/WMEC)

Name	No	Builders	Commissioned	F/S	Home Port
RELIANCE	WMEC 615	Todd Shipyards	20 June 1964	AA	Kittery, ME
DILIGENCE	WMEC 616	Todd Shipyards	26 Aug 1964	AA	Wilmington, NC
VIGILANT	WMEC 617	Todd Shipyards	3 Oct 1964	AA	Cape Canaveral, FL
ACTIVE	WMEC 618	Christy Corp	17 Sep 1966	PA	Port Angeles, WA
CONFIDENCE	WMEC 619	Coast Guard Yard, Baltimore	19 Feb 1966	AA	Cape Canaveral, FL
RESOLUTE	WMEC 620	Coast Guard Yard, Baltimore	8 Dec 1966	AA	St Petersburg, FL
VALIANT	WMEC 621	American Shipbuilding Co	28 Oct 1967	AA	Miami, FL
STEADFAST	WMEC 623	American Shipbuilding Co	25 Sep 1968	AA	Astoria, OR
DAUNTLESS	WMEC 624	American Shipbuilding Co	10 June 1968	AA	Galveston, TX
VENTUROUS	WMEC 625	American Shipbuilding Co	16 Aug 1968	AA	St Petersburg, FL
DEPENDABLE	WMEC 626	American Shipbuilding Co	22 Nov 1968	AA	Cape May, NJ
VIGOROUS	WMEC 627	American Shipbuilding Co	2 May 1969	AA	Cape May, NJ
DECISIVE	WMEC 629	Coast Guard Yard, Baltimore	23 Aug 1968	AA	Pascagoula, MS
ALERT	WMEC 630	Coast Guard Yard, Baltimore	4 Aug 1969	PA	Astoria, OR

Displacement, tons: 1,129 full load (WMEC 620-630)
1,110 full load (WMEC 618, 619)
Dimensions, feet (metres): 210.5 × 34 × 10.5
(64.2 × 10.4 × 3.2)
Main machinery: 2 Alco 16V-251 diesels; 6,480 hp *(4.83 MW)*
sustained; 2 shafts; LIPS cp props
Speed, knots: 18
Range, n miles: 6,100 at 14 kt; 2,700 at 18 kt
Complement: 75 (12 officers)

Guns: 1 Boeing 25 mm/87 Mk 38 Bushmaster; 200 rds/min
to 6.8 km *(3.4 n miles)*. 2—12.7 mm MGs.
Combat data systems: SCCS-210.
Radars: Surface search: Hughes/Furuno SPS-73; I-band.

Helicopters: 1 HH-65A or MH-68A embarked as required.

Modernisation: All 14 cutters underwent a Major
Maintenance Availability (MMA) from 1987-94. The
exhausts for main engines, ship service generators and
boilers were run in a new vertical funnel which reduces
flight deck size. 76 mm guns were replaced by 25 mm
Mk 38. A Mission Effectiveness Project was initiated in
2005. Work, to extend service lives, includes engineering
and habitability measures. *Dependable* is the first
to be refitted and all of the class are to be similarly
upgraded.
Structure: Designed for search and rescue duties. Design
features include 360° visibility from bridge; helicopter
flight deck (no hangar); and engine exhaust vent at

ACTIVE   *10/2003, Frank Findler* / 0572762

stern which has been replaced by a funnel during
MMA. Capable of towing ships up to 10,000 tons. Air
conditioned throughout except engine room; high
degree of habitability.

Operational: Normally operate within 500 miles of the
coast. Primary roles are SAR, law enforcement homeland
security and defence operations.
Sales: *Reliance* sold to Sri Lanka in 2004.

0 + (25) OFFSHORE PATROL CUTTERS (PSOH/WMSM)

Displacement, tons: 3,715
Dimensions, feet (metres): 359.9 × 54.1 × 20.0 *(109.7 × 16.5 × 6.1)*
Main machinery: CODAD; 4 diesels; 9,655 hp *(7.2 MW)*; 2 shafts; cp props; bow thruster
Speed, knots: 25. **Range, n miles:** 9,000 at 9 kt
Complement: 91 (16 officers)
Guns: 1—57 mm.
Radars: To be announced.
Helicopters: 2 HH-65C or 4 HV-911 or 1 HH-65C and 2HV-911.

Programmes: Contract for accelerated design signed with Northrop Grumman Ship
Systems on 10 June 2004. Lockheed Martin responsible for co-development of
engineering design and system integration. Construction of the first of class is expected
to start in 2007 for entry into service in 2010.
Structure: Similar capabilities and equipment as National Security Cutter (WMSL). Stern
ramp for rapid launch and recovery of 2 LRI/SRP. Two helicopter hangars. Enhanced
sea-keeping capability through roll stabilisation.
Operational: Although designed to deploy 230 days per year, deployments are likely to be
of the order of 185 days away from homeport through an augmented crew concept.

ALEX HALEY   *12/1999, USCG* / 0084198

1 DIVER CLASS (PSO/WMEC)

Name	No	Builders	USN Comm	F/S	Home Port
ACUSHNET	WMEC 167	Basalt Rock Co,	5 Feb 1944	PA	Ketchikan, AK
(ex-*Shackle*)	(ex-WAGO 167,	Napa, CA			
	ex-WAT 167, ex-ARS 9)				

Displacement, tons: 1,557 standard; 1,745 full load
Dimensions, feet (metres): 213 × 41 × 15 *(64.9 × 12.5 × 4.6)*
Main machinery: 4 Fairbanks-Morse diesels; 3,000 hp *(2.24 MW)* sustained; 2 shafts
Speed, knots: 15.5
Range, n miles: 9,000 at 8 kt
Complement: 75 (9 officers)
Guns: 2—12.7 mm MGs.
Radars: Navigation: 2 Raytheon SPS-73; I-band.

Comment: Large, steel-hulled salvage ship transferred from the Navy to the Coast Guard
and employed in tug and oceanographic duties. Modified for handling environmental
data buoys and reclassified WAGO in 1968 and reclassified WMEC in 1980. Major
renovation work completed in 1983 and now used for SAR homeland security and law
enforcement operations.

OFFSHORE PATROL CUTTER   *2/2005, NGSS* / 1127296

1 EDENTON CLASS (PSOH/WMEC)

Name	No	Builders	Commissioned	F/S	Home Port
ALEX HALEY	WMEC 39	Brooke Marine, Lowestoft	23 Jan 1971	PA	Kodiak, AK
(ex-*Edenton*)	(ex-ATS 1)				

Displacement, tons: 3,000 full load
Dimensions, feet (metres): 282.6 × 50 × 15.1 *(86.1 × 15.2 × 4.6)*
Main machinery: 4 Caterpillar 3516 DITAWJ diesels; 6,000 hp(m) *(4.41 MW)*; 2 shafts;
cp props; bow thruster
Speed, knots: 18. **Range, n miles:** 10,000 at 13 kt
Complement: 99 (9 officers)
Guns: 2 McDonnell Douglas 25 mm/87 Mk 38; 200 rds/min to 6.8 km *(3.4 n miles)*.
2—12.7 mm MGs.
Radars: Surface search: Hughes/Furuno SPS-73; I-band.
Combat data systems: SCCS-282.
Helicopters: Platform for 1 HH-65A or 1 HH-60J.

Comment: Former Navy salvage ship paid off in 1996 and taken on by the Coast Guard in
November 1997 for conversion. All diving and salvage gear removed, flight deck installed, and
upgraded navigation and communications. Armed with 25 mm guns. Used in the Bering Sea,
Gulf of Alaska and North Pacific as a multi-mission cutter from 16 December 1999.

ACUSHNET   *9/2000, Sattler/Steele* / 0105723

1 STORIS CLASS (PSO/WMEC)

Name	No	Builders	Commissioned	F/S	Home Port
STORIS	WMEC 38	Toledo Shipbuilding	30 Sep 1942	PA	Kodiak, AK
(ex-*Eskimo*)	(ex-WAGB 38)				

Displacement, tons: 1,715 standard; 1,925 full load
Dimensions, feet (metres): 230 × 43 × 15 *(70.1 × 13.1 × 4.6)*
Main machinery: Diesel-electric; 3 GM EMD diesel generators; 1 motor; 3,000 hp *(2.24 MW)*; 1 shaft
Speed, knots: 14. **Range, n miles:** 22,000 at 8 kt
Complement: 78 (10 officers)
Guns: 1 Boeing 25 mm/87 Mk 38 Bushmaster. 2 — 12.7 mm MGs.
Radars: Navigation: 2 Raytheon SPS-73; I-band.

Comment: Laid down on 14 July 1941; launched on 4 April 1942 as ice patrol tender. Strengthened for ice navigation but no longer employed as icebreaker. Employed in Alaskan service for search, rescue Homeland Security and law enforcement. Completed a major maintenance availability in June 1986, during which main engines were replaced with EMD diesels and living quarters expanded. Gun changed in 1994. To be decommissioned in 2007 when she is to be relieved in Kodiak by *Munro*.

STORIS　　　　　　　　　　　*3/1998, van Ginderen Collection* / 0053416

SHIPBORNE AIRCRAFT

Numbers/Type: 95 EADS HH-65C.
Operational speed: 160 kt *(296 km/h)*.
Service ceiling: 11,810 ft *(3,600 m)*.
Range: 400 n miles *(741 km)*.
Role/Weapon systems: Short-range rescue and recovery (SRR) helicopter. Sensors: Bendix RDR 1300 radar and Collins mission management system. Equipped with CDU-900G control displays and MFD-255 multifunctional displays. Following a series of in-flight engine failures which began in 2003, operational flight restrictions were imposed. Conversion of all A and B models to C configuration, with Turbomeca Arriel 2C2 engines began in 2004. All to be converted by 2007. Conversion includes extended heat shields, reconfigured cockpit and improved avionics to facilitate multimission cutter operations. Weapons: 1 — 7.62 mm MG.

HH-65　　　　　　　　　　　*10/2003, Frank Findler* / 0572760

Numbers/Type: 42 Sikorsky HH-60J Jayhawk.
Operational speed: 170 kt *(315 km/h)*.
Service ceiling: 13,000 ft *(3,961 m)*.
Range: 600 n miles *(1,111 km)*.
Role/Weapon systems: Coast Guard version of Seahawk, first flew in 1988. A life-extension programme began in 2005 and will upgrade the entire fleet to MH-60T configuration, capable of deploying on NSC and OPC. Sensors: Bendix RDR-1300C weather/search radar. AAQ-15 FLIR. Weapons: 1 — 7.62 mm MG.

HH-60J　　　　　　　　　　　*3/2003, Adolfo Ortigueira Gil* / 0572761

Numbers/Type: 8 Agusta A 109 MH-68A Stingray.
Operational speed: 168 kt *(310 km/h)*.
Service ceiling: 20,000 ft *(6,100 m)*.
Range: 200 n miles *(370 km)*.
Role/Weapon systems: All-weather, short-range interdiction helicopter selected as follow on to Enforcer to counter high-speed smuggling/drug-running craft. All eight aircraft procured in 2001. All based at Jacksonville, FL.

MH-68A　　　　　　　　　　　*2000, USCG* / 0105721

LAND-BASED MARITIME AIRCRAFT

Notes: (1) The Bell Helicopter Textron HV-911 Eagle Eye tiltrotor selected by Integrated Coast Guard Systems as the Vertical Unmanned Aerial Vehicle (VUAV) to be part of the Integrated Deepwater System. Operable from land, it is also planned to deploy two VUAV in the new National Security and Offshore Patrol Cutters. Sensors are likely to include the FLIR Systems Safire and a radar. Capable of 210 kt, the aircraft can be recovered in up to Sea State 5. Having passed its Critical Design Review (CDR) phase in January 2005, up to 45 units are planned to enter service from 2006.
(2) A High Altitude Endurance Unmanned Air Vehicle (HAE-UAV) is planned to enter service from 2016 although this date may be brought forward. Equipped with high-resolution sensors (EO/FLIR, SAR, ISAR, GMT), the HAE-UAV is to provide long-range surveillance over large areas for extended periods of time. With a loiter altitude of up to 65,000 ft, they are to be capable of transmitting data and EO/IR imagery to shore-based command and control centres to contribute to the Common Operational Picture (COP). The programme is likely to be informed by the USN's BAMS (Broad Area Maritime Surveillance) programme, contenders for which include the Northrop Grumman RQ-4A Global Hawk. Four aircraft are planned.
(3) Four P-3B Orions are used for AEW by US Customs.

HV-911　　　　　　　　　　　*1/2006*, Ed Garza/Bell Helicopter* / 1154061

Numbers/Type: 2 Casa CN-235 200.
Operational speed: 210 kt *(384 km/h)*.
Service ceiling: 24,000 ft *(7,315 m)*.
Range: 2,000 n miles *(3,218 km)*.
Role/Weapon systems: First two of up to 36 maritime patrol aircraft ordered on 18 February 2004 and to be delivered in 2006. To be employed on general maritime patrol missions including SAR, law enforcement, ice patrol and environmental protection. Sensors: Synthetic aperture radar and electro-optic sensors. CBR detection sensors.

CN-235　　　　　　　　　　　*6/2004, CASA* / 1043638

Numbers/Type: 1 Gulfstream C-37A.
Operational speed: 459 kt *(850 km/h).*
Service ceiling: 51,000 ft *(15,540 m).*
Range: 5,600 n miles *(10,370 km).*
Role/Weapon: Military version of Gulfstream V which replaced a C-20B Gulfstream III in
May 2002. Based at Air Station Washington DC. Serves as a long-range command and
control aircraft for Coast Guard command officials.

GULFSTREAM G 550   *6/2003, Paul Jackson* / 0568402

Numbers/Type: 4/7/6 AMD-BA HU-25 A/HU-25 C/HU-25 D Guardian Falcon.
Operational speed: 420 kt *(774 km/h).*
Service ceiling: 42,000 ft *(12,800 m).*
Range: 1,940 n miles *(3,594 km).*
Role/Weapon systems: Medium-range maritime surveillance role. 17 are operational;
21 are in storage or support aircraft. Sensors: APS-127 weather/search radar. Weapons:
unarmed.

HU-25 FALCON   *6/2001, Adolfo Ortigueira Gil* / 0529903

Numbers/Type: 23/8 Lockheed HC-130H/HC-130J.
Operational speed: 325 kt *(602 km/h).*
Service ceiling: 33,000 ft *(10,060 m).*
Range: 4,100 n miles *(7,592 km)*; 5,500 n miles *(1,018 km)* (HC-130J).
Role/Weapon systems: Long-range maritime reconnaissance role. Twenty-two are
operational; five are in maintenance and modification. Sixteen HC-130Hs undergoing
upgrade to deliver Deepwater requirement for Long Range Search (LRS) capability and
provision of heavy air transport for Maritime Safety & Security Teams (MSSTs), Port
Security Units (PSUs), and National Strike Force (NSF). Delivery of first of new HC-130J
started in 2003. Six HC-130J to be further modernised by Lockheed Martin following
contract in September 2005. Upgrade to begin in January 2007, is to include installation
of EDO EL/M 2022A(V)3 maritime surface search radar, mounted beneath the plane's
fuselage, a nose-mounted APN-241 weather radar, electro-optical/infrared-FLIR Systems
Star Safire III, DF-430 UHF/VHF Direction Finder System, and SAAB TransponderTech AB
R4A Airborne Automatic Identification System (AIS). Delivery of all six aircraft 2007-08.
These variants will have 90 per cent C4ISR commonality with CASA CN235-300M.
Sensors (current): APS-137 or APS-125 weather/search radar. FLIR. Weapons: unarmed.

HC-130H   *10/2002, M Mazumdar* / 0529904

PATROL FORCES

0 + (58) FAST RESPONSE CUTTERS (PBO/WPC)

Displacement, tons: 325 full load
Dimensions, feet (metres): 140 × 21.8 × 7.33 *(42.7 × 6.6 × 2.2)*
Main machinery: 2 diesels; 3,650 hp *(2.72 MW)*
Speed, knots: 30+. **Range, n miles:** 4,230 at 10 kt
Complement: 15
Guns: 1 — 25 mm. 4 — 12.7 mm MGs.

Comment: In July 2004, contract awarded to begin preliminary design phase of WPC
cutters to enter service from 2008. The requirement is to be capable of independent
deployment in support of law enforcement, port security, search and rescue, and defense
operations missions. Typical missions to include offshore fishery protection, choke point
interdiction, barrier patrols, and presence in high-risk areas. Design features include
reduced signature through shaping, active fin stabilisation system, an integrated bridge
with 360° visibility and a stern ramp to launch new Short Range Prosecutor (SRP) patrol craft.
A successful Systems Requirement Review was completed on 27 April 2005.

FAST RESPONSE CUTTER   *2/2005*, NGSS* / 1127295

5 CYCLONE CLASS (PATROL COASTAL SHIPS) (WPC/PB)

Name	No	Builders	Commissioned	Home Port
TEMPEST	WPB 2 (ex-PC 2)	Bollinger, Lockport	21 Aug 1993	Pascagoula, MS
MONSOON	WPB 4 (ex-PC 4)	Bollinger, Lockport	22 Jan 1994	San Diego, CA
ZEPHYR	WPB 8 (ex-PC 8)	Bollinger, Lockport	15 Oct 1994	San Diego, CA
SHAMAL	WPC 13 (ex-PC 13)	Bollinger, Lockport	27 Jan 1996	Pascagoula, MS
TORNADO	WPC 14 (ex-PC 14)	Bollinger, Lockport	15 May 2000	Pascagoula, MS

Displacement, tons: 360 full load
Dimensions, feet (metres): 179 × 25.9 × 7.9 *(54.6 × 7.9 × 2.4)*
Main machinery: 4 Paxman Valenta 16RP 200M diesels; 13,400 hp *(10 MW)* sustained;
4 shafts
Speed, knots: 35. **Range, n miles:** 2,500 at 12 kt
Complement: 27 (2 officers)
Guns: 2 McDonnell Douglas 25 mm/87 Mk 38. 4 — 12.7 mm M60 MGs.
Combat data systems: SCCS-Lite.
Radars: Navigation: Hughes/Furuno SPS-73; I-band.

Comment: Contract awarded by USN for eight in August 1990 and five more in
July 1991. Design based on Vosper Thornycroft Ramadan class modified for USN
requirements including 1 in armour on superstructure. The craft have a slow speed
loiter capability. These five vessels were modified to incorporate a semi-dry well,
boat ramp and stern gate to facilitate deployment and recovery of a fully loaded
RIB while the ship is making way. Transferred to the USCG 2004-05. These are to
fill a gap in Coast Guard resources. To be returned to the US Navy in 2008. Eight
unconverted (without stern-ramps) vessels remain in USN service.

CYCLONE CLASS   *9/2002, Winter & Findler* / 0529974

44 GUARDIAN CLASS (TPSB/YP)

Displacement, tons: 3 full load
Dimensions, feet (metres): 24.6 × 8.2 × 0.4 *(7.5 × 2.5 × 0.4)*
Main machinery: 2 Evinrude outboards; 350 hp *(261 kW)*
Speed, knots: 35
Complement: 4
Guns: 1 — 12.7 mm MG. 2 — 7.62 mm MGs.
Radars: Navigation: Raytheon; I-band.

Comment: Transportable Port Security Boats (TPSB) which serve with the six Port Security
Units and a Training Detachment. Can be transported by aircraft.

GUARDIAN   *7/2000, Hachiro Nakai* / 0105727

GUARDIAN   *4/2001, Guy Toremans* / 0131265

HARBOUR TUGS

11 65 ft CLASS (WYTL)

Name	No	Home Port
CAPSTAN	WYTL 65601	Philadelphia, PA
CHOCK	WYTL 65602	Portsmouth, VA
TACKLE	WYTL 65604	Rockland, ME
BRIDLE	WYTL 65607	Southwest Harbor, ME
PENDANT	WYTL 65608	Boston, MA
SHACKLE	WYTL 65609	South Portland, ME
HAWSER	WYTL 65610	Bayonne, NJ
LINE	WYTL 65611	Bayonne, NJ
WIRE	WYTL 65612	Saugerties, NY
BOLLARD	WYTL 65614	New Haven, CT
CLEAT	WYTL 65615	Philadelphia, PA

Displacement, tons: 72 full load
Dimensions, feet (metres): 65 × 19 × 7 *(19.8 × 5.8 × 2.1)*
Main machinery: 1 Caterpillar 3412TA diesel; 400 hp *(298 kW)* sustained; 1 shaft
Speed, knots: 10. **Range, n miles:** 2,700 at 10 kt
Complement: 6
Radars: Navigation: Raytheon SPS-69; I-band.

Comment: Built between 1961 and 1967. The tugs provide icebreaking services to several east coast areas. Re-engined 1993-96.

HAWSER *7/2000, Hachiro Nakai* / 0105731

RESCUE AND UTILITY CRAFT

Notes: Craft of several different types. All carry five or six figure numbers of which the first two figures reflect the craft's length in feet.

172 UTILITY BOATS (YAG/UTB)

Displacement, tons: 13.4 full load
Dimensions, feet (metres): 41.3 × 14.1 × 4.1 *(12.6 × 4.3 × 1.3)*
Main machinery: 2 diesels; 680 hp *(507 kW)* sustained; 2 shafts
Speed, knots: 26. **Range, n miles:** 300 miles at 18 kt
Complement: 3

Comment: 205 built by Coast Guard Yard, Baltimore 1973-83. Aluminium hull with a towing capacity of 100 tons. Used for fast multimission response in weather conditions up to moderate.

41422 *7/2000, Hachiro Nakai* / 0105732

41385 *4/2003, Declerck/Steeghers* / 1043680

117 + (83) MOTOR LIFEBOATS (MLB/SAR)

Displacement, tons: 20 full load
Dimensions, feet (metres): 47.9 × 14.5 × 4.5 *(14.6 × 4.4 × 1.4)*
Main machinery: 2 Detroit diesels; 850 hp *(634 kW)* sustained; 2 shafts
Speed, knots: 25. **Range, n miles:** 220 at 25 kt
Complement: 4

Comment: Built by Textron Marine, New Orleans. The prototype completed trials in mid-1991. Five production boats delivered in 1994. More ordered in September 1995. Replaced the fleet of 44 ft lifeboats. Aluminium hulls, self-righting with a 9,000 lb bollard pull and a towing capability of 150 tons. Primarily a lifeboat but it has a multimission capability. A total of 200 planned by 2010.

MLB 47267 *2/2006*, Julio Montes* / 1154060

381 + 69 DEFENDER CLASS (RESPONSE BOATS) (PBF)

Displacement, tons: 2.7 full load
Dimensions, feet (metres): 25.0 × 8.5 × 8.8 *(7.6 × 2.6 × 2.7)*
Main machinery: 2 Honda outboard motors; 450 hp *(335 kW)*
Speed, knots: 46. **Range, n miles:** 175 at 35 kt
Complement: 4
Guns: 1 — 12.7 mm MG.
Radars: Furuno; I-band.

Comment: High-speed inshore patrol craft of aluminium construction and foam collar built by SAFE Boats International, Port Orchard, Washington. First delivery in July 2003 to replace nearly 300 non-standard shore based boats and provide a standardised platform for the USCG's new Maritime Safety and Security Teams (MSST), established as a result of the 11 September 2001 terrorist attacks. Up to 700 may be procured by 2010. Transportable in a C-130.

DEFENDER CLASS *10/2003, Frank Findler* / 0572753

8 + 83 SHORT RANGE PROSECUTOR CRAFT (SRP)

Displacement, tons: 9
Dimensions, feet (metres): 25.2 × ? × ? *(7.7 × ? × ?)*
Main machinery: 1 inboard diesel waterjet; 315 hp *(235 kW)*
Speed, knots: 33
Complement: 2 crew plus 8 passengers

Comment: First of two classes of RIB being introduced for Deepwater cutters. Trials completed in April 2003 at Coast Guard Station Curtis Bay, MD. The first SRP was delivered to the newly converted 123 ft *Matagorda* on 1 March 2004. Launched and recovered via a stern launch and recovery system. Further to enter fleet as each modernised WPB delivered. A fleet of 91 is projected by 2021.

SRP *10/2004, Jeff Murphy, USCG* / 1121007

0 + (33) LONG RANGE INTERCEPTOR CRAFT (LRI)

Displacement, tons: 15
Dimensions, feet (metres): 35 × ? × ? *(10.7 × ? × ?)*
Main machinery: Twin inboard diesels with waterjet
Speed, knots: 45
Complement: 14 crew and passengers

Comment: First expected to enter service by 2007. A total of 33 is planned by 2021. Launched and recovered via a stern launch and recovery system.

LRI *10/2004, Jeff Murphy, USCG* / 1121008

NATIONAL OCEANIC AND ATMOSPHERIC ADMINISTRATION (NOAA)

Headquarters Appointments

Under Secretary of Commerce for Oceans and Atmosphere:
  Vice Admiral Conrad Lautenbacher Jr USN (ret)
Director, Office of Marine and Aviation Operations and NOAA Commissioned Officer Corps:
  Rear Admiral Samuel P De Bow Jr
Director, Marine and Aviation Operations Centers:
  Rear Admiral Richard R Behn

Establishment and Missions

NOAA is the largest bureau of the US Department of Commerce, with a diverse set of responsibilities in environmental sciences. NOAA components include Office of Marine and Aviation Operations; the National Ocean Service; the National Weather Service; the National Marine Fisheries Service; the National Environmental Satellite, Data and Information Service; and the office of Oceanic and Atmospheric Research. NOAA's research vessels conduct operations in hydrography, bathymetry, oceanography, atmospheric research, fisheries assessments and research, and related programmes in marine resources. Larger research vessels operate in international waters, and smaller ones primarily in Atlantic and Pacific coastal waters, and the Gulfs of Mexico and Alaska. NOAA conduct diving operations. It also operates fixed-wing and rotary aircraft for hurricane research and reconnaissance; oceanographic and atmospheric research; marine mammal observations; hydrologic forecasts; and aerial mapping and charting. NOAA's active fleet numbers 18 ships, and now includes seven former Navy ships. Two other ex-Navy T-AGOS ships (*Assertive* and *Capable*) have been acquired and will be converted to conduct research. *Capable*, which is to be commissioned *Okeanos Explorer*, is the first to be converted and will be committed to ocean exploration. A new oceanographic research ship, *Ronald H Brown* (ex-AGOR 26), was commissioned in 1997. Of the seven ex-naval ships, five are T-AGOS vessels: one has been converted for oceanographic research (*Ka'imimoana*), two for fisheries research (*Gordon Gunter, Oscar Elton Sette*), and two for coastal oceanographic research (*McArthur II* and *Hi'ialakai*). *Sette* replaced *Townsend Cromwell* and *McArthur II* replaced *McArthur* in 2003. *Hi'ialakai* (formerly *Vindicator*), homeported in Hawaii, was commissioned in 2004 and is an addition to the fleet. The former naval T-AGS hydrographic survey ship *Littlehales* was transferred to NOAA in 2003 and recommissioned *Thomas Jefferson*, replacing *Whiting*. A former naval YTT (Yard Torpedo Test) vessel was converted for coastal research and became operational in 2003 as *Nancy Foster*, replacing *Ferrel*. The hydrographic survey ship *Fairweather* was decommissioned in 1988, refurbished, and reactivated in 2004. A new class of fisheries survey vessels has been designed to NOAA specifications and international standards. *Oscar Dyson*, the first of four planned FSVs, was completed in late 2004 and commissioned in May 2005. The second FSV, *Henry B Bigelow*, was launched in July 2005 and is to become operational in 2007. Construction of the third FSV started in July 2005. In 2004, NOAA exercised an option under an existing contract with VT Halter Marine Inc. to develop a contract design of a small-waterplane-area twin-hull ship that, if constructed, will conduct hydrographic surveys.

Ships

The following ships may be met at sea.
  Oceanographic Research Ships: *Ronald H Brown, Ka'imimoana.*
  Multipurpose Oceanographic/Coastal Research Ships: *McArthur II, Nancy Foster, Hi'ialakai*
  Hydrographic Survey Ships: *Rainier, Rude, Thomas Jefferson, Fairweather.*
  Fisheries Research Ships: *Miller Freeman, Oregon II, Albatross IV, Delaware II, David Starr Jordan, John N Cobb, Gordon Gunter, Oscar Elton Sette, Oscar Dyson.*

Personnel

2006: 283 officers plus 12,000 civilians

Bases

Major: Norfolk, VA and Seattle, WA.
Minor: Woods Hole, MA; Pascagoula, MS; Honolulu, HI; Charleston, SC; San Diego, CA; Ketchikan, AK, Kodiak, AK.

OSCAR DYSON   *5/2005*, NOAA* / 1154059

THOMAS JEFFERSON   *6/2003, NOAA* / 0572818

OSCAR ELTON SETTE   *6/2002, NOAA* / 0543400

RONALD H BROWN   *12/2004, Globke Collection* / 1043679

Uruguay

Country Overview

The Oriental Republic of Uruguay is situated in south-eastern South America. With an area of 68,037 square miles it has borders to the north with Brazil and to the west with Argentina. It has a coastline of 356 n miles with the south Atlantic Ocean and River Plate. There are some 675 n miles of navigable internal waterways. The capital, largest city and principal port is Montevideo. Territorial Seas (12 n miles) and an EEZ (200 n miles) are claimed.

Headquarters Appointments

Commander-in-Chief of the Navy:
  Vice Admiral Tabare Daners Eyras
Fleet Commander:
  Rear Admiral Oscar Debali de Palleja
Commander Coast Guard:
  Rear Admiral Heber Fernández Maggio

Diplomatic Representation

Naval Attaché in London:
  Captain Ney Escandón

Personnel

(a) 2006: 5,700 (700 officers) (including 450 naval infantry, 300 naval air and 1,950 Coast Guard)
(b) Voluntary service

Prefectura Nacional Naval (PNN)

Established in 1934 primarily for harbour security and coastline guard duties. In 1991 it was integrated with the Navy, although patrol craft retain Prefectura markings. There are three regions: Atlantic, Rio de la Plata, and Rio Uruguay.

Bases

Montevideo: Main naval base with two dry docks (A new naval base is under construction at Punta Lobos and will replace the current harbour facilities.)
La Paloma: Naval station *(Ernesto Motto)*
Fray Bentos: River base
Laguna del Sauce, Maldonado: Naval air station *(Capitan Carlos A Curbelo)*

Marines

Cuerpo de Fusileros Navales consisting of 450 men in three rifleman companies and one combat support company plus a command company of 100.

Prefix to Ships' Names

ROU

DELETIONS

Frigates

2005 *General Artigas*

Survey and Research Ships

2002 *Comandante Pedro Campbell*

FRIGATES

Notes: Discussions about the acquisition of two Descubierta class corvettes from Spain took place in 2004 but did not lead to a contract.

2 COMMANDANT RIVIÈRE CLASS (FF)

Name	No	Builders	Laid down	Launched	Commissioned	Recommissioned
URUGUAY (ex-*Commandant Bourdais*)	1	Lorient Naval Dockyard	Apr 1959	15 Apr 1961	10 Mar 1962	20 Aug 1990
MONTEVIDEO (ex-*Amiral Charner*)	3	Lorient Naval Dockyard	Nov 1958	12 Mar 1960	14 Dec 1962	28 Jan 1991

Displacement, tons: 1,750 standard; 2,250 full load
Dimensions, feet (metres): 336.9 × 38.4 × 14.1 *(102.7 × 11.7 × 4.3)*
Main machinery: 4 SEMT-Pielstick 12 PC series diesels; 16,000 hp(m) *(11.8 MW)*; 2 shafts
Speed, knots: 25. **Range, n miles:** 7,500 at 15 kt
Complement: 159 (9 officers)

Guns: 2 DCN 3.9 in *(100 mm)*/55 Mod 1953 automatic ❶; dual purpose; 60 rds/min to 17 km *(9 n miles)* anti-surface; 8 km *(4.4 n miles)* anti-aircraft; weight of shell 13.5 kg. 2 Hispano-Suiza 30 mm/70 ❷.
Torpedoes: 6—21.7 in *(550 mm)* (2 triple) tubes ❸ ECAN L3; anti-submarine; active homing to 5.5 km *(3 n miles)* at 25 kt; warhead 200 kg; depth to 300 m *(985 ft)*.
A/S mortars: 1 Mortier 305 mm 4-barrelled launcher ❹.
Countermeasures: ESM: NS 9010-UR; radar warning.
Weapons control: C T Analogique. Sagem DMAA optical director.
Radars: Air/surface search: Thomson-CSF DRBV 22A ❺; D-band.
Navigation: Racal Decca 1226 ❻; I-band.
Fire control: Thomson-CSF DRBC 32C ❼; I-band.
Sonars: EDO SQS-17; hull-mounted; active search; medium frequency.
Thomson Sintra DUBA 3; active attack; high frequency.

Programmes: First one bought from France through SOFMA on 30 September 1988, second pair 14 March 1990. All refitted before transfer.
Structure: Exocet and Dagaie removed before transfer. SSM casings removed from *Montevideo* refit 1999/2000.
Operational: Can carry a Flag Officer and staff. In French service this class sometimes embarked up to 80 soldiers and two LCPs. The A/S mortar is non-operational. *Uruguay* was in refit 2000-2004. *General Artigas* decommissioned in April 2005 and used as spares. The ships form the Escort Division based at Montevideo.

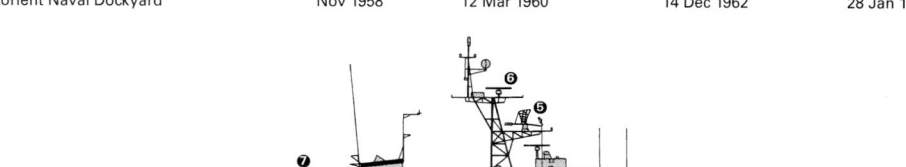

MONTEVIDEO *(Scale 1 : 900), Ian Sturton* / 1044203

MONTEVIDEO *10/2002, Mario R V Carveiro* / 0534050

MONTEVIDEO *3/2002, Robert Pabst* / 0534051

LAND-BASED MARITIME AIRCRAFT

Notes: (1) There are plans to acquire a CN-235 Persuader maritime patrol aircraft which would complement the one Beech B 200T in service.
(2) In addition there are six helicopters (four Westland Wessex HC Mk 2, one Wessex W-60 and one Bell 47G). There are also three fixed-wing aircraft, two Beech T-34C and two Jetstream T2. The latter were bought from the UK in 1998.
(3) An UH 13 AS 355 Esquilo is to be acquired from Brazil for operation from *General Artigas*.

B-200T   *2001, Uruguay Navy* / 0121422

JET STREAM   *2001, Uruguay Navy* / 0121423

WESSEX   *2/2003, A E Galarce* / 0569796

Numbers/Type: 1 Grumman S-2G Tracker.
Operational speed: 140 kt *(260 km/h).*
Service ceiling: 25,000 ft *(7,620 m).*
Range: 1,350 n miles *(2,500 km).*
Role/Weapon systems: Ex-Israeli aircraft. ASW and surface search with improved systems. Sensors: Search radar, MAD, sonobuoys. Weapons: ASW; torpedoes, depth bombs or mines. ASV; rockets underwing.

GRUMMAN S-2G   *2000, Uruguay Navy* / 0105735

PATROL FORCES

Notes: Plans to acquire three 35 m offshore patrol vessels appear to be in abeyance.

1 WANGEROOGE CLASS (PBO/AG)

Name	No	Builders	Commissioned
MALDONADO (ex-*Norderney*)	23 (ex-A1455)	Schichau, Bremerhaven	15 Oct 1970

Displacement, tons: 854 standard; 1,024 full load
Dimensions, feet (metres): 170.6 × 39.4 × 12.8 *(52 × 12.1 × 3.9)*
Main machinery: Diesel-electric; 4 MWM 16-cyl diesel generators; 2 motors; 2,400 hp(m) *(1.76 MW);* 2 shafts
Speed, knots: 14
Range, n miles: 5,000 at 10 kt
Complement: 24
Guns: 1 Bofors 40 mm/70.

Comment: Built as a salvage tug with ice-strengthened hull. Transferred from the German Navy on 21 November 2002. Employed as a support ship and for offshore patrol duties.

MALDONADO (German colours)   *6/2001, Martin Mokrus* / 0130283

3 VIGILANTE CLASS (LARGE PATROL CRAFT) (PBO)

Name	No	Builders	Commissioned
15 de NOVIEMBRE	5	CMN, Cherbourg	25 Mar 1981
25 de AGOSTO	6	CMN, Cherbourg	25 Mar 1981
COMODORO COÉ	7	CMN, Cherbourg	25 Mar 1981

Displacement, tons: 190 full load
Dimensions, feet (metres): 137 × 22.4 × 8.2 *(41.8 × 6.8 × 2.4)*
Main machinery: 2 MTU 12V 538 TB91 diesels; 4,600 hp(m) *(3.4 MW)* sustained; 2 shafts
Speed, knots: 28
Range, n miles: 2,400 at 15 kt
Complement: 28 (5 officers)
Guns: 1 Bofors 40 mm/70.
Weapons control: CSEE Naja optronic director.
Radars: Surface search: Racal Decca TM 1226C; I-band.

Comment: Ordered in 1979. Steel hull. First launched 16 October 1980, second 11 December 1980 and third 27 January 1981. Based at La Paloma.

15 DE NOVIEMBRE   *7/2001, A E Galarce* / 0534052

2 CAPE CLASS (LARGE PATROL CRAFT) (PB)

Name	No	Builders	Commissioned
COLONIA (ex-*Cape Higgon*)	10	Coast Guard Yard, Curtis Bay	14 Oct 1953
RIO NEGRO (ex-*Cape Horn*)	11	Coast Guard Yard, Curtis Bay	3 Sep 1958

Displacement, tons: 98 standard; 148 full load
Dimensions, feet (metres): 95 × 20.2 × 6.6 *(28.9 × 6.2 × 2)*
Main machinery: 2 GM 16V-149TI diesels; 2,322 hp *(1.73 MW)* sustained; 2 shafts
Speed, knots: 20
Range, n miles: 2,500 at 10 kt
Complement: 14 (1 officer)
Guns: 2—12.7 mm MGs.
Radars: Surface search: Raytheon SPS-64; I-band.

Comment: Designed for port security and search and rescue. Steel hulled. During modernisation in 1974 received new engines, electronics and deck equipment. Superstructure modified or replaced, and habitability improved. Transferred from the US Coast Guard 25 January 1990. Both based at Fray Bentos.

COLONIA   *2/2004, A E Galarce* / 1044207

3 RIVER PATROL CRAFT (PBR)

URUGUAY 3-5

Displacement, tons: 6 full load
Dimensions, feet (metres): 37.1 × 10.7 × 2.6 *(11.3 × 3.25 × 0.8)*
Main machinery: 2 Volvo Penta diesels
Speed, knots: 32
Complement: 6
Guns: 3—7.62 mm MGs.

Comment: Two built by Astillero KLASE A, Buenos Aires and delivered to Uruguayan Navy in 2002. A third delivered in 2004. Deployed to Congo-Brazzaville as part of UN force.

1 COASTAL PATROL CRAFT (PB)

Name	No	Builders	Commissioned
PAYSANDU	12 (ex-PR 12)	Sewart, USA	Nov 1968

Displacement, tons: 58 full load
Dimensions, feet (metres): 83 × 18 × 6 *(25.3 × 5.5 × 1.8)*
Main machinery: 2 GM 16V-71 diesels; 811 hp *(605 kW)* sustained; 2 shafts
Speed, knots: 22
Range, n miles: 800 at 20 kt
Complement: 8
Guns: 1 — 12.7 mm MGs. 2 — 7.62 mm MGs.
Radars: Surface search: Raytheon 1500B; I-band.

Comment: Formerly incorrectly listed under Coast Guard. Based at Montevideo.

PAYSANDU *2/2004, A E Galarce* / 1044206

3 COAST GUARD PATROL CRAFT (WPB)

70   71   72

Displacement, tons: 90 full load
Dimensions, feet (metres): 72.2 × 16.4 × 5.9 *(22 × 5 × 1.8)*
Main machinery: 2 GM diesels; 400 hp *(298 kW)*; 2 shafts
Speed, knots: 12
Complement: 8

Comment: Built in 1957 at Montevideo.

PREFECTURA 70 *6/2005*, A E Galarce* / 1133603

2 RIVER PATROL CRAFT (PBR)

URUGUAY 1   URUGUAY 2

Displacement, tons: 5 full load
Dimensions, feet (metres): 38.7 × 11.8 × 3.2 *(11.8 × 3.6 × 1)*
Main machinery: 3 Volvo AD41P 220MOP diesels
Speed, knots: 32
Range, n miles: 1,500 at 24 kt
Complement: 4
Guns: 2 — 12.7 mm MGs.

Comment: Built by Nuevos Ayres yacht builders. Deployed to Congo as part of UN force during 2001.

URUGUAY 1 *2001, Uruguay Navy* / 0121420

9 TYPE 44 CLASS (WPB)

441-449

Displacement, tons: 18 full load
Dimensions, feet (metres): 44 × 12.8 × 3.6 *(13.5 × 3.9 × 1.1)*
Main machinery: 2 Detroit 6V-38 diesels; 185 hp *(136 kW)*; 2 shafts
Speed, knots: 14. **Range, n miles:** 215 at 10 kt
Complement: 3

Comment: Acquired from the US in 1999 and operated by the Coast Guard primarily as SAR craft.

PREFECTURA 442 *6/2005*, A E Galarce* / 1133602

MINE WARFARE FORCES

3 KONDOR II CLASS (MINESWEEPERS — COASTAL) (MSC)

Name	No	Builders	Launched	Commissioned
TEMERARIO (ex-*Riesa*)	31	Peenewerft, Wolgast	2 Oct 1972	11 Oct 1991
FORTUNA (ex-*Bernau*)	33	Peenewerft, Wolgast	3 Aug 1972	11 Oct 1991
AUDAZ (ex-*Eisleben*)	34	Peenewerft, Wolgast	2 Jan 1973	11 Oct 1991

Displacement, tons: 310 full load
Dimensions, feet (metres): 186 × 24.6 × 7.9 *(56.7 × 7.5 × 2.4)*
Main machinery: 2 Russki/Kolomna Type 40-DM diesels; 4,408 hp(m) *(3.24 MW)* sustained; 2 shafts; cp props
Speed, knots: 17. **Range, n miles:** 2,000 at 15 kt
Complement: 31 (6 officers)
Guns: 1 Hispano-Suiza 30 mm/70.
Mines: 2 rails.
Radars: Surface search: TSR 333 or Raytheon 1900; I-band.

Comment: Belonged to the former GDR Navy. Transferred without armament. Minesweeping gear retained including MSG-3 variable depth sweep device. A fourth of class sunk after a collision with a merchant ship on 5 August 2000.

AUDAZ *2/2004, A E Galarce* / 1044205

SURVEY AND RESEARCH SHIPS

1 HELGOLAND (TYPE 720B) CLASS (AGS)

Name	No	Builders	Commissioned
OYARVIDE (ex-*Helgoland*)	22 (ex-A 1457)	Unterweser, Bremerhaven	8 Mar 1966

Displacement, tons: 1,310 standard; 1,643 full load
Dimensions, feet (metres): 223.1 × 41.7 × 14.4 *(68 × 12.7 × 4.4)*
Main machinery: Diesel-electric; 4 MWM 12-cyl diesel generators; 2 motors; 3,300 hp(m) *(2.43 MW)*; 2 shafts
Speed, knots: 17. **Range, n miles:** 6,400 at 16 kt
Complement: 34
Radars: Navigation: Raytheon; I-band.
Sonars: High definition, hull-mounted for wreck search.

Comment: Former German ocean-going tug launched on 25 November 1965. Paid off in 1997 and recommissioned on 21 September 1998 after being fitted out as a survey ship. Oceanographic equipment reported to have been fitted in 2002. Ice strengthened hull. Fitted for twin 40 mm guns.

OYARVIDE *6/2002, A E Galarce* / 0529549

1 INSHORE SURVEY CRAFT (AGSC)

TRIESTE

Displacement, tons: 12 full load
Dimensions, feet (metres): 39.7 × 11.8 × 3.3 (12.1 × 3.6 × 1)
Main machinery: 2 Kamewa waterjets
Speed, knots: 16. **Range, n miles:** 500 at 16 kt
Complement: 4
Sonars: Elac Compact Mk II; 180 kHz. Elac LAZ 4721; 200 kHz.

Comment: Formerly owned by the Academia Maritime Internacional de Trieste. Donated by Italian government in 2000.

TRIESTE   *2001, Uruguay Navy* / 0121418

TRAINING SHIPS

Notes: *Bonanza* is a 26 ton sail training vessel built in UK in 1984 and commissioned in July 1997.

1 SAIL TRAINING SHIP (AXS)

Name	No	Builders	Commissioned
CAPITÁN MIRANDA	20 (ex-GS 10)	SECN Matagorda, Cádiz	1930

Displacement, tons: 839 full load
Dimensions, feet (metres): 209.9 × 26.3 × 12.4 (64 × 8 × 3.8)
Main machinery: 1 GM diesel; 750 hp (552 kW); 1 shaft
Speed, knots: 10
Complement: 49
Radars: Navigation: Racal Decca TM 1226C; I-band.

Comment: Originally a diesel-driven survey ship with pronounced clipper bow. Converted for service as a three-masted schooner, commissioning as cadet training ship in 1978. Major refit by Bazán, Cadiz from June 1993 to March 1994, including a new diesel engine and a 5 m extension to the superstructure. Now has 853.4 m² of sail.

CAPITÁN MIRANDA   *6/2005*, Martin Mokrus* / 1133601

AUXILIARIES

Notes: (1) ROU 73 *(Grito de Asencio)* is an 18 m harbour tug.
(2) *Comar II* is a motor yacht used by the Commander-in-Chief.

COMAR II   *8/2005*, A E Galarce* / 1133600

2 LCVPs

LD 45   **LD 46**

Displacement, tons: 15 full load
Dimensions, feet (metres): 46.5 × 11.6 × 2.7 (14.1 × 3.5 × 0.8)
Main machinery: 1 GM 4-71 diesel; 115 hp (86 kW) sustained; 1 shaft
Speed, knots: 9. **Range, n miles:** 580 at 9 kt
Military lift: 10 tons

Comment: Built at Naval Shipyard, Montevideo and completed 1980.

LD 45 (PNN 631 alongside)   *12/1997, Hartmut Ehlers* / 0016610

1 PIAST CLASS (PROJECT 570) (SALVAGE SHIP) (ARS)

Name	No	Builders	Commissioned
VANGUARDIA	26 (ex-A 441)	Northern Shipyard, Gdansk	29 Dec 1976
(ex-*Otto Von Guericke*)			

Displacement, tons: 1,732 full load
Dimensions, feet (metres): 240 × 39.4 × 13.1 (73.2 × 12 × 4)
Main machinery: 2 Zgoda diesels; 3,800 hp(m) (2.79 MW); 2 shafts; cp props
Speed, knots: 16. **Range, n miles:** 3,000 at 12 kt
Complement: 61
Radars: Navigation: 2 TSR 333; I-band.

Comment: Acquired from Germany in October 1991 and sailed from Rostock in January 1992 after a refit at Neptun-Warnow Werft. Carries extensive towing and firefighting equipment plus a diving bell forward of the bridge. Armed with four 25 mm twin guns when in service with the former GDR Navy.

VANGUARDIA   *8/2004, A E Galarce* / 1044204

1 BUOY TENDER (ABU)

SIRIUS 21

Displacement, tons: 290 full load
Dimensions, feet (metres): 115.1 × 32.8 × 5.9 (35.1 × 10 × 1.8)
Main machinery: 2 Detroit 12V-71TA diesels; 840 hp (626 kW) sustained; 2 shafts
Speed, knots: 11
Complement: 15

Comment: Buoy tender built at Montevideo Naval Yard and completed on 5 February 1988. Endurance, five days.

SIRIUS   *6/1999, Uruguay Navy* / 0084228

2 LCM CLASS (ABU)

LD 41   **LD 42**

Displacement, tons: 24 light; 57 full load
Dimensions, feet (metres): 56.1 × 14.1 × 3.9 (17.1 × 4.3 × 1.2)
Main machinery: 2 Gray Marine 64 HN9 diesels; 330 hp (264 kW); 2 shafts
Speed, knots: 9. **Range, n miles:** 130 at 9 kt
Complement: 5
Military lift: 30 tons

Comment: First one transferred on lease from USA October 1972. Lease extended in October 1986. Second built in Uruguay.

LD 42   *2/2003, A E Galarce* / 0569791

1 LÜNEBURG CLASS (SUPPORT SHIP) (ARL)

Name	No	Builders	Commissioned
GENERAL ARTIGAS (ex-*Freiburg*)	4 (ex-A 1413)	Blohm + Voss	27 May 1968

Displacement, tons: 3,900 full load
Dimensions, feet (metres): 388.1 × 43.3 × 13.8 *(118.3 × 13.2 × 4.2)*
Main machinery: 2 MTU MD 16V 538 TB90 diesels; 6,000 hp(m) *(4.1 MW)* sustained; 2 shafts; cp props; bow thruster
Speed, knots: 17. **Range, n miles:** 6,000 at 14 kt
Complement: 95 (15 officers)
Cargo capacity: 1,100 tons
Guns: 4 Bofors 40 mm/70 (2 twin).
Countermeasures: Decoys: 2 Breda 105 mm SCLAR launchers.

Helicopters: AS 355 Esquilo.

Comment: Former auxiliary transferred to Uruguay on 12 April 2005. Used as a support ship for the Bremen class in German service, she was lengthened by 14.3 m in 1984 to accommodate a flight deck and a port-side crane. Her replenishment-at-sea capability will provide a much needed enhancement to Uruguayan operational capability. Other details are as for the ship in German service.

GENERAL ARTIGAS *10/2005*, Mario R V Carneiro* / 1133599

TUGS

1 COASTAL TUG (YTB)

Name	No	Builders	Commissioned
BANCO ORTIZ (ex-*Zingst*, ex-*Elbe*)	27 (ex-7, ex-Y 1655)	Peenewerft, Wolgast	10 Sep 1959

Displacement, tons: 261 full load
Dimensions, feet (metres): 100 × 26.6 × 10.8 *(30.5 × 8.1 × 3.3)*
Main machinery: 1 R6 DV 148 diesel; 550 hp(m) *(404 kW)*; 1 shaft
Speed, knots: 10
Complement: 12
Guns: 1 — 12.7 mm MG.

Comment: Ex-GDR Type 270 tug acquired in October 1991. 10 ton bollard pull.

BANCO ORTIZ *10/2000, A E Galarce* / 0105807

Vanuatu

Country Overview

The Republic of Vanuatu, formerly the New Hebrides, was jointly administered by Britain and France until it gained independence in 1980. Situated in the southwestern Pacific Ocean, some 1,100 n miles southeast of Papua New Guinea, the country comprises a group of about 80 islands, of which 67 are inhabited, which run generally north-south. The four main islands are Espiritu Santo (the largest), Malekula, Efate and Tanna. Others include Epi, Pentecost, Aoba, Maewo, Erromanga and Ambrym. The capital, largest town and principal port is Port-Vila on Efate. An archipelagic state, territorial seas (12 n miles) are claimed. An Exclusive Economic Zone (EEZ) (200 n miles) is also claimed but limits have not been fully defined by boundary agreements. Disputed sovereignty of Matthew and Hunter Islands, both uninhabited, is one complication.

Headquarters Appointments

Commander, Maritime Wing:
  Superintendent Tari Tamata

Bases

Port Vila, Efate Island

POLICE

1 PACIFIC CLASS (LARGE PATROL CRAFT) (PB)

Name	No	Builders	Commissioned
TUKORO	02	Australian Shipbuilding Industries	13 June 1987

Displacement, tons: 165 full load
Dimensions, feet (metres): 103.3 × 26.6 × 6.9 *(31.5 × 8.1 × 2.1)*
Main machinery: 2 Caterpillar 3516TA diesels; 4,400 hp *(3.28 MW)* sustained; 2 shafts
Speed, knots: 18. **Range, n miles:** 2,500 at 12 kt
Complement: 18 (3 officers)
Guns: 1 — 12.7 mm MG. 1 — 7.62 mm MG.
Radars: Navigation: Furuno 1011; I-band.

Comment: Under the Defence Co-operation Programme Australia has provided one Patrol Craft to the Vanuatu government. Training and operational and technical assistance is also given by the Royal Australian Navy. Ordered 13 September 1985 and launched 20 May 1987. A half-life refit was carried out in 1995 and, following extension of the Pacific Patrol Boat programme by the Australian government, a life-extension refit was carried out at Townsville in 2004. The ship is employed on Exclusive Economic Zone (EEZ) fishery patrol and surveillance, including customs duties.

TUKORO *8/2005*, (Chris Sattler)* / 1129574

Venezuela

ARMADA DE VENEZUELA

Country Overview

The Republic of Venezuela is situated in northern South America. With an area of 352,144 square miles, it has borders to the east with Guyana, to the south with Brazil and to the west with Colombia. It has a 1,512 n mile coastline with the Caribbean Sea and Atlantic Ocean. Margarita is the principal offshore island, of which there are 70. The capital and largest city is Caracas which is served by the port of La Guaira. Other ports include Puerto Cabello, and Maracaibo. The chief port on the Orinoco River is Puerto Ordaz. Territorial Seas (12 n miles) are claimed. An EEZ (200 n miles) has also been claimed but the limits have not been fully defined by boundary agreements.

Headquarters Appointments

Commander General of the Navy (Chief of Naval Operations):
  Vice Admiral Armando Laguna Laguna
Chief of Naval Staff:
  Vice Admiral Bernardo Alberto Bastardo Carreyo

Headquarters Appointments — *continued*

Inspector General:
  Vice Admiral Benigno Remigio Calvo Díaz
Commander Operations:
  Vice Admiral Luís Alberto Chirinos Medina

Diplomatic Representation

Defence Attaché in London:
  Rear Admiral Luis Mérida Galindo

Personnel

(a) 2006: 15,800
(b) 2 years' national service

Fleet Organisation

The fleet is split into 'Type' squadrons – frigates (except GC 11 and 12), submarines, light and amphibious forces. Service Craft Squadron composed of RA 33, BO 11 and BE 11. The Fast Attack Squadron of the Constitución class is subordinate to the Fleet Command.

Marines

Following restructuring, the Marines are formed into a division, *General Simón Bolívar*, which consists of two amphibious brigades. The 1st Amphibious Brigade comprises four infantry battalions: *Rafael Urdaneta* (Puerto Cabello), *Francisco de Miranda* (Punto Fijo), *Renato Beluche* (Maracaibo) and *Manuel Ponce Lugo* (Puerto Cabello). The 2nd Amphibious Brigade comprises three battalions: *General Simón Bolívar* (Maiquetía), *Mariscal Antonio José de Sucre* (Cumaná) and *General José Francisco Bermúdez* (Carúpano). Additionally, there is an Engineer Brigade with three construction battalions; a Fluvial Brigade with the Fluvial Frontier Command at Puerto Ayacucho (Amazonas State) and several posts on border rivers.

Coast Guard

Formed in August 1982. It is part of the Navy. Its Headquarters are at La Guaira (Vargas State). Its primary task is the surveillance of the 200 mile Exclusive Economic Zone and other jurisdictional areas of Venezuelan waters. Coast Guard Squadron includes the frigates GC 11 and GC 12 and several patrol craft.

Naval Aviation

Headquarters are at Puerto Cabello (Carabobo State). Under the command of a Rear Admiral, there are four Squadrons: Training, ASW, Patrol and Transport.

Naval Bases

Caracas: Navy Headquarters and *La Carlota* Naval Aviation Facility.
Vargas State: Division de Infantería HQ and Naval Academy at Mamo; OCHINA (Hydrography) and OCAMAR (Marines Support) HQ and the Coast Guard Command HQ at La Guaira. *Simón Bolívar* International Airport Naval Aviation Facility and Naval Police Training Centre at Maiquetía.
Puerto Cabello (Carabobo State): Fleet Command HQ. Two battalions of 1st Amphibious Brigade at *Contralmirante Agustín Armario* Naval Base and Naval Aviation

Command at *General Salom* Airport, Naval Schools and Dockyard.
Punto Fijo (Falcón State): Western Naval Zone HQ, Patrol Ships Squadron and Infantry Battalion 'Francisco de Miranda' at *Mariscal Juán Crisóstomo Falcón* Naval Base.
Carúpano (Sucre State): Eastern Naval Zone HQ. Two battalions of the 2nd Amphibious Brigade and Marines Training Centre.
Ciudad Bolívar (Bolívar): Fluvial Brigade HQ at *Capitán de Fragata Tomás Machado* Naval Base, with several Naval Posts along the Orinoco River.
Turiamo (Aragua State): *Generalísimo Francisco de Miranda* Marines Special Operation Command at the *Capitán de Fragata Tomás Vega* Naval Station.
Puerto Ayacucho (Amazonas State): Fluvial Frontier Command *General de Brigada Franz Rízquez Iribarren* with several Naval Posts along Orinoco, Atabapo, Negro and Meta rivers.

El Amparo (Apure State): Fluvial Frontier Command HQ *Teniente de Navío Jacinto Muñoz*, with several Naval Posts along Arauca and Barinas rivers.
Puerto de Nutrias (Barinas State): River Post.
San José de Macuro (Delta Amacuro State): Atlantic naval post.
La Orchila (Caribbean Sea): Minor Naval Base and Naval Aviation Station.
Puerto Hierro (Sucre State): Minor Naval Base.
Maracaibo (Zulia State), Güiria (Sucre State), Guanta (Anzoátegui State) and Margarita Island (Nueva Esparta State): Main Coast Guard Stations.
Los Monjes (Gulf of Venezuela), Los Testigos, Aves de Sotavento, La Tortuga and La Blanquilla Island (Caribbean Sea): Secondary Coast Guard Stations.

Prefix to Ships' Names

ARV (Armada de la República de Venezuela)

SUBMARINES

Notes: Acquisition of three new submarines, to replace the current force, is reported to be under consideration. Contenders include the German Type 214, the Franco-Spanish Scorpene class and the Russian Amur class. Calls for bids are expected in 2006.

2 SÁBALO (209) CLASS (TYPE 1300) (SSK)

Name	No	Builders	Laidown	Launched	Commissioned
SÁBALO	S 31 (ex-S 21)	Howaldtswerke, Kiel	2 May 1973	1 July 1975	6 Aug 1976
CARIBE	S 32 (ex-S 22)	Howaldtswerke, Kiel	1 Aug 1973	6 Nov 1975	11 Mar 1977

Displacement, tons: 1,285 surfaced; 1,600 dived
Dimensions, feet (metres): 200.1 × 20.3 × 18
(61.2 × 6.2 × 5.5)
Main machinery: Diesel-electric; 4 MTU 12V 493 AZ80 GA31L diesels; 2,400 hp(m) *(1.76 MW)* sustained; 4 alternators; 1.7 MW; 1 Siemens motor; 4,600 hp(m) *(3.38 MW)* sustained; 1 shaft
Speed, knots: 10 surfaced; 22 dived
Range, n miles: 7,500 at 10 kt surfaced
Complement: 33 (5 officers)

Torpedoes: 8—21 in *(533 mm)* bow tubes. AEG SST 4; anti-surface; wire-guided; active/passive homing to 12 km *(6.6 n miles)* at 35 kt or 28 km *(15.3 n miles)* at 23 kt; warhead 260 kg. 14 torpedoes carried. Swim-out discharge.
Countermeasures: ESM: Thomson-CSF DR 2000; intercept.
Weapons control: Atlas Elektronik ISUS TFCS.
Radars: Navigation: Terma Scanter Mil; I-band.
Sonars: Atlas Elektronik CSU 3-32; hull-mounted; passive/active search and attack; medium frequency.
Thomson Sintra DUUX 2; passive ranging.

Programmes: Type 209, IK81 designed by Ingenieurkontor Lübeck for construction by Howaldtswerke, Kiel and sale

CARIBE *6/1999* / 0084231

by Ferrostaal, Essen, all acting as a consortium. Both refitted at Kiel in 1981 and 1984 respectively.
Modernisation: Carried out by HDW at Kiel. *Sábalo* started in April 1990 and left in November 1992 without fully completing the refit. *Caribe* docked in Kiel throughout 1993 but was back in the water in mid-1994, and completed in 1995. The hull is slightly lengthened and new engines, fire control, sonar and attack periscopes fitted. Refit of *Sábalo* began at Dianca Shipyard in October 2003 and is to be completed in 2006. Refit of *Caribe* is also in progress

and is to be completed in 2007. The upgrade includes new batteries and weapon control systems.
Structure: A single-hull design with two main ballast tanks and forward and after trim tanks. The additional length is due to the new sonar dome similar to German Type 206 system. Fitted with snort and remote machinery control. Slow revving single screw. Very high-capacity batteries with GRP lead-acid cells and battery-cooling. Diving depth 250 m *(820 ft).*
Operational: Endurance, 50 days patrol.

FRIGATES

6 MODIFIED LUPO CLASS (FFGHM)

Name	No	Builders	Laid down	Launched	Commissioned
MARISCAL SUCRE	F 21	Fincantieri, Riva Trigoso	19 Nov 1976	28 Sep 1978	10 May 1980
ALMIRANTE BRIÓN	F 22	Fincantieri, Riva Trigoso	June 1977	22 Feb 1979	7 Mar 1981
GENERAL URDANETA	F 23	Fincantieri, Riva Trigoso	23 Jan 1978	23 Mar 1979	8 Aug 1981
GENERAL SOUBLETTE	F 24	Fincantieri, Riva Trigoso	26 Aug 1978	4 Jan 1980	5 Dec 1981
GENERAL SALOM	F 25	Fincantieri, Riva Trigoso	7 Nov 1978	13 Jan 1980	3 Apr 1982
ALMIRANTE GARCIA (ex-*José Felix Ribas*)	F 26	Fincantieri, Riva Trigoso	21 Aug 1979	4 Oct 1980	30 July 1982

Displacement, tons: 2,208 standard; 2,520 full load
Dimensions, feet (metres): 371.3 × 37.1 × 12.1
(113.2 × 11.3 × 3.7)
Main machinery: CODOG; 2 Fiat/GE LM 2500 gas turbines; 50,000 hp *(37.3 MW)* sustained; 2 GMT A230.20M or 2 MTU 20V 1163 (F 21 and F 22) diesels; 8,000 hp(m) *(5.97 MW)* sustained; 2 shafts; LIPS cp props
Speed, knots: 35; 21 on diesels. **Range, n miles:** 5,000 at 15 kt
Complement: 185

Missiles: SSM: 8 Otomat Teseo Mk 2 TG1 ❶; active radar homing to 80 km *(43.2 n miles)* at 0.9 Mach; warhead 210 kg; sea-skimmer for last 4 km *(2.2 n miles).*
SAM: Selenia Elsag Albatros octuple launcher ❷; 8 Aspide; semi-active radar homing to 13 km *(7 n miles)* at 2.5 Mach; height envelope 15—5,000 m *(49.2—16,405 ft);* warhead 30 kg.
Guns: 1 OTO Melara 5 in *(127 mm)*/54 ❸; 45 rds/min to 16 km *(8.7 n miles);* weight of shell 32 kg.
4 Otobreda 40 mm/70 (2 twin) ❹; 300 rds/min to 12.5 km *(6.8 n miles);* weight of shell 0.96 kg.
Torpedoes: 6—324 mm ILAS 3 (2 triple) tubes ❺. Whitehead A244S; anti-submarine; active/passive homing to 7 km *(3.8 n miles)* at 33 kt; warhead 34 kg (shaped charge).
Countermeasures: Decoys: 2 Breda 105 mm SCLAR 20-barrelled trainable ❻; chaff to 5 km *(2.7 n miles);* illuminants to 12 km *(6.6 n miles).* Can be used for HE bombardment.
ESM: Elisra NS 9003/9005; intercept.
Combat data systems: Selenia IPN 10. Elbit ENTCS 2000 (F 21 and F 22).
Weapons control: 2 Elsag NA 10 MFCS. 2 Dardo GFCS for 40 mm.
Radars: Air search: Selenia RAN 10S or Elta 2238 (F 21 and 22) ❼; E/F-band.
Air/surface search: Selenia RAN 11X; I-band.
Fire control: 2 Selenia Orion 10XP ❽; I/J-band.
2 Selenia RTN 20X ❾; I/J-band.
Navigation: SMA 3RM20; I-band.
Tacan: SRN 15A.
Sonars: EDO SQS-29 (Mod 610E) or Northrop Grumman 21 HS-7 (F 21 and F 22); hull-mounted; active search and attack; medium frequency.

Helicopters: 1 AB 212ASW ❿.

ALMIRANTE BRIÓN *(Scale 1 : 900), Ian Sturton* / 0529541

GENERAL URDANETA *7/1996* / 0050730

Programmes: All ordered on 24 October 1975. Similar to ships in the Italian and Peruvian navies.
Modernisation: F 21 and F 22 were scheduled to start a refit by Ingalls Shipyard in September 1992 but contractural problems delayed start until January 1998. Refits included upgrading the gas turbines, replacing the diesels, improving the combat data system, updating sonar and ESM, and overhauling all weapon systems. The ships were

redelivered in mid-2002. Neither is believed to be fully operational. F 23 and F 24 have been upgraded by Dianca, Puerto Caballo, and returned to service in December and October 2003 respectively. Work included modernisation of the main machinery, air-conditioning and weapon systems. F 25 and F 26 began similar refits at Dianca in 2004.
Structure: Fixed hangar means no space for Aspide reloads. Fully stabilised.

ALMIRANTE BRIÓN

6/2001, Northrop Grumman Ingalls / 0096360

PATROL FORCES

Notes: Replacement of the Constitución class began in February 1999 whan an Invitation to Tender was issued for six 30 kt craft. One was ordered from Bazán in September 1999 but funding withdrawn at last moment. The contract for the procurement of four 73 m offshore patrol boats, probably based on the Serviola class, and four 92 m corvettes was signed with the Spanish government on 29 November 2005. These are likely to be built in partnership with a Venezuelan shipyard.

6 CONSTITUCIÓN CLASS (FAST ATTACK CRAFT—MISSILE AND GUN) (PBG/PG)

Name	No	Builders	Laidown	Launched	Commissioned
CONSTITUCIÓN	PC 11	Vosper Thornycroft	Jan 1973	1 June 1973	16 Aug 1974
FEDERACIÓN	PC 12	Vosper Thornycroft	Aug 1973	26 Feb 1974	25 Mar 1975
INDEPENDENCIA	PC 13	Vosper Thornycroft	Feb 1973	24 July 1973	20 Sep 1974
LIBERTAD	PC 14	Vosper Thornycroft	Sep 1973	5 Mar 1974	12 June 1975
PATRIA	PC 15	Vosper Thornycroft	Mar 1973	27 Sep 1973	9 Jan 1975
VICTORIA	PC 16	Vosper Thornycroft	Mar 1974	3 Sep 1974	22 Sep 1975

Displacement, tons: 170 full load
Dimensions, feet (metres): 121 × 23.3 × 6 *(36.9 × 7.1 × 1.8)*
Main machinery: 2 MTU MD 16V 538 TB90 diesels; 6,000 hp(m) *(4.4 MW)* sustained; 2 shafts
Speed, knots: 31. **Range, n miles:** 1,350 at 16 kt
Complement: 20 (4 officers)

Missiles: SSM: 2 OTO Melara/Matra Teseo Mk 2 TG1 *(Federación, Libertad* and *Victoria)*; active radar homing to 80 km *(43.2 n miles)* at 0.9 Mach; sea-skimmer for last 4 km *(2.2 n miles)*; warhead 210 kg.

Guns: 1 OTO Melara 3 in *(76 mm)*/62 compact *(Constitución, Independencia* and *Patria)*; 85 rds/min to 16 km *(8.7 n miles)*; weight of shell 6 kg.
1 Breda 30 mm/70 *(Federación, Libertad* and *Victoria)*; 800 rds/min; weight of shell 0.37 kg.
2—12.7 mm MGs.
Weapons control: Elsag NA 10 Mod 1 GFCS *(Constitución, Independencia* and *Patria)*. Alenia Elsag Medusa optronic director *(Federación, Libertad* and *Victoria)*.
Radars: Surface search: SMA SPQ-2D; I-band.
Fire control: Selenia RTN 10X (in 76 mm ships); I/J-band.
Navigation: Racal; I-band.

Programmes: Transferred from the Navy in 1983 to the Coast Guard but now back again with Fleet Command.
Modernisation: Single Breda 30 mm guns replaced the 40 mm guns in the missile craft in 1989. All were refitted at Puerto Cabello 1992-1995.
Operational: It is planned to replace these ships with new offshore patrol vessels. Meanwhile it is reported that their propulsion systems have been refitted.

VICTORIA (missile craft)

7/1999, Venezuelan Navy / 0084235

SHIPBORNE AIRCRAFT

Notes: There are five operational Bell 412EP helicopters. Four acquired in 1999 and three more delivered in 2003 of which one has been lost. There is also one Bell 206B which is used for training.

Numbers/Type: 7 Agusta AB 212ASW.
Operational speed: 106 kt *(196 km/h).*
Service ceiling: 14,200 ft *(4,330 m).*
Range: 230 n miles *(426 km).*
Role/Weapon systems: ASW helicopter with secondary ASV role. Sensors: APS-705 search radar, Bendix AQS-18A dipping sonar. Weapons: ASW; two Mk 46 or A244/S torpedoes or depth bombs. ASV; mid-course guidance to Teseo Mk 2 missiles.

AB 212ASW   *6/1999, Venezuelan Navy* / 0084233

LAND-BASED MARITIME AIRCRAFT (FRONT LINE)

Notes: (1) There are also two Beech King Air and three Cessnas used for training and transport.
(2) Two CASA CN-235 maritime patrol aircraft were ordered in April 2005. The contract was signed on 29 November 2005.

Numbers/Type: 3/2/3 CASA C-212 S 43/S 200/S 400 Aviocar.
Operational speed: 190 kt *(353 km/h).*
Service ceiling: 24,000 ft *(7,315 m).*
Range: 1,650 n miles *(3,055 km).*
Role/Weapon systems: Medium-range MR and coastal protection aircraft; limited armed action. Acquired in 1981-82 and 1985-86. Three modernised and augmented in 1998 by S 400 type. Previous numbers have reduced. Sensors: APS-128 radar. Weapons: ASW; depth bombs. ASV; gun and rocket pods.

C-212   *6/2002, CASA/EADS* / 0529548

AMPHIBIOUS FORCES

Notes: It is reported that several hovercraft are to be built at Dianca in collaboration with a UK company.

4 CAPANA (ALLIGATOR) CLASS (LSTH)

Name	No	Builders	Commissioned
CAPANA	T 61	Korea Tacoma Marine	24 July 1984
ESEQUIBO	T 62	Korea Tacoma Marine	24 July 1984
GOAJIRA	T 63	Korea Tacoma Marine	20 Nov 1984
LOS LLANOS	T 64	Korea Tacoma Marine	20 Nov 1984

Displacement, tons: 4,070 full load
Dimensions, feet (metres): 343.8 × 50.5 × 9.8 *(104.8 × 15.4 × 3)*
Main machinery: 2 SEMT-Pielstick 16 PA6 V 280 diesels; 12,800 hp(m) *(9.41 MW)*; 2 shafts
Speed, knots: 14. **Range, n miles:** 5,600 at 11 kt
Complement: 117 (13 officers)
Military lift: 202 troops; 1,600 tons cargo; 4 LCVPs
Guns: 2 Breda 40 mm/70 (twin). 2 Oerlikon 20 mm GAM-BO1.
Weapons control: Selenia NA 18/V; optronic director.
Helicopters: Platform only.

Comment: Ordered in August 1982. Version III of Korea Tacoma Alligator type. Each has a 50 ton tank turntable and a lift between decks. *Goajira* was out of service from June 1987 to May 1993 after a serious fire. T 62 and T 63 reported to have been refitted in 2003 and T 61 and T 62 are likely also to be upgraded.

CAPANA   *6/1998, Venezuelan Navy* / 0084236

ESEQUIBO   *3/1999* / 0084237

2 AJEERA CLASS (LCU)

Name	No	Builders	Commissioned
MARGARITA	T 71	Swiftships Inc, Morgan City	20 Jan 1984
LA ORCHILA	T 72	Swiftships Inc, Morgan City	11 May 1984

Displacement, tons: 428 full load
Dimensions, feet (metres): 129.9 × 36.1 × 5.9 *(39.6 × 11 × 1.8)*
Main machinery: 2 Detroit 16V-149 diesels; 1,800 hp *(1.34 MW)* sustained; 2 shafts
Speed, knots: 13. **Range, n miles:** 1,500 at 10 kt
Complement: 26 (4 officers)
Military lift: 150 tons cargo; 100 tons fuel
Guns: 3—12.7 mm MGs.
Radars: Navigation: Raytheon 6410; I-band.

Comment: Both serve in Fluvial Command. Have a 15 ton crane.

MARGARITA   *6/1999, Venezuelan Navy* / 0084238

SURVEY SHIPS

1 SURVEY AND RESEARCH SHIP (AGOR)

Name	No	Builders	Launched	Commissioned
PUNTA BRAVA	BO 11	Bazán, La Carraca	9 Mar 1990	14 Mar 1991

Displacement, tons: 1,170 full load
Dimensions, feet (metres): 202.4 × 39 × 12.1 *(61.7 × 11.9 × 3.7)*
Main machinery: 2 Bazán-MAN 7L20/27 diesels; 2,500 hp(m) *(1.84 MW)*; 2 shafts; bow thruster
Speed, knots: 13. **Range, n miles:** 8,000 at 13 kt
Complement: 49 (6 officers) plus 6 scientists
Radars: Navigation: ARPA; I-band.

Comment: Ordered in September 1988. Developed from the Spanish Malaspina class. A multipurpose ship for oceanography, marine resource evaluation, geophysical and biological research. Equipped with Qubit hydrographic system. Carries two survey launches. EW equipment is fitted. Assigned to the OCHINA (Hydrographic department).

PUNTA BRAVA   *4/2001* / 0114821

2 SURVEY CRAFT (AGSC)

Name	No	Builders	Commissioned
GABRIELA (ex-*Peninsula de Araya*)	LH 11	Abeking & Rasmussen	5 Feb 1974
LELY (ex-*Peninsula de Paraguana*)	LH 12	Abeking & Rasmussen	7 Feb 1974

Displacement, tons: 90 full load
Dimensions, feet (metres): 88.6 × 18.4 × 4.9 *(27 × 5.6 × 1.5)*
Main machinery: 2 MTU diesels; 2,300 hp(m) *(1.69 MW)*; 2 shafts
Speed, knots: 20
Complement: 9 (1 officer)

Comment: LH 12 laid down 28 May 1973, launched 12 December 1973 and LH 11 laid down 10 March 1973, launched 29 November 1973. Acquired in September 1986 from the Instituto de Canalizaciones. Both assigned to the Fluvial Command.

GABRIELA (alongside *Alcatraz* PG 32)   *1/1994, Maritime Photographic* / 0506180

TRAINING SHIPS

1 SAIL TRAINING SHIP (AXS)

Name	No	Builders	Launched	Commissioned
SIMÓN BOLÍVAR	BE 11	AT Celaya, Bilbao	21 Nov 1979	6 Aug 1980

Displacement, tons: 1,260 full load
Measurement, tons: 934 gross
Dimensions, feet (metres): 270.6 × 34.8 × 14.4 *(82.5 × 10.6 × 4.4)*
Main machinery: 1 Detroit 12V-149T diesel; 875 hp *(652 kW)* sustained; 1 shaft
Speed, knots: 10
Complement: 93 (17 officers) plus 102 trainees

Comment: Ordered in 1978. Three-masted barque; similar to *Guayas* (Ecuador), *Cuauhtemoc* (Mexico) and *Gloria* (Colombia). Sail area (23 sails), 1,650 m². Highest mast, 131.2 ft *(40 m)*. Has won several international sail competitions including Cutty Sark '96. A refit is to be completed in 2005.

SIMÓN BOLÍVAR   *6/2001, A Campanera I Rovira* / 0534070

AUXILIARIES

Notes: There is one navigational aids tender *Macuro* BB-11.

1 LOGISTIC SUPPORT SHIP (AORH)

Name	No	Builders	Commissioned
CIUDAD BOLÍVAR	T 81	Hyundai, Ulsan	2001

Displacement, tons: 9,750 full load
Dimensions, feet (metres): 451.8 × 59 × 21.7 *(137.7 × 18 × 6.6)*
Main machinery: 2 Caterpillar 3616 diesels; 2 shafts; LIPS cp props
Speed, knots: 18. **Range, n miles:** 4,500 at 15 kt
Complement: 104
Guns: 2 Bofors 40 mm/70. 2 — 12.7 mm MGs.

Comment: Ordered from Hyundai, South Korea, in February 1999. Delivered in October 2001. Capable of carrying 4,400 tons of fuel and 900 tons of cargo. Two replenishment stations on each beam. Hangar and deck for medium size helicopter. Replenishment operations reported conducted with both French and Netherlands units. Armament is not yet fitted.

CIUDAD BOLÍVAR   *10/2002, Mario R V Carveiro* / 0534069

OCEAN TUG (ATA)

Name	No	Builders	Laid down	Launched	Commissioned
GENERAL FRANCISCO DE MIRANDA (ex-*Almirante Bruzuar*)	RA 11	Damen, Gorinchem and DIANCA, Puerto Caballo, Venezuela	Apr 2004	2005	2005

Displacement, tons: 700 full load
Dimensions, feet (metres): 213.2 × 39.3 × 19.7 *(65.0 × 12.0 × 6.0)*
Main machinery: 2 CAT 3606TA diesels; 5,400 hp *(4 MW)*; 2 shafts
Speed, knots: 16
Range, n miles: 7,000 at 10 kt
Complement: To be announced
Radars: Navigation: I-band.

Comment: DIANCA, a shipyard owned and operated by the Venezuelan Navy, contracted in early 2004 to build an ocean-going tug with technical assistance from Damen Shipyards. Built of aluminium and steel, the ship is to be used for a variety of tasks including counter-drug, counter-piracy and counter-pollution operations as well as general sea-safety duties. It has a cargo capacity of 150 tons and is planned to be completed by 2006. A second ship is expected.

COAST GUARD

Notes: Procurement of two new classes of patrol craft is in progress. Three 36 m patrol craft are to be built in Venezuela while four patrol craft are under construction in the US.

7 RIVER PATROL CRAFT (PBR)

MANAURE PF 21	TAMANACO PF 24	YARACUY PF 33
MARA PF 22	TEREPAIMA PF 31	SOROCAIMA PF 34
GUAICAIPURO PF 23		

Displacement, tons: 15 full load
Dimensions, feet (metres): 54.1 × 14.1 × 4.3 *(16.5 × 4.3 × 1.3)*
Main machinery: 2 diesels; 2 shafts
Speed, knots: 10
Complement: 8
Guns: 1 — 12.7 mm MG.
Radars: Surface search: Raytheon 6410; I-band.

Comment: River craft used by the Marines. Details given are for four Manaure class. There are also three Terepaima class which are 10 m long and capable of 45 kt.

MANAURE   *6/1998, Venezuelan Navy* / 0050737

1 + 14 DIANCA PATROL CRAFT (PB)

Displacement, tons: To be announced
Dimensions, feet (metres): 75.5 × 16.4 × ? *(23.0 × 5.0 × ?)*
Main machinery: To be announced
Speed, knots: 32
Complement: 10
Guns: To be announced.
Radars: To be announced.

Comment: Dianca Project P 698. First of class entered service in 2004 and a class of 15 is projected. Aluminium construction.

2 ALMIRANTE CLEMENTE CLASS (WFS)

Name	No	Builders	Laidown	Launched	Commissioned
ALMIRANTE CLEMENTE	GC 11	Ansaldo, Livorno	5 May 1954	12 Dec 1954	1956
GENERAL JOSÉ TRINIDAD MORAN	GC 12	Ansaldo, Livorno	5 May 1954	12 Dec 1954	1956

Displacement, tons: 1,300 standard; 1,500 full load
Dimensions, feet (metres): 325.1 × 35.5 × 12.2
(99.1 × 10.8 × 3.7)
Main machinery: 2 GMT 16-645E7C diesels; 6,080 hp(m)
(4.47 MW) sustained; 2 shafts
Speed, knots: 22. **Range, n miles:** 3,500 at 15 kt
Complement: 142 (12 officers)

Guns: 2 Otobreda 3 in *(76 mm)*/62 compact ❶; 85 rds/min
to 16 km *(8.7 n miles)*; weight of shell 6 kg.
2 Breda 40 mm/70 (twin) ❷; 300 rds/min to 12.5 km
(6.8 n miles); weight of shell 0.96 kg.
Torpedoes: 6—324 mm ILAS 3 (2 triple) tubes ❸. Whitehead
A 244S; anti-submarine; active/passive homing to 7 km
(3.8 n miles) at 33 kt; warhead 34 kg (shaped charge).
Depth charges: 2 throwers.
Weapons control: Elsag NA 10 Mod 1 GFCS.
Radars: Air search: Plessey AWS 4 ❹; E/F-band.
Surface search: Racal Decca 1226 ❺; I-band.
Fire control: Selenia RTN 10X ❻; I/J-band.
Sonars: Plessey PMS 26; hull-mounted; active search and
attack; 10 kHz.

Programmes: Survivors of a class of six ordered in 1953.
Modernisation: Both ships were refitted by Cammell Laird/
Plessey group in April 1968. 4 in guns replaced by 76 mm.
Both refitted again in Italy in 1984-85, prior to transfer to
Coast Guard duties in 1986.
Structure: Fitted with Denny-Brown fin stabilisers and air
conditioned throughout the living and command spaces.
Operational: Both reported operational.

ALMIRANTE CLEMENTE   *(Scale 1 : 900), Ian Sturton* / 0506215

GENERAL JOSÉ TRINIDAD MORAN   *10/1998, E & M Laursen* / 0050734

ALMIRANTE CLEMENTE   *4/2001* / 0114820

4 PETREL (POINT) CLASS (WPB)

Name	No	Builders	Commissioned
PETREL (ex-*Point Knoll*)	PG 31	US Coast Guard Yard, Curtis Bay	26 June 1967
ALCATRAZ (ex-*Point Judith*)	PG 32	US Coast Guard Yard, Curtis Bay	26 July 1966
ALBATROS (ex-*Point Franklin*)	PG 33	US Coast Guard Yard, Curtis Bay	14 Nov 1966
PELÍCANO (ex-*Point Ledge*)	PG 34	US Coast Guard Yard, Curtis Bay	18 July 1962

Displacement, tons: 68 full load
Dimensions, feet (metres): 83 × 17.2 × 5.8 *(25.3 × 5.2 × 1.8)*
Main machinery: 2 Caterpillar diesels; 1,600 hp *(1.19 MW)*; 2 shafts
Speed, knots: 23.5
Range, n miles: 1,500 at 8 kt
Complement: 10 (1 officer)
Guns: 2—12.7 mm MGs.
Radars: Surface search: Raytheon SPS-64; I-band.

Comment: *Petrel* transferred from USCG on 18 November 1991 and *Alcatraz* on
15 January 1992, *Albatros* on 23 June 1998 and *Pelícano* on 3 August 1998. The transfer
of four further craft is unlikely. Most of the class are believed to be operational.

12 GAVION CLASS (WPB)

GAVION	PG 401	CORMORAN	PG 405	NEGRON	PG 409
ALCA	PG 402	COLIMBO	PG 406	PIGARGO	PG 410
BERNACLA	PG 403	FARDELA	PG 407	PAGAZA	PG 411
CHAMAN	PG 404	FUMAREL	PG 408	SERRETA	PG 412

Displacement, tons: 45 full load
Dimensions, feet (metres): 80 × 17 × 4.8 *(24.4 × 5.2 × 1.5)*
Main machinery: 2 Detroit 12V-92TA diesels; 2,160 hp *(1.61 MW)* sustained; 2 shafts
Speed, knots: 25. **Range, n miles:** 1,000 at 12 kt
Complement: 10
Guns: 2—12.7 mm MGs. 2—7.62 mm MGs. 1—40 mm Mk 19 grenade launcher.
Radars: Surface search: Raytheon R1210; I-band.

Comment: Ordered from Halter Marine 24 April 1998 and delivered from late 1999 to early 2000.
Aluminium construction. Four craft refitted in 2003 and all believed to be operational.

ALCATRAZ   *4/1999* / 0084242

ALCA   *10/1999, Halter Marine* / 0084243

2 UTILITY CRAFT (YAG)

LOS TAQUES LG 11 **LOS CAYOS** LG 12

Displacement, tons: 350 full load
Dimensions, feet (metres): 87.3 × 23.3 × 4.9 (26.6 × 7.1 × 1.5)
Main machinery: 1 diesel; 850 hp(m) (625 kW); 1 shaft
Speed, knots: 8
Complement: 10
Guns: 1—12.7 mm MG.

Comment: Former trawlers. Commissioned 15 May 1981 and 17 July 1984 respectively. Used for salvage and SAR tasks.

LOS CAYOS *3/1999, Venezuelan Navy* / 0084244

18 INSHORE PATROL BOATS (PBR)

CONSTANCIA LRG 001 **HONESTIDAD** LRG 003 **INTEGRIDAD** LRG 005 **+12**
PERSEVERANCIA LRG 002 **TENACIDAD** LRG 004 **LEALTAD** LRG 006

Displacement, tons: 11 full load
Dimensions, feet (metres): 39.4 × 9.2 × 5.6 (12 × 2.8 × 1.7)
Main machinery: 2 diesels; 640 hp(m) (470 kW); 2 shafts
Speed, knots: 38
Complement: 4
Guns: 2—7.62 mm MGs.
Radars: Surface search: I-band.

Comment: First three speed boat type with GRP hulls delivered from a local shipyard in December 1991. Fourth completed in August 1993. Details given are for *Integridad* which is the first of two built at Guatire, and delivered in 1997/98. GRP construction. The twelve un-named craft are Boston Whaler Guardian class capable of 25 kt, mounting 2—12.7 mm and 2—6.72 mm MGs, and with Raytheon radars. These were donated by the US. All of these craft are used by Marines.

GUARDIAN INSHORE PATROL BOAT *4/1999, Venezuelan Navy* / 0084245

8 PUNTA MACOLLA CLASS (PB)

PUNTA MACOLLA LSM 001 **BAJO BRITO** LSM 004 **VELA DE COBO** LSM 007
FARALLÓN CENTINELA LSM 002 **BAJO ARAYA** LSM 005 **CAYO MACEREO** LSM 008
CHARAGATO LSM 003 **CARECARE** LSM 006

Displacement, tons: 5 full load
Dimensions, feet (metres): 41.7 × 9.2 × 6.6 (12.7 × 2.8 × 2)
Main machinery: 2 diesels; 2 shafts
Speed, knots: 30
Complement: 4
Guns: 1—12.7 mm MG.
Radars: Surface search: Raytheon; I-band.

Comment: Built in Venezuela by Intermarine. Used by OCHINA (Hydrographic department) and for SAR. First six delivered by 1997 and last two in 2000.

BAJO ARAYA *3/1999, Venezuelan Navy* / 0084246

7 POLARIS CLASS (PBF)

POLARIS LG 21 **ALDEBARAN** LG 24 **CANOPUS** LG 26
SIRIUS LG 22 **ANTARES** LG 25 **ALTAIR** LG 27
RIGEL LG 23

Displacement, tons: 5 full load
Dimensions, feet (metres): 26 wl × 8.5 × 2.6 (7.9 × 2.6 × 0.8)
Main machinery: 1 diesel outdrive; 400 hp(m) (294 kW)
Speed, knots: 50
Complement: 4
Guns: 1—12.7 mm MG.
Radars: Surface search: Raytheon; I-band.

Comment: Built by Cougar Marine and delivered in 1987. Used by the Coast Guard for drug interdiction. Two more reported operational.

ALDEBARAN *4/1999, Venezuelan Navy* / 0084247

PROTECTOR 3612 CLASS (PB)

CHICHIRIVICHE LG 31 **CARUANTA** LG 32

Displacement, tons: 11 full load
Dimensions, feet (metres): 36.1 × 13.1 × 1.6 (11.1 × 4.0 × 0.5)

Comment: Built by SeaArk Marine, Monticello, and delivered in 1994.

1 SUPPORT SHIP (AKSL)

Name	No	Builders	Commissioned
FERNANDO GOMEZ (ex-*José Felix Ribas*, ex-*Oswegatchie*)	RP 21 (ex-R 13)	Commercial Iron Works, Portland	14 Dec 1945

Displacement, tons: 245 full load
Dimensions, feet (metres): 100.1 × 25.9 × 9.5 (30.5 × 7.9 × 2.9)
Main machinery: 2 diesels; 1,270 hp (947 kW); 1 shaft
Speed, knots: 10
Complement: 12
Guns: 2—12.7 mm MGs.
Radars: Navigation: Raytheon; I-band.

Comment: Former tug, originally acquired from the US in 1965. Out of service for some years but now employed as a logistic support ship and for occasional patrol and SAR.

FERNANDO GOMEZ *6/1998, Venezuelan Navy* / 0050738

2 RIVER TRANSPORT CRAFT (LCM)

CURIAPO LC 21 **YOPITO** LC 01

Displacement, tons: 115 full load
Dimensions, feet (metres): 73.7 × 21 × 5.2 (22.5 × 6.4 × 1.6)
Main machinery: 2 Detroit diesels; 850 hp (625 kW); 2 shafts
Speed, knots: 9
Complement: 5
Cargo capacity: 60 tons or 200 Marines
Guns: 2—12.7 mm MGs.

Comment: Details given are for *Curiapo* which is a former LCM. *Yopito* is a former LCU of 18 m. Both are used by the Marines. There are also 12 11 m LCVPs.

YOPITO *7/1999, Venezuelan Navy* / 0084248

NATIONAL GUARD (GUARDIA NACIONAL)

Notes: (1) There are also a large number of US and Canadian built river craft of between 6 and 9 m length, which are armed with MGs.
(2) Four intercept launches were delivered in 2003; two in July 2003 and two in October 2003.
(3) Some 60 Pirana class river patrol craft have been ordered. The first 15 were delivered in August 2003.

10 RIO ORINOCO II CLASS (PBF)

B 9801 series

Displacement, tons: 30 full load
Dimensions, feet (metres): 54 × 14 × 4.6 *(16.5 × 4.3 × 1.4)*
Main machinery: 2 MTU 12V 183 TE93 diesels; 2,268 hp(m) *(1.67 MW)* sustained; 2 shafts
Speed, knots: 36. **Range, n miles:** 500 at 25 kt
Complement: 5
Guns: 2—12.7 mm MGs. 2—7.62 mm MGs.
Radars: Surface search: Raytheon R1210; I-band.

Comment: Ordered from Halter Marine 24 April 1998. All delivered by late 1999. Aluminium construction. Some of the similar sized Orinoco I craft built in the 1970s are still in limited use.

ORINOCO II   *1/1999, Halter Marine* / 0050739

12 PUNTA CLASS (PB) and 12 PROTECTOR CLASS (PB)

A 8201 and B 8421 series

Displacement, tons: 15 full load
Dimensions, feet (metres): 43 × 13.4 × 3.9 *(13.1 × 4.1 × 1.2)*
Main machinery: 2 MTU Series 183 diesels; 1,500 hp *(1.1 MW)*; 2 shafts
Speed, knots: 34
Range, n miles: 390 at 25 kt
Complement: 4
Guns: 2—12.7 mm MGs.
Radars: Navigation: Raytheon; I-band.

Comment: Details given for the Punta class. Ordered 24 January 1984. Built by Robert E Derecktor, Mamaroneck, NY. Names begin with *Punta*. Aluminium hulls. Completed from July-December 1984. Re-engined in 1996-97. The Protector class are the same size, but are slower at 28 kt. They were built by SeaArk Marine and completed in 1984. Some are probably non-operational. Names begin with *Rio*.

PROTECTOR   *2/1996, van Ginderen Collection* / 0084249

Vietnam

Country Overview

The Socialist Republic of Vietnam was established in 1976 when the Democratic Republic of Vietnam in the north and the Republic of Vietnam in the south became one nation. The country had been divided at the 17th parallel from the end of French colonial rule in 1954 and during the ensuing Vietnam War. Located on the east coast of the Indochina peninsula, it has an area of 127,844 square miles and is bordered to the north by China and to the west by Cambodia and Laos. It has a 1,858 n mile coastline with the South China Sea. Hanoi is the capital while Ho Chi Minh City (formerly Saigon) is the largest city and a major port. There are further ports at Haiphong and Da Nang. Territorial seas (12 n miles) are claimed. An EEZ (200 n miles) has also been claimed but the limits have not been defined.

Headquarters Appointments

Chief of Naval Forces:
   Vice Admiral Mai Xuan Binh
Deputy Chief of Naval Forces:
   Captain Tran Quang Khue

Personnel

(a)   2006: 9,000 regulars
(b)   Additional conscripts on three to four year term (about 3,000)
(c)   27,000 naval infantry

Organisation and Bases

The Vietnamese Navy is part of the People's Army of Vietnam (PAVN) and is formally known as the PAVN Navy. The fleet is organised into four regions based on, from north to south, Haiphong (HQ), Da Nang, Nha Trang and Cân Tho. There are other bases at Cam Ranh Bay, Hue and Ha Tou.

Coast Guard

A Coast Guard was formed on 1 September 1998. It is subordinate to the Navy and may take on Customs duties.

SUBMARINES

2 YUGO CLASS (MIDGET SUBMARINES) (SSW)

Displacement, tons: 90 surfaced; 110 dived
Dimensions, feet (metres): 65.6 × 10.2 × 15.1 *(20 × 3.1 × 4.6)*
Main machinery: 2 diesels; 320 hp(m) *(236 kW)*; 1 shaft
Speed, knots: 12 surfaced; 8 dived
Range, n miles: 550 at 10 kt surfaced; 50 at 4 kt dived
Complement: 4 plus 6/7 divers

Comment: Transferred from North Korea in 1997. May be fitted with two short torpedo tubes and a snort mast, but used primarily for diver related operations. The conning tower acts as a wet/dry diver compartment. Operational status is doubtful.

YUGO (North Korean colours)
6/1998, Ships of the World
0052525

FRIGATES

Notes: The Barnegat class frigate (ex-seaplane tender) *Pham Ngu Lao* HQ 01 has probably been decommissioned.

0 + 2 (2) GEPARD (PROJECT 11661) CLASS (FFGM)

Displacement, tons: 1,560 standard; 1,930 full load
Dimensions, feet (metres): 334.6 × 44.6 × 14.4
(102 × 13.6 × 4.4)
Main machinery: CODOG; 2 gas turbines; 30,850 hp(m)
(23.0 MW); 1 Type 61D diesel; 7,375 hp(m) *(5.5 MW)*;
2 shafts; cp props
Speed, knots: 26 (18 on diesels)
Range, n miles: 5,000 at 10 kt
Complement: 110 (accommodation for 131)

Missiles: SSM: 8 Zvezda SS-N-25 (KH 35 Uran) (2 quad);
IR or radar homing to 130 km *(70.2 n miles)* at 0.9 Mach;
warhead 145 kg; sea-skimmer.
SAM: 1 SA-N-4 Gecko twin launcher; semi-active radar
homing to 15 km *(8 n miles)* at 2.5 Mach; warhead 50 kg.
20 weapons.

Guns: 1—3 in *(76 mm)*/60 AK-176; 120 rds/min to 15 km
(8 n miles); weight of shell 6.9 kg.
2—30 mm/65 AK-630; 6 barrels per mounting; 3,000 rds/min
combined to 2 km.
Torpedoes: 4—21 in *(533 mm)* (2 twin) tubes.
A/S mortars: 1 RBU 6000 12-tubed trainable.
Mines: 2 rails. 48 mines.
Countermeasures: Decoys: 4 PK 16 chaff launchers.
ESM/ECM: 2 Bell Shroud. 2 Bell Squat. Intercept and jammers.
Weapons control: 2 Light Bulb datalink. Hood Wink and
Odd Box optronic systems. Band Stand datalink.
Radars: Air/surface search: Cross Dome; E/F-band.
Fire control: BassTilt; H/I-band (for guns). Pop Group; F/H/I-
band (for SAM). Garpun-B (for SSM); I/J-band.
Navigation: Nayada; I-band.
IFF: 2 Square Head. 1 Salt Pot B.

GEPARD CLASS *7/2002*, Military Parade* / 0528304

Sonars: Ox Yoke; hull-mounted; active search and attack;
medium frequency.
OxTail; VDS; active search and attack; medium frequency.

Programmes: Contract signed with Rosoboronexport
in late 2005 for the construction of two Gepard class
frigates at Zelenodolsk Shipyard. Construction of the

first ship is likely to start in 2006. Components may be
supplied for the construction of two further ships at
Ho Chi Minh City.
Operational: Details of weapons and sensors are
speculative and based on those originally designated for
the ships in Russian naval service.

5 PETYA (PROJECT 159A) CLASS (FFL)

HQ 09, 11 (Type III)   **HQ 13,15, 17 (Type II)**

Displacement, tons: 950 standard; 1,180 full load
Dimensions, feet (metres): 268.3 × 29.9 × 9.5
(81.8 × 9.1 × 2.9)
Main machinery: CODAG; 2 gas turbines; 30,000 hp(m)
(22 MW); 1 Type 61V-3 diesel; 5,400 hp(m) *(3.97 MW)*
sustained; centre shaft; 3 shafts
Speed, knots: 32. **Range, n miles:** 4,870 at 10 kt; 450 at 29 kt
Complement: 98 (8 officers)

Guns: 4 USSR 3 in *(76 mm)*/60 (2 twin); 90 rds/min to 15 km
(8 n miles); weight of shell 6.8 kg.
4—37 mm (2 twin) (HQ 11). 4—23 mm (2 twin) (HQ 11).
Torpedoes: 3—21 in *(533 mm)* (triple) tubes (Petya III).
SAET-60; passive homing to 15 km *(8.1 n miles)* at 40 kt;
warhead 400 kg.
5—16 in *(406 mm)* (1 quin) tubes (Petya II). SAET-40;
active/passive homing to 10 km *(5.5 n miles)* at 30 kt;
warhead 100 kg.
A/S mortars: 4 RBU 6000 12-tubed trainable (Petya II);
range 6,000 m; warhead 31 kg.
4 RBU 2500 16-tubed trainable (Petya III); range 2,500 m;
warhead 21 kg.
Depth charges: 2 racks.
Mines: Can carry 22.
Countermeasures: ESM: 2 Watch Dog; radar warning.
Radars: Air/surface search: Strut Curve; F-band.
Navigation: Don 2; I-band.
Fire control: Hawk Screech; I-band.
IFF: High Pole B. 2 Square Head.
Sonars: Vychada MG 311; hull-mounted; active attack; high
frequency.

Programmes: Two Petya III (export version) transferred
from USSR in December 1978 and three Petya IIs, two in
December 1983 and one in December 1984. Petya II HQ
13 was reported decommissioned in 1996 but may have
been refitted.
Modernisation: Refitted and updated 1994 to 1999. The
RBUs replaced by 25 mm guns and the torpedo tubes
by 37 mm guns in some of the class. *HQ 17* completed
major overhaul at Ba Son Shipyard in 2001.

HQ 17 (PETYA II) *11/2001* / 0131341

HQ 09 *9/1995, G Toremans* / 0506261

Structure: The Petya IIIs have the same hulls as the Petya IIs
but different armament.

Operational: Reported active between the coast and the
Spratly Islands.

LAND-BASED MARITIME AIRCRAFT

Notes: Air Force Su-27 Flankers and Su-22 Fitter-H can be used for maritime surveillance.

Numbers/Type: 2 PZL Mielec M-28 B1R Bryza.
Operational speed: 181 kt *(335 km/h)*.
Service ceiling: 13,770 ft *(4,200 m)*.
Range: 736 n miles *(1,365 km)*.
Role/Weapon systems: Polish-built aircraft originally based on the USSR Cash light
transport. Contract in October 2003 for the procurement of up to ten aircraft configured
for maritime surveillance. First two to have been delivered by late 2004. Sensors:
MSC-400 mission system, ARS-400 radar (with SAR/ISAR) modes). Weapons: to be
announced.

M-28 (Polish colours)
6/2003*, J Cislak
0567493

For details of the latest updates to *Jane's Fighting Ships* online and to discover the additional
information available exclusively to online subscribers please visit
jfs.janes.com

Numbers/Type: 3 Beriev Be-12 Mail.
Operational speed: 328 kt (608 km/h).
Service ceiling: 37,000 ft (11,280 m).
Range: 4,050 n miles (7,500 km).
Role/Weapon systems: Long-range ASW/MR amphibian. Sensors: Short Horn search radar, MAD, EW. Weapons: ASW; 5 tons of depth bombs, mines or torpedoes. ASV; limited missile and rocket armament.

MAIL (Russian colours)   7/1996, J Cislak / 0084250

CORVETTES

Notes: Ex-US Admirable class HQ 07 is an alongside training hulk.

2 BPS 500 (PROJECT 12418) CLASS (FSGM)

HQ 381   +1

Displacement, tons: 517 full load
Dimensions, feet (metres): 203.4 × 36.1 × 8.2 (62 × 11 × 2.5)
Main machinery: 2 MTU diesels; 19,600 hp(m) (14.41 MW); 2 Kamewa waterjets
Speed, knots: 32
Range, n miles: 2,200 at 14 kt
Complement: 28

Missiles: SSM: 8 Zvezda SS-N-25 (KH-35 Uran) (2 quad) ❶; active radar homing to 130 km (70.1 n miles) at 0.9 Mach; warhead 145 kg.
SAM: SA-N-10. 24 missiles.
Guns: 1—3 in (76 mm)/60 ❷; 120 rds/min to 15 km (8 n miles); weight of shell 7 kg.
1—30 mm/65 AK 630 ❸; 6 barrelled; 3,000 rds/min combined to 2 km.
2—12.7 mm MGs.
Mines: Rails fitted.
Countermeasures: Decoys: 2 chaff launchers ❹.
Weapons control: Optronic director ❺.
Radars: Air/surface search: Cross Dome ❻; E/F-band.
Navigation: I-band.
Fire control: Bass Tilt ❼; H/I-band.

Comment: Severnoye design (improved Pauk) ordered in 1996 and two ships subsequently delivered in kit form to Ba Son Shipyard, Ho Chi Minh City. First unit launched in June 1998 and became operational in late 2001. Missile systems yet to be fitted. The second unit may have been built but this has not been confirmed.

BPS 500   (not to scale), Ian Sturton / 0530054

HQ 381   11/2001 / 0131340

4 + 8 TARANTUL CLASS (PROJECT 1241) (FSGM)

HQ 371   HQ 372   HQ 373   HQ 374

Displacement, tons: 385 standard; 450 full load
Dimensions, feet (metres): 184.1 × 37.7 × 8.2 (56.1 × 11.5 × 2.5)
Main machinery: 2 Nikolayev Type DR 77 gas turbines; 16,016 hp(m) (11.77 MW) sustained; 2 Nikolayev Type DR 76 gas turbines with reversible gearboxes; 4,993 hp(m) (3.67 MW) sustained; 2 shafts
Speed, knots: 36
Range, n miles: 2,000 at 20 kt; 400 at 36 kt
Complement: 41 (5 officers)

Missiles: SSM: 4 SS-N-2D Styx; IR homing to 83 km (45 n miles) at 0.9 Mach; warhead 513 kg; sea-skimmer at end of run.
SAM: SA-N-5 Grail quad launcher; manual aiming; IR homing to 6 km (3.2 n miles) at 1.5 Mach; warhead 1.5 kg.
Guns: 1—3 in (76 mm)/60; 120 rds/min to 15 km (8 n miles); weight of shell 7 kg.
2—30 mm/65 AK 630; 6 barrels per mounting; 3,000 rds/min combined to 2 km.
Countermeasures: Decoys: 2 PK 16 chaff launchers.
Weapons control: Hood Wink optronic director.
Radars: Air/surface search: Plank Shave; E-band.
Navigation: Pechora; I-band.
Fire control: Bass Tilt; H/I-band.
IFF: Salt Pot, Square Head A.
Sonars: Foal Tail; active; high frequency.

Programmes: First pair ordered in October 1994. These were new hulls exported at a favourable price and completed by 1996. Some delay in delivery because of late payments, but both were in service by April 1996. Two further vessels were reported to have been ordered in 1999 for delivery in 2000. Imagery of HQ 374 suggests that the contract may have been completed although this may be the result of a change in pennant numbers. Current numbers of vessels are thus uncertain. A contract was signed in March 2004 for the supply of ten further Tarantul IV, armed with SS-N-25 (Kh 35 Uran). At least two of these are to be built at Vympel Shipyard, Rybinsk, with the balance to be constructed in Vietnam.
Operational: Based at Da Nang.

HQ 374   6/2004, M Mazumdar / 1043705

PATROL FORCES

Notes: (1) At least one Shanghai II class PC may still be operational.(2) Some of the craft listed may be transferred to the Coast Guard and Maritime Police.

2 + 2 (6) SVETLYAK (PROJECT 1041.2) CLASS (PGM)

HQ 261   HQ 262

Displacement, tons: 365 full load
Dimensions, feet (metres): 162.4 × 30.2 × 7.9 (49.5 × 9.2 × 2.4)
Main machinery: 3 diesels; 15,900 hp(m) (11.85 MW) sustained; 3 shafts; cp props
Speed, knots: 30
Range, n miles: 2,200 at 13 kt
Complement: 28 (4 officers)
Missiles: SAM: SA-N-10; shoulder launched and (manual aiming); IR homing to 5 km (2.7 n miles) at 1.7 Mach; warhead 1.5 kg.
Guns: 1—3 in (76 mm)/60 AK-176M; 120 rds/min to 15 km (8 n miles); weight of shell 7 kg.
1—30 mm/65 AK 630; 6 barrels; 3,000 rds/min combined to 2 km.
Countermeasures: Decoys: 2 chaff launchers.
Weapons control: Hood Wink optronic director.
Radars: Air/surface search: Peel Cone; E-band.
Fire control: Bass Tilt; H/I-band.
Navigation: Palm Frond B; I-band.

Comment: Contract for two craft signed with Almaz, St Petersburg in November 2001. First vessel launched on 17 July 2002 and second on 30 July 2002. Following acceptance on 17 October 2002, both vessels were shipped from St Petersburg on 14 December 2002. Two more are expected to be delivered in 2006 and there is reported to be an option for a further six vessels.

SVETLYAK   9/2002, Almaz / 0530061

8 OSA II CLASS (FAST ATTACK CRAFT—MISSILE) (PTFG)

HQ 354-361

Displacement, tons: 245 full load
Dimensions, feet (metres): 126.6 × 24.9 × 8.8 *(38.6 × 7.6 × 2.7)*
Main machinery: 3 Type M 504 diesels; 10,800 hp(m) *(7.94 MW)* sustained; 3 shafts
Speed, knots: 37. **Range, n miles:** 500 at 35 kt
Complement: 30
Missiles: SSM 4 SS-N-2B Styx; active radar or IR homing to 46 km *(25 n miles)* at 0.9 Mach; warhead 513 kg.
Guns: 4 USSR 30 mm/65 (2 twin); 500 rds/min to 5 km *(2.7 n miles)*; weight of shell 0.54 kg.
Radars: Surface search: Square Tie; I-band.
Fire control: Drum Tilt; H/I-band.
IFF: High Pole. 2 Square Head.

Comment: Transferred from USSR: two in October 1979, two in September 1980, two in November 1980 and two in February 1981. All based at Da Nang. Operational status doubtful.

OSA II 354   *5/2000, Bob Fildes* / 0105740

5 TURYA (PROJECT 206M) CLASS
(FAST ATTACK CRAFT—HYDROFOIL) (PCK)

HQ 321, HQ 331-332, HQ 334-335

Displacement, tons: 190 standard; 250 full load
Dimensions, feet (metres): 129.9 × 29.9 (41 over foils) × 5.9 (13.1 over foils)
(39.6 × 7.6 (12.5) × 1.8 (4))
Main machinery: 3 Type M 504 diesels; 10,800 hp(m) *(7.94 MW)* sustained; 3 shafts
Speed, knots: 40. **Range, n miles:** 600 at 35 kt foilborne; 1,450 at 14 kt hullborne
Complement: 30
Guns: 2 USSR 57 mm/70 (twin, aft); 120 rds/min to 8 km *(4.4 n miles)*; weight of shell 2.8 kg.
2 USSR 25 mm/80 (twin, fwd); 270 rds/min to 3 km *(1.6 n miles)*; weight of shell 0.34 kg.
Torpedoes: 4—21 in *(533 mm)* tubes (not in all).
Depth charges: 2 racks.
Radars: Surface search: Pot Drum; H/I-band.
Fire control: Muff Cob; G/H-band.
IFF: High Pole B. Square Head.
Sonars: Foal Tail (not in all); VDS; high frequency.

Comment: Transferred from USSR: two in mid-1984, one in late 1984, two in January 1986. Two more acquired from Russia. Two of the five do not have torpedo tubes or sonar. Two scrapped so far, the remainder are probably non-operational.

TURYA 331   *5/2000, Bob Fildes* / 0105741

3 SHERSHEN (PROJECT 206) CLASS
(FAST ATTACK CRAFT) (PTFM)

HQ 301 series

Displacement, tons: 145 standard; 170 full load
Dimensions, feet (metres): 113.8 × 22 × 4.9 *(34.7 × 6.7 × 1.5)*
Main machinery: 3 Type 503A diesels; 8,025 hp(m) *(5.9 MW)* sustained; 3 shafts
Speed, knots: 45. **Range, n miles:** 850 at 30 kt; 460 at 42 kt
Complement: 23
Missiles: SAM: 1 SA-N-5 Grail quad launcher; manual aiming; IR homing to 6 km *(3.2 n miles)* at 1.5 Mach; altitude to 2,500 m *(8,000 ft)*; warhead 1.5 kg.
Guns: 4 USSR 30 mm/65 (2 twin); 500 rds/min to 5 km *(2.7 n miles)*; weight of shell 0.54 kg.
Torpedoes: 4—21 in *(533 mm)* tubes (not in all).
Depth charges: 2 racks (12).
Mines: Can carry 6.
Radars: Surface search: Pot Drum; H/I-band.
Fire control: Drum Tilt; H/I-band.
IFF: High Pole A. Square Head.

Comment: A total of 16 transferred from USSR: two in 1973, two in April 1979 (without torpedo tubes), two in September 1979, two in August 1980, two in October 1980, two in January 1983 and four in June 1983. Most have been cannibalised for spares.

SHERSHEN (refitting in Haiphong)   *8/2000, P Marsan* / 0105742

4 + (12) STOLKRAFT CLASS (PBR)

HQ 56-59

Displacement, tons: 44 full load
Dimensions, feet (metres): 73.5 × 24.6 × 3.9 *(22.4 × 7.5 × 1.2)*
Main machinery: 2 MTU 12V 183 TE93 diesels; 2,301 hp(m) *(1.69 MW)* sustained; 2 Doen waterjets
1 Volvo Penta diesel; 360 hp(m) *(265 kW)*; 1 shaft
Speed, knots: 30
Complement: 7
Guns: 1 Oerlikon 20 mm.

Comment: Four built by Oceanfast Marine, Western Australia and delivered in early 1997. Trimaran construction forward, transforming into a catamaran at the stern. Shallow draft needed for inshore and river operations. The centreline single shaft is used for loitering. The craft show the colours of the Customs department. Up to 12 more may have been built in Vietnam but this has not been confirmed.

STOLCRAFT   *8/2005*, Kuvel/Marsan* / 1154063

14 ZHUK (PROJECT 1400M) CLASS (PB)

T 864	T 874	T 880	T 881	+10

Displacement, tons: 39 full load
Dimensions, feet (metres): 78.7 × 16.4 × 3.9 *(24 × 5 × 1.2)*
Main machinery: 2 Type M 401B diesels; 2,200 hp(m) *(1.6 MW)* sustained; 2 shafts
Speed, knots: 30. **Range, n miles:** 1,100 at 15 kt
Complement: 11 (3 officers)
Guns: 4—14.5 mm (2 twin) MGs.
Radars: Surface search Spin Trough; I-band.

Comment: Transferred: three in 1978, three in November 1979, one in November 1981, one in May 1985, three in February 1986, two in December 1989, two in January 1990, three in January 1996, two in January 1998 and two in April 1998. So far seven have been deleted but operational numbers are uncertain. Some may be allocated to the Coast Guard.

4 MODIFIED ZHUK CLASS (PB)

HQ 37	HQ 55	+2

Displacement, tons: 38 full load
Dimensions, feet (metres): 95.1 ×? × ? *(29.0 × ? × ?)*
Main machinery: 2 Saab Scania diesels; 2,500 hp(m) *(18.64 MW)* sustained; 2 shafts
Speed, knots: 30
Complement: 11 (3 officers)
Guns: 2—12.7 mm MGs (2 twin).
Radars: Navigation: I-band.

Comment: Built in Vietnam to design based on Zhuk class.

HQ 55 (under construction)   *8/2000, P Marsan* / 0105744

3 BP-29-12-01 PATROL CRAFT (PB)

BP-29-12-01   BP-33-11-01   BP-33-12-01

Displacement, tons: To be announced
Dimensions, feet (metres): To be announced
Main machinery: 2 diesels; 2 shafts
Speed, knots: To be announced
Guns: 2—12.7 mm MGs.
Radars: Navigation: I-band.

Comment: Indigenously-built patrol craft of an unknown type.

PATROL CRAFT   *11/2004*, Marcel/Marsan* / 1154064

2 POLUCHAT (PROJECT 368) CLASS
(COASTAL PATROL CRAFT) (PB/YPT)

Displacement, tons: 100 full load
Dimensions, feet (metres): 97.1 × 19 × 4.8 *(29.6 × 5.8 × 1.5)*
Main machinery: 2 Type M 50 diesels; 2,200 hp(m) *(1.6 MW)* sustained; 2 shafts
Speed, knots: 20. **Range, n miles:** 1,500 at 10 kt
Complement: 15
Guns: 2—12.7 mm MGs.
Radars: Navigation: Spin Trough; I-band.

Comment: Both transferred from USSR in January 1990. Can be used as torpedo recovery vessels.

POLUCHAT (Russian colours)   *7/1993, Hartmut Ehlers* / 0506181

RIVER PATROL CRAFT

Comment: There are large numbers of river patrol boats, mostly armed with MGs. A 14.5 m craft ordered from Singapore TSE in 1994. More are being built locally with Volvo Penta engines.

RIVER PATROL BOAT   *8/2000, P Marsan* / 0105743

AMPHIBIOUS FORCES

3 POLNOCHNY (PROJECT 771) CLASS (LCM)

HQ 511   HQ 512   HQ 513

Displacement, tons: 760 standard; 834 full load
Dimensions, feet (metres): 246.1 × 31.5 × 7.5 *(75 × 9.6 × 2.3)*
Main machinery: 2 Kolomna Type 40-D diesels; 4,400 hp(m) *(3.2 MW)* sustained; 2 shafts
Speed, knots: 19
Complement: 40
Guns: 2 or 4 USSR 30 mm/65 (1 or 2 twin). 2—140 mm rocket launchers.
Radars: Surface search: Spin Trough; I-band.
Fire control: Drum Tilt; H/I-band.

Comment: Transfers from USSR: one in May 1979 (B), one in November 1979 (A) and one in February 1980 (B). Details are for Polnochny B class. All are reported to be in poor condition.

HQ 512 and 513   *6/1995, Giorgio Arra* / 0084254

1 LST 1-510 CLASS (LST) and 2 LST 512-1152 CLASS (LST)

TRAN KHANH DU (ex-Da Nang, ex-*Maricopa County* LST 938) HQ 501
VUNG TAU (ex-*Cochino County* LST 603) HQ 502
QUI NONH (ex-*Bulloch County* LST 509) HQ 503

Displacement, tons: 2,366 beaching; 4,080 full load
Dimensions, feet (metres): 328 × 50 × 14 *(100 × 15.2 × 4.3)*
Main machinery: 2 GM 12-567A diesels; 1,800 hp *(1.34 MW)*; 2 shafts
Speed, knots: 11. **Range, n miles:** 6,000 at 10 kt
Complement: 110
Guns: 8 Bofors 40 mm/60 (2 twin, 4 single). 4 Oerlikon 20 mm.

Comment: Built in 1943-44. Transferred from US to South Vietnam in mid-1960s. Seldom seen at sea.

TRAN KHANH DU   *8/2000* / 0105745

30 LANDING CRAFT (LCM and LCU)

Comment: About five LCUs, 12 LCM 8 and LCM 6, and three LCVPs remain of the 180 minor landing craft left behind by the USA in 1975. In addition there are about 10 T4 LCUs acquired from the USSR in 1979.

LCU   *6/2001* / 0131363

MINE WARFARE FORCES

2 YURKA (RUBIN) (PROJECT 266) CLASS
(MINESWEEPERS—OCEAN) (MSO)

HQ 851   HQ 885

Displacement, tons: 540 full load
Dimensions, feet (metres): 171.9 × 30.8 × 8.5 *(52.4 × 9.4 × 2.6)*
Main machinery: 2 Type M 503 diesels; 5,350 hp(m) *(3.91 MW)* sustained; 2 shafts
Speed, knots: 17. **Range, n miles:** 1,500 at 12 kt
Complement: 45
Guns: 4 USSR 30 mm/65 (2 twin); 500 rds/min to 5 km *(2.7 n miles)*; weight of shell 0.54 kg.
Mines: 10.
Radars: Surface search: Don 2; I-band.
Fire control: Drum Tilt; H/I-band.
Sonars: Stag Ear; hull-mounted; active minehunting; high frequency.

Comment: Transferred from USSR December 1979. Steel-hulled, built in early 1970s.

YURKA (Egyptian colours)   *10/1998, F Sadek* / 0017818

4 SONYA (YAKHONT) (PROJECT 1265) CLASS
(MINESWEEPERS/HUNTER—COASTAL) (MHSC)

HQ 861   HQ 862   HQ 863   HQ 864

Displacement, tons: 450 full load
Dimensions, feet (metres): 157.4 × 28.9 × 6.6 *(48 × 8.8 × 2)*
Main machinery: 2 Kolomna 9-D-8 diesels; 2,000 hp(m) *(1.47 MW)* sustained; 2 shafts
Speed, knots: 15. **Range, n miles:** 3,000 at 10 kt
Complement: 43
Guns: 2 USSR 30 mm/65 AK 630. 2—25 mm/80 (twin).
Mines: 8.
Radars: Surface search: Nayada; I-band.
Sonars: MG 69/79; active; high frequency.

Comment: First one transferred from USSR 16 February 1987, second in February 1988, third in July 1989, fourth in March 1990. Two based at Da Nang.

SONYA 862   *5/2000, R Fildes* / 0105746

2 YEVGENYA (KOROND) (PROJECT 1258) CLASS
(MINEHUNTERS—INSHORE) (MHI)

Displacement, tons: 90 full load
Dimensions, feet (metres): 80.7 × 18 × 4.9 *(24.6 × 5.5 × 1.5)*
Main machinery: 2 Type 3-D-12 diesels; 600 hp(m) *(440 kW)* sustained; 2 shafts
Speed, knots: 11. **Range, n miles:** 300 at 10 kt
Complement: 10
Guns: 2 USSR 25 mm/80 (twin).
Mines: 8.
Radars: Surface search: Spin Trough; I-band.
Sonars: MG 7; active; high frequency.

Comment: First transferred from USSR in October 1979; two in December 1986. One deleted in 1990.

YEVGENYA (Russian colours)   *1993, B Lemachko* / 0506182

5 K 8 (PROJECT 361T) CLASS (MINESWEEPING BOATS) (PBR)

Displacement, tons: 26 full load
Dimensions, feet (metres): 55.4 × 10.5 × 2.6 *(16.9 × 3.2 × 0.8)*
Main machinery: 2 Type 3-D-6 diesels; 300 hp(m) *(220 kW)* sustained; 2 shafts
Speed, knots: 18
Complement: 6
Guns: 2—14.5 mm (twin) MGs.

Comment: Transferred from USSR in October 1980. Probably used as river patrol craft.

SURVEY SHIPS

Notes: A new survey ship of 2,500 tons is required.

1 KAMENKA (PROJECT 870) CLASS (AGS)

Displacement, tons: 760 full load
Dimensions, feet (metres): 175.5 × 29.8 × 8.5 *(53.5 × 9.1 × 2.6)*
Main machinery: 2 Sulzer diesels; 1,800 hp(m) *(1.32 MW)*; 2 shafts; cp props
Speed, knots: 14
Range, n miles: 4,000 at 10 kt
Complement: 25
Radars: Navigation: Don 2; I-band.

Comment: Transferred from USSR December 1979. Built at Northern Shipyard, Gdansk in the late 1960s. May be civilian manned.

KAMENKA (Russian colours)   *1984* / 0506127

AUXILIARIES

Notes: In addition to the vessels listed below there are two YOG 5 fuel lighters, two floating cranes, two ex-USSR unarmed Nyryat 2 diving tenders, a Sorum class ocean-going tug (BD 105) and approximately ten harbour tugs.

1 VODA (PROJECT 561) CLASS (WATER TANKER) (AWT)

BO 82

Displacement, tons: 2,115 full load
Dimensions, feet (metres): 267.4 × 37.7 × 14.1 *(81.5 × 11.5 × 4.3)*
Main machinery: 2 diesels; 1,600 hp *(1.2 MW)*; 2 shafts
Speed, knots: 12
Range, n miles: 3,000 at 10 kt
Complement: 38
Radars: Navigation: Don 2; I-band.

Comment: Built by Yantar, Kaliningrad, in the 1950s. Probably an ex-Russian Pacific Fleet unit transferred in about 1996. Carries about 1,000 tons of water.

17 OFFSHORE SUPPLY VESSELS (AKL)

TRUONG HQ 966	HQ 618	HQ 669
BD 621-622	HQ 619	HQ 670
BD 630-632	HQ 643	HQ 671
HQ 601	HQ 651	HQ 673
HQ 614	HQ 661	

Measurement, tons: 1,000 dwt
Dimensions, feet (metres): 231.6 × 38.7 × 13.1 *(70.6 × 11.8 × 4)*
Main machinery: 1 diesel; 1 shaft
Speed, knots: 12
Complement: 30

Comment: Details are for HQ 966 launched at Halong Shipyard in June 1994. This is one of a group of 20 freighters reported as used by the Navy for coastal transport, and to service the Spratleys garrison. BD pennant numbers have been assigned to Spratly Islands service. The ships are of various sizes and include fishing vessels adapted for supply tasks. All are likely to be armed with machine guns.

BD 621 (old number)   *3/1997* / 0050742

2 FLOATING DOCKS

Comment: One has a lift capacity of 8,500 tons. Transferred from USSR August 1983. Second one *(Khersson)* has a lift capacity of 4,500 tons and was supplied in 1988.

Virgin Islands (UK)

Country Overview

A British dependency, the British Virgin Islands are situated in the eastern Caribbean Sea at the northern end of the Leeward Islands in the Lesser Antilles chain. Puerto Rico lies some 52 n miles to the west. Comprising a group of 36 islands, 16 of them inhabited, and more than 20 islets and cays there are four main islands: Tortola (21 square miles);

Anegada (15 square miles); Virgin Gorda (8 square miles); and Jost Van Dyke (3.5 square miles). Other inhabited islands include Peter Island, Cooper Island, Beef Island, Salt Island, and Norman Island. The capital, only town and principal port is Road Town, Tortola. Territorial seas (3 n miles) and a Fishery Zone (200 n miles) are claimed. The remainder of the Virgin Islands form a separate external territory of the US.

Headquarters Appointments

Commissioner of British Virgin Islands Police:
 Barry W Webb

Bases

Road Town, Tortola

POLICE

Notes: (1) Following the withdrawal of *St Ursula* from service in 2003, procurement of a replacement craft is expected.
(2) There are also a 12 m Scarab, fitted with three 225 hp outboard motors, and a 10 m Mako with two 150 hp outboards.
(3) Two Dauntless class 12 m patrol boats are operated by the US Virgin Islands whose waters are also patrolled by USCG craft.

Yemen

Country Overview

The Republic of Yemen was formed in 1990 through the union of the People's Democratic Republic of Yemen and the Yemen Arab Republic. The country includes the islands of Socotra, Kamaran and Perim. With an area of 207,285 square miles, it is situated on the south-west coast of the Arabian Peninsula and is bordered to the north by Saudi Arabia and to the east by Oman. It has a 1,030 n mile coastline with the Red Sea and the Gulf of Aden, which are linked by a strategic strait, the Bab el Mandeb. The capital and largest city is Sanaa while the principal ports are Aden

and Al Hudaydah. Territorial seas (12 n miles) are claimed. A 200 n mile EEZ has been claimed but the limits have only been partly defined by boundary agreements.

Personnel

2006: 1,700 naval plus 500 marines

Bases

Main: Aden, Hodeida
Secondary: Mukalla, Perim, Socotra, Al Katib

Coast Defence regions: Al Ghaydah, Aden and Cameron Island

Coast Defence

Two mobile SS-C-3 Styx batteries. Some 100 mm guns installed in tank turrets at Perim Island.

PATROL FORCES

Notes: (1) In addition there are two 'Osa IIs', 122 and 124. One is in a poor state of repair and may have been decommissioned. The other was sighted in a floating dock in mid-2002 and may be seaworthy, although the SSM system is probably not operational.
(2) Five ex-USCG life boats were reported to have been delivered in 2004.
(3) Ten patrol boats were reportedly ordered from Lürssen Werft in 2005.

1 TARANTUL I CLASS (PROJECT 1241) (FSGM)

124 (ex-971)

Displacement, tons: 385 standard; 580 full load
Dimensions, feet (metres): 184.1 × 37.7 × 8.2 *(56.1 × 11.5 × 2.5)*
Main machinery: 2 Nikolayev Type DR 77 gas turbines; 16,016 hp(m) *(11.77 MW)* sustained; 2 Nikolayev Type DR 76 gas turbines with reversible gearboxes; 4,993 hp(m) *(3.67 MW)* sustained; 2 shafts
Speed, knots: 36
Range, n miles: 400 at 36 kt; 2,000 at 20 kt
Complement: 50

Missiles: SSM: 4 SS-N-2C Styx (2 twin) launchers; active radar or IR homing to 83 km *(45 n miles)* at 0.9 Mach; warhead 513 kg; sea-skimmer at end of run.
SAM: SA-N-5 Grail quad launcher; manual aiming; IR homing to 10 km *(5.4 n miles)* at 1.5 Mach; altitude to 2,500 m *(8,000 ft)*; warhead 1.1 kg.
Guns: 1—3 in *(76 mm)*/60; 120 rds/min to 7 km *(3.8 n miles)*; weight of shell 7 kg.
2—30 mm/65 AK 630; 6 barrels per mounting; 3,000 rds/min to 2 km.
Countermeasures: Decoys: 2 PK 16 chaff launchers.
Weapons control: Hood Wink optronic director.
Radars: Air/surface search: Plank Shave (also for missile control); E-band.
Navigation: Spin Trough; I-band.
Fire control: Bass Tilt; H/I-band.
IFF: Square Head. High Pole.

Programmes: Two export versions of the ship originally delivered from the USSR. First one on 7 December 1990, second on 15 January 1991. One decommissioned by 2001.
Operational: Facilities for servicing missiles in Aden were destroyed in mid-1994. This remaining ship is still in a reasonable state of repair although probably without missiles.

TARANTUL 124 *10/1995* / 0016612

2 ZHUK CLASS (PROJECT 1400M)

202   **203**

Displacement, tons: 39 full load
Dimensions, feet (metres): 78.7 × 16.4 × 3.9 *(24 × 5 × 1.2)*
Main machinery: 2 Type M 401B diesels; 2,200 hp(m) *(1.6 MW)* sustained; 2 shafts
Speed, knots: 30. **Range, n miles:** 1,100 at 15 kt
Complement: 11 (3 officers)
Guns: 4—14.5 mm (2 twin) MGs.
Radars: Surface search: Spin Trough; I-band.

Comment: Two delivered from USSR in December 1984 and three in January 1987. Three have been cannibalised for spares. One based at Aden, one at Al Katib. Used as utility craft including target towing.

ZHUK *3/1990* / 0084258

6 BAKLAN CLASS (HSIC)

BAKLAN 1201	**ZUHRAB** 1203	**HUNAISH** 1205
SIYAN 1202	**AKISSAN** 1204	**ZAKR** 1206

Displacement, tons: 12 full load
Dimensions, feet (metres): 50.9 × 9.8 × 2.6 *(15.5 × 3 × 0.8)*
Main machinery: 2 diesels; 2 surface drives
Speed, knots: 55. **Range, n miles:** 400 at 30 kt
Complement: 4
Guns: 2—12.7 mm MGs.
Radars: Surface search: Furuno; I-band.

Comment: Ordered from CMN Cherbourg on 3 March 1996. First five were delivered 1 August 1996 and the last one in mid-1997. Top speed in Sea States up to 3. Composite hull construction.

BAKLAN CLASS *8/1996, C M N Cherbourg* / 0084259

3 HUANGFEN (TYPE 021) CLASS
(FAST ATTACK CRAFT—MISSILE) (PTFG)

126	127	128

Displacement, tons: 171 standard; 205 full load
Dimensions, feet (metres): 126.6 × 24.9 × 8.9 *(38.6 × 7.6 × 2.7)*
Main machinery: 3 Type 42—160 diesels; 12,000 hp(m) *(8.8 MW)* sustained; 3 shafts
Speed, knots: 35. **Range, n miles:** 800 at 30 kt
Complement: 28
Missiles: SSM: 4 YJ-1 (Eagle Strike) (C-801); inertial cruise; active radar homing to 40 km *(22 n miles)* at 0.9 Mach; warhead 165 kg; sea-skimmer.
Guns: 4 30 mm/(2 twin AK 230); 500 rds/min to 5 km *(2.7 n miles)*.
Radars: Surface search: Square Tie; I-band.
Fire control: Rice Lamp; H/I-band.
IFF: 2 Square Head. High Pole A.

Comment: Modified Huangfen type. Delivered on 6 June 1995 at Aden having been built by the China Shipbuilding Corporation and completed in 1993. Payment was delayed by the Yemeni civil war. Based at Al Katib. *128* ran aground in September 1997 but was salvaged and may be operational again. *126* is in a reasonable state of repair but is not armed with missiles.

HUANGFEN 126 *5/1995* / 0506339

10 AUSTAL PATROL SHIPS (PB)

P 1022-1031

Displacement, tons: 90 full load
Dimensions, feet (metres): 123.0 × 23.6 × 7.2 *(37.5 × 7.2 × 2.2)*
Main machinery: 2 Caterpillar 3512 diesels; 3,500 hp *(2.61 MW)*; 2 shafts
Speed, knots: 29. **Range, n miles:** 1,000 at 25 kt
Complement: 19 (3 officers)
Guns: 1—25 mm; 2—12.7 mm MGs.

Comment: Contract with Austal Ships on 9 June 2003 for a total of 10 patrol craft. All were shipped to Yemen in February 2005. Of aluminium construction, the design is based on the Bay class Australian Customs vessels. The contract includes engineering and practical training for 60 Yemeni crew.

P-1022 *6/2004, Kade Rogers, RAN* / 0583301

AMPHIBIOUS FORCES

Notes: Ropucha 139 is an alongside hulk.

1 NS-722 CLASS (LSMM)

BILQUIS

Displacement, tons: 1,383 full load
Dimensions, feet (metres): 295.4 × 31.8 × 7.9 *(90 × 9.7 × 2.4)*
Main machinery: 2 Caterpillar diesels; 5,670 hp *(4.2 MW)*; 2 shafts
Speed, knots: 18. **Complement:** 49
Military lift: 5 T-72 tanks and 111 marines
Missiles: SAM: SA-16 or ZM Mesko.
Guns: 4 ZSU-23-2MR Wrobel 23 mm (2 twin).

Comment: Ordered in late 1999 for delivery in 2002, development of the Polnochny class built by Naval Shipyard Gdynia, Poland. Shipped from Poland to Yemen on 24 May 2002. Roles include disaster relief and cadet training as well as amphibious warfare.

BILQUIS *10/2001, J Cislak* / 0131343

3 DEBA CLASS (PROJECT NS-717) (LCU)

HIMYER (ex-*Dhaffar*)   SABA   ABDULKORI (ex-*Thamoud*)

Displacement, tons: 221 full load
Dimensions, feet (metres): 134.5 × 23.3 × 5.6 *(41 × 7.1 × 1.7)*
Main machinery: 2 Cummins diesels; 2 shafts
Speed, knots: 15. **Range, n miles:** 500 at 14.5 kt
Complement: 10
Military lift: 16 tons and 50 troops
Guns: 2 ZU-23-2MR Wrobel 23 mm/87 (1 twin).
2—12.7 mm MGs.
Radars: Navigation: I-band.

Comment: Ordered from Poland in October 1999 and delivered in mid-2001. AK-630 CIWS may also be fitted at a later date.

ABDULKORI (on transport ship) *5/2001, J Cislak* / 0131342

2 ONDATRA (PROJECT 1176) CLASS (LCU)

13	14

Displacement, tons: 145 full load
Dimensions, feet (metres): 78.7 × 16.4 × 4.9 *(24 × 5 × 1.5)*
Main machinery: 1 diesel; 300 hp(m) *(221 kW)*; 1 shaft
Speed, knots: 10
Range, n miles: 500 at 5 kt
Complement: 4
Military lift: 1 MBT
Radars: Navigation: Spin Trough; I-band.

Comment: Transferred from USSR January 1983. Has a tank deck of 45 × 13 ft.

ONDATRA 14 *1990* / 0506128

1 T4 CLASS (LCM)

134

Displacement, tons: 93 full load
Dimensions, feet (metres): 65.3 × 18.4 × 4.6 *(19.9 × 5.6 × 1.4)*
Main machinery: 2 diesels; 316 hp(m) *(232 kW)*; 2 shafts
Speed, knots: 10
Complement: 4

Comment: Reported to have paid off in 1995 but still in service.

T4 134 *1/1990* / 0016614

MINE WARFARE FORCES

1 NATYA CLASS (PROJECT 266ME)
(MINESWEEPER—OCEAN) (MSO)

201

Displacement, tons: 804 full load
Dimensions, feet (metres): 200.1 × 33.5 × 10.8 *(61 × 10.2 × 3)*
Main machinery: 2 Type M 504 diesels; 5,000 hp(m) *(3.67 MW)* sustained; 2 shafts; cp props
Speed, knots: 16
Range, n miles: 3,000 at 12 kt
Complement: 67
Guns: 4—30 mm/65 (2 twin); 500 rds/min to 5 km *(2.7 n miles)*; weight of shell 0.54 kg.
4—25 mm/80 (2 twin); 270 rds/min to 3 km *(1.6 n miles)*; weight of shell 0.34 kg.
A/S mortars: 2 RBU 1200 five-tubed fixed launchers; range 1,200 m; warhead 34 kg.
Mines: 10
Countermeasures: MCM: Carries contact, acoustic and magnetic sweeps.
Radars: Surface search: Don 2; I-band.
Sonars: MG 69/79; hull-mounted; active minehunting; high frequency.

Comment: Transferred from USSR in February 1991. Operational status doubtful. A second of class was delivered to Ethiopia in October 1991 but sheltered in Aden for a time in 1992.

NATYA 201 *6/2002, Rahn/Globke* / 0530089

5 YEVGENYA (PROJECT 1258) CLASS (MINEHUNTERS) (MHC)

11   12   15   20   +1

Displacement, tons: 90 full load
Dimensions, feet (metres): 80.7 × 18 × 4.9 *(24.6 × 5.5 × 1.5)*
Main machinery: 2 Type 3-D-12 diesels; 600 hp(m) *(440 kW)* sustained; 2 shafts
Speed, knots: 11. **Range, n miles:** 300 at 10 kt
Complement: 10
Guns: 2—25 mm/80 (twin).
Radars: Navigation: Spin Trough; I-band.
Sonars: MG 7 small transducer lifted over stern on crane.

Comment: GRP hulls. Two transferred from USSR in May 1982, third in November 1987 and three more in March 1990. One deleted in 1994. Two based at Aden and three at Al Katib. At least two are fully operational.

YEVGENYA 20 *2/1997* / 0016615

AUXILIARIES

Notes: (1) A 4,500 ton Floating Dock acquired from the USSR.
(2) A 14 m Hydrographic craft acquired from Cougar Marine in 1988.
(3) An oil-pollution control craft acquired in 1999.
(4) Two Toplivo class tankers, *135* and *140*, are reported to have been decommissioned.

Zimbabwe

Country Overview

The Republic of Zimbabwe gained independence on 17 April 1980. Formerly the British colony of Southern Rhodesia and, between 1953 and 1963, part of the Federation of Rhodesia and Nyasaland (now Malawi), a unilateral declaration of independence on 11 November 1965 precipitated a turbulent period of guerilla war. This eventually led to a peace settlement in 1979 and elections in 1980. A landlocked country with an area of 150,873 square miles, it is situated in central southern Africa and is bordered to the north by Zambia, to the east by Mozambique, to the south by South Africa and to the west by Botswana and Namibia. It has a shoreline of approximately 350 n miles with Lake Kariba, artificially formed by the Kariba Dam, from which the country gets much of its electric power.

The capital, largest city and commercial centre is Harare (formerly Salisbury). The railway system is linked to the port of Beira in Mozambique.

Bases

Kariba, Binga.

PATROL FORCES

2 RODMAN 46HJ CLASS (PB)

Displacement, tons: 12.5 full load
Dimensions, feet (metres): 45.9 × 12.5 × 2.0 *(14.0 × 3.8 × 0.6)*
Main machinery: 2 Caterpillar 3280 diesels; 850 hp *(633 kW)*
Speed, knots: 30
Range, n miles: 350 at 18 kt
Complement: 4

Comment: GRP hull. Built in 1999 by Rodman, Vigo. Operated by Zimbabwe Police.

RODMAN 46 *6/1999, Rodman* / 0570998

3 RODMAN 38 CLASS (PB)

Displacement, tons: 10 full load
Dimensions, feet (metres): 36.1 × 12.8 × 2.3 *(11.0 × 3.9 × 0.7)*
Main machinery: 2 diesels; 2 waterjets
Speed, knots: 28
Range, n miles: 300 at 15 kt
Complement: 4

Comment: GRP hull. Built in 1999 by Rodman, Vigo. Operated by Zimbabwe Police.

RODMAN 38 *6/1999, Rodman* / 0571000

5 RODMAN 790 CLASS (PB)

Displacement, tons: 2.4 full load
Dimensions, feet (metres): 26.6 × 8.9 × 2.3 *(8.1 × 2.72 × 0.7)*
Main machinery: 2 Volvo Penta TAMD diesels
Speed, knots: 30
Complement: 2

Comment: GRP hull. Built in 1999 by Rodman, Vigo. Operated by Zimbabwe Police.

RODMAN 790 *6/1999, Rodman* / 0570999

INDEXES

Indexes
Country abbreviations

Alb	Albania	DR	Dominican Republic	Lat	Latvia	SAr	Saudi Arabia
Alg	Algeria	Ecu	Ecuador	Lby	Libya	Sen	Senegal
Ana	Anguilla	Egy	Egypt	Leb	Lebanon	Ser	Serbia and Montenegro
Ang	Angola	ElS	El Salvador	Lit	Lithuania	Sey	Seychelles
Ant	Antigua and Barbuda	EqG	Equatorial Guinea	Mac	Macedonia, Former Yugoslav Republic of	Sin	Singapore
Arg	Argentina	Eri	Eritrea			SL	Sierra Leone
Aus	Austria	Est	Estonia	Mad	Madagascar	Slo	Slovenia
Aust	Australia	ETim	East Timor	Mex	Mexico	Sol	Solomon Islands
Az	Azerbaijan	Fae	Faroe Islands	MI	Marshall Islands	Spn	Spain
Ban	Bangladesh	Fij	Fiji	Mic	Micronesia	Sri	Sri Lanka
Bar	Barbados	FI	Falkland Islands	Mld	Maldives	StK	St Kitts
Bel	Belgium	Fin	Finland	Mlt	Malta	StL	St Lucia
Ben	Benin	Fra	France	Mlw	Malawi	StV	St Vincent and the Grenadines
Bhm	Bahamas	Gab	Gabon	Mly	Malaysia	Sud	Sudan
Bhr	Bahrain	Gam	Gambia	Mor	Morocco	Sur	Suriname
Blz	Belize	GB	Guinea-Bissau	Moz	Mozambique	Swe	Sweden
Bmd	Bermuda	Ger	Germany	Mrt	Mauritius	Swi	Switzerland
Bol	Bolivia	Geo	Georgia	Mtn	Mauritania	Syr	Syria
Bru	Brunei	Gha	Ghana	Myn	Myanmar	Tan	Tanzania
Brz	Brazil	Gn	Guinea	Nam	Namibia	Tld	Thailand
Bul	Bulgaria	Gra	Grenada	NATO	NATO	Tkm	Turkmenistan
Cam	Cameroon	Gre	Greece	Nic	Nicaragua	Tog	Togo
Can	Canada	Gua	Guatemala	Nig	Nigeria	Ton	Tonga
Cay	Cayman Islands	Guy	Guyana	Nld	Netherlands	TT	Trinidad and Tobago
Chi	Chile	HK	Hong Kong	Nor	Norway	Tun	Tunisia
CI	Cook Islands	Hon	Honduras	NZ	New Zealand	Tur	Turkey
CtI	Côte d'Ivoire	Hun	Hungary	Omn	Oman	Tuv	Tuvalu
Cmb	Cambodia	Ice	Iceland	Pak	Pakistan	Twn	Taiwan
Col	Colombia	Ind	India	Pal	Palau	UAE	United Arab Emirates
Com	Comoros	Indo	Indonesia	Pan	Panama	UK	United Kingdom
ConD	Congo, Democratic Republic	Iran	Iran	Par	Paraguay	Ukr	Ukraine
CPR	China, People's Republic	Iraq	Iraq	Per	Peru	Uru	Uruguay
CpV	Cape Verde	Ire	Irish Republic	Plp	Philippines	US	United States of America
CR	Costa Rica	Isr	Israel	PNG	Papua New Guinea	Van	Vanuatu
Cro	Croatia	Ita	Italy	Pol	Poland	Ven	Venezuela
Cub	Cuba	Jam	Jamaica	Por	Portugal	VI	Virgin Islands
Cypr	Cyprus (Republic)	Jor	Jordan	Qat	Qatar	Vtn	Vietnam
Den	Denmark	Jpn	Japan	RoK	Korea, Republic of (South)	Yem	Yemen
Dji	Djibouti	Kaz	Kazakhstan	Rom	Romania	Zim	Zimbabwe
Dom	Dominica	Ken	Kenya	Rus	Russian Federation		
DPRK	Korea, Democratic People's Republic (North)	Kir	Kiribati	SA	South Africa		
		Kwt	Kuwait	Sam	Samoa		

Named ships

For details of the latest updates to *Jane's Fighting Ships* online and to discover the additional information available exclusively to online subscribers please visit

jfs.janes.com

Named classes

Aircraft by countries